WHEN THEY READ

MANUSCRIPTS

How the manuscript's form and contents depict the idea

A writing style that informs, entertains, and touches the reader

Verifiable research facts (in nonfiction)

Anecdotes and quotes from your interviews with people

How the manuscript will serve their readers and the market

***Perfect* copy; SASE enclosed**

1986 WRITER'S MARKET®

WHERE TO SELL WHAT YOU WRITE

Edited by Paula Deimling

Assisted by Kathleen Vonderhaar

Writer's Digest Books
Cincinnati, Ohio

Distributed in Canada by Prentice-Hall of Canada Ltd., 1870 Birchmount Road, Scarborough, Ontario M1P 2J7, and in Australia and New Zealand by Bookwise (Aust.) Pty. Ltd., Box 296, Welland, S.A. 5007, Australia.

Managing Editor, Market Books Department: Constance J. Achabal

Library of Congress Catalog Number 31-20772
International Standard Serial Number 0084-2729
International Standard Book Number 0-89879-198-7

Contents

The Profession

The Markets

The Profession

Introduction

It may be glorious to write
   Thoughts that will glad the two or three
High souls, like those far stars that come in sight,
   Once in a century;
But better far it is to speak
   One simple word . . .

                    —J.R. Lowell

As a writer, you probably want to speak to the world. Most writers spend lifetimes looking for an audience, looking for words that will inspire, sparkle, and last like Halley's tail. There are no formulas for freelancing, though, except maybe:
                    Think deeply. Write simply. Sell carefully.
                    Keep searching for an audience.
   Writer's Market can help. This 57th edition lists more than 4,000 markets. We've spent the year looking for new markets and old markets with new needs. A double dagger (‡) denotes new listings and those that have returned to our book after a year or more of absence. If a market isn't listed, there can be several reasons why; see page four for an explanation of our selection process. Also you won't find a poetry section in this edition of *Writer's Market* since we've compiled a far more comprehensive list and now published the *1986 Poet's Market*. Just as our fiction markets grew into a separate book, *Fiction Writer's Market*, so have the poetry markets. But we haven't eliminated poetry completely from *Writer's Market*—see the Poetry subheadings in many of the listings.
   You are *our* audience who put us on Waldenbooks' and B. Dalton's bestseller lists last year (thank you!). We've worked especially hard to give you new information this year. We have explored issues not addressed in previous *Writer's Markets*, like subsidy publishing and a self-help approach to dealing with editors. We've traveled to New York City to talk with editors and writers. We've surveyed editors, writers, and agents for opinions on agents and reading fees. We've tried to answer the questions you've asked in your letters.
   Another goal this year was to make the complicated process of selling your work easier for you. Our "What Editors Look For" chart on the inside front cover, we hope, will help you evaluate a submission before you mail it. Our new Query Checklist in the Appendix outlines the process of preparing this sales tool. (The process varies with each submission, but the checklist defines many of the steps that selling writers use.)

One of the highlights of this year's edition is three upfront articles by publishing pros—Sol Stein, Donna Buys Wilson, and L.M. Rosenberg—who practice their craft daily and who have found audiences. They show you how to get editors to notice your book, how to develop an article writing/selling approach, and how to write great, publishable fiction.

Whether you earned no or nine bylines last year, the following features will help you know what editors want in 1986.

● What Editors Say, What Writers Say, What Agents Say. We asked their views on writing and selling. You'll enjoy their well-thought-out and sometimes off-the-cuff comments.

● Anecdotes. Editors, writers, and agents have shared anecdotes on how writers have landed or lost assignments. These little stories are distributed throughout the book.

● Close-up interviews with editors and writers. Many of our featured *guests* like Isaac Asimov and Lewis H. Lapham work in both capacities. The Close-ups also spotlight markets we think you'll want to learn more about—*Playboy, Highlights for Children*, Overlook Press and others.

● New details on book publishers. We asked book publishers additional questions this year and incorporated their answers into the listings: What is the average print order for a writer's first book, what percentage of the books that you publish are from first-time authors, and what percentage of books come from unagented writers? The answers to these questions and the use of the Book Publisher Subject Index should aid your search for a publisher.

● More information on magazines' dealings with freelancers. We asked editors if writers had a better chance of breaking in to their publications with fillers or short, lesser-paying articles (rather than with major features). Some said yes—they use small articles as a gauge of a writer's abilities; others said no; some said sometimes. You'll find this information in the listings. Also, *Writer's Market* now reports if a magazine pays writers' expenses while on assignment or sometimes does. If the editor doesn't pay assignment expenses or didn't answer the question, the listing won't mention assignment expenses.

● More on rights. We asked magazine editors to clarify what rights they buy to material. To avoid misinterpretations, each editor received a list of rights definitions as *we* define them in our Appendix.

● Appendix and Glossary with updated information on manuscript mechanics, submission procedures, postal chart, payment rates for writing jobs, and terms of the trade.

● Submissions recordkeeper. Once your submission has all the elements an editor looks for, then flip to the back inside cover to record where and when you submit it.

This year can be a special one, not because Halley's Comet adds another sight to the night sky you ponder, but because you've chosen to work with this book. *Writer's Market* is a commitment to finding audiences, to selling your words, to trying to tell stories "once in a century" that might last. You needn't wish upon any star. Think deeply. Write simply. You will have spoken.

—*Paula Deimling*

How to Use *Writer's Market*

Looking for what *the editor* wants in each listing will help you get the most (satisfaction and pay) from your freelancing efforts. Read and reread each listing. Send only the type of material that editors request; don't send a manuscript to an editor who requests queries. Respect editor's needs even if you don't agree with their preferences.

• Information about the emphasis and audience of a publication should be incorporated into the slant and style of your submission.

• Send queries or manuscripts to one magazine at a time unless the editor has indicated in the listing that simultaneous submissions are OK. Openness to photocopied submissions does not imply that simultaneous submissions are acceptable.

• Figures listing the number of freelance manuscripts purchased are approximations, but they indicate a market's openness. With new magazines, these figures may change dramatically, depending on the submissions they receive or sudden changes in policy.

• Figures for manuscript lengths preferred by editors are limits to keep in mind when submitting material or suggesting manuscript length in a query letter. However, a story should be told in the space it requires—no more and no less.

• Look for markets that pay on acceptance, *not* "on publication." Payment here is immediate, and not dependent on when your story appears in print. Also, some magazines pay more for assigned stories than for complete manuscripts sent over the transom. Querying for an assignment in these cases is the best move.

• Look, too, for markets that don't buy all rights, and don't make "work-for-hire" contract agreements (in which the market, and not the author, owns the article's copyright). Retain rights you might be able to resell.

• Don't abuse phone queries. Use this route only when your "hot" story will be chilled by usual submission procedures.

• Check a market's receptiveness to computer printout and electronic submissions. Editors do not object to manuscripts typed by computer printers if the pages look like they have come from a typewriter. What has prompted some editors to dislike printouts are the dot-matrix submissions without descenders and with faint and poorly spaced dots. While most editors won't object to the newer kind of dot-matrix (where the dots are nearly imperceptible), follow the computer information in each listing. If a listing does not mention printout or disk preferences, the editor is leery of such submissions.

• Times listed are approximate. When an editor gave us a range of reporting and publishing times, say four to six weeks, we listed the time as six weeks. Give editors about six extra weeks on reporting time before following up politely on queries or submissions.

• Enclose a self-addressed, stamped envelope (SASE) in *any* correspondence with editors. Enclosing a SASE without enough postage to get a manuscript back to its owner is like not sending a SASE—and that's poor etiquette for a writer. Use International Reply Coupons (IRCs) with a return envelope for all Canadian and foreign submissions. U.S. (return) postage is useless in Canada and foreign countries.

• Address a cover letter or query to a specific editor by name. If the name is not easily recognizable as to gender, use the full name (e.g., Dear Dale Smith:).

• If the editor advises in the listing that a sample copy is available for a price and a SASE—but does not specify the size of the SASE—look at the publication's description. If it is a tabloid, newspaper or magazine, you'll need to enclose a 9x12 SASE with three first class stamps affixed. Generally speaking, if a sample copy is available for a price (without SASE), postage is included in the price. Most guidelines are available for a business-size envelope with one first-class stamp (unless otherwise specified).

Key to Symbols Used in *Writer's Market Listings:*

‡ *New Listing in all sections*
* *Subsidy publisher in Book Publishers section*
● *Company publication in Consumer and Trade, Technical, and Professional Journals sections*
□ *Cable TV market in Scriptwriting section*

Urgent

● Listings are based on editorial questionnaires and interviews. They are *not* advertisements (publishers do not pay for their listings) *nor* are markets endorsed by *WM* editors.

● All listings have been verified prior to the publication of this book. If a listing has not changed from last year, then the editor has told us that his needs have not changed—and that the previous listing still accurately reflects what he buys. We require documentation in our files for each listing and *never* run a listing without its editorial office's approval.

● Information in listings is as current as possible, but editors change jobs, companies and publications move, and editorial needs change between the publication date of *Writer's Market* and the day you buy it. Listings for new markets and changes in others can be found throughout the year in *Writer's Digest*, the monthly magazine for freelancers. If you know of a market not listed in this book, send us the market's name and address and editor's name; we will contact them for the next edition.

● When looking for a specific market, check the index. A market might not be listed for one of these reasons: 1) It doesn't solicit freelance material. 2) It has gone out of business. 3) It doesn't pay for material (we have, however, included nonpaying listings in the journalism and lifestyles categories because publication in these magazines could be valuable to a writer). *Some* magazines in the In-flight section, however, compensate writers with coupons for air travel. 4) It has failed to verify or update its listing for the 1986 edition. 5) It requests not to be listed. 6) Complaints have been received about it, and it hasn't answered *Writer's Market* inquiries satisfactorily. (To the best of our ability—and with our readers' help—we try to screen out any dishonest listings.) 7) It buys few manuscripts, thereby constituting a very small market for freelancers. 8) It was in the midst of being sold at press time, and rather than disclose premature details, we chose not to list it.

● *Writer's Market* reserves the right to exclude any listing.

Selling Your Book: How to Get Editors to Notice Your Work

BY SOL STEIN

A writer has two jobs, and it's astonishing how similar they are. Both require close attention to an audience.

The first job is to think of what your audience is expecting. The reader of fiction wants an emotional experience. The novelist has to envision the effect of every scene on his reader. The nonfiction writer must remember that his audience wants to learn something in every chapter.

But once the writer has finished his first job (writing the book to satisfy an audience), he must think about his very first reader—the editor who receives his manuscript or inquiry. What is that editor expecting?

Appearance Counts

After more than 30 years of receiving submissions, I am still influenced by the appearance of a manuscript. There is one agent whose submissions always snare my attention because he has most of his authors' manuscripts retyped in clear, black, double-spaced easy-to-read pages. Appearance matters *even more* when receiving manuscripts directly from authors because, at minimum, we want to know that the envelope we are opening was sent by a *professional*. You needn't have sold anything to appear like a pro. What are the signs?

A professional will not bind or staple his pages. He knows that editors are used to reading separate double-spaced pages with ample margins at top, bottom, and both sides. Use a pica rather than an elite size type face, if possible (*never* script or fancy type faces). Editors value their eyesight more than most people. Don't use weak dot-matrix type or a ribbon that should have been thrown out. They guarantee your manuscript will get short shrift.

A professional's cover letter will be short, to the point, and intriguing by its content. It will *not* say, "My work is copyrighted." (All work, as soon as it is written, is protected by copyright; professionals aren't afraid of their work being stolen.) A professional will not say, "I have designed a jacket for my book"; he knows that's the sign of an amateur. Publishers have art departments. They expect writers to stick to writing.

A professional with an academic background will never say, "I wrote my dissertation on so-and-so and would like to rewrite it as a book for the general reader." Prove it by submitting a sample of what the finished trade manuscript will be like.

A professional will include return postage and an envelope large enough to hold the manuscript. It's amazing how many authors affix postage to an envelope too small to hold the manuscript. Keep in mind that a publisher may process at least

Sol Stein *has been editor-in-chief and president of Stein and Day Publishers since its founding 23 years ago. He is the author of seven successful novels, all of which were published by other publishers. Stein is also a prize-winning playwright, produced both on and off Broadway, and has written screenplays as well as published articles, poetry, and reviews in national, literary, and scholarly publications. His novel* Other People *was recently selected by the West Coast Review of Books as "one of the greatest books of the decade."*

500 manuscripts for each one that may be publishable. The cost of processing the 500 rarely equals the profit to be made on the publishable one. Editors will not look favorably on a submission that expects the publisher to bear the additional cost of returning unwanted manuscripts. Many won't return material not accompanied by a SASE.

My editors concur that the biggest nuisance in their lives is telephone inquiries. When you've been interrupted by an unwanted call during dinner, you know what an editor working on a manuscript feels like when he gets an author's inquiry by telephone.

Yesterday a writer phoned my office four times. My secretary told him I was busy preparing for the next day's sales conference. The man said he wanted to submit a partial novel to me because he read my introduction to another novel that my company had recently republished in paperback (it was a first by an unknown that became a national bestseller). Would I read his manuscript before it was finished? My secretary explained that I preferred to read the first three pages—or, at most, ten pages—because that's all a customer in a bookstore will read of a novel before putting it down or taking it to the cash register. The author asked if I would consider contracting for a novel before it was finished. Even Jack Higgins, who has had ten bestsellers in a row, finishes his novels before sending them to Mr. Stein, my secretary told him. "But," the unpublished novelist persisted, "isn't that point negotiable if Stein really likes my book?" She didn't have time to argue the point or tell him of my unhappy experience as a young editor when I signed up a first novel after reading 100 excellent pages and it went downhill in a way no editor could fix. We can't buy a *part* of a novel any more than the author could buy part of a living dog in a pet shop. Only the whole is publishable.

Warnings for Novelists

In your cover note of inquiry, don't say, "I have just written a fiction novel." A novel *is* fiction and that frequently-heard phrase is a giveaway that the writer is an amateur who doesn't know what the words mean.

Don't say, "I have just finished a 150,000-word novel." A professional knows that an average novel today runs 75,000-100,000 words. Beyond that length the publisher would have to charge more than the market will stand. The marketplace rarely *sees* exceptions like . . . *And Ladies of the Club.* Don't use the long novel written by well-known authors as a basis of comparison; their books have large first printings that enable the publisher to keep down the price.

Remember that a short or long synopsis of a *plot* won't tell the editor how well you write. Fiction depends entirely on the author's special skills of handling language and developing characters out of which plots grow.

Don't say, "My novel really gets going on page 30." If it does, discard the first 30 pages; start your novel on page 30.

Don't say in your cover note that "I am enclosing my third novel" unless the other two have been published. In that case, you should name the publishers and the year of publication. Otherwise your note will be interpreted to mean that you have written two unpublishable novels and you are now submitting a third. An editor can't help being prejudiced by repeated failure.

Don't say, "I am willing to rewrite with editorial guidance." That is assumed if you are a pro. All my bestselling novelists get edited and do rewrites as needed. Although I've written seven novels, the eighth is now in draft number nine *before* I'll show it to a prospective publisher—whose editor will probably have further suggestions for changes.

If you are sending an inquiry to a firm that doesn't want to see complete manuscripts, make sure that your plot summary doesn't take more than 30 seconds to read. The salesperson who will eventually sell your novel to the bookstore will have no more than 30 seconds to tell what it's about. If your novel can't be summarized in 30 seconds, you're a genius who doesn't need practical advice or a novelist who doesn't understand the publishing and marketing process.

If you want to be absolutely sure that your manuscript will not be taken seriously, start your cover letter with "My book is a guaranteed bestseller. . . ." As a publisher who has had books on the bestseller lists for 18 consecutive years, I can tell you that no author who isn't already a "name brand" can guarantee bestsellerdom, and even those sometimes go amiss.

Nonfiction Expertise

When I and other editors consider nonfiction proposals, we are most excited by the seeming contradiction of newness and reliability. Most doctors, lawyers, accountants, and engineers can't write as well as writers, but I know two doctors who weren't writers but had books published successfully.

The first was a pediatrician who thought he was writing short stories for children. Editor Patricia Day recognized that the doctor had a fresh approach to child care for the better-educated parent (that's a good sign, because better-educated people buy more books). This doctor, Marvin Gersh, quoted Dr. Benjamin Spock as saying that when you give a baby a first bath, take your wristwatch off. Gersh said, "If you have to be told to take your wristwatch off, maybe you shouldn't be having babies." A sense of humor that's pointed frequently grabs an editor. One of the important observations in his book was that there are only two signs—difficulty in breathing and unstoppable bleeding—that required *immediate* attention; for everything else, time was not that pressing. What a relief to the worried, inexperienced parent! Patricia Day extracted a book from the pediatrician that was selected by 28 book clubs and is still in print after 18 years.

Last year we received an unagented manuscript from a doctor who had developed the first unified theory on the causes and prevention of cancer. It had to be rewritten almost line by line. Was it worth it? Certainly. Yet books on medical subjects by laymen are not usually given consideration because the bookstores won't stock them unless a well-known doctor writes an introduction.

The Quality of the Mind Behind the Book

As an editor I respond most eagerly to superior handling of the language. Here is the beginning of a proposal that sounds arrogant, but the quality of the language caught an editor's attention:

Food in History is a pioneer work on a deceptively simple theme. Its purpose is to examine the forces which have shaped the nature of man's diet throughout the course of thirty thousand years, and to show, without special pleading, something of the way in which the pursuit of more and better food has helped to direct—sometimes decisively, more often subtly—the movement of history itself. To demonstrate, in effect, that in some senses at least food *is* history.

This is an important example because the author was not an anthropologist or a professional historian, but the language conveyed the presence of a mind. The editor went on reading.

As far as I am aware, this type of panoramic view has never been attempted before even on a national, far less on a world scale. Nor do I know of any other work which has tried to correlate the information revealed in recent years by new disciplines in archeology and anthropology, in biology, ecology, economics, technology and zoology. Such material is diffuse and often narrowly technical, but much of it throws valuable light on the role of food in the past.

What those two paragraphs tell me as an editor is that I am in the hands of an author who is trying something original and I want to know if she can carry it off. She did. *Food in History*, by a previously unknown author, Reay Tannahill, became a main selection of the Book-of-the-Month Club, sold some 165,000 copies in hardcover, and has been selling as a trade paperback for more than a decade. It is considered a classic, that is, a book that has a chance of outliving its author and its editor.

Practical Books

Books of instruction that are read for their content, not their style, are a very big part of American publishing. We look for subject matter first (Has it been done? Has it been done well by someone else?) and the clarity of the prose style. *How to Teach Your Baby to Swim* was an easy choice because the author had been teaching babies to swim; the subject hadn't been covered before; and it was clearly and concisely written. That book is now in its 15th printing.

How-to-do-it for the home fixer-upper is a big and growing field. Just as the recession was beginning, we grabbed a well-illustrated manuscript called *Mend It!* because we sensed that what the writer felt was true: That people were concentrating more on fixing everything they could instead of throwing it away. The Literary Guild agreed. The author had a winner because the book was not only well done but *timely*.

I remember how taken I was by a car book proposal in which the author said, "Once a month, or whenever you have a problem with your car, spread out newspaper in your driveway and park your car over the newspapers overnight. In the morning, back your car off the papers and if there is a leak, you'll be able to tell whether it's coming from the front, middle, or back of the car, and from the color you can tell (with the help of this book) *what* is leaking so that you can steer the mechanic quickly to the trouble spot." (Unfortunately, the author never completed that book, and it's still waiting to be written.)

Over the course of several decades, I have learned that there are categories of books that are popular abroad, but generally the market in this country is poor for them, even if well done. They are memoirs (Americans prefer biography rather than autobiography); travel books (Americans will buy guide books but not books about one's travels, though the British love such books); and, alas, poetry (the market for a book of poetry, on the average, is no more than 800 copies, far below the breakeven point).

Getting Help

Once upon a time when I or my editors received a proposal or a manuscript that required more editorial work (usually a complete rewrite under detailed direction) than a publisher is willing to invest, we rejected the book. Now there are editorial services listed in the *Literary Market Place* which employ professional editors who can help a writer fix a manuscript to the point where a publisher is willing to contract for it. These services are compensated, but if a project is promising enough, some will lower fees in exchange for a percentage of the advance and royalties if the book is sold.

In conclusion, the most important advice I can offer from editorial meetings where thousands of manuscripts have been rejected (and hundreds accepted) *after* having been proposed by an editor, is for the writer to think of the market. Who will buy this book if I write it? Why will they buy it? How many such people are there? How will they get to know about the book—is the subject publicizable in interviews, and can I do such interviews effectively? If I were an editor instead of a writer, would I read this proposal after the first paragraph? Why? The vast majority of writers I've talked to do *not* ask themselves these questions and write or rewrite their proposals or cover letters accordingly, which is why their proposals go unaccepted.

The chances of getting a book accepted are not high. If you follow the guidelines in this article, you'll at least have placed your submission at the top of the pile where the editor will seriously consider your book.

Article Writing: How to Develop an Approach That Sells____

BY DONNA BUYS WILSON

Writing articles that sell requires so much more than knowing how to write. As frustrating and unfair as it seems, only one-third of a writer's time is spent writing. The rest of the time, a writer must be a sales and business person. If a writer ignores the sales and business ends of writing, there will be no financial reward. A professional writer wants to make a living with his craft and *must* write for money. You will earn more by writing on assignment. Assignments go to the writers who thoroughly research a publication.

Know Your Market

Do not write with only a hope of selling the results somewhere. The days when you could write an article that would fit into any of a dozen general magazines are gone. Magazines are highly specialized and targeted for specific audiences. Even the so-called women's magazines which appear to be vying for the same market have subtle differences that govern their particular editorial content. One women's magazine, for example, may not want articles about children under a certain age. Another may want only articles that provide a service message. And these rules change; you must keep up with them to successfully sell to these markets.

Be familiar with the magazines you wish to write for was a message drilled into me ever since I attended my first writers' conference in 1971. One of the speakers described how he had cataloged 12 years of *Reader's Digest* articles on index cards. He did a lot of work, but since this magazine sometimes pays several thousand dollars for an article, such an investment was worthwhile for him.

I don't think it's necessary to be that familiar with a magazine's history; most writers and editors recommend studying this year's and last year's issues. For a well-paying magazine, research time can result in a healthy sale. For lesser paying markets, you can select magazines that interest you, and send for writer's guidelines if you need more specific information.

Without studying a magazine, you take the chance of looking like an amateur. I was embarrassed not long ago when I queried an airline magazine for a "destination" piece on Kenya. The editor wanted only articles on the destinations to which the airline flew—Cairo, Athens, London, and others, but not Nairobi. If I'm lucky, the editor won't remember my name the next time I pitch a piece; you can bet I'll do better research.

Develop Personal Contacts

I made one of my first sales to a magazine editor I met on a bus. We were in Philadelphia attending a large health meeting when he commented on the magazine dis-

Donna Buys Wilson *has been a writer for 15 years specializing in the medical and behavioral sciences. She is currently a contributing editor to* Physician's Weekly, *a Los Angeles correspondent for* Physicians' Radio Network, *and a frequent contributor to* Cardiology World News. *Her articles have appeared in* Family Circle, Glamour, Psychology Today, Parents, Health, Family Weekly, American Baby *and others.*

played on my name badge. We exchanged cards and follow-up letters. Many months later when I was contemplating a job change, I contacted him to see if he had any openings. He offered me a freelance assignment on a subject he knew I had expertise in. (I have a Bachelor of Science degree in nursing.)

Later when I was without a job, this same editor encouraged me to attend a cardiology meeting in Atlantic City. I dreaded driving there from New York City but forced myself. The meeting became a turning point in my writing career.

I was introduced to Duke Yates, managing editor of *Medical World News*, who invited me to send a résumé and writing samples.

By the next morning, I had my samples, résumé, and letter in the mail. A few days later, Yates invited me to lunch. By the end of the lunch, I had an assignment to write a piece on nurses.

Yates told me later he talks to dozens of writers each week who say they want to write for *Medical World News*, but most never follow up. He was impressed that I had sent the samples immediately and that I respected deadlines. I received more assignments and, within several months, was named a contributing editor.

Look for New Markets

Once I'd established myself with medical trade publications, I decided to try more competitive, higher-paying consumer markets. After seeing a National Institutes of Health symposium program on memory, I sent a query (a sales pitch), an outline and samples to the editor of *Family Health*, now *Health*. I realize now that my outline was too long; I'm fortunate that the editor didn't discard it. Instead, Caroline Stevens wrote me a polite letter: "Your suggestion for an article on memory is intriguing but a little unfocussed. I wonder if you could come up to the office sometime next week to discuss it in more detail."

After our talk, she sent me an outline to follow and a letter confirming the assignment. Her outline was half as long as mine and was very specific about points she wanted me to stress and questions I should research.

Soon after the *Family Health* article on memory was published, the editor of *Glamour* asked if I'd write a similar one for her magazine. Such assignments led to more assignments with those and other magazines.

What to Write

Ideas are everywhere, but developing them into salable articles takes patience, research and imagination. "Think of a gimmick," advised the late Mort Weisenger, a founding member of the American Society of Journalists and Authors (and a role model for me). For example, you can take any question of importance and call ten or more experts to comment on it. He did a roundup article—ten college professors tell the one mistake parents make in preparing their children for college.

One day Weisenger was listening to a talk show. A former Miss America said she uses Vaseline on her teeth to make them gleam. This led to an article, "What T.V. Doesn't Tell You About the Miss America Contest." He then wrote the novel, *The Contest*.

I once got an idea while reading the sports section of the newspaper—something I rarely do. A headline about a bionic arm of a Dodger baseball player caught my eye. The article was about an operation performed on Tommy John, then a Dodger pitcher. The surgeon was someone I had interviewed two weeks earlier on another subject for Physicians' Radio Network. I got the assignment from *Family Weekly* to write a human-interest story about a baseball player's comeback.

Give Editors What They Want

Editors have very definite ideas about what they want to publish, how they want to handle it, and when they feel it's appropriate to publish it. That doesn't mean you can't give them ideas. Your ideas have to be ones that are potential editorial material for the magazine you're pitching, and you must do your research on that magazine. Give editors fantastic ideas and don't feel badly if they don't use them all. They will realize your potential and assign to you the ideas they want to see as articles.

I don't argue with editors about the content of an article. If they want an article written a certain way, including or excluding certain information, follow their instructions. They know more about the magazine and their readers than you do. And they are paying the bill. Of course, if they have an idea that's way off base, and you know it because of your expertise on a certain subject, tell them. What I usually do is get back to them after I've researched the point in question and tell them what I've discovered in my research. I realize that I'm not infallible; sometimes they have new information that I don't know about. Get all the facts before you argue with an editor on content.

Build an Article

Here are a few basic tips I use in structuring an article:

● To get the attention of readers, I start with a riveting or dramatic anecdote, a personal story that relates to the subject.

● At the beginning of the article (certainly within the first two or three paragraphs) I make a topic statement of what the article is about and what the reader can expect to learn. In my article on memory for *Glamour*, for example, I began with an anecdote about the murder of two girls and how the crime was solved when a witness remembered a license plate number through hypnosis. Soon after, I made the statement, "How the brain stores and retrieves information has been the subject of intensive study for years." I then described the research on how the brain stores and retrieves information.

● In the body of the article, prove your topic statement. I refer back to this statement often to avoid straying from the topic. You may be tempted to include very interesting information, but, if it's not related to your main theme, it will only distract the reader and weaken the article's structure.

● Conclude the article with a summary statement or paragraph on what has been covered.

Writing to sell takes practice, persistence, and perception on how the reader and editor will react to your words.

Writers and writing instructors will say that you can't teach someone how to write. Yet you *can* learn to pay attention to grammar and write sentences that are clear. Ask a friend or another writer if your message is understood; graciously accept comments.

Sell Your Writing Again and Again

Once you research a subject, think of angles that will work for different magazines. By rewriting the lead, you can sell essentially the same research. An article, for example, on how to buy a used car could be slanted differently and sold to many publications. One writer I know sells the same article to a dozen foreign markets.

Also, if you send samples of published articles with your queries for original articles, the editor might come back to you with a proposal that you write a completely different article on the same subject as one of your published samples.

Some magazines, like *Reader's Digest*, publish reprints. If you have a published article that might be appropriate for a reprint market, send it to the publication with a brief note. Editors will appreciate your thoughtfulness. Even if the editors don't reprint that article, it may lead to an assignment.

Writing Fiction: Silence, Exile and Cunning

BY L.M. ROSENBERG

I'm going to try answering a hard question: How does one write great and publishable fiction?

Let's say somebody squawks, "But I don't *care* about great fiction. I just want to write *publishable* stuff." That writer (I use the generic "he") is probably in the wrong field and certainly the wrong essay. When we fail to aspire, we fail; no good can come of it. No writer should aspire to mere publishability any more than a pianist ought to labor over "Chopsticks" or a chef devote his life to slamming out hamburger patties.

The squawker has assumed that great fiction *isn't* publishable. Certainly, it takes longer to write great fiction, and sometimes longer to sell, but great fiction has a longer life. In 1850, for instance, publication year of *The Scarlet Letter* and *Moby-Dick*, the runaway bestseller was *Helen's Babies*. So let's assume we *want* to write wonderful fiction—fiction that makes us laugh or cry or forget the time of day. How do we go about doing it? What weapons and tools does a writer have?

Stephen Dedalus, in *A Portrait of the Artist as a Young Man*, declares, "...I will try to express myself in some mode of life or art as freely as I can and as wholly as I can, using for my defense the only arms I allow myself to use—silence, exile and cunning."

This is a good place to begin: with silence, exile and cunning.

Silence

Silence comes first for the writer, and it is difficult. Silence requires patience, and most writers aren't naturally patient (or silent). The amateurish writer lunges at his stories, as if in mortal terror of the blank page. He has no skill in patience, no room for silence. He doesn't wait to see if, in fact, he must write at all or, more importantly, wait to discover *what* he must write, and what's important to him.

Unearthing material takes time and a certain genius for holding quietly attentive. Poet William Stafford says, "I get pen and paper, take a glance out of the window (often it is dark out there) and wait. It is like fishing."

Every fisherman knows that you can't catch a fish if you keep throwing beer cans and paper plates into the water. You can't listen while you're chattering. The fiction writer must listen to the world, be open to whatever is out there as well as what lies within. "To work in silence and with all one's heart, that is the writer's lot," says Sarah Orne Jewett, who wrote the classic, *The Country of the Pointed Firs*.

Sooner or later, every writer must relinquish personal ambition—that is, ambition for himself rather than the work. He must learn to forget what he's been taught to see and think, and think for himself; begin afresh.

L.M. Rosenberg *has worked at* The New Yorker, T.Y. Crowell Books, Redbook, *and various little magazines. She has published fiction, poetry and essays in publications such as* The Atlantic Monthly, The New York Times, *and* The New Republic. *Since 1979, she has taught creative writing at the State University of New York at Binghamton.*

Exile

I'm not advocating complete withdrawal from the world. Far from it. The writer of great fiction is unafraid of the world, as well as of himself. And in simple daily ways we all need company and help. There are benefits of a good writing workshop or literature class (a bad one may do more harm than nothing at all); a helpful conference or informal writer's group; a few trustworthy readers (no liars allowed); not to mention the whole community of writers around us, living and dead. We all need community.

Early in their careers, writers are encouraged to find this community in Tolstoy, Dickens, and Shakespeare. It would take a great dolt not to admire at least *one* of these writers. But in fairness to readers, we must write what we love to read. "No tears in the writer, no tears in the reader," Robert Frost warned. Let me turn that around. No pleasure for the writer, no pleasure for the reader.

Perhaps the one genius required of a writer is a genius for self-honesty. If you love Henry James or Batman comics, sitcoms or *Charlotte's Web*, acknowledge it, and make it part of your work, keeping in mind that *as* a writer, if nowhere else, we always aspire to be our own best self. Not the slouch half-comatose in front of the television, not the nasty fellow who snickers at off-color jokes, but the secret child-like self who has always remained true, for instance, to Swiss-Family-Robinson-type adventure stories.

This sounds easier than it is. We are always being told whom to admire or study or imitate, instructed about "what sells"—which always means "what sold last year." And even worse than other people's instructions and expectations are our own instructions and expectations for ourselves.

Novelist Bernard Malamud says most people want to *have written* a novel, not to actually write one. If you love the idea of being a writer, but loathe the act of writing, then writing is not for you. If you want instant success, writing isn't it. And if you yearn to be rich and, famous you'd be better off in a dozen other fields.

This doesn't mean we can't hope, pine or daydream. Writers make a living from fine-tuned daydreaming, what John Gardner called "the vivid and continuous dream." We may want to be rich, famous, wise, witty, to wear funny hats and have our pictures on the cover of the *New York Times Book Review* section, but when we sit down to write, we must leave that baggage behind. Otherwise, there is no room for the important daydreaming, the dream of the fiction itself. In a tale by Isak Dinesen, one character warns the character Marcus Corcoza, not to fret "too much about Marcus Corcoza," for to do so is to be "his slave and his prisoner." The writer must be free. To be attached to nothing but the truth—this is a form of exile that takes great courage and ability.

Cunning

Ability brings me, at last, to cunning. We speak of great writers as "masters of craft" and of great con men as "crafty." Cunning *is* craft; it is resourcefulness. A writer must dodge nimbly in and out of the great iron bars of grammar and syntax. He must learn to dissolve or construct a sentence, to move a character from Japan to Boise, to give an impression of speed or weight or breathlessness or panic to a string of chicken-tracks on a white page.

No one can be a great writer—and certainly not a published one—unless he's in command of his own language. Some writers must learn grammar explicitly, by studying good grammar books like W.W. Watt's *An American Rhetoric*, or by learning to diagram sentences, or giving themselves exercises (try those at the end of John Gardner's *The Art of Fiction*). Others learn intuitively, by osmosis. These are almost invariably life-long voracious readers. They know the best, most elegant way to craft a story because they've seen it a thousand times, by a thousand master craftsmen.

Skill is what's learnable—from great teachers, intuition, or books on writing like John Gardner's *On Becoming a Novelist*. There are even ways to learn how to use silence; Dorothea Brande has some suggestions in her book, *Becoming a Writer.* Cunning is the joke that saves Joyce's "silence, exile and cunning" from bitterness; it is the delight of the magician in his trick, the joy of doing a difficult thing with seeming ease.

Practical Advice

It is under the heading of cunning that it's possible to offer some practical advice about publishing. These are suggestions, not rules, and I only ask that you think twice before discarding all of them.

1) Don't publish before you're ready. How do you know? Some people never do, just as some poor souls walk around on Main Street in pink slip and yellow hat, feeling elegant. If you are the self-deluded type, at least you'll be happy with yourself, if sometimes frustrated by the doltish world.

Most of us only pretend to be deluded. We try to convince ourselves we're ready to publish before we are. Here are a few tests of fire: Read your fiction aloud to someone you not only like, but trust and admire. If the very idea scares you, you're not ready to publish. If, as you read aloud, you skim over certain awkward passages, your shoulders keep hunching toward your ears, or you find yourself breathless, thinking, "maybe this will get by, and he won't notice," then you need to revise your work before submitting it to editors.

2) Know the fiction markets. When I freelanced at *Redbook* years ago, reading unsolicited manuscripts, people sent everything from war novels to dirty limericks. Don't get the name of a magazine or book publisher from a list. Go to your local library and take time to browse among the periodicals. If you pick up a magazine and think, *Jeez, I can write better than this junk*—forget it. Tasteless editors are too tasteless to publish you. If you find a magazine you like and about which you can honestly say, *my work belongs here*, then you've found a potential market. A shortcut is to read through some yearly anthologies of fiction (*Best American Short Stories*, *The Pushcart Prize*) and when you find a story you love, look to see who published it. Chances are, you'll find yourself stopping at the same magazine time after time. Its address will be listed at the back of the book. Get hold of a few issues, or subscribe. If after reading the magazine you still feel you've found the right home for your work, submit it.

3) Learn to take *no* for an answer. If a magazine or book publisher keeps sending form rejection slips, he's really not interested. But if you get personal notes from the editor (as long as they're not accompanied by requests for large sums of money), keep trying until doomsday. Just make sure you wait sufficient intervals (a few *months*, not a few *days*) between efforts. No editor writes a personal note unless he means it. It takes time to correspond personally, and most editors don't waste time.

4) Write at least a few pages every day. Remember, if you don't write, you are not a writer. For some, five or six pages per day is a realistic goal. For others, it's two or three. I find this more helpful than setting aside periods of time, since with a page limit, you have *something* written in a day, whether it takes you fifteen minutes or five hours.

If two or three pages seem impossibly skimpy, consider this: If you write steadily, six days a week (even writers need a day's rest), in a week you'll have 12 to 18 pages. In a month you'll have at least 48 pages. Try *not* to revise while you're hammering out the first draft or at least work in long sections with breathing periods of re-reading and revising between bouts of steady writing. Always write a half page beyond your limit, such as two-and-a-half pages or four-and-a-half pages, so that when you sit down to work the next day, you already have *something* in front of you. If possible, limit your initial revising to that half page leftover from the day before. There's time to work on the fine detail later. This general method is the only way *I* know of to get through a novel, but every novelist is different.

5) Many short story writers worry about writing novels. They feel they *should* write one; I'm not sure why. Stanly Elkin defines a short story as an "acute" problem,

a novel as a "chronic" one. It's almost impossible to tell a novelist how to write a short story instead of a novel. Novelists tend to be long-winded, dreamy, rambling writers, forever digging to get at the bottom of something. Trying to turn a novelist into a short story writer is like trying to turn a bonfire into a firecracker.

Short story writers, on the other hand, sometimes do become novelists, and short stories themselves turn into novels. Your first clue is when the thing gets too long to be a short story; let's say 41 pages. When you go back to revise it, instead of making it more concise, you keep discovering things you left out, scenes you want to include, characters who demand their own brothers and sisters. Chances are you are writing a novel. The main thing is not to worry about it, either way. Most musicians don't yearn to be dancers. So it should be with short story writers and novelists.

6) Keep a writer's notebook. Push the Dear-Diary material down to a minimum. Record overheard scraps of conversation, place, names, dreams, bits of information, ideas, images and metaphors. Try to carry a small notebook with you wherever you go.

7) Never be afraid to know anything even if it proves your assumptions wrong—maybe *especially* if it does. Nothing that is possible to human nature should be a secret to the fiction writer. In the world of art, knowledge is power of the best kind.

8) Be true to the story. Fiction writing is a process of discovering truth. What matters is not your gorgeous prose, your pretty yellow hair, or the hope your grandfather had of a literary grandchild. What matters is the work itself. Writing is an exercise in human perfectability. *Aim* for perfection; try, in novelist Larry Woiwode's words, "to get it right." Then you will find yourself coming full circle at last from cunning back to silence.

"When the storyteller is loyal . . . to the story, there in the end, silence will speak. When the story has been betrayed, silence is but emptiness," (storyteller) Isak Dinesen wrote. "But we, the faithful, when we have spoken our last word, will hear the voice of silence."

What Editors Say . . .

The joy, definitely, is seeing the many days of nonstop work that go into a single monthly issue being "worth it" when the finished product appears. The irony is that it looks so effortless! Some writers lack an understanding of the volume of correspondence (queries, manuscripts, etc.) that is typical at a magazine such as ours, and display impatience when their idea or story is not given top priority.

—Lidia de Leon
Delta Sky Magazine

Remember when you are writing that you are speaking only to one person. Even if your feature will be read by millions, it's a matter of one-to-one contact between writer and individual reader.

—Tommie Pinkard
Texas Highways Magazine

Writers seem to miss the fact that editors are people who are in a position to know their market and are able (if they are unhampered) to make the writer look like a genius, by editing the work to a brilliant shine.

—Thomas A. Noton
The Christian Writer

There are only two reasons we read anything willingly: because it's significant or because it's funny.

—Jack Garlington
Western Humanities Review

We receive hundreds of *bad* query letters from illegible scrawled notes on a slip of note paper to poor photocopies with no address. Almost all have several grammar or spelling errors in the first sentence. They go in the trash. What makes these people think they can write a book if they can't write a letter?

—Steve Davis
Steve Davis Publishing

There is no such thing as writer's block. Simply put something—anything on paper—then you have something to revise.

—Advice from the editor of *Sunset Magazine*

What is usually missing when I reject a manuscript that *almost* fits my needs? The manuscript is frequently "too linear." The narrative runs from point A through point Z without exploring some of the psychological or social aspects of the adventure.

—George Thomas
Canoe Magazine

In personal experience pieces, the emphasis is on "unusual"—we receive literally dozens of "my favorite pet" stories per month, and the one striking thing about most of them is that they are all the same. I need to find the article that is different, the experience that is *not* shared by every reader, who have all had "their first dog," "their first show," or "their first dog death."

—Moira Anderson
Dog Fancy

A lot of manuscripts are flat. And if they're flat, there's nothing I can do with them—I can't rewrite for color.

—Robert Yates
ABA Journal

Once a writer has roughed out an article, he should go back and consider what reader response he hopes to evoke in each section of the story. The article should then be revised to capture those emotions and reactions, so it builds block by block to the ending.

—Elinor Allcott Griffith
Reader's Digest

"Cute" does not substitute for quality.

—Shirley P. Rogers
Roseburg Woodsman

The deadline monster sits on my right shoulder and the rewrite monster on my left. Between them the brain is sorting material while the mouth and ear are busy answering the phone. The right hand is writing and the left hand is searching for that letter the eyes saw just a moment ago . . . the one necessary for a speedy conclusion to the phone call . . .ad infinitum.

—Barbara A. Johnston
Pro/Comm

When I reject a manuscript that *almost* fits my needs, what is usually missing?. . .A selection of quotes from a broad cross-section of people *in* the industry to buttress points made in the article.

—Jerry Roche
HBJ Publications

All too frequently in today's pressured academic environment, manuscripts are submitted for publication too soon; the authors have not thoroughly digested their material nor spent the necessary time polishing their arguments or their writing.

—Cynthia Miller
Catholic University Press

Although *Omni* is the top-paying market in science fiction and the competition *is* tough, I encourage unpublished writers to submit their manuscripts. I *do* publish unknowns. So far this year I've published two first stories. Although at first you probably will get form rejections, if you keep at it, chances are, you'll eventually start getting personal letters, advice from me on other markets, and possibly a critique.

—Ellen Datlow
Omni Magazine

Editors have one primary goal: Make the writer's copy more exciting, interesting, and applicable to the readers' needs.

—Robert Walker
Christian Life

I think more writers need a sense of story—you're not writing a piece, you're telling a story. Give the editor a story line to follow—not a "just the facts, ma'am" series of paragraphs.

—Knute Berger
Washington Magazine

We deal with author's agents, but I tend not to publish material submitted by agents. I would rather use *Oui* as a forum for unproven talent that needs one or two opportunities to get started. Of the 12 or so fiction pieces *Oui* publishes per year, 11 or more were unsolicited.

—Barry Janoff
Oui Magazine

Write to the needs of the magazine. If you are not comfortable with its requirements, then don't write for it.

—Phyllis Starr Wilson
Self Magazine

Learn to adapt to a wide range of styles. When you get an assignment, write it in the magazine's style, rather than depending upon the magazine to adapt to yours. Magazines are no longer showcases for writers' talents. They have a perspective. The writer must adapt.

—Coleman A. Lollar
Frequent Flyer

Most often absent from an unsalvageable near-miss is a simple item ignored in our editorial guidelines. For instance, my lead time for manuscripts is about seven months, and if an entire feature is geared to the wrong time, I just can't use it, no matter how good it is.

—Art Michaels
Pennsylvania Angler

My favorite writers are the ones who study our style—right down to whether we say "Dr." or "MD"—and submit manuscripts that don't need a lot of fine tuning from us. My favorites of the favorite writers are the ones who take the time to come up with a clever or witty title for their pieces, one that we can use.

—Joan Lippert
Health Magazine

Read your copy as if you are the last to see it. Don't assume editors up the line will catch spelling errors, typos, or other problems. A simple spelling error can call into question how careful a writer or reporter you are.

—Renie Schapiro
The New Physician

Some writers reflect the two-dimensional cardboard characteristics in their writing much in the same way some screenwriters do when building their characterizations. They're phony—thus, they have no depth—they're not three-dimensional.
—Gerald J. LePage
The American Screenwriter

Manuscripts have come to us with every other word misspelled or typos in every paragraph. I don't feel like editing an entire story to where it becomes my story instead of theirs.

—Lee Darrigrand
Western & English Fashions

The topic may be fine, but if *a lot* of editing needs to be done, the manuscript is returned. Most rejected manuscripts that almost fit our needs are usually missing any of the following considerations: topic, timeliness of article, neatness, or good command of the English language.

—Rhonda Wilson
National Research Bureau

The joys and frustrations of being an editor center on the fact that I do everything—from deciding what goes into each issue to researching and writing some of the articles, soliciting/accepting and editing all the others, doing every layout and some of the art, selecting and cropping photos, copyfitting and adjusting to space limits, pasting up, proofreading, and ordering each contributor's check.

—Earl V. Fischer
American Drycleaner

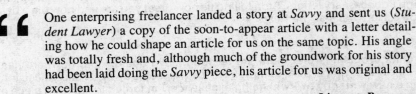

One enterprising freelancer landed a story at *Savvy* and sent us (*Student Lawyer*) a copy of the soon-to-appear article with a letter detailing how he could shape an article for us on the same topic. His angle was totally fresh and, although much of the groundwork for his story had been laid doing the *Savvy* piece, his article for us was original and excellent.

Lizanne Poppens
Student Lawyer

What Agents Say . . .

Buying tendencies are influenced by so many things that authors should just go about their business of writing what they want to write and worry about the market later, or not at all. Hot, trendy subjects get attention, then glut the market and burn themselves out. Literature is the only staple. Fine writing is the only criteria.

—David L. Meth

The problem is screening clients to find genuine new talent—writers who can write what is wanted today, not those under the illusion that they can write the Great American Novel on the first try.

—Daniel P. King

Go to as many agents as you have to—to evoke interest. Don't try to nag a reluctant agent into representing you; similarly, don't use bribes of various kinds (including thinly-veiled or not-veiled sexual offers) or gimmicks. Multiple submissions are fine, but make them look individually written. Never, never refer to a personal letter from a publisher as a "rejection slip."

—James Seligmann Agency

The primary communication between the agent and the author is the query letter. A clear, provocative and brief query letter goes a long way toward making that author rememberable. Immediately, it will induce us to read some pages (perhaps a chapter) of the material submitted, and this, of course, is the acid test. From our point of view, there is no inducement that takes the place of good writing.

—James Warren

Writers generally do not fully appreciate the fact that agents work on speculation and therefore the time invested by the agent is frequently not commensurate with the commission if there is a sale.

—Gloria Stern Agency

Ultimately, it is the love affair between the agent and his material that motivates him to seek far and wide for the right market. "Romancing" an agent (gifts and wining and dining) is of no value whatever. It is only first-rate talent and craftsmanship that counts, and those things are self-evident.

—Alice Hilton

Most editors know that literary agents are a necessary evil, needing us to screen manuscripts for them so they can operate; writers should realize that we are business people and don't have the time to spend hours on the phone or in reading and answering unnecessary letters. Stop telling us how great you are and how big a bestseller you have. That's all we hear.

—Gene Lovitz

My chief problem is that there are far too many hopefuls and nowhere near enough time. For the most part, I simply have to turn people away. If I am enticed into taking on a new writer by overwhelming excellence, I'm forced to lop off a piece of deadwood, to make room.

—Virginia Kidd

Having been a writer, I'm not in favor of reading fees. My feeling on critiques for a fee is that most of the time the writer would be better off enrolling in an adult education writing course at any university, where for a fee much smaller than for a critique, one can usually get 12 weeks of advice and help.

—Ray Peekner Literary Agency

Editors should approach agents, as well as the other way around. Writers should realize that agents are very busy and work on speculation.

—Jane Jordan Browne

We are in the middle of a communications revolution that must affect books but how or how soon is impossible to predict.

—Frances Collin

In nonfiction, we find that writers seldom do enough advance research to determine if their treatment of a subject is fresh and original compared to books already published.

—James Heacock

Unknown writers are not too popular these days, unless they can produce exciting material and fresh slants.

—Ann Elmo

 Alex Haley said he was totally intimidated by his first book. He had been writing magazine articles, and the idea of a book—400 pages instead of 3,000 words—was frightening. But then he figured that each chapter in a book is like a magazine article. He knew how to write a magazine article, he said, so he just wrote each chapter in his book as if it were a magazine article.

What Writers Say . . .

Every unpublished writer is convinced that there is a malevolent conspiracy to prevent his getting that first needed major byline. It's a comparatively harmless paranoia. You *will* get that first needed byline.

—Murray Teigh Bloom

Writing is a very private business. You can share your frustrations with other writers, but the work is your own. No one can do it for you, and no one will ever know how much you struggle with every single idea you publish.

—Shirley Biagi

Hiring an agent is the sort of problem a beginning writer should *not* think about. Don't waste your mental energy worrying about agents—concentrate on finding yourself and what you care about and improving your style and, above all, studying the writers you admire.

—Maurice Zolotow

I go to as great a length to secure payment as any other professional who has rendered services and not been paid. It seems to me that as long as writers lie down and let themselves be walked on, we'll have editors who pirate our work.

—Lee Jolliffe

My favorite quote is: "Inspiration may strike unexpectedly but I like to be sitting at my desk every day so that I don't miss its arrival."

—Evelyn Kaye

Write only about topics that you feel passionate about. Unless you really care, your readers won't care.

—Karen O'Connor

Writers must be professional about their writing if they expect to sell. Vanity is best left to the Victorians. Today's writer must be willing to put in his or her time to learn the *skills* first. Today's writer must present his or her material in a professional manner to the proper market . . . and be prepared to suffer criticism, slights, isolation and late payments. If writers don't enjoy the process, they should be word processors or computer specialists.

—Annie Moldafsky

" The advice that helped me break into a freelancing career came from Ellen Stein, editor of *Ohio Magazine*. I had been a "closet" writer for years. Stein suggested (at a writers' roundtable) that aspiring freelancers aim a little lower. Don't expect to sell a full-length feature to an editor who's never worked with you before, she said. Target a short piece to an appropriate section of the magazine. Editors are much more willing to risk a small piece falling through than a major one. (It worked. I sold *Ohio* a short piece on an all-mysteries bookstore and less than a year later, I was freelancing fulltime.) "

The Markets

Book Publishers ⸺⸺⸺⸺⸺

Two sorts of writers possess genius:
those who think and those who cause others to think.
　　　　　　　　　　　　　　　　—Roux

Are you thinking about writing a book? Then think, by putting words on paper. Every book starts this way. Slowly at first, but soon you have a first draft to rewrite. You revise, enhance, and sometimes delete your favorite thoughts and lines. This careful thinking shapes your book.

But the thinking doesn't stop when you write the last chapter. Another more objective type of thinking must take over when you try to sell your work—you must think like a business person. "Creativity is only part of the process for the writer who wants to share his literary genius," said one writer who uses *Writer's Market*. "He must shed his artistic mantle and don the three-piece tailoring of a salesperson."

Too often writers think publishers should be eager to consider a book that has taken so much effort and time to write. But your book must cause editors to think—and to think that now is the time for this book to be in print. Your approach must be logical as a story plot and self-reliant as a character who braves staggering odds. Editors don't have time for writers crying in the transom.

An estimated 47,000 new books will go to press this year. Yours can be one of them—if you think of new ways to touch readers and editors.

When we asked editors and literary agents what kind of year 1986 would be for the book industry, we received mixed reactions. One agent said, "1986 will be a poor year and for some years to come. All of the publishers combined, even though they yearly gross over seven billion (an inflationary figure meaning how poorly they are doing instead of how well), can't even outgross one fast-food company in a maze of many."

Still, few writers and publishers would trade books for hamburgers. "I think any year is a good year to sell a marketable book and any year is a bad one to sell one that's not marketable," said another agent.

Everyone in the industry agrees, though, on one point: There is time, energy, and interest any year for *great* books. While the average book may sell 5,000 to 10,000 copies annually, great books buck the averages. At the same time, there are books that are never called *great*, but they delight and teach readers—and continue to be stocked on bookstore shelves over the years. What is important is that you write what you think and feel with the market and an audience in mind. Those are the books that sell.

Trends that may affect what editors buy this year include the following:

• self-help and how-to books. They continue to be popular as readers turn to books to learn everything from how to deal with depression to how to write a will. If your occupation specializes in a subject that affects readers' lives, editors will be interested. Too many writers want to write books on subjects that they are *only familiar with*, you *must know* the subject you want to write about.

• computer books. The field has moved from "jump on the bandwagon" to more realistic thinking. Now, companies have statistics based on book sales to decide which computer books sell best. Readers have more expertise in computers than they did five years ago. The need for neophyte computer books has somewhat leveled off. Publishers, though, still want books that convey technical details in an interesting, accurate way. Companies, like Tandy Corp., will pay a generous amount for the *right* book.

• technical books. Professionals in most fields rely on books to supplement their educations and to learn more about their trades. Observed one publisher, "Technical books tend to be more specialized and must offer solid information to compete."

• books about and by *celebrities* or "experts" in a field. People like to read about people, especially those they see on movie and television screens. Simon & Schuster's plans to publish a magazine loosely based on "Entertainment Tonight" indicates that celebritydom is still at a peak.

• books as films and docudramas. Book publishers can't help but think of possible movie and television rights when they find a captivating story. Viewers are seeing current and pre-TV-days books on the screen such as *Lace* and *Anna Karenina*. "Many areas are opening up in subsidiary rights, such as audio and video," observed one agent.

• fiction. Though mysteries usually have a constant readership, there has been a noticeable surge of interest in the last year. Publishers are also showing more interest in science fiction and fantasy with occasional new imprints for them. (Science fiction purists are seeing more fantasy than science in science fiction.) Many science fiction novels are now regarded as mainstream books. Of course, publishers are always looking for the listbuster mainstream novel.

• romance. Romance readers are seeing a shift to inspirational romances and romantic intrigue. Another development in the field is Dell Publishing's and other companies' initiation of women's fiction programs. Some publishers are encouraging well-developed genre and mainstream romances that don't follow a formula.

• books for young people. Some young adult publishers have created new imprints which encompass multiple/reader choice books and problem novels. Other publishers are looking for pre-school books that can help parents teach their children.

• headline-inspired books. Many readers want extensions of news articles in book form; others want to read investigative findings on various topics. In either case, people are curious about front-page news, such as terrorism, espionage and medical breakthroughs. If a writer can approach these subjects from an informed and well-thought-out viewpoint, there may be a market for the book.

• the next craze. Writers can start a trend or shift one to another level of awareness. Your day-to-day contact with people sometimes tells you what is important and what is lacking in peoples' lives. A book that caters to these concerns will be worth the cover price for readers and publishers.

Of course, the kinds of books that will sell best in 1986 or 1987 remain to be seen. There is probably an author somewhere (you?) who is writing a book that doesn't fit in any category; the book could be next season's favorite. That's the magic of the industry.

No matter what type of book you've written, this Book Publisher section can help you contact editors. You'll find more than 800 publishers who want writers to contact them. Not all publishers buy the kind of work you write, but the Subject Index for nonfiction and fiction will tell you which ones do.

Reading each listing, you can select two or three publishers that buy what you're writing. Send for catalogs and manuscript preparation guidelines from these publishers. Read a couple of their books. Once you decide on a specific publisher, try to find out the editor assigned to your subject area (sometimes a receptionist will give out this information), then address your submission to this editor. In most cases, submit queries and manuscripts to the editor whose name appears in the listing.

Some writers study publishing companies as if they were going to submit a sealed bid to a construction firm. Not all bids will earn a contract, but you'll want to know a prospective publisher before making contact. Know whether a publisher produces books on a royalty or subsidy basis. (The difference may affect your bank account.) Because many writers don't do this pre-selling research, you'll have an advantage if you do so. Of course, knowledge about a company won't sell a poor product.

One drawback to authors is that each publisher prefers a different way of receiving submissions. Some want complete manuscripts; some want outlines/synopses and sample chapters; others want a one-page proposal. Publishers in this book tell you what they prefer; follow each publisher's guidelines. Don't expect an editor to make exceptions for *your* book. Think like an editor—who has stacks of books and proposals in front of him.

Subsidy Publishers

When you've been submitting the most important thing in your life—your book—to publishers, nonresponses and rejections become discouraging. Sometimes writers receive a letter from an editor complimenting the book, but also saying, "With the current economic conditions in book publishing, we would like you to share some of the risks involved. . . ." The company asks for $1,000 or, say, $5,000.

The editor's note is not the acceptance letter you had dreamed of, but it isn't a rejection slip either. What does a writer do?

Before answering this editor's letter, you'll want to analyze the contract terms and the company offering them. Actually, it's best to do this analysis before you submit a manuscript. A publisher can launch or limit your book's potential. Only you, who know the book best, can make the decision. Here are some considerations to help you decide.

Most publishers pay writers for a book through a royalty arrangement. Authors receive anywhere from 3 to 25 percent of the wholesale or retail price. These publishers, who don't ask writers to subsidize the costs, need books that will sell to a special-interest audience or to the general book buyer.

We encourage writers to work with publishers that pay writers for their work. "If the publisher has already received a lot of money from the author, there's no incentive for him to spend any of his profit selling the book to the general public," said *Literary Markets* newsletter editor/publisher Bill Marles. We have placed asterisks in front of "subsidy" book publishers, so you know which publishers ask writers to share the publishing risks for a book.

Sometimes, though, a "royalty" publisher will offer a subsidy arrangement to an author whose talent outweighs the marketing potential of a book. In the listings you'll find out what percentage of titles has been subsidy published and sometimes how a publisher chooses the titles to be subsidy published. This percentage tells you whether the publisher is predominately a royalty or subsidy publisher. Publishers whose work is one-hundred percent subsidized by writers are listed after the "royalty" publishers.

Some publishers require a subsidy but don't expect the writer to pay this cost. "A writer should seek subsidy publishing when the content is important, but the sales are not large enough to enable a publisher to recover the initial investment," pointed out Herbert H. Lambert of CBP Press. "We do this for about one or two books in ten, and the subsidy usually comes from friends, foundations, or church agencies.''

In some countries, Canada for example, books are subsidized by government grants.

When you discuss a subsidy arrangement with a publisher, find out what terms would be in *your* contract. The problem is that often there are too many terms for the concept of subsidy publishing and too few explanations as to how each arrangement will affect the writer and the book.

"Subsidy publishing makes possible the publication of books that meet rigorous quality criteria; vanity publishing puts out anything that the author is willing to pay for,'' commented one book publisher.

Writers who call the *Writer's Market* office often ask if a publisher is a subsidy or vanity press. We don't distinguish between the two terms; we call any publishing effort that asks the writer for all or part of the costs—a subsidy publisher.

Recently, we've been hearing about publishers who call themselves self-publishers. They call subsidy publishing a racket and claim to offer an alternative. "Self-publishing doesn't seem to carry the same 'taint' as subsidized publishing, and I know of more successes among self-published books than subsidized ones,'' said Sanford G. Thatcher, editor-in-chief of Princeton University Press. "Self-publishing is probably preferable to subsidized publishing, although the only difference is that the latter involves paying someone else to do what one undertakes to do oneself in self-publishing.''

Writers can approach a small press publisher and agree to split the cost of a press run. Another option is to contract with a local printer for such-and-such-a-price. Many printers produce books for families, companies, foundations and churches. If you choose this route, though, you'll need to promote and distribute your book. Otherwise, your den, dining room or closets will become warehouses for your book.

"Done properly, self-publishing is an exciting and viable way to get your book into print,'' say Marilyn and Tom Ross, authors of *The Complete Guide to Self-Publishing* (Writer's Digest Books).

No matter which publishing route you choose for your book, remember that the writing of a good book comes first. Again, if you want to sell your work, write with the reader and market in mind. After all, that's what publishing means—writing for a public.

Also, don't spend years writing a book and only a few days looking for a publisher. Give that book the best publisher possible. For some writers, *the best* is a publisher whose books constantly appear on bestseller lists. For others, *the best* is a small press where each author gets personal attention from the editor.

You must decide. The choice is tough but can be fun, too. Haven't you always dreamed of the time when you had a book or book idea to sell? Yes? Then enjoy and *think* positively.

ABBEY PRESS, St. Meinrad IN 47577. (812)357-8011. Publisher: Keith McClellan, O.S.B. Publishes original paperbacks. Averages 8 titles/year; receives 600 submissions annually. 50% of books from first-time authors; 100% of books from unagented writers. Average print order for a writer's first book is 10,000. Pays definite royalty on net sales. Publishes book an average of 1 year after acceptance. Computer printout submissions acceptable; prefers letter-quality to dot-matrix. Query with outline and sample chapter. Reviews artwork/photos. Reports in 3 weeks. SASE.

Nonfiction: "Books that contribute to the healing, support, enrichment, and celebration of marriage and family life through the application of Judeo-Christian values. Manuscripts on personal, marital, and family spirituality

---

*Asterisk preceding a listing indicates that individual subsidy publishing or co-publishing (where author pays part or all of publishing costs) is also available. Those firms that specialize in total subsidy publishing are listed at the end of the book publishers' section.

sought particularly. Perspective must be Roman Catholic and/ or Mainline Christian."
Recent Nonfiction Title: *Goodbye, My Son, Hello,* by Adolfo Quezada.
Tips:"Anything in the area of Christian spirituality as it relates to individuals and their interpersonal relationships sells best. We expect substance and clarity in all submissions."

ABINGDON PRESS, 201 8th Ave. S., Box 801, Nashville TN 37202. (615)749-6403. Director of Publishing: Ronald P. Patterson. Director, Support Services: Robert Hill, Jr. Executive Editor Trade Books: R. Donald Hardy. Senior Editor/Reference Books: Carey J. Gifford. Editor of Lay Books: Mary Ruth Howes. Editor of Family Books: Ernestine Calhoun. Publishes paperback originals and reprints; church supplies. Published 100 titles last year; receives approximately 725 submissions annually. 95% of books from unagented writers. Average print order for a writer's first book is 4,000-5,000. Pays royalty. Publishes book an average of 18 months after acceptance. Electronic submissions OK—"we have a Shaffstall converter and like to receive sample diskettes early." Computer printout submissions acceptable; prefers letter-quality to dot-matrix. Query with outline and samples. Write for ms submission guide. Reports in 6 weeks. SASE.
Nonfiction: Religious-lay and professional, children's books and academic texts. Length: 32-300 pages.
Recent Nonfiction Title: *Solid Living in a Shattered World,* by William H. Hinson.
Fiction: Juveniles only. Reviews artwork/photos.
Recent Fiction Title: *When James Allen Whitaker's Grandfather Came to Stay,* by Martha Whitmore Hickman.
Tips: "A short, pithy book is ahead of the game. Long, rambling books are a luxury few can afford. Religious nonfiction work geared to church professionals is the area in which we see our best sales."

HARRY N. ABRAMS, INC., Subsidiary of Times Mirror Co. 100 5th Ave., New York NY 10011. (212)206-7715. President, Publisher and Editor-in-Chief: Paul Gottlieb. Publishes hardcover and "a few" paperback originals. Averages 65 titles/year; receives "thousands" of submissions annually. 5% of books from first-time authors; 25% of books from unagented writers. "We are one of the few publishers who publish almost exclusively illustrated books. We consider ourselves the leading publishers of art books and high-quality artwork in the US." Offers variable advance. Publishes book an average of 1-2 years after acceptance. Photocopied submissions OK. Computer printout submissions acceptable; no dot-matrix. SASE. Reports in 3 months. Free book catalog.
Nonfiction: Art, nature and science, and outdoor recreation. Needs illustrated books for art and art history, museums. Submit outline/synopsis and sample chapters and illustrations. Reviews artwork/photos.
Recent Nonfiction Title: *Renoir, His Life, Art, and Letters,* by Barbara Ehrlich White.
Tips:"We publish *only* high-quality illustrated art books. i.e., art, art history, museum exhibition catalog, written by specialists and scholars in the field. Once the author has signed a contract to write a book for our firm the author must finish the manuscript to agreed-upon high standards within the schedule in the contract."

ACADEMY CHICAGO, 425 N. Michigan Ave., Chicago IL 60611. (312)644-1723. Editorial Director/ Senior Editor: Anita Miller. Publishes hardcover and paperback originals and reprints. Averages 40 titles/year; receives approximately 1000 submissions annually. 3% of books from first-time authors; 25% of books from unagented writers. Average print order for a writer's first book 1,500-3,500. Pays 7-10% royalty; no advance. Publishes book an average of 1 year after acceptance. Photocopied submissions OK. Computer printout submissions acceptable; no dot-matrix. Reports in 2 months. SASE.
Nonfiction: Adult, travel, and historical. No how-to, cookbooks, self-help, etc. Query and submit first four consecutive chapters. Reviews artwork/photos.
Recent Nonfiction Title: *Young Man in Paris,* by John Weld.
Fiction: "Mysteries, Mainstream novels." No "romantic" fiction, or religious or sexist material; nothing avant-garde. "We can no longer do children's books or young adults."
Recent Fiction Title: *Everything in the Garden,* by Elizabeth North.
Tips: "We are very interested in good nonfiction history and biography. We are also interested in quality fiction and will consider once-published books that deserve reprinting."

ACCENT BOOKS, A division of Accent Publications, 12100 W. 6th Ave., Box 15337, Denver CO 80215. (303)988-5300. Managing Editor: Mary B. Nelson. Publishes evangelical Christian paperbacks, the majority of which are nonfiction (including teacher training books), though superior fiction books are considered if they contain underlying Christian message. Averages 18 titles/year; receives 500-550 submissions annually. 30% of books from first-time authors; 100% of books from unagented writers. Average print order for a writer's first book is 5,000-10,000. Pays royalty on cover price. Publishes book an average of 9 months after acceptance. Computer printout submissions acceptable; no dot-matrix. SASE. Query or submit 2 sample chapters and a brief synopsis of each chapter, together with contents page. Do not submit full ms unless requested. Reports in 3 months. Ms guidelines for SASE.
Recent Nonfiction Title: *Missing.*

Recent Fiction Title: *The Man Who Would Kill God.*
Tips: "We issue very few contracts on the basis of unwritten work."

ACE SCIENCE FICTION, The Berkley Publishing Group, 200 Madison Ave., New York NY 10016. (212)686-9820. Publishes paperback originals and reprints. Publishes 120 titles/year.
Fiction: Science fiction and fantasy. Query with outline and 3 sample chapters. Reports in 3 months. SASE.

ACROPOLIS BOOKS, LTD., Subsidiary of Colortone Press, 2400 17th St. NW, Washington DC 20009. (202)387-6805. Publisher: Alphons J. Hackl. Publishes hardcover and trade paperback originals. Averages 25 titles/year. Pays individually negotiated royalty. Publishes book an average of 7 months after acceptance. Electronic submissions OK, but requires hard copy also. Computer printout submissions acceptable; prefers letter-quality to dot-matrix. SASE. Reports in 2 months. Free book catalog.
Nonfiction: How-to, reference and self-help. Subjects include health, beauty/fashion and money management. "We will be looking for manuscripts dealing with fashion and beauty, and self development. We also will be continuing our teacher books for early childhood education. Our audience includes general adult consumers, professional elementary school teachers and children." Submit outline/synopsis and sample chapters. Reviews artwork/photos as part of ms package.
Recent Nonfiction Title: *Earn College Credit for What You Know*, by Susan Simosko.

ACS PUBLICATIONS, INC., Box 16430, San Diego CA 92116-0430. (619)297-9203. Editorial Director: Maritha Pottenger. Publishes trade paperback originals and reprints. Averages 10 titles/year; receives 400 submissions annually. 50% of books from first-time authors; 95% of books from unagented writers. Average print order for a writer's first book is 3,000. Pays 15-20% royalty "on monies received through wholesale and retail sales." No advance. Publishes book an average of 18 months after acceptance. Photocopied submissions OK "if neat." Electronic submissions OK if CP/M compatible with Cromemco, DEC VT180, IBM CPM-86, Osborne, and Xerox (5¼" diskettes; 9 track, 800 bpi, ½ inch magnetic tape; ASCII also acceptable). Prefers hard copy first to evaluate. Computer printout submissions acceptable; prefers letter-quality to dot-matrix. SASE. Reports in 1 month on queries; 2 months on mss. Free book catalog. Writer's guidelines for 9x12 SAE and 4 first class stamps.
Nonfiction: Self-help, astrology and New Age. Subjects include holistic health alternatives, psychology, numerology, and psychic understanding. "Our most important market is astrology. We are seeking pragmatic, useful, immediately applicable contributions to field; prefer psychological approach. Specific ideas and topics should enhance people's lives. Research also valued. No determinism ('Saturn made me do it.') No autobiographies. No airy-fairy 'space cadet' philosophizing. Keep it grounded, useful, opening options (not closing doors) for readers." Query or submit outline/synopsis and 3 sample chapters.
Recent Nonfiction Title: *Expanding Astrology's Universe*, by Zipporah Dobyns.
Tips: "Our readers are astrology students and professionals plus the general public interested in increased fulfillment through nontraditional paths." The writer has the best chance of selling a book on astrological topics compatible with our philosophy of personal responsibility. We are not interested in fatalistic books."

BOB ADAMS, INC., 840 Summer St., Boston Ma 02127. (617)268-9570. Contact: Submissions Editor. Publishes hardcover and trade paperback originals and software. Averages 10 titles/year. Pays variable royalty. Publishes book an average of 3 months after acceptance. Simultaneous and photocopied submissions OK. Electronic submissions OK, but requires hard copy also. Computer printout submissions acceptable. SASE. Reports in 1 month on queries; 2 months on mss.
Nonfiction: Specializes in career and job-hunting books. "We are interested in seeing outlines of all manuscripts related to careers, career planning, and job-hunting. We have also published books in other subject areas and will consider titles in all categories of nonfiction. Submit query first and only send manuscript upon request. We cannot assume responsibility for unsolicited manuscripts." Reviews artwork/photos as part of ms package.
Recent Nonfiction Title: *The Greater Atlanta Job Bank*, by Adams and Fiedler (local employment guide in series).

‡AFFIRMATION BOOKS, 22 The Fenway, Boston MA 02215. (617)266-8792. Executive Editor: Marie Kraus. Publishes trade paperback originals. Publishes 4 titles/year; receives 50 submissions annually. 50% of books from first-time authors; 100% of books from unagented writers. Pays 5-10% royalty on retail or wholesale price. Publishes book an average of 1 year after acceptance. Simultaneous and photocopied

 The double dagger before a listing indicates that the listing is new in this edition. New markets are often the most receptive to freelance contributions.

submissions OK. Computer printout submissions acceptable; no dot-matrix. SASE. Reports in 3 weeks on queries; 2 months on mss. Book catalog for #10 SAE and 1 first class stamp.

Nonfiction: Self-help. Subjects include psychology (combined with religion) and religion (combined with psychology; Christian, no dogma). "Affirmation Books is part of the ministry of the House of Affirmation, international therapeutic residential centers for clergy and religious suffering from emotional unrest (not alcohol or drug problems). We need books for an audience that is primarily clergy and religious or lay people working in or for the church. Topics on healthy emotional living that will help people improve the quality of their lives. Not pop psychology; some research or mention of previous literature in the field." No personal journeys, alcohol or drug problems, or books aimed at parents only. Query or submit outline/synopsis and sample chapters. Reviews artwork/photos.

Recent Nonfiction Title: *Midlife Wanderer: The Woman Religious in Midlife Transition*, by Sheila Murphy.

Tips: "We are primarily a mail-order business although we are looking to expand our bookstore outlets. Because we have a specific audience, clergy, men and women religious, lay people, none of our backlist has gone out of print. We are interested in expanding our audience."

AGLOW PUBLICATIONS, A ministry of Women's Aglow Fellowship International, Box 1, Lynnwood WA 98046-1557. (206)775-7282. Editor: Gwen Weising. Publishes mass market paperback originals. Averages 10 titles/year, receives 100 submissions annually. 50% of books from first-time authors; 100% of books from unagented writers. Average print order of a writer's first book is 10,000. Pays up to $7^1/_2$% maximum royalty on retail price "depending on amount of editorial work needed"; buys some mss outright. No advance. Publishes book 1 year after acceptance. Photocopied submissions OK. Computer printout submissions acceptable; prefers letter-quality to dot-matrix. SASE. Reports in 1 month on queries; 2 months on mss. Free book catalog. Guidelines for SASE.

Nonfiction: Bible studies, self-help and cookbooks. Subjects include religion (Christian only). Familiarize yourself with our materials before submitting. Our needs and formats are very specific." Query or submit outline/synopsis and first 3 sample chapters.

Recent Nonfiction Title: *Forgiveness—A Two-way Street*, by JoAnne Sekowsky.

Fiction: "We are a Christian women's publishing house and are looking for manuscripst for both teenage girls and women. No secular material or material directed toward a men's audience." Query or submit outline/synopsis and sample chapters.

Tips: "Our books are largely bought by evangelical, charismatic Christian women, although many, especially cookbooks, have a much larger audience."

AHSAHTA PRESS, Boise State University, Dept. of English, 1910 University Dr., Boise ID 83725. (208)385-1246. Co-Editor: Tom Trusky. Publishes trade paperback originals. Averages 3 titles/year. Pays 25% royalty on retail price. "Royalty commences with third printing." Publishes books an average of 10 months after acceptance. Simultaneous and photocopied submissions OK. Computer printout submissions acceptable; prefers letter-quality to dot-matrix. SASE. Reports in 2 weeks on queries; 3 months on mss.

Poetry: Contemporary Western American (cultural ecological or historical) poetry collections. No "rhymed verse, songs of the sage, buckaroo ballads, purple mountain's majesty, coyote wisdom; Jesus-in-the-prairie, or 'nice' verse." Accepts poetry translations from native American languages, Spanish and Basque. Submit 15 samples with SASE between February and April. "Write incredible, original poetry."

Recent Poetry Title: *The Dark Is A Door*, by Susan Deal (Pushcart prizewinner).

ALASKA NORTHWEST PUBLISHING CO., Box 4-EEE, Anchorage AK 99509. Editor and Publisher: Robert A. Henning. Publishes primarily paperback originals. Averages 12 titles/year. Most contracts call for 10% royalty. "Rejections are made promptly, unless we have three or four possibilities in the same general field, and it's a matter of which one gets the decision. That could take three months." Publishes book an average of 2 years after acceptance. Computer printout submissions acceptable; prefers letter-quality to dot-matrix. SASE. Free book catalog.

Nonfiction: "Alaska, northern British Columbia, Yukon, Northwest Territories and northwest U.S. are subject areas. Emphasis on life in the last frontier, history, biography, cookbooks, travel, field guides, juveniles and outdoor subjects. Writer must be familiar with area first-hand. We listen to any ideas." Query with outline, sample chapters, and any relevant photographs preferred. Reviews artwork/photos as part of ms package.

ALBA HOUSE, 2187 Victory Blvd., Staten Island, New York NY 10314. (212)761-0047. Editor-in-Chief: Anthony L. Chenevey. Publishes hardcover and paperback originals and reprints. Specializes in religious books. "We publish shorter editions than many publishers in our field." Pays 10% royalty on retail price. Averages 15 titles/year. Query. State availability of photos/illustrations. Simultaneous and photocopied submissions OK. SASE. Reports in 1 month. Free book catalog.

Nonfiction: Publishes philosophy, psychology, religion, sociology, textbooks and Biblical books. Accepts nonfiction translations from French, German or Spanish. Submit outline/synopsis and 1-2 sample chapters.

Recent Nonfiction Title: *The Making of a Pastoral Person*, by Gerald Niklas.
Tips: "We look to new authors." Queries/mss may be routed to other editors in the publishing group.

‡**THE ALBAN INSTITUTE, INC.**, 4125 Nebraska Ave. NW, Washington DC 20016. (202)244-7320.
Director of Publications: Celia A. Hahn. Publishes trade paperback originals. Averages 6-8 titles/year. Pays 7%
royalty; $50 on publication for 2- to 8-page articles relevant to congregational life—practical—ecumenical.
SASE. Reports in 2 months. Prefers queries. Free book catalog.
Nonfiction: Religious—focus on local congregation—ecumenical. Must be accessible to general reader.
Research preferred. Needs mss on the task of the ordained leader in the congregation, the career path of the
ordained leader in the congregation, problems and opportunities in congregational life, and ministry of the laity
in the world and in the church. No sermons, devotional, anecdotal, inspirational type or prayers. Query or
submit outline/synopsis and sample chapters.
Recent Nonfiction Title: *So You're on the Search Committee*, by Bunty Ketcham.
Tips: "Our audience is intelligent, probably liberal mainline Protestant and Catholic clergy and lay leaders,
executives and seminary administration/faculty—people who are concerned with the local church at a practical
level and new approaches to its ministry."

‡**ALBATROSS PUBLISHING HOUSE**, 66 Crosby St., New York NY 10012. Editor: Candace Maté.
Publishes hardcover originals. Averages 4 titles/year. Pays 5-15% royalty on retail price; offers "open"
advance. Simultaneous submissions OK. SAE and IRCs. Reports in 2 weeks on queries; 1 month on mss.
Nonfiction: How-to and reference (nautical). "We're looking for practical books on any aspect of sailing, boat
building, seamanship, navigation, and the related fields." No cruising stories. Query or submit outline/
synoposis and sample chapters.
Recent Nonfiction Title: *Shipshape*, by Ferenc Maté.

‡***ALCHEMY BOOKS**, Suite 531, 681 Market St., San Francisco CA 94105. (415)777-2197. Submissions
Editor: Graham Philips. Publishes hardcover, trade paperback, and mass market paperback originals. Averages
35 titles/year. Over 50% of books from first-time authors; 99% of books from unagented authors. Subsidy
publishes 20% of books based on nature of book, internal staff schedule requirements, and management budget
considerations. "Frequently we will make these sorts of arrangements with knowledgeable authors who have
written specialized nonfiction to a target audience." Pays varying royalty on wholesale price; no advance.
Publishes book an average of 4 months after acceptance. Simultaneous and photocopied submissions OK.
SASE. Reports in 4 months. Free book catalog.
Nonfiction: "Coffee table" book, cookbook, humor, juvenile, self-help and technical. Subjects include art,
business and economics, cooking and foods, history, music, nature, philosophy, photography, politics,
religion, sociology and legal. "We are not limited to any specific needs and wish to encourage a wide variety of
all kinds of nonfiction." Submit complete ms. Reviews artwork/photos.
Recent Nonfiction Title: *The Law and the Travel Industry*, by Alexander Anolik (legal).
Fiction: Adventure, experimental, fantasy, gothic, historical, horror, humor, mainstream, mystery, religious,
romance, science fiction, suspense and western. "We are interested in all kinds of fiction, adult and juvenile.
We want more good science fiction." Submit complete ms.
Recent Fiction Title: *The Crooked Side of Hell*, by Coralia Nelson (suspense).
Poetry: "We are not looking *for* poetry, although we will look *at* anything." Submit 5 poems.
Recent Poetry Title: *Next Step*, by Margrete Heising and Fritz Wilhelm.
Tips: "We sell to a broad cross-section of the population. We deliberately do not limit our audience. Sometimes
we will select a specialized target audience and publish specialized nonfiction books aimed at their field. We
would like to see more science fiction, more political books, more thoughtful material regarding mankind's
evolution and perspective on the universe. We are always seeking nonfiction of a specialized nature, technical
and nontechnical, or any subject."

ALFRED PUBLISHING CO., INC., 15335 Morrison St., Box 5964, Sherman Oaks CA 91413. (818)995-
8811. Senior Editor: Joseph Cellini. Publishes Alfred Handy Guides, full-size trade paperbacks and software.
Averages 40 titles/year. Pays variable royalty; buys some mss outright; offers negotiable advance. Publishes
book an average of 8 months after acceptance. Simultaneous submissions OK. Electronic submissions OK on
either double-sided, double-density IBM configured disk or capture keystrokes via modem from author; but
requires hard copy also. Computer submissions acceptable; "use good ribbon." SASE. Reports in 2 months.
Free book catalog.
Nonfiction: How-to. Subjects include computers and business. Length: 15,000 words minimum. Submit
outline/synopsis and 1 sample chapter. Reviews artwork/photos as part of ms package.
Recent Nonfiction Title: *Ready To Run Accounting With Lotus 123 and Symphony*, by Urschel.
Tips: "Freelance writers should be aware of the continued tightening of the computer book market. Publishers
with whom I've spoken are being much more selective because booksellers no longer can stock everything."

ALLEGHENY PRESS, Box 220, Elgin PA 16413. Editor: Bonnie Henderson. Publishes hardcover originals, trade paperback originals and reprints. Averages 4 titles/year; receives 260 submissions annually. 50% of books from first-time authors; 100% of books from unagented writers. Average print order for a writer's first book is 2,000. Pays 10-20% royalty on wholesale price. Publishes book an average of 4 months after acceptance. Simultaneous and photocopied submissions OK. Computer printout submissions acceptable; prefers letter-quality to dot-matrix. SASE. Reports in 2 weeks on queries; 1 month on mss.
Nonfiction: Animals and nature. Especially needs college lab manuals and nature/outdoor books. Publishes for college students, outdoor enthusiasts, and armchair geographers. Submit outline/synopsis and sample chapters.
Recent Nonfiction Title: *Along Penn's Waterways*, by Carsten Ahrens.
Tips: "Potential authors should at least look at one Allegheny Press book before submitting material to our company."

ALLEN & UNWIN, INC., 50 Cross St., Winchester MA 01890. (617)729-0830. Vice President/General Manager: Katherine L. Zarker. Publishes hardcover and paperback originals. Averages 150 titles/year. Publishes book an average of 1 year after acceptance. Simultaneous and photocopied submissions OK. Computer printout submissions acceptable. SASE. Reports in 3 weeks. Book catalog for SASE.
Nonfiction: Business/economics, history, literature, literary criticism, philosophy, politics, reference, science, sociology, technical and textbooks. Especially needs advanced university material; must be of international interest. Submit outline/synopsis and sample chapters.

ALLEN PUBLISHING CO., 7324 Reseda Blvd., Reseda CA 91335. Publisher: Michael Wiener. Publishes paperback originals. Averages 3 titles/year. Pays 10% royalty on net price; no advance. Publishes book an average of 6 months after acceptance. Simultaneous and photocopied submissions OK. Computer printout submissions acceptable; prefers letter-quality to dot-matrix. "Author queries welcome from new or established writers. Do not send manuscript or sample chapter." Reports in 2 weeks. SASE "essential." One-page author guidelines available for SASE.
Nonfiction: Self-help material, 25,000-50,000 words, aimed at wealth-builders. "We want to reach the vast audience of opportunity seekers who, for instance, purchased *Lazy Man's Way to Riches*, by Joe Karbo. Material must be original and authoritative, not rehashed from other sources. Most of what we market is sold via mail order in softcover book form. No home fix-it, hobby hints, health or 'cure' books, or 'faith' stories, poetry or fiction. We are a specialty publisher and will not consider any book not fitting the above description." Reviews artwork/photos as part of ms package.
Recent Nonfiction Title: *How To Give Yourself a Fresh Start*.
Tips: "Self-help books are always needed. There never seems to be enough."

ALMAR PRESS, 4105 Marietta Dr., Binghamton NY 13903. (607)722-0265. Editor-in-Chief: A.N. Weiner. Managing Editor: M.F. Weiner. Publishes hardcover and paperback originals and reprints. Averages 6 titles/year; receives 50 submissions annually. 75% of books from first-time authors; 100% of books from unagented writers. Average print order for a writer's first book is 2,000. Pays 10% royalty; no advance. Publishes book an average of 6 months after acceptance. Prefers exclusive submissions; however, simultaneous (if so indicated) and photocopied submissions OK. Electronic submissions OK if compatible with IBM-PC. Computer printout submissions acceptable; prefers letter-quality to dot-matrix. Reports in 1 month. SASE must be included. Catalog for SASE.
Nonfiction: Publishes business, technical, and consumer books and reports. "These main subjects include general business, financial, travel, career, technology, personal help, hobbies, general medical, general legal, and how-to. *Almar Reports* are business and technology subjects published for management use and prepared in $8^{1}/_{2}x11$ and book format. Publications are printed and bound in soft covers as required. Reprint publications represent a new aspect of our business." Submit outline/synopsis and sample chapters. Reviews artwork/photos as part of ms package. Looks for information in the proposed book that makes it different or unusual enough to attract book buyers. Reviews artwork/photos.
Recent Nonfiction Title: *How to Buy, Install and Maintain Your Own Telephone Equipment*, by La Carrubba and Zimmer.
Tips: "We look for timely subjects. The type of book the writer has the best chance of selling to our firm is something different or unusual-*no* poetry or fiction, also *no* first-person travel or family history. The book must be complete and of good quality."

*ALPINE PUBLICATIONS, INC., 1901 S. Garfield St., Loveland CO 80537. Managing Editor: B.J. McKinney. Publishes hardcover and paperback originals. Averages 4 titles/year; receives 20-50 submissions annually. 80% of books from first-time authors; 100% of books from unagented writers. Average print order for a writer's first book is 2,000. Subsidy publishes 25% of books. Pays 7-15% royalty. Publishes book an average of 30 months after acceptance. Simultaneous submissions OK "when we are informed." Computer printout submissions acceptable; no dot-matrix. SASE. Reports in 2 months. Catalog and guidelines for SASE.
Nonfiction: "Alpine Publications is seeking book-length nonfiction manuscript with illustrations on the care,

management, health, training or characteristics of various breeds of dogs, birds and cats. We specialize in books for the owner/breeder, so they must be written by persons knowledgable in these fields or be well-researched and documented. Our books provide in-depth coverage, present new techniques, and specific 'how-to' instruction. We are not interested in books about reptiles or exotic pets." Query with SASE. Prefers outline/synopsis and 3-5 chapters or complete ms. Reviews artwork/photos as part of ms package.

Recent Nonfiction Title: *A Breeder's Guide to Canine Reproduction*, by Holst.

Tips: A freelancer has the best chance of selling "nonfiction breed books on purebred dogs or cats or related topics for breeders/owners/exhibitors; 80% of our market is directed to purebred dog fanciers."

ALYSON PUBLICATIONS, INC., 40 Plympton St., Boston MA 02118. (617)542-5679. Publisher: Sasha Alyson. Publishes trade paperback originals and reprints. Averages 20 titles/year; receives 600 submissions annually. 60% of books from first-time authors; 80% of books from unagented writers. Average print order for a writer's first book is 6,000. Pays 8-15% royalty on net price; buys some mss outright for $200-1,000; offers average $600 advance. Publishes book an average of 1 year after acceptance. Computer printout submissions acceptable; no dot-matrix. SASE. Reports in 2 weeks on queries; 5 weeks on mss. Looks for "writing ability and content suitable for our house." Book catalog and ms guidelines for business-size SAE and 3 first class stamps.

Nonfiction: Subjects include gay/lesbian. "We are especially interested in nonfiction providing a positive approach to gay/lesbian issues." Accepts nonfiction translations. Submit one-page synopsis. Reviews artwork/photos as part of ms package.

Recent Nonfiction Title: *The Men With the Pink Triangle*, by Heinz Heger (history).

Fiction: Gay novels. Accepts fiction translations. Submit one-page synopsis.

Recent Fiction Title: *Between Friends*, by Gillian E. Hanscombe (lesbian fiction).

Tips: "We publish many books by new authors."

‡*AMEREON LTD.**, Box 1200, Mattituck NY 11952. (516)298-5100 or 298-4247. Subsidiaries include J.M. Carroll & Co., Box 44, Bryan TX 77806, and Amereon House. Editor: Kay B. Russell. Publishes mostly hardcover reprints. Averages 90 titles/year; receives 50 submissions annually. 100% of books from unagented writers. Subsidy publishes 5% of books. Pays 3-10% royalty on wholesale price or makes outright purchase of $500. Publishes book an average of 2 years after acceptance. Photocopied submissions OK. Electronic submissions OK, if compatible with IBM MS-DOS, AM CompEdit. Computer printout submissions acceptable; prefers letter-quality to dot-matrix. SASE. Reports in 3 weeks on queries; 3 months on mss. Free book catalog; ms guidelines for SASE.

Nonfiction: Biography, how-to, humor, reference and self-help. Subjects include Americana (Western, military, Custer, Civil War); cooking and foods; and history (Western American, military, Custer, Civil War); Query.

Recent Nonfiction Title: *Thomas A. Edison, The Wizard of Menlo Park*, by Lawrence A. Frost (album).

Fiction: Adventure, fantasy, gothic, historical, humor, mainstream, mystery, religious, romance, science fiction, suspense and western. No gratuitous sex nor sex used in poor taste. Submit outline/synopsis and sample chapters.

Recent Fiction Title: *The Victory of Connie Lee and Other Stories*, by Bess Streeter Aldrich (short story collection).

Tips: "Writers have the best chance of selling books to us with very broad appeal—because our main customers are libraries."

AMERICAN ASTRONAUTICAL SOCIETY, (Univelt, Inc., Publisher), Box 28130, San Diego CA 92128. (619)746-4005. Editorial Director: H. Jacobs. Publishes hardcover originals. Averages 8-10 titles/year; receives 20 submissions annually. 5% of books from first-time authors; 5% of books from unagented writers. Average print order for a writer's first book is 600-2,000. Pays 10% royalty on actual sales; no advance. Publishes book an average of 4 months after acceptance. Simultaneous and photocopied submissions OK. Computer printout submissions acceptable; prefers letter-quality to dot-matrix. Reports in 1 month. SASE. Free book catalog; ms guidelines for SAE and 39¢ postage.

Nonfiction: Proceedings or monographs in the field of astronautics, including applications of aerospace technology to Earth's problems. "Our books must be space-oriented or space-related. They are meant for technical libraries, research establishments and the aerospace industry worldwide." Submit outline/synopsis and 1-2 sample chapters. Reviews artwork/photos as part of ms package.

Recent Nonfiction Title: *Soviet Lunar and Planetary Exploration*, by N.L. Johnson.

AMERICAN CATHOLIC PRESS, 1223 Rossell Ave., Oak Park IL 60302. (312)386-1366. Editorial Director: Father Michael Gilligan. Publishes hardcover originals and hardcover and paperback reprints. "Most of our sales are by direct mail, although we do work through retail outlets." Pays by outright purchase of $25-100; no advance. Publishes book an average of 8 months after acceptance. Simultaneous and photocopied submissions OK. Computer printout submissions acceptable. Reports in 2 months. SASE. Free book catalog.

Nonfiction: "We publish books on the Roman Catholic liturgy—for the most part, books on religious music and educational books and pamphlets. We also publish religious songs for church use, including Psalms, as well as choral and instrumental arrangements. We are very interested in new music, meant for use in church services. Books, or even pamphlets, on the Roman Catholic Mass are especially welcome. We have no interest in secular topics and are not interested in religious poetry of any kind." Query.
Recent Nonfiction Title: *The Role of Music in the New Roman Liturgy*, by W. Herring (educational).

AMERICAN COUNCIL FOR THE ARTS, 570 7th Ave., New York NY 10018. (212)354-6655. Editor-in-Chief: Robert Porter. Publishes hardcover and trade paperback originals. Averages 5-8 titles/year; 50-100 submissions annually. 75% of books from first-time authors; 100% of books from unagented writers. Average print order of a writer's first book is 3,000. Pays 10-15% royalty on wholesale or retail price. Publishes book an average of 1 year after acceptance. Simultaneous and photocopied submissions OK. Electronic submissions OK if compatible with DECmate II, but requires hard copy also. Computer printout submissions acceptable. SASE. Reports in 1 month on queries; 2 months on mss. Free book catalog.
Nonfiction: How-to, reference, technical, textbook and professional books on business and economics—nonprofit management, recreation, sociology, and travel—all as they pertain to the arts. Books on the arts in areas of management, reference, public policy, and role in society (i.e., city life, travel, recreation, education, etc.). Especially needs books on nonprofit management skills, especially the arts (i.e., marketing, planning); public policy in the arts; resource directories for the arts; and practical discussions of ways the arts can be integrated into specific aspects of everyday life. Publishes for artists, professionals, and trustees of arts organizations and agencies; university faculty and students; professionals and trustees of nonprofit institutions. No mss on the aesthetics of specific arts disciplines or biographies. Query or submit outline/synopsis and 3-4 sample chapters. Reviews artwork/photos as part of ms package.
Recent Nonfiction Title: *Financial Management Strategies for Arts Organizations*, by Frederick J. Turk and Robert P. Gallo.

THE AMERICAN PSYCHIATRIC PRESS, INC., (associated with the American Psychiatric Association), 1400 K St. NW, Washington DC 20005. (202)682-6268. Editor: Tim Clancy. Publishes hardcover and trade paperback originals and software. Averages 35 titles/year, 6-10 trade books/year in its new line. Pays 10% minimum royalty based on all money actually received, maximum varies; offers average $5,000-7,500 advance. Publishes book an average of 1 year after acceptance. Simultaneous and photocopied submissions OK (if made clear in cover letter). Electronic submissions OK but requirements vary depending on type of project, but requires hard copy also. Computer printout submissions acceptable; prefers letter-quality to dot-matrix. SASE. Reports in 6 weeks "in regard to an *initial* decision regarding our interest. A *final* decision requires more time (8-12 weeks)." Book catalog for business size SAE and 1 first class stamp.
Nonfiction: Reference, self-help, technical, textbook and general nonfiction. Subjects include psychology/psychiatry and sociology (as it relates to psychiatry). Especially looking for books that discuss major psychiatric topics for the general public. Also interested in books for children. No first-person accounts of mental illness or anything not clearly related to psychiatry. Query with outline/synopsis and sample chapters.
Recent Nonfiction Title: *Getting Tough on Gateway Drugs: A Guide for the Family*, by Robert L. DuPont, Jr., M.D.
Tips: "Our trade line is aimed at educated lay readers—people who need help dealing with the psychiatric problems that can plague them and their friends and family. These problems range from drug abuse to anorexia nervosa to major psychiatric disorders. Besides these trade books, we publish many professional titles. The purpose of the trade books is to communicate with and educate the public. Since the reading public has become increasingly aware of psychiatric disorders, we anticipate healthy sales. If I were a writer trying to market a book today, I would make absolutely sure I am writing about an important topic and my approach is fresh and innovative. Authors should have a professional background in social science or health (preferably a medical doctor). Professional writers may wish to approach a psychiatrist to be a co-author."

AMPHOTO, 1515 Broadway, New York NY 10036. (212)764-7300. Senior Editor: Marisa Bulzone. Publishes hardcover and paperback originals. Averages 20 titles/year. Pays royalty, or makes outright purchase; offers variable advance. Publishes book an average of 9 months after acceptance. Simultaneous and photocopied submissions OK. Electronic submissions OK, but requires hard copy also. Computer printout submissions acceptable; prefers letter-quality to dot-matrix. Reports in 1 month. SASE. Free book catalog.
Nonfiction: "Photography instruction only. We cover all technical and how-to aspects. Few portfolios or picture books." Submit outline/synopsis, sample chapters and sample photos. Reviews artwork/photos as part of ms package. Looks for "practical value to the readers, marketing information."
Recent Nonfiction Title: *Secrets of Studio Still Life Photography*, by Gary Perweiler.
Tips: "Consult the photo magazines for book ideas."

*ANDERSON PUBLISHING CO., Suite 501, 602 Main St., Cincinnati OH 45201. (513)421-4393. Editorial Director: Jean Martin. Publishes hardcover, paperback originals, journals and software and reprints.

Publishes 14 titles/year. Subsidy publishes 10% of books. Pays 15-18% royalty; "advance in selected cases." Publishes book an average of 7 months after acceptance. Simultaneous and photocopied submissions OK. Computer printout submissions acceptable; prefers letter-quality to dot-matrix. Reports in 2 months. SASE. Free book catalog.
Nonfiction: Law and law-related books, and criminal justice criminology texts (justice administration legal series). Query or submit outline/chapters with vitae.
Recent Nonfiction Title: *Corportate Crime*, by Frank Cullen, Grey Cavender and William Makastaad.

*AND/OR PRESS, Box 522, Berkeley CA 94701. Contact: Ronin Publishing, Box 1035, Berkeley CA 94201. (415)540-6278. Publisher: Sebastian Orfali. Publishes paperback originals, and hardcover and paperback reprints. Averages 8 titles/year. Specializes in "nonfiction works with young urban professional interest. We function as an alternative information resource. 75% are funded by investors and author receives small advance. 25% are funded by author; Ronin works with author to produce, promote and distribute. Also obtains foreign and domestic subsidiary rights." Pays 5-10% royalty; offers average advance of 10% of first print run. Publishes ms an average of 9 months after acceptance. Electronic submissions OK. Computer printout submissions acceptable. Reports in 2 weeks to 3 months. SASE. Prefers outline with 1-3 sample chapters.
Nonfiction: Publishes appropriate technology, human potential, the future, health and nutrition, travel and psycho-pharmacology books. Also alternative lifestyle books. Reviews artwork/photos as part of ms package.
Recent Nonfiction Title: *Beating Job Burnout*, by Dr. Beverly Potter.
Tips: "Ronin recognizes that the author is not merely an outside vendor but is an integral part of all phases of the publishing process. Ronin uses a decentralized form—relying on freelance professionals: artists, editors, etc. Ronin uses a novel distribution approach in addition to the traditional."

ANDREWS, McMEEL AND PARKER., 4400 Johnson Dr., Fairway KS 66205. Editorial Director: Donna Martin. Publishes hardcover and paperback originals. Averages 30 titles/year. Pays royalty on retail price. "Not currently reading unsolicited mss. Publishing program mainly related to features of Universal Press Syndicate, for which Andrews, McMeel & Parker is the book-publishing arm."

*ANGEL PRESS/PUBLISHERS, 561 Tyler, Monterey CA 93940. (408)372-1658. Editor: Ruby Grace. Publishes hardcover originals and reprints and mass market paperback originals. Averages 2-4 titles/year; receives 600-700 submissions annually. 10% of books from first-time authors; 80% of books from unagented writers. Average print order from a writer's first book is 2,000. Subsidy publishes 50% of books. Pays negotiable royalty; cash return (actual). No advance. Publishes book an average of 1 year after acceptance. Simultaneous and photocopied submissions OK. Computer printout submissions acceptable; prefers letter-quality to dot-matrix. SASE. Reports in 3 weeks on queries; "several" months on mss.
Nonfiction: Biography, how-to, humor, self-help and spiritual/metaphysical. Subjects include Americana, animals, health, history, hobbies, nature, philosophy, photography, politics, psychology, recreation, religion and sociology. Especially needs "well-written, well-conceived books in the areas of controversy, feminist, humor, satire; plus any book that is unusually well-written and is potentially a good seller in its field." Query before submitting ms. Reviews artwork/photos as part of ms package.
Recent Nonfiction Title: *Living with Angels*, by Dorie D'Angelo (spiritual/inspirational).
Fiction: Adventure, fantasy, humor, mainstream, metaphysical, and human potential. "Fiction is not our main thrust." Query before submitting ms.
Recent Fiction Title: *Re'lize Whut Ahm Talkin' 'Bout?*, by Steve Chennault (black English).
Tips: Spiritual/metaphysical or holistic health books have the best chance of selling to this firm.

‡APPALACHIAN MOUNTAIN CLUB, 5 Joy St., Boston MA 02108. (617)523-0636. Editorial Director: Mr. Aubrey Botsford. Imprint includes AMC Books. Publishes hardcover and trade paperback originals. Averages 3-6 titles/year; receives 10-15 submissions annually. 80% of books from first-time authors; 99% of books from unagented writers. Pays 5-10% royalty on retail price; offers $500-1,000 advance. Publishes book an average of 6 months after acceptance. Simultaneous and photocopied submissions OK. Computer printout submissions acceptable; prefers letter-quality to dot-matrix. SASE. Reports in 6 weeks on queries; 3 months on mss. Book catalog for SAE.
Nonfiction: "Coffee table" book, how-to, illustrated book, reference and guidebook. Subjects include history (Northeast, mountains), nature, photography, recreation, sports "self-propelled" outdoors activities, and travel. "We want manuscripts about the outdoors, ecology, the environment, mountains and their history and culture, non-motorized recreation, and guidebooks and field guides. We would also like to see semi-philosophical works on the outdoors." No physical fitness manuals. Query or submit outline/synopsis and sample chapters. Reviews artwork/photos.
Recent Nonfiction Title: *River Rescue* , by Les Bechdel and Slim Ray.
Tips: "We are expanding into the Southeast (North Carolina, South Carolina, Washington DC, Maryland, Virginia, West Virginia), with basically the same interests as herein New England. Be patient. The AMC makes decisions slowly, mainly because it cannot afford to take financial risks."

APPLE-WOOD BOOKS, INC., Box 2870, Cambridge MA 02139. (617)923-9337. Editorial Director: Phil Zuckerman. Publishes hardcover and trade paperback originals. Averages 12 titles/year. Pays 10-15% royalty on wholesale price; offers $250-2,500 advance. Publishes book an average of 18 months after acceptance. Simultaneous and photocopied submissions OK. Computer printout submissions acceptable. SASE. Reports in 3 weeks on queries; 3 months on mss. Book catalog for 8½x11 SAE and 2 first class stamps.
Nonfiction: Subjects include biography, history, politics, literature and humor. "We publish books for people who grew up in the 1950s and 1960s."
Recent Nonfiction Title: *A Guide to Writer's Homes in New England*, by Miriam Levine (guidebook).
Fiction: "We don't consider fiction by category, but by quality. We publish the future great American writers." Query or submit outline/synopsis, sample chapters and SASE.
Recent Fiction Title: *The Personal History, Adventures, Experiences & Observations of Peter Leroy*, by Eric Kraft.

‡**APPLEZABA PRESS**, Box 4134, Long Beach CA 90804. (213)591-0015. Publisher: D.H. Lloyd. Publishes trade paperback originals. Averages 3-4 titles/year; receives 800-1,000 submissions annually. 20% of books from first-time authors; 100% of books from unagented writers. Pays 8-12% royalty on retail price plus several author copies. Seldom offers advance. Publishes book an average of 3 years after acceptance. Simultaneous and photocopied submissions OK. Computer printout submissions acceptable; prefers letter-quality to dot-matrix. SASE. Reports in 1 month on queries; 2 months on mss. Free book catalog (when available).
Nonfiction: Cookbook and humor. Subjects include cooking and foods. "Our needs are not great here. However, we are working on a 'poets' cookbook at present and are soliciting contributions. We need individual recipes from poets as well as a few short, upbeat poems relating to food, recipes, restaurants, etc." No how-to, reference, sports or self-help books. Query. Reviews artwork/photos.
Fiction: Experimental, humor, mainstream, novella and short story collections. "We prefer to see short, novella length, or short story collections. No confession, gothic, horror or western manuscripts. Submit outline/synopsis and sample chapters.
Recent Fiction Title: *Mog & Glog*, by D.H. Lloyd (short stories).
Poetry: "The poetry that attracts us is *usually* short, conversational prose poems. We don't let this limit us, however." No traditional forms. Submit complete ms.
Recent Poetry Title: *Madonna Who Shifts For Herself*, by Lyn Lifshin (conversational/feminist).
Tips: The freelancer has the best chance of publishing collections of poetry or short fiction. "They are economical enough for us to produce, and we have developed a market for them."

‡**THE AQUARIAN PRESS LTD.**, Denington Estate, Wellingborough, Northamptonshire NN8 2RQ England. Editor-in-Chief: Michael Cox. Hardcover and paperback originals. Pays 8-10% royalty. Photocopied submissions OK. Computer printout and disk submissions acceptable; prefers letter-quality to dot-matrix. SAE and International Reply Coupons. Reports in 1 month. Free book catalog.
Nonfiction: Publishes books on comparative religion, magic, metaphysics, mysticism, occultism, parapsychology and esoteric philosophy. Length: 30,000-100,000 words.
Tips: "We look for a clear indication that the author has thought about his market; a fundamental ability to *communicate* ideas—authority in combination with readability."

ARBOR HOUSE, Subsidiary of Hearst Corp., 235 E. 45th St., New York NY 10017. Publisher: Eden Collinsworth. Editor-in-Chief: Ann Harris. Publishes hardcover and trade paperback originals and selected reprints. Pays standard royalty; offers negotiable advance. Publishes book an average of 9 months after acceptance. Computer printout submissions acceptable; prefers letter-quality to dot-matrix. SASE. Free book catalog.
Nonfiction: Autobiography, cookbook, how-to and self-help. Subjects include Americana (possibly), art (possibly), business and economics, cooking and foods, health, history, politics, psychology, recreation, inspiration and sports. Query first to "The Editors." Reviews artwork/photos as part of ms package.
Recent Nonfiction Title: *What Did I Do Wrong? Mothers, Children, Guilt*, by Lynn Caine.
Fiction: "Quality fiction—everything from romance to science fiction, fantasy, adventure and suspense." Query or submit outline/synopsis and sample chapters to "The Editors."
Recent Fiction Title: *Glitz*, by Elmore Leonard.
Tips: "Freelance writers should be aware of a greater emphasis on agented properties and market resistance to untried fiction."

ARCHER EDITIONS PRESS,318 Fry Branch Rd., Lynnville TN 38472. Editorial Director: Wanda Hicks. Publishes hardcover and paperback originals and paperback reprints. Pays 15% royalty on wholesale price; occasionally offers $250-750 advance. Averages 1-6 titles/year. Simultaneous and photocopied submissions OK. Reports in 3 months. SASE. Free book catalog.
Nonfiction: "We are interested in books that could go to the academic and public library market in the fields of history, literature and art. We would especially like biographies in this field." Query.

Recent Nonfiction Title: *Thomas Francis Meagher*, by W.F. Lyons (Civil War reprint); and *Lost Sandstones and Lonely Skies*, by Jesse Stuart (essays).
Fiction: "We are doing a limited amount of fiction of a somewhat academic nature by established authors."
Recent Fiction Title: *The Autobiography of Cassandra; Princess and Prophetess of Troy*, by Ursule Molinaro.

ARCHITECTURAL BOOK PUBLISHING CO., INC., 10 E. 40th St., New York NY 10016. (212)689-5400. Editor: Walter Frese. Averages 10 titles/year; receives 400 submissions annually. 80% of books from first-time authors; 95% of books from unagented writers. Average print order for a writer's first book is 5,000. Royalty is percentage of retail price. Publishes book an average of 10 months after acceptance. Computer print-out submissions acceptable; no dot-matrix. Prefers queries, outlines and 2 sample chapters with number of illustrations. Reports in 2 weeks. SASE.
Nonfiction: Publishes architecture, decoration, and reference books on city planning and industrial arts. Accepts nonfiction translations. Also interested in history, biography, and science of architecture and decoration. Reviews artwork/photos.

ARCO PUBLISHING, INC., 215 Park Ave. S., New York NY 10003. Senior Editor, Consumer Books (trade): Madelyn Larsen. Pays advance against royalties. Simultaneous submissions OK; "inform us if so." Computer printout submissions acceptable; no dot-matrix. Materials submitted without sufficient postage will not be returned.
Nonfiction: Publishes needle crafts, pet care and training, horses (all aspects); project-oriented science (young adult); how-to; and militaria. "Our readers are people who want information, instruction and technical know-how from their books. They want to learn something tangible." No fiction, poetry, cookbooks, biographies, autobiographies, religion or personal "true" accounts of persons or pets. Prefers letter of inquiry with a contents page and 1 sample chapter. Educational Books, Linda Bernbach, Editor; Career guidance, test preparation and study guides, Ellen Lichtenstein, Editor. Same requirements as for consumer books.

ARCsoft PUBLISHERS, Box 132, Woodsboro MD 21798. (301)845-8856. Publisher: Anthony R. Curtis. Publishes trade paperback originals. Averages 20 titles/year. Pays 10% royalty on net sales; offers variable advance. Publishes book an average of 6 months after acceptance. Computer printout submissions acceptable; no dot-matrix. SASE. Reports in 1 month on queries; 10 weeks on mss. Free book catalog.
Nonfiction: Technical. "We publish hobby books including personal computing, electronics projects, model railroading, stamps, photography, etc., especially for beginners." Accepts nonfiction translations. Query or submit outline/synopsis and 1 sample chapter. Reviews artwork/photos as part of ms package.
Recent Nonfiction Title: *IBM PCjr Games Programs*, by Howard Bridges.
Tips: "We look for the writer's ability to cover our desired subject thoroughly, writing quality and interest."

*M. ARMAN PUBLISHING, INC., 28 N. Ridgewood Ave., Rio Vista, Ormond Beach FL 32074. (904)673-5576. Mailing address: Box 785, Ormond Beach FL 32074. Contact: Mike Arman. Publishes trade paperback originals, reprints and software. Averages 6-8 titles/year; receives 20 submissions annually. 20% of books from first-time authors; 100% of books from unagented writers. Average print order for a writer's first book is 1,500. Subsidy publishes 20% of books. Pays 10% royalty on wholesale price. No advance. Publishes book (on royalty basis) an average of 8 months after acceptance; 6 weeks on subsidy basis. Photocopied submissions OK. "We now set type directly from author's disks. Our equipment can read many CPM 5¼ formats, and can read IBM disks if the file is ASC II. We can do this for our own books, and we can save subsidy publishers 40-50% on their typesetting bills." Computer printout submissions acceptable. SASE. Reports in 1 week on queries; 3 weeks on mss. Book catalog for business size SAE with 39¢ postage.
Nonfiction: How-to, reference, technical, and textbook. "Motorcycle and aircraft technical books only." Accepts nonfiction translations. Publishes for enthusiasts. Submit complete ms. Reviews artwork/photos as part of ms package.
Recent Nonfiction Title: *A Guide to Autogyros*, by Crowe (construction, flight training, operation of autogyros).
Fiction: "Motorcycle or aircraft-related only." Accepts fiction translations. Immediate needs are "slim," but not non-existent. Submit complete ms.
Recent Fiction Title: *Motorcycle Summers*, by Gately (G-rated short stories about motorcycling).
Tips: "The type of book a writer has the best chance of selling to our firm is how-to fix motorcycles—specifically Harley-Davidson. We have a strong, established market for these books."

ART DIRECTION BOOK COMPANY, 10 E. 39th St., New York NY 10016. (212)889-6500. Editorial Director: Don Barron. Senior Editor: Loren Bliss. Publishes hardcover and paperback originals. Publishes 15-20 titles/year. Pays 10% royalty on retail price; offers average $1,000 advance. Publishes book an average of 1 year after acceptance. Photocopied submissions OK. Computer printout submissions acceptable; no dot-matrix. SASE. Reports in 3 months. Free book catalog.

Nonfiction: Commercial art, ad art how-to and textbooks. Query first with outline/synopsis and 1 sample chapter. "We are interested in books for the professional advertising art field—that is, books for art directors, designers, etc.; also entry level books for commercial and advertising art students in such fields as typography, photography, paste-up, illustration, clip-art, design, layout and graphic arts." Reviews artwork/photos as part of ms package.
Recent Nonfiction Title: *How To Prepare Roughs, Comps, and Mock-Ups*, by John Marqvand.

ASHTON-TATE PUBLISHING GROUP, Division Ashton-Tate, 10150 W. Jefferson Blvd., Culver City CA 90230. (213)204-5570. Editor: Bill Jordan. Publishes trade paperback originals. Averages 30 titles/year. Pays royalty on cash received. Simultaneous and photocopied submissions OK. SASE. Reports in 3 weeks on queries; 1 month on mss. Free book catalog.
Nonfiction: Technical, microcomputer-related. Especially looking for microcomputer hardware and software topic areas for introductory through advanced readers. No non-computer related material. Submit outline/synopsis and sample chapters.
Recent Nonfiction Title: *Up and Running: Adventures of Softwares Entrepreneurs*, by Charles E. Sherman.
Tips: Audience is "specific software end-users, software application developers, and general audience/microcomputer enthusiasts."

*ASSOCIATED BOOKSELLERS, 147 McKinley Ave., Bridgeport CT 06606. (203)366-5494. Editor-in-Chief: Alex M. Yudkin. Publishes hardcover and paperback originals, and reprints. Averages 8 titles/year. 5% of books from first-time authors; 1% of books from unagented writers. Average print order for a Writer's first book is 3,000. Subsidy publishes 10% of books. Subsidy publishing is offered "if the marketing potential is limited." Pays 10% royalty on wholesale or retail price; offers average $500 advance. Simultaneous and photocopied submissions OK. Computer printout submissions acceptable; no dot-matrix. Query. Reports in 1 month. Book catalog for SAE and 1 first class stamp.
Nonfiction: Publishes how-to, hobbies, recreation, self-help, sports books and cookbooks. Reviews artwork/photos.
Recent Title: *New Canadian High Energy Diet Book*.

‡DEAN ASTER PUBLISHING CO., Box 10752, Merrillville IN 46411. (219)947-1418. Editor-in-Chief: Dr. Donald D. Macchia. Publishes hardcover, trade paperback and mass market paperback originals. Averages 6-9 titles/year. 10% of books from first-time authors ("we hope to increase this percentage"); 100% of books from unagented writers. Pays 5-15% royalty on retail price. Offers average $500 advance. Publishes book an average of 9 months after acceptance. Simultaneous submissions OK. Computer printout submissions acceptable; no dot-matrix. SASE. Reports in 6 weeks on queries; 2 months on mss. Book catalog $1; ms guidelines for SASE.
Nonfiction: How-to, illustrated book, reference, self-help, technical and textbook. Subjects include health (medical education); psychology (biofeedback, etc.); recreation (sports, athletic training); and science information. "We are particularly interested in medical or health education books written for the health care professional. Self-help books for the lay audience are also needed. We will consider academic texts, science information books, and books written for the sports athlete." No historical, music, art, cookbooks, political, or books of a humorous nature." Query. Reviews artwork/photos.
Recent Nonfiction Title: *Mind Over Fatter*, by Dr. Mary F. Asterita (self-help, weight management).
Fiction: Science fiction. "Although we have yet to publish fiction, we may consider good science fiction." Query.
Tips: "Our books are read by medical, science or psychology students, health care professionals, people interested in improving their health or outlook on life, and people who desire to learn more about modern science and technology. We are writing for a more educated audience. Our readers demand more information regarding the underlying anatomical and physiological reasons for the exercise routines, diets and rest requirements they read in print."

ATHENEUM PUBLISHERS, 115 5th Ave., New York NY 10003. Editor-in-Chief: Thomas A. Stewart. Receives 10,000 submissions annually. 5% of books from first-time authors; 1% of books from unagented writers. Average print order for a writer's first book is 5,000. Publishes book an average of 1 year after acceptance. Simultaneous and photocopied submissions OK. Electronic submissions OK, but requires hard copy also. Computer printout submissions acceptable; prefers letter-qualtiy to dot-matrix. SASE. Reports in 6 weeks. Writer's guidlines for SASE.
Nonfiction: General trade material dealing with politics, psychology, history, cookbooks, sports, biographies and general interest. Length: 40,000 words minimum. Query or submit outline/synopsis and a sample chapter.
Recent Nonfiction Title: *Son*, by Jack Olsen.
Tips: "We would prefer not to have artwork or photographs accompany unsolicited manuscripts."

ATHENEUM PUBLISHERS, INC., Juvenile Department, 115 5th Ave., New York NY 10003. Editor: Jean Karl. Publishes hardcover originals and paperback reprints. Averages 75 titles/year; receives 3,500-4,000 submissions annually. 8% of books from first-time authors; 40% of books from unagented writers. Average print order for a writer's first book is 5,000. Publishes book an average of 18 months after acceptance. Computer printout submissions acceptable; prefers letter-quality to dot-matrix. SASE. Book catalog for 9x12 SAE with 44¢ postage. Reports in 6 weeks.
Nonfiction: Juvenile books for ages 3-16. Picture books for ages 3-8. "We have no special needs; we publish whatever comes in that interests us." Reviews artwork/photos "of professional quality" as part of ms package.
Tips: "Most submissions are too ephemeral. Think deeper and learn to put words on paper in a way that conveys that depth to readers, without being didactic."

ATHLETIC PRESS, Box 80250, Pasadena CA 91108. (213)283-3446. Editor-in-Chief: Donald Duke. Publishes paperback originals. Averages 3 titles/year. Pays 10% royalty; no advance. Publishes book an average of 1 year after acceptance. Query or submit complete ms. "Illustrations will be requested when we believe manuscript is publishable." Simultaneous and photocopied submissions OK. Computer printout submissions acceptable. Reports in 1 month. SASE. Free book catalog.
Nonfiction: Specializes in sports conditioning books.

ATLANTIC MONTHLY PRESS, 8 Arlington St., Boston MA 02116. (617)536-9500. New York Office: 420 Lexington Ave., New York NY 10170. (212)687-2424. Editor-in-Chief: Harold Evans. Executive Editor: Upton Birnie Brady. Editor-in-Chief, children's books: Melanie Kroupa. Senior Editors: Peter Davison, Joyce Johnson and Edward Weeks. Associate Editors: C. Michael Curtis, Amy Meeker (children's books). Averages 50 titles/year; receives 3,000-5,000 submissions annually. 20% of books from first-time authors; 10% of books from unagented writers. "Advance and royalties depend on the nature of the book, the stature of the author, and the subject matter." Publishes book and average of 9 months after acceptance. Computer printout submissions acceptable; no dot-matrix. SASE.
Nonfiction: Publishes general nonfiction, biography, autobiography, science, philosophy, the arts, belles lettres, history and world affairs. Looks for "intelligence, coherence, organization, good writing (which comes first), neatness of presentation—and a covering letter." Length: 70,000-200,000 words. Reviews artwork/photos.
Recent Nonfiction Title: *Visions of America: How We Saw the 1984 Election*, by Williams A. Henry III.
Fiction: Publishes general fiction, juveniles and poetry. Length: 70,000-200,000 words.
Recent Fiction Title: *A Game of Pawno*, by L. Christian Balling

*ATLANTIS PUBLISHING COMPANY, 5432 Hallandale Beach Blvd., Hollywood FL 33023. (305)981-1009. President: Dr. Arthur G. Haggis. Publishes hardcover, trade paperback and mass market paperback originals and software. Averages 5 titles/year; receives 250 submissions annually. 10% of books from first-time authors; 10% of books from unagented writers. Average print order for writer's first book is 500. Subsidy publishes 10% of books based on "book subjects and how well written." Pays 7-15% royalty on wholesale price; offers no advance. Simultaneous submissions OK with notation as to other publishers contacted. Computer printout submissions acceptable; no dot-matrix. SASE. Reports in 1 month. Book catalog for SAE and 60¢ postage.
Nonfiction: How-to, self-help, and textbooks. Subjects include health, spelling, beginning language and numbers, and computers. "We have no plans to publish nonfiction books other than present series of health, spelling, beginning language and number development, and computer texts." Submit outline/synopsis and sample chapters or complete ms.
Recent Nonfiction Title: *Atlantis Beginning Language and Number Development Program Book 1*, by Dr. Arthur G. Haggis and Lewanna S. Haggis (pre-kindergarten-grade 1).
Tips: "Our books are for preschool through grades 12, remedial education, adult basic education, and home study programs (book style)."

AUGSBURG PUBLISHING HOUSE, 426 S. 5th St., Box 1209, Minneapolis MN 55440. (612)330-3432. Director, Book Department: Roland Seboldt. Publishes hardcover and paperback originals and paperback reprints. Publishes 45 titles/year; receives 5,000 submissions annually. 20% of books from first-time authors; 95% of books from unagented writers. Average print order for a writer's first book is 5,000. Pays 10-15% royalty on retail price; offers variable advance. Publishes book an average of 1 year after acceptance. Simultaneous and photocopied submissions OK. Computer printout submissions acceptable; no dot-matrix. Reports in 6 weeks. SASE.
Nonfiction: Health, psychology, religion, self-help and textbooks. "We are looking for manuscripts that apply scientific knowledge and Christian faith to the needs of people as individuals, in groups and in society;" also good contemporary stories with a Christian theme for the young readers in age categories 8-11, 12-14, and 15 and up." Query or submit outline/synopsis and a sample chapter or submit complete ms. Reviews artwork/photos.
Recent Nonfiction Title: *Bringing Out the Best in People*, by Alan Loy McGinnis.

AVALON BOOKS, Thomas Bouregy & Co., Inc., 401 Lafayette St., New York NY 10003. Editor: Rita Brenig. Publishes 60 titles/year. Pays $400 advance which is applied against sales of the first 3,500 copies of the book. Computer printout submissions acceptable; no dot-matrix. SASE. Reports in 3 months. Tip sheet for SASE.
Fiction: "We want well-plotted, fast-moving light romances, romance-mysteries, gothics, westerns, and nurse-romance books of about 50,000 words." Submit one-page synopsis or submit complete ms. No sample chapters or long outlines. SASE.
Recent Fiction Title: *Love's Secret Game*, by Susan E. Kirby.
Tips: "We like writers to focus on the plot, drama, and characters, not the background."

AVANT BOOKS, Slawson Communications, Inc., 3719 6th Ave., San Diego CA 92103. Publisher: Leslie Smith. Publishes trade paperback originals. Averages 8 titles/year; receives 200 submissions annually. 1% of books from first-time authors; 5% of books from unagented writers. Print order for a writer's first book ranges from 3,000-15,000. Pays 10-20% royalty on wholesale price. Publishes book an average of 6-12 months after acceptance. Simultaneous (if so advised) and photocopied submissions OK. Electronic submissions OK if compatible with IBM PC, Kaypro 4, or MSDOS WordStar, but requires hard copy also. Computer printout submissions acceptable; prefers letter-quality to dot-matrix. SASE. Reports in 2 months on queries. Book catalog $1.50 and SAE with 39¢ postage.
Nonfiction: Subjects include art, health, nature, psychology and social sciences. "Books dealing with global culture, and vital ecological issues. Also some how-to and self-help titles." No esoteric, political, single-group or viewpoint orientation. Submit outline/synopsis and sample chapters only. Reviews artwork/photos as part of ms package.
Recent Nonfiction Title: *Arcosanti*, by Paolo Soleri.

*AVI PUBLISHING CO., 250 Post Rd. E., Box 831, Westport CT 06881. (203)226-0738. Editor-in-Chief: James R. Ice, Ph.D. Publishes hardcover and paperback originals. Publishes 30 titles/year; receives fewer than 100 submissions annually. 50% of books from first-time authors; 100% of books from unagented writers. Subsidy publishes 10% of books. "Subsidy publishes symposia; subject matter within the areas of food, nutrition, agriculture and health, endorsed by appropriate professional organizations in the area of our specialty." Pays 10% royalty based on list price on the first 3,000 copies sold; offers average $5,000 advance (paid only on typing and art bills). Publishes book an average of 18 months after acceptance. Computer printout submissions acceptable; no dot-matrix. SASE. Reports in 1 month. Free book catalog and ms guidelines.
Nonfiction: Specializes in books on foods, agriculture, nutrition and health, scientific, technical, textbooks and reference works. Accepts nonfiction translations. Query or "submit a 500-word summary, a preface, a table of contents, estimated number of pages in manuscript, 1-2 sample chapters, when to be completed and a biographical sketch." Reviews artwork/photos as part of ms package.
Recent Nonfiction Title: *Site Engineering for Landscape Architects*, by Stum and Nathan.

AVON BOOKS, 1790 Broadway, New York NY 10019. President/Publisher: Walter Meade. Editorial Director: Page Cuddy. Publishes paperback originals and paperback reprints. Averages 300 titles/year. Buys 10-20 unsolicited mss/year. Pay and advance are negotiable. Publishes ms an average of 2 years after acceptance. Simultaneous and photocopied submissions OK. Computer printout submissions acceptable; prefers letter-quality to dot matrix. SASE. Reports in 2 months. Book catalog for SASE.
Nonfiction: Animals, biography, business/economics, cookbooks/cooking, health, history, hobbies, how-to, humor, juveniles, music, nature, philosophy, photography, politics, psychology, recreation, reference, religion, science, self-help, sociology and sports. No textbooks. Submit outline/synopsis and first three chapters. SASE.
Recent Nonfiction Title: *The Working Photographer*, by Marija and Tod Bryant.
Fiction: Adventure, fantasy, gothic, historical, mainstream, mystery, religious, romance, science fiction, suspense and western. Submit outline/synopsis, first three sample chapters and SASE.
Recent Fiction Title: *Chastity Morrow*, by Rosanne Kohake.

AZTEX CORP., 1126 N. 6th Ave., Box 50046, Tucson AZ 85703. (608)882-4656. Publishes hardcover and paperback originals. Averages 15 titles/year; receives 250 submissions annually. 100% of books from unagented writers. Average print order for a writer's first book is 3,500. Pays 10% royalty. Publishes book an average of 18 months after acceptance. Electronic and disk submissions OK but inquire about compatibility; requires hard copy also. Computer printout submissions acceptable; prefers letter-quality to dot-matrix. SASE. Reports in 3 months. Free catalog. *Author-Publisher Handbook* for $3.95.
Nonfiction: "We specialize in transportation subjects (how-to and history) and early childhood education." Accepts nonfiction translations. Submit outline/synopsis and 2 sample chapters or complete ms. Reviews artwork/photos as part of ms package.
Recent Nonfiction Title: *MGA—A History and Restoration Guide*, by Robert Vitrikas.
Tips: "We look for accuracy, thoroughness and interesting presentation."

‡**BAEN ENTERPRISES**, 8-10 W. 36th St., New York NY 10018. (212)947-8244. Senior Editor: Elizabeth Mitchell. Publishes hardcover trade paperback and mass market paperback originals, mass market paperback reprints and software. Averages 65-90 titles/year; receives 1,000 submissions annually. 5% of books from first-time authors; 2% of books from unagented writers. Pays 6-12% royalty on cover price or makes outright purchase. Simultaneous and photocopied submissions OK. Computer printout submissions acceptable; prefers letter-quality to dot-matrix. SASE. Reports in 2 weeks on queries; 2 months on mss. Ms guidelines for SASE.
Nonfiction: Technical (computer). No high tech science; computer titles and futuristic topics such as space technology, artificial intelligence, etc. Submit outline/synopsis and sample chapters or complete ms.
Recent Nonfiction Title: *The Future of Flight*, by Leik Myrabo/Dean Ing (high tech).
Fiction: Fantasy and science fiction, high tech and computer. Submit outline/synopsis and sample chapters or complete ms.
Recent Fiction Title: *The Game of Empire*, by Paul Anderson (science fiction).
Tips: "Our audience includes those who are interested in *hard* science fiction and quality fantasy pieces that instruct as well as entertain."

BAKER BOOK HOUSE COMPANY, Box 6287, Grand Rapids MI 49506. (616)676-9185. Editorial Director: Dan Van't Kerkhoff. Publishes hardcover and paperback originals, paperback reprints and software. Averages 80 titles/year; receives 1,500 submissions annually. 20% of books from first-time authors; 80% of books from unagented writers. Average print order for a writer's first book is 5,000. Pays 10% royalty. Also buys booklet-length mss by outright purchase: $250-500. No advance. Publishes book an average of 8-16 months after acceptance. Simultaneous and photocopied submissions OK. Computer printout submissions acceptable "if legible"; prefers letter-quality to dot-matrix. SASE. Reports in 1 month. Book catalog for large SAE and $1.20 postage.
Nonfiction: Humor, juvenile, philosophy, psychology, religion, self-help and textbook. "All must be of religious nature." Submit outline/synopsis and 2-3 sample chapters (more, if chapters are brief) or submit complete ms. Reviews artwork/photos.
Recent Nonfiction Title: *We Need Each Other*, by Guy Greenfield.
Fiction: Juvenile or adult. Limited, but submissions welcome.

‡**BAKER STREET PRODUCTIONS LTD.**, 502 Range St., Box 3610, Mankato MN 56001. (507)625-2482. Contact: Karyne Jacobsen. Publishes hardcover and trade paperback originals and software. Averages 8 titles/year; receives 300 submissions annually. 25% of books from first-time authors; 100% of books from unagented writers. Publishes book an average of 6-12 months after acceptance. Photocopied submissions OK. Computer printout submissions acceptable; prefers letter-quality to dot-matrix. SASE. Reports in 1 month on queries; 2 months on mss. Free book catalog.
Fiction: Adventure, fantasy, humor and mystery. Needs juvenile materials, grades 1-3. No science fiction. Submit outline/synopsis and sample chapters. Reviews artwork/photos.
Recent Fiction Title: *Everything Is Special*, by Neese (guidance).

BALE BOOKS, Box 2727, New Orleans LA 70176. Editor-in-Chief: Don Bale Jr. Publishes hardcover and paperback originals and reprints. Averages 10 titles/year; receives 25 submissions annually. 50% of books from first-time authors; 90% of books from unagented writers. Average print order for a writer's first book is 1,000. Offers standard 10-12½-15% royalty contract on wholesale or retail price; sometimes purchases mss outright for $500. Offers no advance. Publishes book an average of 3 years after acceptance. "Most books are sold through publicity and ads in the coin newspapers." Will consider photocopied submissions. Computer printout submissions acceptable. "Send manuscript by registered or certified mail. Be sure copy of manuscript is retained." SASE. Book catalog for SAE and 39¢ postage.
Nonfiction: Numismatics. "Our specialty is coin and stock market investment books; especially coin investment books and coin price guides. We are open to any new ideas in the area of numismatics. The writer should write for a teenage through adult level. Lead the reader by the hand like a teacher, building chapter by chapter. Our books sometimes have a light, humorous treatment, but not necessarily." Looks for "good English, construction and content, and sales potential." Submit outline/synopsis and 3 sample chapters.
Recent Nonfiction Title: *How to Find Valuable, Old Scarce Coins*.

BALLANTINE/DEL REY/FAWCETT BOOKS, Division of Random House, 201 E. 50th St., New York NY 10022. "Science fiction and fantasy should be sent to Judy-Lynn del Rey, editor-in-chief, Del Rey Books. Proposals for trade books, poster books, calendars, etc., should be directed to Joelle Delbourgo, editor of trade books. Proposals including sample chapters for contemporary and historical fiction and romances should be sent to Ann LaFarge, senior editor of Ballantine or Barbara Dicks, senior editor of Fawcett." Publishes trade and mass market paperback originals and reprints. Royalty contract varies. Published 350 titles last year; about 25% were originals.
Nonfiction: General nonfiction. "Not interested in poetry; books under 50,000 words are too short for consideration. Since we are a mass market house, books which have a heavy regional flavor would be

inappropriate for our list."
Fiction: General fiction, science fiction and fantasy.
Recent Titles: *Tough Guys Don't Dance*, by Norman Mailer (Ballantine). *The Wheel of Fortune*, by Susan Howatch (Fawcett). *Job: A Comedy of Justice*, by Robert A. Heinlein (Del Rey).

BALLINGER PUBLISHING CO., 54 Church St., Harvard Square, Cambridge MA 02138. (617)492-0670.
President: Carol Franco. Publishes hardcover originals. Averages 60 titles/year. Pays royalty by arrangement.
Simultaneous and photocopied submissions OK. Computer printout submissions acceptable; prefers letter-quality to dot-matrix. SASE. Reports in 1 month. Free book catalog.
Nonfiction: Professional and reference books in economics, business, finance, high technology, and international relations. Submit outline/synopsis and sample chapters or submit complete ms.
Recent Nonfiction Title: *The Reagan Record* , by John Palmer and Isabel Sawhill.

BANKERS PUBLISHING CO., 210 South St., Boston MA 02111. (617)426-4495. Executive Editor: Robert I. Roen. Publishes hardcover originals. Averages 7 titles/year; receives 20-30 submissions annually. 50% of books from first-time authors; 100% of books from unagented writers. Average print order for a writer's first book is 2,000. Pays 10-15% royalty on both wholesale and retail price; buys some mss outright for negotiable fee. Publishes book an average of 8 months after acceptance. Computer printout submissions acceptable; prefers letter-quality to dot-matrix. SASE. Reports in 2 months. Book catalog and ms guidelines for $5^1/_2$x$8^1/_2$ SAE and 2 first class stamps.
Nonfiction: How-to reference texts on banking only for banking professionals. "Because of their nature, our books remain useful for many years (it is not unusual for a title to remain in print for 5-10 years). However, some of our technical titles are revised and updated frequently." Looks for "the ability of the author to communicate practical, how-to technical knowledge to the reader in an understanding way." Submit outline/synopsis and 2 sample chapters.
Recent Nonfiction Title: *Bank Audits and Examination*, by John Savage.
Tips: "As long as a book contains technical, necessary information about doing a particular banking job, it does well. We try to provide bankers with information and guidance not available anywhere else. Most of our writers are experienced bankers, but we are willing to consider a professional researcher/writer for some projects. We seek to work with new authors."

BANTAM BOOKS, INC., 666 5th Ave., New York NY 10103. Imprints include Skylark, For Young Readers, Sweet Dreams, Peacock Press, Loveswept, New Age Books, Spectra Windstone, and Bantam Classics. (212)765-6500. President/CEO: Lou Wolfe. Executive Vice President/COO: Alberto Vitale. Vice President/Publisher/Editor-in-Chief: Linda Grey. Editorial Director/Adult Fiction and Nonfiction Books: Steve Rubin. Publishes mass market, trade paperback, and hardcover books for adults, young adults (ages 12-17), and young readers (ages 8-12), fiction and nonfiction reprints and originals. Pays variable royalty and advance. Publisher does not accept queries or unsolicited manuscripts.
Nonfiction: Linda Cunningham, Executive Editor, Religious and Inspirational Books; Toni Burbank, Executive Editor (women's studies, school and college); Fred Klein, Vice President and Executive Editor/Media; Senior Editors: (cookbooks, mysteries, health); Linda Cunningham (business, finance); LuAnn Walther (school and college, classics); Tobi Sanders (science); Nessa Rapoport (Bantam Jewish Bookshelf).
Fiction: Sol Skolnick—Trade and HC Association Publisher; Peter Guzzardi (sports and general fiction); Carolyn Nichols (Loveswept); Lou Aronica, Editor, Spectra Science Fiction and Fantasy; Kate Miciak, Administrative Editor (general fiction, mysteries); Elizabeth Barrett, Associate Editor, Loveswept. Young Adult titles: Judy Litenstein, books for young readers. Nina Hoffman (Director of Subsidiary Rights), Linda Biagi (Manager of Subsidiary Rights), Kenzi Sugihara (Director Bantam Electronic Publishing), Alicia Condon, Senior Editor Loveswept. Also considers submissions for war series.

BARNES & NOBLE, Division of Harper & Row, 10 E. 53rd St., New York NY 10022. (212)207-7000.
Editorial Director: Irving Levey. Editor: Jeanne Flagg. Assistant Editor: Daniel Bial. Special Projects: Lourdes Font. Publishes paperback originals and paperback reprints. Averages 40 titles/year. Pays standard paperback royalties for reprints; offers variable advance. Simultaneous and photocopied submissions OK. Computer printout submissions acceptable. SASE. Reports in 1 month.
Nonfiction: Education paperbacks including "College Outline Series" (summaries of college subjects) and Everyday Handbooks (self-teaching books on academic subjects, and skills and hobbies). Query or submit outline/synopsis and sample chapters. Looks for "an indication that the author knows the subject he is writing about and that he can present it clearly and logically."
Recent Nonfiction Title: *Girltalk: All the Stuff your Sister Never Told You*, by Carol Weston.

BARRON'S EDUCATIONAL SERIES, INC., 113 Crossways Park Dr., Woodbury NY 11797. Publishes hardcover and paperback originals and software. Publishes 170 titles/year. 10% of books from first-time authors; 90% of books from unagented writers. Pays royalty, based on both wholesale and retail price. Publishes book an average of 9 months after acceptance. Simultaneous and photocopied submissions OK. Computer printout acceptable; prefers letter-quality to dot-matrix. Reports in 3 months. SASE. Book catalog $5. "Only writers with contracts receive guidelines."

Nonfiction: Adult education, art, cookbooks, foreign language, review books, guidance, pet books, travel, literary guides, juvenile, sports, test preparation materials and textbooks. Accepts artwork/photos. Query or submit outline/synopsis and 2-3 sample chapters. Accepts nonfiction translations.

Recent Nonfiction Titles: *The Joy of Ice Cream*, by Matthew Kline; *The Five Senses*, children's series by J.M. Parramon and J.J. Puigi; *The Traveler's Dictionary*.

Tips: "The writer has the best chance of selling us a book that will fit into one of our series."

BASIC BOOKS, INC., 10 E. 53rd St., New York NY 10022. (212)207-7057. Editorial Director: Martin Kessler. Publishes hardcover originals, and paperback reprints from its backlist only. Publishes approximately 60 titles/year. Pays standard royalty; negotiates advance depending on projects. SASE. Reports in 3 months.

Nonfiction: Political science, economics, behavioral sciences, and some popular science for universities and trade. Prefers submission of propectus, outline, synopsis, and/or sample chapters.

Recent Nonfiction Title: *Metamagical Phemes*, by Douglas Hofstadter.

BC STUDIO PUBLICATIONS, Box 5908, Huntington Beach CA 92615. Executive Editor: Shirleen Kaye. Publishes booklets and reports. Averages 50 titles/year; receives 200-400 submissions annually. 100% of books from unagented writers. Pays 8-10% on wholesale price; will possibly negotiate outright purchase; buys b&w art for $10-250. No advance. Publishes book an average of 6 months after acceptance. Simultaneous submissions OK; photocopied submissions preferred. Computer printout submissions acceptable. SASE. Reports in 1 month on queries; 6 weeks on mss. Samples and art and writers guidelines for $2 and 2 loose first class stamps.

Nonfiction: Softcover booklets up to 28 pages (no full length books): business directory, how-to, juvenile, mail order, reference, self-help and technical. Subjects include business and money making, cooking and foods, diets, health, hobbies, philosophy, psychology and recreation. "We are interested in any short report from 2-28 pages that shows people how to solve a problem, make more money, start a business, build something, improve themselves or their lives, or find sources for their needs through low cost softcover directories. No partisan politics, religion, fiction or purely recreational type reading." Prefers complete ms after reading guidelines.

Recent Title: *325 Ways to Make Money Living in the Country*, by B. Camp (paperback report 8x11").

Tips: "Our booklets and reports are for people who are interested in self-improvement, income improvement, dollar stretching, and those interested in mailorder or small business. We also will publish for some hobbyists and collectors."

BEACON HILL PRESS OF KANSAS CITY, Box 527, Kansas City MO 64141. Book division of Nazarene Publishing House. Coordinator: Betty Fuhrman. Editorial Associate: Evelyn Stenbock. Publishes hardcover and paperback originals. Averages 65-70 titles/year. Offers "standard contract (sometimes flat rate purchase). Advance on royalty is paid on first 1,000 copies at publication date. On standard contract, pays 10% on first 10,000 copies and 12% on subsequent copies at the end of each calendar year." Publishes book an average of 2 years after acceptance. Computer printout submissions acceptable; prefers letter-quality to dot-matrix. SASE. Reports in 4-8 months unless immediately returned. "Book Committee meets quarterly to select from the manuscripts which will be published."

Nonfiction: Inspirational, Bible-based. Doctrinally must conform to the evangelical, Wesleyan tradition. Conservative view of Bible. No autobiography, poetry, devotional collections, or children's picture books. Accent on holy living; encouragement in daily Christian life. Popular style books usually under 128 pages. Query. Textbooks "almost exclusively done on assignment." Full ms or outline/sample chapters. Length: 20,000-40,000 words.

Recent Nonfiction Title: *Beware The Little Animals*, by Jane Brewington.

BEACON PRESS, 25 Beacon St., Boston MA 02108. (617)742-2110. Director: Wendy J. Strothman. Publishes hardcover originals and paperback reprints. Averages 32 titles/year; receives 250 w submissions annually. Average print order for a writer's first book is 3,000. Offers royalty on net retail price; advance varies. Publishes book an average of 7-9 months after acceptance. Simultaneous and photocopied submissions OK. Computer printout submissions acceptable; prefers letter-quality to dot-matrix. Return of materials not guaranteed without SASE. Reports in 2 months. Query or submit outline/synopsis and sample chapters to Nancy Lattanzio, editorial assistant.

Nonfiction: General nonfiction including works of original scholarship, religion, women's studies, philosophy, current affairs, literature communications, sociology, psychology, history, political science, art and some counseling.

Recent Nonfiction Title: *Bread Not Stone: The Challenge of Feminist Biblical Interpretation*, by Elizabeth Schussler Fiorenza.

Tips: "No fiction or poetry submissions invited. No children's books."

*BEAR AND CO., INC., Drawer 2860, Santa Fe NM 87504-2860. (505)983-9868. Acquisitions/PR: Barbara Clow. Publishes trade paperback originals and trade paperback reprints. Averages 9 titles/year; receives 300 submissions annually. 20% of books from first-time authors; 80% of books from unagented writers. Average print order for a writer's first book is 3,000. Subsidy publishes 10% of books. Pays 8-10% royalty on wholesale price; offers no advance. Publishes book an average of 1 year after acceptance. No simultaneous or photocopied submissions. Computer printout submissions acceptable; prefers letter-quality to dot-matrix. SASE. Reports in 2 weeks on queries; 2 months on mss. Free book catalog; writer's guidelines for SAE and 50¢ postage.
Nonfiction: Reference. Subjects include theology, philosophy, art, history, music, politics, psychology, religion, sociology and science. "We publish works coming out of Matthew Fox's creation-centered theology, a school of contemporary Catholicism. We are looking for books on creation-centered mystics AD-2,000 AD. Write to Bear and Co., for specific sources we want to publish. No lightweight theology, history, new science or art books. No classical Catholic religious works." Query only with outline/synopsis and sample chapters. Reviews artwork/photos as part of ms package.
Recent Nonfiction Title: *Original Blessing*, by Matthew Fox, OP (theology).
Tips: "Books with depth and quality are sought now. Our audience is comprised of individuals from all cultures who are seriously investigating sources of spirituality from Western roots."

BEAU LAC PUBLISHERS, Box 248, Chuluota FL 32766. Publishes hardcover and paperback originals. SASE.
Nonfiction: "Military subjects. Specialist in the social side of service life." Query.
Recent Nonfiction Titles: *Mrs. NCO; Mainly Military but Not Entirely*, all by Mary Preston Gross; *Florida's Fantastic Fauna and Flora*, by Leslie Fletcher.

BEAUFORT BOOKS, INC., 9 E. 40th St., New York NY 10016. (212)685-8588. Editor-in-Chief: Susan Suffes. Publishes hardcover and trade paperback originals. Averages 70-80 titles/year; receives 1,000 submissions annually. 10% of books from unagented writers. Pays $7^1/_2$-15% royalty on retail price; offers variable advance. Publishes book an average of 1 year after acceptance. Simultaneous and photocopied submissions OK. Letter-quality submissions preferred. SASE. Reports in 2 weeks on queries; 1 month on mss. Book catalog for 6x9 SAE and 2 first class stamps.
Nonfiction: Subjects include biography, health, business, sports, travel, history, music, and recreation. Query, or submit outline/synopsis and 3 sample chapters or complete ms.
Recent Nonfiction Title: *Jagger*, by Carey Schofield.
Fiction: Mystery, thrillers, contemporary and literary novels. "No first novels, no science fiction." Accepts fiction translations from French. Query or submit complete ms.
Recent Fiction Title: *Deathwatch*, by Ellesten Trevor.

THE BENJAMIN COMPANY, INC., One Westchester Plaza, Elmsford NY 10523. (914)592-8088. President: Ted Benjamin. Publishes hardcover and paperback originals. Averages 10-12 titles/year. Buys mss by outright purchase. Offers advance. Simultaneous and photocopied submissions OK. Computer printout submissions acceptable; prefers letter-quality to dot-matrix. Reports in 2 months.
Nonfiction: Business/economics, cookbooks, cooking and foods, health, hobbies, how-to, self-help, sports and consumerism. "Ours is a very specialized kind of publishing—for clients (industrial and association) to use in promotional, PR, or educational programs. If an author has an idea for a book and close connections with a company that might be interested in using that book, we will be very interested in working together with the author to 'sell' the program and the idea of a special book for that company. Once published, our books do get trade distribution through a distributing publisher, so the author generally sees the book in regular book outlets as well as in the special programs undertaken by the sponsoring company. Normally we do not encourage submission of manuscripts. We usually commission an author to write for us. The most helpful thing an author can do is to let us know what he or she has written, or what subjects he or she feels competent to write about. We will contact the author when our needs indicate that the author might be the right person to produce a needed manuscript." Query. Submit outline/synopsis and 1 sample chapter. Looks for "possibility of tie-in with sponsoring company or association."
Recent Nonfiction Title:*Protect Your Business*, for Council of Better Business Bureaus.

BENNETT & MCKNIGHT PUBLISHING CO., Division of Glencoe Publishing Co. 809 W. Detweiller Dr., Peoria IL 61615. (309)691-4454. Vice President/Editorial: Michael Kenny. Publishes hardcover and paperback originals. Specializes in textbooks and related materials. Pays up to 10% royalty for textbooks "based on cash received, less for supplements"; no advance. Publishes book an average of 2 years after acceptance. Averages 20 titles/year. Query "with 1-2 sample chapters that represent much of the book; not a general introduction if the ms is mostly specific 'how-to' instructions." Photocopied submissions OK. Computer printout submissions acceptable. Reports in 2-4 weeks. SASE. Free book catalog.
Nonfiction: Publishes textbooks and related items for home economics, industrial education, career education,

and art programs in schools, junior high and above. Wants "content with good coverage of subject matter in a course in one of our fields; intelligent organization; and clear expression."

Recent Nonfiction Titles: *Energy Power and Transportation Technology,* and *Production Technology.*

THE BERKLEY PUBLISHING GROUP, (publishers of Berkley/Berkley Trade Paperbacks/Jove/Charter/Second Chance at Love/To Have and To Hold/Tempo young adult fiction/Ace Science Fiction), 200 Madison Ave., New York NY 10016. (212)686-9820. Vice President/Publisher: Roger Cooper. Editor-in-Chief: Nancy Coffey. Publishes paperback originals and reprints. Publishes approximately 900 titles/year. Pays 6-10% royalty on retail price; offers advance. Publishes book an average of 18 months after acceptance. "We don't accept unsolicited material."

Nonfiction: How-to, inspirational, family life, philosophy and nutrition.

Recent Nonfiction Title: *The One Minute Manager.*

Fiction: Adventure, historical, mainstream men's adventure, young adult, suspense, western, occult, romance and science fiction. Submit outline/synopsis and first 3 chapters for Ace Science Fiction only).

Recent Fiction Title: *. . . And Ladies of the Club.*

Young Adult Fiction Title: *T.L.C., Tender Loving Care.*

BETHANY HOUSE PUBLISHERS, 6820 Auto Club Rd., Minneapolis MN 55438. (612)944-2121. Managing Editor: Carol Johnson. Publishes hardcover and paperback originals and paperback reprints. "Contracts negotiable." Averages 50 titles/year. Publishes book an average of 18 months after acceptance. Simultaneous and photocopied submissions OK. Computer printout submissions acceptable. Reports in 1-2 months. Free book catalog on request.

Nonfiction: Publishes reference (lay-oriented), devotional (evangelical, charismatic), and personal growth books. "No poetry, please." Submit outline and 2-3 sample chapters. Looks for "provocative subject, quality writing style, authoritative presentation, unique approach, sound Christian truth." Reviews artwork/photos as part of ms package.

Recent Nonfiction Title: *The Bethany Parallel Commentary* (reference).

Fiction: Well-written stories with a Christian message. Submit synopsis and 2-3 sample chapters. SASE. Guidelines available. SASE.

Recent Fiction Title: *Jenny,* by Marcia Mitchell (young adult romance).

BETTER HOMES AND GARDENS BOOKS, 1716 Locust St., Des Moines IA 50336. Editor: Gerald Knox. Publishes hardcover originals and reprints. Publishes 30 titles/year. "Ordinarily we pay an outright fee for work (amount depending on the scope of the assignment). If the book is the work of one author, we sometimes offer royalties in addition to the fee." Will consider photocopied submissions. Reports in 6 weeks. SASE.

Nonfiction: "We publish nonfiction in many family and home service categories, including gardening, decorating and remodeling, sewing and crafts, money management, entertaining, handyman's topics, cooking and nutrition, and other subjects of home service value. Emphasis is on how-to and on stimulating people to action. We require concise, factual writing. Audience is primarily husbands and wives with home and family as their main center of interest. Style should be informative and lively with a straightforward approach. Stress the positive. Emphasis is entirely on reader service. We approach the general audience with a confident air, instilling in them a desire and the motivation to accomplish things. Food book areas that we have already dealt with in detail are currently overworked by writers submitting to us. We rely heavily on a staff of home economist editors for food books. We are interested in nonfood books that can serve mail order and book club requirements (to sell at least for $9.95 and up) as well as trade. Rarely is our first printing of a book less than 100,000 copies. Publisher recommends careful study of specific *Better Homes and Gardens* book titles before submitting material." Prefers outlines and 1 sample chapter, but will accept complete ms. Will consider photocopied submissions.

Tips: Queries/mss may be routed to other editors in the publishing group.

BETTERWAY PUBLICATIONS, INC., General Delivery, White Hall VA 22987. (804)823-5661. Senior Editor: Robert F. Hostage. Publishes hardcover and trade paperback originals. Averages 12-14 titles/year; receives 1,000 submissions annually. 50-60% of books from first-time authors; 100% of books from unagented writers. Average print order for a writer's first book is 5,000-10,000. Pays 10-15% royalty on wholesale price. Advance averages $500. Publishes book an average of 6 months after acceptance. Simultaneous and photocopied submissions OK. Computer printout submissions acceptable; no dot-matrix. SASE. Reports in 3 weeks on queries; 1 month on mss. Free book catalog and writer's guidelines with 9x12 SAE and 56¢ postage.

Nonfiction: Cookbook, how-to, reference, self-help, health and crafts. Subjects include small business and personal finance, cooking and foods, health, childcare and parenting, crafts resources and homemaking. Especially wants "small and home business books; crafts resource guides practical and inspirational books for women who want personal/business fulfillment and a strong home and family life; books on parenting and child care; and health and nutrition." Submit outline/synopsis and sample chapters. Reviews artwork/photos as part

of ms package.
Recent Nonfiction Title: *Organize Your Personal Finances—Turn Choas into Cash.*
Tips: Trends in book publishing that freelance writers should be aware of include "the dynamically increasing number of book published and publishing ventures founded every month, and the resulting need for aspiring authors to research their subject category markets, to ensure that there is a market niche for their proposed work."

BIBLI O'PHILE PUBLISHING CO., Box 5189, New York NY 10022. (212)888-1008. Contact: Cathy Frumerman: Publishes hardcover and trade paperback originals. Averages 2-3 titles/year. Pays 5-10% royalty on wholesale price. Computer printout submissions acceptable; no dot-matrix. SASE. Reports in 2 months. Free book catalog.
Nonfiction: Biography, cookbook, how-to and self-help. Subjects include business and economics (lay person's guide); cooking and food; and health. Especially looking for biographies, autobiographies, self-help, financial guides for laypersons, books on inner and outer beauty, and health/vegetarian cookbooks. Submit complete ms.
Recent Nonfiction Title: *The Hip High-Prote, Low Cal, Easy-Does-It Cookbook*, by Hayden (cookbook).

*BINFORD & MORT PUBLISHING, 2536 SE 11th Ave., Box 42368, Portland OR 97242. (503)238-9666. Publisher: James Gardenier. Publishes hardcover and paperback originals and reprints. Receives 500 submissions annually. 60% of books from first-time authors; 90% of books from unagented writers. Average print order for a writer's first book is 5,000. Pays 10% royalty on retail price; offers variable advance (to established authors). Publishes about 10-12 titles annually. Occasionally does some subsidy publishing (10%), at author's request. Publishes book an average of 1 year after acceptance. Reports in 2-4 months. Computer printout submissions acceptable; prefers letter-quality to dot-matrix. SASE.
Nonfiction: Books about the Pacific Coast and the Northwest. Western Americana, biography, history, nature, recreation, reference, and travel. Query. Reviews artwork/photos as part of ms package.
Recent Nonfiction Title: *Oregon Shipwrecks*, by Don Marshall.
Fiction: Low priority. No needs at this time.
Tips: "Books about the Pacific Coast and the Northwest still best, because that is the type of book we publish."

JOHN F. BLAIR, PUBLISHER, 1406 Plaza Dr., Winston-Salem NC 27103. (919)768-1374. Editor-in-Chief: John F. Blair. Publishes hardcover originals, trade paperbacks and occasionally reprints; receives 1,300 submissions annually. 10-20% of books from first-time authors; 100% of books from unagented writers. Average print order for a writer's first book is 3,500. Royalty to be negotiated. Publishes book an average of 2 years after acceptance. Free book catalog. Submit synopsis/outline and first 3 chapters or complete ms. Computer printout submissions acceptable; no dot-matrix. Reports in 3 months. SASE. Book catalog and ms guidelines for large manila SAE and 56¢ postage.
Nonfiction: Especially interested in well-researched adult biography and history. Preference given to books dealing with Southeastern United States. Also interested in environment and Americana; query on other nonfiction topics. Looks for utility and significance. Reviews artwork/photos as part of ms package.
Recent Nonfiction Title: *South Carolina's Historic Restaurants and Their Recipes*, by Dawn O'Brien and Karen Mulford.
Fiction: "We are most interested in serious novels of substance and imagination. Preference given to material related to Southeastern United States. No category fiction. Juveniles should be for ages 9-14; no picture books. We are accepting few poetry mss at this time."
Recent Fiction Title: *The Silence of Snakes*, by Lewis W. Green.

BOOKCRAFT, INC., 1848 W. 2300 South, Salt Lake City UT 84119. (801)972-6180. Managing Editor: H. George Bickerstaff. Publishes (mainly hardcover) originals and reprints. Pays standard 10-12½-15% royalty on retail price; "we rarely give a royalty advance." Averages 30-35 titles/year. Will send general information to prospective authors on request. Query. Publishes book an average of 6 months after acceptance. Will consider photocopied submissions. Computer printout submissions acceptable; prefers letter-quality to dot-matrix. "Include contents page with ms." Reports in about 2-4 months. SASE.
Nonfiction: "We publish for members of The Church of Jesus Christ of Latter-Day Saints (Mormons) and do not distribute to the national market. All our books are closely oriented to the faith and practices of the LDS church, and we will be glad to review such mss. Mss which have merely a general religious appeal are not acceptable. Ideal book lengths range from about 64 to 176 pages or so, depending on subject, presentation, and age level. We look for a fresh approach—rehashes of well-known concepts or doctrines not acceptable. Mss should be anecdotal unless truly scholarly or on a specialized subject. Outlook must be positive. We do not publish anti-Mormon works. We don't publish poetry, plays, personal philosophizings, family histories, or personal histories. We also publish short and moderate length books for Mormon youth, about ages 14 to 19, mostly nonfiction. These reflect LDS principles without being 'preachy'; must be motivational. 20,000-30,000 words is about the right length, though good longer mss are not entirely ruled out. This is a tough area to write

in, and the mortality rate for such mss is high. We publish only 1 or 2 new juvenile titles annually."
Recent Nonfiction Title: *The Light and The Life*, by Artist Kapp and Judith Smith.
Fiction: Must be closely oriented to LDS faith and practices.
Recent Fiction Title: *One Song for Two*, by Kristen Randle.

THE BORGO PRESS, Box 2845, San Bernardino CA 92406. (714)884-5813. Publisher: Robert Reginald. Editor: Mary A. Burgess. Publishes hardcover and paperback originals. Averages 35 titles/year; receives 200+ submissions annually. 10% of books from first-time authors; 80% of books from unagented writers. Pays royalty on retail price: "10% of gross, with a 12% escalator." No advance. Publishes book an average of 1-2 years after acceptance. "Most of our sales are to the library market." Computer printout submissions acceptable; no dot-matrix. "Will accept diskettes compatible with IBM PC using MS—Dos 2.1 with WORDSTAR; requires hard copy also." Reports in 2 months. SASE. Book catalog and writer's guidelines for SAE and 39¢ postage.
Nonfiction: Publishes literary critiques, bibliographies, historical research, film critiques, theatrical research, interview volumes, biographies, social studies, political science, and reference works for library and academic markets. Query with letter or outline/synopsis and 1 sample chapter. "All of our books, without exception, are published in open-ended, numbered, monographic series. Do not submit proposals until you have looked at our catalogs and publications. This is not a market for fiction, poetry, popular nonfiction, artwork, or anything else except scholarly monographs."
Recent Nonfiction Title: *Analytical Congressional Directory*, by R. Reginald and J.M. Elliot.

*DON BOSCO PUBLICATIONS, 475 N. Ave., Box T, New Rochelle NY 10802. (914)576-0122. Subsidiaries include Salesiana Publishers. Editorial Director: John Malloy. Publishes hardcover and trade paperback originals. Averages 6-10 titles/year; receives 100 w submissions annually. 5% of books from first-time authors; 100% of books from unagented writers. Average print order for a writer's first book is 3,000. Subsidy publishes 10% of books. "We judge the content of the manuscript and quality to be sure it fits the description of our house. We subsidy publish for nonprofit and religious societies." Pays 5-10% royalty on retail price; offers average $100 advance. Publishes book an average of 9 months after acceptance. Computer printout submissions acceptable; no dot-matrix. SASE. Reports in 2 weeks on queries; 2 months on mss. Free book catalog.
Nonfiction: Biography, juvenile and textbook on Roman Catholic religion and sports. "Biographies of outstanding Christian men and women of today. Sports for youngsters and young adults. We are a new publisher with wide experience in school marketing, especially in religious education field." Accepts nonfiction translations from Italian and Spanish. Query or submit outline/synopsis and 2 sample chapters. Reviews artwork/photos.
Recent Nonfiction Title: *The Falcon and the Dove*, by Peter Lappin.
Fiction: "We are not considering fiction in the coming year."
Tips: Queries/mss may be routed to other editors in the publishing group.

‡THE BOSTON MILLS PRESS, 98 Main St., Erin Ontario N0B 1T0 Canada. (519)833-2407. President: John Denison. Publishes hardcover and trade paperback originals. Averages 12 titles/year; receives 100 submissions annually. 75% of books from first-time authors; 100% of books from unagented writers. Pays 6-10% royalty on retail price; no advance. Publishes book an average of 8 months after acceptance. Simultaneous and photocopied submissions OK. Electronic submissions OK if compatible with IBM PC (Volks writer, but requires hard copy also. Computer printout submissions acceptable. SASE. Reports in 2 weeks on queries; 4 weeks on mss. Free book catalog.
Nonfiction: Illustrated book. Subjects include history. "We're interested in anything to do with Canadian or American history—especially transportation. We like books with a small, strong market." No autobiographies. Query. Reviews artwork/photos.
Recent Nonfiction Title: *Stone Houses*, by Plaxton and Moffat (architecture).
Tips: "We can't compete with the big boys so we stay with short-run specific market books that bigger firms can't handle. We've done well this way so we'll continue in the same vein. We tend to accept books from completed manuscripts."

THOMAS BOUREGY AND CO., INC., 401 Lafayette St., New York NY 10003. Editor: Rita Brenig. Offers advance on publication date. Averages 60 titles/year. Reports in 3 months. Computer printout submissions acceptable; no dot-matrix. SASE.
Imprints: *Avalon Books* (fiction).
Fiction: Romances, nurse/romances, westerns and gothic novels. Avoid sensationalist elements. Send one-page query with SASE. No sample chapters. Length: about 50,000 words.
Recent Fiction Title: *Nurse Stacy's Puzzle*, by Mary Curtis Bowers.

R.R. BOWKER CO., 205 E. 42nd St., New York NY 10017. (212)916-1600. Editor-in-Chief, Book Division: David B.Busel. Pays negotiable royalty. Reports in 2 months. SASE.

Nonfiction: Publishes books for the book trade and library field, professional books, reference books and bibliographies. Query; "send in with your idea a very thoroughly developed proposal with a table of contents, representative chapters, and analysis of the competition."
Recent Nonfiction Title: *Library Automations; OFF-AIR Video Taping In Education.*

MARION BOYARS PUBLISHERS INC., 262 W. 22nd St., New York NY 10011. (212)807-6574. Managing Editor: Ken Hollings. Publishes hardcover and trade paperback originals and hardcover and trade paperback reprints. Averages 30 titles/year. "Standard advance against royalty on retail price is the only method we employ." Pays 15% maximum royalty on retail price; offers ½ of royalty on first printing as advance. SASE. "All submissions must be through a recognized literary agent." Computer printout submissions not acceptable. Book catalog for 9x12 SAE and 2 first class stamps.
Nonfiction: Biography, belles lettres. Subjects include business and economics, feminism, history, music, nature, philosophy, politics, psychology, and sociology. Especially looking for materials on "serious topical issues and matters of international concern in feminisim, health, energy, literature, sociology, language." No cookery, children's. Query to Marion Boyars, 24 Lacy Rd., London SW 15 I NL, England, (01)788-9522, through agent only.
Recent Nonfiction Title: *Stargazing: Andy Warhol's World and his Films.*
Fiction: Ethnic, experimental, general and thrillers. Query through agent only.
Recent Fiction Title: *Jenny Morton's Last Night at the Jungle Inn.*

BRADBURY PRESS., (affiliate of Macmillan, Inc.), 866 3rd Ave. New York NY 10022. (212)702-1409. Publisher: Richard Jackson. Executive Editor: Norma Jean Sawicki. Publishes hardcover originals for children and young adults. Averages 28 titles/year. Pays 10% royalty or 5% on retail price to author, 5% to artist; offers average $3,000 advance. Reports in 3 months. SASE. Book catalog for SAE and 88¢ postage.
Fiction: Picture books, contemporary fiction, adventure and humor. Also "stories about real kids; special interest in realistic dialogue." No adult ms. No fantasy or religious material. Submit complete ms.
Recent Fiction Title: *The Pain and the Great One*, by Judy Blume (picture book).
Tips: "Blockbusters make it *possible* to take risks; we still do first novels."

BRANDEN PRESS, INC., 17 Station St., Box 843, Brookline Village MA 02147. (617)734-2045. President: Adolph Caso. Subsidiaries include International Pocket Library and Popular Technology. Publishes hardcover and trade paperback originals, hardcover and trade paperback reprints and software. Averages 15 titles/year; receives 200 submissions annually. 50% of books from first-time authors; 90% of books from unagented writers. Average print order for a writer's first book is 3,000. Pays 5-10% royalty on wholesale price; offers $1,000 maximum advance. Publishes book an average of 1 year after acceptance. Electronic submissions OK if compatible with IBM PC, but requires hard copy also. Computer printout submissions acceptable; prefers letter-quality to dot-matrix. Inquiries only with SAE and 1 first class stamp. Reports in 1 week on queries; 2 months on mss. Free book catalog.
Nonfiction: Biography, illustrated book, juvenile, reference, technical and textbook. Subjects include Americana, art, health, history, music, photography, politics, sociology and classics. Especially looking for "about 10 mss on national and international subjects, including biographies of well-known individuals." No religion or philosophy. Query. Reviews artwork/photos as part of ms package.
Recent Nonfiction Title: *R.F. Kennedy, Biography of a Compulsive Politician*, by Roberts.
Fiction: Adventure (well-written, realistic); ethnic (histories, integration); historical (especially biographies); mainstream (emphasis on youth and immigrants); religious (historical-reconstructive); romance (novels with well-drawn characters); and books about computers and software. No science, mystery or pornography. Query.
Recent Fiction Title: *Erebus Child of Chaos*, by Sam Saladino.
Poetry: No religious, humorous or autobiographical poetry books. Submit 5 poems.
Recent Poetry Title: *Dante's Inferno*, by Kilmer and Martinez.
Tips: "Branden publishes only manuscripts determined to have a significant impact on modern society. Our audience is a well-read general public, professionals, college students, and some high school students. If I were a writer trying to market a book today, I would thoroughly investigate the number of potential readers interested in the content of my book."

GEORGE BRAZILLER, INC., 1 Park Ave., New York NY 10016. 25% of books from first-time authors; 10% of books from unagented writers. Average print order for a writer's first book is 3,000. Offers standard 10-12½-15% royalty contract; offers variable advance depending on author's reputation and nature of book. Publishes book an average of 1 year after acceptance. Computer printout submissions acceptable; prefers letter-quality to dot-matrix. SASE. No unsolicited mss. Reports in 6 weeks.
Fiction and Nonfiction: Publishes general fiction and nonfiction; subjects included literature, art, philosophy and history. Accepts nonfiction, fiction and poetry translations "provided clearance from foreign publisher is

obtained." Query. Submit outline/synopsis and 2 sample chapters. Reviews artwork/photos.
Recent Nonfiction Title: *Childhood*, by Nathalie Sarrante.
Recent Fiction Title: *Lanark*, by Alasdair Gray.

‡*BRETHREN PRESS, 1451 Dundee Ave., Elgin IL 60120. (312)742-5100. Owned and managed by The Church of the Brethren General Board. Book Editor: David Eller. Publishes hardcover and trade paperback originals, and trad paperback reprints. Averages 12 titles/year; receives 250 queries/submissions annually. 30% of books from first-time authors; 90% of books from unagented writers. "We occasionally do 'shared risk' publications in which the author or other publishing partner shares financially in the start-up costs. This varies according to the over-estimated cost; could be up to 50% or several thousand dollars. The publishing partner agrees to buy back unsold inventory after three years. This is a rare arrangement, usually made only when a denominational program unit requires a book on a certain subject." Payment depends on target market. Typical contract: Flat fee for first 2,500 copies (average page $500-750); 5% to 10% 2,501 to 5,000. 10% over 5,000. "We are considering going to a % of the net price." Publishes book an average of 9 months after acceptance. Simultaneous and photocopied submissions OK. Electronic submissions OK on IBM PC/DOS (inquire), but requires hard copy also. Computer printout submissions acceptable; prefers letter-quality to dot-matrix. SASE. Reports in 2 months on queries; 3-6 months (hopefully) on mss. Free book catalog.
Nonfiction: Biography, cookbook, juvenile, self-help and textbook. Subjects include business and economics, cooking and foods, health, history, philosophy, politics, psychology, religion and sociology. All titles should be from a faith perspective. Needs theology, doctrines, devotional, peace-related, simple living, family life and women's issues, "Plain People" heritage, and current and international events. No how-to books. Query or submit outline/synopsis and sample chapters. Reviews artwork/photos.
Recent Nonfiction Title: *What About the Russians?*, by Dale Brown (trade, anthology).
Fiction: Religious. "The only fiction published in recent years were inspirational, with historical settings in "Pennsylvania Dutch"/Plain People context." No romances. Query.
Tips: "We prefer timely issues with solid theological content, well- written for average reader. Adhere to Chicago Manual style and Church of the Brethren Handbook of Style."

BREVET PRESS, INC., Box 1404, Sioux Falls SD 57101. Publisher: Donald P. Mackintosh. Managing Editor: Peter E. Reid. Publishes hardcover and paperback originals and reprints. Receives 40 submissions annually. 50% of books from first-time authors; 100% of books from unagented writers. Average print order for a writer's first book is 5,000. Pays 5% royalty; advance averages $1,000. Query; "after query, detailed instructions will follow if we are interested." Publishes book an average of 1 year after acceptance. Simultaneous and photocopied submissions OK. Computer printout submissions acceptable. SASE. Reports in 1-2 months. Free book catalog.
Nonfiction: Specializes in business management, history, place names, and historical marker series. Americana (A. Melton, editor); business (D.P. Mackintosh, editor); history (B. Mackintosh, editor); and technical books (Peter Reid, editor). Reviews artwork/photos. Send copies if photos/illustrations are to accompany ms.
Recent Nonfiction Title: *Challenge*, by R. Karolevitz (history).
Tips: "Write with market potentail and literary excellance. Keep sexism out of the manuscripts by male authors."

BRIARCLIFF PRESS PUBLISHERS, 11 Wimbledon Ct., Jericho NY 11753. Editorial Director: Trudy Settel. Senior Editor: J. Frieman. Publishes hardcover and paperback originals. Averages 5-7 titles/year; receives 100 submissions annually. 10% of books from first-time authors; 60% of books from unagented writers. Average print order for a writer's first book is 5,000. Pays $4,000-5,000 for outright purchase; offers average of $1,000 advance . Publishes book an average of 3 months after acceptance. "We do not use unsolicited manuscripts. Ours are custom books prepared for businesses, and assignments are initiated by us." Computer printout submissions acceptable; prefers letter-quality to dot-matrix. SASE.
Nonfiction: How-to, cookbooks, sports, travel, fitness/health, business and finance, diet, gardening and crafts. "We want our books to be designed to meet the needs of specific businesses." Query. Submit outline and 2 sample chapters. Accepts nonfiction translations from French, German and Italian. Reviews artwork/photos as part of ms package.
Recent Nonfiction Title: *Amana Microwave Oven Cookbook*, by C. Adams.

‡**BRICK HOUSE PUBLISHING CO.**, 3 Main St., Andover MA 01810. (617)475-9568. Publisher: Robert Runck. Publishes hardcover and trade paperback originals. Averages 20 titles/year; receives 100 submissions annually. 20% of books from first-time authors; 100% of books from unagented writers. Pays 7½-15% royalty on wholesale or retail price. Offers average $1,000 advance. Publishes book an average of 6 months after acceptance. Simultaneous and photocopied submissions OK. Electronic submissions OK, but requires hard copy also. Computer printout submissions acceptable; prefers letter-quality to dot-matrix. SASE. Reports in 2 weeks on queries; 3 months on mss. Book catalog for SAE; ms guidelines for SASE.
Nonfiction: How-to, reference, technical and textbook. Subjects include business, home design, remodeling

and repair. "We are looking for writers to do books in the following areas: practical guidance and information for people running small businesses, consumer trade books on money and job topics, and how-to books on home design, remodeling and repair." Query.

Recent Nonfiction Title: *New House Planning and Idea Book*, by Alberta (how-to).

BRIDGE PUBLISHING, INC., 2500 Hamilton Blvd., South Plainfield NJ 07080. (201)754-0745. Executive Editor: Lloyd B. Hildebrand. Imprints include Logos (pentecostal/charismatic), Haven (evangelical), and Open Scroll (pentecostal/charismatic and evangelical). Contact Stephen Dunham, assistant editor for imprint submissions. Publishes trade and mass market paperback originals and reprints. Averages 25 titles/year; receives 100 submissions annually. 25% of books from first-time authors. Average print order for a writer's first book is 7,500. Pays negotiable royalty or makes outright purchase. Offers finder's fees for books in public domain (if we publish them). We buy American rights on books published abroad; we assign projects to writers. Offers negotiable advance. Publishes book an average of 8 months after acceptance. Photocopied submissions OK. Computer printout submissions acceptable; prefers letter-quality to dot-matrix. SASE. Reports in 1 month on queries; 2 months on mss. Free book catalog.

Nonfiction: How-to, self-help and religious/Christian (nondenominational). Subjects include health, religion, and personal testimony written in a "teaching," self-help style. Especially looking for books with spiritual emphasis. Query with outline/synopsis and at least 3 sample chapters or submit complete ms.

Recent Nonfiction Title: *Christian Heroes of the Holocaust*, by Joseph J. Carr.

Fiction: Religious and inspirational. Query.

Recent Fiction Title: *Lydia, Seller of Purple*, by Robert W. Faid (biblical novel).

Tips: "If I were a writer trying to market a book today, I would write personal letters to one editor at a time on my list. The letter would tell what audiences the manuscript is addressed to and would explain the theme and other pertinent information."

‡BRIGHAM YOUNG UNIVERSITY PRESS, Scholarly Publications, Box 140 TNRB, Provo UT 84602. Senior Editor: Howard A. Christy. Publishes hardcover and paperback originals. Averages 2-3 titles/year. "We subsidy publish all of our books. We seek books of high merit which may have little potential for repaying the cost of publication. Our objective is therefore to make a contribution to scholarship, not whether or not we recoup costs or make a profit." Pays royalties ranging from 0-15% of wholesale price, or net sales. Reports in 6 weeks. SASE.

Nonfiction: Scholarly nonfiction. "We are interested in high-quality work from any discipline, but we focus mainly on Western regional studies, law (emphasis constitutional issues), the social sciences, and histories/anthropological studies dealing with the American Indian. No length preferences. We do not publish fiction or children's literature." Query. Requests outline/synopsis, 2 sample chapters, and author curriculum vita.

Recent Nonfiction Title: *On Being a Christian and a Lawyer*, by Thomas Shaffer.

WILLIAM C. BROWN CO., PUBLISHERS, 2460 Kerper Blvd., Dubuque IA 52001. President, College and Professional Division: Lawrence E. Cremer. Publishes 125 titles/year. 99% of books from unagented writers. Pays variable royalty on net price. Publishes book an average of 1 year after acceptance. Electronic submissions OK on IBM or Apple compatible, but requires hard copy also. Computer printout submissions acceptable; prefers letter-quality to dot-matrix. Ms must be provided both in hard copy and on diskettes or magnetic tape. SASE. Free guidelines. Reviews artwork/photos.

Nonfiction: College textbooks and general trade in select markets. "Be aware of the reading level for the intended audience." Query. Submit outline/synopsis and 2 sample chapters.

Recent Nonfiction Title: *Philip Allsen's Total Fitness for Life*, (book and book/diskette combination).

Tips: Queries/mss may be routed to other editors in the publishing group.

*BRUNSWICK PUBLISHING CO., Box 555, Lawrenceville VA 23868. (804)848-3865. Publisher: Marianne S. Raymond. Publishes hardcover originals, trade and mass market paperback originals. Averages 8-12 titles/year. 90% of books from first-time authors; 90% of books from unagented writers. Subsidy publishes 90% of books based on "author-publisher dialogue." Payment is based on "individual contracts according to work." Publishes book an average of 8 months after acceptance. Photocopied submissions OK. Computer printout submissions acceptable. SASE. Reports in 2 weeks on queries; 3 weeks on mss. Book catalog for business size SAE.

Nonfiction: Biography, "coffee table" book, cookbook, how-to, humor, illustrated book, juvenile, reference, self-help, technical and textbook. Subjects include Americana, animals, business and economics, cooking and foods, health, history, hobbies, music, nature, philosophy, politics, psychology, religion, sociology, travel, and black and ethnic experience. "Not limited to any particular subject but interested in Third World authors and subjects to continue Third World Monograph series." Query or submit outline/synopsis and sample chapters. Reviews artwork/photos as part of ms package.

Recent Nonfiction Title: *The Lagos Plan of Action vs. the Berg Report*, by Robert S. Browne and Robert J. Cummings.

Fiction: "Will consider fiction mainly on subsidy basis—not limited to special topics." Adventure, erotica, ethnic, historical, humor, mainstream and romance. Query or submit outline/synopsis and sample chapters.
Poetry: "Poetry published only on subsidy basis as of now—not limited to any particular subject."
Recent Poetry Title: *Magic of Life*, by Philip Louis Gabriel.
Tips: "Try to be very original in material or presentation. Offer your readers excellent advice (how-to, self-help). Don't take one person's opinion of what constitutes a 'good' or 'bad' manuscript as final. We look for quality, originality and utility."

BUCKNELL UNIVERSITY PRESS, Lewisburg PA 17837. (717)524-3674. Distributed by Associated University Presses. Director: Mills F. Edgerton, Jr. Publishes hardcover originals. Averages 18-20 titles/year. Pays royalty. Publishes book an average of 2 years after acceptance. Photocopied submissions OK. Computer printout submissions acceptable. Reports in 1 month on queries; 6 months on mss. Free book catalog.
Nonfiction: Subjects include scholarly art, history, music, philosophy, politics, psychology, religion and sociology. "In all fields, our criterion is scholarly presentation; manuscripts must be addressed to the scholarly community." Query.
Recent Nonfiction Title: *New Americans: The Westerner and the Modern Experience in the American Novel*, by Glen A. Love.

*BYLS PRESS, Department of Bet Yoatz Library Services, 6247 N. Francisco Ave., Chicago IL 60659. (312)262-8959. President: Daniel D. Stuhlman. Publishes trade paperback originals. Averages 3 titles/year; receives 10-20 submissions annually. Subsidy publishes variable percentage of books. Pays 7½-15% on wholesale price; no advance. Photocopied submissions OK. Electronic submissions OK, on North Star 5¼" SD, IBM compatible or modem. Computer printout submissions acceptable; prefers letter-quality to dot-matrix. SASE. Reports in 1 week on queries; reporting time on mss "depends on material." Free book catalog.
Nonfiction: How-to (for teachers), and juvenile. Subjects include baking and religion ("stories aimed at children for Jewish holidays"). "We're looking for children's books for Jewish holidays that can be made into computer personalized books. In particular we need books for Sukkot, Shabbat and Purim. We need titles for our teacher education series." Query; "no agents, authors only. Do not submit ideas without examining our books and ask yourself if a book idea fits what we are looking for."
Recent Nonfiction Title: *My Own Hanukah Story*, by D. Stuhlman (children's).
Fiction: Religious (stories for Jewish children). No expository fiction. "All unsolicited manuscripts are returned only if return postage is included."

C Q PRESS, 1414 22nd St. NW, Washington DC 20037. (202)887-8642. Director: Joanne Daniels. Publishes hardcover and paperback originals. Pays standard college royalty on wholesale price; offers college text advance. Publishes book an average of 5 months after acceptance. Simultaneous and photocopied submissions OK. SASE. Reports in 3 months. Free book catalog on request.
Nonfiction: College text. "We are one of the most distinguished publishers in the area of political science." Submit outline and sample chapter.
Recent Nonfiction Title: *The Elections of 1984*, by Michael Nelson, editor.

‡CADDYLAK PUBLISHING, Subsidiary of Caddylak Systems, Inc., 60 Shames Dr., Westbury NY 11590. (516)333-7440. Executive Vice President: Edward Werz. Publishes softcover originals (sold almost exclusively through direct marketing). Averages 26 titles/year; receives 25 submissions annually. 100% of books from unagented writers. "Most of our authors are first-time authors when they begin working with us but write several subsequent books for us. Payment for each project is treated individually, but generally, the rights to smaller works (up to about 25,000 words) are purchased on a flat fee basis, and rights to larger works are purchased on a royalty basis." Advance varies by project. Publishes books an average of 4-6 months after acceptance. Simultaneous and photocoied submissions OK. Computer printout submissions acceptable; prefers letter-quality to dot-matrix. Ms returned only if requested. "We prefer to keep a writer's sample on file for possible future assignments." Reports negative results in 2 weeks on queries; 4 weeks on mss. Free book catalog.
Nonfiction: How-to and reference. Subjects include business (general) and management reports. "We plan to do 40 to 50 new titles during the next two years. The list will consist of individual business titles, more technical management reports, and longer, more comprehensive books that will be published in binder format. All subject matter must be appropriate to our broad audience of middle-level corporate managers. No sensational, jazzy nonfiction without solid research behind it." Submit outline/synopsis and sample chapters.
Recent Nonfiction Titles: *Research Any Business Question—Fast and Professionally*, by Ronald Roel (business how-to).
Tips: "The deciding factors in whether or not we publish a certain book are: (1) we believe there will be a very sizeable demand for the book, (2) the outline we review is logically structured and very comprehensive, and (3) the sample chapters are concisely and clearly written and well-researched."

CAMARO PUBLISHING CO., 90430 World Way Center, Los Angeles CA 90009. (213)837-7500. Editor-in-Chief: Garth W. Bishop. Publishes hardcover and paperback originals. Pays royalty on wholesale price. "Every contract is different. Many books are bought outright." Published 9 titles last year. SASE.
Nonfiction: Books on travel, food, wine, health and success. Query.
Recent Nonfiction Title: *California Wine Catalog.*

CAMBRIDGE, THE ADULT EDUCATION COMPANY, 888 7th Ave., New York NY 10106. (212)957-5300. Vice President Editorial: Brian Schenk. Publishes paperback originals in adult education. Averages 25 titles/year. Pays usually flat fee only; occasionally pays 6% royalty on institutional net price; offers small advance. Publishes book an average of 1 year after acceptance. Photocopied submissions OK. Computer printout submissions acceptable; prefers letter-quality to dot-matrix. SASE. Reports in 1 month. Free book catalog.
Nonfiction: Basic skills—adult education only—emphasizing alternative programs. Vocational, pre-GED, and ESL. Submit prospectus and sample lesson only. No phone calls. Looks for "marketability (how broad and how stable the market is for the program); understanding of adult students (learning styles and needs); thoroughness of design of program (will it require substantial editing? How does the design relate to current educational practice); and cost factors, possible production problems." Reviews artwork/photos as part of ms package. Best known for GED preparation material.
Recent Nonfiction Title: *Snapshots: A Collection of Readings for Adults* (ABE reading program).

CAMBRIDGE UNIVERSITY PRESS, 32 E. 57th St., New York NY 10022. Editorial Director: Colin Day. Publishes hardcover and paperback originals. Publishes 700 titles/year. Pays 12% royalty on retail price; 8% on paperbacks; no advance. Query. Computer printout submissions acceptable. SASE. Reports in 2 weeks to 6 months.
Nonfiction: Anthropology, archeology, economics, life sciences, mathematics, psychology, upper-level textbooks, academic trade, scholarly monographs, biography, history, and music. Looking for academic excellence in all work submitted. Department Editors: Elizabeth Maguire (humanities); Susan Milmoe (psychology); Frank Smith (history, political science); Susan Allen-Mills (social anthropology, sociology), Ellen Shaw (English as second language), Colin Day (economics); James DeMartino (life sciences); Jonathan Sinclair-Wilson (philosophy); Peter-John Leone (earth sciences); David Emblidge (religious studies)..
Recent Nonfiction Title: *Energy Policy in America Since 1945: A Study of Business-Govenment Relations*, by Richard H. K. Vietor.

‡***CAMDEN HOUSE, INC.**, Drawer 2025, Columbia SC 29202. (803)788-8689. President: Dr. James Hardin. Publishes hardcover originals and hardcover reprints. Averages 6-10 titles/year; receives 20-30 submissions annually. 50% of books from first-time authors; 90% of books from unagented writers. Subsidy publishes 70% of books. Pays 15-20% royalty on net sales; offers $100 advance. Publishes book an average of 6-8 months after acceptance. Photocopied submissions OK. Electronic submissions OK on IBM compatible. Computer printout submissions acceptable; no dot-matrix. SASE. Reports in 2 weeks on queries; 1-2 months on mss. Free ms guidelines and book catalog.
Nonfiction: Biography and scholarly. Subjects include (in series) English and American literature, linquistics, culture, philosophy and religion; German literature, linquistics and culture; and sports (reprints of baseball classics). Publishes scholarly books in series. Query or submit complete ms. Reviews artwork/photos.
Recent Nonfiction Titles: *The Well Springs of Literary Creation*, by Ursula Mahlendorf, (scholarly German).
Tips: "We are a small publisher for books of *high quality* in our series and reprints. Our authors receive personal and individual attention."

CAMELOT BOOKS, Children's Book Imprint of Avon Books, a division of the Hearst Corp., 1790 Broadway, New York NY 10019. (212)399-1383. Senior Editor: Ellen Krieger. Publishes paperback originals and reprints. Averages 36 titles/year; receives 1,500-2,000 submissions annually. 10-15% of books from first-time authors; 10-15% of books from unagented writers. Pays 6-8% royalty on retail price; offers minimum advance $1,500. Publishes book an average of 18 months after acceptance. Simultaneous and photocopied submissions OK. Computer printout submissions acceptable; prefers letter-quality to dot-matrix. SASE. Reports in 10 weeks. Free book catalog; ms guidelines for SAE and 98¢ postage.
Fiction: Subjects include adventure, fantasy, humor, mainstream, mystery, science fiction ("very selective with mystery and science fiction") and suspense. Submit entire ms or 3 sample chapters and outline. Reviews artwork/photos.
Recent Fiction Title: *Behind the Attic Wall*, by Sylvia Cassedy.

***ARISTIDE D. CARATZAS, PUBLISHER**, Box 210, 481 Main St., New Rochelle NY 10802. (914)632-8487. Managing Director: Marybeth Sollins. Publishes hardcover and paperback originals and hardcover and paperback reprints. Averages 20 titles/year; receives 250 submissions annually. 25% of books from first-time authors; 95% of books from unagented writers. Average print order for a writer's first book is 1,500. Subsidy publishes 5% of books based on ms "commercially marginal, though of importance to a particular field." Publishes book an average of 18 months after acceptance. Photocopied submissions OK. Computer printout submissions acceptable; prefers letter-quality to dot-matrix. SASE. Reports in 3 months. Free book catalog on request.

Nonfiction: Subjects include art, history, philosophy and religion. Query first. Unsolicited mss are not returned; "we cannot be responsible for lost unsolicited mss." Looks for "suitability with our publications program; credentials of the author; and quality and economic justification of the work." Accepts nonfiction translations from German, French, Italian and modern Greek. Reviews artwork/photos.

Recent Nonfiction Title: *The Rediscovery of Greece*, by F. M. Tsigakou.

Tips: "The writer has the best chance of selling nonfiction, scholarly books: fields include archaeology: art history; classics, history; religion (early Christianity-Mediaeval); some comparative literature, neo-hellenica."

CAREER PUBLISHING, INC., 910 N. Main St., Box 5486, Orange CA 92667. (714)771-5155. Contact: Senior Editor. Publishes paperback originals and software. Averages 6-23 titles/year; receives 300 submissions annually. 80% of books from first-time authors; 90% of books from unagented writers. Average print order for a writers first book is 1,500. Pays 10% royalty on wholesale price; no advance. Publishes book an average of 6 months after acceptance. Simultaneous (if so informed with names of others to whom submissions have been sent) and photocopied submissions OK. Electronic submissions OK on Basic IBM P/C, Apple and Commodore TRS-80; but requires hard copy also. Computer printout submissions acceptable; prefers letter-quality to dot-matrix. Reports in 2 months. SASE. Book catalog for 25¢; ms guidelines for SAE and 1 first class stamp.

Nonfiction: Microcomputer material, educational software, word processing, guidance material, allied health, dictionaries, etc. "Textbooks should provide core upon which class curriculum can be based: textbook, workbook or kit with 'hands-on' activities and exercises, and teacher's guide. Should incorporate modern and effective teaching techniques. Should lead to a job objective. We also publish support materials for existing courses and are open to unique, marketable ideas with schools in mind. Reading level should be controlled appropriately—usually 8th-9th grade equivalent for vocational school and community college level courses. Any sign of sexism or racism will disqualify the work. No career awareness masquerading as career training." Submit outline/synopsis, 2 sample chapters/and table of contents or complete ms. Reviews artwork/photos as part of ms package.

Recent Nonfiction Title: *Motorcycle Dictionary/Terminology*, by William H. Kosbab.

Tips: "Authors should be aware of vocational/career areas with inadequate or no training textbooks, submit ideas and samples to fill the gap. Trends in book publishing that freelance writers should be aware of include education—especially for microcomputers."

CAROLINA BIOLOGICAL SUPPLY CO., 2700 York Rd., Burlington NC 27215. (919)584-0381. Head, Scientific Publications: Dr. Phillip L. Owens. Publishes paperback originals. Averages 15 titles/year. Pays 10% royalty on sales. Simultaneous and photocopied submissions OK. SASE. Reports in 2 weeks on queries.

Nonfiction: Self-help, technical, textbook on animals, health, nature, biology and science. "We will consider short (10,000 words) manuscripts of general interest to high school and college students on health, computers, biology, physics, astronomy, microscopes, etc. Longer manuscripts less favored but will be considered." Query first. Reviews photos/artwork as part of ms package.

Recent Nonfiction Title: *Microfilaments*, by Vivianne T. Nachmias.

CARROLL & GRAF PUBLISHERS, INC., 260 5th Ave., New York NY 10001. (212)889-8772. Contact: Kent Carroll. Publishes hardcover, trade paperback, and mass market paperback originals, and hardcover, trade paperback, and mass market paperback reprints. Averages 60 titles/year. Pays 6-10% royalty on retail price. Publishes book an average of 1 year after acceptance. Photocopied submissions OK. Computer printout submissions acceptable; prefers letter-quality to dot-matrix. SASE. Reports in 2 weeks on queries; 1 month on mss. Free book catalog.

Nonfiction: Biography and fiction. Query. Reviews artwork/photos as part of ms package. All unsolicited mss are returned unopened.

Fiction: Adventure, erotica, fantasy, humor, mainstream, mystery, and suspense. Query. All unsolicited mss are returned unopened.

CARSTENS PUBLICATIONS, INC., Hobby Book Division, Box 700, Newton NJ 07860. (201)383-3355. Publisher: Harold H. Carstens. Publishes paperback originals. Averages 5 titles/year. 90% of books from unagented writers. Pays 10% royalty on retail price; offers average advance. SASE. Electronic submissions OK if compatible with ASCII-5¼" floppy disk, TRS 80 or Modem. Computer printout submissions acceptable; prefers letter-quality to dot-matrix. Book catalog for SASE.

Nonfiction: Model railroading, toy trains, model aviation, railroads and model hobbies. "We have scheduled or planned titles on several railroads as well as model railroad and model airplane books. Authors must know their field intimately since our readers are active modelers. Our railroad books presently are primarily

photographic essays on specific railroads. Writers cannot write about somebody else's hobby with authority. If they do, we can't use them." Query. Reviews artwork/photos as part of ms package.
Recent Nonfiction Title: *Electrical Handbook for Model RR*, by Paul Mallery.
Tips: "No fiction. We need lots of good b&w photos. Material must be in model, hobby, railroad field only."

CATHOLIC TRUTH SOCIETY, 38/40 Eccleston Square, London SW1V 1PD England. (01)834-4392. Editorial Director: David Murphy. Publishes hardcover and paperback originals and reprints. Averages 80 titles/year; receives 250 submissions annually. An estimated 20% of books from first-time authors; 100% from unagented writers. Average print order for a writer's first book is 5,000. Pays in outright purchase of $50-400; no advance. Publishes book an average of 3 months after acceptance. Simultaneous and photocopied submissions OK. Computer printout submissions acceptable; prefers letter-quality to dot-matrix. Reports in 1 month. SAE with IRCs. "Do not send U.S. Mail stamps for return of manuscript." Free book catalog and ms guidelines.
Nonfiction: Books dealing with how to solve problems in personal relationships, parenthood, teen-age, widowhood, sickness and death, especially drawing on Christian and Catholic tradition for inspiration; simple accounts of points of interest in Catholic faith, for non-Catholic readership; and books of prayer and devotion. Query, submit outline/synopsis and sample chapter, or submit complete ms. Reviews artwork/photos as part of ms package.
Recent Nonfiction Title: *A Catechism of Church Law*, edited by Catholic Truth Society.
Tips: Catholic Truth Society publishes nothing but Catholic books.

CATHOLIC UNIVERSITY OF AMERICA PRESS, 620 Michigan Ave. NE, Washington DC 20064. (202)635-5052. Director: Dr. David J. McGonagle. Marketing Manager: Cynthia Miller. Averages 10-15 titles/year; receives 100 submissions annually. 50% of books from first-time authors; 100% of books from unagented writers. Average print order for a writer's first book is 1,000. Pays variable royalty on net receipts. Publishes book an average of 1 year after acceptance. Electronic submissions OK; but requires hard copy also. Computer printout submissions acceptable; no dot-matrix. Reports in 2 months.
Nonfiction: Publishes history, biography, languages and literature, philosophy, religion, church-state relations, political theory and social studies. No unrevised doctoral dissertations. Length: 200,000-500,000 words. Query with sample chapter plus outline of entire work, along with curriculum vitae and list of previous publications. Reviews artwork/photos.
Recent Nonfiction Title: *Metaphysical Themes in Thomas Aquinas*, by John F. Wippel.
Tips: Freelancer has best chance of selling "scholarly monographs and works suitable for adoption as supplementary reading material in courses."

‡*CAY-BEL PUBLISHING COMPANY, Thompson-Lyford Bldg., 2nd Fl., 45 Center St., Brewer ME 04412. (207)989-3820. Editor-in-Chief: John E. Cayford. Imprints include C&H Publishing Co. Publishes hardcover and trade paperback originals, and hardcover and trade paperback reprints. Averages 8 titles/year; receives 250 queries; 50 mss annually. 90% of books from first-time authors; 100% of books from unagented writers. Average print order for a writer's first book is 2,000-5,000. Subsidy publishes 10% of books when authors "want us to put their manuscript in a book form, to typeset it and print it, but want to handle their own sales." Pays 10-15% royalty on retail price. Publishes book an average of 6-8 months after acceptance. Simultaneous and photocopied submissions OK. Computer printout submissions acceptable; prefers letter-quality to dot-matrix. SASE. Reports in 2 weeks on queries; 1 month on mss. Free book catalog. Ms guidelines for $1.
Nonfiction: Biography, cookbook, reference and maritime. Subjects include Americana, cooking and foods, history, religion, and vital records and genealogy. "Our book schedule is fairly well filled for the next year, but we will give very careful consideration to any book about a Maine personage or to a Maine history." No poetry or pornography. Query first, then submit complete ms. Reviews artwork/photos.
Recent Nonfiction Titles: *Fort Knox—Fortress in Maine*, by J. Cayford.
Fiction: "We have planned a series of books written by a Maine author in the 1920s, however these will be reprints and an in-house project. We plan no fiction—unless it is exceptionally good and has a Maine theme."
Tips: "Our books are sold to libraries, schools, colleges, and to book stores. They are used as reference tools or teaching aids. The technical field is our bread and butter—short runs with high profit. Writers with books about any phase of Maine industry—i.e., shipping, ice, brickmaking, canning, clocks, weapons, etc., are very desirable. Our staff will work with authors on these subjects. We are very flexible in scheduling, however, we do require a completed mss before setting a printing date."

‡*CBP PRESS, (formerly Bethany Press), Subsidiary of Christian Board of Publication, Box 179, St. Louis MO 63166. (314)371-6900. Editor: Herbert H. Lambert. Publishes trade paperback originals and trade paperback reprints. Averages 12 titles/year; receives 400 submissions annually. 50% of books from first-time authors; 100% of books from unagented writers. "We subsidy publish about one or two books in ten, and the subsidy usually comes from friends, foundations, or church agencies." An author should be subsidy published "when projected sales are under 3,000, and the book is needed." Pays 17% royalty on wholesale price; offers

no advance. Publishes book an average of 1 year after acceptance. Simultaneous and photocopied submissions OK. Computer printout submissions acceptable; prefers letter-quality to dot-matrix. SASE. Reports in 6 weeks. Free book catalog.

Nonfiction: Biography, how-to, humor, and self-help on religion. "We are looking for books on Bible theology spirituality, worship, and practical Christianity. These books may be primarily for clergy or laity of main-line Protestant and Roman Catholic groups." Submit outline/synopsis and sample chapters.

Recent Nonfiction Title: *The Love Commandment*, by Mary W. Patrick

Tips: "Deal with some current theme that has not been adequately discussed in other books. We look for books on personal devotions or lay Christianity that have a unique approach."

CELESTIAL ARTS, Box 7327, Berkeley CA 94707. (415)524-1801. Editorial Director: George Young. Editor: Paul Reed. Publishes paperback originals. Publishes 20 titles/year; receives 12,000 submissions annually. 50% of books from first-time authors; 90% of books from unagented writers. Average print order for a writer's first book is 5,000. Publishes book an average of 9 months after acceptance. Simultaneous and photocopied submissions OK. Computer printout submissions acceptable; prefers letter-quality to dot-matrix. SASE. Reports in 3 months. Free book catalog.

Nonfiction: Publishes biography, cookbooks/cooking, health, humor, psychology, recreation, new age philosophy, gay, and self-help. No poetry. "Submit 2-3 sample chapters and outline; no original copy. If return requested, include postage." Reviews artwork/photos.

Recent Nonfiction Title: *Love Is Letting Go of Fear*, by Jerry Jampolsky.

Tips: "Celestial Arts is a subsidiary of *Ten Speed Press*, and the same guidelines apply. We do not want to see the same manuscripts submitted to both Ten Speed and Celestial."

‡*THE CHRISTOPHER PUBLISHING HOUSE**, 106 Longwater Dr., Norwell MA 02061. (617)878-9336. Managing Editor: Susan Lukas. Publishes hardcover and trade paperback originals. Averages 10-20 titles/year; receives over 100 submissions annually. 30% of books from first-time authors; 100% of books from unagented writers. Subsidy publishes 50% of books based on subject matter and marketability. Pays 5-30% of royalty on wholesale price; offers no advance. Publishes book an average of 6-9 months after acceptance. Simultaneous and photocopied submissions OK. Electronic submissions OK; will arrange for online translation at time of transmission but requires hard copy also. Computer printout submissions acceptable; prefers letter-quality to dot-matrix. SASE. Reports in 1 month. Free book catalog; ms guidelines for SASE.

Nonfiction: Biography, how-to, reference, self-help, textbook and religious. Subjects include Americana, animals, art, business and economics, cooking and foods (nutrition), health, history, philosophy, politics, psychology, religion, sociology and travel. "We will be glad to review all nonfiction manuscripts, particularly college textbook and religious-oriented. Submit complete ms. Reviews artwork/photos.

Recent Nonfiction Title: *Whither America: Will There Be a Tricentennial*, by Arthur Munk (philosophy).

Poetry: "We will review all forms of poetry." Submit complete ms.

Recent Poetry Title: *Drumbeats & Whispers*, by Thomas V. Simpkins.

Tips: "Our books are for a general audience, slanted toward college-educated readers. There are specific books targeted towards specific audiences when appropriate."

CITADEL PRESS, 120 Enterprise Ave., Secaucus NJ 07094. (212)736-0007. Editorial Director: Allan J. Wilson. Publishes hardcover originals and paperback reprints. Receives 800-1,000 submissions annually. 7% of books from first-time authors; 50% of books from unagented writers. Average print order for a writer's first book is 5,000. Pays 10% royalty on hardcover, 5-7% on paperback; offers average $3,000 advance. Publishes book an average of 2 months after acceptance. Simultaneous and photocopied submissions OK. Computer printout submissions acceptable; no dot-matrix. Reports in 2 months. SASE. Catalog for $1.

Nonfiction: Biography, film, psychology, humor and history. Also seeks "off-beat material," but no "poetry, religion, politics." Accepts nonfiction and fiction translations. Query. Accepts outline/synopsis and 3 sample chapters. Reviews artwork/photos.

Recent Nonfiction Title: *Arrogant Aussie*, by Michael Leapman.

Tips: "We concentrate on biography, popular interest, and film with limited fiction (no romance, religion, poetry, music)."

‡*CLEANING CONSULTANT SERVICES, INC.**, 1512 Western Ave., Seattle WA 98101. (206)682-9748. President: William R. Griffin. Publishes trade paperback originals and trade paperback reprints. Averages 4-6 titles/year; receives 15 submissions annually. 75% of books from first-time authors; 100% of books from unagented writers. Subsidy publishes 10% of books. "If they [authors] won't sell it and won't accept royalty contract, we offer our publishing services and often sell the book along with our books." Pays 5-15% royalty on retail price or outright purchase, $100-2,500, depending on negotiated agreement. Publishes book an average of 6-12 months after acceptance. Photocopied submissions OK. Computer printout submissions acceptable; prefers letter-quality to dot-matrix. SASE required if author asks for ms back. Reports in 6 weeks on queries; 3 months on mss. Free book catalog; ms guidelines for SASE.

Nonfiction: How-to, illustrated book, reference, self-help, technical, textbook and directories. Subjects include business, health, and cleaning and maintenance. Needs books on anything related to cleaning, maintenance, self-employment or entrepreneurship. Query or submit outline/synopsis and sample chapters or complete ms. Reviews artwork/photos.
Recent Nonfiction Title: *How to Sell and Price Contract Cleaning*, by John Graham (how-to).
Tips: "Our audience includes those involved in cleaning and maintenance service trades, opportunity seekers, schools, property managers, libraries—anyone who needs information on cleaning and maintenance. How-to and self-employment guides are doing well for us in today's market."

‡**COACH HOUSE PRESS, INC.**, Box 458, Morton Grove IL 60053. (312)967-1777. Publisher/President: David Jewell. Publishes trade paperback originals. Averages 3-8 titles/year; receives 150-200 submissions annually. 50% of books from first-time authors; 95% of books from unagented writers. Pays 10% royalty on receipts from book sales; 50% royalty on performance. Publishes book an average of 3-12 months after acceptance. Simultaneous and photocopied submissions OK. Electronic submissions OK on ASCII. Computer printout submissions acceptable; prefers letter-quality to dot-matrix. SASE. Reports in 1 month on queries; 3 months on mss. Free script catalog.
Nonfiction: Drama production guides and aids.
Recent Nonfiction Title: *Acting Up! An Innovative Guide to Creative Drama for Older Adults*, by Telander, Verson and Quinlan.
Fiction: Plays for children's theatre, one-act plays for high school contest and plays for senior adults. Query or submit complete ms.
Recent Fiction Title: *Blue Horses*, by Kathryn Schultz-Miller (playscript).
Tips: "Plays which sell best to today's producers, respect children as intelligent, alert and informed, and *avoid* stereotyping any group as evil, stupid or immature. If I were a writer trying to market a book today, I would get a first-class production of my play, and then watch the audience react and adjust my play accordingly."

‡**COLES PUBLISHING CO., LTD.**, 90 Ronson Dr., Rexdale, Ontario, Canada M9W 1C1. (416)249-9121. Manager of Publishing/Editorial Director: Gary O'Connell. Publishes hardcover and paperback originals and reprints. Averages 25 titles/year; receives 100 submissions annually. 20% of books from first-time authors; 100% of books from unagented writers. Average print order for a writer's first books is 5,000. "We are a subsidiary company of 'Coles, the Book People,' a chain of 235 bookstores throughout Canada and America." Pays by outright purchase of $500-$2,500; advance averages $500. Publishes book an average of 8 months after acceptance. Buys Canadian rights only. Simultaneous and photocopied submissions OK. Reports in 1 month. SAE and International Reply Coupons. Book catalog $3.
Nonfiction: "We publish in the following areas: education, language, science, math, pet care, gardening, cookbooks, medicine and health, occult, business, reference, technical and do-it-yourself, crafts and hobbies, antiques, games, and sports. We also publish a complete line of literary study aids sold worldwide." No philosophy, religion, history or biography. Submit outline/synopsis and sample chapters.
Recent Nonfiction Title: *Food Processor Magic*; *Enjoying Cruising Under Sail*.
Tips: "The writer has the best chance of selling us wide appeal, practical self-help books."

COLLECTOR BOOKS, Box 3009, Paducah KY 42001. Editor: Steve Quertermous. Publishes hardcover and paperback originals. Publishes 25-30 titles/year. 50-75% of books from first-time authors; 100% of books from unagented writers. Average print order for a writer's first book is 5,000. Pays 5% royalty on retail; no advance. Publishes book an average of 8 months after acceptance. Send prints or transparencies if illustrations are to accompany ms. Computer printout submissions acceptable; no dot-matrix. SASE. Reports in 1 month. Free book catalog.
Nonfiction: "We only publish books on antiques and collectibles. We require our authors to be very knowledgeable in their respective fields and have access to a large representative sampling of the particular subject concerned." Query. Accepts outline/synopsis and 2-3 sample chapters. Reviews artwork/photos as part of ms package.
Recent Nonfiction Title: *Character Toys*, by D. Longest.

COLLEGE-HILL PRESS, 4284 41st St., San Diego CA 92105. (619)563-8899. Promotions Manager: Karen Jackson. Publishes hardcover and trade paperback originals. Averages 50 titles/year. Pays average 10% royalty on invoiced amount. Reports in 1 week. SASE. Free book catalog.
Nonfiction: Reference, textbook, and medical. Subjects include speech, hearing, language, special education, and medicine. Query and request "editorial and marketing questionnaire."
Recent Nonfiction Title: *Children in Crises* , by Sharon R. Morgan.

COLLIER MACMILLAN CANADA, INC., 50 Gervais Dr., Don Mills, Ontario M3C 3K4 Canada. Publishes originals and reprints in hardcover and paperback, and software. Published 15 titles last year; receives 500 submissions annually. 75% of books from first-time authors; 95% of books from unagented writers. Advance varies, depending on author's reputation and nature of book. Computer printout submissions acceptable; prefers letter-quality to dot-matrix. Reports in 6 weeks. SAE and IRCs. Publishes book an average of 9 months after acceptance.

Nonfiction: "Vocational—technical, family studies, language arts, (for Canadian high school curricula). Query.

Tips: "Writers have the best chance of selling us young adult fiction and textbooks for grades 7 through 12 (controlled vocabulary)."

COLORADO ASSOCIATED UNIVERSITY PRESS, Box 480, 1344 Grandview Ave., University of Colorado, Boulder CO 80309. (303)492-7191. Editor: Frederick Rinehart. Publishes hardcover and paperback originals. Averages 10 titles/year; receives 350 submissions annually. 50% of books from first-time authors; 99% of books from unagented writers. Average print order for a writer's first book is 500-1,000. Pays 10-12$^1/_2$-15% royalty contract on wholesale or retail price; "no advances." Publishes book an average of 1 year after acceptance. Will consider photocopied submissions "if not sent simultaneously to another publisher." Electronic submissions OK but "inquire first"; requires hard copy also. Computer printout submissions acceptable; prefer letter-quality to dot-matrix. Reports in 3 months. SASE. Free book catalog.

Nonfiction: Scholarly, regional and environmental subjects. Length: 250-500 pages. Query first with table of contents, preface or opening chapter. Reviews artwork/photos as part of ms package.

Recent Nonfiction Title: *Dr. Webb of Colorado Springs*, by Helen Clapesattle (medical science).

*COLUMBIA PUBLISHING CO., INC., Frenchtown NJ 08825. (201)996-2141. Editorial Director: Bernard Rabb. Publishes hardcover originals. Receives 500 submissions annually. 20% of books from first-time authors; 90% of books from unagented writers. Average print order for a writer's first book is 3,000. Subsidy publishes 5% of books. "Subsidy publishing is rarely offered and then only if we feel the book to be worthy to have our name on it." Pays 10% royalty; offers average advance. Publishes book an average of 9 months after acceptance. Simultaneous and photocopied submissions OK. Electronic submissions OK on IBM PC or DOS 2.1, but requires hard copy also. Computer printout submissions acceptable; no dot-matrix. Reports in 6 months or longer. SASE.

Nonfiction: Biography, theater, film, dance, classical music, political science, business, recreation, and nature/ecology. Accepts nonfiction and fiction translations from French and German. "We do not want spy novels, westerns, romances, science fiction, mysteries, fad books, religious titles or academic books not applicable to a lay audience." Submit complete ms. Reviews artwork/photos as part of ms package.

Recent Nonfiction Title: *New York and the China Trade*, by Howard.

Fiction: Alternative fiction. Literary novels—serious fiction only. Submit complete ms.

Recent Fiction Title: *Odyssey of Revenge*, by Diamond.

COMMUNICATION SKILL BUILDERS, INC., Box 42050, Tucson AZ 85733. (602)323-7500. Acquisitions/Editorial Manager: Ronald H. Weintraub. Publishes paperback originals, kits, games, software and audio cassettes. Averages 60 titles/year; receives 85 submissions annually. 100% of books from unagented writers. Pays negotiable royalty on wholesale or retail price. Publishes book an average of 9 months after acceptance. No simultaneous submissions; photocopied submissions OK. Electronic submissions OK, if IBM-PC compatible or telecommunicated through modem, but requires hard copy also. Computer printout submissions acceptable. SASE. Reports in 2 months. Free book catalog—Speech-Language/Special Education; ms guidelines for SAE and 56¢ postage.

Nonfiction: Speech-Language/Special Education material: Articulation therapy, language remediation and development; hearing impaired; adult communicative disorders; physically handicapped/developmentally delayed; early childhood education; professional resources; assessment materials. Reviews artwork/photos as part of ms package. "If a material is illustrated, costs for the photographs or drawings are the responsibility of the author."

Recent Nonfiction Title: *Let's Communicate*.

COMMUNICATIONS PRESS, INC., 1346 Connecticut Ave. NW, Washington DC 20036. (202)785-0865. President: Mary Louise Hollowell. Publishes hardcover, trade paperback, and professional/text paperback originals. Averages 6-10 titles/year. Pays royalty or honorarium; offers "nominal, if any" advance. Publishes book an average of 9 months after acceptance. Computer printout submissions acceptable; no dot-matrix. SASE. Reports in 1 month. Free book catalog.

Nonfiction: Reference, technical and textbook. Subjects include business and economics (communications); journalism and communications; performing arts; politics and sociology (science/technology, public affairs and communications). Submit outline/synopsis and 2 sample chapters.

Recent Nonfiction Title: *Acting in the Million Dollar Minute: The Art and Business of Performing in TV Commercials*, by Tom Logan.

COMPCARE PUBLICATIONS, 2415 Annapolis Lane, Minneapolis MN 55441. Publisher: Arnold Keuning. Publishes hardcover and trade paperback originals and reprints. Averages 6-8 titles/year. Receives 200 submissions annually. 75% of books from first-time authors; 60% of books from unagented writers. Average print order for a writer's first book is 5,000. Pays negotiable royalty; offers negotiable advance. Publishes book an average of 1 year after acceptance. Simultaneous and photocopied submissions OK. Computer printout submissions acceptable; prefers letter-quality to dot-matrix. SASE. Reports in 2 months. Free book catalog; ms quidelines for SASE.

Nonfiction: Personal growth books on alcoholism/chemical dependency, weight control, personal relationships, stress management and parenting. "Prefer to hear from writers with credentials in the field they are writing about. Very little chance of publication for divorce experiences or personal recovery from alcoholism or drug addiction." Query. Reviews artwork/photos.

Recent Nonfiction Title: *Stress Breakers*, by Helene Lerner withRoberta Elins.

Tips:"Avoid material that is not new and not positive and problem solving."

‡**COMPUBIBS**, Subsidiary of Vantage Information Consultants, Inc., 358 Willis Ave., Mineola NY 11501. (516)877-1333. Acquisitions Editor: Herbert Regenstreif. Publishes trade paperback originals and software. Averages 8-10 titles/year; receives 25 submissions annually. 40% of books from first-time authors; 100% of books from unagented writers. Makes $100-300 outright purchase plus payment of flat rate/copy if minimum number is exceeded; offers no advance. Publishes ms an average of 4-6 months after acceptance. Photocopied submissions OK. Computer printout submissions acceptable; prefers letter-quality to dot-matrix. Reports in 1 month on queries; 6 weeks on mss.

Nonfiction: Reference and bibliographies. Subjects include business and economics, history, psychology, sports, computers and libraries. Query.

Recent Nonfiction Titles: *Library Automation: A Systems and Software Sampler*, by Charlotte L. Levy and Sara Robbins (reference book).

Tips: "Reference books for a general or professional audience have the best chance of selling to our firm. In completing a book for us, author must honor time provision. Our books are valuable in part because of their currency. If information becomes stale, some titles are less valuable."

COMPUTE! BOOKS, A Division of COMPUTE! Publications, Inc., Affiliate of ABC Publishing Companies, Box 5406, Greensboro NC 27403. (919)275-9809. Book editor: Stephen Levy. Publishes trade paperback originals and software. Averages 36-48 titles/year. Pays 15% of gross wholesale receipts as royalty on one-author books; pro rata (per page) share of 7½% of gross receipts, plus one-time fee as royalty on collections. Photocopied submissions OK. Publishes ms an average of 6 months after acceptance. Electronic submissions OK if prior arrangements made. Computer printout submissions acceptable (dot-matrix OK if clear). Reports in 1 month.

Nonfiction: Books on computers. "We publish books for the home computer user and are always looking for reference books, teaching books, and books of useful programs for small computers. Books must be aimed at the users of a *specific* computer with a specific and limited purpose in mind. For instance, our *Mapping the 64* covers Commodore 64 memory locations clearly and completely with general tips for using them but does not attempt to provide any full-fledged programs. If you have unusual expertise or inside knowledge of a particular subject, then we might well be interested in a highly technical reference book on the order of *Atari BASIC Sourcebook*, but usually we try to aim our books at nontechnical users who are learning programming in their own way and at their own pace. Writers should think of their audience as intelligent people who want their computers to improve their lives and the lives of their loved ones. We are also interested in entertainment programs and programming; home applications; educational programs; and books that teach programming at different levels—if a family or individual would find them useful and interesting." No highly technical books or hardware books. Submit proposal first, which may be a letter or outline and synopsis with sample chapters. "We will always require a detailed outline before we issue a contract, but we like to start at the proposal stage and sometimes work with promising authors to develop the outline we want to see. Writers who are known to us through articles in *COMPUTE! Magazine* and *COMPUTE!'s Gazette* already have our trust—we know they can come through with the right material—but we have often bought from writers we did not know, and from writers who had never published anything before."

 My worst experience was with an author whose work I liked so much that I read the 112 pages of fiction he sent (which was an unreasonable amount for him to have sent), and then when I accepted a story and showed interest in his novel, he told me the story had been accepted elsewhere. I felt my trust was betrayed.

—Morty Sklar
The Spirit That Moves Us Press

Recent Nonfiction Title: *The Second Book of Machine Language*, by Richard Mansfield.

Tips: "If I were trying to create a marketable computer book today, I would become intimately familiar with one computer, then define a specific area to explain to less-familiar computer users, and write a clear, concise outline of the book I meant to write, along with a sample chapter from the working section of the book (not the introduction). Then I would send that proposal to a publisher whose books you believe are excellent and who targets the same audience you are aiming at. Once the proposal was in the mail, I'd forget about it. Keep learning more about the computer and develop another book proposal. *Don't write a book without a go-ahead from a publisher.* The chances are too great that you will spend 6 months writing a book, only to discover that there are nine on the market with the same concept by the time your manuscript is ready to send out."

COMPUTER SCIENCE PRESS, INC., 11 Taft Ct., Rockville MD 20850. (301)251-9050. President: Barbara B. Friedman. Editor-in-Chief: Dr. Arthur D. Friedman. Publishes hardcover and paperback originals and software. Averages 20 titles/year. 25% of books from first-time authors; 98% of books from unagented writers. Average print order for a writer's first book is 3,000. Pays royalty on net price; no advance. Publishes book an average of 6 months after acceptance. Simultaneous and photocopied submissions OK. Computer printout submissions acceptable. Reports ASAP. SASE. Free book catalog.

Nonfiction: "Technical books in all aspects of computer science, computer engineering, computer chess, electrical engineering, computers and math, and telecommunications. Both text and reference books. Will also consider public appeal 'trade' books in computer science, manuscripts and diskettes for computer education at all levels: elementary, secondary and college." Also publishes bibliographies in computer science areas and the quarterly *Journal of VLSI Systems & Computations* and *Journal of Telecommunication Networks*. Query or submit complete ms. "We prefer 3 copies of manuscripts." Looks for "technical accuracy of the material and reason this approach is being taken. We would also like a covering letter stating what the author sees as the competition for this work and why this work is superior."

Recent Nonfiction Title: *Computational Aspects of VLSI*, by Jeff Ullman.

CONCORDIA PUBLISHING HOUSE, 3558 S. Jefferson Ave., St. Louis MO 63118-3968. Averages 50 titles/year; receives approximately 1,000 submissions annually. 25% of books from first-time authors; 100% of books from unagented writers. Average print order for a writer's first book is 7,500-10,000. Pays royalty on retail price; outright purchase in some cases. Publishes book an average of 2 years after acceptance. Electronic submissions OK on IBM-PC; but requires hard copy also. Computer printout submissions acceptable; no dot-matrix. Reports in 3 months. SASE. Writers guidelines for SASE.

Nonfiction: Publishes Protestant, general religious, theological books and periodicals. No poetry; little adult fiction, juveniles. "As a religious publisher, we look for manuscripts that deal with ways that readers can apply Christian beliefs and principles to daily living. Any manuscript that deals specifically with theology and/or doctrine should conform to the tenets of the Luterhan Church-Missouri Synod." Query preferred or submit outline and sample chapter.

Fiction: Juvenile picture and beginner books. "We look for manuscripts that deal with Bible stories, Bible history and Christian missions." Submit complete ms.

Recent Adult Fiction Title: *Moses: Prince, Servant, Prophet.*

CONTEMPORARY BOOKS, 180 N. Michigan Ave., Chicago IL 60601.(312)782-9181. Publisher: Harvey Plotnick. Executive Editor: Nancy Crossman. Adult Education Director: Wendy Harris. Publishes hardcover and trade paperbacks. Averages 110 titles/year. Pays sliding scale of royalties for cloth; most frequently 7½% for paperback. Offers small advance. Simultaneous submissions OK, if so advised. Reports in 3 weeks, longer on complete ms.

Nonfiction: Sports instructional, fitness and health, how-to, self improvement, leisure activities, hobbies, practical business, women's interest, and cookbooks. Also publishes GED and adult basic education materials. Prefers query first with outline/synopsis and sample chapter. "We look at everything; and we do, in fact, publish occasional titles that come in over the transom." Looks for "clarity, insight, high regard for the reader."

Recent Nonfiction Title: *The Truth Hurts*, by Jimmy Piersall.

DAVID C. COOK PUBLISHING CO., Chariot Books, 850 N. Grove, Elgin IL 60120. (312)741-2400. Managing Editor: Catherine L. Davis. Associate Editors: Julie Smith and Lorabeth Norton. Publishes hardcover and paperback originals and paperback reprints for children and teens. Averages 40-45 titles/year. Pays royalty on retail price. No unsolicited ms. Query only. Computer printout submissions acceptable; prefers letter-quality to dot-matrix. SASE required. Reports in 3 months. Writer's guidelines for 9x12 SASE.

Nonfiction: "We're particularly interested in books that teach the child about the Bible in fun and interesting ways—not just Bible story rehashes. Also books that help children understand their feelings and problems; books about animals, sports, science, or true stories of young people whose Christian faith is a vital part of an interesting life." Query. "We prefer a 2- to 4-page synopsis and first 2 chapters." No unsolicited mss.

Recent Nonfiction Title: *Storybooks for Caring Parents*, series by Dave Jackson.

Fiction: "We want books with a spiritual dimension that is an integral inevitable part of the story. The plot should involve spiritual as well as external conflict, and the characters should resolve these conflicts through faith in God. Yet the stories should be entertaining and compelling. We are always looking for books that are humorous and books that can be part of a series. For the Pennypincher series we need sports or space fiction for the 10- to 14-year-old boy, and romances for 10- to 14-year-old girls. Also need more titles for the Making Choices series for both 9-12 year-olds and 6-8 year-olds, in which reader is main character, and story has many possible endings.
Recent Fiction Title: *Potter*, by Walter Wangerin.
Tips: "The author should sell us his manuscript, not only providing a sampling of the book, but also explaining the book's uniqueness, why the book will sell, and citing key competition in the market."

CORDOVAN PRESS, Division of Scripps-Howard Business Publications, 5314 Bingle Rd., Houston TX 77092. (713)688-8811. Publisher: Delton Simmons. Publishes hardcover and paperback originals and reprints. Averages 5 titles/year. Pays negotiable royalty. Publishes book an average of 1 year after acceptance. Computer printout submissions acceptable.
Nonfiction: Professional business and finance, and business self-help. Regional trade, on Western and Southwestern history, Texas and Southwestern travel and guidebooks. Query.

CORNELL MARITIME PRESS, INC., Box 456, Centreville MD 21617. Managing Editor: Willard A. Lockwood. Imprint includes Tidewater Publishers. Publishes original hardcover and quality paperbacks. Averages 10 titles/year; receives 150 submissions annually. 41% of books from first-time authors; 99% of books from unagented writers. Payment is negotiable but royalties do not exceed 10% for first 5,000 copies, 12 1/2% for second 5,000 copies, 15% on all additional. Royalties for original paperbacks and regional titles are invariably lower. Revised editions revert to original royalty schedule. Publishes book an average of 10 months after acceptance. Computer printout submissions acceptable; no dot-matrix. Send queries first, accompanied by writing samples and outlines of book ideas. Reports in 1 month. SASE. Free book catalog and ms guidelines.
Nonfiction: Marine subjects (highly technical); manuals; and how-to books on maritime subjects. Tidewater Publishers imprint publishes books on regional history, folklore and wildlife of the Chesapeake Bay and the Delmarva Peninsula.
Recent Nonfiction Title: *Celestial Navigation Planning*.

CORTINA LEARNING INTERNATIONAL, INC., 17 Riverside Ave., Westport CT 06880. (203)227-8471. General Editor: MacDonald Brown. Pays on a fee or a royalty basis. Published 27 titles last year. "Do not send unsolicited manuscripts; send outline and sample chapter." Reports in 2 months or less.
Nonfiction: Publishes foreign language and ESL teaching textbooks for self-study and school; language teaching phonograph records and tapes; materials of special ESL interest; and how-to books on writing fiction and nonfiction, writing for radio and TV, photography and art. Word length varies.

‡**COUGAR BOOKS**, Box 22246, Sacramento CA 95822. Editorial Director: Ruth Pritchard. Publishes paperback originals. Averages 5 titles/year. Pays 7-10% royalty on wholesale or retail price; outright purchases negotiable. Simultaneous and photocopied submissions OK. Computer printout and disk submissions OK; "query first to be sure disk is compatible or use modem." SASE. Reports in 2 months. Book catalog sent for ✿10 SASE.
Nonfiction: Trends in nutrition, health, child care, parenting. Accepts artwork/photos. "We're picking up subject areas in which California is pioneering." Query first or submit outline/synopsis and 2 sample chapters.
Recent Nonfiction Titles: *Mommy, I'm Hungry-How to Feed Your Child Nutritiously*, by P. McIntyre; *Alternative Birth*, by K. Anderson; *Midwife Murder Case*, by J. Bowers and Rosalie Tarpening; *Mommy & Me Exercises*, by Christie Costanzo.

‡**COUNCIL OF PLANNING LIBRARIANS**, 1313 E. 60th St., Chicago IL 60637-2897. (312)947-2007. Editor: Robert W. Dameron. Publishes 25 titles/year; receives 250 submissions annually. 50% of books from first-time authors; 100% of books from unagented writers. Makes outright purchase of $100. Publishes book an average of 6 months after acceptance. Simultaneous and photocopied submissions OK. Computer printout submissions acceptable; prefers letter-quality to dot-matrix. SASE. Reports in 1 month. Book catalog for 9x12 SAE and 3 first class stamps; ms guidelines for SASE.
Nonfiction: "Bibliographies (only), preferably annotated, in the field of planning, which includes architecture, economics, education, environmental science, health science, history, law, library science, psychology, and sociology as they deal with concerns of planners." No articles offering *one* person's views on a subject. Query.
Recent Nonfiction Title: *Demographic Factors in Urban Planning*, by Dale E. Casper, Ph.D. (bibliography).
Tips: "Our audience consists of professional planners, educators, and librarians in specialized libraries. An annotated bibliography of recent (last 10 years) monographs in specific aspect of planning has the best chance of selling to us. Keep in mind that the citations should be accessible by reader."

COWARD McCANN, INC., Imprint of G.P. Putnam's Sons, 200 Madison Ave., New York NY 10016. (212)576-8900. President and Publisher: Phyllis Grann. Publishes hardcover originals. Averages 60 titles/year. Pays 10-15% royalty on retail prices. No unsolicited mss. No response without SASE.
Nonfiction: Animals, biography, health, history, how-to, juveniles, nature, politics, psychology, recreation, science, self-help, sociology and sports. "We are looking for nonfiction books on topics of current and/or lasting popular interest, for general, not specialized audiences. Our scope is broad; our needs are for quality manuscripts marketable in the hardcover arena. We do not want manuscripts in specialized or technical fields that require extensive design and art work that lead to high cover prices." Query with SASE only.
Recent Nonfiction Title: *Haven*, by Ruth Gruber.
Fiction: Adventure, mainstream, mystery, romance and suspense. "We also want espionage thrillers and mysteries, although the market for these is not as strong as it once was. We do not want science fiction, fantasy or experimental novels." Query with SASE only.
Recent Fiction Title: *Mortal Matters*, by Penelope Gilliatt.

CRAFTSMAN BOOK CO. OF AMERICA, 6058 Corte Del Cedro, Box 6500, Carlsbad CA 92008. (619)438-7828. Editor-in-Chief: Laurence D. Jacobs. Publishes paperback originals and software. Averages 10 titles/year; receives 40 submissions annually. 90% of books from first-time authors; 99% of books from unagented writers. Average print order for a writer's first book is 5,000. Pays royalty of 12¹/₂% of gross revenues, regardless of quantity sold. "More than 60% of our sales are directly to the consumer, and since royalties are based on gross revenues the author's share is maximized." Publishes book an average of 15 months after acceptance. Will consider photocopied submissions. Computer printout submissions acceptable; prefers letter-quality to dot-matrix. SASE. Reports in 2 weeks. Free catalog and ms guidelines.
Nonfiction: "We publish practical references for professional builders and are aggressively seeking manuscripts related to construction, the building trades, civil engineering, construction cost estimating and construction management. Ours are not how-to books for homeowners. Emphasis is on step-by-step instructions, illustrations, charts, reference data, checklists, forms, samples, cost estimates, estimating data, rules of thumb, and procedures that solve actual problems in the field or in the builder's office. Each book covers a limited subject fully, becomes the owner's primary reference on that subject, has a high utility-to-cost ratio, and helps the owner make a better living in his profession. We like to see ideas and queries for books in their early stages; we work with first-time authors, prefer an outline or query, and look for completeness in the coverage of the topic, and clear, simple writing." Query or submit outline. Reviews artwork/photos as part of ms package.
Recent Nonfiction Title: *Paint Contractor's Manual*, by Dave Matis and Jobe H. Toole.

CRAIN BOOKS, 740 Rush St., Chicago IL 60611. Director: Jack Graham. Publishes hardcover and paperback originals. Averages 6-8 titles/year. Pays royalty on net revenues; makes an advance only under exceptional circumstances. Publishes book an average of 1 year after acceptance. Reports in 2 months. SASE. Free book catalog.
Nonfiction: Publishes business books exclusively both for the professional and academic markets. Subjects include advertising and marketing, insurance, finance and investment, business management, and international business. Basically interested in "practical, nuts-and-bolts, how-to approach by experts in the field." Wants to see "outline, table of contents (down to B heads), and 2-3 sample chapters." Reviews artwork/photos as part of ms package. Send contact sheet if photos/illustrations are to accompany ms.
Recent Nonfiction Title: *Marketing Research People*, by Jack J. Honomichl.

CREATIVE ARTS BOOK COMPANY, Donald S. Ellis, San Francisco; Black Lizard Books; Life and Health Books; Creative Arts Communications Books; 833 Bancroft Way, Berkeley CA 94710. (415)848-4777. Publisher: Donald S. Ellis. Senior Editor: Dona Budd. Business Manager: Anne Fuller. Publishes hardcover and paperback originals and paperback reprints. Averages 16 titles/year. Pays 5-10% royalty on retail price or buys some mss outright for $500-10,000. Offers minimum $500 advance. Publishes book an average of 12-18 months after acceptance. Simultaneous and photocopied submissions OK. Computer printout submissions acceptable. SASE. Reports in 3 weeks. Free book catalog.
Nonfiction: Alternative health and foods, cookbooks, how-to, biographies and essays, but open to anything *brilliant* (except poetry). Reviews artwork/photos as part of ms package.
Recent Nonfiction Title: *Just Being At the Piano*, by Mildred Chase.
Fiction: "Looking for serious literary fiction of broad appeal."
Recent Fiction Title: *A Woman Named Solitude*, by Andre Schwarz-bart.

THE CROSSING PRESS, Box 640, Trumansburg NY 14886. Co-Publishers: Elaine Gill, John Gill. Publishes hardcover and trade paperback originals. Averages 10-12 titles/year. Pays royalty. Publishes book an average of 1 year after acceptance. Simultaneous and photocopied submissions OK. Electronic submissions acceptable if 8" disks, but requires hard copy also. Computer printout submissions acceptable. Reports in 1 month on queries; 2 months on mss. Free book catalog.

Nonfiction: Cookbook, how-to, literary and feminist. Subjects include cooking, health, gays and feminism. Accepts nonfiction, fiction and poetry translations. Submissions to be considered for the feminist series must be written by women. Submit outline and sample chapter. Reviews artwork/photos as part of ms package.
Recent Nonfiction Title: *Reclaiming Birth.*
Fiction: Feminism (good literary material). Submit outline and sample chapter.
Recent Fiction Title: *Abeng, Connecticut Countess.*

CROSSROAD/CONTINUUM, (Formerly Continuum Publishing Corp.), 370 Lexington Ave., New York NY 10017. (212)532-3650. Contact: The Editors. Crossroad is a religious publishing program. Continuum is a nonfiction program in the area of human development, current affairs, social and literary concerns. Publishes hardcover and paperback originals and paperback reprints. Publishes 30 titles/year; receives 2,000 submissions annually. 25% of books from first-time authors; 95% of books from unagented writers. Average print order for a writer's first book is 2,500. Pays average 10-12$1/2$-15% royalty on hardcover; 7$1/2$% on retail paperback; sometimes offers an advance. Publishes book an average of 1 year after acceptance. Photocopied submissions OK. Computer printout submissions acceptable; no dot-matrix. SASE. Reports in 2 months. Query. Free book catalog.
Recent Crossroad Title: *Changes,* by John Michael Talbot.
Recent Continuum Title: *Dear Cherry: Questions and Answers on Eating Disorders,* by Cherry Boone O'Neill.

CROSSWAY BOOKS, 9825 W. Roosevelt Rd., Westchester IL 60153. Subsidiary of Good News Publishers. Managing Editor: Ted Griffin. Publishes hardcover and trade paperback originals. Averages 25 titles/year. 5% of books from first-time authors; 50% of books from unagented writers. Average print order for a writer's first book is 3,000. Pays negotiable royalty; offers negotiable advance. Publishes book an average of 1 year after acceptance. Computer printout submission acceptable; prefers letter-quality to dot-matrix. SASE. Reports in 2 months. Book catalog for 9x12 SAE and 90¢ postage.
Nonfiction: Subjects include issues on Christianity in contemporary culture, Christian doctrine, and church history. Accepts translations from European languages. "All books must be written out of Christian perspective or world view." No unsolicited ms. Query by letter first.
Recent Nonfiction Title: *Basic Christian Faith,* by C. Donald Cole.
Fiction: Mainstream; science fiction; fantasy (genuinely creative in the tradition of C.S. Lewis, J.R.R. Tolkien and Madeleine L'Engle); and juvenile age 6 and up to young adult. No formula romance. Query by mail first. "All fiction must be written from a genuine Christian perspective."
Recent Fiction Title: *The Sword and the Flame,* by Stephen R. Lawhead.

CROWN PUBLISHERS, INC., 1 Park Ave., New York NY 10016. (212)532-9200. Imprints include Clarkson N. Potter, Arlington House, Barre, Harmony and Julian Press. Editor-in-Chief: Betty A. Prashker. Publishes hardcover and paperback originals. Publishes 250 titles/year. Simultaneous submissions OK. Computer printout submissions acceptable; no dot-matrix. SASE. Reports in 6 weeks.
Nonfiction: Americana, animals, art, biography, cookbooks/cooking, health, history, hobbies, how-to, humor, juveniles, music, nature, philosophy, photography, politics, psychology, recreation, reference, science, self-help and sports. Query with letter only.
Recent Title: *Mistral's Daughter,* by Judith Krantz.

DANTE UNIVERSITY OF AMERICA PRESS, INC., Box 635, Weston MA 02193. Contact: Manuscripts Editor. Publishes hardcover originals and reprints, and trade paperback originals and reprints. Averages 3-5 titles/year; receives 50 submissions annually. 50% of books from first-time authors; 50% of books from unagented writers. Average print order for a writer's first book is 3,000. Pays royalty; offers negotiable advance. Publishes book an average of 10 months after acceptance. Simultaneous and photocopied submissions OK. Electronic submissions OK on Altos 8000, but requires hard copy also. Computer printout submissions acceptable. SASE. Reports in 6 weeks on queries; 2 months on mss. Book catalog for business size SAE and 1 first class stamp.
Nonfiction: Biography, reference, reprints, and nonfiction and fiction translations from Italian and Latin. Subjects include general scholarly nonfiction, Renaissance thought and letter, Italian language and linguistics, Italian-American history and culture, and bilingual education. Query first with SASE. Reviews artwork/photos as part of ms package.
Recent Nonfiction Title: *The Inferno,* by Dante (new translation by Nicholas Kilmer; 34 modern illustrations by Benjamin Martinez).
Poetry: "There is a chance that we would use Renaissance poetry translations."

DAPHNEAN PRESS, Suite 301, 737 N. LaSalle St., Chicago IL 60610. (312)944-2525. President: Michael Gross. Publishes hardcover and trade paperback originals and hardcover and trade paperback reprints. Averages 5-10 titles/year; receives 1,000 submissions annually. Pays 5-10% royalty on paperback wholesale price and hardcover retail price. Publishes book an average of 6-8 months after acceptance. Simultaneous and photo-copied (if good quality) submissions OK. Electronic submissions OK on IBM PC, but requires hard copy also. Computer printout submissions acceptable, preferably double-struck; prefers letter-quality to dot-matrix. SASE. Reports in 4 weeks on queries; 10 weeks on mss. Free book catalog.

Nonfiction: General and scholarly academic. Subjects include Americana, biography, reference, anthropology, history, philosophy, photography, political science, psychology, religion, sociology and Judaica. "We are particularly interested in the humanities and the social sciences. We are also looking for manuscripts in a specialized nonfiction field which might be called 'academic hobbies.' This field includes reference works for those who pursue an academic field such as history, or psychology as a hobby. In other words, we are looking for academic level books that would be marketable to a more general audience. Nonfiction of academic, scholarly and textbook quality is also of great interest." No how-to, occult or martial arts. Query only.

Tips: "Our audience is academic and semiacademic. The niche that we see for ourselves is between scholarly and popular, emphasizing quality nonfiction."

DARTNELL CORP., 4660 N. Ravenswood Ave., Chicago IL 60640. (312)561-4000. Senior Vice-President: John P. Steinbrink. Averages 7 titles/year; receives 150-200 submissions annually. 50% of books from first-time authors; 99% of books from unagented writers. Average print order for a writer's first book is 2,000. Pays in royalties on sliding scale based usually on retail price. Publishes book an average of 1 year after acceptance. Electronic submissions OK on Penta, but requires hard copy also. Computer printout submission acceptable; no dot-matrix. Reports in 1 month. SASE. Free ms guidelines for SASE.

Nonfiction: Publishes business manuals, reports and handbooks. Interested in new material on business skills and techniques in management, sales management, marketing, supervision, administration, advertising, etc. Submit outline and sample chapter.

Recent Nonfiction Title: *Successful Telemarketing*, by Peg Fisher.

DARWIN PUBLICATIONS, 850 N. Hollywood Way, Burbank CA 91505. (818)848-0944. Executive Editor: Victoria Darwin. Publishes hardcover and trade paperback originals and reprints. Averages 3-4 titles/year; receives 500 submissions annually. 60% of books from first-time authors; 95% of books from unagented writers. Pays 10% royalty on retail price. Publishes book an average of 1 year after accepance. Simultaneous and photocopied submissions OK. Computer printout submissions acceptable (printout paper should be separated and collated with sprocket holes detached); no dot-matrix. SASE. Reports in 2 weeks on queries; 1 month on mss. Free book catalog and ms guidelines for SASE.

Nonfiction: "Coffee table" books, how-to, illustrated books, reference and technical. Subjects include Americana, regional history, hobbies, nature, railroading and recreation. "Manuscripts on adventurous topics, with interesting photos, (mostly b&w). In-depth research with casual writing style." Query. Accepts outline/synopsis and 1-2 sample chapters. "We look at overall scope and treatment of the topic, the author's writing style, how photos and illustrations complement the text, and how much editing it will require in light of its salability (its editorial cost-effectiveness). Author is expected to contribute marketing input." Reviews artwork/photos as part of ms package.

Recent Nonfiction Title: *Recreational Gold Prospecting*, by Jim Martin (how-to).

Tips: "It is increasingly expensive to produce hardcover, illustrated books that pertain to limited audiences. Writers should either broaden their scope for such books or lower their expectations for production specifications."

DATA AND RESEARCH TECHNOLOGY CORP., D.A.R.T. Corp., 1102 McNeilly Ave., Pittsburgh PA 15216. Editor: K.K. McNulty. Publishes software. Receives 25-50 submissions annually. 80% of books from first-time authors; 100% of books from unagented writers. Average print order for a writer's first book is 2,500. Pays 10% royalty; buys some mss outright. Publishes ms an average of 6 months after acceptance. Electronic submissions OK via IBM-PC DOS, but requires hard copy also. Computer printout submissions acceptable; prefers letter-quality to dot-matrix. SASE. Reports in 3 weeks.

Nonfiction: Publishes the "Answers" (series of select bibliographies). Current and original bibliographies as reference sources for specific audiences like telecommunications managers, condominium owners, or people interested in computer applications, etc. "To be accepted for publication, the quality must meet the approval of any serious researcher or librarian. The references must include a brief abstract, title, publisher, pages, price. The bibliography should include not only books, but periodicals, tapes, any audiovisuals, videotapes and disks, trade associations, etc." Also looks at any authoritative, specific manuscripts in the field of bibliography. Query with SASE. Accepts outline/synopsis and 1 sample chapter. Reviews artwork/photos.

‡*DATAMOST, INC.**, 19821 Nordhoff St., Northridge CA 91325. (818)709-1202. Managing Editor: Lorraine Coffey. Publishes trade paperback originals and software. Averages 20-30 titles/year; receives 250 submissions annually. 80% of books from first-time authors; 95% of books from unagented writers. Subsidy publishes 15% of books. Pays 6-10% royalty on wholesale price or retail price; offers negotiable advance. Publishes book an average of 3-6 months after acceptance. Simultaneous and photocopied submissions OK.

Electronic submissions OK on Apple with standard DOS format. Computer printout submissions acceptable. SASE. Reports in 4 weeks on queries; 6 weeks on mss. Free book catalog; writer's guidelines for SASE.
Nonfiction: How-to, reference, technical and textbook. Subjects include hobbies and computers. "Our manuscript needs are based on the computer industry. We are always looking for books on the newest machine, software utility or hardware. Our books are aimed toward the home user (children and adults) with little or no computer knowledge." Query or submit outline/synopsis and sample chapters. Reviews artwork/photos.
Recent Nonfiction Title: *Apple Thesaurus*, by Aaron Filler (hardware/software reference).
Fiction: "We have not published any titles in this category, but we are always willing to review queries for possible submissions." We are currently exploring this area. Query or submit outline/synopsis and sample chapters.
Tips: "The freelancer has the best chance of selling us machine (computer) specific instructional books. We like to see *advanced* topic books, if they are written clearly. We want complete books. We stand behind our books, so if your book includes programming, test it before you send it. We try to act quickly when we receive a new manuscript or query. Although our books have always been computer-related, we are always willing to look at different types of manuscripts."

‡HARLAN DAVIDSON, INC., 3110 N. Arlington Heights Rd., Arlington Heights IL 60004. (312)253-9720. Subsidiary includes The Forum Press, Inc. Editor-in-Chief: Maureen Gilgore Hewitt. Publishes hardcover and paperback originals. Averages 12 titles/year; receives 200 submissions annually. 5% of books from first-time authors; 100% of books from unagented writers. Pays royalty on net price. Publishes book an average of 9 months after acceptance. SASE. Reports in 1 month on queries; 3 months on mss. Free book catalog.
Nonfiction: Textbook. Subjects include business and economics, history, philosophy, politics, psychology, and sociology. Particularly looking for history mss. Submit outline/synopsis and sample chapters.
Recent Nonfiction Title: *A History of American Business*, by C. Joseph Pusateri (textbook).
Tips: "Books that do well for us are introductory, very clearly written, and lively in style. Students today seem to respond best to material that gets to the point quickly, yet entertainingly. If I were a writer trying to market a book today, I would be persistent. Things often fail to move in publishing simply because too many things cry for attention at once. A quiet, polite, follow-up note (or two or three) can keep a project alive through to acceptance or redirection."

DAVIS PUBLICATIONS, INC., 50 Portland St., Worcester MA 01608. (617)754-7201. Acquisitions Editor: Wyatt Wade. Averages 5-10 titles/year. Pays 10-15% royalty. Publishes book an average of 1 year after acceptance. Computer printout submissions acceptable; prefers letter-quality to dot-matrix. SASE. Write for copy of guidelines for authors.
Nonfiction: Publishes art, design and craft books. Accepts nonfiction translations. "Keep in mind the intended audience. Our readers are visually oriented. All illustrations should be collated separately from the text, but keyed to the text. Photos should be good quality original prints. Well selected illustrations should explain, amplify, and enhance the text. We average 2-4 photos/page. We like to see technique photos as well as illustrations of finished artwork. Recent books have been on papermaking, airbrush painting, jewelry, design, puppets, quilting, and watercolor painting." Submit outline, sample chapters and illustrations. Reviews artwork/photos as part of ms package.

STEVE DAVIS PUBLISHING, Box 190831, Dallas TX 75219. Publisher: Steve Davis. Publishes hardcover and trade paperback originals. Averages 5 titles/year. Pays 10-15% royalty on net price. Publishes book an average of 9 months after acceptance. "Disk submissions compatible with TI Professional 5¼" MS-DOS, (or CPM-80). ASCII files OK, only *after* project is accepted from query; should be accompanied by hardcopy printout and should not use extensive special formatting codes." Computer printout submissions acceptable; query first and use fresh ribbon. "We expect manuscripts to be professionally proofed for style, grammar and spelling before submission." Reports in 3 weeks on queries *if interested*. Not responsible for unsolicited material. Does not publish fiction.
Nonfiction: Books on applications of personal computers, modern technology and communications, and current social issues. "We are very selective about our list. We look for material that is professionally prepared, takes a fresh approach to a timely topic, and offers the reader helpful information." No religious or occult topics, no sports, and no mass market material such as diet books, cookbooks, joke books, exercise books, etc. "Our publishing schedule is filled through June of 1986." Query should include phone number, a description of the project and its potential market, an outline and a couple of sample pages. "We can only respond to projects that interest us."
Recent Nonfiction Title: *Programs for the PCjr*.

DAW BOOKS, INC., 1633 Broadway, New York NY 10019. Editor: Donald A. Wollheim. Publishes science fiction paperback originals and reprints. Publishes 62 titles/year. Pays 6% royalty; offers $2,500+ advance. Simultaneous submissions "returned at once, unread." Computer printout submissions acceptable; prefers letter-quality to dot-matrix. SASE. Reports in 6 weeks. Free book catalog.

Fiction: "We are interested in science fiction and fantasy novels only. We do not publish any other category of fiction. We are not seeking collections of short stories or ideas for anthologies. We do not want any nonfiction manuscripts." Submit complete ms.
Recent Fiction Title: *City of Sorcery*, by Marion Zimmer Bradley.

JOHN DE GRAFF, INC., Distributed by International Marine Publishing Co., Camden ME 04843. Editorial: Clinton Corners NY 12514. (914)266-5800. President: John G. DeGraff. Publishes hardcover originals. Averages 2-3 titles/year. Pays 10% royalty on retail price. Publishes book an average of 10 months after acceptance. Simultaneous and photocopied submissions OK. Computer printout submissions acceptable. SASE. Reports in 2 weeks on queries; 1 month on mss. Free book catalog.
Nonfiction: Nautical (pleasure boating). "Our books are for yachtsmen, boat builders and naval architects. We're interested in the how-to aspects rather than boating experiences." Submit complete ms. Reviews artwork/photos as part of ms package.
Recent Nonfiction Title: *Successful Sunfish Racing*, by Derrick Fries.

DELACORTE PRESS, 245 E. 47th St., New York NY 10017. (212)605-3000. Editor-in-Chief: Jackie Farber. Publishes hardcover originals. Publishes 20 titles/year. Pays 10-12½-15% royalty; average advance. Publishes book an average of 24 months after acceptance. Simultaneous and photocopied submissions OK. Computer printout submissions acceptable; prefers letter-quality to dot-matrix. SASE. Reports in 2 months.
Fiction and Nonfiction: Query, outline or brief proposal, or complete ms accepted only through an agent; otherwise returned unopened. No mss for children's or young adult books accepted in this division.
Recent Nonfiction Title: *Go For It!*, by Dr. Irene C. Kassorla.
Recent Fiction Title: *Changes*, by Danielle Steel.

DELMAR PUBLISHERS, INC., 2 Computer Dr., W., Box 15015, Albany NY 12212-5015. (518)459-1150. Vice President of Publishing: G.C. Spatz. Publishes hardcover and paperback textbooks and educational software. Averages 50 titles/year; receives 150 submissions annually. 35% of books from first-time authors; 100% of books from unagented writers. Average print order for a writer's first book is 5,000. Pays royalty on wholesale price. Publishes book an average of 3 years after acceptance. SASE. Electronic submissions acceptable on IBM PC or WordStar, but requires hard copy also. Computer printout submissions acceptable; no dot-matrix. Reports in 2 weeks on queries; 2 months on submissions. Free book catalog.
Nonfiction: Subjects include business and data processing, allied health/nursing, childcare, mathematics, agriculture/horticulture texts, and textbooks for most vocational and technical subjects. Books are used in secondary and postsecondary schools. Query and submit outline/synopsis and 2-3 sample chapters. Reviews artwork/photos as part of ms package.
Recent Nonfiction Title: *Fundamentals of CAD*, by Gary Bertdine.
Tips: Vocational textbooks have the best chance of selling for *Delmar Publishers*. Queries/mss may be routed to other editors in the publishing group.

DELTA BOOKS, Division of Dell Publishing Co., 1 Dag Hammarskjold Plaza, New York NY 10017. (212)605-3000. Editor-in-Chief: Jackie Farber. Publishes trade paperback reprints and originals. Averages 10 titles/year. Pays 6-7½% royalty; offers advance. Simultaneous and photocopied submissions OK. Computer printout submissions acceptable; prefers letter-quality to dot-matrix. SASE. Reports in 2 months. Book catalog for 8½x11 SASE.
Nonfiction: Consciousness, health, how-to, humor, music, New Age, photography, politics, recreation, reference, science, self-help and sports. "We would like to see books on the arts, social history, social criticism and analysis, and child care. We do not want to see biography, philosophy, academic books, textbooks, juveniles, or poetry books." Query or submit outline/synopsis and sample chapters. Prefers submissions through agents.
Recent Nonfiction Title: *Holy Terror*, by Flo Conway and Jim Siegelmann.
Fiction: "We are looking for original, innovative and contemporary novels." Submit through an agent.
Recent Fiction Title: *The Feud*, by Thomas Berger.

‡**DEMBNER BOOKS**, 80 8th Ave., New York NY 10011. (212)924-2525. Subsidiary of Red Dembner Enterprises, Corp. Associate Editor: Therese Eiben. Publishes hardcover and trade paperback originals, and hardcover and trade paperback reprints. Averages 10-15 titles/year; receives 500-750 submissions annually. 25% of books from first-time authors; 85% of books from unagented writers. Pays 10-15% royalty on hardcover; 6-7½% royalty on paperback, both on retail price. Offers average $1,000-5,000 advance. Publishes book an average of 1 year after acceptance. Simultaneous and legible photocopied submissions OK. Computer printout submissions acceptable; prefers letter-quality to dot-matrix. SASE. Reports in 2 weeks on queries; 10 weeks on mss. Book catalog for #10 SAE and 1 first class stamp.
Nonfiction: How-to, reference, self-help and workbooks. Subjects include animals, health, history (popular), music, psychology, sports and social causes. "We want books written by knowledgable authors that focus on a problem area (health/home/handicapped) and offer an insightful guidance toward solutions." No surveys or

collections—books that do not focus on one specific, promotable topics. Also, no books on heavily published topics, such as weight loss and exercise programs. Query or submit outline/synopsis and sample chapters. SASE a must. Reviews artwork/photos.
Recent Nonfiction Title: *For Sasha, With Love, An Alzheimer's Crusade*, by G. Holland (memoir, useful information).
Fiction: Adventure, mystery, suspense, western and literary. "We look for genre fiction (mystery, suspense, etc.), that keeps pace with the times, deals with contemporary issues, and has three-dimensional characters. Occasionally we publish literary novels, but the writing must be of excellent quality." No indulgent, self-conscious fiction. Query or submit outline/synopsis and sample chapters. SASE a must.
Recent Fiction Title: *The Kamchatka Incident*, by Robert McKinney.
Tips: "Dembner Books has been publishing for ten years. We take a great deal of pride in the books we publish. We are interested in serving a need as well as entertaining. We publish books worth reading and even worth keeping. Small hardcover houses such as ourselves are being very careful about the books they choose for publication primarily because secondary rights sales have dropped, and the money is less. Quality is of utmost importance."

T.S. DENISON & CO., INC., 9601 Newton Ave., S. Minneapolis MN 55431. Editor-in-Chief: W.E. Rosenfelt. Publishes teacher aid materials; receives 500 submissions annually. 90% of books from first-time authors; 100% of books from unagented writers. Average print order for a writer's first book is 500. Royalty varies, usually $80-100 per 1,000 sold, 8-10% on occasion; no advance. Publishes book an average of 1-2 years after acceptance. Photocopied submissions OK. Computer printout submissions acceptable; no dot-matrix. SASE. Reports in 1 month. Book catalog and ms guidelines for SASE.
Nonfiction: Specializes in preschool teaching aids. Send prints if photos are to accompany ms. Submit complete ms. Reviews artwork/photos as part of ms package.

DENLINGER'S PUBLISHERS, LTD., Box 76, Fairfax VA 22030. (703)631-1500. Publisher: William W. Denlinger. Publishes hardcover and trade paperback originals, hardcover and trade paperback reprints. Averages 12 titles/year; receives 200 submissions annually. 50% of books from first-time authors; 90% of books from unagented writers. Average print order for a writer's first book is 300. Pays variable royalty. No advance. Publishes book an average of 18 months after acceptance. Simultaneous and photocopied submissions OK. Computer printout submissions acceptable; prefers letter-quality to dot-matrix. SASE. Reports in 1 week on queries; 6 weeks on mss. Book catalog and ms guidelines for SASE.
Nonfiction: How-to and technical books on dogs and Americana. Query. Reviews artwork/photos.
Recent Nonfiction Title: *Bird Dogs and Upland Game Birds*, by Jack Stuart.
Fiction: Southern historical.
Recent Fiction Title: *Mandingo*.

DETSELIG ENTERPRISES LTD., Box G399, Calgary, Alberta T3A 2G3 Canada. President: T.E. Giles. Publishes hardcover and trade paperback originals. Averages 6-8 titles/year. "The quality of the material and writing must be of a very high standard." Pays 8-13% royalty on wholesale price. No advance. Publishes book an average of 10 months after acceptance. Simultaneous and photocopied submissions OK. Computer printout submissions acceptable; prefers letter-quality to dot-matrix. SASE. Reports in 1 month on queries; 4 months on mss. Free book catalog.
Nonfiction: Biography, "coffee table" books, cookbooks, reference, technical and textbooks. Subjects include business and economics, cooking and foods, health, history, hobbies, psychology and sociology. "Most of our books will emphasize the Canadian scene." Immediate needs are university and college textbooks. No radical politics and religion. Query.
Recent Nonfiction Title: *Dog Training for Law Enforcement*, by R.S. Eden.

*DEVIN-ADAIR PUBLISHERS, INC., Distributor of The Chatham Press, 6 N. Water St., Greenwich CT 06830. (203)531-7755. Editor: Jane Andrassi. Publishes hardcover and paperback originals, reprints and software. Averages 20 titles/year; receives up to 500 submissions annually. 30% of books from first-time authors; 80% of books from unagented writers. Average print order for a writer's first book is 7,500. Subsidy publishes 5% of books. Royalty on sliding scale, 5-25%; "average advance is low." Publishes book an average of 9 months after acceptance. No simultaneous submissions. Electronic submissions OK, but requires hard copy also. Computer printout submissions acceptable; prefers letter-quality to dot-matrix. SASE. Free book catalog.
Nonfiction: Publishes Americana, business, how-to, conservative politics, history, medicine, nature, economics, sports and travel books. New lines: personal computer books and homeopathic books. Accepts translations. Query or submit outline/synopsis and sample chapters. Looks for "early interest, uniqueness, economy of expression, good style, and new information." Reviews artwork/photos as part of ms package.
Recent Nonfiction Title: *Mike Quill—Himself*, by Shirley Quill.
Tips: "We seek to publish books of high quality manufacture. We spend 8% more on production and design

than necessary to insure a better quality book. Trends include increased specialization and a more narrow view of a subject. General overviews in computer publishing are now a thing of the past. Better a narrow subject in depth than a wide superficial one."

*DHARMA PUBLISHING, 2425 Hillside Ave., Berkeley CA 94704. (415)548-5407. Editor: Elizabeth Cook. Publishes hardcover and paperback originals and paperback reprints. Publishes 10 titles/year; receives 150-200 submissions annually. 100% of books from unagented writers. Average print order for a writer's first book is 3,000. Pays 5-7% royalty on retail price; no advance. Subsidy publishes 5% of books. Electronic submissions OK on CPM, but requires hard copy also. Computer printout submissions acceptable. SASE. Reports in 1-2 months. Book catalog $3.50.
Nonfiction: Art (Tibetan and other Buddhist); biography (Buddhist); history (Asia and Buddhism); philosophy (Buddhist); photography (Buddhist); psychology (Buddhist); religion (Buddhism); and self-help. "We want translations of Buddhist texts from Tibetan or Sanskrit. No original discussions of Buddhist topics." Query. Reviews artwork/photos.
Recent Nonfiction Title: *Knowledge of Freedom: Time to Change*, by Tarthany Tulku (1985).
Tips: "The writer has the best chance of selling books on Buddhism to us. We are a small, nonprofit company dedicated to preserving the Buddhist tradition."

DIAL BOOKS FOR YOUNG READERS, Division of E.P. Dutton, 2 Park Ave., New York NY 10016. (212)725-1818. Associate Editor: Paula Wiseman. Imprints include Dial Easy-to-Read Books, Out-and-About Books, and Dial Very First Books. Publishes hardcover originals. Averages 50 titles/year; receives 20,000 submissions annually. 10% of books from first-time authors. Pays variable royalty and advance. Simultaneous and photocopied submissions OK, but not preferred. Computer printout submissions acceptable; no dot-matrix. SASE. Reports in 2 weeks on queries; 3 months on mss. Book catalog and ms guidelines for SASE.
Nonfiction: Juvenile picture books and young adult books. Subjects include animals, history, and nature. Especially looking for "quality picture books and well-researched young adult and middle-reader mss." Not interested in alphabet books, riddle and game books, and early concept books." Query with outline/synopsis and sample chapters. Reviews artwork/photos.
Recent Nonfiction Title: *Mountains*, by Clive Catchpole (picture book).
Fiction: Adventure, fantasy, historical, humor, mystery, romance (appropriate for young adults), and suspense. Especially looking for "lively and well written novels for middle grade and young adult children involving a convincing plot and believable characters. The subject matter or theme should not already be overworked in previously published books. The approach must not be demeaning to any minority group, nor should the roles of female characters (or others) be stereotyped, though we don't think books should be didactic, or in any way message-y." No "topics inappropriate for the juvenile, young adult, and middle grade audiences. No plays or poetry." Submit complete ms.
Recent Fiction Title: *The Man in the Woods*, by Rosemary Wells (novel).
Tips: "Our readers are anywhere from preschool age to teenage. Picture books must have strong plots, lots of action, unusual premises, or universal themes treated with freshness and originality. Humor works well in these books. A very well thought out and intelligently presented book has the best chance of selling. Genre isn't as much of a factor as presentation."

DILLON PRESS, INC., 500 S. 3rd St., Minneapolis MN 55415. (612)333-2691. Editorial Director: Uva Dillon. Senior Editor: Tom Schneider. Juvenile Fiction Editor: Ann-Louise Taylor. Nonfiction Editor: Jan Zelasko. Publishes hardcover originals. Averages 25-30 titles/year; receives 3,000 submissions annually. 50% of books from first-time authors; 90% of books from unagented writers. Average print order for a writer's first book is 3,000-5,000. Pays royalty and by outright purchase. Publishes book an average of 9 months after acceptance. Computer printout submissions acceptable; no dot-matrix. Reports in 6 weeks. SASE.
Nonfiction: "We are actively seeking mss for the juvenile educational market." Subjects include foreign countries, contemporary biographies for elementary and middle grade levels, unusual approaches to science topics for primary grade readers, wildlife, crafts/outdoor activities, and contemporary issues of interest and value to young people. Submit complete ms or outline and 1 sample chapter. Reviews artwork/photos as part of ms package.
Recent Nonfiction Title: *Poland: Land of Freedom Fighters*, by Christine Pfeiffer.
Fiction: "We are looking for fiction mss that appeal to kindergarten through ninth grade readers." Subjects include mysteries, adventure, fantasy, science fiction, contemporary problems, and girls' sports stories. Especially interested in historical fiction based on an actual event.
Recent Fiction Title: *Stripe Presents the ABCs*, by Dorothy Decker.
Tips: "Writers can best tailor their material to our needs by studying our most current books and by researching the need and markets for their own book proposals."

DIMENSION BOOKS, INC., Box 811, Denville NJ 07834-0811. (201)627-4334. Contact: Thomas P. Coffey. Publishes 25 titles/year; receives 700 submissions annually. 20% of books from first-time authors; 90%

Close-up

Allen T. Klots
Senior Editor
Dodd, Mead & Co.

When Allen Klots began work with Dodd, Mead, he wrote press releases and jacket copy. "I can remember Dos Passos—he came in and cut every adjective I'd written about him (complimentary ones). It was amazing," Klots recalls. "He said beginning writers should stop using adjectives. I've always remembered that."

Now nearly 40 years later, Klots is deleting *the adjectives* and at the same time is mindful that "good writers have a style of their own which should not be tampered with."

Actually, he still writes jacket copy (all Dodd, Mead editors write this copy for the books they edit). "We follow through very closely every manuscript for which we are responsible," he says. "Next to the author, the editor knows the book better than anybody else."

Klots enjoys working with authors who write with "clarity and imagination.

"It's a combination of knowing your subject and the authority with which you write," says the native New Yorker, who has inherited a British accent from his mother. "You should write about what you know in both fiction and nonfiction."

The writer benefits most from the editor's questioning of his work and from the editor's honesty.

Recently an agent told Klots he had observed "a lessening of the very close rapport between editor and author in the industry." Dodd, Mead publishes 150 to 175 titles annually, but its editors try to maintain a small-press rapport with writers. "We have a strong heritage that goes back to Agatha Christie," says Klots. The company dates back to 1839 when Moses Dodd founded it to print sermons.

Much of the editors' work at Dodd is geared toward the once-a-week editorial meeting where they discuss submitted book ideas. The sales manager also attends the meeting. "Very often the material looks as if it is publishable, but before we sign a contract, we make up a profit/loss statement," he points out. They estimate what the first printing and sales figures might be. "We try not to publish a book unless the margin of profit comes out to 50 percent or more." Occasionally, though, there are exceptions.

Most of Dodd's nonfiction books are bought on the basis of proposals with a detailed outline and perhaps a sample chapter. Giving the editor "the spirit of the writing" as part of the proposal aids the decision-making process. For fiction, editors hesitate to sign a contract until they read the entire book.

The majority of books published by Dodd has been submitted by agents, but editors do read queries submitted by writers. There are books on its list that wouldn't be there if they didn't read the unsolicited mail, says Klots.

He encourages writers to keep writing and to practice various forms of writing—articles, commentaries, stories. Realize there are trends that make certain subjects more salable at certain times.

Keep the market in mind, but, above all, "write what you feel," says Klots (with conviction and without adjectives). "It would be a mistake for a writer to write *just* to be published if he has the gifts to write a book of quality that can contribute to the literature of the language."

of books from unagented writers. Pays "regular royalty schedule" based on retail price; advance is negotiable. Publishes book an average of 3-5 months after acceptance. Computer printout submissions acceptable; no dot-matrix. SASE. Book catalog for SAE and 2 first class stamps. Reports in 1 week.

Nonfiction: Publishes general nonfiction including religion, principally Roman Catholic. Also psychology. Accepts nonfiction translations. Query. Accepts outline/synopsis and 3 sample chapters. Length: 40,000 words minimum. Reviews artwork/photos.

Recent Nonfiction Title: *The Enneagram: A Journey of Self-Discovery*, by Beesing, Nogosek, and O'Leary.

DODD, MEAD & CO., 79 Madison Ave., New York NY 10016. (212)685-6464. Senior Editors: Jerry Gross, Allen T. Klots, Margaret Norton and Cynthia Vartan. Managing Editor: Chris Fortunato. Averages 200 titles/year. Pays 10-15% royalty; advances vary, depending on the sales potential of the book. A contract for nonfiction books is offered on the basis of a query, a suggested outline and a sample chapter. Write for permission before sending mss. Adult fiction, history, philosophy, the arts, current events, management and religion should be addressed to Editorial Department. Publishes book an average of 9 months after acceptance. Electronic submissions OK "only on exceptional occasions when submission can be used on equipment of our suppliers." Reports in 6 weeks. SASE.

Fiction and Nonfiction: Publishes book-length mss. Length: 70,000-100,000 words average. Looks for high quality; mysteries and romantic novels of suspense, biography, popular science, travel, yachting and other sports, music and other arts. Very rarely buys photographs or poetry. Publishes books for juveniles. Children's Books Editor: Jo Ann Daly. Length: 1,500-75,000 words.

Tips: "Freelance writers should be aware of trends toward nonfiction and the difficulty of publishing marginal or midlist fiction."

DOLL READER, Subsidiary of Hobby House Press, Inc., 900 Frederick St., Cumberland MD 21502. (301)759-3770. Subsidiaries include *Doll Reader, The Teddy Bear and Friends Magazine*, and *Dolls Values Quarterly*. Publisher: Gary R. Ruddell. Publishes hardcover originals. Averages 18 titles/year. 20% of books from first-time authors; 90% of books from unagented writers. Pays royalty. Publishes book an average of 18 months after acceptance. Simultaneous and photocopied submissions OK. Computer printout submissions acceptable; prefers letter-quality to dot-matrix. SASE. Reports in 2 weeks. Free book catalog.

Nonfiction: Doll related books. "We publish books pertaining to dolls and teddy bears as a collector's hobby; we also publish pattern books. The *Doll Reader* is published 8 times a year dealing with the hobby of doll collecting. We appeal to those people who are doll collectors, miniature collectors, as well as people who sew for dolls. Our magazine has a worldwide circulation of close to 50,000." Query or submit outline/synopsis. Reviews artwork/photos as part of ms package. *The Teddy Bear and Friends Magazine* is published quarterly.

Recent Nonfiction Title: *6th Blue Book of Dolls and Values*, by Jan Foulke (price guide for dolls).

‡**DORCHESTER PUBLISHING CO., INC.**, Suite 900, 6 E. 39th St., New York NY 10016. (212)725-8811. Editorial Director: Jane Thornton. Imprint includes Leisure Books. Publishes mass market paperback originals and reprints. Averages 130 titles/year; receives thousands submissions annually. 50% of books from first-time authors; 60% of books from unagented writers. Pays royalty on retail price or makes outright purchase. Offers average $1,000 advance. Publishes book an average of 1 year after acceptance. Simultaneous and photocopied submissions OK. Computer printout submissions acceptable; no dot-matrix. SASE. Reports in 6 weeks on queries; up to 4 months on mss. Free book catalog; ms guidelines for SASE.

Nonfiction: Biography and humor. "Our needs are minimal as we publish perhaps four nonfiction titles a year." Query.

Fiction: Historical (120,000% words); horror (100,000% words); mainstream (100,000% words); mystery (50,000-60,000 words); and suspense (50,000-60,000 words). We are strongly backing the horror/occult, historical romance, contemporary women's fiction and short mystery." No sweet romance, science fiction, western, erotica or male adventure. Query or submit outline/synopsis and sample chapters.

Recent Fiction Title: *Thorn of Love*, by Robin Lee Hatcher (historical romance).

Tips: "Horror/occult and historical romance are our best sellers."

DOUBLEDAY & CO., INC., Dept. AA-M, 245 Park Ave., New York NY 10167. Publishes hardcover and paperback originals. Offers royalty on retail price; offers variable advance. Reports in 2½ months. "At present, Doubleday and Co. is *only* able to consider fiction for mystery/suspense, science fiction, and romance imprints." Send *copy* of complete manuscript (60,000-80,000 words) to Crime Club Editor, Science Fiction Editor, or Starlight Romance Editor as appropriate. Sufficient postage for return via fourth class mail must accompany manuscript.

DOUBLEDAY CANADA, LTD., 105 Bond St., Toronto, Ontario M5B 1Y3 Canada. (416)977-7891. Senior Editor: Denise Schon. Publishes hardcover originals. Publishes 15-20 titles/year; receives 1,700 submissions annually. 10% of books from first-time authors; 50% of books from unagented writers. Pays royalty on retail price; advance "varies." Publishes book an average of 9 months after acceptance. Simultaneous and photocopied submissions OK. Computer printout submissions acceptable; no dot-matrix. Reports in 3 months. Book catalog and ms guidelines for SAE and IRC.

Nonfiction: General interest. "We do not specialize, but the major part of our list consists of biography, popular history, and subjects of contemporary interest. Our main concern is to publish books of particular interest to the Canadian market, although our books are published in the U.S. as well. We will consider any nonfiction proposal." Query or submit outline/synopsis and 3 or 4 sample chapters. Reviews artwork/photos as part of ms package "if pertinent, but photocopies will suffice—*do not* send original artwork in the mail."

Recent Nonfiction Title: *Glenn Gould Variations*, by Himself and His Friends.

Fiction: "No particular preferences as to style or genre. We publish both 'literary' and 'commercial' books. Once again, we are most interested in adult fiction with a Canadian angle (author, setting, subject). Of course, we hope they have North American potential as well." Query or submit outline/synopsis and opening chapters.

Recent Fiction Title: *Among Friends*, by L.R. Wright.

Tips: Looks for "identification of genre of work; straightforward description of what book is about; indication of whether work is completed or in progress; covering letter detailing writer's publishing history, any credentials or experience that particularly qualifies him/her to do the proposed book." In fiction, studies plot summary and brief sketch of major characters. Queries/mss may be routed to other editors in the publishing group.

‡DOUGLAS & MCINTYRE PUBLISHERS, 1615 Venables St., Vancouver, British Columbia V5L 2H1 Canada. (604)254-7191. Manuscript Editor: Shaun Oakey. Imprints include Groundwood Books. Publishes hardcover originals and trade paperback originals; and trade paperback reprints. Averages 50 titles/year; receives 600 submissions annually. 50% of books from first-time authors; 90% of books from unagented writers. Pays 8-15% royalty on retail price; offers average $500 advance. Simultaneous and photocopied submissions OK. SASE. Reports in 1 month on queries; 2 months on mss. Free book catalog.

Nonfiction: Biography, cookbook, illustrated book, juvenile and Canadian history. Subjects include Canadiana, art, business and economics, cooking and foods, history, and Canadian politics. No how-to; outdoor guides; or medical/health books. Query and submit outline/synopsis and sample chapters or complete ms.

Recent Nonfiction Title: *The World of Canadian Wine*, by John Schreiner.

Fiction: Ethnic, experimental, historical and literary/women's. "Will begin fiction list in fall '86; we will be interested only in literary works." No mass market-type material—romance, gothic, etc. Submit outline/synopsis and sample chapters or complete ms.

Tips: "For our fiction and general trade lists we prefer Canadian authors."

DOW JONES-IRWIN, (Business and Finance) 1818 Ridge Rd., Homewood IL 60430. (312)798-6000. Editorial Director: Ralph Rieves. Publishes originals only. Royalty schedule and advance negotiable. Averages 100 titles/year. Reports in 1 month. SASE.

Nonfiction: Business and financial subjects. Query with outline.

Recent Nonfiction Title: *Money Market: Myth, Reality and Practice*, by Marcia Stigum.

Tips: Queries/mss may be routed to other editors in the publishing group.

DOWN EAST BOOKS, Subsidiary of Down East Enterprise, Inc., Box 679, Camden ME 04843. (207)594-9544. Editor: Karin Womer. Publishes hardcover and trade paperback originals and trade paperback reprints. Averages 10-16 titles/year; receives 450 submissions annually. 50% of books from first-time authors; 95% of books from unagented writers. Average print order for a writer's first book is 2,500. Pays 10-15% on wholesale price. Offers average $200 advance. Publishes book an average of 18 months after acceptance. Simultaneous and photocopied submissions OK. Computer printout submissions acceptable; prefers letter-quality to dot-matrix. SASE. Reports in 2 weeks on queries; 2 months on mss. Book catalog and ms guidelines for SASE.

Nonfiction: Biography, "coffee table" books, cookbooks, illustrated books, juvenile, reference and guidebooks. Subjects include Americana, art, cooking and foods, history, nature, traditional crafts and recreation. "Our books have a Maine or New England emphasis." Query. Reviews artwork/photos as part of ms package.

Recent Nonfiction Title: *Mount Washington in Winter*, by Winston Pote.

Fiction: "We publish no fiction except for an occasional juvenile title (average 1/year)."

Recent Fiction Title: *Miracle at Egg Rock: The Story of Puffin Q7*, by Doris Gove.

THE DRAGONSBREATH PRESS, 10905 Bay Shore Dr., Sister Bay WI 54234. Editor: Fred Johnson. Publishes hardcover and trade paperback originals only in handmade limited edition form, no mass-market. "The Dragonsbreath Press is a small press producing handmade limited edition books including original artwork meant for collectors of fine art and books who appreciate letterpress printing. This audience accepts a handmade book as a work of art." Averages 1 title/year; receives 500 submissions annually. Payment conditions "to be arranged"; no advance. Simultaneous and photocopied submissions OK. Computer printout submissions acceptable; prefers letter-quality to dot-matrix. SASE. Reports in 2 months on queries; 3 months on mss.

Nonfiction: Biography, humor and illustrated books. Subjects include Americana, art, history and photography. "We're interested in anything suited to handmade book production—short biography, history, original artwork, photography." Query first; do not submit ms. Reviews artwork/photos as part of ms package.

Fiction: Adventure, erotica, experimental, fantasy, horror, humor, mystery and science fiction. "We are looking for short, well written stories which lend themselves to illustration and deserve to be made into fine, handmade books." *No long, novel length manuscripts* or *children's books*. Query first; do not submit ms.

Poetry: "We're looking for good readable poetry that is unique. No religious, sweet Hallmark style or divorce poems." Submit 3 samples with query; submit complete ms "only when requested."

Tips: "We are not currently reading any manuscripts. Please do not submit manuscripts unless they have been requested. Do not send novels. Our typical book would consist of one or two short stories, not a whole collection. Always include SASE if reply wanted."

DRAMA BOOK PUBLISHERS, 821 Broadway, New York NY 10003. (212)228-3400. Contact: Ralph Pine or Judith Holmes. Publishes hardcover and paperback originals and reprints and software. Averages 15 titles/year. Royalty varies; advance varies; negotiable. Publishes book an average of 9-12 months after acceptance. Electronic submissions for Read CP/M Unix (tape only) OK; but requires hard copy also. Computer printout submissions acceptable; prefers letter-quality to dot-matrix. Reports in 1 to 2 months. SASE.

Nonfiction: Books—texts, guides, manuals, directories, reference—for and about performing arts theory and practice: acting, directing; voice, speech, movement, music, dance, mime; makeup, masks, wigs; costumes, sets, lighting, sound; design and execution; technical theatre, stagecraft, equipment; stage management; producing; arts management, all varieties; business and legal aspects; film, radio, television, cable, video; theory, criticism, reference; playwriting; theatre and performance history. Accepts nonfiction, drama and technical works in translations also. Query; accepts 1-3 sample chapters; no complete mss. Reviews artwork/photos as part of ms package.

Fiction: Plays and musicals.

DUNDURN PRESS LTD., Box 245, Station F, Toronto, Ontario, M4Y 2L4 Canada. (416)368-9390. Publisher: Kirk Howard. Publishes hardcover, trade paperback and hardcover reprints. Averages 15 titles/year; receives 250 submissions annually. 20% of books from first-time authors; 100% of books from unagented writers. Average print order for a writer's first book is 2,000. Pays 10% royalty on retail price; 8% royalty on some paperback children's books. Publishes book an average of 1 year after acceptance. "Easy-to-read" photocopied submissions OK. Computer printout submissions acceptable; prefers letter-quality to dot-matrix.

Nonfiction: Biography, "coffee table" books, how-to, juvenile, literary and reference. Subjects include Canadiana, art, history, hobbies, Canadian history and literary criticism. Especially looking for Canadian biographies. No religious or soft science topics. Query with outline/synopsis and sample chapters. Reviews artwork/photos as part of ms package.

Recent Nonfiction Title: *Emma Albani, Victorian Diva*.

Tips: "Publishers want more factual books written in better prose styles. If I were a writer trying to market a book today, I would visit book stores and watch what readers buy and what company publishes that type of book 'close' to my manuscript."

DUQUESNE UNIVERSITY PRESS, 600 Forbes Ave., Pittsburgh PA 15282. (412)434-6610. Averages 9 titles/year; receives 400 submissions annually. 25% of books from first-time authors; 90% of books from unagented writers. Average print order for a writer's first book is 2,000. Pays 10% royalty on net sales; no advance. Publishes book an average of 1 year after acceptance. Electronic submissions OK but check with publisher; but requires hard copy also. Computer printout submissions acceptable; no dot-matrix. Query. Reports in 3 months. Free writer's guidelines.

Nonfiction: Scholarly books in the humanities, social sciences for academics, libraries, college bookstores and educated laypersons. Length: open. Looks for scholarship.

Recent Nonfiction Title: *Contemporary Psychology: Revealing and Obscuring the Human*, by Maurice Friedman (psychology).

DURST PUBLICATIONS, 29-28 41st Ave., Long Island City NY 11101. (212)706-0303. Owner: Sanford Durst. Publishes hardcover and trade paperback originals and reprints. Averages 20% titles/year; receives 100 submissions annually. Average print order for a writer's first book is 2,500. Pays variable royalty. Publishes book an average of 6 months after acceptance. Computer printout submissions acceptable; no dot-matrix. SASE. Reports in 1 month. Book catalog for business-size SAE and 75¢ postage.

Nonfiction: How-to and reference on Americana, art, business and economics, cooking and foods, hobbies—primarily coin collecting, stamp collecting, antiques and legal. Especially needs reference books and how-to on coins, medals, tokens, paper money, art, antiques—illustrated with valuations or rarities, if possible. Publishes for dealers, libraries, collectors and attorneys. Submit outline/synopsis and sample chapters. Reviews artwork/photos as part of ms package.

Recent Nonfiction Title: *Buying & Selling Country Land*, by D. Reisman (practical/legal).

Tips: "Write in simple English. Do not repeat yourself. Present matter in logical, orderly form. Try to illustrate."

E.P. DUTTON, 2 Park Ave., New York NY 10016. (212)725-1818. Publisher, Children's Books: Ann Durell. Averages 40 titles/year. Pays royalty on list price; offers variable advance. Considers unsolicited mss. Computer printout submissions acceptable; prefers letter-quality to dot-matrix. "Please send query letter first on all except picture book manuscripts."
Fiction: Picture books; Smart Cats (beginning readers); stories for ages 8-12; Skinny Books (Hi-lo for ages 12 and up). Reviews artwork/photos as part of ms package. Emphasis on books that will be current and popular as well as well-written.
Tips: Queries/mss may be routed to other editors in the publishing group.

EAKIN PUBLICATIONS, INC., Box 23066, Austin TX 78735. (512)288-1771. Imprints include Nortex. Editorial Director: Edwin M. Eakin. Publishes hardcover and paperback originals and reprints. Averages 40 titles/year; receives 300 submissions annually. 60% of books from first-time authors; 99% of books from unagented writers. Average print order for a writer's first book is 2,000. Pays 10-12-15% in royalty. Publishes book an average of 12 months after acceptance. Simultaneous and photocopied submissions OK. Computer printout submissions acceptable; prefers letter-quality to dot-matrix. SASE. Reports in 3 months. Free book catalog and ms guidelines for SASE.
Nonfiction: History, juvenile history, contemporary, and regional. Specifically needs biographies of well-known Texas people, current Texas politics and history for grades 3-9. Query first or submit outline/synopsis and sample chapters.
Recent Nonfiction Title: *The Cowboy Chronicles, A Sports Writer's View of America's Most Celebrated Team*, by Carlton Stowers.
Fiction: Historical fiction for school market. Specifically need juveniles that relate to Texas. Query or submit outline/synopsis and sample chapters.
Recent Fiction Title: *Where the Pirates Are*, by Tom Townsend.

EAST WOODS PRESS, (Trade name of Fast & McMillan Publishers, Inc.), 429 East Blvd., Charlotte NC 28203. (704)334-0897. Editorial Director: Sally Hill McMillan. Publishes hardcover and paperback originals and hardcover and paperback reprints. Publishes 10-15 titles/year. Pays 5-12% royalty on retail price. Offers average $500 advance. "Submissions must be on hard copy. If accepted, we can work with disks to edit and produce." Computer printout submissions acceptable. Reports in 6 weeks on queries; 8 weeks on mss. SASE. Book catalog for 9x12 SAE and 2 first class stamps.
Nonfiction: "Coffee table" books, cookbooks, how-to, self-help and travel guides. No business or humor. "We are mainly interested in travel and the outdoors. Regional guidebooks are our specialty, but anything on travel and outdoors will be considered." Query. "A list of competitive books should be submitted, along with specific reasons why this manuscript should be published. Also, maps and art should be supplied by the author."
Recent Nonfiction Title: *Wildflower Folklore*, by Laura C. Martin.

*EASTVIEW EDITIONS, Box 783, Westfield NJ 07091. (201)964-9485. Subsidiary includes Glenn Associates. Manager: Mr. N. Glenn. Publishes hardcover and trade paperback originals and reprints. Averages 12 titles/year; receives 50 submissions annually. 95% of books from first-time authors; 100% of books from unagented writers. Average print order for a writer's first book is 2,500. Pays standard royalty contract. Publishes book an average of 6 months after acceptance. Simultaneous and photocopied submissions OK. Computer printout submissions acceptable; prefers letter-quality to dot-matrix. SASE. Reports in 6 weeks. Book catalog for 75¢ postage.
Nonfiction: Illustrated books on all of the arts; also history, hobbies, music, nature, photography, design, dance and antiques. Also does limited editions of nature and art books. Considers all material for domestic and international publication. Submit outline and 2-3 sample chapters, table of contents; "description of the book, what the author envisions." Reviews artwork/photos as part of ms package. "Send copies of materials—we cannot be responsible for original materials." Will distribute to book trade and libraries; (national and international) books privately printed. Will cooperate with author/artist/photographer in producing mss and books for publication and distribution.
Recent Nonfiction Title: *Great Walls of China*, by Franc Palaia.

THE ECCO PRESS, Subsidiaries include *Antaeus*, 18 W. 30th St., New York NY 10001. (212)685-8240. Editor: Daniel Halpern. Associate and Managing Editor: Megan Ratner. Publishes hardcover and trade paperback originals and reprints. Averages 12 titles/year; receives 1,000-2,000 submissions annually. 1% of books from first-time authors; 20% of books from unagented writers. Pays 5-15% royalty on retail price; offers average $300 advance. Publishes book an average of 9 months after acceptance. Photocopied submissions OK. Computer printout submissions acceptable; prefers letter-quality to dot-matrix. SASE. Reports in 1 week on queries; 2 months on mss. Free book catalog; ms guidelines for SASE.
Nonfiction: Cookbook and literary criticism. "Can do only one or two books." No scientific, historical or sociological mss. Query.

Recent Nonfiction Title: *Twentieth Century Pleasures*, by Robert Hass.
Fiction: Experimental, mainstream and serious or 'literary' fiction. "Can do one or possibly two novels or short story collections." Query.
Recent Fiction Title: *A Bolt of White Cloth*, by Leon Noolie.
Poetry: One or two new collections. No religious, inspirational, etc. Submit 4-6 samples.
Recent Poetry Title: *Singing*, by Dennis Schmitz.

‡*ECW PRESS, Subsidiaries include Emerson House, Poetry Canada Review, Essays on Canadian Writing, 307 Coxwell Ave., Toronto, Ontario M4L 3B5 Canada. (416)694-3348. President: Jack David. Imprints include ECW Press. Publishes hardcover and trade paperback originals. Publishes 12-15 titles/year; receives 120 submissions annually. 50% of books from first-time authors; 80% of books from unagented writers. Subsidy publishes up to 5% of books. Pays 10% royalty on retail price. Simultaneous and photocopied submissions OK. Electronic submissions OK on CP/M, but requires hard copy also. Computer printout submissions acceptable; prefers letter-quality to dot-matrix. Reports in 2 weeks. Free book catalog.
Nonfiction: Reference and Canadian literary criticism. "ECW is interested in all literary criticism aimed at the undergraduate and graduate university market." Query. Reviews artwork/photos as part of ms package.
Recent Nonfiction Title: *North of America*, by James Doyle (literary criticism).
Tips: "The writer has the best chance of selling literary criticism to our firm because that's our specialty and the only thing that makes us money."

‡EDITS PUBLISHERS, Box 7234, San Diego CA 92107. (619)488-1666. Editorial Director: Robert R. Knapp. Publishes hardcover and paperback originals. Averages 4 titles/year. Pays variable royalty on retail price; no advance. Photocopied submissions OK. Reports in 2 months. SASE. Book catalog for SASE.
Nonfiction: "Edits publishes scientific and text books in social sciences, particularly counseling and guidance, psychology, statistics and education." Query or submit sample chapters.
Recent Nonfiction Title: *Actualizing Therapy*, by E. Shostrom (therapy text).

*EDUCATION ASSOCIATES, Division of The Daye Press, Inc., Box 8021, Athens GA 30603. (404)542-4244. Editor, Text Division: D. Keith Osborn. Publishes hardcover and trade paperback originals. Averages 2-6 titles/year; receives 150 submissions annually. 1% of books from first-time authors. Subsidy publishes 50% of books. "We may publish a textbook which has a very limited audience . . . but we still believe that the book will make a contribution to the educational field." Buys mss "on individual basis." Photocopied submissions OK. Computer printout submissions acceptable; no dot-matrix. SASE. Reports in 4 weeks on queries.
Nonfiction: How-to and textbook. Subjects include psychology and education. "Books in the fields of early childhood and middle school education. Do not wish basic textbooks. Rather, are interested in more specific areas of interest in above fields. We are more interested in small runs on topics of more limited nature than general texts." Query with one-page letter. If interested will request synopsis and sample chapters. No reply unless SASE is enclosed.
Recent Nonfiction Title: *Cognition in Early Childhood*, by J.D. Osborn.
Tips: College textbooks—usually dealing with early childhood, middle school, or child development—have the best chance of selling to *Education Associates*.

WILLIAM B. EERDMANS PUBLISHING CO., Christian University Press, 255 Jefferson Ave. SE, Grand Rapids MI 49503. (616)459-4591. Editor-in-Chief: Jon Pott. Publishes hardcover and paperback originals and reprints. Averages 65 titles/year; receives 3,000-4,000 submissions annually. 25% of books from first-time authors; 95% of books from unagented writers. Average print order for a writer's first book is 4,000. Pays 7½-10% royalty on retail price; usually no advance. Publishes book an average of 1 year after acceptance. Simultaneous and photocopied submissions OK. Computer printout submissions acceptable; no dot-matrix. SASE. Reports in 3 weeks for queries; 4 months for mss. Looks for "quality and relevance." Free book catalog.
Nonfiction: Reference, textbooks and tourists guidebooks. Subjects include history, philosophy, psychology, religion, sociology, regional history and geography. "Approximately 80% of our publications are religious—specifically Protestant—and largely of the more academic or theological variety (as opposed to the devotional, inspirational or celebrity-conversion type of book). Our history and social studies titles aim, similarly, at an academic audience; some of them are documentary histories. We prefer that writers take the time to notice if we have published anything at all in the same category as their manuscript before sending it to us." Accepts nonfiction translations. Query. Accepts outline/synopsis and 2-3 sample chapters. Reviews artwork/photos.
Recent Nonfiction Title: *The Naked Public Square*, by Richard John Neuhaus.

‡ELEPHANT WALK, 2544 N. Monticello Ave., Chicago IL 60647. (312)342-3338. Senior Editor: Gene Lovitz. Paperback imprint of The Little House Press, Division of The Little House Group. Publishes trade paperback originals. "Our first list should be around ten titles." Pays 10% royalty on retail price. Offers variable advance. Simultaneous and photocopied submissions OK. Computer printout submissions acceptable.

SASE. Reports in 2 weeks on queries; 1 month on mss.

Nonfiction: Gift market, "coffee table" books, humor, magic, 64-page chapbooks, and sex. "On the serious side, we are looking for topical subjects, real trials and cases, nonfiction novels, quality mss we can publish under the Elephant Walk imprint in paperback as well as in hardcover under the Little House imprint."

Fiction: 450-page historical romances with explicit sex, 300-page regency romances with nonexplicit sex, super-hero bang-bang books (especially if a series), science fiction, mystery, horror, and Doc Savage type of soldier of fortune books on mercenaries. "If you have a series, submit two or three mss of the series with the same central characters."

Juveniles: Stories should appeal to both boys and girls, ages 4 to 15. Subjects include animals, mystery, biography, adventure, magic, circus and Tolkien kinds of fantasy.

Tips: "Don't contact us with proposals, but only if you have a completed manuscript or one near completion. If unpublished, send query first. List any publishers or agents contacted, and to what extent. Keep correspondence and phone calls to a minimum. No pen pals."

EMC PUBLISHING, EMC Corporation, 300 York Ave., St. Paul MN 55101. (612)771-1555. Editor: Rosemary J. Barry. Publishes hardcover originals and software. Averages 20 titles/year. Pays variable royalty or makes variable outright purchase. Publishes book an average of 1 year after acceptance. Simultaneous and photocopied submissions OK. Computer printout submissions acceptable; prefers letter-quality to dot-matrix. Reports in 2 weeks on queries; 1 month on mss.

Nonfiction: Textbook. Subjects include business and economics, career/consumer education, language arts and foreign language. Especially looking for "language arts skill material. No religious or adult material. We publish strictly for schools." Query. All unsolicited mss are returned unopened.

Recent Nonfiction Title: *Decisions*, by Brenneke and Hamill (consumer economics textbook).

Fiction: "No religious or adult material; we publish *only* for schools." Query. All unsolicited mss are returned unopened.

‡ENRICH CORPORATION,, Subsidiary of Ohaus, 2325 Paragon Dr., San Jose CA 95131. (408)263-7111. Publisher: Henry C. Goldenberg. Pubishes trade and mass market paperback originals. Averages 40 titles/year; receives 50 submissions annually. 10-15% of books from first-time authors; 100% of books from unagented writers. Pays 5-7% royalty on wholesale price or makes outright purchase. Publishes book an average of 6-18 months after acceptance. Simultaneous and photocopied submissions OK. Computer printout submissions acceptable; prefers letter-quality to dot-matrix. SASE. Reports in 1 month on queries; 2 months on submissions. Free book catalog.

Nonfiction: How-to, humor, juvenile, and children's educational activity books. Subjects include children's coping skills. Especially needs "books that help children (ages 2-12) learn basic readiness skills in a fun and unique way (illustrated)." No topics that appeal only to a select few. Query or submit outline/synopsis and sample chapters. Reviews artwork/photos.

Recent Nonfiction Title: *Kindergarten Readiness*, by Quinn (work book).

Fiction: Has not published fiction but will consider humor for children ages 2-12. Query or submit outline/synopsis and sample chapters.

Tips: "Our audience includes parents, teachers, and relatives of families who have children. We look for uniqueness that captures our attention and hopefully the buyer's."

ENSLOW PUBLISHERS, Bloy St. and Ramsey Ave., Box 777, Hillside NJ 07205. (201)964-4116. Editor: Ridley Enslow. Publishes hardcover and paperback originals. Averages 30 titles/year. Pays 10-15% royalty on retail price or net price; offers $500-5,000 advance. Publishes book an average of 8 months after acceptance. Photocopied submissions OK. Computer printout submissions acceptable. SASE. Reports in 2 weeks. Free book catalog.

Nonfiction: Biography, business/economics, health, hobbies, how-to, juveniles, philosophy, psychology, recreation, reference, science, self-help, sociology, sports and technical. Accepts nonfiction translations. Submit outline/synopsis and 2 sample chapters. Reviews artwork/photos as part of ms package.

Recent Nonfiction Title: *Cloning and the New Genetics*, by Hyde (science).

ENTERPRISE PUBLISHING CO., INC., 725 Market St., Wilmington DE 19801. (302)654-0110. Publisher: T.N. Peterson. Editor: Ann Faccenda. Publishes hardcover and paperback originals, "with an increasing interest in newsletters and periodicals." Averages 4 titles/year. Pays royalty on wholesale or retail price. Offers $1,000 average advance. Publishes book an average of 6 months after acceptance. Simultaneous and photocopied submissions OK, but "let us know." Computer printout submissions acceptable; prefers letter-quality to dot-matrix. SASE. Catalog and writer's guidelines for SASE.

Nonfiction: "Subjects of interest to small business owners/entrepreneurs. They are highly independent and self-sufficient, and of an apolitical to conservative political leaning. They need practical information, as opposed to theoretical: self-help topics on business, including starting and managing a small enterprise,

advertising, marketing, raising capital, public relations, tax avoidance and personal finance." Business/
economics, legal self-help and business how-to. Query. All unsolicited mss are returned unopened.
Recent Nonfiction Title: *Taxwise Investing*, by Vernon K. Jacobs.

*PAUL S. ERIKSSON, PUBLISHER, 208 Battell Bldg., Middlebury VT 05753. (802)388-7303; Summer:
(802)247-8415. Publisher/Editor: Paul S. Eriksson. Associate Publisher/Co-Editor: Peggy Eriksson. Publishes
hardcover and paperback trade originals and paperback trade reprints. Averages 5-10 titles/year; receives 1,500
submissions annually. 25% of books from first-time authors; 95% of books from unagented writers. Average
print order for a writer's first book is 3,000-5,000. Subsidy publishes 5% of books. Pays 10-15% royalty on
retail price; advance offered if necessary. "We have to like the book and probably the author." Publishes book
an average of 6 months after acceptance. Photocopied submissions OK. Computer printout submissions
acceptable; prefers letter-quality to dot-matrix. SASE. Reports in 3 weeks. Free book catalog.
Nonfiction: Americana, birds (ornithology), art, biography, business/economics, cookbooks/cooking/foods,
health, history, hobbies, how-to, humor, music, nature, philosophy, photography, politics, psychology,
recreation, self-help, sociology, sports and travel. Submit outline/synopsis and sample chapters.
Recent Nonfiction Title: *Steal This Plot: A Writer's Guide to Story Structure and Plagiarism*, by June and
William Noble.
Fiction: Mainstream. Submit outline/synopsis and sample chapters.
Recent Fiction Title: *The Headmaster's Papers*, by Richard A. Hawley.
Tips: "We look for intelligence, excitement and salability. We prefer manuscripts written out of deep, personal
knowledge or experience."

‡*ESPRESS, INC., 5605 16th St. NW, Box 8606, Washington DC 20011. (202)723-4578. President: Rev.
Henry J. Nagorka. Publishes trade paperback originals and reprints. Averages 6-12 titles/year. Subsidy
publishes 50% of books. "We publish only works which are totally exceptional, which mark a new era of
development. The judgment is made by our staff and highly qualified advisors." Pays 15-35% royalty on retail
price. Photocopied submissions OK. SASE. Reports in 3 weeks on queries; 2 months on mss. Free book catalog
and ms guidelines.
Nonfiction: Biography, juvenile and reference. Subjects include philosophy, religion, parapsychology and
psychotronics. Query.
Recent Nonfiction Title: *Who's the Matter With Me?*, by Alice Steadman (self-help).
Tips: "Our audience consists of a large segment of the younger mature adults searching for new philosophical
concepts, a loyal and committed group of students and adults of parapsychological specialization and professionals in metaphysics and psychotronics, including instructors, researchers and practitioners. We also publish
the bimonthly *Psychic Observer*. Same requirements hold for articles."

*ETC PUBLICATIONS, Drawer ETC, Palm Springs CA 92263. (619)325-5352. Editorial Director: LeeOna
S. Hostrop. Senior Editor: Dr. Richard W. Hostrop. Publishes hardcover and paperback originals. Averages 12
titles/year; receives 100% submissions annually. 75% of books from first-time authors; 90% of books from
unagented writers. Average print order for a writer's first book is 2,500. Subsidy publishes 5-10% of books.
Offers 5-15% royalty, based on wholesale and retail price. No advance. Publishes book an average of 1 year
after acceptance. Simultaneous and photocopied submissions OK. Computer printout submissions acceptable;
prefers letter-quality to dot-matrix. SASE. Reports in 3 weeks. Book catalog $2.
Nonfiction: Business management, educational management, gifted education, books for writers and
textbooks. Accepts nonfiction translations in above areas. Submit complete ms. Reviews artwork/photos as
part of ms package.
Recent Nonfiction Title: *The Forbidden Apple—Sex in the Schools*, by Victor Ross and John Marlowe
(education).
Tips: "ETC will seriously consider textbook manuscripts in any knowledge area in which the author can
guarantee a first-year adoption of not less than 500 copies. Special consideration is given to those authors who
are capable and willing to submit their completed work in camera-ready, typeset form."

EVANS AND CO., INC., 216 E. 49 St., New York NY 10017. Editor-in-Chief: Herbert M. Katz. Publishes
hardcover originals. Royalty schedule to be negotiated. Averages 30 titles/year. 5% of books from unagented
writers. Publishes book an average of 8 months after acceptance. Will consider photocopied submissions.
Computer printout submissions OK; no dot-matrix. "No mss should be sent unsolicited. A letter of inquiry is
essential." Reports in 8 weeks. SASE essential.
Nonfiction and Fiction: "We publish a general trade list of adult fiction and nonfiction, cookbooks and
semireference works. The emphasis is on selectivity since we publish only 30 titles a year. Our fiction list
represents an attempt to combine quality with commercial potential. Our most successful nonfiction titles have
been related to health and the behavioral sciences. No limitation on subject. A writer should clearly indicate
what his book is all about, frequently the task the writer performs least well. His credentials, although
important, mean less than his ability to convince this company that he understands his subject and that he has the

ability to communicate a message worth hearing." Reviews artwork/photos.

Tips: "Writers should review our catalog (available for 9x12 envelope with 3 first class stamps) or the *Publishers Trade List Annual* before making submissions."

EXANIMO PRESS, 23520 Hwy. 12, Segundo CO 81070. Editor: Dean Miller. Publishes hardcover and trade paperback originals. Averages 4-10 titles/year; receives 30% submissions annually. 100% of books from first-time authors; 100% of books from unagented writers. Average print order for a writer's first book is 5,000. Pays 10% minimum royalty on retail price; buys some mss outright for $500-1,500; no advance. Publishes ms an average of 6 months after acceptance. Photocopied submissions OK. Computer printout submissions acceptable if legible; prefers letter-quality to dot-matrix. SASE. Reports in 1 month on queries; 2 weeks on mss. Book catalog for SAE and 1 first class stamp.

Nonfiction: How-to and technical. Subjects include prospecting; small mining; treasure hunting; self-employment; dowsing (water witching); and self- or family-improvement from a financial point of view. "We are concentrating on books that graphically tell how to get out of debt and into profitable self-employment. Our *Owlhooter's Manual—The Poor Man's Guide To Financial Independence* is the first of 25 scheduled volumes. Volume 2 deals with 'cottage industries' or profitable work at home. We want books that detail the conversion of hobbies or avocations into profitable businesses." Likes 8x10 pages, 40-104 pages. Prefers a profusely illustrated book, has in-house artist. Needs mss on flea-marketeering and garage/yard sales. No copy artistry or read-and-rewrites. Query. Submit outline and synopsis, 1 sample chapter and intended table of contents. Reviews artwork/photos as part of ms package.

Recent Nonfiction Title: *Coinshooter's Manual—How To Use Your Metal Detector Profitably.*

Tips: "Develop a reputation for technically accurate mss and success will follow. We have found that many would-be authors with superb writing aptitude are not aware that their local libraries are usually crammed with technical reference data."

‡*EXPOSITION PRESS OF FLORIDA**, 1701 Blount Rd., Pompano Beach FL 33069. (305)979-3200. Vice President: Adam Uhlan. Imprints include Exposition-Trade, Exposition Lochinor, University Books, and Testament. Publishes hardcover, trade paperback and mass market paperback originals, and hardcover and trade paperback reprints. Averages 300 titles/year. 50% of books from first-time authors; 80% of books from unagented writers. Subsidy publishes 70% of books. Pays royalty on retail price. Offers average $5,000 advance. Publishes book an average of 5 months after acceptance. Simultaneous and photocopied submissions OK. Computer printout submissions acceptable; prefers letter-quality to dot-matrix. SASE. Reports in 1 week on queries; 2 weeks on mss. Book catalog for 8½x11 SAE and 4 first class stamps.

Nonfiction: Biography, "coffee table" book, cookbook, how-to, humor, illustrated book, juvenile, reference, self-help, technical, and textbook. Subjects include Americana, animals, art, business and economics, cooking and foods, health, history, hobbies, music, nature, philosophy, photography, politics, psychology, recreation, religion, sociology, sports and travel. All types with commercial or specialized appeal. No pornography or anti-ethnic. Query, submit outline/synopsis and sample chapters, complete ms or through agent. Reviews artwork/photos.

Recent Nonfiction Title: *Nutritional Guide to Fast Food*, by Robert Haas.

Fiction: Adventure, confession, erotica, ethnic, experimental, fantasy, gothic, historical, humor, mainstream, mystery, religious, romance, science fiction, suspense and western. All innovative and original types. Needs specialized and mainstream fiction. No anti-ethnic. Submit outline/synopsis and sample chapters or complete ms.

Recent Fiction Title: *Scarlett O'Hara Can Go to Hell*, by Miriam Center (humorous biography).

Poetry: We welcome all types of poetry. Submit complete ms.

Recent Poetry Title: *Ebony Rhythm*, by Beatrice Murphy (Black poetry).

FABLEWAVES PRESS, Box 7874, Van Nuys CA 91409. (213)322-0236. Editor: Claude Lanaux. Publishes trade paperback originals. Averages 3 titles/year. Pays 6-7½% royalty on retail price. Simultaneous and photocopied submissions OK. Computer printout submissions acceptable; prefers letter-quality to dot-matrix. SASE. Reports in 2 months on queries; 5 months on requested mss.

Fiction: Experimental and mainstream. Also short stories and literary—"to encourage creative writing for our offbeat/bizarre Anthology series; fiction of 'electrifying literary merit' for our highly selective Where Does Literary Acclaim Originate in America? series." Send for free guidelines catalog. "Present needs: imaginatively written novels and short stories that reflect the vices and follies of our time. Don't send deadwood-formula type manuscripts if you want to catch our interest. Be inventive at heart. Project your soul and guts. No pro-macho, pro-war, pro-wealth, pro-power or pro-materialistic visions." Query or submit outline/synopsis.

Recent Fiction Title: *Intrepid Visions*, by Jacques Carrié (short stories).

Tips: "Our audience is young-at-heart and curious about the unusual and unexpected."

‡**FACTS ON FILE, INC.**, 460 Park Ave. S., New York NY 10016. (212)683-2244. Editorial Director: Eleanora Schoenebaum. Publishes hardcover originals (75%) and reprints (25%). Averages 120 titles/year.

Offers "usually 15% royalty of net proceeds, sometimes 10% of list price." Also buys some mss by outright purchase: $2,000-50,000. Advance averages $7,000. Simultaneous and photocopied submissions OK. SASE. Reports in 1 month. Book catalog for SASE.

Nonfiction: Reference for libraries and trade in art; business/economics; history; music; nature; energy; politics; psychology; science; self-help; sociology; and travel. "All books must be essentially reference or information-oriented, but given that, the subject matter can be almost anything." Does *not* want "juvenile books, textbooks, Ph.D. theses, opinionated books." Submit outline/synopsis and sample chapters. Looks for "organization, comphrensiveness, clarity."

Recent Nonfiction Title: *Encyclopedia of Birds*, by Christopher Perrins and Dr. Alex L.A. Middleton.

*FAIRCHILD BOOKS & VISUALS, Book Division, 7 E. 12th St., New York NY 10003. Manager: E.B. Gold. Publishes hardcover and paperback originals. Offers standard minimum book contract; no advance. Pays 10% of net sales distributed twice annually. Averages 12 titles/year. Subsidy publishes 5% of books. Publishes book an average of 1 year after acceptance. Photocopied submissions OK. SASE. Free book catalog.

Nonfiction: Publishes business books and textbooks relating to fashion, electronics, marketing, retailing, career education, advertising, home economics and management. Length: Open. Query, giving subject matter, brief outline and at least 1 sample chapter. Reviews artwork/photos as part of ms package.

Recent Nonfiction Title: *Furniture Marketing: From Product Development to Distribution*, by Bennington.

*FAIRLEIGH DICKINSON UNIVERSITY PRESS, 285 Madison Ave., Madison NJ 07940. (201)377-4050. Chairperson, Editorial Committee: Harry Keyishian. Publishes hardcover originals. Averages 35 titles/year; receives 300 submissions annually. 33% of books from first-time authors; 100% of books from unagented writers. Average print order for a writer's first book is 1,000. Subsidy publishes less than 10% of books. "Contract is arranged through Associated University Presses of Cranbury, New Jersey. We are a *selection* committee only." Publishes book an average of 18 months after acceptance. Computer printout submissions acceptable; prefers letter-quality to dot-matrix. Reports in 2 weeks on queries; 4 months on mss. Free book catalog.

Nonfiction: Reference and scholarly books. Subjects include art, business and economics, history, literary criticism, music, philosophy, politics, psychology, sociology and women's studies. Looking for scholarly books in all fields. No nonscholarly books. Query with outline/synopsis and sample chapters. Reviews artwork/photos as part of ms package.

Recent Nonfiction Title: *Transcendentalism and the Western Messenger: A History of the Magazine and its Contributors*, by Robert D. Habich.

Tips: "Research must be up to date. Poor reviews result when authors' bibliographies and notes don't reflect current research."

‡FAIRMONT PRESS INC., Box 14227, Atlanta GA 30324. (404)447-5314. Director of Operations: L. Hutchings. Publishes hardcover originals. Averages 4-8 titles/year. Pays 5-12% royalty. SASE. Reports in 6 weeks. Free book catalog.

Nonfiction: How-to, reference, science, self-help, technical. Subjects include energy, plant engineering, environment, safety. Submit outline/synopsis and sample chapters.

Recent Nonfiction Title: *Guide to New Natural Gas Utilization Technologies*, by American Gas Association (edited by Nelson Hay).

*THE FAMILY ALBUM, Rt. 1, Box 42, Glen Rock PA 17327. (717)235-2134. Contact: Ron Lieberman. Publishes hardcover originals and reprints and software. Averages 4 titles/year; receives 150 submissions annually. 30% of books from first-time authors; 100% of books from unagented writers. Average print order for a writer's first book is 1,000. Subsidy publishes 20% of books. Pays royalty on wholesale price. Publishes book an average of 10 months after publication. Simultaneous and photocopied submissions OK. Electronic submissions OK on 5¼ floppy disk—CP/M. Computer printout submissions acceptable; prefers letter-quality to dot-matrix. SASE. Reports in 2 months.

Nonfiction: "Significant works in the field of (nonfiction) bibliography. Worthy submissions in the field of Pennsylvania-history, biography, folk art and lore. We are also seeking materials relating to books, literacy, and national development. Special emphasis on Third World countries, and the role of printing in international development." No religious material. Submit outline/synopsis and sample chapters.

‡FARM JOURNAL BOOKS, W. Washington Sq., Philadelphia PA 19105. (215)829-4805. Subsidiary of *Farm Journal*. Managing Editor: Nancy Steele. Publishes hardcover and trade paperback originals. Averages 4-12 titles/year. Pays 5-8% royalty on retail price; offers average $3,000 advance. SASE. Computer printout and disk submissions OK. Reports in 2 weeks on queries; 1 month on mss. Queries/mss may be routed to other editors in the publishing group.

Nonfiction: Cookbook, how-to. Immediate needs include original craft books, especially books for people

who sew. No rural nostalgia. Query. Accepts outline/synopsis and 2 sample chapters.
Recent Nonfiction Title: *Let's Make More Patchwork Quilts*, by Jessie MacDonald (how-to).

FARRAR, STRAUS AND GIROUX, INC., 19 Union Sq. W., New York NY 10003. Children's Editor: Stephen Roxburgh. Publishes hardcover originals. Receives 1,000 submissions annually. Pays royalty; advance. Publishes book an average of 18 months after acceptance. Photocopied submissions OK. Computer printout submissions acceptable; prefers letter-quality to dot-matrix. SASE. Reports in 3 months. Catalog for SAE and 56¢ postage.
Nonfiction and Fiction: "We are primarily interested in fiction picture books and novels for children and young adults." Submit outline/synopsis and sample chapters. Reviews artwork/photos as part of ms package.
Recent Nonfiction Title: *Boy: Tales of Childhood*, by Roald Dahl.
Recent Fiction Title: *Wish You Were Here*, by Hilma Wolitzer.
Recent Picture Book Title: *The Winter Wren*, by Brock Cole.
Tips: Fiction of all types has the best chance of selling to this firm. Farrar, Straus and Giroux publishes a limited number of nonfiction titles.

THE FEMINIST PRESS, The City University of New York, 99 Hudson St., New York NY 10013. (516)997-7660. Publishes paperback originals and reprints of literature. Averages 12-15 titles/year. Pays 10% royalty on net sales; no advance. Simultaneous and photocopied submissions OK. Reports in 3 months. Query or submit outline/synopsis and sample chapters.
Nonfiction: Florence Howe, President/Co-Director. Feminist books for a general trade and women's studies audience. "We publish biographies, reprints of lost feminist literature, women's history, bibliographies and educational materials. No material without a feminist viewpoint. No contemporary adult fiction, drama, poetry, or doctrinal dissertation." Looks for "feminist perspective, interesting subject, potential use in women's studies classroom, sensitivity to issues of race and class, clear writing style, general grasp of subject."
Recent Nonfiction Title: *The Cross Cultural Study of Women*, by Betty Schmitz.
Tips: "Submit a proposal for an important feminist work that is sophisticated in its analysis, yet popular in its writing style. Both historical and contemporary subjects will be considered. We are especially interested in works that appeal to both a trade audience and a women's studies classroom market."

FIESTA CITY PUBLISHERS, 740 Sky View Dr., Box 5861, Santa Barbara CA 93150-5861. (805)969-2891. President: Frank E. Cooke. Publishes hardcover and mass market paperback originals. Averages 3 titles/year; receives 50 submissions annually. 80% of books from first-time authors; 100% of books from unagented writers. Average print order for a writer's first book is 1,000. Pays 5-15% royalty on retail price. No advance. Publishes book an average of 10 months after acceptance. Simultaneous and photocopied submissions OK. Computer printout submissions acceptable; no dot-matrix. SASE. Reports in 2 weeks on queries; 1 month on mss. Book catalog for 4x9½ SAE and 39¢ postage.
Nonfiction: Cookbook, self-help and musical subjects. "How-to books on playing instruments, writing music, marketing songs; any music-related material (including bios or autobios of famous music world personalities). Nothing personalized or dull." Query or submit complete ms. Reviews artwork/photos as part of ms package.
Recent Nonfiction Title: *Cooking With Music*, by Frank E. Cooke and Ann Cooke (cookbook with original music).
Tips: "Know what is commercial; attempt to understand what subjects and methods have lasting value; avoid short-term fads."

‡DONALD I. FINE, INC., 128 E. 36th St., New York NY 10016. (212)696-1838. Vice President/Assistant Publisher: Deborah Wilburn. Publishes hardcover and trade paperback originals. Averages 50-60 titles/year; receives 500 submissions annually. 10% of books from first-time authors; 10% of books from unagented writers. Prefers to receive agented submissions. Pays negotiable royalty on retail price; offers negotiable advance. Publishes book an average of 6-9 months after acceptance. Simultaneous and photocopied submissions OK. Exclusive preferred. Computer printout submissions acceptable on 8½x11 sheets. SASE. Reports in 2-3 months. Free book catalog.
Nonfiction: Biography, cookbook, how-to and self-help. Subjects include Americana, cooking and foods, health, history, politics, psychology, religion and sports. Needs manuscripts on current issues, exposés. Self-help must be fresh. Query or submit outline/synopsis and sample chapters.
Recent Nonfiction Title: *Bless Me Father, for I Have Sinned*, by Donoghue and Shapiro (religious).
Fiction: Adventure, experimental, fantasy, historical, horror, humor, mainstream, mystery, religious, romance, science fiction, suspense and western. "We are open to novels of almost any kind. We are looking for young talent to develop." No junk novels derived from the latest commercial bestseller. No formula category novels. Query or submit outline/synopsis and sample chapters.
Recent Fiction Title: *Tom O'Bedlam*, by Robert Silverberg (science fiction).
Tips: "For nonfiction, author's credentials must be excellent for the subject matter. Commercial hardcover fiction and nonfiction and novels of distinct literary merit have the best chance of selling to our firm.

‡**FITZHENRY & WHITESIDE, LTD.**,195 Allstate Parkway, Markham, Ontario L3R 4T8 Canada. (416)477-0030. Vice-President: Robert Read. Publishes hardcover and paperback originals and reprints. Chiefly educational materials. Royalty contract varies; advance negotiable. Publishes 50 titles/year. Photocopied submissions OK. Reports in 1-3 months. Enclose return postage.
Nonfiction: "Especially interested in topics of interest to Canadians, and by Canadians." Textbooks for elementary and secondary schools, biography, business, history, health and art, social studies, language arts and science. Submit outline and sample chapters. Length: open.
Recent Title: *Private Realms of Light, The Canadians*, by Andrew Malcolm.

FLARE BOOKS, Young Adult Imprint of Avon Books, a division of the Hearst Corp., 1790 Broadway, New York NY 10019. (212)399-1384. Senior Editor: Ellen Krieger. Publishes mass market paperback originals and reprints. 20% of books from unagented writers. Pays 6-8% royalty; offers average $2,000 advance. Publishes book an average of 18 months after acceptance. Simultaneous and photocopied submissions OK. Computer printout submissions acceptable; prefers letter-quality to dot-matrix. SASE. Reports in 10 weeks. Ms guidelines for SASE.
Nonfiction: General. Query or submit outline/synopsis and 6 sample chapters. "We are *very* selective with young adult nonfiction." Reviews artwork/photos.
Recent Nonfiction Title: *Battle Off Midway Island*, by Theodore Taylor.
Fiction: Adventure, ethnic, experimental, fantasy, humor, mainstream, mystery, romance, suspense and contemporary. "We are very selective with science fiction, fantasy and mystery." Mss appropriate to ages 12-18. Query or submit complete ms.
Recent Fiction Title: *Downtown*, by Norma Fox Mazer.

FLEET PRESS CORP., 160 5th Ave., New York NY 10010. (212)243-6100. Editor: Susan Nueckel. Publishes hardcover and paperback originals and reprints. Royalty schedule and advance "varies." Publishes book an average of 1 year after acceptance. SASE. Reports in 8 weeks. Free book catalog.
Nonfiction: History, biography, arts, religion, general nonfiction and sports. Length: 45,000 words. Publishes juveniles. Stresses social studies and minority subjects; for ages 8-15. Length: 25,000 words. Query with outline; no unsolicited mss.

FLORA AND FAUNA PUBLICATIONS, Suite 100, 4300 NW 23rd Ave., Gainesville FL 32606. (904)371-9858. Editor/Publisher: Ross H. Arnett, Jr. Book publisher/packager. Publishes hardcover and trade paperback originals. Averages 8-10 titles/year; receives 50 submissions annually. 75% of books from first-time authors; 90% of books from unagented writers. Average print order for a writer's first book is 500. Pays 15% royalty on list price; usually no advance because of high royalty. Publishes book an average of 1 year after acceptance. Photocopied submissions OK. Computer printout submissions acceptable; prefers letter-quality to dot-matrix. SASE. Reports in 2 weeks on queries; 3 months on mss. Free book catalog.
Nonfiction: Reference, technical, textbook and directories. Subjects include plants and animals (for amateur and professional biologists), and natural history. Looking for "books dealing with kinds of plants and animals, especially insects. No nature stories or 'Oh My' nature books." Query with outline/synopsis and 3 sample chapters. Reviews artwork/photos as part of ms package.
Recent Nonfiction Title: *Plants and Insects*, by P. Jolivet (natural history).
Tips: "Well-documented books, especially those that fit into one of our series, have the best chance of selling to our firm."

‡**J. FLORES PUBLICATIONS**, Box 14, Rosemead CA 91770. (818)287-2195. Editor: Eliezer Flores. Publishes trade paperback originals and reprints. Averages 10 titles/year. Pays 10-15% royalty on net sales; no advance. Simultaneous and photocopied submissions OK. Computer printout submissions acceptable; prefers letter-quality to dot-matrix. SASE. Reports in 1 month on queries; 6 weeks on mss. Free book catalog; writer's guidelines for SAE and 1 first class stamp.
Nonfiction: How-to, illustrated book and self-help. "We need original nonfiction manuscripts on military science, weaponry, improvised weaponry, self-defense, survival, police science, the martial arts, guerrilla warfare and silencers. How-to manuscripts are given priority." No pre-World War I material. Query with outline and 2-3 sample chapters. Reviews artwork/photos. "Photos are accepted as part of the manuscript package and are strongly encouraged."

Market conditions are constantly changing! If this is 1987 or later, buy the newest edition of *Writer's Market* at your favorite bookstore or order directly from Writer's Digest Books.

Recent Nonfiction Title: *Full Auto Conversion Manual* (illustrated how-to).
Tips: "Trends include illustrated how-to books on a specific subject. Be thoroughly informed on your subject and technically accurate."

FODOR'S TRAVEL GUIDES, 2 Park Ave., New York NY 10016. (212)340-9800. President and Publisher: James Louttit. Publishes paperback travel guides. Averages 100 titles/year.
Nonfiction: "We are the publishers of periodic travel guides—regions, countries, cities, and special tourist attractions. We do not solicit manuscripts on a royalty basis, but we are interested in travel writers and/or experts who will and can cover an area of the globe for Fodor's for a fee." Submit credentials and samples of work.
Recent Nonfiction Title: *Fodor's Fun In Puerto Rico.*

FOLCROFT LIBRARY EDITIONS/NORWOOD EDITIONS, 842 Main St., Darby PA 19023. (215)583-4550. President: Hassie Weiman. Publishes hardcover originals (library bound). Publishes 50 titles/year. Pays standard royalty rates; offers variable advance. Simultaneous and photocopied submissions OK. SASE. Reports in 3 months.
Nonfiction: Scholarly materials in the humanities by scholars and active researchers associated with universities. Submit complete ms.
Recent Nonfiction Title: *The Kibbutz and Anthropological Study*, by Shepher.

FORMAN PUBLISHING INC., Suite 206, 11661 San Vicente Blvd., Los Angeles CA 90049. (213)820-8672. President: Len Forman. Publishes hardcover and mass market paperback originals. Averages 6 titles/year; receives 300 submissions annually. 100% of books from first-time authors; 100% of books from unagented writers. Average print order for a writer's first book is 10,000 (hardcover), 100,000 (softcover). Pays standard royalty. Publishes book an average of 1 year after acceptance. Photocopied submissions OK. Computer printout submissions acceptable; prefers letter-quality to dot-matrix. SASE. Reports in 1 month. Ms guidelines with SASE.
Nonfiction: Cookbook, how-to and self-help. Accepts nonfiction translations. Submit outline/synopsis and 3 sample chapters. Reviews artwork/photos.
Recent Nonfiction Title: *PMS Self-Help Book*, by Dr. Susan Lark.

FORTRESS PRESS, 2900 Queen Lane, Philadelphia PA 19129. (215)848-6800. Editorial Director: Harold W. Rast. Publishes hardcover and paperback originals. Receives 1,000 submissions annually. 10% of books from first-time authors; 95% of books from unagented writers. Average print order for a writer's first book is 3,500. Pays 7½% royalty on paperbacks; 10% on hardcover; modest advance. Publishes book an average of 1 year after acceptance. Photocopied submissions OK. Computer printout submissions acceptable; prefers letter-quality to dot-matrix. Reports in 90 days. SASE. Free book catalog; ms guidelines for SAE and 50¢ postage.
Nonfiction: Publishes theology, religious and counseling books. Specializes in general religion for laity and clergy; academic texts and monographs in theology (all areas). Accepts nonfiction translations. Mss must follow Chicago *Manual of Style* (13th edition). Query. Accepts outline/synopsis and 2 sample chapters. No religious poetry or fiction.
Recent Nonfiction Title: *The Rise of Christianity*, by W.H.C. Frend.

FRANCISCAN HERALD PRESS, 1434 W. 51st St., Chicago IL 60609. (312)254-4462. Editor: The Rev. Mark Hegener, O.F.M. Imprints include Synthesis Booklets and Herald Biblical Booklets. Publishes hardcover and paperback originals and reprints. Averages 40 titles/year; receives 150 submissions annually. 5% of books from first-time authors; 98% of books from unagented writers. Average print order for a writer's first book is 2,000. Pays 8-12% royalty on both wholesale and retail price; offers $200-1,000 advance. Photocopied submissions OK. Electronic submissions OK on disk, but requires hard copy also. Computer printout submissions acceptable; no dot-matrix. SASE. Reports in 2 weeks. Free book catalog; ms guidelines for SASE.
Nonfiction: "We are publishers of Franciscan literature for the various branches of the Franciscan Order: history, philosophy, theology, Franciscan spirituality and biographies of Franciscan saints and blessed." Accepts nonfiction translations from German, French, Italian and Spanish. Query or submit outline/synopsis and 1 sample chapter.
Recent Nonfiction Title: *The Way of the Lord Jesus: Catholic Moral Principles*, by Germain Grisez, PhD.

‡**THE FRASER INSTITUTE**, 626 Bute St., Vancouver, British Columbia V6E 3M1 Canada. (604)688-0221. Assistant Director: Sally Pipes. Publishes trade paperback originals. Averages 7-10 titles/year; receives 4 submissions annually. 100% of books from unagented writers. Pays honorarium. Publishes book an average of 6 months after acceptance. Simultaneous and photocopied submissions OK. Electronic submissions OK, but requires hard copy also. Computer printout submissions acceptable; no dot-matrix. SAE and IRC. Reports in 6 weeks. Free book catalog.
Nonfiction: Analysis, opinion, on economics, social issues and public policy. Subjects include business and

economics, politics, religion and sociology. "We will consider submissions of high-quality work on economics, social issues, economics and religion, public policy, and government intervention in the economy." Submit complete ms.

Recent Nonfiction Title: *Industrial Innovation: Its Place in the Public Policy Agenda*, by Kristian Palda.

Tips: "Our books are read by well-educated consumers, concerned about their society and the way in which it is run. Our readers feel they have some power to improve society and view our books as a source of the information needed to take steps to change unproductive and inefficient ways of behavior into behavior which will benefit society. Recent trends in book publishing include taxation, health care, property regulation, zoning, and inflation. A writer has the best chance of selling us a high-quality book of 200-400 pages on government, economics, finance, or social issues."

‡**SAMUEL FRENCH, INC.**, 45 W. 25th St., New York NY 10010. (212)206-8990. Subsidiaries include Samuel French Ltd. (London); Samuel French (Canada) Ltd. (Toronto); Samuel French, Inc. (Hollywood); and Baker's Plays, (Boston). Editor: Lawrence Harbison. Publishes paperback acting editions of plays. Averages 80-90 titles/year; receives 1,200 submissions annually, mostly from unagented playwrights. Pays 10% book royalty on retail price. Pays 90% stock production royalty; 80% amateur production royalty. Offers variable advance. Simultaneous and photocopied submissions OK. SASE. Reports immediately on queries; from 6 weeks to 8 months on mss. Book catalog $1.25, postpaid; ms guidelines $3.

Nonfiction: Acting editions of plays.

Tips: "Broadway and Off-Broadway hit plays, light comedies and mysteries have the best chance of selling to our firm. Our market is theater producers—both professional and amateur and actors. Read as many plays as possible of recent vintage to keep apprised of today's market; write small-cast plays with good female roles; and be one hundred percent professional in approaching publishers and producers (see guidelines)."

THE FREE PRESS, Division of the Macmillan Publishing Co., Inc., 866 3rd Ave., New York NY 10022. President/Publisher: Erwin A. Glikes. Averages 65 titles/year. Royalty schedule varies. Publishes book an average of 9 months after acceptance. "Prefers camera-ready copy to machine-readable media." SASE. Reports in 3 weeks.

Nonfiction: Professional books and textbooks. Publishes college texts, adult nonfiction, and professional books in the social sciences, humanities and business. Reviews artwork/photos as part of ms package "but we can accept no responsibility for photos or art." Looks for "identifiable target audience, evidence of writing ability." Accepts nonfiction translations. Send 1-3 sample chapters, outline, and query letter before submitting mss.

‡**C.J. FROMPOVICH PUBLICATIONS**, RD 1, Chestnut Rd., Coopersburg PA 18036. (215)346-8461. Contact: Publisher. Publishes trade and mass market paperback originals. Averages 3 titles/year. Pays 10% royalty on wholesale price. No advance. Reports in 1 month. Book catalog for business size SAE and 1 first class stamp.

Nonfiction: Self-help, technical on natural nutrition. Submit outline/synopsis and sample chapters.

Recent Nonfiction Title: *Feeding Baby Naturally From Pregnancy On . . .*, by Catherine J. Frompovich, DSc., ND., (Ph.D.).

FRONT ROW EXPERIENCE, 540 Discovery Bay Blvd., Byron CA 94514. (415)634-5710. Editor: Frank Alexander. Publishes trade paperback originals. Averages 2-3 titles/year; receives 20 submissions annually. 90% of books from first-time authors; 100% of books from unagented writers. Average print order for a writer's first book is 500. Pays 5-10% royalty on net sales. Publishes book an average of 1 year after acceptance. Simultaneous and photocopied submissions OK. Computer printout submissions acceptable; no dot-matrix. "We return submissions but not without a SASE." Reports in 1 week on queries; 1 month on mss. Free book catalog.

Nonfiction: How-to, reference, curriculum guides for movement education, special education, educational games, and perceptual-motor development. Especially needs innovative curriculum guides. Publishes for elementary physical education directors, elementary, junior high, and preschool teachers, YMCA activity directors, occupational therapists, physical therapists, curriculum directors, and childhood development professionals in general. Accepts nonfiction translations from any language in subject areas we specialize in. No mss outside of movement education, special education, educational games, and perceptual-motor development. Reviews artwork/photos as part of ms package. Query. Submit outline/synopsis and 3 sample chapters.

Recent Nonfiction Title: *Games We Should Play in School*, by Frank Aycox.

GAMING BOOK DISTRIBUTORS, (formerly SRS Enterprises, Inc./Scientific Research Services), Division of Gambling Times, Inc., 1018 N. Cole Ave., Hollywood CA 90038. (213)466-5261. Nationally distributed by Lyle Stuart Inc., Seacaucus NJ. Director of Publishing: Robert Ames. Publishes hardcover and trade paperback originals. Averages 40 titles/year. Pays 4-15% royalty on retail price; no advance. Publishes book an

average of 1 year after acceptance. SASE. Reports in 6 weeks on queries; 3 months on mss.
Nonfiction: How-to. Subjects cover only gambling and gaming. "We're looking for books on all types of gambling and gambling-related activities." Submit outline/synopsis and sample chapters. Reviews artwork/photos as part of ms package.
Recent Nonfiction Title: *Million Dollar Blackjack*, by Ken Uston (how to play and win at 21).
Fiction: Query.

GARBER COMMUNICATIONS, INC., (affiliates: Steinerbooks, Spiritual Fiction Publications, Spiritual Science Library, Rudolf Steiner Publications, Freedeeds Books, Biograf Publications), 5 Garber Hill Rd., Blauvelt NY 10913. (914)359-9292. Editor: Bernard J. Garber. Publishes hardcover and paperback originals and reprints. Averages 15 titles/year; receives 250 submissions annually. 10% of books from first-time authors; 100% of books from unagented writers. Average print order for a writer's first book is 500-1,000 copies. Pays 5-7% royalty on retail price; offers average $500 advance. Publishes book an average of 1 year after acceptance. Will consider photocopied submissions. Reports in 2 months. SASE. Free book catalog; ms guidelines for SAE and 25¢ postage.
Nonfiction: Spiritual sciences, occult, philosophical, metaphysical and ESP. These are for our Steiner Books division only. Serious nonfiction. Philosophy and Spiritual Sciences: Bernard J. Garber. Query with outline and first, middle and last chapters for nonfiction.
Recent Nonfiction Title: *Frederick Nietzsche*, by Rudolf Steiner.
Fiction: Patricia Abrams, editor, the new genre called Spiritual Fiction Publications. "We are now looking for original manuscripts or rewrites of classics in modern times."
Recent Fiction Title: *The Farthermost City*, by Thomas Miles.

GARDEN WAY PUBLISHING, Storey Communications, Inc., Schoolhouse Rd., Pownal VT 05261. (802)823-5811. Editor: Roger Griffith. Publishes hardcover and paperback originals. Publishes 12 titles/year; receives 2,000 submissions annually. 50% of books from first-time authors; 50% of books from unagented writers. Average print order for a writer's first book is 7,500. Offers a flat fee arrangement varying with book's scope, or royalty, which usually pays author 6% of book's retail price. Advances are negotiable, but usually range from $1,500 to $3,000. "We stress continued promotion of titles and sales over many years." Emphasizes direct mail sales and sales to specialty stores, plus sales to bookstores through Harper and Row. Publishes book an average of 9 months after acceptance. Photocopied submissions OK. Computer printout submissions acceptable; no dot-matrix. Enclose return postage.
Nonfiction: Books on gardening, cooking, animal husbandry, homesteading, country living, country business, house and small building construction and energy conservation. Emphasis should be on how-to. Length requirements are flexible. "The writer should remember the reader will buy his book to learn to do something, so that all information to accomplish this must be given. We are publishing specifically for the person who is concerned about natural resources and a deteriorating life style and wants to do something about it." Query with outline and 2-3 sample chapters. Reviews artwork/photos as part of ms package.
Recent Nonfiction Title: *The Joy of Gardening Cookbook*, by Janet Ballantyne.

GARLAND PUBLISHING, INC., 136 Madison Ave., New York NY 10016. (212)686-7492. Vice President: Gary Kuris. Publishes hardcover originals. Averages 120 titles/year. Pays 10-15% royalty on wholesale price. "Depending on marketability, authors may prepare camera-ready copy." Publishes book an average of 3 months after acceptance. Simultaneous and photocopied submissions OK. Computer printout submissions acceptable; prefers letter-quality to dot-matrix. Reports in 2 weeks on queries; 1 month on mss. Free book catalog.
Nonfiction: Reference books for libraries. Humanities and social sciences. Accepts nonfiction translations. "We're interested in reference books—bibliographies, sourcebooks, indexes, etc.—in all fields." Submit outline/synopsis and 1-2 sample chapters. Reviews artwork/photos as part of ms package.
Recent Nonfiction Title: *Ulysses*, by James Joyce (a synoptic edition).

GAY SUNSHINE PRESS, Box 40397, San Francisco CA 94140. (415)824-3184. Editor: Winston Leyland. Publishes hardcover and trade paperback originals and trade paperback reprints. Averages 10 titles/year. Pays royalty or makes outright purchase. Photocopied submissions OK. SASE. Reports in 3 weeks on queries; 1 month on mss. Book catalog $1.
Nonfiction: How-to and gay lifestyle topics. "We're interested in innovative literary nonfiction which deals with gay lifestyles." No long personal accounts (e.g. "how I came out"), academic or overly formal titles. No books that are too specialized (e.g., homosexuality in the ancient world). Query. "After query is returned by us, submit outline/synopsis and sample chapters. All unsolicited mss are returned unopened."
Recent Nonfiction Title: *Gay Sunshine Interviews*, Volume 2, edited by W. Leyland (gay literary/political interviews).
Fiction: Erotica, ethnic, experimental, historical, mystery, science fiction and gay fiction in translation. "Interested in well-written novels on gay themes; also short story collections. We have a high literary standard for

fiction." Query. "After query is returned by us, submit outline/synopsis and sample chapters. All unsolicited mss are returned unopened."

Recent Fiction Title: *Thirsty Evil*, by Gore Vidal (short fiction).

*GENEALOGICAL PUBLISHING CO., INC., 1001 N. Calvert St., Baltimore MD 21202. (301)837-8271. Editor-in-Chief: Michael H. Tepper, Ph.D. Publishes hardcover originals and reprints. Subsidy publishes 10% of books. Averages 80 titles/year; receives 400 submissions annually. 50% of books from first-time authors; 100% of books from unagented writers. Average print order for a writer's first book is 2,000-3,000. Offers straight 10% royalty on retail price. Publishes book an average of 6 months after acceptance. Photocopied submissions OK. Computer printout submissions acceptable; no dot matrix. Reports "immediately." Enclose SAE and return postage.

Nonfiction: Reference, genealogy, and immigration records: "Our requirements are unusual, so we usually treat each author and his subject in a way particularly appropriate to his special skills and subject matter. Guidelines are flexible, but it is expected that an author will consult with us in depth. Most, though not all, of our original publications are offset from camera-ready typescript. Since most genealogical reference works are compilations of vital records and similar data, tabular formats are common. We hope to receive more ms material covering vital records and ships' passenger lists. We want family history compendia, basic methodology in genealogy, heraldry, and immigration records. Prefers query first, but will look at outline and sample chapter or complete ms. Reviews artwork/photos as part of ms package.

Recent Nonfiction Title: *American Ancestors and Relatives of the Princess of Wales.*

‡GENERAL HALL, INC., 23-45 Corporal Kennedy St., Bayside NY 11360. (718)423-9397. Publisher: Ravi Mehra. Publishes hardcover and trade paperback originals for the college market. Averages 5-6 titles/year; receives 100-300 submissions annually. 10% of books from first-time authors; 100% of books from unagented writers. Pays 10-15% royalty. Publishes book an average of 10 months after acceptance. Simultaneous and photocopied submissions OK. Computer printout submissions acceptable; no dot-matrix. SASE. Reports in 6 weeks. Reviews artwork/photos.

Nonfiction: Reference and textbook. Subjects include Americana, blacks, business and economics, politics, psychology and sociology. Submit complete ms.

Recent Nonfiction Title: *The Future of Women*, by Rona M. Fields.

THE J. PAUL GETTY MUSEUM, Subsidiary of The J. Paul Getty Museum Trust, Box 2112, Santa Monica CA 90406. (213)459-2306. Editor: Sandra Knudsen Morgan. Publishes hardcover and trade paperback originals and reprints. Averages 10 titles/year; receives 30 submissions annually. 20% of books from first-time authors; 100% of books from unagented writers. Average print order for a writer's first book is 1,500. Pays 6-12% royalty on retail price; buys some mss outright; offers average $2,000 honorarium. Publishes book an average of 18 months after acceptance. Photocopied submissions OK. Electronic submissions OK IBM, but requires hard copy also. Computer printout submissions acceptable; prefers letter-quality to dot-matrix. SASE. Reports in 2 month. Free book catalog and ms guidelines.

Nonfiction: Reference and scholarly on art and history. "Scholarly titles and well-researched general and children's titles on topics related to the museum's seven collections: Greek and Roman art and architecture (especially the Villa dei Papiri), illuminated manuscripts, drawings and paintings from the Renaissance through the nineteenth century, European sculpture decorative arts of the Regence through Napoleonic periods, and photographs." No nonEuropean art. Query. Reviews artwork/photos as part of ms package.

Recent Nonfiction Title: *Selections from the Decorative Arts in the JPGM*, by G. Wilson.

‡THE C.R. GIBSON COMPANY, 32 Knight St., Norwalk CT 06856. (203)847-4543. Senior editor: Jayne Bowman. Publishes hardcover originals. Averages 25 titles/year; receives 230 submissions annually. Pays royalty or outright purchase. Publishes book an average of 18 months after acceptance. Simultaneous and photocopied submissions OK. SASE. Reports in 3 weeks on queries; 2 months on mss. Free book catalog.

Nonfiction: Juvenile and gift books. Subject includes religion/inspiration. Query or submit outline/synopsis and sample chapter. Reviews artwork/photos.

Tips: "Religious inspirational books or books suitable for special occasion gift-giving have the best chance of selling to our firm."

‡GIFTED EDUCATION PRESS, The Reading Tutorium, 10201 Yuma Ct., Box 1586, Manassas VA 22110. (703)369-5017. Publisher: Maurice D. Fisher. Publishes mass market paperback originals. Averages 3-5 titles/year; receives 6 submissions annually. 75% of books from first-time authors; 100% of books from unagented writers. Pays 10-11% on retail price. Publishes book an average of 3 months after acceptance. Simultaneous and photocopied submissions OK. Computer printout submissions acceptable; prefers letter-quality to dot-matrix. SASE. Reports in 1 month on queries; 3 months on mss. Free book catalog.

Nonfiction: How-to. Subjects include philosophy, psychology, education of the gifted; and how to teach children to read. "Need books on how to educate gifted children—both theory and practice. Also, we are searching for books on using computers for the gifted, and how to teach children with learning problems to read. Need rigorous books on procedures, methods, and specific curriculum for the gifted." Query.

Recent Nonfiction Title: *Teaching Philosophy to Gifted Students*, by James LoGiudice (course of study).

Tips: "If I were a writer trying to market a book today, I would develop a detailed outline based upon intensive study of my field of interest. Present creative ideas in a rigorous fashion. Be knowledgeable about and comfortable with ideas."

THE K.S. GINIGER CO., INC., 235 Park Ave., S., New York NY 10003. (212)533-5080. President: Kenneth Seeman Giniger. Book publisher and independent book producer/packager. Publishes hardcover, trade and paperback originals. Averages 8 titles/year; receives 500 submissions annually. 10% of books from first-time authors; 10% of books from unagented writers. Average print order for a writer's first book is 7,500. Pays royalty on wholesale or retail price. Publishes book an average of 1 year after acceptance. Computer printout submissions acceptable; prefers letter-quality to dot-matrix. SASE. Reports in 2 weeks.

Nonfiction: Biography, how-to, reference and self-help. Subjects include Americana, art, health, history, hobbies, religion, sports and travel. Query with SASE. Accepts outline/synopsis; 1 sample chapter. Reviews artwork/photos as part of ms package. All unsolicited mss are returned unread "if postage is enclosed."

Recent Nonfiction Title: *Sotheby's Guide to Buying and Selling at Auction*, by Hugh Hildesley.

Tips: "We look for a good idea and power of expressing it with clarity and interest."

GINN AND CO., 191 Spring St., Lexington MA 02173. (617)861-1670. Senior Vice President, Publications: Mary Ansaldo. Royalty schedule: from 10% of net on a secondary book to 3% on elementary materials. "We are doing a significant number of books on a work-for-hire or fee basis." Averages 200 titles/year. Sample chapters, complete or partially complete mss will be considered. Electronic submissions OK. Computer printout submissions acceptable. Reports in 2 to 6 weeks. Enclose return postage.

Nonfiction: Publishers of textbooks and instructional materials for elementary and secondary schools.

Tips: Queries/mss may be routed to other editors in the publishing group.

THE GLOBE PEQUOT PRESS, INC., Old Chester Rd., Box Q, Chester CT 06412. (203)526-9571. Vice President/Publications Director: Linda Kennedy. Publishes hardcover and paperback originals (95%) and paperback reprints (5%). Averages 15 titles/year; receives 2,000 submissions annually. 20% of books from first-time authors; 75% of books from unagented writers. Average print order for a writer's first book is 5,000. Offers 7½-10% royalty on net price; advances offered "for specific expenses only." Publishes book an average of 1 year after acceptance. Simultaneous and photocopied submissions OK. Computer printout submissions acceptable; prefers letter-quality to dot-matrix. SASE. Reports in 3 weeks. Book catalog for SASE.

Nonfiction: The Northeast-Americana, recreation (outdoor books), and travel (guide books). Some regional history and cookbooks. "Guide books are especially promising today, with a guide book people can plan travel itineraries in advance, save time and money. Books with a New England or Northeastern focus will be considered most seriously." No doctoral theses, genealogies or textbooks. Submit outline/synopsis and sample chapters. Reviews artwork/photos.

Recent Nonfiction Title: *Special Museums of the Northeast*.

*THE GOLDEN QUILL PRESS, Avery Rd., Francestown NH 03043. (603)547-6622. Owner: Edward T. Dell Jr. Publishes hardcover originals. Averages 25 titles/year; receives 250 submissions annually. 50% of books from first-time authors. Average print order for a writer's first book is 750. Subsidy publishes 90% of books "depending on past sales records." Pays 10% maximum royalty on retail price. Publishes book an average of 6 months after acceptance. Photocopied submissions OK. Electronic submissions OK, 1200 Baud—modem supplied, but requires hard copy. Computer printout submissions acceptable; prefers letter-quality to dot-matrix. SASE. Reports in 2 weeks on queries; 1 month on mss. Free book catalog.

Nonfiction: Biography. Query or submit complete ms. Reviews artwork/photos as part of ms package.

Poetry: All types. Submit complete ms.

GOLDEN WEST BOOKS, Box 80250, San Marino CA 91108. (213)283-3446. Editor-in-Chief: Donald Duke. Managing Editor: Vernice Dagosta. Publishes hardcover and paperback originals. Pays 10% royalty contract; no advance. Simultaneous and photocopied submissions OK. Reports in 2-4 weeks. SASE. Free book catalog.

Nonfiction: Publishes selected Western Americana and transportation Americana. Query or submit complete ms. "Illustrations and photographs will be examined if we like manuscript."

GOLDEN WEST PUBLISHERS, 4113 N. Longview, Phoenix AZ 85014. (602)265-4392. Editor: Hal Mitchell. Publishes trade paperback originals. Averages 4 titles/year; receives 200 submissions annually. 50% of books from first-time authors; 100% of books from unagented writers. Average print order for a writer's first book is 5,000. Pays 6-10% royalty on retail price or makes outright purchase of $500-2,500. No advance. Publishes book an average of 6 months after acceptance. Simultaneous and photocopied submissions OK.

Electronic submissions OK—A/M 425 to Comp Edit, but requires hard copy also. Computer printout submissions acceptable; no dot-matrix. SASE. Reports in 2 weeks on queries; 1 month on mss. Book catalog for business size SAE and 1 first class stamp.
Nonfiction: Cookbooks, how-to, guide books and self-help books. Subjects include cooking and foods, health, history, the outdoors, travel and the West or Southwest. Query or submit outline/synopsis and sample chapters. Prefers query letter first. Reviews artwork/photos as part of ms package.
Recent Title: *Fool's Gold,* by Robert Sikorsky.

GRAPHIC ARTS CENTER PUBLISHING CO., 3019 NW Yeon Ave., Box 10306, Portland OR 97210. (503)226-2402. General Manager and Editor: Douglas Pfeiffer. Publishes hardcover originals. Averages 3-6 titles/year. Pays outright purchase averaging $3,000. Simultaneous and photocopied submissions OK. Reports in 3 weeks. SASE.
Nonfiction: "All titles are pictorials with text. Text usually runs separately from the pictorial treatment, and authors are selected to complement the pictorial essay." Query.

*GRAPHIC IMAGE PUBLICATIONS, Box 1740, La Jolla CA 92038. (619)755-6558. President: Hurb Crow. Publishes trade and mass market paperback originals and software. Averages 5 titles/year. Subsidy publishes 10% of books based on "length of experience and success of prior works." Pays 5-15% royalty on wholesale price; advance negotiable. Publishes book an average of 1 year after acceptance. Query with outline/synopsis and 2 sample chapters to the attention of Judy Delp, managing editor. Must have SASE for response. Reports in 2 months. Simultaneous and photocopied submissions OK. Computer printout submissions acceptable; no dot-matrix.
Nonfiction: How-to, computer software programs and travel. "We publish for people with a desire to learn on their own; and for people who love to travel and to know about the areas they visit."
Recent Nonfiction Title: *Cabo San Lucas,* by Susan H. Crow.
Fiction: Romance.
Recent Fiction Title: *Night Vision,* by Erin Hahn (suspense).
Tips: "Be professional in your query, and let us know a little about yourself, be positive." Queries/mss may be routed to other editors in the publishing group.

GRAY'S PUBLISHING, LTD., Box 2160, Sidney, British Columbia V8L 3S6 Canada. (604)652-5911. Editor: Maralyn Horsdal. Publishes hardcover and paperback originals and reprints. Averages 4 titles/year. Offers standard royalty contract on retail price. Query with outline and 3-4 sample chapters. Reports in 10 weeks. SAE and IRCs.
Nonfiction: Wants "nonfiction, Canadiana," especially Pacific Northwest. Subjects include biography, natural history, history and nautical. Looks for "good writing and worthwhile marketable topic." Reviews artwork/photos as part of ms package. Length: 60,000-120,000 words.
Recent Nonfiction Title: *Molly the Dog that Wouldn't Quit,* by Perkins (Animal).

GRAYWOLF PRESS, Box 142, Port Townsend WA 98368. (206)385-1160. Editor/Publisher: Scott Walker. Imprints include Graywolf Short Fiction Series. Publishes hardcover and trade paperback originals, and trade paperback reprints. Averages 10-16 titles/year. Pays 7-10% royalty on retail price. Photocopied submissions OK. SASE. Reports in 2 weeks on queries; 1 month on mss. Free book catalog.
Fiction: Short fiction collections. "Limited to direct solicitation only." Query through agent only.

GREAT OCEAN PUBLISHERS, 1823 N. Lincoln St., Arlington VA 22207. (703)525-0909. President: Mark Esterman. Publishes hardcover and trade paperback originals and hardcover reprints. Averages 3 titles/year; receives 350 submissions annually. 10% of books from first-time authors; 50% of books from unagented writers. Average print order for a writer's first book is 3,000-5,000. Pays 8-10% hardcover royalty; 6-8% paperback on retail price; occasionally offers advance. Publishes book an average of 1 year after acceptance. Simultaneous (if so indicated) and photocopied submissions OK. Computer printout submissions acceptable; prefers letter-quality to dot-matrix. Reports in 3 weeks.
Nonfiction: Biography, how-to, illustrated book, reference, self-help and technical. Subjects include art, business and economics, child care/development, health, history, music, philosophy, politics and religion. "Any subject is fine as long as it meets our standards of quality." Submit outline/synopsis and sample chapters. "SASE *must* be included with all material to be returned." Looks for "1) good writing, 2) clear evidence that manuscript is intended as a *book,* not a long collection of weakly organized small pieces, and 3) good organization—not to mention a worthwhile, interesting subject." Accepts nonfiction translations—query first. Reviews artwork/photos. Reviews artwork/photos.
Recent Nonfiction Title: *Beethoven Remembered.*
Tips: Nonfiction with a real theme and a mature knowledgeable point of view have the best chance of selling to Great Ocean. If you have to ask . . .

‡*WARREN H. GREEN, INC., Subsidiaries include Fireside Books and Zeus Publishers, 8356 Olive Blvd., St. Louis MO 63132. (314)991-1335. President: Warren H. Green, Ph.D. Publishes hardcover originals. Averages 40 titles/year; receives over 300 submissions annually. 50% of books from first-time authors; 100% of books from unagented writers. Subsidiary publishes 10% of books based on subject matter. Pays 10-17½% on sales receipts; offers no advance. Publishes book an average of 9 months after acceptance. Simultaneous and photocopied submissions OK. Computer printout submissions acceptable; prefers letter-quality to dot-matrix. SASE. Reports in 1 week on queries; 3 weeks on mss. Free book catalog and ms guidelines.
Nonfiction: Reference. Subjects include health, history, medical, philosophy, psychology, sociology and education. Query or submit outline/synopsis and sample chapters.
Recent Nonfiction Title: *Health Care & the Social Services*, by Dr. Richard Estes (sociology).
Tips: Audience consists of medics (clinical and research), philosophers, educators, social workers, nurses and historians. "Best sales are in state-of-the-art diagnostic and clinical medicine. Make certain your book is new, different, needed, and not just an addition to paper pollution. Manuscripts should be fully documented and contain state-of-the-art materials, and not be a rehash of currently available information. No essays, collections or proceedings of symposia."

THE STEPHEN GREENE PRESS/LEWIS PUBLISHING, 15 Muzzey St., Lexington MA 02173. (802)257-7757. Editorial Director: Thomas Begner. Publishes hardcover and paperback originals (99%); hardcover and paperback reprints (1%). Averages 30 titles/year. Royalty "variable; advances are small." Send contact sheet or prints to illustrate ms. Photocopied submissions OK. Reports in 3 months. SASE.
Nonfiction: How-to (self-reliance); nature and environment; recreation; self-help; sports (outdoor and horse); popular technology; popular psychology and social science; and regional (New England). "We see our audience as mainly college-educated men and women, 30 and over. They are regular book buyers and readers. They probably have pronounced interests, hobby or professional, in subjects that our books treat. Authors can assess their needs by looking critically at what we have published."
Recent Nonfiction Title: *Improving Your Running*, by Bill Squires and Ray Krise.

GREENLEAF CLASSICS, INC., Box 20194, San Diego CA 92120. Managing Editor: Ralph Vaughan. Publishes paperback originals. Publishes 450 titles/year. Pays by outright purchase about 3 months after acceptance. Publishes book an average of 4 months after acceptance. Reports in 1-2 months. "No manuscripts will be returned unless accompanied by return postage." Writer's guidelines for SASE.
Fiction: Specializes in adult erotic novels. "All stories must have a sexual theme. They must be contemporary novels dealing with the serious problems of everyday people. All plots are structured so that characters must get involved in erotic situations. Write from the female viewpoint (third person). Request our guidelines before beginning any project for us." Preferred length: 35,000 words. Send complete ms (preferred); or at least 3 sample chapters.

‡**GREENWOOD PRESS**, Box 5007, Westport CT 06881. (203)226-3571. Executive Vice President: James Sabin. Averages 280 titles/year; receives 1,000-2,000 submissions annually. 50% of books from first-time authors; 90% of books from unagented writers. Average print order for a writer's first book is 1,000-2,000. Pays negotiable royalty; offers negotiable advance. Publishes book an average of 12 months after acceptance. Simultaneous and photocopied submissions OK. "We encourage authors under contract to submit manuscripts on disk or mag tape. We accept from a range of different systems." Computer printout submissions acceptable; no dot-matrix. SASE. Reports in 6 weeks. Free book catalog. Guidelines issued upon contract signing.
Nonfiction: Reference (dictionaries and handbooks); professional books in business and law (the Quorum Books imprint); and scholarly monographs. Query or submit prospectus, 1 sample chapter and vita. Reviews artwork/photos.
Recent Nonfiction Title: *Dictionary of Mexican-American History*, by Matt Meier and Feliciano Rivera.
Tips: "The writer has the best chance of selling our firm non-fiction references, and professional materials because of better market conditions. Once the author has signed a contract to write a book for us, the writing pitfall the author must avoid is writing a book significantly different from that placed under contract."

‡**GROUNDWOOD BOOKS**, 3F, 26 Lennox St., Toronto, Ontario M6G 1J4 Canada. (416)537-2501. Children's Publisher: Patricia Aldana. Imprint of Douglas & McIntrye. Publishes hardcover originals and trade paperback originals. Averages 15 titles/year; receives 500 submissions annually. 40-60% of books from first-time authors; 80% of books from unagented writers. Pays 10% royalty on retail price. Offers average $1,000 advance. Publishes book an average of 1 year after acceptance. Simultaneous submissions OK. Computer printout submissions acceptable; prefers letter-quality to dot-matrix. SASE. Reports in 2 weeks on queries; 8 weeks on mss.
Fiction: Juvenile. Subjects include adventure, fantasy, historical, humor, mainstream, mystery and science fiction. "We are looking for good *Canadian* fiction." Submit outline/synopsis and sample chapters.
Recent Fiction Title: *Angel Square*, by Brian Doyle (juvenile novel).

GROUPWORK TODAY, INC., Box 258, South Plainfield NJ 07080. Editor-in-Chief: Harry E. Moore Jr. Publishes hardcover and paperback originals. Averages 4-6 titles/year; receives 40-50 submissions annually. 90% of books from first-time authors; 100% of books from unagented writers. Average print order for a writer's first book is 1,000. Offers $100 advance against royalties on receipt of contract and completion of ms ready for publication; 10% of gross receipts from sale of book. Publishes book an average of 9 months after acceptance. Computer printout submissions acceptable; prefers letter-quality to dot-matrix. SASE. Books are marketed by direct mail to Groupwork Agency executives and professionals (YMCA, YWCA, Scouts, Salvation Army, colleges, directors of organized camps, and libraries). "Also will answer specific questions from an author considering us as a publisher." No simultaneous submissions. Reports in 6-8 weeks. Book catalog for SAE with 50¢ in stamps.

Nonfiction: "We are publishers of books and materials for professionals and volunteers who work with people in groups. Titles are also used by colleges for texts and resources. Some of our materials are also suited to the needs of professionals who work with individuals. Groupwork agency management, finance, program development and personnel development are among the subjects of interest to us. Writers must be thoroughly familiar with 'people work' and have fresh insights to offer. New writers are most welcome here. Lengths are open but usually run 40,000-60,000 words." Readers are mainly social agency administrators and professional staff members. Groupwork materials are also read by volunteers serving in the social agencies. Mss are judged by experienced professionals in social agencies. The company is advised on policy direction by a council of advisors from national agencies and colleges across the nation. "We also are publishing our 'monogram' series to deal with the most important problems with which social work agencies must deal today. We are also in the market for papers, 15-35 double-spaced pages, for a Management Workbook Series. Papers must deal with finance, program development, communication, organizational planning or some other subject directed to the problems of nonprofit, human services organizations. We pay a $35 advance against a 10% royalty on gross sales." Submit outline and 3 sample chapters for nonfiction. Reviews artwork/photos as part of ms package.

Recent Nonfiction Title: *Meaning Well is Not Enough: Perspectives on Volunteering*, by Jane Mallory Park.

Tips: "If a writer will send material only on which he or she has done as much work as possible to make a good outline, a sample chapter or two to indicate writing ability, and the idea is a contribution to our field, we will spend all kinds of time guiding the author to completion of the work."

‡**GRYPHON HOUSE, INC.**, 3706 Otis St., Box 275, Mt. Rainier MD 20712. (301)779-6200. President Editor: Larry Rood. Publishes trade paperback originals. Averages 3 titles/year; receives 250-400 submissions annually. 80% of books from first-time authors; 100% of books from unagented writers. Average print order for a writer's first book is 3,000-4,000. Pays 10-12½% royalty on retail price; offers average $300 advance. Photocopied submissions OK. Computer printout submissions OK; prefers letter-quality to dot-matrix. SASE. Reports in 2 weeks. Book catalog for 9x12 SAE and 2 first class stamps. Writer's guidelines for SASE.

Nonfiction: How-to and creative educational activities for teachers to do with preschool children, ages 1-5. "We are specialty publishers and do not consider anything at present out of the above category. Our audience includes teachers in preschools, nursery schools, day care centers and kindergartens." Query or submit outline/synopsis and 1 sample chapter. Looks for "brevity, clarity and an explanation of how this book is unique."

Recent Nonfiction Title: *Hug a Tree and Other Things to do Outdoors with Young Children*, by Rockwell, et.al.

***GUERNICA EDITIONS**, Box 633, Station N.D.G., Montreal, Quebec H4A 3R1 Canada. (514)481-5569. President/Editor: Antonio D'Alfonso. Publishes hardcover and trade paperback originals, hardcover and trade paperback reprints and software. Averages 10 titles/year; receives 1,000-2,000 submissions annually. 5% of books from first-time authors. Average print order for a writer's first book is 750-1,000. Subsidy publishes 50% of titles. "Subsidy in Canada is received only when the author is established, Canadian-born and active in the country's cultural world. The others we subsidize ourselves." Pays 3-10% royalty on retail price. Makes outright purchase of $200-5,000. Offers 7¢/word advance for translators. Photocopied submissions OK. IRCs required. "American stamps are of no use to us in Canada." Reports in 1 month on queries; 6 weeks on mss. Free book catalog.

Nonfiction: Biography, humor, juvenile, reference and textbook. Subjects include art, history, music, nature, philosophy, photography, politics, psychology, recreation, religion and Canadiana. "We are looking for essays on history, philosophy, religion, politics, film, and other topics which can be used as discussion books." Query.

Fiction: Erotica, ethnic, historical, mystery, science fiction and suspense. "We wish to open up into the fiction world. No country is a country without its fiction writers. Canada is growing some fine fiction writers. We'd like to read you. No first novels." Query.

Poetry: "We wish to have writers in translation. Any writer who has translated Italian poetry is welcomed. Full books only. Not single poems by different authors, unless modern, and used as an anthology. First books will have no place in the next couple of years." Submit samples.

Recent Poetry Title: *Embers and Earth*, by Gaston Miron.

GUIDANCE CENTRE, Faculty of Education, University of Toronto, 10 Alcorn Ave., Toronto, Ontario M4V 2Z8 Canada. (416)978-3210. Editorial Director: L. Miller. Coordinating Editor: Gethin James. Publishes hardcover and paperback originals. Averages 15 titles/year. Pays in royalties. Reports in 1 month. Submissions returned "only if Canadian postage is sent." Free book catalog.
Nonfiction: "The Guidance Centre is interested in publications related to career planning and guidance and in measurement and evaluation. Also general education. No manuscripts which have confined their references and illustrations to United States material." Submit complete ms. Consult Chicago *Manual of Style*.
Recent Nonfiction Title: *Loneliness*, by Bulka.

*GULF PUBLISHING CO., Box 2608, Houston TX 77001. (713)529-4301. Vice President: C.A. Umbach Jr. Editor-in-Chief: William J. Lowe. Imprints include Lone Star Books (regional Texas books). Publishes hardcover and large format paperback originals and software. Averages 40-50 titles/year. Subsidy publishes 5% of books. Pays 10% royalty on net income; offers $300-2,000 advance. Publishes book an average of 1 year after acceptance. Simultaneous and photocopied submissions OK. Computer printout submissions OK; no dot-matrix. Reports in 2 months. SASE. Free book catalog.
Nonfiction: Business, reference, regional trade, scientific and self-help. "We are the world's largest specialized publisher to the energy industries." Submit outline/synopsis and 1-2 sample chapters. Reviews artwork/photos as part of ms package.
Recent Nonfiction Title: *Managing Project Cost Control*, by Bill Tompkins.

H.P. BOOKS, Subsidiary of Knight-Ridder Newspapers, Box 5367, Tucson AZ 85703. Publisher: Rick Bailey. Publishes hardcover and paperback originals. Averages 40-45 titles/year. Pays royalty on wholesale price; advance negotiable. Publishes ms an average of 9 months after acceptance. Simultaneous and photocopied submissions OK. "We delight in disk submissions but must be 8" diskette compatible with Wang VS 100 system or transfer directly to computer via telephone modem." Reports in 2-4 weeks. SASE. Free book catalog.
Nonfiction: Specializes in how-to books in several fields, all photo-illustrated. Cookbooks, cooking and foods, gardening, hobbies, how-to, leisure activities, photography, automotive, health, recreation, self-help, art techniques, computer and technical books. Most books are 160 pages minimum; "word count varies with the format." Query only and state number and type of illustrations available. Submit introduction and 1 sample chapter. "We *require* author to supply photos and illustrations to our specifications."
Recent Nonfiction Title: *The Complete Cook*, by Pat Jester.

‡H.W.H. CREATIVE PRODUCTIONS, INC., 87-53 167th St., Jamaica NY 11432. (212)297-2208. President: Willis Hogan, Jr. Imprints include Phase One Graphic (nonfiction and fiction), Contact Maxine Bayliss about imprints. Publishes hardcover and trade paperback originals. Averages 5 titles/year. Pays 10-15% royalty on wholesale price; offers average $200 advance. Photocopied submissions OK. SASE. Reports in 1 month on queries; 2 months on mss.
Nonfiction: Biography, cookbook, humor, illustrated book and self-help. Subjects include Americana, animals, art, cooking and foods, health, hobbies, nature, photography (as a creative art form), recreation, travel and energy. Particularly interested in cookbooks, personalities, self portraits, new forms of energy, high technology. Submit outline/synopsis and sample chapters.
Recent Nonfiction Title: *Now a Word About Marriage*.
Fiction: Confession, ethnic, experimental, fantasy, humor, mainstream, romance, science fiction, suspense and plays. "Mindblowing science fiction, clean romance, experimental writing on any subject, children's stories." Submit outline/synopsis and sample chapters.
Recent Fiction Title: *Cat Torture*.

*ROBERT HALE LIMITED, Clerkenwell House, 45/47 Clerkenwell Green, London EC1R 0HT England. (01)251-2661. Managing Director: John Hale. Chief Editor: Carmel Elwell. Publishes hardcover and trade paperback originals, and hardcover reprints. Averages 600 titles/year. Subsidy publishes 50% of books. Pays royalty on retail price. Publishes book an average of 9 months after acceptance. Photocopied submissions OK. Computer printout submissions acceptable. SASE. Reports in 1 week on queries; 6 weeks on mss. Book catalog for $1 (postage). ("Send dollar bills or checks for postage and *not*; postage stamps, postal coupons, money orders, etc.")
Nonfiction: Biography, "coffee table" book, cookbook, how-to, humor, illustrated book, reference and self-help. Subjects include animals, art, cooking and foods, health, history, hobbies, music, nature, photography, politics, recreation, religion, sports and travel. No autobiography of unknown persons, verse, philosophy, American history, education or technical material. Submit outline/synopsis and sample chapters. Reviews artwork/photos as part of ms package.
Recent Nonfiction Title: *Ava*, by Roland Flamini (biography).
Fiction: Adventure, gothic, historical, mainstream, mystery, romance, suspense and western. "We are seeking anything between the lengths of 40,000 and 100,000 words for the adult reader." No Americana, confession,

erotica, ethnic, experimental, fantasy, horror, humor, religious or science fiction. Submit outline/synopsis and sample chapters.
Recent Fiction Title: *The Shadow King*, by Roberta J. Dewa (historical).

‡**ALEXANDER HAMILTON INSTITUTE**, 1633 Broadway, New York NY 10019. (212)397-3580. Senior Editor: Rick Wolff. Publishes hardcover originals and software. Averages 18 titles/year. 30% of books from first-time authors; 90% of books from unagented writers. "We pay advance against negotiated royalty or straight fee (no royalty)." Offers average $2,000 advance. Simultaneous submissions OK. Computer printout submissions acceptable; no dot-matrix. SASE. Reports in 3 weeks on queries; 7 weeks on mss. Ms guidelines for SASE.
Nonfiction: How-to, reference and self-help. Subjects include business and economics and management. "Our needs are in the leading edge of business/management field. Since we publish only a specific type of book, we have very select needs. We want only 'how-to' books in the management area. We do *not* want traditional textbooks." Query or submit outline/synopsis and sample chapters. Reviews artwork/photos.
Recent Nonfiction Title: *Fire Me and I'll Sue*, by Thomas Condon (how-to).
Tips: "We sell exclusively by direct mail to managers and executives around the world. A writer must know his/her field and be able to teach its principles clearly and concisely."

‡**HANLEY & BELFUS, INC.**, 210 S. 13th St., Philadelphia PA 19107. (215)546-4995. President: John J. Hanley. Executive Vice President: Linda C. Belfus. Publishes hardcover and trade paperback originals. Averages 10 titles/year; receives 200 submissions annually. 50% of books from first-time authors; 100% of books from unagented writers. Pays 10% royalty on retail price. Publishes book an average of 9 months after acceptance. Simultaneous and photocopied submissions OK. Electronic submissions OK on Apple Macintosh PC; but requires hard copy also. Computer printout submissions acceptable; prefers letter-quality to dot-matrix. SASE. Reports in 1 week on queries; 2 weeks on mss. Free ms guidelines.
Nonfiction: Reference, textbook, medical manuals and atlases. Subjects include health. Especially looking for textbooks for medical students, nursing students and allied health students, and selected reference books for practicing doctors. Query or submit outline/synopsis and sample chapters. Reviews artwork/photos.

HARCOURT BRACE JOVANOVICH, 1250 6th Ave., San Diego CA 92101. Director of Trade Books Department: Peter Jovanovich. Publishes hardcover and paperback originals and reprints. SASE.

HARCOURT BRACE JOVANOVICH LEGAL & PROFESSIONAL PUBLICATIONS, INC., Subsidiary of Harcourt Brace Jovanovich, Inc., 14415 S. Main St., Gardena CA 90248. (213)321-3275. Subsidiaries include Law Distributors, Gilbert Printing, Gilbert Law & Legalines, Bar/Bri Law Reviews. President: Meyer Fisher. Publishes trade paperback originals, trade paperback reprints and software. Averages 6 titles/year. Pays 7-10% royalty on wholesale price. Offers $1,000-6,000 advance. Publishes ms an average of 6 months after acceptance. Simultaneous submissions OK. Electronic submissions OK, but requires hard copy also. Computer printout submissions acceptable. SASE. Reports in 3 weeks on queries; 2 months on mss. Free book catalog.
Nonfiction: How-to, reference law books for minors, self-help, technical, textbook, law outlines and study aids. Subjects include business and economics, psychology, professional law, C.P.A., and criminal justice. Especially needs books on "juvenile laws, psychology for law people, law for lay people. Does not want biography, cookbooks, health, humor, politics or religious books." Submit outline/synopsis and 6 sample chapters. Reviews artwork/photos as part of ms package.
Recent Nonfiction Title: *Herbert Legal Series: Multistate Bar Examination, Volume One*.
Tips: Queries/mss may be routed to other editors in the publishing group.

HARLEQUIN BOOKS, 225 Duncan Mill Rd., Don Mills, Ontario M3B 3K9 Canada. (416)445-5860. Imprints include Harlequin Romance, Harlequin Presents, Superromances, Harlequin American Romance, Harlequin Temptation and Harlequin Intrigue. Publishes paperback originals. Pays royalty on retail price; offers advance. Publishes book an average of 18 months after acceptance. Photocopied submissions OK. SAE and IRCs. Reports in 2-3 months.
Fiction: For Harlequin Romance and Harlequin Presents submit to Maryan Gibson, senior editor. Outline/synopsis and sample chapters OK. For Superromance submit to Lauren Bauman, senior editor. Outline/synopsis and sample chapters OK. For Temptation submit to Margaret Carney. For Harlequin American Romance to Debra Matteucci, senior editor, Harlequin Books, 300 E. 42nd St., 6th Floor, New York NY 10017. For Harlequin Intrigue submit to Reva Kindser, editor, (also at the New York address). Outline/synopsis OK. Complete mss only.

HARPER & ROW PUBLISHERS, INC., 10 E. 53rd St., New York NY 10022. (212)207-7000. Imprints include Barnes & Noble; Harper & Row-San Francisco (religious books only); Perennial Library; and Torchbooks. Managing Editor: Katharine Kirkland. Publishes hardcover and paperback originals, and paperback reprints. Publishes 300 titles/year. Pays standard royalties; advances negotiable. No unsolicited queries or mss. Reports on solicited queries in 6 weeks.

Nonfiction: Americana, animals, art, biography, business/economics, cookbooks, health, history, how-to, humor, music, nature, philosophy, photography, poetry, politics, psychology, reference, religion, science, self-help, sociology, sports and travel. "No technical books."

Fiction: Adventure, fantasy, gothic, historical, mainstream, mystery, romance, science fiction, suspense, western and literary. "We look for a strong story line and exceptional literary talent."

THE HARVARD COMMON PRESS, 535 Albany St., Boston MA 02118. (617)423-5803. President: Bruce P. Shaw. Publishes hardcover and trade paperback originals and reprints. Averages 8 titles/year; receives "thousands" of submissions annually. 75% of books from first-time authors; 75% of books from unagented writers. Average print order for a writer's first book is 7,500. Pays royalty; offers average $1,000 advance. Publishes book an average of 9 months after acceptance. Simultaneous and photocopied submissions OK. Computer printout submissions acceptable; no dot-matrix. SASE. Reports in 1 month. Book catalog for 9x11 1/2 SAE and 56¢ postage; ms guidelines for SASE.

Nonfiction: Travel, cookbook, how-to, reference and self-help. Subjects include Americana, business and economics, cooking and foods, health, history, hobbies, music, nature, politics, psychology, recreation and sociology. "We want strong, practical books that help people gain control over a particular area of their lives, whether it's family matters, business or financial matters, health, careers, food or travel. An increasing percentage of our list is made up of books about travel and travel guides; in this area we are looking for authors who are well traveled, and who can offer a different approach to the series guidebooks. We are open to good nonfiction proposals that show evidence of strong organization and writing, and clearly demonstrate a need in the marketplace. First-time authors are welcome." Accepts nonfiction translations. Submit outline/synopsis and 1-3 sample chapters. Reviews artwork/photos.

Recent Nonfiction Title: *The Teenagers Guide to the Best Summer Opportunities*, by Jan Greenberg.

HARVARD UNIVERSITY PRESS, 79 Garden St., Cambridge MA 02138. (617)495-2601. Director: Arthur J. Rosenthal. Editor-in-Chief: Maud Wilcox. Publishes hardcover and paperback originals and reprints. Publishes 120 titles/year. Publishes ms an average of 1 year after acceptance. Electronic submissions OK "at the discretion of our production department," but requires hard copy also. Computer printout submissions acceptable; no dot-matrix. Free book catalog.

Nonfiction: "We publish only scholarly nonfiction." No fiction.

*HARVEST HOUSE PUBLISHERS, 1075 Arrowsmith, Eugene OR 97402. (503)343-0123. Managing Editor: Eileen L. Mason. Publishes hardcover, trade paperback and mass market originals. Averages 50 titles/year; receives 1,000 submissions annually. 5% of books from first-time authors; 100% of books from unagented writers. Pays 10% minimum royalty on wholesale price. Publishes book an average of 6 months after acceptance. Simultaneous and photocopied submissions OK. Computer printout submissions acceptable; no dot-matrix. SASE. Reports in 4-6 weeks. Book catalog for 8 1/2x11 SAE and $1.22 postage; ms guidelines for SAE and 1 first class stamp.

Nonfiction: "coffee table" book, humor, how-to, reference and self-help. Subjects include politics (from Christian perspective); psychology (from Christian perspective); and religion. "No poetry, autobiography or textbooks—or any topic which we have already given extensive coverage to on our list." Query or submit outline/synopsis and sample chapters.

Recent Nonfiction Title: *The God Makers*, by Dave Hunt (religion).

Fiction: Historical (romance with a Christian emphasis) and mystery/suspense (with characters who deal with situations from a Christian belief system/message of salvation or growth in the Christian life). Query or submit outline/synopsis and sample chapters.

Recent Fiction Title: *Mist Over Morro Bay*, by Carole Gift Page (mystery).

Tips: Audience is women, ages 25-45. We look for professional presentation of work on fresh, innovative material within the scope of our publishing goal: to publish books which help the hurts of people. Avoid religious clichés."

HASTINGS HOUSE PUBLISHERS, INC., 10 E. 40th St., New York NY 10016. (212)689-5400. Editor: Walter Frese. Hardcover and paperback originals (80%) and reprints (20%). Averages 60 titles/year; receives 3,000 submissions annually. 40% of books from first-time authors; 80% of books from unagented writers. Average print order for a writer's first book is 5,000-7,500. 10% minimum royalty. Publishes book an average of 9 months after acceptance. Computer printout submissions acceptable; no dot-matrix. Reports in 1-2 weeks. SASE. Free book catalog.

Nonfiction: Publishes Americana, graphic arts, biography, cookbooks, cooking and foods, history, juveniles, photography, recreation, sports and travel. Accepts nonfiction translations. Query or submit outline/synopsis and 2 sample chapters. Reviews artwork/photos as part of ms package.

Recent Nonfiction Title: *Graphic Designers Production Handbook*, by Sanders/Bevington.

*HAWKES PUBLISHING, INC., 3775 S. 5th W., Salt Lake City UT 84115. (801)262-5555. President: John Hawkes. Publishes hardcover and trade paperback originals. Averages 24 titles/year; receives 200 submissions annually. 70% of books from first-time authors; 90% of books from unagented writers. Average print order for a writer's first book is 2,000. Subsidy publishes 25% of books/year based on "how promising they are." Pays varying royalty of 10% on retail price to 10% on wholesale; no advance. Publishes book an average of 6 months after acceptance. Photocopied submissions OK. Computer printout submissions acceptable; prefers letter-quality to dot-matrix. SASE. Reports in 1 month on queries; 3 months on mss. Free book catalog.
Nonfiction: Cookbook, how-to and self-help. Subjects include cooking and foods, health, history, hobbies and psychology. Query or submit outline/synopsis and sample chapters. Reviews artwork/photos.
Recent Nonfiction Title: *Migrant's Road,* by Reba Lazenby.

HAYDEN BOOK CO., 10 Mulholland Dr., Hasbrouck Heights NJ 07604. (201)393-6000. Editorial Director: Michael Violano. Publishes hardcover and paperback originals and software. Averages 100 titles/year; receives 250 submissions annually. 15% of books from first-time authors; 90% of books from unagented writers. Average print order for a writer's first book is 5,000-20,000. Pays 12-15% royalty; offers advance. Publishes book an average of 5 months after acceptance. Simultaneous (if so identified) and photocopied submissions OK. Electronic submissions OK on 5¼" and 8" disks from microcomputer systems, but requires 3 hard copies also. Reports in 6 weeks. SASE. Free book catalog; ms guidelines for SASE.
Nonfiction: Publishes technician-level and engineering texts and references on microcomputers, digital electronics, electricity and robotics; computer science; texts; and books on programming and applications for popular microcomputers.

HAZELDEN FOUNDATION, Dept. of Educational Materials, Box 176, Center City MN 55012. (612)257-4010. Managing Editor: Linda Peterson. Publishes hardcover and trade paperback originals and pamphlets. Predominantly direct mail. Averages 70 titles/year. Pays 7-9% royalty on retail price; buys some mss outright; offers $150-300% advance. Publishes ms an average of 10 months after acceptance. Simultaneous and photocopied submissions OK. Computer printout submissions acceptable. SASE. "We immediately acknowledge receipt. A decision is usually made within 2 months."
Nonfiction: Reference, self-help, psychology, sociology and addictions. "We are seeking manuscripts of pamphlet or booklet length. The subject matter, ideally, will center around alcoholism, drug abuse or other addictions. The focus would be on the prevention, recovery from, or understanding of an addiction." Publishes for people recovering from an addiction and those close to them; people seeking information about alcoholism/drug abuse; and professionals who help such people. No personal stories or poetry. Submit outline/synopsis, introduction and 2 sample chapters.
Recent Nonfiction Title: *A Teenager's Guide to Living With an Alcoholic Parent,* by Lynn Hornik-Beer.

HEALTH PROFESSION DIVISION, McGraw-Hill Book Co., 1221 Avenue of the Americas, New York NY 10020. Editorial Director: B.J. Clark. Publishes 60 titles/year. Pays on royalty basis. SASE.
Nonfiction: Textbooks, major reference books and continuing education materials in the field of medicine.
Recent Nonfiction Title: *Neurosurgery,* 1st Edition, by Wilkins-Regachary.

*HEART OF THE LAKES PUBLISHING, 2989 Lodi Rd., Interlaken NY 14847-0299. (607)532-4997. Contact: Walter Steesy. Publishes hardcover and trade paperback originals and hardcover and trade paperback reprints. Averages 10-15 titles/year; receives 10-15 submissions annually. 100% of books from unagented writers. Average print order for a writer's first book is 500-1,000. Subsidy publishes 50% of books, "depending on type of material and potential sales." Payment is "worked out individually." Publishes book an average of 1 year after acceptance. Simultaneous and photocopied submissions OK. Electronic submissions OK; contact in advance for information. Computer printouts acceptable. SASE. Reports in 1 week on queries; 2 weeks on mss. Current books flyer for business size SAE and 1 first class stamp; full catalog $3.
Nonfiction: New York state and New England history and genealogy. Query. Reviews artwork/photos.
Recent Nonfiction Title: *Their Own Voices: Oral History Recorded in 1840 in Washington County, New York,* by Asa Fitch, c 1840 (edited by Wiston Adler).
Fiction: "Not looking for any, but will review any that deal with New York state historical subjects."

D.C. HEATH & CO., 125 Spring St., Lexington MA 02173. (617)862-6650. President: Loren Korte.College Division Editor-in-Chief: Bruce Zimmerli. General Manager Lexington Books: Robert D. Bovenschulte. College Div. Editorial Director—Hardside: Thomas Flaherty. College Division Editorial Director—Softside: Barbara Piercecchi. Vice President/General Manager—Electronics Publishing Division: Thomas Haver. Editor-in-Chief—School Division: Roger Rogalin. Publishes hardcover and paperback textbooks (grades kindergarten through college), professional scholarly, and software. Averages 300 titles/year. Offers standard royalty rates. Query. Publishes book an average of 1 year after acceptance. Electronic submissions OK if compatible with Wang and IBM. Computer printout submissions acceptable; prefers letter-quality to dot-matrix. SASE.

Textbooks: "Texts at the college level in history, political science, chemistry, math, biology, physics, economics, modern languages, English, business, and computer science. Also publishes professional reference books: "Advanced-level research studies in the social sciences, library science, and in technical fields (Lexington Books)." Length varies.

Tips: Queries/mss may be routed to other editors in the publishing group.

HEINLE & HEINLE PUBLISHERS, INC., Subsidiary of Linguistics International, Inc., 286 Congress St., Boston MA 02210. (617)451-1940. President: Charles H. Heinle. Editor: Stanley Galek. Publishes books and software. Averages 15 titles/year. 75% of books from first-time authors; 100% of books from unagented writers. Pays 6-15% royalty on net price; no advance. Publishes book an average of 18 months after acceptance. SASE. Reports immediately on queries; 2 weeks on mss. Free book catalog; ms. guidelines for SASE.
Nonfiction: Textbook. "Foreign language and English as a second or foreign language text materials. Before writing the book, submit complete prospectus along with sample chapters, and specify market and competitive position of proposed text."
Recent Nonfiction Title: *Vamos*, by Kenneth Chastain.

‡HELIX PRESS, 4410 Hickey, Corpus Christi TX 78413. (512)852-8834. Editor: Aubrey R. McKinney. Publishes hardcover originals. Averages 3 titles/year. 100% of books from first-time authors; 100% of books from unagented writers. Pays 3-10% royalty on wholesale price. Publishes book an average of 6 months after acceptance. Simultaneous and photocopied submissions OK. Computer printout submissions acceptable; prefers letter-quality to dot-matrix. SASE. Reports in 4 weeks.
Nonfiction: Adult, science oriented. Subjects include physical science, natural science and cosmology, written for the layman. Emphasize the sciences—physical, natural (conservation, ecology, natural history), and field adventures. Query or submit outline/synopsis and sample chapters. Reviews artwork/photos.
Recent Nonfiction Title: *The Slender Thread*, by McKinney.

HENDRICKSON PUBLISHERS, INC., 137 Summit St., Box 3473, Peabody MA 01961-3473. (617)532-6546. Executive Editor: Dr. Ben Aker. Publishes hardcover and trade paperback originals, and hardcover and trade paperback reprints. Averages 6-12 titles/year. Pays 5-15% royalty on wholesale and retail price. Average advance depends on project. Publishes book an average of 6 months after acceptance. Simultaneous (if so notified) and photocopied submissions OK. Computer printout submissions acceptable. SASE. Reports in 4 weeks on queries; 6 weeks on mss. Free book catalog.
Nonfiction: Religious. "We will consider any quality manuscripts within the area of religion, specifically related to Biblical studies and related fields." Submit outline/synopsis and sample chapters or complete ms.
Recent Nonfiction Title: *The Spirit and the Church: Antiquity*, by Dr. Stanley Burgess.

HERE'S LIFE PUBLISHERS, INC., Subsidiary of Campus Crusade for Christ, Box 1576, San Bernardino CA 92404. (714)886-7981. Editorial Director: Les Stobbe. Publishes hardcover and trade paperback originals and mass market paperback originals. Averages 30 titles/year; receives 400 submissions annually. 25% of books from first-time authors; 100% of books from unagented writers. Average print order for a writer's first book is 5,000. Pays 15% royalty on wholesale price. Offers $1,000-2,000 advance. Publishes book an average of 9 months after acceptance. Simultaneous and photocopied submissions OK. SASE. Electronic submissions OK if IBM compatible on disk; no special requirements on modem. Requires hard copy also. Reports in 1 month on queries; 3 months on mss. Writer's guidelines for SASE.
Nonfiction: Biography, how-to, illustrated book, reference and self-help. Subjects include religion and sports (religious). Needs "books in the areas of evangelism, Christian growth and family life; must reflect basic understanding of ministry and mission of Campus Crusade for Christ. No metaphysical or missionary biography." Query or submit outline/synopsis and sample chapters. Reviews artwork/photos.
Recent Nonfiction Title: *His Image . . . My Image*, by Josh McDowell.
Tips: "We are interested in a book that meets a specific felt need for a definable target market, written by an author who has some platform for publicity."

*HERITAGE BOOKS, INC., 3602 Maureen, Bowie MD 20715. (301)464-1159. Editorial Director: Laird C. Towle. Publishes hardcover and paperback originals (50%) and reprints (50%). Averages 10 titles/year; receives 50 submissions annually. 25% of books from first-time authors; 100% of books from unagented writers. Subsidy publishes 5% of books. Pays 10% royalty on retail price; occasional advance. Publishes book an average of 9 months after acceptance. Simultaneous and photocopied submissions OK. Computer printout submissions acceptable; prefers letter-quality to dot-matrix. Reports in 1 month. SASE. Free book catalog.
Nonfiction: "We particularly desire nonfiction titles dealing with history and genealogy including how-to and reference works, as well as conventional histories and genealogies. The titles should be either of general interest or restricted to Eastern US. We prefer writers to query, submit an outline/synopsis, or submit a complete ms, in that order, depending on the stage the writer has reached in the preparation of his work." Reviews artwork/photos.

Recent Nonfiction Title: *Federal Census of Provincetown, Mass., 1860*, by Ferguson.
Tips: "The quality of the book is of prime importance; next is its relevance to our fields of interest."

‡**HEYDAY BOOKS**, Box 9145, Berkeley CA 94709. (415)549-3564. Publisher: Malcolm Margolin. Publishes hardcover and trade paperback originals, trade paperback reprints. Averages 4-6 titles/year; receives 50 submissions annually. 50% of books from first-time authors; 100% of books from unagented writers. Pays 8-15% royalty on retail price; offers average $1,000 advance. Publishes book an average of 8 months after acceptance. Reports in 1 week on queries; up to 5 weeks on mss. Book catalog for business size SASE and 1 first class stamp.
Nonfiction: How-to and reference. Subjects include Americana, history, nature and travel. "We publish books about native Americans, natural history, history, and recreation, with a strong California focus." Query. Reviews artwork/photos.
Recent Nonfiction Title: *Roads to Ride*, by Grant Peterson.
Fiction: Historical. Must have strong regional (California) focus. Query.
Recent Fiction Title: *Yamino-Kwiti*, by Donna Preble.
Tips: "Give good value, and avoid gimmicks."

HOLIDAY HOUSE, INC., 18 E. 53rd St., New York NY 10022. (212)688-0085. Editorial Director: Margery Cuyler. Publishes hardcover originals. Averages 35-40 titles/year. Pays in royalties based on retail price; offers variable advance. Photocopied submissions OK. Computer printout submissions acceptable. Reports in 2 months. SASE.
Nonfiction and Fiction: General fiction and nonfiction for young readers—pre-school through high school. "It's better to submit the ms without art." Submit outline/synopsis and 3 sample chapters or complete ms. "No certified, insured or registered mail accepted."
Recent Nonfiction Title: *The Statue of Liberty*, by Leonard Everett Fisher.
Recent Fiction Title: *Stagefright*, by Ann M. Martin.

HOLLOWAY HOUSE PUBLISHING CO., 8060 Melrose Ave., Los Angeles CA 90046. (213)653-8060. Editorial Director: Robert Leighton. Publishes paperback originals (95%) and reprints (5%). Averages 30 titles/year; receives 300-500 submissions annually. 50% of books from first-time authors; 80% of books from unagented writers. Average print order for a writer's first book is 15,000-20,000. Pays royalty based on retail price. Publishes book an average of 6 months after acceptance. Photocopied submissions OK. Electronic submissions OK on or compatible with IBM PC WordStar, but requires hard copy also. Submit outline and 3 sample chapters. SASE. Reports in 6 weeks. Free book catalog and ms guidelines for SASE.
Nonfiction: Gambling and game books—from time to time publishes gambling books along the line of *How to Win*, *World's Greatest Winning Systems*, *Backgammon*, *How to Play and Win at Gin Rummy*, etc. Send query letter and/or outline with one sample chapter. SASE. Length: 60,000 words. Reviews artwork/photos.
Recent Nonfiction Title: *Eddie Murphy*, by Marianne Ruuth (biography).
Fiction: "Holloway House is the largest publisher of Black Experience literature. We are in the market for hard-hitting contemporary stories with easily identifiable characters and locations. Dialogue must be realistic. A strain of sex is acceptable but not essential. Action, people and places must be thoroughly depicted and graphically presented." Black romance line newly launched—Holloway House Heartline Romances, designed to appeal to middle class black women paralleling other romance lines designed for white readers. Reviews artwork/photos.
Recent Fiction Title: *Harlem*, by Tim McCanlies.

*****HOLMES & MEIER PUBLISHERS, INC.**, 30 Irving Place, New York NY 10003. (212)254-4100. Publisher: Max J. Holmes. Associate Publisher: Barbara Lyons. Editor: Naomi Lipman. Publishes hardcover and paperback originals (50%) and reprints (50%). Publishes 80 titles/year. Subsidy publishes 2% of books. Pays variable royalty. Publishes book an average of 8 months after acceptance. Computer printout submissions acceptable; prefers letter-quality to dot-matrix. SASE. Reports in 3 months. Free book catalog.
Nonfiction: Americana, Africana, art, biography, business/economics, education, history, Judaica, Latin American studies, literary criticism, music, nature, politics, psychology, reference, sociology, textbooks and women's studies. Accepts nonfiction translations. "We are noted as a scholarly publishing house and are pleased with our reputation of excellence in the field. However, while we will continue to publish books for academic and professional audiences, we are expanding our list to reach the broader non-academic intellectual community. We will continue to build on our strengths in the social sciences, humanities and natural sciences. We do not want how-to and self-help material." Reviews artwork/photos as part of ms package. Query first and submit outline/synopsis, sample chapters, curriculum vitae and idea of intended market/audience.
Recent Nonfiction Title: *The Destruction of the European Jews*, by Raul Hilberg.

HOLT, RINEHART & WINSTON OF CANADA, LTD., 55 Horner Ave., Toronto, Ontario M8Z 4X6 Canada. (416)255-4491. School Editor-in-Chief: William Park. College Editor-in-Chief: Ron Munro.

Publishes hardcover and paperback text originals for the El-Hi, community college and university markets. Royalty varies according to type of book; pays $200-500 for anthologies. No advance. Simultaneous and photocopied submissions OK. Reports in 1-3 months. SAE and IRCs. Free book catalog.
Nonfiction: Education texts. Query.
Recent Nonfiction Title: *Music Canada*, by Penny Louise Brooks, general editor.

HORIZON PRESS, 156 5th Ave., New York NY 10010. Averages 24 titles/year; receives 400-500 submissions annually. 15% of books from first-time authors; 90% of books from unagented writers. Average print order for a writer's first book is 5,000. Pays royalty based on both wholesale and retail price. Royalty schedule standard scale from 10% to 15%. Publishes book an average of 10 months after acceptance. Computer printout submissions acceptable; prefers letter-quality to dot-matrix. SASE. Reports in 3 months. Free book catalog.
Nonfiction: History, literature, science, biography, the arts and general. Length: 40,000 words and up. Accepts nonfiction translations. Reviews artwork/photos as part of ms package. Query with full description.
Recent Nonfiction Title: *William Glackens and "The Eight"*.
Fiction: Query with full description. *"We rarely publish fiction."*
Recent Fiction Title: *Countrymen of Bones*.

HOUGHTON MIFFLIN CO., 2 Park St., Boston MA 02108. (617)725-5000. Editor-in-Chief: Nan A. Talese. Managing Editor: Linda Glick Conway. Hardcover and paperback originals (90%) and paperback reprints (10%). Royalty of 6% on retail price for paperbacks; 10-15% on sliding scale for standard fiction and nonfiction; advance varies widely. Publishes book an average of 18 months after acceptance. Publishes 110 titles/year. Simultaneous and photocopied submissions OK. Computer printout submissions acceptable; no dot-matrix. "Proposals will not be returned without SASE." Reports in 6-8 weeks. SASE.
Nonfiction: Americana, natural history, animals, biography, cookbooks, health, history, how-to, politics, psychology and self-help. Query.
Recent Nonfiction Title: *House*, by Tracy Kidder.
Fiction: Historical, mainstream, mystery, science fiction and suspense. Also publishes poetry. Query.
Recent Fiction Title: *The Nurses*, by Richard Frede.

HOUGHTON MIFFLIN CO., Children's Trade Books, 2 Park St., Boston MA 02108. Contact: Editor. Publishes hardcover originals and trade paperback reprints (some simultaneous hard/soft). Averages 45-50 titles/year. Pays standard royalty; offers advance. Computer printout submissions acceptable; no dot-matrix; and no justified right margins. SASE. Reports in 1 month on queries; 2 months on mss. Free book catalog.
Nonfiction: Submit outline/synopsis and sample chapters. Reviews artwork/photos as part of ms package.
Fiction: Submit complete ms.

HOUNSLOW PRESS, A Division of Anthony R. Hawke Limited, 124 Parkview Ave., Willowdale, Ontario M2N 3Y5 Canada. (416)225-9176. President: Anthony Hawke. Publishes hardcover and trade paperback originals and reprints. Averages 6 titles/year; receives 500 submissions annually. 5% of books from first-time authors; 80% of books from unagented writers. Average print order for a writer's first book is 1,000. Pays 5-15% royalty on retail price; offers average $500 advance. Publishes book an average of 18 months after acceptance. Simultaneous and photocopied submissions OK. Reports in 2 weeks on queries; 1 month on mss. Free book catalog.
Nonfiction: Biography, "coffee table" book, cookbook, how-to, humor, illustrated book, juvenile, reference, self-help on animals, art, business and economics, cooking and foods, health, history, hobbies, nature, philosophy, photography, politics, psychology, recreation, religion and travel. Publishes for a general audience. "We do well with cookbooks and photography books about Canadian themes." Query. Submit outline/synopsis and 4 sample chapters. Reviews artwork/photos.
Recent Nonfiction Title: *Sorry Daddy—A Father's Guide to Toddlers*, by Marvin Ross and David Shaw.
Fiction: Adventure, humor and mainstream. Query.
Poetry: Query.
Recent Poetry Title: *Mirages*, by Ludwig Zeller and Susanna Wald.
Tips: "Humor, self-help and controversial topics sell the best for us."

‡**HOWELL-NORTH BOOKS**, Subsidiary of Darwin Publications, 850 N. Hollywood Way, Burbank CA 91505. (818)848-0944. Editorial Director: Victoria Darwin. Publishes hardcover and trade paperback originals, and hardcover and trade paperback reprints. Averages 8 titles/year; receives 300 submissions annually. 50% of books from first-time authors; 95% of books from unagented writers. Pays 5-15% royalty on retail price. Publishes book an average of 18 months after acceptance. Computer printout submissions acceptable; prefers letter-quality to dot-matrix. SASE. Simultaneous and photocopied submissions OK. Reports within 2 weeks on queries; 6 weeks on mss. Free book catalog.
Nonfiction: Biography, "coffee table" book, and illustrated book. Subjects include Americana, history,

hobbies, nature, recreation and travel (modes of transportation, specifically railroading). "We wish to broaden nonrailroad area; adventure, maritime and recreation will receive higher priority. Histories will not be considered unless they have a strong contemporary market." No personal travel guides, tips, etc., for Europe; autobiographies. Query strongly preferred or submit outline/synopsis and sample chapters. "Mss and queries will not be answered without SASE." Reviews artwork/photos.

Recent Nonfiction Title: *Rail City: Chicago, USA*, by George H. Douglas (history).

Tips: "Manuscript must be clean (good spelling, grammar, etc.) and research accurate. Problems in these areas cost time and money. Writer must be capable of following through with details as needed."

HUDSON HILLS PRESS, INC., Suite 301, 220 5th Ave., New York NY 10001. (212)889-3090. President/ Editorial Director: Paul Anbinder. Publishes hardcover and paperback originals. Averages 6-8 titles/year; receives 50-100 submissions annually. 15% of books from first-time authors; 90% of books from unagented writers. Average print order for a writer's first book is 3,000. Offers royalties of 5-8% on retail price. Average advance: $5,000. Publishes book an average of 1 year after acceptance. Simultaneous and photocopied submissions OK. Computer printout submissions acceptable; prefers letter-quality to dot-matrix. SASE. Reports in 1 month. Free book catalog.

Nonfiction: Art and photography. "We are only interested in publishing books about art and photography, or collections of photographs (photo essays or monographs)." Query first, then submit outline/synopsis and sample chapters. Reviews artwork/photos.

Recent Nonfiction Title: *San Francisco Museum of Modern Art: The Painting and Sculpture Collection.*

‡HUMAN SCIENCES PRESS, INC., 72 5th Ave., New York NY 10011. (212)243-6000. Promotion Manager: Barbara Perrin. Vice President/Editor-in-Chief: Norma Fox. Publishes hardcover and paperback originals. Averages 52 titles/year. Pays standard royalites; sometimes offers advance. No simultaneous submissions; 3 photocopied submissions OK. SASE. Reports in 1 month. Free book catalog.

Nonfiction: Behavioral and social sciences for professional text references. Submit complete ms.

HUMANICS LIMITED, 1389 Peachtree St. NE, Atlanta GA 30309. (404)874-2176. President: Gary B. Wilson. Publishes softcover, educational and trade paperback originals. Averages 10 titles/year; receives 500 submissions annually. 20% of books from first-time authors; 100% of books from unagented writers. Average print order for a writer's first book is 5,000. Pays average 10% royalty on net sales; buys some mss outright. Publishes book an average of 1 year after acceptance. Reports in 3 months. Free book catalog; ms guidelines for SASE.

Nonfiction: Juvenile, self-help, textbook and teacher resource books. Subjects include cooking and foods, health, psychology, sociology, education, parenting, business and New Age. Submit outline/synopsis and at least 3 sample chapters. Reviews artwork/photos as part of ms package.

Recent Nonfiction Title: *Tao of Leadership*, by John Heider (New Age).

Tips: "We are very open in the areas of education—infant development, early childhood, parent involvement, and New Age."

‡CARL HUNGNESS PUBLISHING, Box 24308, Speedway IN 46224. (317)244-4792. Editorial Director: Carl Hungness. Publishes hardcover and paperback originals. Pays "negotiable" outright purchase. Reports in 3 weeks. SASE. Free book catalog.

Nonfiction: Stories relating to professional automobile racing. No sports car racing or drag racing material. Query.

Recent Nonfiction Title: *Indianapolis 500 Yearbook*, by C. Hungness and others (historical).

‡*HUNTER HOUSE, INC., PUBLISHERS, Box 1302, Claremont CA 91711. General Manager: K.S. Rana. Publishes hardcover and trade paperback originals. Averages 12 titles/year; receives 100 submissions annually. 50% of books from first-time authors; 50% of books from unagented writers. Subsidy publishes 16% of books. "We determine whether an author should be subsidy published based upon subject matter, quality of the work, and if a subsidy is available." Pays 7½-12½% royalty on retail price. Offers $50 advance. Publishes book an average of 12-18 months after acceptance. Simultaneous and photocopied submissions OK. Electronic submissions OK on Osborne SSDD or transferrable formats. Computer printout submissions acceptable. SASE. Reports in 2 months on queries; 6 months on mss. Free book catalog.

Nonfiction: How-to, juvenile, and self-help. Subjects include health, psychology and "new science." Needs mss on "family and health, especially emerging areas in women's health, men's opening up and single parenting, older people, young adult, especially on health and intergenerational concerns." No evangelical, right-wrong political, Americana or esoteric. Query or submit outline/synopsis and sample chapters. Reviews artwork/photos.

Recent Nonfiction Title: *Couples in Collusion*, by Jürg Willi, MD (marital therapy).

Fiction: Erotica and ethnic fiction, fantasy and science fiction by women. Needs one or two historical/mythical/fantasy books by and for women. Query or submit outline/synopsis and sample chapters.

Recent Fiction Title: *On the Road to Baghdad*, by Güneli Gün.
Tips: "Manuscripts on family and health, or psychology for an aware public do well for us. Write simply, with established credentials and imagination. We respect writers and do not mistreat them. We ask for the same consideration."

HUNTINGTON HOUSE, INC., 1200 N. Market St., Shreveport LA 71107. (318)221-2767. President: Bill Keith. Publishes hardcover, trade paperback, and mass market paperback originals, trade paperback reprints and software. Averages 10-20 titles/year; receives 100-150 submissions annually. 75% of books from first-time authors; 90% of books from unagented writers. Average print order for a writer's first book is 10,000. Pays 10-15% royalty on wholesale and retail price, or $50; offers $100-2,500 advance. Publishes book an average of 6 months after acceptance. Simultaneous and photocopied submissions OK. Computer printout submissions acceptable. SASE. Reports in 2 months on queries; 3 months on mss. Free book catalog and ms guidelines.
Nonfiction: Biography, self-help and religious. "We publish self-help books and Christian growth books oriented to the Christian community." No New Age, occult, humanism or liberal theology. Query. Reviews artwork/photos.
Recent Nonfiction Title: *The Hidden Dangers of the Rainbow*, by Constance Cumbey.
Fiction: Query.
Tips: "Write clear, crisp, exciting self-help or teaching manuscripts."

HURTIG PUBLISHERS LTD., 10560 105th St., Edmonton, Alberta T5H 2W7 Canada. (403)426-2359. Editor-in-Chief: Elizabeth Munroe. Hardcover and paperback originals (80%) and reprints (20%). Averages 12 titles/year. Typically pays 10% royalty on first 7,500 copies; 12% on next 7,500; 15% thereafter. Offers $500-1,000 advance on first book. Photocopied submissions OK. Computer printouts acceptable; "will read anything legible—must be hard copy printout." Prefers letter of inquiry first. Reports in 2-3 months. SASE. Free book catalog.
Nonfiction: Publishes biographies of well-known Canadians, Canadian history, humor, nature, topical Canadian politics and economics, reference (Canadian), and material about native Canadians "aimed at the nationalistic Canadian interested in politics, the North and energy policy." No poetry or original fiction. Query or submit outline/synopsis and 1-2 sample chapters; or submit complete ms. Very few unsolicited mss published. Looks for "suitability of topic to general publishing program; market interest in topic; qualifications of writer to treat that topic well; quality of writing." State availability of photos and/or illustrations to accompany ms.
Recent Nonfiction Title: *Pitseolak: A Canadian Tragedy*, by David F. Raine.

ICARUS PRESS, INC., Suite 906, 120 W. LaSalle St., Box 1225, South Bend IN 46624. (219)233-6020. Editorial Director: Bruce M. Fingerhut. Publishes hardcover and paperback originals. Averages 20 titles/year. Offers 12-17% royalty based on wholesale price. Average advance: $2,000. Simultaneous and photocopied submissions OK (if so indicated). SASE. Reports in 1-2 months. Free book catalog.
Nonfiction: Americana, biography, history, recreation, sports, and travel (regional). Accepts nonfiction translations. "Our interests in sports, whether of the self-help, coaching, or history genre, remain high. As to history, biography, current affairs, etc., such manuscripts as we publish must be real trade titles—with national appeal. We do *not* want to see poetry, photography, art, hobbies (other than those immediately connected with sports), or cookbooks." Reviews artwork/photos as part of ms package. Query first, then submit outline/synopsis and 2-4 sample chapters. Looks for "originality, flair of style, writing competence."
Recent Nonfiction Title: *Chicago Ragtime: Another Look at Chicago, 1880-1920*, by Richard Lindberg.

IDEALS PUBLISHING CORP., Nelson Place at Elm Hill Pike, Box 14130, Nashville TN 37214-1000. Director, Publishing: Patricia Pingry. Publishes hardcover and paperback juvenile books, cookbooks, greeting booklets, and *Ideals* periodical. Pays on royalty and buy-out basis; offers advance only on assigned projects. Photocopied submissions OK. SASE. Reports in 4-6 weeks.
Nonfiction: Cookbooks. Length: 300 recipes.
Recent Nonfiction Title: *Wok Cookbook*.
Fiction: "Juveniles fall into one of 3 categories: seasonal (holiday theme), religious, or of some educational or moral value. They must stress the same traditional values as *Ideals* periodicals." Query. Length varies.

ILLUMINATI, Suite 203, 8812 W. Pico Blvd., Los Angeles CA 90035. Editor: P. Schneidre. Publishes hardcover and trade paperback originals. Imprints include Tadbooks (poetry); PictoGrams (illustrated gift books); Tall Tales (each is a single piece of short fiction). Averages 21 titles/year; receives 3,000 submissions annually. 50% of books from first-time authors; 100% of books from unagented writers. Average print order for a writer's first book is 1,000. Pays 10-12½% royalty on retail price. Offers average $150 advance. Publishes book an average of 1 year after acceptance. Photocopied submissions OK. SASE. Reports in 2 weeks on queries; 3 weeks on mss. Book catalog for 9x12 SAE and 3 oz. postage, 1st class.

Nonfiction: Literature and art. Submit complete ms. Reviews artwork/photos.
Poetry: No light verse or haiku. Submit complete ms.
Recent Poetry Title: *The Orange Piano*, by David St. John.

INCENTIVE PUBLICATIONS, INC, 3835 Cleghorn Ave., Nashville TN 37215. (615)385-2934. Editor: Jennifer Goodman. Publishes paperback originals. Averages 15-20 titles/year. Pays royalty or makes outright purchase. Publishes book an average of 1 year after acceptance. Photocopied submissions OK. Computer printout submissions acceptable; prefers letter-quality to dot-matrix. SASE. Reports in 2 weeks on queries; 3 weeks on mss. Free book catalog.
Nonfiction: Teacher resources and books on educational areas relating to children. Submit outline/synopsis and sample chapters. Reviews artwork/photos as part of ms package.
Recent Nonfiction Title: *The Tabletop Learning Series*, by Imogene Forte.

*INDIANA UNIVERSITY PRESS, 10th & Morton Sts., Bloomington IN 47405. (812)337-4203. Director: John Gallman. Publishes hardcover and paperback originals (75%) and paperback reprints (25%). Averages 90-100 titles/year. 30% of books from first-time authors. 98% from unagented writers. Average print order for a writer's first book is 1,500. Subsidy publishes 10% of books. Pays maximum 10% royalty on retail price; offers occasional advance. Publishes book an average of 18 months after acceptance. Photocopied submissions OK. Electronic submissions OK if IBM compatible, but requires hard copy also. Computer printout submissions acceptable; no dot-matrix. Reports in 2 months. SASE. Free book catalog and ms guidelines.
Nonfiction: Scholarly books on humanities, history, philosophy, religion, Jewish studies, Black studies, translations, semiotics, public policy, film, music, linguistics, social sciences, regional materials, African studies, women's studies, and serious nonfiction for the general reader. Query or submit outline/synopsis and sample chapters. "Queries should include as much descriptive material as is necessary to convey scope and market appeal to us." Reviews artwork/photos.
Recent Nonfiction Title: *Semiotics and the Philosophy of Language*, by Umberto Eco.
Fiction: Query or submit outline/synopsis.

‡INFORMATION RESOURCES PRESS, A Division of Herner and Company, Suite 700, 1700 N. Moore St., Arlington VA 22209. (703)558-8270. Vice President/Publisher: Ms. Gene P. Allen. Publishes hardcover originals. Averages 6 titles/year; receives 12 submissions annually. 50% of books from first-time authors; 100% of books from unagented writers. Pays 10-15% royalty on net cash receipts after returns and discounts. Publishes book an average of 1 year after acceptance. Simultaneous and photocopied submissions OK. Electronic submissions OK on Wang VS, but requires hard copy also. Computer printout submissions acceptable; no dot-matrix. SASE. Reports in 2 weeks on queries; 2 months on mss. Free book catalog and ms guidelines.
Nonfiction: Reference, technical and textbook. Subjects include health and library and information science. Needs basic or introductory books on information science, library science, and health planning that lend themselves for use as textbooks. Preferably, the mss will have been developed from course notes. No works on narrow research topics (nonbasic or introductory works). Submit outline/synopsis and sample chapters or complete ms.
Recent Nonfiction Title: *Online Information Systems*, by Brenda Gerrie (text, reference).
Tips: "Our audience includes libraries (public, special, college and university); librarians, information scientists, college-level faculty; schools of library and information science; health planners, graduate-level students of health planning, and administrators; economists."

INFOSOURCE, INC., 771 Dunlap Circle, Winter Springs FL 32708. (305)365-9990. Book packager producing 10 titles/year. President: D. Michael Werner. Publishes hardcover and trade paperback originals. Receives 50 submissions annually. 100% of books from unagented writers. Average print order for a writer's first book is 5,000. Pays 10-20% on retail price or makes outright purchase of $100-5,000. Offers average $50-2,000 advance. Publishes book an average of 6 months after acceptance. Simultaneous and photocopied submissions OK. Electronic submissions OK on "any CP/M or IBM compatible," but requires hard copy also. Computer printout submissions acceptable. SASE. Reports in 2 weeks on queries; 1 month on mss. Book catalog for legal-size SAE and 3 first class stamps.
Nonfiction: How-to, reference and technical. Subjects include business and computers. "We envision sophisticated business managers with no computer background as our audience for computer books, and middle-level managers as our audience for business books. Looking immediately for contributors for volumes on Apple and IBM-PC computers and on all business topics. Looking in the next 1-2 years for books on portable computers, public data bases, small business and marketing, and for contributors for volumes on Apple and IBM-PC computers and on business topics." Query. Reviews artwork/photos.
Recent Nonfiction Title: *Micros, Minis and Mainframes*, by Werner/Warrner (how-to).
Tips: "If I were a writer trying to market a book today, I would concentrate 100% of my time on writing 'how-to' and instructional materials geared to increased productivity on a personal computer."

*INSTITUTE FOR THE STUDY OF HUMAN ISSUES, (ISHI Publications), 210 S. 13th St., Philadelphia PA 19102. (215)387-9002. Director of Publications: Betty Crapivinsky-Jutkowitz. Associate Director: Edward A. Jutkowitz. Managing Editor: Brad Fisher. Publishes hardcover and paperback originals (85%) and paperback reprints (15%). Averages 18 titles/year. Publishes 10% of books by partial subsidy. Pays 10-12$\frac{1}{2}$% royalty on wholesale price; no advance. Photocopied submissions OK. Computer printout submissions acceptable; no dot-matrix. Reports in 3 months. SASE. Free book catalog.

Nonfiction: Books on political science, history, anthropology, folklore, sociology, economics and drug studies, suitable for students and scholars in these fields. Accepts nonfiction translations. Submit outline/synopsis for initial consideration. Reviews artwork/photos as part of ms package.

Recent Nonfiction Title: *The French Socialist Experiment*, edited by John Ambler.

INTERCULTURAL PRESS, INC., Box 768, Yarmouth ME 04096. (207)846-5168. Contact: David S. Hoopes, Editor-in-Chief, 130 North Rd., Vershire VT 05079. (802)685-4448. Publishes hardcover and trade paperback originals. Averages 5-15 titles/year. Pays royalty; occasionally offers small advance. Simultaneous and photocopied submissions OK. Computer printout submissions acceptable; prefers letter-quality to dot-matrix. SASE. Reports in "several weeks" on queries; 2 months on mss. Free book catalog and writer's guidelines.

Nonfiction: How-to, reference, self-help, textbook and theory. Subjects include business and economics, philosophy, politics, psychology, sociology, travel, or "any book with an international or domestic intercultural, multicultural or cross-cultural focus, i.e., a focus on the cultural factors in personal, social, political or economic relations. We want books with an international or domestic intercultural or multicultural focus, especially those on business operations (how to be effective in intercultural business activities) and education (textbooks for teaching intercultural subjects, for instance). Our books are published for educators in the intercultural field, business people who are engaged in international business, and anyone else who works in an international occupation or has had intercultural experience. No manuscripts that don't have an intercultural focus." Accepts nonfiction translations. Query "if there is any question of suitability (we can tell quickly from a good query)," or submit outline/synopsis. Do not submit mss unless invited.

Recent Nonfiction Title: *Survival Kit for Overseas Living*, by Robert Kohls (how-to).

INTERGALACTIC PUBLISHING CO., Box 5013, Cherry Hill NJ 08034. (609)665-7577. Contact: Samuel W. Valenza, Jr. Intergalactic is now a subsidiary of Regal Communications Corporation, publishers of *Lottery Magazine* averages 3-10 titles/year on the subject of lottery. Receives 5-20 submissions annually. 100% of books from first-time authors; 100% of books from unagented writers. Average print order for a writer's first book is 1,000-5,000. The publisher invites mss dealing with lottery in general and *systems of play* in particular. The company also produces and sells lottery and gaming related products and games, and invites submissions of ideas for same. Publishes book an average of 1 year after acceptance. Letter quality submissions are preferred.

Recent Nonfiction Title: *A History of: From Roman Times to Present; Almanac and Traveler's Guide to Lottery*, (annual).

INTERNATIONAL MARINE PUBLISHING CO., 21 Elm St., Camden ME 04843. Editor-in-Chief: Philip Mason. Publishes hardcover and paperback originals. Averages 15 titles/year. Pays standard royalties, based on net price, with advances. Publishes book an average of 9 months after acceptance. Computer printout submission acceptable; prefers letter-quality to dot-matrix. Reports in 6 weeks. Return postage necessary. Free mail-order catalog.

Nonfiction: "Marine nonfiction only—but a wide range of subjects within that category: boatbuilding, boat design, yachting, seamanship, boat maintenance, maritime history, etc." All books are illustrated. "Material in all stages welcome. We prefer queries first with 2-3 sample chapters." Reviews artwork/photos as part of ms package.

Recent Nonfiction Title: *Catboats*, by Stan Grayson.

Tips: "Freelance writers should be aware of the need for clarity, accuracy and interest."

INTERNATIONAL PUBLISHING & COMPUTER SERVICES, INC., (formerly *Lancaster Miller and Schnobrich Publishers*), Box 3056, Berkeley CA 94703. (415)652-6004. Editor and Publisher: Thomas Miller. Imprints include Interpub. Publishes trade hardcover, paperback originals and software. Averages 6-7 titles/year. Pays 6-8% royalty on paperbacks; 10-12% on hardcover; offers $1,000-30,000 advance. Computer printout submissions acceptable. SASE. Reports in 2 weeks. Free book catalog.

Nonfiction: Computer books only.

Recent Nonfiction Title: *Logo Not Just For Children*.

INTERNATIONAL SELF-COUNSEL PRESS, LTD., 306 W. 25th St., North Vancouver, British Columbia V7N 2G1 Canada. (604)986-3366. President: Diana R. Douglas. Senior Editor: Pat Robertson. Publishes trade paperback originals. Averages 10-15 titles/year; receives 100 submissions annually. 50% of books from first-time authors. Average print order for a writer's first book is 4,000. Pays 10% royalty on wholesale price; no advance. Publishes book an average of 6 months after acceptance. Simultaneous and photocopied submissions OK. Computer printout submissions acceptable; prefers letter-quality to dot-matrix. Reports in 4-6 weeks. SASE (Canadian), IRCs. Free book catalog.

Nonfiction: Specializes in self-help and how-to books in law, business and finance for lay person. Submit outline/synopsis and sample chapters. Follow Chicago *Manual of Style*.

Recent Nonfiction Title: *Medical Law Handbook*, by T. David Marshall.

*THE INTERNATIONAL UNIVERSITY PRESS, Subsidiary of The International University Foundation, 1301 S. Noland Rd., Independence MO 64055. (816)461-3633. Editor: Dr. John Wayne Johnston. Publishes hardcover originals and trade and mass market paperback originals. Averages 100 titles/year; receives 1,000-1,500 submissions annually. 75% of books from first-time authors; 95% of books from unagented writers. Average print order for a writer's first book is 250. Subsidy publishes 50% of books. "Such decisions are made by a committee based on internal criteria." Pays "percentage, based on size of first run." Publishes book an average of 1 year after acceptance. Simultaneous and photocopied submissions OK. Computer printout submissions acceptable; no dot-matrix. SASE. Reports in 6 weeks on queries; 6 months on mss.

Nonfiction: Biography, reference, technical, textbook on art, business and economics, health, history, music, philosophy, politics, psychology, religion, sociology and sports. Especially needs "any manuscript that exhibits coherence, originality, adequate command of the language, and few, if any, mechanical errors. Must have serious intent and some market appeal." Publishes for a "small, select group of readers of quality work." No poorly written work on any topic. Accepts poetry translations from Spanish. Submit complete ms.

Recent Nonfiction Title: *Playwriting Principles*, by Philip P. Shaps.

Fiction: Fantasy, gothic, historical, horror, humor, mainstream, mystery, romance, science fiction, suspense and western. "We hope to review a large number of fiction manuscripts with an eye to publishing a growing volume of such works. No erotica or any work of questionable general interest to a sober, serious reading audience." Submit complete ms.

Poetry: "We will consider poetry manuscripts of 50 pages or more either in form of long, epic poems or a collection of shorter works." Submit complete ms. Accepts poetry translations from Spanish.

‡INTERNATIONAL WEALTH SUCCESS, Box 186, Merrick NY 11566. (516)766-5850. Editor: Tyler G. Hicks. Averages 10 titles/year; receives 25 submissions annually. 95% of books from first-time authors; 100% of books from unagented writers. Average print order for a writer's first book "varies from 500 and up, depending on the book." Pays 10% royalty on wholesale or retail price. Buys all rights. Usual advance is $1,000, but this varies, depending on author's reputation and nature of book. Publishes book 2-4 months after acceptance. Photocopied and dot-matrix submissions OK. Electronic submissions OK on Apple and IBM PC disks, but requires hard copy also. Query. Reports in 4 weeks. Enclose return postage. Free book catalog.

Nonfiction:*Self-Help and How-to:* "Techniques, methods, sources for building wealth. Highly personal, how-to-do-it with plenty of case histories. Books are aimed at the wealth builder and are highly sympathetic to his and her problems." Financing, business success, venture capital, etc. Length 60,000-70,000 words. Reviews artwork/photos as part of ms package.

Recent Nonfiction Title: *How to Grow Rich in Real Estate*, by Nielsen.

Tips: "Concentrate on practical, hands-on books showing people how to build wealth today, starting with very little cash. Most of the manuscripts we get today assume that everyone has money to invest in gold, rare coins, stocks, etc. This is not so. There are millions who haven't made it yet. This is *our* audience, an audience that can build great wealth for a writer who tells these people what to do, where to do it and how to do it. Forget theories; concentrate on the day-to-day business of making money from one's own business, and you've got it made. Don't get too involved with your personal life story—instead, concentrate on telling your reader how he or she can get rich in their own business."

*THE INTERSTATE PRINTERS & PUBLISHERS, INC., 19-27 N. Jackson St., Box 594, Danville IL 61832-0594. (217)446-0500. Acquisitions/Managing Editor: Ronald L. McDaniel. Hardcover and paperback originals and software. Publishes about 50 titles/year. 100% of books from unagented writers. Subsidy publishes 5% of books. Usual royalty is 10%; no advance. Markets books by mail and exhibits. Publishes book an average of 9 months after acceptance. Computer printout submissions acceptable; prefers letter-quality to dot-matrix. Reports in 1-2 months. SASE. Free book catalog.

Nonfiction: Publishes high school and undergraduate college-level texts in vocational education, agriculture, trade and industrial education, home economics and business education. Also publishes professional references, texts, and supplementary materials in special education (including speech-language pathology, audiology, learning disabilities, neurological impairment.) "We favor, but do not limit ourselves to, works that are designed for class—quantity rather than single-copy sale." Query or submit outline/synopsis and 2-3 sample chapters. Reviews artwork/photos as part of ms package.

Recent Nonfiction Title: *Agricultural Computer Guide and Directory*.

Tips, "Freelance writers should be aware of strict adherence to the use of nonsexist language; fair and balanced representation of the sexes and of minorities in both text and illustrations; and discussion of computer applications wherever applicable."

INTERURBAN PRESS/TRANS ANGLO BOOKS, Box 6444, Glendale CA 91205. (213)240-9130. President: Mac Sebree. Publishes hardcover and trade paperback originals. Averages 10 titles/year; receives 50-75 submissions yearly. 35% of books from first-time authors; 99% of books from unagented writers. Average print order for a writer's first book is 2,000. Pays 5-10% royalty on retail price; offers no advance. Computer printout submissions acceptable. SASE. Reports in 2 weeks on queries; 2 months on mss. Free book catalog.
Nonfiction: Western Americana and transportation. Subjects include Americana, business and economics, history, hobbies and travel. "We are interested only in manuscripts about railroads, local transit, local history, and western American (gold mining, logging, early transportation, etc.). Also anything pertaining to preservation movement, nostalgia." Query. Reviews artwork/photos.
Recent Nonfiction Title: *Silver Short Line*, by Demoro/Wurm (history).
Tips: "We stick strictly to the topics already enumerated. Our audience is comprised of hobbyists in the rail transportation field ("railfans"); those interested in Western Americana (logging, mining, etc.); and students of transportation history, especially railroads and local rail transit (streetcars)."

INTERVARSITY PRESS, Box 1400, Downers Grove IL 60515. (312)964-5700. Editorial Director: James W. Sire. Publishes hardcover and paperback originals. Averages 45 titles/year. Pays 10% royalty on retail price; offers averages $750 advance. Publishes book an average of 1 year after acceptance. "Indicate simultaneous submissions." Computer printout submissions acceptable; prefers letter-quality to dot-matrix. Reports in 16 weeks. SASE. Free book catalog.
Nonfiction: "InterVarsity Press publishes books geared to the presentation of Biblical Christianity in its various relations to personal life, art, literature, sociology, psychology, philosophy, history and so forth. Though we are primarily publishers of trade books, we are cognizant of the textbook market at the college, university and seminary level within the general religious field. The audience for which the books are published is composed primarily of university students and graduates; stylistic treatment varies from topic to topic and from fairly simple popularizations for college freshmen to scholarly works primarily designed to be read by scholars." Accepts nonfiction translations. Query or submit outline/synopsis and 2 sample chapters.
Recent Nonfiction Title: *The Gravedigger File*, by Os Guinness.

*IOWA STATE UNIVERSITY PRESS, 2121 S. State Ave., Ames IA 50010. (515)294-5280. Director: Merritt Bailey. Managing Editor: Judith Gildner. Hardcover and paperback originals. Averages 35 titles/year; receives 350 submissions annually. 98% of books from unagented writers. Average print order for a writer's first book is 2000. Subsidy publishes 10-50% of titles, based on sales potential of book and contribution to scholarship. Pays 10-12½-15% royalty on wholesale price; no advance. Simultaneous submissions OK, if advised; photocopied submissions OK. Computer printout submissions acceptable; prefers letter-quality to dot-matrix. Reports in 2-4 months. SASE. Free book catalog; ms guidelines for SASE.
Nonfiction: Publishes biography, history, scientific/technical textbooks, the arts and sciences, statistics and mathematics, and medical and veterinary sciences. Accepts nonfiction translations. Submit outline/synopsis and several sample chapters, preferably not in sequence; must be double-spaced throughout. Looks for "unique approach to subject; clear, concise narrative; and effective integration of scholarly apparatus." Send contrasting b&w glossy prints to illustrate ms. Reviews artwork/photos.
Recent Nonfiction Title: *Roswel Garst: A Biography*, by Harold Lee.

ISHIYAKU EUROAMERICA, INC., Subsidiary of Ishiyaku Publishers, Inc., Tokyo, Japan: 11559 Rock Island Court, St. Louis MO 63043. (314)432-1933. President: Manuel L. Ponte. Publishes hardcover originals. Averages 6 titles/year; receives 50 submissions annually. 10% of books from first-time authors; 100% of books from unagented writers. Average print order for writer's first book is 3,000. Pays 10% minimum royalty on retail price or pays 35% of all foreign translation rights sales. Offers average $1,000 advance. Simultaneous submissions OK. Computer printout submissions acceptable. SASE. Reports in 2 weeks on queries; 1 week on mss. Free book catalog.
Nonfiction: Reference and medical/dental/nursing textbooks. Subjects include art, health (medical and dental); psychology (nursing); and psychiatry. Especially looking for "all phases of nursing education, administration and clinical procedures. I do not wish to see additional dental books in 1986." Query, or submit outline/synopsis and sample chapters or complete ms. Reviews artwork/photos.
Recent Nonfiction Title: *Occlusion-Principles and Concepts*, by J. dos Santos Jr (dental text).

‡ISI PRESS, Subsidiary of Institute for Scientific Information, 3501 Market St., Philadelphia PA 19104. (215)386-0100. Director: Robert A. Day. Publishes hardcover and paperback originals. Averages 6 titles/year. Pays 10% royalty on retail price; offers average $500 advance. No computer printout or disk submissions. SASE. Reports in 1 week on queries; 6 weeks on mss.

Nonfiction: How-to and technical on communications. "We are developing a strong professional writing series. In general, we publish scholarly and professional books concerned with communications: writing, editing, publishing, etc." Query or submit outline/synopsis and 1 sample chapter.
Recent Nonfiction Title: *How to Write Papers About Computer Technology*, by Charles H. Sides.

ITHACA HOUSE, 108 N. Plain St., Ithaca NY 14850. (607)272-1233. Subsidiaries include *Chiaroscuro: A Magazine of Poetry.* Editor: John Latta. Publishes trade paperback originals. Averages 3-5 titles/year. Pays in copies; 40% discount on purchases. Publishes book an average of 1 year after acceptance. Simultaneous and photocopied submissions OK (if notified). Computer printout submissions acceptable; no dot-matrix. SASE. Reports in 3 weeks on queries; 4 months on mss. Free book catalog.
Poetry: "We will publish 3-5 volumes of contemporary poetry—literary work of the highest order." Submit 5-10 poems.
Recent Poetry Title: *All That Autumn*, by Eileen Silver-Lillywhite (contemporary).

‡**JAMESTOWN PUBLISHERS, INC.**, Box 6743, Providence RI 02940. (401)351-1915. Senior Editor: Ted Knight. Publishes paperback supplementary reading text/workbooks and software. Averages 25-30 titles/year; receives 100+ submissions annually. 10% of books from first-time authors; 100% of books from unagented writers. Average print order for writer's first book is 10,000. Pays 10% royalty on retail price; buys some mss outright; offers variable advance. Publishes book an average of 1 year after acceptance. Electronic submissions OK on Apple II and (disk); DEC mainframe (modem), but requires hard copy also. Computer printout submissions acceptable; prefers letter-quality to dot-matrix. SASE. Reports in 1 month. Free book catalog.
Nonfiction: Textbook. "Materials for improving reading and study skills for kindergarten through twelfth grade, college, or adult education." Submit outline/synopsis and sample chapters. Reviews artwork/photos as part of ms package.
Recent Nonfiction Title: *How to Study in High School*, by Jean Snider.
Fiction: "We occasionally use original fiction as the basis for comprehension exercises and drills." Submit outline/synopsis and sample chapters.

JH PRESS, Box 294, Village Station, New York NY 10014. (212)255-4713. Publisher: Terry Helbing. Publishes trade paperback originals. Averages 3 titles/year. Pays 6-10% royalty on retail price; offers average $100 advance. Publishes book an average of 9 months after acceptance. Simultaneous and photocopied submissions OK. SASE. Reports in 2 weeks. Free book catalog.
Nonfiction: Subjects include drama and theatre. Studies of gay theater or gay plays. Query. Reviews artwork/photos as part of ms package.
Recent Nonfiction Title: *Gay Theatre Alliance Directory of Gay Plays*, by Terry Helbing.
Fiction: Drama and theater. "Gay plays that have been produced but not previously published." Query.
Recent Fiction Title: *Last Summer at Bluefish Cove*, by Jane Chambers (play).

JOHNS HOPKINS UNIVERSITY PRESS, Suite 275, 701 West 40th St., Baltimore MD 21211. Editorial Director: Anders Richter. Publishes mostly clothbound originals and paperback reprints; some paperback originals. Publishes 100 titles/year. Payment varies; contract negotiated with author. Publishes book an average of 10 months after acceptance. Electronic submission, OK but requires hard copy also. Computer printout submissions acceptable; prefers letter-quality to dot-matrix. SASE. Reports in 2 months.
Nonfiction: Publishes scholarly books and journals, biomedical sciences, history, literary theory and criticism, wildlife biology and management, psychology, political science, regional material and economics. Accepts nonfiction translations. Length: 50,000 words minimum. Query. Accepts outline/synopsis and 2-3 sample chapters. Reviews artwork/photos as part of ms package.
Recent Nonfiction Title: *The Nursing Home In American Society*, by Colleen L. Johnson and Leslie A. Grant.
Fiction: Occasional fiction by invitation only.

JOHNSON BOOKS, 1880 S. 57th Ct., Boulder CO 80301. (303)443-1576. Editorial Director: Michael McNierney. Publishes hardcover and paperback originals and reprints. Publishes 8-10 titles/year; receives 350 submissions annually. 60% of books from first-time authors; 100% of books from unagented writers. Average print order for a writer's first book is 5,000. Royalties vary. Publishes book an average of 1 year after acceptance. Computer printout submissions acceptable; prefers letter-quality to dot-matrix. SASE. Reports in 1-2 months. Free book catalog; ms guidelines for SASE.
Nonfiction: General nonfiction, how-to, Western history, environmental subjects, science, geology, archaeology nature, outdoor recreation and sports. Accepts nonfiction translations. "We are primarily interested in books for the informed popular market, though we will consider vividly written scholarly works. As a small publisher, we are able to give every submission close personal attention." Query first or call. Accepts outline/synopsis and 3 sample chapters. Looks for "good writing, thorough research, professional presentation and appropriate style. Marketing suggestions from writers are helpful. Reviews artwork/photos."
Recent Nonfiction Title: *How to Create a Water Crisis*, by Frank Walsh.

JONATHAN DAVID PUBLISHERS, 68-22 Eliot Ave., Middle Village NY 11379. (212)456-8611. Editor-in-Chief: Alfred J. Kolatch. Publishes hardcover and paperback originals. Averages 25-30 titles/year. Pays standard royalty. Reports in 3 weeks. SASE.
Nonfiction: Adult nonfiction books for a general audience. Americana, cookbooks, cooking and foods, how-to, recreation, reference, self-help and sports. "We specialize in Judaica." Query.
Recent Nonfiction Title: *The Baseball Book of Why*, by Dan Schlossberg.

JOSSEY-BASS, INC., PUBLISHERS, 433 California St., San Francisco CA 94104. (415)433-1740. Editorial Director: Steven Piersant. Publishes hardcover and paperback originals. Averages 100 titles/year; receives 1,000 submissions annually. 5% of books from first-time authors; 99% of books from unagented writers. Average print order for a writer's first book is 3,000. Pays 10-15% royalty on net receipts; no advance. Computer printout submissions acceptable; no dot-matrix. Reports in 4 weeks. SASE. Free book catalog; ms guidelines for SASE.
Nonfiction: Professional, scholarly books for managers, senior administrators, faculty, researchers, graduate students, and professionals in private practice. Research-based books developed for practical application. "We do not want undergraduate texts or collections of previously published materials." Submit outline/synopsis and 3-4 sample chapters.
Recent Nonfiction Title: *The Neurotic Organization*, by Manfred F.R. Kets de Vries and Danny Miller.

JUDSON PRESS, Valley Forge PA 19481. (215)768-2116. Manuscript Editor: Phyllis A. Frantz. Publishes hardcover and paperback originals. Averages 40 titles/year; receives 500 submissions annually. 40% of books from first-time authors; 95% of books from unagented writers. Average print order for a writer's first book 3,500. Generally 10% royalty on retail price. "Payment of an advance depends on author's reputation and nature of book." Publishes book an average of 9 months after acceptance. Computer printout submissions acceptable; no dot-matrix. Query with outline and 2-3 sample chapters. Reports in 3 months. Enclose return postage. Free book catalog; ms guidelines for SASE.
Nonfiction: Adult religious nonfiction of 30,000-80,000 words. "Our audience is mostly church members who seek to have a more fulfilling personal spiritual life and want to do a better job as Christians in their church and other relationships." Reviews artwork/photos as part of ms package.
Recent Nonfiction Title: *Letters to a Retired Couple*, by David and Vera Mace.

KALIMAT PRESS, Suite 700, 10889 Wilshire Blvd., Los Angeles CA 90024. (213)208-8559. Managing Editor: Anthony A. Lee. Publishes hardcover and trade paperback originals and hardcover reprints. Averages 10 titles/year; receives 100 submissions annually. 10% of books from first-time authors; 100% of books from unagented writers. Average print order for a writer's first book is 2,000. Pays 10% royalty on wholesale price; usually offers no advance. Publishes book an average of 12-18 months after acceptance. Photocopied submissions OK. Computer printout submissions acceptable; prefers letter-quality to dot-matrix. SASE. Reports in 3 weeks on queries; 8-10 weeks on mss. Free book catalog; ms guidelines for SASE.
Nonfiction: Biography, juvenile and academic. Subjects include history (Middle East) and religion (Baha'i faith). "We want books on the Baha'i Faith only. No non-Baha'i books." Submit outline/synopsis and sample chapters. Reviews artwork/photos as part of ms package.
Recent Nonfiction Title: *Circle of Unity: Baha'i Approaches to Current Social Issues*, by Lee.
Fiction: Adventure, confession, historical, humor, religious, romance and suspense (Baha'i orientation *only*). Submit outline/synopsis and sample chapters.
Recent Fiction Title: *Fire and Blood*, by Garlington.

KAR-BEN COPIES INC., 6800 Tildenwood Ln., Rockville MD 20852. (301)984-8733. President: Judy Groner. Publishes hardcover and trade paperback originals. Averages 6 titles/year; receives 75 submissions annually. 50% of books from first-time authors; 100% from unagented writers. Average print order for a writer's first book is 5,000. Pays 3-10% royalty on retail price; makes negotiable outright purchase; offers average $1,000 advance. Publishes book an average of 1 year after acceptance. Computer printout submissions acceptable. SASE. Reports in 1 week on queries; 4 weeks on mss. Free book catalog.
Nonfiction: Jewish juvenile. Subjects include religion and Jewish history texts. Especially looking for books on Jewish history, holidays, and customs for children—"early childhood and elementary." Query with outline/synopsis and sample chapters or submit complete ms. Reviews artwork/photos as part of ms package.
Recent NonfictionTitle: *The Children We Remember*, by Chana Abells (photoessay on children of the Holocaust).
Fiction: Adventure, fantasy, historical and religious (all Jewish juvenile). Especially looking for Jewish holiday and history-related fiction for young children. Submit outline/synopsis and sample chapters or complete ms.
Recent Fiction Title: *The Passover Parrot*, by Evelyn Zusman (juvenile fiction).
Tips: "We envision Jewish children and their families and juveniles interested in learning about Jewish subjects as our audience."

KENT STATE UNIVERSITY PRESS, Kent State University, Kent OH 44242. (216)672-7913. Director: Paul H. Rohmann. Publishes hardcover and paperback originals and some reprints. Averages 12-15 titles/year. Standard minimum book contract on net sales; rarely offers advance. "Always write a letter of inquiry before submitting manuscripts. We can publish only a limited number of titles each year and can frequently tell in advance whether or not we would be interested in a particular manuscript. This practice saves both our time and that of the author, not to mention postage costs. If interested we will ask for complete manuscript. Decisions based on in-house readings and two by outside scholars in the field of the study." Computer printout submissions acceptable; prefers letter-quality to dot-matrix. Reports in 10 weeks. Enclose return postage. Free book catalog.
Nonfiction: Especially interested in "scholarly works in history of high quality, particularly any titles of regional interest for Ohio. Also will consider scholarly biographies, literary studies, archeological research, the arts, and general nonfiction."
Recent Nonfiction Title: *First Lady: The Life of Lucy Webb Hayes*, by Emily Geer (biography, history).

‡**KERN INTERNATIONAL INC.**, (formerly *Kern Publications*), 433 Washington St., Box 1029, Duxbury MA 02331. (617)934-0445. Senior Editor: Pam Korites. Publishes trade paperback originals and microcomputer software. Averages 6 titles/year; receives 50 submissions annually. 50% of books from first-time authors. Average print order for a writer's first book is 500. Pays 15-25% royalty on wholesale price. Publishes book an average of 6 months after acceptance. Simultaneous and photocopied submissions OK. Electronic submissions OK on IBM PC, but requires hard copy also. Computer printout submissions acceptable; prefers letter-quality to dot-matrix. SASE. Reports in 2 weeks. Book catalog and ms guidelines for SASE.
Nonfiction: How-to, technical, textbook and computer software in book form. Subjects include business, science and engineering. We are interested in books that include computer program listings. Of special interest are how-to books in this area. We are also interested in nontechnical books and programs, such as business applications, as long as they relate to microcomputers. Of special interest are computer-aided design and manufacturing, robotics, computer graphics, and computer-aided instruction. Also, our publications must be of immediate interest to the computer and educational communities and must be highly professional in technical content. No mss of merely academic interest." Query or submit outline/synopsis and sample chapters. Reviews artwork/photos.
Recent Nonfiction Title: *Graphics for the IBM PC*.

‡**KEY PORTER BOOKS LIMITED**, 2nd Floor, 70 The Esplanade, Toronto, Ontario M5E 1R2 Canada. (416)862-7777. Editorial Director: Lorraine Durham. Publishes trade and mass market paperback originals. Averages 30 titles/year. 5% of books from first-time authors; 30% of books from unagented writers. Pays in royalties or outright purchase. Advance varies widely. Publishes book 1-2 years after acceptance. Simultaneous and photocopied submissions OK. Computer printout submissions acceptable; prefers letter-quality to dot-matrix. SASE. Free book catalog.
Nonfiction: Biography, "coffee table" book, cookbook, how-to, humor, illustrated book and self-help. Subjects include Americana, animals, art, business and economics, cooking and foods, health, history, hobbies, music, nature, photography, politics, recreation, sports and travel. No fiction or juvenile books. Submit outline/synopsis and sample chapters or complete ms.
Recent Nonfiction Title: *North American Wildlife*, by Loral Dean (natural history).

KIDS CAN PRESS, 585½ Bloor St. W., Toronto, Ontario M6G 1K5 Canada. (416)534-3141. Contact: Ricky Englander. Publishes hardcover and trade paperback originals. Averages 8 titles/year; receives 1,000 submissions annually. The percentage of books from first-time authors varies. Average print order for a writer's first book is 5,000. Pays 10% maximum royalty on retail price. Publishes book an average of 1-2 years after acceptance. Computer printout submissions acceptable; no dot-matrix. SAE and IRC. Reports in 2 months on mss. Free book catalog.
Nonfiction: Juvenile. Subjects include Canadiana, cooking and foods, health, history, hobbies, music and nature. Readers range from preschoolers to 15 year-olds.
Fiction: Adventure, historical (Canadian), humor, mystery, romance and science fiction. Submit complete ms.
Tips: "All material must be authored by Canadian citizen or landed immigrant and be from Canadian view."

‡**KIRKLEY PRESS, INC.**, 7677 Canton Center Dr., Baltimore MD 21224. Editor: Jay Weitzel. Publishes paperback 16-page booklets and paycheck stuffer folders; receives 30 wsubmissions annually. 10% of books from first-time authors. Average print order for a writer's first book is 20,000-50,000. "We buy manuscripts outright and pay upon acceptance. Payment (total) varies between $200 and $300, depending on subject and strength with which written. Sample of our material sent on request." Publishes book an average of 6 months after acceptance. No disk submissions. Computer printout submissions acceptable; prefers letter-quality to dot-matrix. Send complete ms. Enclose return postage.
Nonfiction: "We publish small booklets which are sold to businesses for distribution to employees and newsletters which are mailed monthly to business executives. They attempt to stimulate or motivate employees

to improve work habits. Basically they are pep talks for employees. We need writers who are so close to the problems of present-day employee attitudes that they can take one of those problems and write about it in a warm, human, understanding, personal style and language that will appeal to the employee and which the employer will find to his advantage to distribute to the employees." Length: 2,400-2,600 words. Reviews artwork/photos.

Recent Nonfiction Title: *If You Were the Boss*, by D. Shiel.

Tips: Newsletter articles accepted on business letter techniques; in-house and external newsletters; direct mail techniques; electronic and subliminal communications; effective public speaking and graphic techniques. "The type of material the writer has the best chance of selling to our firm deals with motivation of employees."

B. KLEIN PUBLICATIONS, Box 8503, Coral Springs FL 33065. (305)752-1708. Editor-in-Chief: Bernard Klein. Hardcover and paperback originals. Specializes in directories, annuals, who's who type of books, bibliography, business opportunity, reference books. Averages 15-20 titles/year. Pays 10% royalty on wholesale price, "but we're negotiable." Advance "depends on many factors." Markets books by direct mail and mail order. Simultaneous and photocopied submissions OK. Reports in 1-2 weeks. SASE. Book catalog for SASE.

Nonfiction: Business, hobbies, how-to, reference, self-help, directories and bibliographies. Query or submit outline/synopsis and sample chapters or complete ms.

Recent Nonfiction Title: *Guide to American Directories*.

THE KNAPP PRESS, Knapp Communications Corp., 5900 Wilshire Blvd., Los Angeles CA 90036. (213)937-3454. Associate Editor: Patricia Connell. Publishes hardcover originals. Averages 20 titles/year. Pays royalty, makes outright purchase or combination payment depending on the book. Simultaneous and photocopied submissions OK. SASE. Reports in 1 month. Free book catalog.

Nonfiction: Large format illustrated books, cookbooks and how-to. Subjects include Americana, animals, art, cooking and entertaining, collecting, hobbies, photography, interior design, architecture, home redecorating and remodeling, and travel.

Recent Nonfiction Title: *The Best of Bon Appetit*, Vol. II.

‡**KNIGHTS PRESS**, Box 454, Pound Ridge NY 10576. Publisher: Elizabeth G. Gershman. Publishes trade paperback originals. Averages 12-18 titles/year; receives 500 submissions annually. 50% of books from first-time authors; 75% of books from unagented writers. Pays 10-15% (escalating) royalty on retail price; offers average $1,500 advance. Publishes book an average of 6-9 months after acceptance. Photocopied submissions OK. Computer printout submissions acceptable; prefers letter-quality to dot-matrix. SASE. Reports in 1 month on queries; 3 months on mss. Book catalog and ms guidelines for business size SAE and 1 first class stamp.

Fiction: Adventure, confession, erotica (very soft-core considered), ethnic, experimental, fantasy, gothic, historical, horror, humor, mystery, romance, science fiction, suspense and western. "We publish only gay men's fiction; must show a positive gay lifestyle or positive gay relationship." No young adult or children's; pornography; formula plots, especially formula romances; or hardcore S&M. Query. Submit outline/synopsis and sample chapters.

Recent Fiction Title: *The World Can Break Your Heart*, by Daniel Curzon (contemporary).

Tips: "We are interested in well-written, well-plotted gay fiction. We are looking only for the highest quality gay literature available."

ALFRED A. KNOPF, INC., 201 E. 50th St., New York NY 10022. (212)751-2600. Senior Editor: Ashbel Green. Children's Book Editor: Ms. Frances Foster. Publishes hardcover and paperback originals (90%) and paperback reprints (10%). Published 182 titles in 1984. Royalties and advance "vary." Simultaneous (if so informed) and photocopied submissions OK. Reports in 2-4 weeks. Book catalog for SASE.

Nonfiction: Book-length nonfiction, including books of scholarly merit. Preferred length: 40,000-150,000 words. "A good nonfiction writer should be able to follow the latest scholarship in any field of human knowledge, and fill in the abstractions of scholarship for the benefit of the general reader by means of good, concrete, sensory reporting." Query.

Recent Nonfiction Title: *Distant Neighbors*, by A. Riding (current affairs).

Fiction: Publishes book-length fiction of literary merit by known or unknown writers. Length: 30,000-150,000 words. Submit complete ms.

Recent Fiction Title: *The Lonely Silver Rain*, by J.D. MacDonald.

KNOWLEDGE INDUSTRY PUBLICATIONS, INC., 701 Westchester Ave., White Plains, NY 10604. (914)328-9157. Vice President/Executive Editor: Barbara Miller. Publishes hardcover and paperback originals. Averages 30 titles/year; receives 150 submissions annually. 60% of books from first-time authors; 100% of books from unagented writers. Average print order for a writer's first book is 2,500. Offers 5-10% royalty on wholesale price; also buys mss by outright purchase for minimum $500. Offers negotiable advance. Publishes book an average of 6 months after acceptance. Photocopied submissions OK. Computer printout submissions acceptable; prefers letter-quality to dot-matrix. SASE. Reports in 2 weeks. Free book catalog; ms guidelines for SASE.

Nonfiction: Business and economics. Especially needs "communication and information technologies, TV and video, library and information science, office automation and office productivity." Query first, then submit outline/synopsis and sample chapters. Reviews artwork/photos as part of ms package.

Recent Nonfiction Title: *Video Editing and Post—Production* by Gary H. Anderson.

JOHN KNOX PRESS, 341 Ponce de Leon Ave. NE, Atlanta GA 30365. (404)873-1549. Editorial Director: Walter C. Sutton. Acquisitions Editor: John G. Gibbs. Averages 24 nonfiction titles/year. Pays royalty on income received; no advances. 20% of books from first-time authors; 90% of books from unagented writers. Publishes book an average of 9-12 months after acceptance. Electronic submissions OK on Wang US 90. Computer printout submissions acceptable. Free catalog and "Guidelines for a Book Proposal" on request with SASE.

Nonfiction: "We publish textbooks, resource books for ministry, and books to encourage Christian faith, in subject areas including biblical studies, theology, ethics, psychology, counseling, worship, and the relationship of science and technology to faith." Query or submit outline/synopsis and sample chapters.

KARL KRAMER VERLAG GMBH & CO., Rotebuhlstrasse 40, D-7000, Stuttgart, Germany. 49-711-62-08-93. President/Editorial Director: Karl H. Kramer. Publishes hardcover and paperback originals. Averages 15 titles/year. Pays 10% minimum royalty; offers $500-$1,000 advance. SASE. Reports in 2 months. Free book catalog.

Nonfiction: Architecture. Submit outline/synopsis and sample chapters or complete ms.

Recent Nonfiction Title: *Space and Form*, by Juergen Joedicke.

THE KRANTZ COMPANY PUBLISHERS, 2210 N. Burling, Chicago IL 60614. (312)472-4900. Publisher: L. Krantz. Publishes hardcover and trade paperback originals. Averages 4-5 titles/year; receives 100 submissions annually. 50% of books from first-time authors; 90% of books from unagented writers. Average print order for a writer's first book is 5-10,000. Pays royalty or makes outright purchase. Publishes book an average of 6-12 months after acceptance. Simultaneous submissions OK. SASE. Reports in 1 month. Free book catalog.

Nonfiction: Coffee table book, how-to, reference, self-help and general nonfiction in the areas of art and photography, and some science. Query. Accepts artwork/photos. No unsolicited mss accepted. Reviews artwork/photos.

Recent Title: *Antiques—Best of the Best*, by Marjorie Glass (general nonfiction).

ROBERT E. KRIEGER PUBLISHING CO. INC., Box 9542, Melbourne FL 32902-9542. (305)724-9542. Executive Assistant: Ann M. Krieger. Publishes hardcover and paperback originals as well as reprints. Averages 120 titles/year. Pays royalty on net realized price. Electronic submissions OK if IBM. Computer printout submissions acceptable; prefers letter-quality to dot-matrix. Reports in 1 month. Free book catalog.

Nonfiction: College reference, technical, and textbook. Subjects include business and economics, history, music, philosophy, psychology, recreation, religion, sociology, sports, chemistry, physics, engineering and medical.

Recent Nonfiction Title: *Human Existence and Philosophical Experience*, by Thomas R. Koenig.

LACE PUBLICATIONS INC., Box 10037, Denver CO 80210-0037. (303)778-7702. Managing Editor: Artemis OakGrove. Publishes trade paperback originals and reprints. Plans to publish 5 titles in 1985; receives 100 submissions annually. 75% of books from first-time authors; 75% of books from unagented writers. Average print order for a writer's first books is 2,000. Pays royalty. "Each project is negotiated on an individual basis. We will eventually offer advances." Publishes book an average of 15 months after acceptance. Simultaneous and photocopied submissions OK. Computer printout submissions acceptable; prefers letter-quality to dot-matrix. SASE. Reports in 1 month on queries; 2 months on mss.

Fiction: Adventure, erotica, ethnic, fantasy, gothic, historical, humor, mystery, romance, science fiction and western. "All submissions must have lesbian themes and main characters. Erotica for our Lady Winston series is especially appreciated. We plan to do some quality erotic art and photography and will be looking for work to fill that need. Entertainment is our main emphasis." No poetry or horror. "We specifically wish to avoid material that is political in nature or designed to make our readers question their inner needs or selves and be left with a negative sense about their lifestyles." Query or submit outline/synopsis and sample chapters. "Male Authors need not apply because our audience will *not* accept them."

Recent Fiction Title: *Just Hold Me*, by Linda Parks (lesbian novel).

Tips: "Audience consists of lesbians and all other women interested in sexuality out of the norm. It isn't likely that our books will appeal to men except in the prurient sense. We stress strong character development and well-thought-out plots."

DAVID S. LAKE PUBLISHERS, (formerly *Pitman Learning*), 19 Davis Dr., Belmont CA 94002. Publisher: Mel Cebulash. Averages 50-80 titles/year. Pays royalty or fee outright. Photocopied submissions OK. Computer printout submissions acceptable; prefers letter-quality to dot-matrix. SASE. Query or submit outline/synopsis for nonfiction. Reports in 1 month. Free book catalog.
Recent Nonfiction Title: *The Reading Triangle*, by Clinard.
Fiction: "We are looking for easy-to-read fiction suitable for middle school and up. We prefer the major characters to be young adults or adults. Solid plotting is essential." Length: 20,000 words maximum. Submit complete ms.
Recent Fiction Title: *Dangerous Waters*, by Ken Girard.

LAKE VIEW PRESS, Box 578279, Chicago IL 60657. (312)935-2694. Director: Paul Elitzik. Publishes hardcover and paperback originals. Averages 6 titles/year; receives 200 submissions annually. 20% of books from first-time authors; 100% of books from unagented writers. Average print order for a writer's first book is 3,000. Pays 8-10% royalty on retail price. No advance. Publishes book an average of 1 year after acceptance. Computer printout submissions acceptable; no dot-matrix; do not send insured. SASE. Reports in 2 months. Free catalog with SAE, and 2 first class stamps.
Nonfiction: Films, Middle East, Afro-American, labor, women, and Asia. Accepts nonfiction translations. "Our audience interest is current affairs, politics and the contemporary cultural scene." Submit outline, and author biography.
Recent Nonfiction Title: *Reflections: A Writer's Life, A Writer's Work*, by Harry Mark Petrakis.

LAKEWOOD BOOKS, 4 Park Ave., New York NY 10016. Editorial Director: Donald Wigal, Ph.D. Publishes 64-page "Impulse" originals. "We are not trade books publisher." Publishes up to 38 titles/year; receives 1,000 submissions annually. 1% of books from first-time authors. Average print order for a writer's first book is 10,000. Pays on a "qualified" work-for-hire basis. "Few exceptions." Publishes book an average of 1 year after acceptance. Simultaneous and photocopied submissions OK. Computer printout submissions acceptable; prefers letter-quality to dot-matrix. Reports in 2 months. SASE.
Nonfiction: "Our books are apparently bought by women who have families, or are attracted to a rather middle-of-the-road life style. Our titles are mainly self-help (exercise, diet) and informational (finances, how-to). We avoid controversial topics. Nonfiction which ties in with specific products welcomed by query (e.g., '100 Tips on Using Brand X in the Garden')." No fiction, poetry, astrology, puzzle, cookbook or sport titles needed at present. Query. Author should have "an awareness of our format (limitations and potential), and sensitivity to the mass market. Concise overview best."
Recent Nonfiction Title: *Shape Up Hips and Thighs*.
Tips: "Freelance writers should be aware that an author's word processing ability is becoming standard and presumed by editors. I have to be assured the work is on tape or disk ready for fast editing and that revised copy is quickly available. Freelance editing is becoming more popular. Nearly all the unsolicited works we receive should have been sent to trade publishers or to mass market publishers. We publish only 64-page Impulse buyer's titles."

LANDMARK BOOKS, 2200 66th St. W., Minneapolis MN 55423. Editor-in-Chief: Joyce Hovelsrud. Publishes hardcover and paperback originals. Averages 6-10 titles/year; receives 35 submissions annually. 20% of books from first-time authors; 80% of books from unagented writers. Average print order for a writer's first book is 7,500. Pays standard royalty. Publishes book an average of 18 months after acceptance. Computer printout submissions acceptable. SASE. Reports in 6 weeks. Free book catalog and writer's guidelines.
Nonfiction: "We're a religious market looking for manuscripts on subjects of current issues and interest which are appropriate for both religious and general markets. Material must be scripturally sound. We do not publish watered down religion and are interested in material with impact." Looks for "subjects that are timely and timeless." Wants to see "the thrust of the subject in synopsis; the comment the author is making; where he is going with a subject and how he's going to develop it in his outline." In the completed ms wants "something of impact, order, relevance, *good* writing, and a recognizable style." Accepts translations. Query or submit complete ms. Reviews artwork/photos as part of ms package.
Recent Nonfiction Title: *My Diary—A Christmas Journey*, by A Toff.

‡*PETER LANG PUBLISHING, INC.**, 34 E. 39th St., New York NY 10016. (212)692-9009. Subsidiary of Verlag Peter Lang AG, Bern, Switzerland. Editor-in-Chief: Jay Wilson. Publishes hardcover and trade paperback originals, and hardcover and trade paperback reprints. Averages 120 titles/year; receives 600 submissions annually. 75% of books from first-time authors; 98% of books from unagented writers. Subsidiary publishes 25% of books. All subsidies are guaranteed repayment plus profit (if edition sells out) in contract. Subsidy published if ms is highly specialized and author relatively unknown. Pays 10-30% royalty on retail price. Translators get flat fee plus percentage of royalties. No advance. Publishes book an average of 1 year after acceptance. Photocopied submissions OK. Computer printout submissions acceptable; prefers letter-quality to dot-matrix. SASE. Reports in 2 months on queries; 4 months on mss. Book catalog free on request.

Ms guidelines for SASE.

Nonfiction: Biography, reference, textbook and scholarly monograph. Subjects include Americana, art, business and economics, health (rarely), history, music, philosophy, politics, psychology, religion, sociology and sports. All books are scholarly monographs, textbooks, reference books, reprints of historic texts, critical editions or translations. "We are expanding and are receptive to any scholarly project in the humanities and social sciences." No mss shorter than 150 pages; elementary and high school textbooks. Submit complete ms.

Recent Nonfiction Title: *People of the High Country*, by Gary Wright (archaeology).

Fiction: Critical editions and English translations of classics in any language. "We publish primarily nonfiction." Submit outline/synopsis and complete ms.

Recent Fiction Title: *Summer Tales*, by Johann Beer (short story collection).

Poetry: Scholarly critical editions only. Submit complete ms.

Recent Poetry Title: *The Poetry of Dino Frescobaldi*, by Joseph Alessia.

Tips: "Besides our commitment to specialist academic monograhs, we are one of the few U.S. publishers who publish books in most of the modern languages."

LARANMARK PRESS, Box 253, Neshkoro WI 54960. (414)293-4377. President/Editor-in-Chief: Larry D. Names. Contact: Peggy Eagan. Publishes hardcover and paperback originals and fiction reprints. Averages 6-12 titles/year; receives 10,000 submissions annually. 75% of books from first-time authors; 50% of books from unagented writers. Average print order for a writer's first book is 15,000. Pays 6% royalty on the first 50,000 copies; 8% on the next 50,000; 10% thereafter; 12% on hardcover; sometimes offers $150-1,000 advance. Publishes book an average of 1-2 years after acceptance. Electronic submissions OK on IBM PC Compatible and Honeywell PC, but requires hard copy also. Computer printout submissions acceptable; make dot-matrix dark enough. Ms guidelines for SASE.

Nonfiction: Adult books for hardcover line on sports, cooking, Americana, history, and how-tos. Accepts nonfiction translations. Query with outline/synopsis and 3 sample chapters, or submit through agent. Reviews artwork/photos as part of ms package.

Recent Nonfiction Title: *Dear Pete: The story of Pete Rose and His Fans*, by Helen Fabbri.

Fiction: "We are not accepting *any* fiction until January 1987. We are booked up. We are concentrating on good nonfiction."

Recent Fiction Title: *Summers of the Ferris Wheel*, by James V. McMakin.

Tips: "We are looking for nonfiction that can be aimed at a specific group of people, (i.e., sailors) and regional (any, not just Wisconsin or Midwest) nonfiction."

LARKSDALE, 133 S. Heights Blvd., Houston TX 77007. (713)869-9092. Publisher: James Goodman. Editor-in-Chief: Nancy B. Adleman. General trade publisher. Imprints include The Linolean Press (religious), The Lindahl Press (general), and Harle House (mass market paperback). Publishes hardcover and paperback originals. Averages 40 titles/year; receives 800 submissions annually. 30% of books from first-time authors; 95% of books from unagented writers. Average print order for a writer's first book is 2,000. Pays standard royalty contract; no advance. Publishes book an average of 14 months after acceptance. Electronic submissions OK on ASCII Files (modem)—CPM 2.2 DSQD 5¼ (disk). Computer printout submissions acceptable. "SASE means stamped container for return, *not* stamps or a check for postage." Reports in 2 months.

Nonfiction: All types including, how to, self help, and health. Religious area includes Christian Doctrine and Inspirational. No off-color work accepted. Submit complete ms to publisher. Reviews artwork/photos as part of ms package.

Recent Nonfiction Title: *How to Write How-to Books*, by J. Frank Brumbaugh.

Fiction: Contemporary and poetry.

Recent Fiction Title: *The Healing Gift*, by Mary Wyche Estes (mainstream).

LARSON PUBLICATIONS, INC., Subsidiary of Bokforlaget Robert Larson A.B., Sweden; 4936 Route 414, Burdett NY 14818. (607)546-9342. Director: Paul Cash. Publishes hardcover and trade paperback originals and hardcover and trade paperback reprints. Averages 4-5 titles/year; receives 400 submissions annually. 70% of books from first-time authors; 75% of books from unagented writers. Average print order for a writer's first books is 3,000-4,000. Pays 10% minimum royalty of cash received, flexible maximum on wholesale price. Offers advance of ⅓ of first year's expected royalty on some titles. Photocopied submissions OK. Electronic submissions OK if compatible with IBM-PC/Final Work. Computer printout submissions acceptable; dot-matrix OK if double-strike. SASE. Reports "as soon as possible—no full-time reader."

Nonfiction: How-to and self-help. Subjects include alternative education, astrology, cooking and foods, health, parenting, philosophy and religion. Query only; do not send complete ms.

Recent Nonfiction Title: *The Notebooks of Paul Brunton: Perspectives*, by Paul Brunton (philosophy/spiritual).

Fiction: Fantasy, mystical allegory, religious and science fiction. "We are just beginning to explore this area." No mss unrelated to spiritual self-discovery. Query only; do not send unsolicited ms.

Tips: "Our audience is independent, spiritually-minded, all ages."

‡**LEARNING ENDEAVORS**, 13262 Europa Court, Apple Valley MN 55124. (612)432-0710. Editor: Elizabeth Swiderski. Publishes hardcover and trade paperback originals and mass market paperback originals. Averages 1-3 titles/year; receives 15 submissions annually. Pays 10% maximum royalty on wholesale price. Publishes manuscript an average of 6 months after acceptance. Photocopied submissions OK. SASE. Reports in 3 weeks on queries; 2 months on mss.

Nonfiction: Education and special education textbooks. "We use material which is used by the teacher of students with learning difficulties. Books should be usable in the classroom and pointed toward a single or multiple grades." Query.

Recent Nonfiction Title: *Study Skills: Learning Made Easier*, by Swiderski/Zettel (study guide).

LEARNING PUBLICATIONS, INC., Box 1326, Holmes Beach FL 33509. (616)372-1045. Editor: Danna Downing. Publishes hardcover and trade paperback originals. Averages 15 titles/year; receives 500 w submissions annually. 75% of books from first-time authors; 80% of books from unagented writers. Average print order for a writer's first book is 1-2,000. Pays 5% royalty on income received from sales. No advance. Publishes book an average of 18 months after acceptance. Photocopied submissions OK. Computer printout submissions acceptable; prefers letter-quality to dot-matrix. SASE. Reports in 3 weeks on queries; 3 months on mss. Free book catalog.

Nonfiction: How-to (for professionals), reference, self-help (for general public, technical, textbooks on art, psychology, sociology, reference books for counselors, teachers and school administrators. Books to help parents of children with reading problems and special needs (impaired, gifted, etc.); or art activity books for teachers. Query or submit outline synopsis and sample chapters. Reviews artwork/photos.

Recent Nonfiction Title: *Teaching Basic: Thirty Lesson Plans, Activities and Quizzes*, by Vonk and Erickson.

LEATHER STOCKING BOOKS, Box 19746, West Allis WI 53219. (414)778-1120. Editor: Carlton Sitz. Publishes hardcover and original paperbacks. Average 7-8 titles/year. Pays 10% royalty on wholesale price; no advance. Publishes book an average of 2 years after acceptance. Electronic submissions OK, but requires hard copy also. Computer printout submissions acceptable. SASE. Reports in 2 months.

Nonfiction: Frontier history, guns, outdoor (how-to), and military. Reviews artwork/photos as part of ms package. Query.

Recent Nonfiction Title: *Gunslinger*, by Carl Breihan.

LEE'S BOOKS FOR YOUNG READERS, 813 West Ave., Box 111, O'Neil Professional Bldg., Wellington TX 79095. (806)447-5445. Independent book producer/packager. Publisher: Lee Templeton. Publishes hardcover originals. Averages 8 titles/year; receives 25 submissions annually. 20% of books from first-time authors; 100% of books from unagented writers. Average print order for a writer's first book is 1,000. Pays 10% minimum royalty on wholesale price. No advance. Publishes book an average of 1 year after acceptance. Computer printout submissions acceptable; prefers letter-quality to dot-matrix. SASE. Free book catalog.

Nonfiction: Biography. "Our books are nonfiction history of young heroes. All our books are written for 'reluctant' readers in junior high school market (10-14 age group), to be sold to junior (middle) school libraries. We will consider queries about young American heroes, male or female, that historians overlooked." All unsolicited mss are returned unopened.

Recent Nonfiction Title: *LaFayette, America's 19 Year Old General*.

LEXIKOS, 1012 14th St., San Francisco CA 94114. (415)861-4916. Editor: Robin Kirk. Publishes hardcover and trade paperback originals and trade paperback reprints. Averages 5-7 (growing each season) titles/year; receives 500 submissions annually. 50% of books from first-time authors; 100% of books from unagented writers. Average print order for a writer's first book is 5,000. Royalties vary from 8-12½% according to book sold. "Authors asked to accept lower royalty on high discount (50% plus) sales." Offers average $1,000 average. Publishes book an average of 1 year after acceptance. Simultaneous and photocopied submissions OK. Computer printout submissions acceptable; no dot-matrix. SASE. Reports in 1 month. Book catalog for 6x9 SAE and 2 first class stamps.

Nonfiction: "Coffee table" book, illustrated book. Subjects include regional, outdoors, oral histories, Americana, history and nature. Especially looking for 50,000-word "city and regional histories, anecdotal in style for a general audience; books of regional interest about *places*; adventure and wilderness books; annotated reprints of books of Americana; Americana in general." No health, sex, European travel, diet, broad humor, fiction, quickie books (we stress backlist vitality), religion, children's or nutrition. Submit outline/synopsis and sample chapters. Reviews artwork/photos.

Recent Nonfiction Title: *River Pigs and Cayuses: Oral Histories from the PNW*, by Ron Strickland.

Tips: "A regional book has the best chance of selling to Lexikos. Submit a short, cogent proposal; follow up with letter queries. Give publisher reason to believe you will help him *sell* the book (identify the market, point out availability of mailing lists, distinguish book from competition. Avoid grandiose claims. Establish faith (in letters, proposals) of your ability to *write*, take editing. We stress high production values, durability and intelligent writing."

LIBERTY PUBLISHING COMPANY, INC., 50 Scott Adam Rd., Cockeysville MD 21030. (301)667-6680. Publisher: Jeffrey B. Little. Imprints include Liberty Personal Counsel Library, J. Little, publisher. Publishes hardcover and mostly trade paperback originals and software. Averages 10-15 titles/year; receives 500 submissions annually. 90% of books from first-time authors; 95% of books from unagented writers. Average print order for a writer's first book is 4,000-6,000. Pays 6-12% royalty on wholesale or retail price; buys some mss outright for $500-1,500; offers average $400 advance. Publishes book an average of 6-12 months after acceptance. Computer printout submissions acceptable; prefers letter-quality to dot-matrix. Reports in 3 weeks on queries; 1-2 months on mss. "Exclusive distribution arrangements with self-publishers possible."

Nonfiction: biography, cookbook, how-to, illustrated book and self-help. Subjects include Americana, business and economics, cooking and foods, history, hobbies, photography (b&w only), recreation, sports, travel; educational, and parent guides. Accepts nonfiction translations. "How-to or self-help books dealing with concrete advice written by people qualified to address the subject. Extensive graphic possibilities preferred. No self improvement books dealing with psychology and mind improvement. No poetry, please." Query with author biography or submit outline/synopsis and 3 sample chapters. Reviews artwork/photos as part of ms package.

Recent Nonfiction Title: *Understanding Wall Street*, by J. Little (business guide for the layman investor).

Tips: Freelancer has best chance of selling business, how-to; "This is an area for which we are known."

*LIBRA PUBLISHERS, INC., Suite 207, 4901 Moreno Blvd., San Diego CA 92117. (619)273-1500. Contact: William Kroll. Publishes hardcover and paperback originals. Specializes in the behavioral sciences. Averages 15 titles/year. 10-15% royalty on retail price; no advance. Subsidy publishes 15% of books (those which have obvious marketing problems or are too specialized). Publishes book an average of 8 months after acceptance. Computer printout submissions acceptable; prefers letter-quality to dot-matrix. Reports in 2 weeks. SASE. Free book catalog.

Nonfiction: Mss in all subject areas will be given consideration, but main interest is in the behavioral sciences. Submit outline/synopsis and 3 sample chapters. Reviews artwork/photos as part of ms package.

Recent Nonfiction Title: *The Glimpse*, by Joyce Mae Iver.

LIBRARIES UNLIMITED, Box 263, Littleton CO 80160. (303)770-1220. Editor-in-Chief: Bohdan S. Wynar. Publishes hardcover and paperback originals (95%) and hardcover reprints (5%). Averages 30-40 titles/year; receives 100-200 submissions annually. 10-20% of books from first-time authors. Average print order for a writer's first book is 2,000. Specializes in library science and reference books. 10% royalty on net sales; advance averages $500. Publishes book an average of 1 year after acceptance. Marketed by direct mail to 40,000 libraries and schools in this country and abroad. Query or submit outline/synopsis and sample chapters. All prospective authors are required to fill out an author questionnaire. Query if photos/illustrations are to accompany ms. Reports in 2 months. SASE. Free book catalog and ms guidelines.

Nonfiction: Publishes reference and library science text books. Looks for professional experience.

Recent Nonfiction Title: *Guide to American Literature*, by Valmai Kirkham Fenster.

LIGHTBOOKS, Box 1268, Twain Harte CA 95383. (209)533-4222. Publisher: Paul Castle. Publishes hardcover and paperback originals. Averages 4-6 titles/year; receives 10-15 submissions annually. 100% of books from first-time authors; 100% of books from unagented writers. Average print order for a writer's first book is 2,000-3,000. Pays 10-15% royalty on wholesale or retail price; no advance. Publishes book an average of 3-6 months after acceptance. Simultaneous and photocopied submissions OK. Computer printout submissions acceptable; prefers letter-quality to dot-matrix. SASE. Reports in 1 month.

Nonfiction: Photography. "We are always interested in good manuscripts on technique and/or business of photography. We especially want manuscripts on *marketing* one's photography. We don't want manuscripts on art criticism of photography, collections of art photos, basic photo teaching books, or anything other than books on the technique and/or business of photography. Query; if the idea is good, we'll ask for outline/synopsis and sample chapters." Reviews artwork/photos as part of ms package. "Artwork/photos are essential to acceptance."

Recent Nonfiction Title: *The Master Book of Portraiture and Studio Management*, by Don Peterson.

Tips: "We need more anecdotes and illustrations (word) to amplify the writer's points. We particularly look for skilled photographers who are doing something very well and can communicate their expertise to others. We are willing to work with such individuals on extensive re-write and editing, if what they have to say is valuable."

LIGUORI PUBLICATIONS, Book and Pamphlet Dept., 1 Liguori Dr., Liguori MO 63057. (314)464-2500. Editor-in-Chief: Rev. Christopher Farrell, C.SS.R. Managing Editor: Roger Marchand. Publishes paperback originals. Specializes in Catholic-Christian religious materials. Averages 30 titles/year; receives about 100 submissions annually. About 50% of books from first-time authors; 95% of books from unagented writers. Average print order for a writer's first book is 10,000-16,000. Pays royalty on books; flat fee on pamphlets and teacher's guides. Publishes book an average of 8 months after acceptance. Electronic submissions on TRS-80

Model III in a 1.3 system/1.0 version OK "if sent with computer printout." Computer printout submissions acceptable; no dot-matrix. Query or submit outline/synopsis and 1 sample chapter; "never submit total book." Reports in 3-5 weeks. SASE. Free book catalog and ms guidelines.

Nonfiction: Publishes doctrinal, inspirational, Biblical, self-help and educational materials. Looks for "thought and language that speak to basic practical religious concerns of contemporary Catholic Christians." **Recent Nonfiction Title:** *Inner Calm: Christian Answer to Modern Stress.*

Tips: "People seek light on real-life concerns. Writers, in clear language expressing well-founded views, lead and educate in light of Good News shared in faith-community. Write book that is: short in length, written in plain language, on a subject most people can relate to. It meets a need and will be bought."

LINCH PUBLISHING, INC., Box 75, Orlando FL 32802. (305)647-3025. Vice President: Gary L. Porter. Publishes hardcover and trade paperback originals. Pays 10-15% royalty on wholesale price. Rarely pays advances. Simultaneous and photocopied submissions OK. Reports in 3-6 weeks. Book catalog for $1 and regular size SAE with 39¢ postage.

Nonfiction: Specializes in books on estate planning and legal how-to books which must be applicable in all 50 states. "We are interested in a recordkeeping book for heirs, how to get through probate and settle an estate, and minimizing federal estate and/or state inheritance taxes; also, how to incorporate and raise money for a small business and how to get an adoption." Query first before submitting mss. "We could have already have accepted a manuscript and be in the process of publishing one of the above."

Recent Nonfiction Title: *It's Easy to Avoid Probate.*

LITTLE, BROWN AND CO., INC., 34 Beacon St., Boston MA 02106. Contact: Editorial Department, Trade Division. Publishes hardcover and paperback originals and paperback reprints. Averages 100% titles/year. "Royalty and advance agreements vary from book to book and are discussed with the author at the time an offer is made." Submissions only from authors who have had a book published or have been published in professional or literary journals, newspapers or magazines." Computer printout submissions acceptable; prefers letter-quality to dot-matrix. Reports in 10-12 weeks for queries/proposals. SASE.

Nonfiction: "Some how-to books, distinctive cookbooks, biographies, history, science and sports." Query or submit outline/synopsis and sample chapters. Reviews artwork/photos as part of ms package.

Recent Nonfiction Title: *The Living Planet*, by David Attenborough.

Fiction: Contemporary popular fiction as well as fiction of literary distinction. "Our poetry list is extremely limited; those collections of poems that we do publish are usually the work of poets who have gained recognition through publication in literary reviews and various periodicals." Query or submit outline/synopsis and sample chapters.

Recent Fiction Title: *Victory over Japan*, by Ellen Gilchrist.

*THE LITTLE HOUSE PRESS, 2544 N. Monticello Ave., Chicago IL 60647. (312)342-3338. Senior Editor: Gene Lovitz. Publishes trade hardcover (Little House) and trade paperback (Elephant Walk) originals. "We intend to average twenty titles a year as new publishers once we get under way." ; receives 2,000 w submissions annually. 60% of books from first-time authors; 95% of books from unagented writers. Average print order for a writer's first book is 10,000. Pays 10% minimum royalty on hardcover retail price; maximum royalty negotiable. Average advance varies with author or quality of book and market. Simultaneous and photocopied submissions OK. Computer printout submissions acceptable; prefers letter-quality to dot-matrix. SASE. Reports in 2 weeks on queries; 1 month on mss.

Nonfiction: Biography, how-to, humor, juvenile, reference, self-help and metaphysics. Subjects include animals, business and economics, cooking and foods, health, homes and politics. Reviews artwork/photos.

Fiction: Mainstream, adventure, spy, espionage, fantasy, gothic, horror, mystery, far-out, experimental, and intellectual (think of Thomas Mann) "We welcome the serious novelist. Fast paced melodrama is what we are looking for; also cliff-hangers; books we could publish both in hardcover and paperback. Courtroom drama, big business, Washington politics, Malibu/Paris/'Dallas' ambience; but also . . . *And Ladies Of The Club* kinds of manuscripts."

Poetry: Only completed books of verse. Queries only.

Tips: "One manuscript at a time. Stay off the phone, and don't bog us down with correspondence. List any other publisher or agent that has been contacted about the material sent, and to what extent. We only contract for completed manuscripts. However, We want the text on par with the *Manual of Style*. We will reject a novel on sight if it is masses of narrative with little dialog. We prefer published authors to send the completed manuscript; unpublished authors to query us first And, Verily, verily I say unto thee/ It is blessed to send SASE."

LIVE OAK PUBLICATIONS, Box 2193, Boulder CO 80306. (303)530-1087. Publisher: Tom Ellison. Publishes trade paperback originals. Averages 3-6 titles/year. Negotiable payment, depending on the work. Offers average $500-$1,000 advance. Photocopied submissions OK. SASE. Reports in 2 weeks. Free book catalog.

Nonfiction: How-to. Subjects include business and self-help. "We are actively seeking manuscripts for how-to books on specific self-employment opportunities, career change, new ways of working and work in general, but we will consider any how-to topics." Query.

Recent Nonfiction Title: *Ideas That WORK*, by Susan Elliot (how-to).

Tips: "Our readers want books which can show them how to assume more control over their lives. If you have any ideas let us hear from you."

‡*LLEWELLYN PUBLICATIONS**, Subsidiary of Chester-Kent, Inc., Box 64383-WM86, St. Paul MN 55164-0383. (612)291-1970. President: Carl L. Weschcke. Publishes hardcover and trade paperback originals and reprints and software. Averages 12-15 titles/year; receives 100-150 submissions annually. 50% of books from first-time authors; 95% of books from unagented writers. Subsidy publishes 10% of books "generally the book is well-written and makes a valuable contribution to the subject area, but we feel the market potential to be too small for our investment in publication, or the book is too expensive or too slow in turnover." Pays 10-15% royalty. Publishes book an average of 6-18 months after acceptance. Simultaneous and photocopied submissions OK. Computer printout submissions acceptable; prefers letter-quality to dot-matrix. Reports in 3 months. Book catalog $2; ms guidelines for $1 and SASE.

Nonfiction: "Coffee table" book, how-to, reference, self-help and textbook. Subjects include astrology and occultism. Especially looking for self-help through astrology and occultism, with the emphasis on practicality, readability, and wide market. No psuedo or "pop" approaches to the subjects; no "satanism." Submit outline/synopsis and sample chapters.

Recent Nonfiction Title: *The Llewellyn Guide to Magical States of Consciousness*, by Denning and Phillips (Qabalah and meditation).

Tips: "Our books are for people of all ages and interests, with a special interest in personal growth, awareness of inner potentials, conscious of other dimensions, and a conviction that life is meaningful. We see a continuing movement towards 'real' books in these subject areas as contrasted to 'pop' appraoches; less interest in 'celebrity' books, more interest in direct involvement and personal experience."

LODESTAR BOOKS, Division of E. P. Dutton, 2 Park Ave., New York NY 10016. (212)725-1818. Editorial Director: Virginia Buckley. Hardcover originals. Publishes juveniles, young adults, fiction and nonfiction; no picture books. Averages 20 titles/year; receives 800 submissions annually. 10-20% of books from first-time authors; 25-30% of books from unagented writers. Average print order for a writer's first book is 4,000-5,000. Pays royalty on invoice list price; advance offered. Publishes book an average of 18 months after acceptance. Photocopied submissions OK. Electronic submissions OK, but requires hard copy also. Computer printout submissions acceptable; prefers letter-quality to dot-matrix. Reports in 2-4 months. SASE. Ms guidelines for SASE.

Nonfiction: Query or submit outline/synopsis and 2-3 sample chapters including "theme, chapter-by-chapter outline, and 1 or 2 completed chapters." State availability of photos and/or illustrations. Queries/mss may be routed to other editors in the publishing group. Reviews artwork/photos as part of ms package.

Fiction: Publishes only for young adults and juveniles: adventure, fantasy, humorous, contemporary, mystery, science fiction, suspense and western books. Submit complete ms.

Tips: "A young adult novel that is literary, fast-paced, well-constructed (as approved to a commercial novel) and well-written nonfiction on contemporary issues have the best chance of selling to our firm.

LOIRY PUBLISHING HOUSE, Suite 301, 226 W. Pensacola St., Tallahassee FL 32301. (904)681-0019. Executive Editor: William S. Loiry. Publishes hardcover and trade paperback originals. Pays negotiable royalty. No advance. Simultaneous and photocopied submissions OK. SASE. Reports in 1 month.

Nonfiction: How-to, juvenile, reference, self-help, and textbook. "Loiry Publishing House is rapidly expanding and looking for high-quality manuscripts with a market that can be identified and reached. We publish in three main areas: Human Relations: personal growth, sexuality, effective parenting, and race relations; Children and Youth: the conditions of, importance of, policies affecting, advocacy for, and activism of (looking for manuscripts on child abuse, missing children, children in poverty, latchkey children, and school improvement, emphasizing solutions and how they can be attained); and Politics: what is really going on in politics and government and why and what citizens can do to make a difference (looking for manuscripts on the impact of U.S. foreign policy, especially in Central America, and manuscripts on the impact of the Reagan Administration on American life). We will also consider nonfiction manuscripts on other categories. For manuscripts we cannot publish, we refer them to our Author Consulting Program where we advise authors on how to self-publish." Query.

Recent Nonfiction Title: *The Impact of Youth: A History of Children and Youth With Recommendations for the Future*, by William S. Loiry.

LONGMAN, INC., 1560 Broadway, New York NY 10036. (212)764-3950. Executive Vice President: Bruce S. Butterfield. Publishes hardcover and paperback originals. Publishes 100 titles/year. Pays variable royalty; offers variable advance. Photocopied submissions OK. SASE. Reports in 6 weeks.

Nonfiction: Textbooks only (elementary/high school, college and professional): world history, political science, economics, communications; social sciences, education, English, Latin, foreign languages, English as a second language. No trade, art or juvenile.

LOOMPANICS UNLIMITED, Box 1197, Port Townsend WA 98368. Book Editor: Michael Hoy. Publishes trade paperback originals. Publishes 12 titles/year; receives 50 submissions annually. 40% of books from first-time authors; 100% of books from unagented writers. Average print order for a writer's first book is 1,000. Pays 7¹/₂-20% royalty on wholesale or retail price; or makes outright purchase of $100-1,200. Offers average $500 advance. Publishes book an average of 6 months after acceptance. Simultaneous and photocopied submissions OK. Computer printout submissions acceptable; prefers letter-quality to dot-matrix. SASE. Reports in 6 weeks. Free book catalog.
Nonfiction: How-to, reference and self-help. Subjects include business and economics, philosophy, politics, travel, and "beat the system" books. "We are looking for how-to books in the fields of espionage, investigation, the underground economy, police methods, how to beat the system, crime and criminal techniques. No cookbooks, inspirational, travel, or cutesy-wutesy stuff." Query, or submit outlines/synopsis and sample chapters. Reviews artwork/photos.
Recent Nonfiction Title: *Methods of Disguise*, by John Sample (how-to).
Tips: "Our audience is young males looking for hard-to-find information on alternatives to 'The System'."

*LORIEN HOUSE, Box 1112, Black Mountain NC 28711. Editor: David A. Wilson. Publishes trade paperback originals. Averages 2-4 titles/year; receives 50 submissions annually. 50% of books from first-time authors; 100% of books from unagented writers. Average print order for a writer's first book is 1,000. Subsidy publishes 20% of books. "Rather than subsidy, we do a co-op publishing, sharing costs with the author." Pays 10-15% royalty on retail price. No advance. Publishes book an average of 18 months after acceptance. Computer printout submissions acceptable; prefers letter-quality to dot-matrix. SASE. Reports in 1 week on queries. Book catalog 50¢.
Nonfiction: How-to, technical and literary. Subjects include history (American); nature (wild foods, ecology); and philosophy (metaphysics). "We are open to any subject as long as it is well done and treated as a literary and technical piece at the same time." No photo essays or children's books. Submit outline/synopsis. Reviews artwork/photos as part of ms package.
Recent Nonfiction Title: *Gemstones, Crystals & Healing*, by Thelma Isaacs (geology/metaphysics).

LOTHROP, LEE & SHEPARD BOOKS, Division of William Morrow Company, 105 Madison Ave., New York NY 10016. (212)889-3050. Editor-in-Chief: Dorothy Briley. Hardcover original children's books only. Royalty and advance vary according to type of book. Averages 55 titles/year; receives 4,000 submissions annually. Less than 2% of books from first-time authors; 25% of books from unagented writers. Average print order for a writer's first book is 6,000. State availability of photos to accompany ms. Publishes book an average of 2 years after acceptance. Photocopied submissions OK, but originals preferred. No simultaneous submissions. Computer printout submissions acceptable; no dot-matrix. SASE. Responds in 4-6 weeks. Book catalog for SAE.
Fiction and Nonfiction: Publishes picture books, general nonfiction, and novels. Submit outline/synopsis and sample chapters for nonfiction. Juvenile fiction emphasis is on novels for the 8-12 age group. Submit complete ms for fiction. Looks for "organization, clarity, creativity, literary style."
Recent Title: *The Story of Jumping Mouse*, by John Steptoe.
Tips: "Trends in book publishing that freelance writers should be aware of include the demand for books for children under age 3 and the shrinking market for young adult books, especially novels."

‡LOTUS PRESS, INC., Box 21607, Detroit MI 48221. (313)861-1280. Editor/Publisher: Naomi Madgett. Imprint includes Penway Books. Publishes hardcover and trade paperback originals. Averages 4-7 titles/year; receives 200 submissions annually. 30% of books from first-time authors; 100% of books from unagented writers. Pays in copies. "Authors are given 25 free copies and may (but are not required) order additional copies at a discount. It is the best we can do." Publishes book an average of 2 years after acceptance. Photocopied submissions OK. Computer printout submissions acceptable; prefers letter-quality to dot-matrix. Reports in 6 weeks. Free book catalog and ms guidelines; SASE appreciated.
Nonfiction: Publishes textbook on poetry. "We do not want to see ANY nonfiction. We publish poetry exclusively except for the one textbook under the Penway imprint." Reviews artwork/photos.
Poetry: "We are already committed for the next two years. We are most committed to the consideration of black poets." No amateur variety poetry; poetry imitative of other poets' styles and attitudes; or poetry whose vocabulary is in poor taste. Submit 3-5 poems.
Recent Poetry Title: *The Watermelon Dress: Portrait of a Woman*, by Paulette Childress White (lyric).
Tips: "Our audience is college-educated, black and white, poetry lovers; those who appreciate the possibilities of language."

LOUISIANA STATE UNIVERSITY PRESS, Baton Rouge LA 70803. (504)388-6618. Associate/Executive Editor: Beverly Jarrett. Director: L.E. Phillabaum. Averages 60 titles/year; receives 200-300 submissions annually. 75% of books from first-time authors; 85-90% of books from unagented writers. Average print order for a writer's first book is 1,000-1,500. Pays royalty on wholesale price; no advance. Publishes book an average of 12-18 months after acceptance. Photocopied submissions OK. Electronic submissions OK, varied capacity, but requires hard copy also. Computer printout submissions acceptable; no dot-matrix. SASE. Reports in 1 month on queries; 1-6 months on mss. Free book catalog; free ms guidelines for SASE.

Nonfiction: "We would like to have manuscripts on humanities and social sciences, with special emphasis on Southern history and literature; Southern studies; French studies; political philosophy; and music, especially jazz." Query.

Recent Nonfiction Title: *The Awakening Twenties*, by Gorham Munson.

Tips: "The writer has the best chance of selling us books on scholarly study in history, literary criticism, or political philosophy because we are a university press."

‡**LOYOLA UNIVERSITY PRESS**, 3441 N. Ashland Ave., Chicago IL 60657. (312)281-1818. Editorial Director: George A. Lane. Imprints include Campion Books. Publishes hardcover and trade paperback originals, and hardcover and trade paperback reprints. Receives 100 submissions annually. 40% of books from first-time authors; 95% of books from unagented writers. Pays 5-10% royalty on wholesale price; offers no advance. Publishes book an average of 1 year after acceptance. Simultaneous and photocopied submissions acceptable. Electronic submissions OK on TRS-805" disks. Models 3&4 and CompuScan OCR, but requires hard copy also. Computer printout submissions acceptable; prefers letter-quality to dot-matrix. SASE. Reports in 1 month on queries; 1 month on mss. Book catalog for 7x10 SAE.

Nonfiction: Biography and textbook. Subjects include art (religious), history (church) and religion. The four subject areas of Campion Books include Jesuitica (Jesuit history, biography and spirituality); Literture-Theology interface (books dealing with theological or religious aspects of literary works or authors); contemporary Catholic concerns (books on morality, spirituality, family life, pastoral ministry, prayer, worship, etc.); and Chicago/art (books dealing with the city of Chicago from historical, artistic, architectural, or ethnic perspectives, but with religious emphases). Query before submitting ms. Reviews artwork/photos.

Recent Nonfiction Titles: *Hollywood and The Catholic Church*, by Les and Barbara Keyser.

Tips: "Our audience is principally the college-educated reader with religious, theological interest.

‡**McCLELLAND AND STEWART-BANTAM LTD.**, (Seal Books), #601, 60 St. Clair Ave. E., Toronto, Ontario M4T 1N5 Canada. (416)922-4970. Vice President/Publisher: Janet Turnbull. Publishes trade paperback and mass market paperback originals and mass market paperback reprints. Averages 24 titles/year; receives 2,000 submissions annually. 10% of books from first-time authors; 80% of books from unagented writers. "All authors published by this firm must be Canadian citizens, residents of Canada, or their subject matter must be (in part) of Canadian content." Pays royalty on retail price; offers average $4,000 (Canadian) advance. Publishes book an average of 1 year after acceptance. Simultaneous submissions OK. Computer printout submissions acceptable; prefers letter-quality to dot-matrix. SASE or SAE, IRC. Reports in 6 weeks.

Nonfiction: How-to and self-help. Subjects include Canadiana, health, nature, politics and sports. Submit outline/synopsis and sample chapters.

Recent Nonfiction Title: *Fungo Blues*, P. van Rjndt (sports).

Fiction: Adventure, historical, horror, mainstream, mystery, romance and suspense. Submit outline/synopsis and sample chapters.

Recent Fiction Title: *Murder on Ice*, by Ted Wood (mystery).

Tips: "Nonfiction backlist (how-to) or genre fiction have the best chance of selling to our firm."

MARGARET K. McELDERRY BOOKS, Atheneum Publishers, Inc., 115 5th Ave., New York NY 10003. Editor: Margaret K. McElderry. Publishes hardcover originals. Publishes 20-25 titles/year; receives 1,200-1,300 submissions annually. 8% of books from first-time authors; 75% of books from unagented writers. The average print order is 3,500 for a writer's first teen book; 7,500 for a writer's first picture book. Pays royalty on retail price. Publishes book an average of 1½ years after acceptance. Reports in 6 weeks. Computer printout submissions acceptable; no dot-matrix. SASE; ms guidelines for SASE.

Nonfiction and Fiction: Quality material for preschoolers to 16-year-olds. Looks for "originality of ideas, clarity and felicity of expression, well-organized plot (fiction) or exposition (nonfiction) quality." Reviews artwork/photos as part of ms package.

Recent Title: *Jonah and the Great Fish*, by Warwick Hutton.

Tips: "There is not a particular 'type' of book that we are interested in above others; rather, we look for superior quality in both writing and illustration." Freelance writers should be aware of the swing away from teen-age problem novels to books for young readers.

McFARLAND & COMPANY, INC., PUBLISHERS, Box 611, Jefferson NC 28640. (919)246-4460. President: Robert Franklin. Business Manager: Rhonda Herman. Publishes hardcover and "quality" paperback originals; a non-"trade" publisher. Averages 50 titles/year; receives 600 submissions annually. 70% of books from first-time authors; 98% of books from unagented writers. Average print order for a writer's first book is 1,000. Pays 10-12½% royalty on gross receipts; no advance. Publishes book an average of 14 months after acceptance. Computer printout submissions acceptable; prefers letter-quality to dot-matrix. Reports in 2 weeks. **Nonfiction:** Scholarly monographs, reference, technical and professional. Subjects include Americana, art, business, chess, drama/theatre, health, cinema/radio/TV (very strong here), history, literature, librarianship (very strong here), music, parapsychology, religion, sociology, sports/recreation, women's studies, and world affairs. "We will consider *any* scholarly book—with authorial maturity and competent grasp of subject." Reference books are particularly wanted—fresh material (i.e., not in head-to-head competition with an established title). We don't like mss of fewer than 200 double-spaced typed pages. Our market consists mainly of libraries, and a few college textbooks. Our film books make it into book clubs frequently. They are the only ones we send to bookstores." No memoirs, poetry, children's books, devotional/inspirational works or personal essays. Query or submit outline/synopsis and sample chapters. Reviews artwork/photos as part of ms package. **Recent Nonfiction Title:** *Sports Quotations*, by Andrew J. Maikovich (reference). **Tips:** "We do *not* accept novels or fiction of any kind. Don't worry about writing skills—we have editors. What we want is well-organized *knowledge* of an area in which there is not good information coverage at present, plus reliability so we don't feel we have to check absolutely everything."

McGRAW-HILL BOOK CO., College Division, 1221 Avenue of the Americas, New York NY 10020. (212)997-2271. Editorial Director: William J. Willey. Editor-in-Chief, Engineering, Math and Science: B.J. Clark. Editor-in-Chief, Social Sciences and Humanities: Philip Butcher. Editor-in-Chief, Business and Economics: Joseph Marcelle. Publishes hardcover and softcover technical material and software for the college market.
Nonfiction: The College Division publishes textbooks. The writer must know the college curriculum and course structure. Also publishes scientific texts and reference books in business and economics, computers, engineering, social sciences, physical sciences, nursing, and mathematics. Material should be scientifically and factually accurate. Most, but not all, books should be designed for existing courses offered in various disciplines of study. Books should have superior presentations and be more up-to-date than existing textbooks.

DAVID McKAY CO., INC., 2 Park Ave., New York NY 10016. Editor: James Louttit. Publishes hardcover and paperback originals. Averages 20 titles/year. "No unsolicited manuscripts or proposals considered or acknowledged."

MACMILLAN OF CANADA, Suite 685, 146 Front St. W., Toronto, Ontario M5J 1G2 Canada. Publisher: Douglas M. Gibson. Editor-in-Chief: Anne Holloway. Publishes hardcover originals and paperback reprints. Averages 25 titles/year; receives 3,000 submissions annually. 10% of books from first-time authors; 50% of books from unagented writers. 10% royalty on retail price. Publishes book an average of 1 year after acceptance. Computer printout submissions acceptable; prefers letter-quality to dot-matrix. Reports in 10 weeks. SAE and IRCs. Book catalog for SAE and IRCs.
Nonfiction: "We publish Canadian authors on all sorts of subjects and books of all sorts that are about Canada. Biography, history, art, current affairs, how-to and juveniles. Particularly looking for good topical nonfiction." Submit translations. Accepts outline/synopsis and 3, 4 or 5 sample chapters "depending on length of total manuscript." Reviews artwork/photos.
Recent Nonfiction Title: *P.Q.: Rene Levesque and the Parti Quebecois in Power*, by Graham Fraser (current affairs).
Fiction: Query.
Recent Fiction Title: *Since Daisy Creek*, by W.O. Mitchell.

MACMILLAN PUBLISHING COMPANY, 866 3rd Ave., New York NY 10022. Publishes hardcover and paperback originals and reprints. Averages 130 titles/year. Will consider juvenile submissions only. Fiction and nonfiction. Address mss to Children's Book Department. Enclose return postage.

MCPHERSON & COMPANY, Box 638, New Paltz NY 12561. Editor: Bruce McPherson. Imprints include: Treacle Press, Documentext. Publishes hardcover and paperback originals, and paperback reprints. Averages 5 titles/year; receives 400+ submissions annually. 20% of books from first-time authors; 90% of books from unagented writers. Average print order for a writer's first book is 2,000. Pays royalty. Publishes book an average of 10 months after acceptance. Computer printout submissions acceptable; no dot-matrix. No unsolicited mss—query first with SASE. Reports in 3 weeks to 2 months.
Fiction and Nonfiction: "We issue novels, anthologies, books of literary criticism, anthropology, avant garde, film studies, etc., and plan to expand into the areas of alternative lifestyle and contemporary politics." Accepts fiction translations. Sometimes reviews artwork/photos.
Recent Fiction Title: *A Transparent Tree*, by Robert Kelly.

‡*MA/AH PUBLISHING, Military Affairs and Aerospace Historian, Eisenhower Hall, Kansas State University, Manhattan KS 66506. (913)532-6733. Publications Director: Patricia Clark. Publishes trade paperback originals and trade paperback reprints. Averages 12-15 titles/year; receives 25+ submissions annually. 90% of books from first-time authors; 100% of books from unagented writers. Subsidy publishes 50% of books. Pays 10% royalty on retail price. Publishes book an average of 6 months after acceptance. Computer printout submissions acceptable; prefers letter-quality to dot-matrix. SASE. Reports in 1 week on queries; 1 month on ms. Free book catalog and ms guidelines.

Nonfiction: Biography, reference and textbook. Subjects include Americana (Western American history); and history (military, naval, American). Prefers manuscripts on military subjects: memoirs, studies of battle action, and technological advances. No undocumented studies. Query or submit outline/synopsis and sample chapters or complete ms.

Recent Nonfiction Title: *The Infantry Brigade in Combat*, by D.A. Wolf (military history—Vietnam).

Tips: "Our audience includes scholars and history buffs."

MADRONA PUBLISHERS, INC., Box 22667, Seattle WA 98122. (206)325-3973. President: Daniel J. Levant. Editorial Director: Sara Levant. Publishes hardcover and paperback originals (90%) and paperback reprints (10%). Averages 6 titles/year; receives 1,000 submissions annually. 75% of books from first-time authors; 95% of books from unagented writers. Average print order for a writer's first book is 5,000. Pays 7½-15% royalty on wholesale or retail price; offers $1,000 average advance. Publishes book an average of 1 year after acceptance. Computer printout submissions acceptable; prefers letter-quality to dot-matrix. SASE. Reports in 8 weeks.

Nonfiction: Americana, biography, cookbooks, cooking and foods, health, history, hobbies, how-to, humor, photography, politics, psychology, recreation, self-help and travel. Query, submit outline/synopsis and at least 2 sample chapters or complete ms. Accepts nonfiction and fiction translations. Reviews artwork/photos (if appropriate) as part of ms package.

Recent Nonfiction Title: *What Was Good About Today*, by Carol Kruckeberg.

‡THE MAIN STREET PRESS, William Case House, Pittstown NJ 08867. (201)735-9424. Editorial Director: Martin Greif. Publishes hardcover and trade paperback originals. Averages 20 titles/year; receives 100 submissions annually. 10% of books from first-time authors; 100% of books from unagented writers. Pays 3-15% royalty on wholesale or retail price; offers average $4,000 advance. Publishes book an average of 1 year after acceptance. Simultaneous and photocopied submissions OK. Computer printout submissions acceptable; prefers letter-quality to dot-matrix. SASE. Reports in 2 months on queries; 3 months on mss. Reviews artwork/photos. Book catalog $1.50.

Nonfiction: "Coffee table" book, how-to, illustrated book and reference. Subjects include Americana, art, cooking and foods, hobbies, travel, gardening, film, architecture, and design. "We publish *heavily illustrated* books on almost all subjects; we publish *only* illustrated books." Especially needs how-to quilting books. "We do not want to consider any nonfiction book wth fewer than 75 illustrations." Query or submit outlines/synopsis and sample chapters.

Recent Nonfiction Title: *Folk Quilts and How to Recreate Them*, by Audrey and Douglas Wiss (quilting).

Tips: "Our books are for the "carriage trade.""

*MARATHON INTERNATIONAL PUBLISHING COMPANY, INC., Dept. WM, Box 33008, Louisville KY 40232. (502)245-1566. President: Jim Wortham. Publishes hardcover originals, and trade paperback originals, trade paperback reprints. Averages 10 titles/year. Pays 10% royalty on wholesale. Publishes book an average of 10 months after acceptance. Simultaneous and photocopied submissions OK. Computer printout submissions acceptable. SASE. Reports in 1 week on queries; 2 weeks on mss. Book catalog for 6x9 SAE and 4 first class stamps.

Nonfiction: Cookbooks, how-to, self-help on business and economics, and offbeat humor. Especially needs how-to make extra money-type mss; self-improvement; how a person can be happier and more prosperous. No biography or textbooks. Query. Reviews artwork/photos as part of ms package.

Recent Nonfiction Title: *How to Make Money in Penny Stocks*, by Jim Scott (financial).

Poetry: Will consider poetry mss for subsidy publication only.

‡*MAVERICK PUBLICATIONS, Drawer 5007, Bend OR 97708. (503)382-6978. Book publisher and independent book producer/packager. Publisher: Ken Asher. Publishes hardcover and trade paperback originals. Averages 15 titles/year; 100 submissions annually. "Like every other publisher, the number of books we can publish is limited. We would like to suggest to any writer who has a timely manuscript and is having trouble getting it published to consider publishing it themselves. We will be glad to discuss this alternative with anyone who might be interested." 40% of books from first-time authors; 100% of books from unagented writers. Pays 15% royalty on net selling price. Publishes book an average of 3 months after acceptance. Simultaneous and photocopied submissions OK. Computer printout submissions acceptable; prefers letter-quality to dot-matrix. Reports in 2 weeks on queries; 3 weeks on mss. Book catalog $5. "Our book catalog is a permanent three-ring

binder. Punched full-color flyers are issued as books are published."
Nonfiction: Biography, cookbook, illustrated book, self-help and technical. Subjects include Americana, cooking and foods, health, history, hobbies, music and travel. Query.
Recent Nonfiction Title: *Sacred Cows at the Public Trough*, by Denzel and Nancy Ferguson (environmental).
Fiction: Adventure, historical, mystery and science fantasy. "We have no specific needs, but prefer stories based on facts." Submit outline/synopsis and sample chapters.
Recent Fiction Title: *Skyhawk*, by Ted Tate (mystery).
Tips: "Book publishing trends include direct marketing by independent publishers of quality material to an intelligent public. A timely, well-researched exposé of national or at least regional importance has the best chance of selling to our firm."

MCN PRESS, Box 702073, Tulsa OK 74170. (918)743-6048. Publisher: Jack Britton. Publishes hardcover and trade paperback originals. Averages 5-7 titles/year. Pays 10% royalty on wholesale or retail price; offers no advance. Computer printout submissions acceptable. SASE. Reports in 10 weeks. Free book catalog.
Nonfiction: Biography, illustrated book and reference. Subjects include history and hobbies. "Our audience includes collectors, military personnel and military fans." Submit outline/synopsis and sample chapters or complete ms.
Recent Nonfiction Title: *Medals, Military and Civilian of U.S.*, by Borthick and Britton (reference).

‡**MEADOWBROOK PRESS**, 18318 Minnetonka Blvd., Deephaven MN 55391. (612)473-5400. Senior Editor: Marge Hughes. Publishes trade paperback originals (with small print-runs of hardcover copies). Averages 8-12 titles/year. Pays variable royalty; buys some mss outright or by assigning them as works-for-hire. Simultaneous and photocopied submissions OK. SASE. Book catalog for SASE.
Nonfiction: How-to, juvenile, self-help and consumer reference. Subjects include cooking and foods; health (on dieting, nutrition); travel; parenting; consumer interest (on money-saving); children's activities. No standard cookbooks; technical books; biographies or memoirs. "We prefer a query first; then we will request an outline and/or sample material."
Recent Nonfiction Title: *Economy Motel Guide*, by The Meadowbrook Reference Group.
Tips: "Note that the majority of our books are produced in-house, *not* by authors. In addition, most of our concepts are developed by the staff."

MEDICAL ECONOMICS BOOKS, Division of Medical Economics Co., 680 Kinderkamack Rd., Oradell NJ 07649. Editor-in-Chief, Medicine & Nursing: Elizabeth A. Stueck. Editor-in-Chief, Practice & Financial Management: Reuben Barr. Publishes hardcover, paperback, and spiral bound originals. Company also publishes magazines and references for doctors, nurses, pharmacists and laboratorians. Averages 36 titles/year. Pays by individual arrangement. Publishes book an average of 11 months after acceptance. Simultaneous and photocopied submissions OK. Electronic submissions "accepted on selective basis; inquire first," but requires hard copy also. Computer printout submissions acceptable; prefers letter-quality to dot-matrix. SASE. Reports in 6 weeks. Free book catalog. Ms guidelines for SASE. Tests freelancers for rewriting, editing, and proofreading assignments.
Nonfiction: Clinical and practice-financial management references, handbooks, and manuals. Medical—primary care—all fields; obstetrics and gynecology, laboratory medicine and management. Critical care nursing. Submit table of contents and prospectus. Reviews artwork/photos as part of ms package.
Recent Nonfiction Title: *Guide to Interpreting 12-Lead ECGs*, by J. Marcus Wharton, M.D. and Nora Goldschlager, M.D.
Tips: "Our mission is to provide the practicing health care professional with high quality, clearly-written, practical and useful books." Queries/mss may be routed to other editors in the publishing group.

MED-PSYCH PUBLICATIONS, Pine Mountain Press, Inc., Box 7553, Brandenton FL 33507. Aquisitions Editor: Marilyn A. Brilliant. Publishes hardcover and paperback originals. Averages 6-8 titles/year. Pays 10% royalty on wholesale price; no advance. Publishes book an average of 2 years after acceptance. Electronic submissions OK, but requires hard copy also. Computer printout submissions acceptable. SASE. Reports in 2 months. Book catalog $1.
Nonfiction: Health, how-to psychology and self-help. "We would like to see more para-psychology, folk medicine and counseling material. We do not want any text books." Reviews artwork/photos as part of ms package. Query.
Recent Nonfiction Title: *Humor As Therapy*, by Daniel Keller, Ph.D.

‡**MEMPHIS STATE UNIVERSITY PRESS**, Memphis State University, Memphis TN 38152. (901)454-2752. Editor-in-Chief: J. Ralph Randolph. Publishes hardcover and paperback originals. Averages 5 titles/year. Each contract is subject to negotiation. Will consider photocopied submissions. No computer printout or disk submissions. Query. Accepts outline/synopsis and 2 sample chapters. Reports in 3-6 months. SASE. Free book catalog and writer's guidelines.

General Nonfiction: Regional emphasis. "We publish scholarly and trade nonfiction, books in the humanities, social sciences, and regional material. Interested in nonfiction material within the lower Mississippi River Valley. Tennessee history, and regional folklore."
Recent Nonfiction Title: *Home Place*, by Robert Drake (growing up in west Tennessee).
Tips: Considering new material on a very limited basis until 1986.

MENASHA RIDGE PRESS, INC., Rt. 3, Box 450, Hillsborough NC 27278. (919)732-6661. Managing Editor: R.W. Sehlinger. Publishes hardcover and trade paperback originals. Averages 10-15 titles/year; receives 600 submissions annually. 50% of books from first-time authors; 90% of books from unagented writers. Average print order for a writer's first book is 4,000. Pays 10% royalty on wholesale price or purchases outright; offers average $1,000 advance. Simultaneous and photocopied submissions OK. Electronic submissions OK on IBM PC/300 or 1200 Baud; sometimes requires hard copy. SASE. Reports in 1 month. Free book catalog.
Nonfiction: How-to, reference, self-help, consumer, outdoor recreation, travel guides and small business. Subjects include business and economics, health, hobbies, recreation, sports, travel and consumer advice. Especially looks for mss in small business, how-to and consumer affairs. No biography or religious copies. Submit outline/synopsis and sample chapters. Reviews artwork/photos.
Recent Nonfiction Title: *Shipwrecks: Diving the North Carolina Coast*, by Farb (scuba diving/history).
Tips: Audience: age 25-60, 14-18 years' education, white collar and professional, $22,000+ median income, 75% male, 75% east of Mississippi River.

*MERCURY HOUSE INC., Suite 700, 300 Montgomery St., San Francisco CA 94104. (415)981-1434. President: William M. Brinton. Publishes hardcover originals. Averages 6 titles/year; receives 50-60 submissions annually. 50% of books from first-time authors; 100% of books from unagented writers. Average print order for a writer's first book is 2,500. Subsidy publishes "only if there is a good market and author has something to say and can say it well." Pays standard royalties; advances negotiable. "Will consider negotiating with author who pays a percentage of cost of printing, publishing, selling book, a tax-oriented transaction." Publishes book an average of 5 months after acceptance. Simultaneous and photocopied submissions OK. Computer printout submissions acceptable; no dot-matrix. SASE. Reports in 3 weeks on queries; 6 weeks on mss.
Nonfiction: Subjects include business and economics and politics. Nonfiction needs are very limited. "We do not want to see nonfiction topics unless written by well-known author." Query with outline synopsis and sample chapters. All unsolicited mss are returned unopened.
Fiction: Political and financial world and suspense. Query with outline/synopsis and sample chapters. All unsolicited mss are returned unopened.
Recent Fiction Title: *The Alaska Deception*.
Tips: "Our audience is adult laymen and professionals. Mercury House expects to use electronic marketing of its titles through computer users, thus reducing need for wholesale distributors and increasing direct sales to end-users, i.e., the reader."

MERIWETHER PUBLISHING LTD., 885 Elkton Dr., Colorado Springs CO 80907. (303)594-4422. Editor/President: Arthur L. Zapel. Publishes trade paperback originals and reprints. Averages 30-50 titles/year; receives 350 submissions annually. 85% of books from first-time authors; 95% of books from unagented writers. Pays 10% royalty on wholesale or retail prices or outright purchase. Publishes books an average of 6 months after acceptance. Simultaneous and photocopied submissions OK. Reports in 3 weeks on queries; 2 months on mss. Book catalog for 8½x11 SAE and 75¢ postage. Ms guidelines for either $1 or SASE.
Nonfiction: How-to, self-help, textbook and one-act plays. Subjects include religion, speech, drama and English. "We specialize in books dealing with the communication arts: drama, speech, theatre, English, etc. Also we publish how-to books for youth activities." No cookbooks, philosophy, sociology, etc. Query. Reviews artwork/photos. "We occasionally make work-for-hire assignments; usually only with writers we have published before."
Recent Nonfiction Titles: *Theatre Games for Young Performers*, by Maria C. Novelly.
Fiction: Religious plays or comedy one-act plays or comedy musicals.
Tips: "We cater to the educational, church and youth market. Most of our books are sold to teachers or church leaders in youth activity."

CHARLES E. MERRILL PUBLISHING CO., a Bell & Howell Co., 1300 Alum Creek Dr., Columbus OH 43216. (614)890-1111. Publishes hardcover and paperback originals and software. Averages 400 titles/year. "Royalties and contract terms vary with the nature of the material. They are very competitive within each market area. Some projects are handled on an outright purchase basis." Will accept simultaneous submissions if notified. Computer printout submissions acceptable; prefers letter-quality to dot-matrix. SASE. Submit outline/synopsis and 3 sample chapters. Reports in 1-3 months.
Education Division: Editor-in-Chief: Ann Turpie. Publishes texts, workbooks, software, and other suplementary materials for elementary, junior high and high schools in all subject areas, primarily language arts and lit-

erature, mathematics, science and social studies (no juvenile stories or novels). Bilingual materials (Spanish) are also published for mathamatics and science. Reviews artwork/photos.

College Division: Editor-in-Chief, Education, Special Education and Humanities, Business, Mathematics, Science and Technology: Franklin Lewis. Publishes college texts and related materials. Reviews artwork/photos.

METAMORPHOUS PRESS, Subsidiary of Metamorphosis, Inc., 7 Mt. Jefferson Terrace, Box 1712, Lake Oswego OR 97034. (503)635-6709. Editor: Victor Roberge. Publishes hardcover, trade paperback originals and hardcover and trade paperback reprints. Averages 6-8 titles/year; receives 600 submissions annually. 100% of books from first-time authors; 100% of books from unagented writers. Average print order for a writer's first book is 2,000-5,000. Pays minimum 10% profit split on wholesale prices. No advance. Publishes book an average of 8 months after acceptance. Simultaneous and photocopied submissions OK. Electronic submissions OK, but requires hard copy also. Computer printout submissions acceptable; prefers letter-quality to dot-matrix. SASE. Free book catalog; ms guidelines for SASE.

Nonfiction: Biography, how-to, illustrated book, reference, self-help, technical and textbook—all related to behavioral science and personal growth. Subjects include business and sales, health, psychology, sociology, education, children's books, science and new ideas in behavioral science. "We are interested in any well-proven new idea or philosophy in the behavioral science areas. Our primary editorial screen is 'will this book further define, explain or support the concept that we create our reality literally or assist people in gaining control of their lives.' " Submit idea, outline, and table of contents only. Reviews artwork/photos as part of ms package.

Recent Nonfiction Title: *Alchemy of Intelligence*, by Warren Doheman (mind and education).

‡***MEYERBOOKS, PUBLISHER**, Box 427, Glenwood IL 60425. (312)757-4950. Publisher: David Meyer. Publishes hardcover and trade paperback originals and hardcover and trade paperback reprints. Averages 3 titles/year; receives 1-5 submissions annually. 25% of books from first-time authors; 100% of books from unagented writers. Subsidy publishes 25% of all books. "Subject matter and intended audience determine whether an author should be subsidy published. If we cannot correctly identify the market for the subject, but the author can, we consider this kind of project suitable for subsidy treatment." Pays 5-10% royalty, on wholesale price or retail price. Makes outright purchase for minimum $500. Offers average $250 advance. Publishes book an average of 12 months after acceptance. Simultaneous and photocopied submissions OK. Computer printout submissions acceptable; prefers letter-quality to dot-matrix. SASE. Reports in 1 month on queries; 6 months on mss. Book catalog for #10 SASE and 1 first class stamp.

Nonfiction: Cookbook, reference and self-help. Subjects include Americana, cooking and foods, health (natural healing), history (theatre), hobbies (magic) and nature. "We publish books for limited, specialized markets." Books have been contracted on herbal aphrodisiacs, the history of Mormon printng in Navoo, Illinois, a bibliography of Illinois imprints, and a monograph on stage magic history. "No technical book, esoteric subjects, or books which might be better published by large New York publishers." Query or submit outline/synopsis and sample chapters. Reviews artwork/photos.

Recent Nonfiction Title: *American Folk Medicine*, by Clarence Meyer (health).

Tips: "Choose carefully the subject you intend to spend a year or more of your time and effort in completing. Consider whether your book project realistically has an audience sufficient enough to warrant publication and satisfactory sales. You might convince yourself that a slapdash manuscript or an obscure subject will be of interest to people, but you must convince more than yourself—you must convince a publisher."

‡**THE MGI MANAGEMENT INSTITUTE, INC.**, 378 Halstead Ave., Harrison NY 10528. (914)835-5790. President: Dr. Henry Oppenheimer. Averages 15 titles/year. 50% of books from first-time authors; 100% of those books from unagented writers. Pays 3-5% royalty on retail price (price is usually in $100 range). Publishes book an average of 3 months after acceptance. Electronic submissions OK on IBM PC, Wordstar, but requires hard copy also. Computer printout submissions acceptable. Reports in 2 weeks. Free book catalog.

Nonfiction: How-to, technical and correspondence courses. Subjects include business and economics, electrical engineering, computer, and manufacturing-related topics. Needs correspondence courses in manufacturing management, computers, artificial intelligence and marketing professional services. All nonfiction must relate to architecture, engineering or manufacturing. Query. Reviews artwork/photos.

Recent Nonfiction Title: *Shop Floor Control*, by W. Wassweiler (correspondence course).

Tips: Our audience includes graduate engineers and architects, manufacturing supervisors and managers, and real estate investors.

MICROTREND, BOOKS, (formerly Microtrend, Inc.), Slawson Communications, Inc., 3719 6th Ave., San Diego CA 92103. (619)291-9126. Publishes trade paperback originals and software. Averages 12 titles/year; receives 100 submissions annually. 10% of books from first-time authors; 20% of books from unagented writers. Average print order for a writer's first book is 5,000-50,000. Pays 10-20% royalty on wholesale price. Offers variable advance. Publishes book an average of 6 months after acceptance. Simultaneous and photocopied submissions OK. Electronic submissions OK via MSDOS with Word Star, but requires hard copy also. Computer printout submissions acceptable; prefers letter-quality to dot-matrix. SASE. Reports in 2 weeks on queries; 1 month on mss. Ms guidelines for SASE.

Nonfiction: How-to, self-help, and technical—only microcomputer subjects. Query. Reviews artwork/photos as part of ms package.

Recent Nonfiction Title: *How to Use Radio Shack Printers*, by William Barden.

‡**MILADY PUBLISHING CORPORATION**, Subsidiary of MPC Educational Publishers, 3839 White Plains Rd., Bronx NY 10467. (212)881-3000. President: Thomas R. Severance. Publishes technical books, particularly for occupational education. Averages 10 titles/year; receives 12 submissions annually. 25% of books from first-time authors; 100% of books from unagented writers. Pays 8-12% royalty on wholesale price. Offers average $750 advance. Publishes book an average of 1 year after acceptance. Photocopied submissions OK. Computer printout submissions acceptable; prefers letter-quality to dot-matrix. SASE. Reports in 6 weeks. Book catalog for $1.

Nonfiction: How-to, reference, textbook, workbooks and exam reviews on occupational education. No academic. Query or submit outline/synopsis and sample chapters. Reviews artwork/photos.

Recent Nonfiction Titles: *Office Procedures and Technology*, by Moon (text).

Tips: "Our audience is vocational students."

MILLER BOOKS, 2908 W. Valley Blvd., Alhambra CA 91803. (213)284-7607. Subsidiaries include *San Gabriel Valley Magazine*, Miller Press and Miller Electric. Publisher: Joseph Miller. Publishes hardcover and trade paperback originals, hardcover reprints and software. Averages 4 titles/year. Pays 10-15% royalty on retail price; buys some mss outright. Simultaneous and photocopied submissions OK. Computer printout submissions acceptable. SASE ("no returns on erotic material"). Reports in 2 weeks on queries; 2 months on mss. Free book catalog.

Nonfiction: Cookbook, how-to, self-help, textbook and remedial textbooks. Subjects include Americana, animals, cooking and foods, history, philosophy and politics. "Remedial manuscripts are needed in most fields." No erotica. Submit complete ms. Reviews artwork/photos as part of ms package. "Please don't send letters. Let us see your work."

Recent Nonfiction Title: *Every Feeling is Desire*, by James Smith, M.D.

Fiction: Adventure, historical, humor, mystery and western. No erotica. Submit complete ms.

Recent Fiction Title: *The Magic Story*, by F.V.R. Dey (positive thinking).

Tips: "Write something good about people, places and our country. Avoid the negative—it doesn't sell."

MOON PUBLICATIONS, Box 1696, Chico CA 95927. (916)345-5473/345-5413. Editors: Deke Castleman and Mark Morris. Publishes trade paperback originals. Averages 3 titles/year. Pays 10% royalty on retail price; offers average $700-1,500 advance. Publishes book an average of 1 year after acceptance. Photocopied and electronic submissions OK on CPM, TRS DOS, but requires hard copy also. Computer printout submissions acceptable. SASE. Reports in 3 weeks. Book catalog 39¢ postage; ms guidelines for SASE.

Nonfiction: Travel guidebook titles. Subjects include recreation and travel. "We will consider any guidebook, on virtually any country or travel destination area in the world. We specialize in Asia and the Pacific. Writers should first write for a copy of our guidelines. No travelogue super-subjective or 'narrative' travel writing." Query with outline/synopsis, table of contents, and sample chapters. Reviews artwork/photos.

Recent Nonfiction Title: *Finding Fiji*, by David Stanley (guidebook).

Tips: "Our books are for the general public. We find all socio-economic classes buying them. They are aimed for the independent, budget-minded, do-it-yourself traveler but appeal to all travelers because they are the comprehensive guides to the areas they cover."

MOREHOUSE-BARLOW CO., INC., 78 Danbury Rd., Wilton CT 06897. Editorial Director: Stephen S. Wilburn. Publishes hardcover and paperback originals. Averages 20 titles/year. Pays 10% royalty on retail price. Publishes book an average of 8 months after acceptance. Computer printout submissions acceptable; prefers letter-quality to dot-matrix. SASE.

Nonfiction: Specializes in Anglican religious publishing. Theology, ethics, church history, pastoral counseling, liturgy and religious education. Accepts outline/synopsis and 2-4 sample chapters. No poetry or drama. Reviews artwork/photos as part of ms package.

Recent Nonfiction Title: *The Killing, Suffering, Sex, and Other Paradoxes*.

WILLIAM MORROW AND CO., 105 Madison Ave., New York NY 10016. Publisher: Sherry W. Arden. Imprints include Greenwillow Books (juveniles), Susan Hirschman, editor. Lothrop, Lee and Shepard (juveniles), Dorothy Briley, editor. Morrow Junior Books (juveniles), David Reuther, editor. Quill (trade paperback), Allison Brown-Cerier, Managing Editor. Affiliates include Hearst Books (trade). Editorial Director: Joan Nagy. Hearst Marine Books (nautical). Publisher: Paul Larsen. Beech Tree Books, James D. Landis, Publisher. Receives 10,000 submissions annually. 30% of books from first-time authors; 5% of books from unagented writers. Payment is on standard royalty basis. Publishes book an average of 1-2 years after

acceptance; prefers letter-quality to dot-matrix. Query letter on all books. No unsolicited mss or proposals. Mss and proposals should be submitted through a literary agent. Computer printout submissions acceptable.
Nonfiction and Fiction: Publishes adult fiction, nonfiction, history, biography, arts, religion, poetry, how-to books and cookbooks. Length: 50,000-100,000 words.
Recent Fiction Title: *If Tomorrow Comes*, by Sidney Sheldon.

MORROW JUNIOR BOOKS, 105 Madison Ave., New York NY 10016. (212)889-3050. Editor-in-Chief: David L. Reuther. Senior Editors: Pamela Pollack and Andrea Curley. Publishes hardcover originals. Publishes 50 titles/year. All contracts negotiated separately; offers variable advance. Computer printout submissions acceptable; prefers letter-quality to dot-matrix. SASE. Reports in 6 weeks. Free book catalog.
Nonfiction: Juveniles (trade books). No textbooks. Query. Reviews artwork/photos as part of ms package.
Fiction: Juveniles (trade books).

MOSAIC PRESS MINIATURE BOOKS, 358 Oliver Rd., Cincinnati OH 45215. (513)761-5977. Publisher: Miriam Irwin. Publishes hardcover originals. Averages 11 titles/year; receives 150-200 submissions annually. 49% of books from first-time authors. Average print order for a writer's first book is 2,000. Buys mss outright for $50. Publishes book an average of 30 months after acceptance. Computer printout submissions acceptable; no dot-matrix. SASE. Reports in 2 weeks; "but our production, if manuscript is accepted, often takes 2 or 3 years." Book catalog $3.
Nonfiction: Biography, cookbook, humor, illustrated book and satire. Subjects include Americana, animals, art, business and economics, cooking and foods, health, history, hobbies, music, nature, sports and travel. Interested in "beautifully written, delightful text. If factual, it must be extremely correct and authoritative. Our books are intended to delight, both in their miniature size, beautiful bindings and excellent writing." No occult, pornography, science fiction, fantasy, haiku, or how-to. Query or submit outline/synopsis and sample chapters or complete ms. Reviews artwork/photos as part of ms package.
Recent Nonfiction Title: *Musical Boxes*, by Mark Palkovic.
Tips: Factual—Freelancer has best chance of selling a factual ms; "I want a book to tell me something I don't know."

MOTORBOOKS INTERNATIONAL PUBLISHERS & WHOLESALERS, INC., Box 2, Osceola WI 54020. Director of Publications: William F. Kosfeld. Senior Editor: Barbara K. Harold. Hardcover and paperback originals. Averages 10-12 titles/year. 100% of books from unagented writers. Offers 7-15% royalty on wholesale or retail price. Offers average $1,500 advance. Publishes book an average of 7-10 months after acceptance. Simultaneous and photocopied submissions OK. Electronic submissions OK, but requires hard copy also. Computer printout submissions acceptable; prefers letter-quality to dot-matrix. Reports in 2-3 months. SASE. Free book catalog. Ms guidelines for SASE.
Nonfiction: Publishes biography, history, how-to, photography, and motor sports as they relate to cars, trucks, motorcycles, motor sports and aviation (domestic and foreign). No repair manuals. Submit outline/synopsis, 1-2 sample chapters and sample of illustrations. "State qualifications for doing book." Reviews artwork/photos as part of ms package. Accepts nonfiction translations from German/Italian.
Recent Nonfiction Title: *The Harley-Davidson Motor Company*, by David Wright.
Tips: "Trends in book publishing that freelance writers should be aware of include higher trade discounts resulting in less total royalties."

MOTT MEDIA, INC., PUBLISHERS, 1000 E. Huron, Milford MI 48042. Senior Editor: Leonard George Goss. Associated with Evangelical Book Club. Hardcover and paperback originals (90%) and paperback reprints (10%). Averages 20-25 titles/year; receives 300 submissions annually. 25% of books from first-time authors; 90% of books from unagented writers. Average print order for a writer's first book is 3,500-5,000. Pays variable royalty on retail, depending on type of book. Publishes book an average of 10 months after acceptance. Computer printout submissions acceptable. Reports in 1 month. SASE. Free book catalog; ms guidelines for SASE.
Nonfiction: Specializes in religious books, including trade and Christian school textbooks.Publishes Americana (religious slant); biography (for juveniles on famous Christians, adventure-filled; for adults on Christian people, scholarly, new slant for marketing); how-to (for pastors, Christian laymen); juvenile (biographies, 30,000-40,000 words); politics (conservative, Christian approach); religious (conservative Christian); self-help (religious); and textbooks (all levels from a Christian perspective, all subject fields). No preschool materials. Main emphasis of all mss must be religious. Wants to know "vocation, present position and education of author; brief description of the contents of the book; basic readership for which the manuscript was written; brief explanation of why the manuscript differs from other books on the same subject; the author's interpretation of the significance of this manuscript." Query or submit outline/synopsis and sample chapters. Reports in 1 month.
Recent Nonfiction Title: *The Christian Legal Advisor*, by John Eidsmoe.
Fiction: "We're beginning to consider a limited amount of fiction for the Christian consumer. No overt moral or crisis decision necessary, but fiction must demonstrate a Christian perspective."

*MOUNTAIN PRESS PUBLISHING CO., 1600 North Ave. W, Missoula MT 59806. Publisher: David P. Flaccus. Hardcover and paperback originals (90%) and reprints (10%). Averages 12 titles/year; receives 60 submissions annually. 50% of books from first-time authors; 90% of books from unagented writers. Average print order for a writer's first book is 3,000-5,000. Royalty of 12% of net amount received; no advance. Subsidy publishes less than 5% of books. "Top-quality work in very limited market only." Publishes book an average of 6 months after acceptance. Computer printout submissions acceptable. Reports in 2-4 weeks. SASE. Free book catalog.

Nonfiction: Publishes history (western Americana); hobbies; how-to (angling, hunting); nature (geology, habitat and conservation); outdoor recreation (backpacking, fishing, etc.); technical (wood design and technology); and textbooks. Looks for "target audience, organization, quality of writing and style compatibility with current list and goals." Accepts nonfiction translations. State availability of photos and/or illustrations to accompany ms. Reviews artwork/photos as part of ms package.

Recent Nonfiction Title: *The Baron, the Logger, the Miner and Me,* (western Americana).

THE MOUNTAINEERS BOOKS, 306-2nd Ave W., Seattle WA 98119. (206)285-2665. Manager: Donna DeShazo. Publishes hardcover and trade paperback originals (85%) and reprints (15%). Averages 10-15 titles/year; receives 150-250 submissions annually. 25-30% of books from first-time authors; 98% of books from unagented writers. Average print order for a writer's first book is 2,000-5,000. Offers 17½% royalty based on net sales. Offers advance on occasion. Publishes book an average of 1 year after acceptance. Dot-matrix submissions are acceptable with new ribbon and double spaced. SASE. Reports in 6-8 weeks. Free book catalog and ms guidelines for SASE.

Nonfiction: Recreation, non-competitive sports, and outdoor how-to books. "We specialize only in books dealing with mountaineering, hiking, backpacking, skiing, snowshoeing, canoeing, bicycling, etc. These can be either how-to-do-it, where-to-do-it (guidebooks), or accounts of mountain-related experiences." Does *not* want to see "anything dealing with hunting, fishing or motorized travel." Submit outline/synopsis and minimum of 2 sample chapters. Accepts nonfiction translations. Looks for "expert knowledge, good organization."

Recent Nonfiction Title: *Trekking in Nepal*, by Stephen Bezruchka (guidebook).

Fiction: "We might consider an exceptionally well-done book-length manuscript on mountaineering." Does *not* want poetry or mystery. Query first.

Tips: "The type of book the writer has the best chance of selling our firm is an authoritative guidebook (*in our field*) to a specific area not otherwise covered; a first-person narrative of outdoor adventure otherwise unduplicated in print."

JOHN MUIR PUBLICATIONS, Box 613, Santa Fe NM 87501. (505)982-4078. Project Co-ordinator: Lisa Cron. Publishes trade paperback originals. Averages 6 titles/year; receives 300-500 submissions annually. 50% of books from first-time authors; 90% of books from unagented writers. Average print order for a writer's first book is 7,500-10,000. Pays 7-9% royalty; offers variable advance. Publishes book an average of 1 year after acceptance. Simultaneous and photocopied submissions OK. Computer printout submissions acceptable; no dot-matrix. SASE. Reports in 1 month on queries; 2 months on mss. Free book catalog.

Nonfiction: How-to, illustrated book, general nonfiction and humor. Subjects include automobile repair manuals, general nonfiction, and travel. "We are interested in manuscripts written with warmth, wit, humor and accuracy. The topic of such a submission is open. We're particularly interested in manuscripts pertaining to automobile repair and maintenance. We don't publish theory books or political treatises or books like 'The History of Tennis Memorabilia'; topics must either have a practical application or be of current interest." Submit outline/synopsis and at least 3 sample chapters. Reviews artwork/photos as part of ms package.

Recent Nonfiction Title: *Road & Track's Used Car Classics*, edited by Peter Bohr.

Tips: *Please* take a look at our books before submitting a manuscript. It is friendliness and humor that set our books apart. Also we often get queries for 'the children's book editor' or 'the poetry editor' when a bit of research would reveal we publish neither children's nor poetry books."

‡MULTNOMAH PRESS, 10209 SE Division St., Portland OR 97220. (503)257-0526. Associate Editor: Margaret Norton. Publishes hardcover and trade paperback originals, and trade paperback reprints. Averages 40 titles/year; receives 500 submissions annually. 30% of books from first-time authors; 100% of books from unagented writers. Pays royalty on wholesale price. Publishes books an average of 9 months after acceptance. Photocopied submissions OK. Electronic submissions OK on MSDOS or PCDOS compatible, but requires hard copy also. Computer printout submissions acceptable; no dot-matrix. SASE. Reports in 6 weeks on queries; 10 weeks on mss. Free book catalog; ms guidelines for SASE.

Nonfiction: "Coffee table" book and self-help. Subjects include religion. "We publish issue-related books linking social/ethical concerns and Christianity; books addressing the needs of women from a Christian point of view; books addressing the needs of the traditional family in today's society; and books explaining Christian theology in a very popular way to a lay audience." No daily devotional, personal experience, Scripture/photo combinations or poetry. Submit outline/synopsis and sample chapters. Reviews artwork/photos.

Recent Nonfiction Title: *Christian Mindset in a Secular Society*, by Carl F. H. Henry (Christian social-ethical).

Tips: "We are looking for well-developed, researched and documented books addressing a critical issue from a theologically conservative point of view. We have a reputation for tackling tough issues from a Biblical view; we need to continue to deserve that reputation. Avoid being too scholarly or detached. Although we like well-researched books, we do direct our books to a popular market, not just to professors of theology."

MUSEUM OF NEW MEXICO PRESS, Box 2087, Santa Fe NM 87503. (505)827-6454. Director: James Mafchir. Editor-in-Chief: Sarah Nestor. Hardcover and paperback originals (90%) and reprints (10%). Averages 4-6 titles/year; receives 100 submissions annually. 50% of books from first-time authors; 75% of books from unagented writers. Average print order for a writer's first book is 2,000-5,000. Royalty of 10% of list after first 1,000 copies; no advance. Publishes book an average of 1 year after acceptance. Computer printout submissions acceptable; no dot-matrix. Reports in 1-2 months. SASE. Free book catalog.

Nonfiction: "We publish both popular and scholarly books on regional anthropology, history, fine and folk arts; geography, natural history, the Americas and the Southwest; regional cookbooks; art, biography (regional and Southwest); music; nature; reference, scientific and technical." Accepts nonfiction translations. Prints preferred for illustrations; transparencies best for color. Sources of photos or illustrations should be indicated for each. Query or submit outline/synopsis and sample chapters to Sarah Neston, Editor-in-Chief. Mss should be typed double-spaced, follow Chicago *Manual of Style*, and be accompanied by information about the author's credentials and professional background. Reviews artwork/photos as part of ms package.

MUSEUM OF NORTHERN ARIZONA PRESS, Box 720, Rt. 4, Flagstaff AZ 86001. (602)774-5211. Publisher: Eugenia M. Horstman. Publishes hardcover and trade paperback originals. Averages 6-8 titles/year. Pays one-time fee on acceptance of ms. No advance. Queries only. No computer printout or disk submissions. SASE. Reports in 1 month. Free catalog.

Nonfiction: Coffee table book, reference, technical on Southwest, art, nature, science. Especially needs ms "relating directly to the culture and history of the Colorado Plateau for people interested in the Southwest—science, the arts and culture." Query or submit outline/synopsis and 3-4 sample chapters. Accepts artwork/photos.

Recent Nonfiction Title: *Images on Stone* (rock art).

MUSIC SALES CORP., 24 E. 22nd St., New York NY 10010. (212)254-2100. Imprints include Acorn, Amsco, Anfor, Ariel, Award, Consolidated, Embassy, Oak, Yorktown, Music Sales Ltd., London: Wise Pub., Ashdown Ltd., and Music Sales, Australia. Editor-in-Chief: Eugene Weintraub. President (NY office): Barry Edward. Publishes paperback originals (95%) and reprints (5%). Publishes 75 titles/year. Standard publishing contracts. Simultaneous and photocopied submissions OK.

Nonfiction: Instructional music books; also technical, theory, reference and pop music personalities. Music Sales Corporation publishes and distributes a complete line of quality music instruction books for every musician from beginner to professional.

Recent Nonfiction Title: *The Complete Piano Player*, (series of books from beginner to advanced), by Kenneth Baker.

‡**MUSTANG PUBLISHING CO.**, Box 9327, New Haven CT 06533. (203)624-5485. President: Rollin Riggs. Publishes hardcover and trade paperback originals. Averages 4 titles/year; receives 100 submissions annually. 50% of books from first-time authors; 100% of books from unagented writers. Pays 7-10% royalty on retail price. Publishes book an average of 1 year after acceptance. Simultaneous and photocopied submissions OK. No electronic submissions. Computer printout submissions acceptable; prefers letter-quality to dot-matrix. SASE. Reports in 1 month. Book catalog available from our distributor: Kampmann & Company, 9 E. 40th St., New York NY 10016.

Nonfiction: How-to, humor and self-help. Subjects include Americana, hobbies, recreation, sports and travel. "Our needs are very general—humor, travel, etc.—for 18 to 35-year-old market." Query or submit outline/synopsis and sample chapters.

Recent Nonfiction Title: *Europe: Where the Fun Is*, by Jacobsen and Riggs (travel guide).

Tips: "If it's clever, interesting and marketable, I'll take a look at it."

THE NAIAD PRESS, INC., Box 10543, Tallahassee FL 32302. (904)539-9322. Editorial Director: Barbara Grier. Publishes paperback originals. Averages 12 titles/year; receives 255 submissions annually. 20% of books from first-time authors; 99% of books from unagented writers. Average print order for a writer's first book is 12,000. Pays 15% royalty on wholesale or retail price; no advance. Publishes book an average of 8-12 months after acceptance. Reports in 2 months. SASE. Book catalog and ms guidelines for SAE and 39¢ postage..

Fiction: "We publish lesbian fiction, preferably lesbian/feminist fiction. We are not impressed with the 'oh woe' school and prefer realistic (i.e., happy) novels." Query. "We emphasize fiction and are now heavily

reading manuscripts in that area. We are working in a lot of genre fiction—mysteries, science fiction, short stories, fantasy—all with lesbian themes, of course."
Recent Fiction Title: *The Swashbuckler*, by Lee Lynch.

NATIONAL BOOK COMPANY, 333 SW Park Ave., Portland OR 97205-3784. (503)228-6345. Imprints include Halcyon House. Editorial Director: Carl W. Salser. Senior Editor: John R. Kimmel. Manager of Copyrights: Lucille Fry. Publishes hardcover and paperback originals (95%), paperback reprints (2%), and software. Averages 28 titles/year. Pays 5-15% royalty on wholesale or retail price; no advance. Publishes book an average of 1 year after acceptance. Computer printout submissions acceptable. SASE. Reports in 2 months. Free catalog for 9"x12" SAE with 2 first class stamps.
Nonfiction: Only materials suitable for educational uses in all categories. Art, business/economics, health, history, music, politics, psychology, reference, science, technical and textbooks. "The vast majority of titles are individualized instruction/Mastery Learning programs for educational consumers. Prospective authors should be aware of this and be prepared for this type of format, although content, style and appropriateness of subject matter are the major criteria by which submissions are judged. We are most interested in materials in the areas of the language arts, social studies and the sciences." Query, submit outline/synopsis and 2-5 sample chapters or complete ms. Reviews artwork/photos as part of ms package.
Recent Nonfiction Title: *Biology Dictionary*, by Dr. R.B. St. Pierre.

THE NATIONAL GALLERY OF CANADA, Publications Division, Ottawa, Ontario K1A 0M8 Canada. (613)990-0540. Head: Peter L. Smith. Publishes hardcover and paperback originals. Averages 15 titles/year. Pays in outright purchase of $1,500-2,500; offers averages $700 advance. Photocopied submissions OK. Reports in 3 months. SASE. Free sales catalog.
Nonfiction: "In general, we publish only *solicited* manuscripts on art, particularly Canadian art, and must publish them in English and French. Exhibition catalogs are commissioned, but we are open (upon approval by Curatorial general editors) to manuscripts for the various series, monographic and otherwise, that we publish. All manuscripts should be directed to our Editorial Coordinator, who doubles as manuscript editor. Since we publish translations into French, authors have access to French Canada and the rest of Francophonia. Because our titles are distributed by University of Chicago Press, authors have the attention of European as well as American markets."
Recent Nonfiction Title: *Eugéne Atget*, by James Borcoman.

‡*NATIONAL LITERARY GUILD, Suite 204, 210 N. Pass Ave., Burbank CA 91505. (818)845-2680. Contact: Chuck Colburn in the Acquisitions Department. Publishes hardcover and trade paperback originals. Averages 15 titles/year; receives approximately 500 submissions annually. Cooperatively publishes 60% of books. 80% of books from first-time authors; 90% of books from unagented writers. "We are not a subsidy publisher; we are a cooperative. If we accept a book on that basis, we invest in the book as much as the author. If our acquisition editor recommends we publish an unpublished author, we determine our budget and submit a contract to the author asking for approximately 50% of the funding to publish the book." Pays 10-25% royalty on retail price; offers no advances on trade contract. Publishes books an average of 1 year after acceptance. Simultaneous submissions OK. Computer printout submissions acceptable; no dot-matrix. SASE. Reports in 1 week; queries. Book catalog and ms guidelines for 8½x11 SAE and 3 first class stamps.
Nonfiction: Biography, "coffee table" book, cookbook, how-to and self-help. Subjects include cooking and foods, and religion. No political books. Submit complete ms. Reviews artwork/photos.
Recent Nonfiction Titles: *Clinker Islands*, by Lillian Otterman.
Fiction: Adventure, confession, fantasy, humor, mystery, religious, science fiction and suspense. No pornography. Submit complete ms.
Recent Fiction Title: *Courthouse*, by Senator Glen M. Stadler.
Tips: "If I were a writer trying to market a book today, I would find a good public relations firm to make the author highly visible to all media. Book publishing is a strong guessing game with unpublished authors. We have had books which we weren't sure of sell well and ones which we thought were sure sales go flop on the market. Public relations seem to be the big factor. How-to books sell well."

‡NATIONAL PRESS, INC., 7508 Wisconsin Ave., Bethesda MD 20814. (301)657-1616. Publisher: Joel D. Joseph. Publishes hardcover and trade paperback originals, and hardcover and trade paperback reprints and software. Averages 10-12 titles/year. 50% of books from first-time authors; 80% of books from unagented writers. Pays 5-15% royalty on retail price. Offers variable advance. Publishes book an average of 9 months after acceptance. Computer printout submissions acceptable; prefers letter-quality to dot-matrix. Simultaneous and photocopied submissions OK. SASE. Reports in 1 month. Free book catalog.
Nonfiction: Consumer guides, cookbook, how-to, humor, illustrated book, juvenile, reference and self-help. Subjects include Americana, animals, business and economics, cooking and foods, health, recreation, sports and travel. Query and/or submit outline/synopsis and sample chapters.
Recent Nonfiction Titles: *Handbook of Employee's Rights*, by Joel Joseph (how-to).

NATIONAL TEXTBOOK CO., 4255 W. Touhy Ave., Lincolnwood IL 60646-1975. (312)679-5500. Editorial Director: Leonard I. Fiddle. Publishes softcover originals for education and trade market, and software. Averages 20-30 titles/year; receives 200 w submissions annually. 10% of books from first-time authors; 80% of books from unagented writers. Mss purchased on either royalty or buy-out basis. Publishes book an average of 6-12 months after acceptance. Computer printout submissions acceptable; no dot-matrix. Enclose return postage. Book catalog and writer's guidelines for SAE and 2 first class stamps. Send sample chapter and outline or contents. Reports in 4 months.
Nonfiction: Textbook. Major emphasis being given to foreign language and language arts areas, especially secondary level material. Gay E. Menges, Language Arts Editor. Michael Ross, Foreign language and ESL. Barbara Wood Donner, Career Guidance.
Recent Nonfiction Title: *Building Real Life English Skills*, by Penn and Storkey (survival reading and writing).

NATUREGRAPH PUBLISHERS, INC., Box 1075, Happy Camp CA 96039. (916)493-5353. Editor: Barbara Brown. Quality trade books. Averages 5 titles/year; receives 200 submissions annually. 75% of books from first-time authors; 100% of books from unagented writers. Average print order for a writer's first book is 2,500. "We offer 10% of wholesale; 12½% after 10,000 copies are sold. To speed things up, queries should include: 1) summary, 2) detailed outline, 3) comparison to related books, 4) 2 sample chapters, 5) availability and samples of any photos or illustrations, and 6)author background. Send manuscript only on request." Publishes book an average of 18 months after acceptance. Photocopied submissions OK. Computer printout submissions acceptable; prefers letter-quality to dot-matrix. Reports in 1-2 months. SASE. Free book catalog; ms guidelines for SASE.
Nonfiction: Primarily publishes nonfiction for the layman in 7 general areas: natural history (biology, geology, ecology, astronomy); American Indian (historical and contemporary); outdoor living (backpacking, wild edibles, etc.); land and gardening (modern homesteading); crafts and how-to; holistic health (natural foods and healing arts); and PRISM Editions (Baha'i and other new age approaches to harmonious living). All material must be well-grounded; author must be professional, and in command of effective style. Our natural history and American Indian lines can be geared for educational markets." Reviews artwork/photos.
Recent Nonfiction Title: *Oaks of North America*, by Miller and Lamb.

NAVAL INSTITUTE PRESS, Annapolis MD 21402. Acquisitions Editors: Richard R. Hobbs, and Deborah Guberti. Press Director: Thomas F. Epley. Averages 30 titles/year; receives 100 submissions annually. 40% of books from first-time authors; 99% of books from unagented writers. Average print order for a writer's first book is 3,000. Pays 14-18-21% royalty based on net sales; modest advance. Publishes book an average of 1 year after acceptance. Computer printout submissions acceptable; no dot-matrix. SASE. Reports in 2 weeks (queries); 6 weeks (others). Free book catalog; ms guidelines for SASE.
Nonfiction: "We are interested in naval and maritime subjects: tactics, strategy, navigation, naval history, biographies of naval leaders and naval aviation." Reviews a selection of artwork/photos as part of ms package.
Fiction: Limited, very high quality fiction on naval and maritime themes.
Recent Title: *The Hunt for Red October*, by Tom Clancy.

NC PRESS, 31 Portland St., Toronto, Ontario M5V 2V9 Canada. (416)593-6284. Editorial Director: Caroline Walker. Publishes hardcover and paperback originals and reprints and a full line of children's books. Averages 10-15 titles/year; receives 500 submissions annually. 50% of books from first-time authors; 80% of books from unagented writers. Average print order for a writer's first book is 2,500. Pays royalty on list under 50% discount. Electronic submissions OK on IBM PC, CP/M 8" diskettes, but requires hard copy also. Computer printout submissions acceptable. SASE (Canadian) IRCs. Ms guidelines for SASE.
Nonfiction: "We generally publish books of social/political relevance either on contemporary topics of concern (current events, ecology, etc.), or historical studies and popular health books. We publish primarily Canadiana. Cannot publish U.S. authors without U.S. co-publisher." Accepts nonfiction translations from French. Submit outline/synopsis and 1-2 sample chapters.
Recent Nonfiction Title: *Choice Cooking*, by The Canadian Diabetes Association.

THOMAS NELSON PUBLISHERS, Nelson Place at Elm Hill Pike, Nashville TN 37214. (615)889-9000. Editorial Director: Bruce A. Nygren. Publishes hardcover and paperback originals and reprints. Averages 125 titles/year. Pays royalty or by outright purchase; sometimes in advance. Publishes book an average of 1 year after acceptance. Computer printout submissions acceptable. SASE. Reports in 8 weeks. Book catalog for SASE.
Nonfiction: Reference, academic, archeology, and religious—adult and children's (must be orthodox Christian in theology). Accepts outline/synopsis and 3 sample chapters. Reviews artwork/photos as part of ms package.
Recent Nonfiction Title: *Answers to 200 of Life's Most Probing Questions*, by Pat Robertson.
Fiction: Publishes Promise Romance (inspirational and children's).

Recent Fiction Title: *In Name Only*, by Irene Hannon (Promise Romance).
Recent Academic Title: *The Catacombs*, by James Stevenson.
Recent Children's Title: *The Hand-Me-Down Cap*, by Charlotte Graeber and Joe Boddy (MR. T & Me Series).

NELSON-HALL PUBLISHERS, 111 N. Canal St., Chicago IL 60606. (312)930-9446. Editorial Director: Harold Wise, PhD. Publishes hardcover and paperback originals. Averages 105 titles/year. Pays 15% maximum royalty on retail price; average advance. Photocopied submissions OK. SASE. Reports in 1 month. Free book catalog.
Nonfiction: Textbooks and general scholarly books in the social sciences. Query.
Recent Nonfiction Title: *Sociology: the Science of Human Organization*, by Jonathan H. Turner.

NEW AMERICAN LIBRARY, 1633 Broadway, New York NY 10019. (212)397-8000. Imprints include Signet, Mentor, Signet, Classics, Plume, Meridian, E.P. Dutton, Dew Books, and NAL Books. Publisher: Elaine Koster. Editor-in-Chief: Maureen Baron. Editor-in-Chief/Trade Books: Arnold Dolin. Editor-in-Chief/Hardcover: Michaela Hamilton. Publishes hardcover and paperback originals and hardcover reprints. Publishes 350 titles/year. Royalty is "variable"; offers "substantial" advance. Simultaneous and photocopied submissions OK. Computer printout submissions acceptable. Reports in 3 months. SASE. Free book catalog.
Tips: Queries/mss may be routed to other editors in the publishing group.

‡**THE NEW ENGLAND PRESS, INC.**, Box 575, Shelburne VT 05482. (802)863-2520/985-2569. President: Alfred Rosa. Publishes hardcover and trade paperback orignals and trade paperback reprints. Averages 6-10 titles/year; receives 200 + submissions annually. 50% of books from first-time authors; 75% of books from unagented writers. Pays 10-15% royalty on wholesale price. Publishes ms an average of 9 months after acceptance. Photocopied submissions OK. Computer printout submissions acceptable; no dot-matrix. SASE. Reports in 1-2 weeks on queries; 1 month on mss. Free book catalog.
Nonfiction: Biography, cookbook, how-to, humor and illustrated book. Subjects include Americana (Vermontiana and New England); cooking and foods, history (New England orientation); and essays (New England orientation). No juvenile or psychology. Query or submit outline/synopsis chapters. Reviews artwork/photos.
Recent Nonfiction Title: *Of Cabbages and Kings*, by Marguerite Hurrey Wolf (Vermontiana essays).
Fiction: Historical (New England orientation), and humor. No novels. Query.
Recent Fiction Title: *The Joys of Cheap Wine*, by Henry Billings (humor).
Tips: "As a small but emerging company we attempt to emphasize personalized service and establishing a good rapport with our authors. Although we are small, we do believe in advertising—TV included in our regional area."

NEW LEAF PRESS, INC., Box 311, Green Forest AR 72638. Editor-in-Chief: Cliff Dudley. Hardcover and paperback originals. Specializes in charismatic books. Publishes 10 titles/year; receives 250 submissions annually. 20% of books from first-time authors; 80% of books from unagented writers. Average print order for a writer's first book is 10,000. Pays 10% royalty on first 10,000 copies, paid once a year; no advance. Send photos and illustrations to accompany ms. Publishes book an average of 10 months after acceptance. Simultaneous and photocopied submissions OK. Computer printout submissions acceptable. SASE. Reports in 3 months. Free book catalog and ms guidelines for SASE. Reviews artwork/photos.
Nonfiction: Biography and self-help. Charismatic books; life stories, and how to live the Christian life. Length: 100-400 pages. Submit complete ms.
Recent Nonfiction Title: *The Marriage Game*, by Pat and Shirley Boone.

NEW READERS PRESS, Publishing division of Laubach Literacy International, Box 131, Syracuse NY 13210. Senior Editor: Kay Koschnick. Reading, writing and ESOL; Senior Editor: Mary Ann Lapinski, Math, Social Studies and Science. Publishes paperback originals. Averages 15 titles/year; receives 200 submissions annually. 40% of books by first-time authors; 100% of books by unagented writers. Average print order for a writer's first book is 5,000. "Most of our sales are to high school classes for slower learners, special education, and adult basic education programs, with some sales to volunteer literacy programs, private human-services agencies, prisons, and libraries with outreach programs for poor readers." Pays royalty on retail price, or by outright purchase. "Rate varies according to type of publication and length of manuscript." Advance is "different in each case, but does not exceed projected royalty for first year." Publishes book an average of 1 year after.acceptance. Photocopied submissions OK. Electronic submissions OK if IBM-PC compatible, but requires hard copy also. Computer printout submissions acceptable; prefers letter-quality to dot-matrix. Reports in 2 months. SASE. Free book catalog.
Nonfiction: "Our audience is adults and older teenagers with limited reading skills (6th grade level and below). We publish basic education materials in reading and writing, math, social studies, health, science, and English-as-a-second-language for double illiterates. We are particularly interested in materials that fulfill curriculum requirements in these areas. Manuscripts must be not only easy to read (3rd-6th grade level) but mature

in tone and concepts. We would consider submissions in the curriculum areas of reading skills development, writing, grammar, spelling, reasoning skills, listening skills, study skills, practical math, social studies (geography and U.S. history), science, self-awareness and interpersonal relations, and adapting to U.S. culture (for functionally illiterate English-as-a-second language students). We would also consider materials for specialized audiences of nonreaders, such as the learning disabled or speakers of nonstandard dialects. We would welcome humor or short plays suitable for classroom use. We are not interested in biography, poetry, or anything at all written for children." Accepts outline/synopsis and 1-3 sample chapters "depending on how representative of the total they are." Reviews artwork/photos as part of ms package.
Recent Nonfiction Title: *Government Today*, by Beverly Vaillancourt.
Fiction: "We are not currently accepting fiction submissions."

NEW YORK UNIVERSITY PRESS, Washington Square, New York NY 10003. (212)598-2886. Contact: Editor. Publishes hardcover and scholarly paperback originals. Averages 60 titles/year. Pays negotiable royalty. No advance. Reports in 3 weeks. Free book catalog.
Nonfiction: Scholarly works in the areas of economics, political science, history, New York City regional history, philosophy, politics, and literary criticism. Submit precis and vita.
Recent Nonfiction Title: *Puerto Rico*, by Raymond Carr.

NEW YORK ZOETROPE, INC., 80 E. 11th St., New York NY 10003. (212)420-0590. Contact: James Monaco. Publishes hardcover and trade paperback originals, hardcover and trade paperback reprints and software. Averages 25 titles/year. Pays 10-20% royalty on wholesale prices or makes outright purchase of $500-1,000. Offers average $200 advance. Publishes book an average of 1 year after acceptance. Simultaneous and photocopied submissions OK. Computer printout submissions acceptable. SASE. Reports in 2 weeks on queries; 2 months on mss.
Nonfiction: "Coffee table" book, reference, technical and textbook. Subjects include business and economics, travel and media. Interested especially in film and computer subjects. No fiction. Query.
Recent Nonfiction Title: *Making Ghostbusters: The Annotated Screenplay*.

NEWCASTLE PUBLISHING CO., INC., 13419 Saticoy, North Hollywood CA 91605. (213)873-3191. Editor-in-Chief: Alfred Saunders. Publishes trade paperback originals and trade paperback reprints. Averages 8 titles/year. 50% of books from first-time authors; 95% of books from unagented writers. Average print order for a writer's first book is 3,000-5,000. Pays 5-10% royalty on retail price; no advance. Publishes book an average of 6-8 months after acceptance. Simultaneous and photocopied submissions OK. Computer printout submissions acceptable; prefers letter-quality to dot-matrix. SASE. Reports in 3 weeks on queries; 6 weeks on mss. Free book catalog.
Nonfiction: How-to, self-help, metaphysical and new age. Subjects include health (physical fitness, diet and nutrition), psychology and religion. "Our audience is made up of college students and college-age nonstudents; also, adults ages 25 and up." No biography, travel, children's books, poetry, cookbooks or fiction. Query or submit outline/synopsis and sample chapters. Looks for "something to grab the reader so that he/she will readily remember that passage."
Recent Nonfiction Title: *Tarot for Your Self*, by Mary K. Greer(occult/self-help).

‡*NEWCONCEPT PRESS**, Box 124, Emerson NJ 07630. (201)265-0002. President: Judith Abrams. Publishes hardcover and paperback originals. Averages 10 titles/year. "We will not consider subsidy publishing unless work is scholarly and sponsored by a recognized foundation or other institution." Pays variable royalty on total receipts—domestic; special sales, mail order, etc., subject to change. Simultaneous and photocopied submissions OK. Computer printout submissions acceptable. SASE. Reports in 2 months. Free book catalog.
Nonfiction: Reference, self-help, technical, textbook, and professional. Subjects include health, psychology, sociology, and life-span development. "We need books on human behavior—pyschology, psychotherapy, etc.—written for the educated lay reader or professional; child-development books to be used in home or nursery school settings and adult development, and family relations. Submit outline/synopsis and sample chapters.
Recent Nonfiction Titles: *Cure Through Madness*, by Robert Langs, M.D. (hardcover trade).

NICHOLS PUBLISHING CO., Box 96, New York NY 10024. Editorial Director: Linda Kahn. Publishes hardcover originals. Averages 25-30 titles/year. Simultaneous and photocopied submissions OK. Computer printout submissions acceptable. Reports in 6 weeks. SASE. Book catalog for SASE.
Nonfiction: Professional/academic materials in architecture, business, education, engineering, international affairs, investment, and energy topics. Query with outline, table of contents and 2 sample chapters. Reviews artwork/photos as part of ms package.
Recent Nonfiction Title: *Producing Instructional Systems*, by A.J. Romisowski.

NIMBUS PUBLISHING LIMITED, Subsidiary of H.H. Marshall Ltd., Box 9301, Station A, Halifax, Nova Scotia B3K 5N5 Canada. (902)454-8381. Contact: Elizabeth Eve. Imprints include: Petheric Press (nonfiction and fiction). Publishes hardcover and trade paperback originals (90%) and trade paperback reprints. Averages 5 titles/year; receives 200 submissions annually. 50% of books from first-time authors; 100% of books from unagented writers. Average print order for a writer's first book is 3,000. Pays 4-10% royalty on retail price. Publishes book an average of 2 years after acceptance. Photocopied submissions OK. Electronic submissions OK, but requires hard copy also. Computer printout submissions acceptable. SAE, IRCs. Reports in 2 months on queries; 4 months on mss. Free book catalog.
Nonfiction: Biography, "coffee table" books, cookbooks, how-to, humor, illustrated books, juvenile, books of regional interest on art, cooking and foods, history, nature, travel and regional. "We do some specialized publishing; otherwise, our audience is the tourist and trade market in Nova Scotia." Query or submit outline/synopsis and a minimum of 1 sample chapter. Reviews artwork/photos as part of ms package.
Recent Nonfiction Title: *Saint John*, by George Schuyler (history).

‡**NITTY GRITTY COOKBOOKS**, 447 E. Channel Rd., Box 2008, Benicia CA 94510. (707)746-0800. President: Earl Goldman. Publishes trade and mass market paperback originals. Averages 4 titles/year; 200 submissions annually. 50% of books from first-time authors; 100% of books from unagented writers. Pays negotiable royalty. Offers average $500 advance. Publishes book an average of 6 months after acceptance. Simultaneous and photocopied submissions OK. Computer printout submissions acceptable. SASE. Reports in 2 weeks. Free book catalog and ms guidelines.
Nonfiction: Books on cooking and foods. "We publish cookbooks only." Query or submit outline/synopsis and sample chapters.
Tips: "Any idea is a possible cookbook."

NORTH LIGHT, Imprint of Writer's Digest Books, 9933 Alliance Rd., Cincinnati OH 45242. (513)984-0717. Editor: David Lewis. Publishes hardcover originals and trade paperback originals. Averages 10-12 titles/year. Pays 10% royalty on net receipts. Offers $1,000-3,000 advance. Simultaneous submissions and photographs of artwork OK. SASE. Reports in 3 weeks on queries; 2 months on mss. Free book catalog.
Nonfiction: How-to art instruction and graphic arts books. Subjects include instructional art. Interested in books on watercolor painting, oil painting, basic drawing, pen and ink, airbrush, markers, basic design, color, illustration techniques, layout and typography. Does not want "prestige-type art books not focusing on how-to art instruction." Query or submit outline/synopsis and examples of artwork.
Recent Nonfiction Title: *Exploring Color*, by Nita Leland (art instruction-all levels).

*****NORTHEASTERN UNIVERSITY PRESS**, 17 Cushing Hall, Northeastern University, 360 Huntington Ave., Boston MA 02115. (617)437-2783. Editors: Deborah Kops and Nancy Waring. Publishes hardcover originals, and hardcover and paperback reprints. Averages 10 titles/year. 80% of books from first-time authors; 100% of books from unagented writers. Average print order for a writer's first book is 3,000. Subsidy publishes 20% of books. Pays 7-10% royalty on wholesale price. Publishes book an average of 1 year after acceptance. SASE. Reports in 1 month on queries; 3 months on mss.
Nonfiction: Biography, reference and scholarly. Subjects include history, music, politics, criminal justice, literary criticism, women's studies, New England regional and scholarly material. "We are looking for scholarly works of high quality, particularly in the fields of American history, criminal justice, literary criticism, French literature, music and women's studies. Our books are read by scholars, students, and a limited trade audience." Submit outline/synopsis and 2-3 sample chapters. Reviews artwork/photos as part of ms package.
Recent Nonfiction Title: *Partial Justice: Women in State Prisons 1800-1935*, by Nicole Rafter.
Poetry: "We will consider translations, particularly of French poetry." Submit complete ms.
Recent Poetry Title: *Renard the Fox*, by Patricia Terry (translation from the Old French).
Tips: "Scholarly books have the best chance of selling to Northeastern—we're a university press. For *Writer's Market* readers, regional books are a good bet."

NORTHERN ILLINOIS UNIVERSITY PRESS, DeKalb IL 60115. (815)753-1826/753-1075. Director: Mary L. Lincoln. Pays 10-15% royalty on wholesale price. SASE. Free catalog.
Nonfiction: "The NIU Press publishes mainly history, political science, literary criticism and regional studies. It does not consider collections of previously published articles, essays, etc., nor do we consider unsolicited poetry." Accepts nonfiction translations. Query with outline/synopsis and 1-3 sample chapters.
Recent Nonfiction Title: *Chicago Divided: The Making of a Black Mayor*, by Paul Klappner.

*****NORTHLAND PRESS**, Box N, Flagstaff AZ 86002. (602)774-5251. Hardcover and paperback originals (80%) and reprints (20%). Advance varies. Averages 10 titles/year. Subsidy publishes 25% of books. Pays royalty on wholesale or retail price. Publishes book an average of 8 months after acceptance. Computer printout submissions acceptable; no dot-matrix. Simultaneous and photocopied submissions OK. Reports in 6-8 weeks.

SASE. Free book catalog.

Nonfiction: Publishes western Americana, Indian arts and culture, Southwestern natural history and fine photography with a western orientation. Query. "Submit a proposal including an outline of the book, a sample chapter, the introduction or preface and sample illustrations. Include an inventory of items sent." Looks for "clearly developed treatment of subject; tightly constructed presentation; an outline of author's background; pertinent research reference. Author should include assessment of intended audience (potential buyers and market) and other books published on same subject matter." Transparencies and contact sheet required for photos and/or illustrations to accompany ms.

Recent Nonfiction Title: *Zane Gray's Arizona*, by Candace C. Kant.

‡**NORTHWESTERN UNIVERSITY PRESS**, 1735 Benson Ave., Evanston IL 60201. (312)492-5313. Editor: Jonathan Brent. Imprint includes Northwestern Press Paperbacks. Publishes hardcover originals and hardcover and trade paperback reprints. Averages 10-15 titles/year; receives 300 submissions annually. 10% of books from first-time authors; 50% of books from unagented writers. Pays variable royalty or outright purchase. Offers average $500-2,500 advance. Publishes book an average of 9-12 months after acceptance. Simultaneous and photocopied submissions OK. SASE. Reports in 3 months on queries; 6 weeks on mss. Free book catalog. Ms guidelines for SASE.

Nonfiction: Biography, humor, reference, textbook and scholarly. Subjects include Americana, art, business and economics, history, music, philosophy, politics, psychology, religion, sociology, and literary criticism (aesthetics). Especially needs books on literary criticism, philosophy, art history, and translations of Eastern European authors. "No student's doctoral theses." Query. Reviews artwork/photos.

Recent Nonfiction Title: *Flawed Texts and Verbal Icons*, by Hershel Parker (literary criticism).

Fiction: Publishes reprints of "classics" in fiction. No original mss. Query.

Recent Fiction Title: *The Confidence Man: His Masquerade*, The Writings of Herman Melville. Vol. 10.

Tips: Scholarly, intellectual books have the best chance of selling to this press.

NORTHWOODS PRESS, Box 88, Thomaston ME 04861. (207)354-6550. Editor-in-Chief: R.W. Olmsted. Publishes hardcover and trade paperback originals. Averages 30 titles/year; receives 1,000 submissions annually. 100% of books from unagented writers. Average print order for a writer's first book is 350-500. Pays 10% royalty on amount received by publisher. Offers no advance. Publishes book an average of 6 months after acceptance. Simultaneous submissions OK; photocopied submissions on plain bond only. Electronic submissions OK if compatible with Compugraphic Editwriter 7300, Sanyo computer or 1160 TI 99/4A Computer printout submissions acceptable. SASE. Reports in 3 weeks. Book catalog for 6x9 SAE and 1 first class stamp; ms guidelines for SASE.

Nonfiction: Biography, cookbook, and how-to. Subjects include Americana, cooking and foods, history, hobbies, nature, philosophy, politics, psychology, recreation, sociology and travel. "We consider anything but pornographic and evangelical material." Reviews artwork/photos.

Recent Nonfiction Title: *Selected Letters of Don Marquis*, edited by Bill McCollum Jr. (American literature).

Poetry: Good, serious work. No "Edgar A. Guest type poetry, no versy stuff that rhymes—no 'typewriter' poetry."

Recent Poetry Title: *Answers To A Bowing Moon*, by Ann Zoller.

‡*****NORTHWORD**, Box 5634, Madison WI 53705. (608)231-2355. Editor: Jill Weber Dean. Publishes hardcover and trade paperback originals and trade paperback reprints. Averages 2-3 titles/year. Subsidy publishes 10% of books. "We have done very little subsidy publishing and don't seek more. We have two projects where a university engaged our services to produce a book and paid for production costs. *Rarely*, we receive a manuscript that deserves to be published but shows no potential for commercial success." Pays 15% royalty on wholesale price. Offers average $250 advance. Publishes book an average of 1 year after acceptance. Computer printout submissions acceptable; prefers letter-quality to dot-matrix. SASE. Simultaneous submissions OK *only* if we are so informed. "It takes me literally forever to reply to most submissions. I do not object to polite periodic reminders, however." Free book catalog.

Nonfiction: Biography, "coffee table" book, cookbook, how-to, humor, illustrated book and self-help. Subjects include cooking and foods, history, nature, photography, recreation, sports and travel. "We publish *only* titles of *genuine* focus and appeal for the geographical area centered on Wisconsin and the neighboring states (especially Minnesota and Michigan). We are always looking for guidebooks of various types to our region—travel, recreation, sporting activities, historical sights, natural landmarks, etc." No religion. Submit outline/synopsis and sample chapters. Reviews artwork/photos.

Recent Nonfiction Title: *Fire & Ice*, by Davenport & Wells (historic disaster epics).

Tips: "In general, our audience is a literate, curious, fairly well-educated group interested in enjoying life in our region to the fullest. We are a tiny but serious firm, and what little publishing we do, we do well."

W.W. NORTON CO., INC., 500 5th Ave., New York NY 10110. (212)354-5500. Managing Editor: Sterling Lawrence. Royalty varies on retail price; advance varies. Publishes 213 titles/year. Photocopied and

simultaneous submissions OK. Computer printout submissions acceptable. Submit outline and/or 2-3 sample chapters for fiction and nonfiction. Return of material not guaranteed without SASE. Reports in 4 weeks.
Nonfiction and Fiction: "General, adult fiction and nonfiction of all kinds on nearly all subjects and of the highest quality possible within the limits of each particular book." Last year there were 56 book club rights sales; 30 mass paperback reprint sales; "innumerable serializations, second serial, syndication, translations, etc." Looks for "clear, intelligent, creative writing on original subjects or with original characters."
Recent Nonfiction Title: *The Minimal Self: Psychic Survival in Troubled Times*, by Christopher Lash.
Recent Fiction Title: *Under the Lake*, by Stewart Woods.
Tips: "Long novels are too expensive—keep them under 350 pages (manuscript pages)."

NOYES DATA CORP., (including Noyes Press and Noyes Publications), Noyes Bldg., Park Ridge NJ 07656. Publishes hardcover originals. Averages 60 titles/year. Pays 10%-12% royalty on retail price; advance varies, depending on author's reputation and nature of book. Free book catalog. Query Editorial Department. Reports in 1-2 weeks. Enclose return postage.
Nonfiction: (Noyes Press) "Art, classical studies, archeology, and history. Material directed to the intelligent adult and the academic market." Technical: (Noyes Publications) Publishes practical industrial processing science; technical, economic books pertaining to chemistry, chemical engineering, food, textiles, energy, electronics, pollution control—primarily those of interest to the business executive. Length: 50,000-250,000 words.

OAK TREE PUBLICATIONS, INC., Subsidiary of Leisure Dynamics, Suite 202, 9601 Aero Dr., San Diego CA 92123. (916)560-5163. Editorial/Production Manager: Beth Ingram. Publishes hardcover and trade paperback originals and hardcover and trade paperback reprints. Publishes 25 titles/year; receives 1,000 submissions annually. 50% of books from first-time authors; 50% of books from unagented writers. Pays 10% royalty on retail price; 5% royalty on wholesale price. Variable advance. Publishes book an average of 1 year after acceptance. Simultaneous and photocopied submissions OK. Computer printout submissions acceptable; no dot-matrix. SASE. Reports in 2 months. Free book catalog and ms guidelines.
Nonfiction: Humor, illustrated book, juvenile, reference, and self-help. Subjects include health, recreation, sports, and travel. "We are looking for informative and entertaining manuscripts for the areas listed previously. Submit outline/synopsis and sample chapters. Reviews artwork/photos.
Recent Nonfiction Title: *SPIKE, The Story of the Victorious U.S. Volleyball Team*, by Doug Beal (sports).
Fiction: Children's. "We are looking for highly illustratable children's literature, for ages 2-11 with an educational and entertaining perspective." No juvenile fiction. Submit complete ms.
Recent Fiction Title: *I Wish I Had a Computer that Makes Waffles*, by Dr. Fitzhugh Dodson (children's).

OCCUPATIONAL AWARENESS, Box 948, Los Alamitos CA 90720. Editor-in-Chief: Edith Ericksen. Publishes originals and software. Averages 10 titles/year. Offers standard contract. Average advance $1,500. Publishes book an average of 1 year after acceptance. Photocopied submissions OK. Electronic submissions OK, but requires hard copy also. Computer printout submissions acceptable. SASE.
Nonfiction: Materials on behavior/adjustment (no TA), textbooks, workbooks, kits, career guidance, relating careers to curricula, special education and tests. Submit outline and 3 sample chapters for professional books and textbooks. Reviews artwork/photos as part of ms package.

OCTAMERON ASSOCIATES, 820 Fontaine St., Alexandria VA 22302. (703)836-1019. Editorial Director: Karen Stokstad. Publishes trade paperback originals. Averages 10 titles/year; receives 25 submissions annually. 100% of books from unagented writers. Average print order for a writer's first book is 8,000-10,000. Pays 8% royalty on retail price. Publishes book an average of 2 months after acceptance. Simultaneous submissions OK. SASE. Computer printout submissions acceptable; prefers letter-quality to dot-matrix. Reports in 1 week. Free book catalog.
Nonfiction: Reference, self-help, career and post-secondary education subjects. Especially interested in "paying-for-college and college admission guides." Query. Submit outline/synopsis and 2 sample chapters. Reviews artwork/photos.
Recent Nonfiction Title: *Financial Aid Officers*, by Donald Moore.

ODDO PUBLISHING, INC., Box 68, Beauregard Blvd., Fayetteville GA 30214. (404)461-7627. Managing Editor: Genevieve Oddo. Publishes hardcover and paperback originals; receives 100+ submissions annually.

 The double dagger before a listing indicates that the listing is new in this edition. New markets are often the most receptive to freelance contributions.

50% of books from first-time authors; 100% of books from unagented writers. Average print order for a writer's first book is 3,500. Scripts are usually purchased outright. "We judge all scripts independently." Royalty considered for special scripts only. Publishes book an average of 2 years after acceptance. Computer printout submissions acceptable; no dot-matrix. Reports in 3-4 months. Book catalog $1.07. "Manuscript will not be returned without SASE."

Nonfiction: Publishes juvenile books in language arts, workbooks in math, writing (English), photophonics, science (space and oceanography), and social studies for schools, libraries, and trade. Interested in children's supplementary readers in the areas of language arts, math, science, social studies, etc. "Texts run from 1,500 to 3,500 words. Ecology, space, oceanography and pollution are subjects of interest. Books on patriotism. Manuscript must be easy to read, general, and not set to outdated themes. It must lend itself to full color illustration. No stories of grandmother long ago. No love angle, permissive language, or immoral words or statements." Submit complete ms, typed clearly. Reviews artwork/photos as part of ms package.

Recent Nonfiction Title: *Let's Walk Safely.*

OHARA PUBLICATIONS, INC., 1813 Victory Place, Box 7728, Burbank CA 91510-7728. Contact: Editor. Publishes trade paperback originals. Averages 12 titles/year. Pays royalty. Photocopied submissions OK. SASE. Write for guidelines. Reports in 3 weeks on queries; 8 weeks on mss.

Nonfiction: Martial arts. "We decide to do a book on a specific martial art, then seek out the most qualified martial artist to author that book. 'How to' books are our mainstay, and we will accept no manuscript that does not pertain to martial arts systems (their history, techniques, philosophy, etc.)" Query first, then submit outline/synopsis and sample chapter. Include author biography and copies of credentials.

Recent Nonfiction Title: *Ninja*, by Steven Hays.

OHIO STATE UNIVERSITY PRESS, 1050 Carmack Rd., Columbus OH 43210. (614)422-6930. Director: Peter J. Givler. Pays royalty on wholesale or retail price. Averages 20 titles/year. Query letter preferred with outline and sample chapters. Reports in 2 months. Ms held longer with author's permission. Enclose return postage.

Nonfiction: Publishes history, biography, science, philosophy, the arts, political science, law, literature, economics, education, sociology, anthropology, geography, and general scholarly nonfiction. No length limitations.

Recent NonfictionTitle: *Paintings from Books: Art and Literature in Britain, 1760-1900*, by Richard D. Altick.

*OHIO UNIVERSITY PRESS, Scott Quad, Ohio University, Athens OH 45701. (614)594-5505. Imprints include *Ohio University Press* and *Swallow Press*. Director: Patricia Elisar. Associate Director: Holly Panich. Publishes hardcover and paperback originals (97%) and reprints (3%). Averages 25-30 titles/year. Subsidy publishes 6% of titles, based on projected market. Pays in royalties starting at 1,500 copies based on wholesale or retail price. No advance. Photocopied submissions OK. Reports in 3-5 months. SASE. Free book catalog.

Nonfiction: "General scholarly nonfiction with particular emphasis on 19th century literature and culture. Also history, social sciences, philosophy, business, western regional works and miscellaneous categories." Query.

Recent Nonfiction Title: *Forms of Feelings in Victorian Fiction*, by Barbara Hardy.

‡OOLICHAN BOOKS, Box 10, Lantzville, British Columbia V0R 2H0 Canada. (604)390-4839. Publisher: Ron Smith. Publishes hardcover and trade paperback originals. Averages 8 titles/year; receives 80-100 submissions annually. 40% of books from first-time authors; 100% of books from unagented writers. Pays 10% royalty on retail price. Publishes book an average of 12-18 months after acceptance. Photocopied submissions OK. Computer printout submissions acceptable; no dot-matrix. SASE. Reports in 2 months on queries; 2 months on mss. Book catalog for 9x12 SASE.

Nonfiction: Biography and regional history. Subjects include history (regional, specifically Pacific Northwest); philosophy (on aesthetics/poetics); and politics. "We need nonfiction in the humanities and social sciences, with emphasis on the Pacific Northwest, and quality poetics of any length, as we print pamphlets and chapbooks. Query. Reviews artwork/photos.

Recent Nonfiction Title: *Forever Green*, by Hector Richmond (autobiography/forest conservation).

Fiction: Experimental and mainstream (literary, quality fiction). "We publish two to four new fiction titles a year. We consider book-length fiction of literary merit by known and unknown writers." Query.

Recent Fiction Title: *A First Class Funeral*, by Sonia Birch-Jones (short stories).

Poetry: "We publish two to four quality free/open verse books a year by known and unknown authors." No rhymed verse; no philosophical or political diatribes. Submit complete ms.

Recent Poetry Title: *Confabulations*, by Sharon Thesen (free verse poem).

Tips: "Our audience is small but devoted to quality, literary writing. We have no illusions about a desire to compete with the commercial presses, although we hope some of our writers might publish with them in the future." A freelancer has the best chance of selling a fiction manuscript, as "we are attempting to develop our fiction list."

OPEN COURT PUBLISHING CO., Box 599, LaSalle IL 61301. Publisher: M. Blouke Carus. Heywood. Director, General Books: Dr. Andre Carus. Averages 20-30 titles/year. Royalty contracts negotiable for each book. Electronic submission OK IBM or compatible PC, PC-XT, PC-AT, but requires hard copy also. Computer printout submissions acceptable; prefers letter-quality to dot-matrix. Query. Enclose return postage.
Nonfiction: Philosophy, psychology, science and history of science, mathematics, comparative religion, education, orientalia, and related scholarly topics. Accepts nonfiction translations from German and French. "This is a publishing house run as an intellectual enterprise, to reflect the concerns of its staff and as a service to the world of learning." Submit outline/synopsis and 2-3 sample chapters. Reviews artwork/photos as part of ms package.
Recent Nonfiction Title: *A History of Engineering in Classical and Medieval Times*, by Donald Hill.

OPTIMUM PUBLISHING INTERNATIONAL INC., 2335 Sherbrooke St., West Montreal, Quebec H3H 1G6 Canada. (514)932-0776. Managing Director and Editor-in-Chief: Michael S. Baxendale. Hardcover and paperback originals and reprints. Averages 21 titles/year; receives 1,000 w submissions annually. 10% of books from first-time authors; 50% of books from unagented writers. Pays royalty or fee; negotiated with author or agent depending on project involved. Publishes in both official Canadian languages (English and French). Publishes book an average of 1 year after acceptance. Photocopied submissions OK. Electronic submissions OK, but query first; but requires hard copy also. Computer printout submissions acceptable; no dot-matrix. Reports in 4-6 weeks. SAE and IRCs.
Nonfiction: Biography, cookbooks, cooking and foods, gardening, history, natural history, how-to, health, nature, crafts, photography, art, self-help, crime, sports, and travel books. Query or submit outline/synopsis and sample chapters. Reviews artwork/photos.
Recent Nonfiction Title: *Four Seasons Menu Cook Book*, by Margo Oliver.

ORBIS BOOKS, Maryknoll NY 10545. (914)941-7590. Editor-in-Chief: John Eagleson. Publishes paperback originals. Publishes 35 titles/year. 7-8½-10% royalty on retail prices; offers average $1,000 advance. Query with outline, 2 sample chapters, and prospectus. Electronic submissions OK. Reports in 4 to 6 weeks. Enclose return postage.
Nonfiction: "Religious developments in Asia, Africa and Latin America. Christian missions. Justice and peace. Christianity and world religions."
Recent Nonfiction Title: *The Power of the Poor in History*, by Gustavo Gutierrez.

OREGON STATE UNIVERSITY PRESS, 101 Waldo Hall, Corvallis OR 97331. (503)754-3166. Hardcover and paperback originals. Averages 5 titles/year; receives 100 submissions annually. 75% of books from first-time authors; 100% of books from unagented writers. Average print order for a writer's first book is 3,000. Pays royalty on wholesale price. No advance. Publishes book an average of 9-12 months after acceptance. Computer printout submissions acceptable; no dot-matrix. SASE. Reports in 1 month. Free book catalog for SASE.
Nonfiction: Publishes scholarly books in history, biography, geography, literature, social science, marine and freshwater sciences, life sciences, geology, education, and bibliography, with strong emphasis on Pacific or Northwestern topics. Submit outline/synopsis and sample chapters.
Recent Nonfiction Title: *Regionalism and the Pacific Northwest*, edited by William G. Robbins, Robert J. Frank, and Richard E. Ross.

ORYX PRESS, 2214 N. Central Ave., Phoenix AZ 85004. (602)254-6156. President/Editorial Director: Phyllis B. Steckler. Publishes hardcover and paperback originals. Averages 35 titles/year; receives 300 submissions annually. 40% of books from first-time authors; 100% of books from unagented writers. Average print order for a writer's first book is 1,000. Pays 10-15% royalty on net receipts; no advance. Publishes book an average of 9 months after acceptance. Electronic submissions OK on IBM compatible, 1600 BPI ASC II format, but requires hard copy also. Computer printout submissions acceptable; prefers letter-quality to dot-matrix. SASE. Reports in 2 months. Free book catalog; and ms guidelines.
Nonfiction: Bibliographies, directories, general reference, library and information science, business reference, health care, gerontology, automation, and agriculture monographs. Publishes nonfiction for public, college and university, junior college, school and special libraries; agriculture specialists, health care deliverers; and managers. Query or submit outline/synopsis and 1 sample chapter, or complete ms. Queries/mss may be routed to other editors in the publishing group.
Recent Nonfiction Title: *Evolution vs Creationism: The Public Education Controversy*, ed. by Zetterberg (resource for teachers and librarians).

Close-up

Mark Gompertz
Editor-in-Chief and Vice President
The Overlook Press

The view from Overlook's 12th floor office is interesting; you can see the Empire State Building. The ceilings are high, the windows tall; there is lots of sunlight. But only a visitor will notice. At this small press, time is spent on books, not window-watching.

It's 5 p.m.; most people outside are heading toward subways and cars. Editor-in-chief Mark Gompertz is working . . . editing, proofreading, acquiring new books, writing promotional copy, preparing for sales conferences. Still, Gompertz worries about the writers who are wondering *what is taking so long.* "That writer works on something, hands it in and waits," he says. "It is really hard to call an author and say I plan to get to your manuscript at the end of the week and then 20 million things happen."

Three people (with the help of freelance copyeditors) edit, produce and market Overlook's 25 to 30 books annually. The "eclectic" list includes art and architecture books, literary fiction, books imported from England, and a martial arts book that became a bestseller, *A Book of Five Rings.*

Serious reviewers won't overlook books just because they have been published by a small house, he believes. Neither should authors in deciding where to send their books; many times authors get more attention and have more say at small presses. "The decision-making happens a lot more quickly although it may take a long time for us to get to reading something; there's not a hierarchy of ten vice-presidents who have to approve it."

Founded in a converted apple shack on Overlook Mountain in Woodstock, New York, this family-owned company sells books by mail order from the Woodstock office. Three people in this (Woodstock) office seek untapped markets for Overlook's backlist books through direct mail and special sales. Viking Penguin Inc. distributes Overlook Press books, including them in its catalog. When a writer sends a query, the book must fulfill both markets. Even at the query stage, Overlook editors think about what they might tell Viking and buyers about a particular book. But once editors decide *this is a book for us,* "we do not give up on a book; we cannot afford to."

Gompertz feels badly when he receives a query for a highly subjective, personal book from a person who has time to write but isn't a writer; "you *know* the pain this person is feeling." But *personal* stories like *Beyond the Chestnut Trees* do find their way onto Overlook's list when the writer researches and tells a special tale. "If a person has a story that he thinks will transcend the diary aspect, a single sheet of facts with thoughts on marketing helps in comparisons," says Gompertz.

He tries to balance the workload—to not slight writers and to get books to press on schedule. "There is only so much time at night, though, that you can devote or on weekends," explains Gompertz. "It becomes a real problem and one we have not been able to solve."

OSBORNE/McGRAW-HILL, Division of McGraw-Hill, Inc., 2600 10th St., Berkeley CA 94710. (415)548-2805. Editor-in-Chief: Judith Ziajka. Publishes trade paperback originals. Receives 400 submissions annually. 15% of books from first-time authors; 99% of books from unagented writers. Publishes book an average of 5 months after acceptance. Electronic submissions OK, but requires hard copy also. Computer printout submissions acceptable. SASE. Reports in 1 week on queries; 2-3 weeks on mss. Free book catalog and ms guidelines.
Nonfiction: Technical. "We are interested in books about popular microcomputer hardware and software, as well as technical books written for computer professionals." Submit outline/synopsis and sample chapters. Reviews artwork/photos.
Recent Nonfiction Title: *Apple II User Guide*, 3rd edition, by Lon Poole, Marty McNiff, and Steven Cook(technical).
Tips: "We envision home and business users of microcomputers, programmers and aspiring programmers as our audience."

OTTENHEIMER PUBLISHERS, INC., 300 Reisterstown Rd., Baltimore MD 21208. (301)484-2100. President: Allan T. Hirsh Jr. Vice-President; Allan T. Hirsh III. Managing Editor: Emeline Kroiz. Publishes hardcover and paperback originals. Publishes 250 titles/year; receives 500 submissions annually. Less than 1% of books from first-time authors; 100% of books from unagented writers. Average print order for a writer's first book is 15,000. Negotiates royalty and advance. Publishes book an average of 6 months after acceptance. Photocopied submissions OK. Computer printout submissions acceptable; prefers letter-quality to dot-matrix. Reports in 1 month.
Nonfiction: Cookbooks, reference, gardening, home repair and decorating, automotive and medical for the layperson. Submit outline/synopsis and sample chapters or complete ms. Reviews artwork/photos.
Tips: "We're looking for nonfiction adult books on the how-to information area, for mass market—we're a packager."

OUR SUNDAY VISITOR, INC., 200 Noll Plaza, Huntington IN 46750. (219)356-8400. Managing Editor: Robert Lockwood. Publishes paperback originals and reprints. Averages 20-30 titles a year. Pays variable royalty on net receipts; offers average $500 advance. Reports in 1 month on most queries and submissions. SASE. Free author's guide and catalog.
Nonfiction: Catholic viewpoints on current issues, reference and guidance, Bibles and devotional books, and Catholic heritage books. Prefers to see well-developed proposals as first submission with "annotated outline, three sample chapters, definition of intended market."
Recent Nonfiction Title: *Strange Gods: Contemporary Religious Cults in America*, by William Whalen.

OUTBOOKS INC., 217 Kimball Ave., Golden CO 80401. Contact: William R. Jones. Publishes trade paperback originals and reprints. Averages 10 titles/year. Pays 5% royalty on retail price. Computer printout submissions acceptable; no dot-matrix. SASE. Reports in 1 month on queries only. Free book catalog "as available."
Nonfiction: Regional books on Americana, history, nature, recreation and travel. Publishes for "lay enthusiasts in American history, outdoors, and natural history, ecology, and conservation." Query.
Recent Nonfiction Title: *Evidence and the Custer Enigma*, by Jerome A. Greene.

*OUTDOOR EMPIRE PUBLISHING, INC., Box C-19000, Seattle WA 98109. Publishes trade paperback originals (25%) and reprints (75%). Averages 25 titles/year. Subsidy publishes 50% of books based on market potential of subject. Buys some mss outright for $500, or by special contract depending upon project. Publishes book an average of 3 months after acceptance. Computer printout submissions acceptable "if good quality." SASE. Reports in 1 month.
Nonfiction: How-to, self-help, textbook, and workbook-texts on recreation and sports for ages 10 through adult. "Contemporary how-to treatment of various subjects in the areas of outdoor recreation: boating, fishing, hunting, camping, bicycling, mopeds, 4-wheel drives, all terrain vehicles, survival, and emergency preparedness." No mss on professional team sports, or outdoor travel journals. Reviews artwork/photos as part of ms package. Query or submit outline/synopsis and sample chapters or complete ms.

THE OVERLOOK PRESS, Distributed by Viking/Penguin, 12 W. 21st St., New York NY 10010. (212)807-7300. Editor-in-Chief: Mark Gompertz. Imprints include Tusk Books. Publishes hardcover and trade paperback originals and hardcover reprints. Averages 25 titles/year. Pays 3-15% royalty on wholesale or retail price. Queries only. SASE. Reports in 2 months. Free book catalog.
Nonfiction: How-to and reference. Subjects include Americana, business and economics, history, hobbies, nature, recreation, sports, and travel. No pornography. Query only.
Recent Nonfiction Title: *The Merchants: the Big Business Families of Saudi, Arabia*, by Michael Field.
Fiction: Adventure, ethnic, fantasy/science fiction, historical, mainstream, mystery/suspense. "We tend not to publish commercial fiction."

Recent Fiction Title: *Walter*, by David Cook.
Poetry: "We like to publish poets who have a strong following—those who read in New York City regularly or publish in periodicals regularly." No poetry from unpublished authors. Submit complete ms.
Recent Poetry Title: *The Book of Fortune*, by Daniel Mark Epstein.
Tips: "We are a very small company that will never publish more than 15-25 books each year. If authors want a very quick decision, they should go to another company first and come back to us. We try to be as prompt as possible, but it sometimes takes over 3 months for us to get to a final decision."

‡**OWL CREEK PRESS**, The Montana Review, Box 2248, Missoula MT 59806. Editor: Rich Ives. Publishes hardcover, trade paperback and mass market paperback originals; and mass market paperback reprints. Averages 5-10 titles/year; receives 2,000 submissions annually. 50% of books from first-time authors; 95% of books from unagented writers. Pays 10-20% royalty on wholesale price (cash or equivalent in copies). If paid in copies, royalty is advanced. Photocopied submissions OK. Computer printout submissions acceptable; prefers letter-quality to dot-matrix. SASE. Reports in 2 months. Book catalog for standard size SAE and 1 first class stamp.
Nonfiction: Photography. "Our selections are made solely on the basis of lasting artistic quality." No cookbooks, how-to, juvenile, self-help, technical or reference. Submit outline/synopsis and sample chapters.
Fiction: "We seek writing of lasting artistic merit in all areas. Writing genre is irrelevant, although we avoid easy approaches and formula work. We are not interested in writing that attempts to fulfill genre requirements or comply with preconceived notions of mass market appeal. If it's work of lasting quality we will try to find and build a market for it." Submit outline/synopsis and sample chapters.
Poetry: "We publish both full-length and chapbook titles. Selections are based solely on the lasting quality of the manuscripts. No manuscripts where genre category or preconceived ideas of mass market appeal dominate the work." Submit complete ms, unsolicited through contests only.
Recent Poetry Title: *Small Mercies*, by Elizabeth Weber.
Tips: "We attempt to reach the reader with a somewhat discerning taste first. Future plans include further expansion into fiction and translated titles (both poetry and fiction) as well as maintaining a continued series of both full-length and chapbook poetry originals."

OXFORD UNIVERSITY PRESS, INC., 200 Madison Ave., New York NY 10016. (212)679-7300. Publishes hardcover originals and paperback reprints. Publishes over 100 titles/year. Pays standard royalty; offers variable advance. Photocopied submissions OK. SASE. Free book catalog.
Nonfiction: History, music, political science, literature, philosophy, religion, science, medicine and reference books. Submit outline/synopsis and sample chapters.
Recent Nonfiction Title: *Franklin D. Roosevelt and American Foreign Policy* (political history).

OXMOOR HOUSE, (Division of The Southern Progress Corp.), Box 2262, Birmingham AL 35201. Editor-in-Chief: John Logue. Vice President/General Manager: Tom Angelillo. Publishes hardcover and paperback originals. Averages 13 titles/year. Pays on royalty basis or fee. Reports in 1 month. SASE.
Nonfiction: "Publishes books of general interest to Southern readers—cookbooks, garden books, books on crafts, sewing, photography, art, outdoors, antiques and how-to topics. Submit outline and sample chapter.
Recent Nonfiction Title: *The Southern Heritage Cookbook Library*.

P.P.I. PUBLISHING, 7016 Corporate Way, Box 335, Dayton OH 45459. (513)433-2709. Vice President: Kim Brooks. Publishes mass market paperback originals (booklets). Averages 45-50 titles/year; receives 300 submissions annually. 45% of books from first-time authors; 100% of books from unagented writers. Average print order for a writer's first book is 500. Pays 10% royalty on retail selling price to customer (some customer's discounts). Publishes book an average of 3 months after acceptance. Simultaneous and photocopied submissions OK. Computer printout submissions acceptable but not preferable; no dot-matrix. SASE. Reports in 3 weeks on queries; 10 weeks on mss. Book catalog with or without guidelines for SAE and 2 first class stamps; ms guidelines only for SAE and 1 first class stamp.
Nonfiction: Juvenile and teens, and self-help. Subjects include health and sociology. "We publish nonfiction booklets of 15,000 words or larger for junior and senior high schools, libraries, colleges, universities and other specialized markets such as social service organizations. Our main subjects include controversial issues and times in the news. Items that students are preparing for research papers or debates are of particular interest. We keep our markets informed on what's happening today in the judicial court system, in the home, in schools, and in the future. Some recent topics that were published include how to deal with freshman stress for the college student, euthanasia, prescription drug abuse, teens and drinking and driving, food irradiation, teenage suicide, the Klan, teens and drugs, television, etc. We are especially looking for 15,000-word manuscripts or larger on current events—items that students are interested in or that affect them. We're not interested in how-to, technical material, travel or cookbooks." Submit outline/synopsis, sample chapters or complete ms. "For new authors we prefer outlines or queries to save them time and trouble." Reviews artwork/photos as part of ms pack-

age on a limited basis.

Recent Nonfiction Titles: *Teenage Drinking and Driving: A Deadly Duo*, by Elaine Fantle Shimberg.

Tips: "Find out what students and library patrons are interested in today's news, what's happening with the teen and how world events affect us, and what the future outlook is for social issues, world issues and family."

‡**PACIFIC PRESS PUBLISHING ASSOCIATION**, Book Division, Seventh-Day Adventist Church, Box 7000, Boise ID 83707. (208)467-7400. Vice President of Editorial Development: Herbert D. Douglass. Publishes hardcover and trade paperback originals and hardcover and trade paperback reprints. Averages 50 titles/year; receives 800 submissions annually. Up to 50% of books from first-time authors; 100% of books from unagented writers. Pays 5-7% royalty on retail price. Offers average $100 advance. Publishes books an average of 6 months after acceptance. Photocopied submissions OK. Electronic submissions Ok, but "Contact us prior to submission to establish compatibility with your hardware." Requires hard copy also. Computer printout submissions acceptable; prefers letter-quality to dot-matrix. Reports in 1 month on queries; 2 months on mss. Ms guidelines for SASE.

Nonfiction: Biography, cookbook (vegetarian), how-to, juvenile, self-help and textbook. Subjects include cooking and foods (vegetarian only), health, nature, religion, and family living. "We are an exclusively religious publisher. We are looking for practical, how-to-oriented manuscripts on religion, health, and family life that speak to human needs, interests and problems from a Biblical perspective. We don't want anything totally secular or written from other than a Christian perspective." Query or submit outline/synopsis and sample chapters.

Recent Nonfiction Title: *God Cares*, by Mervyn Maxwell (devotional/expository study of Book of Revelation).

Tips: "Our primary audiences are members of our own denomination (Seventh-day Adventist), the general Christian reading market, and the secular or nonreligious reader. Books that are doing well for us are those that relate the Biblical message to practical human concerns and those that focus more on the experimental rather than the theoretical aspects of Christianity."

‡**PADRE PRODUCTIONS**, Box 1275, San Luis Obispo CA 93406. Editor-in-Chief: Lachlan P. MacDonald. Publishes hardcover and paperback originals (90%) and reprints (10%). Pays minimum 6% royalty. Offers $200-1,000 advance. Averages 4-8 titles/year; receives 400 submissions annually. 50% of books from first-time authors; 90% of books from unagented writers. Publishes book an average of 36-48 months after acceptance. Average print order for a writer's first book is 3,000. State availability of photos and/or illustrations or include contact sheet or stat. Simultaneous submissions OK. Computer printout submissions acceptable; prefers letter-quality to dot-matrix. Reports in 2-6 months. Mss and queries without SASE are not answered. Book catalog and ms guidelines for SASE.

Nonfiction: Subjects include Americana (antiques); art; business and economics (opportunities) hobby (collectibles); cookbook; history (California); how-to; money and finances (investments for the layman); nature (with illustrations); photography; poetry; publishing; recreation; reference; self-help; and travel. Query or submit outline and 2-3 sample chapters. "Include ample packaging; type all material; don't send slides unless asked." Looks for "literacy, flair, intelligence." Reviews artwork/photos as part of ms package.

Recent Nonfiction Title: *Chrona—A Time Segment*, by Aaron Corob.

Fiction: Subjects include (in order of preference): fantasy, contemporary and juvenile. Juveniles for ages 10-14 years, (about 160 pages with strong illustrative possibilities). Submit complete ms.

Tips: "The writer has the best chance of selling to our firm complete manuscripts with illustrations as local area guide."

THE PAGURIAN CORPORATION LIMITED, 13 Hazelton Ave., Toronto, Ontario M5R 2E1 Canada. (416)968-0255. Editor-in-Chief: Christopher Ondaatje. Publishes paperback and hardcover originals and reprints. Averages 2 titles/year. Offers negotiable royalty contract. Advance negotiable. Publishes book an average of 6 months after acceptance. Photocopied submissions OK. Computer printout submissions acceptable; prefers letter-quality to dot-matrix. Submit 2-page outline, synopsis or chapter headings and contents. Reports "immediately." SAE, IRC.

Nonfiction: Publishes general interest trade and art books. Will consider fine arts, outdoor and cookbook. Length: 40,000-70,000 words. Reviews artwork/photos as part of ms package.

Tips: "We are publishing *fewer* books, and all are Canadian art or art history themes."

PALADIN PRESS, Box 1307, Boulder CO 80306. (303)443-7250. President/Publisher: Peder C. Lund. General Manager: Kim R. Hood. Editorial Director: Rose-Marle Strasburg. Publishes hardcover and paperback originals (80%) and paperback reprints (20%). Averages 25 titles/year. Pays 10-12-15% royalty on net sales. Publishes book an average of 1 year after acceptance. Simultaneous and photocopied submissions OK. Computer printout submissions acceptable. Reports in 1 month. SASE. Free book catalog.

Nonfiction: "Paladin Press primarily publishes original manuscripts on military science, weaponry, self-defense, the martial arts, survival, police science, guerrilla warfare and fieldcraft, and within the last two years, humor. How-to manuscripts, as well as pictorial histories, are given priority. Manuals on building weapons, when technically accurate and cleanly presented, are encouraged. If applicable, send sample photographs and line drawings with outline and sample chapters." Query or submit outline/synopsis and sample chapters. Reviews artwork/photos as part of ms package.

Recent Nonfiction Title: *Commando Dagger: The Complete Illustrated History of the Fairbourn-Sykes Fighting Knife*, by Leroy Thompson.

Tips: "We need concise, instructive material aimed at our market and accompanied by sharp, relevant illustrations and photos."

‡**PANDA PRESS**, Panda Pictures Corp., 79 Milk St., Boston MA 02109. (617)574-0650. Editorial Director: Nathan Forrest. Publishes hardcover and trade paperback originals and trade paperback reprints. Averages 16 titles/year; receives 700 submissions annually. 75% of books from first-time authors; 75% of books from unagented writers. Pays 10-15% royalty from retail price. Offers average 5,000 advance. Publishes book an average of 5 months after acceptance. Computer printout submissions acceptable; no dot-matrix. SASE. Photocopied submissions OK. "We prefer return-postage stamps instead of crunched-up envelopes (SASE's)." Reports in 2 weeks on queries; 6 weeks or longer for unsolicited mss. Free book catalog; ms guidelines for SASE or 1 first class stamp.

Nonfiction: Wade Hampton, nonfiction editor. Biography, cookbook, how-to, illustrated book and reference. Subjects include Americana, animals, art, cooking and food, history, nature, photography and travel. "We do not want to see anything that has been beaten to death. Our audience is curious and intelligent, affluent and involved. We will lean heavily towards imaginative travel books, how-to's, new ways of looking at familiar places, people and things, memorable biography, even juvenile titles if exceptional for their educational value. We publish very little 'juvenile' nonfiction because most of the submissions we receive in this area do not merit publication. We want interesting material, but nothing too technical." Submit outline/synopsis and sample chapters. Reviews artwork/photos.

Recent Nonfiction Title: *Final Dawn*, by Cole (historical narrative).

Fiction: Henry Heth, fiction editor. Aventure, experimental, historical, horror, humor, mainstream, mystery, science fiction and suspense. "Whatever we touch, we expect to advertise and promote quite heavily. We focus our budget and our efforts on material which we feel will stand the test of time. We tend to shy away from anything which comes across as being less than memorable. Panda titles must have lasting appeal, which especially means no love stories, gothics, romances, confessions, or anything overly sentimental or superficial. One consideration is the potential for a manuscript to be developed into a motion picture." Submit complete ms.

Recent Fiction Title: *The Staretz*, by Gene Cetrone (biographical novel).

Poetry: "We would like to see fresh use of language and imaginative themes which communicate clearly— nothing off the deep end, which would have very limited appeal. Nothing overly sentimental; nothing which fails to communicate; no cliches or stale images; no love poems; nothing too trite." Submit complete ms.

Recent Poetry Title: *The Stranger*, by Tom Pacheco (lyrical verse).

Tips: "Panda is a thinking-man's press. We are after an intellectually-oriented audience, without trying to appear highbrow about it. We publish nothing geared toward short attention spans. Panda concentrates all of its resources on selecting the very best material and then we give it everything we've got, with each and every title. The writer today should offer editors the best that they have to offer."

PANJANDRUM BOOKS, Suite 1, 11321 Iowa Ave., Los Angeles CA 90025. (213)477-8771. Subsidiaries include Panjandrum Books Inc. Editor/Publisher: Dennis Koran. Publishes hardcover and trade paperback originals. Averages 4-5 titles/year. Pays 7-10% royalty on retail price. Computer printout submissions acceptable. SASE. Reports in 2 weeks on queries; 2 months on mss. Book catalog for 7x10 SAE and 2 first class stamps.

Nonfiction: Biography, cookbook, how-to, juvenile and reference. Subjects include cooking health, history, hobbies, music, philosophy, recreation, theater and drama, herbs, vegetarianism, and childhood sexuality. "We're looking for manuscripts of cookbooks, health books, music (how-to), drama, and critical/history, and are open to queries on other subjects." No religious or humorous. Query or submit outline/synopsis and sample chapters.

Recent Nonfiction Title: *Alfred Jarry: The Man with the Axe*, by Lennon (literary biography).

Fiction: Avant-garde, experimental, fantasy, gothic (not romance), and translations of European literature (not previously translated into English). Query with sample chapter.

Recent Fiction Title: *Fighting Men*, by Manus (post-Vietnam novel).

Poetry: Submit maximum 5 poems.

Recent Poetry Title: *Visions of the Fathers of Lascaux*, by Eshleman.

PANTHEON BOOKS, Division of Random House, Inc., 201 E. 50th St., New York NY 10022. Averages 90 + titles/year. Pays royalty on invoice price (retail price minus freight pass-through, usually 50¢). Publishes book an average of 1 year after acceptance (longer if ms not written/completed when contract is signed). Address queries to Adult Editorial Department (28th Floor). "We prefer to work with experienced writers who

have already published at least one book or several articles. In addition to a description of the book, queries must include a brief market study detailing how the book proposed will be different from other books available on the subject." Computer printout submissions acceptable; prefers letter-quality to dot-matrix. SASE.
Nonfiction: Emphasis on Asia, international politics, radical social theory, history, medicine, women's studies, and law. Recreational guides and practical how-to books as well. Query letters only. No mss accepted. Publishes some juveniles. Address queries to Juvenile Editorial Department (6th floor).
Recent Nonfiction Title: *The Good War*, by Studs Terkel.
Fiction: Publishes fewer than 5 novels each year, primarily mysteries. Queries on fiction not accepted.

PAULIST PRESS, 997 Macarthur Blvd., Mahwah NJ 07430. (201)825-7300. Publisher: Rev. Kevin A. Lynch. Managing Editor: Donald Brophy. Publishes hardcover and paperback originals (90%) and paperback reprints (10%). Averages 100 titles/year; receives 500 submissions annually. 5-8% of books from first-time authors; 95% of books from unagented writers. Pays royalty on retail price. Occasionally offers advance. Publishes book an average of 8 months after acceptance. Photocopied submissions OK. Electronic submissions OK, but requires hard copy also. Computer printout submissions acceptable; prefers letter-quality to dot-matrix. SASE. Reports in 4 weeks.
Nonfiction: Philosophy, religion, self-help and textbooks (religious). Accepts nonfiction translations from German, French and Spanish. "We would like to see theology (Catholic and ecumenical Christian), popular spirituality, liturgy, and religious education texts." Submit outline/synopsis and 2 sample chapters. Reviews artwork/photos as part of ms package.
Recent Nonfiction Title: *The Ground Is Holy, the Sanctuary Movement in the U.S.*, by Ignatius Bau

PEACHTREE PUBLISHERS, LTD., 494 Armour Circle NE, Atlanta GA 30324. (404)876-8761. Executive Editor: Chuck Perry. Publishes hardcover and trade paperback originals. Averages 12-15 titles/year; receives up to 1,000 submissions annually. 75% of books from first-time authors; 95% of books from unagented writers. Average print order for a writer's first book is 5,000-10,000. Publishes book an average of 9-12 months after acceptance. Computer printout submissions acceptable; prefers letter-quality to dot-matrix. Reports in 1 week on queries; 3 months on mss. Free book catalog; ms guidelines for SASE.
Nonfiction: Cookbook and humor. Subjects include cooking and foods, history, recreation and religion. No business, technical, reference, art and photography, juvenile or animals. Submit outline/synopsis and sample chapters. Reviews artwork/photos as part of ms package.
Recent Nonfiction Title: *Elvis is Dead and I Don't Feel So Good Myself*, by Lewis Grizzard (humor).
Fiction: Historical, humor and mainstream. "We are particularly interested in fiction with a Southern feel." No fantasy, juvenile, science fiction or romance. Submit outline/synopsis and sample chapters.
Recent Fiction Title: *The Whisper of the River*, by Ferrol Sams (general fiction).
Tips: "We're looking for mainstream fiction and nonfiction of Southern interest; although our books are sold throughout the United States, our principal market is the Southeastern region—Virginia to Texas."

THE PENNSYLVANIA STATE UNIVERSITY PRESS, 215 Wagner Bldg., University Park PA 16802. (814)865-1327. Editor-in-Chief: Jack Pickering. Publisher hardcover and paperback originals. Specializes in books of scholarly value, and/or regional interest. Averages 40 titles/year. Pays 10% royalty on wholesale price. Offers no advance. Maintains own distribution company in England which serves the British Empire, Europe, etc. Submit outline/synopsis and 2 sample chapters plus endorsement by a scholar at a university or research institution. Publishes book an average of 8 months after acceptance. Electronic submissions OK, but requires hard copy also. Computer printout submissions acceptable; prefers letter-quality to dot-matrix. Reports in 2-4 months. SASE. Free book catalog.
Nonfiction: Publishes scholarly books on agriculture, art, business and economics, history, medicine and psychiatry, music, nature, philosophy, politics, psychology, religion, science and technology, sociology, technology, women's studies, black studies, and *Keystone Books* (a paperback series concentrating on topics of special interest to those living in the mid-Atlantic states). Accepts translations. Reviews artwork/photos as part of ms package. Looks for "content and form acceptable to scholars (as attested by a recognized scholar)."
Recent Nonfiction Title: *Rivers of Pennsylvania*, by T. Palmer (nature, conservation, history).

PENNWELL BOOKS, Box 1260, Tulsa OK 74101. (918)663-4220. Editorial Director: Kathryne Pile. Publishes hardcover originals. Averages 30 titles/year. 40% of books from first-time authors; 99% of books from unagented writers. Pays 10-13% royalty on net receipts. Offers no advance. Publishes book an average of 7 months after acceptance. Electronic submissions OK on IBM and Compatibles, Word Star, but requires hard copy also. Computer printout submissions acceptable; no dot-matrix. SASE. Reports in 1 week on queries; 2 weeks on mss. Free book catalog and ms guidelines.
Nonfiction: Technical books and software for petroleum engineering, dental practice management, computer technology and laser technology. Submit outline/synopsis and sample chapters.

‡**PENTAGRAM**, Fathom Press, Box 379, Markesan WI 53946. Editor/publisher/Printer: Michael Tarachow. Publishes trade paperback originals. Averages 0-5 titles/year; receives 50 submissions annually. 50% of books from first-time authors; 100% of books from unagented writers. Payment varies. Publishes book an average of 2 years after acceptance. Photocopied submissions OK. SASE. Reports in 1 week. Always query with SASE before sending mss. Free book catalog.

Poetry: Query with SASE before sending mss.

Recent Poetry Title: *Blossoms and bones*, by Christopher Buckley.

Tips: "Pentagram publishes books by letterpress; handset metal type on mould-made and/or hand-made papers. We are looking for readers who experience books with their five or more senses."

***PEREGRINE SMITH BOOKS**, Box 667, Layton UT 84041. (801)544-9800. Editorial Director: Buckley C. Jeppson. Publishes hardcover and paperback originals (80%) and reprints (20%). Subsidy publishes 10% of books. Receives 100 + submissions annually. 50% of books from first-time authors; 90% of books from unagented writers. Average print order for a writer's first book is 5,000. Pays 10% royalty on wholesale price. Offers no advance. Publishes book an average of 1 year after acceptance. Photocopied submissions OK. Reports in 3 months. SASE. Book catalog 56¢.

Nonfiction: "Subjects include western American history, natural history, American architecture, art history and fine arts. "We consider biographical, historical, descriptive and analytical studies in all of the above. Much emphasis is also placed on pictorial content. Many of our books are used as university texts." Query or submit outline/synopsis and 2 sample chapters. Accepts nonfiction translations from French. Consult *Chicago Manual of Style*. Reviews artwork/photos as part of ms package.

Recent Nonfiction Title: *Lawrence in Oaxaca: A Search for the Novelist in Mexico*, by Ross Parmenter.

Fiction: "We mainly publish reprints or anthologies of American writers." Query or submit outline/synopsis and 2 sample chapters. "No unsolicited manuscripts accepted. Query first." Looks for "style, readable, intelligent, careful writing. Must be geared to a competitive commercial market." Accepts fiction translations from French.

Tips: "Write seriously. If fiction, no potboilers, bestseller movie tie-in type hype books and no science fiction. We like Pynchon and Gaddis. If nonfiction, only serious, well-researched critical, historical or craft-related topics."

THE PERFECTION FORM CO., Suite 15, 8350 Hickman Rd., Des Moines IA 50322. (515)278-0133. Editor: M. Kathleen Myers. Publishes paperback originals for sale in secondary schools and software. Publishes 10 titles/year. Receives 150 submissions annually. 50% of books from first-time authors; 90% from unagented writers. Average print order for a writer's first book is 5,000. Pays royalty; offers small advance on publication. Publishes book an average of 2-3 years after acceptance. Computer printout submissions acceptable; prefers letter-quality to dot-matrix. SASE. Reports in 3 months.

Nonfiction: Publishes supplementary educational materials, grades kindergarten-12 social studies and language arts. Also publishes CAI language arts and social studies on software.

Fiction: Original mss of approximately 20,000-30,000 words written for young adult audiences ages 12-18. Wholesome, high interest books. Adventure stories, humor, mystery, supernatural, personal conflict and choice, sports, family, courage and endurance. Submit chapter and outline or complete ms.

PETERSON'S GUIDES, INC., Box 2123, Princeton NJ 08540. (609)924-5338. Publisher/President: Peter W. Hegener. Editorial Director: Karen C. Hegener. Publishes paperback originals and software (for the educational/guidance market. Averages 25 titles/year. Receives 150-200 submissions annually 50% of books from first-time authors; 90% from unagented writers. Average print order for a writer's first books is 5,000-12,000. Pays 5-10% royalty on net sales; offers advance. Publishes book an average of 9 months after acceptance. Photocopied submissions OK. Computer printout submissions acceptable; prefers letter-quality to dot-matrix.. Reports in 3 months. Free catalog.

Nonfiction: Educational and career reference and guidance works for professionals, libraries, and trade. Submit complete ms or detailed outline and sample chapters. Looks for "appropriateness of contents to our market, accuracy of information and use of reliable information sources, and writing style suitable for audience." Reviews artwork/photos as part of ms package.

Recent Nonfiction Title: *Peterson's Competitive Colleges*, edited by Karen C. Hegener.

PETROCELLI BOOKS, INC., Research Park, 251 Wall St., Princeton NJ 08540. (609)924-5851. Editorial Director: O.R. Petrocelli. Senior Editor: Rick Batlan. Publishes hardcover and paperback originals. Publishes 20 titles/year. Offers 12½-18% royalties. No advance. Simultaneous and photocopied submissions OK. Computer printout submissions acceptable; prefers letter-quality to dot-matrix. SASE. Reports in 1 month. Free book catalog.

Nonfiction: Business/economics, reference, technical, and textbooks. Submit outline/synopsis and 1-2 sample chapters.

Recent Nonfiction Title: *Applications in Artificial Intelligence*, edited by Stephen J Andriole.

PHILOMEL BOOKS, Division of The Putnam Publishing Group, 51 Madison Ave., New York NY 10010. (212)689-9200. Editor-in-Chief: Ann Beneduce. Editor: Christine Grenz. Publishes quality hardcover originals. Publishes 12-20 titles/year. Pays standard royalty. Advance negotiable. SASE. Reports in 1 month on queries. Request book catalog from marketing department of Putnam Publishing Group.
Nonfiction: Young adult and children's picture books. No alphabet books or workbooks. Query first. Looks for "interesting theme; writing quality; suitability to our market."
Recent Nonfiction Title: *Sight and Seeing: A World of Light and Color*, by Hilda Simon.
Fiction: Young adult and children's book on any topic. Query to Christine Grenz.
Recent Fiction Title: *A Little Love*, by Virginia Hamilton.
Tips: Unsolicited ms will be returned unopened. "We regret this change in procedure; we cannot afford the time required to process manuscripts unless we have authorized their submission in response to a previously submitted query letter."

POCKET BOOKS, 1230 Avenue of the Americas, New York NY 10020. Imprints include Washington Square Press (high-quality mass market), Poseidon Press (hardcover fiction and nonfiction), Tapestry (historical romance), and Wallaby (trade paperbacks). Publishes paperback originals and reprints. Averages 300 titles/year. Pays royalty on retail price. Query only. No unsolicited mss.
Nonfiction: History, biography, reference and general nonfiction.
Recent Nonfiction Title: *Balls*, by Graig Nettles and Peter Golenbock.
Fiction: Adult, (mysteries, science fiction, romance, westerns).
Recent Fiction Title: *Smart Women*, by Judy Blume.

POLARIS PRESS, 16540 Camellia Terrace, Los Gatos CA 95030. (408)356-7795. Editor: Edward W. Ludwig. Publishes paperback originals; considers reprints, depending upon reputation of author. Specializes in science fiction and college-level books with appeal to general public. Averages 3 titles/year; receives 300 submissions annually. 10% of books from first-time authors; 75% of books from unagented writers. Average print order for a writer's first book is 5,000. Pays 6% royalty on retail price; offers averages $300-500 advance. Publishes book an average of 6 months after acceptance. Send contact sheets or prints if photos and/or illustrations are to accompany ms. Computer printout submissions acceptable; no dot-matrix. Reports in 2 weeks. SASE. Free book catalog for SAE and 3 first class stamps.
Fiction: Fantasy and science fiction 60,000-90,000 words. "Please, *no* manuscripts which require extensive (and expensive) use of color in inner pages." No juvenile general fiction or experimental. Reviews artwork/photos as part of ms package. Query.
Recent Fiction Title: *The Seven Shapes of Solomon*, by Ludwig (anthology of previously published science and science fantasy stories).
Tips: "Query to determine immediate needs, which are usually specialized. List briefly main interests and qualifications. We will accept two sample chapters plus synopsis. There is little chance that an unsolicited manuscript will be accepted spontaneously."

PORTER SARGENT PUBLISHERS, INC., 11 Beacon St., Boston MA 02108. (617)523-1670. Publishes hardcover and paperback originals, reprints, translations and anthologies. Averages 3 titles/year. Pays royalty on retail price. "Each contract is dealt with on an individual basis with the author." Send query with brief description, table of contents, sample chapter and information regarding author's background. Computer printout submissions acceptable. Enclose return postage. Looks for "originality and clear and concise treatment and availability of subject." Free book catalog.
Nonfiction: Reference, special education and academic nonfiction. "Handbook Series and Special Education Series offer standard, definitive reference works in private education and writings and texts in special education. The Extending Horizons Series is an outspoken, unconventional series which presents topics of importance in contemporary affairs and the social sciences." This series is particularly directed to the college adoption market. Accepts nonfiction translations from French and Spanish. Contact: Gale T. Pryor.
Recent Nonfiction Title: *Workplace Democracy and Social Change*, by Frank Lindenfeld and Joyce Rothschild-Whitt, editors (political science).

†POSEIDON PRESS, Division of Pocket Books, 1230 Avenue of the Americas, New York NY 10020. (212)246-2121. Vice President/Publisher: Ann E. Patty. Publishes hardcover and trade paperback originals (100%). Averages 10-12 titles/year. Pays 10-15% royalty on hardcover retail price. Simultaneous and photocopied submissions OK. Computer printout submissions acceptable; no dot-matrix. SASE. Reports in 6 weeks.
Nonfiction: Biography, cookbook, reference and self-help. Subjects include business and economics, health, history, psychology and sociology. No religious/inspiration, humor. Query or submit outline/synopsis and/sample chapter.
Fiction: Literary, historical, contemporary and mainstream. Query or submit outline/synopsis and sample chapter.

POTENTIALS DEVELOPMENT FOR HEALTH & AGING SERVICES, 775 Main St., Buffalo NY 14203. (716)842-2658. Publishes paperback originals. Averages 6 titles/year; receives 20-30 submissions annually. 75% of books from first-time authors; 100% of books from unagented writers. Average print order for a writer's first book is 1,500. Pays 5-8% royalty on sales. Publishes book an average of 1 year after acceptance. Computer printout submissions acceptable; no dot-matrix. SASE. Reports in 6 weeks. Free book catalog and ms guidelines for SASE.
Nonfiction: "We seek material of interest to those working with elderly people in the community and in institutional settings. We need tested, innovative and practical ideas." Query or submit outline/synopsis and 3 sample chapters to J.A. Elkins. Looks for "suitable subject matter, writing style and organization." Reviews artwork/photos as part of ms package.
Recent Nonfiction Title: *Edible Activities* by C. Suchan.
Tips: "The writer has the best chance of selling us materials of interest to those working with elderly people in nursing homes, senior and retirement centers. Our major market is activity directors. Must be willing to be flexible with submitted material to fit actual, not percieved, needs of activity directors."

CLARKSON N. POTTER, INC., 1 Park Ave., New York NY 10016. (212)532-9200. Vice President/Editorial Director: Carol Southern. Director of Operations: Michael Fragnito. Publishes hardcover and trade paperback originals. Averages 35 titles/year. Pays 10% royalty on hardcover; 5-7½% on paperback; 5-7% on illustrated hardcover, varying escalations; advance depends on type of book and reputation or experience of author. No unagented mss can be considered. Photocopied submissions OK. Reports in 4 weeks. SASE. Free book catalog.
Nonfiction: Publishes Americana, art, autobiography, biography, cooking and foods, history, how-to, humor, juvenile, nature, photography, self-help, style and annotated literature. Accepts nonfiction translations. "Manuscripts must be cleanly typed on 8½x11 nonerasable bond; double-spaced. Chicago *Manual of Style* is preferred." Query or submit outline/synopsis and sample chapters. Reviews artwork/photos as part of ms package.
Recent Nonfiction Title: *Smart Women, Foolish Choices*, by Connell Cowan and Melvyn Kinder.
Recent Fiction Title: *Black Water: A Book of Fantastic Literature*, edited by Alberto Kangud.

THE PRAIRIE PUBLISHING COMPANY, Box 264, Postal Station C, Winnipeg, Manitoba R3M 3S7 Canada. (204)885-6496. Publisher: Ralph Watkins. Publishes trade paperback originals. Averages 4 titles/year; receives 25 submissions annually. 4% of books from first-time authors; 85% of books from unagented writers. Average print order for a writer's first book is 2,000. Pays 10% royalty on retail prices. Photocopied submissions OK. Computer printout submissions acceptable; no dot-matrix. SASE. Reports in several weeks. Free book catalog; ms guidelines for SASE. Reviews artwork/photos as part of ms package.
Nonfiction: Biography and cookbook. Subjects include cooking and foods. "We would look at any submissions."
Recent Nonfiction Title: *My Name Is Marie Anne Gabaury*, by Mary Jordan.

‡**PRAKKEN PUBLICATIONS, INC.**, Box 8623, Ann Arbor MI 48107. (313)769-1211. Executive Editor: Alan H. Jones. Publishes hardcover and trade paperback originals. Averages 3 titles/year; receives 10 submissions annually. 50% of books from first-time authors; 100% of books from unagented writers. Pays 10% royalty on net price. Simultaneous and photocopied submissions OK. Computer printout submissions acceptable; prefers letter-quality to dot-matrix. SASE. Reports in 2 weeks on queries; 1 month on mss. Free book catalog.
Nonfiction: Technical and textbook (vocational). Subject includes technical education. "We are interested in manuscripts with broad appeal in any of the specific subject areas of the industrial arts and vocational-technical education field." Submit outline/synopsis and sample chapters. Reviews artwork/photos as part of ms package.
Recent Nonfiction Title: *Basic Mathematics*, by A.L. Hambley (textbook).

PRENTICE-HALL, Children's Book Division, Englewood Cliffs NJ 07632. Editor-in-Chief: Barbara Francis. Manuscripts Editor: Rose Lopez. Publishes hardcover and paperback originals and paperback reprints. Publishes 30 hardcovers/year,15 paperbacks/year. Pays royalty. Offers advance. SASE. Reports in 6 weeks. Book catalog for SASE.
Nonfiction: All subjects, all age groups but special interest in topical science and technology, art, social sciences, history (any unusual approaches), humor (no jokes or riddles but funny fiction), music (keen interest in basic approaches, no biographies), sociology (8-12), and sports (6-9), puzzle and participation (6-8). Query. Accepts outline/synopsis and 5-6 sample chapters from published writers; entire ms from unpublished writers. Prefers to see portfolio separate from ms except when illustrator is making the submission or when clarity requires that ms be accompanied by photos or rough illustrations.
Recent Nonfiction Title: *The Marvelous Music Machine: A Story of the Piano*, by Mary Blocksma, illustrated by Mischa Richter.
Fiction: Gothic, humor, mainstream and mystery. Submit outline/synopsis and sample chapters.

Recent Fiction Title: *Stagedoor to Terror: A Miss Mallard Mystery*, by Robert Quackenbush (detective mystery, ages 6-9).
Picture Books: Accent on humor.
Recent Picture Book: *A Weekend in the Country*, by Lee Lorenz; *Joey*, By Jack Kent.

PRENTICE-HALL CANADA, INC., Educational Book Division, 1870 Birchmount Road, Scarborough, Ontario M1P 2J7 Canada. (416)293-3621. Executive Editor: Rob Greenaway.
Nonfiction: Publishes texts, workbooks, and instructional media including computer courseware for elementary, junior high and high schools. Subjects include business, computer studies, geography, history, language arts, mathematics, science, social studies, technology, and French as a second language.

PRENTICE-HALL CANADA, INC., Trade Division, 1870 Birchmount Road, Scarborough, Ontario M1P 2J7 Canada. (416)293-3621. Acquisitions Editor: Iris Skeoch. Publishes hardcover and trade paperback originals and software. Averages 10 titles/year; receives 250-300 submissions annually. 40% of books from first-time authors; 40% of books from unagented writers. Negotiates royalty and advance. Publishes book an average of 9 months after acceptance. Computer printout submissions acceptable; prefers letter-quality to dot-matrix. SAE and IRCs. Reports in 10 weeks. Ms guidelines for SASE.
Nonfiction: Subjects of Canadian and international interest; art, politics and current affairs, business, travel, health and food. Send sample chapters or outlines.
Recent Nonfiction Title: *The Joy of Bridge*, by Audrey Grant and Eric Rodwell.

‡**PRENTICE-HALL, INC.**, Business & Professional Books Division, Gulf & Western, Inc., Sylvan Ave., Englewood Cliffs NJ 07632. (201)592-2000. Product Manager: Ted Nardin. Publishes hardcover and trade paperback originals. Averages 150 titles/year; receives 1,000+ submissions annually. 50% of books from first-time authors; 95% of books from unagented writers. Pays in royalty: 5% on cash received on *mail order*; 10-15% on all *trade* sales. Offers $3,000-5,000 advance. Publishes book an average of 9 months after acceptance. Simultaneous and photocopied submissions OK. Electronic submissions OK, but requires hard copy also. Computer printout submissions acceptable; prefers letter-quality to dot-matrix. SASE. Reports in 3 weeks. Free book catalog; writer's guidelines for SASE.
Nonfiction: How-to, reference, self-helf and technical. Subjects include business and economics, recreation, sports, real estate, law, accounting, computers and education. Needs business, professional, technical and educational references for sale primarily via direct mail. Query or submit outline/synopsis and sample chapters. Reviews artwork/photos as part of ms package
Recent Nonfiction Title: *Product Safety Engineering*, by M. Seiden (how-to reference).
Tips: "We seek high-level, practical references that command high prices and that can be sold to targeted markets via direct mail."

THE PRESERVATION PRESS, National Trust for Historic Preservation, 1785 Massachusetts Ave. NW, Washington DC 20036. Editor: Diane Maddex. Publishes nonfiction books and periodicals on historic preservation (saving and reusing the "built environment"). Averages 6 titles/year. Books are often commissioned by the publisher.
Nonfiction: Subject matter encompasses architecture and architectural history, building restoration and historic preservation. No local history. Query. Looks for "relevance to national preservation-oriented audience; educational or instructional value; depth; uniqueness; need in field."
Recent Nonfiction Title: *What Style Is It? A Guide to American Architecture*.

PRESIDIO PRESS, 31 Pamaron Way, Novato CA 94947. (415)883-1373. Editor-in-Chief: Adele Horwitz. Senior Editor: Joan Griffin. Publishes hardcover and paperback originals. Pays 15% royalty on net price. Offers nominal advance. Publishes book an average of 18 months after acceptance. Photocopied submissions OK. Computer printout submissions acceptable; prefers letter-quality to dot-matrix. SASE. Reports in 3 months. Free book catalog.
Nonfiction: Military history and regional books. No scholarly. Fiction with military background considered. Accepts nonfiction translations. Query or submit outline/synopsis and 3 sample chapters. Reviews artwork/photos as part of ms package.
Recent Nonfiction Title: *The Rise and Fall of an American Army: U.S. Ground Forces, Vietnam, 1965-1973*, by Shelby L. Stanton.

‡**PRESS GANG PUBLISHERS**, 603 Powell St., Vancouver, British Columbia V6A 1H2 Canada. (604)253-2537. Publishes trade paperback originals. Averages 2 titles/year. Pays royalty. Offers no advance. Simultaneous and photocopied submissions OK. SASE. Reports in 1 month on queries; 2 months on mss. Book catalog for business size SAE and 50¢ (Canadian funds).
Nonfiction: Women's politics. "We are a feminist press, interested in analytical and historical work." No mss without relevance to women's liberation. Preference to Canadian mss. Submit outline/synopsis and sample

chapters.
Recent Nonficton Title: *Falling From Grace*, by E. Van de Walle;
Fiction: Short stories, novels (by/about women), and nonsexist children's books. No mss without relevance to women's liberation. Submit complete ms.

PRICE/STERN/SLOAN INC., PUBLISHERS, 410 N. La Cienega Blvd., Los Angeles CA 90048. Imprints include Serendipity Books, Bugg Books, Wee Sing Books, Troubador Press and Laughter Library. Associate Editor: Claudia Sloan. Publishes trade paperback originals. Averages 100-120 titles/year; receives 6,000+ submissions annually. 20% of books from first-time authors; 60% of books from unagented writers. Pays royalty on wholesale price, or by outright purchase. Offers small or no advance. Publishes book an average of 1 year after acceptance. Simultaneous and photocopied submissions OK. Computer printout submissions acceptable; no dot-matrix. SASE. Reports in 3 months. Ms guidelines for SASE.
Nonfiction: Juveniles. Subjects include humor self-help (limited), and satire (limited). Submit outline/synopsis and sample chapters only. "Most titles are unique in concept as well as execution and are geared for the so-called gift market." Reviews artwork/photos as part of ms package.
Tips:"Humor and satire were the basis of the company's early product and are still the mainstream of the company."

‡**PRINCETON ARCHITECTURAL PRESS**, 40 Witherspoon St., Princeton NJ 08540. (609)924-7911. Associate Editor: Judith McClain-Twombly. Publishes hardcover and trade paperback originals and hardcover reprints. Averages 8 titles/year; receives 20 submissions annually. 50% of books from first-time authors; 100% of books from unagented writers. Pays 6-12% royalty on wholesale price. Simultaneous and photocopied submissions OK. Electronic submissions OK on IBM and Altos compatibles, but requires hard copy also. Computer printout submissions acceptable; no dot-matrix. SASE. Reports in 1 month. Free book catalog.
Nonfiction: "Coffee table" book, illustrated book and textbook. Subjects include art, history and architecture. Needs texts on architecture, landscape architecture, architectural monographs, and texts to accompany a possible reprint, architectural history and urban design. Submit outlines/synopsis and sample chapters or complete ms. Reviews artwork/photos.
Recent Nonfiction Title: *The Danteum*, by Thomas Schumacher (architectural history).
Tips: "Our audience is architects, designers, urban planners, architectural theorists, and architectural-urban design historians. Also many academicians and practitioners. In architecture, write about postmodern thought; in design, focus on historical precedent."

*****PRINCETON UNIVERSITY PRESS**, 41 William St., Princeton NJ 08540. (609)452-4900. Editor-in-Chief: Sanford G Thatcher. Publishes hardcover and trade paperback originals and reprints. Averages 140 titles/year; receives 5,000 submissions annually. 50% of books from first-time authors; 99% of books from unagented writers. Average print order for writer's first book is 1,250. Subsidy assists 50% of books, "when we don't break even on the first printing." Pays 10% maximum royalty on retail price. Rarely offers advance. Publishes book an average of 1 year after acceptance. Simultaneous submissions OK, if notified; photocopied submissions OK. Electronic submissions OK on Penta with Telemedia interface, compatible with Radio Shack TRS-80, IBM PC, and Wang. Requires hard copy also. Computer printout submissions acceptable; no dot-matrix. SASE. Reports in 2 weeks on queries; 1 month on ms "if unsuitable" or 6 months "if suitable and put through entire review process". Ms guidelines for SASE.
Nonfiction: Biography, reference and technical. Subjects include art history, literary criticism, history, philosophy, religion, political science, economics, anthropology, sociology, science and poetry.
Recent Nonfiction Title: *Churchill and Roosevelt: The Complete Correspondence*, edited by Warren F. Kimball.
Poetry: "Poetry submissions (original and in translation) are judged in competition. Write to Robert Brown. Submit complete ms.
Tips:"A work of original scholorship that significantly contributes to the advance of knowledge in its field via new data or new interpretations, or both, has the best chance of selling. We do not often offer advance contracts; most books we accept are already completed.

PRINTEMPS BOOKS, INC., Box 746, Wilmette IL 60091. (312)251-5418. Secretary/Treasurer: Beatrice Penovich. Publishes trade paperback originals. Averages 3 titles/year. Pays royalty or makes outright purchase, "to be agreed upon." Offers no advance. SASE. Reports in 1 month on mss.
Fiction: Adventure, ethnic, fantasy, humor, mystery, suspense, and children's stories (short). "Our aim is to both entertain and educate students who have less than average reading skills. We envision publication of a collection of stories suitable for high school students who have a very limited vocabulary." Publishes for school systems and over-the-counter purchases. Submit complete ms.

‡**PROBUS PUBLISHING CO.**, 118 N. Clinton, Chicago IL 60606. (312)346-7985. Vice President: J. Michael Jeffers. Publishes hardcover originals. Averages 20-30 titles/year; receives 50+ submissions annually.

70% of books from first-time authors; 100% of books from unagented writers. Pays 10-15% royalty on wholesale price. Offers average $1,500 advance. Publishes book an average of 1-2 months after acceptance. Simultaneous and photocopied submissions OK. Electronic submissions OK on MS-DOS. Computer printout submissions acceptable; no dot-matrix. SASE. Reports in 1 week on queries; 2 weeks on mss. Free book catalog; ms guidelines for SASE.

Nonfiction: How-to and technical. Subjects include business and economics and investments. "We will only look at quality business books that take a responsible point of view." Submit outline/synopsis and sample chapters.

Recent Nonfiction Title: *Investor's Equation*, by Bowen (business).

Tips: "Serious investors, businessmen and entrepreneurs are our readers."

‡**PRODUCTIVITY PRESS**, Box 814, Cambridge MA 02238. (617)497-5146. Acquisitions Editor: Patricia Slote. Book publishing division of Productivity, Inc., Box 16722, Stamford CT 06905. (203)967-3500. President/Publisher: Norman Bodek. Publishes business books and tapes on quality and productive management skills and techniques. Books are aimed at corporate executives and middle managers with ways to improve productivity, product and service quality, innovation and quality of worklife for employees. Published two new titles in 1984; 4-6 planned for 1985. Royalties, advances, all contract terms negotiable. Simultaneous and photocopied submissions OK. SASE. Responds to queries and abstracts within 1 month. Query with abstract of 2-3 paragraphs, telling what will be covered in the book; combined with an outline (3-5 pages) of subject matter, chapter by chapter. One or more sample chapters preferred (photocopied originals, we will assume no responsibility for loss or damage of mss), along with a brief letter explaining how your book differs from others on the subject and a resume or biographical data sheet.

Nonfiction: "We specialize in books for and about business management, what works and what doesn't. As the sponsor of several study missions to the Far East, we are cognizant of the Japanese economic phenomenon but are more interested in explaining the nut-and-bolts aspects of how their system—or any management system anywhere—works in the factory or office. We're looking for tomorrow's trends. Our readers learned about Quality Circles, Just-In-Time inventory methods and lifetime employment programs long before they read about them in the general business press. We are after ideas that are about to shake up an industry or stir new debate on the subject."

Fiction: "We haven't yet published any fiction, but that's not to say we won't. We're currently looking at a novel that could click, not because it has a 'business' setting, but because it's well-written and teaches about management systems as it entertains."

Recent Nonfiction Title: *Managerial Engineering*, by Ryuji Fukuda.

PROMETHEUS BOOKS, INC., 700 E. Amherst St., Buffalo NY 14215. (716)837-2475. President/Editor-in-Chief: Paul Kurtz. Vice President/Director of Advertising and Promotion: Victor Gulotta. Publishes hardcover and trade paperback originals. Averages 30 titles/year; receives 1,000+ submissions annually. 10-20% of books from first-time authors; 75% from unagented writers. Pays 5-10% royalty on wholesale price; offers negotiable advance. Publishes book an average of 6 months after acceptance. Computer printout submissions acceptable; no dot-matrix. SASE. Reports in 2 months. Free book catalog.

Nonfiction and Fiction: Textbook and trade. Subjects include philosophy, science, psychology, religion, sociology, medical ethics, biography, literature and criticism. "Prometheus is an independent publishing house with a commitment to maximizing the availability of books of high scholarly merit and popular interest. We welcome manuscript proposals suitable to our publishing program, which focuses on the humanities and social and natural sciences. One area of specialization in which we have experienced tremendous growth is scientific criticism of 'paranormal phenomena.' We also are interested in examining proposals for competitive college texts, both primary and supplementary." Accepts nonfiction translations. Submission of popular trade nonfiction is also encouraged. Submit outline/synopsis and/or "at least the first few" chapters. Reviews artwork/photos as part of ms package.

Recent Title: *Religion, State and the Burger Court*, by Leo Pfeffer.

PRUETT PUBLISHING CO., 2928 Pearl, Boulder CO 80301. Managing Editor: Gerald Keenan. Averages 20 titles/year; receives 200 submissions annually. 75% of books from first-time authors; 100% of books from unagented writers. Average print order for a writer's first book is 2,000-3,000. Pays royalty contract on wholesale price. "Most books that we publish are aimed at special interest groups. As a small publisher, we feel most comfortable in dealing with a segment of the market that is very clearly identifiable, and one we know we can reach with our resources." Publishes book an average of 10 months after acceptance. Legible photocopies acceptable. Any disk submissions would have to interface with present typesetting system, but requires hard copy also. Computer printout submissions acceptable; no dot-matrix. Reports in 4 weeks. SASE. Free catalog on request; ms guidelines for SASE.

Nonfiction: Publishes general adult nonfiction and textbooks. Subjects include pictorial railroad histories, outdoor activities related to the Intermountain West, and some western Americana. Textbooks with a regional (intermountain) aspect for preschool through college level. Does not want to see anything with the personal

reminiscence angle or biographical studies of little-known personalities. "Like most small publishers, we try to emphasize quality from start to finish, because, for the most part, our titles are going to a specialized market that is very quality conscious. We also feel that one of our strong points is the personal involvement ('touch') so often absent in a much larger organization." Accepts outline/synopsis and 3 sample chapters. Mss must conform to the Chicago *Manual of Style*. Reviews artwork/photos as part of ms package.
Recent Nonfiction Title: *San Juan Country*, by Griffiths.

PSG PUBLISHING CO., INC.,545 Great Rd., Littleton MA 01460. (617)486-8971. President/Publisher: Frank Paparello. Publishes hardcover and paperback originals. Pays royalty on net revenues. Specializes in publishing medical and dental books, newsletters and journals for the professional and student markets. Pays 10-15% royalty. Simultaneous submissions OK. Reports in 1 month. SASE. Free book catalog.
Nonfiction: Medical and dental books, newsletter and journals. Request proposal form. Query or submit complete ms. Reviews artwork photos as part of ms package.
Recent Nonfiction Title: *Clinical Psychopharmacology*, by Jerrold Bernstein, M.D.
Tips: Queries/mss may be routed to other editors in the publishing groups.

PUCKERBRUSH PRESS, 76 Main St., Orono ME 04473. (207)581-3832/866-4808. Publisher/Editor: Constance Hunting. Publishes trade paperback originals. Averages 2-3 titles/year; receives 500-1,000 submissions annually. 60% of books from first-time authors; 50% of books from unagented writers. Average print order for a writer's first book is 500-1,000. Pays 10-15% royalty on retail price. Publishes book an average of 1 year after acceptance. Simultaneous submissions OK. Computer printout submissions acceptable; prefers letter-quality to dot-matrix. SASE. Reports in 1 month. Free book list.
Nonfiction: Literary. Subject includes religion ("lively, interesting; no Bible verse listing"). Submit outline/synopsis and sample chapters or complete ms.
Recent Nonfiction Title: *The Rocking Horse*, by Douglas Young (sermons for children).
Fiction: Literary—"anything fresh, written (as opposed to confused or automated)." No California fantasy or Midwest realism. Submit outline/synopsis and sample chapters or complete ms.
Recent Fiction Title: *The Police Know Everything*, by Sanford Phippen (downeast, bizarre stories).
Poetry: "Anything nontemporary." No "confessional, feminist, or 20th century imitation." Submit complete ms.
Recent Poetry Title: *Palace of Earth*, by Sonya Dorman (Pushcart Foundation Small Press Promotion selection).
Tips: "We have a small, literate, widely-read audience."

PURDUE UNIVERSITY PRESS, South Campus Courts, D., West Lafayette IN 47907. (317)494-2035. Director: William J. Whalen. Managing Editor: Verna Emery. Publishes hardcover and paperback originals. Specializes in scholarly books from all areas of academic endeavor. Pays 10% royalty on list price. Offers no advance. Publishes 7-8 titles/year. Publishes book an average of 1 year after acceptance. Photocopied submissions OK "if author will verify that it does not mean simultaneous submission elsewhere." Reports in 4 months. SASE. Free book catalog.
Nonfiction: Publishes agriculture, Americana, art (but no color plates), biography, communication, economics, engineering, history, horticulture, literature, philosophy, political science, psychology, science, sociology, and literary criticism. "Works of scholarship only." Submit complete ms only.
Recent Nonfiction Title: *Deconstruction Reframed*, by Floyd Merrell.

Q.E.D. INFORMATION SCIENCES, INC., 170 Linden St., Box 181, Wellesley MA 02181. (617)237-5656. Manager of Publishing/Software: Jerry Murphy. Publishes computer books for MIS professionals and software. Averages 20 titles/year. Pays 10-15% royalty on net receipts. Publishes book an average of 6 months after acceptance. Electronic submissions OK on IBM PC. Computer printout submissions OK. SASE. Preliminary reports in 1 week on queries; 3 weeks on mss. Free book catalog.
Nonfiction: Technical. Subjects include computers, personal computing, and database technology. "Our books are read by data processing managers and technicians." Submit outline/synopsis and 2 sample chapters. Reviews artwork/photos as part of ms package.
Recent Nonfiction Title: *Data Analysis: The Key to Data Base Design*, by R. Perkinson.

QUARTET BOOKS INC., Subsidiary of The Namara Group, Suite 2005, 215 S. Park Ave., New York NY 10003. (212)254-2277. Director: Marilyn Warnick. Editor: Catherine Norden. Subsidiaries include The Womens Press and Namara Publications and Robin Clark. Publishes hardcover and trade paperback originals and hardcover and trade paperback reprints. Averages 40 titles/year in US, 200 in UK. Pays 6-12% royalty; offers average $2,000 advance. Simultaneous submissions OK. SASE. Reports in 3 weeks on queries; 6 weeks on mss. Book catalog for 7x9 SAE and 2 first class stamps.
Nonfiction: Biography, "coffee table" book, and illustrated book. Subjects include animals, business and economics, history, jazz, philosophy, photography, politics, psychology, sociology and Middle Eastern

politics, culture and society. Especially looking for "well-written, thoroughly researched books on most serious topics and people who will be of interest to both the English and American reader. No World War II experiences, cookery, health, do-it-yourself, keep-fit, astrology, or anything sexist or racist. Submit outline/synopsis and sample chapters.

Recent Nonfiction Title: *The Transformation of Spain.*

Fiction: Adventure, erotica (only if very literary), mainstream, crime, and feminist. No romances, science fiction, westerns, horror, or any genre books other than crime. Submit through agent only.

Recent Fiction Title: *Distant View of a Minaret*, by Alisa Risaat.

Tips: "If I were a writer trying to market a book today, I would try to come up with something fresh rather than imitating current bestsellers. We are looking for titles that can be published by our sister company, Quartet Books Ltd. in London, as well as by the U.S. company so the books must appeal to both markets."

QUE CORPORATION, 7999 Knue Rd., Indianapolis IN 46250. (317)842-7162. Editorial Director: David F. Noble. Publishes trade paperback originals, hardware and software products guides, software for books on computer spreadsheets, and software. Published 20 titles in 1984; 45 titles anticipated in 1985; receives 700 submissions annually. 80% of books from first-time authors; 100% of books from unagented writers. Pays 8-15% escalating royalty on wholesale price; buys some mss outright. Simultaneous (if so advised) and photocopied submissions OK. Electronic submissions OK on CP/M 8" or IBM PC compatible; requires hard copy also. Computer printout submissions acceptable; prefers letter-quality to dot-matrix. SASE. Reports in 1 month. Free book catalog; ms guidelines for SASE.

Nonfiction: How-to, technical, and reference books relating to microcomputers; textbooks on business use of microcomputers; software user's guides and tutorials; operating systems user's guides; computer programming language reference works; books on microcomputer systems, spreadsheet software business applications, word processing, data base management, time management, popular computer programs for the home, computer graphics and game programs, hobbies (microcomputers), networking, communications, languages, educational uses of microcomputers, computer-assisted instruction in education and business and course-authoring applications. "We will consider books on most subjects relating to microcomputers." Query, submit outline/synopsis and sample chapters, or send complete ms.

Recent Nonfiction Title: *Using dBASE III*, by George Chou, Ph.D.

QUICKSILVER PRODUCTIONS, Box 340, Ashland OR 97520. (503)482-5343. Manager: Laurie McAlister. Publishes mass market paperback originals. Averages 4 titles/year. Pays 7½-8% royalty. Computer printout submissions OK. Free book catalog.

Nonfiction: Cookbooks, and calendars on astrology.

Recent Nonfiction Title: *Celestial Influences 85*, by Jim Maynard (wall calendar).

‡**QUILL, A Division of William Morrow and Co., Inc.**, Subsidiary of The Hearst Corporation, 105 Madison Ave., New York NY 10016. (212)889-3050. Managing Editor: Alison Brown Cerier. Publishes trade paperback originals and reprints. Averages 50 titles/year. 40% of books from first-time authors; 10% of books from unagented writers. Pays royalty on retail price. Offers variable advance. Publishes ms an average of 1 year after acceptance. Simultaneous and photocopied submissions OK. Computer printout submissions acceptable; prefers letter-quality to dot-matrix. No unsolicited mss or proposals; mss and proposals should be submitted through a literary agent. Reports in 4 weeks.

Nonfiction: Biography and trade books. Subjects include cooking and foods, history, music, psychology, science, and puzzles and games. Needs nonfiction trade paperbacks with enduring importance; books that have backlist potential and appeal to educated people with broad intellectual curiosities. No fitness, diet, how-to, self-help or humor. Query.

Recent Nonfiction Title: *Vita*, by Victoria Glendinnig (biography).

QUINTESSENCE PUBLISHING CO., INC., 8 S. Michigan Ave., Chicago IL 60603. (312)782-3221. Publisher: H.W. Haase. Vice President, Editorial: Tomoko Tsuchiya. Publishes hardcover and trade paperback originals. Averages 22 titles/year. Pays average 10% royalty. Computer printout submissions acceptable. SASE. Reports in 2 weeks.

Nonfiction: Technical (on all aspects of dentistry). Submit outline/synopsis and 2-4 sample chapters. Reviews artwork/photos as part of ms package.

RAINBOW BOOKS, Box 1069, Moore Haven FL 33471. (813)946-0293. Publishes hardcover and trade paperback originals. Averages 8-10 titles/year. Reports in 1 week. Queries only, addressed to B. Lampe, Associate. Book catalogue $1.

Nonfiction: Reference and resource books plus some well-targeted how-to.

Recent Nonfiction Title: *How to Enjoy Retirement*, by Watson.

RAINTREE PUBLISHERS INC., 330 E. Kilbourn Ave., Milwaukee WI 53202. (414)273-0873. Editor-in-Chief: Russell Bennet. Publishes hardcover originals. Averages 20-50 titles/year. Pays royalty or makes outright purchase. Simultaneous and photocopied submissions OK. Computer printout submissions acceptable; prefers letter-quality to dot-matrix. SASE. Reports in 2 months. Free book catalog.
Nonfiction: Juvenile and reference. Subjects include animals, health, history, nature and photography. "We publish school and library books in series." Query with outline/synopsis and sample chapters. Reviews artwork/photos as part of ms package.
Fiction: Adventure, historical and science fiction. Query with outline/synopsis and sample chapters.

‡**REFERENCE SERVICE PRESS**, Suite 310, 3540 Wilshire Blvd., Los Angeles CA 90010. (213)251-3743. President: Dr. Gail Schlachter. Publishes hardcover and paperback originals. 5 titles planned for 1986; 10-20 titles/year thereafter. Receives 30-50 submissions annually. 90% of books from unagented writers. Average print order for a writer's first book is 1,000. Pays 10-20% royalty on net price, depending upon form of submission. Publishes book an average of 9 months after acceptance. Photocopied submissions OK. Disk submissions OK, but "must be prepared according to our specifications; check with us before submitting." Computer printout submissions acceptable; prefers letter-quality to dot-matrix. SASE. Reports in 45 days. Ms guidelines for SASE.
Nonfiction: Reference works (directories, dictionaries, handbooks, guides, bibliographies, encyclopedias, almanacs, serials, etc.) in any subject area and monographs on topics of interest to reference librarians. Query or submit outline/prospectus and 2-3 sample chapters. Reviews artwork/photos as part of ms package.
Recent Nonfiction Title: *Directory of Financial Aids for the Disabled, 1986-87*, by Gail A. Schlachter.

REGAL BOOKS, Division of Gospel Light Publications, 2300 Knoll Dr., Ventura CA 93003. Managing Director Acquisitions: J. Edward Hastings. Publishes hardcover and paperback originals. Averages 25 titles/year receives 5,000 submissions annually. 20% of books from first-time authors, 90% of books from unagented writers. Average print order for writer's first book is 5,000. Pays 10% royalty on paperback titles, 10% net for curriculum books. Publishes book an average of 11 months after acceptance. Buys all rights. Computer printout submissions acceptable; prefers letter-quality to dot-matrix. SASE. Reports in 3 months. Ms guidelines for SAE and 50¢ postage.
Nonfiction: Bible studies (Old and New Testament), Christian living, counseling (self-help), contemporary concerns, evangelism (church growth), marriage and family, youth, inspirational/devotional, communication resources, teaching enrichment resources, Bible commentary for Laymen Series, and missions. Query or submit detailed outline/synopsis and 2-3 sample chapters; no complete mss.
Recent Nonfiction Title: *Unleashing the Church*, by Frank Tillapaugh.
Recent Fiction Title: *Johnny Come Home*, by R.C. Sproul.

REGENTS PUBLISHING CO., INC., 2 Park Ave., New York NY 10016. 5% of books from first-time authors; 100% of books from unagented writers. Average print order for a writer's first book is 10,000. ESL Acquisitions Editor: John Chapman. Computerized Instruction Editor: David Tillyer. Publishes English as a second language textbooks, computer-assisted instruction programs for the same market, and software. Averages 50 titles/year; receives 250 submissions annually. Prefers complete proposals, including description of target market, comparison with similar materials already on the market, description of age/grade/difficulty level, as well as table of contents and at least 3 sample units. Publishes book an average of 1 year after acceptance. Electronic submissions OK on Apple IIE or IBM PC, but requires hard copy also. Computer printout submissions acceptable; no dot-matrix.
Nonfiction: Textbooks. Publishes ESL/EFL and Spanish language textbooks for all ages. Produces ESP materials for business, science, etc.
Recent Nonfiction Title: *Spectrum* (an adult notional/functional ESL series).
Tips: Freelance writers should be aware of English as second language trends and market needs in education.

REGNERY/GATEWAY, INC., 44 E. Superior St., Chicago IL 60610. President: Clyde P. Peters. Chairman: Henry Regnery. Publishes hardcover and paperback originals (50%) and paperback reprints (50%). Averages 6-12 titles/year. Pays royalty. Simultaneous and photocopied submissions OK. Computer printout submissions acceptable. SASE. Reports in 1 month. Free book catalog.
Nonfiction: Biography, economics, history, philosophy, politics, psychology, religion, science, sociology and education (teaching). Accepts nonfiction translations. "We are looking for books on current affairs—of either political, legal, social, environmental, educational or historical interest. Books heavy on sex and obscene brutality should not be submitted. No fiction, verse or children's literature." Queries preferred. Additional information if requested. No unsolicited mss accepted. Looks for "a novel approach to the subject, expertise of the author, clean, respectable writing, salability of the proposed work."
Recent Nonfiction Title: *The Coercive Utopians*, by Rael Jean Isaac.

‡**RELIGIOUS EDUCATION PRESS**, 1531 Wellington Rd., Birmingham AL 35209. (205)879-4040. Editor: James Michael Lee. Publishes trade paperback originals. Averges 5 titles/year; receives 50 submissions annually. 40% of books from first-time authors; 100% of books from unagented writers. Pays 10% royalty on actual selling price. "Many of our books are work for hire. We do not have a subsidy option. Offers no advance. Photocopied submissions OK. Information on request for electronic submissions. Computer printout submissions OK; no dot-matrix. SASE. Reports in 3 weeks on queries; 8 weeks on mss. Free book catalog.
Nonfiction: Technical and textbook. Scholarly subjects on religion and religious education. "We publish serious significant and scholarly books on religious education and pastoral ministry." No mss under 200 pages, books on Biblical interpretation, or "popular" book. Query. Reviews artwork/photos as part of ms package.
Recent Nonfiction Title: *The Spiritualism of the Religious Educator*, by Lee (religion/psychology).
Tips: "Write clearly, reason exactly and connectively, and meet deadlines."

***RESOURCE PUBLICATIONS, INC.**, #290, 160 E. Virginia St., San Jose CA 95112. Editorial Director: Kenneth E. Guentert. Publishes paperback originals. Publishes 10 titles/year; receives 100-200 submissions annually. 30% of books from first-time authors; 99% of books from unagented writers. Average print order of a writer's first book is 1,500. Subsidy publishes 25% of books. "If the author can present and defend a personal publicity effort or otherwise demonstrate demand and the work is in our field, we will consider it." Pays 8% royalty; offers no advance. Publishes book an average of 12-18 months after acceptance. Photocopied submissions (with written assurance that work is not being submitted simultaneously) OK. Electronic submissions OK if CP/M 8" single density disks, but requires hard copy also. Computer printout submissions acceptable; prefers letter-quality to dot-matrix. SASE. Reports in 2 months.
Nonfiction: "We look for creative source books for the religious education, worship, religious art, and architecture fields. How-to books, especially for contemporary religious art forms, are of particular interest (dance, mime, drama, choral reading, singing, music, musicianship, bannermaking, statuary, or any visual art form). No heavy theoretical, philosophical, or theological tomes. Nothing utterly unrelated or unrelatable to the religious market as described above. "We're starting a new line of how-to books for personal computer applications." Query or submit outline/synopsis and sample chapters. "Prepare a clear outline of the work and an ambitious schedule of public appearances to help make it known and present both as a proposal to the publisher. With our company a work that can be serialized or systematically excerpted in our periodicals is always given special attention." Accepts translations. Reviews artwork/photos as part of ms package.
Recent Nonfiction Title: *Banners and Such*, by Ortegel (how-to).
Fiction: "Light works providing examples of good expression through the religious art forms. Any collected short works in the areas of drama, dance, song, stories, anecdotes or good visual art. Long poems or illustrated light novels which entertain while teaching a life value which could be useful in religious education or to the religious market at large." Query or submit outline/synopsis and sample chapters.
Recent Fiction Title: *Balloons! Candy! Toys!*, by Daryl Olszewski (stories).
Tips: "Books that provide readers with practical, usable suggestions and ideas pertaining to worship education and the religious arts has the best chance of selling to our firm. We are opening an editorial department for books dealing with small computers. It represents a real opportunity for the author active in small computers."

FLEMING H. REVELL CO., Central Ave., Old Tappan NJ 07675. Imprints include Power Books and Spire. Vice President/Editor-in-Chief: Gary A. Sledge. Managing Editor: Norma F. Chimento. Publishes hardcover and paperback originals and reprints. Averages 80 titles/year. Pays royalty on retail price; sometimes offers advance. No unsolicited mss. Book catalog for SASE.
Nonfiction: Religion and inspirational. "All books must appeal to Protestant-evangelical readers." Query.
Recent Nonfiction Title: *David*, by Mel White with Marie Rothenberg.
Fiction: Protestant-evangelical religion and inspiration. Query.
Recent Fiction Title: *Journey of No Return*, by Bette M. Ross.

REVIEW AND HERALD PUBLISHING ASSOCIATION, 55 West Oak Ridge Dr., Hagerstown MD 21740. Vice President for Editors: Richard W. Coffen. Publishes hardcover and paperback originals and software. Specializes in religious-oriented books. Averages 30-40 titles/year; receives 300 submissions annually. 15% of books from first-time authors; 100% of books from unagented writers. Average print order for a writer's first book is 6,000-7,500. Pays 5-10% royalty on retail price; offers averages $100 advance. Publishes book an average of 1 year after acceptance. Computer printout submissions acceptable; prefers letter-quality to dot-matrix. SASE. Reports in 4 months. Free brochure; ms guidelines for SASE.
Nonfiction: Juveniles (religious-oriented only; 20,000-60,000 words; 128 pages average); nature (128 pages average); and religious (20,000-60,000 words; 128 pages average). Query or submit outline/synopsis and 2-3 sample chapters but prefers to do own illustrating. Looks for "literary style, constructive tone, factual accuracy, compatibility with Adventist theology and life style, and length of manuscript." Reviews artwork/photos as part of ms package.
Recent Nonfiction Title: *On My Back, Looking Up*, by Evelyn Orser.

Tips: "Familiarize yourself with Adventist theology because Review and Herald Publishing Association is owned and operated by the Seventh-Day Adventist Church. We are accepting fewer but better-written manuscripts."

REYMONT ASSOCIATES, 6556 SW Maple Lane, Boca Raton FL 33433. Editor-in-Chief: D.J. Scherer. Managing Editor: Felicia Scherer. Publishers paperback originals. Receives 30 submissions annually. 20% of books from first-time authors; 100% of books from unagented writers. Average print order for a writer's first book is 1,000. Pays 10-12-15% royalty on wholesale price; no advance. Publishes book an average of 3 months after acceptance. Computer printout submissions acceptable. Reports in 2 weeks. SASE. Report catalog for SASE.
Nonfiction: Publishes business reports, how-to, unique directories, and bibliographies. " 'Net' writing; no rhetoric. Aim for 7,500-10,000 words." Submit outline/synopsis and 2 sample chapters. Reviews artwork/photos as part of ms package.
Recent Nonfiction Title: *How to Make Money with Pen & Ink Drawings..*
Tips: Trends in book publishing that freelance writers should be aware of include "the need for sharply focused single-subject reports of 7,000-8,000 words in length."

RICHBORO PRESS, Box 1, Richboro PA 18954. (215)364-2212. Editor: George Moore. Publishes hardcover, trade paperback originals and software. Averages 6 titles/year; receives 500 submissions annually. 90% of books from unagented writers. Average print order for a writer's first book is 500. Pays 10% royalty on retail price. Publishes book an average of 1 year after acceptance. Electronic submissions OK on MS DOS, PC DOS, TRS DOS, and UNIX, but requires hard copy also. Computer printout submissions acceptable. SASE. Reports in 6 weeks on queries; 3 months on mss. Free book catalog; ms guidelines $1 with SASE.
Nonfiction: Cookbook, how-to and gardening. Subjects include cooking and foods. Query.
Recent Nonfiction Title: *Italian Herb Cooking*, by Daneo.

THE RIVERDALE COMPANY, INC., PUBLISHERS, #102, 5506 Kenilworth Ave., Riverdale MD 20737. (301)864-2029. President: John Adams. Publishes hardcover originals. Averages 8-12 titles/year. Pays 15% maximum royalty on wholesale price. Publishes book an average of 6 months after acceptance. Computer printout submissions acceptable; prefers letter-quality to dot-matrix. SASE. Reports in 1 week on queries; 2 months on mss. Free book catalog.
Nonfiction: "We publish technical and social science for scholars, students, policy makers; and tour, restaurant and recreational guides for the mass market." Subjects include economics, history, politics, psychology, sociology and travel. Especially needs social science mss on South Asia or South Asia-Africa. Will consider college text proposals in economics and Third World studies; travel guides of any sorts. Query. Accepts outline/synopsis and 2-3 sample chapters.

‡*RONIN PUBLISHING INC., Box 1035, Berkeley CA 94701. (415)540-6278. Publisher: Sebastian Orfal. Publishes originals and trade paperback reprints. Averages 4 titles/year; receives 50+ submissions annually. 25% of books from first-time authors; 100% of books from unagented writers. Buys 10-20% royalty on wholesale price; if co-published with author, royalties are negotiable. Offers $500 advance (sometimes). Simultaneous and photocopied submissions OK. Electronic submissions OK on IBM PC, but requires hard copy also. Computer printout submissions acceptable. SASE. Reports in 2 months. Free book catalog.
Nonfiction: How-to (business), humor, and illustrated book. Subjects include business and economics, health, nutrition and psychology (business). "We are primarily interested in management psychology how-to." Query or submit outline/synopsis and sample chapters. Reviews artwork/photos as part of ms package.
Recent Nonfiction Title: *Beating Job Burnout*, (3rd ed.), by B. Potter.
Fiction: Humor. Primarily interested in illustrated humor. Query or submit outline/synopsis and sample chapters.
Recent Fiction Title: *Out of the Closet & Off The Wall: An Illustrated History of The Coat Hanger*, by Weber & Weber.

THE ROSEN PUBLISHING GROUP, 29 E. 21st St., New York NY 10010. (212)777-3017. President: Roger Rosen. Imprints include Pelion Press (music titles). Publishes hardcover originals. Entire firm averages 46 titles/year; young adult division averages 35 titles/year. 60% of books from first-time authors; 80% of books from unagented writers. Pays royalty or makes outright purchase. Publishes book an average of 9 months after acceptance. Simultaneous and photocopied submissions OK. Computer printout submissions acceptable; prefers letter-quality to dot-matrix. SASE. Reports in 4 weeks. Free book catalog; ms guidelines for SASE.
Nonfiction: Young adult, reference, self-help and textbook. Subjects include art, health (coping), and music. "Our books are geared to the young adult audience whom we reach via school and public libraries. Most of the books we publish are related to career guidance and personal adjustment. We also publish material on the theater, music and art, as well as journalism for schools. Interested in supplementary material for enrichment of school curriculum." Mss in the young adult nonfiction areas include of vocational guidance, personal and so-

cial adjustment, journalism and theatre. For Pelion Press, mss on classical music, emphasis on opera and singing." Query or submit outline/synopsis and sample chapters. Reviews artwork/photos as part of ms package.
Recent Nonfiction Title: *Coping with Academic Anxiety*, by Ottens.

ROSS BOOKS, Box 4340, Berkeley CA 94704. President: Franz Ross. Publishes hardcover and paperback originals (85%), paperback reprints (15%), and software. Averages 7-10 titles/year. 85% of books from first-time authors; 90% of books from unagented writers. Average print order for a writer's first book is 5,000-10,000. Offers 8-12% royalty on net price. Offers average advance 2% of the first print run. Publishes book an average of 1 year after acceptance. Simultaneous and photocopied submissions OK. Electronic submissions OK on TRS 80 model L/6 or IBM PC. Computer printout submissions acceptable; prefers letter-quality to dot-matrix. SASE. Reports in 1 month. Free book catalog.
Nonfiction: General career finding, bicycle books, popular how-to science, garden books, music, general how-to, some natural foods, and Eastern religion. Especially wants general career finding, popular how-to science and how-to's. No political or children's books. Accepts nonfiction translations. Submit outline/synopsis and 2 sample chapters with SASE. Reviews artwork/photos as part of ms package.
Recent Nonfiction Title: *300 Years at the Keyboard*.

*ROSSEL BOOKS, 44 Dunbow Dr., Chappaqua NY 10514. (914)238-8954. President: Seymour Rossel. Publishes hardcover originals, trade paperback originals, reprints and software. Averages 6-8 titles/year; receives 150-200 submissions annually. 15% of books from first-time authors; 90% of books from unagented writers. Average print order for a writer's first book is 2,500. "We subsidy publish only books which have been sponsored by foundations, organizations, etc." Pays royalty on wholesale or retail price. Offers negotiable advance. Publishes book an average of 1 year after acceptance. Photocopied submissions OK. Electronic submissions OK on IBM PC, DOS compatible. Computer printout submissions acceptable; prefers letter-quality to dot-matrix. SASE. Reports in 2 weeks on queries; 1 month on mss. Book catalog for business size SAE and 39¢ postage.
Nonfiction: Jewish cookbook, how-to, illustrated book, juvenile, reference, textbook, and Judaica in all fields—art, cooking and foods, history, philosophy, photography, politics, psychology, religion, sociology and travel. "We currently seek juvenile nonfiction manuscripts on Jewish subjects; adult manuscripts on being Jewish in America, Jews on the frontier, interesting anecdotal histories with Jewish content, and collections of American Jewish photos. We do not publish adult Jewish fiction. However, we do wish to see juvenile fiction in the Judaica field." Submit outline/synopsis and sample chapters. Reviews artwork/photos as part of ms package.
Recent Nonfiction Title: *Torah From Our Sage*, by J. Nevsner (commentary on Jewish classic, Pirke Avot).
Fiction: Juvenile Jewish adventure, ethnic, historical, mystery, religious, romance and science fiction. Submit outline synopsis and sample chapters.
Tips: "Within the next year, Rossel Books will be initiating a new publishing imprint, Longhorn Books. Longhorn will seek to do Texas-oriented material for the Texas regional marketplace. We would be glad to see submissions for this new imprint as well."

ROUTLEDGE & KEGAN PAUL, INC., Routledge & Kegan Paul PLC (UK), 9 Park St., Boston MA 02108. (617)742-5863. U.S. Editor: Stratford Caldecott. Eight subject editors in the U.K. Editorial Director: Malcolm Campbell. Imprints include Ark, Arkana and Pandora Press. Pandora Press publishes both fiction and nonfiction and deals with topics of interest to women. Arkana publishes primarily books on popular religious topics, especially Eastern religions and occult. Publishes hardcover and trade paperback originals and reprints. Averages 200 titles/year; receives 5,000+ submissions annually. 10% of books from first-time authors; 50-70% of books from unagented writers. Pays 7½-10% royalty on retail price; offers average $1,000 advance. Publishes book an average of 1 year after acceptance. Inquire about electronic submissions. Simultaneous and photocopied submissions OK. Computer printout submissions acceptable; prefers letter-quality to dot-matrix. SASE. Reports in 3 weeks on queries; 6 weeks on mss. Book catalog 73¢; ms guidelines for SASE.
Nonfiction: Academic monograph and textbook. Subjects include biography, illustrated book, reference, self-help, social sciences, philosophy, history, travel psychology women's studies, mind/body/spirit, education, geography, economics and literary criticism. Monograph length: 100,000 words maximum. Query and/or submit outline/synopsis and sample chapters.
Recent Nonfiction Title: *Rough Guide to Greece*, by Mark Ellingham (travel).
Fiction: Routledge & Kegan Paul no longer publishes fiction. Fiction appears only under its imprint, Pandora Press. Ethnic, historical and mainstream. No fiction that is not of particular interest to women. Query.
Recent Fiction Title: *This Place*, by Andrea Freud Lowenstein.

*ALAN ROWE PUBLICATIONS., 3906 N. 69th St., Milwaukee WI 53216. (414)527-0555. Subsidiaries include The Diver's Bookstore and Aquatronics. Administrative Editor: Alan Rowe. Publishes trade paperback originals. Averages 8-10 titles/year. Subsidy publishes 10% of books. "If the book appears to have a limited scope or is totally regional in nature, we might arrange a limited run edition to test the market. In such a case, author contributes." Pays 10% royalty. Photocopied submissions OK. Computer printout submissions acceptable. SASE. Reports in 1 month. Book catalog $1.

Nonfiction: How-to, reference and technical. Subjects include Americana, history, recreation, sports and travel. "All subjects should relate to dive/marine themes. At present we are a specialty house. We invite submissions. Looking for material concerning the diver (scuba). We review submissions from around the world. We are interested in seeing manuscripts dealing with how-to, informational, marine history, regional guides, and dive adventure." Accepts nonfiction translations from German and French. Query or submit outline/synopsis and 2-3 sample chapters. Reviews artwork/photos as part of ms package.

Recent Nonfiction Title: *Make Money in Diving*, by Jon-Paul Giguere;

Tips: Queries/mss may be routed to other editors in the publishing group.

ROWMAN & ALLANHELD, PUBLISHERS, Division of Littlefield Adams & Co., 81 Adams Dr., Totowa NJ 07512. Vice President/Publisher: Matthew Held. Publishes hardcover and paperback originals and hardcover and paperback reprints. Pays 5-12½% royalty on net sales; offers no advance. Simultaneous submissions OK. SASE. Reports in 2 months. Free book catalog.

Nonfiction: Technical and textbooks. Subjects include art, business/economics, health, philosophy, politics, reference, science and sociology. "We publish scholarly studies in these fields with special emphasis on international studies (development, Third World, trade, finance, agricultural), labor economics and agricultural science, economics and philosophy. Our authors are typically academics writing for other professionals, for government bodies and other organizations which utilize primary research." Submit outline/synopsis and sample chapters.

Recent Nonfiction Title: *Equality and Liberty*, by Kai Nielson

ROYAL PUBLISHING CO., Subsidiary of ROMC (Recipes of the Month Club), Box 5027, Beverly Hills CA 90210. (213)550-7170. President: Mrs. Harold Klein. Publishes hardcover, trade, and mass market paperback originals. Averages 4 titles/year. Pays 8-12% royalty on retail price; buys some mss outright. Photocopied submissions OK. SASE. Free book catalog.

Nonfiction: Cookbook. "We especially need cookbooks, diet, food history and specialty cookbooks." Submit complete ms.

Recent Nonfiction Title: *Wining and Dining*, by Riess.

RPM PRESS, INC., Box 157, Verndale MN 56482. (218)631-4707. Publisher: David A. Hietala. Publishes trade paperback originals (50%), and audio-cassette (with workbook) training programs (50%). Averages 18-24 titles/year; receives 75-150 submissions annually. 75% of books from first-time authors; 100% of books from unagented writers. Average print order for a writer's first book is 1,000-5,000. Pays 5-15% royalty on retail price or makes outright purchases of $200-1,500. Offers average advance to established authors of $500. Publishes book/training program an average of 6-9 months after acceptance. Simultaneous and photocopied submissions okay. Electronic submissions OK any ASC II file, but requires hard copy also. Computer printout submissions OK; no dot-matrix. SASE. Reports in 5 weeks on queries; 2 months on mss (usually sooner for both). Book catalog for 9x12 SAE and 88¢ postage; ms guidelines for SASE.

Nonfiction: How-to, reference, technical, and audio-cassette training programs on business, applied management, finance, and engineering geared toward managing the nonprofit workcenter (for the handicapped). "We are looking for how-to books and audio-tape training programs that tell how to set up new business ventures, or improve present management practice in this specialized setting, or how-to training program on setting up quality assurance program or marketing rehabilitation services. People who buy our books and training programs are managers and concerned professionals looking to improve the management practice of their nonprofit business enterprise, so we obviously like to hear from writers who have spent some time in the management of business organizations (or who can speak assertively as if they had). We realize that few writers have the hard-won experience that we are looking for—that's why we offer *extensive* editorial assistance to the few authors we end up working with. If you want to work with us, please note the sort of marketplace we're serving and the type of material we seek. We receive hundreds of query letters each year that are outside our area of specific interest. We have no upper limit on the number of books we publish annually—our limit is based on the number of on-target manuscripts we have available. We are entirely receptive to hearing all ideas and are interested in working with new or established authors who, once they establish themselves with us, are willing to work with us on a long-term basis." Query.

Recent Nonfiction Title:*Market Planning Handbook*, by D. Weinrauch.

RUTGERS UNIVERSITY PRESS, 30 College Ave., New Brunswick NJ 08903. Averages 50 titles/year; receives 600 submissions annually. 30% of books from first-time authors; 90% of books from unagented writers. Average print order for a writer's first book is 2,000. Pays royalty on retail price. Publishes book an average of 1 year after acceptance. Electronic submissions OK, but requires hard copy also. Computer printout submissions acceptable; no dot-matrix. Final decision depends on time required to secure competent professional

reading reports. SASE. Free book catalog; ms guidelines for SASE.
Nonfiction: Scholarly books in history, literary criticism, film studies, art history, anthropology, sociology, women's studies and criminal justice. Regional nonfiction must deal with mid Atlantic region with emphasis on New Jersey. Length: 60,000 words minimum. Query. Reviews artwork/photos as part of ms package.
Recent Nonfiction Title: *Leon Golub, Existential/Activist Painter*, by Donald Kuspit.

‡RYND COMMUNICATIONS, National Health Publishing, National Law Publishing, 99 Painters Mill Rd., Owingsmills MD 21117. (301)363-6400. Acquisitions Editor: Elanore Lampner. Publishes hardcover originals. Averages 5-10 titles/year and quarterly subscription service. Receives 20 submissions annually. 30% of books from first-time authors; 100% of books from unagented writers. Pays 10-12% royalty on retail price. Offers average $250 advance. Publishes book an average of 1 year after acceptance. Electronic submissions OK on IBM compatible. Computer printout submissions acceptable; prefers letter-quality to dot-matrix. SASE. Reports in 2 weeks on queries; 6 weeks on mss. Free book catalog.
Nonfiction: Reference, technical and textbook. Subjects include business and economics (health-related); health (administration); and heath law. Needs textbooks in hospital and nurse management and administration; alternative health care delivery systems; medical ethics and liability; health care marketing and economics. Nothing clinical; prefers works that can be used as both references and textbooks; no trade books. Query or submit outline/synopsis and sample chapters.
Recent Nonfiction Title: *Home Health Care*, by Allen Spiegel, Ph.D. (reference/text).
Tips: "We are a growing house devoted to health care. We welcome new authors, whether or not they have already published; we look for academic and experience background and a clear writing style."

S. C. E.-EDITIONS L'ETINCELLE, 65 Hillside Ave., Westmount, Montreal, Quebec H3Z 1W1 Canada. (514)935-1314. President: Robert Davies. Imprints include L'Etincelle (nonfiction and fiction) and Memoire Vive (microcomputer books). Publishes trade paperback originals. Averages 12 titles/year; receives 200 submissions annually. 10% of books from first-time authors; 80% of books from unagented writers. Average print order for a writer's first book is 4,000. Pays 8-12% royalty on retail price; offers average $1,000 advance. Publishes book an average of 1 year after acceptance. Simultaneous and photocopied submissions OK. Electronic submissions OK on ASC II and EBDCIC, but requires hard copy also. Computer printout submissions acceptable. SASE. Reports in 2 months on queries; 3 months on mss. Free book catalog.
Nonfiction: Biography, cookbook, how-to, humor, reference and self-help. Subjects include animals, business and economics, cooking and foods, health, history, hobbies, microcomputers, nature, philosophy, politics, psychology, recreation, sociology, sports and travel. Accepts nonfiction translations. "We are looking for about five translatable works of nonfiction, in any popular field. Our audience includes French-speaking readers in all major markets in the world." No topics of interest only to Americans. Query or submit outline/synopsis and 3 sample chapters. Reviews artwork/photos or part of ms package.
Recent Nonfiction Title: *Lay Bare the Heart, Relaxation Techniques for Children.*

ST. ANTHONY MESSENGER PRESS, 1615 Republic St., Cincinnati OH 45210. Editor-in-Chief: The Rev. Norman Perry, O.F.M. Publishes paperback originals. Averages 12 titles/year. Pays 6-8% royalty on retail price; offers average $500 advance. Publishes book an average of 8 months after acceptance. Books are sold in bulk to groups (study clubs, high school or college classes) and in bookstores. Photocopied submissions OK if they are not simultaneous submissions to other publishers. Electronic submissions OK, but requires hard copy also. Computer printout submissions acceptable; prefers letter-quality to dot-matrix. SASE. Free catalog.
Nonfiction: Religion. "We try to reach the Catholic market with topics near the heart of the ordinary Catholic's belief. We want to offer insight and inspiration and thus give people support in living a Christian life in a pluralistic society. We are not interested in an academic or abstract approach. Our emphasis is on popular writing with examples, specifics, color and anecdotes." Length: 25,000-40,000 words. Query or submit outline and 2 sample chapters.
Recent Nonfiction Title: *Fundamentalism: What Every Catholic Needs to Know*, by Anthony E. Gilles.

ST. LUKE'S PRESS, Mid-Memphis Tower, 1407 Union, Memphis TN 38104. (901)357-5441. Subsidiaries include Raccoon Books, Inc. (literary nonprofit), and American Blake Foundation (scholarly nonprofit). Consulting Editor: Roger Easson, Ph.D. Averages 8-10 titles/year; receives 3,000 submissions annually. 50% of books from unagented writers. Average print order for a writer's first book is 5,000. Pays 10% minimum royalty on invoice; offers average $100-200 advance. Publishes book an average of 2 years after acceptance. Electronic submissions OK on TRS 80, but requires hard copy also. Computer printout submissions acceptable. SASE. Reports in 3 months. Book catalog $1.
Nonfiction: Biography. Accepts translations. Submit story line and 3 sample chapters. Reviews artwork/photos as part of ms package.
Recent Nonfiction Title: *Absolutely, Positively Overnight*, by Robert Sigafoos.
Fiction: Submit story line and 3 sample chapters.
Recent Fiction Title: *Covenant at Coldwater*, by John Osier.

‡*ST. VLADIMIR'S SEMINARY PRESS, 575 Scarsdale Rd., Crestwood NY 10707. (914)961-8313. Managing Editor: Theodore Bazil. Publishes hardcover and trade paperback originals, and hardcover and trade paperback reprints. Averages 15 titles/year. Subsidy publishes 20% of books. Market considerations determine whether an author should be subsidy published. Pays 7% royalty on retail price. Offers average $1,000+ advance. Simultaneous and photocopied submissions OK. Computer printout submissions acceptable; prefers letter-quality to dot-matrix. SASE. Reports in 3 months on queries; 6 months on mss. Free book catalog and ms guidelines.
Nonfiction: Religion dealing with Eastern Orthodox theology. Query. Reviews artwork/photos as part of ms package.
Recent Nonfiction Title: *The Sacrament of Love*, by Paul Evdokimov (theology of marriage).
Tips: "We have an interest in books that stand on firm theological ground; careful writing and scholarship are basic."

HOWARD W. SAMS & CO., INC., 4300 W. 62nd St., Indianapolis IN 46268. (317)298-5400. Manager of Acquisitions: James S. Hill. Payment depends on quantity, quality and salability. Pays royalty or makes outright purchase. Prefers queries, outlines and sample chapters. SASE. Usually reports within 1 month.
Nonfiction: Technical and engineering books on computers, electronics, security, robots, video and telecommunications.

SAYBROOK PUBLISHING CO., 3518 Armstrong, Dallas TX 75205. (214)521-3757. Managing Editor: Nathan Mitchell. Publishes hardcover and trade paperback originals and reprints. Averages 4-5 titles/year; receives 700 submissions annually. 25% of books from first-time authors; 50% of books from unagented writers. Average print order for a writer's first book is 5,000. Pays 6-12% royalty on retail price. Simultaneous and photocopied submissions OK. Computer printout submissions acceptable; prefers letter-quality to dot-matrix. SASE. Reports in 3 months. Ms guidelines for SASE.
Nonfiction: Biography, juvenile, and literary human science. Subjects include Americana, art, business and economics, health, nature, philosophy, politics, psychology, religion, sociology, women's studies and environmental studies. "Especially interested in scholarly studies in the human sciences which are also exciting, marketable dramatic literature written for substantial sales in the trade." Submit outline/synopsis and sample chapters. Reviews artwork/photos as part of ms package.
Recent Nonfiction Title: *My Quest for Beauty*, by Rollo May.
Fiction: Scholarly work in the human sciences. Especially looking for "books which reveal in a scholarly way specific, essential truths about human beings, e.g., Isaac Bashevis Singer. No books whose *only* purpose is to sell." Submit outline/synopsis and sample chapters.
Tips: "Our books are for the intelligent, curious, general reader. We publish freelance submissions. Seek to tell the truth about human beings by any means. The times in which we live demand it. There are enough readers who hunger for it. If your submission is important and you can convince us that you are determined to do the very best work you are capable of, we will work with you all the way for as long as it takes."

SCARECROW PRESS, INC., 52 Liberty St., Metuchen NJ 08840. Editor in Chief: Bill Eshelman. Senior Editor: Barbara Lee. Publishes hardcover originals. Averages 110 titles/year; receives 500 submissions annually. 70% of books from first-time authors; 100% of books from unagented writers. Average print order for a writer's first book is 1,000. Pays 10% royalty on list price of first 1,500 copies; 15% of list price thereafter. Offers no advance. Publishes book an average of 11 months after receipt of ms. Photocopied submissions OK. Computer printout submissions acceptable; no dot-matrix. SASE. Reports in 2 weeks. Free book catalog.
Nonfiction: Books about music. Needs reference books and meticulously prepared annotated bibliographies, indexes, women's studies and movies. Query. Occasionally reviews artwork/photos as part of ms package.

*SCHENKMAN PUBLISHING CO., INC., 190 Concord Ave., Cambridge MA 02138. (617)492-4952. Editor-in-Chief: Joseph Q. Schenkman. Publishes hardcover and paperback originals. Specializes in textbooks and professional and technical books. Averages 60 titles/year. Subsidy publishes 3% of books. Royalty varies on net sales, but averages 10%. "In some cases, no royalties are paid on first 2,000 copies sold." No advance. State availability of photos and/or illustrations. Publishes book an average of 1 year after acceptance. Computer printout submissions acceptable. Reports in 1-2 months. SASE. Free book catalog.
Nonfiction: Publishes economics, history, psychology, sociology, textbooks and professional and technical books. Reviews artwork/photos as part of ms package. Query.
Recent Nonfiction Title: *Crime and Nation Building*, by Cynthia Mahabir.

*SCHIRMER BOOKS, Macmillan Publishing Co., Inc., 866 3rd Ave., New York NY 10022. Senior Editor: Maribeth Payne. Publishes hardcover and paperback originals, paperback reprints and some software. Publishes 20 books/year; receives 250 submissions annually. 40% of books from first-time authors; 95% of books from unagented writers. Average print order for a writer's first book is 3,000-5,000. Subsidy publishes 5-10% of books. Pays royalty on wholesale or retail price; offers small advance. Submit photos and/or illustrations "if central to the book, not if decorative or tangential." Publishes book an average of 1 year after acceptance. Electronic submissions OK, but requires hard copy also. Computer printout submissions acceptable; prefers letter-quality to dot-matrix. Reports in 6 weeks. SASE; free ms guidelines. Book catalog for SASE.

Nonfiction: Publishes books on the performing arts specializing in music, dance and theatre, college texts, biographies, reference and how-to. Needs texts or scholarly mss for college or scholarly audience. Submit outline/synopsis and sample chapters and current vita. Reviews artwork/photos as part of ms package.

Recent Nonfiction Title: *Deep Song: The Dance Story of Martha Graham*, by Ernestine Stodelle.

SCHOCKEN BOOKS, INC., 62 Cooper Sq., New York NY 10003. (212)475-4900. Managing Editor: Patricia Woodruff. Publishes hardcover and paperback originals and paperback reprints. Publishes 56 titles/year. Pays standard royalty; offers variable advance. Photocopied submissions OK. SASE. Reports in 6 weeks. Free book catalog.

Nonfiction: Needs books of Jewish interest, academic sociology, and children's (mythology and folktales). Submit outline/synopsis and sample chapters.

Recent Nonfiction Title: *Peace is Possible*, by Franz Alt.

SCHOLARLY RESOURCES, INC., 104 Greenhill Ave., Wilmington DE 19805. (302)654-7713. Managing Editor: Philip G. Johnson. Publishes hardcover and trade paperback originals. Averages 15 hardcover titles/year; receives 100 submissions annually. 75% of books from first-time authors; 99% of books from unagented writers. Average print order for a writer's first book is 1,500. Pays 5-15% royalty on retail price. Publishes book an average of 9 months after acceptance. Simultaneous and photocopied submissions OK. Computer printout submissions acceptable; prefers letter-quality to dot-matrix. SASE. Reports in 2 weeks on queries; 2 months on mss. Free book catalog; ms guidelines for SASE.

Nonfiction: Reference. Subjects include history, sociology and political science. "We are interested in bibliography and other reference material as well as historical research and interpretative works on modern America, modern China, and diplomatic history. Our audience includes university and public libraries; some course adoption." Query or submit outline/synopsis and sample chapters. Reviews artwork/photos as part of ms package.

Recent Nonfiction Title: *Race, Economics, and Corporate America*, by John W. Work.

SCHOLASTIC, INC., 730 Broadway, New York NY 10003. (212)505-3000. Editor: Ann Reit. Imprints include Wildfire and Sunfire. Publishes trade paperback originals and software. Averages 36 titles/year. Pays 6% royalty on retail price. Computer printout submissions acceptable; no dot-matrix. Reports in 3 months. Ms guidelines for business size SASE.

Fiction: Romance (Wildfire line), and historical romance (Sunfire). Wildfire books should be 40,000-45,000 words, for girls ages 12-15 who are average to good readers." Query. Request ms guidelines and follow carefully before submitting outline and 3 sample chapters.

Tips: Queries/mss may be routed to other editors in the publishing group.

SCHOLASTIC-TAB PUBLICATIONS, 123 Newkirk Rd., Richmond Hill, Ontario L4C 3G5 Canada. (416)883-5300. Subsidiary of Scholastic, Inc. Acquisitions Editor: Peggy Foy. Imprints include North Winds Press (nonfiction and fiction). Publishes hardcover, trade paperback and mass market paperback originals (80%), and paperback reprints (20%). Averages 35 titles/year in English and French. Pays royalty on list price; advance "depends on probable print run." Publishes book an average of 18 months after acceptance. Computer printout submissions acceptable; prefers letter-quality to dot-matrix. SASE. Reports in 3 weeks on queries; 3 months on mss.

Nonfiction: How-to, humor and juvenile. Subjects include animals, hobbies, crafts, puzzle books, mystery and adventure stories; Canadian authors preferred. Submit outline/synopsis and sample chapters with basic storyline; looking for "an engaging story with a compelling and imaginative storyline, strong and convincing characters, and an immediate, lively writing style," or complete ms. Reviews artwork/photos as part of ms package.

Recent Nonfiction Title: *Seeds & Weeds, A Book of Country Crafts*, by Mary Alice Downie and Jillian Gilliland.

Fiction: Adventure, fantasy, humor, mainstream, mystery, romance, science fiction and suspense, suitable for ages 4-16, Canadian authors preferred. Submit outline/synopsis and sample chapters or complete ms.

Recent Fiction Title: *Ms. Terry Wonderful*, by Marlyn Godfrey.

CHARLES SCRIBNER'S SONS, 115 5th Ave., New York NY 10003. President/Publisher: Mildred Marmur. Publishes hardcover originals and hardcover and paperback reprints. Average 300 titles/year; receives 1,000+ submissions annually. 20% of books from first-time authors; 10% of books from unagented writers. "Our contract terms, royalties and advances vary, depending on the nature of the project." Publishes book an average of 18-24 months after acceptance. Electronic submissions OK on IBM PC, but requires hard copy also.

Computer printout submissions acceptable; no dot-matrix. SASE. Reports in 2 months. Free ms guidelines.
Nonfiction: Publishes adult general fiction and nonfiction, practical books, science for the layman, and health and business books. Queries only.
Recent Fiction Title: *Meditations in Green*, by Stephen Wright.

CHARLES SCRIBNER'S SONS, Children's Books Department, 115 5th Ave., New York NY 10003. (212)486-4035. Editorial Director, Children's Books: Clare Costello. Publishes hardcover originals and paperback reprints of own titles. Averages 40 titles/year. Pays royalty on retail price; offers advance. Publishes book an average of 1 year after acceptance. Computer printout submissions acceptable. SASE. Free book catalog.
Nonfiction: Subjects include animals, art, biography, health, hobbies, humor, nature, photography, recreation, science and sports. Query. Reviews artwork/photos as part of ms package.
Recent Nonfiction Title: *Wolfman*, by Lawrence Pringle.
Fiction: Adventure, fantasy, historical, humor, mainstream, mystery, science fiction and suspense. Submit outline/synopsis and sample chapters.
Recent Fiction Title: *The Wild Children*, by Felice Holmen.

SECOND CHANCE AT LOVE, 200 Madison Ave., New York NY 10016. (212)686-9820. Subsidiary of Berkley Publishing Group. Senior Editor: Ellen Edwards. Publishes mass market paperback original category romances. Averages 72 titles/year. Pays 2-6% royalty. Photocopied submissions OK. Computer printout submissions acceptable; prefers letter-quality to dot-matrix. Reports in 6 weeks. Free ms guidelines.
Fiction: Contemporary romance. Accepts 3 sample chapters and detailed chapter-by-chapter outline, but prefers complete ms from unpublished writers. Query and request ms guidelines.
Recent Fiction Title: *Ain't Misbehaving*, by Jeanne Grant.

SECOND CHANCE PRESS/PERMANENT PRESS, Rd. A2, Noyac Rd., Sag Harbor NY 11963. (516)725-1101. Editor: Judith Shepard. Publishes hardcover and trade paperback originals, hardcover trade paperback, and mass market paperback reprints. Averages 12 titles/year; receives 1,500 submissions annually. 25% of books from first-time authors; 80% of books from unagented writers. Average print order for a writer's first book is 2,000. Pays 10% maximum royalty on wholesale price; offers average $200 advance. Publishes book an average of 18 months after acceptance. Simultaneous and photocopied submissions OK. Computer printout submissions acceptable; prefers letter-quality to dot-matrix. SASE. Reports in 2 weeks on queries; 3 months on mss.
Nonfiction: Biography, cookbook, self-help and current events. Subjects include Americana, cooking and foods, health, history, philosophy, politics, psychology and religion. No scientific and technical material or academic studies. Query.
Recent Nonfiction Title: *Kal Flight 007: The Hidden Story*, by Oliver Clubb.
Fiction: Adventure, confession, erotica, ethnic, experimental, fantasy, gothic, historical, humor, mainstream, mystery, romance, and suspense. Especially looking for fiction with a unique point of view—"original and arresting", suitable for college literature classes. No mass market romance. Query.
Recent Fiction Title: *Hermanos*, by William Herrick.
Tips: "Second Chance Press devotes itself exclusively to re-publishing fine books that are out of print and deserve continued recognition."

SELF-COUNSEL PRESS, INC., Subsidiary of International Self-Counsel Press, Ltd., 1303 N. Northgate Way, Seattle WA 98133. (206)522-8383. Senior Editor: Patricia Robertson. Publishes trade paperback originals. Averages 15 new titles/year; receives 200 submissions annually. 30% of books from first-time authors; 95% of books from unagented writers. Average print order for a writer's first book is 5,000. Pays 10% royalty on wholesale price. Publishes book an average of 6-9 months after acceptance. Computer printout submissions acceptable; no dot-matrix. SASE. Reports in 6 weeks on queries; 2 months on mss. Free book catalog and ms guidelines.
Nonfiction: How-to and reference on law, business and economics. Books on starting and running specific businesses applicable to both Canada and the U.S. Do-it-yourself and self-help law books for lay people. New line in psychology self-help books. Query or submit outline/synopsis and sample chapters.
Recent Nonfiction Title: *Keyboarding for Kids*, by Barbara Aliaga.

SERVANT PUBLICATIONS, 840 Airport Blvd., Box 8617, Ann Arbor MI 48107. (313)761-8505. Editor: Bert Ghezzi. Publishes hardcover, trade and mass market paperback originals and trade paperback reprints. Averages 25 titles/year. Pays 10% royalty on retail price. Computer printout submissions acceptable. Reports in 1 month. Free book catalog.
Nonfiction: Subjects include religion. "We're looking for practical Christian teaching, scripture, current problems facing the Christian church, and inspiration." No heterodox or non-Christian approaches. Query or

submit brief outline/synopsis and 1 sample chapter. Reviews artwork/photos as part of ms package. All unsolicited mss are returned unopened.
Recent Nonfiction Title: *A Lamp for My Feet*, by Elisabeth Elliot.

‡*SEVEN LOCKS PRESS, INC.**, 7425 MacArthur Blvd., Box 72, Cabin John MD 20818. (301)320-2130. Publisher: Calvin Kytle. Publishes hardcover and trade paperback originals, and hardcover and trade paperback reprints. Averages 6 titles/year; receives 100 submissions annually. 50% of books from first-time authors; 50% of books from unagented writers. Subsidy publishes 50% of books. Whether an author should be subsidy published depends on the "type of manuscript and cost of production." Pays 10% royalty of gross sales. Simultaneous and photocopied submissions OK. Computer printout submissions acceptable; no dot-matrix. SASE. Reports in 1 month on queries; 3 months on mss. Free book catalog.
Nonfiction: Biography, juvenile, reference and textbook. Subjects include Americana, business and economics, history, nature, politics, religion and sociology. Especially needs "books that promise to enlighten public policy; also, books of regional interest that are entertaining. Query or submit outline/synopsis and sample chapters. Reviews artwork/photos as part of ms package.
Recent Nonfiction Title: *Myths That Cause Crime*, by H. Pepinsky and P. Jesilow (criminal justice).
Tips: "Literate, intelligent, socially conscious men and women are our readers."

SEVEN SEAS PRESS, Subsidiary of Davis Publications, 524 Thames St., Newport RI 02840. (401)847-1683. Editor: James Gilbert. Publishes hardcover originals. Averages 12 titles/year. 75% of books from first-time authors; 90% of books from unagented writers. Average print order for a writer's first book is 3,000. Pays 8-12¹/₂% on gross receipts. Offers average $1,500 advance. Publishes book an average of 14 months after acceptance. Computer printout submissions acceptable; prefers letter-quality to dot-matrix. SASE. Reports in 1 month.
Nonfiction: "Coffee table" book, cookbook, how-to, humor, illustrated book, reference and technical. "All our titles are in the nautical/marine field. We specialize in informative books that help cruising sailors, in particular, enjoy their sport." Also publishes a line of nonfiction nautical high adventure books. Query or submit outline/synopsis and sample chapters. Reviews artwork/photos as part of ms package.
Recent Nonfiction Title: *The Handbook For Non-Macho Sailors*, by Katy Burke (boating).

‡**SHADOW MOUNTAIN**, Subsidiary of Deseret Book Company, 40 E. South Temple, Box 30178, Salt Lake City UT 84130. (801)534-1515. Editor: Jack Lyon. Publishes hardcover and trade paperback originals, and hardcover and trade paperback reprints. Averages 10 titles/year; receives 100 submissions annually. 100% of books from first-time authors; 100% of books from unagented writers. Pays negotiable royalty on retail price—usually about 10%. Offers negotiable advance. Simultaneous and photocopied submissions OK. Computer printout submissions acceptable; prefers letter-quality to dot-matrix. SASE. Reports in 6 weeks. Free book catalog and ms guidelines.
Nonfiction: Cookbook, how-to, reference, self-help, trade nonfiction and professional. Subjects include business and economics, cooking and foods, health, hobbies, psychology, recreation and sports. Especially need books on parenting, marriage and family relations, education, health, exercise, diet, cooking, homemaking, business, self-help, family entertainment motivational, etc. No pornography. Query and/or submit outline/synopsis and sample chapters or complete ms. Reviews artwork/photos as part of ms package.
Recent Nonfiction Title: *Teaching Children Joy*, by Linda and Richard Eyre.
Tips: "We are very open to new ideas and are looking for authors who know their subjects thoroughly and can put together good, solid books that will sell well for a long time. If I were a writer trying to market a book today, I would focus on the needs of a particular market that I am well acquainted with and write to fill the needs of that market."

HAROLD SHAW PUBLISHERS, 388 Gundersen Dr., Box 567, Wheaton IL 60189. (312)665-6700. Managing Editor: Megs Singer. Publishes hardcover and paperback originals (80%) and paperback reprints (20%). Averages 24 titles/year; receives 1,600 submissions annually. 5% of books from first-time authors; 90% of books from unagented writers. Average print order for a writer's first book is 5,000. Offers 5-10% royalty on retail price. Offers average $300-400 advance (only with established authors). Publishes book an average of 2 years after acceptance. Computer printout submissions acceptable; prefers letter-quality to dot-matrix. SASE. Reports in 6 weeks. Book catalog for SAE and 3 first class stamps.
Nonfiction: How-to, juveniles, poetry, literary, religion and self-help. Especially needs "manuscripts dealing with the needs of Christians in today's changing world that give Christians practical help and challenge for living out their faith. If it is not for the Christian market, we don't want to see it. We do not want to see poetry unless the poet is already established and has a reading audience. Manuscripts must be high in quality and creativity." Query first, then submit outline/synopsis and 2-3 sample chapters.
Recent Nonfiction Title: *Where the Wind Begins*, by Paula D'Arcy.
Tips: "Trends in book publishing that freelance writers should be aware of include the need to use nonsexist language without going to extremes.

‡*SHINING STAR PUBLICATIONS, Subsidiary of Good Apple Inc., Box 1329, Jacksonville OR 97530. (503)899-7121. Editor: Becky Daniel. Averages 120 titles/year; receives 1,500 submissions annually. 50% of books from first-time authors; 100% of books from unagented writers. Subsidy publishes 16% of books. Pays by outright purchase. No advance. Publishes book an average of 1 year after acceptance. Photocopied submissions OK. Computer printout submissions acceptable; prefers letter-quality to dot-matrix. SASE. Reports in 1 month. Book catalog for 9x12 SAE and 2 first class stamps. Ms guidelines for SASE.
Nonfiction: Workbooks on religion. Submit complete ms.
Recent Nonfiction Title: *Life of Jesus Series*, by Rebecca Daniel (workbook).
Fiction: Religious (Bible-based stories). Submit complete ms.
Tips: "Submissions should be single spaced with art suggestions."

SIERRA CLUB BOOKS, 2034 Fillmore St., San Francisco CA 94115. (415)931-7950. Editor-in-Chief: Daniel Moses. Publishes hardcover and paperback originals (95%) and reprints (5%). Averages 20 titles/year. Pays 7-12½% royalty on retail price. Offers average $5,000 advance. Computer printout submissions acceptable. SASE. Reports in 2 months. Free book catalog.
Nonfiction: Animals, health, history (natural), how-to (outdoors), juveniles, nature, philosophy, photography, recreation (outdoors, nonmechanical), science, sports (outdoors), and travel (by foot or bicycle). "The Sierra Club was founded to help people to explore, enjoy and preserve the nation's forests, waters, wildlife and wilderness. The books program looks to publish quality trade books about the outdoors and the protection of natural resources. Specifically, we are interested in undeveloped land (not philosophical but informational), nuclear power, self-sufficiency, natural history, politics and the environment, and juvenile books with an ecological theme." Does *not* want "personal, lyrical, philosophical books on the great outdoors; proposals for large color photographic books without substantial text; how-to books on building things outdoors; books on motorized travel; or any but the most professional studies of animals." Query first, submit outline/synopsis and sample chapters.
Recent Nonfiction Title: *A Bitter Fog: Herbicides and Human Rights*, by Carol Van Strum (a book about the effects of pesticide spraying on a rural community in Oregon).
Fiction: Adventure, historical, mainstream and science fiction. "We do very little fiction, but will consider a fiction manuscript if its theme fits our philosophical aims: the enjoyment and protection of the environment." Does *not* want "any manuscript with animals or plants that talk; apocalyptic plots." Query first, submit outline/synopsis and sample chapters, or submit complete ms.
Recent Fiction Title: *The River Why*, by David James Duncan.

SILHOUETTE BOOKS, 300 E. 42nd St., New York NY 10017. (212)682-6080. Editor-in-Chief: Karen Solem. Imprints include Silhouette Romances, Silhouette Romances, Silhouette Special Editions, Silhouette Desires, Silhouette First Loves, and Silhouette Intimate Moments. Publishes mass market paperback originals. Averages 312 titles/year; receives 4,000 submissions annually. 10% of books from first-time authors; 25% of books from unagented writers. Pays royalty. Publishes book an average of 1 year after acceptance. Computer printout submissions acceptable; no dot-matrix. No unsolicited mss. Send query letter; 2 page synopsis and SASE to head of line. Ms guidelines for SASE.
Imprints: Silhouette Romances (contemporary adult romances), Roz Noonan, editor; 53,000-58,000 words. Silhouette Special Editions (contemporary adult romances), Mary Clare Kersten, senior editor; 75,000-80,000 words. Silhouette Desires (contemporary adult romances), Isabel Swift, editor; 55,000-65,000 words. Silhouette Intimate Moments (contemporary adult romances), Leslie Wainger, senior editor; 80,000-85,000 words. Silhouette First Loves (contemporary young adult romances), Nancy Jackson, senior editor; 45,000-50,000 words.
Fiction: Romance (contemporary romance for adults and young adults). "We are interested in seeing submissions for all our lines. No manuscripts other than contemporary romances of the type outlined above." Mss should "follow our general format, yet have an individuality and life of its own that will make it stand out in the readers' minds."
Recent Fiction Title: *Sarah's Child*, by Linda Howard.
Tips: "The contemporary romance market is constantly changing and developing, so when you read for research, read the latest books and those that have been recommended to you by those knowledgable in the genre."

SIMON & SCHUSTER, Trade Books Division, 1230 Avenue of the Americas, New York NY 10020. "If we accept a book for publication, business arrangements are worked out with the author or his agent and a contract is drawn up. The specific terms vary according to the type of book and other considerations. Royalty rates are more or less standard among publishers. All unsolicited mss will be returned unread. Only mss submitted by agents or recommended to us by friends or actively solicited by us will be considered. In such cases, our requirements are as follows: All mss submitted for consideration should be marked to the attention of a specific editor. It usually takes at least three weeks for the author to be notified of a decision—often longer. Sufficient postage for return by first-class registered mail, or instructions for return by express collect, in case of rejection, should be included. Mss must be typewritten, double-spaced, on one side of the sheet only. We suggest margins of about one and one half inches all around and the standard 8"x11" typewriter paper." Prefers complete mss. Computer printout submissions acceptable; prefers letter-quality to dot-matrix.

Nonfiction and Fiction: "Simon and Schuster publishes books of general adult fiction, history, biography, science, philosophy, the arts and popular culture, running 50,000 words or more. Our program does not, however, include school textbooks, extremely technical or highly specialized works, or, as a general rule, poetry or plays. Exceptions have been made, of course, for extraordinary manuscripts of great distinction or significance."

Tips: Queries/mss may be routed to other editors in the publishing group.

*SLAVICA PUBLISHERS, INC., Box 14388, Columbus OH 43214. (614)268-4002. President/Editor: Charles E. Gribble. Publishes hardcover and paperback originals, reprints and software. Averages 20 titles/year; receives 50-70 submissions annually. 50%+ of books from first-time authors; 100% of books from un-agented writers. Subsidy publishes 33-50% of books. "All manuscripts are read for quality; if they pass that test, then we talk about money. We *never* accept full subsidies on a book, and we *never* publish anything that has not passed the scrutiny of expert readers. Most subsidies are very small (usually in the range of $200-800)." Offers 10-15% royalty on retail price; "for some books, royalties do not begin until specified number has been sold." Publishes book an average of 1 year after acceptance. "Only in exceptional circumstances will we consider simultaneous submissions, and only if we are informed of it. We strongly prefer good photocopied submissions rather than the original." Electronic submissions OK on any CP/M or MSDOS 5¼, but requires hard copy also. Computer printout submissions acceptable; prefers letter-qualtiy to dot-matrix. SASE. Query first. Reports in 1 week to 4 months (more in some cases). Free book catalog.

Nonfiction: Biography, history, reference, textbooks, travel, language study, literature, folklore and literary criticism. "We publish books dealing with almost any aspect of the peoples, languages, literatures, history, cultures of Eastern Europe and the Soviet Union, as well as general linguistics and Balkan studies. We do not publish original fiction and in general do not publish books dealing with areas of the world other than Eastern Europe, the USSR and the Balkans (except for linguistics, which may deal with any area)." Accepts nonfiction translations from Eastern European languages. Query first. Looks for authors of scholarly and textbooks who know their fields and write clearly. Reviews artwork/photos as part of ms package.

Recent Nonfiction Title: *Tyrant and Victim in Dostoevsky*, by Gary Cox.

Tips: "A large percentage of our authors are academics, but we would be happy to hear from other authors as well. Very few of our books sell well enough to make the author much money, since the field in which we work is so small. The few that do make money are normally textbooks."

THE SMITH, 5 Beekman St., New York NY 10038. Managing Editor: Tom Tolnay. Publishes hardcover and paperback originals. The Smith is owned by the Generalist Association, Inc., a nonprofit organization which gives to writers awards averaging $500 for book projects. Averages 3-4 titles/year. A sizeable percentage of books from first-time authors; 85% of books from unagented writers. Average print order for a writer's first book is 1,500. Publishes book an average of 1 year after acceptance. Publishing relationship sometimes first established through magazine, *Pulpsmith*, which includes stories, poetry, novel excerpts and essays. Computer printout submissions acceptable; prefers letter-quality to dot-matrix. Reports in 2 months. SASE. Free book catalog; ms guidelines for SASE.

Nonfiction and Fiction: "Original fiction—no specific schools or categories; for nonfiction, controversial social and cultural issues." Send query first for nonfiction; sample chapter preferred for fiction. Reviews artwork/photos as part of ms package.

Recent Title: *Hearing Out James T. Farrell* (selected lectures).

SOS PUBLICATIONS, Subsidiary of Bradley Products, 4223-25 W. Jefferson Blvd., Los Angeles CA 90016. (213)730-1815. Publisher: Paul Bradley. Publishes mini-bound originals and re-prints. Averages 4 titles/month; receives 800-1,000 submissions annually. 40% of books from first-time authors; 40% of books from unagented writers. Average print order for a writer's first book is 30,000. Pays royalty on wholesale price. Publishes book an average of 6 months after acceptance. Photocopied submissions OK. Computer printout submissions acceptable; no dot-matrix. SASE which will *enclose* the manuscript must accompany submission. Any queries must also include SASE. "Due to both the large number of manuscripts received and our limited reading staff, we report as soon as possible, but allow approximately 3-4 months." No guidelines for SASE.

Fiction: Contact: Fiction Editor. Mystery, romance and suspense. "Our Private Library Collection will soon usher in the Mini-Bound, a hardcover book the size of a mass-market paperback. It will showcase original titles, illustrations and new authors. There will be four categories: The novel, mystery, romance, and adventure. Two further categories are anticipated: Science fiction and westerns. Send complete ms.

‡THE SOURCEVIEW PRESS, Subsidiary of The SourceView Corp., 835 Castro St., Martinez CA 94553. (415)228-6228. Editor: Michael Dean. Publishes trade paperback originals and software. Averages 2-5 titles/year; 100 software titles/year. Pays 6-9% royalty on wholesale price. SASE. Reports in 2 weeks on mss; does not respond to queries.

Nonfiction: Reference and technical. Computer software only. Needs books on computer languages, disk operating systems, theory of writing software, etc. No how-to books in application areas geared to specific software. Submit outline/synopsis and sample chapters or complete ms; prefers agented submissions.

Tips: "Our audience includes college-educated managerial persons with day-to-day involvement with microcomputers. We are a new publisher—any helpful suggestions you folks can give us would be appreciated."

SOUTH END PRESS, 116 St. Botolph, Boston MA 02118. (617)266-0629. Publishes trade paperback and hardcover originals and trade paperback reprints. Averages 22 nonfiction titles/year. Pays 8% royalty on retail price. Simultaneous submissions OK. Computer printout submissions acceptable; no dot-matrix. Reports in 2 months. Free book catalog.

Nonfiction: Subjects include politics, economics, feminism, social change, radical cultural criticism, explorations of race, class, and sex oppression and liberation. No conservative political themes. Submit outline/synopsis and 1-2 sample chapter(s).

Fiction: Not accepting unsolicited fiction manuscripts or queries.

SOUTHERN ILLINOIS UNIVERSITY PRESS, Box 3697, Carbondale IL 62901. (618)453-2281. Director: Kenney Withers. Averages 50 titles/year. Pays 10-12 1/2% royalty on net price. Publishes book an average of 1 year after acceptance. Computer printout submissions acceptable; no dot-matrix. SASE. Reports in 6 weeks. Free book catalog.

Nonfiction: "We are interested in humanities, social sciences and contemporary affairs material. No dissertations or collections of previously published articles." Accepts nonfiction translations from French, German, Scandinavian and Hebrew. Query.

Recent Nonfiction Title: *Thomas Pynchon*, by Cowart (literary criticism).

SOUTHERN METHODIST UNIVERSITY PRESS, Dallas TX 75275. (214)692-2263. Director: Trudy McMurrin. Averages 7 titles/year; receives 300 submissions annually. 20% of books from first-time authors; 95% of books from unagented writers. Average print order for writer's first book is 1,500. Payment is on royalty basis; contracts variable. No advance. Publishes book an average of 15 months after acceptance. Computer printout submissions acceptable "as long as copy is clear and double-spaced; no dot-matrix." Requires query letter with outline, vita, and 1-2 sample chapters. Reports "tend to be slow for promising manuscripts requiring outside reading by authorities." SASE. Free book catalog.

Nonfiction: Regional and scholarly. Subjects include history, biography, folklore literature, anthropology, geology, international and constitutional law, American studies, and the performing arts. Length: open. Reviews artwork/photos as part of ms package.

Recent Nonfiction Title: *Owen Wister: Chronicles of the West, Gentleman of the East*, by Darwin Payne.

Tips: "Books are not commissioned. Advance contracts are sometimes awarded for works-in-progress or collections of original essays."

SOVEREIGN PRESS, 326 Harris Rd., Rochester WA 98579. Senior Editor: Marguerite Pedersen. Publishes hardcover and trade paperback originals. Averages 5 titles/year. Pays by individual agreements. "Payments before publishing are bonus rather than advance." Simultaneous and photocopied submissions OK. Computer printout submissions acceptable. SASE. Reports in 1 month. Book catalog for $1. "We have a unique dedication to the culture of individual sovereignty and put out a special catalog that gives full details of our publishing policy. We want no inquiries and no submissions from anyone not acquainted with our unique orientation."

Nonfiction: Social orientation books on history, philosophy, politics and religion (individual sovereignty only). Publishes for "those seeking a way to integrate personal ideals with universal realities." Especially needs "works effectively promoting the *culture* of individual sovereignty." Submit complete ms.

Recent Nonfiction Title: *Six Disciplines of Man's Being*, by Melvin Gorham.

Fiction: "Historical novels and fictional projections that promote the *culture* of individual sovereignty." Especially needs "perceptively conceived historical novels of Northern European life before the culture was corrupted by theocracy; fictional projections for a *practical* society of sovereign individuals." Submit complete ms.

Recent Fiction Title: *Camp 38*, by Jill von Konen.

‡**SPINSTERS INK**, 803 DeHaro, San Francisco CA 94107. (415)647-9360. Editor/Publisher: Sherilyn Thomas. Publishes trade paperback originals and reprints. Averages 7-10 titles/year; receives 108 submissions annually. 50% of books from first-time authors; 90% of books from unagented writers. Pays 8-12% royalty on retail price. Publishes book an average of 9 months after acceptance. Photocopied submissions OK. Computer printout submissions acceptable; prefers letter-quality to dot-matrix. SASE. Reports in 3 weeks on queries; 2 months on mss. Free book catalog.

Nonfiction: Self-help and feminist analysis for positive change. Subjects include health, history, philosophy, politics, psychology, sociology, feminist and lesbian. "We would like to see an incisive and clear work on an issue of import in the lesbian and feminist communities. No sexist, racist or homophobic work—in general, any work based on oppression of any people is not wanted. Submit outline/synopsis and sample chapters. Reviews artwork/photos as part of ms package.
Recent Nonfiction Title: *The Highest Apple*, by Judy Grahn (critical analysis of lesbian poetry).
Fiction: Ethnic and feminist-lesbian. Submit outline/synopsis and sample chapters.
Recent Fiction Title: *The Woman Who Owned The Shadows*, by Paula Gunn Allen (native American novel).
Poetry: Minimal. Submit complete ms.
Recent Poetry Title: *We Say We Love Each Other*, by Minnie Bruce Pratt (Southern lesbian).

ST PUBLICATIONS, Book Division, 407 Gilbert Ave., Cincinnati OH 45202. (513)421-4050. Book Division Coordinator: Carole Singleton. Publishes hardcover and trade paperback originals and hardcover reprints. Averages 3-5 titles/year; receives 15-20 submissions annually. 50% of books from first-time authors; 100% of books from unagented writers. Pays royalty on wholesale price: 10-12½ escalating from initial sales of book, or 20% (after recovery of production costs). Publishes book an average of 9 months after acceptance. Photocopied submissions OK. Computer printout submissions acceptable. SASE. Reports in 6 weeks on queries; 2 months on mss. Free book catalog; ms guidelines for SASE.
Nonfiction: How-to, reference, technical and textbook. Subjects include art (collections of copyright-free artwork suitable for sign, display or screen printing industries). "We need technical, how-to books for professionals in three specific industries: the sign industry, including outdoor advertising, electric and commercial signs; the screen printing industry, including the printing of paper products, fabrics, ceramics, glass and electronic circuits; and the visual merchandising and store design industry. We are not interested in submissions that do not relate specifically to those three fields." Submit outline/synopsis and sample chapters. Reviews artwork/ photos as part of ms package.
Recent Nonfiction Title: *Neon Techniques and Handling*, by Samuel Miller (how-to, technical).
Tips: "Our audience consists of professionals in the sign, screenprinting, and visual merchandising and store design industries. Request a copy of our book catalog and related magazines (*Signs of the Times*, *Visual Merchandising*, or *Screen Printing*) to get a feel for the technical level of the books we publish and the audience(s) for which they are intended."

STACKPOLE BOOKS, Box 1831, Harrisburg PA 17105. Editorial Director: Chet Fish. Publishes hardcover and paperback originals. Publishes approximately 50 titles/year. "Proposals should begin as a one-page letter, leading to chapter outline only on request. If author is unknown to Stackpole, supply credentials." Publishes book an average of 9 months after acceptance. Computer printout submissions acceptable; prefers letter-quality to dot-matrix. SASE. Ms guidelines for SASE.
Nonfiction: Outdoor-related subject areas—firearms, fishing, hunting, military guides, wildlife, and outdoor skills. Reviews artwork/photos as part of ms package.

*STANDARD PUBLISHING, 8121 Hamilton Ave., Cincinnati OH 45231. (513)931-4050. Publisher/Vice President: Ralph M. Small. Publishes hardcover and paperback originals (85%) and reprints (15%). Specializes in religious books. Averages 60 titles/year; receives 2,000 submissions annually. 25% of books from first-time authors; 90% of books from unagented writers. Average print order for a writer's first book is 7,500. Subsidy publishes 5% of books. Pays 10% usual royalty on wholesale price. Offers $200-1,500 advance. Publishes book an average of 1 year after acceptance. Computer printout submissions acceptable; prefers letter-quality to dot-matrix. SASE. Reports in 1-2 months. Ms guidelines for SASE.
Nonfiction: Publishes how-to; crafts (to be used in Christian education); juveniles; reference; Christian education; quiz; puzzle and religious books; and college textbooks (religious). All mss must pertain to religion. Query or submit outline/synopsis and 2-3 sample chapters. Reviews artwork/photos as part of ms package.
Recent Nonfiction Title: *Older, Wiser, Better in Almost Every Way*, by Jeanette Lockerbie.
Fiction: Religious, devotional books.
Recent Fiction Title: *The Bradford Adventure Series*, by Jerry Jenkins.
Tips: Freelancer has best chance of selling children's books and Christian education methods or programs.

STANFORD UNIVERSITY PRESS, Stanford CA 94305. (415)497-9434. Editor: William W. Carver. Averages 55 titles/year; receives 900 submissions annually. 40% of books from first-time authors, 95% of books from unagented writers. Pays up to 15% royalty; sometimes offers advance. Photocopied submissions OK. Computer printout submissions acceptable; prefers letter-quality to dot-matrix. SASE. Reports in 3 weeks on queries; 5 weeks on mss. Free book catalog.
Nonfiction: Scholarly books in the humanities, social sciences, and natural sciences; history and culture of China, Japan, and Latin America; European history; biology and taxonomy; literature, criticism, and literary theory; anthropology and linguistics; archaeology and geology; political science, sociology, and economics; psychology; women's studies; classical studies. Also syntheses, high-level textbooks, and serious nonfiction

for a more general audience. Query. Reviews artwork/photos as part of ms package.
Recent Nonfiction Title: *The Letters of Anthony Trollope*, edited by N. John Hall.
Tips: "We work hard on manuscripts and expect authors to do likewise."

STEIN AND DAY PUBLISHERS, Scarborough House, Briarcliff Manor NY 10510. Averages 100 titles/year. Offers standard royalty contract. No unsolicited mss without querying first. Nonfiction, send outline or summary and sample chapter. *Must* furnish SASE with all fiction and nonfiction queries.
Nonfiction & Fiction: Publishes general adult fiction and nonfiction books; no juveniles or college. All types of nonfiction except technical. Quality fiction. Minimum length: 65,000 words.
Recent Nonfiction Title: *The Beverly Hills Style*, by Judy Mazel.
Recent Fiction Title: *Confessional*, by Jack Higgens.

STEMMER HOUSE PUBLISHERS, INC., 2627 Caves Rd., Owings Mills MD 21117. (301)363-3690. President: Barbara Holdridge. Publishes hardcover originals. Averages 25 titles/year; receives 1,000 submissions annually. 10% of books from first-time authors; 90% of books from unagented writers. Average print order for a writer's first book is 4,000-10,000. Pays royalty on wholesale price. Publishes book an average of 18 months after acceptance. Computer printout submissions acceptable; no dot-matrix. SASE. Reports in 2 weeks on queries; 3 months on mss. Book catalog for 9x12 SAE and 56¢ postage.
Nonfiction: Biography, cookbook, illustrated book, juvenile and design books. Subjects include Americana, animals, art, cooking and foods, history and nature. Especially looking for "literary novels of sustained quality, biography, history, and art and design." No humor. Query or submit outline/synopsis and sample chapters. Reviews artwork/photos as part of ms package.
Recent Nonfiction Title: *An Italic Calligraphy Handbook*, by Mary Leister (natural history).
Fiction: Adventure, ethnic, historical, mainstream and philosophical. "We want only manuscripts of sustained literary merit. No popular-type manuscripts written to be instant bestsellers." Query.
Recent Fiction Title: *The Fringe of Heaven*, by Margaret Sutherland (contemporary novel).
Tips: "If I were a writer trying to market a book today, I would not imitate current genres on the bestseller lists, but strike out with a subject of intense interest to me." Freelancer has best chance of selling a book with a universal theme, either for adults or children, exceptionally well written, and marketable internationally. "Our goal is a list of perennial sellers of which we can be proud."

STERLING PUBLISHING, 2 Park Ave., New York NY 10016. (212)532-7160. Acquisitions Manager: Sheila Anne Barry. Publishes hardcover and paperback originals (75%) and reprints (25%). Averages 80 titles/year. Pays royalty; offers advance. Publishes book an average of 8 months after acceptance. Computer printout submissions acceptable; prefers letter-quality to dot-matrix. Reports in 6 weeks. SASE. Book catalog for SASE.
Nonfiction: Alternative lifestyle, fiber arts, games and puzzles, health how-to and medicine, business, foods, hobbies, how-to, children's humor, music, occult, pets, photography, recreation, reference, self-help, sports, theatre (how-to), technical, collecting, wine and woodworking. Query or submit complete chapter list, detailed outline/synopsis and 2 sample chapters with photos if necessary. Reviews artwork/photos as part of ms package.
Recent Nonfiction Title: *Hardcore Bodybuilding*, by Robert Kennedy.

*STIPES PUBLISHING CO., 10-12 Chester St., Champaign IL 61820. (217)356-8391. Contact: Robert Watts. Publishes hardcover and paper originals. Averages 25 titles/year. 100% of books from unagented writers. Subsidy publishes 2% of books, "determined by scholarly contribution of the book." Pays 15% maximum royalty on retail price. Publishes book an average of 3-5 months after acceptance. Computer printout submissions acceptable; prefers letter-quality to dot-matrix. SASE. Reports in 2 weeks on queries; 2 months on mss.
Nonfiction: Technical (some areas), textbooks on business and economics, music, agriculture/horticulture, and recreation and physical education. "All of our books in the trade area are books that also have a college text market." No "books unrelated to educational fields taught at the college level." Submit outline/synopsis and 1 sample chapter.
Recent Nonfiction Title: *Manual of Woody Landscape Plants*, by Michael Dirr (college text and general reference).

STOEGER PUBLISHING COMPANY, 55 Ruta Court, S. Hackensack NJ 07606. (201)440-2700. Subsidiary includes Stoeger Industries. Publisher: Robert E. Weise. Publishes trade paperback originals. Averages 12-15 titles/year. Royalty varies, depending on ms. Simultaneous and photocopied submissions OK. SASE. Reports in 1 month on queries; 3 months on mss. Free book catalog.
Nonfiction: Cookbook, how-to and self-help. Subjects include sports, outdoor sports, cooking and foods, and hobbies. Especially looking for how-to books relating to hunting, fishing, or other outdoor sports. Submit outline/synopsis and sample chapters.
Recent Nonfiction Title: *Advanced Muzzleloading*, by Toby Bridges.

STONE WALL PRESS, INC., 1241 30th St., NW, Washington DC 20007. President/Publisher: Henry Wheelwright. Publishes hardcover and trade paperback originals. Averages 2-5 titles/year; receives 50 submissions annually. 75% of books from first-time authors; 95% of books from unagented writers. Average print order for a writer's first book is 3,000-4,000. Pays standard royalty; offers minimal advance. Publishes book an average of 6 months after acceptance. Computer printout submissions acceptable; no dot-matrix. SASE. Reports in 2 weeks. Book catalog for business size SAE and 1 first class stamp.
Nonfiction: How-to and environmental/outdoor. "Unique, practical, illustrated how-to outdoor books (nature, camping, fishing, hiking, hunting, etc.) and environmental books for the general public." Query. Looks for "concise, sharp writing style with humorous touches; a rough table of contents for an idea of the direction of the book, a new approach or topic which hasn't been done recently." Accepts outline/synopsis and several sample chapters. Reviews artwork/photos as part of ms package.
Recent Nonfiction Title: *Swimming Flies, A Revolutionary Approach to Successful Fly Fishing*, by Georges Odier.

STONEYDALE PRESS PUBLISHING CO., 304 Main St., Stevensville MT 59870. (406)777-2729. Publisher: Dale A. Burk. Publishes hardcover and trade paperback originals. Averages 4-6 titles/year; receives 100-125 submissions annually. 20% of books from first-time authors; 100% of books from unagented writers. Pays 10-12% on actual price or makes outright purchase. Offers average $500 advance. Electronic submissions OK on CPM, but requires hard copy also. SASE. Reports in 1 month. Book catalog for SAE and 56¢ postage.
Nonfiction: Biography, "coffee table" book and how-to on Americana, art, history, nature, recreation, travel and Montana topics. "We're looking for good outdoor recreation book ideas for our area (northern Rocky Mountains, Pacific Northwest); historical ideas from the same region not overly done in the past. Also open to 'coffee table' format books, if we can be convinced a market exists for a specific idea." Query. Reviews artwork/photos as part of ms package.
Recent Nonfiction Title: *Elk Hunting in Northern Rockies*, by Ed Wolff.

STRAWBERRY HILL PRESS, 2594 15th Ave., San Francisco CA 94127. President: Jean-Louis Brindamour, Ph.D. Senior Editors: Donna L. Osgood, Joseph Lubow, Carolyn Soto, Robin Witkin. Publishes paperback originals. Publishes 12 titles/year. Receives over 5,000 submissions annually. 90% of books written by first-time authors; 98% of books from unagented writers. Average print order for a writer's first book is 5,000. "We are a small house, proud of what we do, and intending to stay relatively small (that does not mean that we will do a less-than-professional job in marketing our books, however). The author-publisher relationship is vital, from the moment the contract is signed until there are no more books to sell, and we operate on that premise. We do no hardcovers, and, for the moment at least, our format is limited strictly to 6x9 quality paperbacks, prices between $4.95-10.95. We seldom print fewer than 5,000 copies in a first printing, with reprintings also never falling below that same figure." Pays 10% royalty on wholesale price; no advance. Publishes book an average of 2 years after acceptance. Photocopied submissions OK. Electronic submissions OK on TRS 80 Model III system. Computer printout submissions acceptable; no dot-matrix. Reports in 2 months. SASE. Book catalog for SAE and 2 first class stamps.
Nonfiction: Self-help, inspiration (not religion), cookbooks, health and nutrition, aging, diet, popular philosophy, metaphysics, alternative life style,; Third World, minority histories, oral history and popular medicine. Accepts nonfiction and fiction translations. No religion, sports, craft books, photography or fine art material. Submit outline/synopsis and 1 sample chapter.
Recent Nonfiction Title: *Living Up the Street*, by Gary Soto.
Recent Fiction Title: *Dowry of Death*, by Melvin A. Casberg, M.D.

LYLE STUART, INC., 120 Enterprise Ave., Secaucus NJ 07094. (201)866-0490, (212)736-1141. Subsidiaries include Citadel Press and University Books. President: Lyle Stuart. Editor-in-Chief: Tom Roberts. Publishes hardcover and trade paperback originals, and trade paperback reprints. Averages 70 titles/year. Pays 10-12% royalty on retail price; offers "low advance." SASE.
Nonfiction: Biography, "coffee table" book, how-to, humor, illustrated book and self-help. Subjects include Americana, art, business and economics, health, history, music and politics. "The percentage of acceptable over-the-transom manuscripts has been so low during the years that we are no longer reading unsolicited material."
Recent Nonfiction Title: *The Films of Woody Allen*.

‡*SUCCESS PUBLISHING**, 8084 Nashua Dr., Lake Park FL 33410. (305)626-4643. President: Allan H. Smith. Publishes trade paperback originals. Averages 8-10 titles/year; receives 50 submissions annually. 50% of books from first-time authors; 65% of books from unagented writers. Subsidy publishes 25% of books. Pays variable royalty on wholesale price (10% minimum) or makes minimum outright purchase of $1,000. Publishes book an average of 4 months after acceptance. Simultaneous submissions OK. SASE. Computer printout submissions acceptable; prefers letter-quality to dot-matrix. Reports in 4 weeks on queries; 6 weeks on

mss. Book catalog for SAE and 1 first class stamp.

Nonfiction: How-to, juvenile, self-help and craft. Subjects include business and economics and hobbies. Especially looking for mss interesting to home-based businesspeople; middle and high school children, and those interested in sewing and crafts. No poetry, cult, religious or technical books. Query and/or submit outline/synopsis and sample chapters.

Recent Nonfiction Title: *Sewing for Profits*, by Judith and Allan Smith.

*SUN PUBLISHING CO., Box 5588, Santa Fe NM 87502-5588. (505)255-6550. Editor-in-Chief: Skip Whitson. Publishes paperback originals and reprints. Averages 10 titles/year; receives 500 + submissions annually. 50% of books from first-time authors; 100% of books from unagented writers. Average print order for a writer's first book is 100-1,000. Pays 8% royalty; no advance. Will subsidy publish "if we think the book is good enough, and if we have the money to do it, (very unlikely), we'll publish it on our own; otherwise, the author will have to put up the money." Query or submit outline/synopsis, 2 sample chapters and table of contents. "Do not send complete manuscript unless requested to do so." Send photocopies if photos/illustrations are to accompany ms. Simultaneous and photocopied submissions OK. Computer printout submissions acceptable; no dot-matrix. Reports in 4 months. SASE. Book list for SASE.

Nonfiction: Metaphysical, Oriental and new age. "40-200-page lengths are preferred." Looks for brevity and clarity. Reviews artwork/photos as part of ms package.

Recent Nonfiction Title: *Earth Changes Survival Handbook*, by Page Bryant.

Tips: "We are looking for manuscripts on the coming earth changes, for outright purchase."

THE SUNSTONE PRESS, Box 2321, Santa Fe NM 87504-2321. (505)988-4418. Editor-in-Chief: James C. Smith Jr. Publishes paperback originals; few hardcover originals. Averages 16 titles/year; receives 300 submissions annually. 70% of books from first-time authors; 95% of books from unagented writers. Average print order for writer's first book is 2,000-5,000. Pays royalty on wholesale price. Computer printout submissions acceptable. Prefers letter-quality to dot-matrix. SASE. Reports in 2 months.

Nonfiction: How-to series craft books. Books on the history and architecture of the Southwest; poetry. Looks for "strong regional appeal (Southwestern). Length: open. Reviews artwork/photos as part of ms package.

Recent Nonfiction Title: *How to Paint and Sell Your Art*, by Marcia Muth (how-to).

Fiction: Publishes "for readers who use the subject matter to elevate their impressions of our world, our immediate society, families and friends."

Recent Fiction Title: *Bride of the Santa Fe Trail*, by Jean Burroughs.

Poetry: Traditional or free verse. Poetry book not exceeding 64 pages. Prefers Southwestern theme.

Recent Poetry Title: *Runners*, by Gerald Hausman.

SYBEX, INC., 2344 6th St., Berkeley CA 94710. (415)848-8233. Editor-in-Chief: Dr. Rudolph S. Langer. Acquisitions Editor: Carole Alden. Publishes paperback originals. Averages 60 titles/year. Royalty rates vary. Average $2,500 advance. Publishes book an average of 3 months after acceptance. Simultaneous and photocopied submissions OK. "We prefer hard copy for proposal evaluations and encourage our authors to submit Wordstar diskettes upon completion of their manuscripts. Wordstar word processor diskettes preferred. Computer printout submissions acceptable. Reports in 2 months. Free book catalog.

Nonfiction: Computer and electronics. "Manuscripts most publishable in the field of personal computers, personal computer applications, microprocessors, hardware, programming, languages, applications, and telecommunications." Submit outline/synopsis and 2-3 sample chapters. Accepts nonfiction translations from French or German. Looks for "clear writing; technical accuracy; logical presentation of material; and good selection of material, such that the most important aspects of the subject matter are thoroughly covered; well-focused subject matter; and well-thought-out organization that helps the reader understand the material. And marketability." Reviews artwork/photos as part of ms package.

Recent Nonfiction Title: *Mastering Symphony*.

Tips: Queries/mss may be routed to other editors in the publishing group.

SYRACUSE UNIVERSITY PRESS, 1600 Jamesville Ave., Syracuse NY 13210. (315)423-2596. Director: Luther Wilson. Averages 25 titles/year. Pays royalty on net sales. Simultaneous and photocopied submissions OK "only if we are informed." Computer printout submissions acceptable. SASE. Reports in 2 weeks on queries; "longer on submissions." Free book catalog.

Nonfiction: "The best opportunities in our nonfiction program for freelance writers are of books on New York state. We have published regional books by people with limited formal education, but they were thoroughly acquainted with their subjects, and they wrote simply and directly about them. No vague descriptions or assumptions that a reference to a name (in the case of a biography) or place is sufficient information. The author must make a case for the importance of his subject." Query. Accepts outline/synopsis and at least 2 sample chapters.

Recent Nonfiction Title: *Marietta Holley: Life With "Josiah Allen's Wife"*, by Kate Winter.

T.F.H. PUBLICATIONS, INC., 211 W. Sylvania Ave., Neptune City NJ 07753. (201)988-8400. Managing Editor: Neal Pronek. Publishes hardcover originals. Averages 30 titles/year. Buys most mss outright. Publishes book an average of 8 months after acceptance. Simultaneous and photocopied submissions OK. Computer printout submissions acceptable; prefers letter-quality to dot-matrix. SASE. Reports "immediately." Book catalog for 9x12 SAE and $1.90 postage.
Nonfiction: How-to on animals (especially pets) and nature, illustrated book, juvenile, reference, technical (fish taxonomy) for owners of pet animals, tropical fish hobbyists, and textbook. Especially needs "books that tell people how to care for and (where applicable) breed animals (dogs, cats, fresh and saltwater fish, and birds) kept as pets." Query or submit outline/synopsis and 1 sample chapter.
Recent Nonfiction Title: *The Book of the Cocker Spaniel*, by Joan Brearley.
Tips: "Nonfiction manuscript needs for the next year or two include pet books on marketable subjects (dogs, cats, birds, fish) suitable as pets. We must have *photo* illustrations, preferably in color."

T.L. ENTERPRISES, INC., **Book Division**, 29901 Agoura Rd., Agoura CA 91301. (818)991-4980. Editor-in-Chief: Michael Schneider. Assistant Manager: Gail Lerman. Publishes trade and mass market paperback originals. Averages 2 titles/year. Pays 5-10% royalty on retail price. Publishes book an average of 1 year after acceptance. Computer printout submissions acceptable; no dot-matrix. SASE if you need materials returned.. Reports in 1 month.
Nonfiction: How-to, reference, technical and travel/touring related to owning a recreational vehicle. Subjects include cooking and foods, hobbies, nature, recreation and travel. "We *do* read all queries, and we will mail test titles of promise; test winners will receive an immediate home. At present, our book market consists primarily of RV owners, plus motorcycle and bicycle touring enthusiasts and photographers. For now, our book audience is our magazine audience—the million or more people who read *Trailer Life*, *Motor Home*, *Rider*, Bicycle Rider, and Darkroom Photography, et al—together with the 450,000 families who belong to our Good Sam (RV owners) Club." Query with outline/synopsis. Reviews artwork/photos as part of ms package.
Recent Nonfiction Title: *52 Great RV Backroads of America*, by Bob Longsdorf.

TAB BOOKS, INC., Blue Ridge Summit PA 17214. (717)794-2191. Vice President: Ray Collins. Publishes hardcover and paperback originals and reprints. Publishes 200 titles per year; receives 520 submissions annually. 50% of books from first-time authors; 95% of books from unagented writers. Average print order for writer's first book is 10,000. Pays variable royalty; buys some mss outright for a negotiable fee. Offers advance. Photocopied submissions OK (except for art). Electronic submissions OK on IBM PC, Word Star. Computer printout submissions acceptable; no dot-matrix. SASE. Reports in 6 weeks. Free book catalog and ms guidelines.
Nonfiction: TAB publishes titles in such fields as computer hardware, computer software, business, solar and alternate energy, marine line, aviation, automotive, music technology, consumer medicine, electronics, electrical and electronics repair, amateur radio, shortwave listening, model railroading, toys, hobbies, drawing, animals and animal power, practical skills with projects, building furniture, basic how-to for the house, building large structures, calculators, robotics, telephones, model radio control, TV servicing, audio, recording, hi-fi and stereo, electronic music, electric motors, electrical wiring, electronic test equipment, video programming, CATV, MATV and CCTV, broadcasting, photography and film, appliance servicing and repair, advertising, antiques and restoration, bicycles, crafts, farmsteading, hobby electronics, home construction, license study guides, mathematics, metalworking, reference books, schematics and manuals, small gasoline engines, two-way radio and CB, and woodworking. Accepts nonfiction translations. Reviews artwork/photos as part of ms package.
Tips: "How-to or business books have the best chance of selling to our firm."

‡**TANDY CORPORATION**, 900 Two Tandy Center, Fort Worth TX 76102. (817)390-3446. Director, Technical Publications: David S. Gunzel. Publishes trade paperback originals. Averages 2-15 titles/year; receives 20-50 submissions annually. 20% of books from first-time authors; 100% of books from unagented writers. Pays 4-25% royalty on wholesale price; offers average $15,000 advance. Publishes book an average of 4 months after acceptance. Electronic submissions OK on Tandy Model II, Scripsit, but requires hard copy also. Computer printout submissions acceptable; no dot-matrix. Reports in 2 weeks on queries; 1 month on mss. Tandy/Radio Shack catalogs available from all stores.
Nonfiction: Technical. Subjects include computers and electronics. Needs books on Tandy computers, applications, languages and systems; books on technology and consumers (phones, video). Query. Reviews artwork/photos as part of ms package.
Recent Nonfiction Title: *Using Your Radio Shack Printer*, by William Barden, Jr. (computer).
Tips: "Computer books with a new approach sell very well, with a two or three year life cycle."

TAPLINGER PUBLISHING CO., INC., 132 W. 22nd, New York NY 10011. (212)741-0801. Editors: Ms. Bobs Pinkerton and Roy E. Thomas. Imprints include Crescendo (music) and Pentalic (calligraphy). Publishes hardcover originals. Publishes 75 titles/year; 2% of books from first-time authors; 1% of books from unagented

writers. Average print order for a writer's first book is 3,000-5,000. Pays standard royalty; offers variable advance. Publishes book an average of 1 year after acceptance. Simultaneous and photocopied submissions OK. Computer printout submissions acceptable; no dot-matrix. Reports in 10 weeks. SASE.
Nonfiction: Art, biography, history, theatre, general trade and belles-lettres. No juveniles. Query.
Fiction: Serious contemporary quality fiction. Accepts fiction translations. No juveniles.

JEREMY P. TARCHER, INC., 9110 Sunset Blvd., Los Angeles CA 90069. (213)273-3274. President/Editor-in-Chief: Jeremy P. Tarcher. Publishes hardcover and trade paperback originals. Averages 15 titles/year; receives 700 submissions annually. 50% of books from first-time authors; 25% of books from unagented writers. Average print order for a writer's first book is 7,000. State availability of photos and/or illustrations. Pays 10-12½-15% royalty on hardcover list price; offers advance "competitive in the industry." Publishes book an average of 7 months after acceptance. Simultaneous and photocopied submissions OK. Computer printout submissions acceptable; parefers letter-quality to dot-matrix. SASE. Reports in 6 weeks. Book catalog for 69¢ (bookrate) or $1.07 (first class). Ms Guidelines for SASE.
Nonfiction: Publishes popular psychology and sociology, health and fitness, alternative medicine, consciousness, cooking, and science. Submit outline/synopsis and sample chapters.
Tips:"The writer has the best chance of selling our firm books on creativity; science for the layperson; psychology/personal development; health and medicine; fitness/sports; 'serious' cookbooks; social trends; and women's concerns. Once the author has signed a contract the pitfall that must be avoided is not taking the editor seriously or regarding the input as adversarial. We are trying to help the writer produce a marketable book of high quality. Often writers cannot step back from their work and be objective."

TAYLOR PUBLISHING CO., Subsidiary of Insilco, Box 597, Dallas TX 75221. (214)637-2800. Editorial Director: J. Nelson Black. Senior Editor: Robert Frese. Publishes hardcover and trade paperback originals. Averages 20-30 titles/year; receives 4,000-5,000 submissions annually. 33% of books from first-time authors; 80% of books from unagented writers. Average print order for a writer's first book is 7,500. Pays 10-12½-15% royalties. Offers variable advance. Publishes book an average of 6-8 months after acceptance. Electronic submissions OK on IBM compatible. Computer printout submissions acceptable; prefers letter-quality to dot-matrix. SASE. Reports in 6 weeks on queries; 4 months on mss. Book catalog for SAE and 44¢ postage.
Nonfiction: Biography, "coffee table" book, cookbook, how-to, illustrated book, reference and self-help. Subjects include sports, gardening, lifestyles, art/photography, regional and general interest. Interested in books with broad general appeal and authoritative content and with traditional and nontraditional sales potential. Query or submit outline/synopsis and sample chapters. Reviews artwork/photos as part of ms package.
Recent Nonfiction Title:*Fantasy: The Incredible Cabbage Patch Phenomenon*, by William Hoffman.
Tips:"Beyond the casual writer's desire to knock off a quick bestseller, we're looking for writers with depth, authority, organizational skills, and a distinctive talent for writing—in short, writers who can create books that readers will want to buy."

*TEACHERS COLLEGE PRESS, 1234 Amsterdam Ave., New York NY 10027. (212)678-3929. Director: Carole P. Saltz. Publishes hardcover and paperback originals (90%) and reprints (10%). Averages 75 titles/year. Subsidy publishes 10% of books. Pays royalty; offers advance. Publishes book an average of 1 year after acceptance. Reports in 6 months. SASE. Free book catalog.
Nonfiction: "This university press concentrates on books in the field of education in the broadest sense, from early childhood to higher education: good classroom practices, teacher training, special education, innovative trends and issues, administration and supervision, film, continuing and adult education, all areas of the curriculum, comparative education, computers, guidance and counseling and the politics, economics, nursing, philosophy, sociology and history of education. The press also issues classroom materials for students at all levels, with a strong emphasis on reading and writing." Submit outline/synopsis and sample chapters.
Recent Nonfiction Title: *Reading Without Nonsense*, 2nd edition, by Frank Smith.

TECHWRITE ™, 5545 L.W. Raymond, Indianapolis IN 46241. (317)875-5232. Publisher: Jack Rooney. Techwrite is a trademark of the Docutech Corporation, Indianapolis, Indiana. Publishes trade paperback originals and trade paperback reprints. Averages 10-20 titles/year. Receives 30-50 submissions annually. 80% of books from first-time authors; 90% of books from unagented writers. Average print order for a writer's first book is 10,000. Pays 10-15% royalty on wholesale price or makes outright purchase ($5/page minimum, $10/page maximum). Publishes book an average of 6 months after acceptance. Simultaneous and photocopied submissions OK. Electronic submissions OK via 1200 baud, but requiers hard copy also. Computer printout submissions acceptable; prefers letter-quality to dot-matrix. SASE. Reports in 1 month on queries; 2 weeks on mss.
Nonfiction: How-to, reference, technical, textbook and computer documentation. Subjects include technical information. "Some of *TECHwrite*'s specialty areas include electronics, computers, industrial equipment and machinery, robotics, medical equipment, security systems, communication systems, and aerospace." Especially looking for books involving state-of-the-art technology. Query with outline/synopsis and sample chap-

ters, or submit complete ms. Reviews artwork/photos.
Recent Nonfiction Title: *Heat Transfer Pump Handbooks*, by Dean Brothers (reference manual).
Fiction: Experimental fiction mss "as long as they are technically oriented."
Tips: "We envision persons desiring information on various technical subjects, involving new developments and/or innovative procedures in computer technology and other sciences as our audience. If I were a writer trying to market a book today, I would check out and target the high-technology market."

TEMPLE UNIVERSITY PRESS, Broad and Oxford Sts., Philadelphia PA 19122. (215)787-8787. Editor-in-Chief: Michael Ames. Publishes 35 titles/year. Pays royalty of up to 10% on wholesale price. Publishes book an average of 9 months after acceptance. Electronic submissions OK, but requires hard copy also. Computer printout submissions acceptable. SASE. Reports in 3 months. Free book catalog.
Nonfiction: American history, public policy and regional (Philadelphia area). "All books should be scholarly. Authors are generally connected with a university. No memoirs, fiction or poetry." Uses Chicago *Manual of Style*. Reviews artwork/photos as part of ms package. Query.
Recent Nonfiction Title: *Democratic Vistas: Post Offices and Public Art in the New Deal*, by Marlene Park and Gerald Markowitz.

TEMPO BOOKS, A division of The Berkley Publishing Group, 200 Madison Ave., New York NY 10016. (212)686-9820. Publishes hardcover reprints and paperback originals. Fiction titles for young adults. Buys manuscripts on royalty basis. Computer printout submissions acceptable; no dot-matrix. Submit 3 chapters and synopsis. SASE. Reports in 2 months. Guidelines for SASE.
Fiction: Contemporary romances and problem novels for ages 10 to 14. "We are looking for contemporary young adult fiction dealing in all subjects." Submit outline/synopsis and sample chapters.
Recent Fiction Title: *Ready, Set, Love*, by Judith Enderle.

TEN SPEED PRESS, Box 7123, Berkeley CA 94707. Publisher: P. Wood. Editors: G. Young and P. Reed. Owns subsidary publishing company, CELESTIAL ARTS. Publishes trade paperback originals and reprints. Averages 20 titles/year; receives 15,000 submissions annually. 50% of books from first-time authors; 90% of books from unagented writers. Average print order for a writer's first book is 5,000-7,000. Offers standard royalty of 10% of list price; 12½% after 100,000 copies are sold. Offers average $3,000 advance. Publishes book an average of 8 months after acceptance. Computer printout submissions acceptable; prefers letter-quality to dot-matrix. SASE. Reports in 1 month. Free book catalog.
Nonfiction: Americana, gardening, careers, cookbooks, business, cooking and foods, life guidance, history, humor, law, gay, nature, self-help, how-to, hobbies, recreation and travel. Subjects range from bicycle books to business. "We will consider any first-rate nonfiction material that we feel will have a long shelf life and be a credit to our list." No set requirements. Submit outline and sample chapters. Reviews artwork/photos as part of ms package.

TEXAS A&M UNIVERSITY PRESS, Drawer C, College Station TX 77843. (409)845-1436. Director: Lloyd G. Lyman. Publishes 30 titles/year. Pays in royalties. Publishes book an average of 1 year after acceptance. Electronic submissions OK, but requires hard copy also. Computer printout submissions acceptable; prefers letter-quality to dot-matrix. SASE. Reports in 1 week on queries 1 month on submissions. Free book catalog.
Nonfiction: History, natural history, environmental history, economics, agriculture and regional studies (including fiction). Receives artwork/photos as part of ms package. "We do not want poetry." Query. Accepts outline/synopsis and 2-3 sample chapters. Reviews artwork/photos as part of ms package.
Recent Nonfiction Title: *In the Deep Parts Core: Life, Letters and Texas.* by Craig Clifford.

TEXAS CHRISTIAN UNIVERSITY PRESS, Box 30783, TCU, Fort Worth TX 76129. (817)921-7822. Director: Keith Gregory. Editor: Judy Alter. Publishes hardcover originals, some reprints. Averages 12 titles/year. Pays royalty. Publishes book an average of 1 year after acceptance. Computer printout submissions acceptable; prefers letter-quality to dot-matrix. Reports "as soon as possible."
Nonfiction: American studies, Texana, theology, literature and criticism, and young adult regional fiction. "We are looking for good scholarly monographs, other serious scholarly work and regional titles of significance." Reviews artwork/photos as part of ms package. Query.
Recent Nonfiction Title: *Warning: Writer at Work, The Best Collectibles of Larry L. King.*
Recent Fiction Title: *The Times It Never Rained*, by Kelton (reprint).

TEXAS MONTHLY PRESS, INC., Subsidiary of Mediatex Communications Corp., Box 1569, Austin TX 78767. (512)476-7085. Editorial Director: Scott Lubeck. Publishes hardcover and trade paperback originals (80%), and trade paperback reprints (20%). Averages 16-20 titles/year. Pays royalty; offers average $2,500 advance. Publishes book an average of 18 months after acceptance. Simultaneous and photocopied submissions OK. Electronic submissions OK, but requires hard copy also. Computer printout submissions acceptable.

SASE. Reports in 2 weeks on queries; 2 months on mss. Free book catalog.
Nonfiction: Biography, "coffee table" book, cookbook, humor, guidebook, illustrated book and reference. Subjects include Texana, art, business and economics, cooking and foods, history, nature, photography, politics, recreation, sports and travel. Texas-related subjects only. "Especially interested in biographies of distinguished Texans in all fields." Query or submit outline/synopsis and 3 sample chapters. Reviews artwork/photos as part of ms package.
Recent Nonfiction Title: *Landscaping with Native Texas Plants*, by Sally Wasowski and Julie Ryan.
Fiction: Adventure, ethnic, mainstream, mystery, and suspense. "All stories must be set in Texas." No experimental, erotica, confession, gothic, romance or poetry. Query or submit outline/synopsis and 3 sample chapters. No unsolicited mss.
Recent Fiction Title: *Stange Sun Light*, by Peter LaSalle.

TEXAS WESTERN PRESS, The University of Texas at El Paso, El Paso TX 79968. (915)747-5688. Director/Editor: Hugh W. Treadwell. Publishes hardcover and paperback originals. Publishes 6-7 titles/year. "We are a university press, not a commercial house; therefore, payment is in prestige more than money. Our audience consists of serious readers of serious nonfiction." Will consider photocopied submissions. Free book catalog. Reports in 1 to 3 months.
Nonfiction: Scholarly books. Historic and cultural accounts of the Southwest (West Texas, southern New Mexico, northern Mexico and Arizona). Some literary works, occasional scientific titles. "Our *Southwestern Studies* use manuscripts of 20,000 words. Our hardback books range from 30,000 words up. The writer should use good exposition in his work. Most of our work requires documentation. We favor a scholarly, but not overly pedantic, style. We specialize in superior book design." Query. Follow *MLA Style Sheet*.
Recent Nonfiction Title: *American Indian Ecology*, by J. Donald Hughes.

‡**THEATRE COMMUNICATIONS GROUP**, 355 Lexington Ave., New York NY 10017. (212)697-5230. Editor: Laura Ross. Publishes hardcover and trade paperback originals and trade paperback reprints. Averages 8 titles/year; receives 20 submissions annually. 80% of books from unagented writers. Pays 7-10% royalty on retail price; offers average $1,500 advance. Publishes book an average of 1 year after acceptance. Simultaneous and photocopied submissions OK. Electronic submissions (diskettes) OK, but requires hard copy also. Computer printout submissions acceptable; prefers letter-quality to dot-matrix. SASE. Reports in 2 months. Free book catalog.
Nonfiction: "Coffee table" book, how-to, illustrated book, reference, technical and textbook. Subjects include theatre and performing arts (including plays, anthologies, how-to, reference, etc.). "We are looking for new books in the area of the performing arts—critical, reference, play anthologies, how-to for actors, directors, playwrights, administrators and designers. Occasionally we'll entertain an idea for a play collection (i.e., we published a collection of Vietnam plays last spring)." Query (preferred) or submit outline/synopsis and sample chapters. Reviews artwork/photos as part of ms package.
Recent Nonfiction Title: *American Set Design*, by Arnold Aronson (illustratd reference). Query.
Fiction: Query.
Recent Fiction Title: *New Plays USA*, by James Levere (ed.) (anthology).
Tips: "We will be branching out more and more from just reference works to more general interest titles."

*****THE THEOSOPHICAL PUBLISHING HOUSE**, Subsidiary of The Theosophical Society in America, 306 W. Geneva Rd., Wheaton IL 60189. (312)665-0123. Senior Editor: Shirley Nicholson. Imprint includes Quest (nonfiction). Publishes trade paperback originals. Averages 12 titles/year; receives 750-1,000 submissions annually. 50% of books from first-time authors; 95% of books from unagented writers. Average print order for a writer's first book is 5,000. Subsidy publishes 40% of books based on "author need and quality and theme of manuscript." Pays 10-12% royalty on retail price; offers average $1,500 advance. Publishes book an average of 8 months after acceptance. Simultaneous and photocopied submissions OK. Computer printout submissions acceptable; prefers letter-quality to dot-matrix. SASE. Reports in 2 weeks on queries, 2 months on mss. Free book catalog; ms guidelines for SASE.
Nonfiction: Subjects include self-development, self-help, philosophy (holistic), psychology (transpersonal), Eastern and Western religions, comparative religion, holistic implications in science, health and healing, yoga, meditation and astrology. "TPH seeks works which are compatible with the theosophical philosophy. Our audience includes the 'new age' consciousness community seekers in all religions, general public, professors, and health professionals. No material which does not fit the description of needs outlined above." Accepts nonfiction translations. Query or submit outline/synopsis and sample chapters. Reviews artwork/photos as part of ms package. SASE required.
Recent Nonfiction Title: *Spiritual Aspects of Male/Female Relations*, by Scott Miners.

THISTLEDOWN PRESS, 668 E. Place, Saskatoon, Saskatchewan S7J 2Z5 Canada. (306)477-0556. Editor-in-Chief: Paddy O'Rourke. Publishes hardcover and trade paperback originals. Average 6-8 titles/year; receives 150 submissions annually. 50% of books from first-time authors; 100% of books from unagented writers. Average print order for a writer's first book is 750. Pays standard royalty on retail price. Publishes book an average of 18-24 months after acceptance. Computer printout submissions acceptable; no dot-matrix. SAE, IRC. Reports in 2 weeks on queries; 8 weeks on mss. Free book catalog; ms guidelines for SASE.

Fiction: Literary. Solicited fiction only. All unsolicited mss are returned unopened.

Recent Fiction Title: *The Way to Always Dance*, by Gertrude Story (literary—short stories).

Poetry: "Author should make him/herself familiar with our publishing program before deciding whether or not her/his work is appropriate." No poetry by people *not* citizens and residents of Canada. Submit complete ms.

Recent Poetry Title: *Fielding*, by Dennis Cooley (contemporary Canadian).

Tips: "We prefer a book that has literary integrity and distinct voice."

‡**THOMAS PUBLICATIONS**, Subsidiary of Thomas Graphics, Suite 1, 937 Reinli, Austin TX 78751. (512)452-3877. Contact: Ralph D. Thomas. Publishes trade paperback originals and trade paperback reprints. Averages 8-10 titles/year; receives 30 submissions annually. 80% of books from first-time authors; 75% of books from unagented writers. Pays 10-15% royalty on wholesale or retail price, or makes outright purchase of $500-2,000. Publishes book an average of 6 months after acceptance. Simultaneous and photocopied submissions OK. Electronic submissions OK on Kaypro; but requires hard copy also. Computer printout submissions acceptable; prefers letter-qualtiy to dot-matrix. SASE. Reports in 2 weeks on queries; 4 weeks on mss. Book catalog $1; free ms guidelines.

Nonfiction: How-to, reference and textbook. Subjects include sociology and investigation and investigative techniques. "We are looking for hardcore investigative methods books, manuals on how to make more dollars in private investigation, private investigative marketing techniques, and specialties in the investigative professions." Query or submit outline/synopsis and sample chapters. Reviews artwork/photos as part of ms package.

Recent Nonfiction Title: *How to Find Anyone Anywhere*, by Ralph Thomas (investigation).

Tips: "Our audience includes private investigators, those wanting to break into investigation, related trades such as auto repossessors, private process servers, news reporters, and related security trades."

THORNDIKE PRESS, One Mile Rd., Box 159, Thorndike ME 04986. (207)948-2962. Senior Editor: Timothy A. Loeb. Publishes hardcover and paperback originals (25%) and reprints (75%). Averages 100 titles/year; receives 500 submissions annually. 10% of books from first-time authors; 80% of books from unagented writers. Average print order for writer's first book is 2,000. Offers 10-15% of wholesale receipts; or makes outright purchase for $500-2,000. Offers average $1,000 advance. Publishes book an average of 1 year after acceptance. Electronic submissions OK on IBM PC, WordStar, Writing Asst., PC-Write-, or Easy Writer 1.1. Computer printout submissions acceptable; prefers letter-quality to dot-matrix. SASE. Reports in 2 months. Book catalog for SAE and 54¢ postage.

Nonfiction: Americana (especially Maine and the Northeast), animals, humor, nature, and all subjects of regional interest. Especially needs "manuscripts relating to the wilderness and oudoor recreation (hunting, fishing, etc.) in the Northeast U.S." No poetry, young adult or children's books. Submit outline/synopsis and 2-3 sample chapters. Reviews artwork/photos as part of ms package.

Recent Nonfiction Title: *Trout and Salmon Fishing in Northern New England*, by Al Raychard.

Fiction: Mystery, humor (New England), nostalgia, and regional interests (Maine and New England). "We will always consider exceptional manuscripts in our areas of interest, but 80% of the submissions we receive are not appropriate to our line. We prefer short works." No young adult or children's books; no poetry. Submit outline/synopsis and 2-3 sample chapters.

Recent Fiction Title: *Port and Star Boarder*, by B.T. Morison (mystery).

Tips: "We are moving away from Maine-only books and looking for a wider audience. The majority of our publishing consists of large print editions of current best sellers for the visually impaired (88 titles a year). For original books, we seek outdoor/nature guides, New England humor, nostalgia, mystery and general fiction of a high degree of literary merit. We are *not* publishing poetry, children's or young adult, adventure/suspense, cookbooks, science fiction, erotica, mass-market fiction, or romances."

THORSONS PUBLISHERS, LTD, Denington Estate, Wellingborough, Northamptonshire NN8 2RQ England. Editor-in-Chief: J.R. Hardaker. Publishes hardcover and paperback originals and reprints. Pays 7½-10% royalty. Publishes book an average of 9 months after acceptance. Photocopied submissions OK. Computer printout submissions acceptable; prefers letter-quality to dot-matrix. SAE, IRCs. Reports in 4 weeks. Free book catalog.

Nonfiction: Natural health and healing, natural food and vegetarian cookery, alternative medicine, hypnotism and hypnotherapy, practical psychology, inspiration, mind training, personal improvement, self-help themes, books for women, special diets, animal rights, public speaking topics, and yoga and related disciplines. Submit outline/synopsis and 3 sample chapters. Reviews artwork/photos as part of ms package.

Tips: Queries/mss may be routed to other editors in the publishing group.

THREE CONTINENTS PRESS, 1346 Connecticut Ave. NW, Washington DC 20036. Publisher/Editor-in-Chief: Donald E. Herdeck. General Editor: Norman Ware. Publishes hardcover and paperback originals (90%) and reprints (10%). Receives 200 submissions annually. 15% of books from first-time authors; 60% of books from unagented writers. Average print order for writers first book is 1,000. Pays 10% royalty; advance "only on delivery of complete manuscript which is found acceptable; usually $300." Photocopied (preferred) and simultaneous submissions OK. State availability of photos/illustrations. Computer printout submissions acceptable; prefers letter-quality to dot-matrix. SASE. Reports in 6 months. Free book catalog.
Nonfiction and Fiction: Specializes in African, Caribbean and Middle Eastern (Arabic and Persian) literature and criticism and translation, Third World literature and history. Scholarly, well-prepared mss; creative writing. Fiction, poetry, criticism, history and translations of creative writing. "We search for books which will make clear the complexity and value of African literature and culture, including bilingual texts (African language/English translations) of previously unpublished authors from less well-known areas of Africa. We are always interested in genuine contributions to understanding African and Caribbean culture." Length: 50,000-125,000 words. Query. "Please do not submit manuscript unless we ask for it." Reviews artwork/photos as part of ms package.
Recent Nonfiction Title: *So Spoke the Uncle*, by Jean Price-Mars.
Recent Fiction Title: *Tales from the Cameroon*, René Philombe, Trans. by Richard Bjornson.
Tips: "We need a *polished* translation, or original prose or poetry by non Western authors *only*."

‡**THREE TREES PRESS**, 2 Silver Ave., Toronto Ontario M6R 3A2 Canada. (416)534-4456. Assistant to the Publisher: Joy Parks. Publishes hardcover and trade paperback originals. Averages 8 titles/year; receives 500 submissions annually. 50% of books from first-time authors; 100% of books from unagented writers. Pays 5-10% royalty. Publishes book an average of 18-24 months after acceptance. "Clean" photocopied submissions OK. SASE. No Multiple submissons. Computer printout submissions acceptable; no dot matrix. Reports on queries in 1 week; 1 month on mss. Free book catalog and ms outline. SASE.
Nonfiction: Illustrated book and juvenile. "In the future we hope to do some nonfiction for children in the areas of history, science and the future." Query and submit outline/synopsis and sample chapters or complete ms. Reviews artwork/photos.
Fiction: Historical (for young adult); science fiction (for young adults); all children's and young adult. "We are very open to all fantasy, new fairy tales, picture books, adventure, science fiction, young adult historical novels. We do not want to see books dealing with social realism or children of divorce; also no stories for small children that have too much copy." Query and submit outline/synopsis and sample chapters or complete ms.
Recent Fiction Title: *Love - 15*, by Dennis McCloskey (young adult).
Poetry: "We publish very little poetry, we need quality children's verse and story poems." No nonsense limmericks. Submit 10 poems.
Recent Poetry Titles: *Time is Flies*, by George Swede (mostly haiku).
Tips: "Read the books previously published by a certain company before submitting your manuscript to them. We only publish writing by Canadians, living in Canada or abroad." We also only accept completed mss.

‡**THRESHOLD BOOKS**, R.D. 3, Box 1350, Putney VT 05346. (802)387-4586, 254-8300. Director: Edmund Helminski. Publishes hardcover and trade paperback originals. Averages 2-3 titles/year; receives 15 submissions annually. 20% of books from first-time authors; 100% of books from unagented writers. Pays 7-15% royalty on wholesale price. Publishes book an average of 8-10 months after acceptance. Simultaneous and photocopied submissions OK. Computer printout submissions acceptable. SASE. Reports in 3 weeks on queries; 2 months on mss. Free book catalog.
Nonfiction: Biography, literary and philosophical. Subjects include philosophy, spiritual, psychology, religion, poetry and literary translation. Needs philosophy, history of religion, the arts, sufism, and mysticism. Query.
Recent Nonfiction Title: *Steps to Freedom*.
Fiction: Philosophical/international, Third World. Query.
Poetry: "We will consider translations of the great poets, of any culture or era." Submit complete ms.
Recent Poetry Title: *Open Secret Versions of Rumi*, by Barks and Moyne (13th century Persian).
Tips: "Books with spiritual significance and quality writing have the best chance of selling to our firm."

THUNDER'S MOUTH PRESS, Box 780, New York NY 10025. (212)866-4329. Publisher: Neil Ortenberg. Publishes hardcover and trade paperback originals and reprints. Averages 6 titles/year; receives 1,000 submissions annually. 75% of books from unagented writers. Average print order for a writer's first book is 2,000. Pays 5-10% royalty on retail price; offers average $200 advance. Publishes book an average of 8 months after acceptance. Reports in 3 weeks on queries; 2 months on mss. Book catalog for SAE and 22¢ postage.
Nonfiction: Biography, cookbook, how-to, self-help on cooking and foods, history, philosophy, politics and sociology. Publishes for "college students, academics, politically left of center, ethnic, social activists, women, etc. We basically do poetry and fiction now, but intend to start doing nonfiction over the next few years. How-to books, or biographies, history books, cookbooks would be fine." No cat books. Query or submit out-

line/synopsis and sample chapters.

Fiction: Erotica, ethnic, experimental, historical, humor, science fiction and political. "We are interested in doing anywhere from 3-5 novels per year, particularly highly literary or socially relevant novels." No romance. Query or submit outline/synopsis and sample chapters.

Recent Fiction Title: *The Red Menace*, by Michael Anania.

Poetry: "We intend to publish 3-5 books of poetry per year." No elitist, rhymes or religious poetry." Submit complete ms.

Recent Poetry Title: *Echoes Inside the Labyrinth*, by Tom McGrath.

TIMBER PRESS, Box 1631, Beaverton OR 97075. (503)292-2606. Editor: Richard Abel. Publishes hardcover and paperback originals. Publishes 20 titles/year; receives 300-400 submissions annually. 90% of books from first-time authors; 100% of books from unagented writers. Pays 10-20% royalty; sometimes offers advance to cover costs of artwork and final ms completion. Publishes book an average of 8 months after acceptance. Electronic submissions OK on most micros and word processors using disks, but requires hard copy also. Computer printout submissions acceptable; prefers letter-quality to dot-matrix. SASE. Reports in 2 months. Free book catalog; ms guidelines for SASE.

Nonfiction: Arts and crafts, natural history, Northwest regional material, forestry and horticulture. Accepts nonfiction translations from German. Query or submit outline/synopsis and 3-4 sample chapters. Reviews artwork/photos as part of ms package.

Recent Nonfiction Title: *Complete Book of Roses*, by Krussmann (horticulture).

TIME-LIFE BOOKS INC., 777 Duke St., Alexandria VA 22314. (703)838-7000. Editor: George Constable. Publishes hardcover originals. Publishes 40 titles/year. "We have no minimum or maximum fee because our needs vary tremendously. Advance, as such, is not offered. Author is paid as he completes part of contracted work." Books are almost entirely staff-generated and staff-produced, and distribution is primarily through mail order sale. Query to the Director of Corporate Development. SASE.

Nonfiction: "General interest books. Most books tend to be heavily illustrated (by staff), with text written by assigned authors. We very rarely accept mss or book ideas submitted from outside our staff." Length: open.

Recent Nonfiction Title: *Civil War Series*.

TIMES BOOKS, Division of Random House, Inc., 130 Fifth Ave., New York NY 10011. (212)620-5900. Vice President, Editor-in-Chief: Jonathan B. Segal. Senior Editors: Kathleen Moloney, Elisabeth Scharlatt and Hugh O'Neill. Publishes hardcover and paperback originals (75%) and reprints (25%). Publishes 45 titles/year. Pays royalty; average advance. Publishes book an average of 1 year after acceptance. Computer printout submissions acceptable.

Nonfiction: Business/economics, science and medicine, history, biography, women's issues, the family, cookbooks, current affairs, cooking, self-help and sports. Accepts only solicited manuscripts. Reviews artwork/photos as part of ms package.

Recent Nonfiction Title: *The Canadian*, by Andrew H. Malcolm.

*TOMPSON & RUTTER INC., Box 297, Grantham NH 03753. (603)863-4392. President: Frances T. Rutter. Publishes trade paperback originals. Averages 3 titles/year; receives 35-40 submissions annually. 30% of books from first-time authors; 100% of books from unagented writers. Average print order for a writer's first book is 1,000-1,500. Subsidy publishes 5% of books. Pays average 10% royalty on wholesale price. No advance. Publishes book an average of 1 year after acceptance. Simultaneous submissions OK. Computer printout submissions acceptable; no dot-matrix. Reports in 1 month. Included in Shoe String Press catalog.

Nonfiction: Local history and New England folklore. Query with 1-page sample of published writing.

Recent Nonfiction Title: *Sarah Josepha Hale, A New England Pioneer, 1788-1879*, by Sherbrooke Rogers.

TOR BOOKS, 9th Floor, 49 W. 24th St., New York NY 10010. (212)564-0150. Managing Editor: Nancy Wiesenfeld. Publishes mass market hardcover and trade paperback originals (75% "and growing") and reprints (25%). Averages 72 books/year. Pays 6-8% royalty; offers negotiable advance.

Fiction: Horror, science fiction, occult, and some fantasy. In the near future: thrillers. Prefers agented mss or proposals.

Recent Fiction Title: *Artifact*, by Gregory Benford.

Tips: "We're pretty broad in the occult, horror and fantasy but more straightforward in science fiction and thrillers, tending to stay with certain authors and certain types of work."

*TRANSACTION BOOKS, Rutgers University, New Brunswick NJ 08903. (201)932-2280. President: I.L. Horowitz. Publisher: Scott Bramson. Book Division Director: Dalia Buzin. Publishes hardcover and paperback originals (65%) and reprints (35%). Specializes in scholarly social science books. Averages 85 titles/year; receives 400-500 submissions annually. 15% of books from first-time authors; 85% of books from unagented writers. Average print order for a writer's first book is 1,000. Subsidy publishes 10% of books. Royalty "de-

pends almost entirely on individual contract; we've gone anywhere from 2-15%." No advance. Publishes book an average of 8 months after acceptance. Electronic submissions OK, but requires hard copy also. Computer printout submissions acceptable; prefers letter-quality to dot-matrix. Reports in 4 months. SASE. Free book catalog; ms guidelines for SASE.
Nonfiction: Americana, art, biography, economics, history, law, medicine and psychiatry, music, philosophy, politics, psychology, reference, scientific, sociology, technical and textbooks. "All must be scholarly social science or related." Query or submit outline/synopsis. "Do not submit sample chapters. We evaluate complete manuscripts only." Accepts nonfiction translations. Use Chicago *Manual of Style.* Looks for "scholarly content, presentation, methodology, and target audience." State availability of photos/illustrations and send one photocopied example. Reviews artwork/photos as part of ms package.
Recent Nonfiction Title: *The Politics of the American Civil Liberties Union*, by William A. Donohue.

‡**TRANS-CANADA PRESS**, Division of the Cardamon Corp., 161 Davenport Rd., Toronto, Ontario M5R 1J1 Canada. (416)968-2714. President: Evelyn Davidson. Publishes hardcover and trade paperback originals. Averages 5 titles/year. Publishes book an average of 3 months after acceptance. Simultaneous submissions OK. Electronic submissions OK via Xerox 820, 860, but requires hard copy also. Computer printout submissions acceptable; prefers letter-quality to dot-matrix. SASE. Reports in 1 month.
Nonfiction: Biography. Subjects include business (management) and economics, and biographical information (who's who). Needs mss on food business/management only. Query.
Recent Nonfiction Title: *Seizing the Future: Opportunity for Canada in the 80's*, Ralph Fisher and A. Davidson (reference/business).

TRIBECA COMMUNICATIONS INC., Suite 1907, 401 Broadway, New York NY 10013. (212)226-6047. Publisher: Jim Mann. Book publisher/packager. Publishes hardcover and trade paperback originals. Averages 25 titles/year. Royalty and advance negotiable. Publishes book an average of 18 months after acceptance. Simultaneous and photocopied submissions OK. Computer printout submissions acceptable; prefers letter-quality to dot-matrix.
Nonfiction: "Coffee table" book, cookbook, humor and juvenile. Subjects include animals, business and economics, cooking and foods, health, history, recreation, sports, travel and computers. Especially looking for "original ideas for computer books, humor books, children's books that 'teach' some kind of skill; we are interested in almost all nonfiction areas." Submit outline/synopsis and sample chapters, and sample art. Cannot return unsolicited material.
Recent Nonfiction Title: *The Second Nine Months*, by Judith Gansberg and Arthur Mostel, M.D.

TROUBADOR PRESS, A division of Price/Stern/Sloan, Publishers, Inc., Suite 205, 1 Sutter St., San Francisco CA 94104. (415)397-3716. Editorial Director: Malcolm K. Whyte. Publishes paperback originals (occasional hardcover editions). Averages 6 titles/year; receives 300 submissions annually. 50% of books from unagented writers. Average print order for a writer's first book is 10,000. Pays royalty. Offers average $500 advance. Publishes book an average of 6 months after acceptance. Computer printout submissions acceptable; prefers letter-quality to dot-matrix. Reports in 1 month. SASE. Book catalog and ms guidelines for SASE.
Nonfiction: "Troubador Press publishes mainly, but is not limited to, children's activity books: coloring, cutout, mazes, games, paper dolls, etc. All titles feature original art and exceptional graphics. Primarily nonfiction. Interested in expanding on themes of 80 current titles. We like books which have the potential to develop into series." Query or submit outline/synopsis and 2-3 sample chapters with conciseness and clarity of a good idea. Reviews artwork/photos as part of ms package.
Recent Nonfiction Title: *Huggs and Cuddles Teddy Bear Paper Dolls*, by Malcolm Whyte and Terra Muzick.
Tips: "We continue to publish new authors along with established writers/artists and licensed properties. We feel the mix is good and healthy." Queries/mss may be routed to other editors in the publishing group.

TURNSTONE PRESS LTD., Denington Estate, Wellingborough, Northamptonshire NN8 2RQ England. Editors: John Hardaker and Michael Cox. Publishes hardcover and paperback originals and reprints. Pays 7½% royalty on paperbacks; 10% on hardcovers. Photocopied submissions OK. Computer printout submissions acceptable; prefers letter-quality to dot-matrix. SAE, IRC. Reports in 2 months. Free book catalog.
Nonfiction: Pre-history, archaeology (alternative), earth mysteries, psychology, personal development, health and healing, ecology, lifestyle, new age topics and social issues. Submit outline/synopsis and 3 sample chapters.
Tips: Queries/mss may be routed to other editors in the publishing group.

*****CHARLES E. TUTTLE CO., INC.**, Publishers & Booksellers, Suido 1-chome, 2-6, Bunkyo-ku, Tokyo, Japan 112. Publishes originals and reprints. "Handles all matters of editing, production and administration including royalties, rights and permissions." Averages 30 titles/year. Subsidy publishes 30% of books. Pays $500 against 10% royalty on retail price; advance varies. Send complete mss or queries accompanied by outlines or sample chapters and biographical data to Tokyo. U.S. and Canada distributors: Publishers and

Booksellers, Drawer F, 26-30 Main St., Rutland VT 05701. Publishes book an average of 2 years after acceptance. Computer printout submissions acceptable; no dot-matrix. Reports in 6 weeks. SASE. Book catalog $1.
Nonfiction: Specializes in publishing books about Oriental art, culture, language and sociology as well as history, literature, cookery, sport, martial arts, and children's books which relate to Asia, the Hawaiian Islands, Australia and the Pacific areas. Also interested in Americana, especially antique collecting, architecture, genealogy and Canadiana. No poetry and fiction except that of Oriental themes. Accepts translations. Normal book length only. Looks for "subject matter related to Asia, particularly Japan; authority of the author; balance and logical order in the structure of the manuscript; presentation—minimum of spelling/grammatical errors, double-spaced typing." Reviews artwork/photos as part of ms package.
Recent Nonfiction Title: *Chinese Chess*, by H. T. Lau.

TWAYNE PUBLISHERS, A division of G.K. Hall & Co., 70 Lincoln St., Boston MA 02111. (617)423-3990. Publishes hardcover and paperback originals. Publishes 120 titles/year; receives 1,000 submissions annually. 5% of books from first-time authors; 10% of books from unagented writers. Average print order for a writer's first book is 1,000. Pays royalty. Query only with SASE, outline and 2 sample chapters. Reports in 5 weeks. No unsolicited mss—query first.
Nonfiction: Publishes scholarly books and volumes in and out of series for the general reader. Literary criticism, biography, history; women's studies, art history, current affairs and science.
Recent Nonfiction Title: *Mothers and More: American Women in the 1950s*, by Eugenia Kaledin.
Tips: Queries may be routed to other editors in the publishing group. Unsolicited mss will not be read.

TWENTY-THIRD PUBLICATIONS, INC., 185 Willow St., Box 180, Mystic CT 06355. (203)536-2611. Acquisitions: Patricia Kluepfel. Publishes trade paperback originals. Averages 30 titles/year; receives 250 submissions annually. 25% of books from first-time authors; 90% of books from unagented writers. Average print order for a writer's first book is 5,000. Pays average 10% royalty on net receipts. Publishes book an average of 15 months after acceptance. SASE. Reports in 3 weeks. Book catalog for 9x12 SAE and 2 first class stamps.
Nonfiction: Religious education and adult education (Roman Catholic). "Our audience is teachers, mainstream and educators." Query.
Recent Nonfiction Title: *Morality of Capital Punishment*, by R. Endres.

*TYNDALE HOUSE PUBLISHERS, INC., 336 Gundersen Dr., Wheaton IL 60187. (312)668-8300. Editor-in-Chief/Acquisitions: Wendell Hawley. Publishes hardcover and trade paperback originals (90%) and hardcover and mass paperback reprints (10%). Publishes 100 titles/year; receives 3,000 submissions annually. 25% of books from first-time authors; 98% of books from unagented writers. Average print order for a writer's first book is 7,000-10,000. Subsidy publishes 2% of books. Pays 10% royalty; offers negotiable advance. Publishes book an average of 18 months after acceptance. Computer printout submissions acceptable; no dot-matrix. Reports in 6 weeks. SASE. Free book catalog; ms guidelines for SASE.
Nonfiction: Religious books only: personal experience, family living, marriage, Bible reference works and commentaries, Christian living, devotional, inspirational, church and social issues, Bible prophecy, theology and doctrine, counseling and Christian psychology, Christian apologetics and church history. Submit table of contents, chapter summary, preface, first 2 chapters and 1 later chapter.
Fiction: Bible and contemporary novels. Christian romance, western and adventure. Junior high fiction. Submit outline/synopsis and sample chapters.

ULTRALIGHT PUBLICATIONS, INC., Box 234, Hammelstown PA 17036. (717)566-0468. Editor: Michael A. Markowski. Imprints includes Aviation Publishers and Medical Information Systems. Publishes hardcover and trade paperback originals. Averages 8 titles/year; receives 20 submissions annually. 10% of books from first-time authors; 100% of books from unagented writers. Average print order for a writer's first book is 5,000. Pays 10-15% royalty on wholesale price; buys some mss outright. Offers average $1,000 advance. Simultaneous and photocopied submissions OK. Computer printout submissions acceptable; no dot-matrix. SASE. Reports in 3 weeks on queries; 2 months on mss. Book catalog and ms guidelines for SASE.
Nonfiction: How-to, technical on hobbies (model airplanes) and aviation. Publishes for "aviation buffs, dreamers and enthusiasts. We are looking for titles in the homebuilt, ultralight, sport and general aviation fields. We are interested in how-to, technical and reference books of short to medium length that will serve recognized and emerging aviation needs." Also interested in automotive historical, reference and how-to; popular health, medical, and fitness for the general public. Self-help, motivation and success are also areas of interest. Query or submit outline/synopsis and 3 sample chapters. Reviews artwork/photos as part of ms package.
Recent Nonfiction Title: *Composite Construction*, by Lambie (how-to).

UMI RESEARCH PRESS, University Microfilms International, Xerox, 300 N. Zeeb Road, Ann Arbor MI 48106. Contact: Editor-in-Chief. Publishes hardcover originals and revised dissertations. Averages 100 titles/year; receives 100 submissions annually. 80% of books from first-time authors; 100% of books from unagented writers. Average print order for a writer's first book is 500. Pays 5% royalty on net sales. Offers average $100 advance. Photocopied submissions OK. Electronic submissions OK on IBM PC, Wang and Xerox, but requires hard copy also. Computer printout submissions acceptable "if good quality." Ms guidelines available.

Nonfiction: Marie D. Low, Ph.D., Editor-in-Chief. Scholarly and professional research and critical studies. Subjects include architecture; cinema (theory and aesthetics); art; theatre (history and theory); business and economics, musicology; computer science; photography (theory); material culture; cultural anthropology; psychology (clinical); urban planning and history; and literary criticism. Especially looking for "scholarly works, original conclusions resulting from careful academic research. Primarily aimed at graduate, post-graduate and professional level. Academics, research librarians, art and music communities, business and computer science professionals are our audience." No mass market books. Query.

Recent Nonfiction Title: *American Material Culture and Folklife*, ed. by S. Bronner (essays).

Tips: "Send letters of inquiry to appropriate publishers *before* devoting hours to a manuscript. Get feedback at the outline/prospects stage."

UNIVELT, INC., Box 28130, San Diego CA 92128. (619)746-4005. Editorial Director: H. Jacobs. Publishes hardcover originals. Averages 8 titles/year; receives 20 submissions annually. 5% of books from first-time authors; 5% of books from unagented writers. Average print order for a writer's first book is 1,000-2,000. Pays 10% royalty on actual sales; no advance. Publishes book an average of 4 months after acceptance. Computer printout submissions acceptable; prefers letter-quality to dot-matrix. Reports in 4 weeks. SASE. Book catalog and ms guidelines for SASE.

Nonfiction: Publishes in the field of aerospace, especially astronautics and technical communications, but including application of aerospace technology to Earth's problems. Submit outline/synopsis and 1-2 sample chapters. Reviews artwork/photos as part of ms package.

Recent Nonfiction Title: *Handbook of Soviet Manned Space Flight.*

Tips: "Freelancer has best chance of selling manuscripts on the history of astronautics (we have a history series) and astronautics/space/light subjects. We publish for the American astronautical society." Queries/mss may be routed to other editors in the publishing group.

UNIVERSE BOOKS, 381 Park Ave. S., New York NY 10016. (212)685-7400. Editorial Director: Louis Barron. Publishes hardcover and paperback originals (95%) and reprints (5%). Averages 45 titles/year; receives 1,000+ submissions annually, 25% of books from first-time authors; 75% of books from unagented writers. Average print order for a writer's first book is 3,000-4,000. Offers 10-15% royalty on retail price (hardbound books). "On a few extra-illustrated art books and on special studies with a limited market we may pay a smaller royalty." Offers $1,000-4,000 advance . "If a book makes a genuine contribution to knowledge but is a commercial risk, we might perhaps accept a subsidy from a foundation or other organization, but not directly from the author." Publishes book an average of 9 months after acceptance. Simultaneous and photocopied submissions OK. Computer printout submissions acceptable; no dot-matrix. "Will not return material without postage-paid SAE." Reports in 2 weeks. Book catalog for 3 first-class stamps (not SASE).

Nonfiction: Animals, art, economics, history, linguistics, nature, performing arts, politics, reference and science. Universe also pays secondary attention to biography, health and how-to. Also uses "discussions of specific animal, bird or plant species; social histories of specific types of artifacts or social institutions; art histories of specific types of artifacts or symbols. We publish books in the following categories: antiques, crafts and collectibles, art, architecture and design, history, life, physical and agricultural sciences, ballet, music, contemporary problems, and social sciences (especially books on survival, appropriate technology, and the limits to growth). We do not publish fiction, poetry, cookbooks, criticism or belles lettres." Accepts nonfiction French and German translations. Submit outline/synopsis and 2-3 sample chapters. Reviews artwork/photos as part of ms package.

Recent Nonfiction Titles: *Judgment in Berlin*, by Herbert J. Stern; *Growing Hybrid Orchids Indoors*, by Jack Kramer.

UNIVERSITY ASSOCIATES, INC., 8517 Production Ave., San Diego CA 92121. (619)578-5900. President: J. William Pfeiffer. Publishes paperback originals (65%) and reprints (35%). Specializes in practical materials for human resource development, consultants, etc. Pays average 10% royalty; no advance. Publishes book an average of 6 months after acceptance. Markets books by direct mail. Simultaneous submissions OK. Computer printout submissions acceptable; no dot-matrix. SASE. Reports in 4 months. Free book catalog.

Nonfiction: Richard Roe, Vice-President, Publications. Publishes (in order of preference) human resource development and group-oriented material, management education and community relations and personal growth, and business. No materials for grammar school or high school classroom teachers. Use *American Psychological Association Style manual.* Query. Send prints or completed art or rough sketches to accompany ms.

Recent Nonfiction Title: *The 1985 Annual Developing Human Resources*, by J.W. Pfeiffer and L.D. Good-stein.

UNIVERSITY OF ALABAMA PRESS, Box 2877, University AL 35486. Director: Malcolm MacDonald. Publishes hardcover originals. Published 40 titles last year. "Pays maximum 10% royalty on wholesale price; no advance." Computer printout submissions acceptable. SASE. Free book catalog.
Nonfiction: Biography, business and economics, history, music, philosophy, politics, religion and sociology. Considers upon merit almost any subject of scholarly interest, but specializes in linguistics and philology, political science and public administration, literary criticism and biography, philosophy and history. Accepts nonfiction translations.
Recent Nonfiction Title: *Female Crime and Delinquency*, (criminology).

THE UNIVERSITY OF ALBERTA PRESS, 141 Athabasca Hall, Edmonton, Alberta T6G 2E8 Canada. (403)432-3662. Director: Norma Gutteridge. Imprint includes Pica Pica Press. Publishes hardcover and trade paperback originals, and trade paperback reprints. Averages 10 titles/year; receives 200-300 submissions annually. 60% of books from first-time authors; 100% of books from unagented writers. Average print order for a writer's first book is 1,500. Pays 10% royalty on retail price. Publishes book an average of 1 year after acceptance. Electronic submissions OK on IBM Compatible, but requires hard copy also. Computer printout submissions acceptable; no dot-matrix. SASE Reports in 1 week on queries; 3 months on mss. Free book catalog and ms guidelines.
Nonfiction: Biography, how-to, reference, technical textbook, and scholarly. Subjects include art, history, nature, philosophy, politics, and sociology. Especially looking for "biographies of Canadians in public life, and works analyzing Canada's political history and public policy, particularly in international affairs. No pioneer reminiscences, literary criticism (unless in Canadian literature), reports of narrowly focused studies, unrevised theses." Submit complete ms. Reviews artwork/photos as part of ms package.
Recent Nonfiction Title: *Shadow and Substance in British Foreign Policy 1895-1939*, by B.J. McKercher and J. Moss (British history).
Tips: "We are interested in original research making significant contribution to knowledge in the subject."

UNIVERSITY OF ARIZONA PRESS, 1615 E. Speedway, Tucson AZ 85719. (602)621-1441. Director: Stephen Cox. Publishes hardcover and paperback originals and reprints. Averages 40 titles/year; receives 300-400 submissions annually. 60% of books from first-time authors; 90% of books from unagented writers. Average print order for a writer's first book is 1,500. Royalty terms vary; usual starting point is after sale of first 1,000 copies. Publishes book an average of 1 year after acceptance. Photocopied submissions OK. Electronic submissions OK on IBM PC with WordStar, but requires hard copy also. Computer printout submissions acceptable; no dot-matrix. Reports in three months. SASE. Free catalog and ms guidelines.
Nonfiction: Serious books about the American West, Mexico and natural history, and about subjects strongly identified with the universities in Arizona—anthropology, philosophy, arid lands studies, space sciences, Asian studies, Southwest Indians, and Mexico. Query and submit outline and sample chapters. Reviews artwork/photos as part of ms package.
Recent Nonfiction Title: *The Politics of Meaning: Power and Explanation in the Construction of Social Reality*, by Peter C. Sederberg.

*UNIVERSITY OF ILLINOIS PRESS, 54 E. Gregory, Champaign IL 61820. (217)333-0950. Director/Editor: Richard L. Wentworth. Publishes hardcover and trade paperback originals, and hardcover and trade paperback reprints. Averages 50-60 titles/year. Subsidy publishes 20-25% of books. "We decide whether an author should be subsidy published by determining which manuscripts can't be published without the expectation of deficite larger than we can afford." Pays 0-15% royalty on net sales; offers average 1,000-1,500 advance (rarely). Simultaneous and photocopied submissions OK. Computer printout submissions acceptable; prefers letter-quality to dot-matrix. SASE. Reports in 1 week on queries; 4 months on mss. Free book catalog.
Nonfiction: Biography, reference and scholarly books. Subjects include Americana, business and economics, history (especially American history), music (especially American music), politics, sociology, sports and literature. Always looking for "solid scholarly books in American history, especially social history; books on American popular music, and books in the broad area of American studies." Query with outlines/synopsis.
Recent Nonfiction Title: *Theirs Be the Power: The Moguls of Eastern Kentucky*, by Harry M. Caudill (polemical history).
Fiction: Ethnic, experimental and mainstream. "We publish four collections of stories by individual writers each year. We do not publish novels." Query.
Recent Fiction Title: *Home Fires*, by David Long (short stories).
Tips: "Serious scholarly books that are broad enough and well-written enough to appeal to non specialists are doing well for us in today's market. Writers of nonfiction whose primary goal is to earn money (rather than get promoted in an academic positon) are advised to try at least a dozen commercial publishers before thinking about offering the work to a university press."

UNIVERSITY OF IOWA PRESS, 307 E. College, Iowa City IA 52242. (319)353-3181. Director: Paul Zimmer. Publishes hardcover and paperback originals. Averages 15-20 titles/year; receives 300-400 submissions annually. 30% of books from first-time authors; 95% of books from unagented writers. Average print order for a writer's first book is 1,500. Pays 7-10% royalty on retail price. "We market mostly by direct mailing of fliers to groups with special interests in our titles and by advertising in trade and scholarly publications." Publishes book an average of 1 year after acceptance. Electronic submissions OK for tape, but requires hard copy also. Readable computer printout submissions acceptable. Reports in 4 months. Free book catalog and ms guidelines.

Nonfiction: Publishes anthropology, archaeology, British and American literary studies, history (Victorian, U.S., German, medieval, Latin American), natural history and scientific books. Currently Publishes the Iowa School of Letters Award for Short Fiction. Looks for "evidence of original research; reliable sources; clarity of organization, complete development of theme with documentation and supportive footnotes and/or bibliography; and a substantive contribution to knowledge in the field treated." Query or submit outline/synopsis. Use Chicago *Manual of Style*. Reviews artwork/photos as part of ms package.

Recent Nonfiction Title: *Alternative Literary Publishing: Five Modern Histories*, by Sally Dennison.

UNIVERSITY OF MASSACHUSETTS PRESS, Box 429, Amherst MA 01004. (413)545-2217. Director: Bruce Wilcox. Acquisitions Editor: Richard Martin. Publishes hardcover and paperback originals (95%) reprints and imports (5%). Averages 25-30 titles/year; receives 600 submissions annually. 20% of books from first-time authors; 90% of books from unagented writers. Average print order for a writer's first book is 1,500. Royalties depend on character of book; if offered, generally at 10% of net income. Advance rarely offered. No author subsidies accepted. Publishes book an average of 10 months after acceptance. Computer printout submissions acceptable; prefers letter-quality to dot-matrix. Preliminary report in 1 month. SASE. Free book catalog.

Nonfiction: Publishes Afro-American studies, art and architecture, biography, criticism, history, natural history, philosophy, poetry, psychology, public policy, sociology and women's studies in original and reprint editions. Accepts nonfiction translations. Submit outline/synopsis and 1-2 sample chapters. Reviews artwork/photos as part of ms package.

Recent Nonfiction Title: *Thoreau's Seasons*, by Richard Lebeaux (criticism).

Tips: "As members of AAUP, we sometimes route (queries/mss) to other university presses."

UNIVERSITY OF MICHIGAN PRESS, 839 Greene St., Ann Arbor MI 48106. (313)764-4394. Editorial Director: Walter E. Sears. Senior Editor: Mary C. Erwin. Publishes hardcover and paperback originals (95%) and reprints (5%). Averages 35-40 titles/year. Pays 10% royalty on retail price but primarily on net; offers advance. Electronic submissions OK, but requires hard copy also. Computer printout submissions acceptable; no dot-matrix. SASE. Reports in 2 weeks. Free book catalog.

Nonfiction: Americana, art, business/economics, health, history, music, philosophy, photography, psychology, recreation, reference, science, sociology, technical, textbooks and travel. No dissertations. Query first.

Recent Nonfiction Title: *Nuclear Power: Technology on Trial*, by J. Duderstadt and C. Kikuchi.

UNIVERSITY OF MISSOURI PRESS, 200 Lewis Hall, Columbia MO 65211. (314)882-7641. Director: Edward D. King. Associate Director: Susan McGregor Denny. Publishes hardcover and paperback originals and paperback reprints. Averages 30 titles/year; receives 300 submissions annually. 100% of books from first-time authors; 100% of books from unagented writers. Average print order for a writer's first book is 1,000. Pays 10% royalty on net receipts; no advance. Publishes book an average of 6-8 months after acceptance. Photocopied submissions OK. Electronic submissions OK on IBM PCxt, but requires hard copy also. Computer printout submissions acceptable; prefers letter-quality to dot-matrix. Reports in 6 months. SASE. Free book catalog; ms guidelines for SASE.

Nonfiction: Scholarly publisher interested in history, literary criticism, political science, social science, music, art, art history, and original poetry. Also regional books about Missouri and the Midwest. No mathematics or hard sciences. Query or submit outline/synopsis and sample chapters. Consult Chicago *Manual of Style*.

Recent Nonfiction Title: *Richard Crashow: An Annotated Bibliography of Criticism, 1632-1980*, by John R. Roberts.

Fiction: "Fiction, poetry and drama manuscripts are taken into submission only in February and March of odd-numbered years. We publish original short fiction in Breakthrough Series, not to exceed 35,000 words. May be short story collection or novella. We also publish poetry and drama in the same series. No limitations on subject matter." Query.

Recent Fiction Title: *Off in Zimbabwe*, by Rod Kessler (stories).

UNIVERSITY OF NEBRASKA PRESS, 901 N. 17th St., Lincoln NE 68588-0520. Editor-in-Chief: Willis G. Regier. Publishes hardcover and paperback originals (60%) and hardcover and paperback reprints (40%). Specializes in scholarly nonfiction, some regional books; reprints of Western Americana; and natural history. Averages 50 new titles, 30 paperback reprints (*Bison Books*)/year; receives 700 submissions annually. 25% of books from first-time authors; 95% of books from unagented writers. Average print order for a writer's first book is 1,000. Royalty is usually graduated from 10% on wholesale price for original books; no advance. Computer printout submissions acceptable; prefers letter-quality to dot-matrix. SASE. Reports in 4 months. Free book catalog; ms guidelines for SASE.

Nonfiction: Publishes Americana, biography, history, nature, photography, psychology, sports, literature, agriculture and American Indian themes. Accepts nonfiction and fiction translations. Query. Accepts outline/synopsis, 2 sample chapters and introduction. Looks for "an indication that the author knows his subject thoroughly and interprets it intelligently." Reviews artwork/photos as part of ms package.

Recent Nonfiction Title: *The Tourist*, by John Jakle.

UNIVERSITY OF NEVADA PRESS, Reno NV 89557. (702)784-6573. Director: John Stetter. Editor: Nicholas M. Cady. Publishes hardcover and paperback originals (90%) and reprints (10%). Averages 6 titles/year; receives 200 submissions annually. 20% of books from first-time authors; 100% of books from unagented writers. Average print order for a writer's first book is 2,000. Pays 10% royalty on retail price. Publishes book an average of 2 years after acceptance. Computer printout submissions acceptable; no dot-matrix. Preliminary reports in 2 months. Free book catalog and ms guidelines.

Nonfiction: Specifically needs regional history and natural history, anthropology, biographies and Basque studies. "We are the first university press to sustain a sound series on Basque studies—New World and Old World." No juvenile books. Submit complete ms. Reviews artwork/photos as part of ms package.

Recent Nonfiction Title: *Trees of the Great Basin: A Natural History*, by Ronald Lanner.

*UNIVERSITY OF NEW MEXICO PRESS, Journalism 220, Albuquerque NM 87131. (505)277-2346. Senior Editor: Elizabeth C. Hadas. Publishes hardcover and trade paperback originals and hardcover and trade paperback reprints. Averages 50 titles/year. 40% of books from first-time authors; 90% of books from unagented writers. Average print order for writer's first book is 1,500. Subsidy publishes 5% of books "depending upon nature of manuscript." Pays maximum 10% royalty on wholesale price. Publishes book an average of 18 months after acceptance. Electronic submissions OK, but requires hard copy also. Computer printout submissions acceptable; prefers letter-quality to dot-matrix. SASE. Reports in 2 weeks on queries; 6 months on mss. Free book catalog.

Nonfiction: Scholarly and regional books covering Americana, art, history, nature and photography. Query. Reviews artwork/photos as part of ms package.

Recent Nonfiction Title: *Textiles of the Prehistoric Southwest*, by Kate Kent (illustrated monograph).

Fiction: "No original fiction. Any fiction manuscripts will be returned unread if accompanied by SASE. Otherwise, they will be discarded."

THE UNIVERSITY OF NORTH CAROLINA PRESS, Box 2288, Chapel Hill NC 27514. (919)966-3561. Editor-in-Chief: Iris Tillman Hill. Publishes hardcover and paperback originals. Specializes in scholarly books and regional trade books. Averages 50 titles/year. Royalty schedule "varies." No advance. "As a university press, we do not have the resources for mass marketing books." Send prints to illustrate ms only if they are a major part of the book. Photocopied submissions OK. Electronic submissions OK, but requires hard copy also. Publishes book an average of 9-12 months after acceptance. Reports in 5 months. SASE. Free book catalog.

Nonfiction: "Our major fields are American and European history." Also scholarly books on Americana, classics, oral history, political science, urban studies, religious studies, psychology and sociology. History books on law and music. Books on nature, particularly on the Southeast; literary studies. Submit outline/synopsis and sample chapters. Must follow Chicago *Manual of Style*. Looks for "intellectual excellence and clear writing. We do *not* publish poetry or original fiction."

Recent Nonfiction Title: *Turing's Man: Western Culture in the Computer Age*, by J. David Bolter.

UNIVERSITY OF OKLAHOMA PRESS, 1005 Asp Ave., Norman OK 73019. (405)325-5111. Editor-in-Chief: John Drayton. Publishes hardcover and paperback originals (85%); and reprints (15%). Averages 50 titles/year. Pays royalty comparable to those paid by other publishers for comparable books. Publishes book an average of 12-18 months after acceptance. Electronic submissions OK, but requires hard copy also. Computer printout submissions acceptable; prefers letter-quality to dot-matrix. Reports in 4 months. SASE. Book catalog $1.

Nonfiction: Publishes American Indian studies, Western US history and classical studies. No poetry and fiction. Query, including outline, 1-2 sample chapters and author resume. Chicago *Manual of Style*. Reviews artwork/photos as part of ms package.

Recent Nonfiction Title: *Colorado Ghost Towns and Mining Camps*, by Sandra Dallas.

*UNIVERSITY OF PENNSYLVANIA PRESS, Blockley Hall, 418 Service Dr., Philadelphia PA 19104. (215)898-6261. Director: Thomas M. Rotell. Publishes hardcover and paperback originals (90%) and reprints (10%). Averages 45 titles/year. Subsidy publishes 10% of books. Subsidy publishing is determined by: evaluation obtained by the press from outside specialists; work approved by Press Editorial Committee; subsidy approved by funding organization. Royalty determined on book-by-book basis. State availability of photos and/ or illustrations to accompany ms, with copies of illustrations. Photocopied submissions OK. Computer printout submissions acceptable; no dot-matrix. Reports in 3 months. SASE. Free book catalog.

Nonfiction: Publishes Americana, biography, business, economics, medicine, biological sciences, computer science, physical sciences, law, anthropology, folklore and literary criticism. "Serious books that serve the scholar and the professional." Follow the Chicago *Manual of Style*. Query with outline and 1-4 sample chapters, addressed to the editor.

Recent Nonfiction Title: *Passing the Time in Ballymenone*, by Henry Glassie.

Tips: Queries/mss may be routed to other editors in the publishing group.

UNIVERSITY OF PITTSBURGH PRESS, 127 N. Bellefield Ave., Pittsburgh PA 15260. (412)624-4110. Director: Frederick A. Hetzel. Managing Editor: Catherine Marshall. Publishes hardcover and paperback originals. Publishes 32 titles/year; receives 430 submissions annually. 30% of books from first-time authors; 95% of books from unagented writers. Average print order for a writer's first book is 1,000-2,500. Pays 12½% royalty on hardcover, 8% on paperback; no advance. Photocopied submissions OK. Computer printout submissions acceptable; prefers letter-quality to dot-matrix. Reports in 4 months. SASE. Free book catalog.

Nonfiction: Scholarly nonfiction. No textbooks or general nonfiction of an unscholarly nature. Submit outline/ synopsis and 1 sample chapter. Reviews artwork/photos as part of ms package.

Recent Nonfiction Title: *Cuba Between Empires, 1878-1902*, by Louis A. Pérez Jr..

THE UNIVERSITY OF TENNESSEE PRESS, 293 Communications Bldg., Knoxville TN 37996-0325. Contact: Acquisitions Editor. Averages 30 titles/year; receives 500 submissions annually. 50% of books from first-time authors; 99% of books from unagented writers. Average print order for a writer's first book is 1,250. Pays negotiable royalty on retail price. Photocopied submissions OK. "We can only review hard copy." Computer printout submissions acceptable; no dot-matrix. Reports in 2 week on queries; "in 1 month on submissions we have encouraged." Book catalog 75¢; writer's guidelines for SASE.

Nonfiction: American history, political science, film studies, sports studies, literary criticism, Black studies, women's studies, Caribbean, anthropology, folklore and regional studies. Prefers "scholarly treatment and a readable style. Authors usually have Ph.D.s." Submit outline/synopsis, author vita, and 2 sample chapters. No fiction, poetry or plays. Reviews artwork/photos as part of ms package.

Recent Nonfiction Title: *Nightly Horrors: Crisis Coverage in Television Network News*, by Dan Nimmo and James E. Combs.

Tips: "Our market is in several groups: scholars; educated readers with special interests in given scholarly subjects; and the general educated public interested in Tennessee, Appalachia and the South. Not all our books appeal to all these groups, of course, but any given book must appeal to at least one of them."

UNIVERSITY OF TEXAS PRESS, Box 7819, Austin TX 78713. Managing Editor: Barbara Spielman. Averages 60 titles/year; receives 1,000 submissions annually. 50% of books from first-time authors; 99% of books from unagented writers. Average print order for a writer's first book is 1,000. Pays royalty usually based on net income; occasionally offers advance. Publishes book an average of 18 months after acceptance. Electronic submissions OK, but requires hard copy also. Computer printout submissions acceptable; no dot-matrix. SASE. Reports in 2 months. Free book catalog and writer's guidelines.

Nonfiction: General scholarly subjects: astronomy, natural history, economics, Latin American and Middle Eastern studies, native Americans, classics, films, medical, biology, contemporary architecture, archeology, Chicano studies, physics, health, sciences, international relations, linguistics, photography, twentieth-century and women's literature. Also uses specialty titles related to Texas and the Southwest, national trade titles, and regional trade titles. Accepts nonfiction and fiction translations. Query or submit outline/synopsis and 2 sample chapters. Reviews artwork/photos as part of ms package.

Recent Nonfiction Title: *Peppers: The Domesticated Capsicums*, by Jean Andrews.

Tips: "It's difficult to make a manuscript over 400 double-spaced pages into a feasible book. Authors should take special care to edit out extraneous material." Looks for sharply focused, in-depth treatments of important topics.

UNIVERSITY OF UTAH PRESS, University of Utah, 101 University Services Bldg., Salt Lake City UT 84112. (801)581-6771. Director: Stephen H. Hess. Publishes hardcover and paperback originals and reprints. Averages 12 titles/year; receives 500 submissions annually. 30% of books from first-time authors; 100% of books from unagented writers. Average print order for writer's first book is 1,000. Pays 10% royalty on net sales on first 2,000 copies sold; 12% on 2,001 to 4,000 copies sold; 15% thereafter. Publishes book an average of 18 months after acceptance. Computer printout submissions acceptable; no dot-matrix. Reports in 8-10 weeks. SASE. Free book catalog; ms guidelines for SASE.

Nonfiction: Scholarly books on Western history, philosophy, anthropology, Mesoamerican studies, folklore, and Middle Eastern studies. Accepts nonfiction translations. Popular, well-written, carefully researched regional studies for Bonneville Books Series. Query with outline and 3 sample chapters. Author should specify

page length in query. Reviews artwork/photos as part of ms package.
Recent Nonfiction Title: *Saltair*, by Nancy D. McCormick and John S. McCormick.

UNIVERSITY OF WISCONSIN PRESS, 114 N. Murray St., Madison WI 53715. (608)262-4928 (telex: 265452). Director: Allen N. Fitchen. Acquisitions Editors: Peter J. Givler and Gordon Lester-Massman. Publishes hardcover and paperback originals, reprints and translations. Averages 40-50 titles/year. Pays standard royalties on retail price. Reports in 3 months. SASE.
Nonfiction: Publishes general nonfiction based on scholarly research. Looks for "originality, significance, quality of the research represented, literary quality, and breadth of interest to the educated community at large." Accepts nonfiction translations. Follow Chicago *Manual of Style*. Send complete ms.
Recent Nonfiction Title: *A Century of American Print Making, 1880-1980*, by James Watrous.

UNIVERSITY PRESS OF AMERICA, 4720 Boston Way, Lanham MD 20706. (301)459-3366. Editorial Director: James E. Lyons. Publishes hardcover and paperback originals (95%) and reprints (5%). Averages 450 titles/year. Pays 5-15% royalty on wholesale price; no advance. Computer printout submissions acceptable. Reports in 6 weeks. SASE. Free book catalog.
Nonfiction: Scholarly monographs, college, and graduate level textbooks in history, economics, business, psychology, political science, African studies, black studies, philosophy, religion, sociology, music, art, literature, drama and education. No juvenile or el-hi material. Submit outline.
Recent Nonfiction Title: *Vietnam as History*, by Peter Braestrup.

UNIVERSITY PRESS OF KANSAS, 329 Carruth, Lawrence KS 66045. (913)864-4154. Editor: Fred Woodward. Hardcover and paperback originals. Averages 20 titles/year; receives 500-600 submissions annually. 25% of books from first-time authors; 95% of books from unagented writers. Royalties negotiable; no advance. Markets books by advertising and direct mail, chiefly to libraries and scholars. "State availability of illustrations if they add significantly to the manuscript." Publishes book an average of 10 months after acceptance. Computer printout submissions acceptable; no dot-matrix. Reports in 4 months. SASE. Free book catalog; ms guidelines for SASE.
Nonfiction: Publishes biography, history, psychology, philosophy, politics, regional subjects (Kansas, Great Plains, Midwest), and scholarly.Reviews artwork/photos as part of ms package. Query.
Recent Nonfiction Title: *The Radical Politics of Thomas Jefferson* (political science).

UNIVERSITY PRESS OF MISSISSIPPI, 3825 Ridgewood Rd., Jackson MS 39211. (601)982-6205. Director: Barney McKee. Acquisitions Editor: Seetha Srinivasan. Publishes hardcover and paperback originals (90%) and reprints (10%). Averages 18 titles/year. Customarily pays 10% net royalty on first printing and 10% net on additional printings. No advance. Publishes book an average of 9 months after acceptance. Computer printout submissions acceptable. SASE. Reports in 2 months. Free book catalog.
Nonfiction: Americana, biography, business and economics, history, politics, psychology, sociology, literary criticism and folklore. Especially needs regional studies and literary studies, particularly mss on William Faulkner and Eudora Welty. Submit outline/synopsis and sample chapters and curriculum vita. Reviews artwork/photos as part of ms package.
Recent Nonfiction Title: *Conversations with Walker Percy*, ed. by Lewis A. Lawson and Victor A. Kramer.

*UNIVERSITY PRESS OF NEW ENGLAND, 3 Lebanon St., Hanover NH 03755. (603)646-3349. "University Press of New England is a consortium of university presses. Some books—those published for one of the consortium members—carry the joint imprint of New England and the member: Dartmouth, Brandeis, Brown, Tufts, Clark, Universities of Connecticut, New Hampshire, Vermont and Rhode Island." Director: Thomas L. McFarland. Editor: Charles Backus. Publishes hardcover and trade paperback originals (90%) and trade paperback reprints (10%). Averages 30 titles/year. Subsidy publishes 80% of books. Pays standard royalty; occasionally offers advance. Electronic submissions OK, but requires hard copy also. Computer printout submissions acceptable. SASE. Reports in 1 month. Free book catalog.
Nonfiction: Americana (regional—New England), art, biography, history, music, nature, politics, psychology, reference, science, sociology, and regional (New England). No festschriften, memoirs, unrevised doctoral dissertatious, or symposium collections. Submit outline/synopsis and 1-2 sample chapters.
Recent Nonfiction Title: *Bogs of the Northeast*, by Charles W. Johnson.

*UNIVERSITY PRESS OF VIRGINIA, Box 3608, University Station, Charlottesville VA 22903. (804)924-3468. Editor-in-Chief: Walker Cowen. Publishes hardcover and paperback originals and reprints. Averages 45 titles/year. 70% of books from first-time authors; 100% of books from unagented writers. Average print order for a writer's first book is 1,000. Royalty on retail depends on the market for the book; sometimes none is made. "We subsidy publish 40% of our books, based on cost versus probable market." Publishes book an average of 10 months after acceptance. Computer printout submissions acceptable; no dot-matrix. Returns rejected material within a week. Reports on acceptances in 2 months. SASE. Free catalog; ms guidelines for SASE.

Nonfiction: Publishes Americana, business, history, law, medicine and psychiatry, politics, reference, scientific, bibliography, and decorative arts books. "Write a letter to the director, describing content of the manuscript, plus length. Also specify if maps, tables, illustrations, etc., are included." No educational, sociological or psychological mss. Accepts nonfiction translations from French. Reviews artwork/photos as part of ms package.

Recent Nonfiction Title: *China: Seventy Years after the 1911 Hsin-hai Revolution*, edited by Hungdah Chiu with Shao-chuan Leng.

*UNIVERSITY PRESSES OF FLORIDA, 15 NW 15th St., Gainesville FL 32603. (904)392-1351. Director: Phillip Martin. Publishes hardcover and trade paperback originals and trade paperback reprints. Averages 30 titles/year. Subsidy publishes 15% of books. "We must break even on direct costs of manufacture." Pays 0-12½% royalty on net sales receipts; no advance. Simultaneous and photocopied submissions OK. Electronic submissions OK, but confer with editor in advance. Computer printout submissions acceptable. SASE. Reports in 4 weeks on queries; 6 months on mss. Free book catalog.

Nonfiction: Biography, "coffee table" book, cookbook, reference and scholarly monographs. Subjects include Americana, animals, anthropology, art, business and economics, history, nature, philosophy, politics, psychology, archaeology and literary theory. Especially looking for "learned works on serious subjects lucidly written for the general, educated reader. No astrology, faith healing, folk medicine, handicraft or education textbooks." Query.

Recent Nonfiction Title: *Philosophy of the Literary Symbolic*, by Hazard Adams (literary theory).

UTAH STATE UNIVERSITY PRESS, Utah State University, Logan UT 84322. (801)750-1362. Director: Linda Speth. Publishes hardcover and trade paperback originals and hardcover and trade paperback reprints. Averages 6 titles/year; receives 170 submissions annually. 8% of books from first-time authors. Average print order for a writer's first book is 1,500. Pays 10-15% royalty on retail price; no advance. Publishes book an average of 18 months after acceptance. Electronic submissions OK on Televideo 803, but requires hard copy also. Computer printout submissions acceptable; prefers letter-quality to dot-matrix. SASE. Reports in 2 weeks on queries; 2 months on mss. Free book catalog; ms guidelines for SASE.

Nonfiction: Biography, reference and textbook on Americana, history, politics and science. "Particularly interested in book-length scholarly manuscripts dealing with Western history, Western literature (Western Americana). All manuscript submission must have a scholarly focus." Submit complete ms. Reviews artwork/photos as part of ms package.

Recent Nonfiction Title: *Blazing Crosses in Zion: The Ku Klux Klan in Utah*, by Larry R. Gerlach.

Poetry: "At the present time, we have accepted several poetry manuscripts and will not be reading poetry submissions for one year."

Recent Poetry Title: *Stone Roses: Poems from Transylvania*, by Keith Wilson.

VANCE BIBLIOGRAPHIES, 112 N. Charter, Box 229, Monticello IL 61856. (217)762-3831. Publisher: Judith Vance. Imprints include Architecture Series: Bibliography and Public Administration Series: Bibliography, Judith Vance, Publisher. Publishes trade paperback originals. Averages 480 titles/year. 240/imprints; receives 500 submissions annually. 10% of books from first-time authors; 100% of books from unagented writers. Average print order for a writer's first book is 250. Pays $100 honorarium and 10-20 author's copies. Publishes book an average of 4 months after acceptance. Photocopied submissions OK. Computer printout submissions acceptable; prefers letter-quality to dot-matrix. Reports in 1 week on queries; 2 weeks on mss. Free book catalog; and ms guidelines.

Nonfiction: Reference bibliographies on public administration and/or architecture and related subject areas. Publishes for "graduate students and professionals in the field; primary customers are libraries." Query or submit complete ms.

Recent Nonfiction Title: *Pedestrian Facilities Design in Architecture*, by R.B. Harmon.

VEHICULE PRESS, Box 125, Place du Parc Station, Montreal, Quebec H2W 2M9 Canada. (514)844-6073. President/Publisher: Simon Dardick. Imprints include Signal Editions (poetry) and Dossier Quebec (history, memoirs). Publishes trade paperback originals. Average 8 titles/year. Pays 10-15% royalty on retail price; offers $200-500 advance. Photocopied submissions OK. SAE. "We would appreciate receiving an IRC rather than U.S. postage stamps which we cannot use." Reports in 2 weeks on queries; 2 months on mss. Free book catalog.

Nonfiction: Biography and memoir. Subjects include Canadiana, history, politics, social history and literature. Especially looking for Canadian social history. Query. Reviews artwork/photos as part of ms package.

Recent Nonfiction Title: *The Life of a Document: A Global Approach to Archives and Records Management*, by Carol Couture and J-Y Rousseau.

Fiction: Short stories only. Query.

Recent Fiction Title: *Voyage to the Other Extreme*, by Marilu Mallet (short stories).

Poetry: Contact Michael Harris, editor. Looking for Canadian authors. Submit complete ms.
Recent Poetry Title: *Veiled Countries*, by Marie-Clair Blais.
Tips: "We are only interested in Canadian authors."

VGM CAREER HORIZONS, (Division of National Textbook Co.), 4255 W. Touhy Ave., Lincolnwood IL 60646-1975. (312)679-4210. Editorial Director: Leonard Fiddle. Senior Editor: Barbara Wood Donner. Publishes hardcover and paperback originals. Averages 20-30 titles/year; receives 200+ submissions annually. 10% of books from first-time authors; 80% of books from unagented writers. Mss purchased on either royalty or buy-out basis. Publishes ms an average of 6-12 months after acceptance. Computer printout submissions acceptable; no dot-matrix. SASE. Reports in 6 weeks. Book catalog and ms guidelines for large SASE.
Nonfiction: Publishes career guidance books. "We are interested in all professional and vocational areas. Our titles are marketed to a junior and senior high school, college and trade audience, so readability and reading level of books in the series is especially important. VGM books are used by students and others considering careers in specific areas, and contain basic information of the history and development of each career field; its educational requirements; specialties and working conditions; how to write a resume, interview, and get started in the field; and salaries and benefits. Additionally, we expect to be producing more general career guidance and development materials in the next year or two. We are open to all suggestions in this area, although all proposals should be of relevance to young adults, as well as to older career changers. Since our titles are largely formatted, potential writers should always query first, requesting information on already-published titles and format and structure." Looks for "a comprehensive, orderly synthesis of the material, and an interesting presentation that is clear and accurate."
Recent Nonfiction Title: *Opportunities in Microelectronics*, by Richard Moran and D. Mark Hornung.
Tips: "On most projects, we prefer writers who have considerable personal background and knowledge of their subjects, although freelance writers who research well are also considered. Although the content of most titles is similar, the ability to present comprehensive, factual information in an upbeat, interesting manner is particularly in an author's favor."

VICTOR BOOKS, Box 1825, Wheaton IL 60187. (312)668-6000. Executive Editor: James R. Adair. Publishes trade paperbacks, mass market paperbacks and hardcover originals. Averages 50 titles/year; receives 1,046 submissions annually. 10% of books from first-time authors; 100% of books from unagented writers. Average print order for a writer's first book is 12,000. Pays "competitive royalties on retail price with advances." Publishes book an average of 1 year after acceptance. Computer printout submissions acceptable; prefers letter-quality to dot-matrix. Reports in 2 months. SASE. Free book catalog and ms guidelines.
Nonfiction: Only religious themes. "Writers must know the evangelical market well and their material should have substance. Many of our books are by ministers, Bible teachers, seminar speakers, counselors and subject experts. Freelancers can team with nonwriting experts to ghost or co-author books to fit our line. We prefer to see a brief outline to show where the book is going, accompanied by at least 2 sample chapters to give an indication of writing and content. Writing must have a popular touch, clearly communicate, and be biblically based." Also publishes reference books with religious themes for children and adults. Prefers outline/synopsis and sample chapters, but queries are acceptable.
Recent Nonfiction Title: *When a Good Man Falls*, by Erwin Lutzer.
Fiction: "Fiction queries are being considered, both children and adults."

‡**VOLCANO PRESS, INC.**, 330 Ellis St., San Francisco CA 94102. (415)664-5600. President: Ruth Gottstein. Publishes trade paperback originals. Averages 4 titles/year; receives 100+ submissions annually. 95% of books from first-time authors; 100% of books from unagented writers. Average print order for a writer's first book is 5,000. Publishes some mss by author participation (co-venture). Pays royalty; buys some mss outright. Publishes book an average of 18-24 months after acceptance. Simultaneous and photocopied submissions OK. Computer printout submissions acceptable; no dot-matrix. SASE. Reports in 3 months. Book catalog for business size SAE and 1 first class stamp.
Nonfiction: Women and social change. Subjects include business and economics, health, history, philosophy, politics, psychology, sociology and travel. Query or submit outline/synopsis (½ page description) and sample chapters. "No telephone solicitations." Reviews artwork/photos as part of ms package.
Recent Nonfiction Title: *Menopause, Naturally*, by Sadja Greenwood, M.D.
Tips: "The writer has the best chance of selling our firm women's nonfiction—emerging issues of social interest."

‡**WADSWORTH PUBLISHING COMPANY**, Division of Wadsworth, Inc., 10 Davis Dr., Belmont CA 94002. (415)595-2350. Subsidiaries include Brooks/Cole Pub. Co., Kent Pub. Co., Prindle, Weber and Schmidt Pub. Co., and others. Editor-in-Chief: Stephen D. Rutter. Publishes hardcover and paperback originals and software. Publishes 600 titles/year. 50% of books from first-time authors; 100% of books from unagented writers. Pays 5-15% royalty, on net price. Advances not automatic policy. Publishes ms an average of 1 year after acceptance. Simultaneous and photocopied submissions OK. Electronic submissions OK, but

requires hard copy also. Computer printout submissions acceptable; prefers letter-quality to dot-matrix. SASE. Reports in 2 weeks. Ms guidelines available.
Nonfiction: Textbook: higher education only. Subjects include business and economics, health, music, philosophy, photography, politics, psychology, religion, sociology and all academic subjects in higher education. "We need books that use fresh teaching approaches to all courses taught at schools of higher education throughout the U.S. and Canada. We specifically do not publish textbooks in art and history." Query or submit outline/synopsis and sample chapters. Sometimes reviews artwork/photos as part of ms package.
Recent Nonfiction Title: *Calculus and Analytic Geometry*, by Mizrahi and Sullivan (college textbook).
Tips: "Our audience is college professors and their students, and adults interested in continuing professional education."

J. WESTON WALCH, PUBLISHER, Box 658, Portland ME 04104. (207)772-2846. Managing Editor: Richard S. Kimball. Editor: Jane Carter. Computer Editor: Robert Crepeau. Publishes paperback originals and software. Averages 120 titles/year; receives 300 submissions annually. 23% of books from first-time authors; 100% of books from unagented writers. Average print order for a writer's first book is 700. Offers 10-15% royalty on gross receipts; buys some titles by outright purchase for $100-1,000. No advance. Publishes book an average of 18 months after acceptance. Electronic submissions OK on most microcomputers, Apple preferred, but requires hard copy also. Computer printout submissions acceptable; prefers letter-quality to dot-matrix. SASE. Reports in 3 weeks. Book catalog $1.05.
Nonfiction: Subjects include art, business, computer education, economics, English, foreign language, government, health, history, mathematics, music, psychology, recreation, science, social science, sociology, special education and sports. "We publish only supplementary educational material for sale to secondary schools throughout the U.S. and Canada. Formats include books, posters, ditto master sets, visual master sets (masters for making transparencies), cassettes, filmstrips, microcomputer courseware and mixed packages. Most titles are assigned by us, though we occasionally accept an author's unsolicited submission. We have a great need for author/artist teams and for authors who can write at third- to tenth-grade levels. We do *not* want basic texts, anthologies or industrial arts titles. Most of our authors—but not all—have secondary teaching experience. I cannot stress too much the advantages that an author/artist team would have in approaching us and probably other publishers." Query first. Looks for "sense of organization, writing ability, knowledge of subject, skill of communicating with intended audience." Reviews artwork/photos as part of ms package.
Recent Nonfiction Title: *The Complete Newspaper Resource Book*, by Jane Lamb.

WALKER AND CO., 720 5th Ave., New York NY 10019. Contact: Submissions Editor. Hardcover and paperback originals (90%) and reprints (10%). Averages 150 titles/year; receives 3,500 submissions annually. Pays 10-12-15% royalty on retail price or by outright purchase. Advance averages $1,000-2,500 "but could be higher or lower." Query or submit outline/synopsis and sample chapter. Submit photocopy samples of photos/illustrations to accompany ms. Photocopied submissions OK. SASE. Free book catalog. Do not telephone submissions editions.
Nonfiction: Publishes Americana, art, biography, business, histories, how-to, juveniles, science and history, medicine and psychiatry, music, nature, parenting, psychology, recreation, reference, popular science, and self-help books.
Recent Nonfiction Title: *How to Make Your Child a Winner*, by Dr. Victor B. Cline (parenting).
Fiction: Mystery, romantic suspense, regency romance, historical romance, western, and action adventure.
Recent Fiction Title: *Blunt Darts*, by Jeremiah Healy.

WALLACE—HOMESTEAD BOOK CO., American Broadcasting Company, Inc., 580 WatersEdge, Lombard IL 60148. (312)953-1100. General Manager: William N. Topaz. Publishes hardcover and trade paperback originals. Averages 30 titles/year; receives 300 submissions annually. 50% of books from first-time authors; 100% of books from unagented writers. Pays royalty on net price. Publishes book an average of 8 months after acceptance. "Consult with production manager about electronic submissions." Computer printout submissions acceptable; prefers letter-quality to dot-matrix. Simultaneous and photocopied submissions OK. SASE. Reports in 4 weeks. Free book catalog and ms guidelines.
Nonfiction: Cookbook, how-to and reference. Subjects include Americana, art, business and economics, cooking and food, hobbies and crafts, photography, needlecraft, agriculture, antiques and collectibles. Especially looking for mss on antiques, collectibles, memorabilia, quilting, cookbooks, agriculture/farm, agriculture, business and other specialty areas. No school or textbook material. Submit outline/synopsis and

sample chapters. Reviews artwork/photos as part of ms package.

Recent Nonfiction Titles: *Super Quilter II*, by Carla Hassel (quilting).

Tips: "Our books are intended for an adult nontechnical audience."

WAYNE STATE UNIVERSITY PRESS, 5959 Woodward Ave., Detroit MI 48202. (313)577-4600. Acting Director: Richard Kinney. Editor: J. Owen. Publishes hardcover and paperback originals. Publishes 24 titles/year. Pays standard royalty schedule on wholesale price; no advance. Publishes book an average of 20 months after acceptance. Computer printout submissions acceptable; no dot-matrix. Reports in 6 months. SASE. Free book catalog.

Nonfiction: Publishes Americana, art and architecture history, Michigana, classical studies, biography, economics, history, law, folklore studies, ethnic studies, aphasia and learning disabilities, philosophy, politics, psychology, and literature books. Submit outline/synopsis and sample chapters. "Do not send photos unless requested, or send photocopies."

Recent Nonfiction Title: *Courier from Warsaw*, by Jan Nowak.

WESTERN MARINE ENTERPRISES INC., Box Q, Ventura CA 93002. (805)644-6043. Editor: William Berssen. Publishes hardcover and trade paperback originals. Averages 6 titles/year. Pays 15% royalty on net price. Offers no advance. Computer printout submissions acceptable; prefers letter-quality to dot-matrix. SASE. Reports in 3 week.

Nonfiction: Boating. Subjects include recreation, sports and travel. "We specialize in boating books—mainly how-to and when-to." No "simple narrative accounts of how someone sailed a boat from here to there!" First-time book authors should submit complete ms.

Recent Nonfiction Title: *Cruising Guide to California's Channel Islands*, by Brian M. Fagan (sail and powerboat guide).

WESTERN PRODUCER PRAIRIE BOOKS, Box 2500, Saskatoon, Saskatchewan S7K 2C4 Canada. Manager: Rob Sanders. Publishes hardcover and paperback originals (95%) and reprints (5%). Specializes in historical nonfiction, natural history, and young adult novels with emphasis on Western Canadian region. Publishes book an average of 20 months after acceptance. Averages 15 titles/year; receives 400 submissions annually. 20% of books from first-time authors; 80% of books from unagented writers. Average print order for a writer's first book is 400. Pays negotiable royalty on list price. Submit contact sheets or prints if illustrations are to accompany ms. Electronic submissions OK on Micom or Wang, but requires hard copy also. Computer printout submissions acceptable; no dot-matrix. Reports in 4 months. SAE, IRC. Free book catalog; ms guidelines for SASE (Canada), IRC.

Nonfiction: Publishes history, nature, photography, biography, reference, agriculture, economics, politics and cookbooks. Accepts nonfiction and fiction translations. Submit outline, synopsis and 2-3 sample chapters. Reviews artwork/photos as part of ms package.

Recent Nonfiction Title: *Land of Earth and Sky*, by Ronald Rees.

WESTERN TANAGER PRESS, 1111 Pacific Ave., Santa Cruz CA 95060. (408)425-1111. Publisher: Hal Morris. Publishes hardcover and trade paperback originals (50%), and hardcover and trade paperback reprints (50%). Averages 3 titles/year; receives 50-100 submissions annually. 25% of books from first-time authors; 100% of books from unagented writers. Average print order for a writer's first book is 2,000. Publishes book an average of 6 months after acceptance. Computer printout submissions acceptable; prefers letter-quality to dot-matrix.

Nonfiction: Biography and history. "We are looking for works of local and regional history dealing with California. This includes biography, natural history, art and politics. Also interested in travel, hiking, biking guides and touring books." Query. Looks for "a well-written, well-thought-out project with a specific audience in mind." Reviews artwork/photos as part of ms package.

WESTERNLORE PRESS, Box 35305, Tucson AZ 85740. Editor: Lynn R. Bailey. Publishes 6-12 titles/year. Pays standard royalties on retail price "except in special cases." Query. Reports in 2 months. Enclose return postage with query.

Nonfiction: Publishes Western Americana of a scholarly and semischolarly nature: anthropology, history, biography, historic sites, restoration, and ethnohistory pertaining to the greater American West. Republication of rare and out-of-print books. Length: 25,000-100,000 words.

*WESTVIEW PRESS, 5500 Central Ave., Boulder CO 80301. (303)444-3541. Publisher/President: F.A. Praeger. Hardcover and paperback originals (90%), lecture notes, reference books, and paperback texts (10%). Specializes in scholarly monographs or conference reports with strong emphasis on applied science, both social and natural. 0-10% royalty on net price, depending on market. Accepts subsidies for a small number of books, "but only in the case of first class scholarly material for a limited market when books need to be priced low, or when the manuscripts have unusual difficulties such as Chinese or Sanskrit characters; the usual quality

standards of a top-flight university press apply, and subsidies must be furnished by institutions, not by individuals." Averages 300 titles/year. Markets books mainly by direct mail. State availability of photos and/or illustrations to accompany manuscript. Reports in 1-4 months. SASE. Free book catalog.
Nonfiction: Agriculture/food, agricultural economics, public policy, energy, natural resources, international economics and business, international law, international relations, area studies, development, science and technology policy, sociology, anthropology, reference, military affairs, national security, health, Asia and the Pacific, comparative politics, social impact assessment, women's studies, Latin America and Caribbean, Soviet Union and Eastern Europe, Middle East, Africa, and Western Europe. Looks for "scholarly excellence and scientific relevance." Query and submit 2 sample chapters and tentative table of contents and Curriculum Vitae. Use Chicago *Manual of Style*. "Unsolicited manuscripts receive low priority; inquire before submitting projects."
Recent Nonfiction Title: *The Business of Book Publishing*, by Geiser.

*WHITAKER HOUSE, Pittsburgh and Colfax Sts., Springdale PA 15144. (412)274-4440. Managing Editor: Donna C. Arthur. Paperback originals (40%) and reprints (60%). Publishes 30-35 titles/year. Subsidy publishes 25% of books. "We publish only Christian books." Royalty negotiated based on the cover price of the book. Publishes book an average of 6 months after acceptance. "We market books in Christian book stores and in rack-jobbing locations such as supermarkets and drug stores." Looking for teaching books with illustrations, anecdotes, and personal experiences used throughout, typed, double-spaced, about 300 pages in length. Query first. Computer printout submissions acceptable; prefers letter-quality to dot-matrix. SASE. Unsolicited mss returned. Ms guidelines for SASE.
Nonfiction: Publishes mostly how-to books ("how to move on in your Christian walk"; 90,000 words); and religious ("don't want heavy theology"; 90,000 words). "Please note that we want teaching books that give the author's life experiences as well as solid Christian teaching." Looks for "well-written informative work that *follows our specifications*." Accepts outline/synopsis and 2-3 sample chapters. Reviews artwork/photos as part of ms package.
Recent Nonfiction Title: *The Diet Alternative*, by Diane Hampton.

THE WHITSTON PUBLISHING CO., Box 958, Troy NY 12181. (518)283-4363. Editorial Director: Jean Goode. Publishes hardcover originals. Averages 20 titles/year; receives 100 submissions annually. 100% of books from unagented writers. Pays 10-12-15% royalty on wholesale price; no advance. Publishes book an average of 30 months after acceptance. Computer printout submissions acceptable; no dot-matrix. Reports in 1 year.
Nonfiction: "We publish scholarly and critical books in the arts, humanities and some of the social sciences. We also publish reference books, bibliographies, indexes, checklists and monographs. We do not want author bibliographies in general unless they are unusual and unusually scholarly. We are, however, much interested in catalogs and inventories of library collections of individuals, such as the catalog of the Evelyn Waugh Collection at the Humanities Research Center, the University of Texas at Austin; and collections of interest to the specific scholarly community, such as surveys of early black newspapers in libraries in the US, etc." Accepts poetry translations from French and Spanish. Query or submit complete ms. Reviews artwork/photos as part of ms package.
Recent Nonfiction Title: *Marcel Duchamp: Eros C'est la Vie*, by A. Marquis (biography).

WILDERNESS PRESS, 2440 Bancroft Way, Berkeley CA 94704. (415)843-8080. Editorial Director: Thomas Winnett. Publishes paperback originals. Averages 4 titles/year; receives 150 submissions annually. 20% of books from first-time authors; 95% of books from unagented writers. Average print order for a writer's first book is 5,000. Pays 8-10% royalty on retail price; offers average $500 advance. Publishes book an average of 6 months after acceptance. Computer printout submissions acceptable; prefers letter-quality to dot-matrix. Reports in 2 weeks. SASE. Book catalog for SASE.
Nonfiction: "We publish books about the outdoors. Most of our books are trail guides for hikers and backpackers, but we also publish how-to books about the outdoors and perhaps will publish personal adventures. The manuscript must be accurate. The author must thoroughly research an area in person. If he is writing a trail guide, he must walk all the trails in the area his book is about. The outlook must be strongly conservationist. The style must be appropriate for a highly literate audience." Query, submit outline/synopsis and sample chapters, or submit complete ms demonstrating "accuracy, literacy, and popularity of subject area." Reviews artwork/photos as part of ms package.
Recent Nonfiction Title: *South Bay Trails*, by Frances Spangle and Jean Rusmore.

JOHN WILEY & SONS, INC., 605 3rd Ave., New York NY 10158. (212)850-6000. Publishes hardcover and paperback originals and software. Publishes 1,000 titles/year. Pays variable royalties on wholesale price. Follow *MLA Style Sheet*. Simultaneous and photocopied submissions OK. Electronic submissions OK. "We are actively seeking software authors, particularly in the engineering field." Publishes software in engineering, social science, computer science, business, life science, politics, law and medicine. Reports in 6 months.

SASE. Free book catalog.

Nonfiction: Publishes college textbooks, professional reference titles, trade books, journals. Query or submit outline/synopsis and 2 sample chapters.

Recent Nonfiction Title: *Resumé Writing, Comphrensive How-to-do-it Guide.*

Tips: Queries/mss may be routed to other editors in the publishing group.

WILLIAMSON PUBLISHING CO., Box 185, Church Hill Rd., Charlotte VT 05445. (802)425-2102. Editorial Director: Susan Williamson. Publishes trade paperback originals. Averages 10-12 titles/year; receives 250 submissions annually. 50% of books from first-time authors; 90% of books from unagented writers. Average print order for a writer's first book is 5,000-10,000. Pays 10-12% royalty on sales dollars received or makes outright purchase if favored by author. Offers average $1,000-1,500 advance. Publishes book an average of 12-18 months after acceptance. Simultaneous and photocopied submissions OK. Computer submissions acceptable; prefers letter-quality to dot-matrix. SASE. Reports in 4 weeks on queries; 6 weeks on mss. Book catalog for SAE and 2 first class stamps.

Nonfiction: Cookbook, how-to, illustrated book and self-help. Subjects include landscaping, building, animals, business, education, cooking and foods, health, hobbies, nature and travel. "Our areas of concentration are people-oriented business books, cookbooks, small-scale livestock raising, family housing (all aspects), health and education." No children's books, photography, politics, religion, history, art or biography. Query with outline/synopsis and sample chapters. Reviews artwork/photos as part of ms package.

Recent Nonfiction Title: *The Termination Trap: Best Strategies for A Job Going Sour*, by Stephen Cohen, MD.

Tips: "In our specialized area, the more solid how-to information on important subjects in people's lives the better."

WILSHIRE BOOK CO., 12015 Sherman Rd., North Hollywood CA 91605. (213)875-1711. Editorial Director: Melvin Powers. Publishes paperback originals (50%) and reprints (50%). Publishes 50 titles/year; receives 6,000 submissions annually. 25% of books from first-time authors; 75% of books from unagented writers. Average print order for a writer's first book is 5,000. Pays standard royalty; offers variable advance. Computer printout submissions acceptable; no dot-matrix. SASE. Reports in 2 weeks. Book catalog for SASE.

Nonfiction: Health, hobbies, how-to, psychology, recreation, self-help, entrepeneurship, how to make money, and mail order. "We are always looking for self-help and psychological books such as *Psycho-Cybernetics* and *Guide to Rational Living*. We need manuscripts teaching mail order, entrepreneur techniques, how to make money and advertising. We publish 70 horse books. "All that I need is the concept of the book to determine if the project is viable. I welcome phone calls to discuss manuscripts with authors." Reviews artwork/photos as part of ms package.

Recent Nonfiction Title: *How to Self-Publish Your Book and Have the Fun and Excitement of Being a Best-Selling Author*, by Melvin Powers.

*WIMMER BROTHERS BOOKS, 4210 B.F. Goodrich Blvd., Box 18408, Memphis TN 38118. (901)362-8900. Editorial Director: Richard Anderson. Senior Editor: Kay Boundy. Publishes hardcover and paperback originals. Averages 4-5 titles/year. Subsidy publishes 50% of books. Offers 10-15% royalty on wholesale price; no advance. Publishes book an average of 15 months after acceptance. Computer printout submissions acceptable; no dot-matrix. SASE. Reports in 2 months. Book catalog for SASE.

Nonfiction: Cookbooks, cooking and foods, and how-to. Especially needs specialized cookbooks and how-to books dealing with home entertainment. Looks for "interesting angle, well-edited recipes in the book and good grammar." Submit complete ms. Reviews artwork/photos as part of ms package.

Recent Nonfiction Title: *Wining and Dining with John Grisanti*, by John Grisanti.

WINCHESTER PRESS, Imprint of New Century Publishers, Inc., 220 Old New Brunswick Rd., Piscataway NJ 08854. Consulting Editor: Robert Elman. Publishes hardcover and paperback originals. Averages 15-20 titles/year. Pays 10-12½-15% royalty on retail price; offers average $2,500 advance. "Submit sample photos and some idea of total number projected for final book." Simultaneous and photocopied submissions OK. SASE. Reports in 3 months. Free book catalog.

Nonfiction: Main interest is in leisure activities, outdoor sports, crafts and related subjects. Publishes cookbooks related to fish and game; how-to (sports and sporting equipment); pets (hunting dogs); recreation (outdoor); sports (hunting, fishing, etc.); and technical (firearms, boats and motors, fishing tackle, etc.). Looks for "good organization, defined audience potential, original and accurate information and good photographs." Submit outline/synopsis and sample chapters.

Recent Nonfiction Title: *The Book of the Black Bear*, by Richard P. Smith.

Tips: "The writing of leisure-activities books—particularly how-to books—has vastly improved in recent years. Manuscripts must now be better written and must reflect new ideas and new information if they are to be considered for publication by Winchester Press. Recreational equipment and opportunities have expanded, and writers must also be up-to-date journalists."

Close-up

Betsy Perry
Editor
John Wiley & Sons, Inc.

"Put yourself in the shoes of the editor or manuscript reviewer—then give me as much information as I need to make a decision." And give Betsy Perry *specific* information, not claims that your book is a natural follow-up to such-and-such-a-bestseller.

What Perry looks for are "well-thought-out, articulate proposals describing the book, the audience or market, and the competition." Many times the information about the book's competition is sketchy or not in the proposal. "If the author has a good analysis of how the book is similar or different from competing books, that's very helpful to me," says Perry, who reads all trade nonfiction proposals.

She likes to see a detailed table of contents with chapter headings and subheadings and information on what qualifies the writer to write the book. The ability to write well, clearly, and in an interesting manner is essential, she stresses.

In reading proposals, Perry evaluates a writer's commitment to his work. "For most nonfiction trade books, you're not going to get wealthy unless you write several, so there's got to be a commitment and enthusiasm and interest in the writing process and in developing the book," says Perry.

Perry sends manuscripts that are being seriously considered to a content reviewer and discusses them with the publisher and Wiley's sales and marketing groups. "The author and publisher are actually working toward the same end; we both want the best books we can publish," she points out.

Writers whose books are accepted for publication should realize that silence isn't golden. "I'm impressed with authors who ask questions like what will happen after the book is written," she says. "It shows they really care about their writing and the quality of the book."

At this 179-year-old company, a manuscript accepted for publication goes to two content editors who know the book's subject and who review it for accuracy and appropriateness. Next, it goes to a developmental editor who looks at the book's style and organization. The editors prepare a written report for Perry who then conveys the information to the writer.

Writers with an expertise (such as in architecture or computers or any specialty) should inquire about becoming manuscript reviewers for publishers, especially those in the textbook field, she suggests. "Reading other people's proposals is one of the best ways to get experience—to see and critique what people have written."

She finds herself reviewing writers' proposals in the evenings but isn't complaining. "Most people get into publishing because they like books and the publishing world," says Perry, who first worked as a book sales representative for Prentice-Hall. "Publishing is not as glamorous as people might think; it's a lot of long hours."

Despite a busy schedule, she stays in contact with the authors whose books she is editing—to keep them on deadline and to offer "encouragement and enthusiasm.

"You try to be sensitive to their needs and to what a priority this book is in their lives at this time," she says. "I know how difficult the writing process is."

‡**WINDSOR BOOKS**, Subisidary of Windsor Marketing Corp., Box 280, Brightwaters NY 11718. (516)666-4631. Managing Editor: Stephen Schmidt. Publishes hardcover and trade paperback originals, reprints, and very specific software. Averages 8 titles/year; receives approximately 20 submissions annually. 60% of books from first-time authors; 100% of books from unagented writers. Pays 10% royalty on retail price; 5% on wholesale price (50% of total cost); offers variable advance. Publishes book an average of 9 months after acceptance. Simultaneous and photocopied submissions OK. Computer printout submissions acceptable; prefers letter-quality to dot-matrix. SASE. Reports in 2 weeks on queries; 3 weeks on mss. Free book catalog.
Nonfiction: How-to and technical. Subjects include business and economics (investing in stocks and commodities). Interested in strategies, methods for investing in the stock market, options market, and commodity markets. Query or submit outline/synopsis and sample chapters. Reviews artwork/photos as part of ms package.
Recent Nonfiction Title: *How to Triple Your Money Every Year with Stock Index Futures*, by George Angell (hardcover).
Tips: "Our books are for serious investors; we sell through direct mail to our mailing list and other financial lists. Writers must keep their work original; this market tends to have a great deal of information overlap among publications."

WINGBOW PRESS, Subsidiary of Bookpeople, 2929 Fifth St., Berkeley CA 94710. (415)549-3030. Editor: Randy Fingland. Publishes hardcover and trade paperback originals and trade paperback reprints. Averages 3-4 titles/year; receives 500. 20% of books from first-time authors; 100% of books from unagented writers. Average print order for a writer's first book is 7,500. Pays 7-10% royalty on retail price; offers average $500 advance. Publishes book an average of 18 months after acceptance. Electronic submissions OK on IBM and Epson, but requires hard copy also. Computer printout submissions acceptable. SASE. Reports in 3 weeks on queries; 9 weeks on mss. Free book catalog.
Nonfiction: How-to, reference, psychology and sociology. Especially needs regional guides to San Francisco Bay area. Query or submit outline/synopsis and 1-5 sample chapters. Reviews artwork/photos as part of ms package.
Recent Nonfiction Title: *Working Inside Out: Tools for Change*, by by Margo Adair (psychology/women's spirituality).
Tips: "We are currently not seeking poetry or original fiction. The writer has the best chance of selling regional guidebooks, psychology/health/self-sustenance, and women's books. That's where our marketing strength lies. We usually want to see a completed manuscript before signing a contract; if not, manuscript must be readable, grammatical, and author must be willing to be edited."

WINGRA WOODS PRESS, Box 9601, Madison WI 53715. Acquisitions Editor: M.G. Mahoney. Book packager producing 6-10 titles/year. Publishes trade paperback originals. Pays 10-12% royalty on retail price. Simultaneous and photocopied submissions OK. Computer printout submissions acceptable. SASE. Reports in 6 weeks.
Nonfiction: Cookbook, how-to, juvenile, self-help. Subjects include Americana, popular history and science, animals, art, and nature. Especially looking for popularized book-length treatments of specialized knowledge; interested in proposals from academics and professionals. Query with outline/synopsis. Do not send complete mss.
Recent Nonfiction Title: *The Christmas Cat.*

WINSTON PRESS, INC., CBS Educational Publishing, 430 Oak Grove, Minneapolis MN 55403. (612)871-7000. Editor-in-Chief: Janice M. Johnson. General Books Editor: Tom Grady. Curriculum Editor: Yvette Nelson. Religious Books Editor: Jim Bitney. Publishes hardcover and paperback originals (90%) and reprints (10%). Publishes 40 trade titles/year; receives 1,000 submissions annually. 20% of books from first-time authors. Average print order for a writer's first book is 5,000. Pays royalty on net price; advance varies. Publishes book an average of 18 months after acceptance. Photocopied submissions OK. Computer printout submissions acceptable. SASE. Reports in 2 months. Mss guidelines for SASE.
Nonfiction: Religion, human development and family. Curriculum materials in religion or related topics for preschool through adult education. Specialized and general trade books, gift and photography books. Query or submit outline/synopsis. Looks for "a clear, popular writing style, responsible scholarship (but not a scholarly style), and fresh ideas." Accepts nonfiction translations. Prefers proposal and sample chapters for inquiry. Accepts artwork/photos as part of ms package.
Recent Nonfiction Title: *Baby Hunger*, by Lois Davitz.

***WINSTON-DEREK PUBLISHERS**, Pennywell Dr., Box 90883, Nashville TN 37209. (615)329-1319 or 356-7384. Publisher: James W. Peebles. Publishes hardcover, trade and mass market paperback originals. Averages 25-35 titles/year; receives 1,200 + submissions annually. 60% of books from first-time authors; 50% of books from unagented writers. Average print order for writer's first book is 3,000-5,000. "We will co-publish exceptional works of quality and style only when we reach our quota in our trade book division." Pays 10-15%

royalty on retail price; advance varies. Simultaneous and photocopied submissions OK. Electronic submissions acceptable; prefers letter-quality to dot-matrix. SASE. Reports in 1 month on queries; 6 weeks on mss.
Nonfiction: Biography, behavioral science and health. Subjects include Americana; philosophy (contemporary format); cookbooks; religion (noncultism); and inspirational. Length: 50,000 words or less. Submit outline/first 2 or 4 consecutive chapters. Reviews artwork/photos as part of ms package. No political or technical material.
Recent Nonfiction Title: *To Be the Bridge: Black/White Catholicism, U.S.A.*, by Sandra Smithson, O.S.F.
Fiction: Ethnic (non-defamatory); religious (theologically sound); suspense (highly plotted); and Americana (minorities and whites in positive relationships). Length: 50,000 words or less. "We can use fiction with a semi-historical plot; must be based or centered around actual facts and events—Americana, religion, gothic, and science fiction. Juvenile: "We are looking for books on relevant aspects of growing up and understanding life's situations. No funny animals talking." Children's books must be of high quality. Submit outline/synopsis and first 2 or 4 consecutive chapters. Unsolicited mss will be returned unopened. "We do not discuss manuscripts via telephone." Reviews artwork/photos as part of ms package.
Recent Fiction Title: *Night Wood*, by Darlene Goodenow (an Althea Bantree mystery selection).
Recent Children's Book Title: *The Hey God Series*, by Roxie Cawood Gibson.
Poetry: "Should be inspirational and divine—poetry that is suitable for meditation. We will accept unusual poetry book of exceptional quality and taste." Submit complete ms for all poetry.
Recent Poetry Title: *Thoughts From a Friend*, by Eric Dlugokinski.
Tips: "The American audience is looking for less violent material. Outstanding biographies are quite successful, as are books dealing with the simplicity of man and his relationship with his environs. Our new imprint is *Scythe Books*, the children's division of Winston-Derek Publishers. We need material for adolescents within the 9-13 age group. These manuscripts should help young people with motivation for learning and succeeding, goal setting and character building. Biographies of famous women and men are always welcome. Stories must have a new twist and be provocative."

*WOODSONG GRAPHICS, INC., Stoney Hill Rd., Box 238, New Hope PA 18938. (215)794-8321. Editor: Ellen P. Bordner. Publishes hardcover and trade paperback originals. Averages 6 titles/year; receives 1,500 submissions annually. 40% of books from first-time authors; 100% of books from unagented writers. Average print order for writer's first book is 2,500-5,000. Subsidy publishes 15% of books. Will occasionally consider subsidy publishing based on "quality of material, motivation of author in distributing his work, and cost factors (which depend on the type of material involved), plus our own feelings on its marketability." Pays royalty on net price; offers average $100 advance. Publishes book an average of 1 year after acceptance. Simultaneous submissions OK. Computer printout submissions acceptable; prefers letter-quality to dot-matrix. SASE. Reports in 2 weeks on queries; reports on full mss *can* take several months, depending on the amount of material already in the house. "We do everything possible to facilitate replies, but we have a small staff and want to give every manuscript a thoughtful reading." Book catalog for SAE and 1 first class stamp.
Nonfiction: Biography, cookbook, how-to, humor, illustrated book, juvenile, reference, and self-help. Subjects include cooking and foods, hobbies, philosophy and psychology. "We're happy to look at anything of good quality, but we're not equipped to handle lavish color spreads at this time. Our needs are very open, and we're interested in seeing any subject, provided it's handled with competence and style. Good writing from unknowns is also welcome." No pornographic; only minimal interest in technical manuals of any kind. Query or submit outline/synopsis and at least 2 sample chapters. Reviews artwork/photos as part of ms package.
Recent Nonfiction Title: *Living in a Motor Home*, by Laura Wolfe.
Fiction: Adventure, experimental, fantasy, gothic, historical, humor, mainstream, mystery, romance, science fiction, suspense and western. "In fiction, we are simply looking for books that provide enjoyment. We want well-developed characters, creative plots, and good writing style." No pornography or "sick" material. Submit outline/synopsis and sample chapters.
Poetry: "We are unable to take on any new poetry manuscripts for the time being."
Tips: "Good nonfiction with a specific target market and a definite slant has the best chance of selling to our firm. We rarely contract in advance of seeing the completed manuscript."

WORD BEAT PRESS, Box 10509, Tallahassee FL 32302-2509. Editor: Allen Woodman. Publishes trade paperback originals and trade paperback reprints. Averages 3-5 titles/year; receives 500 submissions annually. 50% of books from first-time authors; 80% of books from unagented writers. Average print order for a writer's first book is 500-1,000. Pays 10% royalty on wholesale price. Offers average $100 advance. Publishes book an average of 1 year after acceptance. Computer printout submissions acceptable; prefers letter-quality to dot-matrix. SASE. Reports in 5 weeks on queries; 3 months on mss. Book catalog for legal size SAE and 1 first class stamp.
Nonfiction: "We will look at any book that would be of interest to fiction writers, how-to, self-help, reference, and other books about writing." Reviews artwork/photos as part of ms package.
Fiction: Short story collections and novellas; "open to fine writing in any category. We are planning a series of perfect-bound short story collections and novellas of between 40-90 typed, double-spaced manuscript pages."

Query first.
Tips: "We hold annual fiction book competitions judged by nationally recognized writers. Past judges have included George Plimpton, Eve Shelnutt and Janet Burroway. Send SASE for details. Freelancer has best chance of selling short story collections and books of interest to professional writers."

WORD BOOKS PUBLISHER, Division of Word Inc., subsidiary of ABC, 4800 W. Waco Dr., Waco TX 76703. (817)772-7650. Managing Editor: Al Bryant. Publishes hardcover and trade paperback originals, and hardcover, trade paperback, and mass market paperback reprints. Averages 50 titles/year. Pays 7½-15% royalty on retail price; offers average $2,000 advance. Photocopied submissions OK. Computer printout submissions acceptable; prefers letter-quality to dot-matrix. Reports in 1 month on queries; 2 months on mss. Free book catalog.
Nonfiction: Biography, "coffee table" book, cookbook, how-to, reference, self-help, and textbook. Subjects include health, history (church and Bible), philosophy, politics, psychology, religion, sociology, and sports. Especially looking for "religious books that help modern-day Christians cope with the stress of life in the 20th century. We welcome queries on all types of books." Query with outline/synopsis and sample chapters.
Recent Nonfiction Title: *Love Must Be Tough*, by James Dobson.
Fiction: Religious, romance and science fiction. "We are considering the romance field and also children's fiction." No non-religious fiction. Submit outline/synopsis and sample chapters.
Recent Fiction Title: *Winterflight*, by Joe Bayly.

WORDWARE PUBLISHING, INC., Suite 104, 1104 Summit Ave., Plano TX 75074. (214)423-0090. Editor: Jeff Anderson. Publishes mass market paperback originals and software. Averages 100 titles/year; receives 400 submissions annually. 20% of books from first-time authors; 100% of books from unagented writers. Average print order for writer's first book is 10,000. Pays 7½% minimum royalty, negotiable maximum. Advance negotiated. Publishes book an average of 4 months after acceptance. Electronic submissions OK on WordStar, but requires hard copy also. Computer printout submissions acceptable; prefers letter-quality to dot-matrix. SASE. Reports in 2 weeks.
Nonfiction: How-to, illustrated book, reference, self-help, technical and textbook. Subjects include business and economics, history, hobbies, politics and computers. "In general, our books are aimed at self-help and education. However, we are evolving our editorial direction and wish to avoid a restricting genre."
Recent Nonfiction Title: *Writing And Publishing On Your Microcomputer*, by R.A. Stultz (computer how-to).
Tips: "Basically, we seek to appeal to the individual who is interested in a variety of subjects and wishes to have them provided to him/her in easy-to-understand terms."

WORLD ALMANAC PUBLICATIONS, 200 Park Ave., New York NY 10166. (212)692-3824. Editor-in-Chief: Hana Umlauf Lane. Senior Editor: Rob Fitz. Publisher of *The World Almanac*. Publishes hardcover and trade paperback originals. Averages 30 titles/year. Pays 5-15% on retail price. Publishes book an average of 1 year after acceptance. Computer printout submissions acceptable; prefers letter-quality to dot-matrix. SASE. Reports in 3 weeks. Free book catalog.
Nonfiction: Reference. "We look for information books, like *The World Almanac*, but popular and entertaining. We expect at least a synopsis/outline and sample chapters, and would like to see the completed manuscript." Reviews artwork/photos as part of ms package.

WORLD NATURAL HISTORY PUBLICATIONS, Division of Plexus Publishing, Inc., 143 Old Marlton Pike, Medford NJ 08055. (609)654-6500. Editorial Director: Thomas Hogan. Publishes hardcover and paperback originals. Averages 4 titles/year. Pays 10-20% royalty on wholesale price; buys some booklets outright for $250-1,000. Offers $500-1,000 advance. Simultaneous and photocopied submissions OK. SASE. Reports in 2 months. Book catalog for SASE.
Nonfiction: Animals, biography of naturalists, nature and reference. "We are looking for manuscripts of about 300-400 pages for our series *Introduction to* ... some group of plants or animals designed for high school and undergraduate college use and for amateur naturalists. We will consider any book on a nature/biology subject, particularly those of a reference (permanent) nature. No philosophy or psychology; no gardening; generally not interested in travel, but will consider travel that gives sound ecological information." Also interested in mss of about 20 to 40 pages in length for feature articles in *Biology Digest* (guidelines for these available with SASE). Always query.
Recent Nonfiction Title: *Working for Life: Careers in Biology*.
Tips: "Write a book that is absolutely accurate and that has been reviewed by specialists to eliminate misstatement of fact."

WRITER'S DIGEST BOOKS, 9933 Alliance Rd., Cincinnati OH 45242. (513)984-0717. Editor-in-Chief: Carol Cartaino. Publishes hardcover and paperback originals (nonfiction only) about writing, photography, music, and other creative pursuits; as well as general-interest subjects. Pays advance and variable royalty depending upon type of book. Published 47 titles in 1984. Simultaneous (if so advised) and photocopied submissions OK. "Computer printout submissions OK; prefers letter-quality to dot-matrix. Publishes book an average of 1 year after acceptance. Enclose return postage. Book catalog for SASE.

Nonfiction: "We're seeking up-to-date, how-to treatments by authors who can write from successful experience. Should be well-researched, yet lively and readable. Query or submit outline/synopsis and sample chapters. Be prepared to explain how the proposed book differs from existing books on the subject. We are also very interested in republishing self-published nonfiction books and good instructional or reference books that have gone out of print before their time. No fiction or poetry! Send sample copy, sales record, and reviews if available." If you have a good idea for a book that needs updating often, try us. We're willing to consider freelance compilers of such works. Reviews artwork/photos as part of ms package.

Recent Nonfiction Title: *How to Find Another Husband . . . by Someone Who Did.*

YANKEE BOOKS, Main St., Dublin NH 03444. (603)563-8111. Subsidiary of Yankee Publishing Inc. Editor: Clarissa M. Silitch. Publishes trade paperback and hardcover originals. Averages 8-10 titles/year. 60% of books from first-time authors; 85% of books from unagented writers. Average print order for a writer's first book is 5,000-10,000. Pays royalty with $1,000-5,000 advance. Publishes book an average of 18 months after acceptance. Electronic submissions OK if compatible with IBM PC, DD, DS, but requires hard copy also. Computer printout submissions acceptable; prefers letter-quality to dot-matrix. SASE. Reports in 4 weeks on queries; 6 weeks on mss. Free book catalog.

Nonfiction: Cookbooks, how-to, country matters, nature, subjects related in one way or another to New England: nostalgia, Americana antiques, cooking, crafts, house and home, gardening, the outdoors, essays, folklore and popular history, photographs, today and old-time, travel in the Northeast U.S., the sea, boats, sailors, et al. No scholarly history, even slightly off-color humor, highly technical works, or biographies of persons not strikingly interesting. Query or submit outline/synopsis and sample chapters or complete ms. Reviews artwork/photos as part of ms package.

Recent Nonfiction Title: *The Friendship Quilt Book*, by Mary Garden.

‡**YORK PRESS LTD.**, Box 1172, Fredericton, New Brunswick E3B 5C8 Canada. (506)454-6109. General Manager/Editor: Dr. S. Elkhadem. Publishes trade paperback originals. Averages 8 titles/year; receives 25 submissions annually. 10% of books from first-time authors; 100% of books from unagented writers. Pays 5-10% royalty on wholesale price. Publishes book an average of 6 months after acceptance. Photocopied submissions OK. Computer printout submissions acceptable; prefers letter-quality to dot-matrix. SASE. Reports in 1 week on queries; 4 weeks on ms. Free book catalog; ms guidelines $1.50.

Nonfiction: Reference, textbook and scholarly. Subjects include literary criticism. Especially needs literary criticism, comparative literature and linguistics. Query.

Recent Nonfiction Title: *Ernest Hemingway*, by R.S. Nelson (literary criticism).

Tips: "If I were a writer trying to market a book today, I would spend a considerable amount of time examining the needs of a publisher *before* sending my manuscript to him. Scholarly books are the only kind we publish. The writer must adhere to our style manual and follow our guidelines exactly."

‡**YOURDON PRESS**, Subsidiary of Yourdon Inc., 1501 Broadway, New York NY 10036. (212)391-2828. Acquisitions Editor: Dan Mausner. Publishes hardcover and trade paperback originals. Averages 10 titles/year; receives 35 submissions annually. 50% of books from first-time authors; 100% of books from unagented writers. Pays 15% royalty on net receipts. Publishes book an average of 6 months after acceptance. Electronic submissions OK for accepted books; Unix typesetting from diskettes. Computer printout submissions acceptable. SASE. Reports in 1 month on queries; 2 months on mss. Free book catalog.

Nonfiction: Technical. Subjects in the area of development of computer systems. Especially interested in following topics: structured programing, software engineering, project management, information modelling and data base design, planning in data processing departments; information centers, prototyping and fourth generation languages. No highly esoteric, academic or obscure mss. Query or submit outline/synopsis and sample chapters. Reviews artwork/photos as part of ms package.

Recent Nonfiction Title: *Systems Development Without Pain*, by Paul Ward.

Tips: "Our books are read by programmers, systems analysts, data processing managers, information systems managers, and business executives. Highly readable, sophisticated, and practical books in our subject areas have the best chance of selling to us."

ZEBRA BOOKS, Subsidiary of Norfolk Publishing Co., 475 Park Ave. S., New York NY 10016. (212)889-2299. Editorial Director: Leslie Gelbman. Publishes mass market paperback originals and reprints. Averages 150 titles/year; receives thousands of submissions annually. 60% of books from first-time authors; 60% of books from unagented writers. Pays royalty on retail price or makes outright purchase. Simultaneous and photocopied submissions OK. Computer printout submissions acceptable; no dot-matrix. SASE. Reports in 3 months on queries; 4 months on mss. Book catalog for business size SAE and 39¢ postage.

Nonfiction: Biography, how-to, humor and self-help. Subjects include health, history and psychology. "We are open to many areas, especially self-help, stress, money management, child-rearing, health, war (WWII,

Vietnam), and celebrity biographies." No nature, art, music, photography, religion or philosophy. Query or submit outline/synopsis and sample chapters.

Recent Nonfiction Title: *The Telephone Survival Guide*, by Dawn B. Sova.

Fiction: Adventure, confession, erotica, gothic, historical, horror, humor, mainstream, romance and suspense. Tip sheet on historical romances, gothics, family sagas, adult romances and women's contemporary fiction is available. No poetry or short story collections. Query with synopsis and several sample chapters. SASE is a must.

Recent Fiction Title: *Betray Not My Passion*, by Sylvie F. Sommerfield.

THE ZONDERVAN CORP., 1415 Lake Drive, SE, Grand Rapids MI 49506. (616)698-6900. Executive Editor: Cheryl Forbes. Publishes hardcover and trade and mass market paperback originals (60%), and trade and mass market paperback reprints (40%). Averages 100 titles/year; receives 2,500 submissions annually. 30% of books from first-time authors; 98% of books from unagented writers. Average print order for a writer's first book is 5,000. Pays royalty of 14% of the net amount received on sales of cloth and softcover trade editions and 12% of net amount received on sales of mass market paperbacks. Offers variable advance. Electronic submissions OK on IBM compatible and Wang. Computer printout submissions are acceptable; prefers letter-quality to dot-matrix. The author should separate the perforated pages. SASE. Reports in 8 weeks on queries. Book catalog for 9x12 SAE and $1.22 postage. Ms guidelines for SASE.

Nonfiction: Biography, "coffee table" book, how-to, humor, illustrated book, reference, devotional and gift, self-help, youth books, Bible study, inspirational romance, history, books for charsimatics; textbooks on philosophy, psychology, religion and sociology. All from religious perspective (evangelical). Immediate needs include "books that take a fresh approach to issues and problems in the evangelical community; that offer new insights into solving personal and interpersonal problems; and that encourage readers to mature spiritually." No mss written from an occult point of view. Query or submit outline/synopsis and 2 sample chapters.

Recent Nonfiction Title: *Blood Brothers*, by Elias Charcour with David Hazard (autobiography).

Fiction: Books that deal realistically and creatively with relevant social and religious issues. No mss for new children's books. Query or submit outline/synopsis and 2 sample chapters.

Recent Fiction Title: *The Water is Wide*, by Elizabeth Gibson (Northern Ireland).

Subsidy Book Publishers

The following publishers produce one-hundred percent of their books on a subsidy basis. What they charge and what they offer to each writer varies, so you'll want to judge each publisher on its own merit. Because subsidy publishing can cost you several thousand dollars, make sure the number of books, the deadlines, and services offered by a publisher are detailed in *your* contract. Some writers employ an attorney to review the contract; this step prevents misunderstandings between you and your prospective publisher. *Don't ever agree to terms you don't understand.* For more information on subsidy publishing, consult the Book Publishers introduction in this book.

De Young Press, Box 7252, Spencer, IA 57301-7252.

Dorrance & Company, 828 Lancaster Ave., Bryn Mawr PA 19010.

New Media Books, 3530 Mound View Ave., Studio City CA 91604.

Peter Randall Publisher, 500 Market St., Box 4726, Portsmouth NH 03801.

Southern Tennessee Publishing, Box 91, Waynesboro TN 38485.

Summa Publications, Box 20725, Birmingham, AL 35216.

Vantage Press, 516 W. 34th St., New York NY 10001.

Book Publishers Subject Index

Nonfiction

To help you know the types of books each publisher *needs* in 1986, we've compiled this index. Remember that while a publisher may be listed under the Art and Architecture category, the company may be interested in only one type of art book, say, how-to or art history. By consulting each company's listing (and, later, its books), you'll know what aspect of that subject is its specialty.

Agriculture/Horticulture. AVI; Delmar; Interstate; Oryx; Penn. State Univ.; Purdue Univ.; Roman & Allanheld; Stipes; Universe; Univ. of Nebraska; Univ. Press of America; Wallace-Homestead; Western Producer Prairie; Westview.

Alternative Lifestyles. And/Or; Avant; Brick House; Celestial Arts; McPherson; Naturegraph; South End; Sterling; Strawberry Hill; Thorsons; Turnstone.

Americana. Amereon; Angel; Arbor House; Binford & Mort; John F. Blair; Branden; Brevet; Brunswick; Camden House; Cay-Bel; Christopher; Coward McCann; Crown; Daphnean; Darwin; T.S. Denison; Denlinger's; Devin-Adair; Douglas & McIntyre; Down East; Dragonsbreath; Durst; Paul S. Eriksson; Exposition; Donald I. Fine; General Hall; K.S. Giniger; Globe Pequot; Golden West Books; H.W.H. Creative Productions; Harper & Row; Harvard Common; Hastings House; Heyday; Houghton Mifflin; Hounslow; Howell-North; Icarus; Interurban/Trans Anglo; Jonathan David; Key Porter; Knapp; Peter Lang; Laranmark; Lexikos; Liberty; McFarland; MA/AH; Madrona; Main Street; Maverick; Meyerbooks; Miller; Mosaic; Moth Media; Mustang; National Press; Northland; Northwestern Univ.; Northwoods; Outbooks; Padre; Clarkson N. Potter; Purdue Univ.; Rainbow; Alan Rowe; Saybrook; Second Chance/Permanent; Seven Locks; Stemmer House; Stoneydale; Lyle Stuart; Sun; Taylor; Ten Speed; Thorndike; Transaction; Charles E. Tuttle; Univ. of Illinois; Univ. of Michigan; Univ. of Nebraska; Univ. of New Mexico; Univ. of North Carolina; Univ. of Pennsylvania; Univ. Press of Mississippi; Univ. Press of New England; Univ. Press of Virginia; Univ. Presses of Florida; Utah State Univ.; Walker; Wallace-Homestead; Westernlore; Wingra Woods; Yankee.

Animals. Allegheny; Alpine; Angel; Arco; Avon; Barron's Educational Series; Brunswick; Carolina Biological Supply; Christopher; Coles; David C. Cook; Crown; Dembner; Denlinger's; Dial for Young Readers; Paul S. Eriksson; Exposition; Flora and Fauna; Garden Way; H.W.H. Creative Productions; Robert Hale; Harper & Row; Houghton Mifflin; Iowa State Univ.; Key Porter; Knapp; Little House; Miller; Mosaic; National Press; Quartet; Raintree; S.C.E.-Editions L'Etincelle; Scholastic-Tab; Charles Scribner's; Sierra Club; Stemmer House; Sterling; T.F.H.; Tab; Thorndike; Thorsons; Tribeca; Universe; Univ. of Michigan; Univ. Presses of Florida; Williamson; Wingra Woods; World Natural History.

Anthropology/Archealogy. Brigham Young Univ. Press; Cambridge Univ.; Daphnean; Inst. for Study of Human Issues; Johnson; Kent State Univ.; McPherson; Museum of New Mexico; Noyes Data; Ohio State Univ.; Princeton Univ.; Rutgers Univ.; Southern Methodist Univ.; Stanford Univ.; Turnstone; UMI Research; Univ. of Arizona; Univ. of Iowa; Univ. of Nevada; Univ. of Tennessee; Univ. of Texas; Univ. of Utah; Univ. Presses of Florida; Westernlore; Westview.

Art & Architecture. Harry N. Abrams, Inc.; Alchemy; Arbor House; Archer Editions; Architectural Book; Art Direction; Avant; Barron's Educational Series; Beacon; Bear; Bennett & McKnight; Branden; George Braziller; Bucknell Univ.; Aristide D. Caratzas; Christopher; Crown; Davis; Delta; Dharma; Douglas & McIntyre; Down East; Dragonsbreath; Dundurn; Durst; Eastview; Exposition; Facts on File; Fairleigh Dickinson Univ.; Fitzhenry & Whiteside; Fleet; J. Paul Getty Museum; K.S. Giniger; Great Ocean; Guernica; H.P.; H.W.H. Creative Productions; Robert Hale; Harper & Row; Hastings House; Hounslow; Hudson Hills; Illuminati; International Univ.; Intervarsity; Iowa State Univ.; Ishiyaku Euroamerica; Kent State Univ.; Key

Porter; Knapp; Karl Kramer Verlag GMBH; Krantz; Peter Lang; Learning; Loyola Univ.; McFarland; Macmillan of Canada; Main Street; William Morrow; Mosaic; Museum of New Mexico; Museum of Northern Arizona; National; National Gallery of Canada; Nichols; North Light; Northwestern Univ.; Noyes Data; Ohio State Univ.; Optimum; Oxmoor; Padre; Pagurian; Penn. State Univ.; Peregrine Smith; Clarkson N. Potter; Prentice-Hall; Preservation; Princeton; Purdue Univ.; Resource; Rossel; Rowman & Allanheld; Rutgers Univ.; Saybrook; Charles Scribner's; Simon & Schuster; ST; Stemmer House; Sterling; Stoneydale; Lyle Stuart; Sun; Taplinger; Taylor; Transaction; Troubador; Charles E. Tuttle; UMI Research; Universe; Univ. of Alberta; Univ. of Iowa; Univ. of Massachusetts; Univ. of Michigan; Univ. of Missouri; Univ. of New Mexico; Univ. Press of New England; Univ. Presses of Florida; Vance Bibliographies; Viking Penguin; Weston Walch; Walker; Wallace-Homestead; Wayne State Univ.; Western Tanager; Whitston; Wingra Woods; Winston-Derek.

Astrology/Psychic Phenomena. ACS; Aquarian; Coles; Espress; Front Row Experience; Garber; Larson; Llewellyn; Med-Psych; Newcastle; Porter Sargent; Sterling; Strawberry Hill; Sun; Theosophical; Turnstone.

Autobiography. Arbor House; Atlantic Monthly; Bibli O'Phile; Fiesta City; Clarkson N. Potter.

Bibliography. R.R. Bowker; Computer Science; Council of Planning Librarians; Data and Research Technology; Family Album; Feminist; Garland; B. Klein; Oregon State Univ.; Oryx; Reymont; Scarecrow; Scholarly Resources; Univ. Press of Virginia; Vance Bibliographies; Whitston.

Biography. Academy Chicago; Alaska Northwest; Amereon; Angel; Apple-Wood; Archer Editions; Architectural Book; Atheneum; Atlantic Monthly; Avon; Beaufort; Bibli O'Phile; Binford & Mort; John F. Blair; Borgo; Don Bosco; Marion Boyars; Branden; Brethren; Brunswick; Cambridge Univ.; Camden House; Catholic Univ. of Amer.; Cay-Bel; CBP; Celestial Arts; Christopher; Citadel; Columbia; Coward McCann; Creative Arts; Crossroad/Continuum; Crown; Dante Univ. of Amer.; Daphnean; Detselig; Dharma; Dodd, Mead; Dorchester; Doubleday Canada; Douglas & McIntyre; Down East; Dragonsbreath; Dundurn; Eakin; Enslow; Paul S. Eriksson; Espress; Exposition; Facts on File; Family Album; Feminist; Fiesta City; Donald I. Fine; Fitzhenry & Whiteside; Fleet; Franciscan Herald; K.S. Giniger; Golden Quill; Gray's; Great Ocean; Guernica; H.W.H. Creative Productions; Robert Hale; Harper & Row; Harvest House; Hastings House; Here's Life; Horizon; Houghton Mifflin; Hounslow; Howell-North; Huntington House; Hurtig; Icarus; International Univ.; Iowa State Univ.; Kalimat; Kent State Univ.; Key Porter; Peter Lang; Lee's Books; Liberty; Little, Brown; Little House; Loyola Univ.; MA/AH; Macmillan of Canada; Madrona; Maverick; MCN; Metamorphous; William Morrow; Mosaic; Motorbooks International; Mott-Media; Museum of New Mexico; National Literary Guild; Naval Institute; New Leaf; Nimbus; Northeastern Univ.; Northwestern Univ.; Northwoods; Northword; Ohio State Univ.; Oolichan; Optimum; Pacific Press; Panjandrum; Pocket Books; Poseidon; Clarkson N. Potter; Prairie; Princeton Univ.; Prometheus; Purdue Univ.; Quartet; Quill; Regnery/Gateway; Routledge & Kegan; S.C.E.-Editions L'Etincelle; St. Luke's; Saybrook; Charles Scribner's; Second Chance/Permanent; Seven Locks; Simon & Schuster; Slavica; Southern Methodist Univ.; Stemmer House; Stoneydale; Lyle Stuart; Sun; Taplinger; Texas Monthly; Threshold; Thunder's Mouth; Transaction; Trans-Canada; Twayne; Universe; Univ. of Alabama; Univ. of Alberta; Univ. of Illinois; Univ. of Massachusetts; Univ. of Michigan; Univ. of Nebraska; Univ. of Nevada; Univ. of Pennsylvania; Univ. Press of Kansas; Univ. Press of Mississippi; Univ. Press of New England; Univ. Presses of Florida; Vehicule; Walker; Wayne State Univ.; Western Producer Prairie; Western Tanager; Westernlore; Whitaker House; Winston-Derek; Woodsong Graphics; Word Books; World Natural History; Zondervan.

Business & Economics. Bob Adams; Alchemy; Alfred; Allen; Allen & Unwin; Almar; Amer. Council for the Arts; Arbor House; Avon; Ballinger; Bankers; Bantam; Basic Books; BC Studio; Beaufort; Benjamin; Betterway; Bibli O'Phile; Marion Boyars; Brethren; Brevet; Briarcliff; Brick House; Brunswick; Caddylak; Cambridge Univ.; Christopher; Cleaning Consultant Services; Coles; Columbia Communications; Cordovan; Crain; Dartnell; Harlan Davidson; Delmar; Detselig; Devin-Adair; Douglas & McIntyre; Dow Jones-Irwin; EMC; Enslow; Enterprise; Paul S. Eriksson; ETC; Exanimo; Exposition; Facts on File; Fairchild; Fairleigh Dickinson Univ.; Fitzhenry & Whiteside; Fraser Institute; Free; General Hall; Great Ocean; Greenwood; Gulf; Alexander Hamilton Institute; Harcourt Brace Jovanovich Legal & Professional; Harper & Row; Harvard Common; D.C. Heath; Hounslow; Humanics; Infosource; Inst. for Study of Human Issues; Intercultural; International Self-Counsel; International Univ.; International Wealth Success; Interurban/Trans Anglo; Johns Hopkins Univ.; Jossey-Bass; Key Porter; Kirkley; B. Klein; Knowledge Industry; Robert E. Krieger; Peter Lang; Liberty; Linch; Little House; Live Oak; Longman; Loompanics; McFarland; McGraw-Hill; Marathon International; Menasha Ridge; Mercury House; Charles E. Merrill; Metamorphous; MGI

Management Institute; Mosaic; National; National Press; New York Univ.; New York Zoetrope; Nichols; Northwestern Univ.; Noyes Data; Ohio Univ.; Oryx; Overlook; Padre; Penn. State Univ.; Petrocelli; Poseidon; Prentice-Hall; Prentice-Hall Canada; Princeton Univ.; Probus; Purdue Univ.; Quartet; Regnery/Gateway; Reymont; Riverdale; Roman & Allanheld; Ronin; Routledge & Kegan; RPM; S.C.E.-Editions L'Etincelle; Saybrook; Schenkman; Charles Scribner's; Self-Counsel; Seven Locks; Shadow Mountain; South End; Southern Methodist Univ.; Stanford Univ.; Sterling; Stipes; Lyle Stuart; Success; Tab; Taylor; Teachers College; Ten Speed; Texas Monthly; Times; Transaction; Trans-Canada; Tribeca; UMI Research; Universe; University Associates; Univ. of Alabama; Univ. of Arizona; Univ. of Michigan; Univ. of Pennsylvania; Univ. of Texas; Univ. Press of Amer.; Univ. Press of Mississippi; Univ. Press of Virginia; Univ. Presses of Florida; Wadsworth; Weston Walch; Walker; Wallace-Homestead; Wayne State Univ.; Western Producer Prairie; John Wiley & Sons; Williamson; Windsor; Wordware.

Career Guidance. Bob Adams; Almar; Arco; Barron's Educational Series; Career; Collier Macmillan Canada; EMC; Fairchild; Guidance Centre; Interstate; Live Oak; McFarland; Milady; Octameron; Rosen; Ross; Teachers College; VGM Career Horizons.

Chapbooks. Elephant Walk.

Coffee Table Books. Alchemy; Appalachian Mountain Club; Brunswick; Darwin; Detselig; Down East; Dundurn; Exposition; Robert Hale; Harvest House; Hounslow; Howell-North; Key Porter; Krantz; Llewellyn; Main Street; Multnomah; Museum of Northern Arizona; National Literary Guild; Nimbus; Northword; Quartet; Seven Seas; Texas Monthly; Theatre Communications; Word Books.

Communications. Avant; Beacon; Career; College-Hill; Communication Skill Builders; Communications; Drama; ISI; Kirkley; Knowledge Industry; Longman; Merriwether; New York Zoetrope; Oryx; Padre; Purdue Univ.; Regal; Univelt; University Associates; Writer's Digest.

Community. Groupwork Today; Indiana Univ.; Loiry; Macmillan of Canada; NC; Temple Univ.; University Associates; Vance Bibliographies; Westview.

Computers/Electronics. Alfred; ARCsoft; Atlantis; Baen; Career; Carolina Biological Supply; Compute!; Computer Science; Datamost; Steve Davis; Delmar; Fairchild; Graphic Image; Hayden; D.C. Heath; Infosource; International Publishing & Computer Services; Kern International; McGraw-Hill; Microtrend; New York Zoetrope; Noyes Data; Osborn/McGraw-Hill; Prentice-Hall Canada; Q.E.D. Information Services; Que; Regents; Howard W. Sams; Sourceview; Sybex; Tab; Tandy; Techwrite; Tribeca; Univ. Press of Virginia; Weston Walch; John Wiley & Sons; Wordware; Yourdon.

Consumer Affairs. Almar; EMC; Meadowbrook; Menasha Ridge.

Cooking/Foods/Nutrition. Aglow; Alaska Northwest; Alchemy; Angel; Applezaba; Arbor House; Associated Booksellers; Atheneum; AVI; Avon; Bantam; Barron's Educational Series; BC Studio; Benjamin; Berkley; Better Homes and Gardens; Betterway; Bibli O'Phile; Brethren; Briarcliff; Brunswick; Camaro; Cay-Bel; Celestial Arts; Christopher; Coles; Compact; Contemporary; Cougar; Creative Arts; Crossing; Crown; Dante Univ. of Amer.; Detselig; Douglas & McIntyre; Down East; Ecco; Paul S. Eriksson; Evans; Exposition; Farm Journal; Fiesta City; Donald I. Fine; Forman; C.J. Frompovich; Garden Way; Globe Mini Mags; Globe Pequot; Golden West Publishers; H.P.; H.W.H. Creative Productions; Robert Hale; Harper & Row; Harvard Common; Hastings House; Hawkes; Houghton Mifflin; Hounslow; Humanics; Ideals; Jonathan David; Key Porter; Kids Can; Knapp; Laranmark; Liberty; Little, Brown; Little House; Madrona; Main Street; Marathon International; Maverick; Meadowbrook; Meyerbooks; Miller; William Morrow; Mosaic; Museum of New Mexico; National Literary Guild; National Press; Nimbus; Nitty Gritty Cookbooks; Northwoods; Northword; Optimum; Ottenheimer; Oxmoor; Pacific Press; Padre; Pagurian; Panjandrum; Peachtree; Poseidon; Clarkson N. Potter; Prairie; Prentice-Hall Canada; Quicksilver; Quill; Richboro; Ross; Rossel; Royal; S.C.E.-Editions L'Etincelle; Second Chance/Permanent; Seven Seas; Shadow Mountain; Stackpole; Stemmer House; Sterling; Strawberry Hill; Sun; T.L.; Jeremy P. Tarcher; Taylor; Ten Speed; Texas Monthly; Thorsons; Thunder's Mouth; Times; Tribeca; Troubador; Univ. Press of Virginia; Vehicule; Walker; Wallace-Homestead; Western Producer Prairie; Williamson; Wimmer; Winchester; Woodsong Graphics; Word Books; Yankee.

Counseling. Barron's Educational Series; Beacon; Career; Edits; Fortress; Groupwork Today; Interstate; John Knox; Learning; Med-Psych; Morehouse-Barlow; Mott-Media; New Leaf; Occupational Awareness; Teachers College; Tyndale House.

Crafts. Arco; Better Homes and Gardens; Betterway; Briarcliff; Collector Books; Davis; Doll Reader; Farm Journal; Naturegraph; Optimum; Oxmoor; Scholastic-Tab; Stackpole; Standard; Success; Sunstone; Tab; Timber; Troubador; Universe; Wallace-Homestead; Winchester; Yankee.

Datebooks/Calendars. Quicksilver.

Educational. Acropolis Books; American Catholic; Arco; Bantam; Barnes & Noble; Barron's Educational Series; Brigham Young Univ.; Cambridge, Adult Education; Career; CBP; Coles; Collier-Macmillan Canada; Communication Skill Builders; Cortina Learning International; Crossroad/Continuum; Eakin; Edits; Education Associates; EMC; Enrich; ETC; Feminist; Warren H. Green; Guidance Centre; Holt, Rinehart & Winston of Canada; Humanics; Incentive; Intercultural; Interstate; Jamestown; David S. Lake; Larson; Learning; Learning Endeavors; Liberty; Liguori; Longman; Charles E. Merrill; MGI Management Institute; Morehouse-Barlow; National; New Readers; Nichols; Occupational Awareness; Octameron; Ohio State Univ.; Open Court; Oregon State Univ.; Oryx; Prentice-Hall; Que; Regents; Regnery/Gateway; Religious Education; Resource; Routledge & Kegan; Shadow Mountain; Teachers College; Weston Walch; Williamson; Winston.

Ethnic. Brunswick; Dante Univ. of Amer.; Dharma; Fleet; Genealogical; General Hall; Guernica; Heart of the Lakes; Holloway House; Indiana Univ.; Inst. for Study of Human Issues; Kar-Ben Copies; Museum of New Mexico; Museum of Northern Arizona; Naturegraph; Northland; Open Court; Penn State Univ.; Rossel; Schocken; Slavica; Strawberry Hill; Sun; Texas Western; Three Continents; Charles E. Tuttle; Univ. of Arizona; Univ. of Massachusetts; Univ. of Nebraska; Univ. of Nevada; Univ. of Oklahoma; Univ. of Pennsylvania; Univ. of Tennessee; Univ. of Utah; Univ. Press of America; Wayne State Univ.; Westernlore; Yankee.

Fashion & Beauty. Acropolis Books, Ltd.; Fairchild.

Feminism. Crossing; Feminist; South End; Spinsters Ink.

Film/Cinema/Stage. Atlantic Monthly; Borgo; Citadel; Coach House; Columbia; Communications; Drama; Samuel French; Indiana Univ.; JH; Lake View; McFarland; McPherson; Main Street; Panjandrum; Scarecrow; Schirmer; Sterling; Tab; Taplinger; Theatre Communications; Twayne; UMI Research.

Games/Entertainment. Coles; Contemporary; Gaming Book Distributors; H.P.; Holloway House; Intergalactic; McFarland; Quill; Sterling; Tab; Troubador; Winchester.

Gardening/Plants. Better Homes and Gardens; Betterway; Briarcliff; Coles; Delmar; Garden Way; H.P.; Main Street; Naturegraph; Optimum; Ottenheimer; Oxmoor; Richboro; Ross; Jeremy P. Tarcher; Taylor; Ten Speed; Timber; Universe; Walker; Yankee.

Gay/Lesbian. Alyson; Crossing; Gay Sunshine; JH; Spinsters Ink; Ten Speed; Thorsons.

General Nonfiction. Academy Chicago; Amer. Psychiatric; Atheneum; Atlantic Monthly; Ballantine/Del Rey/Fawcett; Beacon; George Braziller; Computer Science; Delacorte; Doubleday Canada; Evans; Flare; Fleet; Horizon; Johnson; Kent State Univ.; Krantz; Landmark; Larksdale; William Morrow; John Muir; New American Library; W.W. Norton; Pocket Books; Pruett; Charles Scribner's; Smith; Stein and Day; Taplinger; Time-Life; Viking Penguin.

Government/Politics. Alchemy; Allen & Unwin; Angel; Apple-Wood; Arbor House; Atheneum; Avon; Basic Books; Beacon; Bear; Borgo; Marion Boyers; Branden; Brethren; Brunswick; Bucknell Univ.; CQ; Christopher; Columbia; Communications; Coward McCann; Crown; Daphnean; Harlan Davidson; Delta; Devin-Adair; Douglas & McIntyre; Eakin; Paul S. Eriksson; Exposition; Facts on File; Fairleigh Dickinson Univ.; Donald I. Fine; Fraser Institute; General Hall; Great Ocean; Guernica; Robert Hale; Harper & Row; Harvard Common; Harvest House; D.C. Heath; Houghton Mifflin; Hounslow; Hurtig; Inst. for Study of Human Issues; Intercultural; International Univ.; Johns Hopkins Univ.; Key Porter; Lake View; Peter Lang; Little House; Loiry; Longman; Loompanics; Louisiana State Univ.; McClelland and Stewart-Bantam; McPherson; Madrona; Mercury House; Miller; Mott-Media; National; NC; New York Univ.; Northeastern Univ.; Northern Illinois Univ.; Northwestern Univ.; Northwoods; Ohio State Univ.; Oolichan; Oxford Univ.; Penn. State Univ.; Prentice-Hall Canada; Princeton Univ.; Quartet; Rainbow; Regnery/Gateway; Riverdale; Rossel; Rowman & Allanheld; S.C.E.-Editions L'Etincelle; Saybrook; Scholarly Resources; Second Chance/Permanent; Seven Locks; South End; Sovereign; Stanford Univ.; Lyle Stuart; Sun; Teachers College; Texas Monthly; Thunder's Mouth; Transaction; Universe; Univ. of Alabama; Univ. of Alberta; Univ. of

Illinois; Univ. of Massachusetts; Univ. of North Carolina; Univ. of Pennsylvania; Univ. of Tennessee; Univ. of Texas; Univ. Press of America; Univ. Press of Kansas; Univ. Press of Mississippi; Univ. Press of New England; Univ. Press of Virginia; Univ. Presses of Florida; Utah State Univ.; Vehicule; Wadsworth; Weston Walch; Wayne State Univ.; Western Tanager; John Wiley & Sons; Word Books; Wordware.

Health/Medicine. Acropolis Books, Inc.; ACS; Almar; Amer. Psychiatric; And/Or; Angel; Arbor House; Dean Aster; Atlantis; Augsburg; Avant; AVI; Avon; Bantam; BC Studio; Beaufort; Benjamin; Better Homes and Gardens; Betterway; Branden; Brethren; Briarcliff; Bridge; Brunswick; Camaro; Cambridge Univ.; Career; Carolina Biological Supply; Celestial Arts; Christopher; Cleaning Consultant Services; Coles; College-Hill; Compact; Compcare; Contemporary; Cougar; Coward McCann; Creative Arts; Crossing; Crown; Delmar; Delta; Detselig; Devin-Adair; Enslow; Paul S. Eriksson; Evans; Exposition; Donald I. Fine; Fitzhenry and Whiteside; K.S. Giniger; Globe Mini Mags; Golden West Pulbishers; Great Ocean; Warren H. Green; H.P.; H.W.H. Creative Productions; Robert Hale; Hanley & Belfru; Harper & Row; Harvard Common; Hawkes; Hazelden; Health Profession Division; D.C. Heath; Houghton Mifflin; Hounslow; Humanics; Information Resources; International Univ.; Iowa State Univ.; Ishiyaku Euroamerica; Johns Hopkins Univ.; Key Porter; Kids Can; Robert E. Krieger; Peter Lang; Larksdale; Little House; McClelland and Stewart-Bantam; McFarland; Madrona; Maverick; Meadowbrook; Medical Economics; Med-Psych; Menasha Ridge; Metamorphous; Meyerbooks; Mosaic; National; National Press; Naturegraph; NC; New Readers; Newcastle; Newconcept; Oak Tree; Optimum; Oryx; Ottenheimer; Oxford Univ.; Pacific Press; Panjandrum; Pantheon; Penn. State Univ.; Poseidon; Potentials Development for Health & Aging Services; Prentice-Hall; Prentice-Hall Canada; PSG; Quintessence; Raintree; Ronin; Rosen; Rowman & Allanheld; S.C.E.-Edition L'Etincelle; Saybrook; Charles Scribner's; Second Chance/Permanent; Shadow Mountain; Sierra Club; Strawberry Hill; Lyle Stuart; Jeremy P. Tarcher; Teachers College; Theosophical; Thorsons; Times; Transaction; Tribeca; Turnstone; Universe; Wadsworth; Weston Walch; Walker; Westview; John Wiley & Sons; Williamson; Wilshire; Word Books; Zebra.

History. Academy Chicago; Alaska Northwest; Allen & Unwin; Amereon; Angel; Appalachian Mountain Club; Apple-Wood; Arbor House; Archer Editions; Architectural Book; Atheneum; Atlantic Monthly; Avon; Beacon; Bear; Beaufort; Binford & Mort; John F. Blair; Borgo; Boston Mills; Marion Boyars; Branden; George Braziller; Brethren; Brevet; Brigham Young Univ.; Brunswick; Cambridge Univ.; Aristide D. Caratzas; Catholic Univ. of Amer.; Cay-Bel; Christopher; Citadel; Cordovan; Coward McCann; Crossroad/Continuum; Crossway; Crown; Daphnean; Darwin; Harlan Davidson; Detselig; Devin-Adair; Dharma; Dial for Young Readers; Doubleday Canada; Douglas & McIntyre; Down East; Dragonsbreath; Dundurn; Eakin; Eastview; William B. Eerdmans; Paul S. Eriksson; Exposition; Facts on File; Fairliegh Dickinson Univ.; Farrar, Straus and Giroux; Donald I. Fine; Fitzhenry & Whiteside; Fleet; J. Flores; Franciscan Herald; Genealogical; J. Paul Getty Museum; K.S. Giniger; Globe Pequat; Golden West Publishers; Gray's; Great Ocean; Warren H. Green; Guernica; Robert Hale; Harper & Row; Harvard Common; Hastings House; Hawkes; Heart of the Lakes; D.C. Heath; Heritage; Heyday; Horizon; Houghton Mifflin; Hounslow; Howell-North; Hurtig; Icarus; Indiana Univ.; Inst. for Study of Human Issues; International Marine; International Univ.; Interurban/Trans Anglo; Intervaristy; Iowa State Univ.; Johns Hopkins Univ.; Johnson; Kalimat; Kar-Ben Copies; Kent State Univ.; Key Porter; Kids Can; Robert E. Krieger; Peter Lang; Laranmark; Leather Stocking; Lee's Books; Lexicos; Liberty; Little, Brown; Longman; Lorien; Louisiana State Univ.; Loyola Univ.; McFarland; MA/AH; Macmillan of Canada; Madrona; Maverick; MCN; Memphis State Univ.; Meyerbooks; Miller; William Morrow; Mosaic; Motorbooks International; Mountain; Museum of New Mexico; Museum of Northern Arizona; National; Naturegraph; Naval Institute; NC; New Readers; New York; Nimbus; Northeastern Univ.; Northern Illinois Univ.; Northwestern Univ.; Northwoods; Northword; Noyes Data; Ohio State Univ.; Ohio Univ.; Oolichan; Optimum; Oregon State Univ.; Outbooks; Overlook; Oxford Univ.; Padre; Paladin; Panjandrum; Pantheon; Peachtree; Penn. State Univ.; Peregrine Smith; Pocket Books; Poseidon; Clarkson N. Potter; Prentice-Hall; Prentice-Hall Canada; Preservation; Princeton Univ.; Purdue; Quartet; Quill; Rainbow; Raintree; Regnery/Gateway; Riverdale; Rossel; Routledge & Kegan; Alan Rowe; Rutgers Univ.; S.C.E.-Editions L'Etincelle; Schenkman; Scholarly Resources; Second Chance/Permanent; Seven Locks; Simon & Schuster; Slavica; Southern Methodist Univ.; Sovereign; Stanford Univ.; Stemmer House; Stoneydale; Strawberry Hill; Lyle Stuart; Sun; Sunstone; Taplinger; Temple Univ.; Ten Sped; Texas Monthly; Texas Western; Three Continents; Thunder's Mouth; Times; Tompson & Rutter; Transaction; Tribeca; Turnstone; Charles E. Tuttle; UMI Research; Universe; Univ. of Alabama; Univ. of Alberta; Univ. of Illinois; Univ. of Iowa; Univ. of Massachusetts; Univ. of Missouri; Univ. of Nebraska; Univ. of Nevada; Univ. of New Mexico; Univ. of North Carolina; Univ. of Oklahoma; Univ. of Pennsylvania; Univ. of Tennessee; Univ. of Utah; Univ. Press of America; Univ. Press of Kansas; Univ. Press of Mississippi; Univ. Press of New England; Univ. Press of Virginia; Univ. Presses of Florida; Utah State Univ.; Vehicule; Weston Walch; Walker; Wayne State Univ.; Western Producer Prairie; Western Tanager; Westernlore; Wingra Woods; Word Books; Wordware; Yankee; Zebra.

Hobby. Almar; Angel; Arco; ARCsoft; Associated Booksellers; Avon; Bale; Barnes & Noble; BC Studio; Benjamin; Brunswick; Carstens; Coles; Collector Books; Contemporary; Crown; Darwin; Datamost; Detselig; Doll Reader; Dundurn; Eastview; Enslow; Paul S. Eriksson; Expositon; K.S. Giniger; H.P.; H.W.H. Creative Productions; Robert Hale; Harvard Common; Hawkes; Hounslow; Howell-North; Interurban/Trans Anglo; Key Porter; Kids Can; B. Klein; Knapp; Liberty; Madrona; Main Street; Maverick; MCN; Menasha Ridge; Meyerbooks; Mosaic; Mountain; Mustang; Northwoods; Overlook; Oxmoor; Padre; Panjandrum; S.C.E.-Editions L'Etincelle; Scholastic-Tab; Charles Scribner's; Shadow Mountain; Sterling; Success; T.L.; Tab; Ten Speed; Ultralight; Walker; Wallace-Homestead; Williamson; Wilshire; Woodsong Graphics; Woodware.

Home/Family Life. Abbey Press; Bennett & McKnight; Berkley; Better Homes and Gardens; Betterway; Catholic Truth Society; Collier Macmillan Canada; Compcare; Cougar; Delmar; Delta; Fairchild; Great Ocean; Gryphon House; Here's Life; Humanics; Interstate; John Knox; Lakewood; Loiry; Meadowbrook; Newconcept; Ottenheimer; Pacific Press; Regal; Shadow Mountain; Harold Shaw; Sterling; Tab; Times; Tyndale House; Williamson; Wimmer.

How-to. Acropolis Books, Inc.; Albatross; Alfred; Allen; Almar; Amereon; American Council for the Arts; Amphoto; Angel; Appalachian Mountain Club; Arbor House; ARCsoft; Arman; Art Direction; Dean Aster; Atlantis; Avon; Barnes & Noble; BC Studio; Berkley; Betterway; Bibli O'Phile; Brick House; Bridge; Brunswick; Caddylak; Catholic Truth Society; CBP; Christopher; Cleaning Consultant Services; Compact; Contemporary; Cornell Maritime; Coward McCann; Creative Arts; Crossing; Crown; Darwin; Datamost; John De Graff; Delta; Dembner; Denlinger's; Devin-Adair; Dundurn; Durst; Enrich; Enslow; Paul S. Eriksson; ETC; Examino; Exposition; Fairmont; Farm Journal; Fiesta City; Donald I. Fine; J. Flores; Forman; Front Row Experience; Gay Sunshine; K.S. Giniger; Golden West Publishers; Graphic Image; Great Ocean; Stephen Greene/Lewis; Gryphon House; H.P.; Robert Hale; Alexander Hamilton Institute; Harcourt Brace Jovanovich Legal & Professional; Harper & Row; Harvard Common; Harvest House; Hawkes; Here's Life; Heritage; Heyday; Houghton Mifflin; Infosource; Intercultural; International Self-Counsel; International Wealth Success; ISI; Johnson; Jonathan David; Kern International; Key Porter; B. Klein; Knapp; Krantz; Laranmark; Larksdale; Larson; Learning; Leather Stocking; Liberty; Lightbooks; Linch; Little, Brown; Little House; Live Oak; Llewellyn; Loiry; Loompanics; Lorien House; McClelland and Stewart-Bantam; Macmillan of Canada; Madrona; Main Street; Meadowbrook; Med-Psych; Menasha Ridge; Merriwether; Metamorphous; MGI Management Institute; Milady; Miller; William Morrow; Motorbooks International; Mott-Media; Mountain; Mountaineers; John Muir; Music Sales; Naturegraph; Newcastle; Nimbus; North Light; Northwoods; Northword; Optimum; Outdoor Empire; Overlook; Oxmoor; Pacific Press; Padre; Panjandrum; Pantheon; Clarkson N. Potter; Prentice-Hall; Probus; Que; Rainbow; Resource; Reymont; Richboro; Ronin; Ross; Rossel; RPM; Schirmer; Scholastic-Tab; Self-Counsel; Seven Seas; Shadow Mountain; Harold Shaw; Sierra Club; ST; Standard; Stone Wall; Success; Sun; Sunstone; T.F.H.; T.L.; Tab; Taylor; Techwrite; Ten Speed; Theatre Communications; Thomas; Thorsons; Thunder;s Mouth; Ultralight; Univ. of Alberta; Wallace-Homestead; Western Marine; Williamson; Wilshire; Wimmer; Winchester; Windsor; Wingbow; Wingra Woods; Woodsong Graphics; Word Beat; Word Books; Wordware; Writer's Digest; Yankee; Zebra; Zondervan.

Humanities. Amer. Council for the Arts; Duquesne Univ.; Folcraft/Norwood; Free; Garland; Indiana Univ.; Louisiana State Univ.; Prometheus; Southern Illinois Univ.; Univ. of Texas; Whitston.

Humor. Alchemy; Amereon; Angel; Apple-Wood; Applezaba; Avon; Baker; Celestial Arts; Citadel; Crown; Delta; Dorchester; Dragonsbreath; Elephant Walk; Enrich; Paul S. Eriksson; Exposition; Farrar, Straus and Giroux; Guernica; H.W.H. Creative Productions; Robert Hale; Harper & Row; Harvard Common; Hounslow; Hurtig; Key Porter; Little House; Madrona; Marathan International; Mosaic; Mustang; National Press; Nimbus; Northwestern Univ.; Northword; Oak Tree; Paladin; Peachtree; Clarkson N. Potter; Prentice-Hall; Price/Stern/Sloan; Princeton Univ.; Rainbow; Ronin; S.C.E.-Editions L'Etincelle; Scholastic Tab; Charles Scribner's; Seven Seas; Sterling; Lyle Stuart; Ten Speed; Texas Monthly; Thorndike; Tribeca; Woodsong Graphics; Zebra; Zondervan.

Illustration. Appalachian Mountain Club; Dean Aster; Boston Mills; Brunswick; Cleaning Consultant Services; Douglas & McIntyre; Down East; Dragonsbreath; Elephant Walk; Exposition; J. Flores; Graphic Arts Center; Robert Hale; Here's Life; Howell-North; Key Porter; Knapp; Liberty; Main Street; Maverick; MCN; Metamorphous; John Muir; National Press; Nimbus; Northword; Oak Tree; Optimum; Quartet; Ronin; Routledge & Kegan; Self-Counsel; Seven Seas; Southern Methodist Univ.; Texas Monthly; Theatre Communications; Three Trees; Transaction; Univ. Press of Virginia; Wayne State Univ.; John Wiley & Sons.

Juvenile. Abingdon Press; Alaska Northwest; Alchemy; Atheneum Publishers, Inc.; Augsburg; Avon; Baker; Bantam; BC Studio; Bookcraft; Don Bosco; Branden; Brethren; Brunswick; Concordia; Coward McCann; Crown; T.S. Denison; Dial for Young Readers; Douglas & McIntyre; Down East; Dundurn; Enrich; Enslow; Espress; Exposition; Farrar, Straus and Giroux; Feminist; Donald I. Fine; Fleet; C.R. Gibson; Gryphon House; Guernica; Hastings House; Holiday House; Incentive; Kalimat; Kar-Ben Copies; Kids Can; Lee's Books; Little House; Lodestar; Loiry; Lothrop, Lee & Shepard; Margaret K. McElderry; Macmillan; Macmillan of Canada; Meadowbrook; Morrow Junior; National Press; Nimbus; Oak Tree; Oddo; Pacific Press; Panjandrum; Pantheon; Philomel; Clarkson N. Potter; Prentice-Hall; Raintree; Review and Herald; Rossel; Saybrook; Schocken; Scholastic-Tab; Charles Scribner's; Seven Locks; Harold Shaw; Sierra Club; Standard; Stemmer House; Success; Three Trees; Tribeca; Viking Penguin; Walker; Wingra Woods; Winston-Derek; Woodsong Graphics.

Labor. Crain; Dartnell; Groupwork Today; Jossey-Bass; Kirkley; Que; RPM; University Associates.

Language/Literature. Allen & Unwin; Apple-Wood; Archer Editions; Atlantis; Bantam; Barron's Educational Series; Beacon; George Braziller; Cambridge, Adult Education; Camden House; Catholic Univ. of Amer.; Coles; College-Hill; Collier/Macmillan Canada; Communication Skill Builders; Crossroad/Continuum; Dante Univ. of Amer.; EMC; Fitzhenry & Whiteside; D.C. Heath; Heinle & Heinle; Horizon; Illuminati; Indiana Univ.; Intervarsity; Johns Hopkins Univ.; Kent State Univ.; Longman; Lorien House; Louisiana State Univ.; McFarland; Merriwether; Charles E. Merrill; National Textbook; New Readers; New York Univ.; Oddo; Ohio State Univ.; Oregon State Univ.; Oxford Univ.; Prentice-Hall; Princeton Univ.; Prometheus; Purdue Univ.; Regents; Slavica; Stanford Univ.; Southern Methodist Univ.; Taplinger; Texas Christian Univ.; Three Continents; Charles E. Tuttle; Univ. of Alabama; Univ. of Illinois; Univ. of Nebraska; Univ. of Texas; Univ. of America; Univ. Press of Mississippi; Utah State Univ.; Vehicule; Weston Walch; Word Beat; York.

Literary Criticism. Allen & Unwin; Borgo; Dundurn; Ecco; ECW; Fairleigh Dickinson Univ.; Johns Hopkins Univ.; McPherson; Northeastern Univ.; Northern Illinois Univ.; Northwestern Univ.; Prometheus; Puckerbrush; Routledge & Kegan; Rutgers Univ.; Slavica; Stanford Univ.; Texas Christian Univ.; Three Continents; Twayne; UMI Research; Univ. of Alabama; Univ. of Massachusetts; Univ. of Missouri; Univ. of North Carolina; Univ. of Tennessee; Univ. Presses of Florida; York.

Marine Subjects. Cay-Bel; Cornell Maritime; Gray's; International Marine; Naval Institute; Alan Rowe; Seven Seas.

Military. Arco; Beau Lac; Leather Stocking; MCN; Paladin; Presidio; Stackpole; Westview.

Money & Finance. Acropolis Books, Ltd.; Almar; Bale; Bankers; Bantam; BC Studio; Ballinger; Benjamin; Better Homes and Gardens; Contemporary; Cordovan; Dow Jones-Irwin; Enterprise; Harcourt Brace Jovanovich Legal and Professional; International Self-Counsel; International Wealth Success; Lakewood; Linch; Marathon International; Medical Economics; Nichols; Padre.

Music/Dance. Alchemy; American Catholic; Avon; Bear; Beaufort; Marion Boyars; Branden; Brunswick; Bucknell Univ.; Cambridge Univ.; Columbia; Communications; Concordia; Crown; Delta; Dodd, Mead; Drama; Eastview; Paul S. Eriksson; Exposition; Facts on File; Fairleigh Dickinson Univ.; Fiesta City; Fleet; Front Row Experience; Great Ocean; Guernica; Robert Hale; Harper & Row; Harvard Common; Horizon; International Univ.; Key Porter; Kids Can; Robert E. Krieger; Peter Lang; Louisiana State Univ.; McFarland; Maverick; William Morrow; Mosaic; Museum of New Mexico; Music Sales; National; Northeastern Univ.; Northwestern Univ.; Ohio State Univ.; Oxford Univ.; Pagurian; Panjandrum; Penn. State Univ.; Players; Prentice-Hall; Princeton Univ.; Quill; Resource; Rosen; Ross; Scarecrow; Schirmer; Simon & Schuster; Sterling; Stipes; Lyle Stuart; Transaction; Twayne; UMI Research; Universe; Univ. of Alabama; Univ. of Missouri; Univ. of North Carolina; Univ. Press of America; Univ. Press of New England; Wadsworth; Weston Walch; Walker; Whitston.

Nature/Environment. Harry N. Abrams, Inc.; Alaska Northwest; Alchemy; Allegheny; Angel; Appalachian Mountain Club; Avant; Avon; Binford & Mort; John F. Blair; Marion Boyars; Brick House; Brunswick; Carolina Biological Supply; Colorado Associated Univ.; Columbia; Coward McCann; Crown; Darwin; Devin-Adair; Dial for Young Readers; Down East; East Woods; Eastview; Paul S. Eriksson; Exposition; Facts on File; Fairmont; Flora and Fauna; Garden Way; Gray's; Stephen Greene/Lewis; Guernica; H.W.H. Creative Productions; Robert Hale; Harper & Row; Harvard Common; Helix; Heyplay; Hounslow; Howell-North; Hurtig;

Johns Hopkins Univ.; Johnson; Key Porter; Kids Can; Robert E. Krieger; Lexikos; Lorien House; McClelland and Stewart-Bantam; Meyerbooks; Mosaic; Mountain; Mountaineers; Museum of New Mexico; Museum of Northern Arizona; Naturegraph; NC; New York Univ.; Nichols; Nimbus; Northland; Northwoods; Northword; Noyes Data; Oddo; Optimum; Oregon State Univ.; Outbooks; Outdoor Empire; Overlook; Oxmoor; Pacific Press; Padre; Pagurian; Penn. State Univ.; Pennwell; Peregrine Smith; Clarkson N. Potter; Purdue Univ.; Raintree; Regnery/Gateway; Review and Herald; S.C.E.-Editions L'Etincelle; Saybrook; Charles Scribner's; Seven Locks; Sierra Club; Stackpole; Stanford Univ.; Stemmer House; Stipes; Stone Wall; Stoneydale; T.F.H.; T.L.; Ten Speed; Texas Monthly; Thorndike; Timber; Troubador; Turnstone; Universe; Univ. of Alberta; Univ. of Iowa; Univ. of Massachusetts; Univ. of Michigan; Univ. of Nebraska; Univ. of Nevada; Univ. of New Mexico; Univ. of North Carolina; Univ. of Wisconsin; Univ. Press of New England; Univ. Presses of Florida; Walker; Western Producer Prairie; Western Tanager; Westview; Wilderness; Wingra Woods; World Natural History.

Philosophy. Alba; Alchemy; Allen & Unwin; And/Or; Angel; Aquarian; Atlantic Monthly; Avon; Baker; BC Studio; Beacon; Bear; Berkley; Marion Boyars; George Braziller; Brethren; Brunswick; Bucknell Univ.; Camden House; Aristide D. Caratzas; Catholic Univ. of Amer.; Celestial Arts; Christopher; Crossroad/Continuum; Crown; Dante Univ. of Amer.; Daphnean; Harlan Davidson; Dharma; William B. Eerdmans; Enslow; Paul S. Eriksson; Espress; Exposition; Fairleigh Dickinson Univ.; Farrar, Straus and Giroux; Franciscan Herald; Garber; Great Ocean; Warren H. Green; Guernica; Harper & Row; Hazelden; Hounslow; Indiana Univ.; Intercultural; International Univ.; Intervarsity; Robert E. Krieger; Peter Lang; Larson; Little House; Loompanics; Lorien House; Louisiana State Univ. Press; New York Univ.; Northwestern Univ.; Northwoods; Ohara; Ohio State Univ.; Ohio Univ.; Oolichan; Open Court; Oxford Univ.; Panjandrum; Paulist; Penn. State Univ.; Princeton Univ.; Prometheus; Purdue Univ.; Quartet; Regnery/Gateway; Rossel; Rowman & Allanheld; S.C.E.-Editions L'Etincelle; Saybrook; Second Chance/Permanent; Sierra Club; Simon & Schuster; South End; Sovereign; Strawberry Hill; Teachers College; Theosophical; Threshold; Thunder's Mouth; Transaction; Univ. of Alabama; Univ. of Alberta; Univ. of Arizona; Univ. of Massachusetts; Univ. of Michigan; Univ. of Pennsylvania; Univ. of Utah; Univ. Press of America; Univ. Press of Kansas; Univ. Presses of Florida; Volcano; Wadsworth; Wayne State Univ.; Winston-Derek; Woodsong Graphics; Word Books.

Photography. Alchemy; Amphoto; Angel; Appalachian Mountain Club; ARCsoft; Art Direction; Avon; Branden; Crown; Daphnean; Delta; Dharma; Dodd, Mead; Down East; Dragonsbreath; Eastview; Paul S. Eriksson; Exposition; Graphic Image; Guernica; H.P.; H.W.H. Creative Productions; Robert Hale; Harper & Row; Hastings House; Hounslow; Hudson Hills; Key Porter; Knapp; Kranta; Liberty; Lightbooks; Madrona; Motorbooks International; Optimum; Oxmoor; Padre; Clarkson N. Potter; Quartet; Raintree; Rossel; Charles Scribner's; Sierra Club; Sterling; Tab; Taylor; Texas Monthly; UMI Research; Univ. of Michigan; Univ. of Nebraska; Univ. of New Mexico; Univ. of Texas; Univ. Press of Mississippi; Viking Penguin; Wadsworth; Wallace-Homestead; Western Producer Prairie; Winston; Writer's Digest; Yankee.

Psychology. ACS; Affirmation Books; Alba; Amer. Psychiatric; Angel; Aquarian; Arbor House; Dean Aster; Atheneum; Augsburg; Avant; Avon; Baker; Basic Books; Beacon; Bear; Marion Boyars; Brethren; Brunswick; Bucknell Univ.; Cambridge Univ.; Celestial Arts; Christopher; Citadel; Coward McCann; Crossroad/Continuum; Crown; Daphnean; Harlan Davidson; Delta; Dembner; Deselig; Dharma; Dimension; Edits; Education Associates; William B. Eerdmans; Enslow; Paul S. Eriksson; Evans; Exposition; Facts on File; Fairleigh Dickinson Univ.; Farrar, Straus and Giroux; Donald I. Fine; General Hall; Warren H. Green; Stephen Greene/Lewis; Guernica; Harcourt Brace Jovanovich Legal & Professional; Harper & Row; Harvard Common; Harvest House; Hawkes; Hazelden; Houghton Mifflin; Hounslow; Human Sciences; Humanics; Intercultural; International Univ.; Intervarsity; Ishiyaku Euroamerica; Johns Hopkins Univ.; John Knox; Robert E. Krieger; Peter Lang; Learning; Libra; Madrona; Med-Psych; Metamorphous; National; Newcastle; Newconcept; Northwestern; Northwoods; Open Court; Penn. State Univ.; Poseidon; Prometheus; Purdue Univ.; Quartet; Quill; Rainbow; Regnery/Gateway; Riverdale; Ronin; Rossel; Routledge & Kegan; S.C.E.-Editions L'Etincelle; Saybrook; Schenkman; Second Chance/Permanent; Shadow Mountain; Stanford Univ.; Jeremy P. Tarcher; Theosophical; Threshold; Transaction; Turnstone; UMI Research; Univ. of Massachusetts; Univ. of Michigan; Univ. of Nebraska; Univ. of North Carolina; Univ. of Pennsylvania; Univ. Press of America; Univ. Press of Kansas; Univ. Press of Mississippi; Univ. Presses of Florida; Volcano; Wadsworth; Weston Walch; Walker; Wilshire; Wingbow; Woodsong Graphics; Word Books; Zebra; Zondervan.

Real Estate. Prentice-Hall.

Recreation. Harry N. Abrams, Inc.; Amer. Council for the Arts; Angel; Appalachian Mountain Club; Arbor House; Associated Booksellers; Dean Aster; Avon; BC Studio; Beaufort;

Binford & Mort; Celestial Arts; Columbia; Coward McCann; Crown; Darwin; John De Graff; Delta; Down East; East Woods; EMC; Enslow; Paul S. Eriksson; Exposition; Front Row Experience; Globe Pequot; Stephen Greene/Lewis; Guernica; H.P.; H.W.H. Creative Productions; Robert Hale; Harvard Common; Hastings House; Hounslow; Howell-North; International Marine; Johnson; Jonathan David; Key Porter; Leather Stocking; Liberty; McFarland; Madrona; Menasha Ridge; Moon; Mountain; Mountaineers; Mustang; National; Northwoods; Oak Tree; Outbooks; Outdoor Empire; Overlook; Padre; Panjandrum; Pantheon; Peachtree; Prentice-Hall; Riverdale; Ross; Alan Rowe; S.C.E.-Editions L'Etincelle; Charles Scribner's; Shadow Mountain; Sierra Club; Stackpole; Sterling; Stipes; Stone Wall; Stoneydale; T.L.; Taylor; Ten Speed; Texas Monthly; Thorndike; Tribeca; Univ. of Michigan; Weston Walch; Walker; Wilderness; Williamson; Wilshire; Winchester.

Reference. Acropolis Books, Ltd.; Bob Adams; Albatross; Allen & Unwin; Amereon; Amer. Council for the Arts; Amer. Psychiatric; Anderson; Appalachian Mountain Club; Architectural Book; ARCsoft; Arman; Dean Aster; AVI; Avon; Ballinger; Bankers; BC Studio; Bear; Bethany; Betterway; Binford & Mort; Borgo; R.R. Bowker; Branden; Brick House; Brunswick; Caddylak; Career; Cay-Bel; Christopher; Cleaning Consultant Services; Coles; College-Hill; Communications; Compute!; Computer Science; Craftsman; Crown; Dante Univ. of Amer.; Darwin; Datamost; Delta; Dembner; Detselig; Down East; Drama; Dundurn; Durst; ECW; Edits; William B. Eerdmans; Enslow; Espress; ETC; Exposition; Facts on File; Fairleigh Dickinson Univ.; Fairmont; Free; Garland; Genealogical; General Hall; J. Paul Getty Museum; K.S. Giniger; Great Ocean; Warren H. Green; Greenwood; Guernica; Gulf; Robert Hale; Alexander Hamilton Institute; Hanley & Belfus; Harcourt Brace Jovanovich Legal & Professional; Harper & Row; Harvard Common; Harvest House; Hayden; Hazelden; Health Profession Division; D.C. Heath; Here's Life; Heritage; Heyday; Human Sciences; Hurtig; Information Resources; Infosource; Intercultural; International Univ.; Ishiyaku Euroamerica; Jonathan David; B. Klein; John Knox; Robert E. Krieger; Peter Lang; Learning; Libraries Unlimited; Little House; Llewellyn; Loiry; Loompanics; McFarland; McGraw-Hill; MA/AH; Main Street; MCN; Medical Economics; Menasha Ridge; Metamorphous; Meyerbooks; Milady; Museum of New Mexico; Museum of Northern Arizona; National; National Press; Thomas Nelson; New York Zoetrope; Newconcept; Northeastern Univ.; Northwestern Univ.; Oak Tree; Octameron; Oregon State Univ.; Ottenheimer; Overlook; Oxford Univ.; Padre; Panjandrum; Pennwell; Petrocelli; Pocket Books; Poseidon; Prentice-Hall; Princeton Univ.; Que; Rainbow; Raintree; Rosen; Rossel; Routledge & Kegan; RPM; Scarecrow; Schirmer; Scholarly Resources; Seven Locks; Seven Seas; Slavica; Sourceview; ST; Standard; Sterling; Taylor; Techwrite; Texas Monthly; Theatre Communications; Thomas; Transaction; Universe; Univ. of Alberta; Univ. of Illinois; Univ. Press of New England; Univ. Presses of Florida; Wallace-Homestead; Western Producer Prairie; John Wiley & Sons; Wingbow; Woodsong Graphics; Word Beat; Word Books; Wordware; World Almanac; World Natural History; Writer's Digest; Yankee; York; Zondervan.

Regional. Alaska Northwest; Appalachian Mountain Club; Binford & Mort; John F. Blair; Brigham Young Univ.; Cay-Bel; Collier/Macmillan Canada; Colorado Associated Univ.; Cordovan; Doubleday Canada; Douglas & McIntyre; Down East; Dundurn; Eakin; East Woods; William B. Eerdmans; Family Album; Fitzhenry & Whiteside; Globe Pequot; Golden West Books; Golden West Publishers; Gray's; Stephen Greene/Lewis; Guernica; Gulf; Heart of the Lakes; Heritage; Hurtig; Indiana Univ.; Interurban/Trans Anglo; Johns Hopkins Univ.; Johnson; Kent State Univ.; Kids Can; Lexikos; Louisiana State Univ.; Macmillan of Canada; Memphis State Univ.; Moon; Mountain; Museum of New Mexico; Museum of Northern Arizona; NC; Nimbus; Northeastern; Northern Illinois Univ.; Northland; Northword; Ohio Univ.; Oolichan; Oregon State Univ.; Outbooks; Oxmoor; Penn. State Univ.; Peregrine Smith; Prentice-Hall Canada; Preservation; Presidio; Pruett; Quartet; St. Luke's; Southern Methodist Univ.; Stoneydale; Sunstone; Syracuse Univ.; Taylor; Temple Univ.; Texas Christian Univ.; Texas Monthly; Texas Western; Thorndike; Timber; Tompson & Rutter; Charles E. Tuttle; Univ. of Arizona; Univ. of Illinois; Univ. of Nevada; Univ. of New Mexico; Univ. of Tennessee; Univ. of Texas; Univ. of Wisconsin; Univ. Press of Kansas; Univ. Press of Mississippi; Univ. Press of New England; Utah State Univ.; Vehicule; Westernlore; Wingbow; Yankee.

Religion. Abingdon Press; Accent Books; Affirmation Books; Aglow; Alban Inst.; Alchemy; American Catholic; Angel; Aquarian; Augsburg; Avon; Baker; Bantam; Beacon; Beacon Hill of Kansas City; Bear; Bethany; Bookcraft; Don Bosco; Brethren; Bridge; Brunswick; Bucknell Univ.; Camden House; Aristide D. Caratzas; Catholic Truth Society; Catholic Univ. of Amer.; Cay-Bel; CBP; Christopher; Concordia; David C. Cook; Crossroad/Continuum; Crossway; Daphnean; Dharma; Dimension; William B. Eerdmans; Espress; Exposition; Donald I. Fine; Fleet; Fortress; Franciscan Herald; Fraser Institute; C.R. Gibson; K.S. Giniger; Great Ocean; Guernica; Robert Hale; Harvest House; Hendrickson; Here's Life; Hounslow; Huntington House; Indiana Univ.; International Univ.; Intervarsity; Jonathan David; Judson; Kalimat; Kar-Ben Copies; John Knox; Robert E. Krieger; Landmark; Peter Lang; Larksdale; Larson; Liguori; Loyola Univ.; McFarland; Merriwether; Morehouse-Barlow; William Morrow; Mott-Media; Multnomah; National Literary Guild; Thomas Nelson; New Leaf; Newcastle; Northwestern Univ.; Open Court; Orbis; Our Sunday Visitor; Oxford Univ.; Pacific Press;

Paulist; Peachtree; Penn. State Univ.; Princeton Univ.; Prometheus; Puckerbrush; Regal; Regnery/Gateway; Religious Education; Resource; Fleming H. Revell; Ross; Rossel; St. Anthony Messenger; St. Vladimir's Seminary; Saybrook; Second Chance/Permanent; Servant; Seven Locks; Harold Shaw; Sovereign; Standard; Theosophical; Threshold; Tyndale House; Univ. of Alabama; Univ. of Michigan; Univ. of North Carolina; Univ. Press of America; Univ. Press of New England; Victor; Wadsworth; Wayne State Univ.; Whitaker House; Winston; Winston-Derek; Word Books; Zondervan.

Scholarly. Brigham Young Univ.; Bucknell Univ.; Cambridge Univ.; Camden House; Catholic Univ. of Amer.; Colorado Associated Univ.; Dante Univ. of Amer.; Daphnean; Duquesne Univ.; Fairleigh Dickinson Univ.; Folcraft/Norwood; J. Paul Getty Museum; Greenwood; Harvard University; International Univ.; ISI; Johns Hopkins Univ.; Jossey-Bass; Kalimat; Kent State Univ.; Alfred A. Knopf; McFarland; Memphis State Univ.; Nelson-Hall; New York Univ.; Nichols; Northeastern Univ.; Northern Illinois Univ.; Northwestern Univ.; Noyes Data; Ohio Univ.; Open Court; Oregon State Univ.; Penn. State Univ.; Princeton Univ.; Purdue Univ.; Religious Education; Roman & Allanheld; Rutgers Univ.; Saybrook; Schirmer; Schocken; Scholarly; Southern Methodist Univ.; Temple Univ.; Texas Christian Univ.; Texas Western; Transaction; Twayne; UMI Research; Univ. of Alabama; Univ. of Alberta; Univ. of Arizona; Univ. of Illinois; Univ. of Iowa; Univ. of Massachusetts; Univ. of Michigan; Univ. of Missouri; Univ. of Nebraska; Univ. of Nevada; Univ. of New Mexico; Univ. of North Carolina; Univ. of Oklahoma; Univ. of Pennsylvania; Univ. of Pittsburgh; Univ. of Tennessee; Univ. of Texas; Univ. of Utah; Univ. of Wisconsin; Univ. Press of America; Univ. Press of Kansas; Univ. Press of New England; Univ. Press of Virginia; Univ. Presses of Florida; Utah State Univ.; Wayne State Univ.; Western Tanager; Westernlore; Westview; Whitston; York.

Science/Technology. Harry N. Abrams, Inc.; Allen & Unwin; Almar; American Astronautical Society; And/Or; Arco; Dean Aster; Atlantic Monthly; Avon; Ballinger; Bantam; Bear; Cambridge Univ.; Carolina Biological Supply; Coles; Collier/Macmillan Canada; Computer Science; David C. Cook; Coward McCann; Crown; Steve Davis; Delmar; Delta; Dodd, Mead; Enslow; Facts on File; Fairmont; Farrar, Straus and Giroux; Fitzhenry & Whiteside; Stephen Greene/Lewis; Gulf; H.W.H. Creative Productions; Harper & Row; D.C. Heath; Helix; Horizon; Iowa State; Johnson; Knowledge Industry; John Knox; Krantz; Robert E. Krieger; Little, Brown; McGraw-Hill; Medical Economics; Charles E. Merriwether; MGI Management Institute; Museum of New Mexico; Museum of Northern Arizona; National; New Readers; Nichols; Noyes Data; Oddo; Ohio State Univ.; Open Court; Oregon State Univ.; Oryx; Oxford Univ.; Penn. State Univ.; Prentice-Hall; Princeton Univ.; Prometheus; Purdue Univ; Quill; Rainbow; Regnery/Gateway; Ross; Rowman & Allanheld; Howard W. Sams; Charles Scribner's; Sierra Club; Simon & Schuster; Sun; Tab; Times; Transaction; Univelt; Universe; Univ. of Arizona; Univ. of Iowa; Univ. of Michigan; Univ. of Pennsylvania; Univ. of Texas; Univ. Press of New England; Utah State Univ.; Weston Walch; Walker; John Wiley & Sons; Wingra Woods; Wordware.

Self-help. Acropolis Books, Inc.; ACS; Affirmation Books; Aglow; Alchemy; Allen; Almar; Amereon; Amer. Psychiatric; Associated Booksellers; Dean Aster; Atlantis; Augsburg; Avon; Baker; BC Studio; Benjamin; Bethany; Betterway; Bibli O'Phile; Brethren; Bridge; Brunswick; Carolina Biological Supply; CBP; Chrisopher; Cleaning Consultant Services; Compcare; Contemporary; Coward McCann; Crossroad/Continuum; Crown; Delta; Dembner; Dharma; Enslow; Paul S. Eriksson; Examino; Exposition; Facts on File; Fairmont; Fiesta City; Forman; C.J. Frompovich; K.S. Giniger; Golden West Publishers; Grean Ocean; Stephen Greene/Lewis; Gulf; H.P.; H.W.H. Creative Productions; Alexander Hamilton Institute; Harcourt Brace Jovanovich Legal & Professional; Harper & Row; Harvest House; Hawkes; Hazelden; Here's Life; Houghton Mifflin; Hounslow; Humanics; Huntington House; Intercultural; International Self Counsel; International Wealth Success; Jonathan David; Key Porter; B. Klein; Krantz; Lakewood; Larksdale; Larson; Learning; Liberty; Liguori; Little House; Live Oak; Llewellyn; Loiry; Loompanics; McClelland and Stewart-Bantam; Madrona; Marathon International; Maverick; Meadowbrook; Med-Psych; Menasha Ridge; Merriwether; Metamorphous; Meyerbooks; Mott-Media; John Muir; Multnomah; Mustang; National Literary Guild; National Press; New Leaf; Newcastle; Newconcept; Northword; Oak Tree; Octameron; Ohara; Optimum; Outdoor Empire; Pacific Press; Padre; Paladin; Paulist; Poseidon; Clarkson N. Potter; Prentice-Hall; Price/Stern/Sloan; Rainbow; Rosen; Routledge & Kegan; Second Chance/Permanent; Shadow Mountain; Harold Shaw; Spinsters Ink; Sterling; Strawberry Hill; Success; Sun; Taylor; Ten Speed; Thorsons; Times; Walker; Whitaker House; Williamson; Wilshire; Woodsong Graphics; Word Beat; Word Books; Wordware; Yankee; Zebra; Zondervan.

Social Science. Avant; Brigham Young Univ.; Catholic Univ. of Amer.; Crossroad/Continuum; Delta; Duquesne Univ.; Edits; Evans; Fitzhenry & Whiteside; Fleet; Free; Garland; Stephen Greene/Lewis; Groupwork Today; D.C. Heath; Indiana Univ.; Iowa State Univ.; McGraw-Hill; Memphis State Univ.; Charles E. Merrill; Nelson-Hall; New Readers;

Oddo; Ohio Univ.; Porter Sargent; Prentice-Hall; Riverdale; Routledge & Kegan; Southern Illinois Univ.; Stanford Univ.; Transaction; Turnstone; Twayne; Univ. of Missouri; Univ. of Texas; Volcano; Weston Walch; Westview; Whitston; John Wiley & Sons.

Sociology. Alba; Alchemy; Allen & Unwin; Amer. Council for the Arts; Amer. Psychiatric; Angel; Avon; Basic Books; Beacon; Bear; Marion Boyars; Branden; Brethren; Brunswick; Bucknell Univ.; Christopher; Communications; Coward McCann; Daphnean; Harlan Davidson; Dembner; Detselig; William B. Eerdmans; Enslow; Paul S. Eriksson; Exposition; Facts on File; Fairleigh Dickinson Univ.; Farrar, Straus and Giroux; Fraser Institute; General Hall; Warren H. Green; Harper & Row; Harvard Common; Hazelden; Human Sciences; Humanics; Inst. for Study of Human Issues; Intercultural; International Univ.; Intervarsity; Robert E. Kriger; Peter Lang; Learning; Longman; McFarland; Metamorphous; Newconcept; Northwestern Univ.; Northwoods; Ohio State Univ.; Pantheon; Penn. State Univ.; Poseidon; Prentice-Hall; Princeton Univ.; Prometheus; Purdue Univ.; Quartet; Rainbow; Regnery/Gateway; Riverdale; Rossel; Rowman & Allanheld; Rutgers Univ.; S.C.E.-Editions L'Etincelle; Saybrook; Schenkman; Schoken; Scholarly Resources; Seven Locks; Stanford Univ.; Jeremy P. Tarcher; Teachers College; Thomas; Thunder's Mouth; Transaction; Charles E. Tuttle; Univ. of Alberta; Univ. of Illinois; Univ. of Massachusetts; Univ. of Michigan; Univ. of North Carolina; Univ. Press of Mississippi; Univ. Press of New England; Univ. Presses of Florida; Vehicule; Volcano; Wadsworth; Weston Walch; Wayne State Univ.; Westview; Wingbow; Word Books; Zondervan.

Sports. Appalachian Mountain Club; Arbor House; Associated Booksellers; Atheneum; Athletic; Avon; Barron's Educational Series; Beaufort; Benjamin; Don Bosco; Briarcliff; Camden House; Coles; Contemporary; David C. Cook; Coward McCann; Crown; Delta; Dembner; Devin-Adair; Dodd, Mead; Enslow; Paul S. Eriksson; Exposition; Donald I. Fine; Fleet; K.S. Giniger; Stephen Greene/Lewis; Robert Hale; Harper & Row; Harvard Common; Hastings House; Here's Life; Carl Hungness; Icarus; International Univ.; Interstate; Johnson; Jonathan David; Key Porter; Robert E. Krieger; Peter Lang; Laranmark; Lexikos; Liberty; Little, Brown; McClelland and Stewarts-Bantam; McFarland; Menasha Ridge; Mosaic; Motorbooks International; Mountain; Mountaineers; Mustang; National Press; Northword; Oak Tree; Ohara; Ohio State Univ.; Optimum; Outdoor Empire; Overlook; Prentice-Hall; Alan Rowe; S.C.E.-Editions L'Etincelle; Charles Scribner's; Shadow Mountain; Sierra Club; Sterling; Stone Wall; Jeremy P. Tarcher; Taylor; Texas Monthly; Times; Tribeca; Ultralight; Univ. of Illinois; Univ. of Nebraska; Univ. of Tennessee; Weston Walch; Walker; Western Marine; Wilshire; Winchester; Word Books.

Technical. Alchemy; Allen & Unwin; Almar; American Council for the Arts; Amer. Psychiatric; Amphoto; ARCsoft; Arman; Dean Aster; AVI; Aviation; Baen; BC Studio; Branden; Brevet; Brick House; Brunswick; Carolina Biological Supply; Cleaning Consultant Services; Compute!; Cornell Maritime; Craftsman; Darwin; Datamost; Detselig; Enslow; ETC; Exposition; Fairmont; Flora and Fauna; J. Flores; C.J. Frompovich; Great Ocean; H.P.; Harcourt Brace Jovanovich Legal & Professional; D.C. Heath; Information Resources; Infosource; International Univ.; Iowa State Univ.; ISI; Kern International; Robert E. Krieger; Learning; Lorien House; Metamorphous; MGI Management Institute; Mountain; Museum of New Mexico; Museum of Northern Arizona; New York Zoetrope; Newconcept; Noyes Data; Oregon State Univ.; Osborne/McGraw-Hill; Pennwell; Petrocelli; Prakken; Prentice-Hall; Probus; Q.E.D. Information Sciences; Que; Quintessence; Religious Education; Riverdale; Rowman & Allanheld; RPM; Howard W. Sams; Schenkman; Seven Seas; Sourceview; ST; T.F.H.; T.L.; Tandy; Taylor; Techwrite; Theatre Communications; Ultralight; Univelt; Univ. of Alberta; Univ. of Michigan; Windsor.

Textbook. Abingdon Press; Alba; Allen & Unwin; Amer. Psychiatric; Anderson; ARCsoft; Arman; Art Direction; Dean Aster; Atlantis; Augsburg; AVI; Baker; Bennett & McKnight; Don Bosco; Branden; Brethren; Brick House; Wm. C. Brown; Brunswick; CQ; Caddylak; Career; Carolina Biological Supply; Christopher; Cleaning Consultant Services; College-Hill; Collier Macmillan Canada; Communications; Computer Science; Cortina Learning International; Crain; Datamost; Harlan Davidson; Delmar; Detselig; Down East; Education Associates; William B. Eerdmans; EMC; ETC; Exposition; Flora and Fauna; Free; General Hall; Ginn; Guernica; Hanley & Belfus; Harcourt Brace Jovanovich Legal & Professional; Hayden; Health Profession Division; D.C. Heath; Heinle & Heinle; Holt, Rinehart & Winston of Canada; Human Sciences; Humanics; Information Resources; Interstate; Kern International; John Knox; Robert E. Krieger; Peter Lang; Learning; Learning Endeavors; Libraries Unlimited; Llewellyn; Loiry; Longman; Lotus; Loyola Univ.; McGraw-Hill; MA/AH; Merriwether; Charles E. Merrill; Metamorphous; Milady; Mott-Media; Mountain; National; National Textbook; Nelson-Hall; New York Zoetrope; Newconcept; Northwestern Univ.; Occupational Awareness; Outdoor Empire; Pacific Press; Paulist; Petrocelli; Potentials Development for Health & Aging Services; Prakken; Prentice-Hall; Prometheus; Pruett; Regents; Religious Education; Riverdale; Rosen; Routledge & Kegan; Rowman & Allanheld; Schirmer; Seven Locks; Slavica; ST; Standard;

Stanford Univ.; Stipes; Taylor; Techwrite; Theatre Communications; Thomas; Univ. of Alberta; Univ. of Michigan; Wadsworth; Weston Walch; John Wiley & Sons; Word Books; Wordware; York; Zondervan.

Translations. Dante Univ. of Amer.; Davis; Dharma; Dimension; ETC; Forman; Fortress; Franciscan Herald; Garland; Iowa State Univ.; Johns Hopkins Univ.; Lake View; Museum of New Mexico; Northeastern Univ.; Paulist; Penn. State Univ.; Porter Sargent; Threshold.

Transportation. American Astronautical Society; Aviation; Darwin; John De Graff; Golden West Books; H.P.; International Marine; Motorbooks International; John Muir; Ottenheimer; Outdoor Empire; Pruett; Ross; Tab; Ultralight.

Travel. Academy Chicago; Alaska Northwest; Almar; American Council for the Arts; And/Or; Appalachian Mountain Club; Barron's Educational Series; Beaufort; Binford & Mort; Briarcliff; Brunswick; Camaro; Christopher; Devin-Adair; Dodd, Mead; East Woods; William B. Eerdmans; Paul S. Eriksson; Exposition; Facts on File; Fodor's Travel Guides; K.S. Giniger; Globe Pequot; Golden West Publishers; Graphic Image; H.W.H. Creative Productions; Robert Hale; Harper & Row; Harvard Common; Hastings House; Heyday; Hounslow; Howell-North; Icarus; Intercultural; Interurban/Trans Anglo; Key Porter; Knapp; Lexikos; Liberty; Loompanics; Madrona; Main Street; Maverick; Meadowbrook; Menasha Ridge; Moon; Mosaic; John Muir; Mustang; National Press; New York Zoetrope; Nimbus; Northwoods; Northword; Oak Tree; Optimum; Outbooks; Overlook; Padre; Prentice-Hall Canada; Regnery/Gateway; Riverdale; Rossel; Routledge & Kegan; Alan Rowe; S.C.E.-Editions L'Etincelle; Sierra Club; Slavica; Stoneydale; T.L.; Ten Speed; Texas Monthly; Tribeca; Univ. of Michigan; Walker; Western Marine; Winston-Derek; Yankee.

Women. Bantam; Beacon; Contemporary; Feminist; Indiana Univ.; Northeastern Univ.; Pantheon; Penn. State Univ.; Routledge & Kegan; Rutgers Univ.; Saybrook; Scarecrow; South End; Thorsons; Thunder's Mouth; Times; Twayne; Univ. of Tennessee; Volcano.

World Affairs. Atlantic Monthly; Avant; Ballinger; Beacon; Family Album; Intercultural; Lake View; Landmark; NC; Nichols; Orbis; Pantheon; Prentice-Hall Canada; Regnery/Gateway; Roman & ALlanheld; Southern Illinois Univ.; Stanford Univ.; Strawberry Hill; Univ. of Utah; Westview.

Young Adult. Arco; Dial for Young Readers; Farrar, Straus and Giroux; Holiday House; Lodestar; Regal; Rosen; Success.

Fiction

This subject index for fiction will help you pinpoint fiction markets without having to scan nonfiction listings. The parenthetical phrases (following publishers' names) tell you what type of fiction within a particular genre the publisher is interested in. As with the nonfiction markets, read the complete listing for a publisher for advice on what types of fiction the company buys. For more detailed advice and fiction markets (that offer a royalty payment, *or* copies as payment), consult *Fiction Writer's Market* (Writer's Digest Books).

Adventure. Alchemy; Amereon; Angel; Arbor House; Avon; Baker Street Productions; Berkley; Bradbury; Branden; Brunswick; Camelot; Charles River; Coward McCann; Dembner; Dial for Young Readers; Dragonsbreath; Elephant Walk; Exposition; Farrar, Straus and Giroux; Donald I. Fine; Flare; Groundwood; Robert Hale; Harper & Row; Hounslow; Kalimat; Kar-Ben Copies; Kids Can; Lace; Little House; Lodestar; Lothrop, Lee & Shepard; McClelland and Stewart-Bantam; Maverick; Miller; Mountaineers; National Literary Guild; Overlook; Perfection Form; Printemps; Quartet; Rainbow; Raintree; Rossel; Scholastic-Tab; Charles Scribner's; Second Chance/Permanent; Seven Seas; Sierra Club; Stemmer House; Texas Monthly; Walker; Wingbow; Woodsong Graphics; Zebra.

Confession. Charles River; Exposition; H.W.H. Creative Productions; Kalimat; National Literary Guild; Second Chance/Permanent; Wingbow; Zebra.

Erotica. Brunswick; Dragonsbreath; Exposition; Gay Sunshine; Graphic Image; Greenleaf; Guernica; Lace; Quartet; Second Chance/Permanent; Thunder's Mouth; Wingbow; Zebra.

Ethnic. Marion Boyars; Branden; Brunswick; Charles River; Exposition; Flare; Gay Sunshine; Guernica; H.W.H. Creative Productions; Lace; Little House; Overlook; Printemps; Rainbow; Rossel; Routledge & Kegan; Second Chance/Permanent; Spinsters Ink; Stemmer House; Texas Monthly; Thunder's Mouth; Univ. of Illinois; Winston-Derek.

Experimental. Alchemy; Applezaba; Marion Boyars; Charles River; Dragonsbreath; Ecco; Exposition; Donald I. Fine; Flare; Gay Sunshine; H.W.H. Creative Productions; Little House; Oolichan; Panjandrum; Second Chance/Permanent; Techwrite; Thunder's Mouth; Univ. of Illinois; Woodsong Graphics.

Fantasy. Ace Science Fiction; Alchemy; Amereon; Angel; Arbor House; Avon; Baen; Baker Street Productions; Ballantine/Del Rey/Fawcett; Camelot; Crossway; Daw; Dial for Young Readers; Dragonsbreath; Exposition; Farrar, Straus and Giroux; Donald I. Fine; Flare; Groundwood; H.W.H. Creative Productions; Harper & Row; International Univ.; Kar-Ben Copies; Lace; Larson; Little House; Lodestar; Lothrop, Lee & Shepard; Maverick; National Literary Guild; Overlook; Padre; Panjandrum; Polaris; Printemps; Scholastic-Tab; Charles Scribner's; Second Chance/Permanent; Tor; Wingbow; Woodsong Graphics.

Feminist. Crossing; Quartet; South End; Spinsters Ink.

Gay/Lesbian. Alyson; Gay Sunshine; JH; Knights; Naiad; Spinsters Ink.

Gothic. Alchemy; Amereon; Avalon; Avon; Bethany; Exposition; Robert Hale; Harper & Row; International Univ.; Lace; Little House; Panjandrum; Prentice-Hall; Scholastic; Second Chance/Permanent; Woodsong Graphics; Zebra.

Historical. Alchemy; Amereon; Avon; Berkley; Branden; George Braziller; Brunswick; Charles River; Denlinger's; Dial for Young Readers; Dorchester; Dundurn; Eakin; Exposition; Farrar, Straus and Giroux; Donald I. Fine; Gay Sunshine; Groundwood; Guernica; Robert Hale; Harper & Row; Harvest House; Heyday; Houghton Mifflin; Huntington House; International Univ.; Kalimat; Kar-Ben Copies; Kids Can; Lace; Little House; Lothrop, Lee & Shepard; McClelland and Stewart-Bantam; Maverick; Miller; Overlook; Peachtree; Poseidon; Rainbow; Raintree; Rossel; Routledge & Kegan; Charles Scribner's; Second Chance/Permanent; Sierra Club; Sovereign; Stemmer House; Thunder's Mouth; Vehicule; Wingbow; Woodsong Graphics; Zebra.

Horror. Alchemy; Dorchester; Dragonsbreath; Elephant Walk; Exposition; Donald I. Fine; International Univ.; Little House; McClelland and Stewart-Bantam; Second Chance/Permanent; Seven Seas; Tor; Zebra.

Humor. Alchemy; Amereon; Angel; Applezaba; Baker Street Productions; Bradbury; Brunswick; Camelot; Charles River; David C. Cook; Dial for Young Readers; Dragonsbreath; Enrich; Farrar, Straus and Giroux; Donald I. Fine; Flare; Groundwood; H.W.H. Creative Productions; Hounslow; International Univ.; Kalimat; Kids Can; Lace; Lodestar; Lothrop, Lee & Shepard; Merriwether; Miller; National Literary Guild; Peachtree; Perfection Form; Prentice-Hall; Printemps; Rainbow; Ronin; Scholastic-Tab; Charles Scribner's; Second Chance/Permanent; Thorndike; Thunder's Mouth; Woodsong Graphics; Zebra.

Juvenile. Abingdon Press; Atlantic Monthly; Baker; Bantam; John F. Blair; Bradbury; David C. Cook; Crossway; Dial for Young Readers; Dillon; Down East; E.P. Dutton; Eakin; Farrar, Straus and Giroux; Groundwood; H.W.H. Creative Productions; Holiday House; Ideals; Kar-Ben Copies; Kids Can; Lothrop, Lee & Shepard; Margaret K. McElderry; Macmillan; Morrow Junior; Oak Tree; Padre; Philomel; Prentice-Hall; Printemps; Rossel; Scholastic-Tab; Charles Scribner's; Victor; Word Books.

Literary. Beaufort; Columbia; Creative Arts; Dembner; Doubleday Canada; Ecco; Harper & Row; Alfred A. Knopf; Peter Lang; Little, Brown; Little House; Oolichan; Poseidon; Puckerbrush; Stemmer House; Taplinger; Thistledown; Thunder's Mouth.

Mainstream. Academy Chicago; Alchemy; Amereon; Angel; Applezaba; Avon; Beaufort; Berkley; John F. Blair; Bradbury; Branden; George Braziller; Brunswick; Camelot; Coward McCann; Crossway; Delta; Dillon; Dorchester; Doubleday Canada; Ecco; Evans; Exposition; Farrar, Straus and Giroux; Donald I. Fine; Flare; Groundwood; H.W.H. Creative Productions; Robert Hale; Harper & Row; Houghton Mifflin; Hounslow; International Univ.; Jamestown; Larksdale; Little, Brown; Little House; McClelland and Stewart-Bantam; William Morrow; W.W. Norton; Oolichan; Overlook; Padre; Peachtree; Poseidon; Prentice-Hall; Quartet; Rainbow;

Routledge & Kegan; Scholastic-Tab; Charles Scribner's; Second Chance/Permanent; Sierra Club; Simon & Schuster; Smith; Stein and Day; Stemmer House; Texas Monthly; Univ. of Illinois; Vehicle; Viking Penguin; Wingbow; Woodsong Graphics; Zebra.

Military/War. Bantam.

Mystery. Academy Chicago; Alchemy; Amereon; Avalon; Avon; Baker Street Productions; Bantam; Beaufort; Camelot; Coward McCann; Dembner; Dillon; Dodd, Mead; Dorchester; Doubleday; Dragonsbreath; Elephant Walk; Exposition; Farrar, Straus and Giroux; Donald I. Fine; Flare; Gay Sunshine; Groundwood; Guernica; Robert Hale; Harper & Row; Harvest House; Houghton Mifflin; Huntington House; International Univ.; Kids Can; Lace; Little House; Lodestar; Lothrop, Lee & Shepard; McClelland and Stewart-Bantam; Maverick; Miller; National Literary Guild; Overlook; Pantheon; Pocket Books; Prentice-Hall; Printemps; Rainbow; Rossel; Scholastic-Tab; Charles Scribner's; Second Chance/Permanent; Seven Seas; SOS; Texas Monthly; Thorndike; Vehicle; Walker; Wingbow; Woodsong Graphics.

Nostalgia. Thorndike.

Occult. Berkley; Tor.

Picture Books. Bradbury; Concordia; Dial for Young Readers; E.P. Dutton; Prentice-Hall.

Plays. Coach House; Drama; Exposition; H.W.H. Creative Productions; JH; Merriwether.

Poetry. Ahsahta; Atlantic Monthly; Branden; George Braziller; Brunswick; Christopher; Dragonsbreath; Ecco; Golden Quill; Guernica; Houghton Mifflin; Hounslow; Illuminati; International Univ.; Ithaca House; Peter Lang; Larkdsdale; Marathon International; William Morrow; Northeastern Univ.; Northwoods; Overlook; Princeton Univ.; Puckerbrush; Resource; St. Luke's; Harold Shaw; Sunstone; Thistledown; Three Continents; Univ. of Massachusetts; Univ. of Missouri; Vehicle; Wingbow; Winston-Derek; Woodsong Graphics.

Regional. Cay-Bel; Doubleday Canada; Dundurn; Garber; Peachtree; St. Luke's; Sunstone; Thistledown; Thorndike.

Religious. Aglow; Alchemy; Amereon; Avon; Baker; Bookcraft; Branden; Brethren; Bridge; Charles River; Concordia; David C. Cook; Exposition; Donald I. Fine; Huntington House; Ideals; Kalimat; Kar-Ben Copies; Larson; Mott-Media; National Literary Guild; Rainbow; Resource; Fleming H. Revell; Rossel; Standard; Tyndale House; Victor; Winston-Derek; Word Books; Zondervan.

Romance. Alchemy; Amereon; Arbor House; Avalon; Avon; Berkley; Bethany; Branden; Brunswick; David C. Cook; Coward McCann; Dial for Young Readers; Dodd, Mead; Doubleday; Elephant Walk; Exposition; Farrar, Straus and Giroux; Donald I. Fine; Flare; Graphic Image; H.W.H. Creative Productions; Robert Hale; Harlequin; Harper & Row; Harvest House; Holloway House; Huntington House; International Univ.; Kalimat; Kids Can; Lace; McClelland and Stewart-Bantam; Merriwether; Pocket Books; Rainbow; Rossel; Scholastic; Scholastic-Tab; Second Chance at Love; Second Chance/Permanent; Seven Seas; Silhouette; SOS; Tempo; Woodsong Graphics; Word Books; Zebra.

Science Fiction. Ace Science Fiction; Alchemy; Amereon; Arbor House; Dean Aster; Avon; Baen; Ballantine/Del Rey/Fawcett; Bantam; Berkley; Camelot; Crossway; Daw; Dillon; Doubleday; Dragonsbreath; Elephant Walk; Exposition; Farrar, Straus and Giroux; Donald I. Fine; Flare; Gay Sunshine; Groundwood; Guernica; H.W.H. Creative Productions; Harper & Row; Houghton Mifflin; International Univ.; Kids Can; Lace; Larson; Lodestar; Lothrop, Lee & Shepard; National Literary Guild; Overlook; Pocket Books; Polaris; Rainbow; Raintree; Rossel; Scholastic-Tab; Charles Scribner's; Second Chance/Permanent; Sierra Club; Thunder's Mouth; Tor; Wingbow; Woodsong Graphics; Word Books.

Short Story Collections. Applezaba; Graywolf Press; Word Beat Press.

Spiritual. Larson.

Sports. Bantam; David C. Cook; Dillon; Perfection Form.

Suspense. Alchemy; Amereon; Arbor House; Avon; Berkley; Marion Boyars; Camelot; Coward McCann; Dembner; Dial for Young Readers; Dorchester; Doubleday; Exposition; Farrar, Straus and Giroux; Donald I. Fine; Flare; Guernica; H.W.H. Productions; Robert Hale;

Harper & Row; Harvest House; Houghton Mifflin; International Univ.; Kalimat; Little House; Lodestar; Lothrop, Lee & Shepard; McClelland and Stewart-Bantam; Mercury House; National Literary Guild; Overlook; Printemps; Rainbow; Scholastic-Tab; Charles Scribner's; Second Chance/Permanent; Seven Seas; SOS; Texas Monthly; Walker; Wingbow; Winston-Derek; Woodsong Graphics; Zebra.

Western. Alchemy; Amereon; Avalon; Avon; Berkley; Exposition; Farrar, Straus and Giroux; Donald I. Fine; Robert Hale; Harper & Row; International Univ.; Lace; Lodestar; Miller; Pocket Books; Rainbow; Walker; Woodsong Graphics.

Young Adult. Bantam; Berkley; Bethany; Bradbury; Branden; David C. Cook; Crossway; Dial for Young Readers; Farrar, Straus and Giroux; Holiday House; Kids Can; David S. Lake; Peter Lang; Lodestar; Margaret K. McElderry; Perfection Form; Philomel; Scholastic; Scholastic-Tab; Silhouette; Temp.

 One freelance writer very imperiously demanded we spell out precisely specifics of an assignment, made us sign an agreement, then turned in material that was different than what we'd agreed upon. **"**

Consumer Publications _____

Half my lifetime I have earned my living
by selling words and, I hope, thoughts.
—Winston Churchill

When you write for magazines, your business is to sell words. But, actually, it's how you've combined words and what they say that make the sale. Whether you're writing fiction or personal-experience articles, the editor wants a good story *told well*.

A story needs depth, newness and examples that give meaning to ideas. "Sometimes I can see why a manuscript or subject *should* be interesting or entertaining, but if the author hasn't tapped the subject's potential, it won't sell," pointed out one editor. Too many writers think grammatically worded quotes and facts will impress an editor. They do, but you can't forget the human side of any story. Before writing on a topic, ask yourself: How will my treatment of this subject affect my readers' lives? Stories must touch and/or teach readers. Why else would an editor buy a story? Certainly not to feed a byline-hungry writer.

Once you've thought of the reader and the editor, *think of yourself* as a person in business to sell a product. You might never write a self-help article on any subject, but adopt a self-help approach in dealing with editors.

Most freelance writers thrive on the prospect of completing article assignments; they love putting the best of their writing skills and research into each story. They enjoy getting paid for a job that doesn't require an 8-to-5 commitment, five days a week (though they might write 60 hours a week).

But when a manuscript isn't returned or a check for a story arrives late or doesn't arrive, some writers look for someone to blame, someone "to come to the rescue." A few writers contact attorneys, writers' clubs, and *Writer's Market*, expecting them to be their collection agency. What many writers forget is that freelancing entails risks. If you can't risk rejection notes, nonresponse, and delayed payment, then maybe freelancing is not for you. (For more information on "The Business of Freelancing," see the Appendix in the back of this book.)

Many of the problems writers encounter with magazines can be avoided if you know the publications you query. "If you can't take the time to read my magazine, why should I take the time to read your story," many editors say.

When an editor receives a query from a writer about doing an article on, say, Bill Cosby and the magazine published an interview with him three months earlier, the editor knows he is dealing with a lazy freelancer. If you send a short story about a musician to a magazine that publishes only *articles* about music, likewise, you'll be writing your own rejection slip.

Sometimes a magazine, such as *Friends*, will shift its editorial focus and the type of material it buys. Don't judge a magazine from what you remember. What editors need varies from year to year, so read before you write. And don't send material to a publication you haven't seen for awhile; last year writers saw *Geo* and many computer magazines suspend publication. Some magazines don't survive beyond a few issues; some are published for years, then fold.

Another reason that you'll want to see a magazine is to evaluate what kind of consumer publication it is. Publications, remember, can be published by major corporations or by one industrious person. The Consumer Publications section includes four-color magazines, newsletters, tabloids, newspapers, and "little" magazines. One writer last year was disappointed when she had sent a story to a magazine published by a person using a high-quality photocopier; there were no pictures or "color" in the magazine, she complained. See each magazine; if you like its format, submit your material.

Every year, we see trends and ideas that affect magazine formats and story choices. We've also asked editors for their thoughts. After all, they've *seen* 1986 already; many of them are working on 1987 issues right now. Here are some of the industry trends that affect writers:

● emphasis on self-improvement. Readers want to improve their lives, looks, home, talents, etc. Editors, catering to these readers, want material to show them how. Articles with *very* specific information sell best. What the improvements will cost is important, too, unless the magazine caters to an affluent audience. If you can find new ways to make difficult jobs easy for the reader and get expert opinions from many sources, you'll be able to write for many types of markets.

● emphasis on *people* stories. It's a trend that continues in magazines, books, television and movies. *Rolling Stone*, for instance, was depicted in the movie, "Perfect"; it's a film about a *person* doing a story about various *people*. *The Star* has gone from a tabloid to magazine format. A prototype for a new magazine loosely based on the TV show, "Entertainment Tonight" is being tested with possible plans of initiating such a magazine. Of course, most magazines "cover" people involved in the art, sport or subject of the publication. Many magazines are interested in stories about courageous people who are not celebrities—people who have accomplished something locally that would inspire readers in any town.

● specialty magazines. Whether your interest is teddy bears or traveling in Europe, magazines give readers information they can't get in *general* publications. Health and computer publications are some of today's most popular specialty publications. Travel-related magazines seem to be on the upswing. Last year Caesars World initiated *Seven* for its affluent guests. Among other new travel magazines are *Travelling on Business* and *Europe for Travelers*. You'll also see additional inflight magazines in this year's *Writer's Market*.

● fiction in "nonfiction" magazines. We've noticed that some editors are considering fiction as a break in their predominately nonfiction publications. The PEN Syndicated Fiction Project has encouraged magazine editors to publish the project's top fiction submissions. With the premiere of the TV show, Amazing Science Fiction Stories (the name is taken from the magazine), it may stir more interest than ever in the genre. Home Box Office (HBO) is telecasting The Ray Bradbury Theater.

● article/photo packages. At major magazines, editors expect writers to only write; the company hires professional photographers to handle photo assignments. But at a number of magazines, editors want "packages" with a manuscript and photos. Some writer/photographers send photos with a submission to illustrate the object or place they propose to write about (even if the editor later hires a photographer to take the final prints). Writers who know how to use a camera have an additional tool to help them get assignments. Also, take a break from writing occasionally to develop a photographer's eye for detail. If you never send a photo to an editor, you can use a camera to visually record scenes and subjects to later write about.

If you read *Writer's Digest, Publishers Weekly, Folio*, and magazines that report on magazines, you'll be able to spot trends. Professional writers know the announcement of a new magazine or special edition helps them get assignments.

Writers must watch for the details—in the marketplace, in stories, and in negotiations with editors. Professionals also know "the little things," like the tone of a query or ideas backed by anecdotes, are what land or lose assignments.

One detail, though, that you'll want to forget when writing or selling is any rejection note you've received. Learn from your rejections, but keep them in the past. Each story and contact with an editor is a *new* transaction, a new chance to sell your words—and your thoughts.

● *Bullet preceding a listing indicates a company publication.*

Animal

Editors at animal publications want material that *helps* animal owners and trainers. "The article has to address the readers, presenting information that is either of interest or value to 'pet' people, or unique or different, or exceptionally entertaining," points out one editor. Animal magazine editors don't need "a recitation of what the author knows about the subject." They get too many gruesome stories about animals, "first pet" articles, and "talking animals" stories. The publications in this section deal with pets, racing and show horses, other pleasure animals and wildlife. Magazines about animals bred and raised for the market are classified in the Farm category. Publications about horse racing can be found in the Sports section.

AMERICAN FARRIERS JOURNAL, The Laux Company Publishers, Inc., Box 700, Ayer MA 01432. (617)772-4890. Editor: Joanne Lowry. Bimonthly (with an additional annual edition) magazine covering horseshoeing, horse health related to legs and feet of horses and metalworking for a professional audience of full-time horseshoers, veterinarians and horse trainers. Circ. 5,000. Pays on publication. Byline given. Buys all rights. Submit seasonal/holiday material 6 months in advance. Computer printout submissions acceptable: dot-matrix submission accepted only when double-spaced. Reports in 4 weeks on queries; 2 weeks on mss. Sample copy $6; writer's guidelines for SAE and 1 first class stamp.
Nonfiction: Book excerpts, general interest, historical/nostalgic, how-to, interview/profile, new product, personal experience, photo feature and technical. No material about horseshoers that is degrading or negative. Buys 30 mss/year. Send complete ms. Length: 800-3,000 words. Pays $50-450.
Photos: Send photos with ms. Reviews b&w contact sheets, b&w negatives, 35mm color transparencies, and 8x10 b&w or color prints. Captions and identification of subjects required. Buys one-time rights.

ANIMAL KINGDOM, New York Zoological Park, Bronx NY 10460. (212)220-5121. Editor: Eugene J. Walter Jr. Bimonthly magazine for members of zoological societies, individuals interested in wildlife, zoos and aquariums. Pays on acceptance. Publishes ms an average of 1 year after acceptance. Byline given. Buys all rights. Usually pays 25% kill fee but it varies according to length, amount of work involved, etc. Computer printout submissions acceptable; no dot-matrix. Reports in 8 months. SASE. Writer's guidelines for SAE and 1 first class stamp.
Nonfiction: Wildlife articles dealing with wildlife, natural history, conservation or behavior. Also included are articles about animals in history, art and culture. Articles must be scientifically well-grounded, but written for a general audience, not scientific journal readers. No pets, domestic animals or botany. Length: 1,000-2,500 words (sometimes 3,000-4,000 words). Pays $350-1,000. Rarely pays expenses of writers on assignment.
Photos: State availability of photos. Payment for photos purchased with mss negotiable.
Tips: "It helps to be a working scientist studying animals in the wild, or a scientist working in a zoo such as a staff member here at the New York Zoological Society. I cannot be too encouraging to anyone who lacks field experience. Many authors who send us unsolicited manuscripts are nonscientists who are doing their research in libraries. They're simply working from scientific literature and writing it up for popular consumption. There are a fair number of others who are backyard naturalists, so to speak, and while their observations may be personal, they are not well grounded scientifically. It has nothing to do with whether or not they are good or bad writers. In fact, some of our authors are not especially good writers, but they are able to provide us with fresh, original material and new insights into animal behavior and biology. That sort of thing is impossible from someone who is working from books. Write from a personal point of view and avoid technical jargon. We do not accept fillers; short stories, yes."

ANIMALS, MSPCA, 350 S. Huntington Ave., Boston MA 02130. Editor: Susan Burns. Bimonthly magazine for members of the MSPCA. Circ. 15,000. Pays on acceptance. Buys first serial rights. Photocopied and previously published submissions OK but less likely to be accepted. Computer printout submissions acceptable. Reports in 2 weeks. Sample copy $1.75 with 8½x11 SASE; writer's guidelines for letter size SASE.
Nonfiction: Uses practical articles on animal care; humane/animal protection issues, animal profiles, true pet stories (*not mawkish*), and research essays on animal protection. Nonsentimental approach. Length: 300-3,000 words. Pays 2¢/word.
Photos: Pays $10 for 5x7 or larger b&w prints; $30 for color transparencies with accompanying ms or on assignment. Uses photo essays and original photos of artistic distinction for Gallery department.

‡**ARABIAN HORSE TIMES**, Adams Corp., Rt. 3, Waseca MN 56093. (507)835-3204. Editor: Patti Drennan. Managing Editor: Marian Studer-Johnson. 20% freelance written. Monthly magazine about Arabian

horses. Editorial format includes hard news (veterinary, new products, book reports, etc.), lifestyle and personality pieces, and bloodline studies. Circ. 19,000. Pays on publication. Publishes ms an average of 6 months after acceptance. Byline given. Offers 33% kill fee. Buys first serial rights. Submit seasonal/holiday material 3 months in advance. Simultaneous queries OK. Computer printout submissions acceptable; prefers letter-quality to dot-matrix. SASE. Reports in 3 weeks on queries; 6 weeks on mss. Free sample copy and writer's guidelines.

Nonfiction: General interest, how-to, interview/profile, new product and photo feature. Buys at least 12 mss/year. Query with published clips. Length: 1,000-5,000 words. Pays $75-350. Pays expenses of writers on assignments.

Photos: Prefers 5x7 color prints. Payment depends on circumstances. Captions and identification of subjects required. Buys one-time rights.

Fiction: Will look at anything about horses except erotica. Buys 1-2 mss/year. Send complete ms. Length: 1,500-5,000 words. Pays $75-250.

Poetry: Horse-related poetry only. Buys 1-2 poems/year. Submit maximum of 1 poem. Pays $50-100.

Fillers: Buys 12/year. Length: 100-500 words. Pays $10-75.

Tips: "As our periodical is specific to Arabian horses, we are interested in anyone who can write well and tightly about them. Send us something timely."

BIRD TALK, Dedicated to Better Care for Pet Birds, Fancy Publications, Box 6050, Mission Viejo CA 92690. (714)240-6001. Editor: Linda W. Lewis. Managing Editor: K.C. Chuberka. Monthly magazine covering the care and training of cage birds for men and women who own any number of pet or exotic birds. Estab. 1984. Circ. 40,000. Pays latter part of month in which article appears. Byline given. Buys first North American serial rights. Submit seasonal/holiday material 4 months in advance. Simultaneous queries, and photocopied and previously published submissions OK. SASE. Reports in 3 weeks on queries; 6 weeks on mss. Sample copy $3; writer's guidelines for 9x12 SAE and 1 first class stamp.

Nonfiction: General interest (anything to do with pet birds); historical/nostalgic (of bird breeds, owners, cages); how-to (build cages, aviaries, playpens and groom, feed, breed, tame); humor; interview/profile (of bird and bird owners); new product; how-to (live with birds—compatible pets, lifestyle, apartment adaptability, etc.); personal experience (with your own bird); photo feature (humorous or informative); travel (with pet birds or to see exotic birds); and articles giving medical information, legal information, and description of breeds. No juvenile or material on wild birds not pertinent to pet care; everything should relate to *pet* birds. Buys 30 mss/year. Query or send complete ms. Length: 500-3,000 words. Pays 3-5¢/word.

Photos: State availability of photos. Reviews b&w contact sheets. Pays $50-100 for color transparencies; $10 minimum for 8x10 b&w prints. Model release and identification of subjects required. Buys one-time rights.

Columns/Departments: Editorial (opinion on a phase of owning pet birds) and Small Talk (short news item of general interest to bird owners). Buys 4 mss/year. Send complete ms. Length: 100-250 words. Pays 3¢/word and up.

Fiction: "Only fiction with pet birds as primary focus of interest." Adventure, fantasy, historical, humorous, mystery, suspense. No juvenile, and no birds talking unless it's their trained vocabulary. Buys 6 mss/year. Send complete ms. Length: 2,000-3,000 words. Pays 3¢/word and up.

Tips: "Send grammatical, clean copy on a human-interest story about a pet bird or human/pet bird relationship. We also need how-tos on feather crafts; cage cover making; aviary, perch and cage building; and planting plants in aviaries safe and good for birds. Keep health, nutrition, lack of stress in mind regarding pet birds. Study issues of *Cat Fancy*, *Dog Fancy* or *Horse Illustrated* to learn our style."

CALIFORNIA HORSE REVIEW, The Largest All-Breeds Horse Magazine in the Nation, 2437, Fair Oaks CA 95628. (916)961-0815. Publisher/Editor: Jackie Hester. Assistant Editor: Carolee Webster. 70% freelance written. Monthly magazine covering all equines, for "professional trainers, breeders and amateurs whose main interest is in caring for, breeding, showing and riding their horses. Articles provide entertainment and factual information to these readers. Emphasis is on equines in the West and most particularly in California." Circ. 8,000. Pays within 30 days of publication. Publishes ms an average of 3 months after acceptance. Byline given. No kill fee. Buys one-time rights. Submit seasonal/holiday material 3 months in advance. Photocopied submissions OK. Computer printout submissions acceptable; prefers letter-quality to dot-matrix. SASE. Reports in 1 month. Sample copy $1; writer's guidelines for business size SAE and 1 first class stamp.

Nonfiction: Historical/nostalgic, how-to, veterinary medicine, humor, inspirational, interview/profile, personal experience, photo feature, technical and travel. "We want material for major articles concerning health, training, equipment, breeding, and interviews with well-known personalities in the equine field. No general-interest articles or articles not aimed at Western horse owners, trainers or breeders." Buys 200 mss/year. Query; no unsolicited mss. Length: 1,200-3,000 words. Pays $35-125. Sometimes pays the expenses of writers on assignment.

Photos: "Photos are purchased usually as a part of the editorial package."

Tips: "We are more apt to purchase material from horsemen who have some writing skill than from writers who have little horse knowledge. Interviews of trainers, breeders or others well known in the horse world are always sought. Readers want factual information written in clear, understandable fashion. Photos are necessary to illustrate many nonfiction articles."

‡**THE CANADIAN HORSE**, Suite 210, 7240 Woodbine Ave., Markham Ontario L3R 1A4 Canada. (416)495-7722. Associate Publisher: Harry Weston. For thoroughbred horsemen. Monthly magazine. Circ. 5,500. Pays on publication. Buys all rights. Query first, "with a letter that demonstrates your knowledge of and familiarity with our magazine." Enclose SAE and International Reply Coupons.
Nonfiction: Material on Thoroughbred racing and breeding. Pays approximately 20¢/word.

CANINE CHRONICLE, Routledge Publications, Inc., Box 115, Montpelier IN 47359. (317)728-2464. Publisher: Ric Routledge. Editor: Francis M. Bir. 10% freelance written. Twice weekly tabloid covering purebred dogs for people who breed and show them. Circ. 7,000. Publishes mss an average of 2 weeks after acceptance. Pays on acceptance. Byline given. Buys all rights. Submit seasonal/holiday material 3 months in advance. Simultaneous queries and photocopied and previously published submissions OK. Computer printout submissions acceptable; no dot-matrix. SASE. Reports in 3 weeks on queries and mss. Free sample copy.
Nonfiction: How-to (on grooming, feeding, handling, breeding, kennels); history; interviews and features about the people behind the dogs. Buys 25 mss/year. Send complete ms. Pays average of $100 for 1,500 words, "although we are not a stickler on length if the subject is covered."
Photos: State availability of photos. "Technical how-tos should be illustrated if possible." Reviews 5x7 b&w prints. Captions and identification of subjects required. Buys all rights.
Columns/Departments: Query or send complete ms.
Fiction: "We use a limited amount of fiction. Stay away from 'Boy meets dog.' " Buys 5 mss/year. Send complete ms.

CAT FANCY, Fancy Publications, Inc., Box 6050, Mission Viejo CA 92690. (714)240-6001. Editor: Linda W. Lewis. 80-90% freelance written. Monthly magazine for men and women of all ages interested in all phases of cat ownership. 80 pages. Circ. 130,000. Pays after publication. Publishes ms an average of 6 months after acceptance. Buys first American serial rights. Byline given. Submit seasonal/holiday material 4 months in advance. Computer printout submissions acceptable. SASE. Reports in 6 weeks. Sample copy $3; writer's guidelines for SASE.
Nonfiction: Historical, medical, how-to, humor, informational, personal experience, photo feature and technical. Buys 5 mss/issue. Query or send complete ms. Length: 500-3,000 words. Pays 3-5¢/word.
Photos: Photos purchased with or without accompanying ms. Pays $10 minimum for 8x10 b&w glossy prints; $50-100 for 35mm or 2¹/₄x2¹/₄ color transparencies. Send prints and transparencies. Model release required.
Fiction: Adventure, fantasy, historical and humorous. Nothing written with cats speaking. Buys 1 ms/issue. Send complete ms. Length: 500-3,000 words. Pays 3¢/word.
Poetry: Avant-garde, free verse, haiku, light verse and traditional. Buys 5 poems/issue. Length: 5-50 lines. Pays $10.
Fillers: Newsworthy or unusual; items with photo and cartoons. Buys 10 fillers/year. Length: 100-500 words. Pays $20-35.
Tips: "We receive more filler-type articles than we can use. It's the well-researched, hard information article we need."

CATS MAGAZINE, Box 10766, Southport NC 28461. Executive Editor: Jean Amelia Laux. (919)457-5072. Co-Editor: Linda J. Walton, Box 37, Port Orange FL 32019. Monthly magazine for men and women of all ages; cat enthusiasts, vets and geneticists. Circ. 75,000. Pays on publication. Byline given. Buys first North American serial rights and Japanese first rights. Submit seasonal/Christmas material 6 months in advance. Reports in 2 months. SASE. Free sample copy.
Nonfiction: "Cat health, cat breed articles, articles on the cat in art, literature, history, human culture, cats in the news. Cat pets of popular personalities. In general how cats and cat people are contributing to our society. We're more serious, more scientific, but we do like an occasional light or humorous article portraying cats and humans, however, as they really are. No talking cats. Would like to see something on psychological benefits of cat ownership; how do cat-owning families differ from others?" Byline given. Length: 800-2,500 words. Pays $15-75.
Photos: Photos purchased with or without accompanying ms. Captions optional. Pays $10 minimum for 4x5 or larger b&w photos; $150 minimum for color (cover). Prefers 2x2 minimum, but can use 35mm (transparencies only). "We use color for cover only. Prefer cats as part of scenes rather than stiff portraits." Send transparencies to Box 37, Port Orange FL 32019. Mark each transparency with name and address.
Fiction: Science fiction, fantasy and humorous fiction; cat themes only. Length: 800-2,500 words. Pays $15-$100.

Poetry: Poetry in traditional forms, blank or free verse, avant-garde forms and some light verse; cat themes only. Length: 4-64 lines. Pays 50¢/line.
Tips: "We sometimes hold articles due to a backlog. Let us know if you have a time limit."

‡**THE CHRONICLE OF THE HORSE**, The Chronicle of the Horse, Inc., Box 46, Middleburg VA 22117. (703)687-6341. Editor: Peter Winants. Managing Editor: Nancy Comer. 80% freelance written. Weekly magazine about horses. "We cover English riding sports, including horse showing, grand prix jumping competitions, steeplechase racing, foxhunting, dressage, endurance riding and combined training. We are the official publication for the national governing bodies of many of the above sports. We feature news of the above sports, and we also publish how-to articles on equitation and horse care, and interviews with leaders in the various fields." Circ. 20,100. Pays for features on acceptance; news and other items on publication. Publishes ms an average of 3 months after acceptance. Byline given. Offers negotiable kill fee. Buys first North American rights and makes work-for-hire assignments. Submit seasonal/holiday material 3 months in advance. Computer printout submissions acceptable only if double spaced, 8 1/2x11 format; no dot-matrix. Simultaneous queries and photocopied submissions OK. SASE. Reports in 2 weeks. Free sample copy and writer's guidelines.
Nonfiction: General interest; historical/nostalgic (history of breeds, use of horses in other countries and times, art, etc); how-to (trailer, train, design a course, save money, etc.); humor (centered on living with horses or horse people); interview/profile (of nationally known horsemen or the very unusual); technical (horse care, articles on feeding, injuries, care of foals, shoeing, etc.); and news (of major competitions, clear assignment with us first). Special issues include Racing over Fences; Grand Prix Jumping; Combined Training; Dressage; Hunt Roster; Junior and Pony; and Christmas. No Q&A interviews, clinic reports, western riding articles, personal experience, or wild horses. Buys 300 mss/year. Query or send complete ms. Length: 300-1,225 words. Pays $25-200.
Photos: State availability of photos. Reviews 5x7 b&w prints. Pays $10-15. Identification of subjects required. Buys one-time rights.
Columns/Departments: Dressage, Combined Training, Horse Show, Horse Care, Polo, Racing, Racing over Fences, Young Entry (about young riders, geared for youth), Horses and Humanities, and Hunting. Query or send complete ms. Length: 300-1,225 words. Pays $25-200.
Poetry: Light verse and traditional. No free verse. Buys 100 mss/year. Length: 5-30 lines. Pays $15.
Fillers: Anecdotes, short humor, newsbreaks and cartoons. Buys 250 mss/year. Length: 50-175 lines. Pays $10-25.
Tips: "Get our guidelines. Our readers are sophisticated, competitive horsemen. Articles need to go beyond common knowledge. Freelancers often attempt too broad or too basic a subject. We welcome well-written news stories on major events, but clear the assignment with us."

DOG FANCY, Fancy Publications, Inc., Box 6050, Mission Viejo CA 92690. (714)240-6001. Editor: Linda Lewis. 75% freelance written. Monthly magazine for men and women of all ages interested in all phases of dog ownership. Circ. 80,000. Pays after publication. Publishes ms an average of 9 months after acceptance. Buys first American serial rights. Byline given. Submit seasonal/holiday material 4 months in advance. Computer printout submissions acceptable. SASE. Sample copy $3; free writer's guidelines.
Nonfiction: Historical, medical, how-to, humor, informational, interview, personal experience, photo feature, profile and technical. Buys 5 mss/issue. Query or send complete ms. Length: 500-3,000 words. Pays 3-5¢/word.
Photos: Photos purchased with or without accompanying ms. Pays $10 minimum for 8x10 b&w glossy prints; $50-100 for 35mm or 2 1/4x2 1/4 color transparencies. Send prints and transparencies. Model release required.
Fiction: Adventure, fantasy, historical and humorous. Buys 5 mss/year. Send complete ms. Length: 500-3,000 words. Pays 3¢/word.
Fillers: "Need short, punchy photo fillers and cartoons." Buys 10 fillers/year. Pays $20-35.
Tips: "The most rewarding aspect of working with freelance writers is finding a writer who not only knows how to write, but does it with feeling, conviction, and sensitivity to his audience."

‡**FAMILY PET**, Box 22964, Tampa FL 33622. Editor-in-Chief: M. Linda Sabella. 50% freelance written. Quarterly magazine about pets and primarily for pet owners in Florida. "Our readers are all ages; many show pets, most have more than one pet, and most are in Florida." Averages 16-24 pages. Circ. 3,000. Pays on publication. Buys one-time rights. Computer printout submissions acceptable; no dot-matrix. SASE. Reports in 2 months. Sample copy and writer's guidelines for 9x12 SAE with 56¢ postage affixed.
Nonfiction: Historical (especially breed histories); how-to (training and grooming hints); humor (or living with pets); informational; personal experience; photo feature; and travel (with pets). Buys 1-2 mss/issue. Send complete ms. Length: 500-1,000 words. Pays $5-20. Maximum $20 for article/photo package.
Photos: Purchased with or without accompanying ms. Captions required. Pays $3-5 for 5x7 b&w glossy prints used inside. Send prints. Pays $10 for photos used on cover.
Columns/Departments: New Books (reviews of recent issues in pet field). Send complete ms. Length: 200-

400 words. Pays $3-5. Open to suggestions for new columns/departments.
Poetry: Light verse, prefers rhyme. Buys 1/issue. Length: 12-16 lines preferred. Pays $3-5.
Fillers: Jokes, gags, anecdotes, puzzles and short humor. Buys 4-5 fillers/year. Length: 100-350 words. Pays $2-5.
Tips: "We like to include variety so sometimes we will buy several small (shorter) articles instead of one long one."

HORSE AND HORSEMAN, Box HH, Capistrano Beach CA 92624. Editor: Mark Thiffault. 75% freelance written. For owners of pleasure horses; predominantly female with main interest in show/pleasure riding. Monthly magazine; 74 pages. Circ. 96,000. Buys all rights. Byline given. Buys 40-50 mss/year. Pays on acceptance. Sample copy $2; writer's guidelines for SASE. Submit special material (horse and tack care; veterinary medicine pieces in winter and spring issues) 3 months in advance. Reports in 1 month. Query or submit complete ms. SASE.
Nonfiction: Training tips, do-it-yourself pieces, grooming and feeding, stable management, tack maintenance, sports, personalities, rodeo and general horse-related features. Emphasis must be on informing, rather than merely entertaining. Aimed primarily at the beginner, but with information for experienced horsemen. Subject matter must have thorough, in-depth appraisal. Interested in more Western (show) riding/training copy, plus special horse areas like Tennessee Walkers and other gaited breeds. More factual breed histories. Uses informational, how-to, personal experience, interview, profile, humor, historical, nostalgia, successful business operations, technical articles. Length: 2,500 words average. Pays $75-200.
Photos: B&w photos (4x5 and larger) purchased with or without mss. Pays $4-10 when purchased without ms. Uses original color transparencies (35mm and larger). No duplicates. Pays $100 for cover use. Payment for inside editorial color is negotiated.

‡**HORSE & RIDER MAGAZINE**, Rich Publishing, Inc., 41919 Moreno Rd., Temecula CA 92390. (714)676-5712. Editor: Ray Rich. Managing Editor: Judy Kizler. 90% freelance written. Monthly magazine for horse owners, riders, breeders and trainers. "Our readers look to us for articles that deal with every aspect of horse care, conditioning, training and performance. We therefore emphasize practical information and prefer subject matter the reader can apply to enjoying his horse. This includes interviews with successful trainers and breeders, veterinarians, competitive riders, and other experts." Circ. 97,500. Pays prior to publication. Publishes ms an average of 3 months after acceptance. Buys all rights. Submit seasonal/holiday material 3 months in advance. Computer printout submissions acceptable; prefers letter-quality to dot-matrix. SASE. Reports in 1 week on queries. Sample copy $2; free writer's guidelines.
Nonfiction: Historical/nostalgic (Old West); how-to (training horses); humor (cowboy-type); interview/profile (trainer); new product; and personal experience (riding). "We also publish annuals: *Horse Women*, *Horse Action*, *Horse Care*, *Horse Lover's*, *All-Western Yearbook*." Buys 220 mss/year. Query or send complete ms. Length: 500-2,500 words. Pays $100-360.
Photos: Laurie Guidero, photo editor. State availability of photos or send photos with query or ms. Pays $10-25 for 8x10 b&w prints; $50-100 for 8x10 color prints. Captions and identification of subjects required. Buys one-time rights.
Columns/Departments: Dan Cotterman, column/department editor. Buys 48 mss/year (regular contributors).
Tips: "Organizing and presenting an informative, entertaining article usually requires considerable effort. Good composition demands at least one rewrite during which the writer trims and polishes what will exist as the finished product. Have your article tech-checked by the trainer or veterinarian you have interviewed. This is best done before typing the final copy to send to us."

‡**THE HORSE DIGEST, The News and Business Journal of the Horse Industry**, XIT Robinwood, Inc., 4 Loudon St. SE, Leesburg VA 22075. (703)777-6508. Editorial Director: Bob Naylor. Managing Editor: Kathy Laws. 40-80% freelance written, "including reprints from other horse publications, for which we usually pay writer $35." Monthly magazine covering all aspects of all breeds and disciplines of the horse industry, with primary focus on North America. "We reach subscribers nationwide and in Canada; average age 32.5; average household income $31,288; 61.3% female; 85.71% own horses." Circ. 40,300. Pays on publication. Publishes ms an average of 3 months after acceptance. Byline given. Kill fees paid only under special prior arrangement. Buys one-time rights. Submit seasonal/holiday material 3 months in advance. Simultaneous queries, and simultaneous, photocopied, and previously published submissions OK. Computer printout submissions acceptable; prefers letter-quality to dot-matrix. Reports in 6 weeks. Free sample copy and writer's guidelines.
Nonfiction: Book excerpts; expose; general interest; historical/nostalgic (only a few); how-to (horse management, training, health, conditioning, equipment, showing, and farm or horse business management); humor (rarely, except for short items); interview/profile (of well-known celebrities who have horses; question and answers with trendsetters in the horse industry); new product (query us first); photo feature (sometimes); and technical. Special issues include breeding (January); horse sales and auctions (March); and others to be scheduled. "No first-person pieces on writer's love affair or experiences with Old Dobbin; no articles too specific to one breed, region or discipline or addressed to unsophisticated audience." Buys 36 mss/year. Query

with published clips. Length: 800-1,500. Pays $50-150. "We also pay for news tips." Pays expenses above $10 of writers on assignment.

Photos: State availability of photos with query or ms. Reviews contact sheets, 8x10 b&w glossy prints and 2¹/₄x2¹/₄ color transparencies. Pays $150-200 color (cover); $10-50 b&w prints. Identification of subjects required. Buys one-time rights.

Columns/Departments: Interview (questions and answers with equine industry pacesetters, trendsetters); Faces (profiles of non-horse world celebrities who are seriously involved with horses—focusing on horse aspects of their lives); Experts Speak (3 experts' approaches to common problem); and The Topic Is (5-7 different perspectives on trends or events in or affecting the industry). Buys 40-50 mss/year. Query with published clips. Length: 750-1,000 words. Pays $75-100; "often pay some documented phone expenses, too."

Fillers: Roger Hyneman, associate editor. Clips, anecdotes and newsbreaks. Buys approximately 50/year, "but mostly from regular correspondents." Length: 100-250 words. "We usually rewrite them." Pays $5-50.

Tips: "Writers have a better chance of breaking in with short, lesser-paying articles and fillers because we use more of them and we are always hungry for news items—trends spotted in the bud, scams and scandals, mergers, high-dollar syndications or sales, etc. Also, send us a résumé and best clips (no more than six). We may need you as a regional correspondent. Correspondents feed us clippings, items picked up through contacts and press releases; help research regional aspects of national stories upon request; and handle one to three feature assignments per year."

HORSE ILLUSTRATED, Fancy Publications, Inc., Box 6050, Mission Viejo CA 92690. (714)240-6001. Editor: Jill-Marie Jones. 90% freelance written. Monthly magazine for men and women of all ages interested in all phases of horse ownership. Circ. 50,000. Pays after publication. Publishes ms an average of 4 months after acceptance. Buys first North American serial rights. Submit seasonal/holiday material 4 months in advance. Computer printout submissions acceptable. SASE. Sample copy $3; free writer's guidelines.

Nonfiction: Medical, how-to, humor, informational, interview, photo feature, profile, technical and sport. Buys 5 mss/issue. Length: 500-2,500 words. Pays 3-5¢/word.

Photos: Photos purchased with or without accompanying ms. Pays $10 minimum for 8x10 b&w glossy prints; $50-100 for 35mm 2¹/₄x2¹/₄ color transparencies. Send prints and transparencies. Model release required.

Fiction: Adventure and humor. Buys 5 mss/year. Send complete ms. Length: 500-2,000 words. Pays 3-5¢/word.

Fillers: Newsworthy or unusual items with photo and cartoons. Buys 10/year. Pays $20-35.

Tips: "We believe very strongly in working with new/young journalists with talent, and support them by giving them more and more assignments. The most annoying aspect of working with freelance writers is not meeting deadlines. Writers often don't realize editors/publishers have unforgiving timetables; and if a writer misses a deadline even once, we are very gun shy about using him/her again."

HORSEMAN MAGAZINE, 5314 Bingle Rd., Houston TX 77092. (713)688-8811. Editor: Linda Blake. 60% freelance written. Monthly magazine for people who own and ride horses for pleasure and competition. Majority own western stock horses and compete in western type horse shows as a hobby or business. Many have owned horses for many years. Circ. 146,000. Rights purchased vary with author and material. Pays on publication. Buys first North American serial rights. Byline given. Computer printout submissions acceptable; no dot-matrix. Submit seasonal material 4 months in advance. Reports in 3 weeks. SASE. Free sample copy and writer's guidelines.

Nonfiction: "How-to articles on horsemanship, training, grooming, exhibiting, horsekeeping, and history dealing with horses. We really like articles from professional trainers, or articles about their methods written by freelancers. The approach is to educate and inform readers as to how they can ride, train, keep and enjoy their horses more." Query. Length: 1,000-2,500 words. Pays up to 7-10¢/word.

Photos: Photos purchased with accompanying ms or on assignment. Captions required. Pays $10 minimum for 5x7 or 8x10 b&w prints; 35mm or 120 negatives. Pays $25 for inside color. Prefers transparencies. Buys all rights.

Tips: "Send article ideas with very narrow focus. Indicate depth. Use know-how from top experts or send us good, concise articles about specific training problems with detailed explanation of correction. Otherwise, stick to fringe articles: humor, photo essay, Horseman Travelog. The articles need to be packed with information, but we don't always mean step-by-step how-to. Make them readable."

HORSEMEN'S YANKEE PEDLAR NEWSPAPER, Box 785 Southbridge St., Auburn MA 01501. (617)832-9638. Publisher: Nancy L. Khoury. Associate Editors: Suzy Lucine, Kyrill Schabert. 40% freelance written. "All-breed monthly newspaper for horse enthusiasts of all ages and incomes, from one-horse owners to large commercial stables. Covers region from New Jersey to Maine." Circ. 12,000. Pays on publication. Buys all rights for one year. Submit seasonal/holiday material 3 months in advance of issue date. Publishes ms an average of 5 months after acceptance. SASE. Reports in 1 month. Sample copy $1.75.

Nonfiction: Humor, educational and interview about horses and the people involved with them. Pays $2/published inch. Buys 50 mss/year. Submit complete ms or outline. Length: 1,500 words maximum.

Photos: Purchased with ms. Captions and photo credit required. Buys 3 cover photos/year; pays $25. Submit b&w prints. Pays $5.

Columns/Departments: Area news column. Buys 85-95/year. Length: 1,200-1,400 words. Pays 75¢/column inch. Query.

Tips: "Query with outline of angle of story, approximate length and date when story will be submitted. Stories should be people oriented and horse focused. Send newsworthy, timely pieces, such as stories that are applicable to the season, for example: foaling in the spring or how to keep a horse healthy through the winter. We like to see how-tos, features about special horse people and anything that has to do with the preservation of horses and their rights as creatures deserving a chance to survive."

HORSEPLAY, Box 545, Gaithersburg MD 20877. (301)840-1866. Editor: Cordelia Doucet. 20% freelance written. Monthly magazine covering horses and English horse sports for a readership interested in horses, show jumping, dressage, combined training, hunting, and driving. 60-80 pages. Circ. 47,000. Pays end of publication month. Publishes ms an average of 3 months after acceptance. All rights reserved. Pays kill fee. Byline given. Submit all material 2 months in advance. SASE. Reports within 6 weeks. Sample copy $2.75; free writer's and photographer's guidelines.

Nonfiction: How-to (various aspects of horsemanship, course designing, stable management, putting on horse shows, etc.); interview; photo feature; profile and technical. Length: 1,000-3,000 words. Pays 9¢/word, all rights.

Photos: Cathy Heard, art director. Purchased on assignment. Write captions on separate paper attached to photo. Query or send contact sheet, prints or transparencies. Pays $10-20 for 8x10 b&w glossy prints; $175 for color transparencies for cover; $45 for inside color.

Tips: Don't send fiction, western riding, or racing articles.

HORSES ALL, Rocky Top Holdings, Ltd., Box 550, Nanton Alberta T0L 1R0 Canada. (403)646-2144. Editor: Jacki French. 30% freelance written. Monthly tabloid for horse owners, 75% rural, 25% urban. Circ. 11,200. Pays on publication. Publishes ms an average of 6 months after acceptance. Buys one-time rights. Phone queries OK. Submit seasonal material 3 months in advance. Simultaneous, photocopied (if clear), and previously published submissions OK. Computer printout submissions acceptable. Reports on queries in 5 weeks; on mss in 6 weeks. Sample copy $2.

Nonfiction: Interview, humor and personal experience. Query. Pays $20-100.

Photos: State availability of photos. Captions required.

Columns/Departments: Length: 1-2 columns. Query. Open to suggestions for new columns/departments. Send query to Doug French.

Fiction: Historical and western. Query. Pays $20-100.

Tips: "We use more short articles. The most frequent mistakes made by writers in completing an article assignment for us are poor research, wrong terminology, and poor (terrible) writing style."

‡**HORSES WEST**, Horses West, Inc., Box 1590, Boulder CO 80306-1590. (303)443-7442. Editor-in-Chief: Jaymee Brandt. Managing Editor: Joanna Neff. 30% freelance written. Monthly tabloid covering regional and national news and current information on the training, feeding and care of horses. "*Horses West* is an all-breed regional newspaper serving the Rocky Mountain states and also subscribers in the South, Midwest, New England, and on the West Coast. Our readers are primarily horse breeders, horse owners and advertisers in the horse industry." Estab. 1984. Circ. 12,000. Pays within 30 days after publication. Publishes ms an average of 1 month after acceptance. Byline given. Offers 20% kill fee. Buys all rights, first rights (primary), and second serial (reprint) rights. Submit seasonal/holiday material 3 months in advance. Simultaneous queries, and simultaneous, photocopied, and previously published submissions OK. Computer printout submissions acceptable; prefers letter-quality to dot-matrix. SASE. Reports in 6 weeks. Sample copy for $1, 9x12 SAE and 6 first class stamps; writer's guidelines for business size SAE and 1 first class stamp.

Nonfiction: Book excerpts (from horse training and care books); expose (controversial topics in the horse industry); general interest (regional and national news on well-known events and/or horses and personalities; horsekeeping and stable management; showing techniques; breeding programs); historical/nostalgic (relating to horses); how-to; humor (cartoons, short anecdotes relating to horses); interview/profile (all-discipline, successful trainers and exhibitors—highlighting techniques, methods or practical approaches to solving a horse problem); opinion (on happenings in the horse world); personal experience (human-interest stories: working-student training, well-known horses, national/regional); photo feature (how-to, training, human interest, humorous, the unusual); technical (riding, training, updates on veterinary treatments; horsekeeping, stable management; tack and equipment—explain use); helpful hints on time-saving horse care techniques—any of value to horse owners. Special issues include April lampoon issue; cartoons, short anecdotes and fillers are needed. Buys 20-30 mss/year. Query. Length: 500-3,000 words. Pays $1-2/column inch.

Photos: State availability of photos with query. Reviews 5x7 and 8x10 b&w and color glossy prints. Payment for photos included in payment for ms. Captions, model release and identification of subjects required. Buys one-time rights.

Columns/Departments: Marketplace (new items and services of interest to horse people). "We are on the lookout for new columns dealing with aspects of horse ownership such as horsekeeping tips, a column on shoeing by a farrier, legal aspects of horse ownership, and area news columns." Buys 12-20 mss/year. Query. Length: 500-1,000 words. Pays $1-2/column inch.

Fiction: Adventure, fantasy, historical, humorous, mainstream, mystery, novel excerpts, science fiction, suspense and western. "No tear-jerkers." Also needs fiction pieces for special April lampoon issue. Query. Length: 1,000-2,500 words. "We will serialize top-quality stories of more than 3,000 words." Pays $1-2/column inch.

Poetry: Free verse, light verse and traditional. "No greeting-card-level poetry." Submit maximum 5 poems. Length: 28 lines maximum. Pays $5-15.

Fillers: Clippings, jokes, gags, anecdotes, short humor and newsbreaks. Buys 12-20/year. Length: 100-1,000 words. Pays $5-25.

Tips: "We are looking for skillfully written articles in a feature-style, photojournalistic format. Interviews, general interest, fiction, humor/cartoons and regional/national news—all on the subject of all-breed, training, feeding and care of horses—are the areas most open to freelancers."

‡**JUNIOR RIDERS, The Magazine for Young People Who Love Horses**, Flegel Publishing Co., Box 50384, St. Louis MO 63105. (314)966-4330. Publisher: G.A. Smith. 80-90% freelance written. Bimonthly magazine covering the sport of horseback riding. "Our target audience is the 12- to 14-year old who has been riding for some time. Subjects include horse care, training, understanding your horse, various horseback riding activities." Estab. 1984. Circ. 1,700. Pays on publication. Publishes ms an average of 1-3 months after acceptance. Byline given. Buys first North American serial rights. Simultaneous queries, and simultaneous, photocopied and previously published submissions OK. SASE. Reports in 1 month. Sample copy for SASE and 5 first class stamps; writer's guidelines for SASE.

Nonfiction: Book excerpts, general interest, historical/nostalgic, how-to, humor, interview/profile, personal experience, photo feature, technical, and travel. Buys 50-60 mss/year. Query. Length: 1,500-2,500 words. Pays $25 minimum. Pays some expenses of writers on assignment (photo, reasonable travel, other); publisher must be notified.

Photos: State availability of photos with query. Send photos with query or ms. Captions, model releases and identification of subjects required. Buys one-time rights. "We will pay for film, photo processing, etc."

Columns/Departments: Hoofprints in History, The Vet's Bag, and Dear Appy. Need columns on projects, books, reviews, etc. Buys 20 mss/year. Query. Length: 900-1,500 words. Pays $25 minimum.

Fiction: Adventure, condensed novels, historical, humorous and western. Buys 5-6 mss/year. Query. Length: 1,200-2,500 words. Pays $25 minimum.

Poetry: Pays $5-15.

Tips: "If you know horses, how to write and how to write for a young audience, we would like to hear from you. Though young, our audience is discriminating. Articles must be factual and accurate, well thought out and well presented. *Junior Riders* is just starting out. Publisher used to freelance, and makes a commitment to freelancers—stick with me now, help me get started, I'll pay better later."

THE MORGAN HORSE, American Morgan Horse Association, Box 1, Westmoreland NY 13490. (315)735-7522. Acting Editor: Avo Kiviranna. Article Contact: James Bloonquist. 60% freelance written. Monthly breed journal covering the training, showing, and vet care of Morgan horses. Circ. 10,000. Pays on publication. Publishes ms an average of 3 months after acceptance. Byline given. Rights vary with submission. Submit seasonal/holiday material 3 months in advance. Simultaneous queries and simultaneous, photocopied, and previously published submissions OK (subject to editor's discretion). Computer printout submissions acceptable; prefers letter-quality to dot-matrix. SASE. Reports in 3 months. Sample copy $3; writer's guidelines for business size SAE and 1 first class stamp.

Nonfiction: How-to (trailering, driving, training, etc.); human interest (if highly unusual); interview/profile (of respected Morgan personalities); veterinary articles. Special issues include Morgan Grand National, Stallions, Versatility, Driving, Mare, Youth, Western, Gelding, Foal, International, Horse Buying. No articles with less-than-national interest or material dealing with half-bred Morgans. "We have few fillers we can print but always seem to receive more than our share of them." Buys 15-20 mss/year. Query with clips of published work. Length: 500-3,000 words. Pays 5¢/word and up. Sometimes pays the expenses of writers on assignment.

Photos: Send photos with ms. Pays $5 minimum for 8x10 b&w prints, $20 for color. Captions, model release and identification of subjects required.

Tips: "We like to see completed manuscripts from new writers and welcome articles on veterinary breakthroughs and training. We do develop a stable and encourage new contributors to grow into our group after proving themselves with a few articles."

PAINT HORSE JOURNAL, American Paint Horse Association, Box 18519, Fort Worth TX 76118. (817)439-3400. Editor: Bill Shepard. 10% freelance written. For people who raise, breed and show paint horses. Monthly magazine. Circ. 12,000. Pays on acceptance. Publishes ms an average of 3 months after acceptance. Buys first North American serial rights. Pays negotiable kill fee. Byline given. Phone queries OK, but prefers written query. Submit seasonal/holiday material 3 months in advance. Photocopied and previously published submissions OK. Computer printout submissions acceptable; no dot-matrix. SASE. Reports in 1 month. Sample copy, $1; writer's guidelines for SAE and 1 first class stamp.

Nonfiction: General interest (personality pieces on well-known owners of paints); historical (paint horses in the past—particular horses and the breed in general); how-to (train and show horses); and photo feature (paint horses). Buys 4-5 mss/issue. Send complete ms. Pays $50-250.

Photos: Send photos with ms. Offers no additional payment for photos accepted with accompanying ms. Uses 3x5 or larger b&w glossy prints; 35mm or larger color transparencies. Captions required.

Tips: *"PHJ* needs breeder-trainer articles from areas throughout U.S. and Canada. Photos with copy are almost always essential. Well-written first person articles welcome. Humor, too. Submit well-written items that show a definite understanding of the horse business. Use proper equine terminology and proper grounding in ability to communicate thoughts."

PERFORMANCE HORSEMAN, Gum Tree Store Press, Inc. Gum Tree Corner, Unionville PA 19375. (215)857-1101. Editor-in-Chief: Pamela Goold. Articles Editor: Miranda D. Lorraine. 33% freelance written. Monthly magazine covering Western horsemanship and horse care. Circ. 30,000. Pays on acceptance. Byline given. Offers negotiable kill fee. Buys all rights; makes work-for-hire assignments. Computer printout submissions acceptable; prefers letter-quality to dot-matrix. SASE. Reports in 1 month on queries; 6 weeks on mss. Sample copy for 12x14 SAE; free writer's guidelines.

Nonfiction: How-to. Buys 8-12 mss/year. Query with published clips. Length: 3,000-4,500 words. Pays $300 and up; payment depends on individual assignment.

Photos: State availability of photos with query. Pays $35-125 for 35mm color transparencies; $10-25 for 5x7 b&w prints. Identification of subjects required.

‡**PRACTICAL HORSEMAN,** Gum Tree Store Press Inc., Gum Tree Corner, Unionville PA 19375. (215)857-1101. Editor-in-Chief: Pamela Goold. Articles Editor: Miranda Lorraine. 20% freelance written. Monthly magazine for knowledgeable horsemen interested in breeding, raising and training Thoroughbred and Thoroughbred-type horses for show, eventing, dressage, hunting, and pleasure riding. Circ. 52,000. Pays on acceptance. Publishes ms an average of 3 months after acceptance. Byline given. Buys all rights; makes work-for-hire assignments. Simultaneous submissions OK. Computer printout submissions acceptable; no dot-matrix. SASE. Reports in 1 month on queries; 6 weeks on mss. Sample copy for 12x14 SAE; free writer's guidelines.

Nonfiction: How-to. Articles on show and field hunters, jumpers, combined training and dressage. Buys 8-12 mss/year. Query with published clips. Length: 3,000-4,500 words. Pays $300 and up. Sometimes pays expenses of writers on assignment.

Photos: State availability of photos. Pays $35-125 for 35mm color transparencies; $10-25 for 5x7 b&w prints. Identification of subjects required. Buys all rights.

Tips: "We base all articles on expert knowledge. Few writers can sustain the depth, focus and detail that we require through a full-length story. Good clips and queries are a better idea than a full-length story that may misfire. We don't accept generalities, and so our writers must have sufficient working knowledge of horses to know whether the interviewee has answered a question or skirted the point. *How* and *why* must be constant features of any article we publish; writers sometimes allow themselves to be satisfied too easily."

PURE-BRED DOGS AMERICAN KENNEL GAZETTE, American Kennel Club, Inc., 51 Madison Ave., New York NY 10010. (212)696-8332. Editor: Ms. Pat Beresford. 40% freelance written. Official publication of the American Kennel Club, a monthly magazine covering pure-bred dogs. "Reaches breeders of pure-bred dog owners. All articles published must be related to the pure-bred dog fancy—dog showing, judging, breeding, health and medicine, grooming, training, and the dog in art or literature." Circ. 50,000. Pays on publication. Publishes ms an average of 12-18 months after acceptance. Byline given. Buys first North American serial rights. Submit seasonal/holiday material 6 months in advance. Reports in 1 month. Free sample copy and writer's guidelines.

Nonfiction: General interest, how-to, photo feature, technical, medical, and must relate to the canine. Buys about 25 mss/year. Send complete ms. Length: 750-3,000 words. Pays $50-250 and up "depending on article."

Photos: Send photos with accompanying query or ms. Reviews 8x10 b&w and color prints or slides. Pay depends on entire article. Model release and identification of subjects required.

Tips: "We simply like to have complete outlines of manuscripts on any ideas submitted. If we like the work or see potential, we will contact the writer. Only editorial features section is open to freelancers. We like to see in-depth coverage of dogs with good photo illustrations."

PURRRRR! THE NEWSLETTER FOR CAT LOVERS, The Meow Company, Suite 187, 89 Massachusetts Ave., Boston MA 02115. Editor: Carol Frakes. 90% freelance written. A bimonthly newsletter for the av-

erage cat owner, *not* breeders. "The publication is designed to amuse while providing cat lovers with information about the care, feeding and enjoyment of house cats." Circ. 2,000 + . Pays on publication. Publishes ms an average of 10 months after acceptance. Byline given. Buys first serial rights and second serial (reprint) rights. Submit seasonal/holiday material 6 months in advance. Photocopied and previously published submissions OK unless it's been published in a competing publication, such as *Cats* and *Cat Fancy*. Computer printout submissions acceptable; no dot-matrix. SASE. Reports in 2 weeks. Sample copy $2; writer's guidelines for business size SAE and 1 first class stamp.
Nonfiction: General interest; historical; how-to; literary cat lovers (have featured Colette, Mark Twain and May Sarton); humor; interview/profile; new product; travel, off-beat unusual. "We want a humorous slant wherever possible; writing should be tight and professional. Avoid the first person." Special Christmas issue. No shaggy cat stories, sentimental stories, "I taught Fluffy to roll over" cutsie material. Buys 50/mss year. Query with published clips, or send complete ms. Do not call. Length: 250-1,500 words. Pays: $15-100.
Photos: Avoid "cute" photos. State availability of photos. Pays $5-10 for 5x8 b&w prints. Model release and identification of subjects required. Buys one-time rights.
Fillers: Clippings, anecdotes, short humor and newsbreaks. Buys 20/year. Length: 25-75 words. Pays $5.
Tips: "The most frequent mistakes made by writers in completing an article assignment for us are not following instructions and persisting in making pieces too personal and too sentimental. We want practical articles, such as recent articles on pet insurance, pros and cons of declawing, etc."

THE QUARTER HORSE JOURNAL, Box 32470, Amarillo TX 79120. (806)376-4811. Editor-in-Chief: Audie Rackley. 10% freelance written. Official publication of the American Quarter Horse Association. Monthly magazine. Circ. 82,000. Pays on acceptance. Publishes ms an average of 3 months after acceptance. Buys all rights or first North American serial rights. Submit seasonal/holiday material 2 months in advance. Computer printout submissions acceptable; prefers letter-quality to dot-matrix. SASE. Reports in 2 weeks. Free sample copy and writer's guidelines for 2 first class stamps.
Nonfiction: Historical ("those that retain our western heritage"); how-to (fitting, grooming, showing, or anything that relates to owning, showing, or breeding); informational (educational clinics, current news); interview (feature-type stories—must be about established horses or people who have made a contribution to the business); new product; personal opinion; and technical (equine updates, new surgery procedures, etc.). Buys 30 mss/year. Length: 800-2,500 words. Pays $50-250.
Photos: Purchased with accompanying ms. Captions required. Send prints or transparencies. Uses 5x7 or 8x10 b&w glossy prints; 2¼x2¼ or 4x5 color transparencies. Offers no additional payment for photos accepted with accompanying ms.
Tips: Writers have a better chance of breaking in at this publication with short, lesser-paying articles and fillers (rather than with major features) because "most writers are not familiar enough with the horse business to give it the right touch."

SHOWHORSE,(formerly *Northeast Horseman*), Henley Sales, Ltd., Box 1270, Bangor ME 04401. (207)947-0126. Publisher: Stephen Kinney. Editor: Janet Danforth. 65% freelance written. A monthly magazine specifically for those breeds for which saddle seat riding was developed, Morgans, Saddlebreds, Arabians, and their allied breeds. Covers these breeds wherever and however they are used in competition. Pays on publication. Publishes ms an average of 4 months after acceptance. Computer printout submissions acceptable; prefers letter-quality to dot-matrix. Unsolicited mss not returned. Writer's guidelines for SAE and 1 first class stamp.
Nonfiction: Feature-oriented. Uses question-and-answer interviews, opinion pieces, farm and personality profiles and how-to pieces. Send resume and clippings (not returned); mss on assignment only. Sometimes pays the expenses of writers on assignment.
Tips:"We prefer phone queries from freelancers."

TROPICAL FISH HOBBYIST, "The World's Most Widely Read Aquarium Monthly", TFH Publications, Inc., 211 W. Sylvania Ave., Neptune City NJ 07753. (201)988-8400. Editor: John R. Quinn. Managing Editor: Neal Pronek. 75% freelance written. Monthly magazine covering the tropical fish hobby. "We favor articles well illustrated with good color slides and aimed at both the neophyte and veteran tropical fish hobbyist." Circ. 50,000. Pays on acceptance. Publishes ms an average of 4 months after acceptance. Byline given. Buys all rights. Submit seasonal/holiday material 4 months in advance. Photocopied submissions OK. Computer printout submissions acceptable; no dot-matrix. SASE. Reports in 2 weeks. Sample copy $2.50; free writer's guidelines.
Nonfiction: General interest, how-to, photo feature, technical, and articles dealing with beginning and advanced aspects of the aquarium hobby. No "how I got started" in the hobby articles that impart little solid information. Buys 20-30 mss/year. Length: 500-2,500 words. Pays $25-100.
Photos: John R. Quinn, photo editor. State availability of photos or send photos with ms. Pays $10 for 35mm color transparencies. Identification of subjects required. "Originals of photos returned to owner, who may market them elsewhere."

Fiction: "On occasion, we will review a fiction piece relevant to the aquarium hobby."
Tips: "We cater to a specialized readership—people knowledgable in fish culture. Prospective authors should be familiar with subject; photography skills are a plus. It's a help if an author we've never dealt with queries first or submits a short item."

THE WESTERN HORSEMAN, Box 7980, Colorado Springs CO 80933. Editor: Randy Witte. 40% freelance written. Monthly magazine covering western horsemanship. Circ. 155,220. Pays on acceptance. Publishes ms an average of 5 months after acceptance. Buys first-time rights. Byline given. Submit seasonal/holiday material 3 months in advance. SASE. Reports in 3 weeks. Sample copy $1.75.
Nonfiction: How-to (horse training, care of horses, tips, etc.); and informational (on rodeos, ranch life, historical articles of the West emphasizing horses). Length: 1,500 words. Pays $85-135; "sometimes higher by special arrangement."
Photos: Send photos with ms. Offers no additional payment for photos. Uses 5x7 or 8x10 b&w glossy prints and 35mm transparencies. Captions required.
Tips: "Submit clean copy with professional quality photos. Stay away from generalities. Writing style should show a deep interest in horses coupled with a wide knowledge of the subject."

Art

Art magazines vary as much as the types and trends in the art world that they report. The artist with an interest in writing about art should query these publications. Some of them want step-by-step art instruction articles; others need articles on exhibiting and selling artwork. Listed here are publications of and about art, art history, and specific art forms written for art patrons and artists. Publications addressing the business and management concerns of the art industry are listed in the Art, Design, and Collectibles category of the Trade Journals section.

THE AMERICAN ART JOURNAL, Kennedy Galleries, Inc., 40 W. 57th St., 5th Floor, New York NY 10019. (212)541-9600. Editor-in-Chief: Jane Van N. Turano. Scholarly magazine of American art history of the 17th, 18th, 19th and 20th centuries, including painting, sculpture, architecture, decorative arts, etc., for people with a serious interest in American art, and who are already knowledgeable about the subject. Readers are scholars, curators, collectors, students of American art, or persons who have a strong interest in Americana. Quarterly magazine; 96 pages. Circ. 2,000. Pays on acceptance. Buys all rights. Byline given. Photocopied submissions OK. SASE. Reports in 2 months. Sample copy $8.
Nonfiction: "All articles are historical in the sense that they are all about some phase or aspect of American art history." No how-to articles or reviews of exhibitions. No book reviews or opinion pieces. No human interest approaches to artists' lives. No articles written in a casual or "folksy" style. *Writing style must be formal and serious.* Buys 25-30 mss/year. Submit complete ms "with good cover letter." Length: 2,500-8,000 words. Pays $300-400.
Photos: Purchased with accompanying ms. Captions required. Uses b&w only. Offers no additional payment for photos accepted with accompanying ms.
Tips: "Actually, our range of interest is quite broad. Any topic within our time frame is acceptable if it is well-researched, well-written, and illustrated. Whenever possible, all mss must be accompanied by b&w photographs which have been integrated into the text by the use of numbers."

AMERICAN INDIAN ART MAGAZINE, American Indian Art, Inc., 7314 E. Osborn Dr., Scottsdale AZ 85251. (602)994-5445. Managing Editor: Roanne P. Goldfein. 97% freelance written. Quarterly magazine covering Native American art, historic and contemporary, including new research on any aspect of Native American art. Circ. 15,000. Pays on publication. Publishes ms an average of 8 months after acceptance. Byline given. Buys one-time and first rights. Submit seasonal/holiday material 6 months in advance. Simultaneous queries OK. Reports in 2 weeks on queries; 2 months on mss. Writer's guidelines available.
Nonfiction: New research on any aspect of Native American art. No previously published work or personal interviews with artists. Buys 12-18 mss/year. Query. Length: 1,000-2,500 words. Pays $75-300.
Tips: "We are devoted to the great variety of textiles, ceramics, jewelry and artifacts of Native American artists—in articles (with bibliographies) appealing to laymen and professionals."

ART NEW ENGLAND, A Resource for the Visual Arts, 353 Washington St., Brighton MA 02135. (617)782-3008. Editors: Carla Munsat, Stephanie Adelman. Visual arts tabloid published 10 times/year. Provides "a comprehensive index for regional exhibitions, lectures and films. Articles focus on different aspects of painting, sculpture, graphics, crafts, photography, and architecture; features include interviews and profiles on new or established artists, curators and other leaders in the art community. Articles on the business of art and collecting are also included." Circ. 15,000. Pays on publication. Byline given. Submit seasonal/holiday material 2 months in advance. SASE. Sample copy $1.75; free writer's guidelines.
Nonfiction: Book excerpts and book reviews (fine arts, photography, crafts, architecture); interview/profile (on new and established artists, curators and other members of the art community); opinion (on artists' rights, etc.); personal experience (from artist's or curator's point of view); and photo feature (art). No articles or reviews *not* related to the visual arts. "We are only interested in art-related subjects." Buys 30 mss/year. Query with resume and clips. Length: 900-1,500 words (features only). Pays $50 maximum features only; reviews less.
Tips: "Features and reviews are most open to freelancers."

‡**ART TIMES, Cultural and Creative News**, Box 730, Mount Marion NY 12456. (914)246-5170. Editor: Raymond J. Steiner. 10% (just fiction and poetry) freelance written. Monthly tabloid covering the arts (visual, theatre, dance, etc.). "*Art Times* covers the art fields and is distributed in locations most frequented by those enjoying the arts. Our 15,000 copies are distributed throughout three upstate New York counties rich in the arts as well as in most of the galleries in Soho, 57th Street and Madison Avenue in the metropolitan area; locations include theatres, galleries, museums, cultural centers and the like. Our readers are mostly over 40, affluent, art-conscious and sophisticated." Estab. 1984. Circ. 15,000. Pays on publication. Publishes ms an average of 4 months after acceptance. Byline given. Not copyrighted. Buys first serial rights. Submit seasonal/holiday material 3 months in advance. Simultaneous queries, and simultaneous and photocopied submissions OK. SASE. Reports in 1 month on queries; 3 months on mss. Sample copy for SAE and 3 first class stamps; writer's guidelines for business size envelope and 1 first class stamp.
Fiction: "We're looking for short fiction that aspires to be *literary*. No excessive violence, sexist, off-beat, erotic, sports, or juvenile fiction." Buys 8-10 mss/year. Send complete ms. Length: 1,500 maximum. Pays $15 maximum (honorarium).
Poetry: Poet's Niche. Avant-garde, free verse, haiku, light verse, and traditional. "We prefer well-crafted 'literary' poems. No excessively sentimental poetry." Buys 30-35 poems/year. Submit maximum 6 poems. Length: 80 lines maximum. Offers contributor copies.
Tips: "Be familiar with *Art Times* and its special audience. *Art Times* has literary leanings with articles written by a staff of scholars knowledgable in their respective fields. Our readers expect quality. Although an 'arts' publication, we observe no restrictions (other than noted) in accepting fiction/poetry other than a concern for quality writing—subjects can cover anything and not specifically arts."

THE ARTIST'S MAGAZINE, F&W Publishing Co., 9933 Alliance Rd., Cincinnati OH 45242. Editor: Michael Ward. 60% freelance written. Monthly magazine covering art instruction. "Ours is a highly visual approach to teaching the serious amateur artist techniques that will help him improve his skills and market his work. The style should be crisp and immediately engaging." Estab. 1984. Circ. 150,000. Pays on acceptance. Publishes ms an average of 6 months after acceptance. Byline given. Offers 20% kill fee. Buys first North American serial rights and second serial (reprint) rights. Submit seasonal/holiday material 6 months in advance. Simultaneous queries, and photocopied and previously published submissions OK "as long as noted as such." Computer printout submissions acceptable; no dot-matrix. SASE. Reports in 1 month. Sample copy $2 with 9x12 SAE plus postage; free writer's guidelines.
Nonfiction: Book excerpts; how-to (every aspect of technique for painting, drawing and business of art; use new product or media); and inspirational (how an artist may have succeeded through hard work, determination, etc.). No unillustrated articles. Buys 60 mss/year. Query. Length: 500-2,500 words. Pays $50-350. Sometimes pays expenses of writers on assignment.
Photos: "Photos are required with every sort of article and are essential in any instructional piece." Reviews 35mm color slides or 3x5 transparencies. Payment is for the "package" of slide, text and captions. Captions required. Buys one-time rights.
Columns/Departments: Book reviews; The Artist's Life (brief items about art and artists); and P.S. (1-page humorous look at art). Buys 100 mss/year. Send complete ms. Length: 200 words for book reviews; 400-600 words for the The Artist's Life; 300-400 words for P.S. Pays $30 for book reviews; $50-100 for The Artist's Life; and $50-100 for P.S.
Tips: "Look at several issues carefully and read the author's guidelines carefully. We are especially happy to get excellent visuals which illustrate the article and the four-color separations for such visuals."

ARTS MAGAZINE, 23 E. 26th St., New York NY 10010. (212)685-8500. Editor: Richard Martin. Monthly, except July and August. Journal of contemporary art, art criticism, analysis and history, particularly for artists, scholars, museum officials, art teachers and students, and collectors. Circ. 28,500. Pays on publication. Buys all rights. SASE.

Nonfiction: Art criticism, analysis and history. Topical reference to museum or gallery exhibition preferred. Query. Length: 1,500-2,500 words. Pays $100, with opportunity for negotiation.

Photos: B&w glossies or color transparencies customarily supplied by related museums or galleries.

FORMAT: ART & THE WORLD, Seven Oaks Press, 405 S. 7th St., St. Charles IL 60174. (312)584-0187. Editor: Ms. C.L. Morrison. 70% freelance written. Quarterly magazine covering art and society. "Our audience consists of three groups: artists wanting to know more about survival and their effectiveness in the current art system (visual and other arts); women exploring their role, opportunities, and situation in the art world; and writer/editors involved in the small-press literary community. We are practical, straight-talking and nonsexist—not a glossy coffee-table art magazine, but instead a budget-conscious vehicle by which creative people can communicate ideas, experiences and proposals for change. Subscribers are 30% Midwest, 20% West Coast, 20% East Coast, with the rest scattered in the US and a tiny segment of Europe." Circ. 700. Pays on publication. Publishes ms an average of 1 month after acceptance. Byline given. "We copyright for the author; some assignments are on a work-for-hire basis." Buys first serial rights. Photocopied submissions OK. SASE. Reports in 1 month. Sample copy $3.

Nonfiction: Opinion, personal experience, and some historical subjects involving a new interpretation. "Subjects we are particularly interested in now include: artists as workers (self-employment and being an employee); artist's social role; proposals for education of artists; how artists make their work known; using art-knowledge in everyday life; how artists can affect the direction of industry and consumer preference; opinions about government funding; how current society affects current art; how past society and living conditions affected past art; and artists' personal experiences with one thing or another—i.e., real life episodes. No articles that say, 'I don't understand modern art—it's all a bunch of junk stuff,' or murder mysteries in which the hard working cop is uplifted by the artist-victim's work." Send complete ms. Length: 300-3,000 words. Pays $5-15 plus up to 1 pound of contributor copies.

Fiction: "Art-related, or 'odd' subjects." Buys 10 mss/year. Length: 250-1,000 words. Pays $5-15 and/or 1 pound of contributor copies.

Poetry: Avant-garde, free verse and traditional. Poetry should be subject-oriented. Subjects are social critique, art and sex-role identity. No "romantic, organic sense-impressions, word-pictures, pure language, and so forth." Buys 25 poems/year. Submit maximum 10 poems. Length: 8-40 lines. Pays 1 pound of contributor copies.

Tips: "A writer can break in with us by being straightforward, outspoken, original, well-informed, individualistic, concerned. Our general tone, however, is not angry. We are often quite light and humorous. Try to avoid 'complaining' and feature concrete observation, evaluation and proposals. We would like to receive more articles and interviews—well-written and not repeats of information published 1,000 times before. If the writer has no real-life experience (i.e., is all textbooks and academia), forget it. Material should be knowledgable, but not so remote as to lack everyday application."

GLASS CRAFT NEWS, The Monthly Magazine for Stained Glass Enthusiasts, Edge Publishing Group, Room 1310, 270 Lafayette St., New York NY 10012. (212)966-6694. Editor: David Ostiller. Bimonthly magazine covering stained glass. "Our readers are stained glass hobbyists. We are interested in articles that are useful to them, rather than merely interesting." Circ. 40,000. Pays on publication. Byline given. Offers $25 kill fee. Buys first North American serial rights. Simultaneous queries, and simultaneous, photocopied and previously published submissions OK. Computer printout submissions acceptable. SASE. Reports in 2 weeks on queries; 1 month on mss. Sample copy for 9x12 SAE and 71¢ postage; writer's guidelines for 4x9½ SAE and 1 first class stamp.

Nonfiction: How-to (anything related to stained glass); interview/profile (of stained glass craftsmen); new product; and technical. "We like articles on techniques, features on individuals who are doing interesting work in glass (with emphasis on the technical aspects of their work), and marketing tips. We also want articles on subjects other than glass, which would be of use to hobbyists, e.g., cabinetmaking, lighting techniques and glass photography. We are not interested in nonpractical articles, such as stories about church windows or Louis Tiffany." Buys 30 mss/year. Query. Length: 750-2,000 words. Pays $50-200.

Photos: State availability of photos. Pays $5-25 for color contact sheets, transparencies and 8x10 prints. Identification of subjects required. Buys one-time rights.

Tips: "Freelancers should have a reasonable understanding of the crafts field, particularly stained glass. We get too many articles from people who are not familiar with their subject."

METALSMITH, Society of North American Goldsmiths, 6707 N. Santa Monica Blvd., Milwaukee WI 53217-3940. Editor: Sarah Bodine. Editorial address: 1 Penn Lyle Rd., Princeton Jct. NJ 08550. Quarterly magazine covering craft metalwork and metal arts for people who work in metal and those interested in the field, including museum curators, collectors and teachers. The magazine covers all aspects of the craft including historical and technical articles, business and marketing advice and exhibition reviews. Circ. 3,000. Pays on publication. Byline given. Buys first North American serial rights. Submit seasonal/holiday material 6 months in advance. Photocopied and previously published submissions (foreign) OK. Computer printout submissions acceptable; prefers letter-quality to dot-matrix. SASE. Reports in 1 month on queries; 6 weeks on mss.

Nonfiction: Expose (metals, markets, theft); historical/nostalgic; how-to (advanced-level metalsmithing techniques); humor; inspirational; interview/profile; opinion (regular column); personal experience; photo feature; technical (research); and travel (Metalsmith's Guides to Cities). Special issues include Annual Summer Program Listing and Suppliers Listing. Buys 15 mss/year. Recent article example: "Beyond the Bench: Production Jewelers and How They Survive" (1984). Query with clips of published work and indicate "experience in the field or related fields." Length: 1,000-3,500 words. Pays $25-400/article.

Columns/Departments: Exhibition reviews; Issues: Galleries, Marketing and Business Advice, Metalsmith's Guides to Cities and Regions, and Book Reviews. Buys 20 mss/year. Query with clips of published work. Length: 250-3,000 words. Pays $25-100/article.

Tips: "The discovery of new talent is a priority—queries about innovative work which has not received much publicity are welcome. Almost all our writing is done by freelancers. Those knowledgable in the field and who have previous experience in writing analysis and criticism are most sought after. *Metalsmith* is looking to build a stable of crafts writers and so far have found these few and far between. Those who have both a feeling for metalwork of all kinds and a sharp pencil are sought. Articles must have some substance. We do run two-page spreads, so an idea submitted must have thematic unity and depth. We are not looking for pretty pictures of metalwork, but analysis, presentation of new or undiscovered talent and historical documentation. A few lines of explanation of a story idea are therefore helpful."

THE ORIGINAL ART REPORT, Box 1641, Chicago IL 60690. Editor and Publisher: Frank Salantrie. 1% freelance written. Emphasizes "visual art conditions from the visual artists' and general public's perspectives." Newsletter; 6 pages. Pays on publication. Publishes ms an average of 2 months after acceptance. SASE. Reports in 4 weeks. Sample copy $1.25 and 1 first class stamp.

Nonfiction: Expose (art galleries, government agencies ripping off artists, or ignoring them); historical (perspective pieces relating to now); humor (whenever possible); informational (material that is unavailable in other art publications); inspirational (acts and ideas of courage); interview (with artists, other experts; serious material); personal opinion; technical (brief items to recall traditional methods of producing art); travel (places in the world where artists are welcome and honored); philosophical, economic, aesthetic, and artistic. "No vanity profiles of artists, arts organizations, and arts promoters' operations." Buys 4-5 mss/year. Query or submit complete ms. Length: 1,000 words maximum. Pays 1¢/word.

Columns/Departments: New column: In Back of the Individual Artist. "Artists express their views about non-art topics. After all, artists are in this world, too"; WOW (Worth One Wow), Worth Repeating, and Worth Repeating Again. "Basically, these are reprint items with introduction to give context and source, including complete name and address of publication. Looking for insightful, succinct commentary." Submit complete ms. Length: 500 words maximum. Pays ½¢/word.

Tips: "I get excited when ideas are proposed which address substantive problems of individual artists in the art condition and as they affect the general population. Send original material that is direct and to the point, opinionated and knowledgable. Write in a factual style with clarity. No straight educational or historical stuff, please. All material must be original or unique." Recent article example: "On the Mysteries of Success" (vol. 8, no. 1). Send SASE with 1 first class stamp for sample copy.

PLATE WORLD, The Magazine of Collector's Plates, Plate World Ltd., 6054 W. Touhy, Chicago IL 60648. (312)763-7773. Acting Editor: Alyson Sulaski Wyckoff. Feature Editor: Richard Lalich. 5% freelance written. Bimonthly magazine. "We write exclusively about limited-edition collector's plates—artists, makers, dealers and collectors. Our audience is involved in plates mostly as collectors; also dealers, makers or producers." Circ. 75,000. Pays on acceptance. Publishes ms an average of 3 months after acceptance. Byline given. Offers 50% kill fee. Buys various rights. Submit seasonal/holiday material 5 months in advance. Computer printout submissions acceptable; prefers letter-quality to dot-matrix. Reports in 1 month on queries; 2 weeks on mss. Sample copy $3.50; free writer's guidelines. Pays some expenses of writers on assignment—"travel plus phone."

Nonfiction: Interview/profile (how artists create, biography of artist, profile of exceptional plate collector); exceptional plate collectors or short dealer profiles for our departments. Also, we have a back-of-the-book department (Backstamp) where we publish short items of interest." No critical attacks on industry. No articles on antique plates. Buys 10 mss/year. Query and send samples of work. Pays $100-500.

Photos: Albert Scharpov, art director. Human interest, technical. State availability of photos. Reviews transparencies. Pays negotiable rate. Identification of subjects required. Usually buys all rights, occasionally buys one-time rights.

Tips: Profiles of artists working in plates is the area most open to freelancers. "The most frequent mistakes made by writers in completing an article for use are: not enough research, profiles not objective, articles too promotional. Also, writers must understand our editorial content—*only* limited-edition collector's plates (no antiques, etc.)"

SOUTHWEST ART, Box 13037, Houston TX 77219. (713)850-0990. Editor: Susan Hallsten McGarry. 80% freelance written. Emphasizes art—painting and sculpture. Monthly. Pays on tenth of the month of publication. Publishes ms an average of 8 months after acceptance. Buys all rights to ms (not artwork). Photocopied submissions OK. Computer printout submissions acceptable; no dot-matrix. SASE. Reports in 4 months. Sample copy $6.
Nonfiction: Informational, interview, personal opinion and profile. "We publish articles about artists and art trends, concentrating on a geographical area west of the Mississippi. Articles should explore the artist's personality, philosophy, media and techniques, and means by which they convey ideas." Buys 100 mss/year. Must submit 20 color prints/transparencies along with a full biography of the artist. If artist is accepted, article length is 1,800-2,000 words minimum. Pays on sliding scale to $300. Sometimes pays the expenses of writers on assignment.
Tips: The writer has a better chance of breaking in at *Southwest Art* with short, lesser-paying articles and fillers (rather than with major features) because "short pieces, skillfully handled, are an excellent gauge of feature writing potential. Submit both published and unpublished samples of your writing. An indication of how quickly you work and your availability on short notice is helpful."

Association, Club and Fraternal

Association publications enable writers to write for national audiences while covering a local story of national interest. If your town has a Kiwanis, Lions, or Rotary Club chapter, one of its projects might merit a story in the club's magazine. Some association magazines circulate worldwide. These publications link members who live continents from one another or in the same town. They keep members, friends and institutions informed of the ideals, objectives, projects, and activities of the sponsoring club. Club-financed magazines that carry material not directly related to the group's activities (for example, *The American Legion Magazine* in the General Interest section) are classified by their subject matter in the Consumer and Trade Journals sections of this book.

‡● **BFG TODAY**, The BFGoodrich Company, 500 S. Main St., Akron OH 44318. (216)374-2255. Editor: Janice L. Frobes. 25% freelance written. Quarterly magazine for employees and retirees of the BFGoodrich Company, manufacturer of chemicals, plastics, tires and engineered products. "*BFG Today* seeks to help readers understand how the company operates and how internal issues and trends affect it. Circ. 40,000. Pays on acceptance. Publishes ms an average of 3 months after acceptance. Byline given. Makes work-for-hire assignments. Submit seasonal/holiday material 6 months in advance. No simultaneous queries, or simultaneous, photocopied, or previously pulished submissions. Computer printout submissions acceptable; prefers letter-quality to dot-matrix. SASE. Reports in 1 month. Free sample copy and guidelines.
Nonfiction: General interest, how-to, humor, interview/profile, new product and technical. Buys 8 mss/year. Query with published clips. Length: 600-2,500 words. Pays $300 minimum. Pays expenses of writers on assignment.
Tips: "Query the magazine with business, industry or how-to story ideas that will be of interest to our readers. Include samples of published writing, preferably previously published in other corporate magazines."

CALIFORNIA HIGHWAY PATROLMAN, California Association of Highway Patrolmen, 2030 V St., Sacramento CA 95818. (916)452-6751. Editor: Carol Perri. 80% freelance written. Monthly magazine. Circ. 20,000. Pays on publication. Publishes ms an average of 6 months after acceptance. Buys one-time rights. Computer printout submissions acceptable. SASE. Reports in 2 months. Free sample copy and writer's guidelines.
Nonfiction: Publishes articles on transportation safety, driver education, consumer interest, humor and general interest. "Topics can include autos, boats, bicycles, motorcycles, snowmobiles, recreational vehicles and pedestrian safety. We are also in the market for California travel pieces and articles on early California. We are *not* a technical journal for teachers and traffic safety experts, but rather a general interest publication geared toward the layman." Pays 2½¢/word.
Photos: "Illustrated articles always receive preference." Pays $2.50/b&w photo. Captions required.

CATHOLIC FORESTER, Catholic Order of Foresters, 425 W. Shuman Blvd., Naperville IL 60566. (312)983-4920. Editor: Barbara Cunningham. 50% freelance written. A bimonthly magazine of short, general interest articles and fiction for members of the Order which is a fraternal insurance company. Family type audience, middle class. Circ. 150,000. Pays on acceptance. Publishes ms an average of 6 months after acceptance. Byline given. Buys one-time rights, second serial (reprint) rights, and simultaneous rights. Submit seasonal/holiday material 6 months in advance. Simultaneous queries, and simultaneous, photocopied, and previously published submissions OK. SASE. Reports in 3 weeks on queries; 6 weeks on ms. Sample copy for 8¹/₂x11 SAE and 73¢ postage; free writer's guidelines.
Nonfiction: General interest; historical/nostalgic; how-to (carpentry, cooking, repairs, etc.) humor; inspirational; interview/profile; new product; opinion; personal experience; photo feature; technical (depends on subject); and travel. No blatant sex nor anything too violent. Query with published clips, or send complete ms. Length: 1,000-3,000 words. Pays $50 minimum.
Photos: Prefers something of unusual interest or story-telling. State availability of photos, or send photos with query or ms. Reviews any size b&w and color prints. Payment to be determined. Captions, model releases, and identification of subjects required. Buys one-time rights.
Columns/Departments: Needs unusual items on what is going on in the world; new, interesting products or discoveries. Query or send complete ms. Length: 1,000 words. Payment to be determined.
Fiction: Adventure, historical, humorous, mainstream, mystery, religious (Catholic), romance, suspense and western. No sex or extreme violence. Length: 1,200-5,000 words. Pays $50 minimum.
Poetry: Free verse, Haiku, light verse, traditional. Submit maximum 5 poems. Payment to be determined.
Fillers: Jokes, anecdotes, short humor. Length: 300-500 words. Payment to be determined.
Tips: "Short feature articles of interest to the all-American type are most open to freelancers."

CBIA NEWS, Journal of the Connecticut Business and Industry Association. CBIA Service Corp., 370 Asylum St., Hartford CT 06103. (203)547-1661. Editor: Mara Braverman. 30% freelance written. A monthly tabloid (except combined July/August issue) covering business in Connecticut for approximately 6,500 member companies. Half of the *News* is about the association and written in-house. Other half is about how to run your business better; interesting businesspeople in Connecticut, and business trends here. These are sometimes written by freelancers. Circ. 7,200. Pays on acceptance. Publishes ms an average of 5 months after acceptance. Byline given. Offers 20% kill fee. Buys variable rights; can be negotiable. Photocopied and previously published submissions OK if not published in competing publication. Computer printout submissions acceptable; prefers letter-quality to dot-matrix. SASE. Reports in 2 weeks. Free sample copy.
Nonfiction: Book excerpts, how-to (how to run your business better in some specific way); interview/profile (must be a Connecticut person). Buys approximately 20 mss/year. Query with published clips. Length and payment vary with the subject.
Photos: State availability of photos with query or ms. Reviews b&w contact sheets. Pays negotiable rate. Model release and identification of subjects required.
Tips: "Write to me including resume and clips. They do *not* have to be from business publications. If I'm interested, I'll contact you and describe fees, rules, etc. The most frequent mistakes made by writers are relying too heavily on one or two sources and letting sources promote themselves in the article."

CHARIOT, Ben Hur Life Association, Box 312, Crawfordsville IN 47933. (317)362-4500. Editor: Loren Harrington. A quarterly magazine covering fraternal activities plus general interest items. Circ. 11,000. Pays on acceptance. Publishes ms an average of 2 months after acceptance. Byline given. Not copyrighted. Buys variable rights. Submit seasonal/holiday material 10 months in advance. Simultaneous queries, and simultaneous and photocopied submissions OK. Computer printout submissions acceptable; prefers letter-quality to dot-matrix. SASE. Reports in 2 weeks on queries; 1 month on mss. Sample copy for 9x12 SAE and 4 first class stamps—for *serious* inquiries only; writer's guidelines for business size SASE and 2 first class stamps.
Nonfiction: General interest, historical and how-to. "Absolutely *nothing* of a smutty, sexually-oriented, gay, etc. nature. Only items of benefit to our readers and/or family would be considered." Rarely buys mss. Query with or without published clips, or send complete ms. Length: 300-3,500 words. Pays 3-20¢/word.
Photos: State availability of photos with query letter or ms. "We would like to have quality photo with query. We will return if rejected." Reviews b&w and color contact sheets and b&w and color prints. Payment for photos included in payment for mss. Captions, model release and identification of subjects required. Buys one-time rights.
Columns/Departments: Columns are editorial or insurance-related. "Would consider a query piece, but it would have to be extremely applicable."
Fiction: "Absolutely *nothing* of a smutty, sexually-oriented, gay etc. nature. Only stories of benefit to our readers and/or family would be considered." Query with or without published clips or send complete ms. Length: 300-2,500 words. Pays 3-20¢/word.
Poetry: Light verse and traditional. "Poetry not normally used, but would consider short snappy poems as filler material." Length: open. Pays 3-20¢/word.
Fillers: Jokes, gags, anecdotes, short humor and newsbreaks. Rarely buys fillers. Length: open. Pays $1-20.

Tips: "Our requirements are very tightly edited and professionally written with a wide appeal to our particular audience, self-help volunteer and charity. Those items that we can give our local units to encourage their fraternal participation and projects would be considered more than any other single submitted features. Only on rare occasions in the past have we looked to outside submitted features. Our current procedures, however, will probably tend to encourage such things in the future."

‡**D.A.C. NEWS**, Detroit Athletic Club, 241 Madison Ave., Detroit MI 48226. Editor: John H. Worthington. 3% freelance written. For business and professional men. Much of the magazine is devoted to member activities, including social events and athletic activities at the club. Magazine published 9 times/year. Pays after publication. Publishes ms an average of 2 months after acceptance. Buys first rights. Byline given. SASE. Reports in 1 month. Sample copy for 9x12 SASE.
Nonfiction: General interest articles, usually male-oriented, about sports (pro football, baseball, squash, golf, skiing and tennis); travel (to exclusive resorts and offbeat places); drama; personalities; health (jogging, tennis elbow, coronary caution); and some humor, if extremely well-done. Some nostalgia (football greats, big band era are best examples). "We would like to see articles on eccentric millionaires, sunken treasure, the world's biggest yacht, old English pubs, the economy, football's greatest games, offbeat resorts and gourmet foods." Buys 5-6 unsolicited mss/year. Send complete ms. Length: 750-3,000 words. Pays $50-250.
Photos: Send photos with ms. Offers no additional payment for photos accepted with mss.
Tips: "Tell us your story idea and where you have been published previously. Give us a brief synopsis of one idea. Quality, not length is the factor. Express a cheerful willingness to rewrite along our lines."

THE ELKS MAGAZINE, 425 W. Diversey, Chicago IL 60614. Managing Editor: Herbert Gates. 50% freelance written. Emphasizes general interest with family appeal. Magazine published 10 times/year. 48 pages. Circ. 1,600,000. Pays on acceptance. Publishes mss an average of 6 months after acceptance. Buys first North American serial rights. Computer printout submissions acceptable; no dot-matrix. SASE. Reports in 6 weeks. Free sample copy and writer's guidelines.
Nonfiction: Articles of information, business, contemporary life problems and situations, or just interesting topics, ranging from medicine, science, and history, to sports. "The articles should not just be a rehash of existing material. They must be fresh, provocative, thought provoking, well researched and documented. No fiction, travel or political articles, fillers or verse. Buys 2-3 mss/issue. Written query a must. No phone queries. Length 2,000-3,000 words. Pays $150-500.
Photos: Purchased with or without accompanying manuscript (for cover). Captions required. Query with b&w photos or send transparencies. Uses 8x10 or 5x7 b&w glossies and 35mm or 2¹/₄x2¹/₄ color transparencies (for cover). Pays $250 minimum for color (cover). Offers no additional payment for photos accepted with mss.
Tips: "Requirements are clearly specified in our guidelines and our repeat contributors follow them closely. Loose, wordy pieces are not accepted. A submission, following a query letter go-ahead would do best to include several b&w prints, if the piece lends itself to illustration."

4-H LEADER, The National Magazine for 4-H, (formerly *The National 4-H News*), 7100 Connecticut Ave., Chevy Chase MD 20815. (301)656-9000, ext. 203. Editor: Suzanne C. Harting. 20% freelance written. Monthly magazine for "volunteers of a wide range of ages who lead 4-H clubs; most with college education whose primary reason for reading us is their interest in working with kids in informal youth education projects, ranging from aerospace to sewing, and almost anything in between." Circ. 70,000. Pays on acceptance. Publishes ms an average of 3 months after acceptance. Buys first serial rights or one-time rights. Submit seasonal material 1 year in advance. Computer printout submissions acceptable. SASE. Reports in 1 month. Free sample copy and writer's guidelines.
Nonfiction: Education and child psychology from authorities, written in light, easy-to-read fashion with specific suggestions how the layman can apply principles in volunteer work with youth; how-to pieces about genuinely new and interesting crafts of any kind. "Carft articles must be fresh in style and ideas, and tell how to make something worthwhile . . . almost anything that tells about kids having fun and learning outside the classroom, including how they became interested, most effective programs, etc., always with enough detail and example, so reader can repeat project or program with his or her group, merely by reading the article. Speak directly to our reader (you) without preaching. Tell them in a conversational manner how they might work better with kids to help them have fun and learn at the same time. Use lots of genuine examples (although names and dates are not important) to illustrate points. Use contractions when applicable. Write in a concise, interesting way. Our readers have other jobs and not a lot of time to spend with us. Will not print personal reminiscences, stories on 'how this 4-H club made good' or about state or county fair winners." Length: 3-8 pages, typewritten, double-spaced. Payment up to $200, depending on quality and accompanying photos or illustrations.
Photos: State availability of photos. "Photos must be genuinely candid, of excellent technical quality and preferably shot in 'available light' or in that style; must show young people or adults and young people having fun learning something. How-to photos or drawings must supplement instructional texts. Photos do not necessarily have to include people. Photos are usually purchased with accompanying ms, with no additional payment. Captions required. If we use an excellent single photo, we generally pay $25 and up."

Tips: "We are very specialized, and unless a writer has been published in our magazine before, he more than likely doesn't have a clue to what we can use. When query comes about a specific topic, we often can suggest angles that make it usable." There will be more emphasis on interpersonal skills, techniques for working with kids, more focus on the family. Write for a sample copy. I judge a writer's technical skills by the grammer and syntax of his query letter; I seldom ask for a manuscript I think will require extensive reorganization or heavy editing."

●**GRACE DIGEST**, W.R. Grace & Co., 1114 Avenue of Americas, New York NY 10036. (212)819-6003. Editor: Joyce Cole. A semiannual magazine covering Grace products and people; company divisions and subsidiaries. "Articles are written in lay terms for shareholders and all Grace employees." Circ. 125,000. Computer printout submissions acceptable; no dot-matrix. SASE. Free sample copy.
Nonfiction: Interview/profile, and technical (in lay terms). Buys 4 mss/year. Query with published clips. Pays competitive rates.
Photos: State availability of photos. Captions, model release and identification of subjects required.

KIWANIS, 3636 Woodview Trace, Indianapolis IN 46268. Executive Editor: Chuck Jonak. 90% of feature articles freelance written. Magazine published 10 times/year for business and professional men and their families. Circ. 300,000. Pays on acceptance. Buys first North American serial rights. Pays 20-40% kill fee. Publishes ms an average of 6 months after acceptance. Byline given. Computer printout submissions acceptable "if clear, paper is of good quality, and print is of typewriter quality." Separate sheets before submission. SASE. Reports in 1 month. Sample copy and writer's guidelines for 9x12 SAE and 75¢ postage.
Nonfiction: Articles about social and civic betterment, business, education, religion, family, sports, health, recreation, etc. Emphasis on objectivity, intelligent analysis and thorough research of contemporary problems. Concise, lively writing, absence of cliches, and impartial presentation of controversy required. Especially needs articles on business and professional topics that will directly assist the readers in their own businesses (generally independent retailers and companies of less than 25 employees) or careers. "We have an increasing need for articles of international interest and those that will enlighten our readers about the needs of underprivileged children." Length: 2,500-3,000 words. Pays $300-750. "No fiction, personal essays, fillers or verse of any kind. A light or humorous approach welcomed where subject is appropriate and all other requirements are observed. Detailed queries can save work and submission time."
Photos: "We often accept photos submitted with manuscripts, but we do not pay extra for them; they are considered part of the price of the manuscript. Our rate for a manuscript with good photos is higher than for one without." Model release and identification of subjects required. Buys one-time rights.
Tips: "Feature section is open to freelancers. First, obtain writer's guidelines and sample copy. Study for general style and content. Present well-researched, smoothly written manuscript. When querying, present detailed outline of proposed manuscript's focus, direction, and editorial intent. Indicate expert sources to be used for attribution, as well as article's tone and length."

THE LION, 300 22nd St., Oak Brook IL 60570. (312)986-1700. Editor-in-Chief: Roy Schaetzel. Senior Editor: Robert Kleinfelder. 40% freelance written. Covers service club organization for Lions Club members and their families. Monthly magazine; 56 pages. Circ. 670,000. Pays on acceptance. Publishes ms an average of 5 months after acceptance. Buys all rights. Byline given. Phone queries OK. Photocopied submissions OK. SASE. Reports in 2 weeks. Free sample copy and writer's guidelines.
Nonfiction: Informational (stories of interest to civic-minded men) and photo feature (must be of a Lions Club service project). No travel, biography, or personal experiences. No sensationalism. Prefers anecdotes in articles. Buys 4 mss/issue. Query. Length: 500-2,200. Pays $50-400.
Photos: Purchased with or without accompanying ms or on assignment. Captions required. Query for photos. B&w and color glossies at least 5x7 or 35mm color slides. Total purchase price for ms includes payment for photos, accepted with ms. "Be sure photos are clear and as candid as possible."
Tips: "Incomplete details on how the Lions involved actually carried out a project and poor quality photos are the most frequent mistakes made by writers in completing an article assignment for us."

THE MODERN WOODMEN, 1701 1st Ave., Rock Island IL 61201. (309)786-6481. Editor: Gloria Bergh. "Our publication is for families who are members of Modern Woodmen of America. Modern Woodmen is a fraternal life insurance society, and most of our members live in smaller communities or rural areas throughout the United States. Various age groups read the magazine." 100% freelance written. Quarterly magazine, 24 pages. Circ. 350,000. Not copyrighted. Pays on acceptance. Publishes ms an average of 6 months after acceptance. Buys one-time rights and simultaneous rights. Photocopied and simultaneous submissions OK. Reports in one month if SASE included. Computer printout submissions acceptable. Sample copy and guidelines for SAE and 2 first class stamps.
Nonfiction: For children and adults. We seek lucid style and rich content. We want articles that appeal to young families, emphasize family interaction, community involvement, family life. We also consider educational, historical and patriotic articles. We don't want religious articles or teen romances. $50 minimum. Length:

1,000-1,200 words.
Photos: B&w and color photos purchased with ms. Captions optional. Payment varies with quality and need.
Fiction: Most of the fiction we publish is for children and teens. We stress plot and characterization. A moral is a pleasant addition but not required.
Tips: "Focus on people, whether the article is about families, or is educational, historical or patriotic. We don't choose articles because we've published that author before. If the material and style are right, we use it—if not, we don't."

THE OPTIMIST MAGAZINE, Optimist International, 4494 Lindell Blvd., St. Louis MO 63108. (314)371-6000. Editor: Dennis R. Osterwisch. Assistant Editor: Kathy Robertson. 20% freelance written. Monthly magazine about the work of Optimist clubs and members for the 148,000 members of the Optimist clubs in the United States and Canada. Circ. 152,000. Pays on acceptance. Publishes ms an average of 4 months after acceptance. Buys first North American serial rights. Submit seasonal material 3 months in advance. Photocopied and previously published submissions OK. Computer printout submissions acceptable; prefers letter-quality to dot-matrix. SASE. Reports in 1 week. Sample copy and writer's guidelines for SAE and 4 first class stamps.
Nonfiction: General interest (people, places and things that would interest men dedicated to community service through volunteer work); interview (members who have in some way distinguished themselves). No articles of a negative nature. "We are always looking for articles about Optimist Club activities and individuals who are members. Good action photos are always a plus. We are also open to articles of a motivational nature; motivating our readers to succeed in their Optimist work, their profession, and their personal life. No religious-oriented material." Buys 2-3 mss/issue. Query. "Submit a letter that conveys your ability to turn out a well-written article and tells exactly what the scope of the article will be and whether photos are available." Length: 1,000-1,500 words. Pays $100-150.
Photos: State availability of photos. Payment negotiated. Captions preferred. Buys all rights. "No mug shots or people lined up against the wall shaking hands. We're always looking for good color photos relating to Optimist activities that could be used on our front cover. Colors must be sharp and the composition must be suitable to fit an 8^{1}/$_{2}$x11 cover."
Tips: Find out what the Optimist clubs in your area are doing, then find out if we'd be interested in an article on a specific club project. All of our clubs are eager to talk about what they're doing. Just ask them and you'll probably have an article idea.

PERSPECTIVE, Pioneer Clubs, Division of Pioneer Ministries, Inc., Box 788, Wheaton IL 60189-0788. (312)293-1600. Editor: Lorraine Mulligan Davis. 5% freelance written. "All subscribers are volunteer leaders of clubs for girls and boys in grades 1-12. Clubs are sponsored by evangelical churches throughout North America." Quarterly magazine; 32 pages. Circ. 24,000. Pays on acceptance. Publishes ms an average of 6 months after acceptance. Buys first North American serial rights and second serial (reprint) rights to material originally published elsewhere. Submit seasonal/holiday material 9 months in advance. Simultaneous submissions OK. Computer printout submissions acceptable if double-spaced; no dot-matrix. SASE. Reports in 6 weeks. Writer's packet $1.50; includes writer's guidelines and sample magazine.
Nonfiction: How-to (projects for clubs, crafts, cooking, service);informational (relationships, human development, mission education, outdoor activities); inspirational (Bible studies, adult leading youths); interview (Christian education leaders); personal experience (of club leaders). Buys 4-10 mss/year; 3 unsolicited/year. Byline given. Query. Length: 200-1,500 words. Pays $10-60.
Columns/Departments: Storehouse (craft, game, activity, outdoor activity suggestions—all related to club projects for any age between grades 1-12). Buys 4-6 mss/year. Submit complete ms. Length: 150-250 words. Pays $8-20.
Tips: "We only assign major features to writers who have proven previously that they know us and our constituency. Submit articles directly related to club work, practical in nature, i.e., ideas for leader training in communication, Bible knowledge, teaching skills. They must have practical application. We want substance— not ephemeral ideas. In addition to a summary of the article idea and evidence that the writer has knowledge of the subject, we want evidence that the author understands our purpose and philosophy. We're doing more and more inhouse writing—less purchasing of any freelance."

‡**PRIVILEGE**, Published exclusively for ABC Members, Allied Consumer Services, 3906 Church Rd., Mount Laurel NJ 08054. (609)778-9400. Managing Editor: J.K. Bucsko. 60% freelance written. Quarterly magazine for members of Associated Bank Cardholders group. "Our readers are middle Americans, married, credit card holders; many have a college degree. Our purpose is to provide information that increases or enhances their knowledge of ABC membership benefits available to them; to offer advice and guidance about spending and investments; and to aid in planning and decision-making regarding purchases, leisure pursuits, financial management, etc." Circ. 115,000. Pays on acceptance. Publishes ms an average of 4 months after acceptance. Byline given. Buys simultaneous rights, and first serial rights. Submit seasonal/holiday material 3 months in advance. Simultaneous queries, and simultaneous, photocopied and previously published submis-

sions OK. Computer printout submissions acceptable; prefers letter-quality to dot-matrix. SASE. Reports in 2 weeks. Sample copy for 9x12 SAE and 6 first class stamps. Writer's guidelines for SAE and 1 first class stamp.

Nonfiction: Barbara A. Gauntt, articles editor. General interest, financial, how-to, humor, photo feature and travel. "Light humor pieces, particularly those that touch on family-oriented topics, or current trends, are always suitable." Buys 40 mss/year. Query. Length 1,200-3,500 words. Pays 20¢/word.

Photos: State availability of photos. Reviews color transparencies. Payment included with ms only. Buys one-time rights.

Columns/Departments: Barbara A. Gauntt, column/department editor. Finance and investments, homemaking and cooking, specific products and comparison shopping, household repairs and safety, and fashion. Buys 24/year. Send complete ms. Length: 1,200-1,500 words. Pays 20¢/word.

‡**REVIEW**, A Publication of North American Benefit Association, North American Benefit Association, 1338 Military St., Box 5020, Port Huron MI 48061-5020. (313)985-5191, ext. 77. Editor: Virginia E. Farmer. Associate Editor: Patricia Pfeifer. 15% freelance written. Quarterly trade journal on insurance/fraternal deeds. Family magazine. Circ. 35,000. Pays on acceptance. Publishes ms an average of 2 years after acceptance. Byline given. Not copyrighted. Buys one-time rights, simultaneous rights, and second serial (reprint) rights. Submit seasonal/holiday material 6 months in advance. Simultaneous, photocopied and previously published submissions OK. Computer printout submissions acceptable; no dot-matrix. SASE. Reports in 6 weeks. Sample copy for SAE.

Nonfiction: General interest, historical/nostalgic, how-to (improve; self-help); humor; inspirational; personal experience; and photo feature. No political/controversial. Buys 4-10 mss/year. Send complete ms. Length: 600-1,500 words. Pays 3-5¢/word.

Photos: Prefers ms with photos if available. Send photos with ms. Reviews b&w 5x7 or 8x10 prints. Pays $10-15. Model release and identification of subjects required. Buys one-time rights.

Fiction: Adventure, humorous and mainstream. Buys 2-4 mss/year. Send complete ms. Length: 600-1,500 words. Pays 3-5¢/word.

Tips: "We like articles with accompanying photos; articles that warm the heart; stories with gentle, happy humor. Give background of writer as to education and credits. Manuscripts and art material will be carefully considered, but received only with understanding that North American Benefit Association shall not be responsible for loss or injury."

THE ROTARIAN, Official Magazine of Rotary International, 1600 Ridge Ave., Evanston IL 60201. (312)328-0100. Editor: Willmon L. White. 50% freelance written. For Rotarian business and professional men and their families; for schools, libraries, hospitals, etc. Monthly. Circ. 488,000. Usually buys all rights. Pays on acceptance. Computer printout submissions acceptable; prefers letter-quality to dot-matrix. SASE. Reports in 1 month. Sample copy for SAE and 7 first class stamps; writer's guidelines for SAE and first class stamp.

Nonfiction: "The field for freelance articles is in the general interest category. These run the gamut from guidelines for daily living to such concerns as world hunger, the nuclear arms race, and preservation of environment. Recent articles have dealt with international illiteracy, energy, dehumanization of the elderly, and worldwide drug abuse and prevention. Articles should appeal to an international audience and should in some way help Rotarians help other people. An article may increase a reader's understanding of world affairs, thereby making him a better world citizen. It may educate him in civic matters, thus helping him improve his town. It may help him to become a better employer, or a better human being. We are interested in articles on unusual Rotary club projects or really unusual Rotarians. We carry debates and symposiums, but are careful to show more than one point of view. We present arguments for effective politics and business ethics, but avoid expose and muckraking. Controversy is welcome if it gets our readers to think but does not offend ethnic or religious groups. In short, the rationale of the organization is one of hope and encouragement and belief in the power of individuals talking and working together." Query preferred. Length: 1,000-2,000 words. Payment varies.

Photos: Purchased with mss or with captions only. Prefers $2\frac{1}{4}$x$2\frac{1}{4}$ or larger color transparencies, but also uses 35mm. B&w prints and photo essays. Vertical shots preferred to horizontal. Scenes of international interest. Color cover.

‡**THE SERTOMAN**, Sertoma International, 1912 E. Meyer Blvd., Kansas City MO 64132. (816)333-8300. Editor: Patrick W. Burke. Quarterly magazine with "service to mankind" as its motto edited for business and professionals. Circ 35,000. Pays on acceptance. Byline given. Buys one-time rights. Submit seasonal material 3 months in advance. Simultaneous, photocopied and previously published submissions OK. SASE. Reports in 2 weeks. Free sample copy.

Nonfiction: General interest (social civic issues, energy, finance, retirement, alcohol, drug abuse); and humor (in daily living). "We're especially interested in articles on speech and hearing, Sertoma's international sponsorship." Buys 2 mss/issue. Query with clips of previously published work. Length: 500-2,000 words. Pays $25-100.

Photos: Pays $5 minimum/5x7 b&w glossy prints. Captions and model release required. Buys one-time rights.

THE TOASTMASTER, Box 10400, Santa Ana CA 92711. (714)542-6793. Editor-in-Chief: Tamara Nunn. 40-50% freelance written. Covers communication and leadership techniques; self-development for members of Toastmasters International, Inc. Monthly magazine; 32 pages. Circ. 100,000. Pays on acceptance. Buys all rights. Byline given. Photocopied submissions and previously published work OK. SASE. Reports in 3 weeks. Free sample copy and writer's guidelines.
Nonfiction: How-to (improve speaking, listening, thinking skills; on leadership or management techniques, etc., with realistic examples); humor (on leadership, communications or management techniques); interviews (with communications or management experts offering advice that members can directly apply to their self-development efforts; should contain "how to" information). No articles on fear of speaking, time management, meeting planning or basic speaking techniques. Buys 20-30 mss/year. Query. Length: 1,800-3,000 words. Pays $25-150.
Photos: Purchased with or without ms. Query. Pays $10-50 for 5x7 or 8x10 b&w glossy prints; $35-75 for color transparencies. Offers no additional payment for photos accepted with ms.
Tips: "The most annoying aspect of working with freelance writers is their insistence on calling to find out when we'll publish their work. Trends in magazine publishing that freelance writers should be aware of include a tendency toward specialization—stories that require a writer to have personal knowledge (indepth) of a topic. Also, word processing can make or break a freelancer. One freelancer said his income has *tripled* since he acquired a word processor."

VACATION TIMES AND BUSINESS TRAVEL, Evening Star Inc. dba Airline Discount Club-International, Box 616, Parker CO 80134. (303)841-4337. Editor: Richard A. Bodner. 15% freelance written. A quarterly magazine available only to club members covering discounted accommodations, travel and other savings available through ADC-I. "We offer airline employee 'discount' prices to our members on a variety of accommodations, flights, car rentals and activities. Our format features money-saving tips for vacation and destination features for the areas in which we have properties available. Readers are mature adults with above average incomes." Circ. 2,000 +. Pays on acceptance. Publishes ms an average of 6 months after acceptance. Byline given. Buys one-time rights, simultaneous rights and second serial (reprint) rights. Submit seasonal/holiday material 6 months in advance. Simultaneous, photocopied, and previously published submissions OK. Computer printout submissions acceptable; prefers letter-quality to dot-matrix. SASE. Reports in 3 weeks. Sample copy $3; writer's guidelines 25¢.
Nonfiction: Historical/nostalgic, how-to, personal experience and travel. "Articles should relate to saving money while on vacation, features about destination, activities, background/history of area(s), bargain purchases, how to plan a vacation, tips for the business traveler, and others of interest to the vacationer. Do not send articles that are unrelated to areas in which we have properties available. No articles about camping, hunting, fishing." Buys 12-16 mss/year. Send complete ms. Length: 300-1,200 words. Pays $40-125. Photos are required with most articles.
Photos: Brad Margritz, photo editor. State availability of photos. Pays $5-15 for b&w slides and 3x4 prints. Captions and model release required. Buys one-time rights.
Tips: "All articles should be geared to the vacationer or business traveller interested in saving money or pertain to areas in which we offer discounted accommodations. We have added a number of hotels/motels in the U.S., Europe and the Caribbean that extend a direct discount to our members."

WOODMEN OF THE WORLD MAGAZINE, 1700 Farnam St., Omaha NE 68102. (402)342-1890, ext. 302. Editor: Leland A. Larson. 20% freelance written. Published by Woodmen of the World Life Insurance Society for "people of all ages in all walks of life. We have both adult and child readers from all types of American families." Monthly. Circ. 467,000. Not copyrighted. Buys 20 mss/year. Pays on acceptance. Byline given. Buys one-time rights. Publishes ms an average of 2 months after acceptance. Will consider photocopied and simultaneous submissions. Computer printout submissions acceptable; prefers letter-quality to dot-matrix. Submit seasonal material 3 months in advance. Reports in 5 weeks. SASE. Free sample copy.
Nonfiction: "General interest articles which appeal to the American family—travel, history, art, new products, how-to, sports, hobbies, food, home decorating, family expenses, etc. Because we are a fraternal benefit society operating under a lodge system, we often carry stories on how a number of people can enjoy social or recreational activities as a group. No special approach required. We want more 'consumer type' articles, humor, historical articles, think pieces, nostalgia, photo articles." Buys 15-24 unsolicited mss/year. Submit complete ms. Length: 2,000 words or less. Pays $10 minimum. 5¢/word depending on count.
Photos: Purchased with or without mss; captions optional "but suggested." Uses 8x10 glossy prints, 4x5 transparencies ("and possibly down to 35mm"). Payment "depends on use." For b&w photos, pays $25 for cover, $10 for inside. Color prices vary according to use and quality with $150 maximum. Minimum of $25 for inside use; up to $150 for covers.
Fiction: Humorous and historical short stories. Length: 1,500 words or less. Pays "$10 minimum or 5¢/word, depending on count."

Astrology and Psychic

Some writers explore life from an astrological or psychic perspective. If you want to write for these publications, read them first since each has an individual personality and approach to these phenomena. The following publications regard astrology, psychic phenomena, ESP experiences, and related subjects as sciences or as objects of serious study.

DOORWAYS TO THE MIND, Aries Productions, Inc., Box 29396, Sappington MO 63126. Editor: Beverly C. Jaegers. Managing Editor: G. Weingart. 80-90% freelance written. Quarterly magazine covering mind development, PSI, practical ESP, stock-prediction and Wall Street; working with ESP, predictions; contests, dowsing and pendulum work. For a general audience interested in mental development and self-help/ESP using Russian/U.S. methods. Pays on publication. Publishes ms an average of 6 months after acceptance. Byline given. Buys second serial (reprint) rights and all rights. Not copyrighted. Buys one-time rights. Submit seasonal/holiday material 4 months in advance. Simultaneous queries, and simultaneous, photocopied, and previously published submissions OK. Computer printout submissions acceptable; prefers letter-quality to dot-matrix. SASE. Reports in 6 weeks. Sample copy for $1, 6x9 SAE, and 69¢ postage; writer's guidelines for business size SAE and 2 first class stamps.
Nonfiction: Michael Christopher, articles editor. Book excerpts, general interest, inspirational, interview/profile, opinion. Not interested in articles on witchcraft, the occult, UFOs, space creatures or space vehicles, etc. Buys 10-15 mss/year. Send complete ms. Length: 1,000-2,500 words. Pays $10 minimum.
Columns/Departments: Michael Christopher, column/department editor. News & Notes, Book Reviews. Buys 10-12 mss/year. Send complete ms. Length: 200-350 words. Pays $5 minimum.
Poetry: Light verse, traditional. Buys 3-4 poems/year. Submit maximum 5 poems. Pays in 10 contributor copies.
Fillers: Newsbreaks. Buys variable number/year. Length: 200-550 words. Pays $2 minimum.
Tips: "Write realistically; avoid wordiness and overuse of 'I'. Research and include helpful data on ESP development, mind control, and psychic research, dowsing and pendulum, special studies such as graphoanalysis, astrology, archeology, and crime detection with ESP."

FATE, Clark Publishing Co., 500 Hyacinth Place, Highland Park IL 60035. Editor: Mary Margaret Fuller. 70% freelance written. Monthly. Buys all rights; occasionally North American serial rights only. Byline given. Pays on publication. Query. Reports in 2 months. SASE.
Nonfiction and Fillers: Personal psychic experiences, 300-500 words. Pays $10. New frontiers of science, and ancient civilizations, 2,000-3,000 words; also parapsychology, occultism, witchcraft, magic, spiritual healing miracles, flying saucers, etc. Must include complete authenticating details. Prefers interesting accounts of single events rather than roundups. "We very frequently accept manuscripts from new writers; the majority are individuals' first-person accounts of their own psychic experience. We do need to have all details, where, when, why, who and what, included for complete documentation." Pays minimum of 5¢/word. Fillers should be fully authenticated. Length: 100-300 words.
Photos: Buys good glossy prints with mss. Pays $5-10.

‡**METAPSYCHOLOGY, The Journal of Discarnate Intelligence**, MetaCom Corp., Box 30022, Philadelphia PA 19103. Editor: Tam Mossman. 80% freelance written. Quarterly journal/review on channeling—transmission of spirit writings and messages through Ouija board, automatic writing, trance, etc. For those interested in Jane Roberts' Seth books and other wisdom from spirit entities. Estab. 1985. Circ. 2,500. Pays on publication. Publishes ms an average of 3 months after acceptance. Byline given. Buys all rights for Q & A section and first serial rights. Submit seasonal/holiday material 6 months in advance. Simultaneous queries, and simultaneous and photocopied submissions OK. Computer printout submissions acceptable; no dot-matrix. SASE. Reports in 1 week on queries; 2-3 weeks on mss. Sample copy $5; free writer's guidelines (included in sample issue).
Nonfiction: Book excerpts (first serial); channeled essays; how-to (only by trance psychics); encounters with spirits; interview/profile (of trance psychics); personal experience; and use of mind for personal evolution. "No self-aggrandizement, religious treatises, articles with a religious axe to grind (pro or con), personal opinion pieces, or pointless voyages into autobiographical thickets." Buys 25 mss/year, most are channeled material. Query with clips of channeled material. Length: 2,000 words. "We serialize book-length pieces." Pays 3¢/word, depending on length, quality.
Photos: Photos used only on cover. We do not want unsolicited photos/art.
Columns/Departments: Questions and Answers—trance psychics should write for guidelines. Book reviews—write, with previous review clips. Psychometrists should write in if their impressions are particularly

vivid and accurate. Buys 100+ mss/year. Query with published clips. Length: 100-5,000 words. Pays 3¢/word.

Tips: "First, read a sample copy of *Metapsychology*. If your material, or writing, or insight, is up to our standards, then you have an excellent chance of getting published—especially if you channel spirit messages yourself. Few other publications accept trance material at all. Interviews with 'professional' channelers would be welcome. Interviews with spirit guides would be preferred, however. We also want interviews with psychiatrists and psychologists who are supportive of channeling."

‡**MYSTERIES OF LIFE, The Unknown Visited and Explained**, National Publishing, Box 8042, Van Nuys CA 91409. (818)366-1090. Editor: Hank Krastman. 90% freelance written. Quarterly newsletter of the occult, astrology, mystic. Circ. 10,000. Pays on acceptance. Publishes ms an average of 3 months after acceptance. Byline given. Buys all rights. Submit seasonal/holiday material 3 months in advance. Simultaneous queries, and simultaneous and photocopied submissions OK. Computer printout submissions acceptable; prefers letter-quality to dot-matrix. SASE. Reports in 2 weeks. Sample copy for 8½x11 SAE.
Nonfiction: General interest, how-to, photo feature, and travel. "We also accept book manuscripts, same subjects." Buys 12 mss/year. Send complete ms. Length: open. Pays 3-5¢/word. Sometimes pays the expenses of writers on assignment.
Photos: Cherry Krastman, photo editor. Send photos with query or ms. Reviews 8½x11 b&w prints. Pays $5-10. Captions, model release and identification of subjects required. Buys all rights.
Tips: "Send us manuscripts of unexplained phenomena and all related subjects in the US and world."

‡**NEW REALITIES**, Suite 408, 680 Beach St., San Francisco CA 94109. (415)776-2600. Editor: James Bolen. 20% freelance written. For general public interested in total wellness, personal growth and in holistic approach to living. Straightforward, entertaining material on new environments, the healing arts, new spirituality, consciousness research, and the frontiers of human potential and the mind. Bimonthly. Pays on publication. Publishes manuscript an average of 6 months after acceptance. Reports in 6 weeks. Computer printout submissions acceptable. SASE.
Nonfiction: "Documented articles on mental, physical and spiritual holistic dimensions of humankind. Balanced reporting, no editorializing. No personal experiences as such. Accepts profiles of leaders in the field. Must have documented evidence about holistic leaders, healers, researchers. Short bibliography for further reading." Query. Length: 1,500-3,500 words. Pays $75-250. Accepts photos. Sometimes pays the expenses of writers on assignment.
Tips: "The writer may have a better chance of breaking in at our publication with short articles and fillers since this gives us the opportunity to become familiar with their writing style. The most frequent mistakes made by writers in completing an article for us are incomplete research, subjective reporting, facts not documented, and poor grammatic structure."

PREDICTION, The Magazine for Astrology and the Occult, Link House Magazines (Croydon) Ltd., Link House, Dingwall Ave., Croydon, CR9 2TA, England. 01-686-2599. Editor: Jo Logan. 90% freelance written. Monthly magazine. Circ. 35,000. Pays on acceptance. Byline given. Buys first British serial rights. SAE and IRCs. Reports in 1 month. Free sample copy.
Nonfiction: New product (within confines of magazine); personal experience (of an occult nature only); and technical (astrology, tarot, palmistry, alternative medicine, etc.). Buys 50 mss/year. Send complete ms. Length: 1,000-2,000 words. Pays £20-80.
Columns/Departments: Astrology. Buys 12 mss/year. Length: 750 words. Pays £20.
Fillers: Clippings, anecdotes and newsbreaks.
Tips: "Feature articles with an occult slant and astrological profiles (with charts) of personalities living or dead are most open to freelancers."

Automotive and Motorcycle

Economy, luxury, and just-for-fun vehicles of all makes and models are showcased in these magazines. Publications in this section detail the maintenance, operation, performance, racing and judging of automobiles and recreational vehicles. Publications that treat vehicles as means of transportation or shelter instead of as a hobby or sport are classified in the Travel, Camping, and Trailer category. Journals for teamsters, service station operators, and auto and motorcycle dealers will be found in the Auto and Truck classification of the Trade Journals section.

AMERICAN MOTORCYCLIST, American Motorcyclist Association, Box 6114, Westerville OH 43081-6114. (614)891-2425. Executive Editor: Greg Harrison. For "enthusiastic motorcyclists, investing considerable time and money in the sport. We emphasize the motorcyclist, not the vehicle." Monthly magazine. Circ. 134,000. Pays on publication. Rights purchased vary with author and material. Pays 25-50% kill fee. Byline given. Query. Submit seasonal/holiday material 4 months in advance. SASE. Reports in 1 month. Sample copy $1.25.
Nonfiction: How-to (different and/or unusual ways to use a motorcycle or have fun on one); historical (the heritage of motorcycling, particularly as it relates to the AMA); interviews (with interesting personalities in the world of motorcycling); photo feature (quality work on any aspect of motorcycling); and technical or how-to articles. No product evaluations or stories on motorcycling events not sanctioned by the AMA. Buys 20-25 mss/year. Query. Length: 500 words minimum. Pays minimum $3/published column inch.
Photos: Purchased with or without accompanying ms, or on assignment. Captions required. Query. Pays $15 minimum per photo published.
Tips: "Accuracy and reliability are prime factors in our work with freelancers. We emphasize the rider, not the motorcycle itself. It's always best to query us first and the further in advance the better to allow for scheduling."

AUTOMOBILE QUARTERLY, 221 Nassau St., Princeton NJ 08542. (609)924-7555. Editor-in-Chief: L. Scott Bailey. Emphasizes automobiles and automobile history. Quarterly hardbound magazine; 112 pages. Circ. 30,000. Pays on acceptance. Buys all rights. Pays expenses as kill fee. Byline given. SASE. Reports in 3 weeks. Sample copy $13.95.
Nonfiction: Authoritative articles relating to the automobile and automobile history. Historical, interview and nostalgia. Buys 5 mss/issue. Query. Length: 2,000-20,000 words. Pays $200-800.
Photos: Purchased on assignment. Captions required. Query. Uses 8x10 b&w glossy prints and 4x5 color transparencies. "Payment varies with assignment and is negotiated prior to assignment."
Tips: "Familiarity with the magazine a *must*."

AUTOWEEK, Crain Communications, Inc., 1400 Woodbridge, Detroit MI 48207. (313)446-6000. Managing Editor: Ed Peabody. 20% freelance written. Emphasizes automobile racing and the auto industry, domestic and international. Weekly tabloid. Circ. 150,000. Pays on publication. Byline "generally given." Buys first North American serial rights or by agreement with author. Submit seasonal material 2 months in advance. Computer printout submissions acceptable. SASE. Reports in 2-4 weeks. Publishes ms an average of 6 weeks after acceptance. Free sample copy and writer's guidelines.
Nonfiction: Wide variety of articles from nostalgia to news reports, driving impressions to technical analyses, personality profiles to 'sneak' previews of future products. "We maintain a fulltime staff in Detroit, with a group of regular correspondents around the country and overseas. We do, however, solicit manuscripts from literate, knowledgeable writers." Recent article example: Steve Cropley's "The Porsche 944 Turbo Story" in the March 4, 1985 issue. Buys 24 mss/year. Length: 1,000-2,500 words. Query. Pays negotiable rates.
Photos: Pays $15/b&w; $35/color transparency.

‡**CADILLAC TIMES**, Progressive Communications, Inc., 905 N. Orange Ave., Orlando FL 32801. (305)843-6180; (800)327-4797. Editor: Craig Christman. 20% freelance written. Monthly company newsletter covering automobiles—primarily Cadillacs. Our newsletters consist of part automotive news and part general interest articles. Our audience is between 35 and 65 years old. Articles should be upbeat, short, and about topics of wide-range interests such as health, travel, human interest and trivia." Circ. 15,000. Pays on acceptance. Publishes ms an average of 2 months after acceptance. Byline given. Not copyrighted. Buys first rights and second serial (reprint) rights. Submit seasonal/holiday material 3 months in advance. Computer printout submissions acceptable; prefers letter-quality to dot-matrix. SASE. Reports on mss in 2 months. Free sample copy.
Nonfiction: General interest; how-to (automobile upkeep tips, tips on cleaning or fixing upholstery, wheels, etc); travel (must be of interest to people in all regions of US); and health (must be upbeat). "Each year we produce a December holiday issue. It must include Christmas and Hanukkah. Buys 12 mss/year. Send complete ms. Length: 250-400 words. Pays $50-100.
Photos: State availability of photos with query letter or manuscript or send photos with ms. Prefers b&w contact sheets.
Tips: "The most frequent mistake made by freelancers is writing articles aimed at readers too young for the audience. Keep articles short, concise, upbeat, and aimed toward the income and age bracket of Cadillac owners."

CAR AND DRIVER, 2002 Hogback Rd., Ann Arbor MI 48104. (313)994-0055. Editor/Publisher: David E. Davis Jr. For auto enthusiasts; college-educated, professional, median 24-35 years of age. Monthly magazine; 160 pages. Circ. 900,000. Pays on acceptance. Rights purchased vary with author and material. Buys all rights or first North American serial rights. Buys 10-12 unsolicited mss/year. Submit seasonal material 4 months in advance. Reports in 2 months. SASE.

Nonfiction: Non-anecdotal articles about the more sophisticated treatment of autos and motor racing. Exciting, interesting cars. Automotive road tests, informational articles on cars and equipment; some satire and humor. Personalities, past and present, in the automotive industry and automotive sports. "Treat readers as intellectual equals. Emphasis on people as well as hardware." Informational, how-to, humor, historical, think articles, and nostalgia. Query with clips of previously published work. Length: 750-2,000 words. Pays $200-1,500. Also buys mini-features for FYI department. Length: about 500 words. Pays $100-500.

Photos: B&w photos purchased with accompanying mss with no additional payment.

Tips: "It is best to start off with an interesting query and to stay away from nuts-and-bolts stuff since that will be handled in-house or by an acknowledged expert. Our goal is to be absolutely without flaw in our presentation of automotive facts, but we strive to be every bit as entertaining as we are informative."

CAR COLLECTOR/CAR CLASSICS, Classic Publishing, Inc., Suite 144, 8601 Dunwoody Pl., Atlanta GA 30338. Editor: Donald R. Peterson. 90% freelance written. For people interested in all facets of collecting classic, milestone, antique, special interest and sports cars; also mascots, models, restoration, garaging, license plates and memorabilia. Monthly magazine; 76 pages. Circ. 45,000. Pays on publication. Publishes ms an average of 4 months after acceptance. Submit seasonal/holiday material 4 months in advance. Photocopied submissions OK. Computer printout submissions acceptable; no dot-matrix. SASE. Reports in 2 months. Sample copy for $2; writer's guidelines for SAE and 1 first class stamp.

Nonfiction: General interest, historical, how-to, humor, inspirational, interview, nostalgia, personal opinion, profile, photo feature, technical and travel. Fiction article example: "The Royal Cars of India" (April 1985). Buys 75-100 mss/year. Query with clips of published work. Buys 24-36 unsolicited mss/year. Length: 300-2,500 words. Pays 5¢/word minimum.

Photos: "We have a continuing need for high-quality color positives (e.g., 2¼ or 35mm) *with* copy." State availability of photos with ms. Offers additional payment for photos with accompanying mss. Uses b&w glossy prints; color transparencies. Pays a minimum of $75 for cover and centerfold color; $10 for inside color; $5 for inside b&w. Buys one-time rights. Captions and model release required.

Columns/Departments: "Rarely add a new columnist but we are open to suggestions." Buys 36/year. Query with clips of published work. Length: 2,000 maximum; prefer 1,000-2,000 words. Pays 5¢/word minimum.

Tips: "The most frequent mistakes made by writers are writing to a 'Sunday supplement' audience rather than to a sophisticated audience of car collectors and submitting stories that are often too basic and assume no car knowledge at all on the part of the reader."

CAR CRAFT, Petersen Publishing Co., 8490 Sunset Blvd., Los Angeles CA 90069. (213)657-5100, ext. 345. Editor: Jeff Smith. For men and women, 18-34, "enthusiastic owners of 1949 and newer muscle cars." Monthly magazine; 132 pages. Circ. 400,000. Study past issues before making submissions or story suggestions. Pays generally on publication, on acceptance under special circumstances. Buys all rights. Buys 2-10 mss/year. Computer printout submissions acceptable. Query. SASE.

Nonfiction: How-to articles ranging from the basics to fairly sophisticated automotive modifications. Drag racing feature stories and some general car features on modified late model automobiles. Especially interested in do-it-yourself automotive tips, suspension modifications, mileage improvers and even shop tips and homemade tools. Length: open. Pays $100-200/page.

Photos: Photos purchased with or without accompanying text. Captions suggested, but optional. Reviews 8x10 b&w glossy prints; 35mm or 2¼x2¼ color negotiable. Pays $30 for b&w, color negotiable. "Pay rate higher for complete story, i.e., photos, captions, headline, subtitle: the works, ready to go."

‡**CAR REVIEW**, Popular and Performance, Dobbs Publications, Drawer 7157, Lakeland FL 33807. (813)644-0449. Editor; Donald Farr. 30% freelance written. Monthly magazine covering American performance cars, 1950-1974. "*Car Review* caters to owners and enthusiasts of 1950-74 American performance cars, focusing primarily on the 'muscle cars' of the middle to late 60s." The magazine includes features (both b&w and color), how-tos, show coverage, historical, etc. Estab. 1984. Circ. 97,800. Pays on publication. Publishes ms an average of 4 months after acceptance. Byline given. Offers variable kill fee. Buys one-time rights. Submit seasonal/holiday material 4 months in advance. Photocopied submissions OK; acceptance of previously published work depends on where and when published. Computer printout submissions acceptable; prefers letter-quality to dot-matrix. SASE. Reports in 2 weeks. Free sample copy.

Nonfiction: Historical/nostalgic, how-to, interview/profile (someone involved in the design or evolution of a performance car); photo feature (related to "muscle cars"); and technical (how to rebuild a car or how to improve its performance or appearance). Buys 48-60 mss/year. Query. Length: 200-2,500 words. Pays $50-500. Sometimes pays expenses of writers on assignment.

Photos: Send photos with query. Pays $10 for b&w contact sheets; $20-30 for color transparencies. Captions and identification of subjects required.

Tips: *Car Review* uses second-person articles. Photo features are most open to freelancers. Writers must have a knowledge of American high-performance cars.

CARMAG, CARM Publishing, Inc., 23 Leslie St., Toronto Ontario M4M 3H9 Canada. (416)461-0761. Editor: Ed Belitsky. 60% freelance written. Bimonthly automotive magazine for the practical motorist. Circ. 55,000. Pays on publication. Publishes ms an average of 2 months after acceptance. Byline given. Offers $50-100 kill fee. Buys first rights. Computer printout submissions acceptable; prefers letter-quality to dot-matrix. Submit seasonal/holiday material 2 months in advance. SASE. Reports in 1 month. Free sample copy.
Nonfiction: How-to, interview/profile, photo feature, technical. Buys 30 mss/year. Query or send complete ms. Length: 600-1,200 words. Pays $100-300. Sometimes pays the expenses of writers on assignment.
Photos: Send photos with ms. Reviews 35mm color transparencies; 5x7 or 4x5 color prints. Captions, model release, and identification of subjects required. "We do not buy manuscripts without photos if applicable. Only the very big publications can afford to send people to photograph an article individually. Today's freelancer has to be a photographer too."
Tips: "We emphasize quality of content, not quality of graphics. Our writers must research their subjects well. A brief note with an idea outline is probably the best way to begin. The editor may then offer a preferred angle of approach to the subject."

CORVETTE FEVER, Prospect Publishing Co., Inc., Box 55532, Ft. Washington MD 20744. (301)839-2221. Publisher: Patricia E. Stivers. 40% freelance written. Bimonthly magazine; 64-84 pages. Circ. 35,000. Pays on publication. Publishes ms an average of 4 months after acceptance. Buys first and second serial (reprint) rights. Byline given. Phone queries OK. Submit seasonal/holiday material 4 months in advance. Photocopied submissions OK. SASE. Reports in 4 weeks. Sample copy and writer's guidelines $2.
Nonfiction: General interest (event coverage, personal experience); historical (special or unusual Corvette historical topics); how-to (technical and mechanical articles, photos are a must); humor (Corvette-related humor); interview (with important Corvette persons, race drivers, technical persons, club officials, etc.); nostalgia (relating to early Corvette car and development); personal experiences (related to Corvette car use and experiences); profile (prominent and well-known Corvette personalities wanted for interviews and articles); photo feature (centerspread in color of Corvette and female Vette owner; photo essays on renovation, customizing and show cars); technical (any aspect of Corvette improvement or custom articles); and travel (relating to Corvette use and adventure). Buys 4-6 mss/issue. Query or send complete ms. Length: 500-2,500 words. Pays $40-300.
Photos: Send photos with ms. Pays $5 for 5x7 b&w glossy prints; $10 for color contact sheets and transparencies. Captions preferred; model release required.
Columns/Departments: Innovative Ideas, In Print, Model Shop, Pit Stop, and Tech Vette. Buys 3 mss/issue. Send complete ms. Length: 300-800 words. Pays $24-200.
Fiction: "Any type of story as long as it is related to the Corvette." Buys 1-2 mss/issue. Send complete ms. Length: 500-2,500 words. Pays $40-200.
Fillers: Clippings, jokes, gags, anecdotes, short humor and newsbreaks. Buys 2-3/issue. Length: 25-150 words. Pays $2-15.

CYCLE, Ziff-Davis Publishing, Co., 780-A Lakefield Rd., Westlake Village CA 91361. (818)889-4360. Editor: Phil Schilling. Managing Editor: Allyn Fleming. 10% freelance written. Monthly magazine covering motorcycles for motorcycle owners (mostly men). Circ. 450,000. Pays on publication. Publishes ms an average of 4 months after acceptance. Byline given. Buys first North American serial rights. Submit seasonal/holiday queries 4 months in advance. Simultaneous queries and photocopied submissions OK. Computer printout submissions acceptable. SASE. Reports in 1 month.
Nonfiction: Investigative, historical, interview/profile (of racing personalities or others in the industry); photo feature; technical (theory or practice); travel (long-distance trips anywhere in the world); and reports on racing. Query "with references." Length: 2,000-4,000 words. Pays $400-700.
Photos: Pays $20-100 for b&w prints; $50-200 for 35mm color transparencies. Model release and identification of subjects required. Buys one-time rights.

CYCLE NEWS, WEST, 2201 Cherry Ave., Box 498, Long Beach CA 90801. (213)427-7433. Editor: John Ulrich. Publisher: Sharon Clayton. 50% freelance written. Emphasizes motorcycle news for enthusiasts plus local event coverage west of Mississippi River. Weekly tabloid; 48 pages. Circ. 50,000. Pays on 15th of month for work published in issues cover-dated the previous month. Publishes ms an average of 6 months after acceptance. Buys all rights. Computer printout submissions acceptable. SASE. Reports in 1 month. Free writer's guidelines.
Nonfiction: Expose; how-to; historical; humor; informational; interview (racers); personal experience (racing, nonracing with a point); personal opinion (land use, emission control, etc.); photo feature; profile (personality profiles); technical; and travel (off-road trips, "bikepacking"). Buys 1,000 mss/year. Submit complete ms. Pays minimum $2/column inch. Sometimes pays the expenses of writers on assignment.
Photos: Purchased with or without accompanying manuscript. Captions required. Submit contact sheet, prints, negatives or transparencies. Pays $10 minimum for 5x7 or 8x10 glossy prints; $50 minimum for 35mm slides or 2¼x2¼ color transparencies. Model release required.

CYCLE WORLD, 1499 Monrovia Ave., Newport Beach CA 92663. Editor: Paul Dean. 15% freelance written. For active motorcyclists, "young, affluent, educated, very perceptive." Subject matter includes "road tests (staff-written), features on special bikes, customs, racers, racing events; technical and how-to features involving mechanical modifications." Monthly. Circ. 350,000. Pays on publication. Publishes ms an average of 4 months after acceptance. Buys all rights. Electronic submissions OK via IBM XY WRITE. Computer printout submissions acceptable. SASE. Sample copy $2; free writer's guidelines.
Nonfiction: Buys informative, well-researched, technical, theory and how-to articles; interviews; profiles; humor; and historical pieces. Buys 100 mss/year. Query. Length: 800-5,000 words. Pays $100-150/published page. Sometimes pays the expense of writers on assignment.
Photos: Purchased with or without ms, or on assignment. "We need funny photos with a motorcycle theme." Captions optional. Pays $50 for 1 page; $25-35 for half page. 8x10 b&w glossy prints, 35mm color transparencies.
Columns/Department: Round Up. "Pieces relating to motorcycle industry." Length: 40-200 lines/piece. Pays negotiable rates.
Fiction: "Exceptional" humorous stories. No racing fiction or "rhapsodic poetry." Length: 1,500-3,000 words.

THE EJAG MAGAZINE, EJAG Publications, Box J, Carlisle MA 01741. (617)369-5531. Editor: Lori R. Toepel. 50% freelance written. Monthly magazine covering "everything about Jaguar and Daimler autos for readers ranging from corporate presidents to local car-fixers; Sunday mechanics—all Jaguar-Daimler fans." Circ. 30,000. Pays on acceptance. Publishes ms an average of 3 months after acceptance. Byline given. Offers $10-25 kill fee. Buys all rights unless otherwise negotiated. Submit seasonal/holiday material 3 months in advance. Computer printout submissions acceptable "if easily readable"; prefers letter-quality to dot-matrix. SASE. Reports in 1 month. Free sample copy and writer's guidelines.
Nonfiction: General interest (on auto field in general); historical/nostalgic (on Jaguars of previous eras, in U.S. and abroad); how-to (do it yourself pieces in depth for maintenance, repair, restoration); interview/profile (of Jag owners, racers, factory people, collectors); new product (anything applicable to Jaguars); personal experience; photo feature (on beautiful Jaguars, technical procedures, restorations); technical (do-it-yourself or general tech background). "No club news or club meets (we have direct lines to these). No technical articles that sound like manuals." Buys 25 or more unsolicited mss/year. Query. Length: 1,200-5,000 words. "Longer articles accepted—for splitting into several months installments." Pays 5-8¢/word for general topics, 10-15¢/word for technical and do-it-yourself. Sometimes pays the expenses of writers on assignment.
Photos: State availability of photos. Pays $5 maximum for 35mm, 3x3 color transparencies and 3x5 and 5x7 b&w prints. Caption, model release and identification of subjects (if possible) required. Buys all rights unless otherwise negotiated.
Fillers: "We buy many fillers so they are always welcomed."
Tips: "We welcome unpublished writers *but* you must know the subject."

FOUR WHEELER MAGAZINE, 21216 Vanowen St., Canoga Park CA 91303. (213)992-4777. Publisher: Dave Cohen. Senior Editor: Rich Johnson. Executive Editor: Bruce W. Smith. 20% freelance written. Emphasizes four-wheel-drive vehicles, competition, off-road adventure. Monthly magazine; 200 pages. Circ. 195,000. Pays on publication. Publishes ms an average of 6 months after acceptance. Buys first North American serial rights. Written queries only. Submit seasonal/holiday material at least 4 months in advance. SASE. Sample copy $2.50 plus $1.50 postage.
Nonfiction: 4WD competition and adventure articles, technical ideas, how-to's, and vehicle features about a unique 4WD vehicle. "We like adventure: mud-running through treacherous timber trails, old desert ghost town four-wheeling trips, coverage of ice-racing jeeps; and unusual 4WD vehicles such as customized trucks, 4WD conversions. See features by Willie Worthy, Rich Johnson and Bruce Smith." Query before sending complete ms. Length: 2,500 words maximum; average 3-5 pages when published. Pays $100/page for complete package. Sometimes pays the expenses of writers on assignment.
Photos: Requires excellent quality photos, e.g., 10 b&w glossy 8x10s, 20 color transparencies. Captions required. Prefers Kodachrome 64 or 2¹/₄.
Tips: "Technical material is difficult to come by. A new writer has a better chance of success with us if he can offer new technical articles, maintenance and performance tips. Also, we like unique custom 4x4 vehicle features. The short 'vehicle features' are the easiest written and show us the writer/photographer's potential."

FRIENDS MAGAZINE, Ceco Communications, Inc., 30400 Van Dyke Blvd., Warren MI 48093. (313)575-9400. Editor: Herman Duerr. "*Friends* is a magazine for Chevrolet owners; Chevrolet products are the 'hook' to all of our stories." 75% freelance written. Monthly magazine; 32 pages. Circ. 1,000,000. Pays on acceptance. Publishes ms an average of 6 months after acceptance. Rights vary. Computer printout submissions acceptable; no dot-matrix. Submit seasonal/holiday material 6 months in advance. Simultaneous and photocopied submissions OK. SASE. Reports in 2 months. Free sample copy and writer's guidelines.
Nonfiction: Travel (by automobile; U.S. only); celebrity profiles (of Chevrolet owners); unusual use of

Close-up

Friends Magazine
A Magazine for
Chevrolet Owners

Herman Duerr is steering *Friends'* new editorial policy away from its long-time general-interest focus. The 47-year-old magazine (published for Chevrolet dealers by Ceco Communications) now focuses on material with a "Chevy tie-in." Good places on the North American continent that travelers can reach by car, recreational activities, and well-known people who own Chevrolet products are potential subjects for *Friends.* "The stories can be on any topic—but they have to tie-in in some way with Chevrolet or in some way celebrate the automobile," Duerr says.

Sometimes the Chevy tie-in is more vague. *Friends* recently published an article on the miniseries, *Space,* as its cover story. (Chevrolet's sponsorship of the miniseries made it a *Friends* story.)

Another aim of the new *Friends* model is to appeal more to the Chevrolet dealers. They decide who receives the magazine. Some dealers send it to customers buying certain models of Chevrolet cars; others send *Friends* to all their customers. Based on statistics furnished by dealers, *Friends* has the strongest following with rural dealerships. "There is a certain loyalty to small town dealers." This trend is considered when editing the magazine.

The publication needs writers who can do more than state facts. Add "color" to your stories, suggest the editors. "What we like is a complete package— story and photos. If you're a writer who happens to be a good photographer, that's good," says Duerr, who recently replaced former editor Tom Morrisey.

Friends relies on freelancers for feature articles. Technical Chevrolet product articles are done on assignment by writers in the Warren, Michigan area who spend time with engineers to ensure accuracy. Though the articles are technical in nature, the writers aren't technical writers. *Friends* editors want technical copy to have the viewpoint of a novice, making stories easier for the average reader to understand.

No matter how good the story or writing is, though, an article can't be used without getting permission from anyone quoted or photographed. Another problem for *Friends* editors is copy that is too general and geared toward the old editorial policy, like travel articles not involving cars.

State immediately in your query the type of article you are proposing, later in the letter include the specifics of your story, and whether photos are available, recommend the editors of *Friends.* "I think that all editors probably are one-page readers in that they're willing to look at one page, be it the query letter page or the first page of a manuscript." The worst queries attempt to be cute or tricky. No editor likes to wade through verbiage simply to find that they don't want the story anyway.

Give the story you're proposing a second thought, advise *Friends'* editors. "Probably a thousand other writers have the same idea. On your second thought, you might be able to notice some aspect of your story other writers didn't."

—Katherine Jobst

Chevrolet products; humor (auto-related); entertainment (programs and events sponsored by Chevrolet); and photo features (strong Chevrolet-tied photo essays). "We're looking for freelancers who can focus and produce lively copy—people who can see beyond the 'Aunt Martha's Chevy' story that we've seen 10,000 times, and produce a story that will interest or excite the general reader while ringing in the Chevrolet name. If you wouldn't *really* want to read it, why bother writing it?" Query by mail only. Releases required for all persons named or quoted in story. Sometimes pays expenses on assignment.

Photos: State availability of photos. Pays $200/page. Transparencies only. "About the only time we'll consider black and white is when the article is an early historical piece." Captions and model release required.

HIGH PERFORMANCE PONTIAC, JHS Publishing Co., 29 Grove St., South Hackensack NJ 07606. (201)440-2770. Editor: Cliff Gromer. Bimonthly magazine on Pontiac automobiles for Pontiac enthusiasts. Circ. 60,000. Pays on publication. Byline given. Buys all rights. Submit seasonal/holiday material 3 months in advance. No simultaneous queries, or simultaneous, photocopied or previously published submissions. SASE. Reports in 2 weeks on queries; 3 weeks on mss. Sample copy for SASE.

Nonfiction: Historical/nostalgic and how-to (technical information on restoring and hopping up Pontiacs); interview/profile; new product; personal experience; photo feature; technical; travel; and "anything to do with high performance Pontiac automobiles." Buys 50 mss/year. Query. Length: 800-2,000 words. Pays $75-300.

Photos: State availability of photos or send photos with query. Reviews b&w and color transparencies and prints. Captions and identification of subjects required.

Tips: "Must have excellent photos with every article."

‡**HOT BIKE**, McMullen Publishing Co., 2145 W. Le Palme, Ancheim CA 92632. (714)635-9040. Editor: Paul Garson. 10-35% freelance written. Monthly magazine that is a serious, tech-oriented, high performance motorcycle publication with emphasis on Harley-Davison motorcycles, plus coverage of race events, classics and exotics. Circ. 80,000. Pays on publication. Publishes ms an average of 3 months after acceptance. Byline given. Buys one-time rights. Submit seasonal/holiday material 3 months in advance. Photocopied submissions OK. Computer printout submissions acceptable; no dot-matrix. SASE. Reports in 2 weeks. Sample copy $1.25; writer's guidelines for SAE with 1 first class stamp.

Nonfiction: Historical/nostalgic (classic bikes and events); how-to (tech article, high performance engine, suspension, etc.); interview/profile (top racers and builders); new products (for new product section); photo feature (high-performance street and track machine); and travel (unusual touring articles). Buys 40 mss/year. Send complete ms. Length: 500-3,000 words. Pays $50-300. Sometimes pays the expenses of writers on assignment.

Photos: "For cover consideration, a female model helps—no nudes—keep it sexy but tasteful. Photos should be dramatic if they are race oriented." Pays $20-50 for b&w contact sheets, negatives and prints (5x7 or 8x10); $30-100 for color transparencies (35mm or 2¼). Captions, model releases and identification of subjects required.

Tips: "Have a hot subject, hot photos, clear and concise writing. Bad photos ruin most freelance submissions. Read the magazine and study format style and subject matter. We are always willing to give you new writers a chance."

HOT ROD, Petersen Publishing Co., 8490 Sunset Blvd., Los Angeles CA 90069. (213)657-5100. Editor: Leonard Emanuelson. For readers 10 to 60 years old with automotive high performance, street rod, truck, drag racing and street machine interest. Monthly magazine; 120 pages. Circ. 900,000. Buys all rights. Byline given. Pays on acceptance. Free editorial guidelines. Submit seasonal material 4 months in advance. Reports on accepted and rejected material "as soon as possible." SASE.

Nonfiction: Wants how-to, new product and technical pieces. Length: 2-12 ms pages. Pays $100-225/printed page. "Freelance quantity at *Hot Rod* will undoubtedly decline; staff will originate most material. Foresee more need for photo essays, less for the written word. We accept very little unsolicited (written) freelance or nontechnical material."

Photos: Photos purchased with or without accompanying ms and on assignment. Sometimes offers no additional payment for photos accepted with ms. Captions required. Pays $25 for b&w prints and $25 minimum for color.

Tips: "Freelance approach should be tailored for specific type and subject matter writer is dealing with. If it is of a basic automotive technical nature, then story slant and info should be aimed at the backyard enthusiasts. What we do is attempt to entertain while educating and offering exceptional dollar value."

‡**JAGS UNLIMITED**, Jags Unlimited, Inc., 1306 S. Pope, Benton IL 62812. (618)439-9595. Editor: Cecilia Kirkpatrick. Monthly magazine on Jaguar automobiles. Pays on publication. Byline given. Simultaneous queries, and simultaneous, photocopied, and previously published submissions OK. SASE. Reports in 4 weeks.

Nonfiction: Book excerpts; general interest; historical/nostalgic; how-to (restore your car, find your part or service); humor; interview/profile; new product; opinion; personal experience; photo feature ("Show My Jag" section); technical (tried and true methods); and Jaguar events. All mss Jaguar related. Payment negotiable (usually 4-10¢/word).

Photos: Cover photos need to be color, vertical shots in enlarged prints, transparencies, or 35mm slides. Photos accompanying articles may be b&w or color. Each photo should have a name and address label affixed to the back of the photo. Captions and identification of subjects required.

Tips: "All manuscripts from devoted Jaguar enthusiasts are welcomed. However, we are interested in quality of material rather than number of words. The only formal requirement is that manuscripts be typed and double-spaced. Photos enhance all articles."

KEEPIN' TRACK OF VETTES. Box 48, Spring Valley NY 10977. (914)425-2649. Editor: Shelli Finkel. 70% freelance written. Monthly magazine; 60-68 pages. For Corvette owners and enthusiasts. Circ. 38,000. Pays on publication. Publishes ms an average of 3 months after acceptance. Buys all rights. Byline given. Submit seasonal/holiday material 3 months in advance. Computer printout submissions acceptable; prefers letter-quality to dot-matrix. SASE. Reports in 3-4 weeks. Free sample copy and writer's guidelines.

Nonfiction: Expose (telling of Corvette problems with parts, etc.); historical (any and all aspects of Corvette developments); how-to (restorations, engine work, suspension, race, swapmeets); humor; informational; interview (query); nostalgia; personal experience; personal opinion; photo feature; profile (query); technical; and travel. Buys 8-10 mss/issue. Query or submit complete ms. Pays $50-200. Sometimes pays the expenses of writers on assignment.

Photos: Send photo with ms. Pays $10-35 for b&w contact sheets or negatives; $10-50 for 35mm color transparencies; offers no additional payment for photos with accompanying ms.

‡**MARHABA,** The Magazine for Avis Rent A Car in the Middle East, Age Communications Ltd., Parkway-House, Sheen Lane, London SW14 8LS England. Editor: Joseph R. Yogerst. Assistant Editor: Jules MacMahon. Art Director: Jan Lehne. A quarterly "in-car" magazine for covering motor racing, classic cars, automobile touring, and other aspects of driving. Circ. 18,000. Pays on publication. Byline given. Buys first Mideast serial rights in both English and Arabic. Submit seasonal/holiday at least 4 months in advance. Simultaneous queries, and photocopied or previously published submissions OK. SAE with IRC. Reports in 1 month.

Nonfiction: Anything related to driving or speed sports. The emphasis need not be on the Middle East. Types of articles published include long-distance driving (i.e. Kathmandu to Istanbul, Cape to Cairo); motor touring in the Middle East (i.e. Driving Through Oman etc.); motor sports (interviews with race drivers, articles on specific races or types of races); nostalgia (early auto pioneers, land speed record attempts, famous race drivers etc.); historical (related to specific makes of cars i.e. Rolls Royce, Cadillac, Corvette etc.); how-to (with a specific desert driving slant); profiles (of famous people in the motor industry); and photo features (on motor sports, classic cars etc.). Length: 1,500-2,000 words. Pays £80 sterling (estimated $95) per 1,000 words. Query or send complete mss. Buys 3-5 mss/issue.

Photos: State availability of photos. Captions required. Pays minimum of £20 for 35mm or larger format color transparencies; pays £150 for cover photos. Buys first Mideast rights.

THE MERCEDES BENZ STAR, Magazine of the Mercedes-Benz Club of America. Toad Hall Motorbooks, Inc., 1235 Pierce St., Lakewood CO 80214. (303)235-0116. Editor: Frank Barrett. A bimonthly club magazine covering Mercedes-Benz automobiles. "Our readers are not just Mercedes-Benz owners but *enthusiasts* interested in the cars' history, how to maintain their cars properly, how to enjoy them more, and in knowing more about interesting Mercedes-Benz cars and people." Circ. 18,000. Pays on publication. Byline given. Buys first rights. Submit seasonal/holiday material 4-6 months in advance. Simultaneous queries, and simultaneous, photocopied and previously published submissions OK. Computer printout submissions acceptable; no dot-matrix. SASE. Reports in 2 weeks on queries; 1 month on mss. Sample copy $3.

Nonfiction: Book excerpts, historical, how-to, humor, interview/profile, personal experience, photo feature, technical and travel. "All must relate strongly to Mercedes-Benz and be of commensurate quality." Buys 6-10 mss/year. Query with published clips. Length: 1,000-7,000 words. Pays $50-300.

Photos: State availability of photos with query or ms. Reviews b&w contact sheets, 35mm up to 4x5 color transparencies, and 8x10 full-frame b&w prints. Pays negotiable rate. Buys one-time rights.

Columns/Departments: Buys 12 mss/year. Query with published clips. Length: 500-1,500 words. Pays variable rate; $150 maximum.

Tips: "We like factual articles on interesting cars and people. How-to technical articles are most appreciated, along with event coverage, but we could also use some good humor.

MOTOR TREND, Petersen Publishing Co., 8490 Sunset Blvd., Los Angeles CA 90069. (213)657-5100. Editor: Tony Swan. 15-20% freelance written. For automotive enthusiasts and general interest consumers. Monthly. Circ. 750,000. Buys all rights. "Fact-filled query suggested for all freelancers." Computer printout submissions acceptable; prefers letter-quality to dot-matrix. Reports in 30 days. SASE.

Nonfiction: Automotive and related subjects that have national appeal. Emphasis on domestic and imported cars, roadtests, driving impressions, auto classics, auto, travel, racing, and high-performance features for the enthusiast. Packed with facts. Freelancers should confine queries to feature material; road tests and related activity handled inhouse.

Photos: Buys photos, particularly of prototype cars and assorted automotive matter. Pays $25-250 for b&w glossy prints or color transparencies.

Fillers: Automotive newsbreaks, humorous short takes, automotive cartoons, featurettes. 500 words maximum.

MOTORCYCLIST MAGAZINE, Petersen Publishing, 8490 Sunset Blvd., Los Angeles CA 90069. (213)657-5100. Editor-in-Chief: Art Friedman. Managing Editor: James Cowell. 10% freelance written. Emphasizes motorcycles or motorcycle enthusiasts. Monthly magazine; 100 pages. Circ. 225,000. Pays on publication. Publishes ms an average of 6 months after acceptance. Buys all rights. Byline given. Written queries preferred. SASE. Reports in 3 months. Free writer's guidelines.

Nonfiction: How-to, humor, informational, interview, new product, photo feature, profile and technical. Buys 12-25 mss/year. Length: 500-2,000 words. Pays $25-1,000.

Photos: Reviews contact sheets and negatives. Pays $25-100 for 8x10 b&w prints; $75-200 for 35mm color transparencies. Captions, model release and identification of subjects required.

Columns/Departments: Hotline (short news items); Last Page (humorous, bizarre, tip-type items); Sport (features on competitions, racers—timeliness is important). Buys 10/year. Send complete ms. Length: 50 words minimum.

Fiction: Adventure, fantasy, humorous. Buys 1-2 mss/year. Send complete ms.

Fillers: Short humor and newsbreaks. Buys 20/year. Length: 50-250 words. Pays $25-50.

NISSAN DISCOVERY, The Magazine for Datsun Owners, Donnelley Marketing, Box 4617, N. Hollywood CA 91607. (213)877-4406. Editor: Wayne Thoms. Bimonthly magazine for Datsun owners and their families. Circ. 500,000. Pays on acceptance. Byline given. Not copyrighted. Buys first North American serial rights. Submit seasonal/holiday material 5 months in advance. Photocopied and previously published submissions OK. SASE. Reports in 1 month. Sample copy $1.50 in cash or stamps, 9x12 SAE, and 80¢ postage; writer's guidelines for business-size SAE and 20¢ postage.

Nonfiction: Historical/nostalgic, humor, photo feature, travel. "We need general family interest material with heavy emphasis on outstanding color photos: travel, humor, food, lifestyle, sports, entertainment." No food articles. Buys 25 mss/year. Query. Length: 1,300-1,800 words. Pays $300-1,000.

Photos: State availability of photos. Reviews 2¼" and 35mm color transparencies. No b&w photos. "Payment usually is part of story package—all negotiated." Captions and identification of subjects required. Buys one-time rights.

Tips: "A freelancer can best break in to our publication by submitting a brief idea query with specific information on color slides available. Offer a package of copy and art."

NORTHEAST RIDING, Paul Essenfeld, 209 Whitney St., Hartford CT 06105. (203)236-6604. Editor: Paul Essenfeld. 70% freelance written. Monthly magazine "to entertain and inform the road and street motorcyclists of the Northeast, who ride for recreation and commuting. Area events, good roads to ride, and club activities are featured along with information on camping, service, safety, and political issues affecting riding in the area." Circ. 20,000. "Payment is negotiable prior to acceptance. Payment made on publication." Publishes ms an average of 3 months after acceptance. Byline given. Buys first rights. Submit seasonal/holiday material 6 months in advance. Simultaneous queries, and simultaneous, photocopied, and previously published submissions OK. Computer printout submissions acceptable. SASE. Reports in 2 weeks. Sample copy for 9x12 SAE and 90¢ postage.

Nonfiction: General interest (places to ride); historical/nostalgic (on vintage bikes); interview/profile (unusual biker); new product (accessories); opinion (legislation); personal experience (riding/touring); photo feature (motorcycles with people); technical (repair/service/testing); travel (mostly New England); and articles on safety. Buying very small amount of material; most is donated. No material on dirt bikes, enduros, or trials. Send complete ms. Length: 500-2,000 words. Payment is minimal. Sometimes pays the expenses of writers on assignment.

Photos: Send photos with query or manuscript. Reviews 4x5 b&w prints. Captions required. Buys one-time rights.

Columns/Departments: Safety, Legal, Technical, Favorite Ride. Send complete ms. Length 500-1,000 words. Payment is negotiable prior to acceptance. Payment made on publication.

Tips: "Submit ms and photos ready to use. Articles must be of interest to Northeastern motorcyclists, and photos should include motorcycles *and* people. The Favorite Ride department is most open to freelancers. Write about New England locations, specific description of route. Include at least one b&w photo of area *with* motorcycle."

OFF-ROAD MAG, Argus Publishing, Suite 316, 12301 Wilshire Blvd., Los Angeles CA 90025. (213)820-3601. Editor: Mike Parris. Monthly magazine covering off-pavement vehicles, particularly 4-wheel drive, utility, and pickup trucks; and off-road racing and rallying vehicles. Readers are owners and people who aspire to own off-road vehicles, as well as those who intend to modify engines and other components for off-road use. Circ. 120,000. Pays on publication. Byline given. Buys all rights, "but may reassign rights upon request." Submit seasonal/holiday material 4 months in advance. Computer printout submissions acceptable; prefers letter-quality to dot-matrix. SASE. Reports in 1 month. Writer's guidelines for business size SAE and 1 first class stamp.

Nonfiction: Technical (modification); travel (and adventure in the continental U.S.); off-road groups; and land-closures. "The key to writing for us is technical expertise. You must be knowledgeable on the subject." Buys 50 mss/year. Send complete ms and photos or diagrams. Length: 2,000-3,000 words. Pays $125-400.

Photos: Send photos with ms. Reviews 35mm color transparencies and 8x10 b&w glossy prints.

Fillers: Fix it, How-to. Buys 25/year. Length: 750-1,000 words. Pays $50-100.

Tips: "Freelance writers should be aware that: word processing is a must; clean writing *isn't* enough; and photographic skills should be polished."

ON TRACK MAGAZINE, The Auto Racing Newsmagazine, O.T. Publishing, Paul Oxman Publisher, Unit M, Box 8509, 17165 Newhope St., Fountain Valley CA 92708. (714)966-1131. Managing Editor: Jane Pappalau. Bimonthly magazine covering auto racing. Circ. 25,000. Pays on publication. Byline given. Not copyrighted. Buys first North American serial rights. Simultaneous queries, and simultaneous and photocopied submissions OK. SASE. Reports in 6 weeks.

Nonfiction: General interest, how-to, interview/profile, opinion, personal experience, photo feature, technical—all related to auto racing. Query. Length: 250-3,000 words. Pays 50¢/column inch; some rates negotiable.

Photos: Anne Peyton, art director. State availability of photos. Pays $75 for 35mm color transparency, $10 for 5x7 or 8x10 b&w print. Buys one-time rights.

PETERSEN'S 4-WHEEL & OFF-ROAD, Petersen Publishing Company, 8490 Sunset Blvd., Los Angeles CA 90069. (213)657-5100. Editor: Michael Coates. Managing Editor: Cecily Chittick. 10-15% freelance written. Monthly magazine covering automotive four-wheel drive vehicles. "We appeal to the off-road enthusiast who plays hard and likes to have fun with his or her 4x4. Our approach is slanted toward showing how to do-it-yourself when it comes to maintaining or modifying an off-road vehicle." Pays on acceptance. Publishes ms an average of 6 months after acceptance. Byline given. Buys all rights. Submit seasonal/holiday material 6 months in advance. Electronic submissions OK—call Jack Cooke/Photocomp, (213)657-5100, ext. 477; requires hard copy also. Computer printout submissions acceptable: no dot-matrix. SASE. Reports in 1 month. Writer's guidelines for SAE and 1 first class stamp.

Nonfiction: How-to (modify a vehicle); photo feature (modified vehicles); and technical (modification of a vehicle). No first-person accounts of anything; no travel features. Buys 6-10 mss/year. Query or send complete ms. Length: 300-1,500 words. Pays $50-500. Sometimes pays expenses of writers on assignment, but "has to be negotiated beforehand."

Photos: Barry Wiggins, photo editor. Pays $10-75 for color transparencies; $5-25 for 8x10 b&w prints. Captions, model release, and identification of subjects required. Buys all rights.

Columns/Departments: Tailgate (miscellaneous automotive news); Focus (political news, opinions of relevance to four-wheelers). Buys 6 mss/year. Send complete ms. Length: 20-100 words. Pays $10-25.

Tips: "The best way to break in is with a well-photographed, action feature on a modified vehicle. Study our magazine for style and content. We do not deviate much from established editorial concept. Keep copy short, information accurate, and photos in focus."

PICKUPS & MINI-TRUCKS MAGAZINE, Petersen Publishing Co., 8490 Sunset Blvd., Los Angeles CA 90069. (213)657-5100. Editor: John J. Jelinek. Managing Editor: Chriss Bonhall. 10% freelance written. Covers street pickups. Monthly magazine. Circ. 155,000. Pays on publication. Publishes ms an average of 4 months after acceptance. Buys all rights. Pays kill fee "depending on assignment." Byline given. Submit seasonal/holiday material 4 months in advance. Photocopied submissions OK "with guarantee of exclusivity." Computer printout submissions acceptable; no dot-matrix. SASE. Reports 1-2 months. Writer's guidelines for SAE and 1 first class stamp.

Nonfiction: How-to (modifications to light duty trucks, such as extra seats, tool storage, body and mechanical repairs, modifications, etc.); historical/nostalgic (restored trucks); technical and travel (2-wheel drive travel only, must show vehicle being used). Buys 1-2 mss/per issue. Submit complete ms. Query and request writer's guidelines ("Contributor's Memo"). Length: 1,000-3,000 words. Pays $75/published page. Sometimes pays expenses of writers on assignment.

Photos: Purchased with accompanying manuscript or on assignment. Captions required. Query for photos. Pays $10-75 for 8x10 b&w glossy prints; $25-75 for 35mm or 2¼x2¼ color transparencies; offers no additional payment for photos accepted with ms. Model release required.

‡**POPULAR CARS**, The Complete Street Machine Magazine, McMullen Publishing, Inc., 2145 W. La Palma, Anaheim CA 92801-1785. (714)635-9040. Managing Editor: Hib Halverson. 25% freelance written.

Monthly magazine on contemporary, high performance automobiles. "Our main emphasis is on 'street machines' and 60's and 70's 'muscle' cars and related subjects." Circ. 75,000. Pays on publication. Publishes ms an average of 4 months after acceptance. Byline given. Kill fee negotiated in advance. Buys first serial rights. Submit seasonal/holiday material 3 months in advance. Photocopied submissions OK. Computer printout submissions acceptable. SASE. Reports in 3 weeks on queries; 1 month on mss. Sample copy $2.50; free writer's guidelines.

Nonfiction: B. Hatano, feature editor; U.B. Sherman, technical editor and H. Halverson, other. Historical/nostalgic (60's, 70's muscle cars); how-to (street performance and "street machining"); interview/profile (of people associated with automotive performance subjects); new product (new cars—2 page maximum, performance cars *only*); photo feature (on people's street machines); technical (street performance); and drag race and street machine event coverage. Special issues on Ford '64-'70 Mustangs and Corvettes. No new car tests. Buys 36-40 mss/year. Query with published clips. Length: 435-1,175 words. Pays $75-300.

Photos: H. Halverson and Brian Hatano, photo editors. Reviews 35mm color transparencies and 5x7 prints. Pays $20-75 for transparencies; $0-20 for prints. Captions, model release, and identification of subjects required. Buys all rights.

Tips: "A freelancer can best break into our publication by a query, submission of past work, good quality manuscripts, reputation, and good 'car features'."

ROAD & TRACK, 1499 Monrovia Ave., Newport Beach CA 92663. Editor: John Dinkel. 10% freelance written. For knowledgeable car enthusiasts. Monthly magazine. Publishes ms up to 2 years after acceptance. Buys all rights. Computer printout submissions acceptable. Reports in 6 weeks. SASE.

Nonfiction: "The editor welcomes freelance material, but if the writer is not thoroughly familiar with the kind of material used in the magazine, he is wasting both his time and the magazine's. *Road & Track* material is highly specialized and that old car story in the files has no chance of being accepted. We publish more serious, comprehensive and in-depth treatment of particular areas of automotive interest." Query. Pays 12-25¢/word minimum depending upon subject covered and qualifications and experience of author.

Tips: "Freelancer must have intimate knowledge of the magazine. Unless he can quote chapter and verse for the last 20 years of publication he's probably wasting his time and mine."

ROAD KING MAGAZINE. Box 250, Park Forest IL 60466. Editor-in-Chief: George Friend. 10% freelance written. Truck driver leisure reading publication. Quarterly magazine; 72 pages. Circ. 226,515. Pays on acceptance. Publishes ms an average of 1 month after acceptance. Buys all rights. Byline given "always on fiction—if requested on nonfiction—copyright mentioned only if requested." Submit seasonal/holiday material 3 months in advance. Simultaneous and photocopied submissions OK. Computer printout submissions acceptable; prefers letter-quality to dot-matrix. SASE. Sample copy for 7x10 SAE with 73¢ postage or get free sample copy at any Union 76 truck stop.

Nonfiction: Trucker slant or general interest, humor, and photo feature. No articles on violence or sex. Name and quote release required. No queries. Submit complete ms. Length: 500-2,500 words. Pays $50-150.

Photos: Submit photos with accompanying ms. No additional payment for b&w contact sheets or 2¼x2¼ color transparencies. Captions preferred. Buys first rights. Model release required.

Fiction: Adventure, historical, humorous, mystery, rescue-type suspense and western. Especially about truckers. No stories on sex and violence. "We're looking for quality writing." Buys 4 mss/year. Submit complete ms. Length: approximately 1,200 words. Pays up to $400.

Fillers: Jokes, gags, anecdotes and short humor about truckers. Buys 20-25/year. Length: 50-500 words. Pays $5-100.

Tips: No collect phone calls or postcard requests. "We don't appreciate letters we have to answer." No certified, insured or registered mail. No queries. "Do not submit manuscripts or art or photos using registered mail, certified mail or insured mail. Publisher will not accept such materials from the post office. Publisher will not discuss refusal with writer. Nothing personal, just legal. Do not write and ask if we would like such and such article or outline. We buy only from original and complete manuscript submitted on speculation. Do not ask for writer's guidelines. See above and/or get copy of magazine and be familiar with our format before submitting anything. Never phone for free copy as we will not have such phone calls."

ROAD RIDER, Box 6050, Mission Viejo CA 92690. Editor: Bob Carpenter. 20% freelance written. Covers touring and camping on motorcycles for a family-oriented audience. Monthly magazine; 72 pages. Circ. 80,000. Pays on publication. Publishes ms an average of 6 months after acceptance. Buys all rights. Submit seasonal/holiday material 1 year in advance. Computer printout submissions acceptable; prefers letter-quality to dot-matrix. SASE. Reports in 1 month. Sample copy $3; free writer's guidelines with SASE.

Nonfiction: "We will consider any articles providing they are of sound base so far as motorcycling knowledge is concerned. Must be cycle-oriented. How-to's usually are of technical nature and require experience. We would love to see more humorous cycle experience type of material. Cycling personalities are also big here. We try to do three or four historical pieces per year. All evaluation/testing pieces are done in house. Travel pieces need good photos; same thing is true on historical or nostalgia material." No beginner articles. Buys 48 mss/

year. Query or send complete ms. Length: 300-1,500 words. Pays $100-200.
Photos: Send photos with ms. Offers no additional payment for photos accepted with accompanying ms. Prefers 5x7 b&w glossy prints or 35mm color transparencies. Captions and model release required.
Tips: "We are an enthusiast publication—as such, it is virtually impossible to sell here unless the writer is also an enthusiast and actively involved in the sport. A good, well-written, brief item dealing with a motorcycle trip, accompanied by top quality b&w and color photos receives prime time editorial attention. We are always on the lookout for good material from eastern seaboard or Midwest. Best way to hit this market is to buy and study a sample issue prior to submitting. Most of our contributors are Road Rider People. If you are unsure as to what Road Rider People refers, you will probably not be able to sell to this magazine. We continue to be overstocked on following: beginner articles (all ages, sexes, etc.), journal-format travel articles (not welcome) and travel articles from Southwestern U.S."

STOCK CAR RACING MAGAZINE,Box 715. Ipswich MA 01938. Editor: Dick Berggren. For stock car racing fans and competitors. Monthly magazine: 100 pages. Circ. 400,000. Pays on publication. Buys all rights. Byline given. SASE. Reports in 6 weeks.
Nonfiction:"Uses nonfiction on stock car drivers, cars, and races. We are interested in the story behind the story in stock car racing. We want interesting profiles and colorful, nationally interesting features." Query. Buys 50-60 mss/year. Length: 100-6,000 words. Pays $10-350.
Photos: State availability of photos. Pays $20 for 8x10 b&w photos; $50-250 for 35mm or larger color transparencies. Captions required.
Tips:"We get more queries than stories. We just don't get as much material as we want to buy. We have more room for stories than ever before. We are an excellent market with 12 issues per year."

‡STREET RODDING ILLUSTRATED, McMullen Publishing, 2145 W. LaPalma Ave., Anaheim CA 92801. (714)635-9040. Editor: Philippe Danh. Associate Publisher: Jerry Dexter. Up to 25% freelance written. Bimonthly magazine on modified auto built prior to 1949. Circ. 85,000. Pays on publication. Byline given. Buys all rights. Computer printout submissions acceptable: prefers letter-quality to dot-matrix. SASE. Sample copy $1. Free writer's guidelines.
Nonfiction: How-to (build street rods); technical (all types, auto related). "Freelancer must know about street rods or will sound foolish to our readers." Send complete ms. Rarely pays the expenses of writers on assignment.
Photos: Reviews b&w contact sheets, negatives, and 8x10 prints; 2¹/₄ color transparencies. Captions, model release and identification of subjects required.
Columns/Departments: Buys 36 mss/year. Send complete ms. Length: 750-1,500 words. Pays $150-750.
Tips: "We will use anything from anyone as long as it suits our needs."

SUPER CHEVY, Argus Publishing, Suite 316, 12301 Wilshire Blvd., Los Angeles CA 90025. (213)820-3601. Editor: Doug Marion. Feature Editor: Jeff Tann. Monthly magazine covering Chevrolet automobiles for anyone associated with Chevys—owners, mechanics, car builders and racing drivers. Circ. 160,000. Pays on acceptance. Byline given. Buys all rights. Submit seasonal/holiday material 4 months in advance. Simultaneous queries OK. Reports in 2 weeks on queries; 1 week on mss. Free sample copy.
Nonfiction: Historical (classic Chevy); interview; race coverage (drag, stock and sprint car). Buys 25 mss/year. Query by phone or letter. Length: 300-1,500 words. Pays $75-100/printed page.
Photos: State availability of photos. Pays $25-60/35mm color transparency; $10 minimum/5x7 or 8x10 b&w glossy print. Captions and model release required.

‡3 WHEELING MAGAZINE, The Original All Terrain Vehicle Magazine, Wright Publishing Co., 2949 Century Pl., Box 2260, Costa Mesa CA 92626. (714)979-2560. Editor: Bruce Simurda. Managing Editor: Rick Busenkell. 5% freelance written. Monthly magazine covering all terrain vehicles. Circ. 65,000. Pays on publication. Publishes ms an average of 3 months after acceptance. Byline given. Buys all rights. Submit seasonal/holiday material 3 months in advance. Simultaneous queries and simultaneous submissions OK. SASE. Reports in 1 month. Sample copy for 9x12 SAE and 5 first class stamps.
Nonfiction: General interest, how-to, new product, personal experience, technical and travel. Buys 10 mss/ year. Query. Length: 600-900 words. Pays $60-90. Sometimes pays the expenses of writers on assignment.
Photos: State availability of photos. Reviews b&w contact sheets and 35mm color transparencies. Captions, model release and identication of subjects required.
Columns/Departments: All freelance columns on contract basis only. Buys 36 mss/year. Query. Length: 600-650 words. Pays $60-90.

VETTE MAGAZINE, CSK Publishing Co., 29 Grove St., South Hackensack NJ 07606. (201)440-2770. Editor: Cliff Gromer. Bimonthly magazine on Corvette automobiles for Corvette enthusiasts. Circ. 85,000. Pays on publication. Byline given. Buys all rights. Submit seasonal/holiday material 3 months in advance. SASE. Reports in 2 weeks on queries; 3 weeks on mss. Sample copy for SASE.

Nonfiction: Expose (auction frauds); general interest; historical/nostalgic; how-to (car modifications for more performance); interview/profile (Corvette people); new product; opinion; personal experience; photo feature; technical; travel or "anything that has to do with Corvette lifestyle." Buys 50 mss/year. Query. Length: 1,200-2,000 words. Pays $75-300.

Photos: State availability of photos or send photos with query. Reviews b&w and color transparencies and 5x7 prints. Captions and model release required.

Tips: "Must submit excellent photos with every article."

• **VOLKSWAGEN'S WORLD**, (formerly *Small World*), Volkswagen of America, 88 W. Big Beaver Rd., Box 3951, Troy MI 48099. Editor: Ed Rabinowitz. Magazine published 5 times/year for Volkswagen owners in the United States. Circ. 250,000. Pays on acceptance. Buys all rights. Byline given. Computer printout submissions acceptable. Reports in 6 weeks. SASE. Free writer's guidelines.

Nonfiction: "Interesting stories on people using Volkswagens; useful owner modifications of the vehicle; travel pieces with the emphasis on people, not places; Volkswagenmania stories, personality pieces, inspirational and true adventure articles. VW arts and crafts, etc. The style should be light. Our approach is subtle, however, and we try to avoid obvious product puffery, since *Volkswagen's World* is not an advertising medium. We prefer a first-person, people-oriented handling. No basic travelogues; articles on older VWs; stay away from Beetle stories. With all story ideas, please query first. All unsolicited manuscripts will be returned unopened. Though queries should be no longer than 2 pages, they ought to include a working title, a short, general summary of the article, and an outline of the specific points to be covered. We strongly advise writers to read at least 2 past issues before working on a story." Buys 10-12 mss/year. Length: 1,000 words maximum; "shorter pieces, some as short as 450 words, often receive closer attention." Pays $150 per printed page for photographs and text; otherwise, a portion of that amount, depending on the space allotted. Most stories go 2 pages; some run 3 or 4.

Photos: Submit photo samples with query. Photos purchased with ms; captions required. "We prefer color transparencies, 35mm or larger. All photos should carry the photographer's name and address. If the photographer is not the author, both names should appear on the first page of the text. Where possible, we would like a selection of at least 40 transparencies. It is recommended that at least one show the principal character or author. Quality photography can often sell a story that might be otherwise rejected. Every picture should be identified or explained." Model releases required. "Remember, you are writing to an up-scale audience." Pays $300 maximum for front cover photo.

Fillers: "Short, humorous anecdotes about Volkswagens." Pays $15.

Tips: "Style of the publication and its content are being structured toward more upscale, affluent buyer. VW drivers are not the same as those who used to drive the Beetle."

VW & PORSCHE, Argus Publishers, Suite 316, 12301 Wilshire Blvd., Los Angeles CA 90025. (213)820-3601. Editor: C. Van Tune. 60% freelance written. Bimonthly magazine covering VW, Porsche and Audi cars for owners. Circ. 75,000. Pays one month before publication. Publishes ms an average of 6 months after acceptance. Byline given. Kill fee varies. Buys all rights. Submit seasonal/holiday material 4 months in advance. Computer printout submissions acceptable; prefers letter quality to dot-matrix. SASE. Reports in 2 weeks on queries. Free sample copy.

Nonfiction: How-to (restore, maintain or tune-up); Special, modified or restored VWs and Porsches. Buys 30-35 mss/year. Query. Length: 1,000-2,500 words. Pays $75-100/printed page. "More if color pictures are used." Sometimes pays the expenses of writers on assignment.

Photos: "We require crisp, well-lit b&w and color prints and slides; great variety in angles and settings." State availability of photos. Reviews 8x10 glossy prints. Identification and/or signed release of subjects required.

Tips: "All of our articles deal with VWs, Porsches and Audis in a technical light, therefore a strong technical knowledge is critical; short articles used may occasionally be humorous, not so 'techy.'"

Aviation

Airline deregulation is the one trend that will affect the type of material that aviation magazine editors buy. "Competition (resulting from deregulation) means that commercial air travel is forever changing," said one editor. "That's what the readers want to know about." Editors at aviation magazines sometimes find unsolicited material too elementary for their audiences who *know* commercial aviation. "Many appropriate topics are handled with inappropriate basics, while lacking complexities," also points out this editor. Professional and private pilots, and aviation enthusiasts read the publications in this section. Magazines intended for passengers of commercial airlines are grouped in the In-Flight category. Technical aviation and space journals and publications for airport operators, aircraft dealers and others in aviation businesses are listed under Aviation and Space in the Trade Journals section.

AERO, Fancy Publications, Box 6050, Mission Viejo CA 92690. (714)240-6001. Editor: Dennis Shattuck. 50% freelance written. For owners of private aircraft. "We take a unique, but limited view within our field." Circ. 75,000. Buys first North American serial rights. Buys about 20-30 ms/year. Pays after publication. Sample copy $3; writer's guidelines for SASE. Will consider photocopied submissions if guaranteed original. Reports in 2 months. Query. SASE.
Nonfiction: Material on aircraft products, developments in aviation, specific airplane test reports, travel by aircraft, development and use of airports. All must be related to general aviation field. Length: 1,000-4,000 words. Pays $75-250.
Photos: Pays $15 for 8x10 b&w glossy prints purchased with mss or on assignment. Pays $150 for color transparencies used on cover.
Columns/Departments: Weather flying, instrument flight refresher, new products.
Tips: "Freelancer must know the subject about which he is writing; use good grammar; know the publication for which he's writing; remember that we try to relate to the middle segment of the business/pleasure flying public. We see too many 'first flight' type of articles. Our market is more sophisticated than that. Most writers do not do enough research on their subject. Would like to see more material on business-related flying, more on people involved in flying."

AIR LINE PILOT, 1625 Massachussetts Ave. NW, Washington DC 20036. (202)797-4176. Editor-in-Chief: C.V. Glines. Managing Editor: Anne Kelleher. 20% freelance written. Covers commercial aviation issues for members of Air Line Pilots Association (ALPA). Monthly magazine: 48-64 pages. Circ. 45,000. Pays on acceptance. Publishes ms an average of 1 month after acceptance unless on assignment. Buys all rights. Computer printout submissions acceptable; no dot-matrix. Submit seasonal material 4 months in advance. SASE. Reports in 1 month. Sample copy and writer's guidelines with SASE.
Nonfiction: Historical (aviation/personal or equipment, aviation firsts); informational (aviation safety, related equipment or aircraft aids); interview (aviation personality); nostalgia (aviation history); photo feature; profile (airline pilots; must be ALPA members); and technical. No book reviews or advice on piloting techniques. Buys 15 mss/year. Query. Length: 1,000-2,500 words. Pays $100-500.
Photos: State availability of photos with query. Purchased with or without accompanying ms. Captions required. Pays $10-25 for 8x10 b&w glossy prints; $20-250 for 35mm or 2¼x2¼ color transparencies. Covers: Pays $250.
Tips: "Unless a writer is experienced in the technical aspects of aviation, he is more likely to score with a pilot profile or aviation historical piece."

‡**AOPA PILOT**, 421 Aviation Way, Frederick MD 21701. (301)695-2350. Editor: Edward G. Tripp. For aircraft owners, pilots, and the complete spectrum of the general aviation industry. Official magazine of the Aircraft Owners and Pilots Association. Monthly. Circ. 260,000. Pays on acceptance. Reports in 2 months. No computer disk submissions. SASE. Sample copy $2.
Nonfiction: Factual articles up to 2,500 words that will inform, educate and entertain pilots and aircraft owners ranging from the student to the seasoned professional. These pieces should be generously illustrated with good quality photos, diagrams or sketches. Quality and accuracy essential. Topics covered include maintenance, operating technique, reports on new and used aircraft, avionics and other aviation equipment, places to fly (travel), governmental policies (local, state and federal) relating to general aviation. Additional features on weather in relation to flying, legal aspects of aviation, flight education, pilot fitness, and aviation history are used occasionally. No commonplace first-solo or fly-in/local-event stories. Query. Pays $400 maximum.
Photos: Pays $25 minimum for each photo or sketch used. Original b&w negatives or color slides should be made available.

‡**AVIATION/USA**, Randall Publishing Company, Box 2029, Tuscaloosa AL 35403. (205)349-2990. Editor: Claude Duncan. 25-50% freelance written. Trade journal. Weekly tabloid on general aviation (small planes, not jets). "Most of our readers are private pilots who like to read about other pilots, their planes, equipment and adventures." Estab. 1985. Circ. 10,000. Pays on acceptance. Publishes ms an average of 1 month or less after acceptance. Byline given. Offers 100% kill fee. Not copyrighted. Simultaneous and previously published (updated) submissions OK. Computer printout submissions acceptable; prefers letter-quality to dot-matrix. Reports in 2 weeks. Free sample copy and writer's guidelines.
Nonfiction: General interest (with general aviation angle); historical/nostalgic (except combat stories); how-to

(overcome flight problems); humor (with pilot angle); interview/profile (with general aviation angle); personal experience (with pilots); technical (planes); travel (related to small planes); and small local airports. Buys 100 mss/year. Send complete ms. Length: 250-750 words. Pays $10-50. Pays expenses of writers on assignment.

Photos: Send photos with query or ms. Prefers b&w prints; commercially processed OK if sharp. Pays $5.

Tips: "We encourage multiple submissions. Submitting art with copy gives a definite edge. Nothing is too local if it's interesting."

‡**CESSNA OWNERS MAGAZINE**, Cessna Owners Organization, 163-D Citation Ct., Birmingham AL 35209. (205)942-9579. Editor: John Cargile. Managing Editor: Bob Green. 10% freelance written. Monthly magazine covering Cessna airplanes for Cessna airplane owners (Skyhawk, Skylane, and Centurion). "We are into an exchange of information and ideas concerning flying, maintenance and modification. Our members provide for lively discussions, but we are now interested in features/profiles/interviews with people within our industry. We are not interested in general aviation articles." Circ. 5,000. Pays on publication. Publishes ms an average of 1 month after acceptance. Byline given. Not copyrighted. Buys first North American serial rights. Submit seasonal/holiday material 3 months in advance. Simultaneous queries and submissions OK. Computer printout submissions acceptable; prefers letter-quality to dot-matrix. SASE. Reports in 2 weeks on queries; 1 month on mss. Sample copy and writer's guidelines for 9x12 SAE and 73¢ postage.

Nonfiction: Historical/nostalgic, how-to, humor, inspirational, interview/profile, new product, opinion, personal experience, photo feature, technical and travel. Buys 11 mss/year. Query. Length: 300-1,500 words. Pays $20-100.

Photos: Send photos with query. Pays $10-15 for b&w prints; $25-50 for color prints. Captions, model release and identification of subjects required.

FLIGHT REPORTS, Peter Katz Productions, Inc., 1280 Saw Mill River Rd., Yonkers NY 10710. (914)423-6000. Editor: Mary Hunt. Managing Editor: Peter J. Katz. 50% freelance written. Monthly travel magazine for pilots and aircraft owners. Pays on publication. Byline given. Buys all rights. Submit seasonal/holiday material 2 months in advance. SASE. Reports in 2 weeks. Sample copy $1.

Nonfiction: Destination reports include what to do, where to stay, and airport facilities for domestic travel and Canada only. No foreign travel. Buys variable number of mss/year. Query. Length: 750-1,500 words. Pays $25-50.

Photos: State availability of photos. Pays $5 for 3½x5½ b&w and color prints. Captions required.

Tips: "Pilot's license and cross country flying experience is helpful. Some aviation background is required."

FLYING, CBS Magazine, 1 Park Ave., New York NY 10016. (212)503-4000. Editor-in-Chief: Richard L. Collins. Editorial Coordinator: Mary McDonnell. 5% freelance written. For private and commercial pilots involved with, or interested in, the use of general-aviation aircraft (not airline or military) for business and pleasure. Monthly magzine; 116 pages. Circ. 370,000. Pays on acceptance. Buys one-time rights. Submit seasonal/holiday material 4 months in advance of issue date. SASE. Reports in 3 weeks.

Nonfiction: How-to (piloting and other aviation techniques); and technical (aviation-related). No articles on "My Trip" travel accounts, or historical features. Buys about 12 mss/year. Submit complete ms. Length: 750-3,500 words. Pays $50-1,000.

Columns/Departments: "I Learned About Flying From That" personal experience. Pays $100 minimum.

Tips: "New ideas and approaches are a must. Tone must be correct for knowledgeable pilots rather than the non-flying public. Facts must be absolutely accurate."

FREQUENT FLYER, Dun & Bradstreet, 888 7th Ave., New York NY 10106. Editor: Coleman A. Lollar. 75% freelance written. Monthly magazine covering business travel (airlines/airports/aviation) for mostly male high-level business executive readership. Circ. 300,000. Pays on acceptance. Publishes ms an average of 6 months after acceptance. Byline given. Offers $75 kill fee. Buys all rights. Submit seasonal/holiday material 6 months in advance. Computer printout submissions acceptable; no dot-matrix. SASE. Reports in 2 months on queries; 1 month on mss. Free sample copy and writer's guidelines.

Nonfiction: Book excerpts, expose, new product, technical, travel, and news reporting, in particular on airports/aircraft/airlines/hotel/credit card/car rental. Not interested in queries on stress or anything written in the first person; no profiles, humor or interviews. "*FF* reports on travel as part of an executive's job. We do not assume that he enjoys travel, and neither should the freelancer." Buys 100 mss/year. Query with published clips. Length: 800-3,000 words. Pays $100-500. Sometimes pays the expenses of writers on assignment.

Photos: Eve Cohen, articles editor. "We accept both b&w and color contact sheets, transparencies and prints; rates negotiable." Buys one-time rights.

Tips: "We publish very little destination material, preferring articles about how deregulation, airport developments, etc., have affected air services to a destination, rather than descriptive articles. We avoid all travel articles that sound promotional. We publish general business/economic features when they directly relate to the reader as a *mobile* businessman (portable computers, foreign banking, credit card/traveler's check development, etc.). We do not report on other business topics. We like service articles, but not in the usual 'how-to' format: our readers travel too much (average of almost 50 roundtrips a year) to be told how to pack a bag, or how to stay in touch with the office. In service articles, we prefer a review of how frequent travelers handle certain situations rather than how they *should* handle them. Unrequested manuscripts will probably not be read. Give us a good, solid story idea. If accepted, expect a fairly detailed assignment from us. We rewrite heavily. Overly sensitive authors may want to avoid us."

GENERAL AVIATION NEWS, Box 110918, Carrollton TX 75006. (214)446-2502. Editor: Bob Johnson. 10-20% freelance written. For pilots, aircraft owners, aviation buffs, aircraft dealers, and related business people. Weekly tabloid; 24-28 pages. Circ. 30,000. Pays on publication. Publishes ms an average of 1 month after acceptance. Buys all rights. Byline on all features and most news stories. Phone queries OK. Submit seasonal/holiday material 1 month in advance. Simultaneous submissions okay if prior arrangements made with editor. SASE. Computer printout submissions acceptable; prefers letter-quality to dot-matrix. Sample copy $1. Proposal or rejection within 1 month.
Nonfiction: General aviation stories of interest to nationwide audience of persons connected to aviation. Articles on any aspect of aviation will be considered provided they are of interest to those in the general aviation community. "We are a *general aviation* (no airlines, no military) publication." Buys 10-20 unsolicited mss/year. Length: about 1,000 words maximum. Pays up to $50 per published article, less for shorter articles. Sometimes pays expenses of writers on assignment.
Photos: Send photo material with accompanying mss. Pays $5 for b&w or color prints. Captions required. Buys all rights.
Tips: "Writers should read *GAN* before sending mss; also recommend that writers read other aviation publications/periodicals, to have a grasp of current trends and attitudes in the general aviation world. *GAN* publishes approximately 30-40 stories per issue, most of which are no more than 3-5" in length. Follow the advice in the front of *Writer's Market*. *GAN* is a good place for beginning freelancers to try their hand."

‡**KITPLANES**, "Featuring Fast-Build Aircraft for the Home Craftsman."Fancy Publications, Box 6050, Mission Viejo CA 92690. (714)240-6001. Editor: Dennis Shattuck. Managing Editor: April Hay. 60% freelance written. Monthly magazine covering self-construction of private aircraft for pilots and builders. Estab. 1984. Circ. 45,000. Pays on publication. Publishes ms an average of 6 months after acceptance. Byline given. Offers negotiable kill fee. Buys first North American serial rights. Submit seasonal/holiday material 6 months in advance. Computer printout submissions acceptable; dot-matrix must be caps and lower case printing. SASE. Reports in 2 weeks on queries; 6 weeks on mss. Sample copy $3; writer's guidelines for business size SAE..
Nonfiction: How-to, interview/profile, new product, personal experience, photo feature technical general interest, historic/nostalgic and travel. "We are looking for articles on specific construction techniques, the use of tools, both hand and power, in aircraft building, the relative merits of various materials, conversions of engines from automobiles for aviation use, installation of instruments and electronics." No general-interest aviation articles, or "My First Solo" type of articles. Buys 80 mss/year. Query. Length: 500-5,000 words. Pays $100-400.
Photos: Send photos with query or ms or state availability of photos. Pays $10-75 for b&w prints; $20-150 for color transparencies and color prints. Captions and identification of subject required. Buys one-time rights.
Fiction: Buys 2 ms/year. Send complete ms. Length: 500-5,000 words. Pays $75-500.
Tips: "*Kitplanes* contains very specific information—a writer must be extremely knowledgeable in the field. Major features are entrusted only to known writers. I cannot emphasize enough that articles must be directed at the individual aircraft constructor. We will not accept or even consider articles about personal experiences in flight."

PRIVATE PILOT, Fancy Communications Corp., Box 6050, Mission Viejo CA 92690. (714)240-6001. Editor: Dennis Shattuck. 60% freelance written. For owner/pilots of private aircraft, for student pilots and others aspiring to attain additional ratings and experience. "We take a unique, but limited view within our field." Circ. 85,000. Buys first North American serial rights. Buys about 30-60 mss/year. Pays on publication. Sample copy $3; writer's guidelines for SASE. Will consider photocopied submissions if guaranteed original. No simultaneous submissions. Computer printout submissions acceptable "if double spaced and have upper and lower case letters." Reports in 2 months. Query. SASE.
Nonfiction: Material on techniques of flying, developments in aviation, product and specific airplane test reports, travel by aircraft, development and use of airports. All must be related to general aviation field. No personal experience articles. Length: 1,000-4,000 words. Pays $75-300.
Photos: Pays $15 for 8x10 b&w glossy prints purchased with mss or on assignment. Pays $150 for color transparencies used on cover.
Columns/Departments: Business flying, homebuilt/experimental aircraft, pilot's logbook. Length: 1,000 words. Pays $50-125.
Tips: "Freelancer must know the subject about which he is writing; use good grammar; know the publication for which he's writing; remember that we try to relate to the middle segment of the business/pleasure flying

public. We see too many 'first flight' type of articles. Our market is more sophisticated than that. Most writers do not do enough research on their subject. Would like to see more material on business-related flying, more on people involved in flying."

SPORT FLYER, (formerly *Ultralight Flyer*), Ultralight Flyer, Inc., Box 98786, Tacoma WA 98499. (206)588-1743. Managing Editor: Bruce Williams. 50% freelance written. Monthly tabloid covering sport and recreational aviation nationwide. Provides upbeat coverage of sport flying news activities, and politics. Circ. 30,000. Pays on publication. Publishes ms an average of 1 month after acceptance. Byline given. Buys first North American serial rights, one-time rights, and second serial (reprint) rights to material published elsewhere. Submit seasonal/holiday material 3 months in advance. Simultaneous queries, and photocopied and previously published submissions (from non-competitive publications) OK. Computer printout submissions acceptable; prefers letter-quality to dot-matrix. Inquire about electronic submissions. SASE. Reports in 2 weeks on queries; 1 month on mss. Sample copy $2; writer's guidelines for business size SAE and 56¢ postage.
Nonfiction: General interest, historical/nostalgic, how-to (safety practices, maintenance), humor, inspirational, interview/profile, new product, opinion (letters to editor), personal experience, photo feature, technical, travel. "*Aviation* is technical and we are looking for material for people who know the industry. No 'gee whiz' type articles aimed at non-pilot audiences." Buys 100-200 mss/year. Query or send complete ms. Length: 250-1,500 words. Pays $3/printed column inch maximum. Sometimes pays the expenses of writers on assignment.
Photos: "Good pics a must." Send photos with ms. Pays negotiable rates for color transparencies; $10 for b&w pictures used. Submit negatives and prints. Identification of subjects required.
Tips: "We are always looking for the story with photos of the unusual homebuilt plane, women in aviation, or young people interested in flying. We also use many short items of the news variety."

WESTERN FLYER, N.W. Flyer, Inc., Box 98786, Tacoma WA 98499. (206)588-1743. Managing Editor: Bruce Williams. 30% freelance written. Biweekly tabloid covering general aviation. Provides "upbeat coverage of aviation news, activities, and politics of general and sport aviation." Circ. 25,000. Pays on publication. Publishes ms an average of 1 month after acceptance. Byline given. Buys one-time rights and first North American seral rights, on occasion second serial (reprint) rights. Submit seasonal/holiday material 2 months in advance. Simultaneous queries and photocopied and previously published submissions (from noncompetitive publications) OK. Computer printout submissions acceptable. Inquire about electronic submissions. SASE. Reports in 2 weeks on queries; 1 month on mss. Sample copy $2; writer's guidelines for business size SAE and 56¢ postage.
Nonfiction: General interest, historical/nostalgic, how-to (safety practices, maintenance), humor, inspirational, interview/profile, new product, opinion (letters to editor), personal experience. photo feature, technical, travel. "Every other issue is a special issue. Send for list. No 'gee-whiz' type articles aimed at non-pilot audiences." Buys 100 mss/year. Query or send complete ms. Length: 250-1,500 words. Pays $3/printed column inch maximum.
Photos: "Good pics a must." Send photos with ms. Pays $10 for b&w pictures used. Submit negatives, and prints. Identification of subjects required. Query on color photos and slides.
Tips: "We always are looking for features on places to fly to and interviews on people doing interesting and unusual things in aviation. Places to fly to should include an airport and have information about things to do in the area. The interviews might be with people who use aviation to enhance their business interests, i.e., the salesman who flies throughout his territory instead of driving."

‡**WINGS OF VERMONT**, Montair Flight Service, Inc., 1160 Airport Dr., South Burlington VT 05401. (802)862-2247. Editor: Mr. Kim P. Tomlinson. 100% freelance written. Semiannual magazine on general aviation for pilots and aviation enthusiasts. Estab. 1984. Circ. 350. Pays on publication. Publishes ms an average of 6 months after acceptance. Byline given. Buys simultaneous rights, first rights, and second serial (reprint) rights. Submit seasonal/holiday material 6 months in advance. Simultaneous queries, and simultaneous, and previously published submissions OK. Computer printout submissions acceptable; no dot-matrix. SASE. Reports in 4-6 weeks on queries; 6 months on mss. Sample copy $2.50; writer's guidelines for #10 SAE and 1 first class stamp.
Nonfiction: Book excerpts (general aviation, private pilot); general interest (aviation hobbies, aircraft collectors); historical/nostalgic (wartime aviation, especially propeller aircraft, specific plane biographies, famous flyers/pilots); how-to (flight instruction, better performance for the private pilot, flying techniques, procedures, methods); humor (tasteful, nothing, crass or humor encouraging lack of safety—no 'crash' humor); inspirational; interview/profile (well-known pilots, aviation businessmen); personal experience (specific flying stories); technical (better care of privately owned aircraft); and travel (how to travel cheaply, airline and travel industry information). No articles with opinions on aircraft/airline crashes—anything relating to unprofessional behavior, exposes; anything slanderous or anti-aviation safety.Buys 4-6 mss/year. Query or send complete ms. Length: 500-2,500 words. Pays $10-50.
Columns/Departments: Book/film/TV show reviews, aviation only. Instructor's Compass (training tips to the private pilot by certified flight instructors) Examiner's Corner (by FAA Pilot Examiner only—trends in pilot

checkrides, techniques for private pilot). Buys 2 mss/year. Query or send complete ms. Length: 500-1,500 words. Pays $10-25.

Fillers: Anecdotes and newsbreaks. Length: 250 words. Pays $5.

Tips: "Writer should be conscious of "aviation comraderie." Should be technically accurate, demonstrate clear understanding of aviation principles and aviation's beauty and addictive nature. Nonfiction area is most open to freelancers. Articles should be of interest to small aircraft owners, as well as to the business aircraft owner as well as the aviation enthusiast. ."

WINGS MAGAZINE, Division of Corvus Publishing Group, Ltd., Suite 158, 1224 53rd Ave. NE, Calgary Alberta T2E 7E2 Canada. (403)275-9457. Publisher: Paul Skinner. Covers commercial and military aviation. Readers are age 15-70 and are predominantly people employed in aviation. Bimonthly magazine. Circ. 10,500. Pays on publication. Buys first rights. Phone queries OK. SAE and IRCs. Sample copy $2.50.

Nonfiction: Historical (mainly Canadian history); how-to (technical); informational (technical aviation); interview (Canadian personalities in aviation circles); new product, photo feature; profile (Canadian individuals); technical; aircraft handling tests and technical evaluation of new products. No poetry or cartoons. Query; include phone number (with area code). Length: 500-2,000 words. Pays $50-200.

Photos: State availability of photos in query. Purchased with or without accompanying ms. Captions required. Offers no additional payment for photos accepted with ms. Pays $5-20 for 5x7 b&w glossy prints; $25-50 for 35mm color transparencies.

Tips: The writer must have a technical grounding in aviation, be employed in aviation, be a knowledgeable buff or a licensed pilot. Be sure story idea is unique and would be of interest to a Canadian audience. The audience has a high level of technical insight and needs reading material that is newsworthy and informative to the industry executive, aviation expert and worker.

Business and Finance

General interest business publications give executives and consumers information from different perspectives—from local reports to national overviews. The Home State Savings crisis in Ohio and interstate acquisitions of banks and lending institutions may prompt consumers to seek more business—and finance-related information this year. National and regional publications are listed below in separate categories. Those in the national grouping cover business trends nationwide, computers in business, and include some material on the general theory and practice of business and financial management for consumers and members of the business community. Those in the regional grouping report on the business climates of specific regions. Magazines that use material on national business trends and the general theory and practice of business and financial management, but which have a technical slant, are classified in the Trade Journals section, under the Business Management, Finance, Industrial Operation and Management, or Management and Supervision categories.

National

BARRON'S NATIONAL BUSINESS AND FINANCIAL WEEKLY, 22 Cortlandt St., New York NY 10007. (212)285-5243. Editorial Director and Publisher: Robert M. Bleiberg. Editor: Alan Abelson. Managing Editor: Kate Welling. 25% freelance written. For business and investment people. Weekly. Buys all rights. Pays on publication. Publishes ms an average of 1 month after acceptance. Computer printout submissions acceptable; prefers letter-quality to dot-matrix. SASE. Free sample copy.

Nonfiction: Articles about various industries with investment point of view; shorter articles on particular companies, their past performance and future prospects. "Must be suitable for our specialized readership." Length: 1,000-2,500 words. Pays $500-1,000 for articles. Articles considered on speculation only.

Columns/Departments: News and Views, pays $200-400. Book Reviews, pays $150.

BETTER BUSINESS, National Minority Business Council, Inc., 235 E. 42nd St., New York NY 10017. (214)573-2385. Editor: John F. Robinson. 50% freelance written. Quarterly magazine covering small/minority

business. Circ. 9,200. Pays on publication. Publishes ms an average of 2 months after acceptance. Byline given. Buys first North American serial rights and all rights. Submit seasonal material 1 month in advance. Computer printout submissions acceptable; prefers letter-quality to dot-matrix. SASE. Sample copy $3 and 9x12 SAE with $1.50 postage; free writer's guidelines.
Nonfiction: Interview/profile, technical. Buys 10 mss/year. Query with clips. Length: 3,000-5,000 words. Pays $200-250.
Photos: State availability of photos. Reviews b&w prints. Captions required. Buys all rights.

COMMODITY JOURNAL, American Association of Commodity Traders, 10 Park St., Concord NH 03301. Editor: Arthur N. Economou. For investors interested in commodity trading based on cash and forward markets, financial instruments and foreign currencies. Bimonthly tabloid. Circ. 220,000. Pays on publication. Buys all rights. Byline given. Written queries OK. SASE. Reports in 2 months. Free sample copy and writer's guidelines.
Nonfiction: Technical (commodity and foreign currency trading, investing and hedging; commodity markets and foreign currency trends; written intelligibly for investors). "We are not interested in articles concerning the conventional futures market, except insofar as the spot or cash-based markets provide a better alternative." Buys 2 mss/issue. Query. Length: 1,000-2,000 words. Pays 10¢/word.

COMPUTING FOR BUSINESS, (formerly *Interface Age*), MWJ Publishing, 7330 Adams St., Paramount CA 90723. (213)408-0909. Editorial Director: Les Spindle. Associate Editorial Director: Shelia Ball. 30% freelance written. Monthly magazine covering microcomputers in business. Focus is toward the business computer user. Readers receive up-to-the-minute reports on new products, applications for business, and programs they can apply to their own personal computer." Circ. 100,000. Pays on publication. Publishes ms an average of 6 months after acceptance. Byline given. Kill fee varies. Buys all rights. Submit seasonal/holiday material 4 months in advance. Simultaneous queries, and simultaneous and photocopied submissions OK. Electronic submissions OK; call ahead for compatibility. Computer printout acceptable "after phone-consulting with editors." Reports in 4-6 weeks on mss. Sample copy $3.75; free writer's guidelines.
Nonfiction: How-to, new product, opinion, personal experience, photo feature, technical. No agency- or company-written articles. "Articles should pertain to microcomputing applications in business, law, medicine, unique breakthroughs. We seek interviews/profiles of people making unusual use of microcomputers. Computer programs and sample listings must be printed with a new ribbon to get the best quality reproduction in the magazine." Buys 60 mss/year. Query with clips of published work or send complete ms. Length: 1,000-5,000 words. Pays $50 and more (negotiable)/printed page including photos, charts, programs, and listings. Sometimes pays the expenses of writers on assignment.
Photos: Send photos, charts, listings and programs with ms. Photos included in purchase price of article. Captions, model release and identification of subjects required.
Tips: "Case study articles specifying how a particular type of business (law firm, retail store, office, etc.) implemented a computer to improve efficiency and not-yet-reviewed product reviews stand the best chance for acceptance. Hardware and software appraisals by qualified reviewers are desirable. Practical and business applications, rather than home/hobbyist pursuits, are encouraged. Focus tightly on 'Computing for Business' theme."

D&B REPORTS, Dun & Bradstreet, 299 Park Ave., New York NY 10171. (212)593-6723. Editor: Patricia W. Hamilton. 10% freelance written. Bimonthly magazine for owners and top managers of small businesses (average sales of $9 million annually.) Circ. 71,630. Pays on acceptance. Publishes ms an average of 2 months after acceptance. Byline given. Buys all rights. Simultaneous queries OK. Computer printout submissions acceptable; prefers letter-quality to dot-matrix. SASE. Reports in 2 weeks. Free sample copy and writer's guidelines.
Nonfiction: How-to (small business management, cash management, finance); interview/profile (of innovative managers); new product (how developed and marketed). "Articles provide concrete, hands-on information on how to manage more effectively. Articles on scientific developments or social change with implications for business are also of interest." Buys 8-12 mss/year. Query with clips of published work. Length: 2,000-3,000 words. Pays $500 minimum.
Tips: "The most rewarding aspect of working with freelance writers is discovering new talent, then being able to use it on a regular basis for article assignments."

 The double dagger before a listing indicates that the listing is new in this edition. New markets are often the most receptive to freelance contributions.

DOLLARS & SENSE, National Taxpayers Union, 325 Pennsylvania Ave. SE, Washington DC 20003. Editor-in-Chief: Tom G. Palmer. 10% freelance written. Emphasizes taxes and government spending for a diverse readership. Monthly newspaper; 12 pages. Circ. 120,000. Pays on publication. Publishes ms an average of 1 month after acceptance. Buys first serial rights and all rights. Submit seasonal/holiday material 1 month in advance. Previously published submissions OK. Computer printout submissions acceptable. SASE. Free sample copy and writer's guidelines.
Nonfiction: Exposé dealing with wasteful government spending and excessive regulation of the economy. Buys 7 mss/year. Query. Length: 500-1,500 words. Pays $25-100.
Tips: "We look for original material on subjects overlooked by the national press and other political magazines. Probably the best approach is to take a little-known area of government mismanagement and examine it closely. The articles we like most are those that examine a federal program that is not only poorly managed and wasteful, but also self-defeating, hurting the very people it is designed to help. We are also interested in the long-term harm done by different kinds of taxation. Articles on IRS harassment and abuses are always needed and welcome. We have no use for financial or investment advice or broad philosophical pieces."

DUN'S BUSINESS MONTH, Technical Publications Co., A Division of Dun & Bradstreet Corp., 875 3rd Ave., New York NY 10022. (212)605-9400. Editor: Arlene Hushman. Editorial Director: Clem Morgello. Emphasizes business, management and finances for a readership "concentrated among senior executives of those companies that have a net worth of $1 million or more." Monthly magazine. Circ. 284,000. Pays on acceptance. Buys all rights. Submit seasonal/holiday material 3 months in advance. Photocopied submissions OK. Reports in 1 month. Sample copy $2.50.
Nonfiction: Business and government, historical (business; i.e., law or case history), management (new trends, composition), finance and accounting, informational, interview, personal opinion and company profile. Buys 12 mss/year. Query first. Length: 1,200-2,500 words. Pays $200 minimum.
Photos: Art Director. Purchased with accompanying ms. Query first. Pays $75 for b&w photos; $150 for color.
Tips: "Make query short and clearly to the point. Also important—what distinguishes proposed story from others of its type."

THE EXECUTIVE FEMALE, NAFE, 1041 Third Ave., New York NY 10021. (212)371-0740. Editor: Susan Strecker. Associate Editor: Susan Kain. 30% freelance written. Emphasizes "upbeat and useful career and financial information for the upwardly mobile female." 30% freelance written. Bimonthly magazine; 60 pages. Circ. 150,000. Byline given. Pays on publication. Publishes ms an average of 6 months after acceptance. Written queries only. Submit seasonal/holiday material 6 months in advance. Buys first rights, first North America serial rights, one-time rights, all rights, simultaneous rights and second serial (reprint) rights to material originally published elsewhere. Simultaneous and photocopied submissions OK. Computer printout submissions acceptable. SASE. Reports in 3 months. Sample copy $1.50; free writer's guidelines.
Nonfiction: "Articles on any aspect of career advancement and financial planning are welcomed." Sample topics: managerial work issues, investment, coping with inflation, trends in the work place, money-saving ideas, financial planning, trouble shooting, business communication, time and stress management, and career goal setting and advancement. No negative or radical material. Article length: 1,000-2,500 words. Pays $50-$100 minimum. Sometimes pays the expenses of writers on assignment.
Columns/Departments: Profiles (interviews with successful women in a wide range of fields, preferably non-traditional areas for women); Entrepreneur's Corner (successful female business owners with unique ideas); Horizons (career planning, personal and professional perspectives and goal-setting); More Money (specific financial issues, social security, tax planning); and Your Executive Style (tips on health and lifestyle). Department length: 800-1,200 words. Pays $25-50 minimum.
Tips: "Write with more depth. I have the feeling that most authors are just writing off the tops of their heads to have articles 'out there.'"

FACT, The Money Management Magazine, 305 E. 46th St., New York NY 10017. Editor-in-Chief: Daniel M. Kehrer. 50% freelance written. Monthly personal money management and investment magazine for sophisticated readers. Circ. 150,000. Pays on acceptance. Publishes ms an average of 2 months after acceptance. Byline given. Offers 25% kill fee. Buys first rights and nonexclusive (reprint) rights. Simultaneous queries OK. Computer printout submissions acceptable; prefers letter-quality to dot-matrix. SASE. Reports in 6 weeks. Free sample copy.
Nonfiction: General interest (specific money management topics); how-to (invest in specific areas); and new product. No business articles; no "how-to-balance your checkbook" articles. Writers must be knowledgeable and use lots of sidebars and tables. Buys 75 mss/year. Query with published clips. Length: 1,000-2,500 words. Pays $250-700.
Photos: Contact the art director. State availability of photos. Pays $25-250 for color transparencies. Captions, model release and identification of subjects required. Buys one-time rights.
Columns/Departments: Stocks, mutual funds, precious metals, bonds, real estate, collectibles, taxes, insurance, cash management and banking. Buys 50-60 mss/year. Query with published clips. Length: 1,500-

1,800 words. Pays $250-600.

Tips: "Show writing credentials and expertise on a subject. Try something fresh, with photo possibilities. Read the magazine. Our readers are sophisticated about investments and money management."

FORBES, 60 5th Ave., New York NY 10011. (212)620-2200. Managing Editor: Sheldon Zalaznick. "We occasionally buy freelance material. When a writer of some standing (or whose work is at least known to us) is going abroad or into an area where we don't have regular staff or bureau coverage, we have given assignments or sometimes helped on travel expenses." Pays negotiable kill fee. Byline usually given.

FORTUNE, 1271 Avenue of the Americas, New York NY 10020. Staff-written. Occasional contract.

INC MAGAZINE, The Magazine for Growing Companies, INC Publishing Corp., 38 Commercial Wharf, Boston MA 02110. (617)227-4700. Editor: George Gendron. Executive Editor: Bo Burlingham. Managing Editor: Sara P. Noble. Senior Editor, Submissions: Mark K. Metzger. 15% freelance written. A monthly business magazine for chief executive officers and managers of growing companies up to $100 million in sales. Circ. 600,000. Pays on acceptance. Publishes ms an average of 2 months after acceptance. Byline given. Offers 33% kill fee. Buys all rights. Submit seasonal/holiday material 3 months in advance. Computer printout submissions acceptable. Reports in 6 weeks on queries; 1 month on mss.
Nonfiction: Interview/profile and opinion. Buys 25 mss/year. Query with published clips. Length: 350-4,000 words. Pays $150-2,500. Pays expenses of writers on assignment.
Columns/Departments: Insider, Hands On, Spotlight, and Work Style. Buys 20 mss/year. Query with published clips. Length: 350-1,200 words. Pays $150-800.

INFO AGE MAGAZINE, Canada's Business Micro Magazine, Plesman Publications, 703 2 Lansing Square, Willowdale, Ontario M2J 4P8 Canada. (416)497-9562. Editor: Gord Campbell. Managing Editor: Bill Knapp. 95% freelance written. Monthly magazine on business microcomputers. "Our readers are mainly business people, professionals or corporate employees with microcomputers used for business purposes. Our editorial material is written in a down-to-earth style and in plain English as much as possible for novice- or intermediate-level computer users." Circ. 20,000. Pays on publication. Publishes ms an average of 2 months after acceptance. Byline given. Offers $50 kill fee. Buys first rights. Submit seasonal/holiday material 3 months in advance. No simultaneous queries, or simultaneous, photocopied or previously published submissions. Computer printout submissions acceptable. SASE. Reports in 1 week. Sample copy for $2.95; free writer's guidelines.
Nonfiction: Book excerpts; how-to (involving computers; usually assigned); interview/profile (outstanding companies or individuals in Canadian computer industry); new product (short pieces on new hardware or software); technical (computer-related; usually assigned). No personal experience, "humorous" pieces, highly technical pieces, jargon or program listings. Buys 120 mss/year. Query with published clips. Length: 1,500-2,500 words. Pays $150-350.
Photos: Pays $25 maximum for 8x10 b&w prints. Identification of subjects required. Buys one-time rights.
Tips: "It's not difficult to break into *InfoAge*—we are actively seeking writers. Send a letter indicating your availability, areas of expertise and samples. If you have a proposal for an article, it should be included in the form of a concise outline. Computer magazines used to be quite technical because readers were technically adept. As more people buy computers for what they can do as opposed to how they can be made to do them, magazines are adapting and have become less arcane."

MONEY, Time-Life Bldg., Rockefeller Center, New York NY 10020. Managing Editor: Marshall Loeb. For the middle- to upper-income, sophisticated, well-educated reader. Major subjects: personal investing, financial planning, spending, saving and borrowing, careers, travel. Some freelance material.

THE MONEYPAPER, A Financial Publication for Women, Temper of the Times Communications, Inc., Rm. 209, 2 Madison Ave., Larchmont NY 10538. (914)833-0270. Editor: Vita Nelson. Executive Editor: Marjorie Connaver. A monthly newsletter covering financial issues, particularly as they relate to women. Complicated financial concepts are presented in straightforward language." Circ. 17,000. Pays on publication. Byline given. Offers $25 kill fee. Makes work-for-hire assignments. Submit seasonal/holiday material 1 month in advance. Simultaneous queries and photocopied submissions OK. Computer printout submissions acceptable. SASE. Reports in 2 weeks on queries; 1 month on mss. Sample copy for SAE and 2 first class stamps.
Nonfiction: How-to (personal finance); interview/profile (prominent women); and new product (investing, financial services). Buys 15 mss/year. Query with published clips. Pays $75/column.
Columns/Departments: Taxes, Jobs, Investing, and Owning a Business. "Professionals in the field preferred as authors." Buys 36 mss/year. Length: 750/words. Pays $50 honorarium.

Tips: "We do respond to queries, but a telephone follow-up is good for the writer. We like to direct the focus of the articles, so a dialogue is often necessary. Feature articles are most open to freelancers. We look for thorough research and practical advice on ways to make and save money."

SYLVIA PORTER'S PERSONAL FINANCE MAGAZINE, 380 Lexington Ave., New York NY 10017. (212)557-9100. Editor: Patricia Estess. Executive Editor: Elana Lore. Managing Editor: Greg Daugherty. 50% freelance written. Bimonthly magazine covering personal finance and consumer economics. Pays on acceptance. Publishes ms an average of 3 months after acceptance. Byline given. Offers 20% kill fee. Buys a combination of all rights and second serial (reprint) rights. Submit seasonal/holiday material 4 months in advance. No simultaneous queries. No simultaneous, photocopied or previously published submissions. Computer printout submissions acceptable; no dot-matrix. SASE. Reports in 2 months. Free sample copy; writer's guidelines for SAE and 1 first class stamp.

Nonfiction: General interest (financial). Only articles dealing with personal finance; no financially technical articles. Query with published clips. Length: 1,000-1,500 words. Pays negotiable rates. Sometimes pays the expenses of writers on assignment.

Tips: "The magazine is grounded on the personal relationship between reader and writer. Writers and editors have the responsibility of giving the reader the impression that an article was written 'for me'—and, indeed, it will have been. Send a cover letter with original ideas or slants about personal finance articles you'd like to do for us, accompanied by clippings of your previously published work. The features section is most open to freelancers. We will be covering topics such as financial planning, saving, investing, real estate, taxes, in each issue. It's most important for us that our writers be familiar with the trends in their own special areas of personal finance so our magazine can be as up to date as possible. Features must be accurate, and reflect the editors' and readers' sense that financial matters are fascinating. Articles and fillers give us the opportunity to assess a writer's work. Frequent mistakes made by writers are not following original plan or not staying in close contact with supervising editor."

TECHNICAL ANALYSIS OF STOCKS AND COMMODITIES, The Traders Magazine, Box 46518, Seattle WA 98146. (206)938-0570. Editor: Jack K. Hutson. 80% freelance written. Bimonthly magazine covering trading stocks, bonds and commodities (futures), options, mutual funds, and precious metals. Circ. 1,500. Pays on publication. Publishes ms an average of 3 months after acceptance. Byline given. Offers 50% kill fee. Buys first rights and "both the author and *TA* have the right to reprint." Photocopied and previously published submissions OK. Electronic submissions via phone 300/1200 baud or Apple II/IBM PC computer disk, but requires hard copy also. Computer printout submissions acceptable; prefers letter-quality to dot-matrix. SASE. Reports in 3 weeks on queries; 1 month on mss. Sample copy $5; detailed writer's guidelines for business size SAE and 1 first class stamp.

Nonfiction: Reviews (new software or hardware that can make a trader's life easier; comparative reviews of books, articles, etc.); how-to (make a trade); technical (trading and software aids to trading); utilities (charting or computer programs, surveys, statistics, or information to help the trader study or interpret market movements); humor (unusual incidents of market occurrences, cartoons). No newsletter-type, buy-sell recommendations. The article subject must relate to a technical analysis charting or numerical technique used to trade securities or futures. Buys 60 mss/year. Query with published clips if available or send complete ms. Length: 1,500-4,000 words. Pays $100-500. (Applies base rate and premium rate—write for information). Sometimes pays expenses of writers on assignment.

Photos: Christine M. Napier, photo editor. State availability of photos. Pays $15-50 for 8½x11 b&w glossy prints or color slides. Captions, model release and identification of subjects required. Buys one-time rights.

Columns/Departments: Buys 10 mss/year. Query. Length: 800-1,600 words. Pays $50-200.

Fillers: Carol J. Holman, fillers editor. Jokes. Must relate to trading stocks, bonds, options or commodities. Buys 50/year. Length: 100-500 words. Pays $10-50.

Tips: "Describe how to use chart work and other technical analysis in day-to-day trading of stocks, bonds, options or commodities. A blow-by-blow account of how a trade was made, including the trader's thought processes, is, to our subscribers, the very best received story. One of our prime considerations is to instruct in a manner that the lay person can comprehend. We are not hyper-critical of writing style. The completeness and accuracy of submitted material is of the utmost consideration. Write for detailed writer's guidelines."

TRAVEL SMART FOR BUSINESS, Communications House, 40 Beechdale Rd., Dobbs Ferry NY 10522. (914)693-8300. Editor/Publisher: H.J. Teison. Managing Editor: L.M. Lane. 20% freelance written. Monthly newsletter covering travel and information on keeping travel costs down for business travelers and business travel managers. Circ. 2,000. Pays on publication. Publishes ms an average of 6 weeks after acceptance. No byline given. "Writers are listed as contributors." Buys first North American serial rights. Computer printout submissions acceptable; prefers letter-quality to dot-matrix. SASE. Reports in 6 weeks. Sample copy for business size SAE, and 2 first class stamps; writer's guidelines free for business size SAE and 1 first class stamp.

Nonfiction: Expose (of "inside" travel facts and companies dealing in travel); how-to (pick a meeting site, save money on travel); reviews of facilities and restaurants; analysis of specific trends in travel affecting business travelers. No general travel information, backgrounders, or non-business-oriented articles. "We're looking for value-oriented, concise, factual articles." Buys 20 mss/year. Query with clips of published work. Length: 250-1,500 words. Pays $20-150.

Tips: "We are primarily staff written, with a few regular writers. Contributions to 'Deal Alert' are welcome and can take the form of clips, etc. Know the travel business or have business travel experience. People with a specific area of experience or expertise have the inside track."

WEEKDAY, Enterprise Publications, Suite 3417, 20 N. Wacker Dr., Chicago IL 60606. For the average employee in business and industry. Circ. 30,000. Buys all rights. Byline given. Pays on acceptance. SASE.
Nonfiction and Photos: Uses articles slanted toward the average person, with the purpose of increasing his understanding of the business world and helping him be more successful in it. Also uses articles on "How to Get Along With Other People," and informative articles on meeting everyday problems—consumer buying, legal problems, community affairs, real estate, education, human relations, etc. Length: approximately 1,000 words maximum. Pays $20-50. Uses b&w human interest photos.

Regional

BOULDER BUSINESS REPORT, Our Readers Are Leaders, Boulder Business Report, 2141 14th St., Boulder CO 80302. (303)440-4952. Editor: Suzanne Gripman. 75% freelance written. Monthly newspaper covering Boulder area business issues. Offers "in-depth news tailored to a monthly theme and read by Boulder, Colorado businesspeople and investors nationwide. Philosophy: Colorful, well-written prose of educational value." Circ. 6,000. Pays on completion of assignment. Publishes ms an average of 1 month after acceptance. Byline given. Offers 10% kill fee. Buys one-time rights and second serial (reprint) rights. Simultaneous queries and photocopied submissions OK. Electronic submissions OK via Apple III. Computer printout submissions acceptable; no dot-matrix. SASE. Reports in 1 month on queries; 2 weeks on mss. Sample copy $1.50; free writer's guidelines.
Nonfiction: Book excerpts, interview/profile, new product, photo feature of company, person or product. "All our issues are 'special issues' in that material is written around a monthly theme. No articles are accepted in which the subject has not been pursued in depth and both sides of an issue presented in a writing style with flair." Buys 48 mss/year. Query with published clips. Length: 250-2,000 words. Pays $25-200.
Photos: State availability of photos with query letter. Reviews b&w contact sheets; prefers "people portraits." Pays $10 maximum for b&w contact sheet. Identification of subjects required. Buys one-time rights and reprint rights.
Tips: "It would be difficult to write for this publication if a freelancer was unable to localize a subject. In-depth articles are what we are looking for, written by assignment. The freelancer located in the Boulder, Colorado, area has an excellent chance here, but there are so few writers who go beyond dry reporting that we are willing to take any localized writing with flair that we can get."

‡BUSINESS ATLANTA, The Magazine of Southern Business. Communication Channels Inc., 6255 Barfield Rd., Atlanta GA 30328. (404)256-9800. Editor: David C. Foster. Managing Editor: Luann Nelson. 95% freelance written. Monthly magazine. "*Business Atlanta* is a horizontally circulated magazine directed toward the Atlantan or Georgian involved or interested in local business. Our audience is mostly composed of business owners or executives with corporations either based here or with offices here. Our objective is to inform and entertain these readers." Circ. 26,000. Pays on publication. Publishes ms an average of 4 months after acceptance. Byline given. Offers 10% kill fee. Buys first North American serial rights and second serial (reprint) rights. Submit seasonal/holiday material 4 months in advance. Computer printout submissions acceptable; no dot-matrix. SASE. Reports in 3 months on queries; 6 months on mss. Free writer's guidelines.
Nonfiction: Expose (local government); historical/nostalgic (state or Southern business-related); humor (business-related); interview/profile (local business or government); and photo feature (local business or industry or Atlanta or Georgia life or culture). No opinion or personal experience. Buys 280-300 mss/year. Query with published clips. Length: 2,000-5,000 words. Pays $250-1,000.
Columns/Departments: Profile, Enterprise, Marketing, Management Technology, Finance, Public Affairs, Southern Stocks, and Coffeebreak. Buys 200 mss/year. Query with published clips. Length: 1,750-3,000 words. Pays $250-350.
Tips: "Our policy is to employ local writers only—the majority live in Atlanta, with a few elsewhere in Georgia. If, after we see a writer's clips, we feel the person has potential as a writer for *Business Atlanta*, we will interview the person at our offices and possibly make him or her an assignment. For the most part, all story ideas are generated by the editorial staff. The entire magazine is open to freelancers, but new writers are used for the first few assignments solely for back-of-book material."

BUSINESS TO BUSINESS, Tallahassee's Business Magazine, Business to Business, Inc., Box 6085, Tallahassee FL 32314. (904)222-7072. Editor: Howard Libin. 70% freelance written. Monthly tabloid covering business in the North Florida-South Georgia Big Bend region. Circ. 16,000. Pays on acceptance. Publishes ms an average of 3 months after acceptance. Byline given "generally." Offers 30% kill fee. Buys all serial rights. Submit seasonal/holiday material 4 months in advance. Photocopied and previously published submissions OK. Electronic submissions OK via SS SD. Computer printout submissions acceptable; prefers letter-quality to dot-matrix. SASE. Reports in 2 weeks on queries; 3 weeks on mss. Sample copy for 9x12 SAE and 4 first class stamps; writer's guidelines for SAE and 1 first class stamp.

Nonfiction: Book excerpts (reviews of business related books—*Megatrends*, *Positioning*); In Search of Excellence (topics of interest to business-minded people); historical/nostalgic (only pertaining to the Big Bend); how-to (select the right typewriter, adding machine, secretary, phone system, insurance plan); new products; technical (articles on finance marketing, investment, advertising and real estate as it applies to small business). Special "inserts" planned: advertising, office of the future, consulting, taxes. "No really basic material. Writers must assume that readers have some idea of business vocabulary. No new business profiles, or material without local handle." Have started an "After Work" section and can use a wide array of "lifestyle" pieces—health, food, hobbies, travel, recreation, etc. Buys 30-50 mss/year. Query with published clips if available. Length: 600-2,000 words. Pays $40-250.

Photos: Steve Bradley, Bob O'Lary, photo editors. State availability of photos. Pays $5-20 for b&w contact sheet and b&w prints. Identification of subjects required.

Columns/Departments: "Shorts accepted on all aspects of doing business. Each story should tackle one topic and guide reader from question to conclusion. General appeal for all trades and industries." Buys 50-70 mss/year. Query with published clips if available. Length: 600-1,000 words. Pays $40-90.

Tips: "Send a query with past writing sample included. If it seems that a writer is capable of putting together an interesting 500-800 word piece dealing with small business operation, we're willing to give him/her a try. Meeting deadlines determines writer's future with us. We're open to short department pieces on management, finance, marketing, investments, real estate. Must be tightly written—direct and to the point; yet keep it casual."

BUSINESS VIEW OF SOUTHWEST FLORIDA, Collier County Magazines, Inc., Box 1546, Naples FL 33939. (813)263-7525. Editor: Mark Brown. Monthly magazine for business, financial, and investment community of southwest Florida. "The editorial material is factual, succinct and thought-provoking." Circ. 14,200. Pays on publication. Byline given. Offers $25 kill fee. Buys second serial (reprint) rights. Submit seasonal/holiday material 2 months in advance. Simultaneous queries, and simultaneous and previously published submissions OK "only if not locally simultaneously submitted." Computer printout submissions acceptable. SASE. Reports in 6 weeks. Sample copy $2; writer's guidelines for business-size SAE and 1 first class postage stamp.

Nonfiction: How-to (business-related management); interview/profile (regional/Florida business leaders); opinion (business-related); personal experience (business-related); technical (business-related). "We like charts, graphs and statistics. We try to present the facts with an interesting format. Our topics have tie-in to southwest Florida." Query with published clips. Length: 1,750-3,500 words. Pays $100-175. "Special assignments can pay more."

Columns/Departments: Eleanor K. Sommer, column/department editor. Columns of interest to the business, financial, retail, real estate, and investment community of southwest Florida. Buys 24-36 mss/year. Send complete ms. Length: 750-1,500 words. Pays $25-75.

Fillers: Short humor and newsbreaks (business-related). Buys 25-50 mss/year. Length: 200-600 words. Pays $5-25.

Tips: "We like tight, sophisticated writing that gets right to the point. It can be sprinkled with intelligent humor and puns. Our readers are busy business professionals in one of the fastest growing areas in the nation. Columns with management and legal tips for businesses, computer hints, equipment advances, etc., are open to freelancers."

BUSINESSWOMAN, THA, Inc., Box 23276, San Jose CA 95153-3276. (408)226-3311. Editor: Netha Thacker. 75% freelance written. A bimonthly magazine for Northern California businesswomen. "*Business-Woman* is aimed at executive-level, upwardly mobile, businesswomen. It is first and foremost a business magazine, and secondly a woman's magazine." Circ. 6,000. Pays on publication. Publishes ms an average of 3 months after acceptance. Byline given. Buys first North American serial rights. Submit seasonal/holiday material 8 months in advance. Simultaneous queries, and simultaneous, photocopied and previously published submissions OK. Computer printout submissions acceptable. SASE. Reports in 2 months. Sample copy and writer's guidelines for large manilla envelope with 4 first class stamps. .

Nonfiction: Book excerpts; general interest (to businesswomen); how-to; interview/profile; new product; personal experience; technical; travel; and computers. Articles should be directed to Northern California businesswomen. Each issue focuses on a theme. Past themes include Law, Media and Marketing, Balancing Home and Career and Entrepreneurs. Most articles are assigned; send article ideas specific to certain issue 6-8 months before cover date. No fashion, make-up, sewing, cooking, reviews of arts, out-of-state focus. Buys 60-75 mss/year. Query with published clips, or send complete ms. Length: 500-2,500 words. Pays $10-25.

Columns/Departments: Netha Thacker. Travel-tips (for business travel); Computer (how-to product surveys, new trends). Buys 12-20 mss/year. Query with published clips, send complete ms. Length: 500-1,000 words. Pays $10-25.

Tips: Write queries specific to theme of issue 6-8 months in advance of cover date, include clips and resumé or description of background and expertise. Profiles, features, how-to, trends, travel, and computer departments are most open to freelancers. "The most frequent mistake made by writers in completing an article is not targeting our audience. We prefer articles which quote successful business women and men in the regional area."

COMMERCE MAGAZINE, 200 N. LaSalle St., Chicago IL 60601. (312)580-6900. Editor: Carol Johnson. For top businessmen and industrial leaders in greater Chicago area. Also sent to chairmen and presidents of *Fortune* 1,000 firms throughout United States. Monthly magazine; varies from 100 to 300 pages, (8½x11½). Circ. 15,000. Buys all rights. Buys 30-40 mss/year. Pays on acceptance. Query. SASE.

Nonfiction: Business articles and pieces of general interest to top business executives. "We select our freelancers and assign topics. Many of our writers are from local newspapers. Considerable freelance material is used but almost exclusively on assignment from Chicago—area specialists within a particular business sector."

CRAIN'S CLEVELAND BUSINESS, 140 Public Square, Cleveland OH 44114. (216)522-1383. Editor: Brian Tucker. Weekly tabloid about business in the 7 county area surrounding Cleveland and Akron for upper income executives, professionals and entrepreneurs. Circ. 26,000. Average issue includes 2-3 freelance news or feature articles. Pays on publication. Byline given. Buys first North American serial rights. Phone queries OK. Reports in 3 weeks. Free writer's guidelines.

Nonfiction: "We are interested in business and political events and their impact on the Cleveland area business community. We also want local news developments and trends of significance to business life in the Cleveland-Akron-Lorain area." Buys 2-3 mss/issue. Query. Length: 500-1,200 words. Pays $5 column inch for news stories; $3/column inch for special section features.

Photos: State availability of photos. Reviews 5x7 b&w glossy prints. Pays $10/photo used. Captions required. Buys one-time rights.

EXECUTIVE, Airmedia, 2973 Weston Rd., Box 510, Weston Ontario M9N 3R3 Canada. (416)741-1112. Publisher: Donald Coote. Editor: Patricia Anderson. Monthly business magazine covering financial, political, company profiles for presidents and senior management. Circ. 53,000. Pays on acceptance. Byline given. Buys first rights. Reports as soon as possible. Free sample copy.

Nonfiction: Query with clips of published work.

Photos: Reviews photos. Identification of subjects required. Buys one-time rights.

EXECUTIVE REPORT, Riverview Publications, Suite 624, Bigelow Sq., Pittsburgh PA 15219. (442)471-4585. Publisher: Charles W. Shane. 65% freelance written. Monthly magazine concentrating on the business, industry and finance of western Pennsylvania. Circ. 16,000. Pays within 30 days of publication. Publishes ms an average of 4 months after acceptance. Byline given. Buys first serial and second serial (reprint) rights to the same material. Submit seasonal/holiday material 3 months in advance. Simultaneous queries, and photocopied, simultaneous, and previously published submissions OK. Dot-matrix submissions are acceptable if legible. SASE. Sample copy $2; free writer's guidelines.

Nonfiction: Deborah Leff, Managing Editor. Expose, interview/profile, new product, opinion, personal experience, travel. Buys 10-14 mss/year. Query with clips of published work. Length: 1,000-3,000 words. Pays $100-500. Sometimes pays the expenses of writers on assignment.

Tips: "The most frequent mistake made by writers in completing an article assignment for us is not giving the article sufficient local slant; we are a regional publication. The writer may have a better chance of breaking in at our publication with short articles and fillers because we like a writer to establish a 'track record' before major assignments are made."

THE FINANCIAL POST MAGAZINE, Maclean Hunter, Ltd., 777 Bay St., Toronto, Ontario M5W 1A7 Canada. (416)596-5658. Editor: Paul A. Rush. Monthly magazine covering personal money. Circ. 225,000. Pays on acceptance. Byline given. Offers 50% kill fee. Buys first North American serial rights. Submit seasonal/holiday material 3 months in advance. Simultaneous queries OK. SAE, IRC. Reports in 1 month. Free sample copy.

Nonfiction: Book excerpts, interview/profile and new product. No articles on women in management, stress, travel, US politics and money, or fashion. Canadian angle required.

‡**ILLINOIS BUSINESS**, Crain Communications, Inc., 740 N. Rush, Chicago IL 60611. (312)280-3163. Editor: Joe Cappo. Managing Editor: Alan Rosenthal. 90% freelance written. Quarterly business publication for company presidents, owners, board chairmen, state officials. Circ. 25,000. Pays on acceptance. (All articles are on a work-for-hire basis.) Publishes ms an average of 3 months after acceptance. Simultaneous queries OK "if so advised." Computer printout submissions acceptable. Reports in 1 month.
Nonfiction: "Anything to do with Illinois business and economics." Buys 64 mss/year. (All articles are commissioned.) Query with published clips. Length: 2,500 words maximum. Pays $300 and up; average feature-length article pays $1,000. Sometimes pays the expenses of writers on assignment.
Tips: "Read our publication before submitting a query. All material must be about Illinois business. The magazine is seeking Illinois writers and photographers who can cover Illinois business subjects."

KANSAS BUSINESS NEWS, Kansas Business Publishing Co., Inc., Suite 124, 3601 S.W. 29th, Topeka KS 66614. (913)293-3010. Editor: Dan Bearth. 30% freelance written. Monthly magazine about Kansas business for the business owner, executives and professionals who want to how what is going on in the state that will affect the way they do business, their profits, labor requirements, etc. All submissions must relate to local business conditions. Circ. 15,000. Pays on publication. Publishes ms an average of 6 months after acceptance. Buys all rights. Phone queries OK. Submit seasonal material 3 months in advance. Simultaneous and previously published submissions OK. Computer printout submissions acceptable. SASE. Free sample copy.
Nonfiction: How-to, humor, interview, profile, and technical. Query only. Pays $25-250. Sometimes pays expenses of writers on assignment.
Photos: Marsh Galloway, editor. State availability of photos or send photos with ms. Reviews b&w contact sheets and negatives. Offers no additional payment for photos accepted with ms. Captions preferred; model release required. Buys all rights.
Columns/Departments: Management, Finance, Government, Personnel Management, Taxes, Small Business, Computers and Technology, Insurance, Labor Relations and Investment. Query only. Pays $25 minimum.

KENTUCKY BUSINESS LEDGER, Box 3508, Louisville KY 40201. (502)636-0551. Editor: Philip F. Van Pelt. 30-70% freelance written. Emphasizes Kentucky business and finance. Monthly tabloid. Circ. 14,500. Pays on publication. Publishes ms an average of 1 month after acceptance. Buys all rights. Byline given at editor's option. Phone queries OK. Submit seasonal/holiday material 3 months in advance of issue date. Computer printout submissions acceptable; prefers letter-quality to dot-matrix. SASE. Reports in 24 hours. Sample copy $1.80; free writer's guidelines.
Nonfiction: How-to (tips for businesses on exporting, dealing with government, cutting costs, increasing profits—*must* have specific Kentucky angle); interview (government officials on issues important to Kentucky businesspersons); new uses for existing products or commodities, such as coal, tobacco, etc. "We are not interested in every company's new flange or gasket"); profile (of Kentucky businesspersons); and articles on the meanings of government laws and regulations to Kentucky businesses. "We get too many industry-wide trend stories, which we use hardly at all. We must have a strong Kentucky link to any story." No humor, book reviews or personal advice. Buys 40-50 mss/year. Query. Length: 800-1,000 words. Pays $2/inch.
Photos: State availability of photos with query. Pays $10-15 for b&w glossy prints.
Tips: "On technical subjects from unknown freelancers, we need a statement of expertise and/or previous work within the subject area. Also, we need stringers in major Kentucky cities, particularly in the eastern half of the state."

THE MANHATTAN COOPERATOR, The Co-Op & Condo Monthly. 23 Leonard St., New York NY 10013. (212)226-0808. Editor: Vicki Chesler. 20% freelance written. A monthly tabloid covering real estate trends, taxation, legislation, interior design, management and maintenance for apartment owners. Circ. 100,000. Pays on publication. Publishes ms an average of 3 months after acceptance. Byline given. Buys second serial (reprint) rights. Submit seasonal/holiday material 2 months in advance. Simultaneous queries, and simultaneous, photocopied, and previously published submissions OK. Computer printout submissions acceptable; prefers letter-quality to dot-matrix. Reports in 1 month. Free writer's guidelines.
Nonfiction: General interest (related to NYC metro area and within 200 miles); how-to (for apartment owners); interview/profile (on New Yorkers of interest preferably to apartment owners); new product (related to home ownership, security, energy conservation); technical (related to home improvement or real estate ownership); travel (within 300 miles of NYC or special areas); real estate; legal; taxation; and interior design. Special issues include Home Improvement/Vacation Condos (June); Interior Design (Oct.); Fuel Conservation (Nov.); and Financial Planning (Dec.). Query with or without published clips. Length: 750-1,500 words. Pays $50-175 (more with photos). Sometimes pays expenses of writers on assignment.
Photos: State availability of photos or send photos with query or ms. Pays $10-150 for 8x10 b&w prints. Identification of subjects required. Buys one-time and re-use rights.
Columns/Departments: Owner Profile (NYC apartment owner with interesting career); Insurance Advisor

(related to apartment ownership); Maintenance (buildings over 30 units); Financial Finesse (investing); Building Management (over 30 units); Interior Design; Fuel Conservation; Letter of the Law; Tax Tips; Market Trends; and Security & Safety.

MEMPHIS BUSINESS JOURNAL, Mid-South Communications, Inc., Suite 322, 4515 Poplar St., Memphis TN 38117. (901)685-2411. Editor: Barney DuBois. 20% freelance written. Weekly tabloid covering industry, trade, agribusiness and finance in west Tennessee, north Mississippi, east Arkansas, and the Missouri Bootheel. "Articles should be timely and relevant to business in our region." Circ. 10,400. Pays on acceptance. Publishes ms an average of 2 weeks after acceptance. Byline given. Pays $50 kill fee. Buys one-time rights, second serial (reprint) rights, and makes work-for-hire assignments. Submit seasonal/holiday material 2 months in advance. Publishes ms an average of 2 weeks after acceptance; prefers letter-quality to dot-matrix. Simultaneous queries and submissions OK. Computer printout submissions acceptable. SASE. Reports in 2 weeks. Free sample copy.
Nonfiction: Expose, historical/nostalgic, interview/profile, business features and trends. "All must relate to business in our area." Buys 130 mss/year. Query with or without clips of published work or send complete ms. Length: 750-2,000 words. Pays $80-200. Sometimes pays the expenses of writers on assignment.
Photos: State availability of photos or send photos with ms. Pays $25-50 for 5x7 b&w prints. Identification of subjects required. Buys one-time rights.
Tips: "We are interested in news—and this means we can accept short, hard-hitting work more quickly. We also welcome freelancers who can do features and articles on business in the smaller cities of our region. We are a weekly, so our stories need to be timely."

MINNESOTA BUSINESS JOURNAL, For Decisionmakers of Growing Companies, Dorn Communications, 7831 E. Bush Lake, Minneapolis MN 55435. (612)835-6855. Editor: Donald R. Nelson. Managing Editor: Terry Fiedler. 75% freelance written. A monthly regional business magazine covering general business and Minnesota companies with revenue of less than $25 million per year for managers of small, growing, Minnesota-based companies. Circ. 26,000. Pays on publication. Publishes ms an average of 3 months after acceptance. Byline given. Offers kill fee of 25% of agreed-upon price. Not copyrighted. Buys first serial rights and makes work-for-hire assignments. Simultaneous queries and simultaneous submissions OK. Computer printout submissions acceptable; prefers letter-quality to dot-matrix. Reports in 2 weeks on queries; 1 month on mss. Free sample copy.
Nonfiction: How-to (anything related to running a company efficiently, often written within the context of a company profile); and interview/profile (Minnesota business leaders, company profiles with how-to slant). "Articles all feature a how-to slant, how to manage people, how to cut costs, how to solve family business problems, how to arrange financing, etc." Buys 36 mss/year. Query with published clips. Length: 1,500-3,500 words. Pays $50-500. Computer printout submissions acceptable; prefers letter-quality to dot-matrix.
Tips: Accepts queries and submissions only from Minnesota-based writers. "We cover only Minnesota-based companies (no subsidiaries, franchises, or distributorships). Focus is on entreprenurial ventures, especially in high-tech areas. We are not a Chamber of Commerce newsletter, but a magazine about (not necessarily for) business."

OHIO BUSINESS, Business Journal Publishing Co., 425 Hanna Bldg., Cleveland OH 44115. (216)621-1644. Editor: Robert W. Gardner. Managing Editor: Michael E. Moore. 10% freelance written. A monthly magazine covering general business topics. "*Ohio Business* serves the state of Ohio. Readers are business executives in the state engaged in manufacturing, agriculture, mining, construction, transportation, communications, utilities, retail and wholesale trade, services, and government." Circ. 35,000. Pays for features on acceptance; news on publication. Byline sometimes given. Kill fee can be negotiated. Buys one-time rights, and second serial (reprint) rights; depends on projects. Submit seasonal/holiday material 3-4 months in advance. Simultaneous queries, and simultaneous, photocopied, and previously published submissions OK. Computer printout submissions acceptable; prefers letter-quality to dot-matrix. SASE. Reports in 2 weeks on queries; 1 month on mss. Sample copy $2; writer's guidelines for SAE and 1 first class stamp.
Nonfiction: Book excerpts, general interest, how-to, interview/profile, opinion and personal experience. "In all cases, write with an Ohio executive in mind. Stories should give readers useful information on business within the state, trends in management, ways to manage better, or other developments which would affect them in their professional careers." Buys 14-20 mss/year. Query with published clips. Length: 100-2,500 words. Pays $25 minimum. Sometimes pays expenses of writers on assignment.
Photos: State availability of photos. Reviews b&w and color transparencies and prints. Captions and identification of subjects required. Buys variable rights.
Columns/Departments: News; People (features Ohio business execs); High-Tech (leading edge Ohio products and companies); Made in Ohio (unusual Ohio product/services). Query with published clips. Length 100-600 words. Pays $50 minimum.
Tips: "Features are most open to freelancers. Come up with new ideas or information for our readers: Ohio

executives in manufacturing and service industries. Writers should be aware of the trend toward specialization in magazine publishing with strong emphasis on people in coverage."

OREGON BUSINESS, MIF Publications, Suite 404, 208 SW Stark, Portland OR 97204. (503)223-0304. Editor: Robert Hill. 50% freelance written. Monthly magazine covering business in Oregon. Circ. 20,000. Pays on publication. Publishes ms an average of 4 months after acceptance. Byline given. Buys first rights. Submit seasonal/holiday material 3 months in advance. Photocopied and previously published submissions OK. Computer printout submissions acceptable; prefers letter-quality to dot-matrix. SASE. Reports in 1 month. Sample copy for business size SAE and $1.05 postage.
Nonfiction: General interest (real estate, business, investing, small business); interview/profile (business leaders); and new products. Special issues include tourism, world trade, finance. "We need articles on real estate or small business in Oregon, outside the Portland area." Buys 24 mss/year. Query with published clips. Length: 900-2,000 words. Pays 10¢/word minimum; $200 maximum. Sometimes pays expenses of writers on assignment.

PHOENIX BUSINESS JOURNAL, SCRIPPS HOWARD BUSINESS JOURNAL, Suite 100, 1817 N. 3rd St., Phoenix AZ 85004. (602)271-4712. Editor: Chambers Williams. General Manager: Jim Gressinger. 40% freelance written. Weekly tabloid covering business economics for CEOs and top corporate managers. Circ. 15,000. Pays on publication. Publishes ms an average of 3 weeks after acceptance. Byline given. Buys all rights. Submit seasonal/holiday material 1 month in advance. Computer printout submissions acceptable. SASE. Reports in 2 weeks. Sample copy free.
Nonfiction: Interview/profile (of entrepreneurs); and "news affecting all types of Phoenix area corporations, large and small. Our audience is all local." Buys 250 mss/year. Length: open. Pays average flat rate of $75/20 column inches.

REGARDIES: THE MAGAZINE OF WASHINGTON BUSINESS, 1010 Wisconsin Ave., NW, Washington DC 20007. (202)342-0410. Senior Editor: Henry Fortunato. 95% freelance written. Monthly magazine covering business in the Washington DC metropolitan area for Washington business executives. Circ. 32,000. Pays within 30 days after publication. Publishes ms an average of 3 months after acceptance. Byline given. Pays variable kill fee. Buys first serial rights and second serial (reprint) rights. Computer printout submissions acceptable. Submit seasonal/holiday material 3 months in advance. Reports in 3 weeks.
Nonfiction: Profiles (of business leaders), investigative reporting, real estate, advertising, politics, lifestyle, media, retailing, communications, labor issues, and financial issues—all on the Washington business scene. "If it isn't the kind of story that could just as easily run in a city magazine or a national magazine like *Harper's*, *Atlantic*, *Esquire*, etc., I don't want to see it." Buys 90 mss/year. Length: 4,000 words average. Buys 5-6/issue. Pays negotiable rate. Sometimes pays the expenses of writers on assignment.
Columns/Departments: Length: 1,500 words average. Buys 8-12/issue. Pays negotiable rates.
Tips: "The most frequent mistake writers make is not including enough information and data about business, which with public companies is easy enough to find. This results in flawed analysis and a willingness to accept the "official line.""

TIDEWATER VIRGINIAN, Suite A, 711 W. 21st, Norfolk VA 23517. Executive Editor: Marilyn Goldman. 80% freelance written. Published by two Tidewater area chambers of commerce. Monthly magazine for business management people. Circ. 9,000. Buys first serial rights and second serial (reprint) rights to material originally published elsewhere. Byline given. Buys 60 mss/year. Pays on publication. Publishes ms an average of 2 months after acceptance. Sample copy $1.95. Photocopied and simultaneous submissions OK. Computer printout submissions acceptable; prefers letter-quality to dot-matrix. Reports in 3 weeks. Query or submit complete ms. SASE.
Nonfiction: Articles dealing with business and industry in Virginia, primarily the surrounding area of southeastern Virginia (Tidewater area). Profiles, successful business operations, new product, merchandising techniques and business articles. Recently published article: "High-Tech Telephony," (communication tools that have become faster, smaller, longer-ranged and packed with greater capabilities). Length: 500-2,500 words. Pays $25-150. Sometimes pays the expenses of writers on assignment.

‡TUCSON BUSINESS DIGEST, 3520 S. Dodge, Tucson AZ 85717. (602)571-1744. Editor: Keith Ray. Bimonthly magazine for businessmen. Circ. 18,000. Pays on publication. Byline given. Buys first North American rights. Submit seasonal/holiday material 6 months in advance. Photocopied and electronic submissions OK; "Please query with SASE. We will forward access numbers and codes." Computer printout submissions acceptable. SASE. Reports in 1 month. Sample copy $5.
Nonfiction: How-to, interview/profile, photo feature and technical (computers). "Articles should be relative to Tucson business: trends, analysis, success, etc." Buys 40 mss/year. Send Query. Length: 500-2,000 words. Pays $50-400.

Photos: Send photos with ms. Reviews b&w and color contact sheets and color prints. Model release and identification of subjects required.

Tips: Tucson writers and Tucson business oriented stories only. No fiction, fillers or poetry.

WASHINGTON BUSINESS JOURNAL, Scripps-Howard Business Journals, 8321 Old Courthouse Rd., Vienna VA 22180. (703)442-4900. Editor: Susan E. Currier. 20% freelance written. Weekly tabloid covering business in the District of Columbia, suburban Maryland and Northern Virginia areas for business persons in middle management as well as chief executive officers. Circ. 20,000. Pays on publication. Publishes ms an average of 1 month after acceptance. Byline given. Not copyrighted. Buys all rights. SASE. Computer printout submissions acceptable; prefers letter-quality to dot-matrix. Sample copy $1.

Nonfiction: Interview/profile (of a local figure—public or small entrepreneur); new product (inventions or patents from area people); business. Special issues are published frequently. Editorial calendar available on request. No generic or *national* business topics. Query with published clips or submit complete ms. Length: 600-1,800 words. Pays $3.50-$4.50/column inch.

Photos: State availability or send photos with ms. Pays negotiable rates for 8x10 b&w prints. Identification of subjects required.

Tips: "Queries should have decent writing samples attached. Manuscripts should be well researched, well written and thorough. Neatness and quality of presentation is a plus, as is accurate spelling and grammar. *WBJ* is interested in all business topics including: technology, real estate, accounting, associations, science, education, government, etc. Information sources should be high level and subject should be timely. Accompanying sidebars, photographs and graphs are also well received."

WESTERN INVESTOR, Western States Investment Information, Willamette Publishing, Inc., Suite 1115, 400 SW 6th Ave., Portland OR 97204. (503)222-0577. Editor/Publisher: S.P. Pratt. Managing Editor: Donna Walker. 5% freelance written. Quarterly magazine for the investment community of the 13 western states. For stock brokers, corporate officers, financial analysts, trust officers, CPAs, investors, etc. Circ. 16,000. Pays on publication. Publishes ms an average of 6 months after acceptance. Byline given. Buys one time and second serial (reprint) rights and makes work-for-hire assignments. Simultaneous queries and simultaneous, photocopied and previously published submissions OK. Computer submissions acceptable; prefers letter-quality to dot-matrix. SASE. Sample copy $1.50 with SAE and $1.24 postage.

Nonfiction: General business interest ("trends, people, public, listed in our instrument data section"). "Each issue carries a particular industry theme." Query. Length: 200-2,000 words. Pays $50 minimum.

Photos: State availability of photos. Pays $10 minimum for 5x7 (or larger) b&w prints. Buys one-time rights.

Tips: "All editorial copy must pertain or directly relate to companies and/or industry groups included in our listed companies. Send us a one-page introduction including your financial writing background, story ideas, availability for assignment work, credits, etc. What we want at this point is a good working file of authors to draw from; let us know your special areas of interest and expertise. Newspaper business page writers would be good candidates. If you live and work in the west, so much the better."

WESTERN NEW YORK MAGAZINE, Buffalo Area Chamber of Commerce, 107 Delaware Ave., Buffalo NY 14202. (716)849-6689. Editor: J. Patrick Donlon. 10% freelance written. Monthly magazine of the Buffalo-Niagara Falls area. "Tells the story of Buffalo and Western New York, with special emphasis on business and industry and secondary emphasis on quality of life subjects." Circ. 8,000. Pays on acceptance. Publishes ms an average of 3 months after acceptance. Byline given. Offers $150 kill fee. Not copyrighted. Buys all rights. Submit seasonal/holiday material 3 months in advance. Simultaneous queries OK. Computer printout submissions acceptable; no dot-matrix. SASE. Reports in 1 month. Sample copy for $2, 9x12 SAE and 3 first class stamps; writer's guidelines for business size SAE and 1 first class stamp.

Nonfiction: General interest (business, finance, commerce); historical/nostalgic (Buffalo, Niagara Falls); how-to (business management); interview/profile (community leader); and Western New York industry, quality of life. "Broad-based items preferred over single firm or organization. Submit articles that provide insight into business operations, marketing, finance, promotion, and nuts-and-bolts approach to small business management. No nationwide or even New York statewide articles or pieces on specific companies, products, services." Buys 30 mss/year. Query with published clips. Length: 1,000-2,500 words. Pays $150-300. Sometimes pays the expenses of writers on assignment.

Photos: Amy P. Wopperer, art director. State availability of photos. Reviews contact sheet. Pays $10-25 for 5x7 b&w prints.

Market conditions are constantly changing! If this is 1987 or later, buy the newest edition of *Writer's Market* at your favorite bookstore or order directly from Writer's Digest Books.

Career, College and Alumni

"Students in general are more career-oriented," observes one editor. "They are also less concerned about issues and more preoccupied with relationships." To help students prepare for the job market, many of these magazines are looking for practical career information that readers can use. Some publications also cover issues and relationships. Three types of magazines are listed in this section: university publications written for students, alumni, and friends of a specific institution; publications about college life, and publications on career and job opportunities.

ALCALDE, Box 7278, Austin TX 78713. (512)476-6271. Editor: Ernestine Wheelock. 50% freelance written. Bimonthly magazine. Circ. 44,000. Pays on publication. Publishes ms an average of 6 months after acceptance. Buys all rights. Submit seasonal/holiday material 5 months in advance. Electronic submissions OK via Xerox 860 disk or Macintosh disk. Computer printout submissions acceptable; prefers letter-quality to dot-matrix. SASE. Reports in 1 month.
Nonfiction: General interest; historical (University of Texas, research, and faculty profile); humor (humorous University of Texas incidents or profiles that include background data); interviews (University of Texas subjects); nostalgia (University of Texas traditions); profile (students, faculty or alumni); and technical (University of Texas research on a subject or product). No subjects lacking taste or quality, or not connected with the University of Texas. Buys 18 mss/year. Query. Length: 1,000-2,400 words. Pays according to importance of article.

THE BLACK COLLEGIAN, The National Magazine of Black College Students, Black Collegiate Services, Inc., 1240 S. Broad St., New Orleans LA 70125. (504)821-5694. Editor: James Borders. 40% freelance written. Magazine for black college students and recent graduates with an interest in black cultural awareness, sports, news, personalities, history, trends, current events and job opportunities. Published bimonthly during school year; (4 times/year). 160 pages. Circ. 190,000. Buys one-time rights. Byline given. Pays on publication. Offers 1/3 kill fee. Photocopied, previously published and simultaneous submissions OK. Computer printout submissions acceptable. Submit seasonal and special material 2 months in advance of issue date (Careers in Sciences, August; Computers/Grad School, November; Engineering and Travel/Summer Programs, January; Finance and Jobs, March; Medicine, May). SASE. Reports in 3 weeks on queries; 1 month on mss. Sample copy for 9x12 SAE and 3 first class stamps; writer's guidelines for #10 SAE and 1 first class stamp.
Nonfiction: Material on careers, sports, black history, news analysis. Articles on problems and opportunities confronting black college students and recent graduates. Book excerpts, exposé, general interest, historical/nostalgic, how-to (develop employability), opinion, personal experience, profile, inspirational, humor. Buys 40 mss/year, 6 unsolicited. Query with published clips or send complete ms. Length: 500-2,500 words. Pays $25-350.
Photos: State availability of photos with query or ms, or send photos with query or ms. B&w photos or color transparencies purchased with or without mss. 8x10 b&w prints preferred. Captions, model releases and identification of subjects required. Pays $35/b&w; $50/color.
Tips: "Career features area is most open to freelancers."

‡**CAMPUS VOICE, The National College Magazine**, 13-30 Corporation, 505 Market St., Knoxville TN 37902. (615)521-0646. Editor: Keith Bellows. Managing Editor: Barbara Penland. 80% freelance published. Bimonthly magazine. "The purpose of *Campus Voice* is to define and reflect the college experience of the '80s; to mirror the college culture; and to be jingoistic about college just as a city or regional magazine is jingoistic about its community." Estab. 1984. Circ. 1.2 million. Pays on acceptance. Publishes ms an average of 2 months after acceptance. Byline given. Offers 33 1/3% kill fee. Buys first North American serial rights. Submit seasonal/holiday material 6 months in advance. Computer printout submissions acceptable; no dot-matrix. SASE. Reports in 3 weeks. Sample copy $2, 10x12 SAE and 6 first class stamps. Writer's guidelines for letter size SAE and 1 first class stamp.
Nonfiction: Book excerpts, expose, general interest, how-to (careers/academics with news angles), humor, interview/profile, personal experience, photo feature and travel. Special issue includes In Celebration of College—major theme issue showcasing the people, places, events, traditions, ideas and achievements that make college special. To be published Feb. '86; most material assigned to major national writers—most, but not all. No inspirational, obvious college-oriented, ideas. Buys 100 mss/year. Query with published clips. Length: 750-4,000 words. Pays $500-5,000. Pays expenses of writers on assignment.

Tips: "Don't think of our readers as students—they're 18-to-24-year olds with sophisticated taste. If you pitch a college-based idea make it original. Area most open to freelancers is Campus Beat. Be relevant, offbeat, original. Look for news/entertainment ideas with a twist."

COLLEGE OUTLOOK AND CAREER OPPORTUNITIES, Special editions include Business, Education, Nursing, Academic Honors, Computer/High Tech, Christian, Minority, and Junior College Transfer, Townsend-Kraft Publishing Co., Box 239, Liberty MO 64068. (816)781-4941. Editor: Ellen Parker. 20% freelance written. Student information publications on subjects of interest to college or college-bound students. *"College Outlook* attempts to inform students on college admissions, financial aid, career opportunities, academic subjects, study techniques and other topics of interest to college-bound students." Circ. 2.5 million regular, plus special editions. Pays on acceptance. Publishes ms an average of 3 months after acceptance. Byline given. Buys all rights and second (reprint) rights. Computer printout submissions acceptable; prefers letter-quality to dot-matrix. Reports as soon as possible. Sample copy for SAE and 90¢ postage; writer's guidelines for business size SAE and 1 first class stamp.
Photos: State availability of photos. "We prefer to see photos with focus on students." Model release required. Buys all rights.
Fillers: Newsbriefs. Buys up to 4 mss/year. Length: 100-500 words. Pays 10¢/word.

COLLEGIATE CAREER WOMAN, For Career Minded Women, Equal Opportunity Publications, Inc., 44 Broadway, Greenlawn NY 11740. (516)261-8917. Editor: James Schneider. Magazine published 3 times/year (fall, winter, spring) covering career-guidance for college women. Strives "to aid women in developing career abilities to the fullest potential; improve job hunting skills; present career opportunities; provide personal resources; help cope with discrimination." Audience is 92% college juniors and seniors; 8% working graduates. Circ. 10,500. "Controlled circulation, distributed through college guidance and placement offices." Pays on publication. Byline given. Buys all rights. "Deadline dates: fall, August 5; winter, November 3; spring, February 8. Simultaneous queries, and simultaneous, photocopied and previously published submissions OK. Computer printout submissions acceptable; prefers typed mss. SASE. Free sample copy and writer's guidelines available on request.
Nonfiction: Book excerpts (on job search techniques, role models, success stories, employment helps); general interest (on special concerns of women); historical/nostalgic (on women's achievements, progress, and hopes for the future); how-to (on self-evaluation, job-finding skills, adjustment, coping with the real world); humor (student or career related); interview/profile (of successful career women, outstanding students); new product (new career opportunities); opinion (on women's progress, male attitudes, discrimination); personal experience (student and career experiences); technical (on career fields offering opportunities for women); travel (on overseas job opportunities); and contributions to the development of the whole person. Prefers not to see general stories about women's issues, but those specifically related to careers. Wants more profiles of successful career women. Special issues include career opportunities for women in industry and government in fields such as nursing and health care, communication, sales, marketing, banking, insurance, finance, engineering and computers, as well as opportunities in the government, military, and defense. Query or send complete ms. Length: 1,250-3,000 words.
Photos: Anne Kelly, photo editor. Prefers 35mm color slides, but will accept b&w. Captions, model release and identification of subjects required. Buys all rights. More pictures needed.
Tips: Articles should focus on career-guidance, role model, and industry prospects for women.

THE COMPUTER & ELECTRONICS GRADUATE, The Entry-Level Career & Information Technology Magazine for CS, Systems and EE Graduates, Equal Opportunity Publications, Inc., 44 Broadway, Greenlawn NY 11740. (516)261-8917. Editor: James Schneider. A quarterly career-guidance magazine for computer science/systems and electrical/electronics engineering students and professionals. "We strive to aid our readers in developing career abilities to the fullest potential; improve job-hunting skills; present career opportunities; provide personal resources." Circ. 26,000 (controlled circulation, distributed through college guidance and placement offices). Pays on publication. Byline given. Buys all rights. Deadline: fall, July 1; winter, Oct. 5; spring, Jan. 15; summer, May 3. Simultaneous queries and simultaneous, photocopied, and previously published submissions OK. Computer printout submissions acceptable; no dot-matrix. SASE. Reports in 1 month. Sample copy and writer's guidelines for 8½x11 SAE and 60¢ postage.
Nonfiction: Book excerpts (on job search techniques, role models, success stories, employment helps); general interest (on special concerns to computer science/systems, and electrical/electronics engineering students and professionals); how-to (on self-evaluation, job-finding skills, adjustment, coping with the real world); humor (student or career related); interview/profile (of successful computer science/systems and electrical/electronics engineering students and professionals); new product (new career opportunities); personal experience (student and career experiences); technical (on career fields offering opportunities); travel on overseas job opportunities; and coverage of other reader interests. Special issues include careers in industry and government in computer science, computer systems, electrical engineering, software systems, robotics, artificial intelligence, as well as opportunities in the military and in defense. "We are planning to devote one issue to professionals."

No sensitive or highly technical material. Buys 20-25 mss/year. Query. Length: 1,250-3,000 words. Pays 10¢/word.

Photos: Ann Kelly, photo editor. State availability of photos or send photos with query or mss. Prefers 35mm color slides, but will accept b&w. Captions, model releases, and identification of subjects required.

Tips: "Articles should focus on career-guidance, role model, and industry prospects for computer science, computer systems and electrical and electronics engineering students and professionals."

EQUAL OPPORTUNITY, The Nation's Only Multi-Ethnic Recruitment Magazine for Black, Hispanic, Native American & Asian American College Grads, Equal Opportunity Publications, Inc., 44 Broadway, Greenlawn NY 11740. (516)261-8917. Editor: James Schneider. 50% freelance written. Magazine published 3 times/year (fall, winter, spring) covering career-guidance for minorities. "Our audience is 90% college juniors and seniors, 10% working graduates. An understanding of educational and career problems of minorities is essential." Circ. 15,000. "Controlled circulation, distributed through college guidance and placement offices." Pays on publication. Publishes ms an average of 1 month after acceptance. Byline given. Buys all rights. Deadline dates: fall, August 5; winter, November 3; spring, February 8. Simultaneous queries, and simultaneous, photocopied and previously published submissions OK. Computer printout submissions acceptable; prefers typed mss. SASE. Free sample copy and writer's guidelines for SAE and 3 first class stamps.

Nonfiction: Book excerpts and articles (on job search techniques, role models); general interest (on specific minority concerns); how-to (on job-hunting skills, personal finance, better living, coping with discrimination); humor (student or career related); interview/profile (minority role models); new product (new career opportunities); opinion (problems of minorities); personal experience (professional and student study and career experiences); technical (on career fields offering opportunities for minorities); travel (on overseas job opportunities); and coverage of Black, Hispanic, American Indian and Asian American interests. Special issues include career opportunities for minorities in industry and government in fields such as banking, insurance, finance, communications, sales, marketing, engineering and computers, as well as careers in the government, military and defense. Query or send complete ms. Length: 1,250-3,000 words.

Photos: Prefers 35mm color slides and b&w. Captions, model release and identification of subjects required. Buys all rights.

Tips: Articles should focus on career-guidance, role model, and industry prospects for minorities.

‡GENERATION, A Weekly Magazine, Sub-Board One, Inc., Box G, Harriman Hall, Buffalo NY 14214. (716)831-2248. Editor: Eric F. Coppolino. Associate Editor: A. Galarneau. A campus community publication. A highly diverse weekly magazine with emphasis on social issues. Circ. 10,000. Payment negotiable. Byline given. Buys first North American serial rights. Submit seasonal/holiday material 2 months in advance. Simultaneous queries, and simultaneous, photocopied, and previously published submissions OK. Computer printout submissions acceptable; prefers letter-quality to dot-matrix. SASE. Reports in 4 weeks. Sample copy for 5 first class stamps.

Nonfiction: General interest, humor, interview/profile, personal experience and travel. Special issue: *reach*, The real Student Handbook. Acquires 60 mss/year. Send complete ms. Length: 750-3,000 words. Pays in copies.

Fiction: Acquires 30 mss/year. Send complete ms. Length: 1,000-3,000 words. Pays in copies.

Poetry: John Matthews, poetry editor. Free verse, haiku and light verse. No foreign language. Acquires 60-70/year. Submit maximum 5 poems. Length: 4-50 lines. Pays in copies.

Fillers: Debbie Steckler, fillers editor. Clippings, jokes, gags, anecdotes, short humor and newsbreaks. Acquires 25/year. Length: 50-100 words. Pays in copies.

Tips: "Feature and investigative writing are most open to freelancers."

HIS, Box 1450, Downers Grove IL 60515. (312)964-5700. Editor: Verne Becker. 90% freelance written. Issued monthly from October-May for collegiate students, faculty, administrators and graduate students interested in the evangelical Christian persuasion. "It is an interdenominational, Biblical presentation, combining insights on Scripture and everyday life on campus. We need sophisticated humor, outstanding fiction with a Christian base, articles of interest to non-Christian readers." Pays on acceptance. Publishes ms an average of 2 years after acceptance. Buys first rights and second (reprint) rights to material originally published elsewhere. Reports in 3 months. Computer printout submissions acceptable; prefers letter-quality to dot-matrix. SASE.

Nonfiction and Fiction: "Articles dealing with practical aspects of Christian living on campus, relating contemporary issues to Biblical principles. Should show relationship between Christianity and various fields of study, Christian doctrine, or missions." Submit complete ms. Buys 55 unsolicited mss/year. Recent article example "Why Can't I Get a Job?" (June 1985). Length: 2,000 words maximum. Pays $50-100.

Poetry: Pays $20-35.

Tips: "Direct your principles and illustrations at the college milieu. Avoid preachiness and attacks on various Christian ministries or groups; share your insights on a peer basis."

JOB CORPS IN ACTION, Meridian Publishing Co. Inc., Box 10010, Ogden UT 84409. Associate Editor: Caroll McKanna Halley. A monthly magazine covering Job Corps Centers throughout the United States. "We publish *upbeat* stories about successful individuals and programs that benefit our communities. Job Corps people and program stories only." Estab. 1984. Pays on acceptance. Byline given. Buys first rights and nonexclusive reprint rights. Submit seasonal/holiday material 6 months in advance. Simultaneous queries, and photocopied and previously published submissions OK. SASE. Reports in 3 weeks. Sample copy for $1 and 9x12 SAE; writer's guidelines for business size SAE and 1 first class stamp.
Nonfiction: Book excerpts (if applicable to labor, job, vocational training); historical/nostalgic (only in regard to Job Corps); inspirational (only in the sense of Job Corps success stories or help to communities); interview/profile; personal experience; photo feature; and technical. No expose, nothing depressing, no non-labor, non-education, non-job corps pieces. Buys 30 mss/year. Query with or without published clips or send complete ms. "All considered seriously." Length: 800-1,200 words. Pays 15¢/word.
Photos: State availability of photos, or send photos with query or ms. Pays $35 minimum for color slides to 8x10 transparencies and prints; negotiates payment for covers. Captions required. Buys one-time rights.
Fillers: Newsbreaks in related area. Length: 300-800 words. Pays 15¢/word.
Tips: "Make a *clear* query about Job Corps individuals or programs; make a good presentation—good spelling, grammer and logic. Be sincere, informed on your topic and sure that you have illustration/ideas or photos—color only. There's enough bad press about disadvantaged youth—we want our readers to hear success stories about people who have made a change in their lives for the better through Job Corps training. If you have an idea for a story, write immediately. We're eager for freelancers. If your idea is sound we'll work with you."

THE JOHNS HOPKINS MAGAZINE, The Johns Hopkins University, 203 Whitehead Hall, Baltimore MD 21218. (301)338-7645. Editor: Elise Hancock. Associate Editor: Edward C. Ernst. A bimonthly alumni general interest magazine with features on those subjects interesting Hopkins grads, i.e., medicine, literature, etc. Circ. 85,000. Pays on acceptance. Byline given. Offers $200 kill fee usually. Buys one-time rights and first rights. Submit seasonal/holiday material 4 months in advance. Simultaneous queries, and simultaneous and photocopied submissions OK. Electronic submissions OK if compatible with DEC Mate (Digital) word processors. Computer printout submissions acceptable. SASE preferred. Reports in 3 months. Sample copy for $1.50, 9x12 SAE, and 90¢ postage; free guideline letter.
Nonfiction: General interest, how-to, humor, and photo feature, all *Hopkins related stories*—medical, music, physics, arts and sciences, engineering, continuing education, astronomy. Also interview/profile (alumni of Hopkins), and personal experience (if related to Hopkins). Buys approximately 9 mss/year. Query with published clips or send complete ms. Length: 5,000 words maximum. Pays $25-1,000.
Photos: State availability of photos. Reviews b&w contact sheets. Model release and identification of subjects required. Buys one-time rights.
Fillers: Cartoons.
Tips: Contributions must be general enough (non-technical) to appeal to wide audience, yet at a level which is apropos for a university graduate. (Humor and personal facts help too). The whole magazine is most open to freelancers. Features and cartoons are most welcomed. Trends in alumni magazines are towards color, so promise of exciting color spreads lends the article to publication. Many general feature stories are people-oriented, with personal insights by writer. Most welcome, of course, are articles by or about Hopkins people. A careful study of what schools are at Hopkins reveals what the readership will be interested in. They like brain twisters or thought provoking ethical issues or articles on new techniques in their field."

MAKING IT!, Careers Newsmagazine, Rm. 25, 250 W. 94th St., New York NY 10025. (212)222-3338. Editor: Karen Rubin. Magazine published 4 times/year covering career opportunities for professionals and managers; specifically entry-level opportunities for college and graduate school students and strategic moves for employed professionals. "We are a newsmagazine with a news-feature format; we discourage generalized 'how-to' articles in favor of in-depth profiles of companies, agencies and industries. We will be looking for writers who have specialty in a particular area or interest and can become regular contributors." Circ. 30,000. Pays on publication (in most cases). Byline given. Offers 20% kill fee. Makes work-for-hire assignments. Computer printout submissions acceptable; prefers letter-quality to dot-matrix. SASE. Reports in 2 months. Sample copy $1.50 and 4 first class stamps; writer's guidelines for business size SAE and 1 first class stamp.
Nonfiction: How-to ("we accept only a few, but these should relate to resume, interview, strategies for getting jobs); interview/profile (success stories and profiles about people who have "made it"); and personal experience (strategies for getting the job you want). No superficial or general articles about careers or getting jobs. Buys variable number mss/year. Query with or without published clips. Length: 1,000-2,000 words. Pays $50-250. Sometimes pays the expenses of writers on assignment.
Photos: "Photos that show young people in the work environment." State availability of photos. Pays $5-20 for contact sheets and 8x10 b&w prints. Captions and identification of subjects required. Buys one-time rights.

MISSISSIPPI STATE UNIVERSITY ALUMNUS, Mississippi State University, Alumni Association, Editorial Office, Box 5328, Mississippi State MS 39762. (601)325-3442. Editor: Linsey H. Wright. 10%

freelance written ("but welcome more"). Emphasizes articles about Mississippi State graduates and former students. For well-educated and affluent audience. Quarterly magazine; 36 pages. Circ. 16,443. Pays on publication. Publishes ms an average of 6 months after acceptance. Buys one-time rights. Pays 25% kill fee. Byline given. Phone queries OK. Submit seasonal/holiday material 3 months in advance. Simultaneous, photocopied and previously published submissions OK. Publishes ms an average of 6 months after acceptance. Computer printout submissions acceptable; prefers letter-quality to dot-matrix. SASE. Reports in 1 month. Free sample copy.

Nonfiction: Historical, humor (with strong MSU flavor; nothing risque), informational, inspirational, interview (with MSU grads), nostalgia (early days at MSU), personal experience, profile and travel (by MSU grads, but must be of wide interest to other grads). Recent article example: "The River's Not Too Wide for Morrison." "The story dealt with an MSU graduate in nuclear engineering who is now a country-western songwriter in Nashville." Buys 2-3 mss/year ("but welcome more submissions.") Send complete ms. Length: 500-2,000 words. Pays $50-150 (including photos, if used).

Photos: Offers no additional payment for photos purchased with accompanying ms. Captions required. Uses 5x7 and 8x10 b&w photos and color transparencies of any size.

Columns/Departments: Statesmen, "a section of the *Alumnus* that features briefs about alumni achievements and professional or business advancement. We do not use engagements, marriages or births. There is no payment for Statesmen briefs."

Tips: "All stories *must* be about Mississippi State University or its alumni. We welcome articles about MSU grads in interesting occupations and have used stories on off-shore drillers, miners, horse trainers, etc. We also want profiles on prominent MSU alumni and have carried pieces on Senator John C. Stennis, comedian Jerry Clower, professional football players and coaches, and Eugene Butler, editor-in-chief of *Progressive Farmer* magazine. We feature three alumni in each issue, alumni who have risen to prominence in their fields or who are engaged in unusual occupations or who are involved in unusual hobbies. We're using more short features (500-700 words) to vary the length of our articles in each issue. We pay $50-75 for these, including 1 b&w photo."

NATIONAL FORUM: THE PHI KAPPA PHI JOURNAL, The Honor Society of Phi Kappa Phi, East Tennessee State University, Box 19420A, Johnson City TN 37614. (615)929-5347. Editor: Stephen W. White. Managing Editor: Elaine M. Smoot. Quarterly interdisciplinary, scholarly journal. "We are an interdisciplinary journal that publishes crisp, nontechnical analyses of issues of social and scientific concern as well as scholarly treatments of different aspects of culture." Circ. 110,000. Pays on publication. Byline given. Buys all rights. Submit seasonal/holiday material 6 months in advance. Computer printout submissions acceptable; can accept 5¼" diskettes compatible with Lanier No-Problem Word Processor. Telecommunications capabilities if author has compatible equipment/software. SASE. Reports in 6 weeks on queries; 2 months on mss. Sample copy 65¢; free writer's guidelines.

Nonfiction: General interest, interview/profile and opinion. No how-to or biographical articles. Each issue is devoted to the exploration of a particular theme. Upcoming theme issues: "Why Celebrate the Constitution? Toward the Bicentennial of the Constitution," Liberal Education, the Decline of Writing and Trends Analysis. Recent article example: "The Next Industrial Revolution." Query with clips of published work. Buys 15 unsolicited mss/year. Length: 1,500-2,000 words. Pays $50-200.

Photos: State availability of photos. Identification of subjects required. Buys one-time rights.

Columns/Departments: Educational Dilemmas in the 80s and Book Review Section. Buys 8 mss/year for Educational Dilemmas, 40 book reviews. Length: Book reviews—400-800 words. Educational Dilemmas—1,500-1,800 words. Pays $15-25 for book reviews; $50/printed page, Educational Dilemmas.

Fiction: Humorous and short stories. Buys 2-4 mss/year. Length: 1,500-1,800 words. Pays $50/printed page.

Poetry: Professor Daniel Fogel, poetry editor. Avant garde, free verse, haiku, light verse, traditional. No love poetry. Buys 20 mss/year. Submit 5 poems maximum. Prefers shorter poems.

NOTRE DAME MAGAZINE, University of Notre Dame, Room 415, Administration Bldg., Notre Dame IN 46556. (219)239-5335. Editor: Walton R. Collins. Managing Editor: James Winters. 75% freelance written. Quarterly magazine covering news of Notre Dame and education and issues affecting the Roman Catholic Church. "We are interested in the moral, ethical and spiritual issues of the day and how Christians live in today's world. We are universal in scope and Catholic in viewpoint and serve Notre Dame students, alumni, friends and constituencies." Circ. 92,000. Pays on acceptance. Publishes ms an average of 6 months after acceptance. Byline given. Kill fee negotiable. Buys first rights. Simultaneous queries OK. Electronic submissions OK with IBM, Phillips on Apple Micro compatability, but requires hard copy also. Computer printout submissions acceptable; prefers letter-quality to dot-matrix. SASE. Reports in 3 weeks. Free sample copy.

Nonfiction: Opinion, personal experience, religion. "All articles must be of interest to Christian/Catholic readers who are well educated and active in their communities." Buys 35 mss/year. Query with clips of published work. Length: 600-2,000 words. Pays $500-1,500. Sometimes pays the expenses of writers on assignment.

Photos: State availability of photos. Reviews b&w contact sheets, color transparencies, and 8x10 prints.

Model release and identification of subjects required. Buys one-time rights.

Tips: "Use of jargon, absence of concreteness, and insufficient legwork for a complete story are the most frequent mistakes made by writers in conpleting an article for us."

OSU OUTREACH, Room 313A, Public Information Bldg., Oklahoma State University, Stillwater OK 74078. (405)624-6009. Editor: Doug Dollar. 5% freelance written. Quarterly magazine for OSU alumni. Circ. 12,500. Pays on acceptance. Byline given. Buys one-time rights. Submit seasonal/holiday material 3 months in advance. Simultaneous, photocopied and previously published submissions OK. Publishes ms an average of 4 months after acceptance. Computer printout submissions acceptable. SASE. Reports in 2 weeks. Free sample copy for 9x12 SASE.

Nonfiction: General interest; humor (with strong OSU tie); interview (with OSU grads); historical/nostalgic (OSU traditions, early days events, people, the campus); interview/profile (OSU subjects); personal experience; and photo feature. "Subjects must have strong connection to OSU, and must be of interest to alumni." Buys 5 mss/year. Query with clips of published work or send complete ms. Length: 500-2,000 words. Pays $15-25 (including photos, if used).

Photos: State availability of photos. Pays $5-15 for 5x7 b&w prints; reviews b&w contact sheets. Captions required. Buys one-time rights.

Columns/Departments: Campus, sports, alumni. Buys 30 mss/year. Send complete ms. Length: 100-300 words. Pays $5-10.

Tips: "Items on alumni personalities are of great value if they have strong human-interest appeal. We prefer a tight style."

PRINCETON ALUMNI WEEKLY, Princeton University Press, 41 William St., Princeton NJ 08540. (609)452-4885. Editor: Charles L. Creesy. Managing Editor: Margaret M. Keenan. 50% freelance written. Biweekly (during the academic year) magazine covering Princeton University and higher education for Princeton alumni, students, faculty, staff and friends. "We assume familiarity with and interest in the university." Circ. 50,000. Pays on publication. Publishes ms an average of 3 months after acceptance. Byline given. Offers $100 kill fee. Buys first serial rights and one-time rights. Submit seasonal/holiday material 2 months in advance. Simultaneous queries or photocopied submissions OK. Electronic submissions OK but requirements must be clarified with publisher—"too complex to summarize here." Computer printout submissions acceptable; prefers letter-quality to dot-matrix. Reports "as soon as possible." Publishes ms an average of 3 months after acceptance. Sample copy for 9x12 SAE and 71¢ postage.

Nonfiction: Book excerpts, general interest, historical/nostalgic, interview/profile, opinion, personal experience, photo feature. "Connection to Princeton essential. Remember, it's for an upscale educated audience." Special issue on education and economics (February). Buys 20 mss/year. Query with clips of published work. Length: 1,000-6,000 words. Pays $75-450. Pays expenses of writers on assignment.

Photos: State availability of photos. Pays $25-50 for 8x10 b&w prints; $50-100 for color transparencies. Reviews (for ordering purposes) b&w contact sheet. Captions and identification of subjects required.

Columns/Departments: "Columnists must have a Princeton connection (alumnus, student, etc.)." Buys 50 mss/year. Query with clips of published work. Length: 750-1,500 words. Pays $50-150.

THE PURDUE ALUMNUS, Purdue Alumni Association, Purdue Memorial Union 160, West Lafayette IN 47907. (317)494-5184. Editor: Gay L. Totten. 25% freelance written. Magazine published 9 times/year (except February, June, August) covering subjects of interest to Purdue University alumni. Circ. 60,000. Pays on publication. Publishes ms an average of 2 months after acceptance. Byline given. Buys first rights and makes work-for-hire assignments. Submit seasonal/holiday material 3 months in advance. Simultaneous queries, and simultaneous, photocopied, and previously published submissions OK. Computer printout submissions acceptable; prefers letter-quality to dot-matrix. SASE. Reports in 1 week on queries; 2 weeks on mss. Free sample copy.

Nonfiction: Book excerpts, general interest, historical/nostalgic, humor, interview/profile, personal experience. Focus is on campus news, issues, opinions of interest to 60,000 members of the Alumni Association. Feature style, primarily university-oriented. Issues relevant to education. Buys 12-20 mss/year. Length: 3,000 words maximum. Pays $25-250. Sometimes pays expenses of writers on assignment.

Photos: State availability of photos. Reviews b&w contact sheet or 5x7 prints.

Tips: "We're always anxious for new material, and depend rather heavily on freelancers. We prefer to work by assignment, and appreciate query with ideas, possibly writing samples. We don't pay much, but we do credit and have a well-educated, worldwide audience."

SCORECARD, Falsoft, Inc., 9529 US Highway 42, Box 385, Prospect KY 40059. (502)228-4492. Editor: John Crawley. Assistant Editor: Wayne Fowler. 40% freelance written. A weekly tabloid sports fan magazine covering University of Louisville sports only. Circ. 3,000. Pays on publication. Publishes ms an average of 1 month after acceptance. Byline given. Buys first rights. Submit seasonal/holiday material 1 month in advance. Previously published submissions OK "rarely." Computer printout submissions acceptable; prefers letter-quality to dot-matrix. Reports in 2 weeks. Sample copy for $1 and SAE.

Nonfiction: Assigned to contributing editors. Buys 100 mss/year. Query with published clips. Length: 750-1,500 words. Pays $20-50. Sometimes pays expenses of writers on assignment.

Photos: State availability of photos.

Columns/Departments: Notes Page (tidbits relevant to University of Louisville sports program or former players or teams). Buys 25 mss/year. Length: Approximately 100 words. Pay undetermined.

Tips: "Be very familiar with history and tradition of University of Louisville sports program. Contact us with story ideas. Know subject."

THE STUDENT, 127 9th Ave. N., Nashville TN 37234. Editor: W. Howard Bramlette. 20% freelance written. Publication of National Student Ministries of the Southern Baptist Convention. For college students; focusing on freshman and sophomore levels. Published 12 times during the school year. Circ. 25,000. Buys all rights. Payment on acceptance. Publishes ms an average of 9 months after acceptance. Mss should be double spaced on white paper with 50-space line, 25 lines/page. Reports usually in 6 weeks. Computer printout submissions acceptable; no dot-matrix. SASE. Free sample copy and guidelines.

Nonfiction: Contemporary questions, problems, and issues facing college students viewed from a Christian perspective to develop high moral and ethical values. The struggle for integrity in self-concept and the need to cultivate interpersonal relationships directed by Christian love. Prefers complete ms rather than query. Length: 600 words maximum. Pays 4¢/word after editing with reserved right to edit accepted material.

Fiction: Satire and parody on college life, humorous episodes; emphasize clean fun and the ability to grow and be uplifted through humor. Contemporary fiction involving student life, on campus as well as off. Length: 1,000 words. Pays 4¢/word.

WPI JOURNAL, Worcester Polytechnic Institute, 100 Institute Rd., Worcester MA 01609. Editor: Kenneth McDonnell. 20% freelance written. A quarterly alumni magazine covering science and engineering/education/business personalities for 16,000 alumni, primarily engineers, scientists, managers; parents of students, national media. Circ. 22,500. Pays on publication. Publishes ms an average of 3 months after acceptance. Byline given. Buys one-time rights. Submit seasonal/holiday material 3 months in advance. Simultaneous queries, and simultaneous, photocopied and previously published submissions OK. Electronic submissions OK via disk compatible with DEC or NBI, but requires hard copy also. Computer printout submissions acceptable; prefers letter-quality to dot-matrix. Reports in 2 weeks on queries; 1 month on mss.

Nonfiction: Book excerpts; expose (education, engineering, science); general interest; historical/nostalgic; how-to (financial, business-oriented); humor; interview/profile (people in engineering, science); personal experience; photo feature; and technical (with personal orientation). Query with published clips. Length: 1,000-4,000 words. Pays negotiable rate. Sometimes pays the expenses of writers on assignment.

Photos: State availability of photos with query or ms. Reviews b&w contact sheets. Pays negotiable rate. Captions required.

Fillers: Cartoons. Buys 4/year. Pays $75-100.

Tips: "Submit outline of story and/or ms of story idea or published work. Features are most open to freelancers."

Cartoon and Comic Books

Cartoonists and comic book artists, eager to draw and sell *funnies* or to learn about the craft of cartooning, turn to these publications. Comic book firms looking for writers are also listed in this section. For publications specifically on humor, see the Humor category. Cartoonists and syndicates that buy gaglines can be found in the Gag Writing section in the back of the book.

CARTOON WORLD, Hartman Publishing Co., Box 30367, Lincoln NE 68503. (402)435-3191. Editor: George Hartman. Monthly newsletter for amateur and professional cartoonists with cartoon market news, tips, instruction, new markets and "hints for making money at cartooning locally and nationally. Buys only from paid subscribers. Mostly staff-written, but exceptional work considered. Circ. 150-300. Pays on acceptance. Byline given. Buys second (reprint) rights to material originally published elsewhere. Not copyrighted. Submit seasonal/holiday material 3 months in advance. Simultaneous submissions OK. Publishes ms an average of 1 month after acceptance. Computer printout submissions acceptable; no dot-matrix. SASE. Reports in 1 month.

Sample copy $5.
Nonfiction: How-to, inspirational, new product. "We will accept only material about cartooning and gag writing; nothing negative." Buys 10 mss/year. Query. Length: 1,000 words. Pays $5/page minimum.
Fillers: Clippings and short humor. Buys 10/year. Pays $5 minimum/8½x11 page.

ECLIPSE COMICS, Box 199, Guerneville CA 95446. (707)869-9401. Publisher: Dean Mullaney. Editor-in-Chief: Catherine Yronwode. 100% freelance written. Publishers of various four-color comic books. *Eclipse* publishes comic books with high-quality paper and color reproduction, geared toward the discriminating comic book fan; and sold through the "direct sales" specialty store market. Circ. varies (35,000-85,000). Pays on acceptance. Publishes ms an average of 1 month after acceptance. Byline given. Buys first North American serial rights, second serial (reprint) rights with additional payment, and first option on collection and non-exclusive rights to sell material to South American and European markets (with additional payments). Simultaneous queries, and simultaneous and photocopied submissions OK. Computer printout submissions acceptable; no dot-matrix. SASE. Reports in 1 month. Sample copy $1.50, writer's guidelines for business-size SAE and 1 first class stamp.
Fiction: "All of our comics are fictional." Adventure, fantasy, mystery, romance, science fiction, horror, western. "No sexually explicit material, please." Buys approximately 150 mss/year (mostly from established comics writers). Send sample science fiction or horror script or plot synopsis. Length: 8-11 pages. Pays $30 minimum/page.
Tips: "At the present time we are publishing as many adventure and super-heroic series as our schedule permits. Because all of our comics are 'creator-owned,' we do not buy fill-in plots or scripts for these books. We do have two comics open to new writers, however. These are *Alien Encounters*, bimonthly science fiction anthology, and *Tales of Terrors*, a bimonthly anthology. The stories in these titles vary from 1-page fillers to short stories of 8 or more pages each, with a maximum length of 11 pages. Plot synopsis of less than a page can be submitted; we will select promising concepts for development into full script submissions. All full script submissions should be written in comic book or 'screenplay' form for artists to illustrate. Science fiction themes we need include outer-space, ufos, alien invasions, time travel, inter-dimensional travel, nuclear holocaust aftermath, future-science exploration, robots, cyborgs, end-of-world, etc. Horror themes we need include vampires, werewolves, zombies, walking dead, monsters in the sewers, revenge from beyond the grave, 'murder will out' stories, and assorted slimy, creepy, gooey, demonic and horrific stuff. 85% of the stories in these anthologies have downbeat twist endings of the kind popularized by O. Henry and the EC comic books of the 1950s. The other 15% start off in that mold but lead to an unexpected upbeat resolution. Our special needs at the moment are for moody, romantic, character-oriented pieces with overtones of humanism, morality, political opinion, philosophical speculation, and/or social commentary. Comic book adaptations (by the original authors) of previously published science fiction and horror short stories are definitely encouraged."

‡FIRST COMICS, INC., includes *American Flagg!*, *Jon Sable*, *Grimjack*, *Nexus*, 1014 Davis St., Evanston IL 60201. (312)864-5330. Managing Editor: Mike Gold. 100% freelance written. Comic book magazines published monthly, bimonthly, one-shot and trade paperbacks. "Our average reader is between ages 18 and 30 years, college educated, male." Circ. 4,000,000. Pays between acceptance and publication. Publishes ms an average of 6 months after acceptance. Byline given. Buys negotiable rights. Submit seasonal/holiday material 9 months in advance. Simultaneous queries OK. Computer printout submissions acceptable; prefers letter-quality to dot-matrix. SASE. "We only respond to new writer queries—brief, with SASE. Reports in 6 months.
Fiction: In comic art format, subjects include adventure, experimental, fantasy, historical, humorous, mystery, science fiction and suspense. Query. Payment negotiable.
Tips: Writer has a better chance of breaking in with short, lesser-paying articles and fillers. "We make regular on-going assignments, generally to the creators of the features."

MARVEL COMICS, 387 Park Ave. S., New York NY 10016. (212)576-9200. Editor-in-Chief: James Shooter. 98% freelance written. Publishes 40 comics and magazines per month, 6-12 graphic novels per year, and specials, storybooks, industrials, and paperbacks for all ages. 7 million copies sold/month. Pays a flat fee for most projects, or an advance and incentive, or royalty. Pays on acceptance. Publishes manuscript an average of 6 months after acceptance. Byline given. Rights purchased depend upon format and material. Submit seasonal/holiday material 8 months in advance. SASE.
Fiction: Comic plots and scripts. Adventure, fantasy, horror, humorous, romance, science fiction and western. No "noncomics." Buys 600-800 mss/year. Submit brief plot synopses *only*. Do not send scripts, short stories or long outlines. A plot synopsis should be less than two typed pages. Send two synopses at most. "Using Marvel characters is best." Sometimes pays the expenses of writers on assignment.
Tips: "Marvel Comics wants new talent. We want to maintain our leadership of the graphic storytelling medium, and grow."

Child Care and Parental Guidance

Most people learn how to care for their children from their own parents, but research and new options are changing generation-ago practices. Today many career-oriented couples are starting families. Parents in the '80s are hearing terms that their parents didn't—single-parent households, gifted children, bonding, etc. Child care magazines address these and other issues. Readers want information on new research—on pregnancy, infancy, childhood, and family—written for people who care for children. "Do not submit general topics, such as teaching kids to read or getting ready for school," says one editor. "Submit fresh topics or at least fresh angles." Other markets that buy articles about child care and the family are included in the Education, Religious, and Women's sections of this book.

AMERICAN BABY MAGAZINE, For Expectant and New Parents, 575 Lexington Ave., New York NY 10022. (212)752-0775. Editor-in-Chief: Judith Nolte. Managing Editor: Phyllis Evans. A monthly magazine covering pregnancy, infant health/care, early childhood. "Readership is composed of women in late pregnancy (6-9 months) and early new motherhood (baby age 1-6 months). Most readers are first-time parents; some have older children (2-4 years). Many fathers also read the magazine." Circ. 1,000,000. Pays on acceptance. Publishes ms an average of 4 months after acceptance. Byline given. Submit seasonal/holiday material 4 months in advance. Simultaneous queries, and simultaneous, photocopied, and previously published submissions OK. Computer printout submissions acceptable; prefers letter-quality to dot-matrix. SASE. Reports in 3 weeks on queries; 2 months on mss. Sample copy for 9x12 SAE and $1 postage; writer's guidelines for business size SAE and 1 first class stamp.
Nonfiction: F. Holland George, articles editor. Book excerpts, how-to (some aspect of pregnancy or child care); interview/profile (expert in maternal/infant health, child-care expert); and personal experience (should give advice to new parents or parents to be). No "hearts and flowers," or fantasy pieces. Buys 90 mss/year. Query with or without published clips or send complete ms. Length: 500-2,000 words. Pays $100-400.
Photos: Reviews 8x10 b&w photos. Identification of subjects required. Buys one-time rights.
Columns/Departments: F. Holland George, columns/departments editor. My Own Experience (covers common problem of child raising/pregnancy with solutions). "Discuss personal experience (not diary style)—give advice on practical/psychological subject." Buys 12 mss/year. Send complete ms. Length: 1,000-2,000 words. Pays $100-150.
Fillers: Chuckles from Cherubs (kid's quotes); Tricks of the Trade (helpful hints). Buys 100/year. Length: 50-250 words. Pays $5-100.
Tips: "Send very brief biography with submissions. My Own Experience column and articles giving good advice are areas most open to freelancers."

BABY TALK, 185 Madison Ave., New York NY 10016. Editor: Patricia Irons. 30% freelance written. Monthly. For new and expectant parents. Circ. 950,000. Pays on acceptance. Publishes ms an average of 6 months after acceptance. Buys one-time rights. Computer printout submissions acceptable if letter-quality. SASE.
Nonfiction: Articles on all phases of baby care. Also true, unpublished accounts of pregnancy, life with baby or young children. Buys 50-60 unsolicited mss/year. Submit complete ms. Payment varies.
Photos: B&w and color photos are sometimes purchased with or without ms.

‡**THE CRIB SHEET**, A Family Magazine, Caronn Publications, 14101 NE 76th St., Vancouver WA 98662. (206)892-3037. Editor: Karen La Clergue. 95% freelance written. Monthly magazine on birthing and newborn news. Circ. 5,000. Pays within two weeks after publication. Publishes ms an average of 3 months after acceptance. Byline given. Offers $5 kill fee. Not copyrighted. Buys simultaneous rights, first serial rights, and second serial (reprint) rights. Submit seasonal/holiday material 3 months in advance. Simultaneous, photocopied, and previously published submissions OK. SASE. Reports in 3 weeks. Sample copy for legal size SAE and 2 first class stamps. Writer's guidelines for SAE and 1 first class stamp.
Nonfiction: Book excerpts; general interest (anything of interest to women—especially those with young children); how-to (handcrafted items, etc); humor (as it pertains to family life, birthing, rearing children); personal experience (birthing/coaching, rearing children, teaching, etc.); photo feature (family life—on the farm, in the city, etc.); travel (what to do when traveling with infants and young children with/without entertainment, etc.); and medical advances in natal and prenatal. Buys 20-50 mss/year. Send complete ms. Length: 500-1,500. Pays $2.50-5.
Photos: Send photos with query or ms. Reviews b&w and color prints, but color is printed as b&w. Pays $1.

Captions required. Buys one-time rights.

Fiction: Adventure, fantasy (especially read aloud for young children); historical; mystery; romance; science fiction; serialized novels; suspense; and all types of children's fiction—also artwork for children up to 8 years of age. All material should be family-oriented—no erotica or excessive language. Buys 10-20 mss/year. Send complete ms. Length: 500-1,500 words. Pays $2.50-5.

Poetry: Buys 5-15/year. Submit maximum 10 poems. Length: open. Pays $2.50.

Tips: "Artwork accompanying children's stories will get priority; make it exciting for them."

EXPECTING, 685 3rd Ave., New York NY 10017. Editor: Evelyn A. Podsiadlo. Assistant Editor: Grace Lang. Issued quarterly for expectant mothers. Circ. 1,500,000. Buys all rights. Byline given. Pays on acceptance. Reports in 2-4 weeks. Free writer's guidelines. SASE.

Nonfiction: Prenatal development, layette and nursery planning, budgeting, health, fashion, husband-wife relationships, naming the baby, minor discomforts, childbirth, expectant fathers, working while pregnant, etc. Length: 800-1,600 words. Pays $200-300 for feature articles.

Fillers: Short humor and interesting or unusual happenings during pregnancy or at the hospital; maximum 100 words, $10 on publication; submissions to "Happenings" are not returned.

Poetry: Occasionally buys subject-related poetry; all forms. Length: 12-64 lines. Pays $10-30.

GIFTED CHILDREN MONTHLY, For the Parents of Children with Great Promise, Box 115, Sewell NJ 08080. (609)582-0277. Editor: Dr. James Alvino. Managing Editor: Robert Baum. 50% freelance written. Monthly newsletter covering parenting and education of gifted children for parents. Circ. 40,000. Pays on acceptance. Publishes ms an average of 6 months after acceptance. Buys all rights and first rights. Submit seasonal/holiday material 4 months in advance. Simultaneous queries, and simultaneous, photocopied, and previously published submissions OK. Computer printout submissions acceptable; prefers letter-quality to dot-matrix. SASE. Reports in 1 month on queries; 2 months on mss. Sample copy and writer's guidelines for 9x12 SAE and 51¢ postage.

Nonfiction: Book excerpts; personal accounts; how-to (on parenting of gifted kids); research into practice; outstanding programs; interview/profile; and opinion. Also puzzles, brainteasers and ideas for children's Spin-Off section. "Our Special Reports and Idea Place sections are most accessible to freelancers." Query with clips of published work or send complete ms. Buys 36 unsolicited mss/year. Length: Idea Place 500-750 words; Special Reports 1,000-2,500 words. Pays $10-200.

Tips: "It is helpful if freelancers provide copies of research papers to back up the article."

GROWING PARENT, 22 N. 2nd St., Lafayette IN 47902. Editor: Nancy Kleckner. 85% freelance written. Readers have children under 6 years old (majority under 3 years of age). Writers guidelines and sample issue for 6x9 SASE.

Nonfiction: Articles to 1,500 words with a focus toward parents—the choices, problems and issues they face as their children grow and develop. No personal experience, poetry, articles on child development, humorous pieces or photos. Informational articles based on careful research and written in an easy-to-read style. Pays 8-15¢/word on acceptance. Query.

HOME LIFE, Sunday School Board, 127 9th Ave. N., Nashville TN 37234. (615)251-2271. Editor-in-Chief: Reuben Herring. 40-60% freelance written. Emphasizes Christian family life. For married adults of all ages, but especially newlyweds and middle-aged marrieds. Monthly magazine: 64 pages. Circ. 800,000. Pays on acceptance. Publishes ms an average of 18 months after acceptance. Buys first serial rights, first North American serial rights and all rights. Byline given. Phone queries OK, but written queries preferred. Submit seasonal/holiday material 1 year in advance. Computer printout submissions acceptable; prefers letter-quality to dot-matrix. SASE. Reports in 6 weeks. Free sample copy and writer's guidelines.

Nonfiction: How-to (good articles on marriage and child care); informational (about some current family-related issue of national significance such as "Television and the Christian Family" or "Whatever Happened to Good Nutrition?"); personal experience (informed articles by people who have solved family problems in healthy, constructive ways). "No column material. We are not interested in material that will not in some way enrich Christian marriage or family life." Buys 150-200 mss/year. Query or submit complete ms. Length: 600-2,400 words. Pays 4¢/word.

Fiction: "Fiction should be family-related and should show a strong moral about how families face and solve problems constructively." Buys 12-20 mss/year. Submit complete ms. Length: 1,000-2,400 words. Pays 4¢/word.

Tips: "Study the magazine to see our unique slant on Christian family life. We prefer a life-centered case study approach, rather than theoretical essays on family life. Our top priority is marriage enrichment material."

‡**KIDS KIDS KIDS, The Santa Clara Newspaper for Parents**, Kids Kids Kids Publications, Inc., Box 2277, Saratoga CA 95070. Editor: Lynn Berado. 90% freelance written. Monthly tabloid of resource information for parents and teachers. Circ 40,000. Pays on publication. Publishes ms an average of 3 months

after acceptance. Byline given. Buys one-time rights. Submit seasonal/holiday material 3 months in advance. Simultaneous, photocopied, and previously published submissions OK. Electronic submissions OK on IBM. Computer printout submissions acceptable. SASE. Free sample copy and writer's guidelines.

Nonfiction: Book excerpts (related to our interest group); expose (health, psychology); historical/nostalgic ("History of Diapers"); how-to (related to kids/parenting); humor; interview/profile; photo feature; and travel (with kids, family). Special issues include Music (February); Art (March); Kid's Birthdays (April); Summer Camps (May); Family Fun (June); Pregnancy and Childbirth (July); Fashion (August); Health (September); and Mental Health (October). No opinion or religious articles. Buys 36-50 mss/year. Query or send complete ms. Length: 150-1,500 words. Pays $5-40. Sometimes pays expenses of writers on assignments.

Photos: State availability of photos. Prefers b&w contact sheets and/or 3x5 b&w prints. Pays $5-20. Model release required. Buys one-time rights.

Columns/Departments: Child Care; Family Travel; Birthday Party Ideas; Baby Page. Buys 36 mss/year. Send complete ms. Length: 800-1,000 words. Pays $5-25.

Fiction: Humorous.

Tips: "Submit new, fresh information concisely written and accurately researched."

L.A. PARENT, The Magazine for Parents in Southern California, Pony Publications, Box 65795, Los Angeles CA 90065. (818)240-PONY. Editor: Jack Bierman. Managing Editor: Greg Doyle. 80% freelance written. Monthly tabloid covering parenting. Circ. 75,000. Pays on publication. Publishes ms an average of 4 months after acceptance. Byline given. Buys all rights. Submit seasonal/holiday material 3 months in advance. Simultaneous queries and previously published submissions OK. SASE. Reports in 1 month. Sample copy $1; free writer's guidelines.

Nonfiction: Steve Linder, articles editor. General interest, how-to. "We focus on southern California activities for families, and do round-up pieces, i.e., a guide to private schools, fishing spots." Buys 10-15 mss/year. Query with clips of published work. Length: 700-1,200 words. Pays $75 plus expenses.

LIVING WITH CHILDREN, Baptist Sunday School Board, 127 9th Ave. N., Nashville TN 37234. (615)251-2229. Editor: SuAnne Bottoms. 50% freelance written. Quarterly magazine covering parenting issues for parents of elementary-age children (ages 6 through 11). "Written and designed from a Christian perspective." Circ. 50,000. Pays on acceptance. Publishes ms an average of 2 years after acceptance. Byline given. "We generally buy all rights to mss; first serial rights on a limited basis. First and reprint rights may be negotiated at a lower rate of pay." Submit seasonal/holiday material 1 year in advance. Previously published submissions (on limited basis) OK. Computer printout submissions acceptable: no dot-matrix. SASE. Reports in 1 month on queries; 2 months on mss. Free sample copy and writer's guidelines.

Nonfiction: How-to (parent), humor, inspirational, personal experience, and articles on child development. No highly technical material or articles containing more than 15-20 lines quoted material. Buys 60 mss/year. Query or send complete ms (queries preferred). Length: 800-1,800 words (1,450 words preferred). Pays 5¢/word (beginning Oct. 1, 1985).

Photos: "Submission of photos with mss is strongly discouraged."

Fiction: Humorous (parent/child relationships); and religious. "We have very limited need for fiction." Buys maximum of 4 mss/year. Length: 800-1,450 words. Pays 5¢/word.

Poetry: Light verse and inspirational. "We have limited need for poetry and buy only all rights." Buys 15 poems/year. Submit maximum 3 poems. Length: 4-30 lines. Pays $1.75 (for 1-7 lines) plus $1 for each additional line; pays $4.50 for 8 lines and more plus 65¢ each additional line.

Fillers: Jokes, anecdotes and short humor. Buys 15/year. Length: 100-400 words. Pays $5 minimum, 5¢/word.

Tips: "Articles must deal with an issue of interest to parents. A mistake some writers make in articles for us is failing to write from a uniquely Christian perspective; that is very necessary for our periodicals. Material should be 850, 1,450, or 1,800 words in length. All sections, particularly articles, are open to freelance writers. Only regular features are assigned."

LIVING WITH PRESCHOOLERS, Baptist Sunday School Board, 127 9th Ave. N., Nashville TN 37234. (615)251-2229. Editor: SuAnne Bottoms. 50% freelance written. Quarterly magazine covering parenting issues for parents of preschoolers (infants through 5-year-olds). The magazine is "written and designed from a Christian perspective." Circ. 146,000. Pays on acceptance. Publishes manuscript an average of 2 years after acceptance. Byline given. "We generally buy all rights to manuscripts. First and reprint rights may be negotiated at a lower rate of pay." Submit seasonal/holiday material 2 years in advance. Previously published submissions (on limited basis) OK. Computer printout submissions acceptable; no dot-matrix. SASE. Reports in 1 month on queries; 2 months on mss. Free sample copy and writer's guidelines.

Nonfiction: How-to (parent), humor, inspirational, personal experience, and articles on child development. No highly technical material or articles containing more than 15-20 lines quoted material. Buys 60 mss/year. Query or send complete ms (queries preferred). Length: 800-1,800 words (1,450 words preferred). Pays 5¢/word maximum (beginning Oct. 1, 1985).

Photos: "Submission of photos with mss is strongly discouraged."

Fiction: Humorous (parent/child relationships); and religious. "We have very limited need for fiction." Buys maximum of 4 mss/year. Length: 800-1,450 words. Pays 5¢/word (beginning Oct. 1, 1985).
Poetry: Light verse and inspirational. "We have limited need for poetry and buy only all rights." Buys 15 poems/year. Submit maximum 3 poems. Length: 4-30 lines. Pays $1.75 (for 1-7 lines) plus $1 for each additional line; pays $4.50 for 8 lines and more plus 65¢ each additional line.
Fillers: Jokes, anecdotes and short humor. Buys 15/year. Length: 100-400 words. Pays $5 minimum, 5¢/word maximum.
Tips: "Articles must deal with an issue of interest to parents. A mistake some writers make in writing an article for us is failing to write from a uniquely Christian perspective; that is very necessary for our periodicals. Material should be 850, 1,450, or 1,800 words in length. All sections, particularly articles, are open to freelance writers. Only regular features are assigned."

NETWORK, The Paper for Parents, National Committee for Citizens in Education, 410 Wilde Lake Village Green, Columbia MD 21044. (301)997-9300. Editor: Chrissie Bamber. 10% freelance written. Tabloid published 8 times during the school year covering parent/citizen involvement in public schools. Circ. 6,000. Pays on publication. Publishes ms an average of 1 year after acceptance. Byline given. Buys first serial rights, first North American serial rights; one-time rights, second serial (reprint) rights, simultaneous rights, all rights and makes work-for-hire assignments. Submit seasonal/holiday material 3 months in advance. Simultaneous queries and photocopied submissions OK. Computer printout submissions acceptable. SASE. Reports in 6 weeks. Free sample copy; writer's guidelines for #10 SAE and 39¢ postage.
Nonfiction: Book excerpts (elementary and secondary public education); exposé (of school systems which attempt to reduce public access); how-to (improve schools through parent/citizen participation); humor (related to public school issues); opinion (school-related issues); personal experience (school-related issues). "It is our intention to provide balanced coverage of current developments and continuing issues and to place the facts about schools in a perspective useful to parents. No highly technical or scholarly articles about education; no child rearing articles or personal opinion not backed by research or concrete examples." Buys 4-6 mss/year. Query with clips of published work or send complete ms. Length: 1,000-1,500 words. Pays $25-100. Sometimes pays the expenses of writers on assignment.
Tips: "Readers want articles of substance with information they can use and act on, not headlines which promise much but deliver only the most shallow analysis of the subject. Information first, style second. A high personal commitment to public schools and preferably first-hand experience is the greatest asset. A clear and simple writing style, easily understood by a wide range of lay readers is a must. The most frequent mistake made by writers in completing an article for us is not backing up opinion with concrete, detailed examples or facts, statistics."

PARENTS MAGAZINE, 685 3rd Ave., New York NY 10017. Editor: Elizabeth Crow. 25% freelance written. Monthly. Circ. 1,670,000. Pays on acceptance. Publishes ms an average of 8 months after acceptance. Usually buys first serial rights or first North American serial rights; sometimes buys all rights. Byline given "except for Almanac." Pays $100-350 kill fee. Computer printout submissions acceptable; prefers letter-quality to dot-matrix. SASE. Reports in approximately 6 weeks.
Nonfiction: "We are interested in well-documented articles on the development and behavior of preschool, school-age, and adolescent children and their parents; good, practical guides to the routines of baby care; articles that offer professional insights into family and marriage relationships; reports of new trends and significant research findings in education and in mental and physical health; and articles encouraging informed citizen action on matters of social concern. Especially need articles on women's issues, pregnancy, birth, baby care and early childhood. We prefer a warm, colloquial style of writing, one which avoids the extremes of either slang or technical jargon. Anecdotes and examples should be used to illustrate points which can then be summed up by straight exposition." Query. Length: 2,500 words maximum. Payment varies; pays $400 minimum; $50 minimum for Almanac items. Sometimes pays the expenses of writers on assignment.
Fillers: Anecdotes for "Parents Exchange," illustrative of parental problem-solving with children and teenagers. Pays $20 on publication.

PEDIATRICS FOR PARENTS, The Newsletter for Caring Parents, Pediatrics for Parents, Inc., 176 Mt. Hope Ave., Bangor ME 04401. (207)942-6212. Editor: Richard J. Sagall, M.D. 20% freelance written. Monthly newsletter covering medical aspects of raising children and educating parents about children's health. Circ. 2,800. Pays on publication. Publishes ms an average of 2 months after acceptance. Byline given. Buys first North American serial rights, first and second rights to the same material, and second (reprint) rights to material originally published elsewhere. Rights always include right to publish article in our books on "Best of . . ." series. Submit seasonal/holiday material 6 months in advance. Simultaneous queries, and simultaneous, photocopied and previously published submissions OK. Electronic submissions OK compatible with Apple-PFS or Appleworks. Computer printout submissions acceptable. Reports in 1 month on queries; 6 weeks on mss. SASE. Sample copy for $2; writer's guidelines for business size SAE and 1 first class stamp.
Nonfiction: Book reviews; how-to (feed healthy kids, exercise, practice wellness, etc.); new product; technical

(explaining medical concepts in shirtsleeve language). No general parenting articles. Query with published clips or submit complete ms. Length: 25-1,000 words. Pays 2-5¢/edited word.

Columns/Departments: Book reviews; Please Send Me (material available to parents for free or at nominal cost); Pedia-Tricks (medically-oriented parenting tips that work). Send complete ms. Pays $15-250. Pays 2¢/edited word.

Tips: "We are dedicated to taking the mystery out of medicine for young parents. Therefore, we write in clear and understandable language (but not simplistic language) to help people understand and deal intelligently with complex disease processes, treatments, prevention, wellness, etc. Our articles must be well researched and documented. Detailed references must always be attached to any article for documentation, but not for publication. We strongly urge freelancers to read one or two issues before writing."

PRE-PARENT ADVISOR and NEW PARENT ADVISOR, A Guide to Getting Ready for Birth/A Guide to Life With A New Baby, 13-30 Corporation, 505 Market St., Knoxville TN 37902. (615)521-0600. Editor: Wayne Christensen. "The New Parent Series of annual magazines provides information about the physical, psychological, and emotional concerns to expectant parents (*PPA*), and parents with an infant from one-week to three-months of age (*NPA*), which is done in a manner that suggests the magazines are *for* parents rather than *about* babies." Circ. 1.2 million (each). Pays on acceptance. Byline given. Offers 25% kill fee. Buys first North American serial rights. Simultaneous queries OK. SASE. Reports in 3 weeks. Sample copy for 3x11 SAE and $1.10 postage; free writer's guidelines.

Nonfiction: How-to (many pieces service-oriented such as "how-to breastfeed"); interview/profile (with exceptionally well-known baby authorities); and personal experience ("This adds a great deal to our magazine."). "To assure the consistent delivery of the concept from year to year, the following blend of articles appear in each issue: *PPA*: physical concerns, prenatal emotions, practical preparations, finances, labor and delivery, parent's roles and siblings. *NPA*: parents' roles, baby care, mother care, infant health and development, second-time concerns, unexpected outcomes and day care. Buys 30 full-length features/year. Query with published clips. Length: 1,000-3,000 words. Pays $500-1,500.

Columns/Departments: Pregnancy Today (a collection of short news, items on latest trends in pregnancy). Buys 5 mss/year. Query with published clips. Length: 150-400 words. Pays $75-200.

Tips: "We look for very experienced writers—if you're a beginner your cover letter will have to show a great deal of polish. Our stories rely heavily on letting our readers talk. Any articles must have extensive quotes from readers and experts."

‡**SEATTLE'S CHILD**, Box 22578, Seattle WA 98122. (206)322-2594. Editor: Ann Bergman. Managing Editor: Eleanor Weston. 80% freelance written. Monthly tabloid of articles related to being a parent of children ages 12 and under. Directed to parents and professionals involved with children 12 and under. Circ. 10,000. Pays on acceptance. Publishes ms an average of 2 months after acceptance. Byline given. Offers 50% kill fee. Buys first North American serial rights or all rights. Submit seasonal/holiday material 6 months in advance. Simultaneous queries, and simultaneous and photocopied submissions OK. Electronic submissions OK via IBM PC, 1200 baud, but requires hard copy also. Computer printout submissions acceptable; no dot-matrix. SASE. Reports in 6 weeks on queries; 4 weeks on mss. Sample copy $1.50; writer's guidelines for business size SAE and 1 first class stamp.

Nonfiction: Expose, general interest, historical/nostalgic, how-to, humor, interview/profile, new product, opinion, personal experience, travel, record tape and book reviews, and educational and political reviews. Articles must relate to parents and parenting. Buys 120 mss/year. Send complete ms (preferred) or query with published clips. Length: 400-2,500 words. Pays $25-500.

Photos: Robert Cole, photo editor. Send photos with query or ms. Reviews 5x7 b&w prints. Pays $25-125. Model release required. Buys one-time rights or all rights.

Fillers: Gags. Buys 500/year. Length: 50-250 words. Pays 20¢/word.

Tips: "Don't talk down to audience. Consider that the audience is well-educated, sophisticated and well-read."

THE SINGLE PARENT, Parents Without Partners, Inc., 7910 Woodmont Ave., Bethesda MD 20814. (301)654-8850. Assistant Editor: Liz Bostick. 5% freelance written. Magazine, published 10 times/year; 32 pages. Emphasizes single parenting, family, divorce, widowhood and children. Distributed to members of Parents Without Partners, plus libraries, universities, psychologists, psychiatrists, subscribers, etc. Circ. 20,000. Pays on publication. Publishes ms an average of 6 months after acceptance. Buys one-time rights. Simultaneous, photocopied, and previously published submissions OK. Computer printout submissions acceptable; no dot-matrix. SASE. Reports in 2 months. Sample copy and writer's guidelines for SASE.

Nonfiction: Informational (parenting, legal issues, single parents in society, programs that work for single parents, children's problems); how-to (raise children alone, travel, take up a new career, cope with life as a new or veteran single parent; short lists of how-to tips). No first-hand accounts of bitter legal battles with former spouses. Buys 20 unsolicited mss/year. Query. Length: 1,000-2,000 words. Payment negotiable.

Columns/Departments: "We are starting a new section, F.Y.I., for short news items, reports on research, and tips on how to do things better.

Photos: Purchased with accompanying ms. Query. Pays negotiable rates. Model release required.
Tips: "We get far too many articles that are too general. We are the only magazine for single parents, and we have to be much more specific for our readers. We already know about 'Children and Divorce'; we need to know about 'Divorce and Bad Parent Guilt—What to Do'. We need specific, fresh ideas."

‡**STEP-LIFE, The Problems & Joys of Step-parenting & Remarriage**, Wall Publications, 901 Ivy Ct., Eaton OH 45320. (513)456-6611. Editor: Carla Wall. Bimonthly newsletter on step-parenting and remarriage. Estab. 1985. Publishes ms an average of 2 months after acceptance. Byline given. Buys first North American serial rights and second serial (reprint) rights. Submit seasonal/holiday material 4 months in advance. Simultaneous queries OK. Computer printout submissions acceptable; prefers letter-quality to dot-matrix. SASE. Reports in 2 weeks. Free sample copy.
Nonfiction: How-to, humor, inspirational, interview/profile and personal experience—anything on step-parenting and remarriage subjects. Query. Length: 500-2,500 words. Pays 2-5¢/word.
Photos: State availability of photos with query. Reviews b&w contact sheets. Captions, model release, identification of subjects required. Buys one-time rights.
Columns/Departments: Deena Sharpe, column/department editor. Between You and Me (on remarriages). Query or send complete ms. Length: 1,000-1,500 words. Pays 2-5¢/word.
Fiction: Fiction having to do with step-parenting and remarriage. Pays 2-5¢/word.
Poetry: Poetry that is "bright with hope and happiness." Traditional. Submit 5 poems maximum.
Fillers: Clippings, jokes, gags, anecdotes, short humor and newsbreaks. Length: 50-500 words. Pays $1-5.
Tips: "We are very open to new writers with little publishing experience—especially step-parents. Write from the heart, and let it be about anything having to do with helping the step-family. The Between You and Me column (on helping remarriages become stronger) is most open to freelancers."

‡**TWINS, The magazine for parents of multiples**, Twins Magazine, Inc., Box 12045, Overland Park KS 66212. (913)722-1090. Editor: Barbara C. Unell. 100% freelance written. Bimonthly magazine covering the parenting of multiples. "The magazine gives professional guidance to help parents know more about twin facts and research, as well as help them feel less isolated emotionally, mentally, and physically about being parents of multiples in a world dominated by parents of singletons." Estab. 1984. Circ. 25,000. Pays on publication. Publishes ms an average of 9 months after acceptance. Byline given. Buys all rights and second serial (reprint) rights. Submit seasonal/holiday material 6 months in advance. Simultaneous queries and simultaneous, photocopied, and previously published submissions OK. Computer printout submissions acceptable; prefers letter-quality to dot-matrix. SASE. Reports in 6 weeks on queries; 2 months on mss. Sample copy $3.50 plus $1.50 postage and handling; writer's guidelines for #10 SAE and 1 first class stamp.
Nonfiction: Book excerpts (twin-specific parenting books); general interest (on women's and men's health, on being parents of twins, on marriage, and family life); how-to (on making life easier while parenting twins—all kinds of parenting issues with a twin-specific slant such as giving birthday parties, dressing twins, rooms for twins, discipline, starting school); humor (for Twice as Funny column—focusing on the unintentionally funny side of being a twin or raising twins); interview/profile (a look at parents' views about rearing twins for our On Being Parents of Twins column or for our On Being Twins column, interviews with adult twins as they look back at being a twin as a child and an adult, interviews with well-known parents of twins or personalities doing novel work or in unusual situations with twins); and photo feature (famous twins, twins in unusual situations such as 10 sets on the same street). Special issues include second anniversary issue planned for July/August 1986. No "articles substituting the word 'twin' for 'child'—those that simply apply the same research to twins that applies to singletons without any facts backing up the reason to do so." Buys 150 mss/year. Query with published clips. Length: 1,250-3,000 words. Pays $75 minimum. Sometimes pays the expenses of writers on assignment.
Photos: Send photos with query. Reviews 8x10 and 5x7 b&w prints. Captions, model release and identification of subjects required.
Columns/Departments: Twin Parenting, Research, Resources, Supertwins, Prematurity, Adulthood, Family Health, Questions & Answers, Twice As Funny, On Being Twins, On Being Parents of Twins, Organizations, Pregnancy, Infancy, Toddlerhood, Middle Years, Adolescence, Preschoolers, and Supersavers (saving time and money). Buys 70 mss/year. Query with published clips. Length: 1,250-2,000 words. Pays $75 minimum.
Fillers: Anecdotes and short humor. Buys 12 fillers/year. Length: 500-1,200 words. Payment varies.
Tips: "Send resume, SASE, samples of published work and areas of special interest (personally and professionally), with queries or outlines for story ideas. Make sure you include any facts relating to multiples that qualifies you to write to parents of multiples and professionals who work with them. We prefer a warm, colloquial style of writing, one which avoids the extremes of either slanginess or technical jargon, except where necessary in discussing a particular issue. Relevant viewpoints from both professionals and parents and anecdotes and examples should be used to illustrate points which can then be summed up by straight exposition."

Consumer Service and Business Opportunity

Readers of these publications want to get the most for their money. Some magazines are geared to persons wanting to invest earnings or start a new business; others show readers how to make economical purchases. For some publications, entrepreneurship is an important topic. Publications for business executives and consumers interested in business topics are listed under Business and Finance. Those on how to run specific businesses are classified in Trade, Technical and Professional Journals.

BC REPORTS, BC Studio Publications, Box 5908, Huntington Beach CA 92615. Editor: Shirleen Kaye. Up to 50% freelance written. Short softbound reports (similar to newsletter) on any subject or problem that consumer, hobbyist or small business person needs to have solved, e.g., how-to, hobby, self-help, mailorder. "We publish on speculation. Pay if sells 500 + ; then we have recovered cost and will probably earn for both us and author." Publishes ms an average of 6 months after acceptance. Byline not usually given. Prefers all rights, but might consider simultaneous and second serial (reprint) rights; also makes work-for-hire assignments. Prefers photocopied submissions; simultaneous and previously published submissions OK. Computer printout submissions acceptable; dot-matrix must be "dark and readable." SASE. Reports in 1 month on queries; 6 weeks on mss. Several samples and guidelines for $2, business size SAE and 2 loose first class stamps.
Nonfiction: Expose (consumer, health, money schemes, business); how-to (home, business, hobby, inventions, etc.); inspirational (not religious but self-help); new product (formulas wanted for new and old products); personal experience (if started a business, sideline or solved a problem in ways others could); and technical (how-to for home, business, hobby, inventions, etc.). All are one-shot type reports and booklets. No religion, partisan politics, or extremely controversial material. Buys approximately 50 mss/year. Send complete ms. Length: 2-28 typed pages, single or double spaced. Pays $500 maximum for large report (10-28 pages); 8% begins when over 500 copies sold, to 10%.
Photos: B&w if illustrates how to use or build. Pays $10-25 for 3¹/₂x5 b&w prints. Captions, model release and identification of subjects required. Buys one-time rights.
Fillers: Clippings. "We might buy news or magazine clips that could be expanded into a report or folio. How-to, recipe (unusual only), diets, business and mailorder sales tips, etc." Buys up to 50/year. Length: open. Pays $7-25.
Tips: "Send us short reports of 2-28 pages on any subject for which a person might pay to find out answers, learn techniques, solve business or home problems. We want simple writing, and everything suggested must be actually workable."

BUSINESS TODAY, Meridian Publishing, Box 10010, Ogden UT 84409. Editor: Wayne DeWald. 80% freelance written. Monthly magazine covering all aspects of business. *Business Today* is geared toward small- and medium-size businesses with articles on all aspects of commerce. Particularly interested in profiles of corporate executives. Estab. 1984. Pays on acceptance. Publishes ms an average of 6 months after acceptance. Byline given. Buys first North American serial rights, first rights, and nonexclusive reprint rights. Computer printout submissions acceptable. SASE. Reports in 1 month. Sample copy for $1 and 9x12 SAE; writer's guidelines for legal-size SAE and 1 first class stamp.
Nonfiction: How-to, interview/profile, and personal experience. Buys 40-50 mss/year. Query. Length: 1,000-1,200 words. Pays 15¢/word.
Photos: State availability of photos or send photos with query. "Photos should illustrate, not merely accompany, articles." Pays $35 for 35mm color transparencies. Identification of subjects required. Buys one-time rights.
Fillers: Anecdotes, short humor and newsbreaks. Buys 6/year. Length: 100-250 words. Pays 15¢/word.
Tips: "A freelancer can best break in to our publication by sending a tantalizing query, followed by a tightly written article within our word limits."

CATALOG SHOPPER MAGAZINE, EGW International Corp., #8, 1300 Galaxy Way, Concord CA 94520. (415)671-9852. Editor: Ellen DasGupta. Quarterly magazine covering mail-order catalogs in over 40 categories. "Our magazine provides a unique way to shop at home from catalogs in over 40 categories. Included are many hard-to-find items. It is designed to help our readers by satisfying their hobby needs and making their lives more interesting through knowledge of the variety of specialty catalogs available to them." Circ. 50,000. Pays on publication. Publishes ms an average of 3 months after acceptance. Buys first North American serial rights. Submit seasonal/holiday material 6 months in advance. Simultaneous queries and

photocopied submissions OK. Computer printout submissions acceptable; prefers letter-quality to dot-matrix. SASE. Reports in 2 weeks on queries; 8 weeks on mss. Sample copy $1.50; writer's guidelines for SAE.
Columns/Department Length: 250 words maximum for each original contribution. Doing It Yourself, My Hobby, Life At A Glance, For Better Health, Investment Sidelights, Discovery & Science and High Tech Tidbits. Maximum length 50 words for our Questions To Ponder and for jokes, ancedotes, short humor, puzzle or light verse in Take It Easy. Maximum length 100 words in our Point Of Interest and for items including traveling, scenery, historical sites, or other points of interest in our Point Of Interest. Contributions to our Culinary Delights should list all ingredients and measurements. Choose a recipe that has an interesting story to go with it. Pays 4¢ a word.
Photographs: Seeks colorful outdoor, seasonal photographs for magazine cover. Should be either 35mm negative color slide or 4 x 5 transparency. Prefers vertical photos. Will return material if requested; enclose SAE and adequate postage. When submitting work, include a brief note about yourself and the place where the picture was taken. This will be edited as a "cover photo" note if your photo is published. Pays $50 upon publication.

CONSUMER ACTION NEWS, V&V Enterprises, 1579 Lexington Ave., Springfield OH 45505. (513)325-5822. Editor: Victor Pence. 10% freelance written. A monthly newsletter circulated in state of Ohio for readers who are interested in knowing how to handle consumer complaints: everything from electricity bills to mail order. "We handle consumer complaints and publish results in newsletter." Circ. 500. Pays on acceptance. Publishes ms an average of 2 months after acceptance. Byline given. Copyrighted. Buys one-time rights. Submit seasonal/holiday material minimum 2 months in advance. Simultaneous queries, and simultaneous, photocopied, and previously published submissions OK. Computer printout submissions acceptable; prefers letter-quality to dot-matrix. SASE. Reports in 3 weeks. Sample copy for 10 SAE and 22¢ postage.
Nonfiction: Exposé (material has to be documented or supported with some type of evidence that is legally sound); general interest (could include experiences with a company—must name company, etc.); interviews ("We do not endorse any company, product or service, nor do we accept money from any company. But, in order to let consumers see the human side of the business people they deal with we will run profiles on interesting people"); how-to (anything that could help consumers get better use from the products they buy. For example: a new slant on car care, repairing washer/drier, etc. Has to be very different, not the type of thing found in *Popular Mechanics*, etc.). No material that is not consumer "protection" oriented. Send complete ms. Length: 2,000 words maximum. For articles material suitable for booklets of 10-30 pages flat rate or percentage of sales, may consider combination of both. Pays $10-100. Sometimes pays the expenses of writers on assignment.
Columns/Departments: "We will consider ideas." Send complete ms. Pays $10-100.
Tips: "Every area is open to freelancers. Our type of publication is new in that we print complaints of consumers and name names of the companies involved. We give credit where it is due—good or bad. When we write something bad about a company we give them every chance to correct the problem. We also want interviews of business people. These articles are printed with the understanding that we are not promoting the company or endorsing it."

CONSUMERS DIGEST MAGAZINE, Consumers Digest, Inc., 5705 N. Lincoln Ave., Chicago IL 60659. (312)275-3590. Editor: Frank Bowers. 75% freelance written. Emphasizes anything of consumer interest. Bimonthly magazine. Circ. 1,000,000. Pays on acceptance. Publishes ms an average of 1 month after acceptance. Buys all rights. Computer printout submissions acceptable. SASE. Reports in 1 month. Free guidelines for SAE and 1 first class stamp to published writers only.
Nonfiction: Product-testing, evaluating; general interest (on advice to consumers, service, health, home, business, investments, insurance and money management); new products and travel. Query. Length: 1,200-3,000 words. Also buys shorter, more topical pieces (400-800 words) for Consumer Scope, Health Digest. Fees negotiable. First-time contributors usually are paid 25¢/word. Expenses paid.
Tips: "Send short query with samples of published work. Assignments are made upon acceptance of comprehensive outline."

CONSUMERS' RESEARCH, 517 2nd St. NE, Washington DC 20002. Executive Editor: Maureen Bozell. 70% freelance written. Monthly. Byline given "except when the article as written requires extensive editing, improvement or amplification. Buys first serial rights, second serial (reprint) rights and all rights. Query. Publishes ms an average of 3 months after acceptance. Computer printout submissions acceptable; no dot-matrix. SASE. Sample copy for SAE and 4 first class stamps.
Nonfiction: Articles of practical interest to consumers concerned with tests and expert judgment of goods and services they buy. Must be accurate and well-supported by professional knowledge of subject matter of articles, for instance, consumer economic problems, investments and finance. Recent article example: "Long-Distance Companies Begin Equal Access?" (February 1985). Pays approximately $100/page.

Tips: "The most frequent mistakes made by writers in completing an article assignment for us are: they write on their own authority without quoting sources; they editorialize when we strive to present an objective look at an issue; and they generalize where we like Facts."

ECONOMIC FACTS, The National Research Bureau, Inc., 424 N. 3rd St., Burlington IA 52601. Editor: Rhonda Wilson. Editorial Supervisor: Doris J. Ruschill. Magazine for industrial workers of all ages. 25% freelance written. Published 4 times/year. Pays on publication. Buys all rights. Byline given. Submit seasonal/holiday material 7 months in advance of issue date. Previously published submissions OK. Publishes ms an average of 1 year after acceptance. Computer printout submissions acceptable; prefers letter-quality to dot-matrix. SASE. Reports in 1 week. Free sample copy and writer's guidelines.
Nonfiction: General interest (private enterprise, government data, graphs, taxes and health care). Buys 3-5 mss/year. Query with outline of article. Length: 400-600 words. Pays 4¢/word.

ENTREPRENEUR MAGAZINE, 2311 Pontius, Los Angeles CA 90064. (213)473-0838. Publisher: Ron Smith. 40% freelance written. For a readership looking for highly profitable opportunities in small businesses, as owners, investors or franchisees. Monthly magazine. Circ. 200,000. Pays 60 days after acceptance. Publishes ms an average of 3 months after acceptance. Buys all rights. Byline given. Submit seasonal/holiday material 4 months in advance of issue date. Photocopied submissions OK. Computer printout submissions acceptable; no dot-matrix. SASE. Reports in 1 month. Sample copy $3; free writer's guidelines.
Nonfiction: How-to (in-depth start-up details on 'hot' business opportunities like tanning parlors or computer stores). Buys 50 mss/year. Query with clips of published work. Length: 1,200-2,000 words. Payment varies. Sometimes pays expenses of writers on assignment.
Photos: "We need good b&w glossy prints or color transparencies to illustrate articles." Offers additional payment for photos accepted with ms. Uses 8x10 b&w glossy prints or standard color transparencies. Captions preferred. Buys all rights. Model release required.
Columns/Departments: New Products; New Ideas; Promo Gimmicks. Query. Length: 200-500 words. Pays $25-100.
Tips: "It's rewarding to find a freelancer who reads the magazine *before* he/she submits a query—and who turns in a piece that's exactly what you've told him/her you want—especially if it doesn't have to be rewritten several times. We get so many queries with the wrong 'angle.' I can't stress enough the importance of reading and understanding our magazine and who our audience is before you write. We're looking for writers who can perceive the difference between *Entrepreneur* and 'other' business magazines."

FDA CONSUMER, 5600 Fishers Lane, Rockville MD 20857. (301)443-3220. Editor: William M. Rados. 10% freelance written. Monthly magazine. For "all consumers of products regulated by the Food and Drug Administration." A federal government publication. December/January and July/August issues combined. Circ. 15,000. Pays after acceptance. Publishes ms an average of 3 months after acceptance. Byline given. Not copyrighted. Pays 50% kill fee. "All purchases automatically become part of public domain." Buys 9-10 freelance mss a year. "We cannot be responsible for any work by writer not agreed upon by prior contract." Electronic submissions OK via Lanier. Computer printout submissions acceptable; prefers letter-quality to dot-matrix.
Nonfiction: "Articles of an educational nature concerning purchase and use of FDA regulated products and specific FDA programs and actions to protect the consumer's health and pocketbook. Authoritative and official agency viewpoints emanating from agency policy and actions in administrating the Food, Drug and Cosmetic Act and a number of other statutes. All articles subject to clearance by the appropriate FDA experts as well as acceptance by the editor. Articles based on health topics with the proviso that the subjects be connected to food, drugs, medicine, medical devices, and other products regulated by FDA. All articles based on prior arrangement by contract." Query. Length: 2,000 words. Pays $1,200 average. Sometimes pays the expenses of writers on assignment.
Photos: B&w photos are purchased on assignment only.

FINANCIAL INDEPENDENCE, A Digest for the Self-Employed, (formerly *Independence*), Agora Inc., 824 E. Baltimore St., Baltimore MD 21202. (301)234-0515. Editor-in-Chief: Elizabeth W. Philip. 10% freelance written. Monthly tabloid covering time-saving, money-saving information for the self-employed person who believes in being independent—philosophically, financially and personally. Circ. 16,000. Pays on acceptance. Publishes ms an average of 3 months after acceptance. Byline given. Buys first serial rights, first North American serial rights and all rights. Simultaneous queries and photocopied and previously published submissions OK. Computer printout submissions acceptable; prefers letter-quality to dot-matrix. SASE. Reports in 1 month on queries; 6 weeks on mss. Sample copy $2 and 2 first class stamps; writer's guidelines for business size SAE and 1 first class postage stamp.
Columns/Departments: Legal; Investment Notes; New Business Opportunities; Business Management; Saving Money; Personal Motivation. Length: 800-1,000 words; prefers 800 words. Should conform to *Associated Press Style Guide*. Pays $50-500.

Tips: "The most frequent mistake made by writers in completing an article for us is that the material is vague. We need well-researched factual material, interviews, and innovative financing techniques."

INCOME OPPORTUNITIES, 380 Lexington Ave., New York NY 10017. Editor: Stephen Wagner. Managing Editor: Tom Demske. 90% freelance written. Monthly magazine. For all who are seeking business opportunities, full- or part-time. Publishes magazine an average of 3 months after acceptance. Buys all rights. Two special directory issues contain articles on selling techniques, mail order, import/export, franchising and business ideas. SASE. Reports in 2 weeks.

Nonfiction and Photos: Regularly covered are such subjects as mail order, direct selling, franchising, party plans, selling techniques and the marketing of handcrafted or homecrafted products. Wanted are ideas for the aspiring entrepreneur; examples of successful business methods that might be duplicated. No material that is purely inspirational. Buys 50-60 mss/year. Query with outline of article development. Length: 800 words for a short; 2,000-3,000 words for a major article. "Payment rates vary according to length and quality of the submission." Sometimes pays expenses of writers on assignment.

Tips: "Study recent issues of the magazine. Best bets for newcomers: Interview-based report on a successful small business venture."

LOTTERY PLAYER'S MAGAZINE. National Lottery List, Intergalactic Publishing Company, Box 188, Clementon NJ 08021. (609)783-0910. News Editor: Crys Crystall. 60% freelance written. Monthly tabloid covering lottery news in legalized lottery and all non-lottery states, lottery games, gaming, travel, recreation associated with the lottery. Circ. 150,000. Pays on publication. Publishes ms an average of 10 weeks after acceptance. Byline given. Offers 10% kill fee. Buys simultaneous, first, and second serial (reprint) rights; also makes work-for-hire assignments. Submit seasonal/holiday material 3 months in advance. Simultaneous queries, and simultaneous, photocopied, and previously published submissions OK. Electronic submissions OK, but query for equipment compatibility. Computer printout submissions acceptable; prefers letter-quality to dot-matrix. Reports in 1 month on queries; 2 months on mss. Sample copy free if SAE (with four first class stamps) is sent.

Nonfiction: Book excerpts, expose, general interest, historical/nostalgic, how-to, humor, interview/profile, new product, opinion, personal experience, travel. All mss must pertain to lotteries, games of chance, lottery operations and their directors, popular gaming places (Las Vegas, Atlantic City, Monte Carlo, etc.), and lottery winners and losers. Special issues include Annual Traveler's Guide to the Lotteries, a list of winning numbers and relevant analysis for previous year. Buys 6-10 mss/year. Query with clips of published work or send complete ms. Length: 200-1,500 words. Pays $60-250.

Photos: Send photos with mss. Pays $10-25 for b&w prints; reviews contact sheet. Captions, model release and identification of subjects required. Buys one-time rights.

Columns/Departments: Numerology column (discussing relationship of numbers to everyday life—lucky numbers, etc.); reviews of books on gaming, games of chance. Buys variable number mss/year. Query with clips of published work or send complete ms. Length: 200-400 words. Pays $60-100.

Fiction: Adventure, fantasy, historical, humorous, and romance—associated with lottery. Buys 1-2 mss/year. Query with clips of published work. Length: 1,000-2,500 words. Pays $200-500.

Fillers: Clippings, jokes, gags, and anecdotes. Buys 20-40 fillers/year. Length: 25-100 lines. Pays $20-50.

Tips: "We would like to establish contact with photojournalists in states with lotteries for the express purpose of covering millionaire and other big chance drawings on a regular basis. We will pay regular rates and agreed upon expenses. States include New Hampshire, New York, Nevada, Connecticut, Pennsylvania, Massachusetts, Michigan, Maryland, Rhode Island, Maine, Illinois, Ohio, Delaware, Vermont, Colorado, Arizona, Oregon, California, Missouri, West Virginia, District of Columbia, and Washington."

MONEY MAKER, Your Guide to Financial Security & Wealth, Consumers Digest, Inc., 5705 N. Lincoln Ave., Chicago IL 60659. (312)275-3590. Editor: John Manos. 75% freelance written. Bimonthly magazine covering investment markets for unsophisticated investors. "Instructions for neophyte investors to increase their capital." Circ. 450,000. Pays on publication. Publishes ms an average of 3 months after acceptance. Byline given. Offers 50% kill fee. Buys all rights. Simultaneous queries and photocopied submissions OK. Computer printout submissions acceptable; prefers letter-quality to dot-matrix. Reports in 6 weeks on queries; 3 months on mss. Free sample copy and writer's guidelines.

Nonfiction: How-to (on investment areas); analysis of specific markets. "Indicate your areas of financial expertise." Buys 60 mss/year. Query with clips of published work if available. Length: 1,000-3,000 words. Pays $200-600%. Sometimes pays the expenses of writers on assignment.

Tips: "The most frequent mistake made by writers in completing an article for us is doing insufficient research."

‡**THE NEWSLETTER OF SUPER-SUCCESSFUL SERVICE BUSINESSES**, Cunningham Publishing Co., 701 Washington, Box 1345, Buffalo NY 14205. (519)587-5143. Editor: Peter Cunningham. Managing Editor: Peter G. Jovanovich. Monthly newsletter on super successful business opportunities. Geared to

"aspiring" and "self-made" tycoons (smart-aggressive men/women) who are keen on operating super-successful businesses—primarily in the "service" field. Looking for opportunities that require more "guts" than "money" to start. Estab. 1984. Circ. 8,500. Pays on acceptance. Byline given. Buys all rights. Photocopied submissions OK. SASE. Reports in 2 weeks. Sample copy $3, with SAE and 2 first class stamps.
Nonfiction: How-to (start/operate home business in the service field with ultimate million dollar potential); interview/profile (successful, tycoons only need apply); new product (must have mass market appeal/licensing opportunities); personal experience (individual success stories accepted pertaining to money/business); successful marketing/promotional strategies and how to exploit media. No chain letters, no envelope stuffing plans, pie-in-the-sky opportunities, no expensive-to-start enterprises. No wild or risky schemes. Buys 25 mss/year. Send complete ms. Length: 500-800 words. Pays $25-400. "The more unique the business opportunity, the more we pay."
Photos: Send photos with query or ms. Prefers photos to emphasize a product or promotion. Reviews 3x5 b&w prints (2 photos only). Purchase price includes photos and ms. Model release required.

PUBLIC CITIZEN, Public Citizen, Inc., Box 19404, Washington DC 20036. Editor: Elliott Negin. 5% freelance written. Quarterly magazine covering consumer issues for "contributors to Public Citizen, a consortium of five consumer groups established by Ralph Nader in the public interest: Congress Watch, the Health Research Group, the Critical Mass Energy Project, the Litigation Group, and the Tax Reform Group. Our readers have joined Public Citizen because they believe the consumer should have a voice in the products he or she buys, the quality of our environment, good government, and citizen rights in our democracy." Circ. 45,000. Pays on publication. Publishes ms an average of 4 months after acceptance. Byline given. Buys first rights. Submit seasonal/holiday material 4 months in advance. Computer printout submissions acceptable; prefers letter-quality to dot-matrix. SASE. Reports in 1 month on queries; 2 months on mss. Publishes ms an average of 3 months after acceptance. Sample copy available. "Freelance material rarely used because Public Citizen is a public interest group with a modest budget."
Nonfiction: Exposé (of government waste and inaction and corporate wrongdoing); general interest (features on how consumer groups are helping themselves); how-to (start consumer groups such as co-ops, etc.); interview/profile (of business or consumer leaders, or of government officials in positions that affect consumers); and photo feature (dealing with consumer power). "We are looking for stories that go to the heart of an issue and explain how it affects individuals. Articles must be in-depth investigations that expose poor business practices or bad government or that call attention to positive accomplishments. Send us stories that consumers will feel they learned something important from or that they can gain inspiration from to continue the fight for consumer rights. All facts are double checked by our fact-checkers." No "fillers, jokes or puzzles." Query or send complete ms. Length: 500-10,000 words. Pays $1,000 maximum/article. Sometimes pays the expenses of writers on assignment.
Photos: State availability of photos. Reviews 5x7 b&w prints. "Photos are paid for with payment for ms." Captions required. Buys one-time rights.
Columns/Departments: Reliable Sources ("book reviews"). Query or send complete ms—"no clips." Length: 500-1,000 words. Pays $125 maximum/article.
Tips: No first-person articles, political rhetoric, or "mood" pieces; *Public Citizen* is a highly factual advocacy magazine. Knowledge of the public interest movement, consumer issues, and Washington politics is a plus.

TOWERS CLUB, USA NEWSLETTER, The Original Information-By-Mail, Direct-Marketing Newsletter, Towers Club Press, Box 2038, Vancouver WA 98668. (206)699-4428. Editor: Jerry Buchanan. 5% freelance written. Newsletter published 10 times/year (not published in August or December) covering entrepreneurism (especially selling useful information by mail). Circ. 5,000. Pays on publication. Publishes ms an average of 1 month after acceptance. Byline given. Buys one-time rights. Submit seasonal/holiday material 10 weeks in advance. Simultaneous, photocopied, and previously published submissions OK. Computer printout submissions or 7" diskettes with TRS-80 Scriptsit software OK. SASE. Reports in 2 weeks. Sample copy for $3 and 39¢ postage.
Nonfiction: Exposé (of mail order fraud); how-to (personal experience in self-publishing and marketing). "Welcomes well-written articles of successful self publshing/marketing ventures. Must be current, and preferably written by the person who actually did the work and reaped the rewards. There's very little we will not consider, *if* it pertains to unique money-making enterprises that can be operated from the home." Buys 10 mss/year. Send complete ms. Length: 500-1,000 words. Pays $10-35. Pays extra for b&w photo and bonus for excellence in longer manuscript.
Tips: "The most frequent mistake made by writers in completing an article for us is that they think they can simply rewrite a newspaper article and be accepted. That is only the start. We want them to find the article about a successful self-publishing enterprise, and then go out and interview the principles for a more detailed how-to article, including names and addresses. We prefer that writers actually interview a successful self-publisher. Articles should include how idea first came to subject, how they implemented and financed and promoted the project. How long it took to show a profit and some of the stumbling blocks they overcame. How many

persons participated in the production and promotion. How much money was invested (approximately) and other pertinent how-to elements of the story. Glossy photos of principles at work in their offices will help sell article. B&w only."

VENTURE, The Magazine for Entrepreneurs, Venture Magazine, Inc., 1st Floor, 521 5th Ave., New York NY 10175. (212)682-7373. Editor-in-Chief: Carl Burgen. Monthly magazine about entrepreneurs for people owning their own businesses, starting new businesses or wanting to do so.
Nonfiction: "We use stories on new startups of companies and current news on venture capital and entrepreneurs by assignment only." No unsolicited material. Query.

Detective and Crime

Fans of detective stories want to read accounts of actual espionage and criminal cases. Most of the following magazines buy nonfiction. Markets for *only* criminal fiction (mysteries) are listed in Mystery publications.

DETECTIVE CASES, Detective Files Group, 1440 St. Catherine St. W., Montreal, Quebec H3G 1S2 Canada. Editor-in-Chief: Dominick A. Merle. Art Director: Art Ball. Bimonthly magazine. See *Detective Files*.

DETECTIVE DRAGNET, Detective Files Group, 1440 St. Catherine St. W., Montreal, Quebec H3G 1S2 Canada. Editor-in-Chief: Dominick A. Merle. Art Director: Art Ball. Bimonthly magazine; 72 pages. See *Detective Files*.

DETECTIVE FILES, Detective Files Group, 1440 St. Catherine St. W., Montreal, Quebec H3G 1S2 Canada. Editor-in-Chief: Dominick A. Merle. Art Director: Art Ball. 100% freelance written. Bimonthly magazine; 72 pages. Pays on acceptance. Publishes ms an average of 3 months after acceptance. Buys all rights. Photocopied submissions OK. SASE. Reports in 4 weeks. Free sample copy and writer's guidelines.
Nonfiction: True crime stories. "Do a thorough job; don't double-sell (sell the same article to more than one market); and deliver, and you can have a steady market. Neatness, clarity and pace will help you make the sale." Query. Length: 3,500-6,000 words. Pays $175-300.
Photos: Purchased with accompanying ms; no additional payment.

ESPIONAGE MAGAZINE, Leo II Publications, Ltd., Box 1184, Teaneck NJ 07666. (201)569-4072. Editor: Jackie Lewis. 100% freelance written. A bimonthly magazine "totally devoted to spy stories of international intrigue, suspense, blackmail, confused loyalties, deception, and other things immoral. Fiction and nonfiction stories by top writers in the world of espionage." Estab. 1984. Pays on publication. Publishes ms usually many months after acceptance. Byline given. Buys one-time rights, all rights, first serial rights, first North American serial rights and second serial (reprint) rights. "Since we are a new publication, we have not restricted ourselves as to specific rights; we are open to many types." Photocopied and previously published submissions OK. Computer printout submissions acceptable; no dot-matrix. SASE. Reports in 1 month. Sample copy for $2.50, 6x9 SAE, and 90¢ postage; writer's guidelines for business-size SAE and 1 first class stamp.
Nonfiction: Spy oriented only: book excerpts, expose, historical/nostalgic, humor, interview/profile and personal experience. Anything relating to spy stories. Buys approximately 10 mss/year. Send complete ms. Length: 1,000-10,000 words. Pays 5-6¢/word depending on the amount of editing needed.
Fiction: Spy oriented only: adventure, condensed novels, confession, fantasy, historical, humorous, mystery, excerpts from published novels, romance, science fiction, serialized novels, suspense and western. Anything relating to intrigue, international suspense about spies. Buys 100 mss/year. Send complete ms. Length: 1,000-10,000 words. Pays 5-6¢/word depending on the amount of editing needed.
Fillers: Spy oriented only: anecdotes, newsbreaks. Length: 20-100 words. Pays $5. Also games, crossword puzzles. Pays from $10-20.
Tips: "We are interested in any writer of fiction or nonfiction who writes spy stories. We will not accept explicit sex or gratuitous gore." First person stories are preferred, but stories from any perspective will be considered. Heroes can be any age, nationality, or walk of life. Fiction short stories are most open to freelancers. "Send no subject however unless it is spy oriented."

FRONT PAGE DETECTIVE, INSIDE DETECTIVE, Official Detective Group, R.G.H. Publishing Corp., 20th Floor, 460 W. 34th St., New York NY 10001. (212)947-6500. Editor-in-Chief: Art Crockett. Editor of Front Page and Inside: Rose Mandelsberg.
Nonfiction: The focus of these two publications is similar to the others in the Official Detective Group. "We now use post-trial stories; rarely are pre-trial ones published." Byline given. For further details, see *Official Detective*.

HEADQUARTERS DETECTIVE, Detective Files Group, 1440 St. Catherine St. W., Montreal, Quebec H3G 1S2 Canada. Editor-in-Chief: Dominick A. Merle. Art Director: Art Ball. Bimonthly magazine; 72 pages. See *Detective Files*.

MASTER DETECTIVE, Official Detective Group, R.G.H. Publishing Corp., 460 W. 34th St., New York NY 10001. Editor-in-Chief: Art Crockett. Managing Editor: Christos K. Ziros, 100% freelance written. Monthly. Circ. 350,000. Buys 9 mss/issue. See *Official Detective*.

OFFICIAL DETECTIVE, Official Detective Group, R.G.H. Publishing Corp., 460 W. 34th St., New York NY 10001. (212)947-6500. Editor-in-Chief: Art Crockett. Managing Editor: Christos Mirtsopoulos. 100% freelance written. Monthly magazine "for detective story or police buffs whose tastes run to *true*, rather than fictional crime/mysteries." Circ. 500,000. Pays on acceptance. Buys all rights. Byline given. SASE. Reports in 2 weeks.
Nonfiction: "Only *fact* detective stories. We are actively trying to develop new writers, and we'll work closely with those who show promise and can take the discipline required by our material. It's not difficult to write, but it demands meticulous attention to facts, truth, clarity, detail. Queries are essential with us, but I'd say the quickest rejection goes to the writer who sends in a story on a case that should never have been written for us because it lacks the most important ingredient, namely solid, superlative detective work. We also dislike pieces with multiple defendants, unless all have been convicted." Buys 150 mss/year. Query. Length: 5,000-6,000 words. Pays $250.
Photos: Purchased with accompanying mss. Captions required. Send prints for inside use; transparencies for covers. Pays $12.50 minimum for 4 x 5 b&w glossy prints. Pays $200 minimum for $2^{1}/_{4}$x$2^{1}/_{4}$ or 35mm transparencies. Model release required for color photos used on cover.
Tips: Send a detailed query on the case to be submitted. Include: locale; victim's name; type of crime; suspect's name; status of the case (indictment, trial concluded, disposition, etc.); amount and quality of detective work; dates; and availability and number of pictures. "We're always impressed by details of the writer's credentials."

STARTLING DETECTIVE, Detective Files Group, 1440 St. Catherine St. W., Montreal, Quebec H3G 1S2 Canada. Editor-in-Chief: Dominick A. Merle. Art Director: Art Ball. Bimonthly magazine; 72 pages. See *Detective Files*.

TRUE DETECTIVE, Official Detective Group, R.G.H. Publishing Corp., 460 W. 34th St., New York NY 10001. (212)947-6500. Editor-in-Chief: Art Crockett. Managing Editor: Christos Mirtsopoulos. Monthly. Circ. 500,000. Buys 10 mss/issue. Byline given. See *Official Detective*.

TRUE POLICE CASES, Detective Files Group, 1440 St. Catherine St. W., Montreal, Quebec H3G 1S2 Canada. Editor-in-Chief: Dominick A. Merle. Art Director: Art Ball. Bimonthly magazine; 72 pages. See *Detective Files*.

Ethnic/Minority

Traditions are kept alive, and new ones become established because of ethnic publications. Some ethnic magazines seek material that unites people of all races. "We solicit material that points out the similarity in the lives of all of us regardless of ethnic or racial background," said one editor. "Without mutual respect, we believe mankind is doomed." Ideas, interests and concerns of nationalities and religions are voiced by publications in this category. General interest lifestyle magazines for these groups are also included. Additional markets for writing with an ethnic orientation are located in the following sections: Book Publishers; Career, College, and Alumni; Juvenile; Men's; and Women's.

AIM MAGAZINE, AIM Publishing Company, 7308 S. Eberhart Ave., Chicago IL 60619. (312)874-6184. Editor: Ruth Apilado. Managing Editor: Dr. Myron Apilado. 75% freelance written. Quarterly magazine on social betterment that promotes racial harmony and peace for high school, college and general audience. Circ. 10,000. Pays on publication. Publishes ms an average of 3 months after acceptance. Offers 60% of contract as kill fee. Not copyrighted. Buys one-time rights. Submit seasonal/holiday material 6 months in advance. Simultaneous queries, and simultaneous and photocopied submissions OK. SASE. Reports in 6 weeks on queries. Writer's guidelines for $3.00, 8½x11 SAE and 65¢ postage.
Nonfiction: Expose (education); general interest (social significance); historical/nostalgic (Black or Indian); how-to (help create a more equitable society); and new product (one who is making social contributions to community). No religious material. Buys 16 mss/year. Send complete ms. Length: 500-800 words. Pays $25-35. Sometimes pays the expenses of writers on assignment.
Photos: Reviews b&w prints. Captions and identification of subjects required.
Fiction: Ethnic, historical, mainstream, and suspense. Fiction that teaches the brotherhood of man. Buys 20 mss/year. Send complete ms. Length: 1,000-1,500 words. Pays $25-35.
Poetry: Avant-garde, free verse, light verse. No "preachy" poetry. Buys 20 poems/year. Submit maximum 5 poems. Length: 15-30 lines. Pays $3-5.
Fillers: Jokes, anecdotes and newsbreaks. Buys 30/year. Length: 50-100 words. Pays $5.
Tips: "Interview anyone of any age who unselfishly is making an unusual contribution to the lives of less fortunate individuals. Include photo and background of person. We look at the nation of the world as part of one family. Short stories and historical pieces about blacks and Indians are the areas most open to freelancers. Articles and stories showing the similarity in the lives of people with different racial backgrounds are trends that writers should be aware of."

‡**THE AMERICAN CITIZEN ITALIAN PRESS**, 8262 Hascall St., Omaha NE 68124. (402)391-2012. Editor: Gene Failla. Managing Editor: Victor A. Failla. 40% freelance written. Quarterly newspaper of Italian-American news/stories. Circ. 5,600. Pays on publication. Publishes ms an average of 3 months after acceptance. Byline given. Not copyrighted. Buys first North American serial rights. Submit seasonal/holiday material 2 months in advance. Previously published submissions OK. SASE. Reports in 4 week. Free sample copy.
Nonfiction: Book excerpts, general interest, historical/nostalgic, opinion and photo feature. Query with published clips. Length: 400-900 words. Pays $25-50. Sometimes pays the expenses of writers on assignment.
Photos: State availability of photos. Reviews b&w prints. Pays $5. Captions and identification of subjects required. Buys all rights.
Columns/Departments: Query.
Fiction: Query. Pays $25-50.
Poetry: Traditional. Buys 4-5/year. Submit maximum 2 poems. Pays $5-10.
Tips: Human interest stories most open to freelancers.

AMERICAN DANE MAGAZINE, Danish Brotherhood in America, Box 31748, Omaha NE 68131. (402)341-5049. Acting Administrative Editor: Jerome L. Christensen. Acting Editor-In-Chief: Pamela K. Dorau. Submit only material with Danish ethnic flavor. Monthly magazine. Circ. 11,000. Pays on publication. Publishes ms an average of 2 months after acceptance. Buys all rights. Submit seasonal/holiday material 12 months in advance (particularly Christmas). Photocopied or previously published submissions OK with signed permission of the contributor. Computer printout submissions acceptable; prefers letter-qualtiy to dot-matrix. SASE. Byline given. Reports in 2 months. Sample copy $1 and 50¢ postage. Writer's guidelines for SAE and 1 first class stamp. .
Nonfiction: Historical; humor (satirical, dry wit notoriously Danish); informational (Danish items, Denmark or Danish-American involvements); inspirational (honest inter-relationships); interview; nostalgia; personal experience; photo feature and travel. Buys 10-15 unsolicited mss/year. Length: 3,000 words maximum. Pays $25-50.
Photos: Purchased on assignment. Pays $10-25 for b&w. Total purchase price for ms includes payment for photos. Model release required.
Fiction: Danish adventure, historical, humorous, mystery, romance and suspense. Must have Danish appeal. Buys 12 mss/year. Query. Length: 500-3,000 words. Pays $25-50.
Fillers: Puzzles (crossword, anagrams, etc.) and short humor. Query. Length: 50-300 words.

AN GAEL, Irish Traditional Culture Alive in America Today, The Irish Arts Center, 553 W. 51st St., New York NY 10019. (212)757-3318. Editor: Kevin McEneaney. Quarterly magazine covering the heritage of the Irish people with emphasis on the Irish-American experience. Material in the Irish language, as well as English is welcome. Written for all those who want to maintain or actively pursue Irish arts, history and language. Circ. 2,500. Pays on acceptance. Byline given. Submit seasonal/holiday material 6 months in advance. Photocopied submissions OK. "We cannot return submissions." Reports in 1 month. Sample copy for SASE.
Nonfiction: Humor, photo feature. Articles include periodic features on Irish language; traditional music,

dance and visual arts; Irish-American community profiles; fiction and poetry in both English and Irish; interviews with and profiles of cultural figures; and reviews of cultural activities, drama, books, films and records. Buys 30 mss/year. Send complete ms. Length: 1,000 words maximum. Pays $10.
Photos: Descriptive of traditional Irish subject matter. Reviews 8x10 b&w glossy prints. Identification of subject required. Buys one-time rights.

ARARAT, The Armenian General Benevolent Union, 585 Saddle River Rd., Saddle Brook NJ 07662. Editor-in-Chief: Leo Hamalian. 80% freelance written. Emphasizes Armenian life and culture for Americans of Armenian descent and Armenian immigrants. "Most are well-educated; some are Old World." Quarterly magazine. Circ. 2,400. Pays on publication. Publishes ms an average of 1 year after acceptance. Buys first North American serial rights and second (reprint) rights to material originally published elsewhere. Submit seasonal/holiday material at least 3 months in advance. Photocopied and previously published submissions OK. Computer printout submissions acceptable. SASE. Reports in 6 weeks. Sample copy $3 plus $1 postage
Nonfiction: Historical (history of Armenian people, of leaders, etc.); interviews (with prominent or interesting Armenians in any field, but articles are preferred); profile (on subjects relating to Armenian life and culture); personal experience (revealing aspects of typical Armenian life); and travel (in Armenia and Armenian communities throughout the world and the US). Buys 3 mss/issue. Query. Length: 1,000-6,000 words. Pays $25-100.
Columns/Departments: Reviews of books by Armenians or relating to Armenians. Buys 6/issue. Query. Pays $25. Open to suggestions for new columns/departments.
Fiction: Any stories dealing with Armenian life in America or in the old country. Buys 4 mss/year. Query. Length: 2,000-5,000 words. Pays $35-75.
Poetry: Any verse that is Armenian in theme. Buys 6/issue. Pays $10.
Tips: "Read the magazine, and write about the kind of subjects we are obviously interested in, e.g., Kirlian photography, Aram Avakian's films, etc. Remember that we have become almost totally ethnic in subject matter, but we want articles that present (to the rest of the world) the Armenian in an interesting way. The most frequent mistake made by writers in completing an article for us is that they are not sufficently versed in American history/culture. The articles are too superficial for our audience."

BALTIMORE JEWISH TIMES, 2104 N. Charles St., Baltimore MD 21218. (301)752-3504. Editor: Gary Rosenblatt. 25% freelance written. Weekly magazine covering subjects of interest to Jewish readers. "*Baltimore Jewish Times* reaches 20,000 Baltimore-area Jewish homes, as well as several thousand elsewhere in the US and Canada; almost anything of interest to that audience is of interest to us. This includes reportage, general interest articles, personal opinion, and personal experience pieces about every kind of Jewish subject from narrowly religious issues to popular sociology; from the Mideast to the streets of Brooklyn, to the suburbs of Baltimore. We run articles of special interest to purely secular Jews as well as to highly observant ones. We are Orthodox, Conservative, and Reform all at once. We are spiritual and mundane. We are establishment and we are alternative culture." Circ. 20,000. Pays on publication. Publishes ms an average of 2 months after acceptance. Byline given. Buys one-time rights. Submit seasonal/holiday material 2 months in advance. Simultaneous queries, and photocopied and previously published submissions OK. Computer printout submissions acceptable; prefers letter-quality to dot-matrix. "We will not return submissions without SASE." Reports in 6 weeks. Sample copy $2.
Nonfiction: Barbara Pash, editorial assistant. Book excerpts, expose, general interest, historical/nostalgic, humor, interview/profile, opinion, personal experience and photo feature. "We are inundated with Israel personal experience and Holocaust-related articles, so submissions on these subjects must be of particularly high quality." Buys 100 mss/year. "Established writers query; others send complete manuscript." Length: 1,200-6,000 words. Pays $25-150.
Photos: Kim Muller-Thym, graphics editor. Send photos with ms. Pays $10-35 for 8x10 b&w prints.
Fiction: Barbara Pash, editorial assistant. "We'll occasionally run a high-quality short story with a Jewish theme." Buys 6 mss/year. Send complete ms. Length: 1,200-6,000 words. Pays $25-150.

BLACK ENTERPRISE MAGAZINE, For Black Men and Women Who Want to Get Ahead. Earl G. Graves Publishing Co., 130 5th Ave., New York NY 10011. (212)242-8000. Editor: Earl G. Graves. Managing Editor: Sheryl Hilliard. Monthly magazine covering black economic development and business for a highly-educated, affluent, black, middle-class audience interested in business, politics, careers and international issues. Circ. 250,000. Pays on acceptance. Byline given. Offers negotiable kill fee. Buys all rights. Submit seasonal/holiday material 4 months in advance. Simultaneous queries OK. No unsolicited mss. Reports in 4-6 weeks on queries. Sample copy and writer's guidelines free.
Nonfiction: Expose, general business, career and personal finance interest, how-to, interview/profile, technical, travel, and short, hard-news items of Black business, career and personal finance interest. "We emphasize the how-to aspect." Special issues include: Careers, February; Top 100 Black Businesses, June; Money Management, October; and Arts Guides, November. "No fiction or poetry; no 'rags-to-riches,' ordinary-guy stories, please." Buys 30-40 feature length mss/year. Query with clips of published work. Send "a short,

succinct letter that lets us know the point of the piece, the elements involved, and *why* our readers would want to read it." Length: 600-3,000 words. Buys 40 mss/year. Pays $100-800/article.

Columns/Departments: Ken Smikle, associate editor. In the News (short, hard-news pieces on issues of black interest); and Verve (lifestyle and leisure articles. Ed Smith, Verve editor). Query with clips of published work. Length: 300-1,000 words. Pays $75-300/article.

Tips: "We have stayed away from trivia and first-person pieces on the belief that our readers want hard-nosed reporting and innovative analysis of issues that concern them. *Black Enterprise* has a mission of informing, educating and entertaining an upscale, affluent audience that wants issues addressed from its unique perspective. We are most open to 'In the News,' an expression of a sensitivity to issues/events/trends that have an impact on black people."

CONGRESS MONTHLY, American Jewish Congress, 15 E. 84th St., New York NY 10028. (212)879-4500. Editor: Maier Deshell. 90% freelance written. Magazine published 7 times/year covering topics of concern to the American Jewish community representing a wide range of views. Distributed mainly to the members of the American Jewish Congress; readers are intellectual, Jewish, involved. Circ. 27,000. Pays on publication. Publishes ms an average of 3 months after acceptance. Byline given. Copyrighted. Buys one-time rights. Submit seasonal/holiday material 2 months in advance. No photocopied or previously published submissions. Computer printout submissions acceptable; no dot-matrix. Reports in 2 months.

Nonfiction: General interest ("current topical issues geared toward our audience"). No technical material. Send complete ms. Length: 2,000 words maximum. Pays $100-150/article.

Photos: State availability of photos. Reviews b&w prints. "Photos are paid for with payment for ms."

Columns/Departments: Book, film, art and music reviews. Send complete ms. Length: 1,000 words maximum. Pays $100-150/article.

EBONY MAGAZINE, 820 S. Michigan Ave., Chicago IL 60605. Editor: John H. Johnson. Managing Editor: Charles L. Sanders. 10% freelance written. For black readers of the US, Africa, and the Caribbean. Monthly. Circ. 1,800,000. Buys first North American serial rights and all rights. Buys about 10 mss/year. "We are now fully staffed, buying few manuscripts." Pays on publication. Publishes ms an average of 3 months after acceptance. Submit seasonal material 2 months in advance. Query. Reports in 1 month. SASE.

Nonfiction: Achievement and human interest stories about, or of concern to, black readers. Interviews, profiles and humor pieces are bought. Length: 1,500 words maximum. "Study magazine and needs carefully. Perhaps one out of 50 submissions interests us. Most are totally irrelevant to our needs and are simply returned." Pays $200 minimum. Sometimes pays the expenses of writers on assignment.

Photos: Purchased with mss, and with captions only. Buys 8x10 glossy prints, color transparencies, 35mm color. Submit negatives and contact sheets when possible. Offers no additional payment for photos accepted with mss.

ESSENCE, 1500 Broadway, New York NY 10036. (212)730-4260. Editor-in-Chief: Susan L. Taylor. Editor: Audrey Edwards. Executive Editor: Cheryl Everette. Senior Editor: Elaine C. Ray. Emphasizes black women. Monthly magazine; 150 pages. Circ. 800,000. Pays on acceptance. Makes assignments on work-for-hire basis. 3 month lead time. Pays 25% kill fee. Byline given. Submit seasonal/holiday material 6 months in advance. Computer printout submissions acceptable. SASE. Reports in 2 months. Sample copy $1.50; free writer's guidelines.

Features: "We're looking for articles that inspire and inform black women. Our readers are interested and aware; the topics we include in each issue are provocative. Every article should move the *Essence* woman emotionally and intellectually. We welcome queries from good writers on a wide range of topics: general interest, health and fitness, historical, how-to, humor, self-help, relationships, work, personality interview, personal experience, political issues, and personal opinion." Buys 200 mss/year. Query. Length: 1,500-3,000 words. Pays $500 minimum.

Photos: Folayemi Debra Wilson, art director. State availability of photos with query. Pays $100 for b&w page; $300 for color page. Captions and model release required.

Columns/Departments: Query department editors: Contemporary Living (home, food, lifestyle, consumer information): Curtia James, Contemporary Living, editor; Arts & Entertainment: Pamela Johnson; Health & Fitness: Marjorie Whigham; Careers; Janine Coveney; Travel: Elaine C. Ray. Query. Length: About 1,000 words. Pays $100 minimum. We accept poetry.

Tips: "We're looking for quality fiction; more self-improvement pieces, 'relationship' articles, career information and issues important to black women."

GREATER PHOENIX JEWISH NEWS, Phoenix Jewish News, Inc., Box 26590, Phoenix AZ 85068. (602)870-9470. Executive Editor: Flo Eckstein. Managing Editor: Leni Reiss. 20% freelance written. Weekly tabloid covering subjects of interest to Jewish readers. Circ. 7,000. Pays on publication. Publishes ms an average of 3 months after acceptance. Byline given. Submit seasonal/holiday material 3 months in advance. Simultaneous queries, and simultaneous, photocopied, and previously published submissions OK. Computer

printout submissions acceptable; prefers letter-quality to dot-matrix. (Must be easy to read, with upper and lower case.) SASE. Reports in 1 month. Sample copy $1.50 writer's guidelines for SAE and 1 first class stamp.
Nonfiction: General interest, issue analysis, interview/profile, opinion, personal experience, photo feature and travel. Special issues include Fashion and Health, House and Home, Back to School; Summer Camps; Party Planning; Bridal; and Jewish Holidays. Buys 25 mss/year. Query with published clips or send complete ms. Length: 1,000-2,500 words. Pays $15-100 for simultaneous rights; $1.50/column inch for first serial rights.
Photos: Send photos with query or ms. Pays $10 for 8x10 b&w prints. Captions required.
Tips: "Our newspaper reaches across the religious, political, social and economic spectrum of Jewish residents in this burgeoning southwestern metropolitan area. We look for fairly short (maximum 1,500 words) pieces of a serious nature, written with clarity and balance. We stay away from cute stories as well as ponderous submissions."

GREEK ACCENT, Greek Accent Publishing Corp., 41-17 Crescent St., Long Island City NY 11101. (718)784-2986. Executive Editor: Steven Phillips. 50% freelance written. Bimonthly magazine. "We are a publication for and about Greek-Americans and philhellenes." Circ. 20,000. Pays on publication. Publishes ms an average of 6 months after acceptance. Byline given. Offers 20% kill fee. Buys first North American serial rights. Submit seasonal/holiday material 1 year in advance. Photocopied submissions OK. Computer printout submissions acceptable but not preferred; prefers letter-quality to dot-matrix. SASE. Reports in 1 month on queries; 3 months on mss. Sample copy $3.25 with 9x12 SAE and $1 postage; Writer's guidelines for SAE and 1 first class stamp.
Nonfiction: Michael Richard, articles editor. Book excerpts; expose; historical/nostalgic (historical more than nostalgic); how-to (only with a Greek slant, about Greece or Greeks); humor; interview/profile; new product (made or manufactured by Greeks or Greek-Americans); and travel. No " 'My Trip to Samothraki' articles or 'Greece Through the Eyes of a Non-Greek.' We publish articles on Greeks and Greece, on Greek-Americans who have succeeded at their work in some important way or who are doing unusual things, and on general interest subjects that might specifically interest our audience, such as the role of Greek Orthodox priests' wives, the crisis in Greek-US political relations, the Cyprus problem, Greek school education in the US, and large Greek-American communities like Astoria, New York." Query with clips of published work. "We buy almost no unsolicited articles—we work exclusively from queries." Length: 3,000-5,000 words. Pays $200-300.
Photos: Anna Lascari, art director. State availability of photos. Pays $10 for 8x10 prints or contact sheets; $15 for color transparencies. Model release and identification of subjects required. Buys one-time rights. Sometimes pays the expenses of writers on assignment.
Fiction: Ethnic, fantasy, historical, humorous, mainstream, and mystery. No novels, or Greek or Greek-American stereotyping. All fiction must in some way have a Greek theme. Send complete ms. Length: 1,500-3,000 words. Pays $100-200.
Tips: "Try to deal with problems and concerns peculiar to or of specific interest to Greek-Americans, rather than concentrating solely on Greece. With regard to Greece, heritage-historical-genealogical articles are of interest. The most frequent mistakes result from writers' superficial knowledge of Greek history and heritage, and especially Greek—American history. Writers often do not realize our readers are very knowledgable when it comes to these areas. We'd rather have investigative, informative articles than paeans to the glory that was Greece. Probably the easiest way to get published here is to do a good, in-depth piece on a large, active Greek-American community in the Midwest, West, or South, and back it up with pictures. The more we get from outside the tri-state area, the happier we'll be. Fillers and departments like Observations and On People are written in house."

THE HIGHLANDER, Angus J. Ray Associates, Inc., Box 397, Barrington IL 60010. (312)382-1035. Editor: Angus J. Ray. Managing Editor: Ethyl Kennedy Ray. 20% freelance written. Bimonthly magazine covering Scottish history, clans, genealogy, travel/history, and Scottish/American activities. Circ. 32,000. Pays on acceptance. Publishes ms an average of 6 months after acceptance. Byline given. Buys first North American serial rights and second serial (reprint) rights to material originally published elsewhere. Submit seasonal/holiday material 6 months in advance. Photocopied and previously published submissions OK. Computer printout submissions acceptable; no dot-matrix. SASE. Reports in 1 month. Sample copy and writer's guidelines free.
Nonfiction: Historical/nostalgic. "No fiction; no articles unrelated to Scotland." Buys 20 mss/year. Query. Length: 750-2,000 words. Pays $75-125.
Photos: State availability of photos. Pays $5-10 for 8x10 b&w prints. Reviews b&w contact sheets. Identification of subjects required. Buys one-time rights.
Tips: "Submit something that has appeared elsewhere."

‡**THE HISPANIC MONITOR**, El Observador Hispano (The Hispanic Monitor), Inc., Room 232, 250 W. 57th St., New York NY 10107. (212)757-6557. Editor: Rafael Ruiz. Managing Editor: Geoffrey Fox. 40-60% freelance written. Monthly newspaper covering news of all Hispanic communities in the US. "Our readership at present is primarily academics, journalists and political or community activists; we plan to increase business

people readership as well." Estab. 1984. Circ. 1,000. Pays on publication. Publishes ms an average of 1 month after acceptance. Byline given. Buys first North American serial rights. Simultaneous queries and photocopied submissions OK. Computer printout submissions acceptable; no dot-matrix. SASE. Reports in 1-2 weeks. Sample copy for SAE and 2 first class stamps. Writer's guidelines for business-sized SAE and 1 first class stamp.

Nonfiction: General interest (Hispanic communities); interview/profile (Hispanic political or business figures); and political reporting and analysis. No "puff" pieces, unsubstantiated opinion (facts must be checked and people of opposing viewpoints contacted), or reviews of cultural events unless these include some analysis of socioeconomic context. Buys 40-50 mss/year. Query with published clips. Length: 500-1,200 words; (occasionally up to 2,200). Pays $25-75; ($100 or more for exceptional, longer pieces from writers familiar to us). Sometimes pays the expenses of writers on assignment.

Columns/Departments: Research Notes, written entirely by executive editor Geoffrey Fox, "we are interested in establishing one of short items on business, labor and economy generally (no title yet)."

Tips: "We need more articles on nationalities (such as Colombians, Ecuadorians) and on some of the smaller communities in the country that we have given little coverage so far. If we like your writing but can't use your idea, we may suggest another approach."

INSIDE, The Jewish Exponent Magazine. Federation of Jewish Agencies of Greater Philadelphia, 226 S. 16th St., Philadelphia PA 19102. (215)895-5700. Editor: Jane Biberman. Managing Editor: Robert Leiter. 100% freelance written (by assignment). Quarterly Jewish community magazine—for a 25 years and older general interest Jewish readership. Circ. 85,000. Pays on acceptance. Publishes ms an average of 3 months after acceptance. Byline given. Offers 20% kill fee. Buys one-time rights. Submit seasonal/holiday material 2 months in advance. Simultaneous queries OK. Computer printout submissions acceptable. SASE. Reports in 2 weeks on queries; 3 weeks on mss. Sample copy $2; free writer's guidelines.

Nonfiction: Book excerpts, general interest, historical/nostalgic, humor, interview/profile, and travel. Philadelphia angle desirable. No personal religious experiences or trips to Israel. Buys 15-20 mss/year. Query. Length: 1,500-3,000 words. Pays $200-600.

Fiction: Short Stories.

Photos: State availability of photos. Reviews color and b&w transparencies. Identification of subjects required.

Tips: "Personalities—very well known—and serious issues of concern to Jewish community needed."

JADE, The Asian American Magazine. Box 291367, Los Angeles CA 90029. (213)935-1410. Editor/Publisher: Gerald Jann. Managing Editor: Edward T. Foster. 50% freelance written. Quarterly magazine covering Asian-American people and events for Asian-Americans. Circ. 30,000. Pays on publication. Byline given. Offers 25% kill fee. Buys first North American serial rights only. Submit seasonal/holiday material 6 months in advance. Simultaneous queries and photocopied submissions acceptable. Computer printout submissions acceptable; prefers letter-quality to dot-matrix. SASE. Reports in 3 weeks. Publishes ms an average of 3 months after acceptance. Sample copy $1; writer's guidelines for business size SAE and 1 first class stamp.

Nonfiction: Interview/profile (Asian-Americans in unusual situations or occupations, especially successful people active in communities). Buys 15 unsolicited mss/year. Send complete ms. Length: 4,000 words maximum. Pays $25-200.

Photos: Photos are a *must* with all stories. Send photos with ms. Reviews 35mm color transparencies and 5x7 color and b&w glossy prints. Model release and identification of subjects required. Buys one-time rights.

Columns/Departments: Open to new suggestions for columns/departments.

Fillers: Newsbreaks. Pays $10-25.

Tips: "We're especially interested in hearing from writers who are not on the West Coast."

THE JEWISH MONTHLY, 1640 Rhode Island Ave. NW, Washington DC 20036. (202)857-6645. Editor: Marc Silver. Published by B'nai B'rith. 75% freelance written. Monthly magazine. Buys North American serial rights only. Pays on publication. Computer printout submissions acceptable. SASE.

Nonfiction: Quality articles of interest to the Jewish community: economic, demographic, political, social, biographical, cultural and travel. No immigrant reminiscences. Queries (with clips of published work) should be direct, well-organized and map out the story. Buys 5-10 unsolicited mss/year. Length: 4,000 words maximum. Pays up to 25¢/word.

Tips: "Writers should be familiar with the style and focus of our magazine. We seek well-written stories with a fresh approach to Jewish life—new faces, trends and communal activities; or explorations of holidays and traditions that feature an unusual or little known angle."

JEWISH NEWS, Suite 240, 20300 Civic Center Dr., Southfield MI 48076. (313)354-6060. Editor: Gary Rosenblatt. News Editor: Alan Hitsky. A weekly tabloid covering news and features of Jewish interest. Circ. 17,000. Pays on publication. Byline given. No kill fee "unless stipulated beforehand." Buys first North

American serial rights. Simultaneous queries and photocopied submissions OK. Computer printout submissions acceptable; prefers letter-quality to dot-matrix. SASE. Reports in 2 weeks on queries; 1 month on mss. Sample copy for $1 and SASE.

Nonfiction: Book excerpts, humor, and interview/profile. Buys 10-20 mss/year. Query with or without published clips, or send complete ms. Length: 500-2,500 words. Pays $20-75.

Fiction: Ethnic. Buys 1-2 mss/year. Send complete ms. Length: 500-2,500 words. Pays $20-75.

LECTOR, The Review Journal for Spanish Language and Bilingual Materials, Hispanic Information Exchange, Box 4273, Berkeley CA 94704. (415)893-8702. Editor: Roberto Cabello-Argandona. Managing Editor: Vivian M. Pisano. 75% freelance written. A bimonthly magazine covering reviews of Spanish language and bilingual materials. "For people who work with Hispanic communities in the U.S. or those interested in knowing what the current concerns are among U.S. Hispanics, mainly professionals: librarians, bilingual educators, Spanish teachers and professors, ethnic studies specialists, and administrators who are directly involved or concerned with U.S. Hispanics." Circ. 500. Pays on publication. Publishes ms an average of 4 months after acceptance. Byline given. Offers kill fee. Buys all rights. Submit seasonal/holiday material 3 months in advance. Simultaneous queries, and simultaneous, photocopied and previously published submissions "on occasion" OK. Computer printout submissions acceptable; prefers letter-quality to dot-matrix. SASE. Reports in 2 weeks on queries; 1 month on mss. Free sample copy and writer's guidelines.

Nonfiction: Charlotte A. Bagby, articles editor. General interest (related to Hispanic culture), interview/profile (of authors, publishers, and other professionals); new product (new books, etc.); opinion (related to serving U.S. Hispanic community); personal experience (related to U.S. Hispanics). "Articles related to the Hispanic culture are always welcome. Articles of professional interest are also sought as long as they are not so technical that they would be boring to anyone not directly related to that field. Particularly of interest are stories about publishers and writers of Spanish language or bilingual materials." No very scholarly articles. Buys 12-18 mss/year. Query with published clips. Length: 1,500-2,500 words. Pays $50-100.

Photos: Charlotte A. Bagby, photo editor. State availability of photos with query or mss. Reviews b&w snapshots. Identification of subjects required. Buys one-time rights.

Columns/Departments: Charlotte A. Bagby, column/department editor. Publishers Corner (articles or interviews about publishers, writers, etc.); Perspective (interviews or first person articles about serving Hispanic community); and Events in Profile (current events related to Hispanic community). Buys 12-18 mss/year. Query with published clips. Length: 1,500-2,500 words. Pays $50-100. Sometimes pays expenses of writers on assignment.

Tips: "*Lector* is very open to freelancers. The best way to break in is to present a well-written, well-researched article written at a general reading level that will not insult our readers' intelligence. Our readers are professionals, but they want lively, interesting reading material that is related to their field without being overly-technical. We have had problems with articles directed at too narrow an audience containing too much professional jargon."

MAINSTREAM AMERICA MAGAZINE, The Hemill Company, Inc., 2714 W. Vernon Ave., Los Angeles CA 90008. (213)290-1322. Editor: Diane Clark. Managing Editor: Adriene Diane L. Corbin. 90% freelance written. A monthly Black magazine for upwardly mobile professionals, businessmen, etc. Circ. 50,000. Pays on publication. Publishes ms an average of 4 months after acceptance. Byline given. Buys all rights. Submit seasonal/holiday material 3 months in advance. Simultaneous queries and submissions OK. Computer printout submissions acceptable; prefers letter-quality to dot-matrix. SASE. Reports in 1 month on queries; 2 months on mss. Free writer's guidelines.

Nonfiction: Expose (government, education, business as it impacts on Black Americans); general interest; historical/nostalgic; how-to (succeed in business, career, how to become a successful entrepreneur); inspirational; interview/profile; personal experience (in business, corporate, career). "Features should be upbeat as an example for those striving toward success: political, Black enterprise, positive self image, education, etc." Buys 200 mss/year. Query with or without published clips, or send complete ms. Length: 500-2,000 words. Pays 6-8¢/word. Sometimes pays the expenses of writers on assignment.

Photos: State availability of photos or send photos with query or ms. Pays $10-15 for 8x10 b&w prints. Captions, model releases, and identification of subjects required. Buys one-time rights.

Tips: "The most frequent writer mistakes are failure to meet deadlines and lack of investigative detail; also far too many articles are too long. Read the magazine, follow format, and note subjects of interest. We're receptive to all well written material from known and unknown writers."

MALINI, Pan-Asian Journal for the Literati, Box 195, Claremont CA 91711. (714)625-2914. Editor: Chitra Chakraborty. Quarterly ethnic literary magazine covering Pan-Asian (India to Japan including some Pacific islands) literature and culture. 30% freelance written; 10-25% of material published is poetry. Byline given. Buys all rights. Publishes ms an average of 6 months after acceptance. Submit seasonal/holiday material 4 months in advance. Computer printout submissions acceptable; no dot-matrix. SASE. Reports in 1 month.

Sample copy $1.39; writer's guidelines for legal-size SAE and 1 first class stamp.

Nonfiction: Book excerpts, expose, general interest, historical/nostalgic, humor and personal experience. Does not want to see anything that does not concern Pan-Asian group. Buys 6-10 mss/year. Query. Length: 750-1,200 words. Pays $35-100 (on acceptance).

Fiction: Ethnic. Buys 2-3 mss/year. Query. Length: 750-1,200 words. Pays $25-100 (on acceptance).

Poetry: Avant-garde, free verse, haiku, light verse, traditional and translations. No monologues or profanity. First-time typed, original submissions only. Buys 18-20 poems/year. Submit maximum 6 poems. Poetry submissions should be single-spaced within stanzas, double-spaced between stanzas, with a cover letter stating that the poems are indeed first-time submissions to MALINI. Length: 3-33 lines. Pays $10-100 (on acceptance). Buys all rights.

Tips: "Anybody with ethnic awareness or sensitivity and literary talent can write for us. Ordering a sample copy will be of tremendous help to prospective contributors since there is no other magazine like *Malini* in the United States. Please do not send stories or articles without querying first. All submissions must include a cover letter indicating the status of the submission, i.e., whether they are first-time submissions or not."

MIDSTREAM, A Monthly Jewish Review, 515 Park Ave., New York NY 10022. Editor: Joel Carmichael. 90% freelance written. Monthly. Circ. 14,000. Buys first North American serial rights. Byline given. Pays after publication. Publishes ms an average of 6 months after acceptance. Computer printout submissions acceptable; no dot-matrix. Reports in 2 months. SASE.

Nonfiction: "Articles offering a critical interpretation of the past, searching examination of the present, and affording a medium for independent opinion and creative cultural expression. Articles on the political and social scene in Israel, on Jews in Russia and the U.S.; generally it helps to have a Zionist orientation. If you're going abroad, we would like to see what you might have to report on a Jewish community abroad." Buys historical and think pieces, primarily of Jewish and related content. Pays 5¢/word.

Fiction: Primarily of Jewish and related content. Pays 5¢/word.

Tips: "A book review would be the best way to start. Send us a sample review or a clip, let us know your area of interest, suggest books you would like to review. The author should briefly outline the subject and theme of his article and give a brief account of his background or credentials in this field. Since we are a monthly, we look for critical analysis rather than a 'journalistic' approach."

MOMENT, Jewish Educational Ventures, 462 Boylston, Boston MA 02116. (617)536-6252. Editor: Leonard Fein. Managing Editor: Nechama Katz. 30% freelance written. Monthly (except Jan/Feb & July/August, when bimonthly). Magazine on Jewish affairs. "Moment is a lively, liberal, independent magazine of Jewish affairs." Circ. 25,000. Pays on publication. Publishes ms an average of 3 months after acceptance. Byline given. Offers 25% kill fee. Buys first North American serial rights. Submit seasonal/holiday material 3 months in advance. Photocopied submissions OK. Electronic submissions OK via Decmate II WPS. Computer printout submissions acceptable. SASE. Reports in 6 weeks on queries; 2 months on mss. Sample copy $3.50; free writer's guidelines.

Nonfiction: Book excerpts, historical and personal experience. "We are looking for high-quality journalism presenting critical thinking and reportage about the range of issues facing today's intelligent, liberal American Jew. We are looking for freelancers who can help us enrich the quality of Jewish discussion and debate." Buys 30 mss/year. Query with published clips or send complete ms. Pays $100-400. Sometimes pays the expenses of writers on expenses.

Photos: State availability of photo. Reviews b&w prints. Pays $35. Captions required. Buys one-time rights.

Fiction: Ethnic (only very well-written stories exploring the questions of Jewish industry and Jewish history); and religious (Jewish). "We have an over-abundance of Holocaust-related and 'grandmother' stories. We use very little fiction, so would encourage only the very highest quaity submissions." Buys 3 mss/year. Query with published clips. Length: 2,500-5,000 words. Pays $100-400/words.

Tips: "A detailed query letter, with clips, will help us respond to article ideas."

‡**NIGHTMOVES, Chicago's Free Biweekly**, Nightmoves Publishing Co., Suite 1100, 105 W. Madison, Chicago IL 60602. (312)346-7765. Editor: Howard Wilson. Managing Editor: Gayle Soucek. 80% freelance written. Biweekly tabloid of politics, entertainment, and social issues. "We reach a black, primarily urban audience ages 18-40." Circ. 50,000. Pays on publication. Publishes ms an average of 4 months after acceptance. Byline given. Not copyrighted. "We rarely kill an article without giving the writer ample opportunity to re-write it." Buys first rights and second serial (reprint) rights. Submit seasonal/holiday material 2 months in advance. Photocopied and previously published submissions OK. Computer printout submissions acceptable; prefers letter-quality to dot-matrix. SASE. Reports in 3 weeks on queries; 1 month on mss. Sample copy for 9x12 SAE and 3 first class stamps. Writer's guidelines for #10 SAE and 1 first class stamp.

Nonfiction: Expose (almost any subject, but must be carefully documented); general interest; humor (mostly sophisticated, such as political satire); and interview/profile. No personal opinion or travel. "While we enjoy articles of national interest, our distribution is in the Chicago area only, so we cannot use articles on local issues from other areas, *unless* they relate closely to a broader theme." Buys 120+ mss/year. Query or send complete ms (prefers queries). Length: 750-2,500 words. Pays 3-5¢/word.

Photos: State availability of photos with query letter or ms. "We are a very visually-oriented publication, so photos are welcome, but they must be good quality. Good photos will help sell us on a story idea." Prefers 5x7 or 8x10 b&w prints. Pays $10-20. Captions and model releases required. Buys one-time rights.

Columns/Departments: Movie and Theatre Reviews, Chicago-area restaurant reviews, etc. "This is a limited area for freelancers, and we prefer queries only." Buys 10-15 mss/year. Query. Length: 750-1,250 words. Pays 3-5¢/word.

Tips: "We receive too much 'light' material and not enough well-researched, hard-hitting cover story material. Articles are usually too vague and all-encompassing, lacking a definite focus and adequate research and documentation."

PALM BEACH JEWISH WORLD, Jewish World Publishing, Box 3343, West Palm Beach FL 33402. (305)833-8331. Editor: Tina Hersh. 5% freelance written. Weekly tabloid for the Jewish community. Pays on acceptance. Publishes ms an average of 1 year after acceptance. Byline given. Not copyrighted. Buys first North American serial rights and one-time rights. Submit seasonal/holiday material 1 1/2 months in advance. Simultaneous submissions OK. Computer printout submissions acceptable; no dot-matrix. SASE. Reports in 3 month. Sample copy $1; writer's guidelines for 2 first class postage stamps.

Nonfiction: "We staff-write news items, and prefer a creative style for features in keeping with the content. Profiles of individuals, for example, should reflect the reason the person is important to the Jewish community and particularly the south Florida region, whether positive or negative, and give the reader enough background to make a judgment for himself." Query with writing sample. Length: 750-1,200 words. Pays $45-100. Sometimes pays the expenses of writers on assignment.

Photos: "Photos of the subject, or his or her work, should accompany story." Pays $15 minimum for b&w 35mm negatives and 5x7 prints. Captions and identification of subjects required. Buys one-time rights.

Tips: "The writer has a better chance of breaking in at our publication with short articles and fillers since we are currently at capacity for major features. As we continue to grow, major pieces will be welcome."

PRESENT TENSE: The Magazine of World Jewish Affairs, 165 E. 56th St., New York NY 10022. (212)751-4000. Editor: Murray Polner. For college-educated, Jewish-oriented audience interested in Jewish life throughout the world. Quarterly magazine. Circ. 45,000. Buys all rights. Byline given. Buys 60 mss/year. Pays on publication. Computer printout submissions acceptable. Sample copy $4. Reports in 2 months. Query. SASE.

Nonfiction: Quality reportage of contemporary events (a la *Harper's, New Yorker*, etc.). Personal journalism, reportage, profiles and photo essays. Length: 3,000 words maximum. Pays $100-250.

RECONSTRUCTIONIST, 270 W. 89th St., New York NY 10024. (212)496-2960. Editor: Dr. Jacob Staub. A general Jewish religious and cultural magazine. Monthly. Circ. 8,100. Buys all rights. Pays on publication. SASE. Free sample copy.

Nonfiction: Publishes literary criticism, reports from Israel and other lands where Jews live, and material of educational or communal interest. Query. Buys 35 mss/year. Preferred length is 2,000-3,000 words. Pays $36.

Fiction: Uses a small amount of fiction as fillers.

Poetry: Used as fillers.

SCANDINAVIAN REVIEW, American-Scandinavian Foundation, 127 E. 73rd St., New York NY 10021. (212)879-9779. Editor: Patricia McFate. "The majority of our readership is over 30, well educated, and in the middle income bracket. Most similar to readers of *Smithsonian* and *Saturday Review*. Have interest in Scandinavia by birth or education." Quarterly magazine. Circ. 6,000. Pays on publication. Buys all rights. Byline given. Previously published material (if published abroad) OK. SASE. Reports in 2 months. Sample copy $4.

Nonfiction: Historical, informational, interview, photo feature and travel. "Modern life and culture in Scandinavia." No American-Scandinavian memoirs. Recent article example: "The Norwegians Welfare State and Social Mobility" (summer 1985). Send complete ms. Length: maximum 3,500 words. Pays $50-200.

Photos: Purchased with accompanying ms. Captions required. Submit prints or transparencies. Prefers sharp, high contrast b&w enlargements. Total purchase price for ms includes payment for photos.

Fiction: Literature. Only work translated from the Scandinavian. Buys 4-10 mss/year. Send complete ms. Length: 3,000 words maximum. Pays $75-125.

Poetry: Translations of contemporary Scandinavian poetry. Buys 5-20 poems/year. Pays $10.

Tips: "We will be using more Scandinavian authors and American translators and commissioning more articles, so that we are even less open to freelancers."

SPANISH TODAY, An American Magazine of Hispanic Thought, Box 650909, Miami FL 33265. (305)386-5480. Editor: Andres Rivero. Managing Editor: Pilar E. Rivero. Bimonthly magazine covering Hispanic/Spanish market in the U.S. "We reach professional Hispanics, businesspeople, professors, teachers,

leaders and prominent Hispanics." Circ. 10,000. Pays on publication. Byline given. Buys first North American serial rights. Submit holiday/seasonal holiday material 2 months in advance. Simultaneous submissions OK. SASE. Reports in 3 weeks on queries; 5 weeks on mss. Sample copy $3; free writer's guidelines.
Nonfiction: General interest, historical/nostalgic, inspirational, interview/profile, personal experience, photo feature and travel. "We buy anything of interest and concern to Hispanic in the U.S." Buys 20 mss/year. Query. Average length words: 1,200. Pays 8¢/word.
Photos: State availability of photos. Reviews 8x10 prints.
Tips: "We buy articles written in either Spanish or English languages. Only well-written articles in Spanish are considered. No translations."

Food and Drink

Writers with a taste for fine wines and foods will want to shop for publications in this market. Magazines appealing to readers' appreciation of wines and foods are classified here. Journals aimed at food processing, manufacturing, and retailing will be found in Trade Journals. Magazines covering nutrition for the general public are listed in the Health and Fitness category.

THE COOK'S MAGAZINE, The Magazine of Cooking in America, Pennington Publishing, 2710 North Ave., Bridgeport CT 06604. (203)366-4155. Editor: Judith Hill. Managing Editor: Sheila Lowenstein. 80% freelance written. Bimonthly magazine on food and cooking. Down-to-earth, no-nonsense information for cooking enthusiasts. About cooking in America in the 1980s. Trends, restaurants, chefs, new foods and recipes as well as traditional technique and information all covered. Circ. 175,000. Pays on publication. Publishes ms an average of 7 months after acceptance. Byline given. Offers 50% kill fee. Makes work-for-hire assignment. Submit seasonal/holiday material 7 months in advance. Simultaneous queries OK. Computer printout submissions acceptable. SASE. Reports in 2 weeks. Free sample copy and writer's guidelines.
Nonfiction: Mary Caldwell, articles editor. Food. Buys 50 mss/year. Query with published clips. Length: 1,000-2,500 words. Pays $200-400.

‡**FINE DINING**, Connell Publications, Inc., 1897 N.E. 164 St., N. Miami FL 33162. Editor/Publisher: Sean O'Connell. Articles Editor: Joanne Taylor. Emphasizes restaurant dining and gourmet cuisine. Bimonthly magazine; one edition: New York, Florida, Philadelphia, Chicago, Texas, Los Angeles and Washington. Circ. 65,000. Pays on publication. Buys all rights. Byline given. Submit seasonal/holiday material 3 months in advance. Prefer original manuscripts over photocopies. No computer printout or disk submissions. SASE. Reports in 2 months. Sample copy $2.75 (includes postage and handling).
Nonfiction: Restaurant reviews, famous restaurant stories with recipes; famous hotel stories with fine dining rooms; country inns; interviews with chefs; travel/food articles with emphasis on cuisine and recipes; celebrity interviews with recipes. Sophisticated humor about dining out. Buys 6 mss/year. Query with clips of published work. Length: 1,000-1,500 words plus recipes.
Photos: Send photos with ms. Color close-up slides of food and chefs. Exterior shots of inn, restaurant, and indoor dining rooms. Captions required.
Columns/Departments: Wines of Our Times (domestic and imported); Taking Off (short travel getaway with recipes); Celebrity Cook (favorite recipe of celebrity); Cookbook Comments (book reviews and excerpted recipes); International foods.

THE GARDEN GOURMET, A Cooking and Gardening Journal, Opportunity Press, Inc., Suite 1405, 6 N. Michigan Ave., Chicago IL 60602. (312)346-4790. Editor: Mary Ann Hickey. 80% freelance written. Monthly tabloid on cooking and gardening aimed at people interested in cooking with fresh produce and herbs. Circ. 15,000. Pays on publication. Byline given. Buys first North American serial rights and second (reprint) rights to material originally published elsewhere. Submit seasonal/holiday material 4 months in advance. Simultaneous queries and photocopied submissions OK. Computer printout submissions acceptable. Reports in 2 weeks on queries; 1 month on mss. Publishes ms an average of 2 months after acceptance. Sample copy for $2.50, 9x12 SAE, and 5 first class stamps.
Nonfiction: How-to, interview/profile, and new product. Query with published clips. Length: 800-3,500 words. Pays $75-300.

Photos: State availability of photos. Reviews b&w contact sheets and color transparencies. Model release and identification of subjects required. Buys one-time rights.
Tips: "We report on regional cuisine, i.e., local chefs, restaurants, unique cooking methods, people who grow, produce and cook. Interview/profile of chefs and unique individuals growing and cooking their own food are the areas most open to freelancers."

WINE TIDINGS, Kylix International, Ltd., 5165 Sherbrooke St. W., 414, Montreal, Quebec H4A 1T6 Canada. (514)481-5892. Managing Editor: Judy Rochester. Magazine published 8 times/year primarily for men with incomes of over $40,000. "Covers anything happening on the wine scene in Canada." Circ. 28,000. Pays on publication. Byline given. Buys all rights. Submit seasonal/holiday material 3 months in advance. Computer printout submissions acceptable; prefers letter-quality to dot-matrix. Reports in 1 month.
Nonfiction: J. Rochester, articles editor. General interest; historical; humor; interview/profile; new product (and developments in the Canadian and US wine industries); opinion; personal experience; photo feature; and travel (to wine-producing countries). "All must pertain to wine or wine-related topics and should reflect author's basic knowledge of and interest in wine." Buys 20-30 mss/year. Send complete ms. Length: 500-2,000 words. Pays $25-200.
Photos: State availability of photos. Pays $10-100 for color prints; $10 for b&w prints. Identification of subjects required. Buys one-time rights.

WINE WORLD MAGAZINE, Suite 115, 6308 Woodman Ave., Van Nuys CA 91401. (213)785-6050. Editor-Publisher: Dee Sindt. For the wine-loving public (adults of all ages) who wish to learn more about wine. Quarterly magazine; 48 pages. Buys first North American serial rights. Buys about 50 mss/year. Pays on publication. No photocopied submissions. Simultaneous submissions OK "if spelled out." SASE. Send $2 for sample copy and writer's guidelines.
Nonfiction: "Wine-oriented material written with an in-depth knowledge of the subject, designed to meet the needs of the novice and connoisseur alike. Wine technology advancements, wine history, profiles of vintners the world over. Educational articles only. No first-person accounts. Must be objective, informative reporting on economic trends, new technological developments in vinification, vine hybridizing, and vineyard care. New wineries and new marketing trends. We restrict our editorial content to wine, and wine-oriented material. Will accept restaurant articles—good wine lists. No more basic wine information. No articles from instant wine experts. Authors must be qualified in this highly technical field." Query. Length: 750-2,000 words. Pays $50-100.

ZYMURGY, Journal of the American Homebrewers Association, American Homebrewers Association, Box 287, Boulder CO 80306. (303)447-0816. Editor: Charles N. Papazian. Managing Editor: Kathy McClurg. 10% freelance written. Quarterly magazine on homebrewing. Circ. 7,000. Pays on publication. Publishes ms an average of 6 months after acceptance. Buys first serial rights, first North American serial rights, and simultaneous rights. Submit seasonal/holiday material 5 months in advance. Simultaneous queries, and simultaneous, photocopied, and previously published submissions OK. Computer printout submissions acceptable; prefers letter-quality to dot-matrix. SASE. Sample copy $3; free writer's guidelines.
Nonfiction: General interest (beer); historical (breweries); interview/profile (brewers); photo feature; and travel (breweries). Query. Length: 750-2,000 words. Pays $25-75.
Photos: Reviews b&w contact sheets and 8x10 b&w prints. Captions, model releases, and identification of subjects required.
Fiction: Erotica and beer brewing. Buys 1-2 mss/year. Query. Length: 750-2,000 words. Pays negotiable rates.
Tips: The most frequent mistake made by writers is submitting articles that are too superficial and not enough in depth.

Games and Puzzles

If you like to play games—but are serious about them and can describe and create them—the following publications need you. Crossword fans will also find markets here. These publications are written by and for game enthusiasts interested both in traditional games and word puzzles and newer roleplaying adventure and computer and video games. Additional home video game publications are listed in the Theatre, Movie, TV, and Entertainment section. Other puzzle markets may be found in the Juvenile section.

ABYSS, 1402 21st St. NW, Washington DC 20036. (512)477-1704. Editor: David F. Nalle. Managing Editor: Jon Schuller. 30% freelance written. Bimonthly magazine covering games (fantasy, science fiction, historical). "*Abyss* provides game background and theory articles for adult game players interested in expanding their sources and ideas, particularly in the area of interactive role-playing games. Our orientation is toward college-age gamers who take the hobby seriously as an educational and enlightening pursuit. We ask only for an open mind and an active imagination." Circ. 1,200-1,500. Pays on publication. Publishes ms an average of 5 months after acceptance. Byline given. Buys one-time rights and first rights. Submit seasonal/holiday material 8 months in advance. Electronic submissions OK but prefers disk, compatible with Commodore, Apple or IBM and requires hard copy. Computer printout submissions acceptable; prefers letter-quality to dot-matrix. SASE. Reports in 2 weeks on queries; 6 weeks on mss. Sample copy for $2; free writer's guidelines.

Nonfiction: Expose (concentrate on major game companies like TSR, FGU, SJG, etc.); historical (preferably pre-20th century game-oriented); humor (preferably short game or fantasy related); new product reviews (games and small press items only); opinion (any gaming topic); technical (game design, game publishing, game variants); and articles on any gaming-related topic from a range of approaches. "Also bibliographical fantasy." No "why my campaign is wonderful" articles too closely wedded to only one game system." Buys 30 mss/year. Send complete ms. Length: 1,000-5,000 words. Pays $5-100. Sometimes pays the expenses of writers on assignment.

Columns/Departments: John R. Davies, column/department editor. Berserkgang (opinion/expose); Worlds of . . . (fantasy or science fiction bibliographical relevant to gaming); In the Pentacle (demonscopy, send for sample); and In the Speculum (reviews of games, magazines and books). Buys 18 mss/year. Query. Length: 400-3,000 words. Pays $5-40.

Fiction: Adventure, fantasy, historical, horror and dark fantasy, mythology. "No derivative, pastiche or game-based fiction." Buys 8 mss/year. Send complete ms. Length: 1,000-5,000 words. Pays $5-100.

Tips: "The best way to break into *Abyss* is by writing good, short commentary or opinion articles with new information or perspectives. The areas most open to freelancers are In the Speculum (reviews must include copy of product or be assigned) and Worlds of. . . . Most major features are left to staff writers." The most frequent mistakes made by writers are "not querying just to find out current needs or taking a prosaic or too conventional approach."

CHESS LIFE, United States Chess Federation, 186 Route 9W, New Windsor NY 12550. (914)562-8350. Editor: Larry Parr. 15% freelance written. Monthly magazine covering the chess world. Circ. 60,000. Pays variable fee. Byline given. Offers kill fee. Buys first or negotiable rights. Submit seasonal/holiday material 8 months in advance. Simultaneous queries, and simultaneous, photocopied and previously published submissions OK. Computer printout submissions acceptable. SASE. Reports in 1 month. Publishes ms an average of 6 months after acceptance. Free sample copy and writer's guidelines.

Nonfiction: General interest, historical, interview/profile, and technical—all must have some relation to chess. No "stories about personal experiences with chess. Buys 30-40 mss/year. Query with samples "if new to publication." Length: 3,000 words maximum.

Photos: Reviews b&w contact sheet and prints, and color prints and slides. Captions, model release and identification of subjects required. Buys all or negotiable rights.

Fiction: "Chess-related, high quality." Buys 1-2 mss/year. Pays variable fee.

Tips: "Articles must be written from an informed point of view—not from view of the curious amateur. Most of our writers are specialized in that they have sound credentials as chessplayers. Freelancers in major population areas (except New York and Los Angeles, which we already have covered) who are interested in short personality profiles and perhaps news reporting have the best opportunities. We're looking for more personality pieces on chessplayers around the country; not just the stars, but local masters, talented youths, and dedicated volunteers. Freelancers interested in such pieces might let us know of their interest and their range. Could be we know of an interesting story in their territory that needs covering."

COMPUTER GAMING WORLD, Golden Empire Publications, Box 4566, Anaheim CA 92803-4566. (714)535-4435. Editor: Russell Sipe. 50% freelance written. Bimonthly magazine on computer games (Apple, Atari, C-64, IBM). "*CGW* deals with commercially available computer games for the above listed machines; reviews, strategy and tactics, contest, game design articles, etc." Circ. 25,000. Pays on publication. Publishes ms an average of 3 months after acceptance. Byline given. Buys first serial rights. Submit seasonal/holiday material 2 months in advance. Photocopied submissions OK. Electronic submissions OK if compatible with CompuServe, The Source, or Applesoft or IBM text file. Computer printout submissions acceptable. SASE. Reports in 6 weeks. Sample copy $1.50; free writer's guidelines.

Nonfiction: How-to (design computer games), interview/profile, new product, game reviews and strategy articles. Buys 30-40 mss/year. Query. Length: 500-1,500 words. Pays 2-3¢/word.

Columns/Departments: "Other regular columns will be considered if subject is needed." Query with published clips or send complete ms. Length: 1,000-1,500 words. Pays $50 per installment of column.

Fiction: "We use *very little* fiction."

Tips: "Our editorial space is tight and established contributors have first preference."

DRAGON® MAGAZINE, Monthly Adventure Role-Playing Aid, TSR, Inc., Box 110, Lake Geneva WI 53147. (414)248-3625. Editor: Kim Mohan. 90% freelance written. Monthly magazine of role-playing and adventure games and new trends in the gaming industry for adolescents and up. Circ. 120,000. Pays on publication. Publishes ms an average of 6 months after acceptance. Byline given. Buys first North American serial rights for fiction; all rights for most articles. Submit seasonal/holiday material 6 months in advance. Simultaneous queries and photocopied submissions OK. Computer printout submissions acceptable; prefers letter-quality to dot-matrix. SASE. Reports in 2 weeks on queries; 5 weeks on submissions. Sample copy $3; writer's guidelines for business size SAE and 39¢ postage.

Nonfiction: Articles on the hobby of gaming and fantasy role-playing. No general articles on gaming hobby; "our article needs are *very* specialized. Writers should be experienced in gaming hobby and role-playing." Buys 100 mss/year. Query. Length: 1,000-10,000 words. Pays 3½-5¢/word.

Fiction: Patrick Price, fiction editor. Adventure, fantasy, science fiction, and pieces which deal with gaming hobby. No fiction based on a religious, metaphysical or philosophical theme; no rehashes of other authors' work or ideas. Buys 10 mss/year. Query. Length: 3,000-10,000 words. Pays 4-6¢/word.

Tips: "*Dragon Magazine* and the related publications of Dragon Publishing are *not* periodicals that the 'average reader' appreciates or understands. A writer must *be* a reader, and must share the serious interest in gaming our readers possess. It's particularly rewarding helping new writers break in."

‡GAME NEWS, Role-Games, War Games, Other Adult Games, Suite 910, 1010 Vermont Ave. NW, Washington DC 20005. (202)393-5233. Editor: Anne F. Jaffe. Monthly magazine with Game Trade News pull-out supplement in issues sent to retailers, wholesalers, etc. of the game industry. "*Game News* is devoted exclusively to games and game-related products that give gamers 'news you can use.' It reviews current releases of role-games, war games, and other adult games. *Game News* is published in two editions. The regular edition is circulated to both trade and consumers, and contains features of interest to everyone. The trade edition, called *Game Trade News*, is a pull-out supplement carried only in copies of *Game News* circulated to the trade. *Game Trade News* contains information on best-selling games, upcoming releases by manufacturers, a calendar of trade shows and events, and other industry news of interest to manufacturers, retailers, wholesalers, chain store buyers, and other in the trade." Estab. 1985. Circ. 20,000. Pays on acceptance. Byline given. Buys first serial rights and reprint rights for cartoons; makes work-for-hire assignments. Submit seasonal/holiday material 4 months in advance. Simultaneous queries and photocopied submissions OK. SASE. Reports in 1 month. Sample copy $2.50; free writer's guidelines.

Nonfiction: How-to (game and scenario design); interview/profile; and product reviews (following specific format). No articles on games like chess, or general articles on game theory. Query. Length: varies. Payment varies.

Photos: State availability of photos. Reviews contact sheets. Captions, model release, and identification of subjects required. Buys variable rights.

Columns/Departments: Reviews of new games. Query. Length: varies. Payment varies.

Fillers: Clippings and newsbreaks. Length: no limit. Payment varies.

Tips: "Have experience with and knowledge of war games, role-playing games, miniatures, and adult board games."

GAMES, Playboy Enterprises, Inc., 515 Madison Ave., New York NY 10022. Editor: Jacqueline Damian. 50% freelance written. Monthly magazine featuring games, puzzles, mazes and brainteasers for people 18-49 interested in verbal and visual puzzles, trivia quizzes and original games. Circ. 650,000. Average issue includes 5-7 feature puzzles, paper and pencil games and fillers, bylined columns and 1-2 contests. Pays on publication. Publishes ms an average of 6 months after acceptance. Byline given. Offers 25% kill fee. Buys all rights, first rights, first and second rights to the same material, and second (reprint) rights to material originally published elsewhere. Submit seasonal material 6 months in advance. Book reprints considered. Computer printout submissions acceptable; no dot-matrix. Reports in 6 weeks. Free writer's guidelines with SASE.

Nonfiction: "We are looking for visual puzzles, rebuses, brainteasers and logic puzzles. We also want newsbreaks, new games, inventions, and news items of interest to game players." Buys 4-6 mss/issue. Query. Length: 500-2,000 words. Usually pays $110/published page.

Columns/Departments: Wild Cards (25-200 words, short brainteasers, 25-100 wordplay, number games, anecdotes and quotes on games). Buys 6-10 mss/issue. Send complete ms. Length: 25-200 words. Pays $10-100.

Fillers: Will Shortz, editor. Crosswords, cryptograms and word games. Pays $25-100.

GIANT CROSSWORDS, Scrambl-Gram, Inc., Puzzle Buffs International, 1772 State Road, Cuyahoga Falls OH 44223. (216)923-2397. Editors: C.J. Elum and C.R. Elum. Managing Editor: Carol L. Elum. 50% freelance written. Crossword puzzle and word game magazines issued quarterly. Pays on acceptance. Publishes ms an average of 10 days after acceptance. No byline given. Buys all rights. Simultaneous queries OK.

Computer printout submissions acceptable; no dot-matrix. SASE. Reports in several weeks. "We furnish master grids and clue sheets and offer a 'how-to-make-crosswords' book for $6."
Nonfiction: Crosswords only. Query. Pays according to size of puzzle and/or clues.

THE GRENADIER MAGAZINE, The Independent War Game Review, J. Tibbetts & Son, Purveyers, 3833 Lake Shore Ave., Oakland CA 94610. (415)763-0928. Senior Editor: S.A. Jefferis-Tibbetts. 50% freelance written. Bimonthly magazine covering military simulation and history. Circ. 4,500. Pays on publication. Publishes ms an average of 4 months after acceptance. Byline given. Buys all rights. Submit seasonal/holiday material 4 months in advance. SASE. Reports in 2 weeks. Sample copy $3; writer's guidelines for legal size SAE and 1 first class stamp.
Nonfiction: Historical/nostalgic, how-to, new product, opinion and technical. Buys 36 mss/year. Query. Length: 5,000-12,500 words. Pays $25-100. Sometimes pays the expenses of writers on assignment.
Photos: John T. Lamont, photo editor. Send photos with query. Pays $15 minimum for b&w contact sheets and for 8x10 b&w prints. Captions, model releases, and identification of subjects required.
Columns/Departments: Donald Harrison, column/department editor. Solitaire Gaming, Short Reviews of new products, Book Reviews, and Computer Reviews. Buys 108 mss/year. Send complete ms. Length: 150-500 words. Pays $5-15.

OFFICIAL CROSSWORD PUZZLES, DELL CROSSWORD PUZZLES, POCKET CROSSWORD PUZZLES, DELL WORD SEARCH PUZZLES, OFFICIAL WORD SEARCH PUZZLES, DELL PENCIL PUZZLES & WORD GAMES, OFFICIAL PENCIL PUZZLES & WORD GAMES, DELL CROSSWORD SPECIAL, DELL CROSSWORDS AND VARIETY PUZZLES, DELL CROSSWORD YEARBOOK, OFFICIAL CROSSWORD YEARBOOK, Dell Puzzle Publications, 245 E. 47th St., New York NY 10017. Editor: Rosalind Moore. For "all ages from 8 to 80—people whose interests are puzzles, both crosswords and variety features." 95% freelance written. Buys all rights. Computer printout submissions acceptable; prefers letter-quality to dot-matrix. SASE.
Puzzles: "We publish puzzles of all kinds, but the market here is limited to those who are able to construct quality pieces that can compete with the real professionals. See our magazines; they are the best guide to our needs. We publish quality puzzles which are well-conceived and well-edited, with appeal to solvers of all ages and in almost every walk of life. We are the world's leading name in puzzle publications and are distributed in many countries around the world in addition to the continental U.S. However, no foreign language puzzles. Our market for crosswords and anacrostics is very small, since long-time contributors supply most of the needs in those areas. However, we are always willing to see material of unusual quality, or with a new or original approach. Since most of our publications feature variety puzzles in addition to the usual features, we are especially interested in seeing picture features, and new and unusual puzzle features of all kinds. Do not send us remakes of features we are now using. Send only one sample, please, and make sure your name and address are on each page submitted. Nothing without an answer will be considered. Do not expect an immediate reply. Prices vary with the feature, but ours are comparable with the highest in the general puzzle field."

VIDEO GAMES MAGAZINE, Pumpkin Press, 350 5th Ave., New York NY 10118. (212)947-4322. Editor: Roger C. Sharpe. Managing Editor: Patricia Canole. Monthly magazine covering home and arcade video games and computers. Circ. 100,000. Pays on publication. Byline given. Offers 20% kill fee. Buys first North American serial rights. Submit seasonal/holiday material 3 months in advance. Simultaneous queries and photocopied submissions OK. SASE. Reports in 2 weeks. Free sample copy and writer's guidelines.
Nonfiction: Book excerpts; general interest; historical/nostalgic; how-to (game tips and playing strategies); interview/profile; new product; and personal experience. "We look for editorial coverage of the game, toy and computer industries—interviews, game reviews, product reviews and general business trend overviews." Special issues include Special End-of-the-Year Celebration of Games. No poetry. Buys 120 mss/year. Query with published clips. Length: 1,500-2,500 words. Pays $200-400.
Photos: State availability of photos. Pays $10-25 for b&w contact sheet and b&w transparencies; $50-100 for color transparencies. Captions, model release and identification of subjects required. Buys one-time rights.
Columns/Departments: Clips (short news items and mini-features on latest breaking developments); Game Efforts (product reviews); Hard Sell (system reviews); Soft Touch (computer game software reviews); and Book Beat (book reviews). Buys 80 mss/year. Query with published clips. Length: 1,000-3,000 words. Pays $200-450.
Fiction: "We are looking for pieces with an obvious video or computer game slant." Buys 12 mss/year. Query with published clips. Length: 1,500-3,000 words. Pays $300-500.
Tips: "Look at back issues to familiarize yourself with our editorial content and style; then submit ideas which we will respond to. Part of the problem is finding individuals who understand the uniqueness of our publication in terms of subject matter; however, everything is open for those writers who can cover the material."

General Interest

General interest magazines need writers who can address many audiences at one time, but they don't need generalities. "Although a topic such as drunken driving may have been the subject of many articles, it doesn't mean we cannot treat it again," points out one *Reader's Digest* editor. "Look for a fresh approach that focuses on the human interest side of the story, rather than suggesting a broad analysis of the issue." When stories touch teens and senior citizens, wealthy readers and the unemployed, that's general interest. Some general interest publications, however, appeal to an audience of one general (but slightly varying) lifestyle, such as *Connoisseur* or *Grit*. Each magazine develops a "personality"—one that a writer should study before sending material to an editor. Other markets for general interest material in these Consumer categories: Ethnic/Minority, In-Flight, Lifestyles, Men's, Regional, and Women's. Some company publications also cover general interest topics.

THE AMERICAN LEGION MAGAZINE, Box 1055, Indianapolis IN 46206. (317)635-8411. Contact: Editor. Monthly. 95% freelance written. Circ. 2,500,000. Buys first North American serial rights. Computer printout submissions acceptable; prefers letter-quality to dot-matrix. Reports on submissions "promptly." Publishes ms an average of 6 months after acceptance. Byline given. Pays on acceptance. SASE.
Nonfiction: Query first, but will consider unsolicited mss. "Prefer an outline query. Relate your article's thesis or purpose, tell why you are qualified to write it, the approach you will take and any authorities you intend to interview. War remembrance pieces of a personal nature (vs. historic in perspective) should be in ms form." Uses current world affairs, topics of contemporary interest, little-known happenings in American history, 20th century war-remembrance pieces, and 750-word commentaries on contemporary problems and points of view. No personality profiles or regional topics. Buys 60 mss/year. Length: 2,000 words maximum. Pays $100-2,000.
Photos: Chiefly on assignment.
Poetry: Short, humorous verse. Pays $4.50/line, minimum $10.
Fillers: Short, tasteful jokes, humorous anecdotes and epigrams. Pays $10-20.

THE ATLANTIC MONTHLY, 8 Arlington St., Boston MA 02116. (617)536-9500. Editor-in-Chief: William Whitworth. For a professional, academic audience interested in politics, science, arts and general culture. Monthly magazine. Circ. 440,000. Pays soon after acceptance. Buys first North American serial rights. Pays negotiable kill fee "though chiefly to established writers." Byline given. Phone queries OK though written queries preferred. Submit seasonal/holiday material 3-5 months in advance. Simultaneous and photocopied submissions OK, if so indicated. SASE. Reports in 2 months. Sample copy $2.
Nonfiction: General interest, politics, public affairs, science, humor, popular culture, fine arts, and travel. Query with clips of published work or send complete ms. Length: 1,000-6,000 words. Pays $1,000 and up/article.
Fiction: Mainstream. Buys 2 mss/issue. Send complete ms. Length: 2,000-6,000 words. Pays $2,000 and up/story.
Poetry: Avant-garde, free verse, light verse and traditional. "No concrete or haiku poetry." Buys 2-4 poems/issue. Submit in batches of 2-6. Length: 100 lines maximum. Pays $3 and up/line.

A BETTER LIFE FOR YOU, The National Research Bureau, Inc., 424 N. 3rd St., Burlington IA 52601. (319)752-5415. Editor: Rhonda Wilson. Editorial Supervisor: Doris J. Ruschill. 75% freelance written. For industrial workers of all ages. Quarterly magazine. Pays on publication. Publishes ms an average of 1 year after acceptance. Buys all rights. Submit seasonal/holiday material 7 months in advance of issue date. Previously published submissions OK. Computer printout submissions acceptable; prefers letter-quality to dot-matrix. SASE. Reports in 3 weeks. Free writer's guidelines.
Nonfiction: General interest (steps to better health, on-the-job attitudes); and how-to (perform better on the job, do home repair jobs, and keep up maintenance on a car). Buys 10-12 mss/year. Query or send outline. Length: 400-600 words. Pays 4¢/word.
Tips: "Writers have a better chance of breaking in at our publication with short articles and fillers because all of our articles are short."

CAPPER'S WEEKLY, Stauffer Communications, Inc., 616 Jefferson St., Topeka KS 66607. (913)295-1108. Editor: Dorothy Harvey. 15% freelance written. Emphasizes home and family for readers who live in small towns and on farms. Biweekly tabloid. Circ. 415,000. Pays for poetry on acceptance; articles on publication. Buys first North American serial rights only. Submit seasonal/holiday material 2 months in advance. Computer printout submissions acceptable; prefers letter-quality to dot-matrix. SASE. Reports in 3 weeks; 8 months for serialized novels. Sample copy 55¢.
Nonfiction: Historical (local museums, etc.), inspirational, nostalgia, travel (local slants) and people stories (accomplishments, collections, etc.). Buys 25 mss/year. Submit complete ms. Length: 700 words maximum. Pays $1/inch.
Photos: Purchased with accompanying ms. Submit prints. Pays $5-10 for 8x10 b&w glossy prints. Total purchase price for ms includes payment for photos. Limited market for color photos (35mm color slides, please); pays $25 each.
Columns/Departments: Heart of the Home (homemakers' letters, recipes, hints), and Hometown Heartbeat (descriptive). Submit complete ms. Length: 300 words maximum. Pays $2-10.
Fiction: "We have begun to buy some shorter fiction pieces—longer then short stories, shorter than novels." Mystery and romance mss. No explicit sex, violence or profanity. Buys 2-3 mss/year. Query. Pays $150-200.
Poetry: Free verse, haiku, light verse, traditional, nature and inspiration. "The poems that appear in *Capper's* are not too difficult to read. They're easy to grasp. We're looking for everyday events, and down-to-earth themes." Buys 4-5/issue. Limit submissions to batches of 5-6. Length: 4-16 lines. Pays $3-5.
Tips: "Study a few issues of our publication. Most rejections are for material that is too long, unsuitable or out of character for our paper (too sexy, too much profanity, etc.). On occasion, we must cut material to fit column space."

CHANGING TIMES, The Kiplinger Magazine, 1729 H St. NW, Washington DC 20006. Editor: Marjorie White. For general, adult audience interested in consumer information. Monthly. Circ. 1,350,000. Buys all rights. Reports in 1 month. Computer printout submissions acceptable. SASE. Pays on acceptance. Thorough documentation required.
Nonfiction: "Most material is staff-written, but we accept some freelance." Query with clips of published work. No bylines.

COMMENTARY, 165 E. 56th St., New York NY 10022. (212)751-4000. Editor: Norman Podhoretz. Monthly magazine. Circ. 50,000. Byline given. "All of our material is done freelance, though much of it is commissioned." Pays on publication. Query, or submit complete ms. Reports in 1 month. SASE.
Nonfiction: Brenda Brown, editor. Thoughtful essays on political, social and cultural themes; general, as well as with special Jewish content. Length: 3,000 to 7,000 words. Pays approximately $100/printed page.
Fiction: Marion Magid, editor. Uses some mainstream fiction. Length: varies. Pays $100/printed page.

DIALOGUE, The Magazine for the Visually Impaired, Dialogue Publications, Inc., 3100 Oak Park Ave., Berwyn IL 60402. (312)749-1908. Editor: Nolan Crabb. 50% freelance written. Quarterly magazine of issues, topics and opportunities related to the visually impaired. Pays on acceptance. Publishes ms an average of 6 months after acceptance. Byline given. Buys all rights "with generous reprint rights." Submit seasonal/holiday material 6 months in advance. Photocopied submissions OK. Computer printout submissions acceptable; no dot-matrix. SASE. Reports in 2 weeks on queries; 1 month on mss. Free sample copy to visually impaired writers. Writer's guidelines in print for business size SAE and 1 first class stamp; send a 60-minute cassette for guidelines on tape.
Nonfiction: "Writers should indicate nature and severity of visual handicap." How-to (cope with various aspects of blindness); humor; interview/profile; new product (of interest to visually impaired); opinion; personal experience; technical (adaptations for use without sight); travel (personal experiences of visually impaired travelers); and first person articles about careers in which individual blind persons have succeeded. No "Aren't blind people wonderful" articles; articles that are slanted toward sighted general audience. Buys 60 mss/year. Query with published clips or submit complete ms. Length: 3,000 words maximum. Prefers shorter lengths but will use longer articles if subject warrants. Pays $10-50.
Photos: Bonnie Miller, photo editor. Photographs of paintings, sculpture and pottery by visually handicapped artists; and photos taken by visually impaired persons. State availability or send photos with ms. Pays $10-20 for 3½x4¾ b&w prints. Identification of subjects required. Buys one-time rights.
Columns/Departments: ABAPITA ("Ain't Blindness a Pain in the Anatomy")—short anecdotes relating to blindness; Recipe Round-UP; Around the House (household hints); Vox Pop (see magazine); Puzzle Box (see magazine and guidelines); book reviews of books written by visually impaired authors; Beyond the Armchair (travel personal experience); and Backscratcher (a column of questions, answers, hints). Buys 80 mss/year. Send complete ms. Payment varies.
Fiction: "Writers should state nature and severity of visual handicap." Maryellen Owens, fiction editor. Adventure, fantasy, historical, humorous, mainstream, mystery, science fiction, and suspense. No plotless fiction or stories with unbelievable characters; no horror; no explicit sex and no vulgar language. Buys 12 mss/

year. Send complete ms. Length: 3,000 words maximum; shorter lengths preferred. Pays $10-50.

Poetry: "Writers should indicate nature and severity of visual impairment." Maryellen Owens, poetry editor. Free verse, haiku, and traditional. No religious poetry or any poetry with more than 20 lines. Buys 30 poems/ year. Submit maximum 3 poems. Length: 20 lines maximum. Pays $5-20.

Fillers: Jokes, anecdotes, and short humor. Buys few mss/year. Length: 100 words maximum. Payment varies.

Tips: "*Dialogue* cannot consider manuscripts from authors with 20/20 vision or those who can read regular print with ordinary glasses. Any person unable to read ordinary print who has helpful information to share with others in this category will find a ready market. We believe that blind people are capable, competent, responsible citizens, and the material we publish reflects this view. This is not to say we never sound a negative note, but criticism should be constructive. The writer sometimes has a better chance of breaking in at our publication with short articles and fillers because many writers don't bother to study several issues of the magazine to get an idea of what we're looking for. We are interested in material that is written for a general-interest magazine with visually impaired readers. We are *not* interested in scholarly journal-type articles, 'amazing blind people I have known' pieces, articles written by sighted writers, articles and fiction that exceed our 3,000-word maximum length, and material that is too regional to appeal to an international audience."

EASY LIVING MAGAZINE, The Webb Co., 1999 Shepard Rd., St. Paul MN 55116. (612)690-7228. Editor: George Ashfield. 90% freelance written. Emphasizes financial topics—personal finance, career, money management, consumer; and some foreign travel and food articles for a high-income audience 30-60 years of age. Published by Webb Company for financial institutions. Quarterly magazine. Circ. 250,000. Pays on acceptance. Buys one-time rights and nonexclusive reprint rights. Submit seasonal/holiday material 1 year in advance. Photocopied submissions OK. Computer printout submissions acceptable. SASE. Reports on queries and mss in 3-6 weeks. Publishes ms an average of 4 months after acceptance. Free sample copy and writer's guidelines. Nonfiction only. No first person or personal experience. Query. Length: 1,000-2,000 words. Pays $200-600.

Photos: Contact Rudy Schnasse at (612)690-7396 for current rates.

EQUINOX: THE MAGAZINE OF CANADIAN DISCOVERY, Equinox Publishing, 7 Queen Victoria Dr., Camden East, Ontario K0K 1J0 Canada. (613)378-6651. Editor: James Lawrence. Managing Editor: Bart Robinson. Executive Editor: Frank B. Edwards. Bimonthly magazine. "We publish in-depth profiles of people, places and wildlife to show readers the real stories behind subjects of general interest in the fields of science and geography." Circ. 150,000. Pays on acceptance. Byline given. Offers 50% kill fee. Buys first North American serial rights only. Submit seasonal queries 1 year in advance. SAE, IRCs. Computer printout submissions acceptable; prefers letter-quality to dot-matrix. Reports in 6 weeks. Sample copy $5; free writer's guidelines.

Nonfiction: Book excerpts (occasionally), geography, science and art. No travel articles. Buys 40 mss/year. Query. "Our biggest need is for science stories. We do not touch unsolicited feature manuscripts." Length: 5,000-10,000 words. Pays $1,500-negotiated.

Photos: Send photos with ms. Reviews color transparencies—must be of professional quality; no prints or negatives. Captions and identification of subjects required.

Columns/Departments: Nexus, current science that isn't covered by daily media. Habitat, Canadian environmental stories not covered by daily media. "Our most urgent need." Buys 80/year. Query with clips of published work. Length: 500-1,000 words. Pays $175-350.

Tips: Submit Habitat and Nexus ideas to us—the 'only' route to a feature is through these departments if writers are untried."

FORD TIMES, Ford Motor Co., Box 1899, The American Rd., Rm. 765, Dearborn MI 48121-1899. Editor: Arnold S. Hirsch. 85% freelance written. "General-interest magazine designed to attract all ages." Monthly magazine. Circ. 1,200,000. Pays on acceptance. Publishes ms an average of 8 months after acceptance. Buys first rights only. Pays kill fee. Byline given. Submit seasonal material 6 months in advance. SASE. Computer printout submissions acceptable; prefers letter-quality to dot-matrix. Reports in 1 month. Free sample copy and writer's guidelines.

Nonfiction: "Almost anything relating to contemporary American life that is upbeat and positive. Topics include lifestyle trends, vacation ideas, profiles, insights into big cities and small towns, the arts, the outdoors and sports. We are especially interested in subjects that appeal to readers in the 18-35 age group. We also are using some stories with international settings. We strive to be colorful, lively and, above all, interesting. We try to avoid subjects that have appeared in other publications or in our own." Buys 100 mss/year. Length: 1,500 words maximum. Query required unless previous contributor. Pays $450 minimum for full-length articles. Sometimes pays the expenses of writers on assignment.

Photos: "Speculative submission of high-quality color transparencies and b&w photos with mss is welcomed.

We need bright, graphically strong photos showing people. We need releases for people whose identity is readily apparent in photos."
Tips: A frequent mistake made by writers is that factual informational is omitted from articles.

‡**40 +** , 40 + , Inc., Box 98120, Tacoma WA 98498. (206)582-1988. Editor: Lynn Miranda. Editorial Director: Marilyn Thordarson. 50% freelance written. Bimonthly magazine on matters of interest to women (and men) 40 years of age or more. "We deal realistically with issues and topics of interest to women 40 years of age and above. All models used in the magazine are 40 or above. Most contributors are 40 or more." Estab. 1984. Circ. 20,000. Pays on publication. Publishes ms an average of 6 months after acceptance. Byline given. Offers 50% kill fee. Buys first North American serial rights. Submit seasonal/holiday material 6 months in advance. Simultaneous queries and submissions OK. Computer printout submissions acceptable. SASE. Reports in 1 month on queries; 2 months on mss. Sample copy $1.50, and 39¢ postage. Writer's guidelines for SAE and 1 first class stamp.
Nonfiction: Book review (assignments only); general interest (geared to 40 +); humor (short); interview/profile (women over 40; unusual occupations—women of special interest); photo feature; and travel. No arts and crafts, sewing, decorating, radical feminist, and parenting (unless applicable to *40 +*). Buys 42 mss/year. Query with published clips or send complete ms. Length: 700-3,000 words. Pays $100-400; $25-35 for shorts.
Photos: Send photos with ms. Reviews b&w contact sheets; 2¼ or 5x5 color transparency. Pays $10-50 for b&w; $35-100 for color. Captions and model release required. Buys one-time rights and occasionally all rights.
Columns/Departments: Medical; family relationships. Buys 24 mss/year. Send complete ms. Length: 700-1,500 words. Pays $100-200.
Fiction: Adventure (with 40 + character); confession; fantasy; humorous (with characters over 40); mystery; romance (with 40 + character); and western. No erotica, pornography, true confessions or retirement. Buys 6 mss/year. Send complete ms. Length: 1,500-2,000 words. Pays $200-300.
Poetry: Light verse and humorous. Buys 10-12/issue. Submit maximum 5 poems. Length: 20 words maximum. Pays $50-100.
Fillers: Jokes, anecdotes, short humor and cartoons (with 40 + character—not dumpy). Buys 5-7/year. Length: 1-2 lines. Pays $10.
Tips: "Areas most open to freelancers include travel, unique places of interest to women and couple travelers. Also fiction—short, light with characters who are over 40 and general interest. Life changes, family changes, housing changes. Address a group that is active and educated—not ready for retirement."

FRIENDLY EXCHANGE, The Webb Company, 1999 Shepard Rd., St. Paul MN 55116. (612)690-7383. Editor: Adele Malott. 85% freelance written. Quarterly magazine "designed to encourage the sharing or exchange of ideas, information and fun among its readers, for young, traditional families between the ages of 19 and 39 who live in the area west of the Mississippi River and north of the Ohio." For policyholders of the Farmers Insurance Group of companies." Circ. 4.5 million. Pays on acceptance. Publishes ms an average of 5 months after acceptance. Offers 25% kill fee. Buys first North American serial rights and non-exclusive reprint rights for use in other Webb publications. Submit seasonal/holiday material 9 months in advance. Simultaneous queries and photocopied submissions OK. Computer printout submissions acceptable. SASE. Reports in 2 months. Sample copy free for 9x12 SAE and five first-class stamps; writer's guidelines free for business-size SAE and 1 first class stamp.
Nonfiction: General interest (family activities, sports and outdoors, consumer topics); historical/nostalgic (heritage and culture); how-to (decorate and garden); travel (domestic); and family lifestyle. "Whenever possible, a story should be told through the experiences of actual people or families in such a way that our readers will want to share experiences they have had with similar activities or interests. No product-publicity material." Buys 10 unsolicited mss/year. Query. Length: 1,000-2,500 words. Pays $300-700/article, plus agreed-up-on expenses.
Photos: John Baskerville, art director. Send photos with ms. Pays $150-400 for 35mm color transparencies; and $75 for 8x10 b&w prints. Pays on publication.
Columns/Departments: All columns and departments rely on reader-generated ideas, recipes, household hints, etc. Study articles, "Playing With Trains" (Winter 1984) and "Furry, Feathered Fun at the Zoo (Spring 1985)."
Tips: The most frequent mistake made by writers is not listening to the editor closely enough or not reading the assignment letter carefully enough, so they fail to write the article the editor wants."

FUTURIFIC MAGAZINE, 280 Madison Ave., New York NY 10016. (212)684-4913. Editor-in-Chief: Balint Szent-Miklosy. 75% freelance written. Monthly. "*Futurific, Inc.* is a nonprofit organization set up in 1976 to study the future, and *Futurific Magazine* is its monthly report on findings. We report on what is coming in all areas of life from international affairs to the arts and sciences. Readership cuts across all income levels and includes govenment, corporate and religious people." Circ. 10,000. Pays on publication. Publishes ms an average of 1 month after acceptance. Byline given in most cases. Buys one-time rights and will negotiate reprints. Computer printout submissions OK. SASE. Reports within 1 month. Sample copy for 9x12 SAE and 76¢ in postage.

Nonfiction: All subjects must deal with the future: book excerpts, expose, general interest, how to forecast the future—seriously, humor, interview/profile, new product, photo feature and technical. No historical, opinion or gloom and doom. Send complete ms. Length: 5,000 words maximum. Payment negotiable.

Photos: Send photos with ms. Reviews b&w prints. Pays in copies. Identification of subjects required.

Columns/Departments: Medical breakthroughs, new products, inventions, etc. "Anything that is new or about to be new." Send complete ms. Length: 5,000 words maximum.

Poetry: Avant-garde, free verse, haiku, light verse and traditional. "Must deal with the future. No gloom and doom or sad poetry." Buys 6/year. Submit unlimited number of poems. Length: open. Pays in copies.

Fillers: Clippings, jokes, gags, anecdotes, short humor, and newsbreaks. "Must deal with the future." Length: open. Pays in copies."

Tips: "We seek to maintain a light-hearted, professional look at forecasting. Be upbeat and show a loving expectation for the marvels of the future. Take any subject or concern you find in regular news magazines and extrapolate as to what the future will be. Use imagination. Get involved in the excitement of the international developments, social interaction, etc."

GLOBE, Cedar Square, 2112 S. Congress Ave., West Palm Beach FL 33406. News Editor: John Cooke. Celebrity Editor: Alastair Gregor. "For everyone in the family. *Globe* readers are the same people you meet on the street and in supermarket lines, average hard-working Americans who prefer easily digested tabloid news." Weekly national tabloid newspaper. Circ. 2,000,000. Byline given. SASE.

Nonfiction and Fillers: We want features on well-known personalities, offbeat people, places, events and activities. No personal essays. Current issue is best guide. Stories are best that don't grow stale quickly. No padding. Remember—we are serving a family audience. All material must be in good taste. If it's been written up in a major newspaper or magazine, we already know about it." Buys informational, how-to, interview, profile, inspirational, humor, historical, exposé, photo, and spot news. Length: 1,000 words maximum; average 500-800 words. Pays $250 maximum (special rates for "blockbuster" material).

Photos: Ron Haines, photo editor. Photos are purchased with or without ms, and on assignment. Captions are required. Pays $50 minimum for 8x10 b&w glossy prints. "Competitive payment on exclusives."

Tips: "*Globe* is constantly looking for human interest subject material from throughout the United States, and much of the best comes from America's smaller cities and villages, not necessarily from the larger urban areas. Therefore, we are likely to be more responsive to an article from a new writer than many other publications. This, of course, is equally true of photographs. A major mistake of new writers is that they have failed to determine the type and style of our content, and in the ever-changing tabloid field this is a most important consideration. It is also wise to keep in mind that what is of interest to you or to the people in your area may not be of equal interest to a national readership. Determine the limits of interest first. And, importantly, the material you send us must be such that it won't be 'stale' by the time it reaches the readers."

GOOD READING, Henry F. Henrichs Publications, Litchfield IL 62056. (217)324-2322. 65% freelance written. Monthly magazine. Circ. 8,000. Buys 30-50 unsolicited mss/year. Buys first North American serial rights. Pays on acceptance. Publishes ms an average of 8 months after acceptance. Computer printout submissions acceptable; prefers letter-quality to dot-matrix. SASE. Free writer's guidelines.

Nonfiction: Accurate articles on current or factual subjects, adventure or important places or successful people. Material based on incidents related to business or personal experiences that reveal the elements of success in human relationships. Humorous material welcome. Uses one quiz a month. All published material is wholesome and noncontroversial. No "over emphasized or common topics; no how-to articles or expositions." Length: 500-900 words. Pays $20-100.

Photos: Good quality b&w glossy prints illustrating an article are desirable and should be submitted with the article.

Fillers: 200-500 words. Pays $10-20.

Poetry: Does not pay for poetry, but publishes 4-5/month. Prefers pleasantly rhythmic humorous or uplifting material of 4-16 lines.

Tips: "We purchase articles that we have a need for. We are always on the lookout for good biographical articles. A frequent mistake made by writers is not knowing what we're looking for. We prefer to see manuscripts that fit our guidelines, which are available at no charge upon request. In our magazines the trend is toward better-written, more professional-looking manuscripts. We no longer have time to tighten up manuscripts to make them acceptable for publication."

GOODWIN'S, Goodwin's Foundation Inc., Box 1043, Station B, Ottawa, Ontario K1P 5R1 Canada. (613)234-8928. Editor: Ron Verzuh. 75% freelance written. Quarterly magazine on social affairs and issues. *"Goodwin's* puts issues (workplace democracy, sexism, racism, energy, new technology, housing, health care, day care) into a broad alternative perspective by reporting on people's common problems, analyzing the roots of those problems, and showing how they are being tackled across the country." Circ. 4,500. Pays negotiable rates. Publishes ms an average of 4 months after acceptance. Byline given. Offers negotiable kill fee. Buys first North American serial rights only. No photocopied or previously published submissions. Computer printout submissions acceptable; dot-matrix OK if double-spaced. Reports in 1 month. Sample copy $2.50; writer's guidelines for business size SAE and 50¢ postage.
Nonfiction: Book excerpts (investigative), and expose (social or economic issue). No fiction, poetry, strident tracts or unjournalist writing. Buys 12 mss/year. Query with published clips. Length: 300-3,000 words. Pays in copies and up to $500.
Photos: State availability of photos. Pays $5-100 for 35mm color transparencies; $5-100 for 8x10 b&w prints. Captions, model release and identification of subjects required. Buys one-time rights.
Columns/Departments: Buys 12 mss/year. Query with published clips. Length: 750-1,000 words. Pays in copies and up to $100.
Tips: "Query first with clips; be prepared to rewrite. Organizing section (short items on unique organizing efforts by labor, students, women, poor people, natives, and other social movements) is most open to freelancers. Watch for the investigative element when developing story queries and outlines."

GRIT, Stauffer Communications, Inc., 208 W. 3rd St., Williamsport PA 17701. (717)326-1771. Editor: Naomi L. Woolever. 33% freelance written. For a general readership of all ages in small town and rural America. Tabloid newspaper. Weekly. Circ. 650,000. Buys first and second rights to the same material. Byline given. Buys 1,000-1,500 mss/year. Pays on acceptance for freelance material; on publication for reader participation feature material. Publishes ms an average of 2 months after acceptance. Computer printout submissions acceptable; no dot-matrix. Reports in 1 month. SASE. Sample copy $1; free writer's guidelines.
Nonfiction: Contact Joanne Decker, assignment editor. "We want mss about six basic areas of interest: people, religion, jobs (how individuals feel about their work), recreation, spirit of community (tradition or nostalgia that binds residents of a town together), and necessities (stories about people and how they cope—food, shelter, etc.) Also want sociological pieces about rural transportation and health problems or how a town deals effectively with vandalism or crime. Also first-person articles of 300 words or less about a person's narrowest escape, funniest moment, a turning point in life, or recollections of something from the past, i.e., a flood, a fire, or some other dramatic happening that the person experienced." Want good Easter, Christmas and holiday material. Mss should show some person or group involved in an unusual and/or uplifting way. "We lean heavily toward human interest, whatever the subject. Writing should be simple and down-to-earth." No "articles promoting alcoholic beverages, immoral behavior, narcotics, or unpatriotic acts." Query or submit complete ms. Length: 500 words maximum. Pays 12¢/word for first or exclusive rights; 6¢/word for second or reprint rights.
Photos: Photos purchased with or without ms. Looks for photos "outstanding in composition and technical quality." Captions required. No "deep shadows on (photo) subjects." Prefers 8x10 for b&w, but will consider 5x7. Transparencies only for color. Pays $25 for b&w photos accompanying ms; $100 for front cover color photos.
Poetry: Alvin Elmer, poetry editor. Buys traditional forms of poetry and light verse. "We want poems on seasonal, human interest and humorous topics. We'd also like to see poems about the holidays." Length: preferably 20 lines maximum. Pays $6 for 4 lines and under, plus 50¢/line for each additional line.
Tips: "The freelancer would do well to write for a copy of our Guidelines for Freelancers. Everything is spelled out there about how-tos, submission methods, etc. All manuscripts should include in upper right-hand corner of first page the number of words and whether it's first or second rights."

HARPER'S MAGAZINE, 2 Park Ave., Room 1809, New York NY 10016. (212)481-5220. Editor: Lewis H. Lapham. 40% freelance written. For well-educated, socially concerned, widely read men and women who value ideas and good writing. Monthly. Circ. 140,000. Rights purchased vary with author and material. Pays negotiable kill fee. Pays on acceptance. Computer printout submissions acceptable. Reports in 2 weeks. Publishes ms an average of 3 months after acceptance. SASE. Sample copy $2.50.
Nonfiction: "For writers working with agents or who will query first only, our requirements are: public affairs, literary, international and local reporting, and humor." No interviews. Complete mss and queries must include SASEs. No unsolicited fiction or poems will be accepted. Publishes one major article per issue. Length: 4,000-6,000 words. Publishes one major essay per issue. Length: 4,000-6,000 words. "These should be construed as topical essays on all manner of subjects (politics, the arts, crime, business, etc.) to which the author can bring the force of passionately informed statements." Generally pays 50¢-$1/word.
Photos: Deborah Rust, art director. Occasionally purchased with mss; others by assignment. Pays $50-500.

‡**HEALTH & WEALTH**, Harold Publications, Drawer 189, Palm Beach FL 33480. Editor: Mark Adams. A bimonthly of equal entertainment features with more specialized selections relating to personal health and fi-

Close-up

Lewis H. Lapham
Editor
Harper's Magazine

When Lewis Lapham writes his Notebook in *Harper's*, he writes a minimum of three drafts and sometimes four.

What does this process gain for you, we asked, hoping to get his thoughts about rewriting.

"Pleasure," he replied.

Lapham is not an editor *trying* to write but rather a writer who edits a magazine. In fact, he was a contributing writer for *Harper's* and overnight became its editor (Monday, a writer; Tuesday, an editor). "I know the business from the writer's side rather than from the editor's side," said the former newspaper reporter and former contributing writer to *Life* and *The Saturday Evening Post*.

What surprised Lapham as an editor is "how few people write well and how few people take enough care with their writing." He'd always assumed that three to four drafts were part of writing.

Good writers, he finds, are more concerned about their subjects than their images as a writer. "If somebody asks me what do I want a piece about, I say I don't know. I say what do you want to write about, what do you care about," says Lapham, who also writes a newspaper column for the Words By Wire syndicate.

What gives Lapham pleasure as an editor is discussing an idea for an article with a writer and then seeing the article become something that neither the editor nor the writer had foreseen. "The best ideas are those you have that the writer appropriates and changes into something of his or her own," he believes.

Harper's editors generate most of the story ideas and conversations with writers—a process that Lapham describes as "volatile and creative"—but it doesn't matter to him whether he or the writer initiates the idea.

"Our magazine has always been

© Cynthia B. Matthews

open, and I'm extremely open," Lapham points out.

Writers can most easily break into *Harper's* Annotation section. "I like to see people who can write clearly and well and have a degree of wit and perspective, who are not entirely encumbered with ideology."

Lapham (whose second book will be published by Atlantic Monthly Press this year) stresses the importance of writers developing a *voice*. "You develop a voice by writing what you see and think and feel and not by what you think you ought to see and think and feel," he says. Young writers learn by imitation but eventually have to distinguish between what they think and what *other* people think.

"The world of writing is much more open than people think, much more accessible and hospitable, but only really if they are talented," says Lapham. "If I turn down a story, it's a very arbitrary thing. To be rejected by the editor of *Harper's* does not mean anything; the editor of *The Atlantic* may easily take it."

Regardless of the number of rewrites it takes to perfect a story, address *Harper's* readers, not a market. "The audience of *Harper's* is interested in the play of the mind," says Lapham.

Be interested in this and another kind of play—the pleasure of writing and rewriting.

nance. Circ: 75,000. Buys simultaneous rights, first rights, and second serial (reprint) rights. Submit seasonal material 6 months in advance. Simutaneous, photocopied and previously published submissions OK. SASE. Reports 3 months on mss. Sample copy $1 SAE; Writer's guidelines for SAE.

Nonfiction: General interest, humor, motivational, interviewed profile (must include subject's pictures), personal experience, photo feature, travel, lifestyle, fashion, and technical (for lay reader). Buys 50-100 mss 1 year. Send complete ms. Length: 400-1,000 words. Pays 5¢/published word or $25 maximum.

Fiction: Prefers humor. Buys up to 10 mss/year. Length 400-1,000 words. Pays 5¢/word or $25 maximum.

Photos: Send photos or state availability with ms. Pays 5$ for 8x10 b&w glossy prints or color transparencies. Captions preferred; indentification of subjects required. Buys one-time rights.

Cartoons: Buys few. Pays $10.

Tips: "Type manuscript, double-space and *keep a copy* (we sometimes lose them). Edit Yourself—ruthlessly—for grammar, spelling, punctuation & style. Is your story unique? No queries—We simply can't answer them. We receive thousands of manuscripts a year, so no SASE, NO ANSWER, and no apologies. Follow the rules, be *very* patient and keep trying. We want to publish you."

IDEALS MAGAZINE, Thomas Nelson Publishers, Nelson Place at Elm Hill Pike, Nashville TN 37214-1000. Publisher: Patricia Pingry. Editor: Dorothy Gibbs. 50% freelance written. Family-oriented magazine published 8 times/year: Christmas, Thanksgiving, Easter, and five other seasonal issues. Pays on publication. Publishes ms an average of 6 months after acceptance. Byline given. Buys first rights only. Submit seasonal material 6 months in advance. Send copy, not original ms. "We do not assume responsibility for loss of manuscripts." Previously published submissions OK. Although a ms may be retained for further consideration, there is no guarantee it will be used. Computer printout submissions acceptable; no dot-matrix. Sample copy for $1 postage and handling; writer's guidelines for SASE.

Nonfiction: General interest (holidays, seasons, family, nature, crafts); nostalgia (family oriented); profile (notable people); and travel. Buys 2-3 mss/issue. Length: 650-800 words. Query or send complete ms. Pays $50-75.

Photos: State availability of photos with ms. Buys first rights only.

Fiction: Limited use. Length: 650-800 words. Pays $50-75.

Poetry: Short to medium length. Pays $10.

Tips: "Most of our readers are women, age 35-70, living in non-urban areas. Nostalgia, reminiscences of childhood, and humorous anecdotes appeal to our readers. Material must be wholesome, inspirational, and uplifting, in the tradition of the *Ideals* world."

KNOWLEDGE, Official Publication of the World Olympiads of Knowledge, RSC Publishers, 3863 Southwest Loop 820, Drawer 16489, Ft. Worth TX 76133. (817)292-4272. Editor: Dr. O.A. Battista. Managing Editor: N.L. Matous. 90% freelance written. For lay and professional audiences of all occupations. Quarterly magazine; 60 pages. Circ. 1,500. Pays on publication. Publishes ms an average of 6 months after acceptance. Buys all rights. "We will reassign rights to a writer after a given period." Byline given. Submit seasonal/holiday material 6 months in advance. Computer printout submissions acceptable; prefers letter-quality to dot matrix. SASE. Reports in 1 month. Sample copy $5.

Nonfiction: Informational—original new knowledge that will prove mentally or physically beneficial to all readers. Buys 30 unsolicited mss/year. Query. Length: 1,500-2,000 words maximum. Pays $100 minimum. Sometimes pays the expenses of writers on assignment.

Columns/Departments: Journal section uses maverick and speculative ideas that other magazines will not publish and reference. Payment is made, on publication, at the following minimum rates: *Why Don't They*, $50; *Salutes*, $25; *New Vignettes*, $25; *Quotes To Ponder*, $10; and *Facts*, $5.

Tips: "The editors of knowledge welcome submissions from contributors. Manuscripts and art material will be carefully considered but received *only* with the unequivocal understanding that the magazine will not be responsible for loss or injury. Material from a published source should have the publication's name, date, and page number. Submissions cannot be acknowledged and will be returned only when accompanied by a SAE having adequate postage."

LEFTHANDER MAGAZINE, Lefthander International, Box 8249, Topeka KS 66608. (913)234-2177. Managing Editor: Suzan Menendez. 80% freelance written. Bimonthly. "Our readers are lefthanded people of all ages and interests in 50 U.S. states and 10 foreign countries. The one thing they have in common is an interest in lefthandedness." Circ. 15,000. Pays on publication. Publishes ms an average of 4 months after acceptance. Byline usually given. Offers 25% kill fee. Rights negotiable. Submit seasonal/holiday material 6 months in advance. Simultaneous queries OK. Computer printout submissions acceptable; prefers letter-quality to dot-matrix. Query with SASE rather than unsolicited manuscript. Reports on queries in 4 weeks. Sample copy for 8½x11 SAE and $2. Writer's guidelines for legal size SAE and 1 first class stamp.

Nonfiction: Interviews with famous lefthanders; features about lefthanders with interesting talents and occupations; how-to features (sports, crafts, hobbies for lefties); research on handedness and brain dominance; expose on discrimination against lefthanders in the work world; features on occupations and careers attracting lefties; education features relating to ambidextrous right brain teaching methods. Length: Buys 50-60 mss/year. 750-1,000 words for features. Buys 8-12 personal experience shorts/year. Send ms or query with SASE. Length 450-700 words. Pays $25.

Photos: State availability of photos for features. Pays $10-15 for b&w, good contrast b&w glossies. Rights negotiable.

Fiction: Lefty Jr., 4-page insert published 3 times/year. Children's short stories dealing with lefthandedness. Length: 500-750 words. Pays $35-50.

Fillers: Trivia, cartoons, word games for children's insert, interesting and unusual facts. Send on speculation. Buys 25-50/year. Pays $5-20.

Tips: All material must have a lefthanded hook. We prefer quick, practical, self-help and self-awareness types of editorial content; keep it brief, light, and of general interest. More of our space is devoted to shorter pieces. A good short piece gives us enough evidence of writer's style, which we like to have before assigning full-length features. The most frequent mistakes made by writers in completing an article assignment for us are incoherent material written by researchers who don't know how to write for a general-interest magazine and material that does not have lefthanded slant or does not fit our editorial guidelines and including material with themes that have been worked to death or dealt with previously.

LIFE, Time & Life Bldg., Rockefeller Center, New York NY 10020. (212)841-3871. Managing Editor: Richard B. Stolley. Monthly general interest picture magazine for people of all ages, backgrounds and interests. Circ. 1.5 million. Average issue includes one short and one long text piece. Pays on acceptance. Byline given. Offers $500 kill fee. Buys first North American serial rights. Submit seasonal material 3-4 months in advance. Simultaneous and photocopied submissions OK. Computer printout submissions acceptable; prefers letter-quality to dot-matrix. SASE. Reports in 6 weeks on queries; immediately on mss.

Nonfiction: "We've done articles on anything in the world of interest to the general reader and on people of importance. It's extremely difficult to break in since we buy so few articles. Most of the magazine is pictures. We're looking for very high quality writing. We select writers who we think match the subject they are writing about." Buys 1-2 mss/issue. Query with clips of previously published work. Length: 2,000-6,000 words. Pays $3,000 minimum.

Columns/Departments: Portrait (1,800-2,500 word essay on a well-known person). "We like to do these on people in the news." Buys 1 ms/issue. Query with clips of previously published work. Length: 1,800-2,500 words. Pays $2,000.

MACLEAN'S, Maclean Hunter Bldg., 777 Bay St., 7th, Toronto, Ontario M5W 1A7 Canada. (416)596-5386. Contact: Section Editors (listed in masthead). For news-oriented audience. Weekly newsmagazine; 90 pages. Circ. 650,000. Frequently buys first North American serial rights. Pays on acceptance. "Query with 200- or 300-word outline before sending material." Reports in 2 weeks. Electronic submissions OK if MO-PASS. Computer printout submissions acceptable. SAE and IRCs.

Nonfiction: "We have the conventional newsmagazine departments (Canada, world, business, people, plus science, medicine, law, art, music, etc.) with roughly the same treatment as other newsmagazines. We specialize in subjects that are primarily of Canadian interest, and there is now more emphasis on international—particularly US—news. Most material is now written by staffers or retainer freelancers, but we are open to suggestions from abroad, especially in world, business and departments (like medicine, lifestyles, etc.). Freelancers should write for a free copy of the magazine and study the approach." Length: 400-3,500 words. Pays $300-1,500.

NATIONAL GEOGRAPHIC MAGAZINE, 17th and M Sts. NW, Washington DC 20036. Editor: Wilbur E. Garrett. For members of the National Geographic Society. Monthly. Circ. more than 10,000,000. Query.

Nonfiction: *National Geographic* publishes first-person, general interest, heavy illustrated articles on science, natural history, exploration and geographical regions. Almost half the articles are staff-written. Of the freelance writers assigned, most are experts in their fields; the remainder are established professionals. Fewer than one percent of unsolicited queries result in assignments. Query (500 words) by letter, not by phone, to Senior Assistant Editor (Contract Writers). SASE. Do not send manuscripts. Before querying, study recent issues and check a *Geographic Index* at a library since the magazine seldom returns to regions or subjects covered within the past ten years.

Photos: Photographers should query in care of the Illustration Division.

THE NEW YORK ANTIQUE ALMANAC, The New York Eye Publishing Co., Inc., Box 335, Lawrence NY 11559. (516)371-3300. Editor-in-Chief: Carol Nadel. Tabloid published 10 times/year. Emphasizes antiques, art, investments and nostalgia. 30% freelance written. Circ. 52,000. Pays on publication. Buys all rights. Byline given. Phone queries OK. Submit seasonal/holiday material "whenever available." Previously published submissions OK but must advise. SASE. Computer printout submissions acceptable; no dot-matrix. Reports in 6 weeks. Publishes ms an average of 6 months after acceptance. Free sample copy.

Nonfiction: Expose (fraudulent practices); historical (museums, exhibitions, folklore, background of events);

how-to (clean, restore, travel, shop, invest); humor (jokes, cartoons, satire); informational; inspirational (essays); interviews (authors, shopkeepers, show managers, appraisers); nostalgia ("The Good Old Days" remembered various ways); personal experience (anything dealing with antiques, art, investments, nostalgia); opinion; photo feature (antique shows, art shows, fairs, crafts markets, restorations); profile; technical (repairing, purchasing, restoring); travel (shopping guides and tips); and investment (economics, and financial reviews). Buys 9 mss/issue. Query or submit complete ms. Length: 3,000 words maximum. Pays $15-75. "Expenses for accompanying photos will be reimbursed."

Photos: "Occasionally, we have photo essays (auctions, shows, street fairs, human interest) and pay $5/photo with caption."

Fillers: Personal experiences, commentaries, anecdotes. "Limited only by author's imagination." Buys 45 mss/year. Pays $5-15.

Tips: "Articles on shows or antique coverage accompanied by photos are definitely preferred."

THE NEW YORKER, 25 W. 43rd St., New York NY 10036. Editor: William Shawn. Weekly. Circ. 500,000. Reports in 2 months. Pays on acceptance. SASE.

Nonfiction, Fiction and Fillers: Long fact pieces are usually staff-written. So is "Talk of the Town," although ideas for this department are bought. Pays good rates. Uses fiction, both serious and light. About 90% of the fillers come from contributors with or without taglines (extra pay if the tagline is used).

OPENERS, America's Library Newspaper, American Library Association, 50 E. Huron St., Chicago IL 60611. (312)944-6780. Editor: Ann M. Cunniff. Managing Editor: Deborah Robertson. 80% freelance written. Quarterly tabloid covering "what's great to read" books, fitness and sports, art, music, TV and radio, movies, health, etc., as they relate/tie into the library. Avoid first-person articles. Avoid pompous tomes on the importance of reading and libraries. *Openers* is *fun* to read." Distributed free to library patrons. *Openers* is designed to be used outside the library to encourage library use and inside as a bonus to library patrons to help broaden their reading interests. Circ. 250,000. Pays on publication. Publishes ms an average of 6 months after acceptance. Byline given. Buys all rights. Submit seasonal/holiday material 3 months in advance. Simultaneous queries, and simultaneous and photocopied submissions OK. Computer printout submissions acceptable; prefers letter-quality to dot-matrix. SASE. Reports in 2 months. Sample copy for 9x12 SAE.

Nonfiction: General interest, how-to and humor as they tie-in to reading or books. "Send us an outline first." Buys 25+ mss/year. Query with published clips. Length: 200-800 words. Pays $25-100.

PARADE, Parade Publications, Inc., 750 3rd Ave., New York NY 10017. (212)573-7000. Editor: Walter Anderson. Weekly magazine for a general interest audience. 90% freelance written. Circ. 24 million. Pays on acceptance. Publishes ms an average of 3 months after acceptance. Kill fee varies in amount. Buys first North American serial rights. Computer printout submissions acceptable; no dot-matrix. SASE. Reports in 3 weeks on queries. Writer's guidelines free for 4x9 SAE and 1 first class stamp.

Nonfiction: General interest (on health, business or anything of interest to a broad general audience); interview/profile (of news figures, celebrities and people of national significance); and "provocative topical pieces of news value." Spot news events are not accepted, as *Parade* has a 6-week lead time. No fiction, fashion, travel, poetry, quizzes, or fillers. Address queries to Articles Editor. Length: 800-1,500 words. Pays $1,000 minimum. Pays expenses of writers on assignment.

Tips: "Send a well-researched, well-written query targeted to our market. Please, no phone queries. We're interested in well-written exclusive manuscripts on topics of news interest. The most frequent mistake made by writers in completing an article for us is not adhering to the suggestions made by the editor when the article was assigned."

PEOPLE IN ACTION, Meridian Publishing Company, Box 10010, Ogden UT 84409. Articles Editor: Fern Porras. 80% freelance written. A monthly company magazine featuring "people doing something . . . overcoming, winning, enjoying life, helping others." Readers are upscale, mainstream, family oriented. Pays on acceptance. Byline given. Buys first rights and non-exclusive reprint rights. Computer printout submissions acceptable. SASE. Reports in 1 month. Publishes ms an average of 6 months after acceptance. Sample copy for $1 and 9x12 SAE; writer's guidelines for SAE and 20¢ postage.

Nonfiction: Historical/nostalgic (if person oriented); interview/profile (illustrated); and personal experience (occasionally, "but must be terrific"). "Our readers want to be pleasantly diverted with upbeat, positive stories about people with whom they can identify. Bring your subjects to life with their human qualities and show them in action with your words and your photos. If you're writing about someone else—leave yourself out of it unless you do it well and it is vital to the story line. We don't want anything depressing; the risque is out, so is the religious when it's preachy or confessional. Articles *must* have color photography of good quality or the story will not be used. All material must focus on a specific person or group of people." Buys 50 mss/year. Query with or without published clips. Length: 800-1,200 words. Pays 15¢/word.

Photos: State availability of photos or send photos with query or ms. Pays $35 inside photo, $50 cover photo; uses glossy color prints and transparencies (slide to 8x10). Captions required. Buys one-time rights.

Columns/Departments: Regular features: Chef du Jour (an 800-word profile of anyone who likes to cook; a recipe and 1-2 good color transparencies are essential); Wit Stop (humor; 800-1,000 words); and The Arts (fine artists, dancers, musicians, 800-1,200 words). Pays 15¢/word.

Tips: "Every month we buy almost every article and photo from freelance contributors."

READER'S DIGEST, Pleasantville NY 10570. Monthly. Circ. 18 million. Includes general interest features for the broadest possible spectrum of readership. Items intended for a particular feature should be directed to the editor in charge of that feature, although the contribution may later be referred to another section of the magazine as seeming more suitable. Original contributions—which become the property of *Reader's Digest* upon acceptance and payment by *Reader's Digest*—should be typewritten if possible. When material is from a published source, please give the name and date of publication and the page number. Contributions cannot be acknowledged or returned. Please address contributions to the appropriate department editor, *Reader's Digest*, Pleasantville NY 10570.

Columns/Departments: "Life in These United States contributions must be true, unpublished stories from one's own experience, revelatory of adult human nature, and providing appealing or humorous sidelights on the American scene. Maximum length: 300 words. Contact Editor, Life in U.S., Box 200. Payment rate on publication: $300. True and unpublished stories are also solicited for Humor in Uniform, Campus Comedy, and All in a Day's Work. Maximum length: 300 words. Payment rate on publication: $300. Contact Editor, Humor in Uniform, Campus Comedy or All in a Day's Work, Box 190. Toward More Picturesque Speech: The first contributor of each item used in this department is paid $40 ($35 for reprints). Contributions should be dated, and the sources must be given. Contact Editor, Picturesque Speech. For items used in Laughter, the Best Medicine, Personal Glimpses, Quotable Quotes, and elsewhere in the magazine, payment is made at the following rates: to the *first* contributor of each item from a published source, $35. For original material, $20 per *Digest* two-column line, with a minimum payment of $50. Contact Excerpts Editor Box 190."

READERS NUTSHELL, Harold Publications, Drawer 189, Palm Beach FL 33480. Editor: Mark Adams. 30% freelance written. Bimonthly magazine for customers of insurance agents. Insurance-related material; general interest. Circ. 75,000. Buys simultaneous rights, first serial rights, and second serial (reprint) rights. Submit seasonal material 6 months in advance. Simultaneous, photocopied, and previously published submissions OK. Computer printout submissions acceptable; prefers letter-quality to dot matrix. SASE. Reports in 3 weeks on "holding" mss; in 3 months on mss. Sample copy $1 and SAE; writer's guidelines for SAE.

Nonfiction: Insurance-related, general interest (non controversial home, family, and safety articles); humor; and interview (of famous people). Buys 50-100 mss/year. Send complete ms. Length: 400-1,000 words. Pays 5¢/published word or $25 maximum.

Fiction: Prefers humor. Length: 400-1,000 words. Pays 5¢/word or $25 maximum.

Photos: Send photos with ms. Pays $5 for 8x10 b&w glossy prints or color transparencies. Captions and identification of subjects required.

Fillers: Cartoons. Buys few. Pays $10.

Tips:"Type manuscript, double-spaced, and *keep a copy*. Edit yourself ruthlessly for grammar, etc. Make storey unique. No queries, no SASE, no answer—Be patient and keep trying. We want to publish you."

READERS REVIEW, The National Research Bureau, Inc., 424 N. 3rd St., Burlington IA 52601. Editor: Rhonda Wilson. Editorial Supervisor: Doris J. Ruschill. 75% freelance written. "For industrial workers of all ages." Quarterly magazine. Pays on publication. Publishes ms an average of 1 year after acceptance. Buys all rights. Previously published submissions OK. Computer printout submissions acceptable; prefers letter-quality to dot-matrix. Submit seasonal/holiday material 7 months in advance of issue date. SASE. Reports in 3 weeks. Free writer's guidelines.

Nonfiction: General interest (steps to better health, attitudes on the job); how-to (perform better on the job, do home repairs, car maintenance); and travel. No articles on car repair, stress and tension. Buys 10-12 mss/year. Query with outline. Length: 400-600 words. Pays 4¢/word.

Tips: "Writers have a better chance of breaking in at our publication with short articles and fillers because all of our articles are short."Submit complete ms.

THE SATURDAY EVENING POST, The Saturday Evening Post Society, 1100 Waterway Blvd., Indianapolis, IN 46202. (317)634-1100. Editor-in-Chief: Cory SerVaas M.D. Executive Editor: Ted Kreiter. 65% freelance written. For general readership. Magazine published 9 times/year; 112 pages. Circ. 735,000. Pays on publication. Publishes ms an average of 3 months after acceptance. Buys all rights; one-time reprint and first serial rights. Simultaneous and photocopied submissions OK. Computer printout submissions acceptable; prefers letter-quality to dot-matrix. SASE. Reports in 2 months. Free writer's guidelines for SASE.

Nonfiction: Carrie Torres, editorial assistant. How-to (health, general living); humor; informational; people (celebrities and ordinary but interesting personalities); inspirational (for religious columns); interview; personal experience (especially travel, yachting, etc.); personal opinion; photo feature; profile; travel and small magazine "pick-ups." Buys 5 mss/issue. Query. Length: 1,500-3,000 words. Pays $100-1,000.

Photos: Patrick Perry, photo editor. Photos purchased with or without accompanying ms. Pays $25 minimum for b&w photos; $50 minimum for color photos. Offers no additional payment for photos accepted with mss. Model release required.

Columns/Departments: Editorials ($100 each); Food ($150-450); Medical Mailbox ($50-250); Religion Column ($100-250); and Travel ($150-300).

Fiction: Jack Gramling, fiction editor. Adventure, fantasy, humorous, mainstream, mystery, romance, science fiction, suspense and western. Pays on publication. Query. Length: 1,500-5,000 words. Pays $150-750.

Fillers: Jack Gramling, Post Scripts. Jokes, gags, anecdotes, postscripts and short humor. Buys 10-15 Post Scripts/issue; pays $15.

Tips: "We are interested in topics related to science, medicine, the arts, personalities with inspirational careers and humor. We read unsolicited material."

SATURDAY REVIEW, Saturday Review Publishing Co., Suite 460, 214 Massachusetts Ave. NE, Washington DC 20002. (202)547-1106. Editor: Frank Gannon. Bimonthly magazine covering literature and the arts for highly literate audience. Circ. 200,000. Pays within 30 days of publication. Byline given. Submit seasonal/holiday material 6 months in advance. SASE. Reports in 3 weeks. Sample copy for $2.50 and magazine size SASE.

Nonfiction: Book excerpts; interview/profile (with artists and writers); and coverage of cultural or artistic event. Buys 30 mss/year. Send complete ms. Length: 800-3,000 words. Pays $350-1,500. Briefings: 300-500 words. Pays $50-150.

Photos: Model release and identification of subjects required.

Tips: "We'll have more and shorter reviews of books and films and other departments as appropriate. Features should involve a profile of an important artist or writer—preferably one who has just produced or is about to produce an important work. Avoid the obvious and the overdone; we don't want to do the same people everyone else is doing."

SELECTED READING, The National Research Bureau, Inc., 424 N. 3rd St., Burlington IA 52601. Editor: Rhonda Wilson. Editorial Supervisor: Doris J. Ruschill. 75% freelance written. For industrial workers of all ages. Quarterly magazine. Pays on publication. Publishes ms an average of 1 year after acceptance. Buys all rights. Previously published submissions OK. Computer printout submissions acceptable; prefers letter-quality to dot-matrix. SASE. Submit seasonal/holiday material 6-7 months in advance of issue date. Reports in 3 weeks. Free writer's guidelines.

Nonfiction: General interest (economics, health, safety, working relationships); how-to; and travel (out-of-the way places). No material on car repair. Buys 10-12 mss/year. Query. A short outline or synopsis is best. Lists of titles are no help. Length: 400-600 words. Pays 4¢/word.

Tips: "Writers have a better chance of breaking in at our publication with short articles and fillers because all of our articles are short."

‡**SHERATON**,The Magazine for Sheraton Hotels in the Middle East and North Africa, Age Communications Ltd., Parkway House, Sheen Lane, London SW14 8LS England. Editor: Joseph Yogerst. Assistant Editor: Jules MacMahon. Art Director: Jan Lehne. A bimonthly magazine for Sheraton guests and employees covering a wide variety of subjects. Circ. 17,000. Pays on publication. Buys all rights. Submit seasonal/holiday material at least 4 months in advance. Simultaneous queries, and photocopied or previously published submissions not accepted. SAE with IRC. Reports in 1 month.

Nonfiction: General interest articles for Sheraton guests and employees, roughly broken down into half Middle Eastern and half European/American. "The majority of readers are male, 25-50 years of age, with an annual income of $40-60,000." Regular features on Middle East and North African travel (cities or countries where there is a Sheraton hotel); luxury motoring (Rolls Royce, Cadillac, Mercedes etc.); innovation and technology (ranging from cellular phones to captive breeding to contemporary uses of neon); enterprise (profiles of famous entrepreneurs, businessmen, industrialists, artists); jewelry and antiques (corporate profiles of famous manufacturers or designers, or articles about a specific type of item or material, i.e. gold, diamonds, antique clocks etc.); sports and recreation (interview with famous sports stars, how-to articles, photo essays on specific sports, etc.); and Middle Eastern history and culture. Length: 1,500-2,000 words. Pays £80 Sterling (estimated $95) mss per 1,000 words. Query or send complete ms. Buys 30 mss/year.

Photos: State availability of photos. Captions required. Pays minimum of £20 for 35mm or larger format color transparencies. Buys first Middle East rights.

Tips: "We publish articles on anything that might be of interest to a top-level businessman, technician, engineer, and other professionals who pay regular visits to the Middle East and North Africa."

SIGNATURE—The Citicorp Diners Club Magazine, 641 Lexington Ave., New York NY 10022. Editor: Horace Sutton. 95% freelance written. Basically for Diners Club members (but subscriptions open to all)—"businesspersons, urban, affluent and traveled." Monthly. Circ. 815,000. Pays on acceptance. Publishes ms an average of 4 months after acceptance. Buys first rights only. Buys 175 mss/year. Submit seasonal material at least 5 months in advance. Computer printout submissions acceptable; prefers letter-quality to dot-matrix. Query. SASE. Free writer's guidelines.

Nonfiction: Buys virtually all nonfiction from freelance writers. Front-of-the-book pieces deal with photography, sports, fitness, arts, and acquisitions. Length: Generally 1,200-1,500 words. Pays $700-900. "While travel and travel-related pieces are the major portion of the so-called 'well' or central part of the book, we will entertain any feature-length piece that relates to the art of living well or at least living interestingly. That could include such pieces as 'In Search of the Ultimate Deli' to 'Traveling in the State Department plane with the Secretary of State.' Writing is of high quality and while celebrated bylines are sought and used, the market is open to any writer of talent and style. Writers who join the 'stable' are used with frequency." Feature length: 2,000-3,000 words. Pays $1,200 and up.

Photos: "Photographers are assigned to major pieces and often accompany the writer on assignment. In almost no cases are writers expected to take their own photographs. Quality standard in pictures is high and highly selective. Photography rates on request to the art director."

Tips: "While we are heavy on travel in all its phases—that is, far out Ladakh and Yemen and near at hand, e.g., Hemingway's Venice—we do try to embrace the many facets that make up the art of living well. So we are involved with good food, cuisine trends, sport in all forms, the arts, the stage and films and such concomitant subjects as fitness and finance."

SMITHSONIAN MAGAZINE, 900 Jefferson Drive, Washington DC 20560. Articles Editor: Marlane A. Liddell. 90% freelance written. For "associate members of the Smithsonian Institution; 85% with college education." Monthly. Circ. 2 million. Buys first North American serial rights. Payment for each article to be negotiated depending on our needs and the article's length and excellence. Pays on acceptance. Publishes ms an average of 6 months after acceptance. Submit seasonal material 3 months in advance. Computer printout submissions acceptable; prefers letter-quality to dot-matrix. SASE. Reports in 6 weeks. Query.

Nonfiction: "Our mandate from the Smithsonian Institution says we are to be interested in the same things which now interest or should interest the Institution: cultural and fine arts, history, natural sciences, hard sciences, etc." Length: 750-4,500 words. Payment negotiable.

Photos: Purchased with or without ms and on assignment. Captions required. Pays $350/full color page.

THE STAR, 660 White Plains Rd., Tarrytown NY 10591. (914)332-5000. Editor/Publisher: Ian G. Rae. Executive Editor: Phil Bunton. 40% freelance written. "For every family; all the family—kids, teenagers, young parents and grandparents." Weekly magazine 56 pages. Circ. 3.5 million. Buys second serial (reprint) rights, and first North American serial rights. SASE. Free sample copy and writer's guidelines.

Nonfiction: Malcolm Abrams, managing editor. Exposé (government waste, consumer, education, anything affecting family); general interest (human interest, consumerism, informational, family and women's interest); how-to (psychological, practical on all subjects affecting readers); interview (celebrity or human interest); new product; photo feature; profile (celebrity or national figure); travel (how-to cheaply); health; medical; and diet. No first-person articles. Query or submit complete ms. Length: 500-1,000 words. Pays $50-1,500.

Photos: State availability of photos with query or ms. Pays $25-100 for 8x10 b&w glossy prints, contact sheets or negatives; $150-1,000 for 35mm color transparencies. Captions required. Buys one-time, or all rights.

SUNSHINE MAGAZINE, Henry F. Henrichs Publications, Litchfield IL 62056. (217)324-2322. 75% freelance written. For general audience of all ages. Monthly magazine. Circ. 90,000. Buys 120-140 unsolicited mss/year. Buys first North American serial rights. Pays on acceptance. Publishes ms an average of 8 months after acceptance. Submit seasonal material 7 months in advance. Computer printout submissions acceptable; prefers letter-quality to dot-matrix. Reports in 1-2 months. Complimentary copy sent to included authors on publication. Submit complete ms. SASE. Sample copy 50¢; writer's guidelines for SASE.

Nonfiction: "We accept some short articles, but they must be especially interesting or inspirational. *Sunshine Magazine* is not a religious publication, and purely religious material is rarely used. We desire carefully written features about persons or events that have real human interest—that give a 'lift'." Length: 100-300 words. Pays $10-50.

Columns/Departments: My Most Extraordinary Experience—Yes, It Happened to Me. Must be in first person, deal with a very unusual or surprising situation and have a positive approach. Length: 350-500 words. Pays $25. Favorite Meditation and Gem of the Month, inspirational essays not exceeding 200 words. Pays $20.

Fiction: "Stories must be wholesome, well-written, with clearly defined plots. There should be a purpose for each story, but any moral or lesson should be well-concealed in the plot development. Humorous stories are welcome. Avoid trite plots. A surprising climax is most desirable. Material should be uplifting and noncontroversial." Length: 600-1,200 words. Youth story: 400-700 words. Pays $20-100.

Poetry: Buys one poem for special feature each month. Pays $15. Uses several other poems each month but does not purchase these. Prefers pleasantly rhythmic, humorous or uplifting material. Length: 4-16 lines.

Fillers: 100-200 words. Pays $10.

Tips: "We prefer not to receive queries. Enclose a SASE, be neat, accurate and surprising, but wholesome. Do not send anything dealing with alcohol, violence, divorce, death or depression. We judge each submission individually for its quality. If it is suitable, it doesn't matter who wrote it. Our guidelines are quite specific as to what kind of manuscripts we want. Authors make the mistake of not checking our guidelines first and then submit material that we automatically reject because it is too long, too depressing, etc. Guidelines are available upon request at no charge."

‡**TLC MAGAZINE**, TLC Publications, Inc., 1933 Chestnut St., Philadelphia PA 19103. (215)569-3574. Editor: Rebecca Stefoff. Bimonthly general-interest magazine distributed free to hospital patients nationwide. Circ. 250,000. Pays on publication unless arranged otherwise. Publishes ms an average of 10 months after acceptance. Buys second serial rights only. Submit seasonal/holiday material 10 months in advance. Accepts previously published material only. Computer printout submissions acceptable; no dot-matrix. Reports in 3 months. SASE. Sample copy $2; writer's guidelines for SAE and 1 first class stamp.
Nonfiction: Humor; new product (especially fitness-related); travel and food (only if health-oriented). "Good subjects include food, travel, sports and leisure, profiles, Americana/nostalgia, fashion, home and enterainment. We also use serious—but not overly technical—articles on science and the arts. We like humor. We never use inspirational or religious material or anything concerning hospitalization, death or illness." No inspirational or medical material. "We're only interested in reprints; occasionally we run short book excerpts." Buys 45-60 mss/year. Query with published clips. Length: 400-1,200 words. Queries without SASE will not be answered. Payment individually negotiated.
Photos: State availability of photos. Identification of subjects required. Buys one-time rights.
Tips: "Everything in *TLC* must be upbeat and entertaining with a contemporary tone. The emphasis is on service to our readers: providing them with usable information and tools. Although we don't use health or psychological advice articles, we do like articles that emphasizes healthy living—in other words, we use pieces that suggest a healthy, active lifestyle without being overly medical or therapeutic."

TOWN AND COUNTRY, 1700 Broadway, New York NY 10019. (212)903-5000. Managing Editor: Jean Barkhorn. For upper-income Americans. Monthly. Pays on acceptance. Not a large market for freelancers. Always query first. SASE.
Nonfiction: Frank Zachary, department editor. "We're always trying to find ideas that can be developed into good articles that will make appealing cover lines." Wants provocative and controversial pieces. Length: 1,500-2,000 words. Pay varies. Also buys shorter pieces for which pay varies.

WHAT MAKES PEOPLE SUCCESSFUL, The National Research Bureau, Inc., 424 N. 3rd St., Burlington IA 52601. Editor: Rhonda Wilson. Editorial Supervisor: Doris J. Ruschill. 75% freelance written. For industrial workers of all ages. Published quarterly. Pays on publication. Publishes ms an average of 1 year after acceptance. Buys all rights. Previously published submissions OK. Computer printout submissions acceptable; prefers letter-quality to dot-matrix. SASE. Submit seasonal/holiday material 1 month in advance of issue date. Reports in 3 weeks. Free writer's guidelines.
Nonfiction: How-to (be successful); general interest (personality, employee morale, guides to successful living, biographies of successful persons, etc.); experience; and opinion. No material on health. Buys 3-4 mss/issue. Query with outline. Length: 400-600 words. Pays 4¢/word.
Tips: Short articles and fillers (rather than major features) have a better chance of acceptance because all articles are short.

Health and Fitness

Each of the following magazines has a prescription for health and fitness. Whether it's nutrition, exercise or both, writers must understand this prescription and make "dry facts" come alive. "Almost any medical subject is right for us, but we find very few people who can make the subject enticing to readers," says the managing editor of *Health*. "This is often a problem in the health and medical area." The magazines listed here specialize in covering health-and fitness-related topics for a general audience. Magazines covering health topics from a medical perspective are listed in Trade Journals/Medical. Also see the Sports/Miscellaneous section where publications dealing with health and particular sports may be listed. And remember, nearly every general interest publication is a potential market for a health article.

ACCENT ON LIVING, Box 700, Bloomington IL 61702. (309)378-2961. Editor: Betty Garee. 80% freelance written. For physically disabled persons and rehabilitation professionals. Quarterly magazine; 128 pages. Circ. 18,000. Buys first rights and second (reprint) rights to material originally published elsewhere. Byline usually given. Buys 50-60 unsolicited mss/year. Pays on publication. Publishes ms an average of 1 year after acceptance. Photocopied submissions OK. Computer printout submissions aceptable; prefers letter-quality to dot-matrix. Reports in 2 weeks. SASE. Sample copy $2; writer's guidelines for SAE and 1 first class stamp.
Nonfiction: Betty Garee, editor. Articles about new devices that would make a disabled person with limited physical mobility more independent; should include description, availability, and photos. Medical breakthroughs for disabled people. Intelligent discussion articles on acceptance of physically disabled persons in normal living situations; topics may be architectural barriers, housing, transportation, educational or job opportunities, organizations, or other areas. How-to articles concerning everyday living giving specific, helpful information so the reader can carry out the idea himself. News articles about active disabled persons or groups. Good strong interviews. Vacations, accessible places to go, sports, organizations, humorous incidents, self improvement, and sexual or personal adjustment—all related to physically handicapped persons. No religious-type articles. "We are looking for upbeat material." Length: 250-1,000 words. Pays 10¢/word for article as it appears in magazine (after editing and/or condensing by staff). Query.
Photos: Pays $5 minimum for b&w photos purchased with accompanying captions. Amount will depend on quality of photos and subject matter.
Tips: "The most frequent mistake made by writers is that they don't write from the *disabled person's* point of view. Make sure that you are writing for disabled people, not a general audience. Ask a friend who is disabled to read your article before sending it to *Accent.* Make sure that he/she understands your major points and the sequence or procedure."

ALCOHOLISM, The National Magazine, Alcom, Inc., Box 31329, Wallingford Station, Seattle WA 98103. (206)527-8999. Editor: Christina Carlson. 50% freelance written. Bimonthly magazine covering alcoholism, treatment, and recovery. Circ. 30,000. Pays on publication. Byline given. Buys first rights only. Submit seasonal/holiday material 6 months in advance. Simultaneous queries, and simultaneous and photocopied submissions OK. SASE. Reports in 1 month. Publishes ms an average of 2 months after acceptance. Sample copy $5; writer's guidelines for business size SAE and 1 first class stamp.
Nonfiction: How-to, humor, interview/profile, opinion, and "popularizations of research." New interest in business success through recovery. Special issues include Research Focus and Intervention Focus. No "this is how bad I was"; "this is how bad my parents (brother, etc.) were." Stress "the adventure of recovery" instead of the agony of the disease. No fiction. Especially interested in humor. Buys 20 major features/year. Query with clips of published work or send complete ms. Length: 300-2,000 words. Pays 10¢/word; $100/published page.
Photos: State availability of photos. Captions, model release, and identification of subjects required. Buys one-time rights.
Columns/Departments: "Road to Recovery": tips on ways of enhancing recovery. Buys 12-24 items/year. Send complete ms. Length: 500-750 words. Pays 10¢/word; $100/published page.
Poetry: Free verse, light verse, and traditional (lucid). Wants recovery-oriented material only. No "surrealism; alcoholics are rotten; ain't it terrible on skid road. No grim poetry, please." Buys 1-2/ issue. Submit maximum 5 poems. Length: 2-20 lines. Pays $5-25.
Fillers: Short humor and newsbreaks. Pays $5 minimum; 10¢/word "on longer items."
Tips: "We need writers who know something about alcoholism—something more than personal experience and superficial acquaintance—writers who make tough material readable and palatable for a popular and professional audience. We are always on the lookout for well-researched popularizations of research. We try to run one personal experience per issue dealing with recovery—how the alcoholic finds ways to make sobriety worth being sober for." Editors also interested in working with writers outside the US.

AMERICAN HEALTH MAGAZINE, Fitness of Body and Mind, American Health Partners, 80 Fifth Ave., New York NY 10011. (212)242-2460. Editor-in-Chief: T George Harris. Editor: Joel Gurin. 60% freelance written. 10 issues/year. General interest magazine that covers both scientific and "lifestyle" aspects of health, including laboratory research, clinical advances, fitness, holistic healing and nutrition. Circ. 850,000. Pays on acceptance. Publishes ms an average of 6 months after acceptance. Byline given. Offers 25% kill fee. Buys first North American serial rights; "negotiable, in some cases." Computer printout submissions acceptable. SASE. Reports in 2 months. Sample copy for $3; writer's guidelines for 4x9 SAE and 1 first class stamp.
Nonfiction: Mail to Editorial/Features. Book excerpts; how-to; humor (if anyone can be funny, yes); interview/profile (health or fitness related); photo feature (any solid feature or news item relating to health); and technical. No first-person narratives, mechanical research reports, weight loss plans or recipes. "Stories should be written clearly, without jargon. Information should be new, authoritative and helpful to the readers. No first-person narrative about illness or recovery from an illness or accident." Buys 60-70 mss/year. Query

with 2 clips of published work. "Absolutely *no* complete mss." Length: 1,000-3,000 words. Pays $600-2,000 upon acceptance. Sometimes pays the expenses of writers on assignment.

Photos: Mail to Editorial/Photo. Send photos with query. Pays $100-600 for 35mm transparencies and 8x10 prints "depending on use." Captions and identification of subjects required. Buys one-time rights.

Columns/Departments: Mail to Editorial/News. Consumer Alert, Medical News (technological update), Fitness Report, Life Styles, Nutrition Report, Tooth Report, and Skin, Scent and Hair. Other news sections included from time to time. Buys 500-600 mss/year. Query with clips of published work. Prefers 2 pages-500 words. Pays $125-375 upon acceptance.

Fillers: Mail to Editorial/Fillers. Anecdotes and newsbreaks. Buys 30/year. Length: 20-50 words. Pays $10-25.

Tips: "*American Health* has no full-time staff writers; we have chosen to rely on outside contributors for almost all our articles. The magazine needs good ideas, and good articles, from professional journalists, health educators, researchers and clinicians. Queries should be short (no longer than a page), snappy and to the point. Think short; think news. Give us a good angle and a paragraph of background. Queries only. We do not take responsibility for materials not accompanied by SASE."

‡**BEAUTY DIGEST, For Health & Fitness**, Mass Media Associates, 126 5th Ave., New York NY 10011. (212)255-0440. Editor: Diane Robbins. Managing Editor: Lorraine De Pasque. 25% freelance writen. Bimonthly magazine on beauty, health, fitness, diet and emotion self-help. "All articles must be geared to making reader feel better about herself. Audiences are women 25-40 concerned with self-improvement, both physically and emotionally. Our publication is supportive and accepting." Circ. 250,000. Pays on acceptance. Publishes ms an average of 3 months after acceptance. Byline given. Offers 50% kill fee. Buys one-time rights and second serial (reprint) rights; makes work-for-hire assignments. Submit seasonal/holiday material 4 months in advance. Simultaneous, photocopied, and previously published submissions OK. SASE. Reports in 2 months.

Nonfiction: Book excerpts, how-to and personal experience. Special issues include fashion and women's health. No work-oriented, child-care, crafts or recipes. Buys 20 mss/year. Send complete ms. Length: 1,500-3,500 words. Pays $50-100. Sometimes pays the expenses of writers on assignment.

Columns/Departments: I Made Myself Over, 1,200 words with photos of before and after. Buys 6 mss/year. Send complete ms. Length: 1,200 words. Pays $100.

Tips: "Send previously published work as 25% of our magazine is reprints."

BESTWAYS MAGAZINE, Box 2028, Carson City NV 89702. Editor/Publisher: Barbara Bassett. Emphasizes health, diet and nutrition. Monthly magazine; 120 pages. Circ. 300,000. Pays on publication. Buys all rights. Byline given. Submit seasonal/holiday material 6 months in advance. SASE. Reports in 6 weeks. Writer's guidelines for SASE.

Nonfiction: General interest (nutrition, physical fitness, preventive medicine, supplements, natural foods); how-to (diet and exercise); and technical (vitamins, minerals, weight control and nutrition). "No direct or implied endorsements of refined flours, grains or sugar, tobacco, alcohol, caffeine, drugs or patent medicines." Buys 4 mss/issue. Query. Length: 1,500 words. Pays 10¢/word.

Photos: State availability of photos with query. Pays $7.50 for 4x5 b&w glossy prints; $15 for 2¼x2¼ color transparencies. Captions preferred. Buys all rights. Model release required.

‡**BRUCE JENNER'S BETTER HEALTH & LIVING**, Decathlon Corp., 800 2nd Ave., New York NY 10017. (212)986-9026. Editor: Julie Davis. Managing Editor: Laura L. Deutsch. 80% freelance written. Bimonthly magazine on fitness, health and lifestyle. The magazine focuses on "how to make the most of your lifestyle in a healthy way and still enjoy yourself. Moderation is the key." Estab. 1985. Circ. 250,000. Pays by split payment. Publishes ms an average of 4 months after acceptance. Byline given. Offers 25% kill fee. Buys first North American serial rights. Submit seasonal/holiday materal 4 months in advance. Simultaneous queries and submissions OK. SASE. Reports in 1 month. Sample copy $2.50 with SAE and $1.75 postage.

Nonfiction: Book excerpts, general interest, interview/profile, new product, opinion, personal experience, photo feature and travel. No techical writing. Buys 100 mss/year. Query with published clips. Length: 1,500-5,000 words. Pays $250-1,000. Sometimes pays the expenses of writers on assignment.

Photos: Alice Borenstein, art director. State availability of photos. Reviews 35mm b&w and color transparencies. Pays $200, page rate depending on usage. Model release and identification of subjects required. Buys one-time rights.

Columns/Departments: Better Living—items on beauty/grooming, stress management, illustrated health news, Healthwire—hard news items on health, fitness, medicine; Healthtone—trends, fitness news, health info, resorts or spas tied into one area of country or world; Fitworks—new tools, gadgets, videos, books (highly photographed); Fitness to Go—away from home fitness; Kid Shape, Fit Over 40; Back Page—the back. Buys 200 mss/year. Query with published clips. Length: 100-750 words. Pays $50-300.

Tips: "Send query with clips after familiarizing yourself with format. Submissions should be both male/female oriented. Healthwire and Better Living columns are most open to freelancers."

CELEBRATE HEALTH, Bergan Mercy, Inc., 7500 Mercy Rd., Omaha NE 68124. (402)398-6303. Editor: Nancy Garner Ebert. 85% freelance written. Quarterly consumer-oriented magazine focusing on positive, upbeat news and features in the health/medical field. Circ. 30,000. Pays on acceptance. Publishes ms an average of 6 months after acceptance. Byline given. Offers 25% kill fee. Buys variable rights "depending on author and material." Submit seasonal/holiday material 6 months in advance. Simultaneous queries, and simultaneous and photocopied submissions OK. Computer printout submissions acceptable; prefers letter-quality to dot-matrix. SASE. Reports in 6 weeks. Sample copy $1 and a 9x12 envelope with $1.20 postage; writer's guidelines for business size SAE and 1 first class stamp.
Nonfiction: General interest (family health); historical/nostalgic (medical); how-to (exercise, diet, keep fit); interview/profile (of doctors, health experts); and new product (exercise equipment, sports clothing). "Nothing on pro-abortion, sex, sterilization, or artificial birth control; and please, nothing about how awful doctors are or how corrupt the medical establishment is." Buys 20-25 mss/year. "We'd see completed articles rather than queries." Length: 500-2,500 words. Pays $50-500.
Photos: Send photos with query or ms. Pays $25-50 for b&w contact sheets and negatives; $50-100 for 2¼ or 4x5 color transparencies used inside; $100 for color covers. "35mm is OK for color, too, but must be Kodachrome." Captions, model release and identification of subjects required. Buys variable rights.
Columns/Departments: Medical, Living, World of Work, Childhood, Nutrition, and Prime Time (elderly). Buys 10 mss/year. Send complete ms. Length: 500-2,500 words. Pays $50-500.
Tips: "We use first person *rarely*; only when really substantiated with lots of facts. Every day's mail brings another: "My Experience with Cataracts" or "My Experience with Gout." Only put yourself in the article if there's a reason for you to be there. Writing should be crisp, snappy. The publication is edited according to the Associated Press stylebook. Interested in latest developments in health care facilities; all aspects of physical, mental and emotional health. Use authoritative sources. No medical jargon."

FEELING GREAT, Living, Looking and . . Feeling Great, Haymarket Group Ltd., Suite 407, 45 W. 34th St., New York NY 10001. (212)239-0855. Editor: Tim Moriarty. Managing Editor: Peggy Nicoll. 90% freelance written. Monthly magazine on health, fitness and beauty. "We publish upbeat articles directed toward middle-income, middle-of-the-road readers. Nothing too cosmopolitan, New York-Los Angeles, or controversial; straightforward pieces." Estab. 1984. Circ. 250,00. Pays on acceptance. Publishes ms an average of 6 months after acceptance. Byline given. Offers 25% kill fee. Buys first North American serial rights. Submit seasonal/holiday material 4 months in advance. Computer printout submissions acceptable; prefers letter-quality to dot-matrix. SASE. Reports in 6 weeks on queries; 2 months on mss. Sample copy $1.95 and 11x13 SAE; writer's guidelines for SAE and 1 first class stamp.
Nonfiction: Send to managing editor. General interest (psychological, a few relationship items); how-to (fitness related); humor; opinion ("Backtalk"—no pay but byline given); and personal experience (exercise, fitness, health and beauty related). No old news, travel, childrearing, or anything aimed at the over 35-age group. Buys 150 mss/year. Query with published clips. Do not send complete ms. Length: 800-2,000 words. Pays $200-1,000. Pays expenses of writers on assignment.
Columns/Departments: Send to managing editor. Backtalk. Buys 50 mss/year. Query with published clips. Length: 200-1,500. Pays $50-750.
Fillers: Send to editor. Anecdotes. Buys 40/year. Length: 100-400. No payment; byline given.
Tips: "If we're unfamiliar with a writer or unsure of his/her abilities, we're not likely to take a chance on a feature; however, if the idea is good and the query well-written, we'll assign a feature regardless of background. We desperately need good, interesting fitness articles; health topics and serious psychological pieces that haven't been recycled a hundred times. We need upbeat material, and a sense of humor is always appreciated."

FRUITFUL YIELD NEWSLETTER, The Fruitful Yield, Inc., 721 N. Yale, Villa Park IL 60181. (312)833-8288. Editor: Doug Murguia. 90% freelance written. Biannual national newsletter covering natural foods, vitamins and herbs. Features subjects ranging from prenatal care to health and nutrition for all age groups. Circ. 15,000. Pays on publication. Publishes ms an average of 4 months after acceptance. Buys first rights only. Phone queries OK. Submit seasonal material 3 months in advance. Photocopied submissions OK. Computer printout submissions acceptable; prefers letter-quality to dot-matrix. Reports in 6 months. Free sample copy and writer's guidelines only for SAEs with 3 first class stamps.
Nonfiction: "We are interested in three main types of articles: 1) detailed, documented articles written for the layman telling of the latest research findings in the field of nutrition; 2) personal experience articles telling how natural foods, vitamins or herbs help you or a friend overcome or relieve an ailment (should be detailed and describe your program); and 3) recipes using natural foods and/or giving cooking hints." Length: 250-500 words. Send complete ms. Buys 30 mss/year. Pays $10-20. Sometimes pays the expenses of writers on assignment.
Tips: "Be familiar with our content. We're looking for specific detailed, documented articles that make no assumptions. Use direct quotes from authorities."

FRUITION, The Plan, Box 872-WM, Santa Cruz CA 95061. (408)425-1708. Biannual newsletter covering healthful living/creation of public food tree nurseries and relative social and horticultural matters. 10%

freelance written. Circ. 300. Payment method negotiable. Publishes ms an average of 4 months after acceptance. Byline given. Offers negotiable kill fee. Buys all rights. Simultaneous queries, and simultaneous, photocopied and previously published submissions OK. Electronic submissions OK via MacIntosh 3½ mini disk qd ss. Computer printout submissions acceptable. SASE. Reports in 2-4 weeks. Sample copy $2; writer's guidelines for SAE and 39¢ postage.

Nonfiction: General interest, historical/nostalgic, how-to, inspirational, interview/profile, personal experience, photo feature—all must relate to public access—food trees, foraging fruit and nuts, and related social and horticultural matters. No articles "involving gardening with chemicals, or cloning plants. No articles on health with references to using therapies or medicines." Buys 4-6 mss/year. Length: 750-5,000 words. Pays negotiable fee.

Photos: Dennis Nelson, photo editor. State availability of photos. Pays negotiable fee for b&w contact sheet and 5x5 or larger prints. Identification of subjects required. Buys one-time rights.

Poetry: E. Eagle, poetry editor. Avant-garde, free verse, haiku, light verse and traditional. Buys 4-6/year. Submit maximum 6 poems. Length: 2 lines-750 words. Pays negotiable fee.

Fillers: Clippings, short humor and newsbreaks. Buys 2-6/year. Length: 125-400 words. Pays negotiable fee.

Tips: "Get a copy of *Fruition* to see what we publish. The most frequent mistake made by writers is that material submitted does not relate to our publication."

‡**HEALTH PLEX MAGAZINE, The Magazine for Healthier Living**, Methodist Hospital/Childrens Hospital, 8303 Dodge St., Omaha NE 68114. (402)390-4528. Managing Editor: Gini Goldsmith. 50% freelance written. Quarterly magazine on health information and medical subjects. Focuses on current health care topics, wellness-related articles, etc. Circ. 35,000. Pays on acceptance. Byline given. Buys all rights and first serial rights; makes work-for-hire assignments. Submit seasonal/holiday material 3 months in advance. Photocopied submissions OK. Computer printout submissions acceptable; prefers letter-quality to dot-matrix. SASE. Reports in 1 month. Free sample copy.

Nonfiction: Only health/wellness articles. Buys 16 mss/year. Query with published clips or send complete ms. Length: 1,000-3,000 words. Pays $50-200. Sometimes pays the expenses of writers on assignment.

Photos: State availability of photos. Reviews b&w contact sheets and color transparencies. Pays $100-250. Model release required. Buys all rights.

Columns/Departments: Feelin' Good (wellness articles) and Health Updates (short topics on current health topics, new technology, etc).

HOT WATER LIVING, A Consumer's Guide To Spa and Hot Tub Enjoyment, Harcourt Brace Jovanovich, 1700 E. Dyer Rd., Santa Ana CA 92705. (714)250-8060. Editor: John Kilroy. 15% freelance written. A quarterly magazine covering spas, hot tub, saunas and their use and maintenance; also, fitness products. "We educate consumers about benefits of hot water products and maintenance and how spas, etc. tie in with fitness and health." Pays on acceptance. Publishes ms an average of 2 months after acceptance. Byline given. Buys first North American serial rights. Submit seasonal/holiday material 3 months in advance. Simultaneous queries and photocopied submissions OK. Computer printout submissions acceptable; prefers letter-quality to dot-matrix. SASE. Reports in 2 weeks on queries; 1 month on mss. Free sample copy and writer's guidelines.

Nonfiction: How-to (landscape around spa, build decks, maintain equipment); humor; personal experience; and photo feature (beautiful installations). Buys 6 mss/year. Query with published clips. Length: 250-2,000 words. Pays $100-250. Sometimes pays the expenses of writers on assignment.

Photos: Reviews color transparencies. Model releases required. Buys one-time rights.

LET'S LIVE MAGAZINE, Oxford Industries, Inc., 444 N. Larchmont Blvd., Box 74908, Los Angeles CA 90004. (213)469-3901. Editor: Howard Kim. Associate Publisher: Peggy MacDonald. Emphasizes nutrition. 40% freelance written. Monthly magazine; 96 pages. Circ. 135,000. Pays on publication. Publishes ms an average of 3 months after acceptance. Buys first North American serial rights. Byline given. Submit seasonal/holiday material 4 months in advance. Computer printout submissions acceptable; no dot-matrix. SASE. Reports in 3 weeks on queries; 6 weeks on mss. Sample copy $2.25; writer's guidelines for SAE and 1 first class stamp.

Nonfiction: General interest (effects of vitamins, minerals and nutrients in improvement of health or afflictions); historical (documentation of experiments or treatment establishing value of nutrients as boon to health); how-to (acquire strength and vitality, improve health of adults and/or children and prepare tasty health-food meals); inspirational (first-person accounts of triumph over disease through substitution of natural foods and nutritional supplements for drugs and surgery); interview (benefits of research in establishing prevention as key to good health); advertised new product (120-180 words plus 5x7 or glossy of product); personal opinion (views of orthomolecular doctors or their patients on value of health foods toward maintaining good health); and profile (background and/or medical history of preventive medicine, M.D.s or Ph.D.s, in advancement of nutrition). "We do not want kookie first-person accounts of experiences with drugs or junk foods, faddist healers or unorthodox treatments. Manuscripts must be well-researched, reliably documented, and written in a clear, readable style." Buys 10-15 mss/issue. Query with published clips. Length: 750-1,600 words. Pays $50-150. Sometimes pays expenses of writer on assignment.

Photos: State availability of photos with ms. Pays $17.50 for 8x10 b&w glossy prints; $35 for 8x10 color prints and 35mm color transparencies; and $150 for good cover shot. Captions and model releases required.

Columns/Departments: My Story and Interviews (750-1,200 words). Buys 1-2/issue. Query. Pays $50-250. Last Word (700-800 words on some health aspect not usually appropriate for feature-length coverage). Pays $75-150.

Tips: "We want writers with experience in researching nonsurgical medical subjects, interviewing experts with the ability to simplify technical and clinical information for the layman. A captivating lead and structural flow are essential." The most frequent mistakes made by writers are in writing articles that are too technical; in poor style; written for the wrong audience (publication not thoroughly studied) or have unreliable documentation or overzealous faith in the topic reflected by flimsy research and inappropriate tone."

LISTEN MAGAZINE, 6830 Laurel St. NW, Washington DC 20012. (202)722-6726. Editor: Gary B. Swanson. 50% freelance written. Specializes in drug prevention, presenting positive alternatives to various drug dependencies. "*Listen* is used in many high school classes, in addition to use by professionals: medical personnel, counselors, law enforcement officers, educators, youth workers, etc." Monthly magazine, 32 pages. Circ. 120,000. Buys all rights unless otherwise arranged with the author. Byline given. Pays on acceptance. Publishes ms an average of 5 months after acceptance. Computer printout submissions acceptable; prefers letter-quality to dot-matrix. Reports in 4 weeks. SASE. Sample copy $1; send large manila SASE; free writer's guidelines.

Nonfiction: Seeks articles that deal with causes of drug use such as poor self-concept, family relations, social skills or peer pressure. Especially interested in youth-slanted articles or personality interviews encouraging nonalcoholic and nondrug ways of life. Teenage point of view is essential. Popularized medical, legal and educational articles. Also seeks narratives which portray teens dealing with youth conflicts, especially those related to the use or temptation to use harmful substances. Growth of the main character should be shown. "We don't want typical alcoholic story/skid-row bum, AA stories. We are also being inundated with drunk-driving accident stories. Unless yours is unique, consider another topic." Buys 75-100 unsolicited mss/year. Query. Length: 500-1,500 words. Pays 4-7¢/word.

Photos: Purchased with accompanying ms. Captions required. Pays $5-15 per b&w print (5x7, but 8x10 preferred). Color photos preferred, but b&w acceptable.

Poetry: Blank verse and free verse only. Seeks image-invoking, easily illustrated poems of 5-15 lines to combine with photo or illustration to make a poster. Pays $15 maximum.

Fillers: Word square/general puzzles are also considered. Pays $15.

Tips: "True stories are good, especially if they have a unique angle. Other authoritative articles need a fresh approach. In query, briefly summarize article idea and logic of why you feel it's good."

MUSCLE MAG INTERNATIONAL, 52 Bramsteele Rd., Unit 2, Brampton, Ontario L6W 3M5 Canada. Editor: Robert Kennedy. 80% freelance written. For 16 to 40-year-old men and women interested in physical fitness and overall body improvement. Monthly magazine; 100 pages. Circ. 140,000. Buys all rights. Pays on acceptance. Byline given. Buys 80 mss/year. Sample copy $3. Reports in 1 month. Submit complete ms. IRCs.

Nonfiction: Articles on ideal physical proportions and importance of supplements in the diet, training for muscle size. Should be helpful and instructional and appeal to young men and women who want to live life in a vigorous and healthy style. "We would like to see articles for the physical culturist on muscle building or an article on fitness testing." Informational, how-to, personal experience, interview, profile, inspirational, humor, historical, expose, nostalgia, personal opinion, photo, spot news, new product, and merchandising technique articles. Length: 1,200-1,600 words. Pays 10¢/word.

Columns/Departments: Nutrition Talk (eating for top results) and Shaping Up (improving fitness and stamina). Length: 1,300 words. Pays 10¢/word.

Photos: B&w and color photos are purchased with or without ms. Pays $10 for 8x10 glossy exercise photos; $10 for 8x10 b&w posing shots. Pays $100-200 for color cover and $15 for color used inside magazine (transparencies). More for "special" work.

Fillers: Newsbreaks, puzzles, quotes of the champs. Length: open. Pays $5 minimum.

Tips: "The best way to break in is to seek out the muscle-building 'stars' and do in-depth interviews with biography in mind. Color training picture support essential."

‡**NUTRITION FORUM**, George F. Stickley Co., 210 West Washington Sq., Philadelphia PA 19106. (215)922-7126. Editor: Stephen Barrett, M.D. 60% freelance written. Monthly newsletter. "*Nutrition Forum* is an 8-page newsletter written for nutrition and health educators and intelligent laypersons. It reports on legal and political developments related to nutrition; practical applications of nutrition research; and nutrition fads, fallacies and quackery, including investigative reports." Estab. 1984. Circ. 600. Pays on publication. Publishes ms an average of 3 months after acceptance. Byline given. Buys first North American serial rights. Submit seasonal/holiday material 3 months in advance. Simultaneous queries and photocopied submissions

OK. Computer printout submissions acceptable. Reports in 1 week. Free sample copy; writer's guidelines for 4½x9 SAE and 1 first class stamp.

Nonfiction: Expose (of fads and illegal practices); interview/profile (of prominent nutritionalists); and personal experience (of victims or investigators of quackery). Buys 36 mss/year. Query or send complete ms. Length: 400-3,000 words. Pays $40-300 or $6/published column inch (about 10¢/word). Sometimes pays expenses of writers on assignment.

Fillers: Newsbreak. "We carry several hundred per year. Most are developed in-house, but we are willing to use ones from freelancers." Length: 50-200 words. Pays $10-20.

Tips: An area most open to freelancers is undercover investigations of lawbreakers. Everything sent will be read. All correspondence concerning articles should be sent to Stephen Barrett, M.D., Box 1602, Allentown PA 18105)—*not to the publisher.*"

‡**OSTOMY QUARTERLY**, United Ostomy Association, Inc., 2001 W. Beverly Blvd., Los Angeles CA 90057. (213)413-5510. Editor: Kathy Pape, M.S. 20% freelance written. Quarterly magazine on ostomy surgery and living with ostomies. "The OQ is the official publication of UOA and should cover topics of interest to patients who underwent abdominal ostomy surgery (ileostomy; colostomy, urostomy). Most articles should be 'up-beat' in feeling; also, we cover new surgical techniques in ostomy surgery." Circ. 50,000. Pays on publication. Publishes ms an average of 3 months after acceptance. Byline given. Buys first North American serial rights; makes work-for-hire assignments. Submit seasonal/holiday material 3 months in advance. Simultaneous queries and photocopied submissions OK. Computer printout submissions acceptable; prefers letter-quality to dot-matrix. Print must be dark and readable. SASE. Reports in 3 months. Sample copy $2.50; free writer's guidelines and editorial calender.

Nonfiction: General interest (travel, parenting, psychology); humor (coping humorously with problems with ostomies); interview/profile (important MDs in gastroenterology, urology); personal experience (living with abdominal ostomies); technical (new surgical techniques in ostomy); and travel (with ostomies). No testimonials from members, "How I overcame . . . with ostomy and life is great now." Buys 6 mss/year. Query. Length: 800-2,400 words. Usually asks for pages of copy. Pays $50-150 maximum. Sometimes pays the expenses of writers on assignment but no more than $150 total (expenses + fee) per article will be paid. No kill fee offered.

Photos: Reviews b&w and color transparencies. "We like to use photographs with articles, but price for article includes use of photos. We return photos on request." Captions and model release required.

Columns/Departments: Book reviews (on ostomy care, living with ostomies); Ostomy World (any news items relating to ostomy, enterostomal therapy, medical); and Q&A (answers medical questions from members). Primarily staff-written.

Tips: "We will be looking mainly for articles from freelancers about ostomy management, ostomy advances, people important to ostomates. Send different topics and ideas than we have published for 22 years. Be willing to attend free meeting of UOA chapter to get "flavor" of group. UOA is a nonprofit association which accounts for the fees offered. Hopefully, in the future we can offer greater compensation for writer's efforts. We are a good magazine in which new freelancers can try their hand. We want to help them start their careers."

PEOPLE'S MEDICAL SOCIETY NEWSLETTER, People's Medical Society, 14 E. Minor St., Emmaus PA 18049. (215)967-2136. Editor: Karla Morales. A bimonthly newsletter for members of PMS covering health/medical issues, grassroots health actions, and medical politics. "Our readers are interested in preventive medicine, alternatives to standard medical care, and a consumer activist way with the health/medical care system." Circ. 65,000. Pays on acceptance. Byline given. Offers 33% kill fee or as arranged. Not copyrighted. Buys rights by arrangement with author. Submit seasonal/holiday material 4-6 months in advance. Simultaneous queries, and simultaneous, photocopied and previously published submissions OK. Electronic submissions OK at present on 5¼ and 8" CPM 2.2 disks. Computer printout submissions acceptable; prefers letter-quality to dot-matrix. SASE. Reports in 1 month. Sample copy for $1, business-size SAE, and first class stamp.

Nonfiction: Book excerpts, expose, how-to, humor, inspirational, interview/profile, opinion, and personal experience. "All articles must be health related, from a consumer activist standpoint; experiences with the medical establishment, fighting, insensitivity of doctor/hospital-patient relationship." No articles on specific nutritional therapies, or articles with a religious overtone. Query with published clips or send complete ms. Length: 500-1,500 words. Pays $35-125.

Fillers: Cartoons.

Tips: "First-person accounts, interviews, and cartoons are most open to freelancers."

SHAPE, Merging Mind and Body Fitness, Weider Enterprises, 21100 Erwin St., Woodland Hills CA 91367. (818)884-6800. Editor: Christine MacIntyre. 25% freelance written. Monthly magazine covering women's health and fitness. Circ 515,000. Pays on publication. Offers 1/3 kill fee. Buys all rights and reprint rights. Submit seasonal/holiday material 8 months in advance. Reports in 2 months on queries; and mss.

Nonfiction: Book excerpts; expose (health, fitness related); how-to (get fit); interview/profile (of fit women);

travel (spas). "We use health and fitness articles written by professionals in their specific fields. No articles which haven't been queried first." Query with clips of published work. Length: 500-2,000 words. Pays negotiable fee.

SLIMMER, Health and Beauty for the Total Woman, Suite 3000, 3420 Ocean Park Blvd., Santa Monica CA 90405. (213)450-0900. Editor: Lori Berger. 100% freelance written. Bimonthly magazine covering health and beauty and fitness lifestyles for "college-educated single or married women, ages 18-40, interested in physical fitness and weight loss." Circ. 250,000. Pays 30 days after acceptance. Publishes ms an average of 2 months after acceptance. Byline given. Buys simultaneous rights and second serial (reprint) rights. Submit seasonal/holiday queries 6 months in advance. Computer printout submissions acceptable; prefers letter-quality to dot-matrix. SASE. Reports in 1 month.
Nonfiction: Fitness and nutrition. "We look for well-researched material—the newer the better—by expert writers." No fad diets, celebrity interviews/round-ups, fashion or first-person articles. No unsolicited mss. Query with story idea and clips of published work. Length: 2,500-3,000 words. Pays $300. Sometimes pays the expenses of writers on assignment.
Photos: State availability of photos.

TLC, The Magazine for Recuperation and Relaxation, TLC Publications, Inc., 1933 Chestnut St., Philadelphia PA 19103. (215)569-3574. Editor: Rebecca Stefoff. 75% freelance written. Bimonthly magazine with emphasis on lifestyle articles—leisure, sports, food, travel, personal finance, grooming, art, book excerpts, etc. "*TLC* features articles and artwork (mostly reprints) chosen to entertain and divert our audience—hospital patients. Patients receive the magazine free during overnight hospital stays. We avoid health-related material and concentrate on offering general-interest items which will appeal to a demographically diverse readership." Circ. 250,000. Publishes ms an average of 2-12 months after acceptance. Byline given. Buys only second (reprint) rights to material originally published elsewhere. Computer printout submissions acceptable; no dot-matrix. SASE. Reports in 3 weeks on queries; 2 months on mss. Sample copy for 9x12 SAE and $2.05 postage; guidelines for 1 first class stamp.
Nonfiction: Book excerpts, general interest, historical/nostalgic, Americana, humor, interview/profile, lifestyle (food, the arts, etc.), photo feature and travel. No health-related, medical, inspirational or religious articles. Query with published clips. Length: 400-1,200 words. Payment negotiated on an individual basis.
Photos: State availability of photos. Model release and identification of subjects required. Buys one-time rights.
Tips: "We're most interested in brief (2-8 typed pages) items or excerpts for a diverse audience. Material too timely for a long shelf life, or too controversial to appeal to a majority of readers, is inappropriate for our publication."

TOTAL FITNESS, National Reporter Publications, Inc., 15115 S. 76th E. Ave., Bixby OK 74008. (918)366-4441. Editor: Anne H. Thomas. 95% freelance written. Magazine covers fitness topics of interest to women between the ages of 25-55 who are serious about their physical well-being. Magazine published 6-8 times times per year. Circ. 100,000. Pays on acceptance. Publishes ms an average of 6 months after acceptance. Byline given. Computer printout submissions acceptable; prefers letter-quality to dot-matrix. SASE. Reports in 2 months or less. Free writer's guidelines for SAE and 1 first class stamp.
Nonfiction: Special emphasis on exercise pieces (running, rowing, firming and conditioning arms, hips, calves, etc.); and personal experiences (almost anything can be written from the personal angle, but it must be well written). No fluff pieces or unsubstantiated health articles. "Articles are meant to inspire and/or instruct readers in the area of fitness through exercise." Buys 150 mss/year. Two or three paragraph query with clips of published work preferred. Length: 1,500-3,000 words. Pays $75-300.
Tips: "The writer has a better chance of breaking in at *Total Fitness* with short, lesser-paying articles and fillers because that's what we seem to be buying more of these days. Frequent mistakes made by writers are restating the obvious, wordiness and writing about something that is of great personal interest to the writer but has limited general appeal."

VIBRANT LIFE, A Christian Guide for Total Health, (formerly *Your Life and Health*), Review and Herald Publishing Assn., 55 W. Oak Ridge Dr., Hagerstown MD 21740. (301)791-7000. Editor: Ralph Blodgett. 95% freelance written. Bimonthly magazine covering family and health articles (especially with a Christian slant). Circ. 50,000. Pays on acceptance. "The average length of time between acceptance of a freelance-written manuscript and publication of the material depends upon the topics; some immediately used; others up to a year." Byline given. Offers 25% kill fee. Buys first serial rights, first North American serial rights and sometimes second serial (reprint) rights. Computer printout submissions acceptable; no dot-matrix. Submit seasonal/holiday material 6 months in advance. Photocopied (if clear) submissions OK. SASE. Reports in 2 months. Sample copy $1; free writer's guidelines.
Nonfiction: How-to (get out of debt, save time, have a better life); inspirational (articles showing how faith or trust in God helps people live better lives or have a happier family); and interview/profile (with personalities on

the family, marriage, health or church). "We seek practical articles promoting a happier home, better health, and a more fulfilled life. We especially like articles designed to enrich husband/wife and parent/child relationships, features on breakthroughs in medicine, and most aspects of health (physical, mental, emotional, and spiritual). Recently published articles include "10 Steps to a Better Marriage," "Put More Life into Your Life," and "Getting Motivated to Exercise." Buys 90-100 mss/year. Send complete ms. Length: 750-2,800 words. Pays $100-400.

Photos: Send photos with ms. Needs 35mm transparencies.

Tips: "*Vibrant Life* is published for the typical man/woman on the street, age 20-50. Therefore articles must be written in an interesting, easy-to-read style. Information must be reliable; no faddism. We are more conservative than other magazines in our field. Request a sample copy, and study the magazine and writer's guidelines."

WEIGHT WATCHERS MAGAZINE, 360 Lexington Ave., New York NY 10017. (212)370-0644. Editor-in-Chief: Linda Konner. Senior Editor: Cheryl Solimini. 50% freelance written. Monthly publication for those interested in weight loss and weight maintenance through sensible eating and health/nutrition guidance. Circ. 859,000. Buys first North American serial rights only. Buys 18-30 unsolicited mss/year. Pays on acceptance. Publishes ms an average of 6 months after acceptance. Computer printout submissions acceptable; prefers letter-quality to dot-matrix. Reports in 1 month. Sample copy and writer's guidelines $1.50.

Nonfiction: Subject matter should be related to food, fitness, health or weight loss, but not specific diets or recipes. Would like to see researched articles related to the psychological aspects of weight loss and control and suggestions for making the battle easier. Inspirational success stories of weight loss following the Weight Watchers Program or other *sensible* weight-loss regimens also accepted. Send queries with SASE. No full-length mss. Feature ideas, as well as before-and-after weight loss story ideas dealing either with celebrities or 'real people,' should be sent to: Cheryl Solimini, Senior Editor. Length: 1,500 words maximum. Pays $200-600. Sometimes pays the expenses of writers on assignment.

Tips: "It's rewarding giving freelancers the rough shape of how an article should look and seeing where they go with it. It's frustrating working with writers who don't pay enough attention to revisions that have been requested and who send back second drafts with a few changes. We rarely use fillers. Writers can break in if their writing is lively, tightly constructed, and shows an understanding of our audience. Writers too often include information that is too "sophisticated" or specialized for our readers; we prefer a more basic self-help or service-oriented approach. Material should be lively, but not 'cutesy.' "

WHOLE LIFE TIMES, Journal for Personal and Planetary Health, Whole Life Co., 18 Shepard St., Brighton MA 02135. (617)783-8030. Editor: Shelly Kellman. Managing Editor: Ingrid Schorr. Tabloid covering holistic health, environment, and including some material on world peace. Circ. 160,000. Pays 40-60 days after publication. Byline given. Offers 25% kill fee. Buys first North American serial rights, all rights, and second serial (reprint) rights, and makes work-for-hire assignments; depends on topic and author. Submit seasonal/holiday material 4 months in advance. Simultaneous queries, and simultaneous, photocopied, and previously published submissions OK. SASE. Reports in 2 months. Free sample copy and writer's guidelines.

Nonfiction: Book excerpts (health, environment, community activism); general interest (health-sciences, holistic health, environment, alternative economics and politics); how-to (exercise, relaxation, fitness, appropriate technology, outdoors); interview/profile (on assignment); and new product (health, music, spiritual, psychological, natural diet). No undocumented opinion or narrative. Buys 36-40 mss/year. Query with published clips. Length: 1,150-3,000 words. Pays $50-300.

Photos: Jeff Smith, photo editor. Reviews b&w contact sheets, any size b&w and color transparencies and any size prints. Model release and identification of subjects required. Buys one-time rights.

Columns/Departments: Ingrid Schorr and Barbara Bialick, column/department editors. Films, Books, Recipes, Herbs & Health, Nutrition, Whole Health Network, Living Lightly (appropriate technology), Peacefronts, News Views, Whole Life Person, Music, In the Market. Buys 45-55 mss/year. Query with published clips. Length: 150-1,000 words. Pays $25-80.

WHOLISTIC LIVING NEWS, Association for Holistic Living, Box 16346, San Diego CA 92116. (619)280-0317. Editor: Judith Horton. 50% freelance written. Bimonthly newspaper covering the holistic field from a holistic perspective. Circ. 65,000. Pays on publication. Publishes ms an average of 4 months after acceptance. Byline given. Not copyrighted. Buys first rights and second (reprint) rights to material originally published elsewhere. Submit seasonal/holiday material 6 months in advance. Simultaneous queries, and simultaneous, photocopied, and previously published submissions OK. Computer printout submissions acceptable. SASE. Reports in 1 month on queries; 2 months on mss. Sample copy $1.50; free writer's guidelines.

Nonfiction: General interest (holistic or new age overviews of a general topic); and how-to (taking responsibility for yourself—healthwise). No profiles, individual companies or personal experience. Buys 100 mss/year. Query with published clips. Length: 200-1500 words. Pays $5-20.

Photos: Send photos with query. Pays $7.50 for 5x7 b&w prints. Model release and identification of subjects required.

Tips: "Study the newspaper—the style is different from a daily. The articles generally provide helpful information on how to feel your best (mentally, spiritually, physically). Any of the sections are open to freelancers: Creative Living, Health & Fitness, Arts, Nutrition and Network (recent events and upcoming ones). One of the main aspects of the paper is to promote the concept of a holistic lifestyle and help people integrate it into their lives by taking simple steps on a daily basis."

‡**WORKOUT, For Fitness**, Stewart Communications, Inc., Suite 309, 18455 Burbank Blvd., Tarzana CA 91356. (818)345-6362. Editor: Tim Conaway. 25% freelance written. Monthly magazine of fitness-related service features. "*Workout* is interested in all aspects of the sport and fitness lifestyle: weight training, non-weight exercise programs, flexibility, athletic nutrition, diet and weight control, successful attitude and fitness motivation, stress management, sports medicine, equipment and devices, grooming, personal appearance, fashion, the fitness scene in metropolitan areas, celebrities and athletes who practice the fitness lifestyle, and developments on the fitness scene." Circ. 50,000. Pays on acceptance. Publishes ms an average of 4 months after acceptance. Byline given. Offers 33% kill fee. Buys all rights. Submit seasonal/holiday material 6 months in advance. Computer printout submissions acceptable; no dot-matrix. SASE. Reports in 3 weeks on queries; 1 month on mss. Free sample copy and writer's guidelines.
Nonfiction: How-to (exercise routines, diet/menu, stress mgt. techniques, etc.); interview/profile (celebrity or athlete who practices fitness lifestyles); and new product (fitness devices). No "why fitness is good" essay type pieces; current news expose/reportage on fitness; limited scope (regional, single device when several similar exist, etc.) Buys 30-40 mss/year. Query with published clips. Length; 1,000-2,000 words. Pays $200-300. Sometimes pays the expenses of writers on assignment.
Tips: Proposal must have topic, slant and brief description of service information—exercise program, diet or menu or recipes, relaxation techniques, etc. Clips should show ability to write on fitness topics—however, "expertise" in area not required, merely ability to tap expert's knowledge and communicate it. Nutrition, stress management and personality profiles (latter can earn higher fee) are areas most open to freelancers.

THE YOGA JOURNAL, California Yoga Teachers Association, 2054 University Ave., Berkeley CA 94704. (415)841-9200. Editor: Stephan Bodian. 75% freelance written. Bimonthly magazine covering yoga, holistic health, conscious living, spiritual practices, and nutrition. "We reach a middle-class, educated audience interested in self-improvement and higher consciousness." Circ. 25,000. Pays on publication. Byline given. Offers $35 kill fee. Buys first North American serial rights only. Submit seasonal/holiday material 4 months in advance. Simultaneous queries and photocopied submissions OK. SASE. Reports in 6 weeks on queries; 2 months on mss. Publishes ms an average of 6 months after acceptance. Sample copy $2.50; free writer's guidelines.
Nonfiction: Book excerpts; how-to (exercise, yoga, massage, etc.); inspirational (yoga or related); interview/profile; opinion; personal experience; photo feature; and travel (if about yoga). "Yoga is our main concern, but our principal features in each issue highlight other new age personalities and endeavors. Nothing too far-out and mystical. Prefer stories about Americans incorporating yoga, meditation, etc., into their normal lives." Buys 40 mss/year. Query. Length: 750-3,500 words. Pays $35-150.
Photos: Diane McCarney, art director. Send photos with ms. Pays $100-150 for color transparencies; $10-15 for 8x10 b&w prints. Model release (for cover only) and identification of subjects required. Buys one-time rights.
Columns/Departments: Forum; Food (vegetarian, text and recipes); Health; Music (reviews of new age music); and Book Reviews. Buys 12-15 mss/year. Pays $10-25.
Tips: "We always read submissions. We are very open to freelance material and want to encourage writers to submit to our magazine. We're looking for out-of-state contributors, particularly in the Midwest and east coast."

History

History repeats itself without being repetitive as editors of history magazines look for fresh accounts of past events. Some publications cover an era of a region; others deal with historic preservation. "America has flipped over residential restoration," points out the editor of *Historic Preservation*. "We'll want as many lively, anecdotal pieces about interesting restored houses that we can get our hands on—including first-person stories." Listed here are magazines written for historical collectors, genealogy enthusiasts, historic preservationists and researchers. The Hobby and Craft category lists antique and other history markets.

AMERICAN HERITAGE, 10 Rockefeller Plaza, New York NY 10020. Editor: Byron Dobell. 70% freelance written. Bimonthly. Circ. 140,000. Usually buys first North American or all rights. Byline given. Buys 30 uncommissioned mss/year. Pays on acceptance. Publishes ms an average of 1 year after acceptance. Before submitting, "check our 28-year index to see whether we have already treated the subject." Submit seasonal material 1 year in advance. Electronic submissions acceptable; (any disk—to be converted by us in house). Computer printout submissions acceptable; prefers letter-quality to dot-matrix. Reports in 1 month. Query. SASE. Writer's guidelines for SAE and 1 first class stamp.
Nonfiction: Wants "historical articles by scholars or journalists intended for intelligent lay readers rather than for professional historians." Emphasis is on authenticity, accuracy and verve. "Interesting documents, photographs and drawings are always welcome." Style should stress "readability and accuracy." Length: 1,500-5,000 words. Sometimes pays the expenses of writers on assignment.
Tips: "We have over the years published quite a few 'firsts' from young writers whose historical knowledge, research methods and writing skills met our standards. The scope and ambition of a new writer tell us a lot about his or her future usefulness to us. A major article gives us a better idea of the writer's value. Everything depends on the quality of the material. We don't really care whether the author is 20 and unknown, or 80 and famous."

AMERICAN HISTORY ILLUSTRATED, Box 8200, Harrisburg PA 17105. (717)657-9555. Editor: Ed Holm. 75% freelance written. "A magazine of cultural, social, military and political history published for a general audience." Monthly except July/August. Pays on acceptance. Publishes ms an average of 5-15 months after acceptance. Byline given. Buys all rights. Computer printout submissions acceptable; no dot-matrix. SASE required. Reports in 10 weeks on queries; 16 weeks on mss. Writer's guidelines on request for business size SAE and 1 first class stamp; sample copy $3 (amount includes 3rd class postage) or $2.50 (cover price for 1985) and SAE with 4 first class stamps.
Nonfiction: Regular features include Pages from an American Album (brief profiles of interesting personalities); Artifacts (stories behind historical objects); Portfolio (pictorial features on artists, photographers and graphic subjects); Digging Up History (coverage of recent archaeological and historical discoveries); and Testaments to the Past (living history articles on restored historical sites). "Material is presented on a popular rather than a scholarly level." Writers are encouraged to query before submitting ms. "Query letters should be limited to a concise 1-2 page proposal defining your article with an emphasis on its unique qualities." Buys 60 mss/year. Length: 1,000-3,000 words depending on type of article. Pays $100-400. Pays expenses of writers on assignment.
Photos: Occasionally buys 8x10 glossy prints with mss; welcomes suggestions for illustrations. Pays for the reproduced color illustrations that the author provides.
Tips: "Key prerequisites for publication are thorough research and accurate presentation, precise English usage and sound organization, a lively style, and a high level of human interest. The most frequent mistakes made by writers include failure to accurately research materials; failure to provide sources for checking by manuscripts editor; and failure to follow instruction on author guidelines. Editorializing is unacceptable. Author should not insert herself or himself into manuscript."

AMERICAN WEST, 3033 N. Campbell Ave., Tucson AZ 85719. Managing Editor: Mae Reid-Bills. Editor: Thomas W. Pew Jr. Published by the Buffalo Bill Memorial Association, Cody WY. Sponsored by the Western History Association. Bimonthly magazine covering all aspects of the American West, past and present. 80 pages. Mostly freelance written. Circ. 150,000. Pays within 1 month of acceptance. Buys first North American periodical rights, plus anthology rights. Byline given. Submit seasonal/holiday material 6 months in advance. Computer printout submissions acceptable; no dot-matrix. SASE. Reports in 2 months. Query first.
Nonfiction: Lively, nonacademic, but carefully researched and accurate articles of interest to the intelligent general reader, linking the present with the past of the American West; pictorial features (presenting the life and works of an outstanding Old Western painter or photographer). Length: 3,000 words.
Columns/Departments: Shorter regular features range from 850-1,000 words (best bets for unsolicited mss): Gourmet & Grub (historical background of a Western recipe); Shelters & Households (history behind a Western architectural form); Hidden Inns and Lost Trails (history behind Western landmarks and places to stay—no commercial promotion). Pays $200-800.
Photos: Submit with ms. Also Western Snapshots Yesterday and Today (submissions from readers of interesting old and contemporary photos "that tell a story of a bygone day"). Payment on acceptance.
Tips: "We strive to connect what the West was with what it is today and what it is likely to become. We seek dynamic, absorbing articles that reflect good research and thoughtful organization of details around a strong central story line. We define 'the West' as the United States west of the Mississippi River, and, in proper context, Canada and Mexico."

THE ARTILLERYMAN, (formerly *The Muzzleloading Artilleryman*), Century Publications, Inc., 3 Church St., Winchester MA 01890. (617)729-8100. Editor: C. Peter Jorgensen. Quarterly magazine covering antique artillery, fortifications, and crew-served weapons up to 1900 for competition shooters, collectors and living history reenactors using muzzleloading artillery; "emphasis on Revolutionary War and Civil War but includes everyone interested in pre-1900 artillery and fortifications, preservation, construction of replicas, etc." Circ. 3,100. Pays on publication. Byline given. Not copyrighted. Buys one-time rights. Simultaneous queries, and simultaneous, photocopied and previously published submissions OK. SASE. Reports in 3 weeks. Free sample copy and writer's guidelines.

Nonfiction: Historical/nostalgic; how-to (reproduce ordnance equipment/sights/implements tools/accessories, etc.); interview/profile; new product; opinion (must be accompanied by detailed background of writer and include references); personal experience; photo feature; technical (must have footnotes); and travel (where to find interesting antique cannon). Buys 24-30 mss/year. Send complete ms. Length: 300 words minimum. Pays $20-60.

Photos: Send photos with ms. Pays $5 for 5x7 and larger b&w prints. Captions and identification of subjects required.

Tips: "We regularly use freelance contributions for Places-to-Visit, Cannon Safety, The Workshop and Unit Profiles departments. Also need pieces on unusual cannon or cannon with a known and unique history."

BACKWOODSMAN MAGAZINE, The Publication for 20th Century Frontiersmen, Route 8, Box 579, Livingston TX 77351. Editor: Charlie Richie. 75% freelance written. Bimonthly magazine covering buckskinning, 19th century crafts, muzzleloading, homesteading and trapping. Circ. 5,000. Pays on publication. Publishes ms an average of 4 months after acceptance. Byline given. Buys first North American serial rights. Reports in 2 weeks on queries. Sample copy for $2.

Nonfiction: Historical/nostalgic (1780 to 1900); how-to (19th Century crafts); inspirational (wilderness survival); interview/profile (real-life backwoodsmen); new product (buckskinning field); and travel (American historical). "We want 19th century craft how-tos—mostly the simple kinds of everyday woodslore-type crafts." Buys 30-40 mss/year. Send complete ms. Length: 3-4 double-spaced pages. Pays $25 maximum.

Photos: "We prefer that at least one b&w photo or illustration be submitted with ms."

Fiction: Adventure (old time stories or wilderness camping) and historical (1780 to 1900). Length: 3-4 double-spaced pages.

Tips: "We publish articles by real backwoodsmen and prefer that the writer just be himself and not Hemingway."

BLUE & GRAY MAGAZINE, "For Those Who Still Hear the Guns," Blue & Gray Enterprises, Inc., 130 Galloway Rd. Galloway, OH 43119. (614)870-1861. Editor: David E. Roth. 65% freelance written. Bimonthly magazine on the Civil War period and current Civil War-related activities. "Our philosophy is color, quality and broad-based reporting. Included in this 'broad-based' reporting is the full range of Civil War-related topics, such as pure history articles, living history, relic hunting, collectibles, wargaming, book reviews, new discoveries, and tour guides of historical sites. Our distribution is international in scope and appeals to both a popular and scholarly market." Circ. 13,000 (with a 5% growth per issue). Pays on acceptance. Publishes ms an average of 6 months after acceptance. Byline given. Buys all rights. Submit seasonal/holiday material 6 months in advance. Computer printout submissions acceptable. SASE. Reporting time varies with query/manuscripts. Writer's guidelines for SAE with 1 first class stamp.

Nonfiction: Book excerpts (history); expose (history); historical/nostalgic; how-to (history, living history, relic hunting, etc.); interview/profile (Civil War descendant); opinion (history); personal experience (history, re-enacting, relic hunting, etc.); photo feature (history); technical (history, re-enacting, relic hunting, etc.); travel (Civil War sites); or article on Civil War history. Query with or without published clips or send complete ms. Length: 1,000-6,000 words. Pays $25-350.

Photos: State availability of photos, or send photos with query or mss. Captions and identification of subjects required. Buys non-exclusive rights for continued use.

Columns/Departments: Book Reviews, Living History, Wargaming, Relic Hunting, Controversy, Profile, etc. Query with or without published clips, or send complete ms. Length: 1,000-4,000 words. Pays $25-250.

Fiction: Historical fiction only. Query with or without published clips, or send complete ms. Length: 1,000-6,000 words. Pays $25-250.

Poetry: Robin P. Roth, poetry editor. Free verse, light verse and traditional. Length: up to 100 lines. Pays $10-25.

Tips: "Submit an appropriate Civil War-related ms with sources listed (footnotes preferred), and photos or photo suggestions. All areas of our publication are open to freelancers except Tour Guides which is somewhat restricted because of already firm commitments."

BRITISH HERITAGE, Incorporating British History Illustrated, Historical Times, Inc., 2245 Kohn Rd., Box 8200, Harrisburg PA 17105. (717)657-9555. Executive Editor: Gail Huganir. 80% freelance written. Bimonthly magazine covering British history and travel in the British Isles, Commonwealth countries and old Empire. "*British Heritage* aims to present aspects of Britain's history and culture in an entertaining and informative manner." Circ. 65,000. Pays on acceptance. Publishes ms an average of 1 year after acceptance. Buys all rights. Byline given. Makes work-for-hire assignments. Simultaneous queries OK. Computer printout submissions acceptable; no dot-matrix. SASE. Reports in 3 weeks on queries; 14 weeks on mss. Sample copy $4. Writer's guidelines for SAE and 1 first class stamp before submitting work.

Nonfiction: Historical (British history) and travel. "We insist on sound research for both historical and general interest articles and need information for the "For the Visitor" section, such as houses, museums, exhibitions, etc., associated with the main topic. We prefer a popular (but no cliches) to a scholarly style and advocate simplicity and clarity in articles. Because of the great range of subject matter in Britain's history, we cover significant rather than trivial aspects of people, issues, events and places. We have, however, no bias against the little-known or controversial subject *per se* as long as it is interesting." No fiction, personal experience articles or poetry. Buys 30 unsolicited mss/year. Query with clips of published work. Length: 1,000-3,000 words. Pays $65/1,000 words; $400 maximum.

Photos: State availability of photos or send photocopies. "We will consider fine quality photos only." Pays $20 maximum for color transparencies; $10 maximum for b&w prints. Captions and identification of subjects required. Buys one-time rights.

Tips: "No footnotes needed but sources are required. English style and spelling only. Grab the reader's attention as early as possible, and don't be afraid to use humor. We look for accurate research written in a flowing, interesting style with excellent opportunities for illustration. Provide a list of further reading. There will be increased emphasis in the year ahead on shops, stately homes and old buildings, museums, old customs, inns and other areas of tourist interest. We're looking for both 1,000 and 2,000 word pieces—if they're well-written the writer has an equal chance with either short articles or major features."

‡**CANADIAN WEST**, (formerly *History of the Canadian West*), Box 3399, Langley, British Columbia V3A 4R7 Canada. (604)576-6561. Editor-in-Chief: T.W. Paterson. 80-100% freelance written. Emphasizes pioneer history, primarily of British Columbia, Alberta and the Yukon. Quarterly magazine; 40 pages. Circ. 5,000. Pays on publication. Publishes ms an average of 2 months after acceptance. Buys first North American serial rights. Phone queries OK. Computer printout submissions acceptable; prefers letter-quality to dot-matrix. Previously published submissions OK. SASE. Reports in 2 months. Sample copy $1. Writer's guidelines for 32¢ Canadian postage.

Nonfiction: How-to (related to gold panning and dredging); historical (pioneers, shipwrecks, massacres, battles, exploration, logging, Indians and railroads). No American locale articles. Buys 28 mss/year. Submit complete ms. Length: 2,000-3,500 words. Pays $100-300.

Photos: All mss must include photos or other artwork. Submit photos with ms. Payment included in price of article. Captions preferred. "Photographs are kept for future reference with the right to re-use. However, we do not forbid other uses, generally, as these are historical prints from archives."

Columns/Departments: Open to suggestions for new columns/departments.

CIVIL WAR TIMES ILLUSTRATED, 2245 Kohn Rd., Box 8200, Harrisburg PA 17105. (717)657-9555. Editor: John E. Stanchak. Magazine published monthly except July and August. Circ. 120,000. Pays on acceptance. Buys all rights, first rights or one-time rights, or makes work-for-hire assignments. Submit seasonal/holiday material 1 year in advance. SASE. Reports in 2 weeks on queries; 3 months on mss. Sample copy $2; free writer's guidelines.

Nonfiction: Profile, photo feature, and Civil War historical material. "Positively no fiction or poetry." Buys 20 mss/year. Recent article example: "Henry Starley's Two-Sided Adventure: Explorer and Civil War Soldier" (June 1985). Length: 2,500-5,000 words. Query. Pays $75-450.

Photos: Jeanne Collins, art director. State availability. Pays $5-50 for 8x10 b&w glossy prints and copies of Civil War photos; $400-500 for 4-color cover photos; and $100-250 for color photos for interior use.

Tips: "We're very open to new submissions. Querying us after reading several back issues, then submitting illustration and art possibilities along with the query letter is the best 'in.' Never base the narrative solely on family stories or accounts. Submissions must be written in a popular style but based on solid academic research. Manuscripts are required to have marginal source annotations."

‡**FRONTIER TIMES**, Western Periodicals, Inc., Box 2107, Stillwater OK 74075. (405)743-3370. Editor: John Joerschke. 100% freelance written. Magazine on Western American history before 1920. *Frontier Times* alternates months with *True West*. Circ. 100,000 (combined). Pays on acceptance. Publishes ms an average of 4 months after acceptance. Byline given. Buys first North American serial rights. Submit seasonal/holiday material 6 months in advance. Simultaneous queries OK. Computer printout submissions acceptable; prefers letter-quality to dot-matrix. SASE. Reports in 1 month on queries; 6 weeks on mss. Sample copy $1; writer's guidelines for #10 SAE and 1 first class stamp.

Nonfiction: Historical/nostalgic, how-to, photo feature, travel, and western movies. "We do not want rehashes of worn-out stories, historical fiction, or history written in a fictional style." Buys 200 mss/year. Query. Length: 500-4,500 words. Pays $25-450.

Photos: Send photos with accompanying query or manuscript. Pays $10-25 for 5x8 b&w prints. Identification of subjects required. Buys one-time rights.

Columns/Departments: Marcia Simpson, assistant editor. Western Roundup—200-300 short articles on historically oriented places to go and things to do in the West with one b&w print. Buys 12-16/year. Send complete ms. Length: 200-300 words. Pays $35.

Tips: "Do original research on fresh topics. Stay away from controversial subjects unless you are truly knowledgeable in the field. Read our magazines and follow our writers' guidelines. A freelancer is most likely to break in with us by submitting thoroughly researched, lively prose on relatively obscure topics. First person accounts rarely fill our needs."

‡**MILITARY HISTORY**, Empire Press, 485 Carlisle Dr., Herndon VA 22070. (703)471-6193. Editorial Director: Carl Gnam. 95% freelance written. Bimonthly magazine covering all military history of the world. "We strive to give the general reader accurate, highly readable, often narrative popular history, richly accompanied by period art." Estab. 1984. Pays on publication. Byline given. Buys first North American serial rights and first international rights. Submit seasonal/holiday material 6 months in advance. Photocopied submissions OK. Computer printout submissions acceptable; prefers letter-quality to dot-matrix. SASE. Reports in 1 month on queries; 2 months on mss. Sample copy $3; writer's guidelines for SAE with 1 first class stamp.

Nonfiction: Book excerpts (military history book reviews); historical/nostalgic; humor (if appropriate); interview/profile (military figures of commanding interest); personal experience (only occasionally); and travel (with military history of the place). Buys 18 mss, plus 6 interviews/year. Query with published clips. "To propose an article, submit a short, self-explanatory query summarizing the story proposed, its highlights and/or significance. State also your own expertise, access to sources or proposed means of developing the pertinent information." Length: 4,000 words. Pays $400 minimum.

Columns/Departments: Espionage, weaponry, personality, travel, books—all relating to military history. Buys 24 mss/year. Query with published clips. Length: 2,000 words. Pays $200.

Tips: "Read the magazine, discover our style, and avoid subjects already covered. Pick stories with strong art possibilities (*real* art and photos), send photocopies, tell us where to get them. Avoid historical overview, focus upon an event with appropriate and accurate context. Provide bibliography. Tell the story in popular but elegant style."

OLD WEST, Western Periodicals, Inc., Box 2107, Stillwater OK 74076. (405)743-3370. Quarterly magazine. Byline given. See *True West*.

PRESERVATION NEWS, National Trust for Historic Preservation, 1785 Massachusetts Ave. NW, Washington DC 20016. (202)673-4072. Editor: Michael Leccese. Managing Editor: Arnold M. Berke. 10% freelance written. A monthly tabloid covering preservation of historic buildings in the US. "We cover efforts and controversies involving historic buildings and districts. Most entries are news stories, features or essays." Circ. 160,000. Pays on acceptance. Publishes ms an average of 1 month after acceptance. Byline given. Offers variable kill fee. Not copyrighted. Buys one-time rights. Simultaneous queries, and photocopied and previously published submissions OK. Computer printout submissions acceptable; prefers letter-quality to dot-matrix. SASE. Reports in 1 month on queries. Sample copy 50¢ and 42¢ postage; writer's guidelines for SAE and 1 first class stamp.

Nonfiction: Historical/nostalgic, humor, interview/profile, opinion, personal experience, photo feature and travel. Buys 12 mss/year. Query with published clips. Length: 500-1,000 words. Pays $75-200. Sometimes pays the expenses of writers on assignment.

Photos: State availability of photos with query or ms. Reviews b&w contact sheet. Pays $25-100. Identification of subjects required.

Columns/Departments: "We seek an urban affairs reporter who can give a new slant on development conflict throughout the United States and a columnist for people interested in various aspects of historic houses." Buys 6 mss/year. Query with published clips. Length: 600-1,000 words. Pays $75-200.

Tips: "The writer has a better chance of breaking in at our publication with short articles and fillers because we like to try them out first." Don't submit dull articles that lack compelling details.

TRUE WEST, Western Periodicals, Inc., Box 2107, Stillwater OK 74076. (405)743-3370. Editor: John Loerschke. 100% freelance written. Magazine on Western American history before 1920. *True West* alternates months with *Frontier Times*. "We want reliable research on significant historical topics written in lively prose for an informed general audience." Circ. 100,000 (combined). Pays on acceptance. Publishes ms an average of 4 months after acceptance. Byline given. Buys first North American serial rights. Submit seasonal/holiday material 6 months in advance. Simultaneous queries OK. Computer printout submissions acceptable; prefers letter-quality to dot-matrix. SASE. Reports in 1 month on queries; 6 weeks on mss. Sample copy for $1; writer's guidelines for #10 SAE and 1 first class stamp.

Nonfiction: Historical/nostalgic, how-to, photo feature, travel, and western movies. "We do not want rehashes of worn-out stories, historical fiction, or history written in a fictional style. Buys 200 mss/year. Query. Length: 500-4,500 words. Pays $25-450.

Photos: Send photos with accompanying query or manuscript. Pays $10-25 for b&w prints. Identification of subjects required. Buys one-time rights.

Columns/Departments: Marcia Simpson, assistant editor. Western Roundup—200-300 short articles on historically oriented places to go and things to do in the West with one b&w print. Buys 12-16/year. Send complete ms. Length: 200-300 words. Pays $35.

Tips: "Do original research on fresh topics. Stay away from controversial subjects unless you are truly knowledgeable in the field. Read our magazines and follow our writers' guidelines. A freelancer is most likely to break in with us by submitting thoroughly researched, lively prose on relatively obscure topics. First person accounts rarely fill our needs."

VIRGINIA CAVALCADE, Virginia State Library, Richmond VA 23219. (804)786-2312. Primarily for readers with an interest in Virginia history. 90% freelance written. Quarterly magazine; 48 pages. Circ. 12,000. Buys all rights. Byline given. Buys 12-15 mss/year. Pays on acceptance. Publishes ms an average of 10 months after acceptance. Rarely considers simultaneous submissions. Submit seasonal material 15-18 months in advance. Reports in 1-3 months. Query. Computer printout submissions acceptable; prefers letter-quality to dotmatrix. SASE. Sample copy $2; free writer's guidelines.

Nonfiction: "We welcome readable and factually accurate articles that are relevant to some phase of Virginia history. Art, architecture, literature, education, business, technology and transportation are all acceptable subjects, as well as political and military affairs. Articles must be based on thorough, scholarly research. We require footnotes but do not publish them. Any period from the age of exploration to the mid-20th century, and any geographical section or area of the state may be represented. Must deal with subjects that will appeal to a broad readership, rather than to a very restricted group or locality. Articles must be suitable for illustration, although it is not necessary that the author provide the pictures. If the author does have pertinent illustrations or knows their location, the editor appreciates information concerning them." Length: 3,500 words. Pays $100.

Photos: Uses 8x10 b&w glossy prints; color transparencies should be at least 4x5.

Tips: "*Cavalcade* employs a narrative, anecdotal style. Too many submissions are written for an academic audience or are simply not sufficiently gripping."

Hobby and Craft

If you use your writing craft to describe a hobby or craft you know, editors will be eager to get your manuscripts. Craftspeople always need new ideas. As for collectors, they need to know what is most valuable and why. Antique magazine editors, for instance, want the latest research. Collectors, do-it-yourselfers, and craftspeople look to these magazines for inspiration and information. Publications covering antiques and miniatures are also listed here. Publications for electronics and radio hobbyists are included in the Science classification.

AMERICAN BOOK COLLECTOR, 274 Madison Ave., New York NY 10016. (212)685-2250. Editor: Bernard McTigue. 100% freelance written. Bimonthly magazine on book collecting from the 15th century to the present for individuals, rare book dealers, librarians, and others interested in books and bibliomania. Circ. 3,500. Pays on publication. Publishes ms an average of 3 months after acceptance. Submit seasonal material 3 months in advance. Photocopied and previously published submissions OK. Electronic submissions OK if IBM PC, "others by special arrangement." Computer printout submissions acceptable; prefers letter-quality to dot-matrix. SASE. Reports in 6 weeks. Sample copy and writer's guidelines for $3.50.

Nonfiction: General interest (some facet of book collecting: category of books; taste and technique; artist; printer; binder); interview (prominent book collectors; producers of contemporary fine and limited editions; scholars; librarians); and reviews of exhibitions. Buys 5-10 unsolicited mss/year. "We absolutely require queries with clips of previously published work." Length: 1,500-4,500 words. Pays 5¢/word.

Photos: State availability of photos. Prefers b&w glossy prints of any size. Offers no additional payment for photos accompanying ms. Captions and model release required. Buys one-time rights.

Columns/Departments: Contact editor. Reviews of books on book collecting, and gallery exhibitions.

Tips: "Our emphasis is subject matter and we trust that newcomers are just as capable as veterans. Query should include precise description of proposed article accompanied by description of author's background plus indication of extent of illustrations. The most frequent mistakes made by writers in completing an article for us are failure to focus on books and too much 'gee whiz'."

AMERICAN CLAY EXCHANGE, Page One Publications, Box 2674, La Mesa CA 92041. (619)697-5922. Editor: Susan N. Cox. Biweekly newsletter on any subjects relating to American made pottery—old or new—

with an emphasis on antiques and collectibles for collectors, buyers and sellers of American made pottery, earthenware, china, etc. Pays on publication. "We sometimes pay on acceptance if we want the manuscript badly. If article has not been printed within three months, we will pay for it anyway." Byline given. Buys all rights or first rights "if stated when manuscript submitted." Submit seasonal/holiday material 4 months in advance. Computer printout submissions acceptable; no dot-matrix. SASE. Reports in 1 month on queries; 2 months on mss. Sample copy $1.50; free writer's guidelines.

Nonfiction: Book reviews (on books pertaining to American made pottery, china, earthenware); historical/nostalgic (on museums and historical societies in the U.S. if they handle pottery, etc.); how-to (identify pieces, clean, find them); and interviews profile (if artist is up-and-coming). No "I found a piece of pottery for 10¢ at a flea market" types. Buys 30 ms/year. Query or send complete ms. Length: 1,000 words maximum. Pays $125 maximum.

Photos: Janet Culver, photo editor. Send photos with ms. Pays $5 for b&w prints. Captions required. Buys all rights; "will consider one-time rights."

Tips: "Know the subject being written about, including marks and values of pieces found. Telling a reader what 'marks' are on pieces is most essential. The best bet is to write a short (200-300 word) article with a few photos and marks. We are a small company willing to work with writers who have good, salable ideas and know our product. Any article that deals effectively with a little-known company or artist during the 1900-1950 era is most sought after. We have added a section devoted to dinnerware, mostly from the 1900-1950 era—same guidelines."

AMERICANA, 29 W. 38th St., New York NY 10018. (212)398-1550. Editor: Michael Durham. 90% freelance written. Bimonthly magazine featuring contemporary uses of the American past for "people who like to adapt historical ways to modern living." Circ. 400,000. Pays on acceptance. Publishes ms an average of 9 months after acceptance. Byline given. Buys all rights. Submit seasonal material 6 months in advance. Computer printout submissions acceptable; prefers letter-quality to dot-matrix. SASE. Reports in 6 weeks. Sample copy $2.50; writer's guidelines for SAE with 1 first class stamp.

Nonfiction: General interest (crafts, architecture, cooking, gardening, restorations, antiques, preservation, decorating, collecting, people who are active in these fields and museums); and travel (to historic sites, restored villages, hotels, inns, and events celebrating the past). "Familiarize yourself with the magazine. You must write from first-hand knowledge, not just historical research. Send a well thought out idea. Send a few snapshots of a home restoration or whatever you are writing about." Especially needs material for Christmas and Thanksgiving issues. Buys 8 mss/issue. Query with clips of previously published work. Length: 2,000 words minimum. Pays $400 minimum. Pays expenses of writers on assignments.

Columns/Departments: On Exhibit (short piece on an upcoming exhibit, $75-500); How-to (usually restoration or preservation of an historical object, 2,000 words, $400); Sampler (newsy items to fit the whole magazine, 500 words, $75); and In the Days Ahead (text and calendar of events such as antique shows or craft shows, 1,000 words plus listing, $400).

Tips: "One of the most frequent mistakes made by writers in completing an article assignment for us is writing articles based too much on research. We are not a straight history magazine. It's rewarding to discover an able writer with whom we can establish an on-going relationship."

THE ANTIQUARIAN, Box 798, Huntington NY 11743. (516)271-8990. Editor-in-Chief: Marguerite Cantine. Managing Editor: Elizabeth Kilpatrick. Emphasizes antiques and 19th-century or earlier art. Monthly tabloid. 10% freelance written. Circ. 15,000. Pays on publication. Publishes ms an average of 2 months after acceptance. Buys all rights. Pays 10% kill fee. Byline given. Submit seasonal/holiday material 3 months in advance. Computer printout submissions acceptable; prefers letter-quality to dot-matrix. SASE with proper postage. Reports in 6 weeks. Sample copy for 12x15½ SASE with $1.25 postage attached. No checks.

Nonfiction: How-to (refinish furniture, repair glass, restore old houses, paintings, rebind books, resilver glass, etc.); general interest (relations of buyers and dealers at antique shows/sales, auction reports); historical (data, personal and otherwise, on famous people in the arts and antiques field); interview; photo feature (auctions, must have caption on item including selling price); profile (wants articles around movie stars and actors who collect antiques; query); and travel (historical sites of interest in New York, New Jersey, Connecticut, Pennsylvania and Delaware). Wants concise articles, accurate research; no material on art deco, collectibles, anything made after 1900, cutesy things to 'remake' from antiques, or flea markets and crafts shows. Buys 6 mss/year. Submit complete ms. Length: 200-2,000 words. Pays 3¢/word.

Photos: Pays 50¢-$1 for 3½x5 glossy b&w prints. Captions required. Buys all rights. Model release required.

Tips: "Don't write an article unless you *love* this field. Write as though you were carrying on a nice conversation with your mother. No pretentions. No superiority. It's frustrating when freelancers don't read, follow instructions, or send an SASE, call the office and *demand* answers to questions, or act unprofessionally. But once in a blue moon they do get a totally fresh idea."

ANTIQUE MONTHLY, Boone, Inc., Drawer 2, Tuscaloosa AL 35402. (205)345-0272. Editor/Publisher: Gray D. Boone. Associate Publisher: Anita G. Mason. Senior Editor: Cindy Graff Hobson. 20% freelance written. Monthly tabloid covering art, antiques, and major museum shows. "More than half of our audience are college graduates, over 27% have post-graduate degrees; fifty-nine percent are in $35,000 and over income bracket. Average number of years readers have been collecting art/antiques is 20.5." Circ. 65,100. Pays on publication. Publishes ms an average of 4 months after acceptance. Buys all rights. Submit seasonal/holiday material 2 months in advance. Photocopied submissions OK. Computer printout submissions acceptable. SASE. Reports in 1 month on queries and mss. Sample copy 90¢.

Nonfiction: Discussions of current trends in antiques marketplace; coverage of antiques shows and auctions; profiles of important collectors and dealers; descriptions of decorative arts exhibitions; and book reviews. Recent article example: "Federal furniture brought high prices at auction" (March 1985). No personal material. Buys 6-10 unsolicited mss/year. Length: 1,000-1,500 words. Pays $125 minimum/article. Sometimes pays expenses of writers on assignment.

Photos: State availability of photos. Prefers color transparencies or slides and 5x7 b&w prints. "We rarely pay for photos; usually we pay only for costs incurred by the writer, and this must be on prior agreement." Captions required.

Tips: "Freelancers are important because they offer the ability to cover stories that regular staff and correspondents cannot cover. A story is more likely to interest the editors if there is a timely news peg—if the story is related to a recent or current event or trend in the antiques world."

ANTIQUE REVIEW, (formerly *Ohio Antique Review*), Box 538, Worthington OH 43085. Managing Editor: Charles Muller. (614)885-9757. 60% freelance written. For an antique-oriented readership, "generally well-educated, interested in folk art and other early American items." Monthly tabloid. Circ. 8,000 in all 50 states. Pays on publication date assigned at time of purchase. Publishes ms an average of 3 months after acceptance. Buys first North American serial rights, and second (reprint) rights to material originally published elsewhere. Byline given. Phone queries OK. Submit seasonal/holiday material 3 months in advance. Simultaneous, photocopied and previously published submissions OK. Computer printout submissions acceptable; prefers letter-quality to dot-matrix. SASE. Reports in 1 month. Free sample copy and writer's guidelines.

Nonfiction: "The articles we desire concern history and production of furniture, pottery, china, and other antiques of the period prior to the 1880s. In some cases, contemporary folk art items are acceptable. We are also interested in reporting on antique shows and auctions with statements on conditions and prices. We do not want articles on contemporary collectibles." Buys 5-8 mss/issue. Query with clips of published work. Query should show "author's familiarity with antiques and an interest in the historical development of artifacts relating to early America." Length: 200-2,000 words. Pays $80-125. Sometimes pays the expenses of writers on assignment.

Photos: State availability of photos with query. Payment included in ms price. Uses 5x7 or larger glossy b&w prints. Captions required. Articles with photographs receive preference.

Tips: "Give us a call and let us know of specific interests. We are more concerned with the background in antiques than in writing abilities. The writing can be edited, but the knowledge imparted is of primary interest. A frequent mistake is being too general, not becoming deeply involved in the topic and its reserach."

THE ANTIQUE TRADER WEEKLY, Box 1050, Dubuque IA 52001. (319)588-2073. Editor: Kyle D. Husfloen. 25% freelance written. For collectors and dealers in antiques and collectibles. Weekly newspaper; 90-120 pages. Circ. 90,000. Publishes ms an average of 1 year after acceptance. Buys all rights. Buys about 60 mss/year. Payment at beginning of month following publication. Photocopied and simultaneous submissions OK. Computer printout submissions acceptable; no dot-matrix. Submit seasonal/holiday material 4 months in advance. Query or submit complete ms. SASE. Sample copy 50¢; free writer's guidelines.

Nonfiction: "We invite authoritative and well-researched articles on all types of antiques and collectors' items and in-depth stories on specific types of antiques and collectibles. No human interest stories. We do not pay for brief information on new shops opening or other material printed as service to the antiques hobby." Pays $5-50 for feature articles; $50-150 for feature cover stories.

Photos: Submit a liberal number of good b&w photos to accompany article. Uses 35mm or larger color transparencies for cover. Offers no additional payment for photos accompanying mss.

Tips: "Send concise, polite letter stating the topic to be covered in the story and the writer's qualifications. No 'cute' letters rambling on about some 'imaginative' story idea. Writers who have a concise yet readable style and know their topic are always appreciated. I am most interested in those who have personal collecting experience or can put together a knowledgable and informative feature after interviewing a serious collector/authority."

‡ANTIQUING HOUSTON, A Collectors and Buyers Journal, Tabers' Commercial Art Studios, Box 40734, Houston TX 77240. (713)465-9842. Editor: William B. Taber. Managing Editor: Susan C. Taber. 30% freelance written. Bimonthly tabloid "devoted to promoting, enlightening, and informing the public about antiques and collectibles." Estab. 1984. Circ. 10,000. Pays on acceptance. Publishes ms an average of 2 months after acceptance. Not copyrighted. Buys first North American serial rights and second serial (reprint) rights. Submit seasonal/holiday material 4 months in advance. Previously published work OK. SASE. Reports in 1 month. Free sample copy and writer's guidelines.

Nonfiction: Book excerpts; exposé (fake antiques); general interest; historical/nostalgic; how-to (old-time methods); humor; inspirational; interview/profile (collectors, collections, authorities on antiques); new product (care of antiques); opinion; personal experience; photo feature; technical (repair of and information about antiques and collectibles, antique dating); and travel. All material must relate to antiques and collectibles. Buys 20 mss/year. Send complete ms. Length: 300-600 words; feature articles, 600-1,000 words. Pays $5-50.

Photos: Send photos with ms. Pays $3-10 for b&w contact sheet or 3½x5 b&w prints. Captions, model release required.

Columns/Departments: Recent Finds (antique news); antique recipes (old-time recipes and household hints); care for column (care and presentation of antiques). Buys 12 mss/year. Send complete ms. Length: 300-500 words. Pays $5-30.

Fiction: Fantasy (regarding antiques) and humorous (regarding antiques). Buys 3 mss/year. Send complete ms. Length: 300-1,000 words. Pays $5-50.

Poetry: Buys 3 poems/year. Submit maximum 3 poems. Length: 4-20 lines. Pays $5-15.

Fillers: Anecdotes and short humor. Buys 15/year. Length: 4-15 lines. Pays $5-15.

Tips: "The writer sometimes has a better chance of breaking in at our publication with short articles and fillers. Major features require superior writing. Fillers and articles may be accurate, technical, interesting, or humorous, but not superior."

‡**THE ARCHTOPHILE**, Bear-in-Mind, Inc., 20 Beharrell St., Concord MA 01742. (617)369-1167. Editor: Fran Lewis. Managing Editor: Barbara Fivek. 25% freelance written. Quarterly newsletter on Teddy Bears and Teddy Collecting. For adult Teddy Bear collectors who are interested in heartwarming or poignant tales about what Teddys mean to them or how they have helped to share feelings or comfort them in times of needs. Circ. 10,000. Pays on publication. Publishes ms an average of 4 months after acceptance. Byline given. Buys first North American serial rights. Submit seasonal/holiday material 6 months in advance. Simultaneous, photocopied and previously published submissions OK. Computer printout submissions acceptable; prefers letter-quality to dot-matrix. SASE. Reports in 2 months. Sample copy for SAE and 1 first class stamp.

Nonfiction: Book excerpts, historical/nostalgic, humor, inspirational, interview/profile, personal experience and photo feature. Buys 12-24 mss/year. Send complete ms. Length: 300-500 words. Pays 4-6¢/word.

Fiction: Fantasy and humorous. Buys 12-24 mss/year. Send complete ms. Length: 300-500 words. Pays 4-6¢/word.

Poetry: Avant-garde, free verse, haiku, light verse and traditional. Buys 4 poems/year. Submit maximum 2 poems. Length: 6-10 lines. Pays $10-15.

Fillers: Jokes, gags, anecdotes, short humor and newsbreaks—all Teddy related. Buys 8-10/year. Length: 15-30 words. Pays $5-10.

Tips: Articles, and fiction and poetry submissions must be Teddy Bear related.

BANK NOTE REPORTER, Krause Publications, 700 E. State St., Iola WI 54990. (715)445-2214. Editor: Courtney L. Coffing. 50% freelance written. Monthly tabloid for advanced collectors of U.S. and world paper money. Circ. 4,250. Pays on publication. Publishes ms an average of 4 months after acceptance. Byline given. Buys first North American serial rights. Photocopied submissions acceptable. Computer printout submissions acceptable; prefers letter-quality to dot-matrix. SASE. Reports in 2 weeks. Free sample copy.

Nonfiction: "We review articles covering any phase of paper money collecting including investing, display, storage, history, art, story behind a particular piece of paper money and the business of paper money." No news items. "Our staff covers the hard news." Buys 4 mss/issue. Send complete ms. Length: 500-3,000 words. Pays 3¢/word to first-time contributors; negotiates fee for later articles. Sometimes pays the expenses of writers on assignment.

Photos: Pays $5 minimum for 5x7 b&w glossy prints. Captions and model release required.

Tips: "The writer has a better chance of breaking in at our publication with short articles and fillers due to the technical nature of the subject matter and sophistication of our readers. The most frequent mistake made by writers is not being familiar with the subject matter."

THE BLADE MAGAZINE, Box 22007, Chattanooga TN 37422. Editor: J. Bruce Voyles. 90% freelance written. For knife enthusiasts who want to know as much as possible about quality knives and edged weapons. Bimonthly magazine. Pays on publication. Buys all rights. Submit seasonal/holiday material 6 months in advance. Previously published submissions OK. Computer printout submissions acceptable; no dot-matrix. SASE. Reports in 2 months. Sample copy $2.75.

Nonfiction: Historical (on knives and weapons); how-to; interview (knifemakers); new product; nostalgia; personal experience; photo feature; profile and technical. No poetry. Buys 75 unsolicited mss/year. "We evaluate complete manuscripts and make our decision on that basis." Length: 1,000-2,000 words. Pays 5¢/word minimum.

Photos: Send photos with ms. Pays $5 for 8x10 b&w glossy prints, $25-75 for 35mm color transparencies. Captions required.

Tips: "The ideal article for us concerns a knife maker or a historical article on an old factory—full of well-researched long lost facts with entertaining anecdotes, or a piece bringing out the romance, legend, and love of man's oldest tool—the knife. Read the publication beforehand and save us both a lot of wasted time."

CHRISTMAS ALMANAC/CHRISTMAS CROCHET, Harris Publication, 1115 Broadway, New York NY 10010. (212)434-4239. Editor: Barbara Jacksier. An annual holiday crafts magazine covering home-style, country ideas plus instructions on how to do them. Circ. 500,000. Pays on publication. Byline given. Buys one-time rights. Submit seasonal/holiday material 10 months in advance. Computer printout submissions acceptable. SASE. Reports in 2 months.
Nonfiction: How-to (holiday craft or decorating ideas). Buys 30-40 craft projects/year. Send complete ms. Pays $25-150.
Photos: Send photos with accompanying query or ms. Pays $10-20 for 5x7 b&w prints and color transparencies. Buys one-time rights.

‡**THE COIN ENTHUSIAST'S JOURNAL,** (formerly *The Indicator Newsletter*), Box 55, Palos Verdes Estates CA 90274. (213)378-4850. Editor: William J. Cook. 50% freelance written. Monthly newsletter covering numismatics (coin collecting) and bullion trading. "Our purpose is to give readers information to help them make sound investment decisions in the areas we cover and to help them get more enjoyment out of their hobby." Estab. 1984. Circ. 2,000+. Pays on publication. Publishes ms an average of 2 months after acceptance. Byline given. Offers $50-100 kill fee. Buys all rights. Submit seasonal/holiday material 2 months in advance. Simultaneous queries and simultaneous and photocopied submissions OK. Electronic submissions OK on Apple IIe, but requires hard copy. Computer printout submissions acceptable; prefers letter-quality to dot-matrix. SASE. Reports in 2 weeks on queries; 2 weeks on mss. Sample copy for SAE and 2 first class stamps; writer's guidelines for SAE and 1 first class stamp.
Nonfiction: How-to (make money from your hobby and be a better trader); opinion (what is the coin market going to do?); personal experience (insiders' "tricks of the trade"); and technical (why are coin prices going up [or down]?). No "crystal ball" predictions, i.e., "I see silver going up to $200 per ounce by mid-1986." Query with published clips. Length: 750-2,000 words. Buys 36 mss/year. Pays $100-300; fees negotiable. Also looking for "staff writers" who will submit material each month.
Photos: State availability of photos with query. Pays $5-25 for b&w prints. Buys one-time rights.
Tips: "We run very few short articles. Be able to show an in-depth knowledge and experience in numismatics and also show the ability to be creative in developing new ideas for the coin industry." Potential topics include gold and silver ratios, futures markets, advantages of buying silver coins instead of silver bars, what influences current prices, how taxes may affect the collector. "The most frequent mistakes made by writers in completing an article assignment for us are too much 'story telling' and not enough 'hard facts' or ideas. They give more background than is relevent or needed for the point they want to make."

COINS, Krause Publications, 700 E. State St., Iola WI 54990. (715)445-2214. Editor: Arlyn G. Sieber. Monthly magazine about U.S. and foreign coins for all levels of collectors, investors and dealers. Circ. 130,000. Average issue includes 8 features.
Nonfiction: "We'd like to see articles on any phase of the coin hobby; collection, investing, displaying, history, art, the story behind the coin, unusual collections, profiles on dealers and the business of coins." No news items. "Our staff covers the hard news." Buys 8 mss/issue. Send complete ms. Computer printout submissions acceptable; prefers letter-quality to dot-matrix. Length: 500-5,000 words. Pays 3¢/word to first-time contributors; fee negotiated for later articles.
Photos: Pays $5 minimum for b&w prints. Pays $25 minimum for 35mm color transparencies used. Captions and model release required. Buys first rights.

COLLECTOR EDITIONS QUARTERLY, Collector Communications Corp., 170 5th Ave., New York NY 10010. Editor: R. C. Rowe. 35% freelance written. Quarterly magazine for collectors, mostly aged 30-65 in any rural or suburban, affluent area; reasonably well-educated. Quarterly. Circ. 80,000. Rights purchased vary with author and material. Buys first North American serial rights, and sometimes second serial (reprint) rights. Buys 15-30 mss/year. "First assignments are always done on a speculative basis." Pays on publication. Publishes ms an average of 6 months after acceptance. Photocopied submissions OK. Computer printout submissions acceptable; no dot-matrix. Query with sample photos. Reports in 2 months. SASE. Sample copy $2; writer's guidelines for SAE and 1 first class stamp.
Nonfiction: "Short features about collecting, written in tight, newsy style. We specialize in contemporary (postwar) collectibles. Particularly interested in items affected by scarcity; focus on glass and ceramics. Values for pieces being written about should be included." Informational, how-to, interview, profile, expose, and nostalgia. Length: 500-2,500 words. Pays $100-300. Columns cover stamps and coins, porcelain, glass and auction reports. Length: 750 words. Pays $75. Sometimes pays expenses of writers on assignment.
Photos: B&w and color photos purchased with accompanying ms with no additional payment. Captions are re-

quired. "We want clear, distinct, full-frame images that say something."
Tips: "Unfamiliarity with the field is the most frequent mistake made by writers in completing an article for us."

COLLECTORS NEWS & THE ANTIQUE REPORTER, 606 8th St., Box 156, Grundy Center IA 50638. (319)824-5456. Editor: Linda Kruger. 20% freelance written. A monthly tabloid covering antiques, collectibles and nostalgic memorabilia. Circ. 22,000. Publishes ms an average of 1 year after acceptance. Buys 100 mss/year. Byline given. Pays on publication. Buys first rights and makes work-for-hire assignments. Submit seasonal material (holidays) 3 months in advance. Computer printout submissions acceptable; no dot-matrix. SASE. Reports in 2 weeks on queries; 6 weeks on mss. Sample copy for $1.50 and 9x12 SAE; free writer's guidelines.
Nonfiction: General interest (any subject re: collectibles, antique to modern); historical/nostalgic (relating to collections or collectors); how-to (display your collection, care for, restore, appraise, locate, add to, etc.); interview/profile (covering individual collectors and their hobbies, unique or extensive; celebrity collectors, and limited edition artists); technical (in-depth analysis of a particular antique, collectible or collecting field); and travel (coverage of special interest or regional shows, seminars, conventions—or major antique shows, flea markets; places collectors can visit, tours they can take, museums, etc.). Special issues include January and June show/flea market issues; and usual seasonal emphasis. Buys 100-150 mss/year. Query with sample of writing. Length: 1,200-1,600 words. Pays 75¢/ column inch; $1/column inch for color features.
Photos: Reviews b&w prints and 35mm color slides. Payment for photos included in payment for ms. Captions required. Buys first rights.
Tips: Articles most open to freelancers are on celebrity collectors; collectors with unique and/or extensive collections; transportation collectibles; advertising collectibles; bottles; glass, china & silver; primitives; furniture; toys; political collectibles; and movie memorabilia.

CRAFTS 'N THINGS, 14 Main St., Park Ridge IL 60068. (312)825-2161. Editor: Nancy Tosh. Associate Editor: Jackie Thielen. Bimonthly magazine covering crafts for "mostly women, around age 40." Circ. 250,000. Pays on publication. Byline, photo and brief bio given. Buys first North American Serial rights. Submit seasonal/holiday material 6 months in advance. Simultaneous queries, and photocopied and previously published submissions OK ("if so indicated"). SASE. Reports in 1 month. Free sample copy.
Nonfiction: How-to (do a craft project). Buys 7-14 mss/issue. "Send in a photo of the item and complete directions. We will consider it and return if not accepted. Length: 1-4 magazine pages. Pays $50-200, "depending on how much staff work is required."
Photos: "Generally, we will ask that you send the item so we can photograph it ourselves."
Tips: "We're looking harder for people who can craft than people who can write."

CRAFTSWOMAN, Daedalus Publications, Inc., 1153 Oxford Rd., Deerfield IL 60015-3324. (312)945-1769. Editor: Anne Patterson Dee. 80% freelance written. Bimonthly magazine covering craftswomen and their work. Pays on publication. Publishes ms an average of 6 months after acceptance. Byline given. Buys first and second rights to the same material 2 months in advance. Photocopied, simultaneous and previously published submissions OK. Computer printout submissions acceptable. SASE. Reports in 1 month. Sample copy $3.
Nonfiction: General interest (on craftswomen and their work); historical/nostalgic (quilting, stained glass, pottery, weaving, wood, etc.); how-to (run a shop, sell wholesale, do a trade show, promote shows, work with a sales rep, etc.); interview/profile (with successful craftswomen, shop owners, etc.); personal experience ("how I make money selling my designs," etc.) and travel. No "how-to-make-it articles." Buys 30 mss/year. Query or send complete ms if reprint. Length: 500-1,500 words. Pays $15-75.
Photos: Send photos with ms. Reviews 5x6 or 8x10 b&w glossy prints. Buys one-time rights.
Tips: "We need concise, well-written articles with lots of specifics, quotes and accompanying b&w photos."

CREATIVE CRAFTS AND MINIATURES, Carstens Publications, Inc., Box 700, Newton NJ 07860. Editor: Walter C. Lankenau. Bimonthly magazine covering crafts and miniatures for the serious adult hobbyist. "Quality how-to articles, biographical profiles, book and product reviews, events, question and answer columns, product testing and articles requested by readers." Circ. 50,000 + . Pays on publication. Buys all rights. Byline given. Submit seasonal/holiday material 7 months in advance. SASE. Reports in one month. Sample copy and writer's guidelines $2.
Nonfiction: How-to (step-by-step of specific projects or general techniques; instructions must be clearly written and accompanied by b&w procedural photos and/or drawings); and articles dealing with the crafting and collecting aspects of craft projects and miniatures (dollhouses, dolls, etc.). Query. Length: 1,200 words average. Pays $50/magazine page for photo/text package.
Photos: Purchased with accompanying ms.
Tips: "We desire articles written by craftsmen (or collectors) knowledgeable about hobbies/miniatures. We

need quality crafts that offer some challenge to the hobbyist. When photographing miniatures, be sure to include some photos that have a scale relationship, i.e., a coin or hand next to the miniature to give an idea of proportion."

DOLLS, The Collector's Magazine, Collector Communications Corp., 170 5th Ave., New York NY 10010. (212)989-8700. Editor: Krystyna Poray Goddu. Bimonthly magazine covering doll collecting "for collectors of antique, contemporary and reproduction dolls. We publish well-researched, professionally written articles that are illustrated with photographs of high quality, color or black-and-white." Circ. 55,000. Pays on publication. Publishes ms an average of 6 months after acceptance. Byline given. "Almost all first manuscripts are on speculation. We rarely kill assigned stories, but fee would be about 33% of article fee." Buys first serial rights, first North American serial rights ("almost always"), second serial rights if piece has appeared in a non-competing publication. Submit seasonal/holiday material 6 months in advance. Photocopied submissions considered (not preferred); previously published submissions OK. Computer printout submissions acceptable; no dot-matrix. Reports in 2 months. Sample copy $2; writer's guidelines for SAE and 1 first class stamp.

Nonfiction: Book excerpts; historical (with collecting angle); how-to (make doll clothes with clear instructions, diagrams, etc.); interview/profile (on collectors with outstanding collections); new product (just photos and captions; "we do not pay for these, but regard them as publicity"); opinion ("A Personal Definition of Dolls"); technical (doll restoration advice by experts only); and travel (museums and collections around the world). "No sentimental, uninformed 'my doll collection' or 'my grandma's doll collection' stories or trade magazine-type stories on shops, etc. Our readers are knowledgeable collectors." Query with clips. Length: 500-2,500 words. Pays $100-350. Sometimes pays expenses of writers on assignment.

Photos: Send photos with accompanying query or ms. Reviews 4x5 color transparencies; 4x5 or 8x10 b&w prints. "We do not buy photographs submitted without manuscripts unless we have assigned them; we pay for the manuscript/photos package in one fee." Captions required. Buys one-time rights.

Columns/Departments: Doll Views—a miscellany of news and views of the doll world includes reports on upcoming or recently held events; possibly reviews of new books. "*Not* the place for new dolls, auction prices or dates; we have regular contributors or staff assigned to those columns." Query with clips if available or send complete ms. Length: 200-500 words. Pays $25-75. Doll Views items are rarely bylined.

Fillers: "We don't really use fillers but would consider it if we got something very good. Hints on restoring, for example, or a nice illustration." Length: 500 words maximum. Pays $25-75.

Tips: "We need experts in the field who are also good writers. The most frequent mistake made by writers in completing an article assignment for us is being unfamiliar with the field; our readers are very knowledgeable. Freelancers who are not experts should know their particular story thoroughly and do background research to get the facts correct. Well-written queries from writers outside NYC area especially welcome. Non-experts should stay away from technical or specific subjects (restoration, price trends). Short profiles of unusual collectors or a story of a local museum collection, with good photos, might catch our interest. Editors want to know they are getting something from a writer they cannot get from anyone else. Good writing should be a given, a starting point. After that, it's what you know."

EARLY AMERICAN LIFE, Historical Times, Inc., Box 8200, Harrisburg PA 17105. Editor: Frances Carnahan. 70% freelance written. For "people who are interested in capturing the warmth and beauty of the 1600 to 1900 period and using it in their homes and lives today. They are interested in arts, crafts, travel, restoration, and collecting." Bimonthly magazine, 100 pages. Circ. 350,000. Buys all rights. Buys 50 mss/year. Pays on acceptance. Photocopied submissions OK. Free sample copy and writer's guidelines. Reports in 1 month. Query or submit complete ms. SASE.

Nonfiction: "Social history (the story of the people, not epic heroes and battles), crafts such as woodworking and needlepoint, travel to historic sites, country inns, antiques and reproductions, refinishing and restoration, architecture and decorating. We try to entertain as we inform and always attempt to give the reader something he can do. While we're always on the lookout for good pieces on any of our subjects, the 'travel to historic sites' theme is most frequently submitted. Would like to see more how-to-do-it (well-illustrated) on how real people did something great to their homes." Length: 750-3,000 words. Pays $50-400.

Photos: Pays $10 for 5x7 (and up) b&w photos used with mss, minimum of $25 for color. Prefers 2¼x2¼ and up, but can work from 35mm.

Tips: "Our readers are eager for ideas on how to bring the warmth and beauty of early America into their lives. Conceive a new approach to satisfying their related interests in arts, crafts, travel to historic sites, and especially in houses decorated in the early American style. Write to entertain and inform at the same time, and be prepared to help us with illustrations, or sources for them."

EDGES, The Official Publication of the American Blade Collectors, American Blade, Inc., 2835 Hickory Valley Rd., Chattanooga TN 37421. Editor: J. Bruce Voyles. Quarterly tabloid covering the knife business. Circ. 20,000. Pays on publication. Byline given. Buys all rights. Submit seasonal/holiday material 6 months in advance. Simultaneous queries, and photocopied and previously published submissions OK "as long as they are exclusive to our market." SASE. Reports in 5 months. Acknowledges receipt of queries and ms in 2 months. Sample copy $1.

Nonfiction: Book excerpts, expose, general interest, historical (well-researched), how-to, humor, new product, opinion, personal experience, photo feature, and technical. "We look for articles on all aspects of the knife business, including technological advances, profiles, knife shows, and well-researched history. Ours is not a hard market to break into if the writer is willing to do a little research. To have a copy is almost a requirement." Buys 150 mss/year. Send complete ms. Length: 50-3,000 words "or more if material warrants additional length." Pays 5¢/word.

Photos: Pays $5 for 5x7 b&w prints. Captions and model release required (if persons are identifiable).

Fillers: Clippings, anecdotes and newsbreaks.

Tips: "If writers haven't studied the publication, don't bother to submit an article. If they have studied it, we're an easy market to sell to." Buys 80% of the articles geared to "the knife business."

FIBERARTS, The Magazine of Textiles, 50 College St., Asheville NC 28801. (704)253-0467. Editor: Christine Timmons. 50% freelance written. Bimonthly magazine covering textiles as art and craft (weaving, quilting, surface design, stitchery, knitting, crochet, etc.) for textile artists, craftspeople, hobbyists, teachers, museum and gallery staffs, collectors and enthusiasts. Circ. 26,000. Pays on publication. Publishes ms an average of 4 months after acceptance. Byline given. Rights purchased are negotiable. Submit seasonal/holiday material 8 months in advance. Editorial guidelines and style sheet available. Computer printout submissions acceptable; prefers letter-quality to dot-matrix. SASE. Reporting time varies. Sample copy $3; writer's guidelines for SASE with 39¢ postage.

Nonfiction: Book excerpts; historical/nostalgic; how-to; humor; interview/profile; opinion; personal experience; photo feature; technical; travel (for the textile enthusiast, e.g., collecting rugs in Turkey); and education, trends, exhibition reviews and textile news. Buys 25-50 mss/year. Query. "Please be very specific about your proposal. Also an important consideration in accepting an article is the kind of photos—35mm slides and/or b&w glossies—that you can provide as illustration. We like to see photos in advance." Length: 250-1,200 words. Pays $40-250/article. Sometimes (rarely) pays the expenses of writers on assignment.

Tips: "Our writers are very familiar with the textile field, and this is what we look for in a new writer. The writer should also be familiar with *Fiberarts*, the magazine. We outline our upcoming issue in a column called '50 College St.' far enough in advance for a prospective writer to be aware of our future needs in proposing an article. (Also refer to January/February issue each year.)"

FINESCALE MODELER, Kalmbach Publishing Co., 1027 N. 7th St., Milwaukee WI 53233. (414)272-2060. Editor: Bob Hayden. 65% freelance written. Bimonthly magazine "devoted to how-to-do-it modeling information for scale modelbuilders who build non-operating aircraft, tanks, boats, automobiles, figures, dioramas, and science fiction and fantasy models." Circ. 39,500. Buys first and second rights to the same material. Pays on acceptance. Publishes ms an average of 1 year after acceptance. Byline given. Electronic submissions OK, but requires hard copy also. Computer printout submissions acceptable. SASE. Reports in 1 month on queries; 2 months on mss. Sample copy for 9x12 SAE and 3 first class stamps; free writer's guidelines.

Nonfiction: How-to (build scale models); and technical (research information for building models). Query or send complete ms. Length: 750-3,000 words. Pays $30/published page minimum.

Photos: Send photos with ms. Pays $7.50 minimum for color transparencies and $5 minimum for 5x7 b&w prints. Captions and identification of subjects required. Buys one-time rights.

Columns/Departments: FSM Showcase (photos plus description of model); and FSM Tips and Techniques (modelbuilding hints and tips). Buys 25-50/year. Query or send complete ms. Length: 100-1,000 words. Pays $10-75.

Tips: "A freelancer can best break in first through hints and tips, then through feature articles. Most people who write for FSM are modelers first, writers second. This is a specialty magazine for a special, quite expert audience. Essentially, 99% of our writers will come from that audience."

THE FRANKLIN MINT ALMANAC, Franklin Center PA 19091. (215)459-7016. Editor: Samuel H. Young. Associate Editor: Mary C. Slagle. 90% freelance written. Bimonthly magazine covering collecting, emphasizing numismatics, philatelics, porcelain, crystal, books, records and graphics for members of Franklin Mint Collectors Society who are regular customers and others who request. Circ. 1,200,000. Pays on acceptance. Publishes ms an average of 5 months after acceptance. Byline given. Pays negotiable kill fee. Buys one-time rights. Submit seasonal/holiday material 9 months in advance. Simultaneous queries, and simultaneous, photocopied, and previously published submissions OK. Computer printout submissions acceptable; prefers letter-quality to dot-matrix. Reports in 1 week on queries.

Nonfiction: General interest (topics related to products offered by the Franklin Mint); interview/profile (with well-known people who collect or Franklin Mint collectors); and types of collections. Buys 8 mss/year. Query. Length: 1,500-2,000 words. Pays $750 average/article. Pays expenses of writers on assignment.

Photos: State availability of photos.

Tips: "Solid writing credentials and a knowledge of collecting are a plus. A frequent mistake made by writers is poor organization—they haven't thought through the structure and flow of the piece or else they become bogged down in biographical/historical details."

GEMS AND MINERALS, Box 687, Mentone CA 92359. (714)794-1173. Editor: Jack R. Cox. Monthly for the professional and amateur gem cutter, jewelry maker, mineral collector and rockhound. Buys first North American serial rights. Byline given. Pays on publication. Query. Reports in 1 month. SASE. Free sample copy and writer's guidelines.
Nonfiction: Material must have how-to slant. No personality stories. Field trips to mineral or gem collecting localities used; must be accurate and give details so they can be found. Instructions on how to cut gems; design and creation of jewelry. 4-8 typed pages plus illustrations preferred, but do not limit if subject is important. Frequently good articles are serialized if too long for one issue. Buys 75-120 unsolicited mss/year. Pays 50¢/inch for text.
Photos: Pays for b&w prints as part of text. Pays $1/inch for color photos as published.
Tips: "Because we are a specialty magazine, it is difficult for a writer to prepare a suitable story for us unless he is familiar with the subject matter: jewelry making, gem cutting, mineral collecting and display, and fossil collecting. Our readers want accurate instructions on how to do it and where they can collect gemstones and minerals in the field. The majority of our articles are purchased from freelance writers, most of whom are hobbyists (rockhounds) or have technical knowledge of one of the subjects. Infrequently, a freelancer with no knowledge of the subject interviews an expert (gem cutter, jewelry maker, etc.) and gets what this expert tells him down on paper for a good how-to article. However, the problem here is that if the expert neglects to mention all the steps in his process, the writer does not realize it. Then, there is a delay while we check it out. My best advice to a freelance writer is to send for a sample copy of our magazine and author's specification sheet which will tell him what we need. We are interested in helping new writers and try to answer them personally, giving any pointers that we think will be of value to them. Let us emphasize that our readers want how-to and where-to stories. They are not at all interested in personality sketches about one of their fellow hobbyists."

HANDMADE, Lark Communications, 50 College St., Asheville NC 28801. (704)253-0468. Inquiries to: NB/CL Editor. Editor: Rob Pulleyn. 20% freelance written. Bimonthly how-to crafts magazine featuring projects in all crafts (needlework, knitting, sewing, weaving, crafts, woodworking, etc.). Circ. 300,000. Pays on acceptance. Byline given. Offers negotiable kill fee. We make work-for-hire assignments. Buys first rights only. Submit seasonal/holiday material 6 months in advance. Photocopied submissions acceptable. Computer printout submissions OK; prefers letter-quality to dot-matrix. SASE. Reports in 3 weeks. Publishes ms an average of 4 months after acceptance. Sample copy $2; writer's guidelines for business-size SAE and 22¢ postage.
Nonfiction: Historical/nostalgic (crafts-related—traditional crafts, foreign crafts, etc.); how-to (crafts, all kinds with specific information); humor (crafts related); interview/profile (of craftspeople); photo feature (portfolio-type showing items in related, similar or identical media); technical; and travel (visit to foreign places, crafts related). Buys 50-100 mss/year. Query with clips. Length: 100-1,000 words. Pays $25-400.
Photos: Send photos with ms (if possible). Reviews 35mm transparencies. Payment included in total fee. Captions and identification of subjects required. Buys all rights.

HANDS ON, Shopsmith Inc., 6640 Poe Ave., Dayton OH 45414-2591. (513)898-6070. Contact: Freelance Editor. 30% freelance written, but growing. Bimonthly magazine for woodworkers and do-it-yourselfers. Circ. 500,000. Pays on acceptance. Publishes ms an average of 6 months after acceptance. Byline given. Buys one-time rights by agreement. Computer printout submissions acceptable; prefers letter-quality to dot-matrix. Query. SASE. Reports in 3-6 weeks. Writer's guidelines for SASE; if you wish 2 recent past issues, include $1 with request.
Nonfiction: Craftspersons' profiles generally focus on creative use of Shopsmith tools, specific projects, and how to duplicate the project at home. How-to research is crucial, and techniques should be tied to specific projects. Rough sketches OK; supplies professional drafting. General woodworking articles must focus on well-slanted fresh information: wood joinery, turning, choosing and using material, working efficiently, safety, finishing, the therapy of woodworking, and joys and economy of doing it yourself. How-to projects: large or small, generally feature use of Shopsmith tools. Offers an authoritative variety of original, simple to intermediate project plans and tips in each issue. Length: 100-3000 words. Pays $25-500. Sometimes pays the expenses of writers on assignment.
Photos: Send with ms. Likes photos with captions.
Tips: "We aim to make the joys of woodworking and DIY accessible to many. Present information clearly, with authority, and in a nonintimidating manner. Find a 'you can do it' slant. Get to know our tools. There is very little 'new' information in woodworking, but plenty of information that needs fresh presentation. Find a woodworker who has something to say about planning, constructing, finishing. Present project plans following our format (ask for latest issues)."

HANDWOVEN, from Interweave Press, 306 N. Washington, Loveland CO 80537. (303)669-7672. Managing Editor: Jane Patrick. 75% freelance written. Bimonthly magazine (except July) covering handweaving, spinning and dyeing. Audience includes "practicing textile craftsmen. Article should show considerable depth . of knowledge of subject, although tone should be informal and accessible." Circ. 32,000. Pays on publication. Publishes ms an average of 8 months after acceptance. Byline given. Pays 50% kill fee. Buys first North American serial rights. Simultaneous queries and photocopied submissions OK. Computer printout submissions acceptable; prefers letter-quality to dot-matrix. SASE. Sample copy $4.50; writer's guidelines for SASE. Sometimes pays expenses of writer on assignment.

Nonfiction: Historical and how-to (on weaving and other craft techniques; specific items with instructions); and technical (on handweaving, spinning and dyeing technology). "All articles must contain a high level of in-depth information. Our readers are very knowledgeable about these subjects." Query. Length: 500-2,000 words. Pays $35-150.

Photos: State availability of photos. Identification of subjects required.

Tips: "We're particularly interested in articles about new weaving and spinning techniques as well as applying these techniques to finished products."

THE HOME SHOP MACHINIST, The Home Shop Machinist, Inc., 2779 Aero Park Dr., Box 1810, Traverse City MI 49685. (616)946-3712. Editor: Joe D. Rice. 95% freelance written. Bimonthly magazine covering machining and metalworking for the hobbyist. Circ. 19,000. Pays on publication. Publishes ms an average of 10 months after acceptance. Byline given. Buys first North American serial rights only. Simultaneous submissions OK. Computer printout submissions acceptable; prefers letter-quality to dot-matrix. SASE. Reports in 3 weeks. Free sample copy and writer's guidelines.

Nonfiction: How-to (projects designed to upgrade present shop equipment or hobby model projects that require machining); and technical (should pertain to metalworking, machining, drafting, layout, welding or foundry work for the hobbyist). No fiction. Buys 50 mss/year. Query or send complete ms. Length: open— "whatever it takes to do a thorough job." Pays $40/published page, plus $9/published photo; $70/page for camera-ready art; and $40 for b&w cover photo.

Photos: Send photos with ms. Pays $9-40 for 5x7 b&w prints. Captions and identification of subjects required.

Columns/Departments: Welding; Sheetmetal; Book Reviews; New Product Reviews; Micro-Machining; and Foundry. "Writer should become familiar with our magazine before submitting. Query first." Buys 8 mss/year. Length: 600-1,500 words. Pays $40-70.

Fillers: Machining tips/shortcuts. Buys 12-15/year. Length: 100-300 words. Pays $30-48.

Tips: "The writer should be experienced in the area of metalworking and machining; should be extremely thorough in explanations of methods, processes—always with an eye to safety; and should provide good quality b&w photos and/or clear drawings to aid in description. Visuals are of increasing importance to our readers. Carefully planned photos, drawings and charts will carry a submission to our magazine much farther along the path to publication."

‡**KNITTERS**, Golden Fleece Publications, 126 S. Phillips, Sioux Fall SD 57102. (605)338-4333. Editor: Elaine Rowley. 30% freelance written. Biannual magazine covering knitting and products used in knitting. "*Knitters* is published for hobbyists and artists using yarns and knitting needles." Estab. 1984. Pays on publication. Byline given. Offers negotiable kill fee. Buys one-time rights. Submit seasonal/holiday material 6 months in advance. Photocopied submissions OK. Computer printout submissions acceptable; no dot-matrix. SASE. Reports in 6 months. Sample copy $5; writer's guidelines for legal size envelope and 2 first class stamps.

Nonfiction: Book excerpts, historical/nostalgic, how-to, interview/profile, new product, personal experience, photo feature, technical and travel; all pertaining to knitting. No articles unrelated to knitting or knitting products. Query with published clips. Length: 250-1,500 words. Pays $20-100.

Photos: Alexis Xenakis, photo editor. State availability of photos with query. Pays $90-525 for b&w transparencies and prints; $575-775 for color transparencies and prints. Identification of subjects required.

Columns/Departments: Reviews of books and films related to knitting. Query with published clips. Pays 90¢/word.

Fillers: Clippings, jokes, gags, anecdotes, short humor and newsbreaks; only interested in items related to knitting or knitting products.

Tips: How-to projects for knitters are most open to freelancers. "Writers should be expert knitters or fiber craftsmen and be able to explain how to complete a knitting project from beginning to end."

LAPIDARY JOURNAL, Box 80937, San Diego CA 92138. Editor: Pansy D. Kraus. For "all ages interested in the lapidary hobby." 60% freelance written. Monthly. Rights purchased vary with author and material. Buys all rights or first serial rights. Byline given. Pays on publication. Publishes ms an average of 6 months after acceptance. Photocopied submissions OK. Computer printout submissions acceptable; no dot-matrix. Free sample copy and writer's guidelines. Query. SASE.

Nonfiction: Publishes "articles pertaining to gem cutting, gem collecting and jewelry making for the hobby-

ist." Buys informational, how-to, personal experience, historical, travel and technical articles. Pays 1¢/word.
Photos: Buys good contrast b&w photos. Contact editor about color photos. Payment varies according to size.
Tips: "Whether the writer has a chance of breaking in at this publication depends upon the subject matter, the accuracy, and style of writing."

LIVE STEAM, Live Steam, Inc., 2779 Aero Park Dr., Box 629, Traverse City MI 49685. (616)941-7160. Editor: Joe D. Rice. 60% freelance written. Monthly magazine covering steam-powered models and full-size engines (i.e., locomotives, traction, cars, boats, stationary, etc.) "Our readers are hobbyists, many of whom are building their engines from scratch. We are interested in anything that has to do with the world of live steam-powered machinery." Circ. 12,800. Pays on publication. Publishes ms an average of 10 months after acceptance. Byline given. Buys first North American serial rights only. Simultaneous submissions OK. Computer printout submissions acceptable. SASE. Reports in 3 weeks. Free sample copy and writer's guidelines.
Nonfiction: Historical/nostalgic; how-to (build projects powered by steam); new product; personal experience; photo feature; and technical (must be within the context of steam-powered machinery or on machining techniques). No fiction. Buys 50 mss/year. Query or send complete ms. Length: 500-3,000 words. Pays $30/published page—$500 maximum.
Photos: Send photos with ms. Pays $50/page of finished art. Pays $8 for 5x7 b&w prints; $40 for cover (color). Captions and identification of subjects required.
Columns/Departments: Steam traction engines, steamboats, stationary steam, and steam autos. Buys 6-8 mss/year. Query. Length: 1,000-3,000 words. Pays $20-50.
Tips: "At least half of all our material is from the freelancer. Requesting a sample copy and author's guide will be a good place to start. The writer must be well-versed in the nature of live steam equipment and the hobby of scale modeling such equipment. Technical and historical accuracy is an absolute must. Often, good articles are weakened or spoiled by mediocre to poor quality photos. Freelancers must learn to take a *good* photograph."

LOOSE CHANGE, Mead Publishing Corp., 21176 Alameda St., Long Beach CA 90810. (213)549-0730. Publisher: Daniel R. Mead. 90% freelance written. Monthly magazine covering collecting and investing in antique coin-operated machines. Slot machines; trade stimulators; jukeboxes; gumball and peanut vendors; pinballs; scales, etc. "Our audience is predominantly male. Readers are all collectors or enthusiasts of antique coin-operated machines, particularly antique slot machines. Subscribers are, in general, not heavy readers." Circ. 3,000. Pays on acceptance. Publishes ms an average of 2 months after acceptance. Byline given. Prefers to buy all rights, but also buys first and reprint rights. "We may allow author to reprint upon request in noncompetitive publications." Photocopied submissions OK. Previously published submissions must be accompanied by complete list of previous sales, including sale dates. SASE. Computer printout acceptable; prefers letter-quality to dot-matrix. Reports in 1 month on queries; 6 weeks on mss. Sample copy $1; free writer's guidelines.
Nonfiction: Historical/nostalgic, how-to, interview/profile, opinion, personal experience, photo feature and technical. "Articles illustrated with clear, black and white photos are always considered much more favorably than articles without photos (we have a picture-oriented audience). The writer must be knowledgable about his subject because our readers are knowledgeable and will spot inaccuracies." Buys up to 50 mss/year. Length: 900-6,000 words; 3,500-12,000, cover stories. Pays $100 maximum, inside stories; $200 maximum, cover stories.
Photos: "Captions should tell a complete story without reference to the body text." Send photos with ms. Reviews 8x10 b&w glossy prints. Captions required. "Purchase price for articles includes payment for photos."
Fiction: "All fiction must have a gambling/coin-operated-machine angle. Very low emphasis is placed on fiction. Fiction must be exceptional to be acceptable to our readers." Buys maximum 6 mss/year. Send complete ms. Length: 800-2,500 words. Pays $60 maximum.

LOST TREASURE, 15115 S. 76th E. Ave., Bixby OK 74008. Managing Editor: James D. Watts, Jr. 95% freelance written. For treasure hunting hobbyists, relic collectors, amateur prospectors and miners. Monthly magazine; 72 pages. Circ. 55,000. Buys first rights only. Byline given. Buys 100 mss/year. Pays on publication. Will consider photocopied submissions. No simultaneous submissions. Computer printout submissions acceptable. Reports in 2 months. Submit complete ms. Publishes ms an average of 3 months after acceptance. SASE. Free sample copy and writer's guidelines.
Nonfiction: How-to articles about treasure hunting, coinshooting, personal, profiles, and stories about actual hunts. *Avoid* writing about the more famous treasures and lost mines. No bottle hunting stories. Length: 1,000-3,000 words. "If an article is well-written and covers its subject well, we'll buy it—regardless of length." Pays 3¢/word.
Photos: Pays $5-10 for b&w glossy prints purchased with mss. Captions required. Pays $100-150 for color transparencies used on cover; 35mm minimum size.
Tips: "Read *Lost Treasure* before submitting your stories. Our title is a bit ambiguous—we are a magazine for the hobbyist treasure hunter. A frequent mistake is not knowing what we deal with—coinshooting, prospect-

ing. Writers do not ask for a sample copy or keep to a single theme. They believe they must tell an entire history, beginning with the rocks. Good sharply-focused black-and-white photos are a must with stories, and will do a lot to help sell your story."

MINIATURE COLLECTOR, Collector Communications Corp., 170 5th Ave., New York NY 10010. (212)989-8700. Editor: Krystyna Poray Goddu. Managing Editor: Louise Fecher. 40% freelance written. Bimonthly magazine; 64 pages. Circ. 45,000. Byline given. Buys first North American serial rights and occasionally second (reprint) rights to material originally published elsewhere. Pays on publication. Publishes ms an average of 4 months after acceptance. Submit seasonal/holiday material 4 months in advance. Photocopied and previously published submissions OK. Computer printout submissions acceptable; no dot-matrix. SASE. Reports in 2 months. Sample copy $2.
Nonfiction: Louise Fecher, managing editor. How-to (detailed furniture and accessories projects in 1/12th scale with accurate patterns and illustrations); interview (with miniaturists, well-established collectors, museum curators; include pictures); new product (very short-caption type pieces—no payment); photo feature (show reports, heavily photographic, with captions stressing pieces and availability of new and unusual pieces); and profile (of collectors, with photos). Buys 3-6 mss/issue. Query. Length: 600-1,200 words. Pays $100-200. "Most short pieces, such as news stories, are staff written. We welcome both short and long (1,000 words) stories from freelancers." First manuscripts usually on speculation. Sometimes pays the expenses of writers on assignment.
Photos: Louise Recher, managing editor. Send photos with ms; usually buys photo/manuscript package. Buys one-time rights. Captions required.
Tips: "The most frequent mistake made by writers in completing an article for us is that they write with too general a focus; our magazine is for a highly specialized audience, so familiarity with miniatures is a very big plus. Many writers are also unaware of the high quality of the pieces featured in our magazine."

MODEL RAILROADER, 1027 N. 7th St., Milwaukee WI 53233. Editor: Russell G. Larson. For hobbyists interested in scale model railroading. Monthly. Buys exclusive rights. Study publication before submitting material. Reports on submissions within 1 month. Query. SASE.
Nonfiction: Wants construction articles on specific model railroad projects (structures, cars, locomotives, scenery, benchwork, etc.). Also photo stories showing model railroads. First-hand knowledge of subject almost always necessary for acceptable slant. Pays base rate of $54/page.
Photos: Buys photos with detailed descriptive captions only. Pays $7.50 and up, depending on size and use. Color: double b&w rate. Full color cover: $210.

NATIONAL KNIFE MAGAZINE, Official Journal of the National Knife Collectors Association, Box 21070, Chattanooga TN 37421. (615)899-9456. Editor/Publisher: James V. Allday. Monthly magazine covering knife collection, manufacturing, hand crafting, selling, buying, trading; stresses "integrity in all dealings involving knives and bladed tools/weapons." Circ. 15,000. Pays on publication. Byline given. Buys all rights. Submit seasonal/holiday material 3 months in advance. Simultaneous queries OK. Electronic submissions OK on TRS-80 Mod III Scripsit. Computer printout submissions acceptable. SASE. Reports in 4 weeks on queries; 2 weeks on mss. Sample copy for 9x12 SAE and 6 first class stamps; writer's guidelines for business size SAE and 1 first class stamp.
Nonfiction: Analytical pieces, book reviews, general interest, historical, how-to, humor, interview/profile, new product, personal experience, photo feature, technical, and excerpts. Buys 50+ mss/year. Query with clips of published work. Length: 500-1,500 words. Pays 7¢ or more (negotiable)/word. No kill fee.
Photos: State availability of photos. Pays $7 for 5x7 prints. Captions and identification of subjects required.
Fiction: Adventure, fantasy, historical, humorous and, mainstream. No "non-knife-related stuff." Buys 6 mss/year. Query with clips of published work. Length: open. Pays 5-7¢/word.
Fillers: Anecdotes. Buys 10/year. Length: open. Pays $25.
Tips: "Get acquainted with the knife world and knife specialists by attending a knife show or the National Knife Museum in Chattanooga. We're a feature magazine aimed at knife collectors/investors."

NEEDLE & THREAD, Bassion Publishing, 4949 Byers, Ft. Worth TX 76107. (817)732-7494. Editor: Margaret Dittman. Bimonthly how-to magazine covering home sewing of all types for people interested in sewing fashions, home decorations and gifts. Circ. 750,000. Pays on acceptance. Byline given. Buys negotiable rights. Simultaneous queries and submissions OK. Computer printout submissions acceptable "so long as quality is not compromised." Reports in 6 weeks. Sample copy $3.
Nonfiction: How-to (with completed sewing projects); and interview/profile (of outstanding seamstresses and designers). Buys 120 mss/year. Query with snapshots of projects or clips of published work. Pays negotiable fee depending on the project.
Tips: "All projects must be original designs. On garments a manufactured pattern may be used with original decorative techniques."

NOSTALGIAWORLD, for Collectors and Fans, Box 231, North Haven CT 06473. (203)269-8502. Editor: Bonnie Roth. Managing Editor: Stanley N. Lozowski. 50% freelance written. Bimonthly tabloid covering entertainment collectibles. "Our readership is interested in articles on all eras—everything from early Hollywood, the big bands, country/Western, rock 'n' roll to jazz, pop, and rhythm and blues. Many of our readers belong to fan clubs." Circ. 5,000. Pays on publication. Publishes ms an average of 4 months after acceptance. Byline given. Buys all rights, one-time rights, second serial (reprint) rights, and simultaneous rights. Submit seasonal/holiday material 6 months in advance. Simultaneous queries, and simultaneous, photocopied, and previously published submissions OK. Computer printout submissions acceptable; prefers letter-quality to dot-matrix. SASE. Reports in 1 month on queries; 6 weeks on mss. Sample copy $2; writer's guidelines for legal size SAE and 1 first class stamp.
Nonfiction: Historical/nostalgic; how-to (get started in collecting); and interview/profile (of movie, recording, or sport stars). "Articles must be aimed toward the collector and provide insight into a specific area of collecting. *Nostalgiaworld* readers collect records, gum cards, toys, sheet music, movie magazines, posters and memorabilia, personality items, comics, baseball, and sports memorabilia. We do *not* cater to antiques, glass, or other nonentertainment collectibles. Buys 20-30 unsolicited mss/year."
Photos: Send photos with ms. Pays $5-15 for 5x7 b&w prints; reviews b&w contact sheets. Captions and identification of subjects required. Buys all rights.
Columns/Departments: Video Memories (early TV); and 78 RPM-For Collectors Only (advice and tips for the collector of 78 RPM recordings; prices, values, outstanding rarities). Buys varying number of mss/year. Query or send complete ms. Length: 500-1,500 words. Pays $10-25.
Tips: "Most readers are curious to find out what their collectibles are worth. With inflation running at such a high rate, people are investing in nostalgia items more than ever. *Nostalgiaworld* provides a place to buy and sell and also lists conventions and collectors' meets across the country. Our publication is interested in the entertainment field as it evolved in the twentieth century. Our readers collect anything and everything related to this field."

NUMISMATIC NEWS, Krause Publications, 700 E. State St., Iola WI 54990. (715)445-2214. Editor: David C. Harper. 10% freelance written. Tabloid newspaper on collecting U.S. coins. "We publish hobby news, features and research material." Circ. 41,000. Pays on publication. Publishes ms an average of 2 months after acceptance. Byline given. Buys all rights. Computer printout submissions acceptable; no dot-matrix. SASE. Reports in 1 month. Free sample copy.
Nonfiction: Technical/historical/numismatic. Buys 6-12 mss/year. Query. Length: 500-2,500 words. Pays $25.

NUTSHELL NEWS, Boynton and Associates, Clifton House, Clifton VA 22024. (703)830-1000. Editor: Bonnie Schroeder. 75% freelance written. Monthly magazine about miniatures for miniatures enthusiasts, collectors, craftspeople and hobbyists. "*Nutshell News* is the only magazine in the miniatures field which offers readers comprehensive coverage of all facets of miniature collecting and crafting." Circ. 35,000. Pays on publication. Publishes ms an average of 10 months after acceptance. Buys all rights in the field. Phone queries OK, "but would prefer letters and photos." Submit seasonal material 4 months in advance. Previously published submissions OK, ("if they did not appear in a competing magazine"). Electronic submissions OK but requires hard copy also. Computer printout submissions acceptable; prefers letter-quality to dot-matrix. Reports in 2 months. Sample copy $3; writer's guidelines for SASE.
Nonfiction: Interview/profile of craftspeople specializing in miniatures. Research articles on design periods and styles. Articles on private and museum collections of miniatures. How-to articles on decorating, building miniature furniture, dollhouses, rooms and accessories. Show reports, book reviews, and new product information. "We need stringers nationwide to work on an assignment basis, preferably freelancers with knowledge in the miniatures field to cover interviews with craftspeople and report on miniature shows." Buys 15 mss/issue. Query with "photos of the work to be written about. We're looking for craftspeople doing fine quality work, or collectors with top notch collections. Photos give us an idea of this quality." Length: 1,200-1,500 words. Pays 10¢/published word.
Photos: Pays $7.50 minimum for 5x7 b&w glossy prints. Pays $10 maximum for 35mm or larger color transparencies. Captions required.

THE OLD BOTTLE MAGAZINE, Box 243, Bend OR 97709. (503)382-6978. Editor: Shirley Asher. For collectors of old bottles, insulators, and relics. Monthly. Circ. 3,500. Buys all rights. Byline given. Buys 35 mss/year. Pays on acceptance. Current issue sample $2 sent ppd. No query required. Reports in 1 month. SASE.
Nonfiction, Photos and Fillers: "We are soliciting factual accounts on specific old bottles, canning jars, insulators and relics." Stories of a general nature on these subjects not wanted. "Interviews of collectors are usually not suitable when written by noncollectors. A knowledge of the subject is imperative. Would highly recommend potential contributors study an issue before making submissions. Articles that tie certain old bottles to a

historical background are desired." Length: 250-2,500 words. Pays $10/published page. B&w glossy prints and clippings purchased separately. Pays $5.

OLD CARS PRICE GUIDE, Krause Publications, 700 E. State St., Iola WI 54990. (715)445-2214. Editor: Dennis Schrimpf. Quarterly magazine of old car prices for old car hobbyists and investors. Circ. 90,000. Pays on acceptance. Byline given. Buys first North American serial rights. Submit seasonal/holiday material 3 months in advance. Computer printout submissions acceptable. Reports in 1 week. Sample copy $2.25 and 8x10 SASE.

Nonfiction: How-to (buy and sell collector cars); opinion (on car values market); technical (how to fix a car to increase value); and investment angles. "All articles should be car-value related and include information or actual price lists on recent sales (of more than one car). Articles about brands or types of cars *not* covered in regular price lists are preferred. Plenty of research and knowledge of the old car marketplace is usually essential. Photos required with all articles. No historic or nostalgic pieces." Buys 8-12 mss/year. Send complete ms. Length: 600-1,000 words. Pays $75-150.

Photos: Send photos with ms. Pays $50 minimum for 4x4 color transparencies used on cover; $5 for b&w prints; "undetermined for color." Captions and identification of subjects required. Buys one-time rights.

Columns/Departments: Book Review (books on car values or investments). Buys 4 mss/year. Send complete ms. Length: 100-300 words. Pays 3¢/word; $5/photo.

Fillers: Jokes, gags, anecdotes, short humor, and newsbreaks (related to old car values). Pays 3¢/word.

OLD CARS WEEKLY, Krause Publications, 700 E. State St., Iola WI 54990. (715)445-2214. Editor: John Gunnell. 40% freelance written. "Our readers collect, drive and restore everything from 1899 locomobiles to 1976 Cadillac convertibles. They cover all age and income groups." Weekly tabloid; 44-48 pages. Circ. 80,000. Pays on publication. Buys all rights. Phone queries OK. Byline given. SASE. Reports in 2 days. Sample copy 50¢.

Nonfiction: Short (2-3 pages) timely articles on old cars and old car hobby with 1 photo. Buys 20 mss/issue. Query. Pays 3¢/word.

Photos: State availability of photos with query. Pays $5 for 5x7 b&w glossy prints. Captions required. Buys all rights.

Columns/Departments: Book reviews (new releases for hobbyists). Buys 1 ms/issue. Query. Pays 3¢/word.

Fillers: Newsbreaks. Buys 50/year. Pays 3¢/word. Pays $10 bonus for usable news tips.

Tips: "Must know automotive hobby well. One writer caught the editor's eye by submitting excellent drawings with his manuscript."

POPULAR WOODWORKER, 1300 Galaxy Way, Concord CA 94520. (415)671-9852. Editor: Ellen DasGupta. Bimonthly magazine covering woodworking, wood carving, cabinet-making for the small cabinet shop owner, wood craftsperson, advanced hobbyist or wood carver. Circ. 28,000. Pays on publication. Byline given. Buys first North American serial rights. Submit seasonal/holiday material 4 months in advance. Simultaneous queries, and simultaneous and photocopied submissions OK. Computer printout submissions acceptable. SASE. Reports in 1 month on queries; 6 weeks on mss. Sample copy $2, 9x12 SAE and 90¢ postage; writer's guidelines for SAE and 1 first class stamp.

Nonfiction: How-to (descriptions of woodworking techniques); large and small projects with plans (beginner and advanced); shop tips; repairing woodworking mistakes; humor (woodcraft related); inspirational; interview/profile (of successful/prominent woodworkers, especially if accompanied by quality photos); and personal experience (related to running small shop/selling/designing woodcraft products). "Specific topics we would like to see included: special set-ups/jigs for particular woodworking operations, workshop efficiency and shortcuts, homemade tools and equipment, finishing techniques, characteristics of certain woods, and successful marketing techniques." Buys 100 mss/year. Query with or without published clips, or send complete ms. Length 100-1,500 words maximum. Pays $45/published page.

Photos: "We especially like articles accompanied by top quality, black-and-white glossy photos 5x7 or larger. Clear uncluttered pictures of the completed project shot from different angles should be included with any articles telling how to make a project. Illustrations, diagrams and/or plans should be good pen and ink line drawings. We do have a technical illustrator on staff. We also like to see woodworkers demonstrating techniques. We are seeking woodcraft related color photos (35mm color slides or 4x5 color transparencies) for the cover of the magazine." Pays $25 minimum. We prefer that these cover photos tie in with articles in that issue; however, it is not mandatory." Payment for diagrams, plans, illustrations and b&w photos used are included in ms price of $45/published page. Captions required. Photos returned if requested.

Columns/Departments: Jig Journal, Musical Instrument Making, Wooden Boatbuilding, Marketing Techniques, Show Reviews, Shop Tips, Living With Murphy (repairing woodworking mistakes), Techniques, Wood Types, Out of the Woodwork (humorous or thought-provoking anecdotes); and Popular Woodworker Profiles. Query or send complete ms.

‡**THE PRAIRIE WOOL COMPANION**, Golden Fleece Publications, 126 S. Phillips, Sioux Falls SD 57102. (605)338-4333. Editor: A. David Xenakis. Quarterly magazine covering weaving and products used in weaving. "*Prairie Wool Companion* is published for hobbyists and artists using yarns and looms." Circ. 4,300. Pays on publication. Byline given. Offers negotiable kill fee. Buys one-time rights. Submit seasonal/holiday material 6 months in advance. Photocopied submissions OK. SASE. Reports in 6 months. Sample copy $5; writer's guidelines for legal size SAE and 2 first class stamps.
Nonfiction: Book excerpts, historical/nostalgic, how-to, interview/profile, new product, personal experience, photo feature, technical, travel; all pertaining to weaving. Nothing unrelated to spinning, weaving, or working in wool or wool substitutes. Query with published clips. Length: 250-1,200 words. Pays $20-100.
Photos: State availability of photos. Reviews b&w and color transparencies and prints. Identification of subjects required.
Columns/Departments: Reviews of books and films related to weaving. Query with published clips.
Poetry: Style less important than the relevancy to weaving products.
Fillers: Clippings, jokes, gags, anecdotes, short humor and newsbreaks. Only interested in items related to weaving and weaving products.
Tips: "Writers should be expert weavers or fiber craftsmen, and be able to explain how to complete a weaving project from beginning to end. How-to projects for weavers are most open to freelancers."

‡**THE PROFESSIONAL QUILTER**, Oliver Press, 2304 University Ave., St. Paul MN 55114. (612)645-4715. Editor: Jeannie M. Spears. 75% freelance written. Bimonthly magazine on the quilting business. Emphasis on small business, preferably craft or sewing related. Circ. 2,000. Payment negotiated. Publishes ms an average of 6 months after acceptance. Byline given. Buys first North American serial rights, first serial rights, and second serial (reprint) rights. Submit seasonal/holiday material 3 months in advance. Simultaneous queries, and photocopied and previously published submissions OK. Electronic submissions OK on Kaypro CPM, but requires hard copy also. Computer printout submissions acceptable; prefers letter-quality to dot-matrix. SASE. Reports in 2 weeks on queries; 1 month on mss. Sample copy $4; writer's guidelines for #10 SAE and 1 first class stamp.
Nonfiction: Davey M. Spears, articles editor. Book excerpts; historical/nostalgic; how-to (quilting business); humor; interview/profile; new product; opinion; and personal experience. No quilting or sewing *techniques* or quilt photo spreads. Buys 30 mss/year. Query or send complete ms. Length: 200-2,000 words. Pays $20-100.
Tips: "We need personality and experience, especially from people who have been in business for longer than five years. Send a letter describing your quilt, craft or business experience with a query or manuscript."

QUILTER'S NEWSLETTER MAGAZINE, Box 394, Wheatridge CO 80033. Editor: Bonnie Leman. Monthly. Circ. 150,000. Buys first North American serial rights or second rights. Buys 15 mss/year. Pays on acceptance. Free sample copy. Reports in 5 weeks. Submit complete ms. SASE.
Nonfiction: "We are interested in articles on the subject of quilts and quiltmakers *only*. We are not interested in anything relating to 'Grandma's Scrap Quilts' but could use material about contemporary quilting." Pays 3¢/word minimum.
Photos: Additional payment for photos depends on quality.
Fillers: Related to quilts and quiltmakers only.
Tips: "Be specific, brief, and professional in tone. Study our magazine to learn the kind of thing we like. Send us material which fits into our format but which is different enough to be interesting. Realize that we think we're the best quilt magazine on the market and that we're aspiring to be even better, then send us the cream off the top of your quilt material."

RAILROAD MODEL CRAFTSMAN, Box 700, Newton NJ 07860. (201)383-3355. Editor: William C. Schaumburg. 75% freelance written. For model railroad hobbyists, in all scales and gauges. Monthly. Circ. 97,000. Buys all rights. Buys 50-100 mss/year. Pays on publication. Publishes ms an average of 9 months after acceptance. Submit seasonal material 6 months in advance. Computer printout submissions acceptable; prefers letter-quality to dot-matrix. SASE requested for writer's and photographer's information. Sample copy $2; guidelines for SAE and 1 first class postage stamp.
Nonfiction: "How-to and descriptive model railroad features written by persons who did the work are preferred. Almost all our features and articles are written by active model railroaders. It is difficult for non-modelers to know how to approach writing for this field." Minimum payment: $1.75/column inch of copy ($50/page).
Photos: Purchased with or without mss. Buys sharp 8x10 glossy prints and 35mm or larger color transparencies. Minimum payments: $10 for photos or $2/diagonal inch of published b&w photos, $3 for color transparencies and $100 for covers which must tie in with article in that issue. Caption information required.
Tips: The most frequent mistakes made by writers are the photo quality and wordiness in texts.

ROCKY MOUNTAIN MINIATURE JOURNAL, Box 3315, Littleton CO 80161. (303)978-1355. Editor: Norm Nielsen. 70% freelance written. Bimonthly magazine covering miniatures, dollhouses and related topics for collectors and crafters in the miniature hobby. Circ. 1,200. Pays on publication. Publishes ms an average of 2 months after acceptance. Byline given. Buys one-time rights. Submit seasonal/holiday material 2 months in advance. Computer printout submissions acceptable. Sample copy $2.25; SAE with 1 first class stamp for writer's guidelines.

Nonfiction: Articles and how-to's on miniatures, dollhouses, the people who make or collect them, and related miniatures topics. Query first. Pays 3¢/word.

Photos: Send photos with ms. 5x7 or 8x10 b&w glossies preferred, but other sizes acceptable. Color prints with good contrast accepted (to be reproduced in b&w). Photos returned only if requested. Complete identification of photos necessary and return postage included.

Tips: "How-to pieces with patterns and instructions are always in demand by our readers. We are constantly seeking articles about miniatures made by people anywhere in the world. The most rewarding aspect of working with freelance writers is receiving articles from unexpected new sources who write in good style and present fresh or different approaches and making contacts that may result in several articles from the same new person. We need writers to cover miniature shows in other parts of the country that we can't travel to: similarly we'd like to receive more articles on artists who live elsewhere—we are not restricted to the Rocky Mountain area. In our experience, we often receive articles that are too short. We much prefer to receive longer articles— they could be split into a series (which our readers seem to enjoy), or could even be shortened if necessary, but it's better to have too much than too little. While we prefer the longer articles, we also have a need for fillers and have received very few. Scales other than 1" = 1' (½" or ¼" are currently in demand by readers). We emphasize the importance of photos to accompany articles, and they must be completely identified so that proper credit can be given to the creators of the items as well as the photographer."

JOEL SATER'S ANTIQUES & AUCTION NEWS, Box 500, Mount Joy PA 17552. (717)653-9797. Managing Editor: Joel Sater. Editor: Brian Geoghan. For dealers and buyers of antiques, nostalgics and collectibles, and those who follow antique shows and shops. Biweekly tabloid; 24-32 pages. Circ. 60,000. Pays on publication. Buys all rights. Phone queries OK. Submit seasonal/holiday material 3 months in advance. Simultaneous (if so notified), photocopied and previously published submissions OK. SASE. Reports in 6 weeks. Free sample copy (must identify *Writer's Market*).

Nonfiction: Historical (related to American artifacts or material culture); how-to (restoring and preserving antiques and collectibles); informational (research on antiques or collectibles; "news about activities in our field"); interview; nostalgia; personal experience; photo feature; profile; and travel. Buys 100-150 mss/year. Query or submit complete ms. Length: 500-2,500 words. Pays $5-25.

Photos: Purchased with or without accompanying ms. Captions required. Send prints. Pays $2-10 for b&w photos. Offers no additional payment for photos purchased with mss.

SCOTT STAMP MONTHLY, Box 828, Sidney OH 45365. (513)498-2111. Editor: Richard L. Sine. 30% freelance written. For stamp collectors, from the beginner to the sophisticated philatelist. Monthly magazine; 88 pages. Circ. 22,000. Rights purchased vary with author and material; usually buys all rights. Byline given. Buys 8-9 unsolicited mss/year. Pays on publication. Submit seasonal or holiday material 6 months in advance. Computer printout submissions acceptable; no dot-matrix. Reports in 1 month. Query preferred. SASE.

Nonfiction: "We want articles of a serious philatelic nature, ranging in length from 1,500-2,500 words. We are also in the market for articles, written in an engaging fashion, concerning the remote byways and often-overlooked aspects of the hobby. Writing should be clear and concise, and subjects should be well-researched and documented. Illustrative material should also accompany articles whenever possible." Query. Pays about $200.

Photos: State availability of photos. Offers no additional payment for b&w photos used with mss.

Tips: "Although most material deals with stamps, new writers are invited to seek assignments. It's rewarding to find a good new writer with good new material. Because our emphasis is on lively, interesting articles about stamps, including historical perspectives and human interest slants, we are open to writers who can produce the same. Of course, if you are an experienced philatelist, so much the better. We do not want stories about the picture on a stamp taken from a history book or an encyclopedia and dressed up to look like research. We want articles written from a philatelic standpoint. If idea is good and not a basic rehash, we are interested."

‡**SEW NEWS, The newspaper for people who sew**, PJS Publications, Inc., News Plaza, Box 1790, Peoria IL 61656. (309)682-6626. Editor: Barbara Weiland. 90% freelance written. Monthly newspaper covering home-sewing. "Our magazine is for the beginning home sewer to the professional dressmaker. It expresses the fun, creativity, and excitement of sewing." Circ. 100,000. Pays on acceptance. Publishes ms an average of 6 months after acceptance. Byline given. Buys all rights. Submit seasonal/holiday material 6 months in advance. Photocopied submissions OK. Computer printout submissions acceptable; no dot-matrix. SASE. Reports in 2 months. Sample copy $3; writer's guidelines free.

Nonfiction: Historical/nostalgic (fashion, textiles history); how-to (sewing techniques); humor (sewing cartoons); interview/profile (interesting personalities in home-sewing field); and new product (written in-house). Buys 200-240 ms/year. Query with published clips. Length: 500-2,000 words. Pays $25-400. Rarely pays ex-

penses of writer on assignment.
Photos: State availability of photos. Prefers b&w contact sheets and negatives. Payment included in ms price. Identification of subjects required. Buys all rights.
Fillers: Anecdotes. Buys 12/year. Length: 50-100 words. Pays $10-25.
Tips: "Query first with writing sample. Areas most open to freelancers are how-to and sewing techniques; give explicit, step-by-step instructions plus rough art."

SHUTTLE SPINDLE & DYEPOT, Handweavers Guild of America, Inc., 65 La Salle Road, West Hartford CT 06107. (203)233-5124. Editor: Jane Bradley Sitko. Quarterly crafts magazine covering handweaving, handspinning and dyeing. "Our audience is handcrafts-oriented (many professional fiber artists)." Circ. 16,000. Pays on publication. Byline given. Offers negotiable kill fee. Buys one-time rights. Submit seasonal/holiday material 6 months in advance. Simultaneous queries, and photocopied and previously published submissions OK. Computer printout submissions acceptable; prefers letter-quality to dot-matrix. SASE. Reports in 4 weeks on queries; 3 months on mss. Free sample copy; guidelines for SASE.
Nonfiction: How-to (weaving, sewing) and technical (handweaving, handspinning). Buys 30 mss/year. Query. Length: 1,000-3,000 words. Pays $25-100 (award honorarium).
Photos: Send photos with query. Pays variable rates for 4x5 color transparencies. Model releases and identification of subjects required.
Tips: "We are seeking technical manuscripts about weaving but also need reviews on fiber or weaving exhibits and shows which do not require that the writer be familiar with handweaving. A freelancer can best break in by submitting interviews with famous fiber artists; national or international exhibit reviews; and personality pieces."

SPIN-OFF, Interweave Press, 306 N. Washington, Loveland CO 80537. (303)669-7672. Editors: Lee Raven and Anne Bliss. 10-20% freelance written. Quarterly magazine covering handspinning, dyeing, techniques and projects for using handspun fibers. Audience includes "practicing textile/fiber craftsmen. Article should show considerable depth of knowledge of subject, although the tone should be informal and accessible." Circ. 7,000. Pays on publication. Publishes ms an average of 6 months after acceptance. Byline given. Pays 50% kill fee. Buys first North American serial rights. Simultaneous queries and photocopied submissions OK. Computer printout submissions acceptable; prefers letter-quality to dot-matrix. SASE. Sample copy $2.50 and 8½x11 SAE; free writer's guidelines.
Nonfiction: Historical and how-to (on spinning; knitted, crocheted, woven projects from handspun fibers with instructions); interview/profile (of successful and/or interesting fiber craftsmen); and technical (on spinning, dyeing or fiber technology, use, properties). "All articles must contain a high level of in-depth information. Our readers are very knowledgable about these subjects." Query. Length: 2,000 words. Pays $25-125.
Photos: State availability of photos. Identification of subjects required.

SPORTS COLLECTORS DIGEST, Krause Publications, 700 E. State St., Iola WI 54990. (715)445-2214. Editor: Steve Ellingboe. 70% freelance written. Sports memorabilia magazine published 26 times/year. "We serve collectors of sports memorabilia—baseball cards, yearbooks, programs, autographs, jerseys, bats, balls, books, magazines, ticket stubs, etc." Circ. 20,000. Pays after publication. Publishes ms an average of 3 months after acceptance. Byline given. Buys first North American serial rights only. Submit seasonal/holiday material 3 months in advance. Simultaneous queries and photocopied submissions OK. Computer printout submissions acceptable; no dot-matrix. SASE. Reports in 5 weeks on queries; 2 months on mss. Free sample copy and writer's guidelines.
Nonfiction: General interest (new card issues, research on older sets); historical/nostalgic (old stadiums, old collectibles, etc.); how-to (buy cards, sell cards and other collectibles, display collectibles, ways to get autographs, jerseys, and other memorabilia); interview/profile (or well-known collectors, ball players—but must focus on collectibles); new product (new card sets) and personal experience ("what I collect and why"-type stories). No sports stories. "We are not competing with *The Sporting News*, *Sports Illustrated* or your daily paper. Sports collectibles only." Buys 40-60 mss/year. Query. Length: 300-3,000 words; prefers 1,000 words. Pays $10-50.
Photos: Unusual collectibles. State availability of photos. Pays $5-15 for b&w prints. Identification of subjects required. Buys all rights.
Columns/Departments: "We have all the columnists we need but welcome ideas for new columns." Buys 100-150 mss/year. Query. Length: 600-3,000 words. Pays $15-60.
Tips: "If you are a collector, you know what collectors are interested in. Write about it. No shallow, puff pieces; our readers are too smart for that. Only well-researched articles about sports memorabilia and collecting. Some sports nostalgia pieces are OK. Write only about the areas you know about. Many of our writers do not receive payment; they submit articles for satisfaction and prestige and to help their fellow hobbyists. It's that kind of hobby and that kind of magazine."

‡**TREASURE**, Jess Publishing, 6280 Adobe Rd., 29 Palms CA 92277. (619)367-3531. Editor: Jim Williams. Emphasizes treasure hunting and metal detecting. 90% freelance written. Monthly magazine. Circ. 40,000. Pays on publication. Publishes ms an average of 6 months after acceptance. Buys all rights. Byline given. Phone queries OK. Submit seasonal/holiday material 4 months in advance. Previously published submissions OK. Computer printout submissions acceptable; prefers letter-quality to dot-matrix. SASE. Reports in 2 months. Sample copy 40¢; free writer's guidelines for SAE and 1 first class stamp.
Nonfiction: Kathleen Arwick, articles editor. How-to (coinshooting and treasure hunting tips); informational and historical (location of lost treasures with emphasis on the lesser-known); interviews (with treasure hunters); profiles (successful treasure hunters and metal detector hobbyists); personal experience (treasure hunting); technical (advice on use of metal detectors and metal detector designs). Buys 6-8 mss/issue. Send complete ms. Length: 300-3,000 words. Pays $30-200. "Our rate of payment varies considerably depending upon the proficiency of the author, the quality of the photographs, the importance of the subject matter, and the amount of useful information given."
Photos: Offers no additional payment for 5x7 or 8x10 b&w glossy prints used with mss. Pays $50 minimum for color transparencies (35mm or 2¼x2¼). Color for cover only. "Clear photos and other illustrations are a must." Model release required.
Tips: "The most frequent mistakes made by writers in completing an article for *Treasure* are failure to list sources of information and to supply illustrations or photos with a story."

TRI-STATE TRADER, Mayhill Publishing, Box 90, Knightstown IN 46148. Editor: Thomas Hoepf. 90% freelance written. Weekly newspaper covering antiques, auctions, collectibles, genealogy for collectors nationwide interested in history and past lifestyles. Circ. 38,000. Pays on publication. Publishes ms an average of 2 months after acceptance. Byline given. Buys first and second rights to the same material. Submit seasonal/holiday material 3 months in advance. Simultaneous queries and photocopied and previously published submissions OK. Computer printout submissions acceptable; no dot-matrix. SASE. Reports in 3 weeks on queries; 1 month on mss. Free sample copy on request; writer's guidelines SAE and 1 first-class stamp.
Nonfiction: Historical/nostalgic (of interest to collectors). "We're always interested in brief background articles on specific antiques and collectibles, and how today's antiques are used." Buys 175 mss/year. Query. Length: 300-1,100 words. Pays variable rates.
Fillers: History, places, dates, etc. Length: 30-150 words.
Tips: "We're interested in general news relating to collectibles and history. Read the *TST* and know this market. We are open to most any writer, but our readers are knowledgeable on our topics and expect the same from writers. We always have a need for stories about 500 words long for the inside news page."

WESTERN & EASTERN TREASURES, People's Publishing Co., Inc., Box Z, Arcata CA 95521. Editor: Rosemary Anderson. Emphasizes treasure hunting and metal detecting for all ages, entire range in education, coast-to-coast readership. 90% freelance written. Monthly magazine. Circ. 70,000. Pays on publication. Publishes ms an average of 1 year after acceptance. Buys all rights. Computer printout submissions acceptable; prefers letter-quality to dot-matrix. SASE. Reports in 2 months. Sample copy and writer's guidelines for $2.
Nonfiction: How-to "hands on" use of metal detecting equipment, how to locate coins and relics, prospect for gold, where to look for treasures, rocks and gems, etc., "first-person" experiences. "No purely historical manuscripts or manuscripts that require two-part segments or more." Buys 200 unsolicited mss/year. Submit complete ms. Length: maximum 1,500 words. Pays 2¢/word-negotiable. Sometimes pays the expenses of writers on assignment.
Photos: Purchased with accompanying ms. Captions required. Submit b&w prints or 35mm Kodachrome color transparencies. Pays $5 maximum for 3x5 and up b&w glossy prints; $35 and up for 35mm Kodachrome cover slides. Model release required.
Tips: "The writer has a better chance of breaking in at our publication with short articles and fillers as these give the readers a chance to respond to the writer. The publisher relies heavily on reader reaction. Not adhering to word limit is the main mistake made by writers in completing an article for us. Also, not following what the editor has emphasized as needed material to be clearly covered."

THE WOODWORKER'S JOURNAL, Madrigal Publishing Co., Inc., 517 Lichfield Rd., Box 1629, New Milford CT 06776. (203)355-2694. Editor: James J. McQuillan. Managing Editor: Thomas G. Begnal. Bimonthly magazine covering woodworking for woodworking hobbyists of all levels of skill. Circ. 100,000. Pays on acceptance. Byline given. Buys all rights. Submit seasonal/holiday material 3 months in advance. SASE. Reports in 6 weeks. Free sample copy and writer's guidelines.
Nonfiction: "In each issue, we try to offer a variety of plans—some selected with the novice in mind, others for the more experienced cabinetmaker. We also like to offer a variety of furniture styles, i.e., contemporary, colonial, Spanish, etc. We are always in the market for original plans for all types of furniture, wood accessories, jigs, and other shop equipment. We are also interested in seeing carving and marquetry projects." Buys 20-30 mss/year. Send complete ms. Length "varies with project." Pays $80-120/page. "Payment rate is for a complete project submission, consisting of dimensioned sketches, a write-up explaining how the project was

built, and at least one high-quality b&w photo."
Photos: Send photos with ms. Reviews 5x7 b&w prints. "Photo payment is included in our basic payment rate of $80-120/page for a complete project submission." Captions required. Buys all rights.

THE WORKBASKET, 4251 Pennsylvania Ave., Kansas City MO 64111. Editor: Roma Jean Rice. Issued monthly except bimonthly June-July and November-December. Buys first rights. Pays on acceptance. Query. Reports in 6 weeks. SASE.
Nonfiction: Interested in articles of 400-500 words of step-by-step directions for craft projects and gardening articles of 200-500 words. Pays 7¢/word.
Photos: Pays $7-10 for 8x10 glossies with ms.
Columns/Departments: Readers' Recipes (original recipes from readers); and Making Cents (short how-to section featuring ideas for pin money from readers).

WORKBENCH, 4251 Pennsylvania Ave., Kansas City MO 64111. (816)531-5730. Editor: Jay W. Hedden. 95% freelance written. For woodworkers. Circ. 825,000. Pays on acceptance. Buys all rights then returns all but first rights upon request, after publication. Byline given if requested. Computer printout submissions acceptable. SASE. Reports in 1 month. Query. Publishes ms an average of 1 year after acceptance. Free sample copy and writer's guidelines.
Nonfiction: "In the last couple of years, we have increased our emphasis on home improvement and home maintenance, and now we are getting into alternate energy projects. Ours is a nuts-and-bolts approach, rather than telling how someone has done it. Because most of our readers own their own homes, we stress 'retrofitting' of energy-saving devices, rather than saying they should rush out and buy or build a solar home. Energy conservation is another subject we cover thoroughly; insulation, weatherstripping, making your own storm windows. We still are very strong in woodworking, cabinetmaking and furniture construction. Projects range from simple toys to complicated reproductions of furniture now in museums." Pays: $125/published page, up or down depending on quality of submission.
Columns/Departments: Shop tips bring $20 maximum with drawing and/or photo.
Tips: "If you can consistently provide good material, including photos, your rates will go up and you will get assignments. The field is wide open but only if you produce quality material and clear, sharp b&w photos. If we pay less than the rate, it's because we have to supply photos, information, drawings or details the contributor has overlooked. Contributors should look over the published story to see what they should include next time. Our editors are skilled woodworkers, do-it-yourselfers and photographers. We have a complete woodworking shop at the office, and we use it often to check out construction details of projects submitted to us."

WORLD COIN NEWS, Krause Publications, 700 E. State, Iola WI 54990. (715)445-2214. Editor: Colin Bruce. 30% freelance written. Weekly newsmagazine about non-U.S. coin collecting for novices and advanced collectors of foreign coins, medals, and paper money. Circ. 15,000. Pays on publication. Publishes ms an average of 3 weeks after acceptance. Byline given. Buys first North American serial rights only. Submit seasonal material 1 month in advance. Simultaneous and photocopied submissions OK. Computer printout submissions acceptable; no dot-matrix. Reports in 2 weeks. Free sample copy.
Nonfiction: "Send us timely news stories related to collecting foreign coins and current information on coin values and markets." Send complete ms. Buys 30 mss/year. Length: 500-2,000 words. Pays 3¢/word to first-time contributors; fees negotiated for later articles.
Photos: Send photos with ms. Pays $5 minimum for b&w prints. Captions and model release required. Buys first rights and first reprint rights.

YESTERYEAR, Yesteryear Publications, Box 2, Princeton WI 54968. (414)295-3969. Editor: Michael Jacobi. 25% freelance written. For antique dealers and collectors, people interested in collecting just about anything, and nostalgia buffs. Monthly tabloid. Circ. 7,000. Pays on publication. Publishes ms an average of 2 months after acceptance. Buys all rights. Byline given. Submit seasonal/holiday material 3 months in advance. Simultaneous, photocopied and previously published submissions OK. SASE. Reports in 1 month for queries; 1 month for mss. Sample copy $1.
Nonfiction: General interest (basically, anything pertaining to antiques, collectible items or nostalgia in general); historical (again, pertaining to the above categories); and how-to (refinishing antiques, how to collect). The more specific and detailed, the better. "We do not want personal experience or opinion articles." Buys 36 mss/year. Send complete ms. Pays $5-25.
Photos: Send photos with ms. Pays $5 for 5x7 b&w glossy or matte prints; $5 for 5x7 color prints. Captions preferred.
Columns/Departments: "We will consider new column concepts as long as they fit into the general areas of antiques and collectibles and nostalgia." Buys 3 mss/issue. Send complete ms. Pays $5-25.

Home and Garden

Most home and garden magazines not only show readers how other people live but how you can transform your home and garden. Editors look for space- and energy-saving ideas that look and work well. The number of people who are restoring old homes and the interest in "country" designs have added another dimension to home and garden magazines. Some magazines here concentrate on gardens; others on the how-to of interior design. Still others focus upon homes and/or gardens in specific regions.

AUSTIN HOMES & GARDENS, Duena Development Corp., Box 5950, Austin TX 78763. (512)479-8936. Editor: Marsia Hart Reese. 50% freelance written. Monthly magazine emphasizing Austin, Texas homes, people, gardens, and events for current, former, and prospective residents. Circ. 25,000. Average issue includes 16 articles. Pays on publication. Publishes ms an average of 3 months after acceptance. Byline given. "The material that we buy becomes the sole property of AH&G and cannot be reproduced in any form without written permission." Photocopied submissions OK. Computer printout submissions acceptable. SASE. Reports in 1 month. Sample copy $3.
Nonfiction: General interest (interior design and architecture; trends in home furnishings and landscaping; arts and crafts); historical (local); how-to (on home or garden); and fashion feature. Buys 8 mss/issue. Query and samples of published articles. Length: 700-1,500 words. Pays $100 minimum.
Columns/Departments: Departments include Discoveries (unusual local businesses or services); Epicure (outstanding local restaurants); Travel; and Profile (interesting Austin people). Query. Length: 500-1,000 words. Pays $100 minimum.
Tips: "Always looking for good freelancers, but prefer writers who live in our area and are familiar with our publication."

BETTER HOMES AND GARDENS, 1716 Locust St., Des Moines IA 50336. (515)284-3000. Editor (Building): Joan McCloskey. Editor (Furnishings): Shirley Van Zante. Editor (Foods): Nancy Byal. Editor (Crafts): James Williams. Editor (Travel): Barbara Humeston. Editor: (Garden, Outdoor Living): Doug Jimerson. Editor (100s of Ideas, New Products, What's Happening): Steven Coulter. Editor (Health & Education): Paul Krantz. Editor (Money Management, Automotive, Features): Margaret Daly. Editor (Home Electronics): Kathy Stechert. 10-15% freelance written. Pays on acceptance. Buys all rights. "We read all freelance articles, but much prefer to see a letter of query rather than a finished manuscript."
Nonfiction: Travel, education, health, cars, money management, and home entertainment. "We do not deal with political subjects or with areas not connected with the home, community, and family." Pays rates "based on estimate of length, quality and importance."
Tips: Direct queries to the department that best suits your story line.

CANADIAN WORKSHOP, The How-to Magazine, Chrimak Enterprises, Ltd., 100 Steelcase Rd. E., Markham, Ontario L3R 1E8 Canada. (416)475-8440. Editor: Bob Pennycook. 90% freelance written. Monthly magazine covering the "do-it-yourself market including projects, renovation and restoration, gardening, maintenance and decoration. Canadian writers only." Circ. 70,000. Pays on publication. Publishes ms an average of 5 months after acceptance. Byline given. Offers 75% kill fee. Buys first serial rights only. Submit seasonal/holiday material 6 months in advance. Simultaneous queries OK. Computer printout submissions acceptable; no dot-matrix. SASE. Reports in 3 weeks. Sample copy $2; free writer's guidelines.
Nonfiction: How-to (gardening, home and home machinery maintenance, renovation projects, and woodworking projects). Buys 20-40 mss/year. Query with clips of published work. Length: 1,500-4,000 words. Pays $225-600. Pays expenses of writers on assignment.
Photos: Send photos with ms. Pays $20-150 for 2¼x2¼ color transparencies; covers higher; $10-50 for b&w contact sheets. Captions, model release, and identification of subjects required.
Tips: "Freelancers must be aware of our magazine format. Product-types used in how-to articles must be readily available across Canada. Deadlines for articles are 5 months in advance of cover date. How-tos should be detailed enough for the amateur but appealing to the experienced. We work with the writer to develop a major feature. That could mean several rewrites, but we've found most writers to be eager. A frequent mistake made by writers is not directing the copy towards our reader. Stories sometimes have a tendency to be too basic."

COLORADO HOMES & LIFESTYLES, Suite 154, 2550 31st St., Denver CO 80216. (303)433-6533. Editor: Ann Levine. 50% freelance written. Bimonthly magazine covering Colorado homes and lifestyles for upper-middle-class and high income households as well as designers, decorators, and architects. Circ. 30,000. Pays on publication. Publishes ms an average of 6 months after acceptance. Byline given. Buys all rights. Sub-

mit seasonal/holiday material 6 months in advance. Simultaneous queries and photocopied submissions OK. Electronic submissions OK on ASCII (5¼" DD, DS disk), but requires hard copy also. Computer printout submissions acceptable: prefers letter-quality to dot matrix. SASE. Reports in 2 months. Free writer's guidelines.
Nonfiction: Fine home furnishings, interesting personalities and lifestyles, gardening and plants, decorating and design, fine food and entertaining—all with a Colorado slant. Buys 24 mss/year. Send complete ms. Length: 800-1,500 words. "For celebrity features (Colorado celebrity and home) pay is $200-1500. For unique, well-researched pieces on Colorado people, places, etc., pay is 15-50¢/word. For regular articles, 10-20¢/word. The more specialized and Colorado-oriented your article is, the more generous we are." Sometimes pays the expenses of writers on assignment.
Photos: Send photos with ms. Reviews 35mm color transparencies and b&w glossy prints. Identification of subjects required.
Tips: "Our shorter articles are generally done by staff writers. A frequent mistake made by writers is failure to provide material with a style and slant appropriate for the magazine, due to poor understanding of consumer nature and Colorado focus of the magazine."

COUNTRY LIVING, Hearst Corporation, 224 W. 57th Ave., New York NY 10019. (212)262-3621. Editor: Rachel Newman. Managing Editor: Mary Roby. 10% freelance written. Monthly magazine on country homes/ living. Circ. 1,425,000. Pays on acceptance. Byline given. Usually buys all rights; sometimes first rights only. Makes work-for-hire assignments. Submit seasonal/holiday material 1 year in advance. Photocopied submissions OK. Computer printout submissions acceptable. SASE. Reports in 2 weeks on queries; 1 month on mss.
Nonfiction: Mary Seehafer, articles editor. General interest, historical/nostalgic, interview/profile, and any article about living "country-style." No fiction or poetry. Buys 20 mss/year (excluding regular columnists). Query with published clips. Length: 300-1,200 words. Pays $100-350.
Photos: Ellen Schwartz, photo editor. State availability of photos. Reviews b&w contact sheets, color transparencies, and 8x10 b&w and color prints. Captions required. Buys one-time rights.
Columns/Departments: Mary Seehafer, column/department editor. Buys 12 mss/year. Query with published clips. Length: 300-1,200 words. Pays $100-350.
Tips: "Send short typed piece with cover letter—it must relate to country living. Short informative essay on country furniture, pottery, quilts, textiles, or other specialty is the area most open to freelancers."

EARTH SHELTER LIVING, Webco Publishing Inc., Box 268, 110 S. Greeley St., Stillwater MN 55082. (612)430-1113. Contact: Editor. 60% freelance written. Bimonthly magazine on earth sheltering aimed at knowledgeable consumers and some professionals (architects, builders). Circ. 10,000. Pays on acceptance. Publishes ms an average of 3 months after acceptance. Byline given. Offers 10% kill fee. Buys first serial rights. Submit seasonal/holiday material 4 months in advance. Simultaneous queries, and simultaneous, photocopied and previously published submissions OK. Computer printout submissions acceptable. Reports in 3 weeks. Sample copy $3; free writer's guidelines.
Nonfiction: Book excerpts; how-to (earth shelter construction, passive solar or related areas); humor; interview/profile; new product; opinion; personal experience; photo feature and technical. "Present queries or manuscripts on new methods or new angles on old methods. Earth shelterers are interested in anything different. No articles like those we've already used." Buys 20 mss/year. Query. Length: 1,000-2,500 words. Pays $50-125.

‡ENERGY SENSE, Curriculum Innovations, Inc., 3500 Western Ave., Highland Park IL 60035. (312)432-2700. Editor: Margaret Mucklo. Associate Editor: Carole Rubenstein. 95% freelance written. Quarterly magazine on energy awareness. "Our purpose is to provide energy information in an easy-to-read style and to promote energy awareness in the home and workplace." Pays 30 days after acceptance. Publishes ms an average of 3 months after acceptance. Offers 25% kill fee. Makes work-for-hire assignments. Simultaneous queries OK. Computer printout submissions acceptable. SASE. Reports in 1 month. Sample copy for large SAE and 65¢ postage. Writer's guidelines for #10 SAE and 1 first class stamp.
Nonfiction: General interest. "Our greatest need is for queries in November and December." Buys 40 mss/ year. Query with published clips. Length: 1,200-1,600 words. Pays $75-150.

FARMING UNCLE®, Box 91, Liberty NY 12754. Editor: Louis Toro. 25% freelance written. Quarterly magazine on nature, small stock, and gardening. 72 pages (8½"x11").Pays on acceptance. Publishes ms an average of 3 months after acceptance. Byline given. Buys all rights. SASE. Reports in 1 week on queries. Sample copy for $3 and $1.50 postage (first class).
Nonfiction: How-to (poultry, small stock, gardening, shelter building, etc.). Buys 12 mss/year. Send complete ms. Length: 500-750 words. Pays $7.50-10.
Photos: Send photos with ms. Pays $3-4 for b&w prints. Captions and identification of subjects not required.
Poetry: "We publish poetry but do not pay for it."

FLOWER AND GARDEN MAGAZINE, 4251 Pennsylvania, Kansas City MO 64111. Editor-in-Chief: Rachel Snyder. 50% freelance written. For home gardeners. Bimonthly. Picture magazine. Circ. 600,000. Buys first rights only. Byline given. Pays on acceptance. Publishes ms an average of 1 year after acceptance. Computer printout submissions acceptable; no dot-matrix. Free writer's guidelines. Query. Reports in 6 weeks. SASE.

Nonfiction: Interested in illustrated articles on how to do certain types of gardening and descriptive articles about individual plants. Flower arranging, landscape design, house plants, patio gardening are other aspects covered. "The approach we stress is practical (how-to-do-it, what-to-do-it-with). We try to stress plain talk, clarity, and economy of words. An article should be tailored for a national audience." Buys 20-30 mss/year. Length: 500-1,500 words. Pays 7¢/word or more, depending on quality and kind of material.

Photos: Pays up to $12.50/5x7 or 8x10 b&w prints, depending on quality, suitability. Also buys color transparencies, 35mm and larger. "We are using more four-color illustrations." Pays $30-125 for these, depending on size and use.

Tips: "Prospective author needs good grounding in gardening practice and literature. Then offer well-researched and well-written material appropriate to the experience level of our audience. Use botanical names as well as common. Illustrations help sell the story. Describe special qualifications for writing the particular proposed subject."

GARDEN DESIGN, The Fine Art of Residential Landscape Architecture, American Society of Landscape Architects, 1733 Connecticut Ave. NW, Washington DC 20009. (202)466-7730. Editor: Ken Druse. Editor-in-chief: Susan Rademacher Frey. 75% freelance written. Quarterly magazine covering garden making, garden history, garden design emphasizing the *design* aspects of gardening rather than horticulture. "Design elements and considerations are presented in clear, simple language for garden enthusiasts." Circ. 45,000. Pays on publication. Publishes ms an average of 6 months after acceptance. Byline given. Offers negotiable kill fee. Buys one-time rights and makes work-for-hire assignments. Submit seasonal/holiday material 1 year in advance. Computer printout submissions acceptable; no dot-matrix. SASE. Reports in 2 weeks on queries; 5 weeks on mss. Sample copy $5.

Nonfiction: Historical/nostalgic, interview/profile, opinion, personal experience, photo feature, and travel. Photographic and editorial content addresses specific seasons—spring, summer, autumn, winter. No detailed horticultural or technical articles. Buys 20-30 mss/year. Query with published clips. Length: 500-3,000 words. Pays $50-300. Sometimes pays the expenses of writers on assignment.

Photos: Send photos with query or ms. Pays $50-100 for color transparencies and 8x10 b&w prints. Captions, model release and identification of subjects required.

Columns/Departments: Almanac (calendar of events); First Garden (how-to); Plant Page (design applications of plants); The Garden Traveler (public gardens outside U.S.); Focal Point (personal perspectives); Ex Libris (book reviews); and Eclectic (items of interest). Buys 10-15 mss/year. Query with published clips. Length: 100-1,500 words. Pays $50-300.

Tips: "We emphasize the experience of gardening over technique. Our editorial core covers an array of subjects—historical, contemporary, large and small gardens. Departments follow specific subjects—travel, plants, people, etc. Samples of previously published work are welcomed. Outlines or brief article descriptions of specific subjects are helpful. We are willing to work with authors in tailoring specific subjects and style with them."

GARDEN MAGAZINE, The Garden Society, A Division of the New York Botanical Garden, Bronx Park, Bronx NY 10458. Editor: Ann Botshon. 40% freelance written. Emphasizes horticulture, environment and botany for a diverse readership, largely college graduates and professionals united by a common interest in plants and the environment. Most are members of botanical gardens and arboreta. Bimonthly magazine. Circ. 30,000. Buys first North American serial rights, and all rights. Submit seasonal/holiday material 6 months in advance. Photocopied submissions OK. Computer printout submissions acceptable; prefers letter-quality to dot-matrix. SASE. Reports in 2 months. Sample copy $2.50; guidelines for SAE and 1 first class stamp.

Nonfiction: Ann Botshon, editor. "All articles must be of high quality, meticulously researched and botanically accurate." Expose (environmental subjects); how-to (horticultural techniques), must be unusual and verifiable); general interest (plants in art and history, botanical news, ecology); humor (pertaining to botany and horticulture); and travel (great gardens of the world). Buys 15-20 unsolicited mss/year. Query with clips of published work. Length: 1,000-2,500 words. Pays $100-300.

Photos: Anne Schwartz, associate editor. Pays $35-50/5x7 b&w glossy print; $40-150/4x5 or 35mm color transparency. Captions preferred. Buys one-time rights.

Tips: "We appreciate some evidence that the freelancer has studied our magazine and understands our special requirements. Superficial research is the most frequent mistake made by writers in completing an article for us."

GARDENS FOR ALL NEWS, Newsmagazine of the National Association for Gardening, Gardens for All, 180 Flynn Ave., Burlington VT 05401. (802)863-1308. Editor: Ruth W. Page. 65% freelance written. Monthly tabloid covering food gardening and food trees. "We publish not only how-to-garden techniques, but also news that affects gardeners, like science advances. Specific, experienced-based articles with carefully worked-out techniques for planting, growing, harvesting, using garden fruits and vegetables sought. Most of our material is for gardeners with several years' experience." Circ. 225,000. Pays on acceptance. Publishes ms an average of 1 year after acceptance. Byline given. Buys first rights only and occasionally second (reprint) rights to material originally published elsewhere. Submit seasonal/holiday material 4 months in advance. Photocopied and previously published submissions OK. Computer printout submissions acceptable; prefers letter-quality to dot-matrix. SASE. Reports in 2 weeks on queries; 1 month on mss. Sample copy $1; writer's guidelines for SAE and 1 first class stamp.

Nonfiction: How-to, humor, inspirational, interview/profile, new product, personal experience, photo feature and technical. "All articles must be connected with food/gardening." Buys 80-100 mss/year. Query. Length: 300-3,500 words. Pays $30-450/article. Sometimes pays the expenses of writers on assignment.

Photos: Kit Anderson, photo editor. Send photos with ms. Pays $15-25 for b&w photos; $25-40 for color photos. Captions, model releases and identification of subjects required.

Tips: "Wordiness is a frequent mistake made by writers. Few writers understand how to write 'tight'. The most irritating easily correctable problem is careless grammar and poor spelling, often even in otherwise well-written pieces."

GURNEY'S GARDENING NEWS, A Family Newsmagazine for Gurney Gardeners, Gurney Seed and Nursery Co., 2nd and Capitol, Yankton SD 57079. (605)665-4451. Editor: Pattie Vargas. 85% freelance written. Bimonthly newsmagazine covering gardening, horticulture and related subjects for home gardeners. Circ. 30,000. Pays on acceptance. Publishes ms an average of 1 month after acceptance. Byline given. Buys first North American serial rights, but will consider second serial (reprint) rights to material originally published elsewhere. Submit seasonal/holiday material 6 months in advance. Computer printout submissions acceptable; no dot-matrix. SASE. Reports in 1 month on queries; 2 months on mss. Sample copy for 9x12 SAE; writer's guidelines for business size SAE.

Nonfiction: "We are interested in well-researched, well-written and illustrated articles on all aspects of home gardening. We prefer articles that stress the practical approach to gardening and are easy to understand. We don't want articles which sound like a rehash of material from a horticultural encyclopedia or how-to-garden guide. We rarely buy articles without accompanying photos or illustrations. We look for a unique slant, a fresh approach, new gardening techniques that work and interesting anecdotes. Especially need short (300-500 words) articles on practical gardening tips, hints, and methods. We are interested in: how-to (raise vegetables, flowers, bulbs, trees); interview/profile (of gardeners); photo feature (of garden activities); and technical (horticultural-related)." Buys 70 unsolicited mss/year. Query. Length: 700-1,250 words. Pays $50-125. Also buys articles on gardening projects and activities for children. Length: 500-1,000 words. Pays $30-100.

Photos: Purchases photos with ms. Also buys photo features, essays. Pays $10-85 for 5x7 or 8x10 b&w prints or contact sheets. Caption, model release, and identification of subjects required. Buys one-time rights.

Tips: "Time articles to coincide with the proper season. Read Gurney's Seed and Nursery catalogs and be familiar with Gurney's varieties before you submit an article on vegetables, fruits, flowers, trees, etc. We prefer that it be Gurney's. Our readers know gardening. If you don't, don't write for us."

HERB QUARTERLY, Box 275, Newfane VT 05345. Editor: Sallie Ballantine. 90% freelance written. Quarterly magazine for herb enthusiasts. Circ. 22,000. Pays $25 on publication. Publishes ms an average of 1 year after acceptance. Buys first North American serial rights and second (reprint) rights to manuscripts originally published elsewhere. Electronic submissions OK on IBM PC-WordStar. Computer printout submissions acceptable. Query letters recommended. SASE. Reports in 1 month. Sample copy $5; guidelines SAE and 1 first class stamp.

Nonfiction: Gardening (landscaping, herb garden design, propagation, harvesting); how-to (herb businesses, medicinal and cosmetic use of herbs, crafts); cooking; historical (folklore, focused piece on particular period—*not* general survey); interview of a famous person involved with herbs or folksy herbalist; personal experience; and photo essay ("cover quality" 8x10 b&w prints). "We are particularly interested in herb garden design, contemporary or historical." No fiction or poetry. Send double-spaced ms. Length: 1,500-3,000 words. Reports in one month.

Tips: "Our best submissions are narrowly focused on herbs with much practical information on cultivation and use for the gardener."

HOME BUYERS GUIDE, Bryan Publications, Inc., 1550 Bristol St. N., Newport Beach CA 92660. Editor: Greg Gearn. Emphasizes new homes available for homebuyers and homebuilders. Monthly. Circ. 115,000. Pays on publication. Buys first North American serial rights. Photocopied submissions OK. Previously published work OK, but state where and when it appeared. SASE. Reports in 2 months.

Nonfiction: General interest (taxes, insurance, home safety, mortgages); and opinion (by experts in a field, e.g., a CPA on taxes). "Gear all material to the California homeowner and consumer. Write in an informative yet entertaining style. Give examples the reader can identify with." Buys 2 mss/issue. Send complete ms. Length: 500-1,500 words. Pays $75-200.

Photos: Send photos with ms. Uses color transparencies. Offers no additional payment for photos accepted with ms. Captions preferred, model release required. Buys one-time rights.

HOME ILLUSTRATED, 1515 Broadway, New York NY 10036. (212)719-6630. Editor: Joseph R. Provey. Executive Editor: Harry Wicks. Home Workshop Editor: Michael Morris. Monthly magazine for the home and car manager. "Articles on maintenance, repair, and renovation to the home and family car. Information on how to buy, how to select products useful to homeowners/carowners. Emphasis in home-oriented articles is on good design, inventive solutions to styling and space problems, and useful home-workshop projects." Circ. 1.2 million. Buys first North American serial rights. Byline given. Pays on acceptance. SASE. Query.
Nonfiction: Feature articles relating to homeowner/carowner, 1,500-2,500 words. "This may include personal home-renovation projects, professional advice on interior design, reports on different or unusual construction methods, and energy-related subjects; and outdoor/backyard projects, etc. We are no longer interested in high-tech subjects such as aerospace, electronics, photography or military hardware. Most of our automotive features are written by experts in the field, but fillers, tips, how-to repair, or modification articles on the family car are welcome. Workshop articles on furniture, construction, tool use, refinishing techniques, etc., are also sought. Pays $300 minimum for features; fees based on number of printed pages, photos accompanying mss., etc."
Photos: Photos should accompany mss. Pays $600 and up for transparencies for cover. Inside color: Payments vary, starting at $400/doz. Home and Shop Hints illustrated with 1 photo, $35. Captions and model release required.
Fillers: Tips and fillers useful to tool users or for general home maintenance. Pays $35 and up for illustrated and captioned fillers. Pays $75-100 for half-page fillers.
Tips: "If you're planning some kind of home improvement and can write, you might consider doing a piece on it for us. Good how-to articles on home improvement are always difficult to come by."

‡**HOME MAGAZINE**, Harold Publications, Drawer 189, Palm Beach FL 33480. Editor: Mark Adams. A general interest bimonthly magazine featuring domestic themes and family values. Circ. 75,000. Buys simultaneous rights; first rights; and second serial (reprint) rights. Submit seasonal material 6 months in advance. Simultaneous, photocopied and previously published submissions OK. SASE. Reports in 3 weeks on "holding mss", 3 months on mss. Sample copy $1 and SAE. Writer's guidelines for SAE.
Nonfiction: General interest, humor, motivational, interviews/profile (must include subject's picture), personal experience, photo feature, travel lifestyle and fashion. Buys 50-100 mss/year. Send complete ms. Length: 400-1,000 words. Pays 5¢/published word or $25 maximum.
Fiction: Prefers humor. Buys up to 10 mss/year. Length: 400-1,000 words. Pays 5¢/word or $25 maximum.
Photos: Send photos or state availability with mss. Pays $5 for 8x10 b&w glossy prints or color transparencies. Captions preferred; identification of subjects required. Buys one-time rights.
Cartoons: Buys few. Pays $10.
Tips: "Type manuscript, double-space and *keep a copy* (we sometimes lose them.) Edit Yourself—ruthlessly—for grammar, spelling, punctuation and style. Is your story unique? No queries—We simply can't answer them. We receive thousands of manuscripts per year. so no SASE. No answer, and no apologies. Follow the rules, be *very* patient and keep trying. We want to publish you."

HOME MAGAZINE, Publishing Corp., 140 E. 45th St., New York NY 10017. (212)682-4040. Editor: Olivia Buehl. Executive Editor: Louise I. Driben. 80% freelance written. Monthly magazine covering home remodeling, home improving decorating, landscaping, new products, and home building. "*Home* tells homeowners how to remodel, improve, or redecorate an existing home, build a new home, and deal effectively with architects, designers, contractors, and building supply dealers." Circ. 700,000. Pays on acceptance. Byline given. Pays negotiable kill fee. Buys all rights to copy and photocopy. Submit seasonal material 6 months in advance. Computer printout submissions acceptable. SASE. Reports in 3 weeks on queries; 6 weeks on mss. Publishes ms an average of 5 months after acceptance. Sample copy $2.
Nonfiction: How-to (homeowner-oriented, do-it-yourself projects); and financial subjects of interest to homeowners, (taxes, insurance, etc.). Buys 50-60 mss/year. Query with clips of published work. Length: 200-2,500 words. Pays $150-1,500.

THE HOMEOWNER, America's How-to Magazine, Family Media Inc., 3 Park Ave., New York NY 10016. Editor: Jim Liston. Managing Editor: Lorraine Ulrich. 30% freelance written. Monthly (combined Jan/Feb; July/Aug) magazine on home improvement, maintenance. Aimed at men and women who want to successfully complete home improvement (even ambitious remodeling) and repair projects. Circ. 650,000. Pays on acceptance. Publishes ms an average of 10 months after acceptance. Byline given. Offers 50% kill fee. Buys first North American serial rights. Submit seasonal/holiday material 8 months in advance. Computer printout submissions acceptable; no dot-matrix. SASE. Reports in 1 month. Sample copy $1.95 and 8x10 SAE; writer's guidelines for #10 SAE and 1 first class stamp.

Nonfiction: How-to (remodeling, home maintenance); personal experience (hands on experience with building a home, remodeling or carpentry project); and technical (sophisticated or engineering how-to, related to home projects). No humor regarding writer's ineptitude as a do-it-yourselfer. Buys 30 mss/year. Length: 1,500 maximum. Pays $35. Sometimes pays the expenses of writers on assignment.

‡**HOUSE & GARDEN**, The Conde Nast Bldg; 350 Madison Ave., New York NY 10017. Editor-in-Chief: Louis Oliver Gropp. Editors: Denise Otis and Martin Filler. Monthly. Circ. 500,000. Buys first North American rights. Pays on acceptance. Since all its editorial stories are written by staff members or experts, it has no writer's guidelines. It does *not* accept unsolicited manuscripts, photographs, illustrations, or the like. Enclose SASE with query.

HOUSE BEAUTIFUL, The Hearst Corp., 1700 Broadway, New York NY 10019. (212)903-5000. Editor: JoAnn Barwick. Executive Editor: Margaret Kennedy. Editorial Director: Mervyn Kaufman. Director of Copy/Editor: Carol Cooper Garey. (212)903-5236. Emphasizes design, architecture and building. Monthly magazine; 200 pages. Circ. 840,000. Pays on acceptance. Byline given. Submit seasonal/holiday material 4 months in advance of issue date. SASE. Reports in 5 weeks.
Nonfiction: Historical (landmark buildings and restorations); how-to (kitchen, bath remodeling service); humor; interview; new product; and profile. Submit query with detailed outline or complete ms. Length: 300-1,000 words. Pays varying rates.
Photos: State availability of photos with ms.

LOG HOME GUIDE FOR BUILDERS & BUYERS, Muir Publishing Company Ltd., 1 Pacific Ave., Gardenvale, Quebec H9X 1B0 Canada. (514)457-2045. U.S. Editorial Office: Exit 447, I-4D, Hartford TN 37753. (615)487-2256. Editor: Doris Muir. 65% freelance written. Quarterly magazine covering the buying and building of log homes. "We publish for persons who want to buy or build their own log home. The writer should always keep in mind that this is a special type of person—usually a back-to-the-land, back-to-tradition type of individual who is looking for practical information on how to buy or build a log home." Circ. 125,000. Pays on publication. Publishes ms an average of 6 months after acceptance. Byline given. Buys all rights. Submit seasonal/holiday material 4 months in advance. Simultaneous queries, and simultaneous ("writer should explain"), photocopied, and previously published submissions OK. Electronic submissions OK on IBM PC, but requires hard copy. Computer printout submissions acceptable; no dot-matrix. Reports in 2 weeks. Sample copy $3.50 (postage included). Writer's guidelines for SASE.
Nonfiction: General interest; historical/nostalgic (log home historic sites, restoration of old log structures); how-to (anything to do with building log homes); inspirational (sweat equity—encouraging people that they can build their own home for less cost); interview/profile (with persons who have built their own log homes); new product (or new company manufacturing log homes—check with us first); personal experience (author's own experience with building his own log home, with photos is ideal); photo feature (on log home decor, author or anyone else building his own log home); and technical (for "Techno-log" section; specific construction details, i.e., new log buiding details, joining systems). Also, "would like photo/interview/profile stories on famous persons and their log homes—how they did it, where they got their logs, etc." Interested in log commercial structures. "Please no exaggeration—this is a truthful, back-to-basics type of magazine trying to help the person interested in log homes." Buys 25 mss/year. Query with clips of published work or send complete ms. "Prefer queries first with photo of subject house." Length: open. Pays $50-600.
Photos: State availability of photos. Send photos with query "if possible. It would help us to get a real idea of what's involved." Pays $5-25 for b&w, $25-50 for color transparencies. "All payments are arranged with individual author/submitter." Captions and identification of subjects required. Buys all rights unless otherwise arranged.
Columns/Departments: Pro-Log (short news pieces of interest to the log-building world); Techno-Log (technical articles, i.e., solar energy systems; any illustrations welcome); Book-Log (book reviews only, on books related to log building and alternate energy; "check with us first"); Chrono-Log (features on historic log buildings); and Decor (practical information on how to finish and furnish a log house). Buys possible 50-75 mss/year. Query with clips of published work or send complete ms. Length: 100-1,000 words or more. "All payments are arranged with individual author/submitter." Enclose SASE.
Tips: "The writer may have a better chance of breaking in at our publication with short articles and fillers since writing well on log homes requires some prior knowledge of subject. The most frequent mistakes made by writers in completing an article assignment for us are not doing enough research or not having understanding of the subject; not people oriented enough; angled toward wrong audience. They don't study the publication before they submit manuscripts."

METROPOLITAN HOME, 750 3rd Ave., New York NY 10017. Assistant Managing Editor: Charla Lawhon. For city dwellers. 50% freelance written. Monthly magazine; 120 + pages plus. Circ. 750,000. Buys all rights. Pays on acceptance. Publishes ms an average of 6 months after acceptance. Submit seasonal material 6 months in advance. Computer printout submissions acceptable "as long as they are readable." Reports in 2 months. SASE.

Nonfiction: Barbara Graustark, article editor. "Service material specifically for people who live in cities on interior designs, collectibles, equity, wines, liquor and real estate. Thorough, factual, informative articles." Buys 60-100 mss/year. Query. Length: 300-1,000 words. Pays $600-800. Sometimes pays the expenses of writers on assignment.

Photos: B&w photos and color are purchased only on assignment.

Columns/Departments: Collecting, The Right Choice, Wanderlusting, High Spirits (wine and liquor), Equity and Real Estate. Length: 300-1,000 words. Pays $500 and up.

Tips: "The writer may have a better chance of breaking in at our publication with short articles and fillers as this establishes a tone and helps us to learn how one another works—dependability in rewriting, meeting deadlines, etc."

N.Y. HABITAT MAGAZINE, For Co-op, Condominium and Loft Living, The Carol Group, Ltd., 928 Broadway, New York NY 10010. (212)505-2030. Editor: Carol J. Ott. Managing Editor: Tom Soter. 75% freelance written. Bimonthly magazine covering co-op, condo and loft living in metropolitan New York for "sophisticated, affluent and educated readers interested in maintaining the value of their homes and buying new homes." Circ. 10,000. Pays on publication. Publishes ms an average of 10 weeks after acceptance. Byline given. Offers negotiable kill fee. Buys first North American serial rights. Submit seasonal/holiday material 3 months in advance. Computer printout submissions acceptable. SASE. Reports in 3 weeks. Sample copy for $3, 9x12 SAE and 5 first class stamps; writer's guidelines for business-size SAE and 1 first class stamp.

Nonfiction: Only material relating to co-op and condominium living in New York metropolitan area. Buys 20 mss/year. Query with published clips. Length: 750-1,500 words. Pays $25-500.

1001 HOME IDEAS, Family Media, 3 Park Ave., New York NY 10016. Editor-in-Chief: Anne Anderson. Executive Editor: Kathryn Larson. 50% freelance written. "We're primarily an interior design magazine for mainstream America." Monthly. Circ. 1.5 million. Buys variable rights. Pays on acceptance. Publishes ms an average of 6 months after acceptance. Computer printout submissions acceptable. SASE. Sample copy and writer's guidelines for $2 and SASE. Query first. SASE.

Nonfiction: Interior design material and home service articles on food, gardening, and money-saving tips. Length: 2,000 words maximum.

Photos: "Freelance photographs rarely accepted." Interior design queries should include snapshots of room and clear descriptions of the room and its contents. Professional photographers may contact Robert Thornton, art director, about possible assignments. Send SASE with sufficient postage.

Tips: "Our readers are looking for easy, attractive, and cost-effective ideas in a step-by-step format. Persons who want to suggest a room for possible inclusion in the magazine may do so by sending a query with detailed descriptions of the room and snapshots. Don't hire a professional photographer just to show us what the room looks like."

ORGANIC GARDENING, Rodale Press Publications, 33 E. Minor St., Emmaus PA 18049. (215)967-5171. Editorial Director: Steve Daniels. For a readership "interested in growing plants, vegetables and fruits using organic methods in health, and in protecting the environment." 15% freelance written. Monthly magazine; 120-160 pages. Circ. 1,300,000. Buys all rights and the right to reuse in other Rodale Press Publications with agreed additional payment. Pays 25% kill fee, "if we agree to one." Byline given. Buys 200 mss/year. Pays on acceptance. Publishes ms an average of 8 months after acceptance. Reports in 4-6 weeks. Query first with full details. SASE. Free sample copy and writer's guidelines.

Nonfiction: Articles on food and ornamental gardening that are specifically detailed, thoroughly researched and stress organic methods. Also articles on natural foods preparation, biological pest control, soil care, landscaping and lawn care, and the enviroment. Not interested in generalized garden success stories; prefer details on specific varieties and techniques. Articles must be submitted in duplicate with one copy footnoted with references, telephone contracts, etc.

Photos: B&w and color purchased with mss or on assignment. Enlarged b&w glossy print and/or negative preferred. Pays $15-25. 2¼x2¼ (or larger) color transparencies.

Fillers: Fillers on above topics are also used. Length: 150-500 words. Pays $50-100.

Tips: "Read the magazine regularly, like a hawk."

PHOENIX HOME & GARDEN, Arizona Home Garden, Inc., 3136 N. 3rd Ave., Phoenix AZ 85013. (602)234-0840. Editor: Manya Winsted. Managing Editor: Nora Burba. Assistant Editor; Ellie Schultz. 50% freelance written. Monthly magazine covering homes, furnishings, entertainment, lifestyle and gardening for Phoenix area residents interested in better living. Circ. 35,000. Pays on publication. Publishes ms an average of 4 months after acceptance. Byline given. Buys all rights. Submit seasonal/holiday material 6 months in advance. Queries *only*. Simultaneous queries OK. Computer printout submissions acceptable; no dot-matrix. SASE. Reports in 6 weeks on queries. Sample copy $2, plus $2.10 postage.

Nonfiction: General interest (on interior decorating, architecture, gardening, entertainment, food); historical

(on furnishings related to homes); some how-to (on home improvement or decorating); health, beauty, fashion; and travel (of interest to Phoenix residents). Buys 100 or more mss/year. Query with clips of published work. Length: 1,200 words maximum. Pays $75-300/article.
Tips: "It's not a closed shop. I want the brightest, freshest, most accurate material available. Study the magazine to see our format and style. Major features are assigned to staff and tried-and-true freelancers."

‡**RARE Plants NEWSLETTER**, (formerly *Rare Seeds Newsletter*), 1937 Laughlin, Prineville OR 97754. (503)447-3159. Editor: Wally Wagner. 50% freelance written. Quarterly newsletter on seed growing of rare plants, including seeds for sale and growing information. Circ. 4,000. Pays on publication. Publishes ms an average of 2 months after acceptance. Byline given. Buys one-time, simultaneous, first and second serial (reprint) rights. Simultaneous queries, and simultaneous, photocopied, and previously published submissions OK. Computer printout submissions acceptable. SASE. Reports in 2 weeks on queries; 6 weeks on mss. Sample copy $2; writer's guidelines for business size SAE and 1 first class stamp.
Nonfiction: How-to, interview/profile, new product, opinion, personal experience, technical, travel. ("All must be related to rare plants"). "No articles on plants available in most seed catalogs. We need pieces on germination of rare plant seeds." Buys 30 mss/year. Query with or without clips of published work, or send complete ms. Length: 4 pages maximum. Pays $2-100.
Fillers: Clippings, newsbreaks. Pays $2.
Tips: "The most frequent mistakes made by writers in completing an article for us are writing about common plants, and sending articles not having to do with plants or plant culture. We need more major feature articles."

SAN DIEGO HOME/GARDEN, Westward Press, Box 1471, San Diego CA 92101. (714)233-4567. Editor: Peter Jensen. Managing Editor: Dirk Sutro. 50% freelance written. Monthly magazine covering homes, gardens, food, and nearby travel for residents of San Diego city and county. Circ. 36,000. Pays on publication. Publishes ms an average of 3 months after acceptance. Byline given. Buys first North American serial rights only. Submit seasonal material 3 months in advance. Photocopied submissions OK. Computer printout submissions acceptable; prefers letter-quality to dot-matrix. Reports in 1 month. Free writer's guidelines for SASE.
Nonfiction: General interest (service articles with plenty of factual information, prices and "where to buy" on home needs); how-to (save energy, garden, cook); new product (for the house); photo feature (on houses and gardens) and architecture; home improvement; remodeling; and real estate. Articles must have local slant. Buys 10-15 unsolicited mss/year. Query with clips of previously published work. Length: 500-2,000 words. Pays $50-200. Pays expenses of writers on assignment.
Tips: "No out-of-town, out-of-state material. Most freelance work is accepted from local writers. Gear stories to the unique quality of San Diego. We try to offer only information unique to San Diego—people, places, shops, resources, etc."

‡**SELECT HOMES MAGAZINE**, (incorporating *1001 Decorating Ideas*), Select Home Designs, 382 W. Broadway, Vancouver, British Columbia V5Y 1R2 Canada. (604)879-4144. Editor: Pam Miller Withers (West). Toronto address: Carlingview Ct., Unit 1, 151 Carlingview Dr., Rexdale, Ontario M9W 5E7 Canada. Editor: Jim Adair (East). 40% freelance written. Magazine published 8 times/year covering decorating, interior design, energy, and how-to as applied to homes for mostly upper-income single-family homeowners. Circ. 160,000. Pays half on acceptance, half on publication. Publishes ms an average of 5 months after acceptance. Buys 60 or more text/photo packages/year. Byline and photo credits given. Usually buys first Canadian serial rights; simultaneous rights, first rights, or second serial (reprint) rights, if explained. Submit seasonal/holiday material 3-12 months in advance. Simultaneous queries, and simultaneous, photocopied and previously published submissions OK if explained. Computer printout submissions acceptable; no dot-matrix. SASE or SAE, IRCs. Reports in 1 month. Sample copy for $1 and magazine size SAE; writer's guidelines for SAE.
Nonfiction: How-to, humor and personal experience on decorating, interior design, energy, financial matters and architecture. Special sections include kitchen, spring; bathroom, fall. "We prefer economy of words in a step-by-step format wherever possible, with lengthier cutlines for photos." No business profiles, lifestyle articles or articles on home finance written by non Canadians or those without knowledge of the Canadian market. Buys 60 or more mss/year. Query with published clips. Length: 650-1,500 words. Pays $50 (news and some reprints)-600 (occasionally higher). Sometimes pays expenses of writers on assignment.
Photos: State availability of photos. Reviews contact sheets and 2¼x2¼ transparencies. Pays $50-250, color. "We pay mostly on a negotiable per-day rate, but we like to work from stock lists, too. Send stock lists to the Vancouver office." Captions and model release requested. Buys one-time rights.
Columns/Departments: All About (one subject, e.g., bathrooms, kitchens, etc.); Architecture; The Back Porch (essays, light or humorous, home-related); Case History (home building project); Cottages (recreational or retirement home); 1001 Decorating Ideas; Energy; How-To; International Report (new trends in decor or architecture); Maintenance and Repair; Money; Outdoor Projects; Real Estate; Renovation; Spaces (architectural concepts, interior design and home storage); and Special Report. See writer's guidelines for additional details.
Fillers: Newsbreaks. Buys 10/year. Length: 100-500 words. Pays $15-75.

Tips: "Submit clips and outline and tell us what special interests you have (decorating, energy, how-to). Know the magazine well enough to tell us which column your query is aimed at. The editors generate 75% of the magazine's article ideas and assign them to writers whose style or background matches. We actively solicit book excerpts and reprints; please mention if your material is one of these. We retain stringers throughout Canada. See our guidelines to apply."

THE SPROUTLETTER, Sprouting Publications, Box 62, Ashland OR 97520. (503)482-5627. Editor: Jeff Breakey. 50% freelance written. Bimonthly newsletter covering sprouting, live foods and indoor food gardening. "We emphasize growing foods (especially sprouts) indoors for health, economy, nutrition and food self-sufficiency. We also cover topics related to sprouting, live foods and holistic health." Circ. 2,500. Pays on publication. Publishes ms an average of 2 months after acceptance. Byline given. Offers 50% kill fee. Buys first North American serial rights and second (reprint) rights to material originally published elsewhere. Submit seasonal/holiday material 3 months in advance. Previously published submissions OK. Computer printout submissions acceptable; prefers letter-quality to dot-matrix. SASE. Reports in 2 weeks on queries; 3 weeks on mss. Sample copy $2; writer's guidelines for business size SAE and 2 first class stamps.
Nonfiction: General interest (raw foods, sprouting, holistic health); how-to (grow sprouts, all kinds of foods indoors; build devices for sprouting or indoor gardening); personal experience (in sprouting or related areas); and technical (experiments with growing sprouts). No common health food/vitamin articles or growing ornamental plants indoors (as opposed to food producing plants). Buys 4-6 mss/year. Query. Length: 500-2,400 words. Pays $15-50. Trades for merchandise are also considered.
Columns/Departments: Book Reviews (books oriented toward sprouts, nutrition or holistic health). Reviews are short and informative. News Items (interesting news items relating to sprouts or live foods); Recipes (mostly raw foods). Buys 5-10 mss/year. Query. Length: 100-450 words. Pays $3-10.
Poetry: Buys 1-3 poems/year. Submit maximum 3 poems. Length: 10-50 lines. Payment for poems is a half-year subscription.
Fillers: Short humor and newsbreaks. Buys 3-6/year. Length: 50-150 words. Pays $2-6.
Tips: "Writers should have a sincere interest in holistic health and in natural whole foods. We like writing which is optimistic, interesting and very informative. Consumers are demanding more thorough and accurate information. Articles should cover any given subject in depth in an enjoyable and inspiring manner. A frequent mistake is that the subject matter is not appropriate."

TEXAS GARDENER, The Magazine for Texas Gardeners, by Texas Gardeners, Suntex Communications, Inc., Box 9005, Waco TX 76714. (817)772-1270. Editor: Chris S. Corby. Managing Editor: Rita Miller. 80% freelance written. Bimonthly magazine covering vegetable and fruit production, ornamentals and home landscape information for home gardeners in Texas. Circ. 35,000. Pays on publication. Publishes ms an average of 4 months after acceptance. Byline given. Buys all rights. Submit seasonal/holiday material 6 months in advance. Computer printout submissions acceptable; prefers letter-quality to dot-matrix. SASE. Reports in 6 weeks. Sample copy $2.75; writer's guidelines for business size SAE and 1 first class stamp.
Nonfiction: How-to, humor, interview/profile and photo feature. "We use feature articles that relate to Texas gardeners. We also like personality profiles on hobby gardeners and professional horticulturists who are doing something unique." Buys 50-100 mss/year. Query with clips of published work. Length: 800-2,400 words. Pays $50-200.
Photos: "We prefer superb color and b&w photos; 90% of photos used are color." State availability of photos. Pays negotiable rates for 2¼ color transparencies and 8x10 b&w prints and contact sheets. Model release and identification of subjects required.
Tips: "First, be a Texan. Then come up with a good idea of interest to home gardeners in this state. Be specific. Stick to feature topics like "How Alley Gardening Became a Texas Tradition." Leave topics like "How to Control Fire Blight" to the experts. High quality photos could make the difference. We would like to add several writers to our group of regular contributors and would make assignments on a regular basis. Fillers are easy to come up with 'in-house'. We want good writers who can produce accurate and interesting copy. Frequent mistakes made by writers in completing an article assignment for us are that articles are not slanted toward Texas gardening; show inaccurate or too little gardening information; or lack of good writing style."

YOUR HOME, Meridian Publishing Co., Inc., 1720 Washington, Box 10010, Ogden UT 84409. Articles Editor: Fern Poras. 90% freelance written. A monthly company magazine (for approximately 200 companies) covering home/garden subjects for homeowners and renters of all ages. Circ. 90,000. Pays on acceptance. Byline given. Buys first North American serial rights and non-exclusive reprint rights. One year lead time. Computer printout submissions acceptable; prefers letter-quality to dot-matrix. SASE. Sample copy for $1 and 9x12 SAE; writer's guidelines for SAE and 22¢ postage.
Nonfiction: Historical/nostalgic (homes); how-to (home/garden); humor (home/garden); and photo feature (remodeling with some copy). "We're in need of good decorating/remodeling/gardening ideas, with super-quality *color* transparencies, for beginning homeowners, renters, trailer house owners, and *some* well-to-do homes described in photo feature. Buys 50 mss/year. "We rarely make assignments." Query with or without

published clips or send complete ms. Length: 1,000-1,200 words. Pays 15¢/word.
Photos: State availability of photos or send photos with query or ms. Pays $35 for color transparencies (slides to 8x10). "We also need color transparency covers of brides; pay is negotiable." Captions required. Buys one-time rights.
Fiction: Humorous (home/garden). Buys 5-10 mss/year. Send complete ms. Pays 15¢/word.
Tips: "Send good decorating/remodeling/how-to's around the house and garden. Super sharp, clear color transparencies are essential—no snap shots."

Humor

Something hilarious happened in the grocery store; everyone who saw it laughed. Now, try to describe it to your best friend or to write about it. It doesn't seem as funny? That's one of the challenges of the humorist—whether he's telling a true or made-up story. Publications listed here specialize in gaglines or prose humor. Other publications that use humor can be found in nearly every category in this book. Some of these have special needs for major humor pieces; some use humor as fillers; many others are interested in material that meets their ordinary fiction or nonfiction requirements but has a humorous slant. Other markets for humorous material can be found in the Cartoon and Comic Books and Gag Writing sections. For a closer look at writing humor, consult *How to Write and Sell (Your sense of) Humor* by Gene Perret (Writer's Digest Books).

‡**CAMPUS MAGAZINE, The College Lampoon**, Goodbody Publishing, Inc., 12601 Chase St., Garden Grove CA 92645. (213)383-4163. Editor: Dexter T. Goodbody. Managing Editor: Ralph Abernathy. Monthly college humor magazine. "*Campus* Magazine is a regional humor magazine for young men and women in college. Our goal is to lampoon the *entire* college experience. Everything from registration and life in a dormitory to sorority rush and pledging are satired. We are looking for upbeat, mature, and tasteful caricatures of the American college experience." Estab. 1984. Circ. 25,000. Pays on acceptance. Byline given. Buys all rights. Submit seasonal/holiday material 7 weeks in advance. Simultaneous and photocopied submissions OK. SASE. Reports in 2 weeks. Sample copy $1; free writer's guidelines.
Nonfiction: James Taylor, articles editor. Expose (government, education); humor; interview/profile; and photo feature. Special editions include Christmas Student Buyers Guide, Summer Vacation Getaway, and Back To School. No pornography, religious or political articles. Buys 5-10 mss/year. Send complete ms. Length: 500-2,000 words. Pays up to $50 maximum.
Photos: Tatsuya Mitsubishi, photo editor. Send photos with query or ms. Reviews b&w and color negatives. Pays $60 maximum. Captions, model release and identification of subjects required. Buys all rights.
Columns/Departments: John Cochran, column/department editor. Buys 15-20 mss/year. Send complete ms. Length: 500-2,000 words. Pays $50 maximum.
Fiction: Rod Sterling, fiction editor. Anything humorous which deals with college. No pornography. Buys 10-15 mss/year. Send complete ms. Length: 250-1,500 words. Pays $50 maximum.
Fillers: Deborah Kahn, fillers editor. Clippings, jokes, gags, anecdotes and short humor. Buys 20-40/year. Length: 50-200 words. Pays $25 maximum.
Tips: "Since *Campus* is a humor magazine we are looking for comical, satirical, and parodic stories about college and college students. The main criteria is that the material be funny. Our editorial policy will permit adult language only when it enhances the mood of the article and is not used for shock element. If a writer can demonstrate an understanding of these requirements—it is that easy to get published."

HUMOR MAGAZINE, Humor Publications, Inc., 144 Gay St., Philadelphia PA 19127. (215)482-7673. Editor: Edward Savaria, Jr. 90% freelance written. Monthly. Estab. 1984. Circ. 40,000. Pays on publication or sooner "if earmarked for up-coming edition." Publishes ms an average of 6 months after acceptance. Byline given. Buys first North American serial rights, first rights, and second serial (reprint) rights. Submit seasonal/holiday material minimum 3 months in advance. Simultaneous queries, and simultaneous, photocopied, and previously published submissions OK. Computer printout submissions acceptable; prefers letter-quality to dot-matrix. SASE. Reports in 2 weeks on queries; 1 month on mss. Sample copy for $3 writer's guidelines for SAE and 1 first class stamp—attention: writer's guidelines.
Nonfiction: Book excerpts; expose (satire); general interest; historical/nostalgic; how-to (parody); humor; in-

terview/profile (on comedians, directors of comedy); new product (if funny); opinion (humor angle); personal experience (humor); photo feature (humor); and travel. "Everything must be funny or have to do with humor-comedy. No porn (hard), no silly humor, no excess violence." Buys 30 mss/year. Query or send complete ms. Length: 300-1,000 words. Pays $50-300 + . Sometimes pays expenses of writers on assignment.

Photos: Humor angle. Send photos with query or ms. Pays $10-25 + for 8x10 b&w prints.

Columns/Departments: T.V. Reviews and Movie Reviews (reviews of good, funny shows and movies, old and new); General National/World (any tibits or opinions, humor angle). Query or send complete ms. Length 50-300 words. Pays $25-200.

Fiction: Humorous. Any type of fiction with a humorous angle. Buys 15/mss year. Query or send complete ms. Length; 300-1,000 words. Pays $25-300.

Poetry: Light verse. Buys maximum 12 poems/year. Submit maximum 2 long, 20 short poems. Prefers short poems. Pays $5-25.

Fillers: Clippings, jokes, gags, anecdotes, short humor, newsbreaks—humorous. Cartoons (single and strips). Buys 100/year. Length: 10-100 words. Pays $5-50.

Tips: "We are especially interested in reviews of nationally distributed comedy films, books and records; also, play reviews if playing around the Philadelphia, South Jersey, and New York city area. Very welcome are inter-view/profiles on comedians and any other groups or individuals who bring comedy to the world. Column ideas are considered."

‡**HUMOR NEWS, People, Books, Records, Movies & Videos**, Suite 910, 1010 Vermont Ave., Washington DC 20005. (202)393-5233. Editor: James Roland. Monthly magazine with *Humor Trade News* pull-out supplement in copies sent to trade (retailers, wholesalers, publishers) for the humor industry. "Humor News is devoted exclusively to humor and to all types of humor products. It reviews books, records, tapes, movies, videos, greeting cards, gifts, gag items, and other humor-type products." Estab. 1985. Circ. 20,000. Pays on acceptance. Byline given. Buys first serial rights and reprint rights for cartoons; makes work-for-hire assignments. Submit seasonal/holiday material 4 months in advance. Simultaneous queries and photocopied submissions OK. SASE. Reports in 1 month. Sample copy $2.50; free writer's guidelines.

Nonfiction: Humor; interview/profile (with humor professionals); personal experience; photo feature; and product reviews (following specific format). Nothing nonhumorous. Query. Length: varies. Payment varies.

Photos: Reviews contact sheet. Captions, model releases and identification of subjects required. Buys variable rights.

Columns/Departments: Reviews, films, books and records. Query with published clips. Length: varies. Payment varies.

Fiction: Humorous. Query with published clips. Length: varies. Pays $200-300.

Poetry: Light verse and traditional. Humorous. Submit maximum 3 poems. Length: no limit.

Fillers: Jokes, gags, anecdotes and short humor. Length: no limit. Payment varies.

LAUGH FACTORY MAGAZINE, Warner Publisher Services, #214, 400 S. Beverly Dr., Beverly Hills CA 90212. (213)656-1336. Editor: Jamie Masada. Managing Editor: Mindy Schulthers. 80% freelance written. A bimonthly humor magazine. Circ. 225,000. Pays on publication. Publishes ms an average of 4 months after acceptance. Byline given. Buys one-time rights. Submit seasonal/holiday material 3 months in advance. Simultaneous queries, and simultaneous, photocopied, and previously published submissions OK. Computer print-out submissions acceptable; no dot-matrix. SASE. Reports in 6 weeks. Sample copy $3; writer's guidelines for SAE and 1 first class stamp.

Nonfiction: Humor. "We don't want 'humor' articles as such; we want material that makes people laugh out loud." Complete mss OK. "The only restrictions we have are no four-letter words and nothing too gross." Pay rates are negotiable depending on length and quality of the piece.

Photos: State availability of photos with query or mss. Reviews prints. Also uses photos with captions, without accompanying ms.

Fillers: Jokes, gags, cartoons, short humor, parody ads, and other belly-laugh humor.

Tips: "We use more short articles and fillers than major features. A frequent mistake made by writers is that articles are not funny enough—they miss the humor."

LONE STAR HUMOR DIGEST, (formerly *Lone Star: A Magazine of Humor,*) Lone Star Publications of Humor, Suite 103, Box 29000, San Antonio TX 78229. Editor: Lauren I. Barnett Scharf. 50% (or more) freelance written. A humor book-by-subscription for "the general public and 'comedy connoisseur' as well as

 The double dagger before a listing indicates that the listing is new in this edition. New markets are often the most receptive to freelance contributions.

the professional humorist." Circ. 1,200. Pays on publication, "but we try to pay before that." Publishes ms an average of 4 months after acceptance. Buys variable rights. Submit seasonal/holiday material 6 months in advance. Photocopied submissions and sometimes previously published work OK. Computer printout submission acceptable; no dot-matrix. SASE. Reports in 2 months on queries; 3 months on mss. Sample copy $6, (Writers may also purchase back issues for 3.50 (The format of *The Lone Star Humor Digest* will be similar to the format of *The Lone Star: A Magazine of Humor*); writer's guidelines for business size SAE and 1 first class stamp.

Nonfiction: Humor (on anything topical/timeless); interview/profile (of anyone professionally involved in humor); and opinion (reviews of stand-up comedians, comedy plays, cartoonists, humorous books, *anything* concerned with comedy). "Inquire about possible theme issues." Buys 15 mss/year. Query with clips of published work if available. Length: 500-1,000 words; average is 700-800 words. Pays $5-20 and contributor's copy.

Fiction: Humorous. Buys variable mss/year. Send complete ms. Length: 500-1,000 words. Pays $5-20 and contributor's copy.

Poetry: Free verse, light verse, traditional, clerihews and limericks. "Nothing too 'artsy' to be funny." Buys 10-20/year. Submit maximum 5 poems. Length: 4-16 lines. Pays $2-10.

Fillers: Clippings, jokes, gags, anecdotes, short humor and newsbreaks—"must be humorous or humor-related." Buys 20-30 mss/year. Length: 450 words maximum. Pays $1-5.

Tips: "We *do* like to know a writer's professional background. Those with no background sales in humor should feel free to submit their material. The only real criteria are that it be original and *funny*. We recommend that those who are unfamiliar with *Lone Star* purchase a sample issue before submitting their work. However, this is *not* a requirement. We are also seeking funny/interesting letters for our "Letters to Lone Star" column. Letters may be on any subject covered in the magazine or any aspect of humor. There is no payment for a letter—unless it contains short verse—but the writer receives a contributor's copy on publication."

MAD MAGAZINE, E.C. Publications, 485 Madison Ave., New York NY 10022. (212)752-7685. Editors: John Ficarra and Nick Meglin. 100% freelance written. Magazine published 8 times/year on humor, all forms. Circ. 1½ million. Pays on acceptance. Publishes ms an average of 6 months after acceptance. Byline given. Buys all rights. Submit seasonal/holiday material 6 months in advance. Photocopied submissions OK. Computer printout submissions acceptable; prefers letter-quality to dot-matrix. SASE. Reports in 1 month. Sample copy $1.50; writer's guidelines for legal size SAE and 1 first class stamp.

Nonfiction: Humor. No text pieces. "No formats we're already doing or have done to death like . . . 'You know you're _____ when . . .'." Buys 400 mss/year. Query or send complete ms. Pays $300/*MAD* page. Sometimes pays the expenses of writers on assignment.

Columns/Departments: Don Martin and department ideas. Buys 30 mss/year. Send complete ms. Pays $300/MAD page.

Fiction: Humorous. No text pieces. "We're a visually-oriented magazine." Buys 100 mss/year. Query or send complete ms. Pays $300/MAD page.

Poetry: Free verse, light verse, traditional and parody. Buys 20/year. Pays $300/*MAD* page.

Fillers: Short humor. Buys 100/year. Pays $300/*MAD* page.

Tips: "Freelancers can best break into our magazine with nontopical material (no movie or TV spoofs). We like outrageous but *clean* humor."

ORBEN'S CURRENT COMEDY, 1200 N. Nash St., #1122, Arlington VA 22209. (703)522-3666. Editor: Robert Orben. For "speakers, toastmasters, businessmen, public relations people, communications professionals." Biweekly. Buys all rights. Pays at the end of the month for material used in issues published that month. "Material should be typed and submitted on standard size paper. Leave three spaces between each item. Computer printout submissions acceptable. Unused material will be returned to the writer within a few days if SASE is enclosed. We do not send rejection slips. If SASE is not enclosed, all material will be destroyed after being considered except for items purchased."

Fillers: "We are looking for funny, performable one-liners, short jokes and stories that are related to happenings in the news, fads, trends and topical subjects. The accent is on laugh-out-loud comedy. Ask yourself, 'Will this line get a laugh if performed in public?' Material should be written in a conversational style, and if the joke permits it, the inclusion of dialogue is a plus. We are particularly interested in material that can be used by speakers and toastmasters: lines for beginning a speech, ending a speech, acknowledging an introduction, specific occasions, anything that would be of use to a person making a speech. We can use lines to be used at roasts, sales meetings, presentations, conventions, seminars and conferences. Short, sharp comment on business trends, fads and events is also desirable. Please do not send us material that's primarily written to be read rather than spoken. We have little use for definitions, epigrams, puns, etc. The submissions must be original. If material is sent to us that we find to be copied or rewritten from some other source, we will no longer consider material from the contributor." Pays $5.

Tips: "Follow the instructions in our guidelines. Although they are quite specific, we have received everything from epic poems to serious novels."

SMILE AND CHUCKLE INC., Smile and Chuckle, Inc., 108 S. Iris St., Alexandria VA 22304. (703)370-2085. Editor: Dan Boger. Monthly humor tabloid distributed to all residents in a zip code area. Circ. 10,000. Pays on publication. Buys all rights. Phone queries OK. Submit seasonal material 2 months in advance. Simultaneous and photocopied submissions OK, if so indicated. SASE. Reports in 4 months. Sample copy $1; writer's guidelines for SASE.
Nonfiction: Humor. No sex, violence, politics or controversial subjects. Buys 150 mss/year. Send complete ms. Length: 100-500 words. Pays 5¢/word.
Columns/Departments: Light humor. Send complete ms.
Fiction: Humorous. No sex, violence, politics or controversial subjects.
Poetry: Humor. Buys 2 mss/issue. Submit maximum 5 poems. Pays 5¢/word.
Fillers: Jokes, gags and short humor. Buys 100/year. Pays $2 maximum.

‡**STING**, Alpha Publications, Inc., 1079 DeKalb Pike, Blue Bell PA 19422. (215)277-8787. Editor: Lois G. Fad. 50% freelance written. Monthly magazine of humor and satire. "*Sting* reaches national subscribers with editorial cartoons and humor articles on politics and American life." Estab. 1984. Circ. 5,000. Pays on publication. Publishes ms an average of 2 months after acceptance. Byline given. Buys first North American serial rights and second serial (reprint) rights. Submit seasonal/holiday material 2 months in advance. Computer printout submissions acceptable; prefers letter-quality to dot-matrix. Simultaneous queries, and photocopied, simultaneous, and previously published submissions OK. SASE. Reports in 2 weeks on mss. Sample copy $2; writer's guidelines for business size SAE and 1 first class stamp.
Nonfiction: Humor (political satirical), personal experience (funny stories) and photo feature (funny photos). Buys 60 mss/year. Send complete ms. "Examples of writing and cartoons will be accepted, no originals please." Pays $25-350.
Photos: Francis Laping, photo editor. Send photos with mss. Pays $5-10 for 8x10 b&w prints. Captions and identification of subjects required. Buys one-time rights.
Fiction: Humorous. No "smut"/offensive language. Buys 60 mss/year. Length: 3,000 words maximum. Pays $25-350.
Poetry: Humor. Buys 3 poems/year. Submit maximum 10 poems. Length: 100 lines maximum. Pays $25-100.
Fillers: Jokes, gags and short humor. Buys 40 fillers/year. Pays $5-35.
Tips: "We're looking for witty, sharp, intellectual writers of humor and satire, mostly of a very current political topic, or of domestic humor, i.e., dating, home life, work place, etc. Subtlety is more appreciated than ridicule. Good writing is a must. Nonfiction satire and fictional humor are areas we always need to fill with new, upbeat authors. Pieces should be of national interest and should be *funny*. We welcome submissions by unknown authors and are probably one of the few publications that is available for the humor market. We want and need submissions. The writer has a better chance of breaking in at our publication with short articles and fillers since we have several established authors who do our cover stories—we can't afford too many major stories at once. Frequent mistakes made by writers are poor grammar, poor writing, sloppiness and not being funny."

In-Flight

Most major in-flight magazines cater to the business traveler and also to the vacationer who will be reading, during the flight, about the airline's destinations. Editors of these magazines use general interest material in addition to travel and popular aviation articles. Airline mergers and/or closings can affect these magazines. The "in-flight" magazine writer should watch for airline announcements in the news and in ads. "Now flying to Europe" can mean that an editor will need stories on European cities. Newly-sent-for sample copies and writer's guidelines will give you the latest information. In corresponding with in-flight magazines not based in the United States, remember to enclose an International Reply Coupon or an International Postal Money Order for responses. The majority of in-flight magazines pays for articles in cash; there are some, however, that compensate writers with airline coupons, enabling them to travel via the airline that has published their work.

ABOARD, North-South Net, Inc., 135 Madeira, Coral Gables FL 33134. (305)442-0752. Editor: Olga Connors. Bimonthly magazine covering destinations for the Ecuatorian, Dominican, Panamanian, Paraguayan,

Bolivian, Chilean, Salvadoran and Venezuelan national airlines. Entertaining, upbeat stories for the passengers. Circ. 120,000. Pays on publication. Byline given. Buys one-time rights. Simultaneous queries, and simultaneous, photocopied, and previously published submissions OK. Computer printout submissions acceptable. SASE. Reports in 2 weeks. Sample copy for 11x14 SAE and $1.05 postage; writer's guidelines for #10 SAE and 1 first class stamp.

Nonfiction: General interest, how-to, interview/profile, new product, technical, travel, sports, business, science, technology and topical pieces. Nothing "controversial, political, downbeat or in any way offensive to Latin American sensibilities." Buys 20 mss/year. Query. Length: 1,500-3,000 words. Pays $50-150 (with photos).

Photos: State availability of photos with query. Prefers b&w or color prints and color transparencies. Pays $10-50 for 35mm color transparencies; $5-20 for 5x7 b&w prints. Captions required. Buys one-time rights."

Tips: "Study *Aboard* and other inflights, write exciting, succinct stories with an upbeat slant and enclose photos with captions. Break in with destination pieces for the individual airline or those shared by all seven. Writers must be accurate. Photos are almost always indispensable. Manuscripts are accepted either in English or Spanish. Translation rights must be granted. All manuscripts are subject to editing and condensation."

‡**AIRWAYS INFLIGHT**, Oantas Airways Limited, Box 489, Sydney 2001 Australia. (02)236-3636. Editor: William Smith. Managing Editor: John Ward (Director of Public Affairs). 100% freelance written. Bimonthly magazine. "*Airways Inflight* is a magazine for travellers, not a travel magazine; hence our articles are not necessarily about travel. More than anything else we seek to give our passengers a good read." Circ. 300,000. Pays on acceptance. Publishes ms an average of 4 months after acceptance. Byline given. Buys first serial rights. Computer printout submissions acceptable; no dot-matrix. Reports in 3 months on mss. Free writer's guidelines.

Nonfiction: General interest, historical/nostalgic and humor. No first person accounts, "been there, done that" travel articles. Buys 30 mss/year. Send complete ms with professional quality color transparencies. Length: 1,750-2,000 words. Pays $1,000 maximum, Australian dollars; pays in travel coupons.

Photos: Send photos with query or ms. Reviews 35mm and above color transparencies. Payment included in ms. Captions and identification of subjects required. Buys one-time rights.

Tips: "All areas except flight guide details are open to freelancers. Make sure writing and photos are of the highest professional standard."

‡**AMERICAN WAY**, Mail Drop 3A61, Box 619616, Dallas/Fort Worth Airport TX 75261-9616. (817)355-1583. Editor: Walter A. Damtoft. Bimonthly inflight magazine for passengers flying with American Airlines. Pays on acceptance. Buys exclusive world rights; splits reprint fee 50/50 with the author. Simultaneous queries and photocopied submissions OK. Free sample copy; writer's guidelines for SASE.

Nonfiction: Business, the arts and entertainment, sports, personalities, science and medicine, and travel. "We are amenable to almost any subject that would be interesting, entertaining or useful to a passenger of American Airlines." Also humor, trivia, geneology tips and arson detection, and will consider a variety of ideas. "Articles involving current controversies are rarely scheduled; however, we are not Pollyanish. We can and do publish thoughtful articles on serious subjects." Buys 500-550 mss/year. Query with published work clips. Length: 1,500-1,750 words. Pays $400 and up; shorter items earn $100 or more.

Photos: Pays $50 for each published photograph made by a writer while researching an article.

DELTA SKY, Halsey Publishing, 12955 Biscayne Blvd., N. Miami FL 33181. (305)893-1520. Editor: Lidia de Leon. 90% freelance written. Readers are Delta Air Lines passengers. Monthly magazine. Circ. over 3 million monthly. "Unsolicited materials are rarely used, and only text/photo packages are considered." Computer printout submissions acceptable. Details and guidelines for SASE. Publishes unsolicited ms an average of up to 6 months after acceptance.

Tips: "Freelance writers should be aware of heavier emphasis on graphics, necessitating 'tighter' stories, via conveying idea, facts, etc., in a quicker, more provocative manner."

‡**DISCOVERY**, Emphasis (Hong Kong) Limited, 10/F Wilson House, 19-27 Wyndham St., Hong Kong. (5)215392. Editor: Derek A C Davies. Deputy Editor: Lesley Hargreaves. Monthly magazine on travel. "*Discovery* is an English language inflight magazine for airline passengers covering only Cathay-Pacific destinations." Circ. 90,000. Pays on publication. Byline given. Offers 50% kill fee. Buys one-time rights. Simultaneous queries OK. Computer printout submissions acceptable; prefers letter quality to dot-matrix. SASE. Reports in 1 month. Free sample copy.

Nonfiction: Personal experience, photo feature and travel, all related to Cathay Pacific destinations. Business Discovery section includes Travel Talk (essays on aspects of travel) and Insight (business features relevant to Cathay destinations). Buys 100 mss/year. Query with published clips. Length: 1,200-2,500 words. Pays $200-500.

Fiction: Short stories. Length 2,500-4,000 words. Pays $500.

Photos: Send photos with query or ms. Reviews color transparencies. Pays $30-200. Captions required. Buys

one-time rights.
Tips: "We need features with strong narrative and fresh observations. Come up with an interesting new way to cover an old theme or destination. We like nonfiction travel articles to read as well as an elegant piece of short fiction. Be persistent."

GOLDEN FALCON, The Inflight Magazine for Gulf Air, Bryan Richardson & Associates, Parkway House, Sheen Lane, London SW14 8LS England. Editor: Nicky Holford. Assistant Editor: Jules MacMahon. A monthly inflight magazine covering travel. Byline given. Buys first Mideast serial rights. Submit seasonal/holiday material at least 3 months in advance. Previously published submissions OK "providing it has not been/will not be published in the Mideast before we publish it." Computer printout submissions acceptable; no dot-matrix. Reports in 1 month.
Nonfiction: General interest, historical/nostalgic, humor, personal experience, photo feature, technical and travel. No "material containing references to religion, sex, gambling, alcohol or politics which would offend the Muslim world." Buys approximately 100 mss/year. Send complete ms. Length: 1,000-2,000 words. Pays $100-130; £80 Sterling (per 1,000 words).
Photos: Pays $22-30 for "35mm+" color transparencies. Buys first Mideast serial rights.
Tips: "The travel section is most open to freelancers. When writing travel articles, avoid the first-person singular and stay away from brochure style. Articles must be of interest to readers from Middle Eastern countries. This publication has a 'high income' readership. Stories on backpacking are not suitable. Many of the stories we have received from America have been too convoluted and not appropriate for our market."

‡**HORIZONS**, American Ranch & Coast Publishing, Inc., Box 806, Solana Beach CA 92075. (619)481-7659. Editor: Adrian Barnard. Features Editor: Mary Shepardson. 30% freelance written. The monthly inflight magazine of Imperial Airlines and targeted to a sophisticated upper-income readership, primarily in southern California. The publication is a replating of *Ranch and Coast* magazine. Circ. 5,000. Pays on publication. Publishes an average of 3 months after acceptance. Byline given. Offers 20% kill fee. Buys various rights. Submit seasonal/holiday material 4 months in advance. Simultaneous queries and photocopied and previously published submissions OK. Computer printout submissions acceptable; prefers letter-quality to dot-matrix. SASE. Reports in 1 month. Sample copy $1.50; free writer's guidelines.
Nonfiction: Book excerpts, general interest, historical/nostalgic, humor, interview/profile, photo feature, and articles on lifestyle and social events. No articles targeted at unsophisticated audience; budget or how-to. Buys 25-40 mss/year. Length: 350-2,000 words. Pays 10¢/word.
Photos: State availability of photos with query. Prefers high-quality photographs and other illustrations. "We receive many submissions with inadequate 'snapshot quality' illustrations." Pays $15 for 5x7 or 8x10 b&w prints; $25 for 35mm and larger color transparencies. Captions, model release, and identification of subjects required. Buys one-time rights.
Columns/Departments: Most columns/departments are written on regular contract basis. Arts and investments. Buys 8 mss/year. Query with published clips. Length: 500-1,000 words. Pays 10¢/word.
Fiction: Condensed novels, historical, humorous, mainstream, mystery, novel excerpts and serialized novels. No avant-garde fiction. Buys 6 mss/year. Send complete ms. Word length open. Pays 10¢/word.
Tips: "Submissions should be appropriate in style and content. Writers should be familiar with current format of magazine—which has changed markedly in recent years. Travel and interviews with prominent and interesting people are the sectors most open to freelancers. These should have a fresh approach and should be well illustrated."

INFLIGHT, Meridian Publishing Co., Inc., Box 10010, Ogden UT 84409. (801)394-9446. Editor: Wayne DeWald. 90% freelance written. A bimonthly magazine distributed by business and professional firms, particularly commercial airlines. Magazine covers business, sports, entertaining personalities, humor and travel for a predominantly upscale, mainstream, family-oriented audience. Pays on acceptance. Publishes ms an average of 6 months after acceptance. Byline given. Buys first rights and nonexclusive reprint rights. No simultaneous submissions. Computer printout submissions acceptable. SASE. Reports in 1 month. Sample copy for $1 and 9x12 SAE; writer's guidelines for SAE and 21¢ postage.
Nonfiction: General interest, historical/nostalgic, humor, interview/profile, photo feature, sports. Buys 30 mss/year. Query. Length: 1,000-1,200 words. Pays 15¢/word.
Photos: Send photos with query or ms. Pays $35 for color transparencies; covers negotiable. Identification of subjects required.
Tips: "We do not assign articles. We accept them on speculation."

‡**MABUHAY, The Inflight Magazine of Philippine Airlines**, MPH Magazines (S) Pte Ltd., 601 Sims Dr., #03-01/03 Pan-I Warehouse Complex, Singapore 1438. 748-5050. Editor: Arthur Hullett. Monthly magazine on travel destinations. An inflight magazine distributed to passengers on all Philippine Airlines' international flights. Articles deal with the Philippines and PAL destinations. Circ. 50,000. Pays on publication. Byline given. Buys first Asian rights. Submit seasonal/holiday material 6 months in advance. Simultaneous queries and

photocopied submissions OK. Computer printout submissions acceptable; prefers letter-quality to dot-matrix. Reports in 1 month. Free sample copy and writer's guidelines.

Nonfiction: General interest, historical/nostalgic, humor, personal experience, photo feature and travel. Needs travel articles dealing with airline's international destinations. No shotgun articles which try to cover too much territory and others with a limited approach and range of vision. Buys 100 mss/year. Query. Length: 1,000-3,000 words. Pays 11¢ (U.S.)/word.

Photos: Send photos with query or ms. Reviews 35mm color transparencies. Pays $48 (U.S.). Captions required. Buys one-time rights.

Tips: "Either query a subject first or send an interesting article with a selection (at least 50) of first-class, original color transparencies. The whole magazine is open to freelancers. Be original, entertaining, informative. Write good English—do not waffle or pad."

OZARK MAGAZINE, East/West Network, 5900 Wilshire Blvd., Los Angeles CA 90036. Editor: Laura Bennet. 99-100% freelance written. Monthly general interest inflight magazine slanted for a Midwest audience. Pays on acceptance. Publishes ms an average of 2 months after acceptance. Byline given. Offers 10% kill fee. Buys first North American serial rights. Submit seasonal/holiday material at least 6 months in advance, other queries at least 4 months in advance. Simultaneous queries OK but not masses of photocopies. Electronic submissions OK on IBM, but requires hard copy also. Computer printout submissions acceptable; no dot-matrix. SASE. Reports in 3 weeks on queries; 2 weeks on mss. Sample copy $2.

Nonfiction: General interest, humor, interview/profile, personal experience, photo feature, travel, food, fashion and sports. All articles must somehow relate to the Midwest. Buys 70-125 mss/year. Query with published clips or send complete ms. Length: 2,000-2,200 words. Pays $500-600. Pays expenses of writers on assignment.

Photos: State availability of photos, or send photos with ms. Prefers original 35mm transparencies. Identification of subjects and captions required. Buys one-time rights.

Columns/Departments: Hometown, Sports, Business, Lifestyle, The Right Stuff, Outdoors. Buys 60-100 mss/year. Query with published clips or send complete ms. Length: 1,700 words maximum. Pays $250-300.

Tips: "Usually a first-time writer will get an assignment on speculation or must have really good clips to show."

PACE MAGAZINE, Piedmont Airlines Inflight Magazine, Fisher-Harrison Publications Inc., 338 N. Elm St., Greensboro NC 27401. (919)378-6065. Managing Editor: Leslie P. Daisy. 20% freelance written. Monthly magazine covering travel, trends in business for the present and the future and other business-related articles. Circ. 1.3 million. Pays on acceptance. Publishes ms an average of 8 months after acceptance. Byline given. Buys first serial rights. Submit holiday/seasonal material 6 months in advance. Computer printout submissions acceptable; no dot-matrix. SASE. Reports in 2 months. Sample copy for $4 and SAE; writer's guidelines for SAE and 1 first class stamp.

Nonfiction: Travel (within the Piedmont flight route), trends in business, business management, employee relations, business psychology and self-improvement as related to business and other business-related articles. No personal, religious, historical, nostalgic, humor, or interview/profile pieces. No cartoons. Buys 30 mss/year. Send query or complete ms. No telephone queries. Length: 1,500-4,000 words. Pays $75-200.

Photos: Send photos with accompanying ms. Captions required.

Tips: "Major features are assigned; I would rarely accept an unsolicited major feature. Writers frequently do not perceive the audience correctly—they must not be familiar with the magazine."

PAN-AM CLIPPER, East/West Network, 34 E. 51st St., New York NY 10022. (212)888-5900. Editor: Richard Kagan. Associate Editor: Paula Rackow. 80% freelance written. Monthly magazine for passengers of Pan Am Airways (50% U.S., 50% foreign persons travelling on business or pleasure). Circ. 300,000. Pays on acceptance. Buys first world serial rights. Submit seasonal material 4 months in advance. Photocopied submissions OK. SASE. Reports in 1 month.

Nonfiction: General interest; interview (internationally important); profile; travel (destination pieces on unusual people and events of interest); the arts (of worldwide appeal); and sports of international interest. Length: 1,500 words minimum. Query with clips of previously published work. Rarely accepts unsolicited articles.

Photos: John Hair, art director . State availability of photos. Reviews 8x10 b&w glossy prints and 35mm color transparencies. Captions and model release required. Buys one-time rights.

‡**PARADISE**, Air Niugini, Box 7186, Boroko, Papua New Guinea. 273437/273569. Editor: Maria Ariansen. Bimonthly magazine covering life and culture in Papua New Guinea. "*Paradise* magazine is a colorful magazine of very high standard that enjoys worldwide distribution. Its popularity stems from the fact that the articles reflect life and culture of present day Papua New Guinea accompanied by photography that is equal to the best in the world." Circ. 40,000 (subscription), 36,000 (give away). Byline given. Not copyrighted. Submit seasonal/holiday material 4 months in advance. Simultaneous and previously published submissions OK. Free sample copy.

Nonfiction: Book excerpts, general interest, historical/nostalgic, interview/profile, new product, personal experience, photo feature and travel. Query. Length: open. Pays K1.00 per column per 10.5 cm. to be paid in the form of a Miscellaneous Charge Order (MCO) for air travel.

Tips: This English language bimonthly concentrates on life and culture in Papua New Guinea. *Paradise* no longer features one destination piece on places along Air Niugini's routes.

PSA MAGAZINE, East/West Network, Inc., Suite 800, 5900 Wilshire Blvd., Los Angeles CA 90036. (213)937-5810. Editor: Al Austin. 90% freelance written. Monthly magazine; 140 pages. Pays within 60 days after acceptance. Buys first rights only. Pays 25% kill fee. Byline given. Submit seasonal/holiday material 4 months in advance of issue date. Simultaneous and photocopied submissions OK. Computer printout submissions acceptable; prefers letter-quality to dot-matrix. SASE. Publishes ms an average of 3 months after acceptance. Sample copy $2.

Nonfiction: Prefers California/West Coast slant. General interest; interview (top-level government, entertainment, sports figures); new product (trends, survey field); profile and business (with California and West Coast orientation). Buys 6 mss/issue. Query. Length: 500-2,000 words. Pays $150-800.

Photos: State availability of photos with query. Pays ASMP rates for b&w contact sheets or negatives and 35mm or 2¼x2¼ color transparencies. Captions required. Buys one-time rights. Model release required.

Columns/Departments: Business Trends. Buys 1 ms/issue. Query. Length: 700-1,500 words. Pays $250-500.

REPUBLIC, East/West Network, Inc., 5900 Wilshire Blvd., Los Angeles CA 90036. (213)937-5810. Editor: Jerry Lazar. 90-100% freelance written. Monthly in-flight magazine of Republic Airlines covering American popular culture for predominantly business travelers. Circ. 170,000 copies. Pays on acceptance. Publishes ms an average of 3 months after acceptance. Byline given. Pays ⅓ kill fee. Buys first serial rights and second (reprint) rights to material originally published elsewhere. Submit seasonal/holiday material at least 3 months in advance. Computer printout submissions acceptable; no dot-matrix. SASE. Reports in 2 weeks on queries; 1 month on mss. Sample copy and writer's guidelines for $2.

Nonfiction: General interest, humor, interview/profile, photo feature and travel. "Material must be of national interest—topical but noncontroversial." No reviews. Buys 96 mss/year. Query with clips of published work. Length: 2,000-3,000 words. Pays $250-600. Sometimes pays the expenses of writers on assignment.

Photos: Michele Chu, art director. State availability of photos. Pays $75 minimum for color transparencies; $25 minimum for 8x10 b&w glossy prints. Captions preferred. Model releases required "where applicable." Buys one-time rights.

Columns/Departments: "Columns cover business, media, technology, health, law, Americana, sports and fitness. No reviews, but subjects vary widely. We mostly use writers whose work we know." Buys 24 mss/year. Length: 750-1,500 words. Pays $200-400.

Tips: "The writer has a better chance with short articles and fillers because there is more demand, less risk. Freelance writers should be aware of the need for writers to think visually—an awareness of how words will look on the page and what kinds of graphics will accompany them. A frequent mistake is underestimating the sophistication of the audience; failing to perceive that we are targeted for the upscale business traveler."

REVIEW MAGAZINE, Eastern Airline's Inflight Magazine, East/West Network, 34 E. 51st St., New York NY 10022. (212)888-5900. Editor: John Atwood. Associate Editor: Karen Kreps. Monthly magazine featuring reprints of articles previously published in leading consumer magazines, plus book excerpts and original articles. Circ. 1 million. Pays on acceptance. Byline given. Buys one-time rights. Photocopied and previously published submissions should be submitted by original publication, not by individuals. Computer printout submissions acceptable; prefers letter-quality to dot-matrix. SASE. Reports in 2 weeks on queries; 3 weeks on mss. Sample copy $2.

Nonfiction: General interest, historical/nostalgic, humor, interview/profile and photo feature. No how-to, travel, poetry or violence-related material. Buys 40 mss/year. Query. Length: 2,000-3,000 words. Pays $500-750 for original articles.

Photos: Nina Ovryn, photo editor. State availability of photos. Pays $75-600 for color transparencies; $75-500 for b&w prints. Identification of subjects required.

Tips: "We are always on the lookout for 2,000-word service and essay pieces on New York, Boston, and Washington subjects of interest to passengers on Eastern Air-Shuttle."

‡SILVER KRIS, Singapore Airlines Inflight Magazine, MPH Magazine (S) Pte Ltd., Pan-I Warehouse Complex #03-01/03, 601 Sims Dr., Singapore 1438. 748-5050. Editor: Steve Thompson. Monthly magazine. "We publish mainly travel stories, but also arts and crafts, theater, festivals, sports and humor." Circ. 250,000. Byline given. Pays on publication. Offers 50% kill fee. Buys one-time rights and first Asian rights. Submit seasonal/holiday material 4 months in advance. Simultaneous queries, and simultaneous, photocopied, and previously published submissions OK. Reports in 1 month. Free sample copy and writer's guidelines.

Nonfiction: Humor (short anecdotes); personal experience; photo feature and travel. No political, religious or

moral controversy, no "straight" travel writing with routes, prices and tired cliches. Buys 80 mss/year. Send complete ms. Length: 1,500-3,000 words. Pays $200-800.
Photos: Send photos with query or ms. Reviews 35mm color transparencies. Pays $50-75. Identification of subjects required. Buys one-time rights.
Fillers: Anecdotes and short humor. Buys 30/year. Length: 1,000-1,500 words. Pays $125-200.
Tips: "Subjects should be offbeat (I'd rather have a photo essay on the rickshaw paintings of Dacca, for instance, than a story on the best hotels or restaurants there), and style should be light and entertaining. An important criterion in *Silver Kris* is the provision of first-rate original color transparencies. Writers will stand a better chance if they can provide these—or at least suggest other sources."

SKYLITE, Butler Aviation's Corporate Inflight Magazine, Halsey Publishing Co., 12955 Biscayne Blvd., North Miami FL 33181. (305)893-1520. Editor: Julio C. Zangroniz. Monthly magazine for corporate executives. Circ. 25,000. Pays on publication. Byline given. Offers 50% minimum kill fee. Buys first North American serial rights. Submit seasonal/holiday material 6 months in advance. Simultaneous queries OK. Computer printout submissions acceptable. SASE. Reports in 3 months. Sample copy for $3; writer's guidelines for 4x9 SAE with 1 first class stamp.
Nonfiction: General interest; historical/nostalgic; how-to; inspirational; interview/profile (of corporate executives); travel (domestic and overseas); sports; science and consumer. No first person; anything dealing with politics, sex, drugs or violent crime. Buys 84-96 mss/year. Query. Length: 1,500-2,000 words. Pays $300-500.
Photos: State availability of photos. Reviews 35mm color transparencies. Captions required. Buys one-time rights. Pays for text/photo packages.
Tips: "Your query is your personal representative and *only* spokesman with an editor—make sure it is spotless, errorless and concise, a document that says 'I am a professional'. Queries not accompanied by SASE are not likely to get an answer due to manpower/economic limitations."

SUNRISE, The Inflight Magazine for Kuwait Airways Corporation, Bryan Richardson & Associates, Parkway House, Sheen Lane, London SW14 8L5 England. Editor: Nicky Holford. Assistant Editor: Jules MacMahon. 90% freelance written. A monthly inflight magazine broadly orientated with special emphasis on travel, luxury goods and sophisticated living." Circ. 20,000. Pays on publication. Byline given. Buys first Mideast serial rights. Submit seasonal/holiday material at least 3 months in advance. Computer printout submissions acceptable; no dot-matrix.
Nonfiction: General interest, sports, scientific,historical/nostalgic, humor, photo feature, technical and travel. No "material containing references to religion, sex, politics, gambling, or alcohol which would offend the Muslim world." Buys approximately 100 mss/year. Send complete ms. Length: 1,000-2,000 words. Pays $100-130; £80 Sterling (per 1,000 words).
Photos: State availability of photos. Pays $22-30 for "35mm+" color transparencies. Buys first Mideast rights.
Tips: "The travel section is most open to freelancers. When writing travel articles, avoid the first-person singular and stay away from brochure style. Articles must be of interest to readers from Middle Eastern countries. This publication has high income readers. Stories on backpacking are not suitable. Many of the stories we have received from America have been too convoluted and not appropriate in our market. We do not run short articles or fillers—almost everything is of the same length. Frequently writers have no idea how to slant an article for a Mid-East/Arab market—because they don't think beyond an American readership."

TWA AMBASSADOR, (for Trans World Airlines), The Paulson Publishing, Inc., Suite 209, 289 E. 5th St., St. Paul MN 55101. Editor-in-Chief: Bonnie Blodgett. 90% freelance written. "For TWA passengers, top management executives, professional men and women, world travelers; affluent, interested and responsive." Monthly magazine. Circ. 263,000. Pays on acceptance. Buys all rights. Pays 30% kill fee. Byline given. Submit seasonal/holiday material 6 months in advance. SASE. Reports in 1 month. Sample copy $2.
Nonfiction: Subjects dealing with substantive issues, the arts, in-depth profiles, business concerns, straight reporting on a variety of subjects and service pieces. Query. Length: 2,500-5,000 words. Pays $600-1,500.
Columns/Departments: Destinations, Science, Business, Personal Finance, The Arts, Media, Books and The Law. Query to Doug Lice, Managing Editor. Length: 1,800-2,000 words. Pays $150-400.

‡**UNITED**, East/West Network, 34 East 51st St., New York NY 10022. (212)888-5900. Editor: Tom O'Neil. Managing Editor: Joal Hetherington. 90% freelance written. Monthly magazine, a United Airlines inflight publication. Circ. 360,000. Pays on acceptance. Publishes ms an average of 4 months after acceptance. Byline given. Offers 50% kill fee. Buys first North American serial rights. Submit seasonal/holiday material 4-6 months in advance. Computer printout submissions acceptable; no dot-matrix. SASE. Reports in 4 weeks. Sample copy $2; writer's guidelines for SAE.
Nonfiction: Interview/profile (upscale and well-known business owners, restauranteurs, designers, architects, artists, celebrities, etc.); travel (only US, Hong Kong and Japan); and trends. No European travel, how-

to. Buys 100 mss/year. Query with published clips. Length: 750-2,000 words. Pays $500-1,000. Sometimes pays the expenses of writers on assignment.

Columns/Departments: Jennifer Fortenbaugh, column/department editor. Communique: Short newsy items on new products, events, etc. Buys 25/year. Query with published clips. Length: 200-500 words. Pays $100-200.

USAIR MAGAZINE, Halsey Publishing Co., 600 3rd Ave. New York NY 10016. Editor: Richard Busch. Senior Editor: Mark Orwall. 95% freelance written. A monthly general interest magazine published for airline passengers, many of whom are business travelers, male, with high incomes and college educations. Circ. 190,000. Pays on acceptance. Publishes ms an average of 4 months after acceptance. Buys first rights only. Submit seasonal material 6 months in advance. Photocopied submissions OK. Computer printout submissions acceptable; prefers letter-quality to dot-matrix. SASE. Reports in 2 weeks. Sample copy $3; free writer's guidelines with SASE.

Nonfiction: Travel, business, sports, health, food, personal finance, nature, the arts, science/technology and photography. "No downbeat stories or controversial articles." Buys 100 mss/year. Query with clips of previously published work. Length: 1,500-3,500 words. Pays $400-1,000. Sometimes pays expenses of writers on assignment.

Photos: Send photos with ms. Pays $75-150/b&w print, depending on size; color from $100-250/print or slide. Captions preferred; model release required. Buys one-time rights.

Columns/Departments: Sports, food, money, health, business, living and science. Buys 3-4 mss/issue. Query. Length: 1,200-1,800 words. Pays $300-450.

Tips: "Send irresistible ideas and proof that you can write. It's great to get a clean manuscript from a good writer who has given me exactly what I asked for. Frequent mistakes are not following instructions, not delivering on time, etc."

WESTERN'S WORLD, East-West Network, 5900 Wilshire Blvd., Los Angeles CA 90036. Editor: Ed Dwyer. 100% freelance written. Monthly magazine for Western Airlines with newsmakers, entrepreneurs, and "movers and shakers" of the West. "*WW* is a regional magazine with the West as its purview." Circ. 110,000. Pays on acceptance. Publishes ms an average of 2 months after acceptance. Byline given. Offers 20% kill fee. Buys first North American serial rights. Submit seasonal/holiday material 3 months in advance. Electronic submissions OK. Computer printout submissions acceptable; no dot-matrix. SASE. Reports in 6 weeks on queries; 3 weeks on mss. For sample copy send $2 to Diane Thompson, administration. For guidelines send SAE with 1 first class stamp.

Nonfiction: General interest (Western focus, a la city magazine formula); interview/profile (no celebrities or Q&A format); and travel (specific new trends or services in a Western city for Datelines). "Monthly 'Datelines' from around Western's system (e.g., 'Dateline: Hawaii') keep readers posted on valuable insiders' tips on where to go and what to see. Subjects include technology, business, sports, media, fashion and food." No personal travel accounts or financial writing. Buys 50 mss/year. Query with published clips. Feature length: 1,700-2,000 words. Pays $300-800, depending on assignment and writer. Pays expenses of writers on assignment.

Photos: "A dramatic photo 'portfolio' introduces the readers to the natural marvels of the West." Captions required. Buys one-time rights. Query. Do not send originals.

Columns/Departments: Buys 72 mss/year. Query with published clips. Length: 250-750 words. Pays $50-150.

Fiction: Western (excerpts of classics, e.g., Mark Twain, Zane Grey).

Tips: "Send brief, informative query with clips of previous work. Know the market—we are not a travel magazine."

‡**WINDS, The Inflight Magazine of Japan Air Lines**, Japan Air Lines/Emphasis, Inc., Central Roppongi Bldg., 1-4-27 Roppongi, Minato-ku, Tokyo 106 Japan. (03)585-8857. Editor: Tom Chapman. Monthly magazine covering Japan/Asia/Southeast Asia. International inflight magazine devoted to literate and interesting interpretations of Japan and the Japanese, and, now and then, other destinations in Asia of Japan Air Lines. Circ. 280,000. Pays on publication. Byline given. Kill fee negotiable. Buys first Asian serial rights. Submit seasonal/holiday material 6 months in advance. Simultaneous queries and photocopied submissions OK. SAE, IRC. Reports in 3 weeks. Free sample copy and writer's guidelines.

Nonfiction: Book excerpts; interview/profile, personal experience, photo feature and travel. Familiarity with Japan always necessary. Buys 75 mss/year. Query with published clips. Length: 1,000-4,000 words. Pays $300-3,000+.

Photos: State availability of photos. Reviews 35mm color transparencies. Pays $25-150. Captions, model release and identification of subjects required. Buys one-time rights.

Tips: A freelancer can best break into this publication through good writing, understanding of subject, interesting idea as related to Japan and the Japanese, and knowing and caring about subject.

‡**WINGS OF GOLD, Inflight Magazine of Malaysian Airline System**, Public Relations Department/Malaysian Airline System, Ground Floor Simulator Building, MAS, Complex, Subang, Selangor. (03)768555. Editor: Premila Mohanlall. Managing Editor: Mrs. Siew Yong Gnanalingam. Monthly magazine of articles to inform and entertain passengers. An English language magazine, publishes travel, cultural, and lifestyle pieces on MAS destinations and beyond. Circ. 50,000. Pays on publication. Byline given. Buys first serial rights and one-time rights. Submit seasonal/holiday material 3 months in advance. Simultaneous queries and photocopied submissions OK. Computer printout submissions acceptable; no dot-matrix. Reports in 2 weeks on queries; 1 month on mss. Free sample copy and writer's guidelines.

Nonfiction: General interest; business/economics; historical/nostalgic; how-to (go on a jungle trip, "fly" a simulator); humor; religious; politics; interview/profile; expose; personal experience; photo feature; technical (aviation related); and travel. "We highlight stories which enlighten the readers on the culture and lifestyle of the many countries MAS flies to. It may be a festival, a craft or a profile. Or it may be a travel piece, preferably a lesser publicized 'getaway' resort. The style should be light and entertaining. Articles written in humorous vein are also sought. Steer clear of racial or cultural sensitivities." Query with published clips. Length: 800-2,000 words. Pays $300-600 (Malaysian dollars); pays in airline tickets only.

Photos: Send photos with query or ms. Prefers 35mm or 120mm color transparencies. Pays flat rate: $50 (Malaysian dollars/)picture. Captions required. Buys one-time rights.

Columns/Departments: In The Clouds (news on what flying is all about, e.g., about inflight music, passengers; written in a humorous vein), and What's Up Doc (aviation medicine). Buys 24/year. Length: 300-500 words. Pays $300-500 (Malaysian dollars); pays in airline tickets.

Tips: "90% of articles are freelance contributions. Phraseology and analogies must be original and derived preferably from the latest developments and in a way that everyone can relate to. Language should be simple and easy to read. Avoid bombast. Weave people into the story with anecdotes, quotes, interviews or jokes. Writers must provide slides to support the story—the picture will get across the mood you wish to impart."

Juvenile

Just as children change (and grow), so do juvenile magazines. Children's editors stress that writers must read recent *issues*. This section of *Writer's Market* lists publications for children aged 2-12. Magazines for young people 12-18 appear in the Teen and Young Adult category. Many of the following publications are produced by religious groups, and where possible, the specific denomination is given. For the writer with a story or article slanted to a specific age group, the following children's index is a quick reference to markets for each age group. Editors who are willing to receive simultaneous submissions indicate this in their listing. (This is the technique of mailing the same story at the same time to a number of markets of nonoverlapping circulation. In each case, the writer, when making a simultaneous submission, should inform the editor. In fact, some editors prefer a query over a complete manuscript when the writer is considering making a simultaneous submission.) Mass circulation, nondenominational publications included in this section that have good pay rates are not interested in simultaneous submissions and should not be approached with this technique. Magazines that pay good rates expect, and deserve, the exclusive use of material. Writers should also note in some of the listings that editors will buy "second rights" to stories. This refers to a story which has been previously published in a magazine and to which the writer has already sold "first rights." Payment is usually less for the re-use of a story than for first-time publication.

Juvenile Publications Classified by Age

Two- to Five-Year-Olds: *Chickadee, Children's Playmate, Happy Times, Highlights for Children, Humpty Dumpty's, Nature Friend, Our Little Friend, Owl, Story Friends, Turtle Magazine for Preschool Kids, Wee Wisdom, Young American.*

Six- to Eight-Year-Olds: *Chickadee, Child Life, Children's Digest, Children's Playmate, Dash, The Dolphin Log, Ebony Jr!, Highlights for Children, Humpty Dumpty's,*

Jack and Jill, National Geographic World, Nature Friend, Nautica, Odyssey, Owl, Pennywhistle Press, Primary Treasure, R-A-D-A-R, Ranger Rick, Stickers!, Story Friends, 3-2-1 Contact, Touch, Wee Wisdom, Wonder Time, Young American, The Young Crusader.

Nine- to Twelve-Year-Olds: Action, Bible-in-Life Pix, Boy's Life, Childs Life, Children's Digest, Clubhouse, Cobblestone, Counselor, Crusader, Dash, Digit, Discoveries, The Dolphin Log, Ebony Jr!, Highlights for Children, Medical Detective, National Geographic World, Nature Friend, Nautica, Odyssey, On the Line, Owl, Pennywhistle Press, R-A-D-A-R, Ranger Rick, Stickers!, 3-2-1 Contact, Touch, Wee Wisdom, Young American, The Young Crusader.

ACTION, Dept. of Christian Education, Free Methodist Headquarters, 901 College Ave., Winona Lake IN 46590. (219)267-7656. Editor: Vera Bethel. 100% freelance written. Weekly magazine for "57% girls, 43% boys, ages 9-11; 48% city, 23% small towns." Circ. 25,000. Pays on publication. Publishes ms an average of 1 month after acceptance. Rights purchased vary; may buy simultaneous rights, second (reprint) rights or first North American serial rights. Submit seasonal/holiday material 3 months in advance. Simultaneous and previously published submissions OK. Computer printout submissions acceptable; no dot-matrix. SASE must be enclosed. Reports in 1 month. Free sample copy and writer's guidelines.

Nonfiction: How-to (make gifts and craft articles); informational (nature articles with pictures); and personal experience (my favorite vacation, my pet, my hobby, etc.). Buys 50 mss/year. Submit complete ms with photos. Length: 200-500 words. Pays $15.

Fiction: Adventure, humorous, mystery and religious. Buys 50 mss/year. Submit complete ms. Length: 1,000 words. Pays $25. SASE must be enclosed; no return without it.

Poetry: Free verse, haiku, light verse, traditional, devotional and nature. Buys 20/year. Submix maximum 5-6 poems. Length: 4-16 lines. Pays $5.

Tips: "Send interview articles with children about their pets, their hobbies, a recent or special vacation—all with pictures if possible. Kids like to read about other kids. A frequent mistake made by writers is using words too long for a 10-year-old and *too many* long words."

‡BIBLE-IN-LIFE PIX, David C. Cook Publishing Co., 850 N. Grove Ave., Elgin IL 60120. (312)741-2400. Editor: Dave Camburn. Weekly magazine covering Christian-oriented material for children ages 8-11. "Nondenominational Sunday school publication for grades 3-6. Features articles with curricular emphasis which help to apply the Christian faith to lives of children." Pays on acceptance. Byline given. Buys all rights; makes work-for-hire assignments. Submit seasonal/holiday material 1-1½ years in advance. SASE. Sample copy for 8½x11 SAE and 2 first class stamps; free writer's guidelines.

Nonfiction: Historical/nostalgic, how-to, humor, inspirational, interview/profile, personal experience and photo feature. Query with published clips. Length: 600 words. Pays $70.

Fiction: Adventure, historical, humorous, religious. Query with published clips. Length: 1,000 words. Pays $110.

Tips: "We rarely buy unsolicited manuscripts. Most assignments are made to meet specific curricular needs."

BOYS' LIFE, Boy Scouts of America, Magazine Division, 1325 Walnut Hill Lane, Irving TX 75062. (214)659-2000. Editor: Robert Hood. Monthly magazine covering Boy Scout activities for "ages 8-18—Boy Scouts, Cub Scouts, and others of that age group." Circ. 1.5 million. Length: 1,000-3,000 words. Pays on acceptance. Buys one-time rights. Pays $350 minimum. Reports in 2 weeks.

Nonfiction: "Almost all articles are assigned. We do not encourage unsolicited material."

Columns/Departments: How How's (1-2 paragraphs on hobby tips). Buys 60 mss/year. Send complete ms. Pays $5 minimum.

Fillers: Jokes (Think and Grin—1-3 sentences). Pays $1 minimum.

CHICKADEE MAGAZINE, The Magazine for Young Children, The Young Naturalist Foundation, 59 Front St. E., Toronto, Ontario M5E 1B3 Canada. (416)364-3333. Editor: Janis Nostbakken. 25% freelance written. Magazine published 10 times/year (except July and August) for 4-9 year-olds. "We aim to interest (in an entertaining and lively way) children aged nine and under in the world around them." Circ. 84,000. Pays on publication. Byline given. Buys all rights. Submit seasonal/holiday material up to 1 year in advance. Computer printout submissions acceptable. Reports in 2½ months. Sample copy for $1.50 and IRCs; writer's guidelines for IRC.

Nonfiction: How-to (arts and crafts for children); personal experience (real children in real situations); and photo feature (wildlife features). No articles for older children; no religious or moralistic features. Sometimes pays the expenses of writers on assignment.

Photos: Send photos with ms. Reviews 35mm transparencies. Identification of subjects required.
Fiction: Adventure (relating to the 4-9 year old). No science fiction, fantasy, talking animal stories or religious articles. Send complete ms. Pays $100-300.
Tips:"An article—big or small— is either good or it isn't. A frequent mistake made by writers is trying to teach too much—not enough entertainment and fun."

CHILD LIFE, Benjamin Franklin Literary & Medical Society, Inc., 1100 Waterway Blvd., Box 567, Indianapolis IN 46206. Editor: Steve Charles. 90% freelance written. Monthly (except bimonthly issues in February/March, April/May, June/July and August/September) magazine. For youngsters ages 7-11. Pays on publication. Publishes ms an average of 6 months after acceptance. Buys all rights. Byline given. Submit seasonal/holiday material 8 months in advance. Photocopied submissions OK. SASE. Reports in 10 weeks. Sample copy 75¢; writer's guidelines for SASE.
Nonfiction: Specifically needs articles dealing with health, safety, nutrition and exercise (including group sports). Also articles that stimulate a child's sense of wonder about the world. "We prefer not to sound encyclopedic in our presentation and therefore are always on the lookout for innovative ways to present our material. Articles on sports and sports figures are welcome, but they should try to influence youngsters to participate and learn the benefits of participation, both from a social and a physical point of view." In addition to health, seasonal articles are needed. Buys about 6 mss/issue. Submit complete ms; query not necessary. Length: 1,200 words maximum. Give word count on ms. Pays approximately 4¢/word.
Photos: Purchased only with accompanying ms. Captions and model release required. Reviews color and b&w glossies. Buys one-time rights on most photos.
Fiction: Half of the stories accepted emphasize some aspect of health, but not necessarily as a main theme. Seasonal stories also accepted. Adventure, mystery, fantasy and humorous stories are favorites. Buys about 5 mss/issue. Submit complete ms; query not necessary. Length: 500-1,200 words. Give word count on ms. Pays approximately 6¢/word.

CHILDREN'S DIGEST, Children's Better Health Institute, Box 567, Indianapolis IN 46206. (317)636-8881. Editor: Kathleen B. Mosher. Magazine published 8 times/year covering children's health for children ages 8-10. Pays on publication. Byline given. Buys all rights. Submit seasonal/holiday material 8 months in advance. Submit *only* complete manuscripts. "No queries, please." Photocopied submissions acceptable (if clear). SASE. Reports in 2 months. Sample copy 75¢; writer's guidelines for business size SASE.
Nonfiction: Historical, interview/profile (biographical), craft ideas, health, nutrition, hygiene, exercise and safety. "We're especially interested in factual features that teach readers about the human body or encourage them to develop better health habits. We are *not* interested in material that is simply rewritten from encyclopedias. We try to present our health material in a way that instructs *and* entertains the reader." Buys 15-20 mss/year. Send complete ms. Length: 500-1,200 words. Pays 6¢/word.
Photos: State availability of photos. Pays $5-10 for 5x7 b&w glossy prints. Model release and identification of subjects required. Buys one-time rights.
Fiction: Adventure, humorous, mainstream and mystery. Stories should appeal to both boys and girls. "We need some stories that incorporate a health theme. However, we don't want stories that preach, preferring instead stories with implied morals. We like a light or humorous approach." Buys 15-20 mss/year. Length: 500-1,800 words. Pays 6¢/word.
Poetry: Pays $5 minimum.

CHILDREN'S PLAYMATE, 1100 Waterway Blvd., Box 567, Indianapolis IN 46206. (317)636-8881. Editor: Kathleen B. Mosher. 75% freelance written. "We are looking for articles, stories, and activities with a health, safety, exercise, or nutritionally oriented theme. Primarily we are concerned with preventative medicine. We try to present our material in a positive—not a negative—light, and we try to incorporate humor and a light approach wherever possible without minimizing the seriousness of what we are saying." For children ages 5-7. Magazine published 8 times/year. Buys all rights. Byline given. Pays on publication. Publishes ms an average of 8 months after acceptance. "We do not consider outlines. Reading the whole manuscript is the only way to give fair consideration. The editors cannot criticize, offer suggestions, or review unsolicited material that is not accepted." Submit seasonal material 8 months in advance. Computer printout submissions acceptable; prefers letter-quality to dot-matrix. Reports in 2 months. Sometimes may hold mss for up to 1 year, with author's permission. Write for guidelines. "Material will not be returned unless accompanied by a self-addressed envelope and sufficient postage." Sample copy 75¢; free writer's guidelines with SASE. No query.
Nonfiction: Beginning science, 600 words maximum. Monthly "All about . . ." feature, 300-500 words, may be an interesting presentation on animals, people, events, objects or places, especially about good health, exercise, proper nutrition and safety. Include number of words in articles. Buys 30 mss/year. Pays about 6¢/word.
Fiction: Short stories words for beginning readers, not over 700. Seasonal stories with holiday themes. Humorous stories, unusual plots. Vocabulary suitable for ages 5-7. Pays about 6¢/word. Include number of words in stories.

Fillers: Puzzles, dot-to-dots, color-ins, hidden pictures and mazes. Buys 30 fillers/year. Payment varies.
Tips: Especially interested in stories, poems and articles about special holidays, customs and events.

CLUBHOUSE, Your Story Hour, Box 15, Berrien Springs MI 49103. (616)471-3701. Editor: Elaine Meseraull. 75% freelance written. Magazine published 10 times/year covering many subjects with Christian approach. "Stories and features for fun for 9-13 year-olds. Main objectives: Let kids know that God loves them and provide a psychologically 'up' magazine that lets kids know that they are acceptable, 'neat' people." Circ. 15,000. Pays on acceptance. Publishes ms an average of 1 year after acceptance. Byline given. Buys first serial rights or first North American serial rights, one-time rights, simultaneous rights; and second serial (reprint) rights. Simultaneous queries, and simultaneous, photocopied, and previously published submissions OK. Computer printout submissions acceptable. SASE. Reports in 3 weeks. Sample copy for business or larger size SAE and 3 first class stamps; writer's guidelines for business size SAE and 1 first class stamp.
Nonfiction: How-to (crafts), personal experience and recipes (without sugar or artificial flavors and colors). "No stories in which kids start out 'bad' and by peer or adult pressure or circumstances are changed into 'good' people." Send complete ms. Length: 750-800 words ($25); 1,000-1,200 words ($30); feature story 1,200 words ($35).
Photos: Send photos with ms. Pays on publication according to published size. Buys one-time rights.
Columns/Departments: Body Shop (short stories or "ad" type material that is anti-smoking, drugs and alcohol and pro-good nutrition, etc.); and Jr. Detective (secret codes, word search, deduction problems, hidden pictures, etc.). Buys 10/year. Send complete ms. Length: 400 words maximum. Pays $10-30.
Fiction: Adventure, historical, humorous and mainstream. "Stories should depict bravery, kindness, etc., without overt or preachy attitude." No science fiction, romance, confession or mystery. Buys 40-50 mss/year. Send complete ms. Length: 750-800 words ($20); 1,000-1,200 words ($30), feature story ($35).
Poetry: Free verse, light verse and traditional. Buys 2-4/year. Submit maximum 5 poems. Length: 4-24 lines. Pays $5-20.
Fillers: Cartoons. Buys 10-20/year. Pay $10 maximum.
Tips: "All material for any given year is accepted during April-May in the previous year. Think from a kid's point of view and ask, 'Would this story make me glad to be a kid?' Keep the stories moving, exciting, bright and tense. Stay within length guidelines."

COBBLESTONE, Cobblestone Publishing, Inc., 20 Grove St., Peterborough NH 03458. (603)924-7209. Editor-in-Chief: Carolyn P. Yoder. 100% freelance written; (approximately 2 issues/year are by assignment only). Monthly magazine covering American history for children ages 8-14. "Each issue presents a particular theme, approaching it from different angles, making it exciting as well as informative." Circ. 44,000. Pays on publication. Publishes ms an average of 4 months after acceptance. Byline given. Buys all rights; makes work-for-hire assignments. All material must relate to monthly theme. Simultaneous and previously published submissions OK. Computer printout submissions acceptable; prefers letter-quality to dot-matrix. SASE. Sample copy $2.95; writer's guidelines for SASE.
Nonfiction: Historical/nostalgic, how-to, interview and personal experience. "Request a copy of the writer's guidelines to find out specific issue themes in upcoming months." Include SASE. No Revolutionary War memorabilia, particularly hometown guides to monuments. No material that editorializes rather than reports. Buys 5-8 mss/issue. Length: 500-1,200 words. Query with published clips. Pays up to 15¢/word.
Fiction: Adventure, historical, humorous and biographical fiction. Buys 1-2 mss/issue. Length: 800-1,200 words. Request free editorial guidelines that explain upcoming issue themes and give query deadlines. "Message" must be smoothly integrated with the story. Pays up to 15¢/word.
Poetry: Free verse, light verse and traditional. Buys 6 mss/year. Submit maximum 2 poems. Length: 5-100 lines. Pays on an individual basis.
Tips: "All material is considered on the basis of merit and appropriateness to theme. Query should state idea for material simply, with rationale for why material is applicable to theme. Request writer's guidelines (includes themes and query deadlines) before submitting a query. Include SASE."

‡**COUNSELOR**, A Power Line Paper, Scripture Press Publics, Box 632, Glen Ellyn IL 60138. (312)668-6000. Editor: Joyce Gibson. Managing Editor: Grace Anderson. 60% freelance written. 4-page Sunday school take-home paper issued quarterly for weekly distribution on living today by the power God gives, making the Bible practical. Circ. 170,00. Pays on acceptance. Publishes ms an average of 18 months after acceptance. Byline given. Buys one-time rights and all rights. Reports in 2 weeks on queries; 4 weeks on mss. Free sample copy and writer's guidelines.
Nonfiction: Personal experience (first or third peson adult or child [9-12], God at work in their lives—true); and photo feature—kids in action, children ages 9-12 involved in helping others. No nature, science, or historical pieces. Buys 12-20 mss/year. Query with or without published clips or send complete ms. Length: 500-1,200. First rights pays 4-7¢/word; all rights pays 5-10¢/word, depending on quality.
Photos: Send photos with query or ms. Photos only with stories. Reviews b&w contact sheets, 35mm or larger color transparencies, and 5x7 b&w and color prints. Pays $15-35 for transparencies; $3-25 for prints. Model

release and identification of subjects required. Rights purchased depends on story; usually one-time rights. **Tips:** Ask for tips sheet. True Stories is the only area open to freelancers.

CRUSADER MAGAZINE, Box 7244, Grand Rapids MI 49510. Editor: G. Richard Broene. 30% freelance written. Magazine published 7 times/year. "*Crusader Magazine* shows boys (9-14) how God is at work in their lives and in the world around them." Circ. 13,000. Buys 20-25 mss/year. Pays on acceptance. Byline given. Publishes ms an average of 10 months after acceptance. Rights purchased vary with author and material; buys first serial rights, one-time rights, second serial (reprint) rights, and simultaneous rights. Submit seasonal material (Christmas, Easter) at least 5 months in advance. Photocopied and simultaneous submissions OK. Computer printout submissions acceptable; prefers letter-quality to dot-matrix. Reports in 1 month. SASE. Free sample copy and writer's guidelines for SAE and 3 first class stamps.
Nonfiction: Articles about young boys' interests: sports, outdoor activities, bike riding, science, crafts, etc., and problems. Emphasis is on a Christian multi-racial perspective, but no simplistic moralisms. Informational, how-to, personal experience, interview, profile, inspirational and humor. Submit complete ms. Length: 500-1,500 words. Pays 2-5¢/word.
Photos: Pays $4-25 for b&w photos purchased with mss.
Fiction: "Considerable fiction is used. Fast-moving stories that appeal to a boy's sense of adventure or sense of humor are welcome. Avoid preachiness. Avoid simplistic answers to complicated problems. Avoid long dialogue and little action." Length: 750-1,500 words. Pays 3¢/word minimum.
Fillers: Uses short humor and any type of puzzles as fillers.

DASH, Box 150, Wheaton IL 60189. Editor: David Leigh. For boys ages 8-11. Published bimonthly. Most subscribers are in a Christian Service Brigade program. Circ. 24,000. Rights purchased vary with author and material. Pays on publication. Submit seasonal material 6 months in advance. SASE. Sample copy $1.50 plus large SAE and 73¢ postage; writer's guidelines for SAE and 1 first class postage stamp.
Nonfiction: "Our emphasis is on boys and how their belief in Jesus Christ affects their everyday lives." Uses short articles about boys of this age, problems they encounter. Interview and profile. Buys 8-10 mss/year. Query. Length: 1,000-1,500 words. Pays $30-70.
Photos: Pays $25 for 8x10 b&w photos for inside use.
Fiction: Avoid trite, condescending tone. Needs adventure, mystery and action. Christian truth should be worked into the storyline (not tacked on as a "moral of the story"). Length: 1,000-1,500 words. Pays $60-90.
Tips: "Queries must be succinct, well-written and exciting, to draw my interest. Send for sample copies, get a feel for our publication, query with ideas tailored specifically for us."

DIGIT MAGAZINE, The Video/Computing Connection for Young People, Beckwith/Benton Communications, Inc., 2342 North Point, San Francisco CA 94123. (415)931-1885. Editor: Lassie Benton. Managing Editor: Kendra Bonnett. Bimonthly magazine covering computers/high technology for use as an education/classroom tool. "*Digit* is written for young people between the ages of 10 and 16. Much of the information is edited and written by adults, but the material is generated by youngsters." Circ. 50,000. Pays on publication. Byline given. Photocopied submissions OK. SASE. Reports in 1 month on queries. Sample copy $3; free writer's guidelines with SASE.
Nonfiction: Book excerpts (computers for young people); how-to (dealing with technology interesting to young people); humor (for young people); interview/profile (dealing with youngsters and computers); new product (reviews); personal experience (dealing with technology); photo feature (dealing with youngsters); technical (only in a way that can be explained in layman language); and contests (educational). Query with published clips. Length: 1,000-2,500 words. Pays $50-500.
Photos: State availability of photos. Buys one-time rights.

DISCOVERIES, 6401 The Paseo, Kansas City MO 64131. Editor: Libby Huffman. 100% freelance written. For boys and girls ages 9-12 in the Church of the Nazarene. 100% freelance written. Weekly. Publishes ms an average of 1 year after acceptance. Buys first serial rights and second (reprint) rights. "We process only letter-quality manuscripts; word processing with letter-quality printers acceptable. Minimal comments on pre-printed form are made on rejected material." SASE. Reports in 4 weeks. Guidelines for SAE with two first class stamps.
Fiction: Stories with Christian emphasis on high ideals, wholesome social relationships and activities, right choices, Sabbath observance, church loyalty, and missions. Informal style. Submit complete ms. Length: 800-1,000 words. Pays 3.½¢/word for first serial rights and 2¢/word for second (reprint) rights.
Photos: Sometimes buys photos submitted with mss with captions only if subject has appeal. Send quality 8x10 photos.
Tips: "The freelancer needs an understanding of the doctrine of the Church of the Nazarene and the Sunday school material for third to sixth graders."

THE DOLPHIN LOG, The Cousteau Society, 8430 Santa Monica Blvd., Los Angeles CA 90069. (213)656-4422. Editor: Pamela Stacey. 25% freelance written. Quarterly magazine covering marine biology, ecology, environment, natural history, and water-related stories. "The *Dolphin Log* is an educational publication for children ages 7-15 offered by The Cousteau Society. Subject matter encompasses all areas of science, history and the arts which can be related to our global water system. The philosophy of the magazine is to delight, instruct and instill an environmental ethic and understanding of the interconnectedness of living organisms, including people." Circ. 45,000. Pays on publication. Publishes ms an average of 6 months after acceptance. Byline given. "We do not make assignments and therefore have no kill fee." Buys one-time rights. Submit seasonal/holiday material 4 months in advance. Simultaneous queries OK. Computer submissions acceptable. SASE. Reports in 4 weeks on queries; 2 months on mss. Sample copy for $2 with SASE and 56¢ and postage; writer's guidelines for SASE.

Nonfiction: general interest (per guidelines); how-to (water-related crafts or science); interview/profile (of young person involved with aspect of ocean); personal experience (ocean related); and photo feature (per guidelines). "Of special interest are games involving an ocean/water-related theme which develop math, reading and comprehension skills. Humorous articles and short jokes based on scientific fact are also welcome. Experiments that can be conducted at home and demonstrate a phenomenon or principle of science are wanted as are clever crafts or art projects which also can be tied to any ocean theme. Try to incorporate such activities into any articles submitted." No "talking" animals. Buys 4-12 mss/year. Query or send complete ms. Pays $25-150.

Photos: Send photos with query or ms (duplicates only). Prefers underwater animals, water photos with children, photos which explain text. Pays $25 for b&w; $25-100 for 35mm color transparencies. Captions, model release and identification of subjects required. Buys one-time rights.

Columns/Departments: Discovery (science experiments or crafts a young person can easily do at home). Buys 4 mss/year. Send complete ms. Length: 200-750. Pays $25-50.

Fiction: Adventure (with ecological message); historical (how early cultures interacted with environment and/or animals); humorous (personal experiences with animals, ocean or environment); and science fiction (new ideas on future relationship with ocean, animals, environment). No anthropomorphism or "talking" animals. Buys "very few manuscripts but would like to find good ones." Length: 500-1,200 words. Pays $25-150.

Poetry: No "talking" animals. Buys 2 poems/year. Pays $25-100.

Fillers: Jokes, anecdotes, short humor and newsbreaks. Buys 8/year. Length: 100 lines maximum. Pays $25-50.

Tips: "A freelancer can best break in at our publication by researching a topic and writing good, scientifically sound articles. We are delighted with articles which offer new insights into a particular species or relationship in nature, or principle of ecology. Feature sections use clear, simple, factual writing style combined with sound, verifiable information."

EBONY JR!, Johnson Publishing Co., 820 S. Michigan Ave., Chicago IL 60605. (312)322-9272. Managing Editor: Marcia V. Roebuck-Hoard. 50% freelance written. Monthly magazine (except bimonthly issues in June/July and August/September) for all children, but geared toward black children ages 6-12. Circ. 200,000. Pays on acceptance. Publishes ms an average of 4 months after acceptance. Buys all rights, second serial (reprint) rights or one-time rights. Byline given. Submit seasonal/holiday material 4 months in advance. Previously published submissions OK. Computer printout submissions acceptable; prefers letter-quality to dot-matrix. SASE. Acknowledges receipt of material in 4 weeks; reports in 6 weeks. Sample copy $1; writer's guidelines with SAE and 1 first class stamp.

Nonfiction: How-to (make things, gifts and crafts; cooking articles); informational (science experiments or articles explaining how things are made or where things come from); historical (events or people in black history); inspirational (career articles showing children they can become whatever they want); interviews; personal experience (taken from child's point of view); and profiles (of black Americans who have done great things—especially need articles on those who have not been recognized). Buys 25 unsolicited mss/year. Query or submit complete ms. Length: 500-1,500 words. Pays $75-200. Pays expenses of writers on assignment.

Photos: Purchased with or without mss. Must be clear photos; no Instamatic prints. Reviews prints and transparencies. Pays $10-15 for b&w; $25 maximum for color. Model release required.

Columns/Departments: *Ebony Jr!* News uses news of outstanding black children and reviews of books, movies, TV shows, of interest to children. Pays $25-40.

Fiction: Must be believable and include experiences black children can relate to. Adventure, fantasy and historical (stories on black musicians, singers, actors, astronomers, scientists, inventors, writers, politicians, leaders; any historical figures who can give black children positive images). No violence. Buys 2 mss/issue. Query or submit complete ms. Length: 300-1,500 words. Pays $75-200.

Poetry: Free verse, haiku, light verse, and traditional forms of poetry. Buys 2/issue. No specific limit on number of submissions, but usually purchases no more than 2 at a time. Length: 5-50 lines; longer for stories in poetry form. Pays $15-100.

Fillers: Jokes, gags, anecdotes, newsbreaks and current events written at a child's level. Brain teasers, word games, crossword puzzles, guessing games, dot-to-dot games; fun games, yet educational. Pays $15-85.

Tips: "Those freelancers who have submitted material featuring an event or person who is or was relatively unknown to the general public, yet is the type of material that would have great relevance and interest to children in their everyday lives, are usually the successful writers."

HAPPY TIMES, The Magazine That Builds Character and Confidence, Eagle Systems International, 5600 N. University Ave., Provo UT 84604. (801)225-9000. Editor: Colleen Hinckley. Circulation Director: Mark Avery. 50% freelance written. Published 10 times/year for children ages 3-6 with emphasis on educational and moral content. "Each concept presented needs to teach or promote a moral value or educational concept." Circ. 50,000. Pays on publication. Publishes ms an average of 3 months after acceptance. Byline given. Buys all rights; makes work-for-hire assignments. Submit seasonal/holiday material 5 months in advance. Simultaneous queries, and simultaneous, photocopied, and previously published submissions OK. Computer printout submissions acceptable. SASE. Report in 2 weeks on queries; 1 month on mss. Writer's guidelines for SASE; sample copy for 5 first class stamps.
Nonfiction: Quint Randle, articles editor. General interest, historical/nostalgic, how-to, travel, and unique puzzles that instruct children. "Writers must see our publication *before* submitting, or they'll be out in left field. Most articles are less than 150 words long. The concept is more important than the copy; yet the copy must be super, super tight. Each issue has a theme. Themes include working, adventure (the world), courage, mystery, understanding, thanks, light, determination, cheerfulness, and creativity. Query. "Submit several short ideas for articles or activities. We'll let you know what we want and give you further guidelines." Length: 50-300 words. Pays $10-50.
Photos: State availability of photos. Pays negotiable rates for 35mm transparencies. Captions, model release, and identification of subjects required. Rights negotiated.
Columns/Departments: Bedtime Story (monthly column that teaches something of value—not just a fun story; prefers nonfiction biographical sketch or story). Buys 10 mss/year. Query with published clips. Length: 500-1,250 words. Pays $50-100.

HIGHLIGHTS FOR CHILDREN, 803 Church St., Honesdale PA 18431. Editor: Kent L. Brown Jr. 80% freelance written. Magazine published 11 times/year for children ages 2-12. Circ. 1,700,000. Pays on acceptance. Publishes ms an average of 18 months after acceptance. Buys all rights. Computer printout submissions acceptable; prefers letter-quality to dot-matrix. Reports in about 2 months. Free writer's guidelines with SAE and 1 first class stamp. Sample copy $2.25. SASE.
Nonfiction: "We prefer factual features, including history and science, written by persons with rich background and mastery in their respective fields. Contributions always welcomed from new writers, especially engineers, scientists, historians, etc., who can interpret to children useful, interesting and authentic facts, but not of the bizarre type; also writers who have lived abroad and can interpret the ways of life, especially of children, in other countries, and who don't leave the impression that US ways are always the best. Sports material, biographies and articles of interest to children. Direct, simple style, interesting content, without word embellishment; not rewritten from encyclopedias. State background and qualifications for writing factual articles submitted. Include references or sources of information. Recent article example: "The Other Engineers" (April 1985). Length: 900 words maximum. Pays $65 minimum. Also buys original party plans for children ages 7-12, clearly described in 400-700 words, including drawings or sample of items to be illustrated. Also, novel but tested ideas in crafts, with clear directions and made-up models. Projects must require only free or inexpensive, easy-to-obtain materials. Especially desirable if easy enough for early primary grades. Also, fingerplays with lots of action, easy for very young children to grasp and parents to dramatize. Avoid wordiness. Pays minimum $30 for party plans; $15 for crafts ideas; $25 for fingerplays.
Fiction: Unusual, wholesome stories appealing to both girls and boys. Vivid, full of action. "Engaging plot, strong characterization, lively language." Seeks stories that the child ages 8-12 will eagerly read, and the child ages 2-7 will like to hear when read aloud. "We print no stories just to be read aloud. We encourage authors not to hold themselves to controlled word lists. Avoid suggestion of material reward for upward striving. The main character should preferably overcome difficulties and frustrations through her or his own efforts. The story should leave a good moral and emotional residue. We especially need stories in the suspense/adventure/mystery category, and short (200 words and under) stories for the beginning reader, with an interesting plot and a number of picturable words. Also need rebuses, stories with urban settings, stories for beginning readers (500 words), humorous and horse stories. We also need more material of 1-page length (300-500 words), both fiction and factual. We need creative-thinking puzzles that can be illustrated, optical illusions, body teasers, and other 'fun' activities. War, crime and violence are taboo. Some fanciful stories wanted." Length: 400-900 words. Pays $65/minimum.
Tips: "We are pleased that many authors of children's literature report that their first published work was in the pages of *Highlights*. It is not our policy to consider fiction on the strength of the reputation of the author. We judge each submission on its own merits. With factual material, however, we do prefer either authorities in their field or people with first-hand experience. In this manner we can avoid the encyclopedic article that merely restates information readily available elsewhere. We don't make assignments. Query with simple letter to es-

Close-up

Constance McAllister
Senior Editor
Highlights for Children

"Fun with a purpose." That's the editorial philosophy of *Highlights for Children*. The fun, though, is reserved for readers. Writers must work—to create meaningful, accurate and fun stories—if they hope to earn a byline here. "We are very concerned that what children read in *Highlights* is enlightening, interesting, and also fun for them," says senior editor Constance McAllister.

Highlights' editors read all nonfiction with an eye for authenticity; facts are verified by staff members or consulting editors. "Children are learning a lot about life in the material they read," says McAllister, "and even in fiction we sometimes come up against problems. For example, if a story includes an explanation of the working of a car, that information must not be contrary to fact."

McAllister and other *Highlights'* editors plan the magazine in three-month segments. Scheduling will include a balance of fiction and nonfiction for grade school and pre-school subscribers; articles about history, science and engineering are especially popular among readers. Although nonfiction is not geared to the younger children, editors try to include a sidebar or pictures so that even nonreaders can learn something from it.

"We are very careful about violence," says McAllister. "There is enough of that other places, and we don't need it. We want to give children positive stories that reflect positive characteristics."

In recent months, editors' responsibilities at *Highlights* have been restructured to allow for more specialization. McAllister now works more closely with the magazine's fiction.

She described a typical mix of fiction in the three-month plans. "Certainly I would want there to be one mystery story, because it involves the readers and teaches them how to think. It's fun, and I love mystery stories. And I want there to be an adventure story, a sports story, and a funny story—and some kind of problem-in-human-relations story. And a horse story. I wouldn't dare forget that.

"We want stories to have some little core of learning about how children should treat friends, or how they should handle a certain type of situation, but with some little creative twist to it, and characters that sound as if they could really have been alive," says McAllister. "We like stories that appeal to something very basic, or an old theme with a new twist that makes it fun and lively."

Highlights' editors use a formula in selecting fiction for each issue. Stories for the young reader or to be read aloud to children (ages two to eight) go in larger type. "We ordinarily have five pages for those stories," McAllister says. "That would probably be two two-page stories (on opposing page spreads) and a one-page rebus story (we use words as well as the pictures). Then we would probably give six pages to stories for the older reader; that would break down to three two-page stories. That's eleven pages of fiction overall."

In addition to editing the magazine's fiction, McAllister personally reviews some 2,000 entries in the annual fiction contest. She started the contest six years ago. "It has given us the satisfaction of developing and encouraging new writers," she points out. "We've made a lot of friends."

—Pat Beusterien

tablish whether the nonfiction *subject* is likely to be of interest. A beginning writer should first become familiar with the type of material which *Highlights* publishes. We are most eager for easy stories for very young readers, but realize that this is probably the most difficult kind of writing. Include special qualifications, if any, of author. Write for the child, not the editor.''

HUMPTY DUMPTY'S MAGAZINE, Children's Health Publications, 1100 Waterway Blvd., Box 567, Indianapolis IN 46206. Editor: Christine French Clark. Magazine published 8 times/year stressing health, nutrition, hygiene, exercise and safety for children ages 4-6. Combined issues: February/March, April/May, June/July, and August/September. Pays on publication. Buys all rights. Submit seasonal material 8 months in advance. Reports in 10 weeks. Sample copy 75¢; writer's guidelines for SASE.
Nonfiction: "We are open to nonfiction on almost any age-appropriate subject, but we especially need material with a health theme—nutrition, safety, exercise, hygiene. We're looking for articles that encourages readers to develop better health habits without preaching. Very simple factual articles that creatively teach readers about their bodies. Simple crafts, some with holiday themes. We also use several puzzles and activities in each issue—dot-to-dot, hidden pictures, *simple* crosswords, and easy-to-play 'board' games. Keep in mind that most our readers are just *beginning* to learn to read and write, so word puzzles must be very basic." Submit complete ms. "Include number of words in manuscript and Social Security number." Length: 600 words maximum. Pays 6¢/word.
Fiction: "We're primarily interested in stories in rhyme and easy-to-read stories for the beginning reader. Currently we are needing seasonal stories with holiday themes. We use contemporary stories and fantasy, some employing a health theme. We try to present our health material in a positive light, incorporating humor and a light approach wherever possible. Avoid sexual stereotyping. Characters in contemporary stories should be realistic and up-to-date. Remember, many of our readers have working mothers and/or come from single-parent homes. We need more stories that reflect these changing times but at the same time communicate good, wholesome values." Submit complete ms. "Include number of words in manuscript and Social Security number." Length: 600 words maximum. Pays 6¢/word.
Poetry: Short, simple poems. Pays $7 minimum.

INSIGHT, The Young Calvinist Federation, Box 7244, Grand Rapids MI 49510. (616)241-5616. Editor: John Knight. Assistant Editor: Martha Kalk. 20% freelance written. For young people ages 16-21, a Christian youth magazine. Monthly (except June and August) magazine; 28 pages. Circ. 18,500. Pays on publication. Publishes ms an average of 3 months after acceptance. Byline given. Buys simultaneous, second serial (reprint) and first North American serial rights. Submit seasonal/holiday material 6 months in advance. Simultaneous, photocopied and previously published submissions OK. SASE. Sample copy and writer's guidelines for 9x12 SASE.
Photos: Photos purchased without accompanying ms. Pays $15-35/8x10 b&w glossy print; $50-200 for 35mm or larger color transparencies. Total purchase price for ms includes payment for photos.
Fiction: Humorous, mainstream and religious. "Looks for short stories and nonfiction that lead readers to a better understanding of how the Christian faith is relevant to daily life, social issues and the arts. They must do more than entertain—must make the reader see things in a new light." No sentimental, moralistic guidance articles. Buys 1-2 mss/issue. Send complete ms. Length: 1,000-3,000 words. Pays $45-125.
Poetry: Free verse. Buys 10 poems/year. Length: 4-25 lines. Pays $20-25.
Fillers: Youth oriented cartoons, puzzles and short humor. Length: 50-300 words. Pays $10-35.
Tips: "We are looking for shorter contributions and short, short stories."

JACK AND JILL, 1100 Waterway Blvd., Box 567, Indianapolis IN 46206. (317)636-8881. Editor: Christine French Clark. 85% freelance written. Magazine published 8 times/year for children ages 6-8. Pays on publication. Publishes ms an average of 8 months after acceptance. Buys all rights. Byline given. Submit seasonal material 8 months in advance. Computer printout submissions acceptable. Reports in 10 weeks. May hold material seriously being considered for up to 1 year. "Material will not be returned unless accompanied by self-addressed envelope with sufficient postage." Sample copy 75¢; writer's guidelines for SASE.
Nonfiction: "Because we want to encourage youngsters to read for pleasure and for information, we are interested in material that will challenge a young child's intelligence *and* be enjoyable reading. Our emphasis is on good health, and we are in particular need of articles, stories, and activities with health, safety, exercise and nutrition themes. We are looking for well-written articles that take unusual approaches to teaching better health habits and scientific facts about how the body works. We try to present our health material in a positive light—incorporating humor and a light approach wherever possible without minimizing the seriousness of what we are saying." Straight factual articles are OK if they are short and interestingly written. "We would rather see, however, more creative alternative views to the straight factual article. For instance, we'd be interested in seeing a health message or facts presented in articles featuring positive role models for readers. Many of the personalities children admire—athletes, musicians, and film or TV stars—are fitness or nutrition buffs. Many have kicked drugs, alcohol or smoking habits and are outspoken about the danger of these vices. Black and white photos accompanying this type of article would greatly enhance salability." Buys 25-30 nonfiction mss/year.

Length: 500-1,200 words. Pays approximately 6¢ a word.

Photos: When appropriate, photos should accompany ms. Reviews sharp, contrasting b&w glossy prints. Pays $7 for b&w. Buys one-time rights.

Fiction: May include, but is not limited to, realistic stories, fantasy adventure—set in past, present or future. All stories need a well-developed plot, action and incident. Humor is highly desirable. "Currently we need stories with holiday themes. Stories that deal with a health theme need not have health as the primary subject. We would like to see more playlets and biographical fiction." Length: 500-1,500 words, short stories; 1,500 words/installment, serials of two parts. Pays approximately 6¢ a word. Buys 20-25 mss/year.

Fillers: Puzzles (including various kinds of word and crossword puzzles), poems, games, science projects, and creative craft projects. Instructions for activities should be clearly and simply written and accompanied by models or diagram sketches. "We also have a need for recipes. Ingredients should be healthful; avoid sugar, salt, chocolate, red meat, and fats as much as possible. In all material, avoid references to eating sugary foods, such as candy, cakes, cookies and soft drinks.

Tips: "We are constantly looking for new writers who can tell good stories with interesting slants—stories that are not full of out-dated and time-worn expressions. Our best authors are writers who know what today's children are like. Keep in mind that our readers are becoming 'computer literate', living in an age of rapidly developing technology. They are exploring careers possibilities that may be new and unfamiliar to our generation. They are faced with tough decisions about drug and alcohol use. Many of them are latch-key children because both parents work or they come from single-parent homes. We need more stories and articles that reflect these changing times but that also communicate good, wholesome values. Obtain *current* issues of the magazines and *study* them to determine our present needs and editorial style."

MEDICAL DETECTIVE, Children's Better Health Institute, Box 567, Indianapolis IN 46206. (317)636-8881. Editor: Steve Charles. Quarterly medical "mystery" magazine for 6th grade readers. Pays on publication. Byline given. Buys variable rights. Submit seasonal/holiday material 8 months in advance. SASE. Reports in 10 weeks. Sample copy 75¢; writer's guidelines for business size SAE and 1 first class stamp.

Nonfiction: Medical "mysteries". Problems and solutions in area of diseases and illnesses. Will consider historical material. Looking for articles on current medical research and technology. Buys variable number mss/year. Send complete ms. Length: 500-1,500 words. Pays approximately 6¢/word.

Photos: Send photos with ms. Pays $5 minimum for 8x10 b&w prints. Model release and identification of subjects required. Buys one-time rights.

Fiction: Medical "mysteries." Stories in fictional setting which present factual problems or true stories with medical conditions and factual solutions. No hard-boiled detectives or trite solutions to "unreal" problems. Buys variable number mss/year. Send complete ms. Length: 500-1,000 words.

Tips: "Look around and find a medical health problem resulting from a condition or a disease. Lead the reader through the problem (investigation), and provide separate answer or include resolution in story. Include list of sources or references used in manuscript."

‡**NATIONAL GEOGRAPHIC WORLD**, National Geographic Society, 17th & M Sts. NW, Washington DC 20036. (202)857-7000. Editor: Pat Robbins. Associate Editor: Margaret McKelway. Monthly magazine of factual stories of interest to children ages 8-13 years. "*World* is a strongly visual magazine; all stories must have a visual story line; no unillustrated stories are used." Circ. 1.2 million. Pays on publication. No byline given. Offers $50 kill fee. Buys all rights. Submit seasonal/holiday material 1 year in advance. SASE. Reports in 2 weeks. Free sample copy.

Nonfiction: Subject matter is factual. Subjects include animals, conservation, science and technology, geography, history, sports, outdoor adventure and children's activities. No fiction, poetry, book reviews, TV or current events. Humor, shorts, and game ideas are welcome. Query first. "Writing is always done after pictures are in hand. Freelance assignments are made on a contract basis. Those interested in freelance assignments are asked to do a test piece first."

Photos: "Freelance photography is handled in a variety of ways. Photo story submissions are reviewed by the illustrations editor. Photographers who want assignments should send a query letter first. Include a brief description of the proposed story and list the picture possibilities. If the magazine is interested, the illustrations editor will review the photographer's portfolio."

‡**NATURE FRIEND MAGAZINE**, Pilgrim Publishers, 22777 State Rd. 119, Goshen IN 46526. (219)534-2245. Editor: Stanley K. Brubaker. Monthly magazine appreciating God's marvelous creation. Audience includes children ages 4-14 and older of Christian families who hold a literal view of Creation. Circ. 2,100. Pays on publication unless delayed more than 2 months. Byline given. Buys one-time rights. Submit seasonal/holiday material 3 or more months in advance. Simultaneous queries, and simultaneous, photocopied, and previously published submissions OK if notified of other submissions or past use. SASE. Reports in 4 weeks. Sample copy for 8x10 SAE and 56¢ postage; writer's guidelines $1, 6x9 SAE and 56¢ postage.

Nonfiction: General interest (various length articles on popular and odd creatures); how-to (for children in learning or building, working with nature); inspirational (praise; humbled by God's handiwork); new product (each issue has Nature's Workshop product page); personal experience (especially from child's point of view); photo feature (about wildlife or other nature fascinating to *children*); and puzzles, projects, etc. Buys 35-50 mss/year. Send complete ms. Length: 200-1,200 words. Pays $6-25.

Photos: Send photos with ms. Reviews 2¼ 35mm color transparencies and b&w 8x10 prints. Pays $25 maximum for color; $15 maximum for b&w. Captions, model release, and identification of subjects required. Buys one-time rights.

Fiction: Uses some true-to-life nature study stories with animals or other creature as main character (from animal's perspective). Also families enjoying nature discovery. Buys 30-50 mss/year. Length: 200-1,200 words. Pays $5-25.

Tips: "Subscribe to *Nature Friend Magazine* or study back issues—it has a definite targeted market of fundamental Christians. We want all materials to have a cheerful factual reverential mood. Send samples of your work, complete manuscripts, with photos included if a package. Send only your very best. We are always open to fascinating animal and wildlife 'character sketches', whether stories from human point of view or animal's."

NAUTICA, The Magazine of the Sea for Young People, Spinnaker Press, Inc., Pickering Wharf, Salem MA 01970. (617)745-6905. Editors: Wayne C. Wendel and John Kittredge. 65% freelance written. Bimonthly children's magazine covering all aspects of the nautical and water world. Written for children ages 8-14 years. Reading grade level is between 6th and 7th grades. Pays on publication. Publishes ms an average of 6 months after acceptance. Byline given. Buys first North American serial rights. Submit seasonal/holiday material 3 months in advance. Simultaneous, photocopied, and previously published submissions OK. Computer printout submissions acceptable. SASE. Reports in 6 weeks. Free writer's guidelines; sample copy $1.25 and 9x12 SAE.

Nonfiction: Historical/nostalgic (nautical history); how-to (knot tying/rafting/skiing etc.); interview/profile (nautical character); personal experience (adventure); and photo feature (sea animals etc.). Buys 40 mss/year. Query or send complete ms. Length: 1,000-1,800 words. Pays 10-25¢/word. Sometimes pays expenses of writers on assignment.

Photos: Donna Chludzinski, photo editor. Send photos with accompanying query or ms. Pays $25 maximum for b&w contact sheets; $50 maximum for color transparencies.

Columns/Departments: Departments/columns include Living Abroad (the daily life of people and children who live aboard naval ships, cruising sailboats, canal boats, etc.); Port-of-Call (reports the history, romance, daily life, special interests of ports all over the world); Folklore (the lore and legends of the sea); What is It? (a 1-page photo/test educational feature of an interesting or unusual aspect of the sea, sea life, or sailing); Boat-of-the-Month (focuses on a particular boat with a brief history, explanation of design, and uses); Navigation (lessons and the basic how-tos of navigation such as reading a chart, using a compass, etc.); Nautica Lines (news clips and stories); and Book Review (a short review of children's books on the sea, lakes and rivers). Buys 40 mss/year. Query. Length: 100-1,200 words. Pays 10-25¢/word.

Fillers: Cartoons and games. Buys 20/year.

Tips: "All areas of *Nautica* are opened to freelancers. The use of shorter sentences and a somewhat controlled vocabulary is advised. Above all, do not talk down to the reader. Clarity of expression and logical thought are most important. No reports that could have come out of an encyclopedia—be original and personal. Frequent mistakes are articles that are too technical, too much like a high-school report, or too long—not enough attention is paid to word limits."

ODYSSEY, AstroMedia Corp., 625 E. St. Paul Ave., Milwaukee WI 53202. (414)276-2689. Editor: Nancy Mack. 50% freelance written. Monthly magazine emphasizing astronomy and outer space for children ages 8-12. Circ. 100,000. Pays on publication. Publishes ms an average of 4 months after acceptance. Buys all rights or first North American serial rights. Submit seasonal/holiday material 4 months in advance. Photocopied and previously published submissions OK. Computer printout submissions acceptable; prefers letter-quality to dot-matrix. SASE. Reports in 8 weeks. "Material with little news connection may be held up to one year." Sample copy and writer's guidelines for large SAE and $1.24 postage.

Nonfiction: General interest (astronomy, outer space, spacecraft, planets, stars, etc.); how-to (astronomy projects, experiments, etc.); and photo feature (spacecraft, planets, stars, etc.). "No general overview articles; for example, a general article on the Space Shuttle, or a general article on stars. We do not want science fiction articles." Buys 12 mss/year. Query with published clips. Length: 750-2,000 words. Pays $100-350 depending on length and type of article. Sometimes pays expenses of writers on assignment.

Photos: State availability of photos. Buys one-time rights. Captions preferred; model release required. Payment depends upon size and placement.

Tips: "Since I am overstocked and have a stable of regular writers, a query is very important. I often get several manuscripts on the same subject and must reject them. Write a very specific proposal and indicate why it will interest kids. If the subject is very technical, indicate your qualifications to write about it. Frequent mistakes writers make are trying to fudge on material they don't understand, using outdated references, and telling me their articles are assignments for the Institute of Children's Literature."

ON THE LINE, Mennonite Publishing House, 616 Walnut Ave., Scottdale PA 15683-1999. (412)887-8500. Editor: Virginia A. Hostetler. Weekly magazine for children ages 10-14. Circ. 12,000. Pays on acceptance. Publishes ms an average of 1 year after acceptance. Byline given. Buys one-time rights. Submit seasonal/holiday material 6 months in advance. Simultaneous, photocopied, and previously published submissions OK. Computer printout submissions acceptable; prefers letter-quality to dot-matrix. SASE. Reports in 1 month.
Nonfiction: How-to (things to make with easy-to-get materials); and informational (500-word articles on wonders of nature, people who have made outstanding contributions). Buys 95 unsolicited mss/year. Length: 500-1,200 words. Pays $10-24.
Photos: Photos purchased with or without ms. Pays $10-25 for 8x10 b&w photos. Total purchase price for ms includes payment for photos.
Columns/Departments: Fiction, adventure, humorous and religious. Buys 52 mss/year. Send complete ms. Length: 800-1,200 words. Pays $15-24.
Poetry: Light verse and religious. Length: 3-12 lines. Pays $5-15.
Tips: "Study the publication first. We need short well-written how-to and craft articles. State theme and length of material in query."

OUR LITTLE FRIEND, PRIMARY TREASURE, Pacific Press Publishing Association, 1350 Villa St., Mountain View CA 94042. (415)961-2323, ext. 335. Editor: Louis Schutter. 99% freelance written. Weekly for youngsters of the Seventh-Day Adventist church. *Our Little Friend* is for children ages 2-6; *Primary Treasure*, ages 7-9. Buys first serial rights (international); first North American serial rights; one-time rights, second serial (reprint) rights; and simultaneous rights. Byline given. Publishes ms an average of 1 year or more after acceptance. "The payment we make is for one magazine right. In most cases, it is for the first one. But we make payment for second and third rights also." Simultaneous submissions OK. Computer printout submissions acceptable; prefers letter-quality to dot-matrix. "We do not purchase material during June, July and August." SASE.
Nonfiction: All stories must be based on fact, written in story form. True-to-life, character-building stories; written from viewpoint of child and giving emphasis to lessons of life needed for Christian living. True-to-life is emphasized more than plot. Nature or science articles, but no fantasy; science must be very simple. All material should be educational or informative and stress moral attitude and religious principle. Buys 300 unsolicited mss/year.
Photos: 8x10 glossy prints for cover. Photo payment: sliding scale according to quality.
Fiction: Should emphasize honesty, truthfulness, courtesy, health and temperance, along with stories of heroism, adventure, nature and safety. 700-1,000 words for *Our Little Friend*, 600-1,200 words for *Primary Treasure*. Fictionalized Bible stories are not used. Pays 1¢/word.
Poetry: Juvenile poetry. Up to 12 lines.
Fillers: Puzzles.
Tips: "We are in need of 1,200 word manuscripts for the cover of *Primary Treasure*—an adventure story that has a premise or lesson embroidered into the plot. The cover story must have a scene that our illustrator can put his teeth into."

OWL MAGAZINE, The Discovery Magazine for Children, The Young Naturalist Foundation, 59 Front St. E., Toronto, Ontario M5E 1B3 Canada. (416)364-3333. Editor: Sylvia S. Funston. 25% freelance written. Magazine published 10 times/year (no July or August issues) covering natural science. Aims to interest children in their environment through accurate, factual information about the world around them presented in an easy, lively style. Circ. 105,000. Pays on publication. Publishes ms an average of 3 months after acceptance. Byline given. Buys all rights; makes work-for-hire assignments. Submit seasonal/holiday material 1 year in advance. Computer printout submissions acceptable; no dot-matrix. SASE. Reports in 10 weeks. Sample copy $1.50 and IRC; free writer's guidelines.
Nonfiction: How-to (activities, crafts); personal experience (real life children in real situations); photo feature (natural science, international wildlife, and outdoor features); and science and environmental features. "Write for editorial guidelines first; know your topic. Our magazine never talks down to children." No folk tales, problem stories with drugs, sex or moralistic views, fantasy or talking animal stories. Query with clips of published work.
Photos: State availability of photos. Reviews 35mm transparencies. Identification of subjects required.
Tips: "We accept short, well-written articles about up-to-the-minute science discoveries or developments for our Hoot section."

PENNYWHISTLE PRESS, Gannett Co., Inc., Box 500-P, Washington DC 20044. (703)276-3796. Editor: Anita Sama. A weekly tabloid newspaper supplement with stories and features for children ages 6-12. Circ. 2,600,000. Pays on acceptance. Byline given. Buys all rights. Submit seasonal/holiday material 3-6 months in advance. Photocopied submissions OK. Computer printout submissions acceptable. SASE. Reports in 2 months. Sample copy for 50¢, SAE and 2 first class stamps; writer's guidelines for SAE and 1 first class stamp.
Nonfiction: General interest, how-to (sports, crafts), and photo feature (children). Buys 5 mss/year. Length:

500 words maximum. Pays $50 maximum.

Fiction: For children. Buys 25 mss/year. Send complete ms. Length: 250-850 words. Pays variable rate.

Poetry: Traditional poetry for children. Buys 5-10 poems/year. Submit maximum 1 poem. Pays variable rate.

Tips: Fiction is most open to freelancers.

R-A-D-A-R, 8121 Hamilton Ave., Cincinnati OH 45231. (513)931-4050. Editor: Margaret Williams. 75% freelance written. Weekly for children in grades 3-6 in Christian Sunday schools. Rights purchased vary with author and material; prefers buying first serial rights, but will buy second (reprint) rights. Occasionally overstocked. Pays on acceptance. Publishes ms an average of 1 year after acceptance. Submit seasonal material 1 year in advance. Computer printout submissions acceptable; prefers letter-quality to dot-matrix. Reports in 6 weeks. SASE. Free sample copy.

Nonfiction: Articles on hobbies and handicrafts, nature, famous people, seasonal subjects, etc., written from a Christian viewpoint. No articles about historical figures with an absence of religious implication. Length: 500-1,000 words. Pays 2¢/word maximum.

Fiction: Short stories of heroism, adventure, travel, mystery, animals and biography. True or possible plots stressing clean, wholesome, Christian character-building ideas, but not preachy. Make prayer, church attendance and Christian living a natural part of the story. "We correlate our fiction and other features with a definite Bible lesson. Writers who want to meet our needs should send for a theme list." No talking animal stories, science fiction, Halloween stories or first-person stories from an adult's viewpoint. Length: up to 1,000 words. Pays 2¢/word maximum.

RANGER RICK, National Wildlife Federation, 1412 16th St. NW, Washington DC 20036. (703)790-4270. Editorial Director: Trudy D. Farrand. 50% freelance written. Monthly magazine for children from ages 6-12, with the greatest concentration in the 7-10 age bracket. Buys all world rights. Byline given "but occasionally, for very brief pieces, we will identify author by name at the end. Contributions to regular departments usually are not bylined." Pays on acceptance. Publishes ms an average of 18 months after acceptance. Computer printout submissions acceptable; no dot-matrix. Reports in 2 weeks. "Anything written with a specific month in mind should be in our hands at least 10 months before that issue date." SASE.

Nonfiction: "Articles may be written on anything related to nature, conservation, environmental problems or natural science." Buys 20-25 unsolicited mss/year. Query. Pays from $10-350, depending on length and content (maximum length, 900 words).

Fiction: "Same categories as nonfiction plus fantasy and science fiction. The attributing of human qualities to animals is limited to our regular feature, 'The Adventures of Ranger Rick' so please do not humanize wildlife. The publisher, The National Wildlife Federation, discourages keeping wildlife as pets."

Photos: "Photographs, when used, are paid for separately. It is not necessary that illustrations accompany material."

Tips: "Include in query details of what manuscript will cover; sample lead; evidence that you can write playfully and with great enthusiasm, conviction and excitement (formal, serious, dull queries indicate otherwise). Think of an exciting subject we haven't done recently, sell it effectively with query, and produce a manuscript of highest quality. Read past issues to learn successful styles and unique approaches to subjects. If your submission is commonplace in any way we won't want it."

STICKERS! MAGAZINE, For Kids Stuck on Stickers, Ira Friedman, Inc., Suite 1300, 10 Columbus Circle, New York NY 10019. (212)541-7300. Editor: Bob Woods. Quarterly magazine covering all kinds of adhesive-backed stickers, related products, and activities. "Readers are children, generally girls, ages 6-14, who are wild about collecting, trading, and making things with stickers. We also cover other, trendier 'stuff' for kids, such as neon jewelry, jazzy tote bags, and other accessory items. We try to point out humor, education, friendship, sharing, benefits, and other positive aspects of using stickers." Estab. 1983. Circ. 200,000. Pays on publication. Byline given. Buys first North American serial rights. Submit seasonal/holiday material 3 months in advance. Photocopied submissions OK. Computer printout submissions acceptable. SASE. Reports in 3 weeks on queries; 2 weeks on mss. Sample copy and writer's guidelines for SAE.

Nonfiction: Historical/nostalgic; how-to; humor; interview/profile (with collectors, manufacturers, sticker stores); new product; personal experience; and photo feature. Query with published clips. Length: 250-2,000 words. Pays $50 minimum.

Fillers: Games and puzzles employing stickers.

Tips: "Send a letter that details your idea and lets us know you have more than a casual interest in the subject. We need more than just stories about collectors. Areas most open to freelancers: Stickerama, all sorts of sticker stuff; Best Sticker Ideas, generated by readers; and Sticker People, short profiles."

STORY FRIENDS, Mennonite Publishing House, 616 Walnut Ave., Scottdale PA 15683. (412)887-8500. Editor: Marjorie Waybill. 75% freelance written. Published monthly in weekly parts. For children ages 4-9. Not copyrighted. Buys one-time rights and simultaneous rights. Pays on acceptance. Byline given. Submit seasonal/holiday material 6 months in advance. Computer printout submissions acceptable. SASE. Free sample copy with SAE and 25¢ postage.

Nonfiction: "The over-arching purpose of this publication is to portray Jesus as a friend and helper—a friend who cares about each happy and sad experience in the child's life. Persons who know Jesus have values which affect every area of their lives."

Fiction: "Stories of everyday experiences at home, at church, in school or at play can provide models of these values. Of special importance are relationships, patterns of forgiveness, respect, honesty, trust and caring. We prefer short stories that offer a wide variety of settings, acquaint children with a wide range of friends, and mirror the joys, fears, temptations and successes of the readers. *Story Friends* needs stories that speak to the needs and interests of children of a variety of ethnic backgrounds. Stories should provide patterns of forgiveness, respect, integrity, understanding, caring, sharing; increase the children's sense of self-worth through growing confidence in God's love for them as they are; help answer the children's questions about God, Jesus, the Bible, prayer, death, heaven; develop awe and reverence for God the Creator and for all of His creation; avoid preachiness, but have well-defined spiritual values as an integral part of each story; be plausible in plot; introduce children to followers of Jesus Christ; and develop appreciation for our Mennonite heritage." Length: 300-800 words. Pays 3-5¢/word.

Poetry: Traditional and free verse. Length: 3-12 lines. Pays $5.

3-2-1 CONTACT, Children's Television Workshop, One Lincoln Plaza, New York NY 10023. (212)595-3456. Editor: Jonathan Rosenbloom. Senior Editor: Jim Lewis. 40% freelance written. Magazine published 10 times/year covering science and technology for children ages 8-14. Circ. 320,000. Pays on acceptance. Publishes ms 6 months after acceptance. Buys all rights "with some exceptions." Submit seasonal material 6 months in advance. Simultaneous, photocopied, and previously published submissions OK if so indicated. Computer printout submissions acceptable; prefers letter-quality to dot-matrix. SASE. Reports in 1 month. Sample copy $1.25; free writer's guidelines.

Nonfiction: General interest (space exploration, the human body, animals, computers and the new technology, current science issues); profile (of interesting scientists or children involved in science or with computers); photo feature (centered around a science theme); and role models of women and minority scientists. No articles on travel not related to science. Buys 5 unsolicited mss/year. Query with published clips. Length: 700-1,000 words. Pays $150-400. Sometimes pays expenses of writers on assignment.

Photos: Reviews 8x10 b&w prints and 35mm color transparencies. Model release required.

Tips: "I prefer a short query, without manuscript, that makes it clear that an article is interesting. When sending an article, include your telephone number. Don't call us, we'll call you. Many submissions we receive are more like college research papers than feature stories. We like articles in which writers have interviewed kids or scientists, or discovered exciting events with a scientific angle. Library research is necessary; but if that's all you're doing, you aren't giving us anything we can't get ourselves. If your story needs a bibliography, chances are, it's not right for us."

TOUCH, Box 7244, Grand Rapids MI 49510. Editor: Joanne Ilbrink. 60% freelance written. Monthly magazine. Purpose of publication is to show girls ages 8-15 how God is at work in their lives and in the world around them. Circ. 14,000. Pays on acceptance. Publishes ms an average of 2 months after acceptance. Byline given. Buys second serial (reprint) rights and first North American serial rights. Submit seasonal/holiday material 5 months in advance. Simultaneous, photocopied, and previously published submissions OK. Computer printout submissions acceptable; prefers letter-quality to dot-matrix. SASE. Reports in 3 weeks. Free sample copy and writer's guidelines for SASE and 3 first class stamps.

Nonfiction: How-to (crafts girls can make easily and inexpensively); informational (write for issue themes); humor (needs much more); inspirational (seasonal and holiday); interview; travel; personal experience (avoid the testimony approach); and photo feature (query first). "Because our magazine is published around a monthly theme, requesting the letter we send out twice a year to our established freelancers would be most helpful. We do not want easy solutions or quick character changes from bad to good. No pietistic characters. Constant mention of God is not necessary if the moral tone of the story is positive. We do not want stories that always have a good ending." Buys 36-45 unsolicited mss/year. Submit complete ms. Length: 100-1,000 words. Pays 2¢/word, depending on the amount of editing.

Photos: Purchased with or without ms. Reviews 3x5 clear b&w (only) glossy prints. Pays $5-25 on publication.

Fiction: Adventure (that girls could experience in their hometowns or places they might realistically visit); humorous; mystery (believable only); romance (stories that deal with awakening awareness of boys are appreciated); suspense (can be serialized) and religious (nothing preachy). Buys 20 mss/year. Submit complete ms. Length: 300-1,500 words. Pays 2¢/word.

Poetry: Free verse, haiku, light verse and traditional. Buys 10/year. Length: 50 lines maximum. Pays $5 minimum.

Fillers: Puzzles, short humor and cartoons. Buys 3/issue. Pays $2.50-7.

Tips: "Prefers not to see anything on the adult level, secular material or violence. We judge on quality, and if it is good we go for it. Writers frequently over-simplify the articles and often write with a Pollyanna attitude."

TURTLE MAGAZINE FOR PRESCHOOL KIDS, Children's Better Health Institute, Benjamin Franklin Literary & Medical Society, Inc., 1100 Waterway Blvd., Box 567, Indianapolis IN 46206. (317)636-8881. Editor: Beth Wood Thomas. 95% freelance written. Monthly magazine (bimonthly February/March, April/May, June/July, August/September) for preschoolers emphasizing health, safety, exercise and good nutrition. Pays on publication. Publishes ms an average of 1 year after acceptance. Byline given. Buys all rights. Submit seasonal/holiday material 8 months in advance. SASE. Reports in 10 weeks. Sample copy 75¢; writer's guidelines for business size SASE.
Fiction: Fantasy, humorous and health-related stories. "Stories that deal with a health theme need not have health as the primary subject but should include it in some way in the course of events." No controversial material. Buys 40 mss/year. Submit complete ms. Length: 700 words maximum. Pays approximately 6¢/word.
Poetry: "We use many stories in rhyme—vocabularly should be geared to a 3 to 5 year-old. Anthropomorphic animal stories and rhymes are especially effective for this age group to emphasize a moral or lesson without 'lecturing'." Pays variable rates.
Tips: "We are primarily concerned with preventive medicine. We try to present our material in a positive—not a negative—light and to incorporate humor and a light approach wherever possible without minimizing the seriousness of what we are saying. We would like to see more stories, articles, craft ideas and activities with the following holiday themes: New Year's Day, Valentine's Day, President's Day, St. Patrick's Day, Easter, Independence Day, Thanksgiving, Christmas and Hannukah. We like new ideas that will entertain as well as teach preschoolers. Publishing a writer's first work is very gratifying to us. It is a great pleasure to receive new, fresh material"

WEE WISDOM, Unity Village MO 64065. Editor: Verle Bell. 90% freelance written. Magazine published 10 times/year "for children aged 13 and under dedicated to the truth that each person is a child of God and has an inner source of wisdom, power, love and health from the Father that can be applied in a practical manner to everyday life." Publishes ms an average of 8 months after acceptance. Submit seasonal/holiday material 8 months in advance. Pays on acceptance. Byline given. Buys first serial rights only. Computer printout submissions acceptable; prefers letter-quality to dot-matrix. SASE. Free sample copy and editorial policy for SAE and 3 first class stamps.
Nonfiction: Entertaining nature articles or projects/activities to encourage appreciation of all life. Wants only completed mss. Pays 4¢/word minimum.
Fiction: Character-building stories that encourage a positive self-image. Although entertaining enough to hold the interest of the older child, they should be readable by the third grader. "Characters should be appealing but realistic; plots should be plausible, and all stories should be told in a forthright manner but without preaching. Life itself combines fun and humor with its more serious lessons, and our most interesting and helpful stories do the same thing. Language should be universal, avoiding the Sunday school image." Length: 500-800 words. Pay 4¢/word minimum.
Poetry: Very limited. Prefers short, seasonal or humorous poems. Also buys rhymed prose for "read alouds". Pays $15.00 minimum, 50¢ per line after 15 lines.
Fillers: Pays $15.00 minimum for puzzles and games.

WONDER TIME, 6401 The Paseo, Kansas City MO 64131. (816)333-7000. Editor: Evelyn Beals. 75% freelance written. Published weekly by Church of the Nazarene for children ages 6-8. Buys first serial rights, second (reprint) rights; simultaneous rights and all rights for curriculum assignments. Pays on acceptance. Publishes ms an average of 2 years after acceptance. Byline given. Computer printout submissions acceptable; prefers letter-quality to dot-matrix. SASE. Free sample copy.
Fiction: Buys stories portraying Christian attitudes without being preachy. Uses stories for special days—stories teaching honesty, truthfulness, kindness, helpfulness or other important spiritual truths, and avoiding symbolism. "God should be spoken of as our Father who loves and cares for us; Jesus, as our Lord and Savior." Buys 150/mss year. Length: 400-600 words. Pays 3½¢/word on acceptance.
Poetry: Uses verse which has seasonal or Christian emphasis. Length: 4-12 lines. Pays 25¢/line, minimum $2.50.
Tips: "Any stories that allude to church doctrine must be in keeping with Nazarene beliefs. Any type of fantasy must be in good taste and easily recognizable. We are overstocked now with poetry and stories with general themes. A brochure with specific needs available with free sample." Recently published "a story of a little boy whose grandfather dies, showing how his faith in God and belief in heaven helps his grief"; and "a story about a boy talking to his dad about income taxes; relating it to the Biblical command to give to God and to Caesar."

YOUNG AMERICAN, Student News, Young American Publishing Co., Inc., Box 12409, Portland OR 97212. (503)230-1895. Managing Editor: Kristina Linden. A monthly 16-24 page tabloid inserted in 9 suburban newspapers for students, ages 4-16, and the developing reader to whom 2 pages are devoted. "Subjects vary from world politics to children making headlines, and material is easy to digest as well as timely and pertinent." Circ. 108,000. Pays on publication. Byline given. Buys first North American serial rights. Submit seasonal/holiday material at least 3 months in advance. Simultaneous queries OK. Computer printout submissions acceptable; no dot-matrix. SASE. Reports in 2 months. Sample copy for SAE and 37¢ postage; ms guidelines for SAE and 1 first class stamp.

Nonfiction: Exposé (pertaining to children); how-to (make money for kids, 150 words); interview/profile; and technical (science). No violence or any articles which are not written for children under age 16. Buys 48 mss/year. Send complete ms. Length: 150-300 words. Pays 7¢/word.

Photos: Send photos with ms. Pays $5 for b&w prints. Identification of subjects required. Buys one-time rights.

Columns/Departments: World News, You & the News (stories about newsworthy children, schools, or legislation pertaining to children); entertainment (book reviews); Science/Health; Sports; and Fun of It; (poetry 300 lines maximum). Buys 15-25 mss/year. Length: 150-300 words. Pays 7¢/word.

Fiction: Adventure, fantasy, humorous, mystery, science fiction, suspense and western. Also Christmas story (700-950 words). "No condescending material, stories that are poorly written which tend to tell the reader instead of showing; no didactic material." Buys 12 mss/year. Send complete mss. Length: 500-950 words. Pays 7¢/word.

Poetry: Free verse, haiku, light verse and traditional. Buys 10/year. Submit maximum 12 poems. Pays 7¢/word.

Fillers: Jokes, gags and newsbreaks. Buys 8/year. Length: 40-100 lines. Pays 7¢/word.

Tips: "Our manuscripts are short, 4½ pages maximum, so it's best to send complete manuscript with cover letter. Fiction and cover stories are most open to freelancers. Cover story must be about real children who are involved with various subjects that would be of interest to readers: sports, computers, animals, making money, etc. We are seeking superior writers who can hold a child's interest without violence or sensationalism."

‡**THE YOUNG CRUSADER**, 1730 Chicago Ave., Evanston IL 60201. (312)864-1396. Managing Editor: Michael Vitucci. Monthly for children ages 6-12. Not copyrighted. Pays on publication. Submit seasonal material 6 months in advance. Computer printout submissions acceptable. SASE. Free sample copy.

Nonfiction: Uses articles on total abstinence, character-building and love of animals. Also science stories. Length: 600 words. Pays ½¢/word.

Fiction: Should emphasize Christian principles and world friendship. Also science stories. Length: 600 words. Pays ½¢/word.

Poetry: Limit submissions to batches of 3. Pays 10¢/line.

Lifestyles

The reader's lifestyle may be conservative or liberal, affluent or back-to-the-land. Lifestyle publications cater to these and other tastes and philosophies. They offer writers a forum for unconventional views or serve as a voice for a particular audience or cause. Here are magazines for single and widowed people, vegetarians, homosexuals, atheists, survivalists, back-to-the-land advocates, and others interested in alternative outlooks and lifestyles. Also included are "free press" publications that offer contributor's copies as payment.

THE ADVOCATE, Liberation Publications, Inc., Suite 200, 1800 N. Highland Ave., Los Angeles CA 90028. Editor: Lenny Giteck. Biweekly tabloid for gay men and women, ages 21-40; middle-class, college-educated, urban. Circ. 83,000. Pays on publication. Rights purchased vary with author and material. Byline given. SASE. Reports in 6 weeks.

Nonfiction: Emphasis is on the dignity and joy of the gay lifestyle. News articles, interviews and lifestyle features. Major interest in interviews or profiles of gay people whose names can be used. Informational, personal experience, humor, historical, photo feature and spot news. Query with "concrete description and writing sample." Length: open.

Photos: "Payment for b&w photos purchased without ms or on assignment depends on size of the reproduction."

‡**ALBUQUERQUE SINGLES SCENE MAGAZINE**, 8421-H Osuna NE, Albuquerque NM 87111. (505)299-4401. Editor: Jean Jordan. 90% freelance written. Monthly tabloid covering singles lifestyles. Pays on publication. Publishes ms an average of 6 months after acceptance. Byline given. Buys first serial rights or all rights. Submit seasonal/holiday material 3 months in advance. Computer printout submissions acceptable;

prefers letter-quality to dot-matrix. SASE. Reports in 3 months. Sample copy $1, SAE 4 first class stamps. Free writer's guidelines for SAE and 1 first class stamp.

Nonfiction: General interest (to singles); how-to (for singles coping on their own); humor; inspirational; opinion; personal experience; and travel. All articles must be singles-oriented. No suggestive or pornographic material. Buys 100 mss/year. Send complete ms. "Keep a copy of the manuscript for your file as we do not return them. If you have photo(s) and/or illustration(s) to accompany the article, do not send them with your story unless you do not want them returned." Also publishes some fiction. Length: 800-2,600 words. Pays $35-$100.

Photos: State availability of photos with ms. Pays minimum $10 for b&w prints. Captions, model release, and identification of subjects required.

Columns/Departments: Astrology, finance, real estate, travel, relationships and parenting all singles-oriented. Buys 75 mss/year. Send complete ms. Length: 800-900 words. Pays $35.

Tips: "We are looking for articles that deal with every aspect of single living—whether on a local or national level. Our readers are of above-average intelligence, income and education. Subject matter is virtually unlimited with the exception of material we may consider in 'bad taste.' We are not a 'swingers' publication and will not accept articles of this nature."

AMERICAN SURVIVAL GUIDE, (formerly *Survival Guide*), McMullen Publishing, Inc., 2145 W. La Palma Ave., Anaheim CA 92801. (714)635-9040. Editor: Dave Epperson. Associate Editor: Jim Benson. 50% freelance written. Monthly magazine covering "self-reliance, defense, meeting day-to-day threats—survivalism for survivalists." Circ. 92,000. Pays on publication. Publishes ms an average of up to 2 years after acceptance. Byline given. Not copyrighted. Buys first North American serial rights. Submit seasonal/holiday material 5 months in advance. Computer printout submissions acceptable; prefers letter-quality to dot-matrix. SASE. Reports in 3 weeks. Sample copy $2.50; writer's guidelines for SASE.

Nonfiction: Expose (political); how-to; interview/profile; personal experience (how I survived); photo feature (equipment and techniques related to survival in all possible situations); emergency medical; food preservation; water purification; stealth tactics; self-defense; nutrition; tools; shelter; etc. "No general articles about how to survive. We want specifics and single subjects." Buys 60-100 mss/year. Query or send complete ms. Length: 1,500-4,000 words. Pays $125-400.

Photos: Send photos with ms. "One of the most frequent mistakes made by writers in completing an article assignment for us are photo submissions that are inadequate." Pays $5-75 for b&w contact sheet or negatives; $20-100 for 35mm color transparencies or 8x10 b&w prints. Captions, model release and identification of subjects mandatory. Buys all rights.

Tips: "We will be dealing more with weaponry, tactics, urban survival and nuclear considerations than with food preservation, food storage, water purification and like matters. Know and appreciate the survivalist movement. Prepare material of relevant value to individuals who wish to sustain human life no matter what the circumstance. This magazine is a text and reference."

‡**APPALACHIAN NOTES**, Erasmus Press, 225 Culpepper, Lexington KY 40502. Editor: Lawrence S. Thompson. 100% freelance written. Scholarly quarterly magazine on all aspects of history and culture of Appalachia. Circ. 290. Bills subscriber with first issue of each volume. Publishes ms an average of 6 weeks after acceptance. All articles are signed. Reports in 1 month on queries; 6 weeks on mss.

Nonfiction: Scholarly. No payment. Send complete ms. Length: 300-2,500 words. No payment.

Tips: Historical and documented studies are most open to freelancers.

ASCENSION FROM THE ASHES, The Alternative Magazine, AFTA Press, Suite 2, 153 George St., New Brunswick NJ 08901. (201)828-5467. Editor: Bill-Dale Marcinko. Quarterly magazine covering popular culture (TV, film, books and music) political and sexual issues for young adults (ages 18-30) who are interested in rock music, films, literature and political and sexual issues. Circ. 25,000. Pays in copies. Buys one-time rights. Phone queries OK. Submit seasonal material 1 month in advance. Simultaneous, photocopied, and previously published submissions OK. SASE. Reports in 2 weeks. Sample copy $3.50.

Nonfiction: Humor (satires on popular books, TV, films, records and social issues); interview (of authors, TV/film writers or directors, rock musicians and political movement leaders); opinion (reviews and reactions); profile; personal experience; and photo feature (on the making of a movie or TV program, coverage of a rock concert or political demonstration). *AFTA* also buys investigative articles on political, consumer and religious fraud. Buys 75 unsolicited mss/year. Query with published clips. Pays in copies.

Photos: State availability of photos. Reviews b&w prints. Pays in copies.

Columns/Departments: Books, Etc. (book reviews, fiction and nonfiction of interest to a young counterculture audience); Demons in Dustjackets (horror and science fiction book reviews); Medium Banal (TV reviews); Sprockets (film reviews); and Slipped Discs (record reviews). "We use short (3-4 paragraphs) reviews of comic books, underground comics, alternative magazines, recent books, television programs, films and rock albums, especially on gay, lesbian and politically controversial small press magazines and books. Buys 50 mss/year. Query with published clips. Length: 100-1,000 words. Pays in copies.

Fiction: Short stories. Experimental, erotic, humorous, science fiction, suspense and mainstream. Buys 10 mss/year. Query with clips of previously published work. Length: 1,000 words maximum. Pays in copies.
Poetry: Political survival, humorous and erotic subjects. Pays in copies.
Fillers: "We print folk/rock songs on social issues with music. We also have a section in which readers describe their first-time sexual experiences (gay or straight)." Buys 8 mss/year. Pays in copies.
Tips: "Sending for a sample copy is probably the best way to familiarize yourself with the kind of writing in *AFTA*. Write with humor, simplicity, and intensity, first person if possible. Avoid being formal or academic in criticism. Write for a young adult audience. The short stories accepted generally have a style similar to the works of Vonnegut or Tom Robbins, very loose, playful and humorous. *AFTA* doesn't censor language in any submissions and is known for printing material other magazines consider sexually and politically controversial."

‡**BEYOND SCIENCE FICTION**, Cosmic Circus Productions, 414 S. 41st St., Richmond CA 94804. (415)529-0716. Editor: Rey King. 33% freelance written. Annual magazine on survival in the 21st century. "We publish material which may be considered controversial or subversive." Estab. 1984. Circ. 2,000. Pays on publication. Publishes ms an average of 6 months after acceptance. Byline given. Buys one-time rights. Simultaneous queries, and simultaneous, photocopied, and previously published submissions OK. Computer printout submissions acceptable; prefers letter-quality to dot-matrix. SASE. Reports in 3 months on queries; 6 months on mss. Sample copy $10.
Nonfiction: Book excerpts and expose (government, religious, education, etc.). Buys 2-3 mss/year. Query with published clips or send complete ms. Pays $10-50.
Fiction: Condensed novels (illustrated) erotica fantasy novel excerpts religious (occult) science fiction and comics. No romance or western. Buys 1-2 mss/year. Send complete ms. Length: 100-5,000 words. Pays $25-50.
Tips: "We are looking for material on environmental concerns, cults, conspiracies, future trends and galactic evolution. Words should cut like a dagger, ideas should get you in trouble."

THE BOSTON PHOENIX, 100 Massachusetts Ave., Boston MA 02115. (617)536-5390. Editor: Richard M. Gaines. 40% freelance written. Weekly alternative newspaper; 140+ pages. For 18-40 age group, educated post-counterculture. Circ. 139,000. Buys first serial rights. Pays on publication. Offers kill fee. Publishes ms an average of 1 month after acceptance. Byline given. Photocopied submissions OK. Computer printout submissions acceptable. Reports in 6 weeks. SASE. Sample copy $1.50.
Nonfiction: News (local coverage, national, some international affairs, features, think pieces and profiles); lifestyle (features, service pieces, consumer-oriented tips, medical, food, some humor if topical, etc.); Arts (reviews, essays, interviews); and supplements (coverage of special-interest areas, e.g., stereo, skiing, automotive, computers, pro sound, education, home furnishings with local angle). Query section editor. "Liveliness, accuracy, and great literacy are absolutely required." No fiction or poetry. Query letter preferable to ms. Pays 4¢/word and up. Sometimes pays the expenses of writers on assignment.
Tips: The writer has a better chance of breaking in at our publication with short articles and fillers because there's less money invested for the tryout. \

‡**CANADIAN KEY**, (formerly *Canadian Connection*), Canada's oldest and largest swingers club, Box 68, Station L, Toronto, Ontario M4P 2G5 Canada. (416)481-2406. Editor: Dawn Evans. Magazine published every 2 months. "We are interested in articles and stories directed at the new sexual openness that has come about with swingers and group sex." Circ. 20,000. Pays on acceptance. Publishes ms an average of 4 months after acceptance. Byline given. Offers negotiated kill fee. Buys one-time rights or second serial (reprint) rights. Submit seasonal/holiday material 4 months in advance. Simultaneous queries and simultaneous, photocopied, and previously published submissions OK. Computer printout submissions acceptable. SASE, IRCs outside Canada. Reports in 3 weeks. Sample copy for $5 and 9x12 SAE and 96¢ postage; IRCs outside Canada.
Nonfiction: How-to (on anything relating to sex); humor (of a sexual nature); new product (anything relating to sex); personal experience (of a sexual nature); travel (anything for swingers); and swinging. Buys 6 mss/year. Query with published clips or send complete ms. Length: 1,000-3,000 words. Pays $75-200.
Photos: Send photos with ms. Pays $25-50 for color or b&w sheets, 35mm transparencies or prints. Model release and identification of subjects required. Buys one-time rights.
Fillers: Jokes, gags, anecdotes, short humor and newsbreaks. Buys 30/year. Length: open. Pays $10-50. "The writer has a better chance of breaking in at our publication with articles, as we do not emphasize major features."

THE CELIBATE WOMAN, A Journal for Women Who Are Celibate or Considering This Liberating Way of Relating to Others, 3306 Ross Place NW, Washington DC 20008. (202)966-7783. Editor: Martha Allen. 95% freelance written. Irregularly published (annually thus far) special interest magazine on celibacy and women. Publishes ms an average of 6 months after acceptance. Byline given. SASE. Reports in weeks. Sample copy $4.

Nonfiction: Reflections on celibacy and sexuality. "The journal is a forum for presenting another view of sexuality—an opening up of alternatives in a sex-oriented society." Articles, artwork, letters, experiences, ideas and theory are welcome.

CONTACT, Boumain Publishing Co., Inc., Box 9248, Berkeley CA 94709. Editor: Elliott Leighton. 40% freelance written. Monthly magazine on relationships and related activities. Circ. 45,000. Pays on acceptance. Publishes ms an average of 2 months after acceptance. Byline given. Buys first serial rights, second (reprint) rights, and one-time rights. Simultaneous, photocopied, and previously published submissions OK. Computer printout submissions acceptable. SASE. No queries. Reports in 3 months on mss. Sample copy $3; free writer's guidelines.
Nonfiction: Book excerpts (within subject area of relationships), expose, general interest, humor, interview/profile, opinion, personal experience, photo feature and travel. "We prefer short pieces (1,000 to 2,500 words) on subjects of interest to our unmarried readership. We'd like to see more works grounded in personal experience and dealing with one or more of the following subjects: lifestyles, divorce and custody, coping with loneliness, consciousness-raising, the dating game, traveling solo, making contact, body talk, communication, single parenting, surrogate parenting, recovering from difficult relationships, sex roles, dating services and matchmakers, cooking for one, overcoming shyness, the bar scene and alternatives, and health, nutrition and living." No political, religious, erotic, nonrealistic or philosophical material. Buys 10-15 mss/year. Send complete ms. Length: 1,000-4,000 words. Pays $25-200.
Photos: Send photos with ms. Pays $50 maximum for 8½x11 prints. Model release and identification of subjects required. Buys one-time rights.
Columns/Departments: Book Reviews (books dealing with sexuality, relationships, etc. only); and Gazette (news items of interest to singles). Buys 6-12 mss/year. Send complete ms. Length: 100-2,000 words. Pays $10-100.
Fiction: Adventure, confession, humorous, mainstream and romance "as they relate to subject of relationships, lifestyles etc." No erotic, religious, fantasy and science fiction, crime or sexist material. Buys 6-12 mss/year. Send complete ms. Length: 2,500-5,000 words. Pays $25-100.
Poetry: Avant-garde, free verse, haiku, light verse and traditional. No epic (anything over 50 lines) poems. Buys 25 poems/year. Length: 2-50 lines. Pays 0-$10.
Tips: "A freelancer can best break into our publication by following our guidelines on subject areas and manuscripts preparation; by reading what we publish; and by staying close to his/her own personal experience. The straight prose nonfiction article, somewhat confessional leading to insight in ways of relating to others, is the easiest way for a freelancer to break in."

COSMOPOLITAN CONTACT, Pantheon Press, Box 1566, Fontana CA 92335. Editor-in-Chief: Romulus Rexner. Managing Editor: Nina Norvid. Assistant Editor: Irene Anders. 40% freelance written. Magazine irregularly published 2 or 3 times a year. "It is the publication's object to have as universal appeal as possible to students, graduates and others interested in international affairs, cooperation, contacts, travel, friendships, trade, exchanges, self-improvement and widening of mental horizons through multicultural interaction. This polyglot publication has worldwide distribution and participation, including the Communist countries. Writers participate in its distribution, editing and publishing." Circ. 1,500. Buys first serial rights second serial reprint rights and simultaneous rights. Publishes ms an average of 3 months after acceptance. Pays on publication in copies. Byline given. Simultaneous, photocopied, and previously published submissions OK. Computer printout submissions acceptable; no dot-matrix. SASE. Reports in 6 weeks. Sample copy $2.
Nonfiction: Expose (should concentrate on government, education, etc.); how-to; informational; inspirational; personal experience; personal opinion and travel. "Material designed to promote across all frontiers bonds of spiritual unity, intellectual understanding and sincere friendship among people by means of correspondence, meetings, publishing activities, tapes, records, exchange of hospitality, books, periodicals in various languages, hobbies and other contacts." Submit complete ms. Buys 15-30 mss/year. Maximum 500 words.
Poetry: Traditional. Length: maximum 40 lines.
Tips: "Most of the material is not written by experts to enlighten or to amuse the readers, but it is written by the readers who also are freelance writers. The material is didactic, provocative, pragmatic—not art-for-art's sake—and tries to answer the reader's question, 'What can I do about it?' More short articles and fillers are accepted than major features. The addresses of all contributors are published in order to facilitate global contacts among our contributors, editors and readers/members. Instead of writing, e.g., about Lincoln or history, it is better to be an emancipator and to make history by promoting high ideals of mankind. Consequently, the material submitted to us should not be only descriptive, but it should be analytical, creative, action- and future-oriented. We are not interested in any contribution containing vulgar language, extreme, intolerant, pro-Soviet or anti-American opinions." Recent article example: "Mastery of Life" (Vol. XX, No. 34).

‡**CREATIVE PERSON**, Carol Bryan Imagines, 1000 Byus Dr., Charleston WV 25311. (304)345-2378. Editor: Carol Bryan. 50% freelance written. Quarterly "little" magazine covering the creative person,

creativity, and all related aspects. "*Creative Person* is focused to ease that special loneliness of all people who draw intensely from themselves to create." Estab. 1984. Pays on publication. Publishes ms an average of 6 months after acceptance. Byline given. Buys first serial rights. Submit seasonal/holiday material 6 months in advance. Photocopied and previously published submissions OK. Computer printout submissions acceptable; prefers letter-quality to dot-matrix. SASE. Reports in 1 month. Sample copy $3; writer's guidelines for SASE.

Nonfiction: Book excerpts, how-to, inspirational, interview/profile, opinion, personal experience, and technical (psychological aspects related to creative people written by experts in the field). "Nonfiction must deal with aspects which particularly affect creative people. Planned articles deal with rejection, discipline, mentors, and raising a child. Interviews must examine the creative process and habits of the subject, and the deep concerns they have as talented people (one interview was with singer Marilyn Horne). " Buys 12-15 mss/year. Query with published clips or send complete ms if available as a reprint. Pays in contributor's copies or $25 maximum.

Photos: State availability of photos with query or ms. Reviews 5x7 b&w prints. Pays $3. Captions required. Buys one-time rights.

Columns/Departments: "We are interested in sharing particularly unique creative works or effective ideas which relate to the pursuit of an art. Photo or artwork is helpful. Brief thoughts of the creator (50-100 words are required)." Uses 15-20/year. Send complete ms. Length: 50-100 words. Usually pays in contributor's copies.

Fiction: Experimental, fantasy, humorous, mainstream, novel excerpts and suspense. "All fiction *must* illuminate the creative person, the process of creativity or aspects which relate to living with and being driven by talent. Characters should be involved in situations which explain these qualities with a special insight and clarity reality doesn't often convey. Buys 1-2 mss/year. Send complete ms. Length: 800-3,000 words. Pays in contributor's copies or $25 maximum.

Poetry: Free verse, light verse and traditional. Buys 3-4 poems/year. Submit maximum 6 poems. Pays in contributor's copies or $5 maximum.

Tips: "We are always interested in thought-provoking questions for our creativity specialist, who discusses aspects of the creative person in a regular column. Our purpose is not to appeal to everyone, and we won't sacrifice to do that. Our audience is special, our philosophy is special, and both deserve the best we can offer."

D.I.N. NEWSERVICE, D.I.N. Publications, Box 5115, Phoenix AZ 85010. (602)257-0797. Editor: Jim Parker. 25% freelance written. An innovative, alternative newsmagazine covering behavior and health; published by the Do It Now Foundation. Circ. 10,000. Pays on publication. Publishes ms an average of 3 months after acceptance. Byline given. Offers 30% kill fee. Buys first North American serial rights and second (reprint) rights. Simultaneous queries and photocopied submissions OK. Computer printout submissions acceptable. SASE. Reports in 1 month. Sample copy $2.

Nonfiction: "News and features exploring breaking or nonmainstream developments in human health and behavior, and the constellation of issues and events impacting health and behavior." Buys features, profiles, interviews and opinions. Buys 5 mss/issue. Length: 500-3,500 words. Pays $50-400. Also buys news shorts. Length: 50-300 words. Pays $5-25.

Photos: Pays $10-50 for each b&w or color photo purchased with ms. More for assigned photos.

Columns/Departments: Newsfronts (shorts on current developments in health, behavior, substance abuse, consciousness, media, technology, etc.); Informat (specialized information on various behavioral health topics); Backwords (unusual or off-beat shorts and mini-features); Guestcolumn (guest opinion and commentary); and Postscripts (personal commentary on current news and events).

Tips: "Be authoritative but readable. Don't be afraid to be provocative if you have something to say. Study a sample copy for our viewpoint and style. If a topic interests you, chances are that it will interest us, too—unless it's already been run into the ground by major media. Query first. We'll turn down an interview with God if we ran an interview with God in our last issue."

‡**DAY TONIGHT/NIGHT TODAY**, Box 353, Hull MA 02045. Editor: S.R. Jade. 100% freelance written. Magazine published 7 times a year. "We publish women only; nonsexist, nonracist; we try to provide a place for experimental, and vivid writing by and for women." Circ. 1,250 + . Pays in copies. Publishes ms an average of 7 months after acceptance. Byline given. Rights revert to author. Simultaneous queries and simultaneous, photocopied, and previously published submissions OK. Computer printout submissions acceptable; no dot-matrix. SASE. Reports in 1 month. Sample copy $3.25; writer's guidelines for SAE and 1 first class stamp.

Nonfiction: Book excerpts, historical/nostalgic about specific women's lives or lifestyles; and interview/profile. No travel, religious or fillers. Send complete ms. Length: 3,000 words maximum. Pays in copies.

Fiction: Condensed and serialized novels, ethnic, experimental, fantasy and suspense. Acquires about 15 mss/year. Length: 3,000 words maximum. Pays in copies.

Poetry: Avant-garde, free verse, haiku, light verse and traditional. No "gooey, sentimental, rhyming types of poetry." Acquires about 200/year. Submit maximum 6 poems. Pays in copies.

Tips: Poetry section is most open to freelancers. "We are especially interested in publishing works by women of color."

EARTH'S DAUGHTERS MAGAZINE, Box 41, Central Park Station, Buffalo NY 14215. Collective editorship. 99% freelance written. Publication schedule varies from 2-4 times a year. For people interested in literature and feminism. Circ. 1,000. Pays in copies. Publishes ms an average of 10 months after acceptance. Byline given. Acquires first North American serial rights; copyright reverts to author after publication. Clear photocopied submissions and clear carbons OK. Computer printout submissions acceptable; prefers letter-quality to dot-matrix. SASE. Reports "very slowly; please be patient." Sample copy $4 (includes postage); writer's guidelines for SAE and 1 first class stamp.

Fiction: Feminist fiction of any and all modes. "Our subject is the experience and creative expression of women. We require a high level of technical skill and artistic intensity, and we are concerned with creative expression rather than propaganda. On occasion we publish feminist work by men." No anti-feminist material; no "hard-line, but shoddy, feminist work." Submit 1 short story/submission. "If it is a part of a larger work, mention this." Length: 1,500 words maximum. Pays in copies only.

Poetry: All modern, contemporary, and avant-garde forms. Submit maximum 3-4 poems. Length: 40 lines maximum preferred with occasional exceptions.

Tips: "We're doing smaller issues, one of which will be by invitation only to past contributors."

EARTHTONE, Publication Development, Inc., Box 23383, Portland OR 97223. (503)620-3917. Editor: Pat Jossy. Bimonthly publication for a western U.S. readership interested in developing a self-sufficient lifestyle. "Editorial often deals with a back-to-the-land lifestyle but does not exclude those urban dwellers interested in becoming more independent and self-sufficient in their current residence." Circ. 50,000. Pays on publication. Byline given. Buys first North American serial rights. Submit seasonal/holiday material 6 months in advance. Simultaneous queries, and simultaneous and photocopied submissions OK. SASE. Reports in 1 month. Free sample copy; writer's guidelines for SAE and 1 first class stamp.

Nonfiction: General interest (on country living, food, folk art); historical/nostalgic; how-to (crafts, home projects, small-scale low-cost building); humor; interview/profile (on people living this sort of lifestyle); new product (only if very unusual or revolutionary); personal experience (only if informative on various aspects of homesteading or country living and self-sufficient lifestyle); animal husbandry; health; energy; organic gardening and recreation. How-to articles should be accompanied by photos or illustrations. All articles should have a western U.S. angle. Buys 6-10 mss/issue. Query with published clips if available. Length: 500-3,000 words. Pays $50-300.

Tips: "Break in with a clearly written how-to on crafts, gardening, small-scale low-cost building. Also, interesting personality sketches."

EAST WEST JOURNAL, East West Journal, Inc., 17 Station St., Box 1200, Brookline Village MA 02147. (617)232-1000. Editor: Mark Mayell. 40% freelance written. Monthly magazine emphasizing natural living for "people of all ages seeking balance in a world of change." Circ. 70,000. Pays on publication. Publishes ms an average of 4 months after acceptance. Buys first serial rights or second (reprint) rights. Byline given. Submit seasonal/holiday material 5 months in advance. Simultaneous, photocopied, and previously published submissions OK. Computer printout submissions acceptable; prefers letter-quality to dot-matrix. SASE. Reports in 1 month. Sample copy $1; writer's guidelines for SAE and 1 first class stamp.

Nonfiction: Major focus is on issues of natural health and diet; interviews and features (on solar and alternative energies, natural foods and organic farming and gardening, ecological and energy-efficient modes of transportation, natural healing, human-potential movement, whole food and technology). No negative, politically-oriented, or new-age material. "We're looking for original, first-person articles without jargon or opinions of any particular teachings; articles should reflect an intuitive approach." Buys 15-20 mss/year. Query. Length: 1,500-2,500 words. Pays 8-12¢/word. Sometimes pays expenses of writers and assignment.

Photos: Send photos with ms. Pays $15-40 for b&w prints; $15-175 for 35mm color transparencies (cover only). Captions preferred; model release required.

Columns/Departments: Body, Whole Foods, Natural Healing, Gardening, and Cooking across the cultures. Buys 15 mss/year. Submit complete ms. Length: 1,500-2,000 words. Pays 8-12¢/word.

THE EVENER, Consolidated Publishers, Inc., Box 7, Cedar Falls IA 50613. (319)277-3599. Managing Editor: Susan Salterberg. 45% freelance written. Quarterly magazine on draft horses and other draft animals. "*The Evener*" is published primarily for draft horse, mule and oxen enthusiasts. Circ. 9,000. Pays on acceptance. Publishes ms an average of 8 months after acceptance. Byline given. Prefers to buy first serial rights, but will make exceptions. Submit seasonal/holiday material 4 months in advance. Photocopied and previously published submissions OK. Computer printout submissions acceptable; prefers letter-quality to dot-matrix. Reports in 4 weeks on queries; 4 months on mss. Sample copy for 9x12 SAE and $1.07 postage; writer's guidelines for business size SAE and 37¢ postage; both $1.41.

Nonfiction: Book excerpts (from horse, mule, oxen or small farm-related books); historical/nostalgic (farming in the past, feature on a heartwarming event or situation related to draft animals, agricultural history of an area); how-to (making or repairing farm equipment, training a draft animal, breeding, shoeing draft horses, show decorations); humor (draft animal or country life related); interview/profile (people using innovative farming/

training methods or those who are specialists as breeders, trainers, farmers, judges; old-timers' philosophies and recollections); personal experience (draft horse, mule or oxen related, or a country living or farming angle; experience caring for draft horses on the farm); photo feature (draft horse, mule or oxen or country life related); and technical (horse health and economics of large vs. small farming). No vague how-to articles and those not relating to subject matter. Buys 15 mss/year. Send complete ms. Length: 300-3,000 words. Pays 3-15¢/word. Sometimes pays expenses of writers on assignment.
Photos: Send photos with ms. Pays $5-40 for b&w prints. Welcomes contact sheets. Captions and identification of subjects (if applicable or pertinent) required.
Columns/Departments: Yearlings & Colts (children's section—only accepts true stories about child's experience with draft animals); Bits 'n Pieces (helpful hints); Lines & Traces (mythical horse remedies, historical facts about draft horses, mules or oxen); and Product Profile (horse products). Buys 10 mss/year. Send complete ms. Length: 30-250 words. Pays 3-15¢/word or free subscription.
Fiction: Historical, humorous and novel excerpts related to country life and draft animals. "No unbelievable, over-exaggerated stories." Buys only 2 mss/year. Send complete ms. Length: 300-1,500 words. Pays 3-15¢/word.
Poetry: All types of poetry relating to draft animals. Buys 2 poems/year. Submit maximum 5 poems. Pays $5-20 or free subscription.
Fillers: Anecdotes and newsbreaks. Buys 5/year. Length: 25-750 words. Pays 3-10¢/word or free subscription.
Tips: "Thoroughly peruse the freelance guidelines and the magazine, taking note of our readers' personalities. Submit an objective, concise article with good photos. Possibly attend draft horse and mule shows, horse pulls, sales and other related events. These events give you an excellent opportunity to interact with our audience so you understand our focus and aim. Then send us a 1,500-word manuscript with photos or illustrations. We want articles that teach, evoke emotions, and/or challenge our readers. Freelancers can best break into our publication with nonfiction, especially how-to, interview/profile, technical and historical/nostalgic. Be creative, search for a unique angle and be credible."

FARMSTEAD MAGAZINE, Box 111, Freedom ME 04941. Business offices: (207)382-6200. Editorial offices: (207)382-6205. Publisher: George Frangoulis. Managing Editor: Heidi Brugger. 50% freelance written. Magazine published 6 times/year covering home gardening, shelter/construction, alternative energy, recipes, small-scale livestock (breeds and care), tools, homesteading and country lifestyles. Circ. 170,000. Pays on publication. Publishes ms an average of 1 year after acceptance. Buys first serial rights and second serial (reprint) rights. Phone queries OK. Submit seasonal material 1 year in advance. Reports in 3 months. Free sample copy and writer's guidelines with appropriate size SASE.
Nonfiction: General interest (related to rural living and gardening); how-to (gardening, farming, shelter, energy, construction, conservation, wildlife, livestock, crafts, and rural living); interview (with interesting and/or inspirational people involved with agriculture, or self-sufficiency). No sentimentality or nostalgia. Buys 60 mss/year. Submit complete ms. Length: 1,000-5,000 words. Pays 5¢/word.
Photos: State availability of photos with ms. Pay starts at $10 for each 5x7 b&w print used; starts at $25 for color; $100 for each color transparency used on cover.
Tips: "Contribute a thorough well-researched or first-hand experience article. B&w photos of good quality, 35mm color transparencies or careful diagrams or sketches are a boon. We look for an unusual but practical how-to article. Send short factual pieces with good photos. All unsolicted manuscripts must have SASE or we cannot guarantee their return.

FIRST HAND, Experiences For Loving Men, Firsthand, Ltd., 310 Cedar Lane, Teaneck NJ 07666. (201)836-9177. Editor: Brandon Judell. Managing Editor: Jackie Lewis. 50% freelance written. Monthly magazine of homosexual erotica. Circ. 60,000. Pays 6 weeks after acceptance. Publishes ms an average of 6 months after acceptance. Byline given. Buys all rights (exceptions made), and second (reprint) rights. Submit seasonal/holiday material 6 months in advance. Simultaneous queries and photocopied submissions OK. Computer printout submissions acceptable; prefers letter-quality to dot-matrix. SASE. Reports in 3 weeks. Sample copy $3; writer's guidelines for SASE.
Nonfiction: Book excerpts (should be erotic or offer advice); historical/nostalgic (gay life in the past); how-to (advice for homosexuals coming out); interview/profile (gay figure heads); personal experience ("this is our premise"); travel (where gays go); and erotica. No violent or negative articles about gay life. No bestiality or child abuse. Buys 96 mss/year. Query with or without published clips or send complete ms. Length: 1,500-3,000 words. Pays $100-150.
Columns/Departments: Survival Kit (short nonfiction pieces about all aspects of gay life). Buys 48 mss/year. Query with or without published clips or send complete ms. Length: 400-800 words. Pays $25-75.
Fiction: Novel excerpts.
Poetry: Free verse and light verse. Buys 12/year. Submit maximum 5 poems. Length: 10-30 lines. Pays $25.
Fillers: Jokes, gags and anecdotes. Buys 30 mss/year. Length: 24-400 words. Pays $15-25.
Tips: "Half of each issue is written by our readers. In their letters, they share their lusts, hopes, loves and fears stemming from their homosexuality. The main articles which are bought from freelancers should display the

same candor and honesty. *First Hand* is more than a magazine to get off on. It offers a support system to many homosexuals who feel isolated in the heterosexual community. Many of our readers are married. A few have never had gay sex. Most are very loyal and save every issue. A frequent mistake made by writers is writing in cliches. So many writers think they're composing an ode to a Grecian urn—as opposed to a 1980's article."

FLORIDA SINGLES MAGAZINE AND DATE BOOK, Box 83, Palm Beach FL 33480. Editor: Harold Alan. Monthly magazine covering "singles' problems with life, dating, children, etc., for single, divorced, widowed and separated persons who compose over 50% of the adult population over age 18." Circ. 12,000. Pays on publication. Buys second serial (reprint) rights and one-time rights. Simultaneous, photocopied, and previously published submissions OK. SASE. Reports in 4 months.
Nonfiction: "We want any article that is general in nature dealing with any aspect of single life, dating, problems, etc." Buys 1-3 mss/issue. Send complete ms. Length: 800-1,400 words. Pays $10-30. "We are associated with 2 other singles magazines: the East Coast and Louisville KY *Singles Magazine*. We pay up to $30 for the first-time use of an article in the first publication and $15 each for each time reprinted in the other magazines."
Photos: Offers no additional payment for photos accepted with ms. Model release required.
Fiction: "We will look at any manuscript that is general in nature dealing with any aspect of single life, dating, problems, etc."

THE FUTURIST, A Journal of Forecasts, Trends, and Ideas about the Future, World Future Society, 4916 St. Elmo Ave., Bethesda MD 20814. (301)656-8274. Editor: Edward S. Cornish. 80% freelance written. Bimonthly magazine on all aspects of the future for general audience. "*The Futurist* focuses on trends and developments that are likely to have a major impact on the way we live in the years ahead. It explores how changes in all areas—lifestyles, values, technology, government, economics, environmental affairs, etc.—will affect individuals and society in the next five to fifty years. We cover a very broad spectrum of topics—from assessing how a new technology like computers will affect the way people work to how the institution of marriage may change." Circ. 30,000. Publishes ms an average of 3 months after acceptance. Byline given. Acquires variable rights according to the article. Submit seasonal/holiday material 6 months in advance. Simultaneous queries, and simultaneous (if so advised), photocopied, and previously published submissions OK. Electronic submissions OK if approved of in advance. Computer printout submissions acceptable; prefers letter-quality to dot-matrix. SASE. Reports in 6 weeks on queries; 7 weeks on mss. Free sample copy and writer's guidelines.
Nonfiction: Tim Willard, assistant editor. Book excerpts, general interest, how-to, interview/profile, new product and opinion. "We are especially looking for articles on the social areas of the future of human values, relationships, lifestyles, etc. These 'soft' subjects seem to be much more difficult for informed speculation and projection than the hard area of technology and its effects." No "vague articles that say, 'Wouldn't it be nice if the future were like this,' or 'If that happened in the future?' or articles lacking a future orientation." Acquires 45-50 mss/year. Query with published clips or send complete ms. Length: 500-5,000 words. Pays in copies.
Tips: "Feature articles in *The Futurist* are almost entirely freelance written. The Tomorrow in Brief page and the World Trends and Forecasts section are primarily staff written."

‡**GREENER PASTURES GAZETTE, The newsletter dedicated to the search for countryside Edens**, Relocation Research, Box 864, Bend OR 97709. Editor: Bill Seavey. Managing Editor: Mary Seavey. 10% freelance written. Bimonthly newsletter that assists "urban opt outs" to move to the country. Estab. 1985. Circ. 4,000. Pays on acceptance. Publishes ms an average of 3 months after acceptance. Byline given. Offers 50% kill fee. Buys first North American serial rights. Simultaneous queries, and simultaneous, photocopied, and previously published submissions OK. Computer printout submissions acceptable. SASE *required*. Reports in 1 week on queries; 1 month on mss. Sample copy $3.
Nonfiction: Book excerpts (trends in relocation to country); general interest; how-to (tips on find jobs, starting businesses in country); personal experience (success stories); and travel (to small towns desirable to readers). No general travelogs, poetry or fiction. Buys 15+ mss/year. Query with or without published clips. Length: 1,000 words. Pays $25-200.
Photos: State availability of photos or send photos with query. Reviews 3x5 prints and b&w contact sheets. Identification of subjects required. Buys one-time rights.
Columns/Departments: Life in the Slow Lane, Success Story. Living Abroad and Smalltown USA. Buys 7 mss/year. Query with or without published clips. Length: 200-500 words. Pays $10-50.
Fillers: Jokes, gags and ancedotes. Length: 25-100 words. Pays $5-20.
Tips: "If you moved to the countryside from the city, you may have some insight from personal experience that is relevant to this publication. General articles to help people purchase low-cost rural property or find jobs or start businesses in the countryside are most needed from freelancers. The writer has a better chance of breaking in at our publication with short articles and fillers because space is at a premium."

‡**HANDICAP NEWS**, Burns Enterprises, 272 N. 11th Ct., Brighton CO 80601. (303)659-4463. Editor: Phyllis Burns. 20% freelance written. Monthly newsletter on handicaps. *"Handicap News* is written for people with handicaps and those people working with them. Material should be written in an 'upbeat' mode." Estab. 1984. Circ. 500. Pays on publication. Publishes ms an average of 3 months after acceptance. Credit is given for pieces written by handicapped people. In the news section, no credit is given. Not copyrighted. Buys one-time rights. Simultaneous, photocopied, and previously published submissions OK. SASE. Reports in 1 month. Sample copy $1, #10 SAE and 1 first class stamp. Writer's guidelines with sample copy only.
Nonfiction: How-to, humor, inspiration, medical breakthroughs, new product, opinion, personal experience, physical/occupation therapy developments, research findings, technical and travel. "We request a copy of the study, report or news article which was the source of information. We are sometimes asked for more information by the readers so we must have a file copy." No pessimistic articles. Buys 10-20 mss/year. Send complete ms. Length: 75-300 words. Pays in 2 copies of the newsletter in which the article appeared.
Fiction: Fantasy, historical, humorous, mainstream, religious, science fiction and western. "All fiction must deal directly with the subject (handicapped people and how they respond to certain conditions.) We have not as yet printed any fiction but would be interested in seeing some for the future. This section must be written by handicapped people or their families." Query. Length: 500-750 words. Pays in 2 copies of newsletter in which appeared.
Poetry: Will consider any type, length or style as long as it is written by handicapped people or the families. Nothing pessimistic or down beat. Buys 20-30/year. Submit maximum 4 poems. Pays in 2 copies.
Tips: "In the medical, product, travel, and therapy section, any one may study the format and submit the material with their documentation. In the poems, experiences, inspirational, and fiction, the material must come from the handicapped person and family. In the latter, we will accept almost any material as long as it falls within the guidelines and is optimistic. We look forward to receiving material from handicapped writers but wish more of them would learn the basic format to sending articles to publications. We do not appreciate paying postage on material we receive from you. If possible, type it. If not, write in a 'readable' manner."

HARROWSMITH MAGAZINE, Camden House Publishing, Ltd., Camden East, Ontario K0K 1J0 Canada. (613)378-6661. Editor/Publisher: James M. Lawrence. 75% freelance written. Published 6 times/year "for those interested in country life, nonchemical gardening, energy, self-sufficiency, folk arts, small-stock husbandry, owner-builder architecture and alternative styles of life." Circ. 154,000. Pays on acceptance. Publishes ms an average of 4 months after acceptance. Byline given. Buys first North American serial rights. Submit seasonal/holiday material 6 months in advance. Computer printout submissions acceptable; prefers letter-quality to dot-matrix. SAE and IRCs. Reports in 6 weeks. Sample copy $5; free writer's guidelines.
Nonfiction: Expose, how-to, general interest, humor, interview, photo feature and profile. "We are always in need of quality gardening articles geared to northern conditions. No articles whose style feigns 'folksiness.' No how-to articles written by people who are not totally familiar with their subject. We feel that in this field simple research does not compensate for lack of long-time personal experience." Buys 10 mss/issue. Query. Length: 500-4,000 words. Pays $75-750 but will consider higher rates for major stories.
Photos: State availability of photos with query. Pays $50-250 for 8x10 b&w glossy prints and 35mm or larger color transparencies. Captions required. Buys one-time rights. "We regularly run photo essays for which we pay $250-750."
Tips: "We have standards of excellence as high as any publication in the country. However, we are by no means a closed market. Much of our material comes from unknown writers. We welcome and give thorough consideration to all freelance submissions. Our magazine is read by Canadians who live in rural areas or who hope to make the urban to rural transition. They want to know as much about the realities of country life as the dreams. They expect quality writing, not folksy cliches."

‡**HIGH ADVENTURE**, Assemblies of God, 1445 Boonville, Springfield MO 65802. (417)862-2781, ext. 1497. Editor: Johnnie Barnes. Quarterly magazine "designed to provide boys with worthwhile, enjoyable, leisure reading; to challenge them in narrative form to higher ideals and greater spiritual dedication; and to perpetuate the spirit of the Royal Rangers program through stories, ideas, and illustrations." Circ. 70,000. Pays on acceptance. Byline given. Buys one-time rights. Submit seasonal/holiday material 6-9 months in advance. Simultaneous queries, and simultaneous, photocopied, and previously published submissions OK. Reports in 1 month. Sample copy for 8½x11 SAE; free writer's guidelines.
Nonfiction: Historical/nostalgic, how-to, humor and inspirational. Buys 25-50 mss/year. Query or send complete ms. Length: 1,200 words. Pays 2¢/word.
Photos: Reviews b&w negatives, transparencies and prints. Identification of subjects required. Buys one-time rights.
Fiction: Adventure, historical, humorous, religious and western. Buys 25-50 mss/year. Query or send complete ms. Length: 1,200 words maximum. Pays 2¢/word.
Fillers: Jokes, gags and short humor. Pays $2 for jokes; others vary.

HIGH TIMES, Trans-High Corp., 17 W. 60th St., New York NY 10023. (212)974-1990. Editor: John Howell. Monthly magazine for persons under age 35 interested in lifestyle changes, cultural trends, personal freedom, sex and drugs. "Our readers are independent, adventurous free-thinkers who want to control their own consciousness." Circ. 232,000. Pays on publication. Publishes ms an average of 1 month after acceptance. Buys all rights, second serial (reprint) rights or first North American serial rights. Submit seasonal/holiday material 5 months in advance. Computer printout submissions acceptable; prefers letter-quality to dot-matrix. SASE. Reports in 3 months. Sample copy and writers guidelines $3.50.
Nonfiction: Expose (on political, government or biographical behind the scenes); general interest (political or cultural activities); historical (cultural, literary, dope history, political movements); how-to (that aids the enhancement of one's lifestyle); interview (of writers, scientists, musicians, entertainers and public figures); new product (on dope-related or lifestyle enhancing); nostalgia (cultural or dope-related); opinion (only from public figures); photo feature (on dope- or travel-related topics); profile; technical (explorations of technological breakthroughs related to personal lifestyle); and travel (guides to places of interest to a young hip audience). "We want no material on 'my drug bust.' " Buys 5 mss/issue. Query with published clips. Accepts no responsibility for unsolicited mss. Length: 1,000-2,500 words. Pays $150-400.
Photos: Pays $25-150 for 8x10 glossy print per page; $50-250 for 35mm color transparencies per page. Captions preferred; model release required. Buys one-time rights.
Tips: "Think of article ideas that are too outrageous, controversial, visionary, radical or adventurous for any other magazine."

‡**HOLISTIC LIFE MAGAZINE**, Holistic Life Magazine, Inc., #426, 2223 El Cajon Blvd., San Diego CA 92104. (619)298-4569. Editor: William Borby. 100% freelance written. Quarterly magazine on body, mind and spirit growth. "We offer alternative solutions (from conventional wisdom) to the problems in our lifestyles." Circ. 20,000. No payment. Publishes ms an average of 1 month after acceptance. Byline given. Buys first North American serial rights. Submit seasonal/holiday material 3 months in advance. Simultaneous queries, and simultaneous, photocopied, and previously published submissions OK. Computer printout submissions acceptable; prefers letter-quality to dot-matrix. SASE. Reports in 3 weeks. Sample copy $2; free writer's guidelines.
Nonfiction: Book excerpts, general interest, how-to, humor, inspirational and personal experience. No opinion articles. Prints about 60 mss/year. Query or send complete ms. Length: 1,500-4,000 words. No payment.
Tips: "All too often writers take an opinionated rather than a balanced view. Show both pro and con approaches."

‡**I KNOW YOU KNOW: lesbian views & news**, Jernan Ltd., Inc., Suite 14, 5335 N. Tacoma, Indianapolis IN 46220. (317)252-5381. Editor: Jeri Edwards. Managing Editor: Mary Byrne. 50% freelance written. Monthly magazine reflecting the multifaceted lives of women/lesbians—feminist philosophy. "*IKYK* is being published by professionals to meet the needs of our community not currently being met by any single publication. It is strictly a lifestyle publication designed to help women get the most out of their lives." Estab. 1984. Circ. 5,000 + . Pays on publication. Publishes ms an average of 2 months after acceptance. Byline given. Buys first North American serial rights. Submit seasonal/holiday material 4 months in advance. Simultaneous queries, and simultaneous, photocopied, and previously published submissions OK. Computer printout submissions acceptable; no dot-matrix. SASE. Reports in 2 weeks on queries; 1 month on ms. Sample copy $3.50, 9x12 SAE and 5 first class stamps; writer's guidelines with SAE and 1 first class stamp.
Nonfiction: General interest, how-to (home repairs), building own home, humor (cartoons), interview/profile, personal experience, photo feature, travel, sports, finance, business, art reviews, health, legal and political articles. No pornography or editorialized news. Uses 25 articles/month. Query with published clips. Length: 500-2,500 words. Pays in copies. Sometimes pays expenses of writers on assignment.
Photos: State availability of photos with query. "We use photos with or without manuscripts." Reviews contact sheets, negatives, transparencies and prints. Captions and model release required. Buys one-time rights.
Columns/Departments: Art, film and book reviews, sports, finance, personal awareness, health, politics, legal issues, recipes, spirituality and humor. Uses 25 articles/month. Query with or without published clips. Length: 500-2,500 words. Pays in copies.
Fiction: Adventure, condensed novels, confession, erotica, ethnic, experimental, fantasy, historical, horror, humorous, mainstream, mystery, novel excerpts, religious, romance, science fiction, serialized novels, suspense and western. No pornography. Uses about 12/year. Length: 500-2,500 words. Pays in copies.
Poetry: Avant-garde, free verse and light verse. Submit maximum 4 poems. Length: 4-30 lines. Pays in copies.
Fillers: Clippings, jokes, gags, anecdotes, short humor and newsbreaks from a woman's or lesbian point of view. Length: 25-200 words. Pays in copies.
Tips: "Although we are not necessarily interested in being 'politically correct' we reserve the right to reject any material that we find to be sexist, racist, classist, anti-Semitic or homophobic or could be considered offensive to our readers. Make certain your copy has a story to tell; attend to the questions of who, what, where, why, when and how."

‡IN STYLE, For Men, In Touch International, 7216 Varna Ave., North Hollywood CA 91605. (818)764-2288. Publisher: Frank Roedel. Managing Editor: Samir Hachem. 90% freelance written. Monthly magazine covering travel, fashion, how-to, culture and gay lifestyle. Estab. 1984. Circ. 70,000. Pays on acceptance. Publishes ms an average of 2 months after acceptance. Byline given. Offers $25 kill fee. Buys first North American serial rights. Submit seasonal/holiday material 3 months in advance. Computer printout submissions acceptable; letter-quality preferred. SASE. Reports in 1 week. Free sample copy.
Nonfiction: Book excerpts, how-to, interview/profile, photo feature, travel, and gay lifestyle and culture. Buys 80 mss/year. Query with published clips. Length: 2,500-3,000 words. Pays $75-125 maximum plus expenses.
Photos: Ray Webster, art director. State availability of photos with query. Pays $35 for color transparencies and b&w prints. Captions, model release and identification of subjects required. Buys one-time rights.
Columns/Departments: Bill Franklin, travel and fashion editor. Buys 50 mss/year. Query with or without published clips. Length: 2,000-2,500 words. Pays $75 minimum.
Tips: "Fitness, grooming and travel departments are most open to freelancers."

‡IN TOUCH, In Touch International, 7216 Varna, North Hollywood CA 91605-4186. (818)764-2288. Editor-in-Chief: Bob Stanford. 10% freelance written. Magazine of gay male erotica, including "nude male photos, no erection; erotic gay male fiction; erotic gay male humor; cartoons and humorous briefs." Circ. 70,000. Pays on acceptance. Publishes ms an average of 3 months after acceptance. Byline given. Buys first North American serial rights and one-time rights. Submit seasonal/holiday material 3 months in advance. Simultaneous queries, and simultaneous and photocopied submissions OK. Previously published submissions only in special circumstances. Computer printout submissions OK; prefers letter-quality to dot-matrix. SASE. Reports in 1 month. Sample copy $3.95; writer's guidelines for SAE and 1 first class stamp).
Nonfiction: How-to (humorous); humor; interview/profile; personal experience; photo feature and travel. Open to suggestions. All should be gay male-oriented. Special issues include: July: Red, White & Blue issue; August: Rural Gay Life; September: Back-to-School; October: Halloween; November: Anniversary; December: Christmas. Approach is important—nothing sentimental or whiney. Buys 24 mss/year. Query with a few published clips. Length: 2,500 words average; shorter is better. Pays $75, more if unusually long; however, need for long articles limited. Sometimes pays the expenses of writers on assignment.
Columns/Departments: Touch & Go; item titles from issue #105: Dress for Success (semi-nude man on beach boardwalk); O-HI-O (clothing optional resort); Heavenly Nights; Mr. Hardware contest at London's Heaven Disco; A certain Smile (ad for French underwear); Stud Sale in MI/Party Time/B&D in NC (comments on double entendre road signs) etc.
Fiction: Must be erotic. Adventure, confession, erotica, ethnic, experimental (maybe), fantasy, historical, horror, humorous, mystery, romance (but not sentimental), science fiction, suspense and western. Buys 24 mss/year. Send complete ms. Length: 2,500 average, a bit shorter is better. Pays $75.
Poetry: Pays $25-75. "We use very little poetry. Submissions *must* have SASE."
Tips: "We need well-written gay male erotica; there are no limits on sexual explicitness. We prefer a light touch, and humor is always welcome. Nonfiction articles are especially welcome. Typewritten, legible manuscripts are a must. No preaching, please. All sections are open to freelancers."

‡THE INTERNATIONAL AMERICAN, (formerly *Living Abroad*), 201 E. 36th St., New York NY 10016. (212)685-4023. Editor: Alison R. Lanier. 33% freelance written. Monthly newsletter of international information for expatriate Americans. "We need practical information pertinent to overseas Americans wherever they may be. Personal experience articles are needed only if they would be really relevant to others." Estab. 1983. Circ. 5,000. Pays on acceptance. Byline given. Publishes ms an average of 3 months after acceptance. Buys one-time rights. Simultaneous queries and previously published submissions OK. SASE. Reports in 3 weeks. Sample copy $1; writer's guidelines for SAE and 1 first class stamp.
Nonfiction: Material should pertain in some way to working, living, attitudes, experiences, short advice, warnings, humor or interests of overseas Americans. Articles should be broadly relevant, not simply personal. Especially needs advice, warnings and helpful information from experienced expatriate Americans, including all aspects of overseas adjustments. No travel tips or personal stories. Buys 6-12 mss/year. Query or send complete ms. Length: 350-400 words maximum. Pays $15-35.
Tips: "We don't need 'beginners' information; we do want financial, cross-cultural, practical in-country material. Stay within the very short word length limits given; material must be pertinent to our audience and carry real practical first-hand experience. Areas most open to freelancers are Just So You Know, Practical Tips (100-150 words); Families Abroad (up to 400 words); and As you Move About the World, short practical travel pointers.

INTERNATIONAL LIVING, Agora Publishing, 842 E. Baltimore St., Baltimore MD 21208. (301)234-0515. Editor: Elizabeth Philip. 75% freelance written. Monthly newsletter covering international lifestyles, travel, and investment for Americans. Aimed at affluent and not-so-affluent dreamers to whom the romance of living overseas has a strong appeal, especially when it involves money-saving angles. Circ. 42,000. Pays on acceptance. Publishes ms an average of 3 months after acceptance. Byline given. Buys first North American serial rights and all rights. Submit seasonal/holiday material 2 months in advance. Computer printout submissions acceptable; prefers letter-quality to dot-matrix. SASE. Reports in 1 month on queries; 6 weeks on mss. Sample copy $2.50; writer's guidelines for business size SAE and 1 first class stamp.

Nonfiction: Book excerpts (overseas, travel, retirement investment, save money overseas, invest overseas); historical/nostalgic (travel, lifestyle abroad); how-to (save money, find a job overseas); interview/profile (famous people and other Americans living abroad); personal experience; travel (unusual, imaginative destinations, give how-to's and costs); and other (humor, cuisine). "We want pithy, fact-packed articles. No vague, long-winded travel articles on well-trodden destinations." Buys 100 mss/year. Query with published clips or send complete ms. Length: 200-2,000 words. Pays $15-200.

Tips: "We are looking for writers who can combine original valuable information with a style that suggests the romance of life abroad. Break in with highly-specific, well-researched material combining subjective impressions of living in a foreign country or city with information on taxes, cost of living, residency requirements, employment and entertainment possibilities."

JOINT ENDEAVOR, Texas Department of Corrections, Box 32, Huntsville TX 77340. (713)295-6371, ext 655. Editor: John T. Sullivan. Associate Editor: Lonnie Griggs. 30% freelance written. Published quarterly by inmates of Texas Department of Corrections. Covers criminal justice, offender programs, prison legislation and court actions. "Our readers are professionals, inmates, and anyone with an interest in criminal justice. Subject matter deals with crime, corrections and alternatives to corrections." Circ. 3,000. Pays in copies and a 1-year subscription. Publishes ms an average of 2 months after acceptance. Buys first serial rights and second serial (reprint) rights. Rights reassigned upon publication. Submit material 2 months in advance. Simultaneous and photocopied submissions OK. Computer printout submissions acceptable; prefers letter-quality to dot-matrix. Reports in 3 weeks. Sample copy and writer's guidelines for SASE (80¢).

Nonfiction: Articles on corrections, law or alternative programs; historical/nostalgic; prison humor; interview/profile (relating to crime and/or corrections); opinion on crime and corrections; personal experience (must be authentic); and biography. Wants material on rehabilitation, crime, prisons, probation, youth offenders, criminal psychology and re-entry programs. Special issues include Parole Laws, Prisons: Crisis and Alternatives; Diet and Crime and Minorities in Prison. Send complete ms. Length: open. Uses approximately 4 mss /issue.

Photos: Send photos with ms. Prefers b&w prints. Subjects must be identified.

Fiction: Partial to prison writers, but quality is the main concern. Should be criminal justice-related. Humorous, mainstream and mystery. Send complete ms. Length: 5,000 or less.

Poetry: Uses mostly free verse with strong imagery. Needs approximately 20 poems/year.

Tips: "We deal with criminal justice issues, so our eye is toward work in that area; nonfiction, especially, must pertain to some aspect of criminal justice. Poetry is open, but must be good."

LETTERS FAMILY AFFAIRS, Letters Magazine Inc., 310 Cedar Lane, Teaneck NJ 07666. (201)836-9177. Editor: Jackie Lewis. Published 8 times a year. An erotic magazine covering incest. "We are seeking first person sexual adventures that are erotic without being obscene and that sound real." Pays 1 month following month of acceptance. Byline given. Buys all rights. Submit seasonal/holiday material 6 months in advance. Computer printout submissions acceptable; no dot-matrix. SASE. Reports in 3 weeks. Sample copy $3; writer's guidelines for SAE and 1 first class stamp.

Nonfiction: Book excerpts, historical/nostalgic and personal experience. First-person accounts only; no coercive sex. "No rape, adult/child in the present (incest), adult/child other or bestiality." Buys 40 mss/year. Send complete ms. Length: 1,800-2,200 words. Pays $100.

‡LOBSTER TENDENCIES EAST, Lobster Tendencies Press, Apt. 8, 141 Ridge St., New York NY 10002. (212)460-8457. Editor: Michael Kaniezki. 50% freelance written. Newsletter published every 6 weeks about underground lifestyles. "Writing should provide a healthy release of tension/angst for persons/groups who cannot accept mainstream values and wish to resist them. Our politics is American socialist." Estab. 1982. Circ. 800. Pays on acceptance. Publishes ms an average of 2 months after acceptance. Byine given upon request; otherwise name is listed among others in each issue's co-op. Rights remain with author. Submit seasonal/holiday material 3 months in advance. Simultaneous queries, and simultaneous, photocopied, and previously published submissions OK. Computer printout submissions acceptable; prefers letter-quality to dot-matrix. SASE. Reports in 2 weeks on queries; 6 weeks on mss. Sample copy for business size SAE and 37¢ postage.

Nonfiction: Expose, humor, inspirational, interview/profile, opinion and personal experience. No academic. Acquires 140 mss/year. Send complete ms. Length: 1,000 words. Pays in copies.

Fiction: Confession, erotica, experimental, fantasy, horror, humorous, religious and romance. "No unemotional—the kind that puts ideas ahead of feelings and is written for over-educated types. We like writing that finds hope and humanity in the most unlikely places and isn't afraid to tackle disturbing emotions. No fluff." Acquires 140 mss/year. Send complete ms. Length: 1,000 words maximum. Pays in copies.

Poetry: Avant-garde, free verse, haiku and light verse. Anything with an attitude. Something combative yet reconciling. No academic, full of references to the classics, etc. Writing should be rooted in the real life or famous life of contemporary life. Acquires 25/year. Length: 1-60 lines. Pays in copies.

Fillers: Jokes, gags, anecdotes and short humor. Acquires 100/year. Length 1-100 words. Pays in copies.

Tips: "We think we have a mission to define unpopular causes because we hate bullies. This magazine circulates largely through an underground mailing network. We are interested in artists wishing to establish in independent magazines and not the corporate writing-academic establishment."

MODERN SINGLES, Canada's Magazine for Single People, Modern Singles, Box 213, Station W, Toronto, Ontario M6M 4Z2 Canada. Editor: O. Slembeck. 90% freelance written. Bimonthly magazine. Estab. 1984. Pays on acceptance. Publishes ms an average of 3 months after acceptance. No byline given. Buys first North American serial rights and second serial (reprint) rights. Submit seasonal/holiday material 2 months in advance. Photocopied submissions OK. Computer submissions acceptable; prefers letter-quality to dot-matrix. SAE, IRCS. (When submitting articles from outside Canada, include self-addressed envelope with either Canadian stamps of International Postal Coupons.) Sample copy for $3.50 and SAE; free writer's guidelines.

Nonfiction: General interest; how-to (e.g., overcome loneliness, establish new relationships, develop new interests and hobbies); humor; personal experience; travel; and articles on finance management and singles life from psychological point of view. "We also publish articles on single women's issues." Buys 60 mss/year. Send complete ms. Length: 1,000-2,000 words. Pays $100-400.

Fiction: Adventure, erotica, ethnic, experimental, humorous and romance. Buys 30 mss/year. Send complete ms. Length: 1,000-2,000 words. Pays $50-200.

Fillers: Anecdotes and short humor. Buys 20/year. Length: 300-600 words. Pays $30-60.

Tips: "All areas of our publication are open for freelancers."

THE MOTHER EARTH NEWS, Box 70, Hendersonville NC 28791. (704)693-0211. Editor: Bruce Woods. 40% freelance written. Bimonthly magazine. Emphasizes "back-to-basics, how-to for individuals who seek a more rational self-directed way of life." Circ. 1,900,000. Pays on acceptance. "We buy all rights. However, after publication of our edited version, the rights to your original material are reassigned to you. Then you may resell the unedited version as many times as you like." Byline given. Submit seasonal/holiday material 5 months in advance. Computer printout submissions acceptable; prefer letter-qualtiy to dot-matrix. No handwritten mss. SASE. Reports within 3 months. Publishes ms an average of 1 year after acceptance. Sample copy $3; writer's guidelines for SASE and 39¢ postage.

Nonfiction: Roselyn Edwards, submissions editor. How-to, home business, alternative energy systems, low cost—$100 and up—housing, energy-efficient structures, seasonal cooking, gardening and crafts. Buys 300-350 mss/year. Query or send complete ms. "A short, to-the-point paragraph is often enough. If it's a subject we don't need at all, we can answer immediately. If it tickles our imagination, we'll ask to take a look at the whole piece. No phone queries, please." Length: 300-3,000 words. Pays $100/published page minimum. Sometimes pays the expenses of writers on assignment.

Photos: Purchased with accompanying ms. Send prints or transparencies. Uses 8x10 b&w glossies; any size color transparencies. Include type of film, speed and lighting used. Total purchase price for ms includes payment for photos. Captions and credits required.

Columns/Departments: "Contributions to Mother's Down-Home Country Lore and Barters and Bootstraps are paid by subscription. Profiles pays $25-50."

Fillers: Short how-to's on any subject normally covered by the magazine. Query. Length: 150-300 words. Pays $7.50-25.

Tips: "Probably the best way to break in is to study our magazine, digest our writer's guidelines, and send us a concise article illustrated with color transparencies that we can't resist. When folks query and we give a go-ahead on speculation, we often offer some suggestions. Failure to follow those suggestions can lose the sale for the author. We want articles that tell what real people are doing to take charge of their own lives. Articles should be well-documented and tightly written treatments of topics we haven't already covered. The critical thing is length, and our payment is by space, not word count." No phone queries.

THE MOUNTAIN LAUREL, Monthly Journal of Mountain Life, Laurel Publications, Rt. 1, Meadows of Dan VA 24120. (703)593-3613. Editor: Susan Thigpen. Managing Editor: Bob Heafner. 50% freelance written. Tabloid devoted to an "appreciation of mountain heritage. We tell of the everyday life history, traditions and tales of the Blue Ridge Mountains. Half of our readers are in Virginia; the other half are in all remaining states (including Alaska, Hawaii, Puerto Rico), and Canada." Estab. 1983. Circ. 25,000. Pays in copies and subscription. Publishes ms an average of 3 months after acceptance. Byline given. Buys first serial rights. Submit seasonal/holiday material 4 months in advance. Simultaneous, photocopied, and previously published submissions "at times, not often" OK. Computer printout submissions acceptable; prefers letter-quality to dot-matrix. SASE. Reports in 1 month. Sample copy and writer's guidelines for SAE and 4 first class stamps.

Nonfiction: Book excerpts (about the Blue Ridge); historical/nostalgic; humor; interview/profile; and personal experience (especially of older persons). "We like stories on a personal slant covering a specific aspect, not broad, general stories." Send complete ms. Length: 2,000 words maximum. "As we are still a new publication, we aren't at a point of paying our contributors. We hope to be able to do so within a year. We do give a full byline and will list books by the contributor and where they may be purchased."

Photos: Send photos with ms; photos will be returned. Reviews b&w prints. Model release and identification of subjects required. Also uses captioned old photos.

Fiction: Adventure, historical, humorous and novel excerpts. "*No* erotica or horror; no stereotyped 'Hillbilly' stuff—real mountain people are smart." Send complete ms. Length: 2,000 words maximum.

Fillers: Short humor.

Tips: "Write in a down-to-earth (but no bad language, please) way, as if you were telling a story verbally. Shorter articles usually stand a better chance though subject matter and how well-written articles are our first consideration. We print many first articles by new writers. We like stories with honest sentiment in them." Don't send overused subjects such as farm life or one room schools. We want warmth, not just cut-and-dried cold facts."

NEW AGE, (formerly *New Age Journal*), Rising Star Associates, Ltd. Partnership, 342 Western Ave., Brighton MA 02135. (617)787-2005. Editor: Lee Fowler. Managing Editor: Leonora Wiener. 90% freelance written. Monthly magazine covering alternative ideas and focusing on "what individuals can do to help solve the problems of the modern world." Circ. 250,000. Pays one-half on acceptance and one-half on publication. Publishes ms an average of 4 months after acceptance. Byline given. Offers 25% kill fee. Buys first North American rights, first rights, one-time rights, second serial (reprint) rights, and makes work-for-hire assignments. Submit seasonal/holiday material 3½ months in advance. Simultaneous queries, simultaneous and photocopied submissions and previously published work OK. Computer printout submissions acceptable; not dot matrix. SASE. Reports in 6 weeks. Sample copy $2.50. Writer's guidelines for legal size SAE and 1 first class stamp.

Nonfiction: Address queries to articles editor. Book excerpts, general interest, how-to (how to buy a computer for your kid; how to avoid burn-out; how to garden in the city.), humor, inspirational, interview/profile, new product (new product descriptions), opinion (self-discovery columns, reflective pieces), personal experience, photo feature and travel. "We're not interested in uncritical, slanted journalism. We're open to anything that has a balanced and well-researched perspective." Buys 60 mss/year. Query with published clips or send complete ms. Length: 150-3,000. Pays $25-2,500.

Photos: Greg Paul, photo editor. State availability of photos with query or ms. Pays $25-350 for color transparencies (35mm, 2¼ and $25-200 for 8x10 or 11x14 b&w prints. Requires captions, model release, and identificationof subjects. Buys one-time rights.

Columns/Departments: Address queries to column editor. Nature, Soft Tech, Self-Discovery, Ways and Means (how to), Food, Body/Mind, Natural Living (product reviews), book, film theatre, video painting reviews, humor and cartoons. Buys 72 items/year. Query with published clips. Length: 700-1,500 words. Pays $150-500.

Fiction: Address queries to fiction editor. Adventure, ethnic, humorous, mystery, novel excerpts and romance. Buys 3 mss/year. Send complete ms. Length: 600-2,000 words. Pays $100-1,500.

Poetry: Address queries to poetry editor. Avant-garde, free verse, haiku, light verse and traditional. Buys 5 poems/year. Submit 5 poems maximum. Pays $15-50.

Fillers: Address queries to articles editor. Clippings, anecdotes, short humor and newsbreaks. Buys 3/year. Length: 20-1,000. Pays $25-250.

Tips: "The best way to break into *New Age* is to submit a thorough query with clips. Most writers start in our short news section and then are assigned columns and features."

‡**NEW FRONTIER, Magazine of Transformation**, New Frontier Education Society, 129 N. 13th st., Philadelphia PA 19107. (215)567-1685. Editor: Sw. Virato. Managing Editor: Teri Hofer. 20% freelance written. Monthly magazine covering the New Age and holistic health. "The writer must be consciously aware, holisti-

---

" One writer sent us a well-thought-out query on the subject of classic movie posters—which fit in nicely into *Delta Sky*'s collectibles feature department—along with a very specific detailing of color artwork available for the piece, also important due to the magazine's heavy emphasis on four-color graphics. The writer also had the patience to wait several months before the story was published. It turned out to be a beautiful story—and the beginning of a fruitful working relationship. "

cally oriented, familiar with new age subjects." Circ. 25,000. Pays on publcation. Publishes ms an average of 3 months after acceptance. Byline given. Buys one time rights. Submit seasonal/holiday material 3 months in advance. Simultaneous queries, and simultaneous and photocopied submissions OK. Computer printout submissions acceptable; prefers letter-quality to dot-matrix. SASE. Reports in 3 weeks on queries; 2 months on ms. Sample copy $2; writer's guidelines $2.

Nonfiction: General interest, humor, inspirational, opinion, personal experience and photo feature. "We don't want anything aggressive, overtly sexual or negative." Buys 5-10 mss/year. Query with published clips. Length: 750-1,200 words. Pays $35-150. Sometimes pays the expenses of writers on assignment.

Photos: Send photos with query. Pays $10-50 for 5x7 b&w prints. Captions, model release, and identification of subjects required.

Fiction: Fantasy, religious, New Age, metaphysical. Query with published clips. Length: 750-1,500 words. Pays $30-150.

Tips: "Write a piece to stimulate awareness or expand consciousness; continue sending material (a new manuscript) even if was rejected before. We relish short works that have high impact."

‡**NEW JERSEY SINGLES MAGAZINE**, 21st Century Concepts, 265A, 46 W., Totowa NJ 07511. (201)256-2780. Editor: Hope Noah. Managing Editor: Ellen Adams. 40% freelance written. Monthly singles magazine. Pays on publication. Publishes ms an average of 2 months after acceptance. Byline given. Makes work-for-hire assignments. Submit seasonal/holiday material 2 months in advance. Photocopied, simultaneous submissions and previously published work OK. Computer printout submissions acceptable; no dot-matrix. SASE. Reports in 1 month. Free sample copy; writer's guidelines for SAE.

Nonfiction: Book excerpts, expose, general interest, how-to, humor, inspirational, interview/profile, opinion, personal experience, photo feature and travel. "We have planned special issues on dating, single parents and New York city highlights in the next eighteen months." No "depressing" stories. Query with publshed clips. Length: 600-1,200. Pays $10-75. Sometimes pays the expenses of writers on assignment.

Fiction: Adventure, fantasy, humorous and romance. Query with published clips. Length: 600-1,200. Pays $10-50.

Poetry: Avant-garde, free verse, haiku and light verse.

Fillers: Clippings, jokes, gags, anecdotes, short humor and newsbreaks. Length: 50-250. Pays $5-100.

PHILADELPHIA GAY NEWS, (formerly *Gay News*), Masco Communications, 254 S. 11th St., Philadelphia PA 19107. (215)625-8501. Managing Editor: Stan Ward. Publisher: Mark Segal. 50% freelance written. Weekly tabloid covering news and features of interest to the lesbian and gay community. Circ. 15,000. Pays on publication. Publishes ms an average of 2 months after acceptance. Byline given. Offers 33% kill fee. Buys one-time rights. Submit seasonal/holiday material 2 months in advance. Photocopied and previously published submissions OK. Computer printout submissions acceptable; prefers letter-quality to dot-matrix. SASE. Reports in 4 weeks on queries; 6 weeks on mss. Sample copy $1; writer's guidelines for SAE and 1 first class stamp.

Nonfiction: Book excerpts (with lesbian/gay themes or characters); expose (of enemies to lesbian/gay community); historical/nostalgic (gay history, 'herstory'); humor (satire welcome); interview/profile (of entertainment or activist personalities); opinion (about direction of gay movement and how to achieve gay rights); and travel (resorts that welcome gay tourists, i.e., Key West, San Francisco). "Reflect a constructive attitude toward gay issues. Our emphasis is news and investigative reporting, but we also include entertainment, opinion and personality profiles." Feature articles include gay press, gay health problems. No personal sexual experiences. Buys 40-50 mss/year. Query with clips of published work. Length: 750-2,500 words. Pays $20-75.

Photos: Illustrations of the person, place or subject. State availability of photos. Pays $5 maximum for 5x7 b&w prints. Identification of subjects required. Buys one-time rights.

Columns/Departments: Book reviews of books with lesbian/gay themes or characters. Buys 20 mss/year. Query. Length: 750-1,000 words maximum. Pays $20 maximum.

Tips: "It's rewarding to see a variety of viewpoints from freelancers. Each submission is judged strictly on its own merits and our current editorial priorities. Wordiness and lack of economic structure (too loosely structured) are frequent mistakes made by writers—our space is at a premium."

PILLOW TALK, 215 Lexington Ave., New York NY 10016. Editor: I. Catherine Duff. Monthly magazine. "For people interested in all areas of human relationships—meetings, dating, arguing, making up, sex (in all aspects). We're a light, fun, but helpful and reliable publication—a counselor, a friend, a shoulder to lean on, and entertainment." 100% freelance written. Pays on publication. Publishes ms an average of 2 months after acceptance. Buys all rights. Byline given unless author requests otherwise. Computer printout submissions acceptable; prefers letter-quality to dot-matrix. SASE. Reports in 1 month. Sample copy $1.75; writer's guidelines for SASE.

Nonfiction: How-to (romantic and sexual techniques, meeting new people, handling relationships, overcoming emotional hurdles); humor (sexual, romantic); interview (maybe in rare cases); personal experience (sexual/romantic scenarios if they illustrate a specific topic); and medical/technical (lightly done on sex-related health topics). "No out-and-out pornography unless incorporated in our sexual fantasy department. Should be top-class." Buys 11 mss/issue. Query. Length: 1,000-3,000 words. Pays $150-250.

Photos: State availability of photos. Pays $25-50 for b&w; $250 for color covers. Model release required. Buys all rights.

Columns/Departments: Front Entry, unusual and interesting news items. Healthworks, health related topics; Rear Entry, sexual fantasy. Regular columns on alternate lifestyles: The Gay Life, The Swinging Life and The Kinky Life. Query with published clips. Length: 1,250 words. Pays $150. Open to suggestions for new columns/departments.

Fiction: Only sexual fantasy for Rear Entry department. Length: 2,000 words.

‡**PSYCHIC GUIDE**, Island Publishing Co. Inc., Box 701, Providence RI 02901. (401)351-4320. Editor: Paul Zuromski. Managing Editor: John Kramer. 50% freelance written. Quarterly magazine covering New Age, natural living, and metaphysical topics. "Our editorial is slanted toward assisting people in their self-transformation process to improve body, mind and spirit. We take a holistic approach to the subjects we present. They include spirituality, health, healing, nutrition, new ideas, interviews with new age people, travel, books, music, even a psychic weather report. We avoid sensationalizing and present material with the idea that an individual should decide what he should or shouldn't accept or believe." Circ. 100,000. Pays on publication. Publishes ms an average of 6-12 months after acceptance. Byline given. Offers negotiable kill fee. Buys first North American serial rights. Submit seasonal/holiday material 8 months in advance. Simultaneous queries OK. Computer printout submissions acceptable. SASE. Reports in 2 months on queries; 4 months on mss. Sample copy $3.95, SAE and 2 first class stamps; writer's guidelines for SAE and 1 first class stamp.

Nonfiction: Book excerpts, historical/nostalgic (research on the roots of the New Age movement and related topics); how-to (develop psychic abilities, health, healing, proper nutrition, etc., based on holistic approach); inspirational; interview/profile (of New Age people); new product (or services offered in this field—must be unique and interesting); opinion (on any New Age, natural living or metaphysical topic); and travel (example: to Egypt based on past life research). Don't send "My life as a psychic" or "How I became psychic" articles. Buys 5 mss/year. Query with published clips. Length: 3,000 maximum. Pays $25-150. Sometimes pays the expenses of writers on assignment.

Photos: State availability of photos with query. Pays $10-20 for b&w contact sheets. Captions, model release and identification of subjects required. Buys one-time rights.

Fillers: Clippings, anecdotes or newsbreaks on any interesting or unusual New Age, natural living, or metaphysical topic. Busy 15-20 fillers/year. Length: 500 words maximum. Pays $5-10.

Tips: "Examine our unique approach to the subject matter. We avoid sensationalism and overly strange or unbelievable stories. We can become familiar with their work and they with our unique approach to the subject matter."

‡**R F D, A Country Journal for Gay Men Everywhere**, Rt. 1, Box 127-E, Bakersville NC 28705. (704)688-2447. Managing Editor: Ron Lambe. 90% freelance written. Quarterly magazine of rural gay male concerns. "We look for nonsexist, nonexploitive, positive, open-minded explorations of who we are as gay rural men." Circ. 2,000. Pays on publication. Publishes ms an average of 3 months after acceptance. Byline given. Not copyrighted. Buys one-time rights. Submit seasonal/holiday material 3 months in advance. Simultaneous queries, and simultaneous, photocopied, and previously published submissions OK. Computer printout submissions acceptable; prefers letter-quality to dot-matrix. Reports in 3 months on queries. Sample copy $4.25 postpaid.

Nonfiction: Kenneth Hale-Wehmann, articles editor. Expose, how-to, humor, inspirational, interview/profile, opinion, personal experience and travel. No common or trendy pieces. Acquires 8-10 mss/year. Send complete ms. Length: 500-5,000 words. Pays in 2 copies of journal.

Photos: Prefers b&w prints, (color of high contrast); of rural, nature, or male sexuality themes. Pays in 2 copies of journal. Model release and identification of subjects required. Buys one-time rights. Pays in 2 copies of journal.

Fiction: Adventure, erotica, fantasy and romance. No sexist or insensitive exploitative. Acquires 8 mss/year. Send complete ms. Length: 1,000-5,000 words. Pays in 2 copies of jounral.

Poetry: Franklin Abbott, poetry editor. Avant-garde, free verse, haiku, light verse and traditional. Acquires 40 poems/year. Submit maximum 5 poems. Length: 3-100 lines. Pays in 2 copies of journal.

Tips: "Offer original and thematic work. Style is not a major consideration."

RADICAL AMERICA, Alternative Education Project, Inc., #14, 38 Union Square, Somerville MA 02143. (617)628-6585. Editor: John P. Demeter. Managing Editor: Margaret Cerullo. 35% freelance written. Bimonthly political journal of radical history, socialism, feminism, and community and workplace organizing; cultural analysis and commentary. "*RA* is a popularly written, nonacademic journal aimed at feminists, political activists and left academics written from socialist (independent) and feminist perspectives." Circ. 5,000. Pays in copies. Publishes ms an average of 6 months after acceptance. Byline given. Buys all rights. Submit seasonal/holiday material 3 months in advance. Simultaneous queries, and simultaneous, photocopied, and previously published submissions OK. Computer printout submissions acceptable; no dot-matrix. SASE. Reports in 2 weeks on queries; 1 month on mss. Sample copy $2; free writer's guidelines.

Nonfiction: James Stark, articles editor. Political opinion and history. No strictly journalistic accounts without analysis or commentary. Query with published clips. Length: 2,000-7,000 words. Pays in copies.

Photos: Phyllis Ewen, photo editor. State availability of photos. Pays $5-10 for b&w contact sheet. Captions and identification of subjects required. Buys one-time rights.

Poetry: J.S. Smutt, poetry editor. Avant-garde and free verse. No poetry without political or social theme. Length: 10-50 lines.

THE ROBB REPORT, 1 Acton Place, Acton MA 01720. (617)263-7749. Managing Editor: M.H. Frakes. 70% freelance written. Monthly magazine covering leisure interests of the wealthy. Circ. 50,000. Pays on publication. Publishes ms an average of 5 months after acceptance. Byline given. Rights negotiable. Submit seasonal/holiday material 6 months in advance. Simultaneous queries and previously published submissions OK. Computer printout submissions acceptable; prefers letter-quality to dot-matrix. SASE. Reports in 1 month. Sample copy $8.50; writer's guidelines for business size SAE.

Nonfiction: Book excerpts, expose, interview/profile, trend pieces, how-to and travel. "Articles are usually focused in the following areas: automobiles, home and office design, collectibles, travel, investments, fashion, wine and liquors, food and dining, and boating. These articles must be useful and informative to the reader, enabling him to make intelligent action choices with his high level of disposable income." Buys 84 mss/year. Query. Length: 2,500-3,500 words. Pays $500-750.

Tips: "Writing should be lively enough to hold the reader's attention through a long piece. The most frequent mistakes made by writers in completing an article for us are poorly researched and organized material; mundane writing; relying too much on information from books or other articles rather than going to the source; and lacking quotes because they haven't talked to anyone. Unless written by an expert in the field, manuscript should contain quotes from the sources. We're looking for the newest and most interesting subjects, not the same humdrum treatment of the same predictable topics. First-person reminiscences discouraged."

ROOM OF ONE'S OWN, A Feminist Journal of Literature & Criticism, Growing Room Collective, Box 46160, Station G, Vancouver, British Columbia V6R 4G5 Canada. Editors: Gayla Reid, Pat Robertson, Mary Schendlinger, Eleanor Wachtel, Jeannie Wexler and Jean Wilson. 100% freelance written. Quarterly magazine of original fiction, poetry, literary criticism, and reviews of feminist concern. Circ 1,200. Pays on publication. Publishes ms an average of 6 weeks after acceptance. Byline given. Buys first serial rights. Photocopied submissions OK. Computer printout submissions acceptable "if readable and not in all caps"; prefers letter-quality to dot-matrix. SASE. Reports in 2 months. Sample copy $2.75.

Nonfiction: Interview/profile (of authors) and literary criticism. Buys 8 mss/year. Send complete ms. Length: 1,500-6,000 words. Pays $50.

Fiction: Quality short stories by women with a feminist outlook. Not interested in fiction written by men. Buys 12 mss/year. Send complete ms. Length: 1,500-6,000 words. Pays $50.

Poetry: Avant-garde, eclectic free verse and haiku. Not interested in poetry from men. Buys 32 poems/year. Submit maximum 10 poems. Length: open. Pays $10-25.

‡**RSVP**, The Magazine of Good Living, Davick Publications, 828 Fort St. Mall, Honolulu HI 96816. (808)523-9871. Editor: Rita Ariyoshi. Managing Editor: Cheryl Tsutsumi. 30% freelance written. Monthly magazine covering all topics for people who live and desire good life. "*RSVP* is a publication for the upper demographic market of Hawaii. Our readers are affluent, educated, usually professional or entrepreneurial types who have made it big and enjoy the fruits of their labors. It appeals to society types and aspirants. Any articles should be from the perspective of the insider. It is someone with class and money writing for those with class and money. While the tone is irreverant at times, it is never derogatory of the values of the wealthy." Estab. 1984. Circ. 7,000. Pays on publication. Publishes ms an average of 10 months after acceptance. Byline given. Offers negotiable kill fee. Buys all rights. Submit seasonal/holiday material 1 year in advance. Photocopied submissions OK. Computer printout submissions acceptable; no dot-matrix. SASE. Reports in 2 months.

Nonfiction: General interest, humor, art and collectibles. No articles poking fun at the wealthy or from perspective of the "man in the street". Buys 20 mss/year. Query. Length: 1,000-2,500 words. Pays 10¢/word. Sometimes pays the expenses of writers on assignment.

Photos: State availability of photos with query. Pays $50 for color transparencies. Model release and identification of subjects required. Buys one-time rights.

Tips: The most frequent mistakes made by writers in completing an article for us is using the wrong perspective. Authors sometimes write as a voyeur in the land of the rich.

SIMPLY LIVING, Otter Publications Pty/Ltd., 53 Sydney Road, Manly, N.S.W. 2095, Australia. (02)977-8566. Editor: Mr. Pip Wilson. Managing Editor: Verna Simpson. 99% freelance written. Quarterly magazine covering the environment and anti-nuclear, spiritual and natural health topics. Circ. 35,000. Pays on publication. Publishes ms an average of 3 months after acceptance. Byline given. Buys first serial rights, one time rights, and second serial (reprint) rights. Submit seasonal/holiday material 4 months in advance. Simultaneous queries and previously published submissions OK. Computer printout submissions acceptable; prefersl letter-quality to dot-matrix. SASE. Sample guidelines for $3.95 (Australian) and 8½x11½ SAE; writer's guidelines $1 and SAE. Do not send U.S. stamp. IRC.

Nonfiction: Expose (environmental); how-to (environmental, spiritual); humor; bioregion; alternatives; interview/profile; new product (energy conservation) and photo feature. "We are very keen on celebrity interviews on our topics. Buys 24 mss/year. Query with published clips. Length: 1,000-5,000 words. Pays $100/1,000 words (Oz currency). Sometimes pays the expenses of writers on assignment.

Photos: Stephen Costello, photo editor. Send photos with query. Pays $85/page for color transparencies. Captions, model release, and identification of subjects required. Buys one-time rights.

Fiction: Chris Mooney and Pip Wilson, fiction editors. Adventure, fantasy, humorous, religious/spiritual, on environment, animal and anti-nuclear issues. Buys 4 mss/year. Length: 1,500-2,000 words. Pays $100/1,000 words.

Poetry: Avant-garde, free-verse, haiku, light verse and traditional. Buys 8 poems/year. Submit maximum 1 poem. Pays $30-50.

Tips: "We are looking for a global unity perspective. A freelancer can break in to our publication with a soft approach, new angle and commitment to philosophy."

SINGLELIFE (MILWAUKEE) MAGAZINE, SingleLife Enterprises, Inc., 536 W. Wisconsin Ave., Milwaukee WI 53203. (414)271-9700. Editor: Gail Rose. 30% freelance written. Bimonthly magazine covering singles lifestyles. Circ. 17,000. Pays on publication. Publishes ms an average of 6 months after acceptance. Byline given. Submit seasonal/holiday material 4 months in advance. Simultaneous queries, and photocopied and previously published submissions OK. Electronic submissions OK on Apple IIe and Screen Writer. Computer printout submissions acceptable. SASE. Reports in 3 months. Sample copy $3.50.

Nonfiction: Leifa Butrick, articles editor. Book excerpts, general interest, how-to, humor, opinion, photo feature and travel. Columns open to freelancers include Signing In, Getaways, Singles Parenting, book reviews. Buys 15 mss/year. Prefers ms to query, and prefers third person point of view. Length: 1,000-2,500 words. Pays $25-100. Sometimes pays expenses of writers on assignment.

Photos: Send photos with query or ms. Pays $10-100 for b&w contact sheet, 2¼" transparencies and 8x10 prints; pays $20-200 for 2¼" color transparencies and 8x10 prints. Captions, model release and identification of subjects required.

Fiction and Poetry: Leifa Butrick, editor. Buys 4-6 ms of very high quality. Submit any number of poems. Length: open. Pays $10-100.

Tips: "Our major pieces are often written by freelance writers. We are currently looking for writer of a single parenting column. "We are expanding in the Chicago area and are looking for writers familiar with Chicago nightlife and the singles scene."

STALLION MAGAZINE, The Magazine of the Alternate Lifestyle, Charlton Publications, 351 W. 54th St., New York NY 10019. (212)586-4432. Editor: Jerry Douglas. 75% freelance written. Monthly magazine for gay community. Text includes articles and fiction for gay males; pictorially, male nudes. Circ. 80,000. Pays on publication. Publishes ms an average of 4 months after acceptance. Byline given. Buys first North American serial rights. Submit seasonal/holiday material 6 months in advance. Simultaneous queries, and simultaneous and photocopied submissions OK; rarely accepts previously published submissions. Computer printout submissions acceptable; no dot-matrix. SASE. Reports in 4 months on mss. Free writer's guidelines.

Nonfiction: Book excerpts, expose, general interest, historical/nostalgic, inspirational, interview/profile, opinion, personal experience and photo feature. "We publish one piece of fiction in each issue, and while we certainly do not avoid erotic content in the stories, the work must have some other quality besides sexual heat. In other words, we are not looking for 'stroke pose' per se. We have accepted a wide range of fiction pieces, the only common denominator being that the work deal with some aspect of the gay experience." Buys 12 fiction/36 nonfiction mss/year. Send complete ms. Length: 2,000-3,000 words. Pays $200.

Tips: "Although the visual content of the magazine is strictly erotic, the textual content is not, and we seek articles and fiction of interest to the gay community, beyond the strictly erotic. We are more interested in articles than fiction."

TAT JOURNAL, Box 236, Bellaire OH 43906. Editor: Louis Khourey. 75% freelance written. Annual magazine for all interested in depth philosophy, parapsychology, poetry, astrology, esoteric psychology and holistic health. Circ. 3,000. Pays in copies. Publishes ms an average of 9 months after acceptance. Returns copyright to author after publication. Simultaneous, photocopied, and previously published submissions OK. Computer printout submissions acceptable. SASE. Reports in 6 weeks. Sample copy $3; free writer's guidelines with SASE.

Nonfiction: Expose (occult rip-offs, cults and spiritual gimmicks); how-to (psychological self-change techniques); opinion; personal experience (new insights into the unsolved mysteries of the universe); and forum

(short philosophic pieces from a personal viewpoint). "No articles that proselytize a fanatical belief." Accepts 15 mss/issue. Send complete ms. Length: 300-10,000 words. Pays in copies.
Tips: "We want material that stimulates the reader's curiosity, allowing him to come to his own conclusions; a more psychological bent as opposed to New Age or occult."

TELEWOMAN, A Women's Newsletter, Telewoman, Inc., Box 2306, Pleasant Hill CA 94523. Editor: Anne J. D'Arcy. 100% freelance written. Monthly networking newsletter covering women's networking resources, literary/art/photography resources and connections for a lesbian and "woman-identified" readership. Circ. 500. Pays in copies. Publishes ms an average of 1 month after acceptance. Not copyrighted. Simultaneous queries and simultaneous, photocopied, and previously published submissions OK. Computer printout submissions acceptable; prefers letter-quality to dot-matrix. SASE. Reports in 2 weeks on queries; 1 month on mss. Sample copy $2, business size SAE, and 3 first class stamps.
Nonfiction: Book excerpts, interview/profile, personal experience, photo feature and reviews. No erotic, political or separatist slant. Send complete ms. Length: 500 words on reviews; 3,000 on spotlights and novel excerpts.
Photos: Reviews b&w prints.
Fiction: Novel excerpts, religious (women's spirituality), lesbian romance, and serialized lesbian novels. No erotic material.
Poetry: Avant-garde, free verse, haiku, light verse and traditional. No separatist, political or erotic content. Buys 60 poems/year. Submit unlimited number of poems with SASE. Length: 25 lines maximum. Pays in contributor's copies.
Tips: Most open to poetry, book reviews and music reviews. "We provide books and records for book and record reviews."

TORSO, Varsity Communications, Suite 210, 7715 Sunset Blvd., Los Angeles CA 90046. (213)850-5400.. Editor: Chris Volker. A monthly magazine for gay men. "Divergent viewpoints are expressed in both feature articles and fiction, which examine values and behavior patterns characteristic of a gay lifestyle. *Torso* has a continuing commitment to well-documented investigative journalism in areas pertaining to the lives and well-being of homosexuals." Estab. 1982. Circ. 60,000. Pays on publication. Byline given. Offers $50 kill fee. Buys first North American serial rights. Submit seasonal/holiday material 3 months in advance. Simultaneous queries, and simultaneous and photocopied submissions OK. SASE. Reports in 2 weeks on queries; 1 month on mss. Sample copy $5; writer's quidelines for business size SAE.
Nonfiction: Expose, general interest, humor, interview/profile, opinion, personal experience, photo feature and travel. "*Torso* also regularly reports on cultural and political trends, as well as the arts and entertainment, often profiling the people and personalities who affect them. The tone must be positive regarding the gay experience." Buys 12 mss/year. Query with or without published clips or send complete ms (typewritten and double-spaced). Length: 2,000-4,000 words. Pays $100-200.
Fiction: Adventure, erotica, fantasy, humorous, novel excerpts and romance. "No long, drawn-out fiction with no form, etc." Buys 35 mss/year. Query with or without published clips or send complete ms. Length: 2,000-4,000 words. Pays $100-150.
Tips: "Write about what is happening—what you as a gay male (if you are) would care to read."

‡**TV-TS TAPESTRY**, Tiffany Club, Inc., Box 19, Wayland MA 01778. (617)358-5575. Editor: Merissa Sherrill Lynn. 25% freelance written. Quarterly journal covering cross-dressing and, transsexualism. "Our readership is extremely varied, ranging from male and female crossdressers, transsexually inclined persons, persons interested in androgyny and gender expression, helping professionals (doctors, psychologists, social workers, educators, etc.), and persons affected by the transvestite/transsexual phenomena (families, friends, employers, etc.). Circ. 5,000. Pays on acceptance. Publishes ms an average of 3 months after acceptance. Byline given. Buys first serial rights, one-time rights, and second serial (reprint) rights. Simultaneous queries and simultaneous, photocopied, and previously published submissions OK. Computer printout submissions acceptable; prefers letter-quality to dot-matrix. SASE. Reports in 6 weeks. Sample copy $5 (includes postage).
Nonfiction: Expose (legal, societal prejudice); general interest; how-to (pass, make-up, dress, comportment, find medical or professional help, achieve peace of mind, family situations, etc.); humor; interview/profile; opinion (positive and constructive only); personal experience; photo feature; letters and news. "We have a constantly updated directory of organizations, services and events, so we need to be kept informed of who's who and what's happening. We also have a news and special announcement bulletin board so we need news items, and announcements that would be of any interest to any of our readers." No negative, sexually-oriented articles. Buys 16 or more mss/year. Query. Send complete ms. Length: 3,500 words maximum. Pays in copies.
Photos: State availability of photos or send photos with query. Reviews b&w and color prints. Model release required.
Fiction: "We are looking for fiction that is well-written, entertaining, sensitive and intelligent. Make the reader think and feel. Humor, fantasy and novelettes that can be serialized are OK." Condensed novels (must be able to be serialized); confession; fantasy (nonsexual, believable); humorous; serialized novels; and anything related

to a TV-TS theme. Buys 8-16 mss/year. Query or send complete ms. Length: 3,500 words. Pays in copies.
Poetry: Avant-garde, free-verse, light verse and traditional. Buys 8-12 poems/year. Pays in copies.
Fillers: Clippings, anecdotes, short humor, newsbreaks and art. Buys 20 +/year. Pays in copies.
Tips: "Keep in mind that *Tapestry* is a non-profit journal designed to be of service to the TV-TS community and persons affected by that community. Writing should be tasteful thought-provoking, and constructive, catering to persons seeking information and *emotional* support. We consider transvestism and transsexualism to be a natural human phenomena and treat people so inclined with dignity. We want the items submitted for publication to reflect that attitude and be oriented toward the 'real' human experience and have very negative feelings about the cross-dressing issue. We have an abundance of fillers; we need articles."

THE UNSPEAKABLE VISIONS OF THE INDIVIDUAL INC., Box 439, California PA 15419. Editors-in-Chief: Arthur Winfield Knight, Kit Knight. 50% freelance written. Annual magazine/book for an adult audience, generally college-educated (or substantial self-education) with an interest in Beat (generation) writing. Circ. 2,000. Payment (if made) on acceptance. Publishes ms an average of 2 months after acceptance. Buys first North American serial rights. Computer printout submissions acceptable; no dot-matrix. Reports in 2 months. Sample copy $3.
Nonfiction: Interviews (with Beat writers), personal experience and photo feature. "Know who the Beat writers are—Jack Kerouac, Allen Ginsberg, William S. Burroughs, etc." Uses 20 mss/year. Query or submit complete ms. Length: 300-15,000 words. Pays 2 copies, "sometimes a small cash payment, i.e., $10."
Photos: Used with or without ms or on assignment. Send prints. Pays 2 copies to $10 for 8x10 b&w glossies. Uses 40-50/year. Captions required.
Fiction: Uses 10 mss/year. Submit complete ms. Pays 2 copies to $10.
Poetry: Avant-garde, free verse and traditional. Uses 10 poems/year. Submit maximum 10 poems. Length: 100 lines maximum. Pays 2 copies to $10.

VEGETARIAN TIMES, Box 570, Oak Park IL 60303. (312)848-8120. Editor: Paul Barrett Obis Jr. 50% freelance written. Monthly magazine. Circ. 80,000. Rights purchased vary with author and material. Buys first serial rights or all rights ("always includes right to use article in our books or 'Best of' series"). Byline given unless extensive revisions are required or material is incorporated into a larger article. Pays on publication. Publishes ms an average of 4 months after acceptance. Photocopied and simultaneous submissions OK. Computer printout submissions acceptable. Submit seasonal material 6 months in advance. Reports in 1 month. Query. SASE. Sample copy $2.
Nonfiction: Features concise articles related to vegetarian cooking, health foods and articles about vegetarians. "All material should be well documented and researched. It would probably be best to see a sample copy." Informational, how-to, experience, interview, profile, historical, successful health food business operations and restaurant reviews. Length: average 1,500 words. Pays 5¢/word minimum. Will also use 500- to 1,000-word items for regular columns.
Photos: Prefers b&w ferrotype. Pays $15 for b&w; $50 for color.
Tips: "The worst thing about freelance writers is that everybody who can type thinks they are writers. And the less experience a writer has the more he/she hates to be edited. Some novices scream bloody murder when you delete their paragraphs or add words to make the copy flow better. They also think we editors have nothing to do all day but critique their article. Never the less, many writers have broken into print in our magazine." Write query with brevity and clarity.

‡VINTAGE '45, A Uniquely Supportive Quarterly Journal for Women, Vintage '45 Press, Box 266, Orinda CA 94563. (415)254-7266. Editor: Susan L. Aglietti. 100% freelance written. Quarterly magazine for women. "*Vintage '45* is designed for the active, introspective woman who is interested in personal growth and self-development and who has wearied of traditional women's publications. All material is nonjudgmental and supportive of each woman's right to self-development." Pays in one-year subscriptions only. Publishes ms an average of 6 months after acceptance. Byline given. Buys first serial rights. Photocopied and previously published submissions OK; previously published work must be identified as such. Reports in 3 weeks on queries; 2 months on mss. Computer printout submissions acceptable; prefers letter-quality to dot-matrix. SASE. Sample copy $2.50; writer's guidelines for legal size SAE and 1 first class stamp.
Nonfiction: Non fiction articles are generally written by women professionals in various fields (e.g., law, health, mental health) who address specific topic in depth. "I don't want to see anything unless it relates clearly and specifically to the needs, interests and concerns of mid-life women and is written by a woman." How-to and personal experience (coping or success account of how a woman has dealt with a particular situation). Uses 10-15 mss/year. Query. Length: 1,000-1,500 words. Pays in one-year subscriptions.
Poetry: Traditional. "No jingles and cliché-filled doggerel; or verse too abstruse to be understandable without several readings. All poems must relate *clearly* and *specifically* to mid-life women." Uses 10 poems/year. Submit maximum 5 poems. Pays in 1-year subscription.
Tips: "*Vintage '45* is a good outlet for talented women who want to get publishing credit. Include a cover letter

telling a little about your background and interests. Give professional qualifications if you want to contribute nonfiction. Familiarize yourself with this publication—especially article length."

WARRIORS, Self Defense and Survival Today, Condor Books, Inc., 351 E. 54th St., New York NY 10019. (212)586-4432. Editor: Al Weiss. Managing Editor: Alan Paul. A bimonthly magazine covering self defense, survival, weaponry, mercenary activity, martial arts, and police and anti-crime subjects. Circ. 35,000. Pays a few weeks before publication. Byline given. Offers negotiable kill fee. Buys one-time rights. Submit seasonal/holiday material 4 months in advance. Previously published submissions OK. Computer printout submissions acceptable. SASE. Reports in 1 month. Sample copy for $2 and 85¢ postage, writer's guidelines for SAE and 1 first class stamp.
Nonfiction: Herman Petras, articles editor and David Weiss, assistant editor. Book excerpts, exposé, historical, how-to, interview/profile, new product, personal experience, photo feature and technical. Special issues include NINJA (assassins of Japan) and Survival Guide. Buys 40-50 mss/year. Send complete ms. Pays $125-200.
Photos: Bob Weiss, photo editor. Send photos with ms. Pays $5-50 for 8x10 b&w prints; $50-150 for 35mm color slides. Captions, model release and identification of subjects required.
Columns/Departments: David Weiss, column/department editor. Warriors, World (news, unusual items, humorous items); and Tools of the Trade (new products). Buys 50 mss/year. Send complete ms. Length: 50-250 words. Pays $10-50.
Tips: "Submit well-written pieces on subjects of interest to our readers, and include exciting, professional photos. Or submit a query letter on a proposed piece. Be exciting, make a point, don't overembellish! About 90% of all articles in *Warriors* are freelance."

THE WASHINGTON BLADE, Washington Blade, Inc., Suite 315, 930 F St. NW, Washington DC 20004. (202)347-2038. Managing Editor: Lisa M. Keen. 10% freelance written. Weekly news tabloid covering the gay/lesbian community. Articles (subjects) should be written from or directed to a gay perspective." Circ. 20,000. Pays in 30 days. Publishes ms an average of 1 month after acceptance. Byline given. Offers $15 kill fee. Buys first North American serial rights. Submit seasonal/holiday material 1 month in advance. Photocopied submissions OK. SASE. Free sample copy and writer's guidelines.
Nonfiction: Expose (of government, private agency, church, etc., handling of gay-related issues); historical/nostalgic; interview/profile (of gay community/political leaders; persons, gay or nongay, in positions to affect gay issues; outstanding achievers who happen to be gay; those who incorporate the gay lifestyle into their professions); photo feature (on a nationally or internationally historic gay event); and travel (on locales that welcome or cater to the gay traveler). *The Washington Blade* basically covers two areas: news and lifestyle. News coverage of D.C. metropolitan area gay community, local and federal government actions relating to gays, some national news of interest to gays. Section also includes features on current events. Special issues include: Annual gay pride issue (early June). No sexually explicit material. Buys 30 mss/year, average. Query with published clips. Length: 500-1,500 words. Pays 5-10¢/word.
Photos: "A photo or graphic with feature/lifestyle articles is particularly important. Photos with news stories are appreciated." State availability of photos. Reviews b&w contact sheets and 5x7 glossy prints. Pays $15 minimum. Captions preferred; model release required. On assignment, photographer paid mutually agreed upon fee, with expenses reimbursed. Publication retains all rights.
Tips: "Send good examples of your writing and know the paper before you submit a manuscript for publication. We get a lot of submissions which are entirely inappropriate." Greatest opportunity for freelancers resides in current events, features, interviews and book reviews.

WOMEN'S RIGHTS LAW REPORTER, 15 Washington St., Newark NJ 07102. (201)648-5320. Quarterly legal journal emphasizing law and feminism for lawyers, students and feminists. Circ. 1,300. No payment. Buys all rights. SASE. Sample copy $5 individuals; $9 institutions.
Nonfiction: Historical and legal articles. Query or submit complete ms with published clips and education data. Length: 20-100 pages plus footnotes.

Literary and "Little"

"A touch of risk and magic." That's how one literary magazine editor described the extra *touch* in manuscripts accepted for publication. Said another literary editor, "The greatest joy is to come across a story or poem which hits something in my gut that tells me: 'This is it . . . this is what I originally had in mind years ago, about how writing should be, and it's still true for me'."

Literary magazines launch many writers into print for the first time. In some cases, the writer's career outlasts the magazine. Literary editors wish writers would "support" the magazines they want to write for—by just subscribing.

Writers who want to get a story into print in a few months might have to wait a few years. Literary magazines, especially semiannuals, will buy good material and save it for a 1988 edition, for example. Submitting work to a "literary," the writer may encounter frequent address changes or unbusinesslike responses. On the other hand, many editors read submissions several times and send personal notes to writers. Literary and "little" magazine writers will notice that this year's *Writer's Market* does not contain a Poetry section. Writer's Digest Books has expanded its list of poetry markets into a new *Poet's Market*, edited by Judson Jerome, with detailed information just for the poet. For more information about fiction techniques and markets, see *Fiction Writer's Market*, also published by Writer's Digest Books.

‡**ACM, Another Chicago Magazine**, Thunder's Mouth Press, Box 11223, Chicago IL 60611. (312)524-1289. Editors: Lee Webster and Barry Silesky. 98% freelance written. Literary journal published biannually and funded by the National Endowment for the Arts. Circ. 1,100. Pays on acceptance. Publishes ms an average of 6 months after acceptance. Byline given. Buys first serial rights. Simultaneous queries, and simultaneous and photocopied submissions OK. Electronic submissions OK via disk with DOS ASCI file, but requires hard copy also. Computer printout submissions acceptable; prefers letter-quality to dot-matrix. SASE. Reports in 6 weeks. Sample copy $5; writer's guidelines for #10 SAE and 1 first class stamp.
Nonfiction: Interview (contemporary poets and fiction writers) and reviews of small press publications. Buys 1-2 mss/year. Query. Length: 1,000-20,000 words. Pays $5-25.
Fiction: Sharon Solwitz, fiction editor. Erotica, ethnic, experimental, novel excerpts and serious fiction. Buys 10-20 mss/year. Send complete ms. Length: 50-20,000 words. Pays $5-25.
Poetry: Serious poetry. No light verse or inspirational. Buys 100 poems/year. Length: 1-1,000 lines. Pays $5-25.

AMELIA MAGAZINE, Amelia Press, 329 E St., Bakerfield CA 93304. (805)323-4064. Editor: Frederick A. Raborg Jr. 100% freelance written. "*Amelia* is a quarterly international magazine publishing the finest poetry and fiction available, along with expert criticism and reviews intended for all interested in contemporary literature. Amelia also publishes three supplements each year: *Cicada*, which publishes only high quality traditional or experimental haiku and senryu; *SPSM&H*, which publishes the highest quality traditional and experimental sonnets available; and the annual winner of the Charles William Duke Longpoem contest." Circ. 1,000. Pays on acceptance. Publishes ms an average of 2 months after acceptance. Byline given. Offers 50% kill fee. Buys first North American serial rights. Submit seasonal/holiday material 2 months in advance. Computer printout submissions acceptable; prefers letter-quality to dot-matrix. SASE. Reports in 2 months on mss. Sample copy $4.75 (includes postage); writer's guidelines for business size SAE and 1 first class stamp. Sample copy of any supplement $2.
Nonfiction: Historical/nostalgic (in the form of belles lettres); humor (in fiction or belles lettres); interview/profile (poets and fiction writers); opinion (on poetry and fiction only); personal experience (as it pertains to poetry or fiction in the form of belles lettres); travel (in the form of belles lettres only); and criticism and book reviews of poetry and small press fiction titles. "Nothing overtly slick in approach. Criticism pieces must have depth; belles lettres must offer important insights into the human scene." Buys 8 mss/year. Send complete ms. Length: 1,000-2,000 words. Pays $25 or by arrangement. "Ordinarily payment for all prose is a flat rate of $25/piece, more for exceptional work."
Fiction: Adventure; book excerpts (original novel excerpts only); erotica (of a quality seen in Anais Nin or Henry Miller only); ethnic; experimental; fantasy; historical; horror; humorous; mainstream; mystery; novel excerpts; science fiction; suspense; and western. "We would consider slick fiction of the quality seen in *Redbook*." No pornography ("good erotica is not the same thing"). Buys 12-16 mss/year. Send complete ms. Length: 1,000-3,500 words. Pays $25 or by arrangement for exceptional work.
Poetry: Avant-garde, free verse, haiku, light verse and traditional. "No patently religious or stereotypical newspaper poetry." Buys 80-120 poems/year depending on lengths. Prefers submission of at least 3 poems. Length: 3-100 lines. Pays $2-25; additional payment for exceptional work, usually by established professionals. *Cicada* pays $10 each to three "best of issue" poets; *SPSM&H* pays $14 to the "best of issue" sonnet; winner of the long poem contest receives $100 plus copies and publication.
Tips: "We have planned a series of poetry chapbooks at the rate of two per year." Fiction and poetry are most open to freelancers. "*Have something to say* and say it well. If you insist on waving flags or pushing your religion, then do it with subtlety and class. We enjoy a good cry from time to time, too, but sentimentality does

not mean we want to see mush. As in the first issue of *Amelia*, 'name' writers are used, but newcomers who have done their homework suffer no disadvantage here." *Amelia* is designed to feature every contributor. Length is secondary to any decision to purchase. The most mistakes made by writers in completing articles for us are: "Not reading a copy of the magazine prior to submission; sloppy work; indifference to research, and generally a lack of professionalism. So often the problem seems to be that writers feel small press publications allows such a sloughing of responsibility. It is not so."

THE AMERICAN SCHOLAR, 1811 Q St. NW, Washington DC 20009. (202)265-3808. Editor: Joseph Epstein. 5% freelance written. Quarterly magazine for college-educated, mid-20s and older, rather intellectual in orientation and interests. Circ. 30,000. Buys first serial rights; rights stay in author's possession. Byline given. Buys 20-30 mss/year. Pays on acceptance. Publishes ms an average of 9 months after acceptance. No simultaneous submissions. Computer printout submissions acceptable; no dot-matrix. Reports in 1-2 months. SASE. Sample copy $4.50; free writer's guidelines.
Nonfiction: "The aim of *The Scholar* is to fill the gap between the learned journals and the good magazines for a popular audience. We are interested not so much in the definitive analysis as in the lucid and creative exploration of what is going on in the fields of science, art, religion, politics, and national and foreign affairs. Advances in science particularly interest us." Informational, interview, profile, historical, think articles and book reviews. Query with samples, if possible. Length: 3,500-4,000 words. Pays $350/article and $100 for reviews.
Poetry: "We would like to see poetry that develops an image, a thought or event, without the use of a single cliche or contrived archaism. The most hackneyed subject matter is self-conscious love; the most tired verse is iambic pentameter with rhyming endings. The usual length of our poems is 30 lines. From 1-4 poems may be submitted at one time; *no more* for a careful reading. We urge prospective contributors to familiarize themselves with the type of poetry we have published by looking at the magazine." Buys 5 poems/issue. Pays $50 for poetry on any theme.
Tips: "See our magazine in your public library before submitting material to us. Know what we publish and the quality of our articles."

ANTAEUS, The Ecco Press, 18 W. 30th St., New York NY 10001. (212)685-8240. Editor: Daniel Halpern. Managing Editor: Megan Ratner. Semiannual magazine with fiction and poetry. Circ. 5,000. Pays on publication. Byline given. Buys first North American serial rights. Photocopied submissions OK. SASE. Reports in 1 week on queries; 6 weeks on mss. Sample copy $5; free writer's guidelines.
Fiction: Experimental and novel excerpts. Buys 10-15 mss/year. Send complete ms. Length: no minimum or maximum. Pays $5/printed page.
Poetry: Avant-garde, free verse, light verse and traditional. Buys 30-35 poems/year. Submit maximum 8 poems. Pays $5.

ANTIOCH REVIEW, Box 148, Yellow Springs OH 45387. Editor: Robert S. Fogarty. 80% freelance written. Quarterly magazine for general, literary and academic audience. Buys all rights. Byline given. Pays on publication. Publishes ms an average of 10 months after acceptance. Computer printout submissions acceptable; prefers letter-quality to dot-matrix. Reports in 6 weeks. SASE.
Nonfiction: "Contemporary articles in the humanities and social sciences, politics, economics, literature and all areas of broad intellectual concern. Somewhat scholarly, but never pedantic in style, eschewing all professional jargon. Lively, distinctive prose insisted upon." Length: 2,000-8,000 words. Pays $10/published page.
Fiction: Quality fiction only, distinctive in style with fresh insights into the human condition. No science fiction, fantasy or confessions. Pays $10/published page.
Poetry: Concrete visual imagery. No light or inspirational verse. Contributors should be familiar with the magazine before submitting.

‡**THE ASYMPTOTICAL WORLD**, 341 Lincoln Ave., Box 1372, Williamsport PA 17703. (717)322-7841. Editor: Michael H. Gerardi. 50% freelance written. Annual magazine covering psychodramas, science fiction, fantasy and experimental. "*The Asymptotical World* is a collection of short tales which attempts to elucidate the moods, sensations and thoughts of a curious world created in the mind of man. The tales touch upon themes of darkness, desolation and death. From each tale, the reader may relive a personal experience or sensation, and he may find relevance or discomfort. The tales were not written to be satanic or sacrilegious statements. The stories were penned simply to be dark phantasies which would provide bizarre playgrounds for inquisitive minds." Estab. 1984. Circ. 1,300. Pays on acceptance. Publishes ms an average of 6 months after acceptance. Byline given. Buys first North American serial rights. Simultaneous queries and photocopied submissions OK. Computer printout submissions acceptable; prefers letter-quality to dot-matrix. SASE. Reports in 4 weeks on queries; 3 months on mss. Sample copy $6.95 with 9x12 SAE and 7 first class stamps; writer's guidelines for 4x9$^{1}/_{2}$ SAE and 1 first class stamp.
Fiction: Experimental, fantasy, science fiction and psychodrama. Buys 10-15 mss/year. Query with published

clips or send complete ms. Length: 1,000-2,500 words. Pays $20-50.

Poetry: Buys 2-4 poems/year. "We will be expanding this section of *TAW*." Submit maximum 4 poems. Length: 5-100 lines. Pays $5-50.

Tips: "*The Asymptotical World* is definitely unique. It is strongly suggested that a writer review a copy of the magazine to study the format of a psychodrama and the manner in which the plot is left 'open-ended.' The writer will need to study the atmosphere, mood, and plot of published psychodramas before preparing a feature work. The magazine is very young and is willing to explore many fields."

BLOOMSBURY REVIEW, Box 8928, Denver CO 80201. (303)455-0593. Editor: Tom Auer. 75% freelance written. Monthly magazine covering book reviews and essays of interest to book readers. Circ. 8,000. Pays 2 months after publication. Publishes ms an average of 3 months after acceptance. Byline and 1-line biography given. Buys one-time rights; rights revert back to writer on publication. Computer printout submissions acceptable; prefers letter-quality to dot-matrix. SASE. Reports in 3 months on queries and mss. Sample copy $2.50; free writer's guidelines with SASE.

Nonfiction: Historical/nostalgic (related to books and publishing); interview/profile (of prominent people in the book business such as authors and publishers); essays; and book reviews. Query with published clips. Length: average 750 words. Pays $10 minimum."

Poetry: Original and unpublished. Buys 24/year. Pays $5 average.

Tips: "You've got to be a good writer and a better thinker to get in print. Submitting a book review is the best way to break into our publication."

BOOK FORUM, Hudson River Press, 38 E. 76th St., New York NY 10021. (212)861-8328. Editor: Marshall Hayes. Editorial Director: Marilyn Wood. Quarterly magazine: 192 pages. Emphasizes contemporary literature, the arts, and foreign affairs for "intellectually sophisticated and knowledgeable professionals: university-level academics, writers, people in government, and the professions." 95% freelance written. Circ. 5,200. Pays on publication. Publishes ms an average of 4 months after acceptance. Buys first serial rights. Pays 33$^{1}/_{3}$% kill fee. Byline given. Phone queries OK. Photocopied submissions OK. SASE. Reports in 4 weeks. Sample copy $3.

Nonfiction: "We seek highly literate essays that would appeal to the same readership as, say, the *London Times Literary Supplement* or *Encounter*. Our readers are interested in professionally written, highly literate and informative essays, profiles and reviews in literature, the arts, behavior, and foreign and public affairs. We cannot use material designed for a mass readership. Think of us as an Eastern establishment, somewhat snobbish literary and public affairs journal and you will have it right." General interest, interview (with select contemporary writers, scientists, educators, artists, film makers); profiles, and essays about contemporary innovators. Buys 20-40 unsolicited mss/year. Query. Length: 800-2,000 words. Pays $25-100.

Tips: "To break in send with the query letter a sample of writing in an area relevant to our interests. If the writer wants to contribute book reviews, send a book review sample, published or not, of the kind of title we are likely to review—literary, social, biographical, art."

BOSTON REVIEW, 33 Harrison Ave., Boston MA 02111. (617)350-5353. Editor: Nicholas Bromell. 90% freelance written. Bimonthly magazine of the arts, politics and culture. Circ. 10,000. Pays on publication. Publishes ms an average of 4 months after acceptance. Buys first serial rights, second serial (reprint) rights, and one-time rights; makes work-for-hire assignments. Acquires all rights, unless author requests otherwise. Byline given. Photocopied and simultaneous submissions OK. Computer printout submissions acceptable; no dot-matrix. SASE. Reports in 2 months. Sample copy $3.

Nonfiction: Critical essays and reviews, natural and social sciences, literature, music, painting, film, photography, dance and theatre. Buys 20 unsolicited mss/year. Length: 1,000-3,000 words.

Fiction: Length: 2,000-4,000 words. Pays according to length and author, ranging from $50-200.

Poetry: Pays according to length and author.

‡**BUFFALO SPREE MAGAZINE**, Box 38, Buffalo NY 14226. (716)839-3405. Editor: Johanna V. Shotell. Quarterly for "a highly literate readership." Circ. 21,000. Buys first serial rights. Buys 5-8 mss/year. SASE.

Nonfiction and Fiction: Department Editor: Gary Gross. "Intellectually stimulating prose exploring contemporary social, philosophical and artistic concerns. We are not a political magazine. Matters of interest to western New York make up a significant part of what we print." Length: 1,500 words maximum. Pays $100 for a lead article. "We print fiction, but it must be brilliant." Pays approximately $100.

Poetry: Janet Goldenberg, department editor. "Serious, modern poetry of nature and of man's relationship with nature interests us, provided it is of the highest quality." Pays approximately $20.

C.S.P. WORLD NEWS, Editions Stencil, Box 2608, Station D, Ottawa, Ontario K1P 5W7 Canada. Editor-in-Chief: Guy F. Claude Hamel. 100% freelance written. Monthly literary journal emphasizing book reviews. Publishes ms an average of 2 months after acceptance. Buys first serial rights and first North American serial rights. Photocopied submissions OK. Computer printout submissions acceptable; no dot-matrix. SAE, IRCs.

Reports in 2 months. Sample copy $2.
Nonfiction: Sociology and criminology. Buys 12 mss/year. Send complete ms. Length: 2,600 words. Typewritten, double-spaced.
Columns/Departments: Writer's Workshop material. Buys unlimited items/year. Send complete ms. Length: 20-50 words.
Poetry: Publishes avant-garde forms. Submit complete unlimited ms. Length: 6-12 lines.
Fillers: Jokes, gags and anecdotes. Payment negotiated.
Tips: The writer has a better chance of breaking in with short articles and fillers. "We wish to know our writers and give them a chance to know us. A frequent mistake made by writers is their refusal to subscribe—we need their complete support in helping them to publish their work, especially for the first time."

CANADIAN FICTION MAGAZINE, Box 946, Station F, Toronto, Ontario M4Y 2N9 Canada. Editor: Geoffrey Hancock. Quarterly magazine; 148 pages. Emphasizes Canadian fiction, short stories and novel excerpts. Circ. 1,800. Pays on publication. Buys first North American serial rights. Byline given. SASE (Canadian stamps). Reports in 6 weeks. Back issue $5 (in Canadian funds). Current issue $6 (in Canadian funds).
Nonfiction: Interview (must have a definite purpose, both as biography and as a critical tool focusing on problems and techniques) and book reviews (Canadian fiction only). Buys 35 mss/year. Query. Length: 1,000-3,000 words. Pays $10/printed page plus 1-year subscription.
Photos: Purchased on assignment. Send prints. Pays $10 for 5x7 b&w glossy prints; $50 for cover. Model release required.
Fiction: "No restrictions on subject matter or theme. We are open to experimental and speculative fiction as well as traditional forms. Style, content and form are the author's prerogative. We also publish self-contained sections of novel-in-progress and French-Canadian fiction in translation, as well as an annual special issue on a single author such as Mavis Gallant, Leon Rooke, Robert Harlow or Jane Rule. Please note that *CFM* is an anthology devoted exclusively to Canadian fiction. We publish only the works of writers and artists residing in Canada and Canadians living abroad." Pays $10/printed page.
Tips: "Prospective contributors must study several recent issues carefully. *CFM* is a serious professional literary magazine whose contributors include the finest writers in Canada."

CANADIAN LITERATURE, University of British Columbia, Vancouver, British Columbia V6T 1W5 Canada. Editor: W.H. New. 90% freelance written. Quarterly. Circ. 2,000. Not copyrighted. Buys first Canadian rights only. Pays on publication. Publishes ms an average of 2 years after acceptance. Computer printout submissions acceptable; no dot-matrix. Query "with a clear description of the project." SAE, IRCs.
Nonfiction: Articles of high quality on Canadian books and writers only written in French or English. Articles should be scholarly and readable. Length: 2,000-5,500 words. Pays $5/printed page.

CAROLINA QUARTERLY, University of North Carolina, Greenlaw Hall 066A, Chapel Hill NC 27514. (919)933-0244. Editor: Emily Stockard. Managing Editor: Elizabeth Sheppard. 100% freelance written. Literary journal published 3 times/year. Circ. 1,000. Pays on publication. Publishes ms an average of 3 months after acceptance. Byline given. Buys first North American serial rights. Photocopied submissions OK. Computer printout submissions acceptable; prefers letter-quality to dot-matrix. SASE. Reports in 4 months. Sample copy $4 (includes postage); writer's guidelines for SAE and 1 first class stamp.
Nonfiction: Book reviews and photo feature. Publishes 6 reviews/year, 12 photographs/year.
Fiction: "We are interested in maturity: control over language; command of structure and technique; understanding of the possibilities and demands of prose narrative, with respect to stylistics, characterization, and point of view. We publish a good many unsolicited stories; *CQ* is a market for newcomer and professional alike." No pornography. Buys 12-18 mss/year. Send complete ms. Length: 7,000 words maximum. Pays $3/printed page.
Poetry: "*CQ* places no specific restrictions on the length, form or substance of poems considered for publication." Submit 2-6 poems. Buys 60 mss/year. Pays $5/printed poem.
Tips: "Send *one* fiction manuscript at a time; no cover letter is necessary. Address to appropriate editor, not to general editor. Look at the magazine, a recent number if possible."

CHAPMAN, 35 E. Claremont St., Edinburgh EH7 4HT Scotland. (031)556-5863. Editor: Joy M. Hendry. 50% freelance written. Triannual magazine of Scottish literature and culture. Circ. 2,000. Pays on publication. Publishes ms an average of 2 months after acceptance. No byline given. Buys first serial rights. Computer printout submissions acceptable; prefers letter-quality to dot-matrix. SASE. Reports in 2 weeks on queries; 1 month on mss. Sample copy $2.50 and 2 IRCs.
Nonfiction: Literary criticism and linguistic material (Scottish or Gaelic). "Few American writers would be in a position to write about Scotish literature." Buys 15 mss/year. Length: 1,000-4,000 words. Pays $10-50.
Fiction: Buys 15 mss/year. Send complete ms. Length: 1,500-4,000 words. Pays $10-50.
Poetry: Buys 150 poems/year. Pays $5-50.

THE CHARITON REVIEW, Northeast Missouri State University, Kirksville MO 63501. (816)785-4499. Editor: Jim Barnes. 100% freelance written. Semiannual (fall and spring) magazine covering contemporary fiction, poetry, translation and book reviews. Circ. 600. Pays on publication. Byline given. Buys first North American serial rights. Computer printout submissions acceptable; no dot-matrix. SASE. Reports in 1 week on queries; 2 weeks on mss. Sample copy for $2 and 7x10 SAE and 63-cents postage.
Nonfiction: Book reviews. Buys 2-5 mss/year. Query or send complete ms. Length: 1,000-5,000. Pays $15.
Fiction: Ethnic, experimental, mainstream, novel excerpts and traditional. "We are not interested in slick material." Buys 6-8 mss/year. Send complete ms. Length: 1,000-5,000 words. Pays $5/page.
Poetry: Avant-garde, free verse and traditional. Buys 50-55 poems/year. Submit maximum 10 poems. Length: open. Pays $5/page.
Tips: "Read *Chariton* and similar magazines. Know the difference between good literature and bad. Know what magazine might be interested in your work. We are not a trendy magazine. We publish only the best. All sections are open to freelancers. Know your market or you are wasting your time—and mine."

CHICAGO SUN-TIMES SHOW/BOOK WEEK, *Chicago Sun-Times*, 401 N. Wabash Ave., Chicago IL 60611. (312)321-2131. Editor: Scott L. Powers. Weekly newspaper section emphasizing entertainment, arts and books. Circ. 750,000. Pays on publication. Buys all rights. Pays negotiable kill fee except on speculative articles. Submit seasonal/holiday material at least 2 months in advance. Photocopied and previously published work OK. Computer printout submissions acceptable "if readable"; prefers letter-quality to dot-matrix. SASE. Reports in 3 weeks.
Nonfiction: "Articles and essays dealing with all the serious and lively arts—movies; theater (pro, semipro, amateur, foreign); filmmakers; painting; sculpture; and music (all fields, from classical to rock—we have regular columnists in these fields). Our Book Week column has from 6-8 reviews, mostly assigned. Material has to be very good because we have our own regular staffers who write almost every week. Writing must be tight. No warmed-over stuff of fan magazine type. No high-schoolish literary themes." Query. Length: 800-1,000 words. Pays $75-100.

CONFRONTATION, C.W. Post College of Long Island University, Greenvale NY 11548. (576)299-2391. Editor: Martin Tucker. 90% freelance written. Semiannual magazine; 190 pages. Emphasizes creative writing for a "literate, educated, college-graduate audience." Circ. 2,000. Pays on publication. Pays 50% kill fee. Publishes ms an average of 9 months after acceptance. Byline given. Buys first serial rights. Phone queries, simultaneous and photocopied submissions OK. Computer printout submissions acceptable; no dot-matrix. SASE. Reports in 2 months. Sample copy $2.
Nonfiction: "Articles are, basically, commissioned essays on a specific subject." Memoirs wanted. Buys 6 mss/year. Query. Length: 1,000-3,000 words. Pays $10-100. Sometimes pays the expenses of writers on assignment.
Fiction: Martin Tucker, fiction editor. Experimental, humorous and mainstream. Buys 25-30 mss/year. Submit complete ms. Length: open. Pays $15-100.
Poetry: W. Palmer, poetry editor. Avant-garde, free verse, haiku, light verse and traditional. Buys 60/year. Submit maximum 8 poems. No length requirement. Pays $5-50.
Tips: "At this time we discourage fantasy and light verse. We do, however, read all manuscripts. It's rewarding discovering a good manuscript that comes in unsolicited."

THE DENVER QUARTERLY, University of Denver, Denver CO 80208. (303)753-2869. Editor: David Micofsky. Quarterly magazine for generally sophisticated readership. Circ. 600. Pays on publication. Buys first North American serial rights. Phone queries OK. Photocopied submissions OK. Computer printout submissions acceptable; no dot-matrix. SASE. Reports in 10 weeks. Sample copy $3.
Nonfiction: "Most reviews are solicited; we do publish a few literary essays in each number." Send complete ms. Pays $5/printed page.
Fiction: Buys 10-15 mss/year. Send complete ms. Pays $5/printed page.
Poetry: Buys 50 poems/year. Send poems. Pays $10/printed page.
Tips: "We decide on the basis of quality only. Prior publication is irrelevant. Promising material, even though rejected, may receive some personal comment from the editor; some material can be revised to meet our standards through such criticism. I receive more good stuff than *DQ* can accept, so there is some subjectivity and a good deal of luck involved in any final acceptance."

ENCOUNTER, Encounter, Ltd., 59 St. Martin's Lane, London WC2N 4JS England. Editors: Melvin J. Lasky and Richard Mayne. Monthly magazine (except August and September) covering current affairs and the arts. Circ. 17,000. Pays on publication. Buys one-time rights. SASE, IRC. Reports in 2 weeks on queries; 6 weeks on mss. Sample copy $4.50 including surface mail cost.
Nonfiction: Mainly articles on current affairs. Length: 1,500-5,000 words. Pays variable fee, but "averages £20/1,000 words."
Fiction: "Submit just good up-market stories." Length: 1,500-5,000 words. Pays variable fee, averages £20/

1,000 words.

Poetry: "Submit just good up-market poetry." Submit maximum 6 poems. Length: 12-100 lines. Pays variable fee.

Tips: "Study the magazine first. A straight submission will be carefully considered." Stories and poems most open to freelancers.

EPOCH, Cornell University, 251 Goldwin Smith, Ithaca NY 14853. (607)256-3385. Editor: C.S. Griscombe. Literary magazine of original fiction and poetry published 3 times/year. Circ. 1,000. Pays on publication. Byline given. Buys first North American serial rights. SASE. Sample copy $3.50. Send SASE for listing of nearest library carrying *Epoch*.

Fiction: "Potential contributors should *read* a copy or two. There is *no other way* for them to ascertain what we need or like." Buys 15-20 mss/year. Send complete ms. Pays $10/page.

Poetry: "Potential contributors should read magazine to see what type of poetry is used." Buys 20-30 poems/year. Pays $1/line.

EROTIC FICTION QUARTERLY, EFQ Publications, Box 4958, San Francisco CA 94101. Editor: Richard Hiller. 100% freelance written. Small literary magazine for thoughtful people interested in a variety of highly original and creative short fiction with sexual themes. Estab. 1983. Pays on acceptance. Byline given. Buys all rights. Photocopied submissions OK. Computer printout submissions acceptable; prefers letter-quality to dot-matrix. SASE. Writer's guidelines for SASE.

Fiction: Heartful, intelligent erotica, any style. Also, stories—not necessarily erotic—about some aspect of authentic sexual experience. No standard pornography or men's magazine-type stories; no contrived or formula plots or gimmicks; no broad satire or parody; no poetry. Send complete ms. Length: 500-5,000 words, average 1,500 words. Pays $35 minimum.

Tips: "I specifically encourage beginners who have something to say regarding sexual attitudes, emotions, roles, etc. Story ideas should come from real life, not media; characters should be real people. There are essentially no restrictions on content, style, explicitness, etc.; *originality*, *clarity*, and *integrity* are most important."

EVENT, c/o Kwantlen College, Box 9030, Surrey, British Columbia V3T 5H8 Canada. Managing Editor: Vye Flindall. 100% freelance written. Biannual magazine for "those interested in literature and writing." Circ. 1,000. Uses 80-100 mss/year. Small payment and contributor's copy only. Publishes ms an average of 4 months after acceptance. Buys first serial rights. Byline given. Photocopied and simultaneous submissions OK. Computer printout submissions acceptable; prefers letter-quality to dot-matrix. Reports in 4 months. Submit complete ms. SAE, IRCs.

Nonfiction: "High quality work." Reviews of Canadian books and essays.

Fiction: Short stories and drama.

Poetry: Submit complete ms. "We are looking for high quality modern poetry."

FICTION MONTHLY, "The Bay Area's Fiction Magazine," Fiction Monthly, Suite 67, 545 Haight St., San Francisco CA 94117. (415)753-2228. Publisher/Editor: D.C. Gabbard. Managing Editor: Beth Overson. 30% freelance written. Literary tabloid magazine published 10 times/year. "We offer a monthly guide to literary films, events, radio and television in the San Francisco area, as well as short stories, reviews and interviews. We serve the Bay Area community by offering the best short stories available to us. Our audience is well-educated, intelligent and enjoys reading well-crafted fiction." Circ. 4,000. Pays on acceptance. Not copyrighted. Buys first serial rights, first North American serial rights, and second serial (reprint) rights. Publishes ms an average of 4 months after acceptance. Submit seasonal/holiday material 6 months in advance. Photocopied and simultaneous submissions OK. SASE. Reports in 3 weeks on queries; 9 weeks on mss. Sample copy for 9x12 SAE and 7 first class stamps; writer's guidelines for business size SAE and 1 first class stamp.

Nonfiction: Interview/profile of fiction writers with photos. Buys 4-6 mss/year. Query. Length: 2,500-3,500 words. Pays $60-75; $10 per photo, on acceptance.

Columns/Departments: Critical Perspectives (reviews of novels and short story collections, more often than not small press publications). Buys 25-30 mss/year. Query. Length: 250-400 words. Pays $10.

Market conditions are constantly changing! If this is 1987 or later, buy the newest edition of *Writer's Market* at your favorite bookstore or order directly from Writer's Digest Books.

Fiction: Stephen Woodhams, fiction editor. Ethnic, experimental, humorous and mainstream. No science fiction, fantasy or erotica. Buys 15-20 mss/year. Send complete ms. Length: 500-3,000 words. Pays $10-75.
Tips: "In reviews, or whatever that freelancers submit, we suggest that they avoid glibness; be direct, honest and articulate. Well-written pieces will find a place in our magazine, whomever they are from. Those interested in submitting short fiction should send for a copy of the magazine and its guidelines. Study them before sending anything."

FICTION NETWORK MAGAZINE, Fiction Network, Box 5651, San Francisco CA 94101. (415)552-3223. Editor: Jay Schaefer. 100% freelance written. Magazine of short stories. Fiction Network distributes short stories to newspapers, regional magazines, and other periodicals and also publishes *Fiction Network Magazine* (for agents, editors and writers). Circ. 6,000. Pays on publication. Publishes ms an average of 6 months after acceptance. Byline given. Buys first serial rights and second serial (reprint) rights; prefers previously unpublished stories. Each story accepted may appear in several newspapers and magazines through our syndicate. Photocopied submissions OK. Computer printout submissions acceptable; no dot-matrix. SASE. Reports in 3 months. Does not return foreign submissions—notification only. Sample copy $4 USA and Canada; $6.50 elsewhere. Writer's guidelines for business size SAE, and 1 first class stamp.
Fiction: All types of stories and subjects are acceptable; novel excerpts will be considered only if they stand alone as stories. No poetry, essays, reviews or interviews. No children's or young adult material. Buys 100 mss/year. Send complete ms. "Do not submit a second manuscript until you receive a response to the first manuscript." Length: 5,000 words maximum (2,500 words preferred). Pays $25 minimum for magazine and 50% of syndicate fees.
Tips: "We offer both known and unknown writers excellent exposure and reasonable fees while we open up new markets for stories. Our greatest need is for short-short stories." Contributors include Alice Adams, Max Apple, Ann Beattie, Andre Dubus, Lynne Sharon Schwartz and Marian Thurm.

THE FIDDLEHEAD, University of New Brunswick, The Observatory, Box 4400, Fredericton, New Brunswick E3B 5A3 Canada. (506)454-3591. Editor: Roger Ploude. 90% freelance written. Quarterly magazine covering poetry, short fiction, photographs and book reviews. Circ. 1,100. Pays on publication. Publishes ms an average of 1 year after acceptance. Not copyrighted. Buys first North American serial rights. Submit seasonal/holiday material 6 months in advance. Simultaneous queries and photocopied submissions (if legible) OK. Computer printout submissions acceptable; no dot-matrix. SAE, IRCs. Reports in 3 weeks on queries; 2 months on mss. Sample copy $4, Canada: $4.25, U.S.
Fiction: Kent Thompson. "Stories may be on any subject—acceptance is based on quality alone. Because the journal is heavily subsidized by the Canadian government, strong preference is given to Canadian writers." Buys 20 mss/year. Pays $12/page; $100/article.
Poetry: Robert Gibbs. "Poetry may be on any subject—acceptance is based on quality alone. Because the journal is heavily subsidized by the Canadian government, strong preference is given to Canadian writers." Buys average of 60/year. Submit maximum 10 poems. Pays $12/page; $100 maximum.
Tips: "Quality alone is the criterion for publication. Return postage (Canadian, or IRCs) should accompany all manuscripts."

THE GAMUT, A Journal of Ideas and Information, Cleveland State University, 1216 Rhodes Tower, Cleveland OH 44115. (216)687-4679. Editor: Louis T. Milic. 15% freelance written. Triannual magazine with sharply focused, well-documented articles developing a thesis or explaining a problem, process, or discovery of current interest in any field or profession—one of the sciences, arts, or social sciences, business, or industry. Circ. 1,000. Pays on publication. Publishes ms an average of 3 months after acceptance. Byline given. Buys first North American serial rights. Simultaneous queries and photocopied submissions OK. Computer printout submissions acceptable. SASE. Reports in 2 weeks on queries; 6 weeks on mss. Sample copy $2.50, SAE and $1 postage; writer's guidelines for business size SAE and 1 first class stamp.
Nonfiction: Leonard M. Trawick, articles editor. General interest, humor, personal experience and technical (provided it is understandable by the lay reader). "All material must be by Ohio authors or emphasize the *region*." Buys 25 mss/year. Query or send complete ms. Length: 2,000-8,000 words. Pays $25-250.
Photos: State availability of photos or send photos with ms. Reviews 8x10 b&w prints. Captions, model release, and identification of subjects (if applicable) required. Buys one-time rights.
Tips: "Authors should assume that *The Gamut* readers are well educated but not necessarily expert in the particular field of the article. If the piece is good, we'll print it, even if we don't know the writer."

GRAIN, Saskatchewan Writers' Guild, Box 1154, Regina, Saskatchewan S4P 3B4 Canada. (306)522-0811 (daytime). Editor: Brenda Riches. 100% freelance written. "A literary quarterly magazine that seeks to extend the boundaries of convention and challenge readers and writers." Circ. 850. Pays on acceptance. Publishes ms an average of 3 months after acceptance. No byline given. Not copyrighted. Buys one-time rights. Photocopied submissions OK. Computer printout submissions acceptable; prefers letter-quality to dot-matrix. SAE, IRC. Reports in 1 month on queries; 3 months on mss. Sample copy for $3, 5x8 SAE and 65¢ postage.

Nonfiction: Literary essays. Buys up to 4 mss/year. Query. Pays $30-100.

Fiction: Brenda Riches and Bonnie Burnard, fiction editors. "Literary art only. No fiction of a popular nature." Buys 12-15 mss/year. Send complete ms. Length: 300-8,000 words. Pays 30-100.

Poetry: Brenda Riches and Garry Radison, poetry editors. "Only poetry that has substance." Buys 30-60/year. Submit maximum 8 poems. Length: 3-200 lines. Pays $20.

Tips: "Only work of the highest literary quality is accepted. Read several back issues. Get advice from a practicing writer to make sure the work is ready to send. Then send it."

‡**GRANTA, A Paperback Magazine of New Writing**, Granta Publications, Ltd., 44a Hobson St., Cambridge CB1 1NL England. (0223)315290. Editor: William Buford. Managing Editor: Tracy Shaw. U.S. Office: #81, 325 Riverside Dr., New York NY 10025. U.S. Editor: Jon Levi. In U.K., Granta published in association with Penguin Books Ltd.; in the U.S., in association with Viking Penguin, Inc. 90% freelance written. Quarterly literary and political publication covering literate, contemporary culture and politics. "We seek contemporary imaginative writing, political and cultural journalism, travel writing, autobiography, etc." Circ. 35,000. Pays on publication. Publishes ms an average of 4 months after acceptance. Byline given. Offers kill fee if accepted and not published or if commissioned and not published. Buys first serial world rights (English language). Simultaneous and photocopied submissions OK. Computer printout submissions acceptable; prefers letter-quality to dot-matrix. SASE. Reports in 1 week on queries; 6 weeks on mss. Sample copy $6.95.

Nonfiction: William Buford (U.K.); Jon Levi (U.S.), articles editors. Book excerpts (6-9 months lead time); humor (comic/literary writing); interview (literary); opinion (political, cultural); personal experience (autobiography); photo feature (photo essays, photo and text); and travel. Buys 40 mss/year. Query with or without published clips. Length: 300-40,000 words. Pays $100-5,000. Sometimes pays the expenses of writers on assignment.

Fiction: William Buford (U.K.); Jon Levi (U.S.), fiction editors. Novel excerpts (6-9 months lead time); serialized novels; and serious literary fiction. Buys 40 mss/year. Send complete ms. Length: 300-40,000 words. Pays $100-5,000.

Tips: The magazine has included material by Saul Bellow, Paul Theroux and Gabriel Garcia Marquez.

GREAT RIVER REVIEW, 211 W. 7th, Winona MN 55987. Editors: Orval Lund. Monica Drealan, reviews. 100% freelance written. Magazine; 145 pages, published 2 times/year. Publishes ms an average of 3 months after acceptance. Buys first serial rights. Photocopied submissions OK. Computer printout submissions acceptable; prefers letter-quality to dot-matrix. SASE. Reports in 2 months. Sample copy (back issues) $3; current issue $3.50.

Nonfiction: Essays on the region and articles on Midwestern writers. Query first on articles.

Fiction: Experimental and mainstream, but not mass circulation style. Buys 6-7 prose mss/issue, up to 30 poems. Length: 2,000-9,000 words.

‡**HIBISCUS MAGAZINE, Short Stories, Poetry, Art**, Hibiscus Press, Box 22248, Sacramento CA 95822. Editor: Margaret Wensrich. 99% freelance written. Triannual magazine for people who like to read short stories and poetry. Estab. 1984. Circ. 2,000. Pays on acceptance. Byline given. Buys first North American serial rights. Submit seasonal/holiday material 9 months in advance. Photocopied submissions OK. Computer printout submissions acceptable; prefers letter-quality to dot-matrix. SASE. Reports in 6 weeks. Sample copy $3; writer's guidelines for #10 SAE and 1 first class stamp.

Fiction: Adventure, fantasy, historical, horror, humorous, mainstream, mystery, science fiction, suspense and western. No experimental fiction. Buys 12-16 mss/year. Send complete ms. Length: 1,500-3,000 words. Pays $15-25.

Poetry: Joyce Odam, poetry editor. No restrictions on types of poetry. Buys 30 poems/year. Submit maximum 4 poems. Length: open. Pays $5-25.

THE HUDSON REVIEW, 684 Park Ave., New York NY 10021. Managing Editor: Julia A. Stephen. Quarterly. Pays on publication. Reports in 6-8 weeks. SASE for return of submissions.

Nonfiction: Articles, translations and reviews. Length: 8,000 words maximum.

Fiction: Uses "quality fiction". Length: 10,000 words maximum. Pays $2^1/_2$¢/word.

Poetry: 50¢/line for poetry.

Tips: Unsolicited mss will be read according to the following schedule: *Nonfiction:* Jan. 1 through March 31, and Oct. 1 through Dec. 31; *Poetry:* April 1 through Sept. 30; *Fiction:* June 1 through Nov. 30.

IMAGE MAGAZINE, A Magazine of the Arts, Cornerstone Press, Box 28048, St. Louis MO 63119. (314)752-3704. Managing Editor: Anthony J. Summers. General Editor: James J. Finnegan. 100% freelance written. Triannual literary journal "for the educated, open-minded, thinking person." Circ. 600. Pays on publication. Publishes ms an average of 3 months after acceptance. Byline given. Offers negotiable kill fee. Buys one-time and negotiable rights. Simultaneous queries OK. Computer printout submissions acceptable. SASE. Reports in 3 weeks on queries; 7 weeks on mss. Sample copy $3 and 50¢ postage; free writer's guidelines.

Fiction: Erotica, ethnic, experimental, fantasy, horror, humorous, novel excerpts and science fiction. No "cutesy, self-congratulating material." Buys variable number mss/year. Query or send complete ms. Length: open. Pays $1-100.

Poetry: Avant-garde, free verse, haiku, light verse and traditional. No "overly religious, Elvis poetry, 'The world is neat and happy' type, etc." Buys 20-100/year. Submit maximum 10 poems. Length: open. Pays $1-100.

Tips: "We receive very few reviews, interviews, interesting articles on the literary world, as well as plays and experimental material. Try these for a better shot."

‡**INKBLOT**, Inkblot Publications, 1506 Bonita, Berkeley CA 94709. (415)848-7510. Editor: Theo Green. 50% freelance written. Quarterly magazine on experimental/avante garde literature and visuals. "Our readership is throughout the U.S. and Europe." Estab. 1983. Circ. 1,500. Pays on publication. Publishes ms an average of 6 months after acceptance. Byline given. Buys first North American serial rights and one-time rights. Submit seasonal/holiday material 1 year in advance. Simultaneous queries, and simultaneous, photocopied, and previously published submissions OK. SASE. Reports in 2 weeks on queries; 3 months on mss. Sample copy $3.

Nonfiction: Book excerpts, expose, inspirational, interview/profile, opinion, personal experience. Special issues include contempory German literature. (early 1986) and jazz (1985). No humor or anything nonliterary. Buys 2 mss/year. Query. Length: 1,000-2,000 words. Pays $25 maximum.

Fiction: Erotica, ethnic, experimental and novel excerpts. No science fiction or mainstream. Buys 10 mss/year. Query. Length: 1,000-2,000 words. Pays $25 maximum.

Poetry: Avant-garde and free verse. No traditional poetry. Buys 10 poems/year. Submit maximum 6 poems. Length: 2-100 lines. Pays $25 maximum.

Tips: "Write something off the wall, different. Visual writing is preferred. Fiction is most open to freelancers."

THE IOWA REVIEW, 369 EPB, The University of Iowa, Iowa City IA 52242. (319)353-6048. Editor: David Hamilton, with the help of colleagues, graduate assistants, and occasional guest editors. Magazine published 3 times/year. Buys first serial rights. Photocopied submissions OK. SASE. Reports in 3 months.

Nonfiction: "We publish essays, stories and poems and would like for our essays not always to be works of academic criticism." Buys 65-85 unsolicited mss/year. Submit complete ms. Pays $1/line for verse; $10/page for prose.

‡**IRON, From the North-East**, IRON Press, 5 Marden Terrace, Cullercoats, North Shields, Tyne & Wear NE30 4PD United Kingdom. (091)2531901. 80% freelance written. Literary magazine published three times/year including literature (poetry, fiction), and graphics. "We publish new, original writing (poetry prose). No special slant." Circ. 750. Pays on publication. Publishes ms an average of 10 months after acceptance. Byline given. Buys first United Kingdom serial rights. Computer printout submissions acceptable; no dot-matrix. SAE, IRC. Reports in 2 weeks on queries. Sample copy $4.

Fiction: Experimental, fantasy, humorous, mainstream and science fiction. Buys 20 mss/year. Send complete ms. Length: 200-7,000 words. Pays $15-70.

Poetry: Avant-garde, free verse, haiku, light verse and traditional. Nothing in the "greetings card" verse area. Buys 80/year. Submit maximum 5 poems. Length: 1-200 lines. Pays $5-50.

Artwork: Clare Brannen, art editor. "We also pay small amounts to artists for illustrations. These are commissioned, and artists should contact us first with samples of their work."

JAM TO-DAY, Box 249, Northfield VT 05663. Editors: Judith Stanford and Don Stanford. 90% freelance written. Annual literary magazine featuring high quality poetry, fiction and reviews. Especially interested in unknown or little-known authors. Circ. 300. Pays on publication. Publishes ms an average of 6 months after acceptance. Byline given. Buys first rights and nonexclusive anthology rights. Photocopied submissions OK. Computer printout submissions acceptable; prefers letter-quality to dot-matrix. SASE. Reports in 6 weeks. Sample copy $3.50 (includes postage).

Fiction: "We will consider quality fiction of almost any style or genre. However, we prefer not to receive material that is highly allegorical, abstruse, or heavily dependent on word play for its effect." Buys 1-2 mss/year. Send complete ms. Length: 1,500-7,500 words. Pays $5/page.

Poetry: Avant-garde, free verse, haiku and traditional. No light verse. Buys 30-50/year. Submit 5 poems maximum. Length: open. Pays $5/poem; higher payment for poems more than 3 pages in length.

JAPANOPHILE, Box 223, Okemos MI 48864. Editor: Earl Snodgrass. 80% freelance written. Quarterly magazine for literate people who are interested in Japanese culture anywhere in the world. Pays on publication. Publishes ms an average of 5 months after acceptance. Buys first North American serial rights. Previously published submissions OK. Computer printout submissions acceptable; no dot-matrix. SASE. Reports in 4 weeks. Sample copy $3, postpaid. Writer's guidelines with SASE.

Nonfiction: "We want material on Japanese culture in *North America or anywhere in the world*, even Japan. We want articles, preferably with pictures, about persons engaged in arts of Japanese origin: a Michigan naturalist who is a haiku poet, a potter who learned raku in Japan, a vivid 'I was there' account of a Go tournament in California. We use some travel articles if exceptionally well-written, but we are *not* a regional magazine about Japan. We are a little magazine, a literary magazine. Our particular slant is a certain kind of culture wherever it is in the world: Canada, the U.S., Europe, Japan. The culture includes flower arranging, haiku, religion, art, photography and fiction. It is important to study the magazine." Buys 8 mss/issue. Query preferred but not required. Length: 1,200 words maximum. Pays $8-15.

Photos: State availability of photos. Pays $10-20 for 8x10 b&w glossy prints.

Fiction: Experimental, mainstream, mystery, adventure, science fiction, humorous, romance and historical. Themes should relate to Japan or Japanese culture. Length: 1,000-10,000 words. Pays $20. Contest each year pays $100 to best short story.

Columns/Departments: Regular columns and features are Tokyo Scene and Profile of Artists. "We also need columns of Japanese culture in other cities." Query. Length: 1,000 words. Pays $20 maximum.

Poetry: Traditional, avant-garde and light verse related to Japanese culture or in a Japanese form such as haiku. Length: 3-50 lines. Pays $1-100.

Fillers: Newsbreaks, puzzles, clippings and short humor of up to 200 words. Pays $1-50.

Tips: "We prefer to see more articles about Japanese culture in the U.S., Canada and Europe." Lack of convincing fact and detail is a frequent mistake.

KALEIDOSCOPE, International Literary/Fine Art Magazine by Persons with Disabilities, Kaleidoscope Press, 326 Locust St., Akron OH 44302. (216)762-9755, ext. 474. Editor: Carson W. Heiner Jr. 75% freelance written. Semiannual magazine with international collection of literature and art by disabled/nondisabled people for writers, artists, and anyone interested in fine art and literature. Presents work sematic to disability in factual way, but not maudlin." Circ. 3,000. Pays on publication. Byline given. Buys first North American serial rights. Simultaneous queries, and photocopied and previously published submissions OK. Computer printout submissions acceptable. SASE. Reports in 6 months. Publishes ms an average of 6 months after acceptance. Free sample copy; writer's guidelines for SAE and 1 first class stamp.

Nonfiction: Book excerpts, reviews, historical/nostalgic, humor, inspirational, articles spotlighting arts/disability, interview/profile (on prominent disabled people in the arts), opinion, the craft of fiction, personal experience, photo feature and travel. Publishes 14 mss/year; purchases 2 mss/year. Query with clips if available or send complete ms. Length: 10,000 words maximum. Pays in contributor's copies or cash awards for top submissions.

Photos: No pay for photos except annual cash award for top submission and contributor's copies. Photographic art done by disabled artists. Reviews 3x5, 5x7 8x10 b&w and color prints. Captions and identification of subjects required.

Fiction: Experimental, fantasy, historical, horror, humorous, mainstream, mystery, religious, romance, science fiction, suspense. Short stories, plays, novel excerpts. Publishes 16 mss/year; purchases 4/year. Query with clips if available or send complete ms. Length: 10,000 words maximum.

Poetry: Avant-garde, free verse, haiku, light verse and traditional. Publishes 30 poems/year; purchases 4 poems/year. Submit maximum 6 poems. Length: open. Pays in contributor's copies or cash award for top submissions.

Fillers: Anecdotes and short humor. Length: open.

Tips: "Study the magazine and know the editorial requirements. Avoid triteness and stereotypes in all writing. Articles about arts programs for disabled people sought. Fiction and poetry are most open to freelancers. For fiction, have strong, believable characterizations. Poetry should be vivid and free of cliches." Magazine will add a children's literature section and a column about the theatre scene.

LETTERS, Mainspring Press, Box 905 W, Stonington ME 04681. (207)367-2484. Editor-in-Chief: Helen Nash. Publication of the Maine Writers' Workshop. 50% freelance written. Quarterly magazine for general literary audience. Circ. 6,500. Pays on acceptance. Publishes ms up to 10 months after acceptance. Buys all rights. Submit seasonal/holiday material 5 months in advance. Computer printout submissions acceptable; no dot-matrix. Reports in 1 month. SASE. Sample copy with SASE. Back copies are not free.

Nonfiction: "Any subject within moral standards and with quality writing style." Query. Buys 2-10 unsolicited mss/year. Length: 100-1,000 words. Pays 5¢/word. Pays expenses of writers on assignment.

Fiction: No pornography, confession, religious or western. Buys 5 mss/year. Pays 5¢/word.

Poetry: G.F. Bush, poetry editor. Serious and light verse, traditional, blank verse, humorous, narrative and avant-garde. Buys 15/year. Length: 30-42 lines. Pays maximum 50¢/line.

‡**LITERARY SKETCHES**, Box 711, Williamsburg VA 23187. (804)229-2901. Editor: Mary Lewis Chapman. Monthly newsletter for readers with literary interests; all ages. Circ. 500. Not copyrighted. Byline

given. Pays on publication. Photocopied and simultaneous submissions OK. SASE. Reports in 1 month. Sample copy for SASE.

Nonfiction: "We use only interviews of well-known writers and biographical material on past writers. Very informal style; concise. Centennial or bicentennial pieces relating to a writer's birth, death or famous works are usually interesting. Look up births of literary figures and start from there." Buys 12 mss/year. Submit complete ms. Length: 1,000 words maximum. Pays $1/2$¢/word.

LOS ANGELES TIMES BOOK REVIEW, Times Mirror, Times Mirror Sq., Los Angeles CA 90053. (213)972-7777. Editor: Jack Miles. 70% freelance written. Weekly tabloid reviewing current books. Circ. 1.3 million. Pays on publication. Publishes ms an average of 3 weeks after acceptance. Byline given. Offers variable kill fee. Buys first North American serial rights. Computer printout submissions acceptable; prefers letter-quality to dot-matrix. Accepts no unsolicited book reviews or requests for specific titles to review. "Query with published samples—book reviews or literary features." Buys 500 mss/year. Length: 150-1,500 words. Pays $50-250.

THE MALAHAT REVIEW, The University of Victoria, Box 1700, Victoria, British Columbia V8W 2Y2 Canada. Contact: Editor. 100% freelance written. Magazine published 4 times/year covering poetry, fiction, drama and criticism. Circ. 850. Pays on acceptance. Publishes ms up to 18 months after acceptance. Byline given. Offers 100% kill fee. Buys one-time rights. Photocopied submissions OK. Computer printout submissions acceptable; prefers letter-quality to dot-matrix. SASE (Canadian postage or IRC). Reports in 2 weeks on queries; 3 months on mss. Sample copy $6.

Nonfiction: Interview/profile (literary/artistic). Buys 6 mss/year. Send complete ms. Length: 1,000-5,000 words. Pays $30-150.

Photos: Pays $10-50 for b&w prints. Captions required.

Fiction: Buys 20 mss/year. Send complete ms. Length: 1,000-8,000 words. Pays $30-250.

Poetry: Avant-garde, free verse and traditional. Buys 100/year. Pays $12.50.

THE MASSACHUSETTS REVIEW, Memorial Hall, University of Massachusetts, Amherst MA 01003. (413)545-0111. Editors: John Hicks and Mary Heath. Quarterly. Pays on publication. Buys first North American serial rights. Computer printout submissions acceptable; prefers letter-quality to dot-matrix. Reports in 3 months. Mss will not be returned unless accompanied by SASE. Sample copy for $4 plus 50¢ postage.

Nonfiction: Articles on literary criticism, women, public affairs, art, philosophy, music and dance. Length: 6,500 words average. Pays $50.

Fiction: Short stories or chapters from novels when suitable for independent publication. Length: 15-22 typed pages. Pays $50.

Poetry: 35¢/line or $10 minimum.

MICHIGAN QUARTERLY REVIEW, 3032 Rackham Bldg., University of Michigan, Ann Arbor MI 48109. Editor: Laurence Goldstein. 75% freelance written. Quarterly. Circ. 2,000. Publishes ms an average of 1 year after acceptance. Pays on publication. Buys first serial rights. Computer printout submissions acceptable; no dot-matrix. SASE. Reports in 4 weeks for mss submitted in September-May; in summer, 8 weeks. Sample copy $2 with 2 first class stamps.

Nonfiction: "*MQR* is open to general articles directed at an intellectual audience. Essays ought to have a personal voice and engage a significant subject. Scholarship must be present as a foundation, but we are not interested in specialized essays directed only at professionals in the field. We prefer ruminative essays, written in a fresh style and which reach interesting conclusions." Length: 2,000-5,000 words. Pays $80-150, sometimes more.

Fiction and Poetry: No restrictions on subject matter or language. "We publish about 10 stories a year and are very selective. We like stories which are unusual in tone and structure, and innovative in language." Send complete ms. Pays $8-10/published page.

Tips: "Read the journal and assess the range of contents and the level of writing. We have no guidelines to offer or set expectations; every manuscript is judged on its unique qualities. On essays—query with a very thorough description of the argument and a copy of the first page. Watch for announcements of special issues, which are usually expanded issues and draw upon a lot of freelance writing. Be aware that this is a university quarterly that publishes a limited amount of fiction and poetry; that it is directed at an educated audience, one that has done a great deal of reading in all types of literature."

THE MICROPSYCHOLOGY NEWSLETTER, Microsphere Enterprises, 234 Fifth Ave., New York NY 10001. (212)462-8573. Editor: Joan Virzera. Quarterly literary and psychological newsletter for laypeople and professionals. Circ. 3,000. Pays on publication. Byline given. Offers 100% kill fee. Buys first North American serial rights and second serial (reprint) rights. Submit seasonal/holiday material 3 months in advance. Simultaneous queries, and simultaneous, photocopied, and previously published submissions OK. Computer printout submissions acceptable. SASE. Reports in 1 month. Sample copy $3; writer's guidelines for SASE.

Nonfiction: General interest, humor, inspirational, opinion and personal experience. "Nothing that does not conform to the theme—the importance of the seemingly trivial." Buys 25-50 mss/year. Send complete ms. Length: 1,200 words maximum. Pays variable rates and contributor copies.

Fiction: Experimental, humorous, mainstream, novel excerpts and psychological fiction. "High quality, literary with an emphasis on the theme of the newsletter—the importance of the seemingly trivial." Buys 25-50 mss/year. Send complete ms. Length: 2,000 words maximum. Pays variable rates and contributor copies.

Poetry: Avant-garde, free verse, haiku, light verse and traditional. Light verse and didactic poetry preferred. Buys 25-50 poems/year. No limit on number of poems submitted. Length: "short poems preferred."

Fillers: Short humor. Buys 25-50/year. Length: 500 words maximum. Pays variable rates and contributor copies.

Tips: "Micropsychology is an area dealing with the importance of the seemingly trivial, such as minor irritations and daily frustrations that affect people on a level beyond awareness. A significant aspect of micropsychology is humor therapy—seeing problems with humor alleviates associated stress. I am looking for any well-written material conforming to this theme. I will not hesitate to publish never-published writers whose material is of high quality and applicable." No political or vulgar material. Buys art and photography, psychologically-oriented photos, illustrations and cartoons (10-20/year).

MID-AMERICAN REVIEW, Dept. of English, Bowling Green State University, Bowling Green OH 43403. (419)372-2725. Editor: Robert Early. 100% freelance written. Semiannual literary magazine of "the highest quality fiction and poetry." Also publishes critical articles and book reviews of contemporary literature. Pays on publication. Publishes ms an average of 3 months after acceptance. Byline given. Buys one-time rights. Do not query. Photocopied submissions OK. SASE. Reports in 2 months or less. Sample copy $4.50.

Fiction: Character-oriented, literary. Buys 12 mss/year. Send complete ms. Pays $5/page up to $75.

Poetry: Strong imagery, strong sense of vision. Buys 60/year. Pays $5/page. Annual prize for best fiction, best poem.

Tips: "We want quality fiction and poetry—nothing more or less."

MISSISSIPPI ARTS & LETTERS, Persons Publishing, Box 3510, Hattiesburg MS 39403-3510. (601)545-2949. Editor: Alec Clayton. Managing Editor: Gabi Clayton. 75% freelance written. Bimonthly magazine on the arts in Mississippi. Circ. 2,500. Pays on publication. Publishes ms an average of 3 months after acceptance. Byline given. Buys first serial rights and second (reprint) rights. Submit seasonal/holiday material 6 months in advance. Simultaneous queries, photocopied, and previously published submissions OK. Computer printout submissions acceptable; prefers letter-quality to dot-matrix. SASE. Reports in 4 weeks on queries; 2 months on mss. Sample copy for 8x10 SAE and 3 first class stamps; writer's guidelines for business size SAE and 1 first class stamp.

Nonfiction: Historical/nostalgic; how-to (relative to arts, crafts, photos, etc.); interview/profile; and photo feature. Buys 18-20 mss/year. Query with published clips. Length: 500-3,000 words (once in a while longer). Pays average ½¢/word (from copies to $50 maximum).

Photos: State availibility of photos. Reviews 5x7 or 8x10 b&w prints. Captions and identification of subjects required. Buys one-time rights.

Columns/Departments: "All columns done by staff except reviews." Book Reviews and In a Nutshell (short news items on arts). June/July issue is "a special fiction issue featuring writers from the deep South." Buys 18-20 mss/year. Send complete ms. Length: 1,000-5,000 words. Pays approximately ½¢/word for Book Reviews; pays in copies for news items.

Fiction: Experimental, fantasy, historical, horror, humorous, mainstream, mystery, novel excerpts, science fiction and suspense. No genre submissions. June/July issue is "a special fiction issue featuring writers from the deep South." Buys 18-20 mss/year. Send complete ms with cover letter. Length: 500-8,000 words. Pays $5-100.

Poetry: Avant-garde, free verse, haiku, light verse and traditional. No "mushy love poems." Buys 20 poems/year. Submit maximum 10 poems. Pays in copies for minimal amount.

Fillers: Clippings and short humor. "Most short articles and fillers are staff written. We do not have a policy of buying fillers, but you never know."

Tips: "A freelancer can break into our publication with a good personality profile/interview with someone important in the arts with strong connections to the state of Mississippi (i.e., Leontyne Price or Willie Morris); also fiction. We want good writing with a Southern setting."

MISSOURI REVIEW, University of Missouri, 231 Arts & Science, Columbia MO 65211. (314)882-6066. Editor: Speer Morgan. Managing Editor: Greg Michalson. Triannual magazine. Circ. 2,000. Pays on publication. Byline given. Offers negotiable kill fee. Buys first North American serial rights. Simultaneous queries and simultaneous submissions (when indicated by cover letter), and photocopied submissions OK. Reports in 1 month on queries; 10 weeks on mss. Sample copy $4.

Nonfiction: "Informed/informal essays of literary interest" and criticism. Buys 10-12 mss/year. Query with published clips or send complete ms. Pays $10/page minimum to $500 (for a lead essay) maximum.

Fiction: Bill Peden, fiction editor. "We want fiction with a distinctly contemporary orientation." No young adult material. Buys 20-30 mss/year. Send complete ms. Pays $10/page minimum to $300 maximum.
Poetry: Sherod Santos or Garrett Hongs, poetry editors. Buys 100 poems/year. Submit maximum 6 poems. Pays $10 minimum.
Tips: Address submissions to correct department editors. Don't mix genres in a single submission.

NEW OREGON REVIEW, Transition Publications (a nonprofit corporation), 537 NE Lincoln St., Hillsboro OR 97124. (503)640-1375. Editor: Steven Dimeo, Ph.D. 100% freelance written. Semiannual magazine with short stories and poetry. "We seek to publish fiction of lasting literary merit from both unacknowledged and well-established artists who recognize the time-honored values of literary excellence. Our magazine is for the literate and learned who prefer strong, interesting narratives of substance rather than dry academic fiction." Circ. 200. Pays on publication. Publishes ms an average of 15 months after acceptance. Byline given. Buys first North American serial rights. Submit seasonal/holiday material 6 months in advance. Photocopied submissions OK, "but only if they're clear, legible and neat. Submissions must include short bio/bibliographical statement and should be neat and professional." SASE. Reports in 2 months on mss. Sample copy $3 and 56¢ postage; writer's guidelines for business size SAE and 1 first class stamp.
Photos: Send photos with ms. Prefers "imaginative, moody b&w glossies or line drawings, especially nudes, landscapes and portraits." Reviews negatives and prints. Pays $10/photo; $25/cover photo. Model release required. Buys one-time rights.
Fiction: Fantasy, horror, humorous, mainstream, mystery, science fiction, suspense, nostalgia and erotica. "In fiction we're looking primarily for the well-developed tale with thematic depth, skillful characterization, wit, dramatic change, subtle foreshadowing and imaginative symbolism. We want nothing unduly experimental, moralistic or trite. We prefer stories about male/female relationships." Buys 4-6 mss/year. Send complete ms. Length: 3,000-5,000 words (occasionally longer). Pays $25 flat fee. Annual contest for subscribers only.
Poetry: Free verse and traditional. "We're *always* overstocked and consider only poems of exceptional merit, usually from well-established writers, that demonstrate careful attention to rhyme, rhythm, internal tonal integrity, and progressive development from beginning to end. Contributors should write in the tradition of Emily Dickinson, W.B. Yeats, Robert Frost, W.H. Auden, Theodore Roethke, etc. We automatically reject poems encumbered with Cummingsesque affectations (lower-case letters, little or no punctuation, etc.) that do not in some way echo the sense." Buys 6-10 poems/year. Submit maximum 5 poems. Length: 12-40 lines. Pays $10/flat fee.
Tips: "A freelancer can best break into our publication with fiction. Authors we admire include John Collier, Roald Dahl, Kurt Vonnegut, Franz Kafka and Mark Twain. We're always in the market for realistic narratives laced with horror or the fantastic in the manner of William Faulkner's 'A Rose for Emily' or John Cheever's 'The Enormous Radio'. We prefer stories that focus on relationships."

the new renaissance, An International Magazine of Ideas and Opinions, Emphasizing Literature and the Arts, 9 Heath Road, Arlington MA 02174. Editor: Louise T. Reynolds. 92% + freelance written. International biannual literary magazine covering literature, visual arts, ideas, opinions for general literate, sophisticated public. Circ. 1,500. Pays after publication. Publishes ms an average of 16 months after acceptance. Buys all rights. Simultaneous queries and photocopied submissions OK if so notified. Computer printout submissions acceptable; prefers letter-quality to dot-matrix. Does not read any ms without SASE. Answers no queries without SASE or stamped postcards. Does not read mss during July, August and December of any year. Reports in 1 month on queries; 7 months on mss. Sample copy $5.10 for back issues; $4.30 recent issue; $5.60 current issue.
Nonfiction: Interview/profile (literary/performing artists); opinion; and literary/artistic essays. "We prefer expert opinion in a style suitable for a literary magazine (i.e., *not* journalistic). Send in complete manuscript or essays. Because we are biannual, we prefer to have writers query us, with outlines, etc., on political/sociological articles and give a sample of their writing." Buys 2-5 mss/year. Query with published clips. SASE. Length: 11-35 pages. Pays $24-95.
Photos: State availability of photos or send photos with query. Pays $5-7 for 5x7 b&w prints. Captions, model release, and identification of subjects required, if applicable. Buys one-time rights.
Fiction: No fiction before January 1, 1986. Quality fiction, well-crafted, serious; occasionally, experimental. No "formula or plotted stories; no pulp or woman's magazine fiction. We are looking for writing with a personal voice." Buys 5-12 mss/year. Send complete ms. Length: 2-35 pages. On ms 4 pp. or less, send 3 stories *only*; 10 pp. or less, 2 stories only; over 11 pp., send only 1 story. Pays $20-60.
Poetry: Stanwood Bolton, poetry editor. No poetry before January 1, 1986. Avant-garde, free verse, light verse, traditional, and translations (with originals). No heavily academic poetry; we publish only occasional light verse and do not want to see 'Hallmark Card' writing. Submit maximum 6 average length poems; 8 short; 2-3 long poems. Reports in 4 months. Buys 20-49 poems/year. Pays $10-30.
Tips: "Know your markets. We still receives manuscripts that, had the writer any understanding of our publication, would have been directed elsewhere. *tnr* is a unique litmag and should be *carefully* perused. Close reading of one or two issues will reveal that we have a classicist philosophy and want manuscripts that hold up to re-

readings. Fiction and poetry are especially open to freelancers. Writers most likely to break in to *tnr* are serious writers, poets, those who feel'compelled' to write. We don't want to see 'pop' writing, trendy or formula writing. Nor do we want writing where the 'statement' is imposed on the story, or writing where the author shows off his superior knowledge or sensibility. If we've rejected your work and our comments make some sense to you, keep on submitting to us. But always send us your best work. Writers frequently don't know how to structure or organize for greatest impact, and don't feel deeply enough about the subject to revise or re-write. Do not submit anything in July, August or December. Submissions during those months will be returned unread."

THE NEW SOUTHERN LITERARY MESSENGER, The Airplane Press, 400 S. Laurel St., Richmond VA 23220. (804)780-1244. Editor: Charles Lohmann. 100% freelance written. Quarterly literary tabloid featuring short stories and political satire. Circ. 500. Pays on publication. Publishes ms an average of 2 months after acceptance. Byline given. Buys first serial rights and second (reprint) rights. Queries and previously published submissions OK. SASE. Reports in 1 week on queries; 6 weeks on mss. Sample copy for $1, and SAE with 3 first class stamps; writer's guidelines for 4x9 SASE.
Fiction: Short prose and political satire. Avoid fantasy and science fiction. No formula short stories. Buys 16-20 mss/year. Query. Length: 500-2,500 words. Pays $5.
Tips: "Reading computer printout manuscripts, an editor is often troubled by the thought that perhaps the author spent less time writing than the editor does reading."

NIMROD, 2210 S. Main, Tulsa OK 74114. (918)584-3333. Editor: Francine Ringold. 100% freelance written. For readers and writers interested in good literature and art. Semiannual magazine; 120 (6x9) pages. Circ. 1,500. Payment in contributor's copies. Publishes ms an average of 5 months after acceptance. Byline given. Buys first serial rights only. Photocopied submissions OK, but they must be very clear. Computer printout submissions acceptable; no dot-matrix. SASE. Reports up to 3 months.
Nonfiction: Interviews and essays. Buys 150 unsolicited mss/year. Query or submit complete ms. Length: open.
Fiction: Experimental and mainstream fiction.
Poetry: Traditional forms of poetry, blank verse, free verse and avant-garde forms.
Tips: *Nimrods* sponsors unusual Awards in poetry and fiction: Pablo Neruda Prize (poetry) and Katherine Anne Porter Prize (fiction). First prize in each category is $1,000; second prize is $500. Winners and judges are flown to Tulsa for reading and Awards dinner. Entry deadline is April 21. Send SASE for competition guidelines.

THE NORTH AMERICAN REVIEW, University of Northern Iowa, Cedar Falls IA 50614. (319)273-2681. Editor: Robley Wilson Jr. 50% freelance written. Quarterly. Circ. 4,000. Buys all rights for nonfiction and North American serial rights for fiction and poetry. Pays on acceptance. Publishes ms an average of 1 year after acceptance. Computer printout submissions acceptable; prefers letter-quality to dot-matrix. Familiarity with magazine helpful. SASE. Reports in 10 weeks. Sample copy $2.
Nonfiction: No restrictions, but most nonfiction is commissioned by magazine. Query. Rate of payment arranged.
Fiction: No restrictions; highest quality only. Length: open. Pays minimum $10/page. Fiction department closed (no mss read) from April 1 to December 31.
Poetry: Peter Cooley, department editor. No restrictions; highest quality only. Length: open. Pays 50¢/line minimum.

‡**OHIO RENAISSANCE REVIEW**, Infinity Publications, Box 804, Ironton OH 45638. (614)532-0846/533-9276. Editor: James R. Pack. 100% freelance written. Quarterly magazine on general literature. "*Ohio Renaissance Review* combines contemporary poetry; science fiction, fantasy, and mystery prose; and creative art and photography into a total literary statement. We believe so strongly that we can make the magazine a leading voice in literature today that we have awarded life merit subscriptions to a number of famous people all over the world, from poets and novelists to performing artists and world leaders. So far, their response has been warm and congratulatory." Estab. 1984. Circ. 500. Pays on publication. Publishes ms an average of 3 months after acceptance. Byline given. Buys first North American serial rights. Photocopied submissions OK. Computer printout submissions acceptable; no dot-matrix. SASE. Reports in 6 weeks. Sample copy $4; writer's guidelines $1.
Photos: Ariyan, graphics editor. Send photos with query or ms. Reviews b&w 5x7 prints. Pays $10. Buys one-time rights.
Fiction: Experimental, fantasy, horror, mystery, science fiction and suspense. Buys 35 mss/year. Send complete ms. Length: 400-2,000 words. Pays $2.50/full printed column; 5¢/line/partial printed column.
Poetry: Ron Houchin, poetry editor. Free verse. No traditional, rhyming or abstraction. Buys 80 poems/year. Length: open. Pays 25¢/line; $5 maximum.

THE OHIO REVIEW, Ellis Hall, Ohio University, Athens OH 45701. (614)594-5889. Editor: Wayne Dodd. 40% freelance written. Published 3 times/year. "A balanced, informed engagement of contemporary American letters, with special emphasis on poetics." Circ. 2,000. Publishes ms an average of 6 months after acceptance. Rights acquired vary with author and material; usually buys first serial rights or first North American serial rights. Submit complete ms. Unsolicited material will be read only September-May. Computer printout submissions acceptable. SASE. Reports in 10 weeks.

Nonfiction, Fiction and Poetry: Buys essays of general intellectual and special literary appeal. Not interested in narrowly focused scholarly articles. Seeks writing that is marked by clarity, liveliness, and perspective. Interested in the best fiction and poetry. Buys 75 unsolicited mss/year. Pays minimum $5/page, plus copies.

Tips: "Make your query very brief, not gabby—one that describes some publishing history, but no extensive bibliographies. We publish mostly poetry—short fiction, some book reviews. Generally short length material."

ORBIS, An International Quarterly of Poetry and Prose, 199 The Long Shoot, Nuneaton, Warwickshire CV11 6JQ England. Tel. (0203)327440. Editor: Mike Shields. 75% freelance written. Quarterly magazine covering literature in English and other languages. Circ. 500 (in 30 countries). Pays on publication. Publishes ms an average of 6 months after acceptance. Extra prizes totalling 50 pounds in each issue. Byline given. Buys first serial rights. Photocopied submissions OK. Computer printout submissions acceptable; prefers letter-quality to dot-matrix. SAE, IRCs. Reports in 6 weeks. Sample copy $2; writer's guidelines for 3 IRCs (*not* U.S. postage stamps).

Nonfiction: Literary criticism, how to write poetry, and how to develop a literary work. "No excessively literary or academically pretentious work; keep it practical. Wild avant-garde or ultra-traditional work unlikely to be used." Buys few mss/year. "We reject more than 98% of work received for simple lack of space, so don't be disappointed." Send complete ms. Length: 1,200 words maximum. Pays £2.

Columns/Departments: Letters (not paid for); Past Master (not paid for), "poem from the past accompanied by about 100 words on 'why' "; and Poem in Progress (description of how a favorite poem was developed). Pays £2.

Fiction: "We are looking for short (1,200 words) pieces of original and interesting work; prose poems, mood pieces, short stories, etc. No 'magazine' or 'formula' fiction." Buys few mss/year. Send complete ms. Length: 1,200 words maximum. Pays £2.

Poetry: Free verse, light verse and traditional. "We do not specifically exclude any type of poetry, but we feel that there are far too many undistinguished haiku around, and we will not publish the meaningless gobbledegook which has featured in many magazines recently. No unoriginal rhymed poetry. We are looking for original poems which communicate modern thought and expression and show an excellence of language. Length is not a major factor, but we cannot handle *very* long poems. We also use American poetry, long poems, English dialect poems and translated poetry." Buys 250/year. Submit maximum 6 poems. Length: "over 100 lines may be difficult." Pays £2. U.S. stamps cannot be used to return material from the U.K.; IRCs should be enclosed. Acts as sponsor for three major international poetry competitions per year; prizes already paid thousands of pounds total. Also features evaluative index of other magazines, regularly updated.

PARABOLA, 150 5th Ave., New York NY 10011. (212)924-0004. Editor: Lorraine Kisly. Executive Editor: Jeff Zaleski. "Audience shares an interest in exploring the wisdom transmitted through myth and the great religious traditions." Quarterly magazine; 128 pages. Circ. 15,000. Buys all rights. Byline given. Pays on publication. Photocopied submissions OK. Manuscripts should be sent to the attention of the editors. SASE. Writer's guidelines for SASE.

Nonfiction: "We handle work from a wide range of perspectives, mostly related to myth or comparative religion. Don't be scholarly, don't footnote, don't be dry. We want fresh approaches to timeless subjects." Length: 3,500 words maximum. Buys 25 mss/year. Query. Pays $25-150.

Photos: Purchased with or without accompanying ms. No color. Pays $25.

Fiction: Prefers retellings of traditional stories, legends and myths. Length: 1,500 words maximum. Pays "negotiable rates."

Poetry: "Very little and only when theme-related."

THE PARIS REVIEW, 45-39 171st Place, Flushing NY 11358. Editor: George A. Plimpton. Quarterly. Buys all rights. Pays on publication. Address submissions to proper department and address. Computer printout submissions acceptable; no dot-matrix. SASE.

Fiction: Study publication. No length limit. Pays up to $250. Makes award of $500 in annual fiction contest. Submit to 541 E. 72nd St., New York NY 10021.

Poetry: Study publication. Pays $10 to 25 lines; $15 to 50 lines; $25 to 100 lines; $50 thereafter. Poetry mss must be submitted to Jonathan Galassi at 541 E. 72nd St., New York NY 10021. SASE. Sample copy $6.

PARTISAN REVIEW, 141 Bay State Rd., Boston MA 02215. (617)353-4260. Editor: William Phillips. Executive Editor: Edith Kurzweil. 90% freelance written. Quarterly literary journal covering world literature, politics and contemporary culture for an intelligent public with emphasis on the arts and political/social commentary. Circ. 8,200. Pays on publication. Publishes ms an average of 9 months after acceptance. Buys first serial rights. Byline given. Photocopied submissions OK. SASE. Reports in 6 months. Sample copy $4.50; free writer's guidelines.

Nonfiction: Essays and book reviews. Buys 30-40 mss/year. Send complete ms. Pays $50-150.

Fiction: High quality, serious and contemporary fiction. No science fiction, mystery, confession, romantic or religious material. Buys 8-10 mss/year. Send complete ms. Pays $50-150.

Poetry: Buys 20/year. Submit maximum 6 poems. Pays $25.

PIG IRON MAGAZINE, Pig Iron Press, Box 237, Youngstown OH 44501. (216)744-2258. Editors-in-Chief: Jim Villani and Rose Sayre. 90% freelance written. Annual magazine emphasizing literature/art for writers, artists and intelligent lay audience interested in popular culture. Circ. 1,500. Buys one-time rights. Pays on publication. Byline given. Photocopied and previously published submissions OK. Computer printout submissions acceptable. SASE. Reports in 4 months. Publishes ms an average of 18 months after acceptance. Sample copy $2.50; writer's guidelines with SASE.

Nonfiction: General interest, interview, personal opinion, criticism, new journalism and lifestyle/systems. Buys 3 mss/year. Query. Length: 8,000 words maximum. Pays $2/page minimum.

Photos: Submit photo material with query. Pays $2 minimum for 5x7 or 8x10 b&w glossy prints. Buys one-time rights.

Fiction: Fantasy, avant-garde, experimental, psychological fiction and metafiction, humor, western and frontier. Buys 4-12 mss/issue. Submit complete ms. Length: 8,000 words maximum. Pays $2 minimum.

Poetry: Terry Murcko and George Peffer, poetry editors. Avant-garde and free verse. Buys 25-50/issue. Submit in batches of 5 or less. Length: open. Pays $2 minimum.

Tips: "Send one story at a time. Show us your ability to remake the conventions of story telling. We are looking for poetry and fiction by Third World writers: send to Attention, Third World Issue. We are interested in modernistic, surreal, satirical, futuristic and political subjects. Upcoming thematic issues inclue humor, the Wild West, and Third World.

PLOUGHSHARES, Box 529, Dept. M, Cambridge MA 02139. Editor: DeWitt Henry. Quarterly magazine for "readers of serious contemporary literature: students, educators, adult public." Circ. 3,400. Pays on publication. Rights purchased vary with author and material; usually buys all rights or may buy first North American serial rights. Photocopied submissions OK. SASE. Reports in 6 months. Sample copy $5.

Nonfiction, Poetry and Fiction: Highest quality poetry, fiction and criticism. Interview and literary essays. Buys 25-50 unsolicited mss/year. Length: 5,000 words maximum. Pays $50. Reviews (assigned). Length: 500 words maximum. Pays $15. Fiction: experimental and mainstream. Length: 300-6,000 words. Pays $5-50. Poetry: buys traditional forms, blank verse, free verse and avant-garde. Length: open. Pays $10/poem.

PRAIRIE SCHOONER, Andrews Hall, University of Nebraska, Lincoln NE 68588. Editor: Hugh Luke. Poetry Editor: Hilda Raz. 100% freelance written. Quarterly. Pays in copies of offprints and prizes. Publishes ms an average of 1 year after acceptance. Acquires all rights, but rights will be reverted to author upon request after publication. Computer printout submissions acceptable; prefers letter-quality to dot-matrix. Reports in 3 months. SASE.

Nonfiction: Uses 1-2 articles/issue. Subjects of literary or general interest. No academic articles. Length: 5,000 words maximum.

Fiction: Uses several stories/issue.

Poetry: Uses 20-30 poems in each issue of the magazine. These may be on any subject, in any style. Occasional long poems are used, but preference is for shorter length. High quality necessary.

PRISM INTERNATIONAL, Department of Creative Writing, University of British Columbia, Vancouver, British Columbia V6T 1W5 Canada. Editor-in-Chief: Michael Pacey. Managing Editor: Lasha Seniuk. 100% freelance written. Quarterly magazine emphasizing contemporary literature, including translations. For university and public libraries, and private subscribers. Circ. 1,000. Pays on publication. Publishes ms an average of 3 months after acceptance. Buys first North American serial rights. Photocopied submissions OK. Computer printout submissions acceptable; prefers letter-quality to dot-matrix. SAE, IRCs. Reports in 10 weeks. Sample copy $4.

Fiction: Experimental and traditional. Buys 3 mss/issue. Send complete ms. Length: 5,000 words maximum. Pays $15/printed page and 1-year subscription.

Poetry: Avant-garde and traditional. Buys 30 poems/issue. Submit maximum 6 poems. Pays $15/printed page and 1-year subscription.

Drama: One-acts preferred. Pays $15/printed page and 1-year subscription.

Tips: "The writer has a better chance of breaking in at our publication with short articles and fillers."

QUARRY, Quarry Press, Box 1061, Kingston, Ontario K7L 4Y5 Canada. (613)544-5400, ext. 165. Editor: Bob Hilderley. 99% freelance written. Quarterly magazine covering poetry, prose, reviews. "We seek high quality new writers who are aware of their genre and who are committed to their art." Circ. 1,500. Pays on publication. Publishes ms an average of 6 months after publication. Byline given. Buys first North American serial rights. Simultaneous queries and photocopied submissions OK. Computer printout submission acceptable; prefers letter-quality to dot-matrix. SASE. Reports in 3 weeks on queries; 3 months on mss. Sample copy $3; writer's guidelines for business size SAE and 65¢ in IRCs.
Nonfiction: Short stories, poetry and book reviews. "We need book reviews of Canadian work. We are not interested in reviews of American or United Kingdom books. No literary criticism." Buys 100 mss/year. Send complete ms. Length: open. Pays $5-$10/page plus 1 year subscription.
Fiction: Any short fiction of high quality. "No nonliterary fiction." Send complete ms. Length: 10-15 pages maximum. Pays $5-10/page.
Poetry: Avant-garde, free verse, haiku, light verse and traditional. "No amateur, derivative poetry." Buys 200/year. Submit maximum 10 poems. Length: open. Pays $5-10/page.
Tips: "The most annoying aspect of working with freelance writers is Americans who send SASE with U.S. postage, forgetting that Canada is a foreign country."

QUEEN'S QUARTERLY, A Canadian Review, Queen's University, Kingston, Ontario K7L 3N6 Canada. (613)547-6968. Editors: Dr. Grant Amyot and Mrs. Marcia Stayer. Quarterly magazine covering a wide variety of subjects, including: science, humanities, arts and letters, politics, and history for the educated reader. 15% freelance written. Circ. 1,900. Pays on publication. Publishes ms an average of 1 year after acceptance. Byline given. Buys first North American serial rights. Photocopied submissions OK. Computer printout submissions acceptable; prefers letter-quality to dot-matrix. SASE. Reports in 2 weeks on queries; 3 months on mss. Sample copy $4; free writer's guidelines.
Fiction: Fantasy, historical, humorous, mainstream and science fiction. Buys 4-6 mss/year. Send complete ms. Length: 5,000 words maximum. Pays $25-100.
Poetry: Avant-garde, free verse, haiku, light verse and traditional. No "sentimental, religious, or first efforts by unpublished writers". Buys 25/year. Submit maximum six poems. Length: open. Pays $10-25.
Tips: "Poetry and fiction are most open to freelancers. Include curriculum vita and brief description of what's unique about the submission. Don't send less than the best." No multiple submissions. No more than 6 poems or one story per submission. We buy just a few freelance submissions."

RAMPIKE MAGAZINE, An Arts & Writing Journal, 95 Rivercrest Rd., Toronto, Ontario M6S 4H7 Canada. (416)767-6713. Editor: Karl E. Jirgens. Managing Editor: Eddy Nova. 100% freelance written. Triannual magazine covering post-modern (contemporary) art and writing. "*Rampike* is interested in artists and writers who are pioneers in their field. We have a different theme with each issue, and potential collaborators should contact the editors in advance." Circ. 2,000. Pays on publication and as per mutual agreement. Publishes ms an average of 9 months after acceptance. Byline given. Buys first serial rights; "all rights remain with contributor. Submit seasonal/holiday material 1 month in advance. Photocopied submissions OK. Electronic submissions OK, but requires hard copy also. Computer printout submissions acceptable. SASE. Reports in 1 month. Sample copy $5; writer's guidelines for 4x9½ SAE.
Nonfiction: Book excerpts, expose, humor, interview/profile, photo feature, technical, scientific and academic. No material that doesn't fit the theme or does not show awareness of post-modern editorial bias. Buys 50 mss/year. Query with or without published clips or send complete ms (photocopy only). Length: 2,000-6,000 words. Pays 0-$100.
Photos: Fausto Bedoya, photo editor. State availability of photos or send photos with query or ms. Pays 0-$100 for 6x16 b&w prints on theme. Captions, model release, and identification of subjects required. Buys one-time rights.
Fiction: Adventure, confession, erotica, experimental, fantasy, historical, horror, humorous, mystery, novel excerpts, romance, science fiction, serialized novels, suspense, academic and scientific. No material that is not post-modern or not on theme. Buys 50 mss/year. Query with or without published clips or send complete ms (photocopy only). Length: 2,000-6,000 words. Pays 0-$100.
Poetry: Fausto Bedoya, poetry editor. Avant-garde and free verse. No off-theme or nonpostmodern poetry. Buys 50 poems/year. Submit maximum 12 poems. Length: 5-120 lines. Pays 0-$100.
Tips: "Contact editors, have a strong interest in post-modern developments, and be aware of other artists and writers working in contemporary field. We are most interested in experimental or avant-garde fiction."

SECOND COMING, Box 31249, San Francisco CA 94131. Editor-in-Chief: A.D. Winans. 75% freelance written. Semiannual magazine. Circ. 1,000. Pays in copies. Publishes ms an average of 9 months after acceptance. Acquires one-time rights. Query first with an "honest statement of credits." Computer printout submissions acceptable; prefers letter-quality to dot-matrix. SASE. Reports in 4 weeks. Sample copy $3; Second Coming Anthology (ten years in retrospect) $6.95.
Fiction: Experimental (avant-garde) and humorous. Uses 6-12 mss/year. Submit complete ms. Length: 1,000-

3,000 words. Pays in copies.
Poetry: Avant-garde, free verse and surrealism. Uses 100-150/year. Submit maximum 6 poems. No length requirement. Pays in copies.
Photos: Pays $5 token plus copies for b&w photos.
Tips: "We publish mostly veterans of the small press scene. Read at least one back issue."

SEWANEE REVIEW, University of the South, Sewanee TN 37375. (615)598-5931. Editor: George Core. 60% freelance written. Quarterly magazine for audience of "variable ages and locations, mostly college-educated and with interest in literature." Circ. 3,600. Buys first serial rights and second serial (reprint) rights for anthologies. Pays on publication. Publishes ms an average of 9 months after acceptance. Computer printout submissions acceptable; prefers letter-quality to dot-matrix. Reports in 1 month. SASE. Sample copy $4.75, writers guidelines for SAE with 1 first class stamp.
Nonfiction and Fiction: Short fiction (but not drama); essays of critical nature on literary subjects (especially modern British and American literature); and essay-reviews and reviews (books and reviewers selected by the editor). Length: 5,000-7,500 words. Payment varies: averages $12/printed page.
Poetry: Selections of 4 to 6 poems preferred. In general, light verse and translations not acceptable. Maximum payment is 60¢ per line.

‡**SING HEAVENLY MUSE!**, Women's Poetry & Prose, Sing Heavenly Muse!, Box 13299, Minneapolis MN 55414. (612)822-8713. Editor: Sue Ann Martinson. Literary journal published 2 times/year on women's literature. "*Sing Heavenly Muse!* was founded to foster the work of women poets, fiction writers, and artists and to recognize women's diversity, intelligence, and talent, as well as their need to share perspectives. The journal is feminist in an open, generous sense: we encourage women to range freely, honestly, and imaginatively over all subjects, philosophies, and styles." Circ. 1,000. Pays on publication. Byline given. Buys first North American serial rights. Seasonal/holiday material is generally accepted between April 1 and May 1 and August 1 and September 1. SASE. Sample copy $3.50; free writer's guidelines.
Fiction: Women's writing of all types. "We do not wish to confine women to "women's subjects," whether these are defined traditionally, in terms of feminity and domesticity, or modernly, from a sometimes narrow polemical perspective. We look for explanations, questions that do not come with ready-made answers, emotionally or intellectually; and we welcome men's work that shows an awareness of women's consciousness. Buys 10 mss/year. Query. Length: 5,000 words. Pays $20-50.
Poetry: Avant-garde, free verse, haiku and traditional; women's. No sexist poetry. Buys 30-40/year. Submit maximum 10 poems. Length: 200 lines maximum. Pays $20-50.

‡**THE SOUTHERN CALIFORNIA ANTHOLOGY**, The Master of Professional Writing Program, D.C.C. 211, University of Southern California, Los Angeles CA 90089. (213)743-8255. Editor: Michael McLaughlin. Managing Editor: Chris Westphal. 25% freelance written. Annual literary magazine about contemporary literature. "We want honest, heartfelt writing with consistency of tone, regardless of style." Circ. 2,500. Pays on publication. Publishes ms an average of 3 months after acceptance. Rights revert to author. Submit seasonal/holiday material 3 months in advance. Photocopied submissions OK. Computer printout submissions acceptable; no dot-matrix. SASE. Reports in 1 month on queries; 3 months on mss. Sample copy $9.50; writer's guidelines for SAE.
Photos: Accepts only photos which accompany interviews.
Fiction: Steve Corbin, fiction editor. Erotica, ethnic, experimental, humorous and novel excerpts. No mainstream, religious, confession, romance or sci-fi. Buys 15 mss/year. Send complete ms. Length: 500-6,275 words. Pays $25-100.
Poetry: Carole Fuchs, poetry editor. Avant-garde, free verse and haiku. No traditional. Buys 20 poems/year. Submit maximum 8 poems. "If a good epic poem crosses our desks, we'll print it." Pays $10 maximum.
Tips: "The only nonfiction area open for freelancers is interviews."

THE SOUTHERN REVIEW, 43 Allen Hall, Louisiana State University, Baton Rouge LA 70803. (504)388-5108. Editors: James Olney and Lewis Simpson. 90% freelance written. Quarterly magazine for academic, professional, literary, intellectual audience. Circ. 3,000. Buys first serial rights only. Byline given. Pays on publication. Publishes ms an average of 18 months after acceptance. Sample copy $2.50. No queries. Reports in 2 to 3 months. Computer printout submissions acceptable; prefers letter-quality to dot-matrix. SASE.
Nonfiction: Essays with careful attention to craftsmanship and technique and to seriousness of subject matter. "Willing to publish experimental writing if it has a valid artistic purpose. Avoid extremism and sensationalism. Essays exhibit thoughtful and sometimes severe awareness of the necessity of literary standards in our time." Emphasis on contemporary literature, especially Southern culture and history. Minimum number of footnotes. Buys 80-100 mss/year. Length: 4,000-10,000 words. Pays $12/page for prose.
Fiction and Poetry: Short stories of lasting literary merit, with emphasis on style and technique. Length: 4,000-8,000 words. Pays $12/page for prose; $20/page for poetry.

SOUTHWEST REVIEW, Box 4374, Southern Methodist University, Dallas TX 75275. (214)692-3736. Editor: Willard Spiegelman. 96% freelance written. Quarterly magazine for "adults and college graduates with literary interests and some interest in the Southwest, but subscribers are from all over America and some foreign countries." Circ. 1,400. Pays on publication. Buys first North American and all rights. Byline given. Buys 65 mss/year. Reports in 3 months. SASE. Sample copy $2.50.
Nonfiction: "Literary criticism, social and political problems, history (especially Southwestern), folklore (especially Southwestern), the arts, etc. Articles should be appropriate for literary quarterly; no feature stories. Critical articles should consider writer's whole body of work, not just one book. History should use new primary sources or new perspective, not syntheses of old material." Interviews with writers, historical articles, and book reviews of scholarly nonfiction. Query. Length: 1,500 words.
Fiction: No limitations on subject matter for fiction; high literary quality is only criterion. Prefers stories of experimental and mainstream. Submit complete ms. Length: 1,500-5,000 words. The John H. McGinnis Memorial Award of $1,000 made in alternate years for fiction and nonfiction pieces that appeared in *SWR* during preceding two years.
Poetry: No limitations on subject matter. Not particularly interested in broadly humorous, religious or sentimental poetry. Free verse, some avant-garde forms; open to all serious forms of poetry. "There are no arbitrary limits on length, but we find shorter poems are easier to fit into our format." The Elizabeth Matchett Stover Memorial Award of $100 made annually for a poem published in *SWR*. Submit complete ms.
Tips: "The most frequent mistakes we find in work that is submitted for consideration are lack of attention to grammar and syntax and little knowledge of the kind of thing we're looking for. Writers should look at a couple of issues before submitting."

THE SPIRIT THAT MOVES US, The Spirit That Moves Us Press, Inc., Box 1585-W, Iowa City IA 52244. (319)338-7502. Editor: Morty Sklar. 98% freelance written. Semiannual literary magazine of poetry, fiction, artwork publisher of the 1984 Nobel Laureate, in Vo. 8, #1. "We prefer work which is concerned with life and living. We don't like sensational or academic writing." Circ. 800-5,000. Pays on publication. Publishes ms an average of 10 months after acceptance. Byline given. Buys first North American serial rights and second serial (reprint) rights. Simultaneous queries and photocopied submissions OK. Computer printout submissions acceptable; no dot-matrix. "Write first to find out what our current themes are." SASE. Reports in 1 week on queries; 1 month on mss. Sample copy for $3 our choice; $4 for reader. $5 for new all-fiction issue.
Photos: Morty Sklar, photo editor. "Photographs which capture a sense of life, either in mood or energy." Send photos with ms. Pays 1 cloth, 1 paper and 40% off on extras. Buys one-time rights. Include SASE.
Fiction: "Anything goes as long as it shows concern for life and living and is well-written. No sensational or academic material (work which is skillfully written but has little human involvement)." We don't publish articles. Buys 4-20 mss/year. Send complete ms. Length: open. Pays 1 cloth 1 paper and 40% off on extra copies.
Poetry: Any style or "school"; send what you like best. Buys 25-50 poems/year. Submit maximum 5 poems. Length: open. Pays 1 cloth, 1 paper and 40% off on extra copies.
Tips: "Send the work *you* like best, not what you think we'll like."

STORIES, 14 Beacon St., Boston MA 02108. Editor: Amy R. Kaufman. Bimonthly magazine publishing short fiction. "It is designed to encourage the writing of stories that evoke an emotional response—for which, the editor believes, there is a demand." Circ. 2,000. Pays on publication. Byline given. Buys first North American serial rights. Photocopied and simultaneous submissions OK (if so marked). Computer printout submissions acceptable; prefers letter-quality to dot-matrix. No queries. SASE. Reports in 10 weeks on mss. Sample copy $4 (postpaid); writer's guidelines for business size SAE and 1 first class stamp.
Fiction: Contemporary, ethnic, historical (general), humor/satire, literary, serialized/excerpted novel and translations. "We appreciate humor that is sharply perceptive, not merely amusing; political or moral pieces that make a point, not merely hint at one, and that do not proselytize. Ordinarily, romance, mystery, fantasy, political pieces and science fiction do not suit our purposes, but we will not exclude any story on the basis of genre; we wish only that the piece be the best of its genre." Buys 36-48 mss/year. Send complete ms. Length: 750-15,000 words; 4,000-7,000 words average. Pays $150 minimum.
Tips: "We look for characters identifiable not by name, age, profession, or appearance, but by symbolic qualities; timeless themes and styles that are sophisticated but not affected, straightforward but not artless, descriptive but not nearsighted."

SWALLOW'S TALE MAGAZINE, Swallow's Tale Press, Box 4328, Tallahassee FL 32315. (904)224-8859. Editor: Joe Taylor. Managing Editor: Patricia Willey. 100% freelance written. Semiannual magazine focusing on literature that entertains. Circ. 1,000. Pays on publication. Publishes ms an average of 3 months after acceptance. Byline given. Offers 15% kill fee. Buys first North American serial rights. Photocopied submissions OK. Computer printout submissions acceptable; no dot-matrix. SASE. Reports in 2 weeks on queries; 10 weeks on mss. Sample copy $4; writer's guidelines for business size SAE and 1 first class stamp.

Nonfiction: Interview/profile. "We publish only a very few nonfiction articles: book reviews, critical assessments of literary trends, or a contemporary author's work." Buys 15 mss/year. Send complete ms. Length: 750-5,000 words. Pays $15-50.

Fiction: Experimental, fantasy, horror, humorous, literary and mainstream. Buys 25-30 mss/year. Send complete ms. Length: 750-7,500 words. Pays $25-100.

Poetry: Avant-garde, free verse, light verse and traditional. "We look for poetry that extends the personal moment to the universal, resolves well, and, of course, shows an awareness of language and rhythm." Buys 75-100 poems/year. Submit maximum 5 poems. Length: 8 lines minimum. Pays $10-50.

Tips: "We prefer fiction with plot and action, although we have and will continue to publish experimental fiction and minimalist work with an emphasis on language or theme, if well-crafted."

TALES AS LIKE AS NOT . . ., Second Unit Productions, Word Studies Division, 2939 San Antonio Dr., Walnut Creek CA 94598. Editor: Dale Hoover. Associate Editor: Mike Hoover. 100% freelance written. Quarterly magazine of science fiction, fantasy, mystery and horror. "Our philosophy is to provide entertainment that is fresh, original and personal. We are designed specifically for writers of short stories who are strictly amateur. Professionals need not contribute. If you already have a name, you don't need us." Pays on publication. Publishes ms an average of 6 months after acceptance. Buys one-time rights. No seasonal material except for Halloween; submit material 3 months in advance. Computer printout submissions acceptable. SASE. Reports in 1 month on mss. Sample copy $3; Writer's guidelines for 3x12 SAE and 1 first class stamp.

Fiction: Fantasy, horror, mystery and science fiction. "No sex, experimental, mainstream, ethnic or romance. No stories that teach the reader a lesson and nothing more." Buys 36 mss/year. Send complete ms. Length: 1,500-4,000 words. Pays $5 maximum plus contributor's copy.

Tips: "Keep story lines and character development tight and to the point. Don't waste time. Write about what you know and how you feel, but remember that your job as a writer is to entertain and touch the heart of your reader. Don't cry on his shoulder; don't hash over old stories. One thing a reader hates to do after reading a story is say, 'It's been done before.' Don't rely on blood and gore to tell your story. Leave it to the reader's imagination. We don't use articles, fillers or poetry."

TELESCOPE, The Galileo Press, 15201 Wheeler Ln., Sparks MD 21152. Editors: Jack Stephens and Julia Wendell. 50% freelance written. Triannual literary journal of poetry, fiction, essays, book reviews, interviews and graphics. Circ. 500. Pays on publication. Publishes ms an average of 5 months after acceptance. Byline given. Photocopied submissions OK. Computer printout submissions acceptable; prefers letter-quality to dot-matrix. SASE. Reports in 1 week on queries; 2 months on mss. Sample copy $2; writer's guidelines for SAE and 1 first class stamp.

Nonfiction: Interview/profile, personal experience, book reviews and literary criticism. Special issues include Art in the Atomic Age and Cinema's Influence on Literature. Buys 10 mss/year. Send complete ms. Length: open. Pays $6/page.

Graphics: Send tear sheets or photocopies with query letter. Payment negotiable.

Fiction: "Sensitive and intelligent short fiction" and novel excerpts. Length: open. Pays $6/page, 60¢/line.

Poetry: Buys 75/year. Submit maximum 5 poems. Length: open. Pays 50¢/line.

Tips: The editors strongly suggest that writers familiarize themselves with *Telescope* before submitting. They also suggest that writers query before submitting, because of *Telescope*'s special theme issues.

TRIQUARTERLY, 1735 Benson Ave., Northwestern University, Evanston IL 60201. (312)491-3490. Editor: Reginald Gibbons. Published 3 times/year. Publishes fiction, poetry, and essays, as well as artwork. Pays on publication. Buys first serial rights and nonexclusive reprint rights. Computer printout submissions acceptable; prefers letter-quality to dot-matrix. Reports in 8 weeks. Study magazine before submitting; enclose SASE. Sample copy $3.

Nonfiction: Query before sending essays (no scholarly or critical essays except in special issues).

Fiction and Poetry: No prejudice against style or length of work; only seriousness and excellence are required. Buys 20-50 unsolicited mss/year. Pays $12/page.

UNIVERSITY OF WINDSOR REVIEW, Windsor, Ontario N9B 3P4 Canada. (519)253-4232. Editor: Eugene McNamara. Biannual for "the literate layman, the old common reader." Circ. 300+. Buys first North American serial rights. Reports in 4-6 weeks. Sample copy $5 plus postage. Enclose SAE, IRCs.

Nonfiction: "We publish some articles on literature. I think we reflect competently the Canadian intellectual scene and are equally receptive to contributions from outside the country; I think we are good and are trying to get better." Follow *MLA Style Sheet*. Buys 50 mss/year. Length: about 6,000 words. Pays $25.

Photos: Contact Evelyn McLean.

Fiction: Alistair MacLeod, department editor. Publishes mainstream prose with open attitude toward themes. Length: 2,000-6,000 words. Pays $25.

Poetry: John Ditsky, department editor. Accepts traditional forms, blank verse, free verse and avant-garde. No epics. Pays $10.

THE VIRGINIA QUARTERLY REVIEW, 1 W. Range, Charlottesville VA 22903. (804)924-3124. Editor: Staige Blackford. 50% freelance written. Quarterly. Pays on publication. Publishes ms an average of 2 years after acceptance. Byline given. Buys first serial rights. SASE. Reports in 4 weeks. Sample copy $3.
Nonfiction: Articles on current problems, economic, historical; and literary essays. Length: 3,000-6,000 words. Pays $10/345-word page.
Fiction: Good short stories, conventional or experimental. Length: 2,000-7,000 words. Pays $10/350-word page. Prizes offered for best short stories and poems published in a calendar year.
Poetry: Generally publishes 15 pages of poetry in each issue. No length or subject restrictions. Pays $1/line.
Tips: Prefers not to see pornography, science fiction or fantasy.

WESTERN HUMANITIES REVIEW, University of Utah, Salt Lake City UT 84112. (801)581-7438. Managing Editors: Robert Shapard and Nancy Roberts (on leave). 60% freelance written. Quarterly magazine for educated readers. Circ. 1,000. Pays on acceptance. Publishes ms an average of 6 months after acceptance. Buys all rights. Phone queries OK. Simultaneous and photocopied submissions OK. Computer printout submissions acceptable; prefers letter-quality to dot-matrix. SASE. Reports in 4 weeks.
Nonfiction: Barry Weller, editor for nonfiction and reviews. Authoritative, readable articles on literature, art, philosophy, current events, history, religion and anything in the humanities. Interdisciplinary articles encouraged. Departments on film and books. "We commission book reviews." Buys 40 unsolicited mss/year. Pays $50-150. Pays expenses of writers on assignment.
Fiction: Any type or theme. Buys 2 mss/issue. Send complete ms. Pays $25-150.
Poetry: Larry Levis, poetry editor. Avant-garde, free verse and traditional. "We seek freshness and significance. Do not send poetry without having a look at the magazine first." Buys 5-10 poems/issue. Pays $50.
Tips: Articles submitted lack "originality, humor—whatever it is that makes writing stand out. Length is not important, quality is".

WOMEN ARTISTS NEWS, Midmarch Associates, Box 3304 Grand Central Station, New York NY 10163. Editor: Rena Hansen. 70% freelance written. Bimonthly magazine for "artists and art historians, museum and gallery personnel, students, teachers, crafts personnel, art critics and writers." Circ. 5,000. Buys first serial rights only when funds are available. "Token payment as funding permits." Publishes ms an average of 2 months after acceptance. Byline given. Submit seasonal material 2 months in advance. SASE. Reports in 1 month. Sample copy $2.50.
Nonfiction: Features, informational, historical, interview, opinion, personal experience, photo feature and technical. Query or submit complete ms. Length: 500-2,500 words.
Photos: Used with or without accompanying ms. Query or submit contact sheet or prints. Pays $5 for 5x7 b&w prints when money is available. Captions required.

WORDS AND VISIONS, Arts Showcase, Words & Visions Publications, Box 545, Norwood, Adelaide 5067 South Australia. Editor: Adam Dutkiewicz. 100% freelance written. A quarterly magazine covering arts and popular culture with focus on Australian content and some overseas material. Circ. 1,000. Pays on publication. Publishes ms an average of 3 months after acceptance. Byline given. Buys first serial rights. Submit seasonal/holiday material 3 months in advance. Simultaneous, photocopied, and previously published submissions OK. Computer printout submissions acceptable; no dot-matrix. SAE, IRC. Reports in 3 months. Sample copy $4 plus postage; writer's guidelines for SAE.
Nonfiction: Interview/profile. Buys 6 mss/year. Query. Length: 1,200-1,500 words. Pays $20-25.
Fiction: Span Hanna, fiction editor. Erotica, experimental, fantasy, humorous, mainstream, mystery, science fiction and suspense. No pornography. Buys 10 mss/year. Send complete ms. Length: 1,200-3,000 words. Pays $25-50.
Poetry: Martin Brakmanis, poetry editor. Avant-garde, free verse, haiku and traditional. Buys 40 poems/year. Length: 3-130 lines. Pays $15-30.
Tips: "Cover letter appreciated, with some background on writing skills."

THE YALE REVIEW, 1902A Yale Station, New Haven CT 06520. Editor: Kai T. Erikson. Associate Editor: Penelope Laurans. Managing Editor: Wendy Wipprecht. 20% freelance written. Buys first North American serial rights. Pays on publication. Publishes ms an average of 1 year after acceptance. Computer printout submissions acceptable; no dot-matrix. SASE.
Nonfiction and Fiction: Authoritative discussions of politics, literature and the arts. Buys quality fiction. Pays $75-100. Length: 3,000-5,000 words.

‡**ZYZZYVA, The Last Word: West Coast Writers and Artists**, Zyzzyva, Inc., Suite 400, 55 Sutter St., San Francisco CA 94104. (415)387-8389. Editor: Howard Junker. 100% freelance written. Quarterly magazine.

"We feature work by West Coast writers only. We are essentially a literary magazine, but of wide-ranging interests and a strong commitment to nonfiction." Estab. 1985. Circ. 2,500. Pays on acceptance. Publishes ms an average of 3 months after acceptance. Byline given. Buys first North American serial rights and one-time rights. Simultaneous queries, and simultaneous and photocopied submissions OK. SASE. Reports in 1 week on queries; 2 weeks on mss. Sample copy $6.

Nonfiction: Book excerpts, general interest, historical/nostalgic, humor and personal experience. Buys 25 mss/year. Query. Length: open. Pays $25-100.

Fiction: Ethnic, experimental, humorous, mainstream and mystery. "No bad fiction." Buys 30 mss/year. Send complete ms. Length: open. Pays $25-100.

Poetry: "No bad poetry." Buys 40/year. Submit maximum 5 poems. Length: 3-200 lines. Pays $25-50.

Tips: "Keep trying somewhere else to get experience."

Men's

Men's magazines run the gamut from pictorials to service features. Editors will sometimes shift the focus of their publications to meet or rebuff the competition. *Oui Magazine*, for instance, will publish more trend-related material. "*Oui* is doubling its efforts to reach those readers who want to know about coming trends that will affect their lifestyles, not just sexually but in all other ways: financially, mentally, etc.," said executive editor Barry Janoff. Men's magazines are becoming more specialized, not general in theme as *Playboy* and *Penthouse*, says another men's magazine editor. Magazines that also use material slanted toward men can be found in Business and Finance, Lifestyles, Military, and Sports sections.

ADAM, Publishers Service, Inc., 8060 Melrose Ave., Los Angeles CA 90046. Monthly for the adult male. General subject: Human sexuality in contemporary society. Circ. 500,000. Buys first North American serial rights. Occasionally overstocked. Pays on publication. SASE. Writer's guidelines for SASE. Reports in 6 weeks, but occasionally may take longer.

Nonfiction: "On articles, please query first. We like hard sex articles, but research must be thorough." Length: 2,500 words. Pays $100-250.

Photos: All submissions must contain model release including parent's signature if under 21; fact sheet giving information about the model, place or activity being photographed, including all information of help in writing a photo story, and SASE. Photo payment varies, depending upon amount of space used by photo set.

‡**BUF PICTORIAL, The Only Newsstand Magazine Devoted to Enormous Mammas**, G&S Publications, 1472 Broadway, New York NY 10036. (212)840-7224. Editor: Will Martin. Managing Editor: R.B. Kendennis. 70% freelance written. Bimonthly magazine devoted to attractive heavy women. "Stories and articles written for *Buf* should be flattering to attractive heavy women. Short factual features about chubbies and plumpers, contemporary or historical, are especially welcome, as well as fiction and humor." Circ. 100,000. Pays on assignment to a specific issue. Publishes ms an average of 6 months after acceptance. Byline given. Buys all rights. Submit seasonal/holiday material 6 months in advance. SASE. Computer printout submissions acceptable; no dot-matrix. Reports in 2 months on queries; 3 months on mss. Sample copy $3.95; free writer's guidelines.

Nonfiction: "Humor, satire and spoofs of sexual subjects that other magazines treat seriously are welcome. We do not use explicit, graphic descriptions of sex acts, and we've just about had it with violence. No pornography. Buys 5-10 mss/year. Query with published clips or send complete ms. Length: 500-2,500 words. Pays $40-100.

Columns/Departments: Buys 12-24 mss/year. Query with published clips or send complete ms. Length: 300-600 words. Pays $40-60.

Fiction: "We use sex-related but nonpornographic fiction ranging from short-shorts of several hundred words to a maximum of 2,500 or so." Violence is out. No pornography. Buys 12-20 mss/year. Query with published clips or send complete ms. Length: 1,000-2,500 words. Pays $60-100.

Tips: "The writer should know his market and submit material that fits our format."

CAVALIER, Suite 204, 2355 Salzedo St., Coral Gables FL 33134. (305)443-2370. Editor: Douglas Allen. 50% freelance written. Monthly magazine for "young males, ages 18-29, 80% college graduates, affluent, in-

telligent, interested in current events, sex, sports, adventure, travel and good fiction.'' Circ. 250,000. Pays on publication. Publishes ms an average of 3 months after acceptance. Byline given. Buys first serial and second serial (reprint) rights. Buys 44 or more mss/year. See past issues for general approach to take. Submit seasonal material at least 3 months in advance. Computer printout submissions acceptable. SASE. Reports in 3 weeks.
Nonfiction: Personal experience, interview, humor, think pieces, expose and new product. ''Be frank—we are open to dealing with controversial issues.'' No material on Women's Lib, water sports, hunting, homosexuality or travel, ''unless it's something spectacular or special.'' Query. Length: 2,800-3,500 words. Pays maximum $500 with photos.
Photos: Photos purchased with or with captions. No cheesecake.
Fiction: Nye Willden, department editor. Mystery, science fiction, humorous, adventure, and contemporary problems ''with at least one explicit sex scene per story. We are very interested in female fighting.'' Send complete ms. Length: 2,500-3,500 words. Pays $250 maximum, higher for special.
Tips: ''Our greatest interest is in originality—new ideas, new approaches; no tired, overdone stories—both feature and fiction. We do not deal in 'hack' sensationalism but in high quality pieces. Keep in mind the intelligent 18 to 29 year-old male reader. We will be putting more emphasis in articles and fiction on sexual themes. We prefer serious articles, not hack sexual pornography—fiction can be very imaginative and sensational.''

CHIC MAGAZINE, Larry Flynt Publications, Suite 3800, 2029 Century Park E., Los Angeles CA 90067. Contact: Editorial Director. Monthly magazine for men, ages 20-35 years, college-educated and interested in current affairs, entertainment and sports. Circ. 250,000. Pays 1 month after acceptance. Buys exclusive English and English translation world-wide magazine rights. Pays 20% kill fee. Byline given unless writer requests otherwise. SASE. Reports in 2 months.
Nonfiction: Expose (national interest only); interview (personalities in news and entertainment); and celebrity profiles. Buys 36 mss/year. Query. Length: 5,000 words. Pays $750.
Columns/Departments: Dope, and Sex Life: Pays $300. Odds and Ends (front of the book shorts; study the publication first): Pays $50; length: 100-300 words. Close Up (short Q&As) columns: Length: 1,000 words; pays $200.
Fiction: ''At present we are buying stories with emphasis on erotic themes. These may be adventure, action, mystery or horror stories, but the tone and theme must involve sex and eroticism. The main sex scene should be 1½ pages long. However, the erotic nature of the story should not be subordinate to the charactizations and plot; the sex must grow logically from the people and the plot, not be contrived or forced.''
Tips: Prefers not to get humorous material. ''We do not buy poetry, science-fiction, satire or fiction. Refrain from stories with drug themes, sex with minors, incest and blasphemy.''

‡**ESPRIT, The Spirit of Man**, Chicago Publishing Co., Inc., #3E, 921 W. Addison, Chicago IL 60613. (312)472-3735. Editor: Tom Aikins. Monthly tabloid about young men's lifestyles. Estab. 1984. Circ. 150,000. Pays on publication. Byline given. Offers 50% kill fee. Buys first North American serial rights, one-time rights, all rights, simultaneous rights, first serial rights, or second serial (reprint) rights; makes work-for-hire assignments. Submit seasonal/holiday material 6 months in advance. Simultaneous queries and submissions OK. SASE. Reports in 3 weeks on queries; 5 weeks on mss. Sample copy $2; writer's guidelines for #10 SAE and 1 first class stamp.
Nonfiction: Book excerpts; general interest; humor (satire, general); interview/profile (rock, movie, sport celebrities); opinion (political, social); and travel. Buys 30 mss/year. Query with published clips. Length: 2,000-8,000 words. Pays $150-600 (more for established writers with good publishing record).
Photos: State availability of photos. Reviews b&w contact sheets and 5x7 prints; 2¼ color transparencies. Pays $15-100 for b&w; $50-250 for color. Captions, model release, and identification of subjects required. Buys all rights.
Fiction: Adventure, erotica, fantasy, humorous, novel excerpts, science fiction and serialized novels. Buys 20 mss/year. Send complete ms. Length: 2,000 words. Pays $75.
Fillers: Bill Burck, fillers editor. Clippings, anecdotes and short humor. Buys 50/year. Length: 50-250 words. Pays. $20-50.
WM Editor's Note: At press time, we learned that *Esprit* is not being published.

ESQUIRE, 2 Park Ave., New York NY 10016. (212)561-8100. Editorial Director: Betsy Carter. Editor: Lee Eisenberg. 99% freelance written. Monthly. Pays on acceptance. Publishes ms an average of 6 months after acceptance. Usually buys first serial rights. Computer printout submissions acceptable; prefers letter-quality to dot-matrix. Reports in 3 weeks. ''We depend chiefly on solicited contributions and material from literary agencies. We are unable to accept responsibility for unsolicited material.'' Query. SASE.
Nonfiction: Articles vary in length, but features usually average 3,000-7,000 words. Articles should be slanted for sophisticated, intelligent readers; however, not highbrow in the restrictive sense. Wide range of subject matter. Rates run roughly between $300 and $3,000, depending on length, quality, etc. Sometimes pays expenses of writers on assignments.
Photos: April Silver, art director. Payment depends on how photo is used, but rates are roughly $300 for b&w;

$500-750 for color. Guarantee on acceptance. Buys first periodical publication rights.

Fiction: L. Rust Hills, fiction editor. "Literary excellence is our only criterion." Length: about 1,000-6,000 words. Payment: $1,500-5,000.

Tips: The writer sometimes has a better chance of breaking in at *Esquire* with short, lesser-paying articles and fillers (rather than with major features) "because we need more short pieces."

‡**FLING**, Relim Publishing Col, Inc., 550 Miller Ave., Mill Valley CA 94941. (415)383-5464. Editor: Arv Miller. Managing Editor: Ted Albert. 20% freelance written. Bimonthly magazine of men's sophisticate field. Young male audience of adults ages 18-34. Sexual-oriented field. Circ. 100,000. Pays on acceptance. Publishes ms an average of 5 months after acceptance. Buys first North American serial rights and second serial (reprint) rights; makes work-for-hire assignments. Submit seasonal/holiday material 8 months in advance. Computer printout submissions acceptable; prefers letter-quality to dot-matrix. SASE. Reports in 1 week on queries; 2 weeks on mss. Sample copy $4; writer's guidelines for SAE and 1 first class stamp.

Nonfiction: Expose, how-to (better relationships with women, better lovers); interview/profile; personal experience; photo feature; and taboo sex articles. Buys 15 mss/year. Query. Length: 1,500-3,000 words. Pays $150-250. Sometimes pays expenses of writers on assignment.

Photos: Send photos with query. Reviews b&w contact sheets and 8x10 prints; 35mm color transparencies. Pays $10-25 for b&w; $20-35 for color. Model release required. Buys one-time rights.

Columns/Departments: Buys 12 mss/year. Query or send complete ms. Length: 100-200 words. Pays $15-125.

Fiction: Confession, erotica and sexual. No science fiction, western, plotless, private-eye, "dated," or adventure. Buys 20 mss/year. Send complete ms. Length: 2,000-3,000 words. Pays $135-200.

Fillers: Clippings. Buys 50/year. Length: 100-500 words. Pays $5-15.

Tips: "Nonfiction and fiction wide open areas to freelancers. Always query with one-page letter to the editor before proceeding with any writing. Also send a sample photocopy of published material, similar to suggestion."

GALLERY MAGAZINE, Montcalm Publishing Corp., 800 2nd Ave., New York NY 10017. (212)986-9600. President/Publisher: Milton J. Cuevas. Editor-in-Chief: John Bensink. Managing Editor: Marc Lichter. Design Director: Michael Monte. 30% freelance written. Monthly magazine "focusing on features of interest to the young American man." Circ. 500,000. Pays 50% on acceptance, 50% on publication. Publishes ms an average of 3 months after acceptance. Byline given. Pays 25% kill fee. Buys first North American serial rights; makes work-for-hire assignments. Submit seasonal/holiday material 6 months in advance. Photocopied submissions OK. SASE. Reports in 1 month on queries; 8 weeks on mss. Sample copy $3.50 plus $1.75 postage and handling. Free writer's guidelines.

Nonfiction: Investigative pieces, general interest, how-to, humor, interview, new products and profile. "We *do not* want to see articles on pornography." Buys 6-8 mss/issue. Query or send complete mss. Length: 1,000-3,000 words. Pays $200-1,500. "Special prices negotiated."

Photos: Send photos with accompanying mss. Pay varies for b&w or color contact sheets and negatives. Buys one-time rights. Captions preferred; model release required.

Fiction: Adventure, erotica, experimental, humorous, mainstream, mystery and suspense. Buys 2 mss/issue. Send complete ms. Length: 500-3,000 words. Pays $250-1,000.

‡**GEM**, G&S Publications, 1472 Broadway, New York NY 10036. (212)840-7224. Editor: Will Martin. Managing Editor: R.B. Kendennis. 70% freelance written. Bimonthly magazine devoted to attractive heavy women. "Stories and articles written for GEM should be flattering to attractive heavy women. Short factual features about chubbies and plumpers, contemporary or historic, are especially welcome, as well as humor. Circ. 100,000. Pays on assignment to a specific issue. Publishes ms an average of 3-6 months after acceptance. Byline given. Buys all rights. Submit seasonal/holiday material 6 months in advance. Photocopied submissions OK. Computer printout submissions acceptable; no dot-matrix. SASE. Reports in 2 months on queries; 3 months on mss. Sample copy $3.95; free writer's guidelines.

Nonfiction: Humor, satire and spoofs of sexual subjects that other magazines treat seriously are welcome. "We do not use explicit, graphic descriptions of sex acts, and we've just about had it with violence." No pornography. Buys 5-10 mss/year. Query or send complete ms. Length: 500-2,500 words. Pays $40-100.

Columns: Buys 12-24 mss/year. Query or send complete ms. Length: 300-600 words. Pays $40-60.

Fiction: "We use sex-related but nonpornographic fiction ranging from short-shorts of several hundred words to a maximum of 2,500 or so." Violence is out. No pornography. Buys 12-20 mss/year. Send complete ms. Length: 1,000-2,500 words. Pays $60-100.

Tips: "The writer should know his market and submit material that fits our format."

GENT, Suite 204, 2355 Salzedo St., Coral Gables FL 33134. (305)443-2378. Editor: John C. Fox. 75% freelance written. Monthly magazine for men from every strata of society. Circ. 200,000. Buys first North American serial rights. Byline given. Pays on publication. Publishes ms an average of 2 months after acceptance. Computer printout submissions acceptable; prefers letter-quality to dot-matrix. SASE. Reports in 6 weeks. Writer's guidelines for legal size SASE.

Nonfiction: Looking for traditional men's subjects (cars, racing, outdoor adventure, science, gambling, etc.) as well as sex-related topics. Query first. Length: 1,500-2,500 words. Buys 70 mss/year. Pays $100-200. Sometimes pays expenses of writers on assignment.

Photos: B&w and color photos purchased with mss. Captions (preferred). Submit Complete ms. Length: 100 words.

Fiction: Erotic. "Stories should contain a huge-breasted female character, as this type of model is *Gent*'s main focus. And this character's endowments should be described in detail in the course of the story. Some of our stories also emphasize sexy, chubby women, pregnant women and their male admirers." Submit complete ms. Length: 1,500-3,000 words. Pays $100-200.

Tips: "Study sample copies of the magazine before trying to write for it. We like custom-tailored stories and articles."

GENTLEMEN'S QUARTERLY, Condé Nast, 350 Madison Ave., New York NY 10017. Editor-in-Chief: Arthur Cooper. Managing Editor: Eliot Kaplan. 60% freelance written. Circ. 607,000. Monthly magazine emphasizing fashion, general interest and service features for men ages 25-45 with a large discretionary income. Pays on acceptance. Byline given. Pays 25% kill fee. Submit seasonal/holiday material 6 months in advance. Computer printout submissions acceptable; prefers letter-quality to dot-matrix. SASE. Reports in 1 month.

Nonfiction: Politics, personality profiles, lifestyles, trends, grooming, nutrition, health and fitness, sports, travel, money, investment and business matters. Buys 4-6 mss/issue. Query with published clips. Length: 1,500-4,000 words. Pays $750-3,000.

Columns/Departments: Eliot Kaplan, managing editor. Body & Soul (fitness, nutrition and grooming); Money (investments); Going in Style (travel); Health; Music; Tech (consumer electronics); Dining In (food); Wine & Spirits; Hur; Fiction; Games (sports); Books; The Male Animal (essays by men on life); and All About Adam (nonfiction by women about men). Buys 5-8/issue. Query with published clips or submit complete ms. Length: 1,000-2,500 words. Pays $750-2,000.

Tips: "Major features are usually assigned to well-established, known writers. Pieces are almost always solicited. The best way to break in is through the columns, especially Male Animal, All About Adam, Games, Health or Humor."

‡HIGH SOCIETY, High Society, 801 2nd Ave., New York NY 10017. (212)661-7878. Editor: Louis Montesano. Managing Editor: Nina Malkin. 80% freelance written. Monthly magazine of erotic adult entertainment. Circ. 500,000. Pays on acceptance. Publishes ms an average of 6 months in advance. Byline given. Makes work-for-hire assignments. Submit seasonal/holiday material 6 months in adance. Computer printout submissions acceptable; no dot-matrix. SASE. Reports in 2 weeks. Sample copy $3.75; free writer's guidelines.

Nonfiction: Expose (political/entertainment); how-to (sexual, self-help); humor (bawdy); interview/profile (sports, music, politics); opinion (sexual subjects); and personal experience (sexual). Query with published clips. Length: 1,000-3,000 words. Pays $200 minimun. Sometimes pays expenses of writers on assignment.

Photos: State availability of photos or send photo with query. Reviews 1" color transparencies. Model release and identification of subjects required.

Columns/Departments: Silver Spoonfuls: Newsbits, health, reviews. Buys 50 mss/year. Query with published clips. Length: 500-1,000 words. Pays $200-400.

Fiction: Confession (sex oriented), erotica and humorous (sex oriented). Buys 12 mss/year. Query with published clips. Length: 1,000-2,000 words. Pays $150-250.

‡IMPULSE MAGAZINE, Impulse Enterprises, Ltd., F-605, 4621 N. 16th St., Phoenix AZ 85016. (602)279-1224. Editor: Joe Iacuzzo. 90% freelance written. Monthly magazine about men's lifestyles (general). "*Impulse* is a new publication aimed at being both entertaining and informative for a successful and educated male reader." Estab. 1985. Circ. 100,000. Pays on publication. Publishes ms an average of 4 months after acceptance. Byline given. Offers $150 kill fee. Buys first serial rights. Submit seasonal/holiday material 6 months in advance. Photocopied and simultaneous submissions OK. Computer printout submissions acceptable; prefers letter-quality to dot-matrix. SASE. Reports in 2 weeks on queries; 4 weeks on mss. Sample copy for 9x12 SAE and 5 first class stamps; writer's guidelines for 4x10 SAE and 2 first class stamps.

Nonfiction: Book excerpts, expose, general interest, historical/nostalgic, humor, interview/profile, new product, opinion and photo feature. Buys 24 mss/year. Query or send complete ms. Length: 1,200-9,600 words. Pays $150-600. Sometimes pays expenses of writers on assignment.

Photos: Send photos with ms. Reviews b&w contact sheets and 35mm or larger color transparencies. Pays $25 minimum for b&w; $50 minimum for color. Model release required. Buys negotiable rights.

Columns/Departments: Audio/Video (new technology); High Tech (products and ideas on the forefront of technology); Money (anything financial of interest to our readers); and Health and Fitness. Buys 80mss/year. Query or send complete ms. Length: 900-2,000 words. Pays $100-300.

Fiction: Adventure, experimental, historical, humorous, mainstream, mystery, novel excerpts, science fiction

and suspense. Buys 12 mss/year. Query or send complete ms. Length: 2,000-9,600 words. Pays $150-600.
Fillers: Clippings, jokes, gags and newsbreaks. Buys 120/year. Length: 40-300 words. Pays $25-75.
Tips: "We are a new and growing publication and would like to find a pool of writers we can count on in the years to come to provide us with quality work."

NUGGET, Suite 204, 2355 Salzedo St., Coral Gables FL 33134. (305)443-2378. Editor: John Fox. 75% freelance written. Magazine "primarily devoted to fetishism." Pays on publication. Publishes ms an average of 2 months after acceptance. Byline given. Buys first North American serial rights. Computer printout submissions acceptable; prefers letter-quality to dot-matrix. Reports in 6 weeks. SASE.
Nonfiction: Articles on fetishism—every aspect. Buys 20-30 mss/year. Submit complete ms. Length: 2,000-3,000 words. Pays $100-200. Sometimes pays expenses of writers on assignment.
Photos: Erotic pictorials of women—essay types in fetish clothing (leather, rubber, underwear, etc.) or women wrestling or boxing other women or men, preferably semi- or nude. Captions or short accompanying ms desirable. Reviews color or b&w photos.
Fiction: Erotic and fetishistic. Should be oriented to *Nugget's* subject matter. Length: 2,000-3,000 words. Pays $100-200.
Tips: "We require queries on articles only, and the letter should be a brief synopsis of what the article is about. Originality in handling of subject is very helpful. It is almost a necessity for a freelancer to study our magazine first, be knowledgeable about the subject matter we deal with and able to write explicit and erotic fetish material."

OUI MAGAZINE, Laurent Publications, 300 W. 43rd St., New York NY 10036. (212)397-5889. Editor: Jeffrey Goodman. Managing Editor: Barry Janoff. 25% freelance written. A monthly magazine for men ages 18-40, college educated; "audience seeks mental as well as physical stimulation." Circ. 800,000. Pays on publication. Publishes ms an average of 4 months after acceptance. Byline given. Offers variable kill fee. Buys variable rights. Submit seasonal/holiday material 5 months in advance. Computer printout submissions acceptable; perfers letter-quality to dot-matrix. SASE. Reports in 1 month on queries; 7 weeks on mss. Sample copy $5; ms guidelines for business size SAE and 1 first class stamp.
Nonfiction: Expose (political); how-to (make money, survive, protect yourself from fraud, etc.); humor; interview/profile (top or upcoming actresses); technical; and travel (exotic locales with sexual overtones). "No articles on hookers, bordellos, massage parlors, porn stars or porn movies." Buys 18-25 mss/year. Query with published clips. Length: 2,000-3,000 words. Payment varies.
Photos: Send photos with query. Reviews 35mm transparencies. Model release and identification of subjects required.
Fiction: Adventure, erotica, experimental, fantasy, horror, humorous, mystery, science fiction and suspense. Erotic/sexual slant preferred. "Avoid 'typical' situations: hookers, bordellos, massage parlors; writers are encouraged to explore new areas, create and invent new situations." Send complete ms. Length: 1,500-2,500 words. Payment is negotiable.
Fillers: Contact: Openers Editor. Sexually oriented situations, erotic happenings in everyday situations. Query or send news clipping.
Tips: "Nonfiction is an area *Oui* always needs to fill, in particular, hard-hitting exposes or documented undercover work. Query first with some background information, i.e., newspaper/magazine credits, etc. *Oui* gets too many pieces of fiction that are dull, boring, uninteresting, out of step with current trends, etc. Writers should not only be as current as possible but—and here's the trick—be ahead of their time. Set trends instead of copying."

PENTHOUSE, 1965 Broadway, New York NY 10023. Editor-in-Chief: Bob Guccione. 95% freelance written. For male (ages 18-34) audience; upper-income bracket, college-educated. Monthly. Circ. 3,400,000. Pays on acceptance. Publishes ms an average of 8 months after acceptance. Byline given. Offers 25% kill fee. Buys all righs. Photocopied submissions OK. Computer printout submissions acceptable; no dot-matrix. SASE. Reports in 1 month. Query.
Nonfiction: Peter Bloch, department executive editor. Articles on general themes: money, sex, humor, politics, health, crime, etc. Male viewpoint only. Buys 70-80mss/year, including fiction. Length: 5,000 words. General rates: $2,000 minimum.
Photos: Purchased without mss and on assignment. Pays $200 minimum for b&w; $350 for color. Spec sheet available from Richard Bleiweiss, art director.
Fiction: Kathryn Green, editor. Quality fiction. Experimental, mainstream, mystery, suspense and adventure, erotica and science fiction. Action-oriented, central male character. Length: 3,500-6,000 words. Pays $1,500 minimum.

PENTHOUSE VARIATIONS, Penthouse International, Ltd., 1965 Broadway, New York NY 10023. 496-6100. Editor: Victoria McCarty. 100% freelance written. Monthly magazine. "*Variations* is a pleasure guide for everyone who wants to expand his horizons of enjoyment. All forms of sensuality and eroticism appear in its pages, from monogamy to menaging, from bondage to oral sex, from foreplay to anal sex." Circ. 400,000. Pays on acceptance. Publishes ms an average of 6 months after acceptance. Pseudonym given. Buys total rights "to publish and republish the whole or part edited or unedited, internationally." Simultaneous queries OK. "Viewed skeptically, but letter-quality with tight uniform character-spacing rag-right acceptable." Reports in 1 month on queries; 2 months on mss. Free writer's guidelines.

Nonfiction: Personal experience. "We are looking for first-person, true accounts of erotic experiences, squarely focused within *one* of the pleasure variations. No fiction, articles or short stories. No porno, favorite erotica; we are not a dirty-story clearing house." Buys 60 mss/year. Query. Length: 2,500-3,000 words. Pays $400.

Tips: "I am easily swayed by professionally neat manuscript style: clean ribbon, nonerasable paper, double-spacing, margins. I look for complete sentences and an electrically erotic mind sold in a business-like manner."

PLAYBOY, 919 N. Michigan, Chicago IL 60611. Monthly. Pays on acceptance. Offers 20% kill fee. Buys first serial rights and others. Computer printout submissions acceptable. SASE. Reports in 1 month.

Nonfiction: James Morgan, articles editor. "We're looking for timely, topical pieces. Articles should be carefully researched and written with wit and insight. Little true adventure or how-to material. Check magazine for subject matter. Pieces on outstanding contemporary men, sports, politics, sociology, business and finance, music, science and technology, games, all areas of interest to the urban male." Query. Length: 3,000-5,000 words. Pays $3,000 minimum. *Playboy* interviews run between 10,000 and 15,000 words. After getting an assignment, the freelancer outlines the questions, conducts and edits the interview, and writes the introduction. Pays $4,000 minimum. For interviews contact G. Barry Golson, Executive Editor, 747 3rd Ave., New York NY 10017.

Photos: Gary Cole, photography director, suggests that all photographers interested in contributing make a thorough study of the photography currently appearing in the magazine. Generally all photography is done on assignment. While much of this is assigned to *Playboy*'s staff photographers, approximately 50% of the photography is done by freelancers, and *Playboy* is in constant search of creative new talent. Qualified freelancers are encouraged to submit samples of their work and ideas. All assignments made on an all rights basis with payments scaled from $600/color page for miscellaneous features such as fashion, food and drink, etc.; $300/b&w page; $1,000/color page for girl features; cover, $1,500. Playmate photography for entire project: $10,000-13,000. Assignments and submissions handled by associate editors: Jeff Cohen, Janice Moses, and James Larson and Michael Ann Sullivan, Chicago; Marilyn Grabowski and Linda Kenney, Los Angeles. Assignments made on a minimum guarantee basis. Film, processing, and other expenses necessitated by assignment honored.

Fiction: Alice Turner, fiction editor. Both light and serious fiction. "Entertainment pieces are clever, smoothly written stories. Serious fiction must come up to the best contemporary standards in substance, idea and style. Both, however, should be designed to appeal to the educated, well-informed male reader." General types include comedy, mystery, fantasy, horror, science fiction, adventure, social-realism, "problem" and psychological stories. Fiction lengths are 3,000-6,000 words; short-shorts of 1,000 to 1,500 words are used. Pays $2,000; $1,000 short-short. Rates rise for additional acceptances.

Fillers: Party Jokes are always welcome. Pays $50 each. Also interesting items for Playboy After Hours, front section (check it carefully before submission). The After Hours front section pays anywhere from $50 for humorous or unusual news items (submissions not returned) to $500 for original reportage. Subject matter should be new trends, fads, personalities and cultural developments. Has movie, book, record reviewers but solicits queries for short (1,000 words or less) pieces on art, places, people, trips, adventures, experiences, erotica, television—in short, open-ended. Book and record reviews are on assignment basis only. Ideas for Playboy Potpourri pay $75. Query. Games, puzzles and travel articles should be addressed to New York office.

PLAYERS MAGAZINE, Players International Publications, 8060 Melrose Ave., Los Angeles CA 90046. (213)653-8060. Editor: Joseph Nazel, Jr. Associate Editor: Leslie Spencer. Monthly magazine for the black male but "we have a high female readership—perhaps as high as 40%." Circ. 200,000. Pays on publication. Buys all rights. Submit seasonal/holiday material 6 months in advance. Photocopied submissions OK. SASE. Reports in 3 weeks minimum.

Nonfiction: "*Players* is *Playboy* in basic black." Expose, historical, humor, inspirational, sports, travel, reviews of movies, books, records, profile/interview on assignment. Length: 1,000-5,000 words. Pays 10¢/word.

Photos: Photos purchased on assignment. Pays $25 minimum for b&w; $250 maximum per layout. Model release required.

Fiction: Adventure, erotica, fantasy, historical (black), humorous, science fiction and experimental. Length: 1,000-4,000 words. Pays 6¢/word.

Tips: "Follow current style with novel theme in query or article. We are looking for: city, night life of cities other than New York, Chicago, Los Angeles; interviews with black political leaders; and black history."

Close-up

Alice K. Turner
Fiction Editor
Playboy

Photo by Andrew Porter

"Stories of the type that *Playboy* publishes aren't written by many writers," says *Playboy* fiction editor Alice Turner.

One of the top fiction markets in the country, *Playboy* receives 50 to 80 fiction submissions daily. "I really like to start my day with the mail," she says. "I answer it as quickly as I can." She also reads manuscripts early in the day and generally rejects unsuitable stories immediately. In the afternoon, Turner usually works on projects that take more time, such as reading a novel or writing rewrite letters. Unlike many editors, she doesn't limit telephone calls to a specific time of day.

Despite the large number of submissions, *Playboy* editors try to give each submission a careful look. "The manuscripts are opened and handled right away by two freelance readers," Turner explains. In the next stage, manuscripts are read by two assistants, who recommend particular stories.

Agented stories and those from *Playboy*'s regular writers go directly to Turner or Assistant Editor Teresa Grosch.

Turner draws upon her magazine and book editing experience as she reads *Playboy* stories. She was senior editor at *New York Magazine* for three years before coming to *Playboy*, and senior editor at Ballantine Books before that. She has also written criticism and reviews but does little of that nowadays. "A person who is purchasing books from writers should not be reviewing," she believes.

In discussing what she likes in fiction, Turner says there is no "ideal" *Playboy* story. "We look for traditional values in stories. That is, we want a strong story line, and a shape to the story—a beginning, a middle, and an ending," she points out. "We're not experimental or innovative. We don't publish slices of life, literary experiments, vignettes, or open-ended stories."

There are types of stories which Turner can't find enough of. "It's very good for us to find suitable mystery stories. The quality we get is so poor, and we just do not want tired, formulaic reruns of ideas that would have been fresh in the fifties," says Turner. We're not strictly *genre*, either, although we do publish *genre* fiction."

Probably the most difficult area for a writer to break in with is science fiction. "Science fiction is one field in which there are already a lot of good, professional writers and the competition is tough."

Sports stories and short-shorts are good break-in areas for writers who have not written for *Playboy*. "It's surprisingly hard to find good sports stories, and we're always looking for short-shorts," she says. "Most writers can't write short-shorts." *Playboy*, for instance, bought one short-short from the unsolicited pile a few years ago, but that writer hasn't been able to produce another good short-short.

And, yes, *Playboy* stories do sometimes come from the pile of unsolicited manuscripts. "I tell writers that, as far as I know, all magazines read and buy from their slush piles. This is certainly true at *Playboy*."

—*Michael A. Banks*

‡**SAGA**, Lexington Library, Inc., 355 Lexington Ave., New York NY 10017. (212)391-1400. Editors: Stephen Ciacciarelli, Thomas Walsh. 95% freelance written. Annual general interest men's magazine. "We offer an alternative to the many 'skin' magazines across the country in that we give an exciting, contemporary look at America today without the porn. A man's magazine that can be read by the entire family." Circ. 300,000. Pays on acceptance. Publishes ms an average of 2 months after acceptance. Byline given. Buys first North American serial rights. Computer printout submissions acceptable; prefers letter-quality to dot-matrix. SASE. Reports in 1 month. Sample copy $1.75.
Nonfiction: Expose (government), how-to (save money), humor (topical), interview, new product, profile and travel. Buys 12-15 mss/year. Query. Length: 1,500-3,500 words. Pays $250-600.
Photos: Photos purchased with accompanying ms or on assignment. Pays $35 minimum for b&w photos; $75 minimum for 35mm color photos. Query for photos. Captions and model release required.
Tips: "A reduced publication schedule will lessen our need for material."

SCREW, Box 432, Old Chelsea Station, New York NY 10011. Managing Editor: Manny Neuhaus. 95% freelance written. Weekly tabloid newspaper for a predominantly male, college-educated audience; ages 21 through mid-40s. Circ. 125,000. Pays on publication. Publishes ms an average of 3 months after acceptance. Byline given. Buys all rights. Reports in 3 months. Free sample copy and writer's guidelines.
Nonfiction: "Sexually related news, humor, how-to articles, first person and true confessions. Frank and explicit treatment of all areas of sex; outrageous and irreverent attitudes combined with hard information, news and consumer reports. Our style is unique. Writers should check several recent issues." Buys 150-200 mss/year. Submit complete ms for first person, true confession. Length: 1,000-3,000 words. Pays $100-200. Will also consider material for Letter From . . . , a consumer-oriented wrap-up of commercial sex scene in cities around the country; and My Scene, a sexual true confession. Length: 1,000-2,500 words. Pays about $40.
Photos: Reviews b&w glossy prints (8x10 or 11x14) purchased with or without manuscripts or on assignment. Pays $10-50.
Tips: "All mss get careful attention. Those written in *Screw* style on sexual topics have the best chance."

STAG, Swank Corp., 888 7th Ave., New York NY 10106. Editor: Bill Bottiggi. 50% freelance written. Monthly magazine covering men's entertainment with an emphasis on sex for men ages 18-35. Circ. 170,000. Pays on publication. Publishes ms an average of 3 months after acceptance. Byline given. Buys all rights. Submit seasonal/holiday material 6 months in advance. Computer printout submissions acceptable; prefers letter-quality to dot-matrix. SASE. Reports in 1 month. Sample copy $5.
Nonfiction: Photo Features: "Subject matter of any article should lend itself to 4-6 pages of photos." Buys 8-10 noncommissioned mss/year. Query with published clips. Length: 2,500-3,000 words. Pays $350 minimum/article.
Photos: State availability of photos. Reviews 35mm Kodachrome transparencies. Payment varies according to usage rights.
Fiction: Buys 12 mss/year. Send complete ms. Length: 2,000 words average. Pays $300 minimum. "We prefer sexy, light-hearted or humorous subject matter."
Tips: "The writer has a better chance of breaking into our publication with short articles and fillers. We like a query that tips us off to a new sex club, strip joint, love commune etc., that would cooperate with the writer and our photographers for a feature story. For all our articles, photographs or illustrations are essential." Prefers not to see anything not dealing with sex. Read the magazine.

‡**SWANK**, GCR Publishing Corp., 888 7th Ave., New York NY 10106. (212)541-7100. Editor: Eve Ziegler. Managing Editor: Deborah Neumann. 15% freelance written. Monthly magazine on "sex and sensationalism, lurid. High quality adult erotic entertainment." Audience of men ages 18-38, high school and some college education, low to medium income, skilled blue-collar professionals, union men. Circ. 350,000. Pays on publication. Publishes ms an average of 3 months after acceptance. Byline given; pseudonym, if wanted. Pays 10% kill fee. Buys first North American serial rights. Submit seasonal/holiday material 4 months in advance. Computer printout submissions acceptable. SASE. Reports in 3 weeks on queries; 2 months on mss. Sample copy $3.50; writer's guidelines for SAE and 1 first class stamp.
Nonfiction: Expose (researched); personal experience (confession if it's something fascinating and lurid); and photo feature. Be innovative. Buys 8 mss/year. Query with or without published clips. Pays $350-500. Sometimes pays the expenses of writers on assignment.
Photos: Bruce Perez, photo editor. State availability of photos. Model release required.
Fiction: Erotica and suspense. "We want Elmore Leonard-type material." Buys 12 mss/year. Send complete ms. Length: 2,500-3,000 words. Pays $150-350.
Tips: "Pornography should not be hacked out. Skill and expertise in writing is a must."

Military

Development of Western defensive capability and the changing patterns of guerrilla warfare in the Third World will be affecting what some military magazines buy in 1986. Military magazines will continue to report issues that military personnel need to know. At *Soldier of Fortune* magazine, for example, pictures are also part of this reporting. "An extremely high proportion of our readers are military veterans, and they are sensitive to the difference between staged shots and live combat photos," said its senior editor.

Technical and semitechnical publications for military commanders, personnel and planners, as well as those for military families and civilians interested in Armed Forces activities are listed here. These publications emphasize military or paramilitary subjects or aspects of military life.

ARMED FORCES JOURNAL INTERNATIONAL, Suite 104, 1414 22nd St. NW, Washington DC 20037. Editor: Benjamin F. Schemmer. 30% freelance written. Monthly magazine for "senior career officers of the U.S. military, defense industry, Congressmen and government officials interested in defense matters, international military and defense industry." Circ. 35,000. Pays on publication. Publishes ms an average of 2 months after acceptance. Buys all rights. Photocopied submissions OK. SASE. Reports in 1 month. Sample copy $2.75.
Nonfiction: Publishes "national and international defense issues: weapons programs, research, personnel programs and international relations (with emphasis on defense issues). We do not want broad overviews of a general subject; we are more interested in detailed analysis which lays out *both* sides of a specific program or international defense issue. Our readers are decision-makers in defense matters—hence, subject should not be treated too simplistically. Be provocative. We are not afraid to take issue with our own constituency when an independent voice needs to be heard." Buys informational, profile and think pieces. No poetry, biographies, or non defense topics. Bus 30mss/year. Send complete ms. Length: 1,000-3,000 words. Pays $100-200/page. Sometimes pays the expenses of writers on assignment.
Tips: "The most frequent mistakes made by writers are: 1) one-dimensinal and one-sided articles; 2) broad-brush generalities versus specificity; and 3) poorly-written gobbledy gook."

ARMY MAGAZINE, 2425 Wilson Blvd., Arlington VA 22201. (703)841-4300. Editor-in-Chief: L. James Binder. Managing Editor: Mary Blake French. 75% freelance written. Monthly magazine emphasizing military interests. Circ. 170,000. Pays on publication. Publishes ms an average of 6 months after acceptance. Buys all rights. Byline given except for back-up research. Submit seasonal/holiday material 3 months in advance. Photocopied submissions OK. Computer printout submissions acceptable; prefers letter-quality to dot-matrix. SASE. Free sample copy and writer's guidelines.
Nonfiction: Historical (military and original); humor (military feature-length articles and anecdotes); interview; new product; nostalgia; personal experience; photo feature; profile; and technical. No rehashed history. "We would like to see more pieces about interesting military personalities. We especially want material lending itself to heavy, contributor-supplied photographic treatment. The first thing a contributor should recognize is that our readership is very savvy militarily. 'Gee-whiz' personal reminiscences get short shrift, unless they hold their own in a company in which long military service, heroism and unusual experiences are commonplace. At the same time, Army readers like a well written story with a fresh slant, whether it is about an experience in a foxhole or the fortunes of a corps in battle." Buys 12 mss/issue. Submit complete ms. Length: 4,500 words. Pays 12-17¢/word.
Photos: Submit photo material with accompanying ms. Pays $15-50 for 8x10 b&w glossy prints; $35-150 for 8x10 color glossy prints or 2¹/₄x2¹/₄ color transparencies, but will accept 35mm. Captions preferred. Buys all rights.
Columns/Departments: Military news, books, comment (*New Yorker*-type "Talk of the Town" items). Buys 8/issue. Submit complete ms. Length: 1,000 words. Pays $40-150.

ASIA-PACIFIC DEFENSE FORUM, Commander-in-Chief, U.S. Pacific Command, Box 13, Camp H.M. Smith HI 96861. (808)477-5027/6924. Executive Editor: Lt. Col. Paul R. Stankiewicz. Editor: Don Kileup. 12% (maximum) freelance written. Quarterly magazine for foreign military officers in 51 Asian-Pacific, Indian Ocean and other countries; all services—Army, Navy, Air Force and Marines. Secondary audience—government officials, media and academicians concerned with defense issues. "We seek to keep readers abreast of current status of U.S. forces and of U.S. national security policies, and to enhance international professional dialogue on military subjects." Circ. 30,000. Pays on acceptance. Publishes ms an average of 4 months after acceptance. Byline given. Buys simultaneous rights, second serial (reprint) rights or one-time rights. Phone queries OK. Simultaneous, photocopied, and previously published submissions OK. Computer printout submissions OK; prefers letter-quality to dot-matrix. Requires only a self-addressed label. Reports in 3 weeks on queries; 10 weeks on mss. Free sample copy and writer's guidelines (send self-addressed label).

Nonfiction: General interest (strategy and tactics, current type forces and weapons systems, strategic balance and security issues and Asian-Pacific armed forces); historical (occasionally used, if relation to present-day defense issues is apparent); how-to (training, leadership, force employment procedures, organization); interview and personal experience (rarely used, and only in terms of developing professional military skills). "We do not want overly technical weapons/equipment descriptions, overly scholarly articles, controversial policy, and budget matters; nor do we seek discussion of in-house problem areas. We do not deal with military social life, base activities or PR-type personalities/job descriptions." Buys 2-4 mss/year. Query or send complete ms. Length: 1,000-3,000 words. Pays $100-200.

Photos: State availability of photos with query or ms. "We provide nearly all photos; however, we will consider good quality photos with manuscripts." Reviews 5x7 and 8x10 b&w glossy prints or 35mm color transparencies. Offers no additional payment for photos accompanying mss. Photo credits given. Captions required. Buys one-time rights.

Tips: "The most frequent mistake made by writers is writing in a flashy, Sunday supplement style. Our audience is relatively staid, and fact-oriented articles requiring a newspaper/journalistic approach is used more than a normal magazine style. Develop a 'feel' for our foreign audience orientation. Provide material that is truly audience-oriented and easily illustrated with photos."

‡**EAGLE, For the American Fighting Man**, Command Publications, 1115 Broadway, New York NY 10010. (212)807-7100. Editor: Jim Morris. 100% freelance written. Bimonthly magazine on military adventure. "We are a fact magazine dedicated to a bellicose audience. We publish stories on weapons, military equipment and adventure stories of contemporary combat." Circ. 150,000. Pays on acceptance. Publishes ms an average of 2 months after acceptance. Byline given. Buys all rights or negotiable rights. Simultaneous queries, and simultaneous, photocopied and previously published submissions OK. Computer printout submissions acceptable; prefers letter-quality to dot-matrix. SASE. Reports in 1 week. Sample copy for 9x12 SAE and 4 first class stamps.

Nonfiction: Book excerpts, how-to, interview/profile, new product, personal experience and technical. No fiction or historical earlier than Vietnam. Buys 60 mss/year. Send complete ms. Length: 1,000-2,000 words. Pays $150-500.

Photos: Send photos with ms. Reviews 35mm color transparencies and 5x7 b&w prints. Payment normally included in fee for article. Captions and model release required. Buys all rights or negotiable rights.

‡**FAMILY MAGAZINE, The Magazine for Military Wives**, Box 4993, Walnut Creek CA 94596. (415)284-9093. Editor: Mary Jane Ryan. 90% freelance written. Magazine published 10 times/year with stories of particular interest to military wives who are young, high school educated, and move often. Circ. 525,000. Pays on publication. Publishes ms an average of 6-12 months after acceptance. Byline given. Buys first serial rights. Submit seasonal/holiday material 6 months in advance. Simultaneous queries, and simultaneous and photocopied submissions OK. Computer printout submissions acceptable; prefers letter-quality to dot-matrix. SASE. Reports in 2 months. Sample copy $1.25; writer's guidelines for business size envelope and 1 first class stamp.

Nonfiction: "We are interested in any article that speaks to the situation military wives find themselves in. We do not want stories about finding a man (they already have one) retiring or aging (they're too young) or anything too technical. The backbone of *Family* is recipes, travel stories, and human interest stories usually written by military wives to military wives. No singles stories." Buys 50 mss/year. Length: 500-3,000 words. Pays $100-300. Sometimes pays expenses (phone bills) of writers on assignment.

Photos: "We are in the market for both black and white and color photos of food and families—children, adults, men and women." Pays $25 for b&w; payment for color negotiated.

Fiction: Short fiction of interest to military wives. Buys 3-5 mss/year. Length: 500-2,000 words. Pays $100-300.

Tips: "Most of the stories we reject are not badly written, just inappropriate. Study the magazine—we are very specific. Then submit a complete manuscript. Don't send more stories on a wife finding out she is fulfilled in her marriage—I've seen hundreds."

FOR YOUR EYES ONLY, Military Intelligence Summary, Tiger Publications, Box 8759, Amarillo TX 79114. (806)655-2009. Editor: Stephen V. Cole. 5% freelance written. A biweekly newsletter covering military intelligence (post 1980). Circ. 1,200. Pays on publication. Publishes ms an average of 1 month after acceptance. Byline given. Offers variable kill fee. Buys all rights. Simultaneous queries, and simultaneous, photocopied, and previously published submissions OK. Electronic submissions OK on Modem 300 Baud; and Apple 3.3 disk. Computer printout submissions acceptable. SASE. Reports in 2 weeks on queries; 1 month on mss. Sample copy $2; writer's guidelines for SAE and 1 first class stamp.

Nonfiction: Expose, interview/profile, personal experience, technical, how to, arms sales, tests, current research, wars, battles and military data. "We're looking for technical material presented for nontechnical people, but our readership is highly intelligent and sophisticated, so do not talk down to them. Our emphasis is on how and why things work (and don't work)." No superficial or humorous material; nothing before 1981. Buys 20 mss/year. Query. Length: 50-2,000 words. Pays 3¢/word.

Photos: State availability of photos or send photos with ms. Pays $5-35 for b&w prints. Captions required. Buys one-time rights or negotiable rights.

Fillers: Newsbreaks. Buys 50-100/year. Length: 30-150 words. Pays $1-5.

Tips: "Read publication and author's guide; be aware of how much we generate internally. Briefings (100-300 words) and Newsnotes (30-150 words) are most open to freelancers."

INFANTRY, Box 2005, Fort Benning GA 31905-0605. (404)545-2350. Editor: Albert N. Garland. 80% freelance written. Bimonthly magazine published primarily for combat arms officers and noncommissioned officers. Circ. 20,000. Not copyrighted. Buys first serial rights. Pays on publication. Payment cannot be made to U.S. government employees. Publishes ms an average of 1 year after acceptance. Computer printout submissions acceptable; prefers letter-quality to dot-matrix. Reports in 1 month. Free sample copy and writer's guidelines.

Nonfiction: Interested in current information on U.S. military organization, weapons, equipment, tactics and techniques; foreign armies and their equipment; lessons learned from combat experience, both past and present; and solutions to problems encountered in the Active Army and the Reserve Components. Departments include Letters, Features and Forum, Training Notes, and Book Reviews. Uses 70 unsolicited mss/year. Recent article example: "Thinking About Light Infantry" (November-December 1984). Length of articles: 1,500-3,500 words. Length for Book Reviews: 500-1,000 words. Query. Accepts 75 mss/year.

Photos: Used with mss.

Tips: Start with letters to editor, book reviews to break in.

LEATHERNECK, Box 1775, Quantico VA 22134. (703)640-3171. Editor: William V.H. White. Managing Editor: Tom Bartlett. Emphasizes all phases of Marine Corps activities. Monthly magazine. Circ. 90,000. Pays on acceptance. Buys all rights. Phone queries OK. Submit seasonal/holiday material 3 months in advance. SASE. Reports in 2 weeks. Free sample copy and writer's guidelines.

Nonfiction: "All material submitted to *Leatherneck* must pertain to the U.S. Marine Corps and its members." General interest, how-to, humor, historical, interview, nostalgia, personal experience, profile, and travel. "No articles on politics, subjects not pertaining to the Marine Corps, and subjects that are not in good taste." Buys 24 mss/year. Query. Length: 1,500-3,000 words. Pays $50 and up/magazine page.

Photos: "We like to receive a complete package when we consider a manuscript for publication." State availability of photos with query. No additional payment for 4x5 or 8x10 b&w glossy prints. Captions required. Model release required. Buys all rights.

Fiction: Adventure, historical and humorous. All material must pertain to the U.S. Marine Corps and its members. Buys 3 mss/year. Query. Length: 1,000-3,000 words. Pays $50 and up/magazine page.

Poetry: Light verse and traditional. No poetry that does not pertain to the U.S. Marine Corps. Buys 40 mss/year. Length: 16-20 lines. Pays $10-20.

THE MILITARY ENGINEER, 607 Prince St., Alexandria VA 22314. (703)549-3800. Editor: John J. Kern. 80% freelance written. Bimonthly magazine. Circ. 27,000. Pays on publication. Publishes ms an average of 9 months after acceptance. Byline given. Buys all rights. Phone queries OK. Computer printout submissions acceptable. SASE. Reports in 1 month. Sample copy and writer's guidelines $4.

Nonfiction: Well-written and illustrated semitechnical articles by experts and practitioners of civil and military engineering, constructors, equipment manufacturers, defense contract suppliers and architect/engineers on these subjects and on subjects of military biography and history. "Subject matter should represent a contribution to the fund of knowledge, concern a new project or method, be on R&D in these fields; investigate planning and management techniques or problems in these fields, or be of militarily strategic nature." Buys 50-70 unsolicited mss/year. Length: 1,000-2,000 words. Query.

Photos: Mss must be accompanied by 6-10 well-captioned photos, maps or illustrations; b&w, generally. Pays approximately $25/page.

‡**MILITARY LIVING**, Box 4010, Arlington VA 22204. (703)237-0203. Editor: Ann Crawford. For military personnel and their families. Monthly. Circ. 30,000. Buys first serial rights. "Very few freelance features were used last year; most were staff-written." Pays on publication. Sample copy for 50¢ in coin or stamps. "Slow to report due to small staff and workload." Submit complete ms. SASE.

Nonfiction: "Articles on military life in greater Washington D.C. area. We would especially like recreational features in the Washington D.C. area. We specialize in passing along morale-boosting information about the military installations in the area, with emphasis on the military family—travel pieces about surrounding area, recreation information, etc. We do not want to see depressing pieces, pieces without the military family in mind, personal petty complaints or general information pieces. Prefer 700 words or less, but will consider more for an exceptional feature. We also prefer a finished article rather than a query." Payment is on an honorarium basis, 1-1¹/₂¢/word.

Photos: Photos purchased with mss. 5x7 or larger b&w glossy prints only. Payment is $5 for original photos by author.

MILITARY LIVING R&R REPORT, Box 4010, Arlington VA 22204. (703)237-0203. Publisher: Ann Crawford. Bimonthly newsletter for "military consumers worldwide." "Please state when sending submission that it is for the *R&R Report Newsletter* so as not to confuse it with our monthly magazine which has different requirements." Pays on publication. Buys first serial rights but will consider other rights. SASE. Sample copy $1.

Nonfiction: "We use information on little-known military facilities and privileges, discounts around the world and travel information. Items must be short and concise. Stringers are wanted around the world. Payment is on an honorarium basis. 1-1¹/₂¢/word."

MILITARY REVIEW, U.S. Army Command and General Staff College, Fort Leavenworth KS 66027-6910. (913)684-5642. Editor-in-Chief: Lt. Col. Dallas Van Hoose Jr. Features Editor: Major Tom Conrad. Business Manager: Capt. George Cassi. 65% freelance written. Monthly journal emphasizing the military for senior military officers, students and scholars. Circ. 27,000. Pays on publication. Publishes ms an average of 8 months after acceptance. Byline given. Buys one-time rights. Phone queries and photocopied submissions OK. Computer printout submissions acceptable; prefers letter-quality to dot-matrix. SASE. Reports in 1 month. Free writer's guidelines.

Nonfiction: Military history, international affairs, tactics, new military equipment, strategy and book reviews. Prefers not to get material unrelated to defense subjects, poetry or cartoons. Buys 100-120 mss/year. Query. Length: 2,000-4,000 words. Pays $25-100.

Tips: "We need more articles from military personnel experienced in particular specialties. Examples: Tactics from a tactician, military engineering from an engineer, etc. We would appreciate receiving good quality, double-spaced letter-quality computer printout submissions."

NATIONAL GUARD, 1 Massachusetts Ave. NW, Washington DC 20001. (202)789-0031. Editor: Major Reid K. Beveridge. 10% freelance written. Monthly magazine for officers of the Army and Air National Guard. Circ. 69,000. Pays on publication. Publishes ms an average of 6 months after acceptance. Rights negotiable. Byline given. Electronic submissions OK on IBM PC. Computer printout submissions acceptable. SASE. Query.

Nonfiction: Military policy, strategy, training, equipment, logistics, personnel policies; tactics, combat lessons learned as they pertain to the Army and Air Force (and impact on Army National Guard and Air National Guard). Material must be strictly accurate from a technical standpoint. Does not publish exposes, cartoons or jokes. Buys 10-12 mss/year. Query. Length: 2,000-3,000 words. Payment ($75-500/article) depends on originality, amount of research involved, etc. Sometimes pays expenses of writers on assignment.

Photos: Photography pertinent to subject matter should accompany ms.

OFF DUTY, U.S.: Suite C-2, 3303 Harbor Blvd., Costa Mesa CA 92626. Editor: Bruce Thorstad. Europe: Eschersheimer Landstrasse 69, Frankfurt/M, West Germany. Editor: J.C. Hixenbaugh. Pacific: Box 9869, Hong Kong. Editor: Jim Shaw. 50% freelance written. Monthly magazine for U.S. military personnel and their families stationed around the world. Most readers ages 18-35 years. Combined circ. 683,000. Buys first serial rights or second serial (reprint) rights. Pays on acceptance. Publishes ms an average of 6 months after acceptance. Computer printout submissions acceptable. Free writer's guidelines; sample copy $1.

Nonfiction: Three editions—American, Pacific and European. "Emphasis is on off-duty travel, leisure, military shopping, wining and dining, sports, hobbies, music, and getting the most out of military life. Overseas editions lean toward foreign travel and living in foreign cultures. They also emphasize what's going on back home. In travel articles we like anecdotes, lots of description, color and dialogue. American edition uses more American trends and how-to/service material. Material with special U.S., Pacific or European slant should be sent to appropriate address above; material useful in all editions may be sent to U.S. address and will be forwarded as necessary." Buys 30-50 mss/year for each of three editions. Query. Length: 1,500 words average. Also needs 200-word shorties. Pays 13¢/word for use in one edition; 16¢/word for use in 2 or more. Sometimes pays expenses of writers on assignment.

Photos: Bought with or without accompanying ms. Pays $25 for b&w glossy prints; $50 for color transparencies; $100 for full page color; $200 for covers. "Covers must be vertical format 35mm; larger format transparencies preferred."

Tips: "All material should take into account to some extent our special audience—the U.S. military and their dependents. Our publication is subtitled 'The Military Leisuretime magazine,' and the stories we like best are about how to get more out of the military experience. That 'more' could range from more fun to more satisfaction to more material benefits such as military privileges. The magazine will be adding pages and buying more articles in the year ahead. The writer has a better chance of breaking into our publication with short articles and fillers simply because our major features are more important to us, and the military angle we need is more essential. We've got a fairly strict idea by this time of how our main travel feature or our main cooking feature should read, so when we're handing out assignments, we go with a writer we know. Other features are more loosely structured. Generally, by the time I get an article that I've assigned, the writer and I have talked about it enough so that there are really no major surprises. The mistakes are made by the query writers who very often mistake the basic nature of our magazine. If we do an article on running, we'll get a raft of queries for running articles. That's wrong; we're a general interest magazine. If we've just done running, it's going to be quite a while before we do it again. We've got *dozens* of other subjects to cover."

OVERSEAS!, The Leisure Time Magazine for the Military Man in Europe, Military Consumer Today, Inc., 17 Bismarckstrasse. 6900 Heidelberg, West Germany 06221-2543 1/32/33. Editor: Charles L. Kaufman. Managing Editor: Greg Ballinger. 95% freelance written. Monthly magazine. "Overseas! is aimed at the U.S. military in Europe. It is the leading men's military lifestyle magazine slanted towards life in Europe, specifically directed to males ages 18-35. Note: Overseas! is a private firm and is in *no* way connected with the Department of Defense." Circ. 83,000. Pays on acceptance. Publishes ms an average of 3 months after acceptance. Byline given. Offers kill fee depending on circumstances and writer. Buys one-time rights. Submit seasonal/holiday material at least 4 months in advance. Simultaneous queries, and simultaneous, photocopied, and previously published submissions OK. Computer printout submissions acceptable; prefers letter-quality to dot-matrix. SASE, IRCs. Reports in 2 weeks on queries; 1 month on mss. Sample copy for SAE and 4 IRCs; writer's guidelines for SAE and 1 IRC.
Nonfiction: General interest (lifestyle for men and other topics); how-to (use camera, buy various types of video, audio, photo and computer equipment); humor (no military humor; "we want travel/tourist humor like old *National Lampoon* style. Must be humorous"); interview/profile (music, personality interviews; current music stars for young audience); personal experience (relating to travel in Europe); technical (video, audio, photo, computer; how to purchase and use equipment); (European travel, first person adventure; write toward male audience); and men's fashion/lifestyle. Special issues include Video, Audio, Photo, and Military Shopper's Guide. Needs 250-750 word articles on video, audio, photo and computer products. Published in September every year. No articles that are drug- or sex-related. No cathedrals or museums of Europe stories. Buys 3-5 mss/year "but would buy more if we got better quality and subjects." Query with or without pulished clips or send complete ms. Length: 750-2,000 words. Pays 10¢/word. Rarely pays expenses of writers on assignment.
Photos: Send photos with accompanying query or ms. Pays $20 minimum, b&w; $35 color transparencies, 35mm or larger. Photos must accompany travel articles—"color slides, please. Also, we are always looking for photographs of pretty, unposed, dressed, nonfashion, active *women* for our covers." Pays $150 minimum. Identification of subjects required. Buys one-time rights.
Columns/Departments: Back Talk—Potpourri page of humor, cartoons and other materials relating to life in Europe for Americans. Buys 12-20 mss/year. Query with published clips. Length: 1-150 words. Pays $20-75/piece used.
Fiction: Adventure (relating to travel in Europe); experimental ("query or send manuscript. We're always looking for something new."); Humorous (travel in Europe—what it's like being a tourist); and travel ("mix fact with fiction to make adventure travel story read better. Please label as fiction."). No pornography or life in military. Buys 2 mss/year; "would buy more if we received good manuscripts on subjects we require—i.e., travel in Europe."
Tips: Travel writing and articles on video, audio, photo and computer equipment and use are most open to freelancers. Writing should be lively, interesting, with lots of good information. We are always looking for new ways to present material."

PARAMETERS: JOURNAL OF THE US ARMY WAR COLLEGE, U.S. Army War College, Carlisle Barracks PA 17013. (717)245-4943. Editor: COL William R. Calhoun Jr., U.S. Army. Quarterly. Readership consists of senior leadership of U.S. defense establishment, both uniformed and civilian, plus members of the media, government, industry and academia interested in scholarly articles devoted to national and international security affairs, military strategy, military leadership and management, art and science of warfare, and military history (provided it has contemporary relevance). Most readers possess a graduate degree. Circ. 9,000. Not copyrighted; unless copyrighted by author, articles may be reprinted with appropriate credits. Buys first serial rights. Byline given. Pays on publication. Publishes ms an average of 6 months after acceptance. Computer printout submissions acceptable; prefers letter-quality to dot-matrix. Reports in 1 month.
Nonfiction: Articles preferred that deal with current security issues, employ critical analysis, and provide solutions or recommendations. Liveliness and verve, consistent with scholarly integrity, appreciated. Theses, studies and academic course papers should be adapted to article form prior to submission. Documentation in endnotes. Submit complete ms. Length: 5,000 words, preferably less. Pays $100 minimum; $150 average (including visuals).
Tips: "Research should be thorough; documentation should be complete."

PERIODICAL, Council on America's Military Past, 4970 N. Camino Antonio, Tucson AZ 85718. Editor-in-Chief: Dan L. Thrapp. Quarterly magazine emphasizing old and abandoned forts, posts and military installations; military subjects for a professional, knowledgeable readership interested in one-time defense sites or other military installations. Circ. 1,500. Pays on publication. Buys one-time rights. Simultaneous, photocopied, and previously published (if published a long time ago) submissions OK. SASE. Reports in 3 weeks.
Nonfiction: Historical, personal experience, photo feature and technical (relating to posts, their construction/operation and military matters). Buys 4-6 mss/issue. Query or send complete ms. Length: 300-4,000 words. Pays $2/page minimum.
Photos: Purchased with or without ms. Query. Reviews glossy, single-weight 8x10 b&w prints. Offers no additional payment for photos accepted with accompanying ms. Captions required.

‡**R&R ENTERTAINMENT DIGEST**, R&R Werbe GmbH, 17 Bismarckstrasse, 6900 Heidelberg, W. Germany, 06221-25431/32/33. Editor: Mrs. Tory Billard. 50% freelance written. Monthly entertainment guide for military and government employees and their families stationed in Europe "specializing in travel in Europe, audio/video/photo information, music, and the homemaker scene. Aimed exclusively at military/DoD based in Europe—Germany, Britain and the Mediterranean." Circ. 185,000. Pays on publication. Publishes ms an average of 2-6 months after acceptance. Byline given. "We offer 50% of payment as a kill fee, but this rarely happens—if story can't run in one issue, we try to use it in a future edition." Buys first serial rights for military market in Europe only. "We will reprint stories that have run in stateside publications if applicable to us." Submit seasonal/holiday material 3 months in advance. Computer printout submissions acceptable; prefers letter-quality to dot-matrix. Simultaneous queries, and simultaneous, photocopied, and previously published submissions OK. Reports in 3 weeks. Free sample copy and writer's guidelines.
Nonfiction: Humor (limited amount used—dealing with travel experiences in Europe), and travel (always looking for good travel in Europe features). "We prefer articles by writers who have been to these places rather than writers who do travel features from a book. Articles should sound like writer has been there and done these things—a sort of where to go, what to see feature. No travel stories written from our books." No interviews of singers, historical pieces, album/movie/book reviews, or technical stories. Buys 15 mss/year. Query with published clips or send complete ms. Length: 600-1,800 words. Pays in Deutsche Marks—DM 90 (an estimated $28) /page; full payment for partial page.
Photos: State availablility of photos or send photos with query or mss. Pays DM 80 for 35mm color transparencies. Captions required. "We pay once for use with story but can reuse at no additional cost."
Columns/Departments: Monthly audio, video and photo stories. "We need freelancers with solid background in these areas who can write for general public on a variety of topics." Buys 10 mss/year. Query with published clips or send complete ms. Length: 1,300-1,400 words. Pays DM 90/magazine page.
Fiction: Very little fiction accepted. Query. "It has to be exceptional to be accepted." Length: 600-1,200 words. Pays DM 90/page.
Fillers: Cartoons pertaining to television. Buys 5/year. Pays DM 80/cartoon.
Tips: "Prospective freelancers should keep the tone of their articles light and avoid pedestrian, pedantic writing. The shared experience form of narration is often more interesting than a detached, third-person style. They should be informative, entertaining, fun to read, even humorous at times. Clever, snappy writers who submit *clean*, easy-to-read copy (double-spaced) who accompany their manuscript with a good selection of 35mm color slides have a better chance of being accepted in our magazine."

THE RETIRED OFFICER MAGAZINE, 201 N. Washington St., Alexandria VA 22314. (703)549-2311. Editor: Colonel Minter L. Wilson Jr., USA-Ret. 90% freelance written. Monthly for officers of the 7 uniformed services and their families. Circ. 345,000. Pays on acceptance. Publishes ms an average of 6 months after acceptance. Byline given. Buys all rights or first serial rights. Submit seasonal material (holiday stories with a military theme) at least 6 months in advance. Electronic submissions OK on Digital word processor, but requires hard copy also. Computer printout submissions acceptable; prefers letter-quality to dot-matrix. Reports on material accepted for publication within 6 weeks. SASE. Free sample copy and writer's guidelines.
Nonfiction: Recent military history, humor, hobbies, travel, second-career job opportunities and current affairs. Also, upbeat articles on aging, human interest and features pertinent to a retired military officer's milieu. True military experiences are also useful. "We tend to use articles less technical than a single-service publication. We do not publish poetry or fillers." Buys 48 unsolicited mss/year. Submit complete ms. Length: 1,000-2,500 words. Pays $100-400.
Photos: Marjorie J. Seng, associate editor. Reviews 8x10 b&w photos (normal halftone). Pays $15. Original slides or transparencies for magazine cover must be suitable for color separation. Pays up to $150.
Tips: "We're looking for more upbeat articles on Vietnam."

‡**RUSI JOURNAL**, Royal United Services Institute for Defence Studies, Whitehall, London SW1A 2ET England. Editor: Dr. Brian Holden Reid. Quarterly magazine emphasizing defense and military history. For the defense community: service officers, civil servants, politicians, journalists, academics, industrialists, etc.

Circ. 6,500. Pays on publication. Buys all rights. Photocopied submissions OK. SAE, IRC. Sample copy $10 or £5.

Nonfiction: Learned articles on all aspects of defense; historical military articles with particular reference to current defense problems; weapon technology; international relations and civil/military relations. Buys 40 unsolicited mss/year. Query. Length: 2,500-6,000 words. Pays £12.5/printed page.

Photos: No additional payment is made for photos, but they should accompany articles whenever possible.

SEA POWER, 2300 Wilson Blvd., Arlington VA 22201. Editor: James D. Hessman. Issued monthly by the Navy League of the U.S. for naval personnel and civilians interested in naval maritime and defense matters. Pays on publication. Buys all rights. Reports in 6 weeks. SASE. Free sample copy.

Nonfiction: Factual articles on sea power in general, U.S. industrial base, mineral resources, and the U.S. Navy, the U.S. Marine Corps, U.S. Coast Guard, U.S. Merchant Marine and naval services and other navies of the world in particular. Should illustrate and expound the importance of the seas and sea power to the U.S. and its allies. Wants timely, clear, nonpedantic writing for audience that is intelligent and well-educated but not necessarily fluent in military/hi-tech terminology. No historical articles, commentaries, critiques, abstract theories, poetry or editorials. Query first. Length: 500-2,500 words. Pays $100-500 depending upon length and research involved.

Photos: Purchased with ms.

SOLDIER OF FORTUNE, The Journal of Professional Adventurers. Omega Group, Ltd., Box 693, Boulder CO 80306. (303)449-3750. Editor/Publisher: Robert K. Brown. Executive Editor: Dale Dye. 80% freelance written. Monthly magazine covering the military, police and the outdoors. "We take a strong stand on political issues such as maintenance of a strong national defense, the dangers of communism, and the right to keep and bear arms." Circ. 225,000. Pays on publication. Publishes ms an average of 4 months after acceptance. Byline given. Offers 25% kill fee "for proven freelancers." Buys first world rights; makes work-for-hire assignments. Submit seasonal/holiday material 6 months in advance. Computer printout submissions acceptable on North Star Horizon CPM. Computer printout submissions acceptable; prefers letter-quality to dot-matrix. SASE. Reports in 1 month. Sample copy $4; writer's guidelines for SAE.

Nonfiction: Expose (in-depth reporting from the world's hot spots—Afghanistan, Angola, etc.); general interest (critical focus on national issues—gun control, national defense); historical (soldiers of fortune, adventurers of past, history of elite units, Vietnam); how-to (outdoor equipment, weaponry, self-defense); humor (military, police); interview/profile (leaders or representatives of issues); new product (usually staff-assigned; outdoor equipment, weapons); personal experience ("I was there") focus; photo feature; and technical (weapons, weapons systems, military tactics). Buys 75-100 mss/year. Query. Length: 1,000-3,500 words. Pays $175-1,000.

Photos: Photos with ms are integral to package. Separate submissions negotiable. Captions and identification of weapons and military equipment required. Buys first world rights.

Columns/Departments: I Was There/It Happened to Me (adventure and combat stories). Buys 12 mss/year. Send complete ms. Length: 500 words maximum. Pays $50.

Tips: "All authors should have a professional background in the military or police work."

THE TIMES MAGAZINE, Army Times Publishing Company, Springfield, VA 22159-0200. (703)750-8672. Editor: Barry Robinson. Managing Editor: Donna Peterson. 30% freelance written. Monthly magazine covering current lifestyles and problems of career military families around the world. Circ. 330,000. Pays on publication. Publishes ms an average of 4 months after acceptance. Byline given. Offers negotiable kill fee. Buys all rights. Submit seasonal/holiday material 6 months in advance. Double- or triple-spaced computer printout submissions acceptable; no dot-matrix. SASE. Reports in 1 month. Free sample copy and writer's guidelines for 9x12 SAE.

Nonfiction: Expose (current military); how-to (military wives); interview/profile (military); opinion (military topic); personal experience (military only); and travel (of military interest). No poetry, cartoons or historical articles. Buys 100 mss/year. Query with published clips. Length: 1,000-3,000 words. Pays $50-600. Pays expenses of writers on assignment.

Photos: State availability of photos or send photos with ms. Reviews 35mm color contact sheets and prints. Caption, model release, and identification of subjects required. Buys all rights.

Tips: "In query write a detailed description of story and how it will be told. A tentative lead is nice. Just one good story 'breaks in' a freelancer. Follow the outline you propose in query letter and humanize articles with quotes and examples."

‡TUN'S TALES, Geofcom, Ltd., Box 1118, Kulpsville PA 19443. (215)362-8397. Editor: G. Franklin Grimm. 80% freelance written. Bimonthly tabloid for active and reserve Marines. Estab. 1984. Circ. 73,000. Pays on publication. Publishes ms an average of 2 months after acceptance. Byline given. Buys one-time rights. Submit seasonal/holiday material 2 months in advance. Simultaneous queries, and simultaneous and photocopied submissions OK. SASE. Computer printout submissions acceptable; no dot-matrix. Reports in 2 weeks.

Sample copy for 8x10 SAE and 8 first class stamps.
Nonfiction: Historical/nostalgic, how-to, humor, interview/profile, personal experience and photo feature, all pertaining to active and reserve Marines. Only articles that deal with the Marine Corps are accepted. Buys 6 mss/year. Send complete ms. Length: 500-3,500 words. Pays $35-150. Sometimes pays the expenses of writers on assignment.
Photos: Send photos with ms. Pays $50-100 for 5x7 b&w prints. Captions, model release, and identification of subjects required. Buys one-time rights. Sometimes pays the expenses of writers on assignment.
Fiction: Adventure, condensed novels, historical, humorous, mystery and serialized novels.
Fillers: Dianne C. Grimm, fillers editor. Jokes, gags, anecdotes and short humor. Buys 12/year. Length: 200-400 words. Pays $25-45.
Tips: "We are open to all articles, both major and fillers that will be of interest to Marines and their spouses."

Music

Increased use of electronics in music is one trend that will be affecting what some music magazine editors buy this year. When a magazine's readership is highly knowledgable about a music specialty, lack of depth and technical details will disqualify an article.

Music fans follow the latest music industry news in these publications. Musicians and different types of music (such as jazz, opera, rock and bluegrass) are the sole focus of some magazines. Publications geared to music industry professionals can be found in the music section of Trade Journals. Additional music- and dance-related markets are included in the Theatre, Movie, TV, and Entertainment section.

THE ABSOLUTE SOUND, The High End Journal, Harry Pearson Jr., Box 115, Sea Cliff NY 11579. (516)676-2830. Editor: Harry Pearson Jr. Managing Editor: Art Dudley. Quarterly magazine covering the music reproduction business, audio equipment and records for "up-scale, high tech men and women between 20 and 40, toy freaks." Pays on publication. Byline given. Buys all rights. Computer printout submissions acceptable; prefers letter-quality to dot-matrix. Sample copy $7.
Nonfiction: Exposé (of bad commercial audio practices); interview/profile (famous engineers, famous conductors); new product (audio); opinion (audio and record reviews); and technical (how to improve your stereo system). Special Recordings Issue (Autumn). No puff pieces about industry. Query with published clips. Length: 250-5,000 words. Pays $125-1,000.
Columns/Departments: Audio Musings (satires), and Reports from Overseas (audio fairs, celebrities, record companies). Buys 12 mss/year. Query with published clips. Length: 250-750 words. Pays $125-200.
Fillers: Clippings, newsbreaks; "They Say" approach like *The New Yorker*, but audio or recording related. Buys 30/year. Length: 50-200 words. Pays $10-40.
Tips: "Writers should know about audio recordings and the engineering of same—as well as live music. The approach is *literate* witty, investigative—good journalism."

‡**BAM, Rock and Video/The California Music Magazine**, BAM Publications, 5951 Canning St., Oakland CA 94609. (415)652-3810. Senior Editor: Dave Zimmer. Associate Editor: Bill Forman. 60% freelance written. Biweekly tabloid. Circ. 110,000. Pays on publication. Publishes ms an average of 3 months after acceptance. Byline given. Offers negotiable kill fee. Buys first North American serial rights. Submit seasonal/holiday material 3 months in advance. Computer printout submissions acceptable; no dot-matrix. SASE. Reports in 3 weeks. Sample copy $2.
Nonfiction: Book excerpts, interview/profile and new product. Special issue, Annual Video. No personal experience without an interview subject. Buys 100 mss/year. Query with published clips. Length: 1,500-8,000 words. Pays $40-300. Sometimes pays expenses of writers on assignment.
Tips: "*BAM*'s focus in on both the personality and the craft of musicians. Writers should concentrate on bringing out their subject's special traits and avoid bland, cliched descriptions and quotes. Clear, crisp writing is essential. Many potential *BAM* writers try to be too clever and end up sounding stupid. Also, it helps to have a clear focus. Many writers tend to ramble and simply string quotes together."

BAM, The California Music Magazine, BAM Publications, 5951 Canning St., Oakland CA 94609. (415)652-3810. Editor: Dave Zimmer. Assistant editor: Bill Forman. A biweekly contemporary music tabloid.

Circ. 110,000. Pays on publication. Publishes ms an average of 2-6 months after acceptance. Byline given. Offers negotiable kill fee. Submit seasonal/holiday material at least 6 weeks in advance. Computer printout submissions acceptable; no dot-matrix.

Nonfiction: Book excerpts, interview/profile, new product, photo feature, and live reviews and record reviews of musicians. "Most of *BAM*'s articles deal with rock and roll, slanted towards the 18-35 years of age market with frequent pro musician features and some coverage of pop, jazz, country and blues." No self-indulgent, personal experience material. Buys 100-150 mss/year. Query with published clips. Pays $35-200. Sometimes pays the expenses of writers on assignment.

Photos: Richard McCaffrey, photo editor. State availability of photos. Reviews b&w contact sheets. Pays $15-30 for 5x7 or 8x10 b&w prints; $50-150 for 5x7 or 8x10 color prints. Identification of subjects required. Buys one-time rights.

Columns/Departments: Industry News, Radio and Media News, Video, and Film. Buys 20 mss/year. Query with published clips. Length: 1,000-3,000 words. Pays variable rates.

Tips: "A good selection of clips and a crisply written cover letter always get a response. Most of our major profiles are freelance. They are *assigned* however; so query first. Avoid first-person journalism when writing about another individual or group. At the same time, inject plenty of spirit and personality into features. Our main need at this time is in the area of video."

BLUEGRASS UNLIMITED, Bluegrass Unlimited, Inc., Box 111, Broad Run VA 22014. (703)361-8992. Editor: Peter V. Kuykendall. 80% freelance written. Monthly magazine on bluegrass and old-time country music. Circ. 19,000. Pays on publication. Publishes ms an average of 4 months after acceptance. Byline given. Kill fee negotiated. Buys first North American serial rights, one-time rights, all rights, and second serial (reprint) rights. Submit seasonal/holiday material 4 months in advance. Photocopied submissions OK. Computer printout submissions acceptable. SASE. Reports in 2 weeks on queries; 2 months on mss. Free sample copy and writer's guidelines.

Nonfiction: General interest, historical/nostalgic, how-to, interview/profile, personal experience, photo feature and travel. No "fan" style articles. Buys 75-80 mss/year. Query with or without published clips. No set word length. Pays 4-5¢/word.

Photos: State availability of photos or send photos with query. Reviews 35mm color transparencies and 3x5, 5x7, and 8x10 b&w and color prints. Pays $20-30 for b&w transparencies; $40-125 for color transparencies; $20-50 for b&w prints; and $40-125 for color prints. Identification of subjects required. Buys one-time rights and all rights.

Fiction: Ethnic and humorous. Buys 3-5 mss/year. Query. No set word length: Pays 4-5¢/word.

Tips: "We would prefer that articles be informational, based on personal experience or an interview with lots of quotes from subject, profile, humor, etc."

‡**CINEMASCORE, The Film Music Journal**, Fandom Unlimited Entrps., Box 70868, Sunnyvale CA 94086. (415)960-1151. Editor: Randall D. Larson. Magazine published twice annually covering music for motion pictures and television, history and criticism. "We are devoted to the review and appreciation on the art and technique of music for motion pictures, emphasizing interviews with industry professionals." Circ. 1,500. Pays 50% on acceptance; 50% on publication. Publishes ms an average of 1 year after acceptance. Byline given. Offers 50% kill fee. Buys first North American serial rights. Photocopied and previously published submissions (rarely) OK. Electronic submissions OK on IBM-PC/COMPAQ systems with Microsoft WORD w/p software, but requires hard copy also. Computer printout submissions acceptable. SASE. Reports in 3 weeks on queries; 6 weeks on mss. Sample copy $2; writer's guidelines for SAE and 1 first class stamp.

Nonfiction: Interview/profile, technical, critique, musicological analysis and reviews. Special issue #15 includes foreign film music composers. No general-type reviews. "We want *specific*, in-depth reviews and criticism, and perceptive, though not necessariy technical, analysis." Buys 5-10 mss/year. Query with published clips or send complete ms. Word length open. Pays $15-100 for major research articles; pays in subscriptions for shorter pieces and reviews. Sometimes pays expenses of writers on assignment.

Photos: State availability of photos. Prefers b&w prints. Payment considered part of ms. Identification of subjects required. Buys one-time rights.

Tips: "Have an interest in and knowledge of the use, history, and techique of movie music, and be able to contact industry professionals or insightfully examine their music in an analytical article/profile. Writers should be familiar with the publication before trying to break in. Be willing to buy a copy to ensure writer and publication are compatible."

CREEM, Suite 209, 210 S. Woodward Ave., Birmingham MI 48011. (313)642-8833. Editor: Dave DiMartino. Pays on publication. Buys all rights. SASE. Reports in 6 weeks.

Nonfiction: Short articles, mostly music-oriented. "Feature length stories are mostly staff written, but we're open for newcomers to break in with short pieces. Freelancers are used a lot in the Beat Goes On section. Please send queries and sample articles to Bill Holdship, submissions editor. We bill ourselves as 'America's Only Rock 'n' Roll Magazine'." Query. Pays $50 minimum for reviews, $300 minimum for full-length features.

Photos: Freelance photos.

Tips: "You can't study the magazine too much—our stable of writers have all come from the ranks of our readers. The writer can save his time and ours by studying what we do print and producing similar copy that we can use immediately. Send short stuff—no epics on the first try. We really aren't a good market for the professional writer looking for another outlet—a writer has to be pretty obsessed with music and/or pop culture in order to be published in our book. We get people writing in for assignments who obviously have never even read the magazine, and that's totally useless to us."

FRETS MAGAZINE, GPI Publications, 20085 Stevens Creek Blvd., Cupertino CA 95014. (408)446-1105. Editor: Phil Hood. 50% freelance written. Monthly magazine for amateur and professional acoustic string music enthusiasts; for players, makers, listeners and fans. Country, jazz, classical, blues, pop and bluegrass. For instrumentalists interested in banjo, mandolin, guitar, violin, upright bass, dobro, dulcimer and others. Circ. open. Pays on acceptance. Buys first serial rights. Submit seasonal/holiday material 4 months in advance. Computer printout submissions on $8^{1}/_{2}$x11 sheets with legible type acceptable if not a photocopy or multiple submission. "All-caps printout unacceptable." SASE. Reports in 6 weeks. Free sample copy and writer's guidelines.

Nonfiction: General interest (artist-oriented); historical (instrument making or manufacture); how-to (instrument craft and repair); interview (with artists or historically important individuals); profile (music performer); and technical (instrument making, acoustics, instrument repair). Prefers not to see humor; poetry; general-interest articles that really belong in a less-specialized publication; articles (about performers) that only touch on biographical or human interest angles, without getting into the 'how-to' nuts and bolts of musicianship. Buys 14 mss/year. Query with published clips or sample lead paragraph. Length: 1,000-2,500 words. Pays $125-300. Experimental (instrument design, acoustics). Pays $100-175. Sometimes pays expenses of writers on assignment.

Photos: State availability of photos. Pays $25 minimum for b&w prints (reviews contact sheets); $100 and up for cover shot color transparencies. Captions and credits required. Buys one-time rights.

Columns/Departments: Repair Shop (instrument craft and repair); and *Frets* Visits (on-location visit to manufacturer or major music festival). Buys 10 mss/year. Query. Length: 1,200-1,700 words. Pays $75-175, including photos.

Fillers: Newsbreaks, upcoming events and music-related news.

Tips: "Our focus also includes ancillary areas of string music—such as sound reinforcement for acoustic musicians, using personal computers in booking and management, recording techniques for acoustic music, and so on. We enjoy giving exposure (and encouragement) to talented new writers. We do not like to receive submissions or queries from writers who have only a vague notion of our scope and interest. We do not cover electric guitarists."

GUITAR PLAYER MAGAZINE, GPI Publications, 20085 Stevens Creek, Cupertino CA 95014. (408)446-1105. Editor: Tom Wheeler. 60% freelance written. Monthly magazine for persons "interested in guitars, guitarists, manufacturers, guitar builders, bass players, equipment, careers, etc." Circ. 170,000. Buys first serial and limited reprint rights. Pays on acceptance. Publishes ms an average of 4 months after acceptance. Byline given. Computer printout submissions acceptable; prefers letter-quality to dot-matrix. SASE. Reports in 6 weeks. Free sample copy.

Nonfiction: Publishes "wide variety of articles pertaining to guitars and guitarists: interviews, guitar craftsmen profiles, how-to features—anything amateur and professional guitarists would find fascinating and/or helpful. On interviews with 'name' performers, be as technical as possible regarding strings, guitars, techniques, etc. We're not a pop culture magazine, but a magazine for musicians." Also buys features on such subjects as a guitar museum, role of the guitar in elementary education, personal reminiscences of past greats, technical gadgets and how to work them, analysis of flamenco, etc." Buys 30-40 mss/year. Query. Length: open. Pays $100-300. Sometimes pays expenses of writers on assignment.

Photos: Photos purchased. Reviews b&w glossy prints. Pays $35-75. Buys 35mm color transparencies. Pays $250 (for cover only). Buys one time rights.

HIGH FIDELITY/MUSICAL AMERICA, 825 7th Ave., New York NY 10019. Editor: Shirley Fleming. 50% freelance written. Monthly. Circ. 20,000. Pays on publication. Publishes ms an average of 2 months after acceptance. Buys all rights. Computer printout submissions acceptable; no dot-matrix. SASE.

Nonfiction: Articles, musical and audio, are generally prepared by acknowledged writers and authorities in the field, but uses freelance material. Query with published clips. Length: 1,200 words maximum. Pays $150 minimum.

Photos: New b&w photos of musical personalities, events, etc.

ILLINOIS ENTERTAINER, Box 356, Mount Prospect IL 60056. (312)298-9333. Editor: Guy C. Arnston. 95% freelance written. Monthly tabloid covering music and entertainment for consumers within 100-mile radius of Chicago interested in music. Circ. 80,000. Pays on publication. Publishes ms an average of 3 months after acceptance. Byline given. Offers 100% kill fee. Buys first serial rights. Submit seasonal/holiday material 2 months in advance. Simultaneous queries OK. Computer printout submissions acceptable "if letters are clear"; no dot-matrix. SASE. Reports in 1 week on queries; 1 month on mss. Sample copy $2; free writer's guidelines.

Nonfiction: Interview/profile (of entertainment figures). No Q&A interviews. Buys 200 mss/year. Query with published clips. Length: 500-2,000 words. Pays $15-100. Sometimes pays expenses of writers on assignment.

Photos: State availability of photos. Pays $10-20 for 5x7 or 8x10 b&w prints; $100 for color cover photo, both on publication only. Captions and identification of subjects required.

Columns/Departments: Software (record reviews stress record over band or genre); film reviews; and book reviews. Buys 500 mss/year. Query with published clips. Length: 150-250 words. Pays $6-20.

Tips: "Send samples in mail (published or unpublished) with phone number, and be patient. Articles and fillers offer freelancers the best chance of breaking in, as full staff has seniority."

INTERNATIONAL MUSICIAN, American Federation of Musicians, 1500 Broadway, New York NY 10036. (212)869-1330. Editor: J. Martin Emerson. Monthly for professional musicians. Pays on acceptance. Byline given. SASE. Reports in 2 months.

Nonfiction: Articles on prominent instrumental musicians (classical, jazz, rock or country). Send complete ms. Length: 1,500-2,000 words.

IT WILL STAND, Dedicated to the Preservation of Beach Music, It Will Stand Prod., 1505 Elizabeth Ave., Charlotte NC 28204. (704)377-0700. Editor: Chris Beachley. Irregularly published monthly magazine covering beach music (especially soul 1940-present). Circ. 1,700. Pays on acceptance. Byline given. Offers negotiable kill fee. Buys all rights. Submit seasonal/holiday material 2 months in advance. Sample copy $2.

Nonfiction: Historical/nostalgic, interview/profile, opinion, personal experience and photo feature. Buys 5 mss/year. Query with published clips or send complete ms. Length: open. Pays variable fee.

Photos: State availability of photos. Reviews color and b&w contact sheets and prints.

Tips: "Contact us for direction. We even have artists' phone numbers ready for interviews." Magazine will buy more mss as it becomes regular monthly publication.

KEYBOARD MAGAZINE, GPI Publications, 20085 Stevens Creek Blvd., Cupertino CA 95014. (408)446-1105. Editor: Tom Darter. Monthly magazine for those who play piano, organ, synthesizer, accordion, harpsichord, or any other keyboard instrument. All styles of music; all levels of ability. Circ. 67,000. Pays on acceptance. Byline given. Buys first serial rights and second serial (reprint) rights. Phone queries OK. SASE. Reports in 2 weeks. Free sample copy and writer's guidelines.

Nonfiction: "We publish articles on a wide variety of topics pertaining to keyboard players and their instruments. In addition to interviews with keyboard artists in all styles of music, we are interested in historical and analytical pieces, how-to articles dealing either with music or with equipment, profiles on well-known instrument makers and their products. In general, anything that amateur and professional keyboardists would find interesting and/or useful." Buys 20 unsolicited mss/year. Recent article example: "Daryl Hall" (April 1985). Query: letter should mention topic and length of article and describe basic approach. "It's nice (but not necessary) to have a sample first paragraph." Length: approximately 2,000-5,000 words. Pays $100-300.

Tips: "Query first (just a few ideas at a time, rather than twenty). A musical background helps, and a knowledge of keyboard instruments is valuable."

MODERN DRUMMER, 870 Pompton Ave., Ceder Grove NJ 07009. (201)239-4140. Editor-in-Chief: Ronald Spagnardi. Features Editor: Rick Mattingly. Managing Editor: Rick Van Horn. For "student, semi-pro and professional drummers at all ages and levels of playing ability, with varied specialized interests within the field." 60% freelance written. Monthly. Circ. 50,000. Pays on publication. Publishes ms an average of 3 months after acceptance. Buys all rights. Photocopied and previously published submissions OK. Computer printout submissions acceptable; prefers letter-quality to dot-matrix. SASE. Reports in 1 month. Sample copy $2.50; free writer's guidelines.

Nonfiction: How-to, informational, interview, new product, personal experience and technical. "All submissions must appeal to the specialized interests of drummers." Buys 20-30 mss/year. Query or submit complete ms. Length: 5,000-8,000 words. Pays $200-500. Pays expenses of writers on assignment.

Photos: Purchased with accompanying ms. Reviews 8x10 b&w prints and color transparencies.

Columns/Departments: Jazz Drummers Workshop, Rock Perspectives, In The Studio, Show Drummers Seminar, Teachers Forum, Drum Soloist, The Jobbing Drummer, Strictly Technique, Book Reviews, and Shop Talk. "Technical knowledge of area required for most columns." Buys 40-50 mss/year. Query or submit complete ms. Length: 500-2,500 words. Pays $25-150.

‡MODERN PERCUSSIONIST, A Contemporary Magazine for the Serious Drummer/Percussionist, Modern Drummer Publications, Inc., 870 Pompton Ave., Cedar Grove NJ 07009. (201)239-4140. Editor: Rick Mattingly. Managing Editor: Susan Hannum. 50% freelance written. Quarterly magazine on percussion and percussionists. "Our audience includes percussionists at all levels from student to pro. Writers must have a good general knowledge of the field." Estab. 1984. Circ. 15,000. Pays on publication. Publishes ms an average of 6 months after acceptance. Byline given. Offers variable kill fee. Buys all rights. Simultaneous queries, and photocopied and previously published submissions OK. Computer printout submissions acceptable; no dot-matrix. SASE. Reports in 2 weeks on queries; 1 month on mss. Sample copy $2; writer's guidelines for legal size SAE and 1 first class stamp.

Nonfiction: Historical/nostalgic (performers and instruments from the past); how-to (building or repairing percussion instruments); interview/profile (professional players and teachers); new product (new percussion equipment); and technical (percussion techniques). No "fan-magazine" type articles. Buys 20 mss/year. Query with published clips. Length: 5,000-6,000 words. Pays $150-350. Sometimes pays expenses of writers on assignment.

Photos: David Creamer, photo editor. State availability of photos. Reviews b&w contact sheets and 8x10 prints; color transparencies. Pays $10-45 for b&w; $50-100 for color. Captions, model release, and identification of subjects required.

Columns/Departments: Percussion Today (contemporary and avant-garde); Around The World (instruments and techniques from other countries); and Workshop (care and repair). Buys 12-15 mss/year. Query. Length: 1,000-2,000 words. Pays $25-100.

Tips: "Feature interviews with prominent performers is the area most open to freelancers."

MODERN RECORDING & MUSIC, MR&M Publishing Corp., 1120 Old Country Rd., Plainview NY 11803. (516)433-6530. Publisher/Editor: Larry Zide. Monthly magazine covering semi-pro and professional recording of music for musicians, soundmen and recording engineers. Circ. 35,000. Pays second week of publication month. Buys all rights. Submit all material at least 3 months in advance. Photocopied submissions OK. SASE. Reports in 1 week. Provides sample copy "after assignment."

Nonfiction: Historical/nostalgic (recording industry); how-to (basic construction of a device using readily available parts to duplicate an expensive device in small budget studio or at home); humor; and interview/profile (musician, engineer, producer or someone in an affiliated field). Buys 50-60 mss/year. Query with published clips and outline. Length: 2,000 words minimum. Pays $150-250/article.

Photos: Reviews $2\frac{1}{4}$x$2\frac{1}{4}$ or 35mm color transparencies; 8x10 glossy prints or contact sheets. Pays $25 inside color; $15 inside b&w; $75 for color cover; or package payment of $150.

MUSIC CITY NEWS, Suite 601, 50 Music Square W., Nashville TN 37203. (615)329-2200. Editor: Neil Pond. 5% freelance written. Monthly tabloid emphasizing country music. Circ. 100,000. Buys all rights. Phone queries OK. Submit seasonal or holiday material 2 months in advance. Photocopied submissions OK. Computer printout submissions acceptable. SASE. Reports in 10 weeks. Free sample copy.

Nonfiction: "We publish interview articles with country music personalities, narrative/quote, focusing on new and fresh angles about the entertainer rather than biographical histories." Buys 5-10 unsolicited mss/year. Query. Length: 500-1,250 words. Pays $100-125/feature, $75/junior feature, and $50/vignettes.

Photos: Purchased on acceptance by assignment. Query. Pays $10 maximum for 8x10 b&w glossy prints.

MUSIC MAGAZINE, Barrett & Colgrass Inc., Suite 202, 56 The Esplanade, Toronto, Ontario M5E 1A7 Canada. (416)364-5938. Editor: Ulla Colgrass. 90% freelance written. Bimonthly magazine emphasizing classical music. Circ. 11,000. Pays on publication. Publishes ms an average of 4 months after acceptance. Byline given. Buys first North American rights, one-time rights, and second serial (reprint) rights. Phone queries OK. Submit seasonal/holiday material 4 months in advance. Photocopied and previously published submissions (book excerpts) OK. Computer printout submissions (double-spaced) acceptable. SAE, IRCs. Reports in 3 weeks. Sample copy and writer's guidelines $2.

Nonfiction: Interview, historical articles, photo feature and profile. "All articles should pertain to classical music and people in that world. We do not want any academic analysis or short pieces of family experiences in classical music." Query with published clips. Unsolicited articles will not be returned. Length: 1,500-3,500 words. Pays $100-250.

Photos: State availability of photos. Pays $15-25 for 8x10 b&w glossy prints or contact sheets; $100 for color transparencies. No posed promotion photos. "Candid lively material only." Buys one-time rights. Captions required.

Tips: "Send a sample of your writing with suggested subjects. Off-beat subjects are welcome but must be thoroughly interesting to be considered. A famous person or major subject in music are your best bets."

OPERA CANADA, Suite 433, 366 Adelaide St. E., Toronto, Ontario M5A 3X9 Canada. (416)363-0395. Editor: Ruby Mercer. 80% freelance written. Quarterly magazine for readers who are interested in serious music; specifically, opera. Circ. 7,000. Pays on publication. Publishes ms an average of 1 year after acceptance. Byline given. Not copyrighted. Buys first serial rights. Photocopied and simultaneous submissions OK. Computer printout submissions acceptable; no dot-matrix. Reports on material accepted for publication within 1 year. Returns rejected material in 1 month. SAE, IRCs. Sample copy $3.50.

Nonfiction: "Because we are Canada's only opera magazine, we like to keep 75% of our content Canadian, i.e., by Canadians or about Canadian personalities and events. We prefer informative and/or humorous articles about any aspect of music theater, with an emphasis on opera. The relationship of the actual subject matter to opera can be direct or at least related. We accept record reviews (*only* operatic recordings); book reviews (books covering any aspect of music theater); and interviews with major operatic personalities. Please, no reviews of performances; we have staff reviewers." Buys 10 mss/year. Query or submit complete ms. Length (for all articles except reviews of books and records): 1,000-3,000 words. Pays $50-150. Length for reviews: 100-500 words. Pays $10.
Photos: No additional payment for photos used with mss. Captions required.

OVATION, 320 W. 57th St., New York NY 10019. Editor: Sam Chase. 75% freelance written. Monthly magazine for classical music listeners covering classical music and the equipment on which to hear it. Average issue includes 4 features plus departments. Pays on publication. Publishes ms an average of 6 months after acceptance. Byline given. Buys all rights. Submit seasonal material 4 months in advance. Computer printout submissions acceptable; no dot-matrix. SASE. Reports in 1 month. Sample copy $2.79.
Nonfiction: "We are primarily interested in interviews with and articles about the foremost classical music artists. Historical pieces will also be considered." Buys 5 unsolicited mss/year. Query with published clips. Length: 800-4,500 words. Pays $5/inch.
Photos: State availability of photos. May offer additional payment for photos accepted with ms. Captions required. Buys one-time rights.

RELIX MAGAZINE, Music for the Mind, Relix Magazine, Inc., Box 94, Brooklyn NY 11229. (212)645-0818. Editor: Toni A. Brown. 90% freelance written. Bimonthly magazine covering rock 'n' roll music and specializing in Grateful Dead, and other San Francisco and 60's related groups for readers ages 15-45. Circ. 20,000. Pays on publication. Publishes ms an average of 6 months after acceptance. Byline given. Buys all rights. Photocopied submissions OK. Computer printout submissions acceptable; prefers letter-quality to dot-matrix. SASE. Sample copy $2.
Nonfiction: Historical/nostalgic, interview/profile, new product, personal experience, photo feature and technical. Special issues include November photo special. Query with published clips if available or send complete ms. Length open. Pays variable rates. "We are seeking science fiction, rock and roll stories for a potential book."
Columns/Departments: Query with published clips, if available or send complete ms. Length: open. Pays variable rates.
Fiction: Query with clips of published work, if available, or send complete ms. Length: open. Pays variable rates.
Tips: "The most rewarding aspects of working with freelance writers are fresh writing and new outlooks."

ROCKBILL, Rave Communications, Suite 1201, 850 7th Ave., New York NY 10019. (212)977-7745. Editor: Stuart Matranga. Direct all music and column queries to Robert Edelstein, managing editor. Direct all fiction and more esoteric ideas to Robert O'Brian, executive editor. Direct all nonmusic general features to Robert Doherty, senior editor. Direct all photo and illustration queries to Cliff Sloan, art director. 25% freelance written. Monthly magazine focusing on rock music and related topics for distribution at rock music clubs. Circ. 530,000. Pays on publication. Publishes ms an average of 2 months after acceptance. Byline given. Buys one-time rights. Simultaneous queries OK. Computer printout submissions acceptable; no dot-matrix. No guarantee on return of submissions. Free sample.
Nonfiction: Interview/profile, lifestyle and new music articles. "We're primarily interested in new artists on the verge." Buys 50 mss/year. Length: 150-800 words. Pays $25-75.
Photos: Uses color transparencies only. Identification of subjects required. No guarantee of returns.
Columns/Departments: Fashion, electronics, movies, jazz, country music, classical music, international music, classic album reviews, essays on cities, science and technology, new age-related topics, mysteries and the occult, video, radio, essays on youth, brief interviews with notables, satire, travel, etc. Length: 500-800 words.
Fiction: "In each issue we print one short fiction piece in a section called Ficciones. We describe it as such: 'Magical realism, dangerous, imaginings, spontaneous history.' We're not sure what that means, but we admire Borges, Calvino, Marquez and that ilk." Length: 500 words maximum.
Tips: "We try to publish at least one new writer per issue. Our best advice is to keep trying to be as brilliant as possible; think in terms of the big as well as the small, the apparent as well as the hidden, the molecular as well as the universal. The best way into our hearts is to write with integrity about something important to you and to everyone. And, remember, we're a small magazine in page size only. Our mottos are 'More with Less' and 'Dare to be Naive'."

ROLLING STONE, 745 5th Ave., New York NY 10151. Managing Editor: Robert Wallace. 25-50% freelance written. Biweekly tabloid/magazine on contemporary music and lifestyle. "We seldom accept freelance material. All our work is assigned or done by our staff." Byline given. Offers 25% kill fee. Buys first rights only.

Nonfiction: Seeks new general interest topics. Queries must be concise, no longer than 2 pages. Send queries about musicians and music industry to music editor. Writers knowledgeable about computers, VCRs, or sound equipment can submit an idea for the technology column that ranges from 50-word picture captions to 750-word pieces. Does not provide writer's guidelines; recommends reading *Rolling Stone* before submitting query.

THE $ENSIBLE SOUND, 403 Darwin Dr., Snyder NY 14226. Editor/Publisher: John A. Horan. 20% freelance written. Quarterly magazine. "All readers are high fidelity enthusiasts, and many have a high fidelity industry-related job." Circ. 5,200. Pays on acceptance. Publishes ms an average of 3 months after acceptance. Byline given. Buys all rights. Simultaneous, photocopied, and previously published submissions OK. Computer printout submissions OK *if triple spaced*; prefers letter-quality to dot-matrix. SASE. Reports in 2 weeks. Sample copy $2.

Nonfiction: Expose; how-to; general interest; humor; historical; interview (people in hi-fi business, manufacturers or retail); new product (all types of new audio equipment); nostalgia (articles and opinion on older equipment); personal experience (with various types of audio equipment); photo feature (on installation, or how-to tips); profile (of hi-fi equipment); and technical (pertaining to audio). "Subjective evaluations of hi-fi equipment make up 70% of our publication. We will accept 10/issue." Buys 2 mss/issue. Submit outline. Pays $25 maximum. Sometimes pays expenses of writers on assignment.

Columns/Departments: Bits & Pieces (short items of interest to hi-fi hobbyists); Ramblings (do-it-yourself tips on bettering existing systems); and Record Reviews (of records which would be of interest to audiophiles). Query. Length: 25-400 words. Pays $10/page.

‡SHEET MUSIC MAGAZINE, "The only magazine you can play", Shacor, Inc., 352 Evelyn St., Box 933, Paramus NJ 07653-0933. (201)967-9495. Editor: Edward J. Shanaphy. Managing Editor: Josephine Sblendorio. 40% freelance written. Magazine published 9 times/year on pop music, jazz, Broadway tunes, etc. "Our magazine is geared toward appreciation and instruction of music from Tin Pan Alley to the present day." Circ. 250,000. Pays 30 days after acceptance. Publishes ms an average of 3 months after acceptance. Byline given. Buys first North American serial rights. Submit seasonal/holiday material 4 months in advance. Simultaneous queries, and photocopied and previously published submissions OK. Computer printout submissions acceptable; no dot-matrix. SASE. Reports in 4 weeks. Sample copy $2; writer's guidelines for SAE and 1 first class stamp.

Nonfiction: Susan Rodd, articles editor. Book excerpts, general interest, historical/nostalgic, how-to, interview/profile, new product, personal experience and technical. No articles unrelated to the various music fields. Buys 5 mss/year. Query with or without published clips. Length: 800-1,500 words. Pays $100-200.

Columns/Departments: Susan Rodd, column/department editor. Pop Piano, Harmony at the Keyboard, Organ Studio, Getting Started, Where Are They Now? and Artist's Spotlight. (Beginning and advanced technique and instruction plus profiles.) Buys 40 mss/year. Query with published clips. Length: 600-1,000 words. Pays $100-150.

Fillers: Susan Rodd, fillers editor. Clippings, anecdotes, short humor and newsbreaks. Length: 25-100 words. Pays $15-25.

Tips: "How-to instruction columns are most open to freelancers. Articles should cover one specific problem or technique and be geared to either the beginner or the advanced student." Submissions should not be addressed to the publishing company, but to: *Sheet Music Magazine*, 223 Katonah Ave., Katonah NY 10536. Attn: Susan Rodd.

TOWER RECORDS' PULSE!, 900 Enterprise Dr., Sacramento CA 95825. (916)920-4500. Editor: Mike Farrace. 80% freelance written. Monthly tabloid covering recorded music. Circ. 100,000. Pays on publication. Publishes ms an average of 2 months after acceptance. Byline given. Buys first serial rights. Simultaneous and photocopied submissions OK. Computer printout submissions acceptable; prefers letter-quality to dot-matrix. SASE. Reports in 5 weeks. Free sample copy; writer's guidelines for SAE.

Nonfiction: Feature stories and interview/profile (angled toward artist's taste in music. Specifics: Ten favorite albums, first record ever bought, anecdotes about early record buying experiences). Always looking for good hardware reviews, concise news items and commentary about nonpopular musical genres. Buys 200-250 mss/year. Query or send complete ms. Length: 200-2,500 words. Pays $20-500. Sometimes pays expenses of writers on assignment.

Photos: State availability of photos. Reviews b&w prints. Caption and identification of subjects required. Buys one-time rights.

Fillers: Newsbreaks.

Tips: "Break in with 200-500 word news-oriented featurettes on recording artists or on fast breaking, record-related news, personnel changes, unusual match-ups, reissues of great material. Any kind of music. The more obscure genres are the hardest for us to cover, so they stand a good chance of being used. Writers have a better chance writing articles and fillers. Less copy means easier rewrites, and less guilt when we don't like it, thereby making the relationship with the writer easier, more honest and ultimately more productive. We are not only a magazine about records, but one that is owned by a record retailer.''

TRADITION, Prairie Press, 106 Navajo, Council Bluffs IA 51501. (712)366-1136. Editor: Robert Everhart. 20% freelance written. Quarterly magazine emphasizing traditional country music and other aspects of pioneer living. Circ. 2,500. Pays on publication. Not copyrighted. Byline given. Buys one-time rights. Submit seasonal/holiday material 6 months in advance. Simultaneous queries, and simultaneous, photocopied, and previously published submissions OK. Computer printout submissions acceptable. SASE. Reports in 1 month. Free sample copy.

Nonfiction: Historical (relating to country music); how-to (play, write, or perform country music); inspirational (on country gospel); interview (with country performers, both traditional and contemporary); nostalgia (pioneer living); personal experience (country music); and travel (in connection with country music contests or festivals). Query. Length: 800-1,200 words. Pays $25-50.

Photos: State availability of photos with query. Payment is included in ms price. Uses 5x7 b&w prints. Captions and model release required. Buys one-time rights.

Poetry: Free verse and traditional. Buys 4 poems/year. Length: 5-20 lines. Submit maximum 2 poems. Pays $2-5.

Fillers: Clippings, jokes and anecdotes. Buys 5/year. Length: 15-50 words. Pays $5-10.

Tips: ''Material must be concerned with what we term 'real' country music as opposed to today's 'pop' country music. Freelancer must be knowledgeable of the subject; many writers don't even know who the father of country music is, let alone write about him.''

Mystery

What mystery magazine editors want isn't a mystery when you read their magazines. Additional mystery markets can be found in the Literary and "Little" category of this book. Also, consult the fiction subheadings in all the magazine listings; some of them buy mysteries.

ALFRED HITCHCOCK'S MYSTERY MAGAZINE, Davis Publications, Inc., 380 Lexington Ave., New York NY 10017. Editor: Cathleen Jordan. Magazine published 13 times a year emphasizing mystery fiction. Circ. 200,000. Pays on acceptance. Byline given. Buys first serial rights, second serial (reprint) rights and foreign rights. Submit seasonal/holiday material 7 months in advance. Photocopied submissions OK. SASE. Reports in 2 months or less. Writer's guidelines for SASE.

Fiction: Original and well-written mystery and crime fiction. Length: 1,000-14,000 words.

ELLERY QUEEN'S MYSTERY MAGAZINE, Davis Publications, Inc., 380 Lexington Ave., New York NY 10017. Editor: Eleanor Sullivan. 100% freelance written. Magazine published 13 times/year. Circ. 375,000. Pays on acceptance. Publishes ms an average of 10 months after acceptance. Byline given. Buys first serial rights or second serial (reprint) rights. Submit seasonal/holiday material 7 months in advance. Simultaneous, photocopied, and previously published submissions OK. Computer printout submissions acceptable; prefers letter-quality to dot-matrix. SASE. Reports in 1 month. Writer's guidelines for SASE.

Fiction: Special consideration will be given to ''anything timely and original. We publish every type of mystery: the suspense story, the psychological study, the deductive puzzle—the gamut of crime and detection from the realistic (including the policeman's lot and stories of police procedure) to the more imaginative (including 'locked rooms' and impossible crimes). We always need detective stories but do not want sex, sadism or sensationalism-for-the-sake-of-sensationalism.'' No gore or horror; seldom publishes parodies or pastiches. Buys 13 mss/issue. Length: 6,000 words maximum; occasionally higher but not often. Pays 3-8¢/word.

Tips: ''We have a department of First Stories to encourage writers whose fiction has never before been in print. We publish an average of 15 first stories a year.''

‡**HYST'RY MYST'RYs MAGAZINE**, Hyst'ry Myst'ry House, Garnerville NY 10923. Editor: David Allen. 100% freelance written. Bimonthly tabloid covering historical, archaeological mysteries and controversies of research and study. Publishes ms an average of 1 month after acceptance. Byline given. Buys one-time rights and second serial (reprint) rights. Simultaneous queries, and photocopied and previously published submissions OK. SASE. Reports in 3 weeks. Sample copy $4.

Nonfiction: Articles concerning mysterious aspects of history, archeology, stamps, coins, rare documents, etc. No poetry. No UFO or parapsychology. "All our expository articles must be scientifically oriented about supporting fact and evidence. No second-hand, warmed-over pieces taken from other people or magazines. We will consider things published elsewhere before, but they must be solid." Query. Length: open.
Photos: State availability of photos. Reviews prints. Captions, model release, and identification of subjects required.
Columns/Departments: "We will consider columnists in the areas of word origins, genealogy, exploration, or rare document dealings." Query. Length: open.
Fiction: "We are currently serializing a prototype hist'ry myst'ry novel. We will start publishing short stories based upon this format as set up in this novel. But we *will not publish* general fiction. The writer must use our format in writing short stories. The writer must *study* our fictional style, as nothing like it is being published elsewhere and the individual writer cannot have anythng in his trunk that will do."
Fillers: Jokes, gags, anecdotes, and short humor relevant to history. Length: open.

Nature, Conservation and Ecology

These publications promote reader awareness of the natural environment, wildlife, nature preserves and ecobalance. They do not publish recreation or travel articles except as they relate to conservation or nature. Other markets for this kind of material can be found in the Regional, Sports, and Travel, Camping, and Trailer categories, although the magazines listed there require that nature or conservation articles be slanted to their specialized subject matter and audience. Some juvenile and teen publications such as *National Geographic World* buy nature-related material for young audiences. Consult both categories, in particular the Juvenile section. Energy conservation topics for professionals are covered in the Trade Energy category.

AMERICAN FORESTS, American Forestry Association, 1319 18th St. NW, Washington DC 20036. (202)467-5810. Editor: Bill Rooney. 70% freelance written. Monthly magazine. "We are an organization for the advancement of intelligent management and use of our forests, soil, water, wildlife, and all other natural resources necessary for an environment of high quality and the well-being of all citizens." Circ. 50,000. Pays on acceptance. Publishes ms an average of 8 months after acceptance. Byline given. Buys one-time rights. Phone queries OK but written queries preferred. Submit seasonal/holiday material 5 months in advance. Computer printout submissions acceptable; no dot-matrix. SASE. Reports in 6 weeks. Sample copy 98¢; writer's guidelines for SAE and 1 frist class stamp.
Nonfiction: General interest, historical, how-to, humor and inspirational. All articles should emphasize trees, forests, wildlife or land use. Buys 5 mss/issue. Query. Length: 2,000 words. Pays $200-400.
Photos: State availability of photos. Offers no additional payment for photos accompanying ms. Uses 8x10 b&w glossy prints; 35mm or larger color transparencies, originals only. Captions required. Buys one-time rights.
Tips: "Query should have honesty and information on photo support."

THE ATLANTIC SALMON JOURNAL, The Atlantic Salmon Federation, Suite 1030, 1435 St. Alexandre, Montreal, Quebec H3A 2G4 Canada. (514)842-8059. Editor: Joanne Eidinger. 60% freelance written. A quarterly magazine covering conservation efforts for the Atlantic salmon for an "affluent and responsive audience—the dedicated angler and conservationist of the Atlantic salmon." Circ. 20,000. Pays on publication. Publishes ms an average of 6 months after acceptance. Byline given. Buys one-time rights to articles and photos. Submit seasonal/holiday material 2 months in advance. Simultaneous queries, and simultaneous and photocopied submissions OK. Electronic submissions OK on Micom floppy disk, but requires hard copy also. Computer printout submissions acceptable; prefers letter-quality to dot matrix. SASE. Reports in 6 weeks. Sample copy for SAE and 64¢ (Canadian), or SAE with IRC; free writer's guidelines.
Nonfiction: Expose, historical/nostalgic, how-to, humor, interview/profile, new product, opinion, personal experience, photo feature, technical, travel, conservation, cuisine, science and management. "We are seeking articles that are pertinent to the focus and purpose of our magazine, which is to inform and entertain our membership on all aspects of the Atlantic salmon and its environment, preservation and conservation." Buys 12-15 mss/year. Query with published clips and state availability of photos. Length: 1,500-3,000 words. Pays

$100-325.

Photos: State availability of photos with query. Pays $35-50 for 3x5 or 5x7 b&w prints; $35-150 for $2^1/_4$x$3^1/_4$ or 16mm color slides. Captions and identification of subjects required.

Columns/Departments: Perspective (opinion piece on any subject relating to the Atlantic salmon); and First Person (nonfiction, anecdotal, from first person viewpoint, can be humorous). Buys about 12 mss/year. Length: 1,000-1,500 words. Pays $175.

Fiction: Adventure, fantasy, historical, humorous and mainstream. "We don't want to see anything that does not deal with Atlantic salmon directly or indirectly. Wilderness adventures are acceptable as long as they deal with Atlantic salmon." Buys 3 mss/year. Query with published clips. Length: 3,000 words maximum. Pays $150-325.

Fillers: Clippings, jokes, anecdotes and short humor. Length: 100-300 words average. Does not pay.

Tips: "Articles must reflect informed and up-to-date knowledge of Atlantic salmon. Writers need not be authorities, but research must be impeccable. Clear, concise writing is a plus, and submissions must be typed. Anecdote, River Log and photo essays are most open to freelancers."

AUDUBON MAGAZINE, 950 3rd Ave., New York NY 10022. 75% freelance written. "Not soliciting freelance material; practically all articles are done on assignment only. We have a backlog of articles from known writers and contributors. Our issues are planned well in advance of publication and follow a theme." Pays expenses of writers on assignment. Pays negotiable kill fee. Publishes ms an average of 1 year after acceptance. Electronic submissions OK on IBM-PC, DOS 2.00, but requres hard copy also. Computer printout submissions acceptable; prefers letter-quality to dot-matrix. Byline given.

Tips: The Most frequent mistakes made by writers in completing an article assignment for *Audubon* are "encyclopedic didacticism, 'A swamp is . . .'; writing too long; and presuming reader interest."

‡**BIRD WATCHER'S DIGEST**, Pardson Corp., Box 110, Marietta OH 45750. Editor: Mary Beacom Bowers. Bimonthly magazine covering natural history—birds and bird watching. "*BWD* is a nontechnical magazine interpreting ornithological material for amateur observers, including the knowledgeable birder, the serious novice and the backyard bird watcher; we strive to provide good reading and good ornithology." Circ. 45,000. Pays on publication. Publishes ms up to 18 months after acceptance. Byline given. Buys one-time rights, first serial rights and second serial (reprint) rights. Submit seasonal/holiday material 6 months in advance. Previously published submissions OK. Computer printout submissions acceptable; prefers letter-quality to dot-matrix. SASE. Reports in 6 weeks. Sample copy $2; writer's guidelines for #10 SAE and 1 first class stamp.

Nonfiction: Book excerpts, how-to (relating to birds, feeding and attracting, etc.), humor, interview/profile, personal experience and travel (limited—we get many). "We are especially interested in fresh, lively accounts of closely observed bird behavior and displays and of bird watching experiences and expeditions. We often need material of less common species or on unusual or previously unreported behavior of common species." No articles on pet or caged birds; none on raising a baby bird. Buys 75-90 mss/year. Send complete ms. Length: 600-3,500 words. Pays $25-50. Sometimes pays expenses of writers on assignment.

Photos: Send photos with ms. Pays $10 minimum for b&w prints; $25 minimum for color transparencies. Buys one-time rights.

Poetry: Avant-garde, free verse, light verse and traditional. No haiku. Buys 12-18 poems/year. Submit maximum 3 poems. Length 8-20 lines. Pays $10.

Tips: "We are aimed at an audience ranging from the backyard bird watcher to the very knowledgeable birder; we include in each issue material that will appeal at various levels. We always strive for a good geographical spread, with material from every section of the country. We leave very technical matters to others, but we want facts and accuracy, depth and quality, directed at the veteran bird watcher and at the enthusiastic novice. We stress the joys and pleasures of bird watching, its environmental contribution, and its value for the individual and society."

ENVIRONMENTAL ACTION, 1346 Connecticut Ave., Washington DC 20036. Editors: Francesca Lyman, Richard Asinof and Rose Audette. 20% freelance written. Bimonthly magazine emphasizing grass roots citizen action and congressional/governmental activity affecting the environment for a well-educated, sophisticated, politically oriented readership. Circ. 25,000. Pays on publication. Publishes ms an average of 3 months after acceptance. Byline given. Buys first serial rights, first North American serial and second serial (reprint) rights. Computer printout submissions acceptable. SASE. Reports in 6 weeks. Sample copy $2.50.

Nonfiction: Exposé; human interest feature; news feature; and political analysis (on such issues as the urban environment, chemical pollution, public health, alternative energy, and the public interest movement). Less interested in wilderness and wildlife issues. Prefers not to see material on nature appreciation, animal rights/cruelty, or photo essays. Buys 15-20 mss/year. Query with published clips. Length: 1,000-2,500 words. Pays according to length.

Photos: State availability of photos. Pays $15-50 for 8x10 b&w glossy prints. Buys all rights.

Tips: "We are frequently in the market for local stories that have national significance. Because we have virtually no travel budget, we are most receptive to articles that the editors cannot do from Washington. The most frequent mistakes made by writers in completing an article for us is that the story is too local, not enough national significance, or else it's too technical, without enough anecdotes and human interest."

FORESTS & PEOPLE, Official Publication of the Louisiana Forestry Association, Louisiana Forestry Association, Drawer 5067, Alexandria LA 71301. (318)443-2558. Editor: Kathryn T. Johnston. 50% freelance written. Quarterly magazine covering forests, forest industry, wood-related stories, wildlife for general readers, both in and out of the forest industry. Circ. 8,500. Pays on acceptance. Publishes ms an average of 6 months after acceptance. Byline given. Not copyrighted. Submit seasonal/holiday material 2 months in advance. Simultaneous queries, and simultaneous, photocopied, and previously published submissions OK. Reports in 2 weeks on queries; 3 weeks on mss. Sample copy $1.75; free ms guidelines.
Nonfiction: General interest (recreation, wildlife, crafts with wood, festivals); historical/nostalgic (logging towns, historical wooden buildings, forestry legends); interview/profile (of forest industry execs, foresters, loggers, wildlife managers, tree farmers); photo feature (of scenic forest, wetlands, logging operations); and technical (innovative equipment, chemicals, operations, forestland studies, or industry profiles). No research papers. Articles may cover a technical subject but must be understandable to the general public." Buys 12 mss/year. Query with published clips. Length: open. Pays $100.
Photos: State availability of photos. Reviews b&w and color slides. Identification of subjects required.

HIGH COUNTRY NEWS, High Country News Foundation, Box 1090, Paonia CO 81428. (303)527-4898. Editor: Betsy Marston. 80% freelance written. Biweekly tabloid covering environment and natural resource issues in the Rocky Mountain states for environmentalists, politicians, companies, government agencies, etc. Circ. 4,200. Pays on publication. Publishes ms an average of 2 months after acceptance. Byline given. Buys one-time rights. Submit seasonal/holiday material 6 weeks in advance. Computer printout submissions acceptable if "double spaced (at least) and legible"; prefers letter-quality to dot-matrix. SASE. Reports in 1 month. Free sample copy and writer's guidelines.
Nonfiction: Expose (government, corporate); historical/nostalgic; how-to (appropriate technology); humor; interview/profile; opinion; personal experience; and photo feature. Special issues include those on states in the region. Buys 100 mss/year. Query. Length: 3,000 word maximum. Pays 5¢/word. Sometimes pays the expenses of writers on assignment.
Photos: Send photos with ms. Reviews b&w contact sheets and prints. Captions and identification of subjects required.
Poetry: Chip Rawlins, poetry editor, Box 51, Boulder WY 82923. Avant-garde, free verse, haiku, light verse and traditional. Pays in contributor copies.
Tips: "We use a lot of freelance material, though very little from outside the Rockies. Start by writing short, 500-word news items of timely, regional interest."

INTERNATIONAL WILDLIFE, National Wildlife Federation, 1412 16th St. NW, Washington DC 20036. Managing Editor: Jonathan Fisher. 85% freelance written. Bimonthly for persons interested in natural history, outdoor adventure and the environment. Circ. 400,000. Publishes ms an average of 4 months after acceptance. Usually buys all rights to text; usually one-time rights to photos and art. Pays on acceptance. "We are now assigning most articles but will consider detailed proposals for quality feature material of interest to a broad audience." Computer printout submissions acceptable; no dot-matrix. SASE. Reports in 4 weeks.
Nonfiction: Focuses on world wildlife, environmental problems and man's relationship to the natural world as reflected in such issues as population control, pollution, resource utilization, food production, etc. Especially interested in articles on animal behavior and other natural history, first-person experiences by scientists in the field and timely issues. Query. Length: 2,000-3,000 words. Also in the market for short, 750-word "one pagers." Examine past issue for style and subject matter. Pays $750 minimum. Sometimes pays expenses of writers on assignment.
Photos: Purchases top-quality color and b&w photos; prefers packages of related photos and text, but single shots of exceptional interest and sequences also considered. Prefers Kodachrome transparencies for color, 8x10 prints for b&w.

JOURNAL OF FRESHWATER, Freshwater Society, 2500 Shadywood Rd., Box 90, Navarre MN 55392. (612)471-7467. Editor: Linda Schroeder. 10% freelance written. Annual (October) magazine; 32 pages. Always emphasizes freshwater issues. Pays on publication. Publishes ms an average of 6 months after acceptance. Byline given. Buys one-time rights, all rights and second serial (reprint) rights. Written queries only. Reports in 6 weeks. SASE. Sample copy $5; free writer's and photographer's guidelines.
Nonfiction: Scientific, yet easy to read how-to, general interest, humor, interview, nostalgia, photo feature and technical. "We will consider virtually any material dealing with freshwater environment as long as it is well-written and interesting. Entries must clearly and quickly answer the reader's question 'So what's that got to do with me, my pocketbook, or my relatives?'." No "bumper-sticker" philosophies, encyclopedia articles or

unresearched material. No articles about dam controversies, personal travelogs, fish-catching stories, or long pieces of poetry. Buys 2-3 mss/year. Submit complete ms. Length: "2,500 words or less works best." Pays $100 (more with photos or art)/1,000 words used.

Photos: Submit photos with accompanying ms. Payment for photos can be included in purchase price of article. Uses 5x7 minimum b&w glossy photos or 35mm, 2¹/₄x2¹/₄ or larger color transparencies. Captions preferred. Model release required. Buys all rights for cover photos and all or one-time rights for others.

Fiction: "We purchase very little fiction, but we're open to considering it as long as it's very water-related." Pays $100 (more with photos or art)/1,000 words used.

Tips: "Study at least two past issues of the journal. Query us before you write the article, to save your time and ours. Introduce yourself, state story idea and why we should be interested. Give a few key facts, state main sources you expect to use, propose a deadline you can meet, and offer to round up excellent photos to illustrate."

NATIONAL PARKS, 1701 18th St. NW, Washington DC 20009. (202)265-2717. Senior Editor: Michele Strutin. 75% freelance written. Bimonthly magazine for a highly educated audience interested in preservation of National Park System Units, natural areas and protection of wildlife habitat. Circ. 40,000. Pays on acceptance. Publishes ms an average of 6 months after acceptance. Buys first North American serial rights and second serial (reprint) rights. Submit seasonal/holiday material 5 months in advance. Computer printout submissions acceptable if legible; prefers letter-quality to dot-matrix. SASE. Reports in 10 weeks. Sample copy $3; writer's guidelines for SASE.

Nonfiction: Expose (on threats, wildlife problems to national parks); descriptive articles about new or proposed national parks and wilderness parks; brief natural history pieces describing park geology, wildlife, or plants; "adventures" in national parks (crosscountry skiing, bouldering, mountain climbing, kayaking, canoeing, backpacking); and travel tips to national parks. All material must relate to national parks. No poetry or philosophical essays. Buys 6-10 unsolicited mss/year. Query or send complete ms. Length: 1,000-1,500 words. Pays $75-200.

Photos: State availability of photos or send photos with ms. Pays $25-50 for 8x10 b&w glossy prints; $35-100 for color transparencies; offers no additional payment for photos accompanying ms. Captions required. Buys one-time rights.

NATIONAL WILDLIFE, National Wildlife Federation, 1412 16th St. NW, Washington DC 20036. (703)790-4510. Editor: John Strohm. Managing Editor: Mark Wexler. 75% freelance written. Bimonthly magazine on wildlife, natural history and environment. "Our purpose is to promote wise use of the nation's natural resources and to conserve and protect wildlife and its habitat. We reach a broad audience that is largely interested in wildlife conservation and nature photography. We avoid too much scientific detail and prefer anecdotal, natural history material." Circ. 850,000. Pays on acceptance. Publishes ms an average of 6 months after acceptance. Offers 25% kill fee. Buys all rights. Submit seasonal/holiday material 6 months in advance. Photocopied submissions OK. Computer printout submissions acceptable; prefers letter-quality to dot-matrix. SASE. Reports in 6 weeks. Sample copy for magazine size SAE and 4 first class stamps; writer's guidelines for letter size SAE and 1 first class stamp.

Nonfiction: Book excerpts (nature related); general interest (2,500-word features on wildlife, new discoveries, behavior, or the environment); how-to (an outdoor or nature related activity); personal experience (outdoor adventure); photo feature (wildlife); and short 700-word features on an unusual individual or new scientific discovery relating to nature. Buys 50 mss/year. Query with or without published clips. Length: 700-3,000 words. Pays $350-1,500. Pays expenses of writers on assignment.

Photos: John Nuhn, photo editor. State availability of photos or send photos with query. Reviews 35mm color transparencies. Pays $200-575. Buys one-time rights.

Tips: "Writers can break in with us more readily by proposing subjects (initially) that will take only one or two pages in the magazine (short features)."

NATURAL HISTORY, Natural History Magazine, 79th and Central Park W., New York NY 10024. Editor: Alan Ternes. Over 75% freelance written. Monthly magazine for well-educated, ecologically aware audience: professional people, scientists and scholars. Circ. 460,000. Pays on publication. Publishes ms an average of 1 year after acceptance. Byline given. Buys first serial rights and second serial (reprint) rights. Submit seasonal material 6 months in advance. Computer printout submissions acceptable; no dot-matrix. SASE. Sample copy $3.

Nonfiction: Uses all types of scientific articles except chemistry and physics—emphasis is on the biological sciences and anthropology. Prefers professional scientists as authors. "We always want to see new research findings in almost all the branches of the natural sciences—anthropology, archeology, zoology and ornithology. We find that it is particularly difficult to get something new in herpetology (amphibians and reptiles) or entomology (insects), and we would like to see material in those fields. We lean heavily toward writers who are scientists or professional science writers. We expect high standards of writing and research. We favor an ecological slant in most of our pieces, but do not generally lobby for causes, environmental or other. The writer should have a deep knowledge of his subject, then submit original ideas either in query or by manuscript. Should be able to supply high-quality illustrations." Buys 50 mss/year. Query or subit complete ms. Length: 2,000-4,000 words. Pays $400-750, plus additional payment for photos used.

Photos: Uses some 8x10 b&w glossy prints; pays $125/page maximum. Much color is used; pays $250 for inside and up to $350 for cover. Buys one-time rights.

Tips: "Learn about something in depth before you bother writing about it."

OCEANS, Fort Mason, Building E, San Francisco CA 94123. Editor: Jake Widman. 100% freelance written. Publication of The Oceanic Society. Bimonthly magazine; 72 pages. For people who love the sea. Circ. 65,000. Pays on publication. Publishes ms an average of 12 months after acceptance. Byline given. Buys first serial rights; rarely second serial (reprint) rights. Submit seasonal/holiday material 4 months in advance. Simultaneous and photocopied submissions OK. Computer printout submissions acceptable; prefers letter-quality to dotmatrix. SASE. Reports in 8 weeks. Query with SASE. Sample copy $2; free writer's guidelines for SAE with 1 first class postage stamp.

Nonfiction: "We want articles on the world-wide realm of salt water; marine life (biology and ecology), oceanography, maritime history, marine painting and other arts, geography, undersea exploration and study, voyages, ships, coastal areas including environmental problems, seaports and shipping, islands, food-fishing and aquaculture (mariculture), peoples of the sea, including anthropological materials. Writing should be simple, direct, factual, very readable (avoid dullness and pedantry, make it lively and interesting but not cute, flippant or tongue-in-cheek; avoid purple prose). Use careful research, good structuring, no padding. We like factual information in good, narrative style. *Oceans* is authoritative but less technical than *Scientific American*. First person accounts of adventure and scuba tend to be overworked. Diving OK if unusual in results or story angle. We want articles on rarely visited islands, ports or shores that have great intrinsic interest, but not treated in purely travelogue style. We can use more on environmental concerns." Buys 60-70 mss/year. Query with SASE. Length: 1,000-6,000 words. Pays $100/page.

WM Editor's Note: At press time, we learned that *Oceans* would be moving to a new address and would be undergoing numerous changes.

OCEANUS, The International Magazine of Marine Science and Policy, Woods Hole Oceanographic Institution, Woods Hole MA 02543. (617)548-1400, ext. 2386. Editor: Paul R. Ryan. Assistant Editor: Frank Lowenstein. 10% freelance written. "*Oceanus* is an international quarterly magazine that monitors significant trends in ocean research, technology and marine policy. Its basic purpose is to encourage wise, environmentally responsible use of the oceans. In addition, two of the magazine's main tasks are to explain the significance of present marine research to readers and to expose them to the substance of vital public policy questions." Circ. 15,000. Pays on publication. Publishes ms an average of 3 months after acceptance. Byline given. Buys all rights. Simultaneous queries OK. Computer printout submissions acceptable; no dot-matrix. SASE. Reports in 2 months.

Nonfiction: Interview/profile and technical. *Oceanus* publishes 4 thematic issues/year. Most articles are commissioned. Themes for 1985 included underwater archaeology, the oceans and national security, education and the oceans, and the arctic. Length: 2,700-3,500 words. Pays $300 minimum. Sometimes pays expenses of writers on assignment.

Photos: State availability of photos. Reviews b&w and color contact sheets and 8x10 prints. Pays variable rates depending on size; $125 full-page b&w print. Captions required. Buys one-time rights.

Tips: "The writer has a better chance of breaking in at this publication with short articles and fillers. Most of our writers are top scientists in their fields."

OUTDOOR AMERICA, Suite 1100, 1701 N. Ft. Myer Dr., Arlington VA 22209. (703)528-1818. Editor: Carol Dana. 75% freelance written. Quarterly magazine about natural resource conservation and outdoor recreation for 50,000 members of the Izaak Walton League. Circ. 50,000. Pays on publication. Publishes ms an average of 4 months after acceptance. Byline given. Buys all rights or first serial rights, depending on arrangements with author. Submit seasonal material 6 months in advance. Simultaneous and photocopied submissions OK, if so indicated. Computer printout submissions acceptable; prefers letter-quality; no dot-matrix. SASE. Reports in 2 months. Sample copy $1.50; writer's guidelines with SASE.

Nonfiction: "We are interested in thoroughly researched, well-written pieces on current conservation issues (threats to water, fishers, wildlife, wildlife habitat, air, public lands, soil, etc.) and outdoor recreation (fishing, hunting, camping, woodcraft, photography, ethical outdoor behavior, etc.)." Length: 1,500-2,500 words. Payment: minimum 10¢/word.

Columns/Departments: Interested in shorter articles for the following departments: "Hand's-On Conservation" (how-to articles on conservation projects that can be undertaken by individuals or local groups); "From the Naturalist's Notebook" (pieces that give insight into the habits and behavior of animals, fish, birds). Length: 500-600 words. Payment: minimum 7¢/word.

Photos: Reviews 5x7 b&w glossy prints and 35mm and larger color transparencies. Additional payment for photos with ms negotiated. Pays $150 for covers. Caption and model release required. Buys one-time rights.

SEA FRONTIERS, 3979 Rickenbacker Causeway, Virginia Key, Miami FL 33149. (305)361-5786. Editor: Jean Bradfisch. 95% freelance written. Bimonthly. "For anyone with an interest in any aspect of the sea, its conservation, and the life it contains. Our audience is professional people for the most part; people in executive positions and students." Circ. 40,000. Pays on publication. Byline given. Buys all rights. Will consider photocopied submissions "if very clear." Computer printout submissions acceptable; prefers letter-quality to dot-matrix. Reports on material within 2 months. SASE. Sample copy $2.50; writer's guidelines for SASE.

Nonfiction: "Articles (with illustrations) covering interesting and little known facts about the sea, marine life, chemistry, geology, physics, fisheries, mining, engineering, navigation, influences on weather and climate, ecology, conservation, explorations, discoveries or advances in our knowledge of the marine sciences, or describing the activities of oceanographic laboratories or expeditions to any part of the world. Emphasis should be on research and discoveries rather than personalities involved." Buys 40-50 mss/year. Query. Length: 500-3,000 words. Pays $20-30/page.

Photos: Reviews 8x10 b&w glossy prints and 35mm (or larger) color transparencies. Pays $50 for color used on front and $35 for the back cover. Pays $25 for color used on inside covers.

Tips: "Query to include a paragraph or two that tells the subject, the angle or approach to be taken, and the writer's qualifications for covering this subject or the authorities with whom the facts will be checked."

SIERRA, The Sierra Club Bulletin, 530 Bush Street, San Francisco CA 94108. (415)981-8634. Editor-in-Chief: James Keough. Associate Editors: Joan Hamilton and Annie Stine. 75% freelance written. Magazine published 6 times/year; 96-120 pages. Emphasizes conservation and environmental politics for people who are well educated, activist, outdoor-oriented, and politically well informed with a dedication to conservation. Circ. 290,000. Pays on acceptance. Publishes ms an average of 6 months after acceptance. Byline given. Buys first North American serial rights. Photocopied submissions OK. Electronic submissions OK on ASC II files (or XyWrite), but requires hard copy also. Computer printout submissions acceptable; prefers letter-quality to dot-matrix. SASE. Reports in 6 weeks. Writer's guidelines for SAE and 3 first class stamps.

Nonfiction: Expose (well-documented on environmental issues of national importance such as energy, wilderness, forests, etc.); general interest (well-researched pieces on areas of particular environmental concern); historical (relevant to environmental concerns); how-to and equipment pieces (on camping, climbing, outdoor photography, etc.); interview (with very prominent figures in the field); personal experience (by or about children and wilderness); photo feature (photo essays on threatened areas); and technical (on energy sources, wildlife management land use, solid waste management, etc.). No "My trip to . . ." or "why we must save wildlife/nature" articles; no poetry or general superficial essays on environmentalism and local environmental issues. Buys 5-6 mss/issue. Query with published clips. Length: 800-2,500 words. Pays $200-500. Sometimes pays expenses of writers on assignment (up to $50).

Photos: Linda Smith, art and production manager. State availability of photos. Pays $200 maximum for color transparencies; $200 for cover photos. Buys one-time rights.

Columns/Departments: Book reviews. Buys 20-30 mss/year. Length: 800-1,500 words. Pays $100. Query. For Younger Readers, natural history and conservation topics presented for children ages 8 to 13. Pays $200-400. Submit queries to Jonathan King, associate editor.

Tips: "Queries should include an outline of how the topic would be covered and a mention of the political appropriateness and timeliness of the article. Familiarity with Sierra Club positions and policies is recommended. Statements of the writer's qualifications should be included. We don't have articles and fillers in our format. Frequent mistakes made by writers in completing an article for us are failure to thoroughly research complex issues; failure to conform to editorial direction; and unfamiliarity with Sierra Club programs and policies."

SNOWY EGRET, 205 S. 9th St., Williamsburg KY 40769. (606)549-0850. Editor: Humphrey A. Olsen. 75% freelance written. Semiannual for "persons of at least high school age interested in literary, artistic, philosophical and historical natural history." Circ. less than 500. Pays on publication. Publishes ms an average of 6 weeks after acceptance. Byline given. Buys first North American serial rights. Usually reports in 2 months. SASE. Sample copy $2; writer's guidelines for SAE and 1 first class stamp.

Nonfiction: Subject matter limited to material related to natural history (preferably living organisms), especially literary, artistic, philosophical and historical aspects. Criticism, book reviews, essays and biographies. No columns. Buys 40-50 mss/year. Pays $2/printed page. Send nonfiction prose mss and books for review to Humphrey A. Olsen.

Photos: No photos, but drawings acceptable.

Fiction: "We are interested in considering stories or self-contained portions of novels. All fiction must be natural history or man and nature. The scope is broad enough to include such stories as Hemingway's 'Big Two-Hearted River' and Warren's 'Blackberry Winter.'" Length: maximum 10,000 words. Pays $2/printed page. Send mss for consideration and poetry and fiction books for review to Alan Seaburg, poetry and fiction editor, 17 Century St., West Medford MA 02155. "It is preferable to query first."

Poetry: No length limits. Pays $4/printed page, minimum $2.

Personal Computing

Personal computing magazines continue to be the most changeable publications in the marketplace. Many add or eliminate computer models that they report on; the newer publications are still learning about their readers and how they can serve them. Many computer magazines have folded. In fact, last year *Writer's Market* was no sooner in bookstores when we learned that several magazines (that were being published when our book went to press) had suspended publication. Hopefully, the market is stabilizing, but make sure you see the most recent issue of a magazine before submitting material to it.

Owners of personal computers rely on these magazines to learn more about their PC. Business applications for home computers are covered in the Consumer Business and Finance section. Magazines on computer games and recreational computing are in the Games and Puzzles category. Publications for data processing personnel are listed in the Data Processing section of Trade Journals. Uses of computers in specific professions are covered in the appropriate Trade Journals sections. Also, Writer's Digest Books publishes the *1986 Programmer's Market*, a book directed to the writing and marketing of freelance computer programs, and *The Complete Guide to Writing Software User Manuals* by Brad M. McGehee.

A.N.A.L.O.G. COMPUTING, The Magazine for ATARI Computer Owners, A.N.A.L.O.G. Magazine Corp., Box 23, Worcester MA 01603. (617)892-9230. Editors: Michael DesChenes and Lee H. Pappas. Managing Editor: Jon A. Bell. 80% freelance written. Monthly magazine covering the Atari home computer. Pays on publication. Publishes ms an average of 2 months after acceptance. Byline given. Buys all rights. Submit seasonal/holiday material 2 months in advance. Photocopied submissions OK. Electronic submissions OK on 300-1200 baud "as long as the disk is prepared with one of the more common Atari word processing programs." Computer printout submissions acceptable; prefers letter-quality to dot-matrix. Reports in 2 weeks. Sample copy $3; writer's guidelines for business size SASE.
Nonfiction: How-to and technical. "We publish beginner's articles, educational programs, utilities, multi-function tutorials, do-it-yourself hardware articles (such as how to build your own 400 keyboard), and games (preferably arcade-style in Basic and/or Assembly language). We also publish reviews of Atari software and hardware." Buys 150 mss/year. Send complete ms. Length: open. Pays $60/typeset magazine page. Sometimes pays expenses of writers on assignment.
Photos: Send photos with ms. Reviews 5x7 b&w prints. Captions required, "clipped to the photo or taped to the back." Buys all rights.
Columns/Departments: Atari software and hardware reviews. Buys 30 mss/year. Send complete ms. Length: open.
Tips: "Almost all submissions are from people who read the magazine regularly and use the Atari home computers. We have published many first-time authors. We have published programs written in BASIC, ASSEMBLY, PILOT, FORTH, LISP, and some information on PASCAL. When submitting any program over 30 lines, authors must send a copy of the program on magnetic media, either cassette or disk. We strive to publish personable, down-to-earth articles as long as the style does not impair the technical aspects of the article. Authors should avoid sterile, lifeless prose. Occasional humor (detailing how the author uses his or her computer or tackles a programming problem) is welcome."

AHOY!, Ion International Inc., Suite 407, 45 W. 34th St., New York NY 10001. (212)239-0855. Editor: David Allikas. Managing Editor: Robert J. Sodaro. 80% freelance written. A monthly magazine for users of Commodore 64, VIC 20, Plus-4 C-16, C-128 and LCD home computers. Pays on acceptance. Publishes ms a average of 2 months after acceptance. Byline given. Offers variable kill fee. Buys first serial rights. Submit seasonal/holiday material 3 months in advance. Simultaneous queries and simultaneous, photocopied and previously published submissions OK. Electronic submissions OK on disk or cassette for Commodore 64, VIC 20, Plus 4 C-16, C-128 and LCD. Computer printout submissions acceptable; prefers letter-quality to dot-matrix. SASE. Sample copy $2.50; writer's guidelines for SASE.
Nonfiction: Book excerpts (Commodore-related books); general interest (modern technology); how-to (programming, maintaining, repairing, and customizing Commodore computers); humor (computer-related); interview/profile (computer industry leaders); new product (new Commodore-64, Vic-20, Plus-4 C-16, C-128 and LCD software and peripherals); and technical (how-to programming articles, mechanics of computers and peripherals). Buys 40 mss/year and 80 programs. Query with published clips. Length: 250-5,000 words. Pays $500 maximum. Pays expenses of writers on assignment.

Fillers: Gags for cartoons. Pays $15/cartoon gag.

Tips: "We are looking for high-quality articles and programs. Writers tend not to supply thorough documentation. The more complete the instructions to the readers the better the article. Major features go to regular contributors."

ANTIC MAGAZINE, The Atari Resource, Antic Publishing Co., 524 2nd St., San Francisco CA 94107. (415)957-0886. Editor: Nat Friedland. 25% freelance written. Monthly magazine for Atari 400/800, 1200XL, 600XL, 800XL, and 1450LXD computer users and owners of Atari game machines, compatible equipment and software. Circ. 100,000. Pays on publication. Publishes ms an average of 3 months after acceptance. Byline given. Offers $60 kill fee. Buys all rights. Submit seasonal/holiday material 3 months in advance. Simultaneous queries and photocopied submissions OK. Electronic submissions OK on Atari DOS compatible, but requires hard copy also. Computer printout submissions acceptable. SASE. Reports in 2 weeks on queries; 4 weeks on mss. Sample copy $3; free writer's guidelines. Request text files on disks and printout.

Nonfiction: How-to, interview/profile, new product, photo feature and technical. Special issues include Education (October) and Buyer's Guide (December). No generalized, nontechnical articles. Buys 250 mss/year. Query or send complete ms. Length: 500-2,500 words. Pays $20-180.

Photos: State availability of photos or send photos with ms. Reviews color transparencies and b&w prints; b&w should accompany article. Identification of subjects required.

Columns/Departments: Starting Line (beginner's column); Assembly Language (for advanced programmers); Profiles (personalities in the business); and Product Reviews (software/hardware products). Buys 36 mss/year. Query or send complete ms. Length: 1,500-2,500 words. Pays $120-180.

Tips: "Write for the Product Reviews section. Contact Jack Powell, editor. We need 400 to 600-word articles on a new software or hardware product for the Atari 400/800 computers. Give a clear description; personal experience with product; comparison with other available product; or product survey with charts. The most frequent mistakes made by writers in completing an article are failure to be clear and specific, and writing overly-long submissions."

‡BYTE MAGAZINE, 70 Main St., Peterborough NH 03458. (603)924-9281. Editor: Philip Lemmone. Monthly magazine covering personal computers for college-educated, professional users of computers. Circ. 399,000. Pays on publication. Buys all rights. Double-spaced computer disk submissions OK. Computer printout submissions acceptable; prefers letter-quality to dot-matrix. SASE. Reports on rejections in 3 months; 6 months if accepted. Sample copy $2.95; writer's guidelines for SASE.

Nonfiction: How-to (technical information about computers) and technical. Buys 160 mss/year. Query. Length: 3,000-5,000 words. Pay is competitive.

Tips: "Many *Byte* authors are regular readers of the magazine, and most readers use a computer either at home or at work. Back issues of the magazine give prospective authors an idea of the type of article published in *Byte*. Articles can take one of several forms: tutorial articles on a given subject, how-to articles detailing a specific implementation of a hardware or software project done on a small computer, survey articles on the future of microcomputers, and sometimes theoretical articles describing work in computer science (if written in an informal, 'friendly' style). Authors with less technical orientation should consider writing for our other publication, *Popular Computing Magazine*. Author's guides are available for both publications."

CLOSING THE GAP, Random Graphics, Box 68, Henderson MN 56044. (612)248-3294. Editor: Budd Hagen. Managing Editor: Michael Gergen. 25% freelance written. Bimonthly tabloid covering microcomputers for handicapped readers, special education and rehabilitation professionals. "We focus on currently available products and procedures written for the layman that incorporate microcomputers to enhance the educational opportunities and quality of life for the handicapped." Circ. 10,000. Pays on publication. Publishes ms an average of 4 months after acceptance. Byline given. Buys first serial rights. Simultaneous queries, and simultaneous, photocopied, and previously published submissions OK. Electronic submissions OK (disks) on modem ASCII text file, Apple II compatible, but requires hard copy also. Computer printout submissions acceptable (dot-matrix with descenders). Reports in 2 weeks. Free sample copy and writer's guidelines.

Nonfiction: How-to (simple modifications to computers or programs to aid handicapped); interview/profile (users or developers of computers to aid handicapped); new product (computer products to aid handicapped); personal experience (use of microcomputer to aid, or by, a handicapped person); and articles on current research on projects on microcomputers to aid the handicapped. No highly technical "computer hobbyist" pieces. Buys 25 mss/year. Query. Length: 500-2,000 words. Pays $25 and up (negotiable). "Many authors' material runs without financial compensation."

Tips: "Knowledge of the subject is vital, but freelancers do not need to be computer geniuses. Clarity is essential; articles must be able to be understood by a layman. Avoid computer, educator and rehabilitation jargon. All departments are open to freelancers. We are looking for new ideas. If you saw it in some other computer publication, don't bother submitting. *CTG*'s emphasis is on increasing computer user skills in our area of interest, not developing hobbyist or technical skills. The most frequent mistakes made by writers in completing an article for us is that their submissions are too technical—they associate 'computer' with hobbyist, often their own perspective—and don't realize our readers are not hobbyists or hackers.''

COMMODORE MICROCOMPUTERS, Commodore Business Machines, 1200 Wilson Dr., West Chester PA 19380. (215)431-9100. Editor: Diane LeBold. Publisher: Bob Kenney. 90% freelance written. Bimonthly magazine for owners of Commodore computers, using them for business, programming, education, communications, art, etc. Circ. 165,000. Pays on acceptance. Publishes ms an average of 3 months after acceptance. Byline given. Buys all rights; makes work-for-hire assignments. Submit seasonal/holiday material 5 months in advance. Simultaneous queries and previously published submissions OK. Electronic submissions OK on CBM 8032/8050 Format, Wordcraft or Word Pro files, but requires hard copy also. Computer printout submissions acceptable. SASE. Reports in 1 month on queries; 2 months on mss. Free sample copy; writer's guidelines for legal size SAE and 1 first class stamp.
Nonfiction: Book reviews; how-to (write programs, use software); humor; new product (reviews); personal experience; photo feature; and technical. "Write for guidelines." Buys 120 mss/year. Query or send complete ms. Length: 750-2,500 words. Pays $60-100/page.
Photos: Send photos with ms. Reviews 5x7 b&w and color prints. Captions required. Buys all rights.
Tips: "Write or phone the editor. Talk about several specific ideas. Use Commodore computers. We're open to programming techniques and product reviews."

‡**COMMODORE POWER/PLAY**, Commodore Business Machines, 1200 Wilson Dr., West Chester PA 19380. (215)431-9100. Editor: Diane LeBold. 90% freelance written. Bimonthly magazine for owners of Commodore computers. Circ. 165,000. Pays on acceptance. Publishes ms an average of 3 months after acceptance. Byline given. Offers 50% kill fee. Buys all rights. Submit seasonal/holiday material 5 months in advance. Simultaneous queries and submissions OK. Electronic submissions OK on CBM 8032/8050 Word Pro or Word Craft, but requires hard copy also. Computer printout submissions acceptable; prefers letter-quality to dot-matrix. Reports in 1 month on queries; 2 months on mss. Free sample copy; writer's guidelines for SAE and 1 first class stamp.
Nonfiction: Book excerpts; how-to (program, use computer); humor; interview/profile (latest programmer); new product; and technical (application). Commodore is games and recreation oriented. Buys 120 mss/year. Query with or without published clips or send complete ms. Length: 750-2,500 words. Pays $60-100. Sometimes pays the expenses of writers on assignment.
Photos: Send photos with query or ms. Reviews transparencies and prints. Captions and identification of subjects required. Buys all rights.
Tips: "Write or phone editor. Discuss ideas. Clarify articles for the sake of beginners." Programming techniques and reviews are areas most open to freelancers.

COMPUTE! The Leading Magazine of Home, Educational, and Recreational Computing, Compute! Publications, 324 W. Wendover Ave., Greensboro NC 27408. (919)275-9809. Senior Editor: Richard Mansfield. Managing Editor: Kathleen Martinek. 50% freelance written. Monthly magazine covering consumer and personal computing. Circ. 350,000. Pays on acceptance. Publishes ms an average of 4 months after acceptance. Byline given. Buys all rights. Submit seasonal/holiday material 6 months in advance. Simultaneous queries OK. Electronic submissions OK. Computer printout submissions acceptable. SASE. Reports in 2 weeks on queries; 6 weeks on mss. Sample copy $2.95; free writer's guidelines.
Nonfiction: How-to (compute) and technical (programs, games, utility programs for computers). No reviews. Send complete ms. Length: 500 words minimum. Pays $75-600.
Photos: Reviews 5x7 b&w glossy prints.
Tips: "We stress clarity and a tutorial approach and publish computer programs for many popular computers. Write for guidelines."

‡**COMPUTERITER, Microcomputer News and Views for the Writer/Editor**, Creative Business Communications, Box 476, Columbia MD 21045. (301)596-5591. Editor: Linda J. Elengold. Monthly newsletter on computers/word processing. "We like to hear about writers' experiences with specific computers, peripherals and software." Estab. 1984. Circ. 1,000. Pays on acceptance. Byline given. Offers 50% kill fee. Buys one-time rights and second serial (reprint) rights (occasionally). Submit seasonal/holiday material 6 months in advance. Simultaneous queries, and photocopied and previously published submissions OK. SASE. Reports in 2 weeks on queries; 4 weeks on mss. Sample copy $4; writer's guidelines for SAE and 1 first class stamp.
Nonfiction: Book excerpts, how-to (computer use), interview/profile, new product, personal experience and technical. No "Why I chose to use a computer"—wants very specific how-to's and reviews. Buys 24 mss/year. Query with published clips or send complete ms. Length: 100-500 words. Negotiates payment on individual basis; usually makes outright purchase (for one-time rights).
Tips: "Analyze your personal experiences with computers and software and develop some tips or hints other writers could share. We need interviews of prominent or successful writers on their use of computers, personal

experience, reviews and how-to articles. Reviews are assigned. Approximately 50% of the newsletter is staff-written. We are accepting more manuscripts from freelancers. We prefer queries."

COMPUTE!'s GAZETTE, ABC Publishing, Suite 200, 324 W. Wendover Ave., Greensboro NC 27408. (919)275-9809. Editor-in-Chief: Robert Lock. Managing Editor: Kathleen Martinek. 50% freelance edited. Monthly magazine of consumer and personal computing for owners/users of VIC and Commodore 64 computer systems. "Our audience is mostly beginning and novice computer users." Circ. 275,000. Pays on acceptance. Publishes ms an average of 3 months after acceptance. Byline given. Buys all rights. Submit seasonal/holiday material 6 months in advance. Simultaneous queries OK. Electronic submissions OK, but requires hard copy also. Computer printout submissions acceptable. SASE. Reports in 2 weeks on queries; 6 weeks on mss. Sample copy $2.50; free writer's guidelines.
Nonfiction: How-to (compute); personal experience (with programming/computers); and technical (programs, games, utility programs for computers). No reviews. "We stress clarity and a tutorial approach, and publish quality computer programs for Commodore computers. Follow the suggestions in our author's guide. Send complete ms. Length: 500 words minimum. Pays $70 minimum.

DIGITAL REVIEW, The Magazine for DEC Computing, Ziff-Davis Publishing, 160 State St., Boston MA 02109. (617)367-7190. Editor: Patrick Kenealy. Managing Editor: Jane Silks. Monthly magazine covering Digital Equipment Corporation computers and related hardware, software, services, supplies and applications. Circ. 70,000. Pays on acceptance. Byline given. Offers 15% kill fee. Buys first North American serial rights, one-time rights, and all rights; makes work-for-hire assignments. Simultaneous queries OK. Electronic submissions OK on 300/1200 baud async ASCII modem transmissions, DEC Rainbow or IBM PC single-sided diskettes. Computer printout submissions acceptable. Reports in 2 weeks. Free sample copy and writer's guidelines.
Nonfiction: Book excerpts, expose, how-to, interview/profile, new product, personal experience and technical. Buys 100 mss/year. Query with published clips. Length: 2,000-4,000 words. Pays $500-2,500.

80 MICRO, 80 Pine St., Peterborough NH 03458. (603)924-9471. Publisher: C.W. Communications/Peterborough. Editor: Eric Maloney. 85% freelance written. Monthly magazine about microcomputing for owners and users of TRS-80 by Radio Shack. Circ. 191,000. Pays on acceptance. Publishes ms an average of 6 months after acceptance. Buys all rights. Written queries preferred. Photocopied submissions OK. Requires hard copy of articles and disk or tape of programs. Computer printout submissions acceptable. SASE. Reports in 2 months. Sample copy $4; writer's guidelines for SASE.
Nonfiction: Applications programs for business, education, science, home and hobby; utilities; programming techniques; and tutorials. "We're looking for articles that will help the beginning, intermediate, and advanced TRS-80 microcomputer user become a better programmer. We also publish hardware construction projects. We buy about five manuscripts per issue. Query first; we are glutted." Length: 1,000 words average. Pays $60/printed page.
Reviews: Writers interested in reviewing current available software are asked to query the review editor, stating areas of interest and equipment owned. Buys 5-8 reviews/issue.
Photos: Offers no additional payment for photos accepted with ms. Buys all rights.

HOT COCO, The Magazine for TRS-80 Color Computer, C.W. Communications/Peterborough, 80 Pine St., Peterborough NH 03458. (603)924-9471. Editor: Michael E. Nadeau. Managing Editor: Mark Reynolds. 95% freelance written. Monthly magazine covering Tandy-80 Color Computers "to teach Color Computer owners new ways to use their machines, to provide working programs of practical or entertainment value, and to evaluate commercial products related to the Color Computer." Circ. 60,000. Pays on acceptance. Publishes ms an average of 6 months after acceptance. Byline given. Offers 25% kill fee. Buys all rights. Submit seasonal/holiday material 5 months in advance. Computer printout submissions acceptable. Reports in 2 weeks on queries; 3 weeks on mss. Sample copy $2.95; writer's guidelines for SAE and 1 first class stamp.
Nonfiction: How-to (programming techniques, hardware projects). No "How I convinced my wife that my CoCo is really wonderful" articles. Buys 150-200 mss/year. Query. Length: 2,500 words maximum. Pays $50-500. Sometimes pays expenses of writers on assignment.
Tips: "Becauase space is limited we look for short articles. Try to avoid sending bugged programs and incomplete submissions—no cassette of program listing."

INFOWORLD, The Newsweekly for Microcomputer Users, Popular Computing, Inc., (subsidiary of CW Communications, Inc.), Suite 305, 530 Lytton Ave., Palo Alto CA 94301. (415)328-4602. Editor: Stewart Alsop II. News Editor: David Needle. Technical Editor: Rory O'Connor. Applications Editor: Jacqueline Rae. Photo Editor: Gypsy Zaboroskie. 20% freelance written. "*InfoWorld* is the only weekly magazine that covers personal computers, personal computing, and the personal computer industry exclusively and comprehensively. We specialize in news and reviews. Writers interested in reporting for us have to know the industry and the products well and must be able to work fast; those interested in reviewing must understand one or two product categories extremely well." Circ. 130,000. Pays on acceptance. Byline given. Offers negotiable kill fee. Buys all rights. Submit seasonal/holiday material 6 weeks in advance. Electronic submissions OK; first contact Bob Hoskins, systems manager. Computer printout submissions acceptable; prefers letter-quality to dot-matrix. SASE. Sample copy with 8½x11 SAE and free writer's guidelines (specify news or reviews).

Nonfiction: General interest, interview/profile, new product, opinion, photo feature, technical, and application. Hardware, software, on-line services, product reviews commissioned according to strict standards and guidelines. Special issues include show coverage, biannual In Review retrospective, quarterly Special Reports, etc. No program listings, short stories, poetry or personal vendettas. "We've changed substantially in the past year. We're focusing heavily now on being a true news organization, with a beat system and fairly large staff. The new *Infoworld* includes hard news (all staff-written), news features of 1,500-2,000 words analyzing industry trends (difficult to break into), regular columns (by experts) and product reviews. Most of our freelance work is reviewing products, but you have to know what you're doing in order to review products for us." Buys 100 news mss and 350 review mss/year. Query with resume and published clips. Articles can be submitted in either typed hard copy or (preferably) uploaded to Atex system through a modem. Pays $100 to $300/article.

Photos: "*InfoWorld* is very interested in finding photojournalists who know personal computer industry personalities and can supply us with timely photos for our People department and for regular news pages." Query photo editor with resume and sample photos. Reviews 8½x11 prints. Captions, model release, and identification of subjects required. Pays $25-150. Buys 150 photos per year. Buys one-time rights.

Columns: "We have five weekly columns and are not interested in reviewing new columns ideas."

LINK-UP, Communications and the Small Computer, On-Line Communications, Inc., 6531 Cambridge St., Minneapolis MN 55426. (612)927-4916. Editorial Director: Rick Hoskins. 50% freelance written. Monthly magazine on small-computer communications. "Our purpose is to keep readers up to date on the fast growing field of small-computer communications—home and business." Pays on acceptance. Publishes ms an average of 3 months after acceptance. Byline given. Offers negotiable kill fee. Submit seasonal/holiday material 4 months in advance. Simultaneous queries, and simultaneous and photocopied submissions OK. Electronic submissions OK on 4.25" diskette with ASC II files/MS DOS or IBM EasyWriter1.1. Computer printout submissions acceptable. SASE. Reports in 2 weeks on queries; 6 weeks on mss. Sample copy for $3, 10x12 SAE and $1.25 postage; writer's guidelines for business size SAE and 1 first class stamp.

Nonfiction: Book excerpts, how-to (computer/communications), humor, interview/profile, new product, opinion, photo feature and technical. Buys 50-60 mss/year. Query with published clips or send complete ms. Length: 1,000-3,000 words. Pays $200-400.

Photos: Send photos with query or ms. Reviews 35mm and larger color transparencies and (minimum) 5x7 prints. Pays variable/negotiable rates. Captions, model release, and identification of subjects required. Buys one-time rights.

Fillers: Anecdotes, short humor and newsbreaks. Buys few fillers. Length: 50-200 words. Pays $25-100.

Tips: "Study an issue or two; we're dealing with a lot of technical material, but we're *not* a tech-only magazine. Feature articles on small-computer communications for home and business—data bases, information networks, person-to-person-via-computer, etc.—are the areas most open to freelancers."

MACWORLD, The Macintosh Magazine, PC World Communications, Inc., 555 DeHaro St., San Francisco CA 94107. (415)861-3861. Editor: Kearney Rietmann. 70% freelance written. Published 13 times a year. Magazine covering use of Apple's Macintosh computer. Estab. 1984. Circ. 200,000. Pays on acceptance. Publishes ms an average of 6 months after acceptance. Byline given. Offers negotiable kill fee. Buys all rights. Submit seasonal/holiday material 6 months in advance. Electronic submissions on Macintosh disk with MacWhite, IBM PC disk with WordStar, Async comm, via modem, but requires hard copy also. Computer printout submissions acceptable. SASE. Reports in 6 weeks. Sample copy $6. Free writer's guidelines.

Nonfiction: Book excerpts, community, general interest, historical/nostalgic, how-to, humor, hands-on and practical experiences, interview/profile, new product, opinion, personal experience, photo feature, technical and travel. Buys 120 mss/year. Query with published clips. Length: 500-3,500 words. Pays $200-750. Sometimes pays expenses of writers on assignment.

Photos: State availability of photos or send photos with query. Pays $25-50 for color slides and 5x7 or 8x10 b&w prints. Captions, model release, and identification of subjects required. Buys one-time rights.

Tips: "We seek clearly written, useful articles. Send in article proposal first. Short reviews and new items are the best areas to start with."

MICRO MOONLIGHTER NEWSLETTER, 4121 Buckthorn Ct., Lewisville TX 75028. (214)539-1115. Editor: J. Norman Goode. Managing Editor: Mary K. Goode. 25% freelance written. Monthly newsletter covering personal computing. "Hard hitting techniques for establishing, building and maintaining a home-based business using a personal computer." Pays on acceptance. Publishes ms an average of 1 month after acceptance. Byline given. Buys all rights. Electronic submissions OK if compatible with any 5¼" diskettes under IBM PC formats. Computer printout submissions acceptable; prefers letter-quality to dot-matrix. SASE.

Reports in 1 month. Sample copy $3; writer's guidelines for SAE with 2 first class stamps.
Nonfiction: Book excerpts, expose, general interest, how-to, interview/profile, new product, opinion, personal experience, technical, and business case studies. Buys 24 mss/year. Query or send complete ms. Length: 500-6,000 words. Pays 3-5¢/word.
Columns/Departments: Business Case Studies. Buys 12/year. Query or send complete ms. Length: 500-6,000 words. Pays 3-5¢/word.
Tips: "Writers should submit articles of interest to personal computer owners, those who are interested in starting a home business using the personal computer, and/or articles on products associated with personal computers." Especially open to material on cottage industry and entrepreneurship. Business Case Studies is most open to freelancers.

‡MICRO-ROOTS, The Newsletter/Journal for the Micro-Computer/Genealogy Enthusiast, RaeData, Inc., Suite 104, 7411 Riggs Rd., Adelphi MD 20783. (301)439-4743. Editor: Leon H. Raesly. 75% freelance written. Bimonthly newsletter/journal on home/personal computers and family roots. Audience includes individuals interested in their family roots and mirco-computers. Circ. 11,000. Pays 15 days after publication. Offers 10% kill fee and returns all rights; or pays full fee and retains all rights (depending on circumstances). Buys all rights. Submit seasonal/holiday material 4 months in advance. Electronic submissions OK on ASCII Text files, Ward Christianson Protocols, or straight ASCII text file dump. Computer printout submissions acceptable. SASE. Reports in 3 weeks on queries; 8 weeks on mss. Writer's guidelines for #10 SAE and 1 first class stamp.
Nonfiction: General interest, historical/nostalgic, how-to, humor, interview/profile, new product, opinion (software reviews), personal experiences, technical and travel, all relating to home/personal computing and/or genealogy/family roots. Buys 30-50 mss/year. Query or send complete ms. Length: 50 words minimum. Pays 7¢/printed word as counted by Sensible Speller (it counts hyphenated words as two words, etc.). Sometimes pays expenses of writers on assignment.
Photos: State availability of photos. Reviews 5x7 or 8x10 b&w prints only. Captions, model release, and identification of subjects required. Buys all rights.
Columns/Departments: None purchased now, but OK to query.
Tips: "All sections are open to freelancers. Write as if you were talking with a friend and explaining (or showing off) a technique or skill, if sharing with an individual you know. We especially want articles written in layman terms. Technical articles are OK, but *must* explain any terms used. We hope to receive 50-75% from outside sources. However, if writing reviews, etc. *must* know software from really using it."

‡NATIONAL TELECOMPUTING CORP. VIDEOTEX SERVICE, NTC Videotex, National Telecomputing Corp., 39 Jewett Place, Nyack NY 10960. (914)358-2335. Editor: James Clyde. 80% freelance written. Daly videotex on-line magazine for home and business computer use. Estab. 1982. Circ. 2,100 general audience, 300 real estate. Pays on publication. Publishes ms an average of 1 week after acceptance. Byline given. Copyrighted. Writers may copyright submissions. Buys first North American serial rights, one-time rights, simultaneous rights, and first serial rights; also makes work-for-hire assignments. Submit seasonal/holiday material 2 weeks in advance. Simultaneous and previously published submissions OK. Electronic submissions OK via modem (preferred) IBM PC or compatibles, Tandy MOD II, 12, 16; and Radio Shack MOD 100. Media accepted. SASE. Computer printout submissions acceptable. Reports in 1 week. Sample copy (includes sign-up kit, password, instructions); writer's guidelines for 5x7 SAE and 6 first class stamps.
Nonfiction: General interest, how-to, humor, new product, technical, economic trends, real estate, banking, and finance. Buys 50 mss/year. Send complete ms. Length: 100-750 words. Pays $25-100. Sometimes pays expense of writers on assignment.
Columns/Departments: Computers (Radio Shack, IBM, software development, Lotus 123) and real estate (new projects, trends, community reports, analysis, tax topics). Buys 20 mss/year. Query with published clips or send complete ms. Length: 100-750 words. Pays $25-100.
Fillers: Jokes, short humor and newsbreaks. Buys 100/year. Length: 100-250 words. Pays $10-50 and subscription with acceptance of first submission.
Tips: Submit articles, screens, programs, etc., which would appeal to an audience (general) for several months. Timeless articles are sought. Most articles are short. Videotex users pay by the hour. The most frequent mistake writers make in completing an article for us is that they don't impose a surcharge for valuable reports or for novelty items which are frequently accessed. All submissions may carry a $.01 to $99.99 surcharge for access. Areas most open to freelancers are home computer, business computers, real estate and investment techniques. Screen formats may be as important as content."

NIBBLE, The Reference for Apple Computing, Micro-SPARC Inc., 45 Winthrop St., Concord MA 01742. (617)371-1660. Editor: Mike Harvey. Managing Editor: David Szetela. 90% freelance written. Magazine published 12 times/year covering personal computing for Apple computers. Readership is middle/upper-middle income professionals who own Apple or Apple compatible computers. Circ. 80,000. Pays on acceptance. Publishes ms an average of 1 year after acceptance. Byline given. Buys all rights. Submit seasonal/holiday material 8 months in advance. Electronic submission OK if Apple compatible 5¼'' disk; preferred format is a DOS 3.3 textfile without control codes. Requires hard copy also. Computer printout submissions acceptable. Reports in 1 week on queries; 4 weeks on mss. Sample copy $3.50; free writer's guidelines.

Nonfiction: David Krathwohl, programs editor. Apple programs in the areas of business, home, education, games, and programmers' utilities. Buys 400 mss/year. Send complete hardcopy ms and textfile of ms on diskette if possible. Length: 300-15,000 words. Pays $50-500.

Columns/Departments: David Krathwohl, programs editor. Beginning BASIC programming, VisiCalc, Graphics, and Assembly. Language Programming, Legal. Buys 100 mss/year. Send complete hardcopy ms and textfile of ms on diskette if possible. Length: 300-2,000 words. Pays $100-300.

Tips: "Submit original personal computer programs for Apple computers—explain what they do, how to use them, how they work, and how the techniques can be used in the reader's own programs. Write or call for writer's guidelines."

PC WORLD, The Comprehensive Guide to IBM Personal Computers and Compatibles, PC World Communications, Inc., 555 De Haro St., San Francisco CA 94107. (415)861-3861. Editor: Harry Miller. 80% freelance written. Monthly magazine covering IBM Personal Computers and compatibles. Circ. 300,000. Pays on acceptance. Byline given. Offers negotiable kill fee. Buys all rights. Submit material at least 6 months in advance. Electronic submissions OK on ASCII files and WordStar, but requires hard copy also. Computer printout submissions acceptable. SASE. Reports in 6 weeks. Free sample copy and writer's guidelines.

Nonfiction: Book excerpts, general interest, historic/nostalgic, humor, opinion, personal experience, photo feature, how-to, interview/profile, new product and technical. "*PC World* is composed of five sections: State of the Art, Getting Started, Review, Hands On, and Community. In State of the Art, articles cover developing technologies in the computer industry. The Getting Started section is specifically aimed at the growing number of new computer users. In Review, new hardware and software are critically and objectively analyzed by experienced users. Hands On offers 'how-to' articles, giving readers instructions on patching WordStar, setting up 1-2-3 worksheets, inserting memory boards, developing programming skills and other related topics. Community covers a wide range of subjects, focusing on how society is being shaped by the influx of microcomputers in work places, schools and homes." No articles not related to the IBM PC or compatibles. Query with or without published clips or send complete ms. Buys 50 mss/year. Length: 1,500-2,500 words. Pays $35-1,200.

Photos: State availability of photos or send with query or ms. Reviews color transparencies and 8x10 b&w prints. Pays $25-50. Captions, model release, identification of subjects required. Buys one-time rights.

Columns/Departments: REMark (personal opinions about microcomputer-related issues); Compatible News (hardware, software, business and legal developments related to IBM and PC compatible market). Buys 150 mss/year. Query with or without published clips or send complete ms.

Tips: "Familiarity with the IBM PC or technical knowledge about its operations often determines whether we accept a query. Send all queries to the attention of Proposals—Editorial Department. The Hands On section is especially open to freelancers with practical applications to offer."

PCM, The Personal Computing Magazine for Tandy Users, Falsoft, Inc., 9529 U.S. Highway 42, Box 209, Prospect KY 40059. (502)228-4492. Editor: Lawrence C. Falk. Managing Editor: Courtney Noe. 75% freelance written. A monthly (brand specific) magazine for owners of the TRS-80 Model 100 and 200 portable computer and the TRS-80 Model 1000, 1200 and 2000. Circ. 10,000. Pays on publication. Publishes ms an average of 3 months after acceptance. Byline given. Buys first serial rights. Submit seasonal/holiday material 4 months in advance. Photocopied submissions OK. Electronic submissions OK, but requires hard copy also. Computer printout submissions acceptable. Reports in 2 months. Sample copy for SASE; free writer's guidelines.

Nonfiction: Jutta Kapfhammer, submissions editor. How-to. "We prefer articles with programs." No general interest material. Buys 80 mss/year. Send complete ms. "Do not query." Length: 300 words minimum. Pays $40-50/page.

Photos: State availability of photos. Rarely uses photos.

Tips: "At this time we are only interested in submissions for the TRS-80 Model 100 and the TRS-80 Model 2000. Strong preference is given to submissions accompanied by brief program listings. All listings must be submitted on tape or disk as well as in hardcopy form."

 The double dagger before a listing indicates that the listing is new in this edition. New markets are often the most receptive to freelance contributions.

PERSONAL COMPUTING MAGAZINE, Hayden Publishing Company, Inc., 10 Mulholland Dr., Hasbrouck Heights NJ 07604. (201)393-6104. Editor: Chuck Martin. Managing Editor: Fred Abatemarco. 15% freelance written. Monthly magazine on personal computers. "A special-interest magazine that meets the needs of growing users. Editorial content designed to serve business people whose curiosity about the benefits of personal computer use is developing into serious interest and active involvement. Articles and features serve that level of interest without demanding years of experience or advanced knowledge of the technology." Circ. 525,000. Pays on acceptance. Publishes ms an average of 2 months after acceptance. Byline given. Buys first North American serial rights. Submit seasonal/holiday material 2 months in advance. Simultaneous queries, and simultaneous and photocopied submissions OK. Computer printout submissions acceptable; prefers letter-quality to dot-matrix. Reports in 3 weeks. Free writer's guidelines.
Nonfiction: Technical and feature articles on people in computing. No product reviews. Query with or without published clips. Pay varies.

POPULAR COMPUTING MAGAZINE, 70 Main St., Peterborough, NH 03458. (603)924-9281. Editor-in-Chief: Pamela A. Clark. 70% freelance written. McGraw-Hill monthly magazine covering personal computers directed particularly at managers and professionals actively using microcomputers to increase productivity and effectiveness in business and professions. Circ. 300,000. Pays on acceptance. Publishes ms an average of 3 months after acceptance. Buys all rights. Photocopied submissions OK. Electronic submissions OK via the Source, straight ASCII, IBM compatible (no margins, no indents, 1 blank line between paragraphs). Hard copy not necessary but preferred. Computer printout submissions acceptable. SASE. Reports in 2 months. Sample copy $3.25.
Nonfiction: The bulk of editorial is devoted to news and trends in technology, reviews of important computer systems, peripherals, software and on-line services, solution-oriented articles, commentary on issues facing intermediate-level computer users and practical advice on making the computer a more effective productivity tool. No fiction or cartoons. Send detailed query letter to editor-in-chief. Length: 1,000-2,500 words. Pays $250-750.
Tips: "Article proposals that lend themselves to increasing productivity among managers and professionals have the greatest potential for appeal to our audience. The most frequent mistake made by writers in completing an article for us is writing to the wrong audience (hackers or novices are out). Too many articles are directed at novices. Some authors have trouble tailoring articles for our magazine's focus. Articles should be free as much as possible from computer jargon. Author should be a computer user. The writer has a better chance of breaking in at our publication with short articles and fillers. We are more likely to start a writer on Random/Access, book or software reviews."

‡PROFILES, The Magazine for Kaypro Users, Kaypro Corporation, 533 Stevens Ave., Solana Beach CA 92075. (619)481-4300. Editor: Tom Foote. Managing Editor: Diane Ingalls. 75% freelance written. Monthly magazine (except combined issues July/August and December/January) for Kaypro computer owners/users covering technical information and "think" pieces (e.g., impact of micros on American life). "Writers must be familiar with or more models of the Kaypro computers. We offer articles for all levels, from novice to expert, including software reviews, book reviews, consumer tips, technical help, and information on ways people are putting their Kaypros to work. The bulk of our audience is business people, educators and writers." Circ. 90,000. Pays on acceptance. Byline given. Offers 30% kill fee. Buys first world rights. Submit seasonal/holiday material 4 months in advance. Previously published work OK occasionally. "We prefer to receive manuscripts on Kaypro-formatted diskettes in a single-spaced WordStar text file, with margins set at 1 and 55. However, we will accept Perfect Writer, Vedit or other formats as long as we can read and convert them conveniently. We pay $50 bonus if your accepted article arrives on a *conveniently readable* diskette"; requires hard copy also. Computer printout submissions acceptable. SASE. Reports in 1 month. Sample copy for SAE; free writer's guidelines.
Nonfiction: Expose (rarely; must be related to computer issues); how-to (write programs in various languages, incorporate a computer in a specific business); interview/profile (unusual Kaypro owners/users); new product (software; other products covered by columnist); personal experience (unique uses of Kaypro); technical (software reviews. "Prefers comparative or 'round up' reviews."); and book reviews. "No poetry, no 'bringing home baby' articles (pieces for people who've just bought computers), no pieces estolling the virtues of computers (our readers have already bought them)." Query with or without published clips. Length: 1,500-3,000 words. Pays $150-500. Sometimes pays expenses of writers on assignment.
Photos: Eric Mattei, art director. State availability of photos with query. Pays $175-700 for color transparencies (prefers 3¼); $125 minimum for 8x10 b&w prints. Captions, model release and identification of subjects required. Buys one-time rights.
Tips: "Study the magazine and look for topics we haven't covered or new slants we *have* covered. Query with a specific idea. Writers often break in by doing product reviews. We prefer roundups to single-producers. Be sure you're qualified to do the review."

RAINBOW MAGAZINE, Falsoft, Inc., 9529 US Highway 42, Prospect KY 40059. (502)228-4492. Editor: Lawrence C. Falk. Managing Editor: James E. Reed. 60% freelance written. Monthly magazine covering the TRS-80 Color Computer and Dragon 32 computer. Circ. 75,000. Pays on publication. Publishes ms an average of 4 months after acceptance. Byline given. Buys one-time rights and rights for "tape" service reprint as compilation only. Submit seasonal/holiday material 6 months in advance. Electronic submissions on disk or magnetic tape OK, but requires hard copy also. Computer printout submissions acceptable. Reports in 3 months. Sample copy $3.95; free writer's guidelines.
Nonfiction: Jutta Kapfhammer, submissions editor. Technical (computer programs and articles for Rainbow TRS-80 Color Computer or TRS-80 Model 100 Portable Computer. No general "overview" articles. "We want articles *with* programs or tutorials." Buys 300 + mss/year. Send complete ms. Pays $25-50/page.
Fillers: Cartoons (must be Color Computer-related).

soft sector, Falsoft, Inc., 9529 U.S. Highway 42, Box 209, Prospect KY 40059. (502)228-4492. Editor: Lawrence C. Falk. Managing Editor: Jim Reed. "A monthly bound specific magazine for the Sanyo MS-DOS-based, IBM PC data compatible computer." Estab. 1984. Pays on publication. Byline given. Buys first serial rights. Submit seasonal/holiday material 4 months in advance. Simultaneous and photocopied submissions OK. Electronic submissions OK if ASCII file. Reports in 2 months. Free sample copy; writer's guidelines for SAE.
Nonfiction: Interested only in articles and programs specifically for the Sanyo 550-555 computer. "No general interest or computer commentary." Buys 120 mss/year. Send complete ms. Length: 200 words minimum. Pays $50 maximum/printed magazine page.
Tips: "Know specific computer or don't submit."

Photography

If you want to develop a photographer's eye or to write articles about photography, these publications will help you. Readers of these magazines use their cameras for enjoyment and for weekend assignments. Magazines geared to the professional photographer can be found in Trade Journals.

AMERICAN CINEMATOGRAPHER, A.S.C. Holding Corp., Box 2230, Hollywood CA 90078. (213)876-5080. Editor: Richard Patterson. Associate Editor: George Turner. An international journal of film and video production techniques "addressed to creative, managerial, and technical people in all aspects of production. Its function is to disseminate practical information about the creative use of film and video equipment, and it strives to maintain a balance between technical sophistication and accessibility." 120 pages. Circ. 33,000. Pays on publication. Buys all rights. Phone queries OK. Simultaneous and photocopied submissions OK. Computer printout submissions OK "provided they are adequately spaced." SASE.
Nonfiction: Descriptions of new equipment and techniques or accounts of specific productions involving unique problems or techniques; historical articles detailing the production of a classic film, the work of a pioneer or legendary cinematographer or the development of a significant technique or type of equipment. Also discussions of the aesthetic principles involved in production techniques. Recent article example: "Photographic Effects for Indiana Jones," by Richard Patterson, and "Multi Camera Work on Cheers," by David Weiner. Length: 1,500 to 6,000 words. Pays approximately 5¢/word.
Photos: B&w and color purchased with mss. No additional payment.
Tips: "Queries must describe writer's qualifications and include writing samples. We hope to make more use of freelance writers."

DARKROOM PHOTOGRAPHY MAGAZINE, TL Enterprises, 1 Hallidie Plaza, San Francisco CA 94102. (415)989-4360. Editor: Richard Senti. Managing Editor: Kim Torgerson. A photography magazine with darkroom emphasis, published 9 times/year for both professional and amateur photographers "interested in what goes on *after* the picture's been taken: processing, printing, manipulating, etc." Circ. 80,000. Pays on publication; pays regular writers on acceptance. Byline given. Offers 50% kill fee. Buys all rights, but negotiable. Photocopied submissions OK. Computer printout submissions acceptable. SASE. Reports in 6 weeks. Sample copy and writer's guidelines for SASE.
Nonfiction: Historical/nostalgic (some photo-history pieces); how-to (darkroom equipment build-ins); interview/profile (famous photographers); and technical (articles on darkroom techniques, tools, and tricks). No stories on shooting techniques, strobes, lighting, or in-camera image manipulation. Query or send complete

ms. Length: varies. Pays $35-500.

Photos: State availability or send photos with query or ms. Reviews transparencies and 8x10 prints. "Supporting photographs are considered part of the manuscript package."

Columns/Departments: Tools & Tricks, Special Effects, Making Money, and Larger Formats. Query or send complete ms. Length: 800-1,200 words. Pays $100-150.

Tips: "Published darkroom-related 'tips' receive free one-year subscriptions." Length: 100-150 words.

PETERSEN'S PHOTOGRAPHIC MAGAZINE, Petersen Publishing Co., 8490 Sunset Blvd., Los Angeles CA 90069. (213)657-5100. Group Publisher: Paul Tzimoulis. Editor: Karen Geller-Shinn. 25% freelance written. Monthly magazine; 100 pages. Emphasizes how-to photography. Circ. 300,000. Pays on publication. Publishes ms an average of 9 months after acceptance. Buys all rights. Submit seasonal/holiday material 5 months in advance. Photocopied submissions OK. Computer printout submissions acceptable. SASE. Reports in 2 months. Sample copy $2.50.

Nonfiction: Karen Geller-Shinn, editor. How-to (darkroom, lighting, special effects, and studio photography). "We don't cover personalities." Buys 12-30 unsolicited mss/year. Send story, photos and captions. Pays $60/printed page.

Photos: With coupon to Gallery Editor. Photos purchased with or without accompanying ms. Pays $25-35 for b&w and color photos. Model release and technical details required.

Tips: "We are a how-to-do-it magazine which requires clearly detailed text and step-by-step illustration. Write for our writer's and photographer's guide for details of our requirements."

PHOTO INSIGHT, Suite 2, 169-15 Jamaica Ave., Jamaica NY 11432. Managing Editor: Conrad Lovelo Jr. 82% freelance written. Bimonthly newsletter; 12 pages. Emphasizes up-to-date photography contests; for amateur and professional photographers. Circ. 5,036. Pays on publication. Buys one-time rights. Submit seasonal or holiday material 3 months in advance. Simultaneous and previously published submissions OK. SASE. Reports in 2 months. Sample copy $2.

Nonfiction: How-to on winning contests, humor, inspirational and new products (related to photography). No material on the copyright law for photographers. Buys 1 mss/issue. Length: features-2,000 words. Pays $50 for photo-text package. Captions required.

Photos: Portfolios accepted for publication based on themes. One photographer's portfolio/issue: 6-10 photos.

Columns/Departments: Gallery Insight (photo show reviews) and In The News (new products or seminars). Buys 2 mss/issue. Query. Length: 100-300 words. Pays $25. Open to suggestions for new columns/departments.

Poetry: Contact: Poetry Editor. Traditional. Length: 4-12 lines. Pays $5.

Fillers: Jokes, gags and anecdotes. Length: 300 words maximum. Pays $5.

PHOTO LIFE, 100 Steelcase Rd. E, Markham, Ontario L3R 1E8 Canada. (416)475-8440. Editor: Norm Rosen. 60% freelance written. Monthly magazine. "Canada's leading magazine for the amateur photographer, providing information, entertainment and technical tips which help readers develop their interest in photography." Reader participation emphasized through gallery sections, contests and portfolio features. All articles and photography assigned specifically, but most assignments given to readers who contact *Photo Life* with ideas or sample photography. Canadian photos and articles given priority, although features of interest to Canadian photographers but not written or photographed by Canadians will also be considered. Circ. 85,000. Pays on publication. Publishes ms an average of 3 months after acceptance. Byline given. Buys first North American serial rights. Most content assigned 6 months prior to publication. Computer printout submissions acceptable. Sample copy and writer's guidelines for $2 and SASE. Photo guidelines with SAE and 37¢ Canadian postage.

Nonfiction: Interested in all subjects of interest to amateur photographers. Uses 8x10 glossy b&w prints. Pays $25 (Canadian) minimum/photo. Uses 35mm or larger color transparencies or 8x10 color prints, glossy preferred. Unless assigned, covers are derived from content of each issue. Uses vertical format 35mm slides or larger form slides only. Pays $200/cover. Canadian content only. Article ideas are welcome but *no* unsolicited mss please. Payment for articles ranges from $100 Canadian minimum.

Tips: "Contact us prior to sending unsolicited material. We operate by assignment exclusively. Topics suggested by freelancers will be given a target length when assigned."

‡**PHOTOGRAPHY**, Argus Specialist Publications, Ltd., 1 Golden Square, London, W.1, England. Editor: Roger Cook. 65% freelance written. Monthly magazine. Circ. 43,000. Pays on publication. Publishes ms an average of 2 months after acceptance. Buys first British serial rights. Submit seasonal/holiday material 4 months in advance. Computer printout submissions acceptable; no dot-matrix. SASE.

Nonfiction: How-to (photographic topics), photo feature and technical. Buys 2-3 mss/issue. Buys 6 unsolicited mss/year. Query. Length: 500-2,000 words.

Photos: State availability of photos. Offers no additional payment for 8x10 b&w glossy prints or 35mm color transparencies. Buys one-time rights. Captions and model release required.

POPULAR PHOTOGRAPHY, 1 Park Ave., New York NY 10016. Editorial Director: Arthur Goldsmith. 25% freelance written. Monthly. "The magazine is designed for advanced amateur and professional photographers." Circ. 925,000. Also publishes a picture annual and a photography buyer's guide. Pays on acceptance. Publishes ms an average of 4 months after acceptance. Byline given. "Rights purchased vary occasionally but are usually one-time." Submit material 4 months in advance. Computer printout submissions acceptable; prefers letter-quality to dot-matrix. Reports in 1 month. SASE. Query.
Nonfiction: "This magazine is mainly interested in instructional articles on photography that will help photographers improve their work. This includes all aspects of photography, from theory to camera use and darkroom procedures. Utter familiarity with the subject is a prerequisite to acceptance. It is best to submit article ideas in outline form since features are set up to fit the magazine's visual policies. Style should be easily readable but with plenty of factual data when a technique story is involved. We're not quite as 'hardware'-oriented as some magazines. We use many equipment stories, but we often give more space to cultural and aesthetic aspects of the hobby than our competition does." Buys how-to, interviews, profiles, historical articles and photo essays. Buys 35-50 mss/year, "mostly from technical types already known to us." Query. Length: 500-2,000 words. Pays $125/b&w display page; $200/color page.
Photos: Monica Cipnic, picture editor. Interested in seeing portfolios in b&w and color of highest quality in terms of creativity, imagination and technique.

‡**PRACTICAL PHOTOGRAPHY**, EMAP National Publications, Ltd., Bushfield House, Orton Centre, Peterborough PE2 0UW England. 0733-237111. Editor: Dominic Boland. Monthly magazine; 120 pages. Emphasizes amateur photography. Circ. 95,000. Pays on publication. Publishes ms an average of 3 months after acceptance. Buys one-time rights. Phone queries OK. Submit seasonal/holiday material 3 months in advance. Computer printout submissions acceptable; prefers letter-quality to dot-matrix.
Nonfiction: How-to (any aspect of photography) and humor (related to photography). No travelog-type articles. Buys 3-4 mss/issue. Send complete ms. Length: 300-3,000 words. Pays 20 pounds minimum/1,000 words. Sometimes pays expenses of writers on assignment.
Photos: Pays £10 minimum/8x10 b&w glossy print and 35mm color transparency. Captions preferred; model release required.

Politics and World Affairs

Nuclear issues, terrorist attacks, and hostage confrontations have prompted more readers than ever to follow world news.

These publications cover politics for the reader interested in current events. Other categories in *Writer's Market* include publications that will consider articles about politics and world affairs. Some of these categories are Business and Finance, Regional and General Interest. For listings of publications geared toward the professional, see Trade Journals/Government and Public Service and Trade Journals/International Affairs.

AFRICA REPORT, 833 United Nations Plaza, New York NY 10017. (212)949-5731. Editor: Margaret A. Novicki. 60% freelance written. Bimonthly. For U.S. citizens, residents with a special interest in African affairs for professional, business, academic or personal reasons. Not tourist-related. Circ. 10,500. Pays on publication. Publishes ms an average of 2 months after acceptance. Rights purchased vary with author and material; usually buys all rights, very occasionally first serial rights. Offers negotiable kill fee. Byline given unless otherwise requested. SASE. Sample copy for $4; free writer's guidelines.
Nonfiction: Interested in "African political, economic and cultural affairs, especially in relation to U.S. foreign policy and business objectives. Style should be journalistic but not academic or light. Articles should not be polemical or long on rhetoric but may be committed to a strong viewpoint. I do not want tourism articles." Would like to see in-depth topical analyses of lesser known African countries, based on residence or several months' stay in the country. Buys 15 unsolicited mss/year. Pays $150-250.
Photos: Photos purchased with or without accompanying mss with extra payment. Reviews b&w only. Pays $25. Submit 12x8 "half-plate."
Tips: "Read *Africa Report* and other international journals regularly. Become an expert on an African or Africa-related topic. Make sure your submissions fit the style, length, and level of *Africa Report*."

AMERICAN OPINION MAGAZINE, Belmont MA 02178. Managing Editor: Scott Stanley Jr. "A conservative, anti-communist journal of political affairs." 1% freelance written. Monthly except August. Circ. 35,000. Pays on publication. Publishes ms an average of 3 months after acceptance. Byline given. Buys all rights. Offers variable kill fee. Computer printout submissions acceptable; prefers letter-quality to dot-matrix. SASE. Sample copy $2.50.
Nonfiction: Articles on matters of political affairs of a conservative, anti-communist nature. "We favor highly researched, definitive studies of social, economic, political and international problems that are written with verve and originality of style." Length: 1,500-3,000 words. Pays $25/published page. Sometimes pays the expenses of writers on assignment.

AMERICAS, Organization of American States, Editorial Offices, Administration Bldg., 19th St. and Constitution Ave., Washington DC 20006. Managing Editor: A.R. Williams. 50% freelance written. Bimonthly. Official cultural organ of Organization of American States. Audience is persons interested in inter-American topics. Editions published in English and Spanish. Circ. 100,000. Pays on publication. Publishes ms an average of 6 months after acceptance. Byline given. Buys first hemisphere serial rights. Computer printout submissions acceptable; prefers letter-quality to dot-matrix. Articles received on speculation only. Include cover letter with writer's background. Reports in 3 months. Not necessary to enclose SASE. Free sample copy.
Nonfiction: Articles of general New World interest on travel, history, art, literature, theater, development, archeology, travel, etc. Emphasis on modern, up-to-date Latin America. Taboos are religious and political themes or articles with noninternational slant. Photos required. Recent article example: "The Vision of Rubén Blades", (March/April 1985). Buys 20 unsolicited mss/year. Length: 2,500 words maximum. Pays $200 minimum.
Tips: "Send excellent photographs in both color and black and white, keep the article short and address an international readership, not a local or national one. Make it culturally insightful. We don't want Sunday newspaper travel supplement pieces. Our angle is unique. Read recent back issues before you attempt anything."

CALIFORNIA JOURNAL, The California Center, 1714 Capitol Ave., Sacramento CA 95814. (916)444-2840. Editor: Robert Fairbanks. Managing Editor: A.G. Block. 50% freelance written. Monthly magazine; 40 pages. Emphasizes analysis of California politics and government. Circ. 18,000. Pays on publication. Publishes ms an average of 2 months after acceptance. Byline given. Buys all rights. Computer printout submissions acceptable. SASE.
Nonfiction: Profiles of state and local government and political analysis. No outright advocacy pieces. Buys 25 unsolicited mss/year. Query. Length: 900-3,000 words. Pays $75/printed page.

CONSERVATIVE REGISTER, Proud Eagle Press, Box 8453, Riverside CA 92515. (714)785-5180. Publisher/Editor-in-Chief: Paul Birchard. Editor: Alana Cross. 50% freelance written. Bimonthly Christian newspaper covering politics from a conservative viewpoint. Audience aware of current events. Circ. 3,500. Pays on acceptance. Publishes ms an average of 4 months after acceptance. Byline given. Buys all rights. Submit seasonal/holiday material 2 months in advance. Photocopied submissions OK. Computer printout submissions acceptable. SASE. Reports in 1 month. Sample copy $3; writer's guidelines for business size SAE and 1 first class stamp. No material returned without SASE.
Nonfiction: Jay Sulsenbir, assignments. Expose (of government from a conservative viewpoint); general interest; inspirational (from a Christian viewpoint); interview/profile (of religious, government or business leaders); new product (consumer-related); and opinion. "We strongly favor material which cites governmental action and then projects its impact for Christians and/or conservatives in future years." No profanity, racist, bigoted or immoral material. Buys 5 mss/issue. Submit ms. Length: 100-1,000 words. Pays $5-25.
Photos: State availability of photos. Pays $5-15 for b&w 8x10 prints. Captions, model release, and identification of subjects required.
Columns/Departments: J. Sulsenbir, assignments editor. Query. Length: "We occasionally feature a Christian book review. Also, any political 'thought' piece which fits our format is carefully considered. 'Thought' is the key word. Too many overused topics are being submitted. Be fresh." Buys 8 mss/year. 1,000 maximum. Pays $25.
Fillers: J. Sulsenbir, assignments editor. "Interesting factual pieces are most desired. Local religious material with national interest especially welcome." Short factual humor and newsbreaks. Buys 1-2 mss/issue. Length: 25-100 words. Pays $5-10.
Tips: "We are a Christian publication. The emphasis is political but it is crucial to consider impact on Christians, home life, etc. We are an excellent publication for new or unpublished writers. We want circulation-boosting pieces. Documentation is essential, avoid sensationalism. No phone queries. We are somewhat general in format but specific in viewpoint. We will not use any material over 1,000 words. Writers will have more success submitting material between 300-500 words."

CRITIQUE: A JOURNAL OF CONSPIRACIES & METAPHYSICS, Box 11451, Santa Rosa CA 95406. (707)525-9401. Editor: Bob Banner. Managing Editor: M. Banovitch. 60% freelance written. Semiannual journal "that explores conspiracy scenarios, behind-the-scenes news, exposes, and unusual news that frequently creates debacles within the ordinary mind set. *Critique* also explores assumptions, beliefs and hypotheses that we use to understand ourselves, our 'world' and the metaphysical crisis of our time." Circ. 5,000. Pays on publication. Publishes ms an average of 5 months after acceptance. Byline given. Submit seasonal material 4 months in advance. Simultaneous queries, and simultaneous, photocopied, and previously published submissions OK. Electronic submissions OK if compatible with Text Files operable in DOS for Apple IIe, but requires hard copy also. Computer printout submissions acceptable. SASE. Reports in 4 months. Sample copy $4; free writer's guidelines.
Nonfiction: Book excerpts; book reviews; expose (political, metaphysical, cultural); interview/profile (those in the specified area); and personal experience (as it relates to cultural ideology). Not interested in "anything that gets published in ordinary, established media." Buys 8-25 mss/year. Send complete ms with bio/resume. Length: 200-3,000 words. Pays $30 maximum. "We also publish books. Send us your book proposal."
Tips: "We have published articles, reviews and essays that are difficult to categorize in the simplistic, dualistic Left or Right ideological camps. The material's purpose has been, and will be, to provoke critical thinking; to discriminate between valuable and manipulative information; to incite an awareness of events, trends, phases and our roles/lives within the global psyche that no ordinary consumer of ordinary media could even begin to conceive let alone use such an awareness to affect his/her life. The writer has a better chance of breaking in at our publication with short articles and fillers as it gives us the chance to get acquainted, to feel their style. The most frequent mistakes made by writers in completing an article are tedious writing and poor organizational structure. Send for a sample and request writer's guidelines."

EUROPE, 2100 M St. NW, 707, Washington DC 20037. Editor: Webster Martin. 20% freelance written. Bimonthly magazine; 60 pages. For anyone with a professional or personal interest in Western Europe and European/US relations. Circ. 60,000. Pays on acceptance. Publishes ms an average of 2 months after acceptance. Buys first serial rights and all rights. Submit seasonal material 3 months in advance. Computer printout submissions acceptable; prefers letter-quality to dot-matrix. SASE. Reports in 1 month.
Nonfiction: Interested in current affairs (with emphasis on economics and politics), the Common Market and Europe's relations with the rest of the world. Publishes occasional cultural pieces, with European angle. "High quality writing a must. We publish anything that might be useful to people with a professional interest in Europe." Buys 100 mss/year. Query or submit complete ms. Include resume of author's background and qualifications. Length: 500-2,000 words. Pays $100-325.
Photos: Photos purchased with or without accompanying mss. Also purchased on assignment. Buys b&w and color. Pays $25-35 for b&w print, any size; $50 for inside use of color transparencies; $200-300 for color used on cover.

THE FREEMAN, 30 S. Broadway, Irvington-on-Hudson NY 10533. (914)591-7230. Editor: Paul L. Poirot. 60% freelance written. Monthly for "fairly advanced students of liberty and the layman." Buys all rights, including reprint rights. Byline given. Buys 44 mss/year. Pays on publication. Computer printout submissions acceptable; prefers letter-quality to dot-maxtrix. SASE.
Nonfiction: "We want nonfiction clearly analyzing and explaining various aspects of the free market, private enterprise, limited government philosophy, especially as pertains to conditions in the United States. Though a necessary part of the literature of freedom is the exposure of collectivistic cliches and fallacies, our aim is to emphasize and explain the positive case for individual responsibility and choice in a free economy. Especially important, we believe, is the methodology of freedom; self-improvement, offered to others who are interested. We try to avoid name-calling and personality clashes and find satire of little use as an educational device. Ours is a scholarly analysis of the principles underlying a free market economy. No political strategy or tactics." Length: 3,500 words maximum. Pays 5¢/word.
Tips: "It's most rewarding to find freelancers with new insights, fresh points of view. Facts, figures, and quotations cited should be fully documented, to their original source, if possible."

GUARDIAN, Independent Radical Newsweekly, Institute for Independent Social Journalism, 33 W. 17th St., New York NY 10011. (212)691-0404. Editor: William A. Ryan. Weekly newspaper covering US and international news and politics for a broad left and progressive audience. Circ. 25,000. Pays on publication. Byline given. Simultaneous queries, and simultaneous and photocopied submissions OK if indicated. SASE. Reports in 3 weeks on queries; 1 month on mss. Sample copy for $1, 9x12 SAE and 5 first class stamps; writer's guidelines for business size SAE and 1 first class stamp.
Nonfiction: Jill Benderly, articles editor. Expose (of government, corporations, etc.). "About 90% of our publication is hard news and features on current events." Buys 200 mss/year. Query with published clips. Length: 200-1,800 words. Pays $10-90.
Photos: Michael Kaufman, photo editor. State availability of photos. Pays $15 for b&w prints. Captions

required.

Columns/Departments: Women, Labor, The Left, Blacks. Buys 30 mss/year. Query with published clips. Length: 200-700 words. Pays $10-30.

‡**IN THESE TIMES**, Institute for Public Affairs, 1300 W. Belmont Ave., Chicago IL 60657. Editor: James Weinstein. Managing Editor: Sheryl Larson. 50% freelance written. Weekly tabloid covering national and international news. Circ. 30,000. Pays on publication. Publishes ms an average of 1 month after acceptance. Byline given. Buys variable rights. Submit seasonal/holiday material 2 months in advance. Simultaneous queries, and simultaneous, photocopied, and previously published submissions OK. Computer printout submissions acceptable; prefers letter-quality to dot-matrix. SASE. Reports in 6 weeks. Sample copy for SAE and 4 first class stamps.

Nonfiction: Salim Muwakkil, articles editor. Book excerpts, expose, historical, interview/profile and personal experience. "The labor movement community groups, feminist and minority issues, and anti-corporate movements in general receive special emphasis." Buys 100 mss/year. Query. Length: 400-1,600 words. Pays $150 maximum. Sometimes pays the expenses of writers on assignment.

Photos: State availability of photos. Pays $25 maximum for 8x10 b&w prints. Identification of subjects required. Buys one-time rights.

Columns/Departments: Reviews (books, film, etc.). Buys 45 mss/year. Query. Length: 400-1,600. Pays $25.

‡**THE INTELLECTUAL ACTIVIST, In Defense of Individual Rights**, The Intellectual Activist, Inc., Suite 101, 131 5th Ave., New York NY 10003. (212)982-8357. Editor: Peter Schwartz. 33% freelance written. Irregularly published newsletter of political and economic analysis. "Our fundamental theme is the defense of individual rights. We are especially interested in the exploration of issues in their formative stages, when reders can still influence the outcome by expressing their views in appropriate forums." Pays on publication. Byline given. Offers 20% kill fee. Buys all rights. Computer printout submissions acceptable; no dot-matrix. SASE. Sample copy $2.50. Writer's guidelines for #10 SAE and 1 first class stamp.

Nonfiction: Political/economic analysis. Buys 5 mss/year. Query with or without published clips. Length: 2,000-4,000 words. Pays $250-600.

Tips: "Ask for authors guide, then submit well thought-out query. Articles require a firm pro-individual rights orientation."

INTRIGUE, The International Journal of Reportage, Air Crafts Limited, Inc., Box 68, Woodbridge NJ 07095. Editor: Ted Pastuszak Jr. 20% freelance written. Fortnightly newsletter and special occasional papers covering unusual aspects of world affairs and developments compiled from foreign broadcasts and other diverse sources. For "a sophisticated readership consisting of executives, journalists and international investors." Circ. 2,000. Pays on publication. Publishes ms an average of 2 months after acceptance. Byline given. Offers 20% kill fee. Buys first serial rights. Simultaneous queries OK. Computer printout submissions acceptable; prefers letter-quality to dot-matrix. SASE. Reports in 1 month on queries. Sample copy $1; writer's guidelines for SASE. An update book list of source and reference titles that *Intrigue* distributes is also available free on request.

Nonfiction: Contact: In Cold Type Department. Book excerpts and reviews, expose, interview/profile and personal experience. All subjects should pertain to or concern political, social or economic events or developments. "Special issues include Islands of Intrigue, Espionage Special, and a Diplomatic Edition. With regard to our coverage of foreign affairs, we would prefer *not* to receive material that takes a specific political stand without including proper documentation and research. In short, we prefer reporting to editorializing." Buys less than 50 mss/year. Query with published clips. Length: 600-750 words. Pays $60-150. Sometimes pays the expenses of writers on assignment.

Columns/Departments: Border Lines (background notes on current developments in countries and regions around the world) and The World of Intrigue (a compilation of pressing political situations both at home and abroad in a unique diary format). Buys less than 50 mss/year. Query with published clips. Length: 700-750 words; 40-80 words/item. Pays 10-20¢/word.

Fillers: Contact: Inside Information Section. Clippings and newsbreaks. "We're looking for interesting asides to news stories not covered by the major press." Individual department include Air Waves (notes on international radio); Provoca Touring (travel tips to unusual places currently in the news); Capital Ideas (business and financial items of interest); Arms & Ammunition (news pertaining to arms trade and development). Length: 40-80 words. Pays 10-20¢/word.

Tips: "News and information concerning the following subjects can also be found in our departments when applicable: covert action, foreign trade, oilfield development, international security issues, submarine technology, polar region affairs, reportage/journalism, subliminal research and devices. Since *Intrigue* is designed to be a professional fortnightly briefing on important international matters, writing must be concise and to the point. Freelance writers who submit unsolicited material should consider submitting outlines or concepts for articles before committing themselves to writing and sending out completed mss. Our publication is made up of many short items and only one or two major features per issue."

THE NATION, 72 5th Ave., New York NY 10011. Editor: Victor Navasky. Weekly. Buys first serial rights. Computer printout submissions acceptable; prefers letter-quality to dot-matrix. SASE.
Nonfiction: "We welcome all articles dealing with the social scene, particularly if they examine it with a new point of view or expose conditions the rest of the media overlooks." Queries encouraged. Buys 100 mss/year. Length 2,500 words maximum. Payment negotiable. Modest rates.
Tips: "We are firmly committed to reporting on the issues of labor, national politics, business, consumer affairs, environmental politics, civil liberties and foreign affairs. Those issues can never be over-reported."

NATIONAL DEVELOPMENT (DESAROLLO NACIONAL), Intercontinental Publications, Inc., Box 5017, Westport CT 06880. (203)226-7463. Editor-in-Chief: Virginia Fairweather. 80% freelance written. Emphasizes Third World infrastructure. For government officials in Third World—technocrats, planners, engineers and ministers. Published 9 times/year; 120 pages. Circ. 60,000. Pays on acceptance. Publishes ms an average of 6 months after acceptance. Buys all rights. Byline given. Phone queries OK. Previously published submissions OK. Computer printout submissions acceptable; prefers letter-quality to dot-matrix. SASE. Reports in 1 month. Free sample copy and writer's guidelines.
Nonfiction: Technical (construction, government management, planning, power, telecommunications); informational (agriculture, economics, public works, construction management); interview; photo feature and technical. Buys 6-10 mss/issue. Query with "inclusion of suggestions for specific article topics; point out your area of expertise." Length: 1,800 words. Pays $250.
Photos: B&w and color. Captions required. Query. Total price for ms includes payment for photos.
Columns/Departments: Power technology, telecommunications, computer technology (as applied to infrastructure and development projects), water treatment, financial technology (finances as they might affect Third World governments). Buys 4 mss/issue. Query. Length: 750-1,500 words. Pays $250. Open to suggestions for new columns/departments.

NATIONAL JOURNAL, 1730 M St. NW, Washington DC 20036. (202)857-1400. Executive Director: Julia M. Romero. Editor: Richard Frank. "No freelance material accepted because fulltime staff produces virtually all of our material." Byline given.

NEW GUARD, Young Americans for Freedom, Woodland Rd., Sterling VA 22170. (703)450-5162. Editor-in-Chief: Gerald O'Brien. 50% freelance written. Emphasizes conservative political ideas for readership of mostly young people with a large number of college students. Age range 14-39. Virtually all are politically conservative with interests in politics, economics, philosophy and current affairs. Mostly students or college graduates. Quarterly magazine; 48 pages. Circ. 7,500. Pays on publication. Publishes ms an average of 2 months after acceptance. Buys all rights. Byline given. Phone queries OK. Submit seasonal/holiday material 2-3 months in advance. SASE. Reports in 6 weeks. Free sample copy.
Nonfiction: Expose (government waste, failure, mismanagement, problems with education or media); historical (illustrating political or economic points); interview (politicians, academics, people with conservative viewpoint or something to say to conservatives); personal opinion; and profile. Buys 40 mss/year. Submit complete ms. Length: 1,500 words maximum. Pays $40-100.
Photos: Purchased with accompanying manuscript.

NEWSWEEK, 444 Madison Ave., New York NY 10022. (212)350-4547. My Turn Editor: Phyllis Malamud. Although staff-written, it does except unsolicited mss for My Turn, a column of opinion. The 1,000- to 1,100-word essays for the column must be original and contain verifiable facts. Payment is $1,000, on publication, for first rights. Computer printout submissions acceptable; no dot-matrix. Include SASE for answer. Reports in 1 month.

THE PROGRESSIVE, 409 E. Main St., Madison WI 53703. (608)257-4626. Editor: Erwin Knoll. 75% freelance written. Monthly. Pays on publication. Publishes ms an average of 6 weeks after acceptance. Byline given. Buys all rights. Computer printout submissions acceptable "if legible and double-spaced"; prefers letter-quality to dot-matrix. SASE. Reports in 2 weeks. Query.
Nonfiction: Primarily interested in articles which interpret, from a progressive point of view, domestic and world affairs. Occasional lighter features. "*The Progressive* is a *political* publication. General-interest material is inappropriate." Length: 3,000 words maximum. Pays $75-250.
Tips: "Display some familiarity with our magazine, its interests and concerns, its format and style. We want query letters that fully describe the proposed article without attempting to sell it—and that give an indication of the writer's competence to deal with the subject."

‡PUBLIC OPINION, American Enterprise Institute, 1150 17th St. NW, Washington DC 20036. (202)862-5800. Managing Editor: Karlyn Keene. Bimonthly magazine covering public opinion for the public policy community, journalists, and academics interested in public opinion data and its meanings. Circ. 16,000. Pays on publication. Byline given. Buys all rights. Simultaneous queries OK. Reports in 3 months on queries.

Sample copy $5.

Nonfiction: Historical (dealing with polling industry); "public policy issues, opinion polls and their meaning in relation to public policy." Buys 10-15 mss/year. Query with outline. Length: 2,500-3,000 words. Payment varies widely.

REASON MAGAZINE, Box 40105, Santa Barbara CA 93103. (805)963-5993. Editor: Mary Zupan. 50% freelance written. Monthly. For a readership interested in individual liberty, economic freedom, private enterprise alternatives to government services, individualist cultural and social perspectives. Circ. 40,000. Pays on publication. Publishes ms an average of 2 months after acceptance. Rights purchased vary with author and material; may buy all rights, first North American serial rights, or first serial rights. Byline given. Offers kill fee sometimes. Photocopied submissions OK. Double- or triple-spaced, typed mss only. Reports in 2 months. SASE. Sample copy $2.

Nonfiction: "*Reason* deals with social, economic and political issues, supporting both individual liberty and economic freedom. The following kinds of articles are desired: investigative articles exposing government wrongdoing and bungling; investigative articles revealing examples of private (individual, business, or group) ways of meeting needs; individualist analysis of policy issues (e.g., education, victimless crimes, regulation); think pieces exploring implications of individual freedom in economic, political, cultural, and social areas." Query. Buys 50-70 mss/year. Length: 1,000-5,000 words.

REVIEW OF THE NEWS, 395 Concord Ave., Belmont MA 02178. (617)489-0605. Editor: Scott Stanley Jr. 1% freelance written. Weekly magazine covering the news with a conservative and free market orientation. Circ. 60,000. Average issue includes capsulated news items, bylined sports, films, economic advice and overseas and congressional activities. Pays on publication. Publishes ms an average of 3 months after acceptance. Byline given. Offers negotiable kill fee. Buys all rights. Photocopied submissions OK. Computer printout submissions acceptable; prefers letter-quality to dot-matrix. SASE. Reports in 3 weeks on queries; 6 weeks on mss. Sample copy $1.

Nonfiction: Expose (of government bungling); general interest (current events and politics); interview (with leading conservatives and newsmakers, heads of state, congressmen, economists and politicians); humor (satire on the news); and commentary on the news. Buys 3-4 mss/year. Query with short biography and published clips. Length: 1,500-3,000 words. Pays $25/published page. Sometimes pays expenses of writers on assignment.

TEXAS OBSERVER, A Journal of Free Voices, 600 W. 7th, Austin TX 78701. (512)477-0746. Publisher: Ronnie Dugger. Editor: Geoffrey Rips. 60% freelance written. Bimonthly magazine covering Texas politics and culture for small "influential" audience. Circ. 12,000. Pays on publication. Publishes ms an average of 3 months after acceptance. Byline given. Buys first serial rights. Submit seasonal/holiday material 1 month in advance. Simultaneous queries, and simultaneous and photocopied submissions OK. SASE. Reports in 3 weeks. Free sample copy and writer's guidelines.

Nonfiction: Expose, interview/profile, opinion, personal experience and political analysis. Buys 100 mss/year. Query with published clips. Length: 200-2,000 words. Pays $10-75.

Photos: State availability of photos. Pays $10 for b&w prints. Captions, model release, and identification of subjects required. Buys one-time rights.

Tips: "We're interested in Texas literature, politics, and social issues and national issues as they affect life in Texas; we are not interested in other topics."

‡**TIME MAGAZINE**, Rockefeller Center, New York NY 10020. Staff-written.

‡**US NEWS & WORLD REPORT**, 2400 N St. NW, Washington DC 20037. "We are not presently considering unsolicited freelance submissions."

WASHINGTON MONTHLY, 1711 Connecticut Ave., Washington DC 20009. (202)462-0128. Editor-in-Chief: Charles Peters. 35% freelance written. For "well-educated, well-read people interested in politics, the press and government." Monthly. Circ. 35,000. Rights purchased depend on author and material; buys all rights, first rights, or second serial (reprint) rights. Buys 20-30 mss/year. Pays on publication. Sometimes does special topical issues. Query or submit complete ms. Computer printout submissions acceptable; no dot-matrix. Tries to report in 4-6 weeks. Publishes ms an average of 6 weeks after acceptance. SASE. Sample copy $3.

Nonfiction: Responsible investigative or evaluative reporting about the U.S. government, business, society, the press and politics. "No editorial comment/essays." Also no poetry, fiction or humor. Length: "average 2,000-6,000 words." Pays 5-10¢/word.

Photos: Buys b&w glossy prints.

Tips: "Best route is to send 1-2 page proposal describing article and angle. The most rewarding aspect of working with freelance writers is getting a solid piece of reporting with fresh ideas that challenge the conventional wisdom."

WORLD POLICY JOURNAL, World Policy Institute, 777 UN Plaza, New York NY 10017. (212)490-0010. Editor: Sherle Schwenninger. 80% freelance written. A quarterly magazine covering international politics, economics and security issues. "We hope to bring a new sense of imagination, principle and proportion, as well as a restored sense of reality and direction to America's discussion of its role in the world." Estab. 1983. Circ. 10,000. Pays on acceptance. Publishes ms an average of 3 months after acceptance. Byline given. Offers variable kill fee. Buys all rights. Photocopied submissions OK. Computer printout submissions acceptable; prefers letter-quality to dot-matrix. SASE. Reports in 1 month. Sample copy for $4.75 and SAE; free writer's guidelines.
Nonfiction: Articles that "define policies that reflect the shared needs and interests of all nations of the world." Query. Length: 30-40 pages (8,500 words maximum). Pays variable commission rate. Sometimes pays the expenses of writers on assignment.
Tips: "By providing a forum for many younger or previously unheard voices, including those from Europe, Asia, Africa, and Latin America, we hope to replace lingering illusions and fears with new priorities and aspirations. Articles submitted on speculation very rarely suit our particular needs—the writers clearly haven't taken time to study the kind of article we publish."

Regional

All local topics are potential stories—in their own localities—for regional publications. Many editors, though, won't buy a story that has been reported by other media (newspapers, television). If the story has been done, the writer must find a new aspect of that story that will prompt the reader to read about the subject again.

Some regional publications rely on staff-written material; others on freelance writers who live in or know the region. The best regional publication is the one in your hometown; you probably know this market best. It can be a city or state magazine or a Sunday magazine in a newspaper. Listed below are general interest magazines slanted toward residents of and visitors to a particular region. Next, regional publications are categorized alphabetically by state (including the District of Columbia), followed by a Puerto Rico, a Canada, and a foreign category. Many regional publications buy manuscripts on conservation and the natural wonders of their area; additional markets for such material can be found under the Nature, Conservation, and Ecology, and Sports headings. Publications that report on the business climate of a region are grouped in the regional division of the Business and Finance category. Recreation and travel publications specific to a geographical area are listed in the Consumer Travel section.

General

COASTAL JOURNAL, Box 84 Lanesville Sta., Gloucester MA 01930. Publisher: Joe Kaknes. Editor: Jacqueline Bigford. 100% freelance written. Quarterly magazine primarily focusing on coastal New England from Maine to Connecticut. Pays within 1 month of publication. Publishes ms an average of 6 months after acceptance. Buys first serial rights. Submit seasonal material 6 months in advance. Computer printout submissions acceptable; prefers letter-quality to dot-matrix. SASE. Reports in 1 month. Sample copy $5; free writer's guidelines for SAE and 1 first class stamp.
Nonfiction: Social, political and natural history; biography and people profiles; interviews; environmental and other pertinent public policy issues; boating, commercial fishing, and other maritime-related businesses; travel; art; education; and lifestyles. Reviews finished articles with photos. Length: 1,500-2,000 words. Pays approximately $100/article.
Photos: Prefers b&w glossy prints and 35mm color transparencies. Pays on publication; $15 for b&w prints;

$25 for color transparencies. Captions and credit lines required. Photographers (with no accompanying story) should send query/catalog only.

Fiction: "This magazine occasionally runs short fiction up to 3,000 words. Such manuscripts should have some connection to the sea, the coast, or to New England's history or character. No restrictions on style; the main criterion is quality." Query or send complete ms.

Tips: "We publish major features for the most part. We look for the unusual story or angle, the fresh approach, and the review/assessment of coastal New England related issues. The most frequent mistake made by writers in completing an article for us is not having photos. We include art with every feature. Writing exclusively in the first-person voice is also a problem. Avoid overwriting and turgid style; stories should be crisp, well-researched, lively and concise. We'd like to see more contemporary pieces about events, issues or people with whom readers can identify."

COUNTRY MAGAZINE, A Guide—From the Appalachians to the Atlantic, Country Sun, Inc., Box 246, Alexandria VA 22313. (703)548-6177. Publisher: Walter Nicklin. Managing Editor: Philip Hayward. 75% freelance written. Monthly magazine of country living in the mid-Atlantic region. "Our coverage aims at promoting an appreciation of the region, especially through writing about travel, history, outdoor sports, food, nature, the environment, gardening, the arts, and people in these states: Virginia, Maryland, Delaware, West Virginia, North Carolina, Pennsylvania and New Jersey." Circ. 100,000. Pays on publication. Byline given. Buys one-time rights. Submit seasonal/holiday material 6 months in advance. Photocopied submissions OK. Computer printout submissions (double-spaced) acceptable; no dot-matrix. SASE. Reports in 4 weeks. Sample copy for $1, 9x12 SAE, and $1.22 postage; writer's guidelines for business size SAE and 1 first class stamp.

Nonfiction: Book excerpts (of regional interest); historical (mid-Atlantic history with current news peg); how-to (deal with country living: how to buy country property, how to tap a sugar maple, etc.); interview/profile (of mid-Atlantic residents); photo feature (regional); and travel (mid-Atlantic—off the beaten path). Buys 120 mss/year. Query with published clips if available. Length: 1,000-2,000 words. Pays $3.50/column inch.

Photos: State availability of photos. Pays $15-25 for 35mm color transparencies and 5x7 b&w prints. Captions, model release, and identification of subjects required.

Columns/Departments: The Land, The Rivers, and The Bay (Chesapeake)—all deal with the natural features of the region. Buys 36 mss/year. Query with published clips if available. Length: 500-600 words. Pays $3.50/column inch.

Fiction: Historical, mainstream and novel excerpts. No nonregional, noncountry oriented fiction; "we seldom run fiction." Buys 1 ms/year. Query with published clips if available. Length: 1,200-2,000 words. Pays $3.50/column inch.

Poetry: "We seldom publish poetry." Buys 2 poems/year. Submit maximum 3 poems. Length: 50 lines maximum. Pays $25 maximum.

Tips: "We are especially open to how-to, gardening and issue-oriented stories pegged to the mid-Atlantic region." Follow the editor's requirements.

GUEST INFORMANT, 201 N. Robertson Blvd., Beverly Hills CA 90211. (213)274-8165. Editor: Maryanne Larson. Associate Editor: Stephen Dolainski. 80% freelance written, on assignment. An annual hardcover, 4-color in-hotel-room city guidebook for sophisticated travelers who are interested in what the city has to offer: retail establishments, restaurants, sightseeing activities, sports information, arts events, etc. Publishes 31 editions: Los Angeles; Orange County, CA; San Diego; San Francisco; Sacramento; Phoenix; Tucson; Seattle; San Antonio; Dallas; Houston; Twin Cities (Mpls./St. Paul); Milwaukee; Kansas City; Cincinnati; St. Louis; Philadelphia; Pittsburgh; New York; New Orleans; Tampa/St. Petersburg; Miami; Palm Beach/ Gold Coast; Orlando area; Puerto Rico; Detroit; Boston; Atlanta; Chicago; Denver; and Washington, D.C. Some editions are published under the name *Leisureguide*. Circ. (combined for 31 editions) over 97 million. Pays 60 days after receipt of copy. Publishes ms an average of 2 months after acceptance. Byline given. Offers $50 kill free. Buys all rights. Previously published submissions OK. Computer printout submissions acceptable; no dot-matrix. SASE. Reports in 1 month. Sample copy $2.50; writer's guidelines for SASE.

Nonfiction: "Each annual edition is individualized for a particular city, and each has a lead article (usually an overview of the city), visual arts, lively arts, sports and sightseeing. Some of the books have lengthy articles on shopping and fashion. No destination travel pieces; no articles about foreign cities. Buys 75 mss/year. Query with published clips. Length: Depends on article and edition. Leads approx. 1,200 words; articles on the arts or sports, about 800 words. Pays $150-500; varies by article and edition.

Fillers: "Interesting sight or historical information, etc. on a particular city we cover." Buys 1-4 mss/year. Length: 420-825 words. Pays $100-200.

Tips: "It is rare that we would ever accept an unsolicited manuscript. Instead, we work on assignment. We are looking for freelancers who have good writing skills and an in-depth knowledge of their city. It helps if they have background in a particular aspect of the city (i.e., the museums and galleries, sports, the fashion scene, etc). We are always looking for good writers who have an extensive background in fashion and/or retail as applies to our individual cities. We do not send writers to other cities. Once we find a good writer in a city we tend to use him/her again."

● **INLAND, The Magazine of the Middle West**, Inland Steel Co., 30 W. Monroe St., Chicago IL 60603. (312)346-0300. Managing Editor: Sheldon A. Mix. 50% freelance written. Quarterly magazine; 24 pages. Emphasizes steel products, services and company personnel. Circ. 12,000. Pays on acceptance. Publishes ms an average of 1-2 years after acceptance. Buys first serial rights and first North American serial rights. Kill fee: "We have always paid the full fee on articles that have been killed." Byline given. Submit seasonal/holiday material at least 1 year in advance. Simultaneous submissions OK. Computer printout submissions acceptable; prefers letter-quality to dot-matrix. SASE. Reports in 8 weeks. Free sample copy.

Nonfiction: Articles, essays, humorous commentaries and pictorial essays. "We encourage individuality. Half of each issue deals with staff-written steel subjects; half with widely ranging nonsteel matter. Articles and essays related somehow to the Midwest (Illinois, Wisconsin, Minnesota, Michigan, Missouri, Iowa, Nebraska, Kansas, North Dakota, South Dakota, Indiana and Ohio) in such subject areas as history, folklore, sports, humor, the seasons, current scene generally; nostalgia and reminiscence if well done and appeal are broad enough. But subject is less important than treatment. We like perceptive, thoughtful writing, and fresh ideas and approaches. Please don't send slight, rehashed historical pieces or any articles of purely local interest." Personal experience, profile, humor, historical, think articles, personal opinion and photo essays. No "nostalgia that is merely sentimental and that doesn't move the reader, or rehashes of historical personalities and highlights." Buys 10-15 unsolicited mss/year. Length: 1,200-5,000 words. Payment depends on individual assignment or unsolicited submission. Sometimes pays expenses of writers on assignment.

Photos: Purchased with or without mss. Captions required. "Payment for pictorial essay same as for text feature."

Tips: "Our publication particularly needs humor that is neither threadbare nor in questionable taste, and shorter pieces (800-1,500 words) in which word-choice and wit are especially important. The most frequent mistake made by writers in completing an article for us is untidiness in the manuscript (inattentiveness to good form, resulting in errors in spelling and facts, and in gaping holes in information). A writer who knows our needs and believes in himself should keep trying." Recently published material: "Mark Twain: Unlikely Soldier".

ISLANDS, An International Magazine, Islands Publishing Company, 3886 State St., Santa Barbara CA 93105. Editor: Nancy Zimmerman. 100% freelance written. Bimonthly magazine covering islands throughout the world. "We invite articles from many different perspectives: scientific, historical, exploratory, cultural, etc. We ask our authors to avoid the typical travel magazine style and concentrate on stimulating and informative pieces that tell the reader something he or she might not know about a particular island." Circ. 110,000. Pays 50% on acceptance and 50% within 30 days after publication. Publishes ms an average of 8 months after acceptance. Byline given. Buys all rights. Computer printout submissions acceptable; prefers letter-quality to dot-matrix. SASE. Reports in 4 weeks on queries; 6 weeks on ms. Sample copy for $4.65; writer's guidelines with SASE.

Nonfiction: General interest, historical/nostalgic, how-to, interview/profile, personal experience, photo feature, technical, travel, and any island-related material. "Each issue contains a major centerpiece of up to 5,000 words, 5 or 6 feature articles of roughly 3,000 words, and 2 or 3 topical articles for departments, each of which runs approximately 500 words. Any authors who wish to be commissioned should send a detailed proposal for an article, an estimate of costs (if applicable), and samples of previously published work." No "I went here and did this/I went there and ate that" travel articles. Buys 100 mss/year. "The majority of our manuscriptes are commissioned." Query with published clips or send complete ms. Length: 500-4,000 words. Pays $100-1,000. Pays expenses of writers on assignment.

Photos: State availability or send photos with query or ms. Pays $50-300 for 35mm color transparencies. "Fine color photography is a special attraction of *Islands*, and we look for superb composition, image quality and editorial applicability." Label slides with name and address, include abbreviated captions, and submit in protective plastic sleeves. Identification of subjects required. Buys one-time rights.

Columns/Departments: "Columns and departments are generally assigned, but we have accepted short features for our Island Hopping department. These should be highly focused on some travel-oriented aspect of islands." Buys 10-20 mss/year. Query with published clips. Length: 500-2,000 words. Pays $100-500.

Tips: "A freelancer can best break in to our publication with short (1,000-2,000 word) features that are highly focused on some aspect of island life, history, people, etc. Stay away from general, sweeping articles."

NEW ENGLAND MONTHLY, New England Monthly Inc., Box 446, Haydenville MA 01039. (413)268-7262. Editor: Daniel Okrent. Managing Editor: Chris Jerome. 60% freelance written. A monthly magazine covering such topics as recreation, politics, the arts, the outdoors, business and economics, food, people, gardening and sports and education for residents of Maine, New Hampshire, Massachusetts, Vermont, Rhode Island and Connecticut. Estab. 1984. Circ. 75,000. Pays on acceptance. Byline given. Offers 20% kill fee on commissioned work. Buys first North American serial rights and nonexclusive other rights. Submit seasonal/ holiday material 4 months in advance. Simultaneous queries OK. Computer printout submissions acceptable; prefers letter-quality to dot-matrix. SASE. Reports in 4 weeks. Sample copy $1.75; writer's guidelines for #10 SAE and 1 first class stamp.

Nonfiction: Lee Aitken, associate editor. Book excerpts, expose, general interest, photo feature, travel and general reportage. No nostalgic, reminiscence or inspirational articles. Buys 100 mss/year. Query with published clips. Length: 300-4,000 words. Pays $75-1,500. Sometimes pays expenses of writers on assignment.

Photos: Hans Teensma, photo editor.

Columns/Departments: Julie Michaels, column/department editor. "Column subjects purchased from freelancers include sports, outdoors, gardening, education, science, business, politics, performing arts, visual arts, and literature." Buys 40 mss/year. Length: 1,000-1,800 words. Pays $400-700.

Tips: "We always need a peg—it is not sufficient, for instance, to suggest a profile of, say, Paul Newman, simply because he lives in New England. The Region, which includes short (400-1,000 words) reportorial pieces on specific aspects of New England life and society, is the department that's most open to freelancers."

NORTHWEST MAGAZINE, the magazine of *The Oregonian,* 1320 SW Broadway, Portland OR 97201. Editor: Jack Hart. Weekly newspaper Sunday supplement magazine; 24-40 pages. For an upscale, 25-49 year-old audience distributed throughout the Pacific Northwest. Circ. 420,000. Buys first serial rights for Oregon and Washington state. Pays mid-month in the month following acceptance. All mss on speculation. Simultaneous submissions considered. Computer printout submissions acceptable; prefers letter-quality to dot-matrix. Reports in 2 weeks. SASE. Free writer's guidelines.

Nonfiction: Contemporary, regional articles with a strong hook to concerns of the Pacific Northwest. Cover stories usually deal with regional issues and feature "professional-level" reporting and writing. Personality profiles focus on young, Pacific Northwest movers and shakers. Short humor, personal essays, regional destination travel, entertainment, the arts and lifestyle stories also are appropriate. No history without a contemporary angle, boilerplate features of the type that are mailed out en masse with no specific hook to our local audience, poorly documented and highly opinionated issue stories that lack solid journalistic underpinnings, routine holiday features, or gushy essays that rhapsodize about daisies and rainbows. We expect top-quality writing and thorough, careful reporting. A contemporary writing style that features involving literary techniques like scenic construction stands the best chance." Buys 400 mss/year. Query much preferred, but complete ms considered. Length: 800-3,000 words. Pays $75-500/mss.

Photos: Photographs should be professional quality b&w prints, contact sheets with negatives or Kodachrome slides. Pays $25-50.

Poetry: Paul Pintarich, book review editor. "*Northwest Magazine* seeks poetry with solid imagery, skilled use of language and having appeal to a broad and intelligent audience. We do not accept cutesy rhymes, jingles, doggeral or verse written for a specific season, i.e., Christmas, Valentine's Day, etc. We currently are only accepting poems from poets in the Pacific Northwest region (Oregon, Washington, Idaho, Montana, Northern California, British Columbia and Alaska). Poems from Nevada and Hawaii receive consideration. We are looking for a few fine and distinctive poems each week. Poems on dot-matrix printers accepted if near letter-quality only. No handwritten submissions or threats, please." Send at least 3 poems for consideration. Length: 23 lines maximum. Pays $5 on acceptance.

Tips: "Pay rates and editing standards are up, and this market will become far more competitive. However, new writers with talent and good basic language skills still are encouraged to try us. Printing quality and flexibility should improve, increasing the magazine's potential for good color photographers and illustrators."

THE ORIGINAL NEW ENGLAND GUIDE, Historical Times, Inc., 2245 Kohn Rd., Box 8200, Harrisburg PA 17105. (717)657-9555. Managing Editor: Kathie Kull. Consulting Editor: Mimi E.B. Steadman. 70% freelance written. Annual magazine covering New England travel/vacation and vacations. "The Guide" is a complete travel planner and on-the-road guide to the six New England states. It has a strong family focus and spring-summer-fall coverage of destinations, events and attractions." Circ. 170,000. Pays on acceptance. Publishes ms up to 6 months after acceptance. Buys all rights. January 1 deadline for following May publication date. Computer printout submissions acceptable. Reports in 2 weeks. Sample copy for 9x12 SAE and $2.40 postage; writer's guidelines for #10 SAE and 1 first class stamp.

Nonfiction: Photo feature and travel—New England only. No historical or business. Buys 8 mss/year. Query with published chips. Length: 500-1,500 words. Pays $100-400. Sometimes pays mail and telephone expenses.

Photos: State availability of photos. Reviews 35mm color tranparencies and 8x10 prints. Pays $25-75 for b&w; $50-400 for color. Identification of subjects required. Buys one-time rights.

Fillers: Rarely used.

Tips: "Choose New England-related places or activities that appeal to a wide range of readers—active and sedentary, young and old, single and families. Areas most open to freelancers are region-wide features—state specific sidebars. Copy must 'sell' the area or activity to the traveler as worth a special stop or trip. We do not promote commercial establishments in features. We are service-oriented and provide factual information that helps the reader plan a trip, not just descriptions of places and things."

PACIFIC NORTHWEST, 222 Dexter Ave. N., Seattle WA 98109. Editor: Peter Potterfield. Monthly magazine (except January and August) emphasizing the arts, culture, recreation, service, and urban and rural lifestyle in the Pacific Northwest. Buys first serial rights. Simultaneous and previously published submissions OK. SASE. Reports in 6 weeks. Free writer's guidelines.
Nonfiction: Editorial material should entertain, inform or contribute to an understanding of the Pacific Northwest. Subject matter includes travel and exploration, outdoor activities, issues in the region's development, the environment, arts, history, profiles of places and people, and current issues, ideas and events that concern the Northwest. Buys 4 mss/issue. Query with published clips. Length: 600-3,000 words. Pay starts at 10¢/word.
Photos: Send photos with or without ms. Pays $15-50 for b&w prints; $50-200 for color transparencies, 35mm or larger. Captions preferred. Buys one-time rights.
Columns/Departments: Journal (news items); Books; Closer Look (regional issues and profiles); Travel; Food and Lodging; Back Page (photo); Calendar of Events; and Letters. Query.
Tips: "Query should have clear description of topic and relevance to Northwest with clips if writer is new to us. We look for entertaining as well as informative style and format plus original or unusual information and research. Many native, outdoors or history submissions assume a more narrowly interested audience than we are aiming for."

POSH, (Profiles on the Southern Horizon), Box 221269, Charlotte NC 28222. (704)375-8034. Editor: Frederick J. Keitel III. 80% freelance written. A bimonthly southern fashion/lifestyle magazine for an upscale audience. Circ. 35,000. Pays on publication. Publishes ms an average of 3 months after acceptance. Buys first serial rights. Computer printout submissions acceptable; prefers letter-quality to dot-matrix. SASE. Reports in 3 weeks. Sample copy $3.
Nonfiction: Southern profiles (spotlighting successful businesses and people); fashion accessories; beauty; health; and fitness. "We are seeking articles of interest throughout the southern region. Our readers are well educated and stylish, at home and in the workplace." Query or send complete ms. Length: 750-1,500 words. Pays $150-250 for feature articles. Sometimes pays expenses of writers on assignment.
Photos: "We are very interested in photos. All features are accompanied by photos; suggest sources if not including pictures." Buys b&w prints and color transparencies. Pays negotiable rate.
Columns/Departments: "We will consider all types of articles; however, the magazine is a fashion/lifestyle magazine." Length: 750-1,500 words. Pays $75-100.
Fillers: Anecdotes, newsbreaks, humor, preview of events and personalities. Send complete ms. Length: 250-500 words. Pays 5¢/word.

● **RURALITE**, Box 557, Forest Grove OR 97116. (503)357-2105. Editor: Ken Dollinger. 50% freelance written. Monthly magazine primarily slanted toward small town and rural families, served by consumer-owned electric utilities in Washington, Oregon, Idaho, Nevada and Alaska. "Ours is an old-fashioned down-home publication, with something for all members of the family." Circ. 215,000. Pays on acceptance. Publishes ms an average of 1-6 months after acceptance. Buys first North American serial rights, first serial rights, and occasionally second (reprint) rights. Byline given. Submit seasonal material at least 3 months in advance. Computer printout submissions acceptable. SASE. Sample copy $1; writer's guidelines for SASE.
Nonfiction: Walter J. Wentz, nonfiction editor. Primarily human-interest stories about rural or small-town folk, preferably living in areas (Northwest states and Alaska) served by Rural Electric Cooperatives. Articles emphasize self-reliance, overcoming of obstacles, cooperative effort, hard or interesting work, unusual or interesting avocations, odd or unusual hobbies or histories, public spirit or service and humor. Also considers how-to, advice for rural folk, little-known and interesting Northwest history, people or events. "We are looking specifically for energy (sources, use, conservation) slant and items relating to rural electric cooperatives." No "sentimental nostalgia or subjects outside the Pacific Northwest; nothing racy." Buys 15-20 mss/year. Query. Length: 500-1,500 words. Pays $30-100, depending upon length, quality, appropriateness and interest, number and quality of photos. Sometimes pays the expenses of writers on assignment.
Photos: Reviews b&w negatives with contact sheets. Offers no additional payment for photos accepted with ms.

YANKEE, Dublin NH 03444. (603)563-8111. Editor-in-Chief: Judson D. Hale. Managing Editor: John Pierce. Monthly magazine emphasizing the New England region. Circ. 1,000,000. Pays on acceptance. Byline given. Buys all rights, first North American serial rights or one-time rights. Submit seasonal/holiday material at least 4 months in advance. SASE. Reports in 6 weeks. Free sample copy and writer's guidelines.
Nonfiction: Historical (New England history, especially with present-day tie-in); how-to (especially for Forgotten Arts series of New England arts, crafts, etc.); humor; interview (especially with New Englanders who have not received a great deal of coverage); nostalgia (personal reminiscence of New England life); photo fea-

ture (prefers color, captions essential); profile; travel (to the Northeast only, with specifics on places, prices, etc.); current issues; antiques; and food. Buys 50 mss/year. Query with brief description of how article will be structured (its focus, etc.); articles must include a New England "hook." Length: 1,500-3,000 words. Pays $50-700.

Photos: Purchased with ms or on assignment; (without accompanying ms for This New England feature only; color only). Captions required. Reviews prints or transparencies. Pays $25 minimum for 8x10 b&w glossy prints. $125/page for 2¼x2¼ or 35mm transparencies; 4x5 for cover or centerspread. Total purchase price for ms usually includes payment for photos.

Columns/Departments: Traveler's Journal (with specifics on places, prices, etc.); Antiques to Look For (how to find, prices, other specifics); and At Home in New England (recipes, gardening, crafts). Buys 10-12 mss/year. Query. Length: 1,000-2,500 words. Pays $150-400.

Fiction: Deborah Navas, fiction editor. Emphasis is on character development. Buys 12 mss/year. Send complete ms. Length: 2,000-4,000 words. Pays $750.

Poetry: Jean Burden, poetry editor. Free verse or traditional. Buys 3-4 poems/issue. Send poems. Length: 32 lines maximum. Pays $35 for all rights, $25 for first magazine rights. Annual poetry contest with awards of $150, $100 and $50 for three best poems during the preceding year.

Alabama

BIRMINGHAM, Birmingham Area Chamber of Commerce, 2027 First Ave. N., Birmingham AL 35203. (205)323-5461. Managing Editor: Ray Martin. A monthly magazine primarily for residents of the Birmingham area, including area Chamber of Commerce members. Circ. 10,000. Pays on publication. Byline given. Buys first North American serial rights. Submit seasonal/holiday material 4 months in advance. Photocopied submissions OK. Computer printout submissions acceptable; prefers letter-quality to dot-matrix. SASE. Reports in 1 month. Sample copy $1.25.

Nonfiction: General interest (subject and its relationship to Birmingham, including local individuals who are involved with a particular hobby, business, sport, organization or occupation); historical/nostalgic (focus on the Birmingham of the past, often comparing an area's past history and appearance with its current characteristics); interview/profile (individual's personality in addition to mentioning the person's accomplishments and how the accomplishments were attained; individuals with interesting or unusual occupations are often the subjects of profiles); and personal experience (usually relating the unique experiences of Birmingham residents, often humorous; another type is one which presents the writer's reflections on a specific event or experience, such as a feature published recently about a writer's trip on AMTRAK). No stories that have no direct connection with Birmingham. Buys 144 mss/year. Query with published clips. Length: 4-15 double-spaced typed pages. Pays $50-175.

Tips: "We present Birmingham and its people in an informative, entertaining and positive manner. Rather than reshaping current events and competing with other media on stories having current news value, *Birmingham* prefers to take a deeper look at local individuals who are exceptional in some way. The emphasis of *Birmingham* is always on people rather than things. These people might have an unusual career, hobby or business, but their story always has a tangible connection to our area. *Birmingham* strives for a 50-50 mix of quotes and narrative material. Writers are encouraged to present the atmosphere surrounding their subject as well as descriptions of the individual's physical characteristics."

Alaska

NEW ALASKAN, Rt. 1, Box 677, Ketchikan AK 99901. Publisher: R.W. Pickrell. 20% freelance written. Monthly tabloid magazine, 28 pages, for residents of Southeast Alaska. Circ. 5,500. Pays on publication. Publishes ms an average of 4 months after acceptance. Byline given. Rights purchased vary with author and material; buys all rights, first serial rights, one-time rights, simultaneous rights, or second serial (reprint) rights. Photocopied submissions OK. Computer printout submissions acceptable; no dot-matrix. SASE. Sample copy $1.50.

Nonfiction: Bob Pickrell, articles editor. Feature material about Southeast Alaska. Emphasis is on full photo or art coverage of subject. Informational, how-to, personal experience, interview, profile, inspirational, humor, historical, nostalgia, personal opinion, travel, successful business operations and new product. Buys 30 mss/year. Submit complete ms. Length: 1,000 words minimum. Pays 1½¢/word.

Photos: B&w photos purchased with or without mss. Minimum size: 5x7. Pays $5 per glossy used; pays $2.50 per negative. Negatives are returned. Captions required.

Fiction: Bob Pickrell, articles editor. Historical fiction related to Southeast Alaska. Length: open. Pays 1½¢/word.

‡**WE ALASKANS MAGAZINE,** Anchorage Daily News, Box 6616, Anchorage AK 99502. (907)786-4318. Editor: Kathleen McCoy. Managing Editor: Howard C. Weaver. 20% freelance written. Sunday tabloid magazine for daily newspaper. Circ. 60,000. Pays on publication. Publishes ms an average of 2 months after acceptance. Byline given. Buys first North American serial rights. Submit seasonal/holiday material 6 months in advance. Simultaneous queries, and photocopied and previously published submissions OK. Computer printout submissions acceptable. SASE. Reports in 2 weeks on queries; 1 month on mss. Sample copy for SAE and 60¢ postage; writer's guidelines for SAE and 22¢ postage.
Nonfiction: Book excerpts, historical/nostalgic and personal experience. No general interest articles; only material that relates specifically to Alaska. "We prefer warm, human stories." Buys 12 mss/year. Query with published clips. Length: 1,000-2,000 words. Pays $100-300.
Photos: Kathleen McCoy, photo editor. State availability or send photos with query. Reviews b&w negatives and 35mm color transparencies. Captions, model release, and identification of subjects required. Buys one-time rights.
Tips: "Writers have a better chance of breaking in with articles of approximately 1,000 words. Some articles are too general, too clichéd, or don't move the reader."

Arizona

ARIZONA HIGHWAYS, 2039 W. Lewis Ave., Phoenix AZ 85009. (602)258-6641. Editor: Don Dedera. 90% freelance written. State-owned magazine designed to help attract tourists into and through the state. Pays on acceptance. Publishes ms an average of 6 months after acceptance. Computer printout submissions acceptable; prefers letter-quality to dot-matrix. Sample copy for 98¢ postage; writer's guidelines for SAE and 1 first class stamp.
Nonfiction: Managing editor. "Quality writing is what we're looking for so long as it suits our 1,500-2,000 word length." Subjects include narratives and exposition dealing with contemporary events, history, anthropology, nature, special things to see and do, outstanding arts and crafts, travel, profiles, etc.; all must be oriented toward Arizona and the Southwest. Buys 6 mss/issue. Buys first serial rights. Query with "a lead paragraph and brief outline of story. We deal with professionals only, so include list of current credits." Length: 1,500-2,000 words. Pays 20-30¢/word. Sometimes pays expenses of writers on assignment.
Photos: Picture editor. "We will use 2¼), 4x5 or larger, and 35 mm when it displays exceptional quality or content. We prefer Kodachrome in 35mm. Each transparency *must* be accompanied by information attached to each photograph: where, when, what. No photography will be reviewed by the editors unless the photographer's name appears on *each* and *every* transparency." Pays $80-300 for b&w print or color transparencies. Buys one-time rights.
Tips: "Writing must be of professional quality, warm, sincere, in-depth, well-peopled and accurate. Romance of the Old West feeling is important. Avoid themes that describe first trips to Arizona, Grand Canyon, the desert, etc. Emphasis to be on romance and themes that can be photographed. Double check for general accuracy."

ARIZONA MAGAZINE, Box 1950, Phoenix AZ 85001. (602)271-8291. Editor: Paul Schatt. Weekly; 40 pages. For "everyone who reads a Sunday newspaper." 50% freelance written. Circ. 505,000. Pays when article is scheduled for publication. Publishes ms an average of 3 months after acceptance. Byline given. Buys first serial rights, one-time rights, and second serial (reprint) rights. Photocopied submissions OK; simultaneous submissions OK if exclusive regionally. Computer printout submissions acceptable; prefers letter-quality to dot-matrix. Reports in 3 weeks. SASE. Sample copy and writer's guidelines for 50¢.
Nonfiction: General subjects that have an Arizona connection, are of interest to the West or are of universal interest. "We're looking for good writing above all and writer mastery of the subject. They should have an abundance of quotes and anecdotes. Regional travel is needed; also outstanding profiles. We are interested in Arizona, the West and universal subjects, not always in that order. We want to be topical and lively. We want stories that show some creativity in their approach. If story reads like a cliche Sunday Magazine story, redo it. Historical subjects are being overworked. No routine historical pieces; we want to see *the* dynamite story of how it really happened, but not any more routine stuff." Length: 1,000-2,500 words. "There is a trend to slightly shorter lead pieces which likely will make room for more inside articles. Articles of 800-1,500 words will get fair hearings."
Photos: State availability of photos. Pays $50-350. B&w and color photos purchased with or without ms or on assignment. Pays $15-25 for 8x10 b&w glossy prints; $25-80 for color (35mm or larger).
Tips: "The writer may have a better chance of breaking in at our publication with short articles and fillers. This is especially true if the writer doesn't have the experience to produce a major feature that meets professional reporting and writing standards. Find a good personal subject and write about him/her so the reader will feel he is with the subject. Know the subject well enough to react to the material. Describe the subject in anecdotes and let him reveal himself by his quotes. Please include social security and telephone numbers. The most frequent

mistakes made by writers in completing an article for us are inadequate sourcing and mediocre writing. Both are caused by skimping on the time and effort needed to produce a piece that someone else is willing to buy."

‡**PHOENIX LIVING**, 4621 N. 16th St., Phoenix AZ 85016. (602)279-2394. Editor: Brian J. Ward. 30% freelance written. Bimonthly magazine covering housing for newcomers and prospective home buyers. Circ. 70,000. Pays on acceptance. Publishes ms an average of 2 months after acceptance. Byline given. Buys all rights. Submit seasonal/holiday material 4 months in advance. Simultaneous queries, and photocopied and previously published submissions OK. Computer printout submissions acceptable; prefers letter-quality to dot-matrix. Reports in 1 month. Free sample copy. Writer's guidelines for business size SAE and 1 first class stamp.
Nonfiction: General housing information, real estate, Arizona business, employment overviews, custom buildings and apartment living—all locally oriented. Buys 20 mss/year. Query with published clips. Length: 700-1,000 words; longer features are assigned locally. Pays 10-20¢/word. Sometimes pays expenses of writers on assignment.
Photos: State availability of photos. Pays negotiable fee for 8x10 b&w glossy prints. Captions and model release required. Buys all rights.
Tips: "The writer may have a better chance of breaking in at our publication with short articles and fillers. Because we specialize entirely in upbeat articles to stimulate the housing market, we must know that our writers are very familiar with what we do. Frequent mistakes made by writers include failing to focus on the particular facts (with an occasional, well-placed adjective) that will stimulate the housing market and failure to capture the 'character' of a home or related topic in its most positive light."

PHOENIX MAGAZINE, 4707 N. 12th St., Phoenix AZ 85014. (602)248-8900. Editorial Director: Fern Stewart Welch. 50% freelance written. Monthly magazine for professional, general audience. Circ. 40,000. Pays within 2 weeks of publication. Publishes ms an average of 2 months after acceptance. Byline given in most cases. Occasionally offers kill fee. Usually buys all rights. Submit special issue material 3 months in advance. Computer printout submissions acceptable; prefers letter-quality to dot-matrix. Reports in 1 month. SASE. Sample copy $1.95 plus $1.25 for postage; writer's guidelines with SASE.
Nonfiction: Predominantly features subjects unique to Phoenix life: urban affairs, arts, lifestyle, etc. Subject should be locally oriented. Informational, how-to, interview, profile and historical. Each issue also embraces 1 or 2 in-depth reports on crucial, frequently controversial issues that confront the community. January issue: Superguide to what to see and do in area; February issue: Gardening Guide; March issue: Arizona Lifestyle; June issue: Summer SuperGuide; July issue: The Phoenix Book of Lists; August issue: Valley Progress Report; November issue: Home Decorating. Buys 120 mss/year. Query or submit complete ms. Length: 1,000-3,000 words; payment is negotiable; payment for features averages $100-400.
Photos: Photos are purchased with ms with no additional payment, or on assignment.
Tips: "Write for a copy of our writer's guidelines, then study our magazine and send us some ideas along with samples of your work."

Arkansas

ARKANSAS TIMES, Arkansas Writers' Project, Inc., Box 34010, Little Rock AR 72203. (501)375-2985. Editor: Bob Lancaster. 40% freelance written. Monthly magazine. "We are an Arkansas magazine. We seek to appreciate, enliven and, where necessary, improve the quality of life in the state." Circ. 30,000. Pays on acceptance. Publishes ms an average of 4 months after acceptance. Byline given. Not copyrighted. Buys first North American serial rights. Submit seasonal/holiday material 5 months in advance. Simultaneous, photocopied, and previously published submissions OK. Computer printout submissions acceptable. SASE. Reports in 2 weeks on queries; 1 month on mss. Sample copy $3.25; writer's guidelines with SASE.
Nonfiction: Mel White, articles editor. Book excerpts; expose (in investigative reporting vein); general interest; historical/nostalgic; humor; interview/profile; opinion; recreation; and entertainment, all relating to Arkansas. "The Arkansas angle is all-important." Buys 24 mss/year. Query. Length: 250-6,000 words. Pays $100-400.
Photos: Mary Jo Meade, photo editor. State availability of photos. Pays $25-75 for 8x10 b&w or color prints. Identification of subjects required. Buys one-time rights.
Columns/Departments: Mike Trimble, column editor. I Speak Arkansaw (articles on people, places and things in Arkansas or with special interest to Arkansans). "This is the department that is most open to freelancers." Buys 25 mss/year. Query. Length: 250-100 words. Pays $100.
Fiction: Adventure, historical, humorous, mainstream and romance. "All fiction must have an Arkansas angle." Buys 4 mss/year. Send complete ms. Length: 1,250-5,000 words. Pays $200-300.
Tips: "The most annoying aspect of freelance submissions is that so many of the writers have obviously never seen our magazine."

California

BAKERSFIELD LIFESTYLE, 123 Truxtun Ave., Bakersfield CA 93301. (805)325-7124. Editor and Publisher: Steve Walsh. Monthly magazine covering local lifestyles for college educated males/females ages 25-49 in a balanced community of industrial, agricultural and residential areas. Circ. 10,000. Byline and brief bio given. Buys all rights. Simultaneous queries, and simultaneous and photocopied submissions OK. Computer printout submissions acceptable. SASE. Reports in 6 months. Sample copy $2.50.
Nonfiction: General interest (topical issues); travel (up to 1,500 words); and articles on former residents who are now successful elsewhere. No investigative reporting, politics or negative editorial. Buys 12-15 mss/year. Length: 2,500 words maximum. Pays $10.
Photos: Send photos with ms. Pays $1/photo used.
Fiction: "Anything in good taste." Buys 20 mss/year. Length: 3,000 words maximum. Pays $10 maximum.

THE BERKELEY MONTHLY, Klaber Publishing Co., 910 Parker St., Berkeley CA 94710. (415)848-7900. Editor: Tracy J. Johnston. A monthly local, general interest tabloid focusing on East Bay issues and personalities. Circ. 75,000. Pays 15 days after publication. Byline given. Offers $25 kill fee for features. Buys first North American serial rights. Submit seasonal/holiday material 6 months in advance. Simultaneous queries, and photocopied and previously published submissions "outside our market" OK. SASE. Reports in 2 months on queries; 3 months on mss. Sample copy for $2, 9x12 SAE and 2 first class stamps.
Nonfiction: Book excerpts; expose (local political issues; Berkeley, Oakland); humor; and interview/profile (local personalities). No religious material, war stories or anthing outside local area. Buys 50 mss/year. Query with published clips. Length: 800-4,000 words. Pays $25-400.

CALIFORNIA LIVING, (now called *Image*), *San Francisco Examiner*, 110 Fifth St., San Francisco CA 94103. (415)777-7905. Editor: Curtiss Anderson. Executive Editor: Susan Brennaman. 80% freelance written. Magazine of the Sunday *Examiner* and *Chronicle* covering lifestyle, leisure, service, and untold stories with a Bay area and/or regional focus, for newspaper readers. Circ. 750,000. Pays on publication. Publishes ms an average of 4 months after acceptance. Byline given. Buys first North American serial rights, first serial rights, one-time rights, and second serial (reprint) rights. Submit seasonal/holiday material 6 months in advance. Photocopied submissions OK. Computer printout submissions acceptable; prefers letter-quality to dot-matrix. SASE. Reports in 3 weeks. Sample copy "available on newsstands."
Nonfiction: Lifestyle, leisure and service articles, untold stories, and behind-the-scenes news stories; must have a Bay area and/or regional focus. Buys 200 unsolicited mss/year. Query. Length: 1,200-2,500 words. Pays $150-250. Sometimes pays expenses of writers on assignment.
Photos: Veronique Vienne, art director. State availability or send photos with query or ms. Reviews 35mm color transparencies and 8x10 glossy prints. Pays "open fee." Captions, model release, and identification of subjects required. Buys one-time rights.
Fiction: Novel excerpts (relating to the Bay area).
Tips: "If writer knows the magazine well, his/her chances are as good as anyone's in breaking in. Avoid sending what appears to be first draft."

CALIFORNIA MAGAZINE, 11601 Wilshire Blvd., Los Angeles CA 90025. (213)479-6511. Editor: Harold Hayes. Managing Editor: Victoria Cebalo Irwin. 90% freelance written. Monthly magazine about California. Articles should be based on California—lifestyle, the arts, politics, business, crime, education, technology, etc. Circ. 285,000. Pays on acceptance. Publishes ms an average of 3 months after acceptance. Byline given. Offers variable kill fee. Buys first North American serial rights. Submit seasonal/holiday material 3 months in advance. Photocopied submissions OK. Computer printout submissions acceptable; prefers letter-quality to dot-matrix. SASE. Reports in 6 weeks on queries. Sample copy $2.
Nonfiction: Katherine Pandora, articles editor. Book excerpts, expose (environment, government, education, business), general interest, historical/nostalgic, humor, interview/profile, new product, photo feature and travel; *all* must pertain to California. No stories *not* related to California; no inspirational. Buys 40 mss/year. Query with published clips. Length: 800-4,000 words. Pays $100-2,000. Pays expenses of writers on assignment.
Photos: Nancy Duckworth, photo editor. "We assign almost all photos. We will review portfolios." Captions, model release, and identification of subjects required. Buys one-time rights.
Columns/Departments: Open to freelance: Books, Eloges (intimate profiles), Roots (history), Local Color, and New West Notes (familiar essay). Buys 30 mss/year. Query with published clips. Length: 750-2,000 words. Pays $450-750.
Tips: "Query first with clips. *Don't* send complete manuscript. Read the magazine—it has changed a lot recently—to get a feel for it."

‡**GENTRY MAGAZINE, The Magazine of Orange County People**, Orange County GENTRY, Inc., Suite 15, 333 E. 17th, Costa Mesa CA 92627. (714)650-1950. Editor: Nora Lehman. 80% freelance written. Maga-

Close-up

Hal Silverman
Editor and Magazine Consultant

Hal Silverman knows the Sunday magazine field. He has worked on both coasts—in Baltimore, Los Angeles, New York and San Francisco—on newspapers and magazines.

He was in New York and worked with Clay Felker when *New York* magazine was the first to adapt the concept of "a city magazine that happened to come with a Sunday paper." Silverman is a magazine consultant who has watched Sunday magazines creating their own editorial identities around the country.

In his 13 years as editor of *California Living*, the Sunday magazine of the *San Francisco Examiner*, Silverman not only saw a lot of changes, he made a lot of changes. (*California Living* is now a tabloid-size magazine and is getting a new name.)

What advice does Silverman, who is also associate editor of the *Examiner*, have for writers trying to break in to the regional market of city or Sunday magazines?

Don't let "your ego" get involved with responses from an editor, he says. "I turned down a lot of very, very good stuff," he says of his years at *California Living*. "We never commented on whether something was good or bad. All we were interested in was 'Does this help us get where *we're* headed?' Good or bad was not the issue."

New writers for city, regional or Sunday magazines need to identify and then service that publication's readership, Silverman advises. "The way I would figure out what that market wanted would be to get several issues of a magazine and use the current titles on the cover or contents page to make up fantasy titles. You will very quickly learn whether or not they are interested in the 'amazing this or that' or the 'ten ways to do this'."

While editing *California Living*, Silverman received about 100 submissions each week and published first-time writers. After 40 articles that appeared in the magazine became the basis of books for other publishers, Silverman launched California Living Books that received regional and national recognition.

"My ideal query is short and specific, with a sense of the flavor of the piece—the point of view, the spirit," he says. What he does not like is "a 'threat' to do an article. It's amazing how many times you will write back 'Thanks for your query . . . if you want to do it, we'll look at it' and then you never hear from that writer again."

It's easier to sell five $100 articles than one $500 article, Silverman says. "And in the process, you can win an editor's confidence. I don't know of any editors who have the right to assign, who will not assign to writers they have confidence in."

Some of the most important potential markets for regional writers are in the regional editions of national magazines, like *Sports Illustrated* and *Travel & Leisure*. "They're usually looking for material to accommodate that section with the regional ads." And don't forget the trade press, Silverman says; "opportunities are enormous and you can carve out a specialty."

Keep in mind that "Father's Day is Father's Day everywhere," he says of tailoring general-interest articles to individual geographic markets. Then there are some stories that "transcend geographic focus."

"Editors need writers worse than writers need editors," he stresses, "but editors only need writers who are going to make the editor look good."

—*Jean Stokes*

zine published 9 times/year "devoted to the people of Orange County specifically; targeted to the upper income, but not necessarily about them (readers)." Circ. 50,000+. Pays on publication. Byline given. Offers negotiable kill fee. Buys first North American serial rights; makes work-for-hire assignments. Submit seasonal/holiday material 6 months in advance. Previously published submissions OK only under certain circumstances. Computer printout submissions acceptable; prefers letter-quality to dot-matrix. SASE. Reports in 6 weeks. Sample copy $2.50 or 9x12 SAE and $1 postage; writer's guidelines for SAE.

Nonfiction: All articles must be Orange County oriented. Historical/nostalgic (people); interview/profile (about interesting people from any field); photo feaure; and travel. "We cover any subject with *person* orientation. Our *holiday* issue (Christmas) is totally young people oriented. We have included articles about and by people under age 18." No book reviews, music or movie reviews, general interest, etc. Buys 60 mss/year. Query with published clips. Length: 800-3,000 words. Pays 8¢-10¢/word.

Photos: Photo editor. State availability of photos. Prefers 5x7 b&w prints; color transparencies OK if negotiated for. Pays $3-25 for contact sheets; $10 minimum for transparencies. Model release and identification of subjects required. Buys one-time rights and all rights.

Columns/Departments: People profiles from any field of endeavor relating to Orange County. Buys 60-80 mss/year. Query with or without published clips. Length: 1,000-3,500 words. Pays 8¢-10¢/word.

Poetry: Poetry accepted only if about Orange Country. Buys 1 poem/year.

Tips: "We are a very regional magazine. The focus is Orange County and the people in it."

‡**GUIDE MAGAZINE**, Guide Publishing, Inc., 1909 N. Enterprise St., Orange CA 92665. (714)921-0624. Editor: Michael Peters. 50% freelance written. Monthly magazine covering Orange County entertainment "directed toward the philosophers, trends and general interests of the 'baby boomer' generation." Circ. 40,000. Pays on publication. Publishes ms an average of 4 months after publication. Byline given. Buys one-time rights. Submit seasonal/holiday material 2 months in advance. Simultaneous queries, and simultaneous, photocopied, and previously published submissions OK. Computer printout submissions acceptable; prefers letter-quality to dot-matrix. SASE. Reports in 2 weeks. Sample copy for $1.50, 9x12 SAE and 5 first class stamps; writer's guidelines for 4x10 SAE and 1 first class stamp.

Nonfiction: General interest, historical/nostalgic (history); how-to (invest, excel in business, etc.); humor (satire on baby boomer generation); interview/profile; new product; personal experience (problems, attitudes and concerns of being young); photo feature; travel; and activities (biking, skiing, exercise). Special issues include Valentine, spring (April), Halloween and Christmas. No biographies or high-tech material. Buys 12 mss/year. Query with photocopies of past work. Length: 500-2,000 words. Pays $50-200. Sometimes pays expenses of writers on assignment.

Photos: State availability of photos. Uses 5x7 or larger b&w prints and color transparencies. Payment for photos included in ms. Captions required. Buys one-time rights.

Columns/Departments: Weekend Escapes (weekend trips for two or small group); Activities (scuba, hiking, ballooning, etc.); and Health and Beauty. Buys 24 mss/year. Query. Length: 250-500 words. Pays $50-100.

Tips: "Freelancers can best break in by sending query letter with photocopies of past work and SASE; follow-up with another letter or phone call; and speaking to editor about assignment possibilities. Travel, activities, new business trends and features on baby boomer generation are most open to freelancers. The most frequent mistakes made by writers in completing an article assignment for us are missing the deadline and not sending art to accompany article."

IMAGE, see *California Living*, page 466.

LOS ANGELES MAGAZINE, ABC/Capital Cities, 1888 Century Park East, Los Angeles CA 90067. (213)557-7569. Editor: Geoff Miller. 98% freelance written. Monthly magazine about southern California. "The primary editorial role of the magazine is that of a sophisticated, authoritative guide to getting the most of of life in the Los Angeles area." Circ. 162,000. Pays on acceptance. Publishes ms an average of 6 months after acceptance. Byline given. Offers 30% kill fee. Buys first North American serial rights. Submit seasonal/holiday material 3-6 months in advance. Computer printout submissions acceptable; prefers letter-quality to dot-matrix. SASE. Reports in 6 weeks. Sample copy $4; writer's guidelines for SAE and 1 first class stamp.

Nonfiction: Rodger Claire, articles editor. Book excerpts (about L.A. or by famous L.A. author); expose (any local issue); general interest; historical/nostalgic (about L.A. or Hollywood); and interview/profile (about L.A. person). Buys 400 mss/year. Query with published clips. Length: 250-2,000 words. Pays $50-1,200. Sometimes pays expenses of writers on assignment.

Photos: Rodger Claire, photo editor. State availability of photos.

Columns/Departments: Rodger Claire, column/department editor. Buys 170 mss/year. Query with published clips. Length: 250-1,200 words. Pays $50-700.

LOS ANGELES READER, 8471 Melrose Ave., Second Floor, Los Angeles CA 90069. (213)655-8810. Editor: Dan Barton. Arts Editor: Richard Gehr. Assistant Editor: Tom Christie. Weekly tabloid of features, reviews and fiction for "affluent young Los Angelenos interested in the arts and popular culture." Circ. 75,000.

Pays on publication. Byline given. Buys one-time rights. Submit seasonal/holiday material 2 months in advance. Simultaneous queries and photocopied submissions OK. Computer printout submissions acceptable; prefers letter-quality to dot-matrix. SASE. Reports in 2 months. Sample copy $1; free writer's guidelines.
Nonfiction: Expose, general interest, New Age journalism, historical/nostalgic, interview/profile, personal experience and photo features. "No aimless satire." Buys "hundreds" of mss/year. Send complete ms. Length: 200-4,000 words. Pays $10-300.
Fiction: Adventure, experimental, historical, mainstream and novel excerpts. Interested in serious fiction. Buys 4-5 mss/year. Send complete ms. Length: 1,000-4,000 words. Pays $50-200.
Tips: "Break in with submission for our Cityside page: short news items on Los Angeles happenings/semi-hard news. We are nearly entirely a local publication and want only writing about local themes, topics, people by local writers. Anything exciting."

‡**LOS ANGELES TIMES MAGAZINE, People—Places—Pleasures**, Los Angeles Times, Times Mirror Sq., Los Angeles CA 90053. Editorial Director: Wallace Guenther. Articles Editor: Michael Parrish. 75% freelance written. Weekly magazine of regional general interest. Estab. 1985. Circ. 1,300,000 + . Payment schedule varies. Byline given. Buys first North American serial rights. Submit seasonal/holiday material 3 months in advance. Simultaneous queries and submissions OK. SASE. Reports in 1 month. Sample copy for 9x12 SAE and 6 first class stamps. Writer's guidelines for SAE and 2 first class stamps.
Nonfiction: General interest (regional); historical/nostalgic (regional); interview/profile; personal experience and photo feature. Must have Southern California tie-in, but no need to be set in Southern California. Query with published clips. Length: 400-1,800 words. Pays $400-2,000. Sometimes pays the expenses of writers on assignment.
Photo: Query first. Reviews color transparencies and b&w prints. Payment varies. Captions, model release, and identification of subjects required. Buys one-time rights.

MONTEREY LIFE, The Magazine of California's Spectacular Central Coast, Box 2107, Monterey CA 93942. (408)372-9200. Editor: William Morem. Art Director: Lisa W. deGarrido. 90% freelance written. Monthly magazine covering art, photography, regional affairs, music, sports, environment and lifestyles for "a sophisticated readership in the central California coast area." Circ. 20,000. Pays on publication. Publishes ms an average of 3 months after acceptance. Byline given. Offers variable kill fee. Buys first North American serial rights. Submit seasonal/holiday material 4 months in advance. Simultaneous queries, and simultaneous and photocopied submissions OK. Computer printout submissions acceptable; no dot-matrix. SASE. Reports in 3 weeks on queries; 6 weeks on mss. Sample copy for $3.50 and SAE.
Nonfiction: Historical/nostalgic, humor, interview/profile, photo feature and travel. No poetry. "All articles apply to this region except Getaway which covers travel within one day's drive." Buys 75 mss/year. Query with published clips if available. Length: 175-2,500 words. Pays $25-200. Sometimes pays expenses of writers on assignment.
Photos: State availability of photos. Pays $20-100 for color transparencies; $15-25 for 5x7 and 8x10 b&w prints. Captions, model release, and identification of subjects required. Buys one-time rights.
Columns/Departments: Community Focus. Query with published clips. Length: 250-1,000 words. Pays $25-40.
Tips: "Since we have a core of very cafable freelance writers for longer articles, it is easier to break in with short articles and fillers. Ask probing questions."

NORTHCOAST VIEW, Blarney Publishing, Box 1374, Eureka CA 95502. (707)443-4887. Publishers/Editors: Scott K. Ryan and Damon Maguire. 100% freelance written. A monthly magazine covering entertainment, recreation, the arts, consumer news, in-depth news, fiction and poetry for Humboldt County audience, mostly 18-50 year olds. Circ. 20,000. Pays on publication. Publishes ms an average of 1-6 months after acceptance. Byline given. Generally buys all rights, but will reassign. Submit seasonal/holiday material 6 months in advance. Simultaneous queries, and simultaneous (so long as not in our area), photocopied, and previously published (so long as rights available) submissions OK. Electronic submissions OK via Compugraphic 7500, 8" disk, hard-sectered. Computer printout submissions acceptable; prefers letter-quality to dot-matrix. SASE. Reports in 6 weeks on queries; 4 months on mss. Sample copy $1; writer's guidelines for SASE.
Nonfiction: Book excerpts (locally written); expose (consumer, government); historical/nostalgic (local); humor; interview/profile (entertainment, recreation, arts or political people planning to visit county); new product (for arts); photo feature (local for art section); and travel (weekend and short retreats accessible from Humboldt County). "Most features need a Humboldt County slant." Special issues include Kinetic Sculpture Race (May), Christmas (Dec.), and St. Patrick's Day (March). Buys 30-40 mss/year. Query with published clips or send complete ms. Length: 1,250-2,500 words. Pays $25-75.
Photos: State availability of photos with query letter or ms and send proof sheet, if available. Pays $5-15 for 5x7 b&w prints; $25-100 for 35mm Ektachrome slides for color. Captions, model release, and identification of subjects required. Buys all rights but will reassign.
Columns/Departments: A La Carte (restaurant reviews of county restaurants); Ex Libris (books); Reel Views

(film); Vinyl Views (albums); Cornucopia (calendar); Poetry; Rearview (art). Buys 80-100 mss/year. Send complete ms. Length: 500-750 words. Pays $10-25.

Fiction: Adventure, condensed novels, erotica (light), experimental, fantasy, horror, humorous, mystery, novel excerpts (local), science fiction and suspense. "We are open to most ideas and like to publish new writers. Topic and length are all very flexible—quality reading the only criteria." No cliche, contrived or predictable fiction—"we like a twist to stories." Buys 10-15 mss/year. Send complete ms. Length: 600-4,500 words; "longer good piece may run 2-3 months consecutively, if it breaks well."

Poetry: Stephen Miller and Mary Johnson, poetry editors. Avant-garde, free verse, haiku, light verse and traditional. Open to all types. No "sappy, overdone or symbolic poetry." Buys work of 12-20 poets (3-4 poems each)/year. Submit maximum 5 poems. Length: 12-48 lines. Pays $25.

Tips: "Our greatest need always seems to be for reviews—book, album and film. Films need to be fairly current, but remember that some films take a while to get up to Humboldt County. Book and album—we're always looking for somewhat current but lesser known works that are exceptional. The most frequent mistakes made by writers are using too few quotes and too much paraphrasing."

ORANGE COAST MAGAZINE, The Magazine of Orange County, O.C.N.L., Inc., 18200 W. McDurmott, Irvine CA 92714. (714)660-8622. Editor: Katherine Tomlinson. Assistant Editor: Kevin Ostter. 95% freelance written. Monthly. "*Orange Coast* is designed to inform and enlighten the educated, upscale residents of affluent Orange Country, California and is highly graphic and well-researched. Circ. 40,000. Pays on acceptance. Publishes ms an average of 5 months after acceptance. Byline given. Buys first serial rights. Submit seasonal/holiday material 6 months in advance. Simultaneous queries, and simultaneous and photocopied submissions OK. *Please*, no phone queries. Electronic submissions OK on IBM—any ASCII file, SMART modem 1200 and AM CompEdit, Comp Set or IBM PC, but requires hard copy also. Computer printout submissions acceptable; no dot-matrix. SASE. Reports in 2 months. Sample copy $2.50, 10x12 SAE and $2.25 postage; writer's guidelines for SAE and 1 first class stamp.

Nonfiction: Expose (Orange Country government, refugees, politics, business, crime); general interest (anything dealing with Orange County); historical/nostalgic; guides to activities and services; interview/profile (Orange County prominent citizens); local sports; and lifestyle features. Not a market for travel. Special issues include Dining (March); Health and Beauty (January); Finance (October); Home and Garden (June); and Holiday (December). No articles not dealing with Orange County at least peripherally. Buys 100 mss/year. Query or send complete ms. Length: 2,500-4,000 words. Pays $150 maximum.

Columns/Departments: Local Consumer, Investments, Business, Health, Profiles, Adventure, and Consuming Passions. Not open for submission are: Music, Art, Law, Medicine, Film, Restaurant Review ("we have regular reviewers"). Buys 100 mss/year. Query or send complete ms. Length: 1,500-2,000 words. Pays $100 maximum.

Fiction: Buys only under extremely rare circumstances. Send complete ms. Length: 1,000-5,000 words. Must have an Orange County setting. Pays $150 maximum.

Tips: "Most features are assigned to writers we've worked with before. However, we have rearranged editorial schedules to place unsolicited features. Don't try to sell us 'generic' journalism. *Orange Coast* prefers well-written stories with specific and unusual angles that in some way include Orange County. Be professional and write manuscripts that present you as a stylized, creative and caring writer. All features and most departments are open to freelancers except for the celebrity interview which is written in house. The most frequent mistake made by writers is lack of research. Because we are a relatively low-paying market, some writers tend to slough off. Half-finished work is another problem. Finally, a lot of writers miss the Orange County angle. We are a regional publication in a highly competitive market. Our writers *must* concentrate on the local angle. We get far too many generalized manuscripts. It's very rewarding seeing a really bright new talent emerge. There's nothing more refreshing than a writer coming into my office with new ideas, new approaches to the medium and a no-restraints approach to his/her job."

‡**PREVIEWS MAGAZINE, A Community Magazine**, Santa Monica Bay Printing & Publishing Co., #245, 919 Santa Monica Blvd., Santa Monica CA 90401. (213)458-3376. Editor: Jan Loomis. 60% freelance written. Monthly magazine of the community of West Los Angeles. "We are a sophisticated magazine with local events and people as our focus, sent free to the entire community." Circ. 36,000 Pays on publication. Publishes ms an average of 6 months after acceptance. Byline given. Buys first North American serial rights and all rights; makes-work-for-hire assignments. Submit seasonal/holiday material 6 months in advance. Photocopied submissions OK. Electronic submissions OK on IBM PC/Hayes Modern, but requires hard copy also. Computer printout submissions acceptable. SASE. Reports in 1 month on queries. Sample copy and writer's guidelines free.

Nonfiction: Historical/nostalgic, interview/profile, opinion, photo feature and travel. No extreme positions, titilation, pornography, etc. Buys 20 mss/year. Query with published clips. Length: 200-2,500 words. Pays $25-500.

Photos: State availability of photos. Reviews color and b&w contact sheets, 4x4 transparencies and 8x10 glossy prints. Pays $35-50 for b&w; $35-75 for color.

Fiction: Fantasy, humorous and mainstream. No pornography. Buys 2-4 mss/year. Query with published clips. Length: 1,500-2,500 words. Pays $150-500.
Poetry: Light verse and traditional. No long poems. Buys 2-3 poems/year. Submit maximum 6 poems. Length: 35-60 lines. Pays $25-100.
Fillers: Anecdotes and short humor. Buys 7-10/year. Length: 200-250 words. Pays $25-75.
Tips: "We're looking for fiction and interviews. Query with clips of a good idea that would appeal to upscale readers (average income $60,00; average age 39)."

‡**RANCH & COAST**, American Ranch & Coast Publishing, Inc., Box 806, Solana Beach CA 92075. (619)481-7659. Editor: Adrian Barnard. Features Editor: Mary Shepardson. 30% freelance written. Monthly magazine targeted at a sophisticated, upper-income readership, primarily in Southern California. Circ. 25,000. Pays on publication. Publishes ms an average of 3 months after acceptance. Byline given. Offers 20% kill fee. Buys various rights. Submit seasonal/holiday material 4 months in advance. Simultaneous queries, and photocopied, and previously published submissions OK. Computer printout submissions acceptable; prefers letter-quality to dot-matrix. SASE. Reports in 1 month. Sample copy $1.50; free writer's guidelines.
Nonfiction: Book excerpts, general interest, historical/nostaglic, humor (if specifically appropriate), interview/profile, photo feature, travel, and lifestyle (social and chartiable events). No articles aimed at unsophisticated audience, budget or how-to pieces. Buys 25-40 mss/year. Query with published clips. Length: 350-2,000 words. Pays 10¢/word minimum.
Photos: State availability of photos with query. "High-quality photographs and other illustrations are very important to *Ranch & Coast*. Many submissions have inadequate 'snapshot' quality illustrations." Pays $15 and more for 5x7 and 8x10 b&w; $25 and more for color transparencies. Captions, model release, and identification of subjects required. Buys one-time rights.
Columns/Departments: Most columns/departments are written on regular contract basis. Areas include the arts and investments. Buys 8 mss/year. Query with published clips. Length: 500-1,000 words. Pays 10¢/word minimum.
Fiction: Condensed novels, historical, humorous, mainstream, mystery, novel excerpts and serialized novels. Buys 6 mss/year. Send complete ms. Word length open. Pays 10¢/word minimum.
Tips: "Submissions should be appropriate in style and content. Writers should be familiar with current format of magazine which has changed markedly in recent years. We need profiles of prominent and interesting people from freelancers. These should have something new to say and should be well-illustrated."

SACRAMENTO MAGAZINE, Box 2424, Sacramento CA 95811. Editor: Cheryl Romo. 60% freelance written. Monthly magazine emphasizing a strong local angle on politics, local issues, human interest and consumer items for readers in the middle to high income brackets. Pays on acceptance within a 30-day billing period. Publishes ms an average of 3 months after acceptance. Rights vary; generally buys first North American serial rights, rarely second serial (reprint) rights. Original mss only (no previously published submission). Computer printout submissions acceptable; prefers letter-quality to dot-matrix. No phone calls; query by letter. Reports in 6 weeks. SASE. Sample copy $3.50; writer's guidelines for SASE.
Nonfiction: Local issues vital to Sacramento quality of life. Past articles have included "Gasping at Straws" (rice straw burning and its resultant air pollution) and "Missing" (the disappearance of a young sailor). Buys 15 unsolicited feature mss/year. Query first. Length: 2,000-3,000 words, depending on author, subject matter and treatment.
Photos: State availability of photos. Payment varies depending on photographer, subject matter and treatment. Captions (including IDs, location and date) required. Buys one-time rights.
Columns/Departments: Media, parenting, first person essays, local travel, gourmet, profile, sports and city arts (850-1,250 words); City Lights (250 words).

SAN DIEGO MAGAZINE, Box 85409, San Diego CA 92138. (619)225-8953. Executive Editor: Tom Shess. Editor-in-Chief: Edwin F. Self. Emphasizes San Diego. Monthly magazine; 310 pages. Circ. 65,000. Pays on publication. Buys all rights, but will negotiate. Byline given. Submit seasonal/holiday material 6 months in advance of issue date. Simultaneous and photocopied submissions OK. SASE. Reports in 2 months. Sample copy $3.
Nonfiction: Expose (serious, documented); general interest (to San Diego region); historical (San Diego region); interview (with notable San Diegans); nostalgia; photo essay; profile; service guides; and travel. Buys variable number of mss/issue. Prefers query with clips of published work. Send photocopies. Length: 2,000-3,000 words. Pays $500 maximum.
Photos: State availability of photos with query. Pays $25-100 b&w; $40-100 color; $250 minimum for cover. Captions required. Buys all rights. Model release required.
Columns/Departments: Topics include Up and Coming (fine arts); Books; Music and Dance; Films; and Urban Eye (San Diego related short items). Length: 50-100 words. Pays $50-75.
Tips: "Write better lead paragraphs; write shorter, with greater clarity; wit and style appreciated; stick to basic magazine journalism principles."

THE SAN DIEGO UNION, Box 191, San Diego CA 92112. (618)291-3131. Associate Editor: Ed Nichols. 40% freelance written. "The bulk of the material we buy is for our Sunday section, Opinion. Optimum pieces are analytical essays on international, geo-political developments or commentary on domestic social, economic, scientific and political trends. We're looking for in-depth research, some original material in the article, and cogency of thought." Byline given. Pays $125 on publication. Length: 1,200 words. Op-ed page: interested in material on a broad range of topics related to current events and in-depth pieces on world events. Uses the whole spectrum of original writing—but piece must have a purpose (such as humor) or throw new light on an issue. Length: 750 words. Electronic submissions OK, but query first. Computer printout submissions acceptable.

SAN FRANCISCO FOCUS, The Monthly Magazine for the San Francisco Bay Area, KQED Inc., 500 8th St., San Francisco CA 94103. (415)553-2119. Editor: Mark K. Powelson. Managing Editor: Warren Sharpe. A monthly city/regional magazine. Circ. 160,000. Pays on publication. Byline given. Offers 33% kill fee. Buys one-time rights. Submit seasonal/holiday material 5 months in advance. Simultaneous queries and previously published submissions OK. Computer printout submissions acceptable. SASE. Reports in 6 weeks. Sample copy $1.95; free writer's guidelines.
Nonfiction: Expose, humor, interview/profile and travel. All stories should relate in some way to the San Francisco Bay Area (travel excepted). Query with published clips or send complete ms. Length: 750-3,000 words. Pays $75-750.

SAN FRANCISCO MAGAZINE, 950 Battery St., San Francisco CA 94110. (415)777-5555. Editor: David Gon. Monthly magazine covering general interest topics for San Francisco and northern California residents. Circ. 50,000. Pays within 30 days of the issue's appearance on the newsstand. Byline and brief bio given. No kill fee. Buys first North American serial rights. Photocopied submissions OK. Reports in 3 weeks.
Nonfiction: General interest (lifestyles, fashion); humor; interview/profile (of person with a Northern California connection); personal experience (first person pieces); photo feature; consumer; and science. "Topics may be of national scope. We want well researched, well written articles with a northern California fix." Buys fewer than 10 unsolicited mss/year. Query with clips of published work or send complete ms. Length: 2,000-5,000 words. Pays $500 average.
Photos: State availability of photos. Reviews 35mm color transparencies and 8x10 b&w glossy prints. Negotiates pay separately for package of photos or ms/photo package.

THE SAN GABRIEL VALLEY MAGAZINE, Miller Books, 2908 W. Valley Blvd., Alhambra CA 91803. (213)284-7607. Editor-in-Chief: Joseph Miller. 75% freelance written. Bimonthly magazine; 52 pages. For middle- to upper-income people who dine out often at better restaurants in Los Angeles County. Circ. 3,400. Pays on publication. Publishes ms an average of 45 days after acceptance. Buys simultaneous rights, second serial (reprint) rights and one-time rights. Phone queries OK. Submit seasonal/holiday material 1 month in advance. Simultaneous, photocopied, and previously published submissions OK. Computer printout submissions acceptable. SASE. Reports in 2 weeks. Sample copy $1.
Nonfiction: Expose (political); informational (restaurants in the Valley); inspirational (success stories and positive thinking); interview (successful people and how they made it); profile (political leaders in the San Gabriel Valley); and travel (places in the Valley). Interested in 500-word humor articles. Buys 18 unsolicited mss/year. Length: 500-10,000 words. Pays 5¢/word.
Columns/Departments: Restaurants, Education, and Valley News and Valley Personality. Buys 2 mss/issue. Send complete ms. Length: 500-1,500 words. Pays 5¢/word.
Fiction: Historical (successful people) and western (articles about Los Angeles County). Buys 2 mss/issue. Send complete ms. Length: 500-10,000 words. Pays 5¢/word.
Tips: "Send us a good personal success story about a Valley or a California personality. We are also interested in articles on positive thinking."

‡**SIERRA LIFE MAGAZINE, The Magazine of the High Sierra**, Pramann Publishing, 699 W. Line St., Bishop CA 93514. (619)873-3320. Editor: Sandie Pramann. Managing Editor: Marty Forstenzer. 50% freelance written. Bimonthly magazine on the Sierra region. "Our magazine is about the history, current events, people, and recreational opportunities of the Sierra Nevada region." Pays on publication. Publishes ms an average of 6 months after acceptance. Byline given. Buys second serial (reprint) rights. Submit seasonal/holiday material 6 months in advance. Simultaneous queries, and simultaneous, photocopied, and previously published submissions OK. Computer printout submissions acceptable; prefers letter-quality to dot-matrix. SASE. Reports in 3 months. Sample copy $2.50, 9x11 SAE and $1.50 postage; writer's guidelines for #10 SAE and 1 first class stamp.
Nonfiction: Book excerpts; general interest; historical/nostalgic (history of Sierra Nevada region); how-to (about appropriate subjects); interview/profile (about people related to Sierra); personal experience; photo feature; technical; travel; arts; outdoor; and wildlife. All articles must be related to Sierra Nevada region. Also publishes Sierra life hunting guide/fishing guide/hiking guide/four-wheel drive guide. No fiction or fantasy.

Buys 18 mss/year. Length: 500-10,000 words. Pays $20-400. Sometimes pays expenses of writers on assignment.

Photos: Janice Kabala, photo editor. State availability of photos or send photos with query or ms. Reviews 5x7 b&w prints. "We sometimes request color transparencies." Pays $5 for b&w; $10-50 for color. Identification of subjects required. Buys two-time rights.

Poetry: Traditional (on the Sierra). Buys 12/year. Submit maximum 3 poems. Pays $5-25.

Tips: "We buy a number of historical and outdoor sports articles (skiing, backpacking, fishing) each year. Our reading audience is educated and sophisticated. Articles should reflect that."

‡**VALLEY LIFE MAGAZINE**, Omnific Publishing, Inc., 5548 Reseda Blvd., Tarzana CA 91356. (818)344-1800. Editor: Ian Cunningham. 90% freelance written. Bimonthly magazine pertaining to the quality of life in the San Fernando Valley, Southern California. Audience is upper-income, highly educated. Estab. 1983. Circ. 25,000. Pays on publication. Byline given unless ms has been rewritten by staff. Offers 25% kill fee. Buys first North American serial rights. Submit seasonal/holiday material 6 months in advance. Simultaneous queries, and simultaneous and photocopied submissions OK. SASE. Reports in 4 weeks on queries; 6 weeks on mss. Sample copy $2; writer's guidelines for #10 SAE and 1 first class stamp.

Nonfiction: Expose, general interest, historical/nostalgic, humor, inspirational, interview/profile, new product, opinion, personal experience, photo feature, technical, travel and health/fitness/sport nutrition. No confession, fiction. Query (published writers) or send complete ms (unpublished writers). Length: 1,000-3,000 words. Pays 10¢/word.

Photos: State availability of photos. Reviews b&w and color contact sheets, 35mm and 2¼ transparencies, and 8x10 prints. Captions, model release, and identification of subjects required. Buys one-time rights.

Columns/Departments: Reviews—theater, music, film; Potpourri—unusual products, events and people, pertaining to San Fernando. Send complete ms. Length: 200-600 words. Payment negotiable.

Fillers: Anecdotes, short humor and newsbreaks. Also buys cartoons. Length: 300-1,000 words. Payment negotiable.

Tips: Solid research and reportage. Should understand Southern California/San Fernando Valley lifestyles. Do not telephone unless totally necessary.

‡**VALLEY MAGAZINE**, World of Communications, Inc., Suite 275, 16800 Devonshire St., Granada Hills CA 91344. (818)368-3353. Editor: Anne Framroze. 90% freelance written. Monthly magazine. *Valley Magazine* is a general interest, lifestyle magazine catering to the residents of the San Fernando Valley. Circ. 30,000. Pays 6-8 weeks after acceptance. Publishes ms an average of 2 months after acceptance. Byline given. Offers 20% kill fee. Buys first serial rights. Submit seasonal/holiday material 4 months in advance. Simultaneous queries, and simultaneous and photocopied submissions OK. Computer printout submissions acceptable; prefers letter-quality to dot-matrix. SASE. Free sample copy; writer's guidelines for 8x11 SAE and 1 first class stamp.

Nonfiction: Expose (good investigative reporting); general interest (all types); how-to (not the run-of-the-mill); interview/profile (prominent Valley citizens); travel (always open); and short interesting items or unusual products. Special issues include health, fitness, and travel (weekend getaways). No fiction, first person humorous personal accounts, no opinion pieces. Buys 150 mss/year. Query with published clips. Length: 1,000-4,000 words. Pays $200-500. Sometimes pays expenses of writers on assignment.

Photos: Emily Borden, photo editor. State availability of photos or send with query or ms. Captions, model release, and identification of subjects required.

Columns/Departments: Religion, books, theatre, food, music, travel, business (finance), garden and discoveries (light unusual items). Buys 60 mss/year. Query with published clips. Length: 750-2,300 words. Payment depends on piece.

Tips: "Send a strong query letter with clips of previous work. Manuscripts must have some sort of Valley angle, but can be a general interest subject which is of major significance—for instance, the changing field of health care."

VENTURA COUNTY & COAST REPORTER, The Reporter, VCR Inc., Suite 213, 1583 Spinnaker Dr., Ventura CA 93001. (805)658-2244; (805)656-0707. Editor: Nancy Cloutier. Weekly tabloid covering local news. Circ. 25,000. Pays on publication. Byline given. Buys first North American serial rights. SASE. Reports in 3 weeks.

Nonfiction: General interest, humor, interview/profile and travel (local—within 500 miles). Local (Ventura County) slant predominates. Length: 2-5 double-spaced typewritten pages. Pays $10-25.

Photos: State availability of photos with ms. Reviews b&w contact sheet.

Columns/Departments: Boating Experience (Southern California). Send complete ms. Pays $10-25.

VICTOR VALLEY MAGAZINE, Desert Alive Publishing Company, Box 618, Victorville CA 92392. Editor: Grace Hauser. 100% freelance written. Magazine published monthly except January/February and July/August combined. Circ. 5,000. Pays within 1 month of publication. Publishes ms an average of 3 months after acceptance. Byline given. Offers 50% kill fee. Buys first North American serial rights. Submit seasonal/holiday material 3 months in advance. Simultaneous queries, and simultaneous, photocopied, and previously published submissions OK. Computer printout submissions acceptable "if upper and lower case;" prefers letter-quality to dot-matrix. SASE. Reports in 3 months. Free sample copy; writer's guidelines for SAE and 2 first class stamps.

Nonfiction: General interest, historical/nostalgic, how-to, interview/profile, photo feature and travel. Book reviews, film reviews, controversy and political articles acceptable. Buys 50 mss/year. Send complete ms. Length: 600-1,000 words. Pays $20-75. Sometimes pays expenses of writers on assignment.

Photos: Send photos with ms. Pays $25-50 for color transparencies; $5-25 for 4x5 b&w prints. Captions, model release, and identification of subjects required. Buys one-time rights.

Columns/Departments: Desert Alive (stories about the animal and plant life in and around the high desert area: what nature enthusiasts can look for, how desert-dwellers can better live with the local wildlife, etc.); History and Lore (stories about the western development of the high desert area); Family Living Today (dealing with family and social relationships, children, self-improvement, popular culture, etc.); and Desert Personalities (interesting locals, not necessarily of prominence. No first person articles.

Tips: "Our readers have expressed a strong interest in local history (Mojave Desert), interesting personalities, and living better."

WEST, 750 Ridder Park Dr., San Jose CA 95190. (408)920-5602. Editor: Jeffrey Klein. For a general audience. 50% freelance written. Weekly rotogravure newspaper/magazine, published with the *San Jose Mercury News*. Circ. 300,000. Pays on acceptance. Publishes ms an average of 3 months after acceptance. Byline given. Buys first serial rights, and occasionally second serial (reprint) rights. Submit seasonal material (skiing, wine, outdoor living) 3 months in advance. Will consider photocopied and simultaneous submissions if the simultaneous submission is out of their area. Computer printout submissions acceptable; prefers letter-quality to dot-matrix. SASE. Reports in 1 month. Free sample copy.

Nonfiction: A general newspaper-magazine requiring that most subjects be related to California (especially the Bay Area) and the interests of California. Will consider subjects outside California if subject is of broad or national appeal. Length: 1,000-4,000 words. Query with published clips. Pays $250-600. Sometimes pays expenses of writers on assignment.

Photos: Payment varies for b&w and color photos purchased with or without mss. Captions required. Queries should be submitted to the attention of Carol Doup Muller.

WESTWAYS, Automobile Club of Southern California, 2601 S. Figueroa St., Los Angeles CA 90007. (213)741-4760. Editor: Mary Ann Fisher. 95% freelance written. Monthly magazine. "*Westways* is a regional publication on travel in the West and world travel. Emphasis is on pleasing and interest subjects—art, historical and cultural. Our audience is southern California upper income readers who enjoy leisure and culture." Circ. 475,000. Pays 30 days prior to publication. Publishes ms an average of 6 months after acceptance. Byline given. Offers $75 kill fee. Buys first North American serial rights. Submit seasonal/holiday material 6 months in advance. Photocopied submissions OK. Computer printout submissions acceptable; prefers letter-quality to dot-matrix. SASE. Reports in 2 weeks. Sample copy $1; free writer's guidelines.

Nonfiction: General interest, historical, humor, interview/profile, photo feature and travel. "We are always interested in Christmas/holiday suggestions but need them by May/June prior to season. We do not accept political, controversial or first person articles. Buys 120-130 mss/year. Query with or without published clips or send complete ms. Length: 1,500 words maximum. Pays $150 (minimum is for Wit & Wisdom section of 900 words). Sometimes pays expenses of writers on assignment.

Photos: Send photos with query or ms. Reviews 35mm color transparencies. pays $25-50. Captions, model release, and identification of subjects required. Buys one-time rights.

Columns/Departments: "We have regular monthly columnists for sections/columns except Wit & Wisdom." Buys 24-28 mss/year. Send complete ms. Length: 750-900 words. Pays $100-150.

Colorado

BOULDER SUNDAY CAMERA MAGAZINE, Box 591, Boulder CO 80306. (303)442-1202. Sunday Magazine Editor: Ken Doctor. 75% freelance written. Emphasizes subjects of particular interest to Boulder County residents. Weekly tabloid; 32 pages. Circ. 37,000. Pays on publication. Buys first rights and second (reprint) rights to material originally published elsewhere. Byline given. Phone queries OK. Submit seasonal/holiday material 6-8 weeks in advance. Photocopied submissions OK. Computer printout submissions acceptable; no dot-matrix. SASE. Reports in 6 weeks. Publishes ms an average of 1 month after acceptance.

Nonfiction: Expose (anything relevant to Boulder County that needs exposing); informational (emphasis on good writing, warmth and impact); historical (pertaining to Boulder County or Colorado in general); interview and profile (stress local angle); photo feature (featuring Boulder County or areas in Colorado and Rocky Mountain West where Boulder County residents are apt to go). Buys 100 mss/year. Query. Length: 700-2,000 words. Rates and guidelines available on request.

Photos: Purchased with or without mss or on assignment. Captions required. Query. Pays $10 for 8x10 b&w glossy prints; $20 for 35mm or 2¼x2¼ (or larger) color transparencies.

Tips: "We're demanding a more sophisticated style than we have in the past. Trends in magazine publishing that freelance writers should be aware of include use of more graphics—they should think visually."

COLORADO MONTHLY MAGAZINE, (formerly *This Week in Denver*), Queen City Publishing, Suite 103, 3801 Florida, Denver CO 80210. (303)757-8300. Editor: Eileen Wigginton. Managing Editor: Karen Knapper. 100% freelance written. A monthly regional (Colorado) magazine covering fine arts, music, sports and regional features. "Our readers are well educated and affluent." Circ. 30,000. Pays on publication. Publishes ms an average of 2 months after acceptance. Byline given. Buys first serial rights. Submit seasonal/ holiday material 3 months in advance. Simultaneous queries and photocopies, and previously published submissions (with complete disclosure and release) OK. Electronic and computer printout submissions acceptable. Sample copy $3; writer's guidelines for SASE.

Nonfiction: Historical/nostalgia, interview/profile and general interest. Drawings, photos and 35mm slides are welcome. All nonfiction must have a Colorado theme or tie-in. No political, controversial or erotic articles. Query or send complete ms. Length: 500-2,500 words. Pays 5-10¢/word.

Photos: 35mm color slides with or without ms. Pays negotiable rates.

Fiction: Adventure, historical, humorous, mainstream, mystery, suspense and western. Send complete ms. No erotica. Length: 1,000-2,000 words. 5-10¢/word.

Poetry: Avant-garde, free verse, haiku, light verse and traditional. No erotica or political poetry. Length: open. Pays $5 minimum.

Fillers: Cartoons, short humor and serial game or mystery. Pays negotiable rates.

Tips: "We rely heavily on freelancers. Check all facts, figures, dates, etc., for accuracy. *Colorado Monthly Magazine* looks for tight, well-written articles with an interesting or unusual angle that somehow reflect the state of Colorado and/or her people. Quality photos (color preferred) and 35mm color slides to illustrate subject matter are encouraged."

‡**SPRINGS MAGAZINE,** Sunrise Publishing, 716 N. Tejon, Box 9166, Colorado Springs CO 80932. (303)636-2001. Editor: Stewart M. Green. 60% freelance written. Monthly tabloid that covers Pikes Peak region and Colorado. "We are a regional city magazine; our audience is above average in education and income. We want literate writing, well-conceived and executed writing." Estab. 1982. Circ. 20,000. Pays on publication. Publishes ms an average of 2 months. Byline given. Offers 50% kill fee if on assignment basis. Buys one-time rights, first serial rights, and second serial (reprint) rights; makes work-for-hire assignments. Submit seasonal/holiday material 6 months in advance. Simultaneous queries, and simultaneous, photocopied, and previously published submissions OK. Computer printout submissions acceptable, but requires hard copy also. SASE. Reports in 3 weeks. Sample copy for 10x13 SAE and 5 first class stamps; free writer's guidelines.

Nonfiction: Expose, general interest, historical/nostalgic, humor, interview/profile, personal experience, photo feature and travel. Special issues include Western and Outdoor Adventure, in summer. Otherwise Lifestyle sections: Finance, Real Estate, Health Care, Education, Quality of Life, and Skiing. "We rarely use topics/subjects outside Colorado, unless it has a strong regional tie." Buys 150 mss/year. Query with or without published clips, or send complete ms. Length: 1,000-4,000 words. Pays $50-500. "We pay by the 'character' which works out to about $2 per column inch for departments; $2.25 for features. More payment and expenses if travel/research are needed."

Photos: Send photos with query or ms. Prefers strong b&w photos suitable for reproduction. Reviews 35mm color transparencies and 5x7 or 8x10 b&w prints. Pays $15-50 for b&w, $50-150 for color. Captions, model release, and identification of subjects. Buys one-time rights.

Columns/Departments: All columns written by contract writers. Columns include Arts, Performing Arts, Culinary Arts, Travel and Wine. Some short reviews in calendar section. Buys 55 mss/year. Query with or without published clips. Needs to review publication for style and content. Length: 1,000-1,500 words. Pays $2/column inch.

Fiction: "We run fiction occasionally. It has to have strong writing and regional ties to Colorado. No western fiction please." Buys 2-3 mss/year. Send complete ms. Length: 1,000-3,000 words. Pays $2-2.50/column inch.

Tips: "We need good original ideas that relate to Colorado and the Pikes Peak region. We are starting to run more 'mini-features' that are ideal for new writers. We need confidence in your ability to put together a larger story. We like loyal contributers and appreciate their input. New ideas are always needed."

 The double dagger before a listing indicates that the listing is new in this edition. New markets are often the most receptive to freelance contributions.

Connecticut

CONNECTICUT TRAVELER, Official Publication of the Connecticut Motor Club/AAA, Connecticut Motor Club/AAA, 2276 Whitney Ave., Hamden CT 06518. (203)288-7441. Editor: Elke Martin. 10% freelance written. Monthly tabloid covering anything of interest to the Connecticut motorist for Connecticut Motor Club members. Circ. 155,000. Pays on publication. Publishes ms an average of 6 months after acceptance. Byline given. Buys first North American serial rights, first serial rights, and second serial (reprint) rights. Submit seasonal/holiday material 4 months in advance. Photocopied and previously published submissions OK. Computer printout submissions acceptable; prefers letter-quality to dot-matrix. SASE. Reports in 2 weeks on queries; 1 month on mss. Sample copy for 8½x11 SASE; writer's guidelines for legal size SASE.
Nonfiction: How-to (variety, how to make traveling with children fun, etc.); and travel (regional economy or low-budget with specifics, i.e., what accommodations, restaurants, sights, recreation are available). "We are a regional publication and focus on events, traveling and other topics within the New England area. We do not want to see mechanical or highly complicated automotive how-tos or exotic travel stories that would be financially out of reach for the average traveler." Buys 20 mss/year. Query or send complete ms. Length: 500-1,500 words. Pays $25-150.
Photos: Send b&w photos with ms. Does not accept color. Buys 8x10 glossies as part of ms package. Captions, model release, and identification of subjects required. Buys one-time rights.
Tips: "If you can get us a story on a travel destination that's unusual and hasn't been beaten to death and cover the specifics in an interesting and fun-to-read manner, we'll definitely consider the story for publication. We stress a regional slant, suitability (will senior citizen, children, etc., enjoy this trip?), and what makes the particular destination special."

NORTHEAST MAGAZINE, *The Hartford Courant,* 285 Broad St., Hartford CT 06115. (203)241-3700. Editor: Lary Bloom. 50% freelance written. Weekly magazine for a Connecticut audience. Circ. 300,000. Pays on acceptance. Publishes ms an average of 1 month after acceptance. Byline given. Buys one-time rights. Previously published submissions OK. Unsolicited ms or queries accepted; reports in 3 weeks. Computer printout submissions acceptable; prefers letter-quality to dot-matrix. SASE.
Nonfiction: General interest; in-depth investigation of stories behind news; historical/nostalgic; interview/profile (of famous or important people with Connecticut ties); and personal essays (humorous or anecdotal). No poetry. Buys 100-150 mss/year. Length: 750-4,500 words. Pays $200-1,000.
Photos: Most assigned; state availability of photos. "Do not send originals."
Fiction: Well-written, original short stories. Length: 750-4,500 words.

Delaware

DELAWARE TODAY MAGAZINE, Box 3029, Wilmington DE 19804. (302)995-7146. Editor: Peter Mucha. 90% freelance written. Monthly magazine covering subjects of broad interest in Delaware. 100 pages. Circ. 15,000. Pays month of publication. Computer printout submissions acceptable; prefers letter-quality to dot-matrix. SASE necessary. Reports in 6 weeks.
Nonfiction: Features: Human interest articles. "We want lively, vivid writing about people, organizations, communities, lifestyles and trends or events that are of special interest to people in Delaware." Service articles: "Each month we try to run an informative guide to goods or services or leisure activities. Except for travel articles, must have a Delaware tie-in." Short subjects: "We need items that are brief but informative, perceptive or amusing. Must relate to Delaware." In all cases, query first with writing samples. Features pay $125-300; short subjects $15-50. Columns/Departments pays $50-125. Pays expenses of writers on assignment (withing limits).
Photos: All photography is freelance. Pays $15-25 for b&w photo.
Tips: "Study the magazine first and then think big. The more people who might be interested in the subject, the more likely we are to be interested. Be thorough and lively. Avoid a fuzzy focus and poor organization."

District of Columbia

THE WASHINGTON POST, 1150 15th St. NW, Washington DC 20071. (202)334-6000. Travel Editor: Morris D. Rosenberg. Weekly travel section (Sunday). Pays on publication. Byline given. "We are now emphasizing staff-written articles as well as quality writing from other sources. Stories are rarely assigned to freelance writers; all material comes in on speculation; there is no fixed kill fee." Buys first serial rights. Computer printout submissions acceptable if legible; no dot-matrix. Usually reports in 3 weeks.
Nonfiction: Emphasis is on travel writing with a strong sense of place, color, anecdote and history. Query with

published clips. Length: 1,500-2,000 words.
Photos: State availability of photos with ms (b&w only). "Send good travel photos that illustrate and complement the article, not fuzzy vacation snapshots." Captions required.

THE WASHINGTON POST MAGAZINE, *The Washington Post,* 1150 15th St., NW, Washington D.C. 20071. Managing Editor: Stephen Petranek. 50% freelance written. Weekly rotogravure featuring regional and national interest articles (Washington D.C., southern Pennsylvania, Delaware, Maryland, West Virginia and northern Virginia) for people of all ages and all interests. Circ. 1 million (Sunday). Average issue includes 4-6 feature articles and 4-5 columns. Pays on acceptance. Publishes ms an average of 2 months after acceptance. Byline given. Buys all rights or first North American serial rights, depending on fee. Submit seasonal material 4 months in advance. Photocopied submissions OK. Computer printout submissions acceptable; prefers letter-quality to dot-matrix. SASE. Reports in 1 month on queries; 3 weeks on mss. Free sample copy.
Nonfiction: Controversial and consequential articles of regional interest. Subject areas include children, science, politics, law and crime, media, money, arts, behavior, sports, society, and Photo feature. Buys 2 ms/issue. Query with published clips. Length: 1,500-4,500 words. Pays $200-up.
Photos: Reviews 4x5 or larger b&w glossy prints and 35 mm or larger color transparencies. Offers no additional payment for photos accepted with ms. Model release required.
Fiction: Fantasy, humorous, mystery, historical and mainstream. Buys 6 mss/year. Send complete ms. Length: 3,000 words maximum. Pays $200-$750.

Florida

‡**CENTRAL FLORIDA MAGAZINE,** Central Scene Publications, Inc., 341 N. Maitland Ave., Maitland FL 32751. (305)628-8850. Editor: Rowland Stiteler. Monthly magazine covering the lifestyles of central Florida. "Our readers are affluent, recreation and business-oriented area residents who enjoy the good life. Content is positive, upbeat." Circ. 25,000. Pays on publication. Byline given. Offers $25 kill fee. Buys one-time rights; makes work-for-hire assignments. Submit seasonal/holiday material 4 months in advance. Simultaneous queries, and simultaneous, photocopied, and previously published submissions OK. SASE. Reports in 1 month. Sample copy for $1.50, 9x12 SAE and $1.57 postage; writer's guidelines for business size SAE and 1 first class stamp.
Nonfiction: General interest (with local slant); historical/nostalgic (local); interview/profile (local); photo feature (local); and travel. Special issues include interior design, boating and shopping (expensive retail). Buys 20-30 mss/year. Query with published clips if available. Length: 750-2,500 words. Pays $35-750.
Photos: Send photos with query or ms. Pays $25-100 for 35mm color transparencies; $10 for 5x7 and larger b&w prints. Model release and identification of subjects required. Buys negotiable rights.
Fiction: Humorous and mainstream—"only if it has a local tie-in." Buys 1-2 mss/year. Send complete ms. Length: 1,000-3,500 words. Pays $50-300.
Fillers: Clippings, anecdotes, short humor and newsbreaks—"with a local slant."
Tips: "Focus pieces on the activities of people in central Florida. Query with list of five to ten article ideas."

FLORIDA GULF COAST LIVING MAGAZINE, Baker Publications Inc., Suite 109, 1311 N. Westshore Blvd., Tampa FL 33607. Publications Director: Tina Stacy. Executive Editor: Milana McLead Petty. Magazine published 7 times/year covering real estate and related subjects for "newcomers and local residents looking for new housing in the area we cover." Circ. 575,000 annually. Pays on acceptance. Buys all rights. Submit seasonal/holiday material 3 months in advance. Photocopied submissions OK. SASE. Reports in 2 months. Sample copy $2; free writer's guidelines.
Nonfiction: General interest (on housing-related subjects, interior decorating, retirement living, apartment living, moving tips). No personal views. Buys 5-10 mss/year. Query with published clips or send complete ms. Length: 500-1,200 words. Pays $15-125.
Photos: State availability of photos or send photos with ms. "Your package will be more valuable to us if you provide the illustrations. For color work, 35mm is acceptable." Pays $3-10 for color transparencies; $3-5 for 8x10 glossy prints. "I prefer to include photos in the total package fee." Captions and model release required. Buys one-time rights or all rights, depending on the subject.
Columns/Departments: Query with suggestions for new columns or departments.
Tips: "Housing features, retirement living, interiors, home marketplace, products and services, and other ideas, are the departments most open to freelancers. Be sure the subject is pertinent to our magazine. Know our magazine's style and write for it."

FLORIDA KEYS MAGAZINE, FKM Publishing Co., Inc., Box 818, 6161 O/S Hwy., Marathon FL 33050. (305)743-3721. Editor: David Ethridge. 90% freelance written. Bimonthly general interest magazine covering the Florida Keys for residents and tourists. Circ. 10,000. Pays on publication. Publishes ms an average of 3 months after acceptance. Byline given. Buys first serial rights. Submit seasonal/holiday material 3 months in advance. Simultaneous queries and simultaneous and photocopied submissions OK. Computer printout submissions acceptable; prefers letter-quality to dot-matrix. SASE. Reports in 1 month. Sample copy $2.

Nonfiction: General interest; historical/nostalgic; how-to (must be Florida Keys related: how to clean a conch; how to catch a lobster); interview/profile; new product; personal experience; photo feature and local travel. Query with published clips. Length: 400-2,000 words. Pays $3/inch.

Photos: State availability of photos. Reviews 35mm transparencies. Pays $5-20 for 5x7 b&w prints; $15-100 for 5x7 color prints. Identification of subjects required.

GULFSHORE LIFE, Gulfshore Publishing Co., Inc., 3620 Tamiami Trail N., Naples FL 33940. (813)262-6425. Editor: Molly J. Burns. 25% freelance written. Monthly magazine "for an upper-income audience of varied business and academic backgrounds; actively employed and retired; interested in travel, leisure, business, and sports, as well as local environmental issues." Circ. 18,000. Pays on publication. Publishes ms an average of 5 months after acceptance. Byline given. Buys first serial rights and requests permission for subsequent reprint rights in other publications published by the firm. Submit seasonal material 2 months in advance. Photocopied and simultaneous submissions OK. Computer printout submissions acceptable. SASE.

Nonfiction: Local personalities, sports, travel, nature, environment, business, boating and fishing and historical pieces. Everything must be localized to the southwest coast of Florida. No political or controversial articles. Buys 5-10 unsolicited mss/year. Query. Length: 1,500-2,500 words. Pays $75-300.

Tips: "Familiarize yourself with the magazine and the location: Naples, Marco Island, Ft. Myers, Ft. Myers Beach, Sanibel-Captiva, Whiskey Creek, Punta Gorda Isles and Port Charlotte. Submissions accepted at any time."

ISLAND LIFE, The Enchanting Barrier Islands of Florida's Gulf Coast, Island Life Publications, Box X, Sanibel FL 33957. (813)472-4344. Editor: Joan Hooper. Editorial Associate: Susan Shores. 60% freelance written. Quarterly magazine of the Barrier Islands from Longboat Key to Marco Island, for upper-income residents and vacationers of Florida's Gulf Coast area. Circ. 20,000. Pays on publication. Publishes ms an average of 6 months after acceptance. Byline given. Buys first serial rights and second serial (reprint) rights. Submit seasonal/holiday material 6 months in advance. Simultaneous queries, and simultaneous and photocopied submissions OK. Computer printout submissions acceptable; no dot-matrix. SASE. Reports in 2 months on queries; 3 months on mss. Sample copy for $3, 10x13 envelope and 85¢ postage; writer's guidelines for business size SAE and 1 first class stamp.

Nonfiction: General interest, historical/nostalgic, inspirational, interview/profile and travel. No fiction or first person experiences. "Our editorial emphasis is on the history, culture, scenic, sports, social and leisure activities of the area." Buys 30-40 mss/year. Query with published clips. Length: 500-1,500 words. Pays 5¢/word.

Photos: Send photos with query. Pays $5-10 for 2x3 b&w prints; $5-25 for 2x2 or 4x5 color transparencies. Captions, model release, and identification of subjects required.

Tips: "Submissions are rejected if not enough research has gone into the article. Also, we *never* use first person slant."

JACKSONVILLE MAGAZINE, Drawer 329, Jacksonville FL 32201. (904)353-0313. 90% freelance written. Bimonthly. Circ. 13,000. Pays on publication. Buys all rights. Query. Submit seasonal material 3-6 months in advance. Computer printout submissions acceptable; prefers letter-quality to dot-matrix. Reports in 3 weeks. SASE.

Nonfiction: Historical, business and other feature articles pertaining specifically to Jacksonville. Buys 40-45 mss/year. Length: usually 1,500-3,000 words. Pays $100-300.

Photos: Reviews b&w glossy prints with good contrast and color transparencies. Pays $30 minimum for b&w; color terms to be arranged.

Tips: "We are reducing the length of our articles."

THE LOCAL NEWS, The Local News, Inc., Box 466, Windermere FL 32786-0466. (305)298-2401. Associate Editor: Darrell R. Julian. 20% freelance written. A biweekly newsmagazine serving Central Florida. "Our readers tend to fall into two distinct groups: the 25-40 years age group, college educated, upper middle-class from all over the country and the world; and 55 years old or older age group; (perhaps 40% of our readership) most of whom are middle-class retirees from across the nation." Circ. 5,000. Pays on acceptance. Publishes ms an average of 2 months after acceptance. Byline given. Buys one-time rights, first serial rights, and second serial (reprint) rights. Submit seasonal/holiday material 2 months in advance. Photocopied and previously published submissions OK; prefers previously unpublished material. Computer printout submissions acceptable. SASE. Reports in 2 months minimum. Sample copy for 12x15½ SAE, and $1.40 postage, or send postage only; writer's guidelines for business size SAE and 1 first class stamp.

Nonfiction: General interest, humor, interview/profile, opinion and travel. "Although we serve Central Florida, we are not interested in regional material since we develop this work from our staff. All articles must be in good taste; no erotic or tasteless material would be suitable." Buys 30 mss/year. Send complete ms. Length: 750-3,000 words. Pays $20-25.

Photos: Send photos with accompanying ms. Buys one-time rights.

Columns/Departments: "We would like to develop a regular column with wit and humor, and a political column with a conservative orientation." Send complete ms. Pays $20-25.

Fillers: Jokes, anecdotes and short humor. Buys 10/year. Pays $10.

Tips: "The *Local News* plans to become a weekly publication. Articles suited to the Sunday magazine section of a daily newspaper would be desirable. We will consider most material submitted during this transition."

‡**THE MIAMI HERALD, Tropic Magazine**, Knight Ridder Corp., 1 Herald Plaza, Miami FL 33101. (305)376-3432. Editor: Gene Weingarten. Weekly Sunday newspaper magazine for South Florida readers. Circ. 500,000. Pays on publication. Byline given. Buys first serial rights. Submit seasonal/holiday material 3 months in advance. Simultaneous queries, and simultaneous and photocopied submissions OK. SASE. Reports in 6 weeks.

Nonfiction: Tom Shroder, articles editor. General interest, historical/nostalgic, interview/profile, personal experience and photo feature. No fiction, poetry or quizzes. Buys 30 mss/year. Query. Pays $200-800.

Tips: Well-written articles of interest to South Florida or good first person stories are needed.

MIAMI/SOUTH FLORIDA MAGAZINE, (formerly *Miami Magazine*), Box 340008, Coral Gables FL 33134. (305)856-5011. Editor: Erica Rauzin. Managing Editor: Rick Eyerdan. 30% freelance written. Monthly magazine for involved, generally well-educated citizens of South Florida. Circ. 30,000 + . Pays on publication. Publishes ms an average of 2 months after acceptance. Rights purchased vary with author and material; usually buys first serial rights; rarely buys second serial (reprint) rights. Electronic submissions on Apple IIe or III compatible disk OK. Computer printout submissions acceptable. Reports in 2 months. SASE. Sample copy $1.95 and 55¢ postage; free writer's guidelines.

Nonfiction: Investigative pieces on the area; thorough, general features; exciting, in-depth writing. Informational, how-to, interview, profile, local-hook celebrity stories, and repertorial expose. Strong local angle and fresh, opinionated and humorous approach. "No travel stories from freelancers—that's mostly staff generated. We do not like to get freelance manuscripts that are thinly disguised press releases. We don't need film because we have a regular columnist. Writers should READ the magazine first—then they'll know what to send and what not to send." Buys about 30 unsolicited mss/year. Query preferred or submit complete ms. Length: 3,000 words maximum. Pays $100-600. Sometimes pays expenses of writers on assignment (with pre-set limit).

Columns/Departments: Humor, business, books, art (all kinds), profiles and home design. Length: 1,500 words maximum. Pays $100-250.

Tips: "We are regional in our outlook, not just Miami, but also Key West and Ft. Lauderdale."

MIAMI MENSUAL (MIAMI MONTHLY), The International Magazine of South Florida, Quintus Communications Group, 265 Sevilla, Coral Gables FL 33134. (305)444-5678. Editor: Frank Soler. 50% freelance written. City/regional magazine format. "The only Spanish-language monthly city magazine in the U.S. for a sophisticated, decidedly upscale multicultural, multilingual internationally-oriented audience." Circ. 25,000. Pays on publication. Publishes ms an average of 5 months after acceptance. Byline given. Offers 50% kill fee. Buys all rights. Submits seasonal/holiday material 3 months in advance. Simultaneous queries, and simultaneous, photocopied, and previously published submissions OK. Computer printout submissions acceptable; no dot-matrix. SASE. Reports in 2 weeks. Sample copy $1.

Nonfiction: Book excerpts, expose, general interest, humor, interview/profile, opinion, personal experience, photo feature and travel. Buys 50-70 mss/year. Query with published clips or send complete ms. Length: 1,500-3,000 words. Pays variable rates. Pays expenses of writers on assignment.

Photos: Maribel Moore, art director. Send photos with query or ms. Reviews b&w contact sheet, color transparencies and b&w prints. Captions, model release, and identification of subjects required. Buys one-time or all rights.

Columns/Departments: Humor, Opinion, TV, Movies, Audio/Video, Books, Jet Set, and Gastronomy/Wine. "All must be applicable to a highly sophisticated international audience." Buys 50-70 mss/year. Query with published clips or send complete ms. Length: 1,000-1,500 words. Pays variable rates.

Fiction: Adventure and condensed novels. Send complete ms. Length: open. Pays variable rates.

Tips: "We're open to feature stories about or of interest to prominent international figures in business and the arts. Our publication is equivalent to a combination of a glossy city magazine and *Vanity Fair*, *Connoisseur*, and *Town & Country* for Hispanics."

‡**NEW VISTAS**, General Development Corp., Corp. Communications Dept., 1111 S. Bayshore Dr., Miami FL 33131. (305)350-1256. Editor: Robert C. Ross. Managing Editor: Otis Wragg. 50% freelance written. Magazine published 3 times/year on Florida—growth, travel, lifestyle. Reaches residents of General Development's planned communities in Florida (Port Charlotte, Port St. Lucie, Port Malabar, Port LaBelle, Silver Springs Shores, North Port) plus those who own home sites there. Majority of circulation is in Northeast and

Midwest U.S. Interested in people activities, and growth of these communities. Circ. 250,000 + . Pays on publication. Publishes ms an average of 6 months after acceptance. Byline given. Buys first serial rights. Submit seasonal/holiday material 3 months in advance. Computer printout submissions acceptable; prefers letter-quality to dot-matrix. SASE. Reports in 2 weeks. Free sample copy.

Nonfiction: General interest, historical/nostalgic, how-to, photo feature, and travel, all Florida-related. Buys 8 mss/year. Query. Length: 500-2,000 words. Pays $100-600. Sometimes pays expenses of writers on assignment.

Photos: State availability of photos or send photos with query. Reviews 35mm color transparencies. Captions required. Buys one-time rights.

Tips: "Familiarity with Florida, and General Development's planned communities is a plus. We usually buy one Florida travel article per issue. Destinations close to General Development communities are best."

ORLANDO-LAND MAGAZINE, Box 2207, Orlando FL 32802. (305)644-3355. Editor-in-Chief: E.L. Prizer. Managing Editor: Carole De Pinto. Monthly magazine; 144 pages. Emphasizes central Florida information for "a readership made up primarily of people new to Florida—those here as visitors, traveling businessmen, new residents." Circ. 26,000. Pays on acceptance. Byline given. Buys all rights or first North American serial rights. Phone queries OK. Submit seasonal/holiday material 4 months in advance. Photocopied and previously published submissions OK. Computer printout submissions acceptable. SASE. Reports in 6 weeks. Sample copy $3.

Nonfiction: Historical, how-to and informational. "Things involved in living in Florida." Pay $50-150.

Photos: Reviews b&w glossy prints. Pays $5.

Tips: "We are always in need of *useful* advice-type material presented as first person experience that relates to the central Florida area. Also, travel (excursion) pieces to places open to the general public within one day's (there and back) journey of Orlando or experience pieces (hobbies, sports, etc.) that would not be practical for staff writers—sky diving, delta kites, etc. Must be available in central Florida. Specialized topical columns are being added in health, environment, architecture and travel."

‡SOUTH FLORIDA HOME & GARDEN, Meyer Publications, 75 SW 15 Rd., Miami FL 33129. (305)374-5011. Editor: Erica Rauzin. Managing Editor: Maureen Griess-Glabman. 70% freelance written. Monthly magazine of South Florida homes, interior design, architecture, gardening, landscaping, cuisine and home entertainment. "We want beautiful, clever, interesting, practical specific coverage of subjects listed as they relate to South Florida." Estab. 1984. Circ. 17,000. Pays 15 days before publication. Publishes ms an average of 4 months after acceptance. Byline given. Offers $25 kill fee. Buys all rights or first serial rights and reprint rights, depending on story. Submit seasonal/holiday material 6 months in advance. Electronic submissions OK on Apple IIE or III, but requires hard copy also. Computer printout submissions acceptable. SASE. Sample copy $2.50; writers guidelines for #10 SAE and 1 first class stamp.

Nonfiction: General interest (in our subjects); how-to (interior design and gardening for southern Florida climate and cuisine); new product (short); technical (popularized, well-written); and travel (home architecture or garden destinations only). Buys 100 mss/year. Query with or without published clips. Length: 200-1,000 words. Pays $50-300; (rarely more). Pays expenses of writers on assignment.

Photos: Debra Yates, photo editor. State availability of photos or send photos with query. Reviews 35mm, 4x5 or 2" color transparencies or 2" b&w prints. Captions and identification of subjects required. Buys one-time rights plus one re-use of separations.

Columns/Departments: Homecare—specific home how-to; Garden care; Ideas; Cuisine; Home Business; Parties; Architecture; and Florida Artists. Buys 36 mss/year. Query with or without published clips. Length: 200-1,000 words. Pays $75-300.

SOUTH FLORIDA LIVING, Baker Publications, Inc., Suite 102, Bldg. 3, 700 W. Hillsboro Blvd., Deerfield Beach FL 33441. (305)428-5602. Editor: Eugenio J. Olazábal. 70% freelance written. Bimonthly magazine covering real estate market in Dade, Broward, Martin, Palm Beach, St. Lucie and Indian River counties, for newcomers and home buyers. Circ. 80,000 (North edition); 40,000 (South edition). Pays on acceptance. Publishes ms an average of 3 months after acceptance. Byline given. Buy first serial rights; makes work-for-hire assignments. Submit seasonal/holiday material 4 months in advance. Photocopied and previously published submissions OK. SASE. Reports in 2 weeks. Free sample copy and writer's guidelines.

Nonfiction: Real estate industry trends; home security; historical; how-to (finance, build, design); moving tips; landscaping and gardening; banking; interior decorating; retirement living; and apartment living. No personal stories or articles not related to South Florida. Buys 18-20 mss/year. Query letters, "no phone calls, please." Length: 1,500-2,000 words. Pays 10¢/word for local stories.

Photos: State availability of photos. Pays negotiable fee for 35mm color transparencies and 5x7 b&w prints. Captions and model release required. Buys all rights.

Tips: "National assignments on decorating, financing, etc., for all of Baker's city magazines are made by Tina Stacy, publication director. Payment is 20¢/word. Query her at: *Living*, Suite 400, 5757 Alpha Rd., Dallas TX 75240."

SUNSHINE MAGAZINE, The Magazine of the Fort Lauderdale News & Sun-Sentinel, The News & Sun-Sentinel Co., Box 14430, Fort Lauderdale FL 33302. (305)761-4017. Editor: John Parkyn. A general interest Sunday magazine for the newspaper's 600,000 readers in South Florida. Estab. 1983. Circ. 300,000. Pays within 1 month of acceptance. Byline given. Offers 25% kill fee. Buys first serial rights or one-time rights in the state of Florida. Submit seasonal/holiday material 2 months in advance. Simultaneous queries, and simultaneous, photocopied, and previously published submissions OK. SASE. Reports in 2 weeks on queries; 1 month on mss. Free sample copy and writer's guidelines.
Nonfiction: General interest, how-to, interview/profile and travel. "Articles must be relevant to the interests of adults living in South Florida." Buys about 100 mss/year. Query with published clips. Length: 1,000-3,000 words; preferred length 2,000-3,000 words. Pays 20-25¢/word to $750 maximum (occasionally higher).
Photos: State availability of photos. Pays negotiable rate for 35mm color slides and 8x10 b&w prints. Captions, model release, and identification of subjects required. Buys one-time rights for the state of Florida.
Tips: "Do NOT phone—we don't have the staff to handle calls of this type—but do include your phone number on query letter. Keep your writing tight and concise—readers don't have the time to wade through masses of 'pretty' prose. Be as sophisticated and stylish as you can—Sunday magazines have come a long way from the Sunday 'supps' of yesteryear."

TALLAHASSEE MAGAZINE, Marketplace Communications, Inc., Box 12848, Tallahassee FL 32317. (904)385-3310. Editor: William L. Needham. Managing Editor: W.R. Lundquist. 80% freelance written. Quarterly magazine covering people, events and history in and around Florida's capital city. Circ. 16,000. Pays on publication. Publishes ms an average of 3 months after acceptance. Buys first serial rights. Submit seasonal/holiday material 6 months in advance. Simultaneous queries, and photocopied and previously published submissions OK. Computer printout submissions acceptable; prefers letter-quality to dot-matrix. SASE. Reports in 1 month. Sample copy for 9x12 SAE.
Nonfiction: General interest (relating to Florida or Southeast); historical/nostalgic (for Tallahassee, North Florida, South Georgia); and interview/profile (related to North Florida, South Georgia). No fiction, poetry or topics unrelated to area. Buys 20 mss/year. Query. Length: 500-1,400 words. Pays 10¢/word.
Photos: State availability of photos with query. Pays $35 minimum for 35mm color transparencies; $20 minimum for b&w prints. Model release and identification of subjects required. Buys one-time rights.
Tips: "We seek to show positive aspects of life in and around Tallahassee. Know the area. A brief author biographic note should accompany manuscripts."

TAMPA BAY MONTHLY, Florida City Magazines, Inc. 2502 Rocky Point Dr., Tampa FL 33607. Managing Editor: Laura Kelly. Associate Editor: Ellen Goldberg. 85% freelance written. Monthly magazine for upscale Tampa Bay area readers. Circ. 25,000. Pays within 30 days of publication. Publishes ms an average of 6 months after acceptance. Byline given. Buys first serial rights. Submit seasonal/holiday material 3 months in advance. Simultaneous queries OK. Computer printout submissions acceptable; prefers letter-quality to dot-matrix. SASE. Reports in 6 weeks. Free writer's guidelines available upon request.
Nonfiction: In-depth investigative, general interest, humor, historical/nostalgic, and interview/profile—pertaining to the Tampa Bay area reader. Occasionally needs get-away pieces for Bay Area residents, fashion pieces and food/drink articles. Buys 24-36 mss/year. Query with published clips. Length: 300-500 words for short articles; 3,000-5,000 words for feature articles. Pays $50-500. Will consider book or movie reviews. Sometimes pays expenses of writers on assignment.
Photos: Sergio Waksman, creative director. State availability of photos. Reviews contact sheets. Captions, model release, and identification of subjects required. Buys all rights.
Tips: "The writer has a better chance of breaking in at our publication with short articles and fillers because we can test their style to see if it suits our need."

TROPIC MAGAZINE, see *The Miami Herald* on page 479.

Georgia

ATLANTA JOURNAL-CONSTITUTION, Box 4689, Atlanta GA 30302. (404)526-5479. Travel Editor: Colin Bessonette. Weekly section of daily newspaper, covering travel. Circ. 605,000. Byline given. Submit

seasonal/holiday material 1 month in advance. Simultaneous queries OK. SASE required.
Nonfiction: Travel (any mode of transportation). Buys 50 unsolicited mss/year. Query. Length: 1,200-1,600 words. Pays $100-125.
Photos: Reviews any size b&w glossy prints. Identification of subjects required. Buys one-time rights.
Tips: "We prefer practical, useful information woven into stories on popular (not off-the-wall) destinations."

ATLANTA WEEKLY, Atlanta Newspapers, Box 4689, Atlanta GA 30302. (404)526-5415. Editor: Lee Walburn. 80% freelance written. Sunday general interest magazine. Circ. 500,000. Pays on acceptance. Publishes ms an average of 3 months after acceptance. Byline given. Offers 40% kill fee. Buys one-time rights. Submit seasonal/holiday material 6 months in advance. Simultaneous queries and previously published submissions OK. Computer printout submissions acceptable; no dot-matrix. SASE. Reports in 6 weeks. Free sample copy and writer's guidelines.
Nonfiction: Chris Wohlwend, articles editor. Book excerpts and general interest. "Articles should deal with topics of interest around Atlanta, the South and Southeast." Special issues include home decorating issue; fashion issue; and Christmas gift guide. Buys 100 mss/year. Query with published clips if available. Length: 250-3,000 words. Pays $50-800. Pays expenses of writers on assignment.
Photos: Ike Hussey, photo editor. State availability of photos.
Fillers: Contact: ETC editor. Short humor and newsbreaks. Buys 20/year. Length: 100-200 words. Pays $15-50.

‡AUGUSTA SPECTATOR, Box 3168, Augusta GA 30902. (404)733-1476. Publisher: Faith Bertsche. Magazine published 3 times/year about the Augusta, Georgia and Aiken, South Carolina area for readers who are upper middle class residents, Ft. Gordon army post and medical complex personnel and visitors to the Masters Golf Tournament. Circ. 5,000. Pays on publication. Publishes ms an average of 4 months after acceptance. Byline given. Buys first serial rights. Submit seasonal material 6 months in advance. Simultaneous, photocopied, and previously published submissions OK. Computer printout submissions acceptable; prefers letter-quality to dot-matrix. SASE. Sample copy $1; writer's guidelines for SASE.
Nonfiction: General interest (for people interested in golf, horses and local topical issues); historical (issues concerning the Southeast); interview (of outstanding people of local interest); nostalgia (with a Southern flavor); profile; humor (related to the Masters, polo, birddog trials). Buys 4 unsolicited mss/year. Query. Length: 2,500 words maximum. Pays $25.
Fiction: Adventure, humorous, mystery, romance, suspense and historical. No unnecessary violence. Buys 2 mss/issue. Send complete ms. Length: 2,500 words maximum.
Poetry: Dr. John May, editor. Free verse and traditional. Submit maximum 6 poems. Pays in copies.
Tips: "The most frequent mistakes made by writers in completing an article for us are ignoring the word limit and/or having insufficient or poor photos."

GEORGIA JOURNAL, Agee Publishers, Inc., Box 526, Athens GA 30603. (404)548-5269. Editor: Jane Agee. 50% freelance written. Bimonthly magazine covering the state of Georgia. Circ. 5,000. Pays on acceptance. Publishes ms an average of 6 months after acceptance. Byline given. Buys first serial rights. Submit seasonal/holiday material 4-6 months in advance. Photocopied submissions OK. Computer printout submissions acceptable; no dot-matrix. Reports in 1 month. Sample copy $3; writer's guidelines for SAE and 1 first class stamp.
Nonfiction: "We are interested in almost everything going on within the state. Although we specialize in an area, we maintain a general interest format. We do prefer to get pieces that are current that have a human interest slant. We are also very interested in natural science pieces. We do our special focus issues and suggest that writers send for special focus schedule. We are always swamped with historical articles, and we are not interested in sentimental reminiscences, anything risque, specifically political or religious pieces. Buys 50-60 mss/year. Query. Length: 1,200-2,000 words. Pays $20-25. Sometimes pays expenses of writers on assignment.
Photos: State availability of photos or send photos with query or ms. Reviews sharp 8x10 b&w glossies. Captions, model release, and identification of subjects required.
Fiction: Hugh Agee, fiction editor. "Because we are in almost all school systems in the state, fiction must be suitable for all ages." Buys 3-4 mss/year. Send complete ms. Length: 1,200-2,000 words. Pays $25.
Poetry: Peggy Lyles, poetry editor. Free verse, haiku, light verse and traditional. No poetry specifically dealing with another part of the country (out of the South) or anything not suitable for school children. "Most of our school-age readers are middle school and older." Buys 20 poems/year. Submit maximum 4 poems. Length: 25 lines. Pays in copies.
Tips: "We have a section of short pieces (3-8 paragraphs) called Under the Chinaberry Tree where we always need good general interest submissions. These pieces are usually on topics not meriting feature article length. See a sample copy for Chinaberry Tree pieces that have been used. Another area for freelancers is Georgia Makers where we feature very short pieces on individuals in Georgia who have done something of merit or who have a human interest slant. Basically, though, it is merit-oriented."

Hawaii

‡**ALOHA, THE MAGAZINE OF HAWAII AND THE PACIFIC,** Davick Publishing Co., 828 Fort Street Mall, Honolulu HI 96813. Editor: Rita Ariyoshi. 60% freelance written. *Aloha* is a bimonthly regional magazine of international interest. "Most of our audience does not live in Hawaii, although most readers have been to the islands at least once. Even given this fact, the magazine is directed primarily to residents of Hawaii in the belief that presenting material to an immediate critical audience will result in a true and accurate presentation that can be appreciated by everyone. *Aloha* is not a tourist or travel publication and is not geared to such a readership, although travelers will find it to be of great value." Circ. 80,000. Pays on publication. Publishes ms an average of 4 months after acceptance; unsolicited ms can take a year or more. Byline given. Offers variable kill fee. Buys all rights. Submit seasonal/holiday material 1 year in advance. Photocopied submissions OK. Computer printout submissions acceptable; no dot-matrix. SASE. Reports in 2 months. Sample copy $2.50; writer's guidelines for SAE with 1 first class stamp.

Nonfiction: Book excerpts; historical/nostalgic (historical articles must be researched with bibliography); interview/profile; and photo feature. Subjects include the arts, business, people, sports, special places, food, interiors, history and Hawaiian. "We don't want stories of a tourist's experiences in Waikiki or odes to beautiful scenery. We don't want an outsider's impressions of Hawaii, written for outsiders." Buys 24 mss/year. Query with published clips. Length: 1,000-4,000 words. Pays 10¢/word. Sometimes pays expenses of writers on assignment.

Photos: State availability of photos with query. Pays $25 for b&w prints; prefers negatives and contact sheets. Pays $50 for 35mm (minimum size) color transparencies used inside; $50 for color transparencies used as cover art. "*Aloha* features two photo essays in each issue. Beautiful Hawaii, a collection of photographs illustrating that theme, appears in every issue. A second photo essay by a sole photographer on a theme of his/her own choosing is also a regular feature. Queries are essential for the sole photographer essay." Model release and identification of subjects required. Buys one-time rights.

Fiction: Ethnic and historical. "Fiction depicting a tourist's adventures in Waikiki is not what we're looking for. As a general statement, we welcome material reflecting the true Hawaiian experience." Buys 2 mss/year. Send complete ms. Length: 1,000-2,500 words. Pays 10¢/word.

Poetry: Haiku, light verse and traditional. No seasonal poetry and poetry related to other areas of the world. Buys 6 poems/year. Submit maximum 6 poems. Prefers "shorter poetry." Pays $25.

Tips: "Read *Aloha*. Be meticulous in research and have good illustrative material available, i.e., photos in most cases."

HONOLULU, Honolulu Publishing Co., Ltd., 36 Merchant St., Honolulu HI 96813. (808)524-7400. Editor: Brian Nicol. 20% freelance written. Monthly magazine covering general interest topics relating to Hawaii. Circ. 35,000. Pays on acceptance. Publishes ms an average of 5 months after acceptance. Byline given. Offers $50 kill fee. Buys first serial rights. Submit seasonal/holiday material 5 months in advance. Simultaneous queries, and simultaneous and photocopied submissions OK. Computer printout submissions acceptable; prefers letter-quality to dot-matrix. SASE. Sample copy $2, 9x11 SAE and $2.30 postage.

Nonfiction: Marilyn Kim, articles editor. Expose, general interest, historical/nostalgic, and photo feature—all Hawaii-related. "We run regular features on food, fashion, interior design, travel, etc., plus other timely, provocative articles. No personal experience articles." Buys 10 mss/year. Query with published clips if available. Length: 2,500-5,000 words. Pays $250-400. Sometimes pays expenses of writers on assignment.

Photos: Teresa Black, photo editor. State availability of photos. Pays $15 maximum for b&w contact sheet; $25 maximum for 35mm color transparencies. Captions and identification of subjects required. Buys one-time rights.

Columns/Departments: Marilyn Kim, column/department editor. Calabash (light, "newsy," timely, humorous column on any Hawaii-related subject). Buys 15 mss/year. Query with published clips or send complete ms. Length: 250-1,000 words. Pays $25-35.

‡**MAUIAN MAGAZINE, About Maui People,** Sandwich Islands Publishing, Ltd., Box 10669, Lahaina HI 96761. (808)661-5844. Managing Editor: Joe Harabin. 90% freelance written. Monthly magazine about Maui people (resident and visitor). "We are an upbeat, positive magazine about Maui people, places and businesses. As Maui's only regional magazine we are directed to all people who love Maui, America's top Pacific upscale travel destination. In addition, we feature interviews with celebrities, scientists, artists and business people who live in or visit Maui." Estab. 1984. Circ. 65,000. Pays on publication. Publishes ms an average of 2 months after acceptance. Byline given. Buys first North American serial rights (with right to reprint; author may resell). Submit seasonal/holiday material 2 months in advance. Simultaneous queries, and simultaneous, photocopied, and previously published submissions OK. Computer printout submissions acceptable; prefers letter-quality to dot-matrix. SASE. Reports in 2 weeks on queries; 4 weeks on mss. Free sample copy and writer's guidelines.

Nonfiction: Book excerpts, general interest, historical/nostalgic, humor, inspirational, interview/profile, new product, personal experience, photo feature, technical and travel. Buys 80 mss/year. Send complete ms.

Length: 400-3,000 words. Pays $100-300 or 10¢/word.
Photos: Send photos with ms. Reviews b&w contact sheet, negatives and 8x10 prints and color transparencies. Pays $15 for b&w negatives and prints; $25 for transparencies. Captions, model release, and identification of subjects required. Buys rights to use and perhaps re-use.
Columns/Departments: Query or send complete ms. Length: 400-1,500 words. Pays $50-150.
Fillers: Clippings, jokes, gags, anecdotes, short humor and newsbreaks. Buys 10-30/year. Pays 5-10¢.
Tips: Submit all articles with color slides and b&w negatives.

Illinois

CHICAGO MAGAZINE, 3 Illinois Center, Chicago IL 60601. Editorial Director: Don Gold. Editor: John Fink. 40% freelance written. Monthly magazine for an audience which is "95% from Chicago area; 90% college-trained; upper income; overriding interests in the arts, dining, good life in the city and suburbs. Most are in 25-50 age bracket, well-read and articulate. Generally liberal inclination." Circ. 217,000. Buys first serial rights and second serial (reprint) rights for 90 days only. Pays on acceptance. Publishes ms an average of 5 months after acceptance if unassigned; 3 months if assigned. Submit seasonal material 4 months in advance. Computer printout submissions acceptable "if legible"; no dot-matrix. SASE. Reports in 2 weeks. Query; indicate "specifics, knowledge of city and market, and demonstrable access to sources." For sample copy, send $3 to Circulation Dept.; writer's guidelines with SASE.
Nonfiction: "On themes relating to the quality of life in Chicago: past, present, and future." Writers should have "a general awareness that the readers will be concerned, influential longtime Chicagoans reading what the writer has to say about their city. We generally publish material too comprehensive for daily newspapers or of too specialized interest for them." Personal experience and think pieces, interviews, profiles, humor, spot news, historical articles, travel and exposes. Buys about 50 mss/year. Length: 1,000-6,000 words. Pays $100-$2,500. Pays expenses of writers on assignment.
Photos: Reviews b&w glossy prints, 35mm color transparencies or color prints. Usually assigned separately, not acquired from writers.
Fiction: Christine Newman, fiction editor. Mainstream, fantasy and humor. Preferably with Chicago orientation. "Although we receive hundreds of short stories each year, we only publish about a half dozen." No word length limits, but "no novels, please." Pays $1,000-2,000.
Tips: "Submit plainly, be business-like and avoid cliche ideas."

CHICAGO READER, Box 11101, Chicago IL 60611. (312)828-0350. Editor: Robert A. Roth. 80% freelance written. "The *Reader* is distributed free in Chicago's lakefront neighborhoods. Generally speaking, these are Chicago's best educated, most affluent neighborhoods—and they have an unusually high concentration of young adults." Weekly tabloid; 128 pages. Circ. 117,000. Pays "by 15th of month following publication." Buys all rights. Byline given. Phone queries OK. Photocopied submissions OK. Computer printout submissions acceptable; prefers letter-quality to dot-matrix. SASE. Reports "very slow," up to 1 year or more.
Nonfiction: "We want magazine features on Chicago topics. Will also consider reviews." Buys 500 mss/year. Submit complete ms. Length: "Whatever's appropriate to the story." Pays $50-675.
Photos: By assignment only.
Columns/Departments: By assignment only.

ILLINOIS TIMES, Downstate Illinois' Weekly Newspaper, Illinois Times, Inc., Box 3524, Springfield IL 62708. (217)753-2226. Editor: Fletcher Farrar Jr. 50% freelance written. Weekly tabloid covering that part of the state outside of Chicago and its suburbs for a discerning, well-educated readership. Circ. 23,000. Pays on publication. Publishes ms an average of 2 months after acceptance. Byline given. Buys first serial rights and second serial (reprint) rights. Submit seasonal/holiday material 1 month in advance. Simultaneous queries, and simultaneous, photocopied, and previously published submissions OK. Computer printout submissions acceptable. SASE. Reports in 3 weeks on queries; 8 weeks on mss. Sample copy 50¢.
Nonfiction: Book excerpts, expose, general interest, historical, how-to, interview/profile, opinion, personal experience, photo feature, travel ("in our area"), book reviews, politics, environment, energy, etc. "We are not likely to use a story that has no Illinois tie-in." Annual special issues: Lincoln (February); Health & Fitness (March); Gardening (April); Summer (June); Fall Home (September); and Christmas (books). No articles filled with "bureaucratese or generalities; no articles naively glorifying public figures or celebrity stories for celebrity's sake." Buys 50 mss/year. Query or send complete ms. Length: From 1,500 to 2,500 words maximum. Pays 4¢/word; $100 maximum.
Photos: State availability of photos. Pays $15 for 8x10 prints. Identification of subjects required. Buys one-time rights.
Columns/Departments: Guestwork (opinion column, any subject of personal experience with an Illinois angle). Buys 25 mss/year. Send complete ms. Length: 1,500 words maximum. Pays 4¢/word; $60 maximum.

Tips: "The ideal *IT* story is one the reader hates to put down. Good writing, in our view, is not necessarily fancy writing. It is (in the words of a colleague) 'whatever will engage the disinterested reader.' In other words, nothing dull, please. But remember that any subject—even the investment policies of public pension funds—can be made 'engaging.' It's just that some subjects require more work than others. Good illustrations are a plus. As an alternative newspaper we prefer to treat subjects in depth or not at all. Please, no general articles that lack an Illinois angle."

Indiana

INDIANAPOLIS, 32 E. Washington St., Indianapolis IN 46204. (317)639-6600. Editor: Nancy Comiskey. 90% freelance written. Monthly magazine emphasizing Indianapolis-related problems/features or regional related topics. Circ. 20,000. Pays on publication. Publishes ms an average of 4 months after acceptance. Byline given. Buys one-time rights. Queries only. Submit seasonal/holiday material 4 months in advance. Simultaneous, photocopied, and previously published submissions OK. Computer printout submissions acceptable; prefers letter-quality to dot-matrix. SASE. Reports in 1 month. Sample copy $1; writer's guidelines for SASE.
Nonfiction: Expose (interested, but have no specifics; "we're interested in any Indianapolis-related topic including government and education"); historical (Indianapolis-related only); how-to (buying tips); inspirational; interview (Indianapolis-related person, native sons and daughters); nostalgia; photo feature; profile; and travel (within a day's drive of Indianapolis). "We *only* want articles with Indianapolis or central Indiana ties, no subjects outside of our region. No essays or opinions—unless they are qualified by professional credits for an opinion/essay. We aren't very interested in broad-based, national topics without a local angle. National issues can be broken into 'how does it affect Indianapolis?' or 'what does it mean for Indianapolis?' (We're big on sidebars.)" Query. Length: 500-3,500 words. Pays $40-300.
Photos: State availability of photos. Pays $30 for b&w; $50 for color transparencies. Captions required. Buys one-time rights.
Columns/Departments: Business, life style, sports, marketplace, leisure, money, health and people.
Tips: "We are interested in trends and issues facing Indianapolis now. Manuscripts have a *strong* local angle."

MICHIANA, Sunday Magazine of *The South Bend Tribune*, Colfax at Lafayette, South Bend IN 46626. (219)233-6161. Editor: Bill Sonneborn. 80% freelance written. Weekly for "average daily newspaper readers; perhaps a little above average since we have more than a dozen colleges and universities in our area." Circ. 125,000. Pays on publication. Publishes ms an average of 3 months after acceptance. Byline given. Buys first North American serial rights or simultaneous rights providing material offered will be used outside of Indiana and Michigan. Will consider photocopied submissions if clearly legible. Computer printout submissions acceptable; prefers letter-quality to dot-matrix. Reports in 2 weeks. SASE.
Nonfiction: "Items of general and unusual interest written in good, clear, simple sentences with logical approach to subject. We like material oriented to the Midwest, especially Indiana, Michigan, Ohio and Illinois. We avoid all freelance material that supports movements of a political nature. We seldom use first person humor. We use no poetry." Submit complete ms. Buys 100 unsolicited mss/year. Length: 800-3,000 words. Payment is $50-60 minimum, with increases as deemed suitable.
Photos: All mss must be accompanied by illustrations, b&w photos or 35mm or larger color transparencies.

‡**RIGHT HERE, The Hometown Magazine**, Right Here Publications, Box 1014, Huntington IN 46750. Editor: Emily Jean Carroll. 90% freelance written. Bimonthly magazine of general family interest reaching a northern Indiana audience. Estab. 1984. Circ. 2,000. Pays 2 weeks after date of issue. Publishes ms an average of 4 months after acceptance. Byline given. Buys one-time rights, simultaneous rights, and second serial (reprint) rights. Submit seasonal/holiday material 5 months in advance. Simultaneous, photocopied, and previously published submissions OK. Computer printout submissions acceptable; prefers letter-quality to dot-matrix. SASE. Reports in 4 weeks on queries; 2 months on mss. Sample copy $1.25; writer's guidelines for SAE and 1 first class stamp.
Nonfiction: General interest, historical/nostalgic, how-to, humor, inspirational, interview/profile, opinion, and travel. "We are looking for short pieces on all aspects of Hoosier living." Profiles, nostalgia, history, recreation, travel, music and various subjects of interest to area readers. "We can use material for Kid Stuff pages—poems, puzzles, short stories, etc." Buys 18 mss/year. Send complete ms. Length: 900-2,000 words. Pays $5-20.
Photos: Send photos with ms. Reviews b&w prints. Pays $2-5. Model release and identification of subjects required. Buys one-time rights.
Columns/Departments: Listen To This: Opinion pieces of about 1,000 words; Here and There: Travel pieces in or near Indiana; Remember?: Nostalgia, up to 2,000 words; Keeping Up: Mental, spiritual, self-help, uplifting, etc., to 2,000 words; Here's How: Short how-tos, hints, special recipes, instructional; My Space: Writers 19 years old and under, to 1,000 words; and Kid Stuff: puzzles, poems, stories to 1,000 words. Buys 30-40

mss/year. Query or send complete ms. Length: 800-2,000 words. Pays $5-20.

Fiction: Humorous, mainstream, mystery and romance. Needs short stories of about 2,000 words. Buys 6-8 mss/year. Send complete ms. Length: 900-3,000 words. Pays $5-20.

Poetry: Free verse, light verse and traditional. Buys 30-40/year. Submit maximum 6 poems. Length: 4-48 lines. Pays $1-4 for poetry featured separately; free copy for poetry used as filler or on poetry page.

Fillers: Anecdotes and short humor. Buys 6-8/year. Length: 300 words maximum. Pays $3 maximum. Free copy for material under 300 words.

Tips: "All departments are open. Keep it light—keep it tight." Send short cover letter.

Iowa

THE IOWAN MAGAZINE, Mid-America Publishing Corp., 214 9th St., Des Moines IA 50309. (515)282-8220. Editor: Charles W. Roberts. 65% freelance written. Quarterly magazine covering history, people, places and points of interest in Iowa. Circ. 24,000. Pays on publication. Publishes ms an average of 1 year after acceptance. Byline given. Buys one-time rights. Submit seasonal/holiday material 5 months in advance. Photocopied and previously published submissions OK. Computer printout submissions acceptable. Reports in 1 month. Sample copy for $3.75, 9x12 SAE and $1.75 postage; free writer's guidelines.

Nonfiction: General interest; historical (history as in American heritage, not personal reminiscence); interview/profile; and travel. No "articles from nonIowans who come for a visit and wish to give their impression of the state." Buys 32 mss/year. Query with published clips. Length: 750-3,000 words. Pays $75-300. Sometimes pays expenses of writers on assignment.

Photos: Send photos with ms. Pays $10-25 for b&w; $35-50 for color transparency. Captions and identification of subjects required.

Tips: "If you are writing about Iowa, write on a specific topic. Don't be *too* general. Write a query letter with maybe two or three ideas."

Kansas

KANSAS!, Kansas Department of Economic Development, 503 Kansas Ave., 6th Floor, Topeka KS 66603. (913)296-3479. Editor: Andrea Glenn. 90% freelance written. Quarterly magazine; 40 pages. Emphasizes Kansas "faces and places for all ages, occupations and interests." Circ. 48,000. Pays on acceptance. Publishes ms an average of 1 year after acceptance. Byline given. Buys one-time rights. Submit seasonal/holiday material 8 months in advance. Simultaneous, photocopied, and previously published submissions OK. Computer printout submissions acceptable; no dot-matrix. SASE. Reports in 2 months. Free sample copy and writer's guidelines.

Nonfiction: "Material must be Kansas-oriented and well written. We run stories about Kansas people, places and events that can be enjoyed by the general public. In other words, events must be open to the public, places also. People featured must have interesting crafts etc." General interest, interview, photo feature, profile and travel. No exposes. Query. "Query letter should clearly outline story in mind. I'm especially interested in Kansas freelancers who can supply their own photos." Length: 5-7 pages double-spaced, typewritten copy. Pays $75-125. Sometimes pays expenses of writers on assignment.

Photos: "We are a full-color photo/manuscript publication." State availability of photos with query. Pays $25-50 (generally included in ms rate) for 35mm color transparencies. Captions required.

Tips: "History and nostalgia stories do not fit into our format because they can't be illustrated well with color photography."

‡KANSAS CITY MAGAZINE, 3401 Main St., Kansas City MO 64111. (816)561-0444. Editor: Lyn Foister. 75% freelance written. Monthly; 80-96 pages. Circ. 16,000. Freelance material is considered if it is about Kansas City issues, events or people. Publishes ms an average of 3 months after acceptance. Buys all rights. Written queries only; queries and mss should be accompanied by SASE. Electronic submissions OK on AM Comp Edit, but requires hard copy also. Computer printout submissions acceptable; prefers letter-quality to dot-matrix. Reports in 1 month. Sample copy $3.

Nonfiction: Editorial content is issue- or personality-oriented, investigative reporting, profiles, or lengthy news features. Short items of 250-350 words considered for City Window column; pays $25. Longer stories of 2,000-8,000 words pay negotiable depending on story, plus expenses. Columns, which include inside business, travel, lifestyle, dining out, profile, and a Postscript essay, are from 1,600-3,000 words and pay $100-200. All material must have a demonstrable connection to Kansas City. Bylines are always given, except for City Window material. Sometimes pays expenses of writers on assignment.

Tips: Freelancers should show some previous reporting or writing experience of a professional nature. "The writer has a better chance of breaking in at our publication with short articles and fillers. We like to see their work on easier-to-verify stories, such as Lifestyle before committing to a longer, tougher reporting field."

Kentucky

KENTUCKY HAPPY HUNTING GROUND, Kentucky Dept. of Fish and Wildlife Resources, 1 Game Farm Rd., Frankfort KY 40601. (502)564-4336. Editor: John Wilson. 10% freelance written. A bimonthly state conservation magazine covering hunting, fishing, general outdoor recreation, conservation of wildlife and other natural resources. Circ. 35,000. Pays on publication. Publishes ms an average of 2 months after acceptance. Byline given. Buys one-time rights. Submit seasonal/holiday material 3 months in advance. Previously published submissions OK. Computer printout submissions acceptable. SASE. Reports in 3 weeks on queries; 2 months on mss. Free sample copy.
Nonfiction: General interest, historical/nostalgic, how-to, humor, interview/profile, personal experience and photo feature. All articles should deal with some aspect of the natural world, with outdoor recreation or with natural resources conservation or management, and should relate to Kentucky. "No 'Me and Joe' stories (i.e., accounts of specific trips); nothing off-color or otherwise unsuitable for a state publication." Buys 3-6 mss/year. Query or send complete ms. Length: 500-2,000 words. Pays $50-150 (with photos).
Photos: State availability of photos with query; send photos with accompanying ms. Reviews color transparencies (2¼ preferred, 35mm acceptable) and b&w prints (5x7 minimum). No separate payment for photos, but amount paid for article will be determined by number of photos used.
Tips: "We would be much more kindly disposed toward articles accompanied by several good photographs (or other graphic material) than to those without."

Louisiana

‡**SUNDAY ADVOCATE MAGAZINE**, Box 588, Baton Rouge LA 70821. (504)383-1111, ext. 319. Editor: Charles H. Lindsay. Byline given. Pays on publication. SASE.
Nonfiction and Photos: Well-illustrated, short articles; must have local, area or Louisiana angle, in that order of preference. Photos purchased with mss. Rates vary.

Maine

‡**DOWN EAST MAGAZINE**, Camden ME 04843. (207)594-9544. Editor: Davis Thomas. Emphasizes Maine people, places, events and heritage. Monthly magazine. Circ. 70,000. Pays on acceptance for text; on publication for photos. Byline given. Offers 15% kill fee. Buys first North American serial rights. Phone queries OK. Submit seasonal/holiday material 6 months in advance. SASE. Reports in 1 month. Sample copy $2; free writer's guidelines with SASE.
Nonfiction: Submit to Manuscript Editor. All material must be directly related to Maine: profiles, biographies, nature, gardening, nautical, travel, recreation, historical, humorous, nostalgic pieces, and photo essays and stories. Recent article example: "Old Town Canoe Bounces Back," (April 1985). Buys 40 unsolicited mss/year. Length: 600-2,500 words. Pays up to $300, depending on subject and quality.
Photos: Purchases on assignment or with accompanying ms. Accepts 35mm color transparencies and 8x10 b&w. Also purchases single b&w and color scenics for calendars. Each photo or transparency must bear photographer's name. Captions and model release required. Pays page rate of $50.
Columns/Departments: Short Travel (600-1,500 words, tightly written travelogs focusing on small geographic areas of scenic, historical or local interest); I Remember (short personal accounts of some incident in Maine, less than 1,000 words); and It Happened Down East (1-2 paragraphs, humorous Maine anecdotes). Pay depends on subject and quality.
Tips: "We depend on freelance writers for the bulk of our material—mostly on assignment and mostly from those known to us; but unsolicited submissions are valued."

GREATER PORTLAND MAGAZINE, Chamber of Commerce of the Greater Portland Region, 142 Free St., Portland ME 04101. (207)772-2811. Editor: Colin W. Sargent. 100% freelance written. A quarterly magazine covering metropolitan and island lifestyles of Greater Portland. "We cover the arts, night life, islands, people, and progressive business atmosphere in and around Greater Portland." Circ. 10,000. Pays on publication. Publishes ms an average of 2 months after acceptance. Byline given. Buys first North American serial rights. Submit seasonal/holiday material 6 months in advance. Computer printout submissions OK; prefers letter-quality to dot-matrix. Reports in 1 week on queries; 2 weeks on mss. Free sample copy with $1 postage.

Nonfiction: General interest, humor, interview/profile and personal experience. *"Greater Portland* is completely freelance written. We have an in-town lifestyle slant and are looking for complete stories, not just verbal scenery. For example, if you write a story about our luxury ferry, The Scotia Prince, stay overnight and take the readers aboard. We shy away from survey stories. Cover one subject deliciously, instead. First person narratives are welcome." Buys 30 mss/year. Query with published clips or send complete ms. Length: 500-2,000 words. Pays $150 maximum. Sometimes pays expenses of writers on assignment.
Photos: Buys b&w and color slides with or without ms. Captions required.
Fiction: Short, mainstream fiction that takes place in Greater Portland; humorous, suspense, mystery, and historical. Length: 1,000 words maximum.
Tips: "Send some clips with a cover letter or query. We're always looking for good Casco Bay island stories, with lots of anecdotes. Some stories come in that aren't free-wheeling enough. There is too much solemn ('professional') newspaper writing, too much restraint. Have some fun. Throw your personality into the article. I'd rather water things down than water them up."

MAINE LIFE, Box 111, Freedom ME 04901. Editor: George Frangoulis. 80% freelance written. Published 6 times/year. For readers of all ages in urban and rural settings. 50% of readers live in Maine; balance are readers in other states who have an interest in Maine. Circ. 30,000. Pays on publication. Publishes ms an average of 1 year after acceptance. Buys first serial rights and second serial (reprint) rights. Submit seasonal/holiday material 3 months in advance. Computer printout submissions acceptable; no dot-matrix. Reports in 3 months. SASE. Sample copy $1.75.
Nonfiction: Maine travel, home and garden, wildlife and recreation, arts and culture; Maine people, business, energy and environment. Query. Length: 500-2,000 words. Pays 5¢/word.
Photos: B&w and color slides purchased with or without accompanying ms. Captions required.

‡**MAINE MOTORIST**, Maine Automobile Assn., Box 3544, Portland ME 04104. (207)774-6377. Editor: Eric Baxter. 25% freelance written. Bimonthly tabloid on travel, car care, AAA news. "Our readers enjoy learning about travel opportunities in the New England region and elsewhere. In addition, they enjoy topics of interest to automobile owners." Circ. 95,000. Pays on publication. Publishes ms an average of 3 months after acceptance. Byline given. Not copyrighted. Buys simultaneous rights; makes work-for-hire assignments. Submits seasonal/holiday material 3 months in advance. Simultaneous and photocopied submissions OK. Computer printout submissions acceptable; prefers letter-quality to dot-matrix. SASE. Free sample copy and writer's guidelines.
Nonfiction: Historical/nostalgic (travel); how-to (car care, travel); humor (travel); and travel (New England, U.S. and foreign). No exotic travel destinations that cost a great deal. Send complete ms. Length: 500-1,250 words. Pays $50-150.
Photos: State availability of photos. Reviews 5x7 color and b&w transparencies. Pays $10-25 for b&w; $25-100 for color. Captions required. Buys one-time rights.
Fiction: Erotica.
Tips: "Travel (particularly New England regional) material is most needed. Interesting travel options are appreciated. Humorous flair sometimes helps.

Maryland

BALTIMORE MAGAZINE, 26 S. Calvert St., Baltimore MD 21202. (301)752-7375. Editor: Stan Heuisler. 50% freelance written. Monthly magazine; 150 pages. Circ. 52,047. Pays on publication. Publishes ms an average of 3 months after acceptance. Byline given. Submit seasonal/holiday material 3 months in advance. Electronic submission information supplied on request. Computer printout submissions acceptable; prefers letter-quality to dot-matrix. SASE. Reports in 6 weeks. Sample copy $2.34; writer's guidelines with SASE.
Nonfiction: Consumer, profile, life-style, issues, narratives and advocacy. Must have local angle. "We do not want to see any soft, nonlocal features." Buys 4 mss/issue. Length: 1,000-5,000 words. Pays $100-500. Sometimes pays expenses of writers on assignment.
Photos: State availability of photos. Reviews color and b&w glossy prints. Captions preferred.
Columns/Departments: Frontlines (local news tips), Tips (local unusual retail opportunities), Class Cars and Tech Talk (high-tech product advice). Query.

CHESAPEAKE BAY MAGAZINE, Suite 200, 1819 Bay Ridge Ave., Annapolis MD 21403. (301)263-2662. Editor: Betty D. Rigoli. 45% freelance written. Monthly magazine; 80 pages. *"Chesapeake Bay Magazine* is a regional publication for those who enjoy reading about the Bay and its tributaries. Our readers are yachtsmen, boating families, fishermen, ecologists—anyone who is part of Chesapeake Bay life." Circ. 18,000. Pays either on acceptance or publication, depending on "type of article, timeliness and need."

Publishes ms an average of 1 year after acceptance. Buys first North American serial rights and all rights. Submit seasonal/holiday material 4 months in advance. Simultaneous (if not to magazines with overlapping circulations) and photocopied submissions OK. Computer printout submissions acceptable; prefers letter-quality to dot-matrix. SASE. Reports in 1 month. Sample copy $2; writer's guidelines for SASE.

Nonfiction: "All material must be about the Chesapeake Bay area—land or water." How-to (fishing, hunting, and sports pertinent to Chesapeake Bay); general interest; humor (welcomed, but don't send any "dumb boater" stories where common safety is ignored); historical; interviews (with interesting people who have contributed in some way to Chesapeake Bay life: authors, historians, sailors, oystermen, etc.); and nostalgia (accurate, informative and well-paced). No maudlin ramblings about "the good old days"); personal experience (drawn from experiences in boating situations, adventures, events in our geographical area); photo feature (with accompanying ms); profile (on natives of Chesapeake Bay); technical (relating to boating, hunting, fishing); and Chesapeake Bay folklore. "We do not want material written by those unfamiliar with the Bay area, or general sea stories. No personal opinions on environmental issues or new column (monthly) material and no rehashing of familiar ports-of-call (e.g., Oxford, St. Michaels)." Recent article example: "A Treasure Hunter's Paradise" (March '85). Buys 25-40 unsolicited mss/year. Query or submit complete ms. Length: 1,000-2,500 words. Pays $75-85.

Photos: Virginia Leonard, art director. Submit photo material with ms. Reviews 8x10 b&w glossy prints. Pays $100 for 35mm, 2¼x2¼ or 4x5 color transparencies used for cover photos; $15/color photo used inside. Captions and model release required. Buys one-time rights with reprint permission.

Fiction: "All fiction must deal with the Chesapeake Bay and be written by persons familiar with some facet of bay life." Adventure, fantasy, historical, humorous, mystery and suspense. "No general stories with Chesapeake Bay superimposed in an attempt to make a sale." Buys 8 mss/year. Query or submit complete ms. Length: 1,000-2,500 words. Pays $75-90.

Poetry: Attention: Poetry Editor. Free verse and traditional. Must be about Chesapeake Bay. "We want well crafted, serious poetry. Do not send in short, 'inspired' seasick poetry or 'sea-widow' poems." Buys 2 poems/year. Submit maximum 4 poems. Length: 5-30 lines. Pays $10-25. Poetry used on space available basis only.

Tips: "We are a regional publication entirely about the Chesapeake Bay and its tributaries. Our readers are true 'Bay' lovers, and look for stories written by others who obviously share this love. We are particularly interested in material from the Lower Bay (Virginia) area and the Upper Bay (Maryland/Delaware) area."

‡**MARYLAND MAGAZINE**, Department of Economic and Community Development, 45 Calvert St., Annapolis MD 21401. (301)269-3507. Editor: Bonnie Joe Ayers. Managing Publisher: D. Patrick Hornberger. 95% freelance written. Quarterly magazine promoting the state of Maryland. Circ. 45,000. Pays on acceptance. Publishes ms an average of 1 year after acceptance. Byline given. Offers 25% kill fee. Buys all rights. Submit seasonal/holiday material 1 year in advance. Photocopied submissions OK. Computer printout submissions acceptable; no dot-matrix. SASE. Reports in 8 weeks. Sample copy $2.25; writer's guidelines for business size SAE and 1 first class stamp.

Nonfiction: General interest, historical/nostalgic, humor, interview/profile, photo feature and travel. Articles on any facet of Maryland life except conservation/ecology. No poetry, fiction or controversial material or any topic *not* dealing with the state of Maryland; no trendy topics, or one that has received much publicity elsewhere. Buys 32 mss/year. Query with published clips or send complete ms. Length: 850-2,200 words. Pays $115-300. Pays expenses of writers on assignment.

Tips: "All sections are open to freelancers; however, our tendency is to purchase more historically-oriented articles from freelancers. Thoroughly research your topic and give sources (when applicable)."

Massachusetts

BOSTON GLOBE MAGAZINE, *Boston Globe*, Boston MA 02107. Editor-in-Chief: Ms. Ande Zellman. 25% freelance written. Weekly magazine; 64 pages. Circ. 792,750. Pays on publication. Publishes ms an average of 2 months after acceptance. No reprints of any kind. Buys first serial rights. Submit seasonal/holiday material 3 months in advance. Computer printout submissions acceptable; no dot-matrix. SASE must be included with ms or queries for return. Reports in 4 weeks.

Nonfiction: Expose (variety of issues including political, economic, scientific, medicine and the arts); interview (not Q&A); profile; and book excerpts (first serial rights only). No travelogs or personal experience pieces. Buys 65 mss/year. Query. Length: 3,000-5,000 words. Pays $600-900.

Photos: Purchased with accompanying ms or on assignment. Reviews contact sheets. Pays standard rates according to size used. Captions required.

BOSTON MAGAZINE, 300 Massachusetts Ave., Boston MA 02116. (617)262-9700. Contact: Editor. Monthly magazine. For upscale readers eager to understand and participate in the best that New England has to offer; majority are professional, college-educated and affluent. Pays on publication. Buys one-time rights.

Pays 20% kill fee. Written queries mandatory. Submit seasonal/holiday material 5 months in advance. SASE. Reports in 3 weeks.

Nonfiction: Investigative reporting (subject matter varies); profiles (of Bostonians or New Englanders); business stories; and first person accounts of personal experiences. Buys fewer than 10 unsolicited mss/year. Query David Rosenbaum, articles editor. Length: 1,000-6,000 words. Pays $200-1,200; more for exceptional material. For short takes, brief items of interest in Boston or throughout New England to run in the Reporter section, query David Rosenbaum. Pays 10-20¢/word.

Photos: Stan McCray, art director. B&w and color purchased on assignment only. Query. Specifications vary. Pays $25-150 for b&w; average $275 color.

Tips: "There are many freelance writers in the Boston area, and we have a large group of regular contributing writers, so our need for freelance material from writers based outside the New England area is very limited indeed. Most of all, we look for stories that no one else in our region is doing, either because the subject or the treatment of it hasn't occurred to them, or because the writer has expertise that gives her or him a special insight into the story. A *Boston* story must have a strong and specific focus on Boston or New England, be solidly reported, and be of interest to a wide variety of readers."

CAPE COD LIFE, Including Martha's Vineyard and Nantucket, Cape Cod Life, Inc., Box 222, Osterville MA 02655. (617)428-5706. Editor: Brian F. Shortsleeve. Managing Editor: Alison L. Sporborg. 90% freelance written. Magazine published 6 times/year (weighted toward summer publication), focusing on "area lifestyle, history and culture, people and places, business and industry, and issues and answers." Readers are "year-round and summer residents of Cape Cod as well as non residents who spend their leisure time on the Cape." Circ. 40,000. Pays on publication. Byline given. Kill fees are paid at discretion of publisher. Buys first North American serial rights; makes work-for-hire assignments. Submit seasonal/holiday material 6 months in advance. Simultaneous queries and photocopied submissions OK. Computer printout submissions acceptable; prefers letter-quality to dot-matrix. Reports in 2 weeks on queries; 1 month on mss. Sample copy $3; writer's guidelines for SAE and 1 first class stamp.

Nonfiction: General interest, historical/nostalgic, how-to, humor, interview/profile, photo feature, travel, marine, nautical, nature, arts and antiques. Buys 15 mss/year. Query with published clips. Length: 1,200-2,500 words. Pays $3/published column inch (1,000 words equals approximately 30"). Sometimes pays expenses of writers on assignment.

Photos: James Canavan, art director. State availability of photos with query. Pays $7.50-15 for 35mm b&w slides; $10-20 for 35mm color slides. Captions and identification of subjects required. Buys one-time rights.

Poetry: Traditional. "We only accept poetry that has a Cape Cod, Martha's Vineyard or Nantucket theme." Buys 3 poems/year. Length: 30 lines maximum. Pays $50 maximum.

Tips: "Those freelancers who submit *quality* spec articles generally have a good chance at publication. We do like to see a wide selection of writer's clips before giving assignments. We accept more spec work written about Cape and Islands history than any other area."

NEW BEDFORD, 5 S. 6th St., New Bedford MA 02740. Editor: Ms. Dee Giles Forsythe. 100% freelance written. Bimonthly magazine primarily focusing on southeastern Massachusetts. Pays within period of publication. Publishes ms an average of 6 months after acceptance. Buys first serial rights and second serial (reprint) rights. Submit seasonal material 6 months in advance. Computer printout submissions acceptable; prefers letter-quality to dot-matrix. SASE. Reports in 1 month. Sample copy $1.50; writer's guidelines with SASE.

Nonfiction: Social, political and natural history; biography and people profiles; environmental and other pertinent public policy issues; boating, commercial fishing, and other maritime-related businesses; the arts; education; and lifestyles. Query. Length: 1,500-2,500 words. Pays approximately $100.

Photos: Prefers b&w glossy prints; will consider 35mm color transparencies. Pays on publication; negotiable fee. Captions and credit lines required.

Fiction: "This magazine occasionally runs short fiction up to 3,000 words. Such manuscripts should have some connection to the sea, the coast, or to southern New England's history or character. There are no restrictions on style; the main criterion is quality." Query or send complete ms.

Tips: "We look for the unusual story or angle, the fresh approach, pieces about events, issues or people in the southeastern Massachusetts and Rhode Island area with whom readers can identify. Our philosophy is one of personal communication between the writer and reader; informal writing, but of high quality and accuracy, will always find a home at *New Bedford*."

WORCESTER MAGAZINE, Box 1000, Worcester MA 01614. (617)799-0511. Editor: Dan Kaplan. 10% freelance written. Weekly tabloid, 48 pages emphasizing the central Massachusetts region. Circ. 50,000. Pays on acceptance. Publishes ms an average of 3 weeks after acceptance. Byline given. Buys all rights. Submit seasonal/holiday material 2 months in advance. Simultaneous and photocopied submissions OK. Computer printout submissions acceptable. SASE. Reports in 2 weeks. Sample copy $1; free writer's guidelines.

Nonfiction: Expose (area government, corporate); how-to (concerning the area, homes, vacations); interview (local); personal experience; opinion (local); and photo feature. No nonlocal stories. "We leave national and general topics to national and general publications." Buys 30 mss/year. Query with published clips. Length: 1,000-3,500 words. Pays $50-125.

Photos: State availability of photos with query. Pays $25-75 for b&w photos. Captions preferred; model release required. Buys all rights.

Michigan

ANN ARBOR OBSERVER, Ann Arbor Observer Company, 206 S. Main, Ann Arbor MI 48104. Editors: Don and Mary Hunt. 50% freelance written. Monthly magazine featuring stories about people and events in Ann Arbor. Circ. 40,000. Pays on publication. Publishes ms an average of 2 months after acceptance. Byline given. Buys one-time rights. Electronic submissions OK via WordStar. Computer printout submissions acceptable. Reports in 3 weeks on queries; 4 weeks on mss. Sample copy $1.

Nonfiction: Expose, historical/nostalgic, brief vignettes and photo feature. Buys 75 mss/year. Length: 100-7,000 words. Pays up to $1,200/article. Sometimes pays expenses of writers on assignment.

Tips: "If you have an idea for a story write up a 100-200 word description telling us why the story is interesting. We are most open to intelligent, insightful features of up to 5,000 words about interesting aspects of life in Ann Arbor."

GRAND RAPIDS MAGAZINE, Suite 1040, Trust Bldg., 40 Pearl St., NW, Grand Rapids MI 49503. (616)459-4545. Publisher: John H. Zwarensteyn. Editor: John J. Brosky Jr. Managing Editor: William Holm. 45% freelance written. Monthly general feature magazine serving western Michigan. Circ. 13,500. Pays on 15th of month of publication. Buys first serial rights. Phone queries OK. Submit seasonal material 3 months in advance. Photocopied and previously published submissions OK. Computer printout submissions acceptable; prefers letter-quality to dot-matrix. SASE. Reports in 2 months.

Nonfiction: Western Michigan writers preferred. Western Michigan subjects only: government, labor, education, general interest, historical, interview/profile and nostalgia. Inspirational and personal experience pieces discouraged. No breezy, self-centered "human" pieces or "pieces not only light on style but light on hard information." Humor appreciated but specific to region. Buys 5-8 unsolicited mss/year. "If you live here, see Bill Holm before you write. If you don't, send a query letter with published clips or phone." Length: 500-4,000 words. Pays $15-150.

Photos: State availability of photos. Pays $15+/5x7 glossy print and $22+/35 for 120mm color transparencies. Captions and model release required.

Tips: "Television has forced city/regional magazines to be less provincial and more broad-based in their approach. People's interests seem to be evening out from region to region. The subject matters should remain largely local, but national trends must be recognized in style and content. And we must *entertain* as well as inform."

MICHIGAN: The Magazine of the Detroit News, 615 Lafayette, Detroit MI 48231. (313)222-2620. Articles Editor: Lisa Velders. 50% freelance written. Weekly rotogravure featuring the state of Michigan for general interest newspaper readers. Circ. 850,000. Average issue includes 2 feature articles, departments and staff-written columns. Pays on publication. Publishes ms an average of 2 months after acceptance. Byline given. Offers variable kill fee. Buys first Michigan serial rights. Phone queries OK. Submit seasonal material 2 months in advance. Simultaneous and previously published submissions OK, if other publication involved is outside of Michigan. Computer printout submissions acceptable; prefers letter-quality to dot-matrix. Reports in 3 weeks on queries; 1 month on mss.

Nonfiction: Profiles, places, and topics with Michigan connections. Buys 18 unsolicited mss/year. Query with published clips. Length: 750-3,000 words. Pays $100 minimum.

Photos: Pays $50 minimum per 5x7 b&w glossy print. Pays $150-$350 per 35mm or larger color transparency. Captions required.

Tips: "Magazines are looking for more people-oriented stories now than ever before, in roto magazines, specifically. There's a great effort to run articles more in the vein of a city-oriented magazine and less of the old-style 'roto' (a la *Parade*) type pieces."

WEST MICHIGAN MAGAZINE, West Michigan Telecommunications Foundation, 7 Ionia SW, Grand Rapids MI 49503. (616) 774-0204. Editor: Dotti Clune. 80% freelance written. Monthly magazine covering geographical region of West Michigan. Circ. 20,000. Pays on publication. Publishes ms an average of 3 months after acceptance. Byline given. Buys first serial rights. Submit seasonal/holiday material 3 months in advance. Simultaneous queries, and photocopied, and previously published submissions OK. Computer printout submissions acceptable; prefers letter-quality to dot-matrix. SASE. Reports in 2 weeks on queries; 1 month on mss. Send SAE and $1.15 for sample copy and writer's guidelines.

Nonfiction: Arts, business, dining, entertainment, recreation, travel, expose (government/politics), interview/profile and photo feature. Buys 50 mss/year. Query with published clips if available. Length: 500-2,000 words. Pays $25-250.

Photos: State availability of photos.

Tips: "We look for thought-provoking articles ranging from serious examinations of important issues to humorous glimpses at the lighter side of life in West Michigan. We like articles offering taste, style, and compelling reading; articles capturing the personality of West Michigan—the quality of life in the region and the spirit of its people; and articles appealing to a discriminating audience. We look for colorful, specific, lively material. Many writers aren't imaginative enough. Leads and conclusions are often weak."

Minnesota

‡**LAKE SUPERIOR PORT CITIES**, Lake Superior Port Cities, Inc., 325 Lake Ave. S., Duluth MN 55802. (218)722-5002. Editor: Barbara Landfield. 80% freelance written. Quarterly magazine covering Lake Superior region. "Articles should highlight a person, place or event which has or will signicantly affect the Lake Superior area." Circ. 8,000. Pays within 1 month of publication. Publishes ms an average of 3 months after acceptance. Byline given. Offers $25 kill fee. Buys first North American serial rights and second serial (reprint) rights. Submit seasonal/holiday material 6 months in advance. Photocopied submissions OK. Computer printout submissions acceptable; no dot-matrix. SASE. Reports in 3 months. Sample copy $3.50 and $1.92 postage; writer's guidelines for SAE with 1 first class stamp.

Nonfiction: Book excerpts, general interest, historical/nostalgic, humor, interview/profile, photo feature and travel. "Historical articles *must* be well researched; many of our readers have historical training and are quick to point out errors." Buys 40 mss/year. Query with published clips. Length: 300-5,000 words. Pays $25-200.

Photos: Roberta Baker, art director. State availability of photos with query. Pays $10 for 5x7 or 8x10 b&w prints; $15 for color transparencies. Model release and identification of subjects required. Buys first and second rights.

Tips: "We are actively seeking queries from writers in Lake Superior communities." Writers have a better chance of breaking in with short, lesser-paying articles; "major features are usually assigned to writers we know. Provide enough information on why the subject is important to the region and our readers, or why and how something is unique. In short, we want *details*."

MPLS. ST. PAUL MAGAZINE, Suite 1030, 12 S. 6th St., Minneapolis MN 55402. (612)339-7571. Editor: Brian Anderson. Managing Editor: Marla J. Kinney. 90% freelance written. Monthly general interest magazine covering the metropolitan area of Minneapolis/St. Paul and aimed at college-educated professionals who enjoy living in the area and taking advantage of the cultural, entertainments and dining out opportunities. Circ. 46,000. Pays on acceptance. Publishes ms an average of 3 months after acceptance. Byline given. Offers 33% kill fee. Buys first North American serial rights. Submit seasonal/holiday material 4 months in advance. Computer printout submissions acceptable; prefers letter-quality to dot-matrix. SASE. Reports in 1 month. Sample copy $3.50; free writer's guidelines.

Nonfiction: Book excerpts; expose (local); general interest; historical/nostalgic; interview/profile (local); new product; photo feature (local); and travel (local). Buys 250 mss/year. Query with published clips. Length: 1,000-4,000 words. Pays $100-600. Sometimes pays expenses of writers on assignment.

Photos: Bill Bloedow, photo editor.

Columns/Departments: Nostalgic—Minnesota historical; Arts—local; Home—interior design, local; Last Page—essay with local relevance. Query with published clips. Length: 750-2,000 words. Pays $100-200.

Tips: Short People profiles (400 words) and Nostalgia are areas most open to freelancers.

TWIN CITIES READER, News, Opinion & Entertainment Weekly, MCP, Inc., 600 1st Ave. N, Minneapolis MN 55403. (612)338-2900. Editor: Deborah L. Hopp. "We are a general interest weekly tabloid serving the needs of the community via investigative features, local news and profiles, politics, consumer information, lifestyle trends, general arts and entertainment (with special emphasis on film, music and theatre) and food and dining features. We try to address the special needs and interests of our reader, leaving the daily press to cover topics or angles best suited to the general population of Minneapolis/St. Paul. Our readers are 25-44 years old and enjoy largely managerial/professional positions. They are well educated and active; they also participate enthusiastically in the arts and entertainment opportunities of our community and are considered to be both well-read and well-informed." Circ. 140,000. Pays on publication. Byline given. Buys one-time rights. Submit seasonal/holiday material 1 month in advance. Simultaneous queries, and simultaneous and photocopied submissions OK. Computer printout submissions acceptable; no dot-matrix. SASE. Reports in 3 weeks. Sample copy for 10x13 SAE, and $1.22 postage; free writer's guidelines.

Nonfiction: Travel, fitness and health. Special issues include fitness/health, general real estate, and home interiors. Buys 100 mss/year. Send complete ms. Length: 750-1,500 words. Pays $25-100.

Photos: Greg Helgeson, photo editor. Send photos with accompanying ms. Reviews b&w contact sheets. Pays

$10-100 for 5x7 or 8½x11 b&w prints; $50-300 for 5x7 color transparencies. Model release and identification of subjects required.
Columns/Departments: Books. Buys 20 mss/year. Send complete ms. Length: 500-1,250 words. Pays $30-100.
Tips: "Our readers are young (ages 20-45), well-educated, savvy. Do not write for 'general' readers or the unsophisticated. Books, travel, and health and fitness are most open to freelancers. We like a short, light style with a sense of humor."

Mississippi

DELTA SCENE, Box B-3, Delta State University, Cleveland MS 38733. (601)846-1976. Editor-in-Chief: Dr. Curt Lamar. Business Manager: Ms. Sherry Van Liew. 50% freelance written. Quarterly magazine; 32 pages. For an art-oriented or history-minded audience wanting more information (other than current events) on the Mississippi Delta region. Circ. 1,500. Pays on publication. Publishes ms an average of 2 years after acceptance. Buys first serial rights. Byline given. Submit seasonal/holiday material 4 months in advance. Simultaneous, photocopied, and previously published submissions OK. Computer printout submissions acceptable; no dot-matrix. SASE. Reports in 1 month. Sample copy $1.50.
Nonfiction: Historical and informational articles, interviews, profiles, travel, and technical articles (particularly in reference to agriculture). "We have a list of articles free to anyone requesting a copy." Buys 2-3 mss/issue. Query. Length: 1,000-2,000 words. Pays $5-20.
Photos: Purchased with or without ms, or on assignment. Pays $5-15 for 5x7 b&w glossy prints or any size color or transparency.
Fiction: Humorous and mainstream. Buys 1/issue. Submit complete ms. Length: 1,000-2,000 words. Pays $10-20.
Poetry: Traditional forms, free verse and haiku. Buys 1/issue. Submit unlimited number of poems. Pays $5-10.
Tips: "The freelancer should follow our magazine's purpose. We generally only accept articles about the Delta area of Mississippi, the state of Mississippi, and the South in general. We are sponsored by a state university so no articles, poetry, etc., containing profanity or other questionable material. Nonfiction has a better chance of making it into our magazine than short stories or poetry."

Missouri

MISSOURI LIFE, The Magazine of Missouri, Missouri Life Publishing Co., 710 N. Tucker, St. Louis MO 63101. (314)342-1281. Editor: Debra Gluck. Bimonthly magazine covering Missouri people, places and history. Circ. 30,000. Pays on publication. Byline given. Buys all rights. Submit seasonal/holiday material 3 months in advance. Simultaneous queries, and simultaneous, photocopied, and previously published submissions OK. SASE. Reports in 1 month. Sample copy $3.50; writer's guidelines for business size SAE and 1 first class stamp.
Nonfiction: General interest, historical/nostalgic, interview/profile, personal experience, photo feature and travel. Special issues planned for St. Louis, Kansas City and Lake of the Ozarks. Buys 35-40 mss/year. Written query. Length: 1,200-3,000 words. Pays $50.
Photos: State availability of photos. Pays $10-25 for 2x2 color transparencies and 5x7 and 8x10 b&w prints. Identification of subjects required.
Columns/Departments: Missouri Homes—tours of interesting houses and neighborhoods around the state; Southland—stories from the southern part of the state; Voices—profiles of interesting Missourians; Eastside St. Louis—area stories; Westside Kansas City area—stories. Buys 25-30 mss/year. Query. Length: 1,000-2,500 words. Pays $50.
Tips: "All sections of the magazine are open to writers. If the material has anything to do with Missouri, we're interested. Keep the writing unaffected and personal."

‡**SPRINGFIELD MAGAZINE**, Springfield Communications Inc., Box 4749, Springfield MO 65808. (417)882-4917. Editor: Robert C. Glazier. 80% freelance written. Monthly magazine. "This is an extremely local and provincial magazine. No *general* interest articles." Circ. 10,000. Pays on publication. Publishes ms an average of 3 months after acceptance. Byline given. Buys first serial rights. Submit seasonal/holiday material 6-12 months in advance. Simultaneous queries OK. Computer printout submissions acceptable; prefers letter-quality to dot-matrix. SASE. Reports in 3 months on queries; 6 months on mss. Sample copy $15 and SAE.
Nonfiction: Book excerpts (by Springfield authors only); expose (local topics only); historical/nostalgic (top priority but must be local history); how-to (local interest only); humor (if local angle); interview/profile (needs more on females than on males); personal experience (local angle); photo feature (local photos); and travel (1

page per month). No stock stuff which could appeal to any magazine anywhere. Buys 150+ mss/year. Query with published clips or send complete ms. Length: 500-5,000 words. Pays $25-250. Sometimes pays expenses of writers on assignment.

Photos: State availability of photos or send photos with query or ms. Reviews b&w and color contact sheets; 4x5 color transparencies; and 5x7 b&w prints. Pays $5-35 for b&w; $10-50 for color. Captions, model release, and identification of subjects required. Buys one-time rights.

Columns/Departments: Buys 250 mss/year. Query or send complete ms. Length varies widely but usually 500-2,500 words. Pays scale.

Tips: "Freelancer should study the publication and submit queries. The magazine's greatest need is for features which comment on these times in Springfield. We are overstocked with nostalgic pieces right now. We also are much in need of profiles about young women and men of distinction."

Nevada

NEVADA MAGAZINE, Carson City NV 89710-0005. (702)885-5416. Editor-in-Chief: Caroline J. Hadley. Senior Editor: David Moore. 50% freelance written. Bimonthly magazine published by the state of Nevada to promote tourism in the state. Circ. 62,000. Pays on publication. Publishes ms an average of 4 months after acceptance. Byline given. Buys first North American serial rights. Phone queries OK. Submit seasonal/holiday material 6 months in advance. Computer printout submissions acceptable; prefers letter-quality to dot-matrix. SASE. Reports in 2 months. Sample copy $1; free writer's guidelines.

Nonfiction: Nevada topics only. Historical, nostalgia, photo feature, people profile, recreational and travel. "We welcome stories and photos on speculation." Buys 40 unsolicited mss/year. Submit complete ms. Submit queries to features editor Jim Crandall. Length: 500-2,000 words. Pays $75-300.

Photos: Send photo material with accompanying ms. Pays $10-50 for 8x10 glossy prints; $15-75 for color transparencies. Captions required and name and address labeled. Buys one-time rights.

Tips: "Keep in mind that the magazine's purpose is to promote tourism in Nevada. Keys to higher payments are quality and editing effort (more than length). Send cover letter, no photocopy."

THE NEVADAN, *The Las Vegas Review Journal,* Box 70, Las Vegas NV 89101. (702)385-4241. Editor-in-Chief: A.D. Hopkins. 15% freelance written. Weekly tabloid; 16 pages. For Las Vegas and surrounding small town residents of all ages "who take our Sunday paper—affluent, outdoor-oriented." Circ. 100,000. Pays on publication. Publishes ms an average of 3 months after acceptance. Byline given. Buys one-time rights. Phone queries OK. Submit seasonal/holiday material 2 months in advance. Photocopied and previously published submissions OK. Computer printout submissions acceptable; prefers letter-quality to dot-matrix. SASE. Reports in 3 weeks. Free sample copy and writer's guidelines; mention *Writer's Market* in request.

Nonfiction: Historical (more of these than anything else, always linked to Nevada, southern Utah, northern Arizona and Death Valley); personal experience (any with strong pioneer Nevada angle, pioneer can be 1948 in some parts of Nevada). "We buy a very few contemporary pieces of about 2,400 words with good photos. An advance query is absolutely essential for these. No articles on history that are based on doubtful sources; no current show business material; and no commercial plugs." Buys 52 mss/year. Query. Length: Average 2,000 words (contemporary pieces are longer). Usually pays $60.

Photos: State availability of photos. Pays $10 for 5x7 or 8x10 b&w glossy prints; $15 for 35 or 120mm color transparencies. Captions required. Buys one-time rights.

Tips: "Offer us articles on little-known interesting incidents in Nevada history and good historic photos. In queries come to the point. Tell me what sort of photos are available, whether historic or contemporary, black-and-white or color transparency. Be specific in talking about what you want to write."

New Hampshire

NEW HAMPSHIRE PROFILES, Profiles Publishing Co., 81 Hall St., Concord NH 03301. (603)224-5193. Editor: Stephen Bennett. 50% freelance written. Monthly magazine, approximately 96 pages. Articles concentrate on audience ages 25-49, up-scale consumer-oriented readers who want to know more about the quality of life in New Hampshire. Circ. 25,000. Pays on publication. Buys first serial rights. Electronic submissions OK via Digital Decmate. Computer printout submissions acceptable; no dot-matrix. SASE. Reports in 2 months. Sample copy $2; writer's guidelines with SASE.

Nonfiction: Interview, opinion, profile, photo feature and interesting activities. Publishes social, political, economic and cultural articles for and about the state of New Hampshire and people who live in it. Buys 4-5 mss/issue. Query with published clips. Length varies from 1,000-3,000 words, depending on subject matter. Pays $75-350.

Photos: State availability of photos. Pays $15-25 for b&w 5x7 or 8x10 glossy prints; $25-75 for 2¼x2¼ or

35mm color transparencies used as color photos in magazine.
Tips: "Query before submitting manuscript, and don't send us your only copy of the manuscript—photocopy it."

New Jersey

‡**ATLANTIC CITY MAGAZINE**, 1637 Atlantic Ave., Atlantic City NJ 08401. Editor: Bill Tonelli. 70% freelance written. Monthly city magazine; 120 pages. Circ. 50,000. Most work done on assignment; sometimes purchases unsolicited mss. Pays on publication. Publishes ms an average of 3 months after acceptance. Buys first serial rights. Byline given. Submit seasonal/holiday ideas 4 months in advance. Computer printout submissions acceptable; no dot-matrix. SASE. Reports in 4 weeks. Sample copy $2 plus postage.
Nonfiction: Entertainment, business, people, sports, crime, photo feature, politics and trends. Query and send published clips. Length: 500-5,000 words. Pays $25-500. Pays expenses of writers on assignment.
Photos: State availability of photos. Buys b&w prints and color transparencies. Pay varies. Captions preferred.
Columns/Departments: Art, Business, Entertainment, Question and Answer, Nature, Sports, and Real Estate, plus more. Query and send published clips. Length: 1,000-3,000 words. Pays $25-300.
Tips: "Don't approach us with story ideas until you have studied two or three issues of the magazine. Try and propose articles that the magazine just can't live without."

‡**NEW JERSEY REPORTER, A Journal of Public Issues**, The Center for Analysis of Public Issues (nonprofit), 16 Vandeventer Ave., Princeton NJ 08542. (609)924-9750. Editor: Rick Sinding. 33% freelance written. Magazine published 10 times/year covering New Jersey politics, public affairs and public issues. "*New Jersey Reporter* is a hard-hitting and highly respected magazine published for people who take an active interest in New Jersey politics and public affairs, and who want to know more about what's going on than what newspapers and television newscasts are able to tell them. We publish a great variety of stories ranging from analysis to exposé." Circ. 3,000. Pays on publication. Publishes ms an average of 2 months after acceptance. Byline given. Buys all rights. Simultaneous queries and submissions, and photocopied and previously published submissions OK. Computer printout submissions acceptable; prefers letter-quality to dot-matrix. SASE. Reports in 1 month. Sample copy $2.50.
Nonfiction: Book excerpts, expose, interview/profile and opinion. "We like articles from specialists (in planning, politics, economics, corruption, etc.), but we reject stories that do not read well because of jargon or too little attention to the actual writing of the piece. Our magazine is interesting as well as informative." Buys 10 mss/year. Query with published clips or send complete ms. Length: 2,000-6,000 words. Pays $100-250. Sometimes pays expenses of writers on assignments.
Tips: "Queries should be specific about how the prospective story represents an issue that affects or will affect the people of New Jersey. The writer's resume should be included. Stories—unless they are specifically meant to be opinion—should come to a conclusion but avoid a 'holier than thou' or preachy tone. Allegations should be scrupulously substantiated. Our magazine represents a good opportunity for freelancers to acquire great clips. Our publication specializes in longer, more detailed, analytical features. The most frequent mistake made by writers in completing an article for us is too much personal opinion versus reasoned advocacy. We are less interested in opinion than in analysis based on sound reasoning and fact. *New Jersey Reporter* is a well-respected publication, and many of our writers go on to nationally respected newspapers and magazines."

THE SANDPAPER, Jersey Shore Magazine, The SandPaper, Inc., 1816 Long Beach Blvd., Surf City NJ 08008. (609)494-2034. Publisher/Editor: Curt Travers. Managing Editor: Gerry Paul Little. 60% freelance written. Weekly tabloid (monthly in January and February) covering southern New Jersey shore life. "Industries, histories and tourism are of particular interest to us." Circ. 35,000. Pays on publication. Publishes ms an average of 6 weeks after acceptance. Byline given. Offers 100% kill fee. Buys all rights and first North American serial rights. Submit seasonal/holiday material 2 months in advance. Computer printout submissions acceptable. SASE. Reports in 3 weeks. Sample copy 50¢.
Nonfiction: General interest; historical/nostalgic (relating to coverage area); humor; and opinion. Human interest features plus news briefs. "All must somehow relate to life in and around southern Ocean County/Jersey Shore." No first person. "Material must be focused. We don't need a story on fishing. We would use a story on how striped bass quotas have affected the Island's annual fishing tournament." Buys 1,000 mss/year. Send complete ms. Length: 400-3,000 words. Pays $15-100.
Photos: Andy Bolton, photo editor. State availability of photos or send with ms. Reviews 5x7 or 8x10 b&w prints. Pays $5-25. Model release and identification of subjects required. Buys one-time or all rights.

New Mexico

NEW MEXICO MAGAZINE, Bataan Memorial Bldg., Santa Fe NM 87503. (505)827-2642. Editor: V.B. Price. Managing Editor: Polly Summar. 75% freelance written. Monthly magazine; 64-96 pages. Emphasizes New Mexico for a college educated readership, above average income, interested in the Southwest. Circ. 80,000. Pays on publication. Publishes ms an average of 6 months after acceptance. Buys first North American serial rights. Submit seasonal/holiday material 8 months in advance. Computer printout submissions acceptable; no dot-matrix. SASE. Reports in 10 days to 4 weeks. Sample copy $1.75.
Nonfiction: New Mexico subjects of interest to travelers. Historical, cultural, humorous, nostalgic and informational articles. No columns or cartoons, no nonNew Mexico subjects. Buys 5-7 mss/issue. Query. Length: 500-2,000 words. Pays $50-300. Sometimes pays expenses of writers on assignment.
Photos: Purchased with accompanying ms or on assignment. Query or send contact sheet or transparencies. Pays $30-50 for 8x10 b&w glossy prints; $30-75 for 35mm; prefers Kodachrome; (photos in plastic-pocketed viewing sheets). Captions and model release required. SASE. Buys one-time rights.
Tips: "Send a superb short (300 words) manuscript on a little-known event, aspect of history or place to see in New Mexico. Faulty research will immediately ruin a writer's chances for the future. Good style, good grammar, please! No generalized odes to the state or the Southwest. No sentimentalized, paternalistic views of Indians or Hispanics. No glib, gimmicky 'travel brochure' writing."

New York

ADIRONDACK LIFE, Route 86, Box 97, Jay NY 12941. Editor: Jeffery G. Kelly. 95% freelance written. Emphasizes the Adirondack region and the North Country of New York State for readers ages 30-60, whose interests include outdoor activities, history, and natural history directly related to the Adirondacks. Bimonthly magazine; 80 pages. Circ. 40,000. Pays on publication. Publishes ms an average of 1 year after acceptance. Buys one-time rights. Byline given. Submit seasonal/holiday material 4 months in advance. Previously published book excerpts OK. Computer printout submissions acceptable; no dot-matrix. SASE. Reports in 6 weeks. Sample copy $4; free writer's guidelines.
Nonfiction: Outdoor recreation (Adirondack relevance only); natural history, how-to, where-to (should relate to activities and lifestyles of the region); photo feature (all photos must have been taken in the Adirondacks); profile (Adirondack personality); and historical. Buys 24-28 unsolicited mss/year. Query. Length: For features, 3,000 words maximum; for departments, 500-1,000 words. Pays $100-400.
Photos: Purchased with or without ms or on assignment. All photos must be identified as to subject or locale and must bear photographer's name. Submit color slides or b&w prints. Pays $25 for b&w transparencies; $50 for color transparencies; $300 for cover (color only, vertical in format). Credit line given.
Tips: "Manuscripts should be written in a popular, nontechnical style accessible to a general audience. Generalized material lacking specific Adirondack relevance will not be accepted. We're looking for contemporary themes, written with energy."

FOCUS, 375 Park Ave., New York NY 10022. (212)628-2000. Editor: Steven De Arakie. Managing Editor: Kristine B. Schein. Annual publication featuring a guide to New York City and to New York shops for hotel guests and New York residents. Circ. 250,000. Pays on acceptance. Publishes ms an average of 6 months after acceptance. Buys one-time rights. Phone queries OK. Computer print-out submissions OK; prefers letter-quality to dot-matrix. Sample copy $1.50.
Nonfiction: "We want reviews of antique shops, art galleries, home furnishing stores, women's shops, men's shops and restaurants. The writer must interview an owner and write a description to be approved by the owner. This is all done on assignment." Buys 120 mss/issue. Query with published clips. Length: 110 words minimum. Pays $35 minimum.

HUDSON VALLEY MAGAZINE, Box 425, Woodstock NY 12498. (914)679-5100. Editor: Joanne Michaels. 100% freelance written. Monthly. Circ. 26,000. Pays on publication. Publishes ms an average of 6 months after acceptance. Byline given. Buys first North American serial rights, one-time rights, and second serial (reprint) rights. Submit seasonal/holiday material 3 months in advance. Simultaneous submissions OK. Computer printout submissions acceptable; no dot-matrix. SASE. Reports in 1 month on queries.
Nonfiction: Book excerpts; general interest; historical/nostalgic (Hudson Valley); how-to (home improvement); interview/profile (of area personalities); photo feature; and travel. No fiction or personal stories. Length: 1,500-2,000 words. Query. Pays $20-50.
Photos: State availability of photos. Reviews 5x7 b&w prints. Captions required.

‡**NEW YORK ALIVE, The Magazine of Life and Work in the Empire State**, The Business Council of New York State, Inc., 152 Washington Ave., Albany NY 12210. (518)465-7511. Editor: Mary Grates Stoll. 85%

freelance written. Bimonthly magazine about New York state—people, places, events, history. "Devoted to promoting the culture, heritage and lifestyle on New York state. Aimed at people who enjoy living and reading about the New York state experience. All stories must be positive in tone and slanted toward promoting the state." Circ. 35,000. Pays on acceptance. Publishes ms an average of 8 months after acceptance. Byline given. Offers 25% of agreed-upon purchase price kill fee. Buys one-time rights. Submit seasonal/holiday material 4 months in advance. Simultaneous queries and previously published submissions OK. SASE. Reports in 2 months on queries; 1 month on mss. Sample copy $2.45; writer's guidelines for legal size SAE and 1 first class stamp.

Nonfiction: Historical/nostalgic, humor, interview/profile, personal experience, photo feature and travel. In all cases subject must be a New York state person, place, event or experience. No stories of general nature (e.g. nationwide trends); political; religious; nonNew York state subjects. Query with published clips. Buys 30-40 mss/year. Length: 1,500-3,000 words. Pays $150-300. Pays expenses of writers on assignment.

Photos: State availability of photos. Reviews b&w contact sheets, 35mm color transparencies, and b&w prints. Pays $10-25 for b&w and $25-200 for color. Model release and identification of subjects required.

Columns/Departments: Buys 80-100 mss/year. Query with published clips. Length: 500-1,000 words. Pays $50-100.

Tips: "We buy more short articles."

NEW YORK DAILY NEWS, Travel Section, 220 E. 42 St., New York NY 10017. (212)210-1699. Travel Editor: Bert Shanas. 40% freelance written. Weekly tabloid. Circ. 2 million. "We are the largest circulating newspaper travel section in the country and take all types of articles ranging from experiences to service oriented pieces that tell readers how to make a certain trip." Pays on publication. Byline given. Makes work-for-hire assignments. Submit seasonal/holiday material 4 months in advance. Contact first before submitting electronic submissions; requires hard copy also. Computer printout submissions acceptable "if crisp"; prefers letter-qualtiy to dot-matrix. SASE. Reports "as soon as possible." Writer's guidelines for SAE and 1 first class stamp.

Nonfiction: General interest, historical/nostalgic, humor, inspirational, personal experience and travel. "Most of our articles involve practical trips that the average family can afford—even if it's one you can't afford every year. We put heavy emphasis on budget saving trips and budget tips on all trips. We also run stories now and then for the Armchair Traveler, a person taking an exotic and usually expensive trip. We are looking for professional quality work from professional writers who know what they are doing. The pieces have to give information and be entertaining at the same time." No How I Spent My Summer Vacation type articles. No PR hype. Buys 60 mss/year. Query with SASE. Length: 1,500 words maximum. Pays $75-125.

Photos: "Good pictures always help sell good stories." State availability of photos with ms. Reviews contact sheets and negatives. Captions and identification of subjects required. Buys all rights.

Columns/Departments: Short Hops is based on trips to places within a 300 mile radius of New York City. Length: 800-1,000 words. Travel Watch gives practical travel advice.

Tips: "A writer might have some luck gearing a specific destination to a news event or date: In Search of Irish Crafts in March, for example, but do it well in advance."

NEW YORK MAGAZINE, News Group Publications, Inc. 755 2nd Ave., New York 10017. (212)880-0700. Editor: Edward Kosner. Managing Editor: Laurie Jones. Weekly magazine emphasizing the New York metropolitan area. 30% freelance written. Pays on acceptance. Publishes ms an average of 1 month after acceptance. Buys first North American serial rights. Submit seasonal/holiday material 2 months in advance. Photocopied submissions OK. Computer printout submissions acceptable; prefers letter-quality to dot-matrix. SASE. Reports in 1 month.

Nonfiction: Expose, general interest, interview, profile, behavior/lifestyle, health/medicine, local politics and entertainment. Query. Pays $500-1,500.

Tips: "The writer has a better chance of breaking in at our publication with short articles and fillers. The magazine very rarely assigns a major feature to a new writer."

THE NEW YORK TIMES, 229 W. 43rd St., New York NY 10036. (212)556-1234. SASE.

Nonfiction: *The New York Times Magazine* appears in *The New York Times* on Sunday. Views should be fresh, lively and provocative writing on national and international news developments, science, education, family life, social trends and problems, arts and entertainment, personalities, sports and the changing American scene. Freelance contributions are invited. Articles must be timely. They must be based on specific news items, forthcoming events or significant anniversaries, or they must reflect trends. Our full-length articles run approximately 4,000 words, and for these we pay from $1,500 to $2,500 on acceptance. Our shorter pieces run from 1,000-2,500 words, and for these we pay from $750 to $1,500 on acceptance." Unsolicited articles and proposals should be addressed to Articles Editor. *Arts and Leisure* section of *The New York Times* appears on Sunday. Wants "to encourage imaginativeness in terms of form and approach—stressing ideas, issues, trends, investigations, symbolic reporting and stories delving deeply into the creative achievements and processes of artists and entertainers—and seeks to break away from old-fashioned gushy, fan magazine stuff." Length:

4,000 words. Pays $100-250, depending on length. *Arts and Leisure* Editor: William H. Honan.
Photos: Send to Photo Editor. Pays $75 minimum for b&w photos.
Tips: "The Op Ed page is always looking for new material and publishes many people who have never been published before. We want material of universal relevance which people can talk about in a personal way. When writing for the Op Ed page, there is no formula, but the writing itself should have some polish. Don't make the mistake of pontificating on the news. We're not looking for more political columnists. Op Ed length runs about 750 words, and pays about $150."

NEW YORK'S NIGHTLIFE AND LONG ISLAND'S NIGHTLIFE, MJC Publications Inc., 1770 Deer Park Ave., Deer Park NY 11729. (516)242-7722. Publisher: Michael Cutino. Managing Editor: Bill Ervolino. A monthly entertainment magazine. Circ. 50,000. Pays on publication. Byline given. Offers $15 kill fee. Buys first North American serial rights and all rights. Submit seasonal/holiday material 10 weeks in advance. Simultaneous queries and photocopied submissions OK. SASE. Reports in 10 weeks. Free sample copy and writer's guidelines.
Nonfiction: General interest, humor, inspirational, interview/profile, new product, photo feature, travel and entertainment. Length: 500-1,500 words. Pays $25-75.
Photos: Send photos with ms. Reviews b&w and color contact sheets. Pays $10 for color transparencies and b&w prints. Captions and model release required. Buys all rights.
Columns/Departments: Films, Movies, Albums, Sports, Fashion, Entertainment, and Groups. Buys 150 mss/year. Send complete ms. Length: 400-600 words. Pays $25.
Fillers: Clippings, jokes, gags, anecdotes, short humor and newsbreaks. Buys 10/year. Length: 25-100 words. Pays $10.

‡**NEWSDAY**, Long Island NY 11747. Viewpoints Editor: Ilene Barth. 75% freelance written. Opinion section of daily newspaper. Byline given. Computer printout submissions acceptable. SASE.
Nonfiction: Seeks "opinion on current events, trends, issues—whether national or local government or lifestyle. Must be timely, pertinent, articulate and opinionated. Strong preference for authors within the circulation area. It's best to consult before you start writing." Length: 600-2,000 words. Pays $75-500.
Tips: "The writer has a better chance of breaking in at our publication with short articles and fillers since the longer essays are commissioned from experts and well-known writers."

‡**THE NEWSDAY MAGAZINE**, *Newsday*, Long Island NY 11747. (516)454-2308. Executive Editor: John Montorio. Managing Editor: Stanley Green. For well-educated, affluent suburban readers. Sunday magazine. Circ. 600,000. Pays on publication. Byline given. Buys all rights. Electronic submissions OK. Computer printout submissions acceptable. SASE.
Nonfiction: Miriam Smith, graphics director. "We buy only a limited number of freelance pieces, usually when the freelancer has a specific expertise or point of view that isn't available on *Newsday*'s own staff." No poetry or fiction. Length: 2,000-2,500 words. Pays $400-600.
Photos: B&w contact sheets and 35mm transparencies purchased on assignment. Pays $100/page maximum for b&w; $200/page maximum for color, including cover.

OUR TOWN, East Side/West Side Communications Corp., 435 E. 86th St., New York NY 10028. (212)289-8700. Editor: Ed Kayatt. 70% freelance written. Weekly tabloid covering neighborhood news of Manhattan (96th St.-14th St.). Circ. 110,000. Pays on publication. Publishes ms an average of 1 month after acceptance. Byline given. Buys first serial rights. Submit seasonal/holiday material 1 month in advance. SASE.
Nonfiction: Expose (especially consumer ripoffs); historical/nostalgic (Manhattan, 14th St.-96th St.); interview/profile (of local personalities); photo feature (of local event); and animal rights. "We're looking for local news (Manhattan only, mainly 14th St.-96th St.). We need timely, lively coverage of local issues and events, focusing on people or exposing injustice and good deeds of local residents and business people. (Get *full names, spelled right.*)" Special issues include Education (January, March and August); and Summer Camps (March). Query with published clips. Length: 1,000 words maximum. Pays "70¢/20-pica column-inch as published." Sometimes pays expenses of writers on assignment.
Photos: Pays $2-5 for 8x10 b&w prints. Buys all rights.
Tips: "Come by the office and talk to the editor. (Call first.) Bring samples of writing."

‡**SUBURBIA TODAY**, Gannett Newspapers, One Gannett Dr., White Plains NY 10604. (914)694-5024. Editor: Meryl Harris. Weekly Sunday magazine of the Gannett Westchester Rockland Newspapers. Circ. 200,000. Pays on publication. Buys one-time rights. Submit seasonal/holiday material 3 months in advance. Simultaneous queries, and simultaneous (out of circulation area) and previously published submissions OK. Must provide SASE. Reports in 6 weeks. Not responsible for return of unsolicited mss.
Nonfiction: General interest (lifestyle); historical (well-written local area history); interview/profile (of well-known and lesser-known local personalities); and trends. Query with published clips. Length: 1,000-4,000

words. Pays $100-300.

Photos: "Most photos are taken by newspaper staff photographers." State availability of photos. Pay is open. Not responsible for return of unsolicited photographs.

North Carolina

CHARLOTTE MAGAZINE, Box 36639, Charlotte NC 28236. (704)375-8034. Editor: Terri Byrum. 95% freelance written. Monthly magazine emphasizing probing, researched and upbeat articles on local people, places and events. Circ. 10,000. Pays on publication. Publishes ms an average of 2 months after acceptance. Buys first serial rights and second serial (reprint) rights. Computer printout submissions acceptable; prefers letter-quality to dot-matrix. SASE. Reports in 3 weeks. Sample copy $2.25.

Nonfiction: Departments: lifestyles (alternative and typical); business (spotlight successful, interesting business and people); town talk (short, local articles of interest); theater, arts, book reviews and sports. No PR promos. "We are seeking articles indicating depth and research in original treatments of subjects. Our eagerness increases with articles that give our well-educated audience significant information through stylish, entertaining prose and uniqueness of perspective. Remember our local/regional emphasis." Query or send complete ms. Length: 1,000-2,000 words. Pays $150-250 for feature articles. Sometimes pays expenses of writers on assignment.

Photos: State availability of photos. Buys b&w and color prints; pay negotiable. Captions preferred; model release required.

Columns/Departments: "Will consider all types of articles." Buys 6 columns/issue. Query. Length: 1,000-1,500 words. Pays $75-150.

Fillers: Anecdotes, newsbreaks, humor, preview of events, and personalities. Buys 6-8/issue. Length: 250-750 words. Pays 5¢/word.

‡**THE NEWS AND OBSERVER**, 215 S. McDowell St., Raleigh NC 27514. (919)829-4572. Editor: Claude Sitton. Managing Editor: Bob Brooks. Daily newspaper in Research Triangle area and eastern North Carolina. Circ. 135,000 daily; 170,000 Sunday. Pays on publication. Byline given. Buys simultaneous rights. Submit seasonal/holiday material 1 month in advance. Simultaneous queries, and simultaneous and photocopied submissions OK. SASE. Reports in 2 weeks on queries; 1 month on mss. Sample copy for 9x12 SAE and 4 first class stamps.

Nonfiction: Marion Gregory, features editor. Interview/profile and travel. Send complete ms. Length: 1,200-1,500 words. Pays $35-60.

Photos: Send photos with ms. Pays $5 minimum for 8x10 b&w prints. Identification of subjects required. Buys "right to use as we see fit in news pages."

‡**SOUTHERN EXPOSURE**, Box 531, Durham NC 27702. (919)688-8167. Contact: Editor. Bimonthly magazine, 72-230 pages for Southerners interested in "left-liberal" political perspective and the South; all ages; well-educated. Circ. 7,500. Pays on publication. Buys all rights. Offers kill fee. Byline given. Will consider photocopied and simultaneous submissions. Submit seasonal material 2-3 months in advance. SASE. Reports in 2 months. "Query is appreciated, but not required."

Nonfiction: "Ours is probably the only publication about the South *not* aimed at business or upper-class people; it appeals to all segments of the population. *And*, it is used as a resource—sold as a magazine and then as a book—so it rarely becomes dated." Needs investigative articles about the following subjects as related to the South: politics, energy, institutional power from prisons to universities, women, labor, black people and the economy. Informational interview, profile, historical, think articles, expose, opinion and book reviews. Length: 6,000 words maximum. Pays $50-200.

Photos: "Very rarely purchase photos, as we have a large number of photographers working for us." 8x10 b&w preferred; no color. Payment negotiable.

Fiction: "Fiction should concern the South, e.g., black fiction, growing up Southern, etc." Buys 6 short stories or plays/year. Length: 6,000 words maximum. Pays $50-200.

Poetry: All forms of poetry accepted if they relate to the South, its problems, potential, etc. Length: open. Pays $15-100. Buys 24 poems/year.

Market conditions are constantly changing! If this is 1987 or later, buy the newest edition of *Writer's Market* at your favorite bookstore or order directly from Writer's Digest Books.

THE STATE, *Down Home in North Carolina*, Box 2169, Raleigh NC 27602. Editor: W.B. Wright. 70% freelance written. Monthly. Buys first serial rights. Pays on acceptance. Deadlines 1 month in advance. Computer printout submissions acceptable; prefers letter-quality to dot-matrix. SASE. Sample copy $1.
Nonfiction: General articles about places, people, events, history, nostalgia and general interest in North Carolina. Emphasis on travel in North Carolina, (devotes features regularly to resorts, travel goals, dining and stopping places). Will use humor if related to region. Length: 1,000-1,200 words average. Pays $15-50, including illustrations.
Photos: B&w photos. Pays $3-20, "depending on use."

Ohio

‡**BEACON MAGAZINE, Akron Beacon Journal**, 44 E. Exchange St., Akron OH 44328. (216)375-8268. Editor: Sanford Levenson. 25% freelance written. Sunday newspaper magazine of general interest articles with a focus on Ohio and Ohioans. Circ. 225,000. Pays on publication. Publishes ms an average of 2 months after acceptance. Byline given. Offers 50% kill fee. Buys one-time rights, simultaneous rights, and second serial (reprint) rights. Submit seasonal/holiday material 2 months in advance. Simultaneous queries, and simultaneous and previously published submissions OK. Computer printout submissions acceptable; prefers letter-quality to dot-matrix. SASE. Reports in 1 month. Free sample copy.
Nonfiction: General interest, historical/nostalgic, short humor and interview/profile. Buys 50 mss/year. Query with or without published clips. Length: 500-3,000 words. Pays $100-500. Sometimes pays expenses of writers on assignment.
Photos: State availability of photos. Pays $25-50 for 35mm color transparencies and 8x10 b&w prints. Captions and identification of subjects required. Buys one-time rights.
Tips: "Writers' most frequent mistakes in completing an article for us are incomplete information (we must 'interview' the writer to plug gaps); and subject worship (writer gushes forth praises of story subject)."

BEND OF THE RIVER® MAGAZINE, 143 W. Third St., Box 239, Perrysburg OH 43551. (419)874-7534. Publishers: Christine Raizk Alexander and R. Lee Raizk. 60% freelance written. Monthly magazine for readers interested in Ohio history, antiques, etc. Circ. 2,500. Pays on publication. Publishes ms an average of 6 months after acceptance. Byline given. Buys first serial rights only. Submit seasonal material 2 months in advance; deadline for holiday issue is October 15. Computer printout submissions acceptable; no dot-matrix. SASE. Reports in 1 month. SASE. Sample copy 75¢.
Nonfiction: "We deal heavily in Ohio history. We are looking for well-researched articles about local history and modern day pioneers doing the unusual. We'd like to see interviews with historical (Ohio) authorities, travel sketches of little-known but interesting places in Ohio, grass roots farmers, and preservation. Our main interest is to give our readers happy thoughts and good reading. We strive for material that says 'yes' to life, past and present." No personal reflection or nostalgia. Buys 60 unsolicited mss/year. Submit complete ms. Length: 1,500 words. Pays $10-25.
Photos: Purchases b&w photos with accompanying mss. Pays $1 minimum. Captions required.
Tips: "Any Toledo area, well-researched history will be put on top of the heap! Send us any unusual piece that is either cleverly humorous, divinely inspired or thought provoking. We like articles about historical topics treated in down-to-earth conversational tones. We pay a small amount (however, we're now paying more) but usually use our writers often and through the years. We're loyal."

CINCINNATI MAGAZINE, Suite 300, 35 E. 7th St., Cincinnati OH 45202. (513)721-3300. Editor: Laura Pulfer. Monthly magazine, 88-120 pages; emphasizing Cincinnati living. Circ. 30,000. Pays on acceptance. Byline given. Offers 33% kill fee. Buys all rights. Submit seasonal/holiday material 3 months in advance. Simultaneous, photocopied, and previously published submissions OK. SASE. Reports in 5 weeks.
Nonfiction: How-to, informational, interview, photo feature, profile and travel. No humor. Buys 4-5 mss/issue. Query. Length: 2,000-4,000 words. Pays $150-400.
Photos: Kay Ritchie, art director. Photos purchased on assignment only. Model release required.
Columns/Departments: Travel, how-to, sports and consumer tips. Buys 5 mss/issue. Query. Length: 750-1,500 words. Pays $75-150.
Tips: "It helps to mention something you found particularly well done. It shows you've done your homework and sets you apart from the person who clearly is not tailoring his idea to our publication. Send article ideas that probe the whys and wherefores of major issues confronting the community, making candid and in-depth appraisals of the problems and honest attempts to seek solutions. Have a clear and well defined subject about the city (the arts, politics, business, sports, government, entertainment); include a rough outline with proposed length; a brief background of writing experience and sample writing if available. We are looking for critical pieces, smoothly written, that ask and answer questions that concern our readers. We do not run features that are 'about' places or businesses simply because they exist. There should be a thesis that guides the writer and the reader. We want balanced articles about the city—the arts, politics, business, etc."

‡**COLUMBUS DISPATCH SUNDAY MAGAZINE**, 34 South 3rd St., Columbus OH 43216. (614)461-5250. Contact: editor. 50% freelance written. Buys one-time rights. Byline given. Payment after publication. Computer printout or disk submissions OK; prefers letter-quality to dot-matrix printouts. SASE.
Nonfiction: "We accept offerings from beginning writers, but they must be professionally written. A good picture helps." Strong Ohio angle preferred. No history without a modern tie-in. Buys illustrated and non-illustrated articles. Length: 1,000-3,000 words. Pays $50-250. B&w photos only. Pays $10 maximum/photo.

COLUMBUS HOME & LIFESTYLES, Columbus Lifestyles, Inc., Box 21208, Columbus OH 43221. (614)486-2483. Editor: Eugenia Snyder Morgan. Executive Editor: Gerald F. Kolly. 80% freelance written. A bimonthly magazine covering homes and lifestyles in the central Ohio area. "Our editorial mission is to portray Columbus and central Ohio people in an exciting, upbeat manner. Estab. 1984. Circ. 15,000. Pays on publication. Publishes ms an average of 4 months after acceptance. Byline given. Offers 25% kill fee. Buys first serial rights. Submit seasonal/holiday material 5-6 months in advance. No simultaneous submissions. Photocopied and computer printout submissions acceptable. SASE. Reports in 1 month on queries; 6 weeks on mss. Sample copy for $2.50, 9x12 SAE and postage ($1.40 third class); writer's guidelines for business SAE and 1 first class stamp.
Nonfiction: General interest, historical/nostalgic, interview/profile. "Stories need to lend themselves to color photography or other visual accompanient." No how-to articles, first-person essays, or exposes. Buys 4-6 mss/issue. Query with published clips. Length: 800-3,000 words. Pays $35-200.
Photos: State availability of photos. Pays negotiable rate for color transparencies. Captions, model release, and identification of subjects required. Buys one-time rights.
Columns/Departments: Homes and interiors (residential and corporate), fashion, historical perspectives, food and entertaining (no restaurant reviews), sports and outdoor activities, business, collectibles, arts and artists, People & Events. Buys 2-4 mss/issue. Query with published clips. Length: 500-1,500 words. Pays $35-125.
Tips: "All sections of the magazine are open to freelancers; however, articles *must* have a regional angle."

COLUMBUS MONTHLY, 171 E. Livingston Ave., Columbus OH 43215. (614)464-4567. Editorial Director: Lenore E. Brown. Monthly magazine emphasizing subjects of general interest primarily to the people of Columbus and central Ohio. Pays on publication. Buys all rights. Byline given. SASE. Reports in 1 month. Sample copy $2.65.
Nonfiction: "We want general articles which relate specifically to Columbus or the central Ohio area." No humor, essays or first person material. "I like query letters which are well-written, indicate the author has some familiarity with *Columbus Monthly*, give me enough detail to make a decision, and include at least a basic biography of the the writer." Buys 4-5 unsolicited mss/year. Query. Length: 100-4,500 words. Pays $15-400.
Photos: State availability of photos. Pay varies for b&w or color prints. Model release required.
Columns/Departments: Art, business, food and drink, movies, politics, sports and theatre. Buys 2-3 columns/issue. Query. Length: 1,000-2,000 words. Pays $100-175.
Tips: "It makes sense to start small—something for our Around Columbus section, perhaps. Stories for that section run between 400-1,000 words."

DAYTON MAGAZINE, Dayton Area Chamber of Commerce, 1980 Kettering Tower, Dayton OH 45423. (513)226-1444. Editor: Linda Lombard. 90% freelance written. Bimonthly magazine covering the Dayton area and its people; "promotes Dayton-area business, people, places and events through informative, timely features and departments." Circ. 10,000. Pays on publication. Publishes ms an average of 2 months after acceptance. Byline given. Buys first serial rights. Submit seasonal/holiday material 4 months in advance. Computer printout submissions acceptable; no dot-matrix. SASE. Reports in 2 months. Sample copy for SAE and $1.50 postage.
Nonfiction: General interest, historical/nostalgic, how-to, interview/profile, opinion and photo feature. Must relate to Dayton area. No articles lacking local appeal or slant. Buys approximately 36 mss/year. Query with published clips. Length: 1,400-3,000 words.
Photos: Send photos with ms. Reviews b&w and color contact sheets and color transparencies. Payment "depends on feature." Captions, model release, and identification of subjects required. Buys one-time rights.
Columns/Departments: Buys 60/year. Query with published clips. Length: 1,000-1,200 words.

THE ENQUIRER MAGAZINE, The Cincinnati Enquirer (Gannett), 617 Vine St., Cincinnati OH 45201. (513)369-1938. Editor: Betsa Marsh. 35% freelance written. Sunday newspaper magazine covering a wide range of topics. Circ. 300,000. Pays on publication. Publishes ms an average of 4 months after acceptance. Byline given. Pays 20% kill fee. Buys first serial rights. Submit seasonal/holiday material 3 months in advance. Simultaneous queries, and simultaneous, photocopied, and previously published submissions OK. Computer printout submissions acceptable; prefers letter-quality to dot-matrix. SASE. Reports in 2 weeks on queries. Writer's guidelies for SASE.
Nonfiction: Book excerpts, general interest, historical/nostalgic, humor, interview/profile and travel (rarely).

No editorials, how-to, new products, inspirational or technical material. Buys 25-40 mss/year. Send complete ms. Length: 1,000-2,400 words. Pays $100-350.
Photos: State availability of photos. Pays $25 per photo. Identification of subjects required. Buys one-time rights.

THE MAGAZINE, 4th and Ludlow Sts., Dayton OH 45401. (513)225-2360. Editor: Ralph A. Morrow. 30% freelance written. Sunday supplement. Circ. 256,000. Byline given. Pays on publication. Publishes ms an average of 3 months after acceptance. Buys first serial rights and second serial (reprint) rights. Computer printout submissions acceptable. SASE. Reports in 2 weeks.
Nonfiction: Magazine focuses on people, places, trends. No first person or essays. Emphasis is on color transparencies supplemented by stories. No travel. Length: open. *"The Daily News"* will evaluate articles on their own merits. Average payment per article: $125." Payment varies depending on quality of writing.
Photos: Photos should be glossy. Evaluates photos on their own merit. Payment variable depending on quality.

OHIO MAGAZINE, Ohio Magazine, Inc., Subsidiary of Dispatch Printing Co., 40 S. 3rd St., Columbus OH 43215. Editor-in-Chief: Robert B. Smith. Managing Editor: Ellen Stein. 65% freelance written. Monthly magazine; 96-156 pages. Emphasizes news and feature material of Ohio for an educated, urban and urbane readership. Circ. 96,573. Pays on publication. Publishes ms an average of 5 months after acceptance. Buys all rights, second serial (reprint) rights, one-time rights, first North American serial rights, or first serial rights. Byline given except on short articles appearing in sections. Pays 20% kill fee. Submit seasonal/holiday material 5 months in advance. Simultaneous, photocopied, and previously published submissions OK. Computer printout submissions acceptable; no dot-matrix. SASE. Reports in 2 months. Sample copy $2; writer's guidelines for SASE.
Nonfiction: Features: 2,000-8,000 words. Pays $250-700. Cover pieces $600-850; Ohioana and Ohioans (should be offbeat with solid news interest; 50-250 words, pays $15-50); Ohioguide (pieces on upcoming Ohio events, must be offbeat and worth traveling for; 100-300 words, pays $10-15); Diner's Digest ("We are still looking for writers with extensive restaurant reviewing experience to do 5-10 short reviews each month in specific sections of the state on a specific topic. Fee is on a retainer basis and negotiable"); Money (covering business related news items, profiles of prominent people in business community, personal finance—all Ohio angle; 300-1,000 words, pays $50-250); and Living (embodies dining in, home furnishings, gardening and architecture; 300-1,000 words, pays $50-250). "Send submissions for features to Robert B. Smith, editor-in-chief, or Ellen Stein, managing editor; Ohioguide and Diner's Digest to services editor; and Money to Ellen Stein, managing editor. No political columns or articles of limited geographical interest (must be of interest to all of Ohio). Buys 40 unsolicited mss/year. Sometimes pays expenses of writers on assignment.
Columns & Departments: Contact Ellen Stein. Sports, Last Word, travel, fashion and wine. Open to suggestions for new columns/departments.
Photos: Tom Hawley, art director. Rate negotiable.
Tips: "Freelancers should send a brief prospectus prior to submission of the complete article. All articles should have a definite Ohio application."

‡**TOLEDO MAGAZINE**, The Blade, 541 Superior St., Toledo OH 43660. (419)245-6121. Editor: Sue Stankey. Managing Editor: Steve Fisher. 75% freelance written. Weekly general interest magazine that appears in the Sunday edition of newspaper. Circ. 225,000. Pays on publication. Publishes ms an average of 1 month after acceptance. Byline given. Buys one-time rights. Submit seasonal/holiday material 4-6 months in advance. Simultaneous queries and submissions OK. Computer printout submissions acceptable; no dot-matrix. SASE. Reports in 2 weeks on queries; 1 month on mss. Sample copy for SAE.
Nonfiction: General interest, historical/nostalgic, humor, interview/profile and personal experience. Buys 100-200 mss/year. Query with or without published clips. Length: 500-6,000 words. Pays $75-3,000. Sometimes pays expenses of writers on assignment.
Photos: Dave Cron, photo editor. State availability of photos. Reviews b&w and color contact sheets. Payment negotiable. Captions, model release, and identification of subjects required. Buys one-time rights.
Tips: "Submit a well-organized story proposal and include copies of previously published stories."

Oklahoma

OKLAHOMA LIVING MAGAZINE, Criss-Cross Numerical Directory, Inc. Blythe Publications, Box 76179, Oklahoma City OK 73147. (405)943-4289. Managing Editor: Linda Adlof. 5% freelance written. A bimonthly magazine for home buyers and of general interest in central Oklahoma. "We have three magazines within the cover of *Oklahoma Living*: City Living, Home Living, and Apartment Living. Many articles are centered around the building industry." Pays 75 days after acceptance. Buys first serial rights and second serial (reprint) rights. Computer printout submissions acceptable; no dot-matrix.

Nonfiction: "Each magazine has its own cover story. Past features in City Living have included subjects like pardon and parole in Oklahoma, bankruptcy, health and fitness, behind the scenes at an Oklahoma University football game, and passing down of family businesses, as well as fashion and how-to's. We also want and require localized stories and may want a story of national interest and add a side-bar on a local slant of our own." Buys 8-10 mss/year. Query with published clips. Pays $100/published page (4 double-spaced typed pages).
Photos: State availability of photos. Pays $15-20 for 5x7 b&w prints. Captions, model release, and identification of subjects required.
Columns/Departments: "We have our own local columns but would consider columns on related subjects." Query with published clips.

OKLAHOMA TODAY, Oklahoma Department of Tourism and Recreation, Box 53384, Oklahoma City OK 73152. Editor: Sue Carter. Managing Editor: Kate Jones. 90% freelance written. Bimonthly magazine covering travel and recreation in the state of Oklahoma. "We are interested in showing off the best Oklahoma has to offer; we're pretty serious about our travel slant but will also consider history and personality profiles." Circ. 30,000. Pays on acceptance. Publishes ms an average of 4 months after acceptance. Byline given. Buys first serial rights. Submit seasonal/holiday material 1 year in advance "depending on photographic requirements." Simultaneous queries and photocopied submissions OK. "We don't mind letter-quality computer printout submissions at all, provided they are presented in manuscript format, i.e., double spaced and on 8½x11 sheets, or a size close to that. No scrolls, no dot-matrix please." Reports in 2 months. SASE. Sample copy $2; writer's guidelines with SASE.
Nonfiction: Book excerpts (pre-publication only, on Oklahoma topics); photo feature and travel (in Oklahoma). "We are a specialized market; no first person reminiscences or fashion, memoirs, though just about any topic can be used if given a travel slant." Buys 35-40 mss/year. Query with published clips; no phone queries. Length: 1,000-1,500 words. Pays $150-250. Sometimes pays expenses of writers on assignment.
Photos: High-quality color transparencies, b&w prints. "We are especially interested in developing contacts with photographers who either live in Oklahoma or have shot here. Send samples and price range." Free photo guidelines with SASE. Send photos with ms. Pays $50-100 for b&w and $50-250 for color; reviews 2¼ and 35mm color transparencies. Model release, identification of subjects, and other information for captions required. Buys one-time rights plus right to use photos for promotional purposes.
Tips: "The best way to become a regular contributor to *Oklahoma Today* is to query us with one or more story ideas, each developed to give us an idea of your proposed slant. We're looking for *lively* writing—writing that doesn't need to be heavily edited and is newspaper style. We have a two-person editorial staff, and freelancers who can write and have done their homework get called again and again."

Oregon

CASCADES EAST, 716 NE 4th St., Box 5784, Bend OR 97708. (503)382-0127. Editor: Geoff Hill. 100% freelance written. Quarterly magazine; 48 pages. For "all ages as long as they are interested in outdoor recreation in central Oregon: fishing, hunting, sight-seeing, hiking, bicycling, mountain climbing, backpacking, rockhounding, skiing, snowmobiling, etc." Circ. 7,000 (distributed throughout area resorts and motels and to subscribers). Pays on publication. Publishes ms an average of 6 months after acceptance. Buys all rights. Byline given. Submit seasonal/holiday material 6 months in advance. Computer printout submissions acceptable; no dot-matrix. SASE. Reports in 6 weeks. Sample copy $2.
Nonfiction: General interest (first person experiences in outdoor central Oregon—with photos, can be dramatic, humorous or factual); historical (for feature, "Little Known Tales from Oregon History", with b&w photos); and personal experience (needed on outdoor subjects: dramatic, humorous or factual). "No articles that are too general, sight-seeing articles that come from a travel folder, or outdoor articles without the first person approach." Buys 20-30 unsolicited mss/year. Query. Length: 1,000-3,000 words. Pays 3-10¢/word.
Photos: "Old photos will greatly enhance chances of selling a historical feature. First person articles need black and white photos, also." Pays $8-15 for b&w; $15-50 for color transparencies. Captions preferred. Buys one-time rights.
Tips: "Submit stories a year or so in advance of publication. We are seasonal and must plan editorials for summer '86 in the spring of '85, etc., in case seasonal photos are needed."

Pennsylvania

‡**CITY TAB PITTSBURGH**, Pittsburgh People Publication, Business Communications Inc., 2545-47 Brownsville Rd., Pittsburgh PA 15210. (412)885-7600. Editor: Betty Koffler. 75% freelance written. Bimonthly metropolitan entertainment/city life tabloid. Estab. 1983. Circ. 55,000. Pays on 10th month following publication. Publishes ms an average of 2 months after acceptance. Buys all rights. Submit seasonal/holi-

day material 3 months in advance. Photocopied submissions OK. Computer printout submissions acceptable; prefers letter-quality to dot-matrix. SASE. Reports in 1 month. Free sample copy and writer's guidelines.

Nonfiction: Bill Simmons, articles editor. General interest, historical/nostalgic, humor, interview/profile, opinion, photo feature and travel. Buys 200 mss/year. Send complete ms. Length: 400-800 words. Pays 6¢/word.

Photos: Bill Simmons, photo editor. Send photos with ms. Reviews color transparencies and b&w prints. Pays $15 for color; $5 for b&w. Identification of subjects required. Buys all rights.

Columns/Departments: Bill Simmons, column/department editor. Buys 25 mss/year. Send complete ms. Length: 300-500 words. Pays 6¢/word.

Tips: General feature area most open to freelancers. Prefers timeliness in articles.

ERIE & CHAUTAUQUA MAGAZINE, Charles H. Strong Bldg., 1250 Tower Ln., Erie PA 16505. (814)452-6070. Editor: Mary J. Brownlie. 80% freelance written. Quarterly magazine covering the region of Erie (city), Erie County, Crawford County, Warren County, Pennsylvania and Chautauqua County, New York; for upscale readers with above average education and income. Circ. 20,000, three issues; 30,000, Spring Guide Issue. Pays 30 days after publication. Publishes ms an average of 9 months after acceptance. Buys all rights. Will reassign rights to author upon written request after publication. Computer printout submissions acceptable; prefers letter-quality to dot-matrix. SASE. Reports in 1 month. Sample copy $2; writer's guidelines for SASE.

Nonfiction: Feature articles (usually five per issue) on "key issues affecting our coverage area, lifestyle topics, major projects or events which are of importance to our readership, area history with relevance to life today, preservation and restoration, arts and cultural subjects." Also profiles. Length: 3,000 words maximum for articles; 1,500 words maximum for personality profiles. Pays $35/published page. "All material *must* have relevance to our coverage area."

Photos: Color photos for covers by assignment only to local photographer. Will consider 8x10 b&w glossies with stories. Pays $15 per b&w for all rights 30 days after publication. Model release and captions required.

Columns/Departments: Business, education, social life, arts and culture, travel (within 100-200 miles of Erie), food/wine/fashions and medical items written by contributing editors. Will consider new departments on basis of resume showing expertise and two sample columns. Length: 750 words maximum.

Tips: "It's rewarding to see a variety of ideas and styles in freelancers. We enjoy being able to give new writers a start and finding the person with special expertise for a special story. But we regret reviewing inappropriate material guidelines, *WM* listings, etc., and notice a lack of discipline in meeting deadlines and inadequate research—stories without 'meat'."

‡PENNSYLVANIA, Pennsylvania Magazine Co., Box 576, Camp Hill PA 17011. (717)761-6620. Editor: Albert E. Holliday. Managing Editor: Joan Holliday. 90% freelance written. Quarterly magazine. Circ. 21,000. Pays on acceptance. Publishes ms an average of 6 months after acceptance. Byline given. Offers 33% kill fee. Buys first North American serial rights. Computer printout submissions acceptable; prefers letter-quality to dot-matrix. SASE. Reports in 2 weeks on queries; 3 weeks on mss. Sample copy $2.50; writer's guidelines for #10 SAE an 1 first class stamp.

Nonfiction: General interest, historical/nostalgic, inspirational, personal experience, photo feature, and travel. Nothing on Amish topics, hunting or skiing. Buys 50-75 mss/year. Query. Length: 250-2,500 words. Pays $25-250. Sometimes pays the expenses of writers on assignment.

Photos: State availability of photos. Reviews 35mm & color transparencies and 5x7 b&w prints. Pays $5-50 for b&w; $10-100 for color. Captions and identification of subjects required. Buys one-time rights.

Columns/Departments: Panorama—short items about people, unusual events.

PENNSYLVANIA HERITAGE, Pennsylvania Historical and Museum Commission, Box 1026, Harrisburg PA 17108-1026. (717)787-1396. Editor: Douglas H. West. 90% freelance written. Quarterly magazine covering Pennsylvania history and culture. "*Pennsylvania Heritage* introduces readers to Pennsylvania's rich culture and historic legacy, educates and sensitizes them to the value of preserving that heritage and entertains and involves them in such as way as to ensure that Pennsylvania's past has a future. The magazine is intended for intelligent lay readers." Circ. 9,000. Pays on acceptance. Publishes ms an average of 9 months after acceptance. Byline given. Buys all rights. Simultaneous queries, and simultaneous and photocopied submissions OK. Computer printout submissions acceptable; prefers letter-quality to dot-matrix. Reports in 3 weeks on queries; 6 weeks on mss. Sample copy for $2.50; free writer's guidelines.

Nonfiction: Art, science, biographies, industry, business, politics, transportation, military, historic preservation, archaeology, photography, etc. No articles which in no way relate to Pennsylvania history or culture. "Our format requires feature-length articles." Buys 20-24 mss/year. Query. Length: 2,000-3,500 words. Pays $0-100.

Photos: State availability or send photos with query or ms. Pays $25-100 for color transparencies. Captions and identification of subjects required. Buys one-time rights.

Tips: "Because we've just begun to pay freelancers, the opportunity for acceptance is good. We are looking for well-written, interesting material that pertains to any aspect of Pennsylvania history or culture. The most frequent mistake made by writers in completing articles for us is making them either too scholarly or too nostalgic. We want material which educates, but also entertains. Authors should make history readable and entertaining."

PHILADELPHIA MAGAZINE, 1500 Walnut St., Philadelphia PA 19102. Editor: Ron Javers. 30% freelance written. Monthly magazine for sophisticated middle- and upper-income people in the Greater Philadelphia/South Jersey area. Circ. 140,000. Pays on publication or within 2 months. Publishes ms an average of 2 months after acceptance. Buys first serial rights. Pays 20% kill fee. Byline given. Computer printout submissions acceptable; prefers letter-quality to dot-matrix. SASE. Reports in 1 month. Free writer's guidelines for SASE. Queries and mss should be sent to Polly Hurst, managing editor.
Nonfiction: "Articles should have a strong Philadelphia focus but should avoid Philadelphia stereotypes—we've seen them all. Lifestyles, city survival, profiles of interesting people, business stories, music, the arts, sports and local politics, stressing the topical or unusual. No puff pieces. We offer lots of latitude for style, but before you make like Tom Wolfe, make sure you have something to say." Buys 50 mss/year. Length: 1,000-7,000 words. Pays $100-1,000. Sometimes pays expenses of writers on assignment.

PITTSBURGH MAGAZINE, Metropolitan Pittsburgh Public Broadcasting, Inc., 4802 5th Ave., Pittsburgh PA 15213. (412)622-1360. Editor-in-Chief: Martin Schultz. 50% freelance written. "The magazine is purchased on newsstands and by subscription and is given to those who contribute $25 or more a year to public TV in western Pennsylvania." Monthly magazine; 132 pages. Circ. 56,700. Pays on publication. Buys all rights. Pays kill fee. Byline given. Submit seasonal/holiday material 6 months in advance. Computer printout submissions acceptable; prefers letter-quality to dot-matrix. SASE. Reports in 2 months. Publishes ms an average of 4 months after acceptance. Sample copy $2; free writer's guidelines.
Nonfiction: Expose, lifestyle, sports, informational, service, interview, nostalgia and profile. No humorous or first person material. Query or send complete ms. Length: 2,500 words. Pays $50-500. Query for photos. Model release required.
Columns/Departments: Art, books, films, dining, health, sports and theatre. "All must relate to Pittsburgh or western Pennsylvania."
Tips: "Possible new columns coming. It's rewarding to see more varied information and experience in freelancers than staff personnel."

THE PITTSBURGH PRESS SUNDAY MAGAZINE, The Pittsburgh Press Co., 34 Boulevard of the Allies, Pittsburgh PA 15230. (412)263-1510. Editor: Ed Wintermantel. A weekly general interest newspaper magazine for a general audience. Circ. 625,000. Pays on publication. Byline given. Not copyrighted. Buys first serial rights in circulation area. Simultaneous queries acceptable. Computer printout submissions OK. SASE. Reports in 1 month.
Nonfiction: Regional or local interest, humor and interview/profile. No hobbies, how-to or timely events. Buys 40-50 mss/year. Query. "When submitting a manuscript, writer must include his or her social security number. This is a requirement of the Internal Revenue Service since payments for published stories must be reported." Length: 1,000-3,000 words. Pays $100-400.

SUSQUEHANNA MONTHLY MAGAZINE, Susquehanna Times and Magazine, Inc., Box 75A, R.D.1, Marietta PA 17547. (717)426-2212. Editor: Richard S. Bromer. 25% freelance written. Monthly magazine about regional Lancaster County, Pennsylvania, for people in the upper-middle socio economic level who are college educated, ages 25-60, home and family and community oriented, and interested in local history and customs. Circ. 6,000. Pays on publication. Publishes ms an average of 3 months after acceptance. Buys all rights. Phone queries OK. Simultaneous and photocopied submissions OK. Computer printout submissions acceptable; no dot-matrix. SASE. Reports in 2 months. Sample copy $2 in advance.
Nonfiction: General interest (history, arts), and historical (local events and personalities). "This material must have a special relationship to the area we cover: Lancaster County and nearby areas in southeast Pennsylvania. No fiction, personal reminscences, or travelogs, please." Serious and scholarly material. Buys 60 mss/year. Send complete ms. Length: 750-2,500 words. Pays $35-75.
Photos: Offers no additional payment for photos accepted with ms. Captions preferred; model release required.
Tips: "Read several copies of *Susquehanna Magazine* to get a feel for our style and preferred material. Write up fresh material or fresh approach to old material, e.g., historical incidents. We accept 'class' material only (informative, intellectually stimulating, accurate)—nothing trite or term-paper-like."

Tennessee

MEMPHIS, Towery Press, Box 370, Memphis TN 38101. (901)521-9000. Editor: Kenneth Neill. 30% freelance written. Circ. 30,000. Pays on publication. Publishes ms an average of 3 months after acceptance. Byline given. Buys first North American serial rights. Pays $35 kill fee. Simultaneous, photocopied, and previously published submissions OK. Computer printout submissions acceptable; prefers letter-quality to dot-matrix. SASE. Reports in 6 weeks. Sample copy $2.
Nonfiction: Expose, general interest, historical, how-to, humor, interview and profiles. "Virtually all our material has strong Memphis connections." Buys 25 freelance mss/year. Query or submit complete ms or published clips. Length: 1,500-5,000 words. Pays $75-500. Sometimes pays expenses of writers on assignment.
Tips: "The kinds of manuscripts we most need have a sense of story (i.e., plot, suspense, character), an abundance of evocative images to bring that story alive, and a sensitivity to issues at work in Memphis. The most frequent mistakes made by writers in completing an article for us are lack of focus, lack of organization, factual gaps and failure to capture the magazine's style. Tough investigative pieces would be especially welcomed."

MID-SOUTH MAGAZINE, *Commercial Appeal*, Box 334, , Memphis TN 38101. (901)529-2794. Editor: Karen Brehm. 10% freelance written. Sunday newspaper supplement. Circ. 300,000. Pays after publication. Publishes ms an average of 3 months after acceptance. Byline given. Buys one-time rights. Simultaneous queries, and photocopied and previously published submissions (if so indicated) OK. Computer printout submissions acceptable. SASE. Reports in 3 weeks.
Nonfiction: General interest (with regional tie-in). Buys 12 mss/year. Query with published clips. Length: 1,500-2,000 words. Pays $100.
Photos: State availability of photos. Reviews color transparencies and 5x7 b&w glossy prints. Photos are paid for with payment for ms. Buys one-time rights.

Texas

AUSTIN MAGAZINE, Austin Chamber of Commerce, Box 1967, Austin TX 78767. (512)478-9383 or 339-9955. Editor: Hal Susskind. Managing Editor: Laura Tuma. A monthly business and community magazine; 104-200 pages, published by the Chamber of Commerce; dedicated to telling the story of Austin and its people to Chamber of Commerce members and the community. Circ. 15,000. Offers kill fee. Query letter recommended. Editor strongly suggests reading a recent issue since format has been changed during the last year. Sample available on request. Will consider original mss only. Computer printout submissions acceptable; prefers letter-quality to dot-matrix. SASE. Reports within 3 months. Sample copy available on request.
Nonfiction: Articles should deal with interesting people, businesses, organizations, politics, events, or phenomena relating to the Austin community and in particular Chamber of Commerce members. Articles are also accepted on Austin's entertainment scene and the arts. Length: 750-3,000 words. Pays $75-300.
Photos: B&w and color photos are purchased with mss.

DALLAS CITY MAGAZINE, (formerly Westward), *Dallas Times-Herald*, 1101 Pacific, Dallas TX 75202. Managing Editor: Ron Ruggles. 33% freelance written. Weekly magazine. Circ. 400,000. Pays on publication. Publishes ms an average of 2 months after acceptance. Byline given. Buys first serial rights, first North American serial rights, second serial (reprint) rights, or one-time rights. Submit seasonal/holiday material 3 months in advance. Simultaneous queries, and simultaneous (if outside circulation area) and previously published submissions OK. Computer printout submissions acceptable; prefers letter-quality to dot-matrix. SASE. Reports in 2 months.
Nonfiction: Investigative (of Dallas/Fort Worth); interview/profile (outstanding people of D/FW interest); opinion (essays); and photo feature (album style). No service articles. Recent article/story example: "The New Millionaires." Buys 25 unsolicited mss/year. Query. Length: 1,000-2,500 words. Pays $250-750. Sometimes pays expenses of writers on assignment.
Photos: State availability of photos. Reviews 35mm color transparencies and 8x10 b&w glossy prints. Pays negotiable fee. Captions required. Buys one-time rights.
Tips: "The writer has a better chance of breaking in at our publication with short articles and fillers. Familiarity breeds confidence. And because of limited space, we must be highly selective. Our only criterion is that we find the material interesting and well written, although most accepted submissions have a Dallas slant."

DALLAS/FORT WORTH LIVING, Baker Publications, Suite 400, 5757 Alpha Rd., Dallas TX 75240. (214)239-2399. Publication Director: Tina Stacy. Bimonthly magazine covering housing and relocation for persons in the market for houses, apartments, townhouses and condominiums. Circ. 80,000. Pays on publication. Byline given. Buys all rights. Submit seasonal/holiday material 4 months in advance. Simultaneous queries OK. SASE. Reports in 6 weeks. Free sample copy; writer's guidelines for business size SAE and 1 first class stamp.

Nonfiction: How-to (decorate); new product (local "discoveries"); and technical (energy-saving devices/methods). Buys 30 mss/year. Query with published clips "that show flexibility of writing style." Length: 1,000-3,000 words. Pays 20¢/word.

Photos: State availability of photos. Pays negotiable fee for color transparencies and 8x10 b&w glossy prints. Identification of subjects required. Buys all rights.

Columns/Departments: Luxury Living (customizing a new or old home). Query with clips of published work. Length: 1,000 words minimum. Pays 10¢/word.

Tips: "National assignments on decorating, financing, etc. for all of Baker's city magazines are made by Tina Stacy, publication director. Query her at *Living*, Suite 400, 5757 Alpha Rd., Dallas TX 75240."

DALLAS LIFE MAGAZINE, Sunday Magazine of *The Dallas Morning News*, Belo Corporation, Communications Center, Dallas TX 75265. (214)745-8432. Editor: Melissa East. Weekly magazine. "We are a lively, topical, sometimes controversial city magazine devoted to informing, enlightening and entertaining our urban sunbelt readers with material which is specifically relevant to Dallas lifestyles and interests." Pays on "scheduling". Byline given. Buys first North American serial rights or simultaneous rights. Submit seasonal/holiday material 3 months in advance. Simultaneous queries and submissions OK ("if not competitive in our area"). Computer printout submissions acceptable; prefers letter-quality to dot-matrix. SASE. Reports in 1 month on queries; 6 weeks on mss. Sample copy $1.

Nonfiction: Expose ("anything Dallas-related that is fully substantiated"); general interest; humor (short); interview/profile; and new product. "We look for an exciting style in short, lively, fresh material that is written to indulge the reader rather than the writer. All material must, repeat *must*, have a Dallas metropolitan area frame of reference." Special issues include: Spring and fall home furnishings theme. Buys 15-25 unsolicited mss/year. Query with published clips or send complete ms. Length: 750-2,000 words. Pays $200-650.

Photos: State availability of photos. Pays $15-25 for b&w contact sheets; $25-150 for 35mm or larger color transparencies. Captions, model release, and identification of subjects required. Buys one-time rights.

Tips: "We are focusing sharply on an upwardly mobile, achievement-oriented readership in 25-45 year age range."

EL PASO MAGAZINE, El Paso Chamber of Commerce, 10 Civic Center Plaza, El Paso TX 79901. (915)544-7880. Editor: Russell S. Autry. 100% freelance written. Monthly magazine that "takes a positive look at El Paso people and area activities. Readers are owners and managers of El Paso businesses." Circ. 5,000. Pays on publication. Publishes ms an average of 2 months after acceptance. Byline given. Buys first North American serial rights. Submit seasonal/holiday material 3 months in advance. Simultaneous queries, and simultaneous and photocopied submissions OK. Computer printout submissions acceptable; prefers letter-quality to dot-matrix. Reports in 2 months. Free sample copy and writer's guidelines.

Nonfiction: General interest, business, historical/nostalgic, interview/profile and photo feature. Buys 75 mss/year. Query with published clips. Length: 1,000-2,500 words. Pays 7¢/word.

Photos: Send photos with ms. Pays $10/photo; $300 for cover photo. Captions, model release and identification of subjects required. Buys one-time rights.

Tips: "We are actively seeking feature writers. The writer has a better chance of breaking in at our publication with short articles and fillers because I like to see how well the work can meet the publication's needs. They frequently fail to analyze our market."

FORT WORTH Magazine, Ft. Worth Chamber of Commerce, 700 Throckmorton, Ft. Worth TX 76102. (817)336-2491. Editor: Gail Young. A monthly community magazine about people, places and happenings within Tarrant County for an "affluent, well-educated readership including civic leaders, the chief executive officers of local corporations, and out-of-state FORTUNE 500 companies interested in a reflection of the Ft. Worth lifestyle." Circ. 20,000. Pays on acceptance. Byline given. Not copyrighted. Buys all rights and first North American serial rights. Computer printout submissions acceptable. SASE. Reports in 2 months. Sample copy $2.33; free writer's guidelines.

Nonfiction: Historical/nostalgic (Ft. Worth); business (local angle); photo feature (Ft. Worth link); and Ft. Worth and Tarrant County events. No personal experience. Buys 60 mss/year. Query with published clips. Length: 2,000 words. Pays $100.

Photos: Susan Abbenante photo editor. Send photos with accompanying query or ms. Reviews photos of Fort Worth, cover quality. Pays $75 for 35mm slides or transparencies; $15 for 8x10 b&w prints. Captions, model release and identification of subjects required. Buys one-time rights.

Tips: Feature articles are most open to freelancers. "Because of the Ft. Worth Chamber of Commerce's strong involvement in business, the quality of life and tourism, all of these issues are addressed in some way in the planning of the magazine."

HOUSTON CITY MAGAZINE, Southwest Media Corp., Suite 1450, 1800 W. Loop S., Houston TX 77027. (713)850-7600. Publisher: Lute Harmon. Editor: Fred Rhodes. 35% freelance written. Monthly magazine for upscale audience. Circ. 60,000. Pays on publication. Publishes ms an average of 2 months after acceptance. Byline given. Offers 25% kill fee. Buys first North American serial rights. Computer printout submissions acceptable; no dot-matrix.
Nonfiction: Buys 10-15 mss/year. Query. Length: 1,200-3,000 words. Pays $500-1,500.
Photos: Catherine McIntosh, photo editor. State availability of photos. Captions, model release, and identification of subjects required.
Tips: "Major features are assigned to writers known to us with a proven track record. The most frequent mistakes made by writers in completing articles for us are that the topics are too general; they must have Houston angle and local flavor. Travel pieces are done by staff or Houston-based writers. Columns and departments are done by staff and contributing editors only."

INNER-VIEW, The Newsmagazine of Houston's Innercity, Inner-View Publishing Co., Inc., Box 66156, Houston TX 77266. (713)523-NEWS. Editor: Kit van Cleave. 10% freelance written. A monthly general interest tabloid "specifically for 'inside The Loop' in Houston—the artistic, affluent, trendy part of town." Circ. 50,000. Pays on publication. Publishes ms an average of 1 month after acceptance. Byline given. Buys all rights. Submit seasonal/holiday material 3 months in advance. Simultaneous queries, and simultaneous, photocopied, and previously published submissions OK. Computer printout submissions acceptable; no dot-matrix. SASE. Reports in 2 weeks. Sample copy for $1.20 and 9x12 SAE; writer's guidelines for SAE and 1 first class stamp.
Nonfiction: Historical/nostalgic (about Houston only), humor, interview/profile, opinion and travel. "No religious or broad general articles; pieces need to be exceptional or about Texas or Houston." Buys 20 mss/year. Query with or without published clips or send complete ms. Length: 350-700 words. Pays $50-200. Sometimes pays expenses of writers on assignment.
Photos: Jim Caldwell, photo editor. State availability of photos with query letter or ms. Pays variable rate for 8x10 b&w prints; "we don't buy many photos." Captions and identification of subjects required. Buys one-time rights.
Columns/Departments: Humor. Buys 5-10 mss/year. Query or send complete ms. Length: 350-700 words. Pays $50-200.
Tips: "We would be happy to look at nonfiction and newsy pieces of short length, but we're a local consumer general interest publication with content like *New York*, *New West*, *Chicago Reader*, *D Magazine* and *Texas Monthly*. Feature articles on people who live or work in the 'city-center' area of Houston are most open to freelancers. Most people who write us from *Writer's Market* never request a copy of our publication, so they don't have the slightest idea what we're all about."

‡**NIGHTBEAT MAGAZINE**, "Houston's Only Complete Entertainment Magazine", Nightbeat Magazine, Inc., Suite 120, 2055 S. Gessner, Houston TX 77063. (713)785-6233. Editor-in-Chief: Menda Stewart. Managing Editor: Robyn Rivers. 40% freelance written. Monthly magazine covering entertainment in Houston including entertainer's biographies and interviews and restaurant and club listings. Circ. 100,000. Pays on acceptance. Publishes ms an average of 2 months after acceptance. Byline given. Offers $50 kill fee. Makes work-for-hire assignments. Submit seasonal/holiday material 3 months in advance. Simultaneous queries and photocopied submissions OK. Electronic submissions OK via floppy disk compatible with Apple II or Compugraphic. Computer printout submissions acceptable; no dot-matrix. SASE. Reports in 2 weeks on queries; 6 weeks on mss. Sample copy and writer's guidelines for 11x17 SAE.
Nonfiction: General interest (entertainers); humor (entertainment); photo feature (entertainers); and travel. Buys 50 mss/year. Query. Length: 500-1,500 words. Pays $50-150. Sometimes pays expenses of writers on assignment.
Photos: Hank Smith, photo editor. State availability of photos or send photos with query or ms. Reviews contact sheets and transparencies. Pays $20 for 35mm color slides; $18-50 for b&w contact sheets; $25-50 for 5x7 color prints; $25-50 for color contact sheets. Captions, model release and identification of subjects required. Buys rights by individual arrangement.
Columns/Departments: Hank Smith, column/department editor. Film, entertainers, records and events. "All items cover *fun* events." Buys 24 mss/year. Query. Length: 400-1,000 words. Pays $50-100.
Fillers: Robyn Rivers, fillers editor. Jokes, short humor, and newsbreaks (entertainers). Buys 250/year. Length: 100-750 words. Pays $50.
Tips: "Our direction is entertainment. We feature young unknown artists as well as national stars. We need qualified writers to cover concerts, dramas and special events."

‡**SAN ANGELO MAGAZINE**, San Angelo Standard Inc., 34 W. Harris, San Angelo TX 76902. (915)653-1221. Editor: Philip Schoch. Executive Editor: Kandis Gatewood. 10% freelance written. Monthly magazine about San Angelo, Texas and immediate area. "San Angelo magazine is a city magazine with an upscale audience, offering a wide variety of features and profiles." Circ. 7,000. Pays on publication. Publishes ms an aver-

age of 3 months after acceptance. Byline given. Buys first serial rights. Submit seasonal/holiday material 4 months in advance. Computer printout submissions acceptable; prefers letter-quality to dot-matrix. SASE. Reports in 1 month. Sample copy for 9x11 SASE and 4 first class stamps; writer's guidelines for SAE and 1 first class stamp.

Nonfiction: General interest, historical/nostalgic, interview/profile and travel. General interest and historical articles of San Angelo area. A special issue on the elderly in San Angelo is planned. No articles not applicable to San Angelo area. Buys 10 mss/year. Query with published clips. Pays $25-100. Rarely pays expenses of writers on assignment.

SAN ANTONIO HOMES & GARDENS, Suite 785, 1100 N.W. Loop 410, San Antonio TX 78213. (512)342-0162. Editor: June Hayes. Monthly magazine emphasizing San Antonio homes, people, events and gardens for current, former and prospective residents. First issue March 1985. See *Austin Homes & Gardens* for format, departments, rates and requirements.

Tips: "Since this is a new publication, they will be looking for steady freelancers in the San Antonio, Texas, area."

SAN ANTONIO MAGAZINE, Greater San Antonio Chamber of Commerce, Box 1628, San Antonio TX 78296. (512)229-2108. Editor: Sandy Brown. Emphasizes business and quality of life articles about San Antonio. Monthly magazine; 88 pages. Pays on acceptance. Buys all rights. Photocopied submissions OK. SASE. Reports in 1 month. Free sample copy and writer's guidelines.

Nonfiction: "The magazine's purpose is to tell the story of San Antonio, its businesses and its people, primarily to the membership of the Greater San Antonio Chamber of Commerce to the San Antonio community and to prospective businesses and industries. No material about the Alamo, cowboys and Indians, or any non San Antonio topic." Buys 65 mss/year. Query or send complete ms, "query should be readable, typed and give me an element of the story, as well as some idea of the person's writing ability." Length: 800-3,000 words. Pays $75-300.

Photos: Purchased with mss or on assignment. Captions required. Query. Pays $10-25 for 8x10 b&w glossy prints. Prefers to pay according to the number of photos used in an article, a bulk rate.

Tips: "The best way to break in is to be a resident of San Antonio and, therefore, able to write on assignment or to query the editor personally. Again, we are looking for material which is related to the city of San Antonio, its people and the business community. We consider all possible angles and tie-ins. We like to see writers who can tie national economic or business events to San Antonio and support information with figures."

‡**THIRD COAST, The Magazine of Austin**, Third Coast Media Inc., Box 592, Austin TX 78767. (512)472-2016. Editor: John Taliaferro. Managing Editor: Miriam Davidson. 100% freelance written. Monthly magazine covering Austin. "*Third Coast* is designed to give Austinites a broad spectrum of articles about their city. Our audience is mostly in the 25-50 age range, upscale bracket, enjoying a lively, opinionated, and sophisticated point of view." Circ. 17,000. Pays on publication. Publishes ms an average of 3 months after acceptance. Byline given. Offers kill fee of 20% of acceptance price. Buys first North American serial rights. Submit seasonal/holiday material 3 months in advance. Simultaneous queries, and simultaneous and photocopied submissions OK. Electronic submissions OK on IBM, but requires hard copy also. Computer printout submissions acceptable. SASE. Reports in 3 weeks. Sample copy $2; free writer's guidelines.

Nonfiction: Book excerpts, expose, general interest, historical/nostalgic, humor, inspirational, interview/profile, opinion, personal experience, and photo feature. "Articles must have something to do with Austin or Texas state government. We prefer local writers because they have a closeness and an understanding of what's going on." No how-to or technical—or anything trying to sell something." Query with published clips. Length: 200-5,000 words. Pays 10¢/word. Sometimes pays expenses of writers on assignment ("within reason.")

Photos: Ray Helmers, photo editor. Send photos with query. Pays $25-100 for 5x7 b&w prints. Identification of subjects required. Buys one-time rights.

Columns/Departments: David Stansbury, column/department editor. Book reviews, short movie reviews, opinion, humor, personal experience, criticism, and women's issues. Pieces must have an Austin angle to be considered. Query. Length: 800-1,200 words. Pays 10¢/word.

Fiction: "Any kind of fiction is okay, as long as it has something to do with Austin or is written by an Austin writer." Buys 1-2 mss/year. Send complete ms. Length: 800-2,000 words. Pays 10¢/word.

Poetry: "We have never published poetry, but we could be persuaded were it good enough."

Fillers: Anecdotes and short humor. Buys 50/year. Length: 150-700 words. Pays 10¢/word.

Tips: "Our biggest need is for people with a journalistic background or interest who will do in-depth reporting on Austin issues, personalities, and politics—someone who is willing to interview a lot of people and write a comprehensive piece that local readers will not find in the daily paper. A writer has a better chance with short, lesser-paying articles and fillers because we run more of these types of pieces and have more of a need for them. Out-of-town submissions are fine, but we don't publish too many of them because of the wealth of writers in Austin."

ULTRA MAGAZINE,Farb Publications, Inc., Suite 200, 2000 Bering Dr., Houston TX 77057. (713)961-4132. Editor-in-Chief: Tedd Cohen. Executive Editor: Chris Andrews. Managing Editor: Lindsay Mory. Monthly magazine about Texas and Texans, targeted to affluent Texans. Subjects covered include: people, fashion, travel, the arts, food and wine, design interiors, entertainment and social events, all of which must have a strong Texas slant. Circ. 95,000. Pays on acceptance. Byline given. 25% kill fee on assignments not used. Submit material 4 months in advance. Do not submit simultaneous queries. SASE. Reports in 2-3 weeks. Sample copy $4; writer's guidelines for business size SAE and 1 first class stamp.
Nonfiction: General interest, business and investment, interview/profile, photo features and fashion features. No fiction, poetry, "All stories must be of interest to upscale Texans." Buys 50 mss/year. Query with resume or published clips. Length 1,000-2,000 words. Pays $400-1,000. Travel stories must have photos or state availability of photos.
Photos: Veta Redmond, photo editor. Reviews color transparencies. Model release and identification of subjects required.
Columns: Kathryn Means/Bob Daily, column/department editors. Texas people and events, profiles, food and wine, the arts, homes, health, beauty, fashion, jewelry and real estate. Length: 500-1,500 words. Pays $200-500. Query with published clips.

Utah

‡**UTAH HOLIDAY,** Utah Holiday Publishing Company, 419 E. First St., Salt Lake City UT 84111. Editor: Paul Swenson. Monthly magazine; 36-88 pages. Provides provocative, under-the-surface examination of the state of Utah, its peoples, and local affairs. "Readers predominantly live along the Wasatch Front, are college educated, and are in the middle to upper income brackets. They often attend cultural events and restaurants. The readership is diverse, running the gamut from liberal to conservative." Circ. 20,000. Pays on publication. Byline given. Buys first serial rights. Offers 20% kill fee on assigned articles only. Submit seasonal material 6 months in advance. SASE. Reports in 2 months. Free writer's guidelines. Sample copy $3. Query by letter to Editor.
Nonfiction: Regular coverage includes investigative reporting and analysis of local issues, local general interest in entertainment, leisure, lifestyle, people, food, politics, business, travel, photo features, local history and special summer and winter visitor's guides. Length: 1,000-5,000 words. Pays $50-450.
Photos: State availability of photos with query. Captions preferred.
Fiction and Poetry: Length: 1,500-5,000 words. Pays $50-200.
Tips: "If you've never written for us before, include with your query clips or copies of the first few pages of the story itself. It is essential that you study the magazine before trying to write for us."

Vermont

VERMONT LIFE MAGAZINE, 61 Elm St., Montpelier VT 05602. (802)828-3241. Contact: Editor. 90% freelance written. Quarterly magazine. Circ. 120,000. Publishes ms an average of 9 months after acceptance. Byline given. Offers kill fee. Buys first serial rights. Submit seasonal/holiday material 1 year in advance. Simultaneous queries, and simultaneous, photocopied, and previously published submissions OK. Computer printout submissions acceptable; prefers letter-quality to dot-matrix. SASE. Reports in 1 month. Writer's guidelines on request.
Nonfiction: Wants articles on today's Vermont, those which portray a typical or, if possible, unique aspect of the state or its people. Style should be literate, clear and concise. Subtle humor favored. No Vermont dialect attempts as in "Ayup", outsider's view on visiting Vermont, or "Vermont cliches"—maple syrup, town meetings or stereotyped natives. Buys 60 mss/year. Query by letter essential. Length: 1,500 words average. Pays 20¢/word. Sometimes pays expenses of writers on assignment.
Photos: Buys photographs with mss and with captions and seasonal photographs alone. Prefers b&w contact sheets to look at first on assigned material. Color submissions must be 4x5 or 35mm transparencies. Rates on acceptance; color, $75 inside; $200 for cover. Gives assignments but only with experienced photographers. Query in writing. Captions, model release, and identification of subjects required. Buys one-time rights, but often negotiates for re-use rights.
Tips: "Writers who read our magazine are given more consideration because they understand that we want Vermontish articles about Vermont."

VERMONT VANGUARD PRESS, Statewide Weekly, Vanguard Publishing, 87 College St., Burlington VT 05401. (802)864-0506. Editor: Joshua Mamis. Managing Editor: Gail E. Hudson. 70% freelance written. A weekly alternative newspaper, locally oriented, covering Vermont politics, environment, arts, development, etc. Circ. 20,000. Pays on publication. Publishes ms an average of 1½ months after acceptance. Byline given.

Offers 50% kill fee only after written acceptance. Buys first serial rights. Submit seasonal/holiday material 1 month in advance. Simultaneous queries, and simultaneous, photocopied, and previously published submissions OK. SASE. Reports in 1 month.

Nonfiction: Expose and humor. Articles should have a Vermont angle. Buys about 12 mss/year. Query with published clips. Length: 500-2,500 words. Pays $20-100. Sometimes pays expenses of writers on assignment.

Photos: Michael McDermott, photo editor. State availability of photos. Pays $10-20 for b&w contact sheets and negatives. Captions, model release, and identification of subjects required. Buys one-time rights.

Tips: "Short news stories are most open to freelancers. Knowledge of Vermont politics is essential."

Virginia

NORTHERN VIRGINIAN MAGAZINE, 135 Park St., Box 1177, Vienna VA 22180. (703)938-0666. Editor: Goodie Holden. 80% freelance written. Bimonthly magazine concerning the five counties of northern Virginia. Pays first of month following publication. Publishes ms an average of 3 months after acceptance. Byline given. Buys first serial rights and second serial (reprint) rights. Submit seasonal/holiday material 3 months in advance. Simultaneous queries, and simultaneous, photocopied and previously published submissions OK. Computer printout submissions acceptable. SASE. "Send copy of manuscript as we can't guarantee its return." Reports in 2 weeks on queries; 1 month on mss. Sample copy $1; free writer's guidelines.

Nonfiction: "Freelance manuscripts welcomed on speculation. We are particularly interested in articles about or related to northern Virginia." Buys 75 mss/year. Query or send complete ms. Length: 2,500 words minimum. Pays 1½¢/word.

Photos: Prefers good, clear b&w glossy photos. Pays $5/photo or photo creditline. Captions, model release, and identification of subjects required.

Tips: Longer articles preferred, minimum 2,500 words. History articles accepted only if unique.

‡**THE ROANOKER, The Magazine of Western Virginia**, Leisure Publishing Co., 3424 Brambleton Ave., Box 12567, Roanoke VA 24026. (703)989-6138. Editor: Kurt Rheinheimer. 75% freelance written. Monthly magazine covering people and events of Western Virginia. "*The Roanoker* is a general interest city magazine edited for the people of Roanoke, Virginia, and the surrounding area. Our readers are primarily upper-income, well-educated professionals between the ages of 35 and 60. Coverage ranges from hard news and consumer information to restaurant reviews and local history." Circ. 10,000. Pays on publication. Publishes ms an average of 6 months after acceptance. Byline given. Buys all rights; makes work-for-hire assignments. Submit seasonal/holiday material 4 months in advance. Simultaneous queries OK. Computer printout submissions acceptable; prefers letter-quality to dot-matrix. SASE. Reports in 2 months. Sample copy $2.

Nonfiction: Expose (of government tax-supported agencies); historical/nostalgic; how-to (live better in western Virginia); interview/profile (of well-known area personalities); photo feature; and travel (Virginia and surrounding states). "We are attempting to broaden our base and provide more and more coverage of western Virginia, i.e., that part of the state west of Roanoke. We place special emphasis on consumer-related issues and how-to articles." Periodic special sections on fashion, real estate, media, banking, investing. Buys 100 mss/year. Query with published clips or send complete ms. Length: 3,000 words maximum. Pays $35-200. Sometimes pays expenses of writers on assignment.

Photos: Send photos with ms. Reviews color transparencies. Pays $5-10 for 5x7 or 8x10 b&w prints; $10 maximum for 5x7 or 8x10 color prints. Captions and model release required. Rights purchased vary.

Tips: "It helps if freelancer lives in the area. The most frequent mistake made by writers in completing an article for us is not having enough Roanoke area focus: use of area experts, sources, slants, etc."

THE VIRGINIAN, (formerly *Shenandoah/Virginia Town and Country*, Shenandoah Valley Magazine Corp., Box 8, New Hope VA 24469. (703)885-0388. Editor: Hunter S. Pierce, IV. Bimonthly magazine. Circ. 20,000. Pays on publication. Byline given. Offers negotiable kill fee. Buys negotiable rights. Submit seasonal/holiday material 4 months in advance. Simultaneous queries, and simultaneous, photocopied, and previously published submissions OK. SASE. Reports in 1 month. Sample copy $3.50.

Nonfiction: Book excerpts, general interest, historical/nostalgic, food, how-to, humor, inspirational, interview/profile, personal experience, photo feature and travel. Buys 20 mss/year. Query with or without published clips, or send complete ms. Length: 1,000-1,500 words. Pays negotiable rate.

Photos: State availability of photos. Buys one-time rights.

Tips: "Be familiar enough with the magazine to know the tone and character of the feature articles."

Washington

THE SEATTLE WEEKLY, Sasquatch Publishing, 1931 2nd Ave., Seattle WA 98101. (206)441-5555. Editor: David Brewster. 30% freelance written. Weekly tabloid covering arts, politics, food, business, sports and books with local and regional emphasis. Circ. 30,000. Pays 3 weeks after publication. Publishes ms an average of 2 weeks after acceptance. Byline given. Offers variable kill fee. Buys first serial rights. Submit seasonal/holiday material 1 month in advance. Simultaneous queries OK. Computer printout submissions acceptable; no dot-matrix. SASE. Reports in 1 month. Sample copy 75¢; free writer's guidelines.
Nonfiction: Book excerpts; expose; general interest; historical/nostalgic (Northwest); how-to (related to food and health); humor; interview/profile; opinion; travel; and arts-related essays. Buys 25 cover stories/year. Query with published clips. Length: 700-4,000 words. Pays $75-800. Sometimes pays expenses of writers on assignment.

WASHINGTON, The Evergreen State Magazine, Evergreen Publishing Co., 1500 Eastlake Ave. E., Seattle WA 98102. Editor/Publisher: Kenneth A. Gouldthorpe. Managing Editor: Knute O. Berger. 70% freelance written. A bimonthly magazine covering all facets of life in Washington for an in-state audience. Estab. 1984. Circ. 60,000. Pays on acceptance for assigned stories; on publication for "on spec" material. Publishes ms an average of 6 months after acceptance. Byline given. Offers 20% kill fee on accepted stories. Submit seasonal/holiday material 6 months in advance. Electronic submissions OK on disks formatted for Kaypro II. Computer printout submissions acceptable, but leave margins and double-space; prefers letter-quality to dot-matrix. SASE. Reports in 4 weeks on queries; 6 weeks on mss. Sample copy for $2.50; free writer's guidelines.
Nonfiction: Book excerpts (unpublished Washington-related); general interest; historical/nostalgic; humor; interview/profile; personal experience; photo feature; and travel. "Evergreen Publishing Company undertakes book and one-shot publication projects. Washington state ideas encouraged. No political, expose, reviews, or anything not pertaining to Washington or Washingtonians." Query with published clips. Length: features, 1,500-2,500 words; sidebars, 200-600 words. Pays $150-700. Sometimes pays expenses of writers on assignment.
Photos: Carrie Seglin, photo editor. Large format. State availability of photos with query or send photos with query. Pays $50-250 for b&w; $125-325 for 35mm color slides. Captions, model release, and identification of subjects required. Buys one-time rights.
Columns/Departments: As Others See Us (how Washington is viewed by outsiders); Interiors (homes, architecture, decorating, interiors); State of Mind (thoughts and perspectives on the Evergreen State); Washington Post (our letters column); The Attic (our back page potpourri of ads, pictures, curios etc.); Our Town (where we live, from backwoods to small towns and places you've never seen before); Journeys End (inns, lodges, bed and breakfast hideaways); Players (sports and athletes, games and gamesmen); Statewatch (a round-up from all corners: people, quotes and anecdotes from the lighter side of life); Enterprise (business and commerce); Wildside (wildlife, nature); Open air (outdoors and outdoor activities, from backpacking to picnics, from hang gliding to kite flying); Wordsmith (books, writers and wordsmithing); Repasts (great dining, from grand souffles to small cafes); and Almanac (a compendium of history, weather, wit and wisdom). Buys 75 mss/year. Query with published clips. Length: 600-1,200 words. Pays $150-250.
Fillers: Clippings, jokes, gags, anecdotes, short humor and newsbreaks. Length: 50-250 words. Pays $25-100. Must be Washington related.
Tips: "All areas are open, but the writer has a better chance of breaking in at our publication with short articles and fillers since we buy more departmental material. Our articles emphasize people—sometimes writers get sidetracked. We're also looking for original thinking, not tired approaches."

Wisconsin

MADISON MAGAZINE, Box 1604, Madison WI 53701. Editor: James Selk. Monthly magazine; 76-104 pages. General city magazine aimed at upscale audience. Circ. 18,500. Pays on publication. Buys all rights. Reports on material accepted for publication 10 days after acceptance. Returns rejected material immediately. Query. SASE. Sample copy $3.
Nonfiction: General human interest articles with strong local angles. Buys 100 mss/year. Length: 1,000-5,000 words. Pays $25-500.
Photos: Offers no additional payment for b&w photos used with mss. Captions required.

‡MILWAUKEE MAGAZINE, Milwaukee Magazine Ltd., 321 E. Buffalo St., Milwaukee WI 53202. (414)273-1101. Editor: Charles J. Sykes. 60% freelance written. Monthly magazine covering people and events in Wisconsin and the Milwaukee metropolitan area "targeted to affluent, well-educated readers, who want superior, in-depth writing and journalism." Circ. 37,000. Pays on publication. Publishes ms an average of 3 months after acceptance. Byline given. Offers 33% kill fee. Buys one-time rights. Submit seasonal/holi-

day material 3 months in advance. Simultaneous queries OK. Computer printout submissions acceptable; prefers letter-quality to dot-matrix. SASE. Reports in 2 weeks on queries; 3 weeks on mss. Sample copy $2.25.
Nonfiction: Book excerpts, expose (government), general interest, historical/nostalgic, interview/profile, personal experience, photo feature and Midwest travel. Buys 20 mss/year. Query with published clips. Length: 1,000-4,000 words. Pays $275-500. Pays expenses of writers on assignment.
Fiction: Judith Woodburn, fiction editor. Experimental and mainstream. Buys 3 mss/year. Length: 2,000-6,000 words. Pays $250-500.
Tips: "Nonfiction features are most open to freelancers."

WISCONSIN, *The Milwaukee Journal Magazine*, Box 661, Milwaukee WI 53201. (414)224-2341. Editor: Beth Slocum. 50% freelance written. Weekly general interest magazine appealing to readers living in Wisconsin. Estab. 1984. Circ. 530,000. Pays on publication. Publishes ms an average of 4 months after acceptance. Byline given. Buys first serial rights. Submit seasonal/holiday material 4 months in advance. Simultaneous queries OK. Computer printout submissions acceptable; prefers letter-quality to dot-matrix. SASE. Reports in 1 month on queries; 4 months on mss. Sample copy and writer's guidelines for SASE.
Nonfiction: Book excerpts, expose, general interest, humor, interview/profile, opinion, personal experience and photo feature. Special issues planned on fitness, finance. No nostalgic reminiscences. Buys 100 mss/year. Query. Length: 150-2,000 words. Pays $75-500. Sometimes pays expenses of writers on assignment.
Photos: State availability of photos.
Columns/Departments: Opinion, Decorating and Essays. Buys 100 mss/year. Query. Length: 150-300 words. Pays $75-150.

WISCONSIN TRAILS, Box 5650, Madison WI 53705. (608)241-5603. Managing Editor: Susan Pigorsch. 70% freelance written. Bimonthly magazine for readers interested in Wisconsin; its natural beauty, history, recreation, contemporary issues and personalities; and the arts. Circ. 28,000. Buys first rights, and one-time rights sometimes. Pays on publication. Submit seasonal material at least 1 year in advance. Publishes ms an average of 6 months after acceptance. Byline given. Photocopied submissions OK. Computer printout submissions acceptable; prefers letter-quality to dot-matrix. Reports in 1 month. SASE. Writer's guidelines available.
Nonfiction: "Our articles focus on some aspect of Wisconsin life; an interesting town or event, a person or industry, history or the arts and especially outdoor recreation. We do not use first person essays or biographies about people who were born in Wisconsin but made their fortunes elsewhere. No poetry. No articles that are too local for our regional audience, or articles about obvious places to visit in Wisconsin. We need more articles about the new and little-known." Buys 3 unsolicited mss/year. Query or send outline. Length: 1,000-3,000 words. Pays $100-300, depending on assignment length and quality. Sometimes pays expenses of writers on assignment.
Photos: Purchased with or without mss or on assignment. Prefers 2¼" or larger transparencies, 35mm OK. Color photos usually illustrate an activity, event, region or striking scenery. B&w photos usually illustrate a given article. Pays $10-20 each for b&w on publication. Pays $50 for inside color; $100 for covers and center spreads. Captions preferred.
Tips: "We're looking for active articles about people, places, events, and outdoor adventures in Wisconsin. We want to publish one in-depth article of state-wide interest or concern per issue, and several short (1,000-word) articles about short trips, recreational opportunities, restaurants, inns, and cultural activities. We will be looking for more articles about out-of-the-way places in Wisconsin that are exceptional in some way."

Puerto Rico

WALKING TOURS OF SAN JUAN, Magazine/Guide, Caribbean World Communications, Inc., First Federal Building, Office 301, Santurce PR 00909. (809)722-1767. Editor: Al Dinhofer. Managing Editor: Carmen Merino. Magazine published 2 times/year (January and July). Circ. 22,000. Pays on publication. Byline given. Buys one-time rights. SASE. Reports in 1 month. Sample copy $3, 9x12 SAE and $2 postage.
Nonfiction: Historical/nostalgic. "We are seeking historically based articles on San Juan: any aspect of Spanish colonial culture, art, architecture, etc. We must have sources—in fact, we will publish source material at the end of each article for reader reference." Buys 4 mss/year. Query. Length: 2,000-3,000 words. Pays $150.

Canada

CANADIAN GEOGRAPHIC, 488 Wilbrod St., Ottawa, Ontario K1N 6M8 Canada. Publisher: J. Keith Fraser. Editor: Ross Smith. Managing Editor: Ian Darragh. 90% freelance written. Circ. 135,000. Bimonthly magazine. Pays on publication. Publishes ms an average of 3 months after acceptance. Buys first Canadian rights; interested only in first time publication. Computer printout submissions acceptable; prefers letter-quality to dot-matrix. Writer's guidelines on request.

Nonfiction: Buys authoritative geographical articles, in the broad geographical sense, written for the average person, not for a scientific audience. Predominantly Canadian subjects by Canadian authors. Buys 30-45 unsolicited mss/year. Length: 1,500-3,000 words. Pays 20¢/word minimum. Usual payment for articles with illustrations, $500-800 and up. Higher fees reserved for commissioned articles on which copyright remains with publisher unless otherwise agreed.

Photos: Reviews 35mm slides, 2¼ transparencies or 8x10 glossies. Pays $40-175 for color photos, depending on published size; $20-40 for b&w.

Tips: "Refer to our leaflet for guidance of contributors, and pay attention to our requirements."

KEY TO TORONTO, Key Publishers Company, Ltd., 59 Front St. E., Toronto, Ontario M5E 1B3 Canada. (416)364-3333. Editor: Brian Kendall. 60% freelance written. Monthly magazine covering Toronto entertainment, dining and sightseeing. Circ. 80,000. Publishes ms an average of 6 weeks after acceptance. Byline given. Offers 25-50% kill fee. Buys first North American serial rights. Computer printout submissions acceptable; prefers letter-quality to dot-matrix. SASE. Reports in 2 weeks on queries; 1 month on mss. Sample copy $2.50.

Nonfiction: Articles about current-events and happenings of specific interest to visitors. "*Key* appears free in all hotel rooms in the city and provides an informed guide for visitors. Writers must know Toronto to supply an insider's tour of activities and entertainments." Buys 48 mss/year. Length: 1,200-1,400 words. Pays $300.

Photos: State availability of photos.

Tips: Be willing to "change direction or rewrite according to the editor's needs, and do additional research. All articles require color, mood, background, as well as lots of service detail. The articles are meant to give visitors an inside look at our city and urge them to explore it."

OTTAWA MAGAZINE, Ottawa Magazine Inc., 340 Maclaren St., Ottawa, Ontario K2P 0M6 Canada. (613)234-7751. Editor: Louis Valenzuela. 90% freelance written. Monthly magazine covering life in Ottawa and environs. "*Ottawa Magazine* reflects the interest and lifestyles of its readers who tend to be female ages 25-55, upwardly mobile and suburban." Circ. 42,500. Pays on acceptance. Publishes ms an average of 3 months after acceptance. Byline given. "Kill fee depends on agreed-upon fee; very seldom used." Buys first North American serial rights and second serial (reprint) rights. Simultaneous queries, and photocopied and previously published submissions OK. Computer printout submissions acceptable. Reports in 6 weeks. Free sample copy and writer's guidelines.

Nonfiction: Book excerpts (by local authors or about regional issues); expose (federal or regional government, education); general interest; interview/profile (on Ottawans who have established national or international reputations); photo feature (for recurring section called Freezeframe); and travel (recent examples are Bimini, Oxbridge, Mexico). "No articles better suited to a national or special interest publication." Buys 50 mss/year. Query with published clips. Length: 2,000-4,500 words. Pays $350-750; payment under review.

Columns/Departments: James Hale, column/department editor. Lifelines (short editorial style glimpses at the city, including the best (Bull's-Eye) and worst (Bull) aspects of Ottawa. Buys 50 mss/year. Send complete ms. Length: 50-250 words. Pays $25-50.

Tips: "A phone call to our assistant editor is the best way to assure that queries receive prompt attention. Once a query interests me the writer is assigned a detailed 'treatment' of the proposed piece which is used to determine viability of story. Our feature section is the most open. The writer should strive to inject a personal style and avoid newspaper style reportage. We strive for originality. *Ottawa Magazine* doesn't stoop to boosterism and points out the bad along with the good."

THORNHILL MONTH MAGAZINE, Your Community Magazine, Thornhill Publications, Ltd., Box 250, Thornhill, Ontario L3T 3N3 Canada. 40% freelance written. Monthly magazine "of the people, for the people, and by the people of the community of Thornhill." Circ. 18,000. Pays on publication. Publishes ms an average of 1 month after acceptance. Byline given. Photocopied and previously published submissions OK. Computer printout submissions acceptable; prefers letter-quality to dot-matrix. SASE. Reports in 2 weeks.

Nonfiction: Expose, humor, interview/profile, new product and photo feature. Special issues include industry and history. No travel or personal experiences. Stories must have local angle. Buys 80 mss/year. Query with or without published clips. Length: 500-1,500 words. Pays $25-75.

Photos: Send photos with ms. Captions required. Buys one-time rights.

Fiction: 500-1,000 words by local writers only.

Tips: Also publishes *Markham Month* and *Willowdale Month* magazines, community magazines parallel to *Thornhill Month*. "Any article published in one magazine may appear in our sister publication at editor's discretion."

TORONTO LIFE, 59 Front St. E., Toronto, Ontario M5E 1B3 Canada. (416)364-3333. Editor: Marq de Villiers. 100% freelance written. Monthly magazine emphasizing local issues and social trends, short humor/satire, and service features for upper income, well educated and, for the most part, young Torontonians. Uses some fiction. Pays on acceptance. Publishes ms an average of 5 months after acceptance. Byline given. Buys first North American serial rights. Pays 50% kill fee "for commissioned articles only." Phone queries OK. Reports in 3 weeks. SAE IRCs. Sample copy $2.50.

Nonfiction: Uses most types of articles. Buys 17 mss/issue. Query with published clips. Buys about 40 unsolicited mss/year. Length: 1,000-5,000 words. Pays $400-1,500.

Photos: State availability of photos. Uses good color transparencies and clear, crisp b&w prints. Seldom uses submitted photos. Captions and model release required.

Columns/Departments: "We run about five columns an issue. They are all freelanced, though most are from regular contributors. They are mostly local in concern and cover politics, money, fine art, performing arts, movies and sports." Length: 1,200 words. Pays $400-700.

WESTERN PEOPLE, Western Producer Publications, Box 2500, Saskatoon, Saskatchewan S7K 2C4 Canada. (306)665-3500. Editor: R.H.D. Phillips. Managing Editor: Mary Gilchrist. 90% freelance written. Weekly supplement to *The Western Producer*. "*Western People* is about people in western Canada, past and present. Its emphasis is rural but not necessarily agricultural." Circ. 140,000. Pays on acceptance. Publihes ms an average of 9 months after acceptance. Byline given. Not copyrighted. Buys first North American serial rights; rarely buys second serial (reprint) rights. Submit seasonal/holiday material 2 months in advance. Computer printout submissions acceptable; prefers letter-quality to dot-matrix. SASE, IRCs. Reports in 2 weeks on queries; 1 month on mss. Sample copy and writer's guidelines for SAE with 39¢ Canadian postage or IRCs (48¢).

Nonfiction: General interest, profiles of western Canadians, historical/nostalgic, humor, interview/profile, personal experience and photo feature. No opinion or book reviews. Buys 300 mss/year. Send complete ms. Photos increase chance of acceptance. Length: 600-2,500 words. Pays $40-200.

Photos: Photos accompanying ms increase chance of acceptance. Send photos with ms. Pays $10-50/color transparency; $5-25/b&w print and $10-50/color print. Captions and identification of subjects required. Buys one-time rights.

Fiction: Adventure, historical, humorous, mainstream, science fiction, serialized novels, suspense and western. No city stories. "Our readership is rural." Buys 100 mss/year. Send complete ms. Length: 1,000-2,500 words. Pays $50-175.

Poetry: Free verse, light verse and traditional. Buys 50/year. Submit maximum 6 poems. Pays $10-50.

Fillers: Short humor. Buys 50/year. Length: 100-500 words. Pays $10-50.

Tips: "Subject matter must be western Canadian. Writing must be crisp because of format (16 pages, 8x11). Best to send manuscripts rather than queries until editor is familiar with your work." Most open to profiles and contemporary issues in western Canada. "Focus on people, avoid rambling, and bring the reader close to the subject."

THE WESTERN PRODUCER, Box 2500, Saskatoon, Saskatchewan S7K 2C4 Canada. (306)665-3500. Publisher/Editor: R.H.D. Phillips. 15% freelance written. Weekly newspaper with magazine insert; 56-80 pages. Emphasizes agriculture for western Canadian farm families. Circ. 142,968. Pays on acceptance. Byline given. Buys one-time rights. Submit seasonal/holiday material 2 months in advance. Computer printout submissions acceptable. SAE, IRC. Reports in 2 weeks. Free writer's guidelines.

Nonfiction: General interest, historical (western Canada), personal experience, photo feature and profile. "Urban living material is not appreciated; nor is material patronizing farm people." Buys 1,200 mss/year. Submit complete ms. Pays $25-300.

Photos: Pays $15-20 for 5x7 b&w prints. Captions usually required. Buys one-time rights.

Fiction: Adventure, historical, humorous, mainstream, mystery, suspense, and western Canadian subjects. Buys 40 mss/year. Length: 1,500 words maximum. Pays $25-100.

Poetry: Traditional. Buys 51/year. Pays $5-15.

Tips: "Remember that modern farm families are increasingly well-educated, well-travelled and aware of social trends. And they run highly sophisticated businesses."

WINDSOR THIS MONTH MAGAZINE, Box 1029, Station A, Windsor, Ontario N9A 6P4 Canada. (519)966-7411. Editor: Laura Rosenthal. 75% freelance written. "*Windsor This Month* is mailed out in a system of controlled distribution to 19,000 households in the area. The average reader is a university graduate, of middle income, and active in leisure areas." Circ. 22,000. Pays on publication. Buys first North American serial rights. Phone queries OK. Submit seasonal/holiday material 4 months in advance. "We will accept computer printout submissions or industry compatible magnetic media." SAE, IRCs. Reports in 4 weeks.

Nonfiction: Windsor-oriented editorial: issues, answers, interviews, lifestyles, profiles, photo essays and opinion. How-to accepted if applicable to readership. Special inserts: design and decor, gourmet and travel featured periodically through the year. Buys 5 mss/issue. Query. Buys 15 unsolicited mss/year. Length: 500-5,000 words. Pays $20-200.

Photos: State availability of photos with query. Pays $10 for first published and $5 thereafter for b&w prints.

Captions preferred. Buys all rights.

Tips: "If experienced, arm yourself with published work and a list of ten topics that demonstrate knowledge of the Windsor market, and query the editor.

Foreign

GLIMPSES OF MICRONESIA, Box 8066, Tamuning, Guam 96911. Editor: Pedro C. Sanchez. 75% freelance written. Quarterly magazine; 100 pages. "A regional publication for Micronesia lovers, travel buffs and readers interested in the United States' last frontier. Our audience covers all age levels and is best described as well educated and fascinated by our part of the world." Circ. 25,000. Pays on publication. Publishes ms an average of 6 months after acceptance. Byline given. Pays 10% kill fee on assignments. Buys all rights. Submit seasonal/holiday material 8 months in advance. Computer printout submissions acceptable; prefers letter-quality to dot-matrix. SASE. Reports in 1 month. Sample copy $3.

Nonfiction: "Range of subjects is broad, from political analysis of Micronesia's newly emerging governments to examination of traditional culture; historical (anything related to Micronesia that is lively and factual); personal experience (first person adventure, as in our recently published piece about a sailing expedition to the uninhabited islands of the northern Marianas); interviews/personality profiles of outstanding Micronesian or western Pacific individuals; scientific/natural history (in lay terms); photo features (we're very photo-oriented—query us on island or Pacific themes); and travel (we use one per issue about destinations in Asia and the Pacific). No articles from fly-by-night (overnight) visitors to Micronesia." Buys 30 mss/year. Query. Length: 1,500-5,000 words. Pays 5-10¢/word. Sometimes pays expenses of writers on assignment.

Photos: Purchased with or without accompanying ms. Pays minimum $10 for 8x10 b&w prints or $15 for 4x5 color transparencies or 35mm slides. Pay $200-300 for photo essays; $100 for covers. Captions required.

Columns/Departments: Short think pieces on contemporary Micronesia are accepted for the Island Views section. Opinions are welcomed but must be well founded and must reflect the writer's familiarity with the subject. Length: 500-1,200 words. Pays $30.

Poetry: "We use very little but are willing to look at Pacific related themes to be used with photos." Only traditional forms. Pays minimum $10.

Tips: "Writers living in or having first hand experience with Micronesia and the western Pacific are scarce. If you have that experience, have made yourself familiar with *Glimpses*, have a good story idea that is relevant to our region, then we're willing to work with you in developing a good article."

‡**NASSAU, City Review for The Bahamas Capital**, Inter-Continental Publishing Co., Parliament Sq., Box N-1914; Nassau, Bahamas (809)322-1149. Fiction Editor: Barbara Solomon. Managing Editor: Michael A. Symonette. Monthly general interest/literary magazine for a "highly sophisticated resort area." Circ. 50,000. Pays on publication. Buys one-time rights and Bahamas rights. Submit seasonal/holiday material 3 months in advance. Simultaneous and photocopied submissions OK. Computer printout submissions acceptable; no dot-matrix. SASE. Reports in 2 weeks. Sample copy $2; free writer's guidelines.

Nonfiction: Book excerpts, interview/profile, opinion, personal experience and travel. Query. Length: 1,500-3,000 words. Pays $25-125.

Columns/Departments: Book and cinema reviews. Buys 36 mss/year. Query. Length: 1,500-3,000 words. Pays $25-100.

Fiction: Mainstream and novel excerpts. Buys over 60 mss/year. Send complete ms for short stories only. Length: 1,500-3,000 words. Pays $25-125.

Poetry: Free verse and traditional. Buys 40-50 poems/year. Submit 6 poems maximum. Pays $10-26.

Tips: "Well-written short stories (1,500-3,000 words) on serious and contemporary themes have an excellent chance of being published in *Nassau*."

Religious

Some religious magazines report "the Good News of salvation in Jesus Christ with the intent that the reader will be drawn to make a commitment to Christ." Other magazines want just to inspire readers to think of Christ or to help the less fortunate by tithing or volunteering. Each religious magazine relishes certain styles and beliefs. Editors' views on current trends illustrate that the religious market is moving in different directions—depending on each magazine's slant. Such diversity makes reading each magazine essential for the writer hoping to break in. Educational and inspirational material of interest to church members, workers, and leaders within a denomination or religion is needed by the publications in this category. Publications intended to assist lay and professional religious workers in teaching and managing church affairs are classified in Church Administration and Ministry in the Trade Journals section. Religious magazines for children and teenagers can be found in the Juvenile, and Teen and Young Adult classifications.

‡**ADVENT CHRISTIAN WITNESS**, Advent Christian General Conference, Box 23152, Charlotte NC 28212. (704)545-6161. Editor: Robert J. Mayer. 30% freelance written. Monthly religious/denominational magazine. "The Advent Christian Witness is a religious periodical of conservative evangelical pursuasion. It's threefold task focuses on challenging its readers to think about the issues of our time from a Scriptural perspective, promoting Christian missions in Northern America and around the world, and propagating the distinctive doctrines of the Advent Christian General Conference of America." Circ. 5,000. Pays on publication. Publishes ms an average of 6 months after acceptance. Byline given. Buys simultaneous rights, first serial rights, and second serial (reprint) rights; makes work-for-hire assignments. Submit seasonal/holiday material 8 months in advance. Simultaneous queries, and simultaneous, photocopied, and previously published submissions OK. Electronic submissions OK on Kaypro 2X double side-double density disk, and CP/M disk (not IBM compatible), but requires hard copy also. Computer printout submissions acceptable; prefers letter-quality to dot-matrix. SASE. Reports in 6 weeks on queries; 2 months on mss. Sample copy for 9x12 SAE and 4 first class stamps; writer's guidelines for #10 SAE and 1 first class stamp.
Nonfiction: Book excerpts, how-to, inspirational, interview/profile, opinion, personal experience and photo feature. All should relate to Christian themes and issues. Perspective is conservative-evangelical. No mss over 1,000 words or technical theological/doctrinal. Buys 6-8 mss/year. Query with published clips. Length: 400-1,000 words. Pays $15-30. Sometimes pays expenses of writers on assignment.
Photos: State availability of photos. Prefers photos with action and that communicate visually what the writer is attempting to communicate in words. Reviews b&w contact sheets and 5x7 b&w prints. Pays $5-18. Captions required. Buys one-time rights.
Columns/Departments: "We have an 'opinion' section that deals with controversial issues from Christian perspectives." Buys 3 mss/year. Send complete ms. Length: 250-500 words. Pays $15-25.
Tips: "We look for material with content that will stretch people's thinking about the Christian faith. Articles with one or two photographs are especially welcome. Because of our tight budget, we are especially receptive to beginning writers. Feature and opinion articles are most open. Make sure writing is clear, concise, and less than 1,200 words."

AGLOW, Today's Publication for Christian Women, Aglow Publications, Box I, Lynnwood WA 98046-1557. (206)775-7282. Editor: Gwen Weising. 85% freelance written. Bimonthly nondenominational Christian charismatic magazine for women. Pays on acceptance. Publishes ms an average of 6 months after acceptance. Byline given. Buys North American serial rights, and reprint rights for use in *Aglow* magazine in other countries. Submit seasonal/holiday material 6 months in advance. Simultaneous queries and photocopied submissions acceptable. Computer printout submissions OK. SASE. Reports in 2 months. Writer's guidelines for business-size SAE and 1 first class stamp.
Nonfiction: Christian women's spiritual experience articles (first person) and some humor. "Each article should be either a testimony of or teaching about Jesus as Savior, as Baptizer in the Holy Spirit, or as Guide and Strength in everyday circumstances." Send complete ms. "We would like to see material about 'Women of Vision' who have made and are making an impact on their world for God. Query on these first." Length: 1,000-2,000 words. Pays up to 10¢/word. Sends writer's guidelines for more information at time of acceptance.

ALIVE NOW!, The Upper Room, 1980 Grand Ave., Box 189, Nashville TN 37202. (615)327-2700. Editor: Mary Ruth Coffman. Bimonthly magazine including short prose pieces, poetry and essays relating to a theme concerned with Christian life and action, for a general Christian audience interested in reflection and meditation. Circ. 75,000. Pays on publication. Byline given. Pays "negotiated kill fee, when applicable." Rights purchased are negotiated ("may be one-time rights, or newspaper and periodical"). Submit seasonal/holiday material 8 months in advance. Previously published work OK. Computer printout submissions acceptable. SASE. Reports in 2 months on queries; 6 months on mss. Sample copy and writer's guidelines with SASE.
Nonfiction: Book excerpts, humor, inspirational and personal experience. "Send a typed, interesting story or poem that deals with a personal faith journey, relations with other people and the world, questions of meaning, responsibility for the natural world, and/or thoughts on the meaning of existence. Writing should be for the young adult or mature adult, or the adult with a growing faith awareness." No polemic articles. Buys 120 unsolicited mss/year. Send complete ms. Length: 500 words maximum. Pays $5-40.
Photos: Pamela Watkins, photo editor. Send photos with ms. Pays $50-100 for 4x5 color transparencies; $15-

25 for 8x10 b&w prints. Buys one-time rights.

Columns/Departments: Excerpts from devotional classics. Buys 4 mss/year. Query with published clips. Length: 350-800 words. Pays $25-40.

Fiction: Fantasy, humorous and religious. No confession, erotica, horror, romance or western. Buys 10 mss/year. Query with published clips. Length: 100-450 words. Pays $25-40.

Poetry: Avant-garde and free verse. Buys 30 poems/year. Submit maximum 5 poems. Length: 10-45 lines. Pays $5-25.

Tips: "We are seeing *too* many old chestnuts, clippings and plagiarized material now. There used to be very few."

AMERICA, 106 W. 56th St., New York NY 10019. (212)581-4640. Editor: Rev. George W. Hunt. Published weekly for adult, educated, largely Roman Catholic audience. Pays on acceptance. Byline given. Usually buys all rights. Reports in 2-3 weeks. SASE. Free writer's guidelines.

Nonfiction: "We publish a wide variety of material on politics, economics, ecology, and so forth. We are not a parochial publication, but almost all of our pieces make some moral or religious point. We are not interested in purely informational pieces or personal narratives which are self-contained and have no larger moral interest." Articles on literature, current political and social events. Length: 1,500-2,000 words. Pays $50-100.

Poetry: Length: 15-30 lines. Address to Poetry Editor.

‡THE ANNALS OF SAINT ANNE DE BEAUPRE, Redemptorist Fathers, 9597 St. Anne Blvd., St. Anne De Beaupre, Quebec G0A 3C0 Canada. (418)824-4538. Editor: Bernard Mercier. Managing Editor: Roch Archard. 60% freelance written. Monthly magazines on religion. "Our aim is to promote devotion to St. Anne and Christian family values." Circ. 54,000. Pays on acceptance. Publishes ms an average of 1 year after acceptance. Byline given. Buys first North American serial rights. Submit seasonal/holiday material 2½ months in advance. Simultaneous queries and photocopied submissions OK. SASE. Reports in 2 weeks. Free sample copy and writer's guidelines.

Nonfiction: Expose, general interest, inspirational and personal experience. No articles without spiritual thrust. Buys 30 mss/year. Send complete ms. Length: 500-1,200 words. Pays 3-4¢/word.

Fiction: Religious. Buys 15 mss/year. Send complete ms. Length: 500-1,200 words. Pays 3-4¢/word.

Poetry: Traditional. Buys 12/year. Submit maximum 2-3 poems. Length: 12-20 lines. Pays $5-8.

Tips: "Write something educational, inspirational, objective and uplifting. Reporting rather than analysis is simply not remarkable."

AXIOS, 800 S. Euclid St., Fullerton CA 92632. (714)526-2131. Editor: Daniel J. Gorham. 35% freelance written. Monthly journal seeking spiritual articles mostly on Orthodox Christian background, either Russian, Greek, Serbian, Syrian or American. Circ. 4,789. Pays on publication. Publishes ms an average of 4 months after acceptance. Byline given. Offers 50% kill fee. Buys all rights. Submit seasonal/holiday material 4 months in advance. Simultaneous queries, and simultaneous, photocopied, and previously published submissions OK. Electronic submissions OK on MS-DOS, but requires hard copy also. Computer printout submissions acceptable; prefers letter-quality to dot-matrix. SASE. Reports in 1 month. Sample copy $2 and 44¢ postage.

Nonfiction: Book excerpts; expose (of religious figures); general interest; historical/nostalgic; interview/profile; opinion; personal experience; photo feature; and travel (shrines, pilgrimages). Special issues include The Persecution of Christians in Iran, Russia, behind Iron Curtain or in Arab lands; Roman Catholic interest in the Orthodox Church. Nothing about the Pope or general "all-is-well-with-Christ" items. Buys 14 mss/year. Send complete ms. Length: 1,000-3,000 words. Pays 4¢/word minimum. Sometimes pays expenses of writers on assignment.

Columns/Departments: Reviews religious books and films. Buys 80 mss/year. Query.

Tips: "We need some hard hitting articles on the 'political' church—the why, how and where of it and why it lacks the timelessness of the spiritual. Here in *Axios* you can discuss your feelings, your findings, your needs, your growth; give us your outpouring. Don't mistake us for either Protestant or Roman Catholic; we are the voice of Catholics united with the Eastern Orthodox Church, also referred to as the Greek Orthodox Church."

‡BAPTIST LEADER, Valley Forge PA 19482-0851. (215)768-2153. Editor: Linda Isham. For pastors, teachers, and leaders in church schools. 25% freelance written. Monthly; 64 pages. Buys first serial rights. Pays on acceptance. Publishes ms an average of 8 months after acceptance. Deadlines are 8 months prior to date of issue. Computer printout submissions acceptable; prefers letter-quality to dot-matrix. Reports immediately. SASE. Writer's guidelines for SAE with 1 first class stamp.

Nonfiction: Educational topics. How-to articles for local church school teachers and leaders. Length: 1,500-2,000 words. Pays $25-75.

Photos: Purchased with mss. Church school settings; church, worship, children's and youth activities and adult activities. Human interest and seasonal themes. Reviews 8x10 b&w prints. Pays $15-30.

‡**BIBLICAL ILLUSTRATOR**, The Sunday School Board, 127 9th Ave. N., Nashville TN 37234. Editor: Michael J. Mitchell. 5% freelance written. For members of Sunday School classes that use the International Sunday School Lessons and other Bible study lessons, and for adults seeking in-depth Biblical information. Quarterly. Circ. 90,000. Pays on acceptance. Publishes ms an average of 15 months after acceptance. Byline given. Buys all rights. Computer printout submissions acceptable; no dot-matrix. Reports in 2 weeks. SASE.
Nonfiction: Rarely purchases freelance material. Journalistic articles and photo stories researched on Biblical subjects, such as archeology and sketches of Biblical personalities. Material must be written for laymen but research quality must be up-to-date and thorough. Should be written in a contemporary, journalistic style. Query. Pays 5¢/word. Sometimes pays the expenses of writers on assignment.
Photos: B&w and color photos occasionally purchased with ms or on assignment. Pays $35 for b&w, more for color. Captions required.

BRIGADE LEADER, Box 150, Wheaton IL 60189. Editor: David Leigh. 20% freelance written. Quarterly magazine; 32 pages. For leaders in the Christian Service Brigade program throughout U.S. and Canada. Pays on publication. Buys first serial rights or second serial (reprint) rights. Buys 6-8 mss/year. Submit seasonal material 5 months in advance. Photocopied submissions OK. Computer printout submissions acceptable; prefers letter-quality to dot-matrix. Reports in 2 months. Query. SASE. Sample copy for $1.50 and large SAE with 73¢ postage; writer's guidelines for SAE and 1 first class stamp.
Nonfiction: "We are interested in articles about problems in father-son/man-boy relationships, the holistic development of the Christian man, men as role models for boys, and helping boys to cope with their problems." Informational, personal experience, crafts, projects, wildlife and inspirational. Length: 900-1,500 words.
Photos: Photos purchased with or without ms. Pays $25 for b&w, inside; $50-75 for b&w, cover.

THE CATHEDRAL VOICE, St. Willibrord's Press, Box 98, Highlandville MO 65669. Editor: Karl Pruter. 20% freelance written. Quarterly magazine of the World Peace Academy. Covers peace and peace making; "we take the commandment 'Thou Shalt Not Kill' literally." Circ. 1,200. Pays on acceptance. Publishes ms an average of 2 months after acceptance. Byline given. Not copyrighted. Buys first North American serial rights. Submit seasonal/holiday material 2 months in advance. Simultaneous queries and photocopied submissions OK. SASE. Reports in 2 weeks. Sample copy for 5 first class stamps.
Nonfiction: Expose, general interest, historical/nostalgic, inspirational and personal experience. Length: 1,000-4,000 words. Pays $20-40.
Fiction: Religious. Length: 1,000-4,000 words. Pays $20-40.
Poetry: Free verse, light verse and traditional. Length: 24 lines maximum. Pays $10.

CATHOLIC LIFE, 35750 Moravian Dr., Fraser MI 48026. Editor-in-Chief: Robert C. Bayer. 40% freelance written. Monthly (except July or August) magazine; 32 pages. Emphasizes foreign missionary activities of the Catholic Church in Burma, India, Bangladesh, the Philippines, Hong Kong, Africa, etc., for middle-aged and older audience with either middle incomes or pensions. High school educated (on the average), conservative in both religion and politics. Circ. 16,500. Pays on publication. Publishes ms an average of 3 months after acceptance. Buys all rights. Byline given. Submit seasonal/holiday material 4 months in advance. Simultaneous submissions OK. Computer printout submissions acceptable. SASE. Reports in 2 weeks.
Nonfiction: Informational and inspirational foreign missionary activities of the Catholic Church. Buys 20-25 unsolicited mss/year. Query or send complete ms. Length: 1,000-1,500 words. Pays 4¢/word.
Tips: "Query with short, graphic details of what the material will cover or the personality involved in the biographical sketch. Also, we appreciate being advised on the availability of good black-and-white photos to illustrate the material."

CATHOLIC NEAR EAST MAGAZINE, Catholic Near East Welfare Association, 1011 1st Ave., New York NY 10022. (212)826-1480. Editor: Michael Healy. 90% freelance written. Quarterly magazine; 24 pages. For a general audience with interest in the Near East, particularly its religious and cultural aspects. Circ. 130,000. Pays on publication. Publishes ms an average of 4 months after acceptance. Byline given. Buys first North American serial rights. Submit seasonal material (Christmas and Easter in different Near Eastern lands or rites) 6 months in advance. Photocopied submissions OK if legible. Computer printout submissions acceptable; no dot-matrix. SASE. Reports in 1 month. Free sample copy and writer's guidelines.
Nonfiction: "Cultural, territorial, devotional material on the Near East, its history, peoples and religions (especially the Eastern Rites of the Catholic Church). Style should be simple, factual, concise. Articles must stem from personal acquaintance with subject matter, or thorough up-to-date research. No preaching or speculations." Length: 1,200-1,800 words. Pays 10¢/word.
Photos: "Photographs to accompany manuscript are always welcome; they should illustrate the people, places, ceremonies, etc. which are described in the article. We prefer color but occasionally use black and white. Pay varies depending on the quality of the photos."

Tips: "Writers please heed: stick to the Near East. Send factual articles; concise, descriptive style preferred, not too flowery. Pictures are a big plus; if you have photos to accompany your article, please send them at the same time."

CATHOLIC TWIN CIRCLE, Twin Circle Publishing, Suite 900, 6404 Wilshire Blvd., Los Angeles CA 90048. (213)653-2200. Executive Editor: Mary Louise Frawley. 30% freelance written. Weekly tabloid covering Catholic personalities and Catholic interest topics for a mostly female Catholic readership. Circ. 76,000. Pays on publication. Publishes ms an average of 2 months after acceptance. Byline given. Buys all rights. Submit seasonal material 2 months in advance. Simultaneous and photocopied submissions OK, if so indicated. Computer printout submissions acceptable; prefers letter-quality to dot-matrix. SASE. Reports in 2 months on queries; 1 month on mss. Writer's guidelines with SASE. Not responsible for unsolicited mss.
Nonfiction: "We are looking for articles about prominent Catholic personalities in sports, entertainment, politics and business; ethnic stories about Catholics from other countries and topical issues of concern to Catholics. We are interested in writers who are experienced and write on an ongoing basis." No theological issues. Average issue includes 6-7 feature articles. Buys 3-4 mss/issue. Length: 250-1,000 words. Pays 8¢/word. Pays expenses of writers if assigned.
Photos: State availability of photos. Reviews 5x7 b&w glossy prints. Price negotiated. Captions required. Rights vary.
Tips: Writer has a better chance of breaking in with shorter pieces, as "they give a truer example of a writer's style, strengths and weaknesses. Research thoroughly and use quotes from acceptable sources."

CHARISMA, The Magazine About Spirit-Led Living, Strang Communications Co. Inc., 190 N. Westmonte Dr., Altamonte Springs FL 32714. (305)869-5005. Editor/Publisher: Stephen Strang. 60% freelance written. Monthly magazine covering Christianity, especially Charismatic, Pentecostal and Protestant movements. Circ. 150,000. Pays on publication. Byline given. Buys all rights. Submit seasonal material 6 months in advance. Computer submissions acceptable; prefers letter-quality to dot-matrix. SASE. Reports in1 month. Sample copy $1.95; writer's guidelines for 9x12 SAE and 2 first class stamps.
Nonfiction: Contact Steve Haggerty. Narrative miracle (verifiable healings, rescues, etc.), call to action (issues oriented, morality, Christian standards, etc.), Christian family, historical personalities and movements, and seasonal (Mother's Day, Easter, Christmas, Thanksgiving, Valentine's Day). "Articles on Christian personalities, music, colleges and Israel and the Questions and Answers interviews are offered only to established writers with whom we have a working relationship." Special issues include: Bible in January, college in October and March. Christian music in February and July; missions in December. Buys 45 mss/year. Submit completed ms. Length: 1,500-3,000 words. "No queries from writers we do not know." $100-150 for first time authors; more for established "name" authors. Also articles on Charismatic, Pentecostal and Protestant issues and events. Query first. Pays $50-100 on publication.
Tips: "News, miracle articles and family articles are the best place for new writers to break in. Read the magazine before submitting anything."

CHICAGO STUDIES, Box 665, Mundelein IL 60060. (312)566-1462. Editor: Rev. George J. Dyer. 50% freelance written. Magazine published 3 times/year; 112 pages. For Roman Catholic priests and religious educators. Circ. 10,000. Pays on acceptance. Buys all rights. Photocopied submissions OK. Computer printout submissions acceptable. Reports in 2 months. SASE. Sample copy $5.
Nonfiction: Nontechnical discussion of theological, Biblical and ethical topics. Articles aimed at a nontechnical presentation of the contemporary scholarship in those fields. Submit complete ms. Buys 30 mss/year. Length: 3,000-5,000 words. Pays $35-100.

CHOICE MAGAZINE, (formerly *Solo Magazine*), Box 1231, Sisters OR 97759. Editor: Jerry Jones. Assistant Editor: Ann Staatz. Bimonthly magazine. "The Christian magazine about career, lifestyle and relationships." Aimed for those in their 20's and 30's who are evangelical career oriented, college educated. Circ. 40,000. Pays on publication. Submit seasonal material 8 months in advance. Accepts queries only. No unsolicited mss. Reports in 3 months on queries. Sample copy and writer's guidelines $2.50 with large magazine size SASE.
Nonfiction: General interest (articles on adventure appealing to adults in their 20's and 30's); historical (outstanding people in history); how-to (repair, cook, garden, etc.); humor (anything that helps us laugh with others and at ourselves); inspirational (outstanding young adults who have done something inspirational); nostalgia; opinion (from a wide range of people on any topics of interest to baby boomers); travel; new product; personal experience; and personal victory (*Guidepost* style stories about adults who have gone through a specific battle or crisis in life—and have won). "No articles that are not in harmony with Christian principles and Christ's teachings." Buys 20-30 mss/year. Length: 200-2,000 words. Pays 5-10¢/word.
Columns/Departments: Relationships (how to build healthy ones, how to argue, how to break up and how to start new ones); Devotional/Bible Study (anything that would assist in the adult's spiritual growth and development); Single Parenting (anything helpful to the single parent); and Personal Motivation/Self-Help (anything

that would help motivate and challenge people to reach for their maximum). Buys 20-30 mss/year. Query. Length: 200-600 words. Pays 5-10¢/word.

Poetry: Avant-garde, free verse, haiku, light verse and traditional. Buys 4 mss/year. Submit maximum 2 poems. Length: 5-40 lines. Pays $5-$25.

Fillers: Clippings on news and newsbreaks. Buys 36 mss/year. Length: 10-100 words. Pays 5-10¢/word.

Tips: "Get a copy of our magazine to know our market *before* submitting query. Ask friends in their 20's and 30's what kinds of things they would most want to see in a magazine specifically for them, and write about it. Wherever their greatest needs and interests are, there are our stories."

THE CHRISTIAN CENTURY, 407 S. Dearborn St., Chicago IL 60605. (312)427-5380. Editor: James M. Wall. Executive Editor: Dean Peerman. Managing Editor: Linda Marie Delloff. Weekly magazine; 24-32 pages. For ecumenically-minded, progressive church people, both clergy and lay. Circ. 35,500. Pays on publication. Usually buys all rights. Query appreciated, but not essential. SASE. Reports in 1 month. Free sample copy.

Nonfiction: "We use articles dealing with social problems, ethical dilemmas, political issues, international affairs, and the arts, as well as with theological and ecclesiastical matters. We focus on concerns that arise at the juncture between church and society, or church and culture." Length: 2,500 words maximum. Payment varies, but averages $30/page.

CHRISTIAN HERALD, 40 Overlook Dr., Chappaqua NY 10514. (914)769-9000. Editor: David E. Kucharsky. 80% freelance written or commissioned. Monthly magazine; 64 pages. Emphasizes religious living in family and church. Circ. 200,000. Pays on acceptance. Publishes ms an average of 4 months after acceptance. Buys all rights. Submit seasonal/holiday material 6 months in advance. Photocopied submissions OK. Computer printout submissions acceptable; prefers letter-quality to dot-matrix. SASE. Sample copy $2; writer's guidelines with SASE.

Nonfiction: How-to, informational, inspirational, interview, profile and evangelical experience. Buys 10-20 unsolicited mss/year. Query first. Length: 1,500 words. Pays $50 minimum. Pays expenses of writers on assignment.

Photos: Purchased with or without accompanying ms. Reviews 2¼ color transparencies. Pays $10 minimum for b&w; $25 minimum for color.

Poetry: Meaningfully Biblical. Buys 30 poems/year. Length: 4-20 lines. Pays $10 minimum.

Tips: "The writer may have a better chance of breaking in at our publication with short articles and fillers because our challenge is to fit the writer to the assignment and this takes some experience with the writer. The most frequent mistakes made by writers in completing an article for us are not using enough real-life anecdotes and not being sensitive enough to the need for spiritual angles."

‡THE CHRISTIAN HOME, The Upper Room, 1908 Grand Ave., Box 189, Nashville TN 37202. (615)327-2700. Editor: David I. Bradley. Quarterly magazine covering family and marriage. "Our primary audience is families, teenagers and couples, with many of our users being professional people responsible for Christian nurture in the area of family counseling." Circ. 52,000. Pays on acceptance. Byline given. Buys one-time rights, all rights, first serial rights, and second serial (reprint) rights. Submit seasonal/holiday material 1 year in advance. SASE. Reports in 1 week on queries; 1 month on ms. Free sample copy and writer's guidelines.

Nonfiction: General interest, how-to, humor, inspirational, opinion, personal experience and photo feature. Buys 110 mss/year. Send complete ms. Length: 1,200-1,400 words. Pays $20-75.

Photos: State availability of photos. Reviews b&w contact sheets and 2¼x3¼ color transparencies and prints. Model release required. Buys one-time rights.

Columns/Departments: Focuses on specific issues or themes—marriage, parent as priest, single parent, exceptional child, pastor's page. Buys 30-40 mss/year. Length: 100-800 words. Pays $20-55.

Fiction: Adventure, ethnic, historical, humorous and religious. Buys 8 mss/year. Query with published clips. Length: 1,400-1,800 words. Pays $50-75.

Fillers: Jokes, anecdotes, short humor and newsbreaks. Length: 25-100 words. Pays $2-20.

Tips: "We're looking for terse writing, personal experience, and a focus on spiritual growth or how-to."

CHRISTIAN HOME & SCHOOL, Christian Schools International, 3350 East Paris Ave. SE, Box 8709, Grand Rapids MI 49508. (616)957-1070. Editor: Gordon L. Bordewyk. Assistant Editor: Kimberley D. Paxton. 30% freelance written. Magazine published 8 times/year covering family life and Christian education. "The magazine is designed for parents who support Christian education. We feature material on a wide range of topics of interest to parents." Pays on publication. Publishes ms an average of 4 months after acceptance. Byline given. Buys first North American serial rights. Submit seasonal/holiday material 4 months in advance. Simultaneous queries and photocopied submissions OK. Computer printout submissions acceptable; prefers letter-quality to dot-matrix. SASE. Reports in 3 weeks on queries; 1 month on mss. Sample copy for 9x12 SAE and 4 first class stamps.

Nonfiction: Book excerpts, interview/profile, opinion, personal experience, and articles on parenting and school life. "We publish features on issues which affect the home and school and profiles on interesting individuals, providing that the profile appeals to our readers and is not a tribute or eulogy of that person." Buys 40 mss/year. Send complete ms. Length: 500-2,000 words. Pays $25-60.

Photos: "If you have any black-and-white photos appropriate for your article, send them along."

Tips: "Features are the area most open to freelancers. Since our recent format change, we are publishing articles that deal with contemporary issues which affect parents; keep that in mind. Use an informal easy-to-read style rather than a philosophical, academic tone. Try to incorporate vivid imagery and concrete, practical examples from real life."

CHRISTIAN LIFE MAGAZINE, 396 E. St. Charles Rd., Wheaton IL 60188. Editor-in-Chief: Robert Walker. Executive Editor: Janice Franzen. 75% freelance written. Monthly religious magazine with strong emphasis on spiritual renewal. Circ. 100,000. Pays on publication. Buys all rights. Submit seasonal/holiday material 8-12 months in advance. SASE. Reports in 1 month. Free sample copy and writer's guidelines.

Nonfiction: Adventure articles (usually in the first person, told in narrative style); devotional (include many anecdotes, preferably from the author's own experience); general features (wide variety of subjects, with special programs of unique benefit to the community); inspirational (showing the success of persons, ideas, events and organizations); personality profiles (bright, tightly written articles on what Christians are thinking); news (with human interest quality dealing with trends); news feature (providing interpretative analysis of person, trend, events and ideas); and trend (should be based on solid research). Pays $200 maximum.

Fiction: Short stories (with good characterization and mood). Length: 1,500-2,500 words maximum. Pays $125 maximum.

CHRISTIAN SINGLE, Family Ministry Dept., Baptist Sunday School Board, 127 9th Ave. N., Nashville TN 37234. (615)251-2228. Editor: Cliff Allbritton. Monthly magazine covering items of special interest to Christian single adults. "*Christian Single* is a contemporary Christian magazine that seeks to give substantive information to singles for living the abundant life. It seeks to be constructive and creative in approach." Circ. 102,000. Pays on acceptance "for immediate needs"; on publication "for unsolicited manuscripts." Byline given. Buys all rights; makes work-for-hire assignments. Submit seasonal/holiday material 1 year in advance. SASE. Reports in 6 weeks. Free sample copy and writer's guidelines.

Nonfiction: Humor (good, clean humor that applies to Christian singles); how-to (specific subjects which apply to singles; query needed); inspirational (of the personal experience type); personal experience (of single adults); photo feature (on outstanding Christian singles; query needed); and travel (appropriate for Christian singles; query needed). No "shallow, uninformative mouthing off. This magazine says something, and people read it cover to cover." Buys 120-150 unsolicited mss/year. Query with published clips. Length: 300-1,200 words. Pays 5¢/word.

Tips: "We look for freshness and creativity, not duplication of what we have already done. We seek variety targeted to singles' needs. We give preference to Christian single adult writers but publish articles by *sensitive* and *informed* married writers also. Remember that you are talking to educated people who attend church."

‡CHRISTIANITY & CRISIS, 537 W. 121st St., New York NY 10027. (212)662-5907. Editor: Robert G. Hoyt. Managing Editor: Gail Hovey. 10% freelance written. Biweekly Protestant journal of opinion. "We are interested in special issues, foreign affairs, liberation theology and other theological developments with social or ethical implications. As an independent religious journal it is part of *C&C*'s function to discuss church policies from a detached and sometimes critical perspective. We carry no 'devotional' material but welcome solid contemplative reflections. Most subscribers are highly educated, well-informed." Circ. 13,000. Pays on publication. Publishes ms an average of 2 months after acceptance. Byline given. Offers variable kill fee. Submit seasonal/holiday material 2 months in advance. Simultaneous queries and photocopied submissions OK. Computer printout submissions acceptable. SASE. Reports in 1 month. Sample copy $1.35; free writer's guidelines.

Nonfiction: Buys 150 mss/year. Query with or without published clips. Length: 1,000-4,000 words. Pays 3¢/word. Rarely pays expenses of writers on assignment.

CHRISTIANITY TODAY, 465 Gundersen Dr., Carol Stream IL 60188. 25% freelance written. Emphasizes orthodox, evangelical religion. Semimonthly magazine; 55 pages. Circ. 180,000. Pays on acceptance. Publishes ms up to a year after acceptance. Usually buys first rights. Submit seasonal/holiday material at least 8 months in advance. Computer printout submissions acceptable. SASE. Reports in 2 months. Free sample copy and writer's guidelines.

Nonfiction: Theological, ethical and historical and informational (not merely inspirational). Buys 4 mss/issue. Query only. Unsolicited mss not accepted and not returned. Length: 1,000-4,000 words. Pays $100 minimum.

Columns/Departments: Ministries (practical and specific, not elementary); and Refiner's Fire (Christian review of the arts). Buys 12 mss/year. Send complete ms. Length: 800-900 words. Pays $100.

Tips: "We are developing more of our own manuscripts and requiring a much more professional quality of others."

‡**CHRYSALIS**, B-SC Box 38, Birmingham AL 35254. (205)785-9615. Editor: J. Anthony Daniel Jr. 95% freelance written. Quarterly magazine, literary and little, religious. "We are dedicated to the proposition that all art is a creative gift of God. We exist to help the Christian lead a more creative life." Estab. 1984. Circ. 500. Pays on acceptance. Publishes ms an average of 4 months after acceptance. Byline given. Buys one-time rights. Simultaneous and photocopied submissions OK. Computer printout submissions acceptable; prefers letter-quality to dot-matrix. SASE. Reports in 1 month. Sample copy for 6x9 SAE and 1 first class stamp; writer's guidelines for SAE and 1 first class stamp.

Nonfiction: Historical/nostalgic, humor, inspirational, interview/profile and personal experience. "Writers should not limit themselves to religious topics, but should remember that our readership is mostly Christian in one form or another. We like unusual slants in our articles. Please, do not send your testimony. We also frown on pop psychology." Buys 4-5 mss/year. Send complete ms. Length: 10,000 words. Pays $5-10. "We pay poorly—but we do pay. Rates vary according to the editorial judgment of the worth of a piece and the length."

Fiction: Adventure, experimental, fantasy, historical, humorous, mainstream, mystery, religious and science fiction. "We like to see craftsmanship in a story. We see too many obvious first drafts. Lovingly choose your words and we will lovingly publish them." Buys 6-8 mss/year. Send complete ms. Length: 15,000 words maximum. Pays according to length and author.

Poetry: Avant-garde, free verse and traditional. "Please don't send us free verse if you haven't tried traditional. Be specific and restrained with your sentiments. Keep your conversion experience between you and God." Buys 10-15/year. Length: open. Pays $5-10.

Tips: "Send us anything you have written that comes close to art. That is really all we ask. All our material, except for the past masters focus, is freelance. Read us and submit; if you don't ever submit, you are not leading the abundant, creative life Christ has promised you."

CHURCH & STATE, Americans United for Separation of Church and State, 8120 Fenton St., Silver Spring MD 20910. (301)589-3707. Managing Editor: Joseph Conn. 15% freelance written. Monthly magazine; 24 pages. Emphasizes religious liberty and church/state relations matters. Readership "includes the whole religious spectrum, but is predominantly Protestant and well-educated." Circ. 50,000. Pays on acceptance. Publishes ms an average of 2 months after acceptance. Buys all rights. Simultaneous, photocopied, and previously published submissions OK. SASE. Reports in 1 month. Free sample copy and writer's guidelines.

Nonfiction: Expose, general interest, historical and interview. Buys 11 mss/year. Query. Length: 3,000 words maximum. Pays negotiable fee.

Photos: State availability of photos with query. Pays negotiable fee for b&w prints. Captions preferred. Buys one-time rights.

THE CHURCH HERALD, 1324 Lake Dr. SE, Grand Rapids MI 49506. Editor: Dr. John Stapert. 10% freelance written. Published 22 times/year; 32 pages. Publication of the Reformed Church in America. Circ. 58,000. Pays on acceptance. Publishes ms an average of 1 year after acceptance. Buys all rights, first serial rights, or second serial (reprint) rights. Submit material for major Christian holidays 6 months in advance. Photocopied and simultaneous submissions OK. Computer printout submissions acceptable. SASE. Reports in 4 weeks. Sample copy 50¢; free writer's guidelines.

Nonfiction: "We expect all of our articles to be helpful and constructive, even when a point of view is vigorously presented. Subjects include Christianity and culture, government and politics, forms of worship, the media, ethics and business relations, responsible parenthood, marriage and divorce, death and dying, challenges on the campus, evangelism, church leadership, Christian education, Christian perspectives on current issues, spiritual growth, etc." Buys about 60 mss/year. Submit complete ms. Length: 400-1,500 words. Pays 5¢/word.

Photos: Photos purchased with or without accompanying ms. Pays $25 minimum for 8x10 b&w glossy print.

Fiction: Religious. Length: 400-1,500 words. Pays 4½¢/word.

Poetry: Length: 30 lines maximum. Pays $25 minimum.

COLUMBIA, Drawer 1670, New Haven CT 06507. Editor: Elmer Von Feldt. Monthly magazine for Catholic families; caters particularly to members of the Knights of Columbus. Circ. 1,370,812. Pays on acceptance. Buys all rights. Submit seasonal material 6 months in advance. Reports in 4 weeks. SASE. Free sample copy and writer's guidelines.

Nonfiction: Fact articles directed to the Catholic layman and his family dealing with current events, social problems, Catholic apostolic activities, education, ecumenism, rearing a family, literature, science, arts, sports and leisure. Color glossy prints, transparencies or contact prints with negatives are required for illustration. Articles without ample illustrative material are not given consideration. Pays $600 minimum, including photos. Photo stories are also wanted. Buys 30 mss/year. Query or submit complete ms. Length: 2,500-3,500 words.

Photos: Pays $50 per photo used. Pays 10¢/word.

Fiction: Humor or satire should be directed to current religious, social or cultural conditions. Length: 1,000 words. Pays $200.

‡**COMMONWEAL**, 232 Madison Ave., New York NY 10016. (212)683-2042. Editor: Peter Steinfels. Biweekly magazine edited by Roman Catholic laymen. For college-educated audience. Special book and education issues. Circ. 20,000. Pays on acceptance. Submit seasonal material 2 months in advance. "A number of our articles come in over-the-transom. I suggest a newcomer provide sufficient material to establish his or her expertise and let us know something about him/herself (credentials, tearsheets, education or past experience)." SASE. Reports in 3 weeks. Free sample copy.

Nonfiction: "Articles on timely subjects: politics, literature and religion. Original, brightly written mss on value-oriented themes; think pieces. Buys 50 mss/year. Length: 1,000-3,000 words. Pays 2¢/word.

Poetry: Department editors: Rosemary Deen and Marie Ponsot. Contemporary and avant-garde. Length: maximum 150 lines ("long poems very rarely"). Pays $7.50-25.

THE COMPANION OF ST. FRANCIS AND ST. ANTHONY, Conventual Franciscan Friars, Box 535, Postal Station F, Toronto, Ontario M4Y 2L8 Canada. (416)924-6349. Editor-in-Chief: Friar Philip Kelly, OFM Conv. 60% freelance written. Monthly magazine; 32 pages. Emphasizes religious and human values and stresses Franciscan virtues—peace, simplicity, joy. Circ. 10,000. Pays on acceptance. Publishes ms an average of 6 months after acceptance. Buys first North American serial rights. Phone queries OK. Submit seasonal/holiday material 6 months in advance. Computer printout submissions acceptable; prefers letter-quality to dot-matrix. SASE, Canadian postage. Reports in 3 weeks. Writer's guidelines for SAE, IRCs.

Nonfiction: Historical; how-to (medical and psychological coping); informational; inspirational; interview; nostalgia; profile; and family. No old time religion, antiCatholic or pro-abortion material. No poetry. Buys 6 mss/issue. Send complete ms. Length: 800-1,000 words. Pays 6¢/word, Canadian funds.

Photos: Photos purchased with accompanying ms. Pays $8 for 5x7 (but all sizes accepted) b&w glossy prints. Send prints. Total purchase price for ms includes payment for photos. Captions required.

Fiction: Adventure, humorous, mainstream and religious. Canadian settings preferred. Buys 6 mss/year. Send complete ms. Length: 800-1,000 words. Pays 6¢/word, Canadian funds.

Tips: "Manuscripts on human interest with photos are given immediate preference. In the year ahead we will be featuring shorter articles, more Canadian and Franciscan themes, and better photos. Use a good typewriter, good grammar and sense."

‡**CONSCIENCE, The Voice of Pro-Choice Catholics**, Catholics for a Free Choice, 2008 17th St. NW, Washington DC 20009. (202)638-1706. Editor: Susan J. Boyd. Production Editor: Kathleen Regie. 80% freelance written. Bimonthly newsletter covering reproductive rights, specifically abortion rights. "A feminist, pro-choice perspective is a must, and knowledge of Christianity and specifically Catholicism is helpful." Circ. 10,000. Pays on publication. Publishes ms an average of 4 months after acceptance. Byline given. Buys first North American serial rights; makes work-for-hire assignments. Submit seasonal/holiday material 4 months in advance. Simultaneous queries, and simultaneous, photocopied, and previously published submissions OK. Computer printout submissions acceptable; prefers letter-quality to dot-matrix. Reports in 2 months; free sample copy for #10 envelope with 1 first class stamp. Free writer's guidelines for #10 SAE with 1 first class stamp.

Nonfiction: Book excerpts, expose, interview/profile, opinion and personal experience. "Each issue of *Conscience* has a theme. Themes have included "Bioethics," "Pluralism and Abortion 1984," "Reproductive Rights Around the World," and "The Family." No arguments for or against certain bills without thoughtful pro-choice *Catholic* perspective." Buys 6-10 mss/year. Query with published clips or send complete ms. Length: 1,000-3,500 words. Pays $10-100. "Writers should be aware that we are a nonprofit organization." A substantial number of articles is contributed without payment by writers.

Photos: State availability of photos with query or ms. Prefers 3x5 b&w prints. Identification of subjects required. Buys all rights.

Columns/Departments: Book reviews. Buys 6-10 mss/year. Send complete ms. Length: 1,000-2,000 words. Pays $30 maximum.

Fillers: Clippings and newsbreaks. Uses 6/year. Length: 25-100 words. No payment.

Tips: "Say something new on the abortion issue. Thoughtful, well-researched and argued articles needed. Try a book review first. The most frequent mistakes made by writers in completing an article for us are untimeliness and wordiness. When you have shown you can write thoughtfully, we may hire you for other types of articles."

CORNERSTONE, The Voice of This Generation, Jesus People USA, 4707 N. Malden, Chicago IL 60640. Editor: Dawn Herrin. A bimonthly magazine covering contemporary issues in the light of Evangelical Christianity. Circ. 90,000. Pays on publication. Byline given. Buys first serial rights. Submit seasonal/holiday material 6 months in advance. Computer printout submissions acceptable; no dot-matrix.

Nonfiction: Buys 1-2 mss/year. Length: 2,700 words maximum. Pays negotiable rate.

Photos: Send photos with accompanying ms. Reviews 8x10 b&w and color prints and 35mm slides. Identification of subjects required. Buys negotiable rights.

Columns/Departments: Music (interview with artists, mainly rock, focusing on artist's world view and value system as expressed in his/her music); Current Events; Personalities; Film and Book Reviews (focuses on meaning as compared and contrasted to biblical values). Buys 2-6 mss/year. Length: 100-2,500 words (negotiable). Pays negotiable rate.

Fiction: "Articles may express Christian world view but should not be unrealistic or 'syrupy.' Other than smut, the sky's the limit. We want fiction as creative as the Creator." Buys 1-4 mss/year. Send complete ms. Length: 250-2,500 words (negotiable). Pays negotiable rate.

Poetry: Avant-garde, free verse, haiku, light verse and traditional. No limits *except* for epic poetry ("We've not the room!"). Buys 10-50 poems/year. Submit maximum 10 poems. Payment negotiated.

Fillers: Anecdotes, short humor and newsbreaks. Buys 5-15 year. Length: 20-200 words (negotiable). Payment negotiable.

Tips: "A display of creativity which expresses a biblical world view without cliches or cheap shots at non-Christians is the ideal. We are known as the most avant-garde magazine in the Christian market, yet attempt to express orthodox beliefs in language of the '80s. *Any* writer who does this may well be published by *Cornerstone*. Creative fiction is begging for more Christian participation. We anticipate such contributions gladly. Interviews where well-known personalities respond to the gospel are also strong publication possibilities. Much of our poetry and small feature content is published without payment to the writer. This does not mean we do not pay ever, but rather that many of our readers enjoy being published as payment in and of itself. Inform us of a desire for payment and we will contact you before any decision to publish."

THE COVENANT COMPANION, 5101 N. Francisco Ave., Chicago IL 60625. (312)784-3000. Editor-in-Chief: James R. Hawkinson. 25% freelance written. Monthly magazine; 48 pages. Emphasizes Christian life and faith. Circ. 27,500. Pays following publication. Publishes ms an average of 4 months after acceptance. Submit seasonal/holiday material 3 months in advance. Simultaneous, photocopied, and previously published submissions OK. Computer printout submissions acceptable; prefers letter-quality to dot-matrix. SASE. Reports in 3 months. Sample copy $1.50 and $1 postage.

Nonfiction: Humor; informational; inspirational (especially evangelical Christian); interviews (Christian leaders and personalities); and personal experience. "No articles promoting organizations or people not in the church we serve (Evangelical Covenant Church)." Buys 20-30 mss/year. Length: 100-110 lines of typewritten material at 70 characters/line (double-spaced). Pays $15-35.

DAILY MEDITATION, Box 2710, San Antonio TX 78299. Editor: Ruth S. Paterson. Quarterly. Byline given. Rights purchased vary. Submit seasonal material 6 months in advance. Sample copy 50¢.

Nonfiction: "Inspirational, self-improvement and nonsectarian religious articles, 500-1,600 words, showing the path to greater spiritual growth."

Fillers: Length: 400 words maximum. Pays 1-1½¢/word for prose.

Poetry: Inspirational. Length: 16 lines maximum. Pays 14¢/line.

Tips: "All our material is freelance submission for consideration, and we buy approximately 250 manuscripts a year. We must see finished manuscripts; no queries, please. Checking copy is sent upon publication."

DAUGHTERS OF SARAH, 2716 W. Cortland, Chicago IL 60647. (312)252-3344. Editorial Coordinator: Reta Finger. Managing Editor: Annette Huizenga. 40% freelance written. Bimonthly magazine covering Christian feminism. Circ. 3,200. Pays on publication. Publishes ms an average of 8 months after acceptance. Byline given. Offers 33-50% kill fee. Buys first serial rights and first North American serial rights. Submit seasonal/holiday material 4 months in advance. Computer printout submissions acceptable; prefers letter-quality to dot-matrix. Reports in 2 weeks on queries; 2 months on mss. Sample copy $1.75; writer's guidelines for SAE with 1 first class stamp.

Nonfiction: Book excerpts (book reviews on Christian feminist books); historical (on Christian women); humor (feminist); inspirational (biblical articles about women or feminist issues); interview/profile (of contemporary Christian women from feminist point of view); personal experience (women's—or men's—experiences from Christian feminist point of view); and issues of social justice relating to women. Special issues include women and the health care system, inclusive language, patriarchy in the Hebrew scriptures, feminist theology, and women and healing. "No general, elementary aspects of Christian feminism; we've gone beyond that. We particularly do not want pieces about women or women's issues that are not written from a feminist and Christian point of view." Buys 10-15 mss/year. Query with or without published clips work. Length: 500-2,000 words. (Book reviews on Christian feminist books, 100-500 words). Pays $15-60.

Fiction: Christian feminist. Buys 2-4 mss/year. Query with published clips. Length: 500-2,000 words. Pays $15-60.

Tips: "The writer has a better chance of breaking in at our publication with short articles and fillers. Usually we solicit our feature articles on a particular topic that most freelance writers may not be familiar with. The most frequent mistakes made by writers in completing an article for us are writing too-long articles (we have a small magazine); writing on an unrelated topic; or writing about women but not particularly from a feminist point of view."

DECISION MAGAZINE, 1300 Harmon Place, Minneapolis MN 55403. (612)338-0500. Editor: Roger C. Palms. 25% freelance written. Magazine; 44 pages. Conservative evangelical monthly publication of the Billy Graham Evangelistic Association. Circ. 2,000,000. Pays on publication. Publishes ms an average of 1 year after acceptance. Byline given. Buys first serial rights. Computer printout submissions acceptable; no dot-matrix. SASE. Reports in 2 months.

Nonfiction: Uses some freelance material. Best opportunity is in testimony area (1,800-2,200 words); buys 11 unsolicited short testimonies for Where Are They Now? column. Also uses short narratives, 200-400 words and original quotes. "Our function is to present Christ as Savior and Lord to unbelievers and present articles on deeper Christian life and human interest articles on Christian growth for Christian readers. No tangents. Center on Christ in all material." Buys 21 full-length unsolicited ms/year. Pays expenses of writers on assignment.

Poetry: Uses short poems (limit: 24 lines) in Quiet Heart column. Positive, Christ-centered. Uses limited number of poems; send only if considered appropriate for magazine.

Tips: "The purpose of *Decision* is: 1) To set forth the Good News of salvation with such vividness and clarity that the reader will feel drawn to make a commitment to Christ; 2) to strengthen the faith of believers and to offer them hope and encouragement; and 3) to report on the ministries of the Billy Graham Evangelical Association."

THE DISCIPLE, Box 179, St. Louis MO 63166. Editor: James L. Merrell. 10% freelance written. Monthly published by Christian Board of Publication of the Christian Church (Disciples of Christ). For ministers and church members, both young and older adults. Circ. 58,000. Pays month after publication. Publishes ms an average of 9 months after acceptance. Buys first serial rights. Photocopied and simultaneous submissions OK. Computer printout submissions acceptable; no dot-matrix. Submit seasonal material at least 6 months in advance. Reports in 2 weeks to 3 months. SASE. Sample copy $1.25; free writer's guidelines for SAE and 1 first class stamp.

Nonfiction: Articles and meditations on religious themes, short pieces, and some humorous. No fiction. Buys 100 unsolicited mss/year. Length: 500-800 words. Pays $10-50.

Photos: Reviews 8x10 b&w glossy prints. Occasional b&w glossy prints, any size, used to illustrate articles. Occasional color. "We are looking for b&w photos of church activities—worship, prayer, dinners, etc." Pays $10-25; $35-100/cover. Pays for photos at end of month after acceptance.

Poetry: Uses 3-5 poems/issue. Traditional forms, blank verse, free verse and light verse. Length: 16 lines limit. Themes may be seasonal, historical, religious and occasionally humorous. Pays $3-20.

Tips: "We're looking for personality features about lay disciples, churches. Give a good summary of story idea in query. We use articles primarily from disciples, ministers and lay persons since our magazine is written to attract the denomination. We are barraged with features that mainly deal with subjects that don't interest our readers; fillers are more general, thus more easily placed. We work with more secular poets than writers and the poets write in religious themes for us. The most frequent mistakes made by writers in completing an article for us are that the manuscripts are too wordy or the material shows failure to study our publication's style."

‡**DISCIPLESHIP JOURNAL**, NavPress, a division of The Navigators, Box 6000, Colorado Srings CO 80934. (303)598-1212. Editor: E. Calvin Beisner. Managing Editor: Don Simpson. 85% freelance written. Bimonthly magazine of Christian discipleship. "The mission of *Discipleship Journal* is to help people examine, understand, and practice the truths of the Bible, so that they may know Jesus Christ, become like Him, and labor for His Kingdom by gathering other men and women into the fellowship of His committed disciples." Circ. 77,000. Pays on publication. Publishes ms an average of 2 months after acceptance. Byline given. Offers kill fee. Buys first North American serial rights, all rights and second serial (reprint) rights. Submit seasonal/holiday material 6 months in advance. Simultaneous queries, and simultaneous and previously published submissions OK. Computer printout submissions acceptable; no dot-matrix. SASE. Reports in 4 weeks on queries; 3 months on mss. Sample copy and writer's guidelines for 9x12 SAE and $1.24 postage.

Nonfiction: Book excerpts (rarely); how-to (grow in Christian faith and disciplines; help others grow as Christians; serve people in need; understand and apply the Bible); inspirational; interview/profile (of Christian leaders, focusing on discipleship); personal experience; and interpretation/application of the Bible. No personal testimony; humor; anything not directly related to Christian life and faith; politically partisan articles. Buys 85 mss/year. Query with published clips or send complete ms if under 1,000 words. Length: 750-3,000 words. Pays 2¢/word reprint; 7¢/word first rights; 10¢/word permanent rights. Pays the expenses of writers on assignment.

Tips: "Our articles are meaty, not fluffy (we turn down roughly 98% of unsolicited submissions, despite our using few solicited articles) and try to use similar approaches. Don't waste words. Polish before submitting."

‡**ENGAGE/SOCIAL ACTION**, 100 Maryland Ave. NE, Washington DC 20002. (202)488-5632. Editor: Lee Ranck. 2% freelance written. Monthly for "United Methodist clergy and lay people interested in in-depth analysis of social issues, with emphasis on the church's role or involvement in these issues." Circ. 5,500. May buy all rights. Pays on publication. Rights purchased vary with author and material. Photocopied submissions OK, but prefers original. Computer printout submissions acceptable; prefers letter-quality to dot-matrix. Re-

turns rejected material in 4-5 weeks. Reports on material accepted for publication in several weeks. "Query to show that writer has expertise on a particular social issue, give credentials, and reflect a readable writing style." SASE. Free sample copy and writer's guidelines.

Nonfiction: "This is the social action publication of the United Methodist Church published by the denomination's General Board of Church and Society. We publish articles relating to current social issues as well as church-related discussions. We do not publish highly technical articles or poetry. Our publication tries to relate social issues to the church—what the church can do, is doing; why the church should be involved. We only accept articles relating to social issues, e.g., war, draft, peace, race relations, welfare, police/community relations, labor, population problems, drug and alcohol problems." No devotional, 'religious,' superficial material or personal experiences. Buys 50-60 mss/year. Query or submit complete ms. Length: 2,000 words maximum. Pays $50-75. Sometimes pays the expenses of writers on assignment.

Tips: "Write on social issues, but not superficially; we're more interested in finding an expert who can write (e.g., on human rights, alcohol problems, peace issues) than a writer who attempts to research a complex issue."

EPIPHANY JOURNAL, Epiphany Press, Box 14727, San Francisco CA 94114. Editor: Philip Tolbert. 10% freelance written. Quarterly magazine covering religious topics for the contemplative Christian. Circ. 3,000. Pays on publication. Publishes ms an average of 6 months after acceptance. Byline given. Buys first serial rights and one-time rights. Submit seasonal/holiday material 6 months in advance. Simultaneous queries, and simultaneous and previously published submissions OK. Computer printout submissions OK; prefers letter-quality to dot-matrix. SASE. Reports in 1 month on queries; 2 months on mss. "Sample copy and writer's guidelines available for $5, which will be refunded with payment for your first article." Guidelines only for SAE and 1 first class stamp.

Nonfiction: Essays (applications of traditional patristic spirituality for the practicing Christian in the post-modern world and explorations of the embodiment of traditional Christian culture expressed through literature, craft, art and folklore); interviews with current Christian figures; and stories from the lives of the Saints and teachers of the Christian tradition. Buys 4-8 mss/year. Query or send complete ms. Length: 2,000-6,000 words. Pays 2¢/word ($100 maximum). Also book excerpts (from forthcoming or recently published spiritual or religious works).

Columns/Departments: Book reviews (any current literature of interest to the Christian thinker). Buys 10-15 mss/year. Query or send complete ms. Length: 1,000-2,500 words. Pays 2¢/word ($30 maximum).

Tips: "Get to know our magazine, then send us a query letter or ask for an assignment suggestion. We prefer not to see first person/anecdotal accounts. The writer must have a clear grasp of Christian principles and not merely base their views on sentiment; they must be able to contrast these principles with the modern world view in a way that provides a radical critique of contemporary culture while maintaining a pastoral concern for souls. This perspective must be developed in a writer. The most frequent mistakes made by writers in completing an article for us are unclean thought due to poor grasp of principles, lack of penetration into the subject, lack of relevence to daily spiritual life and contemporary problems, and lack of grounding (initiation) in the fullness of the living tradition of orthodox Christianity."

THE EPISCOPALIAN, 1930 Chestnut St., Philadelphia PA 19103. (215)564-2010. Publisher: Richard Crawford. Managing Editor: Judy Mathe Foley. 60% freelance written. Monthly tabloid about the Episcopal Church for Episcopalians. Circ. 250,000. Pays on publication. Publishes ms an average of 1 month after acceptance. Byline given. Submit seasonal/holiday material 2 months in advance. Previously published submissions OK. Computer printout submissions acceptable; prefers letter-quality to dot-matrix. SASE. Reports in 1 month. Sample copy for 3 first class stamps.

Nonfiction: Inspirational, and interview/profile (of Episcopalians participating in church or community activities). "I like action stories about people doing things and solving problems." No personal experience articles. Buys 24 mss/year. Send complete ms. Length: 1,000-1,500 words. Pays $25-200. Sometimes pays expenses of writers on assignment.

Photos: Pays $10 for b&w glossy prints. Identification of subjects required. Buys one-time rights.

Tips: Likes quotes, photos, and active voice.

ETERNITY MAGAZINE, The Evangelical Monthly, Evangelical Ministries, Inc. 1716 Spruce St., Philadelphia PA 19103. (215)546-3696. Editor: William J. Petersen. Managing Editor: Deborah H. Barackman. A monthly magazine intended "to help readers apply God's Word to all areas of life today." Circ. 42,000. Pays on acceptance. Byline given. Offers $25-50 kill fee. Buys first North American serial rights. Submit seasonal/holiday material 6 months in advance. Computer printout submissions acceptable; prefers letter-quality to dot-matrix. SASE. Reports in 6 weeks. Sample copy $2; writer's guidelines for SAE and 1 first class stamp.

Nonfiction: Ken Myers, executive editor. General interest (the Christian in the culture); how-to (apply Scripture to problems); and interview/profile (well known evangelicals). No fiction; no short, devotional fillers. Buys 20 mss/year. Query. Length: 500-1,500 words. Pays $35-150.

Poetry: Lois Sibley, poetry editor. Buys 10-12 poems/year. Submit maximum 3 poems. Length: 10-15 lines.

Pays $20-40.

Tips: "For general articles, begin with an illustration, apply Scriptural principles to current problems/topics and include an application that will help readers. In poetry, we are looking for a good use of imagery, effectively controlled emotion, and words that elicit a sensory response—a memorable poem. And, the poem must be a good expression of Biblical theology."

EVANGEL, Dept. of Christian Education, Free Methodist Headquarters, 901 College Ave., Winona Lake IN 46590. (219)267-7161. Editor: Vera Bethel. 100% freelance written. Weekly magazine; 8 pages. Audience is 65% female, 35% male; married, 25-31 years old, mostly city dwellers, high school graduates, mostly nonprofessional. Circ. 35,000. Pays on publication. Publishes ms an average of 1 year after acceptance. Buys simultaneous rights, second serial (reprint) rights or one-time rights. Submit seasonal/holiday material 3 months in advance. Computer printout submissions acceptable; no dot-matrix. SASE. Reports in 4 weeks. Free sample copy and writer's guidelines.

Nonfiction: Interview (with ordinary person who is doing something extraordinary in his community, in service to others); profile (of missionary or one from similar service profession who is contributing significantly to society); and personal experience (finding a solution to a problem common to young adults; coping with handicapped child, for instance, or with a neighborhood problem. Story of how God-given strength or insight saved a situation). Buys 100 mss/year. Submit complete ms. Length: 300-1,000 words. Pays $10-25.

Photos: Purchased with accompanying ms. Captions required. Send prints. Pays $5-10 for 8x10 b&w glossy prints; $2 for snapshots.

Fiction: Religious themes dealing with contemporary issues dealt with from a Christian frame of reference. Story must "go somewhere". Buys 50 mss/year. Submit complete ms. Length: 1,200-1,500 words. Pays $35-40. SASE required.

Poetry: Free verse, haiku, light verse, traditional and religious. Buys 50/year. Submit maximum 6 poems. Length: 4-24 lines. Pays $5. SASE required.

Tips: "Seasonal material will get a second look (won't be rejected so easily) because we get so little. Write an attention grabbing lead followed by a body of article that says something worthwhile. Relate the lead to some of the universal needs of the reader—promise in that lead to help the reader in some way. Remember that everybody is interested most in himself. Lack of SASE brands author as a nonprofessional; I seldom even bother to read the script. If the writer doesn't want the script back, it probably has no value for me, either."

THE EVANGELICAL BEACON, 1515 E. 66th St., Minneapolis MN 55423. (612)866-3343. Editor: George Keck. 35% freelance written. Denominational magazine of the Evangelical Free Church of America— evangelical Protestant readership; published twice monthly except monthly July, August and December. Pays on publication. Publishes ms an average of 3 months after acceptance. Rights purchased vary with author and material. Buys all rights or first serial rights, and some reprints. Computer printout submissions acceptable; prefers letter-quality to dot-matrix. Reports in 8 weeks. SASE must be included. Sample copy and writer's guidelines for 75¢.

Nonfiction: Articles on the church, Christ-centered human interest and personal testimony articles, well researched on current issues of religious interest. Desires crisp, imaginative, original writing—not sermons on paper. Length: 250-2,000 words. Pays 3¢/word with extra payment on some articles, at discretion of editor.

Photos: Prefers 8x10 b&w photos. Pays $7.50 minimum.

Fiction: Not much fiction used, but will consider. Length: 100-1,500 words.

Poetry: Very little poetry used. Pays variable rate, $3.50 minimum.

Tips: "Articles need to be helpful to the average Christian—encouraging, challenging, instructive. Also needs material presenting reality of the Christian faith to nonChristians. Some tie-in with the Evangelical Free Church of America is helpful but not required."

EVANGELIZING TODAY'S CHILD, Child Evangelism Fellowship Inc., Warrenton MO 63383. (314)456-4321. Editor: Mrs. Elsie Lippy. 75% freelance written. Bimonthly magazine; 72 pages. "Our purpose is to equip Christians to win the world's children to Christ and disciple them. Our readership is Sunday school teachers, Christian education leaders and children's workers in every phase of Christian ministry to children up to 12 years old." Circ. 28,000. Pays within 90 days of acceptance. Publishes ms an average of 6 months after acceptance. Byline given. Offers 30% kill fee if assigned. Buys first serial rights. Submit seasonal/holiday material 6 months in advance. Simultaneous queries and photocopied submissions OK. Computer printout submissions acceptable; no dot-matrix. SASE. Reports in 3 weeks on queries; 2 months on mss. Free sample copy; writer's guidelines with SASE.

Nonfiction: Unsolicited articles welcomed from writers with Christian education training or current experience in working with children. Buys 35 mss/year. Query. Length: 1,800-2,000. Pays 4-7¢/word.

Photos: Submissions of photos on speculation accepted. Needs photos of children or related subjects. Include SASE. Pays $20-25 for 8x10 b&w glossy prints; $50-150 for color transparencies.

FAITH FOR THE FAMILY, Bob Jones University, Greenville SC 29614. (803)242-5100, ext. 7200. Editor: Bob Jones. Managing Editor: Robert W. Franklin. 65% freelance written. Magazine published 10 times/year covering fundamental Christianity. Circ., 60,000. Pays on acceptance. Publishes ms an average of 4 months after acceptance. Byline given. Buys all rights. Submit seasonal/holiday material 4 months in advance. Simultaneous queries submissions OK. Computer printout submissions acceptable; prefers letter-quality to dot-matrix. SASE. Report in 2 weeks on queries; 4 weeks on mss. Free sample copy and writer's guidelines.
Nonfiction: Expose, general interest, historical/nostalgic, how-to and inspirational. Query or send complete ms. Length: 500-1,500 words. Pays 3¢/word minimum.
Photos: Pays $10 minimum for color transparencies and 8x10 b&w prints. Captions, model release, and identification of subjects required. Buys one-time rights.
Fiction: Religious and Christian. Query or send complete ms. Length: 1,000-1,500 words. Pays 3¢/word minumum.
Tips: "Fiction and practical how-to Christian nonfiction are the areas most open for freelancers. *Faith for the Family* uses very few filler articles."

‡**FAMILY FESTIVALS, Celebrating God's World With Families**, Resource Publications, Inc., #290, 160 E. Virginia St., San Jose CA 95112. (408)286-8505. Editor: Sam Mackintosh. 60% freelance written. Bimonthly magazine of family-directed ritual and celebration. "Magazine for Christian parents who wish to celebrate God's presence by way of religious customs, rituals, and traditions in the home." Circ. 16,000. Pays 3 months after publication. Publishes ms an average of 1 year after acceptance. Byline given. Buys all rights. Submit seasonal/holiday material 9 months in advance. Photocopied and previously published submissions OK. Computer printout submissions acceptable; prefers letter quality to dot-matrix. SASE. Reports in 4 weeks on queries; 6 weeks on mss. Sample copy $2.75, 8½x11 SAE and 3 first class stamps; writer's guidelines for #10 SAE and 1 first class stamp.
Nonfiction: Book excerpts; historical/nostalgic ("I Remember" pieces on family traditions); how-to (family rituals, traditions, celebrations); and personal experience ("sharings", what you have done in your home). No fundamentalist material, general family articles not relating to seasons or tradition. Buys 10 mss/year. Query. Length: 1,000 words maximum. Pays $10-20.
Fiction: Religious (stories of Saints or legends).
Tips: "We don't pay enough to encourage freelancers, frankly. Most of our material is written by readers or people whose material will eventually turn into one of our books."

FAMILY LIFE TODAY MAGAZINE, Box 93670, Pasadena CA 91109. (213)791-0039. Publisher/Editor-in-Chief: Clif Cartland. 15% freelance written. Monthly magazine; 48 pages. Emphasizes "building strong marriages and helping Christian families deal with the realities of contemporary life." Circ. 50,000. Pays on publication. Publishes ms an average of 6 months after acceptance. Byline given. Buys first serial rights. Submit seasonal/holiday material 6 months in advance. Computer printouts acceptable "if separated and in regular page order; prefers traditional form." SASE. Reports in 2 months. Sample copy and writer's guidelines for $2 and 9x12 SASE.
Nonfiction: All articles need to reflect a Christian value system. How-to (any family related situation with narrow focus: how to help the hyperactive child, etc.); humor (if wholesome and family related); interview (with person who is recognized authority in area of marriage and family life); personal experience ("when my husband lost his job," etc.); and photo feature (family related). Buys 25 unsolicited mss/year. Query. Length: 300-1,500 words. Pays 5¢/word for original material; 3¢/word for reprints. Pays expenses of writers on assignment.
Tips: "The writer has a better chance of breaking in at our publication with short articles and fillers as our longer articles tend to involve more research and are keyed to special single-subject reports. The most frequent mistakes made by writers in completing articles for us are that they provide no unique insight or specific helpful suggestions. We look for material with practical suggestions on the chosen subject."

FRIDAY (OF THE JEWISH EXPONENT), 226 S. 16th St., Philadelphia PA 19102. (215)893-5745. Editor: Jane Biberman. 98% freelance written. Monthly literary supplement for the Jewish community of Greater Philadelphia. Circ. 100,000. Pays after publication. Publishes ms an average of 6 months after acceptance. Byline given. Pays 25% kill fee. Buys first serial rights. Submit seasonal/holiday material 3 months in advance. Photocopied submissions OK. Computer printout submissions acceptable. SASE. Reports in 3 weeks. Free sample copy and writer's guidelines.
Nonfiction: "We are interested only in articles on Jewish themes, whether they be historical, thought pieces, Jewish travel or photographic essays. Topical themes are appreciated." Buys 25 unsolicited mss/year. Length: 6-20 double-spaced pages. Pays $75 minimum.
Fiction: Short stories on Jewish themes. Length: 6-20 double-spaced pages. Pays $75 minimum.
Poetry: Traditional forms, blank verse, free verse, avant-garde and light verse; must relate to Jewish theme. Length varies. Pays $15 minimum.
Tips: "Pieces on Jewish personalities—artists, musicians and authors—are most welcome." Include illustrative material.

FUNDAMENTALIST JOURNAL, Old-Time Gospel Hour, Langhorne Plaza, Lynchburg VA 24514. (804)528-4112. Executive Editor: Jerry Falwell. Editor: Deborah Wade Huff. 40% freelance written. A Christian magazine (nonprofit organization) published monthly (July/August combined) covering "matters of interest to all Fundamentalists, providing discussion of divergent opinions on relevant issues; also human interest stories and news reports. Audience is 65% Baptist; 35% other denominations; 30% pastors, 70% other. Circ. 70,000. Pays on publication. Publishes ms an average of 6 months after acceptance. Byline given. Offers negotiable kill fee. Buys all rights; makes work-for-hire assignments. Submit seasonal/holiday material 6 months in advance. Previously published submissions OK. Computer printout submissions acceptable. SASE. Reports in 3 months. Free sample copy; writers guidelines for SAE and 1 first class stamp.

Nonfiction: Earlene R. Goodwin, articles editor. Book excerpts; expose (government, communism, education); general interest; historical/nostalgic (regarding the Bible, Christianity, great Christians of old); inspirational, interview/profile; opinion, and personal experience. "Writing must be consistent with Fundamentalist doctrine. We do not want articles that are critical in naming leaders of churches or Christian organizations." Buys 77 mss/year. Send complete ms. Length: 800-2,500 words. Pays 10¢/printed word.

Columns/Departments: W. David Beck, book editor. Book/film reviews of interest to the Christian family or to pastors, profiles of churches/pastors, articles regarding missions, successful teaching ideas and Bible study. Buys 88 mss/year. Query or send complete ms. Length; 300-2,000 words. Pays 10¢/printed word; $25-50 for book reviews.

Tips: "News is usually by assignment; various articles of general interest to Fundamentalist Christian readers, perspective, profiles, missions articles, successful teaching ideas are most open to freelancers. Samples of previously published work would be helpful."

‡THE GEM, Churches of God, General Conference, Box 926, Findlay OH 45839. (419)424-1961. Editor: Marilyn Rayle Kern. Weekly magazine; adult and youth church school take-home paper. "Our readers expect to find true-to-life help for daily living as growing Christians." Circ. 7,500. Pays on publication. Byline given. Not copyrighted. Buys simultaneous rights, first serial rights or second serial (reprint) rights. Submit seasonal/holiday material 3 months in advance. Simultaneous, photocopied and previously published submissions OK. SASE. Reports in 6 months. Sample copy for 4x9 SAE and 1 first class stamp (unless more than 1 copy); writer's guidelines for 4x9 SAE and 1 first class stamp.

Nonfiction: General interest, historical/nostalgic, humor, inspirational and personal experience. No preachy, judgmental, or use of quotes from other sources. Buys 50 mss/year. Send complete ms. Length: 600-1,600 words. Pays $10-15.

Fiction: Adventure, historical, humorous and religious. No mss which are preachy or inauthentic. Buys 50 mss/year. Send complete ms. Length: 1,000-1,600 words. Pays $10-15.

Fillers: Anecdotes and short humor. Buys 40/year. Length: 100-500 words. Pays $5-7.50.

Tips: "Humor, which does not put down people and leads the reader to understand a valuable lesson, is always in short supply."

GOOD NEWS, The Bimonthly Magazine For United Methodists, Box 165, Wilmore KY 40390. (606)858-4661. Editor: James V. Heidinger II. Executive Editor: James S. Robb. 20% freelance written. Bimonthly magazine for United Methodist lay people and pastors, primarily middle income; conservative and Biblical religious beliefs; broad range of political, social and cultural values. "We are the only evangelical magazine with the purpose of working within the United Methodist Church for Biblical reform and evangelical renewal." Circ. 19,000. Pays on acceptance. Byline given. Buys first serial rights, simultaneous rights, and second serial (reprint) rights. Phone queries OK. Submit seasonal/holiday material 6 months in advance. Simultaneous submissions with noncompeting publications OK. Prefers original mss and not photocopies of reprinted material. Computer printout submissions acceptable. SASE. Reports in 3 months. Sample copy $1.50; free writer's guidelines.

Nonfiction: Historical (prominent people or churches from the Methodist/Evangelical United Brethren tradition); how-to (build faith, work in local church); humor (good taste); inspirational (related to Christian faith); personal experience (case histories of God at work in individual lives); and any contemporary issues as they relate to the Christian faith and/or the United Methodist Church. No sermons or secular material. Buys 25 mss/year. Query with a "brief description of the article, perhaps a skeleton outline. Show some enthusiasm about the article and writing (and research). Tell us something about yourself including whether you or the article has United Methodist tie-in." Pays 5-7¢/word, more on occasion for special assignments.

Photos: Extra payment for photos with accompanying ms. Uses fine screen b&w prints. Total purchase price for ms includes payment for photos. Payment negotiable. Captions required.

Tips: "We are looking for manuscripts 1,700-2,500 words in length, pro treatment of issue-oriented material relating the Christian faith to contemporary life, and personality profiles with good photo possibilities; also we are looking for photo illustrated profiles of evangelically-oriented United Methodist churches with dynamic programs."

GOOD NEWS BROADCASTER, Box 82808, Lincoln NE 68501. (402)474-4567. Editor: Warren Wiersbe. 40% freelance written. Monthly interdenominational magazine for adults from 17 years of age and up. Circ. 150,000. Pays on acceptance. Buys first serial rights. Submit seasonal material at least 1 year in advance. Computer printout submissions acceptable if double spaced; no dot-matrix. SASE required. Reports in 5 weeks. Sample copy $1; writer's guidelines with SASE.

Nonfiction: Managing Editor, Norman A. Olson. Articles which will help the reader learn and apply Christian Biblical principles to his life from the writer's or the subject's own experience. Writers are required "to affirm agreement with our doctrinal statement. We are especially looking for true, personal experience 'salvation,' church, children's ages 4-10, missions, 'youth' (17 years and over), 'parents', 'how to live the Christian life' articles, reports and interviews regarding major and interesting happenings and people in fundamental, evangelical Christian circles." Nothing rambling or sugary sweet, or without Biblical basis. Details or statistics should be authentic and verifiable. Style should be conservative but concise. Prefers that Scripture references be from the *New American Standard Version* or the *Authorized Version* or the *New Scofield Reference Bible*. Buys approximately 100 mss/year. Length: 1,500 words maximum. Pays 4-10¢/word. "When you can get us to assign an article to you, we pay nearer the maximum. More manuscripts are now rejected if unaccompanied by photos." Sometimes pays expenses of writers on assignment.

Photos: Pays $25 maximum for b&w glossies; $75 maximum for color transparencies. Photos paid on publication.

Tips: "The basic purpose of the magazine is to explain the Bible and how it is relevant to life because we believe this will accomplish one of two things—to present Christ as Saviour to the lost or to promote the spiritual growth of believers, so don't ignore our primary purposes when writing for us. Nonfiction should be Biblical and timely; at the least Biblical in principle. Use illustrations of your own experiences or of someone else's when God solved a problem similar to the reader's. Be so specific that the meanings and significance will be crystal clear to all readers."

GOSPEL CARRIER, Messenger Publishing House, Box 850, Joplin MO 64802. (417)624-7050. Editor-in-Chief: Roy M. Chappell, D.D. 75% freelance written. Quarterly publication in weekly parts; 104 pages. Denominational Sunday school take-home paper for adults, ages 20 through retirement. Circ. 3,500. Pays quarterly. Publishes ms an average of 1 year after acceptance. Byline given. Buys simultaneous rights, second serial (reprint) rights and one-time rights. Submit seasonal/holiday material 1 year in advance. Simultaneous, photocopied, and previously published submissions OK. SASE. Reports in 3 months. Sample copy and writer's guidelines 50¢ and SAE with 1 first class stamp.

Nonfiction: Historical (related to great events in the history of the church); informational (may explain the meaning of a Bible passage or a Christian concept); inspirational (must make Christian point); nostalgia (religious significance); and personal experience (Christian concept). No puzzles, poems and filler material.

Fiction: Adventure, historical, romance and religious. Must have Christian significance. Buys 13-20 mss/issue. Submit complete ms. Length: 1,500-1,800 words. Pays 1¢/word.

Tips: "The most frequent mistake made by writers in completing an article for us is that they forget we are a Christian publication and will not publish articles that have mentioned subjects we do not accept in our guidelines."

GUIDEPOSTS MAGAZINE, 747 3rd Ave., New York NY 10017. Editor: Van Varner. "*Guideposts* is an inspirational monthly magazine for all faiths in which men and women from all walks of life tell how they overcame obstacles, rose above failures, met sorrow, learned to master themselves, and became more effective people through the direct application of the religious principles by which they live." Pays 25% kill fee for assigned articles. Byline given. "Most of our stories are first person ghosted articles, so the author would not get a byline unless it was his/her story." Buys all rights and second serial (reprint) rights. SASE.

Nonfiction and Fillers: Articles and features should be written in simple, anecdotal style with an emphasis on human interest. Short mss of approximately 250-750 words (pays $25-100) would be considered for such features as Quiet People and general one-page stories. Full-length mss, 750-1,500 words (pays $200-300). All mss should be typed, double-spaced and accompanied by a stamped, self-addressed envelope. Annually awards scholarships to high school juniors and seniors in writing contest. Buys 40-60 unsolicited mss/year.

Tips: "The freelancer would have the best chance of breaking in by aiming for a 1-page or maybe two-page article. That would be very short, say two and a half pages of typescript, but in a small magazine such things are very welcome. A sensitively written anecdote that could provide us with an additional title is extremely useful. And they are much easier to just sit down and write than to have to go through the process of preparing a query. They should be warm, well-written, intelligent and upbeat. We like personal narratives that are true and have some universal relevance, but the religious element does not have to be hammered home with a sledge hammer." Address short items to Edward Pitoniak.

‡**HICALL**, Gospel Publishing House, 1445 Boonville Ave., Springfield MO 65802. (417)862-2781. Editor: William P. Campbell. 100% freelance written. Assemblies of God (denominational) weekly magazine of Christian fiction and articles. Circ. 120,000. Pays on acceptance. Publishes ms an average of 6 months after

acceptance. Byline given. Buys first North American serial rights, one-time rights, simultaneous rights, and second serial (reprint) rights. Submit seasonal/holiday material 1 year in advance. Simultaneous queries, and simultaneous, photocopied, and previously published submissions OK. Computer printout submissions acceptable; prefers letter-quality to dot-matrix. SASE. Reports in 6 weeks. Sample copy for 5x7 SAE and 1 first class stamp; writer's guidelines for SAE.

Nonfiction: Book excerpts; general interest; how-to (deal with various life problems); humor; inspirational; and personal experience. Buys 80-100 mss/year. Send complete ms. Length: 500-2,000 words. Pays 2-3¢/word.

Fiction: Adventure, humorous and religious. Buys 80-100 mss/year. Send complete ms. Length: 500-2,000 words. Pays 2-3¢/word.

Poetry: Free verse, light verse and traditional. Buys 30 poems/year. Length: 10-30 lines. Pays 3¢/word; 25¢/line.

Fillers: Clippings, jokes, gags, anecdotes, short humor and newsbreaks. Buys 30/year. Pays 2-3¢/word.

‡HIGH ADVENTURE, The Assemblies of God, 1445 Boonville Ave., Springfield MO 65802. (417)862-2781, ext. 1497. Editor: Johnnie Barnes. Quarterly; 16 pages. For boys and men. Circ. 70,000. Rights purchased vary with author and material. Pays on acceptance. SASE. Free sample copy and writer's guidelines. Reports in 6 weeks.

Nonfiction: Nature study, and camping and campcraft articles. Buys how-to, personal experience, inspirational, humor and historical articles. Buys 10-12 mss/year. Query or submit complete ms. Length: 500-600 words.

Fiction: Nature, adventure stories and western fiction wanted. Length: 1,200 words. Pays 2¢/word.

Photos: Photos purchased on assignment.

Fillers: Puzzles, jokes and short humor.

INDIAN LIFE, Intertribal Christian Communications, Box 3765, Station B, Winnipeg, Manitoba R2W 3R6 Canada. (204)338-0311. Editor: George McPeek. 70% freelance written. Bimonthly magazine of Christian experience from a native American (Indian) point of view for readers in 30 different denominations and missions. Circ. 12,000. Pays on publication. Publishes ms an average of 6 months after acceptance. Byline given. Buys first serial rights and second serial (reprint) rights. Submit seasonal/holiday material 4 months in advance. Photocopied and previously published submissions OK. Computer printout submissions acceptable; no dot-matrix. Canada: SAE; IRCs outside Canada. Reports in 3 weeks on queries; 6 weeks on mss. Sample copy for 9x12 SAE and $1 Canadian postage; writer's guidelines for $1, business size SAE and 39¢ Canadian postage.

Nonfiction: Historical/nostalgic (with a positive approach); inspirational; interview/profile (of Indian Christian personalities); personal experience; photo feature; general news (showing Indian achievements); and human interest (wholesome, but not necessarily religious). Special edition on the Indian and alcohol (statistics, self-help programs, personal experience, etc.). No political, sexually suggestive, or negative articles on personalities, groups or points of view. "Keep your writing style simple, but not childish. Watch those multi-syllable words and lengthy sentences. Paragraphs should be short." Buys 12 mss/year. Query with published clips. Length: 500-1,500 words. Pays $20-45; less for news items.

Photos: State availability of photos. Pays $3-5 for b&w contact sheets; $10-20 for 35mm slides or other color transparencies; $5-10 for 5x7 b&w prints. Captions, model release, and identification of subjects required. Buys one-time rights.

Fiction: Adventure, confession, historical, religious and legends with Christian applications. No explicit sex or negative themes. Buys 4-6 mss/year. Query with published clips. Length: 500-1,200 words. Pays $20-40.

Fillers: Clippings, jokes, anecdotes, short humor and newsbreaks. Buys 25-30/year. Length: 50-200 words. Pays $3-10.

Tips: "First person stories must be verifiable with references (including one from pastor or minister) attached. Most material is written by Indian people, but some articles by nonIndians are accepted. Maintain an Indian point of view. We seek to build a positive self-image, provide culturally relevant material and serve as a voice for the Indian church."

‡INTERACTION, A Magazine Sunday School Workers Grow By, Concords Publishing House, 3558 S. Jefferson, St. Louis MO 63118. Mail submissions to LCMS, 1333 S. Kirkwood Rd., St. Louis MO 63122-7295. Editor: Martha Streufert Jander. 20% freelance written. Bimonthly magazine of practical, inspirational, theological articles for Sunday school teachers. Material must be true to the doctrines of the Lutheran Church—Missouri Synod. Circ. 17,000. Pays on acceptance. Publishes ms an average of 1 year after acceptance. Byline given. Buys all rights. Submit seasonal/holiday material 7 months in advance. Computer printout submissions acceptable; prefers letter-quality to dot-matrix. SASE. Reports in 1 month on queries; 2 months on mss. Sample copy 90¢; writer's guidelines for 8½x11 SAE (with sample copy); for 4½x9½ SAE (without sample copy).

Nonfiction: How-to (practical helps/ideas used successfully in own classroom); inspirational (to the Sunday school worker—must be in accordance with LCMS doctrine); and personal experience (of a Sunday school classroom nature—growth). No theological articles. Buys 6 mss/year. Send complete ms. Length: 750-2,000 words. Pays $35.

Fillers: Cartoons. Buys 50/year. "*Interaction* buys short items—activities and ideas planned and used successfully in a Sunday school classroom." Buys 50/year. Length: 200 words maximum. Pays $5.

Tips: "Practical, or 'it happened to me' experiences articles would have the best chance. Also short items— ideas used in classrooms, seasonal and in conjunction with our Sunday school material, New Life in Christ."

INTERLIT, David C. Cook Foundation, Cook Square, Elgin IL 60120. (312)741-2400, ext. 322. Editor-in-Chief: Gladys J. Peterson. 90% freelance written on assignment. Quarterly journal; 24 pages. Emphasizes sharpening skills in Christian communications and journalism. Especially for editors, publishers, and writers in the Third World (developing countries). Also goes to missionaries, broadcasters and educational personnel in the U.S. Circ. 9,000. Pays on acceptance. Publishes ms an average of 1 month after acceptance. Buys all rights. Photocopied submissions OK. Computer printout submissions acceptable; prefers letter-quality to dot-matrix. SASE. Reports in 2 weeks. Free sample copy.

Nonfiction: Technical and how-to articles about communications, media and literacy. "Please study publication and query before submitting manuscripts." Also photo features. Buys 7 mss/issue, mostly on assignment. Length: 500-1,500 words. Pays 6¢/word. Sometimes pays expenses of writers on assignment.

Photos: Purchased with accompanying ms only. Uses b&w. Query or send prints. Captions required.

INTERNATIONAL CHRISTIAN NEWS, ICN, International Christian News, Box 489, Rush Springs OK 73082. (405)476-2383. Editor: Joan Hash Cox. Managing Editor: Joanna Watts. 40% freelance written. Monthly Christian tabloid providing informative and entertaining Christian news. "We have a good variety of entertaining and informational material that appeals to the whole family. We desire our newspapers to be a positive, people-pleasing newspaper that will give the whole family that uplifting feeling a Christian should have in life." Estab. 1984. Circ. 2,500. Pays on publication. Publishes ms an average of 6 months after acceptance. Byline given. Buys first serial rights. Submit seasonal/holiday material 4 months in advance. Photocopied and previously published submissions OK; simultaneous submissions OK "only if we are informed." Computer printout submissions acceptable; prefers letter-quality to dot-matrix. SASE. Reports in 6 weeks. Sample copy $1.50; writer's guidelines for SASE.

Nonfiction: Book excerpts (religion); expose (anything considered in opposition to Christian principles); historical/nostalgic ("we thrive on spiritual heritage and nostalgia"); how-to (a few); humor (none offensive to any person); inspirational; interview/profile (if the person has influence on the Christian believers); opinion (some will be considered); personal experience ("we thrive on good Christian experience"); photo essays (picturesque churches from around the world with a paragraph description); travel; Bible notes found in old Bibles or books, helpful hints, crosswords that teach the Bible and recipes. "We will have an annual God & Country special patriotic issue every July 4th. Our Easter and Christmas issues will always be special." No fiction, except children's stories that are used to reach a truth about the Bible or life. Buys 100 mss/year. Send complete ms. Length: 500-2,000 words. Pays $10-100; front page articles with photo $100.

Photos: Tammy Sherylanne Cox, photo editor. State availability of photos with ms. Pays $10-25 for 3x5 or 5x7 b&w prints. Captions, model release, and identification of subjects required. Buys one-time rights.

Columns/Departments: All material must touch on Christian principles except Recipes. Travel, although we prefer it to be somewhere that would interest a Christian; How-To; Letters to the editor; Teen Scene and Care Kids stories, poems, puzzles, letters, dot to dot; Flaming Thought; Opinion; Sunday Dinner Stories; and Spiritual Heritage. Personal experiences and inspirational are the backbone articles of this publication. Query with published clips. Buys 80 mss/year. Length: 500-1,500 words. Pays $10-100.

Fiction: Religious (for children only). Buys 10 mss/year. Send complete ms. Length: 500-750 words. Pays $10-25.

Poetry: Free verse and traditional. No nonsense or erotic poetry. Buys 120-144 poems/year. Submit maximum 5 poems. Length: 4-30 lines. Pays 10¢/word.

Fillers: Anecdotes, short humor and newsbreaks (all pertaining to religion). Buys 50/year. Length: 250-500 words. Pays $5-15.

Tips: "We want moving articles that make a spiritual point. Don't ramble, don't condemn people. We emphasize instructions and examples to teach good Christian character.

‡**KEEPING POSTED**, Union of American Hebrew Congregations, 838 5th Ave., New York NY 10021. (212)249-0100. Editor: Aron Hurt-Manheimer. Managing Editor: Joy Weinberg. 50% freelance written. Magazine published 6 times/year on reform Jewish issues. "*Keeping Posted* is published by the UAHC, a nonprofit Jewish organization, and is distributed to teachers and children in reform Jewish religious schools and other interested readers." Pays on publication. Publishes ms an average of 3 months after acceptance. Byline given. Offers negotiable kill fee. Buys first North American serial rights. Submit seasonal/holiday material 3 months in advance. Photocopied submissions OK. Computer printout submissions acceptable; prefers letter-quality to dot-matrix. SASE. Reports in 2 weeks on queries; 3 weeks on mss. Sample copy $1.

Nonfiction: Book excerpts, expose, general interest, historical/nostalgic, inspirational, interview/profile,

opinion, personal experience. Buys 24 mss/year. Send complete ms. Length: 750-2,000 words. Pays $100-300. Sometimes pays expenses of writers on assignment.
Photos: Send photo with ms. Pays $25-75. Identification of subjects required. Buys one-time rights.
Fiction: Ethnic, humorous, mainstream and religious. Buys 6 mss/year. Send complete ms. Length: 750-2,000 words. Pays $100-200.
Poetry: Free verse. Buys 2 poems/year.

LIGHT AND LIFE, Free Methodist Church of North America, 901 College Ave., Winona Lake IN 46590. Managing Editor: Lyn Cryderman. 35% freelance written. Monthly magazine; 36 pages. Emphasizes evangelical Christianity with Wesleyan slant for a cross section of adults. Circ. 48,000. Pays on publication. Publishes ms an average of 6 months after acceptance. Byline given. Prefers first serial rights; sometimes buys second serial (reprint) rights. Submit seasonal/holiday material 6 months in advance. Previously published submissions OK. Computer printout submissions acceptable; no dot-matrix. SASE. Reports in 6 weeks. Sample copy $1.50; writer's guidelines for SASE.
Nonfiction: "Each issue includes a mini-theme (two or three articles addressing contemporary topics such as death and dying, science and faith, Christians as citizens), so freelancers should request our schedule of mini-theme topics. We also need fresh, upbeat articles showing the average layperson how to be Christ-like at home, work and play. Never submit anything longer than 2,500 words." Submit complete ms. Buys 70-80 unsolicited ms/year. Pays 4¢/word. Sometimes pays expenses of writers on assignment.
Photos: Purchased without accompanying ms. Send prints. Pays $5-35 for b&w photos. Offers additional payment for photos accepted with accompanying ms.

LIGUORIAN, Liguori MO 63057. Editor: the Rev. Norman Muckerman. 50% freelance written. Monthly. For families with Catholic religious convictions. Circ. 525,000. Pays on acceptance. Publishes ms an average of 3 months after acceptance. Byline given "except on short fillers and jokes." Buys all rights but will reassign rights to author *after* publication upon request. Submit seasonal material 6 months in advance. Electronic submissions OK on disk compatible with TRS 80 Model III, "but we ask contributors to send printout first, disk upon acceptance." Computer printout submissions acceptable; prefers letter-quality to dot-matrix. SASE. Reports in 8 weeks.
Nonfiction: "Pastoral, practical and personal approach to the problems and challenges of people today. No travelogue approach or unresearched ventures into controversial areas. Also, no material found in secular publications—fad subjects that already get enough press, pop psychology, negative or put-down articles." Recent article example: "You Can Go Home Again" (March 1984). Buys 60 unsolicited mss/year. Length: 400-2,000 words. Pays 7-10¢/word. Sometimes pays expenses of writers on assignment.
Photos: Photos purchased with mss. Reviews b&w glossy prints.

LIVE, 1445 Boonville Ave., Springfield MO 65802. (417)862-2781. Editor: Kenneth D. Barney. 100% freelance written. Weekly. For adults in Assemblies of God Sunday schools. Circ. 225,000. Pays on acceptance. Publishes ms an average of 1 year after acceptance. Not copyrighted. Submit seasonal material 4 months in advance; do not mention Santa Claus, Halloween or Easter bunnies. Computer printout submissions acceptable; prefers letter-quality to dot-matrix. SASE. Reports on material within 6 weeks. Free sample copy and writer's guidelines for SASE. Letters without SASE will not be answered.
Nonfiction: Articles with reader appeal emphasizing some phase of Christian living presented in a down-to-earth manner. Biography or missionary material using fiction techniques. Historical, scientific or nature material with spiritual lesson. "Be accurate in detail and factual material. Writing for Christian publications is a ministry. The spiritual emphasis must be an integral part of your material." Prefers not to see material on highly controversial subjects. Buys about 100 mss/year. Length: 1,000-1,600 words. Pays 3¢/word for first serial rights; 2¢/word for second serial (reprint) rights, according to the value of the material and the amount of editorial work necessary. "Please do not send large numbers of articles at one time."
Photos: Color photos or transparencies purchased with mss, or on assignment. Pay open.
Fiction: "Present believable characters working out their problems according to Bible principles; in other words, present Christianity in action without being preachy. We use very few serials, but we will consider three to four-part stories if each part conforms to average word length for short stories. Each part must contain a spiritual emphasis and have enough suspense to carry the reader's interest from one week to the next. Stories should be true to life but not what we would feel is bad to set before the reader as a pattern for living. Stories should not put parents, teachers, ministers or other Christian workers in a bad light. Setting, plot and action should be realistic, with strong motivation. Characterize so that the people will live in your story. Construct your plot carefully so that each incident moves naturally and sensibly toward crisis and conclusion. An element of conflict is necessary in fiction. Short stories should be written from one viewpoint only. We do not accept fiction based on incidents in the Bible." Length: 1,200-1,600 words. Pays 3¢/word for first serial rights; 2¢/word for second serial (reprint) rights. "Please do not send large numbers of articles at one time."
Poetry: Traditional, free and blank verse. Length: 12-20 lines. "Please do not send large numbers of poems at

one time." Pays 20¢/line.

Fillers: Brief and purposeful, usually containing an anecdote, and always with a strong evangelical emphasis. Length: 200-600 words.

THE LOOKOUT, 8121 Hamilton Ave., Cincinnati OH 45231. (513)931-4050. Editor: Mark A. Taylor. 50% freelance written. Weekly for the adult and young adult of Sunday morning Bible school. Pays on acceptance. Byline given. Buys first serial rights, second serial (reprint) rights, or simultaneous rights. Simultaneous submissions OK. Computer printout submissions acceptable; prefers letter-quality to dot-matrix. SASE. Reports in 2 months. Sample copy and writer's guidelines 50¢.

Nonfiction: "Seeks stories about real people or Sunday school classes; items that shed Biblical light on matters of contemporary controversy; and items that motivate, that lead the reader to ask, 'Why shouldn't I try that?' or 'Why couldn't our Sunday school class accomplish this?' Articles should tell how real people are involved for Christ. In choosing topics, *The Lookout* considers timeliness, the church and national calendar, and the ability of the material to fit the above guidelines. Tell us about ideas that are working in your Sunday school and in the lives of its members. Remember to aim at laymen." Submit complete ms. Length: 1,200-1,800 words. Pays 4-6¢/word. We also use inspirational short pieces. "About 600-800 words is a good length for these. Relate an incident that illustrates a point without preaching." Pays 4-5¢/word.

Fiction: "A short story is printed in most issues; it is usually between 1,200-1,800 words long and should be as true to life as possible while remaining inspirational and helpful. Use familiar settings and situations. Most often we use stories with a Christian slant."

Photos: Reviews b&w prints, 4x6 or larger. Pays $5-25. Pays $50-150 for color transparencies for covers and inside use. Needs photos of people, especially adults in a variety of settings.

THE LUTHERAN, 2900 Queen Lane, Philadelphia PA 19129. (215)438-6580. Editor: Edgar R. Trexler. 50% freelance written. General interest magazine of the Lutheran Church in America published twice monthly, except single issues in July, August and December. Pays on acceptance. Publishes an average of 9 months after acceptance. "We need informative, detailed query letters. We also accept manuscripts on speculation only, and we prefer not to encourage an abundance of query letters." Buys one-time rights. Computer printout submissions acceptable; prefers letter-quality to dot-matrix. SASE. Free sample copy and writer's guidelines.

Nonfiction: Popularly written material about human concerns with reference to the Christian faith. "We are especially interested in articles in four main fields: Christian ideology; personal religious life, social responsibilities; Church at work; and human interest stories about people in whom considerable numbers of other people are likely to be interested. Write primarily to convey information rather than opinions. Every article should be based on a reasonable amount of research or should explore some source of information not readily available. Most readers are grateful for simplicity of style. Sentences should be straightforward with a minimum of dependent clauses and prepositional phrases." Length: 500-2,000 words. Pays $90-270.

Photos: Buys photos submitted with ms. Reviews good 8x10 glossy prints. Pays $15-25. Also color for cover use. Pays up to $150.

Tips: "A great need exists for personal experience writing that is creative, relevant to these times and written for a wide audience."

LUTHERAN FORUM, 308 W. 46th St., New York NY 10036-3894. (212)757-1292. Editor: Glenn C. Stone. 25% freelance written. Quarterly magazine; 40 pages. For church leadership, clerical and lay. Circ. 4,500. Pays on publication. Publishes ms an average of 3 months after acceptance. Byline given. Rights purchased vary with author and material; buys all rights, first North American serial rights, second serial (reprint) rights, and simultaneous rights. Will consider photocopied and simultaneous submissions. Computer printout submissions acceptable; prefers letter-quality to dot-matrix. Reports in 6 weeks. SASE. Sample copy $1.50.

Nonfiction: Articles about important issues and developments in the church's institutional life and in its cultural/social setting. Special interest in articles on the Christian's life in secular vocations. No purely devotional/inspirational material. Buys 8-10 mss/year. Query or submit complete ms. Length: 1,000-3,000 words. Payment varies; $30 minimum. Informational, how-to, interview, profile, think articles and expose. Length: 500-3,000 words. Pays $25-50.

Photos: Purchased with ms and only with captions. Prefers 4x5 prints. Pays $15 minimum.

THE LUTHERAN JOURNAL, 7317 Cahill Rd., Edina MN 55435. Editor: The Rev. Armin U. Deye. Quarterly magazine; 32 pages. Family magazine for Lutheran Church members, middle age and older. Circ. 136,000. Pays on publication. Byline given. Will consider photocopied and simultaneous submissions. Reports in 2 months. SASE. Free sample copy.

Nonfiction: Inspirational, religious, human interest and historical articles. Interesting or unusual church projects. Informational, how-to, personal experience, interview, humor and think articles. Buys 12-15 mss/year. Submit complete ms. Length: 1,500 words maximum; occasionally 2,000 words. Pays 1-3¢/word.

Photos: B&w and color photos purchased with accompanying ms. Captions required. Payment varies.

Fiction: Mainstream, religious and historical fiction. Must be suitable for church distribution. Length: 2,000 words maximum. Pays 1-1½¢/word.
Poetry: Traditional poetry, blank verse and free verse, related to subject matter.

THE LUTHERAN STANDARD, 426 S. 5th St., Box 1209, Minneapolis MN 55440. (612)330-3300. Editor: The Rev. Lowell G. Almen. 35% freelance written. Semimonthly. For families in congregations of the American Lutheran Church. Circ. 572,000. Pays on acceptance. Publishes ms an average of 9 months after acceptance. Byline given. Usually buys one-time rights. Computer printout submissions acceptable; no dot-matrix. SASE. Reports in 3 weeks. Free sample copy.
Nonfiction: Inspirational articles, especially about members of the American Lutheran Church who are practicing their faith in noteworthy ways, or congregations with unusual programs. Articles "should be written in language clearly understandable to persons with a mid-high school reading ability." Also publishes articles that discuss current social issues and problems (crime, family life, divorce, etc.) in terms of Christian involvement and solutions. No poetry. Buys 30-50 mss/year. Query. Length: limit 1,200 words. Pays 10¢/word.
Tips: "We are interested in personal experience pieces with a strong first person approach. The manuscript may be on a religious and social issue, but with evident human interest using personal anecdotes and illustrations. How has an individual faced a serious problem and overcome it? How has faith made a difference in a person's life? We prefer letters that clearly describe the proposed project. Excerpts from the project or other samples of the author's work are helpful in determining whether we are interested in dealing with an author. We would appreciate it if more freelance writers seemed to have a sense of who our readers are and an awareness of the kinds of manuscripts we in fact publish."

LUTHERAN WOMEN, 2900 Queen Ln., Philadelphia PA 19129. Editor: Terry Schutz. 20% freelance written. Published 10 times/year. Circ. 40,000. Publishes ms an average of 4 months after acceptance. Buys first North American serial rights and second serial (reprint) rights, and simultaneous rights. Prefers to see mss 6 months ahead of issue, at beginning of planning stage; can consider up to 3 months before publication. Computer printout submissions acceptable; no dot-matrix. SASE. Reports in 2 months. Sample copy 75¢.
Nonfiction: Anything of interest to mothers—young or old—professional or other working women related to the contemporary expression of Christian faith in daily life, community action and international concerns. Family publication standards. No recipes or housekeeping hints. Length: 1,500-2,000 words. Some shorter pieces accepted. Pays up to $50 for full length ms with photos.
Photos: Purchased mostly with mss. Should be clear, sharp b&w.
Fiction: Should show deepening of insight; story expressing new understanding in faith; story of human courage, self-giving and building up of community. Length: 2,000 words. Pays $30-40.
Poetry: Very little is used. "The biggest taboo for us is sentimentality. We are limited to family magazine type contributions regarding range of vocabulary, but we don't want almanac type poetry." No limit on number of lines. Pays $20-35/poem.

‡**LUTHERANS IN STEP**, Division of Service to Military Personnel/LCUSA, Suite 300, 122 C St. NW, Washington DC 20001. (202)738-7501. Editor: Bertram C. Gilbert. 15% freelance written. Information/inspirational paper for Lutheran military people, published 5 times/year. "Our slant is church news and commentary for pastors to send to their members in the service." Circ. 40,000. Publishes ms an average of 6 months after acceptance. Byline given. Buys first serial rights. Submit seasonal/holiday material 9 months in advance. Photocopied submissions OK. Computer printout submissions acceptable; no dot-matrix. SASE. Reports in 3 weeks. Free sample copy and writer's guidelines.
Nonfiction: How-to, humor, inspirational, interview/profile, personal experience and travel. "We need articles on subjects of interest to or about young soldiers, sailors and air personnel which relate to the Christian faith or to our particular denomination. Humor and breeziness are desirable. Willingness to express simple faith concepts in a new or double-take-causing way make us happy." No items that are negative about the military experience or not tied to religion in some way. Buys 10 mss/year. Query. Length: 500-1,000 words. Pays $30-50.
Photos: State availability of photos with query. Pays $25 for 6x9 b&w prints. Captions, model release, and identification of subjects required. Buys one-time rights.
Tips: "Authors should not send manuscripts but should send concepts. We are looking for budding writers who know the military scene well enough to make reference to that in up-to-date terms. We are not interested in the fame of the authors so consider ourselves a good place for a novice to get started. In fact several of ours have become quite successful."

MARIAN HELPERS BULLETIN, Eden Hill, Stockbridge MA 01262. (413)298-3691. Editor: Rev. Donald J. Vanalstyne, M.I.C. 90% freelance written. Quarterly for average Catholics of varying ages with moderate religious views and general education. Circ. 1,000,000. Pays on acceptance. Byline given. Not copyrighted. Submit seasonal material 6 months in advance. Reports in 4-8 weeks. SASE. Free sample copy.
Nonfiction: "Subject matter is of general interest on devotional, spiritual, moral and social topics. Use a posi-

tive, practical and optimistic approach, without being sophisticated. We would like to see articles on the Blessed Virgin Mary." Buys informational and inspirational articles. Buys 18-24 mss/year. Length: 300-900 words. Pays $25-35.

Photos: Photos are purchased with or without ms; captions optional. Pays $5-10 for b&w glossy prints.

MARRIAGE & FAMILY LIVING, St. Meinrad IN 47577. (812)357-8011. Managing Editor: Kass Dotterweich. 50% freelance written. Monthly magazine. Circ. 45,000. Pays on acceptance. Publishes ms an average of 1 month after acceptance. Byline given. Buys first North American serial rights, first book reprint option, and control of other reprint rights. Query. Computer printout submissions acceptable; prefers letter-quality to dot-matrix. SASE. Reports in 6 weeks. Sample copy 50¢.

Nonfiction: Uses 1) articles designed to enrich husband/wife and parent/child relationships by expanding and deepening religious and psychological sensitivities (Note: Ecumenically Judeo-Christian); 2) practical informative articles aimed at helping couples cope with problems of modern living; and 3) personal essays relating amusing, heartwarming or insightful incidents which reflect the rich human side of marriage and family life. Length: 2,500 words maximum. Pays 7¢/word. Pays expenses of writers on assignment.

Photos: Attention, art director. Reviews b&w glossy prints (5x7 or larger) and color transparencies or 35mm slides (vertical preferred). Pays $300/4-color cover or center spread photo; uses approximately 6-8 photos (b&w/color) and illustrations inside. Pays variable rate on publication. Photos of couples, families and individuals especially desirable. Model release required.

Poetry: Any style and length. Pays $15 on publication.

Tips: Query with a brief outline of article and opening paragraphs.

‡**MARYKNOLL MAGAZINE**, Maryknoll Fathers, Maryknoll NY 10545. (914)941-7590. Editor: Moises Sandoval. Managing Editor: Frank Maurovich. Monthly magazine of foreign mission concerns. Circ. 1.2 million. Pays on acceptance. Byline given. Buys first North American serial rights and one-time rights; makes work-for-hire assignments. Submit seasonal/holiday material 8 months in advance. SASE. Reports in 3 weeks. Free sample copy and writer's guidelines.

Nonfiction: Inspirational, interview/profile, personal experience and photo feature. Query. Length: 800-1,000 words. Pays $75-200.

Photos: Pays $35-100 for 35mm color transparencies; $15-30 for 5x7 and 8x10 b&w prints.

Tips: Freelancers can best break in "with an article about missionary work or the social, economic or political conditions in the 25 countries where we work."

MESSENGER OF ST. ANTHONY, Prov. Pad. F.M.C. Editore, Basilica del Santo, 35123 Padova, Italy. (049)664-322. Editor: G. Panteghini. 20% freelance written. Monthly magazine covering family, social and religious issues with a Christian outlook. Circ. 20,000. Pays on publication. Publishes ms an average of 1 year after acceptance. Byline given. Offers 30% kill fee. Buys first serial rights and second serial (reprint) rights. Submit seasonal/holiday material 4 months in advance. Simultaneous queries, and simultaneous and photocopied submissions OK. Computer printout submissions acceptable; prefers letter-quality to dot-matrix. SASE. Reports in 1 month on queries; 6 weeks on mss. Free sample copy and writer's guidelines.

Nonfiction: Historical/nostalgic, humor, inspirational, personal experience, photo feature and travel. Special issue on the first five years of Pope John II. No sexist articles. Buys 60 mss/year. Query. Length: 1,000-1,200 words. Pays $60-130.

Photos: Prefers 10x14 or 13x18 cm photos. Send photos with ms. Pays $10-15 for color prints; $5-10 for b&w prints. Identification of subjects required. Buys one-time rights.

Columns/Departments: Religion, health, living together (social issues), religion and art, and science (human dimensions). Buys 40 mss/year. Query with or without published clips. Length: 1,000-1,200 words. Pays $60-130.

Fiction: Confession (religious witness), ethnic, historical, humorous, and religious. "Only fiction with human, social or religious value." Buys 12-15 mss/year. Query. Length: 1,000-1,200 words. Pays $60-130.

THE MIRACULOUS MEDAL, 475 E. Chelten Ave., Philadelphia PA 19144. Editorial Director: The Rev. Robert P. Cawley, C.M. 40% freelance written. Quarterly. Pays on acceptance. Publishes ms an average of 2 years after acceptance. Buys first North American serial rights. Buys articles only on special assignment. SASE. Free sample copy.

Fiction: Should not be pious or sermon-like. Wants good general fiction—not necessarily religious, but if religion is basic to the story, the writer should be sure of his facts. Only restriction is that subject matter and treatment must not conflict with Catholic teaching and practice. Can use seasonal material; Christmas stories. Length: 2,000 words maximum. Occasionally uses short-shorts from 750-1,250 words. Pays 2¢/word minimum.

Poetry: Maximum of 20 lines, preferably about the Virgin Mary or at least with religious slant. Pays 50¢/line minimum.

MODERN LITURGY, Suite 290, 160 E. Virginia St., San Jose CA 95112. Editor: Kenneth Guentert. 80% freelance written. Magazine; 40-48 pages published 9 times/year for artists, musicians and creative individuals who plan group worship, services; teachers of religion. Circ. 15,000. Buys first serial rights. Pays three months after publication. Publishes ms an average of 9 months after acceptance. Byline given. Electronic submissions OK via CPM, but requires hard copy. Computer printout submissions acceptable; prefers letter-quality to dot-matrix. SASE. Reports in 6 weeks. Sample copy $4; free writer's guidelines for SAE and 1 first class stamp.
Nonfiction and Fiction: Articles (historical, theological and practical) which address special interest topics in the field of liturgy; example services; and liturgical art forms (music, poetry, stories, dances, dramatizations, etc.). Practical, creative ideas; and art forms for use in worship and/or religious education classrooms. "No material out of our field." Buys 10 mss/year. Query. Length: 750-2,000 words. Pays $5-30. Sometimes pays expenses of writers on assignment.
Tips: "Don't be preachy, use too much jargon, or make articles too long."

MOODY MONTHLY, The Christian Family Magazine, Moody Bible Institute, 2101 W. Howard St., Chicago IL 60645. (312)274-1879. Managing Editor: Michael Umlandt. 30% freelance written. Monthly magazine covering evangelical Christianity. "Believing the Bible to be God's word, *Moody Monthly* offers Bible-centered departments and articles to evangelical readers looking for help in living as Christians in today's world." Circ. 210,000. Pays on acceptance. Publishes ms an average of 6 months after acceptance. Byline given. Buys first North American serial rights and first serial rights. Submit seasonal/holiday material 6 months in advance. Computer printout submissions acceptable; prefers letter-quality to dot-matrix. SASE. Reports in 1 month on queries; 2 months on mss. Free sample copy and writer's guidelines.
Nonfiction: General interest (related to evangelical Christianity); how-to (living the Christian life); and personal experience (related to living the Christian life). No death or trauma stories. Buys 50 mss/year. Query. Length: 1,200-2,500 words. Pays 10¢/word. Sometimes pays expenses of writers on assignment.
Photos: Pays $35 minimum for color transparencies. Identification of subjects required. Buys one-time rights.
Columns/Departments: Parenting and First Person (testimony). Buys 20/year. Query. Length: 900-1,500 words. Pays 10¢/word.
Tips: "Our First Person department is a good start for freelancers, but writer must study back issues. Use anecdotes, have a focus and use Biblical support."

NATIONAL CHRISTIAN REPORTER, Box 221076, Dallas TX 75222. (214)630-6495. Editor/General Manager: Spurgeon M. Dunnam III. Managing Editor: John A. Lovelace. Weekly newspaper for an interdenominational national readership. Circ. 475,000. Pays on acceptance. Byline given. Not copyrighted. SASE. Free sample copy and writer's guidelines.
Nonfiction: "We welcome short features, approximately 500 words. Articles need not be limited to a United Methodist angle but need to have an explicit Protestant angle. Write about a distinctly Christian response to human need or how a person's faith relates to a given situation." Send complete ms. Pays 4¢/word.
Photos: Purchased with accompanying ms. "We encourage the submission of good action photos (5x7 or 8x10 b&w glossy prints) of the persons or situations in the article." Pays $10.
Poetry: "Good poetry welcome on a religious theme; blank verse or rhyme." Length: 4-20 lines. Pays $2.
Tips: "Read our publications before submitting. First person stories seldom fit our needs, but opinion pieces of no more than 500 words will be considered without pay for My Witness; and Here I Stand."

THE NEW ERA, 50 E. North Temple, Salt Lake City UT 84150. (801)531-2951. Managing Editor: Brian K. Kelly. 60% freelance written. Monthly magazine; 51 pages. For young people of the Church of Jesus Christ of Latter-Day Saints (Mormon); their church leaders and teachers. Circ. 180,000. Pays on acceptance. Publishes ms an average of 1 year after acceptance. Byline given. Buys all rights. Submit seasonal material 1 year in advance. Electronic submissions OK via Wang, but requires hard copy also. Computer printout submissions acceptable; prefers letter-quality to dot-matrix. SASE. Reports in 1 month. Query preferred. Sample copy 90¢; writer's guidelines for SAE and 1 first class stamp.
Nonfiction: Material that shows how the Church of Jesus Christ of Latter-Day Saints is relevant in the lives of young people today. Must capture the excitement of being a young Latter-Day Saint. Special interest in the experiences of young Mormons in other countries. No general library research or formula pieces without the *New Era* slant and feel. Uses informational, how-to, personal experience, interview, profile, inspirational, humor, historical, think pieces, travel and spot news. Length: 150-3,000 words. Pays 3-6¢/word. *For Your Information* (news of young Mormons around the world). Pays expenses of writers on assignment.
Photos: Uses b&w photos and color transparencies with mss. Payment depends on use in magazine, but begins at $10.
Fiction: Experimental, adventure, science fiction and humorous. Must relate to young Mormon audience. Pays minimum 3¢/word.
Poetry: Traditional forms, blank verse, free verse, avant-garde forms, light verse and all other forms. Must relate to editorial viewpoint. Pays minimum 25¢/line.

Tips: "The most frequent mistakes made by writers in completing an article for us are that they aren't familiar with the magazine's personality and don't write specifically to our audience. If someone has studied the magazine, there's no reason they couldn't break in with a major article."

NEW WORLD OUTLOOK, Room 1351, 475 Riverside Dr., New York NY 10115. (212)870-3758. Editor: Arthur J. Moore. Executive Editor: George M. Daniels. 70% freelance written. Monthly magazine (combined issues July/August and November/December); 48 pages. For United Methodist lay people; not clergy generally. Circ. 40,000. Pays on publication. Publishes ms an average of 3 months after acceptance. Buys first serial rights. Electronic submissions OK via Wang or IBM PC 5¼ floppy disk, but requires hard copy also. Computer printout submissions acceptable; no dot-matrix. SASE. Free sample copy and writer's guidelines.
Nonfiction: Articles about the involvement of the church around the world, including the U.S. in outreach and social concerns and Christian witness. "Write with good magazine style. Facts and actualities are important. Use quotes. Relate what Christians are doing to meet problems. Use specifics. We have too much on New York and other large urban areas. We need more good journalistic efforts from smaller places in U.S. Articles by freelancers in out-of-the-way places in the U.S. are especially welcome." Buys 50-60 mss/year. Query or submit complete ms. Length: 1,000-2,000 words. Usually pays $50-150 but more on occasion. "Writers are encouraged to illustrate their articles photographically if possible." Pays expenses of writers on assignment "if it originates with us or if article is one in which we have a special interest."
Photos: Generally use b&w but covers (4-color) will be considered. Photos are purchased separately at standard rates."
Tips: "A freelancer should have some understanding of the United Methodist Church, or else know very well a local situation of human need or social problem which the churches and Christians have tried to face. Too much freelance material we get tries to paint with broad strokes about world or national issues. The local story of meaning to people elsewhere is still the best material. Avoid pontificating on the big issues. Write cleanly and interestingly on the 'small' ones. We're interested in major articles and photos (including photo features from freelancers)."

NORTH AMERICAN VOICE OF FATIMA, Fatima Shrine, Youngstown NY 14174. Editor: Steven M. Grancini, C.R.S.P. 40% freelance written. For Roman Catholic readership. Circ. 3,000. Pays on acceptance. Not copyrighted. Reports in 6 weeks. SASE. Free sample copy.
Nonfiction and Fiction: Inspirational, personal experience, historical and think articles. Religious and historical fiction. Length: 700 words. All material must have a religious slant. Pays 2¢/word.
Photos: B&w photos purchased with ms.

OBLATES MAGAZINE, Missionary Association of Mary Immaculate, 15 S. 59th St., Belleville IL 62222. (618)233-2238. Contact: Managing Editor. Bimonthly religious magazine for Christian families. Circ. 500,000. Pays on acceptance. Byline given. Buys first North American serial rights. Submit seasonal/holiday material 6 months in advance. SASE. Reports in 1 month. Free sample copy and writer's guidelines.
Nonfiction: Inspirational, personal experience and articles on Oblates around the world. Stories should be inspirational, give insight, and present Gospel values. "Don't be preachy or pious." Send complete ms. Length: 500 words. Pays $75.
Poetry: Light verse—reverent, perceptive, traditional. "Nothing that takes too much effort to decipher. Emphasis should be on inspiration, insight and relationship with God." Submit maximum 3 poems. Length: 8-16 lines. Pays $25.
Tips: "Our readership is made up mostly of mature Americans who are looking for comfort, encouragement and applicable Christian direction. They don't want to spend a lot of time wading through theology laden or personal spiritual journey pieces. But if you can take an incident from Christ's life, for example, and in a creative and clever way parallel that with everyday living or personal experience, all in about 500 words, we're holding a couple of pages for you. This formula will also work for any Gospel theme, e.g., forgiveness, selflessness, hope. In other words, make the Gospel message work in today's world."

THE OTHER SIDE, Box 3948, Fredericksburg VA 22402. Editor: Mark Olson. Associate Editor: Kathleen Hayes. Assistant Editors: John Linscheid and William O'Brien. Publisher: Philip Harnden. 67% freelance written. Magazine published 10 times/year focusing on "peace, justice and economic liberation from a radical Christian perspective." Circ. 15,000. Pays on acceptance. Publishes ms an average of 4 months after acceptance. Byline given. Buys all rights. Query about electronic submissions; requires hard copy also. Computer printout submissions acceptable. SASE. Reports in 1 month. Sample copy $2.50; free writer's guidelines.
Nonfiction: Eunice A. Smith, articles editor. Current social, political and economic issues in the U.S. and around the world: personality profiles, interpretative essays, interviews, how-to's, personal experiences and investigative reporting. "Articles must be lively, vivid and down-to-earth, with a radical Christian perspective." Length: 300-4,000 words. Pays $25-250. Sometimes pays expenses of writers on assignment.
Photos: Cathleen Boint, art director. Photos or photo essays illustrating current social, political, or economic

reality in the U.S. and Third World. Pays $15-50 for b&w.

Fiction: Joseph Comanda, fiction editor. "Short stories, humor and satire conveying insights and situations that will be helpful to Christians with a radical commitment to peace and justice." Length: 300-4,000 words. Pays $25-250.

Poetry: Rosemary Camilleri, poetry editor. "Short, creative poetry that will be thought-provoking and appealing to radical Christians who have a strong commitment to peace and justice." Length: 3-50 lines. Pays $15-20.

OUR FAMILY, Oblate Fathers of St. Mary's Province, Box 249, Battleford, Saskatchewan S0M 0E0 Canada. (306)937-2131, 937-7344. Editor-in-Chief: Albert Lalonde, O.M.I. 60% freelance written. Monthly magazine for average family men and women with high school and early college education. Circ. 17,552. Pays on acceptance. Publishes ms an average of 6 months after acceptance. Byline given. Pays 100% kill fee. Generally purchases first North American serial rights; also buys all rights, simultaneous rights, second serial (reprint) rights or one-time rights. Submit seasonal/holiday material 4 months in advance. Simultaneous, photocopied, and previously published submissions OK. Computer printout submissions acceptable; no dot-matrix. "Writer should inquire with our office before sending letter-quality computer printout or disk submissions." SASE. Reports in 1 month. Sample copy $1.50 and SAE, IRC; writer's guidelines for 35¢ (Canadian fund). (U.S. postage cannot be used in Canada).

Nonfiction: Humor (related to family life or husband/wife relations); inspirational (anything that depicts people responding to adverse conditions with courage, hope and love); personal experience (with religious dimensions); and photo feature (particularly in search of photo essays on human/religious themes and on persons whose lives are an inspiration to others). Phone queries OK. Buys 72-88 unsolicited mss/year. Pays expenses of writers on assignment.

Photos: Photos purchased with or without accompanying ms. Pays $25 for 5x7 or larger b&w glossy prints and color photos (which are converted into b&w). Offers additional payment for photos accepted with ms (payment for these photos varies according to their quality). Free photo spec sheet with SASE.

Fiction: Humorous and religious. "Anything true to human nature. No romance, he-man adventure material, science fiction, moralizing or sentimentality." Buys 1-2 ms/issue. Send complete ms. Length: 700-3,000 words. Pays 7-10¢/word minimum for original material. Free fiction requirement guide with SASE.

Poetry: Avant-garde, free verse, haiku, light verse and traditional. Buys 4-10 poems/issue. Length: 3-30 lines. Pays 75¢-$1/line.

Fillers: Jokes, gags, anecdotes and short humor. Buys 2-10/issue.

Tips: "Writers should be aware that if they write nostalgia that not everything in the 'good old days' was good; our readers do not mind a writer who shares, but the approach, 'now I the expert, will tell you, the ignorant one, what you must know, i.e., talking down to the reader is a no-no; and simplicity in poetry is beautiful.'"

OUR SUNDAY VISITOR MAGAZINE, Noll Plaza, Huntington IN 46750. (219)356-8400. Executive Editor: Robert Lockwood. Weekly magazine for general Catholic audience. Circ. 300,000. Pays on acceptance. Byline given. Submit seasonal material 2 months in advance. Reports in 3 weeks. SASE. Free sample copy with SASE.

Nonfiction: Uses articles on Catholic-related subjects. Should explain Catholic religious beliefs in articles of human interest; articles applying Catholic principles to current problems, Catholic profiles, etc. Payment varies depending on reputation of author, quality of work, and amount of research required. Buys 25 mss/year. Query. Length: 1,000-1,200 words. Minimum payment for major features is $100 and minimum payment for shorter features is $50-75.

Photos: Purchased with mss; with captions only. Reviews b&w glossy prints and color transparencies. Pays $125/cover photo story, $75/b&w story; $25/color photo. $10/b&w photo.

PARISH FAMILY DIGEST, Our Sunday Visitor, Inc., 200 Noll Plaza, Huntington IN 46750. (219)356-8400. Editor: Patrick R. Moran. 95% freelance written. Bimonthly magazine; 48 pages. "*Parish Family Digest* is geared to the Catholic family and to that family as a unit of the parish." Circ. 150,000. Pays on acceptance. Byline given. Buys all rights on a work-for-hire basis. Submit seasonal/holiday material 5 months in advance. Photocopied and previously published submissions OK; all mss are retyped as edited. Computer printout submissions acceptable; prefers letter-quality to dot-matrix. SASE. Reports in 2 weeks on queries; 3 weeks on mss. Sample copy and writer's guidelines for 2 first class stamps.

Nonfiction: General interest, historical, inspirational, interview, nostalgia (if related to overall Parish involvement), and profile. No personal essays or preachy first person "thou shalt's or shalt not's." Send complete ms. Recent article example: "St. Anthony to the Rescue" (May/June 1985). Buys 82 unsolicited mss/year. Length: 1,000 words maximum. Pays $5-50.

Photos: State availability of photos with ms. Pays $10 for 3x5 b&w prints. Buys one-time rights. Captions preferred; model release required.

Fillers: Anecdotes and short humor. Buys 6/issue. Length: 100 words maximum.

Tips: "Know thy publication. Query with outline, title, approximate word length and possible photos. Read the magazine, get the feel of our parish family unit or involvement, and keep manuscripts to no more than 1,000 words maximum. Original ideas usually come through as winners for the beginning writer. Avoid reference book biographicals, and write of real persons."

‡**PARTNERSHIP, The Magazine for Wives in Ministry**, Christianity Today, Inc., 465 Gunderson Dr., Carol Stream IL 60188. (312)260-6200. Editor: Ruth Senter. Managing Editor: Eileen Johnson. 50% freelance written. Bimonthly magazine with articles encouraging clergy wives. For pastors' wives and wives of men in ministry to give practical help in dealing with their role, especially where that role has an impact on their own spiritual and personal growth, their families and marriage relationships and their relationships to the local church. Estab. 1984. Circ. 45,000. Pays on acceptance. Byline given. Offers 50% kill fee. Buys first serial rights. Submit seasonal/holiday material 6 months in advance. Simultaneous queries and photocopied submissions OK. SASE. Reports in 2 weeks on queries; 6 weeks on mss. Sample copy for 9x12 SAE; free writer's guidelines.
Nonfiction: Book excerpts, historical/nostalgic, how-to, humor, inspirational, interview/profile, opinion, personal experience and photo feature. No general interest or interviews. Buys 50 mss/year. Query with or without published clips or send complete ms. Length: 300-1,500 words. Pays $15-250. Sometimes pays expenses of writers on assignment.
Photos: State availability of photo or send photos with query or ms. Reviews b&w and color transparencies. Identification of subjects required. Buys one-time rights.
Columns/Departments: Buys 30 mss/year. Query with or without published clips or send complete ms. Length: 500 words maximum.

PENTECOSTAL EVANGEL, The General Council of the Assemblies of God, 1445 Boonville, Springfield MO 65802. (417)862-2781. Editor: Richard G. Champion. 33% freelance written. Weekly magazine; 32 pages. Emphasizes news of the Assemblies of God for members of the Assemblies and other Pentecostal and charismatic Christians. Circ. 290,000. Pays on publication. Byline given. Buys first serial rights, simultaneous rights, second serial (reprint) rights or one-time rights. Submit seasonal/holiday material 6 months in advance. Simultaneous, photocopied, and previously published submissions OK. SASE. Reports in 3 months. Free sample copy and writer's guidelines.
Nonfiction: Informational (articles on home life that convey Christian teachings); inspirational; and personal experience. Buys 5 mss/issue. Send complete ms. Length: 500-2,000 words. Pays 3¢/word maximum.
Photos: Photos purchased without accompanying ms. Pays $7.50-15 for 8x10 b&w glossy prints; $10-35 for 35mm or larger color transparencies. Total purchase price for ms includes payment for photos.
Poetry: Religious and inspirational. Buys 1 poem/issue. Submit maximum 6 poems. Pays 20-40¢/line.
Tips: "Break in by writing up a personal experience. We publish first person articles concerning spiritual experiences; that is, answers to prayer for help in a particular situation, of unusual conversions or healings through faith in Christ. All articles submitted to us should be related to religious life. We are Protestant, evangelical, Pentecostal, and any doctrines or practices portrayed should be in harmony with the official position of our denomination (Assemblies of God)."

PRAIRIE MESSENGER, Catholic Weekly, Benedictine Monks of St. Peter's Abbey, Box 190, Muenster, Saskatchewan S0K 2Y0 Canada. (306)682-5215. Editor: Andrew Britz. 8% freelance written. Saskatchewan and Manitoba Catholic weekly (48 issues/year) covering religion, culture and social change, as well as local, national and international events. Circ. 15,500. Pays on publication. Publishes ms an average of 2 months after acceptance. Byline given. Not copyrighted. Buys first serial rights and second serial (reprint) rights. Submit seasonal/holiday material 2 months in advance. Simultaneous queries and simultaneous, photocopied, and previously published submissions OK. Computer printout submissions acceptable; no dot-matrix. SASE. Reports in 3 weeks on queries; 3 months on mss.
Nonfiction: General interest, humor, inspirational, interview/profile, opinion and personal experience. Buys fewer than 10 mss/year. Send complete ms. Length: 500-800 words. Pays $1.45/column inch.
Photos: Send photos with ms. Pays $1.50 maximum for b&w negatives; $5.50 maximum for b&w prints. Captions and identification of subjects required. Buys one-time rights.
Columns/Departments: Pastoral Perspectives; Politics Today; Theological Review; Social Action (on the religious scene); and Ecumenical Forum. Buys 20 mss/year. Send complete ms. Length: 750 words; 1,000 for center spreads. Pays $1.45/column inch or $22.50 for comment and analysis columns which have been requested.

PRESBYTERIAN RECORD, 50 Wynford Dr., Don Mills, Ontario M3C 1J7 Canada. (416)444-1111. Editor: the Rev. James Dickey. 50% freelance written. Monthly magazine for a church-oriented, family audience. Circ. 75,000. Buys 25 mss/year. Pays on publication. Publishes ms an average of 4 months after acceptance. Submit seasonal material 3 months in advance. Computer printout submissions acceptable; prefers letter-quality to dot-matrix. Reports on ms accepted for publication in 2 months. Returns rejected material in 3 months. Query. SAE and Canadian stamps or IRC. Free sample copy.

Nonfiction: Material on religious themes. Check a copy of the magazine for style. Also, personal experience, interview, and inspirational material. No material solely American in context. Buys 15-20 unsolicited mss/year. Length: 1,000-2,000 words. Pays $45-55.
Photos: Pays $10-15 for b&w glossy photos. Uses positive color transparencies for cover. Pays $50. Captions required.
Tips: "There is a trend away from maudlin, first person pieces redolent with tragedy and dripping with simplistic pietistic conclusions."

PRESBYTERIAN SURVEY, Presbyterian Publishing House, Inc., 341 Ponce de Leon Ave. NE, Atlanta GA 30365. (404)873-1549. Editor: Vic Jameson. Managing Editor: Catherine Cottingham. 65% freelance written. Denominational magazine published 10 times/year covering religion, denominational activities and public issues for members of the Presbyterian Church (U.S.A.). Pays on acceptance. Publishes ms an average of 9 months after acceptance. Byline given. Offers variable kill fee. Buys first North American serial rights. Submit seasonal/holiday material 6 months in advance. Simultaneous submissions OK. Computer printout submissions acceptable; prefers letter-quality to dot-matrix. SASE. Reports in 2 weeks on queries; 1 month on mss. Free sample copy and writer's guidelines.
Nonfiction: Inspirational and Presbyterian programs, issues, people; any subject from a Christian viewpoint. No secular subjects. Buys 65 mss/year. Send complete ms. Length: 800-2,500 words. Pays $50-150. Sometimes pays expenses of writers on assignment.
Photos: Linda Colgrove, photo editor. State availability of photos. Reviews color transparencies and 8x10 b&w prints. Pays $15-25 for b&w; $25-50 for color. Identification of subjects required. Buys one-time rights.
Columns/Departments: The only column not by a regular columnist is an op ed page for readers of the magazine (As I See It). Buys 10 mss/year. Send complete ms. Length: 600-750 words. No payment.

PURPOSE, 616 Walnut Ave., Scottdale PA 15683. (412)887-8500. Editor: James E. Horsch. 95% freelance written. Weekly magazine "for adults, young and old, general audience with interests as varied as there are persons. My particular readership is interested in seeing Christianity work in tough situations." Circ. 18,500. Pays on acceptance. Publishes ms an average of 8 months after acceptance. Byline given. Buys one-time rights. Submit seasonal material 6 months in advance. Photocopied and simultaneous submissions OK. Computer printout submissions acceptable if legible; prefers letter-quality to dot-matrix. Submit complete ms. SASE required. Reports in 6 weeks. Sample copy and writer's guidelines for 6x9 SASE.
Nonfiction: Inspirational articles from a Christian perspective. "I want material that goes to the core of human problems in business, politics, religion, sex and any other area—and shows how the Christian faith resolves them. I want material that's upbeat. *Purpose* is a story paper which conveys truth either through quality fiction or through articles that use the best fiction techniques. Our magazine accents Christian discipleship. Christianity affects all of life, and we expect our material to demonstrate this. I would like to see story-type articles on how individuals, groups and organizations are intelligently and effectively working at some of the great human problems such as overpopulation, hunger, poverty, international understanding, peace, justice, etc., motivated by their faith." Buys 175-200 mss/year. Submit complete ms. Length: 1,200 words maximum. Pays 5¢/word maximum.
Photos: Photos purchased with ms. Pays $7.50-25 for b&w, depending on quality. Must be sharp enough for reproduction; prefers prints in all cases. Can use color prints at the same rate of payment. Captions desired.
Fiction: Humorous, religious and historical fiction related to theme of magazine. "Produce the story with specificity so that it appears to take place somewhere and with real people. It should not be moralistic."
Poetry: Traditional poetry, blank verse, free verse and light verse. Length: 12 lines maximum. Pays 50¢-$1/line.
Fillers: Jokes, short humor, and items up to 600 words. Pays 4¢/word maximum.
Tips: "We are looking for articles which show that Christianity is working at issues where people hurt, but we want the stories told and presented professionally. Good photographs help place material with us."

‡REFORM JUDAISM, Union of American Hebrew Congregations, 838 5th Ave., New York NY 10021. (212)249-0100. Editor: Aron Hert-Manheimer. Managing Editor: Joy Weinberg. 50% freelance written. Quarterly magazine of reform Jewish issues. "*Reform Judaism* is published by the UAHC, a nonprofit Jewish organization, and is distributed to members of reform Jewish congregations and other interested readers." Pays on publication. Publishes ms an average of 3 months after acceptance. Byline given. Offers negotiable kill fee. Buys first North American serial rights. Submit seasonal/holiday material 3 months in advance. Photocopied and previously published submissions OK. Computer printout submissions acceptable; prefers letter-quality to dot-matrix. SASE. Reports in 2 weeks on queries; 3 weeks on mss. Sample copy $1.
Nonfiction: Book excerpt (reviews), expose, general interest, historical/nostalgic, inspirational, interview/profile, opinion, personal experience, photo feature and travel. Buys 60 mss/year. Send complete ms. Submit complete ms. Length: 750-2,000 words. Pays $100-200. Sometimes pays expenses of writers on assignment.
Photos: Send photos with ms. Prefers 8x10 b&w prints. Pays $25-75. Identification of subjects required. Buys one-time rights.

Fiction: Ethnic, humorous, mainstream and religious. Buys 4 mss/year. Send complete ms. Length: 750-2,000 words. Pays $100-200.
Poetry: Free verse. Buys 2 poems/year. Submit maximum 3 poems. Length: 20 lines maximum. Pays $25-50.

REVIEW FOR RELIGIOUS, 3601 Lindell Blvd., Room 428, St. Louis MO 63108. (314)535-3048. Editor: Daniel F.X. Meenan, S.J. 100% freelance written. Bimonthly. For Roman Catholic priests, brothers and sisters. Pays on publication. Publishes ms an average of 9 months after acceptance. Byline given. Buys first serial rights and second serial (reprint) rights. Computer printout submissions acceptable; no dot-matrix. SASE. Reports in 8 weeks.
Nonfiction: Articles on ascetical, liturgical and canonical matters only; not for general audience. Length: 2,000-8,000 words. Pays $6/page.
Tips: "The writer must know about religious life in the Catholic Church and be familiar with prayer, vows and problems related to them."

ST. ANTHONY MESSENGER, 1615 Republic St., Cincinnati OH 45210. Editor-in-Chief: Norman Perry. 55% freelance written. Monthly magazine, 59 pages for a national readership of Catholic families, most of which have children in grade school, high school or college. Circ. 417,000. Pays on acceptance. Publishes ms an average of 9 months after acceptance. Byline given. Buys first North American serial rights. Submit seasonal/holiday material 4 months in advance. Electronic submissions OK if compatible with CPT word processor, but requires hard copy also. Computer printout submissions acceptable; no dot-matrix. SASE. Free sample copy and writer's guidelines.
Nonfiction: How-to (on psychological and spiritual growth, family problems); humor; informational; inspirational; interview; personal experience (if pertinent to our purpose); personal opinion (limited use; writer must have special qualifications for topic); and profile. Buys 35-50 mss/year. Length: 1,500-3,500 words. Pays 12¢/word.
Fiction: Mainstream and religious. Buys 12 mss/year. Submit complete ms. Length: 2,000-3,500 words. Pays 12¢/word.
Tips: "The freelancer should ask why his or her proposed article would be appropriate for us, rather than for *Redbook* or *Saturday Review*. We treat human problems of all kinds, but from a religious perspective. Get authoritative information (not merely library research); we want interviews with experts. Write in popular style."

ST. JOSEPH'S MESSENGER & ADVOCATE OF THE BLIND, Sisters of St. Joseph of Peace, St. Joseph's Home, Box 288, Jersey City NJ 07303. Editor-in-Chief: Sister Ursula Maphet. 25% freelance written. Quarterly magazine; 30 pages. Circ. 40,000. Pays on acceptance. Publishes ms an average of 6 months after acceptance. Buys first serial rights and second serial (reprint) rights, but will reassign rights back to author after publication asking only that credit line be included in next publication. Submit seasonal/holiday material 3 months in advance (no Christmas issue). Simultaneous and previously published submissions OK. Reports in 3 weeks. Free sample copy and writer's guidelines.
Nonfiction: Humor, inspirational, nostalgia, personal opinion and personal experience. Buys 24 mss/year. Submit complete ms. Length: 300-1,500 words. Pays $3-15.
Fiction: "Fiction is our most needed area." Romance, suspense, mainstream and religious. Buys 30 mss/year. Submit complete ms. Length: 600-1,600 words. Pays $6-25.
Poetry: Light verse and traditional. Buys 25 poems/year. Submit maximum 10 poems. Length: 50-300 words. Pays $5-20.
Tips: "It's rewarding to know that someone is waiting to see freelancers' efforts rewarded by 'print'. It's annoying, however, to receive poor copy, shallow material or inane submissions."

SCOPE, 426 S. 5th St., Box 1209, Minneapolis MN 55440. (612)330-3413. Editor: Constance Lovaas. 40% freelance written. Monthly for women of the American Lutheran Church. Circ. 275,000. Pays on acceptance. Publishes ms an average of 6 months after acceptance. Byline given. Buys first serial rights. Submit seasonal material 5 months in advance. Computer printout submissions acceptable; no dot-matrix. SASE. Reports in 4 weeks. Sample copy for SAE and 2 first class stamps.
Nonfiction: "The magazine transmits Bible study material for group meetings and provides articles for inspiration and growth as well as information about the mission and concerns of the church. "We also want articles that tell how the Christian faith relates to current social concerns, especially the lives of women of all ages in their work, leisure and relationships. Writers need not be Lutheran." Buys 200-300 mss/year. Submit complete ms. Length: 500-1,000 words. Pays $25-60.
Photos: Buys 3x5 or 8x10 b&w photos with ms or with captions only. Pays $10-30.
Poetry: Very little poetry used. Pays $15-25.
Fillers: "We can use interesting, brief, pithy, significant or clever filler items. We do not buy cute sayings of children." Pays $10-20.
Tips: "Writers should be aware of the need for inclusive language to avoid discrimination among races, sexes or persons who are disabled or elderly; recognition of women active in all aspects of the marketplace."

SEEK, Standard Publishing, 8121 Hamilton Ave., Cincinnati OH 45231. (513)931-4050, ext. 365. Editor: Leah Ann Crussell. 98% freelance written. Sunday school paper; 8 pages. Quarterly, in weekly issues for young and middle-aged adults who attend church and Bible classes. Circ. 45,000. Pays on acceptance. Publishes ms an average of 1 year after acceptance. Byline given. Buys first serial rights, first North American serial rights, and second serial (reprint) rights. Buys 100-150 mss/year. Submit seasonal material 1 year in advance. Computer printout submissions acceptable; prefers letter-quality to dot-matrix. SASE required. Reports in 10 days. Sample copy and writer's guidelines for SASE.

Nonfiction: "We look for articles that are warm, inspirational, devotional, of personal or human interest; that deal with controversial matters, timely issues of religious, ethical or moral nature, or first person testimonies, true-to-life happenings, vignettes, emotional situations or problems; communication problems and examples of answered prayers. Article must deliver its point in a convincing manner but not be patronizing or preachy. They must appeal to either men or women, must be alive, vibrant, sparkling and have a title that demands the article be read. We always need stories of families, marriages, problems on campus and life testimonies." No poetry. Buys 100-150 mss/year. Submit complete ms. Length: 400-1,200 words. Pays 3¢/word.

Photos: B&w photos purchased with or without mss. Pays $10 minimum for good 8x10 glossy prints.

Fiction: Religious fiction and religiously slanted historical and humorous fiction. Length: 400-1,200 words. Pays 2½¢/word.

Tips: Submit mss which tell of faith in action or victorious Christian living as central theme. "We select manuscripts as far as one year in advance of publication. Complimentary copies are sent to our published writers immediately following printing."

SHARING THE VICTORY, Publication of the Fellowship of Christian Athletes, Fellowship of Christian Athletes (FCA), 8701 Leeds Road, Kansas City MO 64129. (816)921-0909. Editor: Skip Stogsdill. Managing Editor: Jack Roberts. 10% freelance written. Bimonthly magazine aimed at enabling high school and college athletes, and coaches—male and female—to take their faith seriously, on and off the field." Circ. 47,000. Pays on publication. Publishes ms an average of 6 months after acceptance. Byline given. Buys first serial rights. Submit seasonal/holiday material 4 months in advance. Computer printout submissions acceptable; no dot-matrix. SASE. Reports in 2 weeks. Sample copy $1, SAE and 3 first class stamps; free writer's guidelines.

Nonfiction: Interview/profile and personal experience. Buys 6-10 mss/year. Query. Length; 500-1,000 words. Pays $25-50.

Photos: State availability of photos. Pays $15-35 for 5x7 or 8x10 b&w prints; $25-50 for 5x7 or 8x10 color prints and transparencies. Buys one-time rights.

Tips: "Profiles and interviews are most open to freelancers."

‡SIGNS OF THE TIMES, Pacific Press Publishing Association, Box 7000, Boise ID 83707. (208)465-2500. Editor: Kenneth J. Holland. Managing Editor: B. Russell Holt. 40% freelance written. Monthly magazine on religion. "We are a Christian publication encouraging the general public to put into practice the principles of the Bible." Circ. 400,000. Pays on acceptance. Publishes ms an average of 5 months after acceptance. Byline given. Offers $100 kill fee. Buys first North American serial rights and simultaneous rights. Submit seasonal/holiday material 8 months in advance. Simultaneous queries and submissions, and photocopied and previously published submissions OK. Computer printout submissions acceptable; prefers letter-quality to dot-matrix. SASE. Reports in 2 weeks on queries; 1 month on mss. Free sample copy and writer's guidelines.

Nonfiction: General interest (home, marriage, health—interpret current events from a Biblical perceptive); how-to (overcome depression, find one's identity, answer loneliness and guilt, face death triumphantly); humor; inspirational (human interest pieces that highlight a Biblical principle); interview/profile; personal experience (overcome problems with God's help); and photo feature. "We want writers with a desire to share the good news of reconciliation with God. Articles should be people-oriented, well-researched and should have a sharp focus and include anecdotes." Buys 150 mss/year. Query with or without published clips, or send complete ms. Length: 500-3,000 words. Pays $100-400. Sometimes pays expenses of writers on assignment.

Photos: Ed Guthero, photo editor. Send photos with query or ms. Reviews b&w contact sheets; 35mm color transparencies; 5x7 or 8x10 b&w prints. Pays $35-300 for transparencies; $20-50 for prints. Model release and identification of subjects required (captions helpful). Buys one-time rights.

Tips: "One of the most frequent mistakes made by writers in completing an article assignment for us is trying to cover too much ground. Articles need focus, research, and anecdotes. We don't want essays."

SISTERS TODAY, The Liturgical Press, St. John's Abbey, Collegeville MN 56321. Editor-in-Chief: Sister Mary Anthony Wagner, O.S.B. Associate Editor: Sister Barbara Ann Mayer, O.S.B. 90% freelance written. Magazine, published 10 times/year, for religious women of the Roman Catholic Church, primarily. Circ. 10,000. Pays on publication. Publishes ms an average of 1 year after acceptance. Byline given. Buys all rights. Submit seasonal/holiday material 4 months in advance. Computer printout submissions acceptable; no dot-matrix. SASE. Reports in 3 months. Sample copy $1.50.

Nonfiction: How-to (pray, live in a religious community, exercise faith, hope, charity etc.), informational; and inspirational. Also articles concerning religious renewal, community life, worship, and the role of Sisters in

the world today. Buys 33-40 unsolicited mss/year. Query. Length: 500-2,500 words. Pays $5/printed page.
Poetry: Free verse, haiku, light verse and traditional. Buys 3 poems/issue. Submit maximum 4 poems. Pays $10.

SOCIAL JUSTICE REVIEW, 3835 Westminister Place, St. Louis MO 63108. (314)371-1653. Editor: Harvey J. Johnson. 25% freelance written. Monthly. Not copyrighted; "however special articles within the magazine may be copyrighted, or an occasional special issue has been copyrighted due to author's request." Buys first serial rights. Computer printout submissions acceptable. SASE.
Nonfiction: Wants scholarly articles on society's economic, religious, social, intellectual and political problems with the aim of bringing Catholic social thinking to bear upon these problems. Query. Length: 2,500-3,500 words. Pays about $7/column.

SPIRITUAL LIFE, 2131 Lincoln Rd. NE, Washington DC 20002. (202)832-6622. Co-Editors: Rev. Christopher Latimer, O.C.D. and Rev. Stephen Payne, O.C.D. 80% freelance written. Quarterly. "Largely Catholic, well-educated, serious readers. A few are nonCatholic or nonChristian." Circ. 17,000. Pays on acceptance. Publishes ms an average of 1 year after acceptance. Buys first serial rights. "Brief autobiographical information (present occupation, past occupations, books and articles published, etc.) should accompany article." Reports in 2 weeks. SASE. Free sample copy and writer's guidelines.
Nonfiction: Serious articles of contemporary spirituality. High quality articles about our encounter with God in the present day world. Language of articles should be college level. Technical terminology, if used, should be clearly explained. Material should be presented in a positive manner. Sentimental articles or those dealing with specific devotional practices not accepted. Buys inspirational and think pieces. No fiction or poetry. Buys 20 mss/year. Length: 3,000-5,000 words. Pays $50 minimum. "Five contributor's copies are sent to author on publication of article." Book reviews should be sent to Rev. Steven Payne, O.C.D.

SPIRITUALITY TODAY, Aquinas Institute, 3642 Lindell Blvd., St. Louis MO 63108. Editor: The Rev. Christopher Kiesling O.P. 25% freelance written. Magazine "for those interested in a more knowing and intense Christian life in the 20th century." Pays on publication. Publishes ms an average of 1 year after acceptance. Byline given. Buys all rights but reassigned on request without fee. Computer printout submissions acceptable. SASE. Sample copy $1; free writer's guidelines.
Nonfiction: Articles that seriously examine important truths pertinent to the spiritual life, or Christian life, in the context of today's world. Scriptural, biographical, doctrinal, liturgical and ecumenical articles are acceptable. Buys 15 unsolicited mss/year. Submit complete ms. Length: 4,000 words. Pays 1¢/word.
Tips: "Examine the journal. It is not a typical magazine. Given its characteristics, the style of writing required is not the sort that regular freelance writers usually employ."

‡**STANDARD**, Nazarene International Headquarters, 6401 The Paseo, Kansas City MO 64131. (816)333-7000, ext. 460. Editor: Sheila Boggess. 95% freelance written. Weekly inspirational "story paper" with Christian leisure reading for adults. Circ. 177,000. Pays on acceptance. Publishes ms an average of 15 months after acceptance. Byline given. Buys one-time rights and second serial (reprint) rights. Submit seasonal/holiday material 9 months in advance. Computer printout submissions acceptable; prefers letter-quality to dot-matrix. SASE. Reports in 2 weeks on queries; 4 weeks on mss. Free sample copy; writer's guidelines for SAE with 1 first class stamp.
Nonfiction: How-to (grow spiritually); inspirational; and personal experience (with an emphasis on spiritual growth). Buys 100 mss/year. Send complete ms. Length: 300-1,500 words. Pays 3½¢/word for first rights; 2¢/word for reprint rights. Sometimes pays expenses of writers on assignment.
Photos: Send photos with ms. Pays $15-45 for 8x10 b&w prints. Buys one-time rights.
Fiction: Adventure, religious, romance and suspense—all with a spiritual emphasis. Buys 100 mss/year. Send complete ms. Length: 500-1,500 words. Pays 3½¢/word for first rights; 2¢/word for reprint rights.
Poetry: Free verse, haiku, light verse and traditional. No "lengthy" poetry. Buys 50 poems/year. Submit maximum 5 poems. Length: 50 lines maximum. Pays 20¢/line.
Fillers: Jokes, anecdotes and short humor. Buys 52/year. Length: 300 words maximum. Pays same as nonfiction and fiction.
Tips: "Articles should express Biblical principles without being preachy. Setting, plot and characterization must be realistic."

SUNDAY DIGEST, 850 N. Grove Ave., Elgin IL 60120. Editor: Judy C. Couchman. 75% freelance written. Issued weekly for Christian adults, mainly Protestants. "*Sunday Digest* provides a combination of original articles and reprints, selected to help adult readers better understand the Christian faith, to keep them informed of issues and happenings within the Christian community, and to challenge them to a deeper personal commitment to Christ." Pays on acceptance. Publishes ms an average of 9 months after acceptance. Buys first serial rights. Computer printout submissions acceptable; no dot-matrix. SASE. Reports in 6 weeks. Free sample copy and writer's guidelines for 6½x9½ SAE and 2 first class stamps.

Nonfiction: Needs articles applying the Christian faith to personal and social problems, articles of family interest and on church subjects, inspirational self-help, personal experience and anecdotes. Submit complete ms. Length: 500-1,800 words. Pays 7¢/word minimum. Pays expenses of writers on assignment.

Fiction: Uses true-to-life fiction that is hard-hitting, fast-moving, with a real woven-in, not "tacked on", Christian message. Also publishes allegory, fantasy, satire, and other fiction types. Length: 1,000-1,500 words. Pays 7¢/word minimum.

Poetry: Would like uplifting free verse poetry with a Christian message.

Tips: "It is crucial that the writer is committed to high quality Christian communication."

‡**SUNDAY SCHOOL COUNSELOR**, General Council of the Assemblies of God, 1445 Boonville, Springfield MO 65802. (417)862-2781. Editor: Sylvia Lee. 60% freelance written. Monthly magazine on religious education in the local church—the official Sunday school voice of the Assemblies of God channeling programs and help to local, primarily lay, leadership. Circ. 37,000. Pays on acceptance. Publishes ms an average of 9 months after acceptance. Byline given. Offers variable kill fee. Buys first North American serial rights, one-time rights, all rights, simultaneous rights, first serial rights, or second serial (reprint) rights; makes work-for-hire assignments. Submit seasonal/holiday material 7 months in advance. Simultaneous and previously published submissions OK. Computer printout submissions acceptable; prefers letter-quality to dot-matrix. SASE. Reports in 2 weeks on queries; 1 month on mss. Sample copy $1; free writer's guidelines.

Nonfiction: How-to, inspirational, interview/profile, personal experience and photo feature. All related to religious education in the local church. Buys 100 mss/year. Send complete ms. Length: 300-1,800 words. Pays $10-75. Sometimes pays expenses of writers on assignment.

Photos: Send photos with ms. Reviews b&w and color prints. Model release and identification of subjects required. Buys one-time rights.

TODAY'S CHRISTIAN PARENT, 8121 Hamilton Ave., Cincinnati OH 45231. (513)931-4050. Editor: Mrs. Mildred Mast. 70% freelance written. Quarterly. Pays on acceptance. Publishes ms an average of 1 year after acceptance. Buys first North American serial rights and occasionally second (reprint) rights. Computer printout submissions acceptable; prefers letter-quality to dot-matrix. SASE. Free sample copy and writer's guidelines for 7x9 or larger SASE.

Nonfiction: Devotional, inspirational and informational articles for the family. Also articles concerning the problems and pleasures of parents, grandparents and the entire family and Christian childrearing. Timely articles on moral issues, ethical and social situations, in-depth as much as possible in limited space. Length: 600-1,200 words. Can use short items on Christian family living; and fillers serious or humorous. Very little poetry. Study magazine before submitting. Pays up to 2½¢/word.

Tips: "Write about familiar family situations in a refreshingly different way, so that help and inspiration shine through the problems and pleasures of parenthood. Manuscript should be crisp, tightly-written. Avoid wordiness and trite situations or formats. Slant: from a Christian perspective. Enclose SASE for return of manuscript."

THE UNITED BRETHREN, United Brethren in Christ denomination, 302 Lake St., Huntington IN 46750. (219)356-2312. Editor: Steve Dennie. 10% freelance written. Denominational monthly for conservative evangelical Christians, ages 16 and up. Circ. 5,000. Pays on acceptance. Publishes ms an average of 6 months after acceptance. Byline given. Buys one-time rights. Submit seasonal/holiday material 6 months in advance. Simultaneous, photocopied, and previously published submissions OK. Computer printout submissions acceptable; prefers letter-quality to dot-matrix. SASE. Reports in 2 months. Sample copy $2; free writer's guidelines for SAE and 1 first class stamp.

Nonfiction: General interest, how-to, humor, inspirational and personal experience. Must have religious slant. No purely secular pieces. Buys 36 mss/year. Send complete ms. Length: 500-3,000 words. Pays 2-3¢/word.

Photos: Bought normally accompanying ms. Send photos with ms. Pays $5 maximum for 8x10 b&w glossy prints. No color. Buys one-time rights.

Fiction: All types, but religious slant necessary. Length: 500-2,000 words. Buys 5 mss/year. Pays 2¢/word.

THE UNITED CHURCH OBSERVER, 85 St. Clair Ave. E., Toronto, Ontario M4T 1M8 Canada. (416)960-8500. Publisher and Editor: Hugh McCullum. Managing Editor: Muriel Duncan. 40% freelance written. A 60-page monthly newsmagazine for persons associated with the United Church of Canada. Deals primarily with events, trends and policies having religious significance. Most coverage is Canadian, but reports on international or world concerns will be considered. Pays on publication. Byline usually given. Buys first serial rights and occasionally all rights. "Computer printout submissions acceptable; no dot-matrix."

Nonfiction: Occasional opinion features only. Extended coverage of major issues usually assigned to known writers. No opinion pieces, poetry. Submissions should be written as news, no more than 900 words length, accurate and well-researched. Queries preferred. Rates depend on subject, author and work involved. Pays expenses of writers on assignment "as negotiated."

Photos: Buys photographs with mss. B&w should be 5x7 minimum; color 35mm or larger format. Payment varies.
Tips: "The writer has a better chance of breaking in at our publication with short articles and fillers as there are fewer risks to us with people whose work we don't know; it also allows us to try more freelancers. Include samples of previous *news* writing with query. Indicate ability and willingness to do research, and to evaluate that research. The most frequent mistakes made by writers in completing an article for us are organizational problems, lack of polished style, short on research, and a lack of inclusive language."

UNITED EVANGELICAL ACTION, Box 28, Wheaton IL 60189. (312)665-0500. Editor: Christopher Lutes. 75% freelance written. Bimonthly magazine; alternating 16-20 pages. Offers "an objective evangelical viewpoint and interpretive analysis of specific issues of consequence and concern to the American Church and updates readers on ways evangelicals are confronting those issues at the grass-roots level." Circ. 7,600. Pays on publication. Publishes ms an average of 2 months after acceptance. Buys first serial rights. Phone queries OK. Computer printout submissions acceptable. SASE. Reports in 4 weeks. Sample copy and writer's guidelines with SASE.
Nonfiction: Issues and trends in the Church and society that affect the ongoing witness and outreach of evangelical Christians. Content should be well thought through, and should provide practical suggestions for dealing with these issues and trends. Buys 8-10 mss/year. Query. Length: 900-1,000 words. Pays $50-175.
Tips: Editors would really like to see news (action) items that relate to the National Association of Evangelicals. "Keep writing tersely, to the point, and stress practical over theoretical."

UNITED METHODIST REPORTER, Box 660275, Dallas TX 75266-0275. (214)630-6495. Editor/General Manager: Spurgeon M. Dunnam, III. Managing Editor: John A. Lovelace. Weekly newspaper for a United Methodist national readership. Circ. 475,000. Pays on acceptance. Byline given. Not copyrighted. SASE. Free sample copy and writer's guidelines.
Nonfiction: "We welcome short features, approximately 500 words. Articles need not be limited to a United Methodist angle but need to have an explicit Protestant angle. Write about a distinctly Christian response to human need or how a person's faith relates to a given situation." Send complete ms. Pays 4¢/word.
Photos: Purchased with accompanying ms. "We encourage the submission of good action photos (5x7 or 8x10 b&w glossy prints) of the persons or situations in the article." Pays $10.
Tips: "Read our publications before submitting. First person stories seldom fit our needs, but opinion pieces of no more than 500 words will be considered without pay for My Witness and Here I Stand."

UNITY MAGAZINE, Unity Village MO 64065. Editor: Pamela Yearsley. 90% freelance written. Monthly magazine; 64 pages. Publication of Unity School of Christianity. Circ. 430,000. Pays on acceptance. Publishes ms an average of 7 months after acceptance. Buys first serial rights. Computer printout submissions acceptable; prefers letter-quality to dot-matrix. Submit seasonal material 8 months in advance. Reports in 1 month. SASE. Free sample copy and writer's guidelines.
Nonfiction: "Inspirational articles, metaphysical in nature, about individuals who are using Christian principles in their living." Personal experience and interview. "We specialize in religious, inspirational material—anything else is rejected out of hand." Buys 200 mss/year. Submit complete ms. Length: 2,000 words maximum. Pays minimum of 4¢/word. Sometimes pays expenses of writers on assignment.
Photo: Reviews 4x5 or 8x10 color transparencies purchased without ms. "We are using more color photography inside." Pays $75-100.
Poetry: Traditional, blank verse and free verse. Pays 50¢-$1/line.
Tips: "Be innovative and use new twists on old truths."

THE UPPER ROOM, DAILY DEVOTIONAL GUIDE, The Upper Room, 1908 Grand Ave., Nashville TN 37202. (615)327-2700. World Editor: Janice T. Grana. Managing Editor: Mary Lou Redding. 97% freelance written. Bimonthly magazine "offering a daily inspirational message which includes a Bible reading, text, prayer, 'Thought for the Day,' and suggestion for prayer. Each day's meditation is written by a different person and is usually a personal witness about discovering meaning and power for Christian living through some experience from daily life." Circ. 2,225,000 (U.S.); 385,000 outside U.S. Pays on publication. Publishes ms an average of 1 year after acceptance. Byline given. Offers negotiable kill fee. Buys first North American serial rights and translation rights. Submit seasonal/holiday material 14 months in advance. Computer printout submissions acceptable; prefers letter-quality to dot-matrix. SASE. Reports in 3 weeks on queries; 6 weeks on mss. Sample copy and writer's guidelines for SAE and 2 first class stamps.
Nonfiction: Inspirational and personal experience. No poetry, lengthy "spiritual journey" stories. Buys 360 unsolicited mss/year. Send complete ms. Length: 250 words maximum. Pays $10 minimum.
Columns/Departments: Prayer Workshop, "2-page feature which details some meditation or prayer exercise. "We are interested in adaptations of classical spiritual disciplines from Christians of the past with attention to contemporary struggles and problems." Buys 6 mss/year. Query with published clips. Length: 400-600 words. Pays $50-100. "All quoted material used must be documented through standard footnote material for verifica-

tion. Writer should obtain permission for use of previously copyrighted material which is quoted."

Tips: "The best way to break into our magazine is to send a well-written manuscript that looks at the Christian faith in a fresh way. Standard stories and sermon illustrations are immediately rejected. We very much want to find new writers and welcome good material. Daily meditations are most open. Prayer Workshops are usually assigned. Good repeat meditations can lead to work on longer assignments for our other publications, which pay more. We encourage theological diversity and especially welcome faith-perspective approaches to current social problems and controversial issues within the Christian faith."

VIRTUE, Box 850, Sisters OR 97759. (503)549-8261. Managing Editor: Becky Durost. 70% freelance written. Bimonthly Christian magazine for women. Circ. 95,000. Average issue includes 15 feature articles. Pays on publication. Publishes ms an average of 4 months after acceptance. Byline given. Buys first North American rights. Submit seasonal material 6 months in advance. Simultaneous and previously published submissions OK, if so indicated. Computer printout submissions acceptable; prefers letter-quality to dot-matrix. SASE. Reports in 3 weeks on queries. Sample copy $2; free writer's guidelines.
Nonfiction: Interviews with Christian women; *current issues*; how-to (upkeep and organizational tips for home); inspirational (spiritual enrichment); personal experience; and family information for husbands, wives and children. "No mystical or preachy articles." Buys 20 mss/issue. Query. Length: 1,000-1,500 words. Pays 5-7¢/word.
Photos: Reviews 3x5 b&w glossy prints. Offers additional payment for photos accepted with ms. Captions required. Buys all rights or first serial rights.
Columns/Departments: Opinion piece (reader editorial); foods (recipes and entertaining); and crafts, decorating, gardening, fitness, health, and creative projects. Buys 4-8 mss/issue. Query. Length: 1,500-1,800 words. Pays 5-7¢/word.
Fiction: Christian adventure, humor and romance. Buys 1 ms/issue. Send complete ms. Length: 1,500-1,800 words. Pays 5-7¢/word.
Fillers: Anecdotes, short humor, newsbreaks and thought-provoking family stories. Buys 2/issue. Pays 5-7¢/word.
Tips: "We may be increasing our standard magazine size and will be needing more well-researched articles on current issues."

VISTA, Wesleyan Publishing House, Box 2000, Marion IN 46952. Address submissions to Editor of *Vista*. 80% freelance written. Weekly publication of The Wesleyan Church for adults. Circ. 60,000. Pays on publication. Publishes ms an average of 8 months after acceptance. Byline given. Not copyrighted. "Along with manuscripts for first use, we also accept simultaneous submissions, second rights, and reprint rights. It is the writer's obligation to secure clearance from the original publisher for any reprint rights." Submit material 9 months in advance. Computer printout submissions acceptable; prefers letter-quality to dot-matrix. "SASE for sample copy and with all manuscripts." Not responsible for unsolicited mss. Reports in 2 months.
Nonfiction: Devotional, biographical, and informational articles with inspirational, religious, moral or educational values. Favorable toward emphasis on: New Testament standard of living as applied to our day; soul-winning (evangelism); proper Sunday observance; Christian youth in action; Christian education in the home, the church and the college; good will to others; worldwide missions; clean living, high ideals, and temperance; wholesome social relationships. Disapproves of liquor, tobacco, theaters, dancing. Mss are judged on basis of human interest, ability to hold reader's attention, vivid characterizations, thoughtful analysis of problems, vital character message, expressive English, correct punctuation, proper diction. "Know where you are going and get there." Length: 500-1,500 words. Pays 2½¢/word for quality material, 2-3¢/word for second rights and reprints.
Photos: Pays $15-40 for 5x7 or 8x10 b&w glossy print portraying people in action, seasonal emphasis, or scenic value. Various reader age groups should be considered.
Fiction: Stories should have definite Christian emphasis and character-building values, without being preachy. Setting, plot and action should be realistic. Length: 1,500 words; also short-shorts and vignettes. Pays 2½-3¢/word for quality material, 2¢/word for second rights and reprints.
Tips: We often need a 400-600 word filler to complete an issue; and since we don't receive too many of this type of article, those we do get have a greater chance of being published. Our publication is meant to be leisurely Sunday afternoon reading, so we need light-reading inspirational articles that will keep the reader's attention.

‡**VITAL CHRISTIANITY**, Warner Press, Inc., 1200 E. 5th St., Anderson IN 46018. (317)644-7721. Editor-in-Chief: Arlo F. Newell. Managing Editor: Richard L. Willowby. Magazine covering Christian living for people attending local Church of God congregations; published 20 times/year. Circ. 40,000. Pays on acceptance. Byline given. Offers 100% kill fee. Buys first serial rights. Submit seasonal/holiday material 6 months in advance. Simultaneous queries OK. Computer printout and disk submissions OK but not preferable. SASE. Reports in 6 weeks. Sample copy and writer's guidelines with SAE and $1.
Nonfiction: Humor (with religious point); inspirational (religious—not preachy); interview/profile (of

church-related personalities); opinion (religious/theological); and personal experience (related to putting one's faith into practice). Buys 125 mss/year. Query. Length: 1,200 words maximum. Pays $10-150.
Photos: State availability of photos. Pays $50-300 for 5x7 color transparencies; $20-40 for 8x10 b&w prints. Identification of subjects (when related directly to articles) required. Buys one-time rights. Reserves the right to reprint material it has used for advertising and editorial purposes (pays second rights for editorial re-use).
Tips: "Fillers, personal experience, personality interviews and profiles are areas of our magazine open to freelancers. All submissions are reviewed. The best method is to read our publication and submit similar material."

WAR CRY, The Official Organ of the Salvation Army, 799 Bloomfield Ave., Verona NJ 07044. Editor: Henry Gariepy. Biweekly magazine for "persons with evangelical Christian background; members and friends of the Salvation Army; the 'man in the street.' " Circ. 280,000. Pays on acceptance. Buys first serial rights and second serial (reprint) rights. SASE. Reports in 2 months. Free sample copy.
Nonfiction: Inspirational and informational articles with a strong evangelical Christian slant, but not preachy. In addition to general articles, needs articles slanted toward most of the holidays including Easter, Christmas, Mother's Day, Father's Day, etc. Buys 100 mss/year. Length: approximately 1,000-1,400 words. Pays 4¢/word.
Photos: Occasionally buys photos submitted with ms, but seldom with captions only. Pays $15-35 for b&w glossy prints; $50 color prints.
Fiction: Prefers complete-in-one-issue stories, with a strong Christian slant. Can have modern or Biblical setting, but must not run contrary to Scriptural account. Length: 1,100-1,400 words. Pays 4¢/word.
Poetry: Religious or nature poems. Length: 4-24 lines. Pays $5-25.

‡**THE WESLEYAN ADVOCATE**, The Wesleyan Church Corp., Box 2000, Marion IN 46952. (317)674-3301. Editor: Dr. Wayne E. Caldwell. 30% freelance written. Semimonthly magazine of The Wesleyan Church which reflects the devotional and doctrinal commitment of the denomination and is provided primarily for the membership and friends of The Wesleyan Church. Circ. 20,000. Pays on acceptance. Publishes ms an average of 4 months after acceptance. Byline given. Not copyrighted. Buys first serial rights. Submit seasonal/holiday material 4 months in advance. Computer printout submissions acceptable; prefers letter-quality to dot-matrix. SASE. Reports in 2 weeks on queries; 3 months on mss. Sample copy $1; writer's guidelines for SASE.
Nonfiction: Inspirational; interview/profile (of people significant in or to the Wesleyan Church); personal experience (religious); Bible studies; and doctrinal pieces. Special issues include youth, Easter, family, revival, Christmas, and missions. No political endorsements, attacks on churches, etc. Buys 60-75 unsolicited mss/year. Query with published clips. Length: 200-650 words. Pays 1-3¢/published word.
Poetry: No "doggerel and trite rhyme or verse with poor meter." Buys 10/year. Submit maximum 2 poems. Pays $2-5.
Tips: "Freelancers can best break in with a short devotional or inspirational article or through a personal experience article, accompanied by a personal letter with information about the author. We value personal integrity and a warmth that flows through any kind of article."

THE WITTENBERG DOOR, 1224 Greenfield Dr., El Cajon CA 92021. (619)440-2333. Contact: Mike Yaconelli. 40% freelance written. Bimonthly magazine for men and women connected with the church. Circ. 19,000. Pays on publication. Publishes ms an average of 1 year after acceptance. Buys all rights. Computer printout submissions acceptable. SASE. Reports in 3 months.
Nonfiction: Satirical articles on church renewal, Christianity, and organized religion. Few book reviews. Buys about 30 mss/year. Submit complete ms. Length: 1,000 words maximum, 500-750 preferred. Pays $25-100. Sometimes pays expenses of writers on assignments.
Tips: "We look for someone who is clever, on our wave length, and has some savvy about the evangelical church. We are very picky and highly selective. The writer has a better chance of breaking in at our publication with short articles and fillers since we are a bimonthly publication with numerous regular features and the magazine is only 32 pages. The most frequent mistake made by writers is that they do not understand satire. They see we are a humor magazine and consequently come off funny/cute (like *Reader's Digest*) rather than funny/satirical (like *National Lampoon*)."

WORLD ENCOUNTER, 2900 Queen Lane, Philadelphia PA 19129. (215)438-6360. Editor: James Solheim. Quarterly magazine; 32 pages. For persons who have more than average interest in, and understand-

 The double dagger before a listing indicates that the listing is new in this edition. New markets are often the most receptive to freelance contributions.

ing of, overseas missions and current human social concerns in other parts of the world. Circ. 8,000. Pays on publication. Publishes ms an average of 3 months after acceptance. Byline given. 35% kill fee. Buys first serial rights. Photocopied and simultaneous submissions OK, if information is supplied on other markets being approached. Computer printout submissions acceptable; no dot-matrix. SASE. Reports in 1 month. Sample copy $1.

Nonfiction: "This is a religious and educational publication using human interest features and think pieces related to the Christian world mission and world community. Topics include race relations in southern Africa; human rights struggles with tyrannical regimes; social and political ferment in Latin America; and resurgence of Eastern religions. Simple travelogues are not useful to us. Prospective writers should inquire as to the countries and topics of particular interest to our constituents. Material must be written in a popular style but the content must be more than superficial. It must be theologically, sociologically and anthropologically sound. We try to maintain a balance between gospel proclamation and concern for human and social development. We focus on what is happening in Lutheran groups. Our standards of content quality and writing are very high." No religious editorializing or moralizing. Buys 10 mss/year. Query or submit complete ms. Length: 500-1,800 words. Pays $50-200.

Photos: B&w photos are purchased with or without mss or on assignment. Pays $20-50. Captions required.

Tips: "Write the editor, outlining your background and areas of international knowledge and interest, asking at what points they converge with our magazine's interests. In our field writers should be aware of a radically different understanding of Christian missions in the Third World."

Retirement

Most retirement magazine readers don't sit on front porches sipping fruit drinks all day. That's the kind of stereotype that editors want to avoid in retirement magazines. Some people are retiring in their fifties; others are starting a second business—the one they've always dreamed of. Still, other retirement-age readers prefer to travel or pursue hobbies. These publications give readers specialized information. Some want service articles; others want material to make free time more enjoyable.

DYNAMIC YEARS, 215 Long Beach Blvd., Long Beach CA 90802. Executive Editor: Lorena F. Farrell. 90% freelance written. Bimonthly. "*Dynamic Years* is an official publication of the American Association of Retired Persons emphasizing stories relating to the interests of midlife (ages 45-65) career people." Circ. 200,000. Pays negotiable kill fee. Publishes ms an average of 6-8 months after acceptance. Byline given. Pays on acceptance. Buys first North American serial rights. Submit seasonal material 6 months in advance. Computer printout submissions acceptable; no dot-matrix. SASE. Reports in 2 months. Free sample copy. and writer's guidelines.

Nonfiction: General subject matter is financial planning/investment, lifestyle, preretirement planning, health/fitness, humor, the world of work and job-related pieces, second careers, personal adjustment, sports, travel, fashion/beauty, entertaining, generational relationships, "people in action" with unusual activities, hobbies and exciting uses of leisure. No pieces about individuals long retired; no quizzes, poetry, jokes, nostalgia or inspirational preachments. "Our primary concern is superb writing style, depth and accuracy of information." Buys 100 mss/year. Query with published clips (except for humor). Length: 350-3,000 words. Pays $150 for departmental items, $350 minimum for short pieces, $800-2,000 for full-length features. Sometimes pays expenses of writers on assignment.

Photos: State availability of photos with ms. Pays $75 minimum for professional quality b&w. Pays $150 minimum for professional quality color slides or transparencies. Captions required.

Tips: "The writer has a better chance of breaking in at our publication with short articles and fillers because we need to see how they write, how accurately they research their material, how easy they are to work with, etc., before we'll let them tackle a major piece. The exception is a well-known writer with extensive clips. The most frequent mistakes made by writers in completing articles for us are poorly researched material (dates, spelling, facts, etc.) and a poorly written ('dull') lead on close."

50 PLUS, 850 3rd Ave., New York NY 10022. Editor: Bard Lindeman. Managing Editor: Allen Sheinman. Assistant Editor: Marina Hines. "Current demands upon our editorial staff prohibit the reviewing of material that has not been assigned." No unsolicited mss, photographs or query letters.

‡**GOLDEN YEARS MAGAZINE, Golden Years Senior News, Inc.**, 233 E. New Haven Ave., Melbourne FL 32902-0537. (305)725-4888. Editor: Carol Brenner Hittner. 50% freelance written. Monthly magazine covering the 50+ generation. "We serve the needs and interests of Florida's fastest growing generation presented in a postive, uplifting, straight-forward manner." Circ. 500,000. Pays on publication. Publishes ms an average of 5 months after acceptance. Byline given. Buys first serial rights. Submit seasonal/holiday material 3 months in advance. Simultaneous queries, and simultaneous, and photocopied submissions OK. Computer printout submissions acceptable; prefers letter-quality to dot-matrix. SASE. Sample copy $1; writer's guidelines for SAE with 1 first class stamp.

Nonfiction: Profile (Florida senior celebrities), travel, health, exercise and nutrition articles (with recipes). Buys 150 mss/year. Query with published clips or send complete ms. Length: 500 maximum. Pays 8¢/word and up.

Photos: "We like to include a lot of photos." Send photos with query or ms. Pays $25-50 for color transparencies and prints. Captions, model release, and identification of subjects required. Buys one-time rights.

Columns/Departments: Health and nutrition, legislative update real estate and travel. Query or send complete ms.

Fillers: Crosswords and cartoons. Pays $25 for puzzles and $10 for cartoons.

Tips: "We're looking for profiles on Florida people. Our magazine is a small one; all our articles are short and special—that's why we are successful."

MATURE LIVING, The Sunday School Board of the Southern Baptist Convention, 127 9th Ave. N., Nashville TN 37234. (615)251-2274. Editor: Jack Gulledge. Assistant Editor: Zada Malugen. 80% freelance written. Monthly magazine; 52 pages. Christian magazine for retired senior adults 60+. Pays on acceptance. Publishes ms an average of 15 months after acceptance. Byline given. Buys all rights. Submit seasonal/holiday material 15 months in advance. Computer printout submissions acceptable; prefers letter quality to dot-matrix. SASE. Reports in 6 weeks. Free sample copy and writer's guidelines.

Nonfiction: How-to (easy, inexpensive craft articles made from easily obtained materials); informational (safety, consumer fraud, labor-saving and money-saving for senior adults); inspirational (short paragraphs with subject matter appealing to older persons); nostalgia; unique personal experiences; and travel. Buys 7-8 mss/issue. Send complete ms. Length: 450-1,550 words; prefers articles of 925 words. Pays $16-62.

Photos: Some original photos purchased with accompanying ms. Pays $5-15 for b&w glossy prints, depending on size. Model release required.

Fiction: Everyday living, humor and religious. "Must have suspense and character interaction." Buys 1 ms/issue. Send complete ms. Length: 925-1,550 words. Pays 4¢/word.

Fillers: Short humor, religious or grandparent/grandchild episodes. Length: 125 words maximum. Pays $5.

Tips: "We want warm, creative, unique manuscripts. Presentations don't have to be moralistic or religious, but must reflect Christian standards. Don't write *down* to target audience. Speak *to* senior adults on issues that interest them. They like contemporary, good-Samaritan, and nostalgia articles. We buy some light humor. We use 140-word profiles of interesting, unusual, senior adults worthy of recognition, when accompanied by a quality action black and white glossy photo. Pays $25. Query should emphasize the uniqueness of proposed copy."

MATURE YEARS, 201 8th Ave., S., Nashville TN 37202. Editor: Daisy D. Warren. 75% freelance written. Quarterly magazine for retired persons and those facing retirement; persons seeking help on how to handle problems and privileges of retirement. Pays on acceptance. Publishes ms an average of 3 months after acceptance. Rights purchased vary with author and material; usually buys all rights. Submit seasonal material 14 months in advance. Reports in 6 weeks. SASE. Free writer's guidelines.

Nonfiction: "*Mature Years* is different from the secular press in that we like material with a Christian and church orientation. Usually we prefer materials that have a happy, healthy outlook regarding aging. Advocacy (for older adults) articles are at times used; some are freelance submissions. We need articles dealing with many aspects of pre-retirement and retirement living, and short stories and leisure-time hobbies related to specific seasons. Give examples of how older persons, organizations, and institutions are helping others. Writing should be of interest to older adults, with Christian emphasis, though not preachy and moralizing. No poking fun or mushy, sentimental articles. We treat retirement from the religious viewpoint. How-to, humor and travel are also considered." Buys 24 unsolicited mss/year. Submit complete ms. Length: 1,200-2,000 words.

Photos: 8x10 b&w glossy prints purchased with ms or on assignment.

Fiction: "We buy fiction for adults. Humor is preferred. Please, no children's stories and no stories about depressed situations of older adults." Length: 1,000-2,000 words. Payment varies, usually 4¢/word.

Tips: "The most rewarding aspect of working with freelance writers is getting articles on unusual topics."

MODERN MATURITY, American Association of Retired Persons, 215 Long Beach Blvd., Long Beach CA 90801. Editor-in-Chief: Ian Ledgerwood. 75% freelance written. Bimonthly magazine for readership of persons over 50 years of age. Circ. 12 million. Pays on acceptance. Publishes ms an average of 4 months after acceptance. Byline given. Buys all rights. Submit seasonal/holiday material 6 months in advance. Computer printout submissions acceptable; prefers letter-quality to dot-matrix. SASE. Reports in 4 weeks. Free sample copy and writer's guidelines.

Nonfiction: Historical, how-to, humor, informational, inspirational, interview, new product, nostalgia, personal experience, opinion, photo feature, profile and travel. Query or send complete ms. Length: 1,000-2,500 words. Pays $1,000-2,500.

Photos: Photos purchased with or without accompanying ms. Pays $150 and up for color and $75 and up for b&w.

Poetry: All types. Length: 40 lines maximum. Pays $75.

Fillers: Clippings, jokes, gags, anecdotes, newsbreaks, puzzles (find-the-word, not crossword) and short humor. Pays $25 minimum.

Tips: "We are willing to work with less skilled writers who have basic knowledge in the nostalgia category. The most frequent mistake made by writers in completing an article for us is poor follow-through with basic research. The outline is often more interesting than the finished piece."

PRIME TIMES, Grote Deutsch & Co., Suite 120, 2802 International Ln., Madison WI 53704. Executive Director: Steve Goldberg. Managing Editor: Russell H. Grote. Associate Managing Editor: Joan Donovan. 80% freelance written. Quarterly magazine for people who want to redefine retirement and late life. The audience is primarily people over 50 who were or are credit union members and want to plan and manage their retirement. Circ. 75,000. Pays on publication. Buys first serial rights and second serial (reprint) rights. Publishes ms an average of 4 months after acceptance. Submit seasonal material 6 months in advance. Previously published submissions OK as long and they were not in another national maturity-market magazine. Computer printout submissions acceptable; no dot-matrix. SASE. Reports in 2 months. Sample copy only with 9x12 SAE and 5 first class stamps; writer's guidelines for SASE.

Nonfiction: Expose; how-to—new research and updates (related to financial planning methods, consumer activism, health, travel, and working/lifestyle after retirement); interviews of people over 50 who are leading active or important retirements or otherwise redefining late lifestyles; opinion; profile; travel; popular arts; self-image; personal experience; humor; and photo feature. "No rocking chair reminiscing." Articles on health and medical issues and research *must* be founded in sound scientific method and must include current, up-to-date data. "Health related articles are an easy sale, but you must do your homework and be able to document your research. Don't waste your time or ours on tired generalizations about how to take care of the human anatomy. If you've heard it before, so have we. We know stress can kill, that it is a factor in the onset of degenerative diseases such as arthritis, heart and circulatory system failure, endocrine system failure and the like. We want to know why and how. We want to know who is doing new research, what the current findings may be, and what scientists on the cutting edge of new research say the future hold, preferably in the next one to five years. Is anyone doing basic research into the physiology of the aging process? If so, who? And what have they found? What triggers the aging process? Why do some people age faster than others? What are the common denominators? Does genetic coding and recombinant DNA research hold the answers to slowing or halting the aging process? Get the picture? Give us the facts, only the facts, and all of the facts. Allow the scientists and our audience to draw their own conclusions." Buys 30-40 mss/year, about half from new talent. Query with published clips. Length: 500-3,000 words. Pays $50-900. "Be sure to keep a photocopy—just in case gremlins pinch the original."

Photos: Pays $25-50 for 8x10 glossy high-contrast prints; $25-50 for 35mm color transparency, or according to ASMP guidelines or negotiation; $7.50 for cutline. Will not reproduce color prints. Captions and model release required. Buys one-time rights. "Do not send irreplaceable *anything*."

Fiction: Length: 1,500-3,500 words. Pays $150-750.

Tips: Query should state qualifications (such as expertise or society memberships). Special issues requiring freelance work include publications on mature friendship; health and medical research and updates; comparative aging (cross-cultural); second careers; money management; minorities over 50; continuing education; consequences of the ongoing longevity revolution; and the "young-old" vis-a-vis the "old-old". "Whether urban or rural, male or female, if an attempt at humor, lightness or tongue-in-cheek seems off-target to you, it will to us, too. And we don't gloss over important matters. If you identify a problem, try to identify a solution. Remember that there are at least two generations reading *Prime Times*—folks over 50 and folks over 70. Most are not retired (average age: 61), and about 55% of our readers are women. Above all, we are interested in broadcasting mental and visual images of older people. If your work does not promote such dynamic images of people over 50, it will not be on target with us."

‡SILVER CIRCLE, Publication of Home Savings of America/Savings of America, Suite 2039, 4900 Rivergrade Rd., Irwindale CA 91706. (213)369-8398. Editor: Jay Binkly. Quarterly club magazine covering financial topics. "We seek general interest articles and features for older audiences, ages 50 and up." Circ. 450,000. Pays on publication. Byline given. Offers 50% kill fee. Buys one-time rights. Submit seasonal/holiday material 6 months in advance. Simultaneous queries, with simultaneous and photocopied submissions OK. Computer printout submissions acceptable. SASE. Reports in 2 weeks on queries; 4 weeks on ms. Free sample copy.

Nonfiction: Book excerpts, general interest, historical/nostalgic, how-to, humor, interview/profile, new product, personal experience, photo feature, travel, and financial articles, "but remember, we're published by a savings and loan company." No articles about investing. Buys 10-15 mss/year. Query. Length: 500-4,000 words. Pays $75-600.

Photos: Send photos with query. Pays $25-100 for 2¼ b&w transparencies; $50-200 for 2¼ color transparencies. Captions, model release, and identification of subjects required.

Columns/Departments: Health, Financial, Current Affairs, Taxes, Legal Matters, Personal Security, Travel, Food, Entertainment, Book Reviews, and Consumer. Buys 20 mss/year. Query. Length: 500-1,000 words. Pays $25-150.

Fillers: Jokes, anecdotes and short humor. Length: 50-100 words. Pays $5-20.

Tips: "Articles standing the best chance of publication are those that will enhance the lives of our readers who are retired or facing retirement."

‡**3 SCORE AND 10, A Magazine for People Over 70**, 3 Score and 10, RD #2, Box 103, Boswell PA 15531. (814)629-9815 Editor: Joseph Kaufman. 100% freelance written. Monthly magazine serving people over 70. "We seek inspiration, recognition, wisdom, humor and insight." Estab. 1984. Pays on publication. Publishes ms an average of 18 months after acceptance. Byline given. Not copyrighted. Buys one-time rights. Submit seasonal/holiday material 2 months in advance. Simultaneous queries and submissions; and photocopied and previously published submissions OK. Computer printout submissions acceptable. SASE. Sample copy and writer's guidelines for SAE and 2 first class stamps.

Nonfiction: General interest, historical/nostalgic, inspirational, interview/profile, personal experience and travel. No "depressing material". Buys 36-72 mss/year. Length: 250-2,000 words. Pays $5-15.

Photos: Send photos with ms. Prefers b&w prints. Pays $2-5.

Columns/Departments: Inspiration, wisdom, tributes and triumphs, hobbies and pastimes. Buys 24-48 mss/year. Send complete ms. Length: 250-1,500 words. Pays $5-15.

Poetry: Free verse, light verse and traditional. Buys 12-36 poems/year. Pays $3-5.

Tips: "We seek to serve the population over age 70. Articles and ideas on any subject are welcome, especially inspiration and those that give the reader over 70 a sense of community."

Romance and Confession

Whether a story's romantic intrigue has blossomed in real life or in the writer's mind, readers still enjoy *the escape*. Listed here are publications that need these stories and publications that help writers write better romances. Also to help you write better romances is Writer's Digest Books' *Writing Romance Fiction—For Love and Money*, by Helene Schellenberg Barnhart.

AFFAIRE DE COEUR, Leading Publication for Romance Readers and Writers, Affaire de Coeur, Inc., 5660 Roosevelt Pl., Fremont CA 94538. (415)656-4804. Editors/Publishers: Beth Rowe and Barbara N. Keenan. 90% freelance written. Monthly magazine for romance readers and writers. Circ. 8,000. Pays on publication. Publishes ms an average of 6 months after acceptance. Byline given. Buys all rights. Submit seasonal/holiday material 4 months in advance. Simultaneous queries, and photocopied and previously published submissions OK. SASE. Reports in 3 weeks. Sample copy $2; writer's guidelines for SAE and $5 postage and handling.

Nonfiction: Book excerpts (on romantic fiction); how-to (write romantic fiction); and interview/profile (on romance authors). Buys 12 mss/year. Query. Length: varies. Pays $10-25.

Fiction: Beth Rowe, senior editor. Novel excerpts, romance and serialized novels. Buys variable number mss/year. Query. Length: 1,000-1,500 words. Pays $15-25.

Fillers: Beth Rowe, fillers editor. Newsbreaks. Buys 50/year. Length: varies. Pays with credit line.

Tips: "The most frequent mistake made by writers in completing an article for us is that it is too long. Articles should be, at most, 3,000 words."

MODERN ROMANCES, Macfadden Women's Group, Inc., 215 Lexington Ave., New York NY 10016. Editor: Jean Sharbel. 100% freelance written. Monthly magazine; 80 pages for blue-collar, family-oriented women, ages 18-35 years old. Circ. 200,000. Pays the last week of the month of issue. Buys all rights. Submit seasonal/holiday material 6 months in advance. SASE. Reports in 4 months.

Nonfiction: General interest, baby and child care, how-to (homemaking subjects), humor, inspirational, and personal experience. Submit complete ms. Length: 200-1,500 words. Pay depends on merit. "Confession stories with reader identification and a strong emotional tone. No third person material." Buys 14 mss/issue. Submit complete ms. Length: 1,500-8,500 words. Pays 5¢/word.

Poetry: Light, romantic poetry. Buys 36/year. Length: 24 lines maximum. Pay depends on merit.

‡**SECRETS**, Macfadden Women's Group, 215 Lexington Ave., New York NY 10016. (212)340-7500. Vice President and Editorial Director: Florence J. Moriarty. Editor: Jean Press Silberg. 100% freelance written. Monthly magazine for blue-collar family women, ages 18-35. Pays on publication. Publishes ms an average of 5 months after acceptance. Buys all rights. Submit seasonal material 5 months in advance. Computer printout submissions acceptable; prefers letter-quality to dot-matrix. SASE. Reports in 6 weeks.

Nonfiction and Fiction: Wants true stories of special interest to women: family, marriage and romance themes, "woman-angle articles," or self-help or inspirational fillers. "No pornographic material; no sadistic or abnormal angles." Buys 150 mss/year. Submit complete ms. Length: 300-1,000 words for features; 1,500-7,500 words for full-length story. Occasional 10,000-worders. Greatest need: 4,500-6,000 words. Pays 3¢/word for story mss.

Tips: "Know our market."

TRUE CONFESSIONS, Macfadden Women's Group, 215 Lexington Ave., New York NY 10016. Editor: Barbara J. Brett. 90% freelance written. For high-school-educated, blue-collar women, teens through maturity. Monthly magazine. Circ. 250,000. Buys all rights. Byline given on poetry and some articles. Pays during the last week of month of issue. Publishes ms an average of 6 months after acceptance. Submit seasonal material 6 months in advance. Reports in 4 months. Submit complete ms. SASE.

Stories, Articles and Fillers: Timely, exciting, emotional first-person stories on the problems that face today's young women. The narrators should be sympathetic, and the situations they find themselves in should be intriguing, yet realistic. Every story should have a strong romantic interest and a high moral tone, and every plot should reach an exciting climax. Careful study of a current issue is suggested. Length: 2,000-6,000 words; 5,000 word stories preferred; also book lengths of 8,000-10,000 words. Pays 5¢/word. Also, articles and short fillers.

Poetry: Romantic poetry, free verse and traditional, of interest to women. Submit maximum 4 poems. Length: 16 lines maximum. Pays $10 minimum.

‡**TRUE EXPERIENCE**, Macfadden Women's Group, 215 Lexington Ave., New York NY 10016. Contact: Helene Eccleston. Monthly magazine; 80 pages. For young marrieds, blue-collar, high school education. Interests: children, home, arts, crafts, family and self-fulfillment. Circ. 225,000. Pays 30 days after publication. Byline given. Buys all rights. No photocopied or simultaneous submissions. Submit seasonal material 5 months in advance. SASE. Reports in 3 months.

Nonfiction: Stories on life situations, e.g., love, divorce, any real-life problems. Romance and confession, first-person narratives with strong identification for readers. Articles on health, self-help or child care. "Remember that we are contemporary. We deal with women's self-awareness and consciousness of their roles in society." Buys 100 mss/year. Submit complete ms. Length: 250-1,500 words for nonfiction; 1,000-7,500 words for personal narrative. Pays 3¢/word.

Poetry: Only traditional forms. Length: 4-20 lines. Payment varies.

Tips: "Study the magazine for style and editorial content."

TRUE LOVE, Macfadden Women's Group, 215 Lexington Ave., New York NY 10016. (212)340-7500. Editor: Marta Mestrovic. Monthly magazine; 80 pages. For young, blue-collar women. Circ. 225,000. Pays after publication. Byline given. Buys all rights. Submit seasonal material 6 months in advance. SASE. Reports in 2 months.

Nonfiction: Confessions, true love stories (especially young romance); problems and solutions; health problems; marital and child-rearing difficulties. Avoid graphic sex. Stories dealing with reality, current problems, everyday events, with emphasis on emotional impact. Buys 150 mss/year. Submit complete ms. Length: 1,500-8,000 words. Pays 3¢/word. Informational and how-to articles. Length: 250-800 words. Pays 5¢/word minimum.

Tips: "The story must appeal to the average blue collar woman. It must deal with her problems and interests. Characters—especially the narrator—must be sympathetic."

TRUE ROMANCE, Macfadden Women's Group, 215 Lexington Ave., New York NY 10016. (212)340-7500. Editor: Susan Weiner. Monthly magazine. "Our readership ranges from teenagers to senior citizens. The majority are high school educated, married, have young children and also work outside the home. They are concerned with contemporary social issues, yet they are deeply committed to their husbands and children. They have high moral values and place great emphasis on love and romance." Circ. 225,000. Pays on publication. Buys all rights. Submit seasonal/holiday material at least 5 months in advance. SASE. Reports in 3 months.

Nonfiction: How-to and informational. Submit complete ms. Length: 300-1,000 words. Pays 3¢/word, special rates for short features and articles. Confession. "We want *only* true contemporary stories about relationships." Buys 13 stories/issue. Submit complete ms. Length: 2,000-7,500 words. Pays 3¢/word; slightly higher flat rate for short-shorts.

Poetry: Light verse and traditional. Buys 15/year. Length: 4-20 lines. Pays $10 minimum.

Tips: "The freelance writer is needed and welcomed. A timely, well-written story that is told by a sympathetic narrator who sees the central problem through to a satisfying resolution is all that is needed to break into *True Romance*. We are always looking for good love stories."

Science

These publications are edited for laymen interested in technical and scientific developments and discoveries, applied science, and technical or scientific hobbies. Publications of interest to the personal computer owner/user are listed in the Personal Computing category. Journals for scientists, engineers, repairmen, etc., are listed in Trade Journals.

ALTERNATIVE SOURCES OF ENERGY MAGAZINE, 107 S. Central Ave., Milaca MN 56353. Executive Editor: Donald Marier. 15% freelance written. Bimonthly magazine emphasizing alternative energy sources and the exploration and innovative use of renewable energy sources. Audience is predominantly male, age 36, college educated and concerned about energy and environmental limitations. Circ. 23,000. Pays on publication. Publishes ms an average of 4 months after acceptance. Buys first North American serial rights returning full rights after publication. Phone queries OK. Simultaneous, photocopied, and previously published submissions OK, "if specified at time of submission." Computer printout submissions acceptable; prefers letter-quality to dot-matrix. SASE. Reports in 6 weeks. Sample copy $4.25.

Nonfiction: "Freelance articles published cover a broad range, but we especially look for pieces which deal with technical innovations in the fields mentioned below, company profiles, new approaches to financing renewable energy projects, international news, interviews with innovators in the field, progress reports on unique projects, legislative updates, etc. We insist on full addresses for all companies mentioned (unless irrelevant), solid documentation, and a business style. We also advise tight leads, subheaded body copy and short, relevant conclusions." Length: "Articles accepted are generally between 500 and 3,000 words. We are always interested in short pieces on very specific topics. This would typically be a 500 word piece on a new wind, hydro or pv installation with one quality picture. Unless a SASE is included, your article will not be returned. We strongly urge that you forward a short outline prior to beginning a longer article. We'll let you know our level of interest promptly. Pays 7¢/word and two free author copies. If we like the piece, but feel it must be shortened, payment will be based on the printed version.

Photos: $15 per photo or camera ready graphic and two free author copies.

Tips: "Alternative Sources of Energy Magazine (ASE) is 'the magazine of the Independent Power Production industry.' Specifically, we cover those industries involved in the production of electricity from renewable energy, including windpower, hydropower, photovoltaics, biomass and shared savings projects. Writers have a better chance of breaking in at our publication with short articles and fillers because they're tough to get and assure limited 'fluff.' The most frequent mistake made by writers is verbosity. We pay by word."

BIOSCIENCE, American Institute of Biological Sciences, 730 11th St. NW, Washington DC 20001. (703)527-6776. Editor: Ellen W. Chu. Features and News Editor: Laura Tangley. 5% freelance written. Monthly magazine covering biology as well as science and environmental policy. "*BioScience* is written for professional biologists. It goes to them, their professional societies, and libraries. Although most of the magazine consists of scientific papers, the 'Features and News' section accepts freelance news and feature stories on relevant topics, ranging from reviews of current biological research to analyses of controversial science policy issues." Circ. 12,000. Pays on publication. Publishes ms an average of 6 months after acceptance. Byline given. Buys first serial rights. Submit seasonal/holiday material 3 months in advance. Simultaneous queries OK. Electronic submissions OK on Wang WP or OIS; IBM PC or PC/XT, but requires hard copy also. Computer printout submissions acceptable; prefers letter-quality to dot-matrix. SASE. Reports in 1 month. Free sample copy.

Nonfiction: Interview/profile, photo feature (mostly b&w) and technical. "We accept stories *only* related somehow to biologists, biological research, or science and environmental policy." Buys 12 mss/year. Query with published clips. Length: 1,000-4,500 words. Pays $200/page.

Photos: State availability of photos. Captions required. Payment included in page rate.

Tips: "Ideas should be timely—something that is news, or at least unfamiliar, to most biologists. Stories about research have a better chance of acceptance because we follow policy closely here. Presently the *Features-News* section is the *only* one open to freelancers . . . reading through past issues of *BioScience* in the library would give writers a good idea of what we are interested in and what we've already covered. The most frequent mistake made by writers is writing on too low a level. *BioScience*'s audience is made up of professional biologists—not the lay public."

CQ: THE RADIO AMATEUR'S JOURNAL, 76 N. Broadway, Hicksville NY 11801. (516)681-2922. Editor: Alan Dorhoffer. 50% freelance written. For the amateur radio community. Monthly journal. Circ. 100,000. Pays on publication. Buys first rights. Phone queries OK. Submit seasonal/holiday material 3 months in advance. Computer printout submissions acceptable. SASE. Reports in 3 weeks. Publishes ms an average of 1 year after acceptance. Free sample copy.
Nonfiction: "We are interested in articles that address all technical levels of amateur radio. Included would be basic material for newcomers and intermediate and advanced material for oldtimers. Articles may be of a theoretical, practical or anecdotal nature. They can be general interest pieces for all amateurs or they can focus in on specific topics. We would like historical articles, material on new developments, articles on projects you can do in a weekend, and pieces on long-range projects taking a month or so to complete." Length: 6-10 typewritten pages. Pays $35/published page.

‡**THE ELECTRON**, CIE Publishing, 4781 E. 355th St., Willoughby OH 44094. (216)946-9065. Editor: R.C. Westfall. 80% freelance written. Bimonthly tabloid on electronics. Circ. 62,000. Pays on publication. Publishes ms an average of 2 months after acceptance. Byline given. Buys all rights. Simultaneous queries, and photocopied and previously published submissions OK. Computer printout submissions acceptable. SASE. Reports in 1 month.
Nonfiction: How-to, interview/profile, personal experience, photo feature and technical. Query with published clips or send complete ms. Pays $50-500. Pays expenses of writers on assignment.
Photos: State availability of photos. Reviews 8x10 b&w prints. Captions and identification of subjects required.

‡**ELECTRONICS TODAY INTERNATIONAL**, Unit 6, 25 Overlea Blvd., Toronto, Ontario M4H 1B1 Canada . (416)423-3262. Editor: Bill Markwick. 40% freelance written. Monthly magazine; 88 pages. Emphasizes audio, electronics and personal computing for a wide-ranging readership, both professionals and hobbyists. Circ. 27,000. Pays on publication. Byline given. Buys all rights. Phone queries OK. Submit seasonal/holiday material 4 months in advance. Photocopied submissions OK. SAE, IRC. Reports in 4 weeks. Sample copy $3; free writer's guidelines.
Nonfiction: How-to (technical articles in electronics field); humor (if relevant to electronics); new product (if using new electronic techniques); and technical (on new developments, research, etc.). Buys 10 unsolicited mss/year. Query. Length: 600-3,500 words. Pays $75-100/1,000 words.
Photos: "Ideally we like to publish two photos or diagrams per 1,000 words of copy." State availability of photo material with query. Additional payment for photos accepted with accompanying manuscript. Captions required. Buys all rights.
Fillers: Puzzles (mathematical). Buys 10/year. Length: 50-250 words. Pays $15-20.

EQUILIBRIUM, The Science of All Sciences, Eagle Publishing Co., Box 162, Golden CO 80402. Editor: Gary A. Eagle. "Equilibrium is a new scientific theory being proven by published articles. The dissemination of the balancing of the universe is from many aspects or perspectives. Nearly the full contents is known or understood by a general audience. However, these articles are all linked to one concept. One important theme is held throughout the entire contents." Magazine published for "the average intelligent individual." 30% freelance written. Pays on acceptance or publication. Publishes ms an average of 12 months after acceptance. Byline given. Offers 50% kill fee; varies for ghosts. Buys all rights. Computer printout submissions acceptable; no dot-matrix. Simultaneous queries, and simultaneous, photocopied, and previously published submissions OK. SASE. Reports in 1 month on queries; 6 weeks on mss. Sample copy for $3, 9x12 SAE, and 4 first class stamps; writer's guidelines for business size SAE, and 1 first class stamp.
Nonfiction: Historical/nostalgic (history repeats itself); how-to (physics, psychology, political science, medical, evolution, economics, philosophical, religion, actual UFO occurrences with photo); photo feature (any photo to show balance of something, with article or without); and technical. All should have an equilibrium slant—anything to prove our point. Inquire about special issues. Modern events not accepted. No profanity, direct defamation or anything not of the common interest. "Much of our literature is controversial." Buys 20 mss/year. Query. Length: 50-1,000 words; more than 1,000 words if article series. Pays $50-500.
Photos: State availability or send photos with query or ms. Pays $20-40 for 1" b&w and color slides, and b&w and color prints. Captions required.
Columns/Departments: Especially wants editorials; must speak favorably for equilibrium theory. Length: 250 words. Pays $50-100.

Poetry: Light verse, traditional. "None will be accepted if not dealing with the balance of the universe." Submit maximum 10 poems. Length: 5-20 lines. Pays $10-50.

Fillers: Clippings, jokes, gags, short humor, cartoons. Buys 20/year. Length: 5-20 words. Pays $10-50.

Tips: "Article should be written simply even if you are a professional. State what the balancing aspect of the universe is in query." Tell what the "opposite and equal" reaction is plainly. Encourages new writers. "We read everything that comes in. Though our program has been geared toward the philosophical, we are receptive to a variety of subjects . . . our needs are flexible. We're looking for anything to prove this theory of equilibrium—large or small." First-, second- *and* third-person approach OK; controversial material acceptable. "The most frequent mistakes made by writers in completing an article for us are that they fail to illustrate *or* demonstrate the opposites and equals. They also fail to use the common household dictionary."

‡**HANDS-ON ELECTRONICS**, (formerly *Special Projects*), Gernsbach Publishing Co., 200 Park Ave. S., New York NY 10003. (212)777-6400. Editor: Julian S. Martin. Bimonthly magazine for electronics hobbyists in the areas of shortwave listening, amateur radio, project designing and building, antique radio, personal computers, theory buffs, home appliance repair, etc. Circ. 110,000. Pays on acceptance. Byline given. Makes work-for-hire assignments. Submit seasonal/holiday material 6 months in advance. Simultaneous queries, and simultaneous, photocopied, and previously published submissions OK. SASE. Reports on queries within 2 weeks; 3 weeks on mss. Free sample copy.

Nonfiction: Book excerpts, how-to, new product, photo feature and technical. No business, industry or trade articles. Buys 125 mss/year. Query or send complete ms. Length: 50-3,000 words. Pays $100-300.

Photos: Send photos with query or ms. Reviews 5x7 or 8x10 b&w prints. Photos purchased with ms, not individually. Captions, model releases, and identification of subjects required. Buys all rights.

Columns/Departments: Editorial, Bookshelf, New products, and Test bench tips. Departments/columns assigned to professional writers and are not purchased "over the transom." Buys 50 mss/year. Query. Length: determined prior to assignment. Pays $25.

Fillers: Cartoons. Buys 25/year. Length: 50-1,000 words. Pays $25.

Tips: "Be a reader of the magazine and know the subject matter as a hobbyist. Writers should specialize in a minimum of subject areas, and become known to the frequent buyers."

‡**HOME MECHANIX**, (Formerly *Mechanix Illustrated*), 1515 Broadway, New York NY 10036. (212)719-6630. Editor: Joseph R. Provey. Executive Editor: Harry Wicks. Managing Editor: Peter Easton. 50% freelance written. Monthly magazine for the home and car manager. "Articles on maintenance, repair, and renovation to the home and family car. Information on how to buy, how to select products useful to homeowners/car owners. Emphasis in home-oriented articles is on good design, inventive solutions to styling and space problems, useful home-workshop projects." Circ. 1.6 million. Pays on acceptance. Publishes ms an average of 5 months after acceptance. Byline given. Buys first North American copy rights. Computer printout submissions acceptable; prefers letter-quality to dot-matrix. SASE. Query.

Nonfiction: Feature articles relating to homeowner/carowner, 1,500-2,500 words. "This may include personal home-renovation projects, professional advice on interior design, reports on different or unusual construction methods, energy-related subjects, outdoor/backyard projects, etc. We are no longer interested in high-tech subjects such as aerospace, electronics, photography or military hardware. Most of our automotive features are written by experts in the field, but fillers, tips, how-to repair, or modification articles on the family car are welcome. Workshop articles on furniture, construction, tool use, refinishing techniques, etc., are also sought. Pays $300 minimum for features; fees based on number of printed pages, photos accompanying mss., etc." Pays expenses of writers on assignment.

Photos: Photos should accompany mss. Pays $600 and up for transparencies for cover. Inside color: $300/1 page, $500/2, $700/3, etc. Home and Shop hints illustrated with 1 photo, $25. Captions and model release required.

Fillers: Tips and fillers useful to tool users or for general home maintenance. Pays $25 and up for illustrated and captioned fillers. Pays $75 for half-page fillers.

Tips: "The most frequent mistake made by writers in completing an article assignment for *Home Mechanix* is not taking the time to understand its editorial focus and special needs."

MODERN ELECTRONICS, For electronics and computer enthusiasts, Modern Electronics Publishing, Inc., 76 N. Broadway, Hicksville NY 11801. (516)681-2922. 90% freelance written. onthly magazine covering consumer electronics, personal computers, electronic circuitry, construction projects, and technology for readers with a technical affinity. Estab. 1984. Circ. 105,000. Pays on acceptance. Publishes ms an average of 3 months after acceptance. Byline given. Offers 25% kill fee. Buys first North American serial rights; and makes work-for-hire assignments. Submit seasonal/holiday material minimum 4 months in advance. Computer printout submissions acceptable; prefers letter-quality to dot-matrix. SASE. Reports in 1 week on queries; 3 weeks on mss. Sample copy $1.95; writer's guidelines for business size SAE, and 1 first class stamp.

Nonfiction: General interest (new technology, product buying guides); how-to (construction projects, applications); new product (reviews); opinion (experiences with electronic and computer products); technical (features and tutorials: circuits, applications); includes stereo, video, communications and computer equipment. "Articles must be technically accurate. Writing should be 'loose,' not textbookish." No long computer programs. Buys 125+ mss/year. Query. Length: 500-4,000 words. Pays $80-150/published page. Sometimes pays expenses of writers on assignment.

Photos: Send photos with query or ms. Reviews color transparencies and 5x7 b&w prints. Captions, model release, and identification of subjects required. Buys variable rights depending on mss.

Tips: The writer must have technical or applications acumen and well-researched material. Articles should reflect the latest products and technology. Sharp, interesting photos are helpful, as are rough, clean illustrations for re-drawing. Cover 'hot' subjects (avoid old technology). Areas most open to freelancers include feature articles technical tutorials, and projects to build. Some writers exhibit problems with longer pieces due to limited technical knowledge and/or proper organization. We can accept more short pieces.

OMNI, 1965 Broadway, New York NY 10023-5965. Executive Editor: Gurney Williams, III. Monthly magazine of the future covering science fact, fiction, and fantasy for readers of all ages, backgrounds and interests. Circ. 850,000. Average issue includes 3-4 nonfiction feature articles and 1-2 fiction articles; also numerous columns and 2 pictorials. Pays on acceptance. Offers 25% kill fee. Buys exclusive worldwide and first English rights and rights for *Omni* Anthology. Submit seasonal material 4-6 months in advance. Photocopied submissions OK. Computer printout submissions acceptable; prefers letter-quality to dot-matrix. SASE. Reports in 6 weeks. Free writer's guidelines with SASE (request fiction or nonfiction).

Nonfiction: "Articles with a futuristic angle, offering readers alternatives in housing, energy, transportation, medicine and communications. Scientists can affect the public's perception of science and scientists by opening their minds to the new possibilities of science journalism. People want to know, want to understand what scientists are doing and how scientific research is affecting their lives and their future. *Omni* publishes articles about science in language that people can understand. We seek very knowledgable science writers who are ready to work with scientists to produce articles that can inform and interest the general reader." Send query/proposal. Length: 2,500-3,500 words. Pays $1,500-1,750.

Photos: Frank DeVino, graphic director. State availability of photos. Reviews 35mm slides and 4x5 transparencies.

Columns/Departments: Explorations (unusual travel or locations on Earth); Breakthroughs (new products); Mind (by and about psychiatrists and psychologists); Earth (environment); Life (biomedicine); Space (technology); Arts (theatre, music, film, technology); Interview (of prominent person); Continuum (newsbreaks); Antimatter and UFO Update (unusual newsbreaks, paranormal); Stars (astronomy); First/Last Word (editorial/humor); Artificial Intelligence (computers); The Body (medical). Query with clips of previously published work. Length: 1,500 words maximum. Pays $750-850; $150 for Continuum and Antimatter items.

Fiction: Contact Ellen Datlow. Fantasy and science fiction. Buys 3 mss/issue. Send complete ms. Length: 10,000 words maximum. Pays $1,250-2,000.

Tips: "Consider science fact and science fiction pictorials with a futuristic leaning. We're interested in thematic composites of excellent photos or art with exciting copy."

‡**POPULAR COMMUNICATIONS**, Popular Communications, Inc., 76 N. Broadway, Hicksville NY 11801. (516)681-2922. Editor: Tom Kneitel. 25% freelance written. Monthly magazine on shortwave radio monitoring and other communications topics. Circ. 75,000. Pays on publication. Publishes ms an average of 1 year after acceptance. Byline given. Buys first North American serial rights. Submit seasonal/holiday material 5 months in advance. Simultaneous queries and photocopied submissions OK. Computer printout submissions acceptable; prefers letter-quality to dot-matrix. Reports in 1 month on queries; 2 months on mss. Free sample copy and writer's guidelines.

Nonfiction: Book excerpts (from author of book; on any communications topic); historical/nostalgic (old-time radio station or radio people stories); how-to (build projects for antennas and communications equipment); new product (reviews of communications products—tested); what scanner listeners are monitoring; and new radio stations around the world. No personal experience; interviews with TV/radio personalities; personal opinion; or technical. Buys 30-40 mss/year. Query or send complete ms. Pays $35/published page.

Tips: "We prefer third person features on objective radio communication subjects."

POPULAR SCIENCE, 380 Madison Ave., New York NY 10017. Editor-in-Chief: C.P. Gilmore. 40% freelance written. Monthly magazine; 150-200 pages. For the well-educated adult, interested in science, technology, new products. Circ. 1,800,000. Pays on acceptance. Publishes ms an average of 4 months in advance. Byline given. Buys all rights. Pays negotiable kill fee. Free guidelines for writers. Computer printout submissions acceptable; prefers letter-quality to dot-matrix. Submit seasonal material 4 months in advance. Reports in 3 weeks. Query. SASE. Writer's guidelines for SAE and 1 first class postage stamp.

Nonfiction: "*Popular Science* is devoted to exploring (and explaining) to a nontechnical but knowledgable readership the technical world around us. We cover the physical sciences, engineering and technology, and above all, products. We are largely a 'thing'-oriented publication: things that fly or travel down a turnpike, or go on or under the sea, or cut wood, or reproduce music, or build buildings, or make pictures, or mow lawns.

We are especially focused on the new, the ingenious and the useful. We are consumer-oriented and are interested in any product that adds to the enjoyment of the home, yard, car, boat, workshop, outdoor recreation. Some of our 'articles' are only a picture and caption long. Some are a page long. Some occupy 4 or more pages. Contributors should be as alert to the possibility of selling us pictures and short features as they are to major articles. Freelancers should study the magazine to see what we want and avoid irrelevant submissions. No biology or life sciences." Recent article example: "New Powerful Portables—Best Buy in a Personal Computer." Buys several hundred mss/year. Pays $200 a published page minimum. Use both color and b&w photos. Sometimes pays expenses of writers on assignment.

Tips: "Probably the easiest way to break in here is by covering a news story in science and technology that we haven't heard about yet. We need people to be acting as scouts for us out there and we are willing to give the most leeway on these performances. We are interested in good, sharply focused ideas in all areas we cover. Please query first."

RADIO-ELECTRONICS, 200 Park Ave. S., New York NY 10003. (212)777-6400. Editor: Art Kleiman. For electronics professionals and hobbyists. Monthly magazine, 128 pages. Circ. 211,000. Buys all rights. Byline given. Pays on acceptance. Submit seasonal/holiday material 8 months in advance. SASE. Reports in 3 weeks. Send for "Guide to Writing."

Nonfiction: Interesting technical stories on all aspects of electronics, including video, radio, computers, communications, and stereo written from viewpoint of the electronics professional, serious experimenter, or layman with technical interests. Construction (how-to-build-it) articles used heavily. Unique projects bring top dollars. Cost of project limited only by what item will do. Emphasis on "how it works, and why." Much of material illustrated with schematic diagrams and pictures provided by author. Also high interest in how-to articles. Length: 1,000-5,000 words. Pays about $50-500.

Photos: State availability of photos. Offers no additional payment for b&w prints or 35mm color transparencies. Model releases required.

Columns/Departments: Pays $50-200/column.

Fillers: Pays $15-35.

Tips: "The simplest way to come in would be with a short article on some specific construction project. Queries aren't necessary; just send the article, 5 or 6 typewritten pages."

SCIENCE DIGEST, Hearst Magazines Division, Hearst Corp., 888 7th Ave., New York NY 10106. (212)262-7990. Editor-in-Chief: Oliver S. Moore, III. Managing Editor: Margo Crabtree. Monthly magazine; 140 pages. Emphasizes sciences and technologies for all ages with a scientific bent. Circ. 600,000. Pays on acceptance. Byline given. Buys all magazine and periodical rights worldwide but for use only in *Science Digest* in all its editions worldwide. Pays 25% kill fee. Reports in 1 month. Sample copy $2; writer's guidelines with SASE.

Nonfiction: Informational (authentic, timely information in all areas of science). Book excerpts, expose, interview/profile, new product, opinion, photo feature and technical. Also seeking material on computers, innovation and inventors. Length: 500-2,000 words. Buys 200 mss/year. Query with or without published clips or send complete ms.

Columns/Departments: Astronomy. Buys about 40/year. Query with or without published clips or send complete ms. Length: 500-1,000 words.

Photos: Purchased with or without ms or on assignment. Send photos with query or ms. Reviews contact sheets, negatives, color transparencies and prints. Captions, model release, and identification of subjects required. Buys all magazine and periodical rights worldwide but for use only in *Science Digest* in all its editions worldwide.

Tips: "Our goal is to help our readers appreciate the beauty of science and the adventure of technology. Articles are geared toward the alert, inquisitive layman, fascinated by all facets of science."

SCIENCE 86, American Association for the Advancement of Science, 10th Floor, 1101 Vermont Ave. NW, Washington DC 20005. (202)842-9500. Editor: Allen L. Hammond. Managing Editor: Eric Schrier. Mostly freelance written. Monthly magazine covering popular science. Circ. 50,000. Pays on acceptance. Publishes ms an average of 1 month after acceptance. Byline given. Offers 20% kill fee. Buys all rights, shares reprint royalties. Submit seasonal/holiday material 4 months in advance. Computer printout submissions acceptable. SASE. Reports in 1 month. Sample copy $2; free writer's guidelines.

Nonfiction: Lynn Crawford, editorial coordinator. Book excerpts, expose, profile and photo feature—"only if about science or related." Buys 80 mss/year. Query with clips. Length: 1,500-3,000 words. Pays $1,000-2,000.

Columns/Departments: Buys 200 mss/year. Query with clips. Length: 200-1,000 words. Pays $150-800.

Poetry: Bonnie Gordon, poetry editor. Free verse and traditional. "Science-related poetry only." Submit maximum 5 poems. Length: 50 lines maximum. Pays $400.

Tips: Wants well thought-out, well-researched, well-written, succinct query. Section most open to freelancers is Crosscurrent. Looks for grace, intelligence and wit.

73 FOR RADIO AMATEURS, (formerly *73 Magazine*), Peterborough NH 03458. (603)924-9471. Publisher: John C. Burnett. Executive Editor: Susan Philbrick. For amateur radio operators and experimenters. Monthly. Buys all rights. Pays on publication. Reports on submissions within a few weeks. Query. SASE.
Nonfiction: Articles on anything of interest to radio amateurs, experimenters and computer hobbyists—construction projects. Pays $40-50/page.
Photos: Photos purchased with ms.
Tips: Query letter "should be as specific as possible. Don't hold back details that would help us make a decision. We are not interested in theoretical discussions, but in practical ideas and projects which our readers can use."

TECHNOLOGY REVIEW, Alumni Association of the Massachusetts Institute of Technology, Room 10-140, Massachusetts Institute of Technology, Cambridge MA 02139. Editor-in-Chief: John I. Mattill. 20% freelance written. Emphasizes technology and its implications for scientists, engineers, managers and social scientists. Magazine published 8 times/year. Circ. 75,000. Pays on publication. Publishes ms an average of 3 months after acceptance. Buys first rights. Phone queries OK. Submit seasonal/holiday material 6 months in advance of issue date. Simultaneous and photocopied submissions OK. Computer printout submissions acceptable. SASE. Reports in 6 weeks. Sample copy $2.50.
Nonfiction: General interest, interview, photo feature and technical. Buys 5-10 mss/year. Query. Length: 1,000-10,000 words. Pays $50-750. Sometimes pays the expenses of writers on assignment.
Columns/Departments: Book Reviews; Trend of Affairs; Technology and Economics; and "Prospects" (guest column). Also special reports on other appropriate subjects. Query. Length: 750-4,000 words. Pays $50-750.

UFO REVIEW, Global Communications, 316 5th Ave., New York NY 10001. (212)685-4080. Editor: Timothy Beckley. Emphasizes UFOs and space science. 50% freelance written. Published 4 times/year. Tabloid. Circ. 50,000. Pays on publication. Publishes ms an average of 4 months after acceptance. "We syndicate material to European markets and split 50-50 with writer." Phone queries OK. Photocopied submissions OK. SASE. Reports in 3 weeks. Sample copy $1.
Nonfiction: Expose (on government secrecy about UFOs). "We also want articles detailing on-the-spot field investigations of UFO landings, contact with UFOs, and UFO abductions. No lights-in-the-sky stories." Buys 1-2 mss/issue. Query. Length: 1,200-2,000 words. Pays $25-75.
Photos: Send photos with ms. Pays $5-10 for 8x10 b&w prints. Captions required.
Fillers: Clippings. Pays $2-5.
Tips: "Read the tabloid first. We are aimed at UFO fans who have knowledge of the field. Too many submissions are made about old cases everyone knows about. We don't accept rehash. We get a lot of material unrelated to our subject."

Science Fiction

"Science fiction should be and can be as powerful and influential as so-called 'mainstream' fiction," points out *Omni's* fiction editor. "The lines are blurring and I want to blur them even more." Additional science fiction markets are in the Literary and "Little" category.

AMAZING® **Science Fiction Stories**, (Combined with *Fantastic Stories*), Dragon Publishing, Box 110, Lake Geneva WI 53147-0110. Editor: George H. Scithers. Managing Editor: Patrick L. Price. 90% freelance written. Bimonthly magazine of science fiction and fantasy short stories. "Audience does not need to be scientifically literate, but the authors must be, where required. *AMAZING* is devoted to the best science fiction and fantasy by new and established writers. There is no formula. We require the writers using scientific concepts be scientifically convincing, and that every story contain believable and interesting characters and some overall point." Circ. 13,000. Pays on acceptance. Publishes ms an average of 18 months after acceptance. Byline given. Buys first North American serial rights; "single, non-exclusive re-use option (with additional pay)." Photocopied submissions OK. Computer printout submissions acceptable; no dot-matrix. SASE. Reports in 3 weeks. Sample copy for $2.25; writer's guidelines $2, postpaid.
Nonfiction: Historical (about science fiction history and figures); interview/profile and science articles of interest to science fiction audiences; reviews and essays about major science fiction movies written by big names. No "pop pseudo-science trends: The Unified Field Theory Discovered; How I Spoke to the Flying

Saucer People; Interpretations of Past Visits by Sentient Beings, as Read in Glacial Scratches on Granite, etc." Buys 4-8 mss/year. Query with or without published clips. Length: 300-10,000 words. Pays 6¢/word up to 7,500 words; 4¢/word for 12,000 or more words.

Fiction: Fantasy; novel excerpts (rarely—query); science fiction; serialized novels (query first). "No 'true' experiences, media-derived fiction featuring *Star Wars* (etc.) characters, stories based on UFO reports or standard occultism and modern-scene horror." Buys 50-60 mss/year. Send complete ms. Length: 200-20,000 words. "Anything longer, ask." Pays 6¢/word to 7,500 words; 4¢/word for 12,000 or more words.

Poetry: All types are OK. No prose arranged in columns. Buys 20 poems/year. Submit maximum 3 poems. Length: 45 lines maximum; ideal length, 30 lines or less. Pays 50¢-$1/line.

Tips: "Short fiction is the best way for freelancers to break in to our publication. We basically want good stories. We look for larger pieces by established writers, because their names help sell our product. Don't try to especially tailor one for our 'slant.' We want original concepts, good writing, and well-developed characters. Avoid certain obvious clichés: UFO landings in rural areas, video games which become real (or vice-versa), stories based on contemporary newspaper headlines. '*Hard*' science fiction, that is, science fiction. which is based on a plausible extrapolation from real science, is increasingly rare and very much in demand. The standard pseudo-medieval fantasy is very easy to get, but dull because of its standardness. Exceptional originality is required in that area. The most frequent mistakes made by writers in completing articles for us are bad mss format (i.e., single-spacing which makes it hard to add typeset directions or proofreader's marks); exceeding designated length; and not meeting deadline (second chances are rarely given)."

ANALOG SCIENCE FICTION/SCIENCE FACT, 380 Lexington Ave., New York NY 10017. Editor: Dr. Stanley Schmidt. 100% freelance written. For general future-minded audience. Monthly. Buys first North American serial rights and nonexclusive foreign serial rights. Publishes ms an average of 10 months after acceptance. Byline given. Computer printout submissions (with dark ink) acceptable; prefers letter-quality to dot-matrix. Good dot-matrix submissions are acceptable. SASE. Reports in 1 month. Sample copy $2.50 (no SASE needed); free writer's guidelines for SAE and 1 first class stamp.

Nonfiction: Illustrated technical articles dealing with subjects of not only current but future interest, i.e., with topics at the present frontiers of research whose likely future developments have implications of wide interest. Buys about 12 mss/year. Query. Length: 5,000 words. Pays 5.75¢/word.

Fiction: "Basically, we publish science fiction stories. That is, stories in which some aspect of future science or technology is so integral to the plot that, if that aspect were removed, the story would collapse. The science can be physical, sociological or psychological. The technology can be anything from electronic engineering to biogenetic engineering. But the stories must be strong and realistic, with believable people doing believable things—no matter how fantastic the background might be." Buys 60-100 unsolicited mss/year. Send complete ms on short fiction; query about serials. Length: 2,000-60,000 words. Pays 4.0-4.6¢/word for novelettes and novels; 6.0-7.0¢/word for shorts under 7,500 words. $430-525 for intermediate lengths; on acceptance for first North American serial rights.

Tips: "In query give clear indication of central ideas and themes and general nature of story line—and what is distinctive or unusual about it. We have no hard-and-fast editorial guidelines, because science fiction is such a broad field that I don't want to inhibit a new writer's thinking by imposing 'Thou Shalt Not's.' Besides, a really good story can make an editor swallow his preconceived taboos. *Analog* will consider material submitted from any writer and consider it solely on the basis of merit. We are definitely anxious to find and develop new, capable writers. No occult or fantasy."

FANTASY BOOK, Box 60126, Pasadena CA 91106. Executive Editor: Dennis Mallonee. Editor: Nick Smith. 100% freelance written. Quarterly magazine of illustrated fantasy fiction for all ages; "bulk of the readership is in the 17-35 range." Circ. 5,000. Pays on "approval of galleys." Publishes ms an average of 6 months after acceptance. Byline given. Buys first North American serial rights. Submit seasonal/holiday material 6 months in advance. Photocopied submissions OK. Computer printout submissions acceptable. SASE. Reports in 6 weeks on mss. Sample copy $4; writer's guidelines for legal size SAE and 1 first class stamp.

Fiction: "We will consider any story related to fantasy fiction. We look for stories with strong characterization and carefully developed plot." Buys 50 mss/year. Send complete ms. Length: 2,000-10,000 words. Pays 2½-4¢/word.

Poetry: Light verse, traditional. Buys 8/year. Submit maximum 4 poems. Length: open. Pays $5-20.

FANTASY REVIEW, Florida Atlantic University, 500 NW 20th St., Boca Raton FL 33431. (305)393-3839. Editor: Robert A. Collins. Managing Editor: Catherine Fischer. 50% freelance written. A monthly genre literary magazine of fantasy/horror/science fiction for authors, fans, scholars, editors, publishers, dealers, book store owners and students. Circ. 3,500. Pays on publication. Publishes ms an average of 2 months after acceptance. Byline given. Buys first North American serial rights. Submit seasonal/holiday material 4 months in advance. Simultaneous queries, and simultaneous and photocopied submissions OK. Electronic submissions 8" single side, single density CP/M system (sysgen) for disks; 300 baud, CP/M MODEM 9 handholding program for modems, but requires hard copy also. Computer printout submissions acceptable; prefers letter-quality to

dot-matrix. SASE. Reports in 3 weeks on queries; 6 weeks on mss. Sample copy $2; free writer's guidelines.
Nonfiction: General interest (essays directed to fans); historical/nostalgic (about authors, publishers, artist in field); humor (concerning genre literature); interview/profile (of articles and authors in field); new product (new books, films, magazines, art in field); opinion (reviews of books, films, art); personal experience (by authors on getting published); photo feature (fantasy and science fiction events); and surveys of foreign fiction, foreign fandom. "We don't want breezy fluff. We need solid research and reasoning, knowledge of field, plus easy style. No 'little green men invade our city' stuff. Writers must know the field." Buys 36 mss/year. Query or send complete ms. Length: 1,000-5,000 words. Pays $20-100.
Photos: State availability of photos with query letter, send photos with ms. Pays $5-25 for 5x7 or 8x10 b&w prints. Captions, model release, and identification of subjects required. Buys one-time rights.
Columns/Departments: Commentary Department: reviews of *forthcoming* books, films, magazines, art shows; Opinion: topics of fan interest. Other columns are assigned. Buys 50 mss/year. Length: 500-1,000 words. Pays $10-20.
Poetry: Free verse, haiku, light verse, traditional. "Poems must have a fantasy, horror, or science fiction twist. We don't want conventional topics." Buys 12 poems/year. Submit maximum 5 poems. Length: 3-30 lines. Pays $5-25.
Fillers: Clippings, jokes, gags, newsbreaks. Fillers must have genre interest. Length: 50-150 words. Pays $5.
Tips: "We especially need good articles (*solid thinking*, entertaining style) on odd or representative authors, trends, topics within the field; also interviews with up-and-coming authors and artists *with* pictures."

THE HORROR SHOW, Phantasm Press, Star Rte. 1, Box 151-T, Oak Run CA 96069. (916)472-3540. Editor: David B. Silva. 95% freelance written. Quarterly horror magazine. Circ. 2,000. Publishes ms an average of 3 months after acceptance. Buys first serial rights. Computer printout submissions acceptable. SASE. Reports in 3 weeks. Sample copy for $4 and $1 postage; writer's guidelines for SAE and 1 first class stamp.
Columns/Departments: Curses (letters to the editor).
Fiction: Contemporary horror. "Articles should *not* splash over into science fiction or fantasy (sword and sorcery). We are specifically looking for material which contains a twist or shock at the end. Do not over-indulge in sex or violence." Send complete ms. Length: 4,000 words maximum. Pays ½¢/word plus contributor's copy.
Tips: "We enjoy the honor of publishing first stories and new writers, but we always expect a writer's best effort. Read the magazine. Come up with a unique premise, polish every word, then send it our way. A frequent mistake made by writers in completing an article for us is that the article is not directed at the reader. We look for informative articles directly related to the horror genre."

INTERZONE, Imaginative Fiction and Art, Interzone Collective, 21 The Village St., Leeds LS4 2PR England. Editors: Colin Greenland, Simon Ounsley and David Pringle. A quarterly magazine of science fiction, fantasy and related imaginative fiction. Circ. 2,500. Pays on publication. Byline given. Buys first English language serial rights. Photocopied submissions OK. SAE and IRCs. Computer printout submissions acceptable. Sample copy $3 from U.S. agent, 124 Osborne Rd., Brighton, BN1 GLU, England."
Fiction: Fantasy (not sword and sorcery); mainstream (but must have some fantasy/surreal content); and science fiction. Buys 20 mss/year. Send complete ms—"1 story at a time." Length: 1,000-8,000 words. Pays £30-35/1,000 words.
Tips: Read *Interzone* before you submit. Optimum length is 5,000 words. Best to submit disposable double-spaced photocopies with IRCs for our letter of reply. We like to publish fiction which is topical; it should be innovative yet entertaining; science fiction stories should be aware of recent technological advances, not regurgitations of science fiction clichés from past decades.

ISAAC ASIMOV'S SCIENCE FICTION MAGAZINE, Davis Publications, Inc., 380 Lexington Ave. New York NY 10017. (212)557-9100. Editor-in-Chief: Gardner Dozois. 90% freelance written. Emphasizes science fiction. 13 times a year magazine; 192 pages. Circ. 125,000. Pays on acceptance. Buys first North American serial rights and nonexclusive foreign serial rights. "Clear and dark" photocopied submissions OK but no simultaneous submissions. Computer printout submissions acceptable; no dot-matrix. SASE. Reports in 2-6 weeks. Publishes ms an average of 6 months after acceptance. Writer's guidelines for SASE.
Nonfiction: Science. Query first.
Fiction: Science fiction primarily. Some fantasy and poetry. "It's best to read a great deal of material in the genre to avoid the use of some *very* old ideas." Buys 10 mss/issue. Submit complete ms. Length: 100-20,000 words. Pays 4-7¢/word.
Tips: Query letters not wanted, except for nonfiction. "Response time will be somewhat slower than in years past, and I'll be using a higher proportion of 'form' rejection slips."

‡**NIGHT CRY**, Montcalm Publishing Corp., 800 2nd Ave., New York NY 10017-4798. Editors: Michael Blaine and Alan Rodgers. 99% freelance written. Quarterly magazine of horror and dark fantasy. "We publish fiction almost exclusively; our audience is the audience for Stephen King, Peter Straub, James Herbert, and the

Close-up

Isaac Asimov
Author and Editor

"It was such fun," recalls Isaac Asimov, talking about his mystery, *Murder at the ABA.* "But it's science fiction novels that my public wants and that's what I've got to write."

There is no regret in his voice. He would probably write more mysteries if he wanted to. But Asimov has spent nearly a half century, as a science writer and storyteller, writing *for* readers. "If they're going to invest their money out of loyalty to me, I feel I owe them something," he says.

Asimov writes because he likes to. "I'm sorry for any writer who doesn't enjoy his own books even more than the readers," says this author of more than 327 books.

"What motivates me is my selfish desire to enjoy myself—I enjoy the process of writing and always have many projects going simultaneously so I'm rarely compelled to work on something I don't feel like working on," he points out. "Switching from fiction to nonfiction (and vice versa) keeps his work from getting stale, he believes. Asimov works from 8 a.m. to 10 p.m. each day in his midtown Manhattan apartment, with the window shades drawn and books lining each wall. He answers mail promptly, has no hobbies, and occasionally goes to the theatre or to dinner. His wife, psychiatrist and author Janet Jeppson, encourages him to take breaks now and then. "Writing is my way of taking it easy," he says.

He writes quickly in much the same way as he did when he wrote for "pulp" magazines. "People who flourished in the pulp market, as I did, learned to not have to revise," he says. "I don't expect more of my writing than to be clear."

Asimov had been writing professionally for 44 years before his 262nd book, *Foundation's Edge* landed on *The New York Times'* bestseller lists. When author Stephen King wrote to wish him luck on *Foundation's,* Asimov wrote back: "It's as impossible for me to write a bestseller as it is for you to write a non-bestseller." Asimov laughs as he tells this story; he has written books that *he* knows won't make money, like *Asimov's Annotated Don Juan.*

His sales are divided among many types of books—science fiction, literary studies, humor and satire, and books on history, math, chemistry, biology, physics, astronomy and general science—and, if combined, would mean a bestseller every year for Asimov. "It's easier to write one bestseller every year," he admits. "I feel I earn any affluence I may have. I have to work a lot harder."

Asimov's "way with words" has come from reading. "There is only one way to learn how to write and that is to do a lot of reading," he points out. "You absorb the patterns of the English language and its music without even knowing you're doing it; you get so that you can hear words fall into place."

How he gets so many words and his career to fall into place is somewhat of a mystery to the author. The set of diaries he has kept since age 18 doesn't tell him. "I'm curious . . . how I managed to do it," says Asimov. (Perhaps because writing *is such fun?*) "The autobiography didn't tell me or won't tell anyone else; it just happened so gradually that there was never any time when you could say, hey, I made it."

other writers who've done so well in the genre in the last ten years." Estab. 1984. Circ. 30,000. Pays half on acceptance, half on publication. Publishes ms an average of 6 months after acceptance. Byline given. Offers 50% kill fee. Buys first North American serial rights. Submit seasonal/holiday material 8 months in advance. Simultaneous, photocopied, and previously published submissions OK. Computer printout submissions acceptable; no dot-matrix. SASE. Reports in 3 months on mss. Sample copy $2.95; writer's guidelines for #10 SAE and 1 first class stamp.

Fiction: Fantasy, horror and science fiction. Buys 60 mss/year. Send complete ms. Pays 5-10¢/word.

Poetry: Avant-garde, free verse, haiku and traditional. "We don't particularly want to see cutesy poetry. However, if you think it's appropriate to an audience that enjoys stylishly written horror and fantasy, send it in." Submit maximum of 4 poems. Pays $20-150.

PANDORA, Role-Expanding Science Fiction and Fantasy, Empire Books, Box 625, Murray KY 42071. Editors: Jean Lorrah and Lois Wickstrom. 95% freelance written. Magazine published 2 times/year covering science fiction and fantasy. Circ. 600. Pays on acceptance. Publishes ms an average of 6 months after acceptance. Byline given. Offers $10 kill fee. Buys first North American serial rights and second serial (reprint) rights; one-time rights on some poems. Photocopied submissions OK. Readable computer printout submissions on white 8½x11 paper acceptable. SASE. Reports in 6 weeks. Sample copy $3.50; writer's guidelines for SAE with 1 first class stamp.

Columns/Departments: Books briefly. "We buy 200-word reviews of science fiction and fantasy books that a reader truly loves and feels are being ignored by the regular reviewers. Small press titles as well as major press titles are welcome." Buys 3-4 mss/year. Query or send complete ms. Length: 200-250 words. Pays 1¢/word.

Fiction: Experimental, fantasy, science fiction. "No pun stories. Nothing x-rated. No inaccurate science." Buys 15 mss/year. Send complete ms. Length: 1,000-5,000 words "except for controversial stories which may go to 10,000 words." Pays 1¢/word.

Poetry: Ruth Berman, 5620 Edgewater Blvd., Minneapolis MN 55417. Buys 9/year. Length: open.

Tips: "Send us a complete short story. If we like it, we'll send you a critique with suggestions, if we don't want it just the way it is, but would want it with some more work. You don't have to do exactly what we've suggested, but you should fix weak spots in your story. Inexperienced writers often break in with a book or game review. We use very few articles, basically science articles or articles about writing science fiction. People sometimes submit totally unacceptable things they'd know we'd never touch if they'd been reading the magazine. For example, one writer sent a long gossipy scandal article appropriate to a newsstand scandal sheet, naming names and claiming claims. Definitely not for any magazine of our kind, as he'd have known if he had read previous issues."

SPACE AND TIME, 138 W. 70th St., New York NY 10023. Editor: Gordon Linzner. Biannual magazine covering fantasy fiction, with a broad definition of fantasy that encompasses science fiction, horror, swords and sorcery, etc. Circ. 500. 100% freelance written. Pays on acceptance. Publishes ms an average of 2 years after acceptance. Byline given. Buys first North American serial rights. Photocopied submissions OK. Computer printout submissions acceptable; prefers letter-quality to dot-matrix. SASE. Reports in 2 months. Sample copy $4.

Fiction: Fantasy, horror and science fiction. "Submit skillful writing and original ideas. We lean toward strong plot and character. No fiction based on TV shows or movies (*Star Trek*, *Star Wars*, etc.) or popular established literary characters (e.g., Conan) except as satire or other special case. No UFO, gods from space, or material of that ilk, unless you've got a drastically new slant." Buys 24 unsolicited mss/year. Length: 15,000 words maximum. Pays ¼¢/word plus contributor's copies.

Poetry: Free verse, haiku, light verse, traditional and narrative. "No poetry without a definite fantastic theme or content." Buys 12 mss/year. Submit maximum 5 poems. Length: open. Pays in contributor's copies.

Tips: "All areas are open to freelancers, but we would particularly like to see more hard science fiction, and fantasies set in 'real' historical times. No nonfiction or no fiction that cannot be considered science fiction or fantasy. We particularly enjoy uncovering new talent and offbeat stories for which there are few (if any) markets otherwise; seeing *S&T* authors go on to better paying, wider circulating markets. We regret that we can't publish more material more often. A lot of good, interesting stories have to be passed over, and there are few other markets for genre fiction."

‡STARDATE, The Magazine of Science Fiction and Gaming, Editorial Director: Ted White. Game material to: 3316 Woodford Rd., Cincinnati OH 45213. (513)731-8891. Game Editor: Dale L. Kemper. Nongame material to Editor: Dave Bichoff, Suite 910. 1010 Vermont Ave. NW, Washington DC 20005. 75% freelance written. Monthly magazine spotlighting *Star Trek* and general science fiction and focusing on role-playing games. Estab. 1984. Circ. 10,000 +. Pays on publication. Publishes ms an average of 9 months after acceptance. Byline given. Offers 50% kill fee. Buys first North American serial rights. Photocopied submissions OK. Electronic submissions OK on Apple IIe or IBM PC, but requires hard copy also. Computer printout submissions acceptable; prefers letter-quality to dot-matrix. SASE. Reports in 2 weeks on queries; 1 month on mss.

Nonfiction: Interview/profile (science fiction writers and media personalities); new product (FASA game products); technical (understandable astrophysics/astronomy pieces); and *Star Trek* and role-playing game pieces. Buys 40 mss/year. Send complete ms. Length: 1,000-4,000 words. Pays 2-4¢/words.

Columns/Departments: Adventures, "Written in the style of other *Stardate* adventures and FASA adventure books. Query first before writing a piece as long as an adventure." Datafiles, "These are brief pieces centering around one particular item in the Star Trek Universe." Making Your First Million. Ask Starfleet Command, Star Trek: Role-playing games rules column. Star Reviews/Star Games, "Guest reviews are considered and encouraged." Jaynz Ships of the Universe, Ship design column used in conjunction with the Star Trek: Role-playing games Ship Construction Manual. Quartermaster Corps., Covers new equipment, vehicles, trade items. Menagerie, covers new animal types discovered or detailed. Personnel File, describes in great detail one or more particular characters for Star Trek: Role-playing games. Buys 30 mss/year. Send complete ms. Length: 1,000-2,000 words. Pays 10¢/word.

Fiction: Professional science fiction short stories. No time travel pieces, fantasy, or fan fiction. Buys 10 mss/ year. Query. Length: 2,000-6,000 words. Pays 2-4¢/word.

Fillers: Newsbreaks. Buys 20/year. Length: 100-500 words. Pays 1-2¢/word.

Tips: "The two most important points to consider while writing for *Stardate* are originality and detail. Don't copy things you have seen in the movies or read about in books or other magazines (unless you intend to create a situation for Star Trek: Role-playing Games out of that idea and then go farther than that). If you come up with an original idea, develop it fully and explore it thoroughly. Too often shallow material is submitted that started with a good idea. It then has to be rewritten by the author or our staff to be publishable."

STARLOG MAGAZINE, The Science Fiction Universe, Starlog Group, 8th Floor, 475 Park Ave. South, New York NY 10016. (212)689-2830. Editor: Howard Zimmerman. Managing Editor: David McDonnell. 95% freelance written. Monthly magazine covering "the science fiction-fantasy-adventure genre: its films, TV, books, art and personalities. We explore the fields of science fiction and fantasy with occasional forays into adventure (i.e., the James Bond and Indiana Jones films). We concentrate on the personalities and behind-the-scenes angles of science fiction/fantasy films with comprehensive interviews with actors, directors, screenwriters, producers, special effects technicians and, on occasion, composers and stuntmen." Pays on publication *or* after 3 months from deadline date if article held and budget allows. Publishes ms an average of 4½ months after acceptance. Byline given. All contributors are also credited in masthead. Offers $50 kill fee "only to mss *written* or interviews *done*." Buys first North American serial rights, one-time rights, and second serial (reprint) rights. Material chosen for annual Best Of Starlog compilation (from magazine) receives an additional reprint fee. Submit seasonal/holiday material 5 months in advance. Simultaneous queries and photocopied submissions OK. Computer printout submissions acceptable. SASE. Reports in 4 weeks on queries; 6 weeks on mss. Free sample copy; $2.95 "if you don't enclose clips. Be aware: sci fi is mostly considered a derogatory term by our readers."

Nonfiction: Interview/profile (actors, directors, screenwriters who have made past or current contributions to science fiction films or science fiction novelists); photo features; special effects how-tos (on filmmaking only); retrospectives of famous science fiction films and TV series; occasional pieces on science fiction fandom, conventions, etc., and aspects of that area of science fiction fans' lives. "We also cover animation (especially Disney and WB). Two special issues are also open to freelance submissions. One is the anniversary issue, published in June, which includes special interviews and other material in addition to regular featues. The annual film review issue, published in October, includes bylined reviews of the year's films, written by noted genre authors such as Robert Bloch, Norman Spinrad, Arthur C. Clarke and Theodore Sturgeon. We are always looking for other noted 'name' authors to add to our reviewer roster." Otherwise, no personal opinion or views of *Star Wars*, *Star Trek* or memories of when the writer first saw some film. *No* first person. "We prefer article format as opposed to question-and-answer." No reviews (other than in October issue). Buys 150 + mss/ year. Query first with published clips. Length: 500-3,000 words. Pays $25-225.

Photos: State availability of photos. Pays $10-25 for color slide transparencies and 8x10 b&w prints depending on quality. Captions, model release, identification of subjects, and credit line on photos required. Buys all rights.

Columns/Departments: Future Life (science articles for the layman from 500-2,000 words, *very* much needed, think *Omni* or *Science News*;) L.A. Offbeat ("quirky" articles on science fiction/fantasy films/personalities based in California—not quite the normal slant); Fan Network (articles on science fiction fandom and its aspects—now basically staff-written); Log Entries (the news section which regularly includes the three following staff-written items: Booklog—the science fiction/fantasy/horror book news and mini-reviews; Medialog—news of upcoming science fiction films and TV projects; and Videolog—videocassette and disk releases of genre interest). "We also require science fiction news items of note, mini-interviews on new projects with science fiction authors (usually promoting a new book—almost entirely freelance written); Comics Scene items (profiles of upcoming comic books/strips), items on fantasy, science fiction gaming, merchandising items of interest, toys, games and old science fiction film/TV reunion photos/feature material." Buys 24-30 mss/year. Query with published clips. Length: 500-750 words. No kill fee on logs. Log payment $25-35 on publication only.

Fiction: We do *not* publish any fiction.

Tips: The most frequent mistakes made by writers are "gray type on word processed mss. Ignorance of—and no questions or quotes about—one (or more) of interviewee's film credits or history. Misspellings of film crew members' names (and others whose names are hard to research anywhere). Missed deadlines due to inadequacies of (and overreliance on) overnight mail services. Failure to ask obvious questions. WHY? Shoddy research (and inadequate reference material). Not enough direction (at times) from overworked editors. Human nature. Murphy's Law. A writer can best break in through Log Entries with mini-author interviews or news items which show initiative. Another way: get an unusual interview or article that we can't get through normal channels (for example, an interview with Dino De Laurentiis or Stanley Kubrick). We are always looking for *new* angles on *Star Wars, Star Trek* and seek a small number of features investigating aspects (i.e., cast & crew) of series which remain very popular with many readers: *Lost in Space, Space 1999, Battlestar Galactica, The Twilight Zone.* Know science fiction media before you try us. It's easier to find the space to publish short articles and fillers (in one of our sections). Most full-length major assignments go to freelancers we're already dealing with. A writer can more easily prove himself with a short item (and if he screws up in brief, it's less of a tragedy to us). Discovering new freelancers and helping them to break into print is a special joy. We love it. We're fans of this material—and a prospective writer should be, too—but we were *also* freelancers. And if your love for science fiction shows through, we would love to help you break in. And remember that, life itself is science fiction. Think about it."

STARWIND, The Starwind Press, Box 98, Ripley OH 45167. (513)392-4549. Editor: David F. Powell. Managing Editor: Susannah C. West. 75% freelance written. A quarterly magazine "for the young adult (18-25 or thereabouts) who has an interest in science and technology, and who also enjoys reading well-crafted science fiction and fantasy." Circ. 2,500. Pays on publication. Publishes ms an average of 6 months after acceptance. Byline given. Rights vary with author and material; negotiated with author. Usually first serial rights and second serial reprint rights (nonfiction). Photocopied submissions OK. Electronic submissions OK on IBM PC or PC compatible. Computer printout submissions acceptable. Photocopied and dot-matrix submissions OK. "In fact, we encourage disposable submissions; easier for us and easier for the author. Just enclose SASE for our response. We prefer non-simultaneous submissions." SASE. Reports in 3 months. Sample copy for $2.50; writer's guidelines for business size SAE and 1 first class stamp.

Nonfiction: How-to (technological interest, e.g., how to build a robot eye, building your own radio receiver, etc.); interview/profile (of leaders in science and technology fields); and technical ("did you know" articles dealing with development of current technology). "No speculative articles, dealing with topics such as the Abominable Snowman, Bermuda Triangle, etc. At present, nonfiction is staff-written or reprinted from other sources. We hope to use more freelance written work in the future." Query. Length: 1,000-5,000 words. Pays 1-4¢/word.

Photos: Send photos with accompanying query or ms. Reviews b&w contact sheets and prints. Model release and identification of subjects required. "If photos are available, we prefer to purchase them as part of the written piece." Buys negotiable rights.

Fiction: Fantasy and science fiction. "No stories whose characters were created by others (e.g., *Lovecraft, Star Trek, Star Wars* characters, etc.)." Buys 15-20 mss/year. Send complete ms. Length: 2,000-10,000 words. Pays 1-4¢/word. "We prefer previously unpublished fiction."

Tips: "We have changed *Starwind*'s format from that of a strictly literary magazine to one which includes more nonfiction. Almost all our fiction and nonfiction is unsolicited. We rarely ask for rewrites, because we've found that rewrites are often disappointing; although the writer may have rewritten it to fix problems, he/she frequently changes parts we liked, too. We regret that we cannot accept mss that arrive postage due or return mss that enclose no return postage."

THRUST—SCIENCE FICTION AND FANTASY REVIEW, (Formerly *Thrust-Science Fiction in Review*), Thrust Publications, 8217 Langport Terrace, Gaithersburg MD 20877. (301)948-2514. Editor: D. Douglas Fratz. 30% freelance written. A semiannual literary review magazine covering science fiction and fantasy literature. "*Thrust—Science Fiction and Fantasy Review* is the highly acclaimed, Hugo-Award-nominated magazine about science fiction and fantasy. Since 1972, *Thrust* has been featuring in-depth interviews with science fiction's best known authors and artists, articles and columns by the field's most outspoken writers, and reviews of current science fiction books. *Thrust* has built its reputation on never failing to take a close look at the most sensitive and controversial issues concerning science fiction, and continues to receive the highest praise and most heated comments from professionals and fans in the science fiction field." Circ. 1,500. Pays on publication. Publishes ms an average of 6 months after acceptance. Byline given. Buys first North American serial rights, one-time rights and second serial (reprint) rights. Submit seasonal/holiday material 3-6 months in advance. Simultaneous queries, and simultaneous, photocopied and previously published submissions OK. Electronic submissions OK on IBM compatible-MS-DOS/WordStar. Computer printout submissions acceptable; prefers letter-quality to dot-matrix. SASE. Reports in 2 weeks on queries; 1-2 months on mss. Sample copy for $2.50; writer's guidelines for SAE and 1 first class stamp.

Nonfiction: Humor, interview/profile, opinion, personal experience and book reviews. Buys 5-10 mss/year.

Query or send complete ms. Length: 2,000-5,000 words. Pays ½-2¢/word.

Photos: ''We publish only photos of writers being interviewed.'' State availability of photos. Pays $1-10 for smaller than 8x10 b&w prints. Buys one-time rights.

Columns/Departments: Uses science fiction and fantasy book reviews and film reviews. Buys 25-30 mss/year. Send complete ms. Length: 100-1,000 words. Pays ½-1¢/word. (Reviews usually paid in subscriptions, not cash.)

Tips: ''Reviews are best way to break into *Thrust*. Must be on current science fiction and fantasy books. The most frequent mistake made by writers in completing articles for us is writing to a novice audience; *Thrust*'s readers are science fiction and fantasy experts.''

TWILIGHT ZONE, Montcalm Publishing Co., 800 2nd Ave., New York NY 10017. (212)986-9600. Editor: Michael Blaine. Managing Editor: Robert Sabat. 60% freelance written. Bimonthly magazine of fantasy fiction from Stephen King to Isaac Singer—stories within and beyond the Rod Serling tradition. Circ. 150,000. Pays half on acceptance, half on publication. Publishes ms an average of 4 months after acceptance. Byline given. Offers 25% kill fee. Buys first North American serial rights, first serial rights and second serial (reprint) rights. Submit seasonal/holiday material 8 months in advance. Simultaneous and photocopied submissions OK. Computer printout submissions acceptable; prefers letter-quality to dot-matrix. SASE. Reports in 3 months. Sample copy $3.

Fiction: Fantasy, understated horror and some serialism. No sword and sorcery; hardware-oriented science fiction; vampire, werewolf and deals-with-the-devil stories; sadistic stories; or imaginary-world fantasy. Buys 35 mss/year. Send complete ms. Length: 5,000 words maximum. Pays 5¢/word; $150 minimum.

Social Science and Self-Improvement

These publications focus on how and why readers can improve their own outlooks—and how to understand people in general. Each magazine slanted to a particular audience covers a wide range of topics.

APA MONITOR, 1200 17th St. NW, Washington DC 20036. (202)955-7690. Editor: Jeffrey Mervis. Associate Editor: Kathleen Fisher. 5% freelance written. For psychologists and other social scientists and professionals interested in behavioral sciences and mental health area. Monthly newspaper. Circ. 70,000. Pays on publication. Publishes ms an average of 3 months after acceptance. Buys first serial rights. Computer printout submissions acceptable. Free sample copy.

Nonfiction: News and feature articles about issues facing psychology both as a science and a mental health profession; political, social and economic developments in the behavioral sciences area. Interview, profile and historical pieces. No personal views, reminiscences or satire. Buys no mss without query. Length: 300-3,000 words.

Tips: ''Our writers almost need to be longtime readers or science writers to strike the balance between some of the top Ph.D.s in the country and graduate students at small colleges that we try to reach.''

THE HUMANIST, American Humanist Association, 7 Harwood Dr., Box 146, Amherst NY 14226. (716)839-5080. Editor: Lloyd L. Morain. Associate Editor: William J. Harnack. 60% freelance written. Bimonthly magazine covering philosophy, psychology, religion, ethics. ''Discusses social issues and personal concerns in the light of humanistic ideas and developments in philosophy and science.'' Circ. 14,000. Pays on publication. Publishes ms an average of 2 months after acceptance. Byline given. Buys all rights ''unless arranged with author.'' Previously published submissions OK. SASE. Reports in 3 months on mss. Sample copy $2.50.

Nonfiction: General interest, opinion, personal experience, humanistic concerns, philosophy, controversial topics. ''We like creative, upbeat articles.'' Buys 35 mss/year. Send complete ms. Length: 3,000-8,000 words. Pays variable rates from copies to $200 maximum.

Photos: ''Does not buy photos; however, authors are encouraged to submit them with ms.''

Columns/Departments: Humanism in Literature (humanistic slants on literature, especially contemporary). Buys 3 mss/year. Send complete ms. Length: 600-2,500 words. Pays variable rates from copies to $50 maximum.

ROSICRUCIAN DIGEST, Rosicrucian Order, AMORC, Rosicrucian Park, San Jose CA 95191. (408)287-9171, ext. 213. Editor-in-Chief: Robin M. Thompson. 50% freelance written. Monthly magazine emphasizing mysticism, science and the arts. For "men and women of all ages, seeking answers to life's questions." Circ. 70,000. Pays on acceptance. Publishes ms an average of 6 months after acceptance. Buys first serial rights and rights to reprint. Byline given. Submit seasonal or holiday material 5 months in advance. Photocopied and previously published submissions OK. Computer printout submissions acceptable; no dot-matrix. SASE. Reports in 2 months. Free sample copy and writer's guidelines.

Nonfiction: How to deal with life's problems and opportunities in a positive and constructive way. Informational articles—new ideas and developments in science, the arts, philosophy and thought. Historical sketches, biographies, human interest, psychology, philosophical and inspirational articles. No religious, astrological or political material or articles promoting a particular group or system of thought. Buys 20-30 mss/year. Query. Length: 1,000-1,500 words. Pays 6¢/word.

Photos: Purchased with accompanying ms. Send prints. Pays $10/8x10 b&w glossy print.

Fillers: Short inspirational or uplifting (not religious) anecdotes or experiences. Buys 6/year. Query. Length: 25-250 words. Pays 2¢/word.

Tips: "Be specific about what you want to write about—the subject you want to explore—and be willing to work with editor. Articles should appeal to worldwide circulation. The most rewarding aspect of working with freelance writers is to see an article 'grow' from the original 'seed' into something that will touch the lives of our readers."

Sports

Sports coverage may lapse into clichés in local newspapers, but most magazine editors want to give the story behind each sport and athlete. "Is the story unique?" magazine editors ask themselves. "Does it explore an area or state of mind . . . in a way not done before." Some editors do not want "Me'n Joe" stories. Those detailed accounts of a hunting/fishing trip taken by the author and a buddy start with the friends' awakening at dawn and end with their return home, "tired but happy." The publications in this category buy articles for sports fans and activists on how to practice and enjoy both team and individual sports, material on conservation of streams and forests, and articles reporting on and analyzing professional sports. For the convenience of writers who specialize in one or two areas of sport and outdoor writing, the publications are subcategorized by the sport or subject matter they emphasize. Publications in related categories (for example, Hunting and Fishing; Archery and Bowhunting) often buy similar material (in this case articles on bow and arrow hunting). Consequently writers should read through this entire Sports category to become familiar with the subcategories. Publications on horse breeding, hunting dogs or the use of animals in sports are classified in the Animal category, while horse racing is listed here. Publications dealing with automobile or motorcycle racing can be found in the Automotive and Motorcycle category. Markets interested in articles on exercise and fitness are listed in the Health and Fitness section. Outdoor publications that promote the preservation of nature, placing only secondary emphasis on preserving nature as a setting for sport, are in the Nature, Conservation, and Ecology category. Regional magazines are frequently interested in conservation or sports material with a local angle. Camping publications are classified in the Travel, Camping and Trailer category.

Archery and Bowhunting

BOW AND ARROW HUNTING,, Box HH/34249 Camino Capistrano, Capistrano Beach CA 92624. Editorial Director: Roger Combs. 90% freelance written. Bimonthly magazine. For bowhunters. Pays on acceptance. Publishes ms an average of 6 months after acceptance. Buys all rights; and first North American serial rights." Byline given. Reports on submissions in 2 months. Author must have some knowledge of archery terms. SASE.

Nonfiction: Articles: bowhunting, techniques used by champs, how to make your own tackle, and off-trail hunting tales. Likes a touch of humor in articles. "No dead animals or 'my first hunt.' " Also uses one technical and how-to article per issue. Submit complete ms. Length: 1,500-2,500 words. Pays $150-250.
Photos: Purchased as package with mss; 5x7 minimum. Pays $75-100 for cover chromes, 35mm or larger.
Tips: "We've changed our name and Philosophy to 'Bow and Arrow Hunting.' Good b&w photos are of primary importance. Don't submit color prints. We staff-write our shorter pieces."

BOWHUNTER MAGAZINE, 3150 Mallard Cove Lane, Fort Wayne IN 46804. (219)432-5772. Editor: M. R. James. 90% freelance written. Bimonthly magazine; 112 pages. For "readers of all ages, background and experience who share two common passions—hunting with the bow and arrow and a love of the great outdoors." Circ. 160,000. Buys first publication rights. Pays on acceptance. Publishes ms an average of 8 months after acceptance. We include our Bowhunting Annual as part of the subscription package. This means we have seven issues each year including the Annual (on sale in July) which has been designated a Special Deer Hunting Issue." Submit seasonal material 8 months in advance. Reports in 6 weeks. Computer printout submissions acceptable; prefers letter-quality to dot-matrix. SASE. Sample copy $2; writers guidelines for SAE with 1 first class postage stamp.
Nonfiction: "We want articles that inform as well as entertain readers. Writers should anticipate every question a reader may ask and answer questions in the article or accompanying sidebar. Most features deal with big or small game bowhunting (how-to, where-to-go, etc.) and the 'Me and Joe' article is not dead here. We do avoid most technical pieces. Also, we do not cover all aspects of archery—only bowhunting. Unusual experiences are welcome and freshness is demanded, especially when covering common ground. Readers demand accuracy and writers hoping to sell to us must have a thorough knowledge of bowhunting. No writer should attempt to sell material to us without first studying one or more issues of the magazine. We especially like articles that promote responsible bowhunting and combat anti-hunting attacks. Humor, personal experiences, interviews and personality profiles, nostalgia, personal opinions, and historical articles are good bets. No 'See what I bagged—ain't I great' articles." Buys approximately 100 mss/year. Query or submit complete ms. Length: 200-3,500 words. Pays $25-250 or more.
Photos: Photos purchased with or without accompanying ms. Pays $20-35 for 5x7 or 8x10 b&w prints; $50 minimum for 35mm or 2¼x2¼ color. Captions optional.
Tips: "Keep the reader foremost in mind. Write for him, not yourself. Know the sport and share your knowledge. Weave helpful information into the storyline (e.g., costs involved, services of guide or outfitter, hunting season dates, equipment preferred and why, tips on items to bring, where to write for information, etc.). We have no set formula per se, but most features are first person narratives and most published material will contain elements mentioned above. We enjoy working with promising newcomers who understand our magazine and our needs. Most writers submit material 'on spec.' We reserve most assignments for staffers."

Bicycling

BICYCLING, Rodale Press, Inc., 33 E. Minor St., Emmaus PA 18049. Editor and Publisher: James C. McCullagh. 65% freelance written. Publishes 9 issues/year (6 monthly, 3 bimonthly); 180-200 pages. Circ. 260,000. Pays on publication. Byline given. Buys all rights. Submit seasonal/holiday material 5 months in advance. Electronic submissions OK via Wordstar and IBM PC, but requires hard copy also. Computer printout submissions acceptable; prefers letter-quality to dot-matrix. SASE. Writer's guidelines for SAE and 1 first class stamp.
Nonfiction: How-to (on all phases of bicycle touring, bike repair, maintenance, commuting, new products, clothing, riding technique, nutrition for cyclists, conditioning); travel (bicycling must be central here); photo feature (on cycling events of national significance); and technical (component review—query). "We are strictly a bicycling magazine. We seek readable, clear, well-informed pieces. We rarely run articles that are pure humor or inspiration but a little of either might flavor even our most technical pieces. No poetry or fiction." Buys 5-10 unsolicited mss/issue. Query. Length: 1,500 words average. Pays $25-300. Sometimes pays expenses of writers on assignment.
Photos: State availability of photos with query letter or send photo material with ms. Pays $15-50 for b&w prints and $35-250 for color transparencies. Captions preferred; model release required.
Fillers: Anecdotes and other items for People & Places section.
Tips: "Fitness is becoming an increasingly important subject. Also, study some recent issues of our magazine. We continue to evolve."

CYCLING U.S.A., The Official Publication of the U.S. Cycling Federation, 1750 E. Boulder St., Colorado Springs CO 80909. (303)578-4581. Editor: Josh Lehman. 50% freelance written. Monthly magazine covering reportage and commentary on American bicycle racing, personalities, and sports physiology for USCF licensed cyclists. Circ. 17,000. Pays on publication. Publishes ms an average of 4 months after acceptance. By-

line given. Offers 30% kill fee. Buys first serial rights and second serial (reprint) rights. Submit seasonal/holiday material 1 month in advance. Simultaneous queries, and photocopied and previously published submissions OK. Computer printout submissions acceptable; no dot-matrix. SASE. Reports in 2 weeks. Sample copy for 10x12 SAE and 60¢ postage.
Nonfiction: How-to (train, prepare for a bike race); interview/profile; opinion; personal experience; photo feature; technical; and race commentary on major cycling events. No comparative product evaluations. Buys 15 mss/year. Query with published clips. Length: 850-3,000 words. Pays $85-500.
Photos: State availability of photos. Pays $10-25 for 5x7 b&w prints; $125 for color transparencies used as cover. Captions required. Buys one-time rights.
Columns/Departments: Ask the Doctor; and Racing Form—The Coach's Column. Buys 24 mss/year. Query with published clips. Length: 850-1,000 words. Pays $50-100.
Tips: "A background in bicycle racing is important because the sport is somewhat insular, technical and complex. Most major articles are generated in house. Race reports are most open to freelancers. Be concise, informative and anecdotal. The most frequent mistake made by writers in completing an article for us is that it is too lengthy; our format is more compatible with shorter (500-800 word) articles than longer features."

VELO-NEWS, A Journal of Bicycle Racing. Box 1257, Brattleboro VT 05301. (802)254-2305. Editor: Barbara George. 20% freelance written. Monthly tabloid (October-March, biweekly April-September) covering bicycle racing. Circ. 15,000. Pays on publication. Publishes ms an average of 1 month after acceptance. Byline given. Buys all rights. Simultaneous queries, and simultaneous, photocopied, and previously published submissions OK. Computer printout submissions acceptable; also phone transmissions of ASCII at 1200 baud (call for specs). "We would prefer electronic submissions." SASE. Reports in 2 weeks. Sample copy for 9x12 SAE.
Nonfiction: How-to (on bicycle racing); interview/profile (of people important in bicycle racing); opinion; photo feature; and technical. Buys 50 mss/year. Query. Length: 300-3,000 words. Pays $2.75/column inch.
Photos: State availability of photos. Pays $15-30 for 8x10 b&w prints. Captions and identification of subjects required. Buys one-time rights.

Boating

BAY & DELTA YACHTSMAN, Recreation Publications, 2019 Clement Ave., Alameda CA 94501. (415)865-7500. Managing Editor: Dave Preston. 80% freelance written. Emphasizes recreational boating for small boat owners and recreational yachtsmen in northern California. Monthly tabloid newspaper; 90-166 pages. Circ. 22,000. Pays on publication. Byline given. Buys first serial rights. Phone queries OK. Submit seasonal/holiday material 3 months in advance. Photocopied submissions OK. Computer printout submissions OK; prefers letter quality to dot matrix. SASE. Reports in 1 month. Free writer's guidelines.
Nonfiction: Historical (nautical history of northern California); how-to (modifications, equipment, supplies, rigging etc., aboard both power and sailboats); humor (no disaster or boating ineptitude pieces); informational (government legislation as it relates to recreational boating); interview; nostalgia; personal experience ("How I learned about boating from this" type of approach); photo feature (to accompany copy); profile; and travel. Buys 5-10 unsolicited mss/issue. Query. Length: 1,200-2,000 words. Pays $1/column inch.
Photos: Photos purchased with accompanying ms. Pays $5 for b&w glossy or matte finish photos. Total purchase price for ms includes payment for photos. Captions required.
Fiction: Adventure (sea stories, cruises, races pertaining to West Coast and points South/South West.); fantasy; historical; humorous; and mystery. Buys 4 mss/year. Query. Length: 500-1,750 words. Pays $1/column inch.
Tips: "Think of our market area: the waterways of northern California and how, why, when and where the boatman would use those waters. Think about unusual onboard application of ideas (power and sail), special cruising tips, etc. We're very interested in local boating interviews—both the famous and unknown. Write for a knowledgeable boating public."

BOAT PENNSYLVANIA, Pennsylvania Fish Commission, Box 1673, Harrisburg PA 17105-1673. (717)657-4520. Editor: Art Michaels. Bimonthly magazine covering powerboating, canoeing, kayaking, sailing, rafting, and water skiing. Pays on acceptance. Byline given. Buys all rights; but rights can be reassigned after publication on writer's request. Submit seasonal/holiday material 8 months in advance. Computer printout submissions acceptable; prefers letter-quality to dot-matrix. SASE. Reports in 1 week on queries; 2 months on mss. Writer's guidelines for SASE. Sample copy for 9x12 envelope and 73¢ postage.
Nonfiction: How-to, interview/profile, technical, and travel (only in Pennsylvania for boating). No fishing or hunting articles. Buys 36 mss/year. Query. Length: 200-1,500 words. Pays $20-300.
Photos: State availability of photos with query; send photos with accompanying ms. Reviews 35mm or 2¼x2¼ color transparencies and 8x10 b&w prints. Captions, model release, and identification of subjects re-

quired. Buys all rights.
Columns/Departments: Query or send complete ms.
Tips: "The best way to break into print here is to submit a technically detailed, accurate how-to article with professional-quality black and white 8x10 prints or color slides (35mm) on a powerboating, sailing, canoeing, kayaking, rafting, or water skiing subject. Material must be wholly appropriate to Pennsylvania waterways."

CANADIAN YACHTING MAGAZINE, Maclean Hunter Bldg., 7th Floor, 777 Bay St., Toronto, Ontario M5W 1A7 Canada. Editor: Penny Caldwell. 80% freelance written. Monthly magazine aimed at owners of power and sail pleasure boats, both cruising and racing. Circ. 30,000. Pays on acceptance. Publishes ms an average of 6 months after acceptance. Buys first North American serial rights. Previously published submissions OK, but remember "our obligation not to duplicate material published in larger American magazines available in our reader area." Computer printout submissions acceptable; no dot-matrix.
Nonfiction: "Much of our 'entertainment' coverage of important racing events must be handled by U.S. freelancers. Cruise stories are welcome from anyone." Also uses technical pieces, especially on motor maintenance. Buys 40 unsolicited mss/year. Send complete ms. Length: 1,800-2,500 words. Pays $180-500.
Photos: Pays $15-40 for 8x10 b&w prints; $25-200 for 35mm color transparencies.
Tips: "Query should contain writer's experience and reassurance of photo quality (usually sample). In writing for us stick to the outline, keep it Canadian and keep it relevant to our readers."

CANOE MAGAZINE, Canoe America Associates, Box 597, Camden ME 04843. Editor: John Viehman. Managing Editor: Dave Getchell. 90% freelance written. Magazine published six times/year; 96 pages. "*Canoe* is the total resource for canoeing and kayaking information." For an audience ranging from weekend canoe-camper to Olympic caliber flatwater/whitewater racing, marathon, poling, sailing, wilderness tripping or sea-cruising types. Circ. 55,000. Pays on publication or on acceptance by prior arrangement. Publishes ms an average of 2 months after acceptance. Byline given. Offers 25% kill fee. Buys first serial rights. Sample copy and writer's guidelines for $1 and 9x12 SASE. Electronic submissions OK if compatible with IBM-PC; but all submissions should be checked out with editor first. Computer printout submissions acceptable; no dot-matrix. Reports in 2 months. SASE.
Nonfiction and Photos: "We publish a variety of state of the art canoeing and kayaking articles, striving for a balanced mix of stories to reflect all interests in this outdoor activity, recreational or competitive. Also interested in any articles dealing with conservation issues which may adversely affect the sport. Writing should be readable rather than academic; clever rather than endlessly descriptive. Diary type first-person style not desirable. A good, provocative lead is considered a prime ingredient. We want stories about canoeing/kayaking activities in the 50 states and Canada with which canoeists/kayakers of average or better ability can identify. Also interested in articles discussing safety aspects or instructional items. Occasional call for outdoor photography feature as relates to water accessible subjects. Please pick up and study a recent issue before querying. Also study back issues and published index (each issue) to avoid duplication. No hunting/fishing articles with minimal emphasis on the canoes involved." Buys 50+ mss/year. Query or submit complete ms. Length: 1,500-3,000 words. Pays $100-500. Will consider relevant book reviews (pays $25 on publication); length, 200-350 words. Short news and other items of interest, pays $25-100; "payment increases with accompanying photos."
Tips: "We've started a number of regular departmental stories that offer freelancers a good chance to break into our publication. Look for 1985 issues for examples."

CRUISING WORLD, 524 Thames St., Newport RI 02840. (401)847-1588. Editor: George Day. 75% freelance written. For all those who cruise under sail. Monthly magazine; 220 pages. Circ. 120,000. Pays on acceptance. Publishes ms an average of 8 months after acceptance. Rights purchased vary with author and material. Buys first North American serial rights or first world serial rights. Reports in about 8 weeks. Computer printout submissions acceptable; prefers letter-quality to dot-matrix. SASE.
Nonfiction: "We are interested in seeing informative articles on the technical and enjoyable aspects of cruising under sail. Also subjects of general interest to seafarers." Buys 135-140 unsolicited mss/year. Submit complete ms. Length: 500-3,500 words. Pays $50-500. Sometimes pays expenses of writers on assignment.
Photos: 5x7 b&w prints (5x7) and color transparencies purchased with accompanying ms.
Tips: "The most frequent mistakes made by writers in completing an article assignment for us are missing our audience; missing our style; missing the point of the whole exercise; typing single-space; supplying unusable photos; writing too much but saying too little."

‡**HOT BOAT MAGAZINE,** Chuck Pierce & Associates, Box 1708, Lake Havasu City AZ 86403. (602)855-0077. Editor: Randy Scott. 35% freelance written. Monthly magazine covering boating. "The bulk of our magazine is directed to covering major sporting events (drag boating, water-skiing, endurance racing, etc.) and personality features of racers, skiers and known figures in the marine industry." Circ. 35,000. Pays on publication. Publishes ms an average of 2 months after acceptance. Byline given. Buys first North American serial rights. Submit seasonal/holiday material 2 months in advance. Simultaneous queries and photocopied submissions OK. Computer printout submissions acceptable; prefers letter-quality to dot-matrix. SASE. Reports in 3

weeks. Sample copy for 5 first class stamps and 9x12 SAE. Writer's guidelines for #10 SAE and 1 first class stamp.

Nonfiction: General interest; how-to (repairs, water sports, etc.); humor; interview/profile (well-known sports figures, manufacturers, etc.) and technical (engines, boat hulls, fuels, props, etc.). Buys 35-50 mss/year. Query with published clips. "We usually assign major features to writers that we are sure are familiar with our style of writing." Length: 850-2,500 words. Pays $85-400. Sometimes pays the expenses of writers on assignment.

Photos: State availability of photos with query. Pays $25 maximum for transparencies and $5-25 for b&w prints. (Prefers b&w and color slides and 3x5 prints). Captions and identification of subjects required. Buys one-time rights.

Tips: "Send a tantalizing query with clips of published work. We are willing to work with unpublished writers, but in most cases, it would be on a 'speculation' basis for the initial assignment. Articles should be written with an upwardly mobile, affluent audience in mind; aged 20-50. Look for the unusual slant. For instance, we recently had a feature on a racer describing what it feels like to be in the cockpit of a boat going more than 200 mph. The most frequent mistake made by writers in completing an article for us is on sporting events: the story is bogged with too many figures (speeds, etc). Solution: build the story around highlights; there's no need to mention everyone. Also there are usually not enough quotes in articles from personalities or respected authorities. We would also like to see more tech and how-to articles. How-tos could be along the lines of 'repairing your fiberglass hull', 'creating more hp at a modest cost,' and so on. We also have room for occasional humor pieces of good taste and on a boating theme, of course. We are always open for new suggestions and will consider queries on most boating themes."

LAKELAND BOATING, 106 W. Perry St., Port Clinton OH 43452. (419)734-5774. Editor: David G. Brown. 80% freelance written. Monthly magazine emphasizing pleasure boating on freshwater lakes; both sail and power, but more emphasis on power. Circ. 46,000. Pays on publication. Publishes ms an average of 10 months after acceptance. Buys first serial rights. Computer printout submissions acceptable if legible. SASE. Reports in 1 month. Sample copy $1.75 with SAE and 39¢ postage.

Nonfiction: 2-3 "Cruise" stories/issue. May be personal experiences, but reader must get enough details on ports, marinas, dangers, etc. to perform a similar cruise. Include sketches, maps, lists of marinas, access ramps, harbors of refuge. Length: 1,000 to 2,500 words. "We need 'people' stories about individuals living a water lifestyle on the Great Lakes or major inland rivers. Focus should be on the person who is the subject of the story and how boats and boating influence his/her life. We also need stories about waterfront developments such as new harbors, condominiums with dockage and tourist-type attractions which can be visited by boat.' Query first.

Photos: Send photos with ms. 5x7 or 8x10 b&w can also be submitted separately. Send negatives if you cannot have professional quality prints made. Original 35mm or larger transparencies for color stories. Captions required or identification of all pictures, prints or transparencies. "Please stamp every transparency with name and address." Original photo materials are returned.

Tips: "We are a regional publication, so all stories must have a Great Lakes or Midwestern freshwater slant. Cruise stories must give details. We don't want a 'Me 'n Joe' narrative of every breakfast and fuel stop. The waters being cruised and ports being visited are always more important than the people doing the cruising. The writer has a better chance of breaking in at our publication with short articles and fillers as there is greater need for them. Also, much of our editorial material is planned 12 to 24 months in advance. Biggest reason for stories being rejected is failure to meet our regional needs (failure to read our magazine to learn our slant and style). We would rather spend time developing a story right from the beginning than reject an otherwise well-written manuscript."

MOTORBOATING AND SAILING, 224 W. 57th St., New York NY 10019. (212)262-8768. Editor: Peter A. Janssen. Monthly magazine covering powerboats and sailboats for people who own their own boats and are active in a yachting lifestyle. Circ. 140,000. Average issue includes 8-10 feature articles. Pays on acceptance. Byline given. Buys one-time rights. SASE. Reports in 3 months.

Nonfiction: General interest (navigation, adventure, cruising), and how-to (maintenance). Buys 5-6 mss/issue. Query. Length: 2,000 words.

Photos: Reviews 5x7 b&w glossy prints and 35mm or larger color transparencies. Offers no additional payment for photos accepted with ms. Captions and model release required.

NAUTICAL QUARTERLY, Nautical Quarterly Co., 373 Park Ave. S., New York NY 10016. (212)685-9114. Editor: Joseph Gribbins. Managing Editor: Michael Levitt. 75% freelance written. Quarterly hardcover magazine covering yachting, power and sail. "We are specifically a yachting publication—not a maritime or shipping publication—with special emphasis on the best in yachts and small boats, and nautical experience, power and sail, past and present." Circ. 20,000. Pays on acceptable. Publishes ms an average of 9 months after acceptance. Byline given. Buys first North American serial rights and all rights. Simultaneous queries, and simultaneous, photocopied, and previously published submissions OK. Computer printout submissions accept-

able; "letter-quality submissions are very much preferred." SASE. Reports in 2 months. Sample copy $16.
Nonfiction: Historical/nostalgic, interview/profile, opinion, personal experience, photo feature, technical. "No articles on maritime (i.e., non-yachting) subjects such as tugboats, commercial ships, lighthouses, clipper ships, etc." Buys 20-25 mss/year. Query with published clips. Length: 2,500-8,000 words. Pays $500-1,000.
Photos: Marilyn Rose, photo editor. State availability of photos or send photos with ms. Reviews 35mm color transparencies. Payment varies by arrangement with the photographer. Identification of subjects required. Buys one-time rights.
Tips: "A query, accompanied by writing samples, will succeed if both the idea and the samples suit our standards. Frequent mistakes made by writers are articles not structured as magazine pieces—long, rambling, disorganized, not to the point. We just restructure and rewrite these things—and often cut the fat out. As a specialty publication, we accept these pieces because the information we want is there; the writers are experts or intimately familiar with a subject; but they are not writers."

OFFSHORE, New England's Boating Magazine, Offshore Publications, Inc., Box 148, Waban MA 02168. (617)244-7520. Editor: Herbert Gliick. 75% freelance written. Monthly magazine (oversize) covering boating and the New England coast for New England boat owners. Circ. 19,000. Pays within 1 month of acceptance. Publishes ms an average of 2 months after acceptance. Byline given. Offers negotiable kill fee. Buys first North American serial rights. Submit seasonal/holiday material 2 months in advance. Simultaneous queries, and simultaneous, photocopied, and previously published submissions OK. Electronic submissions OK Kaypro disk, ASCI via phone, but requires hard copy also. Computer printout submissions acceptable. SASE. Reports in 1 week. Sample copy for 11x14 SAE and 88¢ postage.
Nonfiction: Articles on boats, boating and New England coastal places and people. Thumbnail and/or outline of topic will elicit immediate response. Buys 125 mss/year. Query with published clips or send complete ms. Length: 1000-3,500 words. Pays $2-3/column inch.
Photos: Reviews photocopies of 5x7 b&w prints. Identification of subjects required. Buys one-time rights.
Tips: "Demonstrate familiarity with boats or New England coast and ability to recognize subjects of interest to regional boat owners. Those subjects need not be boats. *Offshore* does not take itself as seriously as most national boating magazines. The most frequent mistakes made by writers in completing an article for us are failing to build on a theme (what is the point of the story?); use of adjectives, instead of specifics, creating mush."

PACIFIC YACHTING, Power and Sail in British Columbia, S.I.P. Division, Maclean Hunter, Ltd., 1132 Hamilton St., Vancouver, British Columbia V6B 2S2 Canada. (604)687-1581. Editor: Paul Burkhart. Monthly magazine of yachting and recreational boating. Circ. 20,000. 50% freelance written. Pays mostly on publication. Byline given. Buys first and second serial (reprint) rights and makes work-for-hire assignments. Submit seasonal/holiday material 4 months in advance. Simultaneous queries, and simultaneous, photocopied, and previously published submissions OK. Computer printout submissions acceptable; prefers letter-quality to dot-matrix. SAE and IRCs. Reports in 2 months on queries; 6 months on mss. Publishes ms an average of 6 months after acceptance. Sample copy $2.
Nonfiction: Book excerpts, how-to, humor, interview/profile, new product, opinion, personal experience, photo feature, technical, travel. "Freelancers can break in with first-person articles about yachting adventures on the west coast of Canada accompanied by good 35mm photos. We're open to 'how-to' pieces by writers with strong technical backgrounds in the marine recreation field." No "poetry, religious, or first sailing experiences." Buys 150 mss/year. Will buy fewer stories in the year ahead. Query. Length: 100-2,000 words. Pays 10¢/word.
Photos: Send photos with ms. Reviews b&w contact sheets, b&w and color negatives, 35mm color transparencies (preferred) and prints. Captions and identification of subjects required. Buys various rights.
Columns/Departments: Scuttlebutt (news and light items, new gear, book reviews) and Boat Care (how-to). Buys 80 mss/year. Send complete ms. Length: 100-400 words. Pays $10-40.
Fillers: Clippings, newsbreaks. Length: 100-200 words. Pays $10-25.
Tips: "In working with freelancers we enjoy discovering fresh new perspectives in our own backyard. We regret, however, their failure to inquire or check out our magazine style."

PLEASURE BOATING MAGAZINE, Graphcom Publishing, Inc., 1995 NE 150th St., North Miami FL 33181. (305)945-7403. Managing Editor: Joe Greene. 50% freelance written. Monthly magazine of recreational boating and fishing throughout the South including cruising, racing and diving subjects. Circ. 30,000. Pays on publication. Publishes ms an average of 2 months after acceptance. Buys all rights. Computer printout submissions acceptable. SASE. Reports in 1 month. Free sample copy.
Nonfiction: Technical, how-to departments on fishing, electronics, engines, etc. Features designed to entertain and inform readers in the areas of recreational boating and fishing. Pays $100 for department pieces (1,500 words) to $200 for feature-length articles (3,000 words) with color. Buys 15 unsolicited mss/year. Send complete ms. Length: 500-3,000 words. Pays 5-10¢/word.

Photos: Send photos with ms. Reviews photos suitable for cover. Color transparencies requested for use with features; b&w glossies for use with department material. Pays $50-150. Captions and model release required. Buys all rights.

‡**POWERBOAT MAGAZINE**, 15917 Strathern St., Van Nuys CA 91406. Editor: Mark Spencer. For performance-conscious boating enthusiasts. January, West Coast Runabout Performance Trials; February, East Coast Runabout Performance Trials; March, Offshore Performance Trials; April, Water Ski Issue; May, Awards for Product Excellence; June through November/December, Race reporting and various other features on recreational boating. Circ. 75,000. Pays on publication. Buys all rights or one-time North American serial rights. Reports in 2 weeks. Query required. SASE. Free sample copy.
Nonfiction: Uses articles about power boats and water skiing that offer special interest to performance-minded boaters, how-to-do-it pieces with good b&w pictures, developments in boating, profiles on well-known boating and skiing individuals, competition coverage of national and major events. Length: 1,500-2,000 words. Pays $150-250/article.
Photos: Photos purchased with mss. Prefers 35mm Kodachrome slides. Pays $100 for one-time cover use only.

ROWING USA, U.S. Rowing Association, Suite 980, 251 North Illinois St., Indianapolis IN 46204. (317)237-2769. Editor: Kathryn M. Reith. A bimonthly magazine for U.S. Rowing Association members, primarily competitive rowers, plus a substantial number of recreational rowers (mostly sliding seat boats). Circ. 12,000. Pays on publication. Publishes ms an average of 3 months after acceptance. Byline given. Buys one-time rights. Submit seasonal/holiday material 3 months in advance. Simultaneous queries, and simultaneous, photocopied, and previously published submissions OK. Electronic submissions OK via IBM Displaywriter disks only. Computer printout submissions acceptable; prefers letter-quality to dot-matrix. Reports in 2 weeks on queries; 1 month on mss. Writer's guidelines for SAE with 1 first class stamp.
Nonfiction: Historical/nostalgic; how-to (rowing, boat-building, rigging, coaching); interview/profile; opinion; personal experience; and photo feature. "Articles should have relevance to individual members or member organizations." Anticipates buying 7-9 mss/year. Query. Length: 350-3,500 words. Pays $200 maximum. Sometimes pays expenses of writers on assignment.
Photos: Send photos with accompanying query or ms. Pays $40 maximum for b&w prints. Captions and identification of subjects required. Buys one-time rights.
Columns/Departments: Rowing Shorts (humor) and Book/video/film reviews. Query. Length: 350-1,100 words. Pays $50 maximum.
Poetry: Free verse, haiku, light verse and traditional. Rowing-related only. Pays $50 maximum.
Fillers: Anecdotes and short humor. Pays $15 maximum.
Tips: "The writer may have a better chance of breaking in at our publication with short articles and fillers as the topic of the magazine is fairly specialized. A short piece will verify the writer's knowledge. The most frequent mistake made by writers in completing an article for us is not focusing material to the specific audience."

SAIL, 34 Commercial Wharf, Boston MA 02110. (617)227-0888. Editor: Keith Taylor. 60% freelance written. Monthly magazine for audience that is "strictly sailors, average age 35, above average education." Pays on publication. Publishes ms an average of 6 months after acceptance. Buys first North American serial rights. Submit seasonal or special material at least 3 months in advance. Reports in 6 weeks. Computer printout submissions acceptable; prefers letter-quality to dot-matrix. SASE. Free sample copy.
Nonfiction: Patience Wales, managing editor. Wants "articles on sailing: technical, techniques and feature stories." Interested in how-to, personal experience, profiles, historical and new products. "Generally emphasize the excitement of sail and the human, personal aspect. No logs." Special issues: "Cruising issues, chartering issues, fitting-out issues, special race issues (e.g., America's Cup), boat show issues." Buys 200 mss/year (freelance and commissioned). Length: 1,500-3,000 words. Pays $100-800.
Photos: Offers additional payment for photos. Uses b&w glossy prints or Kodachrome 64 color transparencies. Pays $500 if photo is used on the cover.

‡**SAILING MAGAZINE**, 125 E. Main St., Port Washington WI 53074. (414)284-3494. Editor and Publisher: William F. Schanen, III. Monthly magazine; 82 pages. For readers ages 25-44, majority professionals. About 75% of them own their own sailboat. Circ. 35,000. Pays on publication. Photocopied and simultaneous submissions OK. Reports in 6 weeks. SASE. Free writer's guidelines.
Nonfiction: Micca Leffingwell Hutchins, editor. "Experiences of sailing, whether cruising, racing or learning. We require no special style. We're devoted exclusively to sailing and sailboat enthusiasts, and particularly interested in articles about the trend toward cruising in the sailing world." Informational, personal experience, profile, historical, travel and book reviews. Buys 24 mss/year. Query or submit complete ms. Length: open. Payment negotiable. Must be accompanied by photos.
Photos: B&w and color photos purchased with or without accompanying ms. Captions required. Pays flat fee for article.

TRAILER BOATS MAGAZINE, Poole Publications, Inc., Box 2307, Gardena CA 90248. (213)323-9040. Editor: Jim Youngs. Managing Editor: Jean Muckerheide. 30% freelance written. Monthly magazine (November/December issue combined); 80 pages. Emphasizes legally trailerable boats and related activities. Circ. 80,000. Pays on publication. Publishes ms an average of 2 months after acceptance. Byline given. Buys all rights. Submit seasonal/holiday material 3 months in advance. Computer printout submissions acceptable; prefers letter-quality to dot-matrix. SASE. Reports in 4 weeks. Sample copy $1.25; Writer's guidelines for SASE.

Nonfiction: General interest (trailer boating activities); historical (places, events, boats); how-to (repair boats, installation, etc.); humor (almost any boating-related subject); nostalgia (same as historical); personal experience; photo feature; profile; technical; and travel (boating travel on water or highways). No "How I Spent My Summer Vacation" stories, or stories not even remotely connected to trailerable boats and related activities. Buys 18-30 unsolicited mss/year. Query or send complete ms. Length: 500-3,000 words. Pays $50 minimum.

Photos: Send photos with ms. Pays $7.50-50 for 5x7 or 8x10 b&w glossy print; $10-100 for 35mm color transparency. Captions required.

Columns/Departments: Boaters Bookshelf (boating book reviews); Over the Transom (funny or strange boating photos); and Patent Pending (an invention with drawings). Buys 2/issue. Query. Length: 100-500 words. Pays 7¢-10¢/word. Mini-Cruise (short enthusiastic approach to a favorite boating spot). Need map and photographs. Length: 500-750 words. Pays $50. Open to suggestions for new columns/departments.

Fiction: Adventure, experimental, historical, humorous and suspense. "We do not use too many fiction stories but we will consider them if they fit the general editorial guidelines." Query or send complete ms. Length: 500-1,500 words. Pays $50 minimum.

Tips: "Query should contain short general outline of the intended material; what kind of photos; how the photos illustrate the piece. Write with authority covering the subject like an expert. Frequent mistakes are not knowing the subject matter or the audience. Use basic information rather than prose, particularly in travel stories. We've added a new magazine that is a bit more freelance written: *The Western Boatman*—a bimonthly Western regional boating lifestyle magazine—13 Western states. The writer may have a better chance of breaking in at our publication with short articles and fillers if they are typically hard to find articles. We do most major features in house."

WATERWAY GUIDE, 850 3rd Ave., New York NY 10022. (212)715-2629. Managing Editors: Nancy Brokaw and Queene Hooper. 10% freelance written. Annual magazine. "A pleasure-boater's cruising guide to the Intracoastal Waterway, East Coast waters and the Great Lakes." Four regional editions. Computer printout submissions acceptable; prefers letter-quality to dot-matrix.

Nonfiction: "We occasionally have a need for a special, short article on some particular aspect of pleasure cruising—such as living aboard, sailing versus powerboating, having children or pets on board—or a particular stretch of coast—a port off the beaten track, conditions peculiar to a certain area, a pleasant weekend cruise, anchorages and so on." Query with ms.

Photos: State availability of photos. "We have a need for good photographs, taken from the water, of ports, inlets and points of interest." Reviews b&w prints. Payment varies. Guidelines on request with SASE.

Tips: "Keep the query simple and friendly. Include a short bio and boating experience. We prefer to see manuscript sample attached. No personal experiences, i.e., we need information, not reminiscences. We publish very few feature articles."

‡**WOODENBOAT MAGAZINE**, The Magazine for Wooden Boat Owners, Builders, and Designers, WoodenBoat Publications, Inc., Box 78, Brooklin ME 04616. (207)359-4651. Editor: Jon Wilson. Executive Editor: Peter H. Spectre. Editor: Jennifer Buckley. 60% freelance written. Bimonthly magazine for wooden boat owners, builders, and designers. "We are devoted exclusively to the design, building, care, preservation, and use of wooden boats, both commercial and pleasure, old and new, sail and power. We work to convey quality, integrity, and involvement in the creation and care of these craft, to entertain, to inform, to inspire, and to provide our varied readers with access to individuals who are deeply experienced in the world of wooden boats." Circ. 100,000. Pays on publication. Publishes ms an average of 1 year after acceptance. Byline given. Offers variable kill fee. Buys first North American serial rights. Submit seasonal/holiday material 3 months in advance. Simultaneous queries and submissions, (with notification) and photocopied and previously published submissions OK. Computer printout submissions acceptable. SASE. Reports in 3 weeks on queries; 4 weeks on mss. Sample copy $3.50; free writer's guidelines, SAE appreciated.

Nonfiction: Technical (repair, restoration, maintenance, use, design and building wooden boats). No poetry, fiction. Buys 100 mss/year. Query with published clips. Length: 1,500-5,000 words. Pays $6/column inch. Sometimes pays expenses of writers on assignment

Photos: Send photos with query. Negatives must be available. Pays $15-75 for b&w; $25-250 for color. Identification of subjects required. Buys one-time rights.

Columns/Departments: On the Waterfront pays for *information* on wooden boat-related events, projects, boatshop activities, etc. Buys 25/year. "We use the same columnists for each issue." Send complete information. Length: 250-1,000 words. Pays $5-50 for information.

Tips: "We appreciate a detailed, articulate query letter, accompanied by photos, that will give us a clear idea of what the author is proposing. We appreciate samples of previously published work. It is important for a prospective author to become familiar with our magazine first. It is extremely rare for us to make an assignment with a writer with whom we have not worked before. Most work is submitted on speculation. The most common failure is not exploring the subject material in enough depth."

YACHT RACING & CRUISING MAGAZINE, North American Publishing Co., 23 Leroy Ave., Box 1700, Darien CT 06820. Editor: John Burnham. 66% freelance written. Magazine published 12 times/year; 120 pages. Circ. 50,000. Pays on publication. Publishes ms an average of 4 months after acceptance. Buys first North American serial rights. Byline given. Computer printout submissions acceptable; prefers letter-quality to dot-matrix. SASE. Reports in 2 months. Sample copy $2.50.
Nonfiction: How-to for performance racing/cruising sailors, personal experience, photo feature, profile, regatta reports, and travel. No travelogs. Buys 5-10 unsolicited mss/year. Query. Length: 1,000-2,500 words. Pays $150 per equivalent of one magazine page.
Tips: "Send query with outline and include your experience. The writer may have a better chance of breaking in at our publication with short articles and fillers such as regatta news reports from his or her own area."

YACHTING, C B S Magazine Div.; Yachting offices, 5 River Rd., Box 1200, Cos Cob CT 06807. Executive Editor: Marcia Wiley. For yachtsmen interested in powerboats and sailboats. Monthly. Circ. 150,000. Buys first North American serial rights. SASE.
Nonfiction: Nuts-and-bolts articles on all phases of yachting; good technical pieces on engines, electronics, and sailing gear. Buys 50-100 unsolicited mss/year. Length: 2,500 words maximum. Article should be accompanied by 6-8 or more color transparencies.
Photos: Pays $50 for b&w photos, "more for color when used." Will accept a story without photos, if story is outstanding. See magazine for style, content.

Bowling

BOWLERS JOURNAL, 875 N. Michigan, Chicago IL 60611. (312)266-7171. Editor-in-Chief: Mort Luby. Managing Editor: Jim Dressel. 30% freelance written. Emphasizes bowling. Monthly magazine; 100 pages. Circ. 19,000. Pays on acceptance. Buys all rights. Phone queries OK. Submit seasonal/holiday material 3 months in advance of issue date. Photocopied submissions OK. SASE. Reports in 6 weeks. Sample copy $2.
Nonfiction: General interest (stories on top pros); historical (stories of old-time bowlers or bowling alleys); interview (top pros, men and women); and profile (top pros). "We publish some controversial matter, seek out outspoken personalities. We reject material that is too general; that is, not written for high average bowlers and bowling proprietors who already know basics of playing the game and basics of operating a bowling alley." Buys 5-6 unsolicited mss/year. Query. Length: 1,200-3,500 words. Pays $75-175.
Photos: State availability of photos with query. Pays $5-15 for 8x10 b&w prints; and $15-25 for 35mm or 2¼x2¼ color transparencies. Buys one-time rights.

BOWLING, 5301 S. 76th St., Greendale WI 53129. (414)421-6400, ext. 230. Editor: Rory Gillespie. 15% freelance written. Official publication of the American Bowling Congress. Monthly. Pays on acceptance. Publishes ms an average of 2 months after acceptance. Rights purchased vary with author and material; usually buys all rights. Reports in 1 month. Computer printout submissions acceptable; prefers letter-quality to dot-matrix. Byline given.
Nonfiction: "This is a specialized field and the average writer attempting the subject of bowling should be well-informed. However, anyone is free to submit material for approval." Wants articles about unusual ABC sanctioned leagues and tournaments, personalities, etc., featuring male bowlers. Nostalgia articles also considered. No first-person articles or material on history of bowling. Length: 500-1,200 words. Pays $25-150 per article. No poems.
Photos: Pays $10-15/photo.
Tips: "Submit feature material on bowlers, generally amateurs competing in local leagues, or special events involving the game of bowling. Should have connection with ABC membership. Queries should be as detailed as possible so that we may get a clear idea of what the proposed story would be all about. It saves us time and the writer time. Samples of previously published material in the bowling or general sports field would help. Once we find a talented writer in a given area, we're likely to go back to him in the future. We're looking for good writers who can handle assignments professionally and promptly." No articles on professionals.

THE WOMAN BOWLER, 5301 S. 76th St., Greendale WI 53129. (414)421-9000. Editor: Paula McMartin. Monthly (except for combined July/August) magazine; 64 pages. Circ. 155,000. Emphasizes bowling for women bowlers, ages 8-90. Buys all rights. Pays on acceptance. Byline given "except on occasion, when freelance article is used as part of a regular magazine department. When this occurs, it is discussed first with

the author." Submit seasonal/holiday material 2 months in advance. Photocopied and previously published submissions OK. SASE. Reports in 1 month. Free sample copy and writer's guidelines.
Nonfiction: Historical (about bowling and of national significance); interview; profile; and spot news. Buys 25 mss/year. Query. Length: 1,500 words maximum (unless by special assignment). Pays $25-100.
Photos: Purchased with accompanying ms. Identification required. Query. Pays $5-10 for b&w glossy prints. Model release required.

‡**YABA WORLD**, 5301 S. 76th St., Greendale WI 53129. (414)421-4700. Official publication of Young American Bowling Alliance. Editor: Paul Bertling. For boys and girls ages 21 and under. 10% freelance written. Monthly, November through April. Circ. 80,000. Pays on publication. Publishes ms an average of 2 months after acceptance. Buys all rights. Byline given "except if necessary to do extensive rewriting." Reports in 3 weeks. Query. No computer printout or disk submissions. SASE.
Nonfiction and Photos: Subject matter of articles must be based on tenpin bowling and activities connected with Young American Bowling Alliance only. Audience includes youngsters down to 6 years of age, but material should feature the teenage group. "The magazine is designed for and about youth bowlers. We found they are more interested in fillers rather than full-length features." Buys 3-5 unsolicited mss/year. Length: 500-800 words. Accompanying photos or art preferred. Pays $30-100/article. Photos should be 8x10 b&w glossy prints related to subject matter. Pays $5 minimum.
Tips: "We are primarily looking for feature stories on a specific person or activity. The most frequent mistake made by writers is that stories are about bowling in general. We prefer stories about youth bowlers, specifically our members (Young American Bowling Alliance). Stories about a specific person generally should center around the outstanding bowling achievements of that person in an YABA sanctioned league or tournament. Articles on special leagues for high average bowlers, physically or mentally handicapped bowlers, etc. should focus on the unique quality of the league. *YABA World* also carries articles on YABA sanctioned tournaments, but these should be more than just a list of the winners and their scores. Again, the unique feature of the tournament should be emphasized."

Football

FOOTBALL FORECAST, Baltimore Bulletin, 25 Walker Ave., Baltimore MD 21208. (301)653-3690. Editor: Rick Snider. 75% freelance written. Weekly seasonal sports tabloid covering professional and college football. Circ. 30,000 (seasonal). Pays on publication. Publishes ms an average of 1 month after acceptance. Byline given. Not copyrighted. Buys first and second and second serial (reprint) rights; makes work-for-hire assignments. Submit seasonal/holiday material 1 month in advance. Photocopied and previously published submissions OK. Computer printout submissions acceptable; no dot-matrix. SASE. Reports in 1 month. Free sample copy and writer's guidelines.
Nonfiction: Interview/profile (on coaches, players). "Our audience likes backstage life of football." Buys 10 mss/year. Query. Length: 500-2,000 words. Pays $25-100.
Photos: State availability of photos. Needs "action, backstage, artsy" photos. Pays $10-50 for 5x7 b&w prints. Captions and identification of subjects required. Buys reprint rights.
Columns/Departments: Opinion. Buys 5 mss/year. Query. Length: 1,000-2,000 words. Pays $50-100.
Fiction: Sports. Buys 5 mss/year. Query. Length: 750-1,500 words. Pays $50-100.
Poetry: Must pertain to person, event of big-time sports. Buys 5 poems/year. Submit maximum 5 poems. Length: 20-40 lines. Pays $20-40.
Tips: "We're only interested in big-time football."

‡**FOOTBALL NEWS**, 17820 E. Warren, Detroit MI 48224. Publisher: Roger Stanton. 10% freelance written. For avid grid fans. Weekly tabloid published during football season. 20 issues. Circ. 100,000. Not copyrighted. Pays 50% kill fee. Byline given. Buys 12-15 mss a year. Pays on publication. Reports in 1 month. Query first. No computer printout or disk submissions. SASE. Will send sample copy to writer for $1.
Nonfiction: Articles on players, officials, coaches, past and present, with fresh approach. Highly informative, concise, positive approach. Interested in profiles of former punt, pass and kick players who have made the pros. Interview, profile, historical, think articles, and exposes. "USFL league material possible. More background stories in general. Shorter pieces seem more important." No material for general audiences. Length: 800-1,000 words. Pays $50-100/ms.
Tips: "Include information about yourself that qualifies you to do a particular story."

THE JOHNNY UNITAS HUDDLE, Baltimore Bulletin, 25 Walker Ave., Baltimore MD 21208. (301)653-3690. Editor: Rick Snider. 75% freelance written. Weekly seasonal sports tabloid covering professional and college football. Circ. 30,000 (seasonal). Pays on publication. Publishes ms an average of 1 month after acceptance. Byline given. Not copyrighted. Buys first serial rights and second serial (reprint) rights; makes work-for-hire assignments. Submit seasonal/holiday material 1 month in advance. Photocopied and previously published submissions OK. Computer printout submissions acceptable; no dot-matrix. SASE. Reports in 1 month. Free sample copy and writer's guidelines.

Nonfiction: Sports. "Our audience is interested in behind-the-scenes sports look." Buys 10 mss/year. Query. Length: 500-2,000 words. Pays $25-100.

Photos: State availability of photos. Needs "action, artsy, backstage" photos. Pays $10-50 for 5x7 b&w prints. Captions and identification of subjects required. Buys reprint rights.

Columns/Departments: Opinion. Buys 5 mss/year. Query. Length: 500-2,000 words. Pays $25-100.

Fiction: Sports. Buys 5 mss/year. Query. Length: 500-2,000 words. Pays $50-100.

Poetry: Must pertain to person, event of big-time sports. Buys 5 poems/year. Submit maximum 5 poems. Length: 20-40 lines. Pays $20-40.

Tips: "Write tight but descriptive material."

Gambling

POKER PLAYER, Gambling Times Inc., 1018 N. Cole Ave., Hollywood CA 90038. (213)466-5261. Managing Editor: Phil Hevener. 70% freelance written. Biweekly tabloid covering poker games. (This is the only poker publication in the U.S.) Circ. 25,000. Pays on acceptance. Publishes ms an average of 1 month after acceptance. Byline given. Buys all rights. Electronic submissions OK on DOS PLUS - TRS 80 Bell 103 or 212 Protocol for modem, but requires hard copy also. Computer printout submissions acceptable; no dot-matrix. SASE. Reports in 1 month. Sample copy $1; free writer's guidelines.

Nonfiction: Book excerpts; how-to; humor; interview/profile; personal experience; photo feature; and technical (poker strategy). All articles must be poker related. Query. Length: 150-2,000 words. Pays $50 maximum.

Photos: State availability of photos. Reviews b&w prints.

Tips: "A solid, informative and well-written piece will be accepted regardless of length. Writers tend to think they are writing for a bunch of yahoos. Our readers know poker and want solid information. Vernacular is fine, but it can't be used to hide a lack of substance."

MIKE WARREN'S BETTING SPORTS, Baltimore Bulletin, 25 Walker Ave., Baltimore MD 21208. (301)653-3690. Editor: Rick Snider. 50% freelance written. Bimonthly tabloid covering professional sports. "We reach a public that likes to read about the big sports, and we have a gambling readership that likes issues related to pro sports." Circ. 20,000 (weekly). Pays on publication. Publishes ms an average of 1 month after acceptance. Byline given. Not copyrighted. Buys first serial rights and second serial (reprint) rights; makes work-for-hire assignments. Submit seasonal/holiday material 1 month in advance. Simultaneous queries and previously published submissions OK. Computer printout submissions acceptable; no dot-matrix. Reports in 1 month. Free sample copy and writer's guidelines.

Nonfiction: Book excerpts (sports books); expose (sports, drugs, gambling); and interview/profile (on pro players and coaches). Special issue; Football Annual (July) with features on pro and college football. Buys variable number of mss/year. Query. Length: 500-2,000 words. Pays $25-125.

Photos: State availability of photos. Pays $10-50 for 5x7 b&w prints. Captions and identification of subjects required.

Columns/Departments: College and Pro Football, Basketball, and Gambling. Buys 10 mss/year. Query. Length: 500-2,000 words. Pays $50-100.

Fiction: Sports. Buys variable number of mss/year. Query. Length: 500-1,000 words. Pays $25-100.

Poetry: Poems on sports figures and events. Buys very few poems/year. Submit maximum 5 poems. Length: 20-40 lines. Pays $20-40.

Tips: "Be natural and get to the point for news, write descriptively for features. Don't get hung up by the word gambling. Our readers like to read about sports too."

General Interest

CITY SPORTS MAGAZINE, 118 King St, Box 3693, San Francisco CA 94119. Editor: Maggie Cloherty in northern California, and 1120 Princeton Dr., Marina del Rey CA 90291. Editor: Will Balliet. 80% freelance written. Monthly controlled circulation tabloid covering participant sports for active sports participants. Circ. in California 195,000. Two editions published monthly—one covering sports in northern California and the other for southern California's participant sportsmarket. "For the most part, we use separate writers for each magazine." Pays on publication. Publishes ms an average of 2 months after acceptance. Byline and brief bio given. Pays negotiable kill fee. Buys one-time rights. Submit seasonal/holiday material 3 months in advance. Simultaneous queries OK; previously published submissions ("from outside readership area") OK. Computer printout submissions acceptable. SASE. Reports in 1 month on queries. Sample copy $2.

Nonfiction: Interview/profile (of athletes); travel; and instructional and service pieces on sports. Special issues include: April, Tennis; May, Running; June, Outdoors and Biking; July, Water Sports; November, Skiing; December, Cross Country Skiing and Indoor Sports. Buys 60 mss/year. Query with clips of published work. Length: 1,800-2,800 words. Pays $150-400.

Photos: Pays $50-300 for 35mm color; $25-35 for b&w 8x10 glossy prints. Model release and identification of subjects required.

‡**FLORIDA SPORTS!**, Plaeco Publishing, 104 Cardy St., Tampa FL 33606. (813)254-4216. Editor: Bill Chastain. 80% freelance written. Monthly magazine covering sports in the state of Florida for audience 18-45 years old interested in Florida sports and sports personalities. Estab. 1984. Circ. 10,000. Pays on publication. Publishes ms an average of 2 months after acceptance. Byline given. Buys first North American serial rights. Submit seasonal/holiday material 2 months in advance. Simultaneous queries, and simultaneous, photocopied, and previously published submissions OK. Computer printout submissions acceptable. Reports in 2 weeks. SASE. Sample copy for $1.50 and 9x12 SAE.

Nonfiction: Book excerpts (sports related); expose (if slanted toward Florida sports); interview/profile (related to people from Florida or playing sports in Florida); new product (sports medicine, equipment, etc.); personal experience (limited); and photo feature (something unique that pertains to Florida sports). Buys 60 mss/year. Query with published clips. Length: 750-1,500 words. Pays $25-45.

Photos: Send photos with query or ms. Pays $5 minimum for 5x7 or 8x10 b&w prints. Captions and identification of subjects required. Buys one-time rights.

Tips: "We are looking for full coverage of the state of Florida. A freelancer can best break in by sending us a query letter or a specific idea. If the writer wants to take the time, however, he/she may submit a completed manuscript."

‡**NEW YORK SPORTS**, New York Sports Inc., 812 Carroll St., Brooklyn NY 11215. (718)622-3547. Editor: Stephen Hanks. 100% freelance written. Bimonthly magazine covering major spectator sports in the New York metropolitan area "for sophisticated fans of spectator sports who are interested in in-depth, quality writing about sports figures." Circ. 50,000. Pays on publication. Publishes ms an average of 2 months after acceptance. Byline given. Offers variable kill fee. Buys first North American serial rights. Submit seasonal/holiday material 2 months in advance. Simultaneous queries OK. Computer printout submissions acceptable; no dot-matrix. SASE. Reports in 2 months on queries; 3 weeks on mss. Free sample copy.

Nonfiction: Book excerpts (has to deal with past or present New York sports athletes or teams). "No stories on New York sports subjects that were not assigned by our or another magazine." Buys 40-50 mss/year. Query with published clips. Length: 500-3,000 words. Pays $75-600. Sometimes pays the expenses of writers on assignment.

Columns/Departments: Who's Better? (comparison of two New York athletes or New York out of town athlete in same sport); Clinic Time (science of sport article with emphasis on New York athlete or team); Passionate Fan (first-person account of writer's favorite New York sports hero or team). Buys 60-80 mss/year. Query with published clips. Length: 250-1,500 words. Pays $75-300.

Tips: "Unless a freelancer has an established reputation in magazine writing, it would be difficult for us to use writers outside the New York metropolitan area, except for off-season assignments. Writers must have written for established magazines and have experience in sports magazine writing. Queries should be detailed. We prefer one or two long query letters rather than an outline of five ideas in one letter."

OUTDOOR CANADA MAGAZINE, 953A Eglinton Ave. E., Toronto, Ontario M4G 4B5 Canada. (416)429-5550. Editor-in-Chief: Sheila Kaighin. 50% freelance written. Emphasizes noncompetitive outdoor recreation in Canada *only*. Published 8 times/year; magazine; 72-120 pages. Circ. 130,000. Pays on publication. Publishes ms an average of 3 months after acceptance. Buys first rights. Submit seasonal/holiday material 5-6 months in advance of issue date. Byline given. Originals only. Computer printout submissions acceptable; no dot-matrix. *SASE or IRCs or material not returned.* Reports in 1 month. Sample copy $1.50; writer's guidelines 50¢; mention *Writer's Market* in request.

Nonfiction: Expose (only as it pertains to the outdoors, e.g. wildlife management); and how-to (in-depth, thorough pieces on how to select equipment for various subjects, or improve techniques only as they relate to outdoor subjects covered). Buys 35-40 mss/year. Submit complete ms. Length: 1,000-5,000 words. Pays $100-500.

Photos: Submit photo material with accompanying ms. Pays $10-45 for 8x10 b&w glossy prints and $20-175 for 35mm color transparencies; $250/cover. Captions preferred. Buys all rights. Model release required.

Fillers: Outdoor tips. Buys 20/year. Length: 350-500 words. Pays $25-75.

REFEREE, Referee Enterprises, Inc., Box 161, Franksville WI 53126. (414)632-8855. Editor: Tom Hammill. For well-educated, mostly 26- to 50-year-old male sports officials. 40% freelance written. Monthly magazine. Circ. 42,000. Pays on acceptance of completed manuscript. Publishes ms an average of 4 months after acceptance. Rights purchased varies. Submit seasonal/holiday material 6 months in advance. Photocopied and previously published submissions OK. Computer printout submissions acceptable. SASE. Reports in 2 weeks. Free sample copy.

Nonfiction: How-to, informational, humor, interview, profile, personal experience, photo feature and technical. Buys 54 mss/year. Query. Length: 700-2,500 words. Pays 4-10¢/word. "No general sports articles." Recent article example: "High school football official who was denied payment of a same-contract fee when the event was canceled due to a teachers' strike. The official fought all the way to his state association and ultimately was paid." (April 1985)

Photos: Purchased with or without accompanying ms or on assignment. Captions preferred. Send contact sheet, prints, negatives or transparencies. Pays $15-25 for each b&w used; $25-40 for each color used; $75-100 for color cover. Sometimes pays the expenses of writers on assignment.

Columns/Departments: Arena (bios); Law (legal aspects); Take Care (fitness, medical). Buys 24 mss/year. Query. Length: 200-800 words. Pays 4¢/word up to $100 maximum for Law and Take Care. Arena pays about $15 each, regardless of length.

Fillers: Jokes, gags, anecdotes, puzzles and referee shorts. Query. Length: 50-200 words. Pays 4¢/word in some cases; others offer only author credit lines.

Tips: "Queries with a specific idea appeal most to readers. Generally, we are looking more for feature writers, as we usually do our own shorter/filler-type material. It is helpful to obtain suitable photos to augment a story. Don't send fluff—we need hard-hitting, incisive material tailored just for our audience. Anything smacking of public relations is a no sale. Don't gloss over the material too lightly or fail to go in-depth looking for a quick sale (taking the avenue of least resistance)."

SPORT, Sports Media Corp., 119 W. 40th St., New York NY 10018. (212)869-4700. Senior Editor: Peter Griffin. Managing Editor: Neil Cohen. 95% freelance written. Monthly magazine covering primarily college and pro sports—baseball, football, basketball, hockey, boxing, tennis, others—for sports fans. Circ. 1.25 million. Pays on acceptance. Publishes ms an average of 2 months after acceptance. Byline given. Offers 25% kill fee. Buys first North American serial rights. Submit seasonal/holiday material 3 months in advance. SASE. Reports in 2 weeks.

Nonfiction: General interest; interview (sport interview in Q&A format); and investigative reports on the world of sports. Buys 75 mss/year. Query with published clips. No telephone queries. Length: 2,500-3,000 words. Pays $1,000 minimum.

Columns/Departments: Sport Talk (briefs on news or offbeat aspects of sport). Buys 48 mss/year. Length: 250-500 words. Pays $100-150, depending on length and type of piece. Contact Barry Shapiro, associate editor on Columns/Department.

Tips: "Writers should read the magazine to keep up with the broadening subjects we're dealing with."

SPORTING NEWS, 1212 N. Lindbergh Blvd., St. Louis MO 63132. "We do not actively solicit freelance material."

SPORTS ILLUSTRATED, Time & Life Bldg., Rockefeller Center, New York NY 10020. Articles Editor: William Johnson. Weekly. Primarily staff-written, with small but steady amount of outside material. Pays on acceptance. Buys all rights or first North American serial rights. Byline given, except for Scorecard department. Computer printout submissions acceptable. SASE. Reports in 1 month.

Nonfiction: "Material falls into two general categories: regional (text that runs in editorial space accompanying regional advertising pages) and national text. Runs a great deal of regional advertising and, as a result, considerable text in that section of the magazine. Regional text does not have a geographical connotation; it can be any sort of short feature: Shopwalk, Footloose, Viewpoint, Sideline, On Deck, Spotlight, Sports Rx, Replay, Update, and Stats (400 to 1,500 words); Yesterday, Nostalgia, Reminiscence, Perspective, First Person, On the Scene (1,200-2,000 words), but it must deal with some aspect of sports. National text (1,500-6,000 words) also must have a clear sporting connection; should be personality, personal reminiscence, knowing look into a significant aspect of a sporting subject, but national text should be written for broad appeal, so that readers without special knowledge will appreciate the piece." No how-to or instructional material. Pays $500-1,000 for regional pieces, $1,500 and up for national text. Smaller payments are made for material used in special sections or departments. No fiction or poetry.

Photos: "Do not submit photos or artwork until story is purchased."

Tips: "Regional text is the best section for a newcomer. National text is difficult as most of the national sections are staff-written."

SPORTS PARADE, Meridian Publishing Co., Inc., Box 10010, Odgen UT 84409. Editor: Wayne DeWald. A monthly general interest sports magazine distributed by business and professional firms to employees, customers, clients, etc. Readers are predominantly upscale, mainstream, family oriented. Pays on acceptance. Byline given. Buys first North American serial rights. Submit seasonal/holiday material 6 months in advance. SASE. Reports in 2 weeks. Sample copy $1; writer's guidelines for SAE and 1 first class stamp.

Nonfiction: General interest, humor, and interview/profile. "Emphasis is about 2-to-1 in favor of spectator

sports over participant." Buys 40-50 mss/year. Query. Length: 1,200-1,500 words. Pays 15¢/word.
Photos: State availability of photos or send with query or ms. Pays $35 for 35mm color transparencies. Identification of subjects required. Buys one-time rights.

WOMEN'S SPORTS AND FITNESS MAGAZINE, (formerly *Women's Sports Magazine*), Women's Sports Publications, Inc., 310 Town & Country Village, Palo Alto CA 94301. Editor: Martha Nelson. Query Editor: Martha Nelson. 80% freelance written. Monthly magazine; 72 pages. Emphasizes women's sports, fitness and health. Circ. 125,000. Pays on publication. Publishes ms an average of 3 months after acceptance. Generally buys all rights. Submit seasonal/holiday material 3 months in advance. Computer printout submissions acceptable; no dot-matrix. SASE. Reports in 1 month on queries; 6 weeks mss. Sample copy $2; writer's guidelines for SASE.
Nonfiction: Profile, service piece, interview, how-to, historic, personal experience, personal opinion, travel, new product and reviews. "All articles should pertain to women's sports and fitness or health. All must be of national interest." Buys 5 mss/issue. Length: 2,500-3,000 words. Pays $300-600 for features. Sometimes pays the expenses of writers on assignment.
Photos: State availability of photos. Pays about $25-50 for b&w prints; about $100 for 35mm color transparencies. Buys one-time rights.
Columns/Departments: Buys 6-8/issue. Query with published clips. Length: 500-1,500 words. Pays $50 minimum.
Fillers: Health and fitness information. Length: 100-250 words.
Tips: "We prefer queries to manuscripts. The best query letters often start with a first paragraph that could be the first paragraph of the article the writer wants to do. Queries should indicate that the writer has done the preliminary research for the article and has an 'angle' or something to give the article personality. Published clips help too. Freelancers can best break into *Women's Sports and Fitness* by submitting short items for the Sports Pages and Sportif sections or opinion pieces for End Zone. We are not looking for profiles of athletes that lack depth or a real understanding of the athlete; we are looking for items of concern to active women—and we interpret that broadly—from the water she drinks to women to watch or remember, from adventure/travel to event coverage to home exercise equipment."

Golf

AMATEUR GOLF REGISTER, Amateur Golf Association of America, Inc., 2843 Pembroke Rd., Hollywood FL 33024. Managing Editor: Bernard Block. 30% freelance written. A monthly magazine for amateur golfers of all ages. Circ. 25,000 +. Pays on acceptance. Publishes ms an average of 1 month after acceptance. Byline given. Buys all rights. Submit seasonal/holiday material 2 months in advance. Photocopied submissions OK. Computer printout submissions acceptable; no dot-matrix.
Nonfiction: Book excerpts, how-to, interview/profile, new product; photo feature, travel. Topics should be golf-related. Buys variable number of mss/year. Send complete ms. Length: 200-500 words. Pays $15-50.
Photos: State availability of photos. Pays variable rate for 8x10 prints. Captions, model release, and identification of subjects required. Buys all rights.
Columns/Departments: Buys variable number/year. Query. Length: 200-500 words. Pays $15-50.
Fillers: Jokes, short humor, newsbreaks. Length: 50-300 words. Pays $3-25.

GOLF DIGEST, 495 Westport Ave., Norwalk CT 06856. (203)847-5811. Executive Editor: Jerry Tarde. 30% freelance written. Emphasizes golfing. Monthly magazine; 160 pages. Circ. 1.2 million. Pays on acceptance. Publishes ms an average of 6 weeks after acceptance. Buys all rights. Byline given. Submit seasonal/holiday material 4 months in advance. Photocopied submissions OK. Computer printout submissions acceptable; prefers letter-quality to dot-matrix. SASE. Reports in 4-6 weeks.
Nonfiction: Expose, how-to, informational, historical, humor, inspirational, interview, nostalgia, opinion,

 Lost assignments: refusing to rewrite; asking 'Why do I have to write a catchy lead?'; didn't do extra; whining; **Got assignments:** called with a timely idea that fit; showed willingness to work until the piece was right; went extra mile; took a short department and convinced me it had to be a feature by virtue of how well done it was.

profile, travel, new product, personal experience, photo feature and technical; "all on playing and otherwise enjoying the game of golf." Recent article example: "USGA Declares Open Season on Sandbaggers" (May 1984). Query. Length: 1,000-2,500 words. Pays 20¢/edited word minimum.
Photos: Nick DiDio, art director. Purchased without accompanying ms. Pays $10-150 for 5x7 or 8x10 b&w prints; $25-300/35mm color transparency. Model release required.
Poetry: Lois Hains, assistant editor. Light verse. Buys 1-2/issue. Length: 4-8 lines. Pays $25.
Fillers: Lois Hains, assistant editor. Jokes, gags, anecdotes, and cut lines for cartoons. Buys 1-2/issue. Length: 2-6 lines. Pays $10-25.

GOLF MAGAZINE, Times Mirror Magazines, Inc., 380 Madison Ave., New York NY 10017. (212)687-3000. Editor: George Peper. 20% freelance written. Monthly magazine; 150 pages. Emphasizes golf for males, ages 15-80, college-educated, professionals. Circ. 800,000. Pays on acceptance. Publishes ms an average of 4 months after acceptance. Byline given. Buys all rights. Submit seasonal/holiday material 4 months in advance. Photocopied submissions OK. Dot-matrix submissions acceptable if double-spaced. SASE. Reports in 4 weeks. Send mss to specific section editors—feature, instruction, Golf Reports, etc. General mss direct to Desmond Tolhurst, SA Editor. Sample copy $2.
Nonfiction: How-to (improve game, instructional tips); informational (news in golf); humor; profile (people in golf); travel (golf courses, resorts); new product (golf equipment, apparel, teaching aids); and photo feature (great moments in golf; must be special. Most photography on assignment only). Buys 4-6 unsolicited mss/year. Query. Length: 1,200-2,500 words. Pays $500-750. Sometimes pays expenses of writers on assignment.
Photos: Purchased with accompanying ms or on assignment. Captions required. Query. Pays $50 for 8½x11 glossy prints (with contact sheet and negatives); $75 minimum for 3x5 color prints. Total purchase price for ms includes payment for photos. Captions and model release required.
Columns/Departments: Golf Reports (interesting golf events, feats, etc.). Buys 5-10 mss/year. Query. Length: 250 words maximum. Pays $75. Open to suggestions for new columns/departments.
Fiction: Humorous and mystery. Must be golf-related. Buys 1-2 mss/year. Query. Length: 1,200-2,000 words. Pays $500-750.
Fillers: Short humor. Length: 20-35 words. Pays $25.
Tips: "Best chance is to aim for a light piece which is not too long and is focused on a personality. Anything very technical that would require a consummate knowledge of golf, we would rather assign ourselves. But if you are successful with something light and not too long, we might use you for something heavier later. We are looking for detailed knowledge of golf. Shorter items are a good test of knowledge. Probably the best way to break in would be by our Golf Reports section in which we run short items on interesting golf feats, events and so forth. If you send us something like that, about an important event in your area, it is an easy way for us to get acquainted. The most frequent mistake made by writers in completing an article is not having enough information on golf specifics. Also, they are too likely to be a repeat of something we've already done."

GULF COAST GOLFER, Gulf Coast Golfer, Inc., 9182 Old Katy Rd., Houston TX 77055. (713)464-0308. Editor: Bobby Gray. 60% freelance written. Monthly magazine covering results of major area competition, data on upcoming tournaments, reports of new and improved golf courses, and how-to tips for active, competitive golfers in Texas Gulf Coast area. Circ. 30,000. Pays on publication. Publishes ms an average of 2 weeks after acceptance. Byline given. Buys one-time rights. Submit seasonal/holiday material 3 months in advance. Computer printout submissions acceptable; prefers letter-quality to dot-matrix. SASE. Reports in 3 weeks. Sample copy for 9x12 SAE; free writer's guidelines.
Nonfiction: How-to and personal experience golf articles. No routine coverage. Query. Length: by arrangement. Pays negotiable rates.
Tips: Especially wants articles on how-to subjects about golf in Gulf Coast area.

THE LINKS LETTER, The Newsletter for Golfers Who Travel, The Bartlett Group, Inc., 1483 Fairview Road NE, Atlanta GA 30306. Editor: James Y. Bartlett. 5% freelance written. Monthly newsletter covering golf travel, golf resorts and international travel with news of interest to traveling golfers: where to stay, where to play, what else to do and how much. Circ. 3,000. Pays on publication. Publishes ms an average of 2 months after acceptance. Byline given. Buys first North American serial rights. Submit seasonal/holiday material 3-4 months in advance. Computer printout submissions acceptable. SASE. Reports in 3 weeks on queries. Sample copy for $7.50, 5x7 SAE and 1 first class stamp.
Nonfiction: Travel (not just puffs). Annual issues include Florida, Scotland, Fall Foliage and Spring Azalea resorts. "We don't run any flowery travel pieces. Our readers want down and dirty, hard information, recommendations, places to visit and places to avoid." Buys 3-5 mss/year. Query. Length: 500 words maximum. Pays $25 maximum.
Tips: "Read the newsletter for style and content, then query with an idea for someplace we haven't been (and we've been almost everywhere)."

SCORE, Canada's Golf Magazine, Canadian Controlled Media Communications, 287 MacPherson Ave., Toronto, Ontario M4V 1A4 Canada. (416)961-5141. Managing Editor: Lisa A. Leighton. 85% freelance written. Magazine published 8 times/year covering golf. *"Score* magazine provides seasonal coverage of the Canadian golf scene, professional, amateur, senior and junior golf for men and women golfers in Canada, the U.S. and Europe through profiles, history, editorial comment, instruction, photo features, and regular editorial contributions from the Royal Canadian Golf Association, the Canadian Ladies' Golf Association, and the Canadian Professional Golfers' Association (the three national governing bodies of the game in Canada)." Circ. over 170,000. Pays on publication. Publishes ms an average of 3 months after acceptance. Byline given. Offers negotiable kill fee although kill fees are rarely required. Buys all rights and second serial (reprint) rights if applicable. Submit seasonal/holiday material 8 months in advance. Computer printout submissions acceptable; no dot-matrix. SASE or SAE with IRCs. Reports within 1 month. Sample copy for $2 (Canadian), 9x12 SAE and IRCs; writer's guidelines for business size SAE and IRC.

Nonfiction: Book excerpts (golf); historical/nostalgic (golf and golf characters); humor (golf); interview/profile (prominent golf professionals); photo feature (golf); and travel (golf destinations only). The yearly *Golf Annual* (publication issue date April), includes tournament results from Canada, the U.S., Europe, Asia, Australia, etc., history, profile, and regular features. "No personal experience, technical, opinion or general-interest material. Most articles are by assignment only." Buys 25-30 mss/year. Query with published clips or send complete ms. Length: 700-3,500 words. Pays $140-600.

Photos: Send photos with query or ms. Pays $50-100 for 35mm color transparencies (positives) or $30 for 8x10 or 5x7 b&w prints. Captions, model release (if necessary), and identification of subjects required. Buys all rights.

Columns/Departments: Interview (currently prominent PGA or LPGA professional golfer); Profile (historical or current golf personalities or characters); Great Moments ("Great Moments in Canadian Golf"—description of great single moments, usually game triumphs); New Equipment (Canadian availability only); Travel (golf destinations, including "hard" information such as greens fees, hotel accommodations, etc.); Instruction (by special assignment only; usually from teaching golf professionals); The Mental Game (psychology of the game; by special assignment only); humor (golf humor); and History (golf equipment collections and collectors, development of the game, legendary figures and events). Buys 17-20 mss/year. Query with published clips or send complete ms. Length: 700-1,700 words. Pays $140-300.

Fiction: Historical (golf only) and humorous (golf only). No science fiction or adventure. Buys 1-3 mss/year. Query with published clips or send complete ms. Length: 700-1,700 words. Pays $140-300.

Poetry: Light verse and traditional. No free verse (avant-garde). Buys 2-3 poems/year. Submit maximum 5 poems. Length: 4-20 lines. Pays $10-25.

Fillers: Clippings, jokes, anecdotes, short humor and newsbreaks. Buys 5/year. Length: 50-100 words. Pays $10-25.

Tips: "Only writers with an extensive knowledge of golf and familiarity with the Canadian and/or U.S. golf scene(s) should query or submit in-depth work to *Score*. Golf-oriented humor and verse are the only exceptions to this rule. Many of our features are written by professional people who play the game for a living or work in the industry. All areas mentioned under Columns/Departments are most open to freelancers. Most of our *major* features are assignment only. These are given to regular contributors on the basis of past performances and expertise, etc. Writers wishing to break into the magazine are best to 'prove' their capabilities with shorter work to begin with. On queries and unsolicited material, frequent mistakes made by writers are usually faulty or poor presentation, showing a lack of definite direction, poor spelling, grammar and sloppy typing. On assignments, providing the writer is willing to listen to what we need and to discipline him/herself to write accurately and tightly, there shouldn't be major problems. Background research is sometimes not as thorough as we would like."

Guns

THE AMERICAN SHOTGUNNER, Box 3351, Reno NV 89505. Publisher: Bob Thruston. Monthly. Circ. 120,000. Pays on publication. Buys all rights. Submit special material (hunting) 4 months in advance. Reports on material accepted for publication in 1 month. Returns rejected material. SASE. Free sample copy and writer's guidelines.

Nonfiction: Sue Thruston, managing editor. All aspects of shotgunning—rap and skeet shooting and hunting, reloading, shooting clothing, and shooting equipment. Emphasis is on the how-to and instructional approach. "We give the sportsman actual material that will help him to improve his game, fill his limit, or build that duck blind, etc. Hunting articles are used in all issues, year-round." Buys 20-30 mss/year. Query. Length: open. Pays $75-250.

Photos: Reviews original transparencies. "We also purchase professional cover material." No additional payment for photos used with mss.

COMBAT HANDGUNS, Harris Publications 1115 Broadway, New York NY 10010. Editor: Harry Kane. 10% freelance written. Bimonthly magazine covering use of handguns in combat situations, military, police and personal defense. Readers include persons in law enforcement and the military and those interested in the uses and the history of combat firearms. Circ. 80,000. Pays on acceptance. Publishes ms an average of 6 months after acceptance. Byline given. Buys all rights unless otherwise stipulated. Submit seasonal/holiday material 4 months in advance. Simultaneous queries, and photocopied and previously published submissions OK. SASE. Reports in 2 months.
Nonfiction: Book excerpts; general interest (modifications and uses in combat situations; also gun use in every area of personal defense); how-to; profile (of gunsmith schools); opinion; personal experience ("moment of truth"); photo feature; and technical. Recent article examples: any gun test, any tactical scenario. Buys 20 unsolicited mss/year. Query. Length: 1,500-3,500 words. Pays $150-400.
Photos: B&w prints only. "What I really like is photos and plenty of good ones." State availability of photos or send photos with ms. Buys first rights.
Tips: "Potential contributor should know the magazine. They may have a better chance of breaking in at our publication with short articles and fillers. Shorter pieces are easier to fit in. *No* phone calls."

GUN DIGEST, HANDLOADER'S DIGEST, DBI Books, Inc., Suite 315, 1 Northfield Plaza, Northfield IL 60093. (312)441-7010. Editor-in-Chief: Ken Warner. 90% freelance written. Annual journal/magazine covering guns and shooting. Pays on acceptance. Publishes ms an average of 20 months after acceptance. Byline given. Buys all rights. Computer printout submissions acceptable if legible. Reports in 1 month.
Nonfiction: Buys 50 mss/issue. Query. Length: 500-5,000 words. Pays $100-600; includes photos or illustration package from author.
Photos: State availability of photos with query letter. Reviews 8x10 b&w prints. Payment for photos included in payment for ms. Captions required.
Tips: Award of $1,000 to author of best article (juried) in each issue.

‡**GUN WORLD**, 34249 Camino Capistrano, Box HH, Capistrano Beach CA 92624. Editorial Director: Jack Lewis. 50% freelance written. For ages that "range from mid-20s to mid-60s; many professional types who are interested in relaxation of hunting and shooting." Monthly. Circ. 136,000. Buys 80-100 unsolicited mss/year. Pays on acceptance. Publishes ms an average of 6 months after acceptance. Buys first rights. Byline given. Submit seasonal material 4 months in advance. Reports in 6 weeks, perhaps longer. Computer printout submissions acceptable; prefers letter-quality to dot-matrix. SASE. Copy of editorial requirements for SASE.
Nonfiction and Photos: General subject matter consists of "well-rounded articles—not by amateurs—on shooting techniques, with anecdotes; hunting stories with tips and knowledge integrated. No poems or fiction. We like broad humor in our articles, so long as it does not reflect upon firearms safety. Most arms magazines are pretty deadly and we feel shooting can be fun. Too much material aimed at pro-gun people. Most of this is staff-written and most shooters don't have to be told of their rights under the Constitution. We want articles on new development; off-track inventions, novel military uses of arms; police armament and training techniques; do-it-yourself projects in this field." Buys informational, how-to, personal experience and nostalgia articles. Pays up to $300, sometimes more. Purchases photos with mss and captions required. Wants 5x7 b&w. Sometimes pays the expenses of writers on assignment.
Tips: "The most frequent mistake made by writers in completing an article for us is surface writing with no real knowledge of the subject. To break in, offer an anecdote having to do with proposed copy."

GUNS MAGAZINE, 591 Camino de la Reina, San Diego CA 92108. (619)297-5352. Editor: J. Rakusan. 90% freelance written. Monthly magazine for firearms enthusiasts. Circ. 135,000. Pays on publication. Publishes ms an average of 6 months after acceptance. Buys all rights. Computer printout submissions acceptable; prefers letter-quality to dot-matrix. Reports in 3 weeks. Free sample copy.
Nonfiction: Test reports on new firearms; how-to on gunsmithing; reloading; round-up articles on firearms types. Historical pieces. Does not want to see anything about "John and I went hunting" or rewrites of a general nature, or controversy for the sake of controversy, without new illumination. "More short, punchy articles will be used in the next year. Payments will not be as large as for full-length features, but the quantity used will give more writers a chance to get published." Buys 100-150 mss/year. Length: 1,000-2,500 words. Pays $100-350.
Photos: Major emphasis is on good photos. No additional payment for b&w glossy prints purchased with mss. Pays $50-100 for color; 2¼x2¼ minimum.

NEW BREED, The Magazine for Bold Adventurer, New Breed Publications, Inc., 30 Amarillo Dr., Nanuet NY 10954. (914)623-8426. Editor: Harry Belil. Managing Editor: Richard Schwartzberg. 80% freelance written. Bimonthly magazine covering military adventures, new weapons, survival. For persons interested in "where the action is—hot spots on the globe where the voice of adventure calls." Circ. 60,000. Pays on publication. Publishes ms an average of 2 months after acceptance. Byline given. Buys all rights. Photocopied and previously published submissions OK, if so indicated. Computer printout submissions acceptable; no dot-matrix. Would rather have typed copy. SASE. Reports in 2 weeks on queries; 3 weeks on mss. Sample copy for $2, 9x12 SAE, and first class postage; free writer's guidelines.

Nonfiction: "Give us the best possible information on state-of-the-art field weaponry, combat practice and survival techniques for the professional soldier. Material should be slightly right-wing, pro-weapons (including handguns), somewhat hawkish in diplomacy, pro-freedom, pro-constitution, thus, libertarian and capitalist (in the real sense of the term) and consequently anti-totalitarian. Submit mss on all units of the armed forces, as well as soldiers of fortune, police officers and individuals who can be classified as 'New Breed.' " Special annual "combat guns" issue. Buys 80 mss/year. Send complete ms. Length: 3,000-4,000 words. Pays $150-250 for articles with b&w and color photos.

Tips: "The most frequent mistake made by writers in completing an article for us is not studying our publication for format, style and type of material desired. It would help sell the story if some visual material was included."

SHOTGUN SPORTS, Shotgun Sport, Inc., Box 340, Lake Havasu City AZ 86403. (602)855-0100. Editor: Frank Kodl. Managing Editor: Fredi Kodl. 90% freelance written. Monthly magazine covering the sport of shotgunning. Circ. 110,000. Pays on publication. Publishes ms an average of 8 months after acceptance. Byline given. Buys one-time rights. Submit seasonal/holiday material 3 months in advance. Computer printout submissions acceptable. SASE. Reports in 1 month. Free sample copy and writer's guidelines.

Nonfiction: Book excerpts, expose, general interest, historical/nostalgic, how-to, humor, inspirational, interview/profile, new product, opinion, personal experience, photo feature, technical and travel; "all articles must be related directly to shotgunning to include trap, skeet or hunting." Buys 50-70 mss/year. Query or send complete mss. Length: open. Pays $50-200.

Photos: State availability of photos or send photos with ms. Reviews 5x7 b&w prints. "Photos included in payment for ms." Captions required.

‡**SOUTHERN GUNS & SHOOTER**, Victory Publications, Box 104, Oradell NJ 07649. (201)385-2000. Editor: Bob Nesoff. 80% freelance written. Bimonthly magazine on firearms—handguns in particular; hunting. Gun and outdoor magazine aimed at those interested in firearms, both technically, as collectors and for target and sport shooters. Estab. 1984. Circ. 250,000. Pays on publication. Publishes ms an average of 3 months after acceptance. Byline given. Kill fee negotiable. Buys first North American serial rights. Submit seasonal/holiday material 6 months in advance. Simultaneous queries and photocopied and previously published submissions OK (if so noted). Computer printout submissions acceptable; prefers letter-quality to dot-matrix. SASE. Reports in 3 weeks on queries; 1 month on mss. Sample copy for 9x12 SAE and 6 first class stamps. Writer's guidelines for SAE and 1 first class stamp.

Nonfiction: Expose (product quality), general interest, how-to, new product, personal experience, photo feature and technical. Special issues on hunting and handguns planned. No anti-firearms, hunting, etc. Buys 40-60 mss/year. Query or send complete ms. Length: 2,000-5,000 words. Pays $100-300.

Photos: All articles *must* be accompanied by photos. Captions, model release, and identification of subjects required. Buys one-time rights.

Tips: "Our readers know the subject of firearms and so should the writer. Beginners will be given consideration but must demonstrate knowledge and ability. A good descriptive letter mss will open the door. Writers should list previous credits, if any."

Horse Racing

THE BACKSTRETCH, 19363 James Couzens Hwy., Detroit MI 48235. (313)342-6144. Editor: Ann Moss. Managing Editor: Ruth LeGrove. Quarterly magazine; 100 pages. For Thoroughbred horse trainers, owners, breeders, farm managers, track personnel, jockeys, grooms and racing fans who span the age range from very young to very old. Publication of United Thoroughbred Trainers of America, Inc. Circ. 25,000. SASE. Sample copy $2.

Nonfiction: "*Backstretch* contains mostly general information. Articles deal with biographical material on trainers, owners, jockeys, horses and their careers on and off the track, historical track articles, etc. Unless writer's material is related to Thoroughbreds and Thoroughbred racing, it should not be submitted. Articles accepted on speculation basis—payment made after material is used. If not suitable, articles are returned immediately. Articles that do not require printing by a specified date are preferred. There is no special length requirement and amount paid depends on material. It is advisable to include photos, if possible. Articles should be original copies and should state whether presented to any other magazine, or whether previously printed in any other magazine. Submit complete ms. We do not buy crossword puzzles, cartoons, newspaper clippings, fiction or poetry."

‡**THE FLORIDA HORSE**, The Florida Horse, Inc., Box 2106, Ocala FL 32678. (904)629-8082. Editor: F.J. Audette. 25% freelance written. Monthly magazine covering the Florida Thoroughbred horse industry. "We seek contemporary coverage and feature material on the Florida breeding, racing and sales scene." Circ. 12,000. Pays on publication. Publishes ms an average of 2 months after acceptance. Byline given. Buys first North American serial rights. Computer printout submissions acceptable; prefers letter-quality to dot-matrix. SASE. Reports in 2 weeks. Free sample copy.
Nonfiction: Bill Giaugue, articles editor. Articles covering horses and people of the Florida Thoroughbred industry. Buys 18-24 mss/year. Length: 1,500-3,000 words. Pays $125-200. Sometimes pays expenses of writers on assignment.
Photos: Send photos with ms. Pays $15-25 for sharp, well-composed 8x10 color prints. Captions and identification of subjects required. Buys one-time rights.
Columns/Departments: Medically Speaking (veterinarian analysis of equine problems); Legally Speaking (legal analysis of equine legal considerations); and Track Talk (news and features from racetracks—Florida angle only). Buys 24-36 mss/year. Send complete ms. Length: 800-960 words. Pays $35-50.
Tips: "We recommend that writers be at the scene of the action—racetracks, nurseries; provide clean, focused writing from the Florida angle; and submit lively, interesting material full of detail and background."

HOOF BEATS, United States Trotting Association, 750 Michigan Ave., Columbus OH 43215. (614)224-2291. Editor: Dean A. Hoffman. Managing Editor: Edward Keys. 35% freelance written. Monthly magazine covering harness racing for the participants of the sport of harness racing. "We cover all aspects of the sport—racing, breeding, selling, etc." Circ. 26,000. Pays on publication. Publishes ms an average of 3 months after acceptance. Byline given. Buys negotiable rights. Submit seasonal/holiday material 3 months in advance. Computer printout submissions acceptable. Reports in 3 weeks. Free sample copy, postpaid.
Nonfiction: General interest, historical/nostalgic, humor, inspirational, interview/profile, new product, personal experience, photo feature. Buys 15-20 mss/year. Query. Length: open. Pays $100-400. Pays the expenses of writers on assignment "with approval."
Photos: State availability of photos. Pays variable rates for 35mm transparencies and prints. Identification of subjects required. Buys one-time rights.
Fiction: Historical, humorous, interesting fiction with a harness racing theme. Buys 2-3 mss/year. Query. Length: open. Pays $100-400.

HUB RAIL, Hub Rail, Inc., Box 1831, Harrisburg PA 17105. (717)234-5099. Publisher: David M. Dolezal. Managing Editor: Peter E. Lawrence. 75% freelance written. Bimonthly magazine; 120 pages. Emphasizes harness horse racing or breeding. Circ. 7,500. Pays on publication. Publishes ms an average of 3 months after acceptance. Buys all rights. Phone queries OK. Submit seasonal/holiday material 3 months in advance. Simultaneous and photocopied submissions OK. Computer printout submissions acceptable if double-spaced; prefers letter-quality to dot-matrix. SASE. Reports in 1 month. Free sample copy and writer's guidelines.
Nonfiction: General interest, historical, humor and nostalgia. Articles should pertain to harness racing. Buys 10 mss/year. Send published clips. Length: 1,000-5,000 words. Pays $50-200. Sometimes pays expenses of writers on assignment.
Fiction: "We use short stories pertaining to harness racing." Buys 2 mss/year. Send clips of published work. Length: 2,500-7,000 words. Pays $50-200.
Tips: "We are relatively specialized ('narrow' in scope), and a writer who doesn't understand the harness racing business thoroughly shows it clearly. Know who our readers are."

SPEEDHORSE MAGAZINE, Speedhorse, Inc., Box 1000, Norman OK 73070. (405)288-2391. Editor: Margaret S. Jaffe. 60% freelance written. A monthly journal "devoted to those involved with breeding or racing quarter horses. It is *not* a general circulation horse publication." Circ. 9,000. Pays on publication. Publishes ms an average of 2 months after acceptance. Byline given. Offers negotiable kill fee. Buys negotiable rights. Simultaneous queries OK. Computer printout submissions acceptable; prefers letter-quality to dot-matrix. Reports in 1 month. Sample copy $3; free writer's guidelines.
Nonfiction: How-to (directed specifically at racing); interview/profile (of prominent horsemen); and photo feature (of racing). "Our articles address those topics which interest an experienced horseman. Articles dealing with ranch operations, racing bloodlines and race coverage are of special interest." No general interest stories. Special issues include Stallion articles (November, March); Stakes Winner Issue (April); Service Issue, articles on various services offered horsemen, i.e., transportation, trainers, travel, etc. (May); Broodmare Issue (June); Horse sales and auctions (July, August); Racing Wrap-up (September); and Thoroughbred Issue (October). Buys 3 mss/year. Query. Length: 1,000 words minimum. Pays $25-300. Sometimes pays the expenses of writers on assignment.
Photos: Andrew Golden, photo editor. State availability of photos with query or ms. Reviews b&w and color contact sheets. Pays $5-25 for b&w and color. Identification of subjects required. Buys one-time rights.
Columns/Departments: Book Review and Vet Medicine, by assignment only. Buys 1-2 mss/year. Query. Length: 1,000 words. Pays $50-75.

Fiction: Adventure (race related); historical; humorous; and western. "All fiction must appeal to racing industry." Buys 3 mss/year. Query. Length: 1,000 words minimum. Pays $25-200.

Tips: "If the writer has a good working knowledge of the horse industry and access to people involved with the quarter horse racing industry, the writer should call the editor to discuss possible stories. Very few blind articles are accepted. Most stories are assigned with much editorial direction. Most feature stories are assigned to freelance writers who have been regular contributors to *Speedhorse*. They are located in areas of the country with active quarter horse racing. Many are track publicity directors or newspaper sports writers. The most frequent mistake made by writers in completing an article for us is that they do not write for the market. They send general interest articles rather than technical articles."

SPUR, Box 85, Middleburg VA 22117. (703)687-6314. Managing Director: Kerry Phelps. 70% freelance written. Bimonthly magazine covering Thoroughbred horses and the people who are involved in the business and sport of the Thoroughbred industry. Circ. 10,000. Pays on publication. Publishes ms an average of 6 weeks after acceptance. Byline given. Buys all rights. Computer printout submissions acceptable; prefers letter-quality to dot-matrix. SASE. Reports in 2 weeks on queries; 1 month on mss. Sample copy $3.50; writer's guidelines for business size SAE and 1 first class stamp.

Nonfiction: Historical/nostalgic, Thoroughbred care, personality profile, farm, special feature, regional, photo essay, steeplechasing and polo. Buys 30 mss/year. Query with clips of published work, "or we will consider complete manuscripts." Length: 300-4,000 words. Payment negotiable.

Photos: State availability of photos. Reviews color and b&w contact sheets. Captions, model releases and identification of subjects required. Buys all rights "unless otherwise negotiated."

Columns/Departments: Query or send complete ms to Editorial Dept. Length: 100-500 words. Pays $50 and up.

Fillers: Anecdotes, short humor. Length: 50-100 words. Pays $25 and up.

Tips: "Writers must have a knowledge of horses, horse owners, breeding, training, racing, and riding—or the ability to obtain this knowledge from a subject and to turn out a good article."

THE THOROUGHBRED RECORD, Thoroughbred Publishers, Inc., Box 4240, Lexington KY 40544. (606)276-5311. Editor: Timothy T. Capps. Managing Editor: David Heckerman. 5% freelance written. Weekly magazine covering Thoroughbred racing/breeding. Circ. 13,000. Pays on publication. Publishes ms an average of 2 months after acceptance. Byline given. Buys one-time rights. Simultaneous queries and photocopied submissions OK. Computer printout submissions acceptable; no dot-matrix. SASE. Reports in 1 week on queries; 1 month on mss. Sample copy $2.

Nonfiction: Book excerpts, historical/nostalgic, humor, interview/profile, photo feature, and technical. Special issues include several regional and international editions scattered throughout the year. "Best approached by query from author. No first person articles on anything." Query with published clips or send complete ms. Length: 500-3,000 words. Pays $25 minimum; 10¢/word maximum.

Photos: Send photos with ms. Pays $25 for b&w contact sheet if published; negatives OK for submission; $50 for color contact sheet, negatives and 35mm transparencies (preferred); $150 for color cover. Identification of subjects required.

TROT, 233 Evans Ave., Toronto, Ontario M8Z 1J6 Canada. Advertising and Managing Director: Larry Simpson. Editor: Rolly Ethier. 75% freelance written. Official publication of the Canadian Trotting Association. "Quite a number of our readers derive all their income from harness racing." Circ. 20,000. Pays on acceptance. Publishes ms within average of 2 months after acceptance. Buys first North American serial rights. SAE and International Reply Coupons.

Nonfiction: "General material dealing with any aspect of harness racing or prominent figures in the sport. U.S. contributions should note that preference is given to material with a Canadian angle. Proposed story outlines invited. Length: 1,000-1,800 words. Pays $150-250.

Tips: "Many U.S. submissions do not adhere to the Canadian angle. Most of the material used is generally assigned by the editor—roughly 80 percent."

Hunting and Fishing

ALABAMA GAME & FISH, Game & Fish Publications, Inc., Box 741, Marietta GA 30061. (404)953-9222. Editor: Keith Brooks. Monthly how-to, where-to, when-to hunting and fishing magazine covering Alabama. Pays on acceptance. Byline given. Buys one-time rights. Submit seasonal material 8 months in advance. Simultaneous queries, and simultaneous and photocopied submissions OK. Computer printout submissions acceptable; no dot-matrix. SASE. Reports in 2 months. Sample copy for $2.50 and 10x12 SAE; writer's guidelines for SASE.

Nonfiction: How-to (hunting and fishing *only*); humor (on limited basis); interview/profile (of successful hunter/angler); personal experience (hunting or fishing adventure). No hiking, backpacking, camping. No fiction or poems. No "my first deer" articles. Buys 60 mss/year. Query with or without published clips. Length: 1,800-2,200 words. Pays $150.

Photos: State availability of photos. Pays $75 for full-page, color leads; $225 for covers; $25 for b&w photos not submitted as part of story package. Captions and identification of subjects required. Buys one-time rights.

ALASKA OUTDOORS, Swensen's Publishing, Box 8-3550, Fairbanks AK 99708. (907)276-2672. Editor: Christopher Batin. 80% freelance written. Bimonthly magazine covering hunting and fishing in Alaska. Circ. 73,000. Pays on publication. Publishes ms an average of 6 months after acceptance. Byline given. Buys first serial rights. Submit seasonal/holiday material 4 months in advance. Computer printout submissions acceptable; prefers letter-quality to dot-matrix. SASE. Reports in 2 weeks. Sample copy $2; writer's guidelines for 4x9½ SAE and 1 first class stamp.

Nonfiction: How-to, investigative reports on outdoor issues in Alaska, and articles on where to go to fish and hunt in Alaska. "Articles should include a sidebar that will aid the reader in duplicating your adventure. No survival-type articles or personal brushes with death." Buys 75 unsolicited mss/year. Query. Length: 800-1,800 words. Pays $50-300; "$200 minimum for article with photographic support."

Photos: Send photos with ms to the attention of photo editor. Pays $10-25 for b&w contact sheets; $50-200 for 2¼x2¼ or 35mm color transparencies. Captions required. Buys one-time rights.

Tips: "Include more information and more descriptive writing, and less storytelling and Me 'n Joe type articles. No first-person accounts. Most of our writers have visited or live in Alaska. We are more than just a regional publication; we're distributed nationally."

AMERICAN HUNTER, 1600 Rhode Island Ave. NW, Washington DC 20036. Editor: Tom Fulgham. 90% freelance written. For sport hunters who are members of the National Rifle Association. Circ. over 1,200,000. Buys first North American serial rights. Byline given. Free sample copy and writer's guidelines. Computer printout submissions acceptable; prefers letter-quality to dot-matrix. SASE.

Nonfiction: Factual material on all phases of sport hunting. Not interested in material on fishing or camping. Prefers queries. Length: 2,000-3,000 words. Pays $25-400.

Photos: No additional payment made for photos used with mss. Pays $25 for b&w photos purchased without accompanying mss. Pays $40-275 for color.

ARKANSAS SPORTSMAN, Game & Fish Publications, Inc., Box 741, Marietta GA 30061. (404)953-9222. Editor: Keith Brooks. Monthly how-to, where-to, when-to hunting and fishing magazine covering Arkansas. Pays on acceptance. Byline given. Buys one-time rights. Submit seasonal material 8 months in advance. Simultaneous queries, and simultaneous and photocopied submissions OK. Computer printout submissions acceptable; no dot-matrix. SASE. Reports in 2 months. Sample copy for $2.50 and 10x12 SAE; writer's guidelines for SASE.

Nonfiction: How-to (hunting and fishing *only*); humor (on limited basis); interview/profile (of successful hunter/angler); personal experience (hunting or fishing adventure). No hiking, backpacking, camping. No "my first deer" articles. Buys 60 mss/year. Query with or without published clips. Length: 1,800-2,200. Pays $150.

Photos: State availability of photos. Pays $75 for full-page, color leads; $225 for covers; $25 for b&w photos not submitted as part of story package. Captions and identification of subjects required. Buys one-time rights.

BADGER SPORTSMAN, Vercauteren Publishing, Inc., 19 E. Main, Chilton WI 53014. (414)849-4651. Editor: Mike Goc. Managing Editor: Gary Vercauteren. 80% freelance written. Monthly tabloid covering Wisconsin outdoors. Circ. 12,800. Pays on publication. Publishes ms an average of 1 month after acceptance. Byline given. Buys one-time rights. Submit seasonal/holiday material 2 months in advance. Previously published submissions OK. Computer printout submissions acceptable; prefers letter-quality to dot-matrix. SASE. Sample copy for 9x13 SAE and 56¢ postage; free writer's guidelines.

Nonfiction: General interest; how-to (fishing, hunting, etc., in the Midwest outdoors); humor; interview/profile; personal experience; technical. Buys 400-500 mss/year. Query. Length: open. Pays 35¢/column inch ($15-40).

Photos: Send photos with accompanying query or ms. Reviews 3x5 or larger b&w and color prints. Pays by column inch. Identification of subjects required.

Tips: "We publish stories about *Wisconsin* fishing, hunting, camping; outdoor cooking; and general animal stories."

BASSIN', The Official Magazine for the Weekend Angler, (formerly *Pro Bass*), National Reporter Publications, Inc., 15115 S. 76th E. Ave., Bixby OK 74008. (918)366-4441. Managing Editor: André Hinds. 90% freelance written. Magazine published 8 times/year covering freshwater fishing with emphasis on black bass. Publishes ms on an average of 4 months after acceptance. Circ. 170,000 + . Pays on acceptance. Byline given. Buys first serial rights. Submit seasonal material 6 months in advance. Prefers queries but will examine mss accompanied by SASE. Electronic submissions OK Macintosh Disk. Computer printout submissions acceptable.

Reports in 4-6 weeks. Sample copy and writer's guidelines available on request.

Nonfiction: How-to and where-to stories on bass fishing. Prefers queries. Length: 1,000-3,000 words. Pays $150-300 on acceptance.

Photos: Send photos with ms. Pays $25-100 for inside color photos. Pays $250 for color cover. Send b&w prints or color transparencies. Buys one time rights. Photo payment on publication.

Columns/Departments: Send complete ms. Fishing tips, regional lake reports, product reviews. Length: 100-700 words. Pays $30-50 on publication.

Tips:"Reduce the common fishing slang terminology when writing for *Bassin'* (and other outdoor magazines). This slang is usually regional and confuses anglers in other areas of the country. Good strong features will win me over much more quickly than short articles or fillers: The most frequent (and annoying) mistakes are spelling and grammar errors. It seems that many writers simply don't proofread and correct their errors."

BASSMASTER MAGAZINE, B.A.S.S. Publications, Box 17900, Montgomery AL 36141. (205)272-9530. Editor: Dave Precht. 75% freelance written. Bimonthly magazine (monthly January-April) about largemouth, smallmouth, spotted bass and striped bass for dedicated beginning and advanced bass fishermen. Circ. 400,000. Pays on acceptance. Publication date of ms after acceptance "varies—seasonal material could take years" after acceptance. Byline given. Buys all rights. Submit seasonal material 6 months in advance. Simultaneous and photocopied submissions OK, if so indicated. Letter-quality computer printout submissions acceptable, "but we still prefer typewritten material." SASE. Reports in 1 week. Sample copy $2; writer's guidelines for SAE and 1 first class stamp..

Nonfiction: Historical; interview (of knowledgable people in the sport); profile (outstanding fishermen); travel (where to go to fish for bass); how-to (catch bass and enjoy the outdoors); new product (reels, rods and bass boats); and conservation related to bass fishing; "Short Cast/News & Views" (upfront regular feature covering news-related events such as new state bass records, unusual bass fishing happenings, etc.; conservation, new products and editorial viewpoints; 250-400 words). "No 'Me and Joe Go Fishing' type articles." Query. Length: 400-2,100 words. Pays $100-300.

Photos: "We want a mixture of black and white and color photos." Pays $15 minimum for b&w prints. Pays $100-150 for color cover transparencies. Captions required; model release preferred. Buys all rights.

Fillers: Anecdotes, short humor and newsbreaks. Buys 4-5 mss/issue. Length: 250-500 words. Pays $50-100.

Tips: "Editorial direction continues in the short, more direct how-to article. Compact, easy-to-read information is our objective. Shorter articles with good graphics, such as how-to diagrams, step-by-step instruction, etc., will enhance a writer's articles submitted to *Bassmaster Magazine*. The most frequent mistakes made by writers in completing an article for us are poor grammar, poor writing, poor organization and superficial research."

BC OUTDOORS, SIP Division, Maclean Hunter Ltd., 202-1132 Hamilton St., Vancouver British Columbia V6B 2S2 Canada (604)687-1581. Editor: Henry L. Frew. 80% freelance written. Outdoor recreation magazine published 10 times/year. *BC Outdoors* covers fishing, camping, hunting, and the environment of outdoor recreation. Circ. 37,000. Pays on acceptance. Publishes ms an average of 6 months after acceptance. Byline given. Offers negotiable kill fee. Buys first North American serial rights. Submit seasonal/holiday material 6 months in advance. Computer printout submissions acceptable; no dot-matrix. SASE. Reports in 4 weeks on queries; 8 weeks on mss. Free sample copy and writer's guidelines.

Nonfiction: How-to (new or innovative articles on outdoor subjects); personal experience (outdoor adventure); and outdoor topics specific to British Columbia. Buys 80-90 mss/year. Query. Length: 1,200-1,600 words. Pays $125-300. Sometimes pays the expenses of writers on assignment.

Photos: State availability of photos with query. Pays $10-30 on publication for 5x7 b&w prints; $15-50 for color contact sheets and 35mm transparencies. Captions and identification of subjects required. Buys one-time rights.

Tips: "Subject must be specific to British Columbia. We receive many ms written by people who obviously did not know the magazine or market. The writer has a better chance of breaking in at our publication with short lesser-paying articles and fillers, because we have a stable of regular writers in constant touch who produce most of main features."

‡CALIFORNIA ANGLER, (Formerly *Western Saltwater Fisherman*), Hare Publications, Inc., 6200 Yarrow Dr., Carlsbad CA 92008. (619)438-2511. Editor: Tom Waters. 70% freelance written. Monthly magazine covering fresh and saltwater fishing for the California fisherman. Circ. 20,000. Pays on acceptance. Publishes ms an average of 3 months after acceptance. Byline given. Buys first serial rights and one-time rights. Submit material 3 months in advance. Computer printout submissions acceptable. SASE. Reports in 2 weeks. Sample copy and contributor's kit, $5.

Nonfiction: General interest (fishing); how-to (fishing techniques); personal experience (limited); technical (tackle); travel (fishing in the West). "We use material on techniques, species, hot spot locations, etc., for fresh and saltwater fishing in the West, including Alaska, Canada, South Pacific and Mexico. Informative and entertaining pieces on Western fishing opportunities (primarily in California), geared more toward the *experienced* angler than the beginner." Buys over 100 mss/year. Query with or without published clips. Length: 2,000-2,500 words. Pays $200-300.

Photos: Good photos are a *must* with all submitted articles. State availability of photos. Pays $25-50; $150 for cover photos and color transparencies. Captions, model release and identification of subjects required.

CAROLINA GAME & FISH, Game & Fish Publications, Inc., Box 741, Marietta GA 30061. (404)953-9222. Editor: Aaron Pass. 80% freelance written. Monthly how-to, where-to, when-to hunting and fishing magazine covering North and South Carolina. Pays on acceptance. Length of time publishes ms after acceptance "varies." Byline given. Buys one-time rights. Submit seasonal material 10 months in advance. Simultaneous queries OK but no simultaneous photocopied mss. Computer printout submissions acceptable; no dot-matrix. SASE. Sample copy for $2 and 10x12 envelope; writer's guidelines for SAE with 39¢ postage.
Nonfiction: Very state-specific approach; how-to (hunting and fishing *only*); humor/nostalgia (on limited basis); interview/profile (of successful hunter/angler); personal experience (hunting or fishing adventure). No hiking, backpacking or camping. No "my first deer" articles. Buys 75-80 mss/year. Query with or without published clips. Length: 1,800-2,200 words. Pays $150-175.
Photos: State availability of photos. Pays $75 for full-page, color leads; $225 for covers; $25 for b&w photos. Captions and identification of subjects required. Buys one-time rights.
Tips: "We don't use short, lesser-paying articles and fillers. Most unsolicited writer's haven't really understood our market/slant. Assigned articles are seldom a problem—we *make sure* the writer knows what we want. Read our books and find out what we publish."

DEER AND DEER HUNTING, The Stump Sitters, Inc., Box 1117, Appleton WI 54912. (414)734-0009. Editors: Al Hofacker and Dr. Rob Wegner. 75% freelance written. Bimonthly magazine covering deer hunting for individuals who hunt with bow, gun, or camera. Circ. 70,000. Pays on publication. Publishes ms an average of 6 months after acceptance. Byline given. Offers $50 kill fee. Buys first North American serial rights and second serial (reprint) rights. Submit seasonal/holiday material 4 months in advance. Computer printout submissions acceptable; prefers letter-quality to dot-matrix. SASE. Reports in 1 week on queries; 2 weeks on mss. Free sample copy and writer's guidelines.
Nonfiction: Historical/nostalgic; how-to (hunting techniques); interview/profile; opinion; personal experience; photo feature; technical; book review. "Our readers desire factual articles of a technical nature, that relate deer behavior and habits to hunting methodology. We focus on deer biology, management principles and practices, habitat requirements, natural history of deer, hunting techniques, and hunting ethics." No hunting "Hot Spot" or "local" articles. Buys 40 mss/year. Query with clips of published work. Length: 1,000-4,000 words. Pays $40-250. Sometimes pays the expenses of writers on assignment.
Photos: State availability of photos. Pays $100 for 35mm color transparencies; $350 for front cover; $30 for 8x10 b&w prints. Captions and identification of subjects required. Buys one-time rights.
Columns/Departments: Review Stand (reviews of books of interest to deer hunters); Deer Browse (unusual observations of deer behavior). Buys 20 mss/year. Query. Length: 200-800 words. Pays $10-50.
Fillers: Clippings, anecdotes, newsbreaks. Buys 20/year. Length: 200-800 words. Pays $10-40.
Tips: "Break in by providing material of a technical nature, backed by scientific research, and written in a style understandable to the average deer hunter. We focus primarily on white-tailed deer but periodically use material on mule deer."

FISHING WORLD, 51 Atlantic Ave., Floral Park NY 11001. Editor: Keith Gardner. 100% freelance written. Bimonthly. Circ. 285,000. Pays on acceptance. Buys first North American serial rights. Pays on acceptance. Publishes ms an average of 6 months after acceptance. Photocopied submissions OK. Computer printout submissions acceptable. SASE. Reports in 2 weeks. Free sample copy.
Nonfiction: "Feature articles range from 1,000-2,000 words with the shorter preferred. A good selection of color transparencies should accompany each submission. Subject matter can range from a hot fishing site to tackle and techniques, from tips on taking individual species to a story on one lake or an entire region, either freshwater or salt. However, how-to is definitely preferred over where-to, and a strong biological/scientific slant is best of all. Where-to articles, especially if they describe foreign fishing, should be accompanied by sidebars covering how to make reservations and arrange transportation, how to get there, where to stay. Angling methods should be developed in clear detail, with accurate and useful information about tackle and boats. Depending on article length, suitability of photographs and other factors, payment is up to $300 for feature articles accompanied by suitable photography. Color transparencies selected for cover use pay an additional $300. B&w or unillustrated featurettes are also considered. These can be on anything remotely connected with fishing. Query. Length: 1,000 words. Pays $25-100 depending on length and photos. Detailed queries accompanied by photos are preferred.
Photos: "Cover shots are purchased separately, rather than selected from those accompanying mss. The editor favors drama rather than serenity in selecting cover shots. Underwater horizontal portraits of fish are purchased (one-time rights) for centerfold use at the rate of $300 per transparency."

‡**FLORIDA WILDLIFE**. Florida Game & Fresh Water Fish Commission, 620 South Meridian St., Tallahassee FL 32301. (904)488-5563. Editor: John M. Waters, Jr. About 75% freelance written. Bimonthly state magazine covering hunting, fishing and wildlife conservation. "In outdoors sporting articles we seek themes of wholesome recreation. In nature articles we seek accuracy and conservation purpose." Circ. 27,000. Pays on publication. Publishes ms 6 months to 1 year after acceptance. Byline given. Buys first North American serial rights and second serial (reprint) rights. Submit seasonal/holiday material 6 months in advance. Simultaneous queries, and simultaneous, photocopied, and previously published submissions OK. "Inform us if it is previously published work." Computer printout submissions acceptable if double-spaced. SASE. Reports in 6 weeks on queries; variable on mss. Sample copy $1.25; free writer's guidelines.

Nonfiction: General interest (birdwatching, hiking, camping, boating); how-to (hunting and fishing); humor (wildlife related; no anthropomorphism); inspirational (conservation oriented); personal experience (wildlife, hunting, fishing, outdoors); photo feature (Florida species: game, nongame, botany), and technical (rarely purchased, but open to experts). "In a nutshell, we buy general interest hunting, fishing and nature stories. No 'me and Joe' stories, stories that humanize animals, opinionated stories not based on confirmable facts." Buys 50-60 mss/year. Query. Length: 500-2,500 words. Pays $35-250, depending on availability and use of photos.

Photos: John Roberge, photo editor. State availability of photos with query. Prefer 35mm color slides of hunting, fishing, and natural science series of Florida wildlife species. Pays $10 for small inside photos; $75 for front cover photos, $35 for back cover. "We like short, specific captions." Buys one-time rights.

Fiction: "We buy fiction rarely, and then only if it is true to life and directly related to good sportsmanship and conservation. No fairy tales, erotica, profanity, or bathroom humor." Buys 2-3 mss/year. Send complete mss and label "fiction." Length: 500-2,500 words. Pays $50-125.

Tips: "Read and study recent issues for subject matter, style and examples of our viewpoint, philosophy and treatment. The area of hunting is one requiring sensitivity. Blood and guts are out. We look for wholesome recreation, ethics, safety, and good outdoor experience more than bagging the game in our stories. Of special need at this time are well-written hunting and fishing in Florida articles. Articles sent to us on speculation generally fail to be well written and accurate, as well as having reader interest. We get too many articles that read as if they were copied from an encyclopedia."

‡**FLY FISHERMAN**, Historical Times, Inc., 2245 Kohn Rd., Box 8200, Harrisburg PA 17105. (717)657-9555. Editor: John Randolph. Associate Editor: Jack Russell. 90% freelance written. Magazine published 6 times/year on fly fishing. Circ. 137,000. Pays on acceptance. Publishes ms an average of 8 months after acceptance. Byline given. Buys first North American serial rights and (selectively) all rights. Submit seasonal/holiday material 1 year in advance. Electronic submissions OK on Wang, but requires hard copy also. Computer printout submissions acceptable; prefers letter-quality to dot-matrix. SASE. Reports in 3 weeks on queries; 6 weeks on mss. Sample copy for 11x14 SAE and 4 first class stamps. Free writer's guidelines.

Nonfiction: Book excerpts, how-to, humor, interview/profile, technical, essays on, fly fishing fly tying shorts and features, and fishing technique shorts and features. Where-to. No other types of fishing, including spin or bait. Buys 75 mss/year. Query or send complete ms. Length: 50-3,000 words. Pays $35-500.

Photos: State availability of photos or send photos with query or ms. Reviews b&w contact sheets and 35mm transparencies. Pays $35-100 for contact sheets; $25-200 for transparencies; $400 for cover photos. Captions, model release and identification of subjects required. Buys one-time rights.

Columns/Departments: Fly Fisherman's Bookshelf—500 to 1,000-word book reviews ($75 each); reviews of fly fishing video tapes $75, same length. Buys 8 mss/year. Query. Length: 500-1,000 words. Pays $75.

Fiction: Essays on fly fishing, humorous and serious. No long articles, anything over 3,000 words. Buys 4 mss/year. Query with published clips. Length: 1,200-3,000 words. Pays $125-500.

Fillers: Short humor and newsbreaks. Buys 30/year. Length: 25-1,000 words. Pays $25-250.

Tips: "Our magazine is a tightly focused, technique-intensive special interest magazine. Articles require fly fishing expertise and writing must be tight and in many instances well researched. The novice fly fisher has little hope of a sale with us, although perhaps 30 percent of our features are entry-level or intermediate-level in nature. Fly fishing technique pieces that are broadly focused have great appeal. Both features and departments—short features have the best chance of purchase. Accompany submissions with excellent color slides (35mm) or black and white 8x10 prints or line drawing illustrations."

THE FLYFISHER, 1387 Cambridge, Idaho Falls ID 83401. (208)523-7300. Editor: Dennis G. Bitton. 60% freelance written. Quarterly magazine; 64-72 pages. "*The Flyfisher* is the official publication of the Federation of Fly Fishers, a nonprofit organization of member clubs and individuals in the U.S., Canada, United Kingdom, France, New Zealand, Chile, Argentina, Japan and other nations. It serves an audience of conservation-minded fly fishermen." Circ. 10,000. Pays after publication. Publishes ms an average of 3 months after acceptance. Byline given. Buys first North American serial rights. Submit seasonal/holiday material 60 days in advance. Computer printout submissions acceptable. SASE. Reports in 2 weeks. Sample copy $3, available from FFF, Box 1088, West Yellowstone MT 59758. Writer's guidelines for SASE; write to 1387 Cambridge, Idaho Falls ID 83401.

Nonfiction: How-to (fly fishing techniques, fly tying, tackle, etc.); general interest (any type including where to go, conservation); historical (places, people, events that have significance to fly fishing); inspirational (looking for articles dealing with Federation clubs on conservation projects); interview (articles of famous fly fishermen, fly tiers, teachers, etc.); nostalgia (articles of reminiscences on flies, fishing personalities, equipment and places); and technical (about techniques of fly fishing in salt and fresh waters). Buys 6-8 mss/issue. Query. Length: 500-2,500 words. Pays $50-200.

Photos: Pays $15-50 for 8x10 b&w glossy prints; $20-80 for 35mm or larger color transparencies for inside use. $100-150 for covers. Captions required. Buys one-time rights. Prefers a selection of transparencies and glossies when illustrating with a manuscript, which are purchased as a package.

Fiction: (Must be related to fly fishing). Adventure, conservation, fantasy, historical, humorous, and suspense. Buys 2 mss/issue. Query. Length, 500-2,000 words. Pays $75-200.

Tips: "We make every effort to assist a writer with visuals if the idea is strong enough to develop. We will deal with freelancers breaking into the field. Our only concern is that the material be in keeping with the quality established. We prefer articles submitted by members of FFF, but do not limit our selection of good articles."

FUR-FISH-GAME, 2878 E. Main, Columbus OH 43209. Editor: Ken Dunwoody. 65% freelance written. Monthly magazine; 64-88 pages. For outdoorsmen of all ages who are interested in hunting, fishing, trapping, dogs, camping, conservation and related topics. Circ. 180,000. Pays on acceptance. Publishes ms an average of 7 months after acceptance. Byline given. Buys all rights. Prefers nonsimultaneous submissions. Computer printout submissions acceptable; prefers letter-quality to dot-matrix. Reports in 3-5 weeks. Submit complete ms with photos and SASE. Writer's guidelines for SASE; sample copy $1.

Nonfiction: "We are looking for informative, down-to-earth stories about hunting, fishing, trapping, dogs, camping, boating, conservation and related subjects. Nostalgic articles are also used. Many of our stories are 'how to' and should appeal to small-town and rural readers who are true outdoorsmen. Some recent articles have told how to train a gun dog, catch big-water catfish, outfit a bowhunter and trap late-season muskrat. We also use personal experience stories and an occasional profile, such as an article about an old-time trapper. 'Where to' stories are used occasionally if they have broad appeal and include a map and sidebar giving information on travel, lodging, etc. Length: 1,500-3,000 words. Pays $75-225 depending upon quality, photo support, and importance to magazine. Short filler stories pay $35-80. We are increasing our payment scale to writers and photographers and improving the graphics and layout of the magazine."

Photos: Send photos with ms. Photos are part of ms package and receive no additional payment. Prefer b&w but color prints or transparencies OK. Prints can be 5x7 or 8x10. Caption information required. Photos are also purchased without accompanying ms and usually pay $10-15.

Tips: "We are always looking for quality articles that tell how to hunt or fish for game animals or birds that are popular with everyday outdoorsmen but often overlooked in other publications, such as catfish, bluegill, crappie, squirrel, rabbit, crows, etc. We also use articles on standard seasonal subjects such as deer and pheasant, but like to see a fresh approach or new technique. Trapping articles, especially instructional ones based on personal experience, are useful all year. Articles on gun dogs, ginseng and do-it-yourself projects are also popular with our readers. An assortment of photos and/or sketches greatly enhances any ms and sidebars, where applicable, can also help."

GEORGIA SPORTSMAN, Game & Fish Publications, Box 741, Marietta GA 30061. (404)953-9222. Editor: Aaron Pass. Monthly how-to, where-to, when-to hunting and fishing magazine covering Georgia. Pays on acceptance. Byline given. Buys one-time rights. Submit seasonal material 10 months in advance. Simultaneous queries OK; no simultaneous or photocopied submissions. Computer printout submissions acceptable. SASE. Sample copy for $2 and 10x12 SAE; writer's guidelines for SASE.

Nonfiction: Very state-specific approach; how-to (hunting and fishing *only*); humor/nostalgia (on limited basis); interview/profile (of successful hunter/angler); personal experience (hunting or fishing adventure). No hiking, backpacking or camping. No "my first deer" articles. Buys 75-80 mss/year. Query with or without published clips. Length: 1,800-2,200 words. Pays $150-175.

Photos: State availability of photos. Pays $75 for color leads; $225 for covers; $25 for b&w photos. Captions and identification of subjects required. Buys one-time rights.

GRAY'S SPORTING JOURNAL, Box 2549, So. Hamilton MA 01982. Editor: Ed Gray. 95% freelance written. Magazine; 128 pages. Emphasizes hunting, fishing and conservation for sportsmen. Published 4 times/year. Circ. 30,000. Buys first North American serial rights. Byline given. Computer printout submissions acceptable. SASE. Reports in 6 months. Sample copy $7.50; writer's guidelines for SASE.

Nonfiction: Articles on hunting and fishing experiences. Humor, historical, personal experience, opinion, and photo feature. Buys 7 mss/issue. Submit complete ms. Length: 500-5,000 words. Pays $500-1,000 on publication.

Photos: Submit photo material with accompanying ms. Pays $50-300 for any size color transparencies. Captions preferred. Buys one-time rights.

Fiction: Mostly thoughtful and low-key, and humor. No adventure stories. Submit complete ms. Length: 500-5,000 words. Pays $500-1000.

Poetry: Free verse, light verse, and traditional. Buys 1 poem/issue. Pays $50-250.

Tips: Show that you are "someone who knows his material but is not a self-acclaimed expert; someone who can write well and with a sense of humor; someone who can share his experiences without talking down to the readers; someone who can prepare an article with focus and a creative approach to his prose." No how-to or where-to-go articles.

GREAT LAKES FISHERMAN, Great Lakes Fisherman Publishing Co., 1570 Fishinger Rd., Columbus OH 43221. (614)451-9307. Publisher/Executive Editor: Woody Earnheart. Editor: Ottie M. Snyder, Jr. 99% freelance written. Monthly magazine covering how, when and where to fish in the Great Lakes region. Circ. 68,000. Pays on acceptance. Publishes ms an average of 3 months after acceptance. Byline given. Offers $40 kill fee. Buys first North American serial rights. Submit seasonal/holiday material 4-6 months in advance. Computer printout submissions acceptable. SASE. Reports in 5 weeks. Free sample copy and writer's guidelines.

Nonfiction: How-to (where to and when to freshwater fish). "No humor, me and Joe or subject matter outside the Great Lakes region." Buys 84 mss/year. Query with clips of published work. "Letters should be tightly written, but descriptive enough to present no surprises when the ms is received. Prefer b&w photos to be used to illustrate ms with query." Length: 1,500-2,500 words. Pays $125-200.

Photos: Send photos with ms. "Black and white photos are considered part of manuscript package and as such receive no additional payment. We consider b&w photos to be a vital part of a ms package and return more packages because of poor quality photos than any other reason. We look for four types of illustration with each article: scene (a backed off shot of fisherman); result (not the typical meat shot of angler grinning at camera with big stringer but in most cases just a single nice fish with the angler admiring the fish); method (a lure shot or illustration of special rigs mentioned in the text); and action (angler landing a fish, fighting a fish, etc.). Illustrations (line drawings) need not be finished art but should be good enough for our artist to get the idea of what the author is trying to depict." Prefers cover shots to be verticals with fish and fisherman action shots. Pays $100 minimum for 35mm color transparencies; reviews 8x10 b&w prints. Captions, model release and identification of subjects required. Buys one-time rights.

Tips: "Our feature articles are 99.9 percent freelance material. The magazine is circulated in the eight states bordering the Great Lakes, an area where one-third of the nation's licensed anglers reside. All of our feature content is how, when or where, or a combination of all three covering the species common to the region. Fishing is an age-old sport with countless words printed on the subject each year. A fresh new slant that indicates a desire to share with the reader the author's knowledge is a sale. We expect the freelancer to answer any anticipated questions the reader might have (on accommodations, launch sites, equipment needed, etc.) within the ms. We publish an equal mix each month of both warm- and cold-water articles. The most frequent mistakes made by writers in completing articles for us are bad photos—sending in color instead of b&w for story illustration, massive re-writing needed, or sending material too seasonal and past time for our needs."

LOUISIANA GAME & FISH, Game & Fish Publications, Inc., Box 741, Marietta GA 30061. (404)953-9222. Editor: Gordon Whittington. 80% freelance written. Monthly how-to, where-to, when-to hunting and fishing magazine covering Louisiana. Pays on acceptance. Byline given. Buys one-time rights. Submit seasonal material 10 months in advance. Computer printout submissions are acceptable "only if double-spaced." SASE. Reports in 2 months. Sample copy for $2 and 10x12 SAE; writer's guidelines for SAE and 1 first class stamp.

Nonfiction: Where-to (hunting and fishing *only*); humor (on limited basis); interview/profile (of successful hunter/angler); personal experience (hunting or fishing adventure). No hiking, backpacking or camping. No "my first deer" articles. Buys 60 mss/year. Query with or without published clips. Length: 1,800-2,200 words. Pays $150.

Photos: State availability of photos. Pays $75 for full-page, color leads; $225 for covers; $25 for b&w photos. Captions and identification of subjects required. Buys one-time rights.

Tips: "We don't run shorts or fillers. The most frequent mistakes made by writers in completing an article for us are not enough specific *where-to* info in hunting and fishing articles; too much *how-to*."

TOM MANN OUTDOORS MAGAZINE, (Formerly *Tom Mann's Junior Fisherman Magazine*), Rt. 2, Box 84C, Eufaula AL 36027. (205)687-7044. Editor: Suzanne Newsom. 90% freelance written. Magazine published bimonthly on family outdoor-related topics for family and youth audience. Circ. 50,000. Pays on publication. Published ms an average of 3 months after acceptance. Byline given. Kill fee to be determined. Buys first rights. Submit seasonal/holiday material 6 months in advance. Simultaneous queries, and some previously published submissions OK. Electronic submissions via diskette compatible with IBM Displaywriter Textpack 4 OK. Computer printout submissions acceptable. SASE. Sample copy for SAE and $1.50 postage; free writer's guidelines.

Nonfiction: How-to (on fishing, camping, canoeing, and other outdoor activities); humor (some); and Indian lore. Buys 40 mss/year. Query with published clips. Length: 500-1,000 words. Pays $75-100/printed page.

Photos: John D. Andrews, photo editor. Pays $25 for color transparencies; $15 maximum for b&w prints.

Captions and identification of subjects required. Buys one-time rights.

Fillers: Newsbreaks. "We will be adding a new section featuring interesting information and tips on all phases of the outdoors experience. Pay is yet to be determined."

Tips: "We are looking for writers who can relate to young people and families in the great outdoors. Material must be presented in a wholesome, healthy and positive attitude. Fishing and outdoor (hunting, etc.) equipment and good methods and techniques are the areas most open to freelancers."

MICHIGAN OUT-OF-DOORS, Box 30235, Lansing MI 48909. (517)371-1041. Editor: Kenneth S. Lowe. 50% freelance written. Emphasizes outdoor recreation, especially hunting and fishing, conservation and environmental affairs. Monthly magazine; 116 pages. Circ. 110,000. Pays on acceptance. Publishes ms an average of 6 months after acceptance. Byline given. Buys first North American serial rights. Phone queries OK. Submit seasonal/holiday material 6 months in advance. Computer printout submissions acceptable; prefers letter-quality to dot-matrix. SASE. Reports in 1 month. Sample copy $1; free writer's guidelines.

Nonfiction: Expose, historical, how-to, informational, interview, nostalgia, personal experience, personal opinion, photo feature and profile. No humor. "Stories *must* have a Michigan slant unless they treat a subject of universal interest to our readers." Buys 8 mss/issue. Send complete ms. Length: 1,000-3,000 words. Pays $60 minimum for feature stories.

Photos: Purchased with or without accompanying ms. Pays $15 minimum for any size b&w glossy prints; $60 maximum for color (for cover). Offers no additional payment for photos accepted with accompanying ms. Buys one-time rights. Captions preferred.

Tips: "Top priority is placed on true accounts of personal adventures in the out-of-doors—well-written tales of very unusual incidents encountered while hunting, fishing, camping, hiking, etc. The most rewarding aspect of working with freelancers is realizing we had a part in their development. But it's annoying to respond to queries that never produce a manuscript."

MID WEST OUTDOORS, Mid West Outdoors, Ltd., 111 Shore Drive, Hinsdale (Burr Ridge) IL 60521. (312)887-7722. Editor: Gene Laulunen. Emphasizes fishing, hunting, camping and boating. Monthly tabloid. 100% freelance written. Circ. 55,000. Pays on publication. Buys simultaneous rights. Byline given. Submit seasonal material 2 months in advance. Simultaneous, photocopied and previously published submissions OK. SASE. Reports in 3 weeks. Publishes ms an average of 3 months after acceptance. Sample copy $1; free writer's guidelines.

Nonfiction: How-to (fishing, hunting, camping in the Midwest) and where-to-go (fishing, hunting, camping within 500 miles of Chicago). "We do not want to see any articles on 'my first fishing, hunting or camping experiences,' 'Cleaning My Tackle Box,' 'Tackle Tune-up,' or 'Catch and Release.' " Buys 840 unsolicited mss/year. Send complete ms. Length: 1,000-1,500 words. Pays $15-25.

Photos: Offers no additional payment for photos accompanying ms; uses b&w prints. Buys all rights. Captions required.

Columns/Departments: Fishing, Hunting. Open to suggestions for columns/departments. Send complete ms. Pays $20.

Tips: "Break in with a great unknown fishing hole within 500 miles of Chicago. Where, how, when and why. Know the type of publication you are sending material to."

MISSISSIPPI GAME & FISH, Game & Fish Publications, Box 741, Marietta GA 30061. (404)953-9222. Editor: Keith Brooks. Monthly how-to, where-to, when-to hunting and fishing magazine covering Mississippi. Pays on acceptance. Byline given. Buys one-time rights. Submit seasonal material 8 months in advance. Simultaneous queries, and simultaneous and photocopied submissions OK. SASE. Reports in 2 months. Sample copy for $2.50 and 10x12 SAE; writer's guidelines for SASE.

Nonfiction: How-to (hunting and fishing *only*); humor (on limited basis); interview/profile (of successful hunter/angler); personal experience (hunting or fishing adventure). No hiking, backpacking, camping. No fiction or poems. No "my first deer" articles. Buys 60 mss/year. Query with or without published clips. Length: 1,800-2,200 words. Pays $150.

Photos: State availability of photos. Pays $75 for full-page, color leads; $225 for covers; $25 for b&w photos not submitted as part of story package. Captions and identification of subjects required. Buys one-time rights.

‡NORTH AMERICAN WHITETAIL, "The Magazine devoted to the serious trophy deer hunter", Game & Fish Publications, Inc., Suite 136, 2121 Newmarket Pkwy., Marietta GA 30067. (404)953-9222. Editor: David Morris. 90% freelance written. Monthly magazine on hunting and fishing. "*North American Whitetail* is an in-depth magazine covering all aspects of whitetail deer hunting, with special emphasis on trophy bucks. Game & Fish Publications also publishes 9 separate magazines—Georgia, Tennessee, Arkansas and Texas Sportsman and Oklahoma, Louisiana, Mississippi, Alabama and Carolina Game and Fish. The state editions cover the where, when, how and who of hunting and fishing in their respective states." Circ. combined 325,000. Pays 15th day of month 3 months prior to issue month. Publishes ms an average of 3 months after acceptance. Byline given. Buys first North American serial rights. Submit seasonal/holiday material 8 months in advance. Simultaneous queries and submissions OK. SASE. Reports in 2 months. Sample copy $2.50; free writer's guidelines.

Nonfiction: Gordan Whittington, Aaron Pass and Keith Brooks, articles editors. Book excerpts, how-to, humor, interview/profile, personal experience, technical and where-to. Buys 840 mss/year. Query with published clips. Length: 2,000-3,000 words. Pays $150-350.

Photos: State availability of photos. Reviews 35mm color transparencies and 5x7 or 8½x11 b&w prints. Pays $25 for b&w, $75 for color. Captions and identification of subjects required. Buys one-time rights.

Tips: "Our editorial needs are very specific. I suggest studying our publications. We *do* welcome multiple query submissions. They will be held on file and reviewed each time we prepare an editorial outline. Our greatest need is for feature manuscripts."

OHIO FISHERMAN, Ohio Fisherman Publishing Co., 1570 Fishinger Rd., Columbus OH 43221. (614)451-5769. Publisher/Executive Editor: Woody Earnheart. Editor: Ottie M. Snyder, Jr. 99% freelance written. Monthly magazine covering the how, when and where of Ohio fishing. Circ. 45,000. Pays on publication. Publishes ms an average of 3 months after acceptance. Byline given. Offers $40 kill fee. Buys first rights. Submit seasonal/holiday material 4-6 months in advance. Computer printout submissions acceptable; prefers letter-quality to dot-matrix. SASE. Reports in 5 weeks. Free sample copy and writer's guidelines.

Nonfiction: How-to (also where to and when to fresh water fish). "Our feature articles are 99% freelance material, and all have the same basic theme—sharing fishing knowledge. No humorous or 'me and Joe' articles." Buys 84 mss/year. Query with clips of published work. Letters should be "tightly written, but descriptive enough to present no surprises when the ms is received. Prefer b&w photos to be used to illustrate ms with query." Length: 1,500-2,500 words. Pays $100-150.

Photos: 99% of covers purchased are verticals involving fishermen and fish—action preferred." Send photos with query. "We consider b&w photos to be a vital part of a ms package and return more mss because of poor quality photos than any other reason. We look for four types of illustration with each article: scene (a backed off shot of fisherman); result (not the typical meat shot of angler grinning at camera with big stringer, but in most cases just a single nice fish with the angler admiring the fish); method (a lure or illustration of special rigs mentioned in the text); and action (angler landing a fish, fighting a fish, etc.). Illustrations (line drawings) need not be finished art but should be good enough for our artist to get the idea of what the author is trying to depict." Pays $100 minimum for 35mm color transparencies (cover use); also buys 8x10 b&w prints as part of ms package—"no additional payments." Captions and identification of subjects required. Buys one-time rights.

Tips: "The specialist and regional markets are here to stay. They both offer the freelancer the opportunity for steady income. Fishing is an age-old sport with countless words printed on the subject each year. A fresh new slant that indicates a desire to share with the reader the author's knowledge is a sale. We expect the freelancer to answer any anticipated questions the reader might have (on accommodations, launch sites, equipment needed, etc.) within the ms. "The most frequent mistakes made by writers in completing an article for us are bad photos—sending in color instead of b&w prints to accompany stories; massive re-writing needed; or material is too seasonal and past time for our needs."

OKLAHOMA GAME & FISH, Game & Fish Publications, Box 741, Marietta GA 30061. (404)953-9222. Editor: Keith Brooks. A monthly how-to, where-to, when-to hunting and fishing magazine covering Oklahoma. Pays on acceptance. Byline given. Buys one-time rights. Submit seasonal material 8 months in advance. Simultaneous queries, and simultaneous and photocopied submissions OK. SASE. Reports in 2 months. Sample copy for $2.50 and 10x12 SAE; writer's guidelines for SASE.

Nonfiction: How-to (hunting and fishing *only*); humor (on limited basis); interview/profile (of successful hunter/angler); personal experience (hunting or fishing adventure). No hiking, backpacking or camping. No "my first deer" articles. Buys 60 mss/year. Query with or without published clips. Length: 1,800-2,200 words. Pays $150.

Photos: State availability of photos. Pays $75 for full-page, color leads; $225 for covers; $25 for b&w photos not submitted as part of story package. Captions and identification of subjects required. Buys one-time rights.

ONTARIO OUT OF DOORS, 3 Church St., Toronto, Ontario M5E 1M2 Canada. (416)368-3011. Editor-in-Chief: Burton J. Myers. 90% freelance written. Emphasizes hunting, fishing, camping, and conservation. Monthly magazine; 80 pages. Circ. 55,000. Pays on acceptance. Publishes ms an average of 4 months after acceptance. Buys first North American serial rights. Phone queries OK. Computer printout submissions acceptable; no dot-matrix. Submit seasonal/holiday material 5 months in advance of issue date. Reports in 6 weeks. Free sample copy and writer's guidelines; mention *Writer's Market* in request.

Nonfiction: Expose of conservation practices; how-to (improve your fishing and hunting skills); humor; photo feature (on wildlife); travel (where to find good fishing and hunting); and any news on Ontario. "Avoid 'Me and Joe' articles or funny family camping anecdotes." Buys 20-30 unsolicited mss/year. Query. Length: 150-3,500 words. Pays $35-350.

Photos: Submit photo material with accompanying query. No additional payment for b&w contact sheets and 35mm color transparencies. "Should a photo be used on the cover, an additional payment of $250-350 is made."

Fillers: Outdoor tips. Buys 24 mss/year. Length: 20-50 words. Pays $20.

Tips: "We expect our rates to climb and our expectations on quality of submissions to become more demanding. It's rewarding for us to find a freelancer who reads and understands a set of writer's guidelines, but it is annoying when writers fail to submit supporting photography."

PENNSYLVANIA ANGLER, Pennsylvania Fish Commission, Box 1673, Harrisburg PA 17105-1673. (717)657-4520. Editor: Art Michaels. Monthly magazine of fishing, boating and conservation topics. 75% freelance written. Circ. 68,000. Pays on acceptance. Byline given. Buys all rights, but rights can be reassigned after publication on written request. Submit seasonal/holiday material 8 months in advance. Computer printout submissions acceptable; prefers letter-quality to dot-matrix. SASE. Reports in 1 week on queries; 2 months on mss. Publishes ms an average of 7 months after acceptance. Free writer's guidelines for SASE. Sample copy for 9x12 SAE and 73¢ postage.

Nonfiction: How-to and where-to in Pennsylvania fishing and boating. Technical and the latest trends in fishing. No "Me 'n' Joe" fishing articles and no hunting material. Query. Length: 200 words. Pays $50-300.

Photos: Pays $15 minimum for inside color; $5-50 for b&w prints. Pays $100-300 for color cover photos.

Columns/Departments: Short subjects (with photos) related to fishing. Length: 200-250 words.

Tips: "Timeliness and fresh, sharply focused subjects are important for short fishing pieces, and these are the best way new writers can break in to print. Any technical fishing subject appropriate to Pennsylvania waterways is useful, and material should not exceed 200 words. Another way to break in to print here is to know Pennsylvania angling and write a detailed account of fishing a specific waterway."

PENNSYLVANIA GAME NEWS, Box 1567, Harrisburg PA 17105-1567. (717)787-3745. Editor-in-Chief: Bob Bell. 80% freelance written. Emphasizes hunting in Pennsylvania. Monthly magazine; 64 pages. Circ. 210,000. Pays on acceptance. Publishes ms an average of 10 months after acceptance. Byline given. Buys all rights. Phone queries OK. Submit seasonal/holiday material 6 months in advance. Photocopied submissions OK. Computer printout submissions acceptable; no dot-matrix. SASE. Reports in 1 month. Free sample copy and writer's guidelines.

Nonfiction: Historical, how-to, informational, personal experience, photo feature and technical. "Must be related to outdoors in Pennsylvania." No fishing or boating material. Buys 4-8 unsolicited mss/issue. "We rarely assign work." Query. Length: 2,500 words maximum. Pays $250 maximum.

Photos: Purchased with accompanying ms. Pays $5-20 for 8x10 b&w glossy prints. Model release required.

‡**PENNSYLVANIA SPORTSMAN**, Box 5196, Harrisburg PA 17110. Editor: Lou Hoffman. 40% freelance written. Covering hunting, fishing, camping, boating and conservation in Pennsylvania. Pays on publication. Publishes ms an average of 6 months after acceptance. Byline given. Buys one-time rights. Simultaneous and previously published submissions OK. Computer printout submissions acceptable "10pt ds." SASE. Reports in 3 weeks. Sample copy and writer's guidelines for SASE.

Nonfiction: How-to and where-to articles on hunting, fishing, camping and boating. No material *not* related to field sports. Buys 30-40 unsolicited mss/year. Submit complete ms or query with photos. Length 800-1,200 words. Pays $40-100. Sometimes pays the expenses of writers on assignment.

Photos: Pays $10 for 5x7 b&w prints; $75/color cover; $20/color inside. Prefers 35mm slides. Captions and model releases are required.

Fillers: "Fillers welcome. Subjects should be different, e.g., 'How to Make A Fishy Pegbored,' 'A Camp Toaster.' We are also looking for helpful hints." Length: 300-400 words. Pays $25 each; $10 additional for b&w used with article.

PETERSEN'S HUNTING, Petersen Publishing Co., 8490 Sunset Blvd., Los Angeles CA 90069. (213)657-5100. Editor-in-Chief: Craig Boddington. Emphasizes sport hunting. Monthly magazine; 84 pages. 20% freelance written. Circ. 275,000. Pays on acceptance. Buys all rights. Submit seasonal/holiday material 9 months in advance. Computer printout submissions acceptable. SASE. Reports in 2 months. Publishes ms an average of 8 months after acceptance. Sample copy $1.75. Free writer's guidelines.

Nonfiction: How-to (how to be a better hunter, how to make hunting-related items); personal experience (use a hunting trip as an anecdote to illustrate how-to contents). Buys 15 unsolicited mss/year. Query. Length: 1,500-2,500 words. Pays $250-350.

Photos: Photos purchased with or without accompanying ms. Captions required. Pays $25 minimum for 8x10 b&w glossy prints; $50-150 for 2¼x2¼ or 35mm color transparencies. Total purchase price for ms includes payment for photos. Model release required. Ms must include a selection of 8x10 b&w prints and color slides. Ms without photo support will not normally be considered.

Tips: "Write an unusual hunting story that is not often covered in other publications. We enjoy that rare occasion when a complete package with good, clean well-written copy accompanied by good photos appears."

SAFARI MAGAZINE, The Journal of Big Game Hunting, Safari Club International, Suite 1680, 5151 E. Broadway, Tucson AZ 85711. (602)747-0260. Editor: William R. Quimby. 90% freelance written. Bimonthly club journal covering international big game hunting and wildlife conservation. Circ. 11,000. Pays on publication. Publishes ms an average of 1 year after acceptance. Byline given. Offers $100 kill fee. Buys all rights. Submit seasonal/holiday material 1 year in advance. Previously published submissions OK under certain circumstances. Computer printout submissions acceptable; prefers letter-quality to dot-matrix. SASE. Reports in 2 weeks on queries; 1 month on mss. Sample copy $3.50; writer's guidelines for SAE.
Nonfiction: Doug Fulton, articles editor. Historical/nostalgic (big game hunting); photo feature (wildlife); and technical (firearms, hunting techniques, etc.). Special issues will include hunting and wildlife photos, and stories covering Alaska and Canada. "Contributors should avoid sending simple hunting narratives that do not contain certain new approaches." Buys 36 mss/year. Query or send complete ms. Length: 1,500-2,500 words. Pays $200.
Photos: State availability of photos with query or ms, or send photos with query or ms. Pays $35 for 5x7 or larger b&w prints; $50-150 for 5x9 or larger color prints. Captions, model releases, and identification of subjects required. Buys one-time rights.
Tips: "Study the magazine. Send manuscripts and photo packages with query. Make it appeal to affluent, knowledgable, world-travelled big game hunters. Features on conservation contributions from big game hunters around the world are most open to freelancers. We have enough stories on first-time African safaris, ordinary deer hunts, Alaska dall sheep hunts. We need South American and eastern Canada hunting stories plus stories dealing with hunting and conservation.

SALT WATER SPORTSMAN, 186 Lincoln St., Boston MA 02111. (617)426-4074. Editor-in-Chief: Barry Gibson. Emphasizes saltwater fishing. 85% freelance written. Monthly magazine; 120 pages. Circ. 116,000. Pays on acceptance. Publishes ms an average of 6 months after acceptance. Byline given. Buys first North American serial rights. Pays 100% kill fee. Submit seasonal material 8 months in advance. Computer printout submissions acceptable; no dot-matrix. SASE. Reports in 1 month. Sample copy and writer's guidelines for $1.41 postage..
Nonfiction: How-to, personal experience, technical and travel (to fishing areas). "Readers want solid how-to, where-to information written in an enjoyable, easy-to-read style. Personal anecdotes help the reader identify with the writer." Prefers new slants and specific information. Query. "It is helpful if the writer states experience in salt water fishing and any previous related articles. We want one, possibly two well-explained ideas per query letter—not merely a listing." Buys 100 unsolicited mss/year. Length: 1,500-2,000 words. Pays $200 and up.
Photos: Purchased with or without accompanying ms. Captions required. Uses 5x7 or 8x10 b&w prints and color slides. Pays $300 minimum for 35mm, 2¼x2¼ or 8x10 color transparencies for cover. Offers additional payment for photos accepted with accompanying ms.
Tips: "There are a lot of knowledgable fishermen/budding writers out there who could be valuable to us with a little coaching. Many don't think they can write a story for us, but they'd be surprised. We work with writers. Shorter articles that get to the point which are accompanied by good, sharp photos are hard for us to turn down. Having to delete unnecessary wordage—conversation, cliches, etc.—that writers feel is mandatory is annoying. Often they don't devote enough attention to specific fishing information."

SOUTH CAROLINA WILDLIFE, Box 167, Rembert Dennis Bldg., Columbia SC 29202. (803)758-0001. Editor: John Davis. Managing Editor: Tom Poland. For South Carolinians interested in wildlife and outdoor activities. 60% freelance written. Bimonthly magazine; 64 pages. Circ. 64,000. Byline given. Pays on acceptance. Publishes ms an average of 2 months after acceptance. Buys first rights. Free sample copy. Reports in four to six weeks. Submit outline and 1-page explanation. Computer printout submissions acceptable "if double-spaced."
Nonfiction and Photos: Articles on outdoor South Carolina with an emphasis on preserving and protecting our natural resources. "Realize that the topic must be of interest to South Carolinians and that we must be able to justify using it in a publication published by the state wildlife department—so if it isn't directly about hunting, fishing, a certain plant or animal, it must be somehow related to the environment and conservation. Readers prefer a broad mix of outdoor related topics (articles that illustrate the beauty of South Carolina's outdoors and those that help the reader get more for his/her time, effort, and money spent in outdoor recreation). These two general areas are the ones we most need. Subjects vary a great deal in topic, area and style, but must all have a common ground in the outdoor resources and heritage of South Carolina. Review back issues and query with a one-page outline citing sources, giving ideas for graphic design, explaining justification and giving an example of the first two paragraphs." Does not need any column material. Manuscripts or photographs submitted to *South Carolina Wildlife* should be addressed to: The Editor, Box 167, Columbia SC 29202, accompanied by SASE. The publisher assumes no responsibility for unsolicited material. Buys25-30 mss/year. Length: 1,000-3,000 words. Pays and average of $200-400 per article depending upon length and subject matter. Sometimes pays the expense of writers on assignment.
Tips: "We need more writers in the outdoor field who take pride in the craft of writing and put a real effort to-

ward originality and preciseness in their work. We produce fillers and some shorts. Query on a topic we haven't recently done. The most frequent mistake made by writers in completing an article is failure to check details and go in-depth on a subject. We try to correct this in editing stages."

‡**SOUTHERN OUTDOORS MAGAZINE**, B.A.S.S. Publications, Number 1 Bell Rd., Montgomery AL 36141. Editor: Larry Teague. Emphasizes Southern outdoor activities, including hunting, fishing, boating, shooting, camping. 90% freelance written. Published 8 times/year. Circ. 200,000. Pays on acceptance. Publishes ms an average of 1 month after acceptance. Buys all rights. Computer printout submissions acceptable; prefers letter-quality to dot-matrix. SASE. Reports in 1 month. Sample copy $1.
Nonfiction: Articles should be service-oriented, helping the reader be more successful in outdoor sports. Emphasis is on techniques and trends. Some "where-to" stories purchased on Southern destinations with strong fishing or hunting theme. Buys 120 mss/year. Length: 3,000 words maximum. Pays 15¢/word. Sometimes pays the expenses of writers on assignment.
Photos: Usually purchased with manuscripts. Pays $50 for 35mm color transparencies without ms, and $250-350 for covers.
Fillers: Needs short articles (50-500 words) with newsy slant for "Southern Shorts." Emphasis on irony and humor. Also needs humorous or thought-provoking pieces (750-1,500 words) for "S.O. Essay" feature.
Tips: "It's easiest to break in with short features of 1,200-2,000 words on 'how-to' or 'where-to' fishing and hunting topics. We buy very little first person. How-to stories should quote at least three sources, preferably from different parts of the Southeast. Query first, and send sample of your writing if we haven't done business before. Stories most likely to sell: bass fishing, deer hunting, other freshwater fishing, inshore salt-water fishing, bird and small game hunting, shooting, camping and boating. The most frequent mistakes made by writers in completing an article for us are first person usage; clarity of articles; applicability of topic to the South; lack of quotes from qualified sources."

SPORTS AFIELD, 250 W. 55th St., New York NY 10019. Editor: Tom Paugh. Managing Editor: Fred Kesting. 33% freelance written. For people of all ages whose interests are centered around the out-of-doors (hunting and fishing) and related subjects. Monthly magazine. Circ. 518,010. Buys first North American serial rights for features, and all rights for SA Almanac. Pays on acceptance. Publishes ms an average of 6 months after acceptance. Byline given. "Our magazine is seasonal and material submitted should be in accordance. Fishing in spring and summer; hunting in the fall; camping in summer and fall." Submit seasonal material 6 months in advance. Computer printout submissions acceptable; prefers letter-quality to dot-matrix. Reports in 1 month. Query or submit complete ms. SASE.
Nonfiction and Photos: "Informative articles and personal experiences with good photos on hunting, fishing, camping, boating and subjects such as conservation and travel related to hunting and fishing. We want first-class writing and reporting." Buys 15-17 unsolicited mss/year. Recent article example: "Dude Fishing" (April 1985). Length: 500-2,500 words. Pays $750 minimum, depending on length and quality. Photos purchased with or without ms. Pays $50 minimum for 8x10 b&w glossy prints. Pays $50 minimum for 35mm or larger transparencies. Sometimes pays the expenses of writers on assignment.
Fiction: Adventure, humor (if related to hunting and fishing).
Fillers: Send to Almanac editor. Almanac pays $25 and up depending on length, for newsworthy, unusual, how-to and nature items. Payment on publication. Buys all rights.
Tips: "We seldom give assignments to other than staff. Pieces have been rejected because of poor writing."

‡**THE SPORTSMEN MAGAZINE, The National Sportsmen's Show Magazine (Canada)**, W.T. Sports Publishing, Division of CRV Publications Canada, Ltd., 2077 Dundas St. E, Mississauga, Ontario L4X 1M2 Canada. (416)624-8218. Editor: Reg Fife. Annual magazine featuring the outdoor activities of Canadian sportsmen. (Published February. Deadline: Dec. 15). Distributed at eight sportsmen's shows across Canada. "Designed to awaken the interest of persons attending the shows to topics, such as fishing, hunting, conservation, cottaging, boating, canoeing, nature, etc." Circ. 335,000. Pays on publication. Byline given. Buys first rights. Submit seasonal/holiday material 5 months in advance. Simultaneous queries OK. Reports in 1 month on queries; 2 months on mss. Free sample copy and writer's guidelines.
Nonfiction: Photo feature (outdoor sports, nature); wildlife, adventure. "Material should have Canadian slant and appeal." Buys 10 mss/year. Query with or without clips of published work. Length: 1,200-2,000 words. Buys $200-500.
Photos: Send photos with ms. Photos are "usually bought with ms." Reviews b&w contact sheets, and 5x7 prints, and color transparencies. Captions required. Buys one-time rights.
Fiction: Nature fiction. Buys 1-2 mss/year. Query. Length: 1,200-2,000 words. Pays negotiable fee.

TENNESSEE SPORTSMAN, Game & Fish Publications, Box 741, Marietta GA 30061. (404)953-9222. Editor: Aaron Pass. Monthly how-to, where-to, when-to hunting and fishing magazine covering Tennessee. Pays on acceptance. Byline given. Buys one-time rights. Submit seasonal material 10 months in advance. Simultaneous queries, OK, no simultaneous and photocopied manuscripts. Computer printout submissions ac-

ceptable. SASE. Reports in 2 months. Sample copy for $2 and 10x12 SAE; writer's guidelines for SASE.
Nonfiction: Very state-specific approach; how-to (hunting and fishing *only*); humor, nostalgia (on limited basis); interview/profile (of successful hunter/angler); personal experience (hunting or fishing adventure). No hiking, backpacking, camping. No "my first deer" articles. Buys 60 mss/year. Query with or without published clips. Length: 1,800-2,200 words. Pays $150-175.
Photos: State availability of photos. Pays $75 for color leads; $225 for covers; $25 for b&w photos. Captions and identification of subjects required. Buys one-time rights.

THE TEXAS FISHERMAN, A Complete Guide to the Texas Outdoors, Scripps-Howard Magazines, 5314 Bingle Rd., Houston TX 77092. Editor/Manager: Larry Bozka. For freshwater and saltwater fishermen in Texas. Monthly tabloid. 80% freelance written. Circ. 55,899. Rights purchased vary with author and material. Byline given. Usually buys second serial (reprint) rights. Buys 5-8 mss/month. Pays on publication. Publishes ms an average of 3 months after acceptance. Will consider simultaneous submissions. SASE. Reports in 1 month. Query. Free sample copy and writer's guidelines.
Nonfiction and Photos: General how-to, where-to, features on all phases of fishing in Texas. Strong slant on informative pieces. Strong writing. Good saltwater stories (Texas only). Length: 1,500-2,000 words. Pays $75-200, depending on length and quality of writing and photos. Mss must include 4-7 good action b&w photos or illustrations.
Tips: "Query should be a short, but complete description of the story that emphasizes a specific angle. When possible, send black and white photos with manuscripts. Good art will sell us a story that is mediocre, but even a great story can't replace bad photographs, and better than half submit poor quality photos. How-to stories are preferred."

TEXAS SPORTSMAN, Game & Fish Publications, Box 741, Marietta GA 30061. (404)953-9222. Editor: Gordon Whittington. 80% freelance written. Monthly how-to, where-to, when-to hunting and fishing magazine covering Texas. Pays on acceptance. Byline given. Buys one-time rights. Submit seasonal material 10 months in advance. Computer printout submissions acceptable "only if double-spaced."SASE. Reports in 2 months. Sample copy for $2 and 10x12 SASE; writer's guidelines for SASE and 1 first class stamp.
Nonfiction: Where-to (hunting and fishing *only*); humor (on limited basis); interview/profile (of successful hunter/angler); personal experience (hunting or fishing adventure). No hiking, backpacking or camping. No "my first deer" articles. Buys 60 mss/year. Query with or without published clips. Length: 1,800-2,200 words. Pays $150.
Photos: State availability of photos. Pays $75 for full-page, color leads; $225 for covers; $25 for b&w photos. Captions and identification of subjects required. Buys one-time rights.
Tips: "We don't run shorts or fillers. The most frequent mistakes made by writers in completing articles for us are not enough specific *where-to* info in hunting and fishing articles; too much *how-to*."

THE TRAPPER, Spearman Publishing & Printing, Inc., 213 N. Saunders, Box 550, Sutton NE 68979. (402)773-4343. Editor: Rick Jamison. 75% freelance written. A monthly tabloid covering trapping, outdoor occupations, fur farming, medicinal roots and herbs, calling predators and fur markets for both novice and pro audience, male and female, all ages. Circ. 51,000. Pays on publication. Publishes ms an average of 18 months after acceptance. SiByline given. Buys first North American serial rights, one-time rights, and all rights, and makes work-for-hire assignments. Submit seasonal/holiday material 4 months in advance. Computer printout submissions acceptable; no dot-matrix. SASE. Reports in 6 weeks on mss. Sample copy for SAE; writer's guidelines for SAE and 1 first class stamp.
Nonfiction: How-to (trapping, raising fur, etc.); and personal experience (trapping, outdoor-related experiences). "We do not want to see anything that refers to or condones overharvesting, bragging, etc." Buys 120 mss/year. Query. Length: 500-3,000 words. Pays $20-200.
Photos: Send photos with accompanying query or ms. Pays $5-40 for 8x10 b&w, and color prints. Captions required. Buys one-time rights and all rights.
Tips: "A good feature with excellent photos is really needed all the time. We stress good outdoor ethics, conservation and public relations. How-to articles are always needed; look for fresh ideas or different slant. The most frequent mistakes made by writers in completing an article for us is that the articles are too thin or basic; the market is missed (audience not targeted)."

TURKEY, 3941 N. Paradise Rd., Flagstaff AZ 86001. (602)774-6913. Editor: Gerry Blair. 60% freelance written. A monthly magazine covering turkey hunting, biology and conservation of the wild turkey, gear for turkey hunters, where to go, etc. for both novice and experienced wild turkey enthusiasts. "We stress wildlife conservation, ethics, and management of the resource." Estab. 1984. Circ. 30,000. Pays on publication. Publishes ms an average of 4 months after acceptance. Byline given. Computer printout submissions acceptable; prefers letter-quality to dot-matrix.
Nonfiction: Book excerpts (turkey related); how-to (turkey-related); and personal experience (turkey hunting). Buys 75-100 mss/year. "The most frequent mistake made by writers in completing an article for us is in-

adequate photo support." Query. Length: 500-3,000 words. Pays $20-200.

Photos: Send photos with accompanying query or ms. Pays $5-25 for 8x10 b&w, and color prints; $100 for color slides for cover. Sometimes pays the expenses of writers on assignment.

Columns/Departments: "Nearly all columns are done inhouse, but freelancers often do our 'state of the month' column." Buys 12 mss/year. Query. Pays $25-100.

Fillers: Clippings and newsbreaks that relate to or could affect turkey hunting or management. Length: 50-200 words. Pays $10-40.

Tips: "How-to articles, using fresh ideas, are most open to freelancers. We also need more short articles on turkey management programs in all states, and especially need articles on western turkey hunting."

TURKEY CALL, Wild Turkey Bldg., Box 530, Edgefield SC 29824. (803)637-3106. Editor: Gene Smith. 50% freelance written. An educational publication for members of the National Wild Turkey Federation. Bimonthly magazine. Circ. 28,000. Buys one-time rights. Byline given. Publishes ms an average of 6 months after acceptance. Pays on acceptance. Reports in 4 weeks. No queries necessary. Submit complete package. Wants original ms only (no carbons or other copies). No multiple submissions. Computer printout submissions acceptable; prefers letter-qualtiy to dot-matrix. SASE. Sample copy $2 when supplies permit.

Nonfiction and Photos: Feature articles dealing with the hunting and management of the American wild turkey. Must be accurate information and must appeal to national readership of turkey hunters and wildlife management experts. No poetry or first-person accounts of unremarkable hunting trips. May use some fiction that educates or entertains in a special way. Length: 1,200-1,500 words. Pays $25 for items, $50 for short fillers of 400-500 words, $200-300 for illustrated features. "We want quality photos submitted with features." Art illustrations also acceptable. "We are using more and more inside color illustrations." Prefers b&w 8x10 glossies. Color transparencies of any size are acceptable. Wants no typical hunter-holding-dead-turkey photos or setups using mounted birds or domestic turkeys. Photos with how-to stories must make the techniques clear (example: how to make a turkey call; how to sculpt or carve a bird in wood). Pays $10 minimum for one-time rights on b&w photos and simple art illustrations; up to $75 for inside color, reproduced any size. Covers: Most are donated. Any purchased are negotiated.

Tips: "We use more shorties than feature-length pieces."

VIRGINIA WILDLIFE, Box 11104, Richmond VA 23230. (804)257-1000. Editor: Harry L. Gillam. Send manuscripts to Senior Editor, M. White. 75% freelance written. For sportsmen and outdoor enthusiasts. Pays on acceptance. Publishes ms an average of 1 year after acceptance. Buys first North American serial rights and reprint rights. Byline given. Computer printout submissions acceptable; prefers letter-quality to dot-matrix. Free sample copy and writer's guidelines. SASE (8½x11).

Nonfiction: Uses factual outdoor stories, set in Virginia. "Currently need boating subjects, youth in the outdoors, wildlife and nature in urban areas. Always need good fishing and hunting stories—not of the 'Me and Joe' genre, however. Slant should be to enjoy the outdoors and what you can do to improve it. Material must be applicable to Virginia, sound from a scientific basis, accurate and easily readable. No subjects which are too controversial for a state agency magazine to address; poetry and cartoons; sentimental or humorous pieces (not because they're inherently bad, but because so few writers are good at either); 'how I nursed an abandoned _____ back to health' or stories about wildlife the author has become 'pals' with." Submit photos with ms. Length: prefers approximately 1,200 words. Pays 5¢/word.

Photos: Buys photos with mss; "and occasionally buys unaccompanied good photos." Prefers color transparencies, but also has limited need for 8x10 b&w glossy prints. Captions required. Pays $10/b&w photo; $10-15 for color.

Tips: "We are currently receiving too many anecdotes and too few articles with an educational bent—we want instructional, 'how-to' articles on hunting, fishing and outdoor sports, and also want semi-technical articles on wildlife. We are not receiving enough articles with high-quality photographs accompanying them; also, photos are inadequately labeled and protected. Catering to these needs will greatly enhance chances for acceptance of manuscripts. We have more 'backyard bird' articles than we could ever hope to use, and not enough good submissions on trapping or bird hunting. We are cutting back substantially on number of freelance, over-the-transom submissions we purchase, in favor of making assignments to writers with whom we have established relationships and articles written by our own staff. The trend in our magazine is to pay more for fewer, longer, more in-depth, higher-quality stories. As always, a fresh angle sells, especially since we are basically publishing the same topics year after year. The most frequent mistake made by writers in completing an article for us is incorrect information on wildlife and locale."

WASHINGTON FISHING HOLES, Box 499, Snohomish WA 98290. (206)568-4121. Editor: Dave Mach. 65-75% freelance written. Magazine published monthly; 80 pages. For Washington anglers from ages 8-80, whether beginner or expert, interested in the where-to and how-to of Washington fishing. Circ. 10,000. Pays on publication. Buys first North American serial rights and second serial (reprint) rights. Submit material 4 months in advance. Computer printout submissions acceptable. Reports in 3 weeks. Free sample copy and writer's guidelines. SASE. Query essential.

Nonfiction: How-to (angling only) and informational (how-to). "Articles and illustrations *must* be local, Washington angling or readily available within a short distance for Washington anglers." Buys 120 mss/year. Query. Length: 1,000-1,500 words. Pays approximately $90-120.

Photos: Purchased with accompanying ms at $10 each extra. Buys color and b&w glossy prints or 35mm color transparencies with article. Covers $50. Color transparency, ASA 64 film. Captions and model release required.

WATERFOWLER'S WORLD, Waterfowl Publications, Ltd., Box 38306, Germantown TN 38183. (901)754-7484. Editor: Cindy Dixon. 75% freelance written. Bimonthly magazine covering duck and goose hunting for the serious hunter and experienced waterfowler, with an emphasis on improvement of skills. Circ. 35,000. Pays on publication. Publishes ms an average of 1 year after acceptance. Buys first North American serial rights. SASE. Reports in 2 months. Computer printout submissions acceptable; no dot-matrix. Sample copy $2.50; writer's guidelines for $1.

Nonfiction: General interest (where to hunt); how-to written for the serious duck hunter. Query. Length: 1,500 words. Pays $75-200.

Photos: Reviews 8x10 b&w prints and 35mm color transparencies. Pays $50/cover.

Columns/Departments: Fowlweather Gear (outdoor clothes and supplies).

Tips: "The most frequent mistakes made by writers in completing articles for us are not sending SASE for return of manuscript, and not realizing our audience already knows the basics of duck hunting.

WESTERN OUTDOORS, 3197-E Airport Loop, Costa Mesa CA 92626. (714)546-4370. Editor-in-Chief: Burt Twilegar. 75% freelance written. Emphasizes hunting, fishing, camping, boating for 11 Western states only, Baja California, Canada, Hawaii and Alaska. Monthly magazine; 88 pages. Circ. 150,000. Pays on acceptance. Publishes ms an average of 6 months after acceptance. Buys one-time rights. Query (in writing). Submit seasonal material 4-6 months in advance. Photocopied submissions OK. Computer printout submissions are acceptable if double-spaced; prefers letter-quality to dot-matrix. SASE. Reports in 4-6 weeks. Sample copy $1.50; writer's guidelines for SASE.

Nonfiction: Where-to (catch more fish, bag more game, improve equipment, etc.); informational; photo feature. "We do not accept fiction, poetry, cartoons." Buys 70 assigned mss/year. Query or send complete ms. Length: 1,000-1,800 words maximum. Pays $250-500.

Photos: Purchased with accompanying ms. Captions required. Uses 8x10 b&w glossy prints; prefers Kodachrome II 35mm slides. Offers no additional payment for photos accepted with accompanying ms. Pays $150 for covers.

Tips: "Provide a complete package of photos, map, trip facts and manuscript written according to our news feature format. Stick with where-to type articles. Both b&w and color photo selections make a sale more likely. We are beginning new section, 'Best In The West.' Write for details. The most frequent mistake made by writers in completing an article for us is that they don't follow our style. Our guidelines are quite clear."

WESTERN SPORTSMAN, Box 737, Regina, Saskatchewan, S4P 3A8 Canada. (306)352-8384. Publisher: J.B. (Red) Wilkinson. 90% freelance written. For fishermen, hunters, campers and others interested in outdoor recreation. "Please note that our coverage area is Alberta and Saskatchewan." Bi-Monthly magazine; 64-112 pages. Circ. 28,000. Rights purchased vary with author and material. May buy first North American serial rights or second serial (reprint) rights. Byline given. Pays on publication. Sample copy $3; free writer's guidelines. "We try to include as much information as possible on all subjects in each edition. Therefore, we usually publish fishing articles in our winter issues along with a variety of winter stories. If material is dated, we would like to receive articles 2 months in advance of our publication date." Will consider photocopied submissions. Reports in 4 weeks. SAE and IRCs.

Nonfiction: "It is necessary that all articles can identify with our coverage area of Alberta and Saskatchewan. We are interested in mss from writers who have experienced an interesting fishing, hunting, camping or other outdoor experience. We also publish how-to and other informational pieces as long as they can relate to our coverage area. Our editors are experienced people who have spent many hours afield fishing, hunting, camping, etc., and we simply cannot accept information which borders on the ridiculous. We are more interested in articles which tell about the average guy living on beans, guiding his own boat, stalking his game and generally doing his own thing in our part of Western Canada than a story describing a well-to-do outdoorsman traveling by motorhome, staying at an expensive lodge with guides doing everything for him except catching the fish, or shooting the big game animal. The articles that are submitted to us need to be prepared in a knowledgable way and include more information than the actual fish catch or animal or bird kill. Discuss the terrain, the people in-

volved on the trip, the water or weather conditions, the costs, the planning that went into the trip, the equipment and other data closely associated with the particular event in a factual manner. We're always looking for new writers.'' Buys 120 mss/year. Submit complete ms. Length: 1,500-3,000 words. Pays $100-325.
Photos: Photos purchased with ms with no additional payment. Also purchased without ms. Pays $20-25/5x7 or 8x10 b&w print; $175-200/35mm or larger transparency for front cover.

WISCONSIN SPORTSMAN, Great Lakes Sportsman Group, Box 2266, Oshkosh WI 54903. (414)233-1327. Editor: Thomas C. Petrie. Managing Editor: Charles Petrie. 35-40% freelance written. Bimonthly magazine (except for separate March and April issues) covering outdoor hunting, fishing and related sports for active sportsmen in Wisconsin. Circ. 75,000. Pays on acceptance. Publishes ms an average of 1 month after acceptance. Byline given. Kill fee to be determined. Buys first rights and second serial (reprint) rights. Submit seasonal/holiday material 5 months in advance. Simultaneous queries, and photocopied and previously published submissions OK. Computer printout submissions acceptable; prefers letter-quality to dot-matrix. SASE. Reports in 3 weeks. Sample copy for 8½x11 SAE and 95¢ postage; writer's guidelines for SAE with 22¢ postage.
Nonfiction: General interest (outdoors); historical/nostalgic (state history); how-to (hunting and fishing, etc.); humor; and photo feature (wildlife, wild plants, outdoor scenes). ''Chances of acceptance are enhanced when manuscripts are accompanied by good color transparencies.'' Buys 20-30 mss/year. Query or send complete ms. Length: 800-2,000 words. Pays $150-350. Sometimes pays the expenses of writers on assignment.
Photos: State availability or send photos with query or ms. Reviews 35mm color transparencies and 8x10 b&w prints. Payment for photos included in payment for ms. Identification of subjects required. Buys one-time rights.
Fiction: Adventure and humorous. Buys 7-8 mss/year. Query or send complete ms. Pays $200-600.
Fillers: Jokes, gags, anecdotes, short humor and newsbreaks. Buys 40-50/year. Length: 50-200 words. Pays $10-100.
Tips: As a member of the Great Lakes Group, *Wisconsin Sportsman* also buys some material in combination with its sister publications in Minnesota, Michigan and Pennsylvania.

Martial Arts

ATA MAGAZINE, Martial Arts and Fitness, ATA Magazine Co., Inc., Box 240835, Memphis TN 38124-0835. (901)761-2821. Editor: Milo Dailey. Managing Editor: Carla Dailey. 20% freelance written. *ATA Magazine* is the official publication of the American Taekwondo Association and ATA Fitness Centers, Inc. covering general health and fitness with emphasis on martial arts (Taekwondo), aerobics, and Nautilus strength training equipment. Circ. 13,500. Pays on publication. Publishes ms an average of 3 months after acceptance. ''Most of publication copyrighted.'' Buys first North American serial rights unless otherwise arranged. Submit seasonal/holiday material at least 6 months in advance. Sometimes accepts previously published submissions. Computer printout submissions acceptable; dot-matrix submissions OK ''if on non-heat-sensitive paper.'' Reports in 3 weeks. Sample copy $2.25; writer's guidelines for SAE.
Nonfiction: Interview/profile (on persons notable in other fields who train under ATA programs). ''Special slant is that martial arts are primarily for fitness and personal development. Defense and sports aspects are to reinforce primary aims. Freelancers who are not ATA members should concentrate on non-martial arts aspects of fitness or on ATA martial artists' personalities. We're not interested in fads, non-ATA martial arts or overt 'sex' orientation.'' Currently articles are staff-written, assigned to ATA experts or ATA member freelancers; would possibly buy 4-6 outside freelance mss. Query. Length: depends on material. Pays $25-150.
Photos: Payment for photos included in payment for ms. Prefers b&w prints of size appropriate to quality reproduction. Model release and identification of subjects ''with enough information for a caption'' required.
Fiction: ''We would take a look at fiction—but because of the overall magazine subject matter, would be very, very, very leery. It would almost take a writer who is an ATA martial arts member to get the right outlook.''
Tips: ''So far *ATA Magazine* has served as a developmental organ for ATA members who are or wish to be writers. We're willing to work with writers on nontechnical coverage of subjects of interest to our readership—which is mostly 'adult' in its approach to martial arts and fitness in general. The 'ATA Slant,' except in areas of diet, is virtually mandatory. Most ATA centers have a good story. Most martial arts and strength-training articles are staff-written or assigned to association experts. This leaves nutrition and special personality pieces most open to freelancers, along possibly with fiction. But to get the right slant, proximity to ATA sources (which are currently in about 200 communities coast to coast) is almost mandatory. It seems a major problem in writing for most magazines today is to have expert knowledge with ability to communicate at the non-expert level. A middle ground is the 'special interest' magazine such as ours which allows presumption of both interest and a basic knowledge of the subject. Still, it's easy to become too technical and forget that emotion retains readers—not just facts. ''The most frequent mistakes made by writers in completing an article for us are: 1) The most blatant mistake is not reading the entry in *Writer's Market*. We *do not* use karate movie stars or non-ATA martial artists. Other publications answer this interest segment. 2) We're a small staff with a lot of

hats to wear. Unsolicited manuscripts may get dumped by default. Handwritten ones certainly are. 3) Currently all freelance work accepted except for a regular nutrition column are written by those with familiarity with ATA programs. The 'Tips' in our listing starts right off with Key Number One—know the publication. 4) Recent freelance submissions include one on an ATA instructor who is highly ranked in PKA kickboxing; one upcoming is on identical twin sister *ATA* black belts. Others included coverage of ATA martial arts or fitness members or events. These writers all have an 'ATA connection'. (Several realized we'll accept their material after seeing it in *WM*.) 5) If writers actually read our listing, it would save all a lot of time. One well-known martial arts writer queried, determined we're not 'her thing', and we're both happier . . . 6) Some 'dot-matrix' quality has improve so a 10x glass can barely tell it's not a daisywheel . . . We use one here for form letters. (We're currently using non-standard disk formats which kills that medium for us.)"

BLACK BELT, Rainbow Publications, Inc., 1813 Victory Place, Burbank CA 91504. (213)843-4444. Publisher: Michael James. Emphasizes martial arts for both practitioner and layman. Monthly magazine; 128 pages. Circ. 100,000. Pays on publication. Buys all rights. Submit seasonal/holiday material 6 months in advance. Photocopied submissions OK. Computer printout submissions acceptable. SASE. Reports in 1 month. Free sample copy.
Nonfiction: Expose, how-to, informational, interview, new product, personal experience, profile, technical and travel. No biography, material on teachers or on new or Americanized styles. Buys 6 mss/issue. Query or send complete ms. Length: 1,200 words minimum. Pays $10-15/page of manuscript.
Photos: Very seldom buys photos without accompanying mss. Captions required. Pays $4-7 for 5x7 or 8x10 b&w or color transparencies. Total purchase price for ms includes payment for photos. Model release required.
Fiction: Historical. Buys 1 ms/issue. Query. Pays $35-100.
Fillers: Pays $5 minimum.

FIGHTING STARS, Rainbow Publications, 1813 Victory Pl., Box 7728, Burbank CA 91510-7728. (818)843-4444. Executive Editor: Dave Cater. Bimonthly magazine about the history, tradition and training of the ninja warrior. Circ. 60,000. Pays on publication. Buys first North American serial rights. Submit seasonal material 4 months in advance, but best to send query letter first. Simultaneous and photocopied submissions OK. Computer printout submissions acceptable. SASE. Reports in 6 weeks. Writer's guidelines for SASE.
Nonfiction: General interest, history or training articles (with well-known martial artists) on the art of ninjutsu; profiles (on art's top teachers); how-to (on the art of survival). Buys 30-40 unsolicited mss/year. Send query or complete ms. Length: 1,000-2,000 words. Pays $50-200.
Photos: State availability of photos. Most ms should be accompanied by photos. Reviews 5x7 and 8x10 b&w and color glossy prints. Can reproduce prints from negatives. Will use illustrations. Offers no additional payment for photos accepted with ms. Model releases required. Buys all rights.
Fiction: Must be related to ninja or art of ninjutsu.
Tips: "The art of ninjutsu is the fastest growing martial art in the world. As such, we welcome an array of articles dealing with its history, weapon, training and personalities. The writer, however, must use care in selecting the subject for his piece. "Fighting Stars" will feature only those instructors who have received training from Masaaki Hatsumi or students whose teachers have studied with him."

FIGHTING WOMAN NEWS, Martial Arts, Self-Defense, Combative Sports Quarterly, Box 1459, Grand Central Station, New York NY 10163. (212)228-0900. Editor: Valerie Eads. 100% freelance written. Quarterly magazine. "*FWN* combines sweat and philosophy, the deadly reality of street violence and the other worldliness of such eastern disciplines as Zen. Our audience is composed of adult women actually practicing martial arts with an average experience of 4 + years. Since our audience is also 80 + % college grads and 40% holders of advanced degrees we are an action magazine with footnotes. Our material is quite different from what is found in newsstand martial arts publications." Circ. 6,734. Pays on publication. Byline given. Buys one-time rights. Submit seasonal/holiday material 6 months in advance. Simultaneous queries, and simultaneous, photocopied, and previously published submissions OK. "For simultaneous and previously published we *must* be told about it." Computer printout submissions acceptable; prefers letter-quality to dot-matrix. If computer printout submissions "are unreadable we throw them out." SASE. Reports as soon as possible. Sample copy $3.50; writer's guidelines for business size SAE and 37¢ postage.
Nonfiction: Book excerpts, expose (discrimination against women in martial arts governing bodies); historical/nostalgic; how-to (martial arts, self-defense techniques); humor; inspirational (e.g., self-defense success stories); interview/profile ("we have assignments waiting for writers in this field"); new product; opinion; personal experience; photo feature; technical; travel. "All materials *must* be related to our subject matter. No tabloid sensationalism, no 'sweat is sexy too' items, no fantasy presented as fact, no puff pieces for an instructor or school with a woman champion in house." Buys 12 mss/year. Query. Sometimes pays the expenses of writers on assignment. Length: 1,000-5,000 words. Pays in copies or $10 maximum. Expenses negotiated in some cases.
Photos: Muskat Buckby, photo editor. State availability of photos with query or ms. Reviews "technically competent" b&w contact sheets and 8x10 b&w prints. "We negotiate photos and articles as a package. Some-

times expenses are negotiated. Captions and identification of subjects required. The need for releases depends on the situation."

Columns/Departments: Notes & News (short items relevant to our subject matter); Letters (substantive comment regarding previous issues); Sports Reports; and Reviews (of relevant materials in any medium). Query or send complete ms. Length: 100-1,000 words. Pays in copies or negotiate payment.

Fiction: Muskat Buckby, fiction editor. Adventure, fantasy, historical and science fiction. "Any fiction must feature a woman skilled in martial arts." Buys 0-1 mss/year. Query. Length: 1,000-5,000 words. "We will consider serializing longer stories." Pays in copies or negotiates payment.

Poetry: Muskat Buckby, poetry editor. "We'll look at all types. Must appeal to an audience of martial artists. Buys 3-4 poems/year. Length: open. Pays in copy or negotiated payment.

Tips: "Our greatest need is for solid martial arts material. Non-martial-artist writers can be given interview assignments. The writer may have a better chance of breaking in at our publication with short articles and fillers since it's easier to find a spot for a borderline filler. We are tight on article space."

INSIDE KARATE, The Magazine for Today's Total Martial Artist, Unique Publications, 4201 Vanowen Pl., Burbank CA 91505. (818)845-2656. Editor: Joe Bau. 75% freelance written. Monthly magazine covering the martial arts. Circ. 120,000. Publishes ms an average of 3 months after acceptance. Byline given. Offers $25 kill fee. Buys first North American serial rights. Submit seasonal/holiday material 4 months in advance. Simultaneous queries, and simultaneous and photocopied submissions OK. SASE. Reports in 3 weeks on queries; in 6 weeks on mss. Sample copy $2, 9x12 SAE and 5 first class stamps; free writer's guidelines.

Nonfiction: Book excerpts; expose (of martial arts); historical/nostalgic; humor; interview/profile (with approval only); opinion; personal experience; photo feature; and technical (with approval only). *Inside Karate* seeks a balance of the following in each issue: tradition, history, glamour, profiles and/or interviews (both by assignment only), technical, philosophical and think pieces. To date, most "how to" pieces have been done in-house. Buys 70 mss/year. Query. Length: 1,000-2,500 words; prefers 10-12 page mss. Pays $25-125.

Photos: Send photos with ms. Reviews b&w contact sheets, negatives and 8x10 prints. Captions and identification of subjects required. Buys one-time rights.

Tips: "Trends in magazine publishing that freelance writers should be aware of include the use of less body copy, better (and interesting) photos to be run large with 'story' caps. If the photos are poor and the reader can't grasp the whole story by looking at photos and copy, forget it."

INSIDE KUNG-FU, The Ultimate In Martial Arts Coverage!, Unique Publications, 4201 Vanowen Pl., Burbank CA 91505. (818)845-2656. Editor: Mark Shuper. 75% freelance written. Monthly magazine covering martial arts for those with "traditional, modern, athletic and intellectual tastes. The magazine slants toward little-known martial arts, and little-known aspects of established martial arts." Circ. 100,000. Pays on publication. Publishes ms an average of 6 months after acceptance. Byline given. Offers $35 kill fee. Buys first North American serial rights, and second serial (reprint) rights for book excerpts on rare occasions. Submit seasonal/holiday material 4 months in advance. Simultaneous queries, and simultaneous and photocopied submissions OK. Computer printout submissions acceptable; no dot-matrix. SASE. Reports in 3 weeks on queries; 6 weeks on mss. Sample copy $1.75 with 9x12 SAE and 5 first class stamps; free writer's guidelines.

Nonfiction: Expose (topics relating to the martial arts); historical/nostalgic; how-to (primarily technical materials); cultural/philosophical; interview/profile; personal experience; photo feature; and technical. "Articles must be technically or historically accurate." No "sports coverage, first-person articles, or articles which constitute personal aggrandizement." Buys 100 mss/year. Query or send complete ms. Length: 10-15 pages, typewritten. Pays $75-100. "Rarely" pays the expenses of writers on assignment, "but we have done it."

Photos: Send photos with accompanying ms. Reviews b&w contact sheets, b&w negatives and 8x10 b&w prints. "Photos are paid for with payment for ms." Captions and model release required. Buys one-time rights.

Fiction: Adventure, historical, humorous, mystery and suspense. "Fiction must be short (500-2,000 words) and relate to the martial arts. We buy very few fiction pieces." Buys 2-3 mss/year. Length: 500-2,000 words. Pays $75.

Tips: "The writer may have a better chance of breaking in at our publication with short articles and fillers since smaller pieces allow us to gauge individual ability, but we're flexible—quality writers get published period. The most frequent mistakes made by writers in completing an article for us are ignoring photo requirements and model releases (always number one—and who knows why? All requirements are spelled out in writer's guidelines)."

KARATE ILLUSTRATED, Rainbow Publications, Inc., 1813 Victory Place, Burbank CA 91504. (213)843-4444. Publisher: Michael James. Emphasizes karate and kung fu from the traditional and tournament standpoint and training techniques. Monthly magazine. Circ. 80,000. Pays on publication. Buys all rights. Submit seasonal/holiday material 6 months in advance. Simultaneous and photocopied submissions OK. SASE. Reports in 4-6 weeks. Free sample copy.

Nonfiction: Expose, historical, how-to, informational, interview, new product, personal experience, opinion, photo feature, profile, technical and travel. Buys 6 mss/issue. Query or submit complete ms. Pays $35-150.

Photos: Purchased with or without accompanying ms. Submit 5x7 or 8x10 b&w or color photos. Total purchase price for ms includes payment for photos.
Fiction: Historical. Query. Pays $35-150.
Fillers: Newsbreaks. Query. Pays $5.

Miscellaneous

THE AMATEUR BOXER, Diversified Periodicals, Box 249, Cobalt CT 06414. (203)342-4730. Editor: Bob Taylor. Magazine published 10 times/year for boxers, coaches and officials. Circ. 2,000. Pays on publication. Byline given. Buys first rights. Submit material 2 months in advance. Simultaneous queries, and simultaneous, photocopied and previously published submissions OK. SASE. Reports in 2 weeks on queries; 1 month on mss. Sample copy for 9x12 SAE and 56¢ postage.
Nonfiction: Interview/profile (of boxers, coaches, officials); results; tournament coverage; any stories connected with amateur boxing; photo feature; and technical. Buys 35 mss/year. Query. Length: 500-2,500 words. Pays $15-40.
Photos: State availability of photos. Pays $7-25 for b&w prints. Captions and identification of subjects required. Buys one-time rights.
Tips: "We're very receptive to new writers."

BALLS AND STRIKES, Amateur Softball Association, 2801 NE 50th St., Oklahoma City OK 73111. (405)424-5266. Editor: Bill Plummer III. 30% freelance written. Monthly tabloid covering amateur softball. Circ. 254,000. Pays on publication. Publishes ms an average of 2 months after acceptance. Buys first rights. Byline given. Computer printout submissions acceptable; no dot-matrix. SASE. Reports in 3 weeks. Sample copy $1.
Nonfiction: General interest, historical/nostalgic, interview/profile and technical. Query. Length: 2-3 pages. Pays $50-65.
Tips: "We generally like shorter features because we try to get many different features in each issue."

‡**BASKETBALL WEEKLY**, 17820 E. Warren, Detroit MI 48224. (313)881-9554. Publisher: Roger Stanton. Editor: Matt Marsom. 20 issues during season, September-May. Circ. 45,000. Buys all rights. Pays on publication. Sample copy for SASE and $1. Reports in 2 weeks. SASE.
Nonfiction, Photos and Fillers: Current stories on teams and personalities in college and pro basketball. Length: 800-1,000 words. Pays $35-75. 8x10 b&w glossy photos purchased with mss. Also uses newsbreaks. Do not send general basketball information.
Tips: "Include information about your background that qualifies you to do a particular story. More emphasis on television will affect writers in the year ahead."

FLORIDA RACQUET JOURNAL, Racquetball-Sports, Florida Racquet Journal, Inc., Box 11657, Jacksonville FL 32239. (904)721-3660. Editor: Norm Blum. Managing Editor: Kathy Blum. Monthly tabloid covering racquetball in the Southeast. 50% freelance written. Circ. 20,000. Pays on acceptance. Byline given. Makes work-for-hire assignments and buys second (reprint) rights to material originally published elsewhere. Offers $25 kill fee. Submit seasonal/holiday material 3 months in advance. Simultaneous queries, and simultaneous and photocopied and previously published submissions OK. Computer printout submissions acceptable. SASE. Reports in 2 weeks. Sample copy for $1, SAE, and 2 first class stamps.
Nonfiction: Book excerpts (from racquetball books); expose (of racquetball clubs); historical/nostalgic; humor; new product; personal experience. "No how-to or instructional articles." Buys 12-15 mss/year. Query. Length: 400-900 words. Pays $10-40.
Columns/Departments: Horoscope, crossword puzzle, and health items—all for racquetball players. Buys 36 mss/year. Query. Length: 400-800 words. Pays $10-30.
Fiction: Humorous. Buys variable number mss/year. Query. Length: 500-1,500 words. Pays $10-30.
Poetry: Free verse. Buys variable number/year. Length: 30-60 lines. Pays $5-10.
Fillers: Clippings, jokes, gags, anecdotes, short humor, newsbreaks. Length: 30-50 words. Pays $1-5.
Tips: "We don't want your opinion—let the subject tell the story. If we like your first article we'll keep using you."

‡**GYMNASTICS TODAY, National Newspaper of Contemporary Gymnastics**, Ron Dezvour Publishing Group, 2006 Pine St., Philadelphia PA 14103. (215)735-4917. Editor: Ron Alexander. Bimonthly tabloid covering gymnastics and fitness. Circ. 130,000. Pays on publication. Byline given. Offers 50% kill fee. Buys first serial rights. Submit seasonal/holiday material 2 months in advance. Simultaneous queries, and simultaneous and previously published submissions OK. SASE. Reports in 1 month. Sample copy $1; free writer's guidelines.

Nonfiction: Expose, how-to, humor, inspirational, interview/profile, new product, opinion, personal experience and photo feature. Buys 50 mss/year. Send complete ms. Length: 500-700 words. Pays $100-140.
Photos: State availability of photos or send photos with ms. Reviews 5x7 b&w and color prints. Pays $8-10 for b&w; $10-20 for color. Captions, model release, and identification of subjects required. Buys one-time rights.
Columns/Departments: Send complete ms. Length: 500-700 words. Pays $75-125.
Tips: *"Gymnastics Today* covers the world of gymnastics. Editorial departments range from fitness, nutrition, news, information and events for high school, college and Olympic gymnastics. Information on national and regional meets, sports medicine, business, and fashions is published for the gymnast, coach, official, and fan in *Gymnastics Today."*

INDIANA RACQUET SPORTS, 207 S. Main, Box 216, Frankfort IN 46041. (317)654-6721. Editor: Michael Curts. Monthly tabloid newspaper. 10% freelance written. Circ. 8,000. Pays on publication. Byline given. Buys first and second rights to the same material. Submit seasonal/holiday material 2 months in advance. Simultaneous, photocopied and previously published submissions OK. Computer printout submissions acceptable. SASE. Reports in 2 weeks. Publishes ms an average of 1 month after acceptance. Sample copy for 9x12 SAE and 2 first class stamps; writer's guidelines for business size SAE and 1 first class stamp.
Nonfiction: Health/nutrition; any racquet sport with Indiana connection—tennis, platform tennis, squash, table tennis, badminton, racquetball. Length: open. Pays $20.
Photos: Send photos with ms. Pays $5-10 for 5x7 b&w prints. Buys one-time rights.
Columns/Departments: Buys 12 mss/year. Query. Length: open. Pays $20.
Fillers: Buys 50/year. Length: 75 words maximum.

INSIDE RUNNING, 9514 Bristlebrook Dr., Houston TX 77083. Editor/Publisher: Joanne Schmidt. 50% freelance written. Monthly tabloid covering "news and features of interest to runners and joggers. We are a *Texas* magazine and our focus is on runners and running in the state." Circ. 12,000. Rights negotiable. Pays on acceptance. Publishes ms an average of 1½ months after acceptance. SASE. Reports "within six weeks." Sample copy $1.25; writer's guidelines for SAE and 2 first class stamps.
Nonfiction: "Strongly researched service pieces, profiles, race reports, and coverage of developments in the sport. We would like to discover correspondents and writers in Texas who run or have a familiarity with the sport and are looking for assignments in their area. Coverage in north and east Texas badly needed. Running opportunities and scenery throughout state would be very helpful. We want very much to include capsule accounts of races from around the state for our Texas Round-up section. No personal 'How I Ran the Marathon' pieces." Buys 24 unsolicited mss/year. Query, and explain background and photographic experience; include writing samples, if possible. Pays $35-100. "We may pay more if the writer has worked with us before and demonstrated a knowledge of our needs. We will negotiate with established writers as well." Sometimes pays the expenses of writers on assignment.
Photos: "Strong photos earn extra payment." Pays $10 for b&w 5x7 prints; $25 for 4-K covers.
Fiction: Pays $35-100, "depending on length, quality and originality."
Tips: "Report on races in your area, profile a local runner doing something unusual, focus on ways to make running more fun or exciting. Emphasize a Texas locale with running as part of a 'lifestyle.' We will work with writers and offer concrete, specific suggestions if they will follow through. Quotes and good b&w photos will give you the edge. The most frequent mistakes made by writers in completing an article for us are: 1) ideas aren't original; 2) topic doesn't apply to our readership; or 3) inadequate research."

INTERNATIONAL OLYMPIC LIFTER, IOL Publications, 3916 Eagle Rock, Box 65855, Los Angeles CA 90065. (213)257-8762. Editor: Bob Hise. Managing Editor: Herb Glossbrenner. 20% freelance written. Bimonthly magazine covering the Olympic sport of weight lifting. Circ. 10,000. Pays on publication. Publishes ms an average of 3 months after acceptance. Byline given. Offers $25 kill fee. Buys one-time rights or negotiable rights. Submit seasonal/holiday material 5 months in advance. Photocopied submissions OK. Computer printout submissions acceptable; no dot-matrix. SASE. Reports in 6 weeks. Sample copy $2.50; writer's guidelines for SAE and 4 first class stamps.
Nonfiction: Training articles, contest reports, diet—all related to Olympic weight lifting. Buys 6 mss/year. Query. Length: 250-2,000 words. Pays $25-100.
Photos: Action (competition and training). State availability of photos. Pays $1-5 for 5x7 b&w prints. Identification of subjects required.
Poetry: Keith Cain, poetry editor. Light verse, traditional—related to Olympic lifting. Buys 6-10 poems/year. Submit maximum 3 poems. Length: 12-24 lines. Pays $10-20.
Fillers: Gags and anecdotes related to weight lifting. Buys 6 mss/year. Length: 100-150 words. Pays $10-15.

THE MAINE SPORTSMAN, Box 365, Augusta ME 04330. Editor: Harry Vanderweide. 100% freelance written. Monthly tabloid. Circ. 21,000. Pays "during month of publication." Buys first rights. Publishes ms an average of 3 months after acceptance. Byline given. Computer printout submissions acceptable. SASE. Reports in 2-4 weeks.

Nonfiction: "We publish only articles about Maine hunting and fishing activities. Any well-written, researched, knowledgable article about that subject area is likely to be accepted by us." Expose, how-to, general interest, interview, nostalgia, personal experience, opinion, profile, and technical. Buys 25-40 mss/issue. Submit complete ms. Length: 200-2,000 words. Pays $20-80. Sometimes pays the expense of writers on assignment.
Photos: "We can have illustrations drawn, but prefer 1-3 b&w photos." Submit photos with accompanying ms. Pays $5-50 for b&w print.
Tips: "It's rewarding finding a writer who has a fresh way of looking at ordinary events. Specific where-to-go about Maine is needed."

NATIONAL RACQUETBALL, Publication Management, Inc., 4350 DiPaolo Ctr., Glenview IL 60025. Publisher: Hugh Morgan. Editorial Director: Rex Dimick. For racquetball players of all ages. Monthly magazine. 40% freelance written. Circ. 36,000. Pays on publication. Buys all rights. Byline given. Submit seasonal/holiday material 2-3 months in advance. SASE. Publishes ms an average of 2 months after acceptance. Sample copy $2.
Nonfiction: How-to (play better racquetball or train for racquetball); interview (with players or others connected with racquetball business); opinion (usually used in letters but sometimes fullblown opinion features on issues confronting the game); photo feature (on any subject mentioned); profile (short pieces with photos on women or men players interesting in other ways or on older players); health (as it relates to racquetball players—food, rest, eye protection, etc.); and fashion. No material on tournament results. Buys 4 mss/issue. Query with clips of published work. Length: 500-2,500 words. Pays $25-150.
Photos: State availability of photos or send photos with ms. Offers no additional payment for photos accompanying ms. Uses b&w prints or color transparencies. Buys one-time rights. Captions and model releases required.
Fiction: Adventure, humorous, mystery, romance, science fiction and suspense. "Whatever an inventive mind can do with racquetball." Buys 3 mss/year. Send complete ms. Pays $25-150.
Tips: "Break into *National Racquetball* by writing for monthly features—short pieces about racquetball players you know. We need more contributions from all over the country. Our object is national and international coverage of the sport of racquetball."

PRIME TIME SPORTS & FITNESS, GND Prime Time Publishing, Box 6091, Evanston IL 60204. (312)864-8113/276-2143. Editor: Dennis A. Dorner. Managing Editor: Nicholas J. Schmitz. 80% freelance written. A monthly magazine covering racquet and health club sports and fitness. Circ. 35,000. Pays on publication. Publishes ms an average of 2 months after acceptance. Byline given. Buys all rights; will assign back to author in 85% of cases. Submit seasonal/holiday material 3 months in advance. Photocopied and previously published submissions OK. No simultaneous submissions. Computer printout submissions acceptable; prefers letter-quality to dot-matrix. SASE. Reports in 2 weeks. Sample copy for SAE and 3 first class stamps; writer's guidelines for business size SAE and 1 first class stamp.
Nonfiction: Book excerpts (fitness and health); expose (in tennis, fitness, racquetball, health clubs, diets); adult (slightly risque and racy fitness); historical/nostalgic (history of exercise and fitness movements); how-to (expert instructional pieces on any area of coverage); humor (large market for funny pieces on health clubs and fitness); inspirational (on how diet and exercise combine to bring you a better body, self); interview/profile; new product; opinion (only from recognized sources that know what they are talking about); personal experience (definitely—humor); photo feature (on related subjects); technical (on exercise and sport); travel (related to fitness, tennis camps, etc.); news reports (on racquetball, handball, tennis, running events). Special issues: Swimsuit and Resort Issue (March); Summer Fashion (July); Fall Fashion (October); Christmas Gifts and related articles (December). '' We love short articles that get to the point. No articles on local only tennis and racquetball tournaments without national appeal except when from Chicago/Milwaukee area." Buys 50 mss/year. Length: 2,000+ words maximum. Pays $20-150. Sometimes pays the expenses of writers on assignment.
Photos: Eric Matye, photo editor. Send photos with ms. Pays $5-75 for b&w prints. Captions, model release and identification of subjects required. Buys all rights, "but returns 75% of photos to submitter."
Columns/Departments: Linda Jefferson, column/department editor. New Products; Fitness Newsletter; Handball Newsletter; Racquetball Newsletter; Tennis Newsletter; News & Capsule Summaries; Fashion Spot (photos of new fitness and bathing suits); related subjects. Buys 100 mss/year. Send complete ms. Length: 50-250 words ("more if author has good handle to cover complete columns"). Pays $5-25.
Fiction: Joy Kiefer, fiction editor. Erotica (if related to fitness club); fantasy (related to subjects); humorous (definite market); religious ("no God-is-my shepherd, but Body-is-God's-temple OK"); romance (related subjects). "No raunchy or talking down exercise stories, Upbeat is what we want." Buys 10 mss/year. Send complete ms. Length: 500-2,500 words maximum. Pays $20-150.
Poetry: Free verse, haiku, light verse, traditional on related subjects. Length: up to 150 words. Pays $10-25.
Fillers: Linda Jefferson, fillers editor. Clippings, jokes, gags, anecdotes, short humor, newsbreaks. Buys 400/year. Length: 25-200 words. Pays $5-15.
Tips: "Send us articles dealing with court club sports, exercise and nutrition that exemplify an upbeat 'you can

do it' attitude. Good short fiction or humorous articles can break in. Expert knowledge of any related subject can bring assignments; any area is open. A humorous/knowledgable columnist in weight lifting, aerobics, running and nutrition is presently needed. We review the author's work on a nonpartial basis. We consider everything as a potential article, but are turned off by credits, past work and degrees. We have a constant demand for well-written articles on instruction, health and trends in both. Other articles needed are professional sports training techniques, fad diets, tennis and fitness resorts, photo features with aerobic routines. A frequent mistake made by writers is length—articles are too long. When we assign an article, we want it newsy if it's news and opinion if opinion. Too many writers are incapable of this task."

RACING PIGEON PICTORIAL, The Racing Pigeon Publishing Co. Ltd., 19 Doughty St., London WCIN 2PT, England. Editor-in-Chief: Colin Osman. 50% freelance written. Emphasizes racing pigeons for "all ages and occupations; generally 'working class' backgrounds, both sexes." Monthly magazine. Circ. 13,000. Pays on publication. Publishes ms an average of 3 months after acceptance. Buys first rights, first and second rights to the same material, and second (reprint) rights to material originally published elsewhere. Submit seasonal/holiday material 3 months in advance. Photocopied and previously published submissions OK. SAE and IRCs. Reports in 5 weeks. Sample copy $2.
Nonfiction: Michael Shepherd, articles editor. How-to (methods of famous fanciers, treatment of diseases, building lofts, etc.); historical (histories of pigeon breeds); informational (practical information for pigeon fanciers); interview (with winning fanciers); and technical (where applicable to pigeons). "Don't bother, if you're not a specialist!" Buys 4 mss/issue. Submit complete ms. Length: 6,000 words minimum. Pays $30/page minimum. Sometimes pays the expenses of writers on assignment.
Photos: Rick Osman, photo editor. Purchased with or without accompanying ms or on assignment. Captions required. Send 8x10 b&w glossy prints or 2¼x2¼ or 35mm color transparencies.

THE RUNNER, 1 Park Ave., New York NY 10016. Editor-in-Chief: Marc Bloom. Emphasizes the world of running in the broadest scope with its main thrust in jogging, roadrunning and marathoning/fitness and health. 75% freelance written. Monthly magazine. Circ. 275,000. Pays on acceptance. Publishes ms an average of 4 months after acceptance. Buys most first North American serial rights. Pays 20% kill fee. Byline given. Submit seasonal/holiday material 3 months in advance. Electronic submissions OK "but not on unsolicited manuscripts, only on assignment." Computer printout submissions acceptable; prefers letter-quality to dot-matrix. SASE. Reports in 2-3 weeks. Free sample copy.
Nonfiction: Profiles, body science, event coverage, training, lifestyle, sports medicine, phenomena and humor. Buys 5-6 mss/issue. Query with clips of published work. Length: 2,000-4,000 words. Pays usually $500-1,000. Sometimes pays the expenses of writers on assignment.
Photos: State availability of photos. Pay is negotiable for b&w contact sheets and 35mm color transparencies. Buys one-time rights. Captions required.
Columns/Departments: Training, statistical listings, humor, food, medicine, and physiology. Regular columnists used. Buys 3-4/issue. Length: 900-1,200 words. Pays $200 and up.
Warmups: Short news items, whimsical items, and advice on improving running. Length: 100-500 words. Pays $75.
Tips: "The writer may have a better chance of breaking in at our publication with short articles and fillers because we find it risky to commit to larger pieces with people new to us. The most frequent mistakes made by writers in completing an article for us are poor research, out-of-sync tone, misreading our audience, using a self-indulgent first-person style, and poor sources for quotes."

‡**RUNNER'S WORLD**, Rodale Press, 33 E. Minor St., Emmaus PA 18049. Editor: Robert Rodale. Managing Editor: David Bumke. 40% freelance written. Monthly magazine covering the world of recreational and competitive running. Circ. 350,000. Pays on acceptance. Publishes ms an average of 3 months after acceptance. Byline given. Offers 10% kill fee. Buys first serial rights and second serial (reprint) rights. Submit seasonal/holiday material 4 months in advance (query only). Computer printout submissions acceptable; prefers letter-quality to dot-matrix. SASE. Reports in 1 month. Sample copy for SAE; writer's guidelines for SAE.
Nonfiction: How-to (training pieces, stretching exercises, etc.); interview/profile; photo feature (outstanding races or unusual personalities); technical (running mechanics, new developments in shoes); and medical and diet. No inspirational ("our readers already know about the joys and frustrations of running"), fiction or poetry. Buys 36 mss/year. Query with or without published clips. Length: 2,000-4,000 words. Pays $300-2,000. Sometimes pays the expenses of writers on assignment.
Columns/Departments: Contact column/department editor. Guest Spot, usually an expert (shoes, nutrition, fitness); occasionally a reply to a stand we've taken. Runners' Forum, usually first-person accounts of experiences on the road; part of letters section. Buys 40 mss/year. Send complete ms. Length: 300-600 words. Pays $10-50.
Tips: "The key is submitting ideas for features that will be of interest to a nationwide audience of serious, sophisticated runners. The more technical areas are most open to freelancers: features on exercising, diet and nu-

trition, new developments in shoes, and running mechanics. We emphasize that we *must* be queried on feature ideas. Perhaps our biggest source of frustration is the volume of unsolicited manuscripts we receive; a large majority is unsuitable.

RUNNING TIMES, Running Times, Inc., Suite 20, 144146 Jefferson Davis Highway, Woodbridge VA 22191. (703)491-2044. Editor: Edward Ayres. Monthly magazine; 72 pages. Emphasizes running, jogging, holistic health and fitness. Circ. 100,000. Pays on publication. Byline given. Buys all rights. Submit seasonal/holiday material 3 months in advance. Simultaneous and photocopied submissions OK. SASE. Reports in 1 month. Sample copy $2.
Nonfiction: How-to (training techniques, racing techniques, self-treatment of injuries, etc.); humor; interview; photo feature; profile; and technical (written for an educated readership). "We do not want opinions or ideas which are not backed up by solid research." Buys 1-2 mss/issue. Query or send complete ms. Length: 500-2,500 words. Pays $25-400.
Photos: State availability of photos. Pays $20-50 for 5x7 or 8x10 b&w glossy prints; $30-250 for color transparencies. Captions preferred.
Fiction: Adventure, fantasy and humorous. "Subjects must involve runners or running." Buys 10 mss/year. Send complete ms or published clips.Length: 700-2,500 words. Pays $50-200.

SIGNPOST MAGAZINE, 16812 36th Ave. W., Lynnwood WA 98037. Publisher: Washington Trails Association. Editor: Ann L. Marshall. About hiking, backpacking and similar trail-related activities, mostly from a Pacific Northwest viewpoint. 10% freelance written. Monthly. Will consider any rights offered by author. Buys 12 mss/year. Pays on publication. Publishes ms an average of 6 months after acceptance. Free sample copy. Will consider photocopied submissions. Reports in 3 weeks. Query or submit complete ms. Computer printout submissions acceptable; prefers letter-quality to dot-matrix.
Nonfiction and Photos: "Most material is donated by subscribers or is staff-written. Payment for purchased material is low, but a good way to break into print or spread a particular point of view."
Tips: "We cover only *self-propelled* outdoor sports; won't consider mss about trail bikes, snowmobiles, power boats. Since we are so specialized, we look for quality and appropriateness rather than length of item."

SKYDIVING, Box 1520, Deland FL 32721. (904)736-9779. Editor: Michael Truffer. 10% freelance written. Monthly tabloid featuring skydiving for sport parachutists, worldwide dealers and equipment manufacturers. Circ. 7,200. Average issue includes 3 feature articles and 3 columns of technical information. Pays on publication. Publishes ms an average of 2 months after acceptance. Byline given. Buys one-time rights. Simultaneous, photocopied and previously published submissions OK, if so indicated. Electronic submission OK IBM PC. Computer printout submission acceptable. SASE. Reports in 1 month. Sample copy $2; writer's guidelines with SASE and 73¢ postage.
Nonfiction: "Send us news and information on equipment, techniques, events and outstanding personalities who skydive. We want articles written by people who have a solid knowledge of parachuting." No personal experience or human-interest articles. Query. Length: 500-1,000 words. Pays $25-100.
Photos: State availability of photos. Reviews 5x7 and larger b&w glossy prints. Offers no additional payment for photos accepted with ms. Captions required.
Fillers: Newsbreaks. Length: 100-200 words. Pays $25 minimum.
Tips:"The most frequent mistake made by writers in completing articles for us is that the writer isn't knowledgable about the sport of parachuting."

Skiing and Snow Sports

‡**AMERICAN SKATING WORLD, Publication of the American Ice Skating Community**, Business Communications Inc., 2545-47 Brownsville Rd., Pittsburgh PA 15210. (412)885-7600. Editor: Robert A. Mock. Assistant Editor: Doug Graham. 70% freelance written. Monthly tabloid on ice skating. Circ. 15,000. Pays on publication on the tenth day of the following month. Publishes ms an average of 3 months after acceptance. Byline given. Buys all rights. Submit seasonal/holiday material 3 months in advance. Computer printout submissions acceptable; prefers letter-quality to dot-matrix. SASE. Reports in 3 weeks. Sample copy $1; free writer's guidelines.
Nonfiction: Expose; general interest; historical/nostalgic; how-to (technique in figure skating); humor; inspirational; interview/profile; new product; opinion; personal experience; photo feature; technical and travel. Special issues include annual fashion issue (September). No fiction. Buys 200 mss/year. Send complete ms. "Include phone number." Length: 600-1,000 words. Pays $25-100. Sometimes pays the expenses of writers on assignment.
Photos: Bill Simmons, photo editor. Send photos with query or ms. Reviews color transparencies and b&w prints. Pays $5 for b&w; $15 for color. Identification of subjects required. Buys all rights for b&w; one-time

rights for color.

Columns/Departments: Bill Simmons, column/department editor. Buys 60 mss/year. Send complete ms. Length: 500-750 words. Pays $25-75.

Fillers: Clippings and anecdotes. No payment for fillers.

Tips: "Send a well-polished manuscript, detailed without being wordy." Event coverage is most open to freelancers.

‡**THE NEW ENGLAND SKIERS' GUIDE**, Historical Times, Inc., 2245 Kohn Rd., Box 8200, Harrisburg PA 17105. (717)657-9555. Managing Editor: Kathie Kull. 70% freelance written. Annual magazine covering New England recreational skiing and sports, winter travel. Estab. 1983. Circ. 100,000. Pays on acceptance. Publishes ms an average of 6 months after acceptance. Byline given. Offers 25% kill fee. Buys all rights. Seasonal/holiday material queries due in winter, articles due May 1 for October publishing. Photocopied submissions OK. Computer printout submissions acceptable; prefers letter-quality to dot-matrix. Reports in 2 weeks. Sample copy for 9x12 SAE and $2 postage. Writer's guidelines for #10 SAE and 1 first class stamp.

Nonfiction: Photo feature (New England skiing or winter sports); travel (New England in winter); and skiing technique, gear, resorts. Buys 6 mss/year. Query with published clips. Length: 500-1,500 words. Pays $100-400. Pays mail and phone expenses of writers on assignment.

Photos: State availability of photos. Reviews 35mm color transparencies and b&w prints. Pays $25-100 for b&w; $50-400 for color. Buys one-time rights.

Tips: "Articles should include specific information that directs or helps the reader with sidebars of listings, etc. New England regional focus is essential."

POWDER 'the Skiers' MAGAZINE, Box 1028, Dana Point CA 92629. (714)496-5922. Managing Editor: Pat Cochran. 90% freelance written. Published 7/year, including two special issues: pre-season equipment review and photo annual. Circ. 100,000. Pays on publication. Publishes ms an average of 5 months after acceptance. Buys rights one-time. Submit material late spring, early summer for publication the following season. Computer printout submissions acceptable. Reports on material accepted for publication in 2 months. Phone query preferred. Sample copy for $1.50.

Nonfiction: "We want material by or about people who reach out for the limits of the ski experience. Avoid classical ski teaching technique problems, travelogue features, or beginner-oriented articles. We try to emphasize the quality and enjoyment of the ski experience rather than its mechanics, logistics, or purely commercial aspects." Length: 500-2,500 words. Pays approximately 25¢/word.

Photos: *Top quality* b&w and color transparencies purchased with or without mss or on assignment. Pays approximately $75-150 for b&w, full or partial page, $150-350 for color, full or partial page; $500 cover.

Tips: "Be creative in approaches to articles. We look for quality writing, imagination, personality and humor. Review our magazine thoroughly . . . back at least 6 issues . . . before querying."

SKATING, United States Figure Skating Association, 20 First St., Colorado Springs CO 80906. (303)635-5200. Editor-in-Chief: Ian A. Anderson. Monthly magazine; 64 pages. Circ. 31,000. Pays on publication. Buys all rights. Byline given. Phone queries OK. Submit seasonal/holiday material 3 months in advance. Photocopied and previously published submissions OK. SASE. Reports in 1 month. Writer's guidelines for SASE.

Nonfiction: Historical; how-to (photograph skaters, training, exercise); humor; informational; interview; personal experience; personal opinion; photo feature; profile (background and interests of national-caliber amateur skaters); technical; and competition reports. Buys 4 mss/issue. Query or send complete ms. Length: 500-1,000 words. Pays $50.

Photos: Photos purchased with or without accompanying ms. Pays $15 for 8x10 or 5x7 b&w glossy prints and $35 for color transparencies. Query.

Columns/Departments: European Letter (skating news from Europe); Ice Abroad (competition results and report from outside the U.S.); Book Reviews; People; Club News (what individual clubs are doing); and Music column (what's new and used for music for skating). Buys 4 mss/issue. Query or send complete ms. Length: 100-500 words. Pays $35. Open to suggestions for new columns/departments.

SKI, 380 Madison Ave., New York NY 10017. (212)687-3000. Editor: Dick Needham. 15% freelance written. 8 times/year, September through April. Buys first rights in most cases. Pays 50% kill fee. Bylines given. Pays on acceptance. Publishes ms an average of 4 months after acceptance. Computer printout submissions acceptable; no dot-matrix. Reports in 1 month. SASE.

Nonfiction: Prefers articles of general interest to skiers, travel, adventure, how-to, budget savers, unusual people, places or events that reader can identify with. Must be authoritative, knowledgably written, in easy, informative language and have a professional flair. Cater to middle to upper income bracket readers who are college graduates, wide travelers. No fiction or poetry. Length: 1,500-2,000 words. Pays $200-400.

Photos: Buys photos submitted with manuscripts and with captions only. Good action shots (slides only) in color for covers; pays minimum $700. B&w photos, pays $50 each; minimum $150 for photo stories. (Query on these.) Color slides. Pays $75 each; $250/page.

Tips: "Another possibility is our column, Ski People, which runs 300-400-word items on unusual people who ski and have made some unique contribution to the sport. We want to see outline of how author proposes to develop story for *Ski*, sample opening page or paragraph; include previous clippings or published writing samples. Humor is welcome."

SKI RACING MAGAZINE, International Journal of Skiing, Ski Racing International, 2 Bentley Ave., Poultney VT 05764. (802)287-9090. Editor: Don A. Metivier. Tabloid covering major ski competition events worldwide for the serious skier and ski industry person. 70% freelance written. Published 20 times during the ski season (September-April). Circ. 40,000. Pays on publication. Publishes ms an average of 3 days after acceptance. Byline given. Buys one-time rights. Reports "at once, because of the time frame of events we cover." Electronic submissions OK on IMB PC, but requires hard copy also. Computer printout submissions acceptable. Free sample copy.
Nonfiction: "We cover only news and interviews with those making it. Prefer not to get opinion from writers." Buys 200 mss/year. Query with clips of published work. Length: "depends on the story; from minimum of a paragraph and list of top 5 finishers to maximum of 500-750 words." Pays $25-50 for news stories; $50-100 for longer assignments; negotiates fees prior to assignment on interviews. Sometimes pays the expenses of writers on assignment.
Photos: Pays $10-25 for photos; $50 for covers, action photos, and candids for picture pages and interviews. $50 and up for photos (b&w only) used by advertisers.
Tips: "It's frustrating working with freelance writers who miss deadlines. We publish 3 times a month—old news isn't news. The writer has a better chance of breaking in at our publication with short articles and fillers since we have a large group of regular writers anxious to write ski stories. The most frequent mistake made by writers in completing an article is lack of detail. Most writers are not good reporters; they will look up a word, but not recheck facts."

SKIING MAGAZINE, Ziff-Davis Publishing Co., 1 Park Ave., New York NY 10016. (212)503-3900. Editor-in-Chief: Alfred H. Greenberg. Editorial Directors: William Grout, Dinah B. Witchel. 50% freelance written. Published 7 times/year (September-March). Magazine; 175 pages. Circ. 430,000. Pays on acceptance. Buys first rights. Byline given. Submit seasonal/holiday material 4 months in advance. SASE. Publishes ms an average of 1 year after acceptance. Sample copy $2.
Nonfiction: "This magazine is in the market for any material of interest to skiers. Material must appeal to and please the confirmed skier. Much of the copy is staff-prepared, but many freelance features are purchased provided the writing is fast-paced, concise and knowledgable." Buys 10 unsolicited mss/year. Submit complete ms. Feature length: 2,500-3,000 words. Pay is $300 minimum per national magazine page of text; about 12¢/word for regional.
Photos: Erin Kenney, art director. Purchased with or without accompanying ms or on assignment. Send contact sheet or transparencies. Pays $125/full page for 8x10 b&w glossy or matte photos; $300 minimum/full page for 35mm transparencies, pro-rated for partial pages. Model release required.

SNOWMOBILE CANADA, Suite 202, 2077 Dundas St. E., Mississauga, Ontario L4X 1M2 Canada. (416)624-8218. Editor: Reg Fife. Snowmobiling magazine published in September, October and November "to satisfy the needs of Canada's snowmobilers from coast to coast." Circ. 60,000. Pays on publication. Byline given. Buys first rights. Submit seasonal/holiday material "by July for fall publicaction." Simultaneous queries acceptable. Computer printout submissions acceptable. Reports in 1 month on queries; 2 months on mss. Free sample copy.
Nonfiction: Personal experience (on snowmobiling in Canada); photo feature (nature in winter); technical (new snowmobile developments); travel (snowmobile type). "We look for articles on nature as it relates to snowmobile use; trail systems in Canada; wilderness tips; the racing scene; ice fishing using snowmobiles, maintenance tips and new model designs." Buys 12 mss/year. Query or send complete ms. Length: 800-2,000 words. Pays $75-150.
Photos: Captions required. Buys one-time rights.

SNOWMOBILE WEST, 520 Park Ave., Box 981, Idaho Falls ID 83402. Editor: Steve Janes. For recreational snowmobile riders and owners of all ages. Magazine; 48 pages. 5% freelance written. Publishes 4 issues each winter. Circ. 200,000. Buys first North American serial rights. Pays kill fee if previously negotiated at time of assignment. Byline given on substantive articles of two pages or more. Buys 5 mss/year. Pays on publication. Publishes ms an average of 3 months after acceptance. Free sample copy and writer's guidelines. Reports in 2 months. Articles for one season are generally photographed and written the previous season. Query. Computer printout submissions acceptable. SASE.
Nonfiction and Photos: Articles about snowtrail riding in the Western U.S.; issues affecting snowmobilers; and maps of trail areas with good color photos and b&w. Pays 3¢/word; $5/b&w; $10/color. B&w should be 5x7 or 8x10 glossy print; color should be 35mm transparencies or larger, furnished with mss. With a story of 1,000 words, typically a selection of 5 b&w and 5 color photos should accompany. Longer stories in propor-

tion. Length: 500-2,000 words.

Tips: "It's rewarding finding a freelance writer who understands the nature and personality of our publication. It's annoying when writers say they have the story that we *really need* to use."

Soccer

SOCCER AMERICA, Box 23704, Oakland CA 94623. (415)549-1414. Editor-in-Chief: Ms. Lynn Berling-Manuel. For a wide range of soccer enthusiasts. Weekly tabloid. 10% freelance written. Circ. 12,000. Pays on publication. Buys all rights. Byline given. Submit seasonal/holiday material 30 days in advance. SASE. Reports in 2 months. Publishes ms an average of 2 months after acceptance. Sample copy and writer's guidelines $1.

Nonfiction: Expose (why a pro franchise isn't working right, etc.); historical; how-to; informational (news features); inspirational; interview; photo feature; profile; and technical. "No 'Why I Like Soccer' articles in 1000 words or less. It's been done." Buys 1-2 mss/issue. Query. Length: 200-1,500 words. Pays 50¢/inch minimum.

Photos: Photos purchased with or without accompanying ms or on assignment. Captions required. Pays $12 for 5x7 or larger b&w glossy prints. Query.

Tips: "Freelancers mean the addition of editorial vitality. New approaches and new minds can make a world of difference. But if they haven't gotten themselves familiar with the publication . . . total waste of my time and theirs."

Tennis

TENNIS, 495 Westport Ave., Box 5350, Norwalk CT 06856. Publisher: Mark Adorney. Editor: Shepherd Campbell. For persons who play tennis and want to play it better. Monthly magazine. Circ. 500,000. Buys all rights. Byline given. Pays on publication. SASE.

Nonfiction and Photos: Emphasis on instructional and reader service articles, but also seeks lively, well-researched features on personalities and other aspects of the game, as well as humor. Query. Length varies. Pays $200 minimum/article, considerably more for major features. Pays $50-150/8x10 b&w glossies; $75-350/color transparencies.

TENNIS USA, Contact CBS Consumer Publishing, a Division of Family Media Inc., 3 Park Ave. New York NY 10016. Publisher: Bud Dealey.

‡**TENNIS WEEK**, Tennis News, Inc., 1107 Broadway, New York NY 10010. (212)741-2323. Publisher and Founder: Eugene L. Scott. Editor: Linda Pentz. Weekly newspaper; 20-32 pages. Circ. 40,000. Byline given. Pays on acceptance. Photocopied submissions OK. SASE. Reports in 2 weeks. Sample copy 50¢.

Nonfiction: "Articles should concentrate on players' lives off the court." Buys 100 mss/year. Send complete ms. Pays $25-100.

Photos: Send photos with ms. Pays $10/8x10 b&w glossy print.

WORLD TENNIS, Family Media, Inc., 3 Park Ave., New York NY 10016. (212)340-9200. Editor-in-Chief: Neil Amdur. Executive Editor: Grace Lichtenstein. 10% freelance written. Magazine covering tennis and other racket sports. "We are a magazine catering to tennis enthusiasts—both participants and fans—on every level." Circ. 385,000. Pays on acceptance. Publishes ms an average of 6 months after acceptance. Byline given. Offers 20% kill fee. Buys first North American serial rights, and second serial (reprint) rights. Submit seasonal/holiday material 6-8 months in advance. Accepts simultaneous queries, and photocopied submissions. SASE. Computer printout submissions acceptable; prefers letter-quality to dot-matrix. Reports in 1 month on queries. Sample copy for $1.75; writer's guidelines for SAE.

Nonfiction: Needs book excerpts (tennis, fitness, nutrition); how-to (we use our own instructional panel); interview/profile; personal experience; photo feature; technical (we do racket testing); and travel (tennis resorts). Buys 10-30 mss/year. Query. Length: 2,000 words. Pays $250 minimum. Sometimes pays expenses of writers on assignment.

Columns/Departments: Seniority (essays by older players); and About Juniors (short pieces relating to junior game). Buys 12-20 items/year. Query. Length: 750-1,000 words. Pays $100 and up.

Tips: "Query before sending manuscripts. Most of our material is commissioned but we welcome fresh ideas." The Seniority column is most open to freelancers.

Water Sports

DIVER, Seagraphic Publications, Ltd., Suite 210, 1807 Maritime Mews, Granville Island, Vancouver, British Columbia V6H 3W7 Canada. (604)681-3166. Publisher: Peter Vassilopoulos. Editor: Neil McDaniel. 75% freelance written. Emphasizes scuba diving, ocean science and technology (commercial and military diving) for a well-educated, outdoor-oriented readership. Published 9 times/year. Magazine; 48-56 pages. Circ. 25,000. Payment "follows publication." Buys first North American serial rights. Byline given. Query (by mail only). Submit seasonal/holiday material 3 months in advance of issue date. Computer printout submissions acceptable; prefers letter-quality to dot-matrix. SAE and IRCs. Reports in 6 weeks. Publishes ms an average of 2 months after acceptance.
Nonfiction: How-to (underwater activities such as photography, etc.); general interest (underwater oriented); humor; historical (shipwrecks, treasure artifacts, archeological); interview (underwater personalities in all spheres—military, sports, scientific or commercial); personal experience (related to diving); photo feature (marine life); technical (related to oceanography, commercial/military diving, etc.); and travel (dive resorts). No subjective product reports. Buys 40 mss/year. Submit complete ms. Length: 800-2,000 words. Pays $2.50/column inch.
Photos: "Features are mostly those describing dive sites, experiences, etc. Photo features are reserved more as specials, while almost all articles must be well illustrated with b&w prints supplemented by color transparencies." Submit photo material with accompanying ms. Pays $7 minimum for 5x7 or 8x10 glossy b&w prints; $15 minimum for 35mm color transparencies. Captions and model releases required. Buys one-time rights.
Columns/Departments: Book reviews. Submit complete ms. Length: 200 words maximum. Pays $2.50/column inch.
Fillers: Anecdotes, newsbreaks and short humor. Buys 8-10/year. Length: 50-150 words. Pays $2.50/column inch.
Tips: "It's rewarding finding a talented writer who can make ordinary topics come alive. But dealing with unsolicited manuscripts that don't even come close to being suitable for *Diver* is the most frustrating aspect of working with freelancers."

‡THE DIVER, Diversified Periodicals, Box 249, Cobalt CT 06414. (203)342-4730. Editor: Bob Taylor. 10 times a year magazine on springboard and platform diving. Circ. 1,500. Pays on publication. Byline given. Buys first rights. Submit seasonal/holiday material 2 months in advance. SASE. Reports in 2 weeks on queries; 1 month on mss. Sample copy for 9x12 SAE and 56¢ postage.
Nonfiction: Humor; interview/profile (of divers, coaches, officials); personal experience; photo feature; technical. Buys 50 mss/year. Query. Length: 500-2,500 words. Pays $10-40.
Photos: State availability of photos. Pays $5-25 for b&w prints. Captions and identification of subjects required. Buys one-time rights.

‡RIVER RUNNER MAGAZINE, Rancher Publications, Box 2047, Vista CA 92083. (619)744-7170/727-0120. Editor: Gregg A. Payne. Associate Editor: Mark C. Larson. 80% freelance written. Bimonthly magazine covering rafting, canoeing, and kayaking. "Audience is predominantly male, college educated, and approximately 20-45 years old. The editorial slant favors white-water action. Stories reflect the natural beauty and excitement of running rivers." Circ. 15,000. Pays on publication. Publishes ms an average of 2 months after acceptance. Byline given. Buys first North American serial rights. Submit seasonal/holiday material 6 months in advance. Computer printout submissions acceptable only if double-spaced; prefers letter-quality to dot-matrix. SASE. Reports in 2 weeks on queries; 4 weeks on mss. Sample copy $2.50; writer's guidelines for 4x9 SAE and 1 first class stamp.
Nonfiction: Book excerpts (soon-to-be-published books relevant to river running); historical/nostalgic (articles on human history of a river are welcome, as are articles on river running pioneers, and interesting periods in paddling history); how-to (authoritative, well-researched technical pieces offering sound advice to canoers, kayakers, and rafters); interview/profile; (personality profiles of prominent river runners or others of interest to our outdoor-oriented readership); new products (detailed, critical evaluations of boats and gear of interest to river runners); opinion (responsible opinions of interest to river runners); technical (expert commentary on equipment and techniques of interest to river runners); and an occasional feature on sea kayaking. "Solid, well-researched conservation pieces and equipment reviews are also welcome. We have little need for trip logs submitted by neophyte river runners. Don't submit stories that reflect an unfamiliarity with the sport." Buys 42 mss/year. Query with or without published clips or send complete ms. Length: 250-3,500 words. Pays $250. Sometimes pays the expenses of writers on assignment.
Photos: State availability of photos with query letter or ms. Pays $15-35 for color transparencies; $10-15 for b&w contact sheets and prints. "We need good, sharp photographs that prominently portray strong human emotion or natural beauty. Transparencies must have high technical quality." Captions, model release and identification of subjects required. Buys one-time rights.
Columns/Departments: "Damwatch (focus on immediate, specific threats to rivers); Upfront (short, bright, lively commentary of not more than 500 words)." Relevant book reviews are also welcome; pays $10 on publi-

cation. Forum is nonpaid column provided for recognized river spokespersons to voice opinions of interest to the paddling community." Buys 15 mss/year. Send complete ms. Length: 850-1500 words. Pays $25-75.
Fillers: Clippings, anecdotes, short humor and newsbreaks. "We can use any river-related clippings, or outdoor items of interest to an outdoor readership." Buys 20 mss/year. Length: 50-500 words. Pays $5-35.
Tips: "Submit fresh, original story ideas with strong supporting photographs. Be persistent, and constantly on the lookout for new and unused story ideas. The prime need is for original, well-written river feature stories. We have limited use for hair-boating, first descent stories. (If you don't understand what this means, you probably can't write for this publication.) Stories should be written for the intermediate-level paddler. Freelance writers and photographers are a vital part of *River Runner*. We encourage and appreciate your continued submissions."

SAILBOARD NEWS, The International Journal of Boardsailing, Sports Ink Magazines, Inc., Box 159, Fair Haven VT 05743. (802)265-8153. Editor: Mark Gabriel. 50% freelance written. Monthly boardsailing tabloid. Circ. 19,000. Pays 30 days after publication. Publishes ms an average of 2 weeks after acceptance. Byline given. Buys one-time rights. Submit seasonal/holiday material 3 weeks in advance. Simultaneous queries OK. Computer printout submissions acceptable. SASE. Reports in 3 weeks. Free sample copy and writer's guidelines.
Nonfiction: Book excerpts, expose, general interest, historical/nostalgic, how-to, humor, inspirational, interview/profile, new product, opinion, photo feature, technical, travel. Buys 50 mss/year. Send complete ms. Length: 750 words minimum. Pays $50-200.
Photos: Send photos with ms. Reviews b&w negatives and 8x10 prints. Identification of subjects required.
Columns/Departments: Buys 12 mss/year. Query with published clips or send complete ms.

SAILORS' GAZETTE, Main Line Publications, Suite 110, 337 22nd Ave. N., St. Petersburg FL 33704. (813)823-9172. Editor: Alice N. Eachus. 70% freelance written. Monthly magazine covering sailing in the southeastern states for sailboat owners. Circ. 16,000. Pays on publication. Publishes ms an average of 45-60 days after acceptance. Byline given. Offers 50% kill fee. Buys one-time rights. Submit seasonal/holiday material 3 months in advance. Computer printout submissions acceptable. SASE. Reports in 4 weeks on queries; 6 weeks on mss. Sample copy $2; free writer's guidelines.
Nonfiction: Historical/nostalgic (sailboats with direct ties to SE states); interview/profile (with sailboat owners); personal experience (sailboat cruising in SE); photo feature (b&w on sailing or waterfront scenes in SE states); and technical (sailboat maintenance, not general boat maintenance). No poetry; articles about sailboats with no connection to Southeastern states; articles about first-time sailors. Buys 150 mss/year. Query with published clips. Length: 500-1,800 words. Pays $50-250.
Photos: State availability of photos. Pays $10-25 for high contrast 8x10 b&w prints. Captions and identification of subjects required. Buys one-time rights.
Tips: "The manuscripts that we turn down are usually too general and far removed from the Southeastern themes. We're open to where-to and how-to, as it pertains to the Southeast; also interviews with cruising and racing sailors and racing personalities.

SCUBA TIMES, The Active Diver's Magazine, Poseidon Publishing Co., Box 6268, Pensacola FL 32503. (904)478-5288. Managing Editor: Jean Jerigan. Publisher: M. Wallace Poole. 80% freelance written. Bimonthly magazine covering scuba diving. "Our reader is the young, reasonably affluent scuba diver looking for a more exciting approach to diving than he could find in the other diving magazines." Circ. 75,000. Pays 6 weeks after publication. Publishes ms an average of 6 months after acceptance. Byline given. Buys first world serial rights. Simultaneous queries OK. Computer printout submissions acceptable. SASE. Reports in 2 months. Sample copy $3. Writer's guidelines for business size SAE and 1 first class stamp.
Nonfiction: General interest; how-to; interview/profile ("of 'name' people in the sport, especially if they're currently doing something interesting"); new products (how to more effectively use them); personal experience (good underwater photography pieces); and travel (pertaining to diving). Especially want illustrated articles on avant garde diving and diving travel, such as nude diving, singles only dive clubs, deep diving, new advances in diving technology, etc. No articles without a specific theme. Buys 25 mss/year. Query with clips of published work. Length: 1,200-2,000 words. Pay varies with author. Base rate is $100/published page.
Photos: Art Dept. "Underwater photography must be of the *highest* quality in order to catch our interest. We can't be responsible for unsolicited photo submissions." Pays $25-250 for 35mm color transparencies; reviews 8x10 b&w prints. Captions, model release, and identification of subjects required. Buys first world rights.
Tips: "Our current contributors are among the top writers in the diving field. A newcomer must have a style that captures the inherent adventure of scuba diving, leaves the reader satisfied at the end of it, and makes him want to see something else by this same author soon. Writing for diving magazines has become a fairly sophisticated venture. Writers must be able to compete with the best in order to get published. We only use contributors grounded in underwater photojournalism."

‡**SKIN DIVER**, Petersen Publishing Co., 8490 Sunset Blvd., Los Angeles CA 90069. (213)657-5100. Executive Editor: Bonnie J. Cardone. Managing Editor: Connie Johnson. 85% freelance written. Monthly magazine on scuba diving. "*Skin Diver* offers broad coverage of all significant aspects of underwater activity in the areas of underwater recreation, ocean exploration, scientific research, commercial diving, military advancements, and undersea technological developments." Circ. 209,676. Pays on publication. Publishes ms an average of 9 months after acceptance. Byline given. Buys one-time rights. Submit seasonal/holiday material 6 months in advance. No simultaneous submissions. Computer printout submissions acceptable. SASE. Reports in 3 weeks on queries; 3 months on mss. Sample copy $2.50; free writer's guidelines.

Nonfiction: How-to (catch game, modify equipment, etc.); interview/profile; personal experience; travel; local diving; adventure and wreck diving. No Caribbean travel; "how I learned to dive." Buys 200 mss/year. Send complete ms. Length: 300-2,000 words; 1,200 preferred. Pays $50/published page.

Photos: Send photos with query or ms. Reviews 35mm transparencies and 8x10 prints. Pays $50/published page. Captions and identification of subjects required. Buys one-time rights.

Fillers: Newsbreaks and cartoons. Length: 300 words. Pays $15 for cartoons; $50/published page.

Tips: "Forget tropical travel articles and write about local diving sites, hobbies, game diving, local and wreck diving."

SURFING MAGAZINE, Western Empire, 2720 Camino Capistrano, San Clemente CA 92672. (714)492-7873. Editor: David Gilovich. 5% freelance written. Monthly magazine covering all aspects of the sport of surfing. "*Surfing Magazine* is a contemporary, beach lifestyle/surfing publication. We reach the entire spectrum of surfing enthusiasts." Circ. 80,000. Pays on publication. Publishes ms an average of 2 months after acceptance. Byline given. Buys all rights. Submit seasonal/holiday material 4 months in advance. Photocopied submissions OK. Electronic submissions OK " 'Basic' language needed." Computer printout submissions acceptable; prefers letter-quality to dot-marix. SASE. Reports in 2 weeks. Free sample copy and writer's guidelines for SAE.

Nonfiction: Book excerpts (on surfing, beach lifestyle, ocean-related); how-to (surfing-related); interview/profile (of top surfing personality); new product; photo feature (of ocean, beach lifestyle, surfing); travel (to surfing locations only). Buys 50 mss/year. Query with clips of published work or send complete ms. Length: 3,000 words maximum. Pays 10-15¢/word.

Photos: Larry Moore, photo editor. State availability of photos or send photos with ms. Pays $35-500 for 35mm color transparencies; $20-75 for b&w contact sheet and negatives. Identification of subjects required. Buys one-time rights.

Columns/Departments: Bill Sharp, column/department editor. "Currents"—mini-features of current topical interest about surfing. This department includes reviews of books, films, etc. Buys 36 mss/year. Query with clips of published work, if available, or send complete ms. Length: 100-500 words. Pays $75-100.

Fiction: Adventure, humorous. No fantasy fiction. Buys 3 mss/year. Send complete ms. Length: 1,000-4,000 words. Pays 10-15¢/word.

Tips: "Begin by contributing small, mini-news features for our 'Currents' department. New editorial policy suggests that we will be more receptive than ever to bringing in new writers."

‡**SWIM MAGAZINE**, R. Magnus Enterprises, Inc., 523 S. 26th Rd., Arlington VA 22202. (703)549-6388. Editor: Robert M. Hansen. 75% freelance written. Bimonthly magazine. "*Swim* is for adults interested in swimming for fun, fitness and competition. Readers are fitness-oriented adults from varied social and professional backgrounds who share swimming as part of their lifestyle. Reader ages are evenly distributed from 20 to 90, so articles must appeal to a broad age group." Estab. 1984. Circ. 5,000. Pays on publication. Publishes ms an average of 4 months after acceptance. Byline given. Buys all rights. Submit seasonal/holiday material 4 months in advance. Simultaneous queries and photocopied submissions OK. Computer printout submissions acceptable; prefers letter-quality to dot-matrix. SASE. Reports in 1 month on queries; 3 months on ms. Sample copy for $1 or 9x12 SAE with 7 first class stamps; free writer's guidelines.

Nonfiction: How-to (training plans and techniques); humor (sophisticated adult-oriented humor); interview/profile (people associated with fitness and competitive swimming); new product (articles describing new products for fitness and competitive training); personal experience (related to how swimming has become an integral part of one's lifestyle); photo features (will be considered if of general interest to fitness and competitive swimmers); travel (articles on vacation spots where swimming pools, lakes or (warm) ocean are available for training; diet and health (articles on diet, health and self-help that relate to, or include swimming). "Articles need to be informative as well as interesting. In addition to fitness and health articles, we are interested in exploring interesting topics dealing with swimming that have not been covered by past publications. We want to burst the myth that swimming is a boring sport or way to stay in shape." Buys 30-40 mss/year. Send complete ms. Query first on photo features and travel articles. Length: 1,000-5,000 words. Pays $200. "No payment for articles about personal experiences."

Photos: Send photos with ms. Pays $5 for b&w transparencies and prints; $10 for color transparencies and prints. Captions, model release, and identification of subjects required. Buys one-time rights.

Columns/Departments: Buys 20-24 mss/year. Query. Length: 250-2,500 words. Pays $25-200.

Fillers: Anecdotes, short humor and newsbreaks. Length: 50-350 words. No payment for fillers.

Tips: "*Swim* is interested in first-time writers who know about and understand swimming and adult fitness. The best way to break in is to write us with your ideas or a description of your area of expertise. Articles should be informative, factual and entertaining. Shorter articles on specific topics such as new equipment reviews, personality profiles, swimming stroke technique and personal training programs are most likely to be successful. We are buried in 'humor' articles, but always interested in truly funny material provided it is relevant to swimming."

SWIMMING WORLD, 116 W. Hazel St., Inglewood CA 90302. (213)674-2120. Editor: Robert Ingram. 2% freelance written. For "competitors (10-24), plus their coaches, parents, and those who are involved in the enjoyment of the sport." Monthly. Circ. 40,000. Buys all rights. Byline given. Buys 5-7 mss/year. Pays on publication. Query. SASE.

Nonfiction: Articles of interest to competitive swimmers, divers and water poloists, their parents and coaches. Can deal with diet, body conditioning or medicine, as applicable to competitive swimming. Nutrition and stroke and diving techniques. Psychology and profiles of athletes. Must be authoritative. Length: 1,500 words maximum. Pays $50 maximum.

Photos: Photos purchased with mss. Does not pay extra for photos with mss. 8x10 b&w only. Also photos with captions. Pays $20 maximum for b&w.

THE WATER SKIER, Box 191, Winter Haven FL 33882. (813)324-4341. Editor: Duke Cullimore. Official publication of the American Water Ski Association. 50% freelance written. Published 7 times/year. Circ. 18,000. Buys North American serial rights only. Byline given. Buys limited amount of freelance material. Query. Pays on acceptance. Publishes ms an average of 3 months after acceptance. Reports on submissions within 10 days. Computer printout submissions acceptable "if double-spaced and standard ms requirements are followed"; prefers letter-quality to dot-matrix. SASE.

Nonfiction and Photos: Occasionally buys exceptionally offbeat, unusual text/photo features on the sport of water skiing. Will put more emphasis on technique, methods, etc., in the year ahead.

Tips: "Freelance writers should be aware of specializations of subject matter in magazine publishing; need for more expertise in topic; more professional writing ability."

WINDRIDER, The Magazine of Boardsailing, World Publications, Inc., Box 2456, Winter Park FL 32790. (305)628-4802. Editor: Nancy K. Crowell. 50% freelance written. Magazine published 7 times/year (monthly June, July) on boardsailing/a.k.a. "windsurfing" for boardsailors around the world of all skill levels. "Writers absolutely must be skilled boardsailors with extensive knowledge about the sport." Circ. 40,000. Pays 30 days after publication. Publishes ms an average of 6 months after acceptance. Byline given. Buys first rights. Submit seasonal/holiday material 3 months in advance. Computer printout submissions acceptable; prefers letter-quality to dot-matrix. SASE. Reports in 6 weeks on queries; 3 weeks on ms. Sample copy $2.50; writer's guidelines for business size SAE and 1 first class stamp.

Nonfiction: How-to ("we use established boardsailors for this type of article") and technical (must have technical background in the sport). No fiction, poetry, cartoons or "first time on a sailboard" material. Buys 18 mss/year. Query with published clips. Length: 750-2,500 words. Pays $75-250.

Tips: "You must be involved in the boardsailing world to write for our publication—as competitor, manufacturer or engineer, instructor, etc. We occasionally use freelancers for travel on specific areas, but this is only in the event we can't get there ourselves. Probably the best area for freelancers is our Equipment Tip section."

‡**WISCONSIN SILENT SPORTS**, Waupaca Publishing Co., Box 152, Waupaca WI 54981. (715)258-7731. Editor: Greg Marr. 75% freelance written. Monthly magazine on running, cycling, cross-country skiing, canoeing, camping, backpacking, hiking. A regional publication aimed at people who run, cycle, cross-country ski, canoe, camp and hike in Wisconsin. Not a "coffee-table" magazine. "Our readers are participants from rank amateur weekend athletes to highly competitive racers." Estab. 1984. Circ. 10,000. Pays on publication. Publishes ms an average of 3 months after acceptance. Byline given. Offers 20% kill fee. Buys one-time rights. Submit seasonal/holiday material 2 months in advance. Simultaneous queries, and photocopied and previously published submissions OK. Computer printout submissions acceptable; prefers letter-quality to dot-matrix. SASE. Reports in 1 month. Sample copy and writer's guidelines for large SAE and 5 first class stamps.

Nonfiction: General interest, how-to, interview/profile, new product, opinion, technical and travel. No first person unless it is of Edward Abbey/Norman Mailer quality. Buys 25 mss/year. Query. Length: 2,500 words maximum. Pays $15-100. Sometimes pays expenses of writers on assignment.

Tips: "Where-to-go, how-to, and personality profiles are areas most open to freelancers. Writers should keep in mind that this is a regional Wisconsin-based publication. We do drift over into border areas occasionally but center on Wisconsin."

WORLD WATERSKIING MAGAZINE, World Publications, Box 2456, Winter Park FL 32790. (305)628-4802. Publisher: Terry L. Snow. Editor: Theresa T. Temple. Magazine published 8 times/year. Covers various

Close-up

Nancy K. Crowell
Editor
WindRider

"Don't even attempt to write about a sport if you haven't tried it," says writer and editor Nancy K. Crowell. A few years ago, she took her own advice. It led to her job as editor of *WindRider.*

Having worked with *Women's Sports*, *Racquetball*, and *Waterski*, she heard about a forthcoming publication on boardsailing (windsurfing).

"Let me take some lessons and start writing for that magazine," she recalls saying. She did—and her first article in *WindRider* described those lessons. "I really liked sailing, and boardsailing was accessible to me then."

Editor for the last three years, she has guided the seven-times-a-year publication to a worldwide circulation of 38,000. Eighty percent of her magazine is freelance written, and "everybody who writes for this magazine is involved in the sport."

Involvement is the key for writers trying to write for any sports magazine, and also specific knowledge of a sport. "You need to know the lingo," she points out.

"I'm generally very unreceptive to letters that say 'I'm a freelance writer and I can write about this and that.' I *am* receptive to people who say 'I'm a windsurfer and I've had this experience I'd like to share.' " The ideal query letter for her is a story suggestion plus clips of past articles, but Crowell will consider a new writer if enthusiasm shines through. Editors are particularly receptive to queries from writers who know their magazine. Crowell would like to get queries that say, "I've read your magazine, and I think you should do an article on this subject."

Readers of *WindRider* know that the magazine is consumer-oriented with articles on instruction and boardsailing travel destinations. The other two major magazines of the sport are surfer- and photo-oriented.

As a contributor to *Outdoors*, *Sailing*, and *Playboy*, Crowell is sympathetic to writers. "I make things very clear upfront and I'm always available if they have questions." Writers begin to get "a feel for what sort of information you're looking for" after she outlines two or three times the facts she wants.

Crowell nurtures writers she meets at major boardsailing events. "I can usually tell by talking to someone if they're going to be able to write for the magazine. If they can speak well and express themselves I know they can do that on paper if I can just hold their hand and say 'Tell it to me as though I'm sitting there'." Crowell assigns most of *WindRider's* articles for the coming year by December.

Enthusiasm and expertise, good writing skills and meeting deadlines help writers to successfully pitch ideas to sports magazines much like Crowell does when *she* freelances.

—*Jean Stokes*

levels of water skiing. Circ. 57,000. Pays on publication. Byline given. Buys variable rights. Submit seasonal/ holiday material 6 months in advance. Simultaneous queries, and simultaneous, photocopied, and previously published submissions OK. SASE. Reports in 3 weeks.

Nonfiction: Historical/nostalgic (anything dealing with water skiing); how-to (tips on equipment and repair of skis, bindings, etc.); humor ("always looking for a good laugh about water skiing"); inspirational (someone who beat the odds—handicapped skier, for example); interview/profile (only on assignment); photo feature (action or special effects); technical (on assignment only); travel (picturesque water skiing sites); sports medicine. No first-person accounts or fiction. Buys 10-30 mss/year. Query with or without clips of published work. Pays $150-200/feature story; $75/medical, sports medicine; $40/tips.

Photos: Tom King, senior photographer. "We need lots of sharp photos for our annual issue in October. Send photos with ms. Prefers b&w prints or contact sheet, 35mm or 2 ¼ color slides/transparencies. Model release and identification of subjects required. Buys negotiable rights. Buys 5-15 mss/year. Query with clips of published work. Length: 250-300 words. Pays $40-75.

Fillers: Buys 5/year. Length: 100-150 words. Pays $5-15.

Tips: "We would love to hear from good sportswriters with a lively interest in water skiing. We're especially open to features and sports medicine articles. Medical writing would require background in specialized area and proof with resume, etc."

Teen and Young Adult

"Our market (teens 13-19) is very trend-oriented," points out one teen magazine editor. "We need to keep abreast of these ever-changing trends, and our material must reflect them." Editors agree that the stories they buy in 1986 must not overlook these trends. At the same time, teen magazines address problems that teens in every era have faced—growing up, coping with school, friends and family, and dating. The publications in this category are for young people aged 13-19. Publications for college students are listed in Career, College and Alumni.

ALIVE FOR YOUNG TEENS, Christian Board of Publication, Box 179, St. Louis MO 63166. Editor: Mike Dixon. 95% freelance written. Ecumenical, mainline publication with a Protestant slant; aimed at young teens. "We especially appreciate submissions of useable quality from 12- to 15-year-olds. Those in this age range should include their age with the submission. We appreciate use of humor that early adolescents would appreciate. Please keep the age group in mind." Publishes ms an average of 14 months after acceptance. Buys first rights. Computer printout submissions acceptable; prefers letter-quality to dot-matrix. SASE required with all submissions. Sample copy $1.

Nonfiction: "Articles should concern interesting youth, church youth groups, projects and activities. There is little chance of our taking an article not accompanied by at least 3-4 captioned b&w photos." Length: 800-1,000 words. Pays 3¢/word; photos $3-5.

Fiction: "Give us fiction concerning characters in the *Alive for Young Teens* readers' age group (12-15), dealing with problems and situations peculiar to that group." Length: 100-1,200 words. Pays 3¢/word. Uses 6-10 photo features/issue. Pays $5/photo maximum.

Photos: Send photos with ms. Submit in batches. Pays $10-20 for b&w prints.

Poetry: Length: 20 lines maximum. Pays 25¢/line.

Fillers: Puzzles, riddles and daffy definitions. Pays $10 maximum.

Tips: "A most frequent mistake made by writers in completing articles for us is missing the age-range interests."

AMERICAN NEWSPAPER CARRIER, American Newspaper Boy Press, Box 15300, Winston-Salem NC 27103. Editor: Marilyn H. Rollins. 20% freelance written. Usually buys all rights but may be released upon request. Pays on acceptance. Publishes ms an average of 3 months after acceptance. Queries not required. Computer printout submissions acceptable. Reports in 30 days. SASE.

Fiction: Uses a limited amount of short fiction written for teen-age newspaper carriers, male and female. It is preferable that stories be written around newspaper carrier characters. Humor, mystery and adventure plots are commonly used. No drugs, sex, fantasy, supernatural, crime or controversial themes. Length: 1,200 words. Pays $25.

Tips: "Fillers are staff-written, usually."

BOYS' LIFE, Boy Scouts of America, Magazine Division, 1325 Walnut Hill Lane, Irving TX 75062. (214)659-2000. Editor: Robert Hood. 85% freelance written. Monthly magazine covering Boy Scout activities for "ages 8-18—Boy Scouts, Cub Scouts, and others of that age group." Circ. 1.5 million. Pays on acceptance. Publishes ms an average of 6 months after acceptance. Byline given. Computer printout submissions acceptable.

Nonfiction: "Almost all articles are assigned. We do not encourage unsolicited material."

Columns/Departments: Hobby How's (1-2 paragraphs on hobby tips). Buys 60 mss/year. Send complete ms. Pays $5 minimum. Pays expenses of writers on assignment.

Fillers: Jokes (Think and Grin—1-3 sentences). Pays $1 minimum.

Tips: "The most frequent mistake made by writers is failure to read *Boys' Life.*"

BREAD, 6401 The Paseo, Kansas City MO 64131. (816)333-7000, ext. 214. Editor: Gary Sivewright. 10% freelance written. Christian leisure reading magazine for junior and senior high students, published by the Church of the Nazarene. Monthly. Pays on acceptance. Publishes ms an average of 8 months after acceptance. Accepts simultaneous submissions. Computer printout submissions acceptable. Buys first rights, sometimes second rights. Byline given. Free sample copy and editorial specifications sheet for SASE.

Nonfiction: Helpful articles in the area of developing the Christian life; first-person, "this is how I did it" stories about Christian witness. Length: up to 1,500 words. Articles must be theologically acceptable. Looking for fresh approach to basic themes. Also needs articles dealing with doctrinal subjects such as the Holy Spirit, written for the teen reader. Pays 3½¢/word for first rights and 3¢/word for second rights. Works 6 months ahead of publication.

Photos: 8x10 b&w glossy prints of teens in action. Payment is $15 and up. Uses 1 color transparency/month for cover.

Fiction: "Adventure, school, and church-oriented. No sermonizing." Send us fresh, innovative fiction stories. Avoid the same old formula kinds of pieces. We buy more fiction than anything. Make sure dialogue and situations are up to date." Length: 1,500 words maximum. Pays 3-3.5¢/word for first rights and 3¢/word for second rights.

Poetry: Free verse, light verse and traditional. Buys 10 poems/year. Length: 25 lines maximun. Submit poems in batches of 3. Pays 25¢ a line.

Tips: Send complete ms by mail for consideration. Reports in 6-8 weeks. SASE.

CAMPUS LIFE MAGAZINE, Christianity Today, Inc., 465 Gundersen Dr., Carol Stream IL 60188. Executive Editor: Scott Bolinder. Senior Editors: Gregg Lewis and Jim Long. Associate Editor: Verne Becker. 20% freelance written. For a readership of young adults, high school and college age. "Though our readership is largely Christian, *Campus Life* reflects the interests of all young people—music, bicycling, photography, media and sports." Largely staff-written. "*Campus Life* is a Christian magazine that is *not* overtly religious. The indirect style is intended to create a safety zone with our readers and to reflect our philosophy that God is interested in all of life. Therefore, we publish message stories side by side with general interest, humor, etc." Monthly magazine. Circ. 150,000. Pays on acceptance. Publishes ms an average of 6 months after acceptance. Buys one-time rights. Byline given. Submit seasonal/holiday material 6 months in advance. Simultaneous, photocopied and previously published submissions OK. Computer printout submissions acceptable. SASE. Reports in 2 months. Sample copy $2; writer's guidelines for SASE.

Nonfiction: Personal experiences, photo features, unusual sports, humor, short items—how-to, college or career and travel, etc. Query or submit complete manuscript. Length: 500-3,000 words. Pays $100-250.

Photos: Pays $50 minimum/8x10 b&w glossy print; $90 minimum/color transparency; $250/cover photo. Buys one-time rights.

Fiction: Stories about problems and experiences kids face. Trite, simplistic religious stories are not acceptable.

Tips: "The best ms for a freelancer to try to sell us would be a well-written first-person story (fiction or nonfiction) focusing on a common struggle young people face in any area of life—intellectual, emotional, social, physical or spiritual. Most manuscripts that miss us fail in quality or style. Since our style is distinctive, it is one of the biggest criteria in buying an article, so interested writers must study *Campus Life* to get an understanding of our audience and style. Don't submit unless you have *at least* read the magazine."

CHRISTIAN ADVENTURER, Messenger Publishing House, Box 850, Joplin MO 64802. (417)624-7050. Editor-in-Chief: Roy M. Chappell, D.D. Managing Editor: Rosmarie Foreman. A denominational Sunday School take-home paper for teens, 13-19. 75% freelance written. Quarterly; 104 pages. Circ. 3,500. Pays quarterly. Publishes ms an average of 1 year after acceptance. Buys simultaneous, second serial (reprint) or one-time rights. Byline given. Submit seasonal/holiday material 1 year in advance. Photocopied and previously published submissions OK. SASE. Reports in 6 weeks. Sample copy and writer's guidelines 50¢ and 1 first class stamp.

Nonfiction: Historical (related to great events in the history of the church); informational (explaining the meaning of a Bible passage or a Christian concept); inspirational; nostalgia; and personal experience. Send complete ms. Length: 1,500-1,800 words. Pays 1¢/word.

Fiction: Adventure, historical, religious and romance. Length: 1,500-1,800 words. Pays 1¢/word.
Tips: "The most frequent mistake made by writers in completing an article for us is that they forget we are a Christian publication. They also do not follow the guidelines."

CHRISTIAN LIVING FOR SENIOR HIGHS, David C. Cook Publishing Co., 850 N. Grove, Elgin IL 60120. (312)741-2400. Editor: Anne E. Dinnan. "A take-home paper used in senior high Sunday School classes. We encourage Christian teens to write to us." 75% freelance written. Quarterly magazine; 4 pages. Pays on acceptance. Publishes ms an average of 15 months after acceptance. Buys all rights. Byline given. We are not accepting unsolicited mss. Author must query. Computer printout submissions acceptable; prefers letter-quality to dot-matrix. Reports in 3-5 weeks. SASE. Free sample copy and writer's guidelines for SAE and 1 first class postage stamp.
Nonfiction: How-to (Sunday School youth projects); historical (with religious base); humor (from Christian perspective); inspirational and personality (nonpreachy); personal teen experience (Christian); poetry written by teens and photo feature (Christian subject). "Nothing not compatible with a Christian lifestyle. Since this is difficult to define, author must query doubtful topics." Buys 6 mss/issue. Submit complete ms. Length: 900-1,200 words. Pays $80; $40 for short pieces. Sometimes pays the expenses of writers on assignment.
Fiction: Adventure (with religious theme); historical (with Christian perspective); humorous; mystery; and religious. Buys 2 mss/issue. Submit complete ms. Length: 900-1,200 words. Pays $80-100. "No preachy experiences."
Photos: Cindy Carter, photo editor. Photos purchased with or without accompanying ms or on assignment. Send contact sheet, prints or transparencies. Pays $20-35 for 8½x11 b&w photos; $50 minimum for color transparencies.
Tips: "Our demand for manuscripts should increase, but most of these will probably be assigned rather than bought over-the-transom. Authors should query us, sending samples of their work. That way we can keep them on file for specific writing assignments. Our features are always short. Frequent mistake made by writers in completing articles for us is misunderstanding our market. Writing is often not Christian at all, or it's too 'Christian,' i.e. pedantic, condescending and moralistic."

CIRCLE K MAGAZINE, 3636 Woodview Trace, Indianapolis IN 46268. Executive Editor: Karen J. Pyle. 60% freelance written. "Our readership consists almost entirely of college students interested in the concept of voluntary service. They are politically and socially aware and have a wide range of interests." Published 5 times/year. Magazine; 16 pages. Circ. 12,000. Pays on acceptance. Publishes ms an average of 3 months after acceptance. Normally buys first North American serial rights. Byline given. Submit seasonal/holiday material 6 months in advance. Computer printout submissions acceptable; no dot-matrix. SASE. Reports in 4 weeks. Sample copy and writer's guidelines for large SASE.
Nonfiction: Informational (general interest articles on any area pertinent to concerned college students); community concerns (voluntarism, youth, medical, handicapped, elderly, underprivileged). No "first-person confessions, family history or travel." Recent article examples: "Fund Raising with a Flourish" (January/February 1985), "Children Behind Bars" (March 1985). Query or submit complete ms. Length: 1,500-2,500 words. Pays $175-250.
Photos: Purchased with accompanying ms. Captions required. Query. Total purchase price for ms includes payment for photos.
Tips: "Query must be typed and should indicate familiarity with the field and sources."

‡**CURRENT CONSUMER & LIFESTUDIES, The Practical Guide to Real Life Issues**, Curriculum Innovations, Inc., 3500 Western Ave., Highland Park IL 60035. (312)432-2700. Editor: Margaret Mucklo. Associate Editor: Carole Rubenstein. 90% freelance written. Monthly (during the school year) magazine on consumer and psychology issues with emphasis on life skills. "CC&L is an educational periodical for high school students in consumer, psychology, business, social studies, and home economic curricula nationwide." Circ. 80,000. Pays on publication. Byline given. Publishes ms an average of 3 months after acceptance. Offers 25% kill fee. Makes work-for-hire assignments. Simultaneous queries OK. Computer printout submissions acceptable. SASE. Reports in 1 month. Sample copy for large SAE and 65¢ postage. Writer's guidelines for #10 SAE and 1 first class stamp.
Nonfiction: General interest and how-to (e.g., organize important papers). Queries in July and August. Buys 72 mss/year. Query with published clips. Length: 1,200-1,600 words. Pays $100-125.

DOLLY MAGAZINE, Magazine Promotions, 57 Regent St., Chippendale, New South Wales 2008 Australia. (02)699-3622. Editor: Deborah Bibby. 25% freelance written. Monthly magazine. Informed entertainment for girls 14-20. Fashion, beauty, personalities, general interest. Circ. 200,000. Pays on acceptance. Publishes ms an average of 4 months after acceptance. Byline given. Offers 50% kill fee. Buys first, all, or second serial reprint rights (depends on story). Submit seasonal/holiday material 4 months in advance. Simultaneous and previously published submissions OK. Computer printout submissions acceptable; prefers letter-quality to dot-matrix. SAE and IRC. Reports in 2 weeks on queries; 1 month on mss. Sample copy for 37x27 cms SAE and $2 postage.

Nonfiction: General interest (aimed at teenage girls); interview/profile (of pop stars, actors, etc.); photo feature (cover, beauty shots). No heavy sex mss. Buys 50 mss/year. Query with clips of published work or send complete ms. Length: 1,000 2,500 words. Pay "decided on sight."

Photos: Send photos with ms. Pay "depends on sighting" for 2¼x2¼ color transparencies. Captions, model release and identification of subjects required. Buys one-time rights.

Columns/Departments: Decor—ideas for teenage rooms, flats, etc. Buys 150 mss/year. Query with clips of published work. Length: 100-1,000 words. Pay "depends on sighting."

Fiction: Lisa Wilkinson, fiction editor. Adventure (with a touch of romance); very condensed novels; confession; fantasy (not kinky); historical (romance); humor/satire; juvenile; romance (contemporary); suspense/mystery; women's; young adult. "Characters to be between 17 and 20 and unmarried. We like element of romance." Buys 2 mss/issue. Query with clips of published work and IRCs. Length: 1,000-25,000 words; 2,500 words average. Payment "depends on story and content."

EXPLORING MAGAZINE, The Journal for Explorers, Boy Scouts of America, 1325 Walnut Hill Ln., Irving TX 75038-3096. (214)659-2365. Editor: Robert E. Hood. Executive Editor: Scott Daniels. 85% freelance written. Magazine published 4 times/year—January, March, May, September. Covers the educational teen-age Exploring program of the BSA. Circ. 480,000. Pays on acceptance. Publishes ms an average of 6 months after acceptance. Byline given. Buys one-time and first rights. Submit seasonal/holiday material 6 months in advance. Simultaneous queries OK. Computer printout submissions acceptable; prefers letter-quality to dot-matrix. SASE. Reports in 2 weeks. Sample copy for 8½x10 SAE and $1 postage; writer's guidelines for business size SAE and 1 first class stamp.

Nonfiction: General interest, how-to (achieve outdoor skills, organize trips, meetings, etc.); interview/profile (of outstanding Explorer); travel (backpacking or canoeing with Explorers). "Nothing dealing with sex, drugs, or violence." Buys 15-20 mss/year. Query with clips. Length: 800-2,000 words. Pays $300-450.

Photos: Gene Daniels, photo editor. State availability of photos with query letter or ms. Reviews b&w contact sheets. Captions required. Buys one-time rights.

Tips: "Contact the local Exploring Director in your area (listed in phone book white pages under Boy Scouts of America). Find out if there are some outstanding post activities going on and then query magazine editor in Irving TX. Strive for shorter texts, faster starts and stories that lend themselves to dramatic photographs." Write for guidelines and "What is Exploring?" fact sheet.

FREEWAY, Box 632, Glen Ellyn IL 60138. Editor: Cindy Atoji. For "young Christian adults of high school and college age." 90% freelance written. Weekly. Circ. 70,000. Prefers first serial rights but buys some reprints. Purchases 100 mss/year. Byline given. Reports on material accepted for publication in 5-6 weeks. Publishes ms an average of 1 year after acceptance. Returns rejected material in 4-5 weeks. Computer printout submissions acceptable.

Nonfiction: "*FreeWay*'s greatest need is for personal experience stories showing how God has worked in teens' lives. Stories are best written in first person, 'as told to' author. Incorporate specific details, ancedotes, and dialogue. Show, don't tell, how the subject thought and felt. Weave spiritual conflicts and prayers into entire manuscript; avoid tacked-on sermons and morals. Stories should show how God has helped the person resolve a problem or how God helped save a person from trying circumstances (1,000 words or less). Avoid stories about accident and illness; focus on events and emotions of everyday life. (Examples: How I overcame shyness; confessions of a food addict.) Short-short stories are also needed as fillers. We also need self-help or how-to articles with practical Christian advice on daily living, and trend articles addressing secular fads from a Christian perspective. We do not use devotional material, poetry, or fictionalized Bible stories." Pays 4-7¢/word.

Photos: Whenever possible, provide clear 8x10 or 5x7 b&w photos to accompany mss (or any other available photos). Payment is $5-30.

Fiction: "We use little fiction, unless it is allegory, parables, or humor."

Tips: "Write to us for our 'Tips to Writers' pamphlet and free sample copy. Study them, then query or send complete mss. In your cover letter include information about who you are, writing qualifications, and experience working with teens. Include SASE."

GROUP, Thom Schultz Publications, Box 481, Loveland CO 80539. (303)669-3836. Editor: Gary Richardson. 60% freelance written. For leaders of high-school-age Christian youth groups. Magazine published 8 times/year. Circ. 60,000. Pays on acceptance. Publishes ms an average of 2 months after acceptance. Buys all rights. Byline given. Phone queries OK. Submit seasonal/holiday material 5 months in advance. Special Easter, Thanksgiving and Christmas issues. Computer printout submissions acceptable; prefers letter-quality to dot-matrix. SASE. Reports in 3-4 weeks. Sample copy $1; writer's guidelines for SASE.

Nonfiction: How-to (fundraising, membership-building, worship, games, discussions, activities, crowd breakers, simulation games); informational; (drama, worship, youth group projects, service projects); inspirational (ministry encouragement). Buys 7 mss/issue. Query. Length: 1,200-1,700 words. Pays up to $150.

Sometimes pays the expenses of writers on assignment.

Columns/Departments: Try This One (short ideas for games; crowd breakers, discussions, worships, fund raisers, service projects, etc.). Buys 5 mss/issue. Send complete ms. Length: 300 words maximum. Pays $15. News, Trends and Tips (leadership tips). Buys 1 mss/issue. Send complete ms. Length: 500 words maximum. Pays $25.

‡**GROUP MEMBERS ONLY**, Thom Schultz Publications, Box 481, Loveland CO 80539. Editor: Gary Richardson. 60% freelance written. Magazine published 8 times/year. For members of high-school-age Christian youth groups. Circ. 25,000. Pays on acceptance. Publishes ms an average of 2 months after acceptance. Byline given. Buys all rights. Phone queries OK. Submit seasonal/holiday material 5 months in advance. Computer printout submissions acceptable; prefers letter-quality to dot-matrix. Special Easter, Thanksgiving and Christmas issues and college issues. SASE. Reports in 1 month. Sample copy $1; writer's guidelines for SASE.
Nonfiction: How-to (improving self-image and relationships, strengthening faith). Buys 2 mss/issue. Query. Length: 800-1,000 words. Pays up to $150. Sometimes pays expenses of writers on assignment.

GUIDE, 55 W. Oak Ridge Dr., Hagerstown MD 21740. Editor: Penny Estes Wheeler. 90% freelance written. A Seventh-day Adventist journal for junior youth and early teens. "Its content reflects Seventh-day Adventist beliefs and standards. Another characteristic which probably distinguishes it from many other magazines is the fact that all its stories are nonfiction." Weekly magazine; 32 pages. Circ. 52,000. Buys first serial rights, and second (reprint) rights to material originally published elsewhere. Buys about 350 mss/year. Pays on acceptance. Publishes ms an average of 9 months after acceptance." Byline given. Reports in 6 weeks. SASE. Sample copy 40¢.
Nonfiction: Wants nonfiction stories of character-building and spiritual value. All stories must be true and include dialogue. Should emphasize the positive aspects of living obedience to parents, perseverance, kindness, etc. "We use a limited number of stories dealing with problems common to today's Christian youth, such as peer pressure, parents' divorce, chemical dependency, and so forth. We do not use stories of hunting, fishing, trapping or spiritualism." Send complete ms (include word count). Length: 1,500-2,500 words. Pays 3-4¢/word. Also buys serialized true stories. Length: 10 chapters.
Poetry: Buys traditional forms of poetry; also some free verse. Length: 4-16 lines. Pays 50¢-$1/line.
Tips: "We often buy short "fillers," and an author who does not fully understand our needs is more likely to sell with a short-short. Frequently writers do not understand our unique needs. Out target age is 10-15. New authors tend to write "down." We print "up" for the older reader. Also we require a top quality of writing. We want stories with depth."

IN TOUCH, Aldersgate Curriculum, Box 2000, Marion IN 46952. (317)674-3301. Editor: James Watkins. 25% freelance written. Weekly magazine about teen concerns. For teens in evangelical churches. Circ. 30,000. Pays on acceptance. Publishes ms an average of 9 months after acceptance. Byline given. Offers 50% kill fee. Buys one-time rights, simultaneous rights, first serial rights and second serial (reprint) rights. Submit seasonal/holiday material 9 months in advance. Simultaneous, photocopied, and previously published submissions OK. Computer printout submissions acceptable; prefers letter-quality to dot-matrix. SASE. Writer's guidelines for SAE.
Nonfiction: Book excerpts; how-to (anything relating to 13-19 year-olds); humor; interview/profile; and personal experience (as relates to one's faith). Buys 200 mss/year. Send complete ms. No queries. Length: 500-1,500 words. Pays $10-45. Sometimes pays the expenses of writers on assignment.
Photos: Send photos with ms. Reviews 8x10 prints. Pays $15-25. Buys one-time rights.
Fiction: Fantasy (allegories with religious slant. C.S. Lewis-type); and humorous (relating to 13-19 year olds). Buys 50 mss/year. Send complete ms. Length: 500-1,500 words. Pays $10-45.
Tips: "We're hungry for nonfiction, how-tos, allegory, and humor. We've had our fill of religious fiction. Testimonies from teens of how God is working in their life ("as told to") is area most open to freelancers. The more specific, the better the article—not "How to live the Christian life" but "How to live with nonChristian parents."

JUST ABOUT ME (JAM), A Magazine for Kids 10-15, Suite 202, 56 The Esplanade, Toronto M5E 1A7 Canada. (416)364-5938. Publisher: Anne Barrett. Editor: Ulla Colgrass. 95% freelance written. Bimonthly magazine providing information and entertainment for boys and girls ages 10-15. Circ. 35,000. Readership and content are Canadian. Pays on publication. Publishes ms an average of 4 months after acceptance. Byline given. Buys first North American serial rights or first serial rights. Simultaneous queries, and simultaneous, photocopied, and previously published submissions OK. Computer printout submissions acceptable if double spaced. SASE. Sample copy $2.60; writer's guidelines for SAE and 1 first class Canadian stamp.
Nonfiction: Book excerpts (subject: children's 10-15); general interest; historical/nostalgic; how-to (teens project); humor; interview/profile (of people who have had an effect on youths or who are young); new product; opinion (avoid preaching); personal experience (from a youthful perspective); technical (simple); travel (that would be of interest to 10-15 year-olds); and sports. Buys 4-8 mss/year. Query with published clips. Length:

500-1,500 words. Pays $100-200.

Fiction: Adventure, condensed novels, ethnic, fantasy, historical, horror (mild), humorous, mainstream, mystery, novel excerpts, science fiction and suspense. "Material should appeal to boys and girls ages 10-15." Buys 6 mss/year. Send complete ms. Length: 15-20 typed pages. Pays $50 maximum.

Poetry: Avant-garde, free verse, haiku, light verse and traditional. Buys varied number of poems/year. Pays $10 maximum.

‡**NEW DRIVER, The Continuing Guide to Driver Education and Energy Conservation,** Curriculum Innovations, Inc., 3500 Western Ave., Highland Park IL 60035. (312)432-2700. Editor: Margaret Mucklo. Associate Editor: Carole Rubenstein. 90% freelance written. Quarterly magazine on driver education. "*ND* is an educational periodical for high school students in driver education classes." Circ. 40,000. Pays 2 months after acceptance. Publishes an average of 3 months after acceptance. No byline given. Offers 25% kill fee. Makes work-for-hire assignments. Simultaneous queries OK. Computer printout submissions acceptable. SASE. Reports in 1 month. Sample copy for large SAE and 65¢ postage; writer's guidelines for #10 SAE and 1 first class stamp.

Nonfiction: General interest and how-to (maintain a car, drive a car safely). Queries most needed in July and August. Buys 40 mss/year. Query with published clips. Length: 1,200-1,600 words. Pays $100-150.

PROBE, Baptist Brotherhood Commission, 1548 Poplar Ave., Memphis TN 38104. (901)272-2461. Editor-in-Chief: Timothy C. Seanor. 10% freelance written. For "boys age 12-17 who are members of a missions organization in Southern Baptist churches." Monthly magazine; 32 pages. Circ. 48,000. Byline given. Pays on acceptance. Publishes ms an average of 2 months after acceptance. Buys simultaneous rights. Submit seasonal/holiday material 8 months in advance. Simultaneous submissions OK. Computer printout submissions acceptable; prefers letter-quality to dot-matrix. SASE. Reports in 1 month. Free sample copy and writer's guidelines with 9x12 SASE ($1.18 postage).

Nonfiction: How-to (crafts, hobbies); informational (youth, religious especially); inspirational (sports/entertainment personalities); photo feature (sports, teen subjects). No "preachy" articles, fiction or excessive dialogue. Submit complete ms. Length: 500-1,500 words. Pays $15-45.

Photos: Purchased with accompanying ms or on assignment. Captions required. Query. Pays $10 for 8x10 b&w glossy prints.

Tips: "The writer has a better chance of breaking in at our publication with short articles and fillers. Most topics are set years in advance. Regulars and fun articles are current. The most frequent mistake made by writers in completing an article for us is sending preachy articles. They don't read the guide carefully. Aim for the mid-teen instead of younger teen."

PURPLE COW, The Newspaper for Teens, Purple Cow, Inc., 315 Cates Center, 110 E. Andrews Dr. NW, Atlanta GA 30305. (404)233-7618/7654. Editor: Pam Perry. Monthly tabloid (10 issues) covering any subject of interest to the 12-18-year-old. Distributed free to high school and middle school students in metro Atlanta, Tampa, Sarasota and Ft. Meyers, Florida. Circ. 41,000. Pays on acceptance. Byline given. Buys one-time rights. Submit seasonal/holiday material 2 months in advance. Simultaneous queries, and simultaneous, photocopied, and previously published submissions OK. Computer printout submissions acceptable. SASE. Reports in 1 month. Sample copy $1 with SAE and 2 first class stamps. Writer's guidelines for SASE.

Nonfiction: Book excerpts; general interest; how-to (do anything—from dress fashionably to survive exams); humor; interview/profile (of people of interest to teens); personal experience (teen-related); sports (general, anecdotal—no "How to Play Soccer"); coping (different slants on drugs, sex, school, parents, peer pressure, dating, entertainment, money, etc.). Special issues include junion-senior proms and Christmas. No puzzles, games, fiction or first-person nonfiction. Buys 50 mss/year. Query with clips of published work or send complete ms. Length: 500-3,000 words. Pays $10.

Photos: Send photos with ms. Pays $10 for b&w transparencies and contact sheet.

Columns/Departments: Buys 5 mss/year. Length: 150-500 words. Pays $10 maximum.

Fillers: Buys 10-20/year. Length: 150 words maximum. Pays $5.

Tips: "We are written about 80% by high school students. Adult writers must have unique slant to be considered. Know what you're talking about. Don't talk down. Write in a style that is neither cynical nor preachy. Have something new to say."

‡**SCHOLASTIC UPDATE,** Scholastic, Inc., 730 Broadway, New York NY 10003-9538. (212)505-3000. Editor: Eric Oatman. Classroom periodical published 18 times/year (biweekly during the school year). "A public affairs magazine for social studies students in grades 8-12. Each issue covers a specific problem, country, or institution." Circ. 340,000. Pays on publication. Byline given. Offers 50% kill fee. Buys all rights. Submit seasonal/holiday material 4 months in advance. No simultaneous queries, or simultaneous, photocopied or previously published submissions. Computer printout submissions acceptable. SASE. Reports in 2

months. Sample copy $5 and SAE.

Nonfiction: Interview/profile. Buys 20 mss/year. Query with clips of published work. Length: 750-1,500 words. Pays $150/printed page.

SEVENTEEN, 850 3rd Ave., New York NY 10022. Executive Editor: Ray Robinson. Editor: Midge Turk Richardson. Articles Editor: Sarah Crichton. Monthly. Circ. 1,700,000. Buys first rights for nonfiction, features and poetry. Buys first rights on fiction. Pays 25% kill fee. Pays on acceptance. Byline given. Computer printout submissions acceptable; prefers letter-quality to dot-matrix. SASE. Reports in 3 weeks.

Nonfiction: Articles and features of general interest to young women who are concerned with the development of their own lives and the problems of the world around them; strong emphasis on topicality, helpfulness and entertainment. Send brief outline and query, including a typical lead paragraph, summing up basic idea of article. Also like to receive articles and features on speculation. Length: 2,000-3,000 words. Pays $50-500 for articles written by teenagers but more to established adult freelancers. Articles are commissioned after outlines are submitted and approved. Fees for commissioned articles generally range from $350-1,500.

Photos: Melissa Warner, art director. Photos usually by assignment only.

Fiction: Bonni Price, fiction editor. Top-quality stories featuring teenagers—the problems, concerns and preoccupations of adolescence, which will have recognition and identification value for readers. Does not want "typical teenage" stories, but high literary quality. Avoid oversophisticated material; unhappy endings acceptable if emotional impact is sufficient. Humorous stories that do not condescend to or caricature young people are welcome. Best lengths are 2,500-3,000 words. Pays $700-1,000. "We publish a novelette every July (not to exceed 30 doubled-spaced manuscript pages)—sometimes with a suspenseful plot." Conducts an annual short story contest.

Poetry: By teenagers only. Pays $15. Submissions are nonreturnable unless accompanied by SASE.

Tips: "The best way for beginning teenage writers to crack the *Seventeen* lineup is for them to contribute suggestions and short pieces to the You Said It! column, a literary format which lends itself to just about every kind of writing: profiles, puzzles, essays, exposes, reportage, and book reviews."

STRAIGHT, Standard Publishing Co., 8121 Hamilton Ave., Cincinnati OH 45231. (513)931-4050. Editor: Dawn Brettschneider. 90% freelance written. "Teens, age 13-19, from Christian backgrounds generally receive this publication in their Sunday School classes or through subscriptions." Weekly (published quarterly) magazine; 12 pages. Pays on acceptance. Publishes ms an average of 1 year after acceptance. Buys first rights, second serial (reprint) rights or simultaneous rights. Byline given. Submit seasonal/holiday material 1 year in advance. Reports in 3-6 weeks. Free sample copy; writer's guidelines with SASE. Computer printout submissions acceptable. Include Social Security number on ms. SASE.

Nonfiction: Religious-oriented topics, teen interest (school, church, family, dating, sports, part-time jobs), humor, inspirational, personal experience. "We want articles that promote Christian values and ideals." No puzzles. Query or submit complete ms. "We're buying more short pieces these days; 12 pages fill up much too quickly." Length: 800-1,500 words. Pays 2¢/word.

Fiction: Adventure, historical, humorous, religious and suspense. "All fiction should have some message for the modern Christian teen." Fiction should deal with all subjects in a forthright manner, without being preachy and without talking down to teens. No tasteless manuscripts that promote anything adverse to Bible's teachings. Submit complete ms. Length: 1,000-1,500 words. Pays 2-3½¢/word; less for reprints.

Photos: May submit photos with ms. Pays $20-25 for 8x10 b&w glossy prints. Model release should be available. Buys one-time rights.

Tips: "Don't be trite. Use unusual settings or problems. Use a lot of illustrations, a good balance of conversation, narration, and action. Style must be clear, fresh—no sermonettes or sicky-sweet fiction. Take a realistic approach to problems. Be willing to submit to editorial policies on doctrine; knowledge of the *Bible* a must. Also, be aware of teens today, and what they do. Language, clothing, and activities included in mss should be contemporary. We are becoming more and more selective about freelance material and the competition seems to be stiffer all the time."

'TEEN MAGAZINE, 8490 Sunset Blvd., Hollywood CA 90069. Editor: Roxanne Camron. For teenage girls. Predominantly staff-written. Freelance purchases are limited. Monthly magazine; 100 pages. Circ. 1,000,000. Publishes ms an average of 5 months after acceptance. Buys all rights. Reports in 2-4 months. Computer printout submissions acceptable; no dot-matrix. SASE.

Fiction: Dealing specifically with teenagers and contemporary teen issues. More fiction on emerging alternatives for young women. Suspense, humorous and romance. No prom or cheerleader stories. "Young love is all right, but teens want to read about it in more relevant settings." Length: 2,500-4,000 words. Pays $100.

Tips: "No nonfiction; no fiction with explicit language, casual references to drugs, alcohol, sex, or smoking; no fiction with too depressing outcome."

TEEN POWER, Box 632, Glen Ellyn IL 60138. (312)668-6000. Editor: Christopher Grant. 8-page weekly magazine for junior and senior high Christian teens. Circ. 115,000. Pays on acceptance. Byline given. Buys first serial rights. Submit seasonal/holiday material 9 months in advance. Photocopied and previously published submissions OK. Computer printout submissions acceptable; prefers letter-quality to dot-matrix. SASE. Reports in 1 month on queries; 6 weeks on mss. Sample copy and writer's guidelines for business size SAE and 1 first class stamp.

Nonfiction: How-to (issues of Christian maturity); inspirational (young teen); interview/profile (Christian personality); and personal experience (God's interaction). No reviews or nonChristian-oriented material. "We need evidence of mature, Christian integration with life; no tacked-on morals; creative presentation." Buys 40 mss/year. Send complete ms. Length: 800-1,100 words. Pays $40-90.

Photos: "Simple, bold photos illustrating the ms." Send photos with true story ms only. Pays $5-20 for 3x5 b&w prints. Buys one-time rights.

Columns/Departments: Any mss dealing with application of Bible to everyday teen life—personal experience, expository. Buys 40 mss/year. Send complete ms. Length: 250-400 words. Pays $20-60.

Fiction: Adventure, confession (Christian insight), ethnic; fantasy, humorous, religious, and suspense. Only fiction with teen Christian slant. Buys 40 mss/year. Send complete ms. Length: 800-1,100 words. Pays $60-90.

Tips: Shorter word length and search for more varied, contemporary subjects/issues will affect writers in the year ahead. No poetry; filler material.

TEENAGE MAGAZINE, The Magazine for Young Adults, Highwire Assoc., 217 Jackson St., Lowell MA 01853. (617)458-6416. Editor: Andrew Calkins. Managing Editor: Mike Thompson. 40% freelance written. Monthly magazine for youth. *TeenAge* aims at providing America's teenagers, both females and males, with a truly adult, truly sophisticated magazine—and one that's written and edited largely by teenagers. Circ. 200,000. Pays on publication. Publishes ms an average of 4 months after acceptance. Byline given. Offers 25% kill fee. Buys first North American serial rights. Submit seasonal/holiday material 5 months in advance. Simultaneous queries, and simultaneous, photocopied and previously published submissions OK. Computer printout submissions acceptable; prefers letter-quality to dot-matrix. SASE. Reports in 1 month. Sample copy $2.50 and 9x12 SAE and 56¢ postage. Writer's guidelines for SAE.

Nonfiction: Christine MacLean, articles editor. Book excerpts; general interest (to teenagers); how-to (on college, cars, careers, computers, health); humor (school-related; shorts); interview/profile (especially of entertainers); opinion (from teenagers only—300 words); and personal experience. No overly general surveys or how-to's. We need specific information. Buys 25 mss/year. Query with or without published clips. Length: 300-2,500 words. Pays $50-1,000. Sometimes pays the expenses of writers on assignment.

Columns/Departments: Nancy Rourke, column/department editor. Mind & Body, Career's, College, and Wheels (cars). Buys 6 mss/year. Query with published clips. Length: 800-1,200 words. Pays $100-350.

Fiction: Christine MacLean, fiction editor. Adventure, humorous, mystery, novel excerpts, suspense, and youth-related issues, plots, and characters. Buys 3 mss/year. Send complete ms. Length: 1,000-2,500 words. Pays $350 maximum.

Fillers: Nancy Rourke, fillers editor. Anecdotes. Buys 10/year. Length: 25-75 words. Pays $25.

Tips: Areas most open to freelancers Frontlines (opinions by teenagers) and entertainer profiles.

TEENS TODAY, Church of the Nazarene, 6401 The Paseo, Kansas City MO 64131. (816)333-7000. Editor: Gary Sivewright. 25% freelance written. For junior and senior high teens, to age 18, attending Church of the Nazarene Sunday School. Weekly magazine; 8 pages. Circ. 70,000. Publishes ms an average of 8 months after acceptance. Pays on acceptance. Byline given. Buys first rights and second rights. Submit seasonal/holiday material 10 months in advance. Simultaneous, photocopied and previously published submissions OK. Computer printout submissions acceptable. SASE. Reports in 6-8 weeks. Free sample copy and writer's guidelines for SASE.

Photos: Photos purchased with or without accompanying ms or on assignment. Pays $10-30 for 8x10 b&w glossy prints. Additional payment for photos accepted with accompanying ms. Model release required.

Fiction: Adventure (if Christian principles are apparent); humorous; religious; and romance (keep it clean). Buys 1 ms/issue. Send complete ms. Length: 1,200-1,500 words. Pays 3½¢/word, first rights; 3¢/word, second rights.

Poetry: Free verse; haiku; light verse; and traditional. Buys 15 poems/year. Pays 25¢/line.

Tips: "We're looking for quality nonfiction dealing with teen issues: peers, self, parents, vocation, Christian truths related to life, etc."

TIGER BEAT MAGAZINE, D.S. Magazines, Inc., 105 Union Ave., Cresskill NJ 07626. (201)569-5055. Editor: Diane Umansky. 25% freelance written. For teenage girls ages 14 to 18. Monthly magazine; 80 pages. Circ. 400,000. Pays on publication. Publishes ms an average of 3 months after acceptance. Buys all rights. Buys 50+ manuscripts per year. Electronic submissions OK on single-sided CP/M or MS/DOS disks, but requires hard copy also. Computer printout submissions acceptable; no dot-matrix.

Nonfiction: Stories about young entertainers; their lives, what they do, their interests. Also service-type, self-help articles. Quality writing expected, but must be written with the 14-18 age group in mind. "Skill, style, ideas, and exclusivity are important to *Tiger Beat*. If a writer has a fresh, fun idea, or access to something staffers don't have, he or she has a good chance." Length: 100-750 words depending on the topic. Pays $50-100. Send query. SASE. Sometimes pays the expenses of writers on assignment. Also seeks good teenage fiction, with an emphasis on entertainment and romance.

Photos: Pays $25 for b&w photos used with mss; captions optional. Pays $50-75 for color used inside; $75 for cover. 35mm transparencies preferred.

Tips: "A freelancer's best bet is to come up with something original and exclusive that the staff couldn't do or get. Writing should be aimed at a 17- or 18-year-old intelligence level. Trends in magazine publishing that freelance writers should be aware of include shorter articles, segmenting of markets, and much less 'I' journalism. The most frequent mistake made by writers in completing an article for us is a patronizing attitude toward teens or an emphasis on historical aspects of subject matter. Don't talk down to young readers; they sense it readily."

TIGER BEAT STAR, D.S. Magazines, Inc., 105 Union Ave., Cresskill NJ 07626. (201)569-5055. Editor: Lisa Arcella. Associate Editor: Jeanine Walker. 50% freelance written. Monthly teenage fan magazine for young adults interested in movie, TV and recording stars. "It differs from other teenage fan magazines in that we feature many soap opera stars as well as the regular teenage TV, movie and music stars." Circ. 400,000. Average issue includes 20 feature interviews, and 2 or 3 gossip columns. "We have to take each article and examine its worth individually—who's popular this month, how it is written etc. But we prefer shorter articles most of the time." Pays upon publication. Publishes ms an average of 1 month after acceptance. Byline given. Buys all rights. Submit seasonal material 10 weeks in advance. Previously published submissions discouraged. Electronic submissions OK on disk for Victor 9000 system, but requires hard copy also. Computer printout submissions acceptable; no dot-matrix. Reports in 2 weeks.

Nonfiction: Interview (of movie, TV and recording stars). Buys 1-2 mss/issue. Query with clips of previously published work. "Write a good query indicating your contact with the star. Investigative pieces are preferred." Length: 200-400 words. Pays $50-125.

Photos: State availability of photos. Pays $25 minimum for 5x7 and 8x10 b&w glossy prints. Pays $75 minimum for 35mm and 2¼ color transparencies. Captions and model release required. Buys all rights.

Tips: "Be aware of our readership (teenage girls, generally ages 9-17); be 'up' on the current TV, movie and music stars; and be aware of our magazine's unique writing style. We are looking for articles that are clearly and intelligently written, factual and fun. Don't talk down to the reader, simply because they are teenaged. We want to give the readers information they can't find elsewhere. We don't want things that are too "cutesy" or though of as typical teen magazine language. Our readers are showing us that they have more sophisticated tastes. Many writers also forget basics like subheads and headlines."

‡**TRIUMPH**, Randall House Publications, Box 17307, Nashville TN 37217. (615)361-1221. Editor-in-Chief: H.D. Harrison. 5% freelance written. Quarterly teen training manual for church training curriculum. Audience is 10-12 graders in Free Will Baptist churches; conservative theological. Circ. 2,000. Pays on publication. Publishes ms an average of 6 months after acceptance. Byline given. Buys one-time rights. Submit seasonal/holiday material 9 months in advance. Simultaneous and previously published submissions OK. Computer printout submissions acceptable; prefers letter-quality to dot-matrix. SASE. Reports in 1 month. Free sample copy.

Nonfiction: Mrs. Odell Walton, articles editor. Inspirational. Buys 10-20 mss/year. Send complete ms. Length: 500-1,500 words. Pays $20 maximum.

Photos: Send photos with ms. Buys one-time rights.

Fiction: Mrs. Odell Walton, fiction editor. Religious. Prefers fiction teaching moral. Buys 20-30 mss/year. Send complete ms. Length: 500-1,500 words. Pays $20 maximum.

VENTURE MAGAZINE, Box 150, Wheaton IL 60189. Editor: David Leigh. 10% freelance written. Publication of Christian Service Brigade. For young men 12-18 years of age. Most participate in a Christian Service Brigade program. Published bimonthly. Circ. 22,000. Published 6 times/year. Buys first rights on unsolicited material. Buys 1-3 mss/issue. Pays on publication. Publishes ms an average of 3 months after acceptance. Submit seasonal material 6 months in advance. Usually reports in 2-3 weeks. Query. Computer printout submissions acceptable; prefers letter-quality to dot-matrix. SASE. Sample copy $1.50 plus large SAE and 73¢ postage; writer's guidelines for SAE and 1 first class stamp.

Nonfiction: "Religious articles from boys' perspective; teen-age problems, possible solutions. Interested in photo features on innovative teenage boys who do unusual things, also true-story adventures. Assigned articles deal with specific monthly themes decided by the editorial staff. Most material has an emphasis on boys in a Christian or Brigade setting. No trite 'Sunday school' mss." Length: 400-1,200 words. Pays $50-100.

Photos: No additional payment is made for 8x10 b&w photos used with mss. Pays $25 for those purchased on assignment; $50-75 for b&w cover photos of boys.

Fiction: "Action-packed adventures with Christian theme or lesson. No far-fetched, contrived plots or trite themes/settings." Length 1,000-1,800 words. Pays $50-100.

Tips: "Queries must be succinct, well written, and exciting to draw my interest. Send for sample copy; get a feel for our publication; then query with ideas tailored specifically for us."

WORKING FOR BOYS, Box A, Danvers MA 01923. Editor: Brother Alphonsus Dwyer, C.F.X. 37% freelance written. For junior high, parents, grandparents (the latter because the magazine goes back to 1884). Quarterly magazine; 28 pages. Circ. 16,000. Not copyrighted. Buys 30 mss/year. Pays on acceptance. Publishes ms an average of 6 months after acceptance. Submit special material (Christmas, Easter, sports, vacation time) 6 months in advance. Reports in 1 week. Submit only complete ms. Address all mss to the Associate Editor, Brother Alois, CFX, St. John's High School, Main St., Shrewsbury MA 01545. Computer printout submissions acceptable. SASE. Free sample copy.
Nonfiction: "Conservative, not necessarily religious, articles. Seasonal mostly (Christmas, Easter, etc.). Cheerful, successful outlook suitable for early teenagers. Maybe we are on the 'square' side, favoring the traditional regarding youth manners: generosity to others, respect for older people, patriotism, etc. Animal articles and tales are numerous, but an occasional good dog or horse story is okay. We like to cover seasonal sports." Buys informational, how-to, personal experience, historical and travel. Length: 800-1,200 words. Pays 4¢/word.
Photos: 6x6 b&w glossy prints purchased with ms for $10 each.
Fiction: "Fiction should be wholesome and conservative." Mainstream, adventure, religious, and historical fiction. Theme: open. Length: 500-1,000 words. Pays 4¢/word.
Poetry: Length: 24 lines maximum. Pays 40¢/line.

YM, (formerly *Young Miss*), 685 3rd Ave., New York NY 10017. Editor-in-Chief: Phyllis Schneider. 85% freelance written. Published 10 times/year for teen girls, aged 12-19. Pays on acceptance. Byline given. Buys first rights. Editorial requirement sheet for SASE. Query on nonfiction. Reports on submissions in 8 weeks. Publishes mss an average of 1 year after acceptance. All mss must be typed, double-spaced. Computer printout submissions acceptable. Sample copy $2 and 10x13 SASE.
Nonfiction: Deborah Purcell, articles/fiction editor. Psychological concerns and personal growth; contemporary issues and problems involving teenagers; all aspects of relationships; first-person humor; quizzes; profiles. Buys 10-20 unsolicited mss/year. Length: 1,500-2,500 words. Pays $75 and up for fillers (850 words maximum); $250 and up for articles. No illustrations.
Fiction: Deborah Purcell, articles/fiction editor. "All fiction should be aimed at young adults, not children; when in doubt, develop older rather than younger characters. Stories about relationships and unique resolutions of personal dilemmas are particularly welcomed. The protagonist may be either male or female." Length: 2,500-3,500 words. Pays $350 and up.
Tips: "Queries for nonfiction should express original thought; desire and ability to do thorough research where applicable; clear understanding of the interests and needs of young women; fresh angles. We are not interested in lightweight nonfiction material or style except where applicable (e.g., humor). Fitness and health, fashion and beauty, food and lifestyles articles are all done inhouse."

YOUNG AMBASSADOR, The Good News Broadcasting Association, Inc., Box 82808, Lincoln NE 68501. (402)474-4567. Editor-in-Chief: Warren Wiersbe. Managing Editor: Nancy Bayne. 50% freelance written. Monthly magazine emphasizing Christian living for church-oriented teens, ages 12-17. Circ. 80,000. Buys first North American serial rights or second serial (reprint) rights. Publishes ms an average of 10 months after acceptance. Byline given. Phone queries OK. Submit seasonal/holiday material 1 year in advance. Previously published submissions OK. Computer printout submissions acceptable; prefers letter-quality to dot-matrix. SASE. Reports in 8 weeks. Free sample copy and writer's guidelines.
Nonfiction: How-to (church youth group activities); interview; personal experience; photo features; inspirational and informational features on spiritual topics. Needs "material that covers social, spiritual and emotional needs of teenagers and well-researched articles on current trends and issues, science and technology, sports personalities. Interviews with teens who are demonstrating their faith in Christ in some noteworthy way. Biographical articles about teens who have overcome obstacles in their lives." Buys 3-5 mss/issue. Query or send complete ms. Length: 500-1,800 words. Pays 4-7¢/word for unsolicited mss; 7-10¢ for assigned articles. Sometimes pays expenses of writers on assignment.
Fiction: Needs stories involving problems common to teens in which the resolution (or lack of it) is true to our readers' experiences. Needs more stories set in unusual or exotic times and places. Spiritual interest a must, but no preaching. "If the story was written just to make a point, we don't want it. Most of our stories feature a protagonist 14-17 years old." Buys 35 mss/year. Query or send complete ms. Length: 800-2,500 words. Pays 4-7¢/word for unsolicited mss; 7-10¢/word for assigned articles.
Fillers: Puzzles on Biblical themes. Send complete mss. Pays $3-10.
Tips: "Each issue follows a theme. Write for our list of themes for upcoming issues."

YOUNG AND ALIVE, Christian Record Braille Foundation, Inc., Editorial Dept., 4444 S. 52nd St., Lincoln NE 68506. Editor: Richard Kaiser. 90% freelance written. Monthly magazine for blind and visually impaired young adults (16-20) published in braille and large print for an interdenominational Christian audience. Pays on acceptance. Publishes ms an average of 1 year after acceptance. "Dot-matrix submissions are acceptable—if printing is black enough." SASE. Writer's guidelines for SAE and 1 first class stamp.

Nonfiction Stories and Articles: Adventure, biography, camping, health, history, hobbies, nature, practical Christianity, sports, and travel. "All forms of stories (eg. serials, parables, satire) are used. However, we no longer use fiction, per se. Stories and articles must at least be based on true incidents. From a Christian point of view, *Young and Alive* seeks to encourage the thinking, feelings, and activities of persons afflicted with sight impairment. While it's true that many blind and visually impaired young adults have the same interests as their sighted counterparts, the material should meet the needs of the sight-impaired, specifically." Length: Up to 1,400 words. Query. Pays 3-5¢/word upon acceptance.

Photos: Pays $4-5 for b&w glossy prints.

Tips: "I would like to see more colorful descriptions, more emphatic, energetic verbs, and more intense feeling presented in the manuscripts."

YOUNG SALVATIONIST, A Christian Living Magazine, The Salvation Army, 799 Bloomfield Ave., Verona NJ 07044. (201)239-0606. Editor: Capt. Dorothy Hitzka. Editor-in-Chief: Major Henry Gariepy. 75% freelance written. Monthly magazine for high school teens. "Only material with a definite Christian message will be considered." Circ. 43,000. Pays on acceptance. Byline given. Submit seasonal/holiday material 6 months in advance. SASE. Reports in 1 month on mss. Sample copy for 8½x11 SAE with 3 first class stamps; writer's guidelines for business size SAE and 1 first class stamp.

Nonfiction: Inspirational. "Lead articles should carry Christian truth but not in a 'preachy' manner; should deal with 'real life' issues facing teens today; must be factual; and any references to The Salvation Army must be authentic. Articles must have a logical progression of thoughts with a definite conclusion or solution but no tacked-on morals. The lesson or point should be inherent in the article itself." Buys 36 mss/year. Send complete ms. "State whether your submission is for the Young Salvationist or the Young Soldier section." Length: 800-1,200 words. Pays 3-5¢/word.

Columns/Departments: Magazine includes a Young Soldier "pull-out" section for children ages 6-12 with 600-800 word stories (fiction) relating to children rather than teens. "Two-page spreads of activities that relate to the story will be used in each issue. These should emphasize the truth taught but be an activity that the child can complete." Puzzles and related items are also used in each issue. Buys 24 mss/year. Send complete ms. Length: 250-300 words. Pays 3-5¢/word.

Fiction: "Story must have logical and convincing plot with good characterization and should deal with issues facing today's teens. Dialogue must be natural. No 'put on' teen jargon or Biblical fiction. Fiction must carry a strong Christian truth which is to be inherent in the story itself." Length: 1,000-1,200 words.

Fillers: "We have several columns which deal with self-image, marriage, teen leadership in the church, and other related teen topics. These fillers should meet the same criteria for content as nonfiction." Length: 250-300 words.

‡**YOUTH UPDATE**, St. Anthony Messenger Press, 1615 Republic St., Cincinnati OH 45210. (513)241-5615. Editor: Carol Ann Munchel. 75% freelance written. Monthly newsletter of faith life for teenagers. Designed to attract, instruct, guide and challenge Catholics of high school age by applying the Gospel to modern problems/situations. Circ. 60,000. Pays when ready to print. Publishes ms an average of 3 months after acceptance. Byline given. SASE. Reports in 8 weeks. Sample copy for #10 SAE and 1 first class stamp; writer's guidelines for SAE and 1 first class stamp.

Nonfiction: Inspirational, interview/profile, personal experience and spiritual. Buys 12 mss/year. Query. Length: 2,300-2,500 words. Pays $300. Sometimes pays expenses of writers on assignment.

Theatre, Movie, TV and Entertainment

Entertainment magazines aren't only interested in celebrities, although many writers want to break in with celebrity interviews. An exclusive interview with a hard-to-reach entertainer may land a sale for you, but oftentimes the writers, who get assignments to interview celebrities, consistently provide entertainment news and stories for the magazine. Besides celebrity interviews, most publications want solid reporting on trends and upcoming productions that will interest readers.

This category's publications cover live, filmed, or videotaped entertainment, including home video, TV, dance, theatre, and adult entertainment. For those publications with an emphasis on music and musicians, see the Music section. For markets covering video games, see Games and Puzzles.

‡**ADAM FILM WORLD**, 8060 Melrose Ave., Los Angeles CA 90046. (213)653-8060. Editor: Scott Mallory. For fans of X-rated movies and videotapes. 75% freelance written. Magazine published 8 times/year plus 4 special issues. Circ. 250,000. Buys first North American serial rights. Buys about 12 mss/year. Pays on publication. Publishes ms an average of 3 months after acceptance. No photocopied or simultaneous submissions. Reports on mss accepted for publication in 1-2 months. Returns rejected material in 2 weeks. Query. No disk submissions. Computer printout submissions acceptable; no dot-matrix. SASE. Sample copy $1.50.
Nonfiction: "All copy is slanted for fans of X-rated movies and can be critical of this or that picture, but not critical of the genre itself. All in 4-color. Publication's main emphasis is on pictorial layouts, rather than text; layouts of stills from erotic pictures. Any article must have possibilities for illustration. We go very strong in the erotic direction, but *no* hardcore stills. We see too many fictional interviews with a fictitious porno star, and too many fantasy suggestions for erotic film plots. No think-pieces. We would consider articles on the continuing erotization of legitimate films from major studios, and the increasing legitimization of X films from the minors." Length: 1,000-3,000 words. Pays $150-300. Pays the expenses of writers on assignment.
Photos: "We have gone all four-color. If necessary, we can duotone a few black/white photos." Most photos are bought on assignment from regular photographers with studio contacts, but a few 35mm slides are purchased from freelancers for use as illustrations. Pays minimum of $40/color spot photo.
Tips: "We would like to see more personality pieces on people working in the X-rated industry. The most frequent mistake made by writers in completing an article for us is that they don't include enough background information on the subject."

AMERICAN SQUAREDANCE, Burdick Enterprises, Box 488, Huron OH 44839. (419)433-2188. Editors: Stan and Cathie Burdick. 5% freelance written. Monthly magazine of interviews, reviews, topics of interest to the modern square dancer. Circ. 13,000. Pays on publication. Publishes ms an average of 6 months after acceptance. Byline given. Buys all rights. Submit seasonal/holiday material 3 months in advance. Computer printout submissions acceptable. Reports in 2 weeks on queries. Sample copy for 6x9 SAE; free writer's guidelines.
Nonfiction: General interest, historical/nostalgic, humor, inspirational, interview/profile, new product, opinion, personal experience, photo feature, travel. Must deal with square dance. Buys 6 mss/year. Send complete ms. Length: 1,000-1,500 words. Pays $10-35.
Photos: Send photos with ms. Reviews b&w prints. Captions and identification of subjects required.
Fiction: Subject related to square dancing only. Buys 1-2 mss/year. Send complete ms. Length: 2,000-2,500 words. Pays $25-35.
Poetry: Avant-garde, free verse, haiku, light verse, traditional. Square dancing subjects only. Buys 6 poems/year. Submit maximum 3 poems. Pays $1 for 1st 4 lines; $1/verse thereafter.

ARTSLINE, Creative Publications, Inc., Box 24287, Seattle WA 98124. (206)325-4400. Executive Editor: Sonia Grunberg. Editor: Alice Copp Smith. 80% freelance written. Monthly arts magazine serving as program magazine for six Seattle theatres, concert and dance presenters. "We feature performing and visual arts, nationwide but with an emphasis on the Pacific Northwest. *ArtsLine* is a magazine of information and opinion, a showcase for fine artists' work (each cover offers an original piece of fine art, usually by a local artist). It also affords local writers, designers, and photographers an opportunity to be published." Circ. 73,000. Pays on acceptance. Publishes ms an average of 3 months after acceptance. Byline given. Offers 50% kill fee. Buys first North American serial rights. Submit seasonal/holiday material 3 months in advance. Simultaneous queries, and photocopied submissions OK. Computer printout submissions acceptable; prefers letter-quality to dot-matrix. SASE. Reports in 3 weeks. Sample copy for 9x12 SAE and 3 first class stamps; writer's guidelines for SAE and 1 first class stamp.
Nonfiction: Book excerpts; humor; interview/profile (arts-related only); opinion (arts-related only); photo feature (arts-related only); and performing or visual arts features. No crafts; no arts pieces of regional interest only, when region is not Pacific Northwest. Buys 24 features, 48 columns/year. Query with or without published clips or send complete ms. Length: 750-2,000 words. Pays $75-200.
Photos: Send photos with query or ms. Reviews b&w contact sheets. Pays $25-50 for 35mm or 4x5 color transparencies; $25-50 for 8x10 b&w prints. Captions and identification of subjects required. Buys one-time rights. Photo credit given.
Columns/Departments: On Wine; On Food (staff writer); On Broadway (staff writer); On Film; On Record (staff writer); On Dance; On Music; Arts News (staff writer). Buys 48 mss/year. Query with or without published clips or send complete ms. Length: 750-1,000 words. Pays $75-100.
Fillers: Jokes, anecdotes, short humor (arts-related only). Length: 150 words maximum.

Tips: "A freelancer can best break in to our publication by sending well-written material that fits our format. Feature articles are most open to freelancers. First submission from a writer new to us has to be on speculation; thereafter, we're willing to assign. Know your subject and the Northwest arts scene; write with clarity and grace; know our audience (we'll help). Trends in magazine publishing that freelance writers should be aware of include increasing sophistication of Pacific Northwest readers and their strong support of the arts. Also the proliferation of new publishing ventures in the region (not all of which have survived)."

AUSTRALIAN VIDEO AND COMMUNICATIONS,Incorporating *Australian Video Review*, General Magazine Company Pty., Ltd., 9 Paran Place, Glen Iris, Victoria 3146 Australia. (03)25-6456. 50% freelance written. Editor: Geoffrey M. Gold. Monthly magazine covering home video and telecommunications. Circ. 29,000. Pays on publication. Byline given. Offers 25% kill fee. Buys all Australian rights. Submit seasonal/holiday material 4 months in advance. Simultaneous queries, and photocopied and previously published submissions OK. SASE. Reports in 2 weeks. Sample copy $2.
Nonfiction: Book excerpts, historical/nostalgic, humor, interview/profile, new products and services. Special issues include Australian Video and Computer Games Annual; Australian Video Trade LReference Book 1984; Australian Video Review Annual (movies); video-x monthly. No specifically North American material. "We require 'internationalized' material suitable for Australian readers." Buys 100 mss/year. Query with published clips. Length: 500-3,000 words. Pays $25—350.
Photos: State availability of photos. Pays $25-50 for color transparencies; $15-35 for b&w prints. Captions, model release and identification of subjects required.
Columns/Departments: New Products; Network (humorous round-up); video games. Buys 20 mss/year. Query. Length: 50-600 words. Pays $25-75.
Fiction: Buys 3 mss/year. Query.
Tips: "Contact us with suggestions and copy of previously published work. All sections are open. North American writers should become more aware of the wider international market for their material. Our Australian, New Zealand and Pacific region readers insist on locally relevant articles. At the same time, they are highly literate and wise to the international scene and appreciate foreign articles that bridge the 'national' gap. Our publications need to reflect US 'hard news' bias, British 'whimsy' and European 'flair' with Australian/New Zealand information."

BALLET NEWS, The Metropolitan Opera Guild, Inc., 1865 Broadway, New York NY 10023. (212)582-3285. Editor: Robert Jacobson. Managing Editor: Karl F. Reuling. 75% freelance written. Monthly magazine covering dance and the related fields of films, video and records. Circ. 40,000. Average issue includes 4-5 feature articles. "All are accompanied by many photos and graphics. We are writing for a dance audience who wants to better appreciate the art form. We include reviews, calendar, TV previews, and book reviews." Pays on publication. Byline given. Kill fee negotiable. Buys first rights. Photocopied submissions OK. Computer printout submissions acceptable; prefers letter-quality to dot-matrix. SASE. Reports in 1 month. Sample copy $2.50.
Nonfiction: General interest (critical analysis, theatres); historical; interview (dancers, choreographers, entrepreneurs, costumers, stage designers); profile; travel (dance in any location); and technical (staging, practice). Query, send complete ms, or send clips of previously published work. Length: 2,500 words. Pays 11¢/word.
Photos: State availability of photos or send photos with ms. Payment negotiable for b&w contact sheets.

CINEFANTASTIQUE MAGAZINE, The review of horror, fantasy and science fiction films, Box 270, Oak Park IL 60303. (312)366-5566. Editor: Frederick S. Clarke. 100% freelance written. A bimonthly magazine covering horror, fantasy and science fiction films. Circ. 25,000. Pays on publication. Publishes ms an average of 6 months after acceptance. Byline given. Buys all magazine rights. Simultaneous queries and photocopied submissions OK. Computer printout and dot-matrix submissions acceptable. Sample copy $6 plus $1 postage. SASE. Reports in 8 weeks or longer.
Nonfiction: Historical/nostalgic (retrospects of film classics); interview/profile (film personalities); new product (new film projects); opinion (film reviews, critical essays); technical (how films are made). Buys 100-125 mss/year. Query with published clips. Length: 1,000-10,000 words. Sometimes pays the expenses of writers on assignment.
Photos: State availability of photos with query letter or ms.
Tips: "Develop original story suggestions; develop access to film industry personnel; submit reviews that show a perceptive point-of-view."

DALLAS OBSERVER, Observer Publications, Box 190289, Dallas TX 75219. (214)521-9450. Editor: Bob Walton. 80% freelance written. Biweekly tabloid covering arts and entertainment. Circ. 60,000. Pays on publication. Publishes ms an average of 2 months after acceptance. Byline given. Offers 50% kill fee. Buys first serial rights. Submit seasonal/holiday material 2 months in advance. Simultaneous queries and photocopied submissions OK. Computer printout submissions acceptable; prefers letter-quality to dot-matrix. SASE. Reports in 1 month. Sample copy for $1.50, 8x10 SAE and 5 first class stamps.

Nonfiction: Interview/profile (Dallas only) and arts features. "Write intelligently about local Dallas arts and entertainment subjects." Buys 400 mss/year. Query with published clips. Length: 500-5,000 words. Pays $20-200.

Columns/Departments: Local Dallas arts and entertainment news. Buys 100 mss/year. Query with published clips. Length: 500-1,000 words. Pays $20-75.

Tips: "Freelancers can best break in to our publication with thought-provoking essays or short articles."

DANCE MAGAZINE, 33 W. 60th St., New York NY 10023. (212)245-9050. Editor-in-Chief: William Como. Managing Editor: Richard Philp. 40% freelance written. Monthly. *Dance Magazine* is the "oldest continuously published arts magazine in the world." It is aimed at readers whose interest in dance is professional, and at dance audiences. Pays on publication. Publishes ms an average of 6 months after acceptance. Buys first rights. SASE. Sample copy $3.

Nonfiction: How-to for the dancer, health, education, administration, teaching, writing, therapy, choreography, designing and music. "We occasionally do profiles of dancers and companies. A substantial portion of each issue is given to running performance reviews by our critics across the country and abroad and to the monthly news section." Articles must be written in such a manner as to be clear and accessible to the non-dancer, while providing the dance professional with useful information. Query. Articles are accepted on a speculation basis. Pays maximum $400 (for a series running over several months). Average feature article is 2,000 words; news story, 250 words; an out-of-New York review, 300 words per company reviewed.

Photos: "There is a heavy emphasis on photography. Some of the best dance photography finds its way into our pages." Photography is often assigned directly to the photographer, although we welcome and will look at freelance work brought to the office for our examination.

Tips: "It is usually important that a writer have a thorough knowledge of dance, since our readers are the experts and the avid dance-goers."

DANCE TEACHER NOW, SMW Communications, Inc., University Mall, Suite 2, 803 Russell Blvd., Davis CA 95616. (916)756-6222. Editor: Susan Wershing. 100% freelance written. Magazine published 9 times/year for professional teachers of stage, ballroom, and fitness dance in private studios, fitness centers, etc. Circ. 5,000. Average issue includes 6-8 feature articles, departments, and calendar sections. Pays on acceptance. Publishes ms an average of 2 months after acceptance. Byline given. Buys all rights. Submit seasonal material 6 months in advance. Computer printout submissions acceptable; "as long as the covering letter assures us the author is not shotgunning the article to a dozen publications at once." Reports in 2 months. Sample copy $2.25; free writer's guidelines.

Nonfiction: Dance techniques, legal issues, health and dance injuries, business, advertising, taxes and insurance, curricula, student/teacher relations, government grants, studio equipment, concerts and recitals, competitions, departmental budgets, etc. "The writer must choose subject matter suitable to the knowledgable, professional people our readers are." Buys 4-6 mss/issue. Query with published clips. Length: 1,000-3,000 words. Pays $100-300.

Photos: Photos to accompany articles only. Pays $20 minimum for 5x7 b&w glossy prints. Model release required. Buys all rights.

Columns/Departments: Practical Tips (3-4 paragraphs, short items of immediate practical use to the teacher), Building Your Library, and Spotlight on Successful Teachers (1 per issue).

Tips: "We like complete reportage of the material with all the specifics but personalized with direct quotes and anecdotes. The writer should speak one-to-one to the reader but keep the national character of the magazine in mind. To achieve the practical quality in each article, the most important question in any interview is 'How?' We do not want personality profiles. Articles must include material of practical value to reader. We do not want philosophical or 'artsy' articles; straightforward reporting only."

DIAL, The Magazine for Public Television, East/West Network, 34 E. 51st St., New York NY 10022. (212)888-5900. Editor: Jane Ciabattari. Managing Editor: David Doty. Monthly magazine covering public television. "*Dial* goes to 1.3 million subscribers to public television in 14 cities, including New York, Boston, Chicago, Washington D.C., Los Angeles, Dallas, Detroit, Seattle, Tampa, Portland, Miami, Salt Lake City, Indianapolis and New Orleans." Pays on acceptance. Byline given. Offers 25% kill fee. Buys first North American serial rights and promotional rights. Submit seasonal/holiday material 6 months in advance. SASE. Reports in 1 month. Direct queries to editor-in-chief.

Nonfiction: "All material must have some connection with public television programming." Interview/profile; background pieces on shows. "A freelancer can best break into our publication by being aware of upcoming public television programming." Query with published clips. Length: 750-1,500 words. Pays $750-1,000.

THE DRAMA REVIEW, New York University, 300 South Bldg., 51 W. 4th St., New York NY 10003. (212)598-2597. Editor: Michael Kirby. 70% freelance written. Emphasizes avant-garde performance art for professors, students and the general theater and dance-going public as well as professional practitioners in the performing arts. Quarterly magazine; 144 pages. Circ. 6,000. Pays on publication. Query by letter only. Submit material 4 months in advance. Photocopied and previously published (if published in another language) submissions OK. SASE. Reports in 3 months. Publishes ms an average of 6 months after acceptance. Sample copy $5; free writer's guidelines.

Nonfiction: Jill Dolan, managing editor. Historical (the historical avant-garde in any performance art, translations of previously unpublished plays, etc.) and informational (documentation of a particular performance). Buys 10-20 mss/issue. Query. Pays 2¢/word for translations and other material.

Photos: Jill Dolan, managing editor. Photos purchased with accompanying ms on assignment. Captions required. Pays $10 for b&w photos. No additional payment for photos accepted with accompanying ms.

Tips: "No criticism in the sense of value judgments—we are not interested in the author's opinions. We are only interested in documentation theory and analysis. No criticism or scholarly, footnoted work."

DRAMATICS MAGAZINE, International Thespian Society, 3368 Central Pkwy., Cincinnati OH 45225. (513)559-1996. Editor-in-Chief: S. Ezra Goldstein. Associate Editor: Donald Corathers. 30% freelance written. For theatre arts students, teachers and others interested in theatre arts education. Magazine published monthly, September through May; 44-52 pages. Circ. 32,000. Pays on acceptance. Publishes ms an average of 3 months after acceptance. Buys first North American serial rights. Byline given. Submit seasonal/holiday material 3 months in advance. Simultaneous, photocopied and previously published submissions OK. Computer printout submissions acceptable; prefers letter-quality to dot-matrix. SASE. Reports in 3 weeks. Sample copy $2; free writer's guidelines.

Nonfiction: How-to (technical theatre); informational; interview; photo feature; humorous; profile; and technical. Buys 30 mss/year. Submit complete ms. Length: 750-3,000 words. Pays $30-150.

Photos: Purchased with accompanying ms. Uses b&w photos and color transparencies. Query. Total purchase price for ms includes payment for photos.

Fiction: Drama (one-act plays). No "plays for children, Christmas plays, or plays written with no attention paid to the playwriting form." Buys 5-9 mss/year. Send complete ms. Pays $50-200.

Tips: "The best way to break in is to know our audience—drama students and teachers and others interested in theatre—and to write for them. Writers who have some practical experience in theatre, especially in technical areas, have a leg-up here, but we'll work with anybody who has a good idea. Some freelancers have become regular contributors. Others ignore style suggestions included in our writer's guidelines."

DRAMATIKA, 429 Hope St., Tarpon Springs FL 33589. Editors: John Pyros and daughter. Magazine; 40 pages. For persons interested in the theater arts. Published 2 times/year. Circ. 500-1,000. Buys all rights. Pays on publication. Sample copy $2. Query. SASE. Reports in 1 month.

Fiction: Wants "performable pieces—plays, songs, scripts, etc." Will consider plays on various and open themes. Query first. Length: 20 pages maximum. Pays about $25/piece; $5-10 for smaller pieces.

Photos: B&w photos purchased with ms with extra payment. Captions required. Pays $5. Size: 8x11.

‡EMMY MAGAZINE, Suite 800, Academy of Television Arts & Sciences, 4605 Lankershim Blvd., N. Hollywood CA 91602. (213)506-7885. Editor and Publisher: Richard Krafsur. Managing Editor: Lori Kimball. 100% freelance written. Bimonthly magazine on television—a "critical—though not necessarily fault-finding—treatment of television and its effects on society, and how it might be improved." Circ. 10,000. Pays on acceptance. Publishes ms an average of 1½ months after acceptance. Byline given. Offers 20% kill fee. Buys first North American serial rights. Computer printout submissions acceptable; no dot-matrix. SASE. Reports in 2 weeks on queries; 1 month on mss. Free sample copy.

Nonfiction: Expose, historical/nostalgic, humor, interview/profile, opinion—all dealing with television. No fan-type profiles of TV performers. Buys 40 mss/year. Query with published clips. Length: 2,000-3,000 words. Pays $450-800.

Columns/Departments: Opinion or point-of-view columns dealing with TV. Buys 18-20 mss/year. Query with published clips. Length: 800-1,500 words. Pays $200-400.

Tips: "Query with thoughtful description of what you wish to write about. Or call. In either case, we can soon establish whether or not we can do business together. The most frequent mistake made by writers in completing an article for us is that they misread the magazine and send fan-magazine items."

FANGORIA, Starlog Press/O'Quinn Studios, 475 Park Ave. S, New York NY 10016. (212)689-2830. Editors: R. H. Martin/David Everitt. 35% freelance written. Published 8 times/year. Magazine covering horror films. Circ. 100,000. Pays on publication. Byline given. Offers 15% kill fee. Buys first North American serial rights with option for second rights to same material. Submit seasonal/holiday material 5 months in advance. Simultaneous queries OK. Computer printout submissions acceptable. SASE. Reports in 6 weeks. Publishes ms an average of 6 weeks after acceptance. Sample copy $3.

Nonfiction: Book excerpts, interview/profile. No "think" pieces, opinion pieces, reviews, or sub-theme overviews (i.e., vampire in the cinema). Buys 40 mss/year. Query with published clips. Length: 1,000-8,000 words (multipart run in consecutive issues, up to 3). Pays $100-350.

Photos: State availability of photos. Reviews b&w and color transparencies and prints. "No separate payment

for photos provided by film studios." Captions or identification of subjects required. Buys one-time rights.
Columns/Departments: Monster Invasion (news about new productions; must be exclusive, early information). Query with published clips. Length: 100-500 words. Pays $15-35.
Tips: "Other than recommending that you examine one or several copies of *Fangoria*, we can only describe it as a horror film magazine consisting primarily of interviews with technicians and filmmakers in the field. Study the magazine and be sure to stress the interview subjects' words—not your own opinions. We are very interested in small, independent filmmakers working outside of Hollywood. These people are usually more accessible to writers, and more cooperative. Because much of our magazine is written inhouse, the little independents are sometimes hard for us to contact from New York, whereas outside writers may find a local group mounting an independent production."

‡**FILM COMMENT**, Film Society of Lincoln Center, 140 W. 65th St., New York NY 10023. (212)877-1800. Editor: Richard Corliss. Senior Editor: Harlan Jacobson. 98% freelance written. Bimonthly magazine covering cinema. Circ. 38,000. Pays on publication. Publishes ms an average of 2 months after acceptance. Byline given. Buys one-time rights. Submit seasonal material 2 months in advance. No disk submissions. Computer printout submissions acceptable; no dot-matrix. SASE.
Nonfiction: Book excerpts; expose; general interest (film); historical; interview/profile; new product; opinion; photo feature. "We only accept articles by writers extremely knowledgable in film." No personal accounts of working on a film, fictional movie-inspired work. Buys 90 mss/year. Query with clips of published work. Length: 800-6,000 words. Pays $100-500. Sometimes pays the expenses of writers on assignment.
Photos: State availability of photos.
Columns/Departments: Video, Television, Books, Independents, Industry, Journals. Length: 800-2,000 words. Pays $100-250.
Tips: "The best way to break in is to have excellent writing samples or some film credentials, be already published on film somewhere, and come up with an idea well in advance of its timeliness: an interview with someone who has a new movie coming out, for example. Most open to either serious in-depth essays on filmmakers who haven't been profiled, or right-on-the-mark trend stories or think pieces related to current films, or interviews with topical filmmakers."

FILM QUARTERLY, University of California Press, Berkeley CA 94720. (415)642-6333. Editor: Ernest Callenbach. 100% freelance written. Quarterly. Buys all rights. Byline given. Pays on publication. Publishes ms an average of 3 months after acceptance. Query; "sample pages are very helpful from unknown writers. We must have hard-copy printout and don't care how it is produced, but we cannot use dot-matrix printouts unless done on one of the new printers that gives type-quality letters." SASE.
Nonfiction: Articles on style and structure in films, articles analyzing the work of important directors, historical articles on development of the film as art, reviews of current films and detailed analyses of classics, book reviews of film books. Must be familiar with the past and present of the art; must be competently, although not necessarily breezily, written; must deal with important problems of the art. "We write for people who like to think and talk seriously about films, as well as simply view them and enjoy them. We use no personality pieces or reportage pieces. Interviews usually work for us only when conducted by someone familiar with most of a filmmaker's work. (We don't use performer interviews.)" Length: 6,000 words maximum. Pay is about 2¢/word.
Tips: *"Film Quarterly* is a specialized academic journal of film criticism, though it is also a magazine (with pictures) sold in bookstores. It is read by film teachers, students, and die-hard movie buffs, so unless you fall into one of those categories, it is very hard to write for us. Currently, we are especially looking for material on independent, documentary, etc. films not written about in the national film reviewing columns."

‡**FORREST J. ACKERMAN'S MONSTERLAND, *SF MOVIELAND COMICS, FEATURE***, New Media Publishing, Inc., 3530 Mound View Ave., Studio City CA 91604. (818)766-8625. Editors: Forrest J. Ackerman, James Van Hise, and Hal Schuster. 70% freelance written. Magazines of movies, comics, and animation aimed to entertain and inform. "No one is required to read them, they have to want to read them." Circ. 100,000 each. Pays on acceptance. Publishes ms an average of 1 month after acceptance. Byline given. Buys first North American serial rights. Simultaneous queries and photocopied submissions OK. Computer printut submissions acceptable; no dot-matrix. SASE. Reports in 2 weeks on queries; 1 month on mss. Sample copy $4; writer's guidelines for legal size SAE and 50¢ postage.
Nonfiction: Book excerpts, historical/nostalgic (science fiction movies/comics), interview/profile, new product and personal experience. No material not directly relating to central theme. Buys 250 mss/year. Query with published clips. Length: 1,500-4,000 words. Pays $45-500.
Tips: "We can always use good new writers. The particular subject areas of books include current and upcoming science fiction or fantasy movies or television including overview pieces, reports on production or special effects, interviews with actors, directors, producers or production people; current and/or nostalgia pieces on

British-made movies and television especially those with appearance in this country, including interviews, reviews and profile pieces; and interviews with comic book or comic strip artists or animators, profiles of important upcomings products, and similar feature-length pieces."

‡**HORIZON, The Magazine of the Arts**, Boone, Inc., Drawer 30, Tuscaloosa AL 35402. Editor/Publisher: Gray Boone. Editorial Director: Kellee Reinhart. 60% freelance written. Monthly magazine covering the arts (fine arts, architecture, literature, theater, dance, film, music, photography, television, arts-related travel). "*Horizon* is a graphically rich arts magazine giving readers the tools and information necesary to bring the arts into their everyday lives. Our readership is upscale, highly educated, and geographically diverse. They are interested in the arts in a deeply personal way, whether it's going to the theater or collecting art for their home." Pays on publication. Publishes ms an average of 2 months after acceptance. Byline given. Offers kill fee. Buys first North American serial rights. Submit seasonal/holiday material 4 months in advance. "This is important, as many of our articles are timed with openings, etc." SASE. Reports in 1 month. Sample copy $4; writer's guidelines for SASE.
Nonfiction: Jennifer Graham, senior editor. Book excerpts ("relatively few"); expose ("if sound and well-documented"); historical/nostalgic ("rarely"); profiles ("no puff pieces—must be timely and interpretative"); critical essays or surveys ("must relate to something important in the contemporary cultural scene"); and photo features. "We publish no original fiction or poetry." Buys 6 unsolicited mss/year. Recent article example: "Porgy and Bess" (January/February 1985). Query with clips of published work. Length: 1,500-3,500 words. Pays $350-600. Sometimes pays the expenses of writers on assignment.
Photos: Robin McDonald, art director. State availability of photos or send photos with ms. Reviews any size color transparencies or 8x10 prints. Identification of subjects required. Buys one-time rights.
Tips: Most open to "feature articles. When submitting ideas, consider how they could be fleshed out with sidebars, tips, and biographies so that readers could take this article and go beyond what you've written. Query letters should be well researched and to the point (not two pages long) and are best supported with clips of the writer's other publications. Timeliness and a unique angle are vital also. We take queries in writing only. Phone queries are counter-productive, because they annoy our editors, who are working on other things. Flexibility and promptness at deadlines endear writers to us."

‡**MOVIE COLLECTOR'S WORLD**, The Marketplace For Film & Video Collectors, 151 E. Birch St., Annandale MN 55302. (612)274-5230. Editor: Jon E. Johnson. 90% freelance written. Bi-weekly tabloid covering film-collecting and home video: reviews, profiles, features and technical subjects. "We strive to serve the varied interests of our readers, ranging from film and video enthusiasts to still and poster collectors." Circ. 10,000. Pays on publication. Publishes ms an averge of 2 months after acceptance. Byline given. Buys first and second (reprint) rights. Submit seasonal/dated material 3 months in advance. Photocopied submissions OK. Computer printout submissions OK "if close to double-spaced." SASE. Reports in 3 weeks. Free sample copy and writer's guidelines.
Nonfiction: Book excerpts; expose (investigative or extensive profile-type submissions); how-to; new product (uses and technical review); opinion (in the form of reviews or commentary); technical subjects ("one very popular feature we ran was on Cinemascope"). No personal experience/first person articles other than interview, profile or general interest. "We like to see authoritatives pieces of any type that can be readied without a lot of work." Send complete ms or query. Pays 3¢/word or $100 maximum.
Photos: State availability of photos with query or ms. Pays $3-5 for 8x10 b&w prints. Model release required. Buys one-time rights.
Columns/Departments: Book (film/video-related topics) and tape/disc reviews. Send ms or query. Pays $5 minimum for short reviews, word rates for longer pieces.
Tips: "*MCW* uses freelance material for nearly its entire content, and as a result it is very easy for a freelancer to break into the publication, provided his/her material suits our needs and they know what they're writing about. Once writers get a feel for what *MCW* is, and we get an idea of their work, they tend to become one of our 'family' of regular contributors. The most open areas of *Movie Collector's World* are interviews and profiles, reviews and technical/how-to pieces. All areas/sections are open to new, different and fresh writers wishing to express their feelings, expertise and knowledge as it relates to the movie/video/television/personality world. Writers who know and care about their subject should have no problem when it comes to writing for *MCW* (providing it suits our needs). We actually encourage unsolicited submissions. A look at your wares just might land you a quicker sale than if there has to be a lot of counseling, advising or hand-holding involved. With a bi-weekly schedule we work quick."

PERFORMING ARTS IN CANADA, 2nd Fl., 52 Avenue Rd., Toronto, Ontario M5R 2G2 Canada. (416)921-2601. Editor: Mary Ann Pathy. 70% freelance written. Quarterly magazine for professional performers and general readers with an interest in Canadian theatre, dance, music, opera and film. Covers "all five major fields of the performing arts (music, theatre, opera, film and dance), modern and classical, plus articles on related subjects (technical topics, government arts policy, etc.)." Circ. 80,550. Pays 1 month following publication. Publishes ms an average of 3 months after acceptance. Byline given. Offers 30-50% kill fee. Buys first serial rights. Reports in 3-6 weeks. Computer printout submissions acceptable; prefers letter-quality to dot-matrix. SAE, IRCs. Sample copy $1.

Nonfiction: "Lively, stimulating, well-researched articles on Canadian performing artists or groups. We tend to be overstocked with theatre pieces; most often in need of good classical music articles." No nonCanadian, nonperforming arts material. Buys 30-35 mss/year. Query. Length: 1,500-2,000 words. Pays $150-200.

Tips: "Query preferably with an outline. Writers new to this publication should include clippings."

PREVUE, Today's Personalities and Tomorrow's Entertainment, Prevue Entertainment, Box 974, Reading PA 19603. (215)374-7477. Editor: Jim Steranko. 50% freelance written. Bimonthly magazine covering entertainment, films, TV, music and books. "We want factual information on film and TV productions and their stars. Readership is predominantly young and male. We prefer to use opinions of the subjects covered rather than the writer's. Heavy visuals accompany all features. Manly features cover entertainment *in advance* of the event." Circ. 250,000. Pays on acceptance. Publishes ms an average of 1 month after acceptance. Byline given. Buys all rights and first North American serial rights. Offers negotiable kill fee. Makes work-for-hire assignments. Photocopied submissions OK. Computer printout submissions acceptable; prefers letter-quality to dot-matrix. SASE. Reports in 2 weeks. Sample copy for $2.95, 8½x11 SAE, and $1 postage; writer's guidelines with initial assignment.

Nonfiction: Interview/profile (film and TV stars, musicians, personalities). Buys 50-100 mss/year. Query with published clips or send complete ms. Length: 750-6,000 words. Pays negotiable rates. Sometimes pays the expenses of writers on assignment.

Columns/Departments: Film news. Buys 10-20 mss/year.

Tips: "We gravitate toward writers who know grammar, punctuation, syntax, etc.—and *use* them. We like tight, lean copy, a maximum amount of information in a minimum amount of space. A freelancer can best break in to our publication by listing his/her connections to film and TV personalities. Major celebrities and film projects are assigned to regular writers and minor features go to newcomers in most cases. The most frequent mistake made by writers in completing an article for us is that they do not write for the magazine's reader in the style of other features, or tailor the material to be compatible with our format. Most new writers fail to analyze the market for which they are writing. Generally we encourage queries, then discuss approach and format of the feature."

SATELLITE DISH MAGAZINE, Your Complete Satellite TV Entertainment Guide, Satellite Publications, Inc., 460 Tennessee Ave., Box 8, Memphis TN 38101. (901)521-1580. Editor-in-Chief: Kathy Ferguson. 90% freelance written. Biweekly national magazine with TV/movie entertainment news, features, reviews and personality profiles. "We are looking for two basic styles: the lively entertainment feature on current or upcoming TV (satellite/pay/cable/network) programming; and the in-depth, informative article, usually written in first person, about an issue and its relation to the satellite TV or movie/film industry." Circ. 100,000. Pays on publication. Publishes ms an average of 2 months after acceptance. Byline given. Offers negotiable kill fee. Buys first North American serial and second serial (reprint) rights. Submit seasonal/holiday material 3 months in advance. Previously published submissions "sometimes" OK. Computer printout submissions acceptable; no dot-matrix. SASE. Reports in approximately 2 months. Free sample copy and writer's guidelines.

Nonfiction: General interest; historical/nostalgic; interview/profile; opinion (as it relates to a topic or issue); personal experience (as it relates to a topic or issue); technical (satellite TV news, issues). "We also recommend specialized writing on any of the satellite TV programming categories: Adult Programming, Business News, Children's Programming, Consumer Events, Cultural Information, Education, Entertainment Specials, Ethnic Programming, Family Programming, Health, Movies, Music, News, Public Affairs, Public Broadcasting, Religion, Science, Sports, Unique Variety Programmings and Women's Programming. This could be a piece on an upcoming program, or a specific category or subject and how it relates to satellite television." Query with published clips or send complete ms. Length: 800-2,000 words. Pays $150-1,000. Sometimes pays the expenses of writers on assignment.

Photos: State availability of photos and/or send photos with query or mss. Pays $50 minimum for color transparencies; $25 minimum for 8x10 b&w prints; $50 minimum for 8x10 color prints. Captions required. Buys one-time rights.

Columns/Departments: Film/Movie Reviews (on movies premiering on the pay/cable/satellite networks); Books (as they relate to TV/movies); Celebrity/People (on people as they relate to TV/movies). Buys 50-100 mss/year. Query with published clips or send complete ms. Length: 1,000-1,500 words. Pays $150-750.

Tips: "Personality profiles and movie reviews are most open to freelancers."

SATELLITE ORBIT, The Magazine of Satellite Entertainment & Electronics, CommTek Publishing Company, 418 N. River, Box 1048, Hailey ID 83333. (208)788-4936. Publisher: David G. Wolford. Executive Editor: Bruce Kinnaird. 90% freelance written. Monthly magazine covering satellite television for "an audience that is affluent, educated, and interested in reaching beyond the ordinary. Our readers are interested—and knowledgable—in electronics of all types related to entertainment." Circ. 175,000. Pays on publication.

Publishes ms an average of 2 months after acceptance. Byline given. Offers 33% of payment for kill fee. Buys first North American serial rights, one-time rights, all rights, first rights, or makes work-for-hire assignments. Submit seasonal/holiday material 2 months in advance. Electronic submissions OK on 1,200 baud modem. Computer printout submissions acceptable; prefers letter-quality to dot-matrix. SASE. Reports in 2 weeks. Sample copy $5 (includes 1st class mailing); writer's guidelines for business size SAE and 1 first class stamp.

Nonfiction: Humor (if there is an angle); interview/profile (satellite entertainment figure); new product (in field of electronics); opinion (satellite and entertainment related); technical (innovations). Query. "Unsolicited material will receive *no* consideration. No material about how satellite television is booming—we know that. No nostalgia." Buys 50-60 mss/year. Length: 1,000-1,700 words. Pays $75-650.

Photos: State availability of photos with query letter or ms. Reviews 35mm color transparencies and 8x10 b&w prints. Pays negotiable fee. Captions required. Rights negotiable.

Columns/Departments: *Profiles* of name figures who own a satellite antenna for TV reception: 750-1,000 words; short, lively piece on owner, why he bought antenna and what benefits he derives from it. *Celebrities*: 1,000-1,500 word pieces about entertainment newsmakers. Buys 24-30 items/year. Query. Pays $75-500.

Tips: "Do not make phone queries. Learn the terms of the satellite entertainment field and use those terms in a query letter. Keep track of the industry: What's new in programming? What new satellite networks are going up? Who's making news in the field? The field of satellite entertainment is relatively new, but the market for articles of this nature is going to rocket in a year or two. Initial research into the field might be a bit laborious at first, but freelancers looking for a lucrative new market would be well advised to learn the ropes of this one. Also, freelancers should become more versed in libel law. Plaintiffs are currently winning about 80% of their cases."

SOAP OPERA DIGEST, 254 W. 31st St., New York NY 10001. Executive Editor: Meredith Brown. 25% freelance written. Biweekly magazine; 144 pages. Circ. 750,000. Pays on acceptance. Buys all rights. Submit seasonal/holiday material 4 months in advance of issue date. Computer printout submissions acceptable. SASE. Reports in 1 month.

Nonfiction: Lynn Davey, managing editor, freelance material. "Articles only directly about daytime and nighttime personalities or soap operas." Interview (no telephone interviews); nostalgia; photo features (must be recent); profiles; special interest features: health, beauty, with soap opera personalities and industry news, with a strong interest in nighttime soaps. "We are a 'newsy' magazine—not gossip, and are highly interested in timely news stories. No poorly written material that talks down to the audience." Buys 2-3 mss/issue. Query with clips of previously published work. Length: 1,000-2,000 words. Pays $200 and up. Sometimes pays the expenses of writers on assignment.

Photos: State availability of photos with query. Captions preferred. Buys all rights. "Writers must be good at in-depth, personality profiles. Pack as much info as possible into a compact length. Also want humor pieces."

‡SOAP OPERA PEOPLE, Tempo Publishing, Inc., #520, 6565 Sunset Blvd., Los Angeles CA 90028. (213)466-2451. Editor: Lorraine Zenka Tilden. 80% freelance written. Monthly magazine about soap operas/daytime and some prime time. "We deal with personal insights into actors on soaps and the characters they portray. We like to feel we offer something for everyone who watches soaps." Estab. 1984. Circ. 125,000. Pays on publication. Publishes ms an average of 3 months after acceptance. Byline given. Offers 25% kill fee. Buys all rights; makes work-for-hire assignments. Submit seasonal/holiday material 4 months in advance. Simultaneous queries OK. Computer printout submissions acceptable; prefers letter-quality to dot-matrix. Reports within days. "Phone queries welcome (know the field and know who you're calling by name)."

Nonfiction: General interest (campus trends; clubs; re soaps); humor/satire; interview/profile; opinion (essays); photo feature; and roundups (one question asked of 4-10 celebrities). Needs East Coast freelancers most. No esoteric "acting is my life" interviews. Wants to see interviews that reveal the human (down-to-earth) aspect of a soap star. Thoughts, opinions, issues that soap viewers could feel have touched them, too. Buys 10-15/issue. Query with published clips or send complete ms. Length: 500-1,750 words. Pays $75-200.

Photos: State availability of photos.

Tips: "I'm not interested in hearing from fans who only understand 'Erica' and not Susan Lucci. We want interviews that go beyond an actor's biography and the information he/she has already given four other magazines. Include resume."

STARWEEK MAGAZINE, Toronto Star Newspapers, Ltd., 1 Yonge St., Toronto, Ontario M5E 1E6 Canada. (416)367-2425. Editor: John Bryden. Weekly television newspaper supplement covering personalities, issues, technology, etc., relating to all aspects of video programming. Circ. 800,000. Pays by arrangement. Byline given. Offers 50% kill fee. Not copyrighted. Buys first serial rights. Submit seasonal/holiday material 6 weeks in advance. Computer printout submissions acceptable; prefers letter-quality to dot-matrix. SASE. Reports as soon as possible. Sample copy for 8x11 SAE.

Nonfiction: Interview/profile (of TV personalities); and technical. Buys 750 mss/year. Query with published clips. Length: 500-1,000 words. Pays $200-400.

Photos: Send photos with ms. Pays $50-100 for 8x10 b&w prints; $75-250 for 2x5 or 35mm color transparencies. Identification of subjects required. Buys one-time rights.

Tips: "I prefer to commission 'comment' or analysis pieces from writers whose credentials I know."

TUNED IN MAGAZINE, Tuned In, Corp., Suite A, 6867 Nancy Ridge Dr., San Diego CA 92121. (619)450-1630. Editor: Christina F. Paolini. 15% freelance written. Weekly magazine covering TV, including cable, radio and entertainment for "entertainment-oriented San Diegans, usually between the ages of 18 and 50, of a middle-income background." Circ. 50,000. Pays on publication. Publishes ms an average of 1 month after acceptance. Byline given. Buys one-time rights. Submit seasonal/holiday material 6 weeks in advance. Simultaneous and photocopied submissions OK. Computer printout submissions acceptable; prefers letter-quality to dot-matrix. SASE. Reports in 2 weeks on queries; 1 month on mss. San Diego writers preferred.
Nonfiction: General interest (personality stories, TV/radio articles, entertainment); how-to (get involved in the media; to interact and be a part of it); humor (lighthearted looks at the media and entertainment technology, etc.); interview/profile (of San Diegans who made good; visiting celebrities); and new product (technological updates; services such as radio for the blind). "We're looking for sharp, snappy articles that deal with some aspect of the San Diego entertainment field, or entertainment (TV, radio, film) as it *impacts* San Diego. We run 1 freelance article per issue, and 8 columns (staff-written). Query. Length: 2,000-2,500 words. Pays $125.
Photos: Send photos with accompanying ms. Captions required.
Tips: "Think in terms of national trends as they affect the local community, entertainment options that don't get much coverage, public-service articles, and guides."

TV GUIDE, Radnor PA 19088. Editor (National Section): David Sendler. Editor (Local Sections): Roger Youman. Managing Editor: R.C. Smith. Weekly. Circ. 17.1 million. Study publication. Query to Andrew Mills, assistant managing editor. SASE.
Nonfiction: Wants offbeat articles about TV people and shows. This magazine is not interested in fan material. Also wants stories on the newest trends of television, but they must be written in clear, lively English. Length: 1,000-2,000 words.
Photos: Uses professional high-quality photos, normally shot on assignment, by photographers chosen by *TV Guide*. Prefers color. Pays $250 day rate against page rates—$350 for 2 pages or less.

VIDEO TIMES MAGAZINE, Publications International, Ltd., 3841 W. Oakton St., Skokie IL 60076. (312)676-3470. Editor-in-Chief: Matthew White. Editor: Darrell Moore. 75% freelance written. Monthly magazine covering all software available for videotape and videodisc players. "We explore the movies and other aspects of entertainment available for video. Our audience watches a lot of pre-recorded tape. We provide both information (what's new) and ideas. We specialize in movie themes and in video tape reviews." Estab. 1984. Circ. 150,000. Pays on acceptance. Publishes ms an average of 2 months after acceptance. Byline given. Rights bought depend on material. Submit seasonal/holiday material 4 months in advance. Photocopied submissions OK. Computer printout submissions acceptable. SASE. Reports in 4 weeks. Sample copy for $2.95; free writer's guidelines.
Nonfiction: Book excerpts; historical/nostalgic (old movies); interview/profile (no question and answer worked into overview of movies); photo feature; and articles on themes, festivals, or anything from a performer's career to the most ingenious theme possible. "Writers will be judged on their ability to produce genuinely stimulating articles about watching movies. We intend to publish writers who can engage the reader throughout and who can knowingly expand a reader's awareness of film." Limit articles to those movies available on videotape or disc. No articles on theatrical-only movies. Buys 50 mss/year. Query with published clips. Length: 750-1,500 words. Pays 20¢/word.
Photos: State availability of photos. Wants color transparencies and b&w prints "as big as possible." Identification of subjects required. "We only buy photo stills from movies."
Columns/Departments: Darrell Moore, column/department editor. Movie Reviews (minimum 25 freelance 500-word reviews per issue); and Alternative Programming Reviews (exercise, music, etc.). Buys 400 mss/year. Query with published clips. Length: 100-1,000 words. Pays 20¢/word.
Fillers: Anecdotes and "stories behind the movies: casting, problems, script changes, etc." Length: 50-500 words. Pays $35 per anecdote.
Tips: "We need people who can accurately critique material being made specifically for video. We especially want people who watch a lot of videotape/disc—and think about it as its own medium. All areas, except signed columns, are open to freelancers. To write features, a freelancer must have a strong and proven grasp of film, or subject matter. Anecdotes are basically strong research. We have 35 steady freelancers whom we try to keep busy. It is very hard to break into a review pool. Reviews most often are assigned to those who appreciate a certain type of movie (horror, etc.)."

X-IT, A general arts and entertainment magazine, Image Design, Box 102, St. John's, Newfoundland A1C 5H5 Canada. (709)753-8802. Editor: Ken J. Harvey. Managing Editor: Beth Fiander. 80% freelance written. A triannual entertainment magazine concentrating on new ideas and thoughts in arts and literature (written and visual) for the general public. Circ. 3,000. Pays on publication. Publishes ms an average of 3 months after acceptance. Byline given. Buys one-time rights. Submit seasonal/holiday material 2 months in advance. Simultaneous, photocopied, and previously published submissions OK. Computer printout submissions acceptable. SASE. Reports in 3 weeks on queries; 1 month on mss. Sample copy $3 and 2 IRCs.

Nonfiction: All nonfiction is assigned by the editor. Query. Sometimes pays the expenses of writers on assignment.

Fiction: Adventure, erotica, experimental, fantasy, horror, humorous, mystery, science fiction and suspense. "We are open to practically all areas of literature. Our only demand is quality." Buys 12 mss/year. Send complete ms. Length: 1,500-4,800 words. Pays $10-150.

Poetry: Allela English, poetry editor. Avant-garde, free verse, light verse and traditional. Buys 30 poems/year. Submit maximum 10 poems. Length: open. Pays $10-50.

Fillers: Jokes and short humor. Buys 12/year. Length: "preferably short." Pays $5-25.

Tips: "Send along a short bio with submissions and a covering letter describing how work would fit in with the publication. Fiction and poetry are most open to freelancers. The most frequent mistake made by writers is taking the wrong angle—not listening to what I want. Some take matters into their own hands which is bad for the relationship. We need fillers."

‡XTRA MAGAZINE, Xtra Xtra, Inc., Suite 210, 2906 Maple, Dallas TX 75201. (214)871-0730. Editor: John Morthland. Managing Editor: Phyllis Arp. 75-90% freelance written. Monthly magazine covering contemporary music, film, fashion, and art. "We publish profiles, essays and criticism of contemporary pop arts and entertainment." Estab. 1984. Circ. 25,000. Pays on publication. Publshes ms an average of 1 month after acceptance. Byline given. Offers 25% kill fee. Buys first serial rights. Submit seasonal/holiday material 3 months in advance. Simultaneous queries and photocopied submissions OK. SASE. Reports in 1 month. Sample copy for 8x10 SAE and 5 first class stamp.

Nonfiction: Book excerpts (primarily pop music or film); interview/profile (popular artists and executives); new product (record and film reviews); opinion (record and film reviews); and photo feature. "We are open to just about any suggestions within our format." Buys 90-125 mss/year. Query with or without published clips. Length: 1,000-3,000 words. Pays 12-20¢/word. Pays expenses of writers on assignment.

Photos: Captions, model release, and identification of subjects required.

Columns/Departments: Film, book and record reviews on assignment from editor. Buys 100-125 mss/year. Query with or without published clips. Length: 400-800 words. Pays 12-20¢/word.

Travel, Camping and Trailer

Travel agencies and tour companies constantly remind consumers of the joys of traveling. But it's usually the travel magazines that tell potential travelers about the positive and negative aspects of possible destinations. "A good travel writer reads other travel writers voraciously and studies their styles to figure out why their articles moved them so much," said one editor. Freelance writers should also work as a team with photographers "where pictures are so important," pointed out another editor. Publications in this category tell campers and tourists the where-tos and how-tos of travel. Publications that buy how-to camping and travel material with a conservation angle are listed in the Nature, Conservation and Ecology classification. Regional publications are frequently interested in travel and camping material with a local angle. Hunting and fishing and outdoor publications that buy camping how-to material will be found in the Sports category. Those dealing with automobiles or other vehicles maintained for sport or as a hobby can be found in the Automotive and Motorcycle category. Many magazines in the In-Flight category are also in the market for travel articles and photos.

‡AAA WORLD, Hawaii/Alaska, AAA Hawaii, 730 Ala Moana Blvd., Honolulu HI 96813. (808)528-2600. Editor: Thomas Crosby. 15% freelance written. Bimonthly magazine of travel, automotive safety and legislative issues. Orientation is toward stories that benefit members in some way. Circ. 20,000. Pays on publication. Publishes ms an average of 4 months after acceptance. Byline given. Buys one-time rights. Submit seasonal/holiday material 4 months in advance. Photocopied and previously published submissions OK. Computer printout submissions acceptable. SASE. Reports in 1 week on queries; 1 month on mss. Free sample copy.

Nonfiction: How-to (auto maintenance, safety, etc.); and travel (tips, destinations, bargains). Buys 6 mss/year. Send complete ms. Length: 1,500 words. Pays $150 maximum. Sometimes pays the expenses of writers on assignment.
Photos: State availability of photos. Reviews b&w contact sheet. Pays $10-25. Captions required. Buys one-time rights.
Tips: "Find an interesting, human interest story that affects AAA members."

AAA WORLD, The Webb Co., 1999 Shepard Rd., St. Paul MN 55116. (612)690-7304. Editor: Dick Schaaf. Managing Editor: Gayle Bonneville. 80% freelance written. Bimonthly national magazine of the American Automobile Association covering public policy, consumer, safety and travel topics. Twelve AAA clubs in 13 states may add regional copy to their editions of the national magazine. Queries relating to regional interests will be forwarded to the appropriate region. Circ. 1.8 million. Pays on acceptance. Publishes ms an average of 6 months after acceptance. Byline given. Offers 25% kill fee. Buys one-time rights and nonexclusive reprint rights. Submit seasonal/holiday material at least 6 months in advance. Simultaneous queries and photocopied submissions OK. Computer printout submissions are acceptable if they are dark enough to photocopy. SASE. Reports in 1 month on queries; 6 weeks on mss. Sample copy for 9x12 SAE and 73¢ postage; free writer's guidelines.
Nonfiction: Public policy and public affairs; consumer (travel-oriented); how-to (driving safety, driving techniques); destinations (one piece/issue). No long destination pieces; first person stories; highly technical automotive maintenance features; stories aimed at younger audience. Buys 25 mss/year. Query. Length: 700-1,500 words. Pays $300-500." Sometimes pays the expenses of writers on assignment.
Photos: Purchased separately; additional payment made if author's photos are used.
Tips: Best opportunity for queries is travel-oriented consumer, safety, news/analysis and public affairs; worst is destination travel.

ACCENT, Meridian Publishing Inc., 1720 Washington, Box 10010, Ogden UT 84409. Editor: Wayne Dewald. 95% freelance written. A monthly inhouse travel magazine distributed by various companies to employees, customers, stockholders, etc. "Readers are predominantly upscale, mainstream, family oriented." Circ. 100,000. Pays on acceptance. Publishes ms an average of 1 year after acceptance. Byline given. Buys first rights and nonexclusive reprint rights. Previously published submissions OK. Computer printout submissions are acceptable; dot-matrix submissions are acceptable if readable. SASE. Reports in 2 weeks. Sample copy $1 and 9x12 SAE; writer's guidelines for legal size SAE and first class stamp.
Nonfiction: "We're now using destination pieces only." We want upbeat pieces slanted toward the average traveler, but we also welcome some exotic travel." Buys 48-50 mss/year. Query with or without published clips or send complete ms. Length: 1,000-1,200 words. Pays 15¢/word.
Photos: State availability of color photos or send photos with query or ms. Pays $35 for color transparencies (slides to 8x10) and 8x10 glossy color prints. Captions required. Buys one-time rights.
Tips: "Write about interesting places. Super color transparencies are essential. Most rejections are because of poor quality photography or they didn't study the market."

ADVENTURE ROAD, Citicorp Publishing, 641 Lexington Ave., New York NY 10022. (212)888-9450. Editor: Susan Ochshorn. A bimonthly magazine for members of the Amoco Motor Club, the majority of whom are white-collar workers, college-educated, moderately affluent, middle-aged and enthusiastic about travel. "*Adventure Road* conveys information on car care and club benefits as well as vacation planning." Circ. 2 million. Pays on acceptance. Byline given. Offers 25% kill fee. Buys first rights. Submit seasonal/holiday material at least 6 months in advance. SASE. Reports in 1 month on queries; 3 weeks on mss. Sample copy for 8½x10 SAE and 4 first class stamps; writer's guidelines for business size SAE and 1 first class stamp.
Nonfiction: Book excerpts; how-to (travel-related); photo feature; and travel (restricted to domestic destinations). Buys 35 mss/year ("commissioned; rarely, if ever unsolicited"). Query with published clips. Length: 1,500-2,200 words. Pays $300-600.
Tips: "Freelancers can best break into our publication by writing a literate, well-conceived query letter and providing exciting clips. We are looking for an angle and for destinations or kinds of trips that are unusual in some way. Major features are most open to freelancers. Although our articles tend to be seasonal, we do like to provide our readers with material that they will be able to use in making plans for future trips. We are also interested in pieces about the experience of car travel. Features along these lines have included games people play in their cars and a guide to rare on-the-road radio."

‡**AL MUFTAH, The Magazine for Saudi-American Bank's Visa Gold Card Holders in the Middle East**, Age Communications Ltd., Parkway House, Sheen Lane, London SW14 8LS England. Editor: Joseph R. Yogerst. Assistant Editor: Jules MacMahon. Art Director: Jan Lehne. A bimonthly magazine covering all aspects of luxury travel and consumer goods. Circ. 10,000. Pays on publication. Buys first Middle East rights in both English and Arabic. Byline given. Submit seasonal/holiday material at least 6 months in advance. Simultaneous queries, and photocopied or previously published submissions OK as long as they have not or will

not appear in the Middle East. Send SAE with IRC. Reports in 1 month.

Nonfiction: Each issue includes at least four "VISA Gold Destinations" around the world, covering popular travel destinations outside the Middle East. "A luxury or up-market slant is essential, because an estimated 80 percent of our readers are millionaires." *Al Muftah* also carries regular features on charter yachting, private aircraft, high-speed rail and air travel, luxury motoring, exotic ocean cruises, equestrian sports, interior design, property rental and investment, fashion, jewelry and dining. "We want just about anything that could appeal to a millionaire. We also run occasional articles on exclusive private clubs, be it an 18-hole country club in Florida or a beach and tennis club in Tahiti." Length: 1,500-2,000 words. Pays minimum £80 Sterling (estimated $95) per 1,000 words. Query or send complete ms. Buys 60 mss/year.

Photos: State availability of photos. Captions required. Pays minimum of £20 for 35mm or larger format color transparencies; pays £150 for cover photos. Buys first Middle East rights.

AMERICAN TRAVELER, (formerly *September Days*), Days Inns of America, Inc., 2751 Buford Hwy., NE Atlanta GA 30324. (404)325-4000. Editor: Tom Passavant. Quarterly travel magazine for members of the September Days Club, who are 50 and older. Circ. 400,000. Pays on publication. Submit seasonal material 6 months in advance. Simultaneous and photocopied submissions OK. SASE. Reports in 3 weeks. Sample copy $2; writer's guidelines with SASE.

Nonfiction: Travel (in the continental United States, destination stories); and photo feature (of the United States). No poems or historical pieces. Buys 4-5 mss/issue. Send complete ms. Length: 500-2,000 words. Pays negotiable fee; "depends on ms and topic."

Photos: Pays $45 and up for standard color transparencies. Captions preferred; model release required. Buys one-time rights.

Tips: "Send complete ms on speculation only; do not include photos."

ASU TRAVEL GUIDE, ASU Travel Guide, Inc., 1325 Columbus Ave., San Francisco CA 94133. (415)441-5200. Editor: Howard Baldwin. 20% freelance written. Quarterly guidebook covering international travel features and travel discounts for well-traveled airline employees. Circ. 40,000. Pays on acceptance. Publishes ms an average of 18 months after acceptance. Byline given. Offers kill fee. Buys first North American serial rights, first and second rights to the same material, and second serial (reprint) rights to material originally published elsewhere. Makes work-for-hire assignments. Submit seasonal/holiday material 6 months in advance. Simultaneous queries and simultaneous, photocopied and previously published submissions OK. Computer printout submissions acceptable; prefers letter-quality to dot-matrix. Reports in 1 month. Send SASE for writer's guidelines. Unsolicited ms or queries without SASE will not be acknowledged. No telephone queries.

Nonfiction: International travel articles "similar to those run in consumer magazines." Not interested in amateur efforts from inexperienced travelers or personal experience articles that don't give useful information to other travelers. Buys 16-20 mss/year. Destination pieces only; no "Tips On Luggage" articles. "We will be accepting fewer manuscripts and relying more on our established group of freelance contributors." Length: 1,200-1,500 words. Pays $200.

Photos: "Interested in clear, high-contrast photos; we prefer not to receive material without photos." Reviews 5x7 and 8x10 b&w prints. "Payment for photos is included in article price; photos from tourist offices are acceptable."

Tips: "Query with samples of travel writing and a list of places you've recently visited. We appreciate clean and simple style. Keep verbs in the active tense and involve the reader in what you write. Avoid 'cute' writing, excess punctuation (especially dashes and ellipses), coined words and stale cliches. Any article that starts with the name of a country followed by an exclamation point is immediately rejected. The most frequent mistakes made by writers in completing an article for us are: 1) Lazy writing; using words to describe a place that could describe any destination—i.e. "There is so much to do in (fill in destination) that whole guidebooks have been written about it." 2) Including fare and tour package information—our readers make arrangements through their own airline."

AWAY, 888 Worcester St., Wellesley MA 02181. (617)237-5200. Editor: Gerard J. Gagnon. For "members of the ALA Auto & Travel Club, interested in their autos and in travel. Ages range from approximately 20-65. They live primarily in New England." Slanted to seasons. 20% freelance written. Quarterly. Circ. 170,000. Buys first serial rights. Pays on acceptance. Publishes ms an average of 3 months after acceptance. Submit seasonal material 6 months in advance. Reports "as soon as possible." Although a query is not mandatory, it may be advisable for many articles. Computer printout submissions acceptable; no dot-matrix. SASE. Free sample copy.

Nonfiction: Articles on "travel, tourist attractions, safety, history, etc., preferably with a New England angle. Also, car care tips and related subjects." Would like a "positive feel to all pieces, but not the chamber of commerce approach." Buys general seasonal travel, specific travel articles, and travel-related articles; outdoor activities, for example, gravestone rubbing; historical articles linked to places to visit and humor with a point. "Would like to see more nonseasonally oriented material. Most material now submitted seems suitable only for our summer issue. Avoid pieces on hunting and about New England's most publicized attractions, such as Old

Sturbridge Village and Mystic Seaport.'' Length: 800-1,500 words, ''preferably 1,000-1,200.'' Pays approximately 10¢/word.

Photos: Photos purchased with mss. Captions required. B&w glossy prints. Pays $5-10/b&w photo, payment on publication based upon which photos are used. Not buying color at this time.

Tips: ''We have decided to sharply limit purchases of articles and photographs from outside sources; we will now publish more staff-produced material. The most frequent mistakes made by writers in completing an article for us are spelling, typographied errors and questionable statements of facts, which require additional research by the editorial staff.''

BIKEREPORT, Bikecentennial, Inc., The Bicycle Travel Association, Box 8308, Missoula MT 59807. (406)721-1776. Editor: Daniel D'Ambrosio. 75% freelance written. Bimonthly bicycle touring magazine for Bikecentennial members. Circ. 18,000. Pays on publication. Publishes ms an average of 1 year after acceptance. Byline given. Buys first serial rights. Submit seasonal/holiday material 3 months in advance. Simultaneous queries and photocopied submissions OK. Electronic submissions OK on CP/M Morrow, but requires hard copy also. Computer printout submissions acceptable; no dot-matrix. SASE. Reports in 2 weeks on queries; 1 month on mss. Publishes ms an average of 8 months after acceptance. Sample copy and guidelines for $1 postage. Include short bio with manuscript.

Nonfiction: Historical/nostalgic (interesting spots along bike trails); how-to (bicycle); humor (touring); interview/profile (bicycle industry people); personal experience (''my favorite tour''); photo feature (bicycle); technical (bicycle); travel (''my favorite tour''). No articles on activism—biker's rights. Buys 20-25 mss/year. Query with published clips or send complete ms. Length: 800-2,500 words. Pays $35-65/article.

Photos: Bicycle, scenery, portraits. State availability of photos. Pays $5-25 for b&w and color. Model release and identification of subjects required. Buys one-time rights.

Fiction: Adventure, experimental, historical, humorous. Not interested in anything that doesn't involve bicycles. Query with published clips or send complete ms. Length: 800-2,500 words. Pays $35-65/article.

Tips: ''We don't assign articles.''

CAMPERWAYS, 1108 N. Bethlehem Pike, Box 460, Spring House PA 19477. (215)643-2058. Editor-in-Chief: Charles E. Myers. 75% freelance written. Emphasis on recreation vehicle camping and travel. Monthly (except Dec. and Jan.) tabloid. Circ. 33,000. Pays on publication. Publishes ms an average of 6 months after acceptance. Buys first, simultaneous, second serial (reprint) or regional rights. Byline given. Submit seasonal/holiday material 3-4 months in advance. Simultaneous, photocopied and previously published submissions OK. Computer printout submissions acceptable; prefers letter-quality to dot-matrix. Self-addressed envelope and loose postage. Reports in 1 month. Sample copy $2 and free writer's guidelines.

Nonfiction: Historical (when tied in with camping trip to historical attraction or area); how-to (selection, care, maintenance of RVs, accessories and camping equipment); humor; personal experience; and travel (camping destinations within 200 miles of New York-DC metro corridor). No ''material on camping trips to destinations outside stated coverage area.'' Buys 80-100 unsolicited mss/year. Query. Length: 1,000-2,000 words. Pays $40-85.

Photos: ''Good photos greatly increase likelihood of acceptance. Don't send snapshots, polaroids. We can't use them.'' Photos purchased with accompanying ms. Captions required. Uses 5x7 or 8x10 b&w glossy prints. Total purchase price for ms includes payment for photos.

Columns/Departments: Camp Cookery (ideas for cooking in RV galleys and over campfires. Should include recipes). Buys 10 mss/year. Query. Length: 500-1,500 words. Pays $25-50.

Tips: ''Articles should focus on single attraction or activity or on closely clustered attractions within reach on the same weekend camping trip rather than on types of attractions or activities in general. We're looking for little-known or offbeat items. Emphasize positive aspects of camping: fun, economy, etc. We want feature items, not shorts and fillers. Acceptance is based on quality of article and appropriateness of subject matter. The most frequent mistakes made by writers in completing an article for us are failure to follow guidelines or failure to write from the camper's perspective.''

CAMPING CANADA, CRV Publishing Canada Ltd., Suite 202, 2077 Dundas St. East, Mississauga, Ontario L4X 1M2 Canada. (416)624-8218. Editorial Director: Reg Fife. A magazine published 7 times/year, covering camping and RVing. Circ. 100,000. Pays on publication. Byline given. Buys first rights. Submit seasonal/holiday material 3 months in advance. Computer printout submissions acceptable; no dot-matrix. SASE. Reports in 2 months. Free sample copy and writer's guidelines.

Nonfiction: General interest; historical/nostalgic (sometimes); how-to; new product; personal experience; and photo feature; technical; and travel. No material unrelated to Canada and RVing. Buys 50 mss/year. Query. Length: 1,000-2,000 words. Pays $150-300.

Photos: Send photos with query or manuscript. Reviews contact sheets, negatives, transparencies (send duplicates) and prints. Identification of subjects required. Buys first serial rights.

CAMPING TODAY, Official Publication of National Campers & Hikers Association, T-A-W Publishing Co., 1219 Bracy, Greenville MI 48838. (616)754-9179. Editors: David and Martha Higbie. The monthly official membership publication of the NCHA, "the largest nonprofit camping organization in the United States and Canada. Members are heavily oriented toward RV travel, both weekend and extended vacations. A small segment is interested in backpacking. Concentration is on activities of members within chapters, conservation, wildlife, etc." Circ. 30,000. Pays on publication. Byline given. Buys one-time rights. Submit seasonal/holiday material 3 months in advance. Simultaneous, photocopied, and previously published submissions OK. Computer printout submissions acceptable; prefers letter-quality to dot-matrix. SASE. Reports in 1 month. Sample copy and writer's guidelines for SAE.
Nonfiction: Humor (camping or travel related); interview/profile (interesting campers); new product (RV's and related equipment); technical (RV's); and travel (camping, hiking and RV travel). Buys 12-24 mss/year. Send complete ms. Length: 750-1,000 words. Pays $75-100.
Photos: Send photos with accompanying query or ms. Reviews color transparencies and 5x7 b&w prints. Pays $25 maximum for color transparencies. Captions required.
Tips: "Freelance material on RV travel, RV technical subjects and items of general camping and hiking interest throughout the United States and Canada will receive special attention. Color cover every month."

CAPE COD GUIDE, What to do, where to go, things to see while on Cape Cod, MPG Communications, Specialty Publications, Box 959, Plymouth MA 02360. (617)746-5555, ext. 241. Editor/Publisher: Walter Brooks. Office Manager: D. Sellon. 60% freelance written. A tourist magazine digest covering tourism on Cape Cod. Weekly May-Oct.; monthly Nov.-Apr. Circ. 50,000 weekly. Pays on publication. Publishes ms an average of 2 months after acceptance. Byline given. Buys first and second rights to the same material and second (reprint) rights to material originally published elsewhere. Photocopied and previously published submissions OK. Computer printout submissions acceptable. SASE. Reports in 2 months.
Nonfiction: General interest, historical/nostalgic, humor, interview/profile, personal experience. "Articles must be Cape Cod tourist appropriate." Buys 30 mss/year. Send complete ms. Pays $25-40, including art or b&w photo.
Photos: State availability of photos. Reviews b&w contact sheet, and 3x5 and 5x7 b&w prints. Payment negotiated with ms. Captions, model release, and identification of subjects required. Buys reprint rights with ms.
Columns/Departments: Art; Antiques; Hidden Cape (places not heavily publicized by tourist media); and Seafood Recipes; Nite Life. Buys 20-50 mss/year. Query. Length: 500-750 words. Pays $25-40.
Fiction: Adventure, fantasy, historical, horror, humorous. "All must be Cape Cod oriented!" Buys 30 mss/year. Send complete ms. Length: 500-750 words. Pays $25-40, including art or b&w photos.
Tips: "Submit humorous, tongue-in-cheek, anecdotal copy specifically tied to Cape Cod and of interest to Cape Cod tourists. Our features are primarily freelanced each year. We need short miscellaneous editorial fillers of the same description as our primary needs. Historical based fiction, unique happenings on Cape are of special interest. The most frequent mistakes made by writers in completing an article for us is the use of off-Cape location or subjects, also dull, dry copy and articles that are too long."

‡**CHARTERING MAGAZINE**, Chartering Inc., 830 Pop Tilton's Place, Jensen Beach FL 33457. (305)334-2004. Editor: Michael Shepard. 25-50% freelance written. "*Chartering* is a people-oriented travel magazine with a positive approach to yacht chartering. Our focus is yacht charter vacations." Circ. 40,000. Pays on publication. Publishes ms an average of 3 months after acceptance. Buys first North American serial rights. Submit seasonal/holiday material at least 3 months in advance. Simultaneous queries and simultaneous and photocopied submissions, and previously published work (on rare occasion) OK. Electronic submissions OK. Computer printout submissions acceptable. Reports in 2 weeks. Writer's guidelines for #SAE and 1 first class stamp.
Nonfiction: Antonia Thomas, associate editor. General interest (worldwide, charter boat-oriented travel); historical/nostalgic (charter vacation oriented); how-to (bareboating techniques; getting your captains license); interview/profile (charter brokers, charter skippers, positive); new product (would have to be a new type of charter); opinion; personal experience (charter boat related, worldwide, positive people-oriented travel); photo feature (charter boat, worldwide, positive, people-oriented travel); technical (bareboat technique; charter boat IRS; charter boat documentation); travel (charter vacation-oriented); and ancillary topics such as fishing or scuba or underwater photography. Special issues will focus on the Caribbean, diving, and sports fishing. Buys 36-60 mss/year. Query with published clips or send complete ms. Length: 600-3,000 words. Pays $50-300. Sometimes pays expenses of writers on assignment.
Photos: Antonia Thomas, associate editor. State availability of photos or send photos with query or ms. Pays with article for b&w and color negatives, color transparencies (35mm), and b&w and color prints (3x5 or larger). Requires model release and identification of subjects. Buys one-time rights.
Columns/Departments: Joan Lindgard, associate editor. Cruising areas, bareboat techniques (all facets); sail training facilities. Buys 12-20/year. Query with published clips or send complete ms. Length: 500-900 words.
Tips: "We are happy to look at the work of any freelancer who may have something appropriate to offer within

our scope—travel with a charter vacation orientation. We prefer submissions accompanyied by good, professional quality photography. The best first step is a request for editorial guidelines, accompanied by a typed letter and work sample.''

‡**DISCOVERY**, (formerly *Discovery Magazine*), 3701 West Lake Ave., Glenview IL 60025. Editor: Mary Kaye Stray. A quarterly travel magazine for Allstate Motor Club members. Circ. 1,300,000. Buys first North American serial rights. 75% freelance written. Pays on acceptance. Publishes ms an average of 8 months after acceptance. Computer printout submissions acceptable; no dot-matrix. Submit seasonal queries 8-14 months in advance to allow for photo assignment. Reports in 2-5 weeks. Query, don't send mss. Sample copy for 9x12 SAE and $1 postage; free writer's guidelines.
Nonfiction: "The emphasis is on North America and its people." Emphasizes automotive travel, offering a first-hand look at the people and places, and trends and activities that help define the American character. "We're looking for polished magazine articles that are people-oriented and promise insight as well as entertaintment—not narratives of people's vacations. Destination articles must rely less on the impressions of writers and more on the observations of people who live or work or grew up in the place and have special attachments." Recent articles include: "Longwood: the Living Legacy, and "In Love with a Legend," (Spring, 1985 issue). Query. "Submit a thorough proposal suitable for *Discovery*. It must be literate; concise and enthusiastic. Accompany query with relevant published clips and a resume." Buys 15-20 unsolicited mss/year. Length: 1,500-2,000 words, plus a 500 word sidebar on other things to see and do. Rates vary, depending on assignment and writer's credentials; usual range is $350-850. Sometimes pays the expenses of writers on assignment.
Photography: Color transparencies (35mm or larger). Pays day rate. For existing photos, rates depend on use. Photos should work as story; captions required. Send transparencies by registered mail. Buys one-time rights.
Tips: "No personal narratives, mere destination pieces or subjects that are not particularly visual. We have a strong emphasis on photojournalism and our stories reflect this. The most frequent mistakes made by writers in completing an article for us are not writing to assignment, resulting in a weak focus or central theme; poor organization and a lack of development which diminishes the substance of story. Word precision frequently is the difference between a dull and an exciting story. Writers will benefit by studying several issues of the publication before sending queries.''

ENDLESS VACATION, Endless Vacation Publications, Inc., Box 80260, Indianapolis IN 46280-0260. (317)848-0500. Editor-in-Chief: Betsy Sheldon. 5% freelance written. Bimonthly travel magazine for an "audience whose interest and involvement with travel and vacationing is inherent. The readership is almost entirely made up of vacation timeshare owners and those who seek variety and quality from their vacation experiences—affluent executives and professionals." Circ. 420,000. Pays on acceptance. Publishes ms an average of 6 months after acceptance. Byline given. Offers 25% kill fee. Buys variable rights; "mostly first North American and one-time rights." Submit seasonal/holiday material at least 4 months in advance. Simultaneous queries and simultaneous and previously published submissions OK. SASE.
Nonfiction: "At this time, *Endless Vacation* only accepts freelance material for "In Focus," a regularly featured column on photography tips. Subjects should be geared to non-professionals who are, nevertheless, seriously interested in photography. Articles should run between 800 and 1,000 words. Submissions of photos (color slides or other transparencies) to accompany articles is encouraged. Rate for column is $350. Photos are negotiated separately.''

‡**EUROPE FOR TRAVELERS!**, Europe Incorporated, 408 Main St., Nashua NH 03060. (603)888-0633. Editor: Carol Grasso. 80% freelance written. Quarterly magazine on Europe for traveling Americans. "Our publication is nonpolitical and nonreligious including various ways and places for traveling with spirit and zest, lots of practicalities, hotel and restaurant tips, etc." Estab. 1985. Circ. 5,000. Pays on publication. Publishes ms an average of 5 months after acceptance. Byline given. No kill fee. Buys first North American serial rights, one-time rights, first serial rights, or second serial (reprint rights). Submit seasonal/holiday material 5 months in advance. Simultaneous queries, and simultaneous, photocopied, and previously published submissions OK. Computer printout submissions acceptable; prefers letter-quality to dot-matrix. SASE. Reports in 1 month on queries; 6 weeks on mss. Sample copy $2 and 73¢ postage; writer's guidelines with SAE and 22¢ postage.
Nonfiction: Mostly destination pieces. Also how-to (open to proposals); light humor (but not satire or sarcasm); and personal experience. No religious, political, highly technical or complaint-type articles. Buys 12 mss/year. Query (with published clips, preferred), or send complete ms. Any length up to 2,000 words. Pays $10-100.
Columns/Departments: Prefers complete sample column for consideration. No specific length. Pays $10-40.
Fillers: Buys 8/year. Pays $1-10.
Tips: Get a copy of our magazine for style purposes and submit complete package: manuscripts, photos, maps, etc. Manuscript should be a photocopy. SASE. We return photos but request SASE with sufficient postage. For feature articles, the more complete, in terms of illustrative photos both black and white and color, and maps, which enhance the story, the more likely we are to accept it.

‡**EXCURSIONS, The Magazine of the Americas**, Logos Enterprises, Inc., 395-17N South End Ave., New York City NY 10280. (212)466-3443. Editor: Michael S. Weisberg. Assistant Editor: Susan Barbosa. 75% freelance written. Bimonthly magazine covering travel in the Western hemisphere. "*Excursions* is a consumer travel magazine that specializes in destinations in the Western Hemisphere *only*: North, South and Central Americas; the Caribbean countries; the North and South Poles; and any possessions of the countries within this geographic region. *Excursions* primarily zeroes in on one country or region in each bimonthly issue, with a minimum of two articles on the featured destination." Estab. 1984. Circ. 25,000. Pays on publication. Publishes ms an average of 4 months after acceptance. Byline given. Buys first North American serial rights. Submit seasonal/holiday material 4 months in advance. Simultaneous and photocopied submissions OK. Electronic submissions OK; disk must match IBM PC. Computer printout submissions acceptable; prefers letter-quality to dot-matrix. SASE. Reports in 2 months on queries; 3 months on mss. Sample copy for legal size envelope and 7 first class stamps; writer's guidelines for SASE.

Nonfiction: Personal experience, photo feature and travel. "The editors favor stories about the unusual aspects of familiar places. Stories can concern adventure travel (kayaking, mountain climbing, white water rafting, and the like). Writers might want to explore a small town's inns and restaurants or a large city for its museums, galleries, gardens, hotels, and other attractions. Shorter pieces might focus on a landmark or historic site in one place; a longer entry might deal with the entire area. No piece should read like public relations." No first-person, "what I did on my summer vacation" essays that are too narrow in focus and irrelevant as an experience to most readers. Buys 25 mss/year. Send complete ms. Length: 750-2,500 words. Pays $25.

Photos: State availability of photos with ms. Pays $10 for 2¼x2¼ b&w contact sheets and negatives; $10 for color transparencies. Model release and identification of subjects required. Buys one-time rights.

Tips: "The most frequent mistakes made by writers in completing an article for us is writing first-person articles with meaningless adjectives such as 'breathtaking,' 'great,' 'really fun' —without describing what was 'breathtaking' etc."

FAMILY MOTOR COACHING, 8291 Clough Pike, Cincinnati OH 45244-2796. (513)474-3622. Managing Editor: Pamela Wisby. 75% freelance written. Emphasizes travel by motorhome, and motorhome mechanics, maintenance and other technical information. Monthly magazine; 190-260 pages. Circ. 45,000. Pays on acceptance. Buys first-time, 12 months exclusive rights. Byline given. Phone queries discouraged. Submit seasonal/holiday material 5 months in advance. Computer printout submissions acceptable; prefers letter-quality to dot-matrix. SASE. Reports in 2 months. Sample copy $2; free writer's guidelines.

Nonfiction: Motorhome travel and living on the road; travel (various areas of country accessible by motor coach); how-to (modify motor coach features); bus conversions; and nostalgia. Buys 20 mss/issue. Query. Length: 1,000-2,000 words. Pays $50-200.

Photos: State availability of photos with query. Offers no additional payment for b&w contact sheet(s) 35mm or 2¼x2¼ color transparencies. Captions required. B&w glossy photos should accompany nontravel articles. Buys first rights.

Tips: "Keep in mind, stories must have motorhome angle or connection; inclusion of information about FMCA members enhances any travel article. Stories about an event somewhere should allude to nearby campgrounds, etc. The stories should be written assuming that someone going there would be doing it by motorhome. We need more articles from which to select for publication. We need geographic balance and a blend of travel, technical and incidental stories. No first-person accounts of vacations."

FAR EAST TRAVELER, Largest Hotel Magazine in the Far East, Far East Reporters, Inc., 4-28, 1-chome, Moto-Azabu, Minato-ku 106, Tokyo, Japan. (03)452-0705. Managing Editor: Julia Nolet. 90% freelance written. A monthly English-language travel magazine distributed free to guest rooms in 40 first-class hotels in 7 Asian countries. Readership consists primarily of English-speaking tourists and business travelers interested in travel articles on destinations throughout Asia and the Pacific. Circ. 25,000. Pays 1 month following publication. Publishes ms an average of 4 months after acceptance. Byline given. Buys one-time rights, simultaneous rights, and second serial (reprint) rights. Submit seasonal/holiday material 3 months in advance. Simultaneous, photocopied, and previously published submissions OK. Computer printout submissions acceptable; prefers letter-quality to dot-matrix. Reports in 1 month. Sample copy for 5 IRCs for surface post; writer's guidelines for 1 IRC.

Nonfiction: Historical/nostalgic (on interesting or unusual things of Asia's past); how-to (tips on traveling, especially for businessmen); humor (on traveling, customs in Asia, etc.); personal experience (unusual traveling experience); photo feature (photo essays or any Asian subject); and travel (on any destination in Asia except mainland China). "Although most of our readers are businessmen, we work under the assumption that businessmen are people just like everyone else. We therefore like to see articles with a broad base of appeal written for anyone who enjoys traveling. Articles can range from adventure stories to destination pieces, from trekking in Thailand to shopping in Tokyo. Writers should keep in mind that because of our monthly turnover of readership, we are constantly looking for articles on all major and offbeat destinations in Asia. Just because we published an article on Seoul last year doesn't mean we can't use another one this year. Because of the magazine's close ties to Taiwan, we cannot use any articles on mainland China. Also, no boring, encyclopedic-like articles." Buys 60 mss/year. Complete ms preferred, or send query with published clips. Length: 750-3,000 words. Pays U.S. 10¢/word.

Photos: Color only, no b&w. State availability of transparencies or send transparencies with ms. Pays $25-40 for color transparencies; $70-100 for cover. Captions required. Buys one-time rights.

Columns/Departments: Oriental Oddities (unique things in the Orient, such as unusual, exotic or interesting customs, habits, historical events, etc.); Asia in Focus (photo essays, generally a two-page spread, on any destination or subject in Asia); Festivities (an article focusing on any festival in Asia, such as the Sapporo Snow Festival in Japan). Buys 30-40 mss/year. Send complete ms. Length: 500-1,000 words. Pays U.S. 10¢/word.

Tips: "Well-written articles accompanied by good color photography stand a much better chance of being accepted. Specifically, we are looking for travel articles that entertain as well as inform, for articles that have a natural balance of anecdotes, description and information. Traveling itself can be very exciting—yet it's amazing how many writers fail to convey this excitement in their writing. We want writers to tell what it *feels* like to be there, to give our readers smells and sounds and descriptive imagery. To insure up-to-date material, writers must inform us *when* they visited the place they're writing about."

‡**HIDEAWAYS GUIDE**, Hideaways International, Box 1459, Concord MA 01742. (617)369-0252. Editor: Michael F. Thiel. Managing Editor: Betsy Browning. 25% freelance written. Magazine published 3 times/ year—March, May, September. Also publishes 4 quarterly newsletters. Features travel/leisure real estate information for upscale, affluent, educated, outdoorsy audience. Deals with unique vacation opportunities: vacation home renting, buying, exchanging, yacht/houseboat charters, country inns and small resorts. Circ. 8,000. Pays on publication. Publishes ms an average of 4 months after acceptance. Byline given. Offers negotiable kill fee. Buys first North American serial rights, one-time rights and second serial (reprint) rights. Submit seasonal/holiday material 3 months in advance. Previously published submissions OK. Computer printout and disk submissions compatible with Wordstar program OK; prefers letter-quality to dot-matrix printouts. Reports in 2 weeks on queries; 3 weeks on mss. Sample copy $10; free writer's guidelines.

Nonfiction: How-to (with focus on personal experience: vacation home renting, exchanging, buying, selling, yacht and house boat chartering); travel (intimate out-of-the-way spots to visit). Articles on "learning" vacations: scuba, sailing, flying, cooking, shooting, golf, tennis, photography, etc. Buys 10 mss/year. Query. Length: 800-1,500 words. Pays $50-100.

Photos: State availability of photos with query letter or ms or send photos with accompanying query or ms. Reviews b&w prints. Pays negotiable fee. Captions and identification of subjects required. Buys one-time rights.

Tips: "The most frequent mistakes made by writers in completing an article for us is that they are too impersonal with no photos and not enough focus or accomodations."

‡**THE ITINERARY MAGAZINE, "The" Magazine for Travelers with Physical Disabilities**, Whole Person Tours, Inc., Box 1084, Bayonne NJ 07002-1084. (201)858-3400. Editor: Robert S Zywicki. Managing Editor: Elizabeth C. Zywicki. 25-50% freelance written. Bimonthly magazine of travel for the disabled/handicapped. General travel information geared specifically for the disabled—all disabilities covered. Circ. 5,000+. Pays on publication. Publishes ms an average of 4 months after acceptance. Byline given. Buys first North American serial rights, one-time rights, all rights, simultaneous rights, first serial rights, second serial (reprint) rights or negotiable rights depending on story/authors; makes work-for-hire assignments. Simultaneous queries and simultaneous, photocopied and previously published submissions OK. Computer printout submissions acceptable. SASE. Sample copy for 9x12 SAE and 3 first class stamps; writer's guidelines for #10 SAE and 1 first class stamp.

Nonfiction: Book excerpts, how-to (make travel opportunities/arrangements easier for disabled); humor; interview/profile; new products; personal experience; photo feature; travel; and in-depth research on access for disabled (e.g., airlines). Special issues include traveling with oxygen; renting cars with hand controls/adapted RV travel. Buys 18-24 mss/year. Query or send complete ms. Length: 750 words minimum. Pays $100-300. Sometimes pays the expenses of writers on assignment.

Photos: Send photos with query or ms. Reviews b&w contact sheets and 5x7 prints. Pays $10-25. Captions and model release required. Buys one-time rights.

Columns/Departments: Open to ideas. Buys 1-3 mss/year. Query with published clips. Length: 500-1,000 words. Pays $50-200.

Tips: "It is best for writers to be disabled or to have disabled family members or companion for best understanding of the difficulties found by travelers with disabilities. Area most open to freelancers is travelogues. Also first-hand experience with travel opportunities/difficulties of the disabled; access data. We're small but growing rapidly. There is no other publication like us in the *world*."

JOURNAL OF CHRISTIAN CAMPING, Christian Camping International, Box 646, Wheaton IL 60189. Editor: Charlyene Wall. 75% freelance written. Emphasizes the broad scope of organized camping with emphasis on Christian camping. "Leaders of youth camps and adult conferences read our magazine to get practical help in ways to run their camps." Bimonthly magazine; 32-48 pages. Circ. 6,000. Pays on acceptance. Publishes ms an average of 9 months after acceptance. Buys all rights. Pays 25% kill fee. Byline given. Computer printout submissions acceptable; prefers letter-quality to dot-matrix. SASE. Reports in 6 weeks. Sample copy $2.50; writer's guidelines for SASE.

Nonfiction: General interest (trends in organized camping in general and Christian camping in particular); how-to (anything involved with organized camping from motivating staff, to programming, to record keeping, to camper follow-up); inspirational (limited use, but might be interested in practical applications of Scriptural principles to everyday situations in camping, no preaching); interview (with movers and shakers in camping and Christian camping in particular; submit a list of basic questions first); and opinion (write a letter to the editor). Buys 30-50 mss/year. Query required. Length: 600-2,500 words. Pays 5¢/word.

Photos: Send photos with ms. Pays $10/5x7 b&w contact sheet or print; price negotiable for 35mm color transparencies. Buys all rights. Captions required.

Tips: The most frequent mistake made by writers in completing an article for us is that they have not read the printout information in the listing and send articles unrelated to our readers."

MICHIGAN LIVING, Automobile Club of Michigan, 17000 Executive Plaza Drive, Dearborn MI 48126. (313)336-1211. Editor: Len Barnes. 50% freelance written. Emphasizes travel and auto use. Monthly magazine; 48 pages. Circ. 820,000. Pays on acceptance. Publishes ms an average of 4 months after acceptance. Buys first North American serial rights. Pays 100% kill fee. Byline given. Submit seasonal/holiday material 3 months in advance. SASE. Reports in 4-6 weeks. Buys 50-60 unsolicited mss/year. Free sample copy and writer's guidelines.

Nonfiction: Travel articles on U.S. and Canadian topics, but not on California, Florida or Arizona. Send complete ms. Length: 200-1,000 words. Pays $75-300.

Photos: Photos purchased with accompanying ms. Captions required. Pays $25-150 for color transparencies; total purchase price for ms includes payment for b&w photos.

Tips: "In addition to descriptions of things to see and do, articles should contain accurate, current information on costs the traveler would encounter on his trip. Items such as lodging, meal and entertainment expenses should be included, not in the form of a balance sheet but as an integral part of the piece. We want the sounds, sights, tastes, smells of a place or experience so one will feel he has been there and knows if he wants to go back."

THE MIDWEST MOTORIST, AAA Auto Club of Missouri, 12901 North Forty Dr., St. Louis MO 63141. (314)851-3315. Editor: Michael J. Right. Managing Editor: Jean Kennedy. 70% freelance written. Bimonthly magazine on travel and auto-related topics. Primarily focuses on travel throughout the world; prefers stories that tell about sights and give solid travel tips. Circ. 339,000. Pays on acceptance. Publishes ms an average of 8 months after acceptance. Byline given. Offers negotiable kill fee. Not copyrighted. Buys one-time rights, simultaneous rights (rarely), and second serial (reprint) rights. Submit seasonal/holiday material 6-8 months in advance. Simultaneous queries, and simultaneous, photocopied and previously published submissions OK. Computer printout submissions acceptable as long as they are readable and NOT ALL CAPS. SASE. Reports in 1 month. Sample copy for 9x12 SAE and 4 first class stamps. Free writer's guidelines.

Nonfiction: General interest; historical/nostalgic; how-to; humor (with motoring or travel slant); interview/profile; personal experience; photo feature; technical (auto safety or auto-related); and travel (domestic and international), all travel-related or auto-related. March/April annual European travel issue; September/October annual cruise issue. No religious, philosophical arguments or opinion not supported by facts. Buys 30 mss/year. Query with published clips. Length: 500-2,000 (1,500 preferred). Pays $50-200.

Photos: State availability of photos. Prefers color slides and b&w with people, sights, scenery mentioned. Reviews 35mm transparencies and 8x10 prints. Payment included in ms. Captions, model release and identification of subjects required. Buys one-time rights.

Tips: Query should be informative and entertaining, written with as much care as the lead of a story. Feature articles on travel destinations and tips are most open to freelancers.

NATIONAL MOTORIST, National Automobile Club, Suite 300, 1 Market Plaza, San Francisco CA 94105. (415)777-4000. Editor: Jane M. Offers. 75% freelance written. Emphasizes motor travel in the West. Bimonthly magazine; 32 pages. Circ. 233,000. Pays on acceptance for article, layout stage for pix. Buys first publication rights. Byline given. Submit seasonal/holiday material 3 months in advance SASE. Reports in 2 weeks.

Nonfiction: Well-researched articles on care of car, travel by car. Profile/interview (of someone in transportation/energy field); and travel (interesting places and areas to visit in the 11 Western states). Buys 2-3 mss/issue. Query. Length: "around 1,100 words." Pays 10¢/word and up.

Photos: "Suggestions welcome. May accompany ms, but considered separately. Payment either with ms or separately, depending on source. Often procured from source other than author." Captions optional, "but must have caption info for pix." Send prints or transparencies. Pays $20 maximum/8x10 b&w glossy print; $30 minimum/35mm, 2¼x2¼ or 4x5 color transparency. Model release required.

‡**NEWSDAY**, Melville, Long Island NY 11747. Travel Editor: Steve Schatt. Assistant Travel Editor: Barbara Shea. Travel Columnist: Jane Morse. Travel Writer: Eileen Swift. For general readership of Sunday Travel Section. Newspaper. 50% freelance written. Weekly. Circ. 608,000. Buys all rights for the New York area only. Buys 150 mss/year. Pays on publication. Publishes ms an average of 2 months after acceptance. Will consider photocopied submissions. Simultaneous submissions considered if others are being made outside of the New York area. Computer printout submissions acceptable; prefers letter-quality to dot-matrix. Reports in 1 month. Submit complete ms. SASE.

Nonfiction and Photos: Travel articles with strong focus and theme for Sunday Travel Section, but does not accept pieces based on freebies, junkets, discount or subsidies of any sort. Emphasis on accuracy, honesty, service, and quality writing to convey mood and flavor. Destination pieces must involve visit or experience that a typical traveler can easily duplicate. Skip diaries, "My First Trip Abroad" pieces or laundry lists of activities; downplay first person. Length: 600-1,500 words; prefers 800- to 1,100-word pieces. Pays 10-15¢/word. Also, regional "Weekender" pieces of 700-800 words plus service box, but query Eileen Swift first.

NORTHEAST OUTDOORS, Box 2180, Waterbury CT 06722. (203)755-0158. Editor: Howard Fielding. 80% freelance written. Monthly. Circ. 14,000. Buys first serial rights, one-time rights, second serial (reprint) rights or simultaneous rights. Pays on publication. Publishes ms an average of 6 months after acceptance. By-line given. "Queries are not required, but are useful for our planning and to avoid possible duplication of subject matter. If you have any questions, contact the editor." No "unannounced simultaneous submissions." Deadlines are on the 1st of the month preceding publication. Electronic disk submissions OK if compatible with Kaypro II (single-sided), with Perfect Writer. Computer printout submissions acceptable; prefers letter-quality to dot-matrix. Reports in 15-30 days. SASE. Guidelines for letter-size SASE and one first class stamp. Sample copy for 9x12 SASE and 7 first class stamps.

Nonfiction and Photos: Interested in articles and photos that pertain to outdoor activities in the Northeast. Recreational vehicle tips and campgrounds are prime topics, along with first-person travel experiences in the Northeast while camping. No articles on pets, product reviews or endorsements; or features on destinations outside the northeast US. Buys 50-60 unsolicited mss/year. "While the primary focus is on camping, we carry some related articles on outdoor topics like skiing, nature, hiking, fishing, canoeing, etc. One reader-written feature is 'My Favorite Campground'. Payment for this is $15 and writing quality need not be professional. Our pay rate for features is flexible, but generally runs from $30-50 for features without photos, and up to $80 for features accompanied by 2 or more photos. Features should be from 300-1,000 words. Premium rates are paid on the basis of quality, not length. Pays $10/8x10 b&w print."

Tips: "We're overwhelmed with shorts and fillers on how-to subjects, while surveys show our readers want features on places to go camping—destination features. So, I'm much more likely to buy a good destination feature. The most frequent mistake made by writers in completing an article for us is lack of knowledge (or understanding) of the publication and our readers' needs. Usually I can work this out with a second draft of most stories that don't make it the first time. But this is a problem more often with unsolicited manuscripts than with queried articles, where usually the writer has a good idea of what we're about—or I have the opportunity to tell them."

ODYSSEY, H.M. Gousha Publications, Box 6227, San Jose CA 95150. Editor: Bruce Todd. 90% freelance written. Quarterly magazine devoted to travel and leisure with regional national and international coverage. Pays on acceptance. Publishes ms an average of 1 year after acceptance. Buys first North American serial rights. Submit seasonal material 1 year in advance. Computer printout submissions acceptable. SASE. Reports in 1 month. "If no response to query within 6 weeks, writer should feel free to offer idea elsewhere." Free sample copy and writer's guidelines.

Nonfiction: Travel and travel-related features; how-to (get started in a hobby or recreation). "*Odyssey* seeks lively, well-researched articles packed with helpful information, combining historical and cultural highlights with information on where to go and what to see and do including off-the-beaten path points of interest. Descriptive detail should give a strong sense of place. We want readers to see and feel a place. The style should be friendly and not too informal. Personalization and anecdotes, if skillfully done, are helpful. Please study magazine before sending submission." Query with clips of previously published work or send completed ms. Length, major feature: 1,200-1,600 words. Pays $240-320 (first-time contributors) for major features.

Photos: Virginia Parker, photo editor. Send color transparency stock list rather than samples of work. Pays $100-175 for 2¼, 4x5 or 35mm color transparencies. Pays $350 for a front cover that is article related and $250 for a back cover. Requires originals for separation. Payment on publication. Buys one-time rights. Does not assign photos.

Columns/Departments: Cities and Sights (cover U.S. towns, museums, zoos, marketplaces, historic sights or scenic attractions); People in Travel (about someone who travels a great deal in pursuit of career or hobby; must have vertical color transparency); and Driver's Seat (covers driving safety, auto maintenance). Buys about 3 mss/issue. Send complete ms on spec or query with clips of previously published work. Length: 500-600 words. Pays $120 (first-time contributors) for Cities and Sights and People In Travel; $150 for solid, informative Driver's Seat articles.

WM Editor's Note: At press time, we learned that *Odyssey* had ceased publication.

‡**OHIO MOTORIST**, Box 6150, Cleveland OH 44101. Editor: F. Jerone Turk. 15-20% freelance written. For AAA members in 8 northeast Ohio counties. Monthly. Circ. 300,000. Buys one-time publication rights. Byline given. Buys 25 mss/year. Pays on acceptance. Submit seasonal material 2 months prior to season. Reports in 3 weeks. Submit complete ms. SASE. Free sample copy.
Nonfiction and Photos: "Travel, including foreign; automotive, highways, etc.; motoring laws and safety. No particular approach beyond brevity and newspaper journalistic treatment. Articles for travel seasons." Length: 1,500 words maximum. Pays $50-200/article including b&w photos. $125-250 for articles with color photos, transparencies any size. Purchased with accompanying mss. Captions required. "Ohioana is major need."
Poetry: Humorous verse. Length: 4-6 lines. Pays $8-15.

PACIFIC BOATING ALMANAC, Box Q, Ventura CA 93002. (805)644-6043. Editor: William Berssen. For "Western boat owners." Published in 3 editions to cover the Pacific Coastal area. Circ. 25,000. Buys all rights. Buys 12 mss/year. Pays on publication. Sample copy $9.95. Submit seasonal material 3 to 6 months in advance. Reports in 1 month. Query. SASE.
Nonfiction: "This is a cruising guide, published annually in three editions, covering all of the navigable waters in the Pacific coast. Though we are almost entirely staff-produced, we would be interested in well-written articles on cruising and trailer-boating along the Pacific coast and in the navigable lakes and rivers of the Western states from Baja, California to Alaska inclusive." Pays $50 minimum.
Photos: Pays $10/8x10 b&w glossy print.
Tips: "We are also publishers of boating books that fall within the classification of 'where-to' and 'how-to.' Authors are advised not to send manuscript until requested after we've reviewed a two- to four-page outline of the projected books."

ROMANTIC DINING & TRAVEL LETTER, James Dines & Co., Inc., Box 837, Belvedere CA 94920. Editor: James Dines. Monthly newsletter covering food, wine and travel. "In-depth reviews of 'special places' around the world; hotels, restaurants with detailed wine list commentary with a greater emphasis on the U.S. West Coast. Appeals to a very affluent audience." Pays on publication. Buys all rights. Submit seasonal/holiday material 4 months in advance. Simultaneous queries and simultaneous and photocopied submissions OK. Computer printout submissions acceptable; prefers letter-quality to dot-matrix. Reports in 3 weeks. Sample copy $5; free writer's guidelines.
Nonfiction: Travel and dining (special places only, not tourist traps or student hangouts). No budget tips or human interest articles. Buys 10-20 mss/year. Query with clips. Pays $100-500 ("according to quality, not length.")
Photos: State availability of photos with query letter or ms. Photos with query preferred. Reviews any size b&w or color prints. Pays negotiable fee. Identification of subjects required. Buys one-time rights.
Tips: "We are very specialized; if a writer makes a special 'discovery' of a place—a secluded hideaway, romantic restaurant, or a particularly romantic and elegant hotel—we'll want it. We want our articles to be very detailed and useful in their description. If the quality is there we will see it." Major travel features are most open to freelancers.

‡**RV LIFESTYLE MAGAZINE**, Camping Magazine, Inc., 58640 S.R. 15N, Goshen IN 46526. (219)534-3426. Editor: Bill Gisel. Managing Editor: Sherman Goldenberg. 30% freelance written. Monthly magazine covering the recreational vehicle industry and lifestyle. "Our publication is slanted toward those who make RVs, own RVs or are generally interested in the places RVers go and how they get there." Estab. 1984. Circ. 112,500. Pays on acceptance. Publishes ms an average of 1 month after acceptance. Byline given. Offers negotiable kill fee. Buys first North American serial rights and one-time rights. Submit seasonal/holiday material 3 months in advance. Photocopied submissions OK. Electronic submissions OK via Apple II or III compatible. Computer printout submissions acceptable; prefers letter-quality to dot-matrix. SASE. Reports in 3 months. Sample copy for 9x12 SAE and $1.25 postage.
Nonfiction: Book excerpts (of RV, travel or camping); how-to (on travel, RV repair, RV maintenance); humor (RV-related); interview/profile (on RV industry, figures, full-time RVers); new product (tests); personal experience (travel off the beaten path); technical (RV products and accessories); and travel. No state-wide travel, historical essays, or tourist spots. Buys 50 mss/year. Query with or without published clips, or send complete ms. Length: 200-2,500 words. Pays $50-400. Sometimes pays the expenses of writers on assignment.
Photos: State availability of photos or send photos with query or ms. Review b&w contact sheets and 5x7 prints and color transparencies and 5x7 prints. Captions, model release and identification of subjects required. Buys one-time rights.
Tips: "Query with idea for off-the-track travel article illustrated with top-quality color slides. Talk with RVers

about why they enjoy a particular destination. Emphasize the RV lifestyle. Travel features are most open to freelancers. Expose our readers to new adventures within the RV travel experience. We want our readers to know how much an RV adventure will cost them as well as how they will enjoy it."

RV'N ON, 10417 Chandler Blvd., North Hollywood CA 91601. (213)763-4515. Editor/Publisher: Kim Ouimet. Teen Editor: Guy Ouimet. 50% freelance written. Monthly international mini-newspaper, 16-30 pages, about recreational vehicles (motorhomes, campers and trailers, etc.) Circ. 5,500. "Payments are made 60 days after publication." Publishes ms an average of 3 months after acceptance. Buys first rights. Submit seasonal material 3 months in advance. SASE. Reports in 6 weeks. Sample copy $1 plus SASE with 39¢ postage. Query first on *all* submissions; unqueried material will be returned unread.

Nonfiction: General interest; historical; how-to; humor; interview; nostalgia; opinion; travel; new product; personal experience; and technical. Must be geared to RVs or boats. Buys 30 mss/year. Send complete ms. Length: 100-300 words. Pays 2¢ per word.

Columns/Departments: Campfire Tales (fiction or humorous, anecdotes, etc.; Roadwise Driving Tips; Rolling Kitchen; An Unusual Place (places off the road worth visiting); A Most Unusual Person (release required if name used); and "Teen Talk." Buys 12 mss/year. Query first. Length: 100-500 words. Pays in copies.

Fiction: Adventure, fantasy, historical, humorous, and suspense. Must be geared to RVs or boats. No lengthy items. No poetry or children's tales. Buys 6 mss/year. Query. Length: 200-400 words. Pays in copies.

Fillers: Jokes, anecdotes, short humor and newsbreaks, geared to RVs or boats. Buys 12 mss/year. Length: 25-50 words. Pays in copies.

Tips: "Know motorhomes, campers, etc. and what will be of interest to owners, such as storage tips, repairs, tips of traveling with animals and children. We are anxious to have actual RVers submit material. We use only short items—longer items are by our staff writers. We keep receiving general material which is scanned and returned immediately. We cannot send particular or individual replies on returns. We always know when someone is not familiar with RVs. We do not need how-to on photography and keep receiving poorly written photography articles. Our policy of query first must be followed. This will help us and the writers. We have to return unqueried manuscripts because there are so many. Also, the writers try to substitute RV for car or tent."

‡**TACOMA NEWS TRIBUNE**, Tribune Publish Co., Box 11000, Tacoma WA 98411-0008. (206)597-8650. Editor: Don Pugnetti. Managing Editor: John Komen. 50% freelance written. Daily newspaper travel section. Circ. 117,000. Pays on publication. Publishes ms an average of 3 months after acceptance. Byline given. Buys one-time rights, must be exclusive to Puget Sound area. Submit seasonal/holiday material 1 month in advance. Simultaneous queries and simultaneous (if exclusive to area) and photocopied submissions OK. Computer printout submissions acceptable; prefers letter-quality to dot-matrix. SASE. Reports in 6 weeks on queries; 12 months on mss.

Nonfiction: Travel. Al Gibbs, travel editor. Special issues planned on Hawaii, Europe, cruises, Alaska, Reno, Mexico, Pacific Northwest, Canada, U.S., Orient and ski country. All articles must have good to excellent quality photographs, preferably color transparencies 35mm or larger. Color prints are not acceptable. Send complete ms. Length: 200-1,500 words. Pays $50.

Photos: Al Gibbs, photo editor. Send photos with query or ms. Duplicates acceptable if good quality. Reviews 35mm color transparencies and b&w 8x10 prints. Pays $15-30 for transparencies; $15 for prints. Captions and identification of subjects required. Buys one-time rights.

Tips: "Some publications still list us as having a locally edited Sunday magazine. We do not, and there is no market with us for Sunday magazine-type features."

TEXAS HIGHWAYS MAGAZINE, Official Travel Magazine for the State of Texas, State Dept. of Highways and Public Transportation, 11th and Brazos, Austin TX 78701. (512)475-6068. Editor: Franklin T. Lively. Managing Editor: Ms. Tommie Pinkard. 80% freelance written. A monthly tourist magazine covering travel and history for Texas only. Pays on acceptance. Publishes ms an average of 6 months after acceptance. Byline given. Offers $50 kill fee. Not copyrighted. Buys one-time rights. Submit seasonal/holiday material 6 months in advance. Simultaneous queries and submissions OK. Computer printout submissions acceptable; prefers letter-quality to dot-matrix. Reports in 1 week on queries; 1 month on mss. Free sample copy and writer's guidelines.

Nonfiction: Historical/nostalgic, photo feature, travel. Must be concerned with travel in Texas. "No disaster features." Buys 75 mss/year. Query with published clips. Length: 1,200-1,600 words. Pays $400-600.

Photos: Bill Reaves, photo editor. Send photos with query or ms. Pays $80 for less than a page, $160 for a full page, $300 for cover, $200 for back cover. Accepts 4x5, 35mm color transparencies. Captions and identification of subjects required. Buys one-time rights.

Tips: Send material on "what to see, what to do, where to go in *Texas*." Material must be tourist-oriented.

TOURING TIMES, Box 7324, Overland Park KS 66211. (913)345-8888. Editor: Norman F. Rowland. Quarterly magazine covering group travel. Many tours have either agricultural or horticultural emphasis. Publishes 2 editions quarterly—one for people who have traveled with Rural Route Tours International (foreign) or American Group Travel (domestic) of Kansas City; one for Southland Travel Service of Birmingham, Alabama. Circ. 50,000. Pays on acceptance. Publishes ms an average of 2 months after acceptance. Byline given. Offers ⅓ kill fee. Buys first serial, one-time, simultaneous, second serial (reprint) and variable rights. Submit seasonal/holiday material 6 months in advance. Simultaneous queries, and simultaneous, photocopied and previously published submissions OK "if other markets are specified." Computer printout submissions acceptable; no dot-matrix. Reports in 6 weeks. Free sample copy and writer's guidelines.

Nonfiction: Travel. "All material must be travel related to some degree and present group touring in a positive light." No "restaurant reviews or overly sophisticated off-the-beaten-track pieces." Buys 15 or more mss/year. Query with or without published clips. Length: 1,000-2,500 words. Pays $350-500. Pays the expenses of writers on assignment.

Photos: State availability of photos. Do not send unsolicited transparencies. Pays $60-125 for 2¼ or 35mm color transparencies. Captions, model release and identification of subjects required. Buys one-time rights.

Tips: "Send for sample copies in order to study style and tour destinations. Areas we're presently serving include Alaska, Hawaii, Australia, New Zealand, Pacific Northwest, West Coast, Rockies, Canada-New England, Old South, Carolinas-Florida, American Heritage (Washington to Williamsburg), British Isles, Western Europe, Southern Europe, Scandinavia, China, Spain, Caribbean, Israel, Greece and Japan. We're particularly interested in developing working relationships with writers who have excellent photo skills. Best bet for new writers is our Window to the World section. We need more shorts. The most frequent mistake is negative writing."

TRAILBLAZER MAGAZINE, Thousand Trails, Inc., 4800 S. 188th Way, Seattle WA 98188. (206)246-5406. Editor: Gregg Olsen. 70% freelance written. A monthly magazine of Thousand Trails, Inc., a developer/operator of membership campgrounds, for members, who are outdoor-oriented recreational vehicle owners and travelers. Circ. 90,000. Pays on acceptance. Publishes ms an average of 3 months after acceptance. Byline given. Buys first North American serial rights to the same material. Submit seasonal/holiday material 6 months in advance. Simultaneous queries, and simultaneous and photocopied submissions OK. Computer printout submissions acceptable; prefers letter-quality. SASE. Reports in 1 month on queries; 6 weeks on mss. Sample copy for SASE.

Nonfiction: General interest; historical/nostalgic; how-to (relating to RV owner); humor; interview/profile; new product; personal experience; technical; and travel. Write for editorial calendar. Buys 40 mss/year. Query. Length: 500-3,000 words. Pays 10¢/word. Sometimes pays the expenses of writers on assignment.

Photos: Karen Palmer, photo editor. State availability of photos. Reviews b&w contact sheet, and 35mm and 2¼ color slides. Pays variable rate depending on size and use. Captions required.

Tips: Best areas for freelancers are "RV-related articles, travel subjects in close proximity to our resort/campgrounds. Writing should be bright, lively. We seldom use short items from freelancers. We're also looking for profiles on nationally known 55+ people who have enhanced the quality of lives of others."

TRAILER LIFE, TL Enterprises, Inc., 29901 Agoura Rd., Agoura CA 90301. (213)991-4980. Associate Publisher/Editor: Bill Estes. Monthly magazine for owners and potential buyers of travel trailers, campers and motorhomes. Circ. 324,906. Pays on acceptance. Buys first rights. Phone queries acceptable. Submit seasonal material 4 months in advance. Computer printout submissions acceptable. SASE. Reports in 2 weeks on queries; in 3 weeks on mss. Free writer's guidelines.

Nonfiction: Art of using a trailer, camper or motorhome and the problems involved. Length: 2,000 words maximum. How-to articles with step-by-step photos a necessity. Length: 800 words maximum. Combine as many operations in each photo or drawing as possible. Personal experience stories must be truly interesting. Merely living in or traveling by RV is not enough. Uses travel articles with color transparencies about trips that are inexpensive or unusual, into areas which are accessible by a travel trailer or motorhome. Photos must be top quality. Length: 1,000-2,000 words. Also uses short travel pieces, with a couple of photos of interesting places off the established routes. Length: 100-250 words. Allied interest articles are one of main interests, things that RV owners do, like boating, hiking, fishing and spelunking hobbies. A definite tie-in with travel trailers, motorhomes or pickup campers is essential. Tell the reader how RVs fit into the sport and where they can park while there. All travel articles should include basic information on RV parking facilities in the areas, costs, location, and time of year, etc. Payment varies "from $100 to $400 based on the quality of the material submitted and how it's used."

Photos: "We seek scenic photographs suitable for use on our cover. Payment for cover photos ranges up to $300. An RV must appear in the photo, but it need not dominate the photo. We normally work with 35mm Kodachrome film but will consider larger transparencies on other types of film. In most cases we do not have use for photographs unaccompanied by an article (except for the cover). Black and white photos should be 8x10 glossy. Prints should be numbered and identified on an accompanying caption sheet."

TRAILS-A-WAY, 1219 Bracy Ave., Greenville MI 48838. (616)754-9179. Editor: David Higbie. 25% freelance written. Newspaper published 8 times/year on camping in the Midwest (Michigan, Ohio, Indiana and Illinois). "Fun and information for campers who own recreational vehicles." Circ. 53,000. Pays on publication. Byline given. Buys first and second rights to the same material, and second (reprint) rights to material originally published elsewhere. Submit seasonal/holiday material 3 months in advance. Simultaneous queries and submissions OK. Computer printout submissions acceptable; no dot-matrix. SASE. Reports in 1 month. Sample copy 75¢; writer's guidelines for business size SAE and 2 first class stamps.

Nonfiction: How-to (use, maintain recreational vehicles—5th wheels, travel and camping trailers, pop-up trailers, motorhomes); humor; inspirational; interview/profile; new product (camp products); personal experience; photo feature; technical (on RVs); travel. March/April issue: spring camping; September/October: fall camping. Winter issues feature southern hot spots. "All articles should relate to RV camping in Michigan, Ohio, Indiana and Illinois—or south in winter. No tenting or backpacking articles." Buys 16-24 mss/year. Send complete ms. Length: 1,000-1,500 words. Pays $50-100.

Photos: Send photos with ms. Pays $5-10 for b&w and color prints. No slides. Captions required. Buys one-time rights.

Tips: "Recently made the 53,000 circulation into four editions—Ohio edition, Michigan edition, Indiana edition and Illinois edition. Editorial thrust will be closer to state requirements as far as travel stories are concerned. Otherwise same general camping material will be used in all four. Payment is based on total circulation so that articles may appear in all four."

TRAVEL & STUDY ABROAD, (formerly *Transitions*), 18 Hulst Rd., Amherst MA 01002. (413)256-0373. Editor/Publisher: Prof. Clayton A. Hubbs. 80% freelance written. A resource guide to work, study, and special interest travel abroad, for low budget, independent travelers. Bound magazine. Circ. 15,000. Pays on publication. Buys first rights and second (reprint) rights to material originally published elsewhere. Byline given. Written queries only. SASE. Reports in 1 month. Publishes ms an average of 4 months after acceptance. Sample copy $2.50; writer's guidelines for SASE.

Nonfiction: How-to (find courses, inexpensive lodging and travel); interview (information on specific areas and people); personal experience (evaluation of courses, special interest and study tours, economy travel); and travel (what to see and do in specific areas of the world, new learning and travel ideas). Foreign travel only. No travel pieces for businessmen. Few destination pieces. Buys 40 unsolicited mss/issue. Query with credentials. Length: 500-1,500 words. Pays $25-75.

Photos: Send photos with ms. Pays $10-15 for 8x10 b&w glossy prints, higher for covers. No color. Additional payment for photos accompanying ms, photos increase likelihood of acceptance. Buys one-time rights. Captions required.

Columns/Departments: Studynotes (evaluation of courses or programs); Travelnotes (new ideas for offbeat independent travel); and Jobnotes (how to find it and what to expect). Buys 8/issue. Send complete ms. Length: 1,000 words maximum. Pays $10-50.

Fillers: Newsbreaks (having to do with travel, particularly offbeat educational travel and work or study abroad). Buys 5/issue. Length: 100 words maximum. Pays $5-20.

Tips: "We like nuts and bolts stuff. Real practical information, especially on how to work and cut costs abroad. Be specific: names, addresses, current costs. We are particularly interested in educational (offbeat, low-budget) travel and study abroad for adults and senior citizens—a rapidly growing audience."

‡THE TRAVEL ADVISOR, Box 716, Bronxville NY 10708. Editor-in-Chief: Hal E. Gieseking. 50% freelance written. Monthly newsletter; 6-7 pages. Owned by *Travel/Holiday* magazine. Circ. 800,000 (published as part of *Travel/Holiday*). Pays on acceptance. Buys all rights. SASE. Reports in 1 month. Free sample copy and writer's guidelines. No photos used.

Nonfiction: "Send us short, *very candid* items based on the writer's own travel experience—*not* written first-person. Example: a baggage rip-off in Rome; a great new restaurant in Tokyo (with prices)." Expose (candid look at the travel industry); and how-to (good, inside information on how travelers can avoid problems, save money, etc.). Buys 50 unsolicited short 1-2 paragraph mss/year. Length: 20-150 words. Pays $20-30/item. All full-length articles are currently staff written.

Tips: "*Check* facts carefully."

TRAVEL AND LEISURE, 1120 Avenue of the Americas, New York NY 10036. (212)382-5600. Editor-in-Chief: Pamela Fiori. Executive Editor: Ila Stanger. Monthly. Circ. 950,000. Buys first worldwide serial rights. Pays 25% kill fee. Byline given unless material is assigned as research. Pays on acceptance. Reports in 2 weeks. Query. SASE.

Nonfiction: Uses articles on travel and destinations, restaurant, shopping, sports. Nearly all articles are as-

---

 The double dagger before a listing indicates that the listing is new in this edition. New markets are often the most receptive to freelance contributions.

signed. Length: 800-3,000 words. Pays $750-2,000.
Photos: Makes assignments mainly to established photographers. Pays expenses.
Tips: "New writers might try to get something in one of our six regional editions (East, West, South and Midwest, New York Metro, and Southern California). They don't pay as much as our national articles ($600-1,000), but it is a good way to start. We have a need for pieces that run no more than 800-1,000 words. Regionals cover any number of possibilities from a profile of a restored town in a certain state to unusual new attractions."

TRAVEL SMART, Communications House, Inc., Dobbs Ferry NY 10522. (914)693-4208. Editor/Publisher: H.J. Teison. Covers information on "budget, good-value travel." Monthly newsletter. Pays on publication. Buys all rights. Photocopied submissions OK. Computer printout submissions acceptable. SASE. Reports in 6 weeks. Sample copy and writer's guidelines for #10 SASE with 37¢ postage.
Nonfiction: "Interested primarily in great bargains or little-known deals on transportation, lodging, food, unusual destinations that won't break the bank. No destination stories on major Caribbean islands, London, New York, no travelogs, my vacation, poetry, fillers. No photos or illustrations. Just hard facts. We are not part of 'Rosy fingers of dawn . . .' School. More like letter from knowledgable friend who has been there." Query first. Length: 100-1,000 words. Pays "under $100.".
Tips: "Send clippings of ads for bargain airfares, package tours, hotel deals in your area (outside New York only). When you travel, check out small hotels offering good prices, little known restaurants, and send us brief rundown (with prices, phone numbers, addresses) of at least 4 at one location. Information must be current and backed up with literature, etc. Include your phone number with submission, because we sometimes make immediate assignments."

TRAVEL-HOLIDAY MAGAZINE, Travel Magazine, Inc., 51 Atlantic Ave., Floral Park NY 11001. (516)352-9700. Executive Editor: Scott Shane. For the active traveler with time and money to travel several times a year. Monthly magazine; 100 pages. Circ. 816,000. Pays on acceptance. Buys first North American serial rights. Byline given. Submit seasonal/holiday material 6 months in advance. Computer printout submissions acceptable if double-spaced; prefers letter-quality to dot-matrix. SASE. Reports in 2 months. Sample copy $1; free writer's guidelines. No phone queries.
Nonfiction: Interested in travel destination articles. Send query letter/outline; clips of previously published work *must* accompany queries. Only the highest quality writing and photography are considered by the staff. "Don't ask if we'd like to see any articles on San Francisco, France or China. Develop a specific story idea and explain why the destination is so special that we should devote space to it. Are there interesting museums, superb restaurants, spectacular vistas, etc.? Tell us how you plan to handle the piece—convey to us the mood of the city, the charm of the area, the uniqueness of the museums, etc. No food and wine, medical, photo tips, poetry or boring travelogues." Length: featurettes (800-1,300 words), $250 and up; features (1,600-1,800), $400; "Here and There" column (575 words), $150. For "Here and There" column use "any upbeat topic that can be covered succinctly (with one piece of b&w art) that's travel related and deserves special recognition. When querying, please send suggested lead and indicate 'Here and There' in the cover letter."
Photos: B&w prints $25; color converted to b&w will be paid at $25 rate; color transparencies (35mm and larger) pays $75-400 depending upon use. Pays on publication.
Tips: "Feature stories should be about major destinations: large cities, regions, etc. Featurettes can be about individual attractions, smaller cities, side trips, etc. We welcome sidebar service information. Stimulate reader interest in the subject as a travel destination through lively, entertaining and accurate writing. A good way to break in—if we're not familiar with your writing—is to send us a good idea for a featurette (a walking tour of Milan, a trip to Saba, a famous castle, etc. are featurettes we've run recently). Convey the mood of a place without being verbose; although we like good anecdotal material, our primary interest is in the destination itself, not the author's adventures. The format of the magazine has changed—do not query without having first read several recent issues. Style of the magazine has changed—we no longer use any broadbased travel pieces. Each article must have a specific angle. We are assigning articles to the best writers we can find and those writers who develop and produce good material and will continue to work with us on a regular basis. We have also become much more service-oriented in our articles."

‡**TRAVELLING ON BUSINESS, Serving the Canadian Business Traveler**, Baxter Publishing, 310 DuPont St., Toronto, Ontario M5R 1V9 Canada. (416)968-7252. Editor: Timothy Baxter. 50% freelance written. Monthly magazine on business travel. Estab. 1984. Circ. 17,900. Pays on publication. Publishes ms an average of 4 months after acceptance. Byline given. Buys all rights. Submit seasonal/holiday material 6 months in advance. Simultaneous submissions OK. Electronic submissions OK on Kaypro diskettes, but requires hard copy also. Computer printout submissions acceptable. SASE. Reports in 4 weeks. Free sample copy.
Nonfiction: How-to, new product, personal experience and travel, all on business travel. No holiday stories. Buys 50 mss/year. Query with or without published clips or send complete ms. Length: 500 words minimum. Pays $100-250. Sometimes pays expenses of writers on assignment.
Photos: Reviews color prints. Pays $10-35. Captions, model release, and identification of subjects required.

Buys one-time rights or all rights.

Tips: "A writer has a better chance of breaking in with short articles in order to establish a working relationship."

TRAVELORE REPORT, 225 S. 15th St., Philadelphia PA 19102. (215)545-0616. Editor: Ted Barkus. For affluent travelers; businessmen, retirees, well-educated; interested in specific tips, tours, and bargain opportunities in travel. Monthly newsletter; 6 pages. Buys all rights. Buys 10-20 mss/year. Pays on publication. Sample copy $2. Submit seasonal material 2 months in advance. Computer printout and disk submissions acceptable.

Nonfiction: "Brief insights (25-200 words) with facts, prices, names of hotels and restaurants, etc., on offbeat subjects of interest to people going places. What to do, what not to do. Supply information. We will rewrite if acceptable. We're candid—we tell it like it is with no sugar coating. Avoid telling us about places in United States or abroad without specific recommendations (hotel name, costs, rip-offs, why, how long, etc.). No destination pieces which are general with no specific 'story angle' in mind, or generally available through PR departments." Pays $5-20.

‡TRIP & TOUR, Harold Publications, Drawer 189, Palm Beach FL 33840. Editor: Mark Adams. A bimonthly magazine with colorful features and pictorial essays on travel and leisure. Circ. 75,000. Buys simultaneous rights; first rights; and second serial (reprint) rights. Submit seasonal material 6 months in advance. SASE. Reports in 3 weeks on "holiday mss"; 3 months on mss. Sample copy $1 and SAE; free writer's guidelines for SAE.

Nonfiction: Travel, personal experience, general interest, humor, historical/nostalgic, and photo feature. Buys 50-100 mss/year. Send complete ms. Length: 400-1,000 words. Pays 5¢/published word or $25 maxium.

Fiction: Prefers humor. Buys up to 10 mss/year. Length: 400-1,000 words. Pays 5¢/word or $25 maximum.

Photos: Send photos or state availability with ms. Pays $5 for 8x10 b&w glossy prints, color transparencies. Captions preferred; identification of subjects required. Buys one-time rights.

Cartoons: Buys few. Pays $10.

Tips: "Type manuscript, double-space and *keep a copy* (we sometimes lose them). "Edit yourself—ruthlessly—for grammar, spelling, punctuation and style. Is your story unique? No queries—we simply can't answer them. We receive thousands of manuscripts per year, so no sales, no answer, and no apologies. Follow the rules, be *very* patient and keep trying. We want to publish you."

VISTA/USA, Box 161, Convent Station NJ 07961. (201)538-7600. Editor: Patrick Sarver. Managing Editor: Barbara O'Byrne. 90% freelance written. Quarterly magazine of the Exxon Travel Club. "Our publication uses articles on North American areas without overtly encouraging travel. We strive to use as literate a writing as we can in our articles, helping our readers to gain an in-depth understanding of cities, towns and areas as well as other aspects of American culture that affect the character of the nation." Circ. 900,000. Pays on acceptance. Publishes ms an average of 1 year after acceptance. Buys first North American serial rights. Query about seasonal subjects 18 months in advance. Computer printout submissions acceptable; prefers letter-quality to dotmatrix. SASE. Reports in 1 month. Sample copy (enclose a 9x12 or larger SASE) and writer's guidelines.

Nonfiction: General interest (geographically-oriented articles on North America focused on the character of an area; also general articles related to travel and places); humor (related to travel or places); photo features (photo essays on subjects such as autumn, winter, highly photogenic travel subjects; and special interest areas) and some articles dealing with Americana, crafts and collecting. "We buy feature articles on North America, Hawaii, Mexico and the Caribbean that appeal to a national audience." No articles that mention driving or follow routes on a map or articles about hotels, restaurants or annual events. Uses 7-10 mss/issue. Query with outline and clips of previously published work. Length: 1,500-2,500 words. Pays $600 minimum. Pays the expense of writers on assignment.

Photos: Henry M. Pedersen, art director. Send photos with ms. Pays $100 minimum for color transparencies. Captions preferred. Buys one-time rights.

Tips: "We are looking for readable pieces with good writing that will interest armchair travelers as much as readers who may want to visit the areas you write about. Articles should have definite themes and should give our readers an insight into the character and flavor of an area or topic. Stories about personal experiences must impart a sense of drama and excitement or have a strong human-interest angle. Stories about areas should communicate a strong sense of what it feels like to be there. Good use of anecdotes and quotes should be included. Study the articles in the magazine to understand how they are organized, how they present their subjects, the range of writing styles, and the specific types of subjects used. Afterwards, query and enclose samples of your best writing. The most frequent mistake made by writers in completing an article for us is poor writing: insufficient use of quotes and anecdotes, dull style, poor and often choppy organization, lack of original insight, insufficient research, or failure to cover a topic thoroughly."

Union

Union members read about their union and field of work in the following publication.

OCAW REPORTER, Box 2812, Denver CO 80201. (303)987-2229. Editor: Gerald Archuleta. 5% freelance written. Official publication of Oil, Chemical and Atomic Workers International Union. For union members. Bimonthly magazine; 24-32 pages. Circ. 125,000. Not copyrighted. Buys first rights. Pays on acceptance. Publishes ms an average of 4 months after acceptance. Byline given. Computer printout submissions acceptable; prefers letter-quality to dot-matrix. Reports in 1 month. Query. SASE. Free sample copy.
Nonfiction: Labor union materials, political subjects and consumer interest articles, slanted toward workers and consumers, with liberal political view. Interview, profile, think pieces and exposes. Most material is done on assignment. "We have severe space limitations." Length: 300-600 words. Pays $50-75. Sometimes pays the expenses of writers on assignment.
Photos: No additional payment is made for 8x10 b&w glossy photos used with mss. Captions required.
Tips: The writer has a better chance of breaking in at our publication with short articles and fillers because of severe space limitations.

Women's

Housewives are preparing for careers; career women are preparing for families and a life at home. Women—not planning a change—want new tips on how to make life more rewarding. These are some of the reasons women turn to magazines. Today's readers of women's magazines have more options but less time. Readers seek women's publications as diverse as their daily schedules. Magazines that also use material slanted to women's interests can be found in the following categories: Business and Finance; Child Care and Parental Guidance; Food and Drink; Hobby and Craft; Home and Garden; Lifestyles; Religious; Romance and Confession; and Sports.

‡**BRIDAL FAIR**, Meridian Publishing, Inc., Box 10010, Ogden UT 84409. (801)394-9446. Editor: Fern M. Porras. Managing Editor: Wayne DeWald. 40% freelance written. Monthly magazine about wedding etiquette, planning with informative articles for newlywed couples and honeymoon locations. Our magazine is slanted toward the upwardly mobile young couple. Estab. 1985. Circ. 50,000. Byline given. Offers variable kill fee. Buys first North American serial rights, and second serial (reprint) rights. Simultaneous queries, and simultaneous and photocopied submissions OK; previously published work conditional. SASE. Reports in 1 month. Sample copy for $1 and 9x12 SAE; writer's guidelines for SASE.
Nonfiction: General interest; how-to (upscale type how-to's, i.e., selecting your photographer, rings, arranging your reception, etc.); photo feature; and travel. No humor or personal experience. Buys approximately 20 mss/year. Query. Length: 1,000-1,200 words. Pays 15¢/word.
Photos: State availability of photos with query letter or manuscript. Color transparencies and prints are preferred. Pays $35-50 for cover. Captions, model release, and identification of subjects (when possible) required. Buys one-time rights.
Tips: "The articles we accept are usually feature-length articles. We very rarely use fillers."

BRIDE'S, Conde Nast Bldg., 350 Madison Ave., New York NY 10017. (212)880-8800. Editor-in-Chief: Barbara D. Tober. 25% freelance written. For the first- or second-time bride, her family and friends, the groom and his family and friends. Magazine published 6 times/year. Circ. 410,000. Buys all rights. Offers 20% kill fee, depending on circumstances. Buys 30 unsolicited mss/year. Pays on acceptance. Publishes ms an average of 4 months after acceptance. Byline given. Reports in 2 months. Query or submit complete ms. Article outline preferred. Computer printout submissions acceptable; no dot-matrix. Address mss to Features Department. Free writer's guidelines.
Nonfiction: "We want warm, personal articles, optimistic in tone, with help offered in a clear, specific way.

All issues should be handled within the context of marriage. How-to features on all aspects of marriage: communications, in-laws, careers, money, sex, housework, family planning, religion, step-parenting, second marriage, reaffirmation of vows; informational articles on the realities of marriage, the changing roles of men and women, the kinds of troubles in engagement that are likely to become big issues in marriage; stories from couples or marriage authorities that illustrate marital problems and solutions to men and women both; and how-to features on wedding planning that offer expert advice. Also success stories of marriages of long duration. We use first-person pieces and articles that are well researched, relying on quotes from authorities in the field, and anecdotes and dialogues from real couples." Length: 1,000-3,000 words. Pays $300-600.
Poetry: See the "Love" column.
Tips: "Since marriage rates are up and large, traditional weddings are back in style, and since more women work than ever before, do *not* query us on just living together or becoming a stay-at-home wife after marriage. Send us a query or a well-written article that is both easy to read and offers real help for the bride or groom as she/he adjusts to her/his new role. No first-person narratives on wedding and reception planning, home furnishings, cooking, fashion, beauty, travel. We're interested in unusual ideas, experiences, and lifestyles. No 'I used baby pink rose buds' articles."

CHATELAINE, 777 Bay St., Toronto, Ontario M5W 1A7 Canada. Editor-in-Chief: Mildred Istona. Monthly general-interest magazine for Canadian women, from age 20 and up. *Chatelaine* is read by one women in three across Canada, a readership that spans almost every age group but is concentrated among those 25 to 45 including homemakers and working women in all walks of life. Circ. over 1 million. Pays on acceptance. Byline given. Free writer's guidelines. "Writers new to us should query us with ideas for upfront columns on nutrition, fitness, relationships, feelings, and parents and kids." Pays $350 for about 1,000 words. Prefers queries for nonfiction subjects on initial contact plus a resume and writing samples. Reports within 2 weeks. All mss must be accompanied by a SASE (IRCs in lieu of stamps if sent from outside Canada). Sample copy $1.50 and postage.
Nonfiction: Elizabeth Parr, senior editor, articles. Submit a page or two outline/query first. Full-length major pieces run from 2,000 to 3,500 words. Pays minimum $1,000 for acceptable major article. Buys first North American serial rights in English and French (the latter to cover possible use in *Chatelaine*'s sister French-language edition, edited in Montreal for French Canada). "We look for important national Canadian subjects, examining any and all facets of Canadian life, especially as they concern or interest Canadian women. For all serious articles deep, accurate, thorough research and rich detail are required." Also seeks full-length personal experience stories with deep emotional impact. Pays $750. Features on beauty, food, fashion and home decorating are supplied by staff writers and editors, and unsolicited material is not considered.
Fiction: Barbara West, fiction editor. Mainstream fiction of 3,500 words. Pays $1,500 minimum. "Upbeat stories about man/woman relationships are the ones most likely to appeal. The central character should be a woman in the 25-45 age range, and the story should deal with and resolve contemporary problems and conflicts our readers relate to. We look for strong human interest, pace, emotional impact, believable characters, romance, humor. Avoid violence, too-explicit sex, science fiction, avant-garde experiments, short-shorts. Canadian settings and characters are a plus. No query necessary for fiction."

FAIRFIELD COUNTY WOMAN, NEW HAVEN COUNTY WOMAN, HARTFORD WOMAN, Gamer Publishing Group, 15 Bank St., Stamford CT 06901. (203)323-3105. Editor: Ina B. Chadwick. Regional Editor (New Haven): Tricia Buie, 31 Whitney St., New Haven CT 06501. Regional Editor (Hartford): Joy Esterson, 15 Franklin St., Hartford CT 06114. Monthly tabloid for women who are out in the business world, running their own business, and the professional woman. Circ. 40,000 for each publication. Pays on publication. Byline given. Buys first North American serial rights. Submit seasonal/holiday material 6 months in advance. Simultaneous queries, and simultaneous and previously published submissions OK. SASE. Reports in 2 months. Writer's guidelines sent on request. Intimate knowledge of *region*, a must.
Nonfiction: How-to, interview/profile, photo feature and travel. All should relate to the woman in the business world in area, state. Buys 36-50 mss/year. Query with published clips. Length: 500-1,500 words. Pays $25-250.
Photos: State availability of b&w photos. Reviews b&w contact sheets. Pays $5-50. Captions required. Buys one-time rights.
Tips: "Feature articles are most open to freelancers. Articles that help working women simplify their lives are increasingly in demand. Local writers (Connecticut) have best chance."

FAMILY CIRCLE GREAT IDEAS, 488 Madison Ave., New York NY 10022. (212)593-8181. Editor: Marie T. Walsh. Managing Editor: Shari E. Hartford. 20-95% freelance written. Published 9 times/year; 128 pages. Circ. 1,000,000. Pays on acceptance. Publishes ms an average of 3 months after acceptance. Buys all rights. Submit Christmas material 4 months in advance. Computer printout submissions acceptable; no dot-matrix. Writer's guidelines free upon request with SASE. Reports in 2 weeks. Sample copy $2.25.
Nonfiction: How-to (fashion, decorating, crafts, food and beauty) and new product (for home and family). "Writers have their best chance breaking into the *Great Ideas* series with craft ideas. Craft projects are also in-

cluded in the books not specifically devoted to crafts." Will also review regionally-based features. Article queries should be directed to managing editor; must be accompanied by SASE. Buys 2 mss/issue. Query. Pays $150-350.
Tips: "We do not accept fiction or poetry."

FAMILY CIRCLE MAGAZINE, 488 Madison Ave., New York NY 10022. (212)593-8000. Editor: Gay Bryant. 60% freelance written. For women. Published 17 times/year. Usually buys all rights. Pays 25% kill fee. Byline given. Pays on acceptance. Reports in 6-8 weeks. Query. "We are a *service* magazine. Query should stress how-to angle; we want articles that will help our readers. We are especially interested in writers who have a solid background in the areas they suggest." SASE.
Nonfiction: Susan Ungaro, articles editor. Women's interest subjects such as family and social relationships, children, physical and mental health, nutrition, self-improvement, travel. Service articles. For travel, interested mainly in local material. "We look for service stories told in terms of people. We want well-researched service journalism on all subjects." Length: 1,000-2,500 words. Pays $250-2,500.
Fiction: Jame Raab, book editor. Occasionally uses fiction related to women. Buys short stories, short-shorts, vignettes. Length: 2,000-2,500 words. Payment negotiable. Minimum payment for full-length story is $250. Reports in 6 weeks.
Tips: Query letters should be "concise and to the point. We get some with 10 different suggestions—by the time they're passed on to all possible editors involved, weeks may go by." Also, writers should "keep close tabs on *Family Circle* and other women's magazines to avoid submitting recently run subject matter."

FARM WOMAN NEWS, (formerly *Farm Wife News*), Reiman Publications, Box 643, Milwaukee WI 53201. (414)423-0100. Editor: Ann Kaiser. Managing Editor: Ruth Benedict. 65% freelance written. Monthly (with combined July/August issue) magazine on the interests of farm and ranch women. "*Farm Woman News* is for farm and ranch women from all over the U.S. and Canada. It includes a sampling of the diversity that makes up the farm women's lives—love of home, family, community, hobbies, enduring values, humor, attaining new skills and appreciating present, past and future all within the content of the lifestyle that surrounds agriculture and country living." Circ. 360,000. Pays on acceptance. Publishes ms an average of 1 year after acceptance. Byline given. Offers 20% kill fee. Buys first North American serial rights, one-time rights, and second serial (reprint) rights; makes work-for-hire assignments. Submit seasonal/holiday material 4-5 months in advance. Photocopied and previously published (on occasion) submissions OK. Computer printout submissions acceptable; no dot-matrix. SASE. Reports in 1 month on queries; 4-6 weeks on mss. Sample copy $2.50; writer's guidelines for SAE and 1 first class stamp.
Nonfiction: General interest, historical/nostalgic, how-to (crafts, community projects, decorative, antiquing, etc.); humor; inspirational; interview/profile; personal experience; photo feature; and travel, all pertaining to a rural woman's interest. No put downs of rural families, trashy patronizing interviews that treat farm women as something less admirable than any other woman. Buys 100+ mss/issue. Query, or send complete ms. Length: 1,000 words maximum. Pays $ 40-300. Sometimes pays the expenses of writers on assignment.
Photos: Send photos with query or ms. Reviews 35mm or 2¼ transparencies. Pays $25-100 for b&w; $60-200 for color. Captions, model release and identification of subjects required. Buys one-time rights.
Columns/Departments: Why Farm Wives Age Fast (humor), I Remember When (nostalgia), Country Decorating, and Shopping Comparison (new product comparisons). Buys 45 (maximum)/year. Query or send complete ms. Length: 500-1,000 words. Pays $55-200.
Fiction: Adventure, humorous, mainstream, suspense and western. No erotica, confession, fantasy or overtly religious. Buys 5 (maximum) mss/year. Query or send complete ms. Length: 1,000-1,500 words. Pays $75-200.
Poetry: Avant-garde, free verse, light verse and traditional. No trite, Long or overly rhyming (stanza after stanza after stanza!) poems. Buys 40/year. Submit maximum 6 poems. Length: 5-24 lines. Pays $25-60.
Fillers: Clippings, jokes, anecdotes and short humor. Buys 40/year. Length: 40-250 words. Pays $25-40.
Tips: "Write as clearly and with as much zest and enthusiasm as possible. We love good quotes, supporting materials (names, places, etc.) and strong leads and closings. Readers want to be informed and entertained, and that's just exactly why they subscribe. Readers are busy—not too busy to read—but when they do sit down, they want good writing, reliable information and something that feels like a 'reward'. How-to, humor, personal experience and nostalgia are areas most open to freelancers. Profiles, to a certain degree, are also open. Be accurate and fresh in approach."

GLAMOUR, Conde Nast, 350 Madison Ave., New York NY 10017. (212)880-8800. Editor-in-Chief: Ruth Whitney. For college-educated women, 18-35-years old. Monthly. Circ. 1.9 million; 6.5 million readers. Computer printout submissions acceptable "if the material is easy to read." Prefers letter-quality to dot-matrix printouts. SASE. Pays on acceptance. Pays 20% kill fee. Byline given. Reports within 5 weeks. Writer's guidelines available for SASE.
Nonfiction: Janet Chan, articles editor. "Editorial approach is 'how-to' with articles that are relevant in the areas of careers, health, psychology, interpersonal relationships, etc. We look for queries that are fresh and in-

Close-up

Mary Fiore
Managing Editor
Good Housekeeping

"Just because a story is local doesn't mean that it's not interesting to the whole country," says this magazine veteran whose large office, lined with paintings, is in a town where people don't discuss their problems over the back fence.

Finding ideas for *Good Housekeeping*, though, is as easy as talking with neighbors and reading your local newspaper. "There are hundreds of women and men who have done wonderful things and deserve a story," points out Mary Fiore. "It's the writer's job to find them."

One group of writers in Texas subscribes to local newspapers across the country. "They submit real-life stories that are fantastic," she points out.

"We're always looking for new writers—ones who know what *Good Housekeeping* is all about," says Fiore. "Writers should not submit something that's already been done, but try to submit something that would be of interest to the same people who enjoyed the other articles."

Freelancers have a better chance of writing for the magazine if they submit ideas for (non-departmental) features or articles. "A real-life experience—either your own or someone else's where you overcame a problem—is the easiest way to break in," says Fiore, in her 11th year at *Good Housekeeping*.

"Everyone wants to interview celebrities—that seems to be everyone's idea of a dream assignment," she believes. "There are only so many celebrities worth writing about."

Fiore, excited about the changing roles of women, would probably call the broadening of women's magazines a writer's dream. "A lot of women's magazines are broadening the fields they cover because the fields for women are being broadened," she points out.

"Women now can do anything or go into any field and make a go of it; what new fields have opened for men?"

Good Housekeeping editors receive thousands of submissions annually, many of them about the same subjects and problems. What makes a submission stand out are the solutions to a problem and "a very good story line and a good ring of authenticity. The writer seems to know the subject and is enthusiastic and there is nothing like it in the inventory."

Editor-in-chief John Mack Carter and Fiore "agonize for days" over a splendid story that is so similar to one in the inventory. Stories seem to lose their freshness for editors as manuscripts sit in the files.

"The only time we buy ahead is for Christmas stories (mainly nonfiction); it's very hard to find good Christmas stories," says Fiore, who reviews the magazine's articles, features, and book submissions. "When you find a good one, you buy it."

Fiore is adamant on one point in particular: there is no such thing as a *Good Housekeeping* "type" of story. "We do not have a writing formula. We don't like everything to sound as if it came out of the same typewriter," she says. "There are many different kinds of women and many kinds of stories they're interested in."

clude a contemporary, timely angle. Fashion, beauty, decorating, travel, food and entertainment are all staff-written. We use 1,000-1,200 word opinion essays for our Viewpoint section. Pays $400. Our His/Hers column features generally stylish essays on relationships or comments on current mores by male and female writers in alternate months. Pays $800 for His/Hers mss. Buys first North American serial rights." Buys 10-12 mss/issue. Query "with letter that is detailed, well-focused, well-organized, and documented with surveys, statistics and research, personal essays excepted." Reports in 5 weeks. Short articles and essays (1,500-2,000 words) pay $800 and up; longer mss (2,500-3,000 words) pay $1,000 minimum on acceptance.
Tips: "We're looking for sharply focused ideas by strong writers and constantly raising our standards. We are very interested in getting new writers; and we are approachable, mainly because our range of topics is so broad."

GOOD HOUSEKEEPING, Hearst Corp., 959 8th Ave., New York NY 10019. (212)262-5605. Editor-in-Chief: John Mack Carter. Executive Editor: Mina Mulvey. Managing Editor: Mary Fiore. Mass women's magazine. Monthly; 250 pages. Circ. 5,000,000. Pays on acceptance. Buys all rights. Pays 25% kill fee. Byline given. Submit seasonal/holiday material 8 months in advance. SASE. Reports in 6 weeks. Sample copy $1.95. Free writer's guidelines with SASE.
Nonfiction: Joan Thursh, articles editor. How-to-informational; investigative stories; inspirational; interview; nostalgia; personal experience; and profile. Buys 8-10 mss/issue. Query. Length: 1,500-3,000 words. Pays $1,500 on acceptance for full articles from new writers. Regional Editor: Shirley Howard. Pays $250-350 for local interest and travel pieces of 2,000 words.
Photos: Herbert Bleiweiss, art director. Photos purchased on assignment mostly. Some short photo features with captions. Pays $50-350 for b&w; $50-400 for color photos. Query. Model release required.
Columns/Departments: Light Housekeeping & Fillers, edited by Rosemary Leonard. Humorous short-short prose and verse. Jokes, gags, anecdotes. Pays $25-100. The Better Way, edited by Erika Mark. Ideas and in-depth research. Query. Pays $500 and up. "Mostly staff written; only outstanding ideas have a chance here."
Fiction: Naome Lewis, fiction editor. Uses romance fiction and condensations of novels that can appear in one issue. Looks for reader identification. "Presently overstocked." Buys 3 mss/issue. "We get 1,500 short stories a month; a freelancer's odds are overwhelming—but we do look at all submissions." Send complete mss. Length: 1,500 words (short-shorts); 20,000 words (novels); average 4,000 words. Pays $1,000 minimum for fiction short-shorts; $1,250 for short stories.
Poetry: Arleen Quarfoot, poetry editor. Light verse and traditional. "Presently overstocked." Buys 3 poems/issue. Pays $5/line for poetry on acceptance.

HADASSAH MAGAZINE, 50 W. 58th St., New York NY 10019. Executive Editor: Alan M. Tigay. 60% freelance written. Monthly, except combined issues (June-July and August-September). Circ. 370,000. Buys 10 unsolicited mss/year. Buys first rights (with travel articles, we buy all rights). Computer printout submissions acceptable; prefers letter-quality to dot-matrix. Reports in 6 weeks. SASE.
Nonfiction: Primarily concerned with Israel, Jewish communities around the world, and American civic affairs. Length: 1,500-2,000 words. Pays $200-400, less for reviews. Sometimes pays the expenses of writers on assignment.
Photos: "We buy photos only to illustrate articles, with the exception of outstanding color from Israel which we use on our covers. We pay $175 and up for a suitable cover photo. Offers $50 for inside b&w/photo."
Fiction: Contact: Zelda Shluker. Short stories with strong plots and positive Jewish values. No personal memoirs, "schmaltzy" fiction, or women's magazine fiction. Length: 3,000 words maximum. Pays $300 minimum.
Tips: Of special interest are "strong fiction with a Jewish orientation; unusual experiences, with Jewish communities around the world—or specifically Israel."

HARPER'S BAZAAR, 1700 Broadway, New York NY 10019. Editor-in-Chief: Anthony Mazzola. For "women, late 20s and above, middle income and above, sophisticated and aware, with at least 2 years of college. Most combine families, professions, travel, often more than one home. They are active and concerned with what's happening in the arts, their communities, the world." 50% freelance written. Monthly. Circ. 720,000. Publishes ms an average of 4 months after acceptance. All rights purchased. Query first. Computer printout submissions acceptable; no dot-matrix. SASE.
Nonfiction: "We publish whatever is important to an intelligent, modern woman. Fashion questions plus beauty and health—how the changing world affects her family and herself; how she can affect it; how others are trying to do so; changing life patterns and so forth. Query us first."

‡**HYSTERIA**, Little Red Media Foundation, Box 2481, Station B, Kitchener, Ontario N2H 6M3 Canada. (519)576-8094. Editor: Catherine Edwards. 75% freelance written. Quarterly magazine covering social, cultural and artistic/literary issues of interest to women from a feminist perspective. Circ. 1,200. Pays on acceptance. Publishes ms an average of 6 months after acceptance. Byline given. Offers 10% kill fee. Buys first North American serial rights. Simultaneous queries, and simultaneous, photocopied, and previously published

submissions OK. Computer printout submissions acceptable; prefers letter-quality to dot-matrix. SASE or SAE with IRCs. Reports in 1 month on queries; 3 months on mss. Sample copy $2.50 (Canadian); free writer's guidelines.

Nonfiction: Book excerpts, expose (except not U.S. oriented; with multinational interest); humor (cartoons especially); interview/profile (of interesting and innovative women, artists, writers, other); opinion; personal experience; and photo feature (black and white only; art oriented). "We're not interested in material by or about men; aside from that we have catholic tastes." Buys 16 mss/year. Query with or without published clips or send complete ms. Length: 1,500-5,000 words. Pays $15-50 (some extra for illustrations). Sometimes pays the expenses of writers on assignment.

Photos: State availability of photos or send photos with query or ms. Reviews 5x7 b&w prints. Pays $10 for 5x7 b&w prints. Captions required. Buys one-time rights.

Columns/Departments: Reviews (of books by and about women, especially small-press material); Film Reviews (of films available for rental by community groups—(not major releases); and "She's Just Being Hysterical" (a column of personal outrage). Buys 20 mss/year. Query with or without published clips or send complete ms. Length: 750-2,500 words. Pays $10-25.

Fiction: Ethnic, experimental, fantasy (but not mushy fantasy); humorous; mainstream; mystery; and science fiction. "No romance, historical or religious fiction; nothing in which the heroine gets married and lives happily ever after." Buys 4 mss/year. Send complete ms. Length: 2,000-5,000 words. Pays $20-50.

Poetry: Avant-garde, free verse, haiku and traditional. Buys 25 poems/year. Submit maximum 6 poems. Length: 40 lines maximum. Pays $5.

Tips: "We are trying to develop a broader base of writers, and article features are what we need most. If someone shares our goals and interests, we are happy to work with writers developing articles, etc. The most frequent mistakes made by writers in completing an article assignment for us is writing in a chatty style more suitable for a newspaper. Although we are not opposed to newspapers, our readers are looking for a little more depth."

‡**THE JOYFUL WOMAN, For and About Bible-believing Women Who Want God's Best**, The Joyful Woman Ministries, Inc., 3335 Ringgold Rd., Chattanooga TN 37412. (615)698-7318. Editor: Elizabeth Handford. Monthly magazine covering the role of women in home and business. The *Joyful Woman* hopes to encourage, stimulate, teach, and develop the Christian woman to reach the full potential of her womanhood." Circ. 16,000. Pays on publication. Byline given. Buys first rights. Submit seasonal/holiday material 4 months in advance. Photocopied submissions OK. Computer printout submissions acceptable; prefers letter-quality to dot-matrix. SASE. Reports in 3 months. Sample copy for 9x12 SAE with three first class stamps; writer's guidelines for #10 with 1 first class stamp.

Nonfiction: Book excerpts, how-to (housekeeping, childrearing, career management, etc.); inspirational; interview/profile (of Christian women); and personal experience. "We publish material on every facet of the human experience, considering not just a woman's spiritual needs, but her emotional, physical, and intellectual needs and her ministry to others." Buys 80-100 mss/year. Send complete ms. Length: 700-2,500 words. Pays 2¢/word minimum.

Tips: "The philosophy of the woman's liberation movement trends to minimize the unique and important ministries God has in mind for a woman. We believe that being a woman, and a Christian ought to be joyful and fulfilling personally and valuable to God, whatever her situation—career woman, wife, mother, daughter."

LADIES' HOME JOURNAL, 3 Park Ave., New York NY 10016. Editor: Myrna Blyth. 50% freelance written. Monthly magazine. Pays on acceptance. Submit seasonal/holiday material at least 6 months in advance. Prefers story proposals, not completed ms, and does not like multiple submissions. Computer printout submissions acceptable; prefers letter-quality to dot-matrix.

Nonfiction: Jan Goodwin, executive editor: Exposés, issues, reportage, celebrity, major medical and human interest. Sondra Forsyth Enos, executive editor: Psychological, relationships, child care, education, health, first person stories, "A Woman Today" column. Pays the expenses of writers on assignment.

Fiction: Mary Lou Mullen, book and fiction editor. Short stories are only accepted through literary agents.

LADYCOM, Downey Communications, Inc., 1732 Wisconsin Ave. NW, Washington DC 20007. Editor: Hope M. Daniels. 90% freelance written. For wives of military men who live in the U.S. or overseas. Published 10 times a year. Magazine. Circ. 500,000. Pays on publication. Publishes ms an average of 6 months after acceptance. Buys first North American serial rights. Submit seasonal/holiday material 6 months in advance. Computer printout submissions acceptable; prefers letter-quality to dot-matrix. SASE. Reports in 6 weeks. Sample copy $1. Free writer's guidelines.

Nonfiction: "All articles must have special interest for military wives. General interest articles are OK if they reflect situations our readers can relate to." How-to (crafts, food), humor, profiles, personal experience, personal opinion, health, home decor and travel. "Query letter should name sources, describe focus of article, use a few sample quotes from sources, indicate length, and should describe writer's own qualifications for doing the piece." Length: 800-2,000 words. Pays $200-600/article.

Photos: Purchased with accompanying ms and on assignment. Uses 5x7 or 8x10 b&w glossy prints; 35mm or larger color transparencies; stock photo fee payment for photo with accompanying ms. Captions and model releases are required. Query art director Judi Connelly.

Columns/Departments: It Seems to Me—personal experience pieces by military wives. Your Travels—highlights of life at various bases and posts and nearby cities. Also, Your Pet, Your Money and Babycom. Query. Length: 800-1,200 words. Rates vary.

Fiction: Slice-of-life, romance and suspense. "Military family life or relationship themes only." Buys 6-8 mss/year. Query. Length: 1,500-2,500 words. Pays $200-250.

Tips: "Our ideal contributor is a military wife who can write. However, I'm always impressed by a writer who has analyzed the market and can suggest some possible new angles for us. Sensitivity to military issues is a must for our contributors, as is the ability to write good personality profiles and/or do thorough research about military family life. We don't purchase gothic fiction; hints from Heloise-type material (no one does it better than she does, anyway); Erma Bombeck imitations; Vietnam War-era fiction; and parenting advice that is too personal and limited only to the writer's own experience."

McCALL'S, 230 Park Ave., New York NY 10169. (212)551-9500. Editor: Robert Stein. Managing Editor: Don McKinney. 90% freelance written. "Study recent issues." Our publication "carefully and conscientiously services the needs of the woman reader—concentrating on matters that directly affect her life and offering information and understanding on subjects of personal importance to her." Monthly. Circ. 6,200,000. Pays on acceptance. Publishes ms an average of 6 months after acceptance. Pays 20% kill fee. Byline given. Buys first rights only. Computer printout submissions acceptable; no dot-matrix. Reports in 2 months. SASE. Writer's guidelines for SASE.

Nonfiction: Don McKinney, managing editor. No subject of wide public or personal interest is out of bounds for *McCall's* so long as it is appropriately treated. The editors are seeking meaningful stories of personal experience. They are on the lookout for new research that will provide the basis for penetrating articles on the ethical, physical, material and social problems concerning readers. They are most receptive to humor. *McCall's* buys 200-300 articles/year, many in the 1,000- to 1,500-word length. Pays variable rates for nonfiction. Mrs. Helen Del Monte and Andrea Thompson are editors of nonfiction books, from which *McCall's* frequently publishes excerpts. These are on subjects of interest to women: biography, memoirs, reportage, etc. Almost all features on food, household equipment and management, fashion, beauty, building and decorating are staff-written. Query. "All manuscripts must be submitted on speculation, and *McCall's* accepts no responsibility for unsolicited manuscripts." Sometimes pays the expenses of writers on assignment.

Columns/Departments: "The Mother's Page (edited by Maryann Brinley); short items that may be humorous, helpful, inspiring and reassuring. Pays $100 and up. Vital Signs (edited by Judith Stone); short items on health and medical news. Pay varies. Back Talk (edited by Lisel Eisenheimer); 1,000-word essay in which the writer makes a firm statement of opinion, often taking an unexpected or unpopular point of view. Whether humorous or serious in tone, the piece must reflect the writer's strong feelings on the subject. Pays $1,000. VIP-ZIP (edited by Lucy Sullivan); high-demography regional section. Largely service-oriented, it covers travel, decorating and home entertainment. The editors are also interested in short essays (humorous or serious) and in profiles for the Singular Woman feature. The woman spotlighted here has accomplished something not expected of her and is someone our readers can admire." Pay varies.

Fiction: Helen Del Monte, department editor. "Again the editors would remind writers of the contemporary woman's taste and intelligence. Most of all, fiction can awaken a reader's sense of identity, deepen her understanding of herself, etc. *McCall's* looks for stories which will have meaning for an adult reader of some literary sensitivity. *No* stories that are grim, depressing, fragmentary or concerned with themes of abnormality or violence. *McCall's* principal interest is in short stories; but fiction of all lengths is considered." Length: about 3,000 words average. Length for short-shorts: about 2,000 words. Payment begins at $1,500; $2,000 for full length stories.

Poetry: Barbara Sloane, poetry editor. "There's so much wonderful poetry out there. I wish we could use more." Poets with a "very original way of looking at their subjects" are most likely to get her attention. *McCall's* needs poems on love, the family, relationships with friends and relatives, familiar aspects of domestic and suburban life, Americana, and the seasons. Pays $5/line on acceptance. Length: no longer than 30 lines.

Tips: "Except for humor, query first. Material is running shorter than a few years ago. There is a great demand for shorter pieces, although I wouldn't want to rule out longer pieces such as narratives, personal essays. We are much more open to very short pieces, 750 words up. We don't encourage an idea unles we think we can use it."

MADEMOISELLE, 350 Madison Ave., New York NY 10017.

Nonfiction: Kate White, executive editor, articles. 90% assigned to writers whose work is known to the magazine, 90% articles freelance, columns are written by columnists. "Sometimes we give new writers a 'chance' on shorter, less complex assignments." Directed to college-educated, unmarried working women 18-34. Circ. 1,100,000. Reports in 1 month. Buys first North American serial rights. Pays on acceptance; rates vary.

Publishes ms an average of 6 weeks after acceptance. Prefers written query plus samples of published work. "Sometimes we give new writers a 'chance' on shorter, less complex assignments." Computer printout submissions are acceptable "but only letter-quality, double-spaced." SASE. Particular concentration on articles of interest to the intelligent young woman, including personal relationships, health, careers, trends, and current social problems. Articles should be well-researched and of good quality. Length: 1,500-3,000 words.

Art: Kati Korpijaakko, art director. Commissioned work assigned according to needs. Photos of fashion, beauty, travel. Payment ranges from no-charge to an agreed rate of payment per shot, job series or page rate. Buys all rights. Pays on publication for photos.

Fiction: Eileen Schnurr, fiction editor. Quality fiction by both established and unknown writers. "We are interested in encouraging and publishing new writers and welcome unsolicited fiction manuscripts. However we are not a market for formula stories, genre fiction, unforgettable character portraits, surprise endings or oblique stream of consciousness sketches. We are looking for well-told stories that speak in fresh and individual voices and help us to understand ourselves and the world we live in. Stories of particular relevance to young women have an especially good chance, but stories need not be by or from the point of view of a woman—we are interested in good fiction on any theme from any point of view." Buys first North American serial rights. Pays $1,500 for short stories (10-25 pages); $1,000 for short shorts (7-10 pages). Allow 8-10 weeks for reply. SASE required. In addition to year-round unqualified acceptance of unsolicited fiction manuscripts, *Mademoiselle* conducts a once-a-year fiction contest open to unpublished writers, male and female, 18-30 years old. First prize is $1,000 plus publication in *Mademoiselle*; second prize, $500 with option to publish. Watch magazine for announcement, usually in January issue.

MY WEEKLY, The Magazine for Women Everywhere, D.C. Thomson & Co., Ltd., 80 Kingsway E., Dundee DD4 8SL Scotland. Editor: Stewart D. Brown. 95% freelance written. Weekly entertainment magazine for women. "Entertainment means we do not lecture or try to educate our readers." Circ. 713,165. Pays on acceptance. Publishes ms an average of 6 months after acceptance. Byline given. Buys first British serial rights. Previously published submissions OK. Computer printout submissions acceptable; prefers letter-quality. SASE. Reports in 1 month. Free sample copy.

Nonfiction: General interest; humor (feminine, domestic); interview/profile; personal experience; and photo feature. No political articles, explicit sex or anything that "attempts to lecture" the reader. Buys over 300 mss/year. Send complete ms. Length: 800-3,000 words. Pays variable rates. Sometimes pays the expenses of writers on assignment.

Photos: Send photos with ms. Reviews 2¼x2¼ transparencies. Captions, model release and identification of subjects required. Buys one-time rights.

Fiction: Humorous; romance; serialized novels; suspense (with feminine interest); and stories dealing with *real* emotional, domestic problems. No material dealing explicitly with sex, violence or politics. Buys 150 mss/year. Send complete ms. Length: 1,500-6,000 words. Pays variable rates.

Fillers: Short humor (feminine). Length: 800-1,200 words. Pays variable rates.

Tips: "We invite our readers to meet and share the lives and experiences of interesting people—through both first person articles and the interviews our writers supply. Much of this applies to our fiction, too. If our readers read *My Weekly* to 'escape,' it's to escape not into a glossy, unreal world of actresses, millionaires, politicians, but into the 'real' world of other people dealing with the problems of 'ordinary' life with dignity, warmth and humour."

NEW WOMAN, Murdoch Magazines, 215 Lexington Ave., New York NY 10016. (212)685-4790. Editor: Pat Miller. Managing Editor: Karen Walden. 20% freelance written. Monthly magazine of general interest to women. Aimed toward women ages 25-35, general interest, especially self-help in love and work (career); also cover food, fashion, beauty, travel and money. Circ. 1.15 million. Pays on acceptance. Publishes ms an average of 6 months after acceptance. Byline given. Offers 20% kill fee. Buys first North American serial rights plus reprint rights for limited time after publication date. Submit seasonal/holiday material 5 months in advance. Simultaneous queries, and simultaneous, photocopied and previously published submissions OK. Computer printout submissions acceptable; prefers letter-quality to dot-marix. SASE. Reports in 2 weeks on queries; 1 month on mss. Writer's guidelines for SASE.

Nonfiction: Stephanie von Hirschberg and Donna Jackson, articles editor. Book excerpts, opinion, personal experience, travel, health, relationships, psychology, career, and advice on money. Health supplement in September; Money in October; Career & Travel in 1986. No fashion, food and beauty (produced in house). Buys 50-75 mss/year. Query with published clips. Length: 800-3,500 words. Pays 25¢-$1/word. Pays the telephone expenses of writers on assignment.

Columns/Departments: Stephanie von Hirschberg, column/department editor. "We have retained regular columnists for following pages, so we don't need freelancers. FYI: Advice, Money Q&A, Books, Health."

Fiction: Donna Jackson, fiction editor. Mainstream and novel excerpts. No unsolicited mss except through agent. Length: 3,000-5,000 words.

Poetry: Andrea Jarrell, poetry editor. No unsolicited mss except through agent. Buys 12/year.

Tips: "Send a personal letter, with clippings, telling us what you're interested in, what you really like to write about; and your perceptions of *New Woman*. It counts a lot when a writer *loves* the magazine, and responds to it on a personal level. Areas most open to freelancers are psychology and relationships. Best tip: familiarity with magazine. We look for originality, solid research, depth, and a friendly, accessible style.''

PIONEER WOMAN, Magazine of Pioneer Women/Na'amat, the Women's Labor Zionist Organization of America, Pioneer Women/Na'amat, 200 Madison Ave., New York NY 10016. (212)725-8010. Editor: Judith A. Sokoloff. 80% freelance written. Magazine published 5 times/year covering Jewish themes and issues; Israel; women's issues; Labor Zionism; and occasional pieces dealing with social, political and economic issues. Circ. 30,000. Pays on publication. Byline given. Not copyrighted. Buys first North American serial, one-time and first serial rights; second serial (reprint) rights to book excerpts; and makes work-for-hire assignments. SASE. Reports in 1 month on queries, 2 months on mss. Free sample copy and writer's guidelines.
Nonfiction: Book excerpts; expose; general interest (Jewish); historical/nostalgic; interview/profile; opinion; personal experience; photo feature; travel (Israel); art; and music. "All articles must be of interest to the Jewish community." Buys 35 mss/year. Query with clips of published work or send complete ms. Length: 2,000-2,500 words. Pays 8¢/word.
Photos: State availability of photos. Pays $10-30 for b&w contact sheet and 4x5 or 5x7 prints. Captions and identification of subjects required. Buys one-time rights.
Columns/Departments: Film and book reviews with Jewish themes. Buys 20-25 mss/year. Query with clips of published work or send complete ms. Length: 500-1,000 words. Pays 8¢/word.
Fiction: Historical/nostalgic, humorous, women-oriented, and novel excerpts. "Good intelligent fiction with Jewish slant. No maudlin nostalgia or trite humor." Buys 3 mss/year. Send complete ms. Length 1,200-3,000 words. Pays 5¢/word.

PLAYGIRL, 3420 Ocean Park Blvd., Santa Monica CA 90405. (213)450-0900. Executive Editor: Dianne Grosskopf. Senior Editor: Vanda Krefft. 100% freelance written. Monthly entertainment magazine for 20-40 year old females. Circ. 850,000. Average issue includes 4 articles and 2 interviews. Pays 1 month after acceptance. Byline given. Offers 20% kill fee. Buys all rights. Submit seasonal material 4 months in advance. Simultaneous and photocopied submissions OK, if so indicated. SASE. Reports in 1 month on queries; in 2 months on mss. Publishes ms an average of 3 months after acceptance. Free writer's guidelines with SASE. Sample copy $5.
Nonfiction: Vanda Krefft, senior articles editor. Travel pieces; "humor for the modern woman"; exposes (related to women's issues); interview (Q&A format with major show business celebrities); articles on sexuality; hard information on credit and finances; medical breakthroughs; relationships; coping; and careers. Buys 6 mss/issue. Query with clips of previously published work. Length: 2,500-4,000 words. Pays $500-1,000.
Fiction: Mary Ellen Strote, fiction editor. Contemporary romance stories of 2,500 words. Send complete fiction ms. "The important thing to remember is we don't want graphic sex, and no adventure, suspense, science fiction, murder or mystery stories. We want something emotional." Pays $300 and up for fiction.
Tips: "We are not a beginner's nonfiction market. We're looking for major clips and don't really consider nonpublished writers."

REDBOOK MAGAZINE, 224 W. 57th St., New York NY 10019. (212)262-8284. Editor-in-Chief: Annette Capone. Managing Editor: Jennifer Johnson. Health Editor: Jean Maguire. 80% freelance written. Monthly magazine; 200 pages. Circ. 3,800,000. Pays on acceptance. Publishes ms an average of 6 months after acceptance. Rights purchased vary with author and material. Computer printout submissions acceptable; prefers letter-quality to dot-matrix. SASE. Reports in 2 months. Free writer's guidelines for *Redbook* for SASE.
Nonfiction: Karen Larsen, articles editor. "*Redbook* addresses young mothers between the ages of 25 and 44. About half of *Redbook*'s readers work outside the home and have children under 18. The articles in *Redbook* entertain, guide and inspire our readers. A significant percentage of the pieces stress "how-to," the ways a woman can solve the problems in her everyday life. Writers are advised to read at least the last *six* issues of the magazine (available in most libraries) to get a better understanding of what we're looking for. We prefer to see queries, rather than complete manuscripts. Please enclose a sample or two of your writing as well as a stamped, self-addressed envelope." Also interested in submissions for Young Mother's Story. "We are interested in stories for the Young Mother series offering the dramatic retelling of an experience involving you, your husband or child. Possible topics might include: how you have handled a child's health or school problem, or conflicts within the family. For each 1,500-2,000 words accepted for publication as Young Mother's story, we pay $750. Mss accompanied by a large, stamped, self-addressed envelope, must be signed, and mailed to: Young Mother's Story, c/o *Redbook Magazine*. Length: articles, 2,500-3,000 words; short articles, 1,000-1,500 words. Young Mother's reports in 3-4 months." Sometimes pays the expenses of writers on assignment.
Fiction: Kathryne Sagan, fiction editor. "Out of the 35,000 unsolicited manuscripts that we receive annually, we buy about 50 stories/year. We find many more stories that, for one reason or another, are not suited to our needs but are good enough to warrant our encouraging the author to send others. Sometimes such an author's subsequent submission turns out to be something we can use. *Redbook* looks for stories by and about men and women, realistic stories and fantasies, funny and sad stories, stories of people together and people alone, sto-

ries with familiar and exotic settings, love stories and work stories. But there are a few things common to all of them, that make them stand out from the crowd. The high quality of their writing, for one thing. The distinctiveness of their characters and plots; stock characters and sitcom stories are not for us. We look for stories with a definite resolution or emotional resonance. Cool stylistic or intellectual experiments are of greater interest, we feel, to readers of literary magazines than of a magazine like *Redbook* that tries to offer insights into the hows and whys of day-to-day living. And all the stories reflect some aspect of the experience, the interests, or the dreams of *Redbook*'s particular readership.'' Short-short stories (7-9 pages, 1,400-1,600 words) are always in demand; but short stories of 10-15 pages, (3,000-5,000 words) are also acceptable. Stories 20 pages and over have a ''hard fight, given our tight space limits, but we have bought longer stories that we loved. *Redbook* no longer reads unsolicited novels.'' Manuscripts must be typewritten, double-spaced, and accompanied by SASE the size of the manuscript. Payment begins at $850 for short shorts; $1,000 for short stories.

Tips: ''Shorter, front-of-the-book features are usually easier to develop with first-time contributors. It is very difficult to break into the nonfiction section, although we do buy Young Mother's stories, dramatic personal experience pieces (1,500-2,000 words), from previously unpublished writers. The most frequent mistakes made by writers in completing an article for us are 1) Poor organization. A piece that's poorly organized is confusing, repetitive, difficult to read. I advise authors to do full outlines before they start writing so they can more easily spot structure problems and so they have a surer sense of where their piece is headed. 2) Poor or insufficient research. Most *Redbook* articles require solid research and include: full, well-developed anecdotes from real people (not from people who exist only in the writer's imagination); clear, substantial quotes from established experts in a field; and, if possible, additional research such as statistics and other information from reputable studies, surveys, etc.''

SAVVY, The Magazine for Executive Women, 3 Park Ave., New York NY 10016. (212)340-9200. Editor: Wendy Reid Crisp. 75% freelance written. Monthly magazine covering the business and personal aspects of life for highly educated, professional career women. Circ. 300,000. Average issue includes 4-6 features. Pays on acceptance. Publishes ms an average of 4 months after acceptance. Byline given. Buys first North American serial rights. SASE. Reports in 1-2 months.

Nonfiction: General interest. Articles should be slanted toward high level executive women who have a wide range of interests with an emphasis on their professional concerns. No ''food, home, decorating or 'helpful hint' articles. Send in one or two well-developed ideas and some previously published work to show how you carry out your ideas.'' Recent article example: ''Backlash in the Bedroom,'' by Babe Moore Cambell (May 85). ''We require articles on speculation before we make an assignment to a writer not known to us.'' Query with clips of previously published work; letters should be ''concise and to the point, with the angle of the proposed article made very specific and should include SASE.'' Length: 1,500-3,500 words. Pays $450-2,500. Pays the expenses of writers on assignment.

Photos: Wendy Palitz, art director.

Columns/Departments: Tools of the Trade (ideas and strategies for doing business better, 500 words); and Brief Encounters essays on personal lives of worldly women; 750 words. Departments: Career Strategies, Health, Executive Etiquette, Frontlines (short news items), first person, problem solvers and others.

Tips: ''We commission at least 75% of the articles we publish. Unsolicited manuscripts that come to us are generally inappropriate. It is essential that writers have a solid familiarity with the magazine before submitting material. The most frequent mistakes made by writers in completing an article for us are insufficient research, poor writing, illogical conclusions, and trite thinking.''

SELF, Conde-Nast, 350 Madison Ave., New York NY 10017. (212)880-8834. Editor: Phyllis Starr Wilson. Managing Editor: Valorie Weaver. 50% freelance written. Monthly magazine emphasizing self improvement of emotional and physical well-being for women of all ages. Circ. 1,029,315. Average issue includes 12-20 feature articles and 3-4 columns. Pays on acceptance. Publishes an average of 8 months after acceptance. Byline given. Offers 20% kill fee. Buys first North American serial rights. Submit seasonal material 4 months in advance. Simultaneous and photocopied submissions OK. Computer printout submissions acceptable; prefers letter-quality to dot-matrix. SASE. Reports in 1 month. Free (but minimal) writer's guidelines for SASE.

Nonfiction: Well-researched service articles on self improvement, mind, the psychological angle of daily activities, health, careers, nutrition, fitness, medicine, male/female relationships and money. ''We try to translate major developments and complex information in these areas into practical, personalized articles.'' Buys 6-10 mss/issue. Query with clips of previously published work. Length: 1,000-2,500 words. Pays $700-1,500. ''We are always looking for any piece that has a psychological or behavioral side. We rely heavily on freelancers who can take an article on interior decorating, for example, and add a psychological aspect to it. Everything should relate to the whole person.'' Pays the expenses of writers on assignment ''with prior approval.''

Photos: Submit to art director. State availability of photos. Reviews 5x7 b&w glossy prints.

Columns/Departments: Self Issues (800-1,200 words on current topics of interest to women such as nutrition and diet scams, finding time for yourself, and personal decision making); Your Health (800-1,200 words on health topics); and Your Money (800-1,200 words on finance topics). Buys 4-6 mss/issue. Query. Pays $700-1,200.

Tips: "Original ideas backed up by research, not personal experiences and anecdotes, open our doors. We almost never risk blowing a major piece on an untried-by-us writer, especially since these ideas are usually staff-conceived. It's usually better for everyone to start small, where there's more time and leeway for re-writers. The most frequent mistakes made by writers in completing an article for us are swiss-cheese research (holes all over it which the writer missed and has to back and fill in) and/or not personalizing the information applying it to the reader; instead, just reporting it."

SUNDAY WOMAN, The King Features Syndicate, 235 E. 45th, New York NY 10017. Editor: Merry Clark. 90% freelance written. A weekly newspaper supplement which runs in more than 70 markets in the U.S. and Canada with circulation of more than 4 million. Buys first rights, and second (reprint) rights to material originally published elsewhere. Computer printout submissions acceptable; no dot-matrix. Sample issue and writer's guidelines for SASE (8x10).
Nonfiction: Solid, reportorial articles on topics affecting women, their families, lifestyles, relationships, careers, health, money, and business. "We often run a fascinating success story about women in business or about women entrepreneurs." Also uses celebrity cover stories. No beauty, fashion or pet stories. 1,500-2,000 words. National focus. No poetry, fiction or essays. Pays $50-500 upon acceptance. "We are happy to consider first person stories-reprints only—for Outlook column." Reports in 2 weeks. "Submit previously published pieces for second serial publication by us." Include cover letter with address, phone number, and Social Security number; not responsible for mss submitted without SASE. Manuscripts should be typed and double-spaced. "Query, short and to the point, with clips of published material." No phone calls. Sometimes pays the expenses of writers on assignment.
Tips: "Women and women's roles are changing dramatically. *Sunday Woman* is reflecting this. I don't want the same old service piece or 'First Woman' stories. We're moving on from that. Writers must come up with story ideas that also reflect these changes. The most frequent mistakes made by writers in completing an article for us are inadequate preparation, lack of proper research, insufficient attributions."

TODAY'S CHRISTIAN WOMAN, 184 Central Ave., Old Tappan NJ 07675. Editor: Dale Hanson Bourke. Senior Editor: Evelyn Bence. 50% freelance written. A bimonthly magazine for Christian women of all ages, single and married, homemakers and career women. Circ. 175,000. Pays on acceptance. Byline given. Buys first rights only. Submit seasonal/holiday material 6 months in advance. Computer printout submissions acceptable; prefers letter-quality to dot-matrix. SASE. Sample copy $3.50; free writer's guidelines for SASE.
Nonfiction: Book excerpts, how-to and inspirational (a woman's "view"). Query. "The query should include experience, a brief description of the article, a short excerpt and an explanation of its value to our readers. Each issue we publish an article on a woman's turning point. It is based on a change in attitude." Pays 10¢/word.
Fiction: Humorous, religious, romance and mainstream. Query.

VOGUE, 350 Madison Ave., New York NY 10017. (212)880-8800. Editor: Grace Mirabella. Monthly magazine for highly intelligent women. Pays variable rates on acceptance "depending on the material, our needs, and the specialization of the writer." Buys variable rights. Byline given. Computer printouts acceptable; prefers letter-quality to dot-matrix. SASE.
Nonfiction: Contact: Features Editor. Uses articles and ideas for features. Fashion articles are staff-written. Material must be of high literary quality, contain good information. Query a must. Length: 500-2,500 words. "Our readers are interested not only in their appearance, but in what goes on inside them both intellectually and physically. They are contemporary American women who have deep and varied interests." Short reviews of theatre, art, books, movies, TV, music and restaurants. Ideal article length is 1,000-1,500 words. "Read Vogue and you'll see the enormous range of subjects we cover."

WOMAN BEAUTIFUL, Harold Publications, Drawer 189, Palm Beach FL 33480. Editor: Mark Adams. Bimonthly magazine with style and glamour for the fashion-conscious woman; general features. Circ. 75,000. Buys simultaneous rights; first rights; and second serial (reprint) rights. Submit seasonal material 6 months in advance. Simultaneous, photocopied and previously published submissions OK. Computer printout submissions acceptable; prefers letter-quality to dot-matrix. SASE. Reports in 3 weeks on "holiday mss"; 3 months on mss. Sample copy $1 and SAE. Writer's guidelines for SAE.
Nonfiction: Fashion, style, lifestyle, interpersonal, humor, motivational, general interest, photo feature, and interview/profile (must include subject's picture). Buys 50-100 mss/year. Send complete ms. Length: 400-1,000 words. Pays 5¢/published word or $25 maximum.
Fiction: Prefers humor. Buys up to 10 mss/year. Length: 400-1,000 words. Pays 5¢/word or $25 maximum.
Photos: Send photos or state availability with ms. Pays $5 for 8x10 b&w glossy prints or color transparencies. Captions preferred; identification of subjects required. Buys one-time rights.
Cartoons: Buys few. Pays $10.
Tips: "Type manuscript, double-space and *keep a copy* (we sometimes lose them). Edit yourself—ruthlessly—for grammar, spelling, punctuation & style. Is your story unique? No queries—we simply can't answer

them. We receive thousands of manuscripts per year, so no SASE—no answer, and no apologies. Follow the rules, be *very* patient and keep trying. We want to publish you."

WOMAN MAGAZINE, Harris Publishing, 1115 Broadway, New York NY 10010. (212)807-7100. Editor: Sherry Amatenstein. 35% freelance written. Magazine published 6 times/year covering "every aspect of a woman's life. Offers self-help orientation, guidelines on lifestyles, careers, relationships, finances, health, etc." Circ. 395,000. Pays on acceptance. Publishes ms an average of 4 months after acceptance. Byline given. Buys all rights or first rights "if requested." Photocopied and previously published submissions OK. Computer printout submissions acceptable; no dot-matrix. SASE. Reports in 2 weeks on queries; 3 weeks on mss. Sample copy $1.75; writer's guidelines for letter-size SAE and 1 first class stamp.
Nonfiction: Book excerpts (most of magazine is book reprints); how-to; humor; inspirational (how I solved a specific problem); interview/profile (short, 200-1,000 words with successful or gutsy women); and personal experience (primary freelance need: how a woman took action and helped herself—emotional punch, but not "trapped housewife" material). No articles on "10 ways to pep up your marriage"—looking for unique angle. Short medical and legal updates for "Let's Put Our Heads Together" column. Buys 100 mss/year. Query with published clips or send complete ms. Length: 200-1,500 words. Pays $25-125.
Columns/Departments: Bravo Woman (1,000 word interviews with women who overcame numerous obstacles to start their own business); Woman in News (200 word pieces on successful women); and Woman Forum (controversial issues regarding women). Query with published clips or send complete ms. Length: 200-1,000 words. Pays $20-100.
Tips: "We're for all women—ones in and out of the home. We don't condescend, neither should you. Personal experience pieces are your best bet."

WOMAN'S DAY, 1515 Broadway, New York NY 10036. Contact: Editor. 95% freelance written. 15 issues/year. Circ. over 7,000,000. Buys first and second rights to the same material. Pays negotiable kill fee. Byline given. Pays on acceptance. Computer printout submissions acceptable; no dot-matrix. Reports in 2-4 weeks on queries; longer on mss. Submit detailed queries first to Rebecca Greer, articles editor. SASE.
Nonfiction: Uses articles on all subjects of interest to women—marriage, family life, child rearing, education, homemaking, money management, careers, family health, work and leisure activities. Also interested in fresh, dramatic narratives of women's lives and concerns. "These must be lively and fascinating to read." Length: 500-3,500 words, depending on material. Payment varies depending on length, type, writer, and whether it's for regional or national use, but rates are high. *Woman's Day* has started a new page called Reflections, a full-page essay running 1,000 words. "We're looking for both tough, strong pieces and softer essays on matters real concern to women. We're looking for strong points of view, impassioned opinions. The topics can be controversial, but they have to be convincing. We look for significant issues—medical ethics and honesty in marriage—rather than the slight and the trivial."
Fiction: Contact Eileen Jordan, department editor. Uses high quality, genuine human interest, romance and humor, in lengths between 1,500 and 3,000 words. Payment varies. "We pay any writer's established rate, however."
Fillers: Neighbors and Tips to Share columns also pay $50/each for brief practical suggestions on homemaking, child rearing and relationships. Address to the editor of the appropriate section.
Tips: "We are publishing more articles and devoting more pages to textual material. We're departing from the service format once in a while to print 'some good reads.' We're more interested in investigative journalism than in the past."

‡**THE WOMAN'S NEWSPAPER OF PRINCETON, New Jersey's largest publication for women**, The Woman's Newspaper of Princeton, Inc., Box 1303, Princeton NJ 08542. (609)452-8989. Editor: Arri Parker. 100% freelance written. Monthly tabloid on anything of interest to women with two editions: North Jersey and Central Jersey. Circ. 65,000. Pays on publication. Publishes ms an average of 2 months after acceptance. Byline given. Offers $50 kill fee. Buys first rights. Submit seasonal/holiday material 2 months in advance. Simultaneous queries and submissions and photocopied and previously published submissions OK. Computer printout submissions acceptable. Reports in 2 weeks. Free sample copy and writer's guidelines.
Nonfiction: Expose, how-to, interview/profile, personal experience and technical. Nothing superficial or incorrect. Buys 180 mss/year. Query by phone. Length: open. Pays $40-100. Sometimes pays the expenses of writers on assignment.
Photos: State availability of photos. Prefers 5x5 prints. Pays $40. Captions, model release and identification of subjects required. Buys one-time rights.
Fiction: "We accept very little fiction because most is bad. Preferred is the 'fictionalized' personal experience—most of which is good."

WOMAN'S WORLD, The Woman's Weekly, Heinrich Bauer North American, Inc., 177 N. Dean St., Box 671, Englewood NJ 07631. (201)569-0006. Editor-in-Chief: Dennis Neeld. 95% freelance written. Weekly magazine covering "controversial, dramatic, and human interest women's issues" for women across the nation. Pays on acceptance. Publishes ms an average of 8 months after acceptance. Byline given. Offers kill fee. Buys first North American serial rights. Submit seasonal/holiday material 4 months in advance. Simultaneous queries, and simultaneous, photocopied and previously published submissions OK. Computer printout submissions acceptable; prefers letter-quality to dot-matrix. SASE. Reports in 6 weeks on queries; 1-2 months on mss. Sample copy $1 and self-addressed mailing label; writer's guidelines for business-size SAE and 1 first class stamp.

Nonfiction: Well-researched material with "a hard-news edge and topics of national scope." Reports of 1,000 words on vital trends and major issues such as women and alcohol or teen suicide; dramatic, personal women's stories; articles on self-improvement, medicine and health topics; and the economics of home, career and daily life. Features include In Real Life (true stories); Turning Point (in a woman's life); Families (highlighting strength of family or how unusual families deal with problems); True Love (tender, beautiful, touching and unusual love stories). Other regular features are Report (1,500-word investigative news features with national scope, statistics, etc.); Women and Crime (true stories of 1,000-1,200 words on female criminals "if possible, presented with sympathetic" attitude); Between You and Me (600-word humorous and/or poignant slice-of-life essays); and Living Today (800 words on pop psychology or coping). Queries should be addressed to Janel Bladow, senior editor. We use no fillers, but all the Between You and Me pieces are chosen from mail. Sometimes pays the expenses of writers on assignment.

Fiction: Elinor Nauen, fiction editor. Short story, romance and mainstream of 4,500 words and mini-mysteries of 1,200-2,000 words. "Each of our stories has a light romantic theme with a protagonist no older than forty. Each can be written from either a masculine or feminine point of view. Women characters may be single, married or divorced. Plots must be fast moving with vivid dialogue and action, The problems and dilemmas, inherent in them should be contemporary and realistic, handled with warmth and feeling. The stories must have a positive resolution." Not interested in science fiction, fantasy or historical romance. No explicit sex, graphic language or seamy settings. Humor meets with enthusiasm. Pays $1,200 on acceptance for North American serial rights for 6 months. "The mini-mysteries, at a length of 1,700 words, may feature either a 'whodunnit' or 'howdunnit' theme. The mystery may revolve around anything from a theft to a murder. However, we are not interested in sordid or grotesque crimes. Emphasis should be on intricacies of plot rather than gratuitous violence. The story must include a resolution that clearly states the villain is getting his or her come-uppance." Pays $500 on acceptance. Pays approximately 50¢ a published word on acceptance. Buys first North American serial rights. Queries with clips of published work are preferred; accepts complete mss.

Photos: State availability of photos. "State photo leads. Photos are assigned to freelance photographers." Buys one-time rights.

Tips: "Come up with good queries. Short queries are best. We have a strong emphasis on well-researched material. Writers must send research with manuscript including book references and phone numbers for double checking. The most frequent mistakes made by writers in completing an article for us are sloppy, incomplete research, not writing to the format, and not studying the magazine carefully enough beforehand."

WOMEN IN BUSINESS, Box 8728, Kansas City MO 64114. (816)361-6621. Editor: Margaret E. Horan. 20% freelance written. Bimonthly magazine for working women in all fields and at all levels; ages 26-55; primarily members of the American Business Women's Association; national coverage. Circ. 110,000. Pays on acceptance. Publishes ms an average of 2 months after acceptance. Buys all rights. Letter-quality computer printout submissions only. Reports in 2 months. Publishes ms an average of 6 months after acceptance. Sample copy and writer's guidelines for 9x12 SAE with $1 postage.

Nonfiction: General interest, self-improvement, business trends, and personal finance. Articles should be slanted toward the average working woman. No articles on women who have made it to the top or "slice of life opinions/editorials. We also avoid articles based on first-hand experiences (the 'I' stories)." Buys 25 mss/year. Query or submit complete ms. Length: 1,000-1,500 words. Pays $100-200.

Photos: State availability of photos with query or submit with accompanying ms. Pays $50-100 for 8x10 b&w glossy contact sheet; $150-250 for cover color transparency. Captions preferred. Buys all rights. Model release required.

WOMEN'S CIRCLE, Box 428, Seabrook NH 03874. Editor: Marjorie Pearl. 100% freelance written. Monthly magazine for women of all ages. Buys all rights. Pays on acceptance. Byline given. Publishes ms an average of 1 year after acceptance. Submit seasonal material 7 months in advance. Reports in 3 months. SASE. Sample copy $1. Writer's guidelines for SASE.

Nonfiction: How-to articles of 1,000-2,000 words on handicrafts, all kinds of needlework and dolls. Also articles with b&w photos about female entrepreneurs and hobbyists. Informational approach. Needs Christmas crafts for Christmas annual. Buys 200 mss/year. Query or submit complete ms. Length: open. Pays minimum of 3¢/word, extra for photos.

Tips: "We welcome crafts and how-to directions for any media—crochet, fabric, etc."

WORKING MOTHER MAGAZINE, McCall's Publishing Co., 230 Park Ave., New York NY 10169. (212)551-9412. Editor: Vivian Cadden. Managing Editor: Mary McLaughlin. 90% freelance written. For the working mothers in this country whose problems and concerns are determined by the fact that they have children under 18 living at home. Monthly magazine; 140 pages. Circ. 559,000. Pays on acceptance. Publishes ms an average of 4 months after acceptance. Byline given. Buys all rights. Pays 20% kill fee. Submit seasonal/holiday material 6 months in advance. Computer printout submissions acceptable; no dot-matrix. SASE. Reports in 1 month. Sample copy $1.95; writer's guidelines for SASE.

Nonfiction: Service, humor, material pertinent to the working mother's predicament. "Don't just go out and find some mother who holds a job and describe how she runs her home, manages her children and feels fulfilled. Find a working mother whose story is inherently dramatic." Query. Buys 9-10 mss/issue. Length: 750-2,000 words. Pays $300-500. "We pay more to people who write for us regularly."

Fiction: "Stories that are relevant to working mothers' lives." Length: 2,000 words (average). Pays an average of $500/story.

Tips: The most frequent mistakes made by writers in completing an article for us are not keeping our readers (the working mother) in mind throughout the article; material in the article is not properly organized; writing style is stilted or wordy."

WORKING WOMAN, Hal Publications, Inc., 342 Madison Ave., New York NY 10173. (213)309-9800. Executive Editor: Julia Kagan. Editor: Anne Mollegen Smith. 90% freelance written. Monthly magazine for executive, professional and entrepreneurial women. "Readers are ambitious, educated, affluent managers, executives, and business owners. Median age is 33. Material should be sophisticated, witty, not entry-level, and focus on work-related issues." Circ. 700,000. Pays on acceptance. Publishes ms an average of 8 months after acceptance. Byline given. Offers 20% kill fee after attempt at rewrite to make ms acceptable. Buys all rights, first rights for books, and second serial (reprint) rights. Submit seasonal/holiday material 6 months in advance. Computer printout submissions acceptable only if legible; prefers letter-quality to dot-matrix. SASE. Sample copy for $2.50 and 8½x12 SAE; writer's guidelines for SAE with 1 first class stamp.

Nonfiction: Julia Kagan, executive editor. Book excerpts; how-to (management skills, small business); humor; interview/profile (high level executive, political figure or entrepreneur preferred); new product (office products, computer/high tech); opinion (issues of interest to managerial, professional entrepreneur women); pesonal experience; technical (in management or small business field); travel (businesswomen's guide); and other (business). No child-related pieces that don't involve work issues; no entry-level topics; no fiction/poetry. Buys roughly 200 mss/year. Query with clips of published work. Length: 250-3,000 words. Pays $50-750.

Photos: State availability of photos with ms.

Columns: Management/Enterprise, Basia Hellwig; Career/Consumer, Jacqueline Paris-Chitanvis; Lifestyle, food, fitness, Fredd Greenberg; Business Watch, Michele Morris; Law, Technology, Paula Gottlieb. Query with clips of published work. Length: 1,200-1,500 words. Pays $400.

Tips: "Be sure to include clips with queries and to make the queries detailed (including writer's expertise in the area, if any). The writer has a better chance of breaking in at our publication with short articles and fillers as we prefer to start new writers out small unless they're very experienced elsewhere. Columns are more open than features. We do not accept phone submissions."

Trade, Technical and Professional Journals

"That writer does the most, who gives his reader
the most knowledge and takes from him the least time."
—C.C. Colton

Trade journal readers are busy people. They want information quickly: How to do a better job, how to motivate people, how to turn losses into profit. They want specifics: How did this company in Denver put 50 years of recordkeeping into computer files? They want to be shown how, not told. So do trade journal editors when they read submissions.

Because trade editors and readers *know* the subject of their magazine, they rightfully expect a lot. After all, a trade journal can be *the* voice of an industry or one of many important voices. A trade journal can affect the policies of an industry or can report practices that help or hurt a trade. In either case, trade journals need writers who *know* the industry, too.

Reading a trade journal is like walking through an office, plant or field—where people talk *shop* and everyone understands. If you can't understand the terms they use, query a consumer magazine in that field instead. A teacher, bricklayer, or computer programmer will immediately spot inaccuracies about their professions in an article.

The publications in this section are published by associations, companies, publishing firms and agencies. The symbol (●) denotes company publications.

Some trade journals have large staffs with contributing editors who help evaluate submissions. In many cases, an association will hire one person to handle all of its *communications*.

One "director of publications" for a small association, for instance, produces a full-size four-color national magazine and an association newsletter every month. "I have no staff to help me; I'm the managing editor, art director, chief photographer, advertising manager, traffic manager, staff writer, and even typesetter for the whole show," said this publications director.

If a trade journal editor says that your work does not fit his magazine's needs, do not debate his opinion. Editors with or without a staff rarely have time for correspondence not geared to the next issue.

Sometimes when a trade journal editor receives a manuscript that *does* fit the magazine, he might want to contact the interviewees in the article for a number of reasons. "It would help to have source addresses and phone numbers in a cover letter," said one editor. "We often have to contact the original information source for verification or elaboration of some points."

Some writers will criticize editors for adding this kind of material to their articles. Keep in mind the editor knows the audience better than you do. "The writer should not feel embarrassed or insulted that such direct follow-up may be necessary," said one editor.

Like consumer magazine editors, trade editors encounter deadlines and space limitations but also editorial problems characteristic of their trades. "The rapid change of pace in technical fields places greater emphasis on timeliness," said one trade editor.

The most frequent complaint of trade editors is queries that are actually computer-produced form letters. Trade journal editors want queries that show you've read their magazine. Your credentials and/or résumé proving you *know* the trade will help you land assignments. Some editors will review manuscripts, but the majority prefer to assign (and discuss) an article *before* it is written. Sometimes, the editor wants the writer to ask particular questions when interviewing a source.

Trade journals compete with one another. You'll want to know which journals are competitors and which ones have cornered the market. An editor won't want a story that his competitor just published. The only exception is when the writer can revise an original story and give a fresh slant on the subject.

To get the most from your research time, you might consider querying a consumer magazine *and* a trade journal for an assignment on the same subject. You can write two different articles with each one geared to the appropriate audience.

"The greatest joy for an editor is finding a gem of a piece that is slanted to his publication, has a great opening, good follow-up in the middle, and a 'take away' ending," said a trade journal editor. "The biggest problem is wading through piles of manuscripts that were submitted by those persons who fail to research to find the 'just right' market."

Accounting

The accountant wants to learn more efficient ways to do his job—and trends that might affect his job. That's why he reads these trade journals. If you want to write for an accounting magazine, first find out about its readers. Are they accountants in a small firm or corporate treasurers? Reading the magazine will generally give you answers to this question. Also don't assume that an accounting practice in the United States will interest editors of Canadian trade journals. As one magazine editor pointed out, "All submissions must be relevant to *Canadian* accounting."

CA MAGAZINE, 150 Bloor St., W., Toronto, Ontario M5S 2Y2 Canada. Editor: Nelson Luscombe. 10% freelance written. Monthly magazine for accountants and financial managers. Circ. 55,000. Pays on publication for the article's copyright. Buys first rights only. Computer printout submissions acceptable; prefers letter-quality to dot-matrix. Publishes ms an average of 4 months after acceptance.
Nonfiction: Accounting, business, management and taxation. "We accept whatever is relevant to our readership, no matter the origin as long as it meets our standards. No inflation accounting articles or nonbusiness, nonaccounting articles." Length: 3,000-5,000 words. Pays $100 for feature articles, $75 for departments and 10¢/word for acceptable news items.

CGA MAGAZINE, Suite 740, 1176 W. Georgia St., Vancouver, British Columbia V6E 4A2 Canada. (604)669-3555. 50% freelance written. For accountants and financial managers. Magazine published 12 times/year; 72 pages. Circ. 35,000. Pays on acceptance. Publishes ms an average of 3 months after acceptance. Buys first rights. Byline given. Phone queries OK. Simultaneous and photocopied submissions OK. Electronic submissions OK via CP/M, MS-DOS, PC-DOS 5¼ floppy TRSDOS, LPOS, but requires hard copy also. Computer printout submissions acceptable; prefers letter-quality to dot-matrix. SASE. Reports in 2-4 weeks. Free sample copy and writer's guidelines.
Nonfiction: "Accounting and financial subjects of interest to highly qualified professional accountants. All submissions must be relevant to Canadian accounting. All material must be of top professional quality, but at the same time written simply and interestingly." How-to, informational, academic, research, and technical. Buys 36 mss/year. Query with outline and estimate of word count. Length: 1,500-5,000 words. Pays $225-$1,000. Sometimes pays the expenses of writers on assignment.
Illustrations: State availability of photos, tables, charts or graphs with query. Offers no additional payment for illustrations.

● *Bullet preceding a listing indicates a company publication.*

Tips: "Fillers are not used. Frequently writers fail to include the technical information desired by professional accountants and financial managers."

Advertising, Marketing, and PR

Trade journals for advertising executives, copywriters and marketing and public relations professionals are listed in this category. Those whose main interests are the advertising and marketing of specific products (such as Beverages and Bottling, and Hardware) are classified under individual product categories. Journals for sales personnel and general merchandisers can be found in the Selling and Merchandising category.

ADVERTISING AGE, 740 N. Rush, Chicago IL 60611. (312)649-5200. Managing Editor: Richard L. Gordon. Currently staff-produced. Includes weekly sections devoted to one topic (i.e., marketing in southern California, agribusiness/advertising, TV syndication trends). Much of this material is done freelance—on assignment only. Pays kill fee "based on hours spent plus expenses." Byline given "except short articles or contributions to a roundup."

ADVERTISING TECHNIQUES, ADA Publishing Co., 10 E. 39th St., New York NY 10616. (212)889-6500. Managing Editor: Loren Bliss. 30% freelance written. For advertising executives. Monthly magazine; 50 pages. Circ. 4,500. Pays on acceptance. Not copyrighted. Buys first and second rights to the same material. Reports in 1 month. Publishes ms an average of 2 months after acceptance. Sample copy $1.75.
Nonfiction: Articles on advertising techniques. Buys 10 mss/year. Query. Pays $25-50.

AMERICAN DEMOGRAPHICS, American Demographics, Inc., Box 68, Ithaca NY 14851. (607)273-6343. Editor: Cheryl Russell. Managing Editor: Caroline Eckstrom. 50% freelance written. For business executives, market researchers, media and communications people, public policymakers and those in academic world. Monthly magazine; 52 pages. Circ. 12,000. Pays on publication. Buys all rights. Submit seasonal/holiday material 6 months in advance. Simultaneous, photocopied and previously published submissions OK. Electronic submissions OK if 5" disk, text file. Computer printout submissions acceptable; prefers letter-quality to dot-matrix. SASE. Reports in 1 month on queries; in 2 months on mss. Include self-addressed stamped postcard for return word that ms arrived safely. Publishes ms an average of 5 months after acceptance. Sample copy $5.
Nonfiction: General interest (on demographic trends, implications of changing demographics, profile of business using demographic data); and how-to (on the use of demographic techniques, psychographics, understand projections, data, apply demography to business and planning). No anecdotal material or humor.
Tips: "Writer should have clear understanding of specific population trends and their implications for business and planning."

ART DIRECTION, Advertising Trade Publications, Inc., 10 E. 39th St., New York NY 10016. (212)889-6500. Editor: Loren Bliss. 10% freelance written. Emphasis on advertising design for art directors of ad agencies (corporate, in-plant, editorial, freelance, etc.). Monthly magazine; 100 pages. Circ. 12,000. Pays on publication. Buys one-time rights. SASE. Reports in 3 months. Sample copy $3.
Nonfiction: How-to articles on advertising campaigns. Pays $25 minimum.

BARTER COMMUNIQUE, Full Circle Marketing Corp., Box 2527, Sarasota FL 33578. (813)349-3300. Editor-in-Chief: Robert J. Murely. 100% freelance written. Emphasizes bartering for radio and TV station owners, cable TV, newspaper and magazine publishers and select travel and advertising agency presidents. Semiannual tabloid; 48 pages. Circ. 50,000. Pays on publication. Publishes ms an average of 3 months after acceptance. Rights purchased vary with author and material. Phone queries OK. Simultaneous, photocopied and previously published submissions OK. Computer printout submissions acceptable. SASE. Reports in 1 month. Free sample copy and writer's guidelines.
Nonfiction: Articles on "barter" (trading products, goods and services, primarily travel and advertising). Length: 1,000 words. "Would like to see travel mss on southeast US and the Bahamas, and unique articles on

media of all kinds. Include photos where applicable. No manuscripts on barter for products, goods and services—primarily travel and media—but also excess inventory of business to business." Pays $30-50.
Tips: "Computer installation will improve our ability to communicate."

BUSINESS MARKETING, Crain Communications, Inc., 220 E. 42nd St., New York NY 10017. (212)210-0191. Editor: Bob Donath. Monthly magazine covering the advertising, sales and promotion of business and industrial products and services for an audience in marketing/sales middle management and corporate top management. Circ. 35,000. All rights reserved. Send queries first. Submit seasonal material 3 months in advance; 1½ months in advance for spot news. SASE. Computer printout submissions without format coding acceptable. Reports in 2 months on queries. Sample copy $3.
Nonfiction: Expose (of marketing industry); how-to (advertise, do sales management promotion, do strategy development); interview (of industrial marketing executives); opinion (on industry practices); profile; and technical (advertising/marketing practice). "No self promotion or puff pieces." No material aimed at the general interest reader. Buys 30 mss/year. Query. Length: 1,000-2,000 words.
Photos: State availability of photos. Reviews 8x10 b&w glossy prints and color transparencies. Offers no additional payment for photos accepted with ms. Captions preferred; model release required.
Columns/Departments: Query. Length: 500-1,000 words. "Column ideas should be queried, but generally we have no need for paid freelance columnists."
Fillers: Newsbreaks. Buys 2 mss/issue. Length: 100-500 words.

‡**CANADIAN PREMIUMS & INCENTIVES, Selling Ideas in Motivational Marketing**, Maclean Hunter Publishing Company, 777 Bay St., Toronto, Ontario, Canada M5W 1A7. (416)596-5838. Editor: Ed Patrick. Publisher: Ted Wilson. Quarterly magazine covering premium/incentive programs and promotions; incentive travel. Circ. 15,850. Pays on publication. Byline given. Buys first North American serial, one-time, and first rights. Submit seasonal/holiday material 3 months in advance. Simultaneous queries OK. Computer printout submissions OK. SASE or SAE and IRCs. Reports in 1 week. Sample copy $3.
Nonfiction: Case histories of successful incentive promotions in Canada. New product and travel (incentive). Query with clips of published work. Length: 600-1,500 words. Pays $60-200.
Photos: Pays $15-25 for 8x10 b&w prints. Captions and identification of subjects required. Buys one-time rights.

DIRECT RESPONSE PROFIT-LETTER, "Your Private Post-Graduate Course in Target Marketing", PMG Publications/An Operating Division of Pacific Marketing Group, Suite 3-627, 1750 Kalakaua Ave., Honolulu HI 96286. (808)942-3786. Editor: Thom Reiss. 40% freelance written. A monthly newsletter covering direct response marketing/direct mail/mail order for business executives, entrepreneurs, consultants and those involved in the marketing of goods or services by direct marketing. Pays on acceptance. Publishes ms an average of 3 months after acceptance. Byline given. Offers 10% kill fee. Buys all rights and makes work-for-hire assignments. Simultaneous and photocopied submissions OK. Computer printout submissions acceptable; prefers letter-quality to dot-matrix. SASE. Reports in 2 weeks on queries; 1 month on mss. Sample copy for $8, SAE and 1 first class stamp; writer's guidelines for SAE and 1 first class stamp.
Nonfiction: How-to (advertising copy, graphic design, mail-order, marketing, list management, etc.); and new product (suitable for mail order selling). "We publish four Special Research Reports annually. All are freelance written. Query for subject suitability." Buys 4-20 mss/year. Query. Length: 5,000-10,000 words. Pays $500-1,000.
Columns/Departments: Direct Response Copywriting, Direct Mail/Mail Order Graphic Design, Telemarketing, Publicity and Promotion (as they relate to direct marketing). Buys 80-100 mss/year. Send complete ms. Length: 50-400 words. Pays $50-100.
Fillers: Clippings, newsbreaks. Buys 25-50/year. Length: 25-100 words. Pays $10-25.
Tips: "We need material for our Special Research Reports. We are also very open now for interview pieces with very successful mail-order entrepreneurs, stressing 'How they did it'."

DM NEWS, THE NEWSPAPER OF DIRECT MARKETING, DM News Corp., 19 W. 21st St., New York NY 10010. (212)741-2095. Editor: Joe Fitz-Morris. Managing Editor; Ray Schultz. 90% freelance written. Twice-a-month tabloid about direct response marketing for users and producers of direct response marketing throughout the nation. Circ. 30,000. Pays on acceptance. Byline given. Buys first rights and makes work-for-hire assignments. Computer printout submissions acceptable; no dot-matrix. Phone queries OK. Publishes ms an average of 2 weeks after acceptance. SASE.
Nonfiction: "Come up with a newsbeat scoop and check it out with the editor." Query. Pays $50-100.
Photos: Send photos with ms. Reviews 8x10 b&w glossy prints. Offers no additional payment for photos accepted with ms. Captions and model release required. Buys one-time rights.

THE FLYING A, Aeroquip Corp., 300 S. East Ave., Jackson MI 49203. (517)787-8121. Editor-in-Chief: Wayne D. Thomas. 10% freelance written. Emphasizes Aeroquip customers and products. Quarterly magazine; 24-32 pages. Circ. 30,000. Pays on acceptance. Buys first or second rights, depending upon circumstances. Simultaneous submissions OK. Reports in 1 month.

Nonfiction: General interest (feature stories with emphasis on free enterprise, business-related or historical articles with broad appeal, human interest.) "An Aeroquip tie-in in a human interest story is helpful." No jokes, no sample copies; no cartoons, no short fillers. Buys 1-2 mss/issue. Query with biographic sketch and clips of published work. Length: Not to exceed five typewritten pages. Pays $50 minimum.

Photos: Accompanying photos are helpful.

Fillers: Human interest nonfiction. Pays $50 minimum for a two-page article. No personal anecdotes, recipes or fiction. "Suggest the writer contact editor by letter with proposed story outline."

Tips: "We publish a marketing-oriented magazine as opposed to an employee publication. Despite our title, we are *not* an aviation magazine, although we do produce aerospace products."

HIGH-TECH MARKETING, Technical Marketing Corporation, 163 Main St., Westport CT 06880. (203)222-0935. Editor: Philip Maher. 60% freelance written. A monthly magazine covering the marketing of high technology products for senior marketing executives in high technology industries. Circ. 20,000. Pays on acceptance. Publishes ms an average of 3 months after acceptance. Byline given. Offers negotiable kill fee. Buys first North American serial rights. Submit seasonal/holiday material 6 months in advance. Simultaneous queries and photocopied submissions OK. Electronic submissions OK on IBM PC-XT. Prefers letter-quality submissions. SASE. Reports in 2 weeks on queries; 1 month on mss. Sample copy $3; free writer's guidelines.

Nonfiction: Book excerpts (must be on marketing, no texts); how-to (use of techniques, must be aimed at upper level management); interview/profile (of significant individual in marketing); opinion (from practicing marketers *only*); and analyses of marketing strategies based on interviews; and overviews of industry trends. No new product, historical, or academically oriented material; articles must address current problems of marketing strategy and implementation. Buys 50 mss/year. Query with published clips. Length: 1,000-4,000 words. Pays $200-700. Pays expenses of writers on assignment.

Columns/Departments: Normally staff-written.

Tips: "Since we have a strong concept of what we want to do and an editorial calendar planned six months or more in advance, the best way is to call and find out what we're working on, then explain why you're the writer to do a particular piece or contribute a complementary piece. Best possibilities for feature coverage would be single company stories on marketing strategy and interviews with marketing executives. We're looking for people who want to do a first rate job on every article."

IMPRINT, The Magazine of Specialty Advertising Ideas, Advertising Specialty Institute, 1120 Wheeler Way, Langhorne PA 19047. (215)752-4200. Editor: Theresa Crown. 25% freelance written. Quarterly magazine covering specialty advertising. Circ. 50,000 + . Pays on acceptance. Publishes ms an average of 6 months after acceptance. Byline given. Pays $25 kill fee. Buys one-time rights. Submit seasonal/holiday material 6 months in advance. Simultaneous queries OK. Computer printout submissions acceptable; no dot-matrix. Reports in 1 month. Free sample copy.

Nonfiction: How-to (case histories of specialty advertising campaigns); and features (how ad specialties are distributed in promotions). "Emphasize effective use of specialty advertising. Avoid direct-buy situations. Stress the distributor's role in promotions. No generalized pieces on print, broadcast or outdoor advertising." Buys 10-12 mss/year. Query with clips of published work. Length: 750-1,500 words. Pays $50-170. "We pay authorized phone, hotel bills, etc."

Photos: State availability of photos. Pays $10-25 for 5x7 b&w prints. Captions, model release and identification of subjects required.

Tips: "The most frequent mistake writers make is in their misconceptions of what specialty advertising is. Many of them do not understand the medium, or our target audience, which is the end-user and so mistakes occur. Writers are encouraged to look into the medium before attempting to write any articles. Query with a case history suggestion and writing samples. We can provide additional leads. All articles must be specifically geared to specialty advertising (and sometimes, premium) promotions."

THE INFORMATION AGE MARKETING LETTER, A Direct Marketing Tool for Publishers, Communicators and Information Marketers, Champion Marketing, Box 5000-WM, Davis CA 95617. Editor: Mark Nolan. 10-25% freelance written. A monthly newsletter (except Aug. and Dec.) covering advertising and marketing tips for those who deal in information of any type." Estab. 1984. Pays on publication. Publishes ms an average of 3 months after acceptance. Byline given, sometimes depending on length of material. Buys first North American and second serial (reprint) rights. Submit seasonal/holiday material 6 weeks in advance. Simultaneous, photocopied, and previously published submissions OK. Computer printout submissions acceptable. SASE. Reports in 3 weeks. Sample copy $3.

Nonfiction: How-to (advertise or market information, press releases, etc); mail order tips, postal tips, directories available, cottage industry success stories, etc., newsletters; and new product (software, word processors). No long dissertations or editorials; only "short, pithy, impact news, tips and sources." Buys 50-100 mss/year (estimated). Recent articles: "Positioning For Profits," "Bestselling Subject Matter," and "Soft-

ware Marketing." Recently reprinted *Books by Mail: Sell Information with Enthusiasm*, by Luther Brock. Ph.D. (how-to). Send complete ms. Length: 50-150 words. Pays $25-75.
Columns/Departments: New books department: Short reviews on books pertaining to main theme, including those on word processing, advertising techniques, salesmanship, information industry, work-at-home themes, consulting, seminars, etc. Buys 10-25 mss/year. Send complete ms. Length: 50-150 words. Pays $15-25.
Fillers: Clippings and newsbreaks. Buys 10-50/year. Length: 35-75 words. Pays $5.
Tips: "We need short items most of all. News and tips to help busy nonfiction writers and publishers: how to sell more, save money, choose "tools", etc. The most frequent mistake made by writers in completing an article for us is too much fine writing. Our subscribers are mostly writers and publishers. They are very busy and want valuable news, tips and sources with a minimum of wasted words."

MAGAZINE AGE, MPE, Inc., 125 Elm St., Box 4006, New Canaan CT 06840. (203)972-0761. Editor: Robert Hogan. 30 % freelance written. Monthly magazine for advertisers and advertising agencies designed "to examine how they use a wide range of publications, including consumer, business, trade, farm, etc." Circ. 32,000. Pays on acceptance. Publishes ms an average of 3 months after acceptance. Buys all rights. Computer printout submissions acceptable; prefers letter-quality to dot-matrix. Reports in 2 weeks. Sample copy $4; writer's guidelines for SASE.
Nonfiction: "We are interested in magazine advertising success and failure stories. We want marketing pieces, case histories, effective use of magazine advertising and current trends." Buys 4 mss/issue. Query first. Will not respond to handwritten inquiries. Length: 3,000 words maximum. Pays $500 maximum.
Tips: "Find an unusual aspect of print advertising."

MORE BUSINESS, 11 Wimbledon Court, Jerico NY 11753. Editor: Trudy Settel. 50% freelance written. "We sell publications material to business for consumer use (incentives, communication, public relations)— look for book ideas and manuscripts." Monthly magazine. Circ. 10,000. Pays on acceptance. Publishes ms an average of 1 month after acceptance. Buys all rights. Computer printout submissions acceptable; no dot-matrix. SASE. Reports in 1 month.
Nonfiction: General interest, how-to, vocational techniques, nostalgia, photo feature, profile and travel. Buys 10-20 mss/year. Word length varies with article. Payment negotiable. Query. Pays $4,000-7,000 for book mss.

THE PRESS, The Greater Buffalo Press, Inc., 302 Grote St., Buffalo NY 14207. Managing Editor: Mary Lou Vogt. Quarterly tabloid for advertising executives at Sunday newspapers, ad agencies, retail chains and cartoonists who create the Sunday funnies. Circ. 4,000. Pays on acceptance. Buys all rights. Photocopied submissions and previously published submissions OK. SASE. Reports in 1 month. Sample copy 50¢; free writer's guidelines.
Nonfiction: Short biographies of people in advertising, retailing, business or unusual occupations. No travel/ leisure or personal experience articles. Back issues sent upon written request. Buys 4-6 mss/issue. Query. Length: 800-1,500 words. Pays $100-125.
Photos: State availability of photos (with ms only). Uses 35mm transparencies or larger (color preferred). Offers no additional payment for photos accepted with ms. Captions optional. Photos are usually returned after publication. "We do not accept photographs or artwork unless they accompany a ms."

‡**PUBLIC RELATIONS BUSINESS, The Weekly News Service of Public Relations**, Larimi Communications Associations, Ltd., 246 W. 38th St., New York NY 10018. (212)819-9310. Editor: Michael M. Smith. Managing Editor: John S. Brice. 25% freelance written. Weekly newspaper covering public relations and communications functions. "You must have a good grasp of who and what our readers are/and want—get details from the editors and the staff." Estab. 1984. Circ. 1,000. Pays on publication. Publishes ms an average of 2-3 weeks after acceptance. Byline given. Buys all rights. Simultaneous queries OK. Computer printout submissions acceptable. Reports in 1 week. Sample copy $3; free writer's guidelines.
Nonfiction: Expose (profiles of public relations firms, corporate communications departments, etc.); general interest (to our reader); how-to (public relations techniques and strategies); interview/profile; new product or service (relating to public relations); opinion (from people in the business only); and technical (technology of media and public relations). Buys 100 mss/year. Query with published clips ("representation of the type of material we use"). Length: 850 words. Pays $75-150. Sometimes pays the expenses of writers on assignment.
Photos: State availability of photos with query. Pays negotiable rates for 8x10 b&w prints.
Tips: "Write a letter describing your work and writing experience relating to our publication; send clips and a resume."

‡**PUBLIC RELATIONS JOURNAL**, Public Relations Society of America, 845 3rd Ave., New York NY 70022. (212)826-1757. Editor: Michael Winkleman. Managing Editor: Joanne Maio. 33% freelance written. Monthly trade journal covering public relations. Circ. 16,000. Pays on acceptance. Publishes ms an average of 3 months after acceptance. Byline given. Kill fee depends on why not published (0-50%). Makes work-for-hire assignments. Photocopied submissions and previously published work OK. Electronic submissions OK, but

requires hard copy also. Computer printout submissions acceptable; prefers letter-quality to dot-matrix. SASE. Reports in 3 weeks. Sample copy $3; writer's guidelines for #10 SAE and 1 first class stamp.

Nonfiction: Michael Winkleman, articles editor. Book excerpts, how-to, interview/profile, new product, opinion and technical. All articles need senior level public relations angle. Buys 12-20 mss/year. Query with published clips. Length: 250-3,500 words. Pays $25-350. Pays expenses of writers on assignment.

Photos: Susan Yip, photo editor. State availability of photos with query. Reviews b&w contact sheets, and b&w 8x10 prints. Buys one-time rights.

Columns/Departments: Celia Lehrman/Jo Curran, column/department editors. Briefings and workshops. Buys 12-20/year. Query with published clips. Length: 250-1,000 words. Pays $25-150.

SALES & MARKETING MANAGEMENT IN CANADA, Sanford Evans Communications Ltd., Suite 402, 3500 Dufferin St., Downsview, Ontario. (416)633-2020. Editor: Ernie Spear. Monthly magazine. Circ. 13,000. Pays on publication. Byline given. Buys first North American serial rights. Simultaneous queries and photocopied submissions OK. Reports in 2 weeks.

Nonfiction: How-to (case histories of successful marketing campaigns). "Canadian articles only." Buys 3 mss/year. Query. Length: 800-1,500 words. Pays $200 maximum.

‡**SIGNCRAFT, The Magazine for the Sign Artist and Commercial Sign Shop**, SignCraft Publishing Co., Inc., Box 06031, Fort Myers FL 33906. (813)939-4644. Editor: Tom McIltrot. 40% freelance written. Bimonthly magazine of the sign industry. "Like any trade magazine, we need material of direct benefit to our readers. We can't afford space for material of marginal interest." Circ. 13,000. Pays on publication. Publishes ms an average of 4 months after acceptance. Byline given. Offers negotiable kill fee. Buys first North American serial rights or all rights. Simultaneous queries, and simultaneous, photocopied, and previously published submissions OK. Computer printout submissions acceptable. SASE. Reports in 3 weeks. Free sample copy and writer's guidelines.

Nonfiction: Interviews and profiles. "All articles should be directly related to quality commercial signage. If you are familiar with the sign trade, we'd like to hear from you." Buys 20 mss/year. Query with or without published clips. Length: 500-2,000 words. Pays up to $200.

VISUAL MERCHANDISING & STORE DESIGN, ST Publications, 407 Gilbert Ave., Cincinnati OH 45202. Associate Publisher: Pamela Gramke. Editor: Ms. P.K. Anderson. 30% freelance written. Emphasizes store interior design and merchandise presentation. Monthly magazine; 100 pages. Circ. 10,000. Pays on publication. Buys first and second rights to the same material. Simultaneous and previously published submissions OK. Computer printout submissions acceptable. SASE. Reports in 1 month. Publishes ms an average of 3 months after acceptance.

Nonfiction: Expose; how-to (display); informational (store design, construction, merchandise presentation); interview (display directors and shop owners); profile (new and remodeled stores); new product; photo feature (window display); and technical (store lighting, carpet, wallcoverings, fixtures). No "advertorials" that tout a single company's product or product line. Buys 24 mss a year. Query or submit complete ms. Length: 500-3,000 words. Pays $50-200.

Photos: Purchased with accompanying ms or on assignment.

Tips: "Be fashion and design conscious and reflect that in the article. Submit finished manuscripts with photos or slides always. Look for stories on department and specialty store visual merchandisers and store designers (profiles, methods, views on the industry, sales promotions and new store design or remodels). The size of the publication could very well begin to increase in the year ahead. And with a greater page count, we will need to rely on an increasing number of freelancers."

Agricultural Equipment and Supplies

CUSTOM APPLICATOR, Little Publications, Suite 540, 6263 Poplar Ave., Memphis TN 38119. Editor: Tom Griffin. Managing Editor: Rob Wiley. For "firms that sell and custom apply agricultural chemicals." 50% freelance written. Circ. 17,000. Pays on publication. Buys all rights. "Query is best. The editor can help you develop the story line regarding our specific needs." Computer printout submissions acceptable; prefers letter-quality to dot-matrix. SASE.

Nonfiction: "We are looking for articles on custom application firms telling others how to better perform jobs of chemical application, develop new customers, handle credit, etc. Lack of a good idea or usable information

will bring a rejection." Length: 1,000-1,200 words "with 3 or 4 b&w glossy prints." Pays 20¢/word.
Photos: Accepts b&w glossy prints. "We will look at color slides for possible cover or inside use."
Tips: "We don't get enough shorter articles, so one that is well-written and informative could catch our eyes. Our readers want pragmatic information to help them run a more efficient business; they can't get that through a story filled with generalities."

FARM SUPPLIER, Watt Publishing Co., Sandstone Bldg., Mount Morris IL 61054. (815)734-4171. Editor: Beth Miller. For retail farm supply dealers and managers over the U.S. Monthly magazine; 64 pages. Circ. 30,000. Pays on acceptance. Byline given. Buys all rights in competitive farm supply fields. Phone queries OK. Submit seasonal material or query 2 months in advance. SASE. Computer printout submissions acceptable. Reports in 2 weeks.
Nonfiction: How-to, informational, interview, new product and photo feature. "Articles emphasizing product news and how new product developments have been profitably resold or successfully used. We use material on successful farm, feed and fertilizer dealers." No "general how-to articles that some writers blanket the industry with, inserting a word change here or there to 'customize.' " Buys 12 unsolicited mss/year.
Photos: Purchased with accompanying ms. Submit 5x7 or 8x10 b&w prints; 35mm or larger color transparencies. Total purchase price for a ms includes payment for photos.
Tips: "Because of a constantly changing industry, *FS* attempts to work only two months in advance. Freelancers should slant stories to each season in the farm industry and should provide vertical color photos whenever possible with longer features."

FERTILIZER PROGRESS, The Fertilizer Institute, 1015 18th St. NW, Washington DC 20036. (202)861-4900. Publishing Director: Thomas E. Waldinger. Editor: Michael J. Fritz. Assistant to the Editor: Becki K. Weiss. 7% freelance written. Bimonthly magazine covering fertilizer, farm chemical and allied industries for business and management, with emphasis on the retail market. Circ. 29,540. Pays on publication. Publishes ms an average of 3 months after acceptance. Byline given. Offers 2½¢/word kill fee. Buys all rights. Submit seasonal/holiday material 2 months in advance. Photocopied submissions OK. Computer printout submissions acceptable; prefers letter-quality to dot-matrix. SASE. Reports in 2 weeks on queries; 3 weeks on mss. Free sample copy.
Nonfiction: Articles on sales, services, credit, products, equipment, merchandising, production, regulation, research and environment. Also news about people, companies, trends and developments. No "highly technical or philosophic pieces; we want relevance—something the farm retail dealer can sink his teeth into." No material not related to fertilizer, farm chemical and allied industries, or to the retail market. Send complete ms. Length: 400-2,500 words. Pays $40-250. Sometimes pays the expenses of writers on assignment.
Photos: Send photos with ms. Pays $5-20 for 5x7 b&w and color prints. Captions and identification of subjects required.
Columns/Departments: Elements of Success (productive agronomic advice for dealers to use in selling to farmers); Fit to be Tried (ideas that really work); and Worth Repeating (agricultural-related editorial commentary). Send complete ms. Length: 500-750 words. Pays $40-60.
Tips: "Query letter to propose story idea provides best results."

Art, Design, and Collectibles

"It's not necessary to be sloppy to exhibit creativity; a neat manuscript is just as respected . . .," said one editor. The business of art, art administration, architecture, environmental/package design and antique collectibles is covered in these listings. Art-related topics for the general public are located in the Consumer Art category. Antiques magazines are listed in Consumer Hobby and Craft.

ANTIQUES DEALER, 1115 Clifton Ave., Clifton NJ 07013. (201)779-1600. Editor: Nancy Adams. 90% freelance written. For antiques dealers. Monthly magazine. Circ. 7,500. Average issue includes 4 features, 6 columns. Pays on publication. Byline given. Rights purchased vary with author and material; buys all rights. Submit seasonal/holiday material 4 months in advance. Will send free sample copy to writers on request. Query first. No photocopied material. Reports in 3 weeks. SASE.
Nonfiction: "Remember that we are a trade publication and all material must be slanted to the needs and interests of antiques dealers. Only articles of national interest to dealers; may be tutorial if by authority in one specific field (open a dealership, prices of various items, locate a specific antique); otherwise of broad general in-

terest to all dealers and news of the international antiques trade. Emphasis is currently on collectibles (20-50 years old); heirlooms (50-100 years old); as well as antiques (over 100 years old). Buys 2 mss/issue. Length: minimum 500 words (2 pages double-spaced); maximum 1500 words (6 pages double-spaced). Pays approximately $50 full page for features.

Photos: Should always accompany mss. Pays $10 per b&w photo no smaller than 5x7 (glossy). Professional quality only; no slides, color prints or Polaroids.

Fillers: How-to-run-your-shop-better and humor. Length: 500 words. Pays $50 full page.

Tips: "It is more important that the writer know the subject well, as a specialist, or one interviewing a specialist, than demonstrating writing excellence. But I am also looking for good business journalists who can cover shows and interviews well. Send outline of ideas, resume and writing samples."

ART BUSINESS NEWS, Myers Publishing Co., 60 Ridgeway Plaza, Stamford CT 06905. (203)356-1745. Editor: Jo Yanow. Managing Editor: Caroline Myers Just. Monthly tabloid covering news relating to the art and picture framing industry. Circ. 22,500. Pays on publication. Byline given. Buys all rights. Submit seasonal/holiday material 2 months in advance. Photocopied and simultaneous submissions OK. Computer printout submissions acceptable; prefers letter-quality to dot-matrix. Reports in 2 months. Sample copy $2.

Nonfiction: General interest; interview/profile (of persons in the art industry); new product; articles focusing on small business people—framers, art gallery management, art trends; and how-to (occasional article, on "how-to frame" accepted) . Buys 8-20 mss/year. Length: 1,000 words maximum. Query first. Pays $75-250.

ARTS MANAGEMENT, 408 W. 57th St., New York NY 10019. (212)245-3850. Editor: A.H. Reiss. For cultural institutions. Published five times/year. 2% freelance written. Circ. 6,000. Pays on publication. Byline given. Buys all rights. Mostly staff-written. Computer printout submissions acceptable; no dot-matrix. Query. Reports in "several weeks." SASE.

Nonfiction: Short articles, 400-900 words, tightly written, expository, explaining how art administrators solved problems in publicity, fund raising and general administration; actual case histories emphasizing the how-to. Also short articles on the economics and sociology of the arts and important trends in the nonprofit cultural field. Must be fact-filled, well-organized and without rhetoric. Payment is 2-4¢/word. No photographs or pictures.

INDUSTRIAL DESIGN, Design Publications, Inc., 330 W. 42nd St., 11th Fl., New York NY 10036. (212)695-4955. Managing Editor: Steven Holt. 60% freelance written. Subject of this publication is design (of products, packaging, graphics and environments). Bimonthly magazine. Circ. 15,000. Pays on publication. Publishes ms an average of 3 months after acceptance. Byline given. Buys all rights. Phone queries OK. Computer printout submissions acceptable; prefers letter-quality to dot-matrix. SASE. Sample copy $4.50.

Nonfiction: Expose (design related); how-to (all aspects of design); interview (of important people in design); profile (corporate, showing value of design and/or how design is managed); design history; and new product. "The writer gets top pay and a bonus for hard work, extensive research, a 'how-to' sidebar, and a humorous example or two." Buys 6 unsolicited mss/year. Length: 1,800 words. Query with point-by-point outline and clips of published work. Pays $100-600. Sometimes pays the expenses of writers on assignment.

Photos: State availability of photos. Wants very good quality b&w glossy prints, four-color transparencies and contact sheets. Offers no additional payment for photos accepted with ms. Captions required.

Departments: Portfolio (new products); Visual Communications (graphics, packaging); Environments; and News. Query with clips of published work.

Tips: "Show that you are thoroughly familiar with your topic. Read the magazine."

PROGRESSIVE ARCHITECTURE, 600 Summer St., Box 1361, Stamford CT 06904. Editor: John M. Dixon. Monthly. Pays on publication. Buys first-time rights for use in architectural press. SASE.

Nonfiction: "Articles of technical professional interest devoted to architecture, interior design, and urban design and planning and illustrated by photographs and architectural drawings. We also use technical articles which are prepared by technical authorities and would be beyond the scope of the lay writer. Practically all the material is professional, and most of it is prepared by writers in the field who are approached by the magazine for material." Pays $75-300.

Photos: Buys one-time reproduction rights to b&w and color photos.

Auto and Truck

These journals are geared to automobile, motorcycle, and truck dealers; service department personnel; or fleet operators. Publications for highway planners and traffic control experts are listed in the Government and Public Service category.

AMERICAN CLEAN CAR, Serving the Car & Truck Cleaning Industries, American Trade Magazines, 500 N. Dearborn, Chicago IL 60610. (312)337-7700. Editor: Renald Rooney. Associate Editor: Paul Partyka. Bimonthly magazine of the professional car washing industry for owners and operators of car washes. Circ. 20,000. Pays on publication. Offers negotiable kill fee. Buys first rights and second serial (reprint) rights. Submit seasonal/holiday material 3 months in advance. SASE. Reports in 2 weeks. Free sample copy and writer's guidelines.

Nonfiction: How-to (develop, maintain, improve, etc. car washes); interview/profile (industry leaders); new product (concerned with industry—no payment here); and technical (maintenance of car wash equipment). "We emphasize car wash operation and use features on industry topics: utility use and conservation, maintenance, management, customer service and advertising. A case study should emphasize how the operator accomplished whatever he or she did in a way that the reader can apply to his or her own operation. Manuscripts should have no-nonsense, businesslike approach." Buys 18 mss/year. Query. Length: 500-3,000 words. Pays 6-8¢/word.

Photos: State availability of photos. Pays $6-8 for each photo used. Supply b&w contact sheet. Captions required. Buys all rights.

Columns/Departments: "Most of our columnists are from the industry or somehow related." Buys 18 mss/year. Query. Length: 500-1,000 words. Pays $50-55.

Fillers: Clippings and newsbreaks. Buys 6-12/year. Length: 200-300 words. Pays 6-8¢/word.

Tips: "Query about subjects of current interest. Be observant of car wash operations—how they are designed and equipped; how they serve customers; and how (if) they advertise and promote their services. Most general articles are turned down because they are not aimed specifically to audience. Most case histories are turned down because of lack of practical purpose (nothing new or worth reporting)."

‡AUTO GLASS JOURNAL, Grawin Publications, Inc., Suite 101, 303 Harvard E., Box 12099, Seattle WA 98102-0099. (206)322-5120. Editor: Eric Cosentino. 45% freelance written. Monthly magazine on auto glass replacement. National publication for the auto glass replacement industry. Includes step-by-step glass replacement procedures for current model cars as well as shop profiles, industry news and trends. Circ. 4,200. Pays on acceptance. Publishes ms an average of 2 months after acceptance. No byline given. Buys all rights. Computer printout submissions acceptable. SASE. Reports in 2 weeks on queries; 1 week on mss. Sample copy for 6x9 SAE and 56¢ postage. Writer's guidelines for #10 SAE and 1 first class stamp.

Nonfiction: How-to (install all glass in a current model car); and interview/profile. Buys 22-36 mss/year. Query with published clips. Length: 2,000-3,500 words. Pays $75-250, with photos.

Photos: State availability of photos. Reviews b&w contact sheets and negatives. Payment included with ms. Captions required. Buys all rights.

Tips: "Be willing to find sources for auto glass installation features."

AUTO LAUNDRY NEWS, Columbia Communications, 370 Lexington Ave., New York NY 10017. (212)532-9290. Publisher/Editor: Ralph Monti. For sophisticated carwash operators. Monthly magazine; 45-100 pages. Circ. 15,000+. Pays on publication. Buys all rights. Submit seasonal/holiday material 2 months in advance. Computer printout submissions acceptable; no dot-matrix. SASE. Reports in 1 month.

Nonfiction: How-to, historical, humor, informational, new product, nostalgia, personal experience, technical, interviews, photo features and profiles. Buys 15 mss/year. Query. Length: 1,000-2,000 words. Pays $75-175.

Tips: "Read the magazine; notice its style and come up with something interesting to the industry. Foremost, the writer has to know the industry."

AUTO TRIM NEWS, National Association of Auto Trim Shops (NAATS), 1623 N. Grand Ave., Box 86, Baldwin NY 11510. (516)223-4334. Editor: Nat Danas. Associate Editor: Dani Ben-Ari. 25% freelance written. Monthly magazine for auto trim shops, installation specialists, customizers and restylers, marine and furniture upholsterers as well as manufacturers, wholesalers, jobbers, and distributors serving them. Circ. 8,000. Pays on publication. Byline given. Buys first rights only. Simultaneous and previously published submissions OK. SASE. Reports in 1 month. Sample copy $1.50; free writer's guidelines for SAE and 2 first class stamps.

Nonfiction: How-to, interview/profile, photo feature on customizing, restoration, convertible conversions, and restyling of motor vehicles (cars, vans, trucks, motorcycles, boats and aircraft). Query or send complete ms. Length: 500-1,000 words. Pays $50-100.

Photos: State availability of photos. Pays $5 maximum for b&w print. Reviews b&w contact sheet. Captions and identification of subjects required. Buys one-time rights.

Tips: "No material dealing with engines and engine repairs. We are an aftermarket publication."

AUTOBODY AND THE RECONDITIONED CAR, Spokesman Publishing Co., Suite 300, 431 Ohio Pike, Cincinnati OH 45230. (513)528-5530. Editor: Richard Broshar. Associate Editor: Fran Cummins. 50% freelance written. A monthly magazine covering autobody repair, reconditioning and refinishing. Audience includes independent body shops; new and used car dealers and fleet operators with body shops; paint, glass and trim shops; and jobbers and manufacturers of automobile straightening equipment and refinishing supplies. Circ. 20,000. Pays on publication. Publishes manuscript an average of 3 months after acceptance. Byline given. Buys first North American serial rights and one-time rights. Submit seasonal/holiday material 3 months in advance. Simultaneous queries, and simultaneous, photocopied, and previously published (if so indicated) submissions OK. Computer printout submissions acceptable; prefers letter-quality to dot-matrix. Reports in 1 month. Sample copy $1. Writer's guidelines for business-size SAE and 1 first class stamp.

Nonfiction: Book excerpts (autobody repair, small business management); how-to (manage an autobody shop, do a specific autobody repair); interview/profile (bodyshop owner); photo feature (step-by-step repair); and technical (equipment, supplies and processes in an autobody shop). Editorial calendar will be provided with writer's guidelines. No personal experience as a customer of an autobody shop, or how *not* to run a shop. Buys 36 mss/year. Query with published clips or send complete ms. Length: 500-2,500 words. Pays $150-200 with photos.

Photos: State availability of photos and send one sample, or send photos with ms. Reviews color negatives and 4x5 transparencies, and 3½x5 b&w and color prints. Payment for photos included in payment for ms. Captions required. Buys one-time rights.

Tips: "Visit 10 autobody shops and ask the owners what they want to read about; find sources, then send in a query; or send in a letter with 10 article topics that you know you can cover and wait for an assignment. Experience in trade publication writing helps. Area most open to freelancers is technical and management how-tos. Body and fender tips pay $10—good way to break in. We want technical, technical, technical articles. Autobody people work with everything from laser beam measuring benches to catalytic thermoreactors. Be willing to learn about such subjects. The most frequent mistakes made by writers are not understanding the audience or the autobody business."

AUTOMOTIVE BOOSTER OF CALIFORNIA, Box 765, LaCanada CA 91011. (213)790-6554. Editor: Don McAnally. 2% freelance written. For members of Automotive Booster clubs, automotive warehouse distributors, and automotive parts jobbers in California. Monthly. Circ. 3,500. Not copyrighted. Byline given. Pays on publication. Buys first rights only. Submit complete ms. SASE. Publishes ms an average of 1 month after acceptance.

Nonfiction: Will look at short articles and pictures about successes of automotive parts outlets in California. Also can use personnel assignments for automotive parts people in California. Query first. Pays $1.25/column inch (about 2½¢/word).

Photos: Pays $5 for b&w photos used with mss.

THE BATTERY MAN, Independent Battery Manufacturers Association, Inc., 100 Larchwood Dr., Largo FL 33540. (813)586-1409. Editor: Celwyn E. Hopkins. 30% freelance written. Emphasizes SLI battery manufacture, applications and new developments. For battery manufacturers and retailers (garage owners, servicemen, fleet owners, etc.). Monthly magazine. Circ. 6,200. Pays on acceptance. Publishes ms an average of 4 months after acceptance. Buys all rights. Byline given. Submit seasonal/holiday material 3 months in advance. Simultaneous, photocopied and previously published submissions OK. Computer printout submissions acceptable; no dot-matrix. SASE. Reports in 6 weeks. Sample copy $2.50.

Nonfiction: Technical articles. Submit complete ms. Buys 19-24 unsolicited mss/year. Recent article example: "Separators for the 80s" (April 84). Length: 750-1,200 words. Pays 6¢/word.

Tips: "Most writers are not familiar enough with this industry to be able to furnish a feature article. They try to palm off something that they wrote for a hardware store, or a dry cleaner, by calling everything a 'battery store'."

BRAKE & FRONT END, 11 S. Forge St., Akron OH 44304. (216)535-6117. Editor: Jeffrey S. Davis. 10% freelance written. For owners of automotive repair shops engaged in brake, suspension, drivel exhaust and frame repair, including: specialty shops, general repair shops, new car and truck dealers, gas stations, mass merchandisers and tire stores. Monthly magazine; 68 pages. Circ. 28,000. Pays on publication. Publishes manuscript an average of 3 months after acceptance. Byline given. Buys first North American serial rights. Computer printout submissions acceptable; prefers letter-quality to dot-matrix. SASE. Reports immediately. Sample copy and editorial schedule $3; guidelines for SASE.

Nonfiction: Specialty shops taking on new ideas using new merchandising techniques; growth of business, volume; reasons for growth and success. Expansions and unusual brake shops. Prefers no product-oriented material. Query. Length: about 800-1,500 words. Pays 7-9¢/word. Sometimes pays expenses of writers on assignment.

Photos: Pays $8.50 for b&w glossy prints purchased with mss.

THE CHEK-CHART SERVICE BULLETIN, Box 6227, San Jose CA 95150. Editor: Jo L. Phelps. 20% freelance written. Emphasizes trade news and how-to articles on automotive service for professional mechanics. Monthly newsletter; 8 pages. Circ. 20,000. Pays on acceptance. No byline. Buys all rights. Submit seasonal/holiday material 3-4 months in advance. SASE. Reports in 2 weeks. Publishes ms an average of 2 months after acceptance. Free sample copy and writer's guidelines; mention *Writer's Market* in request.

Nonfiction: "The *Service Bulletin* is a trade newsletter, *not* a consumer magazine. How-to articles and service trade news for professional auto mechanics, also articles on merchandising automobile service. No 'do-it-yourself' articles." Also no material unrelated to car service. Buys 6 unsolicited mss/year. Query with samples. Length: 700-1,100 words. Pays $75-125.

Photos: State availability of photos with query. Offers no additional payment for photos accepted with ms. Uses 8x10 b&w glossy photos. Captions and model release required. Buys all rights.

Tips: "Be willing to work in our style. Ask about subjects we would like to have covered in the future."

COLLISION, Kruza Kaleidoscopix, Inc., Box 389, Franklin MA 02038. Editor: Jay Kruza. For auto dealers, auto body repairmen and managers, and tow truck operators. Magazine published every 6 weeks; 66 pages. Pays on acceptance. Buys all rights. Submit seasonal/holiday material 4 months in advance. Simultaneous, photocopied and previously published submissions OK. SASE. Reports in 3 weeks. Sample copy $2; free writer's guidelines.

Nonfiction: Expose (on government intervention in private enterprise via rule making; also how any business skims the cream of profitable business but fails to satisfy needs of motorist); and how-to (fix a dent, a frame, repair plastics, run your business better). No general business articles such as how to sell more, do better bookkeeping, etc. Query before submitting interview, personal opinion or technical articles. "Journalism of newsworthy material in local areas pertaining to auto body is of interest." Buys 20 or more articles/year. Length: 100-1,500 words. Pays $25-125.

Photos: "Our readers work with their hands and are more likely to be stopped by photo with story." Send photos with ms. Pays $25/first, $5/each additional for 5x7 b&w prints. Captions preferred. Model release required if not news material.

Columns & Departments: Stars and Their Cars, Personalities in Auto Dealership, Auto Body Repair Shops, Association News and Lifestyle (dealing with general human interest hobbies or past times). Almost anything that would attract readership interest. "Photos are very important. Stories that we have purchased are: 'Clearing the Farm . . . of Rattlesnakes'; 'Annual Mule Convention in Bishop, California'; and 'Cochise's Hidden Treasure.' " Buys 10/year. Query. Length: 200-500 words. Pays $40-100.

COMMERCIAL CARRIER JOURNAL, for Private Fleets & For Hire Trucking, Chilton Co., Division of American Broadcasting Co., Chilton Way, Radnor PA 19089. (215)964-4513. Editor-in-Chief: Gerald F. Standley. Executive Editor: Carl R. Glines. 2% freelance written. Monthly magazine that provides news and features on trends, technology, legislation and management techniques for management, operations and maintenance executives of the nation's private and for hire truck and bus fleets. Circ. 77,000. Pays on acceptance. Offers negotiable kill fee. Buys all rights. Submit seasonal/holiday material 6 months in advance. No simultaneous queries, or simultaneous, photocopied and previously published submissions. SASE. Reports in 1 month on queries. Publishes ms an average of 6 months after acceptance.

Nonfiction: How-to, interview/profile, photo feature and technical. No "superficial garbage. A writer *must* know something about the industry and/or topic." Buys 2 mss/year. Query or send complete ms. Pays $50-600.

Photos: Send photos with query or ms. Reviews color transparencies and prints. Captions, model releases, and identification of subjects required.

Tips: Call the executive editor "only if you are already an expert on the topic that you want to write about. Concentrate more on content and less on style."

JOBBER/RETAILER, Bill Communications, Box 5417, Akron OH 44313. Managing Editor: Sandie Stambaugh. 10% freelance written. "Readership is the automotive parts jobber who has entered the world of retailing to the automotive do-it-yourselfer and also wholesales to dealer trade. Editorial slant is business, merchandising/marketing-oriented with news secondary." Monthly tabloid; 56 pages. Circ. 31,781. Pays on publication. Publishes ms an average of 6 months after acceptance. Buys all rights. Submit seasonal/holiday material 2-3 months in advance. Simultaneous, photocopied and previously published submissions in noncompetitive publications OK. Computer printout submissions acceptable; no dot-matrix. SASE. Free sample copy and writer's guidelines for SAE with 2 first class postage stamps; mention *Writer's Market* in request.

Nonfiction: How-to (merchandising do-it-yourself auto parts, store layout and design, transforming traditional jobber facilities to retail operations as well); computer usage; financial information; and technical (on do-it-yourself repairs). Buys 24 mss/year. Recent article example: "Ideas for making more sales" (February 1985). Submit complete ms. Length: 500-1,500 words maximum. Pays $100-200. Sometimes pays expenses of writers on assignment.

Tips: "Articles frequently are not geared to our market. We rarely use fillers."

JOBBER TOPICS, 7300 N. Cicero Ave., Lincolnwood IL 60646. (312)588-7300. Articles Editor: Jack Creighton. 1% freelance written. "A digest-sized magazine dedicated to helping its readers—auto parts jobbers and warehouse distributors—succeed in their business via better management and merchandising techniques; and a better knowledge of industry trends, activities and local or federal legislation that may influence their business activities." Monthly. Pays on acceptance. No byline given. Buys all rights. Query with outline. SASE.

Nonfiction: Most editorial material is staff-written. "Articles with unusual or outstanding automotive jobber procedures, with special emphasis on sales and merchandising; any phase of automotive parts and equipment distribution. Especially interested in merchandising practices and machine shop operations. Most independent businesses usually have a strong point or two. We like to see a writer zero in on that strong point(s) and submit an outline (or query), advising us of those points and what he intends to include in a feature. We will give him, or her, a prompt reply." Length: 2,500 words maximum. Pay based on quality and timeliness of feature.
Photos: 5x7 b&w glossies or 4-color transparencies purchased with mss.

MILK AND LIQUID FOOD TRANSPORTER, Dairy Marketing Communications, N80 W12878 Fond du Lac Ave., Box 878, Menomonee Falls WI 53051. (414)255-0108. Editor: Karl F. Ohm III. 50% freelance written. Monthly magazine for owner/operators, trucking firms and management people involved in transporting bulk milk and other liquid food products in the U.S. and Canada. Circ. 15,600. "We need more feature stories (with b&w photos and color slide cover shots) about owner/operators and large fleets, especially in California, the Midwest, Central South (i.e., Kentucky and Tennessee), the Northeast and Canada which haul bulk milk from farms to dairy plants. We also need stories on major liquid food hauling firms. We also welcome feature stories involving dairy plants, cheese factories and other processing firms who haul finished food products in refrigerated trailers." Pays on acceptance. Publishes ms an average of 3 months after acceptance. Byline given. Buys all rights. Submit seasonal material 3 months in advance. No duplicate submissions. Computer printout submissions OK; no dot-matrix. SASE. Reports in 2 weeks on queries; in 2-3 weeks on mss. "We encourage freelance writers to send for free sample copies, sources for story leads, and writer's and photographer's guidelines."
Nonfiction: Expose (government regulation, state and federal); historical; interview; profile; how-to (maintenance); new product (staff written); and technical (truck maintenance). No personal opinion, humor, first person nostalgia, travel or inspirational. "We do interpretative reporting and features on timely issues affecting the business of transporting milk and other liquid food products i.e., vegetable oils, corn sweeteners, liquid sugars and apple and orange juice concentrates. We prefer articles that cover topics unique to haulers in a particular state. Well-written and well-organized articles about innovative milk and liquid food transporters stand a better chance of being accepted." Buys 8-10 mss/year. Query. "I like to know why the writer thinks his/her story is pertinent to my publication. I also would like to know why the writer chose a particular slant." Length: 3,100-3,500 words. Pays $200-400. Sometimes pays the expenses of writers on assignment.
Photos: State availability of photos. Pays for b&w contact sheets and usable photos. Pays extra for color cover shot. Detailed captions and model release required. Photo release forms are available upon request. Buys all rights.
Tips: "If freelancers take the time to study our magazine and develop a good story, they will find out that the *Milk and Liquid Food Transporter* is not a tough market to crack. Most freelance writers need to take the time to fully edit their stories before submissions. We also like to see the photos well organized, along with suggest outline, so the editor can organize the material. Shorter articles or fillers are staff written. If any freelancer produces a good feature (with photos) for the magazine, I will usually give him/her good contacts for generating additional, local stories or a story assignment."

MOTOR MAGAZINE, Hearst Corp., 555 W. 57th St., New York NY 10019. (212)262-8616. Editor: Kenneth Zino. Emphasizes auto repair. "Readers are professional auto repairmen or people who own auto repair facilities." Monthly magazine; 80-90 pages. Circ. 135,000. Pays on acceptance. Pays a kill fee. Byline given. Buys all rights. SASE. Reports in 1 month. Query first.
Nonfiction: How-to. "Writers should be able to relate their own hands-on experience to handling specific repair and technical articles." Buys 6 mss/issue. Recent article examples: "How to Fix Cadillac's V8-6-4 Engine"; "Servicing the Split-Diagonal Brake System of the Escort"; "How to Perform an Accurate Wheel Alignment"; "Diagnosing GM's THM 125 Transaxle"; and "Chevy Valve Guide Restoration". Query. Length: 700-2,000 words. Pays $150-1,000.
Photos: "Photos and/or rough artwork must accompany how-to articles." State availability of photos. Uses 5x7 glossy prints. Offers additional payment for photos accepted with ms. Captions and model releases required.

MOTOR SERVICE, Hunter Publishing Co., 950 Lee, Des Plaines IL 60016. Editor: Fred Gaca. 75% freelance written. Monthly magazine for professional auto mechanics and the owners and service managers of repair shops, garages and fleets. Circ. 131,000. Pays on acceptance. Buys all rights. Pays kill fee. Byline given. Computer printout submissions acceptable. Publishes ms an average of 2 months after acceptance. Free sample copy.
Nonfiction: Technical how-to features in language a mechanic can enjoy and understand; management articles to help shop owners and service managers operate a better business; technical theory pieces on how something

works; new technology roundups, etc. No "generic business pieces on management tips, increasing sales, employee motivation or do-it-yourself material, etc." Recent article includes "Meet GM's Self-diagnosing Computer Command Control System." Length: 1,500-2,500 words. Pays $75 for departmental material, $375-$500 for feature articles. Buys 35-40 mss/year, mostly from regular contributing editors. Query first. "Writers must know our market."

Photos: Photos and/or diagrams must accompany technical articles. Uses 5x7 b&w prints or 35mm transparencies. Offers no additional payment for photos accepted with ms. Captions and model releases required. Also buys color transparencies for cover use. Pays $125-200.

Tips: "We're always looking for new faces but finding someone who is technically knowledgeable in our field who can also write is extremely difficult. Good tech writers are hard to find."

‡**MOTORCYCLE DEALERNEWS**, Harcourt Brace Jovanovich Publications, A250, 1700 E. Dyer Rd., Santa Ana CA 92705. (714)250-8060. Editor: Fred Clements. 15% freelance written. Monthly magazine "dedicated to informing motorcycle dealers of more effective ways of doing business." Circ. 14,000. Pays on publication. Byline given. Offers negotiable kill fee. Buys all rights. Submit seasonal/holiday material 4 months in advance. Photocopied submissions OK. Computer printout submissions acceptable; prefers letter-quality to dot-matrix. SASE. Reports in 1 month. Sample copy for SASE.

Nonfiction: Business articles specific and useful to motorcycle and ATV dealers. "No articles about a personal experience riding motorcycles." Buys 24 mss/year. Query. Length: 1,000-3,000 words. Pays $50-200.

Photos: State availability of photos with query. Reviews 8x10 b&w prints. Buys all rights.

Tips: "We need submissions from experienced motorcycle business people."

O AND A MARKETING NEWS, Box 765, LaCanada CA 91011. (213)790-6554. Editor: Don McAnally. For "service station dealers, garagemen, TBA (tires, batteries, accessories) people and oil company marketing management." Bimonthly. 5% freelance written. Circ. 9,500. Not copyrighted. Pays on publication. Buys first rights only. Reports in 1 week. SASE.

Nonfiction: "Straight news material; management, service and merchandising applications; emphasis on news about or affecting markets and marketers *within the publication's geographic area of the 11 Western states*. No restrictions on style or slant. We could use straight news of our industry from some Western cities, notably Las Vegas, Phoenix, Seattle, and Salt Lake City. Query with a letter that gives a capsule treatment of what the story is about." Buys 25 mss/year. Length: maximum 1,000 words. Pays $1.25/column inch (about 2½¢ a word).

Photos: Photos purchased with or without mss; captions required. No cartoons. Pays $5.

‡**PROFESSIONAL CARWASHING MAGAZINE**, National Trade Publications, 8 Stanley Circle, Latham NY 12110. Editor: Ray Shear. Monthly magazine covering professional vehicle cleaning. "We are a trade magazine and serve as a communications, entertainment, and information medium for carwash owners and operators. We are also read by manufacturers and suppliers of carwash equipment, as well as their distributors." 20% freelance written. Circ. 17,000. Pays on acceptance. Byline given. Buys all rights. Submit seasonal/holiday material 4 months in advance. Simultaneous queries OK. SASE. Reports in 3 weeks. Sample copies and guidelines $2 plus 50¢ postage and handling to National Trade Publication.

Nonfiction: How-to (maintenance marketing); photo feature and technical. "All material submitted should be geared to the carwash industry. Problems of running a self-service or automatic carwash, unique or inspiring stories of success or failure, individual design of buildings, advertising and methods of marketing are good topics." No beautiful carwash stories, historic, humor, product comparisons. Buys 6-12 mss/year, but would like to buy more. Query with or without published clips. Length: 1,000-2,500 words. Pays 3-5¢/word. Sometimes pays the expenses of writers on assignment. "Payment depends on how much rewriting and follow-up needs to be done."

Photos: State availability of photos with query. Reviews 5x7 prints. Model release and identification of subjects required.

Tips: "Give us material of interests to the carwash industry, including better or unique management techniques, methods of preventative maintenance, or equipment marketing techniques, unusual design. Writers frequently give too short treatment to the subject assigned because they don't understand the industry. The writer has a better chance of breaking in at our publication with short articles and fillers because the first-time submitter will probably not understand the industry."

REFRIGERATED TRANSPORTER, Tunnell Publications, 1602 Harold St., Houston TX 77006. (713)523-8124. Editor: Gary Macklin. 5% freelance written. Monthly. Not copyrighted. Byline given. Pays on publication. Reports in 1 month. Computer printout submissions acceptable; prefers letter-quality to dot-matrix. SASE.

Nonfiction: "Articles on fleet management and maintenance of vehicles, especially the refrigerated van and the refrigerating unit, shop tips, loading or handling systems—especially for frozen or refrigerated cargo, new equipment specifications, conversions of equipment for better handling or more efficient operations. Prefers articles with illustrations obtained from fleets operating refrigerated trucks or trailers." Pays variable rate, approximately $100 per printed page.

Fillers: Buys newspaper clippings. "Do not rewrite."

SPECIALTY & CUSTOM DEALER, Babcox Publications, 11 S. Forge St., Akron OH 44304. (216)535-6117. Publisher: Jim MacQueen. "Audience is primarily jobbers and retailers of specialty automotive parts and accessories, warehouse distributors and manufacturers. Average reader has been in business for 10 years and is store owner or manager. Educational background varies, with most readers in the high school graduate with some college category." Monthly magazine. Circ. 22,000. Pays on publication. Buys all rights. Submit seasonal or holiday material 4 months in advance. SASE. Reports in 6 weeks. Sample copy $3.

Nonfiction: Publishes informational (business techniques); interview, new product, profile and technical articles. "No broad generalizations concerning a 'great product' without technical data behind the information. Lack of detail concerning business operations." Buys 3-5 unsolicited mss/year. Query. Length: 1,000-2,000 words. Pays $100-250.

Tips: "For the most part, an understanding of automotive products particularly in the high performance and specialty automotive market and business practices is essential. Features on a specific retailer, his merchandising techniques and unique business methods are most often used. Such a feature might include inventory control, display methods, lines carried, handling obsolete products, etc."

‡**SPRAY DUST MAGAZINE, The Information Source For Jersey's Auto Body Industry**, Central Jersey Auto Body Association, Box 1705, Rahway NJ 07065. (201)382-1447. Editor: R. Cullen Fink. Monthly magazine of news that effects auto body industry in New Jersey. "*Spray Dust* is written for the New Jersey auto body shop owner, exclusively. Articles either inform the reader on issues political or otherwise that affect his shop or instruct him on ways to improve his business. The magazine has an action slant to the degree that many pieces either imply or state a need for unification in the industry—a call to action." Circ. 2,000. Pays on publication. Publishes ms an average of 2 months after acceptance. Byline given. Buys first serial rights. Simultaneous queries and photocopied submissions OK. Computer printout submissions acceptable; prefers letter-quality to dot-matrix. SASE. Reports in 3 weeks. Sample copy for 9x12 SAE and 5 first class stamps.

Nonfiction: Interview/profile, new product and technical. Buys 12-15 mss/year. Query with published clips. Length: 1,000-2,500 words. Pays $50-100.

Photos: State availability of photos. Prefers 5x7 or larger b&w prints. Pays $5-10. Buys one-time rights.

Columns/Departments: Let's Get Down to Business (how to be a better businessman), Shop Showcase, and Advertiser Spotlight.

Tips: "We are open in all areas except Shop Showcase or Advertiser Spotlight. The best place for freelancers to begin is Let's Get Down to Business. A writer who is handy with a camera has an edge."

THE SUCCESSFUL DEALER, Kona-Cal, Inc., 707 Lake Cook Rd., Deerfield IL 60015. (312)498-3180. Editor: Denise L. Rondini. Managing Editor: R. Patricia Herron. 30% freelance written. Magazine published 6 times/year covering dealership management of medium and heavy duty trucks, construction equipment, forklift trucks, diesel engines and truck trailers. Circ. 19,000. Pays on publication. Byline sometimes given. Buys first serial rights only. Simultaneous queries, and simultaneous and photocopied submissions OK. Computer printout submissions acceptable; prefers letter-quality to dot-matrix. SASE. Reports in 2 weeks. Publication date "depends on the article; some are contracted for a specific issue, others on an as need basis."

Nonfiction: How-to (solve problems within the dealership); interview/profile (concentrating on business, not personality); new product (exceptional only); opinion (by readers—those in industry); personal experience (of readers); photo feature (of major events); and technical (vehicle componentry). Special issues include: March-April: American Truck Dealer Convention; September-October: Parts and Service. Query. Length: open. Pays $100-150/page.

Tips: "Phone first, then follow up with a detailed explanation of the proposed article. Allow two weeks for our response. Know dealers and dealerships, their problems and opportunities; heavy equipment industry."

TOW-AGE, Kruza Kaleidoscopix, Inc., Box 389, Franklin MA 02038. Editor: J. Kruza. For readers who run their own towing service business. 10% freelance written. Published every 6 weeks. Circ. 12,000. Buys all rights; usually reassigns rights. Buys about 12 mss/year. Pays on acceptance. Publishes ms an average of 3 months after acceptance. Photocopied and simultaneous submissions OK. Reports in 1-4 weeks. Computer printout submissions acceptable; prefers letter-quality to dot-matrix. SASE. Sample copy $1; free writer's guidelines.

Nonfiction: Articles on business, legal and technical information for the towing industry. "Light reading material; short, with punch." Informational, how-to, personal, interview and profile. Query or submit complete ms. Length: 200-800 words. Pays $40-80. Spot news and successful business operations. Length: 100-500 words. Technical articles. Length: 100-1,000 words.

Photos: Pays up to 8x10 b&w photos purchased with or without mss, or on assignment. Pays $25 for first photo; $5 for each additional photo in series. Captions required.

‡**TRUCK CANADA**, Sentinel Business Publications, Unit 8, 6420 Victoria Ave., Montreal, Quebec, Canada H3W 2S7. (514)731-3524. Contact: Editor. For members of the heavy trucking industry. 30% freelance written. Monthly magazine; 40 pages. Circ. 21,500. Pays on publication. Publishes ms an average of 4 months after acceptance. Buys first Canadian rights. Phone queries OK. Submit seasonal/holiday material 3 months in advance. Photocopied submissions and previously published work (if not previously published in Canada) OK. Computer printout submissions acceptable; prefers letter-quality to dot-matrix. SAE and International Reply Coupons. Reports in 3 weeks. Free sample copy and writer's guidelines for $1.48 in IRCs.
Nonfiction: General interest; historical; how-to (on truck maintenance); interview, profile and technical. Buys 18 articles/year. Query. Length: 1,500-2,500. Pays 7¢/word. Sometimes pays the expenses of writers on assignment.
Photos: "We feel articles with photos illustrating them are better accepted by readers." State availability of photos. Pays $5 for b&w contact sheets and $7.50 for color transparencies.

‡**TRUCKERS/USA**, Randall Publishing Co., Box 2029, Tuscaloosa AL 35403. (205)349-2990. Editor: Claude Duncan. 25-50% freelance written. Weekly tabloid for long-haul truck drivers and trucker service industry. "Most of our readers are long-haul truckers. We want stories about these drivers, their trucks, lifestyle and people who serve them, such as truck stops. We want upbeat stories." Circ. 15,000. Pays on acceptance. Publishes ms an average of 1 month after acceptance. Byline given. Offers 100% kill fee. Not copyrighted. Simultaneous and previously published (updated) submissions OK. Computer printout submissions acceptable; prefers letter-quality to dot-matrix. Reports in 2 weeks. Free sample copy and writer's guidelines.
Nonfiction: General interest (with trucker angle); historical/nostaglic (with trucker angle); humor (with trucker angle); interview/profile (with truckers); personal experience (with truckers); technical (re heavy-duty trucks); and crimes involving long-haul truckers. Buys 100 mss/year. Send complete ms. Length: 250-750 words. Pays $10-50. Pays expenses of writers on assignment.
Photos: Send photos with query or ms. Prefers b&w prints; commercially processed accepted if sharp quality. Pays $5. Identification of subjects required.
Tips: "Truckers like to read about other truckers, and people with whom truckers are in frequent contact—truckstop workers, state police, etc. We're looking for localized stories about long-haul truckers. Nothing is too local if it's interesting. We encourage multiple submissions, preferrably with art. Submitting art with copy gives a definite edge."

WARD'S AUTO WORLD, 28 W. Adams, Detroit MI 48226. (313)962-4433. Editor-in-Chief: David C. Smith. Managing Editor: James W. Bush. Senior Editors: Jon Lowell and Richard L. Waddell. Associate Editors: Drew Winter and Michael Arnolt. 10% freelance written. For top and middle management in all phases of auto industry. Also includes heavy-duty vehicle coverage. Monthly magazine; 96 pages. Circ. 75,000. Pays on publication. Pay varies for kill fee. Byline given. Buys all rights. Phone queries OK. Submit seasonal/holiday material 1 month in advance. Computer printout submissions acceptable. SASE. Reports in 2 weeks. Publishes ms an average of 1 month after acceptance. Free sample copy and writer's guidelines.
Nonfiction: Expose, general interest, historical, humor, interview, new product, nostalgia, personal experience, photo feature and technical. Few consumer type articles. No "nostalgia or personal history type stories (like 'My Favorite Car')." Buys 4-8 mss/year. Query. Length: 700-5,000 words. Pay $100-600.
Photos: "We're heavy on graphics." Submit photo material with query. Pay varies for 8x10 b&w prints or color transparencies. Captions required. Buys one-time rights.
Tips: "Don't send poetry, how-to and 'My Favorite Car' stuff. It doesn't stand a chance. This is a business newsmagazine and operates on a news basis just like any other newsmagazine."

Aviation and Space

In this section are journals for aviation business executives, airport operators and aviation technicians. Publications for professional and private pilots are classified with the Aviation magazines in the Consumer Publications section.

AG-PILOT INTERNATIONAL MAGAZINE, Bio-Aeronautic Publishers, Inc., Drawer "R", Walla Walla WA 99362. (509)522-4311. Editor: Tom J. Wood. Executive Editor: Rocky Kemp. Emphasizes agricultural aerial application (crop dusting). "This is intended to be a fun-to-read, technical, as well as humorous and serious publication for the ag pilot and operator. They are our primary target." 20% freelance written. Monthly magazine; 60 pages. Circ. 10,200. Pays on publication. Publishes ms an average of 3 months after acceptance.

Buys all rights. Byline given unless writer requested holding name. No phone queries. Computer printout submissions acceptable; prefers letter-quality to dot-matrix. SASE. Reports in 2 weeks. Sample copy $2.

Nonfiction: Expose (of EPA, OSHA, FAA or any government function concerned with this industry); general interest; historical; interview (of well-known ag/aviation person); nostalgia; personal opinion; new product; personal experience; and photo feature. "If we receive an article, in any area we have solicited, it is quite possible this person could contribute intermittently. The international input is what we desire. Industry-related material is a must. No newspaper clippings." Send complete ms. Length: 800-1,500 words. Pays $25-100. Sometimes pays the expenses of writers on assignment.

Photos: "We would like one color or b&w (5x7 preferred) with the manuscript, if applicable—it will help increase your chance of publication." Four color. Offers no additional payment for photos accepted with ms. Captions preferred, model release required.

Columns/Departments: International (of prime interest, as they need to cultivate this area—aviation/crop dusting-related); Embryo Birdman (should be written, or appear to be written, by a beginner spray pilot); The Chopper Hopper (by anyone in the helicopter industry); Trouble Shooter (ag aircraft maintenance tips); and Catchin' The Corner (written by a person obviously skilled in the crop dusting field of experience or other interest-capturing material related to the industry). Send complete ms. Length: 800-1,500 words. Pays $25-100.

Poetry: Interested in all agri-aviation related poetry. Buys 1/issue. Submit no more than 2 at one time. Maximum length: one 10 inch x 24 picas maximum. Pays $25-50.

Fillers: Short jokes, short humor and industry-related newsbreaks. Length: 10-100 words. Pays $5-20.

Tips: "Writers should be witty and knowledgeable about the crop dusting aviation world. Material *must* be agricultural/aviation-oriented. Crop dusting or nothing! We plan a Spanish language edition to all Spanish-speaking countries."

AIRPORT SERVICES MANAGEMENT, Lakewood Publications, 731 Hennepin Ave., Minneapolis MN 55403. (612)333-0471. Editor: Sher Jasperse. 33% freelance written. Emphasizes management of airports, airlines and airport-based businesses. Monthly magazine. Circ. 20,000. Pays on acceptance. Publishes ms an average of 3 months after acceptance. Buys all rights. Byline given. Phone queries OK. Submit seasonal/holiday material 3 months in advance. Photocopied submissions OK but must be industry-exclusive. Computer printout submissions acceptable; prefers letter-quality to dot-matrix. SASE. Reports in 1 month. Free sample copy and writer's guidelines.

Nonfiction: How-to (manage an airport, aviation service company or airline; work with local governments, etc.); interview (with a successful operator); and technical (how to manage a maintenance shop, snow removal operations, bird control, security operations). "No flying, no airport nostalgia or product puff pieces. We don't want pieces on how one company's product solved everyone's problem (how one airport or aviation business solved its problem with a certain type of product is okay). No descriptions of airport construction projects (down to the square footage in the new restrooms) that don't discuss applications for other airports. All articles that begin with anything like, 'She's cute, petite and dresses like a lady, but by golly she runs the Shangrila Airport with a firm hand' are burned on the spot. Just plain 'how-to' story lines, please." Buys 40-50 mss/year, "but at least half are short (250-750 words) items for inclusion in one of our monthly departments." Query. Length: 250-2,500 words. Pays $50 for most department articles, $100-350 for features.

Photos: State availability of photos with query. Payment for photos is included in total purchase price. Uses b&w photos, charts and line drawings.

Tips: "I rarely commission major assignments to writers unproven in writing for our audience, even if they have excellent clips from other magazines. We're using more shorter feature articles (average 2,000 words) because I find that the longer, in-depth, issue-oriented articles are better when they are staff researched and written. No 'gee-whiz' approaches. Writing style should be lively, informal and straightforward, but the *subject matter* must be as functional and as down-to-earth as possible. Trade magazines are *business* magazines that must help readers do their jobs better. Frequent mistakes are using industry vendors/suppliers rather than users and industry officials as *sources*, especially in endorsing products or approaches, and directing articles to pilots or aviation consumers rather than to our specialized audience of aviation business managers and airport managers."

JET CARGO NEWS, The Management Journal for Air Marketing, 5400 Mitchelldale #B5, Houston TX 77092. (713)688-8811. Editor: Rich Hall. Designed to serve international industry concerned with moving goods by air. "It brings to shippers and manufacturers spot news of airline and aircraft development, air routes, CAB ruling, shipping techniques, innovations and rates." 50% freelance written. Monthly. Circ. 25,000. Buys all rights. Buys up to 50 mss/year. Pays on publication. Publishes ms an average of 2 months after acceptance. Will not consider photocopied or simultaneous submissions. Computer printout submissions acceptable; prefers letter-quality to dot-matrix. Submit seasonal material 1 month in advance. Reports in 1 month if postage is included. Submit complete ms. SASE. Will send a sample copy and writer's guidelines on request.

Nonfiction: "Direct efforts to the shipper. Tell him about airline service, freight forwarder operations, innovations within the industry, new products, aircraft, and pertinent news to the industry. Use a tight magazine style. The writer must know marketing." Buys informational articles, how-to's, interviews and coverage of success-

ful business operations. Length: 1,500 words maximum. Pays $4/inch. Sometimes pays the expenses of writers on assignment.
Photos: 8x10 b&w glossy prints purchased with and without mss; captions required. Pays $10.
Tips: A frequent mistake is missing target readers and their interests. With short articles and fillers the writer exhibits his/her initiative.

ROTOR & WING INTERNATIONAL, PJS Publications Inc., Box 1790, Peoria IL 61656. (309)682-6626. Editor: Don Toler. Managing Editor: David Jensen. 80% freelance written. Monthly magazine covering the international helicopter industry. "Prime audience: civil and military helicopter owners and operators; secondary audience: manufacturers. Covers all phases of the helicopter industry with special interest in military, civil government, and commerical offshore operations; and corporate/business use of rotorcraft." Circ. 40,000 (approximately). Pays on acceptance. Publishes ms an average of 3 months after acceptance. Byline given. Buys all rights. Electronic submissions acceptable via 300/1200 Baud/Asyuc. Computer printout submissions acceptable; prefers letter-quality to dot-matrix. Reports in 2 weeks. Free sample copy and writer's guidelines.
Nonfiction: Interview/profile (key figures of importance to rotorcraft); and technical (rotorcraft piloting and operations). No articles "pertaining to homebuilt rotorcraft or run-of-the mill rescues . . ." Buys 60 mss/year ("however, 98% come from regular freelance staff"). Query with clips. Length: 1,500-2,000 words. Pays $250-550. Pays expenses of writers on assignment.
Photos: State availability of photos. "Photos are considered part of manuscript and not purchased separately." Reviews b&w prints. Identification of subjects required.
Tips: "Convince the editors you have an understanding of the civil helicopter industry and have experience with technical/business writing." General features and some news stringing are most open to freelancers. A frequent mistake is "failure to do adequate research."

Beverages and Bottling

Soft drinks and alcoholic beverages are the livelihood of people who read these publications. They need hard facts, not frothiness. "Stories must have a marketing emphasis because wine sales are flat," pointed out one *Wines and Vines* editor. As for soft drinks, consumers are debating what the "real thing" is. Trade journal editors need a more knowledgeable approach. Manufacturers, distributors and retailers of soft drinks and alcoholic beverages rely on these publications. Publications for bar and tavern operators and managers of restaurants are classified in the Hotels, Motels, Clubs, Resorts and Restaurants category.

BEER WHOLESALER, Dogan Communications, Inc., 75 SE 4th Ave., Delray Beach FL 33444. (305)272-1223. Editor: Kenneth Breslauer. Bimonthly magazine about the beer industry for beer wholesalers, importers and brewers. Circ. 4,300. Pays on publication. Byline given. Buys all rights. Reports in 3 weeks on queries; in 2 months on mss. Sample copy $5.
Nonfiction: General interest, interview, profile, how-to and technical. "Submit articles that are business-oriented and presented in an organized manner. Dig for the unusual; what makes this beer wholesaler different? What new ideas can be used? No consumer-oriented articles such as stories on beer can collecting." Query. Length: 1,200-5,000 words. Pays $100-250.
Photos: Send photos with ms. Offers no additional payment for photos accepted with ms. Captions required. Buys all rights.

‡**BEVERAGE RETAILER WEEKLY**, (Formerly *Beverage Retailer World*), Joseph Matzner Publications, 1661 Rt. 23, Wayne NJ 07470. (201)696-3000. Editor: Joseph Matzner. Managing Editor: Kenneth Pringle. 10% freelance written. Weekly tabloid covering the liquor industry. "We specifically serve retailers, providing news on legal changes, marketing happenings, etc." Circ. 36,000. Pays on publication. Publishes ms an average of 3 weeks after acceptance. Byline given. Buys one-time rights. Submit seasonal/holiday material 1 month in advance. Computer printout submissions acceptable; prefers letter-quality to dot-matrix. SASE. Reports in 2 weeks on queries; 1 month on mss. Free sample copy and writer's guidelines.
Nonfiction: Expose, historical/nostalgic, how-to, interview/profile, new product, opinion, personal experience, photo feature, technical and travel. Send complete ms. Length: 500-2,500 words. Pays $25-50.
Photos: John Merlino, photo editor. Pays $10-20 for b&w prints. Reviews b&w contact sheets. Identification

of subjects required.

Columns/Departments: All About Wine, Marketing Trends, and The Retailers View. Send complete ms. Length: 500-2,500 words. Pays $25-50.

Tips: "Call or write, and exhibit satisfactory skills and a knowledge of industry. The more in-depth the article, the more appreciated."

‡**THE LIQUOR REPORTER**, Smithwrite Communications, Inc., 101 Milwaukee Blvd. S., Pacific WA 98047. (206)833-9642. Editor: Robert Smith. 30% freelance written. Monthly tabloid providing local news about the liquor industry, restaurants, distributing, legislature, taverns, food stores, and shops in Washington state. Circ. 11,500. Pays on publication. Publishes ms an average of 1 month after acceptance. Byline given. Offers 100% kill fee for assigned stories. Not copyrighted. Buys simultaneous rights and second serial (reprint) rights. Simultaneous queries and previously published submissions OK. Electronic submissions OK if compatible with Kapro, Wordstar. Computer printout submissions acceptable; prefers letter-quality to dot-matrix. SASE. Reports in 1 month. Sample copy $1; free writer's guidelines.

Nonfiction: News and news features with emphasis on Washington state; book excerpts. Buys 20 mss/year. Query with published clips. Length: 150-1,000 words. Pays $2/column inch minimum. Sometimes pays the expenses of writers on assignment.

Tips: Writers have a better chance of breaking in with short, lesser-paying articles and fillers. Washington state writers preferred. "We're looking for writers in Vancouver (WA) and central Washington."

MID-CONTINENT BOTTLER, 10741 El Monte, Overland Park KS 66207. (913)341-0020. Publisher: Floyd E. Sageser. 5% freelance written. For "soft drink bottlers in the 20-state Midwestern area." Bimonthly. Not copyrighted. Pays on acceptance. Publishes ms an average of 2 months after acceptance. Buys first rights only. Reports "immediately." SASE. Sample copy with $1 postage; guideline with SASE.

Nonfiction: "Items of specific soft drink bottler interest with special emphasis on sales and merchandising techniques. Feature style desired." Buys 2-3 mss/year. Length: 2,000 words. Pays $15-$100. Sometimes pays the expenses of writers on assignment.

Photos: Photos purchased with mss.

‡**MODERN BREWERY AGE**, Box 5550, East Norwalk CT 06856. Editorial Director: Howard Kelly. For "brewery and beer distribution executives on the technical, administrative, and marketing levels." Buys North American serial rights. Pays on publication. Reports "at once." SASE.

Nonfiction and Photos: "Technical and business articles of interest to brewers and beer distributors." Query. Length: 5-8 double-spaced typewritten pages. Pays $75/printed page (about 3 to 3½ pages double-spaced typewritten ms)." Pays $20/published photo. Captions required.

WINES & VINES, 1800 Lincoln Ave., San Rafael CA 94901. Editor: Philip E. Hiaring. 10% freelance written. For everyone concerned with the grape and wine industry including winemakers, wine merchants, growers, suppliers, consumers, etc. Monthly magazine. Circ. 5,500. Buy first North American serial rights or simultaneous rights. Pays on acceptance. Submit special material (water, January; vineyard, February; Man-of-the-Year, March; Brandy, April; export-import, May; enological, June; statistical, July; marketing, September; equipment and supplies, November; champagne, December) 3 months in advance. Reports in 2 weeks. Publishes ms an average of 3 months after acceptance. SASE. Free sample copy.

Nonfiction: Articles of interest to the trade. "These could be on grape growing in unusual areas; new wine-making techniques; wine marketing, retailing, etc." Interview, historical, spot news, merchandising techniques and technical. No stories with a strong consumer orientation as against trade orientation. Author should know the subject matter, i.e., know proper grape growing/winemaking terminology. Buys 3-4 ms/year. Query. Length: 1,000-2,500 words. Pays $25-50.

Photos: Pays $15 for 4x5 or 8x10 b&w photos purchased with mss. Captions required.

Book and Bookstore Trade

These publications can be a market (if you know the bookstore trade) or a valuable source for the published author and person writing a book. They tell you how and why certain books are successful.

AB BOOKMAN'S WEEKLY, Box AB, Clifton NJ 07015. (201)772-0020. Editor-in-Chief: Jacob L. Chernofsky. Weekly magazine; 200 pages. For professional and specialist booksellers, acquisitions and aca-

demic librarians, book publishers, book collectors, bibliographers, historians, etc. Circ. 8,500. Pays on publication. Byline given. Buys all rights. Phone queries OK. Submit seasonal or holiday material 2-3 months in advance. Simultaneous and photocopied submissions OK. SASE. Reports in 1 month. Sample copy $5.
Nonfiction: How-to (for professional booksellers); historical (related to books or book trade or printing or publishing); personal experiences; nostalgia; interviews and profiles. Query. Length: 2,500 words minimum. Pays $60 minimum.
Photos: Photos used with mss.

AMERICAN BOOKSELLER, Booksellers Publishing, Inc., 122 E. 42nd St., New York NY 10168. (212)867-9060. Editor: Ginger Curwen. 10% freelance written. This publication emphasizes the business of retail bookselling and goes to the 5,700 members of the American Booksellers Association and to more than 2,400 other readers nationwide, most of whom are involved in publishing. Monthly magazine; 48 pages. Circ. 7,800. Pays on publication. Publishes ms an average of 4 months after acceptance. Buys first serial rights. Pays 25% kill fee. Byline given "except on small news stories." Submit seasonal/holiday material 3 months in advance. Electronic submissions OK via IBM PC, but requires hard copy also. Computer printout submissions acceptable; prefers letter-quality to dot-matrix. SASE. Reports in 3 months. Sample copy $3.
Nonfiction: General interest (on bookselling); how-to (run a bookstore, work with publishers); interview (on authors and booksellers); photo feature (on book-related events); and solutions to the problems of small businesses. Buys 2 mss/issue. Query with clips of published work and background knowledge of bookselling. Length: 750-2,000 words. Pays $75-300. Sometimes pays the expenses of writers on assignment.
Photos: State availability of photos. Uses b&w 5x7 matte prints and contact sheets. Pays $10-20. Uses 35mm color transparencies. Pays $10-50. Captions and model releases required.
Tips: "While we buy a number of articles for each issue, very few come from freelance writers. Since the focus of the magazine is on the business of bookselling, most of our contributors are booksellers who share their *first-hand* experience with our readers. 85% of these articles are assigned; the rest are unsolicited—but those come mainly from booksellers as well."

‡**BOOKSTORE JOURNAL, The How-To Magazine**, Christian Booksellers Association, Box 200, Colorado Springs CO 80901. (303)576-7880. Editor: Steve Rabey. Managing Editor: Dave Somers. Monthly magazine of the Christian bookselling industry. The purpose of Bookstore Journal is to provide material whereby Christian booksellers can improve their professional retail skills, find information on the products they sell, and read significant news related to their industry. Circ. 7,800. Pays on publication. Byline given. Offers $100 kill fee. Buys first serial rights. Submit seasonal/holiday material 4 months in advance. Simultaneous queries OK. SASE. Reports in 1 month. Sample copy $6; free writer's guidelines.
Nonfiction: General interest (features on Christian bookstores or publishers); how-to (concerning retail management); inspirational (pertaining to how Christian books have inspired author); interview/profile (of authors/artists in the Christian industry); new product (news releases only of product with inspirational emphasis); opinion (editorials on aspects of Christian publishing and/or bookselling); and personal experience (as it relates to Christian bookselling). Buys 100 mss/year. Query with published clips. Length: 1,000-2,000 words. Pays $100-350.
Photos: State availability of photos. Reviews 5x7 b&w prints. Pays $15-25. Identification of subjects required. Buys all rights.
Tips: "Most articles are assigned to people who have expertise in business or bookstore management and can communicate clearly in writing. Freelance writers are used occasionally for reporting on industry events, for special assignments, or for interviewing selected authors, artists, suppliers, and booksellers."

CHRISTIAN BOOKSELLER, 396 E. St. Charles Rd., Wheaton IL 60188. (312)653-4200. Editor: Karen Tornberg. Emphasizes "all aspects of Christian bookselling." 50% freelance written. Monthly mangazine; 68 pages. Circ. 10,000. Pays on publication. Publishes ms an average 3 months after acceptance. Buys all rights; "but we are happy to give second rights upon written request." Phone queries OK. Submit seasonal/holiday material 6 months in advance. Computer printout submissions acceptable; no dot-matrix. SASE. Reports in 4-6 weeks. Writer's guidelines available for SAE with 5 first class stamps.
Nonfiction: "*Christian Bookseller* is a trade magazine serving religious bookstores. Needs articles on bookstore management, marketing, merchandising, personnel, finance, ministry, advertising, profiles of successful and unique bookstores, in-depth interviews with authors and publishers and interviews with musicians." Buys 36-48 mss/year. No fiction. Query. Length: 1,000-2,500 words. Pays $25-150. Sometimes pays the expenses of writers on assignment.
Photos: "Photos are to accompany all articles." State availability of photos with query. Reviews 5x7 b&w glossy prints and contact sheets. Offers no additional payment for photos accompanying ms. Uses 2-3 b&w photos/story. Captions preferred. Buys all rights.
Fillers: Short, filler-type articles dealing with the publishing, bookseller or librarian fields. The writer has a better chance of breaking in at our publication with short articles and fillers (rather than with major features) because it gives us the chance to "get to know them and their style."

Tips: "In queries get to the point; cut the hype; state credentials factually—tell me what you're going to write. All manuscripts must be substantial in content, authoritatively written, and well documented where called for. Writers must exhibit knowledge and understanding of the religious retailing business and industry."

COLLEGE STORE EXECUTIVE, Box 1500, Westbury NY 11590. (516)334-3030. Editor: Stephanie Wood. 5% freelance written. Tabloid, 40 pages, published 10 times/year. Emphasizes merchandising and marketing in the college store market. Publishes 10 issues/year. Circ. 8,500. Pays on publication. Publishes ms an average of 3 months after acceptance. Byline given. Buys all rights. Submit seasonal/holiday material 3 months in advance. Photocopied submissions OK. SASE. Reports in 3 weeks. Must include SASE for writer's guidelines. For sample copy, use large manilla envelope only.
Nonfiction: Expose (problems in college market); general interest (to managers); how-to (advertise, manage a college store); store profile of new or remodeled location; personal experience (someone who worked for a publisher selling to bookstores); personal opinion (from those who know about the market); photo feature (on specific college bookstores in the country or outside); and technical (how to display products). No articles on typical college student or general "how-to" articles. Buys 8-10 mss/year. Query. Length: 1,000 words. Pays $2/column inch.
Photos: State availability of photos with query. Pays $5 for b&w prints. Captions preferred. Buys all rights.
Tips: "No general business advice that could apply to all retail establishments—articles must deal directly with college stores. This is a good place for someone to start—but they have to understand the market." No interviews with managers on their theories of life or public relations pieces on specific products.

FINE PRINT, The Review for the Arts of the Book, Fine Print Publishing Co., Box 3394, San Francisco CA 94119. (415)776-1530. Editor: Sandra D. Kirshenbaum. Quarterly magazine covering the arts of the book plus history of books and publishing, including printing, typography, type design, graphic design, calligraphy, bookbinding and papermaking. "We seek to cover contemporary fine book making and all related arts for printers, librarians, graphic artists, book collectors, publishers, booksellers, bookbinders, typographers, etc." Circ. 3,000. Pays on publication. Byline given. Buys first North American serial rights and "rights to publish in collections." Submit seasonal/holiday material 9 months in advance. Simultaneous queries, and simultaneous and photocopied submissions OK. SASE. Reports in 3 months on queries; 6 months on mss. Sample copy $10; free writer's guidelines.
Nonfiction: Interview/profile (of contemporary book artists and printers); new product (relating to printing, bookbinding, etc.); personal experience ("Book Arts Reporter" covering book events, conferences, workshops, lectures, etc.); technical (related to books, printing, typography, etc.); and exhibit reviews (of book-related exhibits in libraries, museums, galleries). Buys 4-5 mss/year. Query. Length: 2,000-4,000 for lead articles. Pays $150 for lead articles only; pays in copies for other articles.
Photos: State availability of photos with ms. Identification of subjects required. Buys one-time rights.
Columns/Departments: On Type (essays on typography and type design, contemporary and historical); Book Arts Profile; The Featured Book Binding; Exhibit Reviews; and Recent Press Books (reviews of fine limited edition books). Query. Length: 500-1,300 words. No payment "except review copies of fine books."
Fillers: Newsbreaks. Shoulder Notes—In Brief (short notices and descriptions of events, personalities and publications dictating to book arts).

‡**THE HORN BOOK MAGAZINE**, The Horn Book, Inc., 31 St. James Ave., Boston MA 02116. (617)482-5198. Editor: Anita Silvey. Bimonthly magazine covering children's literature for librarians, booksellers, professors, and students of children's literature. Circ. 18,000. Pays on publication. Byline given. Buys one-time rights. Submit seasonal/holiday material 6 months in advance. Simultaneous queries, and simultaneous, photocopied, and previously published submissions OK. Computer printout submissions acceptable; no dot-matrix. SASE. Reports in 6 weeks on queries; 2 months on mss. Free sample copy; writer's guidelines for SAE with 1 first class stamp.
Nonfiction: Interview/profile (children's book authors and illustrators). Buys 20 mss/year. Query or send complete ms. Length: 1,000-2,800 words. Pays $25-250.
Tips: "Writers have a better chance of breaking into our publication with a query letter on a specific article they want to write."

INTERRACIAL BOOKS FOR CHILDREN BULLETIN, Council on Interracial Books for Children, Inc., 1841 Broadway, New York NY 10023. (212)757-5339. Managing Editor: Ruth Charnes. A magazine published 8 times/year covering children's literature/school materials. "Our publication reaches teachers, librarians, editors, authors and parents. It focuses on issues on bias/equity in children's literature and school materials." Circ. 5,000. Pays on publication. Byline given. Offers variable kill fee. Buys first North American serial rights and one-time rights. Submit seasonal/holiday material 6 months in advance. Computer printout submissions acceptable; prefers letter-quality to dot-matrix. Simultaneous queries, and photocopied submissions OK. SASE. Reports in 1 month on queries; 3 months on mss. Sample copy $2.95; writer's guidelines for SAE and 1 first class stamp.

Close-up

John F. Baker
Editor-in-Chief
Publishers Weekly
and *Small Press*

John Baker is an editor and writer but also a chronicler of the (big and small) publishing industry. He follows the moves of publishing conglomerates and one-man presses. He tells readers what moves may be next.

"It's our motto here never to do a story on anything that's already been advertised so we have to be sure we have the first word in the editorial columns," says this editor-in-chief of *Publishers Weekly* and *Small Press.*

Distributing books at the right time and "letting people know about the books they've got" are problems writers might not guess that publishers face. "You have to depend largely on first having the book reviewed in time . . . and developing a word-of-mouth excitement about the book," points out Baker.

"Authors tend to think the publisher forgets about a book after it's published. That's not true," Baker believes. Sometimes if a book doesn't sell, in, say, two or three months, the bookseller will return the books for full credit. "Returns are universal throughout the trade."

Most small press publishers will keep books in print indefinitely as a backlist. Writers with book ideas that would appeal to a small, loyal audience should consider small presses. "Most larger publishers won't bother with a book that's likely to sell less than 5,000 copies. It's simply not economical for them," points out Baker. "If you've got a project on a subject that you know nothing good on already exists and you have a clear idea of how the market can be reached, then by all means take it to a small publisher."

He has seen bestsellers and nonsellers come and go. "Remember there are 50,000 books published a year and not more than 100 or so books in a given year ever make it to the bestseller list so writers can see the odds against them are rather considerable," says Baker, in the publishing field for 30 years.

"You have to come up with a genuinely new angle on an old subject," he suggests. "Aim small first; build up some kind of a readership, some sort of reputation for expertise in a given area, and it's possible you'll be able to parlay that knowledge, that experience, that readership into a bestselling book."

Baker believes most bestsellers aren't dependent on writing ability. "They depend far more on the ability to promote oneself, to promote one's ideas, to sell the editor, publisher and agent.

"If I was urging someone to try a book that would be more easily published than anything else, it would be an intelligent novel written to appeal to somebody between the ages of 13 and 18," he says.

As with authors looking for markets for their books, writers who wish to sell articles to *Publishers Weekly* and *Small Press* must have "a certain amount of knowledge of the publishing scene and the players in it."

Baker looks for writers "who deliver a lot of interesting facts within a very short compass and an apparent authority in the style with which it is written."

Seated behind a crowded desk with a word processor *and* old typewriter at his side, *he* delivers a lot of interesting facts and opinions. . . . Writers can hear more by reading *Publishers Weekly* and *Small Press.*

Nonfiction: Personal experience (strategies for teaching/encouraging equity); interview/profile (of authors/illustrators/teachers/others seeking bias-free children's materials); and analysis of children's material (textbooks, literature, etc.). Buys 25 mss/year. Query. Length: 1,500-2,500 words. Pays $50-200.

Columns/Departments: Review of children's books and AV materials, resources for adults. "Our policy is that books about various groups, e.g., feminists, Third World people, older people, disabled people, etc., be reviewed by members of that group." Buys 100 mss/year. Query with or without published clips. Length: 250-350 words. Pays $10-25.

Tips: "Our goal is a society that is pluralistic and bias-free. We seek the perspectives of groups that have been oppressed by a society dominated by upper class white males. We seek documentation of that oppression in the world of children's books and school learning materials and positive ways to develop awareness of that oppression and ways to conteract it. The primary consideration in writing for the *Bulletin* is sensitivity to racism, sexism, ageism, homophobia, handicapism and other forms of injustice."

NEW PAGES: News & Reviews of the Progressive Book Trade, New Pages Press, 4426 S. Belsay Rd., Grand Blanc MI 48439. (313)743-8055. Editors: Grant Burns and Casey Hill. Triannual tabloid covering independent publishing, libraries and bookstores. Pays on publication. Byline given. Buys first North American serial rights. SASE. Reports in 1 month. Sample copy $3.
Nonfiction: Interview, opinion and book reviews. "We cover the alternative press with articles, news, reviews, listings and useful information for publishers, librarians and booksellers." Query with published clips. Length: (for book reviews) 25-250 words.

PUBLISHERS WEEKLY, 205 E. 42nd Ave., New York NY 10017. (212)916-1877. Editor-in-Chief: John F. Baker. Weekly. Buys first North American serial rights. Pays on publication. Computer printout submissions acceptable; prefers letter-quality to dot-matrix. SASE. Reports "in several weeks."
Nonfiction: "We rarely use unsolicited manuscripts because of our highly specialized audience and their professional interests, but we can sometimes use news items about publishers, publishing projects, bookstores and other subjects relating to books. We will be paying increasing attention to electronic publishing." No pieces about writers or word processors. Payment negotiable; generally $150/printed page.
Photos: Photos occasionally purchased with and without mss.

SMALL PRESS, The Magazine of Independent Publishing, R.R. Bowker Co.-Xerox Corp., 205 E. 42nd St., New York NY 10017. (212)916-1887. Editor-in-Chief: John F. Baker. Executive Editor: Marlene Charnizon. 85% freelance written. A bimonthly magazine covering small presses and independent publishers—book and magazine—for publishers, librarians, bookstores and "dreamers." Circ. 7,000. Pays on publication. Publishes ms an average of 2 months after acceptance. Byline given. Offers kill fee. Buys first North American serial rights. Submit seasonal/holiday material 4 months in advance. Computer printout submissions acceptable; no dot-matrix. Reports in 1 month. Free sample copy.
Nonfiction: Book excerpts (on occasion); how-to; humor; interview/profile; new product; personal experience; and technical. Buys 36 mss/year. Query with or without published clips or send complete ms. Length: 2,000-2,500 words. Pays $100/printed page. Sometimes pays the expenses of writers on assignment.
Photos: State availability of photos. Pays minimum $25 for 5x7 b&w prints. Identification of subjects required. Buys one-time rights.
Columns/Departments: "Columns treat the how-tos of such subjects as printing, paper, distribution, contracts, etc." Buys 36 mss/year. Query with or without published clips or send complete ms. Length: 1,800 words approximately. Pays $100/printed page.
Tips: "Someone really knowledgeable about small presses who writes well, has been published, and respects deadlines is ideal. The most frequent mistakes made by writers in completing an article for us are overwriting and not editing their own work before submitting it."

‡**WESTERN PUBLISHER, A Trade Journal**, WP, Inc., Box 591012, Golden Gate Station, San Francisco CA 94159. (415)221-1964. Editor: Tony D'Arpino. Managing Editor: Paula von Lowenfeldt. 25% freelance written. Monthly tabloid covering publishing and book industry. Audience includes publishers, booksellers, and librarians in Western United States and Pacific Rim nations. Circ. 10,000. Pays on publication. Publishes ms an average of 1 month after acceptance. Byline given. Kill fee negotiable. Buys one-time rights. Submit seasonal/holiday material 3 months in advance; calendar: 6 months. Simultaneous queries, and simultaneous, photocopied, and previously published submissions OK. Computer printout submissions acceptable; prefers letter-quality to dot-matrix. SASE. Reports in 1 week. Sample copy $2.
Nonfiction: Book excerpts (of industry interest), general interest, historical, how-to, interview/profile, new product, opinion, personal experience, photo feature, technical, and short reviews of just published books. No reviews over 500 words. Buys 100 mss/year. Query with or without published clips or send complete ms. Length: open. Pays negotiable rates.
Fillers: Clippings and newsbreaks. Buys 100/year. Length: 100-500 words.

Tips: "The area most open to freelancers is Western Book Round Up (review listings). A freelancer can best break in to our publication with short reviews of forthcoming books, 200-500 words; 250 words, preferred."

Brick, Glass, and Ceramics

‡**AMERICAN GLASS REVIEW**, Box 2147, Clifton NJ 07015. (201)779-1600. Editor-in-Chief: Donald Doctorow. 10% freelance written. Monthly magazine; 24 pages. Pays on publication. Byline given. Phone queries OK. Buys all rights. Submit seasonal/holiday material 2 months in advance of issue date. SASE. Reports in 2-3 weeks. Free sample copy and writer's guidelines; mention *Writer's Market* in request.
Nonfiction: Glass plant and glass manufacturing articles. Buys 3-4 mss/year. Query. Length: 1,500-3,000 words. Pays $40-50.
Photos: State availability of photos with query. No additional payment for b&w contact sheets. Captions preferred. Buys one-time rights.

BRICK AND CLAY RECORD, Cahners Plaza, 1350 E. Touhy Ave., Box 5080, Des Plaines IL 60018. (312)635-8800. Editor-in-Chief: Wayne A. Endicott. For "the heavy clay products industry." Monthly. Buys all rights. Pays on publication. Query first. Reports in 15 days. SASE.
Nonfiction: "News concerning personnel changes within companies; news concerning new plants for manufacture of brick, clay pipe, refractories, drain tile, face brick, glazed tile, lightweight clay aggregate products and abrasives; and news of new products, expansion and new building." Length: 1,500-2,000 words. Pays minimum $75/published page.
Photos: No additional payment for photos used with mss.
Fillers: "Items should concern only news of brick, clay pipe, refractory or abrasives plant operations and brick distributors. If news of personnel, should be only of top-level personnel. Not interested in items such as patio, motel, or home construction using brick; consumer oriented items; weddings or engagements of clay products people, unless major executives; obituaries, unless of major personnel; or items concerning floor or wall tile (only structural tile); of plastics, metal, concrete, bakelite, or similar products; items concerning people not directly involved in clay plant operation." Pays minimum $6 for "full-length published news item, depending on value of item and editor's discretion. Payment is only for items published in the magazine. No items sent in can be returned."

CERAMIC SCOPE, 3632 Ashworth North, Seattle WA 98103. (206)632-7222. Editor: Michael Scott. Monthly magazine covering hobby ceramics business. For "ceramic studio owners and teachers operating out of homes as well as storefronts, who have a love for ceramics but meager business education." Also read by distributors, dealers and supervisors of ceramic programs in institutions. Circ. 8,000. Pays on publication. Byline given unless it is a round-up story with any number of sources. Submit seasonal/holiday material 5 months in advance. Computer printout submissions acceptable. SASE. Reports in 2 weeks. Sample copy $1.
Nonfiction: "Articles on operating a small business specifically tailored to the ceramic hobby field; photo feature stories with in-depth information about business practices and methods that contribute to successful studio operation. We don't need articles dealing primarily with biographical material or how owner started in business."
Photos: State availability of photos or send photos with ms. Pays $5/4x5 or 5x7 glossy b&w print; $25-50/color contact sheets. Captions required.

GLASS DIGEST, 310 Madison Ave., New York NY 10017. (212)682-7681. Editor: Charles B. Cumpston. Monthly. Buys first rights only. Byline given "only industry people—not freelancers." Pays on publication "or before, if ms held too long." Will send a sample copy to a writer on request. Reports "as soon as possible." Enclose SASE for return of submissions.
Nonfiction: "Items about firms in glass distribution, personnel, plants, etc. Stories about outstanding jobs accomplished—volume of flat glass, storefronts, curtainwalls, auto glass, mirrors, windows (metal), glass doors; special uses and values; and who installed it. Stories about successful glass/metal distributors, dealers and glazing contractors—their methods, promotion work done, advertising and results." Length: 1,000-1,500 words. Pays 7¢/word, "usually more. No interest in bottles, glassware, containers, etc., but leaded and stained glass good."
Photos: B&w photos purchased with mss; "8x10 preferred." Pays $7.50, "usually more."
Tips: "Find a typical dealer case history about a firm operating in such a successful way that its methods can be duplicated by readers everywhere."

GLASS MAGAZINE, For the Architectural and Automotive Glass Industries, National Glass Association, Suite 302, 8200 Greensboro Drive, McLean VA 22102. (703)442-4890. Editor: Debbie Levy. 50% freelance written. A monthly magazine covering the architectural and automotive glass industries for members of the glass and architectural trades. Circ. 13,000. Pays on acceptance. Publishes ms an average of 3 months after acceptance. Byline given. Offers varying kill fee. Not copyrighted. Buys first rights only. Computer printut submissions acceptable; prefers letter-quality to dot-matrix. SASE. Reports in 1 week. Sample copy $4; free writer's guidelines.
Nonfiction: Interview/profile (of various glass businesses; profiles of industry people or glass business owners); and technical (about glazing processes). Buys 50 mss/year. Query with published clips. Length: 800 words minimum. Pays $200-1,000.
Photos: State availability of photos. Reviews b&w and color contact sheets. Pays $20-50 for b&w; $50-100 for color. Identification of subjects required. Buys one-time rights.
Tips: "We are looking to set up a network of freelancers who can cover assigned stories."

‡**GLASS NEWS**, (formerly *National Glass Budget*), LJV Corp., Box 7138, Pittsburgh PA 15213. (412)362-5136. Managing Editor: Liz Scott. 5% freelance written. Monthly newspaper covering glass manufacturing, and glass industry news for glass manufacturers, dealers and people involved in the making, buying and selling of glass items and products. Circ. 1,650. Pays on publication. Publishes ms an average of 3 months after acceptance. Makes work-for-hire assignments. Phone queries OK. Submit seasonal material 3 months in advance. Simultaneous and photocopied submissions OK. Electronic submissions OK via 300-1200 baud. Computer printout submissions acceptable; prefers letter-quality to dot-matrix. SASE. Reports in 1 month on queries; 2 months on mss. Free sample copy for 9x12 SAE and 40¢ postage.
Nonfiction: Historical (about glass manufacturers, trademarks and processes); how-to (concerning techniques of glass manufacturers); interview (with glass-related people); profile; new product (glass use or glass); and technical (glass manufacture or use). No glass dealer stories, and rarely glass crafting stories. Buys 3-5 mss/year. Query. Length: 500-10,000 words. Pays $50 minimum.
Photos: State availability of photos. Pays $25 minimum for 8x10 b&w glossy prints. Offers no additional payment for photos accepted with ms. Captions preferred; model release required. Buys one-time rights.
Fillers: Glass-related anecdotes, short humor, newsbreaks and puzzles. Buys 5 mss/year. Pays $15 minimum.
Tips: "Get to know a lot about glass, how it is made and new developments."

Building Interiors

MODERN FLOOR COVERINGS, U.S. Business Press, Inc., 11 W. 19th St., New York NY 10011. (212)953-0940. Editor: Michael Karol. 20% freelance written. Monthly tabloid featuring profit-making ideas on floor coverings, for the retail community. Circ. 28,000. Pays on acceptance. Publishes ms an average of 1 month after acceptance. Byline given. Buys first rights only. Makes work-for-hire assignments. Electronic submissions OK via IBM PC. Computer printout submissions acceptable; prefers letter-quality submissions. SASE. "Better to write first. Send resume and cover letter explaining your qualifications and business writing experience." Writer's guidelines for SAE with 3 first class stamps.
Nonfiction: Interview and features/profiles. Send complete ms. Length: 1,000-10,000 words. Pays $50-250. Sometimes pays the expenses of writers on assignment.
Tips: The most frequent mistake made by writers is that "articles are too general to relate to our audience—which is mainly the floor covering retailer/specialty store."

PAINTING AND WALLCOVERING CONTRACTOR, Finan Publishing, Inc., 130 W. Lockwood, St. Louis MO 63119. (314)961-6644. Under license from the Painting and Decorating Contractors of America, 7223 Lee Hwy., Falls Church VA 22046. (703)534-1201. Publisher and Editor: Tom Finan. Executive Editor: Robert D. Richardson. 50% freelance written. Official monthly publication of the PDCA. Circ. 15,000 "with roughly 85% of that number painting contractors/owners." Emphasis on key aspects of the painting and wallcovering contracting business, aiming for complete coverage of tools, techniques, materials, and business management. Freelance by assignment only. Send resume and sample of work. Pays on publication. Publishes ms an average of 1 month after acceptance. Buys first North American serial rights. Computer printout submissions acceptable; prefers letter-quality to dot-matrix.
Nonfiction: How-to, informational, some technical. Buys 20 mss/year. Pays $150-300. Sometimes pays the expenses of writers on assignment.
Photos: Purchased with accompanying ms. Captions required. Pays $15 for professional quality 8x10 glossy

b&w prints or color slides. Model release required.

Tips: "We're looking to build long term relations with freelancers around the country. If the writer has no sample clips of the painting/wallcovering contractors, send samples showing familiarity with other aspects of the construction industry. Follow up resume/sample with phone call in 2-3 weeks. The writer sometimes has a better chance of breaking in at our publication with short articles and fillers as we need to be sure the writer understands the market we publish for—sometimes we take a chance on those with inappropriate clips. The most frequent mistake made by writers in completing an article for us is misunderstanding the reader's needs, industry and jargon."

‡**WALLS & CEILINGS**, 14006 Ventura Blvd., Sherman Oaks CA 91423. (213)789-8733. Editor-in-Chief: Robert Welch. Managing Editor: Don Haley. 10% freelance written. For contractors involved in lathing and plastering, drywall, acoustics, fireproofing, curtain walls, movable partitions together with manufacturers, dealers, and architects. Monthly magazine; 32 pages. Circ. 11,000. Pays on publication. Buys first North American serial rights. Byline given. Phone queries OK. Submit seasonal/holiday material 3 months in advance of issue date. SASE. Reports in 3 weeks. Sample copy $2.

Nonfiction: How-to (drywall and plaster construction and business management); and interview. Buys 5 mss/year. Query. Length: 200-1,000 words. Pays $75 maximum.

Photos: State availability of photos with query. Pays $5 for 8x10 b&w prints. Captions required. Buys one-time rights.

Business Management

These publications are edited for owners of businesses and top-level business executives. They cover business trends and the general theory and practice of management. Publications that use similar material but have a less technical slant are listed in Business and Finance in the Consumer Publications section. Journals dealing with banking, investment, and financial management can be found in the Trade Finance category. Journals for middle management (including supervisors and office managers) appear in the Management and Supervision section. Those for industrial plant managers are listed under Industrial Operation and Management, and under the names of specific industries such as Machinery and Metal Trade. Publications for office supply store operators are included with the Office Environment and Equipment journals.

ASSOCIATION & SOCIETY MANAGER, Brentwood Publishing Corp., 1640 5th St., Santa Monica CA 90401. (213)395-0234. Editor: Helen N. Kass. 90% freelance written. Bimonthly magazine on management of nonprofit organizations. "Our magazine goes to association and society managers and covers convention and meeting planning, including site selection, price negotiation and program content, as well as 'how-to'—run an association, member benefits, computers, insurance, legislation and finance." Circ. 24,000. Pays by edited word on acceptance. Publishes ms an average of 6 months after acceptance. Byline given. Buys all rights. Submit seasonal/holiday material 6 months in advance. Computer printout submissions acceptable; prefers letter-quality to dot-matrix. SASE. Reports in 1 month. Free sample copy and writer's guidelines.

Nonfiction: How-to (plan conventions and meetings, run an association); interview/profile (of associations and association managers); technical (automation for association management functions); and travel (convention site evaluations, coordination with suppliers, group logistics). No "typical travelogue-type destination pieces or articles plugging a specific product." Buys 50 mss/year. Query with published clips. Length: 1,000-2,500 words. Pays 10-12¢/word.

Columns/Departments: Automation (computer information for association management) and Insurance (specific types to offer members; liability). Buys 20 mss/year. Query with published clips. Length: 1,000-2,000 words. Pays 10-12¢/word.

Tips: "Remember that trade journals are designed to help the professional do his/her job better. Writing must be concise and easy to read; article content must be specific rather than general, with a very narrow focus. We don't entertain our readers; we educate them. Study the publication for format. Follow 'how to' approach; keep to generic approach when discussing services."

COMMUNICATION BRIEFINGS, Encoders, Inc., 806 Westminster Blvd., Blackwood NJ 08012. (609)589-3503, 227-7371. Executive Editor: Frank Grazian. Managing Editor: Anthony Fulginiti. 15% freelance written. A monthly newsletter covering business communication and business management. "Most readers are in middle and upper management. They comprise public relations professionals, editors of company publications, marketing and advertising managers, fund raisers, directors of associations and foundations, school and college administrators, human resources professionals, and other middle managers who want to communicate better on the job." Circ. 13,000. Pays on acceptance. Publishes ms an average of 3 months after acceptance. Byline given sometimes on Bonus Items and on other items if idea originates with the writer. Offers 25% kill fee. Buys one-time rights. Submit seasonal/holiday material 2 months in advance. Previously published submissions OK, "but must be rewritten to conform to our style." Computer printout submissions acceptable; prefers letter-quality to dot-matrix. SASE. Reports in 1 month. Sample copy and writer's guidelines for #10 SAE and 2 first class stamps.

Nonfiction: "Most articles we buy are of the 'how-to' type. They consist of practical ideas, techniques and advice that readers can use to improve business communication and management. Areas covered: writing, speaking, listening, employee communication, human relations, public relations, interpersonal communication, persuasion, conducting meetings, advertising, marketing, fund raising, telephone techniques, teleconferencing, selling, improving publications, handling conflicts, negotiating, etc. Because half of our subscribers are in the nonprofit sector, articles that appeal to both profit and nonprofit organizations are given top priority." *Short Items*: Articles consisting of one or two brief tips that can stand alone. Length: 40-70 words. *Articles*: A collection of tips or ideas that offer a solution to a communication or management problem or that show a better way to communicate or manage. Examples: "How to produce slogans that work," "The wrong way to criticize employees," "Mistakes to avoid when leading a group discussion," and "5 ways to overcome writer's block." Length: 150-200 words. *Bonus Items:* In-depth pieces that probe one area of communication or management and cover it as thoroughly as possible. Examples: "Producing successful special events," "How to evaluate your newsletter," and "How to write to be understood." Length: 1,300 words. Buys 30-50 mss/year. Pays $15-35 for 40- to 250-word pieces; Bonus Items, $200. Sometimes pays the expenses of writers on assignment.

Tips: "Our readers are looking for specific and practical ideas and tips that will help them communicate better both within their organizations and with outside publics. Most ideas are rejected because they are too general or too elementary for our audience. Our style is down-to-earth and terse. We pack a lot of useful information into short articles. Our readers are busy executives and managers who want information dispatched quickly and without embroidery. We omit anecdotes, lengthy quotes and long-winded exposition. The writer has a better chance of breaking in at our publication with short articles and fillers since we buy only six major features (bonus items) a year. We prefer a query before seeing a manuscript. The most frequent mistakes made by writers in completing an article for us are that they do not master the style of our publication and do not understand our readers' needs."

‡**EMPLOYEE RELATIONS REPORT**, Business Communication Services, 2315 Park Ave., Box 671, Richmond VA 23206. (804)355-0214. Editor: Ann Black. 25% freelance written. Monthly newsletter on personnel and public relations. Reports on trends and issues in personnel management and their impact on organizational communication programs. Pays on acceptance. Publishes ms an average of 2 months after acceptance. Buys first North American serial rights. Photocopied submissions OK. SASE. Reports in 3 weeks. Free sample copy and writer's guidelines.

Nonfiction: Interview/profile and case studies based on interviews with company executives. Buys 12 mss/year. Query. Length: 200-1,000 words. Pays $20-100. Sometimes pays expenses of writers on assignment.

Columns/Departments: Employee Relations in Practice (case studies of company employee relations programs based on interviews with PR and personnel executives). Buys 12 mss/year. Query. Length: 500-1,000 words. Pays $50-75.

Fillers: Newsbreaks. Length: 50-200 words. Pays $5-20.

HARVARD BUSINESS REVIEW, Soldiers Field, Boston MA 02163. (617)495-6800. Editor: Kenneth R. Andrews. For top management in business and industry; younger managers who aspire to top management responsibilities; policymaking executives in government, policymakers in nonprofit organizations; and professional people interested in the viewpoint of business management. Published 6 times/year. Pays on publication. Byline given. Buys all rights. SASE. Reports in 6 weeks.

Nonfiction: Articles on business trends, techniques and problems. *"Harvard Business Review* seeks to inform executives about what is taking place in management, but it also wants to challenge them and stretch their thinking about the policies they make, how they make them and how they administer them. It does this by presenting articles that provide in-depth analyses of issues and problems in management and, wherever possible, guidelines for thinking out and working toward resolutions of these issues and problems." Length: 3,000-6,000 words. Pays $500 for full article.

IN BUSINESS, JG Press, Inc., Box 323, Emmaus PA 18049. (215)967-4135. Editor: Jerome Goldstein. Managing Editor: Ina Pincus. Bimonthly magazine covering small businesses, their management and new developments for small business owners or people thinking about starting out. Circ. 60,000. Pays on publication. Buys first North American serial rights. Submit seasonal material 3 months in advance. SASE. Reports in 6 weeks. Sample copy $3; free writer's guidelines.

Nonfiction: Expose (related to small business, trends and economic climate); how-to (advertise, market, handle publicity, finance, take inventory); profile (of an innovative small scale business); and new product (inventions and R&D by small businesses). "Keep how-tos in mind for feature articles; capture the personality of the business owner and the effect of that on the business operations." Buys 5 unsolicited mss/year. Recent article example: "Great Business Ideas That Work" (March 1984). Query with clips of published work. Length: 1,000-2,000 words. Pays $75-200.

Photos: State availability of photos. Pays $25-75. Reviews contact sheets. Captions preferred; model release required.

Tips: "Get a copy of the magazine and read it carefully so you can better understand the editorial focus. Send several specific article ideas on one topic, so we can sharpen the focus. Keep in mind that the reader will be looking for specifics and transferable information."

MAY TRENDS, 111 S. Washington St., Park Ridge IL 60068. (312)825-8806. Editor: John E. McArdle. 20% freelance written. For owners and managers of medium- and small-sized businesses, hospitals and nursing homes, trade associations, Better Business Bureaus, educational institutions and newspapers. Publication of George S. May International Company. 20% freelance written. Magazine published without charge 3 times a year; 28-30 pages. Circulation: 30,000. Buys all rights. Byline given. Buys 10-15 mss/year. Pays on acceptance. Returns rejected material immediately. Query or submit complete ms. Computer printout submissions acceptable; prefers letter quality to dot-matrix. SASE. Reports in 2 weeks. Will send free sample copy to writer on request for SAE with 2 first class stamps.

Nonfiction: "We prefer articles dealing with problems of specific industries (manufacturers, wholesalers, retailers, service businesses, small hospitals and nursing homes) where contact has been made with key executives whose comments regarding their problems may be quoted. We like problem solving articles, *not* success stories that laud an individual company." Focus is on marketing, economic and technological trends that have an impact on medium- and small-sized businesses, not on the "giants"; automobile dealers coping with existing dull markets; and contractors solving cost—inventory problems. Will consider material on successful business operations and merchandising techniques. Length: 2,000-3,000 words. Pays $150-250.

Tips: Query letter should tell "type of business and problems the article will deal with. We specialize in the problems of small (20-500 employees, $500,000-2,500,000 volume) businesses (manufacturing, wholesale, retail and service), plus medium and small health care facilities. We are now including nationally known writers in each issue—writers like the Vice Chairman of the Federal Reserve Bank, the U.S. Secretary of the Treasury; names like Walter Mondale and Murray Wiedenbaum; titles like the Chairman of the Joint Committee on Acreditation of Hospitals; and Canadian Minister of Export. This places extra pressure on freelance writers to submit very good articles. Frequent mistakes: 1) Writing for big business, rather than small, 2) using language that is too professional."

MEETING NEWS, Facts, News, Ideas For Convention and Meeting Planners Everywhere, Gralla Publications, 1515 Broadway, New York NY 10010. (212)869-1300. Editor/Co-Publisher: Peter Shure. Managing Editor: Margie Hazerjian. A monthly tabloid covering news, facts, ideas and methods in meeting planning; industry developments, legislation, new labor contracts, business practices and costs for meeting planners. Circ. 70,400. Pays on acceptance. Byline given. Buys all rights. Computer printout submissions acceptable; prefers letter-quality to dot-matrix. SASE. Reports in 1 month on queries; 2 weeks on mss. Free sample copy.

Nonfiction: Travel; and specifics on how a group improved its meetings or shows, saved money or drew more attendees. "Stress is on business articles—facts and figures." Seven special issues covering specific states as meeting destination—Florida/Colorado/Texas/California/New York/Arizona and also Canada. No general or philosophical pieces. Buys 25-50 mss/year. Query with published clips. Length: varies. Pays variable rates.

Tips: "Special issues focusing on certain states as meeting sites are most open. Best suggestion—query in writing, with clips, on any area of expertise about these states that would be of interest to people planning meetings there. Example: food/entertainment, specific sports, group activities, etc."

NATION'S BUSINESS, Chamber of Commerce of the United States, 1615 H St., NW, Washington DC 20062. (202)463-5650. Editor: Robert Gray. Managing Editor: Henry Altman. 10% freelance written. Monthly magazine of useful information for business people about business issues, managing a business, etc. A pro-business magazine. Audience includes owners and managers at businesses of all sizes, but predominantly at small businesses. Circ. 850,000. Pays on acceptance. Publishes ms an average of 3 months after acceptance. Byline given. Offers $100 or less kill fee. Buys all rights. Submit seasonal/holiday material 6 months in advance. Simultaneous queries, and simultaneous and photocopied submissions OK, but only for exclusive use upon acceptance. Computer printout submissions acceptable; prefers letter-quality to dot-matrix. SASE. Re-

ports in 2 months on queries; 3 months on mss. Sample copy $2.50; free writer's guidelines.
Nonfiction: How-to (run a business); interview/profile (business success stories; entrepreneurs who successfully implement ideas); and business trends stories. Buys 20 mss/year. Query. Length: 650-2,000 words. Pays $175 minimum. Sometimes pays expenses of writers on assignment.
Tips: "Read the magazine first, to understand its easy-to-read style. Slug and number each page of manuscript. Put a phone number as well as an address on first page of manuscript."

PUBLICATIONS LTD, Suite 700, 100 N. LaSalle St., Chicago IL 60602. (312)346-3822. Editor-in-Chief: Franklin E. Sabes. 5% freelance written. For management of small and middle class companies, middle management in larger companies and enterprises. Monthly magazines; produced as house organs. Pays on publication. Buys one-time rights and second (reprint) rights to material originally published elsewhere. Publishes ms an average of 9 months after acceptance. Byline given. Submit seasonal/holiday material 6 months in advance. Simultaneous, photocopied and previously published submissions OK. Computer printout submissions acceptable; prefers letter-quality to dot-matrix. SASE. Reports in 3 months. Free sample copy and writer's guidelines with SAE and 2 first class stamps; mention *Writer's Market* in request.
Nonfiction: How-to (articles that will be of interest to businessmen in the operation of their companies, and ideas that can be adapted and successfully used by others); interview; personal experience (business); profile; and travel. Buys 7 mss/issue. Submit complete ms. Length: 1,000-1,500 words. Pays $15-50.
Tips: "Most articles are reprints. The magazine distribution is limited since all magazines are internal or external house organs for various client/sponsors."

‡**RECORDS MANAGEMENT QUARTERLY**, Association of Records Managers and Administrators, Inc., Box 7070, Silver Spring MD 20907. Editor: Ira A. Penn, CRM, CSP. 10% freelance written. Quarterly magazine covering records and information management. Circ. 9,000. Pays on publication. Publishes ms an average of 6 months after acceptance. Byline given. Buys all rights. Photocopied, simultaneous and previously published submissions OK. Computer printout submissions acceptable. Reports in 1 month on mss. Sample copy $8; free writer's guidelines.
Nonfiction: Professional articles covering theory, case studies, surveys, etc. on any aspect of records and information management. Buys 24-32 mss/year. Send complete ms. Length: 1,500 words minimum. Pays $25-100. Pays a "stipend"; no contract.
Photos: Send photos with ms. Does not pay extra for photos. Prefers b&w prints. Captions required.
Tips: "A writer *must* know our magazine. Most work is written by practitioners in the field. We use very little freelance writing, but we have had some and it's been good."

VETERINARY PRACTICE MANAGEMENT, 13-30 Corporation, 505 Market St., Knoxville TN 37902. (615)521-0633. Group Editor: Thomas Lombardo. 90% freelance written. Semiannual magazine—"a business guide to small animal practitioners." Circ. 30,000. Pays on acceptance. Publishes ms an average 3 months after acceptance. Byline given. Offers $250 kill fee. Buys first serial rights to the same material. Simultaneous queries OK. Electronic submissions OK. Computer printout submissions acceptable; prefers letter-quality to dot-matrix. Free sample copy to experienced business writers.
Nonfiction: Elizabeth H. Dossett, associate editor. How-to, and successful business (practice) management techniques. No "how to milk more dollars out of your clients" articles. Buys 16 mss/year. Query with published clips. Pays $1,000-2,000. Pays expenses of writers on assignment.
Columns/Departments: Management Briefs, and In the Know. "Most items are written in-house, but we will consider ideas." Query with published clips.

Church Administration and Ministry

CHRISTIAN EDUCATION TODAY: For teachers, superintendents and other Christian educators, (formerly *Success: Christian Education Today*), Box 15337, Denver CO 80215. Editor: Edith Quinlan. National Research Editor: Kenneth O. Gangel. 50% freelance written. Quarterly magazine. Pays prior to publication. Publishes ms an average of 6 months after acceptance. Byline given. Buys simultaneous rights with magazines of different circulations. Computer printout submissions acceptable; prefers letter-quality to dot-matrix. SASE. Reports in 1 month. Sample copy and writer's guidelines for $1.
Nonfiction: Articles which provide information, instruction and/or inspiration to workers at every level of

Christian education. May be slanted to the general area or to specific age-group categories such as preschool, elementary, youth or adult. Simultaneous rights acceptable *only* if offered to magazines which do not have overlapping circulation. Length: 1,000-2,000 words. Payment commensurate with length and value of article to total magazine. Sometimes pays expenses of writers on assignment.

Tips: "Often a submitted short article is followed up with a suggestion or firm assignment for more work from that writer."

CHRISTIAN LEADERSHIP, Board of Christian Education of the Church of God, Box 2458, Anderson IN 46018-2458. (317)642-0257. Editor: Donald A. Courtney. 30% freelance written. A monthly magazine (except July and August) covering local church school Sunday school teachers, administrators, youth workers, choir leaders and other local church workers. Circ. 4,160. Pays on publication. Publishes ms an average of 5 months after acceptance. Byline given. Buys first rights and second serial (reprint) rights. Submit seasonal/holiday material 4 months in advance. Simultaneous queries OK. Computer printout submissions acceptable; prefers letter-quality printout to dot-matrix. SASE. Reports in 4 months. Free sample copy and writer's guidelines.

Nonfiction: General interest, how-to, inspirational, personal experience, guidance for carrying out programs for special days, and continuing ministries. No articles that are not specifically related to local church leadership. Buys 90 mss/year. Send complete ms, brief description of present interest in writing for church leaders, background and experience. Length: 300-1,800 words. Pays $5-30.

Photos: Send photos with ms. Pays $10 for 5x7 b&w prints.

Tips: "How-to articles related to Sunday school teaching, program development and personal teacher enrichment or growth, with illustrations of personal experience of the authors, are most open to freelancers."

CHURCH ADMINISTRATION, 127 9th Ave. N., Nashville TN 37234. (615)251-2060. Editor: George Clark. 15% freelance written. Monthly. For Southern Baptist pastors, staff and volunteer church leaders. Uses limited amount of freelance material. Pays on acceptance. Publishes ms an average of 9 months after acceptance. Byline given. Buys all rights. Computer printout submissions acceptable; prefers letter-quality to dot-matrix. SASE. Free sample copy and writer's guidelines for SAE with 2 first class stamps.

Nonfiction: "Ours is a journal for effectiveness in ministry, including church programming, the organizing, and staffing; administrative skills; church financing; church food services; church facilities; communication; and pastoral ministries and community needs." Length: 1,200-1,500 words. Pays 4¢/word.

Tips: "A beginning writer should first be acquainted with the organization and policy of Baptist churches and with the administrative needs of Southern Baptist churches. He/she should perhaps interview one or several SBC pastors or staff members, find out how they are handling a certain administrative problem such as 'enlisting volunteer workers' or 'sharing the administrative load with church staff or volunteer workers.' I suggest writers compile an article showing how *several* different administrators (or churches) handled the problem, perhaps giving meaningful quotes. Submit the completed manuscript, typed 54 characters to the line, for consideration. Freelancers must meet the need of a target audience, with a style and format in compliance."

CHURCH MANAGEMENT—THE CLERGY JOURNAL, Box 1625, Austin TX 78767. (512)327-8501. Editor: Manfred Holck Jr. 100% freelance written. Monthly (except June and December) magazine; 44 pages. For professional clergy and church business administrators. Circ. 20,000. Pays on publication. Byline given. Buys all rights. Offers 50% kill fee. Submit seasonal/holiday material 6 months in advance. Photocopied submissions OK. SASE. Reports in 2 months. Sample copy $2.50.

Nonfiction: How-to (be a more effective minister or administrator); and inspirational (seasonal sermons). No poetry, sermons or personal experiences. Buys 4 mss/issue. Submit complete ms. Length: 1,000-1,500 words. Pays $25-35.

Columns/Departments: Stewardship; Church Administration; Sermons; Tax Planning for Clergy; and Problem Solving. Buys 2/issue. Send complete ms. Length: 1,000-1,500 words. Pays $20-35. Open to suggestions for new columns/departments.

Tips: "Send completed mss. Avoid devotional, personal stories, and interviews. Readers want to know how to be more effective ministers."

CHURCH PROGRAMS FOR PRIMARIES, 1445 Boonville Ave., Springfield MO 65802. Editor: Sinda S. Zinn. Assistant Editor: Deanna Harris. 1% freelance written. Quarterly magazine for teachers of primary age children in a children's church, extended session, story hour, or Bible club setting." Circ. 4,500. Pays on acceptance. Publishes ms an average of 1 year after acceptance. Buys second serial (reprint) rights or first North American serial rights. Submit seasonal/holiday material 12-15 months in advance. Previously published submissions OK "if you tell us." Computer printout submissions acceptable. Reports in 6 weeks. SASE. Free sample copy and writer's guidelines for SAE with 2 first class stamps.

Nonfiction: How-to ("Get Seven Helpers Out of an Old Sock," worship through music, etc.); inspirational; and practical help for the teacher. "The spiritual must be an integral part of your material, and articles should reflect actual experience or observations related to working with 6 to 7 year olds. Articles should be oriented to a church programs setting. Some how-to articles are helpful." Buys 10-12 mss/year. Submit complete ms. Length: 500-1,200 words. Pays $15-36.

Photos: Purchased with mss about handcrafted items. Offers no additional payment for photos accepted with ms.

Tips: "Write requesting a sample of our publication and a copy of our writer's guidelines. Most of the publication is written on assignment. Frequently writers fail to write to the age level and follow instructions."

CHURCH TRAINING, 127 9th Ave. N., Nashville TN 37234. (615)251-2843. Publisher: The Sunday School Board of the Southern Baptist Convention. Editor: Richard B. Sims. 5% freelance written. Monthly. For all workers and leaders in the Church Training program of the Southern Baptist Convention. Circ. 30,000. Pays on acceptance. Publishes ms an average of 18 months after acceptance. Byline given. Buys all rights. Electronic submissions OK on ATEX, but requires hard copy also. Computer printout submissions acceptable; no dot-matrix. Reports in 6 weeks. SASE. Free sample copy and writer's guidelines.

Nonfiction: Articles that pertain to leadership training in the church; success stories that pertain to Church Training; associational articles. Informational, how-to's that pertain to Church Training. Buys 15 unsolicited mss/year. Query with rough outline. Length: 500-1,500 words. Pays 4¢/word.

Tips: "Write an article that reflects the writer's experience of personal growth through church training. Keep in mind the target audience: workers and leaders of Church Training organizations in churches of the Southern Baptist Convention. Often subjects and treatment are too general."

‡**THE CLERGY JOURNAL**, Church Management, Inc., Box 1625, Austin TX 78767. (512)327-8501. Editor: Manfred Holck, Jr. 20% freelance written. Monthly (except June and December) on religion. Readers are Prostentant clergy. Circ. 16,500. Pays on publication. Publishes ms an average of 4 months after acceptance. Byline given. Offers 50% kill fee. Buys all rights. Submit seasonal/holiday material 6 months in advance. Photocopied submissions OK. Computer printout submissions acceptable; prefers letter-quality to dot-matrix. Reports in 2 weeks on queries; 1 month on mss. Sample copy $2.50.

Nonfiction: How-to (be a more efficient and effective minister/administrator). No devotional, inspirational or sermons. Buys 20 mss/year. Query. Length: 500-1,500 words. Pays $25-40. Sometimes pays expenses of writers on assignment.

‡**INNOVATIONS FOR THE CHURCH LEADER**, David C. Cook Publishing Co., 850 N. Grove Ave., Elgin IL 60120. (312)741-2400. Senior Editor: Marlene D. LeFever. Managing Editor: Dave Jackson. 5% freelance written. Quarterly magazine. "*Innovations* provides church leaders with useful, timely information that can bring renewal to the church and the leaders who serve it. It also strives to bring together experts in full-time Christian and secular arenas to share ideas that can be firmly and creatively adapted to each church leader's unique situation." Estab. 1984. Circ. 35,000. Pays on acceptance. Publishes ms an average of 9 months after acceptance. Byline given depending on nature of article. Offers negotiable kill fee. Buys all rights; makes work-for-hire assignments. Submit seasonal/holiday material 1 year in advance. Photocopied submissions OK. Computer printout submissions acceptable. SASE. Reports in 1 month. Free sample copy and writer's guidelines.

Nonfiction: How-to implement innovative church ministries. Recent articles included "Congregations Mature Through Refugee Ministry" (featuring the work of five Free Methodist Churches) and "Men's Ministries Revitalized" (featuring the First Baptist Church of Canyon City, Colorado). No inspirational. Buys 60 mss/year (90% are assigned). Query. Length: 300-1,000 words. Pays 15¢/word.

Columns/Departments: First Person and Forum. Buys 50 mss/year. Send complete ms. Length: 150 words maximum. Pays $25 maximum.

Tips: "We are looking for articles about church ministries. Not only should each article feature innovative ministry, but it should also give guidelines and resources by which other churches could adapt and create a similar program specifically designed to meet their needs."

KEY TO CHRISTIAN EDUCATION, Standard Publishing, 8121 Hamilton Ave., Cincinnati OH 45231. (513)931-4050. Editor-in-Chief: Virginia Beddow. 50% freelance written. Quarterly magazine; 48 pages. For "church leaders of all ages, Sunday school teachers and superintendents, ministers, Christian education professors and youth workers." Circ. 70,000. Pays on acceptance. Publishes ms an average of 2 years after acceptance. Byline given. Buys first North American serial rights. Submit seasonal/holiday material 15 months in advance. Photocopied and previously published submissions OK. Computer printout submissions acceptable; prefers letter-quality to dot-matrix. SASE. Reports in 1 month. Free sample copy and writer's guidelines.

Nonfiction: How-to (programs and projects for Christian education); informational; interview; opinion; and personal experience. Buys 10 mss/issue. Query or submit complete ms. Length: 700-2,000 words. Pays $20-60.

Photos: Purchased with accompanying ms. Submit prints. Pays $5-25 for any size glossy finish b&w prints. Total price for ms includes payment for photos. Model release required.

Fillers: Purchases short ideas on "this is how we did it" articles. Buys 10 mss/issue. Submit complete ms.

Length: 50-250 words. Pays $5-10.
Tips: "Write for guidelines, sample issue and themes. Send 9x12 SASE. Then write an article that fits one of the themes following the guidelines. Be practical. If the article pertains to a specific age group, address the article to that department editor."

‡**MINISTRIES: The Magazine for Christian Leaders**, Strang Communications Co., 190 N. Westmonte Dr., Altamonte Springs FL 32714. (305)869-5005. Editor: Stephen Strang. 80% freelance written. Quarterly magazine covering Pentecostal/Charismatics ministries. Includes practical articles to help church leaders. Circ. 24,000. Pays on publication. Publishes ms an average of 6 months after acceptance. Byline given. Buys all rights. Submit seasonal/holiday material 6 months in advance. Photocopied submissions OK. Computer printout submissions acceptable; prefers letter-quality to dot-matrix. SASE. Reports in 1 month. Sample copy $3, SAE and 1 first class stamp; writer's guidelines for SAE and 39¢ postage.
Nonfiction: Book excerpts, how-to (for pastors), and interview/profile. Writer's must have personal experience in areas they are writing about. Buys 80 mss/year. Query or send complete ms. Length: 1,700-6,000 words. Pays $50-200. Sometimes pays expenses of writers on assignment.
Photos: Carolyn Kiphuth, photo editor.
Columns/Departments: E.S. Caldwell, column/department editor. For Women Only—for women in ministry; Youthful—for youth pastors; Musical Notes—for music ministers; Fire in My Bones—views and opinions; and Book Reviews. Buys 12 mss/year. Send complete ms. Length: 1,000-1,500 words. Pays $50 minimum.
Tips: "Columns are the best place to break in. We need practical, proven ideas with both negative and positive anecdotes. We have a specialized audience—pastors and leaders of Pentecostal and Charismatic churches. It is unlikely that persons not fully understanding this audience would be able to provide appropriate manuscripts."

‡**THE PREACHER'S MAGAZINE**, Nazarene Publishing House, 6401 The Paseo, Kansas City MO 64131. (816)333-7000. Editor: Wesley Tracy. Assistant Editor: Mark D. Marvin. Quarterly magazine of seasonal/miscellaneous articles. "A resource for ministers; Wesleyan-Arminian in theological persuasion." Circ. 17,000. Pays on acceptance. Byline given. Buys first serial rights. Submit seasonal/holiday material 9 months in advance. Simultaneous queries and photocopied submissions OK. SASE. Free sample copy and writer's guidelines.
Nonfiction: How-to, humor, inspirational, opinion and personal experience, all relating to aspects of ministry. No articles that present problems without also presenting answers to them; things not relating to pastoral ministry. Buys 48 mss/year. Send complete ms. Length: 700-2,500 words. Pays $3\frac{1}{2}¢/word.
Photos: Send photos with ms. Reviews 35mm color transparencies and 35mm b&w prints. Pays $25-35. Model release and identification of subjects required. Buys one-time rights.
Columns/Departments: Today's Books for Today's Preacher—book reviews. Buys 24 mss/year. Send complete ms. Length: 300-400 words. Pays $7.50.
Fillers: Anecdotes and short humor. Buys 10/year. Length: 400 words maximum. Pays $3\frac{1}{2}¢/word.
Tips: "Our magazine is a highly specialized publication aimed at the minister. Our goal is to assist, by both scholarly and practical articles, the modern-day minister in applying Biblical theological truths."

THE PRIEST, Our Sunday Visitor, Inc., 200 Noll Plaza, Huntington IN 46750. (219)356-8400. Editor: Father Vincent J. Giese. Associate Editor: Robert A. Willems. 50% freelance written. Monthly magazine (July-August combined issue) covering the priesthood. "Our magazine is basically for priests, although much is now being accepted from laypeople and religious." Circ. 10,050. Pays on acceptance. Publishes ms an average of 5 months after acceptance. Byline given. Not copyrighted. Buys one-time rights. Submit seasonal/holiday material 5 months in advance. Computer printout submissions acceptable; no dot-matrix. SASE. Reports in 1 week on queries; 2 weeks on mss. Free sample copy.
Nonfiction: How-to, inspirational, interview/profile, opinion, personal experience and technical. "Material must deal with the day-to-day problems of the priest in his work in the parish. Don't pad articles." Buys 60 mss/year. Send complete ms. Length: 500-1,500 words. Pays $25-100.
Tips: "Writers frequently don't know the market—priests, pastors and deacons.

‡**YOUR CHURCH**, The Religious Publishing Co., 198 Allendale Rd., King of Prussia PA 19406. (215)265-9400. Editor: Phyllis Mather Rice. 50% freelance written. Bimonthly magazine for ministers and churches "providing practical, how-to articles on every aspect of administering and leading church congregations." Circ. 186,000. Pays on publication. Publishes ms an average of 1 year after acceptance. Byline given. Offers 50% kill fee. Buys one-time rights. Submit seasonal/holiday material 1 year in advance. Simultaneous queries (if informed) and previously published submissions OK. Computer printout submissions acceptable; no dot-matrix. SASE. Reports in 2 months on queries; 3 months on mss. Sample copy $1.50, 9x11 SAE, and 73¢ postage; writer's guidelines for #10 SAE and 22¢ postage.
Nonfiction: How-to (administer and lead church congregations); new product (that churches can use); personal experience (working with congregations); and technical (building churches). No sermons or dissertation-type articles. Buys 60 mss/year. Query or send complete ms. Length: 1,200-3,000 words. Pays $6/typewritten

ms page—$100 total maximum.
Tips: "Freelancers can best break in with articles that have *practical* value to church pastors. We are interested in how-to, readable, interesting copy that flows."

‡**THE YOUTH LEADER**, 1445 Boonville Ave., Springfield MO 65802. Editor: Terry King. Monthly. For church leaders of teenagers (other than in Sunday school): staff, volunteer, appointed lay workers, adult sponsors, counselors, youth ministers. Evangelical Christianity. Secular and sacred holiday emphasis. Circ. 4,500. Pays on acceptance. Byline given. Buys any rights; pays accordingly. Submit seasonal material 4 months in advance. Photocopied submissions OK. SASE. Reports in 6 weeks. Free sample copy.
Nonfiction: How-to articles (e.g., "Basics of Backpacking," "Handling the Bus Trip," "Ten Ways to Better Understand Youth"); skits and role-plays; scripture choruses, ideas for youth services, projects, fund raising and socials; Bible studies and Bible study know-how; discussion starters; and simulation games and activities. Avoid cliches (especially religious ones); practical rather than inspirational emphasis. Buys 35-40 mss/year. Submit complete ms. Length: 100-2,000 words. Pays 3-5¢/word.
Tips: "Lead time is three and a half to four months; writing in summer, think fall, etc. Because the title of our publication is *The Youth Leader*, we get submissions for workers with children as well as teens. Because writers are more familiar with Sunday school than any other phase of church work, they write for Sunday school workers. We use *neither type of submission*."

Clothing

The emphasis must be on current or upcoming styles. Many trade journals work to eliminate misconceptions in their respective industry. *Western and English Fashion*'s editor, for instance, looks for material "that appeals to our trade and yet lets the public know that Western clothing, etc., is not just for cowboys—that it can be fashionable."

APPAREL INDUSTRY MAGAZINE, Shore Publishing, Suite 300-South, 180 Allen Rd., Atlanta GA 30328. Editor: Karen Schaffner. Managing Editor: Ray Henderson. 30% freelance written. Monthly magazine; 64-150 pages. For executive management in apparel companies with interests in equipment, fabrics, licensing, distribution, finance, management and training. Circ. 18,700. Pays on publication. Publishes ms an average of 4 months after acceptance. Byline given. Buys first serial rights. Will consider legible photocopied submissions. Computer printout submissions acceptable. SASE. Reports in 1 month. Sample copy $3; writer's guidelines for SAE with 1 first class stamp.
Nonfiction: Articles dealing with equipment, manufacturing techniques, training, finance, licensing, fabrics, quality control, etc., related to the industry. "Use concise, precise language that is easy to read and understand. In other words, because the subjects are often technical, keep the language comprehensible. Material must be precisely related to the apparel industry. We are not a retail or fashion magazine." Informational, interview, profile, successful business operations and technical articles. Buys 30mss/year. Query. Length: 3,000 words maximum. Pays 15¢/word. Sometimes pays expenses of writers on assignment.
Photos: Pays $5/photo with ms.
Tips: "Frequently articles are too general due to lack of industry- specific knowledge by the writer."

BODY FASHIONS/INTIMATE APPAREL, Harcourt Brace Jovanovich Publications, 545 5th Ave., New York NY 10017. (212)888-4364. Editor-in-Chief: Jill Gerson. 30% freelance written. Monthly tabloid insert, plus 10 regional market issues called *Market Maker*, 24 pages minimum. For merchandise managers and buyers of store products, manufacturers and suppliers to the trade, emphasizing information about men's and women's hosiery: women's undergarments, lingerie, sleepwear, robes, hosiery and leisurewear. Circ. 13,500. Pays on publication. Publishes ms an average of 1 month after acceptance. Buys all rights. Submit seasonal/holiday material 2 months in advance. Computer printout submissions acceptable. SASE. Reports in 1 month.
Columns/Departments: New Image (discussions of renovations of *Body Fashions/Intimate Apparel* department); Creative Retailing (deals with successful retail promotions); and Ad Ideas (descriptions of successful advertising campaigns). Buys 6 features/year. Query. Length: 500-2,500 words. Pays 15¢/word as edited. Sometimes pays expenses of writers on assignment. Open to suggestions for new columns and departments.
Photos: B&w (5x7) photos purchased without mss. Send contact sheet, prints or negatives. Pays $5-25. Captions and model release required.

FOOTWEAR FOCUS, National Shoe Retailers Association, 200 Madison Ave., Room 1409, New York NY 10016. (212)686-7520. Managing Editor: Anisa Mycak. Magazine published 6 times/year about shoes for shoe store owners, buyers and managers from all over the U.S. "Our publication features articles pertaining to new methods, creative ideas and reliable information to help them better operate their businesses." Circ. 20,000. Average issue includes 5 articles/4 departments. Pays on acceptance. Byline given. Makes work-for-hire assignments. SASE. Reports in 1 month. Free sample copy and writer's guidelines.

Nonfiction: Contact: Editor. *Footwear Focus.* Interview (with buyers and store owners); how-to (advertise, display, create interiors, do inventory accounting, and manage data processing systems); new product (shoes and accessories); and technical (new methods of shoe manufacturing). "We want feature articles that are personality interviews or how-to articles. They must be closely related to the shoe industry. All how-tos must pertain to some aspect of shoe retailing such as developing advertising plans, interior displays, setting up an open-to-buy or fashion merchandising." No generic-type articles that can be applied to any industry. No articles on salesmanship, management training, generic items or computers. Buys 5 mss/year. Query with resume and published clips. "We do not accept manuscripts." Length: 900-1,500 words.

Tips: "Freelancers must have knowledge, experience or background in fashion merchandising and retailing, preferably in shoes. Other areas open are advertising and promotion, customer services, and buying and inventory control. We prefer article suggestions to actual manuscripts, as most freelance writing is assigned according to the editor's choice of subject and topic areas. Those writers interested in doing personal interviews and covering regional events in the shoe industry have the best opportunity, since New York City staff writers can cover only local events."

TEXTILE WORLD, Suite 420, 4170 Ashford, Dunwoody Rd. NE, Atlanta GA 30319. Editor-in-Chief: Laurence A. Christiansen. Pays on acceptance. Monthly. Buys all rights. SASE.

Nonfiction: Uses articles covering textile management methods, manufacturing and marketing techniques, new equipment, details about new and modernized mills, etc., but avoids elementary, historical or generally well-known material.

Photos: Photos purchased with accompanying ms with no additional payment, or purchased on assignment.

WESTERN OUTFITTER, 5314 Bingle Rd., Houston TX 77092. (713)688-8811. Editor/Manager: Anne DeRuyter. Assistant Editor: Margaret S. Brenner. Monthly magazine for retailers of Western/English apparel, tack and horse supplies. Circ. 16,000. Pays on acceptance. Buys all rights. Assigned stories only. Free sample copy and writer/photographer guidelines for $1 in postage.

Nonfiction: Interviews with outstanding retailers. "How do they promote? What type of advertising works best for them? What retailing philosophies have made them successful? What problem have they faced and solved? We also need current information on what's new in horse supplies and horse health products. Writing should be informed and business-like." No general pieces. Length: 750-1500 words. Pays $75-200, depending upon quality of article and amount of research involved. "If you have an outstanding Western/English retailer or farm/ranch dealer in your area, determine the key to their success and send us a query." Mss purchased with or without photos. Query.

Photos: "We welcome photo features on effective store displays or successful store pormotions." Query with published clips. Photos must be uncluttered and have strong angles. No static photos or uninteresting mug-shots. Reviews b&w contact sheets. Color used only if it's superior. Pays $50-150.

Tips: "Our magazine is small, but our content and illustrations are top notch. Querying is a must. Presently we need informed pieces on tack and horse care subjects."

Coin-Operated Machines

AMERICAN COIN-OP, 500 N. Dearborn St., Chicago IL 60610. (312)337-7700. Editor: Ben Russell. 30% freelance written. Monthly magazine; 42 pages. For owners of coin-operated laundry and dry cleaning stores. Circ. 19,000. Rights purchased vary with author and material but are exclusive to the field. Pays two weeks prior to publication. Publishes ms an average of 4 months after acceptance. Byline given for frequent contributors. Computer printout submissions acceptable; prefers letter-quality to dot-matrix. SASE. Reports as soon as possible; usually in 2 weeks. Free sample copy.

Nonfiction: "We emphasize store operation and use features on industry topics: utility use and conservation, maintenance, store management, customer service and advertising. A case study should emphasize how the store operator accomplished whatever he did—in a way that the reader can apply to his own operation. Manuscript should have a no-nonsense, business-like approach." Uses informational, how-to, interview, profile,

think pieces and successful business operations articles. Length: 500-3,000 words.
Photos: Pays 6¢/word minimum. Pays $6 minimum for 8x10 b&w glossy photos purchased with mss. (Contact sheets with negatives preferred.)
Fillers: Newsbreaks and clippings. Length: open. Pays $5 minimum.
Tips: "Query about subjects of current interest. Be observant of coin-operated laundries—how they are designed and equipped, how they serve customers and how (if) they advertise and promote their services. Most general articles are turned down because they are not aimed well enough at audience. Most case histories are turned down because of lack of practical purpose (nothing new or worth reporting). A frequent mistake is failure to follow up on an interesting point made by the interviewee—probably due to lack of knowledge about the industry."

ELECTRONIC SERVICING & TECHNOLOGY, Intertec Publishing Corp., Box 12901, Overland Park KS 66212. (913)888-4664. Editor: Conrad Persson. Managing Editor: Rhonda Wickham. 90% freelance written. Monthly magazine for professional servicers and electronic enthusiasts who are interested in buying, building, installing and repairing home entertainment electronic equipment (audio, video, microcomputers, electronic games, etc.) Circ. 60,000. Pays on publication. Publishes ms an average of 6 months after acceptance. Byline given. Buys all rights. Submit seasonal/holiday material 4 months in advance. Simultaneous queries OK. Computer printout submissions acceptable. Reports in 2 weeks on queries; 1 month on mss. Free sample copy and writer's guidelines.
Nonfiction: How-to (service, build, install and repair home entertainment electronic equipment); personal experience (troubleshooting); and technical (home entertainment electronic equipment; electronic testing and servicing equipment). "Explain the techniques used carefully so that even hobbyists can understand a how-to article." Buys 36 mss/year. Send complete ms. Length: 1,500 words minimum. Pays $100-200.
Photos: Send photos with ms. Reviews color and b&w transparencies and b&w prints. Captions and identification of subjects required. Buys all rights. Payment included in total ms package.
Columns/Departments: Marge Riggin, column/department editor. Troubleshooting Tips. Buys 12 mss/year. Send complete ms. Length: open. Pays $30-40.
Tips: "Our readers want nuts-and-bolts type of information on electronics."

PLAY METER MAGAZINE, Skybird Publishing Co., Inc., Box 24970. New Orleans LA 70184. Publisher: Carol Lally. 25% freelance written. Semimonthly Trade magazine, 100 pages, for owners/operators of coin-operated amusement machine companies, e.g., pinball machines, video games, arcade pieces, jukeboxes, etc. Circ. 7,500. Pays on publication. Publishes ms an average of 2 months after acceptance. Byline given. Buys all rights. Submit seasonal/holiday material 2 months in advance. Photocopied and previously published submissions OK. SASE. Query answered in 2 months. Sample copy $2; free writer's guidelines.
Nonfiction: How-to (get better locations for machines, promote tournaments, evaluate profitability of route, etc.); interview (with industry leaders); new product (if practical for industry, not interested in vending machines); unusual arcades (game rooms); and photo features (with some copy). "No 'puff' or 'plug' pieces about new manufacturers. Our readers want to read about how they can make more money from their machines, how they can get better tax breaks, commissions, etc. Also no stories about *playing* pinball or video games. Our readers don't play the games per se; they buy the machines and make money from them." Buys 48 mss/year. Submit complete ms. Length: 250-3,000 words. Pays $30-215. Very rarely pays expenses of writers on assignment.
Photos: "The photography should have news value. We don't want 'stand 'em up-shoot 'em down' group shots." Pays $15 minimum for 5x7 or 8x10 b&w prints. Captions preferred. Buys all rights. Art returned on request.
Tips: "We need feature articles more than small news items or features. Query first."

VENDING TIMES, 545 8th. Avenue, New York NY 10018. Editor: Arthur E. Yohalem. Monthly. For operators of vending machines. Circ. 14,700. Pays on publication. Buys all rights. "We will discuss in detail the story requirements with the writer." SASE.
Nonfiction: Feature articles and news stories about vending operations; practical and important aspects of the business. "We are always willing to pay for good material." Query.

Confectionery and Snack Foods

CANDY INDUSTRY, HBJ Publications, 7500 Old Oak Blvd., Cleveland OH 44130. (216)243-8100. Editor: Pat Magee. 5% freelance written. Monthly. For confectionery manufacturers. Publishes ms an average of 4 months after acceptance. Buys first serial rights. Computer printout submissions acceptable; prefers letter-quality to dot-matrix. SASE. Reports in 2 weeks.
Nonfiction: "Feature articles of interest to large scale candy manufacturers that deal with activities in the fields of production, packaging (including package design), merchandising; and financial news (sales figures, profits, earnings), advertising campaigns in all media, and promotional methods used to increase the sale or distribution of candy." Length: 1,000-1,250 words. Pays 15¢/word; "special rates on assignments."
Photos: "Good quality glossies with complete and accurate captions, in sizes not smaller than 5x7." Pays $5; $20 for color.
Fillers: "Short news stories about the trade and anything related to candy and snacks." Pays 5¢/word; $1 for clippings.

PACIFIC BAKERS NEWS, 16 Peterson Pl., Walnut Creek CA 94595. (415)932-1256. Publisher: C.W. Soward. 50% freelance written. Monthly business newsletter for commercial bakeries in the western states. Pays on publication. No byline given; uses only one-paragraph news items.
Nonfiction: Uses bakery business reports and news about bakers. Buys only brief "boiled-down news items about bakers and bakeries operating only in Alaska, Hawaii, Pacific Coast and Rocky Mountain states. We welcome clippings. We need monthly news reports and clippings about the baking industry and the donut business. No pictures, jokes, poetry or cartoons." Length: 10-200 words. Pays 6¢/word for clips and news used.

Construction and Contracting

Builders, architects, and contractors learn the latest news of their trade in these publications. Journals aimed at architects are included in the Art, Design, and Collectibles section. Those for specialists in the interior aspects of construction are listed under Building Interiors. Also of interest would be the markets in the Brick, Glass, and Ceramics section.

ARCHITECTURAL METALS, National Association of Architectural Metal Manufacturers, 221 N. LaSalle St., Chicago IL 60601. (312)346-1600. Editor: Donald K. Doherty. Editorial Director: August L. Sisco. 10% freelance written. Magazine published winter, spring, summer, and fall covering architectural metal applications for architects, specifiers and other engineers involved in using architectural metal products. Circ. 20,000. Pays on acceptance. Publishes ms an average of 3 months after acceptance. Byline given. Buys first North American serial rights and simultaneous rights on work-for-hire assignments. Simultaneous queries, and simultaneous, photocopied, and previously published submissions OK. Computer printout submissions acceptable; no dot-matrix. Reports in 2 weeks on queries; 1 month on mss. Free sample copy and writer's guidelines.
Nonfiction: "No articles that are too general." Number of mss bought/year "depends on need." Query with published clips or send complete ms. Phone queries preferred. Length: 1,000 words minimum. Pays $150-400/article.
Photos: Send photos with ms. Payment negotiable for quality b&w prints. Captions required.
Tips: "Have a knowledge of architectural metals and write clearly. Applications of hollow metal doors and frames/metal flagpoles/metal bar grating/architectural metal products are all open. Technical details are a must. We enjoy obtaining new sources of quality material from freelancers, but it's difficult to find writers knowledgeable about our industry."

AUTOMATION IN HOUSING & MANUFACTURED HOME DEALER, (formerly *Automation in Housing & Systems Building News*), CMN Associates, Inc., Box 120, Carpinteria CA 93013. (805)684-7659. Editor-in-Chief: Don Carlson. 15% freelance written. Monthly magazine; 88 pages. Specializes in management for industrialized (manufactured) housing and volume home builders. Circ. 25,000. Pays on acceptance. Publishes ms an average of 3 months after acceptance. Buys first North American serial rights. Phone queries OK. Computer printout submissions acceptable; no dot-matrix. SASE. Reports in 2 weeks. Free sample copy and writer's guidelines.

Nonfiction: Case history articles on successful home building companies which may be 1) production (big volume) home builders; 2) mobile home manufacturers; 3) modular home manufacturers; 4) prefabricated home manufacturers; or 5) house component manufacturers. Also uses interviews, photo features and technical articles. "No architect or plan 'dreams'. Housing projects must be built or under construction." Buys 15 mss/year. Query. Length: 500-1,000 words maximum. Pays $300 minimum.

Photos: Purchased with accompanying ms. Query. No additional payment for 4x5, 5x7 or 8x10 b&w glossies or 35mm or larger color transparencies (35mm preferred). Captions required.

Tips: "Stories often are too long, too loose; we prefer 500 to 750 words. We prefer a phone query on feature articles. If accepted on query, usually an article will not be rejected later."

BUILDER, The Magazine of the National Association of Home Builders, Hanley-Wood, Inc., Suite 475, 655 15th St. NW, Washington DC 20005. (202)737-0717. Editor: Frank Anton. Managing Editor: Noreen Welle. 10% freelance written. Monthly magazine of the home building and light commercial industry for those involved with the industry. Circ. 187,000. Pays 60 days after invoice. Publishes ms an average of 2 months after acceptance. Byline given. Offers negotiable kill fee. Buys first North American serial rights. Submit seasonal/holiday material 3 months in advance. Simultaneous queries and photocopied submissions OK. Computer printout submissions acceptable. Reports in 2 weeks on queries; 1 month on mss. Free sample copy and writer's guidelines.

Nonfiction: New product, technical and business needs. No consumer-oriented material. Buys 10 mss/year. Query with published clips. Length: 500-1,200 words. Pays $100-400.

Photos: Send photos with query or ms. Reviews 4x5 color transparencies (slides) and 8x10 color prints. Identification of subjects required. Buys one-time rights.

BUILDER INSIDER, Box 191125, Dallas TX 75219-1125. (214)651-9994. Editor: Mike Anderson. Monthly, covering the entire north Texas building industry for builders, architects, contractors, remodelers and homeowners. Circ. 8,000. Photocopied submissions OK. SASE. Free sample copy.

Nonfiction: "What is current in the building industry" is the approach. Wants "advertising, business builders, new building products, building projects being developed and helpful building hints localized to the Southwest and particularly to north Texas." Submit complete ms. Length: 100-900 words. Pays $30-50.

CATERPILLAR WORLD, Caterpillar Tractor Co., 100 NE Adams AB1470, Peoria IL 61629. (309)675-5829. Editor: Tom Biederbeck. 10% freelance written. Quarterly magazine; 24-32 pages. Emphasizes "anything of interest about Caterpillar people, plants or products. The magazine is distributed to 75,000 Caterpillar people and friends worldwide. It's printed in French and English. Readers' ages, interests and education vary all over the map." Pays on acceptance. Publishes ms an average of 6 months after acceptance. Buys first serial rights and second serial (reprint) rights. Computer printout submissions acceptable. First submission is always on speculation. Free sample copy.

Nonfiction: "Everything should have a Caterpillar tie. It doesn't have to be strong but it has to be there." How-to (buy one piece of equipment and become a millionaire, etc.); general interest (anything that may be of interest to Cat people worldwide); humor (it's hard to find something humorous yet interesting to an international audience; we'd like to see it, however); interview (with any appropriate person: contractor, operator, legislator, etc.); products (large projects using Cat equipment; must have human interest); personal experience (would be interesting to hear from an equipment operator/writer); photo feature (on anything of interest to Cat people; should feature people as well as product); and profile (of Cat equipment users, etc.). Prints occasional lifestyle and health articles (but must apply to international audience). Written approval by the subjects of the article is a must. Query. Length: "What ever the story is worth."

Photos: "The only articles we accept without photos are those obviously illustrated by artwork." State availability of photos in query. Captions and model release required.

Tips: "The best way to get story ideas is to stop in at local Cat dealers and ask about big sales, events, etc."

CONSTRUCTION DIGEST, Construction Digest, Inc., Box 603, Indianapolis IN 46206. (317)634-7374. Senior Editor: Art Graham. Editor: Michael Brown. 10% freelance written. Magazine. "*CD* serves the engineered construction and public works industries in Illinois, Indiana, Ohio, Kentucky and eastern Missouri. It features bids asked, awards, planned work, job photo feature articles, industry trends, legislation, etc." Circ. 14,087. Pays on publication. Publishes ms an average of 2 months after acceptance. Byline given depending on nature of article. Not copyrighted. Makes work-for-hire assignments. Computer printout submissions acceptable; prefers letter-quality to dot-matrix. Reports in 2 weeks. Free sample copy and writer's guidelines.

Nonfiction: How-to, new product, photo feature, technical, and "nuts and bolts" construction jobsite features. No personality/company profiles. Buys 4 mss/year. Send complete ms. Length: 175 typewritten lines, 35 character count, no maximum. Pays $75/published page.

Tips: "We are putting more emphasis on topical features—market trends, technology applied to construction, legislation, etc.—rather than traditional 'nuts & bolts' articles."

CONSTRUCTION EQUIPMENT OPERATION AND MAINTENANCE, Box 1689, Cedar Rapids IA 52406. (319)366-1597. Editor: C.K. Parks. 15% freelance written. Bimonthly. For users of heavy construction equipment. Pays on acceptance. Buys all rights. SASE. Reports in 1 month.
Nonfiction: Articles on selection, use, operation or maintenance of construction equipment; articles and features on the construction industry in general; and job safety articles. Length: 1,000-2,000 words. Also buys a limited number of job stories with photos and feature articles on individual contractors in certain areas of U.S. and Canada. Query. Length varies. Pays $50-200.

CONSTRUCTION SPECIFIER, 601 Madison St., Alexandria VA 22314. (703)684-0200. Editor: Kimberly C. Smith. 50% freelance written. Monthly professional society magazine for architects, engineers, specification writers and project managers. Monthly. Circ. 16,000. Pays on publication. Deadline: 60 days preceding publication on the 1st of each month. Buys North American serial rights. Computer printout submissions acceptable; prefers letter-quality to dot-matrix. "Call or write first." SASE. Model release, author copyright transferral requested. Reports in 3 weeks. Free sample copy.
Nonfiction: Articles on selection and specification of products, materials, practices and methods used in commercial (nonresidential) construction projects, specifications as related to construction design, plus legal and management subjects. Query. Length: 5,000 words maximum. Pays 10¢/published word, plus art.
Photos: Photos desirable in consideration for publication; line art, sketches, diagrams, charts and graphs also desired. Full color transparencies may be used. 8x10 glossies, 3¼ slides preferred. Payment negotiable.
Tips: "We will get bigger and thus will need good technical articles."

‡**CONTRACTORS MARKET CENTER**, Randall Publishing Co., Box 2029, Tuscaloosa AL 35403. (205)349-2990. Editor: Claude Duncan. 25-50% freelance written. Weekly tabloid on heavy-equipment construction industry. "Our readers are contractors, including road contractors, who utilize heavy equipment. We write positive, upbeat stories about their work and their personal success. We like personal stories related to large construction projects." Circ. 18,000. Pays on acceptance. Publishes ms an average of 1 month after acceptance. Byline given. Offers 100% kill fee. Not copyrighted. Submit seasonal/holiday material 1 month in advance. Simultaneous and previously published (updated) submissions OK. Computer printout submissions acceptable; prefers letter-quality to dot-matrix. Reports in 2 weeks. Free sample copy and writer's guidelines.
Nonfiction: General interest (with construction angle); historical/nostalgic (with construction angle); humor (with construction angle); interview/profile (with contractors); personal experience (with construction angle); technical (re: heavy equipment); and business stories related to contractors. Buys 100 mss/year. Send complete ms. Length: 250-750 words. Pays $10-50. Pays expenses of writers on assignment.
Photos: Send photos with ms. Reviews b&w prints; commercially processed OK if sharp. Pays $5. Identification of subjects required.
Tips: "Contractors like to read about other contractors and people with whom they are in frequent contact—suppliers, government regulators, and public works devolopments. We're primarily looking for people-oriented features. Nothing is too local if it's interesting. Submitting art with copy gives definite edge."

FENCE INDUSTRY, 6255 Barfield Rd., Atlanta GA 30328. (404)256-9800. Editor/Associate Publisher: Bill Coker. 60% freelance written. Monthly magazine; 54-80 pages. For retailers and installers of fencing materials. Circ. 15,000. Pays on publication. Publishes ms an average of 2 months after acceptance. Buys all rights. Electronic submissions OK if floppy disks compatible with Rainbow or Digital DECmate. Computer printout submissions acceptable. Reports in 3 months. Free sample copy.
Nonfiction: Case histories, as well as articles on fencing for highways, pools, farms, playgrounds, homes and industries. Surveys and management and sales reports. Interview, profile, historical, successful business operations and articles on merchandising techniques. No how-to articles; "they generally don't apply to installers in our industry." Buys 15-20 unsolicited mss/year. Query. Length: open. Pays 10¢/word.
Photos: Pays $10 for 5x7 b&w photos purchased with mss. Captions required.

FINE HOMEBUILDING, The Taunton Press, Inc., 52 Church Hill Rd., Box 355, Newtown CT 06470. (203)426-8171. Editor: John Lively. Bimonthly magazine covering house building, construction, design for builders, architects and serious amateurs. Circ. 195,000. Pays on publication. Byline given. Offers negotiable kill fee. Buys first rights and "use in books to be published." Computer printout submissions acceptable. Reports as soon as possible. Sample copy $3.50; free writer's guidelines.
Nonfiction: Technical (unusual techniques in design or construction process). Query. Length: 2,000-3,000 words. Pays $150-900.
Columns/Departments: Reports (conferences, workshops, products or techniques that are new or unusual); Great Moments in Building History (humorous, embarrassing, or otherwise noteworthy anecdotes); and Reviews (short reviews on books of building or design). Query. Length: 300-1,000 words. Pays $75-150.

‡**JOURNAL OF COMMERCE**, Box 34080, Station D, Vancouver, B.C., V6J 4M8 Canada . Editorial Director: Brian Martin. Twice-weekly tabloid aimed at a general construction and development audience in west-

ern Canada. Circ. 14,000. Payment on acceptance. Buys first Canadian rights. Enclose SAE,IRCs.
Nonfiction: Specialized stories for specific audiences. Query first. Average length: 1,500 words. Pays 15¢/word (Canadian).
Photos: Pays $5 for 5x7 photos.

LOG HOME AND ALTERNATIVE HOUSING BUILDER, 16 First Ave., Corry PA 16407. (814)664-8624. Editor: M.J. Potocki. 50% freelance written. Bimonthly magazine covering alternative housing including log, dome, solar and underground homes. Circ. 10,000. Pays on publication. Publishes ms an average of 1 month after acceptance. Byline given. Buys all rights. Computer printout submissions acceptable. Reports in 2 weeks on queries; 3 weeks on mss. Free sample copy.
Nonfiction: Energy saving devices and techniques; and unique applications for alternative types of homes and commercial buildings. Restaurants no longer unique. More efficient business management techniques and sales and marketing ideas. "We do not buy articles on how a husband and wife erected their home, or the trials and tribulations of the first-time log or dome home buyer." Buys 6 mss/year. Length: 2,000-4,000 words. Pays $50-200.
Photos: Send photos with ms. Pays $15-30 for 8x10 color prints; $10-25 for 8x10 b&w prints. Captions and identification of subjects required.

METAL BUILDING REVIEW, Nickerson & Collins, 1800 Oakton, Des Plaines IL 60018. (312)298-6210. Editor: Gene Adams. Monthly magazine for contractors, dealers, erectors, architects, designers and manufacturers in the metal building industry. Circ. 22,000. Pays on acceptance. Buys first North American serial rights or all rights. Submit seasonal/holiday material 6 months in advance. Simultaneous queries, and simultaneous, photocopied, and previously published submissions OK. Reports in 3 weeks. Free sample copy.
Nonfiction: How-to, interview/profile, photo feature and technical. Query with or without published clips or send complete ms. Length: 1,000-3,000 words. Pays 3-6¢/word.
Photos: State availability of photos. Pays $5-10 for 5x7 b&w prints; $20-75 for 5x7 color prints. Captions, model release, and identification of subjects required. Buys one-time or all rights.
Tips: "Freelancers can break in with on-the-job-site interviews."

‡MID-WEST CONTRACTOR, Construction Digest, Inc., 3170 Mercier, Box 766, Kansas City MO 64141. (816)931-2080. Editor: Marcia Gruver. 2% freelance written. Biweekly magazine covering the public works and engineering construction industries in Iowa, Nebraska, Kansas and western and northeastern Missouri. Circ. 8,426. Pays on publication. Publishes ms an average of 2 months after acceptance. Byline given depending on nature of article. Not copyrighted. Makes work-for-hire assignments. Computer printout submissions acceptable; prefers letter-quality to dot-matrix. Reports in 2 weeks. Free sample copy.
Nonfiction: How-to, photo feature, technical, "nuts and bolts" construction job-site features. Buys 4 mss/year. Send complete ms. Length: 175 typewritten lines, 35 character count, no maximum. Pays $75/published page. Sometimes pays expenses of writer on assignment.
Tips: "The writer may have a better chance of breaking in at our publication with short articles and fillers because we have very limited space for editorial copy. The most frequent mistake made by writers is that they do not tailor their article to our specific market—the nonresidential construction market in Nebraska, Iowa, Kansas and Missouri. We are not interested in what happens in New York unless it has a specific impact in the Midwest."

P.O.B., Point of Beginning, P.O.B. Publishing Co., Box 810, Wayne MI 48184. (313)729-8400. Editor: Edwin W. Miller. 50% freelance written. Bimonthly magazine featuring articles of a technical, business, professional and general nature for the professionals and technicians of the surveying and mapping community. Circ. 65,500. Pays on publication. Publication date after acceptance "varies with backlog." Byline given "with short biography, if appropriate." Offers 50% kill fee. Buys all rights; makes work-for-hire assignments. Submit seasonal/holiday material 3 months in advance. Simultaneous queries and photocopied submissions OK. Computer printout submissions acceptable; prefers letter-quality (with no right margin justification) to dot-matrix. SASE. Reports in 1 month. Free sample copy for 10x13 SAE and 8 first class stamps; writer's guidelines for SAE and 1 first class stamp.
Nonfiction: Jeanne M. Helfrick, associate editor. Historical/nostalgic; how-to; interview/profile; photo feature; technical (only related to surveying, mapping, construction—profession and business of); and travel (only sites of professional society meetings). Buys 12 mss/year. Submit complete ms. Length: 1,000-4,000 words. Pays $100-400.
Photos: Send captioned photos with ms. Pays $10-50 for color transparencies and prints; $5-25 for 5x7 b&w prints. Model release and identification of subjects required.
Columns/Departments: A Conversation With (interview of people in the field about their professional involvement, point of view); and Picture Profile (profile of people in the field slanted toward their special interest, talent, involvement that is unusual to the profession). Buys 6 mss/year. Query associate editor. Length: 1,000-2,500 words. Payment varies.

Tips: "If an article is good, we'll use it. The most frequent mistake made by writers is that they have not bothered to find out who the readership of our magazine is."

RESTAURANT AND HOTEL DESIGN MAGAZINE, Bill Communications, 633 3rd Ave., New York NY 10017. (212)986-4800, ext. 438, 440. Editor: M.J. Madigan. Managing Editor: Rachel Long. 20% freelance written. Magazine about restaurant/hotel industries for architects, designers and restaurant and hotel executives; published 10 times/year. Circ. 36,000. Pays on acceptance. Publishes ms an average of 3 months after acceptance. Byline given. Buys first North American serial rights. No phone queries. SASE. Reports in 1 month on queries; 2 months on mss.
Nonfiction: Profile. Buys 4-10 mss/year. Query with published clips. Length: 1,500-2,500 words.
Tips: "We generally work with established writers in the design field, directing research and focusing articles. Unsolicited works seldom suit our format. Query should have clarity, brevity, knowledge of the magazine and design language. Quality photography must be submitted with any project query so that we can determine whether or not we can use the story."

ROOFER MAGAZINE, D&H Publications, Box 06253, Ft. Myers FL 33906. (813)275-7663. Editor: Karen S. Parker. 33% freelance written. Monthly magazine covering the roofing industry for roofing contractors. Circ. 16,000. Pays on publication. Publishes ms an average of 4 months after acceptance. Byline given. Buys first serial rights and second serial (reprint) rights. Submit seasonal/holiday material 2 months in advance. Simultaneous queries, and simultaneous and previously published submissions OK. Computer printout submissions acceptable; no dot-matrix. SASE. Reports in 2 weeks on queries; 1 month on mss. Sample copy and writer's guidelines for SAE and 27¢ postage.
Nonfiction: Karen S. Parker, articles editor. Historical/nostalgic; how-to (solve application problems, overcome trying environmental conditions); interview/profile; new product and technical. "Write articles directed toward areas of specific interest; don't generalize too much." Buys 7 mss/year. Query. Length: 3,000-7,000 words. Pays $125-250.
Photos: Send photos with accompanying query. Reviews 8x10 b&w prints and standard size transparencies. Identification of subjects required. Buys all rights.
Columns/Departments: Legal column (contract agreements, litigations, warranties, etc.); technology and application problems; safety; and better business articles. Buys 30-50 mss/year. Query with published clips. Length: 3,000-7,000 words. Pays $125-250.
Tips: "We prefer substantial articles (not short articles and fillers). Slant articles toward roofing contracts. Don't embellish too much."

WORLD CONSTRUCTION, Technical Publishing Co., 875 3rd Ave., New York NY 10022. (212)605-9400. Editorial Director: Ruth W. Stidger. 20% freelance written. Monthly magazine for "English speaking engineers, contractors and government officials everywhere except the U.S. and Canada." Pays on publication. Publishes ms an average of 3 months after acceptance. Byline given unless "the article is less than one page long." Buys all rights. Computer printout submissions acceptable; prefers letter-quality to dot-matrix. SASE. Reports in 1 month. Free sample copy.
Nonfiction: "How-to articles that stress how contractors can do their jobs faster, better or more economically. Articles are rejected when they tell only what was constructed, but not how it was constructed and why it was constructed in that way. No clippings from newspapers telling of construction projects." Query. Length: 1,000-6,000 words. Pays $100-200/magazine page, or 5 typed ms pages, depending on content and quality.
Photos: State availability of photos. Photos purchased with mss; uses 4x5 or larger b&w glossy prints.
Tips: "At the present time we would prefer buying articles dealing with construction projects in overseas locations."

Dairy Products

THE NATIONAL DAIRY NEWS, National Dairy News, Inc., Box 951, Madison WI 53701. (608)222-0777. Publisher: Gerald Dryer. 5% freelance written. Weekly tabloid newspaper covering dairy processing and marketing. Circ. 4,000. Pays on publication. Publishes ms an average of 2 months after acceptance. Byline given. Offers negotiable kill fee. Buys one-time rights. Submit seasonal holiday material 1 month in advance. Simultaneous queries, and simultaneous, photocopied, and previously published submissions OK. Electronic submissions OK; contact publisher. Computer printout submissions acceptable; prefers letter-quality to dot-matrix. SASE. Reports in 1 week on queries; 1 month on mss. Sample copy and writer's guidelines $2.

Nonfiction: Jerry Dryer, articles editor. How-to (improve dairy processing and marketing ventures); humor; interview/profile; new product; photo feature; and technical. Buys 10-40 mss/year. Send complete ms. Length: 50-2,500 words. Pays $25-300. Sometimes pays expenses of writers on assignment.

Photos: Jerry Dryer, photo editor. Send photos with ms. Pays $10-50 for 8x10 b&w prints. Model release and identification of subjects required.

Fillers: Jerry Dryer, fillers editor. Clippings, jokes, gags, anecdotes, short humor and newsbreaks. Length: 25-150 words. Pays $5-25. Avoid general fillers.

Tips: "Our criteria simply calls for a well-written article about a subject of interest to our readers, whatever its length. Frequently the story is poorly researched and many relevant questions aren't answered, usually because writers don't appreciate how sophisticated our readers are. We are not read by dairy farmers; thus, we do not need dairy farmer material."

Data Processing

These publications give computer professionals more data about their trade. While they are not as changeable as computer magazines for consumers, some companies have folded data processing trade journals. "The shake-out in the computer industry involves many last-minute developments," said one computer magazine editor. "It is important for both writers and editors to keep close tabs on the developments that occur daily."

‡ABSOLUTE REFERENCE, The Journal For 1-2-3 And Symphony Users, Que Publishing, Inc., 7999 Knue Rd., Indianapolis IN 46250. (317)842-7162. Editor-in-Chief: Thomas D. Perkins. Managing Editor: P.J. Schemenaur. 80% freelance written. Monthly newsletter covering 1-2-3 and symphony applications, tips, and macros. "Que Publishing is a sister company to Que Corp., one of the world's leading publishers of microcomputer books. Our audience uses *AR* on the job to solve problems that involve Lotus spreadsheet or integrated software use. These readers work for Fortune 500 companies, as well as small for businesses, where *Absolute Reference* is regarded as a tool for 'power' users." Estab. 1983. Circ. 6,900. Payment initiated within 14 days of acceptance. Publishes ms an average of 1 month after acceptance. Byline given. Buys first North American serial rights. Submit seasonal/holiday material 2 months in advance. Photocopied submissions OK. Electronic submissions OK 4 12000 baud Hayes and Crosstalk on X Modem; requires hard copy for disk, no copy for modem. Prefers ¼" floppy disk and hard copy submissions. Computer printout submsisions acceptable. Reports in 2 weeks on queries; 1 month on mss. Sample copy $6; writer's guidelines for #10 SAE and 1 first class stamp.

Nonfiction: How-to (use 1-2-3 or Symphony). "We like to cover tax planning and tax tips using 1-2-3 or Symphony in the March issue to increase productivity on the job)." No articles on Jazz or other software that is not compatible with the IBM PC. No news. Only 1-2-3 and Symphony application articles. Buys 48 mss/year. Query should detail writer's professional experience as it relates to Lotus products or microcomputers. Length: 1,500-3,000 words. Pays 12¢/word.

Photos: We use program listings, tables, and PC printer images to illustrate articles. This 'art' is purchased with the article."

Columns/Department: 1-2-3 Tips: Items on short macros to ease printing, locate files, use pointers, etc.—in short, strings of commnds that save the user time and energy while working in a file. Symphony Tips are also needed, covering any streamlined approach to file usage. Macro Of The Month is a department devoted to lengthier, meatier macros covering more involved execution of file commands. Wish List items detail commands and features that readers wish Lotus had supplied in 1-2-3 or Symphony. Product Reviews focus on 1-2-3 or Symphony-related hardware or software. Buys 96 mss/year. Query on reviews; send complete ms if tip, macro, or wish list item. Length: 175-400 words (tips, wish list); 500-800 words for reviews; 700-1,000 words for macros. Pays $25 minimum for ipts; 12¢/word for reviews; $50-75 for macros.

Tips: "Know 1-2-3 and/or Symphony inside-out. Test the macros; make sure your submission is complete. Suggest a title; label figures and program listings. Write subheads for text; cutlines for figures and listings. Keep in mind the business user—ranging from neophyte to 'old pro.' We use tip writers again and again and encourage them to graduate to writing articles."

ADVANCED COMPUTING (formerly two/sixteen magazine), The journal for business, professional & scientific members of the TRS-80 community, 131 E. Orange St., Lancaster PA 17602. (717)397-3364. Publisher: Richard H. Young. Editor: Nina L. Myers. A bimonthly magazine covering TRS-80 models II, 12,

16, and 6000 microcomputers from Radio Shack with current emphasis on multi-user systems for the 16, 6000, and Model II for people in business, professional and scientific pursuits who use their microcomputers as part of the way they make their living. Circ. 12,500. Pays on publication. Byline given. Buys all rights. Simultaneous queries, and simultaneous and photocopied submissions OK. Electronic submissions OK if single-sided, single- or double-density 8" diskette. WordStar, ASC II or SCRIPSIT format acceptable. Computer printout submissions acceptable except for program listings. SASE. Reports in 1 week on queries; 1 month on mss. Free sample copy and writer's guidelines.

Nonfiction: How-to, new product, personal experience and technical. "We use only hardware specific articles that can be of direct benefit to TRS-80 Model II, 12, 16, and 6000 microcomputer users. No general or theoretical or essay type articles—they must be user-oriented." Query. Buys 120 mss/year. Length: open. Pays $30/published page (6,000 characters/1 page).

Columns/Departments: "We have a Special User Report section where we publish reviews of products that we have not supplied. Be concise, be specific. Don't be too formal. We go for a conversational style. Address readers as 'you' and refer to yourself as 'I.' Buys 120 mss/year. pays $30/published page (6,000 characters/1 page).

Tips: "Our readers are getting more and more sophisticated. No one wants to read about 'my first word processing experience' because they've all been through that by now. They want to learn how to up-grade their computers and their knowledge to get the full capacity from their machines. They want to get their money's worth as well as make some money using the computer."

BUSINESS SOFTWARE, The Computer Magazine for Power Users, M&T Publishing, 2464 Embarcadero Way, Palo Alto CA 94303. (415)424-0600. Editor: Thom Hogan. Managing Editor: Joyce Lane. 50-60% freelance written. Monthly magazine covering the business of computers. "We are not geared toward the pre-purchasers—the people thinking about getting computers—or those just getting a start in computers. Ours is a *highly sophisticated* audience comprised of people who have been using computers in their businesses for years, who are at the leading edge of what's happening in the world of business computing and who want the leverage computers provide to them." Circ. 60,000. Pays on acceptance. Publishes ms an average of 1 month after acceptance. Byline given. Buys first serial rights plus one reprint right. Simultaneous queries and photocopied submissions OK. Electronic submissions OK on 300-1200 baud, 7-8 data bits, 1 stop bit, xmodem transfers. Computer printout submissions acceptable; prefers letter-quality to dot-matrix. SASE. Reports in 4 weeks on queries; 8 weeks on mss. Free sample copy and writer's guidelines.

Nonfiction: Book excerpts; how-to (advanced tutorials on practical software use); opinion (reviews); and technical. No humor or articles not related to business or game reviews. Buys 50-75 mss/year. Query with published clips or send complete ms. Length: 750-3,500 words. Pays $75-100/published page; $500 maximum. Sometimes pays expenses of writers on assignment.

Photos: Send photo with query or ms. Reviews b&w and color contact sheets; payment included in per-page rate. Captions, model release, and identification of subjects required. Buys one-time rights plus one reprint right.

Tips: "Query first, then call after query answered. Timeliness and technical savvy are a must with us. Feature section tutorial section always open to freelancers, but note we are an *advanced* user magazine, not interested in novice, prepurchase, or other introductory material. If articles are technically competent, any length is acceptable to us. Frequent mistakes made by writers are not using enough detailed information about the application being discussed, lack of relevance or inability to relate program to business user and lack of photos, display screen, printouts, reports and sidebars."

COMPUTER DEALER, Gordon Publications, Inc., Box 1952, Dover NJ 07801-0952. (201)361-9060. Editor: David Shadovitz. Monthly magazine of business management ideas for dealers, computer and software stores, systems houses, consultants, consumer electronics outlets and business equipment dealers. Circ. 45,000. Pays on publication. Buys all rights. Phone queries OK. Submit seasonal/holiday material 6 months in advance. Previously published submissions OK. Computer printout submissions acceptable; prefers letter-quality to dot-matrix. SASE. Reports in 1 month. Free sample copy.

Nonfiction: How-to (sell, market, etc.); interview (with computer notables and/or where market is revealed); and articles on capital formation, etc. Writers "must have a knowledge of marketing and the computer industry, and the ability to ferret information or restate information known in other fields in a usable, interesting and particularly applicable way to those persons engaged in selling computers and peripheral products. We prefer not to see general marketing articles." Buys 3-6 mss/issue. Query. Length: 1,000-4,000 words. Pays 8-14¢/word.

Photos: "Photos (artwork) provide and spark greater reader interest and are most times necessary to explicate text." Send photos with ms. Uses b&w 8½x11 glossy prints. Offers no additional payment for photos accepted with ms. Captions and model release required.

Columns/Departments: "Columns are solicited by editor. If writers have suggestions, please query."

COMPUTER GRAPHICS WORLD, 1714 Stockton St., San Francisco CA 94133. (415)398-7151. Publisher/Editor: Randall Stickrod. Monthly magazine covering computer graphics for managers in business, industry, government and institutions; readers are interested in computer graphic application and technology. Circ. 32,000. Pays on publication. Byline and brief bio given. Buys first North American serial rights; "reprints should give us credit." Simultaneous queries and photocopied submissions OK. Reports immediately. Free sample copy; Editorial Highlights available.
Nonfiction: Case studies and success stories in using computer graphics to solve problems. "Articles must be relevant to the needs of persons interested in applying computer graphics." Buys 35 mss/year. Query by phone or brief letter. Length: 1,500 words. Pays $50/printed page.
Photos: Prefers negative transparencies and 8x10 b&w glossy prints. State availability of photos or graphics. Captions required. Buys all rights.

COMPUTER MERCHANDISING, The Magazine for High Technology Retailers, Eastman Publishing, Suite 222, 15720 Ventura Blvd., Encino CA 91436. (818)995-0436. Editor: Mike Hogan. Managing Editor: Larry Tuck. 30% freelance written. Twice monthly magazine covering retailing of computers for home and small business use. "The emphasis of the magazine is to aid the growing number of computer retailers." Circ. 25,000. Pays on acceptance. Publishes ms an average of 3 months after acceptance. Buys first serial rights. Byline given. Submit seasonal/holiday material 3 months in advance. Computer printout submissions acceptable. SASE. Reports in 2 weeks. Sample copy for 9x12 SAE.
Nonfiction: Interview/profile (of industry figures); technical (simple explanation of computers, related products); merchandising suggestions; sales training promotion tips; and case histories. No articles on general topics with no relation to retailing of computers. Buys 60 mss/year. Query. Length: 1,000-2,000 words. Pays $150-450.
Tips: Submit "query which shows research of the specifics of retailing computer products—good grasp of key issues, major names, etc. It's rewarding finding someone who listens to us when we explain what we want and who consistently gives us what we ask for."

COMPUTER RETAILING, W.R.C. Smith Publishing, 1760 Peachtree Rd., Atlanta GA 30357. (404)874-4462. Managing Editor: Marian Thompson. Monthly tabloid emphasizing retailing microcomputers. Circ. 30,000. Pays on acceptance. Byline given. Offers 50% kill fee. Buys first serial righs. Phone queries OK. Submit seasonal/holiday material 2 months in advance. Computer printout submissions acceptable. SASE. Reports in 2 weeks.
Nonfiction: Interested in interviews with local computer/software stores for miniprofile editorial. Also interested in business, vertical or productivity software evaluations. Guidelines provided. Query. Length: 750 words. Pays $100.

COMPUTERWORLD, 375 Cochituate Rd., Box 880, Framingham MA 01701. (617)879-0700. Editor: John C. Whitmarsh. 10% freelance written. Weekly. For management level computer users chiefly in the business community, but also in government and education. Circ. 125,000. Buys all rights. Pays on publication. Publishes ms an average of 2 months after acceptance. Photocopied submissions OK, if exclusive for stated period. Submit special issue material 2 months in advance. Computer printout submissions acceptable; prefers letter-quality to dot-matrix. SASE. Reports in 1 month. Free sample copy, if request is accompanied by story idea or specific query; free writer's guidelines.
Nonfiction: "*Computerworld* is written for professional users and managers of general purpose computer systems. Our audience includes those who direct, manage, supervise and program computers. Primary readers are top systems executives and their staffs, typically Fortune 1000 companies, government agencies and educational organizations. We cover news, product/service announcements and technical/management information. Emphasis is on timely, accurate information of immediate use to data processing professionals. We stress impact on users and need a practical approach. Some knowledge of business computing is required to score with us. Ask yourself: 'How do computer systems support business objectives? How are microcomputers integrated into a corporate environment? How are corporations merging voice and data communications?' Use the most important facts first, then in decreasing order of significance. Include full names, titles of people and configuration of computer systems in use. Buys 100 mss/year. Query, "or call specific editor to ask what's needed at a particular time; establish phone rapport with individual editor." Length: 250-1,200 words. Pays 10¢/word, "except in-depth articles and feature articles for special CW publications, for which payment starts at $100. Consult individual editor."
Photos: 5x7 b&w glossy prints purchased with ms or on assignment. Captions required. Pays $10 minimum.
Fillers: Newsbreaks and clippings. Query. Length: 50-250 words. Pays 10¢/word.
Tips: "The writer has a better chance of breaking in with short articles and fillers as we can judge the quality of the submission quickly, and the writer's investment in time is minimized. The most frequent mistakes made by writers in completing an article for us are not understanding the sophistication of our business users, not reading the publication before querying, and not querying."

COMPUTING CANADA, Canada's Bi-Weekly Data Processing Newspaper, Plesman Publications, Ltd., Suite 703, 2 Lansing Square, Willowdale, Ontario M2J 4P8 Canada. (416)497-9562. Editor: Gordon A. Campbell. Managing Editor: David Paddon. 30% freelance written. Biweekly tabloid covering data processing, the computer industry and telecommunications for data processing management and professionals. Circ. 30,000. Pays on publication. Publishes ms an average of 6 weeks after acceptance. Byline given. Buys first North American serial rights. Submit seasonal/holiday material 1 month in advance. Simultaneous queries and submissions OK. Electronic submissions OK on CP/M 8-inch, MS-DOS, Commodore 300/1200 baud ASCII. Computer printout submissions acceptable; prefers letter-quality to dot-matrix. SASE. Reports in 1 month. Free sample copy and writer's guidelines.

Nonfiction: How-to, interview/profile and current industry news. Special features (software report, office automation, computers in education, etc.) in each issue. Length: 250-1,500 words. Pays $50-200. Sometimes pays expenses of writers on assignment.

Tips: "Suggest a story on an industry event or trend we haven't picked up on. More use of freelance material and more coverage of the microcomputer and office automation markets will affect writers in the year ahead. Ask us for our feature report schedule. Staff writers cover major news. We need freelance for features and less important events. A frequent mistake made by writers is using an excessive public relations slant."

‡**COMPUTING FOR BUSINESS (formerly Interface Age)**, MWJ Publishing, 7330 Adams St., Paramount CA 90723. (213)408-0999. Editorial Director: Les Spindle. Associate Editorial Director: Shelia Ball. Monthly magazine covering microcomputers in business. "In *Computing for Business* there is a distinct focus toward the business person. Readers receive up-to-the-minute reports on new products, applications for business and programs they can apply to their own personal computer." Circ. 100,000. Pays on publication. Byline given. Offers variable kill fee. Buys all rights. Submit seasonal/holiday material 4 months in advance. Simultaneous queries, and simultaneous, photocopied, and previously published submissions OK. Electronic submissions OK only after consulting by phone with the editors. Computer printout submissions acceptable. Reports in 6 weeks on mss. Sample copy $3.75; free writer's guidelines.

Nonfiction: How-to, new product, opinion, personal experience, photo feature and technical. Send for 1985 Editorial Calendar of monthly topics. No agency- or company-written articles. "Articles should pertain to microcomputing applications in business, law, education, medicine, software, unique breakthroughs and future projections. We seek interviews/profiles of people well-known in the industry or making unusual use of microcomputers. Computer programs and sample listings must be printed with a new ribbon to get the best quality reproduction in the magazine." Buys 60 mss/year. Query with published clips or send complete ms. Length: 1,000-5,000 words. Pays $50 and more (negotiable)/printed page including photos, charts, programs and listings.

Photos: Send photos, charts, listings and programs with ms. Photos included in purchase price of article. Captions, model release, and identification of subjects required.

Tips: "Case study articles specifying how a particular type of business (law firm, retail store, office, etc.) implemented a computer to improve efficiency and not-yet-reviewed product reviews stand the best chance for acceptance. Hardware and software appraisals by qualified reviewers are desirable. Practical and business applications, rather than home/hobbyist pursuits, are encouraged. Focus tightly on 'computing for business' theme."

DATA MANAGEMENT MAGAZINE, The Magazine for the Information Management Executive,, Data Processing Management Association (DPMA), 505 Busse Hwy., Park Ridge IL 60068. (312)825-8124. Editor: Bill Zalud. Monthly magazine covering information processing management for professionals with corporate level responsibility for information resource and consulting services, DP service organizations and businesses with emphasis on information processing. Circ. 52,847. Byline given. Submit seasonal/holiday material 3 months in advance. Simultaneous queries OK. Reports in 4 weeks on queries; 3 weeks on mss. Free sample copy and writer's guidelines.

Nonfiction: Interview/profile and technical. "Editorial calendar available upon request. Nothing out-dated—material must be timely." Send complete ms. Length: 1,500-2,000 words. Pays negotiable fee.

Photos: State availability of photos with ms. Reviews 35mm color transparencies and 5x7 b&w prints. Pays negotiable fee. Captions and identification of subjects required.

Tips: "All articles submitted to *Data Management* must contain the point of view of the information processing manager. Authors should keep in mind that our readers are professionals."

DATAMATION, Technical Publishing D & B, 875 3rd Ave., New York NY 10022. Executive Editor: John Kirkley. 80% freelance written. Monthly magazine for scientific, engineering and commercial data processing professionals. Circ. 150,000. Pays on publication. Byline given. Offers negotiable kill fee. Buys all rights. Submit seasonal/holiday material 3 months in advance. Photocopied and previously published submissions ("if indicated where") OK. Computer printout submissions acceptable; prefers letter-quality to dot-matrix. SASE. Reports as soon as possible on queries. Free sample copy and writer's guidelines. "Request our list of themes for the coming year."

Nonfiction: Covers all aspects of computer industry technical, managerial and sociological concerns, as well as computer industry news analysis. No general articles on computers. Buys 60 mss/year. Query with published clips. Length: 2,000-4,000 words. Pays $300-1,000/article. Pays expenses of writers on assignment.

Photos: Reviews 35mm color transparencies and 8x10 b&w prints. No extra payment for photos—included in payment for manuscript.

Tips: "The most frequent mistake made by writers is failure to read the magazine and figure out what we're about."

THE DEC PROFESSIONAL, Professional Press, Inc., 921 Bethlehem Pk., Springhouse PA 19477. (215)542-7008. Publishers: Carl B. Marbach and R.D. Mallery. 95% freelance written. Bimonthly magazine covering Digital Equipment Corp. computers. "We publish highly technical, user-written articles concerning DEC equipment. We are a forum for DEC users worldwide." Circ. 92,000. Publishes ms an average of 3 months after acceptance. Byline given. Buys first North American serial rights. Electronic submissions OK (contact office first), but requires hard copy also. Computer printout submissions acceptable (prefers 800 or 1600 BPI mag tape); prefers letter-quality to dot-matrix. Free sample copy and writer's guidelines.

Nonfiction: Technical (computer related). No articles "not highly technical concerning DEC computers and related topics." Send complete ms. Length: 1,500-5,000 words. Pays $100-300. Sometimes pays expenses of writers on assignment.

Tips: "Please send articles of approximately 1,500-5,000 words, preferably on an 800/1600 BPI mag tape in PIP format, or in WORD-11 or MASS-11. We also accept 5¼" RX50 floppy disks—Rainbow 100, Professional 300 series, or DECmate II compatible. In addition, we can read RT-11 (only), RX01 or RX02 8" floppies. If not available, a letter-quality hardcopy may be forwarded to the editors at Professional Press."

‡DR. DOBB'S JOURNAL, Software Tools for Advanced Programmers, M&T Publishing, Inc., 2464 Embarcadero Way, Palo Alto CA 94303. (415)424-0600. Editor: Michael Swaine. Managing Editor: Frank DeRose. 60% freelance written. Monthly magazine on computer programming. Circ. 40,000. Pays on publication. Publishes ms an average of 9 months after acceptance. Byline given. Buys all rights. Photocopied submissions OK. Electronic submissions OK on IBM PC, but requires hard copy also. Computer printout submissions acceptable; prefers letter-quality to dot-matrix. SASE. Reports in 1 month on queries; 9 weeks on mss.

Nonfiction: How-to and technical. Buys 48 mss/year. Send complete ms. Word length open. Pays $25-500.

Photos: Send photos with ms. Reviews 3x5 prints. Captions required. Buys all rights.

HARDCOPY, The Magazine of Digital Equipment, Seldin Publishing Co., Suite D, 1061 S. Melrose, Placentia CA 92670. (714)632-6924. Editor: Leslie Frohoff. 80% freelance written. Monthly magazine covering Digital Equipment Corporation (DEC) and DEC-compatible computer equipment, software and peripherals primarily for computer-sophisticated users and equipment manufacturers looking for more information on how to sell, distribute or improve their computer products. Circ. 82,000. Pays 30 days from acceptance. Byline given. Buys all rights to new material. "Will negotiate to all North American rights if author is located abroad." Occasionally buys second (reprint) rights. Submit seasonal/holiday material 4 months in advance. Computer printout submissions acceptable. All mss must be double-spaced. SASE. Reports in 2 weeks on queries; 2 months on mss. Sample copy for 9x12 SAE and $1.90 postage; writer's guidelines for business size SAE and 1 first class stamp.

Nonfiction: How-to (sell product; computer-oriented management and business); interview/profile (DEC or DEC-compatible manufacturers); and technical (DEC computer-oriented). No noncomputer related features or computer-oriented features that do not relate in any way to Digital Equipment Corporation. Buys approximately 72 mss/year. Query with published clips. Length: 2,000-3,500 words. Pays $200-500.

Photos: Pays $10-25 for 5x7 b&w prints; $25 for 35mm color transparencies. Identification of subjects required.

Tips: "We need solid technical and how-to features from contributors. Research must be thorough, and the article's main point must somehow relate to DEC. For example, a market trend article should explain how DEC's market will be affected. We suggest you query to receive direction, since our needs are very specific. Before you query, pick up a copy of the magazine and get familiar with the kinds of stories we buy. We don't like to risk holding a large slot open for a feature that doesn't work out. Frequently writers neglect the technical information and vie for style, or vice versa. We want catchy leads and tags as well as a fact-filled body. 'Padding' is also unacceptable."

‡IBM PC UPDATE, New Techniques For Professionals, Que Publishing, Inc., 7999 Knue Rd., Indianapolis IN 46250. (317)842-7162. Editor: Patty Stonesifer. 100% freelance written. Monthly newsletter about IBM PCs and PC-compatible microcomputers. "*Update* is a techniques-oriented journal specializing in providing practical, hands-on information to increase user productivity." Circ. 5,000. Pays on acceptance. Publishes ms an average of 3 months after acceptance. Byline given. Offers $50 kill fee. Buys first North American serial rights. Submit seasonal/holiday material 3 months in advance. Simultaneous queries and submissions OK.

Electronic submissions OK on WordStar; ASC II files, 5¼" disk only, but requires hard copy also. Computer printout submissions acceptable. SASE. Reports in 1 month. Free sample copy and writer's guidelines.
Nonfiction: How-to and technical. Buys 150 mss/year. Query. Length: 2,000-4,000 words. Pays $240-480.
Columns/Departments: Inside WordStar, Inside 1-2-3, Inside dBase, Inside Framework, and Inside Symphony. Buys 60/year. Query. Length: 2,000-4,000 words. Pays $350-450.
Tips: "Writers must have solid microcomputer, IBM-compatible background. The ability to explain procedurally and logically often complex instructions is a must. New applications and techniques are welcomed additions. Case studies and product evaluations are the best place to start—stick with an area *you* know best. Superficiality and fluff are not welcome."

ICP & BUSINESS SOFTWARE REVIEW, International Computer Programs, Inc., 9000 Keystone Crossing, Indianapolis IN 46240. (317)844-7461. Editor-in-Chief: Dennis Hamilton. Editor: Sheila Cunningham. Managing Editor: Louis W. Harm. 5 quarterly magazines and 1 bimonthly magazine covering computer software applications and program use in the business and scientific community. Circ. 198,000. Pays on acceptance. Byline given. Buys all rights. Phone queries OK; written queries preferred. Submit seasonal material 3 months in advance. Simultaneous and photocopied submissions OK. Computer printout submissions acceptable; prefers letter-quality to dot-matrix. Reports in 3 weeks. Free sample copy and writer's guidelines.
Nonfiction: Expose (waste, corruption, misuse of computers); interview (of major computer industry figures); opinion (of computer applications); how-to (computer solutions); new product; personal experience (case studies); technical (application); reviews of individual products. No articles discussing merits of single product. Buys 20 unsolicited mss/year. Length: 1,000-3,000 words. Pays $100-500.

INFORMATION WEEK, (formerly *Information Systems News*, CMP Publications, 600 Community Dr., Manhasset NY 11030. (516)365-4600. Editor: James Moran. 20% freelance written. Weekly news magazine covering hardware, software, computer communication and office automation for managers and staff at U.S. corporations. Circ. over 100,000. Pays within 30 days of acceptance. Publishes ms an average of 1 month after acceptance. Byline given. Buys all rights. Electronic submissions OK via 300 baud. Computer printout submissions acceptable; prefers letter-quality to dot-matrix. SASE. Reports in 1 month.
Nonfiction: "We're looking for articles of business-oriented news for managers of information systems." Buys 50 mss/year. Query by mail. Length: 500 words minimum. Pays the expenses of writers on assignment.
Photos: State availability of color photos.
Tips: "We're looking for experienced magazine writers who can write hard-hitting business stories and still convey a sense of corporate personality. The most frequent mistakes made by writers are bad writing, lousy organization, and not following instructions on focus, length and deadline."

JOURNAL OF SYSTEMS MANAGEMENT, 24587 Bagley Road, Cleveland OH 44138. (216)243-6900. Publisher: James Andrews. 100% freelance written. Monthly. For systems and procedures and management people. Pays on publication. Publishes ms an average of 3 months after acceptance. Byline given. Buys all rights. Computer printout submissions acceptable; prefers letter-quality to dot-matrix. SASE. Reports "as soon as possible." Free sample copy.
Nonfiction: Articles on case histories, projects on systems, forms control, administrative practices and computer operations. No computer applications articles, humor or articles promoting a specific product. Query or submit ms in triplicate. Length: 3,000-5,000 words. Pays $25 maximum.
Tips: Frequent mistakes made by writers are choosing the wrong subject and being too specific regarding a product.

‡LIFELINES/THE SOFTWARE MAGAZINE, Lifelines Publishing, 1651 3rd. Ave., New York NY 10128. (212)722-1700. Managing Editor: Brenda Rodriguez. 75% freelance written. Monthly magazine covering microcomputer software. "Our publication is aimed at business professionals and persons with advanced knowledge of microcomputers, programming and software." Circ. 5,000. Pays on publication. Publishes ms an average of 5 months after acceptance. Byline given. Buys variable rights depending on article and author. Submit seasonal/holiday material 2 months in advance. Simultaneous queries, and simultaneous and photocopied submissions OK. Electronic submissions OK via CP/M 80, 86, 68—IBM-PC, but requires hard copy also. Computer printout submissions acceptable. SASE. Reports in 6 weeks. Free sample copy and writer's guidelines.
Nonfiction: Al Bloch and Brenda Rodriguez, articles editors. How-to, humor, new product and technical. No "articles which oversimplify computers, computer software or the industry." Buys 130-150 mss/year. Query with published clips. Length: 1,000-2,500 words. Pays $60/printed page.
Columns/Departments: Buys 3-5 mss/year. Query with published clips. Length: 1,000-2,500 words. Pays $60/printed page.
Fiction: Humorous (computer technology). Buys 5-10 mss/year. Query with published clips. Length: 1,000-1,500 words. Pays $60/printed page.

Fillers: Brenda Rodriguez and Kate Gartner, fillers editors. Cartoons. Buys 12-24/year. Length: 1,000-1,500 words. Pays $50 (depending on size).
Tips: "A freelancer can best break in by writing articles on new trends, tips, or techniques aimed at our audience. Our nonfiction area is most open to new writers as long as they remain technically correct and communicate directly and conversationally to our audience. The trend that most writers should be aware of, especially in trade journals, is specialization. You must have a good handle on terminology if you want to be credible as a writer for computer industry magazines publishing."

MINI-MICRO SYSTEMS, Cahners Publishing Co., 221 Columbus Ave., Boston MA 02116. (617)536-7780. Editor-in-Chief: George Kotelly. 25% freelance written. Monthly magazine covering minicomputer and microcomputer industries for manufacturers and users of computers, peripherals and software. Circ. 122,000. Pays on publication. Byline given. Publishes ms an average of 3 months after acceptance. Buys all rights. Simultaneous queries and photocopied submissions OK. Computer printout submissions acceptable; prefers letter-quality to dot-matrix. SASE. Reports in 1 month on queries. Free sample copy; writer's guidelines for 4x9 SAE and 1 first class stamp.
Nonfiction: Articles about highly innovative applications of computer hardware and software "firsts". Buys 60-100 mss/year. Query with published clips. Length: 500-2,500 words. Pays $70-100/printed page, including illustrations. Sometimes pays expenses of writers on assignment.
Photos: Send line art, diagrams, photos or color transparencies.
Tips: "The best way to break in is to be affiliated with a manufacturer or user of computers or peripherals."

NEWS/34-38, For Users of IBM Systems 34/36/38, Duke Corporation, Suite 210, 295 E. 29th St., Loveland CO 80537. (303)667-4132. Editor: David A. Duke. Managing Editor: Robert S. Skowron. 50% freelance written. A technically-oriented monthly magazine for data processing uses of IBM Systems 34/36/38. Circ. 20,000. Pays on publication. Publishes ms an average of 3 months after acceptance. Byline given. Buys all rights. Submit seasonal/holiday material 3 months in advance. Simultaneous queries OK. Electronic submissions OK on WordStar and IBM System/36. Computer printout submissions acceptable; prefers letter-quality to dot-matrix. Reports in 1 month. Free sample copy.
Nonfiction: How-to (use Systems 34/36/38); interviews (with users); new product (review); opinion; personal experience (as a DP manager); and technical (tips and techniques). No fluff. Buys 50-100 mss/year. Query with or without published clips. Length: 1,000-5,000 words. Pays $100-500. Sometimes pays expenses of writers on assignment.
Photos: State availability of photos. Send photos with query or ms. Pays $5-10 for b&w prints; $5-20 for color transparencies. Captions, model release, and identification of subjects required. Buys all rights.
Columns/Departments: Technical Tips. Buys 12 mss/year. Query. Length: 50-500 words. Pays $10-100.
Fillers: Newsbreaks. Buys 25/year. Length: 50-500 words. Pays $10-100.
Tips: "We are a very targeted magazine going to a technically-oriented audience. Our writers *must* have a working knowledge of the IBM Systems 34/36/38 computers. Tutorial topics, user stories and management topics are most open to freelancers. We are interested in short feature stories as preferred by our readers. Also, all articles must have immediate benefit to our readers (i.e., if a technique is described, the code must be included so readers can implement the procedure immediately)."

SMALL SYSTEMS WORLD, Hunter Publishing, 950 Lee St., Des Plaines IL 60016. (312)296-0770. Editor: Hellena Smejda. 15% freelance written. Monthly magazine covering applications of IBM minicomputers (S/34/36/38) and IBM PC/AT) in business. Circ. 47,000. Pays on acceptance. Publishes ms an average of 2 months after acceptance. Byline given. Buys all rights. Submit seasonal/holiday material 4 months in advance. Electronic submissions OK Kaypro II—SSDD, but requires hard copy also. Computer printout submissions acceptable. Reports in 2 weeks on queries. Sample copy $5.
Nonfiction: How-to (use the computer in business); and technical (organization of a data base or file system). "A writer who submits material to us should be an expert in computer applications. No material on large scale computer equipment." No poetry. Buys 4 mss/year. Query. Length: 3,000-4,000 words. Sometimes pays expenses of writers on assignment.
Tips: "I only buy long features, mostly ones that I commission specifically. Frequent mistakes are not understanding the audience and not having read the magazine (past issues)."

UNIX/WORLD, Your Guide to the Future of Multiuser Computing System, Tech Valley Publishing, 444 Castro St., Mountain View CA 94041. (415)964-0900. Editor: Philip J. Gill. 40% freelance written. Monthly magazine covering the UNIX operating system (computers) for data processing professionals. Circ. 45,000. Pays on publication. Publishes ms an average of 2 months after acceptance. Byline given. Offers 25% kill fee. Buys first North American serial rights and second (reprint) rights. Submit seasonal/holiday material 6 months in advance. Simultaneous queries, and photocopied and previously published submissions OK. Electronic submissions OK if compatible with 300 baud ASCII format, UUCP (UNIX). Computer printout submissions acceptable. SASE. Reports in 1 month. Sample copy $3; free writer's guidelines.

Nonfiction: Book excerpts; how-to (technical articles on the UNIX system or the C language); interview/profile; new product; technical (see how-to); and product reviews. "All articles should be written for data processing professionals who are encountering the UNIX system for the first time. We are not interested in articles written by marketing departments that push one product line." Buys 100 mss/year. Query with published clips. Length: 2,500-7,000 words. Pays $50-500.

Photos: Send photos with query. Reviews b&w contact sheets. Identification of subjects required. Buys one-time rights.

Columns/Departments: Wizard's Grabbag (tips and techniques that ease the programmer's burden). Buys 100 mss/year. Send complete ms. Length: 100-1,000 words. Pays $25-50.

Tips: "UNIX is a trademark of AT&T Bell Labs. *Unix/World* is not affiliated with AT&T Bell Labs."

Dental

Writers can't only use their observations gleaned from the dentist's chair to write for these journals. "Many freelancers send us manuscripts better suited for the consumer press," said one dental magazine editor. "Articles must contain some specific tools a dentist can utilize in his/her practice."

CONTACTS, Box 407, North Chatham NY 12132. Editor: Joseph Strack. 80% freelance written. Bimonthly. For laboratory owners, managers, and dental technician staffs. Circ. 1,200. Pays on acceptance. Publishes ms an average of 5 months after acceptance. Byline given. Buys first serial rights and second serial (reprint) rights. Reports in 2 weeks. SASE. Free sample copy.

Nonfiction: Writer should know the dental laboratory field or have good contacts there to provide technical articles, how-to, and successful business operation articles. Query. Length: 1,500 words maximum. Pays 5¢/word. Willing to receive suggestions for columns and departments for material of 400-1,200 words. Payment for these negotiable.

DENTAL ECONOMICS, Box 3408, Tulsa OK 74101. Editor: Dick Hale. 60% freelance written. Monthly magazine, 90 pages, emphasizing practice management for dentists. Circ. 103,000. Pays on acceptance. Buys all rights. Byline given. "Occasionally no byline is given when it's an article combining talents of several authors, but credit is always acknowledged." Submit seasonal/holiday material 4 months in advance. Computer printout submissions acceptable, "but we question 'exclusivity'—we must have exclusives in our field." SASE. Reports in 4 weeks. Free sample copy and writer's guidelines.

nonfiction: Expose (closed panels, NHI); how-to (hire personnel, bookkeeping, improve production); humor (in-office type); investments (all kinds); interview (doctors in the news, health officials); personal experience (of dentists, but only if related to business side of practice); profile (a few on doctors who made dramatic lifestyle changes); and travel (only if dentist is involved). Buys 100-120 unsolicited mss/year. Query or submit complete ms. Length: 600-3,500 words. Pays $50-500.

Photos: State availability of photos with query or submit photos with ms. Pays $10 minimum for 8x10 glossy photos; $25 minimum for 35mm color transparencies. Captions and model release required. Buys all rights.

Columns/Departments: Viewpoint (issues of dentistry are aired here). Buys 1 ms/issue. Submit complete ms. Length: 600-1,500 words.

Tips: *DE's* advice to freelancers is: "Talk to dentists about their problems and find an answer to one or more of them. Know the field. Read several copies of *DE* to determine slant, style and length. Write for one dentist, not 100,000. We're growing—we need more submissions and an *objective* look at computers—both hardware and software."

DENTAL MANAGEMENT, The National Business Magazine for Dentists, HBJ Publications, 7500 Old Oak Blvd., Cleveland OH 44130. (216)243-8100. Editor: Belinda Wilson. Managing Editor: Eric Schroder. Monthly magazine covering business and financial aspects of dental practice, practice management, malpractice, insurance, investments and psychological aspects of dentistry for dentists in clinical practice. Circ. 104,000. Pays on publication. Byline given. Buys all rights. SASE. Reports in 3 weeks. Writer's guidelines for SASE.

Nonfiction: Expose (bad investments, tax shelters, poor insurance deals); general interest; how-to (investments, advertising, getting new patients); interview; opinion; and personal experience. No clinical, fiction, cartoons or poetry. Buys 100 mss/year. Query. Length: 3,000 words maximum. Pays $125/published page.

Columns/Departments: "Office Innovations column is most open to freelancers. Interview dentist or staff on tips for dentists on the business/financial aspects of dentistry. Should be innovations actually used by a dental office." Buys 60/year. Send complete ms. Length: 250-500 words. Pays $25/published item.

PROOFS, The Magazine of Dental Sales and Marketing, Box 3408, Tulsa OK 74101. (918)835-3161. Publisher: Joe Bessette. Editor: Mary Elizabeth Good. 10% freelance written. Magazine published 10 times/year; combined issues July/August, November/December. Pays on publication. Byline given. Computer print-out submissions acceptable; prefers letter-quality to dot-matrix. SASE. Reports in 2 weeks. Free sample copy.
Nonfiction: Uses short articles, chiefly on selling to dentists. Must have understanding of dental trade industry and problems of marketing and selling to dentists and dental laboratories. Query. Pays about $75.
Tips: "The most frequent mistakes made by writers are having a lack of familiarity with industry problems and talking down to our audience."

‡**SMILE MAGAZINE**, Atlantic Marketing Group Inc., Box 86, Rockland ME 04841. (207)594-8866. Quarterly magazine on orthodontics. Profiles of orthodontics patients and proper dental hygiene. Circ. 8,000. Pays on acceptance. Byline given. Buys first North American serial rights. Submit seasonal/holiday material 2 months in advance. Simultaneous queries, and simultaneous, photocopied, and previously published submissions OK. Computer printout submissions acceptable; prefers letter-quality to dot-matrix. SASE. Reports in 1 month. Sample copy $1 and 75¢ postage; writer's guidelines for #10 SAE and 1 first class stamp.
Nonfiction: Humor (dental related); personal experience; photo feature (unique braces situations); and travel (related to newsletter). Query. Length: 1,000-2,500 words. Pays $50-200.
Photos: Send photos with query. Reviews 5x7, 8x10 color transparencies and 5x7, 8x10 b&w prints. Pays $20-75. Captions, model release, and identification of subjects required. Buys one-time rights.
Fiction: Humorous, dental related.

TIC MAGAZINE, Box 407, North Chatham NY 12132. (518)766-3047. Editor: Joseph Strack. Monthly magazine for dentists, dental assistants and oral hygienists. 80% freelance written. Pays on acceptance. Publishes ms an average of 4 months after acceptance. Byline given. Buys first serial rights and second serial (reprint) rights. SASE. Reports in 2 weeks.
Nonfiction: Uses articles (with illustrations, if possible) as follows: 1) lead feature: dealing with major developments in dentistry of direct, vital interest to all dentists, 2) how-to pieces: ways and means of building dental practices, improving professional techniques, managing patients, increasing office efficiency, etc., 3) special articles: ways and means of improving dentist-laboratory relations for mutual advantage, of developing auxiliary dental personnel into an efficient office team, of helping the individual dentist to play a more effective role in alleviating the burden of dental needs in the nation and in his community, etc., and 4) general articles: concerning any phase of dentistry or dentistry-related subjects of high interest to the average dentist. Especially interested in profile pieces (with b&w photographs) on dentists who have achieved recognition/success in non-dental fields—business, art, sport, etc. "Interesting, well-written pieces are a sure bet." No material written for patients instead of dentists or "humorous" pieces about pain. Query. Length: 800-3,200 words. Pays 5¢ word/minimum.
Photos: Photo stories: 4-10 pictures of interesting developments and novel ideas in dentistry. B&w only. Pays $10 photo/minimun.
Tips: "We can use fillers of about 500 words or so. They should be pieces of substance on just about anything of interest to dentists. A frequent mistake is failure to keep in mind that our readers are dentists. A psychoanalyst broke in with us recently with pieces relating to interpretations of patients' problems and attitudes in dentistry."

Drugs, Health Care and Medical Products

THE APOTHECARY, Health Care Marketing Services, 153 2nd St., Box AP, Los Altos CA 94022. (415)941-3955. Editor: Jerold Karabensh. Publication Director: Janet Goodman. 100% freelance written. Magazine published 6 times/year about pharmacy. "*The Apothecary* aims to provide practical information to community retail pharmacists." Circ. 65,000. Pays on acceptance. Publishes ms an average of 5 months after acceptance. Byline given. Buys all rights. Submit seasonal material 8 months in advance. Simultaneous queries and photocopied submissions OK. Computer printout submissions acceptable; prefers letter-quality to dot-matrix. SASE. Reports in 6 weeks on queries; 5 months on mss. Free sample copy.

Nonfiction: Janet Goodman, articles editor. How-to (e.g., manage a pharmacy); opinion (of registered pharmacists); and health-related feature stories. "We publish only those general health articles with some practical application for the pharmacist as businessman. No general articles not geared to our pharmacy readership; no fiction." Buys 6 mss/year. Query with published clips. Length: 750-3,000 words. Pays $100-350.
Columns/Departments: Janet Goodman, column/department editor. Commentary (views or issues relevant to the subject of pharmacy or to pharmacists). Send complete ms. Length: 750-1,000 words. "This section is unpaid; we will take submissions with byline."
Tips: "Submit material geared to the *pharmacist* as *business men*. Write according to our policy, i.e., business articles with emphasis on practical information for a community pharmacist. We suggest reading several back issues and following general feature story tone, depth, etc. Stay away from condescending use of language. Though our articles are written in simple style, they must reflect knowledge of the subject and reasonable respect for the readers' professionalism and intelligence."

CANADIAN PHARMACEUTICAL JOURNAL, 101-1815 Alta Vista Dr., Ottawa, Ontario K1G 3Y6 Canada. (613)523-7877. Editor: Jean-Guy Cyr. Assistant Editors: Mary MacDonald and Catherine Partington. 20% freelance written. Monthly journal, 48 pages for pharmacists. Circ. 12,000. Pays on acceptance. Publishes ms an average of 3 months after acceptance. Buys first serial rights. Computer printout submissions acceptable; no dot-matrix. Reports in 2 months. Free sample copy and writer's guidelines.
Nonfiction: Relevant to Canadian pharmacy. Publishes exposes (pharmacy practice, education and legislation); how-to (pharmacy business operations); historical (pharmacy practice, Canadian legislation, education); and interviews with and profiles on Canadian and international pharmacy figures. Length: 200-400 words (for news notices); 800-1,200 words (for articles). Query. Payment is contingent on value; usually 15¢/word. Sometimes pays expenses of writers on assignment.
Photos: B&w (5x7) glossies purchased with mss. Pays $25 first photo; $5 for each additional photo. Captions and model release required.
Tips: "Query with complete description of proposed article, including topic, sources (in general), length, payment requested, suggested submission date, and whether photographs will be included. It is helpful if the writer has read a *recent* (1984) copy of the journal; we are glad to send one if required. The letter should describe the proposed article thoroughly. References should be included where appropriate (this is vital where medical and scientific information is included). Send 2 copies of each ms. Author's degree and affiliations (if any) should be listed; author's writing background should be included (in brief form)."

DRUG TOPICS, 680 Kinderkamack Rd., Oradell NJ 07649. (201)262-3030. Editor: Valentine Cardinale. Executive Editor: Ralph M. Thurlow. Semimonthly magazine for retail drug stores and wholesalers and manufacturers. Circ. over 80,000. Pays on acceptance. Byline given only for features. Buys all rights. Computer printout submissions acceptable. SASE.
Nonfiction: News of local, regional, state pharmaceutical associations, legislation affecting operation of drug stores, news of pharmacists and store managers in civic and professional activities, etc. No stories about manufacturers. Query on drug store success stories which deal with displays, advertising, promotions and selling techniques. Query. Length: 1,500 words maximum. Pays $5 and up for leads, $25 and up for short articles, $100-300 for feature articles, "depending on length and depth."
Photos: May buy photos submitted with mss. May buy news photos with captions only. Pays $10-20.

HOME HEALTH CARE BUSINESS, Cassak Publications, 454 Morris Ave., Springfield NJ 07081. (201)564-9400. Editor: Laurie Cassak. Bimonthly magazine for pharmacists involved in the home health care and DME markets. Circ. 8,000. Pays on publication. Buys all rights. Photocopied and simultaneous submissions OK. SASE. Free sample copy and writer's guidelines.
Nonfiction: Articles about existing home health care centers or opportunities for proprietors; new technologies in the home care field; and helpful hints for the pharmacist engaged in serving the booming consumer/home health care field. "It is essential to understand your reading audience. Articles must be informative but not extremely technical." No human interest stories. Buys informational, how-to, interview and photo articles. Query. Length: 1,000-1,500 words.
Photos: Photos purchased with accompanying ms with no additional payment. Captions optional.

RX HOME CARE, The Journal of Home Health Care and Rehabilitation, Brentwood Publishing Corp., 825 S. Barrington Ave., Los Angeles CA 90049. (213)826-8388. Editor: Martin H. Waldman. Managing Editor: Dana Bigman. 50% freelance written. Monthly magazine covering home health care. "The journal addresses the treatment, medical equipment and supply needs of patients being cared for at home. The primary audience is medical supply dealers. The secondary audience is physical therapists, occupational therapists, nurses, physicians, and other medical professionals in the home health care field." Circ. 15,000. Pays on acceptance. Publishes ms an average of 4 months after acceptance. Byline given. Buys all rights. Submit seasonal/holiday material 6 months in advance. Computer printout submissions acceptable; prefers letter-quality to dot-matrix. SASE. Reports in 1 month on queries; 2 months on mss. Free sample copy and writer's guidelines.

Nonfiction: How-to (market durable medical equipment); interview/profile (of home health care dealerships); and technical (on use of therapies in the home). No "general articles on health-related topics that are not geared specifically to our readership." Buys 60 mss/year. Query with published clips. Length: 1,000-2,000 words. Pays $100-240. Pays expenses of writers on assignment.
Columns/Departments: On Line: covers the use of computers as a business tool for home health care dealers. Topics range from purchasing considerations to tax advantages to facilitating reimbursement from third-party payers. Buys 12 mss/year. Query with published clips. Length: 1,500-2,000 words. Pays $150-240.
Tips: "We have found that our best freelance writers have an understanding of home health care products and reimbursement procedures and write clearly and concisely. We appreciate when writers comform to our style, which is based on the American Medical Association stylebook. A medical background is not necessary to write for *Rx Home Care*, but it is helpful when tackling a technical topic."

Education

Professional educators, teachers, coaches and school personnel—as well as other people involved with training and education—read the journals classified here. One of the main reasons why your favorite educational journal may not be listed is that *Writer's Market* includes only magazines that *pay* for articles. Many journals for educators are nonprofit forums for professional advancement and, thus, writers contribute articles in return for a byline and a few contributor's copies. Education-related publications for students are included in the Career, College, and Alumni, and Teen and Young Adult sections of Consumer Publications.

THE AMERICAN SCHOOL BOARD JOURNAL, National School Boards Association, 1680 Duke St., Alexandria VA 22314. (703)838-6722. Editor: Gregg Downey. Monthly magazine; 52 pages. Emphasizes public school administration and policymaking for elected members of public boards of education throughout U.S. and Canada, and high-level administrators of same. Circ. 42,000. Pays on acceptance. Buys all rights. Phone queries OK. Photocopied submissions OK. Computer printout submissions acceptable. SASE. Reports in 2 months. Free sample copy and guidelines.
Nonfiction: Publishes how-to articles (solutions to problems of public school operation including political problems); and interviews with notable figures in public education. "No material on how public schools are in trouble. We all know that; what we need are *answers*." Buys 20 mss/year. Query. Length: 400-2,000 words. Payment for feature articles varies, "but never less than $75."
Photos: B&w glossies (any size) purchased on assignment. Captions required. Pays $10-50. Model release required.

ARTS & ACTIVITIES, Publishers' Development Corporation, Suite 200, 591 Camino de la Reina, San Diego CA 92108. (619)297-5352. Editor: Dr. Leven C. Leatherbury. Assistant Editor: Maryellen Bridge. 95% freelance written. Monthly (except July and August) art education magazine covering art education at levels from preschool through college for educators and therapists engaged in arts and crafts education and training. Circ. 22,042. Pays on publication. Byline given. Not copyrighted. Buys one-time rights. Submit seasonal/holiday material 4 months in advance. Photocopied submissions OK. Computer printout submissions acceptable; prefers letter-quality to dot-matrix. SASE. Reports in 8 weeks. Sample copy for 9x12 envelope and $2 postage; writer's guidelines for business size SAE and 1 first class stamp.
Nonfiction: Historical/nostalgic (arts activities history); how-to (classroom art experiences, artists' techniques); interview/profile (of artists); opinion (on arts activities curriculum, ideas on how to do things better); personal experience ("this ties in with the how-to—we like it to be *personal*, no recipe style"); and articles on exceptional art programs. Buys 50-80 mss/year. Length: 200-2,000 words. Pays $35-150.
Tips: "Frequently in unsolicited manuscripts writers obviously have not studied the magazine to see what we publish. Everything is considered on an individual basis."

BRITISH JOURNAL OF SPECIAL EDUCATION, (formerly *Special Education: Forward Trends)* 12 Hollycroft Ave., London NW3 7QL England. Editor: Margaret Peter. 40% freelance written. Quarterly. Circ. 6,000. Pays token fee for commissioned articles. Publishes ms an average of 9 months after acceptance. Buys first British rights. Computer printout submissions acceptable; no dot-matrix. SAE, IRCs. Writer's guidelines 60¢ in IRCs.
Nonfiction: Articles on the education of all types of handicapped children. "The aim of this journal of the Na-

tional Council for Special Education is to provide articles on special education and handicapped children that will keep readers informed of practical and theoretical developments not only in education but in the many other aspects of the education and welfare of the handicapped. While we hope that articles will lead students and others to further related reading, their main function is to give readers an adequate introduction to a topic which they may not have an opportunity to pursue further. References should therefore be selective and mainly easily accessible ones. It is important, therefore, that articles of a more technical nature (e.g., psychology, medical, research reviews) should, whenever possible, avoid unnecessary technicalities or ensure that necessary technical terms or expressions are made clear to nonspecialists by the context or by the provision of brief additional explanations or examples. No jargon-filled articles with insubstantial content. Send query that summarizes the proposed content of the article in some detail, i.e., up to 500 words." No material not related to education. Length: 2,200-3,300 words. Payment by arrangement for commissioned articles only.
Tips: "It's not easy for freelancers to break in unless they are practitioners and specialists in special education. If they have the appropriate specialized knowledge and experience, then articles in easily understood, jargon-free language are welcome, provided the depth of analysis and description are also there. Do not describe projects in a different context to that in the United Kingdom."

CHILDBIRTH EDUCATOR, American Baby, 575 Lexington Ave., New York NY 10022. (212)752-0755. Editor: Marsha Rehns. Managing Editor: Trisha Thompson. 80% freelance written. Quarterly magazine providing prenatal education. "Our audience is teachers of childbirth and baby care classes. Articles should have a firm medical foundation." Circ. 22,000. Pays on acceptance. Publishes ms an average of 6 months after acceptance. Byline given. Offers 25% kill fee. Buys first serial rights. Submit seasonal/holiday material 5 months in advance. Simultaneous queries and submissions OK. Computer printout submissions acceptable; no dot-matrix. SASE. Reports in 2 months. Free sample copy.
Nonfiction: Book excerpts (obstetrics, child care, teaching, neonatology); how-to (teaching techniques); and technical (obstetrics, child-rearing, neonatology). Buys 24 mss/year. Query with outline, lead and published clips. Length: 1,500-2,500 words. Pays $300-500. Pays expenses of writers on assignment.
Fillers: Newsbreaks. Buys 10/year. Length: 250-750 words. Pays $50-100. No Byline.
Tips: "Queries should include a detailed outline, first paragraph, and writer's background. Articles should be serious and directed to an intelligent, specially trained reader. Frequently articles are too superficial in medical terms or lacking practical advice in teaching terms."

CLASSROOM COMPUTER LEARNING, 19 Davis Dr., Belmont CA 94002. Editor: Holly Brady. 50% freelance written. Monthly magazine published during school year emphasizing elementary through high school educational computing topics. Circ. 53,000. Pays on acceptance. Publishes ms an average of 4 months after acceptance. Buys all rights or first serial rights. Submit seasonal/holiday material 6 months in advance. Photocopied submissions OK. Electronic submissions OK; "we prefer Apple but we can accommodate others." Computer printout submissions acceptable; prefers letter-quality to dot-matrix. SASE. Reports in 2 months. Writer's guidelines with SAE and 1 first class stamp; sample copy for SAE and 70¢ postage.
Nonfiction: "We publish manuscripts that describe innovative ways of using computers in the classroom as well as articles that discuss controversial issues in computer education." How-to (specific computer-related activities for children in one of three segments of the school population: Kindergarten-5, 6-9, or 10-12); interviews; and featurettes describing fully developed and tested classroom ideas. Recent article example: "How to Turn Your Computer into a Science Lab" (February 1985). Buys 50 mss/year. Query. Length: 600 words or less for classroom activities; 1,000-1,500 words for classroom activity featurettes; 1,500-2,500 words for major articles. Pays $25 for activities; $100-150 for featurettes; varying rates for longer articles. Educational Software Reviews: Assigned through editorial offices. "If interested, send a letter telling us of your areas of inter-

---

 A writer contacted *Modern Drummer* about doing an article on a prominent musician, then tried using his connection with our magazine to get free records, concert tickets, etc., that had no connection with the article he was doing for us. When we found out what he was doing, we cancelled the assignment.

—Rick Mattingly
Modern Drummer

est and expertise as well as the microcomputer(s) you have available to you." Pays $100 per review. Sometimes pays expenses of writers on assignment.

Photos: State availability of photos with query. Also interested in series of photos for posters showing real world use of computers and innovative computer art.

Tips: "The talent that goes in to writing our shorter hands-on pieces is different from that required for features (e.g., interviews, issues pieces, etc.) Write whatever taps you talent best. A frequent mistake is taking too 'novice' or too 'expert' an approach. You need to know our audience well and to understand how much they know about computers. Also, too many manuscripts lack a definite point of view or focus or opinion. We like pieces with clear, strong, well thought out opinions."

COACHING REVIEW, Coaching Association of Canada, 333 River Rd., Ottawa, Ontario K1L 8B9 Canada. (613)748-5624. Editor: Vic MacKenzie. 40% freelance written. Bimonthly magazine in separate English and French issues; 80 pages. For volunteer, community and paid coaches, high school and university sports personnel. Circ. 10,000. Offers on acceptance. Publishes ms an average of 3 months after acceptance. Buys first North American serial rights. Pays 50-75% kill fee. Byline given unless author requests otherwise. Phone queries OK. Submit seasonal/holiday material 3 months in advance. Electronic submissions OK on Macintosh/Micom. Computer printout submissions acceptable; prefers letter-quality to dot-matrix. Reports in 3 weeks. Free sample copy.

Nonfiction: How-to (coach-related of a general interest to all sports); humor (in coaching situations); inspirational (coaching success stories); interview (with top successful coaches); and new product (new ideas and ways of coaching). Wants "authoritative original material on coaching topics." Does not want sports stories with little or no relevance to coaching. Buys 20-30 unsolicited mss/year. Query with complete ms. Length: 1,500-2,500 words. Pays up to $300. Pays expenses of writers on assignment.

Photos: State availability of photos. Pays $5-25 for b&w contact sheets; $15-30 for slide size color transparencies. Captions required. Buys one-time rights.

Tips: "The freelancer can best break in with short articles and fillers so we can appraise the quality of writing and then give an assignment."

COMPUTERS IN EDUCATION, Unit 6, 25 Overlea Blvd., Toronto, Ontario M4H 1B1 Canada. (416)423-3262. Editor: Roger Allen. 80% freelance written. Magazine published 10 times/year; 48+ pages. Articles of interest to teachers, computer consultants and administrators working at the kindergarten to 13 level. Circ. 18,000. Pays on publication. Publishes ms an average of 2 months after acceptance. Byline given. Buys first serial rights, first North American serial rights, one time rights, second serial (reprint) rights, and all rights. Phone queries OK. Photocopied submissions OK. Electronic submissions OK on WordStar and Apple CP/M, but requires hard copy also. Free sample copy and writer's guidelines with SASE or IRC.

Nonfiction: Use of computers in education and techniques of teaching using computers; lesson plans, novel applications, anything that is practical for the teacher. Does not want overviews, "Gee Whizzes," and reinventions of the wheel. Length 700-2,000 words. Pays 6-10¢/word.

Photos: Photos and/or artwork all but mandatory. Pays extra for photos. Captions required.

Tips: "We are looking for practical articles by working teachers. Nothing too general, no overviews, or the same thing that has been said for years."

CURRICULUM REVIEW, Curriculum Advisory Service, 517 S. Jefferson St., Chicago IL 60607. (312)939-3010. Editor-in-Chief: Irene M. Goldman. Managing Editor: Charlotte H. Cox. 80% freelance written. A multidisciplinary magazine for kindergarten-12 principals, department heads, teachers, curriculum planners and superintendents; published 6 times/year. Circ. 10,000. Each issue includes articles in the areas of language arts/reading, mathematics, science, social studies, and the educational uses of computers. A separate feature section varies from issue to issue. Pays on publication. Publishes ms an average of 6 months after acceptance. Byline given. Buys all rights. Photocopies and multiple queries OK, but no multiple submissions. Computer printout submissions acceptable; prefers letter-quality to dot-matrix. SASE. Reports in 6 weeks on queries; 4 months on mss. Free sample copy and writer's guidelines.

Nonfiction: Barbara Berndt, articles editor. How-to articles should consider primarily an audience of secondary educators and describe successful teaching units or courses with practical applications. Articles of interest to kindergarten-8 educators also welcome. Focus should be on innovative or practical programs, teaching units, new curriculum trends, and controversial or stimulating ideas in education. "While we need articles in all four areas (language arts/reading, math, science, social studies), math and science are especially welcome." Buys 45 mss/year. Length: 1,000-2,000 words. Query. Pays $25-100.

Photos: State availability of photos with query. Prefers 35mm color transparencies or 8x10 b&w or color prints. Model release required. Buys all rights with ms; no additional payment.

Columns/Departments: 600 book reviews/year on an assigned basis with educational vita; textbook, supplements, media, and computer software selection in language arts/reading, mathematics, science and social studies. Emphazises secondary level. "We are looking for new and lively treatments of educational topics. Description of specific teaching units or courses are welcome if they have broad implications for other schools. Use fresh, descriptive, plain language—no educationalese." Length: 300-600 words. Pays $20-50.

Tips: "In 1986 we will feature global awareness, learning skills, the classroom of the future, the reading and writing connection, and instructional management systems. Schedule available upon request. The writer has a better chance of breaking in with short articles and fillers since we tend to invite submissions for feature articles to be sure that we have a choice available for feature deadlines."

‡**DAY CARE CENTER**, Diversified Periodicals, Box 249, Cobalt CT 06414. (203)342-4730. Editor: Bob Taylor. 75% freelance written. Bimonthly newspaper about day care centers, nursery schools and pre-schools. "Our audience is day care center owners and directors and experts in child care." Estab. 1985. Circ. target, 10,000. Pays on publication. Publishes ms an average of 3 months after acceptance. Byline given. Offers 33% kill fee. Buys one-time rights. Submit material at least 2 months in advance. Simultaneous queries and submissions, photocopied and previously published submissions OK. Computer printout submissions acceptable. SASE. Reports in 3 weeks on queries; 1 month on mss. Sample copy $1.50 and 9x12 SAE and 3 first class stamps; writer's guidelines for 4x9½ SASE and 1 first class stamp.

Nonfiction: Book excerpts, historical/nostalgic, humor, inspirational, interview/profile, new product, opinion, personal experience, photo feature and technical. Buys 20 mss/year. Query. Length: 200-2,500 words. Pays $15-75.

Photos: State availability of photos with query. Prefers 5x7 or 8x10 b&w prints. Also develops and prints 35mm rolls. Pays $5-30. Captions required. Buys one-time rights.

Fillers: Clipping, jokes, gags, anecdotes, short humor and newsbreaks. Buys 50/year. Length depends on subject. Pays $5-15.

Tips: "We are particularly interested in stories on day care centers as business enterprises but also are interested in preschool education and play. Query with specific story in mind. The areas most open to freelancers are profiles on centers, their owners, directors and staff. Providing that the stories fit our format, we are interested in what freelance writers come up with on their own. We are interested in a mix of styles and will work diligently with a writer."

INSTRUCTOR MAGAZINE, 545 5th Ave., New York NY 10017. (212)503-2888. Editor-in-Chief: Leanna Landsmann. 30% freelance written. Monthly magazine; 180 pages. Emphasizes elementary education. Circ. 269,281. Pays on acceptance. Buys all rights or first North American serial rights. Submit seasonal/holiday material 6 months in advance. Photocopied submissions OK. Computer printout submissions acceptable; prefers letter-quality to dot-matrix. SASE. Reports in 6 weeks. Free writer's guidelines; mention *Writer's Market* in request.

Nonfiction: How-to articles on elementary classroom practice—practical suggestions as well as project reports. Query. Length: 750-2,500 words. Pays $35-300 for articles; $150-250 for short features. Send all queries to Marge Scherer, managing editor/editorial. No poetry.

Tips: "The most frequent mistake made by writers is that the material is better suited for a general audience than for teachers."

LEARNING 85, (formerly *Learning*,) 1111 Bethlehem Pike, Springhouse PA 19477. Editor: Maryanne Wagner. 45% freelance written. Published monthly during school year. Emphasizes elementary and junior high school education topics. Circ. 200,000. Pays on acceptance. Buys all rights. Submit seasonal/holiday material 6 months in advance. Photocopied submissions OK. Computer printout submissions acceptable. SASE. Reports in 3 months. Free writer's guidelines. Sample copy $3.

Nonfiction: "We publish manuscripts that describe innovative, practical teaching strategies or probe controversial and significant issues of interest to kindergarten to 8th grade teachers." How-to (classroom management, specific lessons or units or activities for children—all at the elementary and junior high level, and hints for teaching in all curriculum areas): personal experience (from teachers in elementary and junior high schools); and profile (with teachers who are in unusual or innovative teaching situations). Strong interest in articles that deal with discipline, teaching strategy, motivation and working with parents. Recent articles example: "Teaching Self-Discipline" (August 1985); "Nancie Atwell on How *We* Learned to Write" (March 1985). Buys 250 mss/year. Query. Length: 1,000-3,500 words. Pays $50-350.

Photos: State availability of photos with query. Model release required. "We are also interested in series of photos for teaching posters that present a topic or tell a story that will be of interest to children."

MOMENTUM, National Catholic Educational Association, 1077 30th St., NW, Washington DC 20007. Editor: Patricia Feistritzer. 10% freelance written. Quarterly magazine; 56-64 pages. For Catholic administrators and teachers, some parents and students, in all levels of education (preschool, elementary, secondary, higher). Circ. 14,500. Pays on publication. Buys first rights only. Submit material 3 months in advance. SASE. Reports in 1 month. Free sample copy.

Nonfiction: Articles concerned with educational philosophy, psychology, methodology, innovative programs, teacher training, research, financial and public relations programs and management systems—all applicable to nonpublic schools. Book reviews on educational/religious topics. Avoid general topics or topics applicable *only* to public education. "We look for a straightforward, journalistic style with emphasis on practical examples, as well as scholarly writing and statistics. All references must be footnoted, fully documented. Emphasis is on professionalism." Buys 28-36 mss/year. Query with outline. Length: 1,500-2,000 words. Pays 2¢/word.
Photos: Pays $7 for b&w glossy photos purchased with mss. Captions required.

PHI DELTA KAPPAN, Box 789, Bloomington IN 47402-0789. Editor: Robert W. Cole Jr. 2% freelance written. Monthly magazine; 72 pages. For educators—teachers, kindergarten-12 administrators and college professors. All hold BA degrees; one-third hold doctorates. Circ. 140,000. Buys all rights. Pays on publication. Publishes ms an average of 6 months after acceptance. SASE. Reports in 2 months. Free sample copy.
Nonfiction: Feature articles on education—emphasizing policy, trends, both sides of issues, controversial developments. Also informational, how-to, personal experience, inspirational, humor, think articles and expose. "Our audience is scholarly but hard-headed." Buys 5 mss/year. Submit complete ms. Length: 500-4,000 words. Pays $100-750. "We pay a fee only occasionally, and then it is usually to an author whom *we* seek out. We do welcome inquiries from freelancers, but it is misleading to suggest that we buy very much from them."
Photos: Pays average photographer's rates for b&w photos purchased with mss, but captions are required. Will purchase photos on assignment. Sizes: 8x10 or 5x7 preferred.

SCHOOL ARTS MAGAZINE, 50 Portland St., Worcester MA 01608. Editor: David W. Baker. 85% freelance written. Monthly, except June, July and August. Serves arts and craft education profession, kindergarten-12, higher education and museum education programs. Written by and for art teachers. Pays on publication. Publishes ms an average of 2 months "if timely; if less pressing, can be 1 year or more" after acceptance. Buys first serial rights and second serial (reprint) rights. Computer printout submissions acceptable; prefers letter-quality to dot-matrix. Reports in 3 months. SASE. Free sample copy.
Nonfiction: Articles, with photos, on art and craft activities in schools. Should include description and photos of activity in progress as well as examples of finished art work. Query or send complete ms. Length: 600-1,400 words. Pays $20-100.
Tips: "We prefer articles on actual art projects or techniques done by students in actual classroom situations. Philosophical and theoretical aspects of art and art education are usually handled by our contributing editors. Our articles are renewed and accepted on merit and each is tailored to meet our needs. Keep in mind that art teachers want practical tips, above all. Our readers are visually, not verbally, oriented. Write your article with the accompanying photographs in hand." The most frequent mistakes made by writers are "bad visual material (photographs, drawings) submitted with articles, or a lack of complete descriptions of art processes; and no rational behind programs or activities discarded. It takes a close reading of School Arts to understand its function and the needs of its readers. Some writers lack the necessary familiarity with art education."

SCHOOL SHOP, Prakken Publications, Inc., Box 8623, Ann Arbor MI 48107. Editor: Lawrence W. Prakken. 100% freelance written. A monthly (except June and July) magazine covering issues, trends and projects of interest to industrial, vocational and technical educators at the secondary and post secondary school levels. Special issue in April deals with varying topics for which mss are solicited. Circ. 45,000. Buys all rights. Pays on publication. Publishes ms an average of 6 months after acceptance. Byline given. Prefers authors who have direct connection with the field of industrial and/or technical education. Submit seasonal material 3 months in advance. Simultaneous queries, and simultaneous, photocopied, and previously published submissions OK. Computer printout submissions acceptable. Reports in 6 weeks. SASE. Free sample copy and writer's guidelines.
Nonfiction: Alan H. Jones, managing editor. Uses articles pertinent to the various teaching areas in industrial education (woodwork, electronics, drafting, machine shop, graphic arts, computer training, etc.). "The outlook should be on innovation in educational programs, processes or projects which directly apply to the industrial/technical education area." Buys general interest, how-to, opinion, personal experience, technical and think pieces, interviews, humor, and coverage of new products. Buys 135 unsolicited mss/year. Length: 200-2,000 words. Pays $20-100.
Photos: Alan H. Jones, managing editor. Send photos with accompanying query or ms. Reviews b&w and color prints. Payment for photos included in payment for ms.
Columns/Departments: Alan H. Jones, managing editor. Shop Kinks (brief items which describe short-cuts or special procedures relevant to the industrial arts classroom). Buys 30 mss/year. Send complete ms. Length: 20-100 words. Pays $10 minimum.
Tips: "We are most interested in articles written by industrial, vocational and technical educators about their class projects and their ideas about the field."

SIGHTLINES, Educational Film Library Association, Inc., 45 John St., New York NY 10038. (212)227-5599. Publisher: Marilyn Levin. 80% freelance written. Quarterly magazine; 44 pages. Emphasizes the nontheatrical film and video world for librarians in university and public libraries, independent filmmakers and video makers, film teachers on the high school and college level, film programmers in the community, university, religious organizations and film curators in museums. Circ. 3,000. Pays on publication. Publishes ms an average of 5 months after acceptance. Byline given. Buys all rights. Phone queries OK. Computer printout submissions acceptable; dot-matrix submissions acceptable "if on format of copy guidelines." SASE. Reports in 2 months. Free sample copy for SAE and 4 first class stamps.

Nonfiction: Informational (on the production, distribution and programming of nontheatrical films); interview (with filmmakers who work in 16mm, video; who make documentary, avant-garde, children's, and personal films); new product; and personal opinion (for regular Freedom To View column). No fanzine or feature film material. Buys 4 mss/issue. Query. Length: 4,000-6,000 words. Pay $2\frac{1}{2}$¢/word.

Photos: Purchased with accompanying ms. Offers no additional payment for photos accepted with accompanying ms. Captions and model release required.

Columns/Departments: Who's Who in Filmmaking (interview or profile of filmmaker or video artist who works in the nontheatrical field); Members Reports (open to those library or museum personnel, film teachers, who are members of the Educational Film Library Association and who have creative ideas for programming films or media in institutions, have solved censorship problems, or other nuts-and-bolts thoughts on using film/media in libraries/schools). Buys 1-3 mss/issue. Query. Pays $2\frac{1}{2}$¢/word. Open to suggestions for new columns or departments.

Tips: A frequent mistake made by writers is "not paying attention to editor's suggestions as to focus and intended use to readership."

‡**TEACHER UPDATE, Ideas for Teachers**, Teacher Update, Inc., Box 205, Saddle River NJ 07458. (201)327-8486. Editor: Nicholas A. Roes. 100% freelance written. Monthly (except July and August) newsletter covering early childhood education for preschool teachers. Circ. 10,000. Pays on acceptance. Publishes ms an average of 3 months after acceptance. Byline given. Offers 100% kill fee. Buys all rights. Submit seasonal/holiday material 4 months in advance. Simultaneous queries, and simultaneous, photocopied, and previously published submissions OK. Computer printout submissions acceptable; prefers letter-quality to dot-matrix. SASE. Reports in 6 weeks on queries. Sample copy and writer's guidelines for SASE.

Nonfiction: How-to (suggestions for classroom activities). Query. Pays $20/published page.

Columns/Departments: Special Days and Free Materials. Buys 15 mss/year. Query. Pays $20/published page.

Poetry: Children's poems, fingerplays, etc. Buys 6-10/year. Pays $20/published page.

Tips: "Submit original ideas and make sure submissions are in the *Teacher Update* format."

TEACHING AND COMPUTERS, The Magazine for Elementary Teachers, Scholastic Inc., 730 Broadway, New York NY 10003. (212)505-3051. Editor: Mary Dalheim. 80% freelance written. Monthly magazine covering computers and education, especially how to incorporate the computer into the teacher's everyday curriculum. Circ. 55,000. Pays on acceptance. Publishes ms an average of 5 months after acceptance. Byline given. Offers variable kill fee. Buys all rights. Submit seasonal/holiday material 7 months in advance. Simultaneous queries OK. Computer printout submissions acceptable. SASE. Reports in 3 weeks. Sample copy for $8\frac{1}{2}$x11 SASE; writer's guidelines for #10 envelope and 1 first class stamp.

Nonfiction: How-to (use computers in the classroom); new product; opinion (on computers); and photo feature. No book reviews. Buys 40 mss/year. Send complete ms. Length: 500-2,000 words. Pays $50-300.

Fiction: Short stories and plays about computers for children in grades kindergarten-8. Buys 4 mss/year. Send complete ms. Length: 2,000 words maximum. Pays $50-300.

TODAY'S CATHOLIC TEACHER, 26 Reynolds Ave., Ormond Beach FL 32074. (904)672-9974. Editor-in-Chief: Ruth A. Matheny. 25% freelance written. For administrators, teachers and parents concerned with Catholic schools, both parochial and CCD. Circ. 65,000. Pays after publication. Publishes ms an average of 3 months after acceptance. Byline given. Buys all rights. Phone queries OK. Submit seasonal/holiday material 3 months in advance. SASE required. Sample copy $2; free writer's guidelines for SASE; mention *Writer's Market* in request.

Nonfiction: How-to (based on experience, particularly in Catholic situations, philosophy with practical applications); interview (of practicing educators, educational leaders); personal experience (classroom happenings); and profile (of educational leader). Buys 40-50 mss/year. Submit complete ms. Length: 800-2,000 words. Pays $15-75.

Photos: State availability of photos with ms. Offers no additional payment for 8x10 b&w glossy prints. Buys one-time rights. Captions preferred; model release required.

Tips: "We use many one-page features"

Electricity

These publications are edited for electrical engineers; electrical contractors; and others who build, design, and maintain systems connecting and supplying homes, businesses, and industries with power. Publications for appliance servicemen and dealers can be found in the Home Furnishings and Household Goods classification.

ELECTRIC LIGHT & POWER, Technical Publishing Co., 1301 S. Grove Ave., Barrington IL 60010. (312)381-1840. Editor: Robert A. Lincicome. Managing Editor: Robert W. Smock. Monthly tabloid covering engineering and operations for electric utility executives, managers and engineers. Circ. 42,500. Pays on publication. Byline given. Buys first serial rights. Submit seasonal/holiday material 4 months in advance. Simultaneous queries OK. SASE. Reports in 3 weeks.
Nonfiction: Technical. "No general electricity articles or pieces discussing benefits of electrification, lighting, industrial, commercial or residential uses of electricity." Buys 12-15 mss/year. Query. Length: 4,000 words maximum. Pays $25-200/published page.
Photos: Send photos or copies of photos with ms.
Tips: "Writers must be familiar with electric utility technology and engineering, finance, regulation and operations."

ELECTRICAL BUSINESS, Kerrwil Publications, Ltd., 501 Oakdale Rd., Downsview, Ontario M3N 1W7 Canada. (416)482-6603. Editor-in-Chief: Randolph W. Hurst. 25% freelance written. Monthly magazine for marketing and operations personnel in electrical manufacturing, maintenance and construction as well as distributors. Circ. 22,000. Pays on acceptance. Byline given. Buys first North American serial rights. Offers 10% kill fee. Phone queries OK. Submit seasonal/holiday material 4 months in advance. Previously published submissions "sometimes considered." SAE, IRCs. Reports in 2 weeks. Free sample copy.
Nonfiction: Canadian electrical industry content only. How-to (problem solving, wiring, electrical construction and maintenance); general interest (to the electrical industry); interview (with electrical distributors and maintenance men); new product ("from manufacturers—we don't pay for news releases"); and technical. Query. Length: 500-1,500 words. Pays 10¢/word.
Photos: State availability of photos with query. Pays $5 for b&w photos; negotiable payment for color transparencies. Captions required. Buys one-time rights.

ELECTRICAL CONTRACTOR, 7315 Wisconsin Ave., Bethesda MD 20814. (301)657-3110. Editor: Larry C. Osius. 10% freelance written. Monthly. For electrical contractors. Circ. 59,000. Publishes ms an average of 3 months after acceptance. Byline given. Buys first serial rights, second serial (reprint) rights or simultaneous rights. SASE. Usually reports in 1 month. Free sample copy.
Nonfiction: Installation articles showing informative application of new techniques and products. Slant is product and method contributing to better, faster and more economical construction process. Query. Length: 800-2,500 words. Pays $90/printed page, including photos and illustrative material.
Photos: Photos should be sharp, reproducible glossies, 5x7 and up.

IEEE SPECTRUM, Institute of Electrical and Electronics Engineers, Inc., 345 E. 47th St., New York NY 10017. (212)705-7555. Editor/Publisher: Donald Christiansen. Administrative Editor: Ronald K. Jurgen. Monthly magazine covering electrical/electronics engineering for executive and staff electrical and electronics engineers in design, development, research, production, operations, maintenance in the field of electronic and allied product manufacturing, commercial users of electronic equipment, independent research development firms, government and military departments and service/installation establishments. Circ. 250,000. Pays on acceptance. Buys first serial rights and all rights. Phone queries OK. Submit material 4 months in advance. Photocopied submissions OK. Computer printout submissions acceptable; prefers letter-quality to dot-matrix. Reports in 2 weeks. Free sample copy and writer's guidelines.
Nonfiction: Interview (about socio-technical subjects and energy); technical overviews; historical; and opinion (about careers and management). No elementary business, accounting or management topics. Buys 1 ms/issue. Query. Length: 4,000-5,000 words. Pays $400-$1,500 on work-for-hire articles. Does not pay for articles written by IEEE members.
Columns/Departments: Relate to meetings; industrial developments and publications in the electrical or electronics engineering field. Most departmental material is staff written.
Tips: "Contact the senior editor with story ideas. Be able to exhibit a working knowledge of the magazine's charter."

PUBLIC POWER, 2301 M St. NW, Washington DC 20037. (202)775-8300. Editor: Vic Reinemer. 20% freelance written. Bimonthly. Not copyrighted. Pays on publication. Publishes ms an average of 3 months after acceptance. Byline given. Buys first serial rights. Electronic submissions OK on IBM PC, but requires hard copy also. Computer printout submissions acceptable. Free writer's guidelines.
Nonfiction: Features on municipal and other local publicly-owned electric systems. Payment negotiable.
Photos: Uses b&w and glossy color prints, and slides.

SUNSHINE SERVICE NEWS, Florida Power & Light Co., Box 29100, Miami FL 33102. (305)552-3887. Editor: L.A. Muniz, Jr. 5% freelance written. Monthly employee newspaper for electrical utility . Circ. 15,000. Pays on publication. Publishes ms an average of 3 months after acceptance. Buys first serial rights. Not copyrighted. Computer printout submissions acceptable. Free sample copy.
Nonfiction: Company news, employee news, general interest, historical, how-to, humor and job safety. Company tie-in preferred. Query. Pays $25-100.

Electronics and Communication

Listed here are publications for electronics engineers, radio and TV broadcasting managers, electronic equipment operators, and builders of electronic communications systems and equipment (including stereos, television sets, radio-TV broadcasting, and cable broadcasting systems). Journals for professional announcers or communicators can be found under Journalism and Entertainment and the Arts; those for electric appliance retailers are in Home Furnishings and Household Goods; publications on computer design and data processing systems are listed in Data Processing. Magazines on personal computers appear in the Consumer/Personal Computing section. Publications for electronics enthusiasts or stereo hobbyists can be found in Science or Music in the Consumer Publications section.

ANSWER LINE, On Page Enterprises, Box 439, Sudbury MA 01776. Editor: Stanley J. Kaplan. Managing Editor: Bette Sidlo. 10% freelance written. Bimonthly newsletter focusing on telephone answering services for professional and medical offices, sales and service centers as well as small business people who need telephones monitored when they are not in. Circ. 50,000 initially. Pays on acceptance. Publishes ms an average of 4 months after acceptance. Buys all rights. Phone queries OK. Submit seasonal material 3 months in advance. SASE. Reports in 2 weeks. Free sample copy and writers' guidelines.
Fillers: Clippings, jokes, gags, anecdotes, short humor and newsbreaks. "We are particularly interested in anecdotes in the first person narrative, stories of people and their *positive* answering service experiences and newsbreaks on various developments in business communications as they relate to telephone answering service applications. We particularly seek seasonal material." Buys 10-20 mss/year. Length: 75-150 words. Pays $25-40 minimum.
Tips: Submissions should be geared to telephone answering service clients with emphasis on the advantages of retaining such service. "Submit nothing on answering machines—they compete with our customers' services."

BROADCAST ENGINEERING, Box 12901, Overland Park KS 66212. Editorial Director: Bill Rhodes. 30% freelance written. For "owners, managers, and top technical people at AM, FM, TV stations, cable TV operators, as well as recording studios." Monthly. Circ. 35,000. Buys all rights. Buys 50 mss/year. Pays on acceptance; "for a series, we pay for each part on publication." Publishes ms an average of 3 months after acceptance. Free sample copy and writer's guidelines. Computer printout submissions acceptable. Reports in 6 weeks. SASE.
Nonfiction: Wants technical features dealing with design, installation, modification and maintenance of radio and TV broadcast equipment; interested in features of interest to communications engineers and technicians as well as broadcast management, and features on self-designed and constructed equipment for use in broadcast and communications field. "We use a technical, but not textbook, style. Our publication is mostly how-to, and it operates as a forum. We reject material that is far too general, not on target, not backed by evidence of proof, or is a sales pitch. Our Station-to-Station column provides a forum for equipment improvement and build-it-yourself tips. We pay up to $30. We're especially interested in articles on recording studios and improving facilities and techniques." Buys 10-20 unsolicited mss/year. Query. Length: 1,500-2,000 words for features. Pays $75-200.

Photos: Photos purchased with or without mss; captions required. Pays $5-10 for b&w prints; $10-100 for 2¼x2¼ or larger color transparencies.

BROADCAST TECHNOLOGY, Box 420, Bolton, Ontario L0P 1A0 Canada. (416)857-6076. Editor-in-Chief: Doug Loney. 50% freelance written. Bimonthly magazine; 72 pages. Emphasizes broadcast engineering. Circ. 7,000. Pays on publication. Byline given. Buys all rights. Phone queries OK.
Nonfiction: Technical articles on developments in broadcast engineering, especially pertaining to Canada. Query. Length: 500-1,500 words. Pays $100-300.
Photos: Purchased with accompanying ms. B&w or color. Total purchase price for a ms includes payment for photos. Captions required.
Tips: "Most of our outside writing is by regular contributors, usually employed full-time in broadcast engineering. The specialized nature of our magazine requires a specialized knowledge on the part of a writer, as a rule."

BROADCASTER, 7 Labatt Ave., Toronto, Ontario M5A 3P2 Canada. (416)363-6111. Editor: Barbara Moes. For the Canadian "communications industry—radio, television, cable, ETV, advertisers and their agencies." Monthly. Circ. 7,200. Buys all rights. Byline given. Buys 50-60 mss/year. Pays on publication. Writers should submit outlines and samples of published work; sample issue will be sent for style. Not responsible for unsolicited mss. SAE and IRCs.
Nonfiction: Technical and general articles about the broadcasting industry, almost exclusively Canadian. Length: 1,000-2,000 words. Pays $125-350.
Photos: Rarely purchased.

CABLE COMMUNICATIONS MAGAZINE, Canada's Authoritative International Cable Television Publication, Ter-Sat Media Publications Ltd., 4 Smetana Dr., Kitchener, Ontario N2B 3B8 Canada. (519)744-4111. Editor: Udo Salewsky. 33% freelance written. Monthly magazine covering the cable television industry. Circ. 6,300. Pays on acceptance. Publishes ms an average of 2 months after acceptance. Byline given. Buys all rights. Submit seasonal/holiday material 1 month in advance. Photocopied submissions OK. Computer printout submissions acceptable; no dot-matrix. Reports in 2 weeks on queries; 1 month on mss. Free writer's guidelines; $2 IRCs for sample copy.
Nonfiction: Expose, how-to, interview/profile, opinion, technical articles, and informed views and comments on topical, industry related issues. No fiction. Buys 50 mss/year. Query with published clips or send complete ms. Length: 1,000-4,000 words. Pays $200-800. Pays expenses of writers on assignment.
Columns/Departments: Buys 48 items/year. Query with published clips or send complete ms. Length: 1,000-1,500 words. Pays $200-300.
Tips: "Forward manuscript and personal resume. We don't need freelance writers for articles and fillers. Break in with articles related to industry issues, events and new developments; analysis of current issues and events. Be able to interpret the meaning of new developments relative to the cable television industry and their potential impact on the industry from a growth opportunity as well as a competitive point of view. Material should be well supported by facts and data. Insufficient research and understanding of underlying issues are frequent mistakes."

CABLE MARKETING, The Marketing/Management Magazine for Cable Television Executives, Jobson Publishing, 352 Park Ave. South, New York NY 10010. (212)685-4848. Executive Editor: Nicolas Furlotte. 10% freelance written. Monthly magazine for cable industry executives dealing with marketing and management topics, new trends and developments and their impact. Circ. 15,000. Pays on publication. Publishes ms an average of 2 months after acceptance. Byline given. Buys first North American serial rights. Photocopied submissions OK. Computer printout submissions acceptable; no dot-matrix. Reports in 1 month. Free sample copy.
Columns/Departments: Cable Tech (technology, engineering and new products); Fine Tuning (programming items with emphasis on stand-alone products and alternative forms of programming, also Hollywood/movie studio items); and Cable Scan (news items and marketing featurettes mostly about cable system activities and developments). Buys 20 mss/year. Query with published clips. Length: 200-1,000 words. Pays $50-200.
Tips: "Learn something about the cable TV business before you try to write about it. Have specific story ideas. Have some field of expertise that you can draw upon (e.g., marketing or advertising). Short articles and fillers gives us a chance to better assess a writer's real abilities without exposing us to undue risk, expense, aggravation, etc. on a feature." Not interested in "reviews" of programming. Editorial focus is on the *business* of cable television.

‡**CABLE TELEVISION BUSINESS MAGAZINE**, (formerly *TVC Magazine*), Cardiff Publishing Co., 6430 S. Yosemite St., Englewood CO 80111. (303)694-1522. Editor: Jill Marks. Managing Editor: Chuck Moozakis. 20% freelance written. Semimonthly magazine about cable television for CATV system operators

and equipment suppliers. Circ. 15,000. Pays on publication. Publishes ms an average of 3 months after acceptance. Byline given. Makes work-for-hire assignments. Phone queries OK. Electronic submissions OK via Apple III, Word Juggler software, but requires hard copy also. Computer printout submissions acceptable; no dotmatrix. Reports in 2 weeks on queries; 1 month on mss. Free sample copy.

Nonfiction: Expose (of industry corruption and government mismanagement); historical (early days of CATV); interview (of important people in the industry); profiles (of people or companies); how-to (manage or engineer cable systems); new product (description and application); and case history. "We use articles on all aspects of cable television from programming through government regulation to technical pieces. We use both color and black and white photos, charts and graphs. A writer should have some knowledge of cable television, then send a letter with a proposed topic." Recent article example: "ESPN: Rookie Turns Veteran," (covered programmer, ESPN—February 1, 1985). No first person articles. Buys 5 mss/year. Query. Length: 1,800-3,500 words. Pays $100/page of magazine space. Sometimes pays expenses of writers on assignment.

Photos: State availability of photos. Reviews 35mm color transparencies. Pays $50/page of magazine space for contact sheets. Offers no additional payment for photos accepted with ms. Captions required.

Tips: "The most frequent mistake made by writers in completing an article for us is not being specific enough about what the story topic really means to cable management—i.e., dollars and cents, or operational strategy. Freelancers are only used for major features."

DEALERSCOPE, 115 2nd Ave., Waltham MA 02154. (617)890-5124. Managing Editor: Scott Badler. Monthly magazine covering consumer electronics, home entertainment and major appliances for retailers and manufacturers. Circ. 25,000. Pays on publication. Byline given. Offers 50% kill fee. Submit seasonal material 3 months in advance. Electronic submissions OK but "should call us before sending disk to ensure compatibility with our system." Computer printout submissions acceptable; prefers letter-quality to dot-matrix. SASE. Reports in 1 month. Sample copy for SAE.

Nonfiction: How-to and marketing information for retailers; profiles and interviews of retailers and industry leaders; new product; personal experience in home electronics retailing; technical information relating to new products and sales; and marketing analysis. No hobbyist pieces. Query with published clips. Length: 750-3,000 words. Pays $100-450.

Columns/Departments: Legal, finance, satellite TV, computers and videogames, audio, video (hardware and software), telephones, retailing, electronics accessories and major appliances.

EE'S ELECTRONICS DISTRIBUTOR, Sutton Publishing Company, Inc., 707 Westchester Ave., White Plains NY 10604. (914)949-8500. Editor-in-Chief: Edward J. Walter. 10% freelance written. Monthly tabloid for distributors of electronic parts and equipment (not hi-fi, television or computer). Circ. 15,000. Pays on publication. Publishes ms an average of 2 months after acceptance. Byline given. Buys first North American serial rights. Photocopied submissions OK. Computer printout submissions acceptable; prefers letter-quality to dot-matrix. SASE. Reports in 2 weeks. Free sample copy.

Nonfiction: Stories about specific areas of a distributor's operation such as sales, purchasing, inventory control, etc. No general columns on tax tips, government issues or inventory control. Buys 10 mss/year. Query. Length: 1,250 words typical. Pays $100/7 x 10 page, prorated to fractional pages. Pays expenses of writers on assignment.

Photos: Send photos with ms. Pays $10-15 for b&w contact sheets. Also reviews 5x7 prints. Captions required.

Tips: "We'll be more feature- and less news-oriented in the year ahead. Don't be too general or too basic."

ELECTRONICS WEST, Concept Communications Corp., Publishing, Inc., Suite 105, 2250 N. 16th St., Phoenix AZ 85006. (602)253-9086. Assistant Editor: Cyndy Albanese. 10% freelance written. Monthly magazine covering "a broad spectrum of electronics for middle managers and above associated with the Southwest electronics industry (manufacturing, wholesaling and retailing)." Circ. 20,000. Pays on publication. Byline given. Buys first serial rights. Submit seasonal/holiday material 3 months in advance. Simultaneous queries and photocopied submissions OK. Computer printout submissions acceptable; prefers letter-quality to dot-matrix. SASE. Reports in 3 weeks on queries. Sample copy for SAE and 7 first class stamps; writer's guidelines for SAE and 1 first class stamp.

Nonfiction: Historical/nostalgic (electronics-related); how-to (manage business); humor (unique applications of electronic technology); interview/profile (of businesses and business leaders); personal experience (of managers); photo feature; and technical (written in a nontechnical manner and in a marketing style). Buys 4-5 unsolicited mss/year. Query with published clips. Length: 1,000-2,000 words. Pays 10¢/word maximum.

Photos: State availability of photos. Pays $10 for 8x10 b&w glossy prints. Captions and model release required. Rights purchased are negotiable.

Tips: "We purchase only four to five freelance pieces per year. Major features are written in house or contributed. Submissions are often unrelated to the editorial content of the magazine, i.e., not in *high tech* electronics.

This may be due to the writer's failure to properly research the content of the magazine for which he intends to write." No articles dealing with consumer products—i.e., radio, TV, CB radios, etc., or articles dealing with electricity rather than electronics.

THE INDEPENDENT, Film & Video Monthly, Foundation for Independent Video & Film, 9th Floor, 625 Broadway, New York NY 10012. (212)473-3400. Editor: Martha Gever. 60% freelance written. Monthly magazine of practical information for producers of independent film and video with focus on low budget, art and documentary work from nonprofit sector. Circ. 5,000. Pays on publication. Publishes ms an average of 4 months after acceptance. Byline given. Buys first serial rights. Submit seasonal/holiday material 4 months in advance. Simultaneous queries OK. Computer printout submissions acceptable; no dot-matrix. SASE. Reports in 1 month. Sample copy for 9x12 SAE and 4 first class stamps.
Nonfiction: Book excerpts ("in our area"); how-to; technical (low tech only); and theoretical/critical articles. No reviews. Buys 60 mss/year. Query with published clips. Length: 1,200-3,500 words. Pays $25-100
Tips: "Since this is a specialized publication, it helps to work with writers on short pieces first. A frequent mistake made by writers is unfamiliarity with specific practical and theoretical issues concerning independent film and video."

INTERNATIONAL TELEVISION, The Journal of the International Television Association, Lakewood Publications, Inc., One Park Ave., New York NY 10016. (212)503-5777. Editor: Shonan Noronha. Assistant Editor: Karen Brogno. Monthly magazine covering teleproduction postproduction; equipment/engineering; and video manager topics. Circ. 26,000. Pays on publication. Publishes ms an average of 6 months after acceptance. Byline given. Buys one-time rights. Submit seasonal/holiday material 4 months in advance. Computer printout submissions acceptable (dot-matrix OK if readable and in upper and lower case). SASE. Reports in 1 month on queries; 2 months on mss. Free sample copy and writer's guidelines.
Nonfiction: How-to, (video production case studies, problem-solution approach); inspirational (creative writing or management techniques with how-to approach); and technical (video equipment/engineering topics, e.g., time base correction, system timing with waveform monitor). Query. Length: 1,500-3,000 words. Pays $75/printed page for feature articles.
Columns/Departments: Query. Length: 500-1,000 words. Pays $150 flat rate.

LASERS & APPLICATIONS, High Tech Publications, Inc., 23717 Hawthorne Blvd., Torrance CA 90505. (213)534-3700. Editor: James Cavuoto. 20% freelance written. Monthly magazine of laser and optical industry for engineers and designers. Circ. 30,000. Pays on acceptance. Publishes ms an average of 3 months after acceptance. No byline given. Offers 25% kill fee. Buys all rights. Electronic submissions OK but call first. Computer printout submissions acceptable. SASE. Reports in 1 month. Sample copy $4.
Nonfiction: "We stress new applications of lasers and laser processes in medical, electronics, metalworking, communication, printing, military and other fields. Articles describe how a laser was used to perform a task better or cheaper; and what kind of laser and operating conditions used; and what the prognosis is for selling lasers based on this process. We are particularly interested in applications of lasers in foreign countries." Query with published clips. Length: 250-1,500 words. Pays $100-200.

MASS HIGH TECH, Mass Tech Times, Inc., 755 Mt. Auburn St., Watertown MA 02172. (617)924-2422. Editor: Alan R. Earls. Managing Editor: Patrick Porter. 15% freelance written. Bimonthly trade tabloid covering feature news of electronics, computers, biotech, systems analysis, etc., for high-tech professionals in New England; strong regional angle preferred. Circ. 30,000. Pays on publication. Publishes ms an average of 2 weeks after acceptance. Byline given. Not copyrighted. Buys first North American serial rights. Submit seasonal/holiday material 1 month in advance. Simultaneous queries, and simultaneous, photocopied, and previously published submissions OK "if not in our immediate market." Computer printout submissions acceptable. SASE. Reports in 1 month. Sample copy for 9x12 SAE and 5 first class stamps.
Nonfiction: Book excerpts; historical (technology); humor; interview/profile; new product; opinion (qualified scientist); personal experience; and photo feature (needs technical orientation and strong Boston area orientation). "Material should inform without over simplifying. A light, amusing approach is OK." Increasingly oriented toward news and analysis of items impacting market area. Buys 50 mss/year. Send complete ms. Length: 400-1,200 words. Pays $50-250.
Photos: Send photos with ms. Pays $25 for 5x7 b&w prints. Captions and identification of subjects required (if appropriate). Buys one-time rights.
Columns/Departments: Buys 50 mss/year. Query with idea or send one sample ms. Length: 300-900 words. Pays $50 and up.
Fillers: Anecdotes, short humor and newsbreaks. Buys 100 mss/year. Length: 25-100 words. Pays $10 and up.
Tips: "Know the Boston and New England high-tech scene or have knowledgeable contacts. Material should be plausible to trained professionals. Trends in magazine publishing that freelance writers should be aware of include the need for more sophisticated graphics—photos or drawings are often available free from their corporate subjects (in our market)."

MICROWAVES & RF, 10 Mulholland Dr., Hasbrouck Height NJ 07604. (201)393-6285. Editor: Barry E. Manz. 50% freelance written. Monthly magazine; 200 pages. Emphasizes radio frequency design. "Qualified recipients are those individuals actively engaged in microwave and RF research, design, development, production and application engineering, engineering management, administration or purchasing departments in organizations and facilities where application and use of devices, systems and techniques involve frequencies from HF through visible light." Circ. 60,500. Pays on publication. Buys all rights. Phone queries OK. Photocopied submissions OK. Electronic submissions OK. Computer printouts acceptable "if legible." SASE. Reports in 3 weeks. Free sample copy and writer's guidelines; mention *Writer's Market* in request.
Nonfiction: "We are interested in material on research and development in microwave and RF technology and economic news that affects the industry." How-to (circuit design), new product, opinion; and technical. Buys 70 mss/year. Query. Pays $50/published page.
Fillers: Newsbreaks. Pays $10 minimum.

MICROWAVE SYSTEMS NEWS & COMMUNICATIONS TECHNOLOGY (MSN & CT), (formerly *MSN Microwave Systems News*), EW Communications, Inc., 1170 E. Meadow Dr., Palo Alto CA 94303. (415)494-2800. Editor: Alexander E. Braun. Managing Editor: Cedric R. Braun. Monthly magazine covering developments in the microwave industry: communications, radar, avionics, monolithic integration, testing, etc. "*MSN* reaches an audience composed primarily of electrical engineers, who are interested in solving design problems and in the latest developments in the microwave industry." Circ. 55,000. Pays on publication. Byline given. Buys all rights. Submit seasonal/holiday material 3 months in advance. Computer printout submissions acceptable; prefers letter-quality to dot-matrix. SASE. Reports in 2 weeks. Sample copy for legal size SAE and $3 postage; free writer's guidelines.
Nonfiction: Technical. "No PR-hype or marketing articles." Buys 96 mss/year. Query. Length: 3,500-4,000 words. Pays $200 minimum.
Photos: Send photos with query. Reviews 8x10 b&w and color prints. Payment for photos included in payment for ms. Captions and identification of subjects required.
Tips: "Since our publication goes to a very specialized audience, prospective authors should have a solid technical writing background and possibly an engineering degree. Query first—always. We are always looking for the latest technical developments in the microwave industry. If the proposed article is solid, it'll sell itself."

MULTICHANNEL NEWS, A Fairchild Business Publication, Fairchild Publications, #450, 300 S. Jackson St., Denver CO 80209. (303)393-6397. Editor: Thomas P. Southwick. Managing Editor: Debbie Narrod. 10% freelance written. Weekly newspaper/tabloid covering cable and pay television with hard news only. "We invite stringer queries for markets outside New York, Los Angeles, Washington, Atlanta and Denver." Circ. 15,000. Pays on publication. Publishes ms an average of 1 week after acceptance. Byline given. Buys one-time rights. Photocopied submissions OK. Electronic submissions OK. Computer printout submissions acceptable; no dot-matrix. Reports in 2 weeks on queries. Sample copy $1.
Nonfiction: New product and technical on local cable system news or involvement. Articles by assignment only. Wants news articles; no features. Query, then follow up letter with phone call. Length: 1,000 words maximum. Pays by column inch.
Tips: "A freelancer can break into our publication with hard, breaking news about cable and/or pay TV. Use AP and UPI news style."

ON PAGE, On Page Enterprises, Box 439, Sudbury MA 01776. Editor: Stanley J. Kaplan. Managing Editor: Bette Sidlo. Monthly newsletter about "the beeper industry (radio pocket paging) for professionals, medical people, sales people, small businessmen, municipal employees and any person whose job takes him/her away from the telephone and who must maintain communications." Circ. 100,000. Pays on acceptance. Buys all rights. Submit seasonal material 3 months in advance. Phone queries OK. SASE. Reports in 2 weeks. Free sample copy and writer's guidelines.
Fillers: Clippings, jokes, gags, anecdotes, short humor and newsbreaks. "We are particularly interested in anecdotes for our On Page Forum column in the first person narrative, stories of people and their beeper experiences, and newsbreaks on a variety of communication subjects of interest to people who use beepers. We especially look for seasonal freelance contributions." Buys 10-20 mss/year. Length: 75-150 words. Pays $25-40.
Tips: "Submissions should be geared to beeper users (e.g., subject matter must be related to communications or mobility). No sarcasm or comments insulting those who carry or use a beeper."

‡**OUTSIDE PLANT, Practical Communications, Inc.**, Box 183, Cary IL 60013. (815)455-6006. Editor: Rick Hoelzer. Small percent freelance written. Bimonthly magazine covering construction in the US telephone industry. "We serve construction, maintenance and planning buyers and specifies with Bell and independent telephone companies plus contractors who specialize in such work." Estab. 1983. Circ. 16,000. Pays on publication. Publishes ms an average of 3 months after acceptance. Byline given "if appropriate." Buys all rights. Submit seasonal/holiday material 3 months in advance. Computer printout submissions acceptable; prefers letter-quality to dot-matrix. SASE. Reports in 1 month. Sample copy $5; free writer's guidelines.

Nonfiction: Technical (how to construct, maintain and plan outside telephone system). "Case history type articles are of particular interest." No nonoutside plant telephone material. Buys 3-4/issue. Send complete ms, or "phone us if you have any leads on construction or maintenance articles in telephone industry. Length: 1,200-2,400 words. Pays $100-300. Sometimes pays expenses of writers on assignment.

Columns/Departments: OP Tips & Advice, OP Tomorrow, New Products & Services, OP Literature, and OP Vehicles. Buys 5/issue. Send complete ms. Length: 100-1,000 words. Pays $25-100.

Tips: "Writer has a better chance of breaking in with short, lesser-paying articles because of the higher specialized material we need. The most frequent mistakes made by writer are lack of specific cost figures and overgeneralizing on material."

PERSONAL COMMUNICATIONS MAGAZINE, FutureComm Publications Inc., 4005 Williamsburg Ct., Fairfax VA 22032. (703)352-1200. Editor: Stuart Crump, Jr. Associate Editor: Benn Kobb. 25% freelance written. Monthly magazine covering telecommuncations developments with an emphasis on cellular radio, paging, voice mail, and other new personal communications technologies. "*PCM* is directed toward telecommunication professionals, such as telephone companies, radio common carriers, interconnect companies, and cellular companies." Circ. 25,000. Pays shortly after acceptance. Publishes ms an average of 3 months after acceptance. Byline given. Offers 50% kill fee. Buys first serial rights, one-time rights, or second serial (reprint) rights. "We encourage reprints with proper accreditation." Submit seasonal/holiday material 4 months in advance. Simultaneous queries, simultaneous, photocopied, and previously published submissions OK. Computer printout submissions acceptable. SASE. Reports in 1 month. Sample copy and writer's guidelines for SASE. Include phone number on all submissions.

Nonfiction: General interest (telecommunications); historical/nostalgic (on telecommunications); how-to (select the best telecommunications system, get the most for your money, install a telecommunications system); humor (personal communcations devices and technology); interview/profile (on people or companies in the telecommunications area); new product (telecommunications); opinion (on telecommunications); and personal experience (with devices, services, technologies). Also interested in high-tech articles, interpretive articles for laymen and articles on marketing methods of new radio businesses. No articles which are too general, "even if they concern personal communications. Be sure to read writer's guidelines and magazine first." Buys 20 mss/year. Length: 1,000-2,000 words. Pays $200-400. Sometimes pays expense of writers on assignment.

Photos: Reviews contact sheets, negatives, transparencies and prints. Identification of subjects required. Buys one-time rights.

Columns/Departments: Query first. Length: 1,000-2,000 words. Pays $200-350.

Fiction: Experimental and humorous. Query with or without published clips. Length: 1,000-2,000 words. Pays $200-400.

Fillers: Short humor. Buys 6/year. Length: 500-2,000. Pays $150-300.

Tips: "Concentrate on various personal communications devices such as cellular radio, two-way radio and computer links." We are interested in solid telecommunications articles written with the industry generalist and informed amateur in mind. Our field is new and unique. We advise a query by phone or letter first after reading writer's guidelines so we can guide the writer into submitting what we need."

PRO SOUND NEWS, International News Magazine for the Professional Sound Production Industry, Testa Communications, 220 Westbury Ave., Carle Place NY 11514. (516)334-7880. Editor: Randolph P. Savicky. 50% freelance written. Monthly tabloid covering the recording, sound reinforcement, TV and film sound industry. Circ. 13,000. Pays on publication. Publishes ms an average of 1 month after acceptance. Byline given. Buys first serial rights. Simultaneous queries, and photocopied and previously published submissions OK. Computer printout submissions acceptable. SASE. Reports in 2 weeks.

Nonfiction: Query with published clips. Pays 10¢/word.

PROMOTION NEWSLETTER, Radio and TV, Drawer 50108, Lighthouse Point FL 33064. (305)426-4881. Editor: William N. Udell. 15% freelance written. Monthly newsletter covering promotional activities of radio and television stations. Circ. 580. Pays on acceptance. Publishes ms an average of 2 months after acceptance. Byline may or may not be given. Not copyrighted. Buys one-time rights and nonexclusive reprints; makes work-for-hire assignments. Submit seasonal/holiday material 3 months in advance. Simultaneous queries, and simultaneous and photocopied submissions OK. Computer printout submissions acceptable; prefers letter-quality to dot-matrix. Reports in 2 weeks on queries; 1 month on mss. Free sample copy (while available).

Nonfiction: How-to; interview/profile (of promotional director of a busy station); and photo feature. "We are interested in all promotional activities of radio and TV stations and unusual examples of successful promotional events. We are also looking for special material for all holidays." No "fan" material. Query or send complete ms. Length: 100-500 words, sometimes more. Pays $15-150.

Photos: Reprints of ads and other material acceptable. Send photos with ms. Pays $5 minimum for b&w contact sheets and prints. Identification of subjects required. Buys one-time rights.

Fillers: Clippings and newsbreaks. Length: 100-500 words. Pays $15-150.

Tips: "The type of material we print seldom requires lengthy detail or hype. A frequent mistake is writing for general ('fan') consumption; these readers are professional business operators. No fluff."

SATELLITE DEALER, The Magazine for the Home Satellite Systems Industry, CommTek Publishing Co., Box 2700, Dept. D, Hailey ID 83333. (208)788-9522. Editor: Ron Rudolph. Executive Editor: Bruce Kinnaird. 75% freelance written. Monthly magazine covering the satellite television industry. Circ. 14,000. Pays on publication. Publishes ms an average of 4 months after acceptance. Byline given. Offers 33% kill fee. Buys first North American serial rights, one-time rights, all rights, first serial rights, and second serial (reprint) rights. Submit seasonal/holiday material 4 months in advance. Previously published submissions OK. Electronic submissions on IBM, CPM, and Turbo DOS 8-inch disks. Computer printout submissions acceptable; prefers letter-quality to dot-matrix. SASE. Reports in 5 weeks on queries. Free sample copy and writer's guidelines.

Nonfiction: Book excerpts (possible from new releases in industry); expose (on government communications policy); how-to (on installation of dishes); humor (if there is an angle); interview/profile (on industry leaders and exceptional dealers); personal experience (from TVRO dealers); photo feature (of unusual dish installations); technical (on radio theory as it pertains to satellite TV); and marketing. Special issues include trade show editions. "We print articles concerning the home satellite television industry. We also touch on SMATV (private cable). Everything we print must in some way be valuable to the satellite television dealer's business. Marketing techniques, installation tips, legal explanations and how-to or technical articles are examples of material we often use. All articles should be analytical in nature. No introductory articles on how great this industry is." Buys at least 120 mss/year. Query with published clips and state availability of photos. Length: 700-2,000 words. Pays $75-300. Sometimes pays expenses of writers on assignment.

Photos: State availability of photos with query. Prefers unusual installations, interesting dishes, i.e., landscaped, painted. Reviews contact sheets, and 4x5 and 35mm color transparencies. Pays $10-50 for 8x10 b&w prints; $25-150 for 8x10 color prints. Captions and identification of subjects required. Buys negotiable rights.

Tips: "Exhibit knowledge of either satellite TV or retail sales and a command of the English language. Quality work gets published, regardless of length (within reason). Not grasping the total picture, usually because of incomplete research is the most frequent mistake made by writers. No phone queries."

‡**SOUND & VIDEO CONTRACTOR**, Intertec Publishing Corp., Box 12901, Overland Park KS 66212. (913)888-4664. Editor: Fred Ampel. Managing Editor: Rhonda Wickham. 10% freelance written. Monthly magazine for "qualified professionals involved in various aspects of contracting, design, engineering or construction in the sound and video industries who have operating or specifying authority for equipment, design, engineering, management or service areas." Estab. 1983. Circ. 20,000. Pays on publication. Publishes ms an average of 6 months after acceptance. Buys all rights. Submit seasonal/holiday material 4 months in advance. Simultaneous submissions OK. Computer printout submissions acceptable; prefers letter-quality to dot-matrix. Reports in 1 month. Sample copy $3; free writer's guidelines.

Nonfiction: How-to, interview/profile and technical (all relating to sound/contracting industry); facility profile. No humor. Buys 2 mss/issue. Query. Length: 750 words minimum. Pays $150-300. Sometimes pays expenses of writers on assignment.

Tips: "Call editor or managing editor with article idea or current concept before extensive work is done."

TELEVISION INTERNATIONAL MAGAZINE, Box 2430, Hollywood CA 90028. (213)876-2219. Publisher/Editor: Al Preiss. Magazine published every 2 months for management/creative members of the TV industry. Circ. 16,000 (U.S.); 6,000 (foreign). Pays on publication. Rights purchased vary with author and material. Will consider photocopied submissions. SASE. Reports in 1 month.

Nonfiction: Articles on all aspects of TV programming. "This is not a house organ for the industry. We invite articles critical of TV." Query. Length: 800-3,000 words. Pays $150-500. Column material of 600-800 words. Pays $75. Will consider suggestions for new columns and departments.

Photos: Pays $25 for b&w photos purchased with mss; $35 for color transparencies.

VIDEO SYSTEMS, Box 12901, Overland Park KS 66212. (913)888-4664. Publisher: Cameron Bishop. Editor: David Hodes. 80% freelance written. "Monthly magazine for qualified persons engaged in professional applications of nonbroadcast audio and video who have operating responsibilities and purchasing authority for equipment and software in the video systems field." Circ. 20,500. Pays on acceptance. Buys all rights. Submit seasonal/holiday material 2 months in advance. Photocopied submissions OK. SASE. Reports in 2 months. Free sample copy and writer's guidelines.

Nonfiction: General interest (about professional video); how-to (use professional video equipment); historical (on professional video); new product; and technical. No consumer video articles. Buys 2-6 unsolicited mss/year. Submit complete ms. Length: 1,000-3,000 words. Pays $250.

Photos: State availability of photos with ms. Pay varies for 8x10 b&w glossy prints; $100 maximum for 35mm color transparencies. Model release required.

VIDEOGRAPHY, Media Horizons, 475 Park Ave. S., New York NY 10016. (212)725-2300. Editor: Marjorie Costello. 5% freelance written. Monthly magazine for professional users of video and executives in the videotape and videodisc industries. Circ. 25,000. Pays 1 month after publication. Publishes ms an average of 4 months after acceptance. Buys all rights. Phone queries OK. Computer printout submissions acceptable; prefers letter-quality to dot-matrix. SASE. Reports in 1 month. Sample copy $2.
Nonfiction: Articles about the use of video in business, education, medicine, etc. Especially interested in stories about the use of new video technology to solve production problems. Also stories about cable TV and pay TV services. Buys 2 mss/issue. Query with published clips. Length: 1,000-2,500 words. Pays $300.
Photos: Do not submit photo material with accompanying query. Offers no additional payment for 5x7 b&w glossy prints or color transparencies. Captions required. Buys all rights.
Tips: "Talk to us first. We have specific areas to cover and prefer to oversee the writing of all articles."

‡**VIDEOPRO, Voice of the Industry Professional**, VidPro Publishing Inc., 902 Broadway, New York NY 10010. (212)477-2200. Editor: Carl Levine. 50% freelance written. Monthly magazine about professional video users in broadcast, teleproduction facilities, cable, corporate and advertising industries. "Current, trend setting, state-of-the-art applications." Estab. 1982. Circ. 22,000. Payment on BPA qualification and subscriptions. Publishes ms an average of 3 months after acceptance. Byline given. Offers 50% kill fee. Rights purchased vary. Submit seasonal/holiday material 2 months in advance. Simultaneous queries, simultaneous, photocopied, and previously published submissions only on request. Computer printout submissions acceptable; prefers letter-quality to dot-matrix.
Nonfiction: How-to, humor, new product and photo feature. "I do not want to see any finished articles. All articles are by assignment." Buys 30 mss/year. Query. Length: 250-1,500 words. Pays $100-500. Sometimes pays expenses of writers on assignment.
Photos: Robb Allen, art director. State availability of photos. Reviews production photos showing video equipment in action. Payment varies. Captions and identification of subjects required. Buys one-time rights.
Columns/Departments: Electronic Graphics, Music Video, VideoConference of the Month, In-House Video, and Newsbreaks. Buys 20 mss/year. Query. Length: 500-1,000 words. Pays $150-250.
Tips: Columns and news items are areas most open to freelancers.

VIEW MAGAZINE, The Magazine of TV Programming, View Communications, 80 5th Ave., New York NY 10011. (212)486-7111. Editor: Kathy Haley. Managing Editor: Charline Allen. 60% freelance written. Monthly business magazine covering the TV program market place. Circ. 14,000. Pays 45 days after acceptance. Publishes ms an average of 1 month after acceptance. Byline given. Buys all rights. Computer printout submissions acceptable. Reports in 1 month. Sample copy and writer's guidelines $2.
Nonfiction: General interest (issues facing the industry: pay-per-view programming, ratings and audience measurement, program pricing); and trends (in children's, sports, news and entertainment programming). "We will not consider any unsolicited manuscripts or articles not directly related to the TV industry." Buys 50 mss/year. Query with published clips. Length: 2,500-5,000 words. Pays $450-500 for first-time contributors. Sometimes pays the expenses of writers on assignment.
Tips: No fillers. "*View's* feature articles are written by freelancers who understand the TV programming business. Only writers with experience covering the entertainment industry need query. Best chance: call to discuss your idea."

Energy

Oil, gas, and solar energy topics are covered in addition to energy conservation for industry professionals. Electric energy publications are listed in the Electricity category.

ALTERNATIVE ENERGY RETAILER, Zackin Publications, Inc., Box 2180, Waterbury CT 06722. (203)755-0158. Editor: John Florian. Monthly magazine on selling alternative energy products—chiefly solid fuel burning appliances. "We seek detailed how-to tips for retailers to improve business. Most freelance material purchased is about retailers and how they succeed." Circ. 14,000. Pays on publication. Offers 10% kill fee. Buys first North American serial rights. Submit seasonal/holiday material 4 months in advance. SASE. Reports in 2 weeks on queries. Sample copy for 8½x11 SAE; writer's guidelines for business size SAE.
Nonfiction: How-to (improve retail profits and business know-how); and interview/profile (of successful retailers in this field). No "general business articles not adapted to this industry." Buys 40 mss/year. Query.

Length: 1,500-2,000 words. Pays $200-300.
Photos: State availability of photos. Pays $25 maximum for 5x7 b&w prints and $100 maximum for 5x7 color prints. Reviews color slide transparencies. Identification of subject required. Buys one-time rights.
Tips: "A freelancer can best break in to our publication with features about readers (retailers). Stick to details about what has made this person a success."

BAROID NEWS BULLETIN, Box 1675, Houston TX 77251. Editor-in-Chief: Virginia Myers. 50% freelance written. Emphasizes the petroleum industry for a cross-section of ages, education and interests, although most readers are employed by the energy industries. Quarterly magazine; 36 pages. Circ. 20,000. Pays on acceptance. Publishes ms an average of 1 year after acceptance. Buys first North American serial rights. Byline given. Submit seasonal/holiday material 1 year in advance. Computer printout submissions acceptable; prefers letter-quality to dot-matrix. SASE. Reports in 2 months. Free sample copy and writer's guidelines.
Nonfiction: General interest and historical. No travel articles or poetry. Buys 12 mss/year. Complete ms preferred. Length: 1,000-3,000 words. Pays 8-10¢/word. Sometimes pays the expenses of writers on assignment.
Photos: "Photos may be used in the publication, or as reference for illustration art." Submit b&w prints. No additional payment for photos accepted with ms. Captions preferred. Buys first North American serial rights.
Tips: Manuscripts accompanied by good quality photos or illustrations stand a much better chance of acceptance. "We review on speculation only—no assignments."

FUEL OIL NEWS, Hunter Publishing Co., Box 360, Whitehouse NJ 08888. (201)534-4156. Editor: George Schultz. 20% freelance written. Monthly magazine about the home heating oil market. Circ. 17,000. Pays on publication. Publishes ms an average of 3 months after acceptance. Byline given. Offers $75 kill fee. Makes work-for-hire assignments. Phone queries OK. Submit seasonal material 3 months in advance. Simultaneous, photocopied and previously published submissions OK. Computer printout submissions acceptable. Reports in 2 months. Free sample copy and writer's guidelines.
Nonfiction: Interview (industry); profile (of industry leaders); how-to (on industry methods of delivering fuel or servicing equipment); and technical. No general business articles or new product information. Buys 2 mss/issue. Query. Length: 1,000-3,000 words. Pays $70-200. "Articles should be geared to helping fuel oil dealers maintain viability in the marketplace or to some aspect of home heating or oil delivery."
Photos: State availability of photos. Pays $25 maximum for b&w contact sheets. Captions preferred; model release required. Buys all rights.

FUELOIL AND OIL HEAT, 10 Canfield Rd., Cedar Grove NJ 07009. (201)239-5800. Editor: Paul Geiger. 10% freelance written. For distributors of fuel oil, heating and air conditioning equipment dealers. Monthly. Buys first rights. Pays on publication. Publishes ms an average of 3 months after acceptance. Computer printout submissions acceptable; prefers letter-quality to dot-matrix. Reports in 2 weeks. SASE.
Nonfiction: Management articles dealing with fuel oil distribution and oil heating equipment selling. Cannot use articles about oil production or refining. Length: up to 2,500 words. Pays $50/printed page. "Mostly staff written." Sometimes pays the expenses of writers on assignment.
Tips: The most frequent mistake made by writers in completing an article for us is that they forget our readers are mostly local, family-owned, retail marketers, not big marketers.

HYDROCARBON PROCESSING, Box 2608, Houston TX 77001. Editor: Harold L. Hoffman. 95% freelance written by industry authors. For personnel in oil refining, gas and petrochemical processing; or engineering contractors, including engineering, operation, maintenance and management phases. Special issues: January, Maintenance; April, Natural Gas Processing; July, Energy Management; September, Refining Processes; October, Environmental Management; and November, Petrochemical Processes. Monthly. Buys first rights only. Write for copy of writer's guidelines. SASE.
Nonfiction: Wants technical manuscripts on engineering and operations in the industry that will help personnel. Also nontechnical articles on management, safety and industrial relations that will help technical men become managers. Length: open, "but do not waste words." Pays about $25/printed page.
Tips: "Articles must all pass a rigid evaluation of their reader appeal, accuracy and overall merit. Reader interest determines an article's value. We covet articles that will be of real job value to subscribers. Before writing, ask to see our *Author's Handbook*. You may save time and effort by writing a letter, and outline briefly what you have in mind. If your article will or won't meet our needs, we will tell you promptly."

NATIONAL PETROLEUM NEWS, 950 Lee St., Des Plaines IL 60016. (312)296-0770. Editor: Marvin Reid. For businessmen who make their living in the oil marketing industry, either as company employees or through their own business operations. Monthly magazine; 80 pages. Circ. 18,000. Rights purchased vary with author and material. Usually buys all rights. Buys 3-4 mss/year. Pays on acceptance if done on assignment. "The occasional freelance copy we use is done on assignment." Query. SASE.
Nonfiction: Thomas Olson, managing editor. Material related directly to developments and issues in the oil

marketing industry and "how-to" and "what-with" case studies. Informational, and successful business operations. No unsolicited copy, especially with limited attribution regarding information in story." Length: 2,000 words maximum.

Photos: Pays $150/printed page. Payment for b&w photos "depends upon advance understanding."

‡**OIL AND GAS INVESTOR**, Hart Publications Inc., Suite 400, 1900 Grant, Denver CO 80203. (303)837-1917. Editor: Ron Cooper. Managing Editor: Paulette Whitcomb. 35% freelance written. Monthly magazine covering oil and gas investment with "features and news items of interest to people with money in the oil business." Circ. 11,000. Pays on acceptance. Publishes ms an average of 3 months after acceptance. Byline given. Offers 50% kill fee. Buys all rights. Computer printout submissions acceptable; prefers letter-quality to dot-matrix. SASE. Reports on queries within 2 weeks; 1 month on manuscripts. Sample copy $10.
Nonfiction: Paulette Whitcomb, articles editor. Interview/profiles. Buys 15-20 mss/year. Query with published clips or send complete ms. Length: 2,000-3,000 words. Pays $500-800. Pays expenses of writers on assignment.
Tips: "Financial development in oil and gas are the subjects most open to freelancers. Know something about these subjects, then be able to write."

PETROLEUM INDEPENDENT, 1101 16th St. NW, Washington DC 20036. (202)857-4775. Editor: Joe W. Taylor. For "college educated men and women involved in high risk petroleum ventures. Our readers drill 90% of all the exploratory oil wells in this country. They pit themselves against the major oil companies, politicians, and a dry hole rate of 9 out of 10 to try to find enough petroleum to offset imports. They are in a highly competitive, extremely expensive business and look to this magazine to help them change the political landscape, read about their friends and the activities of the Independent Petroleum Association of America, and be entertained. Contrary to popular opinion, they are not all Texans. They live in almost every state and are politically motivated. They follow energy legislation closely and involve themselves in lobbying and electoral politics." Bimonthly magazine. Circ. 15,000. Pays on acceptance. Buys all rights. Byline given "except if part of a large report compiled in-house." SASE. Reports in 2 weeks. Sample copy $2.
Nonfiction: "Articles need not be limited to oil and natural gas—but must tie in nicely." Expose (bureaucratic blunder); informational; historical (energy-related; accurate; with a witty twist); humor (we look for good humor pieces and have found a few); and interview (with energy decision makers. Center with questions concerning independent petroleum industry. Send edited transcript plus tape); opinion; profile (of Independent Petroleum Association of America members); and photo feature. Buys 30 mss/year. Query with brief outline. SASE. Length: 750-3,000 words. Pays $100-500. Longer articles on assignment; pay negotiable.
Photos: Reviews unusual color and b&w transparencies of oil exploration and development. Purchased with or without accompanying ms or on assignment.
Tips: "Call first, then send outline and query. Don't write with a particular slant. Write as if for a mainstream publication."

PIPELINE & GAS JOURNAL, Box 1589, Dallas TX 75221. (214)691-3911. Editor-in-Chief: Dean Hale. 8% freelance written. Emphasizes energy transportation (oil, natural gas, refined petroleum products and coal slurry) by pipeline. Monthly magazine; 100 pages. Circ. 28,000. Pays on publication. Publishes ms an average of 6 months after acceptance. Buys all rights. Phone queries OK. Photocopied submissions OK. Computer printout submissions acceptable "if sharp, dark and capitals and lower case." SASE. Reports in 10 weeks. Free sample copy.
Nonfiction: Technical. No articles on management. Buys 5-6 mss/year. Query. Length: 800-1,500 words. Pays minimum $50/printed page. Sometimes pays the expenses of writers on assignment.
Photos: State availability of photos with query. No additional payment for 8x10 b&w glossy prints and 5x7 or 8x10 color glossy prints. Captions required. Buys all rights. Model release required.
Tips: "We don't use fillers."

PIPELINE & UNDERGROUND UTILITIES CONSTRUCTION, Oildom Publishing Co. of Texas, Inc., Box 22267, Houston TX 77027. Editor: Oliver Klinger. Managing Editor: Chris Horner. 10% freelance written. Monthly magazine covering oil, gas, water, and sewer pipeline construction for contractors and construction workers who build pipelines. Circ. 13,000. No byline given. Not copyrighted. 10% freelance written. Buys first North American serial rights. Simultaneous queries and photocopied submissions OK. Computer printout submissions acceptable. SASE. Reports in 2 weeks on queries; 3 weeks on mss. Sample copy for $1 and 9x12 SAE.
Nonfiction: How-to. Query with clips of published work. Length: 1,500-2,500 words. Pays $100/printed page "unless unusual expenses are incurred in getting the story."
Photos: Send photos with ms. Reviews 5x7 and 8x10 prints. Captions required. Buys one-time rights.
Tips: "We supply guidelines outlining information we need." The most frequent mistake made by writers in completing articles is unfamiliarity with the field.

PIPELINE DIGEST, Universal News, Inc., Box 55225, Houston TX 77055. (713)468-2626. Editor: Thelma Marlowe. Semimonthly magazine of the worldwide pipeline construction industry for individuals and companies involved in construction and operation of pipelines (gas, oil, slurry, water) worldwide. Includes design and engineering projects and updated listings of projects proposed, awarded and under construction. Circ. 9,500. Pays on publication. Byline given. Previously published submissions OK. SASE. Reports in 2 weeks on queries; 2 months on mss.

Nonfiction: Interview/profile (of people in industry); and new product. All material must relate to the oil and gas industry. Query with clips of published work. Length: 250-1,000 words. Pays negotiable fee.

SAVING ENERGY, 5411 - 117 Ave. SE, Bellevue WA 98006. (206)643-4248. Editor/Publisher: Larry Liebman. 5% freelance written. Emphasizes energy conservation, ideas, and case histories aimed at business, industry and commerce. Monthly newsletter. Pays on acceptance. Publishes ms an average of 10 days after acceptance. Buys all rights. No byline given. Phone queries OK. Computer printout submissions acceptable; prefers letter-quality to dot-matrix. SASE. Reports in 2 weeks. Free writer's guidelines.

Nonfiction: "I need good, tightly written case histories on how industry and commerce are saving energy, listing problems and solutions. The item should present an original energy saving idea. No long stories with art. Include full name and address of business so readers can contact for follow-up." How-to (conserving energy, what the problem was, how it was resolved, cost, how fast the payback was, etc.); and technical (case histories). Buys 25 unsolicited mss/year. Submit complete ms. Length: 200-800 words. Pays $10-25.

Tips: "Take potluck with a well-written item that meets specs, since the item could be shorter than the query letter after editing."

SOLAR ENGINEERING & CONTRACTING, The Business-to-Business Publication of the Solar Industry, Business News Publishing Co., Box 3600, Troy MI 48007. (313)362-3700. Publisher/Executive Editor: Wayne Johnson. Editor: Tim Fausch. A bimonthly magazine for people who design, manufacture, sell, install or maintain solar and other alternative energy systems for profit. Circ. 16,000. Pays on acceptance. Byline given. Offers negotiable kill fee. Buys first rights only. Computer printout submissions acceptable. SASE. Reports in 6 weeks on queries; 1 month on mss. Sample copy for $2.50.

Nonfiction: Interview/profile, new product, opinion, personal experience, photo feature and technical. No do-it-yourself or consumer-oriented articles. Buys 12 mss/year. Query with published clips. Length: 500-2,500 words. Pays $100-250.

Photos: Prefers stages of construction of solar or other alternative energy systems. State availability of photos with query letter or ms. Pays $10-25 for b&w and color prints; $25-300 for b&w and color prints and color transparencies used for covers.

Columns/Departments: National, regional news; financial information; passive solar; and photovoltaics. Buys 10 mss/year. Send complete ms. Length: 50-250 words. Pays $25-100.

Fillers: Clippings and newsbreaks. Buys 10/year. Length: 50-250 words. Pays $5-25.

Tips: "Learn what makes a solar energy system/design unique before you try to pitch us on a story. Know the manufacturers of all equipment in a system and talk to the installers. It is difficult, but not impossible, for writers without a solar background to get published by *SE&C*."

‡**SOONER LPG TIMES**, Suite 114-A, 2910 N. Walnut, Oklahoma City OK 73105. (405)525-9386. Editor: John E. Orr. For "dealers and suppliers of LP-gas and their employees." Monthly. Not copyrighted. Pays on publication. Byline given. Reports in 3 weeks. SASE.

Nonfiction: "Articles relating to the LP-gas industry, safety, small business practices, and economics; anything of interest to small businessmen." Buys 12 mss/year. Length: 1,000-2,000 words. Pays $10-15.

Engineering and Technology

Engineers and professionals with various specialties read the publications in this section. Publications for electrical engineers are classified under Electricity; journals for electronics engineers are classified under the Electronics and Communication heading. Magazines for computer professionals are listed in the Trade/Data Processing section. For magazines on personal computing, see the Consumer/Personal Computing section.

‡**CIVIL ENGINEERING-ASCE**, American Society of Civil Engineers, 345 E. 47th St., New York NY 10017. (212)705-7463. Editor: Virginia Fairweather. Monthly magazine about civil engineering for members

of the American Society of Civil Engineers. Circ. 95,000. Average issue includes 7-10 features. Pays on acceptance. Byline given. Makes work-for-hire assignments. Phone queries OK. Reports in 2 months. Free sample copy and writer's guidelines.

Nonfiction: Technical. "Come up with articles that are timely, well-written and slanted to a Civil Engineering audience. We have an annual special issue in September on the rebuilding of America." Buys marginal freelance. Query. Pays $300-1,500.

Columns/Departments: Editor: Philip DiVietro. "We want reports or news stories on conferences of interest to an engineering audience." Also, new products information. Buys marginal freelance. Query. Pays $100-500.

CONTROL ENGINEERING, Technical Publishing, 1301 S. Grove Ave., Barrington IL 60010. (312)381-1840. Editor: Edward Kompass. Monthly magazine for control engineers—horizontal to industry, product and system-oriented—highly technical. Circ. 91,000. Byline usually given.

Nonfiction: New product, photo feature and technical. "We need submissions from writers who are engineers." No commercial mss. Query or send complete ms. Length: open. Pays $25/page.

DIGITAL DESIGN, Morgan-Grampian Publishing Co., 1050 Commonwealth Ave., Boston MA 02215. (617)232-5470. Editor: John Bond. Managing Editor: Debra Lambert. Monthly magazine of computer electronics for designers and engineers of computer systems, peripherals and components. "Our readers are among the leaders in technical planning and management for computing technology." Circ. 85,000. Pays on publication. Byline given. Buys all rights "except by arrangement with editor." Reports in 2 weeks. Free sample copy and writer's guidelines.

Nonfiction: Debra Lambert, articles editor. How-to (design various types of systems); new product (exclusive articles on unannounced new computer products); and technical. Buys 10 mss/year. Query. Length: 1,500-3,000 words. Pays on individual basis.

Photos: "Relevant photos and other art should be submitted with manuscript. There is no additional payment." State availability of photos. Captions and identification of subjects required.

Tips: "Most of our material is written by engineers about their field of expertise. Nonengineers should at least be conversant in the field about which they are writing and should query an editor about their idea before proceeding. Freelancers should remember that *Digital Design* is a technical publication written specifically to help computer engineers do their job better."

‡GRADUATING ENGINEER, McGraw-Hill, 1221 Avenue of the Americas, New York NY 10020. (212)997-4123. Editor: Howard Cohn. Published September-March "to help graduating engineers make the transition from campus to the working world." Circ. 90,000. Pays on acceptance. Byline given. Buys first North American serial rights. Reports in 2 weeks. Free sample copy for 9x12 SAE and $1 postage.

Nonfiction: General interest (on management, human resources); high technology; and careers, ethics, resumes, future. Special issues include Minority, Women and Computer. Buys 100 mss/year. Query. Length: 2,000-3,000 words. Pays $300-500.

Photos: State availability of photos, illustrations or charts. Reviews 35mm color transparencies, 8x10 b&w glossy prints. Captions and model release required.

LASER FOCUS MAGAZINE, the Magazine of Electro-Optics Technology, 119 Russell St., Littleton MA 01460. (617)486-9501. Publisher/Editor-in-Chief: Dr. Morris Levitt. Managing Editor: Richard Mack. 33% freelance written. A monthly magazine for physicists, scientists and engineers involved in the research and development, design, manufacturing and applications of lasers, laser systems and all other segments of electro-optical technologies. Circ. 41,000. Pays on publication. Publishes ms an average of 6 months after acceptance. Byline given unless anonymity requested. Buys all rights. Computer printout submissions acceptable; prefers letter-quality to dot-matrix. Sample copy on request.

Nonfiction: Lasers, laser systems, fiberoptics, optics and other electro-optical materials, components, instrumentation and systems. "Each article should serve our reader's need by either stimulating ideas, increasing technical competence or improving design capabilities in the following areas: natural light and radiation sources, artificial light and radiation sources, light modulators, optical materials and components, image detectors, energy detectors, information displays, image processing, information storage and processing, subsystem and system testing, support equipment and other related areas." No "flighty prose, material not written for our readership, or irrelevant material." Query first "with a clear statement and outline of why the article would be important to our readers." Pays $30/printed page. Sometimes pays the expenses of writers on assignment.

Photos: Send photos with ms. Reviews 8x10 b&w glossies or 4x5 color transparencies.

Tips: "The writer has a better chance of breaking in at our publication with short articles since shorter articles are easier to schedule, but must address more carefully our requirements for technical coverage. We use few freelancers that are independent professional writers. Most of our submitted materials come from technical experts in the areas we cover. The most frequent mistake made by writers in completing articles for us is that the articles are too commercial, i.e. emphasize a given product or technology from one company. Also articles are not the right technical depth, too thin or too scientific."

THE MINORITY ENGINEER, An Equal Opportunity Career Publication for Professional and Gradu-ating Minority Engineers, Equal Opportunity Publications, Inc., 44 Broadway, Greenlawn NY 11740. (516)261-8917. Editor: James Schneider. 50% freelance written. Magazines published 4 times/year (fall, win-ter, spring, summer professional edition) covering career guidance for minority engineering students and pro-fessional minority engineers. Circ. 16,000. Pays on publication. Publishes ms an average of 3 months after ac-ceptance. Byline given. Buys all rights. "Deadline dates: fall, July 1; winter, September 1; spring, December 15; summer, April 1." Simultaneous, photocopied, and previously published submissions OK. Electronic sub-missions OK, but requires hard copy also. Computer printout submissions acceptable; prefers typed mss; no dot-matrix. SASE. Sample copy and writer's guidelines available on request.
Nonfiction: Book excerpts; articles (on job search techniques, role models); general interest (on specific mi-nority engineering concerns); how-to (land a job, keep a job, etc.); interview/profile (minority engineer role models); new product (new career opportunities); opinion (problems of ethnic minorities); personal experience (student and career experiences); and technical (on career fields offering opportunities for minority engineers). "We're interested in articles dealing with career guidance and job opportunities for minority engineers." Query or send complete ms. Length: 1,250-3,000 words.
Photos: Prefers 35mm color slides but will accept b&w. Captions, model release and identification of subjects required. Buys all rights.
Tips: "Articles should focus on career guidance, role model and industry prospects for minority engineers. Prefer articles related to careers, not politically or socially sensitive."

THE ONTARIO TECHNOLOGIST, Ontario Association of Certified Engineering Technicians and Tech-nologists, Suite 253, 40 Orchard View Blvd., Toronto, Ontario M4R 2G1 Canada. (416)488-1175. Editor: Ruth M. Klein. Bimonthly professional association journal covering technical processes and developments in engineering for association members, educational institutions, government and industry. Circ. 13,342. Pays in membership dues or subscription fee. Byline given. Buys first rights only. Submit seasonal/holiday material 2 months in advance. Photocopied and previously published submissions OK. SASE. Reports in 1 month. Free sample copy and writer's guidelines.
Nonfiction: New product and technical (manpower news). Buys 4 mss/year. Query with clips of published work. Length: 500-1,500 words. Pays 25¢/word.
Photos: State availability of photos. Pays $25 maximum for 8x10 b&w prints. Captions and identification of subjects required. Buys one-time rights.

‡**PARKING MAGAZINE**, National Parking Association, Inc., Suite 2000, 1112-16th St. NW, Washington DC 20036. (202)296-4336. Publisher: Thomas G. Kobus. Executive Editor: George V. Dragotta. 10% freelance written. "The bulk of our readers are owners/operators of off-street parking facilities in major metro-politan areas. The remainder is made up of architects, engineers, city officials, planners, retailers, contractors and service equipment suppliers." Bimonthly magazine. Circ. 6,500. Pays on publication. Buys one-time rights. Submit seasonal/holiday material 3 months in advance of issue date. Simultaneous, photocopied and previously published submissions OK. Reports in 1 month. Sample copy $5.
Nonfiction: General interest (pieces on revitalization of central business districts have a high current priority); how-to (new construction, design, equipment or operational techniques); historical (could deal with some as-pect of history of parking, including piece on historic garage, etc.); new product (parking-related equipment); photo feature (range of facilities in a particular city); and travel (parking in other countries). "No general, neb-ulous pieces or ones not dealing with most current trends in the industry." Buys 6 unsolicited mss/year. Query. Length: 1,000-3,000 words. Pays $50-200, or negotiable.
Photos: State availability of photos with query. Pays $5-25 for 8x10 b&w glossy prints. Captions required. Buys one-time rights. Model release required.

THE WOMAN ENGINEER, An Equal Opportunity Career Publication for Graduating Women and Experienced Professionals, Equal Opportunity Publications, Inc., 44 Broadway, Greenlawn NY 11740. (516)261-8917. Editor: James Schneider. 50% freelance written. Magazine published 4 times/year (fall, win-ter, spring, summer professional edition) covering career guidance for women engineering students and profes-sional women engineers. Circ. 16,000. Pays on publication. Publishes ms an average of 3 months after accept-ance. Byline given. Buys all rights. Deadline dates: fall, July 1; winter, September 1; spring, December 15; summer, April 1. Simultaneous, photocopied, and previously published submissions OK. Computer printout submissions acceptable; prefers typed mss and no dot-matrix. SASE. Sample copy and writer's guidelines available on request.
Nonfiction: Book excerpts and articles (on job search techniques, role models); general interest (on specific women engineering concerns); how-to (land a job, keep a job, etc.); interview/profile (women engineer role

models); new product (new career opportunities); opinion (problems of women engineers); personal experience (student and career experiences); and technical (on career fields offering opportunities for women engineers). "We're interested in articles dealing with career guidance and job opportunities for women engineers." Query or send complete ms. Length: 1,250-3,000 words.

Photos: Prefers 35mm color slides but will accept b&w. Captions, model release and identification of subjects required. Buys all rights.

Tips: "Articles should focus on career guidance, role model and industry prospects for women engineers. Prefer articles related to careers, not politically or socially sensitive."

Entertainment and the Arts

The business of the entertainment/amusement industry (arts, film, dance, theatre, etc.) is covered by these publications. Journals that focus on the people and equipment of various music specialties are listed in the Trade Music section.

AMUSEMENT BUSINESS, Billboard Publications, Inc., Box 24970, Nashville TN 37202. (615)748-8120. Editor: Tom Powell. Weekly tabloid; 32-108 pages. Emphasizes hard news of the amusement and mass entertainment industry. Read by top management. Circ. 15,000. Pays on publication. Byline sometimes given; "it depends on the quality of the individual piece." Buys all rights. Submit seasonal/holiday material 3 weeks in advance. Phone queries OK. SASE.

Nonfiction: How-to (case history of successful promotions); interview; new product; and technical (how "new" devices, shows or services work at parks, fairs, auditoriums and conventions). Likes lots of financial support data: grosses, profits, operating budgets and per-cap spending. No personality pieces or interviews with stage stars. Buys 500-1,000 mss/year. Query. Length: 400-700 words. Pays $3/published inch.

Photos: State availability of photos with query. Pays $3-5 for 8x10 b&w glossy prints. Captions and model release required. Buys all rights.

Columns/Departments: Auditorium Arenas; Fairs, Fun Parks; Food Concessions; Merchandise; Promotion; Shows (carnival and circus); Talent; Tourist Attractions; and Management Changes.

BILLBOARD, The International News Weekly of Music and Home Entertainment, 1515 Broadway, New York NY 10036. (212)764-7300. 9107 Wilshire Blvd., Beverly Hills CA 90210. (213)273-7040. Editor-in-Chief: Adam White. Publisher: Samuel Holdsworth. Special Issues Editor: Ed Ochs. L.A. Bureau Chief: Sam Sutherland. Albums: Sam Sutherland. (All Los Angeles.) Editor: Adam White. Managing Editor: George Finley. Pro Equipment: Steve Dupler. Deputy Editor: Irv Lichtman. Radio/TV Editor: Rollye Bornstein. Black Music: Nelson George. Executive/Classical Editor: Is Horowitz. Video Editor: Tony Seideman. Review-Singles/Campus Editor: Nancy Erlich. (All New York.) Country Music Editor: Kip Kirby (Nashville). International Editor: Peter Jones (London). Weekly. Pays on publication. Buys all rights. SASE.

Nonfiction: "Correspondents are appointed to send in spot amusement news covering phonograph record programming by broadcasters and record merchandising by retail dealers." Concert reviews, interviews with artists, and stories on video software (both rental and merchandising).

BOXOFFICE MAGAZINE, RLD Publishing Corp., Suite 710, 1800 N. Highland Ave., Hollywood CA 90028. (213)465-1186. Editor: Harley W. Lond. 10% freelance written. Monthly business magazine about the motion picture industry for members of the film industry: theater owners, film producers, directors, financiers and allied industries. Circ. 14,000. Pays on publication. Publishes ms an average of 2 months after acceptance. Byline given. Buys one-time rights. Phone queries OK. Submit seasonal material 2 months in advance. Simultaneous, photocopied and previously published submissions OK. Computer printout submissions acceptable; "if dot-matrix, use descenders." SASE. Reports in 1 month. Sample copy $1.

Nonfiction: Expose, interview, nostalgia, profile, new product, photo feature and technical. "We are a general news magazine about the motion picture industry and are looking for stories about trends, developments, problems or opportunities facing the industry. Almost any story will be considered, including corporate profiles, but we don't want gossip or celebrity stuff." Buys 1-2 mss/issue. Query with clips of previously published work. Length: 1,500-2,500 words. Pays $75-150.

Photos: State availability of photos. Pays $10 minimum for 8x10 b&w prints. Captions required.

Tips: "Write a clear, comprehensive outline of the proposed story and enclose a resume and clip samples. We welcome new writers but don't want to be a classroom. Know how to write."

CHRISTIAN MODELS U.S.A. NATIONAL SOURCE DIRECTORY OF TALENT, Christian Business Services Source Book, Dorsey Advertising/Public Relations, Box 64951, Dallas TX 75206-0951. (214)288-8900. Editor: Mr. Lon Dorsey. Semiannual magazine for the hiring of/exposure for Christian Talent by casting, movie, film, recording studios/Christian organizations and businesses. Circ. varies nationally. Pays per agreement. Publishes ms an average of 3 months after acceptance. Byline given. Buys first North American serial rights, one-time rights, and all rights; makes work-for-hire assignments. Queries 4 months in advance for seasonal material. Computer submissions acceptable; no dot-matrix. SASE—prefers stamp inside return envelope. Reports in 1 month on mss; 2 months on queries. Sample copy of directory $14.95 and 9x12 SAE; newsletter $2 and letter size SAE. Writer's guidelines $2 and SAE or free with sample copy.
Nonfiction: Attention Editor: CMUSA National Source Directory. General interest (inquire); how-to (glorify God as Christian talent); humor (in living for Christ); inspirational (victory over hardships); interview/profile (inquire); personal experience (not sticky but true) and photo feature (inquire). No sexual connotations or overtones, no profanity; no crime-to-pulpit testimonies. Query. Length: 250-1,000 words. Pays 4-20¢/word.
Photos: State availability of photos. Reviews contact sheets and small sample prints. Captions, model release and identication of subjects required. Buys variable rights.
Fillers: "Individual may inquire on filler requirements for whatever publications we are working on at the time. We will be happy to try and give info on scheduling."
Tips: "The most frequent mistakes made by writers in completing an article for us are showing more interest in money than in work, and a lack of professional communication habits—lateness and missing deadlines."

THE ELECTRIC WEENIE, Box 882, Honolulu HI 96728. (808)395-9600. Editor: Tom Adams. 10% freelance written. Monthly magazine covering "primarily radio, for 'personalities' worldwide (however, mostly English speaking). We mail flyers mainly to radio people, but obviously no one is excepted if he/she wants a monthly supply of first-rate gags, one liners, zappers, etc." Circ. 1,000. Pays on publication. Publishes ms an average of 6 months after acceptance. No byline given. Buys all rights. Submit seasonal/holiday material 6 months in advance. Computer printout submissions acceptable; prefers letter-quality to dot-matrix. SASE. Sample copy $5, business size SAE and 1 first class stamp.
Fillers: Jokes, gags, short humor, one liners, etc. "Short is the bottom line." Uses 300/month. Pays $1/gag used.
Tips: "We like to receive gags in multiples of one-hundred if possible; not mandatory, just preferred."

ENTERTAINMENT INDUSTRY WEEKLY/ENTERTAINMENT DIGEST, Entertainment Industry Publications, Box 10804, Beverly Hills CA 90213. (213)857-8414. Editor: Lisa Galgon. Managing Editor: Steve Morris. 90% freelance written. Weekly newsletter magazine of the entertainment industry; provides total coverage of entertainment industry from performing to business. Circ. 50,000. Pays on publication. Publishes ms an average of 3 months after acceptance. Byline given. Offers $25 kill fee. Buys all rights. Simultaneous queries, and simultaneous, photocopied and previously published submissions OK. Electronic submissions OK via IBM-PC DOS. Computer printout submissions acceptable. SASE. Reports in 1 month.
Nonfiction: Steve Davis, articles editor. Uses any entertainment industry subject including unions, pay TV, cable, broadcast, film, music, home video, public TV, video tape/disc, advertising, commercials, casting. No fiction. Buys 60-100 mss/year. Send complete ms. Length: Open. Pays variable rates. "We use more short articles."

THE HOLLYWOOD REPORTER, Verdugo Press, 6715 Sunset Blvd., Hollywood CA 90028. (213)464-7411. Publisher: Tichi Wilkerson. Editor: Marcia Borie. Emphasizes entertainment industry, film, TV and theatre and is interested in everything to do with financial news in these areas. 15% freelance written. Daily entertainment trade publication: 25-100 pages. Circ: 25,000. Publishes ms an average of 1 month after acceptance. SASE. Send queries first. Reports in 1 month. Sample copy $1.
Tips: "Short articles and fillers fit our format best. The most frequent mistake made by writers in completing an article for us is that they are not familiar with our publication."

THE LONE STAR COMEDY MONTHLY, Lone Star Publications of Humor, Suite #103, Box 29000, San Antonio TX 78229. Editor: Lauren Barnett Scharf. "Less than one" percent freelance written. Monthly comedy service newsletter for professional humorists—DJs, public speakers, comedians. Includes one-liners and jokes for oral expression. Pays on publication "or before." Publishes ms an average of 1 month after acceptance. Byline given if 2 or more jokes are used. Buys all rights, exclusive rights for 6 months from publication date. Submit seasonal/holiday material 1 month in advance. Photocopied submissions OK. Computer printout submissions acceptable; no dot-matrix. SASE. Reports in 1 month. Sample copy $4.50; 1983 & 1984 issues $3.50 each; writer's guidelines for business size SAE and 1 first class stamp.
Fillers: Jokes, gags and short humor. Buys 20-60/year. Length: 100 words maximum. "We don't use major features in *The Lone Star Comedy Monthly*." Pays $1-5. "Submit several (no more than 20) original gags on one or two subjects only."

OPPORTUNITIES FOR ACTORS & MODELS, "A Guide to Working in Cable TV-Radio-Print Advertising," Copy Group, Suite 315, 1900 N. Vine St., Hollywood CA 90068. Editor: Len Miller. 60% freelance written. A monthly newsletter "serving the interests of those people who are (or would like to be) a part of the cable-TV, radio, and print advertising industries." Circ. 10,000. Pays on acceptance. Publishes ms an average of 2 weeks after acceptance. Byline given. Buys all rights. Simultaneous queries OK. SASE. Reports in 3 weeks. Free sample copy and writer's guidelines.
Nonfiction: How-to, humor, inspirational, interview/profile, local news, personal experience, photo feature and technical (within cable TV). Coverage should include the model scene, little theatre, drama groups, comedy workshops and other related events and places. "Detailed information about your local cable TV station should be an important part of your coverage. Get to know the station and its creative personnel." Buys 120 mss/year. Query. Length: 100-950 words. Pays $50 maximum.
Photos: State availability of photos. Model release and identification of subjects required. Buys one-time or all rights.
Columns/Departments: "We will consider using your material in a column format with your byline." Buys 60 mss/year. Query. Length: 150-450 words. Pays $50 maximum.
Tips: "Good first person experiences, interviews and articles, all related to modeling, acting, little theatre, photography (model shots) and other interesting items" are needed.

PERFORMANCE, 1020 Currie St., Fort Worth TX 76107. (817)338-9444. Editor: Don Waitt. 75% freelance written. The international trade weekly for the touring entertainment industry. "*Performance* publishes tour routing information, updated on a weekly basis. These itineraries, along with box office reports, street news, industry directories, live performance reviews and industry features are of interest to our readers." Weekly magazine; also publishes industry directories once a month. Circ. 20,000. Publishes ms an average of 1 month after acceptance. Buys all rights. Phone queries OK. Submit seasonal/holiday material 2 months in advance. Simultaneous submissions OK. Computer printout submissions acceptable; prefers letter-quality to dot-matrix. SASE. Reports in 1 month. Sample copy and writer's guidelines $3.
Nonfiction: "This is a trade publication, dealing basically with the ins and outs of booking live entertainment. We are interested in adding freelancers from major cities around the U.S. to provide us with hard news and spot information on sound, lighting and staging companies, clubs, ticketing, concert venues, promoters, booking agents, personal managers, and college news relevant to the live entertainment industry. We also publish interviews and overviews of touring in the major cities." Interviews, opinion and profile. Pays 35¢/printed line. Sometimes pays expenses of writers on assignment.
Photos: State availability of photos with ms. B&w photos only. Captions preferred. Buys all rights.
Tips: Needs many short news items, much like a newspaper.

THEATRE CRAFTS MAGAZINE, Theatre Crafts Associates, 135 5th Ave., New York NY 10010. Editor: Patricia MacKay. Magazine of the performing arts, video and film, with an emphasis on production and design. 30% freelance written. Published 10 times/year. "The primary information source for working professionals." Circ. 27,500. Pays on acceptance. Publishes ms an average of 6 months after acceptance. Byline given. Buys variable rights. Simultaneous queries and photocopied submissions OK. Electronic submissions OK via CP/M—Perfectwriter programs or modem, Kaypro II, but requires hard copy also. Computer printout submissions acceptable; prefers letter-quality to dot-matrix. SASE. Reports in 1 month on queries; 2 months on mss. Sample copy $5; free writer's guidelines.
Nonfiction: How-to; new products (and new applications of old products); and technical (advances and developments in administration, design and technology). Buys 18 mss/year. Query. Pays $25-200.
Tips: "Writers have a better chance of breaking in at our publication with short articles and fillers. The most frequent mistake made by writers in completing an article for us is that they have not paid attention to the magazine and its special professional focus."

VANTAGE POINT: ISUES IN AMERICAN ARTS, American Council for the Arts, 570 7th Ave., New York NY 10018. Editor: Bill Keens. Published 6 times/year as 16-page editorial supplement in Horizon Magazine. Bimonthly magazine. Circ. 3,500. Pays on publication. Byline given. Buys first North American serial rights. No telephone queries. Simultaneous queries and simultaneous and photocopied submissions OK. SASE. Reports in 6 weeks. Free sample copy if interested in query or submission—otherwise $2.50, 9x12 SAE and $1 postage.
Nonfiction: Features, profiles, essays and interviews. Buys 12 mss/year. Length: 500-3,000 words. Pays $100-250.
Tips: *Vantage Point* focuses on contemporary issues (social, political, economics and artistic) as they affect the art community on all levels. Readers include high level art executives, trustees, patrons, members of the corporation, foundation and education communities, artists and elected government officials."

VARIETY, 154 W. 46th St., New York NY 10036. Does not buy freelance material.

Farm

Today's farm publication editor wants more than rewrites of USDA and extension press releases. Farm magazines reflect this, and the successful freelance farm writer turns his attention to the business end of farming.

Do you need to be a farmer to write about farming? The general consensus is yes, and no, depending on the topic. For more technical articles, most editors feel that writers should have a farm background (and not just summer visits to Uncle Frank's farm, either) or some technical farm education. But there are writing opportunities for the general freelancer, too. Easier stories to undertake for farm publications include straight reporting of agricultural events; meetings of national agricultural organizations; or coverage of agricultural legislation. Other ideas might be articles on rural living, rural health care, or transportation in small towns.

Always a commandment in any kind of writing, but possibly even more so in the farm field, is the tenet "*Study Thy Market.*" The following listings for farm publications are divided into five categories, each specializing in a different aspect of farm publishing: crops and soil management; dairy farming; general interest farming and rural life (both national and local); livestock; and miscellaneous.

The best bet for a freelancer without a farming background is probably the general interest, family-oriented magazines. These are the *Saturday Evening Posts* of the farm set. The other four categories are more specialized, dealing in only one aspect of farm production.

Where can a writer go for information about farming specialties? Go to a land-grant university; there's one in every state. Also try farming seminars or county extension offices.

Talk with people who know farming best—farmers.

Crops and Soil Management

CRANBERRIES, Diversified Periodicals, Box 249, Cobalt CT 06414. (203)342-4730. Editor: Bob Taylor. 50% freelance written. Monthly magazine covering cranberry growing and processing—anything of interest to growers. Circ. 700. Pays on publication. Publishes ms an average of 4 months after acceptance. Byline given. "No kill fee. If we accept a story, we'll work writer through. Also we'll pay for the story if events make it impossible to run." Buys one-time rights. Submit material 2 months in advance. Simultaneous queries, and simultaneous, photocopied and previously published submissions OK. Computer printout submissions acceptable. SASE. Reports in 1 month on queries; 2 months on mss. Sample copy for 8½x11 SAE and 56¢ postage.
Nonfiction: Humor, interview/profile, personal experience, photo feature and technical. Buys 50 mss/year. Query. Length: 500-2,500 words. Pays $15-40.
Photos: State availability of photos. Pays $7-25 for any size b&w print. Captions and identification of subjects required. Buys one-time rights. Pays $7-35 for illustrations.
Tips: "We're very receptive to new writers." Profiles on growers are open to freelancers. "While we do not pay big bucks, payment is prompt and will increase as the fortunes of the magazine go up. I also like to feel that young or beginning writers get the benefit of patience and good editing. The most frequent mistake made by writers in completing an article for us is not getting all the basic facts."

PECAN SOUTH, Texas Pecan Growers Assn., Drawer CC, College Station TX 77841. (409)775-8300. Bimonthly agribusiness magazine of the Southern pecan industry covering research and technology with some economic, marketing and human-interest stories of industrial interest. Circ. 11,000. Pays on publication. Byline given. Buys one-time and first rights. Submit seasonal/holiday material 4 months in advance. Simultaneous phone queries and simultaneous submissions OK. SASE. Reports in 1 month. Sample copy $3; free writer's guidelines.
Nonfiction: General interest (in the Southeast); how-to (grow, market, promote, handle problems in culture, etc.), interview/profile (of notables or recognized contributors to industries); opinion (of experts only); personal experience (of reputable growers or researchers); and technical (new tools, techniques, plant varieties, chemicals, equipment, etc.). Special issues: irrigation (May); marketing (September); equipment (November). No "home gardening material, commercially slanted stories, or information not of widespread industry interest in the Southeast." Buys variable number mss/year. Query. Length: 900-6,000 words. Pays $25-150.
Photos: Send photos with ms. Pays $10 maximum for b&w contact sheet and 8x10 prints; reviews 8x10 color

prints. Captions required. Buys one-time rights.

Tips: "Discuss material with us by phone before writing; submit completed works well in advance of copy deadlines; include charts, photos and illustrations. We need more grower and related stories in both wholesale and retail categories. Marketing, shipping and economic features are also needed. Very long features (8-10 typed pages) are rarely welcome from freelancers."

POTATO GROWER OF IDAHO, Harris Publishing, Inc., Box 981, Idaho Falls ID 83402. (208)522-5187. Editor: Steve Janes. 25% freelance written. Emphasizes material slanted to the potato grower and the business of farming related to this subject—packing, shipping, processing, research, etc. Monthly magazine; 48-96 pages. Circ. 18,000. Pays on publication. Buys first North American serial rights. Byline given. Phone queries OK. Submit seasonal/holiday material 3 months in advance. Simultaneous queries, and photocopied and previously published submissions OK. Computer printout submissions acceptable. SASE. Reports in 1 month. Sample copy for $1, 8½x11 SAE, and 37¢ postage; writer's guidelines for 5½x7 SAE and 1 first class stamp.
Nonfiction: Expose (facts, not fiction or opinion, pertaining to the subject); how-to (do the job better, cheaper, faster, etc.); informational articles; interviews ("can use one of these a month, but must come from state of Idaho since this is a regional publication; on unique personalities in the potato industry, and telling the nation 'how Idaho grows potatoes' "); all types of new product articles pertaining to the subject; photo features (story can be mostly photos, but must have sufficient outlines to carry technical information); and technical articles (all aspects of the industry of growing, storage, processing, packing and research of potatoes in general, but must relate to the Idaho potato industry). Buys 5 mss/year. Query. Length: 1,000-2,000 words. Pays $15-100.
Photos: B&w glossies (any size) purchased with mss or on assignment; use of color limited. Query if photos are not to be accompanied by ms. Pays $5 for 5x7 b&w prints; $10-50 for 35mm color slides. Captions, model release, and identification of subjects required. Buys one-time rights.
Columns/Departments: Buys 2 mss/year. Query . Length: 750-1,000 words. Pays $20-35.
Fillers: Newsbreaks. Buys 5/year. Length: 50-500 words. Pays $5-15.
Tips: "Choose one vital, but small aspect of the industry; research that subject and slant it to fit the readership and/or goals of the magazine. All articles on research must have a valid source for foundation. Material must be general in nature about the subject or specific in nature about Idaho potato growers. Write a query letter, noting what you have in mind for an article; be specific." Articles on advancement in potato-growing methods or technology are most open to freelancers.

SINSEMILLA TIPS, Domestic Marijuana Journal, New Moon Publishing, 217 SW 2nd, Box 2046, Corvallis OR 97339. (503)757-2532 or 757-8477. Editor: Thomas Alexander. 50% freelance written. Quarterly magazine tabloid covering the domestic cultivation of marijuana. Circ. 8,000. Pays on publication. Publishes ms an average of 2 months after acceptance. Byline given. "Some writers desire to be anonymous for obvious reasons." Buys one-time rights. Submit seasonal/holiday material 2 months in advance. Electronic submissions OK on Osborne 1, HP110 "both have most protocals, but notify in advance." Requires hard copy also. Computer printout submissions acceptable. SASE. Reports in 2 months. Sample copy $4.
Nonfiction: Book excerpts and reviews; expose (on political corruption); general interest; how-to; interview/profile; opinion; personal experience; and technical. Send complete ms. Length: 500-2,000 words. Pays $25-100. Sometimes pays the expenses of writers on assignment.
Photos: Send photos with ms. Pays $10-20 for b&w prints. Captions optional. Model release required. Buys all rights.
Tips: "Sometimes we have too many major articles—usually we hold over to next issue. Writers may have a better chance with short articles and fillers."

SOYBEAN DIGEST, Box 41309, 777 Craig Rd., St. Louis MO 63141-1309. (314)432-1600. Editor: Gregg Hillyer. 75% freelance written. Emphasizes soybean production and marketing. Monthly magazine. Circ. 195,000. Pays on acceptance. Buys all rights. Byline given. Phone queries OK. Submit seasonal material 2 months in advance. Reports in 3 weeks. Sample copy $2; mention *Writer's Market* in request.
Nonfiction: How-to (soybean production and marketing); and new product (soybean production and marketing). Buys over 100 mss/year. Query or submit complete ms. Length: 1,000 words. Pays $50-350.
Photos: State availability of photos with query. Pays $25-100 for 5x7 or 8x10 b&w prints and $50-275 for 35mm color transparencies and up to $350 for covers. Captions and/or manuscript required. Buys all rights.

‡**SOYFOODS, The Magazine About Producing and Marketing Soyfoods**, Box 511, Encinitas CA 92024. (619)753-5979. Editor: Doug Fiske. 33-50% freelance written. Quarterly magazine covering the soyfoods industry, primarily in the U.S.A. "Coverage is primarily of the U.S. soyfoods industry with attention to the worldwide soyfoods industry." Circ. 7,000. Pays on publication. Publishes ms an average of 1½ months after acceptance. Byline given. Offers kill fee. Buys first North American serial rights. Simultaneous queries, and simultaneous, photocopied and previously published submissions OK. Computer printout submissions acceptable; no dot-matrix. SASE. Reports in 2 weeks. Sample copy $6 (U.S., Canada, Mexico; $8 all others).
Nonfiction: Book excerpts, general interest, how-to (produce and/or market soyfoods), new product and tech-

nical. No backwoods or neighborhood, i.e., very small-scale, production/marketing. Buys 15-20 mss/year. Query. Length: 1,000-5,000 words. Pays $100-325. Sometimes pays the expenses of writers on assignment.
Photos: State availability of photos with query. Pays $10-50 for b&w contact sheets and negatives. Identification of subjects required. Buys one-time rights.
Columns/Departments: Institutional Food Service, Restaurant, Retail, Soyfoods World, Soyfoods Market and book reviews. Buys 20-30 mss/year. Query. Length: 100-1,000 words. Pays $10-100.
Tips: "Know the subject; live/work/travel in areas where soyfoods are produced and/or marketed; provide photos with manuscript; submit finished work requiring little or no editing."

WINE WEST, Box 498, Geyserville CA 95441. (703)433-7306. Editor/Publisher: Mildred Howie. 95% freelance written. For entire West Coast and for those who make, grow and enjoy wine. Circ. 3,500. Covers western Mexico through western Canada and as far as east Texas. Buys 35-45 mss/year. Pays on publication. Publishes ms an average of 4 months after acceptance. Byline given. Buys first rights only. Prefers query before submitting ms. Computer printout submissions acceptable; no dot-matrix. SASE. Reports in 1 month. Sample copy 90¢; writer's guidelines for SAE and 1 first class stamp.
Nonfiction: Must be wine oriented. Technical articles on viticulturists and wine ecology. "Features and articles in *Wine West* are involved with Western wine districts, the people, the practices and the lifestyle." No fillers. Length: 300-3,000 words. Pays 10¢/word.
Photos: Pays $10 for b&w photos only purchased with mss.

Dairy Farming

Publications for dairy farmers are listed here. Publications for farmers who raise animals for meat, wool, or hides are included in the Livestock category. Other magazines that buy material on dairy herds are listed in the General Interest Farming and Rural Life classification. Journals for dairy products retailers can be found under Dairy Products.

DAIRY GOAT JOURNAL, Box 1808, Scottsdale AZ 85252. Editor: Kent Leach. 10% freelance written. Monthly for breeders and raisers of dairy goats. Pays on publication. Publishes ms an average of 8 months after acceptance. Buys first rights. Computer printout submissions acceptable; prefers letter-quality to dot-matrix. SASE. Query. Reports in 1 month. Free sample copy.
Nonfiction: Uses articles, items and photos that deal with dairy goats and the people who raise them; goat dairies and shows. How-to articles up to 1,000 words. Buys 12-25 unsolicited mss/year. Pays by arrangement. Sometimes pays the expenses of writers on assignment.
Photos: Buys 5x7 or 8x10 b&w photos for $1-15.
Tips: "In query give the thrust or point of the article, what illustrations may be available, how soon it might be finished—and if payments are expected, state how much or if negotiable."

DAIRY HERD MANAGEMENT, Miller Publishing Co., Box 67, Minneapolis MN 55440. (612)374-5200. Editor: Sheila Widmer Vikla. Emphasizes dairy farming. Monthly magazine; 60 pages. Circ. 108,000. Pays on acceptance. Buys first North American serial rights. Submit seasonal/holiday material 2 months in advance. Photocopied and previously published submissions OK. SASE. Reports in 6 weeks. Free sample copy and writer's guidelines.
Nonfiction: How-to, informational and technical. Buys 2 mss/year. Query. Length: 1,000-3,000 words. Pays $75-200. "Articles should concentrate on useful management information. Be specific rather than general."

THE DAIRYMAN, Box 819, Corona CA 91718. (714)735-2730. Editor: Dennis Halladay. 10% freelance written. Monthly magazine dealing with large-herd commercial dairy industry. Circ. 33,000. Pays on acceptance or publication. Publishes ms an average of 2 months after acceptance. Byline given. Buys first North American serial rights. Submit seasonal material 3 months in advance. Photocopied submissions OK. Computer printout submissions acceptable. SASE. Reports in 2 weeks on queries and mss. Free sample copy; writer's guidelines free with legal size SAE and 1 first class stamp.
Nonfiction: Humor, interview/profile, new product, opinion, and industry analysis. Special issues: Computer issue (February); herd health issues (July and August); and A.I. and breeding issue (November). No religion, nostalgia, politics or 'mom and pop' dairies. Query or send complete ms. Length: 300-500 words. Pays $10-200.
Photos: Send photo with query or ms. Reviews b&w contact sheets and 35mm or 2¼x2¼ transparencies. Pays $10-25 for b&w; $25-60 for color. Requires captions, model releases, and identification of subjects. Buys one-time rights.

Columns/Departments: Herd health, taxes and finances, insurance, dairy safety, economic outlook for dairying. Buys 40/year. Query or send complete ms. Length: 300-1,000 words. Pays $25-100.

Tips: Pretend you're an editor for a moment; now would you want to buy a story without any artwork; neither would I. Writers often don't know modern commercial dairying and they forget they're writing for an audience of *Dairymen*. Publications are becoming more and more specialized . . . you're really got to know who you're writing for and why they're different.

General Interest Farming and Rural Life

These publications are read by farm families or farmers and contain material on sophisticated agricultural and business techniques. Magazines that specialize in the raising of crops are in the Crops and Soil Management classification; publications that deal exclusively with livestock raising are classified in the Livestock category. Magazines for farm suppliers are grouped under Agricultural Equipment and Supplies.

National

ACRES U.S.A., A Voice for Eco-Agriculture, Acres U.S.A., Box 9547, Kansas City MO 64133. (816)737-0064. Editor: Charles Walters, Jr. Monthly tabloid covering biologically sound farming techniques. Circ. 16,000. Pays on acceptance. Byline sometimes given. Not copyrighted. Buys all rights. Submit seasonal/holiday material 3 months in advance. Computer printout submissions acceptable. Reports in 1 month. Sample copy $2.

Nonfiction: Expose (farm-related); how-to; and case reports on farmers who have adopted eco-agriculture (organic). No philosophy on eco-farming or essays. Buys 80 mss/year. Query with published clips. Length: open. Pays 6¢/word.

Photos: State availability of photos. Reviews b&w photos only. Top quality photos only. Pays $6 for b&w contact sheets, negatives and 7x10 prints.

Tips: "We need on-scene reports of farmers who have adopted eco-farming—good case reports. We must have substance in articles and need details on systems developed. Read a few copies of the magazine to learn the language of the subject."

AGWAY COOPERATOR, Box 4933, Syracuse NY 13221. (315)477-7061. Editor: Jean Willis. For farmers. 2% freelance written. Published 9 times/year. Pays on acceptance. Time between acceptance and publication varies considerably. Usually reports in 1 week. Computer printout submissions acceptable. SASE.

Nonfiction: Should deal with topics of farm or rural interest in the Northeastern US. Length: 1,200 words maximum. Pays $100, usually including photos.

Tips: "Fillers don't fit into our format. We do not assign freelance articles."

BLAIR AND KETCHUM'S COUNTRY JOURNAL, Historical Times, Inc., Box 870, Manchester VT 05255. Editor: J. Tyler Resch. Managing Editor: David D. Sleeper. 90% freelance written. Monthly magazine featuring country living for people who live in rural areas or who are thinking about moving there. Circ. 300,000. Average issue includes 8-10 feature articles and 10 departments. Pays on acceptance. Publishes ms an average of 1 year after acceptance. Byline given. Buys first North American serial rights. Submit seasonal material 8 months in advance. Photocopied submissions OK. Computer printout submissions acceptable, prefers letter-quality; "dot-matrix submissions are acceptable if double spaced." SASE. Reports in 1 month. Sample copy $2.50; writer's guidelines for SASE.

Nonfiction: Book excerpts; general interest; opinion (essays); profile (people who are outstanding in terms of country living); how-to; issues affecting rural areas; photo feature. No historical or reminiscence. Buys 8-10 mss/issue. Query with clips of previously published work and SASE. Length: 2,000-3,500 words. Pays $400-500.

Photos: Stephen R. Swinburne, photo editor. State availability of photos. Reviews b&w contact sheets, 5x7 and 8x10 b&w glossy prints and 35mm or larger color transparencies. Captions, model release and identification of subjects required. Buys one-time rights.

Columns/Departments: Listener (brief articles on country topics, how-to's, current events and updates). Buys 10 mss/year. Query with published clips. Length: 200-400 words. Pays approx. $75.

Poetry: Free verse, light verse and traditional. Buys 1 poem/issue. Pays $2.50/line.

Tips: "Be as specific in your query as possible and explain why you are qualified to write the piece (especially for how-to's and controversial subjects). The writer has a better chance of breaking in at our publication with short articles."

BUYING FOR THE FARM, Elmbrook Publishing, Inc., 21100 W. Capitol Dr., Pewaukee WI 53072. (414)783-5157. Editor: H. Lee Schwanz. 30% freelance written. A monthly farming and ranching magazine "concentrating on ways farmers can save money on inputs for crops and livestock production. Prices are compared for classes of inputs." Circ. 25,000. Pays on acceptance. Publishes ms an average of 2 months after acceptance. Byline given. Offers negotiable kill fee. Buys all rights. Submit seasonal/holiday material 2 months in advance. Simultaneous queries OK. Computer printout submissions acceptable; prefers letter-quality to dot-matrix. SASE. Reports in 2 weeks. Sample copy and writer's guidelines for $1.
Nonfiction: Articles related to purchasing for the farm. Buys 50 mss/year. Query with farm writing credentials. Length: 400-800 words. Pays $100-300. Sometimes pays the expenses of writers on assignment.
Photos: Reviews b&w contacts and negatives. Buys one-time rights.
Tips: "We do farmer experience articles and want wide geographical distribution. Writers frequently don't write for the specific type of articles used in *Buying*. We have a unique format."

FARM & RANCH LIVING, Reiman Publications, 5400 S. 60th St., Greendale WI 53129. (414)423-0100. Editor: Roy Reiman. Managing Editor: Bob Ottum. 80% freelance written. A bimonthly lifestyle magazine aimed at families engaged full time in farming or ranching. "*F&RL* is *not* a 'how-to' magazine—it deals with people rather than products and profits." Circ. 230,000. Pays on acceptance. Publishes ms an average of 6 months after acceptance. Byline given. Offers 25% kill fee. Buys first serial rights and second serial (reprint) rights. Submit seasonal/holiday material 6 months in advance. Previously published submissions OK. Computer printout submissions acceptable. SASE. Reports in 6 weeks. Sample copy $2; writer's guidelines for business size SAE and 1 first class stamp.
Nonfiction: Interview/profile, photo feature, historical/nostalgic, humor, inspirational and personal experience. No how-to articles or stories about 'hobby farmers' (doctors or lawyers with weekend farms), or 'hardtimes' stories (farmers going broke or selling out). Buys 50 mss/year. Query first with or without published clips; state availability of photos. Length: 1,000-3,000 words. Pays $150-500 for text-and-photos package. Pays expenses of writers on assignment.
Photos: Scenic. Pays $20-40 for b&w photos; $75-200 for 35mm color slides. Buys one-time rights.
Fillers: Clippings, jokes, anecdotes and short humor. Buys 150/year. Length: 50-150 words. Pays $20 minimum.
Tips: "A freelancer must see *F&RL* to fully appreciate how different it is from other farm publications . . . ordering a sample is strongly advised (not available on newsstands). Query first—we'll give plenty of help and encouragement if story looks promising, and we'll explain why if it doesn't. Photo features (about interesting farm or ranch families); Most Interesting Farmer (or Rancher) I've Ever Met (human interest profile); and Prettiest Place in the Country (tour in text and photos of an attractive farm or ranch) are most open to freelancers. We can make separate arrangements for photography if writer is unable to provide photos."

‡**FARM COMPUTER NEWS**, Meredith Corp., 1716 Locust, Des Moines IA 50336. (515)284-2127. Editor: Gary Vincent. Bimonthly magazine covering farm computerization. "Our readers are farmers who own or are interested in owning a microcomputer." Estab. 1984. Circ. 10,000. Pays on acceptance. Byline sometimes given. Buys all rights. Submit seasonal/holiday material 3 months in advance. Computer printout submissions acceptable; prefers letter-quality to dot-matrix. Reports in 2 weeks on queries; 3 months on mss. Free sample copy.
Nonfiction: Interview/profile (farmers using computers); and technical (direct applications to farming). Buys 50-60 mss/year. Query with published clips. Pays $200-400.

FARM FUTURES, The Farm Business Magazine, AgriData Resources, 330 E. Kilbourn, Milwaukee WI 53202. (414)278-7676. Editor: Claudia Waterloo. Managing Editor: David Pelzer. 25% freelance written. Circ. 160,000. Pays on publication. Publishes ms an average of 3 weeks after acceptance. Byline given. Offers negotiable kill fee. Buys first rights only. Simultaneous queries, and photocopied and previously published submissions OK; no simultaneous submissions. Electronic submissions OK; inquire about requirements. Computer printout submissions acceptable; prefers letter-quality to dot-matrix. Reports in 1 month on queries; 1 month on mss. Free sample copy and guidelines for contributors.
Nonfiction: Practical advice and insights into managing commercial farms, farm marketing how-to's, financial management, use of computers in agriculture, and farmer profiles. Buys 35 mss/year. Query with published clips. Length: 250-2,000 words. Pays $35-400. Sometimes pays the expenses of writers on assignment.
Tips: "The writer has a better chance of breaking in at our publication with short articles and fillers since our style is very particular; our stories are written directly to farmers and must be extremely practical. It's a style most writers have to 'grow into.' The most frequent mistakes made by writers in completing an article for us are lack of thoroughness and good examples; language too lofty or convoluted; and lack of precision—inaccuracies."

FARM INDUSTRY NEWS, Webb Publishing, 1999 Shepard Rd., St. Paul MN 55116. (612)690-7284. Editor: Joseph Degnan. Managing Editor: Kurt Lawton. 10% freelance written. Magazine published 10 times/year in 16 Midwest and Mideast states. Covers product news, high technology, buying information. "We treat high volume farmers as purchasing agents rather than producers. Our stories provide farmers with in-depth information on new products they may consider buying, new developments in agriculture and on other farmers who have invented their own equipment." Circ. 300,000. Pays on acceptance. Publishes ms an average of 2 months after acceptance. Byline given. Buys one-time rights. Computer printout submissions acceptable. SASE. Reports in 3 weeks. Free sample copy and writer's guidelines.
Nonfiction: Interview/profile, new product and technical. No production stories, fiction or poetry. "Please study the publication before submitting stories." Query or send complete ms. Length: 500-1,500 words. Pays $50-400.
Photos: Reviews b&w contact sheets, 35mm color transparencies or 8x10 b&w prints. Payment depends on use and is included with ms. Captions and indentification of subjects required.
Tips: "Read the magazine, then query with specific idea and contacts. Good photographs showing a product and human involvement help in selling an article." Phone queries OK.

FARM JOURNAL, 230 W. Washington Square, Philadelphia PA 19105. Contact: Editor. "The business magazine of American agriculture" is published 14 times/year with many regional editions. Material bought for one or more editions depending upon where it fits. Buys all rights. Byline given "except when article is too short or too heavily rewritten to justify one." Payment made on acceptance and is the same regardless of editions in which the piece is used. SASE.
Nonfiction: Timeliness and seasonableness are very important. Material must be highly practical and should be helpful to as many farmers as possible. Farmers' experiences should apply to one or more of these 8 basic commodities: corn, wheat, milo, soybeans, cotton, dairy, beef and hogs. Technical material must be accurate. No farm nostalgia. Query to describe a new idea that farmers can use. Length: 500-1,500 words. Pays 10-20¢/word published.
Photos: Much in demand either separately or with short how-to material in picture stories and as illustrations for articles. Warm human interest pix for covers—activities on modern farms. For inside use, shots of homemade and handy ideas to get work done easier and faster, farm news photos, and pictures of farm people with interesting sidelines. In b&w, 8x10 glossies are preferred; color submissions should be 2¼x2¼ for the cover, and 35mm for inside use. Pays $50 and up for b&w shot; $75 and up for color.
Tips: *"Farm Journal* now publishes in hundreds of editions reflecting geographic, demographic, and economic sectors of the farm market."

HIGH PLAINS JOURNAL, "The Farmers Paper", High Plains Publishers, Inc., Box 760, Dodge City KS 67801. (316)227-7171. Editor: Galen Hubbs. 5% freelance written. Weekly tabloid with news, features and photos on all phases of farming and livestock production. Circ. 58,000. Pays on publication. Publishes ms an average of 1 month after acceptance. Byline given. Not copyrighted. Buys first rights only. Submit seasonal/holiday material 1 month in advance. Simultaneous queries and photocopied submissions OK. Computer printout submissions acceptable; prefers letter-quality to dot-matrix. SASE. Reports in 3 weeks on queries; 1 month on mss. Sample copy for $1 and SAE with 3 first class stamps; writer's guidelines for SAE and 1 first class stamp.
Nonfiction: General interest (agriculture); how-to; interview/profile (farmers or stockmen within the High Plains area); and photo feature (agricultural). No rewrites of USDA, extension or marketing association releases. Buys 50-60 mss/year. Query with published clips. Length: 10-40 inches. Pays $1/column inch. Sometimes pays the expenses of writers on assignment.
Photos: State availability of photos. Pays $5-10 for 4x5 b&w prints. Captions and "complete" identification of subjects required. Buys one-time rights.
Tips: "Limit submissions to agriculture. Stories should not have a critical time element. Stories should be informative with correct information. Use quotations and bring out the human aspects of the person featured in profiles. Frequently writers do not have a good understanding of the subject. Stories are too long or are too far from our circulation area to be beneficial. Too many writers are just seeking a way to make additional income."

THE NATIONAL FUTURE FARMER, Box 15130, Alexandria VA 22309. (703)360-3600. Editor-in-Chief: Wilson W. Carnes. Bimonthly magazine for members of the Future Farmers of America who are students of vocational agriculture in high school, ranging in age from 14-21 years; major interest in careers in agriculture/agribusiness and other youth interest subjects. Circ. 476,500. Pays on acceptance. Buys all rights. Byline given. Submit seasonal/holiday material 3-4 months in advance. Computer printout submissions acceptable; prefers letter-quality to dot-matrix. SASE. Usually reports in 1 month. Free sample copy and writer's guidelines.
Nonfiction: How-to for youth (outdoor-type such as camping, hunting, fishing); and informational (getting money for college, farming; and other help for youth). Informational, personal experience and interviews are used only if FFA members or former members are involved. Recent article example: "The Road to Success"

(February/March 1985). Buys 15 unsolicited mss/year. Query or send complete ms. Length: 1,000 words maximum. Pays 4-6¢/word.

Photos: Purchased with mss (5x7 or 8x10 b&w glossies; 35mm or larger color transparencies). Pays $7.50 for b&w; $30-40 for inside color; $100 for cover.

Tips: "Find an FFA member who has done something truly outstanding that will motivate and inspire others, or provide helpful information for a career in farming, ranching or agribusiness. We are also very interested in stories on the latest trends in agriculture and how those trends may affect our readers. We're accepting manuscripts now that are tighter and more concise. Get straight to the point."

‡**SPERRY NEW HOLLAND NEWS** Sperry New Holland, 500 Diller Ave., New Holland PA 17557. Editor: Gary Martin. 50% freelance written. Magazine published 8 times/year on agriculture; designed to entertain and inform farm families. Pays on acceptance. Byline usually given. Offers negotiable kill fee. Buys first North American serial rights, one-time rights, and second serial (reprint) rights. Submit seasonal/holiday material 4 months in advance. Simultaneous queries and previously published submissions OK. Computer printout submissions acceptable; prefers letter-quality to dot-matrix. SASE. Reports in 1 month. Free sample copy and writer's guidelines.

Nonfiction: "We need strong photo support for short articles up to 800 words on farm management, farm human interest and agricultural research." Buys 16-20 mss/year. Query. Length: 800 words. Pays $400-700.

Photos: Send photos with query when possible. Reviews color transparencies. Pays $25-200. Captions, model release, and identification of subjects required. Buys one-time rights.

Tips: "The writer must have an emotional understanding of agriculture and the farm family and must demonstrate in the article an understanding of the unique economics that affect farming in North America. We want to know about the exceptional farm managers, those leading the way in use of new technology, new efficiencies—but always with a human touch. Successful writers keep in touch with the editor as they develop the article."

SUCCESSFUL FARMING, 1716 Locust St., Des Moines IA 50336. (515)284-2897. Managing Editor: Loren Kruse. 5% freelance written. Magazine of farm management published for top farmers 13 times/year. Circ. 605,000. Buys all rights. Pays on acceptance. Publishes ms an average of 2 months after acceptance. Reports in 2 weeks. SASE. Sample copy and writer's guidelines for SAE and 5 first class stamps.

Nonfiction: Semitechnical articles on the aspects of farming with emphasis on how to apply this information to one's own farm. "Most of our material is too limited and unfamiliar for freelance writers, except for the few who specialize in agriculture, have a farm background and a modern agricultural education." Recent article example: "Machinery, Labor Savings, Key to No-till Profits" (April, 1985). Buys 50 unsolicited mss/year. Query with outline. Length: about 1,500 words maximum. Pays $250-600.

Photos: Jim Galbraith, art director. Prefers 8x10 b&w glossies to contacts; color should be transparencies, not prints. Buys exclusive rights. Assignments are given, and sometimes a guarantee, provided the editors can be sure the photography will be acceptable.

Tips: "A frequent mistake made by writers in completing articles is that the focus of the story is not narrow enough and does not include enough facts, observations, examples, and dollar signs. Short articles and fillers are usually specific and to the point."

Local

AcreAGE, Malheur Publishing Co., Box 130, Ontario OR 97914. (503)889-5387. Editor: Marie A. Ruemenapp. 20% freelance written. Monthly tabloid covering anything and everything relating to farming and ranching for all rural boxholders in southern Idaho and eastern Oregon. Circ. 42,000. Pays on publication. Publishes ms an average of 3 months after acceptance. Byline given. Buys first serial rights; some exceptions are made; query first. Computer printout submissions acceptable; prefers letter-quality to dot-matrix. SASE. Reports in 3 weeks. Sample copy $1.

Nonfiction: General interest (on farming and ranching); how-to (install fence, irrigate, plant, harvest, etc.); interview/profile (of leaders in agriculture); and personal experience (better ways to farm and ranch). No nostalgic pieces. "About 50% of our articles are technical pieces about such things as ag chemicals, irrigation, etc. These pieces are difficult for writers lacking a good ag background and proximity to a university or research center specializing in such work. No mss on 'how nice (or bad) it is to be a farmer or rancher.'" Buys 24 mss/year. Query or send complete ms. Length: 1,200 words maximum. Pays $1/inch.

Photos: Pays $5-7.50 for 5x7 (minimum) b&w glossy prints. Buys some color slides as cover photos (prefer these with ms). Identification of subjects required.

Tips: "Avoid telling the obvious, e.g., 'Holsteins are a breed of cow that gives lots of milk.' Writers will have better luck breaking in with human interest features (farm-ranch oriented). Past articles have included a power hang-glider (ultralight) pilot who used his machine to check irrigation lines; Landsat satellites for water and crop management; an old-time threshing bee; and a farmer who collects antique farm machinery. The majority of our articles deal with farming and ranching in the southern Idaho, eastern Oregon region. We are a regional publication. The farmers and ranchers in this area have different agricultural practices than their counterparts in other areas of the country. Writers frequently forget this.''

COUNTRY ESTATE, Northern Miner Press Ltd., RR1, Terra Cotta, Ontario L0P 1N0 Canada. (Editorial only). (416)838-2800. Editor: Michael Pembry. 20% freelance written. Quarterly magazine covering country living for upper income country homeowners. "Subjects must inform or entertain this specific audience." Circ. 52,000 (within 50 miles of Toronto). Pays on publication. Publishes ms an average of 1 year after acceptance. Byline given. Buys first North American serial rights. Simultaneous queries and photocopied and simultaneous submissions OK. Electronic submissions OK on Shaftstall converter, but requires hard copy also. Computer printout submissions acceptable. SAE with IRC. Reports in 1 month. Sample copy for $2.50 and 9x11 SAE and 60¢ postage or IRC; writer's guidelines for 30¢ postage or IRC.
Nonfiction: Historical/nostalgic; how-to; humor (on country living); interview/profile (country personalities in southern Ontario); personal experience; and photo feature. "All subjects must relate to country living and people in Ontario, especially areas within 50 miles of Toronto." No "articles written for a very general audience." Buys 30 mss/year. Query. Length: 500-1,500 words. Pays $75-150. Sometimes pays the expenses of writers on assignment.
Photos: State availability of photos with query letter or ms, or send photos with accompanying ms. Reviews transparencies and 5x7 prints. Payment included with article. Captions required. Buys one-time rights.
Tips: "Have a good grasp of our audience. Pick a subject which really relates specifically to country living in Ontario. Submit clean, edited material. Articles with good photos always preferred. The most frequent mistakes made by writers in completing articles for us are that they are too long, too general, or contain too many personal, humorous experiences which are only amusing to the writer, friends or others who know the place and people concerned.''

FLORIDA GROWER & RANCHER, 723 E. Colonial Dr., Orlando FL 32803. Editor: Frank Abrahamson. 10% freelance written. For citrus grove managers and production managers, vegetable growers and managers, field crop and livestock raisers; all agricultural activities in state. Monthly magazine. Circ. 28,000. Buys all rights. Pays on publication. Computer printout submissions acceptable; no dot-matrix. Publishes ms an average of 6 months after acceptance. Reports in 1 month. Query. SASE.
Nonfiction: Articles on production and industry-related topics. In-depth and up-to-date. Writer must know the market and write specifically for it. Informational, how-to, personal experience, interview, profile, opinion and successful business operations. Buys a minimum of outside material due to fulltime staff additions. Length: 500-1,500 words for features; 100 words or less for short items. Pays "competitive rates."
Photos: B&w illustrations desirable with features. Color illustrations purchased only occasionally.

IOWA REC NEWS, Suite 48, 8525 Douglas, Urbandale IA 50322. (515)276-5350. Editor: Karen Tisinger. 15% freelance written. Emphasizes energy issues for residents of rural Iowa. Monthly magazine. Circ. 125,000. Pays on publication. Publishes ms an average of 3 months after acceptance. Buys first rights and second (reprint) rights to material originally published elsewhere. Not copyrighted. Simultaneous, photocopied and previously published submissions OK. Computer printout submissions acceptable. SASE.
Nonfiction: General interest, historical, humor, farm issues and trends, rural lifestyle trends, energy awareness features, and photo features. Recent article example: "What Will I Do With My Farm?" Buys approximately 18 unsolicited mss/year. Send complete ms. Pays $40-60. "Rarely" pays the expenses of writers on assignment.
Tips: "The easiest way to break into our magazine is: include a couple paragraphs about the author, research a particular subject well, and include appropriate attributions to establish credibility, authority. Reading and knowing about farm people is important. Stories that touch the senses or can improve the lives of the readers are highly considered, as are those with a strong Iowa angle. We prefer to tailor our articles to Iowa REC readers and use our staff's skills. We rarely, if ever, publish lengthy articles by freelance writers. Freelancers have the advantage of offering subject matter that existing staff may not be able to cover. Often, however, many articles lack evidence of actual research—they provide lots of information but do not include any sources to give the story any credibility. (Rarely is the author a renowned expert on the subject he's written about.) Inclusion of nice photos is also a plus. The most frequent mistakes made by writers are: lots of typos in copy, uncorrected; story too long, story too biased; no attribution to any source of info; not relevant to electric consumers, farmers.''

‡MAINE ORGANIC FARMER & GARDENER, Maine Organic Farmers & Gardeners Association, Box 2176, Augusta ME 04330. (207)622-3118. Editor: Pam Bell, Box 53, South Hiram ME 04080. 50% freelance written. Bimonthly magazine covering organic farming and gardening for urban and rural farmers and gardeners and nutrition-oriented, environmentally concerned readers. "*MOF&G* promotes and encourages sustainable agriculture and environmentally sound living. Our primary focus is organic sustainable farming, gardening and forestry, but we also deal with local, national and global environmental issues." Circ. 15,000. Pays on publication. Publishes ms an average of 3 months after acceptance. Byline given. Buys first North American serial rights, one-time rights, first serial rights, or second serial (reprint) rights. Submit seasonal/holiday material 4 months in advance. Simultaneous queries, and simultaneous, photocopied, and previously published submissions OK. Computer printout submissions acceptable. SASE. Reports in 3 weeks. Sample copy $1; free writer's guidelines.

Nonfiction: Historical/nostalgic (farming); how-to (farm, garden [organically], forestry, woodlot management and rural skills); interview/profile (farmers, gardeners, government agpeople); personal experience (with livestock plants, trees, energy [renewable], gardens, farms); photo feature; technical (renewable energy, agriculture); and articles on nutrition, and the food system. Buys 30 mss/year. Query with published clips or send complete ms. Length: 1,000-3,500 words. Pays $40-130. Sometimes pays expenses of writers on assignment.

Photos: State availability of photos with query; send photos with ms. Reviews contact sheets and negatives. "We usually work from negatives. Many of our assignment writers send exposed films, and we process and print." Pays $5 for 8x10 b&w prints. Captions, model releases, and identification of subjects required. Buys one-time rights.

Columns/Departments: Food, nutrition and health (1,500-4,000 words); Book Reviews (500-1,000 words). Buys 12-15 mss/year. Query with published clips or send complete ms. Pays $25-50.

Tips: "Freelance writers interviewing existing organic farmers and gardeners, or commercial farmers who are looking for a more organic way should be mindful that interview and profile articles are more than human interest pieces for our readers—they are the backbone of our how-to information. Our readers want to know how-to but they also want to enjoy the reading."

MISSOURI RURALIST, Harvest Publishing, Suite 600, 2103 Burlington, Columbia MO 65202. Editor: Larry Harper. Managing Editor: Joe Link. 20% freelance written. Semimonthly magazine featuring Missouri farming for people who make their living at farming. Pays on acceptance. Publishes ms an average of 6 months after acceptance. Byline given. Buys first North American serial rights and all rights in Missouri. Photocopied submissions OK. Computer printout submissions acceptable; prefers letter-quality to dot-matrix. SASE. Reports in 1 month. Sample copy $2.

Nonfiction: "We use articles valuable to the Missouri farmer, discussing Missouri agriculture and people involved in it, including homemakers. Technical articles must be written in an easy-to-read style. The length depends on the topic." No corny cartoons or poems on farmers. Query. Pays $60/published page. Sometimes pays the expenses of writers on assignment.

Photos: State availability of photos. Pays $5-10 for 5x7 b&w glossy prints. Pays $60 maximum for 35mm transparencies for covers. Captions required.

Fillers: Newsbreaks. Length: 100-500 words. Pays $60/printed page.

Tips: "We're mostly staff written. Contributed material must be Missouri farming oriented and writer must know and understand Missouri agriculture. Usually articles we receive are too general."

NEW ENGLAND FARMER, NEF Publishing Co., Box 391, St. Johnsbury VT 05819. (802)748-8908. Editor: Dan Hurley. Managing Editor: Thomas Gilson. 20% freelance written. Monthly tabloid covering New England agriculture for farmers. Circ. 13,052. Pays on publication. Byline given. Buys all rights and makes-work-for-hire assignments. Submit seasonal/holiday material 2 months in advance. Previously published submissions OK. Computer printout submissions acceptable. SASE. Reports in 3 months. Free sample copy.

Nonfiction: How-to, interview/profile, opinion and technical. No romantic views of farming. "We use on-the-farm interviews with good b&w photos that combine technical information with human interest. No poetics!" Buys 150 mss/year. Send complete ms. Pays $40-100. Sometimes pays the expenses of writers on assignment.

Photos: Send photos with ms. Payment for photos is included in payment for articles. Reviews b&w contact sheet and 8x10 b&w prints.

Tips: "Good, accurate stories needing minimal editing, with art, of interest to commercial farmers in New England are welcome. A frequent mistake made by writers is sending us items that do not meet our needs; generally, they'll send stories that don't have a New England focus."

THE OHIO FARMER, 1350 W. 5th Ave., Columbus OH 43212. (614)486-9637. Editor: Andrew Stevens. For Ohio farmers and their families. 10% freelance written. Biweekly magazine; 50 pages. Circ. 93,000. Usually buys all rights. Buys 5-10 mss/year. Pays on publication. Publishes ms an average of 2 months after acceptance. Will consider photocopied submissions. Reports in 2 weeks. Submit complete ms. Computer printout submissions acceptable; prefers letter-quality to dot-matrix. SASE. Sample copy $1; free writer's guidelines.

Nonfiction: Technical and on-the-farm stories. Buys informational, how-to, and personal experience. Length: 600-700 words. Pays $15.

Photos: Photos purchased with ms with no additional payment, or without ms. Pays $5-25 for b&w; $35-100 for color. Size: 4x5 for b&w glossies; transparencies or 8x10 prints for color.

Tips: "We are now doing more staff-written stories. We buy very little freelance material."

RURAL KENTUCKIAN, Box 32170, Louisville KY 40232. (502)451-2430. Editor: Gary W. Luhr. 75% freelance written. Monthly feature magazine primarily for Kentucky residents. Circulation: 270,000. Pays on acceptance. Publishes ms an average of 8 months after acceptance. Byline given. Not copyrighted. Buys first rights for Kentucky. Submit seasonal/holiday material at least 4 months in advance. Will consider photocopied, previously published and simultaneous submissions if previously published and simultaneous submissions if outside Kentucky. Computer printout submissions acceptable; prefers letter-quality to dot-matrix. SASE. Reports in 2 weeks. Free sample copy.
Nonfiction: Prefers Kentucky-related profiles (people, places or events), history, biography, recreation, travel, lesiure or lifestyle articles or book excerpts; articles on contemporary subjects of general public interest and general consumer-related features including service pieces. Publishes some humorous and first person articles of exceptional quality and opinion pieces from qualified authorities. No general nostalgia. Buys 24-36 mss/year. Query or send complete ms. Length: 800-2000 words. Pays $50-$250. Sometimes pays the expenses of writers on assignment.
Photos: State availability of photos. Reviews color slide transparencies and b&w prints. Identification of subjects required. Payment included in payment for ms. Pays extra if photo used on cover.
Tips: "The quality of writing and reporting (factual, objective, thorough) is considered in setting payment price. We prefer well-documented pieces filled with quotes and anecdotes. Avoid boosterism. Writers need not confine themselves to subjects suited only to a rural audience but should avoid subjects of a strictly metropolitian nature. Well-researched, well-written feature articles, particularly on subjects of a serious nature, are given preference over light-weight material. Despite its name, *Rural Kentuckian* is not a farm publication."

WALLACES FARMER, Suite 501, 1501 42nd Street, W. Des Moines IA 50265. (515)224-6000. Editor: Monte N. Sesker. 2% freelance written. Semimonthly magazine for Iowa farmers and their families. Buys Midwest states rights (Nebraska, Minnesota, Wisconsin, Illinois, Missouri, South Dakota and Iowa). Pays on acceptance. Publishes ms an average of 2 weeks after acceptance. Computer printout submissions acceptable; prefers letter-quality to dot-matrix. Reports in 2 weeks. SASE.
Nonfiction: Occasional short feature articles about Iowa farming accompanied by photos. Buys 10 unsolicited mss/year. Query. Length: 500-1,000 words. Pays about 4-5¢/word.
Photos: Photos purchased with or without mss. Should be taken on Iowa farms. Pays $7-15 for 5x7 b&w; $50-100 for 4x5, 2¼x2¼ color transparencies. See recent issue covers for examples.
Tips: "We are moving toward more staff-produced articles."

WYOMING RURAL ELECTRIC NEWS, 340 West B St., Casper WY 82601. (307)234-6152. Editor: Gale Eisenhauer. 20% freelance written. For audience of rural people, some farmers and ranchers. Monthly magazine; 20 pages. Circ. 58,500. Not copyrighted. Byline given. Buys 12-15 mss/year. Pays on publication. Publishes ms an average of 2 months after acceptance. Buys first rights. Will consider photocopied and simultaneous submissions. Submit seasonal material 2 months in advance. Computer printout submissions acceptable. Reports in 1 month. SASE. Free sample copy with SAE and 3 first class stamps.
Nonfiction and Fiction: Wants energy-related material, "people" features, historical pieces about Wyoming and the West, and things of interest to Wyoming's rural people. Buys informational, humor, historical, nostalgia and photo mss. Submit complete ms. Length for nonfiction and fiction: 1,200-1,500 words. Pays $25-50. Buys some experimental, western, humorous and historical fiction. Pays $25-50.
Photos: Photos purchased with accompanying ms with additional payment, or purchased without ms. Captions required. Pays up to $50 for cover photos. Color only.
Tips: "Study an issue or two of the magazine to become familiar with our focus and the type of freelance material we're using. Submit entire manuscript. Don't submit a regionally set story from some other part of the country and merely change the place names to Wyoming. Photos and illustrations (if appropriate) are always welcomed."

Livestock

Farmers who raise cattle, sheep or hogs for meat, wool or hides are the audience for these journals. Publications for farmers who raise other animals are listed in the Miscellaneous category; many magazines in the General Interest Farming and Rural Life classification buy material on raising livestock. Magazines for dairy farmers are included under Dairy Farming. Publications dealing with raising horses, pets or other pleasure animals are found under Animal in the Consumer Publications section.

BEEF, The Webb Co., 1999 Shepard Rd., St. Paul MN 55116. (612)690-7374. Editor-in-Chief: Paul D. Andre. Senior Managing Editor: Warren Kester. 5% freelance written. Monthly magazine. For readers who have the same basic interest—making a living feeding cattle or running a cow herd. Circ. 125,000. Pays on acceptance. Publishes ms an average of 4 months after acceptance. Buys all rights. Byline given. Phone queries OK. Submit seasonal material 3 months in advance. Computer printout submissions acceptable. SASE. Reports in 2 months. Free sample copy and writer's guidelines.
Nonfiction: How-to and informational articles on doing a better job of producing feeding cattle, market building, managing and animal health practices. Material must deal with beef cattle only. Buys 8-10 mss/year. Query. Length: 500-2,000 words. Pays $25-300.
Photos: B&w glossies (8x10) and color transparencies (35mm or 2¼x2¼) purchased with or without mss. Captions required. Query or send contact sheet or transparencies. Pays $10-50 for b&w; $25-100 for color. Model release required.
Tips: "Be completely knowledgeable about cattle feeding and cowherd operations. Know what makes a story. We want specifics, not a general roundup of an operation. Pick one angle and develop it fully. The most frequent mistake is not following instructions on an angle (or angles) to be developed."

THE CATTLEMAN MAGAZINE, Texas & Southwestern Cattle Raisers Association, 1301 W. 7th St., Ft. Worth TX 76102. (817)332-7155. Editor: Dale Segraves. Managing Editor: Don C. King. Emphasizes beef cattle production and feeding. "Readership consists of commercial cattlemen, purebred seedstock producers, cattle feeders and horsemen in the Southwest." Monthly magazine; 170 pages. Circ. 22,500. Pays on acceptance. Publishes ms an average of 6 months after acceptance. Byline given. Buys all rights. Computer printout submissions acceptable; prefers letter-quality to dot-matrix. SASE. Reports in 3 weeks. Sample copy $1.50; writer's guidelines for business size SAE and 1 first class stamp.
Nonfiction: Need informative, entertaining feature articles on specific commercial ranch operations, cattle breeding and feeding, range and pasture management, profit tips, and university research on beef industry. "We feature various beef cattle breeds most months." Will take a few historical western-lore pieces. Must be well-documented. No first-person narratives or fiction or articles pertaining to areas outside the Southwest or outside beef cattle ranching. Buys 24 mss/year. Query. Length 1,500-2,000 words. Pays $75-200. Sometimes pays the expenses of writers on assignment.
Photos: Photos purchased with or without accompanying ms. State availability of photos with query or ms. Pays $15-25 for 5x7 b&w glossies; $100 for color transparencies used as cover. Total purchase price for ms includes payment for photos. Captions, model release, and identification of subjects required.
Fillers: Cartoons.
Tips: "Submit an article dealing with ranching in the Southwest. Too many writers submit stories out of our general readership area. Economics may force staff writers to produce more articles, leaving little room for unsoliticed articles."

LIMOUSIN WORLD, Limousin World Inc., 6408 S. College Ave., Fort Collins CO 80525. Editor: Wes Ishmael. Managing Editor: Louise Kello. 10% freelance written. A monthly magazine on the Limousin breed of beef cattle for people who breed and raise them. Circ. 13,000. Pays on acceptance. Publishes ms an average of 2 months after acceptance. Byline given. Buys negotiable rights. Submit seasonal/holiday material 2 months in advance. Simultaneous queries, and photocopied and previously published submissions OK. Computer printout submissions acceptable; prefers letter-quality to dot-matrix. SASE. Reports in 2 weeks. Sample copy and writer's guidelines for $2.40.
Nonfiction: How-to (beef herd management equipment); interview/profile (interesting Limousin breeders); new product (limited); and travel (Limousin oriented). "Write interesting, informative, entertaining articles on farm and ranch operations where Limousin breeding has an influence. Management, feeding, breeding, profit producing methods, university research and interesting people are all good topics. Queries should be made on subject for herd features before doing. Short human interest articles on well-known popular personalities who are also breeding Limousin are used." Special issue on Herd Reference. No inflamatory or controversial articles. Query. Length: open. Pays $25-200. Sometimes pays the expenses of writers on assignment.
Photos: Send photos with query or ms. Pays $5-25 for 5x7 and 8x10 b&w prints; $25-100 for 5x7 and 8x10 color prints. Captions required. Buys first-time rights.
Tips: "Our readers are in the cattle breeding and raising business for a living so writing should be directed to an informed, mature audience."

SHEEP! MAGAZINE, Rt. 1, Box 78, Helenville WI 53137. (414)674-3029. Editor: Doris Thompson. 60% freelance written. Monthly magazine. "We're looking for clear, concise, useful information for sheep raisers who have a few sheep to a 1,000 ewe flock." Circ. 8,500. Pays on publication. Publishes ms an average of 1 month after acceptance. Byline given. Offers $30 kill fee. Buys all rights or makes work-for-hire assignments. Submit seasonal/holiday material 3 months in advance. Computer printout submissions acceptable. SASE. Reports in 1 month. Sample copy for 9x12 SAE with postage.
Nonfiction: Book excerpts; information (on personalities and/or political, legal or environmental issues af-

fecting the sheep industry); how-to (on innovative lamb and wool marketing and promotion techniques, efficient record-keeping systems or specific aspects of health and husbandry). "Health and husbandry articles should be written by someone with extensive experience or appropriate credentials (i.e., a veterinarian or animal scientist."); profiles (on experienced sheep producers who detail the economics and management of their operation); features (on small businesses that promote wool products and stories about local and regional sheep producer's groups and their activities); new products (of value to sheep producers; should be written by someone who has used them); and technical (on genetics, health and nutrition). First person narratives. Buys 80 mss/year. Query with clips of published work or send complete ms. Length: 750-2,500 words. Pays $45-150.
Photos: "Color—vertical compositions of sheep and/or people—for our cover. Use only b&w inside magazine. B&w, 35mm photos or other visuals improve your chances of a sale." Pays $50 maximum for 35mm color or transparencies; $5-30 for 5x7 b&w prints. Identification of subjects required. Buys all rights.
Tips: "Send us your best words and photos!"

‡**SHOW RING MAGAZINE**, Box 1399, Albany TX 76430. (915)762-2242. Editor: Mike Martinson. Assistant Editor: Carol Lackey. Approximately 50% freelance written. A national monthly magazine covering the livestock industry (cattle, sheep and swine) with focus on major livestock shows and sales, as well as the purebred breeding industry. Audience includes families and 4-H and FFA groups. "The emphasis of our editorial content is directed toward youth livestock activities, such as state and national livestock shows, youth livestock events, and breeders of livestock for youth." Circ. 5,000. Pays on publication. Publishes ms an average of 2 months after acceptance. Byline given. Not copyrighted. Buys first rights. Submit seasonal/holiday material 3 months in advance. Simultaneous queries OK. Computer printout submissions acceptable; prefers letter-quality to dot-matrix. SASE. Reports in 1 month. Sample copy $1.50.
Nonfiction: General interest (anything on livestock industry); historical/nostalgic (how things have changed in livestock shows or sales); how-to (clip a calf, exhibit an animal); humor (pertaining to livestock); interview/profile (story about prominent ranch or farm "check with us before writing"); new product (any new livestock product); opinion (about any current happening in livestock industry); personal experience (with lifestock, exhibiting animals, etc.; 4-H or FFA experience); photo feature; technical (on embryo transplants, artificial insemination, etc.). Special issues include Show Pig issues (April-Oct.); Sire issue (May); Directory of Agriculture (June/July); and Christmas issue (Dec.). Buys 6 mss/year. Query. Length: 500-2,500 words. Pays $25-100. Sometimes pays the expenses of writers on assignment.
Photos: State availability of photos. Pays $5/3x5 b&w and color prints. Captions and identification of subjects required. Buys one-time rights.
Fiction: "We will not use much fiction. We might be interested if it is humorous or a special story for Christmas, etc. It must pertain to livestock." Buys 1-3 mss/year. Query. Length: 500 words. Pays $25-100.
Tips: "We especially need articles on young people having good experiences showing livestock. How-to articles are also very popular with our readers."

SIMMENTAL SHIELD, Box 511, Lindsborg KS 67456. Publisher: Chester Peterson Jr. Associate Publisher/Editor: Jim Cotton. 30% freelance written. Official publication of American Simmental Association. Readers are breeders of purebred cattle and/or commercial cattlemen. Monthly; 150 pages. Circ. 8,000. Buys all rights. Pays on publication. Publishes ms an average of 3 months after acceptance. Computer printout submissions acceptable. January is AI issue; July is herd sire issue; December is brood cow issue. Submit material 3-4 months in advance. Reports in 1 month. Query first or submit complete ms. SASE. Free sample copy $1.
Nonfiction and Fillers: Farmer experience and management articles with emphasis on ideas used and successful management ideas based on cattleman who owns Simmental. Research: new twist to old ideas or application of new techniques to the Simmental or cattle business. Wants articles that detail to reader how to make or save money or pare labor needs. Buys informational, how-to, personal experience, interview, profile, humor and think articles. Rates vary. Sometimes pays the expenses of writers on assignment.
Photos: Photos purchased with accompanying ms with no additional payment. Interest in cover photos; accepts 35mm if sharp, well exposed.
Tips: "Articles must involve Simmental and/or beef breeding cattle. Be conversant with our lingo and community."

Miscellaneous

GLEANINGS IN BEE CULTURE, Box 706, Medina OH 44258. Editor: Mark Bruner. 40% freelance written. For beekeepers. Monthly. Buys first North American serial rights. Pays on publication. Publishes ms an average of 2 months after acceptance. Reports in 15-90 days. Computer printout submissions acceptable; prefers letter-quality to dot-matrix. SASE. Writer's guidelines available upon request for SAE and 1 first class postage stamp.
Nonfiction: Interested in articles giving new ideas on managing bees. Also uses success stories about commer-

cial beekeepers. No "how I began beekeeping" articles. No highly advanced, technical and scientific abstracts or impractical advice. Length: 3,000 words maximum. "We'll be changing format to allow for approximately 35% more copy space for articles." Pays $23/published page. Sometimes pays the expenses of writers on assignment.

Photos: Sharp b&w photos (pertaining to honeybees) purchased with mss. Can be any size, prints or enlargements, but 4x5 or larger preferred. Pays $3-5/picture.

Tips: "Do an interview story on commercial beekeepers who are cooperative enough to furnish accurate, factual information on their operations. Frequent mistakes made by writers in completing articles are that they are too general in nature and lack management knowledge."

THE SUGAR PRODUCER, Harris Publishing, Inc., 520 Park, Box 981, Idaho Falls ID 83402. (208)522-5187. Editor: Steve Janes. 25% freelance written. Bimonthly magazine covering the growing, storage, use and by-products of the sugar beet. Circ. 19,000. Pays on publication. Publishes ms an average of 3 months after acceptance. Buys one-time rights. Byline given. Phone queries OK. Photocopied and previously published submissions OK. Computer printout submissions acceptable. SASE. Reports in 1 month. Free sample copy and writer's guidelines.

Nonfiction: "This is a trade magazine, not a farm magazine. It deals with the business of growing sugar beets, and the related industry. All articles must tell the grower how he can do his job better, or at least be of interest to him, such as historical, because he is vitally interested in the process of growing sugar beets, and the industries related to this." Expose (pertaining to the sugar industry or the beet grower); how-to (all aspects of growing, storing and marketing the sugar beet); interview; profile; personal experience; and technical (material source must accompany story—research and data must be from an accepted research institution). Query or send complete ms. Length: 750-2,000 words. Pays 3¢/word.

Photos: Purchased with mss. Captions required. Pays $5 for any convenient size b&w; $10 for color print or transparency; $25 for color shot used on cover. Model release required.

Finance

These magazines deal with banking, investment, and financial management. Publications that use similar material but have a less technical slant are listed in Consumer Publications under Business and Finance.

AMERICAN BANKER, 1 State St. Plaza, New York NY 10004. (212)943-0400. Editor: William Zimmerman. Managing Editor: Robert Casey. 30% freelance written. Daily tabloid covering banking and finance for top management of banks, savings banks, savings and loans and other financial service institutions. Circ. 24,000. Pays on publication. Publishes ms an average of 1 month after acceptance. Byline given. Buys all rights. Simultaneous and previously published ("depending on where published") submissions OK. Computer printout submissions acceptable; prefers letter-quality to dot-matrix. Reports in 1 month. Feature calendar on request.

Nonfiction: Patricia Stundza, features editor. Book excerpts and technical (relating to banking/finance). No "nonbanking or nonbusiness-oriented articles—must be specific." Query. Length: 1,500-3,000 words. Pays $75-500. Sometimes pays the expenses of writers on assignment.

Photos: State availability of photos. Pays $100 minimum for 8x10 b&w prints. Captions and identification of subjects required. Buys one-time rights.

BANKING TODAY, (Formerly *Florida Banker*), Box 6847, Orlando FL 32853. Vice President and Executive Editor: William P. Seaparke. 20% freelance written. Monthly magazine; 52 pages. Circ. 7,300. Pays on publication. Publishes ms an average of 3 months after acceptance. Buys all rights; loans usage back to writers on agreement. Pays 50% kill fee. Byline given. Electronic submissions OK if compatible with TRS 80, Model II. Computer printout submissions acceptable. SASE. Reports in 3 months. Sample copy and writer's guidelines $2 prepaid.

 The double dagger before a listing indicates that the listing is new in this edition. New markets are often the most receptive to freelance contributions.

Nonfiction: General interest (banking-oriented); historical (on banking); how-to (anything in banking industry or trade); inspirational (occasionally, must deal with banking); interview; nostalgia; photo feature; profile; technical; and travel. Buys 12-25 unsolicited mss/year. Query. Length: 500-3,000 words. Pays $50-200. Pays expenses of writers on assignment, "if travel is assigned."

Photos: State availability of photos with query. Pays $10-100 for 5x7 b&w glossy prints; $20-200 for 35mm color transparencies. Captions and model release required. Buys all rights. Loans usage back to photographers on agreement.

Columns/Departments: Economy, interviews and technology in banking. Query. Length: 600-3,000 words. Pays $25 minimum.

BENEFITS CANADA, Pension Fund Investment and Employee Benefit Management, Maclean Hunter Ltd., 777 Bay St., Toronto, Ontario M5W 1A7 Canada. (416)596-5958. Editor: John Milne. Magazine published 10 times/year covering money management, investment management, pension fund administration and employee benefits industry for experts in the field. "However, there is a degree of overlap between the investment and benefits sides. Knowledge of each side should be assumed in the readership." Circ. 13,000. Pays on acceptance. Byline given. Buys first North American serial rights. Reports in 2 weeks on queries; 1 month on mss. Free sample copy.

Nonfiction: Interview/profile and opinion (of people in pension fund, investments or employee benefits); and technical (investment or employee benefit administration). Query with published clips or send complete ms. Length: 1,000-2,200 words. Pays $125-300.

CANADIAN BANKER, The Canadian Bankers' Association, Box 348, 2 First Canadian Place, Toronto, Ontario, M5X 1E1 Canada. Editor: Brian O'Brien. 90% freelance written. Emphasizes banking in Canada. Bimonthly magazine. Circ. 37,300. Buys first North American serial rights and second serial (reprint) rights. Publishes ms an average of 2 months after acceptance. Byline given. Electronic submissions OK on Micom, but requires hard copy. SAE and IRCs. Reports in 1 month.

Nonfiction: Informational articles on international banking and economics; interviews, nostalgic and opinion articles; and book reviews. Query. Length: 750-2,000 words. Pays $100-300. "Freelancer should be an authority on the subject. Most contributors are bankers, economists and university professors."

‡**FINANCIAL WORLD, The News Magazine for Investors**, Financial World Partners, 1450 Broadway, New York NY 10001. (212)869-1616. Editor: Kermit Lansner. Managing Editor: Roger B. Harris. Biweekly magazine on investing for professionals and high net worth individuals. "Our objective is to enlighten and instruct our readers about investment opportunities presented by today's multifaceted financial markets. We seek to cover every type of investment vehicle and related subjects of investor interest." Circ. 140,000. Pays on publication. Byline given. Offers variable kill fee. Submit seasonal/holiday material 1 month in advance. Simultaneous queries and photocopied submissions OK. Reports in 1 month. Free sample copy.

Nonfiction: Interview/profile and technical. Buys 12 mss/year. Query with published clips or send complete ms. Length: 1,200-2,000 words. Pays $25-750.

Tips: "We like clear, informed, well-reported financial stories. Send us an excellent piece in our field."

FUTURES MAGAZINE, (formerly *Commodities Magazine*), 219 Parkade, Cedar Falls IA 50613. (319)677-6341. Publisher: Merrill Oster. Editor-in-Chief: Darrell Jobman. For private, individual traders, brokers, exchange members, agribusinessmen, bankers, anyone with an interest in futures or options. 20% freelance written. Monthly magazine; 124-140 pages. Circ. 50,000. Buys all rights. Byline given. Pays on publication. Publishes ms an average of 6 months after acceptance. Photocopied submissions OK. Computer printout submissions acceptable. Reports in 1 month. Query or submit complete ms. SASE. Free sample copy.

Nonfiction: Articles analyzing specific commodity futures and options trading strategies; fundamental and technical analysis of individual commodities and markets; interviews, book reviews, "success" stories; and news items. Material on new legislation affecting commodities, trading, any new trading strategy ("results must be able to be substantiated"); and personalities. No "homespun" rules for trading and simplistic approaches to the commodities market. Treatment is always in-depth and broad. Informational, how-to, interview, profile, technical. "Articles should be written for a reader who has traded commodities for one year or more; should not talk down or hypothesize. Relatively complex material is acceptable." No get-rich-quick gimmicks, astrology articles or general, broad topics. Buys 30-40 mss/year. Length: No maximum or minimum; 1,500 words optimum. Pays $50-1,000, depending upon author's research and writing quality. "Rarely" pays the expenses of writers on assignment.

Tips: "Writers must have a solid understanding and appreciation for futures or options trading. We will have more financial and stock index features as well as new options contracts that will require special knowledge and experience. The writer has a better chance of breaking in at our publication with short articles and fillers since they can zero in on a specific idea without having to know the whole broad area we cover. Fluffy leads or trying to describe whole trading world instead of targeting key issues are frequent mistakes made by writers."

ILLINOIS BANKER, Illinois Bankers Association, Suite 1100, 205 W. Randolph, Chicago IL 60606. (312)984-1500. Director of Publications: Cindy L. Altman. Production Assistant: Anetta Gauthier. Editorial Assistant: Bobbie McDonald. 1% freelance written. Monthly magazine about banking for top decision makers and executives, bank officers, title and insurance company executives, elected officials and individual subscribers interested in banking products and services. Circ. 3,000. Pays on publication. Publishes ms an average of 3 months after acceptance. Byline given. Buys first rights. Phone queries OK. Submit material by the 1st of the month prior to publication. Simultaneous submissions OK. Computer printout submissions acceptable; no dot-matrix. Reports in 2 weeks. Free sample copy and writer's guidelines.

Nonfiction: Interview (ranking government and banking leaders); personal experience (along the lines of customer relations); and technical (specific areas of banking). "The purpose of the publication is to educate, inform and guide its readers in the activities and projects of their banks and those of their fellow bankers, while keeping them aware of any developments within the banking industry and other related fields. Any clear, fresh approach geared to a specific area of banking, such as agricultural bank management, credit, lending, marketing and trust is what we want." Buys 4-5 unsolicited mss/year. Send complete ms. Length: 825-3,000 words. Pays $50-100.

Fillers: Jokes, anecdotes and financial puzzles. Buys 8 mss/year. Pays $15-50.

Tips: "Cutbacks in purchasing have made us more selective."

INDEPENDENT BANKER, Independent Bankers Association of America, Box 267, Sauk Centre MN 56378. (612)352-6546. Editor: Norman Douglas. 15% freelance written. Monthly magazine for the administrators of small, independent banks. Circ. 10,000. Pays on acceptance. Publishes ms an average of 3 months after acceptance. Byline given. Not copyrighted. Buys all rights. Computer printout submissions acceptable. Reports in 1 week. Free sample copy and writer's guidelines.

Nonfiction: How-to (banking practices and procedures); interview/profile (popular small bankers); technical (bank accounting, automation); and banking trends. "Factual case histories, banker profiles or research pieces of value to bankers in the daily administration of their banks." No material that ridicules banking and finance or puff pieces on products and services. Buys 12 mss/year. Query. Length: 2,000-2,500 words. Pays $300 maximum.

Tips: "In this magazine, the emphasis is on material that will help small banks compete with large banks and large bank holding companies. We look for innovative articles on small bank operations and administration."

SAVINGS INSTITUTIONS, U.S. League of Savings Institutions, 111 E. Wacker Dr., Chicago IL 60601. (312)644-3100. Editor: Lee Crumbaugh. 5% freelance written. A monthly business magazine covering management of savings institutions. Circ. 30,000. Pays on acceptance. Publishes ms an average of 2 months after acceptance. Byline given. Buys negotiable rights. Simultaneous queries and photocopied submissions OK. Electronic submissions OK via IBM or compatible ASCII or Multimate file, but requires hard copy also. Computer printout submissions acceptable; prefers letter-quality to dot-matrix. SASE. Reports in 1 month. Free sample copy.

Nonfiction: How-to (manage or improve operations); new products (application stories at savings institutions); and technical (financial management). No opinion or 'puff' pieces. Buys 1-3 mss/year. Query with or without published clips. Length: 3,000-8,000 words. Pays $100/published page. Pays expenses of writers on assignment.

Columns/Departments: Beth Linnen, column/department editor. Operations, Marketing, Personnel, and Wholesale Funds. Buys 10 mss/year. Query with or without published clips. Length: 800-3,000 words. Pays $100/published page.

Tips: "Operations and Marketing departments are most open to freelancers."

Fishing

COMMERCIAL FISHERIES NEWS, Box 37, Stonington ME 04681. (207)367-2396. Managing Editor: Robin Alden Peters. 25% freelance written. Emphasizes commercial fisheries. Monthly newspaper with New England wide coverage; 52 pages. Circ. 8,500. Pays on publication. Publishes ms an average of 3 months after acceptance. Byline given. Buys first rights and one-time rights. Electronic submissions OK via 300 Baud/7 bit, ("we have an Apple III") but requires hard copy also. Computer printout submissions acceptable. SASE. Reports in 2 weeks. Sample copy $1.50.

Nonfiction: "Material strictly limited to coverage of commercial fishing, technical and general; occasional environment, business, etc. articles as they relate to commercial fishing in New England." Buys 5 unsolicited mss/year. Query. Pays $50-150.

Tips: "The writer may have a better chance of breaking in at our publication with short articles and fillers because this shows understanding of a specialized subject. The most frequent mistakes made by writers in completing an article for us are not realizing we are *New England* regional exclusively; not realizing we write for professional fishermen and thus writers must really understand fisheries' subjects to be acceptable."

NATIONAL FISHERMAN, Diversified Communications, 21 Elm St., Camden ME 04843. (207)236-4342. Editor-in-Chief: James W. Fullilove. Managing Editor: Linda S. Stanley. 25% freelance written. Monthly tabloid; 92 pages. For amateur and professional boat builders, commercial fishermen, armchair sailors, bureaucrats and politicians. Circ. 58,000. Pays in month of acceptance. Publishes ms an average of 2 months after acceptance. Byline given. Buys first serial rights only. Phone or letter queries advised. Photocopied submissions OK if good quality. Computer printout submissions acceptable if double spaced; no dot-matrix. SASE. Reports in 1 month. Free sample copy and writer's guidelines; mention *Writer's Market* in request.
Nonfiction: Expose, how-to, general interest, humor, historical, interview, new product, nostalgia, personal experience, opinion, photo feature, profile and technical, but all must be related to commercial fishing in some way. Especially needs articles on commercial fishing techniques (problems, solutions, large catches, busts); gear development; and marine historical and offbeat articles. No articles about sailboat racing, cruising and sportfishing. Buys approximately 35 unsolicited mss/year. Submit complete ms. Length: 100-2,000 words. Sometimes pays the expenses of writers on assignment.
Photos: State availability of photos with ms. "Photos improve chances of being used." Pays $5-15 for 5x7 or 8x10 b&w prints; color cover photo pays $250. Buys one-time rights.
Tips: "We are soliciting historical and human interest articles in addition to business-related articles. The writer may have a better chance of breaking in at our publication with short articles and fillers because our issues are smaller these days, and we can seldom afford to give pages over to lengthy features unless they are exceptionally good. The most frequent mistake made by writers in completing an article for us is failure to provide photos or other relevant illustrations. This is a common occurrence. In some cases, lack of art jeopardizes a story's chance of being published."

PACIFIC FISHING, Special Interest Publications, 1515 NW 51st St., Seattle WA 98107. (206)789-5333. Editors: Ken Talley, Kris Freeman. 30% freelance written. Monthly business magazine for commercial fishermen and others in the West Coast commercial fishing industry. *Pacific Fishing* views the fisherman as a small businessman and covers all aspects of the industry, including harvesting, processing and marketing. Circ. 10,000. Pays on publication. Publishes ms an average of 2 months after acceptance. Byline given. Offers 10-15% kill fee on assigned articles deemed unsuitable. Buys one-time rights. Queries highly recommended. Computer printout submissions acceptable. Reports in 1 month. Free sample copy and writer's guidelines for SAE and 1 first class stamp.
Nonfiction: Interview/profile and technical (usually with a business hook or slant). "Articles must be concerned specifically with *commercial* fishing. We view fishermen as small businessmen and professionals who are innovative and success-oriented. To appeal to this reader, *Pacific Fishing* offers four basic features: technical, how-to articles that give fisherman hands-on tips that will make their operation more efficient and profitable; practical, well-researched business articles discussing the dollars and cents of fishing, processing and marketing; profiles of a fisherman, processor or company with emphasis on practical business and technical areas; in-depth analysis of political, social, fisheries management and resource issues that have a direct bearing on West Coast commercial fishermen." Buys 20 mss/year. Query noting whether photos are available, and enclosing samples of previous work. Length: 1,500-3,000 words. Pays 7-10¢/word.
Photos: "We need good, high-quality photography, especially color, of West Coast commercial fishing. We prefer 35mm color slides. Our rates are $125 for cover; $25-75 for inside color; $15-35 for b&w and $10 for table of contents."
Tips: "Because of the specialized nature of our audience, the editor strongly recommends that freelance writers query the magazine in writing with a proposal. We enjoy finding a writer who understands our editorial needs and satisfies those needs, a writer willing to work with an editor to make the article just right. Most of our shorter items are staff written. Our freelance budget is such that we get the most benefit by using it for feature material. The most frequent mistakes made by writers are not keeping to specified length and failing to do a complete job on statistics that may be a part of the story."

✝ **The double dagger before a listing indicates that the listing is new in this edition. New markets are often the most receptive to freelance contributions.**

Florists, Nurseries, and Landscaping

"Computers will become more of a force in this industry, but so many retailers are still too small to get very involved in computerization," observed one magazine editor. In either case, the writer should explore such businesses with an insider's perspective when writing for these publications. Magazines geared to consumers interested in gardening are listed in the Consumer Home and Garden section.

DESIGN FOR PROFIT, Florafax International, Inc., 4175 S. Memorial Dr., Box 45745, Tulsa OK 74145. (918)622-8415. Editor: Sharon Smith. 30% freelance written. Quarterly magazine covering trends in the floral industry. "The publication is designed to be a creative sales tool for retail florists." Circ. 15,000. Publishes ms an average of 4 months after acceptance. No byline given. Buys all rights. Submit seasonal/holiday material 4 months in advance. Simultaneous queries, and simultaneous and photocopied submissions OK. Computer printout submissions acceptable; prefers letter-quality to dot-matrix. SASE. Reports in 2 weeks on queries; 3 months on mss. Writer's guidelines for two first class stamps.

Nonfiction: Historical/nostalgic (themes tying into floral arranging); how-to (floral designs—how to carry through themes, innovative ideas); interview/profile (prominent individuals in the profession); new product; personal experience (unique, unusual, outstanding in industry); and photo feature. Features or news/features only. Buys variable number of mss/year. Query with published clips. Length: 300-3,000 words. Pays $200 per article. Pays expenses of writers on assignment.

Photos: Send photos with query or ms. Pays negotiable rates for 4x5 transparencies and prints. Captions, model release and identification of subjects required. Buys all rights.

Tips: "Most articles in our publication are long, and in-depth. The most frequent mistake made by writers in completing articles is that the information is not specific enough about the current educational needs of florists."

FLORIST, Florists' Transworld Delivery Association, 29200 Northwestern Hwy., Box 2227, Southfield MI 48037. (313)355-9300. Editor-in-Chief: William P. Golden. Managing Editor: Susan L. Nicholas. 5% freelance written. For retail florists, floriculture growers, wholesalers, researchers and teachers. Monthly magazine; 128 pages. Circ. 25,000. Pays on acceptance. Buys one-time rights. Pays 10-25% kill fee. Byline given "unless the story needs a substantial rewrite." Phone queries OK. Submit seasonal/holiday material 4 months in advance. Simultaneous, photocopied and previously published submissions OK. Computer printout submissions acceptable. SASE. Reports in 1 month.

Nonfiction: How-to (more profitably run a retail flower shop, grow and maintain better quality flowers, etc.); general interest (to floriculture and retail floristry); and technical (on flower and plant growing, breeding, etc.). Buys 5 unsolicited mss/year. Query with clips of published work. Length: 1,200-3,000 words. Pays 20¢/word.

Photos: "We do not like to run stories without photos." State availability of photos with query. Pays $10-25 for 5x7 b&w photos or color transparencies. Buys one-time rights.

Tips: "Send samples of published work with query. Suggest several ideas in query letter."

FLOWER NEWS, 549 W. Randolph St., Chicago IL 60606. (312)236-8648. Managing Editor: Lauren Oates. For retail, wholesale florists, floral suppliers, supply jobbers and growers. Weekly newspaper; 32 pages. Circ. 14,500. Pays on acceptance. Byline given. Submit seasonal/holiday material at least 2 months in advance. Photocopied and previously published submissions OK. SASE. Reports "immediately." Free sample copy and writer's guidelines.

Nonfiction: How-to articles (increase business, set up a new shop, etc.; anything floral related without being an individual shop story); informational (general articles of interest to industry); and technical (grower stories related to industry, but not individual grower stories). No articles on "protecting your business from crime; how to get past due accounts to pay; attitudes for salespeople." Submit complete ms. Length: 3-5 typed pages. Pays $10-20.

Photos: "We do not buy individual pictures. They may be enclosed with manuscript at regular manuscript rate (b&w only)."

GARDEN SUPPLY RETAILER, Miller Publishing, Box 67, Minneapolis MN 55440. (612)374-5200. Editor: Kay Melchisedech Olson. 15% freelance written. Monthly magazine for lawn and garden retailers. Circ. 40,000 + . Pays on acceptance in most cases. Publishes ms an average of 4 months after acceptance. Buys first serial rights, and occasionally second serial (reprint) rights to material originally published elsewhere. Previously published submissions "in different fields" OK as long as not in overlapping fields such as hardware, nursery growers, etc. Computer printout submissions acceptable; prefers letter-quality to dot-matrix. SASE. Reports in 2 weeks on rejections, acceptance may take longer. Sample copy $2.

Nonfiction: "We aim to provide retailers with management, merchandising, tax planning and computer information. No technical advice on how to care for lawns, plants and lawn mowers. Articles should be of interest to *retailers* of garden supply products. Stories should tell retailers something about the industry that they don't already know; show them how to make more money by better merchandising or management techniques; address a concern or problem directly affecting retailers or the industry." Buys 10-15 mss/year. Send complete ms or rough draft plus clips of previously published work. Length: 800-1,000 words. Pays $150-200.

Photos: Send photos with ms. Reviews color negatives and transparencies, and 5x7 b&w prints. Captions and identification of subjects required.

Tips: Previously published submissions "in different fields" are considered only if references and examples apply specifically to the garden supply industry. "We will not consider manuscripts offered to 'overlapping' publications such as the hardware industry, nursery growers, etc. Query letters outlining an idea should include at least a partial rough draft; lists of titles are uninteresting. We seldom use filler material and would find it a nuisance to deal with freelancers for this. The most frequent mistake made by writers in completing an article for us is that the material is not suitable for our audience, being too basic or too general are the most common of mistakes."

‡**INTERIOR LANDSCAPE INDUSTRY, The Magazine for Designing Minds and Growing Businesses**, American Nurseryman Publishing Co., Suite 545, 111 N. Canal St., Chicago IL 60606. (312)782-5505. Editor: Brent C. Marchant. 10% freelance written. Monthly magazine on business and technical topics for all parties involved in interior plantings, including interior landscapers, growers and allied professionals (landscape architects, architects and interior designers). "We take a professional approach to the material and encourage our writers to emphasize the professionalism of the industry in their writings." Estab. 1984. Circ. 10,000. Pays on publication. Publishes ms an average of 5 months after acceptance. Byline given. Buys all rights. Submit material 2 months in advance. Electronic submissions OK on diskettes suitable for IBM PC. Computer printout submissions acceptable. SASE. Reports in 2 weeks on queries; 1 week on mss. Free sample copy.

Nonfiction: How-to (technical and business topics related to the audience); interview/profile (companies working in the industry); personal experience (preferably from those who work or have worked in the industry); photo feature (related to interior projects or plant producers); and technical. No shallow, consumerish-type features. Buys 30 mss/year. Query with published clips. Length: 3 ms pages to 15 ms pages; double spaced. Pays $2/published inch. Sometimes pays expenses of writers on assignment.

Photos: Send photos with query or ms. Reviews b&w contact sheet, negatives, and 5x7 prints; standard size or 4x5 color transparencies. Pays $5-10 for b&w; $15 for color. Identification of subjects required. Buys all rights.

Tips: "Demonstrate knowledge of the field—not just interest in it. Features, especially profiles, are most open to freelancers."

LAWN CARE INDUSTRY, Harcourt Brace Jovanovich, Inc., 7500 Old Oak Blvd., Cleveland OH 44130. (216)243-8100. Editor: Jerry Roche. 10% freelance written. For lawn care/landscape maintenance businessmen. Monthly tabloid; 40 pages. Circ. 12,000. Pays on acceptance. Publishes ms an average of 3 months after acceptance. Buys all rights. Phone queries OK. Submit seasonal/holiday material 3 months in advance. Simultaneous and photocopied submissions OK. Computer printout submissions acceptable. SASE. Reports in 2 weeks. Free sample copy.

Nonfiction: General interest (articles related to small business operation); how-to (run a lawn care business); interview (with lawn care operator or industry notable); new product (helping to better business practices); and profile (of lawn care businessmen). Buys 2 mss/issue. Query. Length: 500-1,000 words. Pays $50-250. Sometimes pays the expenses of writers on assignment.

Photos: State availability of photos with query. Pays $10-100 for 5x7 glossy b&w prints; $50-250 for 35mm color transparencies. Captions required. Buys one-time rights.

Food Products, Processing, and Service

In this section are journals for food wholesalers, processors, warehouses, caterers, institutional managers, and suppliers of grocery store equipment. Publications for grocery store operators are classified under Groceries. Journals for food vending machine operators can be found under Coin-Operated Machines.

FOOD PEOPLE, Olson Publications, Inc., Box 1208, Woodstock GA 30188. (404)928-8994. Editor: Mark W. Pryor. 80% freelance written. Monthly tabloid covering the retail food industry. "We write news and 'news features' about food stores, wholesalers and brokers in the Sunbelt and food manufacturers nationwide." Circ. 25,000. Pays on publication. Publishes ms an average 1 month after acceptance. Byline given. Buys all rights. Submit seasonal/holiday material 6 weeks in advance. Photocopied submissions OK. Computer printout submissions acceptable; prefers letter-quality to dot-matrix. SASE. Reports in 1 month. Sample copy $1.
Nonfiction: Interview/profile (of major food industry figures); photo feature (of food industry conventions, expos and meetings); and news of store/warehouse openings, ad campaigns, marketing strategies, important new products and services. "Articles should be informative, tone is upbeat. Do not send recipes or how-to shop articles; we cover food as a *business*." Buys 120-180 mss/year. Query or send complete ms. Length: 200-1,000 words. Pays $2/published inch. Sometimes pays the expenses of writers on assignment.
Photos: "Photos of people. Photos of displays, or store layouts, etc., that illustrate points made in article are good, too. But stay away from storefront shots." State availability of photos with query or send photos with ms. Pays $10 plus expenses for b&w contact sheets and 5x7 b&w prints; and $30 plus expenses for color transparencies. Captions required. Buys one-time rights.
Columns/Departments: Coast-to-Coast (1-2 paragraph newsbriefs from the Mid-Atlantic, South, West, and Pacific West). Send complete ms. Pays $10.
Tips: "Begin with an area news event—store openings, new promotions. Write that as news, then go further to examine the consequences. Talk with decision makers to get 'hows' and 'whys.' Because we are news-oriented, we have short deadlines for a monthly. We look for contributors who work well quickly and who *always* deliver."

‡FOOD SANITATION MAGAZINE, Serving the Food Processing, Meat Processing and Baking Industries, Post-Harvest Through Consumption, Harcourt Brace Jovanovich Publications, Inc., 7500 Old Oak Blvd., Cleveland OH 44130. (216)243-8100. Editor: Keven M. Cooney. 60% freelance written. Quarterly magazine on food sanitation personnel employed by food storage, transportation and processing companies. A 'how-to' magazine for busy pros dealing with building and equipment sanitation including cleaning, pest control, and microbial control. Estab. 1985. Circ. 7,500. Pays on publication. Publishes ms an average of 8 months after acceptance. Byline sometimes given. Not copyrighted. Buys all rights. Submit seasonal/holiday material 3 months in advance. Simultaneous submissions OK. Computer printout submissions acceptable; prefers letter-quality to dot-matrix. SASE. Reports in 1 month. Sample copy $3, SAE and 3 first class stamps.
Nonfiction: How-to (government compliance sanitation operations); interview/profile (working sanitation, government officials); and technical (equipment procedures as they are *implemented*). No first person pieces, layman stories, generic management pieces, retail pieces, "gee-whiz" profiles, product stories or company stories. No academia. Send complete ms. Length: 4-7 pages double spaced. Pays $50-300 with usable photos. Sometimes pays the expenses of writers on assignment.
Photos: Send photos with query or ms. Reviews 5x7 b&w and color prints. Payment included in ms. Captions, model release and identification of subjects required. Buys all rights.
Fillers: Clippings and anecdotes. Length: 20-100 words. Pays $5-15.
Tips: "Possess, or obtain, good basic background on industry—interview accomplished working sanitation industry figures with emphasis on practical experience, good photos, tight writing. No cutesy, no opinions—good solid omniscient writing. Remember—this is not a janitor's magazine. We're talking FDA/USDA cleanliness. Features—profiles of new facilities, accomplished sanitarians, new techniques, industry trend stories, compliance with federal regulations, pest and microbial stories are areas most open to freelancers."

‡N.A.T.L. NEWS, Official Publication of National Agricultural Transportation League, Suite A, 215 N. Second St., Leesburg FL 32748. (904)326-2188. Editor: Jim Tilly. Managing Editor: Dorothy Doxey. 0-5% freelance written. Bimonthly magazine for produce trucking industry including truckers, truck stops, and truck brokers. "We are exclusively concerned with motor transport of exempt produce (vegetables and fruits) and associated problems of the produce business." Circ. 2,800. Pays on acceptance. Publishes ms an average of 3 months after acceptance. Byline given. Not copyrighted. Buys first North American serial rights. Submit seasonal/holiday material 5 months in advance. Simultaneous queries and photocopied submissions OK. Computer printout submissions acceptable; prefers letter-quality to dot-matrix. SASE. Reports in 2 weeks on queries; 4 weeks on mss. Sample copy $1.50; writer's guidelines for SAE with 1 first class stamp.
Nonfiction: Personal experience (only in produce trucking or related field). "We are looking for short, fact-filled articles dealing with the trucking of produce, produce handling, exempt motor hauling of produce and related subjects and businesses—produce brokers, shippers, buyers and receivers of produce. Essentially any material should deal with the produce business and especially 'exempt hauling' and the problems of that busi-

ness." No articles about "romance of the road" or "trucker heroes" or very technical articles on truck maintenance; no fiction about business. Buys 4-6 mss/year. Query with published clips or send complete ms. Length: 400-1,500 words. Pays $10-50.
Photos: State availability of photos or send photos with query. Uses b&w photos including clear snapshots, related to article.
Columns/Departments: "We seek only factual material on produce trucking, produce handling, exempt motor hauling or produce and related subjects." Buys 3-4 mss/year. Query with published clips. Length: 400-1,200 words. Pays $10-50.
Tips: "Submit only if you are familiar with the produce business, especially the produce trucking business. The shipper or receiver of produce has a chance if the article is well written and knowledgeable about the produce business. We must have sufficient information to print an interesting article: names, dates, etc. We will accept articles about unethical business practices and change names and locations to avoid a libel suit."

QUICK FROZEN FOODS, Harcourt Brace Jovanovich Publications Inc., 7500 Old Oak Blvd., Cleveland OH 44130. (216)243-8100. Editor: John M. Saulnier. Senior Editor: C. Ross Chamberlain. 10% freelance written. For exexcutives of processing plants, distributors, warehouses, transport companies, retailers and food service operators involved in frozen foods. Monthly magazine; 100 pages. Circ. 25,000. Pays on acceptance. Buys all rights. Pays kill fee up to full amount if reasons for kill are not fault of author. Byline given unless it is work-for-hire or ghostwriting. Submit seasonal/holiday material 3 months in advance of issue date. SASE. Reports in 1 week. Free sample copy; mention *Writer's Market* in request.
Nonfiction: Interview, new product, photo feature, profile and technical. Buys 12 mss/year. Query or submit complete ms. Length: 1,500-3,000 words. Pays 5¢/word. "For special circumstances will offer flat rate for package which may be higher than word rate."
Photos: State availability of photos with query or ms. Pays $10 for 4x5 b&w smooth prints. Captions required. Buys all rights.

QUICK FROZEN FOODS INTERNATIONAL, E.W. Williams Publishing Co., 80 8th Ave., New York NY 10011. (212)989-1101. Editor: Sam Martin. 20% freelance written. Quarterly magazine covering frozen foods outside U.S.—"every phase of frozen food manufacture, retailing, food service, brokerage, transport, warehousing, merchandising, providing it is outside the U.S., though we will print stories about U.S. firms that sell abroad, but that must be emphasis." Circ. 10,000. Pays on publication. Publishes ms an average of 3 months after acceptance. Byline given. Offers kill fee: "if satisfactory, we will pay promised amount. If bungled, half." Buys all rights, but will relinquish any rights requested. Submit seasonal/holiday material 6 months in advance. Photocopied submissions OK ("if not under submission elsewhere"). Computer printout submissions acceptable; prefers letter-quality to dot-matrix. SASE. Sample copy for $1 and SAE.
Nonfiction: Book excerpts; general interest; historical/nostalgic; interview/profile; new product (from overseas); personal experience; photo feature; technical; and travel. No articles peripheral to frozen food industry such as taxes, insurance, government regulation, safety, etc. Buys 20-30 mss/year. Query or send complete ms. Length: 500-4,000 words. Pays 3¢/word or by arrangement. "We will reimburse postage on articles ordered from overseas." Sometimes pays the expenses of writers on assignment.
Photos: "We prefer photos with all articles." State availability of photos or send photos with accompanying ms. Pays $7 for 5x7 b&w prints (contact sheet if many shots). Captions and identification of subject required. Buys all rights. "Release on request."
Columns/Departments: News or analysis of frozen foods abroad. Buys 20 columns/year. Query. Length: 500-1,500 words. Pays by arrangement.
Fillers: Newsbreaks. Length: 100-500 words. Pays $5-20.
Tips: "We are primarily interested in feature materials, 1,000-3,000 words with pictures. Always query (though we will buy unsolicited manuscripts if they are suitable). A recent freelancer visited Poland before the crackdown and reported on the state of frozen foods in stores—turned out to be a scoop. Same reporter did the same on recent trip to Israel. Another did the same for China; all queried in advance. A frequent mistake is submitting general interest material instead of specific industry-related stories."

SNACK FOOD, HBJ Publications, Inc., 131 W. 1st St., Duluth MN 55802. (218)723-9343. Executive Editor: Jerry L. Hess. 15% freelance written. For manufacturers and distributors of snack foods. Monthly magazine; 60 pages. Circ. 10,000. Pays on acceptance. Publishes ms an average of 2 months after acceptance. Buys first serial rights. Occasional byline. Phone queries OK. Photocopied submissions OK. Computer printout submissions acceptable. Reports in 2 months. Free sample copy and writer's guidelines.

 **The double dagger before a listing indicates that the listing is new in this edition. New markets are often the most receptive to freelance contributions.**

Nonfiction: Informational, interview, new product, nostalgia, photo feature, profile and technical articles. "We use an occasional mini news feature or personality sketch." Length: 300-600 words for mini features; 750-1,200 words for longer features. Pays 12-15¢/word. Sometimes pays the expenses of writers on assignment.

Photos: Purchased with accompanying ms. Captions required. Pays $20 for 5x7 b&w photos. Total purchase price for a ms includes payment for photos when used. Buys all rights.

Tips: "Query should contain specific lead and display more than a casual knowledge of our audience. The most frequent mistakes made by writers are not writing to our particular audience, lack of a grasp of certain technical points on how the industry functions."

THE WISCONSIN RESTAURATEUR, Wisconsin Restaurant Association, 122 W. Washington, Madison WI 53703. (603)251-3663. Editor: Jan La Rue. Emphasizes restaurant industry for restaurateurs, hospitals, institutions, food service students, etc. Monthly magazine "except December/January combined." Circ. 3,600. Pays on acceptance. Buys all rights or one-time rights. Pays 10% kill fee. Byline given. Phone queries OK. Submit seasonal/holiday material 2-3 months in advance. Previously published work OK; "indicate where." SASE. Reports in 3 weeks. Free sample copy and writer's guidelines with large postpaid envelope.

Nonfiction: Interested in expose, general interest, historical, how-to, humor, inspirational, interview, nostalgia, opinion, profile, travel, new product, personal experience, photo feature and technical articles pertaining to restaurant industry. "No features on nonmember restaurants." Buys 1 ms/issue. Query with "copyright clearance information and a note about the writer in general." Length: 700-1,500 words. Pays $10-20.

Photos: Fiction and how-to article mss stand a better chance for publication if photos are submitted. State availability of photos. Pays $15 for b&w 8x10 glossy prints. Model releases required, captions are not.

Columns/Departments: Spotlight column provides restaurant member profiles. Buys 6/year. Query. Length: 500-1,500 words. Pays $5-10.

Fiction: Likes experimental, historical and humorous stories related to food service only. Buys 12 mss/year. Query. Length: 1,000-3,000 words. Pays $10-20.

Poetry: Uses all types of poetry, but must have food service as subject. Buys 6-12/year. No more than 5 submissions at one time. Length: 10-50 lines. Pays $5-10.

Fillers: Uses clippings, jokes, gags, anecdotes, newsbreaks and short humor. No puzzles or games. Buys 12/year. Length: 50-500 words. Pays $2.50-7.50.

Government and Public Service

Below are journals for people who provide governmental services, either in the employ of local, state, or national governments or of franchised utilities. Journals for city managers, politicians, civil servants, firefighters, police officers, public administrators, urban transit managers, and utilities managers are also listed in this section. Journals for professionals in world affairs can be found in the International Affairs section. Publications for lawyers are in the Law category. Journals for teachers and school administrators can be found in Education. Those for private citizens interested in politics, government, and public affairs are classified with the Politics and World Affairs magazines in the Consumer Publications section.

‡**COMMUNITY ANIMAL CONTROL**, K.B.R. Publications, Box 43488, Tucson AZ 85733. (602)881-1220. Editor: Katherine B. Morgan. 25% freelance written. Bimonthly magazine covering animal welfare/animal control for an "audience of professionals and governmental officials who deal with the public's pets, *not* the pet-owning public." Circ. 7,750. Pays on acceptance. Publishes ms an average of 3 months after acceptance. Byline given. Buys first North American serial rights, simultaneous rights, and second serial (reprint) rights. Submit seasonal/holiday material 4 months in advance. Simultaneous queries, and simultaneous, photocopied, and previously published submissions OK. SASE. Reports in 2 weeks. Free sample copy; writer's guidelines for SAE and 1 first class postage stamp.

Nonfiction: Book excerpts, expose, historical, how-to, interview/profile and technical. "No profiles of dear ladies running animal rescue societies." Buys 6-8 mss/year. Query with or without published clips. Length: 600-2,000 words. Pays $50.

Photos: State availability of photos. Reviews b&w contact sheets. Pays $5-10 for b&w prints. Model release required. Buys one-time rights.

Columns/Departments: Book Reviews. Buys 2 mss/year. Query. Length: 200-1,000 words. Pays $10-25.

Tips: "The most frequent mistake made by writers in completing an article for us is not understanding the terminology in our field. This is understandable and easily corrected in the editing."

‡**FIREHOUSE MAGAZINE**, Firehouse Communications, Inc., 33 Irving Pl., New York NY 10003. (212)935-4550. Editor: Dennis Smith. Executive Editor: John D. Peige. 60% freelance written. Monthly magazine covering fire service and emergency medical service. "*Firehouse* covers major fires nationwide, controversial issues and trends in the fire service, the latest firefighting equipment and methods of firefighting, historical fires, firefighting history and memorabilia." Fire-related books, firefighters with interesting avocations, fire safety education, hazardous materials incidents and the emergency medical services are also covered in the magazine. Circ. 115,000. Pays on pubication. Publishes ms an average of 3 months after acceptance. Byline given. Buys first North American serial rights. Submit seasonal/holiday material 4 months in advance. Simultaneous queries and previously published submissions OK. Computer printout submissions acceptable; prefers letter-quality to dot-matrix. SASE. Reports in 2 weeks. Sample copy for SAE with 7 first class stamps; free writer's guidelines.

Nonfiction: Book excerpts (of recent books on fire, EMS, and hazardous materials); historical/nostalgic (great fires in history, fire collectibles; the fire service of yesteryear); how-to (fight certain types of fires, buy and keep equipment, run a fire department); interview/profile (of noteworthy fire leader; centers, commissioners); new product (for firefighting, EMS); personal experience (description of dramatic rescue; helping one's own fire department); photo feature (on unusual apparatus, fire collectibles, a spectacular fire); technical (on almost any phase of firefighting; techniques, equipment, training, administration); and trends (controversies in the fire service). No profiles of people or departments that are not unusual or innovative, reports of nonmajor fires, articles not slanted toward firefighters' interests. Buys 100 mss/year. Query or send complete ms. Length: 500-3,000 words. Pays $50-400.

Photos: Jon Nelson, photo editor. Send photos with query or ms. Pays $15-45 for 8x10 b&w prints; $30-200 for color transparencies and 8x10 color prints. Captions required. Buys one-time rights.

Columns/Departments: Command Post (for fire service leaders); Training (effective methods); Book Reviews; Fire Safety (how departments teach fire safety to the public); Communicating (PR, dispatching); Arson (efforts to combat it); Doing Things (profile of a firefighter with an interesting avocation; group projects by firefighters); Family Things (activities involving firefighters' families). Query or send complete ms. Length: 750-1,000 words. Pays $100-300.

Fillers: Clippings, jokes, gags, anecdotes, short humor and newsbreaks. Buys 20 fillers/year. Length: 50-100 words. Pays $5-15.

Tips: "Read the magazine to get a full understanding of the subject matter, the writing style and the readers before sending a query or manuscript. Send photos with manuscript or indicate sources for photos. Be sure to focus articles on firefighters."

FOREIGN SERVICE JOURNAL, 2101 E St. NW, Washington DC 20037. (202)338-4045. Editor: Stephen R. Dujack. 80% freelance written. For Foreign Service personnel and others interested in foreign affairs and related subjects. Monthly (July/August combined). Pays on publication. Publishes ms an average of 6 months after acceptance. Byline given. Buys first North American serial rights. Computer printout submissions acceptable. SASE.

Nonfiction: Uses articles on "international relations, internal problems of the State Department and Foreign Service, diplomatic history and articles on Foreign Service experiences. Much of our material is contributed by those working in the fields we reach. Informed outside contributions are welcomed, however." Query. Buys 5-10 unsolicited mss/year. Length: 1,000-4,000 words. Pays 2-6¢/word.

Tips: The most frequent mistakes made by writers in completing an article for us are that the items are not suitable for the magazine, and they don't query.

FOUNDATION NEWS, The Magazine of Philanthropy, Council on Foundations, 1828 L St. NW, Washington DC 20036. (202)466-6512. Editor: Arlie Schardt. Managing Editor: Kathleen Hallahan. 40% freelance written. Bimonthly magazine covering the world of philanthropy, nonprofit organization and their relation to current events. Read by staff and executives of foundations, corporations, hospitals, colleges and universities and various nonprofit organizations. Circ. 15,000. Pays on acceptance. Publishes ms an average of 3 months after acceptance. Byline given. Offers negotiable kill fee. Not copyrighted. Buys all rights. Submit seasonal/holiday material 4 months in advance. Simultaneous queries and previously published submissions OK. Computer printout submissions acceptable; prefers letter-quality to dot-matrix. SASE. Reports in 1 month on queries; 1 month on mss.

Nonfiction: Book excerpts, expose, general interest, historical/nostalgic, how-to, humor, interview/profile and photo feature. Special issue on the role of religion in American life and how religious giving affects social welfare, culture, health conditions, etc. Buys 25 mss/year. Query. Length: 500-3,000 words. Pays $200-2,000. Sometimes pays the expenses of writers on assignment.
Photos: State availability of photos. Pays negotiable rates for b&w contact sheet and prints. Captions and identification of subjects required. Buys one-time rights; "some rare requests for second use."
Columns/Departments: Buys 12 mss/year. Query. Length: 900-1,400 words. Pays $100-500.
Tips: "Writers should be able to put current events into the perspective of how nonprofits affect them and are affected by them."

GRASSROOTS FUNDRAISING JOURNAL, Klein & Honig, Partnership, Box 14754, San Francisco CA 94114. (415)669-1118. Editors: Kim Klein and Lisa Honig. A bimonthly newsletter covering grassroots fund raising for small social change and social service nonprofit organizations. Circ. 3,000. Pays on publication. Byline given. Buys first serial rights. Submit seasonal/holiday material 2 months in advance. Simultaneous queries, and simultaneous, photocopied and (occasionally) previously published submissions OK. SASE. Reports in 2 weeks on queries; 2 months on mss. Sample copy $3.
Nonfiction: Book excerpts; how-to (all fund raising strategies); and personal experience (doing fund raising). Buys 10 mss/year. Query. Length: 2,000-20,000 words. Pays $35 minimum.

THE GRANTSMANSHIP CENTER NEWS, The Grantsmanship Center, 1031 S. Grand Ave., Los Angeles CA 90015. (213)749-4721. Editor: Norton J. Kiritz. 10% freelance written. Emphasizes fundraising, philanthropy, grants process and nonprofit management for professionals in government, foundations and nonprofit organizations. Bimonthly magazine; 88 pages. Circ. 14,000. Pays on publication. Publishes ms an average of 4 months after acceptance. Makes assignments on a work-for-hire basis. Pays variable kill fee. Byline given. Simultaneous, photocopied and previously published submissions OK. Computer printout submissions acceptable; prefers letter-quality to dot-matrix. SASE. Reports in 2 months. Sample copy $4.65.
Nonfiction: Expose, general interest, how-to and interview. "Familiarity with the field is an asset." Buys 1-2 mss/issue. Query with clips of published work. Length: 1,500-10,000 words. Pays $50-350.
Photos: State availability of photos. Uses b&w contact sheets and color transparencies. Offers no additional payment for photos accepted with ms. Captions preferred; model release required. Buys all rights.
Tips: "The most frequent mistake made by writers in completing an article for us is ignoring the special concerns of our readerships."

LAW AND ORDER, Hendon Co., 1000 Skokie Blvd., Wilmette IL 60091. (312)256-8555. Editor: Bruce W. Cameron. 90% freelance written. Monthly magazine covering the administration and operation of law enforcement agencies, directed to police chiefs and supervisors. Circ. 26,000. Pays on publication. Publishes ms an average of 6 months after acceptance. Byline given. Buys first North American serial rights. Submit seasonal/holiday material 3 months in advance. Photocopied submissions OK. No simultaneous queries. Computer printout submissions acceptable; prefers letter-quality to dot-matrix. Reports in 1 month. Sample copy for 9x12 SAE.
Nonfiction: General police interest; how-to (do specific police assignments); new product (how applied in police operation); and technical (specific police operation). Special issues include Buyers Guide (January); Communications (February); Training (March); International (April); Administration (May); Small Departments (June); Police Science (July); Equipment (August); Weapons (September); Mobile Patrol (November); and Working with Youth (December). No articles dealing with courts (legal field) or convicted prisoners. No nostalgic, financial, travel or recreational material. Buys 20-30 mss/year. Length: 2,000-3,000 words. Pays $100-300.

 One freelancer was very persistent, and thus we finally gave her a story. We used the story, but we won't use her again. We got several calls from manufacturers she had contacted saying she had "threatened" them into talking—which is a definite no-no.

—Michael Karol
Modern Floor Coverings

Photos: Send photos with ms. Reviews transparencies and prints. Identification of subjects required. Buys all rights.

Tips: "*L&O* is a respected magazine that provides up-to-date information that chiefs can use. Writers must know their subject as it applies to this field. Case histories are well received. We are upgrading quality for editorial—stories *must* show some understanding of the law enforcement field. A frequent mistake is not getting photographs to accompany article."

MARINE CORPS GAZETTE, Professional Magazine for United States Marines, Marine Corps Association, Box 1775, Quantico VA 22134. (703)640-6161. Editor: Col. John E. Greenwood, USM (Ret.). Managing Editor: Joseph D. Dodd. Monthly magazine. "*Gazette* serves as a forum in which serving Marine officers exchange ideas and viewpoints on professional military matters." Circ. 33,000. Pays on publication. Byline given. Buys first North American serial rights; change to all rights under consideration. Computer printout submissions acceptable. Reports in 3 weeks on queries; 2 months on mss. Sample copy $1; free writer's guidelines.

Nonfiction: Historical/nostalgic (Marine Corps operations only); and technical (Marine Corps related equipment). "The magazine is a professional journal oriented toward hard skills, factual treatment, technical detail—no market for lightweight puff pieces—analysis of doctrine, lessons learned goes well. A very strong Marine Corps background and influence are normally prerequisites for publication." Buys 4-5 mss/year from non-Marine Corps sources. Query or send complete ms. Length: 2,500-5,000 words. Pays $200-400; short features, $50-100.

Photos: "We welcome photos and charts." Payment for illustrative material included in payment forms. "Photos need not be original, nor have been taken by the author, but they must support the article."

Columns/Departments: Book Reviews (of interest and importance to Marines); and Ideas and Issues (an assortment of topical articles, e.g., opinion or argument, ideas of better ways to accomplish task, reports on weapons and equipment, strategies and tactics, etc., also short vignettes on history of Corps). Buys 60 book review and 120 Ideas & Issues mss/year, most from Marines. Query. Length: 500-1,500 words. Pays $25-50 plus book for 750-word book review; $50-100 for Ideas and Issues.

Tips: "Book reviews or short articles (500-1,500 words) on Marine Corps related hardware or technological development are the best way to break in. Sections/departments most open to freelancers are Book Reviews and Ideas & Issues sections—query first. We are not much of a market for those outside U.S. Marine Corps or who are not closely associated with current Marine activities."

PLANNING, American Planning Association, 1313 E. 60th St., Chicago IL 60637. (312)955-9100. Editor: Sylvia Lewis. 25% freelance written. Emphasizes urban planning for adult, college-educated readers who are regional and urban planners in city, state or federal agencies or in private business or university faculty or students. Monthly. Circ. 25,000. Pays on publication. Publishes ms an average of 3 months after acceptance. Buys all rights or first rights. Byline given. Photocopied and previously published submissions OK. Computer printout submissions acceptable; prefers letter-quality to dot-matrix. SASE. Reports in 2 months. Free sample copy and writer's guidelines.

Nonfiction: Expose (on government or business, but on topics related to planning, housing, land use, zoning); general interest (trend stories on cities, land use, government); historical (historic preservation); how-to (successful government or citizen efforts in planning; innovations; concepts that have been applied); and technical (detailed articles on the nitty-gritty of planning, zoning, transportation but no footnotes or mathematical models). Also needs news stories up to 500 words. "It's best to query with a fairly detailed, one-page letter. We'll consider any article that's well written and relevant to our audience. Articles have a better chance if they are timely and related to planning and land use and if they appeal to a national audience. All articles should be written in magazine feature style." Buys 2 features and 1 news story/issue. Length: 500-2,000 words. Pays $50-400. "We pay freelance writers and photographers only, not planners."

Photos: "We prefer that authors supply their own photos, but we sometimes take our own or arrange for them in other ways." State availability of photos. Pays $25 minimum for 8x10 matte or glossy prints and $200 for 4-color cover photos. Captions preferred. Buys one-time rights.

POLICENET MAGAZINE (the Police Network), Personal Computing For Law Enforcement, Educational Learning Systems, Box 225, Tulsa OK 74101. (918)583-0030. Editor-in-Chief: Robert Taylor, Ph.D..Associate Editors: Larry K. Gaines, Ph.D. and James Fagin, Ph.D. Managing Editor: Gerald Griffin. 90% freelance written. A monthly magazine covering use of personal computers by law enforcement depart-

---

Market conditions are constantly changing! If this is 1987 or later, buy the newest edition of *Writer's Market* at your favorite bookstore or order directly from Writer's Digest Books.

ments, officers and their families. Circ. 25,000. Pays on publication. Publishes ms an average of 4 months after acceptance. Byline given. Buys first North American serial rights. Submit seasonal/holiday material 3 months in advance. Simultaneous queries, and simultaneous, photocopied and previously published submissions OK. Electronic submissions OK on 5¼" IBM. Computer printout submissions acceptable. SASE. Reports in 5 weeks. Free sample copy; writer's guidelines for SAE and $1.15 postage stamps.

Nonfiction: Book excerpts (computer); general interest (home use of computers); historical/nostalgic (police history); how-to (write software programs); humor (police stories); interview/profile (with police officers and police department using computers); new product (hardware and software); personal experience (police officer computer usage); photo feature (computer); technical (computer); and travel (vacation). Buys 100 mss/year. Send complete ms. Length: 100-2,000 words. Pays 10-25¢/word. Sometimes pays expenses of writers on assignment.

Photos: Send photos with query or ms. Reviews b&w contact sheets. Pays $5 for 8x10 b&w prints; $15-25 for 8x10 color prints; $5-20 for 8x10 b&w cover shot; $10-100 for 8x10 color cover. Captions required. Buys all rights.

Columns/Departments: Computer News, and Computer Technical. Buys 10 mss/year. Send complete ms. Length: 100-500 words. Pays negotiable rate.

Fillers: Clippings, jokes, gags, anecdotes, short humor and newsbreaks (police or criminal justice related).

POLICE TIMES/COMMAND MAGAZINE, 1100 NE 125th St., North Miami FL 33161. (305)891-1700. Editor: Gerald Arenberg. 95% freelance written. For "law enforcement officers: federal, state, county, local and private security." Magazine published six times/year. Circ. 45,000. Buys all rights. Buys 50-100 mss/year. Pays on acceptance. Publishes ms an average of 4 months after acceptance. Computer printout submissions acceptable. SASE. Reports "at once." Sample copy for $1 postage.

Nonfiction: Interested in articles about local police departments all over the nation. In particular, short articles about what the police department is doing, any unusual arrests made, acts of valor of officers in the performance of duties, etc. Also articles on any police subject from prisons to reserve police. "We prefer newspaper style. Short and to the point. No fiction. Photos and drawings are a big help." Length: 300-1,200 words. Pays $5-15—up to $25 in some cases based on 1¢/word.

Photos: Uses b&w Polaroid and 8x10 b&w glossy prints, "if of particular value." Pays $5-15 for each photo used.

Tips: "We use a newspaper format, long articles are not encouraged. Frequent mistakes made by writers in completing articles for us are that many send opinions or editorial-like articles. Some copy line by line material from local newspapers."

STATE LEGISLATURES, National Conference of State Legislatures, Suite 1500, 1125 17th St., Denver CO 80202. (303)292-6600. Managing Editor: Deborah Brewer. Emphasizes current issues facing state legislatures for legislators, legislative staff members and close observers of state politics and government. Magazine published 10 times/year; 32 pages. Pays on acceptance. Buys all rights. Byline given. SASE. Reports in 1 month. Free sample copy.

Nonfiction: "We're interested in original reporting on the responses of states (particularly state legislatures) to current problems, e.g., tax reform, health care, energy and consumer protection. We seldom publish articles that deal exclusively with one state; our usual approach is to survey and compare the actions of states across the country." Query preferred, but will consider complete ms. Pays $300-500, depending on length.

SUPERINTENDENT'S PROFILE & POCKET EQUIPMENT DIRECTORY, Profile Publications, 220 Central Ave., Box 43, Dunkirk NY 14048. (716)366-4774. Editor: Robert Dyment. 60% freelance written. Monthly magazine covering "outstanding" town, village, county and city highway superintendents and Department of Public Works Directors throughout New York state only. Circ. 2,500. Publishes ms an average of 4 months after acceptance. Pays within 90 days. Byline given for excellent material. Buys first serial rights. Submit seasonal/holiday material 3 months in advance. Simultaneous queries OK. Computer printout submissions acceptable; no dot-matrix. SASE. Reports in 2 weeks on queries; 1 month on mss. Sample copy for 9x12 SAE and 3 first class stamps.

Nonfiction: John Powers, articles editor. Interview/profile (of a highway superintendent or DPW director in NY state who has improved department operations through unique methods or equipment); and technical. Special issues include winter maintenance profiles. No fiction. Buys 20 mss/year. Query. Length: 1,500-2,000 words. Pays $100 for a full-length ms. "Pays more for excellent material. All manuscripts will be edited to fit our format and space limitations." Sometimes pays the expenses of writers on assignment.

Photos: John Powers, photo editor. State availability of photos. Pays $5-10 for b&w contact sheets; reviews 5x7 prints. Captions and identification of subjects required. Buys one-time rights.

Poetry: Buys poetry if it pertains to highway departments. Pays $5-15.

Tips: "We are a widely read and highly respected state-wide magazine, and although we can't pay high rates, we expect quality work. Too many freelance writers are going for the expose rather than the meat and potato type articles that will help readers. We will have a need for more manuscripts and photos because of two new publications being launched. We use more major features than fillers. Frequently writers don't read sample copies first."

TRANSACTION/SOCIETY, Rutgers University, New Brunswick NJ 08903. (201)932-2280, ext. 83. Editor: Irving Louis Horowitz. 10% freelance written. For social scientists (policymakers with training in sociology, political issues and economics). Published every 2 months. Circ. 45,000. Buys all rights. Byline given. Pays on publication. Publishes ms an average of 6 months after acceptance. Will consider photocopied submissions. No simultaneous submissions. Electronic submissions OK; "manual provided to authors." Computer printout submissions acceptable; prefers letter-quality to dot-matrix. Reports in 1 month. Query. SASE. Free sample copy and writer's guidelines.

Nonfiction: Michele Teitelbaum, articles editor. "Articles of wide interest in areas of specific interest to the social science community. Must have an awareness of problems and issues in education, population and urbanization that are not widely reported. Articles on overpopulation, terrorism, international organizations. No general think pieces." Payment for articles is made only if done on assignment. *No payment for unsolicited articles.*

Photos: Joan DuFault, photo editor. Pays $200 for photographic essays done on assignment or accepted for publication.

Tips: "Submit an article on a thoroughly unique subject, written with good literary quality. Present new ideas and research findings in a readable and useful manner. A frequent mistake is writing to satisfy a journal, rather than the intrinsic requirements of the story itself."

VICTIMOLOGY: An International Journal, Box 39045, Washington DC 20016. (703)528-8872. Editor-in-Chief: Emilio C. Viano. "We are the only magazine specifically focusing on the victim, on the dynamics of victimization; for social scientists, criminal justice professionals and practitioners, social workers and volunteer and professional groups engaged in prevention of victimization and in offering assistance to victims of rape, spouse abuse, child abuse, incest, abuse of the elderly, natural disasters, etc." Quarterly magazine. Circ. 2,500. Pays on publication. Buys all rights. Byline given. SASE. Reports in 2 months. Sample copy $5; free writer's guidelines.

Nonfiction: Expose, historical, how-to, informational, interview, personal experience, profile, research and technical. Buys 10 mss/issue. Query. Length: 500-5,000 words. Pays $50-150.

Photos: Purchased with accompanying ms. Captions required. Send contact sheet. Pays $15-50 for 5x7 or 8x10 b&w glossy prints.

Poetry: Avant-garde, free verse, light verse and traditional. Length: 30 lines maximum. Pays $10-25.

Tips: "Focus on what is being researched and discovered on the victim, the victim/offender relationship, treatment of the offender, the bystander/witness, preventive measures, and what is being done in the areas of service to the victims of rape, spouse abuse, neglect and occupational and environmental hazards and the elderly."

YOUR VIRGINIA STATE TROOPER MAGAZINE, Box 2189, Springfield VA 22152. (703)451-2524. Editor: Kerian Bunch. 90% freelance written. Biannual magazine covering police topics for troopers, police, libraries, legislators and businesses. Circ. 10,000. Pays on acceptance. Publishes ms an average of 3 months after acceptance. Byline given. Buys first North American serial rights and all rights on assignments. Submit seasonal/holiday material 2 months in advance. Simultaneous and photocopied submissions OK. Computer printout submissions acceptable; prefers letter-quality to dot-matrix. Reports in 1 month. Writer's guidelines for SAE and 1 first class stamp.

Nonfiction: Book excerpts; expose (consumer or police-related); general interest; nutrition/health; historical/nostalgic; how-to (energy saving); humor; interview/profile (notable police figures); opinion; personal experience; technical (radar); and other (recreation). Buys 40-45 mss/year. Query with clips of published work or send complete ms. Length: 2,500 words. Pays $250 maximum/article (10¢/word). Sometimes pays the expenses of writers on assignment.

Photos: Send photos with ms. Pays $25 maximum/5x7 b&w glossy print. Captions and model release required. Buys one-time rights.

Fiction: Adventure, humorous, mystery, novel excerpts and suspense. Buys 4 mss/year. Send complete ms. Length: 2,500 words minimum. Pays $250 maximum (10¢/word) on acceptance.

Tips: "The writer may have a better chance of breaking in at our publication with short articles and fillers due to space limitations."

Market conditions are constantly changing! If this is 1987 or later, buy the newest edition of *Writer's Market* at your favorite bookstore or order directly from Writer's Digest Books.

Groceries

Owners and operators of retail food stores read these publications. Journals for food wholesalers, packers, warehousers and caterers are classified with the Food Products, Processing, and Service journals. Publications for food vending machine operators can be found in the Coin-Operated Machines category.

CANADIAN GROCER, Maclean-Hunter Ltd., Maclean Hunter Building, 777 Bay St., Toronto, Ontario M5W 1A7 Canada. (416)596-5772. Editor: George H. Condon. 8% freelance written. Monthly magazine about supermarketing and food retailing for Canadian chain and independent food store managers, owners, buyers, executives, food brokers, food processors and manufacturers. Circ 16,000. Pays on publication. Publishes ms an average of 2 months after acceptance. Byline given. Buys first Canadian rights. Phone queries OK. Submit seasonal material 2 months in advance. Previously published submissions OK. Computer printout submissions acceptable; prefers letter-quality to dot-matrix. SAE and IRCs. Reports in 1 month. Sample copy $4.
Nonfiction: Interview (national trendsetters in marketing, finance or food distribution); technical (store operations, equipment and finance); and news features on supermarkets. "Freelancers should be well versed on the supermarket industry. We don't want unsolicited material. Writers with business and/or finance expertise are preferred. Know the retail food industry and be able to write concisely and accurately on subjects relevant to our readers: food store managers, senior corporate executives, etc. A good example of an article would be 'How a Six Store Chain of Supermarkets Improved Profits 2% and Kept Customers Coming.' " Buys 14 mss/year. Query with clips of previously published work. Pays $50-300.
Photos: State availability of photos. Pays $ 10-25 for 8x10 b&w glossy prints. Captions preferred. Buys one-time rights.

ENTRÉE, Fairchild, 7 E. 12th St., New York NY 10003. (212)741-4009. Editor: Tim Davis. Managing Editor: Susan Spedalle. 30% freelance written. Monthly magazine covering "trends in cooking, housewares and food industry news, new products in the gourmet and lifestyle areas for specialty retailers and department store buyers of gourmet housewares and food, and executives and managers in the gourmet product industry." Circ. 15,000. Average issue includes 5-11 features, 5 columns, a calendar, news and 50% advertising. Pays on publication. Publishes ms an average of 2½ months after acceptance. Byline given. Kill fee varies. Buys all rights. Phone queries OK. Computer printout submissions acceptable; no dot-matrix. SASE. Reports in 6 weeks on queries; in 1 week on mss. Sample copy $2.
Nonfiction: Profile (of major retailers); new product ("hot product categories"); photo feature; and technical (cookware and specialty food in terms retailers can apply to their businesses). No first person, humor, cartoons and unsolicited stories on obscure retailers or general pieces of any kind such as accounting or computer stories. Buys 2-3 mss/issue. Query. Length: 1,500-3,000 words. Pays $250-400. Sometimes pays the expenses of writers of on assignment.
Photos: Julia Gorton, art director. Always looking for illustrations and photographs.
Tips: "We've expanded into specialty foods, in addition to gourmet housewares. We're much more interested in experienced *trade* writers rather than experienced consumer magazine writers. We've rejected stories from successful consumer writers because they simply don't meet the requirements of a *business* magazine. *Entrée* is actively searching for qualified, experienced trade writers. We use two to three freelancers every issue and now wish to establish a core of regular writers we can rely on. Our problem is that, while writers are in abundance, experienced *trade* writers are not. We need a writer who can thoroughly analyze a market, whether it be cutlery, cheese, pate or ice cream machines. We need someone who can do in-depth retail profiles with major retailers. Most important, we're not particularly interested in hearing queries. Frequently writers do not have enough business information or understanding. We'd rather interview qualified writers who can accept *our* assignments month after month. A typical feature pays $400."

FLORIDA FOOD DEALER, Retail Grocers Association of Florida, 2810 NE 14th St., Ocala FL 32670. (904)351-2300. Editor: Andy Williams. Assistant Editor: Tyler Ward. 1% freelance written. Monthly magazine covering the Florida retail supermarket and convenience store industry. Circ. 4,000. Publishes ms an average of 3 months after acceptance. Byline given. Offers negotiable kill fee. Buys first North American serial rights. Submit seasonal/holiday material 2 months in advance. Simultaneous queries and photocopied and previously published submissions OK. Computer printout submissions acceptable; prefers letter-quality to dot-matrix. SASE. Reports in 1 week on queries, 2 weeks on mss. Sample copy $1.75.
Nonfiction: Historical/nostalgic; how-to; inspirational; interview/profile; new product; personal experience; technical—Florida angle. "Conservative business-oriented." Special issues include frozen food (March); legislative (April); new equipment (July); beef (May); dairy (June); RGAF convention (October). No coupon han-

dling, consumer tips, recipes. Buys 12 mss/year. Query. Length: 500-1,500 words. Pays $50-150.

Tips: "Know supermarket and convenience store industry from owner's standpoint. The writer has a better chance of breaking in at our publication with short articles and fillers due to space restrictions. The most frequent mistake made by writers is not taking photos themselves, when they have agreed to do so."

GROCER'S SPOTLIGHT, Shamie Publishing Co., 25689 Kelly Rd., Roseville MI 48066. (313)779-4940. News Editor: Ryan Mathews. 10% freelance written. Monthly tabloid about the supermarket industry for operators, chain and independent wholesalers, food brokers and manufacturers. Circ. 75,000. Pays on publication. Byline given. Buys all rights. Phone queries OK. Submit seasonal material 2 months in advance. Simultaneous and photocopied submissions OK. Computer printout submissions acceptable; prefers letter-quality to dot-matrix. SASE. Reports in 3 weeks. Free sample copy and writer's guidelines.
Nonfiction: Interview. Query. Pays $3/column inch; front page, $5/column inch. Sometimes pays expenses of writers on assignment.
Photos: State availability of photos with query. Uses b&w and color.
Columns/Departments: Query. Pays $1/column inch.
Tips: Orienting stories to a consumer rather than business point of view is one of the most frequent mistakes made by writers in completing an article assignment for *Grocer's Spotlight*.

HEALTH FOODS BUSINESS, Howmark Publishing Corp., 567 Morris Ave., Elizabeth NJ 07208. (201)353-7373. Editor-in-Chief: Alan Richman. 20% freelance written. For owners and managers of health food stores. Monthly magazine; 100 pages. Circ. over 8,000. Pays on publication. Byline given "if story quality warrants it." Phone queries OK. "Query us about a good health foods store in your area. We use many store profile stories." Simultaneous and photocopied submissions OK if exclusive to their field. Previously published work OK, but please indicate where and when material appeared previously. Computer printout submissions acceptable if double-spaced and in upper and lower case; prefers letter-quality to dot-matrix. SASE. Reports in 1 month. Sample copy $3; plus $2 for postage and handling.
Nonfiction: Expose (government hassling with health food industry); how-to (unique or successful retail operators); informational (how or why a product works; technical aspects must be clear to laymen); historical (natural food use); interviews (must be prominent person in industry or closely related to the health food industry); and photo features (any unusual subject related to the retailer's interests). Buys 1-2 mss/issue. Query for interviews and photo features. Will consider complete ms in other categories. Length: long enough to tell the whole story without padding. Pays $50 and up for feature stories, $75 and up for store profiles.
Photos: "Most articles must have photos included"; negatives and contact sheet OK. Captions required. No additional payment.

IGA GROCERGRAM, Fisher-Harrison Publications, 338 N. Elm St., Greensboro NC 27401. (919)378-6065. Managing Editor: Leslie P. Daisy. Monthly magazine for independent grocery retailers and wholesalers affiliated with IGA, Inc. Circ. 13,000. Pays on acceptance. Byline given. Buys first rights only. Submit seasonal/holiday material 3 months in advance. SASE. Reports in 6 weeks on queries. Sample copies $2 and SASE. Free writer's guidelines for SASE.
Nonfiction: IGA store profiles; merchandising and marketing ideas. "All articles must concentrate on the independent grocery business." Buys 2-3 mss/year. Query with clips of published work. No telephone queries. Pays $50-200.
Photos: Send photos with ms. Reviews b&w contact sheets and color transparencies. Buys one-time rights.

PENNSYLVANIA GROCER, 1355 Old York Rd., Abington PA 19001. (215)228-0808. Editor: John McNelis. 15% freelance written. For grocers, their families and employees, and store managers; food people in general. Monthly magazine; 16 pages. Circ. 3,000. Byline given. Pays on publication. Publishes ms an average of 3 months after acceptance. Buys first serial rights and second serial (reprint) rights to the same material. Computer printout submissions acceptable; no dot-matrix. SASE. Reports in 1 month. Sample copy $1.
Nonfiction: Articles on food subjects in retail food outlets; mainly local, in Pennsylvania and surrounding areas. Informational, interviews, profiles, historical, successful business operations, new product, merchandising techniques and technical articles. Buys 12-15 unsolicited mss/year. Query or submit complete ms. Length: 500-900 words. Pays $25.
Photos: Pays $25 for 2 b&w photos purchased with ms.
Tips "We need graphics and will use more color."

‡**PROGRESSIVE GROCER**, Progressive Grocer Co., 1351 Washington Blvd., Stamford CT 06902. (203)325-3500. Editor: Ed Walzer. Editorial Director: Larry Schaeffer. 3% freelance written. Monthly magazine covering the retail food industry. "We provide analyses of trends, merchandising ideas and innovations, statistical data, company profiles—all retailer oriented. Audience runs gamut from top executive to department managers." Circ. 87,000. Pays on publication. Publishes ms an average of 3 months after acceptance. Byline given. Buys all rights. Computer printout submissions acceptable; no dot-matrix. Submit seasonal/holi-

day material 3 months in advance. Simultaneous queries and photocopied submissions OK. SASE. Reports in 1 month. Free sample copy.

Nonfiction: General interest, how-to (set up or operate a particular department in supermarket); interview/profile (executive level); and photo feature (interesting store format). No puff pieces or anything in excess of 8 typewritten, double-spaced pages. Buys 3 mss/year. Send complete ms. Length: 500-1,500 words. Pays $200 maximum per magazine page. Sometimes pays the expenses of writers on assignment.

Photos: State availability of photos with ms. Pays $100 maximum for b&w contact sheets; $300 maximum for color contact sheets. Captions, model releases and identification of subjects required.

WHOLE FOODS, The Largest Circulation in the Natural Foods Industry, Whole Foods Communications, Inc., 195 Main St., Metuchen NJ 08840. Publisher: Howard Wainer. 10% freelance written. Monthly magazine edited for health food retailers, wholesalers and manufacturers serving the industry. Byline given on articles and columns; photocredits also. Pays on publication. Publishes ms an average of 4 months after acceptance. Buys first North American serial rights. Submit seasonal material 3 months in advance. Photocopied submissions OK. Computer printout submissions acceptable; no dot-matrix. SASE. Reports in 1 month. Length: 500-2,000 words. Writer's guidelines and sample copy available with 9x12 SASE. "Good freelancers wanted."

Nonfiction: Editorial content targets product knowledge and aids retailers in making responsible and profitable inventory selection through nutritional education, market awareness and merchandising expertise. Feature articles explain products, including manufacturing procedures, proper storage and preparation, as well as nutritional benefits. Industry members speak out about the industry issues in the Debate department. Calendar, book reviews, industry news and product showcase are written in-house. No consumer-oriented pieces other than one-subject consumer tearouts (i.e., "Everything You Need To Know About Tofu . . . or Sprouts . . ."). Not interested in undocumented, unreferenced, experiential pieces unless company or store profile of success (or specifics about failure). Wants "higher quality, compact, documentable work." Testimonials/healing stories *not* wanted."

Photos: Photos desirable with ms. Provide captions and model release if appropriate.

Tips: "We are in the market for qualified freelancers who submit on-target pieces which do not require considerable editing, retyping, etc. Writer should read three issues of the magazine and have observed the operation of a health food store prior to beginning any work. Industry exclusive a must for all submissions. We will provide list of competitors' magazines."

Grooming Products and Services

AMERICAN SALON EIGHTY-SIX, Suite 1000, 100 Park Ave., New York NY 10017. (212)532-5588. Editor: Louise Cotter. Monthly for beauty salon owners and operators. Pays on publication. Buys all rights. Computer printout submissions acceptable; prefers letter-quality to dot-matrix. SASE.

Nonfiction: Profiles, how-to and management. Technical material is mainly staff written. "We are not interested unless material is directly related to the needs of beauty salon professionals."

‡**MODERN SALON**, Vance Publishing, 400 Knightsbridge Pkwy., Lincolnshire IL 60069. (312)634-2600. Editor: Mary Atherton. Managing Editor: Arlene Tolin. 10% freelance written. Monthly magazine covering hairdressing. "Articles slanted toward small business owners, especially owners of beauty salons, are most appropriate." Circ. 100,000. Pays 6 weeks after acceptance or upon publication, whichever comes first. Publishes ms an average of 2 months after acceptance. Buys first North American serial rights. Submit seasonal/holiday material 4 months in advance. Simultaneous queries and photocopied submissions OK. Computer printout submissions acceptable; prefers letter-quality to dot-matrix. SASE. Reports in 3 weeks on queries; 2 months on mss. Sample copy $3.

Nonfiction: How-to (increase business); interview/profile (with a successful salon owner); and business advice and tax tips. No photo tearsheet, opinion pieces, or anything *not* based on research. Buys 20 mss/year. Query with published clips. Length: 1,500-3,500 words. Pays $150-250.

Photos: State availability of photos with query. Pays $5-30 for b&w prints. Captions, model releases and identification of subjects required. Buys all rights.

Tips: "The most frequent mistakes made by writers in completing an article assignment for us are inadequate research and insufficient tailoring to salon industry." Major features are staff-written.

‡**SALON TALK**, Service Publications, Inc., Suite 1000, 100 Park Ave., New York NY 10017. (212)532-5588. Editor: Jody Bryne. 10% freelance written. Bimonthly magazine covering the salon industry/hair and beauty. "*Salon Talk* is published in two sections: *Salon Talk* for professional education and informs cosmetologists. *Salon Talk* for consumers informs consumers of the latest styles and services available in salons." Circ. 20,000. Pays on publication. Publishes ms an average of 3 months after acceptance. Byline given. Buys first North American serial rights; makes work-for-hire assignments. Submit seasonal/holiday material 3 months in advance. Computer printout submissions acceptable; prefers letter-quality to dot-matrix. SASE.
Photos: "Hair fashion photos are extremely desirable." Needs photos of new hair styles or trends. Reviews b&w contact sheets and 8x11 prints. Captions, model release, and identification of subjects required. Buys all rights.

Hardware

Journals for general hardware wholesalers and retailers, locksmiths, and retailers of miscellaneous special hardware items are listed in this section. Journals specializing in the retailing of hardware for a certain trade, such as plumbing or automotive supplies, are classified with the other publications for that trade.

CHAIN SAW AGE, 3435 N.E. Broadway, Portland OR 97232. Editor: Ken Morrison. 1% freelance written. For "mostly chain saw dealers (retailers); small businesses—usually family-owned, typical ages, interests and education." Monthly. Circ. 18,000. Buys "very few" mss/year. Pays on acceptance or publication—"varies." Publishes ms an average of 4 months after acceptance. Will consider photocopied submissions. Query first. Computer printout submissions acceptable; no dot-matrix. SASE. Free sample copy.
Nonfiction: "Must relate to chain saw use, merchandising, adaptation, repair, maintenance, manufacture or display." Buys informational articles, how-tos, personal experience articles, interviews, profiles, inspirational articles, personal opinion articles, photo features, coverage of successful business operations, and articles on merchandising techniques. Length: 500-1,000 words. Pays $20-50 ("2½¢/word plus photo fees").
Photos: Photos purchased with or without mss, or on assignment; captions required. For b&w glossies, pay "varies."
Tips: Frequently writers have an inadequate understanding of the subject area.

HARDWARE MERCHANDISER, The Irving-Cloud Publishing Co., 7300 N. Cicero, Lincolnwood IL 60646. (312)674-7300. Editor: James W. Stapleton. Monthly tabloid covering hardware, home center and hardlines market for owners and managers of hardware stores, home centers and executives of businesses serving them. Circ. 65,000. Pays on acceptance. Buys first North American serial rights. SASE. Reports in 1 month on queries. Free sample copy.
Nonfiction: Profile (of hardware business). Buys 10 mss/year. Query or send complete ms "on speculation; enough to tell the story."
Photos: Send photos with ms. Reviews 35mm or larger color transparencies. "Photos are paid for as part of article payment."

Home Furnishings and Household Goods

Readers rely on these publications to learn more about the home furnishings trade. Included in this section are magazines that focus on specific aspects of home furnishings such as glassware and water beds. Magazines geared to consumers interested in home furnishings are listed in the Consumer Home and Garden section.

APPLIANCE SERVICE NEWS, 110 W. Saint Charles Rd., Box 789, Lombard IL 60148. Editor: William Wingstedt. For professional service people whose main interest is repairing major and/or portable household appliances. Their jobs consist of either service shop owner, service manager or service technician. Monthly "newspaper style" publication. Circ. 41,000. Buys all rights. Byline given. Pays on publication. Will consider simultaneous submissions. Reports in about 1 month. SASE. Sample copy $1.50.

Nonfiction: James Hodl, associate editor. "Our main interest is in technical articles about appliances and their repair. Material should be written in a straightforward, easy-to-understand style. It should be crisp and interesting, with a high informational content. Our main interest is in the major and portable appliance repair field. We are not interested in retail sales." Query. Length: open. Pays $200-300/feature.

Photos: Pays $10 for b&w photos used with ms. Captions required.

CHINA GLASS & TABLEWARE, Ebel-Doctorow Publications, Inc., Box 2147, Clifton NJ 07015. (201)779-1600. Editor-in-Chief: Susan Grisham. 40% freelance written. Monthly magazine for buyers, merchandise managers and specialty store owners who deal in tableware, dinnerware, glassware, flatware and other tabletop accessories. Pays on publication. Publishes ms an average of 4 months after acceptance. Buys one-time rights. Byline given. Phone queries OK. Submit seasonal/holiday material 3 months in advance. SASE. Reports in 3 weeks. Free sample copy and writer's guidelines; mention *Writer's Market* in request.

Nonfiction: General interest (on store successes, reasons for a store's business track record); interview (personalities of store owners; how they cope with industry problems; why they are in tableware); and technical (on the business aspects of retailing china, glassware and flatware). "Bridal registry material always welcomed." No articles on how-to or gift shops. Buys 2-3 mss/issue. Query. Length: 1,500-3,000 words. Pays $40-50/page. Sometimes pays the expenses of writers on assignment.

Photos: State availability of photos with query. No additional payment for b&w contact sheets or color contact sheets. Captions required. Buys first serial rights.

Fillers: Clippings. Buys 2/issue. Pays $3-5.

Tips: "Show imagination in the query; have a good angle on a story—that makes it unique from the competition's coverage and requires less work on the editor's part for rewriting a snappy beginning."

FLOORING MAGAZINE, 545 5th Ave., New York NY 10017. Editor: Dan Alaimo. 10% freelance written. For floor covering retailers, wholesalers, floor covering specifiers, architects, etc. Monthly. Circulation: 22,000. Buys all rights. No byline. Buys 5-6 mss/year. Pays on acceptance. Publishes ms an average of 1 month after acceptance. Query. Reports in 1 month. SASE. Free sample copy.

Nonfiction: "Merchandising articles, new industry developments, unusual installations of floor coverings, etc. Conversational approach; snappy, interesting leads; plenty of quotes." Informational, how-to, interview, successful business operations, merchandising techniques and technical. Recent article example: "Selling to the Yuppie Generation" (January 1985). Length: 1,500-1,800 words. Pays $200-500/feature.

Photos: Photos *must* accompany feature. Captions required.

Tips: "It pays to talk to the subject before sending query letter."

GIFTS & DECORATIVE ACCESSORIES, 51 Madison Ave., New York NY 10010. (212)689-4411. Editor-in-Chief: Phyllis Sweed. 10% freelance written. Published primarily for quality gift retailers. Monthly magazine; 300+ pages. Circ. 33,000. Pays on publication. Publishes ms an average of 6 months after acceptance. No byline. Buys all rights. Submit seasonal/holiday material 6 months in advance. Photocopied submissions OK. Computer printout submissions acceptable; no dot-matrix. SASE. Reports "as soon as possible." Free writer's guidelines.

Nonfiction: "Merchandising how-to stories of quality stores—how they have solved a particular merchandising problem or successfully displayed or promoted a particularly difficult area." Nothing about discount stores or mass merchants. No cartoons, poems or think pieces. Buys 6 unsolicited mss/year. Query or submit complete ms. Length: 500-1,500 words. Pays $75-250. Sometimes pays the expenses of writers on assignment.

Photos: "Photos should illustrate merchandising points made in a story." Pays $7.50-10 for good 5x7 glossy b&w prints; $15-25 for 4x5 color transparencies or 35mm transparencies. Captions required. Buys all rights.

Tips: "The most frequent mistake made by writers is that they write personality pieces rather than business pieces. We're always in the market for a good story from the West or Southwest."

GIFTWARE BUSINESS, 1515 Broadway, New York NY 10036. (212)869-1300. Editor: Rita Guarna. For "merchants (department store buyers, specialty shop owners) engaged in the resale of giftware, china and glass, and decorative accessories." 10% freelance written. Monthly. Circ. 37,500. Buys all rights. Byline given "by request only." Pays on publication. Publishes ms an average of 2 months after acceptance. Will consider photocopied submissions. Computer printout submissions acceptable; prefers letter-quality to dot-matrix. SASE. Query or submit complete ms.

Nonfiction: "Retail store success stories. Describe a single merchandising gimmick. We are a tabloid format—glossy stock. Descriptions of store interiors are less important than sales performance unless display is outstanding. We're interested in articles on aggressive selling tactics. We cannot use material written for the consumer." Buys coverage of successful business operations and merchandising techniques. Length: 750 words maximum.

Photos: Purchased with mss and on assignment; captions required. "Individuals are to be identified." Reviews b&w glossy prints (preferred) and color transparencies.

Tips: "All short items are staff produced. The most frequent mistake made by writers is that they don't know the market. As a trade publication, we require a strong business slant, rather than a consumer angle."

‡**HARDWARE AND HOUSEWARES MERCHANDISING**, (formerly *Hardware Merchandising*), Maclean-Hunter Co., Ltd., 777 Bay St., Toronto, Ontario M52 1A7 Canada. (416)596-5797. For hardware and building supply retailers throughout Canada. 30% freelance written. Circ. 20,000. Contact: Editor-in-Chief. Canadian freelancers should contact the editor at above address for more information. Publishes ms an average of 2 months after acceptance. No computer printout or disk submissions. "Sometimes pays expenses of writers on assignment, but only *some* travel in special circumstances."

Tips: "The most frequent mistake made by writers in completing an article is using poor writing skills—stilted style, unsuited to our readership."

HAPPI, (formerly *Household and Personal Products Industry*), 26 Lake St., Ramsey NJ 07446. Editor: Hamilton C. Carson. 5% freelance written. For "manufacturers of soaps, detergents, cosmetics and toiletries, waxes and polishes, insecticides, and aerosols." Monthly. Circ. 14,000. Not copyrighted. Buys 3 to 4 mss a year, "but would buy more if slanted to our needs." Pays on publication. Publishes ms an average of 2 months after acceptance. Will consider photocopied submissions. Submit seasonal material 2 months in advance. Query. Computer printout submissions acceptable. SASE. Will send a sample copy to writer on request.

Nonfiction: "Technical and semitechnical articles on manufacturing, distribution, marketing, new products, plant stories, etc., of the industries served. Some knowledge of the field is essential in writing for us." Buys informational articles, interviews, photo features, spot news, coverage of successful business operations, new product articles, coverage of merchandising techniques and technical articles. No articles slanted toward consumers. Query with clips of published work. Length: 500-2,000 words. Pays $10-200. Sometimes pays expenses of writers on assignment.

Photos: 5x7 or 8x10 b&w glossies purchased with mss. Pays $10.

Tips: "The most frequent mistake made by writers in completing an article is unfamiliarity with our audience and our industry; slanting articles toward consumers rather than to industry members."

HOME FURNISHINGS, Box 581207, Dallas TX 75258. (214)741-7632. Editor: Tina Berres Filipski. 20% freelance written. Biannual magazine for home furnishings retail dealers, manufacturers, their representatives and others in related fields. Circ. 15,000. Pays on acceptance. Publishes ms an average of 2 months after acceptance. Buys first rights. No simultaneous submissions. Computer printout submissions acceptable; no dot-matrix. SASE.

Nonfiction: Informational articles about retail selling; success and problem solving stories in the retail business; economic and legislative-related issues, etc. "No profiles of people out of our area or nonmembers of the association. No trite, over-used features on trends, lighthearted features." Query. Length: open; appropriate to subject and slant. "Particularly interested in articles related to Southwest furniture retailing." Photos desirable.

HOME LIGHTING & ACCESSORIES, Box 2147, Clifton NJ 07015. (201)779-1600. Editor: Peter Wulff. 10% freelance written. For lighting stores/departments. Monthly magazine. Circ. 7,000. Pays on publication. Publishes ms an average of 3 months after acceptance. Buys all rights. Phone queries OK. Submit seasonal/ holiday material 6 months in advance. Computer printout submissions acceptable; no dot-matrix. SASE. Free sample copy.

Nonfiction: How-to (run your lighting store/department, including all retail topics); interview (with lighting retailers); personal experience (as a businessperson involved with lighting); opinion (about business approaches and marketing); profile (of a successful lighting retailer/lamp buyer); and technical (concerning lighting or lighting design). Buys 20 mss/year. Query. Pays $60/published page. Sometimes pays expenses of writers on assignment.

Photos: State availability of photos with query. Offers no additional payment for 5x7 or 8x10 b&w glossy prints. Pays additional $90 for color transparencies used on cover. Captions required.

Tips: "We don't need fillers—only features."

‡**MART, Business Ideas Today's Retailer Needs to Know**, Gordon Publications, Inc., Box 1952, Dover NJ 07801. (201)361-9060. Editor: Barbara J. Bagley. Managing Editor: Edward E. Ohlbaum. 40% freelance written. Monthly tabloid on retailing, especially consumer electronics, major appliances and electric housewares for retailers, including drugstores, wholesale distributors, and manufacturing district managers and representatives. Circ. 65,000. Pays on acceptance. Publishes ms an average of 3 months after acceptance. Byline given. Offers $50 kill fee. Buys all rights. Submit seasonal/holiday material 5 months in advance. SASE. Computer

printout submissions acceptable; prefers letter-quality to dot-matrix. Reports in 1 month. Sample copy $3; free writer's guidelines.

Nonfiction: General interest, how-to, interview/profile and new product. Buys 50 mss/year. Query with published clips. Length: 800-2,000 words. Pays $100-350.

Tips: "Writers frequently miss getting facts of particular interest to retailers: store volume, selling area, percentage of sales in major appliances, in consumer electronics, etc."

‡**OHIO VALLEY RETAILER**, 11214 Enyart Rd., Loveland OH 45140. (513)683-1615. Editor: Quint Nichols. 25% freelance written. Monthly regional tabloid for retailers and dealers in major goods to consumers (major appliances, TV, audio, personal electronics, computers, satellites, hardware, furniture, flooring and kitchen/bath). Area coverage includes all of Ohio and West Virginia and parts of Pennsylvania, Kentucky, Indiana, Michigan and Virginia. Circ. 12,800. Pays on acceptance. Publishes ms an average of 1 month after acceptance. Byline given. Offers 100% kill fee. Not copyrighted. Buys first serial rights. Simultaneous submissions OK. Computer printout submissions acceptable; prefers letter-quality to dot-matrix. SASE. Reports in several weeks. Free sample copy and writer's guidelines.

Nonfiction: Interview/profile and new product. "We only want stories about successful, retailers of major goods in our area." Buys 20 mss/year. Query with published clips. Length: 300-700 words. Pays $25-50. Sometimes pays expenses of writers on assignment.

Photos: Send photos with query or ms. Prefers 5x7 prints (good color photos accepted). Pays $5-10. Captions required. Buys one-time rights.

Columns/Departments: "We could use a column about furniture, computers, electronics or hardware if there is some connection to our area. Buys 20 mss/year. Query with published clips. Length: 700-1,400 words. Pays $35-50.

Tips: "We would like to hear from writers within our area of coverage. We prefer stories about any store owner who is enjoying a successful year and what is being done to generate this success. Also included in such stories would be the addition (or dropping) of product lines, any expansion of the store, or additonal stores, remodeling, redecorating, etc.—anything that might be of interest to store owners in the same business. Writers can specialize in any category if they wish."

PROFESSIONAL FURNITURE MERCHANT MAGAZINE, The Business Magazine for Progressive Furniture Retailers, Vista Communications, Inc., Suite 300, South, 180 Allen Rd., NE, Atlanta GA 30328. Editor: Gail B. Walker. 35% freelance written. Monthly magazine covering the furniture industry from a retailer's perspective. In-depth features on direction, trends, certain retailers doing outstanding jobs, and analyses of product or service areas in which retailing can improve profits. Circ. 20,000. Pays on publication. Publishes ms an average of 3 months after acceptance. Byline given. Buys first serial rights. Submit seasonal/holiday material 3 months in advance. No simultaneous queries or submissions. Computer printout submissions acceptable; prefers letter-quality to dot-matrix. SASE. Reports in 6 weeks. Sample copy $3.

Nonfiction: Expose (relating to or affecting furniture industry); how-to (business oriented how-to control cash flow, inventory, market research, etc.); interview/profile (furniture retailers); and photo feature (special furniture category). No general articles, fiction or personal experience. Buys 24 mss/year. Send complete ms. Length: 1,000-2,400 words. Pays $150-350. Sometimes pays expenses of writers on assignment.

Photos: State availablity of photos. Pays $5 maximum for 4x5 color transparencies; $5 maximum for 3x5 b&w prints. Captions, model release and identification of subjects required.

Tips: "Read the magazine. Send manuscript specifically geared to furniture retailers, with art (photos or drawings) specified." Break in with features. "First, visit a furniture store, talk to the owner and discover what he's interested in."

● **RAYTHEON MAGAZINE**, Raytheon Company, 141 Spring St., Lexington MA 02173. (617)862-6600, ext. 2415. Editor-in-Chief: Robert P. Suarez. 90% freelance written. Quarterly magazine for Raytheon stockholders, employees, customers, suppliers, plant city officials, libraries and interested persons. "Ours is a company publication that strives to avoid sounding like a company publication. All stories must involve some aspect of Raytheon or its products." Circ. 200,000. Pays on acceptance. Publishes ms an average of 3 months after acceptance. Byline given. Computer printout submissions acceptable; prefers letter-quality to dot-matrix. Free sample copy.

Nonfiction: General interest, humor, interview/profile, new product, nostalgia, photo feature, technical and travel. "This is a corporate publication designed to illustrate the breadth of Raytheon Company in a low key manner through six general-interest articles per issue. Photos are used liberally, top quality and exclusively color. Stories are by assignment only." Buys 4 mss/issue. Query with clips of published work, stating specialties, credentials and other publication credits. Length: 800-1,500 words. Pays $750-1,000/article. Sometimes pays the expenses of writers on assignment.

Tips: "Submit resume and magazine-style writing samples. We are looking for established writers who are capable of crisp, interesting magazine journalism. We are not looking to promote Raytheon, but rather to inform our audience about the company, very subtly. Heavy marketing-style or house organ writing is of no interest to us. A frequent mistake made by writers is not taking the time to truly understand what they're writing about and who the audience is."

RETAILER AND MARKETING NEWS, Box 191105, Dallas TX 75219-1105. (214)651-9959. Editor: Michael J. Anderson. For "retail dealers and wholesalers in appliances, TVs, furniture, consumer electronics, records, air conditioning, housewares, hardware, and all related businesses." Monthly. Circ. 10,000. Photocopied submissions OK. SASE. Free sample copy.
Nonfiction: "How a retail dealer can make more profit" is the approach. Wants "sales promotion ideas, advertising, sales tips, business builders and the like, localized to the Southwest and particularly to north Texas." Submit complete ms. Length: 100-900 words. Pays $30.

SEW BUSINESS, Box 1331, Ft. Lee NJ 07024. Editor: Christina Holmes. For retailers of home sewing, quilting and needlework merchandise. "We are the only glossy magazine format in the industry—including home sewing and the *Art Needlework* and *Quilt Quarterly* supplements." Monthly. Circ. 19,000. Not copyrighted. Pays on publication. Reports in 5 weeks on queries; in 6 weeks on ms. SASE. Free sample copy and writer's guidelines.
Nonfiction: Articles on department store or fabric, needlework, or quilt shop operations, including coverage of art needlework, piece goods, patterns, quilting and sewing notions. Interviews with buyers—retailers on their department or shop. "Stories must be oriented to provide interesting information from a *trade* point of view. Looking for retailers doing something different or offbeat, something that another retailer could put to good use in his own operation. Best to query editor first to find out if a particular article might be of interest to us." Buys 25 unsolicited mss/year. Query. Length: 750-1,500 words. Pays $100 minimum.
Photos: Photos purchased with mss. "Should illustrate important details of the story." Sharp 5x7 b&w glossies. Offers no additional payment for photos accompanying ms.

UNFINISHED FURNITURE MAGAZINE, United States Exposition Corp., 1850 Oak St., Northfield IL 60093. (312)446-8434. Editor: Lynda Utterback. 50% freelance written. Bimonthly magazine for unfinished furniture retailers, distributors and manufacturers throughout the U.S., Canada, England, Australia and Europe. Circ. 6,000. Pays on publication. Publishes ms an average of 2 months after acceptance. Byline given. Buys all rights. Submit seasonal/holiday material 6 months in advance. Simultaneous queries and simultaneous and photocopied submissions OK. Computer printout submissions acceptable. Reports in 3 weeks on queries; 1 month on mss. Free sample copy and writer's guidelines.
Nonfiction: How-to, interview/profile, new product, personal experience and technical (as these relate to the unfinished furniture industry). Production distribution, marketing, advertising and promotion of unfinished furniture and current happenings in the industry. Buys 10 unsolicited mss/year. Send complete ms. Length: 2,000 words. Pays $50-100.
Photos: Pays $5 for b&w photos.
Tips: "We look for professionals in the field (i.e., accountants to write tax articles) to write articles. A frequent mistake made by writers in completing an article for us is not understanding the audience."

Hospitals, Nursing, and Nursing Homes

In this section are journals for nurses; medical and nonmedical nursing homes; clinical and hospital staffs; and laboratory technicians and managers. Journals publishing technical material on new discoveries in medicine and information for physicians in private practice are listed in the Medical category. Publications that report on medical trends for the consumer are in the Health and Science categories.

‡**HOSPITAL GIFT SHOP MANAGEMENT**, Creative Age Publications, 7628 Densmore Ave., Van Nuys CA 91406. (818)782-7232. Editor: Barbara Feiner. 25% freelance written. Monthly magazine covering hospital gift shop management. "*HGSM* presents practical and informative articles and features to assist in expanding the hospital gift shop into a comprehensive center generating large profits." Circ. 15,000+. Pays on acceptance. Publishes ms an average of 4 months after acceptance. Byline given. Buys first North American seri-

al rights. Submit seasonal/holiday material 8 months in advance. Computer printout submissions acceptable. Dot-matrix printers are OK "if readable and double-spaced." SASE. Reports in 1 month. Sample copy and writer's guidelines for $1 postage.

Nonfiction: How-to, interview/profile, photo feature, and management-themed articles. "No fiction, no poetry, no first-person 'I was shopping in a gift shop' kinds of pieces." Buys 12-25 mss/year. Length: 750-2,500 words. Pays $10-100. Query first.

Photos: State availability of photos with query or ms. "If you are preparing a gift shop profile, think of providing gift shop photos." Reviews 5x7 color or b&w prints; payment depends on photo quality and number used. Captions, model releases, and identification of subjects required.

Fillers: Cartoons only; 12+/year. Pays $20.

Tips: "A freelancer's best bet is to let us know you're out there. We prefer to work on assignment a lot of the time, and we're very receptive to freelancers—especially those in parts of the country to which we have no access. Call or write; let me know you're available. Visit your nearby hospital gift shop—it's probably larger, more sophisticated than you would imagine. Specialization is the wave of the future. If there's an untapped market, as the hospital gift shops were not too long ago, you can be sure that a magazine will start up within a reasonable period of time. Many of these trade journals need freelance contributions, so don't close your minds to the possibility of writing for them. It's a great market to break into—and stay with."

HOSPITAL SUPERVISOR'S BULLETIN, Bureau of Business Practice, 24 Rope Ferry Rd., Waterford CT 06386. Editor: Jill Wasserman. 50% freelance written. For non-medical hospital supervisors. Semimonthly newsletter; 8 pages. Circ. 8,000. Pays on acceptance. Publishes ms an average of 4 months after acceptance. Buys all rights. No byline. Submit seasonal/holiday material 6 months in advance. Photocopied submissions OK. Computer printout submissions acceptable; prefers letter-quality to dot-matrix. SASE. Reports in 1 month. Free sample copy and writer's guidelines.

Nonfiction: Publishes interviews with non-medical hospital department heads. "You should ask supervisors to pinpoint current problems in supervision, tell how they are trying to solve these problems and what results they're getting—backed up by real examples from daily life." Also publishes interviews on people problems and good methods of management. People problems include the areas of training, planning, evaluating, counseling, discipline, motivation, supervising the undereducated, getting along with the medical staff, etc., with emphasis on good methods of management. No material on hospital volunteers. We prefer six- to eight-page typewritten articles, based on interviews." Pays 12¢/word after editing.

Tips: "Often stories lack concrete examples explaining general principles. I stress that freelancers interview supervisors (not high-level managers, doctors, or administrators) of non-medical departments. Interviews should focus on supervisory skills or techniques for improving productivity that would be applicable in any hospital department."

HOSPITALS, American Hospital Publishing, Inc., 211 E. Chicago Ave., Chicago IL 60611. (312)951-1100. Editor: Frank Sabatino. 5% freelance written. Bimonthly magazine featuring hospitals and health care systems. Circ. 104,000. Average issue includes 5-6 articles. Pays on acceptance. Publishes ms an average of 3 months after acceptance. Byline given. Buys all rights. Phone queries OK. Submit seasonal material 4 months in advance. Photocopied submissions OK. Electronic submissions OK compatible with Wang, but requires hard copy also. Inquire about electronic submissions. Computer printout submissions acceptable. Reports in 2 weeks on queries; in 2 months on mss. Free sample copy and writer's guidelines.

Nonfiction: How-to and new product. "Articles must address issues of the management of health care institutions." Buys 5-8 unsolicited mss/year. "Moving to staff-written magazine in the year ahead." Query with "reasonably detailed summary or outline of proposed article." Length: 2,000 words maximum. Pays $250-500. Sometimes pays the expenses of writers on assignment.

Columns/Departments: "Columns are published on cost containment, architecture and design, and long-term care. Another column includes short features on innovative hospital programs."

Tips: "We only hire authors experienced in the medical field."

RN, 680 Kinderkamack Rd., Oradell NJ 07649. (201)262-3030. Editor: James A. Reynolds. For registered nurses, mostly hospital-based but also in physicians' offices, public health, schools and industry. 50% freelance written. Monthly magazine; 100 pages. Circ. 275,000. Buys all rights. Pays kill fee for specifically commissioned material. Byline given. Pays on publication. Publishes ms an average of 10 months after acceptance. Submit seasonal/holiday material 8 months in advance. Reports in 2 months. Computer printout submissions acceptable. SASE. Sample copy $3. Free writer's guidelines.

Nonfiction: "If you are a nurse who writes, we would like to see your work. Editorial content: diseases, clinical techniques, surgery, therapy, equipment, drugs, etc. These should be thoroughly researched and sources cited. Personal anecdotes, experiences, and observations based on your relations with doctors, hospitals, patients and nursing colleagues. Our style is simple and direct, not preachy. Do include examples and case histories that relate the reader to her own nursing experience. Talk mostly about people, rather than things. Dashes of humor or insight are always welcome. Include photos where feasible." Buys 100 mss/year. Query or submit complete ms. Length: 1,000-2,000 words. Pays $100-300. Sometimes pays the expenses of writers on assignment.

Photos: "We want good clinical illustration." Send photos with ms. Pays $25 minimum/b&w contact sheet; $35 minimum/35mm color transparency. Captions required; model release required. Buys all rights.

Hotels, Motels, Clubs, Resorts, Restaurants

These publications offer trade tips to hotel and restaurant management, and owners, managers and operators of these establishments. Journals for manufacturers and distributors of bar and beverage supplies are listed in the Beverages and Bottling category. For publications slanted to food wholesalers, processors and caterers, see Food Products, Processing, and Service.

‡**BARTENDER**, Bartender Publishing Corp., Box 593, Livingston NJ 07039. (201)227-4330. Publisher: Raymond P. Foley. Editor: Jaclyn M. Wilson. Emphasizes liquor and bartending for bartenders, tavern owners and owners of restaurants with liquor licenses. 100% freelance written. Bimonthly magazine; 50 pages. Circ. 15,000. Pays on publication. Publishes ms an average of 3 months after acceptance. Buys first serial rights, one-time rights and second serial (reprint) rights. Byline given. Phone queries OK. Submit seasonal/holiday material 3 months in advance. Simultaneous, photocopied, and previously published submissions OK. Computer printout submissions acceptable. SASE. Reports in 2 months. Sample copies $2.50.
Nonfiction: General interest, historical, how-to, humor, interview (with famous ex-bartenders); new products, nostalgia, personal experience, unique bars, opinion, new techniques, new drinking trends, photo feature, profile, travel and bar sports. Send complete ms. Length: 100-1,000 words.
Photos: Send photos with ms. Pays $7.50-50 for 8x10 b&w glossy prints; $10-75 for 8x10 color glossy prints. Caption preferred and model release required.
Columns/Departments: Bar of the Month; Bartender of the Month; Drink of the Month; New Drink Ideas; Bar Sports; Quiz; Bar Art; Wine Cellar Tips of the Month (from prominent figures in the liquor industry); One For The Road (travel); Collectors (bar or liquor related items); Photo Essays. Query. Length: 200-1,000 words. Pays $50-200.
Fillers: Clippings, jokes, gags, anecdotes, short humor, newsbreaks and anything relating to bartending and the liquor industry. Length: 25-100 words. Pays $5-25.
Tips: "To break in, absolutely make sure that your work will be of interest to all bartenders across the country. Your style of writing should reflect the audience you are addressing. The most frequent mistake made by writers in completing an article for us is using wrong subject."

COOKING FOR PROFIT, Metanoia Corp., Box 267, Fond du Lac WI 54935. (414)923-3700. Editor: Bill Dittrich. A monthly magazine covering foodservice operations for restaurants, hospitals and nursing homes, hotels/motels and others in foodservice industry. Circ. 35,000. Pays on publication. Byline given. Buys variable rights. Submit seasonal/holiday material 6 months in advance. Simultaneous submissions OK. Computer printout submissions acceptable. SASE. Reports in 1 month. Sample copy for 9x12 SAE and 40¢ postage; free writer's guidelines.
Nonfiction: Book excerpts, new product, photo feature and technical. "Articles should always go beyond general trends, overviews and theory and offer practical advice and information." No articles on promotions or any front-of-the-house topics. Buys 60-70 mss/year. Query with clips of published work. Length: 500-1,200 words. Pays $100-250.
Photos: Send photos with accompanying query or ms. Pays $50-75 for 8x10 b&w prints; $50-150 for 4x5 or 35mm color slides. Captions, model release and identification of subjects required. Buys one-time rights.
Columns/Departments: Foodservice equipment, energy and maintenance. Query.
Tips: Writers should "send clips of their work; thoroughly describe and, preferably, outline their query and give an idea of what kind of fee they are looking for. Features, particularly restaurant profiles, are most open to freelancers."

FLORIDA HOTEL & MOTEL JOURNAL, The Official Publication of the Florida Hotel & Motel Association, Accommodations, Inc., Box 1529, Tallahassee FL 32302. (904)224-2888. Editor: Mrs. Jayleen

Woods. 10% freelance written. Monthly magazine for managers in the lodging industry (every licensed hotel, motel and resort in Florida). Circ. 6,500. Pays on publication. Publishes ms an average of 2 months after acceptance. Byline given. Offers $50 kill fee. Buys all rights and makes work-for-hire assignments. Submit seasonal/holiday material 3 months in advance. Photocopied submissions OK. Computer printout submissions acceptable; no dot-matrix. SASE. Reports in 1 month. Sample copy for 9x12 SAE and 3 first class stamps; writer's guidelines for business size SAE and 1 first class stamp.

Nonfiction: General interest (business, finance, taxes); historical/nostalgic (old Florida hotel reminiscences); how-to (improve management, housekeeping procedures, guest services, security and coping with common hotel problems); humor (hotel-related anecdotes); inspirational (succeeding where others have failed); interview/profile (of unusual hotel personalities); new product (industry-related and non brand preferential); photo feature (queries only); technical (emerging patterns of hotel accounting, telephone systems, etc.); travel (transportation and tourism trends only—no scenics or site visits); and property renovations and maintenance techniques. Buys 10-12 mss/year. Query with clips of published work. Length: 750-2,500 words. Pays $75-250 "depending on type of article and amount of research." Sometimes pays the expenses of writers on assignment.

Photos: Send photos with ms. Pays $25-100 for 4x5 color transparencies; $10-15 for 5x7 b&w prints. Captions, model release and identification of subjects required.

Tips: "We prefer feature stories on properties or personalities holding current membership in the Florida Hotel & Motel Association. Memberships and/or leadership brochures are available (SASE) on request. We're open to articles showing how Mom & Dad management copes with inflation and rising costs of energy systems, repairs, renovations, new guest needs and expectations. The writer may have a better chance of breaking in at our publication with short articles and fillers because the better a writer is at the art of condensation, the better his/her feature articles are likely to be."

‡**HOTEL AND MOTEL MANAGEMENT**, Harcourt Brace Jovanovich, Inc., 7500 Old Oak Blvd., Cleveland OH 44130. (216)243-8100. Editor: Michael Deluca. Managing Editor: Robert Nuzar. 25% freelance written. Monthly newsmagazine about hotels, motels and resorts in the continental U.S. and Hawaii for general managers, corporate executives, and department heads (such as director of sales; food and beverage; energy; security; front office; housekeeping, etc.) Circ. 41,000. Pays on acceptance. Publishes an average of 2 months after acceptance. Byline given. Buys first North American serial rights. No phone queries. Computer printout submissions acceptable; prefers letter-quality to dot-matrix. SASE. Reports in 3 weeks on queries; do not send mss. Free sample copy.

Nonfiction: "A how-to, nuts-and-bolts approach to improving the bottom line through more innovative, efficient management of hotels, motels and resorts in the continental U.S. and Hawaii. Articles consist largely of specific case studies and interviews with authorities on various aspects of the lodging market, including franchising, financing, personnel, security, energy management, package tours, telecommunications, food service operations, architecture and interior design, and technological advances. We use freelance coverage of spot news events (strikes, natural diasters, etc.). Query with published clips. "Write a query letter outlining your idea and be specific." Length: 800-1,000 words. Sometimes pays expenses of writers on assignment.

Photos: State availability of b&w photos. Captions preferred. Buys one-time rights.

Tips: "The writer may have a better chance of breaking in at our publication with short articles and fillers because we are a newsmagazine that covers an industry of people who don't have time to read longer articles. We need 'hands on' articles which explain the topic."

INDEPENDENT RESTAURANTS, EIP, Inc., 2132 Fordem Ave., Madison WI 53704. (608)244-3528. Editor: Jeanette Riechers. Uses freelance written articles "only occasionally." Monthly magazine covering management and marketing of independently owned and operated restaurants. Circ. 106,000. Pays on acceptance. Publishes ms an average of 4 months after acceptance. No byline given. Offers negotiable kill fee. Buys first North American serial rights. Submit seasonal/holiday material 6 months in advance. Photocopied submissions OK. Computer printout submissions acceptable; prefers letter-quality to dot-matrix. SASE. Reports in 2 months. Sample copy $2.50.

Nonfiction: How-to (improve management of independent restaurant; marketing techniques, promotions, etc.); and interview/profile (with independent restaurateur; needs a strong angle). "Send us a query on a successful independent restaurateur with an effective marketing program, unusual promotions, interesting design and decor, etc." No restaurant reviews, consumer-oriented material, non restaurant-oriented management articles. Buys variable number mss/year. Length: open. Pays variable fee.

Photos: State availability of photos. Captions, model release and identification of subjects required. Buys all rights.

INNKEEPING WORLD, Box 84108, Seattle WA 98124. Editor/Publisher: Charles Nolte. 70% freelance written. Emphasizes the hotel industry worldwide. Published 10 times a year; 12 pages. Circ. 2,000. Pays on acceptance. Publishes ms an average of 3 months after acceptance. Buys all rights. No byline. Submit seasonal/holiday material 1 month in advance. Computer printout submissions acceptable; prefers letter-quality to dot-matrix. SASE. Reports in 1 month. Free sample copy and writer's guidelines for SASE.

Nonfiction: Main topics: Managing—interview with successful hotel managers of large and/or famous hotels/resorts (length: 600-1,200 words); Marketing—interviews with hotel marketing executives on successful promotions/case histories (length: 300-1,000 words); Lodging Classics—stories of famous or highly-rated hotels/inns/resorts, domestic and overseas listing of hotels available from the publisher (length: 300-1,000 words); Bill of Fare—outstanding hotel restaurants, menus and merchandising concepts (length: 300-1,000 words); and ·The Concierge—interviews with the world's most experienced about their experience in guest relations (length: 300-1,000 words). Pays $100 minimum or 15¢/word (whichever is greater) for main topics. Other topics—advertising, creative packages, cutting expenses, frequent guest profile, guest comfort, guest relations, hospitality, ideas, interior design, landscape design, public relations, reports and trends, sales promotion, special guestrooms, staff relations. Length: 50-500 words. Pays 15¢/word.

MEETINGS & CONVENTIONS, Ziff-Davis Publishing Co., 1 Park Ave., New York NY 10016. Editor-in-Chief: Mel Hosansky. 15% freelance written. For association and corporate executives who plan sales meetings, training meetings, annual conventions, incentive travel trips and any other kind of off premises meeting. Monthly magazine; 150 pages. Circ. 80,000. Pays on acceptance. Publishes ms an average of 5 months after acceptance. Buys first rights. Photocopied submissions and previously published work (if not published in a competing publication) OK. Computer printout submissions acceptable; prefers letter-quality to dot-matrix. SASE. Reports in 1-2 months.

Nonfiction: "Publication is basically how-to. We tell how to run better meetings, where to hold them, etc. Must be case history, talking about specific meeting." No destination write-ups. Buys 7-10 unsolicited mss/year. Query. Length: 250-2,000 words. Pays $200-800.

Photos: Uses b&w slides.

‡**NARTA NEWS MAGAZINE, Published for Members of North American Restaurant & Tavern Alliance**, 139 Day St., Newington CT 06111. (203)246-8883. Editor: Carol Repczynski. 40% freelance written. Bimonthly magazine of restaurant/tavern management for owners/managers, featuring news and management advice, operation improvements, merchandising and promotion, and new products. Circ. 5,500. Pays on acceptance. Publishes ms an average of 3 months after acceptance. Byline given. Buys first North American serial rights. Submit seasonal/holiday material 4 months in advance. Simultaneous queries and simultaneous, photocopied and previously published submissions OK. Computer printout submissions acceptable; prefers letter-quality to dot-matrix. SASE. Reports in 3 weeks. Free sample copy.

Nonfiction: General interest (credit card use in restaurants); how-to (manage people, deal with suppliers, beat out competition), new product & equipment; food/beverage trends; personal experience (as bartender or waitperson; as manager); and purchasing, inventory, investments for small businesses. Special issues include holiday pieces on Mother's Day, St. Patrick's Day and New Year's. No studies of rare wines and homey recipes. Buys 18 mss/year. Query with published clips or send complete ms. Length: 900-2,500 words. Pays $35-150. Sometimes pays expenses of writers on assignment.

Photos: State availability of photos. Prefers b&w glossies. Reviews b&w contact sheets and 4x5 prints. Pays $15-30. Buys one-time rights.

Tips: "Send clips and offer to do interviews on assignment; we need stringers in various parts of the country. Analyses of legislative matters important to restaurant/tavern owners and managers would be most welcome, as would articles on turnover of employees, supervision and motivating employees. *NARTA NEWS* has been undergoing expansion and is open to considering well-written material on a wide variety of subjects. Avoid flowery style; we are not a literary magazine; our readers are business people with little time for difficult-to-read material."

RESORT MANAGEMENT MAGAZINE, Western Specialty Publications, Inc., 2431 Morena Blvd., San Diego CA 92110. (619)275-3666. Editor: James McVicar. A magazine published 8 times/year covering the hotel/resort and condo/timeshare industries. "We not reach motels or motor lodges." Pays on publication. Byline given. Offers $50 kill fee. Buys all rights. Submit all material 2 months in advance. Simultaneous queries and photocopied and previously published submissions OK. Computer printout submissions acceptable. SASE. Reports in 3 months. Sample copy $5.

Nonfiction: Book excerpts, expose, general interest, historical/nostalgic, how-to, humor, inspirational, interview/profile, new product, opinion, personal experience, photo feature, technical and travel. Especially interested in state-of-the-art technology and management methods, industry megatrends and instant cost saving devices. Buys 6 mss/year. Query with clips of published work. Length: 500-2,000 words. Pays $50-100.

Photos: Kaaren Slen, art director. Send photos with accompanying query or ms. "Won't return without SASE." Pays $5-10 for b&w and color prints; $10-20 for b&w transparencies; $10-25 for color transparencies. Buys all rights.

RESTAURANT HOSPITALITY, Penton IPC, Penton Plaza, 1111 Chester Ave., Cleveland OH 44114. (216)696-7000. Editor: Stephen Michaelides. 15% freelance written. Monthly magazine covering the foodservice industry for owners and operators of independent restaurants, hotel foodservices, executives of national and regional restaurant chains and foodservice executives of schools, hospitals, military installations and corporations. Circ. 120,000. Average issue includes 10-12 features. Pays on acceptance. Publishes ms an average of 5 months after acceptance. Byline given. Buys exclusive rights. Query first. Computer printout submissions acceptable; prefers letter-quality to dot-matrix. SASE. Reports in 1 week. Sample copy for 9x12 SAE and $1.54 postage.

Nonfiction: General interest (articles that advise operators how to run their operations profitably and efficiently); interview (with operators); and profile. No restaurant reviews. Buys 30 mss/year. Query with clips of previously published work and a short bio. Length: 500-1,500 words. Pays $100/published page. Pays the expenses of writers on assignment.

Photos: Send color photos with manuscript. Captions required.

Tips: "We're accepting fewer queried stories but assigning more to our regular freelancers. We need new angles on old stories, and we like to see pieces on emerging trends and technologies in the restaurant industry. Stories on psychology, consumer behavior, managerial problems and solutions, how-to's on buying insurance, investing (our readers have a high degree of disposable income), design elements and computers in foodservice. Our readers don't want to read how to open a restaurant or why John Smith is so successful. We are accepting 100-150 word pieces with photos (slides preferred; will accept b&w) for our Restaurant People department. Should be light, humorous, anecdotal." Byline given. Pays $75.

‡**THE SERVER**, Business Communications, Inc., 2545-47 Brownsville Rd., Pittsburgh PA 15210. (412)885-7600. Editor: Betty Koffler. 30% freelance written. Monthly newspaper (tabloid) on information geared to all facets of the Pennsylvania food and beverage industry. Includes success stories, happenings in the industry and upbeat focus on restaurant, school, hospital and institutional operations. Circ. 21,500. Pays within 30 days after publication. Publishes ms an average of 3 months after acceptance. Byline given. Publishes all assigned copy. Not copyrighted. Buys one-time rights. Submit seasonal/holiday material 2 months in advance. Simultaneous queries OK. Computer printout submissions acceptable; prefers letter-quality to dot-matrix. SASE. Reports in 2 weeks on queries; 3 weeks on mss. Sample copy and writer's guidelines free.

Nonfiction: Humor, personal experience and photo feature. All must be trade-oriented. No consumer-oriented articles. Buys 24 mss/year. Query. Length: 400-800 words. Pays 6¢/word. Sometimes pays expenses of writers on assignment.

Photos: State availability of photo. Prefers 5x7 or 8x10 b&w prints. Pays $5 each. Captions and identification of subjects required. Buys one-time rights.

Columns/Departments: Buys 36/year. Query. Length: 400-600 words. Pays 6¢/word.

Fillers: Anecdotes and short humor. Length: 300-500 words. Pays 6¢/word.

Tips: "Since *The Server* is a trade publication and our needs are primarily informational, freelancers should have a general knowledge about the food and beverage industry. Areas most open to freelancers are success stories about those involved in restaurants, schools, hotels, institutions, menus, food, decor, etc."

Industrial Operation and Management

Industrial plant managers, executives, distributors and buyers read these journals. Subjects include equipment, supplies, quality control, and production engineering. Some industrial management journals are also listed under the names of specific industries, such as Machinery and Metal Trade. Publications for industrial supervisors are listed in Management and Supervision.

COMPRESSED AIR, 253 E. Washington Ave., Washington NJ 07882. Editor/Publications Manager: S.M. Parkhill. 75% freelance written. Emphasizes general industrial/technology subjects for engineers and managers. Monthly magazine; 48 pages. Circ. 150,000. Buys all rights. Publishes ms an average of 1 month after acceptance. Computer printout submissions acceptable; no dot-matrix. Reports in 6 weeks. Free sample copy, editorial schedule; mention *Writer's Market* in request.

Nonfiction: "Articles must be reviewed by experts in the field." How-to (save costs with air power); and historical (engineering). Recent article example: "Harley-Davidson Fights Back" (April 1985). Buys 48 mss/year. Query with clips of previously published work. Pays negotiable fee. Sometimes pays the expenses of writers on assignment.

Photos: State availability of photos in query. Payment for 8x10 glossy b&w photos is included in total purchase price. Captions required. Buys all rights.

Tips: "We are presently looking for freelancers with a track record in industrial/technology writing. Editorial schedule is developed well in advance and relies heavily on article ideas from contributors. Resume and samples help. Writers with access to authorities preferred; prefer interviews over library research. The magazine's name doesn't reflect its contents; suggest writers request sample copies."

INDUSTRIAL CHEMICAL NEWS, Bill Communications, 633 3rd Ave., New York NY 10025. (212)986-4800. Editor: Irvin Schwartz. Managing Editor: Susan Neale. 15% freelance written. Monthly magazine covering the scientific, business industrial aspects of chemistry for chemists working in industry. Circ. 40,000. Pays on publication. Publishes ms an average of 3 months after acceptance. Byline given. Pays $100 kill fee. Buys all rights. Computer printout submissions acceptable; prefers letter-quality to dot-matrix. SASE. Reports within 1 month. Free sample copy and writer's guidelines.

Nonfiction: Expose (of government or industry matters); interview/profile (related to the chemical industry); personal experience (of a chemist's work life); photo feature (of a chemical development); and technical overviews (chemical or biological). "The features in *ICN* are written in an informative and fresh style. We do not intend to burden our readers with complex technical jargon when the facts can be told more simply, and other publications cover research articles. But neither do we want a basic story; we must tell them something new, something they must know. The features emphasize examples and details of how the research was actually accomplished (equipment used, dollars spent, etc.). Always, the emphasis is our readers: How will the industrial chemist learn from the information?" Buys 3-6 unsolicited mss/year. Query with clips of published work. Length: 1,000-3,000 words. Pays $200-500.

Photos: State availability of photos. "It would be helpful if the author could supply the artwork or recommend material that could be used to clearly portray points made in the written material." Buys one-time rights.

Columns/Departments: Book reviews (new books); employment briefs ("news items on chemical careers"); and news ("broad topic of interest to chemists"). Length: 300-3,000 words.

INDUSTRIAL FABRIC PRODUCTS REVIEW, Industrial Fabrics Assoc., Suite 450, 345 Cedar Bldg., St. Paul MN 55101. (612)222-2508. Editor: Roger Barr. Director of Publications: Carey Bohn. 40% freelance written. Monthly magazine covering industrial textiles for company owners, salespersons and researchers in a variety of industrial textile areas. Circ. 6,000. Pays on publication. Publishes ms an average of 2 months after acceptance. Byline given. Buys all rights. Submit seasonal/holiday material 4 months in advance. Simultaneous queries, and photocopied and previously published submissions OK. Computer printout submissions acceptable; prefers letter-quality to dot-matrix. SASE. Reports in 4 weeks. Sample copy free "after query and phone conversation."

Nonfiction: Technical, marketing and other topics "related to any aspect of industrial fabric industry from fiber to finished fabric product." Special issues include new products, industrial products and equipment. No historical or apparel oriented articles. Buys 12 mss/year. Query with phone number. Length: 1,200-3,000 words. Pays $75/published page. Pays the expenses of writers on assignment.

Photos: State availability of photos. Reviews 8x10 b&w glossy and color prints. Pay is negotiable. Model release and identification of subjects required. Buys one-time rights.

Tips: "Ours is a specialized field; we work hard to develop a stable of writers familiar with our field. But we're always on the lookout for new writers willing to learn the field. The most frequent mistakes made by writers in completing an article for us are that the writing is often soft and the story general because the writers aren't familiar with the subject matter."

INDUSTRY WEEK, Penton/IPC, Inc., 1111 Chester Ave., Cleveland OH 44114, (216)696-7000. Editor-in-Chief: Stanley Modic. 10% freelance written. Emphasizes manufacturing and service industries for top or middle management (administrating, production, engineering, finance, purchasing or marketing) throughout industry. Biweekly magazine; 96 pages. Circ. 350,000. Pays on publication. Publishes ms an average of 6 months after acceptance. Buys all rights. Byline given depending on length of article. Phone queries OK. Submit seasonal or holiday material 3 months in advance. Simultaneous and photocopied submissions OK. Computer printout submissions acceptable. SASE. Reports in 1 month. Sample copy $2.

Nonfiction: John H. Sheridan, feature editor. How-to and informational articles (should deal with areas of interest to executive audience, e.g., developing managerial skills or managing effectively). "No product news or case histories, please." Length: 750-3,000 words. Pays $300/first 1,000 words; $100/additional 1,000 words. Buys 5-10 ms/year. Query. No product news or clippings. Computer printout submissions acceptable; prefers letter-quality to dot-matrix.

Photos: Nick Dankovich, art director. B&w and color purchased with ms or on assignment. Query. Pays $35 minimum. Model release required.

Tips: "Most short items are staff-written. The most frequent mistake made by writers is that emphasis is not directed toward an audience of busy executives. There is shallow treatment of subject matter and weakness on analysis."

INSULATION OUTLOOK, National Insulation Contractors Association, Suite 410, 1025 Vermont NW, Washington DC 20005. (202)783-6278. Editor: Dixie M. Lee. Monthly magazine about general business, commercial and industrial insulation for the insulation industry in the United States and abroad. Publication is read by engineers, specifiers, buyers, contractors and union members in the industrial and commercial insulation field. There is also representative distribution to public utilities, and energy-related industries. Pays on publication. Byline given. Buys first rights only. Phone queries OK. Written queries should be short and simple, with samples of writing attached. Submit seasonal material 6 months in advance. Simultaneous, photocopied and previously published submissions OK. SASE. Sample copy $2; free writer's guidelines. "Give us a call. If there seems to be compatibility, we will send a free issue sample so the writer can see directly the type of publication he or she is dealing with."
Columns/Departments: Query. Pays $50-300.

PLANT MANAGEMENT & ENGINEERING, MacLean Hunter Bldg; 777 Bay St., Toronto, Ontario M5W 1A7 Canada. Editor: Ron Richardson. 10% freelance written. For Canadian plant managers and engineers. Monthly magazine. Circ. 26,000. Pays on acceptance. Publishes ms an average of 6 months after acceptance. Buys first Canadian rights. SAE and IRCs. Computer printout submissions acceptable; prefers letter-quality to dot-matrix. Reports in 3 weeks. Sample copy with SAE only.
Nonfiction: How-to, technical and management technique articles. Must have Canadian slant. No generic articles that appear to be rewritten from textbooks. Buys less than 20 unsolicited mss/year. Query. Pays 12¢/word minimum.
Photos: State availability of photos with query. Pays $25-50 for b&w prints; $50-100 for 2¼x2¼ or 35mm color transparencies. Captions preferred. Buys one-time rights.
Tips: Query first by letter. "Read the magazine. Know the Canadian readers' special needs. Case histories and interviews only—no theoretical pieces. Trends in magazine publishing that freelance writers should be aware of include computers, robots and high tech."

PRODUCTION ENGINEERING, Penton Plaza, Cleveland OH 44114. (216)696-7000. Editor: Donald E. Hegland. Executive Editor: John McRainey. 50% freelance written. For "men and women in production engineering—the engineers who plan, design and improve manufacturing operations." Monthly magazine; 100 pages. Circ. 95,000. Pays on publication. Buys exclusive first North American serial rights. Byline given; "if by prior arrangement, an author contributed a segment of a broader article, he might not be bylined." Phone queries OK. Photocopied submissions OK, if exclusive. Computer printout submissions acceptable. SASE. Reports in 2 weeks. Free sample copy and writer's guidelines.
Nonfiction: How-to (engineering, data for engineers); personal experience (from *very* senior production or manufacturing engineers only); and technical (technical news or how-to). "We're interested in solid, hard hitting technical articles on the gut issues of manufacturing. Not case histories, but no-fat treatments of manufacturing concepts, innovative manufacturing methods, and state-of-the-art procedures. Our readers also enjoy articles that detail a variety of practical solutions to some specific, everyday manufacturing headache." Buys 2-3 mss/issue. Query. Length: 800-3,000 words. Pays $100-300.

PURCHASING EXECUTIVE'S BULLETIN, Bureau of Business Practice, 24 Rope Ferry Rd., Waterford CT 06386. (203)442-4365. Editor: Claire Sherman. Managing Editor: Wayne Muller. For purchasing managers and purchasing agents. Semimonthly newsletter; 4 pages. Circ. 5,500. Pays on acceptance. Buys all rights. Submit seasonal/holiday material 3 months in advance. Reports in 2 weeks. Free sample copy and writer's guidelines.
Nonfiction: How-to (better cope with problems confronting purchasing executives); and direct interviews detailing how purchasing has overcome problems and found better ways of handling departments. No derogatory material about a company; no writer's opinions; no training or minority purchasing articles. "We don't want material that's too elementary (things any purchasing executive already knows)." Buys 2-3 mss/issue. Query. Length: 750-1,000 words.
Tips: "Make sure that a release is obtained and attached to a submitted article."

QUALITY CONTROL SUPERVISOR'S BULLETIN, National Foremen's Institute, 24 Rope Ferry Rd., Waterford CT (800)243-0876. Editor: Steven J. Finn. 100% freelance written. Biweekly newsletter for quality control supervisors. Circ. 10,000. Pays on acceptance. No byline given. Buys all rights. Computer printout submissions acceptable. SASE. Reports in 2 weeks on queries; 1 month on mss. Free sample copy and writer's guidelines.
Nonfiction: Interview and "articles with a strong how-to slant that make use of direct quotes whenever possi-

ble." Buys 70 mss/year. Query. Length: 800-1,100 words. Pays 8-14¢/word.
Tips: "Write for our freelancer guidelines and follow them closely. We're looking for steady freelancers we can work with on a regular basis."

SEMICONDUCTOR INTERNATIONAL, Cahners Publishing Co., 1350 E. Touhy Ave., Box 5080, Des Plaines IL 60018. (312)635-8800. Editor: Donald E. Swanson. 5% freelance written. Monthly magazine covering semiconductor industry processing, assembly and testing technology subjects for semiconductor industry processing engineers and management. "Technology stories that cover all phases of semiconductor product manufacturing and testing are our prime interest." Circ. 35,134. Pays on publication. "News items are paid for upon acceptance." Publishes ms an average of 6 months after acceptance. Byline given. Buys all rights and makes work-for-hire assignments. Computer printout submissions acceptable; no dot-matrix. Reports in 1 month.
Nonfiction: Technical and news pertaining to the semiconductor industry in the U.S. and overseas. No "articles that are commercial in nature or product oriented." Buys 50 mss/year (including feature articles and news). Query with "your interest and capabilities" or send complete ms. Length: 2,500 words maximum.
Photos: State availability of photos or send photos with ms. Reviews 8x10 b&w prints and 35mm color transparencies. Captions and identification of subjects required.
Columns/Departments: "News of the semiconductor industry as it pertains to technology trends is of interest. Of special interest is news of the semiconductor industry in foreign countries such as Japan, England, Germany, France, and the Netherlands." Buys 30-40 mss/year. Query. Length: 200-1,500 words. Pays 15¢/word for accepted, edited copy.
Tips: "The most frequent mistake made by writers in completing an article for us is lack of understanding of the semiconductor fabricating industry."

WEIGHING & MEASUREMENT, Key Markets Publishing Co., Box 5867, Rockford IL 61125. (815)399-6970. Editor: David M. Mathieu. For users of industrial scales and meters. Bimonthly magazine; 32 pages. Circ. 15,000. Pays on acceptance. Buys all rights. Pays 20% kill fee. Byline given. Reports in 2 weeks. Free sample copy.
Nonfiction: Interview (with presidents of companies); personal opinion (guest editorials on government involvement in business, etc.); profile (about users of weighing and measurement equipment); and technical. Buys 25 mss/year. Query on technical articles; submit complete ms for general interest material. Length: 750-2,500 words. Pays $45-125.

Insurance

● **COMPASS**, Marine Office of America Corporation (MOAC), 180 Maiden Lane, New York NY 10038. (212)440-7720. Editor: Irene E. Lombardo. 75% freelance written. Annual magazine of the Marine Office of America Corporation. Magazine is distributed to persons in marine insurance (agents, brokers, risk managers) and the media. Circ. 8,000. Pays half on acceptance, half on publication. Publishes ms an average of 6 months after acceptance. Byline given. Offers $250 kill fee. Not copyrighted. Buys first North American serial rights. Does not accept previously published work or unsolicited mss. Query first. Simultaneous queries OK. Computer printout submissions acceptable; no dot-matrix. Reports in 2 weeks on queries. Free sample copy and writer's guidelines.
Nonfiction: General interest, historical/nostalgic and technical. "Historical/nostalgia should relate to ships, trains, airplanes, balloons, bridges, sea and land expeditions, seaports and transportation of all types. General interest includes marine and transportation subjects; fishing industry; and environmental events—improvements relating to inland waterways, space travel and satellites. Articles must have human interest. Technical articles may cover energy exploration and development—offshore oil and gas drilling, developing new sources of electric power and solar energy; usages of coal, water and wind to generate electric power; and special cargo handling such as containerization on land and sea. Articles must not be overly technical and should have reader interest." No book excerpts, exposes, how-to, humor or opinion. Buys 5 mss/year. Query with or without published clips. Length: 1,500-2,000 words. Pays $1,000 maximum. Sometimes pays the expenses of writers on assignment.
Photos: Robert A. Cooney, photo editor. (212)838-6200. State availability of photos. Reviews b&w and color transparencies and prints. Captions and identification of subjects required. Buys one-time rights.
Tips: "Send a brief outline of the story idea to editor mentioning also the availability of photographs in b&w and color. All articles must be thoroughly researched and original. Articles should have human interest through the device of interviews. We only publish full-length articles—no fillers."

PROFESSIONAL AGENT MAGAZINE, Professional Insurance Agents, 400 N. Washington St., Alexandria VA 22314. (703)836-9340. Editor/Publisher: Janice J. Artandi. 25% freelance written. Monthly magazine covering insurance/small business for independent insurance agents. Circ. 40,000. Pays on acceptance. Byline given. Buys exclusive rights in the industry. Computer printout submissions acceptable. SASE. Reports ASAP. Sample copy for SAE.
Nonfiction: Insurance management for small businesses and self-help. Special issues on life insurance and computer interface. Buys 24 mss/year. Query with published clips or send complete ms. Length: 1,000-3,000 words. Pays $100-500.
Photos: State availability of photos. Pays $35-200 for 5x7 b&w prints; $50-300 for 35mm color transparencies. Captions, model release and identification of subjects required. Buys one-time rights.

International Affairs

These publications cover global relations, international trade, economic analysis and philosophy for business executives and government officials involved in foreign affairs. Consumer publications on related subjects are listed in Politics and World Affairs.

‡**FOREIGN AFFAIRS**, 58 E. 68th St., New York NY 10021. (212)734-0400. Editor: William G. Hyland. 100% freelance written. For academics, businessmen (national and international), government, educational and cultural readers especially interested in international affairs of a political nature. Published 5 times/year. Circ. 90,000. Publishes ms an average of 3 months in advance. Buys all rights. Pays kill fee. Byline given. Buys 45 mss/year. Photocopied submissions OK. Electronic submissions OK via 8" disk: Wang; Modem: 300-1200 Baud), but requires hard copy also. Computer printout submissions acceptable; prefers letter-quality to dot-matrix. Reports in 6 weeks. Submit complete ms. SASE. Pays on publication. Sample copy $5 postpaid.
Nonfiction: "Articles dealing with international affairs; political, educational, cultural, economic, scientific, philosophical and social sciences. Develop an original idea in depth, with a strong thesis usually leading to policy recommendations. Serious analyses by qualified authors on subjects with international appeal." Recent article example: "The President's Choice: Star Wars or Arms Control" (Winter 1984/85). Buys 25 unsolicited mss/year. Length: 5,000 words. Pays approximately $500.
Tips: "We like the writer to include his/her qualifications for writing on the topic in question (educational), past publications, relevant positions or honors), and a clear summation of the article: the argument (or area examined), and the writer's policy conclusions."

‡**JOURNAL OF DEFENSE & DIPLOMACY**, Defense and Diplomacy Inc., 6819 Elm St., McLean VA 22101. (703)448-1338. Editor: Jean-Loup R. Combemale. Managing Editor: Lois M. Blake. 10% freelance written. Monthly publication covering international affairs and defense. "The *Journal* is a sophisticated, slick publication that analyzes international affairs for decision makers—heads of state, key government officials, defense industry executives—who have little time to pore through all the details themselves." Circ. 12,000. Pays on acceptance. Publishes ms an average of 3 months after acceptance. Byline given. Offers 10% kill fee. Buys first rights and second serial (reprint) rights. Simultaneous queries, and simultaneous, photocopied, and previously published submissions OK. Computer printout submissions acceptable; prefers letter-quality to dot-matrix. SASE. Reports in 1 month on queries; 2 months on mss. Sample copy $5 (includes postage); writer's guidelines for business size envelope and 1 first class stamp.
Nonfiction: Book excerpts, general interest (strategy and tactics, diplomacy and defense matters), interview/profile, opinion and photo feature. "Decision makers are looking for intelligent, straightforward assessments. We are looking for clear, concise writing on articles with international appeal. While we have accepted articles that deal with U.S. decisions, there is always an international aspect to the subject." No articles that focus solely on the United States. Buys 24 mss/year. Send complete ms. Length: 2,000-4,000 words. Pays $250. Pays expenses of writers on assignment.
Photos: Reviews color and b&w photos. No additional payment is offered for photos sent with ms.
Columns/Departments: Speaking Out (1,000 to 3,000-word "point of view" piece analyzing any current topic of widespread interest); Materiel (a technical discussion of current and upcoming weapons systems); Books (reviews of books on world politics, history, biography and military matters); interview ("We constantly need interviews with important international figures. We are always looking for the non-U.S. interview."). Buys 6-8 mss/year. Query with published clips. Length: 1,500-3,000 words. Pays $100-250.

Tips: "We depend on experts in the field for most of the articles that we use. As long as a manuscript demonstrates that the writer knows the subject well, we are willing to consider anyone for publication. The most frequent mistake made by writers in completing an article for us is writing in too technical or too official a style. We want to be very readable. We are looking for writers who are able to digest complex subjects and make them interesting and lively. We need writers who can discuss complicated and technical weapons systems in clear nontechnical ways."

‡**THE NATIONAL REPORTER**, (formerly *Counterspy*), Box 647, Ben Franklin Station, Washington DC 20044. (202)328-0178. Editor: John Kelly. 30% freelance written. Bimonthly magazine covering the CIA, IMF, World Bank, foreign policy and corporations. Circ. 6,000. Pays on publication. Publishes ms an average of 2 months after acceptance. Byline given. Buys all rights and makes work-for-hire assignments. Submit seasonal/holiday material 1 month in advance. Photocopied and previously published submissions OK. SASE. Computer printout submissions acceptable; no dot-matrix. Reports in 2 weeks on queries; 3 weeks on mss. Free sample copy and writer's guidelines.
Nonfiction: Expose (government and U.S. corporation), humor, interview/profile, personal experience and photo feature. No "right wing" articles. Buys 10 mss/year. Send complete ms. Length: 2,500-5,000 words. Pays $50 maximum.
Columns/Departments: News Not In the News (important stories ignored by the mainstream media). Buys 10 mss/year. Send complete ms. Length: 1,000 words maximum. Pays $20 maximum.
Fiction: Experimental, historical and novel excerpts. Buys 2 mss/year. Send complete ms. Length: 1,500 words maximum. Pays $25 minimum.
Poetry: Avant-garde and free verse. Buys 7 poems/year. Submit 5 poems maximum. Line length open. Pays $25 maximum.
Fillers: Rose Audette, fillers editor. Clippings, jokes, gags, anecdotes, short humor and newsbreaks. Buys 20 fillers/year. Length: 500 maximum. Pays $10 maximum.
Tips: "We want well written and fully-documented materials."

PROBLEMS OF COMMUNISM, US Information Agency, P/PMP, Room 402, 301 4th St., Washington DC 20547. (202)485-2230. Editor: Paul A. Smith Jr. For scholars and decision makers in all countries of the world with higher education and a serious interest in foreign area studies and international relations. Circ. 28,905 (English language); 5,400 (Spanish language). Not copyrighted. Pays 20% kill fee. Byline given. Buys 60-70 mss/year. Pays on acceptance. Usually buys all rights. Photocopied submissions OK. Reports in 3 months. Free sample copy.
Nonfiction: "*Problems of Communism* is one of a very few journals devoted to objective, dispassionate discourse on a highly unobjective, passionately debated phenomenon: communism. It is maintained as a forum in which qualified observers can contribute to a clearer understanding of the sources, nature and direction of change in the areas of its interest. It has no special emphasis or outlook and represents no partisan point of view. Standards of style are those appropriate to the field of international scholarship and journalism. We use intellectually rigorous studies of East/West relations, and/or related political, economic, social and strategic trends in the U.S.S.R., China and their associated states and movements. Length is usually 5,000 words. Essay reviews of 1,500 words cover new books offering significant information and analysis. Emphasis throughout *Problems of Communism* is on original research, reliability of sources and perceptive insights. We do not publish political statements or other forms of advocacy or apologetics for particular forms of belief." Query or submit complete ms. Pays $600/article; $300/essay reviews.
Photos: Pays minimum $45 for b&w glossy prints.

Jewelry

AMERICAN JEWELRY MANUFACTURER, 8th Floor, 825 7th Ave., New York NY 10019. (212)245-7555. Editor: Steffan Aletti. For jewelry manufacturers, as well as manufacturers of supplies and tools for the jewelry industry; their representatives, wholesalers and agencies. 5% freelance written. Monthly. Circ. 5,000. Buys all rights (with exceptions). Publishes ms an average of 5 months after acceptance. Byline given. Will consider photocopied submissions. Computer printout submissions acceptable. Submit seasonal material 3 months in advance. Reports in 1 month. SASE. Free sample copy and writer's guidelines.
Nonfiction: "Topical articles on manufacturing; company stories; economics (e.g., rising gold prices). Story must inform or educate the manufacturer. Occasional special issues on timely topics, e.g., gold; occasional issues on specific processes in casting and plating. We reject material that is not specifically pointed at our indus-

try; e.g., articles geared to jewelry retailing or merchandising, not to manufacturers." Informational, how-to, interview, profile, historical, expose, successful business operations, new product, merchandising techniques and technical. Buys 5-10 unsolicited mss/year. Query. Length: Open. Payment "usually around $50/printed page."

Photos: B&w photos purchased with ms. 5x7 minimum.

Tips: "The most frequent mistake made by writers in completing an article for us is unfamiliarity with the magazine—retail or merchandising oriented articles are sent in. Query first; we have accepted some general business articles, but not many."

‡**CANADIAN JEWELLER**, 777 Bay St., Toronto, Ontario M5W 1A7 Canada. Editor: Simon Hally. Monthly magazine for members of the jewelry trade, primarily retailers. Circ. 6,000. Pays on acceptance. Buys first Canadian serial rights.

Nonfiction: Wants "stories on the jewelry industry internationally. No stories on the U.S. jewelry business." Query. Length: 200-2,000 words. Pays $40-500.

Photos: Reviews 5x7 and 8x10 b&w prints and 35mm and 2¼x2¼ color transparencies. "We pay more if usable photos accompany ms. Payment is based on space used in the book including both text and photos."

THE DIAMOND REGISTRY BULLETIN, 30 W. 47th St., New York NY 10036. Editor-in-Chief: Joseph Schlussel. 15% freelance written. Monthly newsletter. Pays on publication. Buys all rights. Submit seasonal/holiday material 1 month in advance. Simultaneous and previously published submissions OK. Computer printout submissions acceptable; prefers letter-quality to dot-matrix. SASE. Reports in 3 weeks. Sample copy $5.

Nonfiction: Prevention advice (on crimes against jewelers); how-to (ways to increase sales in diamonds, improve security, etc.); and interview (of interest to diamond dealers or jewelers). Submit complete ms. Length: 50-500 words. Pays $10-150.

Tips: "We seek ideas to increase sales of diamonds."

SOUTHERN JEWELER, 75 3rd St. NW, Atlanta GA 30365. (404)881-6442. Editor: Roy Conradi. 15% freelance written. For Southern retail jewelers and watchmakers. Monthly. Circ. 8,500. Not copyrighted. Buys first rights only. Pays on publication. Publishes ms an average of 3 months after acceptance. Submit seasonal material 2 months in advance. Computer printout submissions acceptable; no dot-matrix. SASE. Sample copy and writer's guidelines for SAE and $1.50 postage.

Nonfiction: Articles related to Southern retail jewelers regarding advertising, management and merchandising. Buys spot news about Southern jewelers and coverage of successful business operations. Prefers *not* to see material concerning jewelers outside the 14 Southern states. No articles on general sales techniques. Recent article example: cover feature on a typical case history article on a retail jeweler in the South (January 1985). Buys 12 unsolicited mss/year. Length: Open. Pays $50-150 for features; $2/clipping.

Photos: Buys b&w glossies. Pays $5.

Tips: "Query should describe specifically the type of article proposed. Writer should be based in the South. Ideally, he/she should have retail jewelry trade background, but a good writer can pick up technical points from us. (Samples of features used in past will be sent upon request.) Write specifically to our audience. We get an unbiased view of the jewelry industry which is the most rewarding/exhilarating aspect of working with freelance writers. Send a sample of your work related to any trade or industry, along with a couple of b&w pictures of the subject character and the establishment. With short articles and fillers we get to know the writer's style before assigning feature stories."

WATCH AND CLOCK REVIEW, 2403 Champa St., Denver CO 80205. (303)296-1600. Managing Editor: Jayne L. Barrick. 20% freelance written. The magazine of watch/clock sales and service. Monthly magazine; 68 pages. Circ. 16,000. Pays on publication. Buys first rights only. Byline given. Submit seasonal/holiday material 3 months in advance. SASE. Reports in 3 weeks. Free sample copy.

Nonfiction: Articles on successful watch/clock manufacturers and retailers; merchandising and display; and profiles of industry leaders. Buys 15 mss/year. Query. Length: 1,000-2,000 words. Pays $100-250.

Photos: Submit photo material with accompanying ms. No additional payment for b&w glossy prints. Captions preferred. Buys first rights. Model release required.

Columns/Departments: Buys 7 mss/issue. Pays $150-200. Open to suggestions for new columns/departments.

Tips: "Brevity is helpful in a query. Find the right subject—an interesting clock shop, a jewelry store with unique watch displays, a street clock of antiquarian interest, etc."

Journalism

Journalism magazines cover the business and creative ends of writing. Even if you never send a query to one, you'll see how other writers approach their work and learn about new marketing strategies and markets. *The Christian Writer*, for example, sees romantic fiction as a trend that may affect what its editors buy. "Fiction, especially romantic (inspirational) fiction, will be changing rapidly in 1986, so we'll be looking at the aspects of writing fiction and how it applies to Christian writers," said editor/publisher Thomas Noton. Journalism magazine editors need writers whose experiences will be an inspiration to new writers. They also need writers who can report new trends and markets for *their* readers. "Usually writers fail to recognize our readership," said *Canadian Author & Bookman* editor Anne Osborne. "Aiming a story about writing for southern U.S. markets at a 95 percent Canadian audience presumes we have no publishers in our own country." Both paying and nonpaying markets of the writing trade are included here. Writers wishing to contribute material to these publications should query about requirements before submitting their work.

‡**ALTERNATIVE MEDIA**, Alternative Press Syndicate, Ansonia Station, Box 1347, New York NY 10023. (212)974-1990. Editor: R.J. Smith. 75% freelance written. Quarterly magazine. "We publish criticism of the major news media and write about the artists, writers and reporters getting less attention than they deserve." Circ. 5,000. Pays on publication. Publishes ms an average of 2 months after acceptance. Byline given. Buys one-time rights. Submit seasonal/holiday material 1 month in advance. Simultaneous queries, and simultaneous, photocopied, and previously published submissions OK. SASE. Reports in 1 month. Sample copy $2.
Nonfiction: Book excerpts, expose, general interest, interview/profile, opinion and personal experience. Buys 35-45 mss/year. Query with or without published clips or send complete ms. Length: 1,000-3,000 words. Pays $25-100,

THE AMERICAN SCREENWRITER, Grasshopper Productions, Inc., Box 67, Manchaca TX 78642. (512)282-2749. Editor: Gerald J. LePage. 25% freelance written. A bimonthly newsletter covering scriptwriting for the screen and TV. "We address scriptwriters who ask for help through our script evaluation program. We aim at writers who are struggling to find their place in the market." Estab. 1984. Circ. 52 and growing. Pays by arrangement with author. Publishes ms an average of 2 months after acceptance. Byline given. Buys all rights. Submit seasonal/holiday material 2 months in advance. Simultaneous queries OK. SASE. Reports in 1 month. Sample copy $3; writer's guidelines for SAE and 1 first class stamp.
Nonfiction: Book excerpts, interview/profile, and personal experience related to scriptwriting. "No sophisticated material that oozes of past films which require reader having seen them." Query with published clips. Length: 300-500 words. Pays 5-10¢/word; interviews pay $30; pays $50/article.
Tips: "The Plight of the Screenwriter section and interviews with other writers are most open to freelancers. We want 'visual' writing—short, comprehensive articles that bring home a problematical point in less than five minute's reading. Suggests writers study publication.

BOOK ARTS REVIEW, The Center for Book Arts, 626 Broadway, New York NY 10012. (212)460-9768. Managing Editor: Bryan R. Johnson. Emphasizes bookbinding, printing and exploring the arts of the book. Quarterly newsletter; 6 pages. Circ. 1,000. Pays in copies. Publishes ms an average of 3 months after acceptance. "Rights revert to artist." Byline given. Submit seasonal/holiday material 3 months in advance. Simultaneous, photocopied and previously published submissions OK. Computer printout submissions acceptable. Reports in 2 months. SASE.
Nonfiction: Reviews (exhibitions, lectures, conferences, shows, etc. dealing with printing, bookbinding, papermaking, calligraphy or preservation); and interview (with book artists). No censorship, fiction, or material dealing with writing. Query. Pays in copies.

BOOK DEALERS WORLD, American Bookdealers Exchange, Box 2525, La Mesa CA 92041. (619)462-3297. Editorial Director: Al Galasso. Senior Editor: Cynthia Schubert. Consulting Editor: Lon Choate. 50% freelance written. Quarterly magazine covering writing, self-publishing and marketing books by mail. Circ. 20,000. Pays on publication. Publishes ms an average of 3 months after acceptance. Byline given. Buys first rights and second (reprint) rights to material originally published elsewhere. Simultaneous and previously published submissions OK. Computer printout submissions acceptable; no dot-matrix. SASE. Reports in 1 month. Sample copy and writer's guidelines for $1.
Nonfiction: Book excerpts (writing, mail order, direct mail, publishing); how-to (home business by mail, ad-

vertising); and interview/profile (of successful self-publishers). Positive articles on self-publishing, new writing angles, marketing, etc. Buys 10 mss/year. Send complete ms. Length: 1,000-1,500 words. Pays $25-50.
Columns/Departments: Print Perspective (about new magazines and newsletters); Small Press Scene (news about small press activities); and Self-Publisher Profile (on successful self-publishers and their marketing stratgey). Buys 20 mss/year. Send complete ms. Length: 250-1,000 words. Pays $5-20.
Fillers: Clippings. "Fillers to do with writing, publishing or books." Buys 6/year. Length: 100-250 words. Pays $3-10.
Tips: "In the year ahead we'll be using more success-oriented pieces on self-publishing and marketing books along with more in-depth interviews. Query first. Get sample copy of the magazine."

BOOKSTORE JOURNAL, The How-to Magazine, Christian Booksellers Association Service Corp., Box 200, 2620 Venetucci Blvd., Colorado Springs CO 80901. (303)576-7880. Editor: Steve Rabey. Monthly magazine for owners and managers of Christian bookstores. Circ. 8,300. Pays on publication. Byline given. Buys all rights; makes work-for-hire assignments. Submit seasonal/holiday material 3 months in advance. Previously published submissions OK (occasionally). SASE. Reports in 1 month on queries; 3 months on mss. Sample copy $3; free writer's guidelines.
Nonfiction: How-to (relating to retail management); new product (for Christian bookstore market); industry-related news and management and marketing information. Buys 120 mss/year. Query with published clips. Length: 800-1,800 words. Pays $100/30 inches of printed copy.
Photos: State availability of photos. Pays $10-25 for 5x7 b&w prints. Model release and identification of subjects required.
Tips: "Send us an informative, comprehensive article on retail business management that meets the needs of Christian booksellers in the U.S.and Canada, and to a lesser extent, the free world."

BYLINE, McCarville Publications, 1148 S. Douglas, Box 30647, Midwest City OK 73140. (405)733-1129. Editor: Mike McCarville. 100% freelance written. A monthly magazine covering poetry and writing. "We stress encouragement of beginning writers." Circ. 2,694. Pays on acceptance. Publishes ms an average of 9 months after acceptance. Byline given. Buys first North American serial rights. Submit seasonal/holiday material 6 months in advance. SASE. Reports in 2 months. Sample copy $2.75; writer's guidelines for SAE and 20¢ postage.
Nonfiction: How-to (write and sell); humor; inspirational; and personal experience. Buys 700 mss/year. Send complete ms. Length: 50-2,500 words. Pays $5-250.
Fiction: Mysteries with a literary setting or twist. No science fiction. Buys approximately 70 mss/year. Send complete ms. Length: 1,000-2,500 words. Pays $50 minimum.
Poetry: Free verse, light verse and traditional. Buys 200 poems/year. Submit maximum 5 poems. Length: 4-36 words. Pays $2 minimum.

CALIFORNIA PUBLISHER, Suite 1040, 1127 11th St., Sacramento CA 95814. (916)443-5991. Editor: Jackie Nava. 5% freelance written. Monthly tabloid read by publishers, journalism teachers, editors and managers in newspaper publishing in California. Publishes ms an average of 2 months after acceptance. Byline given. Buys first and second rights to the same material. Computer printout submissions acceptable; prefers letter-quality to dot-matrix.
Nonfiction: In-depth stories or articles designed to inform and amuse California newspaper publishers. Sample topics include: newsprint shortage, changing role of papers, historical profiles on California journalism greats, success stories, role of minorities in the newspaper field, profiles on California newspapers, and technological advances. No general "humorous" material. "If it isn't specific to *California* journalism, we don't want it." Query. Length: 2,000 words maximum. Pays $25-30.
Photos: Reviews b&w glossy prints.
Tips: "Go on; query us! Stories used will be read by all the newspaper publishers who count in the state of California. We'd like to showcase first effort, good writing talent."

CANADIAN AUTHOR & BOOKMAN, Canadian Authors Association, 24 Ryerson Ave., Toronto, Ontario M5T 2P3 Canada. Editor: Anne Osborne. 75% freelance written. "For writers—all ages, all levels of experience." Quarterly magazine; 32 pages. Circ. 5,000. Pays on publication. Publishes ms an average of 4 months after acceptance. Buys first Canadian rights. Byline given. Written queries only. Computer printout submissions acceptable; no dot-matrix. SASE (Canadian stamps). Sample copy $3.50.
Nonfiction: How-to (on writing, selling; the specifics of the different genres—what they are and how to write them); informational (the writing scene—who's who and what's what); interview (on writers, mainly leading ones, but also those with a story that can help others write and sell more often); and opinion. No personal, lightweight writing experiences; no fillers. Query with immediate pinpointing of topic, length (if ms is ready), and writer's background. Length: 800-1,500 words. Pays 2½¢/word.
Photos: "We're after an interesting-looking magazine, and graphics are a decided help." State availability of photos with query. Offers $5/photo for b&w photos accepted with ms. Buys one-time rights.

Poetry: High quality. "Major poets publish with us—others need to be as good." Buys 40 poems/year. Pays $5.

Tips: "We dislike material that condescends to its reader and articles that advocate an adversarial approach to writer/editor relationships. We agree that there is a time and place for such an approach, but good sense should prevail."

‡**CANADIAN WRITER'S JOURNAL**, Ronald J. Cooke Ltd., 58 Madsen Ave., Beaconsfield, Quebec H9W 4T7 Canada. (514)697-9315. Editor: Ronald S. Cooke. 50% freelance written. A bimonthly digest-size magazine for writers. Estab. 1984. Circ. 3,000. Pays on publication. Byline given. "We seldom use anything pertaining to holidays." Computer printout submissions acceptable. SASE; send coins if no Canadian stamps available. Reports in 2 weeks on queries; 1 month on mss. Sample copy $2.

Nonfiction: How-to articles for writers. Buys 30-35 mss/year. Query. Length: 500-1,000 words.

Tips: "The most frequent mistake made by writers is sending manuscripts that are too long. We prefer short, how-to articles; 1,000 words is our limit and we prefer 700 words."

CHILDREN'S LITERATURE, The Children's Literature Foundation, Box 370, Windham Center CT 06280. (203)456-1900. Editor: Francelia Butler. Managing Editor: John C. Wandell. 90% freelance written. Annual; 250 pages. Circ. 3,500. Pays in reprints. Publishes ms an average of 1 month after acceptance. Byline given. Phone queries OK. Submit seasonal/holiday material 1 year in advance. SASE. Reports in 1 month.

Nonfiction: Scholarly or critical articles *only*—not creative work. Manuscripts must conform to MLA Handbook. Uses 20 mss/issue. Query or send complete ms. Length: 5,000 words.

Photos: State availability of photos. Uses 4x5 or 8x10 b&w glossy prints. Captions and permission to publish required.

Columns/Departments: Book review articles (send to Prof. John Cech, University of Florida, Gainesville FL 32611). Uses 20/year. Query. Length: 3,000 words. Open to suggestions for new columns/departments.

Tips: "This is a scholarly journal."

THE CHRISTIAN WRITER, The Professional Writing Magazine for Christians, Box 5650, Lakeland FL 33807. (813)644-3548. Editor: Thomas A Noton. Associate Editor: Jana Daimmelen. Monthly writing magazine aimed at a Christian audience. "We reach Christians who desire to write or are writers. Our aim is to help create the professional approach to this craft." Circ. 15,000. Acquires first rights; no reprints. Submit seasonal/holiday material 4 months in advance. Simultaneous queries and photocopied submissions OK. Computer printout submissions acceptable; no dot-matrix.SASE. Reports in 1 month on queries; 6 weeks on mss. Sample copy $2 and 9x12 SAE. Writer's guidelines require #10 SAE with 1 first class stamp.

Nonfiction: How-to (specifics on authoring, selling, related subjects); humor (rare); inspirational (limited); interview/profile (top Christian authors); new product (electronic writing); and personal experience (some). Material on conferences, workshops, clubs, etc. for annual Service Guide. "We receive too many 'this is my life' articles. We want more specific articles helping others overcome specialized problems in authoring." Buys 36-50 mss/year. Query with writing credits. Length: 800-2,500 words. Pays $10 minimum for fillers to $150 for feature articles. Payment depends on need and article. Sometimes pays expenses of writer on assignment.

Tips: "We're looking for freelancers who have answers for specific problems in writing, marketing, querying, rewriting, or editing. We are only interested in professionalism as it applies to the craft of writing. Although we use the Christian influence, we do not deal with it directly. We deal with the craft, its problems and answers. The most frequent mistake made by writers is in slant and style—they haven't studied our publication enough."

COLLEGE MEDIA REVIEW, Dept. of Journalism, Ball State University, Muncie IN 47306. Contact: Lillian Lodge-Kopenhaver. Dept. of Communications, Florida International University, North Miami FL 33181. Quarterly magazine for members of College Media Advisers and staffs, editors and faculty advisers of college publications, journalism professors, and others interested in student communication media. Circ. 1,200. Acquires all rights. No payment. Photocopied submissions OK. SASE. Reports in 5 months. Sample copy $2.50; free writer's guidelines.

Nonfiction: Articles by, about and of interest to college publications advisers, staffs and editors. Articles should focus on editing, advising and producing college newspapers, yearbooks and magazines and operating electronic media, including radio, television and cable. "We like to use articles reporting research in publications and journalistic skills and well-thought-out opinion and essays on issues in the student media. Legal research specifically is welcome. Articles should be in a readable style with adequate attribution but without overuse of footnotes." Topical subjects of interest include increasing income, reducing costs, promoting publications, use of new technology, censorship cases at private colleges, tips on purchasing new equipment, how-to articles, and advances in techniques and resources. Query or submit complete ms. Submit 2 copies of all mss. Length: 3,000 words maximum.

Photos: B&w glossy photos used with ms. Captions required.

COLUMBIA JOURNALISM REVIEW, 700 Journalism Bldg., Columbia University, New York NY 10027. (212)280-5595. Managing Editor: Gloria Cooper. "We welcome queries concerning media issues and performance. *CJR* also publishes book reviews. We emphasize in-depth reporting, critical analysis and good writing. All queries are read by editors."

COMPUTER BOOK REVIEW, Comber Press, P.O. Box 37127, Honolulu HI 96837. (808)595-7337. Editor: Carlene Char. 25% freelance written. A monthly magazine that critically reviews and rates microcomputer books. Electronic edition on News Net. Circ. 2,000. Byline given. Publishes ms an average of 1 month after acceptance. Buys all rights; "author may freely use work later, with written permission from Comber Press." Electronic submissions OK on 5¼" floppy disks, IBM-PC DOS format preferred, but prefers hard copy also. Computer printout submissions acceptable. SASE. Reports in 1 week. Sample copy $2; writer's guidelines for SASE.
Nonfiction: Book reviews only. Send complete ms. Length: 250 words. Pays in copies.

CREATIVE YEARS Coronado Publishers, #40, 2490 SW 14th Dr., Gainesville FL 32608. (904)373-7445. Editor: Eloise Cozens Henderson. Associate Editors: Mary Onkka and Rose Mary Pleiman. 20% freelance written. Bimonthly magazine for new and unpublished writers. Circ. 2,000. Pays on publication. Publishes ms an average of 9 months after acceptance. Buys one-time rights. Submit seasonal/holiday material 3 months in advance. Simultaneous submissions OK. SASE. Reports in 3 weeks on queries; 3 months on mss. Sample copy $2; writer's guidelines for SASE.
Nonfiction: General interest, historical/nostalgic, interview, humor, inspirational, opinion and personal experience. "We have an overload of writer's advice. We now feature experiences and articles by disabled people, i.e., 'Profiles in Courage.' " No obscenity, profanity, or liquor/drug related articles. Buys 30 mss/year. Length: 450-500 words. Send complete ms. Pays presently in copies only.
Fiction: Humorous, historical and religious. No obscenity, profanity, liquor/drug related mss. Buys 30 mss/year. Length: 450-500 words. Send complete ms. Pays in copies only.
Poetry: Light verse, traditional. No far out, agnostic, atheist, etc. poetry. Buys 12 poems/year. Pays in copies only.
Tips: "We use mostly material of beginning writers. We especially need Biblical quiz and other puzzle material. We are also seeking short articles about old times in sports (Babe Ruth, Ty Cobb, etc.)."

CROSS-CANADA WRITERS' QUARTERLY, The Canadian Writer's Magazine, Cross-Canada Writers Inc., Box 277, Station F, Toronto, Ontario M4Y 2L7 Canada. (416)690-0917. Editor: Ted Plantos. Associate Editor: Susan Ioannou. 80% freelance written. A quarterly literary writer's magazine covering Canadian writing within an international context. Circ. 2,500. Pays on publication. Publishes ms an average of 1 year after acceptance. Byline given. Buys first North American serial rights. Submit seasonal/holiday material 6 months in advance. Photocopied submissions OK. Computer printout submissions acceptable. SASE. Reports in 3 weeks on queries; 2 months on mss. Sample copy $3.95, 9x12 SAE, and 80¢ Canadian postage or 2 IRCs.
Nonfiction: How-to (literary, slanted for poetry and fiction); and interview/profile (established authors, editors, publishers—in-depth with photos). "Articles and interviews must have depth, be thought-provoking and offer practical advice and background information." No how-to's on nonliterary kinds of writing. Buys 4-10 mss/year. Query or send complete ms. "Each case is different. With an interview, a query could save time and work. A straight article we would have to read."
Photos: State availability of accompanying photos with query or send photos with ms, 5x7 b&w prints. Captions, model release and identification of subjects required. Buys one-time rights.
Fiction: Contact fiction editor. Mainstream. No slight material—mere anecdotes rather than fully developed stories. Buys 4-8 mss/year. Send complete ms. Length: 1,000-3,000 words. Payment on publication.
Poetry: Poetry Editor. Free verse, haiku and traditional (if well-done). No concrete poetry, "diary excerpts" merely, highly obscure private poems or doggerel. Buys 40-50 poems/year. Submit maximum 10 poems. Length: 100 lines maximum "in exceptional cases." Offers contributor copies as payment.
Tips: "The most frequent mistakes made by writers in completing an article for us are misunderstanding of slant, and missing the opportunity for in-depth analysis."

EDITOR & PUBLISHER, 11 W. 19th St., New York NY 10011. Editor: Robert U. Brown. 10% freelance written. Weekly magazine; 60 pages. For newspaper publishers, editors, executives, employees and others in communications, marketing, advertising, etc. Circ. 29,000. Pays on publication. Publishes ms an average of 2 weeks after acceptance. Buys first serial rights only. Computer printout submissions acceptable; prefers letter-quality to dot-matrix. SASE. Sample copy $1.
Nonfiction: John P. Consoli, department editor. Uses newspaper business articles and news items; also newspaper personality features and printing technology. Query.
Fillers: "Amusing typographical errors found in newspapers." Pays $5.

‡**THE EDITORIAL EYE, Focusing on Editorial Standards and Practices**, Editorial Experts, Inc., Suite 400, 85 S. Bragg St., Alexandria VA 22312. (703)823-3223. Editor: Bruce Boston. Managing editor: Eleanor Johnson. 5% freelance written. Monthly professional newsletter on editorial subjects: writing, editing, proofreading, and levels of editing. "Our readers are professional publications people." Use journalistic style." Circ. 1,600. Pays on acceptance. Publishes ms an average of 3 months after acceptance. Byline given. Kill fee determined for each assignment. Buys first North American serial rights. "We retain the right to use article in our training division and in an anthology of collected articles." Submit seasonal/holiday material 3 months in advance. Computer printout submissions acceptable; prefers letter-quality to dot-matrix. Reports in 1 month. Sample copy for SASE and 39¢ postage; writer's guidelines for SAE and 1 first class stamp.
Nonfiction: Editorial problems, issues, standards, practices, and techniques; publication management; publishing technology; style, grammar and usage. No word games, vocabulary building, language puzzles, or jeremiads on how the English language is going to blazes. Buys 3 mss/year. Query. Length: 300-1,000. Pays $25-50.
Tips: "We seek mostly lead articles written by people in the publications field about the practice of publications work. Our back issue list provides a good idea of the kinds of articles we run."

EMPIRE, for the SF Writer, c/o Unique Graphics, 1025 55th St., Oakland CA 94608. (415)655-3024. Editor: Millea Kenin. 99% freelance written. Quarterly magazine covering writing, editing and publishing science fiction and fantasy. "*Empire's* aim is to assist, entertain and inform science fiction and fantasy writers." Circ. 1,500. Pays on publication. Publishes ms an average of 6 months after acceptance. Byline given. Buys first English language serial rights, and occasionally second (reprint) serial rights. Simultaneous queries and photocopied submissions OK if simultaneous are so identified. "We are completely receptive to computer printout submissions as long as they are NOT dot-matrix. Dot-matrix printouts will be returned unread." SASE. Reports in 1 month or less. Sample copy $2, payable to Unique Graphics. Guidelines available for SASE.
Nonfiction: Expose (of publishing industry); how-to (on specific writing and marketing techniques and skills for science fiction & fantasy); humor (about the science fiction writer's life; "If you find any, send it to us."); interview/profile (of writers, editors, agents, publishers, filmmakers involved in the SF genre); personal experience ("how I wrote and sold"); and technical (science fact with application to science fiction). "We use articles about writing, editing and publishing *science fiction and fantasy*; our material is written by professional science fiction writers for would-be professional science fiction writers. We are not interested in general articles for the beginning writer. We take a practical nuts-and-bolts approach." Buys 32 mss/year. Query with proposal if you have not previously written for *Empire*. Length: 1,000-3,500 words. Offers contributor copies as payment and a one-year subscription. Pay negotiable to regular contributors.
Fiction: Crazy Diamonds. "Each issue contains one story which has failed to sell elsewhere and three critiques of the story by professional science fiction writers. We use no other fiction." Buys 4 mss/year. Length: 3,500 words maximum, shorter preferred. Offers contributor copies as payment and subscription.
Poetry: "Short humorous or serious verse about the act of writing science fiction or the science fiction writer's life."
Tips: "If you have not seen a copy of *Empire* and are not closely involved with the science fiction genre, it is better to query with a proposal rather than submitting an unsolicited article."

feed/back, THE CALIFORNIA JOURNALISM REVIEW, 1600 Holloway, San Francisco CA 94132. (415)469-2086. Editor: Shannon Bryony. 50% freelance written. For working journalists, journalism students, professors and news buffs. Magazine; 48 pages. Quarterly. Circ. 1,750. Byline given. Offers subscriptions and copies as payment. Publishes ms an average of 3 months after acceptance. Will consider photocopied and simultaneous submissions. Computer printout submissions acceptable "if good quality with ascenders/descenders." Reports in 2 months. Query. SASE mandatory. Sample copy $3; writer's guidelines for SAE and 1 first class stamp.
Nonfiction: In-depth views of California journalism. Criticism of journalistic trends throughout the country, but with a local angle. Reviews of books concerning journalism. Informational, interview, profile, humor, historical, think pieces, expose, nostalgia, spot news, successful (or unsuccessful) business operations, new product, and technical; all must be related to California journalism. "Articles must focus on the state press and be of interest to professional journalists—they are our audience. We like articles that examine press performance—strengths and weaknesses; we also like personality articles on offbeat or little-known editors and journalists who escape national attention." Rejects articles that are not documented, or those in which the subject matter is not pertinent or those which show personal prejudice not supported by evidence. Length: 1,000-5,000 words.
Photos: B&w glossies (8x10 or 11x14) used with or without mss. Offers subscriptions and/or copies as payment.

FOLIO: The Magazine for Magazine Management, 125 Elm St., Box 4006, New Canaan CT 06840-4006. Editor-in-Chief: J. Hanson. 5% freelance written. Mostly staff written. Publishes ms an average of 3 months after acceptance. Computer printout submissions acceptable. Pays expenses of writers on assignment.
Tips: "In the year ahead we will have more editorial pages and more *assigned* freelance work."

‡**FREELANCE WRITER'S REPORT, The Newsletter for Florida Freelance Writers**, Cassell Communications Inc., Florida Freelance Writers Association, Box 9844, Fort Lauderdale FL 33310. (305)485-9795. Editor: Dana K. Cassell. Monthly newsletter covering writing and marketing advice for freelance writers. Pays on publication. Byline given. Buys one-time rights. Submit seasonal/holiday material 2 months in advance. Simultaneous queries and simultaneous, photocopied, and previously published submissions OK. Computer printout submissions OK. SASE. Reports in 1 month. Sample copy $2.50.

Nonfiction: Book excerpts (on writing profession); how-to (market, write, research); interview (of writers or editors); new product (only those pertaining to writers); photojournalism; promotion and administration of a writing business. No humor, fiction or poetry. Buys 36 mss/year. Query or send complete ms. Length: 500 words maximum. Pays 10¢/edited word.

Tips: "Write in terse newsletter style, eliminate flowery adjectives and edit mercilessly. Send something that will help writers increase profits from writing output—must be a proven method."

THE INKLING LITERARY JOURNAL, Inkling Publications, Inc., Box 128, Alexandria MN 56308. (612)762-2020. Editor: Marilyn Bailey. Associate Editor: Betty Ulrich. Managing Editor: John Hall. 15% freelance written. Monthly journal covering advice, guidance and inspiration for writers and poets. "The *INKLING* is both informative and motivational, providing a forum for writers. Well-written articles and timely market news are the main criteria." Circ. 3,000. Pays on publication. Publishes ms an average of 2 months after acceptance. Byline given. Buys first North American serial rights. Submit seasonal/holiday material 3 months in advance. Simultaneous queries OK. Electronic submissions OK if compatible with TRS 80 model III DOS. Computer printout submissions acceptable; prefers letter-quality to dot-matrix. SASE. Reports in 2 weeks on queries; 1 month on mss. Sample copy $2; writer's guidelines for business size SAE and 1 first class stamp.

Nonfiction: How-to (on the business and approach to writing); motivational; interview/profile; opinion; and personal experience. Buys 20-30 mss/year. Send complete ms. Length: 500-1,500 words. Pays $15-50

Poetry: Avant-garde, free verse, haiku, light verse and traditional. "The *INKLING* runs two poetry contests each year—spring and fall: Winner and 2nd place cash prizes and two honorable mentions." Buys 12-20 poems/year. Submit maximum 3 poems. Length: 25 lines maximum. Pays $4-15.

Tips: "Articles must be *well* written and slanted toward the business (or commitment) of writing and/or being a writer. Interviews with established writers should be in-depth, particularly reporting interviewee's philosophy on writing, how (s)he got started, how (s)he 'does it.' Tape interviews, transcribe, then edit! Monthly 'theme' emphasizes a particular genre or type of writing. Opinion pieces (researched and authoritative) on any of the monthly themes welcomed. (Theme schedule available with guidelines.)"

JOURNALISM EDUCATOR, School of Journalism, University of North Carolina, Chapel Hill NC 27514.(919)962-4084. Editor: Thomas A. Bowers. 100% freelance written. Quarterly for journalism professors, administrators, and a growing number of professional journalists in the U.S. and Canada. Published by the Association for Education in Journalism and Mass Communication. Founded by the American Society of Journalism School Administrators. Does not pay. Byline given. Publishes ms an average of 10 months after acceptance. Computer printout submissions acceptable. Electronic submissions OK on IBM Wordstar. SASE.

Nonfiction: "We do accept some unsolicited manuscripts dealing with our publication's specialized area— problems of administration and teaching in journalism education. Because we receive more articles than we can use from persons working in this field, we do not need to encourage freelance materials, however. A writer, generally, would have to be in journalism/communications teaching or in some media work to have the background to write convincingly about the subjects this publication is interested in. The writer also should become familiar with the content of recent issues of this publication." Nothing not directly connected with journalism education at the four-year college and university level. Length: 2,500 words minimum. No payment.

JOURNALISM QUARTERLY, School of Journalism, Ohio University, Athens OH 45701. (614)594-5013. Editor: Guido H. Stempel III. 100% freelance written. For members of the Association for Education in Journalism and Mass Communication and other academicians and journalists. Quarterly. No payment. Publishes ms an average of 6 months after acceptance. Usually acquires all rights. Circ. 4,200. Photocopied submissions OK. Computer printout submissions acceptable. SASE. Reports in 6 months. Free writer's guidelines.

Nonfiction: Research in mass communication. Recent article includes "Understanding and Recall of TV News." No essays or opinion pieces. Length: 4,000 words maximum. Submit complete ms in triplicate. No payment.

Tips: "Query letters don't really help either the author or me very much. We can't make commitments on the basis of query letters, and we are not likely to reject or discourage the manuscript either, unless it is clearly outside our scope. Do a good piece of research. Write a clear, well-organized manuscript."

MEDICAL COMMUNICATIONS, Journal of the American Medical Writers Association. Back issues, business: AMWA, Suite 410, 5272 River Rd., Bethesda MD 20816. (301)986-9119. Editorial material, manuscripts, queries: 4404 Sherwood Rd., Philadelphia PA 19131. (215)877-1137. Editor: Edith Schwager. 55%

freelance written. For members of the American Medical Writers Association, physicians, nurses, medical libraries, journal and medical news editors, audiovisual, television, film, pharmaceutical and advertising writers and editors, medical journalists, and all other communicators in medical and allied fields. Quarterly Digest size, 32 to 48 pages. Circ. 3,500. Byline. Pays 3 contributor copies. Publishes ms an average of 3 months after acceptance. Query. No dot-matrix or all-caps submissions accepted. SASE.

Nonfiction: Articles on any aspect of medical writing, editing and communication. May be philosophic, scholarly or how-to. "More of a journal than a magazine but with a less formal approach." Prefers fairly serious, simple, straightforward style. Special features acceptable. Article length: 2,500 words maximum. Tables, figures and lists of references used with mss if appropriate.

Tips: "We're especially interested in how-to articles on all aspects of medical writing and editing not usually covered in other journals, including indexing, speaking and translation. We accept few articles resting on a humor or satirical base. Most of our members are highly experienced, literate and literary-minded writers and editors. Only the best writing holds their interest. The most frequent mistakes made by writers in completing an article for us are grammatical, typing and spelling errors; also turgid style, heavy-handed humor or satire."

PHILATELIC JOURNALIST, 154 Laguna Court, St. Augustine Shores FL 32086-7031. (904)797-3513. Editor: Gustav Detjen Jr. 25% freelance written. Bimonthly for "journalists, writers and columnists in the field of stamp collecting. *The Philatelic Journalist* is mainly read by philatelic writers, professionals and amateurs, including all of the members of the Society of Philaticians, an international group of philatelic journalists." Circ. 1,000. Not copyrighted. Pays on publication. Publishes ms an average of 15 days after acceptance. Free sample copy. Submit seasonal material 2 months in advance. Photocopied submissions OK. Computer printout submissions acceptable. Reports in 2 weeks. Query. SASE.

Nonfiction: "Articles concerned with the problems of the philatelic journalist, how to publicize and promote stamp collecting, how to improve relations between philatelic writers and publishers and postal administrations. Philatelic journalists, many of them amateurs, are very much interested in receiving greater recognition as journalists, and in gaining greater recognition for the use of philatelic literature by stamp collectors. Any criticism should be coupled with suggestions for improvement." Buys profiles and opinion articles. Length: 250-500 words. Pays $15-30.

Photos: Photos purchased with ms. Captions required.

PRO/COMM, The Professional Communicator, published by Women in Communications, Inc., Box 9561, Austin TX 78766. (512)346-9875. Managing Editor: Barbara A. Johnston. 95% freelance written, mostly by WICI members and without pay. Monthly January-August; combination September/October and November/December issues; 8-12 pages. Circ. more than 12,000. Publishes ms an average of 3 months after acceptance. Byline given. Buys first serial rights and second serial (reprint) rights. Photocopied and previously published submissions OK. Computer printout submissions acceptable printed on daisy wheel. SASE. Reports in 1 month. Sample copy $1.50.

Nonfiction: General interest (media, freedom of information, legislation related to communications); how-to (improve graphics, take better photos, write a better story, do investigative reporting, sell ideas, start a magazine or newspaper, improve journalism education, reach decision-making jobs, etc.); personal experience (self-improvement, steps to take to reach management level jobs); profile (people of interest because of their work in communications); and technical (advancements in print or electronic media). Query. Length: 1,000-1,500 words.

Photos: Offers no additional payment for photos accepted with mss. State availability of photos with query. Uses b&w photos. Captions required.

Tips: "The writer may have a better chance of breaking in at our publication with short articles and fillers. Many items appearing in the publication feature organizational news. Areas open for other copy vary in size, so fillers appropriate to our sphere of interest are often useful."

‡**PUBLISHED!**, Platen Publishing Company, 14240 Bledsoe St., Sylmar CA 91342. (818)367-9613. Managing Editor: Patricia Begalla. Monthly magazine on writing; for, by and about writers. "We encourage fledgling writers and at the same time solicit submissions from established writers about the writing trade. We are a good market for both established and new authors." Estab. 1985. Circ. 5,000. Pays on acceptance. Byline given. Buys first serial rights and nonexclusive reprint rights. Submit seasonal/holiday material 4 months in advance. Simultaneous queries, and simultaneous, photocopied, and previously published submissions OK. SASE. Acknowledges in 1 week; reports in 2 weeks on queries; 6 weeks on mss. Free sample copy; writer's guidelines for #10 SAE and 1 first class stamp.

Nonfiction: General interest (most articles are writing-related); humor; inspirational (about writing, nothing religious); interview/profile (writers); personal experience (about writing); travel; and book reviews (some general interest, most on writing). No religion, science fiction, fantasy, sex or politics. Buys 100-120 mss/year. Send complete ms. Length: 100-900 words. Pays 5¢/word.

Photos: State availability of photos or send photos with query or ms. Reviews 5x8 b&w prints (other sizes considered). Pays $10. Captions and model release required. Buys one-time rights.

Columns/Departments: Tips for new writers—any good solid information to help fledgling writers. Buys 6-8 mss/year. Send complete ms. Length: 200-400 words. Pays 5¢/word.

Fiction: Will be established in mid-1986. Will feature complete shorts, 900-1,800 words.

Poetry: Free verse, haiku, light verse and traditional. No personal love themes. Buys 20-24/year. Length: 5-20 lines. Pays $10.

Fillers: Jokes, anecdotes and short humor. Length: 10-200 words. Pays $1-10 depending on length.

Tips: "We are a new publication. We encourage every writer. We are still growing. The major thrust of the magazine will be for all writers, with emphasis on new authors. We have put the personal touch back into submitting material and will critique occasionally (free) where we feel writer has potential but not yet good enough to publish."

PUBLISHING TRADE, Serving Non-Consumer Publications, Northfield Publishing, 464 Central Ave., Northfield IL 60093. Editor: Rosanne Ullman. 30% freelance written. Bimonthly magazine covering nonconsumer magazine and tabloid publishing. Circulated to approximately 3,000 publishers, editors, ad managers, circulation managers, production managers and art directors of nonconsumer magazines and tabloids. Circ. 8,000. Publishes ms an average of 2 months after acceptance. Byline given. Buys first North American serial rights and makes work-for-hire assignments. Submit seasonal/holiday material 6 months in advance. SASE. Reports in 2 months on queries. "Do not send manuscript without prior query." Sample copy $4.

Nonfiction: How-to (write, sell advertising, manage production, manage creative and sales people, etc.); interview/profile (*only* after assignment—must be full of "secrets" of success and how-to detail); personal experiences (only after assignment); new product (no payment); and technical (aspects of magazine publishing). "Features deal with every aspect of publishing, including: creating an effective ad sales team; increasing ad revenue; writing effective direct-mail circulation promotion; improving 4-color reproduction quality; planning and implementing ad sales strategies; buying printing; gathering unique information; writing crisp, clear articles with impact; and designing publications with visual impact." No general interest. "Everything must be keyed directly to our typical reader—a 39 year-old publisher/editor producing a trade magazine for 30,000 special interest readers." Buys 12-18 mss/year. Query. Length: 900-3,000 words.

Photos: Send photos with ms. Reviews b&w contact sheets. Captions, model release and identification of subjects required. Buys first rights.

Tips: "Articles must present practical, useful, new information in how-to detail, so readers can do what the articles discuss. Articles that present problems and discuss how they were successfully solved also are welcome. These must carry many specific examples to flesh out general statements."

‡**RISING STAR**, Star/Sword Publications,, 47 Byledge Rd., Manchester NH 03104. (603)623-9796. Editor: Scott E. Green. 50% freelance written. Bimonthly newsletter covering science fiction/fantasy markets for writers and artists. Circ. 250. Pays on publication. Publishes ms an average of 6 months after acceptance. Byline given. Buys first North American serial rights. Simultaneous queries, and photocopied and previously published submissions OK. SASE. Reports in 3 weeks. Sample copy $1; writer's guidelines free for SAE and 1 first class stamp.

Nonfiction: Interview/profile, opinion, personal experience, and reviews of markets. No how-to-write articles. Buys 5 mss/year. Query. Length: 600-1,200 words. Pays $3.

THE ROMANTIST, F. Marion Crawford Memorial Society, Saracinesca House, 3610 Meadowbrook Ave., Nashville TN 37205. (615)292-9695 or 226-1890. Editors: John C. Moran, Don Herron and Steve Eng. Annual magazine emphasizing modern romanticism; especially fantastic literature and art. 100% freelance written; 15% of material published is poetry. Circ. 300, controlled. All rights retained but permission always is given an author for reprints. Publishes ms an average of 1 year after acceptance. Byline given. Photocopied poems and previously published submissions not desired. SASE. Reports in 1 month. Writer's guidelines with SASE.

Nonfiction: No articles without querying first.

Poetry: Traditional; very little free verse. "We prefer rhymed and metered poems, but no homespun doggerel. Prefer the tradition of Swinburne, Poe, Noyes, De la Mare, Masefield, Clark Ashton Smith; especially weird or fantastic verse." Poetry submissions should be double-spaced. Uses 15 unsolicited poems/year.

Tips: Closed currently to poetry.

ST. LOUIS JOURNALISM REVIEW, 8606 Olive Blvd., St. Louis MO 63132. (314)991-1699. Editor/Publisher: Charles L. Klotzer. Monthly tabloid newspaper critiquing St. Louis media, print, broadcasting, TV and cable primarily by working journalists and others. Also covers advertising and public relations. Occasionally buys articles on national media criticism. Circ. 12,000. Buys all rights. Byline given. SASE.

Nonfiction: "We buy material which analyzes, critically, St. Louis area and, less frequently, national media institutions, personalities or trends." No taboos. Payment depends.

SCIENCE FICTION CHRONICLE, Algol Press, Box 4175, New York NY 10163. (718)643-9011. Editor: Andrew Porter. 5% freelance written. Monthly magazine about science fiction publishing for science fiction readers, editors, writers, et. al., who are interested in keeping up with the latest developments and news in science fiction. Publication also includes market reports and media news. Circ. 3,500. Buys first serial rights only. Pays on publication. Publishes ms an average of 3 months after acceptance. Makes work-for-hire assignments. Phone queries OK. Submit seasonal material 4 months in advance. Electronic submissions OK on MS-DOS 1-25. Computer printout submissions acceptable. SASE. Reports in 1 week. Sample copy $1.95.

Nonfiction: Interviews, articles, new product and photo feature. No articles about UFOs, or "news we reported six months ago." Buys 15 unsolicited mss/year. Send complete ms. Length: 200-2,000 words. Pays 1-3¢/word.

Photos: Send photos with ms. Pays $5-15 for 4x5 and 8x10 b&w prints. Captions preferred. Buys one-time rights.

Tips: "News of publishers, booksellers and software related to SF is most needed from freelancers."

‡**SHORT STORY REVIEW CLUB**, Trouvere Company, Rt. 2, Box 290, Eclectic AL 36024. Editor: Brenda Williamson. 95% freelance written. Tri-annual short story writer's club. Newsletter published with critiquing of short stories by members. Estab. 1985. Circ. 75. Pays on acceptance. Publishes ms an average of 4 months after acceptance. Byline given. Buys one-time rights. Submit seasonal/holiday material 6 months in advance. Simultaneous queries, and simultaneous, photocopied, and previously published submissions OK. Computer printout submissions acceptable; prefers letter-quality to dot-matrix. SASE. Reports in 1 month. Sample copy $5; writer's guidelines for 25¢ and #10 SAE and 1 first class stamp.

Nonfiction: How-to (about short story writing). Buys 10 mss/year. Send complete ms. Length: 500-1,500 words. Pays $5-50.

Fiction: Adventure, condensed novels, confession, erotica, ethnic, experimental, fantasy, historical, horror, humorous, mainstream, mystery, novel excerpts, religious, romance, science fiction, serialized novels, suspense and western—any short story. Buys 25 mss/year. Send complete ms. Length: 500-3,000 words. Pays $5-50.

Tips: "Articles are accepted from both subscribers and nonsubscribers. Short stories are only accepted from members."

SMALL PRESS REVIEW, Box 100, Paradise CA 95969. Editor: Len Fulton. Associate Editor: Ellen Ferber. Monthly for "people interested in small presses and magazines, current trends and data; many libraries." Circ. 3,000. Byline given. "Query if you're unsure." Reports in 1 to 2 months. SASE. Free sample copy.

Nonfiction: "News, short reviews, photos, short articles on small magazines and presses." Uses how-to, personal experience articles, interview, profile, spot news, historical articles, think pieces, photo pieces, and coverage of merchandising techniques. Accepts 50-200 mss/year. Length: 100-200 words.

Photos: Uses b&w glossy photos.

● **WDS FORUM**, Writer's Digest School, 9933 Alliance Rd., Cincinnati OH 45242. (513)984-0717. Editor: Kirk Polking. 100% freelance written. Monthly newsletter covering writing techniques and marketing for students of courses in fiction and nonfiction writing offered by Writer's Digest School. Circ. 10,000. Pays on acceptance. Publishes ms an average of 6 months after acceptance. Byline given. Pays 25% kill fee. Buys first rights and second serial (reprint) rights. Submit seasonal/holiday material 3 months in advance. Simultaneous, photocopied and previously published submissions OK. Electronic submissions OK, but requires hard copy also. Computer printout submissions acceptable; no dot-matrix. SASE. Reports in 3 weeks. Free sample copy.

Nonfiction: How-to (write or market short stories, articles, novels, poetry, etc.); and interviews (with well-known authors of short stories, novels and books). Buys 10 mss/year. Phone queries OK. Query. Length: 500-1,000 words. Pays $10-25.

Photos: Pays $5-10 for 8x10 b&w prints of well-known writers to accompany mss. Captions required. Buys one-time rights.

WEST COAST REVIEW OF BOOKS, Rapport Publishing Co., Inc., 1501 N. Hobart Blvd., Hollywood CA 90027. (213)464-2662. Editor: D. David Dreis. Bimonthly magazine for book consumers. "Provocative articles based on specific subject matter, books and author retrospectives." Circ. 80,000. Pays on publication. Byline given. Offers kill fee. Buys one-time rights and second serial (reprint) rights to published author interviews. SASE. Sample copy $2.

Nonfiction: General interest, historical/nostalgic, and profile (author retrospectives). "No individual book reviews." Buys 25 mss/year. Query. Length: open.

Tips: "There must be a reason (current interest, news events, etc.) for any article here. Example: 'The Jew-Haters' was about anti-semitism which was written up in six books; all reviewed and analyzed under that umbrella title. Under no circumstances should articles be submitted unless query has been responded to." No phone calls.

THE WRITER, 120 Boylston St., Boston MA 02116. Editor-in-Chief and Publisher: Sylvia K. Burack. Managing Editor: Elizabeth Preston. Monthly. Pays on acceptance. Buys first serial rights only. Uses little

freelance material. Computer printout submissions acceptable; no dot-matrix. SASE. Sample copy $2.
Nonfiction: Articles of instruction for writers. Length: about 2,000 words. Pays good rates.

‡**WRITERS CONNECTION**, 10601 S. De Anza Blvd., Cupertino CA 95117. (408)973-0227. Editor: Jon Kennedy. 60% freelance written. Monthly magazine covering writing and publishing with strong Bay area/ northern California emphasis for northern California writers. Circ. 2,500. Pays on publication. Publishes ms an average of 6 months after acceptance for articles, much less for column updates. Byline given. Buys one-time serial rights, first rights, or second serial (reprint) rights. Submit seasonal/holiday material 2 months in advance. Simultaneous queries, and simultaneous, photocopied, and previously published submissions OK. Computer printout submissions acceptable; prefers letter-quality to dot-matrix. SASE. Prefers telephone queries. Sample copy and writer's guidelines $2.
Nonfiction: Book excerpts (on writing/publishing); how-to (write and publish, market writing); inspirational (overcoming writer's block, "staying the course"); interview/profile (writers and publishers with how-to slant); new product (books, videotapes, etc. on writing and publishing); and travel writing. "All types of writing from technical to romance novels and article writing are treated." Submit material for California writers conferences by January each year. No personal experience or profiles without a strong how-to slant. Buys 36 mss/year. Query, preferably by telephone, between 11 a.m. and noon. Length: 100-2,500 words. Pays $12-38; "pay is in credit for Writers Connection memberships, seminars, subscriptions and advertising only."
Columns/Departments: Markets/Jobs Update and self-publishing. Buys 24 mss/year. Send complete ms. Length: 100-300 words. Pays $12-25 in subscriptions, ads, or credits on seminars or memberships.
Tips: "Find and report on new markets freelancers can break into, new ways to succeed in the business. We use far more short column items, and we generally have a backlog of features awaiting use."

WRITER'S DIGEST, 9933 Alliance Rd., Cincinnati OH 45242. (513)984-0717. Submissions Editor: Sharon Rudd. (Please note that anything submitted to *Writer's Digest* is automatically considered for publication in *Writer's Yearbook*, so there's no point in submitting to each individually.) 90% freelance written. Monthly magazine about writing and publishing. "Our readers write fiction, poetry, nonfiction, plays and all kinds of creative writing. They're interested in improving their writing skills, improving their sales ability, and finding new outlets for their talents." Circ. 200,000. Pays on acceptance. Publishes ms an average of 7 months after acceptance. Buys first North American serial rights for one-time editorial use, microfilm/microfiche use, and magazine promotional use. Pays 20% kill fee. Byline given. Submit seasonal/holiday material 8 months in advance. Previously published and photocopied submissions OK. "Electronic submissions are possible a few years down the line. We'll accept computer printout submissions, of course—but they *must* be readable. That's the rule behind any submission to any magazine. We strongly recommend letter-quality." SASE. "If you don't want your manuscript returned, indicate that on the first page of the manuscript or in a cover letter." Reports in 1 month. Sample copy $2.50; writer's guidelines for SASE.
Nonfiction: "Our mainstay is the how-to article—that is, an article telling how to write and sell more of what you write. For instance, how to write compelling leads and conclusions, how to improve your character descriptions, how to become more efficient and productive. We like plenty of examples, anecdotes and $$$ in our articles—so other writers can actually see what's been done successfully by the author of a particular piece. We like our articles to speak directly to the reader through the use of the first-person voice. Don't submit an article on what five book editors say about writing mysteries. Instead, submit an article on how you cracked the mystery market and how our readers can do the same. But don't limit the article to your experiences; include the opinions of those five editors to give your article increased depth and authority." General interest (about writing); how-to (writing and marketing techniques that work); humor (short pieces); inspirational; interview and profile (query first); new product; and personal experience (marketing and freelancing experiences). "We can always use articles on fiction and nonfiction technique, and solid articles on poetry or poets are always welcome. No articles titled 'So You Want to Be a Writer,' and no first person pieces that ramble without giving a lesson or something readers can learn from in the sharing of the story." Buys 90-100 mss/year. Queries are preferred, but complete mss are OK. Length: 500-3,000 words. Pays 10¢/word minimum. Sometimes pays expenses of writers on assignment.
Photos: Used only with interviews and profiles. State availability of photos or send contact sheet with ms. Pays $25 minimum for 5x7 or larger b&w prints. Captions required.
Columns/Departments: Chronicle (first-person narratives of writing adventures; length: 1,200-1,500 words; pays 10¢/word); The Writing Life (length: 50-800 words; pays 10¢/word); Tip Sheet (short, unbylined items that offer solutions to writing- and freelance business-related problems that writers commonly face; pays 10¢/word); and My First Sale (an "occasional" department; a first person account of how a writer broke into print; length: 1,000 words; pays 10¢/word). "For First Sale items, use a narrative, anecdotal style to tell a tale that is both inspirational and instructional. Before you submit a My First Sale item, make certain that your story contains a solid lesson that will benefit other writers." Buys approximately 200 articles/year for Writing Life section, Tip Sheet and shorter pieces. Send complete ms.
Poetry: Light verse about "the writing life"—joys and frustrations of writing. "We are also considering poetry other than short light verse—but related to writing, publishing, other poets and authors, etc." Buys 2/issue.

Submit poems in batches of 1-8. Length: 2-20 lines. Pays $10-50/poem.
Fillers: Anecdotes and short humor, primarily for use in The Writing Life column. Uses 2/issue. Length: 50-200 words. Pays 10¢/word.

‡**WRITER'S GAZETTE**, Trouvere Co., Rt. 2, Box 250, Eclectic AL 36024. Editor: Brenda Williamson. 98% freelance written. Quarterly newsletter on writing. Pays on publication. Publishes ms an average of 8 months after acceptance. Byline given. Buys one-time rights. Submit seasonal/holiday material 4 months in advance. Simultaneous queries, and simultaneous and photocopied submissions OK. Computer printout submissions acceptable; prefers letter-quality to dot-matrix. SASE. Reports in 1 month. Sample copy $2.50, #10 SAE and 1 first class stamp; writer's guidelines for #10 SAE and 1 first class stamp.
Nonfiction: How-to (about writing). Buys 25 mss/year. Send complete ms. Length: 100-2,000 words. Pays $1-35.
Fiction: All types. Buys 20 mss/year. Send complete ms. Length: 500-2,000 words. Pays $5-50.
Poetry: Avant-garde, free verse, haiku, light verse and traditional. Buys 200/year. Submit maximum 10 poems. Length: open. Pays 10¢-$50..
Fillers: Jokes, anecdotes and short humor. Buys 10/year. Pays $1-10.
Tips: "Be knowledgable and original."

‡**WRITER'S INFO**, Rhyme Time/Story Time, Box 2377, Coeur d'Alene ID 83814. (208)667-7511. Editor: Linda Hutton. 90% freelance written. Quarterly newsletter on writing. "We provide helpful tips and advice to writers, both beginners and old pros." Estab. 1985. Circ. 200. Pays on acceptance. Publishes ms an average of 6 months after acceptance. Byline given. Buys first North American serial rights and second serial (reprint) rights. Submit seasonal/holiday material 9 months in advance. Simultaneous queries, and simultaneous, photocopied, and previously published submissions OK. Computer printout submissions acceptable; prefers letter-quality to dot-matrix. SASE. Reports in 1 month. Sample copy for #10 SAE and 2 first class stamps; writer's guidelines for #10 SAE and 2 first class stamps.
Nonfiction: How-to, humor and personal experience, all related to writing. No interviews or re-hashes of articles published in other writer's magazines. Buys 10-12 mss/year. Send complete ms. Length: 300 words. Pays $1-10.
Poetry: Free verse, light verse and traditional. No avant-garde or shaped poetry. Buys 25-30/year. Submit maximum 6 poems. Length: 4-20 lines. Pays $1-10.
Fillers: Jokes, anecdotes and short humor. Buys 3-4/year. Length: 100 words maximum. Pays $1-10.
Tips: "Tell us a system that worked for you to make a sale or inspired you to write. All departments are open to freelancers."

‡**WRITER'S JOURNAL**, Lynnmark Publications, Box 2922, Livonia MI 48150. Editor: Robert E. Prodehl. 70% freelance written. Monthly newsletter for writers and poets. "We want to provide encouragement, inspiration, direction and help for all aspiring writers and poets." Circ. 350. Pays on publication. Publishes ms an average of 5 months after acceptance. Byline given. Buys one-time rights. Submit seasonal/holiday material 3 months in advance. Simultaneous queries, and simultaneous, photocopied, and previously published submissions OK. Computer printout submissions acceptable; prefers letter-quality to dot-matrix. SASE. Reports in 3 months. Sample copy $2; writer's guidelines for #10 SAE and 1 first class stamp.
Nonfiction: General interest, historical/nostalgic, how-to, humor, inspirational, interview/profile, opinion and personal experience. Buys 25 mss/year. Send complete ms. Length: 200-1,500 words. Offers 3 contributor's copies.
Poetry: Peggy Mezza, poetry editor. All forms accepted. Subject matter should be in good taste. Buys 80/year. Pays in 3 copies.
Fillers: Clippings. Buys 20/year. Length: 100-300 words. Pays in 3 copies.
Tips: "Our Poet's Page uses a large number and variety of poems. It is a good place to get published. For articles and fillers, tell us about your writing experiences which would help or be of interest to other writers and poets. Our entire publication is open to freelancers. It is best to study a current issue to see the style, format and subjects we publish."

WRITER'S LIFELINE, Box 1641, Cornwall, Ontario K6H 5V6 Canada. Contact: Editor. Bimonthly magazine "aimed at freelance writers of all ages and interests." Buys first serial rights. SAE and IRCs.
Nonfiction: "Articles on all aspects of writing and publishing." Send complete ms. Length: 500 words maximum. Payment: 3 free issues in which article appears.
Fiction: Must be tied in to writing and publishing. Poetry published. Payment: 3 free issues in which story or poem appears.
Tips: "Writer should show evidence of his qualification to write on subject. All articles should be pegged to current concerns of writers: self-publishing, hitting local markets, anecdotes of new writer breaking in, and preparing book reviews are among articles we have published recently."

WRITERS WEST, For Working Writers, Kriss Enterprise, Box 16097, San Diego CA 92116. (619)278-6108. Editor: Francis X. Feighan. Managing Editor: Doug Emry. 90% freelance written. A bi-monthly magazine for the professional writer. "The editorial thrust is away from how-to articles and toward subjects of interest to working writers, whether they are working on a novel or producing short stories, poetry or nonfiction." Circ. 2,500. Pays on acceptance. Publishes ms an average of 3 months after acceptance. Byline given. Buys first North American serial rights, and second (reprint) rights to material originally published elsewhere. Simultaneous queries, and simultaneous, photocopied and previously published submissions OK. Computer printout submissions acceptable. SASE. Reports in 2 weeks. Sample copy $2; writer's guidelines for SAE and 1 first class stamp.
Nonfiction: Expose; interview/profile (well-known authors, writing-related personalities); and opinion (writing related). "No elementary how-tos or how great it is being a writer." Buys 24 mss/year. Query or send complete ms. Length: 2,500 words maximum. "Token payment plus copies."
Photos: "Photos with articles are welcome—preferably with the subject in his/her working environment, or head shots. Include the photographer's credit line." State availability of photos. Reviews 5x7 and larger b&w prints. Payment included in payment for ms. Identification of subjects required. Buys one-time rights.
Columns/Departments: Jerry Hannah, Writing Connection columnist. Writing Connection (news about writers: book length works-in-progress, information on special events, groups, clubs, workshops and organizations). "Please provide dates, phone numbers and mailing addresses." Deadline: 35 days prior to publication date. Length: book descriptions, 2 paragraphs maximum; include mailing address. No payment.
Fiction: "Will consider anything of quality. No trials and tribulations of being a writer." Buys 12 mss/year. Send complete ms; include short biography. Length: 2,500 words maximum.
Poetry: Prefers upbeat, positive poems. Buys 12 poems/year. Length: 50 lines maximum. "Token payment plus copies. Prefers disciplined forms."
Tips: "Writers' most frequent mistakes are misjudging (or *not* judging) WW's intended market: the professional writer (who is not interested in how to budget time in order to write). A writer can break in in any category. WW has published first-time writers; professional treatment of the subject matter is the deciding factor."

WRITER'S YEARBOOK, 9933 Alliance Rd., Cincinnati OH 45242. Submissions Editor: Sharon Rudd. Anything submitted to *Writer's Yearbook*, is automatically considered for publication in *Writer's Digest* so there's no point in submitting to each individually. 90% freelance written. Newsstand annual for freelance writers, journalists and teachers of creative writing. "We provide how-to features and information to help our readers become more skilled at writing and successful at selling their writing." Buys first North American serial rights and (occasionally) reprint rights. Pays 20% kill fee. Byline given. Buys 10-15 mss/year. Pays on acceptance. Publishes ms an average of 6 months after acceptance. "Writers should query in spring with ideas for the following year." Send detailed query or outline of what you have in mind. Previously published (book reprints) and high-quality photocopied submissions OK. Computer printout submissions acceptable; prefers letter-quality to dot-matrix. SASE. "If you don't want your manuscript returned, indicate that on the first page of the manuscript or in a cover letter."
Nonfiction: "We want articles that reflect the current state of writing in America. Trends, inside information and money-saving and money-making ideas for the freelance writer. We try to touch on the various facets of writing in each issue of the *Yearbook*—from fiction to poetry to playwriting, and any other endeavor a writer can pursue. How-to articles—that is, articles that explain in detail how to do something—are very important to us. For example, you could explain how to establish mood in fiction, how to improve interviewing techniques, how to write for and sell to specialty magazines, or how to construct and market a good poem. We are also interested in the writer's spare time—what she/he does to retreat occasionally from the writing wars; where and how to refuel and replenish the writing spirit. 'How Beats the Heart of a Writer' features interest us, if written warmly, in the first person, by a writer who has had considerable success. We also want interviews or profiles of well-known bestselling authors, always with good pictures. Articles on writing techniques that are effective today are always welcome." Recent article example: "The Best Damned Job on Earth," by Gary Provost (1985). Length: 750-4,500 words. Pays 10¢/word minimum. Sometimes pays expenses of writers on assignment.
Photos: Interviews and profiles must be accompanied by high-quality photos. B&w only; depending on use, pays $20-50/published photo. Captions required.

WRITING UPDATE, International Tipsheet for People Who Write, #250, 4812 Folsom Blvd., Sacramento CA 95819. Editor/Publisher: Kimberly A. Edwards. 8% freelance written. A 13-page monthly newsletter covering writing, freelancing, publishing, consulting, in-the-work-place writing, digest of tips, news sources and issues for persons who write for fun, profit or promotion of their careers. "We appeal largely to busy writers of the 80's who see writing as a big part of their personal/professional lives, and at the same time are juggling writing, career and home. Readers want clean, streamlined information they can read over a quick sandwich. They want solid tips they can apply to their lives. They don't want to wade through lengthly articles to get to the good stuff." Publishes ms an average of 2 months after acceptance. Buys one-time rights. Computer printout submissions acceptable; prefers letter-quality to dot-matrix. Mostly staff written. Sample copy $1.95.

Columns/Departments: "Expert Opinion" age. Upbeat, motivational, fact or idea filled articles up to 1,100 words on any aspect of writing or freelancing. Prefers a marketing slant, but is not necessary. Potential contributors should review the publication for tone, style and needs. Pays in 3 copies.

Tips: "The most frequent mistake made by writers in submitting an article to us is sending it cold without seeing our publication. We suggest that writers review us (not just our guidelines on entry in Writer's Market) to get a feel for our needs, tone, style, etc."

Laundry and Dry Cleaning

"Minimally staffed trade magazines such as ours never get enough unsolicited, original material," said the *American Drycleaner*, editor. "We get many general business and management articles that do not directly address our readers, but very few articles or queries that specifically deal with the concerns of our industry." Some journals in the Coin-Operated Machines category are also in the market for material on laundries and dry cleaning establishments.

AMERICAN DRYCLEANER, 500 N. Dearborn St., Chicago IL 60610. (312)337-7700. Editor: Earl V. Fischer. 20% freelance written. For professional drycleaners. Monthly. Circ. 28,000. Buys first North American serial rights or in some cases industry-exclusive simultaneous rights. Pays on publication. Publishes ms an average of 3 months after acceptance. Will send free sample copy to writers with specific queries. Reports "promptly." Computer printout submissions acceptable.

Nonfiction: Articles on all aspects of running a drycleaning business. "These can be narratives about individual drycleaners and how they are handling, say, advertising, counter service, customer relations, cleaning, spot removal, pressing, inspection, packaging, paperwork, or general business management; interpretive reports about outside developments, such as new fabrics and fashions or government regulations affecting drycleaners; or how-to articles offering practical help to cleaners on any facet of their business. The important thing is that the reader find practical benefit in the article, whichever type submitted." No basic advertising and public relations material. "We have regulars for this who know our industry." Pays a minimum of 6¢/published word. Recent article example: "Thoroughness, Savvy Restore Faith in Future" (April 1985).

Photos: Photos purchased with mss; quality 8x10 or 5x7 b&w glossies. Photos should help tell story. No model releases required. Pays $6 minimum.

Tips: "We are happy to receive and frequently publish unsolicited manuscripts. If an advance query is made, it would help to get a theme sentence or brief outline of the proposed article. Also helpful would be a statement of whether (and what sort of) photos or other illustrations are available. Anyone with the type of article that our readers would find helpful can break into the publication. The most frequent mistake made by writers in completing an article for us is writing too superficially on too many aspects of a business. It's better to probe for the really unusual and adaptable practical ideas in practice and find out all about them. Also too many photos are meaningless or their significance is not explained. Find a successful drycleaner—one with unusually satisfied customers, for example, or one that seems to be making a lot of money. Find out what makes that cleaner so successful. Tell us about it in specific, practical terms, so other cleaners will be able to follow suit. Articles should help our readers operate their drycleaning businesses more successfully; the appropriateness and practical value of information given are more important than writing style. We prefer *short* reports about *small* cleaning companies doing *one thing* well enough for others to want to know about it and how they might do the same. Reports can range from less than 250 words up to any length the writer can justify. Our editorial space is steadily increasing; staff help is not. We're glad to use anything suitable for publication (new writers are always welcome)."

INDUSTRIAL LAUNDERER, Suite 613, 1730 M St. NW, Washington DC 20036. (202)296-6744. Editor: David A. Ritchey. 10% freelance written. Monthly magazine; 124 pages for decisionmakers in the industrial laundry industry. Publication of the Institute of Industrial Launderers, Inc. Circ. 2,500. Pays on acceptance. Publishes ms an average of 3 months after acceptance. Buys all rights. Computer printout submissions acceptable. SASE. Reports in 1 week. Sample copies $1; limited sample copies available. Writer's guidelines on request.

Nonfiction: General interest pieces for the industrial laundry industry; labor news, news from Washington; and book reviews on publications of interest to people in this industry. Technical advancements and "people" stories. Informational, personal experience, interview, profile, historical, successful business operations and

merchandising techniques. No "general business articles or articles not specifically related to the industrial laundry industry." Buys 5-10 unsolicited mss/year. Query. Length: 750 words minimum. Payment negotiable.
Photos: No additional payment for 8x10 b&w glossies used with ms. Pays $5 minimum for those purchased on assignment. Captions required.

Law

"We are attempting to develop a stronger core of 'hit 'em where they live' articles in response to our last two readership surveys," pointed out the *Student Lawyer* editor. This publication is also interested in trend stories about the legal marketplace since lawyers' jobs are becoming more difficult to find. Legal clinics and advertising by law firms are other trends that law magazines may be reporting on this year. In any case, make sure the legal issues that you propose to write about would apply to the magazine's readers. Most U.S. law stories, for instance, would not apply to Canadian attorneys.

THE ALTMAN & WEIL REPORT TO LEGAL MANAGEMENT, Altman & Weil Publications, Inc., Box 472, Ardmore PA 19003. (215)649-4646. Editor: Robert I. Weil. 15% freelance written. Monthly newsletter covering law office purchases (equipment, insurance services, space, etc.). Circ. 2,200. Pays on publication. Publishes ms an average of 4 months after acceptance. Byline given. Buys all rights; sometimes second serial (reprint) rights. Photocopied and previously published submissions OK. Computer printout submissions acceptable; prefers letter-quality to dot-matrix. Reports in 1 month on queries; 6 weeks on mss. Sample copy for business size SAE and 1 first class stamp.
Nonfiction: How-to (buy, use, repair); interview/profile; and new product. Buys 6 mss/year. Query. Length: 500-2,500 words. Pays $125/published page.
Photos: State availability of photos. Reviews b&w prints; payment is included in payment for ms. Captions and model release required. Buys one-time rights.

BARRISTER, American Bar Association Press, 750 N. Lake Shore Dr., Chicago IL 60611. (312)988-6056. Editor: Anthony Monahan. For young lawyers who are members of the American Bar Association concerned about practice of law, improvement of the profession and service to the public. Quarterly magazine; 64 pages. Circ. 155,000. Pays on acceptance. Buys all rights, first serial rights, second serial (reprint) rights, or simultaneous rights. Photocopied submissions OK. SASE. Reports in 6 weeks. Free sample copy.
Nonfiction: "As a magazine of ideas and opinion, we seek material that will help readers in their interrelated roles of attorney and citizen; major themes in legal and social affairs." Especially needs expository or advocacy articles; position should be defended clearly in good, crisp, journalistic prose. "We would like to see articles on issues such as the feasibility of energy alternatives to nuclear power, roles of women and minorities in law, the power and future of multinational corporations; national issues such as gun control; and aspects of the legal profession such as salary comparisons, use of computers in law practice." Recent article example: "Are You Meant to Be a Partner?" No humorous court reporter anecdote material or political opinion articles. Buys 15 unsolicited mss/year. Length: 3,000-4,000 words. Query with a working title and outline of topic. "Be specific." Pays $450-750.
Photos: Donna Tashjian, photo editor. B&w photos and color transparencies purchased without accompanying ms. Pays $35-150.
Tips: "We urge writers to think ahead about new areas of law and social issues: sexual habits, work habits, corporations, etc."

CALIFORNIA LAWYER, The State Bar of California, 555 Franklin St., San Francisco CA 94102. (415)561-8286. Editor: Jonathan R. Maslow. Associate Editor: Tom Brom. 80% freelance written. Monthly magazine of law-related articles and general interest subjects of appeal to attorneys. Circ. 200,000. Pays on acceptance. Publishes ms an average of 3 months after acceptance. Byline given. Buys all rights. Simultaneous queries, and simultaneous and photocopied submissions OK. Computer printout submissions acceptable; prefers letter-quality to dot-matrix. Reports in 2 weeks on queries; 3 weeks on mss. Sample copy for 8½x11 SAE and $1.50 postage; writer's guidelines for SAE and 1 first class stamp.
Nonfiction: General interest, historical, interview/profile, opinion, technical, personal finance advice and personal effectiveness. "We are interested in concise, well-written and well-researched articles on recent

trends in the legal profession, legal aspects of issues of current concern, as well as general interest articles of potential appeal and benefit to the state's lawyers. We would like to see a description or outline of your proposed idea, including a list of possible information sources." Buys 36 mss/year. Query with published clips if available. Length: 2,000-3,000 words (features). Pays $400-600.

Photos: Jan Leonard, photo editor. State availability of photos with query letter or manuscript. Reviews prints. Identification of subjects required.

Columns/Departments: Business of Practice; After Hours; Profile; Money; and Effectiveness. Buys 100/year. Query with published clips if available. Length: 1,000-1,500 words. Pays $200-350.

Tips: "Trends in magazine publishing that freelance writers should be aware of include shorter articles, more emphasis on individual magazine styles; stricter guidelines for libel and fact checking."

‡**COMPUTER USER'S LEGAL REPORTER**, Computer Law Group, Inc., 191 Post Rd. W., Westport CT 06880. (203)227-1360. Editor: Charles P. Lickson. 10% freelance written. Monthly newsletter featuring legal issues and considerations facing users of computer and processed data. "The *Computer User's Legal Reporter* is written by a fully qualified legal and technical staffer for nonlaywer readers. It fetaures brief summaries on developments in such vital areas as computer contracts, insurance, warranties, crime, proprietary rights and privacy. Each summary is backed by reliable research and sourcework." Estab. 1984. Circ. 1,000. Pays on publication. Publishes ms an average of 6 weeks after acceptance. Offers 50% kill fee. Buys first North American serial rights. Simultaneous queries and simultaneous, photocopied, and previously published submissions OK. Computer printout submissions acceptable; prefers letter-quality to dot-matrix. SASE. Reports in 2 weeks. Sample copy $5 with # 10 SAE and 5 first class stamps.

Nonfiction: Book excerpts; expose; how-to (protect ideas, etc.); humor (computer law . . . according to Murphy); interview/profile (legal or computer personality); and technical. "No articles not related to computers or high-tech and society." Buys 12 mss/year. Query with published clips. Length: 250-1,000 words. Pays $50; $150 for scenes. Sometimes pays the expenses of writers on assignment.

Columns/Departments: Computer Law . . . . according to Murphy (humorous "laws" relating to computers, definitions, etc.). The editor buys all rights to Murphyisms which may be included in his book, *Computer Law . . . According to Murphy*. Buys 12 mss/year. Length: 25-75 words. Pays $10-50.

Tips: "Send materials with a note on your own background and qualifications to write what you submit. We invite intelligently presented and well-argued controversy within our field. We are considering a technical market letter for lawyers. The need to know how to deal with new technology is a definite trend we expect to be part of."

LEGAL ECONOMICS, A Magazine of the Section of Economics of Law Practice of the American Bar Association, Box 11418, Columbia SC 29211. Managing Editor/Art Director: Delmar L. Roberts. 10% freelance written. For the practicing lawyer. 10 issues/year beginning January 1986. Magazine; 80-100 pages. Circ. 27,000. Rights purchased vary with author and material. Usually buys all rights. Byline given. Pays on publication. Publishes ms an average of 8 months after acceptance. Computer printout submissions acceptable. Query. SASE. Free writer's guidelines. Sample copy $3.50 (make check payable to American Bar Association). Returns rejected material in 90 days, if requested.

Nonfiction: "We assist the practicing lawyer in operating and managing his or her office by providing relevant articles and departments written in a readable and informative style. Editorial content is intended to aid the lawyer by conveying management methods that will allow him or her to provide legal services to clients in a prompt and efficient manner at reasonable cost. Typical topics of articles include timekeeping systems; word processing developments; microcomputer applications; client/lawyer relations; office equipment; computerized research; compensation of partners and associates; information retrieval; and use of paralegals." No elementary articles on a whole field of technology, such as, "why you need word processing in the law office." Pays $75-300.

Photos: Pays $25-50 for b&w photos purchased with mss; $50-75 for color; $75 up for cover transparencies.

Tips: "We occasionally publish thematic issues, such as one issue exclusively on computer hardware and another on software."

‡**LEGAL TIMES**, Law & Business, Inc, a subsidiary of Harcourt Brace Jovanovich, Publishers, 1666 Connecticut Ave. NW, Washington DC 20009. (202)797-9600. Editor: Larry Lempert. Managing Editor: Steve Nelson. Tabloid. 1 national weekly, 1 monthly for DC, and 1 monthly for New York covering the legal profession. "Weekly covers trends, cases, and news developments of interest to sophisticated legal audience, mostly business lawyers, as well as articles about the legal profession per se; monthly includes more feature material about lawyers and law firms." Circ. weekly 6,000; monthlies 30,000-50,000. Pays on publication. Byline given. Buys all rights. Simultaneous queries and photocopied submissions OK. Computer printout submissions acceptable.

Nonfiction: Sherrie Good, associate managing editor. General interest and interview/profile. "All must relate to lawyers, law firms, or trends in the law." Periodic "special sections" on computer litigation support, law office management, and office use of technology. Buys 30 mss/year, but many are from "regulars." Query with published clips and resume. Length: 6,000 words maximum. Pays sliding scale depending on experience. Previous experience required; familiarity with legal practice highly desirable.

LOS ANGELES LAWYER, Los Angeles County Bar Association, Box 55020, Los Angeles CA 90055. (213)627-2727, ext. 265. Editor: Susan Pettit. Monthly (except for combined July/August issue) magazine covering legal profession with "journalistic and scholarly articles of interest to the legal profession." Circ. 17,000. Pays on acceptance. Byline given. Buys first serial rights only. Submit seasonal/holiday material 4 months in advance. Simultaneous queries and photocopied submissions OK. Computer printout submissions acceptable; prefers letter-quality to dot-matrix. Reports in 1 month on queries; 2 months on mss. Sample copy $1.50; free writer's guidelines.
Nonfiction: How-to (tips for legal practitioners); humor; interview (leading legal figures); opinion (on area of law, lawyer attitudes or group, court decisions, etc.); travel (very occasionally); and consumer-at-law feature articles on topics of interest to lawyers. No first person, nonlegal material. Buys 22 mss/year. Query with published clips. Length: 4,000-4,500 words for feature (cover story); 2,000-2,750 words for consumer article. Pays $500-600 for cover story, $200-225 for consumer article.

THE NATIONAL LAW JOURNAL, New York Law Publishing Company, 111 8th Ave., New York NY 10011. (212)741-8300. Editor: Timothy Robinson. Managing Editor: Albert Robbins. 15% freelance written. Weekly newspaper for the legal profession. Circ. 37,000. Pays on publication. Publishes ms an average of 2 months after acceptance. Byline given. Offers $75 kill fee. Buys all rights. Simultaneous queries OK. Electronic submissions OK on 300 or 1200 baud. Computer printout submissions acceptable; prefers letter-quality to dot-matrix. SASE. Reports in 3 weeks on queries; 5 weeks on mss. Sample copy $3.
Nonfiction: Expose (on subjects of interest to lawyers); and interview/profile (of lawyers or judges of note). "The bulk of our freelance articles are 2,000-2,500 word profiles of prominent lawyers, or trend stories relating to the legal profession. We also buy a steady stream of short, spot-news stories on local court decisions or lawsuits; often, these come from legal affairs writers on local newspapers. No articles without a legal angle." Buys 60 mss/year. Query with published clips or send complete ms. Length: 1,500-3,000 words. Pays $300-500. Sometimes pays the expenses of writers on assignment.
Tips: "For those who are not covering legal affairs on a regular basis, the best way into *The National Law Journal* is probably through our On Trial feature. Every week we print a sort of reporter's notebook on some proceeding currently underway in a courtroom. These stories come from all around the country and range from gory murder trials to a night in small claims court. They usually run about 1,000 words and are stylistically quite flexible. We also use op-ed pieces on subjects of legal interest, many of which come from freelancers. Writers interested in doing an op-ed piece should query first."

ONTARIO LAWYERS WEEKLY, The Newspaper for the Legal Profession in Ontario, Butterworth (Canada) Inc., 2265 Midland Ave., Scarborough, Ontario M1P 4S1 Canada. (416)292-1421. Editor: D. Michael Fitz-James. 40% freelance written. A weekly tabloid covering law and legal affairs for a "sophisticated up-market readership of lawyers and accountants." Circ. 10,000. Pays on publication. Publishes ms an average of 1 month after acceptance. Byline given. Offers 50% kill fee. Usually buys all rights. Submit seasonal/holiday material 1 month in advance. Simultaneous queries and submissions, and photocopied submissions OK. Computer printout submissions acceptable; prefers letter-quality to dot-matrix. SAE and IRC. Reports in 1 month. Sample copy $1.50 and 8½x11 SAE.
Nonfiction: Book reviews; expose; general interest (law); historical/nostalgic; how-to (professional); humor; interview/profile (lawyers and judges); opinion; technical; news; and case comments. "We try to wrap up the week's legal events and issues in a snappy informal package with lots of visual punch. We especially like news stories with photos or illustrations. We are always interested in feature or newsfeature articles involving current legal issues, but contributors should keep in mind our audience is trained in English/Canadian Common law—not U.S. law. That means most U.S. constitutional or criminal law stories will not be accepted. Contributors should also keep in mind they're writing for *lawyers* and they don't need to reduce legal stories to simple-minded babble often seen in the daily press." Special Christmas issue. No routine court reporting or fake news stories about commercial products. Buys 200-300 mss/year. Query or send complete ms. Length: 700-1,500 words. Pays $25 minimum, negotiable maximum (have paid up to $250 in the past). Payment in Canadian dollars. Sometimes pays the expenses of writers on assignment.
Photos: State availability of photos with query letter or ms. Reviews b&w contact sheets, negatives, and 5x7 prints. Identification of subjects required. Buys one-time rights.
Columns/Departments: Buys 90-100 mss/year. Send complete ms. Length: 500-1,000 words. Pays negotiable rate.
Fillers: Clippings, jokes, gags, anecdotes, short humor and newsbreaks. Length: 50-200 words. Pays $10 minimum.
Tips: "Freelancers can best break in to our publication by submitting news, features, and accounts of unusual

or bizarre legal events. A frequent mistake made by writers is forgetting the audience we go to is intelligent and learned in law. They don't need the word 'plaintiff' explained to them. No unsolicited mss returned without SASE.

THE PARALEGAL, The Publication for the Paralegal Profession, Paralegal Publishing Corp./National Paralegal Association, 60 E. State St., Box 629, Doylestown PA 18901. (215)348-5575. Editor: William Cameron. Bimonthly magazine covering the paralegal profession for practicing paralegals, attorneys, paralegal educators, paralegal associations, law librarians and court personnel. Special and controlled circulation includes law libraries, colleges and schools educating paralegals, law schools, law firms and governmental agecies, etc. Circ. 4,000. Byline given. Buys all rights. Simultaneous queries, and simultaneous, photocopied and previously published submissions OK. SASE. Reports in 2 weeks on queries; 1 month on mss. Writer's guidelines and suggested topic sheet for business-size SAE.
Nonfiction: Book excerpts, expose, general interest, historical/nostalgic, how-to, humor, interview/profile, new product, opinion, personal experience, photo feature, technical and travel. Suggested topics include the paralegal (where do they fit and how do they operate within the law firm in each specialty); the government; the corporation; the trade union; the banking institution; the law library; the legal clinic; the trade or professional association; the educational institution; the court system; the collection agency; the stock brokerage firm; and the insurance company. Articles also wanted on paralegals exploring "where have they been? Where are they now? Where are they going." Query or send complete ms. Length: 1,500-3,000 words. Pays variable rates. Ask amount when submitting ms or other material to be considered.
Photos: Send photos with query or ms. Captions, model release and identification of subjects required.
Columns/Departments: Case at Issue (a feature on a current case from a state or federal court which either directly or indirectly affects paralegals and their work with attorneys, the public, private or governmental sector); Humor (cartoons, quips, short humorous stories, anecdotes and one liners in good taste and germain to the legal profession); and My Position (an actual presentation by a paralegal who wishes to share with others his/her job analysis). Query.
Fillers: Clippings, jokes, gags, anecdotes, short humor and newsbreaks.

THE PENNSYLVANIA LAWYER, Pennsylvania Bar Association, 100 South St., Box 186, Harrisburg PA 17108. (717)238-6715. Executive Editor: Francis J. Fanucci. Editor: Donald C. Sarvey. 20% freelance written. Magazine published 7 times/year as a service to the legal profession. Circ. 25,000. Pays on acceptance. Publishes ms an average of 4 months after acceptance. Byline given. Buys negotiable rights; generally first rights, occasionally second serial (reprint) rights. Submit seasonal/holiday material 5 months in advance. Simultaneous queries acceptable but not encouraged. Computer printout submissions acceptable; prefers letter-quality to dot-matrix. Reports in 2 weeks. Free sample copy.
Nonfiction: General interest, how-to, humor, interview/profile, new product, and personal experience. All features must relate in some way to Pennsylvania lawyers or the practice of law in Pennsylvania. Buys 12 mss/year. Query. Length: 800-2,500 words. Pays $75-350. Sometimes pays the expenses of writers on assignment.
Tips: "The most frequent mistake made by writers in completing an article for us is failure to 'humanize' stories."

STUDENT LAWYER, American Bar Association, 750 N. Lake Shore Dr., Chicago IL 60611. (312)988-6049. Editor: Lizanne Poppens. Associate Editor: Sarah Hoban. 95% freelance written. Monthly (September-May) magazine; 56 pages. Circ. 45,000. Pays on publication. Buys first rights and second (reprint) rights to material originally published elsewhere. Pays negotiable kill fee. Byline given. Submit seasonal/holiday material 4 months in advance. Photocopied submissions OK. Computer printout submissions acceptable. Reports in 1 month. Publishes ms an average of 3 months after acceptance. Sample copy $2; free writer's guidelines.
Nonfiction: Expose (government, law, education and business); profiles (prominent persons in law-related fields); opinion (on matters of current legal interest); essays (on legal affairs); interviews; and photo features. Recent article examples: "Lawyers for the Bottom Line, (February 1985); "Too Close for Comfort" (September 1984). Buys 5 mss/issue. Query. Length: 3,000-5,000 words. Pays $250-600 for main features.
Photos: State availability of photos with query. Pays $50-75 for 8x10 b&w prints; $50-250 for color. Model release required (please send copy along).
Columns/Departments: Briefly (short stories on unusual and interesting developments in the law); Legal Aids (unusual approaches and programs connected to teaching law students and lawyers); Esq. (brief profiles of people in the law); End Note (very short pieces on a variety of topics; can be humorous, educational, outrageous); Pro Se (opinion slot for authors to wax eloquent on legal issues, civil rights conflicts, the state of the union); and Et Al. (column for short features that fit none of the above categories). Buys 4-8 mss/issue. Length: 250-1,000 words. Pays $75-250.
Fiction: "We buy fiction only when it is very good and deals with issues of law in the contemporary world or offers insights into the inner workings of lawyers. No mystery or science fiction accepted."
Tips: "*Student Lawyer* actively seeks good, new writers. Legal training definitely not essential; writing talent is. The writer should not think we are a law review; we are a features magazine with the law (in the broadest

sense) as the common denominator. Past articles concerned gay rights, prison reform, the media, pornography, capital punishment, and space law. Find issues of national scope and interest to write about; be aware of subjects the magazine—and other media—have already covered and propose something new. Write clearly and well."

VERDICT MAGAZINE Legal Journal of the Association of Southern California Defense Counsel, American Lifestyle Communications Inc., 123 Truxtun Ave., Bakersfield CA 93301. (805)325-7124. Editor: George Martin. Managing Editor: Steve Walsh. A quarterly magazine covering defense law (corporate). Circ. 5,000. Pays on publication. Byline given. Buys first North American serial rights. Submit seasonal/holiday material 4 months in advance. Photocopied submissions OK. Computer printout submissions acceptable. SASE. Reports in 2 months. Sample copy for $2.50, 9x12 SAE and $2 postage; free writer's guidelines.
Nonfiction: How-to (corporate defense law); interview/profile; personal experience; and technical. Buys 12 mss/year. Send complete ms. Length: 1,500-3,000 words. Pays $20-35.
Photos: Send photos with ms. Pays $5-10 for 3x5 b&w prints. Captions required. Buys all rights.
Columns/Departments: Buys 4 mss/year. Send complete ms. Length: 500-750 words. Pays $15-20.
Fiction: Historical and mystery. Buys 4 mss/year. Send complete ms. Length: 1,500-3,000 words. Pays $20-35.

Leather Goods

The "While-You-Wait Concept"—resembling the fast food trend in the restaurant industry in the 1960s and 1970s—is the major trend in the shoe service industry. "Much is at stake in this concept, including the entry of foreign suppliers and machine manufacturers into the U.S. marketplace—an entry which could mean the failure of many U.S. suppliers, manufacturers, and even shoe repairers," said the editor of *Shoe Service*.

SHOE SERVICE, SSIA Service Corp., 154 W. Hubbard St., Chicago IL 60610. (312)670-3732. Editor: Mark Paulson. 50% freelance written. Monthly magazine for business people who own and operate small shoe repair shops. Circ. 6,500. Pays on publication. Publishes ms an average of 3 months after acceptance. Byline given. Buys first serial rights, first North American serial rights, and one-time rights. Submit seasonal/holiday material 3 months in advance. Simultaneous queries, and photocopied and previously published submissions OK. Computer printout submissions acceptable; prefers letter-quality to dot-matrix. SASE. Reports in 6 weeks. Sample copy $1.
Nonfiction: How-to (run a profitable shop); interview/profile (of an outstanding or unusual person on shoe repair); and business articles (particularly about small business practices in a service/retail shop). Buys 12-24 mss/year. Query with published clips or send complete ms. Length: 500-2,000 words. Pays 5¢/word.
Photos: "Quality photos will help sell an article." State availability of photos. Pays $10-30 for 8x10 b&w prints. Uses some color photos, but mostly uses b&w glossies. Captions, model release, and identification of subjects required.
Tips: "Visit some shoe repair shops to get an idea of the kind of person who reads *Shoe Service*. Profiles are the easiest to sell to us if you can find a repairer we think is unusual."

Library Science

AMERICAN LIBRARIES, 50 E. Huron St., Chicago IL 60611. (312)944-6780. Editor: Arthur Plotnik. 5% freelance written. For librarians. "A highly literate audience. They are for the most part practicing professionals with a down-to-earth interest in people and current trends." Published 11 times a year. Circ. 42,500. Buys first North American serial rights. Publishes ms an average of 4 months after acceptance. Pays negotiable kill fee. Byline given. Will consider photocopied submissions if not being considered elsewhere at time of submis-

The double dagger before a listing indicates that the listing is new in this edition. New markets are often the most receptive to freelance contributions.

sion. Computer printout submissions acceptable. Submit seasonal material 6 months in advance. Reports in 10 weeks. SASE.

Nonfiction: "Material reflecting the special and current interests of the library profession. Nonlibrarians should browse recent journals in the field, available on request in medium-sized and large libraries everywhere. Topic and/or approach must be fresh, vital, or highly entertaining. Library memoirs and stereotyped stories about old maids, overdue books, fines, etc., are unacceptable. Our first concern is with the American Library Association's activities and how they relate to the 39,000 reader/members. Tough for an outsider to write on this topic, but not to supplement it with short, offbeat or profoundly significant library stories and features." No fillers. Recent article example: "The Librarian Behind the Bestseller", profiling the librarian who helped develop *In Search of Excellence* (March 1985).

Photos: "Will look at all good b&w, well-lit photos of library situations, and at color transparencies and bright prints for possible cover use." Buys 10-15 mss/year. Pays $25-200 for briefs and articles. Pays $25-75 for b&w photos.

Tips: "You can break in with a sparkling, 300-word report on a true, offbeat library event, use of new technology, or with an exciting photo and caption. Though stories on public libraries are always of interest, we especially need arresting material on academic and school libraries."

EMERGENCY LIBRARIAN, Dyad Services, Box 46258, Stn. G, Vancouver, British Columbia V6R 4G6 Canada. Co-Editors: Carol Ann Haycock and Ken Haycock. Bimonthly magazine. Circ. 3,500. Pays on publication. Photocopied submissions OK. No multiple submissions. SAE and IRCs. Reports in 6 weeks. Free writer's guidelines.

Nonfiction: Emphasis is on improvement of library service for children and young adults in school and public libraries. Also annotated bibliographies. Buys 3 mss/issue. Query. Length: 1,000-3,500 words. Pays $50.

Columns/Departments: Five regular columnists. Also Book Reviews (of professional materials in education, librarianship). Query. Length: 100-300 words. Payment consists of book reviewed.

LIBRARY JOURNAL, 205 E. 42nd St., New York NY 10017. Editor-in-Chief: John N. Berry III. For librarians (academic, public, special). 115-page magazine published 20 times/year. Circ. 30,000. Buys all rights. Buys 50-100 mss/year (mostly from professionals in the field). Pays on publication. Submit complete ms. SASE.

Nonfiction: *"Library Journal* is a professional magazine for librarians. Freelancers are most often rejected because they submit one of the following types of article: 'A wonderful, warm, concerned, loving librarian who started me on the road to good reading and success'; 'How I became rich, famous, and successful by using my public library'; 'Libraries are the most wonderful and important institutions in our society, because they have all of the knowledge of mankind—praise them.' We need material of greater sophistication, dealing with issues related to the transfer of information, access to it, or related phenomena. (Current hot ones are copyright, censorship, the decline in funding for public institutions, the local politics of libraries, trusteeship, etc.)" Professional articles on criticism, censorship, professional concerns, library activities, historical articles, information technology, automation and management, and spot news. Outlook should be from librarian's point of view. Buys 50-65 unsolicited mss/year. Length: 1,500-2,000 words. Pays $50-350.

Photos: Payment for b&w glossy photos purchased without accompanying mss is $30. Must be at least 5x7. Captions required.

MEDIA: CHURCH MEDIA LIBRARY MAGAZINE,127 9th Ave. N., Nashville TN 37234. (615)251-2752. Editor: Floyd B. Simpson. Quarterly magazine; 50 pages. For adult leaders in church organizations and people interested in library work (especially church library work). Circ. 17,500. Pays on publication. Buys all rights. Byline given. Phone queries OK. Submit seasonal/holiday material 14 months in advance. Previously published submissions OK. SASE. Reports in 1 month. Free sample copy and writer's guidelines.

Nonfiction: "We are primarily interested in articles that relate to the development of church libraries in providing media and services to support the total program of a church and in meeting individual needs. We publish personal experience accounts of services provided, promotional ideas, exciting things that have happened as a result of implementing an idea or service; human interest stories that are library-related; and media education (teaching and learning with a media mix). Articles should be practical for church library staffs and for teachers and other leaders of the church." Buys 15-20 mss/issue. Query. Pays 5¢/word.

Market conditions are constantly changing! If this is 1987 or later, buy the newest edition of *Writer's Market* at your favorite bookstore or order directly from Writer's Digest Books.

SCHOOL LIBRARY JOURNAL, 1180 Avenue of the Americas, New York NY 10036. Editor: Lillian N. Gerhardt. For librarians in schools and public libraries. Magazine published 10 times/year; 88 pages. Circ. 43,000. Buys all rights. Pays on publication. Reports in 6 months. SASE.
Nonfiction: Articles on library services, local censorship problems, and how-to articles on programs that use books, films or microcomputer software. Informational, personal experience, interview, expose, and successful business operations. "Interested in history articles on the establishment/development of children's and young adult services in schools and public libraries." Buys 24 mss/year. Length: 2,500-3,000 words. Pays $100.

WILSON LIBRARY BULLETIN, 950 University Ave., Bronx NY 10452. (212)588-8400. Editor: Milo Nelson. 80% freelance written. Monthly (September-June). For professional librarians and those interested in the book and library worlds. Circ. 30,000. Pays on publication. Publishes ms an average of 2 months after acceptance. Buys first North American serial rights only. Sample copies may be seen on request in most libraries. "Manuscript must be original copy, double-spaced; additional photocopy or carbon is appreciated." Computer printout submissions acceptable; prefers letter-quality to dot-matrix. Deadlines are a minimum 2 months before publication. Reports in 3 months. SASE.
Nonfiction: Uses articles "of interest to librarians throughout the nation and around the world. Style must be lively, readable and sophisticated, with appeal to modern professionals; facts must be thoroughly researched. Subjects range from the political to the comic in the world of media and libraries, with an emphasis on the human as well as the technical aspects of any story. No condescension: no library stereotypes." Buys 30 mss/year. Send complete ms. Length: 2,500-6,000 words. Pays about $100-400, "depending on the substance of article and its importance to readers." Sometimes pays the expenses of writers on assignment.
Tips: "The best way you can break in is with a first-rate b&w photo and caption information on a library, library service, or librarian who departs completely from all stereotypes and the commonplace. Libraries have changed. You'd better first discover what is now commonplace."

Lumber and Woodworking

B.C. LUMBERMAN MAGAZINE, Box 34080, Station D, Vancouver British Columbia V6J 4M8 Canada. (604)731-1171. Editorial Director: Brian Martin. 60% freelance written. Monthly magazine; 75 pages. For the logging and saw milling industries of Western Canada and the Pacific Northwest of the United States. Circ. 8,500. Pays on acceptance. Publishes ms an average of 2 months after acceptance. Buys first Canadian serial rights. Submit seasonal/holiday material 2 months in advance. Reports in 2 weeks.
Nonfiction: How-to (technical articles on any aspect of the forest industry); general interest (anything of interest to persons in forest industries in western Canada or U.S. Pacific Northwest); interview (occasionally related to leading forestry personnel); and technical (forestry). No fiction or history. Buys 8 mss/issue. Query first with published clips. Length: 1,500 words average. Pays 15¢/word (Canadian).
Photos: State availability of photos with query. Pays $5-25 for b&w negatives and $50-80 for 8x10 glossy color or prints. Captions required. Buys first Canadian rights.

‡**CANADIAN FOREST INDUSTRIES**, 1450 Don Mills Rd., Don Mills, Ontario, M3B 2X7 Canada. Contact: Editor. 25% freelance written. For forest companies, loggers, lumber-plywood-board manufacturers. Monthly. Circ. 15,000. Pays on publication. Publishes ms an average of 6 months after acceptance. Byline given. Buys first North American serial rights. Reports in 1 month. Computer printout submissions acceptable; prefers letter-quality to dot-matrix. SAE and IRCs. Free sample copy.
Nonfiction: Uses "articles concerning industry topics, especially how-to articles that help businessmen in the forest industries. All articles should take the form of detailed reports of new methods, techniques and cost-cutting practices that are being successfully used anywhere in Canada, together with descriptions of new equipment that is improving efficiency and utilization of wood. It is very important that accurate descriptions of machinery (make, model, etc.) always be included and any details of costs, etc., in actual dollars and cents can make the difference between a below-average article and an exceptional one." Query. Length: 1,200-1,500 words. Pays 20¢/word minimum, more with photos. Pays expenses of writers on assignment.
Photos: Buys photos with mss, sometimes with captions only. Should be 8x10, b&w glossies or negatives.

NORTHERN LOGGER AND TIMBER PROCESSOR, Northeastern Loggers' Association, Box 69, Old Forge NY 13420. (315)369-3078. Editor: Eric A. Johnson. 40% freelance written. Monthly magazine of the forest industry in the northern U.S. (Maine to Minnesota and south to Virginia and Missouri). We are not a purely technical journal, but are more information oriented." Circ. 13,000. Pays on publication. Publishes ms an average of 3 months after acceptance. Byline given. Buys all rights. Submit seasonal/holiday material 3 months in advance. Photocopied and previously published submissions OK. "Any computer printout submission that can be easily read is acceptable." SASE. Reports in 2 weeks. Free sample copy.

Nonfiction: Expose, general interest, historical/nostalgic, how-to, interview/profile, new product and opinion. "We only buy feature articles, and those should contain some technical or historical material relating to the forest products industry." Buys 12-15 mss/year. Query. Length: 500-2,500 words. Pays $25-125.

Photos: Send photos with ms. Pays $20-35 for 35mm color transparencies; $5-15 for 5x7 b&w prints. Captions and identification of subjects required.

Tips: "We accept most any subject dealing with this part of the country's forest industry, from historical to logging, firewood, and timber processing."

● **ROSEBURG WOODSMAN.** Roseburg Lumber Co., % Hugh Dwight Advertising, Suite 101, 4905 SW Griffith Dr., Beaverton OR 97005. Editor: Shirley P. Rogers. 99% (but most rewritten) freelance written. Monthly magazine for wholesale and retail lumber dealers and other buyers of forest products, such as furniture manufacturers. Emphasis on wood products, including company products. Publishes a special Christmas issue. Circ. 8,000. Pays on publication. Publishes ms an average of 9 months after acceptance. Buys first serial rights or one-time rights. No byline given. Submit seasonal material 6 months in advance. Computer printout submissions acceptable; prefers letter-quality to dot-matrix. Reports in 1 week. Free sample copy and writer's guidelines.

Nonfiction: Features on the "residential, commercial and industrial applications of wood products, such as lumber, plywood, prefinished wall paneling, and particleboard, particularly Roseburg Lumber Co. products. We look for unique or unusual uses of wood and stories on hobbyists and craftsmen. No 'clever,' 'wise' or witty contributions unless they tell a fascinating story and are well-illustrated. No fillers, isolated photos or inadequately illustrated articles." Buys 15-20 mss/year. Query or submit complete ms. Length: 250-500 words. Pays $50-$100.

Photos: "Photos are essential. Good pictures will sell us on a story." Rarely uses b&w photos. Will accept prints, but prefers 120 color transparencies or 35mm slides. Pays $25-50/color transparency or color-corrected print; more for cover photo; less for b&w glossy print; purchased only with ms.

Tips: "I sometimes hire a freelancer 'on assignment' at a higher rate. Send letter specifying experience, publications, types of stories and geographic area covered. We have an absolute need for good, striking, interesting photos."

‡**TREE TRIMMERS LOG, A Newsletter For Today's Tree Trimmer**, Tree Trimmers Log, Box 833, Ojai CA 93023. (805)646-9688. Editor: D. Keith. Trade newsletter on tree trimming published 10 times/year. Circ. 400. Pays on acceptance. Publishes ms an average of 2 months after acceptance. Byline given. Offers 25% kill fee. Buys one-time rights. Submit seasonal/holiday material 2 months in advance. Simultaneous queries, and simultaneous, photocopied, and previously published submissions OK. Computer printout submissions acceptable. SASE. Reports in 1 month. Free sample copy and writer's guidelines.

Nonfiction: Book reviews (on trees, pruning, equipment); historical/nostalgic (trees, older trimmer reminiscings); how-to (run small businesses, maintain equipment, be more efficient in work); humor; interview/profile (of a trimmer with a slant; singing trimmer, community concerned trimmer, etc.); new product; personal experience (if you're a working trimmer); photo feature (rescue, action); and technical (taking care of equipment, climbing gear). No "cuteness". Buys 12-15 mss/year. Query or send complete ms. Length: 50-800 words. Pays $5-25.

Photos: State availability of photos. Reviews b&w contact sheets and b&w 3½x5 prints. Pays $5 for contact sheets; $5-10 for prints. Identification of subjects required. Buys one-time rights.

Columns/Departments: Chain Saw (or equipment) Corner and First Aid (50-150 words). "We're open to suggestions." Buys 10/year. Query. Length: 150-350 words. Pays $10.

Fillers: Clippings, jokes, anecdotes, short humor, puzzles, newsbreaks and cartoons. Buys 20/year. Pays $5.

Tips: "Submit a query for an interview with a tree trimmer, a local college horticulturist (trees), etc. Find someone unique, with a good story to tell, or who can offer tips to his fellow trimmers. Being writers, we work with and encourage writers. Our prices are low now, but we invite writers to grow with us."

Machinery and Metal Trade

ASSEMBLY ENGINEERING, Hitchcock Publishing Co., 25W550 Geneva Rd., Wheaton IL 60188. Editor: Wally Maczka. 2% freelance written. Monthly. For design and manufacturing engineers and production personnel concerned with assembly problems in manufacturing plants. Pays on publication. Publishes ms an average of 5 months after acceptance. Buys first serial rights only. Computer printout submissions acceptable; prefers letter-quality to dot-matrix. "Query on leads or ideas. We report on manuscript decision as soon as review is completed and provide edited proofs for checking by author, prior to publication." SASE. Sample copy sent on request.

Nonfiction: Wants features on design engineering and production practices for the assembly of manufactured products. Material should be submitted on "exclusive rights" basis. Subject areas include selection, specification, and application of fasteners, mounting hardware, electrical connectors, wiring, adhesives, joining methods (soldering, welding, brazing, etc.) and assembly equipment; specification of fits and tolerances; joint design; design and shop assembly standards; time and motion study (assembly line); quality control in assembly; layout and balancing of assembly lines; assembly tool and jig design; programming assembly line operations; working conditions, incentives, labor costs, as they relate to assembly line operators; hiring and training of assembly line personnel; and supervisory practices for the assembly line. Also looking for news items on robotic assembly, vision systems, adhesives and tapes, electronic assembly CAD/CAM/CAT, and manufacturing softwave (MRP & MRPII), bar coding AS/RS, AGUS, programmable conveyors and parts feeders, assembly-related subjects, and for unique or unusual "ideas" on assembly components, equipment, processes, practices and methods. "We want only technical articles, not PR releases." Requires good quality photos or sketches, usually close-ups of specific details. Pays $50 minimum/published page.

AUTOMATIC MACHINING, 100 Seneca Ave., Rochester NY 14621. (716)338-1522. Editor: Donald E. Wood. For metalworking technical management. Buys all rights. Byline given. Query. Computer printout submissions acceptable. SASE.
Nonfiction: "This is not a market for the average freelancer. A personal knowledge of the trade is essential. Articles deal in depth with specific job operations on automatic screw machines, chucking machines, high production metal turning lathes and cold heading machines. Part prints, tooling layouts always required, plus written agreement of source to publish the material. Without personal background in operation of this type of equipment, freelancers are wasting time. No material researched from library sources." Length: "no limit." Pays $20/printed page.
Tips: "In the year ahead there will be more emphasis on plant and people news so less space will be available for conventional articles."

‡**CUTTING TOOL ENGINEERING**, 464 Central Ave., Northfield IL 60093. (312)441-7520. Publisher: John William Roberts. Editor: Larry Teeman. For metalworking industry executives and engineers concerned with the metal-cutting/metal-removal/abrasive machining function in metalworking. 25% freelance written. Bimonthly. Circ. 43,000. Pays on publication. Publishes ms an average of 1 month after acceptance. Byline given. Buys all rights. Electronic submissions OK on IBM PC, but requires hard copy also. Computer printout submissions acceptable; no dot-matrix. Query with outline of article and professional background, or submit complete ms. SASE. Will send free sample copy on request.
Nonfiction: "Intelligently written articles on specific applications of all types of metal cutting tools, mills, drills, reamers, etc. Articles must contain all information related to the operation, such as feeds and speeds, materials machined, etc. Should be tersely written, in-depth treatment. In the Annual Diamond/Superabrasive Directory, published in May/June, we cover the use of diamond/superabrasive cutting tools and diamond/superabrasive grinding wheels." Length: 1,000-2,500 words. Pays "$35/published page, or about 5¢/published word."
Photos: Purchased with mss. 8x10 b&w glossies preferred.
Tips: "The most frequent mistake made by writers in completing an article for us is that they don't know the market."

FOUNDRY MANAGEMENT AND TECHNOLOGY, Penton Plaza, Cleveland OH 44114. (216)696-7000. Editor: J.C. Miske. 5% freelance written. Monthly. Publishes ms an average of 1 month after acceptance. Byline given. Buys first serial rights only. Computer printout submissions acceptable; no dot-matrix. SASE. Reports in 2 weeks.
Nonfiction: Uses articles describing operating practice in foundries written to interest companies producing metal castings. Buys 7-10 unsolicited mss/year. Length: 3,000 words maximum. Pays $50/printed page.
Photos: Uses illustrative photographs with article; uses "a great deal of 4-color photos."

INDUSTRIAL MACHINERY NEWS, Hearst Business Media Corp., IMN Division, 29516 Southfield Rd., Box 5002, Southfield MI 48086-5002. (313)557-0100. Editorial: M.M. Ecksel. Monthly tabloid; 200 pages. Emphasizes metalworking for buyers, specifiers, manufacturing executives, engineers, management, plant managers, production managers, master mechanics, designers and machinery dealers. Circ. 80,000. Pays on publication. Buys first North American serial rights. Submit seasonal/holiday material 3 months in advance. Simultaneous, photocopied, and previously published submissions OK. SASE. Reports in 6 weeks. Sample copy $5.

Nonfiction: Articles on "metal removal, metal forming, assembly, finishing, inspection, application of new and used machine tools, technology, measuring, gauging equipment, small cutting tools, tooling accessories, materials handling in metalworking plants, and safety programs. We give our publication a newspaper feel—fast reading with lots of action or human interest photos." Buys how-to. Pays $25 minimum. Length: open.
Photos: Photos purchased with mss; captions required. Pays $5 minimum.
Fillers: Puzzles, jokes and short humor. Pays $5 minimum.
Tips: "We're looking for stories on older machine tools—how they're holding up and how they're being used. We're also interested in metalworking machinery and equipment application articles that illustrate techniques geared to improving efficiency and productivity in the metalworking plant."

MODERN MACHINE SHOP, 6600 Clough Pike, Cincinnati OH 45244. Editor: Ken Gettelman. 25% freelance written. Monthly. Pays 1 month following acceptance. Publishes ms an average of 6 months after acceptance. Byline given. Electronic submissions OK if IBM compatible, but requires hard copy also. Computer printout submissions acceptable; prefers letter-quality to dot-matrix. SASE. Reports in 5 days.
Nonfiction: Uses articles dealing with all phases of metal manufacturing and machine shop work, with photos. No general articles. "Ours is an industrial publication, and contributing authors should have a working knowledge of the metalworking industry." Buys 10 unsolicited mss/year. Query. Length: 800-3,000 words. Pays current market rate. Sometimes pays the expenses of writers on assignment.
Tips: "The use of articles relating to computers in manufacturing is growing."

Maintenance and Safety

EQUIPMENT MANAGEMENT, 7300 N. Cicero Ave., Lincolnwood IL 60646. (312)588-7300. Editor: Greg Sitek. 10% freelance written. Monthly magazine; 76-110 pages. Circ. 55,000. Pays on publication. Rights purchased vary with author and material; usually buys all rights. Computer printout submissions acceptable; prefers letter-quality to dot-matrix. Reports in 1 month. SASE. Free sample copy.
Nonfiction: "Our focus is on the effective management of equipment through proper selection, careful specification, correct application and efficient maintenance. We use job stories, technical articles, safety features, basics and shop notes. No product stories or 'puff' pieces." Buys 12 mss/year. Query with outline. Length: 2,000-5,000 words. Pays $25/printed page minimum, without photos.
Photos: Uses 35mm and 2¹/₄x2¹/₄ or larger color transparencies with mss. Pays $50/printed page when photos are furnished by author.
Tips: "Know the equipment, how to manage it and how to maintain, service, and repair it."

SANITARY MAINTENANCE, Trade Press Publishing Co., 2100 W. Florist Ave., Milwaukee WI 53209. (414)228-7701. Managing Editor: Don Mulligan. Associate Editor: Susan M. Netz. A monthly magazine for the sanitary supply industry covering "trends in the sanitary supply industry; offering information concerning the operations of janitor supply distributors and building service contractors; and helping distributors in the development of sales personnel." Circ. 13,756. Pays on publication. Byline given. Buys first North American serial rights. Photocopied submissions OK. Computer printout submissions acceptable. SASE. Free sample copy and writer's guidelines.
Nonfiction: How-to (improve sales, profitability as it applies to distributors, contractors); and technical. No product application stories. Buys 8-12 mss/year. Query with published clips. Length: 1,500-3,000 words. Pays $75-200.
Photos: State availability of photos with query letter or ms. Reviews 5x7 prints. Payment for photos included in payment for ms. Identification of subjects required.
Tips: Articles on sales and financial information for small businesses are open to freelancers.

SERVICE BUSINESS, Published Quarterly for the Self-Employed Professional Cleaner, Service Business Magazine, Inc., Suite 345, 1916 Pike Place, Seattle WA 98101. (206)622-4241. Publisher/Editor: William R. Griffin. 80% freelance written. Quarterly magazine covering technical and management information relating to cleaning and self-employment. "We cater to those who are self-employed in any facet of the cleaning and maintenance industry who seek to be top professionals in their field. Our readership is small but select. We seek concise, factual articles, realistic but definitely upbeat." Circ. 5,000. Pays between acceptance and publication. Publishes ms an average of 3 months after acceptance. Byline given. Buys first serial rights, second serial (reprint) rights, and all rights; makes work-for-hire assignments. Submit seasonal/holiday material 4 months in advance. Simultaneous queries and previously published work (rarely) OK. Computer printout submissions acceptable; prefers letter-quality to dot-matrix. SASE. Reports in 3 months. Sample copy $3, 9x7½ SAE and 3 first class stamps; writer's guidelines for business size SAE and 1 first class stamp.

Nonfiction: Expose (safety/health business practices); how-to (cleaning, maintenance, small business management); humor (clean jokes, cartoons); interview/profile; new product (must be unusual to rate full article—mostly obtained from manufacturers); opinion; personal experience; and technical. Special issues include "What's New?" (Feb. 10). No "wordy tomes written off the top of the head, obviously without research, and needing more editing time than was spent on writing." Buys 40 mss/year. Query with or without published clips. Length: 500-3,000 words. Pays $5-80. ("Pay depends on amount of work, research and polishing put into article much more than on length.") Sometimes pays the expenses of writers on assignment.

Photos: State availability of photos or send photos with ms. Pays $5-25 for "smallish" b&w prints. Captions, model release, and identification of subjects required. Buys one-time rights and reprint rights. "Magazine size is 8½x7—photos need to be proportionate."

Columns/Departments: "Ten regular columnists now sell four columns per year to us. We are interested in adding a Safety & Health column (related to cleaning and maintenance industry). We are also open to other suggestions—send query." Buys 36 columns/year; department information obtained at no cost. Query with or without published clips. Length: 500-1,500 words. Pays $15-45.

Fillers: Jokes, gags, anecdotes, short humor, newsbreaks and cartoons. Buys 40/year. Length: 3-200 words. Pays $1-20.

Tips: "A freelancer can best break in to our publication with fairly technical articles on how to do specific cleaning/maintenance jobs; interviews with top professionals covering this and how they manage their business; and personal experience. Our readers demand concise, accurate information. Don't ramble. Write only about what you know and/or have researched. Editors don't have time to rewrite your rough draft. Organize and polish before submitting."

Management and Supervision

This category includes trade journals for middle management business and industrial managers, including supervisors and office managers. Journals for business executives and owners are classified under Business Management. Those for industrial plant managers are listed in Industrial Operation and Management.

CONSTRUCTION SUPERVISION & SAFETY LETTER, (CL) Bureau of Business Practice, 24 Rope Ferry Rd., Waterford CT 06386. (203)442-4365. Editor: DeLoris Lidestri. Semimonthly newsletter; 4 pages. Emphasizes all aspects of construction supervision. Buys all rights. Phone queries OK. Submit seasonal material at least 4 months in advance. SASE. Reports in 6 weeks. Free sample copy and writer's guidelines.

Nonfiction: Publishes solid interviews with construction managers or supervisors on how to improve a single aspect of the supervisor's job. Buys 100 unsolicited mss/year. Length: 360-720 words. Pays 10-14¢/word.

Photos: Purchased with accompanying ms. Pays $10 for head and shoulders photo of person interviewed. Total purchase price for ms includes payment for photo.

EMPLOYEE RELATIONS AND HUMAN RESOURCES BULLETIN, Bureau of Business Practice, 24 Rope Ferry Rd., Waterford CT 06386. Supervisory Editor: Barbara Kelsey. For personnel, human resources and employee relations managers on the executive level. Semimonthly newsletter; 8 pages. Circ. 3,000. Pays on acceptance. Buys all rights. No byline. Phone queries OK. Submit seasonal/holiday material 6 months in advance. Photocopied submissions OK. Computer printout submissions acceptable; prefers letter-quality to dot-matrix. SASE. Reports in 1 month. Free sample copy and writer's guidelines.

Nonfiction: Interviews about all types of business and industry such as banks, insurance companies, public utilities, airlines, consulting firms, etc. Interviewee should be a high level company officer—general manager, president, industrial relations manager, etc. Writer must get signed release from person interviewed showing that article has been read and approved by him/her, before submission. Some subjects for interviews might be productivity improvement, communications, compensation, government regulations, safety and health, grievance handling, human relations techniques and problems, etc. No general opinions and/or philosophy of good employee relations or general good motivation/morale material. Buys 3 mss/issue. Query. Length: 700-2,000 words. Pays 10¢/word after editing.

THE FOREMAN'S LETTER, Bureau of Business Practice, 24 Rope Ferry Rd., Waterford CT 06386. (203)442-4365. Editor: Carl Thunberg. 50% freelance written. Semimonthly. For industrial supervisors. Pays on acceptance. Publishes ms an average of 2 months after acceptance. Buys all rights. Interested in regular stringers (freelance). Computer printout submissions acceptable. SASE. Comprehensive guidelines available.

Nonfiction: Interested primarily in direct in-depth interviews with industrial supervisors in the US and Canada. Subject matter would be the interviewee's techniques for becoming a more effective manager, bolstered by illustrations out of the interviewee's own job experiences. Slant would be toward informing readers how to solve a particular supervisory problem. "Our aim is to offer information which readers may apply to their own professional self improvement. No copy that focuses on the theme that 'happy workers are productive workers.' " Buys 15-20 unsolicited mss/year. Length: 600-1,200 words. Pays 8¢-14½¢/word "after editing for all rights."

Photos: Buys photos submitted with mss. Captions needed for identification only. Head and shoulders, any size b&w glossy from 2x3 up. Pays $10.

Tips: "Study our editorial guidelines carefully. Emulate the style of sample issues. Write a how-to article focusing on one specific topic. A new freelancer should be willing to rewrite submissions if necessary. Editor will offer suggestions. An effort will be made to cultivate freelancers who comply the *closest* to editorial guidelines."

HIGH-TECH MANAGER'S BULLETIN, TEM, Bureau of Business Practice, Inc. 24 Rope Ferry Rd., Waterford CT 06386. (203)442-4365. Editor: Isabel Will Becker. 100% freelance written. Bimonthly newsletter for technical supervisors wishing to improve their managerial skills in high technology fields. Pays on acceptance. No byline given. Buys all rights. Computer printout submissions acceptable. Reports in 2 weeks on queries, 6 weeks on mss. Free sample copy and writer's guidelines.

Nonfiction: How-to (solve a supervisory problem on the job); and interview (of top-notch supervisors and managers). "Sample topics could include: how-to increase productivity, cut costs, achieve better teamwork, and help employees adapt to change." No articles about company programs. Buys 72 mss/year. Query. "A resume and sample of work are helpful." Length: 750-1,000 words. Pays 8-14¢/word.

Tips: "We need interview-based articles that emphasize direct quotes. Each article should include a reference to the interviewee's company (location, size, products, function of the interviewee's department and number of employees under his control). Define a problem and show how the supervisor solved it. Write in a light, conversational style, talking directly to technical supervisors who can benefit from putting the interviewee's tips into practice."

LE BUREAU, Suite 1000, 1001 de Maisonneuve W., Montreal, Quebec H3A 3E1 Canada. (514)845-5141. Editor: Paul Saint-Pierre, C.Adm. Published 6 times/year. For "office executives." Circ. 10,600. Pays on acceptance. Byline given. Buys all rights. Submit seasonal material 2 months in advance. SAE and IRCs.

Nonfiction: "Our publication is published in the French language. We use case histories on new office systems, applications of new equipment and articles on personnel problems. Material should be exclusive and above average quality." Buys personal experience articles, interviews, think pieces, coverage of successful business operations and new product articles. Buys about 10 mss/year. Query or submit complete ms. Length: 500-1,000 words. Pays $100-200.

Photos: B&w glossies purchased with mss. Pays $25 each.

MANAGE, 2210 Arbor Blvd., Dayton OH 45439. (513)294-0421. Editor-in-Chief: Douglas E. Shaw. 60% freelance written. Quarterly magazine; 36 pages. For first-line and middle management and scientific/technical managers. Circ. 72,000. Pays on acceptance. Buys North American magazine rights with reprint privileges; book rights remain with the author. SASE. Reports in 1 month. Free sample copy and writer's guidelines.

Nonfiction: "All material published by *Manage* is in some way management oriented. Most articles concern one or more of the following categories: communications, cost reduction, economics, executive abilities, health and safety, human relations, job status, labor relations, leadership, motivation and productivity and professionalism. Articles should be specific and tell the manager how to apply the information to his job immediately. Be sure to include pertinent examples, and back up statements with facts and, where possible, charts and illustrations. *Manage* does not want essays or academic reports, but interesting, well-written and practical articles for and about management." Buys 6 mss/issue. Phone queries OK. Submit complete ms. Length, 600-2,000 words. Pays 5¢/word.

Tips: "Keep current on management subjects; submit timely work."

OFFICE ADMINISTRATION AND AUTOMATION, Geyer-McAllister Publications, Inc., 51 Madison Ave., New York NY 10010. (212)689-4411. Editor: William A. Olcott. Executive Editor: Walter J. Presnick. Monthly business publication covering office systems, equipment, personnel, and management for administrators and systems specialists in charge of office operations. Circ. 55,000. Pays on publication. Byline given. Buys all rights. Photocopied submissions OK. SASE. Reports in 1 month. Sample copy $3.50; free writer's guidelines.

Columns/Departments: Book excerpts, 'Guest Opinion', new products, new literature, case histories, news, plus "of course—features. No "college thesis" articles. Buys 50 mss/year. Query. Length: 500-2,500 words. Pays up to $500.

Photos: Send photos with ms. Captions, model release and identification of subjects required. Buys one-time rights.

Tips: "Analyze and interpret clearly, especially if subject is technical. Assume readers have years of experience in the field."

PERSONNEL ADVISORY BULLETIN, Bureau of Business Practice, 24 Rope Ferry Rd., Waterford CT 06386. (203)442-4365, ext. 355. Editor: Laura Gardner. 75% freelance written. Emphasizes all aspects of personnel practitioners for personnel managers in all types and sizes of companies, both white collar and industrial. Semimonthly newsletter; 8 pages. Pays on acceptance. Publishes ms an average of 4 months after acceptance. Buys all rights. Phone queries OK. Submit seasonal/holiday material 4 months in advance. Computer printout submissions acceptable; no dot-matrix. SASE. Reports in 2 weeks. Free sample copy and writer's guidelines for SAE and 1 first class stamp.

Nonfiction: Interviews with personnel managers or human resource professionals on topics of current interest in the personnel field. No articles on hiring and interviewing, discipline, or absenteeism/tardiness control. Buys 30 mss/year. Query with brief, specific outline. Length: 1,000-1,500 words.

Tips: "We're looking for concrete, practical material on how to solve problems. We're providing information about trends and developments in the field. We don't want filler copy. It's very easy to break in. Just query by phone or letter (preferably phone) and we'll discuss the topic. Send for guidelines first, though, so we can have a coherent conversation."

PRODUCTIVITY IMPROVEMENT BULLETIN, PIB, Bureau of Business Practice, 24 Rope Ferry Rd., Waterford CT 06386. (203)442-4365. Editor: Paula Brisco. 75% freelance written. Semimonthly newsletter covering productivity improvement techniques of interest to middle and top management. Pays on acceptance. Publishes ms an average of 4 months after acceptance. No byline given. Buys all rights. Computer printout submissions acceptable; prefers letter-quality to dot-matrix. Reports in 2 weeks on queries; 1 month on mss. Free sample copy and writer's guidelines.

Nonfiction: Interviews with managers from business or industry detailing how readers can create productivity innovations, based on the interviewees experience. No articles on general management theory. Buys 50 mss/year. Query. Length: 1,000-1,600 words. Pays 8-14¢/word "after editing." Sometimes pays the expenses of writers on assignment.

Columns/Departments: "Personal Productivity column uses interview-based copy explaining specific measures our readers can take to increase their effectiveness." Buys 12 mss/year. Query. Length: 800-1,200 words. Pays 8-14¢/word.

Tips: "Lead story articles *must* cover a 'problem-process-solution-results' format as described in the writer's guidelines. Be willing to rewrite, if necessary. Topics should be well focused. (Check with us before doing the write-up. We like to talk to freelancers.) Writing should be conversational; use the 'you' approach. Use subheads and questions to guide the reader through your piece. Articles on activities of a specific company are subject to its approval."

SALES MANAGER'S BULLETIN, The Bureau of Business Practice, 24 Rope Ferry Rd., Waterford CT 06386. Editor: Paulette S. Withers. 25% freelance written. Newsletter published twice a month; 8 pages. For sales managers and salespeople interested in getting into sales management. Pays on acceptance. Publishes ms an average of 6 months after acceptance. Phone queries from regulars OK. Submit seasonal/holiday material 6 months in advance. Original submissions only. Buys all rights. Computer printout submissions acceptable; prefers letter-quality to dot-matrix. SASE. Reports in 2 weeks. Free sample copy and writer's guidelines only when accompanied by SASE.

Nonfiction: How-to (motivate salespeople, cut costs, create territories, etc.); interview (with working sales managers who use innovative techniques); and technical (marketing stories based on interviews with experts). No articles on territory management, saving fuel in the field, or public speaking skills. Break into this publication by reading the guidelines and sample issue. Follow the directions closely and chances for acceptance go up dramatically. One easy way to start is with an interview article ("Here's what sales executives have to say about . . ."). Buys 5 unsolicited mss/year. Query is vital to acceptance; "send a simple postcard explaining briefly the subject matter, the interviewees (if any), slant, length, and date of expected completion, accompanied by a SASE." Length: 800-1,500. Pays 10-15¢/word.

Tips: "Freelancers should always request samples and writer's guidelines, accompanied by SASE. Requests without SASE are discarded immediately. Examine the sample, and don't try to improve on our style. Write as we write. Don't 'jump around' from point to point and don't submit articles that are too chatty and with not enough real information. The more time a writer can save the editors, the greater his or her chance of a sale and repeated sales, when queries may not be necessary any longer."

SECURITY MANAGEMENT, American Society for Industrial Security, Suite 1200, 1655 N. Fort Myers Dr., Arlington VA 22209. (703)522-5800. Editor-in-Chief: Shari Mendelson Gallery. Senior Editor: Mary Alice Crawford. Managing Editor: Pamela Blumgart. 10% freelance written. Monthly professional magazine of the security business (i.e., protecting assets from loss). Circ. 25,000. Pays on publication. Publishes ms an average of 4 months after acceptance. Byline given. Buys all rights. Submit seasonal/holiday material 6 months in advance. Simultaneous queries and simultaneous, photocopied, and previously published submissions to noncompetitive magazines OK. Computer printout submissions acceptable; prefers letter-quality to dot-matrix. SASE. Reports in 3 weeks on queries; 10 weeks on mss. Sample copy $3; writer's guidelines for business size SAE and 1 first class stamp.
Nonfiction: Mary Alice Crawford, articles editor. Book excerpts, how-to, interview/profile, opinion, personal experience, photo feature and technical. Case studies, analytical pieces and new approaches to persistent security problems such as access control and computer security. No humor. "Send a coherent outline query." Buys 5-10 mss/year. Query with or without published clips. Length: 1,500-5,000 words. Pays 10¢/word; $250 maximum. Sometimes pays the expenses of writers on assignment.
Photos: State availability of photos. Reviews b&w and color contact sheets and prints, and color transparencies.
Fillers: Cecily Roberts, fillers editor. Clippings, anecdotes and newsbreaks. Buys variable number/year. Length: 50-200 words. Pays $5-25.
Tips: "We need more substantive, technical articles, not cursory overviews."

SECURITY MANAGEMENT: PROTECTING PROPERTY, PEOPLE & ASSETS, Bureau of Business Practice, 24 Rope Ferry Rd., Waterford CT 06386. Editor: Alex Vaughn. Semimonthly newsletter; 8 pages. Emphasizes security for industry. "All material should be slanted toward security directors, preferably industrial, but some retail and institutional as well." Circ. 3,000. Pays on acceptance. Buys all rights. Phone queries OK. Photocopied submissions OK. SASE. Reports in 2 weeks. Free sample copy and writer's guidelines.
Nonfiction: Interview (with security professionals only). "Articles should be tight and specific. They should deal with new security techniques or new twists on old ones." Buys 2-5 mss/issue. Query. Length: 750-1,000 words. Pays 10¢/word.

SUPERVISION, 424 N. 3rd St., Burlington IA 52601. Publisher: Michael S. Darnall. Editorial Supervisor: Doris J. Ruschill. Editor: Barbara Boeding. 95% freelance written. Monthly magazine; 24 pages. For first-line foremen, supervisors and office managers. 8½x11 inches. Circ. 8,630. Pays on publication. Publishes ms an average of 1 year after acceptance. Buys all rights. SASE. Reports in 3 weeks. Free sample copy and writer's guidelines; mention *Writer's Market* in request.
Nonfiction: How-to (cope with supervisory problems, discipline, absenteeism, safety, productivity, goal setting, etc.); and personal experience (unusual success story of foreman or supervisor). No sexist material written from only a male viewpoint. Include biography and/or byline with ms submissions. Author photos are used. Buys 12 mss/issue. Query. Length: 1,500-1,800 words. Pays 4¢/word.
Tips: "Query to be brief, but long enough to give a clear picture of material and approach being used. We are particularly interested in writers with first-hand experience—current or former supervisors who are also good writers. Following AP stylebook would be helpful." Uses no advertising.

TRAINING, The Magazine of Human Resources Development, 50 S. Ninth St., Minneapolis MN 55402. (612)333-0471. Editor: Jack Gordon. Monthly magazine for managers and training specialists in business, industry, government and health care. Circ. 49,000. Basically buys first serial rights. Pays on acceptance. Will consider photocopied submissions. Computer printout submissions acceptable; prefers letter-quality to dot-matrix. Works three months in advance. Reports in 6 weeks. SASE. Sample copy for 9x12 SASE and five first class stamps. Writers guidelines for SASE.
Nonfiction: Articles on management and techniques of employee training. Also issues and trends pertaining to job-related training and employee development (legal, legislative and social issues, computer-based training, management tactics, adult learning theory, etc.). Would like to see "articles relating general business concerns to specific training and development functions; interesting examples of successful training and management development programs; articles about why certain types of the above seem to fail; analyses of cost-benefit value of various types of training programs; emerging trends in the training and development field." Informational, how-to. Recent article example: "Customer Education: The Silent Revolution" (January 1985). No puff or "gee whiz" material. Buys 5 unsolicited mss/year. Query only. Feature length: 1,200-3,000 words. Training Today: Reports on research, opinions or events of significance to training specialists or general managers interested in employee development. Length: 300-700 words.
Photos: Prefers b&w or color transparencies, with captions. No extra payment for photos.

UTILITY SUPERVISION, (US) Bureau of Business Practice, 24 Rope Ferry Rd., Waterford CT 06386. (203)442-4365. Editor: DeLoris Lidestri. Semimonthly newsletter; 4 pages. Emphasizes all aspects of utility supervision. Pays on acceptance. Buys all rights. Phone queries OK. Submit seasonal material 4 months in ad-

vance. SASE. Reports in 4-6 weeks. Free sample copy and writer's guidelines.
Nonfiction: Publishes how-to (interview on a single aspect of supervision with utility manager/supervisor concentrating on how reader/supervisor can improve in that area). Buys 100 mss/year. Query. Length: 500-1,000 words. Pays 10-14¢/word.
Photos: Purchased with accompanying ms. Pays $10 for "head and shoulders photo of person interviewed. Total purchase price for ms includes payment for photo.

WAREHOUSING SUPERVISOR'S BULLETIN, WSB, Bureau of Business Practice, Inc. 24 Rope Ferry Rd., Waterford CT 06386. (203)442-4365. Editor: Isabel Will Becker. 75-100% freelance written. Biweekly newsletter covering traffic, materials handling and distribution for warehouse supervisors "interested in becoming more effective on the job." Pays on acceptance. Publishes ms an average of 3 months after acceptance. No byline given. Buys first serial rights only. Computer printout submissions acceptable; prefers letter-quality to dot-matrix. Reports in 2 weeks on queries; 6 weeks on mss. Free sample copy and writer's guidelines.
Nonfiction: How-to (increase efficiency, control or cut costs, cut absenteeism or tardiness, increase productivity, raise morale); interview (of warehouse supervisors or managers who have solved problems on the job). No descriptions of company programs, noninterview articles, textbook-like descriptions or union references. Buys 50 mss/year. Query. "A resume and sample of work are helpful." Length: 800-1,200 words. Pays 8-14¢/word.
Tips: "Interview-based articles must emphasize direct quotes. They should also include a reference to the interviewee's company (location, size, products, function of the interviewee's department and number of employees under his control). Focus articles on one problem, and get the interviewee to pinpoint the best way to solve it. Write in a light, conversational style, talking directly to warehouse supervisors who can benefit from putting the interviewee's tips into practice."

Marine Industries and Water Navigation

BOATING INDUSTRY, 850 3rd Ave., New York NY 10022. Editor/Publisher: Charles A. Jones. Editor: Olga Badillo. 15% freelance written. Monthly for "boating retailers and distributors." Circ. 26,300. Pays on publication. Publishes ms an average of 3 months after acceptance. Byline given. Buys all rights. "Interested in good column material, too. Best practice is to check with editor first on story ideas for go-ahead." Submit seasonal material 4 months in advance. SASE. Reports in 2 months.
Nonfiction: Business-oriented pieces about marine management. Buys 10-15 mss/year. Query. Length: 1,500-4,000 words. No clippings. Pays 9-15¢/word.
Photos: B&w glossy photos purchased with mss.

● **THE COMPASS**, Mobil International Aviation and Marine Sales, Inc., 150 E. 42nd St., New York NY 10017. Editor-in-Chief: R. Gordon MacKenzie. 90% freelance written. 40 pages. Emphasizes marine or maritime activities for the major international deep sea shipowners and ship operators who are Mobil's marine customers. Circ. 20,000. Pays on acceptance. Publishes ms an average of 18 months after acceptance. Byline given. Buys one-time rights. Simultaneous, photocopied, and previously published submissions OK. Computer printout submissions acceptable; prefers letter-quality to dot-matrix. SASE. Reports in 2 weeks. Free sample copy.
Nonfiction: Marine material only. General interest, historical, new product, personal experience and technical. No travelogues. Query or submit complete ms. Length: 2,000-4,000 words. Pays $175-250.
Photos: Purchased with accompanying ms. Reviews 5x7 or larger b&w prints or 35mm color transparencies. Offers no additional payment for photos accepted with ms. Captions preferred. Model release required. Buys one-time rights.

‡**OFFSHORE, International Journal of Ocean Business**, BennWell Publishing Co., Suite 106, 1200 Post Oak, Houston TX 77056. (713)621-9720. Editor: Robert G. Burke. 15% freelance written. Monthly magazine on marine oil and gas operations. Circ. 31,500. Pays on publication. Publishes ms an average of 3 months after acceptance. Byline given. Offers negotiable kill fee. Buys all rights. Submit seasonal/holiday material 3 months in advance. Simultaneous queries and photocopied submissions OK. Computer printout submissions acceptable; prefers letter-quality to dot-matrix. SASE. Reports in 3 weeks. Sample copy for SAE.
Nonfiction: How-to (detailed, technical). Buys 10-15 mss/year. Query. Length: 500-3,000 words. Pays $50-350.

Photos: Send photos with ms. Reviews b&w and color contact sheets, transparencies and prints. Buys all rights.

SEAWAY REVIEW, The Business Magazine of the Great Lakes Seaway System, Harbor Island, Maple City Postal Station MI 49664. Business office: The Seaway Review Bldg., 221 Water St., Boyne City MI 49712. Publisher: Jacques LesStrang. Managing Editor: Michelle Cortright. 10% freelance written. For "the entire Great Lakes/St. Lawrence region maritime community, executives of companies that ship via the Great Lakes, traffic managers, transportation executives, federal and state government officials and manufacturers of maritime equipment." Quarterly magazine. Circ. 16,000. Pays on publication. Buys first North American serial rights. Submit seasonal material 2 months in advance. Photocopied submissions OK. SASE. Reports in 3 weeks. Sample copy $5.
Nonfiction: "Articles dealing with Great Lakes shipping, shipbuilding, marine technology, economics of 8 states in the Seaway region (Michigan, Minnesota, Illinois, Indiana, Ohio, New York, Pennsylvania and Wisconsin), and Canada (Ontario, Quebec), port operation, historical articles dealing with Great Lakes shipping, current events dealing with commercial shipping on lakes, etc." No subjects contrary to our editorial statement. Submit complete ms. Length: 1,000-4,000 words. Pay "varies with value of subject matter and knowledgeability of author, $50-300."
Photos: State availability of photos with query. Pays $10-50 for 8x10 glossy b&w prints; $10-100 for 8x10 glossy color prints or transparencies. Captions required. Buys one-time rights. Buys "hundreds" of freelance photos each year for photo fill.
Fillers: Clippings and spot news relating to ports and the Great Lakes. Buys 3/issue. Length: 50-500 words. Pays $5-50.

Medical

Through these journals, physicians and mental health professionals learn how other professionals help their patients—among other technical topics. Listed here are publications for physicians and health professionals also reporting on new discoveries in medicine and health care plans. Journals for nurses, laboratory technicians, and other medical workers are included with the Hospitals, Nursing, and Nursing Home journals. Publications for druggists and drug wholesalers and retailers are grouped with the Drugs and Health Care Products journals. Publications that report on medical trends for the consumer can be found in the Health and Science categories.

● **ADVANCES FOR MEDICINE**, Hewlett-Packard Medical Products Group, 3000 Minuteman Rd., Andover MA 01810-1085. (617)687-1501, ext. 2027. Editor: Ronna Borenstein. Magazine published 4 times/year for medical professionals—physicians, nurses, biotechnicians, hospital administrators covering Hewlett-Packard's wide range of products and services, with an international emphasis. Circ. 30,000. Pays on acceptance. Publishes ms an average of 3 months after acceptance. Buys one-time rights or makes work-for-hire assignments. Simultaneous queries, and simultaneous, photocopied and previously published submissions OK. Computer printout submissions acceptable; prefers letter-quality to dot-matrix. SASE. Reports in 5 weeks. Sample copy $1.
Nonfiction: Book excerpts; expose; interview/profile; new product releases; personal experience (of medical professionals); and technical (application stories must feature Hewlett-Packard instrumentation). Query with clips of published work or send complete ms. Length: 500-2,500 words. Pays $500 minimum.
Photos: Steve Cahill, photo editor. State availability of photos or send photos with ms. Reviews contact sheets. Captions, model release and identification of subjects required.
Tips: "Submit articles with a human tone on how a specific procedure/HP product has changed (made more efficient, accurate) medical care—stress *unique* applications. Start with a case study of a patient problem, introduce the potential solution, spice with quotations by physicians, and show how the problem is solved and an advancement has been realized—include technological information."

AMERICAN FAMILY PHYSICIAN, 1740 W. 92nd St., Kansas City MO 64114. (816)333-9700. Publisher: Walter H. Kemp. Monthly. Circ. 130,000. Pays on publication. "Most articles are assigned and written by

physicians." Buys all rights. Reports in 2 weeks. SASE.
Nonfiction: Interested only in clinical articles. Query first "with a clear outline plus author's qualifications to write the article." Length: 2,500 words. Pays $100-250.

‡**AMERICAN MEDICAL NEWS**, American Medical Association, 535 N. Dearborn St., Chicago IL 60610. (312)645-5000. Editor: Dick Walt. Executive Editor: Barbara Bolsen. 5-10% freelance written. Weekly tabloid providing nonclinical information for physicians—information on socio-economic, political, and other developments in medicine. "*AMN* is a specialized publication circulating to physicians, covering subjects touching upon their profession, practices, and personal lives. This is a well-educated, highly sophisticated audience." Circ. 375,000 physicians. Pays on acceptance. Publishes ms an average of 4 months after acceptance. Byline given. Offers variable kill fee. Buys all rights. Rights sometimes returnable on request after publication. Simultaneous queries OK. Computer printout submissions acceptable. SASE. Reports in 3 weeks. Free sample copy and writer's guidelines.
Nonfiction: Carol Brierly Golin, articles editor. Interview/profile (occasional); opinion (mainly from physicians); and news and interpretive features. Special issues include "Year in Review" issue published in January. No clinical articles, general-interest articles physicians would see elsewhere, or recycled versions of articles published elsewhere. Buys 100 mss/year. Query. Length: 1,200-2,000 words. Pays $400-700 for features; $150 for opinions and short news items. "We have limited travel budget for freelancers; we pay minimal local expenses."

APA MONITOR, 1200 17th St. NW, Washington DC 20036. (202)955-7690. Editor: Jeffrey Mervis. Associate Editor: Kathleen Fisher. 5% freelance written. Monthly 64-page newspaper for psychologists and other social scientists and professionals interested in behaviorial sciences and mental health area. Circ. 75,000. Pays on publication. Publishes ms an average of 3 months after acceptance. Buys first serial rights. Computer printout submissions acceptable; no dot-matrix. Sample copy $2.40 and large envelope.
Nonfiction: News and feature articles about issues facing psychology both as a science and a mental health profession; political, social and economic developments in the behaviorial science area. Interview, profile and historical pieces. No personal views, reminiscences or satire. Buys no mss without query. Length: 300-3,000 words. Pays expenses of writers on assignment.
Tips: "Our writers almost need to be longtime readers or science writers to strike the balance between some of the top Ph.D.s in the country and graduate students at small colleges that we try to reach."

‡**CARDIOLOGY WORLD NEWS**, Medical Publishing Enterprises, Box 1548, Marco Island FL 33937. (813)394-0400. Editor: John H. Lavin. 50% freelance written. Monthly magazine covering cardiology and the cardiovascular system. "We need news articles *for doctors* on any aspect of our field—diagnosis, treatment, risk factors, etc." Estab. 1985. Pays on acceptance. Publishes ms an average of 2 months after acceptance. Byline given "for special reports and feature-length articles." Offers 20% kill fee. Buys first North American serial rights. Photocopied submissions OK. Computer printout submissions acceptable; no dot-matrix. SASE. Reports in 1 month. Sample copy $1; free writer's guidelines.
Nonfiction: New product and technical (clinical). No fiction, profiles of doctors or poetry. Query with published clips. Length: 250-1,500 words. Pays $50-300; $50/column for news articles. Pays expenses of writers on assignment.
Photos: State availability of photos with query. Pays $50/published photo. Rough captions, model release, and identification of subjects required. Buys one-time rights.
Columns/Departments: Send complete ms. Length: 250-1,000 words. Pays $50-150.
Fillers: Anecdotes. Buys 4-6/year. Length: 100-250 words. Pays $25.
Tips: "Submit written news articles of 250-500 words on speculation with basic source material (not interview notes) for fact-checking. We demand clinical or writing expertise for full-length feature."

‡**CINCINNATI MEDICINE**, Academy of Medicine, 320 Broadway, Cincinnati OH 45202. (513)421-7010. Managing Editor; Cullen Clark. Quarterly membership magazine for the Academy of Medicine of Cincinnati. "We cover socio-economic and political factors that affect the practice of medicine in Cincinnati. For example: How will changes in Medicare policies affect local physicians and what will they mean for the quality of care Cincinnati's elderly patients receive. (Ninety-nine percent of our readers are Cincinnati physicians.)" Circ. 3,000. Pays on acceptance. Byline given. Makes work-for-hire assignments. Simultaneous queries and photocopied submissions OK. Computer printout submissions acceptable; prefers letter-quality to dot-matrix. SASE. Reports in 2 weeks on queries; 1 week on mss. Sample copy for $2 and 9x12 SAE and 7 first class stamps; writer's guidelines for 4½x9½ SAE with 1 first class stamp.
Nonfiction: Historical/nostalgic (history of, or reminiscences about, medicine in Cincinnati); interview/profile (of nationally known medical figures or medical leaders in Cincinnati); and opinion (opinion pieces on controversial medico-legal and medico-ethical issues). "We do not want scientific-research articles, stories that are not based on good journalistic skills (no seat-of-the-pants reporting), or why my 'doc' is the greatest guy in the world stories." Buys 8-10 mss/year. Query with published clips or send complete ms. Length: 800-2,500

words. Pays $100-250. Sometimes pays the expenses of writers on assignment.
Photos: State availability of photos with query or ms. Captions and identification of subjects required. Buys one-time rghts.
Tips: "Send clips of published work; do some short features that will help you develop some familiarity with our magazine and our audience; and show initiative to tackle the larger stories. First-time writers often don't realize the emphasis we place on solid reporting. We want accurate, well-balanced reporting or analysis. Our job is to *inform* our readers."

DIAGNOSTIC IMAGING, Miller Freeman, 500 Howard St., San Francisco CA 94105. Publisher: Thomas Kemp. Editor: Peter Ogle. 10% freelance written. Monthly news magazine covering radiology, nuclear medicine and ultrasound for physicians in diagnostic imaging professions. Circ. 24,000. Average issue includes 4-5 features. Pays on acceptance. Publishes ms an average of 2 months after acceptance. Byline given. Buys all rights. No phone queries. "Written query should be well written, concise and contain a brief outline of proposed article and a description of the approach or perspective the author is taking." Submit seasonal material 1 month in advance. Simultaneous and photocopied submissions OK. Electronic submissions OK on Apple II, IBM PC, and McIntosh, but requires hard copy also. Computer printout submissions acceptable; prefers letter-quality to dot-matrix. SASE. Reports in 2 weeks. Free sample copy.
Nonfiction: "We are interested in topical news features in the areas of radiology, nuclear medicine and ultrasound, especially news of state and federal legislation, new products, insurance, regulations, medical literature, professional meetings and symposia and continuing education." Buys 10-12 mss/year. Query with published clips. Length: 1,000-2,000 words. Pays 15¢/word minimum.
Photos: Reviews 5x7 b&w glossy prints and 35mm and larger color transparencies. Offers $20 for photos accepted with ms. Captions required. Buys one-time rights.

‡**FACETS**, American Medical Association Auxiliary, Inc., 535 N. Dearborn St., Chicago IL 60610. (312)645-4470. Editor: Kathleen T. Jordan. For physicians' spouses. 30% freelance written. Magazine published 5 times/year; 32 pages. Circ. 90,000. Pays on acceptance. Publishes ms an average of 6 months after acceptance. Buys first rights. Simultaneous, photocopied and previously published submissions OK. Computer printout submissions acceptable; prefers letter-quality to dot-matrix. SASE. Reports in 6 weeks. Free sample copy and writer's guidelines.
Nonfiction: All articles must be related to the experiences of physicians' spouses. Current health issues; financial topics; physicians' family circumstances; business management; volunteer leadership how-to's. Buys 10 mss/year. Query with clear outline of article—what points will be made, what conclusions drawn, what sources will be used. No personal experience or personality stories. Length: 1,000-2,500 words. Pays $300-800. Pays expenses of writers on assignment.
Photos: State availability of photos with query. Uses 8x10 glossy b&w prints and 2¼x2¼ color transparencies.
Tips: Uses "articles only on specified topical matter; with good sources, not hearsay or opinion, but credibility. Since we use only nonfiction articles and have a limited readership, we must relate factual material."

GENETIC ENGINEERING NEWS, The Information Source of the Biotechnology Industry, Mary Ann Liebert, Inc., 157 E. 86th St., New York NY 10028. (212)722-3708. Managing Editor: Joan S. Graf. 80% freelance written. Tabloid published 8 times/year featuring articles on industry and research in areas of biotechnology such as recombinant DNA and hybridoma technology. Circ. 14,500. Pays on acceptance. Publishes ms an average of 6 weeks after acceptance. Byline given. Buys all rights. Computer printout submissions acceptable. SASE. Reports in 6 weeks on queries; 1 month on mss. Writer's guidelines for SAE and 1 first class stamp.
Nonfiction: Interview/profile (of corporate executives, academicians or researchers); new product; technical (any articles relating to biotechnology with emphasis on application); and financial (Wall Street analysis, etc.—of new companies). No company personnel changes or rewritten press releases. Buys 150 mss/year. Query with clips of published work. Length: 1,000-1,200 words. "All negotiable." Sometimes pays the expenses of writers on assignment.
Photos: Send photos with ms. Pays negotiable fee for b&w contact sheets. Identification of subjects required.
Tips: "The writer may have a better chance of breaking in at our publication with short articles and fillers, but because biotechnology is a complex area covering molecular biology and economics, and because our readers are primarily professionals in the field, our writers tend to have had some experience writing on biotech before writing for *GEN*. Writers submitting queries *must* be extremely knowledgeable in the field and have direct access to hard news. The most frequent mistake made by writers in completing an article for us is a lack of clarity; writers often fail to develop and explain ideas fully, clearly and accurately. Accuracy is essential."

GERIATRIC CONSULTANT, Medical Publishing Enterprises, Box 1548, Marco Island FL 33937. (813)394-0400. Editor: John H. Lavin. 70% freelance written. Bimonthly magazine covering medical care of the elderly. "We're a clinical magazine directed to doctors and physician assistants. All articles must *help* these health professionals to help their elderly patients. We're too tough a market for nonmedical beginners." Circ.

Close-up

Dodi Schultz
Author, Contributing Editor to *Parents*, and President of the American Society of Journalists and Authors

"Probably one-half million homeowners in this country are harboring a major fire hazard in their chimneys and don't know it."

It's an example of how writers should approach editors, of how Dodi Schultz doesn't waste words when she talks (and writes) about a subject.

"When you're writing a query, you should start with what has interested *you*," she points out. "If the editor feels concerned and feels the readers will be concerned, then you've got your assignment."

As a medical writer, she subscribes to trade journals and watches for re-occurring subjects in the medical trade that would concern the general reader. "You ought to see material that hasn't come to the attention of the public if you want to stay ahead of other writers," says Schultz, pointing out that writers can do this basic research for any trade.

When an editor offers Schultz an assignment by phone, she doesn't begin work until the editor puts the terms in writing. If the editor gets fired or quits work at a company, the written agreement proves that you had an assignment and at least would entitle you to a kill fee.

Before writing an assigned article, Schultz reads several issues of the magazine she'll be writing for. She studies the tone and level at which the magazine generally addresses the readers. "Is it going to be snappy or soothing? Is it going to be matter of fact? Is it going to be a combination of these tones?" she asks herself.

"You must write in the style of the magazine to a certain degree," says Schultz, whose bylines have appeared in *Ladies' Home Journal*, *Self*, *The New York Times Magazine*, and other well-known magazines. "A magazine on the stands represents a certain identity to the reader, and this is why a magazine editor is justified in maintaining a certain tone and asking writers to get that feeling into their work."

The writer doing a book doesn't have these constraints but has more responsibility, this author of more than a dozen books has learned. "When you're writing a book, you can speak for yourself. It's a lot closer to using your own words," she points out. "Of course, you're responsible for what you're doing since book editors do not edit the way magazine editors do."

Schultz enjoys writing books (mostly in collaboration with physicians) and articles simultaneously. She uses a memo board in her home/office to keep track of numerous projects and deadlines.

Editors many times call her about doing assignments. "That point can be reached only when you have done one or more articles for a magazine," says this contributing editor for *Parents*. "There are certain things editors will want to know before they take that first step. They don't know from looking at your work in another magazine how much editing or rewriting was necessary. They only know that when they've worked with you."

Schultz's first job was writing copy for Montgomery Ward catalogs. Having learned to say so much in so little space and to respect editors' wishes, she now chooses the assignments that interest her.

"If you're concerned, probably readers would be concerned," she points out. "The editor wants what he or she believes the reader wants, not that the editor is always right, but that's beside the point."

105,000. Pays on acceptance. Publishes ms an average of 2 months after acceptance. Byline given. Offers 20% kill fee. Buys first North American serial rights. Simultaneous queries OK. Computer printout submissions acceptable; no dot-matrix. Reports in 1 month. Sample copy for $1; free writer's guidelines.

Nonfiction: How-to (diagnosis and treatment of health problems of the elderly) and technical/clinical. No fiction or articles directed to a lay audience. Buys 20 mss/year. Query. Length: 750-3,000 words. Pays $100-300. Pays expenses of writers on assignment.

Photos: State availability of photos. (Photos are not required.) Model release and identification of subjects required. Buys one-time rights.

Fillers: Anecdotes. Buys 6-8/year. Length: 250 words. Pays $25 maximum.

Tips: "Many medical meetings are now held in the field of geriatric care. These offer potential sources and subjects for us."

THE JOURNAL, Addiction Research Foundation of Ontario, 33 Russell St., Toronto, Ontario M5S 2S1 Canada. (416)595-6053. Editor: Anne MacLennan. 50% freelance written. Monthly tabloid covering addictions and related fields around the world. *"The Journal* alerts professionals in the addictions and related fields or disciplines to news events, issues, opinions and developments of potential interest and/or significance to them in their work, and provides them an informed context in which to judge developments in their own specialty/geographical areas." Circ. 24,550. Pays on publication. Publishes ms an average of 3 months after acceptance. Byline given. Kill fee negotiable. Not copyrighted. Buys first serial rights and second serial (reprint) rights. Computer printout submissions acceptable. SAE with Canadian postage; IRC. Reports in 2 months on queries; 3 months on mss. Free sample copy and writer's guidelines.

Nonfiction: Interview/profile and new product. Query with published clips or send complete ms. Length: 1,000 words maximum. Pays 18¢/word minimum.

Photos: Terri Etherington, production editor. State availability of photos. Pays $10-35 for 5x7 or 8x10 b&w prints. Captions, model release, and identification of subjects required. Buys one-time rights.

Columns/Departments: Query with published clips.

Tips: "A freelancer can best break in to our publication with six years reporting experience, preferably with medical/science writing background. We rarely use untried writers."

‡MD MAGAZINE, New Horizons for the Physician, MD Publications, 30 E. 60th St., New York NY 10022. (212)355-5432. Editor: A.J. Vogl. Managing Editor: Barbara Guidos. 80% freelance written. Monthly magazine on culture/travel; a general interest magazine for physicians, covering all aspects of human experience. Circ. 140,000. Pays on acceptance. Publishes ms an average of 6 months after acceptance. Byline given. Offers 33⅓% kill fee. Buys first North American serial rights and second (reprint) rights. Submit seasonal/holiday material 4 months in advance. Photocopied and previously published submissions OK. Computer printout submissions acceptable; prefers letter-quality to dot-matrix. SASE. Reports in 1 month. Sample copy $2; free writer's guidelines.

Nonfiction: Sharon AvRutuick, articles editor. Book excerpts, general interest, historical/nostalgic, interview/profile, photo feature and travel. Buys 100 + mss/year. Query with published clips. Length: 1,000-3,000 words. Pays $350-700. Rarely pays the expenses of writers on assignment.

Photos: Doris Brautigan, photo editor. Send photos with ms. Reviews b&w and color transparencies (35mm or larger) and 8x10 prints and b&w contact sheets. Payment varies. Captions and identification of subjects required. Pays $60-175 for b&w photos; $100-225 for color. Buys one-time rights.

Columns/Departments: Buys 50 + mss/year. Query with published clips. Length: 1,000-1,500 words. Pays $300-350.

Tips: "It is fresh ideas and writing that make things and people come alive."

MEDICAL ECONOMICS, Medical Economics Co., Inc., 680 Kinderkamack Rd., Oradell NJ 07649. (201)262-3030. Editor: Don L. Berg. Managing Editor: Richard Service. Less than 5% freelance written. Biweekly magazine covering topics of nonclinical interest to office-based private physicians (MDs and DOs only). "We publish practice/management and personal/finance advice for office-based MDs and osteopaths." Circ. 167,000. Pays on acceptance. Publishes ms an average of 3 months after acceptance. Byline given. Offers 25% of full article fee as kill fee. Buys all rights and first serial rights. Computer printout submissions acceptable. SASE. Reports in 2 months on queries; 3 weeks on mss. Sample copy for $3 and 9x12 SASE.

Nonfiction: Contact Lilian Fine, chief of Outside Copy Division. How-to (office and personnel management, personal-money management); personal experience (only involving DMs or DOs in private practice); and travel (how-to articles). No clinical articles, hobby articles, personality profiles or office design articles. Buys 8-10 mss/year. Query with published clips. Length: 1,500-3,000 words. Pays $750-1,800. "The payment level is decided at the time go-ahead is given after query."

Photos: Contact Lilian Fine, chief of Outside Copy Division. State availability of photos. Pays negotiable rates for b&w contact sheets and for 35mm color slides. Model release and identification of subjects required. Buys one-time rights.

Tips: "How-to articles should fully describe techniques, goals, options and caveats—in terms that are clear and *realistic* for the average physician. Use of anecdotal examples to support major points is crucial. Our full-time staff is quite large, and therefore we buy only freelance articles that are not already assigned to staff writers. This puts a premium on unusual and appealing subjects."

THE MEDICAL POST, 777 Bay St., Toronto, Ontario M5W 1A7 Canada. Editor: Derek Cassels. Biweekly. For the medical profession. Will send sample copy to medical writers only. Buys first Canadian serial rights. Pays on publication. SAE and IRCs.
Nonfiction: Uses newsy, factual reports of medical developments. Must be aimed at professional audience and written in newspaper style. Length: 300-800 words. Pays 20¢/word.
Photos: Uses photos with mss or captions only, of medical interest; pays $10 up.

MEDICAL TIMES, Romaine Pierson Publishers, Inc. 80 Shore Rd., Port Washington NY 11050. (516)883-6350. Editors: A.J. Bollet, M.D., and A.H.Bruckheim, M.D. Executive Editor: Susan Carr Jenkins. 100% freelance written. Monthly magazine covering clinical medical subjects for primary care physicians in private practice. Circ. 105,000. Pays on acceptance. Publishes ms an average of 1 year after acceptance. Byline given. Buys all rights and makes work-for-hire assignments. Submit seasonal/holiday material 6 months in advance. Simultaneous queries OK. Reports in 1 month on queries; 2 months on mss. Sample copy $5; writer's guidelines for business size SAE and 1 first class stamp.
Nonfiction: "We accept only clinical medical and medico-legal material. It is useless to send us any material that is not related directly to medicine." Buys 100 mss/year (95% from physicians). Query. Length: 500-2,500 words. Pays $25-300.
Photos: State availability of photos. Pays variable rates for 2x2 b&w and color transparencies, and 4x5 or 8x10 b&w and color prints. Model release and identification of subjects required.
Fillers: Anecdotes. "Must be true, unpublished and medically oriented." Buys 25/year. Length: 25-200 words.
Tips: "A query letter is a must. 99% of our material is 'invited.'"

MEDICINE AND COMPUTER MAGAZINE, The Practical Medical Computer Magazine, 470 Mamaroneck Ave., White Plains NY 10605. (914)681-0040. Editor: Jeffrey Rothfeder. Managing Editor: Sally Ketchum. 75% freelance written. Bimonthly magazine covering computer applications in medicine with "a simple nontechnical approach to describing the ways computers are used in medicine by private practitioners." Circ. 50,000. Pays 1-2 months after acceptance. Publishes ms an average of 4 months after acceptance. Offers 10% kill fee. Buys all rights. No simultaneous queries. Photocopied submissions OK. Electronic submissions via disk (IBM-compatible WordStar or Multimate Software) or via modem ("send to our mailbox at Compu-Serve, The Source or MCI Maril") OK. Computer printout submissions acceptable. SASE. Reports in 1 month. Sample copy for $4; free writer's guidelines for SASE.
Nonfiction: Book excerpts (on medical computing); how-to (use software and hardware in the physician's office); interview/profile (with leading medical computing luminaries); new product (review of important computer hardware and software for physicians); opinion (essays on issues that affect physicians and their use of computers); personal experience (first person MD accounts of computerization); photo feature (breakthroughs in medical computing, e.g., DNA modeling—with color slides); and features describing how physicians are using computers from simple applications to more esoteric ones. Special issue includes Practice Management with Computers (feature accounts, application, how-to, etc.). Buys 12 mss/year. Query with published clips. Length: 2,000-3,000 words. Pays $300-1,000. Sometimes pays the expenses of writers on assignment.
Photos: State availability of photos. Pays negotiable rates for 3x5 b&w and color transparencies. Model release and identification of subjects required.
Tips: "Find the most exciting uses of computers in medicine, interview the movers and shakers involved with it, and tell us about it. Do not overwhelm the physicians with your knowledge about the subject; overwhelm them with your ability to impart their knowledge."

THE NEW PHYSICIAN, 1910 Association Dr., Reston VA 22091. Editor: Renie Schapiro. 20% freelance written. For medical students, interns and residents. Published 9 times/year; 56 pages. Circ. 80,000. Buys first serial rights. Buys 6-12 mss/year. Pays on publication. Publishes ms an average of 3 months after acceptance. Will consider simultaneous submissions. Computer printout submissions acceptable. Reports in 3 months. SASE. Free sample copy.
Nonfiction: "Articles on social, political, economic issues in medicine/medical education. Our readers need more than a superficial, simplistic look into issues that affect them. We want skeptical, accurate, professional contributors to do well-researched, comprehensive, incisive reports and offer new perspectives on health care problems." Not interested in material on "my operation," or encounters with physicians, or personal experiences as physician's patient, investment/business advice for physicians, or highly technical or clinical material. Humorous articles and cartoons for physicians-in-training welcome. Informational articles, interviews and exposes are sought. Query and send complete ms. Length: 500-3,500 words. Pays $50-400 with higher fees selected investigative pieces. Sometimes pays expenses of writers on assignment.

Tips: "Our magazine demands real sophistication on the issues we cover because we are a professional journal for readers with a progressive view on health care issues and a particular interest in improving the health system. Those freelancers we publish reveal in their queries and ultimately in their manuscripts a willingness and an ability to look deeply into the issues in question and not be satisfied with a cursory review of those issues."

NUCLEUS SCIENCE JOURNAL, Queens College, Kissena and Melbourne Ave., Flushing NY 11367. Editor: Mark A. Young. Managing Editor: Lisa C. Bogdonoff. Annual scientific journal covering biology, chemistry, medicine and natural science. Circ. 7,000. Pays on publication. Byline given. Buys all rights. Submit seasonal material 3 months in advance. Simultaneous queries, and simultaneous, photocopied and previously published submissions OK. SASE. Reports in 2 weeks on queries; 1 month on mss. Sample copy $1; free writer's guidelines.
Nonfiction: Book excerpts; interview/profile (with scientists who have made significant contributions to furthering an understanding of science); and photo feature. Buys 20 mss/year. Query with or without published clips. Length: open. Pays $50 minimum; sometimes pays in copies; sometimes commissions articles.
Photos: Louis Wegner, photo editor. Reviews b&w contact sheet. Payment depends on photo.
Fillers: A. Simke, fillers editor. Anecdotes and newsbreaks. Buys 10/year. Length: open.
Tips: "Well written scientific 'journal style' articles are what we seek. Articles should be slanted toward laymen and scientists alike. Articles on medical topics written by MDs are especially welcome."

THE PHYSICIAN AND SPORTSMEDICINE, McGraw-Hill, 4530 W. 77th St., Edina MN 55435. (612)835-3222. Editor: Allan J. Ryan, M.D. Executive Editor: Frances Caldwell. Monthly magazine covering medical aspects of sports and exercise. "We look in our feature articles for subjects of practical interest to our physician audience." Circ. 130,000. Pays on acceptance. Byline given. Buys one-time rights. Submit seasonal/holiday material 6 months in advance. Simultaneous queries OK. Reports in 2 weeks. Sample copy for $3; free writer's guidelines.
Nonfiction: Interview/profile (persons active in this field); and technical (new developments in sports medicine). Query. Length: 250-2,500 words. Pays $400-750.
Photos: Marty Duda, photo editor. State availability of photos. Pays ASTM rates for color transparencies. Buys one-time rights.

PHYSICIAN'S MANAGEMENT, Harcourt Brace Jovanovich Health Care Publications, 7500 Old Oak Blvd., Cleveland OH 44130. (216)243-8100. Editor: Bob Feigenbaum. 50% freelance written. Monthly magazine emphasizes finances, investments, malpractice, socioeconomic issues, estate and retirement planning, small office administration, practice management, leisure time, computers, travel, automobiles, and taxes for primary care physicians in private practice. Circ. 110,000. Pays on acceptance. Publishes ms an average of 6 months after acceptance. Buys first serial rights only. Submit seasonal or holiday material 5 months in advance. Computer printout submissions acceptable; no dot-matrix. SASE. Reports in 1 month.
Nonfiction: *"Physician's Management* is a practice management/economic publication, not a clinical one." Publishes how-to articles (limited to medical practice management); informational (when relevant to audience); and personal experience articles (if written by a physician). No fiction, clinical material or satire that portrays MD in an unfavorable light; or soap opera, "real-life" articles. Length: 2,000-2,500 words. Buys 10 mss/issue. Query. Pays $125/3-column printed page. Use of charts, tables, graphs, sidebars and photos strongly encouraged. Sometimes pays the expenses of writers on assignment.
Tips: "Talk to doctors first about their practices, financial interests, and day-to-day nonclinical problems and then query us. Also, the ability to write a concise, well-structured and well-researched magazine article is essential. Freelancers who think like patients fail with us. Those who can think like MDs are successful. Our magazine is growing significantly. The opportunities for good writers will, therefore, increase greatly."

PODIATRY MANAGEMENT, 401 N. Broad St., Philadelphia PA 19108. (215)925-9744. Publisher: Scott C. Borowsky. Editor: Barry Block, D.P.M. Managing Editor: M.J. Goldberg. Business magazine published 8 times/year for practicing podiatrists. "Aims to help the doctor of podiatric medicine to build a bigger, more successful practice, to conserve and invest his money, to keep him posted on the economic, legal and sociological changes that affect him." Circ. 11,000. Pays on publication. Byline given. Buys first North American serial rights and second serial (reprint) rights. Submit seasonal/holiday material 4 months in advance. Simultaneous queries, and simultaneous, photocopied and previously published submissions OK. Send mss to Dr. Block, 225 E. 64th St., New York NY 10021. SASE. Reports in 2 weeks. Sample copy $2; free writer's guidelines.
Nonfiction: General interest (taxes, investments, estate planning, recreation hobbies); how-to (establish and collect fees, practice management, organize office routines, supervise office assistants, handle patient relations); interview/profile; and personal experience. "These subjects are the mainstay of the magazine, but offbeat articles and humor are always welcome." Buys 25 mss/year. Query. Length: 1,000-2,500 words. Pays $150-350.
Photos: State availability of photos. Pays $10 for b&w contact sheet. Buys one-time rights.

RESIDENT & STAFF PHYSICIAN, Romaine Pierson Publishers, Inc., 80 Shore Rd., Port Washington NY 11050. (516)883-6350. Editor: Alfred Jay Bollet, MD. Managing Editor: Anne Mattarella. 15% freelance written. Monthly journal covering clinical medicine and practice management for residents and staff physicians. "*Resident & Staff Physician* goes to hospital-based physicians throughout the country, including practically all residents and the full-time hospital staff responsible for their training." Circ. 100,000. Pays on acceptance. Publishes ms an average of 1 year after acceptance. Byline given. Buys all rights. Submit seasonal/holiday material 1 year in advance. Simultaneous queries and photocopied submissions OK. Reports in 3 weeks on queries; 4 months on mss. Sample copy for $5; free writer's guidelines.
Nonfiction: Historical/nostalgic (medical); new product (medical); and clinical, review-type articles and those for practice management. No case reports. Buys 2 mss/year. Query. Length: 6-8 typewritten pages. Pays $200-300.
Photos: State availability of photos. "Payment is included in manuscript payment." Captions, model release and identification of subjects required. Buys all rights.
Columns/Departments: Medical Mixups (terms patients mix up, e.g., Cadillacs in the eyes instead of cataracts). Buys 5-10 mss/year. Send complete ms. Length: 50 words. Pays $25 maximum.
Fillers: Jokes, anecdotes, short humor and newsbreaks. Buys 5/year. Length: 25-500 words. Pays $25 to $100.
Tips: "A freelancer can best break in to our publication with filler items or humorous anecdotes. Keep the audience in mind. Jokes about high doctor fees are *not* funny to doctors."

SURGICAL ROUNDS, Romaine Pierson Publishers, Inc., 80 Shore Rd., Port Washington NY 11050. (516)883-6350. Editor: Mark M. Ravitch, MD. Executive Editor: Roxane Cafferata. Monthly magazine for surgeons and surgical specialists throughout the country, including all surgical interns, residents, and faculty in medical schools, plus full-time hospital and private practice surgeons and operating room supervisors. Circ. 70,000. Pays on acceptance. Byline given. Buys all rights. Reports in 1 month. Sample copy $5; free writer's guidelines.
Nonfiction: How-to (practical, everyday clinical applications). "Articles for 'The Surgeon's Laboratory' should demonstrate a particular procedure step-by-step and be amply and clearly illustrated with intraoperative color photographs and anatomical drawings." Buys 80 mss/year. Query with published clips. Length: 1,500-2,000 words. Pays $150-400.
Poetry: Only poetry related to hospital, physician, or operative experience. Buys 6/year. Pays $25.

Mining and Minerals

COAL AGE, 1221 Avenue of the Americas, New York NY 10020. Editor: Joseph F. Wilkinson. For supervisors, engineers and executives in coal mining. Monthly. Circ. 24,000. Pays on publication. Buys all rights. SASE. Reports in 3 weeks. SASE.
Nonfiction: Uses some technical (operating type) articles; some how-to pieces on equipment maintenance; and management articles. Query. Pays $200/page.

‡**GOLD PROSPECTOR**, Gold Prospectors Association of America, Box 507, Bonsall CA 92003. (619)728-6620. Editor: Steve Teter. 60% freelance written. Bimonthly magazine covering gold prospecting and mining. "*Gold Prospector* magazine is the official publication of the Gold Prospectors Association of America. The GPAA is an international organization of more than 100,000 members who are interested in recreational prospecting and mining. Our primary audience is people of all ages who like to take their prospecting gear with them on their weekend camping trips, and fishing and hunting trips. Our readers are interested not only in prospecting, but camping, fishing, hunting, skiing, backpacking, etc. And we try to carry stories each issue pertaining to subjects besides prospecting." Circ. 150,000. Pays on publication. Publishes ms an average of 6 months after acceptance. Byline given. Buys first North American serial rights and second serial (reprint) rights. Submit seasonal/holiday material 6 months in advance. Simultaneous queries and photocopied and previously published submissions OK. Computer printout submission acceptable; prefers letter-quality to dot-matrix. SASE. Reports in 3 weeks. Sample copy $1; free writer's guidelines.
Nonfiction: Historical/nostalgic; how-to (prospecting techniques, equipment building, etc.); humor; new product; personal experience; technical; and travel. "One of our publishing beliefs is that our audience would rather experience life than watch it on television—that they would like to take a rough and tumble chance with the sheer adventure of taking gold from the ground or river after it has perhaps lain there for a million years. Even if they don't, they seem to enjoy reading about those who do in the pages of *Gold Prospector* magazine." Buys 75-100 mss/year. Query with or without published clips if available or send complete ms. Length: 1,000-

3,000 words. Pays $25-100.
Photos: State availability of photos with query or ms. Pays $2.50-$10 for 3½x5 b&w prints; $5-25 for 3½x5 color prints. Captions, model release, and identification of subjects required. Buys all rights.
Columns/Departments: Precious metals market report, mining news, and dowsing report. Buys 15-25/year. Query with or without published clips if available or send complete ms. Length: 500-1,000 words. Pays $25-100.
Fillers: Clippings and anecdotes. Buys 25/year. Length: 50-100 words. Pays $5-15.
Tips: "We need manuscripts that accurately describe prospecting techniques, outdoor camping trips and information, and rock hounding techniques, etc."

ROCK PRODUCTS, Maclean-Hunter Publishing Corp., 300 W. Adams, Chicago IL 60606. (312)726-2802. Editor: Richard S. Huhta. Monthly magazine of the nonmetallic mining industry for producers of cement, lime, sand, gravel, crushed stone and lightweight gypsum aggregate. Circ. 23,000. Pays on publication. Byline given. Buys first serial rights. Reports in 2 weeks.
Nonfiction: Technical (maintenance and cement). "All pieces must relate directly to our industry. No general business articles." Buys 5-6 mss/year. Query. Length: 2,000-4,000 words. Pays variable fee.
Photos: No restrictions. Color transfer a plus. No additional fee for ms accompanied by photos.

WORLD MINING EQUIPMENT, Technical Publishing, 875 3rd Ave., New York NY 10022. (212)605-9400. Editorial Director: Ruth W. Stidger. Managing Editor: Frank Petruzalek. 20% freelance written. Monthly magazine on mining, mineral processing and mineral exploration for mine managers and engineers worldwide. Circ. 23,000. Pays on publication. Publishes ms an average of 3 months after acceptance. Byline varies, depending on background. Buys all rights. Submit seasonal/holiday material 4 months in advance. Simultaneous queries, and simultaneous and previously published submissions OK (if not to direct competition). Computer printout submissions acceptable; prefers letter-quality to dot-matrix. Reports in 1 week. Free sample copy and writer's guidelines.
Nonfiction: Book experts (related to mining) how-to (reduce costs, increase production) and technical. Buys 24-30 mss/year. Send complete ms. Length: 1,200-8,000 words. Pays $200-800.
Photos: Mail to editorial director. State availability of photos or send photos with ms. Pays $200 for 35mm and 2¼x2¼ color transparencies; b&w prints $25-100. Captions, model release and identification of subjects required. Buys one-time rights.

Music

CLAVIER, 200 Northfield Rd., Northfield IL 60093. (312)328-6000. Editor: Barbara Kreader. 83% freelance written. Magazine; 48 pages. Published 10 times/year. Pays on publication. Publishes ms an average of 8 months after acceptance. Buys all rights. "Suggest query to avoid duplication." SASE. Free sample copy.
Nonfiction: Wants "articles aimed at teachers of piano and organ. Must be written from thoroughly professional point of view. Avoid, however, the thesis style subject matter and pedantic style generally found in scholarly journals. We like fresh writing, practical approach. We can use interviews with concert pianists and organists. An interview should not be solely a personality story but should focus on a subject of interest to musicians. Any word length. Photos may accompany ms." Buys 65+ unsolicited mss/year. Pays $35/printed page.
Photos: "We need color photos for cover, such as angle shots of details of instruments, other imaginative photos, with keyboard music themes."

MUSIC CONNECTION MAGAZINE, The Alternative Music Trade Publication, Connection Publications, Suite 201, 6640 Sunset Blvd., Hollywood CA 90028. (213)462-5772. Executive Editor: J. Michael Dolan. Senior Editor: Bud Scoppa. 80% freelance written. A biweekly magazine covering the entire music industry for musicians and trade executives. Circ. 40,000. Pays on publication. Publishes ms an average of 2 months after acceptance. Byline given. Makes work-for-hire assignments. Submit seasonal/holiday material 6 weeks in advance. Simultaneous queries and photocopied submissions OK. Computer printout submissions acceptable; prefers letter-quality to dot-matrix. SASE. Reports in 1 month on queries; 2 months on mss. Sample copy for $2; 9x12 SAE and 2 class stamps; writer's guidelines for 9x12 SAE and 2 first class stamps.
Nonfiction: Expose (dealing with major music industry companies or organizations); interview/profile (personalities of interest in popular music); technical (new technological developments in instruments and musical computers); how-to (breaking into the industry, cutting records, etc.); and historical (dealing with the historical

background of the music and record industry). Special issues include: Recording Studios, Video, Nightclubs, and Year-End Review. "All articles must deal with factual and timely occurrences and personalities in the music industry." Buys 120 mss/year. Query with resume and published clips. Length: 800-2,500 words. Pays $30-150. Sometimes pays the expenses of writers on assignment.

Photos: Attention: photo editor. Send photos with accompanying query or ms. Payment negotiable. Identification of subjects required. Buys all rights.

Columns/Departments: Bruce Duff, review editor/club rep. Concert and Nightclub Reviews (acts playing southern California); Record Reviews (recent release LPs, EPs, singles and cassettes); and News & Local Notes (noteworthy happenings in the popular music industry). Buys 500 mss/year. Query with resume and published clips. Length: 100-800 words. Pays $5-40.

Fiction: Bud Scoppa, Editor. Humorous (dealing with the music business and the trials of getting accepted); and mainstream (pertaining to the record industry and the nightclub scene). "We do not want to see anything which is irrelevant to popular music." Buys 1-2 mss/year. Query with resume and published clips. Length: 750-2,500 words. Pays $25-100.

Fillers: Bud Scoppa, senior editor. Clippings, gags, anecdotes and newsbreaks. Buys 5/year. Length 30-300 words. Pays $5-25.

Tips: "Previous experience in the music industry and proven background as a professional writer in related publications are very important. Send as complete a resume as possible, including samples of previously published work, and a cover letter dicussing your musical interests. Feature stories, interviews, and news-article writing are the areas where we most often use freelancers. It is important to take an authoritative and knowledgeable music industry slant when writing these articles. There is no substitute for intensive research when writing a piece for any publication. It becomes painfully obvious to the informed reader when the writer is unsure of his subject matter."

MUSIC EDUCATORS JOURNAL, 1902 Association Dr., Reston VA 22091. (703)860-4000. Editor: Rebecca Taylor. Less than 10% freelance written. Monthly (September-May) magazine for music educators in elementary and secondary schools and universities. Circ. 54,000. Pays only for solicited articles by authors outside the music education field. Publishes ms an average of 6 months after acceptance. Byline given. "We prefer typed manuscripts, but will consider computer printouts." SASE. Reports in 2 months. Free author's guidesheet.

Nonfiction: "*MEJ* is the communications organ for the members of Music Educators National Conference. We publish articles on music education at all levels—not about individual schools, but about broad issues, trends and instructional techniques. Particularly interested in issue-oriented articles, pieces on individual aspects of American and nonWestern music, and up-beat interviews with musicians, composers and innovative teachers." No articles on personal awards or group tours. Length: 1,000-3,000 words. Query the editor.

Tips: "Our readers are experts in music education, so accuracy and complete familiarity with the subject is essential. A selection of appropriate professional quality eight-by-ten black and white glossy prints submitted with a manuscript greatly increases the chances of acceptance."

MUSIC & SOUND OUTPUT, The Magazine for Performers and Producers, Testa Communications, Inc., 220 Westbury Ave., Carle Place NY 11514. (516)334-7880. Editor: Chris Clark. Managing Editor: David Browne. 10% freelance written. Monthly magazine of contemporary music and recording. Audience is mostly working musicians. Prefers technical versus sociological slant in coverage of rock, jazz, R&B, country, pop, blues, and ethnic music. Circ. 93,000. Pays on publication. Publishes ms an average of 3 months after acceptance. Byline given. Offers 10-20% kill fee. Buys all rights. Photocopied submissions OK. Computer printout submissions acceptable; prefers letter-quality to dot-matrix. SASE. Reports in 2 weeks. Sample copy for 9x12 SAE and 6 first class stamps.

Nonfiction: Interview/profile (music performers, producers, engineers, industry executives); technical (recording, and live sound, query first); and reviews of records, concerts. No mss written from a fan's point of view, i.e., features on performers without getting an interview. No how-to articles. Buys 10-20 mss/year. Query with published clips. Length: 250-3,000 words. Pays $25-500. Sometimes pays the expenses of writers on assignment.

Photos: State availability of photos. Prefers exclusive photos. Reviews color transparencies and 8x10 b&w prints. Pays $50-300 for color; $20-200 for b&w. Identification of subjects required. Buys one-time rights.

Columns/Departments: Concert and record reviews (any genre). Buys 10-20 mss/year. Send complete ms. Length: 200-500 words. Pays $20-50.

Tips: "A huge pile of music-related clips is always impressive. We are seeking writers with experience in the music industry as a performer or with extensive technical background in recording. Areas most open to freelancers include record reviews and short (500-1,000 words), profiles of new bands, established musicians with a new direction, producers, engineers and innovators."

MUSICLINE, CCM Publications, Inc., Suite 201, 25231 Paseo De Alicia, Laguna Hills CA 92653. (714)951-9106. Editor-in-chief: John W. Styll. Editor: Thom Granger. Monthly magazine covering the Christian music industry. "Our readers include record company executives, booking agents, artist managers, recording artists, songwriters, church music directors and fans. Our approach is similar to other music trades such as *Billboard*, *Cashbox*, etc., with information as current as possible about news and events as well as current product reviews." Circ. 5,000. Pays on publication. Byline given. Pays 5¢/word kill fee. Buys first North American serial rights. Submit seasonal/holiday material 4 months in advance. Photocopied submissions OK. Computer printout submissions acceptable. SASE. Report in 2 weeks on queries; 1 month on mss. Free sample copy and writer's guidelines.

Nonfiction: General interest (news stories); how-to (ideas for retailers); inspirational; interview/profile (with key industry people); new product; and opinion (guest editorials, book reviews, record reviews). No personality profiles or human interest pieces. Buys 15 mss/year. Query. Length: 300-1,200 words. Pays 8¢/word.

Columns/Departments: Reviews of current Christian albums and reviews of books related to the music industry. "Reviews (we will contact you by phone with assignments) and Bottom Line (inspiration pieces relating to Christian music—submit ms) are the areas most open to freelancers." Buys 200 mss/year. Send published clips. Length: 150-700 words. Pays 8¢/word.

Tips: "A freelancer can best break into our publication with a specific query explaining the article and how and where the article will fit in, with a sample or proposal of ideas (with SASE)."

OPERA NEWS, 1865 Broadway, New York NY 10023. Editor: Robert Jacobson. 75% freelance written. Monthly magazine (May-November); biweekly (December-April). For all people interested in opera; opera singers, opera management people, administrative people in opera, opera publicity people, and artists' agents; people in the trade and interested laymen. Circ. 115,000. Pays on publication. Buys first serial rights only. Pays negotiable kill fee. Byline given. Computer printout submissions acceptable; prefers letter-quality to dot-matrix. SASE. Sample copy $2.50.

Nonfiction: Most articles are commissioned in advance. In summer, uses articles of various interests on opera; in the fall and winter, articles that relate to the weekly broadcasts. Emphasis is on high quality in writing and an intellectual interest in the opera-oriented public. Informational, how-to, personal experience, interview, profile, humor, historical, think pieces, personal opinion and opera reviews. Query; no telephone inquiries. Length: 2,500 words maximum. Pays 13¢/word for features; 10¢/word for reviews.

Photos: Pays minimum of $25 for photos purchased on assignment. Captions required.

SYMPHONY MAGAZINE, American Symphony Orchestra League, 633 E St., NW, Washington DC 20004. (202)628-0099. Editor: Robin Perry Allen. Associate Editor: Chester Lane. 60% freelance written. Bimonthly magazine covering symphony orchestras in North America and the classical music industry for members of the association, including managers, conductors, board members, musicians, volunteer association members, music businesses, schools, libraries, etc. Circ. 17,500. Pays on publication. Publishes ms an average of 6 weeks after acceptance. Byline given. Pays negotiable kill fee. Buys all rights (sometimes negotiable). Simultaneous queries, and photocopied and previously published submissions OK. Computer printout submissions acceptable; facility for electronically transmitted copy (Wang VS-45); no dot-matrix. Reports in 1 month. Free sample copy.

Nonfiction: How-to (manage fundraising, marketing) for symphony orchestra administrative personnel; interview/profile (conductors, philanthropists, managers and personalities in the field); technical (budgeting, tour planning); and "thoughtful, reflective looks at the state of the classical music industry." Buys 25 mss/year. Query with clips of published work. Length: 1,500-3,000 words. Pays $50-400. Sometimes pays the expenses of writers on assignment.

Photos: "We prefer black and white action shots and informal shots." State availability of photos. Captions required.

Office Environment and Equipment

GEYER'S OFFICE DEALER, (formerly *Geyer's Office Dealer Topics*), 51 Madison Ave., New York NY 10010. (212)689-4411. Editor: C. Edwin Shade. 20% freelance written. For independent office equipment and stationery dealers, and special purchasers for store departments handling stationery and office equipment. Monthly. Buys all rights. Pays kill fee. Byline given. Pays on publication. Publishes ms an average of 3 months after acceptance. Computer printout submissions acceptable; prefers letter-quality to dot-matrix. Reports "immediately." SASE.

Nonfiction: Articles on dealer efforts in merchandising and sales promotion; programs of stationery and office equipment dealers. Problem-solving articles related to retailers of office supplies, social stationery items, of-

fice furniture and equipment and office machines. Must feature specified stores. Query. Length: 300-1,000 words. Pays $125 minimum but quality of article is real determinant.
Photos: B&w glossies are purchased with accompanying ms with no additional payment.

WESTERN OFFICE DEALER, 41 Sutter St., San Francisco CA 94104. Editor: Patrick Totty. 5% freelance written. Monthly magazine; 60-70 pages. Circ. 10,000. Byline given. Pays on acceptance. Publishes ms an average of 2 months after acceptance. Buys first serial rights. Submit seasonal (merchandising) material 4 months in advance. Computer printout submissions acceptable; prefers letter-quality to dot-matrix. Reports in 1 week. SASE. Sample copy $2.
Nonfiction: "Our main interest is in how Western retailers of stationery and office products can do a better selling job. We use how-to-do-it merchandising articles showing dealers how to sell more stationery and office products to more people at a greater profit. Seasonal merchandising articles always welcome, if acceptable." Informational, how-to, personal experience, interview, and successful business operations. "We only want material pertaining to successful merchandising activities." Buys 12 mss/year. Query or submit complete ms. Length: 1,000-1,500 words. Pays $100-200.
Photos: Pays $15 for b&w photos used with mss; 3x5 minimum. Captions required.
Tips: "Grade readers prefer specific, real-life examples as a way of illustrating the topic or business practice under discussion."

Packing, Canning, and Packaging

The journal in this category is for shippers, brokers, retailers, and others concerned with methods of growing, merchandising, and shipping foods in general. Other publications that buy similar material can be found under the Food Products, Processing and Service heading.

‡**FOOD & DRUG PACKAGING**, 7500 Old Oak Blvd., Cleveland OH 44140. Editor: Sophia Dilberakis. For packaging decision makers in food, drug, and cosmetic firms. Monthly. Circ. 60,000+. Rights purchased vary with author and material. Pays on acceptance. "Queries only." SASE.
Nonfiction and Photos: "Looking for news stories about local and state (not federal) packaging legislation, and its impact on the marketplace. Newspaper style." Length: 1,000-2,500 words; usually 500-700. Payments vary; usually 5¢/word. Photos purchased with mss. 5x7 glossies preferred. Pays $5.
Tips: "Get details on local packaging legislation's impact on marketplace/sales/consumer/retailer reaction; etc. Keep an eye open to *new* packages. Query when you think you've got one. New packages move into test markets every day, so if you don't see anything new this week, try again next week. Buy it; describe it briefly in a query."

Paint

"Write for a professional audience, not do-it-yourselfers," said one paint magazine editor. "Stories about Uncle Joe, the painter, do not appeal to us."

AMERICAN PAINT & COATINGS JOURNAL, American Paint Journal Co., 2911 Washington Ave., St. Louis MO 63103. (314)534-0301. Editor: Chuck Reitter. 10% freelance written. Weekly magazine; 78 pages. For the coatings industry (paint, varnish, lacquer, etc.); manufacturers of coatings, suppliers to coatings industry, educational institutions, salesmen. Circ. 7,300. Publishes ms an average of 3 months after aceptance. Pays on publication. Pays kill fee "depending on the work done." Buys all rights. Phone queries OK. Simultaneous and photocopied submissions OK. Computer printout submissions acceptable. SASE. Reports in 3 weeks. Free sample copy and writer's guidelines.
Nonfiction: Informational, historical, interview, new product, technical articles and coatings industry news. Buys 2 mss/issue. Query before sending long articles; submit complete ms for short pieces. Length: 75-1,200

words. Pays $5-100. Sometimes pays expenses of writers on assignment.

Photos: B&w (5x7) glossies purchased with or without mss or on assignment. Query. Pays $3-10.

AMERICAN PAINTING CONTRACTOR, American Paint Journal Co., 2911 Washington Ave., St. Louis MO 63103. (314)534-0301. Editor: Rick Hirsch. 20% freelance written. Monthly magazine; 80 pages. For painting and decorating contractors, in-plant maintenance painting department heads, architects and paint specifiers. Circ. 13,000. Publishes ms an average of 2 months after acceptance. Buys all rights. Submit seasonal/holiday material 2 months in advance. SASE. Reports in 1 month. Free sample copy.

Nonfiction: Historical, how-to, humor, informational, new product, personal experience, interviews, photo features and profiles. Buys 10-15 unsolicited mss/year. "Freelancers should be able to write well and have some understanding of the painting and decorating industry. We do not want general theme articles such as 'How to Get More Work Out of Your Employee' unless they relate to a problem within the painting and decorating industry." Length: 1,000-2,500 words. Pays $150-225.

Photos: B&w and color purchased with mss or on assignment. Captions required. Send prints or transparencies.

Tips: "We are not looking for anything but well-researched, major features. The most frequent mistakes made by writers are that articles tend to be too generic and brief—often they do not become familiar with the magazine's content and writing style before submitting manuscripts."

DECORATIVE PRODUCTS WORLD, American Paint Journal Co., 2911 Washington, St. Louis MO 63103. (314)534-0301. Editor: Rick Hirsch. 20% freelance written. Bimonthly magazine about decorating outlets for retailers of paint, wallpaper and related items. Circ. 33,000. Pays on publication. Publishes ms an average of 2 months after acceptance. Byline given. Buys all rights. Submit seasonal material 3 months in advance. Reports in 1 month. Free sample copy and writer's guidelines.

Nonfiction: Profile (of stores). "Find stories that will give useful information for our readers. We are basically a service to our readers and our articles reflect that." Buys 1-2 mss/issue. Length: varies. Query.

Photos: "Photos must accompany a story in order to be published." State availability of photos. Captions required.

Tips: "We are not looking for anything but well-researched, major features. The most frequent mistakes made by writers are that articles tend to be too general and brief—often they do not become familiar with the magazine's content and writing style before submitting manuscripts."

Paper

PAPERBOARD PACKAGING, 7500 Old Oak Blvd., Cleveland OH 44130. (216)243-8100. Editor: Mark Arzoumanian. 15% freelance written. Monthly. For "managers, supervisors, and technical personnel who operate corrugated box manufacturing, folding carton converting and rigid box companies and plants." Circ. 15,000. Pays on publication. Publishes ms an average of 3 months after acceptance. Buys all rights. Photocopied submissions OK. Submit seasonal material 3 months in advance. Computer printout submissions acceptable; no dot-matrix. SASE. Sample copy on request.

Nonfiction: "Application articles, installation stories, etc. Contact the editor first to establish the approach desired for the article. Especially interested in packaging systems using composite materials, including paper and other materials." Buys technical articles. Query. Length: open. Pays "$75/printed page (about 1,000 words to a page), including photos. We do not pay for commercially oriented material. We do pay for material if it is not designed to generate business for someone in our field."

Photos: "Will not pay photography costs, but will pay cost of photo reproductions for article."

Tips: "Freelance writers should be aware that the 'jack of all trades (in the writing sense) is out the window. The need to specialize is paramount today."

PULP & PAPER CANADA, Southam Communications Ltd., Suite 201, 310 Victoria Ave., Montreal, Quebec H3Z 2M9 Canada. (514)487-2302. Editor: Peter N. Williamson. Managing Editor: Graeme Rodden. 5% freelance written. Monthly magazine. Circ. 8,488. Pays on publication. Publishes ms an average of 6 months after acceptance. Byline given. Offers kill fee according to prior agreement. Buys first North American serial rights. Submit seasonal/holiday material 2 months in advance. SASE. Reports in 2 weeks on queries; 3 weeks on mss. Sample copy $4.50 (Canada), $6.50 (other countries); free writer's guidelines.

Nonfiction: How-to (related to processes and procedures in the industry); interview/profile (of Canadian leaders in pulp and paper industry); and technical (relevant to modern pulp and/or paper industry). No fillers, short industry news items, or product news items. Buys 10 mss/year. Query with or without published clips or send complete ms. Articles with photographs (b&w glossy) or other good quality illustrations will get priority review. Length: 1,500-2,000 words (with photos). Pays $130 (Canadian funds)/published page, including photos, graphics, charts, etc.

Pets

Listed here are publications for professionals in the pet industry, wholesalers, manufacturers, suppliers, retailers, owners of pet specialty stores, pet groomers, aquarium retailers, distributors, and those interested in the fish industry. Publications for pet owners are listed in the Animal section of Consumer Publications.

‡**BREED & SHOW**, The Magazine for Champions, ULTRA Data Services, 1115 Vida Dr. Anniston Al 36206. (205)820-9309. Editor: Janet A. Brunson. 50% freelance written. Monthly magazine covering pure-bred dogs. "Readers are professionals (i.e. breeders, exhibitors, judges, owners of pet-related businesses) in the dog world." Estab. 1984. Circ. 4,000. Pays on publication. Publishes ms an average of 6 months after acceptance. Byline given. Offers $10 kill fee. Buys first North American serial rights and second serial (reprint) rights. Submit seasonal/holiday material 6 months in advance. Simultaneous queries, and simultaneous, photocopied, and previously published submissions OK. Computer printout submissions acceptable; prefers letter-quality to dot-matrix. SASE. Reports in 6 weeks. Free sample copy and writer's guidelines.
Nonfiction: Book excerpts; How-to (anything that relates to owning, grooming, showing, breeding or playing with dogs); informational (Cover Story—different featured breed each month, education, new products, methods, travel); technical (medical updates, new surgery procedures, canine midwifery, canine medical problems, medical problems as related to large kennels); inspirational (personal experience, true accounts of noble dogs, interviews/profiles of handicapped exhibitors/breeders); interviews/profiles (judges, obedience instructors/ competitors, breeders, exhibitors, handlers, owners of dog-related businesses); historical/nostalgic; humor; new product; opinion; personal experience. "No sentimental My Dog stories, poems, nonfiction slop about un-real dogs." Buys 40-50 mss/year. Query with published clips. Length: 900-1,750 words. Pays $30-100.
Photos: State availability of photos with query. Photos are purchased as a part of the editorial package. Pays $5-10 for 5x7 b&w prints. Captions required. Buys one-time rights and reprint rights.
Columns/Departments: Business (Speaking of Business... column. Profile of innovative pet businesses/ products and inventors/owners); Book Reviews (short book reviews, approximately 200 words, on new releases. Three-four book reviews accepted each month; Humor (true, amusing stories, On the Lighter Side...); Ring Time; and Regional Directory. Buys 36 mss/year. Query. Length: 500-750 words. Pays $25-35.
Fiction: Adventure, humorous and novel excerpts. No sentimental dog stories. Buys 2 mss/year. Query. Length: 900-1,500 words. Pays $25-60.
Fillers: Clippings, anecdotes, short humor and newsbreaks. Buys 12-36 fillers/year. Length: 200-500 words. Pays $5-20.
Tips: "We like articles from professional breeders, handlers, and judges or articles about their methods/advice written by freelancers. The writer has a better chance of breaking in at our publication with short articles and fillers since book reviews are always needed, so there's more chance of acceptance. The most frequent mistake made by writers in completing an article for us is incorrect length (we specify how long, within a couple hundred words, it should be). We are more apt to purchase material from people active in the dog field with some writing ability than from writers who have little or no dog knowledge."

PET AGE, The Largest Circulation Pet Industry Trade Publication, H.H. Backer Associates, Inc., 207 S. Wabash Ave., Chicago IL 60604. (312)663-4040. Editor: Raymond Gudas. Monthly magazine about the pet industry for pet retailers and industry. Circ. 16,000. Pays on acceptance. Byline given. Buys first serial rights. Submit seasonal material 3 months in advance. Computer printout submissions acceptable; prefers letter-quality to dot-matrix. SASE. Reports in 6 weeks. Sample copy $2.50; free writer's guidelines.
Nonfiction: Profile (of a successful, well-run pet retail operation); how-to; interview; photo feature, and technical—all trade-related. Query first with published clips. Buys 12 mss/year. "Query as to the name and location of a pet operation you wish to profile and why it would make a good feature. No general retailing articles or consumer-oriented pet articles." Length: 1,500-2,500 words. Pays $75-200.
Photos: State availability of photos. Reviews 5x7 b&w glossy prints, contact sheets and color transparencies. Captions and identification of subjects required.
Columns/Departments: Fish Care, Retailing, Government Action, Tax & Finance, Bird Care, New Products

and Industry News. Query with published clips. Length: 1,000-1,500 words.
Tips: "We are interested in profiling successful or otherwise imaginative and/or unique retailing operations. Focus should be on the aspects that make the business successful: history/background of business and owners; description of service/products, sales and marketing strategies, advertising and promotional activities, etc. You must be able to provide 8-10 good b&w photos."

PET BUSINESS, Pet Business, Inc., 7330 NW 66th, Miami FL 33166. Publisher: Robert L. Behme. 20% freelance written. Monthly magazine; 48 pages. For the complete pet industry—retailers, groomers, breeders, manufacturers, wholesalers and importers. Circ. 14,500. Pays on acceptance. Buys first rights only. Publishes ms an average of 3 months after acceptance. Not copyrighted. Previously published submissions OK. Computer printout submission acceptable "as long as it is readable, easy to edit and well written. But there are exceptions—we hate dot-matrix." SASE. Reports in 3 weeks. Sample copy $1; free writer's guidelines.
Nonfiction: General interest (to retailers—what a store is doing, etc.); historical (when there is a reason—death, sale, etc.); how-to (sell more, retailer ideas); interview (with successful stores and manufacturers); opinion (with background); photo feature (on occasion); and news of stores. Buys 15-30 mss/year. "We will consider anything if queried first." Length: 600-1,500 words. Pays $35-250. Pays expenses of writers on assignment.
Photos: State availability of photos. Pays $10 for 5x7 or larger b&w prints; and $30 for any size color prints. Captions required.
Columns/Departments: "We're interested in ideas that relate to retailing, e.g., dogs, cats, small animals—but it must be on a retail, not hobby, level." Open to suggestions for new columns/departments. Query. Pays $100.
Tips: "We are looking at international editions."

THE PET DEALER, Howmark Publishing Corp., 567 Morris Ave., Elizabeth NJ 07208. (201)353-7373. Editorial Director: Alan Richman. 15% freelance written. Monthly magazine; 80 pages. Emphasizes merchandising, marketing and management for owners and managers of pet specialty stores, departments, and pet groomers and their suppliers. Circ. 11,000. Pays on publication. Publication "may be many months between acceptance of a manuscript and publication." Byline given. Phone queries OK. Submit seasonal/holiday material 3 months in advance. Computer printout submissions acceptable; no dot-matrix. SASE. Reports in 1 week. Free sample copy and writer's guidelines.
Nonfiction: How-to (store operations, administration, merchandising, marketing, management, promotion and purchasing). Consumer pet articles—lost pets, best pets, humane themes—*not* welcome. Emphasis is on *trade* merchandising and marketing of pets and supplies. Buys 8 unsolicited mss/year. Length: 800-1,200 words. Pays $50-100.
Photos: Submit photo material with ms. No additional payment for 5x7 b&w glossy prints. "Six photos with captions required." Buys one-time rights.
Tips: "We're interested in store profiles outside the New York, New Jersey, Connecticut and Pennsylvania metro areas. Photos are of key importance. Articles focus on new techniques in merchandising or promotion. Submit query letter first, with writing background summarized; include samples. We seek one-to-one, interview-type features on retail pet store merchandising. Indicate the availability of the proposed article, your willingness to submit on exclusive or first-in-field basis, and whether you are patient enough to await payment on publication."

PETS/SUPPLIES/MARKETING, Harcourt Brace Jovanovich Publications, 1 E. 1st St., Duluth MN 55802. (218)723-9303. Publisher/Editor: David Kowalski. 10% freelance written. Monthly magazine. For independent pet retailers, chain franchisers, livestock and pet supply wholesalers, and manufacturers of pet products. Circ. 14,200. Pays on publication. Buys first rights only. Phone queries OK. Submit seasonal/holiday material 4 months in advance. Photocopied submissions OK. Computer printout submissions acceptable. SASE. Reports in 2 months. Free writer's guidelines. Sample copy $5.
Nonfiction: How-to (merchandise pet products, display, set up window displays, market pet product line); interviews (with pet store retailers); opinion (of pet industry members or problems facing the industry); photo features (of successful pet stores or effective merchandising techniques and in-store displays); profiles (of successful retail outlets engaged in the pet trade); and technical articles (on more effective pet retailing, e.g., building a central filtration unit, constructing custom aquariums or display areas). Business management articles must deal specifically with pet shops and their own unique merchandise and problems. Length: 1,000-2,000 words. Buys 1-2 mss/issue. Query. Pays 10¢/word. Sometimes pays the expenses of writers on assignment.
Photos: Purchased with or without mss or on assignment. "We prefer 5x7 or 8x10 b&w glossies. But we will accept contact sheets and standard print sizes. For color, we prefer 35mm kodachrome transparencies or 2¼x2¼." Pays $10 for b&w; $25 for color. Captions and model release required.
Columns/Departments: Suggestions for new columns or departments should be addressed to the editor. No clippings, please.

Tips: "We want articles which stress professional retailing, provide insight into successful shops, and generally capture the excitement of an exciting and sometimes controversial industry. All submissions are read. However, an initial query could save time and energy and ensure a publishable article."

Photography

AMERICAN CINEMATOGRAPHER, A.S.C. Holding Corp., Box 2230, Hollywood CA 90078. (213)876-5080. Editor: Richard Patterson. Associate Editor: George Turner. Monthly magazine; 120 pages. An international journal of film and video production techniques "addressed to creative, managerial, and technical people in all aspects of production. Its function is to disseminate practical information about the creative use of film and video equipment, and it strives to maintain a balance between technical sophistication and accessibility." Circ. 30,000. Pays on publication. Buys all rights. Phone queries OK. Simultaneous and photocopied submissions OK. Computer printout submissions acceptable "provided they are adequately spaced." SASE.
Nonfiction: Descriptions of new equipment and techniques or accounts of specific productions involving unique problems or techniques; historical articles detailing the production of a classic film, the work of a pioneer or legendary cinematographer or the development of a significant technique or type of equipment. Also discussions of the aesthetic principles involved in production techniques. Recent article example: "Creating a Mermaid for 'Splash' (March 1984). Length: 1,500 to 6,000 words. Pays approximately 5¢/word.
Photos: B&w and color purchased with mss. No additional payment.
Tips: "Queries must describe writer's qualifications and include writing samples. We hope to make more use of freelance writers."

AMERICAN PREMIERE, Penthouse Suite, 8421 Wilshire Blvd., Beverly Hills CA 90211. Editor: Susan Royal. 70% freelance written. Quarterly trade magazine "for and about persons in the film industry—executives, producers, directors, actors, and all others associated." Circ. 25,000. Pays on publication. Publishes ms an average of 3 months after acceptance. Byline given. Pays negotiable kill fee. Buys first North American serial rights. Submit seasonal/holiday material 2 months in advance. Sample copy $4 (address request to "Circulation"); writer's guidelines for business-size SAE and 1 first class stamp.
Nonfiction: Investigative; historical; how-to (incorporate yourself, read a contract, etc.); interview/profile (directors, producers, businesses, top persons in the industry); and other themes associated with the film industry. "Only business-oriented articles." No fan material or gossip. Buys 7-20 unsolicited mss/year. Query with "limited samples" of published work and resume. Length: 1,200-3,000 words. Pays $50-150. Sometimes pays the expenses of writers on assignment.
Tips: "The writer has a better chance of breaking in at our publication with short articles and fillers as they need to learn our style. Writers should be well versed on the workings of the film industry. We're interested in people who can pen statistical, but not boring, articles. The most frequent mistake made by writers in completing an article for us is writing 'down' to our readers."

‡FUNCTIONAL PHOTOGRAPHY, The Magazine of Visual Documentation and Communication for the Scientific, Technical & Medical Image Maker, PTN Publishing Corp. 101 Crossways Park West, Woodbury NY 11797. Senior Editor: David A. Silverman. 70% freelance written. Bimonthly magazine of scientific/medical/technical image producers (doctors, R&D, scientific personnel). Circ. 33,000. Pays on publication. Publishes ms an average of 6 months after acceptance. Byline given. Not copyrighted. Computer printout submissions acceptable; letter-quality or double strike dot-matrix. Prefers no dot-matrix. SASE. Reports in 6 weeks. Sample copy $2; writer's guidelines for #10 SAE and 1 first class stamp.
Nonfiction: How-to, photo feature (related to our market), and technical. "Articles must be of instructive value for our particular type of technical reader." Buys 10-20 mss/year. Query with published clips. Pays $75/published page.
Photos: Send photos with query. Reviews prints. Captions, model release and identification of subjects required. Buys one-time rights.

PHOTO LAB MANAGEMENT, PLM Publishing, Inc., 1312 Lincoln Blvd., Santa Monica CA 90406. (213)451-1344. Editor: Carolyn Ryan. Associate Editor: Arthur Stern. 75% freelance written. Monthly magazine covering process chemistries, process control, process equipment and marketing/administration for photo lab owners, managers and management personnel. Circ. over 10,000. Pays on publication. Publishes ms an average of 5 months after acceptance. Byline and brief bio given. Buys first North American serial rights. Submit seasonal/holiday material 6 months in advance. Computer printout submissions acceptable; no dot-matrix. SASE. Reports on queries in 6 weeks. Free sample copy and writer's guidelines for business-size SAE and 1 first class stamp.

Nonfiction: Personal experience (lab manager); technical; and management or administration. Buys 40-50 mss/year. Query with brief biography. Length: 1,200-1,800 words. Pays $60/published page.

Photos: Reviews 35mm color transparencies and 4-color prints suitable for cover. "We're looking for outstanding cover shots of photofinishing images."

Tips: "Our departments are written in-house and we don't use 'fillers'. Send a query if you have some background in the industry or a willingness to dig out information and research for a top quality article that really speaks to our audience. The most frequent mistakes made by writers in completing an article for us are on the business management side—taking a generic rather than a photo lab approach."

PHOTO WEEKLY, Billboard Publications, Inc., 1515 Broadway, New York NY 10036. (212)764-7415. Editor: Willard Clark. Weekly photography tabloid featuring industry news for photographic retailers and photofinishers. Circ. 15,000. Pays on acceptance. Byline given. Buys one-time rights.

PHOTOFLASH, Models & Photographers Newsletter, Box 7946, Colorado Springs CO 80933. Managing Editor: Ron Marshall. 20% freelance written. Quarterly newsletter of photographic modeling and glamour photography "for models, photographers, publishers, picture editors, modeling agents, advertising agencies, and others involved in the interrelated fields of modeling and photography." Pays on publication. Publishes ms an average of 3 months after acceptance. Byline given. Buys one-time rights and second (reprint) rights. Submit seasonal/holiday material 6 months in advance. Simultaneous queries, and simultaneous, photocopied and previously published submissions OK. Computer printout submissions acceptable. SASE. Reports in 3 months on queries; 4 months on mss. Sample copy $5.

Nonfiction: Interview/profile (of established and rising professionals in the field, especially models); photo feature; and technical (illustrating/explaining photographic and modeling "tricks"). Send complete ms. "We prefer photo-illustrated text packages."

Photos: Send photos with ms. "Payment is for the complete photo-text package; it includes a credit line, contributor copies and up to $15-25 depending on quality, completeness, etc. of the submissions." Reviews 8x10 b&w prints. Captions and model release required.

PHOTOGRAPHER'S MARKET NEWSLETTER, F&W Publications, Inc., 9933 Alliance Rd., Cincinnati OH 45242. (513)984-0717. Editor: Robin Weinstein. 50% freelance written. Monthly newsletter on freelance photography covering "markets and marketing techniques and strategies for amateur and professional photographers who want to begin selling or sell more of their work." Pays on publication. Publishes ms an average of 6 months after acceptance. Byline given. Buys one-time rights. Simultaneous and previously published submissions acceptable. Computer printout submissions acceptable. SASE. Reports in 2 weeks on queries; 1 month on mss. Sample copy $3.50.

Nonfiction: How-to (sell photos); interview/profile (photography professionals); personal experience (in photo marketing); photo feature (previously published work); and technical (must relate to selling). No purely technical material on cameras, film and equipment. Buys 12 mss/year. Query. Length: 1,500-2,000 words plus photos. Pays $75-125.

Photos: State availability of photos. Reviews 8x10 b&w prints; payment included with purchase price. Captions required.

Tips: "We are especially interested in articles which target in on the business of photomarketing. Articles must be geared toward the serious, *knowledgable* photographer who has been in the business a while and knows the field."

‡PHOTOLETTER,, PhotoSource International, Pine Lake Farm, Osceola WI 54020. (715)248-3800 or (800)525-9840. Editor: Beca Land. 10% freelance written. Monthly newsletter on marketing photographs. "*The Photoletter* is a marketing-oriented monthly newsletter of subscribers that range from amateur to professional writers. It is the supplemental issue for two photomarketing services, Photo bulletin and Photomarket, which pair photo buyers with photographers' collections." Circ. 1,622. Pays on acceptance. Publishes ms an average of 2 months after acceptance. Byline given. Buys one-time rights. Submit seasonal/holiday material 6 months in advance. Simultaneous queries, and simultaneous, photocopied, and previously published submissions OK. Electronic submissions OK via the Source (MKT016), Newsnet (NET 6058), MCI Mail (189-2053), and Delphi (Photo101). SASE. Reports in 2 weeks. Sample copy for #10 SAE and 1 first class stamp; free writer's guidelines.

Nonfiction: Book excerpts, how-to (photo marketing), interview/profile, opinion, personal experience, photo feature, technical, travel, and marketing. Buys 15 mss/year. Query. Length: 250-450 words. Pays $25-75.

Columns/Departments: Jeri Engh, column/department editor. At the studio, in nature, as the self-promoter, in the office, as the writer, with the IRS, with people, with models, and through the lens, etc. Buys 7 mss/year. Query. Length: 250-450 words. Pays $25-75.

‡**THE PROFESSIONAL PHOTOGRAPHER, Serving the Entire Professional Market**, Professional Photographers of America, Inc., 1090 Executive Way, Des Plaines IL 60018. (312)299-8161. Editor: Alfred DeBat. 80% freelance written. Monthly magazine of professional portrait, commercial and industrial photography. Describes the technical and business sides of professional photography—successful photo techniques, money-making business tips, legal considerations, selling to new markets, and descriptions of tough assignments and how completed. Circ. 36,000. Publishes ms an average of 9 months after acceptance. Byline given. Buys one-time rights. Submit seasonal/holiday material 6 months in advance. Simultaneous queries, and photocopied and previously published submissions OK. Computer printout submissions acceptable; prefers letter-quality to dot-matrix. SASE. Reports in 2 months. Sample copy $3.25; free writer's guidelines.

Nonfiction: How-to. Professional photographic techniques: How I solved this difficult assignment, How I increased my photo sales, How to buy a studio . . . run a photo business etc. Special issues include February: Portrait Photography; April: Wedding Photography, August: Commercial Photography, and November: Industrial Photography. Buys 8-10 ms/issue. Query. Length: 1,000-3,000 words. "We seldom pay, as most writers are PP of A members and want recognition for their professional skills, publicity, etc."

Photos: State availability of photos. Reviews 35mm color transparencies and 8x10 prints. Captions and model release required. Buys one-time rights.

THE RANGEFINDER, 1312 Lincoln Blvd., Santa Monica CA 90406. (213)451-8506. Editor: Arthur C. Stern. Associate Editor: Carolyn Ryan. Monthly magazine; 80 pages. Emphasizes professional photography. Circ. 50,000. Pays on publication. Publishes ms an average of 3 months after acceptance. Byline given. Buys first North American serial rights. Phone queries OK. Submit seasonal material 4 months in advance. Computer printout submissions acceptable; prefers letter-quality to dot-matrix. SASE. Reports in 6 weeks. Sample copy $2.50; writer's guidelines for SASE.

Nonfiction: How-to (solve a photographic problem; such as new techniques in lighting, new poses or set-ups); profile; and technical. "Articles should contain practical, solid information. Issues should be covered in depth. Look thoroughly into the topic." No opinion or biographical articles. Buys 5-7 mss/issue. Query with outline. Length: 800-1,200 words. Pays $60/published page.

Photos: State availability of photos with query. Captions preferred; model release required. Buys one-time rights.

Tips: "Exhibit knowledge of photography. Introduce yourself with a well-written letter and a great story idea."

STUDIO PHOTOGRAPHY, PTN Publishing Corp., 101 Crossways/Park West, Woodbury NY 11797. (516)496-8000. Editor: Mark Zacharia. 65% freelance written. Monthly magazine. Circ. 65,000. Pays on publication. Publishes ms an average of 6 months after acceptance. Not copyrighted. Buys first serial rights only. Submit seasonal/holiday material 5 months in advance. Computer printout submissions acceptable; prefers letter-quality to dot-matrix. SASE. Reports in 6 weeks.

Nonfiction: Interview, personal experience, photo feature, communication-oriented, technical and travel. No business-oriented articles. Buys 2-3 mss/issue. Length: 1,700-3,000 words. Pays $75 minimum. Sometimes pays expenses of writers on assignment.

Photos: State availability of photos with query. Photos and article in one package.

Columns/Departments: Point of View (any aspect of photography dealing with professionals only). Buys 1/issue. Length: 1,700 words minimum. Pays $35 minimum.

Tips: "No handwritten queries will even be looked at. We look for professional quality in writing. No original photos, only fine quality duplicates. Submit photos with all articles. Only people with definite ideas and a sense of who they are need apply for publication. Read the magazine and become familiar with it before submitting work. Write for sample copy, editorial schedule, and writer/photographer's guidelines."

TECHNICAL PHOTOGRAPHY, PTN Publishing Corp., 101 Crossways Park West, Woodbury NY 11797. Senior Editor: David A. Silverman. 60% freelance written. Monthly magazine; 64 pages. Publication of the "on-staff (in-house) industrial, military and government still, video and AV professional who must produce (or know where to get) visuals of all kinds." Circ. 60,000. Pays on publication. Publishes ms an average of 4 months after acceptance. Buys first North American serial rights. Byline given. Computer printout submissions acceptable; prefers letter-quality to dot-matrix. SASE. Reports in 1 month. Sample copy for #10 envelope and 1 first class stamp.

Nonfiction: How-to; interview; photo feature; profile (detailed stories about in-house operations); and technical. "All manuscripts must relate to industrial, military or government production of visuals." Buys 75-110 mss/year. Query. Length: "as long as needed to adequately cover the subject matter." Pays $75/display page. Sometimes pays the expenses of writers on assignment.

Photos: Offers no additional payment for photos purchased with ms. Query. Captions required.

Plumbing, Heating, Air Conditioning, and Refrigeration

Plumbers and repairmen learn how to do a better job from these publications. Publications for fuel oil dealers who also install heating equipment are classified with the Energy journals.

CONTRACTOR MAGAZINE, 1301 S. Grove Ave., Barrington IL 60010. Editor: John A. Schweizer. 15% freelance written. For mechanical contractors and wholesalers. Newspaper published twice monthly; 50 (11x15) pages. Circ. 46,100. Pays on publication. Publishes ms an average of 2 months after acceptance. Buys first serial rights. Photocopied submissions OK. No simultaneous submissions. Computer printout submissions acceptable. Reports in 1 month. SASE. Sample copy $3.
Nonfiction: Articles on materials, use, policies, and business methods of the air conditioning, heating, plumbing, piping, solar, energy management, and contracting industry. Topics covered include interpretive reports, how-to, informational, interview, profile, think articles, expose, spot news, successful business operations, merchandising techniques and labor. Buys 12 mss/year. Query or submit complete ms. Pays $300 maximum.
Photos: 5x7 b&w glossies purchased with or without ms. Pays $10. Captions required.

DISTRIBUTOR, The Voice of Wholesaling, Technical Reporting Corp., Box 479, Wheeling IL 60090. (312)537-6460. Editorial Director: Ed Schwenn. Managing Editor: Steve Read. Bimonthly magazine on heating, ventilating, air conditioning and refrigeration. Editorial material shows "executive wholesalers how they can run better businesses and cope with personal and business problems." Circ. 10,000. Pays on publication. Byline given. Buys one-time rights. Submit seasonal/holiday material 3 months in advance. "We want material exclusive to the field (industry)." Photocopied submissions OK. Computer printout submissions acceptable; prefers letter-quality to dot-matrix. SASE. Reports in 2 weeks. Sample copy $4; free writer's guidelines with purchased copy of magazine.
Nonfiction: How-to (run a better business, cope with problems); and interview/profile (the wholesalers). No flippant or general approaches. Buys 6 mss/year. Query with or without published clips or send complete ms. Length: 1,000-3,000 words. Pays $100-250 (10¢ a word).
Photos: State availability of photos or send photos with query or ms. Pays $10-25 for color contact sheets; $15-30 for 35mm color transparencies; and $15-30 for 5x7 color prints. Captions and identification of subjects required.
Tips: "Know the industry—come up with a different angle on an industry subject (one we haven't dealt with in a long time). Wholesale ideas, profiles and interviews are most open to freelancers."

DOMESTIC ENGINEERING MAGAZINE, Construction Industry Press, 135 Addison Ave., Elmhurst IL 60126. Editor: Stephen J. Shafer. Managing Editor: David J. Hanks. Monthly magazine; 100 pages. Emphasizes plumbing, heating, air conditioning and piping for contractors, and for mechanical contractors in these specialties. Gives information on management, marketing and merchandising. Circ. 40,000. Pays on acceptance. Buys all rights, simultaneous rights, or first serial rights. Simultaneous, photocopied and previously published submissions OK. SASE. Reports in 1 month. Sample copy $4.
Nonfiction: How-to (some technical in industry areas). Expose, interview, profile, personal experience, photo feature and technical articles are written on assignment only and should be about management, marketing and merchandising for plumbing and mechanical contracting businessmen. Buys 12 mss/year. Query. Pays $25 minimum.
Photos: State availability of photos. Pays $10 minimum for b&w prints (reviews contact sheets) and color transparencies.

FLORIDA FORUM, FRSA Services Corp., Drawer 4850, Winter Park FL 32793. (305)671-3772. Editor: Gerald Dykhuisen. 10% freelance written. Monthly magazine covering the roofing, sheet metal and air conditioning industries. Circ. 8,300. Pays on publication. Publishes ms an average of 2 months after acceptance. Byline given. Buys one-time rights. Submit seasonal/holiday material 2 months in advance. Simultaneous queries, and simultaneous, photocopied, and previously published submissions OK. Electronic submissions OK on Hewlett Packard 3000. Computer printout submissions acceptable. Reports in 2 weeks. Free sample copy.
Nonfiction: General interest, historical/nostalgic, humor, interview/profile, new product, opinion, personal experience and technical. Buys 25 mss/year. Send complete ms. Length: open. Pays variable rates.
Photos: Send photos with ms. Pays variable rates for b&w prints.
Columns/Departments: Buys 12/year. Send complete ms. Length: open. Pays variable rates.

HEATING, PLUMBING, AIR CONDITIONING, 1450 Don Mills Rd., Don Mills, Ontario M3B 2X7 Canada. (416)445-6641. Editor: Ronald H. Shuker. 20% freelance written. Monthly. For mechanical contractors; plumbers; warm air and hydronic heating, refrigeration, ventilation, air conditioning and insulation contractors; wholesalers; architects; consulting and mechanical engineers who are in key management or specifying positions in the plumbing, heating, air conditioning and refrigeration industries in Canada. Circ. 14,500. Pays on publication. Publishes ms an average of 3 months after acceptance. Computer printout submissions acceptable; prefers letter-quality to dot-matrix. Reports in 2 months. For a prompt reply, "enclose a sheet on which is typed a statement either approving or rejecting the suggested article which can either be checked off, or a quick answer written in and signed and returned." Free sample copy.
Nonfiction: News, technical, business management and "how-to" articles that will inform, educate, motivate and help readers to be more efficient and profitable who design, manufacture, install, sell, service, maintain or supply all mechanical components and systems in residential, commercial, institutional and industrial installations across Canada. Length: 1,000-1,500 words. Pays 10-20¢/word. Sometimes pays the expenses of writers on assignment.
Photos: Photos purchased with mss. Prefers 5x7 or 8x10 glossies.
Tips: "Topics must relate directly to the day-to-day activities of *HPAC* readers in Canada. Must be detailed, with specific examples, quotes from specific people or authorities—show depth. We specifically want material from other parts of Canada besides southern Ontario. Not really interested in material from U.S. unless specifically related to Canadian readers' concerns. We primarily want articles that show *HPAC* readers how they can increase their sales and business step-by-step based on specific examples of what others have done."

SNIPS MAGAZINE, 407 Mannheim Rd., Bellwood IL 60104. (312)544-3870. Editor: Nick Carter. 2% freelance written. Monthly. For sheet metal, warm air heating, ventilating, air conditioning and roofing contractors. Publishes ms an average of 3 months after acceptance. Buys all rights. "Write for detailed list of requirements before submitting any work." SASE.
Nonfiction: Material should deal with information about contractors who do sheet metal, warm air heating, air conditioning, ventilation and roofing work; also about successful advertising campaigns conducted by these contractors and the results. Length: "prefers stories to run less than 1,000 words unless on special assignment." Pays 5¢ each for first 500 words, 2¢ each for additional word.
Photos: Pays $2 each for small snapshot pictures, $4 each for usable 8x10 pictures.

WOOD 'N ENERGY, Energy Publications Inc., Box 2008, Laconia NH 03247. (603)528-4285. Editor: Steve Maviglio. Monthly magazine covering wood, coal and solar heating (residential). "*Wood 'n Energy* is mailed to retailers, distributors and manufacturers of wood, coal and solar heating equipment in the U.S. and Canada. A majority of our readers are small businessmen who need help in running their businesses and want to learn secrets to prospering in a field that has seen better days when oil embargoes were daily happenings." Circ. 32,000. Pays on publication. Publishes ms an average of 2 months after acceptance. Byline given. Buys one-time rights and all rights. Submit seasonal/holiday material 4 months in advance. Simultaneous queries OK. Electronic submissions OK if compatible with TRS-80, Model III or IV. Computer printout submissions acceptable; prefers letter-quality to dot-matrix. SASE. Reports in 2 weeks. Sample copy $2.50.
Nonfiction: Interview/profile (of stove dealers, manufacturers, others); photo feature (of energy stores); and technical (nuts and bolts of stove design and operation). Special issue includes Buyers Guide/Retailers Handbook (annual issue with retail marketing articles, "how to run your business," accounting. "The best times of year for freelancers are in our fall issue (our largest) and also in February and March." No "how wonderful renewable energy is" and experiences with stoves. "This is a *trade* book." Buys 25 mss/year. Query with or without published clips or send complete ms. Pays $25-300. Sometimes pays the expenses of writers on assignment.
Photos: State availability of photos or send photos with query or ms. Pays $35 minimum for b&w contact sheets; $125 maximum for color contact sheets. Identification of subjects required. Buys one-time rights.
Columns/Departments: Reports (energy news; potpourri of current incentives, happenings); Regulations (safety and standard news); and Retailers Corner (tips on running a retail shop). "We are also looking for freelancers who could serve in our 'network' around the country. If there's a law passed regulating wood-stove emissions in their town, for example, they could send us a clip and/or rewrite the story. These pay $50 or so, depending on the clip. Contact editor on an individual basis (over the phone is OK) for a green light." Query with or without published clips. Length: 150-500 words. Pays $35-150.
Tips: "Short, hot articles on retailers (500 words and photographs) are desperately needed. We're looking for serious business articles. Freelancers who know the ins and outs of running a business have an excellent shot at being published."

WOODHEAT '86: The Woodstove Directory, Energy Publications Inc., Box 2008, Laconia NH 03247. (603)528-4285. Editor: Steven Maviglio. 40% freelance written. An annual buyer's guide and sourcebook on wood heat, published in August. Circ. 175,000. Pays on variable schedule. Publishes ms an average of 6 months after acceptance. Byline given. Offers variable kill fee. Buys variable rights. Simultaneous queries and submissions OK. Computer printout submissions acceptable; prefers letter-quality to dot-matrix. SASE. Reports in 1 month.

Nonfiction: How-to (installation, etc.); interview/profile (of those in the field, retailers, consumers); new product (new wood energy products); photo feature (of stove installations and/or energy efficient homes); and technical (details on buying and installing). No personal experiences with wood stoves. Buys 5-8 mss/year. Query. Length: 100-2,550 words. Pays $50-500. Pays expenses of writers on assignment.

Photos: State availability of photos with query or ms. Uses all types. Pays $35-250. Captions, model release, and identification of subjects required. Buys variable rights.

Columns/Departments: Reports (potpourri of energy news, wood heat news). Buys 0-10 mss/year. Query. Length: 150-400 words. Pays $35-100.

Tips: "Articles in the magazine must appeal to both current owners and buyers. Personality is a plus in any article; we'd like features on someone who has invented a better burning stove or someone who is handcrafting masonry fireplaces, for example. Article ideas are formulated by mid-January, so query letters should be on hand at that time. Be specific with story ideas. Shorter articles on a wide range of energy issues—in a section called Reports—can be accepted until May. These must be accompanied by a photo. Writing should be spicy, interesting and short. All areas are open to freelancers. We find that freelancers score better with articles with local slants. With 15 million households having wood stoves, there are bound to be many stories to tell."

Printing

"The influence of computer-aided design has changed our type of story, interest and readership," says one design/drafting/reprographics magazine editor. This and other trends will affect publications in this section. These magazines are geared for printers and publishers in various types of plants.

THE ENGRAVERS JOURNAL, The Engravers Journal, Inc., 26 Summit St., Box 318, Brighton MI 48116. (313)229-5725. Managing Editor: Michael J. Davis. 35% freelance written. A bimonthly magazine covering engraving, marking, awards, jewelry, and signage industry. "We provide industry and/or small business related information for the education and advancement of our readers' trade/business." Pays on acceptance. Publishes ms an average of 1 year after acceptance. Byline given "only if writer is recognized authority." Buys all rights (usually). Submit seasonal/holiday material 4-6 months in advance. Photocopied and previously published submissions OK. Computer printout submissions acceptable; prefers letter-quality to dot-matrix. SASE. Reports in 2 weeks. Free sample copy and writer's guidelines.

Nonfiction: General interest (industry related); how-to (e.g., small business subjects, increase sales, develop new markets, use new techniques, etc.); inspirational; interview/profile; new product; photo feature (e.g., a particularly outstanding signage system); and technical. No general overviews of the industry. Buys 12 mss/year. Query with published clips or send complete ms. Length: 1,000-5,000 words. Pays $50-200.

Photos: Send photos with query or ms. Reviews 8x10 prints. Pays variable rate. Captions, model release and identification of subjects required. Buys variable rights.

Tips: "Articles aimed at the small business person offering practical and useful information are most open to freelancers. Steer away from the 'textbook' writing approach."

GRAPHIC ARTS MONTHLY, Technical Publishing Co., 875 Third Ave., New York NY 10022. (212)605-9574. Editor: Roger Ynostroza. Managing Editor: Peter Johnston. 15% freelance written. A monthly magazine covering the printing industry. Circ. 80,000. Pays on publication. Publishes ms an average of 4 months after acceptance. Byline given. Buys all rights. Submit seasonal/holiday material 3 months in advance. Simultaneous queries OK. Computer printout submissions acceptable. SASE. Reports in 1 month. Free sample copy and writer's guidelines for SAE and 2 first class postage stamps.

Nonfiction: New product, photo feature and technical. Buys 15 mss/year. Query. Pays 10¢/word.

Photos: State availability of photos with query or ms. Captions required.

Fillers: Cartoons. Buys 50/year. Pays $15 minimum.

Tips: "The writer may have a better chance of breaking in at our publication with short articles and fillers since a very technical and specialized field means that major features need to be tailored specifically to the audience while shorter pieces can be more general. The most frequent mistakes made by writers in completing an article for us are that topic and writing style are usually much too general to be of direct benefit to our readership.

Many freelance writers seem to want to adapt one topic to several different fields and publications. Also, case-study stories are often success-story descriptions that benefit and interest only the subject company, not the bulk of the readership."

HIGH VOLUME PRINTING, Innes Publishing Co., Box 368, Northbrook IL 60062. (312)564-5940. Editor: Bill Esler. Bimonthly magazine for book, magazine printers, large commercial printing plants with 20 or more employees. Aimed at telling the reader what he needs to know to print more efficiently and more profitably. Circ. 20,000. Pays on publication. Byline given. Buys first and second serial rights. Simultaneous queries OK. Reports in 2 weeks. Writer's guidelines, sample articles provided.
Nonfiction: How-to (printing production techniques); new product (printing, auxiliary equipment, plant equipment); photo feature (case histories featuring unique equipment); technical (printing product research and development); shipping; and publishing distribution methods. No product puff. Buys 12 mss/year. Query. Length: 700-3,000 words. Pays $50-300.
Photos: Send photos with ms. Pays $25-100 for 3x5 and larger b&w prints; $25-150 for any size color transparencies and prints. Captions, model release, and identification of subjects required.
Tips: "Feature articles covering actual installations and industry trends are most open to freelancers. Be familiar with the industry, spend time in the field, and attend industry meetings and trade shows where equipment is displayed."

IN-PLANT PRINTER, Innes Publishing, Box 368, Northbrook IL 60062. (312)564-5940. Editor: Kraig J. Debus. Bimonthly magazine covering in-house print shops. Circ. 35,000. Pays on publication. Byline "usually" given. Buys first and second rights. Submit seasonal/holiday material 2 months in advance. Photocopied and previously published submissions OK. Computer printout submissions OK. Reports in 2 weeks. Free sample copy and writer's guidelines.
Nonfiction: Book excerpts, how-to and case history. "No nebulous management advice; undetailed stories lacking in concrete information. No human interest material." Buys 18 mss/year. Query or send complete ms. Length: 1,500-3,000 words. Pays $100-250.
Photos: Send photos with ms. "No additional payment is made for photos with ms, unless negotiated." Captions required. Buys all rights.

IN-PLANT REPRODUCTIONS, North American Publishing Co., 401 N. Broad St., Philadelphia PA 19108. (215)238-5300. Editor: Ida Crist. Assistant Editor: Amy Phillips. Monthly magazine about in-plant printing management for printing departments in business, government, education and industry. These graphic arts facilities include art, composition, camera, platemaking, press, and finishing equipment, xerographic and other business communications systems. Circ. 40,000. Pays on publication. Byline given. Buys first North American serial rights or all rights. Phone queries OK. SASE. Reports in 1 month. Sample copy $5.
Nonfiction: Interview, profile, how-to and technical. Buys 4 mss/issue. Query. Length: 500-2,500 words. Pays $75-200.

INSTANT AND SMALL COMMERCIAL PRINTER, (formerly *Instant Printer*), Innes Publishing, 425 Huehl Rd., Bldg. 11B, Northbrook IL 60062. (312)564-5940. Editor: Daniel Witte. Bimonthly magazine covering the instant/retail and smaller commercial printing industry for owners/operators of print shops. "We are primarily concerned with ways to be successful, ways to make lots of money, new markets and processes, technological innovations. Basically we try to focus on the needs and concerns of the entrepreneurial type." Circ. 24,000. Pays on publication. Byline given. Buys first North American serial rights with option for future use. Submit seasonal/holiday material 6 months in advance. Photocopied and previously published submissions OK. SASE. Reports in 2 weeks on queries; 1 month on mss. Sample copy $3; free writer's guidelines.
Nonfiction: Book excerpts (primarily on small business-related or graphic arts-related topics); general interest (anything about marketing, promotion, management); how-to (focus on more efficient ways to do everyday things printers do; and technical, business, financial); interview/profile (case histories of successful printers with angle on unique or special services); personal experience (any small printer who has tried marketing some new or unique service, successful or not); technical (any printing-related topic). Buys 18-25 mss/year. Query with or without clips of published work or send complete ms. Pays $200 maximum.
Photos: State availability of photos. Pays $50 maximum for b&w contact sheets, slides or 3x5 prints; $100 maximum for color contact sheets, slides or 3x5 prints. Captions, model release and identification of subjects required. Buys all rights.
Columns/Departments: Promotion—about advertising/promotion techniques used by instant printers (with samples), and Computers—information about computers and software for instant printers. Buys 12 mss/year. Query with or without clips or send complete ms. Length: 1,000 words maxmimum. Pays $75 maximum.
Fillers: Clippings, anecdotes, newsbreaks, and printing or marketing hints. Pays $10 maximum.
Tips: "I would suggest reading copies of our magazine, as well as related graphic arts magazines, for style."

NEWSPAPER PRODUCTION, North American Publishing Co., 401 N. Broad St., Philadelphia PA 19108. (215)238-5300. Demographic edition of *Printing Impressions*. Editor-in-Chief: Fred G. Phillips. For the newspaper industry; production personnel through management to editor and publisher. Bimonthly demographic section magazine; 8-24 pages. Circ. 17,500. Pays on publication. Buys first serial rights. Phone queries OK. Photocopied submissions OK, "no simultaneous submissions." SASE. Reports in 3 weeks.
Nonfiction: Publishes production case histories and how-to articles (production techniques); nothing about the editorial side of newspapers. Length: 1,500 words minimum. Query or submit complete ms. Pays $50-275.
Photos: B&w and color purchased with or without mss, or on assignment. Captions required. Query or submit contact sheet or prints. Additional payment for those used with mss computed into article's length. Model release required.

PLAN AND PRINT, 9931 Franklin Ave., Box 879, Franklin Park IL 60131. (312)671-5356. Editor-in-Chief: James C. Vebeck. 50% freelance written. Monthly magazine for computer-aided design users, commercial reproduction companies, in-plant reproduction, printing, drafting and design departments of business and industry and architects. Circ. 23,000. Pays on publication. Publishes ms an average of 1 month after acceptance. Buys all rights. Byline given. Submit seasonal/holiday material 6 months in advance. Computer printout submissions acceptable; no dot-matrix. SASE. Reports in 2 weeks. Free sample copy and writer's guidelines.
Nonfiction: How-to (how certain problems may have been solved; new methods of doing certain kinds of reproduction and/or design/drafting/computer-aided design work); and technical (must relate to industry). "Strong interest in computer-aided design." Buys 50 mss/year. Query with published clips. Length: 250-5,000 words. Pays $75-400. Sometimes pays the expenses of writers on assignment.
Photos: State availability of photos with query. Pays $5-10 for 8x10 b&w glossy prints. Captions and model release required. Buys all rights.
Columns/Departments: Open to suggestions for new columns/departments.
Poetry: Light verse related to the industry. Buys 6/year. Length: 4-12 lines. Pays $8 maximum.

SCREEN PRINTING, 407 Gilbert Ave., Cincinnati OH 45202. (513)421-2050. Editor: Tamas S. Frecska. 30% freelance written. Monthly magazine; 120 pages. For the screen printing industry, including screen printers (commercial, industrial and captive shops), suppliers and manufacturers, and ad agencies and allied professions. Circ. 11,000. Pays on publication. Publishes ms an average of 2 months after acceptance. Byline given. Buys all rights. Electronic submissions OK on IBM PC, XT. Computer printout submissions acceptable; prefers letter-quality to dot-matrix. Reporting time varies. SASE. Free writer's guidelines.
Nonfiction: "Since the screen printing industry covers a broad range of applications and overlaps other fields in the graphic arts, it's necessary that articles be of a significant contribution, preferably to a specific area of screen printing. Subject matter is fairly open, with preference given to articles on administration or technology, trends and developments. We try to give a good sampling of technical business and management articles; articles about unique operations. We also publish special features and issues on important subjects, such as material shortages, new markets and new technology breakthroughs. While most of our material is nitty-gritty, we appreciate a writer who can take an essentially dull subject and encourage the reader to read on through concise, factual, 'flairful' and creative, expressive writing. Interviews are published after consultation with and guidance from the editor." Interested in stories on unique approaches by some shops. No general, promotional treatment of individual companies. Buys 6-10 unsolicited mss/year. Length: 1,500-3,500 words. Pays minimum of $150 for major features. Sometimes pays the expenses of writers on assignment.
Photos: Cover photos negotiable; b&w or color. Published material becomes the property of the magazine.

‡**SOUTHERN GRAPHICS**, Cody Publications, Box 2028, Kissimmee FL 32742. (305)846-2800. Editor: George Meyer. 50% freelance written. Monthly magazine covering commercial printing and graphic arts. "We write about people and trends in the industry and ideas that will affect the effective management and marketing of commercial printing houses in the South." Circ. 10,000. Pays on acceptance. Publishes ms an average of 2 months after acceptance. Byline given. Offers 20% kill fee. Buys one-time rights. Submit seasonal/holiday material 2 months in advance. Simultaneous queries, and simultaneous, photocopied, and previously published submissions OK. Electronic submissions OK. Computer printout submissions acceptable. SASE. Reports in 2 weeks. Free sample copy and writer's guidelines.
Nonfiction: Book excerpts, historical/nostalgic, humor, interview/profile, new product, personal experience, technical, and anything to do with print communication—products, trends, etc. No religious or extremist politics. Buys 3-5 mss/year. Query with or without published clips or send complete ms. Length: 800-3,000 words. Pays $50-300. Sometimes pays the expenses of writers on assignment.
Photos: State availability of photos or send photos with query or ms. Pays $20-30. Identification of subjects required.
Tips: "We offer a readership that gives freelancers excellent exposure in the publishing industry. Regional topics and regional writers will have an advantage."

THE TYPOGRAPHER, Typographers International Association, Suite 101, 2262 Hall Pl. NW., Washington DC 20007. (202)965-3400. Editor: Geoff Lindsay. Bimonthly tabloid of the commercial typesetting industry for owners and executives of typesetting firms. Circ. 10,000. Pays on publication. Byline given. Buys one-time rights. Simultaneous queries, and simultaneous, photocopied, and previously published submissions OK. Computer printout submissions acceptable. Reports in 1 week. Free sample copy.
Nonfiction: Book excerpts, historical/nostalgic, how-to, interview/profile, new product, opinion, personal experience, photo feature and technical. "All articles should relate to typesetting management." No opinion pieces. Buys 20 mss/year. Query with published clips. Length: 1,000-2,000 words. Pays $50-150.
Photos: State availability of photos. Pays $20-35 for 5x7 b&w prints. Captions and identification of subjects required.

Real Estate

‡**CANADIAN REAL ESTATE**, (formerly *Panorama, The Real Estate Magazine*), The Canadian Real Estate Association, 99 Duncan Mill Rd., Don Mills, Ontario, M3B 1Z2 Canada.(416)445-9910. Editor: E. Mack Parliament. 5% freelance written. Bimonthly real estate newspaper. Circ. 58,000. Pays on publication. Publishes ms an average of 2 months after acceptance. Byline given. Buys all rights. Simultaneous and previously published submissions OK. Computer printout submissions acceptable; no dot-matrix. Reports in 2 weeks on queries; 1 month on mss. Sample copy for 9x12 SAE.
Nonfiction: How-to (make sales and operate a successful real estate business); interview/profile; personal experience; photo feature. No articles on other than real estate subjects. Recent article example: "Here's How Bigger Businesses Are Built." Buys 10 unsolicited mss/year. Send complete ms. Length: 1,000-4,000 words. Pays variable fee; "depends on quality."
Photos: Send photos with ms. Reviews 5x7 b&w and color prints. Captions required. Buys one-time rights.
Tips: "The most frequent mistakes made by writers in completing an article for us are spelling errors and not checking facts."

COMMUNITY DEVELOPMENT PUBLICATIONS, Suite 100, 8555 16th St., Silver Spring MD 20910. (301) 588-6380. Various newsletters for government officials and industry executives in community development; local growth; housing market; managing housing; community and economic development programs; neighborhoods; infrastructure; elderly and taxes. Pays end of month after publication. SASE if return desired. Sample copy and writer's guidelines for SASE.
Fillers: Uses contributions of significant newspaper clippings on housing, community and economic development, infrastructure; elderly and taxes; substantive actions and litigation of interest to housing and development professionals, state and local government, beyond immediate area. Particularly wants regular contributors for multistates, region, or at least a full state, especially state capitals. Buys 500-1,000 clippings. Normally pays $3 for each use of an accepted clipping.

VACATION INDUSTRY REVIEW, (formerly *Time Sharing Industry Review*), Box 4301920, Miami FL 33143. (305)667-0202. Executive Editor: W.L. Coulter. 50% freelance written. Monthly magazine for professionals involved in the vacation, ownership industry. Pays on acceptance. Publishes ms an average of 2 months after acceptance. Buys first rights only. Electronic submissions OK via 300 Baud ASCII. Computer printout submissions acceptable. Reports in 1 month. Publishes ms an average of 1 month after acceptance. Sample copy $1.
Nonfiction: Well-researched news features about new developments, marketing trends, financing, sales strategies, interviews with key industry personalities, etc. Query. Length: 1,000-5,000 words. Pays according to length. Sometimes pays the expenses of writers on assignment.
Photos: Pays extra for photo used.
Tips: "We are an international publication covering every aspect of this dynamic, rapidly growing industry. We need freelance writers with solid feature writing experience in every location where time sharing, camp resorts, condo hotels, and other forms of ownership programs are part of the vacation scene. Send three clips demonstrating your best work, along with a brief resume. We're also interested in story ideas you generate on your own. We are a business-to-business publication; the 'consumer' approach is not appropriate."

Resources and Waste Reduction

PUMPER PUBLICATIONS, Eastern Pumper, Midwest Pumper and Western Pumper, COLE Inc., Drawer 220, Three Lakes WI 54562. (715)546-3347. Editors: Bob Kendall and Pete Lawonn. 5% freelance written. A monthly tabloid covering the liquid waste hauling industry (portable toilet renters, septic tank pumpers, industrial waste haulers, chemical waste haulers, oil field haulers, and hazardous waste haulers). "Our publication is read by companies that handle liquid waste and manufacturers of equipment." Circ. 15,000. Pays on publication. Publishes ms an average of 1 month after acceptance. Byline given. Offers negotiable kill fee. Buys first serial rights. Submit seasonal/holiday material 3 months in advance. Simultaneous queries, and simultaneous, photocopied, and previously published submissions OK. Computer printout submissions acceptable; prefers letter-quality to dot-matrix. Reports in 1 month. Free sample copy.
Nonfiction: Expose (government regulations, industry problems, trends, public attitudes, etc.); general interest (state association meetings, conventions, etc.); how-to (related to industry, e.g., how to incorporate septage or municipal waste into farm fields, how to process waste, etc.); humor (related to industry, especially septic tank pumpers or portable toilet renters); interview/profile (including descriptions of business statistics, type of equipment, etc.); new product; personal experience; photo feature; and technical (especially reports on research projects related to disposal). "We are looking for quality articles that will be of interest to our readers; length is not that important. We publish trade journals. We need articles that deal with the trade." Studies on land application of sanitary waste are of great interest." Query or send complete ms. Pays 7½¢/word. Sometimes pays expenses of writers on assignment.
Photos: Send photos with query or ms. Pays $10-15 for b&w and color prints. "We need good contrast." Captions "suggested" and model release "helpful." Buys one-time rights.
Tips: "We hope to expand the editorial content of our monthly publications. We also have publications for sewer and drainage cleaners with the same format as *The Pumpers*; however, the *Cleaner* has a circulation of 23,000. We are looking for the same type of articles and pay is the same."

RESOURCE RECYCLING, Journal of Recycling, Reuse and Waste Reduction, Resource Recycling, Inc., Box 10540, Portland OR 97210. (503)227-1319. Editor: Jerry Powell. 20% freelance written. Bimonthly magazine covering recycling of paper, metals, glass, etc. for recycling processors. "*Resource Recycling* provides thorough assessments of trends and developments in waste recovery." Circ. 3,000 in 20 countries. Pays on publication. Publishes ms an average of 1½ months after acceptance. Byline given. "We don't assign manuscripts." Buys first North American serial rights, one-time rights, first serial rights, and second (reprint) rights. "No seasonal material in our trade." Simultaneous queries, and simultaneous, photocopied, and previously published submissions OK. Computer printout submissions acceptable; prefers letter-quality to dot-matrix. SASE. Reports in 1 month. Sample copy $1.24; writer's guidelines for SASE.
Nonfiction: Historical/nostalgic, interview/profile, new product, photo feature and technical. No nontechnical or opinion articles. Buys 15-20 mss/year. Query with published clips. "Queries should include a step-by-step outline of the proposed manuscript." Length: 1,500-3,000 words. Pays $100-250. Sometimes pays expenses of writers on assignment.
Photos: State availability of photos. Pays $5-10 for b&w contact sheets, negatives and prints. Identification of subjects required. Buys one-time rights.
Tips: "A freelancer can best break in to our publication with overviews of one recycling aspect in one state (e.g., oil recycling in Alabama). We can supply lists of sources, data, etc. Write with enough sophistication on the subject for our professional audience."

‡**WATER WELL JOURNAL**, Water Well Journal Publishing Co., 500 W. Wilson Bridge Rd., Worthington OH 43085. (614)846-4967. Publisher: Jay H. Lehr. Editor: Anita B. Stanley. 10% freelance written. Monthly magazine about water well drilling and ground water for contractors, suppliers, and manufacturers of equipment. Circ. 30,000. Pays on publication. Publishes ms an average of 3 months after acceptance. Byline given. Makes work-for-hire assignments. Submit seasonal material 6 months in advance. Photocopied submissions OK. Computer printout submissions acceptable. SASE. Reports in 1 month. Sample copy $1; free writer's guidelines.
Nonfiction: Interview, photo feature and technical. "We need major articles such as personality profiles of drillers and articles on pollution problems. We have special issues on pump and pump installation and rural water districts." No general articles on ground water. Buys 1 ms/issue. Query. Pays $50/typeset page.
Fillers: Gloria Swanson, fillers editor. Clippings. Buys 1 ms/issue.
Tips: The most frequent mistake made by writers in submitting an article to us is not knowing enough about the industry.

Selling and Merchandising

Sales personnel and merchandisers interested in how to sell products successfully consult these journals. Journals in nearly every other category of this Trade Journal section also buy sales-related material if it is slanted to the specialized product or industry they deal with, such as clothing or paint. Publications for advertising and marketing professionals can be found under Advertising, Marketing, and PR.

THE AMERICAN SALESMAN, 424 N. 3rd St., Burlington IA 52601. Publisher: Michael S. Darnall. Editorial Supervisor: Doris J. Ruschill. Editor: Barbara Boeding. 95% freelance written. Monthly magazine; 40 pages, (5½x8½). For distribution through company sales representatives. Circ. 2,850. Pays on publication. Publishes ms an average of 4 months after acceptance. Buys all rights. SASE. Free sample copy and writer's guidelines; mention *Writer's Market* in request.
Nonfiction: Sales seminars, customer service and follow-up, closing sales, sales presentations, handling objections, competition, telephone usage and correspondence, managing territory, and new innovative sales concepts. No sexist material, illustration written from only a salesperson's viewpoint. No mss dealing with supervisory problems. Query. Length: 900-1,200 words. Pays 3¢/word. Uses no advertising. Follow AP Stylebook. Include biography and/or byline with ms submissions. Author photos used.

ART MATERIAL TRADE NEWS, The Journal of All Art, Craft, Engineering and Drafting Supplies, Communication Channels Inc., 6255 Barfield Rd., Atlanta GA 30328. (404)256-9800. Editor: Jeffrey Abugel. 30% freelance written. Monthly magazine on art materials. "Our editorial thrust is to bring art materials retailers, distributors and manufacturers information they can use in their everyday operations." Circ. 12,000. Pays on publication. Publishes ms an average of 3 months after acceptance. "All assigned manuscripts are published." Buys first serial rights. Submit seasonal/holiday material 3 months in advance. Photocopied submissions OK. Computer printout submissions acceptable; prefers letter-quality to dot-matrix. SASE. Reports in 6 weeks. Sample copy for 9x12 SAE and $1 postage; writer's guildeines for 4x9½ SAE and 1 first class stamp.
Nonfiction: How-to (sell, retail/wholesale employee management, advertising programs); interview/profile (within industry); and technical (commercial art drafting/engineering). "We encourage a strong narrative style where possible. We publish an editorial 'theme' calendar at the beginning of each year." Buys 36-40 mss/year. Query with published clips. Length: 2,500-3,000 words (prefers 2,500 words). Pays 10¢/word and expenses with prior approval.
Photos: State availability of photos. Pays $10 maximum for b&w contact sheets. Identification of subjects required.
Columns/Departments: Business Talk (the impact of current economic or political events on art materials business). Buys 12-15 mss/year. Query with published clips. Length: 1,000-2,000 words. Pays $75-200.
Tips: "A current, solid background in any one of these areas helps—commercial art, retail selling, wholesale selling, business finance, employee management, interviewing or advertising. We frequently need filler items relating to the art industry. We appreciate clean, concise copy. We do a lot of dealer profiles throughout U.S. They must be written in good conversational tone with complete, accurate background information."

CASUAL LIVING, Columbia Communications, 370 Lexington Ave., New York NY 10164. (212)532-9290. Editor: Ralph Monti. A monthly magazine covering outdoor furniture for outdoor furniture specialists, including retailers, mass merchandiser, and department store buyers. Circ. 11,000. Pays on publication. Byline given. Buys first North American serial rights. Submit seasonal/holiday material 2 months in advance. Computer printout submissions acceptable. SASE. Reports in 1 month. Sample copy and writer's guidelines for 9x12 SAE, and 28¢ postage.
Nonfiction: Interview/profile (case histories of retailers in the industry); new product; opinion; and technical. Buys 12-13 mss/year. Query with or without published clips, then follow up with phone call. Length: 1,000 words average. Pays $200-400.
Photos: State availability of photos with query letter or ms. "Photos are essential with all articles." Reviews b&w contact sheet. Pays $75-100 for b&w prints. Buys all rights.
Tips: "Know the industry, trades and fashions, and what makes a successful retailer."

‡COMPUTER DEALER, Contemporary Business Ideas for Dealers, Retailers and VARS, Gordon Publications, Inc., Box 1952, Dover NJ 07801. (201)361-9060. Editorial Director: David Shadovitz. Editor: John Blackford. 20% freelance written. Monthly magazine on the computer reseller market. Business management magazine for dealers and retailers. Circ. 45,007. Pays on publication. Publishes ms an average of 4 months after acceptance. Offers 50% kill fee. Buys first serial rights. Submit seasonal/holiday material 2 months in ad-

vance. Computer printout submissions acceptable; prefers letter-quality to dot-matrix. SASE. Reports in 1 month. Sample copy and writer's guidelines for 8½x11 SAE.
Nonfiction: Book excerpts, general interest, how-to, interview/profile, new product, opinion, personal experience and photo feature. Buys 40 mss/year. Query with published clips. Length: 1,300-2,500 words. Pays $100-500. Pays expenses of writers on assignment.
Photos: John McLaughlin, photo editor.
Columns/Departments: Elaine Ring, column/department editor. Bits & Pieces: innovative ideas of use to dealers; and This Month in Review: exclusive new reports. Buys 10 mss/year. Query with published clips or send complete ms. Length: 500-1,000 words. Pays $40-200.
Fillers: Elaine Ring, fillers editor. Newsbreaks. Buys 4/year. Length: 500-1,000 words. Pays $40-200.
Tips: Feature length articles are most open to freelancers.

CONVENIENCE STORE NEWS, BMT Publications, Inc., 254 W. 31st St., New York NY 10001. (212)594-4120. Editor: Denise Melinsky. 20% freelance written. Tabloid published 16 times/year. For convenience store chain executives, middle management and owner/operators; franchisors and franchisees; convenience store managers, wholesalers, distributors, service merchandisers, food brokers and manufacturers involved in the food retailing and convenience store business. Circ. 75,000. Pays on publication. Publishes ms an average of 3 months after acceptance. Buys all rights. Phone queries OK. Query for submission of seasonal/holiday material. Computer printout submissions acceptable. Reports on queries in 2 weeks. Free sample copy and writer's guidelines.
Nonfiction: General interest, how-to, interview, profile and photo feature. Interested in news about convenience stores and chains and oil retailers who operate convenience stores, their personnel, operations and product mix trends, promotions and legislative activities on all levels of government that affect the operations of these businesses. Buys 90 unsolicited mss/year. Query. Pays $3/column inch. Pays expenses of writers on assignment.
Photos: Send photos with ms. Pays $5 for b&w glossy prints; $35 for contact sheet and negatives, "provided at least one photo is used." Captions required.
Columns/Departments: Store Managers section. Buys 16-20 mss/issue. Query. Length: 4 double-spaced pages maximum. Pays $3/column inch.
Fillers: Newsbreaks ("in our industry only"). Length: 1-2 pages, double-spaced.
Tips: "We need more in-depth features. The most frequent mistake made by writers in completing an article for us is not getting correct or complete information—a result of not knowing the industry."

‡**HIGH-TECH SELLING, For Telecommunications, Electronics and other High-Tech Industries**, Bureau of Business Practice/Prentice-Hall Publishers, 24 Rope Ferry Rd., Waterford CT 06386. (800)243-0876. Editor: Laura Gardner. Managing Editor: Wayne Muller. 90% freelance written. Monthly newsletter about selling in high-tech industries. Circ. 1,000. Pays on acceptance. Publishes ms an average of 4 months after acceptance. No byline given. Buys all rights. Submit seasonal/holiday material 4 months in advance. Photocopied submissions OK. Computer printout submissions acceptable; prefers letter-quality to dot-matrix. SASE. Reports in 1 week. free sample copy and writer's guidelines.
Nonfiction: How-to, interview/profile (with salespeople involved with high-tech products). "We're looking for interview-based 'success' and 'how-to' stories." Buys 50 mss/year. Query. Length: 1,000 words. Pays 10-15¢/word.
Tips: "Send for writer's guidelines then call or write to discuss specific story ideas."

INFO FRANCHISE NEWSLETTER, 11 Bond St., St. Catharines, Ontario L2R 4Z4 Canada or 728 Center St., Box 550, Lewiston NY 14092. (716)754-4669. Editor-in-Chief: E.L. Dixon, Jr. Managing Editor: Jean Baird. Monthly newsletter; 8 pages. Circ. 5,000. Pays on publication. Buys all rights. Photocopied submissions OK. SASE. Reports in 1 month.
Nonfiction: "We are particularly interested in receiving articles regarding franchise legislation, franchise litigation, franchise success stories, and new franchises. Both American and Canadian items are of interest. We do not want to receive any information which is not fully documented or articles which could have appeared in any newspaper or magazine in North America. An author with a legal background who could comment upon such things as arbitration and franchising or class actions and franchising, would be of great interest to us." Expose, how-to, informational, interview, profile, new product, personal experience and technical. Buys 10-20 mss/year. Length: 25-1,000 words. Pays $10-300.

ON THE UPBEAT, A Few Thoughts to Help People Who Sell for a Living Recharge Their Batteries, The Economics Press, Inc., 12 Daniel Rd., Fairfield NJ 07006. (201)227-1224. Editor: Robert Guder. 25% freelance written. Monthly magazine "serving as a refresher for veteran salespeople and a training tool for new salespeople." Circ. 28,000. Pays on acceptance. Publishes ms an average of 3 months after acceptance. Buys all rights. Submit seasonal/holiday material 3 months in advance. Photocopied submissions OK. Computer printout submissions OK. Reports in 6 weeks if SASE is enclosed. Free sample copy and writer's guidelines.

Nonfiction: Personal Items (incidents involving contemporary figures that highlight a positive personality trait); humor (wholesome jokes, cute stories—any subject); and selling experiences (anecdotes/stories about selling or about a helpful salesperson). Buys 30-40 mss/year. Length: 100-400 words. Pays $25 (jokes)-50.
Fillers: Buys 50-60/year. Length: 10-50 words. Pays $10.
Tips: "True stories/anecdotes about sales experience, either from the salesperson's viewpoint or the buyer's, are always welcome. Story should serve as an example of a principle or technique salespeople should use or stay away from. *On the Upbeat* is a business publication. Stay away from subjects unrelated to working/business, etc. However, jokes and cute stories may be on any *wholesome* subject."

OPPORTUNITY MAGAZINE, (formerly *Salesman's Opportunity* Magazine), 6 N. Michigan Ave., Chicago IL 60602. Managing Editor: Jack Weissman. 30% freelance written. Monthly magazine "for anyone who is interested in making money, full or spare time, in selling or in an independent business program." Circ. 190,000. Pays on publication. Buys all rights. Byline given. Submit seasonal/holiday material 6 months in advance. Computer printout submissions acceptable; prefers letter-quality to dot-matrix. SASE. Free sample copy and writer's guidelines.
Nonfiction: "We use articles dealing with sales techniques, sales psychology or general self-improvement topics." How-to, inspirational, and interview (with successful salespeople selling products offered by direct selling firms, especially concerning firms which recruit salespeople through *Opportunity Magazine*). Articles on self-improvement should deal with specifics rather than generalities. Would like to have more articles that deal with overcoming fear, building self-confidence, increasing personal effectiveness, and other psychological subjects. Submit complete ms. Buys 35-50 unsolicited mss/year. Length: 250-900 words. Pays $20-35.
Photos: State availability of photos with ms. Offers no additional payment for 8x10 b&w glossy prints. Captions and model release required. Buys all rights.
Tips: "Many articles are too academic for our audience. We look for a free-and-easy style in simple language which is packed with useful information, drama and inspiration. Check the magazine before writing. We can't use general articles. The only articles we buy deal with material that is specifically directed to readers who are opportunity seekers—articles dealing with direct sales programs or successful ventures that others can emulate. Try to relate the article to the actual work in which the reader is engaged."

PRIVATE LABEL, The Magazine for House Brands and Generics, E.W. Williams Publishing Co., 80 8th Ave., New York NY 10011. (212)989-1101. Editor: Sam Martin. Managing Editor: Mark Edgar. 10% freelance written. Bimonthly magazine covering food and nonfood private label and generic products. Circ. 25,000. Pays on acceptance. Publishes ms an average of 1 month after acceptance. Byline given. Offers 50-100% kill fee, depending on circumstances. Buys first serial rights and second serial (reprint) rights. Submit seasonal/holiday material 4 months in advance. Photocopied submissions OK if not under submission elsewhere. Computer printout submissions acceptable; no dot-matrix. SASE. Reports in "weeks." Sample copy $1 and SAE.
Nonfiction: Book excerpts (if segments are appropriate); general interest; historical/nostalgic; how-to; interview/profile; personal experience; photo feature; and travel. "We use feature articles showing how retailers promote, buy, display, sell, and feel about their store brands (private label and generic products). We're always interested in coverage of areas more than 300 miles from New York. No articles on peripheral topics such as taxes, insurance, safety, etc." Buys 30-40 mss/year. Query or send complete ms. Length: 500-4,000 words; Pays 3¢/word; "flat fee by special arrangement." Sometimes pays expenses of writers on assignment.
Photos: "We prefer articles with photos." Send photos with ms. Reviews contact sheets (if large selection). Pays $7 minimum for 5x7 b&w prints. Captions and identification of subjects required. Buys all rights; "release on request."
Tips: "We are wide open to freelancers who can line up store permission (preferably headquarters) for feature articles on philosophy, purchase, consumer attitudes, retailer attitudes, display and promotion of private label and generic products."

PROFESSIONAL SELLING, 24 Rope Ferry Rd., Waterford CT 06386. (203)442-4365. Editor: Paulette S. Withers. 33% freelance written. Bimonthly newsletter for sales professionals covering industrial or wholesale sales. "Professional Selling provides field sales personnel with both the basics and current information that can help them better perform the sales function." Pays on acceptance. Publishes ms an average of 6 months after acceptance. No byline given. Buys all rights. Submit seasonal/holiday material 4 months in advance. Computer printout submissions acceptable; prefers letter-quality to dot-matrix. SASE. Reports in 2 weeks. Sample copy and writer's guidelines for business size SAE and 1 first class stamp.
Nonfiction: How-to (successful sales techniques); and interview/profile (interview-based articles). "We buy only interview-based material." Buys 12-15 mss/year. Query. Length: 800-1,000 words.
Tips: "Only the lead article is open to freelancers. That must be based on an interview with an actual sales professional. Freelancers may occasionally interview sales managers, but the slant must be toward field sales, *not* management."

‡**SOUND MANAGEMENT**, Radio Advertising Bureau, 485 Lexington Ave., New York NY 10017. (212)599-6666. Editor: Daniel Flamberg. 20% freelance written. Monthly magazine on radio, advertising sales, and broadcast economics. "We are a business publication reaching the managers and sales managers at every radio station, network, rep firm and allied organizations in the U.S. and Canada." Estab. 1984. Circ. 12,000. Pays on publication. Publishes ms an average of 3 months after acceptance. Byline given. Offers $50 kill fee. Buys one-time rights; makes work-for-hire assignments. Submit seasonal/holiday material 6 months in advance. Photocopied submissions OK. Computer printout submissions acceptable; prefers letter-quality to dot-matrix. SASE. Reports in 2 weeks on queries; 4 weeks on mss. Free sample copy and writer's guidelines.
Nonfiction: Book excerpts (sales & marketing); how-to (sell, motivate, train staff); and interview/profile (radio managers). Buys 20 mss/year. Query with published clips. Length: 500-2,500 words. Pays $250-750. Pays expenses of writers on assignment.
Columns/Departments: On the Books—reviews of management/economics books; and Databank—analysis of client industries. Buys 10 mss/year. Query with published clips. Length: 250-550 words. Pays $100-300.
Tips: Area most open to freelancers is nonfiction features; must be carefully targeted to sophisticated trade audience.

Sport Trade

‡**AEROBICS & FITNESS JOURNAL, The Journal of the Aerobics and Fitness Association of America**, Aerobics and Fitness Association of America, Suite 802, 15250 Ventura Blvd., Sherman Oaks CA 91403. (818)905-0040. Editor: Peg Angsten, R.N. Managing Editor: Harlyn Enholm. 60% freelance written. Bimonthly magazine covering aerobic exercise and sports, health and fitness education. "We need timely, indepth informative articles on health, fitness, aerobic exercise, sports nutrition, sports medicine and physiology." Circ. 20,000. Pays on publication. Publishes ms an average of 4 months after acceptance. Byline given. Offers $50 kill fee. Buys first North American serial rights, and simultaneous rights (in some cases). Submit seasonal/holiday material 4 months in advance. Simultaneous queries and simultaneous, photocopied, and previously published submissions OK. Electronic submissions OK via either Macintosh 512K or IBM PCXT. Computer printout submissions acceptable; prefers letter-quality to dot-matrix. SASE. Reports in 2 weeks. Sample copy for $1 or SAE with 6 first class stamps; writer's guidelines for SAE.
Nonfiction: Book excerpts (fitness book reviews); expose (on nutritional gimmicky); historical/nostalgic (history of various athletic events); humor (personal fitness profiles); inspirational (sports leader's motivational pieces); interview/profile (fitness figures); new product (plus equipment review); opinion (on clubs); personal experience (successful fitness story); photo feature (on exercise, fitness, new sport); and travel (spas that cater to fitness industry). No articles on unsound nutritional practices, popular trends or unsafe exercise gimmicks. Buys 18-25 mss/year. Query. Length: 800-2,500 words. Pays $65-280. Sometimes pays expenses of writers on assignment.
Photos: Sports, action, fitness, aerobic competitions and exercise classes. Pays $30-60 for 8x10 b&w prints; $35-100 for color transparencies. Captions, model release, and identification of subjects required. Buys one-time rights; other rights purchased depend on use of photo.
Columns/Departments: Fitness Industry News, shorts on health and fitness, and profiles on successful fitness figures. Buys 50 mss/year. query with published clips or send complete ms. Length: 50-150 words. Pays 1¢/word.
Poetry: Buys 2 poems/year. Submit maximum 1 poem. Length: 20-80 lines. Pays $20-50.
Fillers: Cartoons, clippings, jokes, short humor and newsbreaks. Buys 12/year. Length: 75-200 words. Pays $20-50.
Tips: "Cover an athletic event, get a unique angle, provide accurate and interesting findings, and write in an intellectual manner. We are looking for new health and fitness reporters and writers. *A&F* is a good place to get started. I have generally been disappointed with short articles and fillers submissions due to their lack of force. Cover a topic with depth."

AMERICAN BICYCLIST, (formerly American Bicyclist and Motorcyclist), 80 8th Ave., New York NY 10011. (212)206-7230. Editor: Konstantin Doren. 30% freelance written. Monthly magazine for bicycle sales and service shops. Circ. 11,025. Pays on publication. Publishes ms an average of 4 months after acceptance. Only staff-written articles are bylined, except under special circumstances. Buys all rights. Computer printout submissions acceptable; no dot-matrix.
Nonfiction: Typical story describes (very specifically) unique traffic-builder or merchandising ideas used with success by an actual dealer. Articles may also deal exclusively with moped sales and service operation within conventional bicycle shop. Emphasis on showing other dealers how they can follow similar pattern and

increase their business. Articles may also be based entirely on repair shop operation, depicting efficient and profitable service systems and methods. Buys 8 mss/year. Query. Length: 1,000-2,800 words. Pays 9¢/word, plus bonus for outstanding manuscript. Pays expenses of writers on assignment.
Photos: Reviews relevant b&w photos illustrating principal points in article purchased with ms; 5x7 minimum. Pays $8/photo. Captions required. Buys all rights.
Tips: "A frequent mistake made by writers is writing as if we are a book read by consumers instead of professionals in the bicycle industry.

AMERICAN FIREARMS INDUSTRY, AFI Communications Group, Inc., 2801 E. Oakland Park Blvd., Ft. Lauderdale FL 33306. 10% freelance written. Monthly magazine specializing in the sporting arms trade. Circ. 30,000. Pays on publication. Publishes ms an average of 2 months after acceptance. Buys all rights. Computer printut submissions acceptable; prefers letter-quality to dot-matrix. Submit all material with SASE. Reports in 2 weeks.
Nonfiction: R.A. Lesmeister, articles editor. Publishes informational, technical and new product articles. No general firearms subjects. Query. Length: 900-1,500 words. Pays $100-150.
Photos: Reviews b&w 8x10 glossy prints. Manuscript price includes payment for photos.

AMERICAN HOCKEY MAGAZINE, (formerly *American Hockey and Arena Magazine*), Amateur Hockey Association of the United States, 2997 Broadmoor Valley Rd., Colorado Springs CO 80906. (303)576-4990. Publisher: Hal Trumble. Managing Editor: Mike Schroeder. 80% freelance written. Monthly magazine covering hockey in general (with amateur/youth hockey emphasis) for teams, coaches and referees of the Amateur Hockey Association of the U.S., ice facilities in the U.S. and Canada, buyers, schools, colleges, pro teams, and park and recreation departments. Circ. 35,000. Pays on publication. Publishes ms an average of 1 month after acceptance. Byline given. Buys first serial rights makes work-for-hire assignments. Phone queries OK. Submit seasonal material 4 months in advance. Photocopied and previously published submissions OK. SASE. Reports in 1 month. Sample copy $2.
Nonfiction: General interest, profile, new product and technical. Query. Length: 500-3,000 words. Pays $50 minimum.
Photos: Reviews 5x7 b&w glossy prints and color slides. Offers no additional payment for photos accepted with ms. Captions preferred. Buys one-time rights.
Columns/Departments: Rebound Shots (editorial); Americans in the Pros (U.S. players in the NHL); College Notes; Rinks and Arenas (arena news); Equipment/Sports Medicine; Referees Crease; Coaches Playbook; For the Record; and Features (miscellaneous). Query.

BICYCLE BUSINESS JOURNAL, 1904 Wenneca, Box 1570, Fort Worth TX 76101. Editor: Levy Joffrion. 10% freelance written. Monthly. Circ. 10,000. Pays on acceptance. Publishes ms an average of 3 months after acceptance. Buys first serial rights. Computer printout submissions acceptable. SASE.
Nonfiction: Stories about dealers who service what they sell, emphasizing progressive, successful sales ideas in the face of rising costs and increased competition. Also includes moped dealerships. Length: 3 double-spaced pages maximum.
Photos: B&w glossy photo a must; vertical photo preferred. Query.
Tips: "We are requesting greater professionalism and more content and research in freelance material."

‡**CORPORATE FITNESS & RECREATION, The Journal for Employee Health and Services Programs**, Brentwood Publishing Corp., (a Prentice-Hall Company), 825 S. Barrington Ave., Los Angeles CA 90049. (213)826-8388. Editor: Martin H. Waldman. Managing Editor: Dana Bigman. 60% freelance written. Bimonthly magazine on employee fitness and recreation. "Our readers are directors of on-site employee fitness and recreation programs." Circ. 12,000. Pays on acceptance. Publishes ms an average of 6 months after acceptance. Byline given. Buys all rights. Submit seasonal/holiday material 6 months in advance. Computer printout submissions acceptable; prefers letter-quality to dot-matrix. SASE. Reports in 1 month on queries; 2 months on mss. Free sample copy and writer's guidelines.
Nonfiction: How-to (plan, implement, supervise, and evaluate employee health and wellness programs); interview/profile (of on-site corporate fitness and recreation programs and facilities); technical (regarding sports medicine, exercise, physiology, and lifestyle improvements—stress management, smoking cessation, employee assistance program, etc.); and analysis of studies conducted on the benefits of employee fitness programs. "No general articles on health-related topics that are not geared specifically to our readership." Buys 30 mss/year. Query with published clips. Length: 1,000-2,000 words. Pays $100-240. Pays expenses of writers on assignment.
Columns/Departments: Sports Medicine: Prevention and Treatment of injuries incurred by participants in employee fitness and recreation programs. Writers should have exercise physiology background. Buys 6 mss/year. Query with published clips. Length: 1,500-2,000 words. Pays $150-240.
Tips: "Queries with clips are appreciated. Submissions should conform to American Medical Association

style and be written clearly and concisely. A medical or exercise physiology background is not necessary, but is helpful when tackling technical subjects. All submissions are reviewed by an editorial advisory board of industry professionals."

FISHING TACKLE RETAILER, B.A.S.S. Publications, 1 Bell Rd., Montgomery AL 36141. (205)272-9530. Editor: Dave Ellison. 70% freelance written. Magazine published 8 times/year. "Designed to promote the economic health of retail sellers of freshwater and saltwater angling equipment." Circ. 22,000. Byline usually given. Publishes ms an average of 3-12 months after acceptance. Buys all rights. Submit seasonal/holiday material 6 months in advance. Electronic submissions OK via 300 or 1200 baud, X-on, X-off protocol. Computer printout submissions acceptable; prefers letter-quality to dot-matrix. SASE. Reports in 6 weeks. Sample copy $2; writer's guidelines for standard size SAE and 1 first class stamp.
Nonfiction: How-to (merchandising and management techniques); technical (how readers can specifically benefit from individual technological advances); and success stories (how certain fishing tackle retailers have successfully overcome business difficulties and their advice to their fellow retailers). Articles must directly relate to the financial interests of the magazine's audience. Buys 100 mss/year. Query with published clips. Length: 50-3,000 words. Pays $10-600. Sometimes pays expenses of writers on assignment.
Photos: State availability of photos. Payment included with ms.
Columns/Departments: Retail Pointers (200-300 words) and Profit Strategy (750-900 words)—how-to tips, should be accompanied by illustration. Buys variable number mss/year.
Tips: "Long stories are usually assigned to writers with whom we have an established relationship. The writer has a better chance of breaking in at our publication with short, lesser-paying articles and fillers.

FITNESS INDUSTRY, Industry Publishers, Inc., 1545 NE 123rd St., North Miami FL 33161. (305)893-8771. Executive Editor: Michael J. Keighley. A magazine about the fitness industry, published 9 times/year. Includes dancercize, running, bicycling, swimming and aerobocize. For retailers and business people in the industry. Circ. 18,500. Pays on publication. Byline given. Buys all rights. Submit seasonal material 2 months in advance. SASE. Reports in 6 weeks. Sample copy $2.50; free writer's guidelines.
Nonfiction: "Content must be general, not featuring one specific manufacturing company or individual shop case-study. Articles can feature products, such as an examination of home-exercise equipment, but must include industry-wide information, not pertaining specifically to the product of one manufacturer. Design, display, merchandising techniques, retailing procedures, shop layout and lighting are among those categories that would be of interest to our readers." Query. Length: 2,000-2,500 words. Pays 5¢/word.

GOLF INDUSTRY, Industry Publishers, Inc., 1545 NE 123rd St., North Miami FL 33161. (305)893-8771. Executive Editor: Michael J. Keighley. Emphasizes the golf industry for country clubs, pro-owned golf shops, real estate developments, municipal courses, military and schools. Bimonthly magazine; 75 pages. Circ. 17,000. Pays on publication. Buys all rights. Submit seasonal/holiday material 3 months in advance. SASE. Reports "usually in 6-8 weeks." Sample copy $2.50. Free writer's guidelines.
Nonfiction: Publishes informational articles "dealing with a specific facet of golf club or pro shop operations, e.g., design, merchandising, finances, etc." Buys 20 mss/year. Submit complete ms. Length: 2,500 words maximum. Pays 5¢/word.
Tips: "Since we don't make freelance assignments, a query is not particularly important. We would rather have a complete manuscript which conforms to our policy of general, but informative, articles about one specific facet of the business of golf merchandising, financing, retailing, etc. Well-written manuscripts, if not used immediately, are often held in our files for use in a future issue. We never publish articles concentrating on one specific manufacturer or extolling the virtues of one product over another. We seldom feature one club or retail outlet. We don't deal with the game itself, but with the business end of the game."

GOLF SHOP OPERATIONS, 495 Westport Ave., Norwalk CT 06856. (203)847-5811. Editor: Nick Romano. 5% freelance written. Magazine published 6 times/year for golf professionals and shop operators at public and private courses, resorts, driving ranges and golf specialty stores. Circ. 12,500. Pays on publication. Publishes ms an average of 1 month after acceptance. Byline given. Submit seasonal material (for Christmas and other holiday sales, or profiles of successful professionals with how-to angle emphasized) 3 months in advance. Photocopied submissions OK. Computer printout submissions acceptable; prefers letter-quality to dot-matrix. Reports in 1 month. Sample copy $1.50.
Nonfiction: "We emphasize improving the golf retailer's knowledge of his profession. Articles should describe how pros are buying, promoting and merchandising and displaying wares in their shops that might be of practical value. Must be aimed only at the retailer." How-to, profile, successful business operation and merchandising techniques. Buys 6-8 mss/year. Phone queries preferred. Pays $165-200. Sometimes pays expenses of writers on assignment.
Photos: "Pictures are mandatory with all manuscript submissions." Captions required.
Tips: "I'm less inclined to assign anything unless the person can handle a camera. The profile pieces must have

decent photos. We're really looking for the freelancers that understand the golf business. This helps us in that we won't have to rewrite a lot or have the writer go back and ask the obvious questions."

PGA MAGAZINE, Professional Golfer's Association of America, 100 Avenue of Champions, Palm Beach Gardens FL 33410. (305)626-3600. Editor: William A. Burbaum. Monthly magazine about golf for 14,000 club professionals and apprentices nationwide. Circ. 38,000. Average issue includes 8-10 articles and 6 departments. Pays on acceptance. Byline given. Phone queries OK. Submit seasonal material 3 months in advance. Photocopied and previously published submissions OK. Reports in 3 weeks. Free sample copy.
Nonfiction: Historical (great moments in golf revisited); personality profiles; off-beat (e.g., golf in stamps, unique collections); inspirational (personal success stories); and photo feature (great golf courses). Buys 15 mss/year. Query with outline and published clips. Length: 900-1,500 words. Pays 15¢/word minimum. "Exhibit knowledge and interest in the professional business and in other needs of today's club professional."
Photos: Pays $25/b&w contact sheets; $75-100/35mm inside color transparencies; $1.50 for cover photos. Captions and model release required.

POOL & SPA NEWS, Leisure Publications, 3923 W. 6th St., Los Angeles CA 90020. (213)385-3926. Editor-in-Chief: J. Field. 40% freelance written. Semimonthly magazine emphasizing news of the swimming pool and spa industry for pool builders, pool retail stores and pool service firms. Circ. 12,000. Pays on publication. Publishes ms an average of 1 month after acceptance. Buys all rights. Photocopied submissions OK. Computer printout submissions acceptable. SASE. Reports in 2 weeks.
Nonfiction: Interview, new product, profile and technical. Phone queries OK. Length: 500-2,000 words. Pays 8-10¢/word. Sometimes pays expenses of writers on assignment.
Photos: Pays $8 per b&w photo used.

RODEO NEWS, Rodeo News Publishing Corp., Box 587, Paul's Valley, OK 73075. (405)238-3310. Editor: Kelly Clark. A monthly special interest magazine devoted to the sport of rodeo and the West. Circ. 15,000. Pays on publication. Byline given. Offers 50% kill fee. Buys first North American serial rights. Submit seasonal/holiday material 3 months in advance. Photocopied submissions OK. Computer printout submissions acceptable. SASE. Reports in 1 month on queries; 2 weeks on mss. Sample copy $3; free writer's guidelines.
Nonfiction: Historical/nostalgic, how-to, humor, interview/profile, new product, personal experience, photo feature and technical. Buys 20 mss/year. Query with published clips. Length: 1,200-5,000 words. Pays $100-500.
Photos: State availability of photos. Pays $25 for 8x10 b&w photos; $75 for color transparencies. Captions and identification of subjects required. Buys all rights.
Fillers: Newsbreaks. Buys 50/year. Length: 500 words. Pays $75 maximum.

THE SHOOTING INDUSTRY, 591 Camino de la Reina, San Diego CA 92108. (619)297-8521. Editor: J. Rakusan. Monthly magazine for manufacturers, dealers and sales representatives of archery and shooting equipment. Pays on publication. Byline given. Buys all rights. SASE. Reports in 3 weeks. Free sample copy.
Nonfiction: Articles that tell "secrets of my success" based on experience of individual gun dealer; and articles of advice to help dealers sell more guns and shooting equipment. Also, articles about and of interest to manufacturers and top manufacturers' executives. Buys about 135 mss/year. Query. Length: 3,000 words maximum. Pays $100-200.
Photos: Photos essential; b&w glossies purchased with ms.

THE SPORTING GOODS DEALER, 1212 N. Lindbergh Blvd., St. Louis MO 63132. (314)997-7111. President/Chief Executive Officer: Richard Waters. Editor: Steve Fechter. 20% freelance written. For members of the sporting goods trade: retailers, manufacturers, wholesalers, and representatives. Monthly magazine. Circ. 27,000. Buys second serial (reprint) rights. Buys about 15 mss/year. Pays on publication. Computer printout submissions acceptable; no dot-matrix. Reports in 2 weeks. Publishes ms an average of 3 months after acceptance. Query. SASE. Sample copy $4 (refunded with first ms); free writer's guidelines.
Nonfiction: "Articles about specific sporting goods retail stores, their promotions, display techniques, sales ideas, merchandising, timely news of key personnel; expansions, new stores, deaths—all in the sporting goods trade. Specific details on how individual successful sporting goods stores operate. What specific retail sporting goods stores are doing that is new and different. We would also be interested in features dealing with stores doing an outstanding job in retailing of baseball, fishing, golf, tennis, camping, firearms/hunting and allied lines of equipment. Query on these." Successful business operations and merchandising techniques. Does not want to see announcements of doings and engagements. Length: open. Rates negotiated by assignment. Also looking for material for the following columns: Terse Tales of the Trade (store news); Selling Slants (store promotions); and Open for Business (new retail sporting goods stores or sporting goods departments). All material must relate to specific sporting goods stores by name, city, and state; general information is not accepted.
Photos: Pays minimum of $3.50 for sharp clear b&w photos; size not important. These are purchased with or

without mss. Captions optional, but identification requested.

Fillers: Clippings. These must relate directly to the sporting goods industry. Pays 1-2¢/published word.

SPORTS MERCHANDISER, W.R.C. Smith Publishing Co., 1760 Peachtree Rd. NW, Atlanta GA 30357. (404)874-4462. Editor: Eugene R. Marnell. 5% freelance written. Monthly tabloid; 100 pages. For retailers and wholesalers of sporting goods in all categories; independent stores, chains, specialty stores, and department store departments. Circ. 30,000. Pays on publication. Publishes ms an average of 3 months after acceptance. Buys all rights. Submit seasonal/holiday material 6 months in advance. Computer printout submissions acceptable; prefers letter-quality to dot-matrix. SASE. Reports in 4 months.

Nonfiction: Articles telling how retailers are successful in selling a line of products, display ideas, successful merchandising programs, inventory operations, and advertising program successes. No articles on business history. Query to be one-page with card (reply) enclosed. Letters to state full name of contact, address, etc. and describe type of business relative to volume, inventory and positioning in local market. Tell particular slant author believes most interesting. Length: 1,000-2,000 words. Pays $75-175.

Photos: State availability of photos with query. Offers no additional payment for 5x7 or 8x10 b&w prints. Captions required. Buys all rights.

Tips: "The retail order season is almost six months opposite the retail buying season (i.e., consumer buying). Lead time for ordering is six months—sometimes more on hardgoods and softgoods. Other products have full-year ordering cycle. The writer has a better chance of breaking into our publication with short, lesser-paying articles because they provide greater detail information on a specific element of store, operator, etc. A query will help everyone."

SPORTS TRADE, Page Publishing Co. Ltd., 501 Oakdale Rd., Downsview, Toronto, Ontario M3N 1W7 Canada. (416)746-7360. Editor: Hugh McBride. 5% freelance written. Magazine published 9 times/year for sporting goods retailers, manufacturers, wholesalers, jobbers, department and chain stores, camping equipment dealers, bicycle sales and service, etc. Circ. 9,800. Pays on publication. Publishes ms an average of 1½ months after acceptance. Buys first serial rights. Computer printout submissions acceptable. Reports in 2 months. SAE, IRCs.

Nonfiction: Technical and informational articles. Articles on successful Canadian business operations, new products, merchandising techniques and interviews. No U.S.-oriented articles. Query. Length: 1,200-2,000 words. Pays 10¢/word or $60/published page. Pays expenses of writers on assignment.

Tips: Submit Canadian-oriented articles only.

SPORTSTYLE, Fairchild Publications, Inc., 7 E. 12th St., New York NY 10003. (212)741-5995. Editor: Mark Sullivan. A bimonthly tabloid covering the sporting goods industry for sporting goods retailers and manufacturers of athletic footwear, apparel and equipment. Circ. 30,000. Pays on publication. Byline given. Offers negotiable kill fee. Computer printout submissions acceptable. Reports in 1 month. Free sample copy.

Nonfiction: "We run business stories only and use a lot of retailer profiles and occasionally manufacturer profiles." Buys 25 mss/year. Query. Length: 2,000 words. Pays $5/column inch.

SWIMMING POOL AGE & SPA MERCHANDISER, Communication Channels, Inc., 6255 Barfield Rd., Atlanta GA 30328. (404)256-9800. Editor: Terri Simmons. Monthly tabloid emphasizing pool, spa and hot tub industry. Circ. 15,000. Pays on publication. Publishes ms an average of 3 months after acceptance. Buys all rights. Phone queries OK. Submit seasonal/holiday material 3 months in advance. Electronic submissions OK on DecMate disk on diskette, but requires hard copy also.

Nonfiction: Expose (if in industry, company frauds); how-to (installation techniques, service and repairs, tips, etc.); interview (with people and groups within the industry); photo feature (pool/spa/tub construction or special use); technical (should be prepared with expert within the industry); industry news; and market research reports. Buys 5-10 unsolicited mss/year. Mss must be double-spaced on white paper. Query. Length: 250-1,500 words. Pays 10¢/word.

Photos: Purchased with accompanying ms or on assignment. Query or send contact sheet. Will accept 35mm transparencies of good quality. Captions required.

TENNIS INDUSTRY, Industry Publishers, Inc., 1545 NE 123 St., North Miami FL 33161. (305)893-8771. Editor: Michael J. Keighley. Emphasizes the tennis industry for department store divisionals, teaching pros, pro shop managers, specialty shop managers, country club managers, coaches, athletic directors, etc. Monthly magazine; 200 pages. Circ. 19,000. Pays on publication. Buys all rights. Submit seasonal/holiday material 3 months in advance. Previously published submissions OK. SASE. Reports "usually in 6-8 weeks." Sample copy $2.50; free writer's guidelines.

Nonfiction: Publishes informational articles dealing "with specific facets of the tennis club or pro shop operation, e.g., design, merchandising, finances, etc." Buys 20 mss/year. Submit complete ms. Length: 2,500 words maximum. Pays 5¢/word.

Tips: "Since we do not make freelance assignments, a query is not particularly important. We would rather have a complete manuscript which conforms to our policy of general but informative articles about one specific facet of the business of tennis merchandising, financing, retailing, etc. Well-done manuscripts, if not used immediately, are often held in our files for use in a future issue. We never publish articles concentrating on one specific manufacturer or extolling the virtues of one product over another. We seldom feature one club or retail outlet. We don't deal with the game itself, but with the business end of the game.''

‡**WILDLIFE HARVEST MAGAZINE, For Game Breeders and Hunting Resorts**, Arrowhead Hunt Club, R#1, Box 28, Goose Lake IA 52750. Editor: John M. Mullin. Monthly magazine of private enterprise game bird hunting resorts and wildlife habitats. Aimed mostly for North American Gamebird Association members. Circ. 1,460. Pays on acceptance. Byline given. Buys one-time serial and first rights. Submit seasonal/holiday material 2 months in advance. Photocopied submissions OK. SASE. Reports in 3 weeks on queries; 2 months on mss. Sample copy $1.25 and 6x9 SAE.
Nonfiction: How-to (pen-rear game birds, develop and operate a bird hunting resort); and photo feature (NAGA member game farms and private enterprise hunting resorts). No general conservation articles or travel articles. Buys 3-4 mss/year. Query. Length: 2,000 words maximum. Pays $40-200.
Photos: Photos should depict private enterprise, commercial game farms or hunting resorts. Send photos with query. Payment for photos included in payment for ms. Reviews 3x5 or 5x7 b&w or color prints (if good contrast). Captions preferred; identification of subjects required.
Tips: "We would buy more articles if they were of the right subject and people." Contact the editor for a listing of NAGA members or game farm enterprises in your state. We are open to picture stories about a *member* game bird farm or member hunting preserve. Most freelance writers don't work well for our magazine. They don't seem to want to go to a specific operation for a story."

WOODALL'S CAMPGROUND MANAGEMENT, Woodall Publishing Co., 500 Hyacinth Pl., Highland Park Il 60035. (312)433-4550. Editor: Mike Byrnes. 66% freelance written. A monthly tabloid covering campground management and operation for managers of private and public campgrounds throughout the U.S. Circ. 17,200. Pays after publication. Byline given. Buys all rights. Submit seasonal/holiday material 4 months in advance. Simultaneous queries OK. Computer printout submissions acceptable. SASE. Reports in 2 weeks on queries; 6 weeks on mss. Free sample copy and writer's guidelines.
Nonfiction: How-to, interview/profile and technical. "Our articles tell our readers how to maintain their resources, manage personnel and guests, market, develop new campground areas and activities, and interrelate with the major tourism organizations within their areas. 'Improvement' and 'profit' are the two key words." Buys 48+ mss/year. Query. Length: 500 words minimum. Pays $50-200. Sometimes pays expenses of writers on assignment.
Photos: Send contact sheets and negatives. ''We pay for each photo used.''
Tips: "Contact us and give us an idea of your ability to travel and your travel range. We sometimes have assignments in certain areas. The best type of story to break in with is a case history type approach about how a campground improved its maintenance, physical plant or profitability."

Stone and Quarry Products

CONCRETE CONSTRUCTION MAGAZINE, 426 South Westgate, Addison IL 60101. Editorial Director: Ward R. Malisch. Monthly magazine, 80 pages average, for general and concrete contractors, architects, engineers, concrete producers, cement manufacturers, distributors and dealers in construction equipment and testing labs. Circ. 82,000. Buys all rights. Pays on acceptance. Bylines used only by prearrangement with author. Photocopied submissions OK. Reports in 2 months. SASE. Free sample copy and writer's guidelines.
Nonfiction: "Our magazine has a major emphasis on cast-in-place and precast concrete. Prestressed concrete is also covered. Our articles deal with tools, techniques and materials that result in better handling, better placing, and ultimately an improved final product. We are particularly firm about not using proprietary names in any of our articles. Manufacturer and product names are never mentioned; only the processes or techniques that might be of help to the concrete contractor, the architect or the engineer dealing with the material. We do use reader response cards to relay reader interest to manufacturers." No job stories or promotional material. Buys 8-10 mss/year. Submit query with topical outline. Pays $200/2-page article. Prefers 1,000-2,000 words with 2-3 illustrations.
Photos: Photos used only as part of complete ms.
Tips: "Condensed, totally factual presentations are preferred."

CONCRETE INTERNATIONAL: DESIGN AND CONSTRUCTION, American Concrete Institute, 22400 W. Seven Mile Rd., Detroit MI 48219. (313)532-2600. Advertising Coordinator: Loretta Edwards. 1% freelance written. Monthly magazine about concrete for design engineers, management and construction people. Circ. 17,000. Pays on publication. Publishes ms an average of 6 months after acceptance. Buys all rights, first serial rights, and second serial (reprint) rights; makes assignments on work-for-hire basis. Submit seasonal material 4 months in advance. Computer printout submissions acceptable; no dot-matrix. SASE. Reports in 3 weeks on queries; in 2 months on mss. Sample copy and writer's guidelines for SASE.

Nonfiction: Historical (concrete structures); how-to (concrete construction, new methods, techniques); new product (concrete-related); and technical (concrete-related). Query (phone queries OK). Length: 300-5,000 words. Pays $100/printed page. Sometimes pays expenses of writers on assignment.

Photos: State availability of photos or send photos with ms. Reviews b&w contact sheets and 5x7 and 8x10 prints. Offers no additional payment for photos accepted with ms. Captions and model release required. Buys one-time rights.

Columns/Departments: Legal (related to concrete construction); Problems, Solutions and Practices; and Management Techniques. Query. Length: 600-1,000 words.

STONE IN AMERICA, American Monument Association, 6902 N. High St., Worthington OH 43085. (614)885-2713. Managing Editor: Bob Moon. Monthly magazine for the retailers of upright memorials in the U.S. and Canada. Circ. 2,600. Pays on acceptance. Buys interment industry rights. Phone queries preferred. SASE. Reports in 1 month. Free sample copy and writer's guidelines.

Nonfiction: How-to (run a monument business); informational (major news within the industry, monuments as an art form); profile (successful retailers); and technical. Buys 30-40 mss/year. Length: 1,500-2,000 words. Query. Pays $100-400.

Photos: Pays $20-50 for 5x7 or 8x10 b&w glossy prints.

Toy, Novelty and Hobby

MODEL RETAILER MAGAZINE, Clifton House, Clifton VA 22024. (703)830-1000. Editor: Geoffrey Wheeler. 40% freelance written. Monthly magazine "for hobby store owners—generally well-established small business persons, fairly well educated, and very busy." Circ. 7,300. Pays on publication. Byline given. Buys one-time rights. Phone queries OK (no collect calls), but prefers written queries. Submit seasonal/holiday material 3 months in advance. Photocopied and previously published submissions OK. Computer printout submissions acceptable; prefers letter-quality to dot-matrix. SASE. Reports in 3 weeks. Free writer's guidelines and sample copy.

Nonfiction: Retailer profiles; articles on store management, marketing, merchandising, advertising; and photo feature (if photos tie in with marketing techniques or hobby store operation, etc.). No company profiles, 'human interest' stories, self-publicity articles, or reports on trade shows. ("We do those ourselves".) Buys 2-4 mss/issue. Query. Length: 1,200-2,500 words. Pays for complete manuscript package of: main copy, side bars (if needed), working headline, and illustrative material (if needed). Range: $125-350, depending on length and degree of specialization.

Photos: "Photos that illustrate key points and are of good quality will help the article, particularly if it concerns business operation. Photos are paid for as part of total article package."

THE STAMP WHOLESALER, Box 706, Albany OR 97321. Executive Editor: Kyle Jansson. 80% freelance written. Newspaper published 28 times/year; 32 pages. For philatelic businessmen; many are part-time and/or retired from other work. Circ. 6,400. Pays on publication. SASE. Byline given. Buys all rights. Reports in 10 weeks. Free sample copy.

Nonfiction: How-to information on how to deal more profitably in postage stamps for collections. Emphasis on merchandising techniques and how to make money. Does not want to see any so-called "humor" items from nonprofessionals. Buys 60 ms/year. Submit complete ms. Length: 1,000-1,500 words. Pays $50 and up/article.

Tips: "Send queries on business stories. Send manuscript on stamp dealer stories. We need stories to help dealers make and save money."

Transportation

‡**INBOUND TRAFFIC GUIDE**, Thomas Publishing Co., 1 Penn Plaza, 26th Fl., New York NY 10019. (212)290-7336. Editor: Richard S. Sexton. 50% freelance written. Quarterly magazine covering the transportation industry. "The *Inbound Traffic Guide* is distributed to people who buy, specify, or recommend inbound freight transportation services and equipment. The editorial matter provides basic explanations of inbound freight transportation, directory listings, how-to technical information, trends and developments affecting inbound freight movements, and expository, case history feature stories." Circ. 42,000. Pays on publication. Publishes ms an average of 3 months after acceptance. Byline given. Buys all rights. Simultaneous queries, and simultaneous and photocopied submission OK. Computer printout submissions acceptable; no dot-matrix. Reports in 2 weeks. Free sample copy and writer's guidelines.
Nonfiction: How-to (basic help for traffic managers) and interview/profile (transportaiton professionals). Buys 15 mss/year. Query with published clips. Length: 750-1,000 words. Pays $300-1,200. Pays expenses of writers on assignment.
Photos: Paula J. Slomer, photo editor. State availability of photos with query. Pays $100-500 for b&w contact sheets, negatives, transparencies and prints; $250-500 for color contact sheets, negative transparencies and prints. Captions and identification of subjects required.
Columns/Departments: Viewpoint (discusses current opinions on transportation topics). Buys 4 mss/year. Query with published clips.
Tips: "Have a sound knowledge of the transportation industry; educational how-to articles get our attention."

Travel

These publications are by and for people who help other people travel. Travel professionals learn about trends, tours, and types of transportation for their customers through trade journals. Magazines about vacations and travel for general readers are listed under Travel in the Consumer section.

AIRFAIR INTERLINE MAGAZINE, The Authority On Interline Travel, Airline Marketing, Inc., 25 W. 39th St., New York NY 10018. (212)840-6714. Editor: Retu Kamlani. Monthly magazine covering travel information for airline employees; describing travel packages by air, land or ship and including information on hotels and restaurants. Circ. 30,000. Pays on publication. Byline given. Buys first North American serial rights. Submit seasonal/holiday material 2 months in advance. Simultaneous queries, and simultaneous and photocopied submissions OK. SASE. Reports in 6 months on queries; 4 months on mss. Free sample copy and writer's guidelines.
Nonfiction: Travel (should concentrate on foreign destinations). Buys 20 mss/year. Query with clips of published work. Length: 2,000 words maximum. Pays $75 maximum.

ASTA TRAVEL NEWS, 488 Madison Ave., New York NY 10022. Editor: Patrick Arton. Managing Editor: Kathi Froio. 75% freelance written. Monthly magazine; 120 pages. Emphasizes travel, tourism and transporta-

---

 The worst mistake that a writer can make in writing?

Copying, consciously or unconsciously. The song from *A Chorus Line*—"I Can Do That"—might be the summation of a too-prevalent attitude in the latter part of the 20th century, namely, that if so-and-so made a million on such-and-such, so can I. The ones who make the millions, or whatever they make, do so by writing from a *personal* vision.

tion. Circ. 21,000. Pays on acceptance. Publishes ms an average of 3 months after acceptance. Buys all rights. Submit seasonal/holiday material 3 months in advance. Photocopied submissions OK. Reports in 1 month.
Nonfiction: How-to, interview, new product, profile, technical and travel. No first person personal experience. Buys 75 mss/year. Query. Length: 500-1,500 words. Pays $50-250. Sometimes pays expenses of writers on assignment.
Photos: Submit photo material with accompanying query. No additional payment for b&w prints or color transparencies. Captions required.

BUS RIDE, Friendship Publications, Inc., Box 1472, Spokane WA 99210. (509)328-9181. Editor: William A. Luke. Magazine published 8 times/year covering bus transportation. Circ. 12,500. Byline given. Not copyrighted. SASE. Sample copy $3; free writer's guidelines.
Nonfiction: How-to (on bus maintenance, operations, marketing); new product; and technical. Only bus transportation material is acceptable. Query. Length: 500-1,500 words. No payment from publication; "writer may receive payment from company or organization featured."
Photos: State availability of photos. Reviews b&w 8x10 prints. Captions required.
Fillers: Newsbreaks. Length: 50-100 words.
Tips: "A freelancer can contact bus companies, transit authorities, suppliers and products for the bus industry to write articles which would be accepted by our publication."

BUS TOURS MAGAZINE, The Magazine of Bus Tours and Long Distance Charters, National Bus Trader, Inc., Rt. 3, Box 349B (Theater Rd.), Delavan WI 53115. (414)728-2691. Editor: Larry Plachno. Editorial Assistant: Dianna Woss. Bimonthly magazine for bus companies and tour brokers who design or sell bus tours. Circ. 9,306. Pays as arranged. Byline given. Not copyrighted. Buys rights as arranged. Submit seasonal/holiday material 9 months in advance. Simultaneous queries OK. Reports in 1 month. Free sample copy and writer's guidelines.
Nonfiction: Historical/nostalgic, how-to, humor, interview/profile, new product, professional, personal experience, and travel; all on bus tours. Buys 10 mss/year. Query. Length: open. Pays negotiable fee.
Photos: State availability of photos. Reviews 35mm transparencies and 6x9 or 8x10 prints. Caption, model release, and identification of subjects required.
Columns/Departments: Bus Tour Marketing; and Buses and the Law. Buys 15-20 mss/year. Query. Length: 1-1½ pages.
Tips: "Most of our feature articles are written by freelancers under contract from local convention and tourism bureaus. Specifications sent on request. Writers should query local bureaus regarding their interest. Writer must have extensive background and knowledge of bus tours."

BUS WORLD, Motor Coach Photo-Feature Magazine, Sunrise Enterprises, Box 39, Woodland Hills CA 91365. (818)710-0208. Editor: Ed Stauss. 75% freelance written. Quarterly trade journal covering the transit and intercity bus industries. "*Bus World* is edited to inform and entertain people who have an interest in buses—bus owners, managers, drivers, enthusiasts and historians. With extensive photographic coverage, *Bus World* describes the function and lore of the bus industry including intercity, transit, tour and charter." Circ. 7,000. Pays on publication. Byline given. Buys first North American serial rights. Electronic submissions OK on IBM PC DOS, but requires hard copy also. Computer printout submissions acceptable; prefers letter-quality to dot-matrix. SASE. Reports in 3 weeks. Sample copy $1; writer's guidelines for SAE and 1 first class stamp.
Nonfiction: Historical/nostalgic, humor, interview/profile, new product, opinion, photo feature and technical. "Author must show an understanding of the bus industry. Coverage includes descriptions of new vehicles, surveys of operating systems, first person experiences with transit and intercity operations, and reviews of historic equipment and systems. Primary coverage is North America." No tourist or travelog viewpoints. Buys 8-12 mss/year. Query. Length: 500-2,000 words. Pays $20-75.
Photos: Photos should be sharp and clear. State availability of photos. "We buy photos with manuscripts under one payment." Reviews 35mm color transparencies and 8x10 b&w prints. Captions required. Buys one-time rights.
Fillers: Cartoons. Buys 4-6/year. Pays $10.
Tips: "Be employed in or have a good understanding of the bus industry. Be enthusiastic about buses—their history and future—as well as current events. Acceptable material will be held until used and will not be returned unless requested by sender. Unacceptable and excess material will be returned only if accompanied by suitable SASE."

CANADIAN RV DEALER, (formerly *Canadian Camping & RV Dealer*), Suite 202, 2077 Dundas St. E., Mississauga, Ontario L4X 1M2 Canada. (416)624-8218. Editor: Peter Tasler. 20% freelance written. Published 7 times/year "to better the development and growth of Canada's recreational vehicle and camping accessory dealers." Circ. 8,000. Pays on publication. Publishes ms an average of 2 months after acceptance. Byline given. Buys first serial rights. SASE (Canadian), SAE, IRC. Reports in 2 months. Free sample copy and writer's guidelines.

Nonfiction: All features must pertain to the Canadian RV dealer and marketplace. Will consider occasional U.S. pieces if applicable to Canada or unusual slant. Would also consider dealer-slanted humor. Self-help management-type articles also OK. Query first.

● **GO GREYHOUND**, The Greyhound Corp., Greyhound Tower - 1810, Phoenix AZ 85077. (602)248-5714. Editor: Donald L. Behnke. 10% freelance written. Quarterly in-house publication for Greyhound shareholders, employees and other interested individuals. Circ. 200,000. Pays on acceptance. Publishes ms an average of 6 months after acceptance. No byline given. Buys one-time rights. Submit seasonal/holiday material 9 months in advance. Simultaneous queries, and simultaneous and photocopied submissions OK. Computer printout submissions acceptable; no dot-matrix. Reports in 3 months. Sample copy and writer's guidelines for 9x12 manila evelope and 4 first class stamps.
Nonfiction: Juanita Soto, public relations representative. Travel (to places reached by Greyhound bus). "We review features about historic, scenic or entertainment attractions that can be reached by Greyhound bus." No personal experience stories. Buys 4 mss/year. Query or send complete ms. Length: 500-800 words. Pays $350 maximum with color pictures.
Photos: Juanita Soto, public relations representative. "Articles must be accompanied by a minimum of 12 good quality color transparencies from which we may choose to illustrate the story." Payment included with purchase of ms. Reviews 35mm and larger color transparencies and 5x7 color prints.
Tips: "Follow our writer's guidelines. We must see accompanying transparencies, and we require excellent color pictures to accompany travel stories. We will only review stories with pictures—professional quality. Articles submitted without required transparencies will not be considered. Do not send personal experience travel on bus."

INCENTIVE TRAVEL MANAGER, Brentwood Publishing Corp., 1640 5th St., Santa Monica CA 90401. (213)395-0234. Editor: Helene N. Kass. 90% freelance written, mostly on assignment. Monthly magazine for corporate executives in charge of incentive travel programs. Circ. 40,000. Pays "by edited word count on acceptance." Publishes ms an average of 6 months after acceptance. Byline given. Buys all rights. Computer printout submissions acceptable; prefers letter-quality to dot-matrix. SASE. Reports "when an assignment is available."
Nonfiction: General interest (incentive travel, planning, promotion, selecting destination, program execution); interview/profile (of executives); and travel (destination updates). Buys 60-70 mss/year. Query with published clips. Length: 1,000-2,500 words. Pays 10-12¢/word.
Tips: "We are not interested in travel articles geared to the average tourist or travel agent. Ours is a very specific focus; you must familiarize yourself with our content and know something about the field."

‡**LEISURE WHEELS MAGAZINE**, Murray Publications Ltd., Box 7302, Station "E", Calgary, Alberta, Canada T3C 3M2. (403)263-2707. Editor: Murray Gimbel. Bimonthly magazine covering Canadian recreational vehicle travel. Circ. 47,700. Pays on publication. Byline given. Buys second serial (reprint) rights. Submit seasonal/holiday material 2 months in advance. SASE. Sample copy 75¢; free writer's guidelines.
Nonfiction: Travel and outdoor leisure-time hobbies. Buys 12 mss/year. Query with published clips. Length: 1,000-2,000 words. Pays $135-200.
Photos: State availability of photos. Pays $15-25 for 5x11 color prints; $10-20 for b&w 5x11 prints. Identification of subjects required. Buys one-time rights.
Columns/Departments: Buys 12 mss/year. Query with or without published clips. Length: 750-1,000 words. Pays $110-150.
Fiction: Adventure and humorous (relating to travel). Buys 6 mss/year. Query with or without publshed clips. Length: 1,000-1,500 words. Pays $135-150.
Fillers: Jokes and anecdotes. Buys 6 mss/year. Length: 500-700 words. Pays $50-70.

NATIONAL BUS TRADER, The Magazine of Bus Equipment for the United States and Canada, Rt. 3, Box 349B (Theater Rd.), Delavan WI 53115. (414)728-2691. Editor: Larry Plachno. Monthly magazine for manufacturers, dealers and owners of buses and motor coaches. Circ. 7,354. Pays on either acceptance or publication. Byline given. Not copyrighted. Buys rights "as required by writer." Simultaneous queries, and simultaneous, photocopied, and previously published submissions OK. Computer printout submissions acceptable. Reports in 1 month. Free sample copy.
Nonfiction: Historical/nostalgic (on old buses); how-to (maintenance repair); new products; photo feature; and technical (aspects of mechanical operation of buses). "We are finding that more and more firms and agencies are hiring freelancers to write articles to our specifications. We are more likely to run them if someone else pays." No material that does NOT pertain to bus tours or bus equipment. Buys 3-5 unsolicited mss/year. Query. Length: varies. Pays variable rate.
Photos: State availability of photos. Reviews 5x7 or 8x10 prints and 35mm transparencies. Captions, model release, and identification of subjects required.
Columns/Departments: Bus maintenance; Buses and the Law; Regulations; and Bus of the Month. Buys 20-

30 mss/year. Query. Length: 1-1½ pages. Pays variable rate.

Tips: "We are a very technical publication. Writers should submit qualifications showing extensive background in bus vehicles. We're always looking for new column ideas. We probably will add more pages in the next year which will require more editorial."

‡**THE OVERNIGHTER**, The Overnighter, Inc., Box 408310, Chicago IL 60640. (312)275-3511. Editor: Philip W. Sunseri. Managing Editor: Eugene B. Biondi. 50% freelance written. Quarterly magazine covering airline crewmembers (flight attendants and pilots). Circ. 7,000. Pays on publication. Publishes ms an average of 3 months after acceptance. Byline given. Buys first serial rights. Submit seasonal/holiday material 6 months in advance. Photocopied and previously published submissions OK. Computer printout submissions acceptable; prefers letter-quality to dot-matrix. SASE. Reports in 4 weeks. Sample copy for $1.50, 6x9 SAE and 4 first class stamps; free writer's guidelines.

Nonfiction: General interest, historical/nostalgic, how-to, humor, interview/profile, opinion, personal experience, photo feature and travel. "We are especially looking for articles of 1,000-3,000 words on travel, industry-related issues, and interviews for a highly mobile and diversified airline crewmember." No articles related to sex or religion. Buys 8 mss/year. Send complete ms. Length: 250-2,500 words. Pays $10-25.

Photos: Send photos with ms. Pays $5-10 for b&w negatives and prints. Captions required. Buys one-time rights.

Columns/Departments: Book Reviews; Health (airline crewmember related); Industry Trends; City Streets (interesting areas of different cities); and Travel Tips. Buys 8-10/year. Send complete ms. Length: 500-2,500 words. Pays $10-25.

Fiction: Condensed novels, confession, historical, mainstream, novel excerpts, romance and suspense. No sex- or religion-related fiction. Buys 4 mss/year. Send compelte ms. Length: 1,000-2,500 words. Pays $10-25.

Fillers: Clippings, anecdotes, short humor and newsbreaks. Buys 15-25/year. Length: 100-500 words. Pays $5-25.

Tips: "Get to know the airline industry as it relates to the crewmember. Understand the lifestyle of the pilot and flight attendant."

RV BUSINESS, TL Enterprises, Inc., 29901 Agoura Rd., Agoura CA 91301. (818)991-4980. Editor: Michael Schneider. Managing Editor: Sheryl Davis. 50% freelance written. Monthly magazine covering the recreational vehicle and allied industries for people of the RV industry—dealers, manufacturers, suppliers, park management, legislators and finance experts. Circ. 25,000. Pays on acceptance. Publishes ms an average of 4 months after acceptance. Byline given. Offers 50% kill fee. Buys first North American serial rights. Submit seasonal/holiday material 6 months in advance. Photocopied submissions OK. Electronic submissions OK (call first), but requires hard copy also. Computer printout submissions acceptable; prefers letter-quality to dot-matrix. SASE. Reports in 3 weeks on queries; 6 weeks on mss. Sample copy for 9x12 SAE and 3 first class stamps; writer's guidelines for business size SAE and 1 first class stamp.

Nonfiction: Expose (carefully done and thoroughly researched); historical/nostalgic (companies, products or people pertaining to the RV industry itself); how-to (deal with any specific aspect of the RV business); interview/profile (persons or companies involved with the industry—legislative, finance, dealerships, park management, manufacturing, supplier); new product (no payment for company promo material—Product Spotlight usually requires interview with company spokesperson, first-hand experience with product. Specifics and verification of statistics required—must be factual; opinion (controversy OK); personal experience (must be something of importance to readership—must have a point: it worked for me, it can for you; or this is why it didn't work for me); photo feature (4-color transparencies required with good captions; photo coverage of RV shows, conventions and meetings not appropriate topics for photo feature); and technical (photos required, 4-color preferred). General business articles may be considered. Buys 75 mss/year. Query with published clips. Send complete ms—"but only read on speculation." Length: 1,000-2,000 words. Pays variable rate up to $500. Sometimes pays expenses of writers on assignment.

Photos: State availability of photos with query or send photos with ms. Reviews 35mm transparencies and 8x10 b&w prints. Captions, model release, and identification of subjects required. Buys one-time or all rights; unused photos returned.

Columns/Departments: Guest editorial; News (50-500 words maximum, b&w photos appreciated); and RV People (color photos/4-color transparencies; this section lends itself to fun, upbeat copy). Buys 100-120 mss/year. Query or send complete ms. Pays $10-200 "depending on where used and importance."

Tips: "Query. Phone OK; letter preferable. Send one or several ideas and a few lines letting us know how you plan to treat it/them. We are always looking for good authors knowledgable in the RV industry or related industries."

THE STAR SERVICE, Sloane Travel Agency Reports, Box 15610, Fort Lauderdale FL 33318. (305)472-8794. Executive Editor: Charles Kulander. 100% freelance written. Editorial manual sold to travel agencies on subscription basis. Pays 15 days prior to publication. Buys all rights. "Write for instruction sheet and sample report form. Initial reports sent by a new correspondent will be examined for competence and criticized as necessary upon receipt; but once established, a correspondent's submissions will not usually be acknowledged until payment is forwarded, which can often be several months, depending on immediate editorial needs." Computer printout submissions acceptable; prefers letter-quality to dot-matrix. Query. SASE. Writer's guidelines for SAE and 1 first class stamp.

Nonfiction: "Objective, critical evaluations of worldwide hotels and cruise ships suitable for North Americans, based on inspections. Forms can be provided to correspondents so no special writing style is required, only perception, experience and judgment in travel. No commercial gimmick—no advertising or payment for listings in publication is accepted." With query, writer should "outline experience in travel and writing and specific forthcoming travel plans, and time available for inspections. Leading travel agents throughout the world subscribe to *Star Service*. No credit or byline is given correspondents due to delicate subject matter often involving negative criticism of hotels. We would like to emphasize the importance of reports being based on current experience and the importance of reporting on a substantial volume of hotels, not just isolated stops (since staying in a hotel is not a requisite) in order that work be profitable for both publisher and writer. Experience in travel writing and/or travel industry is desirable." Buys 4,000 reports/year. Length: "up to 350 words, if submitted in paragraph form; varies if submitted on printed inspection form." Pays $15/report (higher for ships) used. Higher rates of payment and of guaranteed acceptance of set number of reports will be made after correspondent's ability and reliability have been established.

‡**SUCCESSFUL MEETINGS MAGAZINE, The Authority on Meetings and Incentive Travel Management**, Bill Communications, Inc., 633 3rd Ave., New York NY 10017. (212)986-4800. Editor: Charles L. Wrye. Managing Editor: Holly Hughes. Monthly magazine on corporate and association meeting planning. Circ. 77,000. Pays on acceptance. Byline given. Offers 100% kill fee. Buys all rights. Submit seasonal/holiday material 3 months in advance. Reports in 2 months. Sample copy $5; free writer's guidelines.

Nonfiction: Book excerpts (about meeting planning); general interest (trends in this industry); how-to (about meeting management); humor (about business travel/meetings); interview/profile (with industry people); technical (audiovisual); and travel (business group travel). No promotional pieces on hotels or other suppliers. Buys 60-70 mss/year. Query with published clips. Length: 150-800 words. Pays $125-500.

Tips: "Experience in meeting planning is useful. Travel writing or business writing (*not* financial) is also useful. We are willing to interview potential freelancers for a regular ongoing relationship. We see too many dry articles by 'experts'—we need writers who can interview experts and fashion their comments into authoritative overview articles." Site reports and feature stories (topics determined in advance—request editorial calendar) are areas most open to freelancers.

‡**TRAVEL TRADE PUBLICATIONS**, Travel Trade Publications, 6 E. 46th St., New York NY 10017. (212)883-1110. Editor: Joel Abels. Managing Editor: Michael Billig. 90% freelance written. Weekly newspaper covering all areas of the travel industry. "We are the leading weekly newspaper serving the high-pressure travel industry. Most of the stories we cover concern advertisers and readers." Circ. 59,000. Pays on acceptance. Publishes ms an average of 1 week after acceptance. Byline given. Offers negotiable kill fee. Buys first North American serial rights. Submit seasonal/holiday material 4-6 weeks in advance. Simultaneous queries, and simultaneous, photocopied, and previously published submissions OK. Computer printout submissions acceptable; no dot-matrix. Reports in 1 week on queries; 2 weeks on ms. Free sample copy and writer's guidelines.

Nonfiction: Nanettee Lewis Abels, Sr., articles editor. Expose, how-to, humor, interview/profile, new product, opinion, photo feature and travel. "No snobby, effete, 'I-am-the-expert' stories that 'write-down' to readers." Buys 175 + mss/year. Query. Length: 500-2,000 words. Pays $250-1,250 (sometimes higher).

Photos: Kitty Katz, photo editor. State availability of photos. Prefers group shots, people making presentations. Reviews transparencies and prints. Pays $50. Captions, model release, and identification of subjects required. Buys all rights.

Columns/Departments: Lenore Lewis Abels, column/department editor. Traveling With Animals; Traveling With Children; The Black Traveler; and Travel to Israel. Buys 100 mss/year. Query. Length: 300-500 words. Pays $50-100.

Tips: "Our readership is basic, middle America. There is no need to be a Rhodes Scholar. We want facts, fast. We want a writer to be gutsy. We want stories that hit hard. Sometimes this requires a writer to be blunt, that's OK with us. We don't want wishy-washy nothing stories."

TRAVELAGE MIDAMERICA, Official Airlines Guide, Inc., A Dun & Bradstreet Co., Suite 2416, Prudential Plaza, Chicago IL 60601. (312)861-0432. Editor/Publisher: Martin Deutsch. Managing Editor: Linda Ball. 15% freelance written. Biweekly magazine "for travel agents in the 13 midAmerica states and in Ontario and Manitoba." Circ. 17,500. Pays on publication. Publishes ms an average of 2 months after acceptance. Buys one-time rights and second serial (reprint) rights. Submit seasonal/holiday material 3 months in advance. Simultaneous, photocopied, and previously published submissions OK. Computer printout submissions acceptable ("but not pleased with"); prefers letter-quality to dot-matrix. Query first. SASE. Reports in 3 weeks. Free sample copy and writer's guidelines.

Nonfiction: "News on destinations, hotels, operators, rates and other developments in the travel business." Also runs human interest features on retail travel agents in the readership area. No stories that don't contain prices; no queries that don't give detailed story lines. No general destination stories, especially ones on "do-it-yourself" travel. Buys 20 mss/year. Query. Length: 400-1,500 words. Pays $1.50/column inch.
Photos: State availability of photos with query. Pays $1.50/column inch for glossy b&w prints.
Tips: "Our major need is for freelance human interest stories with a marketing angle on travel agents in our readership area. Buying freelance destination stories is a much lower priority."

TRAVELAGE WEST, Official Airline Guides, Inc., 100 Grant Ave., San Francisco CA 94108. Executive Editor: Donald C. Langley. 5% freelance written. Weekly magazine for travel agency sales counselors in the western U.S. and Canada. Circ. 30,000. Pays on publication. Byline given. Buys all rights. Offers kill fee. Submit seasonal/holiday material 2 months in advance. Computer printout submissions acceptable. SASE. Reports in 1 month. Free writer's guidelines.
Nonfiction: Travel. "No promotional approach or any hint of do-it-yourself travel. Emphasis is on news, not description. No static descriptions of places, particularly resort hotels. Buys 40 mss/year. Query. Length: 1,000 words maximum. Pays $1.50/column inch."
Tips: "Query should be a straightforward description of the proposed story, including (1) an indication of the news angle, no matter how tenuous, and (2) a recognition by the author that we run a trade magazine for travel agents, not a consumer book. I am particularly turned off by letters that try to get me all worked up about the 'beauty' or excitement of some place. Authors planning to travel might discuss with us a proposed angle before they go; otherwise their chances of gathering the right information are slim."

Veterinary

MODERN VETERINARY PRACTICE, American Veterinary Publications, Inc., Drawer KK, 300 E. Canon Perdido, Santa Barbara CA 93101. 5% freelance written. Monthly magazine, 90 pages for graduate veterinarians. Circ. 22,000. Pays on publication. Publishes ms an average of 3 months after acceptance. Buys all rights. Phone queries OK. Submit seasonal/holiday material 3 months in advance. Computer printout submissions acceptable; prefers letter-quality to dot-matrix. SASE. Reports in 1 month. Sample copy $2.75.
Nonfiction: How-to (clinical medicine, new surgical procedures, business management); informational (business management, education, government projects affecting practicing veterinarians, special veterinary projects); interviews (only on subjects of interest to veterinarians; query first); and technical (clinical reports, technical advancements in veterinary medicine and surgery). Buys 12-15 unsolicited mss/year. Submit complete ms, but query first on ideas for pieces other than technical or business articles. Pays $50 for first published page; $25 for each additional page.
Photos: B&w glossies (5x7 or larger) and color transparencies (5x7) used with mss. No additional payment.
Tips: "Contact practicing veterinarians or veterinary colleges. Find out what interests the clinician and what new procedures and ideas might be useful in a veterinary practice. Better yet, collaborate with a veterinarian. Most of our authors are veterinarians or those working with veterinarians in a professional capacity. Knowledge of the interests and problems of practicing veterinarians is essential."

NEW METHODS, The Journal of Animal Health Technology, New Methods, Box 22605, San Francisco CA 94122. (415)664-3469. Editor: Ronald S. Lippert, A.H.T. Managing Editor: Charles Linebarger. 8% freelance written. Monthly magazine on animal care in the veterinary field; for employee-related audience of professionals. Circ. 5,400. Pays on publication. Byline given. Buys one-time rights and first rights. Contact editor first before submitting seasonal/holiday material. Computer printout submissions acceptable; prefers letter-quality to dot-matrix. SASE. Reports in 2 weeks on queries; 4 months on mss. Publishes ms an average of 6 months after acceptance. Sample copy for $3.60; 9x12 SAE, and $1.05 postage; writer's guidelines for business-size SAE and 1 first class stamp.
Nonfiction: Book excerpts, expose, general interest, historical/nostalgic, how-to, humor, inspirational, interview/profile, new product, opinion, personal experience, photo feature, technical and travel. "We advise writer to communicate with staff editor before writing for *New Methods*." Special issues include August: Index, October: Convention Special, and February: Convention Special. English speaking and writing requested. Buys 40+ mss/year. Query with published clips or send complete ms. Length: 800-3,200 words. Pays $8-35. Sometimes pays the expenses of writers on assignment.
Photos: Larry Rosenberg, photo editor. State availability of photos or send photos with query or ms. "We prefer b&w photos depicting segments of the article." Call or write for details. Reviews b&w contact sheets, neg-

atives, and 5x7 prints. Captions, model release and identification of subjects required. Buys one-time rights.
Columns/Departments: "We are open to suggestions. Writers should contact Charles Linebarger before submitting material to *New Methods*." Buys 40+ mss/year. Query with or without published clips or send complete ms. Length: 800 words minimum. Pays is determined by publisher, generally $35.
Fiction: Historical and humorous. Buys 12 mss/year. Query with or without published clips or send complete ms. Length: 800 words minimum. Pays $35 maximum.
Poetry: "We are open to all styles as long as content is acceptable." No unrelated themes that are not suitable for *New Methods*. Buys 6 poems/year. Length: varies. Pays $35 maximum.
Fillers: Jokes, short humor and newsbreaks. "We use many but buy few." Length: open. Pays $35 maximum.
Tips: "A simple, straightforward, clean approach is requested. Make every word count. Focus on the reality, humor, and/or gratification of working in the animal health technology field."

VETERINARY COMPUTING, American Veterinary Publications, Inc., Drawer KK, Santa Barbara CA 93102. (800)235-6947 CA, AK or HI (805)963-6561. Editors: Steve Beale and Paul Pratt, VMD. 25% freelance written. Monthly newsletter covering computer applications in veterinary medicine and practice management. "Our readers are veterinary practitioners who have computers or are thinking about buying them. They are looking for information on the best and most cost-effective ways to purchase and use computers in their practices." Pays on publication. Publishes ms an average of 4 months after acceptance. Byline given. Buys all rights. Submit seasonal/holiday material 3 months in advance. Simultaneous queries and photocopied submissions OK. Electronic submissions OK if 5¼" single-sided disks with an Osborne 1 CP/M WordStar, but requires hard copy also. Computer printout submissions acceptable; prefers letter-quality to dot-matrix. SASE. Reports in 3 weeks on queries; 1 month on mss. Publishes ms an average of 4 months after acceptance. Sample copy for 9x12 SAE and 3 first class stamps; free writer's guidelines.
Nonfiction: How-to, new product, book and software reviews, and computer-user tips. No profiles or overly philosophical articles. "We want concrete, practical, usable pieces about how veterinarians can most effectively use computers." Buys 6-12 mss/year. Query or send complete ms (on short articles). Length: 150-2,000 words. Pays $10 (for short tips; $25/printed page for longer articles; printed page equals 1¾ typed double-spaced pages). Sometimes pays expenses of writers on assignment.
Columns/Departments: Book reviews, software reviews, computing tips, new product and news briefs. Buys 6-12 mss/year. Query or send complete ms (for short articles). Length: 150-500 words. Pays $10-50.
Tips: "Make submissions concise, practical, and usable in plain, nontechnical language. We are especially interested in material on how to use canned software such as Lotus 1-2-3, dBase II and WordStar in veterinary practice. Reviews/articles about canned software and money saving computer tips are the areas most open to freelancers in our publication. The writer may have a better chance of breaking in short articles and fillers, though length does not matter as much as practicality. The most frequent mistakes made by writers are lack of depth and lack of how-to information (telling what a vet does with the computer without telling how)."

VETERINARY ECONOMICS MAGAZINE, Box 13265, Edwardsville KS 66113. (913)422-5010. Editor: Mike Sollars. 50% freelance written. Monthly magazine for all practicing veterinarians in the U.S. Buys exclusive rights in the field. Pays on publication. Publishes ms an average of 3 months after acceptance. Computer printout submissions acceptable. SASE.
Nonfiction: Uses case histories telling about good business practices on the part of veterinarians. Also, articles about financial problems, investments, insurance and similar subjects of particular interest to professionals. "We reject articles with superficial information about a subject instead of carefully researched and specifically directed articles for our field." Pays negotiable rates.

 The double dagger before a listing indicates that the listing is new in this edition. New markets are often the most receptive to freelance contributions.

Scriptwriting

"Don't touch the TV screen." You probably heard that warning when you were growing up. But today, for scriptwriters and interactive videodisk users, *touching* is important, though in different ways, for each medium. What all of the following media share is the need for scripts that touch the audience. The dialogue, the characters or narrators, and the setting must create an atmosphere where the audience wants to listen. Media that involve the audience (in a participatory way) more readily hold the audience's attention. Some interactive disk programs, for instance, require that the viewer touch a button *on the screen* to activate them. The writer for stage and screen, on the other hand, must subtly press the audience to feel, think and react emotionally. Some people learn how to write for industry, schools, stage and screen through nonpaying internships or entry-level jobs. The experience can pay off as you gradually switch from understudy to centerstage (at the typewriter or word processor). Before writing a script, ask yourself these questions:

- Who will be your audience?
- What is the purpose of your script?
- Under what circumstances or at what place will the script be produced?
- Who will be paying the bill for the script and its production?
- Will there be producers or companies interested in the script?

Go ahead—touch the screen. Put words on paper. Until you write a script, nobody will be watching *you*.

Business and Educational Writing

"I want to be intrigued in the first ten pages," pointed out one producer. Most unsolicited scripts or the leads of one-page queries don't do that. Because of the high costs of producing audiovisual materials, producers need scripts that will intrigue—their clients and eventually the viewers.

Today's corporations and schools rely on video often to instruct students and employees. People are also using video in their homes to learn new skills like golfing or gourmet cooking. "The expanding home and educational video market provides an excellent opportunity for writers who can produce interesting material with a strong visual slant," said one production manager. "We see this market expanding greatly in the next few years."

An important consideration in writing an instructional script is to design it so an audience might enjoy (and learn from) a second viewing of the film. Especially in the home video market, customers will rent, but not buy video cassettes that don't have lasting value.

As for nonlinear interactive videodisks, the viewer can learn a skill at his own pace. Such programs enable users to learn a particular aspect of a skill by selecting it on a menu, so to speak, then touching the screen or appropriate button as directed by the scriptwriter through a computer. In some cases, the viewer is not even aware that the sequence of the film is controlled by a computer (as activated by the viewer). For scriptwriters interested in interactive scripting, knowledge of this field and computer programs is essential.

Some companies, when they contract to have a video program produced, will provide the scriptwriter to work with the audiovisual production company. In addition to pursuing freelance scriptwriting opportunities, the *experienced* scriptwriter might want to contact companies about such possible assignments, especially if you *know* the industry you'd be writing for.

"Your script must meet customer needs more than ever before," points out one educational film producer. The advice certainly isn't new, but with increased competition among media and media firms, those which please the customer get "top billing."

"Clients want choices," says another producer. With the options of film, video, and multi-image becoming more affordable, business and education representatives want to choose which medium will best serve their audiences and organization's goals.

To be more competitive in the marketplace, some companies are expanding the media services they offer. Scriptwriters must likewise broaden the range of assignments they handle.

With companies entering the software and cable markets, there is an additional need for freelancers. A square (□) to the left of a listing denotes firms interested in cable TV scripts. Reading each *Writer's Market* listing will tell you what companies want and don't want in scripts.

Become familiar with the particular firm you plan to query. What else have they produced? Arrange for a screening that will help you define their audiences, formats and style. Contact local producers directly. Write to out-of-town firms for a list of their clients in your area. If they are interested in your writing, you may be able to view their AV material at a local company or school that uses it. Be sure that your script idea fits with a company's established image. A résumé that establishes you as a writer and writing samples that prove it are very important in this business. Read carefully the market listings detailing how to make initial contact with a production company. Meeting deadlines and doing quality work are essential.

‡ADMASTER, INC., 95 Madison Ave., New York NY 10016. (212)679-1134. Director: Charles Corn. Produces sales and training material. Purchases 50-75 scripts/year. Works with 5-10 writers/year. Buys all rights. No previously published material. Reports in 1 month. Free catalog.
Needs: Charts, film loops (16mm), films (35 and 16mm), filmstrips (sound), multimedia kits, overhead transparencies, slides, tapes and cassettes. "We need material for multi-media industrial and financial meetings." Submit synopsis/outline, complete script or resume. Makes outright purchase of $250-500.

A.V. MEDIA CRAFTSMAN, INC., Suite 600, 110 E. 23rd St., New York NY 10010. (212)228-6644. President: Carolyn Clark. Produces audio visual training material for corporations and educational material for publishers. Works with New York area writers only. Contracts scripts for 10-15 projects per year. Query with samples and resume. Call later. Samples and resumes kept on file.
Needs: "Most of our projects are 10-15 minute training scripts with related study materials for corporations and educational publishers. We create multi-screen presentations for conferences as well." Produces slide shows, sound filmstrips, videos, multiscreen shows, multimedia kits, overhead transparencies, tapes and cassettes. Pays $350-500 per project.
Tips: "Accept changes, do accurate research, and enjoy the subject matter. Send resume and cover letter. State special areas of interest (ie., economics, science, fashion, health, etc.)."

□ **ABS MULTI-IMAGE**, 705 Hinman, Evanston IL 60202. (312)328-8697. President: Alan Soell. "We produce material for all levels of corporate, medical, cable, and educational institutions for the purposes of training and development, marketing, and meeting presentations. We also are developing programming for the broadcast areas. 75% freelance written. We work with a core of three to five freelance writers from development to final drafts." All scripts published are unagented submissions. Buys all rights. Previously produced material OK. Computer printout submissions acceptable. SASE. Reports in 2 weeks on queries.
Needs: Videotape, 16mm films, silent and sound filmstrips, multimedia kits, overhead transparencies, realia, slides, tapes and cassettes, and television shows/series. Currently interested in "sports instructional series that could be produced for the consumer market on tennis, gymnastics, bowling, golf, aerobics, health and fitness, cross-country skiing and cycling. Also home improvement programs for the novice—for around the house—in a series format. These two areas should be 30 minutes and be timeless in approach for long shelf life." Sports audience, age 25-45; home improvement, 25-65. "Cable TV needs include the two groups of programming detailed here. We are also looking for documentary work on current issues, nuclear power, solar power, urban de-

---

□ *Open box preceding a listing indicates a cable TV market.*

velopment, senior citizens—but with a new approach." Query or submit synopsis/outline and resume. Pays by contractual agreement.

Tips: "I am looking for innovative approaches to old problems that just don't go away. The approach should be simple and direct so there is immediate audience identification with the presentation. I also like to see a sense of humor used. Trends in the audiovisual field include interactive video with tape and video disk—for training purposes."

DOM ALBI ASSOCIATES, INC., Suite 1C, 251 W. 92nd St., New York NY 10025. (212)799-2202. President: Dom Albi. Produces material for corporate and business audiences. Buys 20-30 scripts/year. Query or submit resume listing types of clients. Buys all rights.
Needs: Produces 16mm films, multimedia programs, and videotape slide presentations. Payment negotiable.
Tips: "We expect our writers to spend as much time on concept and purpose as they do on the finished script."

ANCO/BOSTON, INC., 441 Stuart St., Boston MA 02116. (617)267-9700. Director, Instructional Systems: R. Hoyt. Produces manuals and AV programs for the industrial and business communities. 15% freelance written. Buys 2-3 scripts/year from unpublished/unproduced writers. All scripts produced are unagented submissions. Submit resume. Computer printout submissions acceptable. SASE. Buys all rights.
Needs: "Technical or business-oriented material on specific subjects for specific customized needs." Produces charts, sound filmstrips, multimedia kits, overhead transparencies, and cassettes and slides.

KEN ANDERSON FILMS, Box 618, Winona Lake IN 46590. (219)267-5774. President: Ken Anderson. Produces material for church-related libraries with evangelical bias; films for all ages, with particular interest in children and teenagers. Previously produced submissions OK. Considers brief, 1-page story synopses only. "We try to maintain a very warm attitude toward writers and will try to give careful consideration to queries. Unsolicited manuscripts will be returned unread. We only produce 4-6 films/year, so our quantity needs are limited." Free catalog.
Needs: Religious material only. "We are constantly looking for good material that is positively Christian and relates realistically to today's life-style. We want true stories for young people and adults; fiction for children." Pays "as low as $100 for basic story idea, which the author could then market elsewhere. But general payment runs more between $250-1,000, depending upon story quality and adaptability for audiovisual production."
Tips: "We are currently looking for filmstrip material appealing to Third World audiences."

ANIMATION ARTS ASSOCIATES, INC., 1100 E. Hector St., Conshohocken PA 19428. (215)825-8530. Contact: Harry E. Ziegler, Jr. For government, industry, engineers, doctors, scientists, dentists, general public, military. 100% freelance written. Send resume of credits for motion picture and filmstrip productions and software. Buys average 12 scripts/year. "The writer should have scriptwriting credits for training, sales, promotion and public relations." SASE.
Needs: Produces 3½-minute 8mm and 16mm film loops; 16mm and 35mm films (ranging from 5-40 minutes); 2¼x2¼ or 4x5 slides; and teaching machine programs for training, sales, industry and public relations. Also produces software—motion picture scripts for training sales promotion and recruitment films. Submit software to Michael Levanios, general manager. Payment dependent on client's budget.
Tips: "Send us a resume listing writing and directing credits for films and sound/slide programs."

☐ **APPALSHOP INC.**, Box 743, Whitesburg KY 41858. (606)633-0108. Producer: Mr. Dee Davis. "Most audiovisuals are educational, thus geared to educational TV, etc. A good part, however, are documentary and of interest to a diversified audience." Currently works with approximately 15 writers, scriptwriters, etc. Buys first serial rights. Previously produced material OK. Computer printout submissions acceptable; no dot-matrix. SASE. Reports in several months. Catalog for SASE; writer's guidelines available.
Needs: 16mm films, sound filmstrips, phonograph records, slides, study prints, tapes and cassettes, television shows/series, and videotape presentations. Query with or without samples or submit synopsis/outline and resume. Pays by outright purchase.

ARZTCO PICTURES, INC., 15 E. 61st St., New York NY 10021. (212)753-1050. President/Producer: Tony Arzt. Produces material for industrial, education, and home viewing audiences (TV specials and documentaries). 80% freelance written. 75% of scripts produced are unagented submissions. Buys 8-10 scripts/year. Buys all rights. Previously produced material OK ("as sample of work only"). Computer printout submissions acceptable; prefers letter-quality to dot-matrix. SASE, "however, we will only comment in writing on work that interests us." Reports in 3 weeks.
Needs: Business films, sales, training, promotional, educational. "Also interested in low-budget feature film scripts." 16mm and 35mm films, videotapes and cassettes, and software. Submit synopsis/outline or completed script and resume. Pays in accordance with Writers Guild standards.
Tips: "We would like writers to understand that we cannot find time to deal with each individual submission in great detail. If we feel your work is right for us, you will definitely hear from us. We're looking for writers with

originality, skill in turning out words, and a sense of humor when appropriate. We prefer to work with writers available in the New York metropolitan area."

ASSOCIATED AUDIO VISUAL, 2821 Central, Evanston IL 60201. (312)866-6780. President/Creative Director: Ken Solomon. Produces material for corporate/industrial/TV commercials and programs. 75% freelance written. Buys 6-12 scripts/year. Buys all rights. Electronic submissions OK on 8" diskette straight ASCII File or IBM PC File 5¼". Computer printout submissions acceptable; prefers letter-quality to dot-matrix. SASE. Reports in 1 month. Catalog for 8x10 SAE and 1 first class stamp.
Needs: Open. Produces 16mm films, slides, tapes and cassettes. "Call first, then send samples." Pays by negotiable outright purchase.
Tips: "Be persistent, have *produced* samples on film or tape rather than scripts." Looks for "intelligence, humor, contemporary, visual and verbal skills; a fast researcher."

AUDIO-VIDEO CORP., 213 Broadway, Menands (Albany) NY 12204. (518)449-7213. Manager of Production Services: Tony Scardillo. Produces material for TV commercial audiences, and sales and informational film screenings. "We purchase 20 scripts annually, with our need increasing." Buys first serial rights. Query with samples or submit resume. SASE. Reports in 6 weeks.
Needs: Scripts for 10 to 30 minute programs for audiences ranging from educational, business and consumer groups to nonprofit organizations. "At least half of the material is of a humorous nature, or is otherwise informative and thought-provoking. We seek imagination, motivation, experience, and after receiving numerous responses from this listing, we would prefer to narrow down our writers' file to those in the New York State-New England area. Menands is a suburb of Albany, New York and we will be providing production services to our offices across the rest of the state. While our market primarily encompasses the Northeast, our requirements span a spectrum of subjects. With our recent expansion, we need access to a pool of freelance writers experienced in producing film scripts that are creative and practical." Produces videotapes, multimedia kits and slide sets. Pays $30-80/minute of finished program.
Tips: "The realities of budgets in the current economy naturally restrict production extravaganzas. It is essential to come up with a clever, concise script that lends itself well to the location and studio budget priorities of the project. Having a visual sense is a bonus and sometimes essential for a 'fresh' approach, but inexperience in this realm should not be a restraint to a good writer."

A/V CONCEPTS CORP., 30 Montauk Blvd., Oakdale NY 11769. (516)567-7227. Contact: P. Solimene or K. Brennan. Produces material for elementary-high school students, either on grade level or in remedial situations. 100% freelance written. Buys 25 scripts/year from unpublished/unproduced writers. Employs both filmstrip and personal computer media. Computer printout submissions acceptable. SASE. Reports on outline in 1 month; on final scripts in 6 weeks. Buys all rights.
Needs: Interested in original educational computer (disk-based) software programs for Apple plus, 48k. Main concentration in language arts, mathematics and reading. "Manuscripts must be written using our lists of vocabularly words and meet our readability formula requirements. Specific guidelines are devised for each level. Length of manuscript and subjects will vary according to grade level for which material is prepared. Basically, we want material that will motivate people to read." Pays $100 and up.
Tips: "Writers must be highly creative and highly disciplined. We are interested in mature content materials."

BARR FILMS, 3490 E. Foothill Blvd., Pasadena CA 91107. (213)793-6153. Contact: Don Barr or Mark Chodzko. "Produces material for all age levels; grades kindergarten through college level as well as in the public library market to the same age span and adult audience. We also have interest in materials aimed at business and industry/management training programs." 20% freelance written. 100% of scripts produced are unagented submissions. Query with samples. Computer printout submissions acceptable. "We will assign projects to qualified writers. We require previous experience in film writing and want to see samples of films previously written and completed for sale in the market." Buys 2-4 scripts/year. SASE. Reports in 1 month. Catalog $1.
Needs: "We produce and distribute 16mm films in all curriculum and subject areas. We prefer a semi-dramatic form of script that entertains and provides information. Avoid excess verbiage—we produce films, not books. The length of our films is 15-24 minutes. We will also consider pure informational subjects with voice over narration. Fees are entirely negotiable. We will accept film treatments and/or completed visual and dialogue scripts. Inquire prior to sending your materials to us."
Tips: "Meet the producer, share previous films, talk film, and be available. Your script must meet customer needs more than ever before."

‡SAMUEL R. BLATE ASSOCIATES, 10331 Watkins Mill Dr., Gaithersburg MD 20879-2935. (301)840-2248. President: Samuel R. Blate. Produces audiovisual material for business and nearby Washington, D.C. government. "We work with two to six writers per year—it varies as to business conditions and demand." Buys first rights when possible. Electronic submissions OK via CP/M-80, SSDD, Kaypro II. Computer printout submissions acceptable; prefers letter-quality to dot-matrix. SASE. Reports in 1 week on queries; 2 weeks on submissions.

Needs: Filmstrips (silent and sound), multimedia kits, slides, and tapes and cassettes. Especially needs short AV productions produced for specific client needs. Query with samples. Payment "depends on type of contract with principal client." Pays expenses of writers on assignment.

Tips: "Writers must have a strong track record of technical and aesthetic excellence. Clarity is not next to divinity—it is above it."

BNA COMMUNICATIONS, INC., 9439 Key West Ave., Rockville MD 20850. (301)948-0540. Producer/ Director: Clifton R. Witt. Produces material primarily for business, industry and government; "client-sponsored films approach specific audiences." 50% freelance written. All scripts produced are unagented submissions. Buys 7-12 scripts, works with 3-4 writers/year. Buys 1 script/year from unpublished/unproduced writer. Buys "usually all rights—but other arrangements have been made." Reports in 1 month. Free catalog.

Needs: "Our needs are presently under control." 16mm films, slides, and tapes, cassettes and videodisks. Query with samples. "Find out what we do before you query." Pays negotiable fee.

Tips: "We're looking for writers with the ability to grasp the subject and develop a relatively simple treatment, particularly if the client is not motion-savvy. Don't overload with tricks . . . unless the show is about tricks. Most good scripts have some concept of a beginning, middle and end. We are interested in good *dialogue* writers."

BOARD OF JEWISH EDUCATION OF NEW YORK, 426 W. 58th St., New York NY 10019. (212)245-8200. Director, Division of Multimedia and Materials Development: Yaakov Reshef. Produces material for Jewish schools, youth groups, temples and synagogues; for audience from kindergarten to old age. Buys 12-15 scripts/year. Submit outline/synopsis. SASE. Reports in 3 months. Buys first rights or all rights.

Needs: General, educational and informational. "Generally, length is up to 20-25 minutes maximum; most material is geared to 10-12 years old and up. Jewish background needed." Produces sound filmstrips, video 16mm films, tapes and cassettes, and slide sets. Pays 10-15% royalty or $1,000 minimum/outright purchase.

BRADY COMMUNICATIONS COMPANY, INC., Routes 197 & 450, Bowie MD 20715. Publishing Director: David T. Culverwell. Produces books for professionals and paraprofessionals in allied health, emergency care and microcomputer science. Will buy rights or sign standard contracts. Free catalog. "We are always eager to develop new writers who write instructively with clarity." Query. Computer printout submissions acceptable. Produces books, manuals, and computer software to accompany books.

Needs: Educational material for allied health, emergency medicine and microcomputer science. "Our company deals with instructional and informational-type projects."

Tips: "Send a resume with samples of writing ability and grasp of subject."

‡**BRADY STUDIOS, INC.**, Box 5220, Westport CT 06881. (203)226-3777. President: Paul Bray, Jr. Produces industrial, education and special aviation material. Buys 6 scripts/year. Buys all rights. No previously produced material. SASE. Reports in 2 weeks on queries. Free catalog.

Needs: Film loops (super 8mm), films (16mm), models, slides, and tapes and cassettes. Query with resume. Makes outright purchase—$800-1,500/10-minute segment.

Tips: "We look for writers with the ability to visualize and express said visualization in words."

ALDEN BUTCHER PRODUCTIONS, 6331 Hollywood Blvd., Hollywood CA 90028. (213)467-6045. Personnel Manager: Cynthia Butcher. Produces material for commercial/industrial and entertainment audiences. Buys 20 scripts/year. Deals mainly with local clients. Uses *only* local writers. Buys all rights. SASE. Reports in 1 month.

Needs: "Our needs depend upon contracts closed." Produces multimedia slide shows, film and video programs. Looks for "the ability to easily communicate with an industrial client and translate that into a script that meets their communication objectives the first time." Query with samples and resume. Computer printout submissions acceptable. Pays "according to production budget on an individual basis."

Tips: "Clients are looking more and more for a production company to provide creative approaches as a part of a bidding process. Often it is important for a writer to be involved in this speculative process prior to writing the actual script. This way they can help develop the style and approach."

‡**CABSCOTT BROADCAST PRODUCTION, INC.**, 517 7th Ave., Lindenwold NJ 08021. (609)346-3400. Contact: Larry Scott/Anne Foster. Produces industrial and broadcast material. Buys 10-12 scripts/year. Buys all rights. No previously produced material. SASE. Reports in 1 month. Free catalog.

Needs: Tapes and cassettes and video. Query with samples. Makes outright purchase.

CATHEDRAL FILMS, INC., 2282 Townsgate Rd., Westlake Village CA 91359. (818)991-3290. Contact: Candace Hunt. Produces material for church and school audiences. Works with variable number of writers/ year. Buys all rights and AV rights. Previously produced material OK "except from other AV media." SASE.

Reports in 1 month on queries; 2 months on mss. Catalog for SAE and 54¢ postage.
Needs: Various Christian, religious, educational and/or dramatic material. All ages. Produces 16mm films, sound filmstrips and video. Submit synopsis/outline or complete script. Pays variable rates.

‡**CLEARVUE, INC.**, 5711 N. Milwaukee Ave., Chicago IL 60646. (312)775-9433. Executive Vice President: W.O. McDermed. Produces material for educational market—grades kindergarten-12. Buys 20-50 scripts/year. Buys all rights. Previously produced material OK. SASE. Reports in 2 weeks on queries; 3 weeks on submissions. Free catalog.
Needs: Filmstrips (silent), filmstrips (sound), multimedia kits, and slides. "Our filmstrips are 35 to 100 frames—8 to 30 minutes for all curriculum areas." Query. Makes outright purchase, $100-5,000.
Tips: "We are interested in mainstream programs—not the exotic or unusual—series rather than singles.

‡**COMMAND PRODUCTIONS**, 62 Bowman Ave., Rye Brook NY 10573. (914)948-6868. Executive Producer: G. Stromberg. Produces material for business clients. Works with 10 writers/year. Submit resume, sample script and long range goals. SASE. Buys all rights.
Needs: Technical and nontechnical business presentations and customized training programs. Produces sound filmstrips, video productions, multimedia kits, overhead transparencies, slides, booklets and brochures. Pays by outright purchase.

CONCEPT 80's, 3409 West Chester Pike, Newtown Square PA 19073. (215)353-5900. Marketing Manager/Producer: Jim Higgins, Jr. Produces material for primarily corporate audiences—approximately 75% technical/industrial, 25% consumer organizations—mostly management, sales force or distributors. Buys 20-25 scripts/year. Buys all rights. No previously produced material. Computer printout submissions acceptable. SASE. Reports in several weeks. Catalog for SAE with 1 first class stamp.
Needs: Charts, silent and sound filmstrips, and multimedia kits, overhead transparencies, slides, videotape presentations, multi-image. "Most projects develop, are produced and delivered within 4-6 weeks." Query with samples or submit resume. Pays by outright purchase, $200-1,000.
Tips: "Writers should have written for audiovisual or print at least 10-20 successful scripts for blue chip corporations."

‡**CONDYNE/THE OCEANA GROUP**, 75 Main St., Dobbs Ferry NY 10522. (914)693-5944. Vice President: Yvonne Heenan. Produces material for legal market, and business and CPA markets. Works with 10-20 writers/year; buys 20 scripts/year. Buys all rights. No previously produced material. SASE. Reports in 2 weeks on queries; 2 months on submissions. Catalog for 7x10 SAE and 3 first class stamps.
Needs: Tapes and cassettes, and video (Betamax). "We are looking for video, ½ hour to one hour length—preview in ½" Beta II, practical, how-to for legal market (lawyers in practice, law students)." Query with samples, submit synopsis/outline, resume, and preview tape and synopsis/outline. Pays royalty or makes outright purchase; $250-500, depending on qualifications; 10% royalty.
Tips: "No phone calls accepted. All submissions must be in writing."

‡**CONSOLIDATED/BARTON**, Box 6834, Jacksonville FL 32205. (904)389-4541. President: Donald E. Barton. Produces material for various audiences. 70% freelance written. Buys 4 scripts/year from unpublished writers. 100% of scripts are unagented submissions. Works with average of 6 writers/year. Buys all rights. Computer printout submissions acceptable; prefers letter-quality to dot-matrix. SASE. Reports in 1 month.
Needs: Sports films, health care, TV commercials, documentary and sales—motivation, material—16mm films and video tapes. Query with samples. Also produces scripts for videos. Pays $850-5,000. Pays expenses of writers on assignment.

CORONADO STUDIOS, #600, 3550 Biscayne Blvd., Miami FL 33137. (305)573-7250. President: Fred L. Singer. Produces material for the general public, various specialized audiences. Buys 50 commercials/year; 15 corporate films/year. "We commission custom scripts that have no value to anyone but our clients." Computer printout submissions acceptable. SASE. Reports in 2 weeks on queries; 1 month on submissions.
Needs: "We will need an indeterminate number of scripts for commercials and corporate films." Produces 16mm films and video tapes. Query with samples. Pays by outright purchase; "depends on nature of job."

‡**CORPORATE COMMUNICATIONS, INC.**, 2950 E. Jefferson Ave., Detroit MI 48207. (313)259-3585. Administrative Manager: Patrick Longe. Produces commercial and industrial material. Works with 15-20 writers/year. Buys all rights. No previously published materal. SASE.
Needs: Films (16 and 35mm), multimedia kits and slides. Pays per project. Send resume and samples for reference.

CORPORATE MEDIA COMMUNICATIONS INC., 2200 Northlake Parkway, Box 261, Tucker GA 30085. (404)491-6300. Vice President: Phil Sehenuk. Produces material for businesses. 80% freelance written. Buys 80-100 scripts/year; also uses print copy. 80% of scripts produced are unagented submissions. Buys all rights. Previously produced material OK, "possibly." Computer printout submissions acceptable. SASE. Reports in 2 weeks. Free catalog.

Needs: Charts, 16mm films, silent and sound filmstrips, multimedia kits, slides, tapes and cassettes, videotape presentations, motivational material, product literature, and promotional material. "We want fresh new material with *human* orientation. We are interested in ideas for motivational show; we also make assignments." Query with samples, submit synopsis/outline, or completed script and resume. Pays negotiable rate/project.

Tips: "Clients want choices. The options of film, video, multi-image are all becoming affordable. Communicators need to be involved in a range of media."

‡**CP FILMS, INC.**, 4431 N. 60th Ave., Omaha NE 68104. (402)453-3200. President: G. Pflaum. Produces religious education material. Works with 4 writers/year. Buys all rights and first serial rights. Accepts previously produced material. SASE. Reports in 1 month. Free catalog.

Needs: Tapes and cassettes (video and audio). Will accept material from other mediums (radio, short story, stage) if author interested in adapting to video play. Submit complete script. Pays royalty; 6-10% on wholesale price of videocassette.

THE CREATIVE ESTABLISHMENT, 115 W. 31st St., New York NY 10001. (212)563-3337. Director of Creative Services: Dale Wilson. Produces material for business meetings and industrial audiences. 30% freelance written. 95% of scripts produced are unagented submissions. Works with approximately 10 writers/year. Buys all rights. SASE. "We don't return unsolicited material; material is held on file." Reports "when needed. Material is always specific to project. We cannot project future needs."

Needs: 8mm and 16mm film loops, 16mm and 35mm films, sound filmstrips, slides, multi-image and live shows. Submit synopsis/outline or completed script and resume. Computer printout submissions acceptable; no dot-matrix. Pays by outright purchase.

***CREATIVE PRODUCTIONS, INC.**, 200 Main St., Orange NJ 07050. (212)290-9075. Contact: Gus Nichols, Bill Griffing. Produces material for industrial, business and medical clients. Buys variable number of scripts/year. Query with resume and "background that is appropriate for specific project we may have." Computer printout submissions OK; prefers letter-quality to dot-matrix printouts. SASE. Buys all rights.

Needs: "We can use staff writers/associate producers with AV experience. We may consider help from time to time on a project basis. The writer must have the ability to create visual sequences as well as narrative. Flexibility is a must; treatments might be technical, humorous, etc." Produces sound filmstrips, 16mm films, slides, video and multi-image shows. Pays salary to writers added to the staff; a negotiable fee to freelancers.

DA SILVA ASSOCIATES, (formerly Raul Da Silva & Other Filmmakers), 137 E. 38th St., New York NY 10016. Creative Director: Raul da Silva. 40% freelance written. Produces material for entertainment audiences. "We strive for excellence in both script and visual interpretation. We produce quality only, and bow to the budget-conscious who cannot or will not afford quality." Submit resume. "Generally we work on assignment only. We have a selection of writers known to us already." 100% of scripts are unagented submission. Cannot handle unsolicited mail/scripts. Computer printout submissions acceptable; prefers letter-quality to dot-matrix. Rights purchased vary. "If possible, we share profits with writers, particularly when resale is involved."

Needs: "We produce both types of material: on assignment and proprietary." Produces video (entertainment only); 35mm films, phonograph records, tapes and cassettes. Also produces material for cable TV (drama/comedy). Pays in accordance with Writers Guild standards. Pays expenses of writers on assignment.

Tips: "We are impressed with scripts that have received recognition in writing competition. We also welcome resumes from writers who have credentials and credits with other producers. From these we will select our future writers." Looks for "knowledge of medium, structure, style, cohesiveness (mastery of continuity), clarity, obvious love for the language and intelligence."

NICHOLAS DANCY PRODUCTIONS, INC., 333 W. 39th St., New York NY 10018. (212)564-9140. President: Nicholas Dancy. Produces media material for corporate communications, general audiences, employees, members of professional groups, members of associations and special customer groups. 80% freelance written. Buys 5-10 scripts/year; works with 5-10 writers/year. 100% of scripts are unagented submissions. Buys all rights. Reports in 1 month. Computer printout submissions acceptable; prefers letter-quality to dot-matrix.

Needs: "We use scripts for videotapes or films from 5 minutes to 1 hour for corporate communications, sales, orientation, training, corporate image, medical and documentary." Format: videotape, 16mm films and slide tape. Query with resume. "No unsolicited material. Our field is too specialized." Pays by outright purchase of $800-5,000. Sometimes pays expenses of writers on assignment.

Tips: "Writers should have knowledge of business and industry and professions, ability to work with clients and communicators, fresh narrative style, creative use of dialogue, good skills in accomplishing research, and a professional approach to production."

ALFRED DE MARTINI EDUCATIONAL FILMS, 414 4th Ave., Haddon Heights NJ 08035. (609)547-2800. President: Alfred De Martini. Produces material for schools, colleges, universities, libraries and museums. 80% freelance written. Buys 12 scripts/year from unpublished/unproduced writers. All scripts produced are unagented submissions. "We're informal, creative, earthy, realistic, productive and perfection-oriented." Submit synopsis/outline. Do not send complete script. Submissions will not be returned. SASE. Reports in 1 month. Buys all rights.
Needs: Subjects include educational material on art, travel and history from secondary to adult level. Produces silent and sound filmstrips, multimedia kits, and tapes and cassettes. Pays in outright purchase of $100-$2,500. "Fee is established in advance with writers."
Tips: Interested in "imagination, brevity, uniqueness of style and ascertaining objectives."

‡**DELPHI PRODUCTIONS**, Suite 309, 1800 30th St., Boulder CO 80301. (303)443-2100. Producer/Director: Oliver Henry. Produces material for educational (grades 3-12); and general public (informational/how-to) amateur sports enthusiasts. Buys 4-5 scripts per year (probably more in the future). Buys all rights. No previously published material. SASE. Reports in 2 weeks on queries (must be accompanied by resume); 1 month on mss.
Needs: Video. "We produce on video for the education and home market. We're looking for any new good ideas that adapt themselves to these markets. We use 80% freelance writers. Instructional/informational with a bit of humor to hold attention is a bias for us now." Query with resume. Pays maximum 10% royalty, makes outright purchase, $200-3,000 or any combination that can be worked out.
Tips: "Experience in film/video script writing is necessary. If you've got a good idea *and* can back up your opinion with good market research, we'd like to look at your idea. We're looking for creative new approaches to a growing market for home viewers."

□ **DIDIK TV PRODUCTIONS**, Box 133, Rego Park NY 11374. (718)843-6839. Produces TV commercials, industrials and government material. Buys 6-8 scripts/year. Rights purchased depend on job. No previously produced material. SASE. Reports in 2 weeks. Catalog for SAE and 1 first class stamp.
Needs: 16 and 35mm films and video tape (¾" and 1"). Submit synopsis/outline. Pays negotiable rates.

‡**NORM DREW ENTERTAINMENT FEATURES**, Suite 608-L, Laurier House, 1600 Beach Ave., Vancouver, British Columbia V6G 1Y6. (604)689-1948. Contact: Norm Drew. "I create, produce, and distribute educational and entertainment features in animated film/video, book, comic strip AV slide, or puppet forms. Buys all rights. Produces material for advertising, training and entertainments. Send resume.
Needs: Looking for fresh, original ½ or 1 hour TV special animated feature script for our cartoon characters, CHIKA, and THE BUSH BABIES. Uses both contemporary themes and traditional values. Pays negotiable fee. Send SAE with IRC for sample sheet.

‡**DUBOIS/RUDDY**, 2145 Crooks, Troy MI 48084. (313)643-0320. Vice President: Chris Ruddy. Produces material for corporations. Works with 20-30 writers/year. Buys all rights. No previously produced material. SASE. Query with resume. No scripts.
Needs: Multi-image and film production. Makes outright purchase; payment negotiable.
Tips: "We will use local writers only. Call and make an appointment."

THE DURASELL CORPORATION, 360 Lexington Ave., New York NY 10017. President: Albert A. Jacoby. Produces AV and video multi-media sales and marketing corporation material for sales presentations, meetings, and training programs—primarily for consumer package goods companies. 100% freelance written. Does not buy scripts from unpublished/unproduced writers. All scripts produced are unagented submissions. Buys 30-50 scripts/year; works with 6-10 writers/year. Buys all rights. Computer printout submissions acceptable; prefers letter-quality to dot-matrix.
Needs: Video, meetings, sound filmstrips, slides and tapes. Must send letter and resume first. Pays by outright purchase. ("Freelancer sets fee.")
Tips: "Freelancers must be fast, creative, organized, enthusiastic, experienced, talented. Demonstrate heavy experience in AV sales meetings scripts and in creative multi-image sales meetings."

‡**DYNACOM COMMUNICIATIONS, INC.**, Box 702, Snowdon Station, Montreal, Quebec H3X 3X8 Canada. Contact: D. Leonard. Buys all rights. No previously produced material. SAE with IRCs.
Needs: Dioramas, multimedia kits, phonograph records, slides, tapes and cassettes, and teaching machine programs. Offers royalty; makes outright purchase.
Tips: "We look for writers with a clear understanding of clients' and audiences' needs."

‡**EDUCATIONAL IMAGES LTD.**, Box 3456, Elmira NY 14905. (607)732-1090. Executive Director: Dr. Charles R. Belinky. Produces material (sound filmstrips, multimedia kits and slide sets) for schools, kindergarten through college and graduate school, public libraries, parks, nature centers, etc. Also produces science-related software material. Buys 50 scripts/year. Buys all AV rights. Query with a meaningful sample of proposed program. Computer printout submissions OK. Free catalog.
Needs: Slide sets and filmstrips on science, natural history, anthropology and social studies. "We are looking primarily for complete AV programs; we will consider slide collections to add to our files. This requires high quality, factual text and pictures." Pays $150 minimum.
Tips: The writer/photographer is given high consideration. "Once we express interest, follow up. Potential contributors lose many sales to us by not following up on initial query. Don't waste our time and yours if you can't deliver."

EDUCATIONAL INSIGHTS, 150 W. Carob St., Compton CA 90220. (213)637-2131. Director of Development: Dennis J. Graham. Educational publisher. 30% freelance written. Averages 50 titles/year. Buys 6 scripts/year from unpublished/unproduced writers. 90% of scripts are unagented submissions. Pays 5% minimum royalty; buys some mss outright. No advance. Simultaneous and photocopied submissions OK. Computer printout submissions acceptable; prefers letter-quality to dot-matrix. SASE. Reports in 1 month. Free catalog.
Needs: Educational areas. Query or submit outline/synopsis and sample chapters or script.

EFC, INC., 5101 F Backlick Rd., Box 1017, Annandale VA 22003. (703)750-0560. Vice President/Script Development: Ruth Pollak. Produces dramatic and documentary film and video for commercial, government, broadcast, schools and communities. 80% freelance written. Buys scripts from published/produced writers only. 50% of scripts produced are unagented submissions. Buys all rights. Computer printout submissions acceptable; prefers letter-quality to dot-matrix. SASE. Reports in 1 month.
Needs: Strong dramatic screenplays, especially for family/children audience. Query with samples. Makes outright purchase or pays by commercial arrangement. Pays expenses of writers on assignment.

EFFECTIVE COMMUNICATION ARTS, INC., 221 W. 57th St., New York NY 10019. (212)333-5656. Vice President: W.J. Comcowich. Produces films, videotapes and interactive videodisks for physicians, nurses and medical personnel. 80% freelance written. Buys 20 scripts/year. Submit complete script and resume. Electronic submissions OK via direct modem or MCI mailbox. Computer printout submissions acceptable; prefers letter-quality to dot-matrix. "Explain what the films accomplished—how they were better than the typical." Buys all rights. Reports in 1 month.
Needs: Multimedia kits, 16mm films, television shows/series, videotape presentations, and interactive videodisks. Currently interested in about 15 films, videotapes for medical audiences; 6 interactive disks for medical audience, 3 interactive disks for point-of-purchase. Makes outright purchase or negotiated rights.
Tips: "Trends in the audiovisual field that freelance writers should be aware of include interactive design."

EMC CORP., 300 York Ave., St. Paul MN 55101. Editor: Rosemary Barry. Produces material for children and teenagers in the primary grades through high school. "We sell strictly to schools and public libraries." Software submissions accepted; educational (most subject areas). 100% freelance written by published/produced writers. All scripts produced are unagented submissions. Buys 2-3 scripts/year. Buys world rights. "The writer, via submitted sample, must show the capability to write appropriately for the educational market." Query with resume and one or more samples of previously produced work. Electronic submissions OK via Apple IIC, TRS-80 III. Computer printout submissions acceptable; prefers letter-quality to dot-matrix. No unsolicited manuscripts accepted. Catalog for 9x12 SASE.
Needs: Career education, consumer education, and special education (as related to language arts especially). "No standard requirements, due to the nature of educational materials publishing." No religious topics. Payment varies.

THE EPISCOPAL RADIO-TV FOUNDATION, INC., 3379 Peachtree Rd. NE, Atlanta GA 30326. (404)233-5419. President/Executive Director: The Rev. Louis C. Schueddig. Produces and distributes materials for educational and religious organizations. Catalog for 8½x11 manila envelope.
Needs: 16mm films, tapes and cassettes, video and VHS.

MARTIN EZRA & ASSOCIATES, 48 Garrett Rd., Upper Darby PA 19082. (215)352-9595 or 9596. Producer: Martin Ezra. Produces material for business, industry and education. Works with 4-5 writers/year. Buys all rights and first rights. SASE. Reports in 3 weeks.
Needs: Educational and informational work. Film loops, films, silent filmstrips, sound filmstrips, multimedia kits, slides, and tapes and cassettes. Query with samples or submit complete script "in writing only." Payment varies with project.

‡**FILM COMMUNICATION, INC.**, Outer Winthrop Rd., Hallowell ME 04347. (207)623-9466. President: Paul J. Fournier. "We are not making assignments to writers."

FILMS FOR CHRIST ASSOCIATION, INC., Suite 1327, 2432 W. Peoria Ave., Phoenix AZ 85029. (602)997-7400. Production Manager: Paul Taylor. Produces material for use by churches (interdenominational); schools (both secular and parochial); and missions. Most films are 20-90 minutes in length. Previously produced submissions OK. Computer printout submissions acceptable; disk submissions OK with Lanier format only. Free catalog.
Needs: Produces 16mm films, videos, sound filmstrips, slides and books, documentaries, and dramas. Particularly interested in scripts or script ideas dealing with such subjects as: Creation vs. evolution, archaeology, science and the Bible, apologetics, Christian living and evangelism. Also interested in good scripts for evangelistic children's films. Query. Prefers brief one-page synopsis. Payment negotiable.

FILMS FOR THE HUMANITIES, INC., Box 2053, Princeton NJ 08540. (609)452-1128. Vice President, Editorial: Stephen Mantell. Produces material for junior high, high school, college, business and industry audience. Buys 50-75 scripts/year; works with 10-15 writers/year. Previously produced material OK. SASE.
Needs: Produces sound filmstrips, multimedia kits, tapes and cassettes. Submit resume and sample material; "we assign topics."
Tips: "We assign writing in line with our curriculum and editorial program needs."

‡**FIRE PREVENTION THROUGH FILMS, INC.**, Box 11, Newton Highlands MA 02161. (617)965-4444. Manager: Julian Olansky. Produces material for audiences involved with fire prevention and general safety: grades kindergarten through 12; colleges and universities; laboratories; industry and home safety. Purchases 5 scripts/year. "We work with several local script writers on a yearly basis." Buys all rights. No previously produced material. SASE. Reports in 3 weeks. Free catalog.
Needs: Films (16mm). "We will need scripts for films dealing with the removal of patients in health care facilities because of fire danger (20 minutes). Also, a film dealing with general safety in an office setting (20 minutes). Query with or without samples. Makes outright purchase.

FLIPTRACK LEARNING SYSTEMS, Division of Mosaic Media, Inc., Suite 200, 999 Main, Glen Ellyn IL 60137. (312)790-1117. Publisher: F. Lee McFadden. Produces training media for microcomputer equipment and business software. 50% freelance written. Buys 25 courses/year; 2-3 from unpublished/unproduced writers. All courses published are unagented submissions. Works with 10-15 writers/year. Buys all rights. Electronic submissions OK on IBM PC with Hayes modem. Computer printout submissions OK. SASE. Reports in 3 weeks. Free product literature.
Needs: Computer courses on disk, video or audio geared to the adult or mature student in a business setting and to the first-time microcomputer user. Produces audio, video, CBT and reference manuals. Query with resume and samples if available. Pays negotiable royalty; makes some outright purchases. Sometimes pays expenses of writers on assignment.
Tips: Looks for "ability to organize lesson content logically, develop carefully sequenced lessons and write step-by-step instruction in narrative form. Experience in writing training material for the adult learner is more important than a deep knowledge of the microcomputer. Business orientation is a help. We are expanding, along with the microcomputer market."

FLORIDA PRODUCTION CENTER, 150 Riverside Ave., Jacksonville FL 32202. (904)354-7000. Vice President: L.J. Digiusto. Produces audiovisual material for general, corporate and government audiences. Buys all rights. No previously produced material. SASE.
Needs: Films (16mm), filmstrips (silent and sound), multimedia kits, overhead transparencies, slides, tapes and cassettes, teaching machine programs, and videos. Query with samples and resume. Makes negotiable outright purchase.

PAUL FRENCH & PARTNERS, INC., Rt. 5, Gabbettville Rd., LaGrange GA 30240. (404)882-5581. Contact: Gene Byrd. 20% freelance written. Query or submit resume. Computer printout submissions acceptable. SASE. Reports in 2 weeks. Buys all rights.
Needs: Wants to see multi-screen scripts (all employee attitude related) and/or multi-screen AV sales meeting scripts or resumes. Produces silent and sound filmstrips, video tapes and cassettes, and slides. Pays in outright purchase of $500-5,000. Payment is in accordance with Writers Guild standards.

□ **FRIED PRODUCTIONS**, 768 Farmington Ave., Farmington CT 06032. (203)674-8221. President: Joel Fried. Executive Producer: Roy Shaw. Production Assistant: David Shearer. "We produce programs that are aimed at the high school/college/cable TV market." Buys all rights. Query; "tell us what your idea is and why you can write on this particular subject." Electronic submissions OK. Computer printout submissions acceptable. SASE. Pays by cash and/or royalty.

Needs: "Education is very important to us. You should be familiar with the market and what subjects are of interest to today's students. We are open to any good idea. Original script ideas for cable production also of interest." Buys 20-40 scripts/yr. Subjects include vocational education and academics, chemistry, career awareness, physics and biology, horticulture, sex education—just about any area. Produces videotapes, 6mm sound filmstrips, overhead transparencies, slides, study prints, teaching machine programs, and multimedia kits. Pays by the project.

Tips: "Please let us hear your ideas. All queries are answered."

‡**GENERAL EDUCATIONAL MEDIA, INC.**, 701 Beaver Valley Rd., Wilmington DE 19803. (302)478-1994. President: David Engler. Produces for business and industry, and general adult audiences. 25% freelance written. Buys 20-30 scripts/year from 5-6 writers. 100% of scripts are unagented submissions. Query with samples. Computer printout submissions acceptable; prefers letter-quality to dot-matrix. SASE. Reports in 6 weeks. Buys all rights.

Needs: Typical length, 15 to 25 minute scripts; subjects, style and format variable. Produces films, video, audio cassettes, slides, computer-based programs, workbooks and trainer's guides. Pays $200-500. Sometimes pays expenses of writers on assignment.

GESSLER PUBLISHING CO., INC., Gessler Educational Software, 900 Broadway, New York NY 10003. (212)673-3113. President: Seth C. Levin. Produces material for students learning ESL and foreign languages. 50% freelance written. Buys about 75 scripts/year. 100% of scripts are unagented submissions. Prefers to buy all rights, but will work on royalty basis. Do not send disk submission without documentation. Electronic submissions OK on Apple IIe/c, Commodore 64, IBM PC/PCjr. Computer printout submissions acceptable; prefers letter-quality to dot-matrix.

Needs: Filmstrips "to create an interest in learning a foreign language and its usefulness in career objectives; also culturally insightful filmstrips on French, German, Italian and Spanish speaking countries." Produces sound filmstrips, multimedia kits, overhead transparencies, games, realia, tapes and cassettes, computer software. Also produces scripts for videos. Submit synopsis/outline or software with complete documentation, introduction, objectives. Makes outright purchase and pays royalties. SASE. Reports in 3 weeks on queries; 2 months on submissions.

Tips: "Be organized in your presentation; be creative but keep in mind that your audience is primarily junior/senior high school students."

GRAPHIC MEDIA, INC., (formerly Photoscope, Inc.), 12th Floor, 12 W. 27th St., Fl. 12, New York NY 10001. (212)696-0880. General Manager: Jody Boltz. Director of Operations: Debra Buchsbaum. Produces material for a corporate audience. 100% freelance written. Buys 10 scripts/year from published/produced writers only. 100% of scripts produced are unagented submissions. Buys all rights. Computer printout submissions acceptable; no dot-matrix. SASE.

Needs: Produces slides and multi-image and offers computer graphic slides. Looks for "imagination, coherency, clarity." Query with samples. Buys scripts outright for negotiable rate.

‡**GRIFFIN MEDIA DESIGN**, (formerly Griffin Communications), 802 Wabash Ave., Chesterton IN 46304. (219)926-8602. Production Manager: Leona Marshall. Produces variety of business and industrial accounts, specifically for the development of advertising, public relations, training programs, marketing, conventions, etc. "We may buy as few as 10 to 50 projects per year." Buys all rights. No previously produced material. SASE. Reports on queries in 3 weeks. Catalog for 9x12 SAE and 2 first class stamps.

Needs: Films, filmstrips (sound), multimedia kits, overhead transparencies, slides, and tapes and cassettes. Query with samples. Makes outright purchase.

Tips: "Potential contributors should make themselves known. It's just as hard for businesses to find good writers as it is for good writers to find work."

HAYES SCHOOL PUBLISHING CO., INC., 321 Pennwood Ave., Wilkinsburg PA 15221. (412)371-2373. 2nd Vice President: Clair N. Hayes, III. Produces material for school teachers, principals, elementary through high school. 25% freelance written. Buys 5-10 scripts/year from unpublished/unproduced writers. 100% of scripts produced are unagented submissions. Buys all rights. Electronic submissions OK via Apple IIe. Computer printout submissions acceptable; prefers letter-quality to dot-matrix. Produces charts, workbooks, teacher's handbooks, posters, bulletin board material, computer software, and liquid duplicating books (grades kindergarten through 12). Also produces educational software. Catalog for SASE and 3 first class stamps.

Needs: Educational material only. Particularly interested in educational material for high school level. Query. Pays $25 minimum.

ICOM INC., 278 N. 5th St., Columbus OH 43215. (614)224-4400. President: Phil Yoder. Produces material for corporate customers, sales people and employees. Buys 40 scripts/year. Buys all rights. Electronic submis-

sions OK via IBM PC WordStar or 8'' WordStar. Computer printout submissions acceptable; no dot-matrix except for rough drafts. SASE. Reports in 2 weeks on query; 1 month on submissions.
Needs: Multimedia kits, slides, videotape presentations, and multi-image. Currently interested in hi-tech, business and sales presentations; training programs. Submit resume. Makes outright purchase $300-2,000.

IDEAL SCHOOL SUPPLY CO., 11000 S. Lavergne Ave., Oak Lawn IL 60453. (312)425-0800. Marketing Manager: Barbara Stiles. Produces material for preschool, primary and elementary students. "The majority of our product line comes from outside sources, most of them practicing classroom teachers. Occasionally these products are edited by freelance talent. Writers and editors are also used for some special development projects." Buys 25 scripts/year from unpublished/unproduced writers. 98% of scripts are unagented submissions. Query with resume which will be filed for future reference. Free catalog.
Needs: Style, length and format vary according to grade level and subject matter of material. Produces software, manipulatives, games, models, printed material, multimedia kits and cassette programs.

IMAGE MEDIA, 1362 LaSalle Ave., Minneapolis MN 55403. (612)872-0578. Creative Director: A.M. Rifkin. Query with samples. SASE. Reports in 2 weeks. Rights purchased "depend on project."
Needs: Produces silent and sound filmstrips, 16mm films, tapes and cassettes and slides. Pays in outright purchase.

‡IMPERIAL INTERNATIONAL LEARNING CORP., 329 E. Court St., Kankakee IL 60901. (815)933-7735. Editor: Patsy Gunnels. Material intended for kindergarten through grade 12 audience. Buys all rights. No previously produced material. SASE. Reports in 2 weeks on queries; 1 month on submissions. Free catalog.
Needs: "Supplemental learning materials of various lengths in the areas of reading, math, social studies, and science with emphasis on using the microcomputer or videotape programs." Produces silent filmstrips, tapes and cassettes, and microcomputer and videotape. Query with samples or submit complete script and resume. Pays negotiable rates.
Tips: "Make time invested in conceptualizing your product time well spent. Make sure that learning objectives are well-defined and instructional technique is well-executed. A writer must know the audience, the subject, and the medium employed. The writer's work must clearly demonstrate that these are brought together into a product that serves each equally well. The demand for traditional AV products will lag behind computer programs for the foreseeable future, but there is growing interest in the use of videotapes, especially used in conjunction with computer programs."

INDUSTRIAL MEDIA, INC., 6660 28th St. SE, Grand Rapids MI 49506. (616)949-7770. Contact: Ed Anderson. Produces instructional aids for vocational schools and industrial in-plant training programs. 50% freelance written. Buys 1 script/year from unpublished/unproduced writers. 2 of scripts are unagented submissions. Buy all rights "usually, but other arrangements are possible." Computer printout submissions acceptable; prefers letter-quality to dot-matrix. SASE. Catalog for 1 first class stamp.
Needs: Slide/cassette and video presentations coordinated with student workbooks and instruction guides for industrial training. "We specialize in materials for training industrial equipment maintenance personnel and apprentices. Topics of particular interest to our customers include: Industrial electricity, electronics, hydraulics, mechanical maintenance, blueprint reading, welding, safety and management skills for plant supervisors. We will consider any topic with broad application in manufacturing training. We prefer to work with writers who can develop an entire, self-contained package, complete with performance objectives, script, workbooks, instruction guide and testing materials." Query. Pays expenses of writers on assignment.

INNOVISION PRODUCTIONS, Box 6391, Lawton OK 73506-0391. (405)357-8558. Assistant Producer: D.J. Griffin. Estab. 1983. "We aim at the 'how-to' market of hobbies and leisure time pursuits. For example, an article in an outdoor magazine brought to life on video tape for home consumers on video cassette is a good place to start. We tend to advertise in the magazine that best fits the product." Works with 3-10 writers/year. "We generate a great deal of material in house." Buys first rights. "We also retain the rights to sell to networks from the original contract." SASE. Reports in 2 weeks on queries; 2 months on submissions. Call for guidelines.
Needs: Topics include flyfishing, skiing, white water sports, backpacking, climbing, boating tips, hobbies and crafts "if they are visually exciting." Produces video cassettes for home use. Query or submit synopsis/outline and resume. "Since we look for a freestyle, it is best to use a detailed outline. The ideas are discussed with us and then the video format is decided upon. The author should also be prepared to appear on camera because it is his ideas that are being sold. Possibly, the most important thing to keep in mind is that we intend to look for the humorous and visually dramatic. We don't mean melodramatic. The idea is for the consumer to buy a tape on his favorite subject and say, 'I really enjoyed that! And I learned something too!' If anything this is our main philosophy." Pays 7-12% royalty; percentage is based on retail *or* wholesale.
Tips: "We are basically looking for expertise in fields where we have none. In preparing a synopsis we need

the author to mix expertise with entertainment. If the subject is active, such as kayaking, we want to make it as visually active as possible. If it's a more tedious subject, then keep it light. We need flexibility above all else; the willingness to try things. Two good programs that we tend to emulate is Bob Vila's *This Old House* on PBS and *American Sportsman* on ABC. Too many programs come off like they are absolutely planned. We want to be free-flowing and somehow enhance the consumer's dream of what this activity is all about. We need form, but a loose form. It is really important that an author be published in the last year, possibly several times. It gives us the ability to springboard from it and gives him the ability to capitalize upon his previous success. Also, call first. We'll be glad to talk it over with authors before they prepare work."

INSIGHT! INC., 100 E. Ohio St., Chicago IL 60611. (312)467-4350. President: Neal Cochran. Produces material for all audiences, depending on type of client. 90% freelance written. Buys scripts from produced writers only. All scripts produced by contract. Buys over 200 scripts/year from more than 30 writers. Buys all rights. Electronic submissions OK via modem ASCOM CP/M or 5¼" disk Apple II + or Eagle II. Computer printout submissions acceptable. SASE.
Needs: "Our needs depend on contracts awarded to Insight! Films, videotapes, filmstrips and, most important, industrial shows of all types." Produces 16mm films, multimedia and "book" shows. No educational materials. Concentrates entirely on film, video and shows. Query with samples. Pays by outright purchase.

INSTRUCTOR BOOKS, 1 E. 1st St., Duluth MN 55802. Editorial Director: John Bradley. "U.S. and Canadian school supervisors, principals, and teachers purchase items in our line for instructional purposes." 35% freelance written. Buys 3 scripts/year from unpublished/unproduced writers. Most scripts produced are unagented submissions. Buys all rights. Writer should have "experience in preparing materials for elementary students, including suitable teaching guides to accompany them, and demonstrate knowledge of the appropriate subject areas, or demonstrate ability for accurate and efficient research and documentation." Computer printout submissions acceptable; prefers letter-quality to dot-matrix. SASE. Free catalog.
Needs: Elementary curriculum enrichment—all subject areas. Display material, copy and illustration should match interest and reading skills of children in grades for which material is intended. Production is limited to printed matter: resource handbooks, teaching guides and idea books. Query. Length: 6,000-12,000 words. Standard contract, but fees vary considerably, depending on type of project.
Tips: "Writers who reflect current educational practices can expect to sell to us."

INTERAND CORPORATION, 3200 W. Peterson Ave., Chicago IL 60659. (312)478-1700. Director of Corporate Communications: Linda T. Phillips. Produces material for industry and business. Buys all rights. Usually no previously published material. SASE. Reports in 2 weeks on queries. Free product information.
Needs: Slides and videotapes. Submit resume. Makes outright purchases.

☐ **INTERNATIONAL MEDIA SERVICES INC.**, 718 Sherman Ave., Plainfield NJ 07060. (201)756-4060. President/General Manager: Stuart Allen. Produces varied material depending on assignment or production in house; includes corporate, public relations, sales, radio/TV, CATV, teleconferencing/CCTV, etc. 60-75% freelance written. 90% of scripts produced are unagented submissions. "We normally issue assignments to writers in the freelance market who specialize in appropriate fields of interest." Buys all rights. No previously produced material. Computer printout submissions acceptable. SASE. Reporting time varies depending on job requirements and specifications.
Needs: Charts, dioramas, 8/16mm film loops, 16/35mm films, silent and sound filmstrips, kinescopes, multimedia kits, overhead transparencies, phonograph records, slides, tapes and cassettes, television shows/series, and videotape presentations. "We routinely hire writers from a freelance resource file." Cable TV needs include educational and entertainment marketplaces. Query with or without samples, or submit synopsis/outline and resume. "All work must be copyrighted and be original unpublished works." Pays in accordance with Writers Guild standards, negotiated contract or flat rate.

☐ **PAUL S. KARR PRODUCTIONS**, 2949 W. Indian School Rd., Box 11711, Phoenix AZ 85017. Utah Division: 1024 N. 250 E., Box 1254, Orem UT 84057. (801)226-8209. (602)266-4198. Produces films and videos for industry, business and education. "*Do not submit material unless requested.*" Buys all rights. Works on coproduction ventures that have been funded.
Needs: Produces 16mm films and videos. Payment varies. Query.
Tips: "One of the best ways for a writer to become a screenwriter is to create a situation with a client that requires a film or video. He then can assume the position of an associate producer, work with an experienced professional producer in putting the production into being, and in that way learn about filmmaking and chalk up some meaningful credits."

KEN-DEL PRODUCTIONS, INC., 111 Valley Rd., Wilmington DE 19804-1397. (302)655-7488. President: Ed Kennedy. Produces material for "elementary, junior high, high school and college level, as well as interested organizations and companies." SASE.

Needs: "Topics of the present (technology, cities, traffic, transit, pollution, ecology, health, water, race, genetics, consumerism, fashions, communications, education, population control, waste, future sources of food, undeveloped sources of living, food, health, etc.); topics of the future; how-to series (everything for the housewife, farmer, banker or mechanic, on music, art, sports, reading, science, love, repair, sleep—on any subject); and material handling." Produces sound filmstrips; 8mm, 16mm, and 35mm films; 16mm film loops; phonograph records; prerecorded tapes and cassettes; slides and videotapes in ¾" U-matic, ½" VHS, ½" BETA cassettes. Query.

KIMBO EDUCATIONAL-UNITED SOUND ARTS, INC., 10-16 N. 3rd Ave., Box 477, Long Branch NJ 07740. (201)229-4949. Contact: James Kimble or Amy Laufer. Produces materials for the educational market (early childhood, special education, music, physical education, dance, and preschool children 6 months and up). 50% freelance written. Buys approximately 12-15 scripts/year; works with approximately 12-15 writers/year. Buys 5 scripts/year from unpublished/unproduced writers. Most of scripts are unagented submissions. Buys all rights or first rights. Previously produced material OK "in some instances." SASE. Reports in 1 month. Free catalog.
Needs: "For the next two years we will be concentrating on general early childhood movement oriented products, new albums in the fitness field and more. Each will be an album/cassette with accompanying teacher's manual and, if warranted, manipulatives." Phonograph records and cassettes; "all with accompanying manual or teaching guides." Query with samples and synopsis/outline or completed script. Pays 5-7% royalty on lowest wholesale selling price, and by outright purchase. Both negotiable. Sometimes pays expenses of writers on assignment.
Tips: "We look for creativity first. Having material that is educationally sound is also important. Being organized is certainly helpful. Fitness is growing rapidly in popularity and will always be a necessary thing. Children will always need to be taught the basic fine and gross motor skills. Capturing interest while reaching these goals is the key."

□ **KOCH/MARSCHALL PRODUCTIONS, INC.**, 1718 N. Mohawk St., Chicago IL 60614. (312)664-6482. Executive Producer: Sally E. Marschall. Produces material for general library audience, high school or college, and mass audience. 20% freelance written. "We read more than a hundred scripts a year. We may buy one a year. We work with one writer at a time." Buys all rights. No previously produced material. SASE. Report in 2 months on queries; 3 months on submissions.
Needs: Produces 16 and 35mm films. "We are looking for feature film ideas that have comedic potential. These can be historical, comtemporary, musical, theatrical, European, American, romantic, thrilling, and/or mysterious." Produces feature-length comedy material for cable TV. "We negotiate payment with each writer."
Tips: "We are looking for original, innovative, nonexploitational, nonderivative screenplays. No first drafts, no student theses. Screenplays must be intelligent, provocative and exciting. Writers must be well-educated, experienced in film writing, and compatible with a team of filmmakers."

‡**DERICK LAWRENCE**, 580 Tremon St., Box 1722, Duxbury MA 02331. (617)934-6561. Executive Producer: Gordon Massingham. Produces television, educational and corporate material. Works with two writers regularly. Purchases average of seven scripts, most of which are commissioned. Buys all rights. No previously produced material. SASE. Reports in 3 weeks on queries; 5 weeks on submissions.
Needs: Film (16, 35mm); filmstrips (sound); slides; and tapes and cassettes. Query. Makes outright purchase or option.
Tips: "We look for a proven record of success, timeliness and accuracy."

BRIEN LEE & COMPANY, 2025 N. Summit Ave., Milwaukee WI 53202. (414)277-7600. President/Creative Director: Brien Lee. Produces custom audiovisual material for business; industry; arts/nonprofit; advertising and public relations agencies; business associations; and special entertainment oriented projects. Buys average 5 scripts/year. Submit example of scripting ability as well as a resume. Buys all rights. Computer printout submissions acceptable; disk OK if compatible. SASE. Reports in 1 month, sometimes leading to an interview and an assignment.
Needs: "We need people who understand what AV is all about . . . words, pictures, sound. Motivational, informational, clear-cut, straightforward . . . writing that is literate, but never so good it could stand on its own without the pictures or sound. It is usually writing for one narrator, plus additional voices and/or characters. No hype." Produces videotapes, multi-image presentations, and mixed media presentations, slide-sound programs and interactive video.
Recent Production: AVL, IVC, dealer meeting.

WILLIAM V. LEVINE ASSOCIATES, INC., 31 E. 28th St., New York NY 10016. (212)683-7177. President: William V. Levine. Presentations for business and industry. 20% freelance written. Buys 4 scripts/year. Firm emphasizes "creativity and understanding of the client's goals and objectives." Will interview writers after submission of resume and/or sample AV scripts. Specifically seeks writers with offbeat or humorous flair. Previously produced material OK. Buys all rights. "We prefer New York City-area based writers only." SASE.

Needs: Business-related scripts *on assignment* for specific clients for use at sales meetings or for desk-top presentations. Also uses theme-setting and inspirational scripts with inherent messages of business interest. Produces sound and silent filmstrips, 16mm films, multimedia kits, tapes and cassettes, slide sets and live industrial shows. Query with resume. Pays $500-2,500.

J.B. LIPPINCOTT CO., Audiovisual Media Department, East Washington Sq., Philadelphia PA 19105. (215)238-4200. Contact: H.M. Eisler. Produces materials for nursing students and medical students. Buys 15-25 scripts/year. Works with approximately 25 writers/year. Buys all rights. Disk submissions OK if compatible with IBM PC and Apple II. SASE. Reports in 2 weeks on queries; 4 weeks on submissions. Free catalog.
Needs: "High-level instruction in medical/surgical topics for pre-service and in-service professional education." Produces 16mm films, sound filmstrips, slides (rarely), video materials and computer software. Query. Negotiates pay.

‡LORI PRODUCTIONS, INC., Suite 1217, 6430 Sunset Blvd., Hollywood CA 90028. (213)466-7567. Produces material for industrial clients. 20% freelance written. Buys 5-10 scripts/year. 99% of scripts are un-agented submissions. Buys all rights. Computer printout submissions acceptable; prefers letter-quality to dot-matrix. SASE. Reports in 3 weeks.
Needs: "We produce industrial films (sales, corporate image, training, safety), which generally run from 30 seconds to 18 minutes in length." Also produces video and cable TV material (varies with customers requirements). Seeks writers with a "clean, concise writing style; a familiarity with film production; and experience with industrial films." Works with Los Angeles area writers *only*. Produces 16mm films, live corporate shows, multi-image presentations, and sales meetings. Query with resume. Pays by outright purchase of $500-2,000. Sometimes pays expenses of writers on assignment.

MARSHFILM ENTERPRISES, INC., Box 8082, Shawnee Mission KS 66208. (816)523-1059. President: Joan K. Marsh. Produces material for elementary and junior/senior high school students. Also produces software and filmstrips. 100% freelance written. Buys 8-16 scripts/year. All scripts produced are unagented submissions. Buys all rights. Computer printout submissions acceptable; prefers letter-quality to dot-matrix.
Needs: 50 frame; 15 minutes/script. Sound filmstrips. Query only. Pays by outright purchase of $250-500/script.

‡MARYLAND PUBLIC TELEVISION, 11767 Bonita Ave., Owings Mills MD 21117. (301)337-4052. Head Writer: Dick George. Produces material "for general public audience; sometimes a specialized audience; people who get college credit by watching our telecourses, farmers who watch Farm Day, our agricultural news show, etc. The vast majority of our scripts are staff-written; however, when our staff is too busy to take on a new project, we do occasionally buy freelance material, perhaps 3 times a year." Buys all rights. No previously produced material. SASE. "We don't take outside submissions unless I've commissioned them." Send resume and samples, etc. Reports in 2 months.
Needs: Films (16mm) and video. "We do documentaries and instructional shows on many different subjects. Right now I need comedy sketches for Crabs, a local comedy show produced and aired live." Makes outright purchase; approximately $100/script minute, with exceptions.
Tips: Send resume and samples. "I'm *not* looking for program ideas—I'm in occasional need of writers to develop *our* program ideas."

ED MARZOLA & ASSOCIATES, 11846 Ventura Blvd., Studio City CA 91604. Vice President: William Case. Produces material for worldwide broadcast. SASE. Reports in 2 weeks.
Needs: "We now produce television programs and feature-length films for theatrical release." Produces 35mm films and videotaped presentations. "We negotiate each case individually." Query with samples or submit resume. Pays according to Writers Guild standards.

‡THE MEDIA GROUP, LTD., 2215 29th St. SE, Grand Rapids MI 49508. (616)247-1364. Producer: Kenneth Schmidt. "We work primarily with two excellent industrial writers." Approximately 120 finished pages/year. Buys all rights. No previously produced material. SASE. Catalog for 8x10 SAE and 53¢ postage.
Needs: Produces film/tape prospects entirely. Industrial—corporate identification; educational, instructive (some interactive disk and tape). Promotional/sales, and occasionally commercial scripts. Style—mainly taking technical information and presenting it understandably to a select audience. Style varies with project. Length: between 6-20 pages (average). Films (16 and 35mm), tapes and cassettes and interactive disk, tape. Query with samples. Submit synopsis/outline, completed script and resume. Pays by outright purchase—$100/finished page (generally), more for more involved writing.
Tips: "Our clients want direct contact with our freelance writers for meetings. Our writers need industry writ-

ing background—technically and production-oriented, and in instructive design. Writers should also be immediately available for meetings with clients. Interactive is on the upswing in training. A good understanding of technical flow-charting and instructive design is essential in that area. We incorporate media tools (digital video effects, computer graphics) into our programs. Writers should have basic understanding of how to write for such elements."

MEDIA LEARNING SYSTEMS, INC., 1532 Rose Villa St., Pasadena CA 91106. (818)449-0006. President: Jim Griffith. Produces "custom" material for corporate, industrial, educational, and product promotional audience. 50% freelance written. Buys 12 scripts/year. Buys 1-2 scripts/year from unpublished/unproduced writers. All of scripts are unagented submissions. Buys all rights. No previously produced material. Computer printout submissions acceptable. SASE. Reports in 1 month. "Writers may contact us via the phone."
Needs: Film loops, filmstrips, multimedia kits, overhead transparencies, phonograph records, slides, tapes and cassettes, and teaching machine programs. Also produces scripts for video for kindergarten through grade 12 learning programs. Sometimes pays expenses of writers on assignment.
Tips: "We are looking for training/instructional material on any subject matter."

☐**MEDIACOM DEVELOPMENT CORP.**, Box 1926, Simi Valley CA 93062. (213)552-9988 or (818)991-5452. Director/Program Development: Felix Girard. Buys all rights or first rights. SASE. Reports in 1 month.
Needs: Produces charts, sound filmstrips, 16mm films, multimedia kits, overhead transparencies, tapes and cassettes, slides and videotape with programmed instructional print materials, broadcast and cable TV programs. Query with samples. Negotiates payment depending on project.
Tips: "Send short samples of work. We are especially interested in flexibility to meet clients' demands and creativity in treatment of precise subject matter. We are looking for good, fresh projects (both special and series) for cable and pay TV markets."

‡**MERIWETHER PUBLISHING LTD. (Contemporary Drama Service)**, Box 457, Downers Grove IL 60515. Editor: Arthur Zapel. "We publish how-to materials in book filmstrip, game and audio cassette formats. We are interested in materials for high school and college level students only." Christian activity book mss accepted. 90% freelance written. Buys 20-25 scripts/year from unpublished/unproduced writers. 95% of scripts are unagented submissions. Query. We will consider elementary level religious materials and plays." Computer printout submissions acceptable; no dot-matrix. Pays royalty; buys some mss outright. Sometimes pays expenses of writers on assignment. Recent titles: *Theatre Games for Young Performers*, by Maria C. Novelly (book).
Tips: "We publish a wide variety of speech contest materials for high school students."

‡**MILADY PUBLISHING CORPORATION**, 3839 White Plains Rd., Bronx NY 10467. (212)881-3000. Business Education Editor: Harry Moon. Produces occupational educational material for students. Buys all rights. "We also have some royalty arrangements in so far as print materials are concerned." No previously produced material. SASE. Reports in 2 weeks on queries; 1 month on submissions.
Needs: Charts, filmstrips (sound), overhead transparencies, slides, tapes and cassettes and video slides. Query. Makes outright purchase. Payment depends on the size and nature of project.

MOTIVATION MEDIA, INC., 1245 Milwaukee Ave., Glenview IL 60025. (312)297-4740. Executive Producer: Frank Stedronsky. Produces customized material for salespeople, customers, corporate/industrial employees and distributors. 50% freelance written. Buys 100 scripts/year from unpublished/unproduced writers. All scripts produced are unagented submissions. Query with samples. SASE. Reports in 1 month. Buys all rights.
Needs: Material for all audiovisual media—particularly marketing-oriented (sales training, sales promotional, sales motivational) material. Produces sound filmstrips, 16mm films, multimedia sales meeting programs, videotapes and cassettes and slide sets. Software should be AV-oriented. Pays $150-5,000.

MRC FILMS & VIDEO, Div. McLaughlin Research Corp., 71 W. 23rd St., New York NY 10010. (212)989-1754. Executive Producer: Larry Mollot. "Audience varies with subject matter, which is wide and diverse." 50% freelance written. Buys 20% of scripts from unpublished/unproduced writers. All scripts produced are unagented submissions. Writer "should have an ability to visualize concepts and to express ideas clearly in words. Realistic, believable dialogue is important. Experience in film or video scriptwriting is desirable. Write us, giving some idea of background. Submit samples of writing. We are looking for new talent. No unsolicited material accepted. Work upon assignment only." Query. SASE.
Needs: Industrial, documentary, educational and television films, as well as TV commercials and public service announcements. Also, public relations, teaching and motivational films and filmstrips. "Some subjects are highly technical in the fields of aerospace and electronics. Others are on personal relationships, selling techniques, ecology, etc. A writer with an imaginative visual sense is important." Produces 16mm films, sound

filmstrips, video programs, audio tapes and cassettes. Fee depends on nature and length of job. Typical fees: $600-1,200 for script for 10-minute film; $1,200-2,000 for script for 20-minute film; $1,500-3,000 for script for 30-minute film. For narration writing only, the range is $300-600 for a 10-minute film; $500-900 for 20-minute film; $600-1,200 for 30-minute film. For scriptwriting services by the day, fee is $80-150/day. All fees may be higher on specific projects with higher budgets.

MULTI-MEDIA PRODUCTIONS, INC., Box 5097, Stanford CA 94305. Program Manager: Mark Vining. Produces audiovisual instructional material for secondary (grades 9-12) schools. 100% freelance written. Buys 20 programs/year; 8 from unpublished/unproduced writers. All scripts produced are unagented submissions. Query with samples, if available. Buys all rights. Computer printout submissions acceptable; prefers letter-quality to dot-matrix. Reports in 6 weeks. Free catalog.
Needs: Sound filmstrip or video material suitable for general high school social studies curricula: history, biography, sociology, psychology, student health, anthropology, archeology and economics. "Style should be straightforward, lively, objective and interactive." Approximate specifications (filmstrip): 50 frames, 10-15 minutes/program part; 1- or 2-part programs. Writer supplies script, slides for filmstrip, and teacher's manual (per our format). Pays royalties quarterly, based on 15% of return on each program sold. "Programs with a central academic theme sell best. Program subjects should adhere to secondary curricula and to student-interactive instructional methods."
Recent Production: *The Pullman Strike* (sound filmstrip).
Tips: "We are looking for programs that engage the viewer with their controversy, timelines, and universal appeal. Sound filmstrips still do best when they challenge the student in an interactive way. This may be by presenting conflicting viewpoints or by directly inviting the student to participate in the program. Programs that challenge students will always find a market."

MULTIVISION INTERNATIONAL INC., 340 W. Huron, Chicago IL 60610. (312)337-2010. Creative Director: Michael Knab. "Most of our work is motivational/corporate image/employee communications." Buys about 50 scripts/year. Buys variable rights. Electronic disk submissions via Exxon System OK. Computer printout submissions acceptable; no dot-matrix. SASE. Reports in 2 weeks.
Needs: 16 and 35mm films, models, multimedia kits, slides, tapes and cassettes, videotape presentations, and all print. Query with samples or submit synopsis/outline. Pays in royalty or outright purchase.
Tips: "We look for quality writing and imagination."

BURT MUNK & COMPANY, 666 Dundee Rd., Northbrook IL 60062. (312)564-0855. President: Burton M. Munk. Produces material for industrial, sales training, product information, and education (schools). 100% freelance written. Works with approximately 10 writers/year. All scripts are unagented submissions. "We deal directly with writers but do not receive submissions of scripts." Buys all rights. Electronic submissions OK via Apple II Plus or Apple IIe, 64K, DOS 3.3. Does not return material; "all our work is 'made to order' for specific client needs—we are a custom house."
Needs: Sound filmstrips, slides, tapes and cassettes, 16mm films and videotapes. Also produces scripts for video. Open for software ideas. "We will contact individual writers who seem suitable for our projects." Makes outright purchase. Sometimes pays expenses of writers on assignment.
Tips: "We have published one very successful software program and are open for more. We will accept unsolicited ideas in disk form (Apple II Plus, 64K, DOS 3.3)."

HENRY NASON PRODUCTIONS, INC., 555 W. 57th St., New York NY 10019. (212)757-5437. President: Henry Nason. Produces custom audiovisual presentations for corporate clients. 90% freelance written. Query with samples or contact for personal interview. Buys all rights. Computer printout submissions acceptable; prefers letter-quality to dot-matrix. SASE. Reports in 1 month.
Needs: Usually 10- to 15-minute scripts on corporate subjects, such as sales, marketing, employee benefits, products, systems, public affairs, etc. Usually freestanding audiovisual modules. "The style should be clear and relaxed, well-researched and organized. Writers must live in the New York City area." Produces slide, multimedia presentations and video scripts. Pays an average of 8-10% of production budget. Sometimes pays expenses of writers on assignment.

‡□ **NETWORK COMMUNICATIONS LTD.**, 14524 85th Ave., Edmonton, Alberta T5R 3Z4 Canada. (403)489-1044. President: R. Schwartz. Produces material for advertising, cable TV, government, etc. 50% freelance written. 100% of scripts are unagented submissions. Submit resume and sample concept or script. Computer printout submissions acceptable; prefers letter-quality to dot-matrix. SASE. Reports in 3 weeks.
Needs: Produces cable programs, industrial films and TV commercials (35mm, 16mm or videotape). Pays by hourly rate, percentage of budget dependent upon project. Sometimes pays expenses of writers on assignment.

‡**NYSTROM**, 3333 N. Elston Ave., Chicago IL 60618. (312)463-1144. Editorial Director: Darrell A. Coppock. Produces material for school audiences (kindergarten through 12th grade). Required credentials depend on topics and subject matter and approach desired. Query. Computer printout and disk submissions OK. SASE. Free catalog.
Needs: Educational material on social studies, earth and life sciences, career education, reading, language arts and mathematics. Produces charts, sound filmstrips, models, multimedia kits, overhead transparencies and realia. Pays according to circumstances.

OCEAN REALM TELEVISION, 2333 Brickell Ave., Miami FL 33129. (305)285-0252. President: Richard H. Stewart. Produces ocean-related material for broad and narrow cast audience. Works with 8 writers/year. Buys all rights and first serial rights. Previously produced material OK. SASE. Reports in 1 month.
Needs: Tapes and cassettes. Query with samples.

OUR SUNDAY VISITOR, INC., Religious Education Dept., 200 Noll Plaza, Huntington IN 46750. (219)356-8400. Director of Religious Education: Joseph Laiacona. Produces material for students (kindergarten through 12th grade), adult religious education groups and teacher trainees. "We are very concerned that the materials we produce meet the needs of today's church." Query. SASE. Free catalog.
Needs: "Proposals for projects should be no more than 2 pages in length, in outline form. Programs should display up-to-date audiovisual techniques and cohesiveness. Broadly speaking, material should deal with religious education, including liturgy and daily Christian living, as well as structured catechesis. It must not conflict with sound Catholic doctrine, and should reflect modern trends in education." Produces educational books, charts, sound filmstrips and multimedia kits. "Work-for-hire and royalty arrangements possible."
Tips: "We're interested in two types of background: audiovisual and religious education. Very few people have both and cannot be expected to perform equally well in each area. We want the best in either field."

PEAK PRODUCTIONS, Box 329, Winter Park CO 80482. (303)726-5881. President: Jim Anderson. Produces all kinds of audiovisual material. Buys all rights, first rights or variable rights. SASE. Reports in 1 month.
Needs: Tapes and cassette, television shows/series, and videotape presentations. Currently interested in the following: education (12-18 minutes); news (all lengths); sports (all lengths); and promotional material. Query with samples. Pays variable rate.

PHOTO COMMUNICATION SERVICES, INC., 6410 Knapp NE, Ada MI 49301. (616)676-1499. President: Michael Jackson. Produces commercial, industrial, sales, training, etc. material. 95% freelance written. Buys 25% of scripts from unpublished/unproduced writers. 95% of scripts produced are unagented submissions. Buys all rights and first serial rights. Electronic submissions OK via IBM PC format, Zenith 96 TPI format (disks); 300 or 1200 Baud Modem, or on the Source, I.D. # BBH782 or MCI Mail. Computer printout submissions acceptable. SASE. Reports in 1 month on queries; 2 weeks on scripts. Writer's guidelines for SAE.
Needs: Multimedia kits, slides, tapes and cassettes, and video presentations. Primarily interested in 35mm multimedia, 1-24 projectors. Query with samples or submit completed script and resume. Pays in outright purchase or by agreement.

PHOTOCOM PRODUCTIONS, Box 3135, Pismo Beach CA 93449. President: Steven C. LaMarine. Produces material for schools, junior high to university level. 25% freelance written. Query with outline/synopsis. Also produces software; tutorials, learning games and simulations that appeal to vocational teachers. "We added educational computer software nearly two years ago and are eager to build this line. Any programs to be considered must be accompanied by documentation and be 'user friendly': TRS 80, Apple, IBM." Buys about 10 scripts/year from unpublished/unproduced writers. All scripts produced are unagented submissions. "Most writing is done in-house or by local talent where interaction with our staff and subject matter experts is easier. However, we are willing to consider projects from any good writer." Buys filmstrip rights. Computer printout submissions acceptable. SASE. Reports in 3 weeks. Free guidelines.
Needs: "We're most interested in how-tos in vocational areas that can be used in high school shop classes or adult education classes. Material that we've been buying is 60-70 frames long and the narration runs about 8-9 minutes." Produces sound filmstrips, multimedia kits and slide sets. Pays 10-15% royalty or $200 minimum/script.
Tips: "Many AV producers are taking on computer software as a logical extension of their services. This is a hot area, but with so many programs becoming available, schools are more discriminating than ever about what they buy."

□ **PHOTOGRAPHIC ILLUSTRATION COMPANY**, 2220 W. Magnolia Blvd., Burbank CA 91505. (818)849-7345. Executive Producer: John Denlinger. Produces material for corporate and public audience. 20% freelance written. Buys 10 scripts/year. Buys all rights. No previously produced material. Electronic sub-

missions OK via IBM Displaywriter. Computer printout submissions acceptable; prefers letter-quality to dot-matrix. SASE. Reports "as requested." Catalog for SAE.
Needs: Charts, films, silent and sound filmstrips and multimedia kits, overhead transparencies, slides, tapes and cassettes, videotape presentations, multimedia. Specific cable TV needs include projects under development. Also needs scripts for video, depending on clients' needs. Query. Pays by outright purchase. Sometimes pays the expenses of writers on assignment.

PREMIER VIDEO FILM & RECORDING CORP., (formerly Premier Film & Recording Corp.), 3033 Locust, St. Louis MO 63103. (314)531-3555. Secretary/Treasurer: Grace Dalzell. Produces material for the corporate community, religious organizations, political arms, and hospital and educational groups. Buys 50-100 scripts/year. Mostly unagented assignments. Buys all rights; "very occasionally the writer retains rights." Previously produced material OK; "depends upon original purposes and markets." Computer printout submissions acceptable. SASE. Reports "within a month or as soon as possible."
Needs: "Our work is all custom produced with the needs being known only as required." 35mm film loops, super 8mm and 35mm films, silent and sound filmstrips, video production, cable TV material, multimedia kits, overhead transparencies, phonograph records, slides, and tapes and cassettes." Submit complete script and resume. Pays in accordance with Writers Guild standards or by outright purchase of $100 or "any appropriate sum."
Tips: "Always place without fail *occupational pursuit*, name, address and phone number in upper right hand corner of resume. We're looking for writers with creativity, good background and a presentable image."

PRENTICE-HALL MEDIA, INC., 150 White Plains Rd., Tarrytown NY 10591. (914)631-8300. Managing Editor: Sandra Carr Grant. Produces material for secondary, postsecondary vocational and science students. Buys 50 scripts/year. Buys all rights. Previously produced material OK. SASE. Reports in 1 month. Catalog for SAE.
Needs: "We will be looking for audiovisual treatments for high technology training." Sound filmstrips. Query with samples or submit synopsis/outline. Pays by outright purchase of $350 minimum.
Tips: "We look for clarity of language, ability to write 'visual' scripts and facility with technical subject matter."

□ **PRIMALUX VIDEO**, 30 W. 26th St., New York NY 10010. (212)206-1402. Director: M. Clarke. Produces industrial and training material; promotional pieces. 70% freelance written. Buys 10 scripts/year; works with 2 writers/year. Buys all rights. No previously produced material. Computer printout submissions acceptable.
Needs: Television show/series and videotape presentations. Produces scripts for video and fashion show material for cable TV. Query with samples. Pays royalty or by outright purchase. Pays expenses of writers on assignment.

BILL RASE PRODUCTIONS, INC., 955 Venture Ct., Sacramento CA 95825. (916)929-9181. President: Bill Rase. Produces material for business education and mass audience. Buys 20 scripts maximum/year. Buys all rights. SASE. Reports "when an assignment is available."
Needs: Produces silent and sound filmstrips, multimedia kits, slides, cassettes, videotapes and video productions. Submit resume, sample page or two of script, and description of expertise. Pays negotiable rate in 30 days.
Tips: "Call and ask for Bill Rase personally. Must be within 100 miles and thoroughly professional."

‡**REGENTS PUBLISHING CO.**, 2 Park Ave., New York NY 10016. (212)889-2780. Acquisitons Editor: John Chapman. "No audiovisual material without textbook. Material is for students of English as a second language/foreign language. No completed manuscripts purchased. Our firm contracts with authors to produce material to our specifications." Buys all rights. No previously produced material. SASE. Reports in 6 weeks on queries. Catalog for business size SAE and 80¢ postage.
Needs: Tapes and cassettes. "Submit resume showing education, writing experience, and teaching experiences. Pays 2-10% royalty.
Tips: "Potential authors must have advanced degree in applied linguistics, language teaching, or other related field. They also must have language teaching experience preferably both in the United States and overseas."

RHYTHMS PRODUCTIONS, Whitney Bldg., Box 34485, Los Angeles CA 90034. President: R.S. White. "Our audience is generally educational, with current projects in elementary early childhood." 50% freelance written. Buys 6 scripts/year from unpublished/unproduced writers. 50% of scripts are unagented submissions. Query. "We need to know a writer's background and credits and to see samples of his work." Computer printout submissions acceptable; prefers letter-quality to dot-matrix. SASE.
Needs: Teacher resource books; phonograph records; video scripts for children's stories and music. "Content

is basic to the resource books; educational background is a necessity. For our phonograph records, we accept only fully produced tapes of a professional quality. If tapes are sent, include return postage.''

SANDY CORP., 1500 W. Big Beaver Rd., Troy MI 48084. (313)649-0800. Manager of Human Resources: David Southworth. Produces material for sales and technical/automotive audiences. Works with 50-200 freelance writers. Buys all rights. SASE. Reports in 1 month on queries.
Needs: Articles up to 500 words on how Chevrolet or GMC truck dealers are doing an outstanding job of selling cars and trucks, servicing cars and trucks, participating in community activities, recognizing employee achievement—can use b&w glossies of story events. Produces various publications (samples on request). Submit outline/synopsis.
Tips: "Submit only if you have good relationship with local Chevrolet or GMC truck dealership and can write copy and take pictures reflecting a professional knowledge of the business."

‡**SAVE THE CHILDREN**, 54 Wilton Rd., Westport CT 06880. (203)226-7272. Producer: Joseph Loya. Generally buys all rights, "but it depends on project. We use work only written for specific assignments." Produces 16mm films, tapes and cassettes, 2¼x2¼ slides, posters and displays.
Needs: General (radio and TV); and education (high school, college and adult). Pays $250-500 minimum/assignment.

SAXTON COMMUNICATIONS GROUP LTD., 605 3rd Ave., New York NY 10158. (212)953-1300. Creative Director: Allen Halpern. Produces material for industrial, consumer and sales audiences, AV presentations and meetings. Submit resume. SASE.
Needs: "We work with more than ten outside writers regularly. We buy copy and scripts for approximately thirty projects a year."

SCIENCE RESEARCH ASSOCIATES, 155 N. Wacker, Chicago IL 60606. (312)984-7000. Script Coordinator: Corey Cather. Buys 30-40 scripts/year; works with 10-15 writers/year. Buys all rights. No previously produced material. Electronic submissions OK. Computer printout submissions acceptable; no dot-matrix. SASE. Reports in 2 weeks. Free writer's guidelines.
Needs: Videotape presentations. Currently interested in "more data processing training videotapes on IBM software products. Tapes will be 7-15 minutes and will have 50-100% animation." Submit treatment and 3 drafts of script/storyboards. Set fee to be determined prior to agreement.

‡**SCOTT RESOURCES, INC.**, Box 2121, Fort Collins CO 80522. (303)484-7445. Produces material for public and private school audiences, kindergarten through grade 12. Supplemental math and science materials. 90% freelance written. Works with 3-5 authors/year. Buys 3-5 scripts/year from unpublished/unproduced writers. 100% of scripts are unagented submissions. Electronic submissions OK. Computer printout submissions acceptable. Free math and science catalog.
Needs: Looking for written or AV material and computer software in earth science/geology and elementary/junior high mathematics. Also produces scripts for videos. Query with samples. Will negotiate equitable royalty.

‡**SCREENSCOPE, INC.**, #204, 3600 M St. NW, Washington DC 20007. (202)965-6900. President: Marilyn Weiner. Produces material for schools, industry, television and theatre. Buys all rights. Submit resume. SASE. Reports in 1 month.
Needs: "For education we need a script which can communicate to many grade levels. Style, format, length, etc. are discussed with producer and client." Produces 16mm and 35mm films and slides. Buys 20 scripts/year. Pays by outright purchase.

SEVEN OAKS PRODUCTIONS, 9145 Sligo Creek Pkwy., Silver Spring MD 20901. (301)587-0030. Production Manager: M. Marlow. 80% freelance written. Produces material for students, civic and professional groups, and PTA chapters. Buys 10-20 scripts from 10 writers/year. 65% of scripts are unagented submissions. Buys all rights or first rights, but rights purchased are negotiable. Query only first. Will not return unsolicited material. Send letter about idea first; will keep on file. Computer printout submissions acceptable; prefers letter-quality to dot-matrix. SASE. Reports in 2 months.
Needs: Educational, medical, safety and general entertainment material. "We look for clarity in style, imagination with the ability to get information across and accomplish objectives, the ability to meet deadlines and to dig if necessary to get sufficient information to make the script better than another on the same subject. Writers should know the film format." Produces 16mm films, video disk computer active programs, multimedia kits, phonograph records, tapes and cassettes, and slide sets. Payment negotiable according to project.

PETER SIMMONS PRODUCTIONS, 660 Main St., Woburn MA 01801. (617)933-6377. Producer: Russ Chapman. Produces material for private corporations—their employees, sales people or potential customers.

"We produce approximately 25 slide shows and/or films and/or videotapes each year, and we're growing." Buys all rights. SASE. Reports in 2 weeks on queries; 1 week on submissions. Free catalog.
Needs: "Our slide shows vary in length from 7 to 25 minutes. Format is generally narration, sometimes interspersed with testimonials from clients, etc. Videotape scripts are more complex, obviously including dialogue. Our clients are a wide variety of companies from the private sector: computer companies, electronics manufacturers, food handlers, colleges." Produces 16mm films, sound filmstrips and slides. Query with samples. Buys by outright purchase.
Tips: "Send us a sample of your work, then follow up with a phone call. We would prefer writers with a background in the visual media and an ability to write a 'visual' script."

□ **SINGER COMMUNICATIONS, INC.**, 3164 Tyler Ave., Anaheim CA 92801. (714)527-5650. Acting President: Natalie Carlton. 40% freelance written. Produces material for foreign organizations; electronic publishing (U.S. and foreign countries). Buys 500 scripts/year; 120 scripts/year from previously unpublished/unproduced writers. 90% of scripts produced are unagented submissions. Works with 200 writers/year; represents publishing companies. 90% of scripts are unagented submissions. Buys syndication or book rights. Previously produced material OK. Electronic submissions OK via IMB, but requires hard copy also. Computer printout submissions acceptable; prefers letter-quality to dot-matrix. SASE. Reports in 2 weeks on queries; 3 weeks on submissions. Catalog for 9x11 SAE and $1 postage; writer's guidelines for 9x11 SAE and $1 postage.
Needs: 16mm films, overhead transparencies, slides, tapes and cassettes, television shows/series, videotape presentations, and educational films for foreign TV. Currently interested in AV material "of worldwide interest only for overseas TV and electronic publishing." Syndicates freelance material for the cable TV market. Query with samples or submit synopsis/outline. Pays negotiable rate. Pays expenses of writers on assignment.
Tips: "Keep international market in mind."

‡**SKAGGS TELECOMMUNICATIONS SERVICE**, Box 27477, Salt Lake City UT 84127. (801)539-1427. Manager of Corporate/Industrial Production: Brent Robison. "Produces material primarily for retail drug and grocery store employees (for parent company, American Stores); however, may also be employees and/or customers of any type of business." Commissions approximately 12 scripts/year. Buys all rights. No previously produced material. SASE. Reports in 2 weeks.
Needs: Videotape. Query with samples. Makes negotiable outright purchases; usually $50-100/finish minute (estimated).
Tips: "Show me a wide variety of scripts written in the past. If writers haven't written for industrial TV, don't bother to query. We look for writers with a thorough awareness of and experience with the techniques of TV scriptwriting; that is, writing for the spoken word, not for the printed page. Also we want awareness of instructional design and how to entertain while informing."

PHOEBE T. SNOW PRODUCTIONS, INC., 240 Madison Ave., New York NY 10016. (212)679-8756. Creative Director: Deborah R. Herr. Produces material for corporate uses, sales force, in-house training, etc. 90% freelance written. Buys 20-40 scripts/year from published/produced writers only. All scripts produced are unagented submissions. Buys all rights. Computer printout submissions acceptable; prefers letter-quality to dot-matrix. SASE. Reports in 2 weeks on queries; 1 month on mss.
Needs: 16mm films, sound filmstrips and slides. Query with samples and resume. Pays by outright purchase.
Tips: "Have some understanding of AV for corporations. This is not the educational field. We're looking for creative writers who work with speed and can take direction. Be aware of short deadlines and some low budgets."

JOE SNYDER & COMPANY LTD., 155 W. 68th St., New York NY 10023. (212)595-5925. Chairman: Joseph H. Snyder. Produces material for corporations, management seminars and employee training. Buys all rights. Submit resume. SASE. Reports in 1 month.
Needs: Subject topics include education, motivation, management, productivity, speaking and writing. Produces multimedia kits, tapes and cassettes, and slides. Payment is in accordance with Writers Guild standards.
Tips: Especially interested in "sharpness and clarity."

SOUTH CAROLINA EDUCATIONAL TELEVISION NETWORK, Drawer L, Columbia SC 29250. (803)758-7261. Associate Director for State Agencies: Ms. Sandra V. Pedlow. Produces material for the general public; training and career development for business and industry; college courses; and on-going adult education in fields of medicine and technical education. Works only with freelancers in the South Carolina area. Buys all rights. Query or submit resume. SASE. Reports in 2 weeks.
Needs: "The Division of Continuing Education works in all media. Since, as a state agency, we work with other state agencies of varying needs, style, format, length, etc. are determined for each individual project." Produces 16mm films, multimedia kits, slides, videotape, live in-studio television productions, telecon-

ferences and related printed materials for training programs. Payment "depends on funding governed by South Carolina state law guidelines."

Tips: "If possible, come in for an interview and bring in samples of previous work."

SPENCER PRODUCTIONS, INC., 234 5th Ave., New York NY 10001. (212)697-5895. General Manager: Bruce Spencer. Produces material for high school students, college students and adults. Occasionally uses freelance writers with considerable talent. Query. SASE.

Needs: 16mm films, prerecorded tapes and cassettes. Satirical material only. Pay is negotiable.

Tips: "For a further insight into our philosophy, read *How to Thrive on Rejection or Don't Get Mad . . . Get Even*, by our executive producer, Alan Abel."

□ **SPINDLER PRODUCTIONS**, 1501 Broadway, New York NY 10036. (212)730-1255. Creative Directors: Richard Cardran and Victor Spindler. Produces material for corporations, ad agencies and upper end of consumer audience. 90% freelance written. Buys 10-20 scripts/year; works with 4-10 writers/year. All of scripts are unagented submissions. Buys all rights. No previously produced material. Electronic submissions OK via TRS 80, Tandy 2000, Telex/Easy Link, 300 Baud, 1 stopbit, 8 bit, no parity. Level 2 or 3 telecopy computer printout submissions acceptable. SASE. Reports in 2 weeks. Catalog for 9x12 SAE and 1 first class stamp.

Needs: TV commercials, industrials, training films, charts, film loops, 16 and 35mm films, multimedia kits, overhead transparencies, slides, tapes and cassettes, teaching machine programs, videotape presentations, and AV presentations. Produces scripts for video—commercials, industrials, training and corporate. Produces material for cable TV (informercials). Query with sample scripts preferably of used/published material or submit outline/synopsis or completed script and resume. Pays by outright purchase. Pays the expenses of writers on assignment.

SPOTTSWOOD STUDIOS, 2524 Old Shell Rd., Box 7061, Mobile AL 36607. (205)478-9387. Co-owner: M.W. Spottswood. "We normally work for sponsors (but not always) who seek public attention." Buys 1-2 scripts/yr. Buys all rights. Query with resume and samples. Computer printout submissions acceptable. SASE. Reports in 2 weeks.

Needs: Business, religious and general. Produces 16mm films and 8mm loops, sound filmstrips, videotape and slide sets. Pays by outright purchase.

AL STAHL ANIMATED, 1600 Broadway, New York NY 10019. (212)265-2942. President: Al Stahl. Produces industrial, sales promotion, educational and television commercial material. Buys first rights. Query. SASE. Free catalog.

Needs: "We specialize in making movies from slides and in converting slide shows and multimedia (three or more screens) into a one-screen movie." Produces 8mm and 16mm films, and multimedia kits. Pays by outright purchase.

‡**STARR/ROSS CORPORATE COMMUNICATIONS**, (formerly Starr Photo Productions, Inc.), 2727 Ponce de Leon, Coral Gables FL 33134. (305)446-3300. Contact: Bob Ross, partner. Produces slide and videotape presentations for corporate audience. Works with 6 writers/year. Buys all rights. Prefers personal inquiries only. Query. Pays $150-1,500 in outright purchase.

Tips: Looks for "professional writers with a track record." Occasionally needs scripts in Spanish.

□ **E.J. STEWART, INC.**, 525 Mildred Ave., Primos PA 19018. (215)626-6500. "Our firm is a television production house providing programming for the broadcast, industrial, educational and medical fields. Government work is also handled." 50% freelance written. Buys 50 scripts/year; buys 5% scripts/year from unpublished/unproduced writers. Buys all rights. Computer printout submissions acceptable. SASE. Reports "when needed."

Needs: "We produce programming for our clients' specific needs. We do not know in advance what our needs will be other than general scripts for commercials and programs depending upon requests that we receive from clients." Cable television material. Videotapes. Submit resume only. Pays in negotiable outright purchase. Sometimes pays expenses of writers on assignment.

Tips: "A trend in the audiovisual field (film, cassette, software, slides, video, etc.) freelancer writers should be aware of is interactive laser disk programming."

SUNTREE PRODUCTIONS, LTD., 220 E. 23rd St., New York NY 10010. (212)686-4111. President: D.W. Funt. Produces material for commercial, industrial and educational audiences. "We bought three scripts last year from two writers. Submit resume; we will call writers with interesting resumes when projects are available." Buys all rights.

Needs: "We are contract producers. Our needs vary from big budget multimedia shows to educational filmstrips. We look for speed, accuracy, flexibility, wit and intelligence." Produces sound filmstrips, videotapes,

tapes and cassettes, and slide sets. "Payment varies according to the project and the writer's experience." **Tips:** To keep pace with trends in this field, "writers must be conceptual as well as verbal."

TALCO PRODUCTIONS, 279 E. 44th St., New York NY 10017. (212)697-4015. President: Alan Lawrence. Vice President: Peter Yung. Produces variety of material for motion picture theatres, TV, clubs, business, etc. Audiences range from young children to senior citizens. 20-40% freelance written. Buys scripts from published/produced writers only. All scripts produced are unagented submissions. Buys all rights. No previously published material. SASE. "We maintain a file of writers and call on those with experience in the same general category as the project in production. We do not accept unsolicited manuscripts. We prefer to receive a writer's resume listing credits. If his/her background merits, we will be in touch when a project seems right." Reports in 3 weeks on queries.
Needs: Films (16-35mm); filmstrips (sound); phonograph records; slides; tapes and cassettes; and videotape. Query. Makes outright purchase/project and in accordance with Writer's Guild standards (when appropriate).
Tips: "Query only with SASE with resume. *Do not send* scripts or published or unpublished material."

‡**TEL-AIR INTERESTS, INC.**, 1755 N.E. 149th St., Miami FL 33181. (305)944-3268. President: Grant H. Gravitt. Produces material for groups and theatrical and TV audiences. Buys all rights. Submit resume. SASE.
Needs: Documentary films on education, travel and sports. Produces films and videotape. Pays by outright purchase.

‡**TELEMATION PRODUCTIONS, INC.**, 7700 E. Iliff Ave., Denver CO 80231. (303)751-6000. Writer/Producer: Richard Schneider. "Telemation is a major video production firm with studios in Denver, Chicago, Phoenix and Seattle. We will forward contacts to the appropriate telemation facility from Denver." Produces material for corporate and industrial video. "All work is done on assignment." Buys all rights. No previously produced material. "We do not accept scripts—assignment only."
Needs: Video tape; interactive video disk programs for the corporate and industrial market—marketing, sales, training, product rollout, etc. Query with samples and resume. Makes outright purchase.
Tips: "Only writers with solid corporate and industrial video experience should contact us. Also, location near one of Telemation's facilities is essential."

‡**TELSTAR, INC.**, 366 N. Prior Ave., St. Paul MN 55104. Editor: Dr. Victor Kerns. Produces video material for adult, college-level audience, in industry and continuing education. Buys video recording rights. Query. Produces instructional videotapes not intended for broadcast.
Needs: Education (curricular materials for small group or independent study); business (training and development material); and communication skills. Looks for "the ability to chapterize/pace the instruction." Pays $100 plus royalties.

FRANCIS THOMPSON, INC., 231 E. 51st St., New York NY 10022. (212)759-4558. Vice President: Byron McKinney. Produces films for varied audiences. Commissions scriptwriting only.

ROGER TILTON FILMS, INC., 315 6th Ave., San Diego CA 92101. (619)233-6513. President: Roger Tilton. Audience varies with client. Submit resume. SASE. "We do not accept unrequested scripts. We will request samples if a writer is being considered." Buys all rights. Computer printout submissions acceptable; prefers letter-quality to dot-matrix. Reports in 2 weeks.
Needs: "Scripts are all on contract basis with specific details supplied by us or our clients. Subjects run full spectrum of topics and audiences." Produces sound filmstrips, 16mm, 35mm and 65mm films, and video cassettes. Makes outright purchase; "depends on project, quoted in advance."
Tips: Writers must demonstrate "ability to work within the constraints of the client."

TRANSTAR PRODUCTIONS, INC., Suite 170, 750 W. Hampden, Englewood CO 80110. (303)761-0595. Producer/Director: Doug Hanes. Produces primarily industrial material. 25% freelance written. Buys 5 scripts/year from unpublished/unproduced writers. 100% of scripts are unagented submissions. Buys 5-6 scripts/year. Buys all rights. No previously produced material. Computer printout submissions acceptable; prefers letter-quality to dot-matrix. SASE. Reporting time varies.
Needs: 8 and 16mm film loops, 16mm films, sound filmstrips, slides, tapes and cassettes, and videotape presentations. Also produces scripts for industrial sales and training. Submit resume. Pays negotiable rate. Sometimes pays expenses of writers on assignment.

TROLL ASSOCIATES, 320 Rt. 17, Mahwah NJ 07430. (201)529-4000. Contact: M. Schecter. Produces material for elementary and high school students. Buys approximately 200 scripts/year. Buys all rights. Query or submit outline/synopsis. SASE. Reports in 3 weeks. Free catalog.
Needs: Produces silent and sound filmstrips, multimedia kits, tapes and cassettes, and (mainly) books. Pays royalty or by outright purchase.

TUTOR/TAPE, 107 France St., Toms River NJ 08753. President: Richard R. Gallagher. Produces and publishes cassettes, filmstrips, software and visual aids including slides and transparencies for the college market. 50% freelance written. Half of scripts produced are unagented submissions. Buys average 5 scripts/year. "We are the largest publisher of prerecorded educational cassettes for the college market. We are capable of handling everything from writer to recording to packaging to marketing in a totally vertically integrated production-marketing publishing organization." Send brief synopsis or short outline stating credentials, education or experience. Computer printout submissions acceptable. SASE. Reports in 1 week.

Needs: 10 to 25 page scripts for 15 to 30 minute educational messages on college topics, including business, management, marketing, personnel, advertising, accounting, economics and other related material. We also seek remedial and study skills material useful to college students and suitable for audio presentation. Pays 15% royalty or by outright purchase.

Tips: "Writers should submit material relevant to students in college who need assistance in passing difficult courses, or interesting material which supplements college textbooks and enhances class work."

UNIVERSITY OF WISCONSIN STOUT TELEPRODUCTION CENTER, 800 S. Broadway, Menomonie WI 54751. (715)232-2622. Director of Instructional Television: Tim Fuhrmann. Produces instructional TV programs for primary, secondary, post secondary and specialized audiences. 10% freelance written. Buys scripts from published/produced writers only. All scripts produced are unagented submissions. "We produce ITV programs for national, regional and state distribution to classrooms around the U.S. and Canada." Buys all rights. Query with resume and samples of TV scripts. Computer printout submissions acceptable; prefers letter-quality to dot-matrix. SASE.

Needs: "Our clients fund programs in a 'series' format which tend to be 8-12 programs each." Produces only with one-inch broadcast quality. "I need materials from writers who have experience in writing instructional TV. I have an immediate need for writers with elementary teaching experience who can write a primary level reading series. Only the 'pros' need apply. We also have a need for writers in Wisconsin and Minnesota whom we can call on to write one or multi-program/series in instructional television."

Recent Production: *Out & About*, (kindergarten social philosophy funding agency: Wisconsin Educational Communications Band).

Tips: "Freelance writers should be aware of the hardware advances in broadcast and nonbroadcast. There are new avenues for writers to pursue in adult learning, computer assisted programming and interactive programming."

VISUAL HORIZONS, 180 Metro Park, Rochester NY 14623. (716)424-5300. President: Stanley Feingold. Produces material for general audiences. Buys 5 programs/year. Query with samples. SASE. Reports in 5 months. Free catalog.

Needs: Business, medical and general subjects. Produces silent and sound filmstrips, multimedia kits, slide sets and videotapes. Payment negotiable.

WREN ASSOCIATES, INC., 208 Bunn Dr., Princeton NJ 08540. Copy Department Head: Barbara Kram. Produces material for employees and sales people, and various sales and corporate presentations for Fortune 500 corporate clients. 20% freelance written. Buys 30-40 scripts/year from previously produced writers only. All scripts produced are unagented submissions. Buys all rights. No previously published material. Electronic submissions OK over CompuServe network, on IBM/Compaq, MS word, and Radio Shack TRS 80 II diskette. Computer printout submissions acceptable. SASE. Reports in 3 weeks. Catalog for #10 SAE and 1 first class stamp.

Needs: Produces 8mm film loops, 16mm films, sound filmstrips, multimedia kits, slides (multiprojector shows); tapes and cassettes, television shows/series (corporate networks); videotape presentations; interactive video on a project-by-project basis for clients and video scripts for industrial specialists on assignment. "We need freelance writers who can assimilate technical or business-oriented subject matter (e.g., telecommunications services, automotive). They must be able to present this material in a clear, entertaining presentation that *sells* the product." Query with samples. Pays $400-7,000/job. Sometimes pays expenses of writers on assignment.

Tips: "Freelance writers should be aware of interactive video disk, tape trend. It's the coming wave in training and P.O.P. sales."

‡**ZELMAN STUDIOS LTD.**, 623 Cortelyou Rd., Brooklyn NY 11218. (718)941-5500. General Manager: Jerry Krone. Produces material for business, education and fund-raising audiences. Query with samples and resume. SASE. Reports in 1 month. Buys all rights.

Needs: Produces film loop, silent and sound filmstrips, films, videotapes, audiocassettes and slides. Pays by outright purchase "by agreement, based on talent and turnaround."

ZM SQUARED, Box C-30, Cinnaminson NJ 08077. (609)786-0612. Contact: Pete Zakroff. "We produce AVs for a wide range of clients including education, business, industry and labor organizations." Buys 10 scripts/year; works with 4-5 writers/year. Buys all rights. No previously produced material. Electronic submissions OK via Apple system. Computer printout submissions acceptable. SASE. Reports in 2 weeks on queries; 1 month on submissions. Free catalog.

Needs: Silent filmstrips, kinescopes, multimedia kits, overhead transparencies, slides, tapes and cassettes, and videotape presentations. Query with or without samples. Pays 3-10% royalty or by outright purchase $150-750.

Playwriting

"What is important is that playwrights think about the world today," stress script editors and directors. A musical may be set in Charlemagne's time (*Pippin*) or a play may recreate the days of Mozart (*Amadeus*), but productions must be about *today*. "Arthur Miller's *The Crucible*, though set during the witch trials centuries ago, showed audiences what was going on in America in 1952," said Samuel French, Inc. editor Lawrence Harbison.

Today, though, playwrights might want to avoid historical plays. With the high costs of salaries, costumes, and sets, producers look for small cast plays. If additional characters don't contribute significantly to the story line, don't include them.

Producers continue to look for scripts with "substantial roles for women." Samuel French, for instance, needs scripts with numerous female roles since the majority of amateur theatre performers are women.

Reading and attending current plays is the best way to know what producers are buying. Too many playwrights' knowledge of theatre comes from reading the classics—"plays by dead Europeans," said Harbison. Knowing both classic and current plays is essential for playwrights. Many scriptwriters begin working for theatres or companies as interns or volunteers. Spend time on and off stage and backstage whenever possible. You must learn the idiosyncrasies of the medium and this learning can occur in New York or at regional theatres on the West Coast or Midwest.

One misconception among amateur theatres is that what succeeds in New York will be successful with their audiences. "What succeeds in New York is novelty," pointed out the Samuel French editor. "What succeeds with amateur theatre audiences is generally that which is familiar."

Don't write off "regional" theatres as minor league. They are often more "professional" than Broadway—and there are more opportunities for new playwrights there, says Harbison.

Attendance at any theatre production gives you insights into how audiences react to particular moments and types of characters. The Theatre Development Fund (Suite 2110, 1501 Broadway, New York NY 10036) enables playwrights to get reduced tickets. Audience Extras (163 W. 23rd St., New York, NY 10011; 1540 N. Highland Ave., Los Angeles, CA 90028; and 1169 Market St., San Francisco, CA 94103) is a source for getting inexpensive tickets after you've paid an annual membership fee. When contacting these organizations, be willing to follow their guidelines. In many cities, high school and college students can get discounts on tickets.

We've heard playwrights stress the importance of getting your work on the stage, but make sure that the production doesn't make your play untouchable for producers and publishers. "If a play is produced Off-Off Broadway under what is called the Actors Equity Showcase Code, the showcase actors have a hold on their roles for three years," said Harbison, "which means a subsequent professional producer must either book them in for his production or pay them off to the tune of three weeks' rehearsal salary—neither of which will he probably do."

Staged readings and productions of your play by colleges or community theatres will enable you to make revisions based on your audiences' reactions, thus, possibly making it more sellable.

"The big question with so many places isn't money," says one playwright.

"What it boils down to is what kinds of rights are they going to want to retain to your work. That's the thing the playwright has to be very, very careful about."

Organizations like New Dramatists (424 W. 44th St., New York, NY 10036) sponsor readings and encourage new talent. "We offer script-in-hand readings of our members' plays, panel discussions, writer studios, free theatre tickets, a national script distribution service and exchanges with theatres," said literary assistant Richard L. LeComte, assistant to the director of Script Development and Marketing.

Aspiring playwrights should also consider joining The Dramatists Guild (234 W. 44th St., New York, NY 10036). You need not have sold a script to be a member. Guild members receive the monthly *Dramatists Guild Newsletter* and *The Dramatists Guild Quarterly*; both contain information about marketing plays.

The closest thing to a playwright's Bible is the *Dramatists Sourcebook* (Theatre Communications Group, 355 Lexington Ave., New York, NY 10017). It lists theatres that consider unsolicited playscripts, play publishers, agents, fellowships, festivals and contests, conferences and workshops, and playwriting opportunities in film, radio and video. A useful directory is the *Theatre Directory* (Theatre Communications Group) listing nearly 275 professional nonprofit theatres. The Alliance of Resident Theatres—New York (formerly the Off-Off Broadway Alliance) will provide general information to playwrights and consultations only for members. The Alliance (Room 315, 325 Spring St., NY, New York 10013) also has information on its 85 member theatres.

Professional Format

Many playwrights use the format of *published* plays as a guideline to typing their unpublished manuscript. In books of plays for the general reader, the publisher puts as many words on a page as possible with a minimum amount of white space. Manuscripts to be studied by publishers, producers and actors should be as readable as possible, separating parenthetical remarks from dialogue in the reader's visual field. An example of proper manuscript format is available in *Guidelines*, available for $3, postpaid, from Samuel French, Inc., 45 W. 25th St., New York, NY 10010. Pica type is preferred by people who evaluate manuscripts.

Put your name, address, *and phone number* on the title page. Place your script in a two- or three-ring binder; some publishers don't like some of the newer clamped binders.

In mailing your submission, don't forget to enclose a self-addressed, stamped envelope with enough postage for the return of the script. (Most producers won't return scripts at their own expense.) Sometimes the evaluation of unsolicited scripts will take six months to a year so don't badger a producer into a quick response that would probably be *no*. Also, if a producer says he reviews only queries, write a query for your completed script. Some playhouses, to review more playwrights' work, will only consider queries with outlines/synopses of plays. Make sure that your submission is appropriate to the theatre or company to which you send it.

ACADEMY THEATRE, 1137 Peachtree St. NE, Atlanta GA 30309. (404)873-2518. Artistic Director: Frank Wittow. Produces 10 plays/year. 20% freelance written. 5% of scripts produced are unagented. Plays performed in Academy Theatre—415 seats thrust stage, and in Academy Lab Theatre, 100 seats, flexible stage. Professional productions tour the Southeast for elementary, high school, college and community audiences. Works with 2-5 unpublished/unproduced writers annually. Submit complete ms. "We accept unsolicited, year-round submissions." Computer printout submissions acceptable. Reports in 4 months. Buys negotiable rights. Pays negotiable royalty. SASE.
Needs: "Full length plays, one acts, children's plays, adaptations, translations, original plays of contemporary significance, plays that go beyond the conventions of naturalism; Transformational plays: actors playing multiple roles. Prefer small cast; unit set. Follow standard playwright submission guidelines and standard preparation of script." No sitcom love affairs, triangles; plays with very large casts. Special programs: "Academy Playwrights Lab is an ongoing program of workshop productions of previously unproduced full length and one

act plays by Southeastern playwrights. Deadline is open. The Atlanta New Play Project is sponsored each June by the Academy and other local theatres. The project includes staged readings, workshops, full productions as plays in progress with a forum for discussion of new works. Southeastern playwrights are specifically desired for this project."

Tips: "Writers should be aware of the obvious trends in funding for the arts; and therefore, submit scripts which might be within reason for production. Few region theatres around the country are in a position to produce large cast, multi-set, multi-media extravaganzas; and what's more *our* theatre audiences don't expect or want that from live theatre productions."

‡**ACTORS THEATRE OF LOUISVILLE**, 316 West Main St., Louisville KY 40202. (502)584-1265. Artistic Director: Jon Jory. Produces/publishes approximately 35 new plays of varying lengths/year. Professional productions are performed for subscription audience from diverse backgrounds. Submit complete ms for one-act plays; agented submissions only for full-length plays. Reports in 6-9 months on submissions. No computer printout submissions. Buys production (in Louisville only) rights. Offers variable royalty. SASE.
Needs: "We accept only one-act plays—unsolicited. No children's shows or musicals. We produce both full-lengths and one-acts."

ALASKA REPERTORY THEATRE, Suite 201, 705 W. 6th Ave., Anchorage AK 99501. (907)276-2327. Artistic Director: Robert J. Farley. Produces 4-5 plays/year. Professional plays performed for Alaskan audiences. Submit complete ms. Reports in 5 months. Pays 3%+ royalty "depending on work." SASE.
Needs: Produces all types of plays.

‡**ALLEY THEATRE**, 615 Texas Ave., Houston TX 77002. A resident professional theatre; large stage seating 798; arena stage seating 296. 15% of scripts are unagented submissions. Works with 10 unpublished/unproduced writers annually. Computer printout submissions acceptable; prefers letter-quality to dot-matrix.
Needs: "Good plays of no more than 2½ hours in length. Cast restriction of no more than 15 actors." Pays variable royalty arrangements. Send synopsis and letter of inquiry. SASE. Reports in 4 months. Produces 10-15 plays/year.
Recent Play Productions: *Starry Night*, by Monte Merrick.
Tips: Trends on the American stage that freelance writers should be aware of include alternatives to realistic style.

AMAS REPERTORY THEATRE, INC., 1 E. 104th St., New York NY 10029. (212)369-8000/8001. Artistic Director: Rosetta LeNoire. Produces 6 plays/year. 1 or 2 scripts produced are unagented submissions. "AMAS is a professional, off-off-Broadway showcase theatre. We produce three showcase productions of original musicals each season; these are presented for a sophisticated New York theatre audience. A number have gone on to commercial productions, the best known of which is *Bubbling Brown Sugar*. We also present two children's theatre productions and one summer tour." Query with synopsis or submit complete script with cassette tape of score or of partial score. Computer printout submissions acceptable; prefers letter-quality to dot-matrix. Reports in 2 months. "Be prepared to wait at least one year or more between acceptance and production. Our standard contract calls for a small percentage of gross and royalties to AMAS, should the work be commercially produced within a specified period."
Needs: "*Musicals only*; in addition, all works will be performed by multi-racial casts. Musical biographies are especially welcome. Cast size should be under 15 if possible, including doubling. Because of the physical space, set requirements should be relatively simple."
Tips: "AMAS is dedicated to bringing all people—regardless of race, creed, color or religion—together through the creative arts. In writing for AMAS, an author should keep this overall goal in mind."

AMERICAN CONSERVATORY THEATRE, Plays-in-Progress Division, 450 Geary, San Francisco CA 94102. (415)771-3880. General Director: William Ball. Director, Plays-in-Progress Division: Janice Hutchins. Produces 9 plays on main stage (Geary Theatre, 1,450 seats) for 18,000 subscribers to repertory season; 3-5 new plays (Playroom Theatre, 50 seats) for 800 subscribers to experimental program. Query with synopsis; submit complete script, submit through agent. "We judge the quality of the play as a whole (theme, characterization, structure, etc.) and for that reason prefer that a playwright send the play itself instead of a synopsis. We accept scripts September through May." Reports in 3 months. "If the script is chosen for production in the experimental, Plays-in-Progress program, the playwright grants A.C.T. an option to enter into a Standard Dramatist Guild Production contract. Option must be exercised within 60 days after final performance at A.T.C." Pays $750 license fee for no less than 7 and no more than 14 separate performances. Offers Playwright-in-Residence Program to playwrights selected for Plays-in-Progress covering duration of rehearsals and performances (about 5 weeks.).
Needs: American realism, comedy/drama/adaptations, farce, satire, abstract. Full length and one acts, but no musicals or children's plays. "As the size of the Experimental Theatre is small, our production elements minimal, we usually produce plays with small casts and production values. We are receptive to many different

forms and structures of the drama. If the manuscript exceeds our producing capabilities in the New Plays Division, and we admire the writing, we attempt to schedule a staged reading as an alternative to production."

AMERICAN THEATRE ARTS, Dept. W, 6240 Hollywood Blvd., Hollywood CA 90028. (213)466-2462. Submit to Literary Manager: Pamela Bohnert. Artistic Director: Don Eitner. Produces 7 plays/year. 15-25% freelance written. Plays performed in 2 Equity Waiver theatres (55 and 70 seats) for the general public. Works with 1-2 unpublished/unproduced writers annually. Submit complete ms. "Submit script-sized SASE for return of manuscript. Submit copies only—not original manuscripts. Submit bound copies, not loose pages secured only with paper clips or rubber bands." Reports in 4 months. "If show goes on to full Equity production, percentage arrangement is worked out with author." Pays $100 minimum royalty. SASE.
Needs: No restrictions as to genres, topics or styles.

ARENA STAGE, 6th and Maine Ave. SW, Washington DC 20024. (202)554-9066. Artistic Director: Zelda Fichandler. Produces 8 plays/year. Works with 1-2 unpublished/unproduced writers annually in "Play Lab," a play development project. Stages professional productions in Washington for intelligent, educated, sophisticated audiences. Prefers query and synopsis plus the first 10 pages of dialogue, or agented submissions. Reports in 4 months. "We obtain option to produce for one year or other term; percentage of future earnings." Pays 5% royalty. Computer printout submissions acceptable "as long as they are easily readible; no dot-matrix." SASE.
Needs: Produces classical, contemporary European and American plays; new plays, translations and adaptations without restrictions. No sitcoms, blank verse, pseudo-Shakespearean tragedies, movies-of-the-week, or soap operas.
Tips: "We can consider large casts, though big plays are expensive and must justify that expense artistically. Be theatrical. Naval-gazing is of little interest. Plays with relevance to the human situation—which cover a multitude of dramatic approaches—are welcome here."

THE ARKANSAS ARTS CENTER CHILDREN'S THEATRE, Box 2137, McArthur Park, Little Rock AR 72203. (501)372-4000. Artistic Director: Bradley Anderson. Produces 5 mainstage plays, 4 tours/year. Mainstage season plays performed at The Arkansas Arts Center for Little Rock and surrounding area; tour season by professional actors throughout Arkansas and surrounding states. Mainstage productions perform to family audiences in public performances; weekday performances for local schools of grades 3 through senior high school. Tour audiences generally the same. Works with 1 unpublished/unproduced writer annually. Submit complete script. Computer printout submissions acceptable; prefers letter-quality to dot-matrix. Reports in several months. Buys negotiable rights. Pays $250-1,500 or negotiable commission. SASE.
Needs: Original adaptations of classic and contemporary works. Also original scripts. "This theatre is defined as a children's theatre; this can inspire certain assumptions about the nature of the work. We would be pleased if submissions did not presume to condescend to a particular audience. We are not interested in 'cute' scripts. Submissions should simply strive to be good theatre literature."
Recent Title: *Great Expectations* (Dickens).
Tips: "We would welcome scripts open to imaginative production and interpretation. Also, scripts which are mindful that this children's theatre casts adults as adults and children as children. Scripts which are not afraid of contemporary issues are welcome."

ART CRAFT PLAY CO., Box 1058, Cedar Rapids IA 52406. (319)364-6311. Averages 5-10 plays/year for junior and senior high school. 100% freelance written. 99% of scripts produced are unagented submissions. Query or send complete ms. Computer printout submissions are acceptable; prefers letter-quality to dot-matrix. Buys amateur rights. Pays $100-1,000.

ARTREACH TOURING THEATRE, 3936 Millsbrae Ave., Cincinnati OH 45209. (513)351-9973. Director: Kathryn Schultz Miller. Produces 4 plays/year to be performed in area schools and community organizations. "We are a professional company. Our audience is primarily young people in schools and their families." Submit complete ms. Reports in 6 weeks. Buys exclusive right to produce for 9 months. Pays $4/show (approximately 150 performances). SASE.
Needs: Plays for children and adolescents. Serious, intelligent plays about contemporary life or history/legend. "Limited sets and props. Can use scripts with only 2 men and 2 women; 45 minutes long. Should be appropriate for touring." No cliched approaches, camp or musicals.
Tips: "We look for opportunities to create innovative stage effects using few props, and we like scripts with good acting opportunities."

ARTS CLUB THEATRE, 1585 Johnston St., Vancouver, British Columbia V6H 3R9 Canada. (604)687-5315. Artistic Director: Bill Millerd. Produces 14 plays/year. 50% freelance written. Works with 1 unpublished/unproduced writer annually. Plays performed in 3 theatres seating 500, 200 and 225 respectively, for a diverse adult audience. Stock professional company operating year-round. Tours British Columbia and occasionally goes on national tours. Submit complete ms. Computer printout submissions acceptable; prefers letter-quality to dot-matrix. Reports in 6 months. "If interested, we ask for first production plus future rights." Pays 8% royalty. SASE or SAE and IRCs.

Needs: Full-length plays for adult audiences. Comedies and plays about concerns of the region. Well-made plays as opposed to experimental; realistic over fantasy. "We are interested in plays that are well-suited to our 200 seat intimate space. Such plays usually are one-set, and have limited number of characters (not more than 8) and have a strong story line."

Recent Production: *Talking Dirty*, by Sherman Snukal ("a sexual satire which takes a close look at the contemporary lifestyles of hip, young sophisticates who inhabit the trendy neighborhoods of Canadian cities").

Tips: "As a theatre that operates in Canada, we are of course more interested in Canadian works. But we are definitely interested in good plays no matter where they are written. We are *not* a theatre that only does Canadian work. We are also very interested in original revue material (both musical and non-musical) to suit our new 225-seat Arts Club Revue Theatre."

ASOLO STATE THEATRE, Postal Drawer E, Sarasota FL 33578. (813)355-7115. Artistic Director: John Ulmer. Produces 7 plays/year. 80% freelance written. About 50% of scripts produced are unagented submissions. A LORT theatre with an intimate performing space. "We play to rather traditional middle class audiences." Works with 2-4 unpublished/unproduced writers annually. "We do not accept unsolicited scripts. Writers must send us a letter and synopsis with self-addressed stamped postcard." Computer printout submissions acceptable; no dot-matrix. Reports in 5 months. Buys negotiable rights. Pays negotiable rate. SASE.

Needs: Play must be *full length*. "We do not restrict ourselves to any particular genre or style—generally we do a good mix of classical and modern works."

Tips: "We have no special approach—we just want well written plays with clear, dramatic throughlines. Don't worry about trends on the stage. Write honestly and write for the stage, not for a publication."

AT THE FOOT OF THE MOUNTAIN THEATER, 2000 S. 5th St., Minneapolis MN 55454. (612)375-9487. Managing Director: Phyllis Jane Rose. 60% freelance written. 2-4 scripts are unagented submissions. "Plays will be performed in our 'black box' theatre by a professional acting company. Plays submitted to our *Broadcloth Series* (a sampler of new scripts by women writers) will be given staged readings by our professional ensemble. The Multi-Cultural Committee is a group of women of color interested in producing work written and performed by people of color." Works with 4-6 unpublished/unproduced writers annually. Submit complete script. Computer printout submissions acceptable; no dot-matrix. Reports in 6 months. Pays $10-30/performance. Submissions returned with SASE.

Needs: All genres: full-length plays, one acts, and musicals by women. Encourages experimental plays. "We are mainly interested in plays by and about women and prefer to produce plays with predominantly female casts. Plays with a feminist approach to the world; plays which work at creating new forms." No sexist or racist plays.

Tips: The theatre prefers small casts and simple sets."

AVILA COLLEGE PERFORMING ARTS DEPT., 11901 Wornall Rd., Kansas City MO 64145. (816)942-8400. Artistic Director: W.J. Louis, PhD. Produces 6 plays/year. 10% freelance written. 33% of scripts produced are unagented submissions. Performs collegiate amateur productions (4 main stage, 2 studio productions) for Kansas City audiences. Query with synopsis. Computer printout submissions acceptable; prefers letter-quality to dot-matrix. Reports in 3 months. Buys rights arranged with author. Pays rate arranged with author. SASE.

Needs: All genres with wholesome ideas and language—musicals, dramas. Length 1-2 hours. Small casts (2-5 characters), women casts; few props, simple staging. No lewd and crude language and scenes.

Tips: Example of play just done: *Towards The Morning*, by John Fenn. Story: "Mentally confused bag lady and 17-year-old egocentric boy discover they need each other; she regains mental stability; he grows up a bit and becomes more responsible. Trends in the American stage freelance writers should be aware of include (1) point-of-view one step beyond theatre of the absurd—theatre that makes light of self-pity; and (2) need for witty, energetic social satire done without smut in the style of *Kid Purple*, by Don Wollner, The 1984 national competition winner of the Unicorn Theatre, Kansas City, MO."

RAN AVNI/JEWISH REPERTORY THEATRE, 344 E. 14th St., New York NY 10003. (212)674-7200. Artistic Director: Ran Avni. "We are an Equity non-profit theatre, Mini-contract." Produces 5 plays/year. Query with synopsis. Reports in 1 month. Pays $25-50/performance. SASE.

Needs: "Plays in English that relate to the Jewish experience."

BAKER'S PLAY PUBLISHING CO., 100 Chauncy St., Boston MA 02111. Editor: John B. Welch. Plays performed by amateur groups, high schools, children's theatre, churches and community theatre groups. "We are the largest publisher of chancel drama in the world." Works with 2-3 unpublished/unproduced writers annually. Submit complete script. Submit complete cassette of music or musical submissions. Computer printout

submissions acceptable. Publishes 18-25 straight plays and musicals; all originals. 80% freelance written. 90% of scripts produced are unagented submissions. Pay varies; outright purchase price to split in production fees. SASE. Reports in 4 months.
Needs: "One-acts (specifically for competition use). Quality children's theatre scripts. Chancel drama for easy staging—voice plays ideal. Long plays only if they have a marketable theme. Include as much stage direction in the script as possible." Emphasis on large female cast desired. No operettas for elementary school production.
Recent Title: *The Beams are Creaking*, by Douglas Anderson.

MARY BALDWIN COLLEGE THEATRE, Mary Baldwin College, Staunton VA 24401. (703)886-6277. Artistic Director: Dr. Virginia R. Francisco. Produces 5 plays/year. 10% freelance written. An undergraduate women's college theatre with an audience of students, faculty, staff and local community (adult, conservative). Query with synopsis or submit complete script. Electronic submissions OK via IBM-PC DOS Text File or Word Perfect File. Computer printout submissions acceptable; prefers letter-quality to dot-matrix. Reports in 3 months. Buys performance rights only. Pays $10-50/performance. SASE.
Needs: Full-length and short comedies, tragedies, musical plays, particularly for young women actresses, dealing with women's issues both contemporary and historical. Experimental/studio theatre not suitable for heavy sets. Cast should emphasize women. No heavy sex; minimal explicit language.

‡**BARTER THEATRE,** Main St., Abingdon VA 24210. Artistic Director/Producer: Rex Partington. 5% freelance written. 1 script is unagented submission. Works with 1 unpublished/unproduced writer annually.
Needs: "Good plays, particularly comedies." Two or three acts, preferably, but will consider good quality plays of shorter length. Pays 5% royalties. Send complete script. SASE.

BERKSHIRE THEATRE FESTIVAL, INC., E. Main St., Stockbridge MA 01262. Artistic Director: Josephine R. Abady. 25% freelance written. Submit complete ms. Reports in 6 months. Produces 10-14 plays a year (5 are mainstage and 5-9 are second spaces). Submissions by agents only.

BROADWAY PLAY PUBLISHING, INC., 249 W. 29th St., New York NY 10001. (212)563-3820. Publishes 15-20 plays/year. 10% of scripts published are unagented submissions. Works with 5 unpublished/unproduced writers annually. Query with synopsis. Computer printout submissions acceptable. Reports on submitted mss in 3 months. Buys stock, amateur, acting edition publishing rights. Pays 10% on book royalty; 90% stock; 80% amateur. SASE.
Needs: New contemporary full-length American plays—use of language. No autobiography, domestic realism, adaptations or translations. Musicals must be accompanied by cassette. No one-acts.

GERT BUNCHEZ AND ASSOCIATES, INC., 7730 Carondelet, St. Louis MO 63105. President: Gert Bunchez. "We feel that the time is propitious for the return of stories to radio. It is our feeling that it is not necessary to 'bring back' old programs and that there certainly should be contemporary talent to write mystery, detective, suspense, children's stories, soap operas, etc. We syndicate radio properties to advertisers and stations. Requirements are plays with sustaining lead characters, 5 minutes to 30 minutes in length, suitable for radio reproduction. Disclaimer letter must accompany scripts." SASE.

‡**CAPITAL REPERTORY COMPANY,** Box 399, Albany NY 12201. (518)462-4531. Artistic Directors: Peter Clough and Bruce Bouchard. Stages 6 productions/season. 15% freelance written. "We are a professional regional theatre with a subscriber audience (broad mix)." Works with 6-10 unpublished/unproduced writers annually. Submit complete ms. Reports in 3 months. Makes outright purchase. Computer printout submissions acceptable; prefers letter-quality to dot-matrix. SASE. All genres, topics, styles, lengths, etc. are needed.
Tips: Send "bound, typed, clean manuscripts."

CATALYST THEATRE, #601, 10136-100 St., Edmonton, Alberta T5J 0P1 Canada. (403)434-1007. Artistic Director: Jan Selman. Produces 4 adult, 3 school, 8 special interest audience plays/year. 40% freelance written. 1 of scripts produced is unagented submission. Plays performed for general Edmonton adult public (some tour Alberta); Alberta schools and conferences, workshops, group homes, worksite, etc. Works with 4 unpublished/unproduced writers annually. Query with synopsis. Computer printout submissions acceptable. Reports in 3 months. Pays 8-10% royalty or $20-40/performance (schools). SASE.
Needs: Special issues. "We're interested in theatre which is a catalyst for discussions—i.e., we do not wish to 'solve' with theatre but we do wish to challenge." General public: full-length; special audience: 30-60 minutes; school: 30-90 minutes. "Some productions tour. We prefer less rather than more." One set or open staging. No extremely complex (technical) plays, essay drama, prescriptive approaches, fluff.
Recent Production: *Talk is Cheap* (interactive for teens and parents).

THE CHANGING SCENE THEATER, 1527½ Champa St., Denver CO 80202. Director: Alfred Brooks. Year-round productions in theatre space. Cast may be made up of both professional and amateur actors. For public audience; age varies, but mostly youthful and interested in taking a chance on new and/or experimental works. No limit to subject matter or story themes. Emphasis is on the innovative. "Also, we require that the playwright be present for at least one performance of his work, if not for the entire rehearsal period. We have a small stage area, but are able to convert to round, semi-round or environmental. Prefer to do plays with limited sets and props." 1-act, 2-act and 3-act. Produces 8-10 nonmusicals a year; all are originals. 90% freelance written. 65% of scripts produced are unagented submissions. "We do not pay royalties or sign contracts with playwrights. We function on a performance share basis of payment. Our theatre seats 76; the first 50 seats go to the theatre; the balance is divided among the participants in the production. The performance share process is based on the entire production run and not determined by individual performances. We do not copyright our plays." Works with 3-4 unpublished/unproduced writers annually. Send complete script. SASE. Reporting time varies; usually several months.
Recent Title: *A Beautiful World*, by David Jones.
Tips: "We are experimental: open to young artists who want to test their talents and open to experienced artists who want to test new ideas/explore new techniques. Dare to write 'strange and wonderful' well-thought-out scripts. We want upbeat ones. Consider that we have a small performance area when submitting."

CHELSEA THEATER CENTER, Third Floor, St. Mary's, 645 W. 46th St., New York NY 10036. Artistic Director: Robert Kalfin. General Manager: Steve Gilger. 50% freelance written. Looking for full-length plays "that stretch the bounds of the theatre in form and content. No limitation as to size of cast or physical production." Works with 1-3 unpublished/unproduced writers annually. Pays for a 6-month renewable option for an off-Broadway production. Works 12 months in advance. No unsolicited mss. Essential to submit advance synopsis. Computer printout submissions acceptable if "readable." SASE.
Recent Production: *Shades of Brown*, by Michael Picardie (man's psycholgical struggle of the aparthied).

CHILDREN'S RADIO THEATRE, 1314 14th St. NW, Washington DC 20005. (202)234-4136. Artistic Director: Joan Bellsey. Produces 10 plays/year. 100% freelance written. "Children's Radio Theatre produces plays to be broadcast on radio nationwide. The plays are intended for a family listening audience." 100% of scripts are unagented submissions. Works with 2-4 unpublished/unproduced writers annually.
Needs: "We like to receive a sample script and specific treatments with SASE." Reports in 3 months. "Each project is negotiated separately. We produce half-hour radio plays covering a wide range of topics including fairy tales, folk tales, musicals, adaptations, pop, original and commissioned plays. We are interested in material targeted for children 5-12. There are character limitations in radio plays—no more then 5 major characters. Contact Children's Radio Theatre before sending *any* material."

CIRCLE IN THE SQUARE THEATRE, 1633 Broadway, New York NY 10019. (212)307-2700. Artistic Director: Theodore Mann. Literary Advisor: Robert Pesola. Produces 3 plays/year. Theatre for subscription audience and New York theatre-going public. Query with 1-page synopsis only. Reports in 3 months. Pays royalty. SASE.
Tips: "We produce classics, revivals, full-length new plays and musicals."

CIRCLE REPERTORY CO., 161 Avenue of the Americas, New York NY 10013. (212)691-3210. Associate Artistic Director: Rod Marriott. Associate Literary Manager: Bill Hemmig. Produces 5 mainstage plays. 5 Projects in Progress/year. Accepts unsolicited mss.

CIRCUIT PLAYHOUSE/PLAYHOUSE ON THE SQUARE, 2121 Madison Ave., Memphis TN 38104. (901)725-0776. Artistic Director: Jackie Nichols. Produces 2 plays/year. 100% freelance written. Professional plays performed for the Memphis/Mid-South area. Member of the Theatre Communications Group. 100% of scripts are unagented submissions. Works with 1 unpublished/unproduced writer annually. A play contest is held each fall. Submit complete ms. Computer printout submissions acceptable. Reports in 3 months. Buys "percentage of royalty rights for 2 years." Pays $500-1,000 in outright purchase.
Needs: All types; limited to single or unit sets. Cast of 20 or fewer.
Tips: "Each play is read by three readers through the extended length of time a script is kept. Preference is given to scripts for the southeastern region of the U.S."

I.E. CLARK, INC., Saint John's Rd., Box 246, Schulenburg TX 78956. (409)743-3232. Publishes 15 plays/year for educational theatre, children's theatre, religious theatre, regional professional theatre, amateur community theatre. 20% freelance written. 25% of scripts produced are unagented submissions. Works with 3-4 unpublished/unproduced writers annually. Submit complete script. Computer printout submissions acceptable; prefers letter-quality to dot-matrix. Reports in 6 months. Buys all available rights; "we serve as an agency as well as a publisher." Pays book and performance royalty, "the amount and percentages dependent upon type and marketability of play." SASE.

Needs: "We are interested in plays of all types—short or long. We seldom publish musicals. We prefer that a play has been produced (directed by someone other than the author); photos and reviews of the production are helpful. No limitations in cast, props, staging, etc.; however, the simpler the staging, the larger the market. Plays with more than one set are difficult to sell. We insist on literary quality. We like plays that give new interpretations and understanding of human nature. Correct spelling, punctuation and grammar (befitting the characters, of course) impress our editors."

Tips: "Don't be afraid to experiment; we like new ideas, new ways of doing things. Theatre is a fine art, and art must be creative. However, the play must be stageable; that's why we seldom publish a play that has not been successfuly performed. The current trend is away from avant-garde. Two-act plays (90-110 minutes) seem to be preferred over the three-act. Two hours is just about the top playing time."

THE CLEVELAND PLAY HOUSE, Box 1989, Cleveland OH 44106. (216)795-7010. Literary Assistant/ Associate to the Director: William Rhys. Plays performed in professional LORT theatre for the general public. Produces 8 musicals (12%) and nonmusicals (88%) a year; 25% are originals. 25% freelance written. Very few scripts produced are unagented submissions. "Cleveland Play House is a long-standing resident company performing in three theatres presenting an eclectic season of commercial plays, musicals, and contemporary and traditional classics with occasional American and world premieres." Works with 2-3 unpublished/unproduced writers annually. Submit letter of inquiry and synopsis. Computer printout submissions acceptable; prefers letter-quality to dot-matrix. Buys stock rights and sometimes first class options. Payment varies. SASE. Reports in 6 months.

Needs: "No restrictions. Vulgarity and gratuitous fads are not held in much esteem. Cast size should be small to moderate. Plays intended for arena stages are not appropriate. Musicals should be geared for actors, not singers. One-act plays are rarely performed. Plays of an extremely experimental nature are almost never selected." No first drafts; works-in-progress; unfinished manuscripts.

COACH HOUSE PRESS, INC., Box 458, Morton Grove IL 60053. (312)967-1777. President: David Jewell. 100% freelance written. All scripts produced are unagented submissions. Publishes trade paperback originals. Averages 3-8 plays/year. Works with 3-5 unpublished writers annually. Pays 5-15% royalty on book receipts; 50% on performance royalty. Simultaneous and photocopied submissions OK. Computer printout submissions acceptable; prefers letter-quality to dot-matrix. SASE. Reports in 3 weeks on queries; 2 months on mss.

Needs: Drama. Plays for children's theatre and older adult theatre. Books on theatre. Publishes for theatre producers and recreation specialists.

Recent Title: *Acting Up!*, by Telander, Quinlan and Verson.

‡**CONTEMPORARY DRAMA SERVICE**, Box 457, Downers Grove IL 60515. Editor: Arthur L. Zapel. Plays performed with amateur performers for age level junior high to adult. "We publish mostly drama but also some how-to books on theatre and speech." Publishes 25-35 plays & musicals/year; 1-act plays, 3-act plays. Both originals and adaptations. 95% freelance written. 90% of scripts are unagented submissions. Works with 30 unpublished/unproduced writers annually. Submit synopsis or complete script. Pays negotiable royalty up to 10%. Letter quality computer printout submissions OK; no dot-matrix. SASE. Reports in 1 month. Catalog for $1 postage.

Needs: "We prefer scripts that can be produced in schools or churches where staging materials are limited. In the church field we are looking for chancel drama for presentation at various holidays: Thanksgiving, Mother's Day, Christmas, Easter, etc. School drama materials can be speech and drama contest plays and monologues, reader's theatre adaptations, drama rehearsal scripts, and musicals. Emphasis on humor. We like a free and easy style. Nothing too formal. We publish elementary material only for church school."

Recent Titles: *Charming Billy* by Peg Kehret (comedy).

Tips: "Be aware of the current styles of comedy writing for stage, screen and television. There is very little written for mime performers. We are trying to find more scripts that may be used by specialist performers of all types."

THE CRICKET THEATRE, 528 Hennepin Ave., Minneapolis MN 55403. (612)333-5241. Associate Artistic Director: Sean Michael Dowse. Audiences consist of adults and students. Works with 2-4 unpublished/unproduced writers annually. Submit complete ms. Computer printout submissions acceptable; no dot-matrix. "Must include SASE." Reports in 6 months minimum. Buys production rights for selected dates. Produces 6 plays, main stage; 5-7 plays, Works-in-Progress; musicals and nonmusicals a year; 40% are originals. 10-20% freelance written. Produces primarily plays by living American playwrights. Only full-length plays will be considered for production.

Needs: "There are no content or form restrictions for scripts of the main season. For Works-in-Progress, any kind of a script is welcomed provided there is a spark of a good play in it. Works-in-Progress presentations are readings, staged readings and stage 2 productions. The focus is on the text and not the fully staged, polished performance as with the main season. All Works-in-Progress playwrights are brought to Minneapolis to join in the play's rehearsal and revision process. Works-in-Progress cannot use plays currently under option or that have had full professional productions. Such plays will be considered only for the main season." No children's plays or large Broadway-type musicals. Cast limit: 9.

Tips: "Trends in the American stage freelance writers should be aware of include the drift from naturalism; the tendency not to give unsolicited manuscripts much attention; the passing of programs to develop new playwrights; the tendency to search for the next hit; and the boredom of two-character plays."

‡**CROSSROADS THEATRE COMPANY**, 320 Memorial Parkway, New Brunswick NJ 08901. (201)249-5625. Artistic Director: Lee Richardson. Produces 6 plays/year. Regional theatre that stages equity professional productions. Query with synopsis. Reports in 6 months. Returns rights to percentage of future productions. Pays royalty. SASE.
Needs: "We need plays involving minority experiences by any writer." Black (Afro-American, African, Caribbean) and interracial plays are preferred. Productions should be suited to a 150-seat theatre.

DELAWARE THEATRE COMPANY, Box 516, Wilmington DE 19899. (302)658-6448. Artistic Director: Cleveland Morris. Produces 5 plays/year. 10% freelance written. "Plays are performed as part of a five-play subscription season in a 300-seat auditorium. Professional actors, directors and designers are engaged. The season is intended for a general audience." 10% of scripts are unagented submissions. Works with 1 unpublished/unproduced writer every two years. Query with synopsis. Computer printout submissions acceptable; prefers letter-quality to dot-matrix. Reports in 6 months. Buys variable rights. Pays 5% (variable) royalty. SASE.
Needs: "We present comedies, dramas, tragedies and musicals. All works must be full-length and fit in with a season composed of standards and classics. All works have a strong literary element. Plays with a flair for language and a strong involvement with the interests of classical humanism are of greatest interest. Single-set, small-cast works are likeliest for consideration."

DENVER CENTER THEATRE COMPANY, 1050 13th St., Denver CO 80204. (303)893-4200. Artistic Director: Donovan Marley. Produces 12 plays/year. Professional regional repertory plays (LORT-B) performed in the only major regional theatre in the Rocky Mountain West. Also, professional tours possible, both regionally and nationally. Submit complete ms. Computer printout submissions acceptable; prefers letter-quality to dot-matrix. Reports in 2 months. Buys negotiable rights. Pays negotiable royalty. SASE.
Needs: "Full-length comedies and dramas. The Denver Center Theatre Company is especially eager to see plays of regional interest."

DODD, MEAD & CO., 79 Madison Ave., New York NY 10016. Senior Editor: Allen T. Klots. "We're only interested in playwrights after professional production, who promise to contribute to the literature of the theatre." Royalty negotiated. Buys book rights only. Reports in 1 month. SASE.

DORSET THEATRE FESTIVAL, Box 519, Dorset VT 05251. (802)867-2223. Artistic Director: Jill Charles. Produces 6 plays/year. 20% freelance written. A professional (equity) theatre, season June-September or October. Audience is sophisticated, largely tourists and second-home owners from metropolitan New York and Boston areas. Query with synopsis and 5-10 pages dialgoue; submit through agent. Computer printout submissions acceptable; prefers letter-quality to dot-matrix. Reports in 2 months. Buys negotiable rights. Pays negotiable rate; minimum $250 for 11 performances. SASE.
Needs: Full length plays (2 acts); any genre, but should have broad audience appeal; generally realistic, but *not* "kitchen dramas." Will consider musicals; must have accompanying cassette. Cast less than 10; single or unit (flexible) settings preferred. "We produce one new play each season and also have a new play reading series of 5 new scripts. We lean toward *positive* plays, whether comedy or drama. No family melodrama."
Tips: "Best time to submit plays is from September to January. (Plays received after March 1 may not be read until fall). Trends on the American stage that freelance writers should be aware of include small casts—stay away from kitchen drama."

THE DRAMATIC PUBLISHING CO., Box 109, Woodstock IL 60098. (815)338-6510. Publishes about 30 new shows a year. 60% freelance written. 40% of scripts published are unagented submissions. "Current growth market is in plays and small cast musicals for stock and community theatre." Also has a large market for plays and musicals for children and for amateur theatre (i.e., junior highs, high schools, colleges, churches and other theatre groups). Works with 4-8 unpublished/unproduced writers annually. Electronic submissions OK via CPM or MSDO—use Word Star. Computer printout submissions acceptable; prefers letter-quality to dot-matrix. Must be at least 30 minutes playing time. Reports in 3 months. Buys stock and amateur theatrical rights as well as rights for cable TV. Pays by usual royalty contract or by occasional outright purchase.
Tips: "Avoid stereotype roles and situations. Submit cassette tapes with musicals whenever possible. Always include SASE if script is to be returned. There is an apparent swing away from sensational situations toward a more carefully developed interrelationship between characters. There is also a length change—one intermission (if any) in a show running up to two hours."

EAST WEST PLAYERS, 4424 Santa Monica Blvd., Los Angeles CA 90029. (213)660-0366. Artistic Director: Mako. 90% freelance written. Produces 5-6 plays/year. Professional plays performed in an Equity waiver house for all audiences. Works with 2-3 unpublished/unproduced writers annually. Query with synopsis or submit complete ms. Reports in 3 weeks on query and synopsis; 2 months on mss. "High majority" of scripts produced are unagented submissions. Buys standard Dramatist's Guild contract rights. Pays $200 in outright purchase or 2-6% of house receipts (ticket prices vary). SASE.

Needs: "We prefer plays dealing with Asian-American themes. The majority of the important roles should be playable by Asian-American actors; our acting company is 98 percent Asian." No fluff, TV sitcom-type material.

Tips: "East West Players was founded by a group of Asian-American actors weary of playing stereotypes in theatre and film. Submitting writers should bear this in mind and refrain from wallowing in 'exoticism.' There appears to be a minor burgeoning of interest in Asian-American writers and themes—witness David Henry Hwang's success on the East Coast, the continuing success and influence of East West Players on the West Coast and establishment theatres developing Asian American material (e.g., The Mark Taper Forum in Los Angeles working on a stage adaptation of Maxine Hong Kingston's works), etc."

ELDRIDGE PUBLISHING CO., Drawer 216, Franklin OH 45005. (513)746-6531. Editor/General Manager: Kay Myerly. Plays performed in high schools and churches; some professional—but most are amateur productions. Publishes plays for all age groups. Publishes 15-20 plays/year; (2%) musicals; 100% originals. 100% freelance written. All scripts produced are unagented submissions. Works with 10-12 unpublished/unproduced writers annually. Send synopsis or complete script. Computer printout submissions acceptable; prefers letter-quality to dot-matrix. Buys all rights "unless the author wishes to retain some rights." Pays $100-125 for 1-act plays; $350 for 3-acts. Also royalty contracts for topnotch plays. SASE. Reports in 60 days.

Needs: "We are looking for good straight comedies which will appeal to high school and junior-high age groups. We do not publish anything which can be suggestive. Most of our plays are published with a hanging indentation—2 ems. All stage, scenery and costume plots must be included." No run-of-the-mill plots. Length: 1-acts from 25-30 minutes; 2-acts of around 2 hours; and skits of 10-15 minutes.

Recent Title: *Dickerson for Senate*, by Ev Miller (comedy-drama).

THE EMPTY SPACE, 95 S. Jackson St., Seattle WA 98104. (206)581-3737. Artistic Director: M. Burke Walker. Produces 6 plays/year. 100% freelance written. Professional plays for subscriber base and single ticket Seattle audience. 1 script is unagented submission. Works with 5-6 unpublished/unproduced writers annually. Query with synopsis before sending script. Computer printout submissions OK; prefers letter-quality to dot-matrix. Response in 3 months. LOA theatre. SASE.

Needs: "Other things besides linear, narrative realism; but we are interested in that as well; no restriction on subject matter. Generally we opt for broader, more farcical comedies and harder-edged, uncompromising dramas. We like to go places we've never been before." No commercial musicals.

ETOBICOKE CHILDREN'S THEATRE, Box 243, Etobicoke, Ontario M9C 1Z1 Canada. (416)626-1963. Artistic Director: Mary E. Miller. Produces 5 plays/year. 50% freelance written. Produces 1 unagented submission each year. Plays are produced professionally with nonunion performers for children, families and seniors. Performed on tour to schools, libraries, senior citizen's homes, community centers, etc. Works with 1 unpublished/unproduced writer annually. Query with synopsis or submit complete ms. Computer printout submissions acceptable; prefers letter-quality to dot-matrix. Reports in 2 months. Rights revert to author. Pays $10-20 for 30-80 performances. SASE.

Needs: "For children—must be entertaining plot plus underlying social or moral values. Any 'lessons' must be learned through what happens, rather than by what is said. For seniors—must be highly entertaining; variety format is good." Length: 45-50 minutes. Cast limited to 3-5 performers. "Plays must require no definite set. Props and costumes must fit into the back of a station wagon."

Tips: "Trends in Canadian stage and screen that freelance writers should be aware of include 'Money is tight'—material must sell—and that a cast of two or three is about all that is being produced by children's touring companies."

THE FIREHOUSE THEATRE, 514 S. 11th St., Omaha NE 68102. (402)346-6009. Artistic Director: Dick Mueller. Produces 7 plays/year.

Needs: "We produce at the Firehouse Dinner Theatre in Omaha. Our interest in new scripts is the hope of finding material that can be proven here at our theatre and then go on from here to find its audience." Submit complete ms. Reporting times vary; depends on work load. Buys negotiable rights. Pays $100/week or negotiable rates. SASE.

Tips: "We are a small theatre. Certainly size and cost are a consideration. Quality is also a consideration. We can't use heavy drama in this theatre. We might, however, consider a production if it were a good script and use another theatre."

FOLGER THEATRE, 201 E. Capitol St. SE, Washington DC 20003. (202)547-3230. Artistic Producer: John Neville-Andrews. Produces 5 plays/year. A Lort D regional theatre for general audience, classically oriented. Query with synopsis; submit through agent. Reports in 3 months. Buys negotiable rights. Pays negotiable rate. SASE.
Needs: Classics and new adaptations of classics only.

‡**SAMUEL FRENCH, INC.**, 45 W. 25th St., New York NY 10010. Editor: Lawrence Harbison. "We publish about 80 new titles a year. We are the world's largest publisher of plays. In addition to publishing plays, we also act as agents in the placement of plays for professional production—eventually in New York. 10 scripts are unagented submissions. Pays on royalty basis. Submit complete ms (bound). "Always type your play in the standard, accepted stageplay manuscript format used by all professional playwrights in the U.S. If in doubt, send $3 to the attention of Lawrence Harbison for a copy of guidelines. We require a minimum of two months to report." SASE.
Needs: "We are willing at all times to read the work of freelancers. As publishers, we prefer simple-to-stage, light, happy romantic comedies or mysteries. If your work does not fall into this category, we would be reading it for consideration for agency representation. No 25-page 'full-length' plays; no children's plays to be performed *by* children; no puppet plays; no adaptations of public domain children's stories; no verse plays; no large-cast historical (costume) plays; no seasonal and/or religious plays; no 'high school' plays; no television, film or radio scripts; no translations of foreign plays requiring large casts."
Recent Title: *A Little Quickie*, by William Van Zandt and Jane Milore (light farce-comedy).

GEORGETOWN PRODUCTIONS, 7 Park Ave., New York NY 10016. Producers: Gerald Van De Vorst and David Singer. Produces 1-2 plays/year for a general audience. Works with 1-2 unpublished/unproduced writers annually. Submit complete ms only. Computer printout submissions acceptable; prefers letter-quality to dot-matrix. Standard Dramatists Guild contract. SASE.
Needs: Prefers plays with small casts and not demanding more than one set. Interested in new unconventional scripts dealing with contemporary issues, comedies, mysteries, musicals or dramas. No first-drafts; outlines; 1-act plays.
Recent Production: *Have I Got A Girl for You!* (the Frankenstein musical) written by Penny Rockwell, Joel Greenhouse and Dick Gallagher.

GEVA THEATRE, 199 Clinton Ave. S., Rochester NY 14607. (716)232-1366. Literary Director: Ann Patrice Carrigan. Produces 6 plays/year. Works with 1-4 unpublished/unproduced writers annually. Query with synopsis. Reports in 6 months. Buys theatre options for 1st- and 2nd-class productions; percentage of author royalties 5 to 10 years from closing production at GeVa Theatre. Pays 5% royalty. Computer printout submissions acceptable; no dot-matrix. SASE.
Needs: "Plays done here run 2-2½ hours. We do one classical piece of world literature, one American classic, three relatively current plays that have made an impact in resident professional theatres across the country and one new work. Those works are normally comedies and dramas in a realistic/impressionist style." Limited to cast of 6 actors, 1-3 set changes. "The priority at GeVa is for scripts that touch people's heads and emotions through vital characterization and a significant storyline. We look for scripts that challenge through entertaining audiences. We are interested in scripts that would stretch the company artistically and the audience imaginatively. We would not be interested in a play whose theme, characterization and structure are not of a piece."
Tips: "Many scripts that come in are scripts for television. The writing is bald and the structure is episodic, and there is the definite logic and texture of a television movie. Writers have to make television writing work in terms of theatre. Often, they do not. People should be writing according to what they are thinking, feeling and responding to rather than *trends*."

HEUER PUBLISHING CO., 233 Dows Bldg., Box 248, Cedar Rapids IA 52406. Publishes 3-5 plays/year. 100% freelance written. 99% of scripts produced are unagented submissions. Amateur productions for schools and church groups. Audience consists of junior and senior high school students and some intermediate groups. Need 1- and 3-act plays. Prefers comedy, farce, mystery and mystery/comedy. Uses 1-act plays suitable for contest work (strong drama). "We suggest potential authors write for our brochure on types of plays." No sex, controversial subjects or family scenes. Prefers 1 simple setting and noncostume plays. Current need is for plays with a large number of characters (16-20). One-act plays should be 30-35 minutes long; 3-act, 90-105 minutes. Most mss purchased outright, with price depending on quality. Minimum of $500 usually. Copyrighted, however, contract stipulates amateur rights only, so author retains professional rights to television, radio, etc. Query with synopsis only. Computer printout submissions acceptable; prefers letter-quality to dot-matrix. SASE. Reports in 6 weeks.
Recent Title: *Gift for Paula*, by Ev Miller (contest work).

HONOLULU THEATRE FOR YOUTH, Box 3257, Honolulu HI 96801. (808)521-3487. Artistic Director: John Kauffman. Produces 6 plays/year. 50% freelance written. Plays are professional productions in Hawaii, primarily for youth audiences (youth aged 2 to 20). Most of scripts are unagented submissions. Works with 2 unpublished/unproduced writers annually. Query with synopsis. Computer printout submissions acceptable; prefers letter-quality to dot-matrix. Reports in 3 months. Buys negotiable rights. Pays $1,000-2,500. SASE.

Needs: Contemporary subjects of concern/interest to young people; adaptations of literary classics; fantasy including space, fairy tales, myth and legend. "HTY wants well-written plays, 60-90 minutes in length, that have something worthwhile to say and that will stretch the talents of professional adult actors." Cast not exceeding 8; *no* technical extravaganzas; *no* full-orchestra musicals; simple sets; props, costumes can be elaborate. No plays to be enacted by children or camp versions of popular fairytales.

Tips: Young people are intelligent and perceptive, if anything more so than lots of adults, and if they are to become fans and eventual supporters of good theatre, they must see good theatre while they are young. Trends on the American stage that freelance writers should be aware of include a growing awareness that we are living in a world community. We must learn to share and understand other people and other cultures.

WILLIAM E. HUNT, 801 West End Ave., New York NY 10025. Interested in reading scripts for stock production, off-Broadway and even Broadway production. 10% freelance written. "Small cast, youth-oriented, meaningful, technically adventuresome; serious, funny, far-out. Must be about people first, ideas second. No political or social tracts." No 1-act, anti-Black, anti-Semitic or anti-Gay plays. "I do not want 1920, 1930 or 1940 plays disguised as modern by 'modern' language. I do not want plays with 24 characters, plays with 150 costumes, plays about symbols instead of people. I do not want plays which are really movie or television scripts." Pays royalties on production. Off-Broadway, 5%; on Broadway, 5%, 7½% and 10%, based on gross. No royalty paid if play is selected for a showcase production. Reports in "a few weeks." Computer printout submissions acceptable; no dot-matrix. Must have SASE or script will not be returned.

Recent Productions: *Spring at Marino*, by Constance Cox. A Loud Bang on June the First, by Wesley Burrowes.

Tips: "Production costs and weekly running costs in the legitimate theatre are so high today that no play (or it is the very rare play) with more than six characters and more than one set, by a novice playwright, is likely to be produced unless that playwright will either put up or raise the money him or herself for the production."

ILLUSION THEATER, 304 Washington Ave. N., Minneapolis MN 55401. (612)339-4945. Artistic Director: Michael Robins. Produces 3-9 plays/year. 90% freelance written. 2-3 scripts are unagented submissions. Works with 1-2 unpublished/unproduced writers annually. "We are a professional acting company performing usually in a studio space seating approximately 90 people. Occasionally productions are moved to larger theatre spaces, and also tour to colleges and high schools. Audience is generally between ages 18-40." Query with synopsis. Letter quality submissions are preferred. Reports in 1 month. "Work we do with playwrights is collaborative. Agreements pertaining to rights are made on an individual basis depending on the project." Pays fee plus royalty. SASE.

Needs: "Our plays range from adaptations of works of literature (*Spring Awakening, Orlando*) to plays created around the history of the acting company's grandparents (*Becoming Memories*) to plays dealing with social issues. The resident company is six actors although the theatre does hire additional artists when needed." Playwrights should send general business letter introducing themselves and their work and include resume if possible.

Tips: "The theatre is not interested in children's plays, religious plays, or plays suitable for the commercial dinner theatre type audiences. Also not interested in plays that are sexist or abusive towards a specific group of people. Our theatre most frequently works with playwrights to collaborate on plays. While the theatre is interested in reading manuscripts to get a sense of the playwright's writing ability and style, the theatre rarely commissions works already complete."

INDIANA REPERTORY THEATRE, 140 W. Washington, Indianapolis IN 46204. (317)635-5277. Artistic Director: Tom Haas. Produces 10 full-length, 9 90-minute Cabarets/year. Plays are professional productions, Lort B and C contracts, in 3 theatres. Mainstage seats 600, Upperstage seats 250, Cabaret seats 150. Subscription audience composed of cross section of Indianapolis community. Query with synopsis. Reports in 3 months. Retains right for first- or second-class production with 60 days after production closes; retains percent on subsequent productions elsewhere. Pays 5% royalty; $500-1,000 nonrefundable advance over royalties. SASE.

Needs: "On our Mainstage we produce exclusively classics, with a heavy emphasis on American work adaptations of classic work or new translations of classic work; also produce one musical yearly (often new musical). Upperstage produces new work of a smaller scale. Cabaret produces exclusively small cast (5 or less) satirical musicals. Prefer under 10 casts, staging which can be adapted—that is, not rigidly realistic; prefer one set or unit set which can be adapted. We tend to be attracted to plays that display an acute interest in using language vigorously, that exhibit an awareness of political thinking without being imitative of political situations. We are interested in epic proportion and in plays that speak very directly to concerns of 1980s. No TV scripts, movie scripts or things that rely on dated techniques like flashbacks; plays which depend on excessive profanity or explicit sexual behavior; one acts."

INVISIBLE THEATRE, 1400 N. 1st Ave., Tucson AZ 85719. (602)882-9721. Artistic Director: Susan Claassen. Produces 5-7 plays/year. 10% freelance written. Semiprofessional regional theatre for liberal, college-educated audiences. Plays performed in 70-100 seat non-equity theatre with small production budget. One script is unagented submission. Query with synopsis. Computer printout submissions acceptable; prefers letter-quality to dot-matrix. Reports in 6 months. Buys non-professional rights. Pays 10% of royalty.
Needs: "Two act plays, generally contemporary, some historical, comedies, drama, small musicals, wide range of topics. Limited to plays with small casts of 10 or less, strong female roles, simple sets, minimal props." No large musicals, complex set designs, casts larger than 15.
Tips: "Trends in the American stage freelance writers should be aware of include substantial roles for women, especially over 35."

LAMB'S PLAYERS THEATRE, 500 Plaza Blvd., Box 26, National City CA 92050. (619)474-3385. Artistic Director: Robert Smyth. Produces 8 plays/year. 30% freelance written. A semi-professional resident company with a year-round production schedule. Audience is varied; high percentage of family and church interest. Works with 2-3 unpublished/unproduced writers annually. Submit complete script. Computer printout submissions acceptable. Reports in 2 months. Buys first production rights, touring option. Pays $250-1,000. SASE.
Needs: "We produce all genres, both one-act and full-length. While not necessarily interested in 'religious' plays, our productions often come from a Christian perspective. With new material, we are primarily interested in work that presents a broad based Christian world-view." Prefers smaller cast (2-10); adaptable staging (arena stage). "We are not interested in material that is 'preachy,' or material that's intention is to shock or titillate with sex, violence or language."
Tips: "Trends freelance writers should be aware of include productions which offer hope without being cliche or sentimental; productions needing small cast and imaginative yet inexpensive sets; and an interest in presentational style pieces—acknowledgment and/or interaction with the audience."

LILLENAS PUBLISHING CO., Box 527, Kansas City MO 64141. (816)931-1900. Editor, Lillenas Drama Resources: Paul Miller. Publishes 4 collections composed of 25 short plays/year (total). 98% freelance written. All scripts published are unagented submissions. "Because we are a religious music and play publisher, most of our works will be performed by churches and church-related schools." Submit query and synopsis or complete ms. "Both are acceptable when the writer is aware of our market." Works with 25 unpublished/unproduced writers annually. Reports in 2 months. "On short plays that become a part of a collection (Christmas, Easter, Mother's Day, etc.) we obtain first rights; on full length plays (or serious one-act plays and sketches) we negotiate with the author. Generally, the work is copyrighted in the author's name." Pays 10% royalty on full length plays and collections by one author, no advance; or pays in outright purchase from $5/double-spaced, typed ms page. Computer printout submissions acceptable; no dot-matrix. SASE. Write for a copy of contributor's guidelines and current need sheets.
Needs: *Full length plays*: "This is a new venture; we are looking for Biblical and contemporary themes. Prefer characterization and thought over settings and large casts." *Short plays and skits*: Primarily seasonal. Children and teen actors (some adults OK). "We are interested in chancel drama, reader's theatre, and choral speaking pieces, as well as traditional staged scripts." Stylistic concerns: Thorough knowledge of proper script format; complete listing of cast, prop, and set requirements; approximate timing. Likes to have a summary paragraph for the reader. Taboos—"good guys" drinking and smoking; put-down of church." No short plays and skits dealing with "the real meaning of Christmas;" a secular approach to Easter and Christmas (Santa Claus, Easter Bunny), fantasy; "religious themes that drip with sentimentality and the miraculous;" plots that depend on the coincidental and plots that have too many subthemes. "We want one strong idea."
Tips: "We are distributed in 10,000 Christian bookstores in North America and other areas of the English-speaking world. We also deal with musicals that have religious themes (again, both Biblical and contemporary)."

LOS ANGELES THEATRE CENTER, 514 S. Spring St., Los Angeles CA 90013. (213)488-1122. Artistic Director: Bill Bushnell. Produces 20-30 plays/year. 90% freelance written. A professional theatre for a general metropolitan audience. 10% of scripts are unagented submissions. Works with 3-5 unproduced writers annually. Query with synopsis plus 10 pages of script. *No unsolicited ms.* Send script inquiries to Mame Hunt, literary manager. Reports in 6 months. Buys first production rights, options to extend and move, subsidiaries. Pays 4-5% royalty. Computer printout submissions acceptable; no dot-matrix. SASE essential.
Needs: Plays with social or political awareness preferred. 10 actors maximum. No "Television scripts or movies pretending to be theatre."
Tips: "The most important and exciting new work in the theatre is non-naturalistic. It takes risks with its subject matter and form and, therefore, it is dramatic writing that cannot be easily transferred to another form, i.e., television or film."

‡**THE MAC-HAYDN THEATRE, INC.**, Box 204, Chatham NY 12037. (518)392-9292 (summer). Producers: Lynne Haydn, Linda MacNish. Produces 6-15 plays/year. "This is a resort area, and our audiences include

rural residents and summer residents from the metropolitan New York City and Albany areas who demand professional quality productions. Submit complete ms; we can only consider a complete script and written score, and would prefer that at least a piano tape be included of the score." Reports in 8 months. Buys exclusive rights to stage production. Pays $25-100/performance. SASE.

Needs: "We are interested in musicals which are wholesome family entertainment; these should be full-length musicals, although we might consider one-act musicals in the future. There is no limitation as to topic, so long as the object is to entertain. We will consider original material as well as adaptations, but any adaptations of copyright material must include proper clearances. We are most interested in legitimate music for trained voices; no rock or fad music. We are looking for scripts which have a story to tell, and which build to a climax; no vignettes, slice of life or character study. We prefer a fast pace and good emotional content, and the score should extend the action, not cause it to stop. We are not interested in political muck-raking or controversy unless it has high entertainment value, and we will not consider obscenity, nudity or bad writing."

Recent Productions: *South Pacific*, by Rodgers and Hammerstein; *Minnie's Boys*, (based on the life of the Marx brothers); *On the 20th Century*, by Comden and Green, music by Cy Coleman.

MAGIC THEATRE, INC., Bldg. D, Fort Mason, San Francisco CA 94123. (415)441-8001. General Director: John Lion. Administrative Director: Marcia O'Dea. Dramaturge: Martin Esslin. "Oldest experimental theater in California." For public audience, generally college-educated. General cross-section of the area with an interest in alternative theater. Plays produced in the off Broadway manner. Cast is part Equity, part non-Equity. Produces 8 plays/year. 50% of scripts produced are unagented submissions. Works with 4-6 unpublished/unproduced writers annually. Submit complete ms. SASE.

Needs: "The playwright should have an approach to his writing with a specific intellectual concept in mind or specific theme of social relevance. We don't want to see scripts that would be television or 'B' movies-oriented. 1- or 2-act plays considered. We pay $500 against 5% of gross."

Recent Productions: *Fool for Love*, by Sam Shepard.

MANHATTAN PUNCH LINE, 3rd Floor, 410 W. 42nd St., New York NY 10036. (212)239-0827. Artistic Director: Steve Kaplan. Produces 6 plays/year. 100% freelance written. Professional off-off Broadway theatre company. 50 scripts are unagented submissions. Works with 1-4 unpublished/unproduced writers annually. Submit complete ms. Reports in 2 months. Buys rights for Broadway and off-Broadway productions, and a share of future subsidiary rights. Pays $325-500. SASE.

Needs: "Manhattan Punch Line is devoted to producing comedies of all types. We are a developmental theatre interested in producing serious plays with a comedic point of view. No comedies aimed at a dinner-theatre audience or television sit-coms."

Tips: "The most important and successful playwrights (Durang, Wasserstein, Innaurato) are all writing comedies. Don't worry about being funny, just try to be honest. Large cast plays are back in."

MANHATTAN THEATRE CLUB, 321 E. 73 St., New York NY 10021. Literary Manager: Jonathan Alper. Produces 10 plays/year. All freelance written. A few of scripts produced are unagented submissions. A two-theatre performing arts complex classified as Off-Broadway, using professional actors. "We present a wide range of new work, from this country and abroad, to a subscription audience. We want plays about contemporary problems and people. Comedies are welcome. No verse plays or historical dramas or large musicals. Very heavy set shows or multiple detailed sets are out. We prefer shows with casts not more than 15. No skits, but any other length is fine." Payment is negotiable. Query with synopsis. Computer printout submissions acceptable; no dot-matrix. SASE. Reports in 6 months.

Recent Production: *Digby*, by Joseph Dougherty.

MIDWEST PLAY LAB PROGRAM, 2301 Franklin Ave., Minneapolis MN 55406. (612)332-7481. Artistic Director: Carolyn Bye. 25% freelance written. "Midwest Play Lab is a 2-week developmental workshop for new plays. The program is held in Minneapolis-St. Paul and is open by script competition to playwrights who live/work in the 13 midwestern states. It is an extensive two-week workshop focusing on the development of a script and the playwright. The plays are given staged readings at the site of the workshop and an additional reading (some staged, some informal) at a prestigious regional theatre." Works with 40 unpublished/unproduced writers annually. In most cases writers should be a member of the Playwrights Center. Submit complete ms—work in progress. Announcements of playwrights in 5 months. Pays a small stipend; room and board; partial travel. Computer printout submissions acceptable; prefers letter-quality to dot-matrix. SASE.

Needs: "We are interested in playwrights with talent, ambitions for a professional career in theatre and scripts which could benefit from an intensive developmental process involving professional dramaturges, directors and actors. A playwright needs to be affiliated with the Midwest (must be documented if they no longer reside in the Midwest); MPL accepts scripts after first of each year. Full lengths and one-acts. No produced materials—"a script which has gone through a similar process which would make our work redundant (O'Neill Conference scripts, for instance)."

NASHVILLE ACADEMY THEATRE, 724 2nd Ave. S., Nashville TN 37210. (615)254-9103. Artistic Director: Dr. Guy Keeton. Produces both amateur and professional productions in a studio situation and in a 696-seat theatre. Age groups performed for are: kindergarten through 4th grade, 5th grade through 8th, and 9th grade to adult. Produces 4 musicals (15%) and nonmusicals (85%) a year; 15% are originals. 15% freelance written. 25% of scripts produced are unagented submissions. "We are considered a family theatre. Although we select plays for different age groups, we feel that any age should enjoy any play we do on some level. In the past we have produced murder mysteries, Shakespeare, plays of the supernatural, fairy tales, *The Mikado* dance-drama, musical comedy, serious drama, chamber theatre, contemporary children's drama—almost anything you can think of." Reports in 2 months. Buys exclusive performance rights for middle Tennessee, one year prior to and during their production. Pays $10-35/performance. Works with 1 unpublished/unproduced writer annually. Computer printout submissions acceptable; no dot-matrix. SASE.
Needs: "We prefer a variety of styles and genres. Length is usually limited to one hour. We are interested in quality new scripts of the old fairy tales for our younger audiences. There is no limit on topics. Interested in musicals also." Wants a richness of language and mood in their productions. No intermissions. Fluid and fast moving. Must have at least some literary merit. No or little obscenity. Cast size: 5-10 players. No limits in staging.

NATIONAL ARTS CENTRE-ENGLISH THEATRE CO., Box 1534, Station B, Ottawa, Ontario K1P 5W1 Canada. (613)996-5051. Theatre Producer: Andis Celms. Produces and/or presents 12 plays/year. 0-5% freelance written. All scripts produced are agented submissions. Professional productions performed in the theatre and studio of the National Arts Centre (also, workshop productions in a new theatre space). Audience ranges from young/middle-aged professionals (especially civil servants) to students. Works with 1-2 unpublished/unproduced writers annually.
Tips: "The general public prefers to see a presentation which has a beginning, a middle and an end."

THE NEW AMERICAN THEATER, 118 S. Main St., Rockford IL 61101. (815)963-9454. Producing Director: J.R. Sullivan. Produces 6 mainstage plays in ten-month season. "The New American Theater is a professional resident theater company performing on a thrust stage with a 270-seat house. It is located in a predominantly middle class midwestern town with significant minority populations." Submit complete ms March through June with replies in 6 months. Buys negotiable rights. Pays royalty based on number of performances. SASE. No limitations, prefer serious themes, contemporary pieces. Open to format, etc. No opera.
Recent Title: *Amadeus, Have You Anything to Declare?*.
Tips: "We look for 'well made' plays exploring past and present American and international social themes. We produce at least 1 premiere each season."

NEW PLAYS INCORPORATED, Box 273, Rowayton CT 06853. (203)866-4520. Publisher: Patricia Whitton. Publishes average 4 plays/year. Publishes plays for producers of plays for young audiences and teachers in college courses on child drama. Query with synopsis. Reports in 2 months. Agent for amateur and semi-professional productions, exclusive agency for script sales. Pays 50% royalty on productions; 10% on script sales. SASE.
Needs: Plays for young audiences with something innovative in form and content. Length: usually 45-90 minutes. "Should be suitable for performance by adults for young audiences." No skits, assembly programs, improvisations or unproduced manuscripts.
Tips: Free catalog available on request.

THE NEW PLAYWRIGHTS' THEATRE OF WASHINGTON, 1742 Church St. NW, Washington DC 20036. (202)232-4527. Artistic Director: Arthur Bartow. Literary Manager: Todd London. Produces 5 musicals and straight plays and 20 readings/year. 100% freelance written. 15% of scripts produced are unagented submissions. "Plays are produced in professional productions in the 125-seat New Playwrights' Theatre in the Dupont Circle area of the city for a subscription audience as well as large single-ticket buying followers. Works with varying number of writers annually; mostly unpublished (approximately 30%), 65% unproduced. Prefers synopsis plus 20 pages of finished scripts, "typed to form, suitably bound." All musicals must be accompanied by cassette tape recording of songs in proper order. Reports in 2 weeks on synopsis; 6-8 months on scripts. "Rights purchased and financial arrangements are individually negotiated." SASE, acknowledgement postcard. No rights requested on readings; buys 7% of playwright's future royalties for 7 years, and first production credit requested for plays or musicals offered as full productions. Pays 6% royalty against a $300/week minimum.
Needs: "All styles, traditional to experimental, straight plays to musicals and music-dramas, revues and cabaret shows, and full-lengths only. No verse plays, children's plays, puppet plays or film scripts. Staging: performance space adaptable.
Tips: "We prefer a strong plot line, be the play realistic, expressionistic or non-realistic, with a positive out-

look on life. We prefer not to receive, but will accept plays of the 'theatre of the infirm.' Would like to find some good, new, funny plays; nothing too far out, surrealistic or avant garde. We will absolutely not accept adaptations or plays written by other than American citizens."

NEW TUNERS THEATRE/PERFORMANCE COMMUNITY, (formerly Performance Community/New Tuners), 1225 W. Belmont Ave., Chicago IL 60657. (312)929-7367. Artistic Director: Byron Schaffer, Jr. Produces 3-4 new musicals/year. 66% freelance written. "Nearly all" scripts produced are unagented submissions. Plays performed in a small off-Loop theatre seating 148 for a general theatre audience, urban/suburban mix. Submit complete ms and cassette tape of the score, if available. Reports in 6 months. Buys exclusive right of production within 80 mile radius. "Submit first, we'll negotiate later." Pays 5-10% of gross. "Authors are given a stipend to cover a residency of at least two weeks." Computer printout submissions acceptable; prefers letter-quality to dot-matrix. SASE.
Needs: "We're interested in traditional forms of musical theatre as well as more innovative styles. We have less interest in operetta and operatic works, but we'd look at anything. At this time, we have no interest in nonmusical plays unless to consider them for possible adaptation—please send query letter first. We are also seeking comic sketches and songs for a 'New Faces' type revue. Our primary interest is in comedic and up-tempo songs, but we will also consider ballads. Cassette tapes of songs should be sent, if possible. Our production capabilities are limited by the lack of space, but we're very creative and authors should submit anyway. The smaller the cast, the better. We are especially interested in scripts using a younger (35 and under) ensemble of actors. We mostly look for authors who are interested in developing their script through workshops, rehearsals and production. No interest in children's theatre. No casts over 15. No one-man shows."
Tips: "Freelance writers should be aware that musical theatre can be more serious. The work of Sondheim and others who follow demonstrates clearly that musical comedy can be ambitious and can treat mature themes in a relevant way. Probably 90 percent of what we receive would fall into the category of 'fluff.' We have nothing against fluff. We've had some great successes producing it and hope to continue to offer some pastiche and farce to our audience; however, we would like to see the musical theatre articulating something about the world around us, rather than merely diverting an audience's attention from that world."

NEWBERRY COLLEGE THEATRE, Dept. of Theatre, Newberry SC 29108. (803)276-5010. Artistic Director: Kenn Robbins. Produces 6 plays/year. Performs plays in Chapel Theatre (175 seats) and Rast Memorial Lab Theatre (flexible seating) for Newberry students and community. Submit complete script (bound only). Reports in 6 weeks. Buys production rights only. Pay 25/50% royalty. SASE.
Needs: "Plays that are suitable for college student performance inside a liberal arts context; we are supported by the Lutheran Church. We are particularly interested in student written plays that qualify for ACTF playwriting awards; also will consider second and third productions. The piece need not be a world premiere." No gratuitous sex or profanity. "Do not care to see plays with propaganda as main motive."

NORTHLIGHT THEATRE, (formerly Northlight Repertory Theatre), 2300 Green Bay Rd., Evanston IL 60201. (312)869-7732. Artistic Director: Michael Maggio. "We are a LORT-D theatre with a subscription audience using professional artistic personnel. Our season runs from September through June. We are committed to developing new plays, translations and adaptations from other literary forms. We produce significant new scripts and second productions from an international repertoire." Audience is primarily college educated, 35-65 years old, with a broad range of socio-economic backgrounds. Query with synopsis. Computer printout submissions acceptable. Reports in 3 months. Produces 5 mainstage a year; 40% are unproduced originals developed inhouse. Rights purchased vary. SASE.
Needs: "New plays and small production music theatre. Plays may vary in genre and topic. Full-length and prefer a cast size of 8 or less without doubling. Though accessibility is an issue, we rate substance as a higher concern for our audience. We have a 298-seat house with a small, extended apron proscenium stage allowing for some use of multiple sets but only the suggestion of levels, e.g. a second story home, etc. Our budget and other resources restrict very elaborate staging but we are fortunate to have talented and creative designers. Solely commercial work or dinner theatre material is not appropriate for our audiences. Trends on the American stage that freelance writers should be aware of include adaptations from other literary forms and new translations of foreign work. We emphasize work which speaks to the human condition and is often contemporary."
Recent Title: *Teibele and Her Demon*, by Isaac B. Singer and Eve Friedman.

ODYSSEY THEATRE ENSEMBLE, 12111 Ohio Ave., Los Angeles CA 90025. (213)826-1626. Artistic Director: Ron Sossi. Produces 12 plays/year. Plays performed in a 3-theatre facility. "All three theatres are Equity waiver; Odyssey 1 and 2 each have 99 seats, while Odyssey 3 has 72-90 seats. We have a subscription audience of 1,800 who subscribe to a six-play season, and are offered a discount on our remaining non-subscription plays. Remaining seats are sold to the general public." Query with synopsis. Reports in 8 months. Buys negotiable rights. Pays 5-7% royalty or $25-35/performance. SASE. "We will *not* return scripts without SASE."

Needs: Full-length plays only with "either an innovative form or extremely provocative subject matter. We desire more theatrical pieces that explore possibilities of the live theatre experience."

OLD GLOBE THEATRE, Box 2171, San Diego CA 92112. (619)231-1941. Artistic Director: Jack O'Brien. Produces 12 plays/year. "We are a LORT B professional house. Our plays are produced for a single ticket and subscription audience of 250,000, a large cross section of southern California, including visitors from the LA area." Submit complete ms through agent only. Reports in 2 months. Buys negotiable rights. Pays 6-10% royalty. SASE.
Needs: "We are looking for contemporary, realistic, theatrical dramas and comedies and request that all submissions be full-length plays at this time." Prefers smaller cast and single sets, and "to have the playwright submit the play he has written rather than to enforce any limitations. No musicals or large cast historical dramas."
Tips: "Get back to theatricality. I am tired of reading screenplays."

OLD LOG THEATER, Box 250, Excelsior MN 55331. Producer: Don Stolz. Produces 2-act and 3-act plays for "a professional cast. Public audiences, usually adult. Interested in contemporary comedies. No more than 2 sets. Cast not too large." Produces about 8 plays/year. Payment by Dramatists Guild agreement. Send complete script. SASE.

ONE ACT THEATRE COMPANY, 430 Mason St., San Francisco CA 94102. (415)421-6162. Artistic Director: Simon L. Levy. Produces 16 plays/year. 10% freelance written. Professional productions performed for a subscription and community audience—35-50 age group, especially. 1-3 scripts are unagented submissions. Works with 1-3 unpublished/unproduced writers annually. Reports in 3 months. Buys negotiable rights. Pays negotiable rate. SASE.
Needs: "One-act plays only: 90 minutes maximum. Comedy and drama, wide stylistic range. We will consider plays with provocative themes."
Tips: "We are interested in 'cafe plays' (those dealing with personal problems in relationships). We are looking for plays that deal with unusual contemporary, political, and racial issues."

O'NEILL THEATER CENTER'S NATIONAL PLAYWRIGHTS CONFERENCE/NEW DRAMA FOR TELEVISION PROJECT, Suite 901, 234 W. 44th St., New York NY 10036. (212)382-2790. Artistic Director: Lloyd Richards. Develops staged readings of 12 stage plays, 3-4 teleplays/year for a general audience. "We accept unsolicited mss with no prejudice toward either represented or unrepresented writers. Our theatre is located in Waterford, Connecticut and we operate under an Equity LORT(C) Contract. We have 3 theatres: Barn-250 seats, Amphitheatre-300 seats, Instant Theater-150." The works which we present are unpublished and unproduced, but the writers who create them are not necessarily unproduced or unpublished." Submit complete bound ms. Decision by late April. "We have an option on the script from time of acceptance until 60 days *after* the four-week summer conference is completed. After that, all rights revert back to the author." Pays minimum $200 stipend plus room, board and transportation. Computer printout submissions acceptable. SASE. "Interested writers should send us a self-addressed-stamped #10 envelope with 22¢ postage and request our updated guidelines in September prior to the following summer's conference. We accept script submissions from Sept. 15-Dec. 1 of each year. Conference takes place during four weeks in July and August each summer."
Needs: "We do staged readings of new American plays. We use modular sets for all plays, minimal lighting, minimal props and no costumes. We do script-in-hand readings with professional actors and directors."

OPERA VARIETY THEATER, 3944 Balboa St., San Francisco CA 94121. (415)566-8805. Director: Violette M. Dale. 85% freelance written. Plays to be performed by professional and amateur casts for a public audience; all ages, generally families; upper educational level. All scripts produced are unagented submissions. Works with 2-5 unpublished/unproduced writers annually. Submit complete script. Produces 2-3 musicals (50% or more) and nonmusicals (1-2) a year; all are originals. "Everyone (cast, author, technical people, publicity, etc.) receives percentage of box office." SASE. Reports in 6 months.
Needs: "Prefer musicals (but must have musically challenging, singable, tuneful material; arranged, ready to cast). Plays or music on most any theme that conservative audiences would enjoy. Must have substantial, believable plot and good characterizations. Must be simple to produce; small cast (10 or less), easy setting, etc. (small backstage area limits cast, props, staging, etc.). Emphasis is on entertainment rather than social reform." Length: 1, 2 or 3 acts. "No vulgarity in language or action; no wordy preaching."
Recent Production: *The Making of Perpeople*, by Hulsebus (comedy on creation story).

ORACLE PRESS, LTD., 5323 Heatherstone Dr., Baton Rouge LA 70820. (504)766-5577. Artistic Director: Cj Stevens. Publishes 10-15 plays/year. 90% freelance written. 90% of scripts produced are unagented submissions. Plays performed by college, high school and other amateur groups. 100% of scripts are unagented submissions. Works with 20-30 unpublished/unproduced writers annually. Query with synopsis. Computer printout submissions acceptable; prefers letter-quality to dot-matrix. Reports in 6 weeks. Copyright in name of playwright; performance rights referred to playwright. Pays 10% royalty. SASE.

Needs: "Production must be playable *on stage*. Will not publish gratuitous filth or obscenity."

Tips: "The trend which we find deplorable is that of writing everything for Broadway; hence, small casts, limited sets. College and high school groups frequently desire just the opposite."

JOSEPH PAPP, PRODUCER, New York Shakespeare Festival/Public Theater, 425 Lafayette St., New York NY 10003. (212)598-7129. Plays and Musicals Department—Gail Merrifield, Director; William Hart, Literary Manager; Elizabeth Holloway, Associate Manager. Interested in full-length plays and musical works. No restrictions as to style, form or historical period. New works produced year-round on five stages at the Public theater complex. Produces 15 plays/musicals a year. Most are originals. Unsolicited material accepted. Standard option and production agreements. Reports in 2 months. SASE.

PEOPLE'S LIGHT & THEATRE COMPANY, 39 Conestoga Rd., Malvern PA 19355. (215)647-1900. Producing Director: Danny S. Fruchter. Produces 5 full-length, 4-5 one-act plays/year. Approximately 10% of scripts produced are unagented submissions. "LORT D Actors' Equity plays are produced in Malvern 30 miles outside Philadelphia in 350-seat main stage and 80-seat second stage. Our audience is mainly suburban, some from Philadelphia. We do a 6-show subscription season which includes a New Play Festival each summer." Works with 2-4 unpublished/unproduced writers annually. Query with synopsis and cast list. Computer printout submissions acceptable; prefers letter-quality to dot-matrix. SASE is a must. Reports in 10 months. Buys "rights to production in our theatre, sometimes for local touring." Pays 2-5% royalty.

Needs: "We will produce anything that interests us." Prefers single set, maximum cast of 12 (for full length), fewer for one act. No musicals, mysteries, domestic comedies.

Tips: "Freelance writers should be aware of trend away from naturalistic family drama and toward smaller cast size."

PIONEER DRAMA SERVICE, 2171 S. Colorado Blvd., Box 22555, Denver CO 80222. (303)759-4297. Publisher: Shubert Fendrich. Plays are performed by high school, junior high and adult groups, colleges and recreation programs for audiences of all ages. "We are one of the largest full-service play publishers in the country in that we handle straight plays, musicals, children's theater and melodrama." Publishes 15 plays/year; (40%) musicals and (60%) straight plays. 20% freelance written. 100% of scripts published are unagented submissions. Submit synopsis or complete script. Computer printout submissions acceptable; prefers letter-quality to dot-matrix. Buys all rights. Pays "usually 10% royalty on copy sales; 50% of production royalty and 50% of subsidiary rights with some limitations on first-time writers." SASE. Reports in 30-60 days.

Needs: "We are looking for adaptations of great works in the public domain or plays on subjects of current interest. We use the standard 1-act and 3-act format, 2-act musicals, melodrama in all lengths and plays for children's theater (plays to be done by adult actors for children)." Length: 1-acts of 30-45 minutes; 2-act musicals and 3-act comedies from 90 minutes to 2 hours; and children's theatre of 1 hour. No "heavily domestic comedy or drama, simplistic children's plays, shows with multiple sets or that hang heavily on special effects, plays with a primarily male cast, highly experimental works, or plays which lean strongly on profanity or sexual overtones."

Recent Title: *Tumbleweeds* (musical based on the Tom Ryan comic strip), by Tim Kelly, Arne Christiansen and Ole Kittleson.

Tips: "We believe writers should obtain the amateur rights to prominent properties—books, television shows, comic strips, etc., adapt and present the material by a local group and then market the show. It is becoming more and more difficult to 'create' a market for material which lacks familiarity."

PLAYERS PRESS, INC., Box 1132, Studio City CA 91604. Senior Editor: Robert W. Gordon. "We deal in all areas and handle works for film, television as well as theatre. But all works must be in stage play format for publication." Also produces scripts for video, and material for cable television. 80% freelance written. 10-12 scripts are unagented submissions. Works with 1-10 unpublished/unproduced writers annually. Submit complete ms. "Must have SASE or play will not be returned, and two #10 SASE for update and correspondence. All submissions must have been produced and should include a flyer and/or program with dates of performance." Reports in 3 months. Buys negotiable rights. "We prefer all area rights." Pays variable royalty "according to area; approximately 10-75% of gross receipts." Also pays in outright purchase of $100-25,000 or $5-5,000/performance.

Needs: "We prefer comedies, musicals and children's theatre, but are open to all genres. We will rework the ms after acceptance. We are interested in the quality, not the format."

Recent Title: *A Matter of Degree*, by Anson Campbell.

PLAYS, The Drama Magazine for Young People, 120 Boylston, Boston MA 02116. Editor: Sylvia K. Burack. Publishes approximately 80 1-act plays each season to be performed by junior and senior high, middle grades, lower grades. Can use comedies, farces, melodramas, skits, mysteries and dramas, plays for holidays and other special occasions, such as Book Week; adaptations of classic stories and fables; historical plays; plays about other lands; puppet plays; folk and fairy tales; creative dramatics; and plays for conservation, ecology or human rights programs. Mss should follow the general style of *Plays*. Stage directions should not be typed in capital letters or underlined. No incorrect grammar or dialect. Characters with physical defects or speech impediments should not be included. Desired lengths for mss are: Junior and Senior high—20 double-spaced ms pages (25 to 30 minutes playing time). Middle Grades—12 to 15 pages (20 to 25 minutes playing time). Lower Grades—6 to 10 pages (8 to 15 minutes playing time). Pays "good rates on acceptance." Reports in 2-3 weeks. SASE. Sample copy $3; send SASE for manuscript specification sheet.

PLAYWRIGHTS' PLATFORM, INC., 43 Charles St., Boston MA 02114. (617)720-3770. Literary Manager: Robert Kinerk. Develops and presents 30 plays/season. "Selected scripts are developed through cold, rehearsed and staged reading, as well as no-frills productions. All activities professional. Audiences general and professional." Indicate with synopsis if Massachusetts or New England writer; submit complete ms if Massachusetts writer. Reports in 5 months. Program credit given only (in case of eventual fall production or publication). Playwright honoraria *average* $20 for script program. Computer printout submissions acceptable; prefers letter-quality to dot-matrix.
Needs: Seeking new voices, unusual visions. Readings and workshops employ minimal props, costumes, lights, sets.
Tips: "Playwrights of real promise afforded access to first-class directors and actors with considerable dramaturgical support available. Theatrical characters and events are *not* ultimately 'real,' but rather of extraordinary human circumstance and values. We're looking for a strong, original voice. We'd rather find someone with something to say and the power to say it than someone aware of trends and skilled at following them."

READ MAGAZINE, 245 Long Hill Rd., Middletown CT 06457. (203)347-7251. Editor: Edwin A. Hoey. 10% freelance written. For junior high school students. Biweekly magazine; 32 pages. Circ. 500,000. Rights purchased vary with author and material. May buy second serial (reprint) rights or all rights. Byline given. Buys 10 mss/year. Pays on publication. Sample copy and writer's guidelines for SASE. Will consider photocopied submissions. No simultaneous submissions. Reports in 6 weeks. Submit complete ms. SASE.
Drama and Fiction: First emphasis is on plays; second on fiction with suspense, adventure or teenage identification themes. "No preachy material. Plays should have 12 to 15 parts and not require complicated stage directions, for they'll be used mainly for reading aloud in class. Remember that we try to be educational as well as entertaining." No kid detective stories or plays. No obscenity. Pays $50 minimum.

ST. BART'S PLAYHOUSE, 109 E. 50th St., New York NY 10022. (212)751-1616. Artistic Director: Tom Briggs. "Will accept synopsis and cassette tape of score of inherently American musicals from which artistic director will solicit scripts, if interested. Do not call." 20% freelance written. 1 script is unagented submission. Works with 1 unpublished/unproduced writer annually. Computer printout submissions acceptable; prefers letter-quality to dot-matrix.

SEATTLE REPERTORY THEATRE, Seattle Center, 155 Mercer St., Seattle WA 98109. (206)447-2210. "The Seattle Repertory Theatre is currently looking for new, unproduced plays for its main stage and for its New Plays in Process Project. Playwrights should not send script but should submit professional resume, plot synopsis and 15 pages of dialogue from the front of the play to Alison Harris, Literary Manager."

SOHO REPERTORY THEATRE, 80 Varick St., New York NY 10013. (212)925-2588. Co-Artistic Directors: Jerry Engelbach and Marlene Swartz. Produces 4-10 full productions and 8-10 staged readings/year. 15% freelance written. All of scripts produced are unagented submissions. Plays performed off-off-Broadway. "The audience is well-educated, mature and composed of regular theatregoers. Our playwrights have usually been produced, and some published, previously." Query with synopsis. "We prefer that queries/synopses be submitted by a director interested in staging the play, but will accept author queries, too." Computer printout submissions acceptable. Reports in 90 days. Rights for full-length plays: percentage of author's royalties on future earnings, credit in published script and on future programs; for staged readings: none. Pays $100 and up for limited run performance rights. Pays $500 and up for future right to option. SASE.
Needs: "Unusual plays not likely to be seen elsewhere; including rarely produced classics; revivals of superior modern works; new plays that utilize contemporary theatre techniques; and musicals and mixed media pieces that are noncommercial. Writers should keep in mind that our stage is a thrust, not a proscenium." Desires "full-length works that are physical, three-dimensional and that use heightened language, are witty and sophisticated, and that demonstrate a high quality of dramatic craft. No sitcoms, featherweight pieces for featherbrained audiences, drawing room plays, pedantic political pieces, works that do not require the audience to think, or pieces more suited to television or the printed page than to the live stage."
Tips: "Most of the plays submitted to us are too conventional. Look us up in the Theatre Communications Group's *Theatre Profiles* to see what kind of work we have done, and use the most unusual productions as a guideline. The most interesting contemporary theatre pieces are stylistically eclectic and very active. Dialogue

is terse and direct. Sets are rarely realistic. The audience's imagination is constantly challenged, and they leave the theatre feeling that they've had a physical, as well as intellectual/aesthetic, experience. Such works are rare, which is why we reject a thousand scripts for each one we produce."

SOUTHEASTERN ACADEMY OF THEATRE AND MUSIC INC., DBA ACADEMY THEATRE, 1137 Peachtree St. NE, Atlanta GA 30309. (404)873-2518. Artistic Director: Frank Wittow. Produces 12-18 plays/year; mainstage subscription series theatre for youth, first stage studio new play series, school of performing art, and lab theatre series. Query with synopsis or agented submissions. Reports in 6 months. Buys "usually sole and exclusive right to produce play within a 100-mile radius of the metro Atlanta area for up to 3 years." Pays 5% royalty or $5-100/performance. SASE.
Needs: "Full-length, small cast shows which provide interesting challenges for actors. Plays which deal with new approaches to naturalism, transformational plays. One-acts considered for lab theatre (minimal royalty)." Cast: 12 maximum. Minimal or simple sets. "Deal with basic, honest emotions. Delve into social issues in a subtle manner. Provide thought-provoking material which deals with the human condition and allows for greater self-awareness." No frivolous, light comedies.
Tips: "The Academy Theatre is devoted to exploring human behavior, through physical and emotional involvement, for the purpose of greater self-awareness, for the purpose of making people more social, more able to live with each other."

STAGE ONE: The Louisville Children's Theatre, 721 W. Main St., Louisville KY 40202. (502)589-5946. Producing Director: Moses Goldberg. Produces 6-7 plays/year. 20% freelance written. 15-20% of scripts produced are unagented submissions (excluding work of Playwright-in-Residence). Plays performed by an Equity company for young audiences aged 4-18; usually does different plays for different age groups within that range. Submit complete ms. Computer printout submissions acceptable. Reports in 4 months. Pays negotiable royalty or $25-50/performance. SASE.
Needs: "Good plays for young audiences of all types: adventure, fantasy, realism, serious problem plays about growing up or family entertainment." Cast: ideally, 10 or less. "Honest, visual potentiality, worthwhile story and characters are necessary. An awareness of children and their schooling is a plus." No "campy material or anything condescending to children. No musicals unless they are fairly limited in orchestration."

CHARLES STILWILL, Managing Director, Community Playhouse, Box 433, Waterloo IA 50704. (319)235-0367. Plays performed by Waterloo Community Playhouse with a volunteer cast. Produces 13 plays (7 adult, 5 children's); 1-3 musicals and 7-12 nonmusicals a year; 1-4 originals. 17% freelance written. Most of scripts produced are unagented submissions. Works with 1-4 unpublished/unproduced writers annually. "We are one of few community theatres with a commitment to new scripts. We do at least one and have done as many as four a year. We are the largest community theatre per capita in the country. We have 5,000 season members." Average attendance at main stage shows is 5,000; at studio shows 2,200. "We try to fit the play to the theatre. We do a wide variety of plays. Looking for good plays with more roles for women than men. Our public isn't going to accept nudity, too much sex, too much strong language. We don't have enough Black actors to do all-Black shows." Theatre has done plays with as few as two characters, and as many as 61. "On the main stage, we usually pay between $300 and $500. In our studio, we usually pay between $50 and $300. We also produce children's theatre. We are looking for good adaptations of name children's shows and very good shows that don't necessarily have a name. We produce children's theatre with both adult and child actors. We also do a small (2-6 actors) cast show that tour the elementary schools in the spring. This does not have to be a name, but it can only be about 35 minutes long." Send synopsis or complete script. Computer printout submissions acceptable. SASE. "Reports negatively within 11 months, but acceptance takes longer because we try to fit a wanted script into the balanced season."
Recent Title: *The Griffin and the Minor Cannon*, by Russell Davis (this year's school tour).

THEATRE THREE, 2800 Routh, Dallas TX 75201. (214)651-7225. Artistic Director: Norma Young. Produces 11-12 plays/year. 8% freelance written. 3 of scripts produced are unagented submissions. Plays in an arena house to a general audience using professional actors. Works with approximately 2 unpublished/unproduced writers annually. Produces a new play festival that includes staged readings of up to 10 new plays. Submit complete script. Computer printout submissions acceptable. Replies in several months. Buys performance/staged reading rights for productions at Theatre Three only. Pays 6% royalty or honorarium for readings. SASE.
Needs: Full-length plays. "We produce a wide range of genre including musicals. Our house is inappropriate for spectacle-type shows. Multiset and large cast shows can be cost prohibitive."

THEATRE VIRGINIA, (formerly Virginia Museum Theatre), Boulevard & Grove Ave., Richmond VA 23221. (804)257-0835. Artistic Director: Terry Burgler. Produces 7 plays/year. LORT company. Submit complete script. Reports in 6 months. Buys negotiable rights, "but usually we share in future earnings from the property, if we produce the premiere." Pays royalty. SASE.

Needs: "We consider all types of plays, but are drawn to materials based on other literary works: adaptations of novels, biographies, courtroom events, etc. No outlines, incomplete works, one-acts, rotten plays."

‡**25TH STREET THEATRE**, Box 542, Saskatoon, Saskatchewan S7K 3L6 Canada. Artistic Director: Andras Tahn. Produces 5 plays/year. 100% freelance written. At least 5 new Canadian plays produced/premiered per season running from September to May. "These are full mainstage professional productions serving a subscription (season ticket) audience of 1,000 per show." 2-4 scripts are unagented submissions. Works with 1 unpublished/unproduced writer annually. Submit complete ms. Reports in 6 weeks. Buys first professional production rights with an option to tour the play and first refusal rights on remounts in the Saskatchewan region to be held for 2 years. Pays 10% of gross; buys some scripts outright for $500-1,500 "depending on whether writer is established or new." Computer printout submissions acceptable; prefers letter-quality to dot-matrix. SASE or SAE and IRCs.
Needs: "Our objective is to produce new plays by new writers with special emphasis on Canadian work. Anything worthy will be produced but only the best new work finds its way onto the mainstage." Prefers to do small cast plays due to budget restrictions. No badly written plays or plays with no writer behind them.
Tips: "In Canada the trend is toward openness. Anything goes. The theatre is hungry for new solid professional work. The audiences are becoming more demanding; plays have to be able to compete on the international market."

VIRGINIA STAGE COMPANY, 108 E. Tazewell St., Norfolk VA 23510. (804)627-6988. Artistic Director: Charles Towers. Produces 7 plays/year. 20% freelance written. 10% of scripts produced are unagented submissions. A professional regional theatre serving the one million people of the Hampton Roads area. Plays are performed in LORT C proscenium mainstage or LORT D flexible second stage. Works with 2 unpublished/unproduced writers annually. Query with synopsis; "sample scene or dialogue may be included." Reports in 2 months. Buys negotiable rights. Pays negotiable rate. SASE.
Needs: "Primarily full-length dramas and comedies which address contemporary issues within a study of broader themes and theatricality. A small cast and limited staging is preferable but not necessary. Material must be inherently theatrical in use of language, staging or character. We do not want to see material which offers simplistic solutions to complex concerns, is more easily suited for television or film or whose scope is *limited to* specific contemporary topical issues."

WEST COAST PLAYS, Suite 621, 849 S. Broadway, Los Angeles CA 90014. (213)622-6727. Editor: Robert Hurwitt. Publishes 14 plays/year (2 volumes, 7 plays each). 100% freelance written. ½-¾ of scripts published are unagented submissions. Plays are for general audience, professional use (through theatres), and academic use (some volumes get used as texts). Works with 7 unpublished/unproduced writers annually. "Half to three-fourths of the writers we publish each year (up to 14) may be previously unpublished." Submit complete script. Reports in 6 months. Buys one-time publication rights with right to reprint. Pays royalty: .7% of list price on first 2,000 copies sold; 1.4% after that. Advance on royalties from $50 for a one-act to $100 for a full-length play. Computer printout submissions acceptable; no dot-matrix. SASE.
Needs: All types: one-acts, full-length plays; children's plays, experimental, epic or realistic; musical, comedy, drama; Third World, women's, gay, straight. "We try to cover the spectrum of what is most exciting in new plays from the Western U.S. We *only* publish plays that have had their first U.S. production in the western United States, roughly anywhere from Denver to Hawaii." No scripts that have not yet had a full-scale production.

WOOLLY MAMMOTH THEATRE COMPANY, 1317 G St. NW, Washington DC 20005. (202)393-3939. Artistic Director: Howard Shalwitz. Literary Manager: Neil Steyskal. Produces 5-6 plays/year. 100% freelance written. Produces professional productions for the general public in Washington, DC. 3-4 scripts are unagented submissions. Works with 1-2 unpublished/unproduced writers annually. Query with synopsis. Reports in 2 weeks on synopsis; 6 weeks on scripts. Buys first and second class production rights. Pays 5% royalty. SASE.
Needs: "We look for plays that depart from the traditional categories in some way. Apart from an innovative approach, there is no formula. Musicals are welcome. One-acts are rarely used." Cast limit of 12; no unusually expensive gimmicks.
Tips: Trends on the American stage that freelance writers should be aware of include rising costs and the difficulty of getting good, older actors in regional theatres.

WORKSHOP WEST PLAYWRIGHTS' THEATRE, 9510-105th Ave., Edmonton, Alberta T5H 0J8 Canada. (403)429-4251. Artistic Director: Gerry Potter. Produces 5 plays/year. 50% freelance written. 20% of scripts produced are unagented submissions. Professional productions performed in 200-300 seat houses for middle-of-the-road urban audiences, many from university. Works with 1 or 2 unpublished/unproduced writers annually. Submit complete ms. Computer printout submissions acceptable; prefers letter-quality to dot-matrix. Reports in 2 months. Buys various rights "though we try for Canadian rights for 1 year." Pays 8-11% royalty vs. guarantee. SASE.

Needs: Canadian plays only. "Various genres, though we avoid commercial comedy, musicals and absurdist work. Interested in innovative works, historical subjects, (especially Canadian or Western Canadian). Normally full-length." Cast: 7 maximum. "Socially-aware drama and modern poetic drama." No Broadway musicals.

Tips: Freelance writers should be aware of "renewed emphasis on story and character, but away from naturalism."

Screenwriting

The road to Emerald City (where producers pay a fortune for your movie scripts) can be a rocky one. Still, that's no reason not to make the journey.

Scriptwriters can write for audiences in their own communities and around the world. There are more opportunities today than just five years ago. While the term, screenwriting, might prompt you to think of movies shown at a theatre, the scriptwriter this year will probably find more success in writing for the TV screen. Even if writing movies for the box office is your goal, you might want to turn your attentions first to television.

Made-for-TV movies, TV shows, and docudramas are outlets for scriptwriters, although the field is a difficult one to break in to. Most producers want material that has been registered with the Writers Guild of America. "In our business, writers think if they have an idea, that is enough for a show," said one TV show producer. "We won't consider anything without funds or set talent."

The cable television market provides a wealth of opportunity for the scriptwriter, depending on whether the writer contacts cable pay channels or local cable franchises.

Cable TV producers will have to give audiences *more* in view of the home video competition, said one producer. Pay cable firms are producing more material lately. Producers either approach cable companies with ideas, or companies are subcontracting with producers for films.

Watch what each cable channel is producing *before* you query one with your ideas. You'll be competing against scriptwriters with track records when you try to crack the national cable market, so follow each company's guidelines and develop ideas that mass audiences will be interested in. Cable networks that serve special-interest audiences, on the other hand, need more specialized material. Producers that consider cable TV material are denoted in this book with the symbol (□). Consult cable TV trade journals, *The New York Times*, and *Variety* to keep up on the latest trends.

The best opportunities for new scriptwriters are in their hometowns. As cable companies vied for each city's franchise in the last few years, the firms began offering local programming (public access) as a selling point. As a result, citizens can receive production studio training and can produce shows using their local cable company's facilities for little or no charge. An estimated 1,100 U.S. cities have one or more community video centers. "Scriptwriters really need to start asking questions in the communities in which they live," suggested Joyce Miller, community programming manager in Cincinnati's Warner Amex office.

Local access programming focuses more on nonfiction than fiction, although citizens are not restricted to doing only community service material. In Cincinnati, local poets were invited to read their work as Miller and citizens produced, "Cincinnati . . .A Place for Poetry."

Citizens groups, colleges, art agencies and community theatres can produce original screenplays using public access facilities. Of course, persons interested in producing such a project would first have to discuss it with the staff at their local cable center. You may want to enroll in a training class for public access production—

to find out what the requirements are—before approaching the cable company or a local group about producing a script. Keep in mind, though, that the citizen, not the cable company, would be the producer for public access programs.

If, for instance, you want to make a documentary about drunken driving, you could approach your local Alcoholism Council for feedback and perhaps active involvement in the production of your script.

The chance to get experience is rare at commercial television stations, pointed out Sue Miller Buske, executive director of the National Federation of Local Cable Programmers. Public access programming offers more freedom than most scriptwriters might guess.

Some people have used the experience they've gained through local access to pursue other TV-related projects. One Manhattan woman who produced a show on Chinese culture will now be producing material *in* China.

Industry sources believe the home video market will be creating a demand for more how-to and feature films. Of course, producers will then be looking for more scriptwriters.

As the prices of video cassette recorders continue to decrease, more consumers are buying them. According to *Home Video Publisher* statistics, an estimated 16 million U.S. households owned a VCR in 1984; projections indicate that after New Year's Eve of 1985, there would be 26 million VCRs in homes.

What these numbers mean is that more consumers will be considering the rental and purchases of cassettes. And as the price of cassettes also drops (due to the greater volume), the emphasis will shift more from the rental of films to purchase.

Fiction on film has always outsold nonfiction at box offices and in video stores, but now people will be turning more often to video tapes to learn facts about a subject or to learn a skill (while continuing to enjoy cassette movies).

One consideration that producers will be watchful of (in reading scripts) is whether it will have a lasting value for viewers. A cooking film, for instance, that teaches the viewer how to make one dish is less useful than one that teaches a variety of cooking skills. Producers want a film to be so useful and so interesting that viewers will return to the film much as they would a how-to book.

Bookstores, in particular Waldenbooks, look for quality, collectibility, and repeatability in selecting videocassette titles, reported *Home Video Publisher*. Sporting goods stores, maternity shops, and even grocery stores may begin selling tapes with how-to information for their specific audiences. "It won't happen immediately; it will build," predicted *HVP* senior editor Leslie Grey.

Two-hour movies (fiction, again) produced for video store distribution rather than movie-house distribution are another trend that will affect scriptwriters. Hollywood films for theatre distribution cost an estimated $10 million to $40 million to produce. The made-for-video-only films are being produced at a cost of $50,000, say, for a drama to $1 million for an action film. Whereas the Hollywood scriptwriter needs a script "package" that sometimes includes a major star's agreement to be in the film, video movies will rely more on the script and on good but lesser-known actors. "Good stories and catchy packaging and artwork" will attract video movie fans to these films, speculated Felix Girard, director of program development for Mediacom Development Corp.

Also, if you have extensive writing credits, you might approach producers of cinema-distributed films. It's a good idea to register your script with the Writers Guild of America (8955 Beverly Blvd., Los Angeles 90048, or 555 W. 57th St., New York, New York 10019) prior to submitting it. Often ideas, rather than entire scripts, are sold to networks or producers—so don't be surprised if *your* dialogue doesn't make it to the screen. Some producers seek only scripts submitted through agents. (See Authors' Agents listings for more information.)

Format for the screenplay call for a typed, single-spaced (triple-spaced between the dialogue of different characters) manuscript. Set margins at 15 and 75 (pica) or 18 and 90 (elite) and allow 125-150 pages for a two-hour feature film (90 pages for 90 minutes).

Working on characterization, dialogue, plot construction, conflict and resolution will help you sell scripts—and help you on your journey to the Emerald City.

ARKOFF INTERNATIONAL PICTURES, 9200 Sunset Blvd., P.H. 3, Los Angeles CA 90069. (213)278-7600. President of Distribution: Billy Fine. 2% freelance written. 100% of scripts produced are agented submissions. "We do not look at unsolicited manuscripts. We work through agents and attorneys only."

‡BONIME ASSOCIATES, LTD., 230 E. 44th St., New York NY 10017. (212)490-2910. President: Andrew Bonime. Produces "feature motion pictures. We develop high quality, moderate-to high-budget feature film projects. We either purchase scripts, book manuscripts, or hire writers on the average of six projects per year (includes rewrites of presently owned material)." 100% freelance written. Works with 1-2 unpublished/unproduced writers annually. Buys theatrical motion picture rights. "We accept only material submitted through recognized agents."
Needs: Submit through "recognized agents." Pays in accordance with Writers Guild standards.
Tips: "We are always looking for new writing talent, but because of sheer time and volume and because of legal reasons, we cannot accept unsolicited material or any material that does not come through recognized agents. We're interested in writers who have an understanding of motion picture technique for writing scripts, ability to create character—drama or comedy—and an understanding of the visual process of film. Freelance writers should be aware of personal/character relationships and unusual concepts."

THE CHAMBA ORGANIZATION, 230 W. 105th St., #2-A, New York NY 10025. President: St. Clair Bourne. Produces material for "the activist-oriented audience; the general audience (PG), and in the educational film market we aim at high school and adult audiences, especially the so-called 'minority' audiences. Assignments are given solely based upon our reaction to submitted material. The material is the credential." 100% freelance written. 10% of scripts produced are unagented submissions. Buys 2-4 scripts/year. Works with 3 unpublished/unproduced writers annually. Query with a brief description of plot, thumbnail descriptions of principal characters and any unusual elements. Computer printout submissions acceptable; prefers letter-quality to dot-marix. SASE.
Needs: "I concentrate primarily on feature film projects and unique feature-length documentary film projects. We prefer submission of film treatments first. Then, if the idea interests us, we negotiate the writing of the script." Also needs scripts for video and material (film) for cable television. Payment negotiable according to Writers Guild standards.
Recent Production: *On the Boulevard* (fiction).
Tips: Trends in the American stage and screen include "a critical examination of traditional American values."

□ **CHRISTIAN BROADCASTING NETWORK**, Virginia Beach VA 23463. (804)424-7777. Executive Producer, Program Development: David Freyss. Produces material for a general mass audience as well as Christian audiences. Second largest cable network in the nation. Producer of *700 Club*. 20% freelance written. 60% of scripts produced are unagented submissions. "We are planning over 12 different programs: some one-shot, some series, women's programs, dramas based on Bible characters and holiday shows. Mostly staff-written but will consider freelance treatments." Buys negotiable rights. Works with 5 unpublished/unproduced writers annually. Previously produced material OK. Computer printout submissions acceptable; prefers letter-quality to dot-matrix. Send to Tom Rogeberg, Director of Operations, CBN Cable Network. SASE. Reports in 2 weeks.
Needs: Secular and Christian. Dramatic, service, educational, children's, feature films, informational shows, film adaptations of books. Query and request release form to submit an idea or script. Buys some ideas outright; flat fee for treatment, outline or script.
Tips: "We're looking for writers with strong television/film background who have screenwriting experience. A basic belief in the *Bible* is necessary."

CINE/DESIGN FILMS, INC., 255 Washington St., Denver CO 80203. (303)777-4222. Producer/Director: Jon Husband. Produces educational material for general, sales training and theatrical audiences. 75% freelance written. 90% of scripts produced are unagented submissions. Buys 8-10 scripts/year. Phone query OK: "original solid ideas are encouraged." Computer printout submissions acceptable. Rights purchased vary.
Needs: "Motion picture outlines in the theatrical, documentary, sales or educational areas. We are seeking theatrical scripts in the low-budget area that are possible to produce for under $1,000,000. We seek flexibility and

---

□ *Open box preceding a listing indicates a cable TV market.*

personalities who can work well with our clients." Produces 16mm and 35mm films. Pays $100-200/screen minute on 16mm productions. Theatrical scripts negotiable.

Tips: "Understand the marketing needs of film production today."

□ **CINETUDES**, 295 W. 4th St., New York NY 10014. (212)966-4600. President: Christine Jurzykowski. Produces material for television, scripts for video and material for cable television. Works with 20 writers/year. 50% freelance written. 5 scripts are unagented submissions. Works with 5 unpublished/unproduced writers annually. Query with samples or submit resume. SASE. Reports in 2 weeks. Buys all rights.

Needs: Feature length screenplays (theatrical/television); theatrical shorts; children's programming. "We look for the willingness to listen and past experience in visual writing." Produces 16mm and 35mm films and videotape. Pays by outright purchase or pays daily rates.

DILLY INTERNATIONAL PRODUCTIONS, 1055 St. Paul Pl., Cincinnati OH 45202. (513)381-8696. Contact: Millard Segal. Produces material for a general TV audience. Buys all rights. Reports "immediately or takes option."

Needs: Magazine-format shows—visually interesting. "You must know the structure of TV scripting. Take college courses to learn before submitting." Submit treatment. Pays negotiable royalty; buys some scripts outright for a negotiable rate; "guaranteed deal for a series."

Tips: "There is not much money in writing for cable TV now, but in a couple of years there will be."

DSM PRODUCERS, Suite 1204, 161 W. 54th St., New York NY 10019. (212)245-0006. Produces material for consumer, trade and executive audiences. Works with 7-12 writers/year. Previously produced material OK. SASE. Reports in 1 month.

Needs: Phonograph records, tapes and cassettes. Currently interested in commercial material for all segments of the music industry i.e., record acts; commercials/film/radio-television/industrial/trade. Submit cassette/video or completed script and resume. Pays in royalty or in accordance with Writers Guild standards.

‡□ **EMBASSY TELEVISION**, 1438 N. Gower Ave., Box 27, Los Angeles CA 90028. Produces scripts for video, and material for cable television. 25% freelance written. "Our shows are mainly staff-written. Occasionally we use outside writers, but legally we can only accept work from writers whose material is submitted through accredited agents." Works with 5 unpublished/unproduced writers annually. Writers Guild of America membership required. Computer printout submissions acceptable; no dot-matrix.

□ **ETERNAL WORD TELEVISION NETWORK**, 5817 Old Leeds Rd., Birmingham AL 35210. (205)956-9537. Director of Programming: Dick Stephen. Produces material with a Catholic focus on everyday living. "Spiritual growth network which also airs family entertainment. Support comes from donations. Founded by Mother Angelica who has an active book ministry." Computer printout submissions acceptable; no dot-matrix. SASE. Reports in 4 months.

Needs: "We would like to see scripts in all forms and formats: drama, talk shows, panel discussions and original ideas." Half-hour programs or specials for cable television with uplifting, inspirational themes. Submit synopsis/outline of script. "May hold the script for up to 1 year."

Tips: "We want scripts that promote strong social values, or with religious themes."

GOLDSHOLL DESIGN & FILM, INC., 420 Frontage Rd., Northfield IL 60093. (312)446-8300. President: M. Goldsholl. Query. Buys all rights.

Needs: Scripts for industrial public relations films. Also interested in original screenplays and short stories to be made into screenplays. "Describe your material before sending it. Do not send 'fantasy' scripts!" Produces sound filmstrips, 16mm and 35mm films, multimedia kits, tapes and cassettes, and 35mm slide sets. Pays 5-10% of budget.

Tips: "Write your ideas clearly. Know the visual world."

LIROL TV PRODUCTIONS, 6335 Homewood Ave., Los Angeles CA 90028. (213)467-8111. Contact: Sandra Murray. Computer printout submissions acceptable. 25% freelance written. Writers worked with "varies from year to year"; published/produced writers only. Buys all rights.

Needs: Nonfiction material, TV syndication, presentations for industrial clients and commercials. Submit synopsis/outline. Pays in accordance with Writers Guild standards.

Market conditions are constantly changing! If this is 1987 or later, buy the newest edition of *Writer's Market* at your favorite bookstore or order directly from Writer's Digest Books.

Close-up

Writers Guild of America

When Writers Guild of America members went on strike last year, newspaper reports began telling TV viewers how the strike might affect their lives. There were reports that the daytime dramas would be affected and that the late evening show producers would resort to reruns during the strike. Viewers (and newspaper readers) perhaps for the first time thought about the writers behind the scenes.

Aside from the strike, though, the Writers Guild works year-round for writers, offering a number of services to members and nonmembers. "We are a labor union representing writers in the *television, radio*, and *motion picture* industry," says WGA-East membership administrator Adrine Stephens-Gordon. "We represent freelance writers and staff writers, protecting them in essential areas such as fees, payment, credits, rights, and arbitrations of dispute."

The guild has offices on both coasts: the Writers Guild of America, East, with headquarters in New York (555 W. 57th St., New York, NY 10019) and the Writers Guild of America, West, based in Los Angeles (8955 Beverly Blvd., Los Angeles, CA 90048). Writers who live east of the Mississippi River join the guild's east office; writers west of this line join at the west office.

Through the WGA, writers—both members and nonmembers—can register their scripts, synopses, outlines, ideas, treatments and scenarios. As with the U.S. Copyright Office, the guild cannot protect titles. "The aim of registration is to prove priority of ownership," the WGA tells scriptwriters, "and that priority cannot be proved if the material is shown to a producer."

Writers register a script by sealing it in a WGA envelope. When the guild receives this envelope, it is dated, given a registration number, and filed. The writer may then indicate on the title page of his script that it is registered with the WGA. The date of registration or the registration number should not be listed on a script submitted to producers.

The Writers Guild charges nonguild members a $15 registration fee for up to 150 pages of material. Students pay $10 to register material. Guild members are charged $5 for script registration. The registration is valid for 10 years but may also be renewed.

Writers Guild of America helps members and nonmembers with information on agents and current payment rates. A writer who has received an offer from a producer can call the guild office to find out what producers are paying writers.

How to Join

"For a writer to become a member, he or she would first have to sell one script," points out the membership administrator.

When the scriptwriter joins the guild, he agrees not to work with independent film producers unless a producer becomes a signatory to the guild agreement.

Approximately 2,500 producers have signed the guild's applicable minimum basic agreement, thus agreeing to pay certain rates, give writers credits for scripts, and also to contribute to the guild's pension, health and welfare plan.

"A lot of producers, I'm told by writers, tell writers they do not hire nonmembers of the guild. This is inaccurate," explains Gordon.

Producers who have signed guild agreements can still work with nonguild writers, but they (the producers) must tell writers they are a WGA signatory and that the writer will be required to join the guild once he has been hired by a signatory.

Writers pay a one-time initiation fee of $1,000 to join the Writers Guild of America and $50 annually in membership dues. "If the writer has any earnings under the guild's jurisdiction, he pays an assessment of one-and-one-half percent of the gross amount (in addition to the annual dues)," says the membership administrator.

In return, the guild represents writers "for the purpose of collective bargaining."

□ **THE LITTLE RED FILMHOUSE**, Box 691083, Los Angeles CA 90069. (213)855-0241. Producer: Larry Klingman. Produces material for kindergarten through adult audience. 60% freelance written. 80% of scripts produced are unagented submissions. Buys 3 scripts/year. Buys all rights and makes work-for-hire assignments. "We purchase specific rights if we are adapting published work." Works with 2-3 unpublished/unproduced writers annually. No previously produced material. Computer printout submissions acceptable. SASE. Reports in 2 weeks on queries; 1 month on submissions. Free catalog.
Needs: Motion pictures, television shows/series. Produces fiction aimed at the following groups: 7-10-year-olds, 11-14-year-olds, young adults. "We are looking for good stories, humor and cross-cultural materials with the potential for serializing." Same requirements for cable television. Query with brief (1-2 paragraphs) outline. Pay varies with the project.
Tips: "Spend more time with the end users to get a feel for the materials they are demanding. Become market driven. Don't tell us what the market *should* want, give us what the market *is demanding*. Do not send script or manuscript prior to query."

□ **LEE MAGID PRODUCTIONS**, Box 532, Malibu CA 90265. (213)858-7282. President: Lee Magid. Produces material for all markets, teenage-adult; commercial—even musicals. 50% freelance written. 80% of scripts produced are unagented submissions. Buys 20 scripts/year; works with 10 writers/year. Works with "many" unpublished/unproduced writers. Buys all rights. Previously produced material OK. Electronic submissions acceptable via VHS video or cassette/audio; requires hard copy also. SASE. Reports in 6 weeks.
Needs: Films, sound filmstrips, phonograph records, television shows/series, videotape presentations. Currently interested in film material, either for video (television) or theatrical. "We deal with cable networks, producers, live-stage productions, etc. Market is still questionable as to monies to be paid." Submit synopsis/outline and resume. Pays in royalty, in outright purchase, in accordance with Writers Guild standards, or depending on author."
Tips: "We like comedy, real-life drama that all can relate to."

□ **MEDIACOM DEVELOPMENT CORP.**, Box 1926, Simi Valley CA 93062. (213)552-9988 or (818)991-5452. Director/Program Development: Felix Girard. 80% freelance written. Buys 10-20 scripts annually from unpublished/unproduced writers. 50% of scripts produced are unagented submissions. Query with samples. Send queries to Box 1926, Simi Valley CA 93062. Computer printout submissions acceptable. SASE. Reports in 1 month. Buys all rights or first rights.
Needs: Produces charts; sound filmstrips; 16mm films; multimedia kits; overhead transparencies; tapes and cassettes; slides and videotape with programmed instructional print materials, broadcast and cable television programs. Publishes software ("programmed instruction training courses"). Negotiates payment depending on project.
Tips: "Send short samples of work. Especially interested in flexibility to meet clients' demands, creativity in treatment of precise subject matter. We are looking for good, fresh projects (both special and series) for cable and pay television markets. A trend in the audiovisual field that freelance writers should be aware of is the move toward more interactive video disk/computer CRT delivery of training materials for corporate markets."

□ **NICKELODEON MTV NETWORKS, INC.**,1133 Avenue of the Americas, New York NY 10036. (212)944-4250. Manager of Program Services and Commercial Clearance: Ann Sweeney. Produces material for age-specific audience aged 2 to 15. Now in 18 million homes. Buys negotiable rights. SASE. Reports in 1 month.
Needs: "Full channel children's programming for cable TV. Value filled, non-violent material desired." Submit resume and programming ideas (2-3 page explanations). Pays variable rate.

PACE FILMS, INC., 411 E. 53rd Ave., New York NY 10022. (212)755-5486. President: R. Vanderbes. Produces material for a general theatrical audience. Buys all rights. Previously produced material OK. SASE. Reports in 2 months.
Needs: Theatrical motion pictures. Produces 35mm films, cable tapes and cassettes. Query with samples; submit synopsis/outline or completed script. Pays in accordance with Writers Guild standards.

‡**PASETTA PRODUCTIONS**, Suite 205, 8322 Beverly Blvd., Los Angeles CA 90048. (213)655-8500. Assistant to President: Vicki LaBrie. "Very seldom do we consider submitted material because of the quality and other requirements." Buys all rights. No previously produced material. SASE. Reports in 6 weeks on queries; 2 months on submissions.
Needs: Television or videotape. "We do shows as we are contracted." Submit synopsis/outline or presentation of project. Pays in accordance with Writers Guild standards.
Tips: "Material must be registered with the WGA. Any funding sources secured or talent set for the show would greatly aid in getting the show produced. Writers think if they have an idea, that is enough for a show. However, we won't consider anything without funds or set talent. The shows we produce are mainly musical/variety and the writers we use are specialized and well-known in the industry."

PAULIST PRODUCTIONS, Box 1057, Pacific Palisades CA 90272. (213)454-0688. Contact: Story Department. 100% freelance written. *Capital Cities Family Specials* are geared toward senior high school students. Buys 4-6 half-hour scripts/year. WGA membership required. Computer printout submissions acceptable; no dot-matrix.
Needs: "We are looking for longer form one- to three-hour television specials and theatrical releases on people who have acted boldly on their moral convictions regarding human and/or Christian values." Submit complete script through agent only. "We are not interested in unsolicited manuscripts."
Tips: "Watch our *Capital Cities Family Specials* enough so that you have a strong sense of the sort of material we produce. We look for wit, originality of theme and approach, an unsentimental, yet strong and positive manner of approaching subject matter—intelligent, literate, un-cliché-ridden writing."

□ **RESTON TELEVISION THEATER**, (formerly Reston Repertory Television Theater), Box 3615, Reston VA 22090. (703)437-0764. Executive Producer: Sharon Cohen. 100% freelance written. Produces material for local cable and PBS audience. Buys 1-2 scripts/year. "We negotiate with playwright on the basis of a percentage of resulting sales." SASE. Reports in 1 month on queries; 4 months on submissions.
Needs: "Original scripts—no adaptations. Production requirements should be simple (no car chases). Playing time may be 30-90 minutes. All scripts considered within the limits of good taste." Submit complete script.
Tips: "Hollywood does fine work, but it serves a different purpose than ours. If you think that your script contains all the elements that would make it a *hot* property in Hollywood, we would probably *not* be interested in reading it."

‡**TELEVISION PRODUCTION SERVICES CORP.**, 381 Horizon Dr., Edison NJ 08817. (201)287-3626. Executive Director/Producer: R.S. Burks. Produces video music materials for major market distributor networks, etc. Buys 50-100 scripts/year. Buys all rights. Previously produced material OK. Computer printout submissions OK; prefers letter-quality to dot-matrix printouts. SASE. Reports in 2 weeks.
Needs: "We do video music for record companies, MTV, HBO, etc. We use treatments of story ideas from the groups management. We also do commercials for over the air broadcast and cable." Submit synopsis/outline or completed script, and resume; include return envelope and postage.
Tips: Looks for rewrite flexibility and availability. "We have the capability of transmission electronically over the phone modem to our printer or directly onto disk for storage."

BOB THOMAS PRODUCTIONS, INC., Box 1787, Wayne NJ 07470. (201)696-7500. New York Office: 60 E. 42nd St., New York NY 10165. (212)221-3602. President: Robert G. Thomas.
Needs: Scripts for "made-for-television" films and *only* through registered agents.

UNITED JEWISH APPEAL/FEDERATION OF JEWISH PHILANTHROPIES, 130 E. 59th St., New York NY 10022. (212)980-1000. Public Relations: Art Portnow. Produces material for people interested in Jewish topics and a Jewish audience. Produces scripts for video. 80% freelance written. 2-3 scripts are unagented submissions. Works with 10 unpublished/unproduced writers annually. Buys negotiable rights. Previously produced material OK. Computer printout submissions acceptable; prefers letter-quality to dot-matrix printouts. Reports in 1 month.
Needs: Audiovisual materials for group showing, scripts for commercial TV and radio programs. "Writer must be well-versed in Judaic tradition and customs." Produces slides/sound shows, video, radio, films. Query with sample or resume and sample of script from a completed program. Does not return samples. Buys scripts outright for $100-500; "varies with length and requirement of the script."
Tips: "Unique ideas are welcome here. New angles on holidays are always of interest. Additional per diem freelance writing assignments for news release work and the like is also available."

Gag Writing ━━━━━━━━━━━━━━━━━━━━━

If you decide to write and sell gags, you'll have another decision to make: Do you want to write gags that people "read" or "hear"?

The cartoonist (who needs gags to "read") and the entertainer (who needs gags to "hear") have different requirements, demands and audiences. Some cartoonists write their own captions. Some comedians write the jokes they perform. But many times, cartoonists and entertainers will collaborate with a writer.

The important "thing" is to decide whether a gag is for print or performance *before* you write it. Cartoons and monologues reach audiences in different ways. What seems funny in the morning's comic strips might not get any laughs that night in a comedy club.

Gags for Print

When we asked cartoonists what characteristics they look for in a gag writer, they said it's "hard to explain." You know a great gag at first reading, they pointed out.

"The ability to describe an idea so I can visualize it well and ideas that are up to date" are characteristics that many cartoonists look for.

They complain that some writers send old material—either dog-eared gags that have been rejected by other cartoonists or gags with yesterday's terms or situations. Remember that people don't disco in 1986; they break (dance).

Cartoonists need visual gags; they can't use gags suited for night-club monologues. "I prefer understated or exaggerated gags where the gag itself is not funny unless and until the reader sees the picture—a marriage of words and drawing—that appeals to a broad audience," said one cartoonist.

To write gags for a cartoonist, you need not be an artist. A submission does not need an elaborate drawing or a paragraph explaining the gag *if* that gag is truly funny, pointed out another cartoonist. Cartoonists like to illustrate a *funny* gagline without seeing someone else's drawing of it. In fact, a gag on a 3x5 card that says, "Man says to woman . . . (the gag)," is sufficient.

Captions—if used—should be simple and universal. You can get more mileage out of a gag by initially directing it toward a specific audience (a farm journal, for example) and altering it somewhat for a more general market, such as a family magazine.

Look for cartoonists' work in books and magazines. Get a feel for their styles. Consult their requirements in *Writer's Market* and write accordingly.

Submit gags on 3x5 cards or slips, one per card. Include an identification number on the upper left-hand corner, and type your name and address on the back of the card. You must also include a self-addressed, stamped envelope any time you send material to a cartoonist. Submitting 10 to 20 gags at one time is standard.

Good gags will prompt people to laugh at—and learn about—themselves and everyday life. Insulting people's religions and nationalities doesn't work, said one gag writer. Instead, most cartoonists want timely gags focusing on audiences' newest crazes.

As for money matters, gag writers are paid after the cartoonist receives a check from the publication. Magazines may pay anywhere from $10 to about $300 per cartoon. The writer usually earns 25% commission on the selling price; 50% if the cartoonist submits a rough sketch and sells only the writer's idea, not the finished cartoon, to a publisher.

To expand the number of markets you sell to, consider other outlets. Magazines buy short humor, anecdotes and jokes. Greeting card publishers need humorous verses. Syndicates will review cartoons with gags. And don't overlook local outlets.

The hometown newspaper may want to editorialize on recent school board actions with a short, to-the-point caption and drawing. Use your creativity in writing and in finding new markets.

Gags for Performance

While seven may be a gambler's lucky number, *three* works best for many comedians. Entertainers generally won't devote an entire monologue to one topic but rather will cover, say, three topics with transitions between them. And usually three jokes per topic are sufficient, though the number can vary. (Ten jokes on one subject will wear out the topic—and the audience's interest.)

Even if a comedian appears to be casually rambling, most monologues have been carefully planned, with the best jokes placed at the beginning and end of the act.

Some comedians will pay a writer to write the entire monologue. Others will buy one-liners, then fit the jokes from different writers into a monologue.

We invited comedians to have a listing in our book. However, some entertainers don't want their audiences to know that they don't write their own material; other comedians who travel frequently do not have the time or staff to screen unsolicited gags. So, most of them declined our offer, but that doesn't mean that you shouldn't approach a comedian you want to write for. Some comedians will talk with fans after a show; the ingenuous gag writer might try to hand gags to a comedian on tour. Also, consider mailing gags to entertainers whose style seems to match your writing style.

Remember, though, that professional approach is essential. Carbon copies of jokes, handwritten gags on bent cards, or typos in your letter of introduction will tell the comedian you are an amateur. Typing each gag on a separate sheet of paper or index card enables the buyer to select the one or ones he likes. Always enclose a self-addressed, stamped envelope for the return of your gags.

Do not send the same batch of jokes to several comedians at the same time. No comedian wants to tell an already-told joke; in fact, comedians are successful *because* their gags and methods of delivery are different than anyone else's in the business.

Wait until you get a response or the return of your gags before sending them to another entertainer. Because you won't know if your gags have reached a comedian's office or agent, you might want to give a deadline date for a response. We generally don't recommend that you give buyers an ultimatum, but you could be waiting for a response and the comedian didn't receive your gags. You might say something like this in your cover letter: "...I look forward to hearing from you soon but realize you have a busy schedule. If you have not returned the enclosed gags by July 1 [give a date four months from your date of mailing], I'll assume that you're not buying gags at this time and will market my work elsewhere."

Before you type or submit gags, though, try them on audiences. And remember that the successful comedian wants listeners to feel they are smarter than him. Comedians try out jokes at nearby comedy clubs before they add them to their nightclub acts. In your hometown, patrons of a local comedy club will tell you (by their reactions) if your material is funny.

Joan Rivers who writes 99 percent of her gags tests them in the office (her staff is the audience) and at comedy clubs. She recommends that comedians tape their performances, then listen to the jokes and reactions to them.

One concern voiced by gag writers is whether entertainers or audiences will steal their material. Joan Rivers keeps records of her jokes on a computer; there she lists whether she or a gag writer wrote the joke. Sometimes her office will receive the same joke from six different parts of the country.

One day in Joan Rivers' office, her staff was laughing at a joke she'd just written. That evening, a Tonight Show guest host told the same joke. "Creative minds at times think of the same idea," said Rivers' secretary.

In Melvin Helitzer's "Comedy Techniques for Writers and Performers" class at Ohio University, students write impromptu jokes on paper, then share them with the class; the jokes must relate to words given by Helitzer at the beginning of class. We saw two students (who sat across the room from one another) come up with the same word association.

Wanting to avoid accusations of stolen material, some entertainers are reluctant to look at writers' work. Before you accuse anyone of stealing a gag, make sure it isn't a coincidence or a joke in public domain.

"Many jokes and commonly repeated stories of a similar kind are in the public domain. A work in the public domain may be used freely by anyone and is no longer subject to any copyright protection," said the U.S. Copyright Office. "However, material of this kind may be copyrighted if it is original or contains a substantial amount of original 'new matter'."

Jokes and stories, including compilations of such material, may be submitted for registration on Form TX (Library of Congress, Washington, D.C. 20559). "It is the particular way in which the author tells the joke or story that is protected, not the idea of the joke or the story itself," according to the copyright office.

Don't think you need a gambler's luck to write for comedians. It may take many years to establish contacts, but if you can produce audience-pleasing material, good comedians will want your gags. Many entertainers started in little clubs and moved into larger arenas. That's what gag writers must also do.

PAUL M. ARCHETKO, Box 90631, Rochester NY 14609. (716)225-8346. Began selling cartoons in 1980. Holds 100 gags/year. Sells to men's publications. Recently sold material to *Hustler*, *Swank*, *Genesis*, *Velvet*, *Letters*, and *High Society*. Works with 6 writers annually. Submit gags on 3x5 slips. Reports in 1 week. Sells cartoons for $75-150. Pays 25% commission. SASE.
Needs: "I deal only in men, girlie magazines and am only interested in this type of gag. Off-the-wall, unusual, short captions do the best; no caption, highly visual do better. Will look at hardcore sex, biker, fetish material etc. Anti-religious gags do nothing for me; no market for generals, etc. Anything from mild to rough sex or related is fine."
Tips: "The shorter the gag the better; get to the point. Drop the 'stage setting' and leave it to the cartoonist. Gags must be funny, highly visual, and unusual or unique in that I wouldn't have thought of it myself. Include 'rejection slip' with gags."

EDGAR ARGO, 6504 Langdale Rd., Baltimore MD 21237. Holds 500 gags/year. Works with 30 gagwriters/year. Sells to a wide range of magazines, newspapers, etc. "Creatively I'm very liberal—I will consider *anything* if there is a market for it." Recently sold to *Penthouse*, *New Woman*, *Review of the News*, and *Private Practice*, etc. Buys 5% of the gags received from freelance writers. Submit gags on 3x5 cards or slips. No limit on number of gags submitted. "Average I receive is 10-20." Reports in 1 week. Sells cartoons for $10-300; pays gagwriters $2.50-75. Pays 25% commission or standard rate at the time. SASE.
Needs: "I work very fast and in a variety of styles. I will illustrate any gag that I think is *funny* and *salable*. There are *no* restrictions. I will consider ideas for syndicated comic strips." The best markets for cartoons/gags will be business, medical, legal, x-rated video, women's magazines, and bikers.
Tips: "Typing is not necessary, but the gags must be legible. I won't struggle to read them. I want economy of words. Humor, originality and simplicity are characteristics I most look for in a gagwriter—because that's what editors look for in a cartoonist." Must have SASE.

EDOUARD BLAIS, 2704 Parkview Blvd., Minneapolis MN 55422. (612)588-5249. Holds 250 gags/year. Works with 10 gagwriters/year. Sells to mens, sports, fitness, health, education, family, outdoor, camping and fishing publications. Recently sold material to *Gallery*, *Curriculum Review*, *New England Running*, and *Your Health and Fitness*. Buys 25-50% of the gags received from freelance writers. Submit gags on 3x5 slips; 10-12 in one batch. Reports in 1 week. Sells cartoons for $5-75. Pays 25% commission. SASE. Writer's guidelines for SASE.
Needs: Erotic, women's magazines, health, fitness, hobbies, education, family, outdoors, camping, and fishing gags, etc. No "science or computer gags or 'in' type humor such as *New Yorker* uses." Looks for sight gags—no captions, or minimum amount of words. "I accept gags I feel match up well with my style of drawing."
Tips: "I would especially like to receive gags on family—especially young married couples, not necessarily

dealing with sex (that's OK, too), but all aspects of young family life. Gag writers should be aware of what's going on in all phases of society, the style of language being used, and new developments (like fast food, microwave, G-spot, etc.). I am relatively new to cartooning (and will complete my fifth year this March).

DAN BORDERS, 191 Alton Rd., Galloway OH 43119. (614)878-3528. Holds 35 gags/year. Works with 5 gagwriters/year. Sells to computer magazines of all kinds, trade journals, many general interest and electronic gags. Recently sold material to *Computer World*, *Info World*, *Dr. Dobb's Journal*, *Radio-Electronics* and *Reader's Digest*. Buys 25% of the gags received from freelance writers. Submit gags on 3x5 cards or slips. Submit 15 gags in one batch. Sells cartoons for $15-50. Pays 25% commission. SASE.
Needs: Electronics and computer gags, and environment, family and angel gags. No "girlie gags." Looks for humorists with dry humor.
Tips: "Many computer magazines are buying computer cartoons. Also electronic 'toons' are selling well. I am always ready to see good, well-thought-out ideas."

BILL BOYNANSKY, Apt. 13/20, Ansonia Hotel, 2109 Broadway, New York NY 10023. Works with 35-60 gagwriters/year. Holds over 1,000 gags/year; sells between 800-900 cartoons/year. Submit 15-20 gags at one time. Reports in 3 days to 2 months. Pays "25% for regular, 35% for captionless; all others—regular payment." SASE.
Needs: General, male, female, sexy, girlie, family, children's, adventure and medical. "No overdone girlie gags, overdone family gags, TV, parking the car, woman nagging husband, etc. Prefer to see captionless gag ideas on all subject matters, but no beginners; only those who know their business. I prefer to deal with cartoonists by letter because it saves me time."
Recent Cartoon: Scene: Man (in great anger) breaking up a TV set with a baseball bat: "I'm sick of this damn violence—on T.V.!!!"

ASHLEIGH BRILLIANT, 117 W. Valerio St., Santa Barbara CA 93101. Sold about 315 cartoons last year. Self-syndicated and licensed to publications and manufacturers worldwide. Reports in 2 weeks. Pays $25.
Needs: "My work is so different from that of any other cartoonist that it must be carefully studied before any gags are submitted. Any interested writer not completely familiar with my work should first send $2 for my catalog of 1,000 copyrighted examples. Otherwise, their time and mine will be wasted."
Recent Cartoon: "I feel much better now that I've given up hope."

LEONARD BRUCE, AKA "LEO", 22A Brianfield Cove, Jackson TN 38305. (901)668-1205. Holds 20 gags/month. Works with 4 gagwriters/year. Sells to newspapers, charity publications, space publications, science fiction and science fiction movie magazines, comic book publications, and animal care publications. Recently sold material to *Starlog*, *Comics Collector*, *Space Age Times*, *Kind Magazine*, *World Wildlife Newsletter* and *Shelter Sense Magazine*. Submit gags on 3x5 cards. Submit 12 gags in one batch. Pays 10% commission. Buys first serial rights. Reports in 2 weeks. SASE.
Needs: Looking for gags on science fiction movie themes, comic book hero themes, themes on computers, space travel, UFOs, life on other planets, "aliens" trying to cope with our world. Also a Berry's World theme; one guy in crazy situations. No political, foreign affairs or white collar themes. Will consider gags for cartoon strips: Leotoons (science fiction "alien" themes); Fred (space exploration themes); and It's a Mad World (crazy situations in our insane world). Looks for offbeat gags, "taking normal situations and turning them into 'sight gags' or word gags. As an example: Berry's World or Herman gag themes."
Tips: "I look for quality and good typing ability in a gagwriter. Gagwriters should be aware that gags *have* to be very funny or the whole cartoon doesn't work or sell. The gag is the main reason a cartoon sells nowadays. I would especially like to receive gags on alien life and science fiction."

JUNIOR CHAMBERS, Apt. 1, 416 W. Division, Villa Park IL 60181. Holds 100 gags/year. Buys 50% of sales from freelance writers. Will work with writers who are professional.
Needs: "New Yorker" type gags. Batch size not important. Pays 25% commission. SASE.

‡DON COLE, Box 917, Dover NJ 07801. (201)328-9153. Holds 25-50 gags/year. Sells to general interest magazines and trade journals. Recently sold material to Shutterbug ads, *Photographic News* and *VFW Magazine*. Submit gags on 3x5 slips; about 12 (or 1 ounce) in one batch. Reports in 3 days. Pays 25% commission. SASE.
Needs: Photographic (but must know the *trade*); general; trade journals; "anything clean and *funny*." No erotic, women's liberation or anti-Christian themes. Will consider strip ideas based on a professional photographer or cartoonist (Mort Walker or Al Capp style—or whatever). Also daily humor plus adventure, continuous. Especially wants "plausibility, humor, good satire, predicaments.'
Tips: "Send *original* work only. No gags from old magazines or cartoon books."

THOMAS W. DAVIE, 28815 4th Place S, Federal Way WA 98003. Buys 75 gags/year. Works with 10 gagwriters/year. Has sold to *Medical Economics*, *Sports Afield*, King Features, *Chevron U.S.A.*, *Rotarian*, *Saturday Evening Post*, *Ladies' Home Journal*, *Playgirl* and *Boys' Life*. Buys 30% of the gags received from freelance writers. Gags should be typed on 3x5 slips. Prefers batches of 5-25. Sells cartoons for $10-450. Pays 25% commission. Reports in 1 month. SASE. No IRC.
Needs: General gags, medicals, mild girlies, sports (hunting and fishing), business and travel gags. No pornography.
Tips: "I'm often overstocked—please don't flood me with gags."

ED DAVIS, 69 Wind Whisper Court, The Woodlands TX 77380. (713)363-9264. Holds 30 gags/year. Works with 25 gagwriters/year. Sells to men's, women's, management and general publications. Recently sold material to *Easy Rider*, *Hustler*, *National Enquirer*, *Graphic Arts Monthly* and *Printer's News*. Buys 10% of the gags received from freelance writers. Submit gags on single cards. Submit reasonable number of gags. Sells cartoons for $30-300; pays gagwriters $7.50-75. Reports in 15 days. Pays 25% commission; "will work out better terms for writers in sync with my humor." SASE.
Needs: "Prefers any gag to deal with American themes. I sell more erotic and 'black' humor material than anything. Also need management/business, printing/graphic arts, cowboy/western, sports, animals, working women (cosmopolitan), medical/healthcare, trade journal, and general material. I have markets for any *good* material."
Tips: "Experience guides me to material I 'feel' will sell. I tend to reject worn-out situations and scenes which are too complicated or require much research. Time is limited." Looks for professional material. "All others will not be considered."

LEE DeGROOT, Box 115, Ambler PA 19002. Pays 25% on sales.
Needs: Interested in receiving studio greeting card ideas. "I draw up each idea in color before submitting to greeting card publishers, therefore, giving the editors a chance to visualize the idea as it would appear when printed . . . and thus increasing enormously the chances of selling the idea." Enclose SASE.

‡**NORM DREW**, Laurier House, Suite 608-L, 1600 Beach Ave., Vancouver, British Columbia V6G 1Y6 Canada. (604)689-1948. Holds 300-500 gags in a year. Currently expanding comic cartoon gag needs. Sells to general urban magazines and daily and weekly newspapers, trade journals, and TV or film. Recently sold to *Globe and Mail*, CBC TV, *Creative Computing*, BCTV, and *West Ender Weekly*, Contenova Cards (created and sold 2 merchandise lines: "Life Lines" and "Daily Grind"). Submit 3x5 cards; 12-20 in a batch. Reports in 1 week on submissions. Pays 25% percentage arrangement. General gags: 25-40% reprint. Makes outright purchase for Chika, Bush Babies. SAE with International Reply Coupons to cover return postage (USA rate). USA stamps not valid here.
Needs: Comic strips, gags, or scripts. Subjects include urban lifestyles, consumer angst, TV viewers, computers, bicycling, photography, home video, insurance, art, accounting, media trades—TV, radio, press, entertainment—film, stock market, current events—Europe/North America, apartment living, travel, hobbies: model building, model railroads, shortwave radio, home movies/video/audio, collectors: stamps, coins, and flea market hunters, gardening, advertising world. Young urbans, senior citizens, and contemporary kids views, foibles. No puns, porn, prurience, 'sick' subjects. Not at present doing sports, family, religion, outdoors, racial, medical, car, boat or general 'girlie' or liberated woman stereotypes. No weak play-on-words or illustrated "jokes". "I look for fresh, originality, healthy humor, astute eye for contemporary urban foibles; subtle, classy observations; accurate inside knowledge of the subject; visual irony, imminent victim gags; good visual situation sense; fresh, zany, slightly irreverent, sassy approach; attuned to current absurdities, timeless uinversal human frailties. Condense punchline to its punchiest minimal. I may reword/restage gag for stronger visual impact. Gag writer still will get 25%."
Tips: "I create and produce animated films and am currently working on a series of short animated 'fillers' for TV. These are captionless, pantomime, visual 'snowball effect' gags on urban life foibles. Think Keaton, Laurel and Hardy, Chaplin. If you always wished you could have written for the silent movies, try your hand at this series. Lot of action, close ups for reactions. Block out same as for Sunday page comics but about 30 panels per minute. Pay is outright purchase."

MIGUEL "MIKE" ESPARZA, 17157 E. Milan Circle, Aurora CO 80013. (303)693-9296. Holds 200 gags/year. Works with 20 gagwriters/year. Has sold to both men's and women's publications, general interest magazines and some trade journals. Buys 4% of the gags received from freelance writers. Submit on 3x5 cards, 12 or more gags in one batch. Sells cartoons for $15-100; pays gagwriters $3.75-25. Pays 25% commission. Reports in 2 weeks. SASE.
Needs: "Material for markets such as *Wall Street Journal*. Also gags for *National Enquirer*." Holds gags for family, business and general markets. Now working on single-panel feature on family life, including husband's work at office. Particularly needs Sunday strip ideas. "I prefer visual gags that are easily understood. Gaglines without visual support are not held."

Tips: "I would especially like to receive gags on family, general interest, business, and women in the work place in 1986. The characteristic I most look for in a gagwriter is consistency. It's refreshing to find an occasional diamond in the rough. But I usually hold at least one from the pros who study markets and know what sells."

‡**CHICK GANDIL**, % Smith Kaufman, 212 E. Third St., Cincinnati OH 45202. Buys 20-75 gags/year. 10% of gags purchased from freelance writers. Performs at conventions and state fairs. Submit on 8½x11 paper, 10-15 in one batch. Reports in 3 months. SASE. Pays $10 minimum, upon acceptance.
Needs: Family doctor jokes, home repair, and "shaggy" jokes. No women's or ethnic jokes.

DAVE GERARD, Box 692, Crawfordsville IN 47933. (317)362-3373. Holds 100 gags/year. Selss 30-40 freelance cartoons per month for magazines and periodicals. Recently sold material to *National Enquirer*, *Friends*, *D.A.C. News*, *Golf Digest*, *Wall Street Journal*, *Good Life*, *Medical Economics*, and King Features' Laff-A-Day. Works with 10 writers annually. Submit gags on 3x5 cards; 10 in one batch. Reports in 2 weeks. Sells cartoons for $50-300. Pays 25% commission. SASE.
Needs: General interest and sports, business, family and upbeat gags on pertinent and timely topics, like taxes, inflation, computers, etc. No "prisoners hanging on wall, kings and queens, talking animals, or put-down humor. I will be frank if material is not what I like. No erotic material."
Tips: "I like good sight gag material and short captions; also no-caption gags. Writers should be aware that subject matter changes along with the lifestyles of Americans, which, of course, change yearly. Gagwriting is stuck, in many cases, on old material."

‡**MEL HELITZER**, Lasher Hall, Ohio University, Athens OH 45701. (614)594-5608. Buys 100-150/year. 20% of gags from freelance writers. Uses gags as a master of ceremonies at banquets. Submit gags on 3x5 cards; 10 or more in a batch. Reports in 1 week. Makes outright purchase of $10 minimum. Pays on acceptance. SASE required.
Needs: University-related material. Subjects include faculty, administration, students and curriculum. Short one-liners or one-paragraph anecdotes. No student drugs, sex or alcohol. No blue language, but double entendres are OK.

CHARLES HENDRICK JR., Old Fort Ave., Kennebunkport ME 04046. (207)967-4412. Buys several gags/year; sold 50-60 cartoons last year. Works with 6 gagwriters/year. Sells to newspapers, magazines and local markets. Buys 5% of the gags received from freelance writers. Submit 8 gags at a time. Sells cartoons for $25-60; pays gagwriters $10-25. Pays 50% net of commission or negotiates commission. Reports in 1 month. SASE.
Needs: General family, trade (hotel, motel, general, travel, vacationers). Safe travel ideas—any vehicle. Gags must be clean; no lewd sex. Mild sex OK.
Recent Cartoon: Laughing Eskimo ladies sitting inside refrigerator. Frantic salesman says "but ladies, that is *not* a mobile home!"

WAYNE HOGAN, Box 842, Cookeville TN 38503. Began selling cartoons in 1982. Holds 200 gags/year. Sells to little press and general interest magazines and trade/professional journals. Recently sold material to *Bitter Sweet*, *The Artist's Magazine*, *Amelia*, *Computerworld*, and *Quarterly Journal of Ideology*. Submit gags on sheets of white typing paper; 10-15 gags in one batch. Reports in 2 weeks. Pays 25% of each paid use of cartooned gag. SASE.
Needs: General gags, art/artist-related gags, computer-related gags, and "mostly any sort of understated humor relating to mundane affairs of life." No "gallows/black" humor or erotica.
Recent Cartoon: Patty Lou, a single-panel cartoon strip "for which I'll consider gags depicting the female character associated with everyday, mundane, off-the-wall activities/events/phenomena."
Tips: "I look for conceptually clever and to-the-point gags."

‡**DAVID R. HOWELL**, Box 170, Porterville CA 93258. (209)781-5885. Holds 100+ gags/year. Sells to magazines, trade journals, etc. Recently sold material to *True Detective*, *TV Guide*, *National Enquirer*, *Woman's World*, King Features, *Cartoons*, etc. Submit gags on 3x5 cards or slips; 6-12 in one batch. Reports in 1 week. Pays 25% commission. SASE.
Needs: Cars, medical, farm, computer, specific topics. No politics, sex, taboo topics. No old stuff. "I need fresh, original approaches."

FRED ("FREJAC") JACKSON III, 70 Illinois, Pontiac MI 48053. Holds 150 gags/year. Works with 100 gagwriters/year. Sells cartoons to book companies (mostly cartoons to illustrate textbooks), girlie magazines, computer magazines, general interest magazines, religious publications, business publications, women's publications, children's magazines, farm magazines. Has sold to *Ahoyl*, *Woman's World*, *Radio-Electronics*, *Computerworld*, *Prentice-Hall Books*, *Wallace's Farmer*, *Creative Computing*, and others. Buys 20% of the gags received from freelance writers. Submit gags on 3x5 slips. Sells cartoons for $10-100. Pays 25-35% commission; 35% for captionless and major market sales. Reports in 1 month. SASE. "I hold unsold gags indefinitely until sold."

Needs: Girlie (both X-rated and softcore), captionless computer, office, general, business, humor through youth, animals, family, farm, video game, captionless, cable and pay TV, liberated woman, the sciences, electronics gags. "No old, tired gags, please. I've seen them all before."

Tips: "I need a constant supply of computer, girlie and humor through family gags. Most gags I receive are unfunny, stale and unoriginal. I look for gags that are very visual, clever sight gags. Girlie gags get top priority."

REAMER KELLER, 4500 S. Ocean Blvd., Palm Beach FL 33480. (305)582-2436.
Needs: Prefers general and visual gags. Pays 25%.

MILO KINN, 1413 SW Cambridge St., Seattle WA 98106. Holds approximately 200 gags/year; sells 100-200 cartoons/year. Has sold to *Medical Economics*, *Computerworld*, *Infoworld*, *Review of the News*, *Charlton* and many farm publications and trade journals, etc. Works with 8-10 writers annually. Buys 25% of the gags received from freelance writers. Sells cartoons for $15-100 "and up, on occasion." Pays 25% commission. SASE.
Needs: Medical, computer, dental, farm, male slant, girlie, woman, captionless, adventure and family gags. Sells girlie, farm, medical, office and general cartoons.
Tips: "The cartoon should be a funny picture or situation—not just 2 people talking. The gag should be a single caption-(not 'he' or 'she')—not just a joke, but a 'comic picture'! Try to slant to certain fields but must also fit 'general' category (not too technical) so they can go to more markets."

FRANK LENGEL, Box 890, Leesville SC 29070. (803)532-3259. Holds 100 gags/year. Works with 15 gagwriters/year. Sells to trade journals, general interest and men's magazines. Recent sales to *Saturday Evening Post*, *ABA Journal*, *Easyrider*, *National Enquirer*, *Hustler* and *Good Housekeeping*. Buys 5% of the gags received from freelance writers. Submit on 3x5 slips in batches of 10-20. But "also would look at a gag submitted on a brown paper bag if it's a gem!" Reports in 1 week. Sells cartoons for $15-300; pays gagwriters $5-100. Pays 33⅓% commission "upon receipt of my check from the publication." SASE. Submit seasonal material 4-6 months in advance.
Needs: General interest, family, business, medical, sex and outrageous satire. "I will look at almost anything if it is fresh and funny." Rarely considers word-play or multi-panel cartoons.
Tips: "My subject matter needs have remained relatively constant. The gagwriter mirrors society in a creative way. As society changes, gags change; however, they must deal with those things that remain constant, i.e., taxes, courts, family, schools, church, etc. I prefer understated or exaggerated gags where the gag itself is not funny unless and until the reader sees the picture—a marriage of words and drawing—that appeals to a broad audience. I like a clever writer. 'Clever' is funny because the gags are so strong that we all say to ourselves 'I should have thought of that one' as soon as we see it." *Recent Cartoon:* "Did you have a rough day darling?" (This line itself is not inherently funny). Scene—Pioneer wife greeting cowboy husband at front door of cabin; husband is stuck full of arrows."

LO LINKERT, 1333 Vivian Pl., Port Coquitlam, British Columbia V3C 2T9 Canada. Works with 20 gagwriters/year. Has sold to most major markets. Buys 1-5% of the gags recieved from freelance writers. Prefers batches of 10-15 gags. Sells cartoons for $50-600; pays gagwriters $20-100. Pays 25% commission. Returns rejected material in 1 week. Enclose SAE and 30¢ U.S. postage.
Needs: Clean, general, topical, medical, family, office, outdoors gags; captionless, pro woman sophisticated ideas. "Make sure your stuff is funny. No spreads." Wants "action gags—not two people saying something funny. No puns, dirty sex, drugs, drunks, racial or handicapped."
Tips: "I look for a gagwriter who sends few, but great, gags. I hate to be swamped by one writer who dumps bundles of gags on me."

LOS ANGELES TIMES SYNDICATE, 218 S. Spring St., Los Angeles CA 90012. (213)972-5198. "We don't hold gags; we contract with cartoonists to produce cartoons, and unless they're unacceptable to newspapers, we use all of them." Sells to newspapers (comics and editorial pages) and newspaper Sunday magazines. Recently sold to major newspapers worldwide . Submit photocopies or stats of 24 daily strips and 4 Sundays. The cartoons can be any size, as long as they're to scale with cartoons running in newspaper. Reports in about 2 months. SASE.
Needs: "We are looking for comic strips, panels and political cartoons. We especially need strips that are funny and well-drawn, and have interesting characters whom readers will love. Also, the work should be original (no imitations of strips or panels already in existence). We need cartoonists who can meet regular and frequent deadlines and are very prolific (a strip cartoonist will produce 52 Sunday strips and well over 300 daily strips per year). On strips and panels, since we sell to newspapers read by entire families, be careful with sex, booze gags, graphic or grotesque violence and so on. Politics is OK if you don't get strident. On political cartoons, the

market is very competitive; you must have your own voice, gag sense and drawing style, or you could be lost in the crowd." Looks for "freshness, economy and lovable characters. Anything that's been overdone will not sell well. Strips are printed 6^7/16x2", panels 3^1/8x4", political cartoons only slightly larger, so be careful with fine details, wordiness, clutter and pattern screens."

Tips: "Too many cartoonists are too eager to please, so their work becomes bland, over-affable, soft and dull. They copy what seems to sell. There was not much like Garfield on the market before that strip started; the same is true of Doonesbury, Peanuts, or many other top strips. Although it's bad to be so wild that the strip is incomprehensible or offensive, being boring is much, much worse. We're very open to hearing from cartoonists. To confer with the comics editor, call between 8 a.m. and 6 p.m. Pacific time and ask for David Seidman (pronounced Seedman). Also, we hardly ever match writers with artists or vice versa; we like submissions to be complete packages."

ART McCOURT, Box 210346, Dallas TX 75211. (214)339-6865. Began selling cartoons in 1950. Works with 12 gagwriters/year. Sells 700 cartoons/year to general/family, medical, farm and male magazines. Recently sold material to *Ford Times*, *Furrow*, *Agway Coop*, *Medical Management*, McNaught Syndicate, *National Enquirer*, *American Legion* and King Features. Buys 25% of the gags received from freelance writers. Submit 15-20 gags at one time on 3x5 cards or slips. Sells cartoons for $10-340. Pays 25% commission. Reports in 2 days. SASE.
Needs: Family/general, medical (no gripes about doctors' bills), male, computers, hunting, fishing, and farm gags. "Something unique and up-to-date." No "crowds, ghouls, TV, mothers-in-law, talking animals or desert islands."
Recent Cartoon: Female stork nagging her husband who has put human baby in the nest: "How many times I gotta tell ya not to bring your work home with you?"
Tips: "I look for original, crisp wordage and fresh approach with minimal descriptions. Don't just send a punchline that has no background. Read the newspapers; be topical. Writers shouldn't be impatient; gags can make the rounds for several years."

‡THERESA McCRACKEN, 910 Constitution NE, Washington DC 20002. (202)547-1373. Holds 100 gags/year. Sells mostly to trade journals, but also to some general interest city magazines and newspapers. Recently sold material to *Creative Computing*, Computer World, *Physician's Management*, *Hospital Supervisor's Bulletin*, *Nutritional Health Review*, *Vegetarian Health*, *Oregon Food Journal*, *Federal Times*, *Public Utilities Fortnightly*, *Artist's Magazine* and *Arizona Republic*. Submit gags on 3x5 cards or slips; 10-20 in one batch. Reports in 1 week if not wanted; 1 month if interested in submission. Pays 25% commission.
Needs: "Since I sell mostly to trade journals in one batch, I prefer to receive 10 to 20 gags on one subject so I can do several cartoons for one market all at the same time. I don't care what the subject is since I live near the Library of Congress and am able to search for publications that deal with just about any imaginable interest. Nothing sexist (i.e., no bad woman-driver gags), or racist gags."
Tips: "I really like cartoons where the humor is in the drawing as opposed to the caption. At any rate, I also prefer short captions. 'In Jokes' in a profession are also welcomed. Be aware of what's going on in the world by reading a good newspaper everday."

ROBERT MAKINSON, GPO Box 3341, Brooklyn NY 11202. (718)855-5057. Began buying gags in 1979; bought 150 least year. "I publish *Latest Jokes* and *Jokes by Contributors*. Jokes are used by comedians, disc jockeys and public speakers." Buys 5% of gags received from freelance writers. Submit gags on 3x5 slips in batches of 10-20. Makes outright purchase of $1/joke. Reports in 2 weeks. "SASE should always be included."
Needs: "We want jokes that relate to current trends but which do *not* mention the names of current famous personalities. Public speakers are getting more and more interested in humor, so contacts in that area would be useful to a gagwriter. I'll look at anything. Keep practicing and submitting."
Tips: "The gags I buy are strong enough to make an audience laugh out loud and do not sound too similar to jokes I've heard before."

MASTERS AGENCY, Box 427, Capitola CA 95010. (408)688-8396. Director: George Crenshaw. Buys 200+ gags/year. Sells to magazines, newsletters, trade journals, house organs and newspapers worldwide. Submit sketches or finished roughs only. Reports in 1 week. Pays $10-15. SASE.
Needs: Banking, hospital, Christmas/holidays, industrial safety, automation/computers, farm and factory gags. "'Oldies' are OK with us if they're funny, but nothing prior to 1960, as humor then is now obsolete. We will also pay $25-30 for *finished roughs*. Especially interested in material of this type."
Tips: "We hope we can use finished roughs as is, but if quality is under-par and we have to re-draw, then rate is minimum of $10-15. We will also purchase already published clips on above outlined topics or *any* other topics, paying $10-15 each on fast acceptance."

ENRIQUE BRAXTON MAY, 511 Washington St., Westfield NJ 07090. (201)232-4473. Submit gags on 3x5 slips. Reports in several months. Pays 25% commission.
Needs: "As a starting cartoonist I'm interested in all sorts of gags, including soccer gags and sports gags for children. Also, I'm interested in ideas for short films and possibly children's stories for creating book/film ideas."
Tips: "I like visual gags that move. I am producing my own short animated films and would like to develop a children's book/film/song package to publish overseas."

REX F. MAY (BALOO), Box 2239, West Lafayette IN 47906. (317)463-3689. Holds 500 gags/year. Works with 15 gagwriters/year. Sells to general interest and some girlie magazines. Recently sold material to *Good Housekeeping, National Enquirer, Hustler, Cavalier, Woman's World, Wall Street Journal*, King Features, *Medical Economics, Saturday Evening Post, Easyriders, Datamation, Leadership, New Woman, Changing Times and Christian Science Monitor*. Buys less than 1% of the gags received from freelance writers. Submit gags on 3x5 slips; no more than 100 in a batch. Sells cartoons for $15-300; pays gagwriters $3.75-75. Pays 25% commission. Reports in 2 weeks. SASE.
Needs: "I don't need many gags. A top gagwriter myself, I write 15,000 gags a year for many top cartoonists. I still use gags by others if they fit my style. You probably should look my style over before you submit. I don't do much background or use many props. It's a very simple style. What I want is general-to-weird material. I sell weird non-girlie stuff to the girlie magazines, so don't send standard girlies. Simplicity and shortness of caption are the way to go.
Tips: "Writers should be mindful of a tendency to overdescribe. ('A woman sitting in an easy chair to husband sitting in another chair reading a newspaper with a surprised expression on his face' can be condensed to 'woman to husband.') Avoid doing material that has already been done; the only way to do this is to destroy any material that you even *suspect* has been done before. You can't get rich writing gags, but it can be a fun, profitable hobby. It takes me about three years currently, to try a cartoon from the top to the bottom markets, so be patient."

RAY MORIN, 140 Hamilton Ave., Meriden CT 06450. (203)237-4500. Holds 5+ gags/year; sells 90+ cartoons/year. Works with 2 writers annually. Has sold to *Boys' Life, Wall Street Journal, National Enquirer, Saturday Evening Post*, McNaught Syndicate and King Features. Buys 3% of the gags received from freelance writers. Submit 7-10 gags at one time. SASE. Sells cartoons for $25-300. Pays 25% commission. Holds gags "indefinitely," trying to redraw the cartoon from a different angle.
Needs: General, family, children's, comic strips, medical and business. "I do 95% of my own gags, but am willing to look."
Tips: "I would especially like to receive gags on kids, domestics and medicine in 1986."
Recent Cartoon: Man and wife emerging from movie theatre. Wife says: "Remember how shocked we were when Clark Gable told Vivien Leigh, 'Frankly Scarlett, I don't give a damn'?"

DAVID MURRIETA, 9302 W. Adams, Tolleson AZ 85353. (602)936-5439. Began selling cartoons in 1982. Works with 6 gagwriters/year. Sells material on general interest, adult humor, Hispanic situations, teenage situations. Recently sold material to *Cartoon Showcase, Computer Truck Dispatch, Phoenix College* and *Westsider Newspaper*. Submit gags on 3x5 slips; 10-20 in one batch. Sells cartoons for $30-100; pays gagwriters $8-25. Pays 25% commission. Reports in 2 weeks. SASE. Guidelines for SAE and 2 first class stamps.
Needs: Gags for general magazine, newspapers, trade journals and ethnic magazines. Any jokes, gags and subjects are acceptable especially on teenagers and business. Looks for "very humorous, easy-to-understand gags."
Tips: "I am very interested in starting a syndicated cartoon panel."

IRV PHILLIPS, 2807 E. Sylvia St., Phoenix AZ 85032. Recently sold material to *Saturday Evening Post, New Yorker, National Enquirer, Modern Maturity*, King Features and McNaught Syndicate. Submit 10-20 gags in one batch. Reports in several weeks. Pays minimum 25% commission.
Needs: General and pantomine gags. No pornography. Looks for funny, offbeat, *visual* gags; short, with new twists. Also interested in book material possibilities.

THOMAS PRISK, Star Rt., Box 52, Michigamme MI 49861. Holds 300 "and up" gags/year. Worked with more than 130 writers last year. Sells to trade journals, newsletters, magazines, etc. Published in *The Bulletin of The Atomic Scientists*, Charlton Publications, *Medical Economics, Creative Computing*, etc. Holds with the *Saturday Evening Post, National Enquirer, Good Housekeeping*, etc. Submit gags on 3x5 slips, 10 or more to a batch. Pays 25% commission. Reports in 2 weeks. SASE. "Foreign writers, use only American postage; I don't have the time or patience for the postal coupons."
Needs: Off-the-wall general humor, medical, dental, computer, office, captionless and with short captions. "I would also like to see religious gags with the Christian slant." No porn or racial prejudice slants.
Tips: "I look for well-written gags that are short and to the point. I like a nice fresh approach to old themes."

Please be sure name and address are on each gag slip, *SASE must be included in batch*. Include blank slip for comments. Unless gags are legibly handwritten, they should be typed out. Writers shouldn't be too impatient with long holds; gags will circulate until sold or until I lose interest in the gag's possibility of being sold. The gags I hold are slanted to my style and market needs. Rejected gags are not necessarily considered unsalable."

ART REYNOLDS, Box 226, Vader WA 98593. (206)295-3736. Began selling cartoons in 1977. Sells to general interest magazines and trade magazines. Recently sold material to Creative Communications Publishers, *The Northern Logger & Timber Processor*, *Timber/West Magazine*, *Loggers World Magazine* and *Christian Logger Magazine*. Submit gags on 3x5 cards; 10-15 in one batch. Pays 25% commission. Reports in 1 week. SASE.
Needs: General and family gags that appeal to *Saturday Evening Post*, *Saturday Review*, *Good Housekeeping* and *Better Homes & Gardens*. Also gags with outdoor emphasis. Presently needing gags pertaining to the logging industry. No overworked themes or sex and girlie-girlie gags. "Inquire with SASE. I'll furnish sample and information on cartoon strips and panels I'm working on. I look for fresh, short and snappy, and funny gags."
Tips: "Try your gag idea on your family before submitting. If you don't get a favorable response from them, you probably won't from me either."

JOAN RIVERS, Box 49774, Los Angeles CA 90049. Write first for a release form. Submit gags on 8½x11" paper, typed in duplicate with name and address on each page. "Must have a release form with each submission." Reports in 2 months. Pays $10/one liner. SASE.
Needs: "Always looking for *new* topics—not usual themes. Anything and everything.
Tips: "Submit good *one-liners*. If it is long, a story, a monologue, a riddle, question and answer, it won't work."

‡**DAN ROSANDICH**, Pilgrim Route, Box 101A, Houghton MI 49931. (906)482-6234. Holds estimated 500 gags/year. "I have had my cartoons published in local papers, newsletters, reprinted work in college textbooks, and send my cartoons to the most obscure trade journals up to the large circulation general-family publications. A California distributor sells my reprints overseas and in South America." Recently sold material to *National Enquirer*, *The Star*, *Physician's Management*, *Medical Economics*, *King Features*, *Laff-A-Day*, *American Medical News*, National Catholic News Service, *Espionage*, *Official Detective Stories*. Have sold full-color cartoons to *Cavalier*, *Chic*, *High Society*, *Harvey*, *Hooker*, *Expose*, *Swank*, *Adam*, and *Velvet*." Submit 3x5 slips or cards (prefers 3x5 slips). "I'd like to see a good supply of gags submitted to make my own conclusions on a writer's consistency." Pays 25%. "I would also buy ideas outright at $1 per gag. The writers should specify this in the submission—I would buy a lot if I saw good material. SASE.
Needs: "Anyone considering sending gags should be aware of the fact that I currently work with several excellent gagwriters, but I'm wide open to newcomers if they can show exceptional work. The field of men's magazines is declining in its use of gag cartoons, probably due to several economic factors, so withhold work in this category. I'd love to find the writer who specializes in captionless themes which could relate to just about to anything under the sun. I sell to a dozen or so agricultural magazines on a monthly basis so am open to farm gags of any kind. I also appreciate seeing timely ideas relating to computers, family and banking gags. I'd like health and medical material; keep the doctor in mind with medicals."
Tips: "A good quality I look for in a gagwriter is if he can think up the wordless idea, of course. But if they can produce a gag that depicts a scenario and a quick line, this is what I enjoy."

TER SCOTT, Box 305, Lake Nebagamon WI 54849. (715)374-2525. Holds 100-300 gags/year. Works with 15 gagwriters/year. Sells to trade journals, newspapers and advertisers. Recently sold material to *Multi-Level Marketing News*, *Salesman's Opportunity*, and *Michigan Health Director*. Submit gags on 3x5 slips; 10-25 in one batch. Sells cartoons for $20-100. Pays 25% commission plus occasional bonuses. Reports in 2 weeks. SASE.
Needs: "I will look at anything but hardcore, girlies and racial prejudice and prefer general, religious, farm, sales and trade journal material. I provide a list of markets and currently submit cartoons to my regular gagwriters as these accounts become stocked or change often. I always need topical and seasonal material for Classified Comics newspaper strip, multi-level marketing trade journals, sales magazines, and ideas for all occcasion cards directed to business and salespeople: sales promotion, announcements, collections, thank you and birthday cards."
Tips: "Gagwriters should try to visualize their idea in cartoon form to know if it's feasible, then toss the caption around a while for best wording. Be aware that I may reword and/or rework a gag to better fit the cartoon on occasion, but the gagwriter will still receive full commission. Send printed or typed material with return address stamped on each submission. I'm also available to work with writers who need a cartoonist for their specific needs such as cartoon markets they've pioneered, ads and story books."

JOSEPH SERRANO, Box 725, Capitola CA 95010. Has sold to most major and middle markets. Pays 25% commission. SASE.
Needs: General and topical material.

GODDARD SHERMAN, 1214 McRee Dr., Valdosta GA 31602. Holds 200 gags/year. Sells to general, medical and youth publications. Recently sold material to *National Enquirer, Saturday Evening Post, Boys' Life, Medical Economics, Modern Maturity* and *Woman's World.* Submit gags on 3x5 slips; 15-20 gags in one batch. Reports in 2 weeks. Pays 33⅓% commission. SASE.
Needs: Prefers captionless gags, or very short captions; funny action in picture. No overly technical settings, e.g., "inside machine shops or steel mills. I have no familiarity with them so I cannot draw them accurately." Gags should be in good taste, on general themes.

JOHN W. SIDE, 335 Wells St., Darlington WI 53530. Interested in "small-town, local happening gags with a general slant." Pays 25% commission. Sample cartoon $1. Returns rejected material "immediately." SASE.

SINGER COMMUNICATIONS, INC., 3164 Tyler Ave., Anaheim CA 92801. (714)527-5650. "Our firm represents over 80 cartoonists. We do not buy gags but many of our participating artists do. We add about 500 cartoons each year." Cartoons sold to all types of publications throughout the world. Recently sold material to *Business Today, She Magazines, Reader's Digest* and *Signature.* Sells cartoons for $5-200. Submit very good copies; no originals. Writer's guidelines for SAE and $1.
Tips: "We accept clippings and tearsheets for reprint in foreign countries."

STEWART SLOCOM, (signs work Stewart), 18 Garretson Road, White Plains NY 10604. (914)948-6682. Holds 25-30 gags/year. Works with 20 gagwriters/year. Sells to general interest, women's and sports publications. Recently sold material to *McCalls, Woman's Day, New Woman, Working Mother, National Enquirer, Golf Journal,* Kings Features and McNaught Syndicate. Buys 1-2% of the gags received from freelance writers. Submit gags on 3x5 slips; 10-15 in one batch. Sells cartoons for $25-325; pays gagwriters $6.25-81.50. Pays 25% commission. Reports in 2 days. SASE.
Needs: General, family, women-in-business, computer and sports gags.
Tips: "I look for *originality* (even on overworked themes) and for the prospect of a funny picture. Writers should be mindful of computers, medical, sports, women's lib (business, home, sports, etc.) and older persons in gagwriting."

SUZANNE STEINIGER, 9373 Whitcomb, Detroit MI 48228. (313)838-5204. Holds 100+ gags/year. Works with 3 gagwriters/year. Sells to farm magazines, sex-type periodicals, women's and general interest magazines and Charlton Publications. Buys 30% of the gags received from freelance writers. Submit gags on 3x5 cards or 3x5 slips. Submit 30 or more gags in one batch. Pays 25% commission. Reports in 1 week. SASE.
Needs: "For the present I would like to see gags *National Lampoon* style. I guess you could say general interest, but I'm looking for crazy *new* ideas. I like to see everything except detailed scenes. Writers should simplify their words and scenes. I am working on a cartoon strip. I will not say what the strip is about for fear of someone accidentally getting the same idea. I am looking for a patient writer, someone I can discuss my idea with and someone to *help*. I do like gags that are funny and less detailed. For example, a writer should say 'man to woman in restaurant' instead of 'man in crowded restaurant, waiter looking surprised to the woman next to him.' There should be less confusion. I like quick and simple gags the best. I would especially like to receive gags on holidays, farm and robots in 1986. The best markets for cartoons and gags in 1986 will be farm magazines."
Tips: "Today the gags are funnier visually. The scene should have fewer props. Fewer props made the great comics such as the Marx Brothers very funny and popular, not to mention Peanuts. There should be fewer details and more concentration on the joke, the entire *gag*. I like writers who do a good job of writing and leave the drawing to us (cartoonists)."

JOHN STINGER, Box 189, Stewartsville NJ 08886. Interested in general business gags. Would like to see more captionless sight gags. Currently doing a syndicated panel on business. Has sold to major markets. "Index cards are fine, but keep gags short." Pays 25% commission; "more to top writers." Bought about 25 gags last year. Can hold unsold gags for as long as a year. SASE.

FRANK TABOR, 2817 NE 292nd Ave., Camas WA 98607. (206)834-3355. Began selling cartoons in 1947. Holds 200 gags/year. Works with 6 gagwriters/year. Sells to trade journals. Recently sold material to *Medical Economics, American Medical News, American Machinist, Basic Computing, Infoworld, Chesapeake Bay, Tooling & Production* and *True Detective.* Buys 5% of the gags received from freelance writers. Submit gags on 3x5 slips; 10 in one batch. Sells cartoons for $25-100; pays gagwriters $6.25-25. Pays 25% commission. Reports in 2 days. SASE.
Needs: Computers, police, detective, fishing, salesman, medical (must be funny for the doctor—no gags on big doctor bills), industrial (slanted to the industry executive) and flower shop gags. "Cartoon spreads are wide

open.'' No gags on subjects not listed above. ''I receive too much material written for the general markets and not nearly enough gags on the subjects I ask for. I look for situations in which the cartoon carries the punch; I don't care for the one-liner or illustrated joke. I need trade gags by writers who know or who will study the trade they're writing about.''

Tips: ''Not enough writers are trying to write for the trades. They're too easily won over by the big rates at the major markets. I have lots of trades paying $35 to $225, and they're begging for cartoons. I am interested in reviewing ideas on strips and panels for syndication.''

ISSAM TEWFIK, #701, 2400 Carling Ave., Ottawa, Ontario K2B 7H2 Canada. (613)828-5239. Holds 300 gags/year. Sells to general interest magazines, trade journals, men's and women's publications and newspapers. Recently sold material to *Hospital Supervisor Bulletin* and *Accent on Living*. Submit gags on 3x5 slips. Submit 10 or more gags in one batch. Reports in 1 week. Pays 25% commission. SASE.
Needs: General, family, erotic, sports, law, military, insurance, medical, computers, children, detective, cars, old age, management, outdoor, money, trucking, etc. Prefers gags that are slanted towards a specific subject and a magazine. Research the magazine and slant towards its requirements. ''I will consider eagerly a well conceived strip or panel with well-defined characters and theme (e.g., family, animal, professional, children and single people).''
Tips: ''Identify a need either in a specific magazine or a syndicate and let us work together to produce something marketable. Slanting to the different publications is the key to success.''

BOB THAVES, Box 67, Manhattan Beach CA 90266. Pays 25% commission. Returns rejected material in 1-2 weeks. May hold unsold gags indefinitely. SASE.
Needs: Gags ''dealing with anything except raw sex. Also buys gags for syndicated (daily and Sunday) panel, *Frank & Ernest*. I prefer offbeat gags for that, although almost any general gag will do.''

MARVIN TOWNSEND, 631 W. 88th St., Kansas City MO 64114. Holds 25-30 gags/year; sells 300 cartoons/year. Sells to trade and business publications and church and school magazines. Works with 20 writers annually. Buys 3-4% of the gags received from freelance writers. Prefers batches of not over 20 gags. Sells cartoons for $70-300. Pays 25% commission. SASE.
Needs: Interested in gags with a trade journal or business slant. Such as office executives, professional engineers, plant managers, supervisors, foremen, safety engineers, etc. ''Religious and children gags also welcome. Captioned or captionless. *No general gags wanted.* Don't waste postage sending general gags or worn-out material.''
Tips: ''Cute or mildly funny ideas don't sell. They must have a real punch or unusual twist to them. I discourage contributions from gag men not capable of creating the particular slant I need.''

‡**BARDULF UELAND**, Halstad MN 56548. Has sold to *Parade*, *Legion*, *New Woman*, King Features, McNaught Syndicate. Works with 12 gagwriters/year. Submit 12-15 gags/batch. Pays 25% commission. Reports in 1-3 days, but holds unsold gags indefinitely unless return is requested. SASE.
Needs: General, family, medical and farm gags. No sex.
Recent Cartoon: Guy to pastor, ''You really hit home today, Reverend, I'm divorcing Alice'' (McNaught Syndicate).

JOSEPH F. WHITAKER, 2522 Percy Ave., Orlando FL 32818. (305)298-8311. Holds 100 gags/year. Works with 6 gagwriters/year. Sells all types of gags. Recently sold material to *Star, National Enquirer, National Catholic News,* McNaught Syndicate and women's magazines. Buys 20% of the gags from freelance writers. Submit gags on 3x5 slips; 10-15 in one batch. Sells cartoons for $4-15; pays gagwriters $12-100. Pays 25% commission. Reports in 4 days. SASE.
Needs: All types of gags. The best markets for cartoons/gags in 1986 will be syndicates, girlie, women, farm and advertising.
Tips: ''I look for captionless gags.''

ART WINBURG, 21 McKinley Ave., Jamestown NY 14701. Has sold to *National Star*, *American Medical News*, *VFW Magazine*, *Physician's Management*, *American Legion*, *Modern Medicine*, *New Woman*, and *Highlights for Children*. Sells cartoons for $15-225. Pays 25% commission. Returns rejected material ''usually within a week, sometimes same day received.'' Will return unsold gags on request. ''Always a possibility of eventually selling a cartoon.'' SASE.
Needs: All types of gags; general, family, trade and professional journals, adventure, sports, medical and children's magazines. Gag writer should ''use variety, be original, and avoid old cliches.'' Would prefer not to see gags about ''smoke signals, flying carpets, moon men, harems or cannibals with some person in cooking pot.''
Tips: ''Most gag writers don't know how to slant. They should see and study what the magazines use. Most gags submitted to me are dull, pointless, some not even a gag.''

MARTIN YOUNG, Box 7415, Orlando FL 32854. (305)898-0690. Holds 250-300 gags/year. Works with 10 gagwriters/year. Sells to men's and women's, general interest magazines, trade journals and newspapers. Recently sold material to M.A.D.D. (Mothers Against Drunk Drivers), *Saturday Evening Post*, *Charisma*, Atari Computer, *Orlando Sentinel* and *Freezing Florida*. Buys 75% of the gags received from freelance writers. Submit gags on 3x5 cards; 15-20 gags in one batch. Sells cartoons for $5-125. Pays 25% of cartoon sale. Reports in 3 days. SASE.

Needs: Computer (home/office); religious (no anti-religious); dieting; *Saturday Evening Post* type; hospital/doctor/nurse; family humor; humor through youth; school/teachers/kids; and off-the-wall general gags. No political or sex gags, no overworked gags or cliches. "Only send funniest material. I currently have a cartoon strip called Fish Tales. It deals with some well established characters that live in the ocean. Please write for further details."

Tips: "I very much like *strong, very funny*, straight-to-the-point gags. I have been getting too many weak, overworked themes. Try to be original. Gagwriters should keep up with the times. Their gags will reflect how current they are on what's happening in the world around them. Characteristics that I look for in a gagwriter include that they be honest, friendly, and will try to please me with their material. I have been selling cartoons long enough to know what sells and what doesn't. I would be willing to work with writers on cartoon strips."

Greeting Card Publishers ————————

When you want to tell someone you care but aren't sure how to say it, you rely on greeting cards. Actually (while you scan the card racks), you're looking for a writer who best conveys your message. That's what greeting card publishers do when they read submissions.

The greeting card market changes, but doesn't change. As a writer for cards, you are always conveying the same message—love, sympathy, or best wishes—but in new words and formats. Today we're seeing cards designed to look like computer printouts (on cardboard, of course), sculptured cards, and cards with simple artwork and messages and plenty of white space. Cards today acknowledge friends' and family members' job promotions, diets, driver's licenses and, even, divorces.

Some publishers are buying what they call *off-the-wall* humor. This includes "insult" cards where the message is a putdown to the recipient. It is too early, though, to say whether these cards will become a staple (like studio cards) in card shops.

Greeting card publishers have shifted from purely sentimental cards to those with more down-to-earth verses. "Flowery sentiments are not in fashion right now," observed Mary M. Hood, creative director for Red Farm Studio. "It is important to show caring and sensitivity, however."

Most companies select cards that will appeal to most card buyers. "A card that can be sent by a man or a woman to a man or a woman is ideal," said Ned Stern, editor of Amberley Greeting Card Co. "A man-to-man card, for example, has a very limited market. This is also true for a 'to my Mother (Brother, Sister, etc.) on her Birthday' type of card." Some firms will add a line or two of trademark cards to appeal to specific buyers, such as working women or people who like animals.

Card publishers in general are buying shorter verses for cards. Many need terse but striking words to complement a card's artwork or cover photo. "If you are artistically inclined, you may wish to enhance your idea with a rough sketch," said one card company. "If not, a brief written description can be just as effective." But publishers agree that excellent artwork won't salvage a poor card idea.

If the company you contact sells boxed assortments of cards, chances are, its editors prefer cards without the words, *we* or *I*, to make them more versatile. If you're designing a card for a specific occasion, make sure that, say, birthday or anniversary, appear on the front of the card.

Important details to remember when writing and selling greeting card ideas are the publishers' lead times. Most firms work a year or more ahead of the customers' need for cards; for card editors, 1986 seems like last year. Because each line of cards is subject to production schedules and is featured in company catalogs, most editors cannot add a card to the line after the deadline no matter how well they like the card. Consult each company's listing to find out how far in advance to submit seasonal material.

Some publishers require writers to sign a submission agreement form before they will look at your work. Such forms are typical, but carefully read the form before signing it.

Greeting card companies usually buy all rights. "The only exceptions are writers who come up with a whole concept for a promotion series (including the actual implementation of the concept with specific card ideas) incorporating a character or other device such as a special theme, and these sales are negotiated," said Kirk Polking, editor of the *Beginning Writer's Answer Book*. When possible, refrain from selling all rights to your work, but if you want to write verses for cards you'll probably have to sell all rights.

To submit conventional greeting card material, type or neatly print your verses on either 4x6 or 3x5 slips of paper or file cards. For humorous or studio card ideas, either fold sheets of paper into card dummies about the size and shape of an actual card, or use file cards. For ideas that use attachments, try to get the actual attachment and put it on your dummy; if you can't, suggest the attachment. For mechanical card ideas, you must make a workable mechanical dummy. Most companies will pay more for attachment and mechanical card ideas.

Neatly print or type your idea on the dummy as it would appear on the finished card. Type your name and address on the back of each dummy or card, along with an identification number (which helps you and the editor in keeping records). Always maintain records of where and when ideas were submitted; use a file card for each idea.

Submit 5 to 15 ideas at a time (this constitutes a "batch"). Quality, not quantity, should be your guideline. Keep the file cards for each batch together until rejected ideas are returned. You may want to code each submission so you can identify how many you have sent and where.

Don't send card verses or ideas to companies without considering their latest lines of cards.

For aspiring verse writers, researching the greeting card market is fun and essential. Study the card racks. Observe which cards people are buying. Read card verses and observe how the verses complement the artwork. (The store clerk will think you're carefully choosing the *right* card when, in fact, you're looking for the right publisher for your verses.) This research helps *you* sell your work—it shows that you care about your prospective *customers*.

AMBERLEY GREETING CARD CO., Box 36159, Cincinnati OH 45236. (513)489-2775. Editor: Ned Stern. Buys 300-400 freelance ideas/year. SASE. Reports in 1 month. Material copyrighted. Buys all rights. Pays on acceptance. Writer's guidelines for business size SAE and 1 first class stamp. Market list is regularly revised.
Needs: Humorous, informal, sensitive and studio. No seasonal material or poetry. Pays $40/card idea.
Tips: "Amberley publishes specialty lines, primarily novelty and humorous studio greeting cards. We accept freelance ideas, including risque and nonrisque. Make it short and to the point. Nontraditional ideas are selling well."

ARTFORMS CARD CORPORATION, 725 County Line Rd., Dearfield IL 60015. (312)272-9844. Editor: Ms. Bluma K. Marder. 50% freelance written. Bought 65 freelance ideas/samples last year; receives an estimated 200 submissions annually. Buys "about 60-70 messages"/year. Submit ideas in batches of 10. Submit seasonal/holiday material 6 months in advance. SASE. Reports in 3 weeks. Buys all rights. Catalog $1.50. Market list available for SASE.
Needs: Conventional; humorous; informal; inspirational; sensitivity; studio; messages for Jewish Greeting Cards such as Bar/Bat Mitzvah, Jewish New Year; Chanukah; and Passover; wedding, engagement, confirmation, new home, new baby, bridal shower, baby shower, terminally ill, friendship, sympathy, anniversary, get well and birthday. No insults or risque greetings. Length: 2 lines minimum, 4 lines maximum. Pays $15-25/card idea.
Other Product Lines: Gift wrap for Chanukah and year 'round use.
Recent Verse: Cover—"For Your Barmitzvah." Inside Message—May the memory/of this special day/enrich your life/in every way!"
Tips: "Do research on Judaism so greeting is not questionable to a religious market; also, if Biblical quotes are used, make sure references are correct. We look for simple messages that pertain directly to subject matter. The shorter the message—the better. It is not necessary for the message to rhyme. Humorous cards are selling well. We will be expanding from Judaic market only to general market."

CAROLYN BEAN PUBLISHING, LTD., 120 2nd St., San Francisco CA 94105. (415)957-9574. Chief Executive Officer: Lawrence Barnett. 90% freelance written. Bought 300 freelance ideas/samples last year; receives an estimated 10,000 submissions annually. Submit seasonal/holiday material 18 months in advance. Buys exclusive card rights; negotiates others. Pays on acceptance or publication. SASE. Reports in 6 weeks. Writer's guidelines for SASE and 49¢ postage.
Needs: Conventional holiday and occasions; humorous; informal; studio; general, occasion-oriented messages. Looks for sophisticated, witty and/or sensitive material. No "Hallmark-type, hearts and flowers" messages or heavy Christian messages. Occasion-oriented cards sell best. Pays $15-30. "These terms are negotiable."
Tips: "The greeting card market has become more traditional in the last year."

BLUE MOUNTAIN ARTS, INC., Dept. WM, Box 1007, Boulder CO 80306. Contact: Editorial Staff. Buys 50-75 items/year. SASE. Reports in 3-5 months. Buys all rights. Pays on publication.
Needs: Inspirational (without being religious); and sensitivity ("primarily need sensitive and sensible writings about love, friendships, families, philosophies, etc.—written with originality and universal appeal"). Pays $150.
Other Product Lines: Calendars, gift books and greeting books. Payment varies.
Tips: "Get a feel for the Blue Mountain Arts line prior to submitting material. Our needs differ from other card publishers; we do not use rhymed verse, preferring instead a more honest person-to-person style. We use unrhymed, sensitive poetry and prose on the deep significance and meaning of life and relationships. A very limited amount of freelance material is selected each year, either for publication on a notecard or in a gift anthology, and the selection prospects are highly competitive. But new material is always welcome and each manuscript is given serious consideration."

BRILLIANT ENTERPRISES, 117 W. Valerio St., Santa Barbara CA 93101. Contact: Editorial Dept. Buys all rights. Submit words and art in black on 5½x3½ horizontal, thin white paper in batches of no more than 15. Reports "usually in 2 weeks." SASE. Catalog and sample set for $2.
Needs: Postcards. Messages should be "of a highly original nature, emphasizing subtlety, simplicity, insight, wit, profundity, beauty and felicity of expression. Accompanying art should be in the nature of oblique commentary or decoration rather than direct illustration. Messages should be of universal appeal, capable of being appreciated by all types of people and of being easily translated into other languages. Since our line of cards is highly unconventional, it is essential that freelancers study it before submitting." No "topical references, subjects limited to American culture or puns." Limit of 17 words/card. Pays $40 for "complete ready-to-print word and picture design."
Recent Verse: "I feel much better now that I've given up hope."

CONTENOVA GIFTS, 1239 Adanac St., Vancouver, British Columbia V6A 2C8 Canada. (604)253-4444. Editor: Jeff Sinclair. 100% freelance written. Bought 60 freelance ideas/samples last year. Submit ideas on 3x5 cards or small mock-ups in batches of 10. Reports in 6 weeks. Buys world rights. Pays on acceptance. Current needs list for SAE and IRC. Do *not* send U.S. postage stamps.
Needs: Humorous and studio. Both risque and nonrisque. "The shorter, the better." Birthday, belated birthday, get well, anniversary, thank you, congratulations, miss you, new job, etc. Seasonal ideas needed for Christmas by March; Valentine's Day by September. Risque and birthday cards sell best. Pays $50.
Tips: "In Canada, the increased rates have affected Christmas card sales. We need to refine the Christmas card line—it's now more competitive."

‡**CRABWALK, INC.**, 648 Broadway, New York NY 10012. (212)260-1901. Editor: Alan Gabay. Seasonal/holiday material should be submitted 1 year in advance. SASE. Reports in 2 months. Not copyrighted. Pays on acceptance. Market list for #10 envelope and 22¢ postage. Market list is regularly revised.
Needs: Humorous, informal, sensitivity, soft line, and studio cards. Pays $30-50.
Other Product Lines: Calendars, gift books, postcards, promotions, pads and gift matches.

CURRENT, INC., Box 2559, Colorado Springs CO 80901. (303)594-4100. Editor: Nancy McConnell. 10% freelance written. Bought 51 freelance ideas/samples last year; receives an estimated 505 submissions annually. Buys 2 or 3 children's book manuscripts/year. Buys 50 greeting card sentiments/year (predominately humor or long verse). Submit seasonal/holiday material 18 months in advance. SASE. Reports in 3 weeks. Buys all rights. Pays on acceptance. "Flat fee only; no royalty." Pays approximately $300 for 1,500-word children's ms. Writer's guidelines for business size SAE and 1 first class stamp.
Needs: Greeting cards (light humor, all occasion), not too risque; children's stories, and children's activity books. Pays $10/sentiment.
Tips: "We tend to pick up on every trend or create our own. We suggest that writers keep abreast of what's selling at retail as we key off those sales results, too. Read our direct mail catalog."

DRAWING BOARD GREETING CARDS, INC., 8200 Carpenter Freeway, Dallas TX 75247. (214)637-0390. Editorial Director: Jimmie Fitzgerald. Submit ideas on 3x5 cards, typed, with name and address on each card. SASE. Reports in 2 weeks. Pays on acceptance.
Needs: Conventional, humorous, informal, inspirational, everyday, seasonal and studio cards. No 'blue' or sex humor. Pays $30-80.
Other Product Lines: Calendars. Pays $200-600.

D. FORER & CO., INC., 105 E. 73rd St., New York NY 10021. (212)879-6600. Editor: Barbara Schaffer. SASE. Reports in 2 weeks. Pays on acceptance. One-time market list for SAE and 1 first class stamp..
Needs: Humorous, studio. Pays $20.

FRAN MAR GREETING CARDS, LTD., Suite 106, 587 Main St., New Rochelle NY 10801. (914)632-2232. President: Stan Cohen. Buys 100-300 items/year. Submit ideas in small batches (no more than 15 in a batch) on 3x5 sheets or cards. SASE. "Copy will not be returned without SASE enclosed with submissions." Reports in 2 weeks. Buys all rights. Pays on the 15th of the month following acceptance. Market list for SASE.
Needs: Invitations (all categories), thank you notes (all categories), humorous pads, camp and juvenile stationery.
Other Product Lines: Stationery, novelty card concepts, captions, and novelty pad captions. Pays minimum $25/card idea.
Recent Verses: Pad concept—pad all green except for 2 eyes at the bottom. Caption—"This is not a pad, somebody squashed my froggie." Invitation—"A surprise party/Come help us surprise the pants off—."
Tips: Send "short copy—with a punch. Pads should be functional and/or funny. Our invitations are printed all on one side, so the gag would have to be on the front. We've done well with humorous risque (on the light side) invitations."

‡**FREEDOM GREETING CARD CO.**, Box 715, Bristol PA 19007. (215)945-3300. Editor: J. Levitt. Submit seasonal/holiday material 1 year in advance. SASE. Reports in 1 month. Material copyrighted. Buys greeting card rights. Pays on acceptance. Writer's guidelines for SASE.
Needs: Announcements, conventional, inspirational, juvenile, sensitive and soft line. Pays per card idea; $10 minimum for 2-8 line card verses.

THE GRAPHIC ARTISAN, LTD., Box 388, 3 Cross St., Suffern NY 10901. Editor: Peter A. Aron. Annual amount of freelance purchases $1,000-5,000. Submit seasonal/holiday material 6-9 months in advance. SASE. Reports in 1 month. Buys all rights (one-time payment). Pays on acceptance.
Needs: Announcements, conventional, humorous, informal, juvenile and studio. Pays $10-25/card idea. Also reviews bumper stickers, calendars, gift books, greeting books, plaques and postcards. "Payment would vary with the complexity and completeness of the individual item."
Tips: "Material must be tasteful. Note that this does *not* mean noncontroversial, nonsexy, or anything like that—must not be libelous or disgusting for the sake of shock. It's a tough world out there—but originality and first rate work still make it."

‡**GREAT LAKES CONCEPTS DESIGNED**, Box 2107, Traverse City MI 49685. (616)941-1372. Buys 12 designs/year. Reports in 3 months. SASE. Buys first and reprint rights. Pays on acceptance. Guidelines for business size SAE and 1 first class stamp.
Needs: Imaginative, humorous and creative artwork for all-occasion notecards. No seasonal material. "This year we are only publishing notecards—no writing or poetry on design or inside." Pays $50 maximum.
Tips: "Submit material that is of simple subjects (one or two only per design), brightly colored and imaginative. We are looking for children's themes."

LEANIN' TREE PUBLISHING CO., Box 9500, Boulder CO 80301. (303)530-1442. Contact: Editor. Submit verses (not more than 15) on 3x5 cards. SASE. Reports in 3 months. May hold good verses indefinitely. Pays $35 on publication; $10 for reuse. Market list and verse writer guidelines for SASE.
Needs: Birthday, friendship, get well, anniversary, thank you, sympathy, wedding, romantic love, Christmas, Valentines, Easter, Mother's Day, Father's Day and all-occasion Christian.
Tips: "We publish western, Christian and contemporary friendship (not studio) cards. Humor preferred in western card line. Please do not send art suggestions. Become familiar with our card lines before submitting."

MAINE LINE CO., Box 418, Rockport ME 04856. (207)236-8536. Editor: Perri Ardman. Buys 200-400 freelance ideas/samples per year. Submit photocopies; submissions not returned. Reports in 2 months. Submit seasonal/holiday material 1 year in advance. Material copyrighted. Buys greeting card rights. Pays on acceptance. Writer's guidelines for business size SAE and 3 first class stamps. Market list is regularly revised and issued one time only.
Needs: Humorous, invitations, inspirational (motivational, notre liqious), and holiday cards for modern women. No juvenile or religious material. Pays $35-50/card idea.
Other Product Lines: Greeting books (pays $35-50); plaques (pays $35-50); and postcards (pays $35-50). Also needs sayings, statements for T-shirts, buttons, mugs & stickers.
Tips: "Don't submit traditional-type material. Study our guidelines. We want greeting card copy with particular appeal to contemporary women of all ages, from all walks of life. Prose is better than verse; humor based on realities of life rather than on word-play most likley to be accepted. Copy that speaks, beneath the humor, a universal truth which women recognize or copy which articulates attitudes, experiences, feelings shared by many, many women is most likely to be accepted. Copy that is suggestive, clever and tasteful is OK, but not necessary. Birthday cards and women-to-women friendship cards dealing with women's concerns are always needed. There is a demand for freelance copy from people who have an interesting perspective on modern life, expressed in a unique way, understood by many. Writers need not submit any visuals with copy but may suggest

visuals. Lack of drawing ability does not decrease chances of having copy accepted; however, we also seek people who can both write and illustrate. Writers who have a contemporary illustrative style are invited to send samples or tearsheets to illustrate copy they're submitting.''

‡**ALFRED MAINZER, INC.**, 27-08 40th Ave., Long Island City NY 11101. (718)392-4200. Art Director: Arwed Baenisch. 15% freelance written. Bought 200 freelance ideas/samples last year. Buys all rights. SASE. **Needs:** Conventional, inspirational, informal and juvenile. All types of cards and ideas. Traditional material. All seasonals and occasionals wanted. Payment for card ideas negotiated on individual basis only.

OATMEAL STUDIOS, Box 138, Rochester VT 05767. (802)767-3325. Editor: Helene Lehrer. 90% freelance written. Buys 200-300 greeting card lines/year. Bought over 200 freelance ideas/samples last year. Submit material for birthday, friendship, anniversary, get well, etc. Also Christmas, Chanukah, Mother's Day, Father's Day, Easter, Valentine's Day, etc. Pays $50. Pays on acceptance. Reports in 6 weeks. Current market list for SASE.
Needs: Humorous material (clever and *very* funny) year-round. "Humorous tongue-in-cheek-type humor, conversational in tone and format, sells best for us.''
Tips: "The greeting card market has become more competitive with a greater need for creative and original ideas. We are looking for writers who can communicate situations, thoughts, and relationships in a funny way and apply them to a birthday, get well, etc., type greeting. We suggest that a writer send for our guidelines to get a clear picture of the type of humor we're looking for.''

‡**THE PARAMOUNT LINE, INC.**, Box 1225, Pawtucket RI 02862. Editorial Director; Dolores Riccio. Submit ideas in batches of no more than 15. Reports in 1 month. Buys all rights. Pays on acceptance. Send SASE for instruction sheet with seasonal reading dates.
Needs: Contemporary me-to-you messages, general or cute/clever, rhymed or unrhymed, short or long, for all everyday and seasonal titles. Address humorous card ideas to Hope Billings, creative planner. Address studio card ideas and studio promotions to Robert Alley, humor coordinator.
Other Product Lines: Promotions.
Tips: "Study the market; use conversational, contemporary language; avoid limitations and heavy sentiment; experiment with natural, new ways of saying what greeting card buyers want to say.''

PORTAL PUBLICATIONS, LTD., 21 Tamal Vista Blvd., Corte Madera CA 94925. (415)924-5652. Editor: Nancy Dunwell. 100% freelance written. Buys 150 greeting card lines/year. SASE. Reports in 2 months. Pays $50/sentiment. Free guidelines.
Needs: Light humor and conversational, prose and verse sentiments. Young adult sending situations. Everyday and seasonal ideas. General birthday and friendship cards sell best. Submit one idea/3x5 card with name and address.
Tips: "Our greeting card products are developed to meet the needs of the young professional woman. This is an expanding market segment. Conversational prose and soft humor are the major types of sentiments we use.''

‡**RED FARM STUDIO**, Box 347, 334 Pleasant St., Pawtucket RI 02862. (401)728-9300. Editor: Mary M. Hood. SASE. Reports in 2 weeks. Buys all rights. Pays on acceptance. Market list for #10 SASE.
Needs: Conventional, inspirational, sensitivity, and soft line cards. "We cannot use risque or insult humor.'' Pays $3 per line of copy.
Tips: "Write verses that are direct and honest. Flowery sentiments are not in fashion right now. It is important to show caring and sensitivity, however.''

REED STARLINE CARDS CO., Box 26247, Los Angeles CA 90026. (213)663-3161. Editor: Barbara Stevens. 100% freelance written. Purchases 200 ideas and artwork/year. Pays on acceptance. Buys international rights. Submit seasonal/holiday material 6 months (for season 2 years ahead publishing) in advance. SASE. Reports in 2 months on submissions. Guidelines for SAE. Market list is regularly revised.
Needs: Humorous and studio cards. "Birthday group cards sell best for us.'' No verse or jingles type material. Pays $40 minimum/card idea.

ROCKSHOTS, INC., 632 Broadway, New York NY 10012. (212)420-1400. Editor: Tolin Greene. "We buy 75 greeting card verse (or gag) lines annually.'' Submit seasonal/holiday material 1 year in advance. SASE. Reports in 1 month. Buys use for greeting cards. Writer's guidelines for SAE and 1 first class stamp.
Needs: Humorous ("should be off-the-wall, as outrageous as possible, preferably for sophisticated buyer''); soft line; combination of sexy and humorous come-on type greeting ("sentimental is not our style''); and insult cards ("looking for cute insults''). . No sentimental or conventional material. "Card gag can adopt a sentimental style, then take an ironic twist and end on an off-beat note.'' Pays up to $50. Prefers gag line on 8x11 paper with name, address, and phone and social security numbers in right corner.
Tips: "Think of a concept that would normally be too outrageous to use, give it a cute and clever wording to

make it drop-dead funny and you will have commercialized a non-commercial message. It's always good to mix sex and humor. Our emphasis is definitely on the erotic. Hard-core eroticism is difficult for the general public to handle on greeting cards. The trend is toward 'light' sexy humor, even cute sexy humor. 'Cute' has always sold cards, and it's a good word to think of even with the most sophisticated, crazy ideas. Remember that your gag line will probably be illustrated by a cartoonist, illustrator or photographer. So try to think visually. If no visual is needed, the gag line *can* stand alone, but we generally prefer some visual representation.''

‡**SUNRISE PUBLICATIONS, INC.**, Box 2699, Bloomington IN 47402. (812)336-9900. Editor: Jill Baker. Usually buys 100 verses per year, although the amount varies. Submit all card ideas by June. SASE. Reports in 1 month. Acquires greeting card rights only. Pays on acceptance. Free writer's guidelines. Market list is regularly revised.
Needs: Conventional, humorous, informal and juvenile. No "off-color humor or lengthy poetry." Pays $20 per card idea.
Tips: "We like short one- or two-line captions, sincere or clever. Our customers prefer this to lengthy rhymed verse. Submit ideas for birthday, get well, friendship, wedding, baby congrats, sympathy, thinking of you, anniversary, belated birthday, and thank yous."

VAGABOND CREATIONS, INC., 2560 Lance Dr., Dayton OH 45409. (513)298-1124. Editor: George F. Stanley, Jr. 30% freelance written. Buys 30-40 ideas annually. Submit seasonal/holiday material 6 months in advance. SASE. Reports in 1 week. Buys all rights. Sometimes copyrighted. Pays on acceptance. Writer's guidelines for business size SAE. Market list issued one time only.
Needs: "Cute, humorous (animated animals or objects in people situations). We will consider illustrations— only on cover; we need short subtle inside tie-in message (some puns permitted)." Do not send poetry. Pays $10-15 per card idea.

WARNER PRESS, INC., Box 2499, Anderson IN 46018. (317)644-7721. Editor: Jane L. Hammond. Buys $2,500-3,500 worth of freelance material/year. Submit seasonal/holiday material 9 months in advance. SASE. Reports in 5 weeks. Prefers to buy all rights. Pays on acceptance. Writer's guidelines for business size SASE. Market list is regularly revised.
Needs: Announcements, conventional, informal, inspirational, juvenile, sensitivity and verses of all types with contemporary Christian message and focus. No off-color humor. Pays $5-40 per card idea.
Other Product Lines: Pays $60-150 for calendars; $30-100 for greeting books; $15-30 for plaques; $5-10 for postcards; $10-50 for posters.
Tips: "Try to avoid use of 'I' or 'we' on card verses. A majority of what we purchase is for box assortments. An estimated 75% of purchases are Christian in focus; 25% good conventional verses. The market is moving away from the longer verses in a variety of card types, though there is still a market for good inspirational verses (i.e. like Helen Steiner Rice). We are always looking for good, fresh writers who write with sensitivity and understanding of the 'hope that is within' without being preachy."

‡**CAROL WILSON FINE ARTS, INC.**, Box 17394, Portland OR 97217. (503)281-0780. Editor: Gary Spector. Purchases 100-200 freelance designs annually. Submit seasonal/holiday material 1 year in advance. SASE. Reports in 3 weeks. Buys negotiable rights. Payment to be discussed.
Needs: Announcements, conventional, humorous, informal, inspirational, invitations, juvenile, sensitivity, soft line and studio cards. Pays $25 per card idea. Royalties to be discussed.
Other Product Lines: Calendars, gift books, postcards and posters.
Tips: "We are particularly interested in expanding the humorous part of our line with work that is laugh-out-loud funny. Birthday cards are always an important category. Cards should be 'personal'—ask yourself 'Is this a card that someone would buy for a specific person?' Keep in mind that the majority of card buyers are women between the ages of 20 and 40."

Syndicates ────────────────────────────

If you're working to get your writing syndicated, it helps to know the number of writers you'll be competing against. If we told you a statistic, we'd be guessing. But if we told you that landing a syndicated column is easy, we'd be lying. What we do know is that most newspaper and magazine columnists want their work to be syndicated. And writers who hope to write a column for any publication want to be syndicated. That means that if you want to write for millions of readers through syndication, you'll have to outwrite thousands of writers.

Getting a syndicate to say *yes*, though, isn't impossible—if you have the *right* idea. A timely idea, a writing style to express it well, and (formal and practical) research showing readers how or why you're telling them something are the sparks for a great column. Also, if you can develop a loyal readership while writing columns for a regional or city-wide publication, a syndicate is more likely to talk with you.

Write about what you know, what you are, or what you do well—always with the reader in mind. Even a column written gratis will get you the clips you need to gain a syndicate's interest. If you are not working for a newspaper, at least read the syndicated columns in as many newspapers as you can. Notice length, style and audience slant.

"We're dealing with fewer undiscovered writers but still do review material," pointed out Don Michel, vice-president and editor of the Los Angeles Times Syndicate.

Some major syndicates still read queries for columns, looking for ideas that go a step beyond what is currently syndicated. "Look for unique concepts that can be continued on a sustaining basis or can form part of a series . . .," suggested Donald Fass, executive editor of Continuum Broadcasting Network.

Editors constantly receive material from Erma Bombeck imitators and writers who want to do travel and celebrity articles. (You don't want editors to notice that you write like someone else.) Develop your own voice and an original writing style so you can offer something syndicates don't have but want.

To be successful, syndicates need material that newspaper, magazine, and trade journal editors are willing to pay for. Syndicated articles must outshine the *free* press release stories and those proposed in queries—to keep editors subscribing to a syndicate.

Contrary to what you might think, though, a syndicated columnist doesn't "have it made." Syndicates will drop a column if it doesn't make money.

Syndicates seem to be synonymous with publishing columns, but they also buy one-shot feature articles, article series, puzzles and games, cartoons, and excerpted or serialized books. Some firms specialize in material on particular subjects, like the environment. Syndicated nonfiction includes advice columns, commentary, humorous articles, and special-interest columns on everything from health to table manners.

Although nonfiction outweighs fiction in the syndicate markets, the PEN Syndicated Fiction Project (listed in the Contests and Awards section) and Fiction Network are finding publications willing to publish good fiction.

We have been hearing about companies syndicating material via computers for customers' home use. Because a firm may not have yet established guidelines, carefully weigh the terms of any contract. When a syndicate editor is not sure who will be subscribing to his service or is currently soliciting the first round of subscribers, you'll want to get more information before committing your material to such a syndicate.

Syndicated material is generally short (500-1,000 words/column), objective, and carefully documented. Since syndicates sell primarily to newspapers, "terse" newspaper style is appropriate, even for features. Remember that smaller syndicates and news services often handle specialized material (health, religion, career, business) for a well-targeted audience.

Syndicates sell your copy for a commission. The writer receives from 40% to 60% of the gross proceeds, though some syndicates pay the writer a salary and others buy material outright. The syndicate's percentage covers costs of promotion, mailing, staff, etc. Writers of top syndicated columns can earn more than $50,000 a year though most syndicated writers can't expect to see anything near that figure.

Once a syndicate begins publishing your work, make sure you receive regular payments. It is best to get the frequency and the estimated percentage amount in writing from the editor. One writer continued to send material and accepted promises of payment until the syndicate had accumulated over 100 columns.

If you know the marketplace well enough (and are willing to start with smaller publications for smaller pay), you can syndicate your own material. But with this option, you'll have to invest money and time into marketing and distributing. You'll have to convince newspaper editors they need your material.

As weekly newspapers continue to be acquired by chains, you might propose a column to run in each of a company's weekly publications. You could also present such a proposal to a noncompeting chain in another region.

Remember, though, your sales pitch must include proof—six to eight columns—that you'll be offering the newspaper readers a valuable service.

Consult the following listings for the topic and form of submissions preferred by syndicates. Listings also cover the syndicate's outlets. Most, as mentioned above, sell to newspapers, but many also sell to magazines, and to radio stations that use syndicated material as "brights"—that is, lively, interesting facts and anecdotes. For more information about the titles of columns and features handled by particular syndicates, consult the *Editor and Publisher Syndicate Directory* (11 W. 19th St., New York, NY 10011). For a list of newspapers published in the U.S. and Canada, see *Ayer Directory of Publications* in your library.

You'll be better able to compete in the syndicate market as you see subjects and styles go in and out of vogue. Developing that intangible sense of what will be "in" next year will help you in this market. Come up with next year's "in" subject (write well, too), and you won't have to worry about the competition for a while.

ADVENTURE FEATURE SYNDICATE, 329 Harvery Dr., Glendale CA 91206. (818)247-1721. Editor; Orpha Harryman Barry. SASE. Reports in 1 month. Buys all rights, first North American serial rights and second serial (reprint) rights. Free writer's guidelines.
Needs: Fiction (spies) and fillers (adventure/travel). Submit complete ms.

‡**ARKIN MAGAZINE SYNDICATE**, 761 NE 180th St., North Miami Beach FL 33162. Editor: Joseph Arkin. 20% freelance written by writers on contract; 5% freelance written by writers on a one-time basis. "We regularly purchase articles from several freelancers for syndication in trade and professional magazines." Submit complete ms. Previously published submissions OK, "if all rights haven't been sold." Computer printout submissions acceptable; no dot-matrix. SASE. Reports in 3 weeks. Buys all North American magazine and newspaper rights.
Needs: Magazine articles (nonfiction; 800-1,800 words, directly relating to business problems common to several (not just one) business firms, in different types of businesses); and photos (purchased with written material). "We are in dire need of the 'how-to' business article." Will not consider article series. Pays 3-10¢/word; $5-10 for photos; "actually, line drawings are preferred instead of photos." Pays on acceptance.
Tips: "Study a representative group of trade magazines to learn style, needs and other facets of the field."

‡**THE ARTISTS AND WRITERS SYNDICATES**, 1034 National Press Building, Washington DC 20045. (202)888-8882. Editor: Marjorie Steitz. Purchases 2 or 3 freelance features annually. Syndicates to newspapers—U.S. and Canada. SASE. Reports in 2 weeks. Writer's guidelines for SASE.
Needs: Newspaper columns (weekly preferred, illustrated). Must be popular subject. "Quality of writing must be first-rate." Query with published clips or photocopies of unpublished work. Pays 50% commission.
Tips: "This is a very difficult field to enter. We suggest trying newspaper syndication only after succeeding (and establishing a good track record) with a newspaper—or two or three newspapers. TV is an awesome rival. "How-to" features are one way to compete. Offer a service readers can't get on TV."

AUTHENTICATED NEWS INTERNATIONAL, ANI, 29 Katonah Ave., Katonah NY 10536. (914)232-7726. Editor: Sidney Polinsky. Syndication and Features Editor: Helga Brink. Supplies book review material to national magazines, newspapers, and house organs in the United States and important countries abroad. Buys exclusive and non-exclusive rights. Previously published submissions OK "at times." Reports in 3 months. SASE.
Nonfiction and Photos: Can use photo material in the following areas: hard news, photo features, ecology and the environment, science, medical, industry, education, human interest, the arts, city planning, and pertinent photo material from abroad. 750 words maximum. Prefers 8x10 b&w glossy prints, color transparencies (4x5 or 2¼x2¼, 35mm color). Where necessary, model releases required. Pays 50% royalty.

BUDDY BASCH FEATURE SYNDICATE, 771 West End Ave., New York NY 10025. (212)666-2300. Editor/Publisher: Buddy Basch. Purchases 10 features/year. Syndicates to print media: newspapers, magazines, house organs, etc. SASE. Reports in 2 weeks or less. Buys first North American serial rights.
Needs: Magazine features, newspaper features, and one-shot ideas that are really different. "Try to make them unusual, unique, real 'stoppers', not the usual stuff." Will consider one-shots and articles series on travel, entertainment, human interest—"the latter, a wide umbrella that makes people stop and read the piece. Different, unusual and unique are the key words, not what the *writer* thinks, but has been done nine million times before." Query. Pays 20-50% commission. Additional payment for photos $10-50. Currently syndicates *It Takes a Woman*, by Frances Scott (woman's feature).
Tips: "Never mind what your mother, fiance or friend thinks is good. If it has been done before and is old hat, it has no chance. Do a little research and see if there are a dozen other similar items in the press—and don't just try a very close 'switch' on them. You don't fool anyone with this. There are less and less newspapers, with more and more people vying for the available space. But there's *always* room for a really good, different feature or story. Trouble is few writers (amateurs especially) know a good piece, I'm sorry to say."

‡**BUSINESS FEATURES SYNDICATE**, Box 9844, Ft. Lauderdale FL 33310. (305)485-0795. Editor: Dana K. Cassell. Estab. 1984. Buys about 100 features/columns a year. Syndicates to trade journal magazines, business newspapers and tabloids. SASE. Buys exclusive rights while being circulated. Writer's guidelines for business size SAE and 1 first class stamp. Reports in 1 month.
Needs: Fillers, magazine columns, magazine features, newspaper columns, newspaper features and news items. Buys single features and article series on generic business, how-to, marketing, merchandising, security, management and personnel. Length: 250-2,500 words. Query or submit complete ms. Pays 50% commission. Sometimes pays 50% on photos. Currently syndicates Retail Market Clinic, by Dana Cassell.
Tips: "We need nonfiction material aimed at the independent retailer or small service business owner. Material must be written for and of value to more than one field, for example: jewelers drug store owners, and sporting goods dealers."

CALLIE-PEARL INTERNATIONAL SYNDICATE FEATURES, Box 56, Sunderland MA 01375. Editor: Wilesse Comissiong. 25% freelance written by writers under contract; 25% freelance written on a one-time basis. Computer printout submissions acceptable. Reports within one month. Query with published clips; no unsolicited mss will be returned. For writer's guidelines or queries include SASE. Payment is individually considered, based on circulation. Contracts generally are 70/30%.
Tips: "We buy innovative, untried features older syndicates cautiously avoid. We publish a syndicate marketing newsletter to apprise writers of marketing techniques and tips. For a sample copy send SASE."

‡**CHRONICLE FEATURES**, Suite 1011, 870 Market St., San Francisco CA 94102. (415)777-7212. Editor/General Manager: Stuart Dodds. Buys 3 features/year. Syndicates to daily newspapers in the U.S. and Canada. SASE. Reports in 1 month. Buys first North American serial and second serial (reprint) rights.
Needs: Newspaper columns and features. "In choosing a column subject, the writer should be guided by the aspirations and lifestyle of today's newspaper reader. We look for originality of expression and, in special fields of interest, a high degree of expertise." Preferred length: 500-750 words. Submit complete ms. Pays 50% revenue from syndication. Offers no additional payment for photos or artwork accompanying ms. Currently syndicates The Nuclear Age, by Lewis Rothlein (op-ed page column).

CITY NEWS SERVICE, Box 39, Willow Springs MO 65793. (417)469-2423. Editor: Richard Weatherington. 25% freelance written by writers on contract; 30% freelance written by writers on a one-time basis. Buys 100+ features/year; 25+ column/department items/year; 75+ fillers/year. Works with 50 previously unpublished writers annually. "We syndicate stories slanted toward small business in all trades." Computer printout submissions acceptable. SASE. Reports in 1 week on queries; 4 months on mss. Buys syndication rights. Writer's guidelines for SAE and 1 first class stamp.
Needs: New product, technical, business articles (1,500-3,000 words). No opinion or first-person narratives. "Will review any column which relates to small business (1,000-1,500 words)." Also uses fillers: Short Business Tips and Inside Techniques (100-250 words). Especially interested in business, finance, law, computer,

security and management material. Query or submit complete ms. Send sample of 3 columns. Pays 50-75% commission on articles and columns; 50% on fillers.

Tips: "We seek material primarily directed toward the small businessman." Subjects should be well researched and specific. "We tailor each story to fit the market we service. We are not a mass syndicate. We are more like a custom editorial service and use the freelance material as a base for tailoring. If the writer knows the subject, we will take care of the tailoring for the specific market."

COLLEGE PRESS SERVICE, 2629 18th St., Denver CO 80211. (303)458-7216. Editor: Bill Sonn. 25% freelance written. "We work with about 15 previously published freelancers a year." Sells to average 600 outlets. Initial written query is imperative. Computer printout submissions acceptable; prefers letter-quality to dot-matrix. SASE. Reports in 1 month. Material is not copyrighted.

Needs: Magazine and newspaper features; news items. "All our material is somehow related to colleges, students, higher education, faculty members, research, etc. We use only reportage, no opinion or commentary pieces." Pays 5¢/word.

CONTINUUM BROADCASTING NETWORK/GENERATION NEWS, INC., Suite 46, 345 W. 85th St., New York NY 10024. (212)580-9525. Executive Editor: Donald J. Fass. Associate Editor: Stephen Vaughn. Broadcast Feature Producer: Deanna Baron. 60% freelance written. 25% written by writers on contract; 35% freelance written by writers on a one-time basis. Buys 300 features/interviews/year. Works with 30-40 previously unpublished writers annually. Syndicates to newspapers and radio. Computer printout submissions acceptable; no dot-matrix. SASE. Reports in 5 weeks. Buys all rights. Writer's guidelines for business size SAE and 2 first-class stamps.

Needs: Newspaper columns (all kinds of weekly regular features for newspapers); radio broadcast material (90-second and 2½-minute regular daily radio features: lifestyle, comedy, music and interview—scripts as well as taped features); 30-minute and 60-minute specials. One-shot features for radio only-for 30- and 60-minute specials; scripts and completed productions. Query with 1 or 2 clips of published work only and 1 page summary on proposed articles. Demo tape and/or full script for broadcast; not necessary to query on tapes, but return postage must be provided. Pays 25-50% commission or $25-175, depending on length. Offers no additional payment for photos accompanying ms. Currently syndicates Getting It Together (weekly youth-oriented music and lifestyle column; American Weekend (radio feature magazine program); Keeping Fit (daily series); Taking Off (daily travel series); The Eighties (daily radio lifestyle features) and On Bleecker Street (weekly program on the sixties—interview and music show hosted by Don Fass and Deanna Baron), and The Great American Trivia Test, (weekly and daily newspaper and radio feature).

Tips: "Chances are very good to excellent, particularly in radio syndication. For both newspaper and radio, it must be a unique or very contemporary concept that can be sustained indefinitely. It is helpful to have a backlog of material and good subject knowledge, combined with good research skills."

COWLES SYNDICATE, INC., (formerly *The Register and Tribune Syndicate, Inc.*), 715 Locust St., Des Moines IA 50304. (515)284-8244. President: Dennis R. Allen. Submission Editor: Thomas E. Norquist. 25% freelance written. Buys material for syndication in 1,700 daily newspapers, television, product licensing outlets. Works with many previously unpublished writers depending on subject matter. Submit complete ms. Submission not returned without SASE. Photocopied submissions required. Computer printout submissions acceptable "if legible and easy to read"; no dot-matrix. Reports in 6 weeks. Buys all rights.

Needs: News items (nonfiction); and photos (purchased with written material); items reflecting topical trends and needs with ability for sustaining on-going column. Especially interested in self-help topic matter. Buys article series "from 500-700 words/column on current topics. Most submissions require at least 6 weeks worth of column copy or artwork in near finish form. Don't send original work." Pays in royalties or commissions. Pays on publication.

Tips: "We prefer column ideas to sustain an on-going column versus one-time publication. Study articles and series currently appearing in newspapers; follow successful format and topic matter for self-help."

CURIOUS FACTS FEATURES, 6B Ridge Ct., Lebanon OH 45036. (513)932-1820. Editor: Donald Whitacre. 43% freelance written. Buys 175 articles, features and fillers/year. Works with 65% previously unpublished writers annually. Syndicates to 55 newspapers; columns that contain oddities of all kinds, especially oddities about laws. Computer printout submissions OK; "typewritten," better. SASE. Reports in 6 weeks. Buys all rights. Writer's guidelines for 4½x9½ SAE and 2 first class stamps.

Needs: Fillers (maximum 50 words; oddities of all types); and newspaper features (maximum 400 words; strange laws of the world; strange animals of the world). "We are always interested in Strange Anomalies of Medicine—Questions and Answers dealing with Oddities in the World. We purchase all kinds of oddities (no copyrighted material)." Pays 50% commission. Submit 4 columns (complete ms).

Photos: No additional payment for photos accepted with ms. Currently syndicates Curious Facts . . . , by Donald Whitacre (oddities of all kinds).

Tips: "We use true oddities, which can be cut if they are too long." Average length: 30-300 words.

EDITORIAL CONSULTANT SERVICE, Box 524, West Hempstead NY 11552. Editorial Director: Arthur A. Ingoglia. 90% freelance written. "We work with 75 writers in the U.S. and Canada," previously published writers only. Adds about 3 new columnists/year. Syndicates material to an average of 60 newspapers, magazines, automotive trade and consumer publications, and radio stations with circulation of 50,000-575,000. Query. Computer printout submissions acceptable; letter-quality submissions preferred. SASE. Reports in 3 weeks. Buys all rights. Writer's guidelines for SASE.
Needs: Magazine and newspaper columns and features; news items; and radio broadcast material. Prefers carefully documented material with automotive slant. Also considers automotive trade features. Will consider article series. No horoscope, child care, lovelorn or pet care. Author's percentage varies; usually averages 50%. Additional payment for 8x10 b&w and color photos accepted with ms. Submit 2-3 columns. Currently syndicates Let's Talk About Your Car, by R. Hite.

FICTION NETWORK, Box 5651, San Francisco CA 94101. (415)552-3223. Editor: Jay Schaefer. 100% freelance written by writers whom have signed contracts. Syndicates to newspapers and regional magazines. Buys 150 features/year. Works with 25 previously unpublished writers annually. Computer printout submissions acceptable; letter-quality only. SASE. Reports in 3 months. Buys first serial and second serial (reprint) rights. Sample catalog of syndicated stories $4; writer's guidelines with SAE and 1 first class stamp.
Needs: All types of fiction (particularly holiday) under 2,500 words. "We specialize in quality literature." Submit complete ms. "Send one manuscript at a time; do not send second until you receive a response to the first." Pays 50% commission. Currently syndicates short fiction only; authors include Alice Adams, Ann Beattie, Max Apple, Andre Dubus, Bobbie Ann Mason, Joyce Carol Oates and others.
Tips: "We seek and encourage previously unpublished authors. Keep stories short, fast-paced and interesting."

FIRST DRAFT, Box 191107, Dallas TX 75219. (214)358-2271. Editor: Sheri Rosen. 75% written by writers on contract; 25% freelance written by writers on a one-time basis. Buys 60 articles/year. Syndicates to corporate and organizational employee publications. Electronic submissions OK—ASCII compatible or MCI Mail. Computer printout submissions acceptable. SASE. Reports in 2 months. Buys all rights. Writer's guidelines for business size SAE and 2 first class stamps.
Nonfiction: News items of 500 words (the effect of what's happening in the world on working people and businesses). May be universal or limited by industry. Buys one-shot features. Query with published clips or submit complete ms. Pays flat rate of $100 on acceptance.
Tips: "Most freelancers we use are business writers or former company publication editors."

GENERAL NEWS SYNDICATE, 147 W. 42nd St., New York NY 10036. (212)221-0043. 20% freelance written; 10% freelance written by writers on a one-time basis. Works with 12 writers/year; average of 3 previously unpublished writers annually. Syndicates to an average of 12 newspaper and radio outlets averaging 20 million circulation; buys theatre and show business people columns (mostly New York theatre pieces). Computer printout submissions acceptable; no dot-matrix. SASE. Reports in 3 weeks. Buys one-time rights.
Needs: Entertainment-related material.

‡**DAVE GOODWIN & ASSOCIATES**, Drawer 54-6661, Surfside FL 33154. Editor: Dave Goodwin. 50% written by writers on contract; 20% freelance written by writers on a one-time basis. Buys about 25 features a year from freelancers. Rights purchased vary with author and material. May buy first rights or second serial (reprint) rights or simultaneous rights. Will handle copyrighted material. Electronic submissions OK via IBM PC. Computer printout submissions acceptable; prefers letter-quality to dot-matrix. Query or submit complete ms. Reports in 3 weeks. SASE.
Nonfiction: "Money-saving information for consumers: how to save on home expenses; auto, medical, drug, insurance, boat, business items, etc." Buys article series on brief, practical, down-to-earth items for consumer use or knowledge. Rarely buys single features. Currently handling Insurance for Consumers. Length: 300-5,000 words. Pays 50% on publication. Submit 2-3 columns.

HARRIS & ASSOCIATES PUBLISHING DIVISION, 615 Carla Way, La Jolla CA 92037. (615)488-3851. President: Dick Harris. 50% written by writers on contract; 25% freelance written by writers on a one-time basis. Works with 10 previously published writers annually. Rights purchased vary with author and material. Buys first North American serial rights. Does not purchase many mss per year since material must be in special style. Pays on acceptance. Not necessary to query. Send sample of representative material. Reports in less than 1 month. SASE.
Nonfiction: Material on driver safety and accident prevention. Pays 15¢/word minimum.
Photos: Action, unposed, 8x10 b&w photos are purchased without features or on assignment. Captions are required. Pays $25 minimum/photo.
Humor: Humor for modern women (not women's lib); humor for sports page. "We like to look at anything in

our special interest areas. Golf and tennis are our specialties. We'll also look at cartoons in these areas. Will buy or contract for syndication. Everything must be short, terse, with humorous approach."
Tips: "Submit *good* photos or art with text."

HERITAGE FEATURES SYNDICATE, 214 Massachusetts Ave. NE, Washington DC 20002. (202)543-0440. Managing Editor: Andy Seamans. 2% freelance written. Buys 3 columns/year. Syndicates to over 100 newspapers with circulations ranging from 2,000-630,000. Works with previously published writers. SASE. Reports in 3 weeks. Buys first North American serial rights. Computer printout submissions acceptable.
Needs: Newspaper columns (practically all material is done by regular columnists). One-shot features. "We purchase 750-800 word columns on political, economic and related subjects." Query. Pays $50 minimum. Currently syndicates Mohr on National Security, by Henry Mohr.
Tips: "Freelance writers can best break in to the syndicate market by being published in a local newspaper, being a working journalist, and gaining some degree of public notice in another media, such as authoring a book."

HISPANIC LINK NEWS SERVICE, 1420 N St. NW, Washington DC 20005. (202)234-0280. Editor/Publisher: Charles A. Ericksen. 50% freelance written by writers on contract; 20% freelance written by writers on a one-time basis. Buys 156 columns and features/year. Works with 50 writers/year; 5 previously unpublished writers. Syndicates to 200 newspapers and magazines with circulations ranging from 5,000 to 300,000. Computer printout submissions acceptable; prefers letter-quality to dot-matrix. SASE. Reports in 2 weeks. Buys second serial (reprint) or negotiable rights. Free writer's guidelines.
Needs: Magazine columns, magazine features, newspaper columns, newspaper features. One-shot features and article series. "We prefer 650-700 word op/ed or features, geared to a general national audience, but focus on issue or subject of particular interest to Hispanic Americans. Some longer pieces accepted occasionally." Query or submit complete ms. Pays $25-150. Currently syndicates Hispanic Link, by various authors (opinion and/or feature columns).
Tips: "This year we would especially like to get topical material and vignettes relating to Hispanic presence and progress in the United States. Provide insights on Hispanic experience geared to a general audience. Eighty-five to ninety percent of the columns we accept are authored by Hispanics; the Link presents Hispanic viewpoints, and showcases Hispanic writing talent to its 200 subscribing newspapers and magazines. Copy should be submitted in English. We syndicate in English and Spanish."

HOLLYWOOD INSIDE SYNDICATE, Box 49957, Los Angeles CA 90049. (213)826-9602. Editor: John Austin. 15% written by writers on contract; 50% freelance written by writers on a one-time basis. Purchases mss for syndication to newspapers in San Francisco, Philadelphia, Detroit, Montreal, London, and Sydney, etc. Works with 2-3 previously unpublished writers annually. Pays on acceptance "but this is also negotiable because of delays in world market acceptance and payment. Query or submit complete ms. Previously published submissions OK, if published in the U.S. and Canada only. Computer printout submissions acceptable; prefers letter-quality to dot-matrix. SASE. Reports in 6 weeks. Buys first rights or second serial (reprint) rights.
Needs: News items (column items concerning entertainment—motion picture—personalities and jet setters for syndicated column; 750-800 words). Also considers series of 1,500-word articles; "suggest descriptive query first. We are also looking for off-beat travel pieces (with pictures) but not on areas covered extensively in the Sunday supplements. We can always use pieces on 'freighter' travel but not luxury cruise liners. We also syndicate nonfiction book subjects—sex, travel, etc., to overseas markets. No fiction." Pay negotiable."
Tips: "Study the entertainment pages of Sunday (and daily) newspapers to see the type of specialized material we deal in. Perhaps we are different from other syndicates, but we deal with celebrities. No 'I' journalism such as 'when I spoke to Cloris Leachman.' Many freelancers submit material from the 'dinner theatre' and summer stock circuit of 'gossip type' items from what they have observed about the 'stars' or featured players in these productions—how they act off stage, who they romance, etc. We use this material."

‡**HYDE PARK MEDIA**, 7158 Lee St., Chicago IL 60648. (312)967-7666. Editor: Anthony DeBartolo. "Volume purchased has been low—5-10 features/year. I could place more material." Syndicates to area newspapers and magazines. SASE. Reports in 3 weeks. Buys first North American serial rights.
Needs: Magazine features (1,500-3,000 words); newspaper features (750-1,500 words); anything with a Chicago hook—a person from Chicago, for example, doing something interesting in another part of the country. Buys single (one-shot) features. Query with published clips. Pays 50% commission on sale.

INDEPENDENT NEWS ALLIANCE, 200 Park Ave., New York NY 10166. (212)602-3713. Executive Editor: Sidney Goldberg. 25% freelance written. Supplies material to leading U.S. and Canadian newspapers, also to South America, Europe, Asia and Africa. Works with 30 previously unpublished writers annually. Rights purchased vary with author and material. May buy all rights, first rights, or second serial (reprint) rights. Pays "on distribution to clients." Previously published submissions OK "on occasion." Query or submit complete

ms. Computer printout submissions acceptable; prefers letter-quality to dot-matrix. Reports in 2 weeks. SASE. **Nonfiction and Photos:** In the market for background, investigative, interpretive and news features. Lifestyle, trends, the arts, national issues that affect individuals and neighborhoods. The news element must be strong and purchases are generally made only from experienced, working journalists and authors. Wants timely news features of national interest that do not duplicate other coverage but add to it, interpret it, etc. Wants first-class nonfiction suitable for feature development. The story must be aimed at newspapers, must be self-explanatory, factual and well condensed. It must add measurably to the public's information or understanding of the subject, or be genuinely entertaining. Broad general interest is the key to success here. Length: 500 to 1,500 words, on occasion longer. Rarely buys columns. Looking for good 1-shots and good series of 2 to 7 articles. Where opinions are given, the author should advise, for publication, his qualifications to comment on specialized subjects. The news must be exclusive to be considered at all. Rate varies depending on interest and news value. Pays $75-300. Buys 8x10 glossy photos when needed to illustrate story; pays $25-50.
Tips: "Be space conscious—newspapers want a quick lead, fast follow-up. No leisurely developed stories. Write tight, clean copy. The target should be page one or the lead feature page of the paper—not 'any old' story."

INTERCONTINENTAL MEDIA SERVICES, LTD., Box 75127, Washington DC 20013. (202)638-5595. Editor: Dr. Edward von Rothkirch. Buys 500 features, 1,200 syndicated columns/year. Syndicates primarily to newspapers, some magazines. "In addition we syndicate 6 radio programs and are now going into 3-6 TV vignettes." SASE. Reports in 1 month. Buys all rights when available. Writer's guidelines for SAE and 1 first class stamp.
Needs: Newspaper columns (travel, collectibles, medical—500 to 700 words); newspaper features (travel, unusual subjects—1,500 words); news items (political backgrounders on foreign countries and personalities); radio broadcast material (travel, book reviews, science—length 2-3 minutes). One-shot (sometimes) and article series. "We will consider 400-1,500 words on foreign politics or personalities, travel to out-of-the-way or unusual places, collectibles of all kinds, science or medical subjects." Submit complete ms. Pays 50% of net; $50-500 (special) flat rate. Pays $25-100 for photos. Currently syndicates Magic Carpet, by Edward R'Church (travel).
Tips: "If the material is well-prepared, the approach is new or different, and there is a substantial segment of potential readers that have an interest in the subject, there is a good chance for syndication. The writer should indicate what the market potential is for the material."

INTERNATIONAL ECO FEATURES SYNDICATE, Box 69193, W. Hollywood, Los Angeles CA 90069. Editor: Janet Bridgers. 100% freelance written by writers on a one-time basis. Syndicates to newspapers. Works with approximately 10 previously unpublished writers annually. Electronic submissions OK, but "we prefer contact by mail first;" hard copy also required. Computer printout submissions acceptable; prefers letter-quality to dot-matrix. SASE. Reports in 2 months. Buys first worldwide serial rights. Writer's guidelines for business size SASE.
Needs: Newspaper columns specializing in environment, ecology and animal rights. Op-ed articles, 800-1,000 words; features, 1,000-2,000 words with photos. Electronic submissions OK, but query with clips of published work. Pays 50% commission. "We will ask a higher price from newspapers when photos are accepted with manuscripts."
Tips: "We specialize in material about ecology, the environment and animal rights. We are not interested in material that is not about these subjects. We are *particularly* interested in op-eds on regional environmental issues."

INTERNATIONAL MEDICAL TRIBUNE SYNDICATE, Suite 700, 600 New Hampshire Ave. NW, Washington DC 20037. (202)338-8866. Editor: Keith Haglund. 50% freelance written; 10% freelance written by writers on a one-time basis. Buys about 100 articles/year. Works with a few previously unpublished writers annually. Syndicates to small- and medium-sized newspapers, daily and weekly; magazines; computer news service; specialty publications in the health field. Electronic submissions OK, but query first. Computer printout submissions acceptable; prefers letter-quality to dot-matrix. SASE. Reports in 1 month. Buys all rights.
Needs: Fillers (250-400 words on medical or health developments); newspaper features (1,000-1,500 words—relatively complete treatment of an area of medicine or health); news items (straight news story filed within one week of event covered, etc., average 500 words). One-shot features on any topic in medicine and health. "Topics that we would especially like to get material on this year include up-to-date medical advances that can tell people how best to stay healthy." Length: 1,000 to 1,500 words. Query with published clips or submit complete ms. "Call with idea." Pays 15¢/word for straight news; 20¢/word for features. Offers kill fee if assigned story. Offers no additional payment for photos accompanying ms.
Tips: "Our syndicate is an excellent opportunity for freelancers, but clear, concise and *lively* writing is a must. Strongly suggest query first, by mail or phone."

INTERPRESS OF LONDON AND NEW YORK, 400 Madison Ave., New York NY 10017. (212)832-2839. Editor: Jeffrey Blyth. 50% freelance written by writers on contract; 50% freelance written by writers on a one-time basis. Works with 3-6 previously unpublished writers annually. Buys British and European rights mostly, but can handle world rights. Will consider photocopied submissions. Previously published submissions OK "for overseas." Computer printout submissions acceptable; prefers letter-quality to dot-matrix. Query or submit complete ms. Pays on publication, or agreement of sale. Reports immediately or as soon as practicable. SASE.

Nonfiction: "Unusual stories and photos for British and European press. Picture stories, for example, on such 'Americana' as a five-year-old evangelist; the 800-pound 'con-man'; the nude-male calendar; tallest girl in the world; interviews with pop celebrities such as Yoko Ono, Michael Jackson, Bill Cosby, Tom Selleck, Cher, Priscilla Presley, Cheryl Tiegs, Eddie Murphy, Liza Minelli, also news of stars on such shows as "Dynasty"/ "Dallas"; cult subjects such as voodoo, college fads, anything amusing or offbeat. Extracts from books such as Earl Wilson's *Show Business Laid Bare*, inside-Hollywood type series ('Secrets of the Stuntmen'). Real life adventure dramas ('Three Months in an Open Boat,' 'The Air Crash Cannibals of the Andes'). No length limits—short or long, but not too long. Payment varies; depending on whether material is original, or world rights. Pays top rates, up to several thousand dollars, for exclusive material."

Photos: Purchased with or without features. Captions required. Standard size prints. Pay $50 to $100, but no limit on exclusive material.

Tips: "Be alert to the unusual story in your area—the sort that interests the American tabloids (and also the European press)."

KING FEATURES SYNDICATE, INC., 235 E. 45th St., New York NY 10017. (212)682-5600. Editor: James D. Head. 10% freelance written. Syndicates material to newspapers. Works with 10 previously unpublished writers annually. Submit "brief cover letter with samples of feature proposals." Previously published submissions OK. Computer printout submissions acceptable. SASE. Reports in 3 weeks. Buys all rights.

Needs: Newspaper features and columns. No travel, wine or general humor columns; restaurant, theatre or movie reviews; or fad-oriented subjects. Pays "revenue commission percentage" or flat fee. Special single article opportunity is Sunday Woman, a weekly supplement distributed nationally. Buys one-time rights to articles on beauty, health, grooming, fashion, coping, money management for women, career guidance, etc. Query with SASE to Merry Clark, senior editor.

Tips: "Be brief, thoughtful and offer some evidence that the feature proposal is viable. Read newspapers—lots of them in big and small markets—to find out what already is out there. Don't try to buck established columns which newspapers would be reluctant to replace with new and untried material."

LOS ANGELES TIMES SYNDICATE, Times-Mirror Square, Los Angeles CA 90053. Vice President/Editor: Don Michel. Special Articles Editor: Dan O'Toole. Syndicates to U.S. and worldwide markets. Usually buys first North American serial rights and world rights, but rights purchased can vary. Submit seasonal material six weeks in advance. SASE. Material ranges from 800-2,000 words.

Needs: Reviews continuing columns and comic strips for U.S. and foreign markets. Send columns and comic strips to Don Michel. Also reviews single articles, series, magazine reprints, and book serials. Send these submissions to Dan O'Toole. Recent special projects include Lee Iacocca, Jane Fonda and Studs Terkel. Send complete mss. Pays 50% commission. Offers no additional payment for photos accompanying ms. Currently syndicates Erma Bombeck, Art Buchwald, Dr. Henry Kissinger, Joseph Kraft and Paul Conrad.

Tips: "We're dealing with fewer undiscovered writers but still do review material."

MINORITY FEATURES SYNDICATE, Box 421, Farrell PA 16146. (412)962-2522. Editor: Sally Foglia. 50% written by freelance on conctact; 50% freelance written by writers on a one-time basis. Works with 50% previously unpublished writers annually. Buys first North American serial rights. Electronic submissions OK via Apple IIe. SASE. Reports in 5 weeks. Writer's guidelines for 44¢ postage.

Needs: Fillers, magazine features, newspaper features. Also needs comic book writers for Bill Murray Productions. Query with published clips. Pays open commission. Pays $25 minimum for photos. Currently syndicates *Sonny Boy*, *Those Browns* and *The Candyman*, by Bill Murray (newspaper features).

Tips: "We are getting into the comic book market. Writers should write for guidelines."

NATIONAL NEWS BUREAU, 2019 Chancellor St., Philadelphia PA 19103. (215)569-0700. Editor: Harry Jay Katz. "We work with more than 200 writers and buy over 1,000 stories per year." Syndicates to more than 1,000 publications. SASE. Reports in 2 weeks. Buys all rights. Writer's guidelines for 9x12 SAE and 54¢ postage.

Needs: Newspaper features; "we do many reviews and celebrity interviews. Only original, assigned material." One-shot features and article series; film reviews, etc. Query with clips. Pays $5-200 flat rate. Offers $5-200 additional payment for photos accompanying ms.

NEW YORK TIMES SYNDICATION SALES CORP., 200 Park Ave., New York NY 10166. (212)972-1070. Vice President/Editorial Director: Paula Reichler. 20% written by writers on contract; 50% freelance written by writers on a one-time basis. Syndicates approximately "three books per month plus numerous one-shot articles." Also included in foreign newspapers and magazines. Buys first serial rights, first North American Serial rights, one-time rights, second serial (reprint) rights, and all rights. Computer printout submissions acceptable; no dot-matrix.
Needs: Wants magazine and newspaper features; magazine and newspaper columns; and book series. "On syndicated articles, payment to author is 50% of net sales. We only consider articles that have been previously published. Send tearsheets of articles published." Photos are welcome with books and articles. "Topics that we would especially like to get material on this year include fitness and holiday themes."
Tips: "Topics should cover universal markets and either be by a well-known writer or have an off-beat quality. Quizzes are welcomed if well researched."

NEWS AMERICA SYNDICATE, 1703 Kaiser Ave., Irvine CA 92714. President/Chief Executive Officer: Richard S. Newcombe. Syndicates material to newspapers. Submit "examples of work with explanatory letter to Submissions Department." SASE. Reports in 2 months. Rights purchased vary. Free writer's guidelines.
Needs: Newspaper columns (should be 500-800 words in length and should appeal to a wide audience. Subject matter should not be too specialized because syndicates sell columns to newspapers all over the U.S. and Canada). Submit minimum 10 columns. Currently syndicates *Ann Landers*, by Ann Landers.

NEWS FLASH INTERNATIONAL, INC., 2262 Centre Ave., Bellmore NY 11710. (516)679-9888. Editor: Jackson B. Pokress. 10% freelance written. Supplies material to Observer newspapers and overseas publications. Works with 6 previously unpublished writers annually. "Contact editor prior to submission to allow for space if article is newsworthy." Photocopied submissions OK. Computer printout submissions acceptable; no dot-matrix. Pays on publication. SASE.
Nonfiction: "We have been supplying a 'ready-for-camera' sports page (tabloid size) complete with column and current sports photos on a weekly basis to many newspapers on Long Island as well as pictures and written material to publications in England and Canada. Payment for assignments is based on the article. It may vary. Payments vary from $20 for a feature of 800 words. Our sports stories feature in-depth reporting as well as book reviews on this subject. We are always in the market for good photos, sharp and clear, action photos of boxing, wrestling, football, baseball and hockey. We cover all major league ball parks during the baseball and football seasons. We are accredited to the Mets, Yanks, Jets and Giants. During the winter we cover basketball and hockey and all sports events at the Nassau Coliseum."
Photos: Purchased on assignment; captions required. Uses "good quality 8x10 b&w glossy prints; good choice of angles and lenses." Pays $7.50 minimum for b&w photos.
Tips: "Submit articles which are fresh in their approach on a regular basis with good quality black and white glossy photos if possible; include samples of work. Articles should have a hard-hitting approach and plenty of quotes and short terse sentences."

NEWSPAPER ENTERPRISE ASSOCIATION, INC., 200 Park Ave., New York NY 10166. (212)557-5870. Editorial Director: David Hendin. Director International Newspaper Operations: Sidney Goldberg. Executive Editor: Diana Drake. Managing Editor, Comics: Sarah Gillespie. "We provide a comprehensive package of features to mostly small- and medium-size newspapers." Computer printout submission acceptable. SASE. Reports in 6 weeks. Buys all rights.
Needs: "Any column we purchase must fill a need in our feature lineup and must have appeal for a wide variety of people in all parts of the country. We are most interested in lively writing. We are also interested in features that are not merely copies of other features already on the market. And the writer must know his or her subject. Any writer who has a feature which meets all of those requirements should simply send a few copies of the feature to us, along with his or her plans for the column and some background material on the writer." Current columnists include Bob Walters, Bob Wagman, Julian Bond, George McGovern, Dr. Peter Gott, Tom Tiede, Murray Olderman, Dick Kleiner, Rusty Brown and William Rusher. Current comics include Alley Oop, Born Loser, Frank & Ernest, Levy's Law, Eek & Meek, Kit 'n' Carlyle, Bugs Bunny, Berry's World, Snake, and Babyman.
Tips: "We get enormous numbers of proposals for first person columns—slice of life material with lots of anecdotes. While many of these columns are big successes in local newspapers, it's been our experience that they are extremely difficult to sell nationally. Most papers seem to prefer to buy this sort of column from a talented local writer."

NUMISMATIC INFORMATION SERVICE, Rossway Rd., Rt. 4, Box 237A, Pleasant Valley NY 12569. Editor: Barbara White. Buys 5 features/year. Query. Computer printout submissions acceptable. SASE. Reports in 2 weeks. Buys all rights.
Needs: Newspaper columns (anything related to numismatics and philately, particularly the technical aspects of the avocations); news items (relative to the world of coin and stamp collecting); and fillers (on individual

coins or stamps, or the various aspects of the hobbies). No fiction or get rich schemes. Pays $5 for 500 word article; 50¢ additional payment for b&w photos accepted with ms.

OCEANIC PRESS SERVICE, Box 6538, Buena Park CA 90622-6538. (714)527-5650. Editor: John Taylor. 25% written by writers on contract; 25% freelance written by writers on a one-time basis. Buys from 12-15 writers annually, "using their published work" for use in some 300 magazines, newspapers or books with a circulation range of 1-15 million. Works with 10 previously unpublished writers annually. Buys timely topics with universal appeal. Buys all rights, or second serial (reprint) rights. Query with published clips. Electronic submissions OK via IBM, but requires hard copy also. Computer printout submissions acceptable; no dot-matrix. SASE. Reports in 3 weeks. Writer's guidelines $1.
Needs: "We like authors and cartoonists, but for our mutual benefit, they must fit into our editorial policies. The following list will give an idea of the kind of materials we want: interviews or profiles (world figures only); recipes, with color transparencies or b&w pictures; home building and home decoration features with photos; hairstyle features with photos; interviews with movie and TV stars with photos; current books to be sold for translation to foreign markets: mysteries, biographies, how to do, self improvement, westerns, science fiction, romance, psychological, and gothic novels; features on family relations, modern women, heroism, and ecology; features on water sports, with color transparencies; and newspaper columns with illustrations. We are always happy to obtain reprint rights, especially book excerpts or serializations. Payment is outright or on a 50/50 basis; range is $25-3,000. We take care of foreign language translations. Submit a varied sampling of columns, tearsheets preferred."

PHOTO ASSOCIATES NEWS SERVICE, INC., Box 306, Flushing NY 11358. (212)619-1700/(718)961-0909. Editor-in-Charge: Rick Moran. Freelance Editor: R.J. Maiman. "We worked with 30 writers last year handling 450 stories for a variety of domestic and international magazines and newspapers." Prefers electronic submissions via phone; 300 Baud or MCI Mail (Telex 75-0809 photo UD; MCI Mail 217-8611). Computer printout submissions acceptable. Query with resume, published clips and SASE. "Also enclose a list of story ideas that you think we would want." Responds within 10 days with writer's guidelines.
Needs: "Our big emphasis is on articles with illustrations or photos. Our client list includes publications in Asia, South America and Europe and virtually all of them want to accompany stories. Topics we have been successful with in the past include entertainment, travel, pop science and psychology and public safety issues (police, fire, paramedics). All sorts of celebrity material is constantly being called for by our clients overseas, as are fresh story ideas that have not already been exploited over the wires. Pet and animal stories have also done very well in the past. Our greatest emphasis is on breaking news and headline stories, feature length, covered with a local angle, but these too must be accompanied by good photos." Pays 65% commission on sale. Payments are made once a month.
Tips: "We are supportive of both National Writers Union and ASMP members. While we prefer writers who have proven track records, we are always looking for new talent with flair."

SINGER COMMUNICATIONS, INC., 3164 Tyler Ave., Anaheim, CA 92801. (714)527-5650. Editor: Natalie Charlton. 100% freelance written by writers on a one-time basis. Buys 500 features, 300 books/year. Works with 20 previously unpublished writers annually. Syndicates to magazines, newspapers, radio, TV, book publishers and businesses. Electronic submissions OK via IBM, but requires hard copy also. Computer printout submissions acceptable; prefers letter-quality to dot-matrix. SASE. Reports in 1 month. Buys all rights, first North American serial, second serial (reprint), and world rights. Writer's guidelines $1.
Needs: Fiction (with universal appeal, contemporary romance, westerns); fillers (gags and jokes); magazine columns; magazine features; newspaper columns (with universal appeal); newspaper features (worldwide interest, no political); radio and TV broadcast material; merchandising and marketing items for manufacturing. One-shot features and article series. "We will consider any feature with a worldwide interest that has a timeless quality. We service the entire free world and therefore stay away from features and columns if they are geared only for U.S. consumption." Query with published clips. "We prefer published work for foreign reprint." Pays 50% commission, or flat rate or minimum guarantee depending on material; books negotiable. Pays additional rate for color transparencies or b&w line drawings. Currently syndicates Solve A Crime, by B. Gordon (crime column) and 100 other columns.
Tips: "Find a niche in a specialized field which is not over-run; interview important people."

‡**SMALL TOWN DEVELOPMENT**, Kent D. Johnson, Box 75, Route 3, Concordia KS 66901. (913)243-7553. Editor: Kent Johnson. Estab. 1984. Syndicates to newspapers. SASE. Computer printout submissions acceptable. Reports in 2 weeks on submissions. Buys first North American serial rights. Guidelines for #10 SAE and 1 first-class stamp.
Needs: Newspaper columns. Purchases single (one-shot) features and article series. Needs material on small town economic development. Submit complete ms. Length: 500 words. Pays flat rate of $50. No additional payment for photos. Currently syndicates Small Town Development, by Kent Johnson.

SYNDICATED WRITERS GROUP, Box 23, Boyertown PA 19512. (215)367-9496. Editor: Daniel Grotta. "Syndicated Writers Group is a unique and revolutionary syndicate in that we are the world's first interactive computerized library databank which editors may access from their computer terminals, select, buy and then download articles and columns. We syndicate to newspapers and magazines, both by computer and by traditional submissions/transmission methods." Electronic submissions OK via disk or modem. Models I, II and IV TRS-80 5" single sided, single density; 40 or 77 track 5" or 8" CP/M format; any submissions acceptable. Reports in 3 months. Maintains exclusive rights for the length of the contract. Writer's guidelines with SASE.
Needs: "We have a need for contract writers in certain subjects such as technology, medicine, pets, lifestyles, politics, computers, consumerism, etc. Because our main sales emphasis is on the library, we are far less interested in regular columns than in individual articles. We would consider accepting a new column only if it is absolutely unique and sensational. Pays 50% commission; 80% when SWG acts as agent for specific assignment; 85% for secondary rights sales, such as books, TV, etc. Maintains exclusive rights for the length of the contract. Pays additional for photos or artwork sold with manuscripts, but only top-quality stuff. At present we cannot consider any separate graphics material. Currently syndicates The Endless Winter, by Ted Heck (ski column); Wanderlust, by Deborah Williams.
Tips: "We are looking for top quality writers with magazine or book backgrounds who are used to presenting substance with style. Our articles and columns are not only informative and interesting, but *entertaining*. We want each piece to be a potential award-winner." SWG is an electronic editorial syndicate, and all our writers and editors will eventually be connected to us by computer. We work *only* with writers under direct contract to us. However, we will consider freelance writers as potential contract writers as vacancies open. Develop a column format with at least 13 (weekly) or 6 (monthly) samples, plus an accurate description of the column, and a biography/resume. Have something very unusual or brilliant to say, with style and consistency. Be expert in your chosen field."

TEENAGE CORNER, INC., 70-540 Gardenia Ct., Rancho Mirage CA 92270. President: David J. Lavin. Buys 122 items/year for use in newspapers. Submit complete ms. Reports in 1 week. Material is not copyrighted.
Needs: 500-word newspaper features. Pays $25.

TRIBUNE MEDIA SERVICES, (formerly Tribune Company Syndicate), 720 N. Orange Ave., Orlando FL 32801. (305)422-8181. Editor: Michael Argirion. Syndicates to newspapers. Reports in 1 month. SASE. Buys all rights, first North American serial rights and second serial (reprint) rights.
Needs: Newspaper columns and features. Buys single features and article series if suitable for newspapers. Query with published clips. Pays 50% commission. Currently syndicates the Mike Royko column.

‡**UNITED CARTOONIST SYNDICATE**, Box 7081, Corpus Christi TX 78415. (512)855-2480. Editor; Pedro R. Moreno. Works with 12 cartoonists annually. Syndicates to newspapers, newsletters, magazines, books or book publishers, and licensing companies. SASE. Reports in 1 week on submissions. Buys all rights. Guidelines $5.
Needs: Newspaper features (comic panel and comic strips in a family entertainment slant). Purchases single (one-shot) features and article series. Will consider meta-physical, UFOs, and human and animal interest stories or articles. Query with clips of published work. Pays author 40%. Additional payment for photos: $10-25. Currently syndicates PUD, by Kelvin Anderson.
Tips: "Have your freelance work published first, then submit clippings to a syndicate with an address where it was published."

UNITED FEATURE SYNDICATE, 200 Park Ave., New York NY 10166. Editorial Director: David Hendin. Director International Newspaper Operations: Sidney Goldberg. Executive Editor: D.L. Drake. Managing Editor, Comics: Sarah Gillespie. Supplies features to 1,700 U.S. newspapers, plus Canadian and other international papers. Works with published writers. Query with 4-6 samples and SASE. Computer printout submissions acceptable. Reports in 6 weeks.
Columns, Comic Strips and Puzzles: Current columnists include Jack Anderson, Judith Martin, Donald Lambro, Ben Wattenberg, Martin Sloane, Barbara Gibbons. Comic strips include Peanuts, Nancy, Garfield, Drabble, Marmaduke, Tarzan, and Robotman. Standard syndication contracts are offered for columns and comic strips.
Tips: "We buy the kind of writing similar to major syndicates—varied material, well-known writers. The best way to break in to the syndicate market is for freelancers to latch on with a major newspaper and to develop a rabid following. Also, cultivate new areas and try to anticipate trends."

UNIVERSAL PRESS SYNDICATE, 4400 Johnson Dr., Fairway KS 66205. Buys syndication rights. Reports normally in 1 month. Returned postage required.

Nonfiction: Looking for features—columns for daily and weekly newspapers. "Any material suitable for syndication in daily newspapers." Currently handling James J. Kilpatrick and others. Payment varies according to contract.

‡**WEEKLY FEATURES SYNDICATE LTD.**, 126 S. 8th St., St. Joseph MO 64501. (816)364-2920. Editor: Linda Bennett. Works with approximately 10 writers/year. "We have 12 overseas agencies that sell our features, plus we market all newspapers and magazines in the United States area." SASE. Reports in 1 month. Buys all rights. Writer's guidelines for 9x12 SAE.

Needs: Short stories (mysteries, romance, doctor-nurse love, western love) and features on home fix-it and decoration ideas. Buys articles series. "We usually want a series of books or features covering the chosen topic of romance, love stories, mysteries, western, doctor and nurse fiction stories." Submit complete ms. "We do not use features represented by other agents. Pays 75% commission. Pays $10-100 for photos accepted with mss. Currently syndicates Larry Bretsnider (Automotive Adviser), edited by Larry Bretsnider.

Services & Opportunities

Authors' Agents ————————————

"I've written a book and need *you*
to recommend a good agent for me."

—Writers, calling *Writer's Market*

When you think you've written something too valuable to stay in a desk drawer, most of you begin a tireless (and tiring) search for a publisher. But for some writers, that search begins by looking for an agent. For other writers, the search for an agent starts after they've received numerous rejections on a book.

In either case, you want to know which agents are best and whether a specific agent will enhance or hinder your writing career.

But it would be unfair for us to say such-and-such-an-agent is right for you. The match-up between writer and agent depends so much on what you've written, your goals as a writer, and how your agent approaches the sale of your work.

An agent can turn a writer into an author but can't make you a writer. The ideas, the writing ability, the sensitivity toward what words are saying to readers must be there first, carefully crafted by many years of writing. Over the years, you'll also want to learn about the marketplace even if you plan to acquire an agent. "One benefits from being involved in this business side of writing, especially at the early stages of one's career," said author Karen O'Connor. "It's important to learn and study *all* aspects of the profession before turning some of them over to an agent or attorney."

When you know the marketplace, it's easier to select an agent. You'll know what questions to ask. "Most writers who are seeking agents simply know very little about the publishing business and about the agent's or even their own responsibilities," pointed out agent David Meth of Writer's Productions.

Problems arise when the writer and agent have different expectations. And the writer who tells an agent he knows nothing about book publishing places himself at the mercy of an agent (especially an unscrupulous one). What such a writer has told the agent is that he won't be able to evaluate the agent's performance. The agent needs to know that the writer will seek the services of another agent if his agent does a poor job. At the same time, the writer needs to know that if he can't produce marketable material, the agent will seek more competent writers to represent.

The role of the agent has been expanding as agents seek new outlets for author's work. With the increase in home video movies, agents will probably be selling more video rights than in the past. Many agents (through their sub-agents) are now selling book rights to foreign publishers. Few writers (even those who know publishing in the United States) can negotiate with foreign markets as an experienced agent can.

In the U.S. market, you can sell a book without an agent. In fact, many good but unknown writers have had to sell their first books before an agent would represent subsequent books. "Sell something. Short stories, whatever. And, if writers are lucky enough to obtain book contract offers, then they should certainly approach an agent for assistance," said agent Virginia Kidd. "A track record is the simplest and most direct proof that a writer has earning potential." Once you've selected an agent, he will handle the marketing of your work giving you more time to do what you know best—write.

An agent is a literary broker, a middleman, who gets your manuscript to the right editor at the right time. Some agents will also set up book auctions for rights, then serve as the auctioneer; other agents prefer that the subsidiary rights person (for a hardcover publisher) conduct the auction. The agent makes the sale and negotiates the best possible deal for you. If you live in the Midwest, for example, and are interested in contacting publishers in New York, you may do well to have an agent. He is often close to the action in the publishing world. Because of his experience in teaching, writing or editing, he knows the ins and outs of the industry. He relies on contacts within the industry to know what a publishing house wants before it makes its announcements public. Some writers consider the services of an agent invaluable.

But an agent is not for everyone. Many writers prefer to do their own marketing. They look for publishers; hire attorneys for advice and contract review; and keep the 10 percent to 15 percent agent commission on domestic sales for themselves.

Few agents will handle anything shorter than a book-length manuscript. Others deal only with scriptwriters who have previous credits. Many are looking for published writers or take on new clients only through referrals from other writers/editors.

How to Contact

When looking for an agent, don't expect immediate offers. If you have good ideas (preferably book-length ones), and if you are persistent, your search can be successful. If several agents decline to represent you, that doesn't say your writing is poor or that you'll not find an agent. Because most agents work on a commission basis, they must feel reasonably sure that they can sell your work. Continue contacting new agents one at a time while trying to sell your material over the transom to publishers (that's OK *until* you've agreed to let an agent represent you). If your writing is marketable, this method will double your chances of acceptance. The most direct approach to contacting an agent is by mail with a brief query letter (not to exceed two single-spaced typewritten pages) in which you describe your work, yourself, and your publishing history. For a nonfiction book, add an outline; for fiction, a few sample chapters (up to 50 typed, double-spaced pages) will tell an agent whether the book is no or go. Generally, treatments or even concepts are preferred for television or films. Your letter should be personalized—not a photocopied form letter with the agent's name typed in—and *always include a self addressed stamped envelope* with enough postage for a reply plus return of materials. If you don't hear from an agent within six weeks, send a polite note asking if the material has been received—and include a photocopy of your original query plus materials and another SASE. If you hear nothing within four months, send a note withdrawing the material—and immediately contact another agent using the same method.

Agents and the Market Today

Literary agencies represent as few as five clients or more than 100 clients depending upon the number of agents and the extent to which they aid writers. "Some agents have skills that others lack," pointed out one agent. Sometimes former book publishing editors become agents, bringing with them a strong *editorial* background. Some agents are attorneys or have one on staff. An agent should not be measured by the number of clients, or even the number of sales made in a given time period, but rather by the number of deals and dollars that he makes for his clients. Agents work for *additional* sales of your manuscripts. No good agent will be satisfied selling your novel to a hardcover publisher, for instance; he'll invest time in selling it to a paperback house, to a movie producer, to a newspaper syndicate for serialization, to a book club, to a foreign publisher. To do this, the agent exercises energy, ideas, connections, and business experience the writer probably doesn't have.

Most agents do not handle magazine articles, poetry or essays. There is not enough revenue generated from such sales to make them worth an agent's time. Most writers develop their own rapport with the people who edit such publications and sell to them directly. Later, when a writer is doing books, his agent may handle such small sales—as a professional courtesy, not an income maker. Autobiography is almost impossible to sell today, unless you are well known in some area of endeavor. Thin books (manuscripts of less than 200-250 pages) do not sell easily either; most agents refuse to handle them because publishers are not likely to be interested. If you are writing genre fiction—such as mysteries, science fiction or romances—you may have to get a couple of book sales behind you before an agent will handle your work. Most publishers who do genre fiction are generally receptive to hearing from authors directly.

Some agents specialize. That's why we asked agents this year what type of writing they specialize in selling. We've added their responses to the listings. The most recent specialists are those agencies representing writers of computer software. Some agencies have broadened their clientele by taking on writers of computer-related books. Other agent specialties are indicated in the listings that follow. Some agents in this section are members of the Independent Literary Agents Association (55 5th Ave., 15th Floor, New York, NY 10003), or the Society of Authors' Representatives (Box 650, Old Chelsea Station, New York, NY 10113).

Should I Pay an Agent?

"Our agency reluctantly, regretfully, has joined the ranks of fellow agents, over 80 percent of whom charge some manner of reading fee to cover the costs of servicing manuscripts from new authors," one agent tells potential clients. "Yet we remain *not* in the business of reading *for* fees."

That's the kind of agent you'll want to deal with—one not in the business to make money from reading manuscripts. Despite this statistic, there *are* agents who charge no fees over and above 10 percent to 15 percent commission. In fact, the agents we've listed here work on a commission basis only.

Reading fees or an agency's policy against them can work for or against the writer (depending on what the writer expects of the agent). Generally, commission-only agencies cannot provide detailed reports or critiques for submissions they don't consider salable. "We don't know how other agents run their businesses, but we doubt any of them have the time to do much new-writer evaluation without a fee," commented one agent. "Probably, they read for acceptance or rejection only, unable to render the service most new writers need and hunger for."

Some agents will recommend that a writer find a freelance editor or take a "writing to sell" class as a less expensive way to get feedback. "To help the writer produce a sustained level of good writing, there is no more effective method than the reader-feedback process," said one agent, who charges a fee. Some agents will forward a manuscript to a professional reader/editor with one-hundred percent of the fee going to this reader, not the agency. Other agencies offer a criticism service where the agents do the critiquing. We also heard of one commission-only agency charging a $100 reading fee to read a 1,000-page manuscript that numerous agents had declined to read. As you might guess, the circumstances for each writer and book are different.

If you decide to pay a reading or criticism fee, realize that the fee in most cases won't prompt the agent to represent you. "Fees have no relationship to future sales," said one agent. "Fees merely compensate an agent for his time in reading a new writer's manuscript. An agent's sales are dependent upon consistent sales."

Before paying a fee, find out what you will get in return. Does a *critique* mean a three-paragraph analysis on how you can improve your book or a page-by-page critique with many comments in the margins and an analysis?

Here are other questions to ask about reading fees:

● Is it a one-time fee, or will you have to pay again on subsequent submissions?

● Will you have to pay the fee again when resubmitting a revised manuscript?

● Will the fee be refunded if the agent decides to represent you?

● Will the agent waive the fee if you have already had work published, or if you have particular expertise in the area you are writing about?

Agents may offer suggestions on how a book might be rewritten to be made salable, but agents in general do *not* edit books. *Editing should be done by editors—after* the book *is sold.*

Also, agents shouldn't sell unsalable work, teach a beginner how to write salable copy; solve the author's personal problems or lend money; be available outside of office hours except by appointment; or perform the functions of press agent, social secretary or travel agent. In other words, having an agent is *not* the final solution to your writing problems. An agent can aid and simplify your career, but ultimately your career is in your hands.

Critiques vs. Sales

Do not confuse literary agents with other individuals or "agencies" that advertise as "consultants" offering manuscript criticism or "literary services" for a fee that may cover a critique, an edit, or a rewrite of your manuscript. In order to offer some "protection" to our readers, *none of the agents listed here charge fees, to the best of our knowledge.* In addition, *Writer's Market* does not include any agent who charges criticism, editing, marketing, or *any* other fees. Ask anyone who claims to be an "agent," or who uses agent-like phrasing ("We like your manuscript and we think it is marketable—of course, some revisions will be necessary to make it professionally acceptable," etc.) when discussing a fee of any sort, to give you a list of *recent* book sales. If an agent has not sold three books to established publishing houses in the previous year, he is probably out of the publishing market mainstream. Make sure you can afford such literary services. Fees may range from several hundred to several *thousand* dollars—and there is no guarantee that the arrangement will result in a sale to recoup your investment. Such firms and individuals may make their profits from reading and editing fees—not from sales to publishers. Consult the *Literary Agents of North America: 1986-87 Marketplace* (for pricing information, write Author Aid/Research Associates International, 340 E. 52nd St., New York, NY 10022) for a list/index of agents (who do and do not charge and *sometimes* charge for their services) in the U.S. and Canada. The book also lists agents and their areas and subjects of specialization.

Should I Sign a Contract?

Agents have differing opinions as to whether they want writers to sign a contract. Some require a contract; others consider it a formality that they don't bother with.

Many writers view a contract with an agent as a guarantee of future representation. "In the signing of a contract, the writer surrenders his option to deal with other agents and with publishers directly," said agents Alice Hilton and James Warren. "Now this may mean little to the unpublished author, but it can mean everything to the published author whose current publisher's contract contains option clauses and who has changed agents in midstream."

Some agents prefer contracts because an author may be shopping around for another agent for the second or third book.

"A contract between author and agent, if fairly drawn, should protect both sides," pointed out one agent. "It should provide for a clean and amicable parting, if they decide to go separate ways."

Be careful in signing any contract with an agent. Some writers will have an attorney review the contract. Know what rights your agent would be handling to your work. Also discuss (and try to get in writing) any possible fees that the agent would require you to pay. Some agencies charge a "marketing fee" or monthly retainer fee for office overhead, etc. If you pay such a fee, you are entitled to see any correspondence that such a marketing endeavor would produce.

The Independent Literary Agents Association has adopted a Code of Ethics recently that requires members to discuss commissions and fees prior to working with a writer. The code tells agents to forward payments from publishers to the writer within 10 working days. (Most often, the royalty checks will be sent to the agent, not the writer.) ILAA members must agree to provide photocopies of royalty statements to the writer and must grant the author access to records of all transactions.

This organization of 80 member agencies has also compiled a list of acceptable expenses that the agent might pass on to authors. An "ethical" agency will charge the author for among other items like legal advice, telex and cable fees, and for copies of a book so that agent might distribute it to film producers in selling movie rights and to other buyers of subsidiary rights.

Unlike attorneys or accountants, agents do not have to have specific training or to be accredited. Thus, there are no official grievance committees or disbarments to deter the incompetent or unscrupulous agent.

Now that ILAA has adopted the ethics code, the next step would be a decision on how the organization might handle complaints against any member (at *Writer's Market* press time, the decision had not been made). "We have never had a member drummed out of the corps," said ILAA president Peter L. Skolnik, explaining that the organization's bylaws permit discretionary action by the ILAA Council but do not prescribe a formal mechanism by which the performance of members might be evaluated.

One writer mistrusts editors or agents who keep complimenting her work. Aggressive, professional salesmanship is what the writer needs from an agent.

Make sure that the agent that represents you is meticulous about knowing what each individual editor prefers. "The better agents know what I'm likely to do, but a lot of agents just send material around on the spiral file," pointed out *Harper's* editor Lewis Lapham. "The manuscript goes from A to B to C and as it gets rejected, they put it on the wheel and would be delighted if it sold anywhere."

"Check with other writers whom the agent represents," suggested one writer. "Ask for names and call them."

Reputable agents won't hesitate to tell you what books they've sold in the last year. Take note of the publishers they've dealt with. Does the agent you're considering deal with publishers you'd hope to sell a book to?

The Independent Literary Agents Association requires that members have sold 10 books within 18 months. Agents also need letters of recommendation from two current ILAA members to be considered for membership.

The Society of Authors' Representatives will provide additional information to writers through the pamphlet, "The Literary Agent" (if you enclose a self addressed, stamped envelope).

 The double dagger before a listing indicates that the listing is new in this edition. New markets are often the most receptive to freelance contributions.

SAR's 55 member agencies subscribe to these ethical practices: Deduct a commission and pay the balance to the author promptly; do not charge authors for normal office expenses but may charge authors for such items as copyright fees, manuscript retyping or photocopies, copies of books or plays for use in the sale of other rights, and long-distance calls and cables; maintain separate bank accounts so each author's funds are not combined with the agency's working funds; and treat the financial affairs of clients as private and confidential. SAR members may or may not require writers to sign an agency's agreement.

One concern voiced frequently by writers is whether agents ever steal work and market it as their own. From what we can determine, such piracy does not occur. Agents don't have the time to re-package your book, and besides, they never know who might have already read it. Sometimes writers will start a book as part of a creative writing class; the person contemplating theft doesn't know if you've had a teacher grade (first-draft) chapters of that book. Perhaps, you'd sent the book to the copyright office. The risks are too great for agents who can make money honestly by selling manuscripts for writers.

Discussing Your Work with an Agent

You'll be disappointed with agents' responses if you expect them to conduct lengthy discussions. Most agents have numerous clients. Keep in mind also that an agent is working on speculation—for no pay—until he sells your work, explained ILAA's president. The more time an agent spends on the phone with writers, the less selling time he has. You'll have to decipher whether an agent is reluctant to discuss your manuscript's marketing problems because he hasn't done much selling on it yet or because he is busy circulating your work and truly doesn't have time to talk.

A good agent will tell you about the marketing problems a manuscript might be having, although you may have to wait for a time that is convenient for the agent. Timing is important in the *selling* of a book so an agent's response time for correspondences with writers may suffer at certain times.

If you have any doubts about where (or whether) your manuscript is being marketed, ask to see the mail between your agent and the publishers he claims to be showing your work to. If you have paid a marketing fee, it is illegal for the agent to withhold a prepaid service longer than three months—unless the customer is allowed to cancel the order and get a refund. An agent who breaks this law can be sued by the writer.

Your agent might become "a sounding board, wailing wall, or cheering section," but don't expect this instant rapport. Business relationships grow as each party is pleased with one another's performance.

Select an agent as carefully as you do words for a story. Analyze the agent's past performances. After all, your agent must have the right touch (and words) to sell, say, 75,000 of your words.

DOMINICK ABEL LITERARY AGENCY, INC., 498 West End Ave., New York NY 10024. (212)877-0710. Member ILAA. Obtains new clients through recommendations and solicitation. Will not read unsolicited mss; will read unsolicited queries and outlines. SASE. Agent receives 10% commission on U.S. sales; 20% on foreign.
Will Handle: Book-length adult fiction and nonfiction. Percentage of mss handled 65% nonfiction books; 35% fiction books.

EDWARD J. ACTON, INC., 928 Broadway, New York NY 10010. (212)675-5400. Contact: Inge Hanson. Member of ILAA. "We 'specialize' in highly commercial fiction or nonfiction." Obtains new clients through referral, generally by editors and other writers. Represents 100 clients. 10% of clients are new/unpublished writers. Will read—at no charge—unsolicited queries and outlines. Reports in 1 week on queries; 3 weeks on submissions. SASE. Agent receives 15% commission on domestic and dramatic sales; 19% on foreign sales.
Will Handle: Nonfiction books and novels. Percentage of mss handled: 60% nonfiction; 40% fiction books.

Tips: "The most frequent reasons for declining to represent a writer are works which are not targeted to a large readership or commercial market, and writing, plot or characterization that is weak."

‡**ALBERT LITERARY AGENCY**, 119 Richard Ct., Aptos CA 95003. (408)688-7535. President: Ken Albert. Obtains new clients through referral and directory listings. Will read—at no charge—unsolicited queries and outlines. Will not read unsolicited mss. SASE. Agent receives 10% commission on domestic sales. **Will Handle:** Nonfiction books (business, how-to, humor, etc.).

DOROTHY ALBERT LITERARY AGENCY, 162 W. 54th St., New York NY 10019. Obtains new clients through recommendations of editors, educational establishments, contacts in the film industry, and inquiries. Writers should send letter of introduction, description of material, and list of previous submissions, if any. Will not read unsolicited mss; will read unsolicited queries and outlines. SASE a must. Agent receives 10% on domestic sales; 15% on Canadian; 20% on foreign. No reading fee.
Will Handle: Novels, motion pictures (completed, no treatments), stage plays (musicals), and TV scripts. No poetry, short stories, textbooks, articles, documentaries, or scripts for established episode shows. "We are interested in novels which are well-plotted suspense; quality drama, adult fiction and human relations. The writer should have some foreknowledge of structure and endurance, whether it be motion pictures, television, or books."

MAXWELL ALEY ASSOCIATES, 145 E. 35th St., New York NY 10016. (212)679-5377. Contact: Ruth Aley. Member ILAA. Represents 37 clients. Prefers to work with previously published authors. Query first with a brief outline, table of contents, 2 sample chapters and biographical background sketch. Do not send complete ms. Computer printout submissions acceptable; no dot-matrix. SASE (include return postage if sending outlines). Reports in 1 month on queries, or sooner if negative. Does not charge fee "unless special circumstances warrant." Agent receives 15% commission on domestic sales; 20% on foreign.
Will Handle: Only exceptional fiction, but preferably nonfiction books, if useful.

ALLEN & YANOW LITERARY AGENCY, Box 5158, Santa Cruz CA 95063. (408)427-1293. President: Mort Yanow. Vice President: David Allen. "Our agency specializes in selling nonfiction (physical and social sciences); and quality fiction." Will read mss, queries, outlines. Computer printout submissions acceptable. SASE. Reports in 2 weeks. Agent receives 10% commission on domestic and dramatic sales; 20% on foreign sales.
Will Handle: Films, nonfiction books, novels (no genre). Percentage of mss handled: 60% nonfiction; 35% fiction; 5% screenplays.

JAMES ALLEN, Literary Agent, (in association with Virginia Kidd Literary Agents), 538 E. Harford St., Milford PA 18337. (717)296-7266. Obtains new clients "preferably by reference from someone already on my list or from an established professional in the field." Represents 32 clients. "Writer must have minimum $3,000 earnings from writing in the previous year; a sale in the area they bring to me is a help, i.e., a mystery writer bringing a mystery novel stands a better chance of being taken on than, say, an anthropologist with publishing credits in his field who brings me a first mystery novel." Will read queries and outlines. Will not read unsolicited mss. SASE. Agent receives 10% commission on domestic sales; 20% on dramatic and foreign sales.
Will Handle: Magazine fiction, nonfiction books and novels. "If the work from a prospective client is a 'near miss' I tell him/her why, in varying degrees of detail; likewise for authors on my list. I do not, per se, have a critiquing service."
Tips: "Get at least a couple of sales, even of shorter-length material, by the writer before seeking representation. For me at least, proper manuscript preparation and careful proofreading before I see material is very important. Manuscripts riddled with errors give a bad impression."

‡**LEE ALLEN AGENCY**, 4571 N. 68th St., Milwaukee Wi 53218. (414)463-7441. Owner: Lee A. Matthias. Obtains new clients through listings in *Scriptwriter's Market*, *Literary Market Place*, various textbooks and WGA agency list. Represents 20 clients. "Material must be registered with the Writers Guild or copyrighted, and the number supplied; be in correct submission form; be accompanied by a SASE, and *preceded* by a mail query." Will read—at no charge—unsolicited queries. SASE. Agent receives 10% on domestic sales; 10% on dramatic sales.
Will Handle: Films, Novels.
Tips: "Fashion your material into a professionally prepared, submitable form. Consider your marketplace. Produce material that speaks to that audience. Make it fresh, lively and compelling. Above all, entertain."

‡**FRED AMSEL & ASSOCIATES**, 291 S. La Cienega Blvd., Beverly Hills CA 90211. (213)844-1200. Contact: Jeffrey Thal. "Last year our clients earned an average of over $20,000." Will read—at no charge—unsolicited queries. Will not read unsolicited mss. SASE. Agent receives 10% commission of domestic sales;

10% on dramatic sales; 10% on foreign sales.
Will Handle: Films and TV scripts (not episodics).
Tips: "Write a good introductory letter, or get a referral from a mutual friend."

MARCIA AMSTERDAM AGENCY, 41 W. 82nd St., New York NY 10024. (212)873-4945. Contact: Marcia Amsterdam. Member of WGA-East. Obtains new clients through client or editor referrals. 60% of clients are new/unpublished writers. Will read queries, partials and outlines. Computer printout submissions acceptable; no dot-matrix. Reports in 3 weeks. SASE. Agent receives 10% commission on domestic sales; 15% on British; 20% on foreign.
Will Handle: Novels, nonfiction books, teleplays, screenplays. Percentages of mss handled: approximately 6% nonfiction; 85% fiction; 2% screenplays; 3% juvenile.

‡**ANIMAL CRACKERS ENTERTAINMENT**, Talent and Literary Agency, 204 Riverside Ave., Newport Beach CA 92663. (714)645-4500. Senior Editor: Robert D. Bills. WGA Signatory. Obtains new clients through referral; also queries by new writers. Represents 14 clients. "Last year our clients earned an average of from $5,000-10,000." Will read—at no charge—unsolicited queries. Will read submissions at no charge but may charge criticism fee. Will not read unsolicited mss. SASE. Agent receives 10% on domestic sales; 10% on dramatic sales; and 20% for foreign sales.
Will Handle: Films (comedies and humorous treatments of current events, social trends) and TV scripts (scripts for current series and sitcoms, series ideas, pilots with comedic themes).
Tips: "Quality writing is our primary condition. Always query first and send SASE. Use WGA teleplay/ screenplay format. Register your material with the WGA before submitting it to anyone. Once accepted by an agent, give him time to do his job."

THE BALKIN AGENCY, 850 W. 176th St., New York NY 10033. President: Richard Balkin. Member ILAA and Authors Guild. Obtains new clients through recommendations, over-the-transom inquiries, and solicitation. Currently represents 45 clients. 10% of clients are new/unpublished writers. Will not read unsolicited mss; will read unsolicited queries, or outlines and 2 sample chapters. Computer printout submissions acceptable; prefers letter-quality to dot-matrix. Reports in 2 weeks on queries; 3 weeks on submissions. SASE. Interested in new/beginning writers. Agent receives 10% commission on domestic sales, 20% on British, 20% on foreign.
Will Handle: Magazine articles (only as a service to clients who primarily write books), nonfiction books, textbooks (college only), and professional books (on occasion). Specializes in adult nonfiction. Percentage of mss handled: 100% nonfiction.
Tips: "Query with description; what is unique about the work; how it differs from competing or overlapping titles; audiences/market; and size and amount of art work, if any; and completion date."

‡**VIRGINIA BARBER LITERARY AGENCY, INC.**, 353 W. 21 St., New York NY 10011. (212)255-6515. Contact: Virginia Barber or Mary Evans. Member of ILAA. Obtains new clients through referral, ordinarily. Represents 75 clients. Will read—at no charge—unsolicited queries and then may ask to see ms. Agents receive 10% commission on domestic sales; 10% on dramatic sales; 20% on foreign sales.
Will Handle: Nonfiction books and novels. "Our authors are generally widely reviewed. We have few who are primarily interested in paperback original publication."

‡**BARMEIER AND COMPANY**, Box 492, Burbank CA 91503. (818)841-9294/506-0994. President: Jim Barmeier. Obtains new clients through solicitation and referrals. Represents 7 clients. "Last year our clients earned an average of $2,000 to 5,000." Will read—at no charge—unsolicited mss, queries and outlines. SASE. Agents receive 10% commission on domestic sales; 20% on foreign sales.
Will Handle: Films, magazine articles, magazine fiction, nonfiction books, novels, stage plays, syndicated material (humor only), and TV scripts (movies, specials, mini-series only; no episodic material). "Our primary interest is in projects which can be translated into film or television. These would include scripts, obviously, but also magazine articles (if you have the rights to the story), magazine fiction, nonfiction books (if there is a story there which can be made into a film or TV project), novels, stage plays, and anything else which could be geared toward the visual media."
Tips: "We will definitely look at new writers and encourage their submissions with a SASE."

BLOOM, LEVY, SHORR & ASSOCIATES, 800 S. Robertson Blvd., Los Angeles CA 90035. (213)659-6160. Obtains new clients only by referral from clients, directors, producers, and studio executives. 50% of clients are new/unpublished writers. SASE. Reports in 1 month. Agent receives 10% commission.
Will Handle: "We will read only completed motion picture screenplays. This may include screenplays for feature films as well as movies made for television. We will not read outlines, treatments, or scripts for episodic or situation comedy television." Percentage of mss handled: 5% fiction; 95% screenplays.

GEORGES BORCHARDT, INC., 136 E. 57th St., New York NY 10022. (212)753-5785. Obtains new clients "mainly through authors already represented by us who refer others." Potential clients "must be highly recommended by someone we know." Reads unsolicited queries from well-established writers. 1% of clients are new/unpublished writers. Reports immediately on queries; 3 weeks on submissions. Interested in new/beginning writers "but we only consider their work if they have been recommended." Currently represents 200 clients. Member SAR. Agent receives 10% commission.
Will Handle: Magazine articles and fiction, novels, and nonfiction books. Specializes in "possibly the kinds of books that might or should win major awards." Percentage of mss handled: 60% nonfiction; 38% fiction; 1% poetry; 1% juvenile.
Tips: "Get your manuscript in the best possible shape and enlist the help of an established author of your acquaintance."

‡**THE BRADLEY-GOLDSTEIN AGENCY**, (formerly The Ruth Hagy Brod Agency), Suite 6-E, 7 Lexington Ave., New York NY 10010. (212)666-6051. (718)672-7924. President: Paul William Bradley. Director: Martha Goldstein. Obtains new clients through referrals, listings in *Writer's Market*, *Literary Market Place*, *Literary Journal*, *Literary Agents of North America*, *Publishers Weekly* and via publishers' recommendations. Represents 75-100 clients. "We are interested in helping new writers become established. Eligibility is based entirely upon merit and marketability." Will read—at no charge—unsolicited mss, queries and outlines; prefers proposal with outline and sample chapters. SASE. Agent receives 15% commission on domestic sales and dramatic sales; 50% minimum on foreign sales.
Will Handle: Nonfiction books, novels; radio, TV and motion picture scripts; stage plays; syndicated material; and textbooks (college, scholarly and reference).
Tips: "Always submit a clear, concisely written query letter and a cleanly typed and copied proposal in advance of a full submission. Those few agents who do consider unsolicited material are flooded—so brevity and clarity are all-important to advancing your chances."

BRANDT & BRANDT LITERARY AGENTS, INC., 1501 Broadway, New York NY 10036. (212)840-5760. Member of SAR. Represents approximately 150 clients. Query. Computer printout submissions acceptable; prefers letter-quality to dot-matrix. SASE. Agent receives 10% commission on domestic rights; 15% on British rights; and 20% on other foreign rights.
Will Handle: Novels and nonfiction books.

BROOKE DUNN OLIVER, Suite 202, 9165 Sunset Blvd., Los Angeles CA 90069. (213)859-1405. Contact: James Brooke. 50% of clients are new/unpublished writers. Member Writers Guild. "Our agency specializes in selling screenplays and plays." Obtains clients through recommendations. Currently represents 10 clients. Reports in 2 weeks on queries; 2 weeks on submissions. Agent receives 10% commission on domestic sales.
Will Handle: Screenplays; TV scripts (movies; no episodic material); stage plays. 25% stage play mss; 75% screenplays.

CURTIS BROWN, LTD., 10 Astor Place, New York NY 10003 (212)473-5400. President: Perry H. Knowlton. Curtis Brown Associates, Ltd: James Oliver Brown, President. Books: Peter L. Ginsberg, Emilie Jacobson, Perry H. Knowlton, Marilyn Marlow, Clyde Taylor, Maureen Walters. Film and TV rights: Timothy Knowlton. Member of SAR. Query by letter only. Computer printout submissions acceptable; prefers letter-quality to dot-matrix. Unsolicited mss will be returned unread. Agent receives 10% commission on domestic rights; 20% on foreign rights; 10% on film rights (film commission sometimes varies in particular circumstances).
Will Handle: Novels and nonfiction books.

‡**NED BROWN, INCORPORATED**, Box 5020, Beverly Hills CA 90210. (213)276-1131. President: Ned Brown. Obtains new clients through referral by clients, editors, publishers and personal contact. Must earn minimum of $10,000 from commercial writing and must have been commercially published for prior 3 years. Will not read unsolicited mss.
Will Handle: Films, nonfiction books, novels and stage plays.

PEMA BROWNE LTD., 185 E. 85th St., New York NY 10028. (212)369-1925. Contact: Pema Browne or Perry J. Browne. "Our agency specializes in selling romance (historical and contemporary); young adult; children's illustrated; various category paperback and nonfiction (how to and business, etc.). Obtains new clients through editors' and authors' referrals and directory listings. Represents 20 clients. 20% of clients are new/unpublished writers. Will read queries or outlines. Computer printout submissions acceptable; prefers letter-quality to dot-matrix. Reports in 1 week on queries; 3 weeks on mss. "Author must send SASE for reply." Agent receives 15% commission on domestic and dramatic sales, 20% on foreign sales. No unsolicited mss.
Will Handle: Films (treatments only); nonfiction books (how-to, illustrated: general subjects); novels (catego-

ry, not "middle books"); stage plays (treatments only); syndicated material (columns, comic strips); and TV scripts (treatments only). No poetry. Percentage of mss handled: 50% nonfiction; 50% fiction.

Tips: "The most frequent reasons for declining to represent a writer are inexperience and viability of manuscript in terms of its commercial possibilities as determined by the marketplace and guidelines for the romance genre writer. Seek the services of a consulting editor before sending manuscript. Obvious pitfalls are thereby avoided, as well as expense of mailing, etc."

‡**HOWARD BUCK AGENCY, LTD.**, Suite 1107, 80 8th Ave., New York NY 10011. (212)807-7855. Associate: Mark Frisk. Obtains new clients mostly through references, sometimes via queries and word of mouth. Represents 23 clients. "Last year our clients earned an average of over $20,000." We will read—at no charge—unsolicited queries and outlines. Will not read unsolicited mss. SASE. Agent receives 15% commission on domestic sales; 20% on foreign sales.

Will Handle: Nonfiction books and novels. "We make a speciality of biography but will consider any solid nonfiction project. We're always on the lookout for literary fiction and genre material as well—mysteries, detective, etc."

Tips: "Present your material as cleanly and professionally as possible. Mistakes and sloppiness can turn an agent off. There are too many people out there who know how to do it right; no one wants to waste time on a person who clearly can't write proper English."

SHIRLEY BURKE AGENCY, 370 E. 76th St., B-704, New York NY 10021. (212)861-2309. Obtains new clients through recommendations. Preferably potential clients must have published at least one book. 5% of clients are new/unpublished writers. Will not read or return unsolicited mss (do not send without approval or SASE); will read unsolicited queries. SASE. Reports within 10 days on queries. Agent receives 15% commission.

Will Handle: Magazine fiction, novels, and nonfiction books. Handles 50% nonfiction and 50% fiction.

‡**CALDER AGENCY**, 4150 Riverside Dr., Burbank CA 91505. (818)845-7434. Contact: Literary Department. Obtains new clients by reading scripts. "Represents properties, not necessarily clients." Will read—at no charge—queries and synopses ("writers should send in a synopsis or call before submitting a screenplay"). Will not read unsolicited mss. SASE. Agent receives 10% commission on domestic sales and 10% on dramatic sales.

Will Handle: Feature-length screenplays and two-hour movies for television.

RUTH CANTOR, LITERARY AGENT, 156 5th Ave., New York NY 10010. Literary Agent: Ruth Cantor. Foreign Rights: Nurnberg. Movies and Television: Al Jackinson. "Our agency specializes in selling "good" fiction, children's books, specialist trade nonfiction. Obtains new clients through recommendations by writers, publishers, editors, and teachers. Potential client "must be of proven competence as a writer. This means either some publishing record or a recommendation from someone likely to be a competent critic of his work—a teacher of writing, another writer, etc." Will not read unsolicited mss; will read unsolicited queries and outlines. Reports in 2 weeks on queries; 2 months on submissions. SASE. "Send a letter giving publishing history and writing experience, plus concise outline of proposed project or of ms you want to send. Do not phone." Agent receives 10% commission on domestic sales; 20% on foreign.

Will Handle: Novels, nonfiction books and children's books. Currently handles 20% nonfiction; 80% fiction.

Tips: "The most frequent reasons for declining to represent a writer are lack of publishing record, off-target material, lack of writing talent, and lack of professionalism."

MARIA CARVAINIS AGENCY INC., 235 West End Ave., New York NY 10023. (212)580-1559. President: Maria Carvainis. Member-at-large of The Authors Guild, Inc., Signatory to Writers Guild of America, East, and member of Romance Writers of America. "Our agency specializes in selling important lead titles of nonfiction and fiction." Obtains new clients "through recommendations of current authors, editors, and letters of query." Represents over 60 clients. 15% of clients are new/unpublished writers. "I look for the strengths of the projects I read for representation and then consider how extensive the market is for these fiction or nonfiction projects. "Will read queries. Computer printout submissions acceptable; no dot-matrix. Reports in approximately 6 weeks on queries; 2 months on submissions, depending on the volume. SASE. No unsolicited mss. Agent receives 15% commission on domestic sales, 10% on dramatic sales (for WGA writers), 20% on foreign sales.

Will Handle: All kinds of fiction from serious to commercial (specializing in contemporary women's fiction and historicals and young adult fiction); nonfiction books (serious to commercial projects); movie and television scripts and treatments (preferably but not exclusively the writer should have some credits); and poetry (writer must have some published poems). Will also handle magazine articles and fiction for book authors represented. Percentage of mss handled: 40% nonfiction; 45% fiction; 10% juvenile; 5% magazine nonfiction.

Tips: "There are many good agents in the field and it is important once an author has confidence in the agent's abilities to carefully assess whether he/she feels comfortable working with that agent in a creative writing and business relationship."

‡**THE TERRY CHIZ COMPANY**, Suite E, 5761 Whitnall Hwy., North Hollywood CA 91601. (818)506-0994. Obtains new clients through friends, clients, etc. Represents 7 clients. "Last year our clients earned an average of less than $2,000 to over $20,000." Will read—at no charge—unsolicited mss, outlines and completed properties. SASE. Agent receives a commission range of 10-15%.
Will Handle: Films, nonfiction books and TV scripts.

HY COHEN LITERARY AGENCY, LTD., 111 W. 57th St., New York NY 10019. (212)757-5237. President: Hy Cohen. Currently represents 25-30 clients. 50% of clients are new/unpublished writers. Obtains new clients through recommendations. Will read unsolicited mss, queries and outlines. Mail mss to 66 Brookfield Rd., Upper Montclair NJ 07043. SASE. Reports almost immediately on queries; 1 month on mss. Interested in new/beginning writers. Agent receives 10% commission.
Will Handle: Magazine articles and fiction, novels, and nonfiction books. Percentage of mss handled: 30% nonfiction books; 70% fiction books.
Tips: "Selecting a subject or characters of *no* interest to anyone. and writing a novel in the first person singular are the worst mistakes an author can make in writing a book."

‡**RUTH COHEN, INC.**, Box 7626, Menlo Park CA 94025. (415)854-2054. President: Ruth Cohen. Member of ILAA. Obtains new clients through references. Represents 45 clients. "Last year our clients earned an average of from $20,000 to $30,000." Will read—at no charge—unsolicited queries and outlines. SASE. Agent receives 15% commission on previously unpublished authors with domestic sales; 15% on domestic sales; and 20% on foreign sales.
Will Handle: Nonfiction books, novels and genre books—romances, mysteries, juveniles, young adult fiction.

‡**JOYCE K. COLE LITERARY AGENCY**, Box 5139, Berkeley CA 94705. (415)548-9648. Contact: Joyce K. Cole. Obtains new clients through recommendations and writers' queries. Represents 45 clients. "Last year our clents earned an average of from $5,000 to $10,000." Will read—at no charge—unsolicited queries, outlines and sample chapters. SASE. Agent receives 10% commission on domestic sales; 10% on dramatic sales; 20% on foreign sales.
Will Handle: Nonfiction books, novels, young adult fiction and nonfiction. Handles magazine articles and magazine fiction only for established clients.

‡**COLUMBIA LITERARY ASSOCIATES, INC.**, 7902 Nottingham Way, Elliott City MD 21043. (301)465-1595. Contact: Linda Hayes, Marketing Director. Obtains new clients through referrals, *Literary Market Place*, and *Literary Agents of North America* listings. Represents 30 clients. "Last year our clients earned an average of from $10,000 to $30,000." Will read—at no charge—unsolicited queries and outlines. SASE mandatory for response. Agent receives 12% commission on domestic sales; 20% on dramatic sales, 20% on foreign sales, sold separately.
Will Handle: Nonfiction books (mass market cookbooks and general nonfiction) and novels (mainstream novels, contemporary romances).
Tips: "Send brief, professional queries (with SASE and noting submissions to publishers and/or other agents. This author/agent relationship is a personal, long-term commitment. Find an agent you're comfortable with both personally and professionally."

‡**DON CONGDON ASSOCIATES, INC.**, 177 E. 70th St., New York NY 10021. (212)570-9090. Vice President: Michael Congdon. President: Don Congdon. Member of SAR. Obtains 95% of new clients through referrals from other clients and editors and 5% unsolicited. Represents 80 clients. "Writers must have been previously published, preferably in book form, but at least in national magazines." Will read—at no charge—unsolicited queries. SASE. Agents receive 10% commission on domestic sales and 19% on foreign sales.
Will Handle: Nonfiction books and novels. "Our agency represents only top-quality, trade fiction and nonfiction writers. We generally do not represent romance novelists, how-to works or textbooks authors."

JOAN DAVES, 59 E. 54th St., New York NY 10022. Contact: Joan Daves. Obtains new clients through recommendation by clients and editors. Represents 80+ clients. Will read—at no charge—queries and outlines; will not read unsolicited mss. SASE. Agent receives 10% commission on domestic and dramatic sales; 20% on stock, amateur and foreign sales.
Will Handle: Nonfiction books and novels.

ANITA DIAMANT: THE WRITERS WORKSHOP, INC., 310 Madison Ave., New York NY 10017. (212)687-1122. President: Anita Diamant. Member of SAR and Writers Guild. Obtains new clients through recommendations by publishers or other clients. Potential clients must have made some professional sales. Will not read unsolicited mss; will read unsolicited queries. Computer printout submissions acceptable; prefers letter-quality to dot-matrix. SASE. Reports in 2 weeks on queries; 1 month on submissions. Interested in new/beginning writers. Agent receives 15% commission to first $20,000; 10% thereafter.
Will Handle: Adult fiction, novels, nonfiction books, motion pictures, and TV scripts. Percentage of mss handled: 40% nonfiction; 60% fiction; "Screenplays handled by our Hollywood representatives."

‡**THE JONATHAN DOLGER AGENCY**, Apt. 9B, 49 E. 96th St., New York NY 10128. (212)427-1853. President/Owner: Jonathan Dolger. Obtains new clients through referral. Represents 60-70 clients. "Last year our clients earned an average of from $10,000 to $20,000. Previously published authors preferred." Will read—at no charge—unsolicited queries. Will not read unsolicited mss. SASE. Agent receives 10-15% commission on domestic sales; 10% on dramatic sales; 20% on foreign sales.
Will Handle: Adult trade nonfiction books and novels and illustrated books.

EDUCATIONAL DESIGN SERVICES INC., Box 253, Wantagh NY 11793. (516)221-0995/(212)539-4107. President: Bertram L. Linder. Vice President: Edwin Selzer. "Our agency specializes in selling educational materials only (large·textual) and at kindergarten through grades 12 and some college market. Obtains new clients through inquiries, referrals and selective advertising. Represents 28 clients. 65% of clients are new/unpublished writers. Will read—at no charge—unsolicited mss, queries and outlines if accompanied by SASE. Reports in 3 weeks. Agent receives 15% commission on domestic sales; 20% on foreign sales.
Will Handle: Textbooks—kindergarten-college, educational materials only. Percentage of mss handled: 100% nonfiction books.

‡**ELEK INTERNATIONAL RIGHTS AGENT**, Box 223, Canal St. Station, New York NY 10013. (212)431-9368. Obtains new clients through recommendations. Represents 15 clients. "Last year our clients earned an average of from $20,000 to $500,000." Will read —at no charge—unsolicited quries and outlines. Will not read unsolicited mss. SASE. Agent receives 15% commission on domestic sales; 20% on foreign sales.
Will Handle: Early child development, adult nonfiction.

ANN ELMO AGENCY, INC., 60 E. 42nd St., New York NY 10165. (212)661-2880. Member SAR. Obtains new clients through writers' queries. 50% of clients are new/unpublished writers. Sales average about a book a month. Will read queries and outlines at no charge. Reports in 1 week on queries; 1 month on submissions. SASE. Agent receives 15% commission for domestic sales and 20% for foreign sales.
Will Handle: Magazine articles (only strong ideas); magazine fiction (very few short stories); novels; nonfiction books; stage plays; and occasional TV scripts. "No query answered without return postage."
Tips: "Lack of credibility and poor delineation of characters are the worst mistakes that a writer can make in writing fiction. In non-fiction, good research of factual data is most important."

JOHN FARQUHARSON LTD., #1914, 250 W. 57th St., New York NY 10107. (212)245-1993. Member of SAR and ILAA. Will read—at no charge—queries. No unsolicited mss. SASE. Agent receives 10% commission on domestic and dramatic sales; 20% on foreign sales.

‡**THE FILM/PUBLISHING GROUP**, 6835 Quinton Lane, Tujunga CA 91042. (818)352-2205. Communications Director: Vincent R. Ducette. Obtains new clients through advertising and word of mouth. Represents 16 clients. "Last year our clients earned an average of from $15,000 to $20,000. Our major criteria is a writer's degree of professionalism and viability in today's film and book market. The writer need not have sold to the present as long as high potential is seen." Will read—at no charge—unsolicited mss, queries and outlines. Will read submissions at no charge, but may charge criticism fee. SASE. Agent receives 10% commission on domestic sales; 10% on foreign sales.
Will Handle: TV and motion picture films reflecting contemporary life, and novels with motion picture potential, TV or "Movie of the Week' viability."
Tips: "Dedication to the craft and single-mindedness of purpose are prerequisites for a successful writing career."

‡**BARTHOLD FLES, LITERARY AGENT**, 501 5th Ave., New York NY 10017. (212)687-7248. Owner: Barthold Fles. Obtains new clients mostly by recommendation (clients, editors), sometimes at writers' conferences. Represents about 50 clients. "Last year our clients earned an average of from $5,000 to $10,000." Will read—at no charge—unsolicited mss, queries and outlines. SASE. Agent receives 10% commission on domestic sales; 20% on foreign sales. "Query first; no simultaneous submissions to agents."
Will Handle: Nonfiction books and novels. No academic subjects. "We do many mysteries and some ro-

mances, juveniles intermediate and teenage but no picture books; and fiction and nonfiction, hardcover and original paperbacks."

Tips: "We prefer writers who have published, though not necessarily books."

THE FOLEY AGENCY, 34 E. 38th St., New York NY 10016. (212)686-6930. Contact: Joan and Joe Foley. Obtains clients through recommendation "and our interest." Currently represents 30 clients. Maximum of 2% of clients are new/unpublished writers. "Query first with *all* details and a self-addressed stamped envelope (no reply without the latter). We handle only books." Will read queries; will not read unsolicited mss. SASE. Reports in 1 month. Agent receives 10% commission on domestic, dramatic, and foreign sales (plus sub-agent 10%).

Will Handle: Nonfiction books and novels. Percentage of mss handled: 75% nonfiction; 25% fiction.

Tips: "We are taking on very few new writers."

‡FRANKLIN/NATHAN LITERARY AGENCY, #1903, 386 Park Ave. S., New York NY 10016. (212)689-1842/(212)685-0808. Contact: Lynn Franklin, Ruth Nathan, Jeff Gerecke. Represents 30-40 clients. Will read—at no charge—queries and outlines. SASE. Agent receives 15% commission on domestic sales; 20% of dramatic sales; 20% on foreign sales.

Will Handle: Nonfiction books and novels.

‡SAMUEL FRENCH, INC., 45 W. 25th St., New York NY 10010. (212)206-8990. Editor: Lawrence Harbison. Member of SAR. Obtains new clients through reading and seeing their plays. Represents "thousands" of clients. "A writer must have written a marketable play." Will read—at no charge—unsolicited mss and queries. SASE. Author receives 10% book royalty; 80% amateur, 90% stock royalties. Guidelines for ms preparation of submissions $3 (postpaid).

Will Handle: Stage plays. If Samuel French, Inc., receives an outstanding play, the firm is interested in submitting the play to producers. Once the play is produced, Samuel French would want to publish the play.

Tips: "Present material professionally. It is important for a playwright to know there is a professional manuscript format."

THE FROMMER PRICE LITERARY AGENCY INC., 185 E. 85th St., New York NY 10028. (212)289-0589. Contact: Diana Price. Obtains new clients "mainly by referral." Represents 60 clients. 10% of clients are new/unpublished writers. "Previously published writers preferred, but will consider any queries." Will read queries and outlines. Reports immediately on queries; 1 month on submissions. SASE. Agent receives 15% commission on domestic and dramatic sales, 20% on foreign sales.

Will Handle: Nonfiction books and novels (adult only). Percentage of mss handled: 75% nonfiction, 25% fiction.

Tips: "The most important criterion is trust."

JAY GARON-BROOKE ASSOCIATES, INC., 415 Central Park West, New York NY 10025. (212)866-3654. President: Jay Garon-Brooke. Member of ILAA. "Specializes in commercial and quality fiction and nonfiction; occasional how-to manuscript." Obtains new clients through referrals. 15% of clients are new/unpublished writers. Will not read unsolicited mss. "New authors must query by mail, providing their backgrounds and outlines of their projects." Reports in 3 weeks on queries; 2 months on submissions.

Will Handle: General fiction and nonfiction suitable for hardcover or paperback publication, as well as paperback mass-market category fiction; theatrical and television film scripts, and computer books. Percentage of mss handled: 20% nonfiction books; 75% fiction books; 1% stage plays; 4% screenplays.

Tips: "The most frequent reasons for declining to represent a writer are the lack of quality of writing, technique or construction, and believable characters."

‡MAX GARTENBERG, LITERARY AGENT, 15 W. 44th St., New York NY 10036. (212)860-8451. Obtains new clients through recommendations and solicitations by authors. Represents 25 clients. Will read—at no charge—unsolicited queries and outlines (of nonfiction books only). Will not read unsolicited mss. SASE. Agent receives 10% commission on domestic sales; 10% on dramatic sales; 15% on foreign sales.

Will Handle: Nonfiction books and novels (excluding "category" fiction such as romances, westerns).

GOODMAN ASSOCIATES LITERARY AGENTS, 500 West End Ave., New York NY 10024. (212)873-4806. Contact: Arnold P. Goodman, Elise Simon Goodman. Member, Governig Board of ILAA. "Our agency specializes in selling general adult fiction and nonfiction. Small, personal agency. One partner is a lawyer." No unsolicited mss. Currently represents 60 clients. "Accepting new clients very selectively. 10% of clients are new/unpublished writers. Query letter should contain brief bio of author and enough about project to interest us." Computer printout submissions acceptable; prefers letter-quality to dot-matrix. Reports in 1 week on

queries; 1 month on submissions. SASE. Percentage of mss handled: 65% nonfiction books; 35% fiction books.
Will Handle: Adult book-length fiction and nonfiction. No textbooks, juveniles, science fiction, plays, screenplays.

‡**IRENE GOODMAN LITERARY AGENCY**, 521 5th Ave., 17th Floor, New York NY 10017. (212)688-4286. Vice President: Alex Kamaroff. Member of ILAA. "Our agency specializes in selling mass market commercial fiction, especially woman's and romances, and popular nonfiction. Obtains new clients through referrals from editors, authors, magazines and unsolicited queries. Represents 120 clients. 10% of clients are new/unpublished writers. "Last year our clients earned an average of from $10,000 to $20,000. Romance authors averaged around $50,000 each." Reports "immediately on queries. Will not read unsolicited mss. Will read—at no charge—unsolicited queries. SASE. Agent receives 15% commission on domestic sales; 20% on foreign sales.
Will Handle: Magazine articles, nonfiction books and novels. 50% nonfiction books; 5% magazine fiction; 45% fiction books.
Tips: "The first deadly sin is boredom. If you can keep me turning those pages, I will forgive a multitude of errors. Also, too many writers take too long to warm up. Hook me immediately in the first two pages. Be aware of the market. Go to bookstores, study bestseller lists."

KEITH GORMEZANO, #7WMLA, 2921 E. Madison St., Seattle WA 98112-4237. (206)322-1431. Member of SAR and ILAA. "Our agency specializes in selling science fiction and fiction short stories." Obtains new clients by word of mouth, advertising, direct mail. Represents 5 clients. 80% of clients are new/unpublished writers. Will read queries "provided business size SASE is enclosed." Will read submissions at no charge, but may charge criticism fee. Will not read unsolicited mss. Reports in 1-6 months. SASE. Agent receives 8-11% commission on domestic sales; 12-14% on dramatic sales; and 17-19% on foreign sales. "Poems and short stories submitted may be published at usual rates in *Brown Review*, which agent is connected with if agent does not want to represent client but desires to give them a break."
Will Handle: Films; magazine articles; magazine fiction; nonfiction books (mass market); novels (historical, erotic); poetry; radio scripts (1940s style); stage plays (contemporary); syndicated material (humor, political, ethnic); textbooks (college); and TV scripts (comedies). Handles 10% nonfiction books; 20% of magazine nonfiction; 20% fiction books; 10% magazine fiction; and 20% poetry.
Tips: "Don't send a form letter, send a resume; it makes you seem more personable."

‡**GRAHAM AGENCY**, 311 W. 43rd St., New York NY 10036. (212)489-7730. Owner: Earl Graham. Member of SAR. Obtains new clients through recommendations and inquiries. Represents 50 clients. Will read—at no charge—unsolicited queries, and scripts requested as result of queries. Will not read unsolicited mss except as outlined previously. Agent receives 10% commission.
Will Handle: Stage play.
Tips: "Write a concise, intelligent letter which gives the gist of the play."

SANFORD J. GREENBURGER ASSOCIATES, 55 5th Ave., New York NY 10003. (212)206-5600. Agents: Heide Lange, Peter L. Skolnik, Diane Cleaver. Member of ILAA. Represents 300 clients of which about 150 are actively writing. Will read—at no charge—queries and outlines. SASE. Agent receives 15% commission on domestic and dramatic sales; 19% on foreign sales (includes 10% to sub-agent in foreign territory).
Will Handle: Nonfiction books and novels.
Tips: "Send a query letter first. Try to work out with an agent—ahead of time—what an agent can or can't do for you in order to establish realistic expectations. Compatibility is helpful."

‡**HHM LITERARY AGENCY**, Box 1153, Rahway NJ 07065. Agent: Haes H. Monroe. Estab. 1985. Obtains new clients through advertising and word of mouth. "I prefer a published writer but will consider an unpublished writer if they can spark my interest." Will read—at no charge—unsolicited mss, queries and outlines. SASE. Agent receives 10% commission on domestic sales; 15% on dramatic sales; 20% on foreign sales.
Will Handle: Magazine articles, films, nonfiction books, novels, stage plays, and movie and TV scripts. "I am interested in a broad range of categories. In all cases, first I prefer to receive a query letter with synopsis or treatment and sample chapters or scenes, then I will respond in all cases to the writer if I am interested or not."

REECE HALSEY AGENCY, 8733 Sunset Blvd., Los Angeles CA 90069. (213)652-2409. Contact: Dorris Halsey. Obtains clients through direct referral from existing clients. Will read—at no charge—queries only. "Do not send *any* material until it is requested." SASE. Agent receives 10% commission on domestic sales.
Will Handle: TV scripts (movies of the week; no episodic series).

‡**THOMAS S. HART LITERARY ENTERPRISES**, 20 Kenwood St., Boston MA 02124. (617)288-8512. Contact: Thomas S. Hart. Obtains new clients through recommendations of clients, etc. Represents 20 clients. Will read—at no charge—mss, queries and outlines. Will not read unsolicited mss. SASE. Agent receives 10% commission on domestic sales; 15% on dramatic sales; 20% on foreign sales.
Will Handle: Nonfiction books and novels ("well-written mainstream or literary fiction and mysteries but little other genre fiction.")

HEACOCK LITERARY AGENCY, INC., Suite 14, 1523 6th St., Santa Monica CA 90401. (213)451-8523/393-6227. Authors' Representatives: James or Rosalie Heacock. "Our agency specializes in selling health and/or healing, women's issues, business expertise, new physics & science, pregnancy/infant care/parenting, biography of celebrities, fitness & exercise and nutrition. Member of ILAA and Association of Talent Agents, Writers Guild Signatory. Obtains new clients through "referrals from publishers, recommendations of our authors, referrals from book publicists and editors, listings in *Writer's Market* and *Literary Market Place*, and from public speaking as times permit. (Also from ILAA membership list.)" Represents 65 clients. 20% (nonfiction only) of clients are new/unpublished writers. "The majority of our clients have been previously published, but we will also read queries from authors who have a strong background in writing and a sense of craft and originality. Unpublished novelists should not query unless their book is finished; partials cannot be considered until you have a publishing track record. A good query letter tells us much about a person's ability to express thoughts. Treat your query with as much care as your manuscript; include brief biographical data and tell us why you wrote the book and why it's important to you." Will read—at no charge—queries, outlines, first 20-30 pages of ms. Computer printout submissions acceptable; no dot-matrix. SASE. Reports in 1 month on queries; 6 weeks on nonfiction mss, 2 months on fiction mss "depending on work load." Agent receives 15% commission on first $50,000 of domestic sales, 25% on foreign sales.
Will Handle: Nonfiction books "of all sorts; we especially like new idea books and new ways to solve old problems, significant books likely to endure"; novels "either literary or well-crafted novels of mass market appeal, and big mainstream novels"; and screenplays. Percentage of mss handled: 90% nonfiction; 5% fiction; 5% screenplays. Recent sales: *DLPA to End Chronic Pain and Depression*, by Dr. Arnold Fox and Barry Fox (Simon and Schuster); and *Napping House*, by Don and Audrey Wood (Harcourt Brace Jovanovich).
Tips: "Revise and polish your manuscript until it shines like a bright jewel before you even consider seeking an agent. The old adage 'Writing is rewriting' is appropriate here. When you're convinced that your book is the best of which you're capable, query with SASE." Free agency brochure for SASE.

HEINLE & HEINLE ENTERPRISES, 29 Lexington Rd., Concord MA 01742. (617)369-4858. Managing Director: Charles A.S. Heinle. President: Beverly D. Heinle. Client contact: Beverly D. Heinle. "Our agency specializes in selling nonfiction." Obtains new clients through word-of-mouth, *Writer's Market*, *Literary Market Place*, and recommendations by clients. Currently represents 40 clients. 80% of clients are new/unpublished writers. Will not read unsolicited mss; will read unsolicited queries, outlines, and full-length proposals. Reports in 2 weeks on queries. No multiple submissions. All submissions and letters must be originals, not photocopies, and must offer an exclusive right to consider the proposal for at least 2 months. Computer printout submissions acceptable; prefers letter-quality to dot-matrix. SASE. "We are particularly interested in writers who take a professional interest in their work." Agent receives 10% commission on regular book placements, although on some special placements, the commission will be 15-20%.
Will Handle: Nonfiction of all kinds, text materials at college and adult levels, and children's and young adult fiction. We do not handle poetry, short stories, or magazine articles. We do not supply criticism or undertake rewrite assignments. We are most interested in materials with a New England theme or slant; past, present, or future; but, of course, good writing is the main consideration. We handle textbooks in the foreign-language area also." 90% nonfiction; 10% fiction.
Tips: "Write a query letter describing the project and including an outline or synopsis. Indicate orientation as a writer, and pertinent background information. Supply sample material only when requested."

‡**HESSELTINE/BAKER ASSOCIATES**, Suite 490, 165 W. 46th St., New York NY 10036. (212)921-4660. Head of Literary Department: Rick Leed. Member of SAR. Obtains new clients through recommendations. Represents 25 clients. "Last year our clients earned an average of over $20,000." Will read—at no charge—unsolicited queries. SASE. Agent receives 10% commission on domestic sales, on dramatics sales, and on foreign sales.
Will Handle: Films, stage plays, and TV scripts.

‡**FREDERICK HILL ASSOCIATES**, 2237 Union St., San Francisco CA 94123. (415)921-2910. President: Frederick Hill. Obtains new clients through referrals from clients, publishers; occasionally through listings. Represents 50 clients. "Last year our clients earned an average of over $20,000." Will read—at no charge—unsolicited queries and outlines. Will not read unsolicited mss. SASE. Agent receives 10% commission on domestic sales; 10% on dramatic sales; 20% on foreign sales.
Will Handle: Nonfiction books and novels.

HINTZ LITERARY AGENCY, (Associated with Larry Sternig Literary Agency and Ray Peekner Literary Agency), 2879 N. Grant Blvd., Milwaukee WI 53210. "Our agency specializes in selling mysteries and thrillers (depends on market)." Obtains new clients through queries and referrals from clients and editors. Currently represents 25 clients. 15% of clients are new/unpublished writers. Will not read unsolicited mss; queries only. Computer printout submissions acceptable; prefers letter-quality to dot-matrix. SASE. Reports in 3 weeks on queries; 1 month on mss. Agent receives 10% commission.
Will Handle: Trade fiction and nonfiction; juvenile. Percentage of mss handled: 20% nonfiction books; 60% fiction books; 5% screenplays; 15% juvenile.
Tips: "Writers should put all their enthusiasm into a query or synopsis and should always include an author's sheet on themselves." Prefers concise, informal queries and no statements like, "This will make both of us a lot of money."

MICHAEL IMISON PLAYWRIGHTS LTD., Suite 1R, 105 W. 7th St., New York NY 10023. (212)874-2671. American Representative: Abbe Levin. Member of SAR. Obtains new clients mostly by personal recommendation. Represents 80 clients. "Before sending scripts writers should submit brief letter about themselves and their material." SASE. Agent receives 10% commission on dramatic sales; 12.5% on foreign sales.
Will Handle: Stage plays, "preferably plays with an international appeal but plays for local U.S. markets also of interest. We do not handle novels or work other than drama."

‡**INTERNATIONAL PUBLISHER ASSOCIATES, INC.**, 746 West Shore, Sparta NJ 07871. (201)729-9321. Executive Vice President: Joseph DeRogatis. Obtains new clients through personal contacts, and our reputation. Represents 27 clients. "Last year our clients earned an average of less than $2,000 to $5,000." Will read—at no charge—unsolicited mss, queries, outlines and ideas and/or proposals. SASE. Agent receives 15% commission on domestic sales and 20% on foreign sales.
Will Handle: Nonfiction books (will accept all ideas, proposals, and manuscripts for any category of nonfiction), and TV scripts (our west coast office specializes in reviewing TV and movie scripts for consideration).
Tips: "Author should be certain that an agent is known by the publishing community and is able to get manuscripts looked at by the editors."

J. DE S. ASSOCIATES, Shagbark Rd., Wilson Pt., South Norwalk CT 06854. (203)838-7571. President: Jacques de Spoelberch. Obtains new clients through other clients, publishers' recommendations and directory listings. Represents 60 clients. Less than 10% of clients are new/unpublished writers. Will read mss, queries and outlines. SASE. Agent receives 15% commission.
Will Handle: Nonfiction books and novels.

‡**ASHER D. JASON ENTERPRISES, INC.**, 111 Barrow St., New York NY 10014. (212)929-2179. Contact: Asher D. Jason. Obtains new clients through referrals. Represents 15 clients. "Last year our clients earned an average of over $20,000." Writers must have published articles or books. Will not read unsolicited mss. Agent receives 15% commission on domestic sales; 15% on dramatic sales; 19% on foreign sales.
Will Handle: Films, nonfiction books and novels.

JET LITERARY ASSOCIATES, INC., 124 E. 84th St., New York NY 10028. (212)879-2578. President: Jim Trupin. "Our agency specializes in selling Harliquin-type contemporary romances, mass market nonfiction." Obtains new clients through referrals. Represents 70 clients. 5% of clients are new/unpublished writers. "Writer must have a book publishing credit." Will read queries. Reports in 2 weeks on queries; 3 weeks on submissions. SASE. Will not read unsolicited mss. Agent receives 15% commission on domestic sales, 20% on dramatic sales, 25% on foreign sales.
Will Handle: Nonfiction books and novels. Percentage of mss handled: 50% nonfiction books; 50% fiction books.
Tips: Lack of publication credits and poor writing are the most frequent reasons for declining to represent a writer.

‡**WILLIAM KERWIN AGENCY**, Suite 202, 1605 N. Cahuenga, Hollywood CA 90028. (213)469-5155. Owner: Bill Kerwin. Obtains new clients by unsolicited scripts, friends of friends, graduate students, etc. Represents 3 clients. "Last year our clients earned an average of over $20,000." Will read—at no charge—unsolicited mss and queries. SASE. Agent receives 10% commission on domestic sales; 10% on dramatic sales; 10% on foreign sales.
Will Handle: Films and TV scripts (no episodic).

VIRGINIA KIDD, Literary Agent, 538 E. Harford St., Milford PA 18337. (717)296-6205/296-7266. "Obtains new clients by referrals, mostly." Represents 30 active clients; 30 mostly inactive. "I prefer that the writer should have earned at least $3,000 through his/her writing during the previous year, and/or have published at least one book, and/or at the very least come to me recommended by someone whose opinion I highly value. (I

probably won't accept, but will recommend to my associates.)" Query. SASE. Will *not* read unsolicited mss. Agent receives 10% commission on domestic sales; 15% on dramatic sales; and 20% on foreign sales.
Will Handle: Magazine articles, magazine fiction, nonfiction books and novels ("I specialize in science fiction but I am not limited to any one field.") "I work through a Hollywood agent for dramatic rights in the literary properties I sell. I do not send out any submission without having read it first and I may critique a given work for a client—never for a nonclient.
Tips: "Don't phone; inquire with SASE, listing your achievements and citing your earnings; do not send a sample unless encouraged to do so. If you are a new unpublished writer, go it alone for a while until you can demonstrate that you are of interest."

‡KIDDE, HOYT AND PICARD, 335 E. 51st St., New York NY 10022. (212)755-9461. Contact; Katharine Kidde, Chief Associate. Obtains new clients through connections in publishing, the *Literary Market Place*, other trade magazines, etc. Represents 50 clients. "Last year our clients earned an average of from $3,000 to $7,500. We prefer that authors have been published with at least one or two short pieces, if not a full-length work." Will read—at no charge—unsolicited queries, outlines and 2 chapters and a synopsis. Agent receives 10% commission on domestic sales, dramatic sales and foreign sales. SASE.
Will Handle: Magazine articles (geared toward magazines with wide national distribution, especially if author has full-length work); magazine fiction (geared toward magazines with wide national distribution, especially if author has a full-length novel); nonfiction books (general, not technical, work—for widely known publishers); and novels (mainstream, literary, and romantic fiction for well-known publishers). No science fiction.
Tips: "First query us by mail telling a little about yourself (high points only), especially with reference to what you've published and describe the work in question clearly."

DANIEL P. KING, LITERARY AGENT, 5125 N. Cumberland Blvd., Whitefish Bay WI 53217. (414)964-2903. Contact: Daniel P. King. Member of Crime Writers' Association (England). "Our agency specializes in selling mystery, true crime, horror and science fiction." Obtains clients by referral from current clients; members of writers' clubs. Currently represents 70 clients. 10% of clients are new/unpublished writers. "We will read all query letters and outlines and if we are interested, we will represent without previous credits. We have a good overseas market for previously published material." Will not read unsolicited mss. Computer printout submissions acceptable. Reports in 1 week on queries; 2 months on submissions. "We like to see a concise query letter—no more than a page typed in a professional and coherent manner." SASE. Agent receives 10% commission on domestic sales; 10% on dramatic sales; 20% on foreign sales.
Will Handle: "While we handle all material, we are especially interested in crime and mystery fiction and nonfiction: book-length or short story/article length." Magazine articles (true crime); magazine fiction (mystery, spy, science fiction); nonfiction books (crime); novels (mystery, spy, science fiction, mainstream). Percentage of mss handled: 10% nonfiction books; 80% fiction books; 10% magazine fiction.
Tips: "The worst mistakes that a writer can make in writing a book are attempting to ape a current author rather than develop one's own style; lack of working with a detailed outline of the book; overuse of flowery prose, words that a reader needs a dictionary to understand and inability to write in simple, straightforward prose."

HARVEY KLINGER, INC., 301 W. 53rd St., New York NY 10019. (212)581-7068. President: Harvey Klinger. Obtains clients through referrals from existing clients and from editors. Currently represents over 50 clients. 10% of clients are new/unpublished writers. "Must have completed or have close to completion a full length novel, screenplay, or nonfiction work." Will read queries and outlines. Computer printout submissions acceptable; no dot-matrix. SASE. Reports in 2 weeks on queries; 6 weeks on submissions. Agent receives 15% commission on domestic and dramatic sales; 25% on foreign sales.
Will Handle: Films (completed screenplay or film treatment); nonfiction books (query first, with complete description of the book); novels (query first; may include brief synopsis); TV scripts (completed script or treatment). Percentage of mss handled: 60% nonfiction; 40% fiction.

PAUL KOHNER AGENCY, 9169 Sunset Blvd., Los Angeles CA 90069. (213)550-1060. Contact: Gary Salt. Obtains new clients through referrals from business contacts or other clients. Occasionally blind queries, phone calls, etc. Represents 40 clients. "Last year our clients earned an average of over $30,000. We expect our writers to have been published or sold in the major market in which they are seeking our representation. No specific income standards apply. We look for long-term professional commitments. Novices or occasional writers should apply elsewhere." Will read—at no charge—unsolicited queries. Will not read unsolicited mss. Agent receives 10% commission on domestic sales; 10% on dramatic sales.
Will Handle: Films (one of our big markets); magazine articles (if it has dramatic rights potential), nonfiction books ("We've had some success placing dramatic rights here"); novels; and TV scripts (our other major market).
Tips: "Never send us anything without a query letter first."

‡**BARBARA S. KOUTS, LITERARY AGENT**, Affiliated with Philip G. Spitzer Agency, 1465 3rd Ave., New York NY 10028. (212)628-0352. Contact: Barbara S. Kouts. Member of ILAA. Obtains new clients through word of mouth, referrals by editors, *Writer's Market*, and *Literary Market Place*. Represents 50 clients. "Last year our clients earned an average of from $2,000 to $5,000." Will read—at no charge—unsolicited queries, outlines, and sample chapters. SASE. Agent receives 10% commission on domestic sales; and 20% on foreign sales.
Will Handle: Magazine fiction, nonfiction books, novels (no romances), poetry and children's book manuscripts. Send query letters.
Tips: "I welcome new writers and look for clarity, conciseness, and craft in writing skills. I try to be as helpful as possible to new writers."

LUCY KROLL AGENCY, 390 West End Ave., New York NY 10024. (212)877-0627. Member of SAR and WGA East and West. "Our agency specializes in selling nonfiction." Obtains new clients through recommendations. Very few clients are new/unpublished writers. Will not read unsolicited mss. Reports in 1 month on queries. SASE. Agent receives 10% commission.
Will Handle: Novels, nonfiction books and stage plays. 60% nonfiction books; 2% fiction books; 10% magazine fiction; 30% stage plays.

‡**BILL KRUGER LITERARY SERVICES**, Box 40997, St. Petersburg FL 33743. (813)381-5348. Contact: William Kruger. Obtains new clients through listings in *Fiction Writer's Market* and listings in *Literary Market Place*. Represents 25 clients. "Last year our clients earned an average of from $2,000 to $5,000." Will read— at no charge—unsolicited queries, outlines and brief proposals. Agent receives 10% commission on domestic sales, 20% on foreign sales; unpublished 12% domestic, 15% Canadian, 25% foreign.
Will Handle: Nonfiction books—how to, humor, cookbooks, technical, juvenile (no pictures), anything unusual; novels—science fiction, fantasy, mystery, romance, Western, humor and sports.
Tips: "Indicate some knowledge of market by studying *Books in Print* and let agent know the status of the material in regard to what's already done."

‡**MICHAEL LARSEN/ELIZABETH POMADA LITERARY AGENTS**, 1029 Jones St., San Francisco CA 94109. (415)673-0939. Contact: Michael Larsen or Elizabeth Pomada. member of ILAA. Obtains new clients primarily by referrals; also through listings in *Literary Market Place*, *Writer's Market*, *Literary Agents of North America*. Represents about 150 clients. "We will consider anyone with talent and fresh ideas." Will read—at no charge—unsolicited queries, outlines, and nonfiction book proposals, or fiction, 30 pages and synopsis. Agent receives 15% commission on domestic sales; 15% on dramatic sales; 20% on foreign sales.
Will Handle: Nonfiction books and novels (literary and commercial, romances and mysteries). "We feel that first novels should be finished and should be written with a fresh new voice. We do work with nonfiction book proposals in an extremely wide range of subjects from computers and cookbooks to scientific and philosophical how-tos."
Tips: "There are more publishers publishing more books than ever before. All publishers and agents are searching for new talent and new ideas. If a writer both polishes his or her craft and submits the best work in a professional way, success will follow."

‡**THE NORMA LEWIS AGENCY**, 521 5th Ave., New York NY 10175. (212)751-4955. Contact: Norma Liebert, Partner. Obtains new clients through listings and recommendations. Will read—at no charge— queries. SASE. Agent receives 15% commission domestic sales; 20% on foreign sales.
Will Handle: Films, nonfiction books, novels, radio scripts, stage plays, textbooks and TV scripts. "We specialize in children's, young adult and educational projects."

‡**WENDY LIPKIND AGENCY**, 225 E. 57 St., New York NY 10022. (212)935-1406. President: Wendy Lipkind. Member of ILAA. Obtains new clients through referrals and author solicitation. Represents 50 clients. Will read—at no charge—unsolicited queries. Will not read unsolicited mss. SASE. Agent receives 10% commission on domestic sales; 10% on dramatic sales; 20% on foreign sales.
Will Handle: Nonfiction books and novels.
Tips: "For first-time novelists, write the *entire* novel."

‡**LITERISTIC, LTD.**, 264 5th Ave., New York NY 10001. (212)696-4770. Member of SAR. Represents 75 clients. Will read—at no charge—unsolicited queries and outlines. Will not read unsolicited mss and will not accept unsolicited mss or other over phone—must write letter. SASE. Agent receives 10% commission on domestic sales, 10% on dramatic sales and 20% on foreign sales.
Will Handle: Magazine articles, magazine fiction, nonfiction books, novels, television and motion picture rights, and screenplays.
Tips: "Be recommended by someone of established reputation: writer, teacher, editor, etc."

‡**PETER LIVINGSTON ASSOCIATES, INC.**, Suite 800, 947 Walnut St., Boulder CO 80302. (303)443-6877. Contact: Alice Price (nonfiction), David Morgan (fiction), agents. Canadian Office: Peter Livingston Associates, Inc., Canada, 143 Collier St., Toronto, M4W 1M2 Canada. (416)928-1019. President: Peter Livingston. Member of ILAA. Obtains new clients primarily through client and editor referrals. Represents 30 clients. "Last year our clients earned an average of over $20,000. We prefer new clients with some professional publishing experience and/or professional expertise, e.g., M.D., Ph.D., etc." Will read—at no charge—unsolicited queries and outlines. Will not read unsolicited mss. SASE. Agent receives 15% on domestic sales; 15% on dramatic sales; and 20% on foreign sales.
Will Handle: Nonfiction books and novels.

THE STERLING LORD AGENCY, INC., 660 Madison Ave., New York NY 10021. (212)751-2533. Vice President: Patricia Berens. Member SAR. Obtains new clients through "recommendation of clients, editors, word of mouth." Will read queries and outlines. Reports immediately on queries. SASE. Agent receives 10% commission on domestic sales, 20% on British, dramatic, and other foreign sales.
Will Handle: Nonfiction books and novels.

‡**BARBARA LOWENSTEIN ASSOCIATES**, Suite 714, 250 W. 57th St., New York NY 10107. (212)586-3825. Literary Agent/Vice President: Eileen Fallon. Member of ILAA. Obtains new clients through referrals by current clients and editors, and through query letters. "Last year our clients earned an average of over $20,000." Will read—at no charge—unsolicited queries. "Write a strong query letter." Will not read unsolicited mss. SASE. Agent receives 15% on domestic sales; 15% on dramatic sales; and 20% on foreign sales.
Will Handle: Nonfiction books and novels (commercial fiction, including romance; literary fiction). "The only condition for eligibility is our feeling that we can successfully represent the project. We have taken on a number of unpublished writers and brought them to publication."

‡**THE LUND AGENCY**, Suite 204, 6515 Sunset Blvd., Hollywood CA 90028. (213)466-8280. President: Cara Lund. Represents 15 clients. "Last year our clients earned an average of over $20,000. Writers should be a member of WGA-W and have published novels, books or produced screenplays. We also have an excellent science fiction department." Will not read unsolicited mss in the science fiction department only. Agent receives 10% commission on domestic sales; 10% on dramatic sales; 20% on foreign sales.
Will Handle: Films (from produced screenwriters only or from published book); science fiction; horror; fantasy; period pieces; true stories (docudramas); magazine fiction (science fiction); novels; textbooks (geneology, medical, archeology, psychology); TV scripts from produced screenwriters only, episodic TV spec scripts for existing shows, movie of the week true stories preferred, good mini-series).
Tips: "Our agency has five literary agents and two attorneys. My advice is to find an agent who has the *time*, *interest*, *manpower*, *finances*, and *knowledge* required to represent your particular area."

‡**DONALD MacCAMPBELL, INC.**, 12 E. 41st St., New York NY 10017. (212)683-5580. Editor: Maureen Moran. Handles published writers only. Will not read unsolicited mss. Agent receives 10% commission on domestic sales; 20% on foreign sales.
Will Handle: Novels only (commercial book-length fiction).
Tips: Send letter of inquiry with SASE.

‡**MCCARTER LITERARY AGENCY**, 823 Park Ave., New York NY 10021. President: Mrs. Renate McCarter. Obtains new clients by word of mouth (clients and editors). Represents 14 clients; maximum wanted 12. Will read—at no charge—unsolicited queries. Will read—at no charge—unsolicited queries. Will not read or return unsolicited mss. Agent receives 10% commission on domestic sales; 10% on dramatic sales and 10% on foreign sales.
Will Handle: Nonfiction books (anthropology) and novels.
Tips: "First contact must be query letter with SASE. We have no time to answer or read unsolicited mss."

‡**MANAGEMENT I**, #590, 6464 Sunset Blvd, Hollywood CA 90028. (213)461-7515. Owner/Agent: Thomas Lietgreen. Member of WGA. Obtains new clients through referrals. Unsolicited material accepted. Will read—at no charge—unsolicited mss, queries and outlines. SASE. Agent receives 10% commission on domestic sales.
Will Handle: Films, novels and TV scripts.

HAROLD MATSON CO., INC., 276 5th Ave., New York NY 10001. (212)679-4490. Query. No unsolicited mss. SASE. Member SAR. Agent receives 10% commission.
Will Handle: Novels and nonfiction books.

‡**CLAUDIA MENZA LITERARY AGENCY**, 237 W. 11th St., New York NY 10014. (212)889-6850. President: Claudia Menza. Obtains new clients through referrals; and listings such as the one in the *Writer's Market*.

Represents 25 clients. Will read—at no charge—unsolicited manuscripts, queries, outlines and sample chapters. SASE. Agent receives a 15% commission on domestic sales; 15% on dramatic sales; 20% on foreign sales.
Will Handle: Films, nonfiction books, novels and TV scripts.
Tips: "We try to give reasons why we are turning down a client. If we do accept a client, we will give critical comments on the manuscript."

GEORGE MICHAUD AGENCY, 10113 Riverside Dr., Toluca Lake CA 91602. (818)508-8314. Literary Agent: Arthur Dreifuss. Obtains clients through Writers Guild publication. "Will consider new writers." Will read—at no charge—queries; "will respond with instructions and requirements." SASE. Reports in 6 weeks on queries; 3-6 months on submissions. Interested in new/beginning writers. Agent receives 10% commission on domestic sales.
Will Handle: TV and movie screenplays and treatments. Percentage of mss handled: 1% stage plays; 99% screenplays.
Tips: Do not send novels or short stories.

‡**MARVIN MOSS INC.**, 9200 Sunset Blvd., Los Angeles CA 90069. (213)274-8483. President: Marvin Moss. "Licensed by State of California Writers Guild, etc." Obtains new clients through referral, sometimes by submission from writer directly. "Last year our clients earned an average of over $20,000. Will accept no scripts, etc., without signed release on *our* form." Agent receives 10% commission on domestic sales; 10% on dramatic sales; 20% on foreign sales (on books).
Will Handle: Films (only complete scripts); nonfiction books (especially, if suitable for movies or TV movies); novels (no genre books); TV scripts (for TV movies).

MULTIMEDIA PRODUCT DEVELOPMENT, INC., 410 S. Michigan Ave., Room 724, Chicago IL 60605. (312)922-3063. President: Jane Jordan Browne. "Our agency specializes in selling nonfiction, mainstream fiction, and category fiction, such as science fiction, historical romances, contemporary romances. Obtains new clients through recommendations and word-of-mouth. Currently represents 95 clients. 5% of clients are new/unpublished writers. "Multimedia handles only works of professional writers who make their living as authors. The rare exceptions are celebrity autobiographies and the 'new idea' nonfiction book." Will read unsolicited queries and outlines. Computer printout submissions acceptable; prefers letter-quality to dot-matrix. SASE. Reports in 2 weeks on queries; 1 month on submissions. Agent receives 15% commission on domestic sales; 20% on foreign.
Will Handle: Novels, nonfiction books, screenplays, juvenile. No poetry, plays, articles or short stories. Percentage of mss handled: 65% nonfiction; 25% fiction; 5% screenplays; 5% juvenile.
Tips: "The most frequent reasons for declining to represent a writer are lack of professional skills or approach or the subject matter is not commercial."

JEAN V. NAGGAR LITERARY AGENCY, 336 E. 73rd St., New York NY 10021. (212)794-1082. Contact: Jean Naggar. Member of ILAA. Obtains new clients through recommendations. Query with outline and brief biographical sketch. Computer printout submissions acceptable; no dot-matrix. SASE. Reports in 2 days on queries; as soon as possible on submissions—"sometimes a long wait. I am taking on *very few* new writers at this time." Agent receives 15% commission on domestic sales; and 20% on foreign sales.
Will Handle: Novels and nonfiction books. Percentage of mss handled: approximately 30% nonfiction; 70% fiction. Specializes in a "broad range of fiction, from literary to historical to science fiction, etc. with many in between. Some prior writing credits are a help." Sales include *The Clan of the Cave Bear*, *The Mammoth Hunters*, *Things Invisible to See*, by Nancy Willard.

‡**CHARLES NEIGHBORS, INC.**, Suite 3607, 7600 Blanco Rd., San Antonio TX 78216. (512)342-5324. Also has New York city branch office. Owner: Charles Neighbors. Obtains new clients mostly through recommendations from editors and clients. Represents 60 clients. "Last year our clients earned an average of from $5,000 to 10,000." Will read—at no charge—unsolicited queries and outlines. Will not read unsolicited mss. SASE. Agent receives 15% commission on domestic sales; 15% on dramatic sales; 20% on foreign sales.
Will Handle: Films (prefer synopses or treatments to finished screenplays); nonfiction books (outlines and author credentials); novels (2-3 chapters and outline).
Tips: "Be prepared for your area of interest. Then study the best, not to copy but to compare. Read. Read. Read."

‡**NEW ENGLAND PUBLISHING ASSOCIATES, INC.**, Box 5, Chester CT 06412. (718)788-6641. President: Elizabeth Frost Knappman. Member of American Book Producers Association. Obtains new clients by word of mouth and *Literary Market Place*. Represents 30 clients. Will read—at no charge—unsolicited mss, queries, and outlines. Agent receives 15% commission on domestic sales; 15% on dramatic sales; and 10% on foreign sales.

Will Handle: Nonfiction books and novels.

Tips: "Call first, then send an outline and chapter. Don't give up."

NEW WAVE, Authors' Representatives, 2544 N. Monticello Ave., Chicago IL 60647. (312)342-3338. Client Contact: Gene Lovitz. Represents over 200 authors. "Interested in promising new writers and ideas providing the text is on par with *The Manual of Style*. Queries, outlines, sample chapters and/or completed mss welcomed *only* if sent with SASE (otherwise they will not be returned)." Reports in 6 weeks. Agent receives 10% commission on domestic sales; 20% on foreign. "We charge no fee. We read for acceptance or rejection only on a non-fee basis. Definitive critiquing service—not to be confused with a 'reading fee'—is available for a nominal charge, should the author want such a written evaluation; but this is not a requirememt for our handling of a manuscript."

Will Handle: Adult trade novels, adult nonfiction, juveniles, gift market, poetry and experimental. "We are especially interested in 400-500 page historic romances, gothic, horror, series developed for mass produced paperback sales, health, TV and film scripts." No articles.

Tips: "New Wave is interested in both hardcover and paperback placements, as well as chapbooks and illustrated material (risque or otherwise)."

‡**THE BETSY NOLAN LITERARY AGENCY,** 215 Park Ave. S., New York NY 10003. (212)420-6000. President: Betsy Nolan. Vice President: Patricia Falco. Obtains new clients through referral and direct contact. Represents approximately 20 clients. "Ms should be one of several potential projects." Will read—at no charge—unsolicited mss, queries and outlines. Will read submissions at no charge, but may charge criticism fee. Agent receives 15% commission on domestic sales; 15% on dramatic sales; and 15% on foreign sales.

Will Handle: Nonfiction books and novels. No romantic fiction.

MARY NOVIK, LITERARY AGENT, 5519 Deerhorn Lane, North Vancouver, British Columbia V7R 4S8 Canada. (604)987-4982. Member of Writer's Union of Canada and observes its published guidelines. 50% of clients are new/unpublished writers. Agent receives 10% commission on North American sales; 20% on foreign sales.

Will Handle: "The agency will read *romance novels* only. No reading fees are charged. Interested writers should submit the first three chapters (or 50 pages) with synopsis of rest. Computer printout submissions acceptable; prefers letter-quality to dot-matrix. Enclose SASE (check or International Reply Coupons since U.S. stamps cannot be used from Canada). Keep in mind that Canadian postage is considerably higher than American. Reports in one month on queries; six weeks on submissions. Writers are advised to study the market carefully before submitting to make sure that their novels keep pace with current trends." Recent sales: *Moon Madness* and *Summer Wine*, by Freda Vasilos (Silhouette) and *A Lasting Kind of Love*, by Catherine Spencer (Harlequin.)

FIFI OSCARD ASSOCIATES, INC., 19 W. 44th St., New York NY 10036. (212)764-1100. Contact: Literary Department. "Our agency specializes in selling nonfiction and nongenre fiction." Member of SAR and Writers Guild. Obtains clients through recommendations. Prefers to work with authors who have previously published articles or books. 10% of clients are new/unpublished writers. Computer printout submissions acceptable; no dot-matrix. SASE. Reports in 1 week on queries; 3 weeks on submissions. Agent receives 15% commission on domestic sales.

Will Handle: Material in all areas. Percentage of ms handled: 60% nonfiction books; 40% fiction books.

Tips: "The most frequent reasons for declining to represent a writer are undeveloped characters, lack of tension in the writing and/or predictable story lines."

‡**JOHN K. PAYNE LITERARY AGENCY, INC.,** (formerly Lenniger Literary Agency, Inc.), Rm. 1101, 175 5th Ave., New York NY 10010. (212)475-6447. President: John K. Payne. Obtains new clients through recommendations. Represents 50 clients. "We prefer writers with one or two book sales." Agent receives 10% commission on domestic sales; 20% on foreign.

Will Handle: Nonfiction books and novels (historicals).

Tips: "I am partial to material with Irish backgrounds and am looking for family sagas, historicals, romantic novels, biographies, and enduring books."

RAY PEEKNER LITERARY AGENCY, 3210 S. 7th St., Milwaukee WI 53215. Contact: Ray Puechner. Associated with Larry Sternig Literary Agency, Hintz Literary Agency, Bill Kruger Agency, Lee Allan Agency (films). Member of MWA, WWA, RWA, SCBW and SFWA. Obtains new clients through referrals from clients and editors. Currently represents 60 clients. 2% of clients are new/unpublished writers. Will not read unsolicited mss. No multiple queries. Computer printout submissions acceptable; no dot-matrix. Reports in 2 weeks on queries; 1 month on submissions. Interested in new/beginning writers "if recommended by an editor,

or well-established writer." Agent receives 10% commission.
Will Handle: Booklengths only, fiction and nonfiction, adult and young adult. Percentage of mss handled: 20% nonfiction; 40% fiction; 40% juvenile.

RODNEY PELTER, 129 E. 61st St., New York NY 10021. (212)838-3432. Contact: Rodney Pelter. Specializes in fiction and nonfiction—self-help, how-to, illustrated books, interior design and the arts. Obtains new clients through referrals from people in publishing (editors, publishers, etc.) plus referrals from writers, etc. Represents 15-20 clients. Query with first 50 pages of ms plus SASE. Agent receives 10-15% commission on domestic sales (graduated scale, depending on size of advance); 10-20% on dramatic sales (depending on size of option or sale); and 20% on foreign sales.
Will Handle: Nonfiction books and novels. Percentage of mss handled: 40% nonfiction, 60% fiction.
Tips: "Write an intelligent query letter (with SASE). Give casual background summary; details of experience in writing or lack of it; no gimmicks, no sales pitch—save it for the book jacket."

‡**AARON M. PRIEST LITERARY AGENCY, INC.**, 556 5th Ave., New York 10017. (212)818-0344. Contact: Aaron Priest or Molly Friedrich. Member of ILAA. Obtains new clients through referral. Represents 35 clients. "Last year our clients earned an average of over $20,000." Will read—at no charge—unsolicited queries and outlines. SASE.
Will Handle: Nonfiction books (outline/3 chapters); novels (outline/3 chapters).

‡**SUSAN ANN PROTTER LITERARY AGENT**, Suite 1408, 110 W. 40th St., New York NY 10018. (212)840-0480. Contact: Susan Protter. Member of ILAA. Obtains new clients through referrals and author queries. Represents 50 clients. Will read—at no charge—unsolicited queries. SASE. Agent receives 15% commission on domestic sales, 25% on foreign sales.
Will Handle: Nonfiction books in the areas of history, biography, health, medicine, science, psychology, business, and self-help. Also serious fiction, thrillers, mysteries, women's fiction and science fiction. Always query first with a summary or proposal and SASE.
Tips: "What I am looking for are writers with a future and a professional attitude toward their work."

‡**HELEN REES**, 308 Commonwealth Ave., Boston MA 02116. (617)262-2401. Contact: Helen Rees. Member of ILAA. Obtains new clients through referrals. Represents 55 clients. "Last year our clients earned an average of from $10,000 to $20,000. Preferably a writer should have some publishing record." Will read—at no charge—unsolicited queries and outlines. Will not read unsolicited mss. Agent receives 15% commission on domestic sales; 15% on dramatic sales; 20% on foreign sales.
Will Handle: Nonfiction books and novels.

‡**RHODES LITERARY AGENCY**, 140 West End Ave., New York NY 10023. (212)580-1300. Owner: Joseph Rhodes and Joan Lewis. Obtains new clients through recommendation or inquiry letters. Made 25 sales in 1984. Will not read unsolicited mss; will read unsolicited queries. SASE. Member ILAA and Writers Guild. Will consider new writers. Agent receives 10% commission.
Will Handle: Novels, nonfiction books, and stage plays.

MARIE RODELL-FRANCES COLLIN LITERARY AGENCY, 110 W. 40th St., New York NY 10018. (212)840-8664. Contact: Frances Collin. Member of SAR. Currently represents 75 clients. 3-5% of clients are new/unpublished writers. Query. Computer printout submissions acceptable; prefers letter-quality to dot-matrix. Reports in 1-2 days on queries; 1 month on submissions. SASE. Agent receives 15% commission for domestic sales; and 25% for foreign.
Will Handle: Trade novels and trade nonfiction books. Percentage of mss handled: 55% nonfiction; 40% fiction; 5% juvenile.

‡**ELEANOR ROSZEL ROGERS**, (formerly Eleanor Merryman Roszel), 1487 Generals Hwy., Crownsville MD 21032. (301)987-8166. Contact: Eleanor Roszel Rogers. Obtains new clients through client referral, publisher referral, *Literary Market Place*, *Writer's Market*. Represents 15 clients. "A writer must have produced something which I find of interest and about which I can be enthusiastic." Will read—at no charge—unsolicited mss, queries, and outlines (always prefer query first). SASE. Agent receives 10% commission on domestic sales; 20% on foreign sales.
Will Handle: Nonfiction books (not highly technical books, but those for a general readership); novels (no horror fiction or science fiction, Harlequin-type romances).
Tips: "In my own business, I strive for a partnership with my clients since we're both after the same goal—the publication of that client's work."

‡**IRENE ROGERS LITERARY REPRESENTATION**, Suite 850, 9701 Wilshire Blvd., Beverly Hills CA 90212. (213)837-3511. President: Irene Rogers. Obtains new clients through personal referrals and occasion-

ally by inquiry. Represents 10 clients. "Last year our clients earned an average of over $20,000." Will read—at no charge—unsolicited queries. Will not read unsolicited mss. SASE. Agent receives 10% commission on domestic sales; 10% on dramatic sales.
Will Handle: Films, nonfiction books and novels.
Tips: "Queries are always to be the first step. If interest is positive, then proceed from there."

ROSENSTONE/WENDER, 3 E. 48th St., New York NY 10017. (212)832-8330. (201)568-8739. Contact: Susan Golomb, Leah Schmidt, John Gersten. Member of Society of Authors' Representatives. Obtains new clients through client inquiries. Will read unsolicited queries, outlines. Reports in 2 months. Agent receives 10% commission on domestic and dramatic sales; 20% on foreign sales.
Will Handle: Films, and stage plays submitted to John Gersten; novels, nonfiction books, and TV scripts submitted to Susan Golomb.

MARY JANE ROSS AGENCY, 85 Sunset Lane, Tenafly NJ 07670. (201)568-8739. Contact: Mary Jane Ross. "Our agency specializes in Protestant Evangelical nonfiction plus other nonfiction, 'good' mysteries, and science fiction. Obtains new clients usually by recommendation. Represents authors and also numerous small publishers on subsidiary rights. 90% of clients are new/unpublished writers. Will read queries at no charge "but must enclose SASE." Reports in 2 weeks on queries; 1 month on submissions. Agent receives 15% commission on domestic and dramatic sales; 25% on foreign sales.
Will Handle: Nonfiction books and novels. No juvenile. Percentage of mss handled: 90% nonfiction books; 1% magazine nonfiction; 9% fiction books.
Tips: "Send query letter first with SASE. Manuscript must be legible, double spaced, but do not send the original; stamps for returning must be enclosed. Writer must be patient while decision is made. I require exclusivity."

JANE ROTROSEN, 226 E. 32nd St., New York NY 10016. (212)889-7133. Member ILAA. Obtains new clients through referrals, both editorial and author; queries, conferences, contacts. Represents approximately 130 clients. Will read—at no charge—unsolicited mss (prefer query first), queries and outlines. SASE. Agent receives 15% commission on domestic sales; 20% on foreign sales.
Will Handle: Nonfiction books and novels. Query first.

GLORIA SAFIER, 244 E. 53rd St., New York NY 10022. (212)838-4868. Contact: Gloria Safier. Member of SAR. Represents 45 clients. 20% of clients are new/unpublished writers. Query. Reports in 1 week on queries. SASE. Agent receives 15% commission.
Will Handle: Trade novels and nonfiction, films and plays. Percentage of mss handled: 10% nonfiction mss; 75% fiction; 10% stage plays; 5% screenplays.
Tips: "Write a good letter, one that describes the book you want the agent to read (never write a letter that says just, 'I've written a book, would you like to read it?'—this sort of letter is useless) and reveals something about your background."

JAMES SELIGMANN AGENCY, Suite 1101, 175 5th Ave., New York NY 10010. Contact: James F. Seligmann. Member SAR. Obtains new clients through recommendation, personal contact, or solicitation. Will not read unsolicited mss; will read unsolicited queries and outlines. Computer printout submissions acceptable; prefers letter-quality to dot-matrix. SASE. Agent receives 15% commission.
Will Handle: Novels and nonfiction books. "Please, no poetry, drama or film or TV scripts, science fiction, mysteries, suspense novels, or books for children under 12."

‡SHUMAKER TALENT AGENCY, 10850 Riverside Dr., N. Hollywood CA 91602. (213)877-3370. Contact: Timothy Shumaker. Obtains new clients through Writers Guild west, and referrals. Represents 10 clients. "Last year our clients earned an average of less than $2,000." Will consider—at no charge—mss, queries, outlines and tapes. SASE. Agent receives 10% commission on domestic sales; 10% on dramatic sales; 10% on foreign sales.
Will Handle: Films, nonfiction books, novels, syndicated material, textbooks and TV scripts.

BOBBE SIEGEL, RIGHTS REPRESENTATIVE, 41 W. 83rd St., New York NY 10024. (212)877-4985. Contact: Bobbe Siegel. Associate: Richard Siegel. "Our agency specializes in selling literary fiction-fantasy, science fiction, historicals, diet, health, and how-to." Obtains clients by referral, usually by editors or writers. Currently represents 50 clients, 35% of clients are new/unpublished writers. Will read mss, queries, outlines, proposals. "Send query letter first." Will not read any submission done in dot-matrix. Reports in 2 weeks on queries; 2 months on submissions. SASE. Agent receives 15% commission on domestic sales; 10% on dramatic sales; 20% on foreign sales (10% of which is for foreign agent).
Will Handle: Nonfiction books, novels. Percentage of mss handled: 65% nonfiction; 35% fiction.
Tips: "The most frequent reasons for declining to represent a writer are poor writing, dot matrix submission,

on copy edited manuscript which needs retyping. The poor writing includes—bad plotting, poor organization, overlong manuscripts, bad editing and too-flowery language. Freelance writers will have a tougher time without an agent. They will have to do more research to establish which houses will view their material without an agent.''

‡**ROSALIE SIEGEL, AUTHOR'S AGENT**, 111 Murphy Dr., Pennington NJ 08534. (609)437-1007. President: Rosalie Siegel. Member of ILAA. Represents 45 clients. Reads "no unsolicited material except queries.'' Will read submissions at no charge, but may charge criticism fee. Will not read unsolicited mss. SASE. Agent receives 10% commission on domestic sales; 10% on dramatic sales; 20% on foreign sales.
Will Handle: Nonfiction books and novels (no romance, westerns, category books).

‡**EVELYN SINGER LITERARY AGENCY**, Box 594, White Plains NY 10602. (914)949-1147/(212)799-5203. Obtains new clients through recommendations. Represents 50 clients. "Writers need to have earned $20,000 from freelance or literary activity and have a recommendation by editors or writing course teachers.'' Will read—at no charge—queries and outlines. No phone queries. SASE. Agent receives 10% commission on domestic sales; 20% on foreign sales.
Will Handle: Nonfiction books (adult and juvenile); novels (adult and juvenile).

SOFTWARE AGENCY, 928 Broadway, New York NY 10010. (212)675-5400. Principal: Edward J. Acton. Obtains new clients by referral. Currently represents 35 clients. Will read ms, queries, outlines. Computer printout submissions acceptable; prefers letter-quality to dot-matrix. SASE. Reports in 2 weeks on queries; varying time on submissions. Agent receives 15% commission.
Will Handle: Computer books, software programs only.

‡**CHARLES M. STERN ASSOCIATION**, Box 32742, 319 Coronet, San Antonio TX 78216. (512)349-6141. Contact: Charles M. Stern. Obtains new clients through recommendations, *Literary Market Place* and *Writer's Market*. Will read—at no charge—unsolicited queries and outlines. Will not read unsolicited mss. SASE. Agent receives 15% commission on domestic sales; 20% on dramatic sales; 20% on foreign sales.
Will Handle: Films, nonfiction books, how-to books and novels.
Tips: "Send query with synopsis. Make sure manuscript is presented in acceptable form. Do not use dot-matrix. Send stamps for return postage.''

GLORIA STERN LITERARY AGENCY, 1230 Park Ave., New York NY 10028. (212)289-7698. Contact: Gloria Stern. Member of ILAA. "Our agency specializes in selling nonfiction: biography, politics, history, medicine and serious fiction. Represents 34 clients. 40% of clients are new/unpublished writers. "For fiction, only serious fiction, authors who have been published in magazines or have had a book published; for nonfiction, the author must have particular expertise in the field he plans to write about.'' Query. No unsolicited mss. Computer printout submissions acceptable; no dot-matrix. SASE. Reports in 3 days on queries; 1 month on submissions. Agent receives 10-15% commissions.
Will Handle: Novels, trade nonfiction books. No self-publications. "Prefers serious literary fiction.'' Percentage of mss handled: 85% nonfiction; 15% fiction.
Tips: "A dull start to a book puts editors off.''

LARRY STERNIG LITERARY AGENCY, 742 Robertson St., Milwaukee WI 53213. (414)771-7677. "I am unable to take on new clients.'' Currently represents 40 clients. Handles 20% nonfiction mss; 80% fiction mss. Will not read unsolicited mss. Agent receives 10% commission.
Handles: Magazine and fiction, novels and nonfiction books.

‡**JO STEWART**, 201 E. 66th St., New York NY 10021. (212)879-1301. Owner/President: Jo Stewart. Obtains new clients through reference by editors or other writers and through letters that potential writers send me. Will read—at no charge—unsolicited mss, queries and outlines. Agent receives 10% commission on domestic sales; 20% on foreign sales; 15% on first-time novelists.
Will Handle: Films, magazine fiction and novels.

GUNTHER STUHLMANN, AUTHOR'S REPRESENTATIVE, Box 276, Becket MA 01223. Contact: Ms. Barbara Ward. Obtains new clients through "personal recommendation from clients, publishers, editors.'' Will not read unsolicited mss. SASE for queries and outlines. Reports in 1 week on queries; 3 weeks on submissions. Agent receives 10% commission on domestic and Canadian sales; 15% on British and 20% overseas.
Will Handle: Novels, nonfiction books, motion picture, TV and serial rights based on established properties only. "We do not handle individual original plays, TV scripts or film scripts. We handle such rights only on the basis of established properties, i.e., as subsidiary rights to books we handle.''

‡**H.N. SWANSON, INC.**, 8523 Sunset Blvd., Los Angeles CA 90069. (213)652-5385. Contact: H.N. Swanson—B.F. Kamsler. Obtains new clients through recommendations, contacts, etc. Represents approximately 100 clients. "Last year our clients earned from $20,000 to $500,000." Writers must have been published or produced. Will read—at no charge—unsolicited queries and outlines. Will not read unsolicited mss. SASE. Agent receives 10% commission on domestic sales; 10% on dramatic sales; and 20% on foreign sales. **Will Handle:** Films, magazine fiction, novels, stage plays and TV scripts. Material must be complete.

ALFONSO TAFOYA, 212, 655 6th Ave., New York NY 10010. (212)929-1090. Director: Alfonso Tafoya. Obtains new clients through referrals. Represents 30 clients. Writers should have some prior publishing. Will read queries at no charge. Agent receives 10% commission on domestic sales; 20% on dramatic and foreign sales.
Will Handle: Films (treatments); dramatic motion pictures and TV scripts (treatments). Author must have "track record" in these areas.
Tips: "Have *one* very good, very polished, completed project. Be patient."

‡**THOMPSON AND CHRIS LITERARY AGENCY**, 3926 Sacramento St., San Francisco CA 94118. (415)386-2443. Contact: Teresa Chris, Partner. Obtains new clients through recommendations, seminars, talks or listings. Represents 45 clients. "Last year our clients earned an average of from $5,000 to $10,000." Will read—at no charge—unsolicited mss, queries, and outlines. SASE. Agent receives 15% commission on domestic sales; 15-20% on dramatic sales; and 15-20% commission on foreign sales.
Will Handle: Nonfiction books (wide range); novels (genre commercial and literary); and children's books.

‡**A TOTAL ACTING EXPERIENCE**, Talent Agency, Suite 3231, 6736 Laurel Canyon, N. Hollywood CA 91606. (818)765-7244. Contact: Dan A. Bellacicco, Agent. Estab. 1984. Will read—at no charge—unsolicited mss, queries, outlines. "Include one page synopsis for all work. Plus resume." SASE. Agent receives 10% commission on domestic sales; 10% on dramatic sales; 10% on foreign sales.
Will Handle: Films, novels, radio scripts, stage plays, syndicated material, and TV scripts. "No heavy violence, drugs or sex. All material must have a harmonious theme and story."
Tips: "We seek new sincere, quality writers for long-term relationships. We would love to see film, television, and stage material that remains relevant and provocative twenty years from today; dialogue that is fresh, and unpredictable; and story, theme and characters that are intelligent, enlightening, humorous, witty, creative, inspiring, and, most of all, entertaining."

TRAID ARTISTS, INC.,(formerly *Adams, Ray & Rosenberg*), 10100 Santa Monica Blvd., Suite 1600, Los Angeles CA 90067. Obtains new clients through recommendation only. 5% of clients are new/unpublished writer. Will not read unsolicited mss. Reports in 2 weeks on queries; 1 month on submissions. Agent receives 10% commission.
Will Handle: Novels (motion picture, publication and TV rights), motion pictures, stage plays (film rights), and TV scripts. Percentage of mss handled: 3% nonfiction; 9% fiction; 3% stage plays; 85% screenplays.

SUSAN P. URSTADT INC., 125 E. 84th St., New York NY 10028. (212)744-6605. President: Susan Urstadt. Member ILAA. Obtains new clients "usually through reference." Represents 20-40 clients. 5% of clients are new/unpublished writers. Will read queries and outlines. Computer printout submissions acceptable; prefers letter-quality to dot-matrix. SASE. Reports in 2 weeks on queries; 6 weeks on submissions. Agent receives 10% commission on domestic sales, 15% on dramatic sales, 20% on foreign sales.
Will Handle: Nonfiction books include history, biography, autobiography, social sciences, current affairs and essays; sports books; specialize in *horses*. Also illustrated books on art, decorative arts, antiques, gardening and horticulture, architecture and cookbooks. Percentage of mss handled: 60% nonfiction books; 40% fiction books.

VASS TALENT AGENCY, (formerly *Frank Vass Talent Agency*, Suite 428, 6404 Hollywood Blvd., Los Angeles CA 90028. (213)481-3828. Owner: Frank Vass. Member of Writers Guild and ATA. Currently represents 50 clients—100% of mss are screenplays and teleplays (TV plays). 10% of clients are new/unpublished writers. Interested in new/beginning writers. Will read—at no charge—mss (80- 120-page screenplays); and synopses. Query first. Reports in 2 months. SASE. Agent receives 10% commission on domestic sales.
Will Handle: Screenplays and teleplays (synopses).

JOHN A. WARE LITERARY AGENCY, 392 Central Park W., New York NY 10025. (212)866-4733. Contact: John Ware. "Our agency specializes in selling biography, history, current affairs 'issues'/investigative journalism, health, sports, and contemporary fiction." Obtains new clients through referrals, speaking engagements, inquiries. Represents approximately 50 clients. 50% of clients are new/unpublished writers. Will read queries and outlines; no unsolicited mss. Reports in 2 weeks on queries; 3 weeks on mss. SASE. Agent re-

ceives 10% commission on domestic and dramatic sales. 20% on foreign sales.
Will Handle: Nonfiction books and novels. Percentage of mss handled: 70% nonfiction; 30% fiction.

‡**ANN WAUGH AGENCY**, 4731 Laurel Canyon Blvd., North Hollywood CA 91607. (818)980-0141. Contact; Steve Jacobson. Obtains new clients through referrals. Represents 8 clients. "Last year our clients earned an average of over $20,000." Will read—at no charge—unsolicited screenplays (only). SASE; must submit first, a small SASE so that we can send a release form. Agent receives 10% commission on domestic sales.
Will Handle: Films and TV scripts.
Tips: "All writers who have not already sold must take screenwriting courses so that they have a specific idea on the proper form a screenplay should take."

‡**RUTH WRESCHNER, AUTHORS' REPRESENTATIVE**, 10 W. 74th St., New York NY 10023. (212)877-2605. Contact: Ruth Wreschner. Obtains new clients through referral, the International Women's Writers Guild, and the American Society of Journalists and Authors. Represents 30 clients. "Last year our clients earned an average of from $5,000 to $20,000. I specialize, although by no means exclusively, in popular medicine and psychology. These *must* be authored by professionals, although frequently writers are assigned." Will read—at no charge—unsolicited queries. Will not read unsolicited mss. Authors should query first. SASE. Agent receives 15% commission on domestic sales; 20% on foreign sales.
Will Handle: Nonfiction books, novels and textbooks.

‡**ANN WRIGHT REPRESENTATIVES, INC.**, 136 E. 57th St., New York NY 10022. (212)832-0110/832-0151. Head of Literary Department: Dan Wright. Member of WGA. Obtains new clients through referrals, inquiry and requested submissions. Represents 35 clients. "Last year our clients earned an average of over $20,000. We specialize in motion picture properties, screenwriters, television writers and novelists." Will read—at no charge—mss, screenplays, treatments and scripts. Queries first. Will not read unsolicited mss. SASE. Agent receives 10% commission on domestic sales; 15% on dramatic sales; 20% on foreign sales; 10% of gross film and TV deals.
Will Handle: Films (screenplays, treatments); novels (for film or TV possibilities); and TV scripts (from experienced TV writers only). "Clients should supply their own duplicate manuscript of screenplays and scripts."

WRITERS AND ARTISTS AGENCY, 162 W. 56th St., New York NY 10019. (212)246-9029. West Coast office: 11726 San Vicente Blvd., Los Angeles CA 90049. Contact: Jonathan Sand, Carol Reich (NY); Joan Scott, Rima Bauer, Marty Adelstein (LA). Obtains clients through reading (solicited only) manuscripts and attending plays. Currently represents 80 clients. Will read 2-page synopsis and resume. Will not read unsolicited mss. Agent receives 10% commission on domestic, dramatic and foreign sales.
Will Handle: Plays, films, and TV scripts (NY office). TV scripts and screenplays (LA office).

WRITERS HOUSE INC., 21 W. 26th St., New York NY 10010. Contact: Ed Ratliff. Member of SAR and Authors Guild. Obtains new clients "mostly by referrals and recommendations." Represents 240 clients. 10% of clients are new/unpublished writers. Will read queries, outlines and sample chapters. Computer printout submissions acceptable; prefers letter-quality to dot-matrix. Reports in 2 weeks on queries; 6 weeks on submissions. SASE. Agent receives 10% commission on domestic sales, 15% on dramatic sales, 20% on foreign sales.
Will Handle: Novels, nonfiction, young adult and juvenile. "Prefer seeing a detailed synopsis and a sample chapter or two." Percentage of mss handled: 40% nonfiction; 30% fiction; 30% juvenile and young adult.

WRITER'S PRODUCTIONS, Box 5152, Westport CT 06881. Contact: David L. Meth. New clients obtained through "word of mouth and professional listings. No phone calls." 50% of clients are new/unpublished writers. Limited client list. Will read ms (sample of 25-50 pages only); queries and outlines. Computer printout submissions acceptable; no dot-matrix. SASE (no postage meter for return envelope. Reports in 1 week on queries; 1 month on submissions. Agent receives 15% commission on domestic and dramatic sales, 20% on foreign sales.
Will Handle: Nonfiction books (intriguing, sensitive subjects, nothing technical); novels (sensitive, provocative fiction of the highest quality). Percentage of mss handled: 10% nonfiction; 90% fiction. Recent Sale: *The Upper Room*, by Mary Menroe (St. Martin's Press 1985).
Tips: "We are looking for writers who deal with their subjects sensitively and compassionately, and whose characters will live beyond the time the book is put down. Sometimes writers make the mistake of talking the story out instead of letting the characters reveal themselves. Does not allow the reader to discover for himself, but tells directly. Always send the *best* work possible as an example of your talent and skill."

‡**MARY YOST ASSOCIATES, INC.**, 59 E. 54th St., New York NY 10025. (212)980-4988. President: Mary Yost. Member of SAR. Obtains new clients through referrals. Represents 75 clients. Will read—at no charge—unsolicited queries. SASE. Agent receives 10% commission on domestic sales; 5% on dramatic sales;

Close-up

Richard Curtis
Literary Agent

Photo by Mark Fadiman

His client list reads like a who's who of contemporary authors, and includes John Jakes, Gregory Benford, and Janet Daly (for whom he recently negotiated a $1.3 million dollar deal with Pocket Books for *The Great Alone*). He's been a literary agent since 1959. In fact, it's the only job he's ever held.

Richard Curtis is also a crusader. "Aside from being an agent, I've tried to be an author's advocate, speaking out not only on behalf of my own authors, but for all authors," he says.

Richard Curtis is a name known to many writers. His column, Agents Corner, appears monthly in *Locus*, a magazine for science fiction authors, and has been picked up for publication by the Romance Writers of America, the Mystery Writers of America, and The Western Writers of America. The column is his forum. "I've decided to take my case to the people, through my column, which I hope will raise consciousness and shape opinion, so that authors themselves will have a better idea of some of the problems I've been trying to deal with," he says.

"Some agents are not afraid to take very strong action on behalf of *their own clients*, but there are some problems in this publishing industry that can only be solved by collective action," Curtis points out.

His book, *How to Be Your Own Literary Agent*, is aimed at professional and semi-professional authors and is another part of his crusade. "It is written for the writer who seeks to understand contracts, royalty statements, negotiation terms, and some of the pitfalls involved in negotiation. This knowledge enables writers to oversee their agents who, after all, are only human."

Curtis has plenty of advice for new writers, especially about marketing books. "Of all the things that you are going to write," he says, "the pitch letter is the most important. For nonfiction, you must establish your credentials, the market for your book, what the book is, and the competition for the book—all in a page and without hardsell." Direct submissions to a specific person at a publishing house, he advises.

If a new writer is offered a contract, the author should get an agent immediately, Curtis believes. "Most agents will be more than happy to take over for an author who has an offer already pending."

Curtis, of course, stresses the importance of an agent in the marketplace. "Most of the time, author submissions will not be taken as seriously as agented submissions; agents have clout and they have entry. A good agent knows the market and has influence on the market," he points out. "If the writer doesn't understand royalty structures, normal advance payout, which rights to keep, which territories to grant, he might as well give his money away, because he will already have done that by signing a contract without knowing what's at stake."

Even for writers without agents, Curtis wants to increase awareness of publishing practices, such as reserves against returns. "Most authors end up having bad experiences with their publishers, because all they care about is getting into print—not money or other considerations."

—*Michael A. Banks*

10% on foreign sales.
Will Handle: Nonfiction books and novels. "Query letter and SASE must be sent."

‡**SUSAN ZECKENDORF ASSOCIATES, INC.**, Apt. 11B, 171 W. 57th St., New York NY 10019. (212)245-2928. President: Susan Zeckendorf. Member of ILAA. Obtains new clients through queries, editors and clients. Represents 35 clients. "Last year our clients earned an average of from $5,000 to $10,000." Will read—at no charge—unsolicited queries and outlines. Will not read unsolicited mss. SASE. Agent receives 15% commission on domestic sales and 10% commission on foreign sales.
Will Handle: Authoritative nonfiction books and novels—no romances, westerns, or other category fiction.

GEORGE ZIEGLER AGENCY, 160 E. 97th St., New York NY 10029. (212)348-3637. Proprietor: George Ziegler. Obtains new clients through referrals and submissions. Represents 24 clients. 20% of clients are new/unpublished writers. "Writers should send query first, with brief synopsis/description of book." SASE. Reports in 1 week on queries; 2 months on submissions. Agent receives 15% commission on domestic and dramatic sales, 20% on foreign sales (if subagent used).
Will Handle: Nonfiction books (for general trade only); novels (non-genre, no romances); stage plays (full-evening-length, contemporary or historical, *realistic*). Percentage of mss handled: 60% nonfiction books; 40% fiction books.
Tips: "It's at least twice as hard as it was seven or eight years ago to get a publisher to take the leap for a talented unknown unless the book is potential top of the list. It's even hard for the writer who has one book under his or her belt if the book didn't get favorable critical attention. Many of the manuscripts I read are competent without being publishable in this competitive marketplace. The special insights, the overall cohesiveness and a professional respect for words are what lift a work out of the mundane, and these, I think, are most frequently lacking."

Contests and Awards ————————————

If the prospect of having writers judge your work sounds appealing, then you'll want to explore the contest market. While editors sometimes judge entries in magazine contests, most contest sponsors hire professional writers to select the winning entries.

When writing a story for a contest or applying for a fellowship, give the judges something (in writing, of course) that will stand out in their minds. This advice sounds obvious, but in judging essays last year for *Writer's Market*, we encountered a few essays that sounded alike; they included useful information, but information we already knew. Entries need images and details that are too vivid and unique to forget. (Remember the chimney sweep who drove a VW—and inspired magazine sales for one writer—in the 1985 *WM* upfront article, "Sweeping Up More Assignments"?)

Contests enable writers to compete with one another where the same rules apply to each writer. Some competitions focus on a form (like the short story, perhaps) or a subject (like human rights). In other awards, the theme or approach doesn't matter; the object for judges is to find *the best*—the best article, play, or first-time novel.

Contests offer writers a variety of benefits. Aside from the monetary rewards from many writing prizes, there is satisfaction and the incentive to excel further. There is exposure and recognition. Distinction in a playwriting contest may lead to staged readings of a script; a major book award may increase the sales of a novel.

Most of the contests listed here are annual competitions. *No contest that charges the writer an entry or reading fee has been included.* Contests for both published and unpublished work are listed. Some competitions do not accept entries or nominations directly from writers; we've included them for their national or literary importance. If you feel that your writing meets the requirements of one of these competitions, tell your publisher/editor about the contest.

We've listed contests by name, address, contact person and type of competition. If a contest sounds interesting to you, send a self-addressed, stamped envelope to the contest contact person (if listed) for contest information and rules. In fact, don't enter any contest without seeking this information; some contests have very detailed instructions and requirements. In contests where writers' names must be concealed in a *titled* envelope, putting your name on the manuscript will disqualify it from consideration.

Another reason for studying contest rules is to find out if you are eligible. Not all contests are for everyone. There are contests for beginning writers and those for professionals; also contests for college and high school students only.

Contest rules will usually state what is meant by *professional* or *amateur* in a particular contest, since there are numerous connotations for these terms. If the rules are not clear, however, send a self-addressed, stamped envelope and note asking for clarification. You might pose a simple question in the note—"Am I eligible to enter your contest if I have sold one short story to *Family Circle*?"—with *yes* and *no* boxes, one of which the contest director could check as a response. Don't send or expect a lengthy letter. Some contests draw thousands of entries.

This year's *Writer's Market* includes a sampling of opportunities for writers interested in pursuing fellowships and grants for their writing projects. Fellowships may include stipends, writing residencies and/or cash awards to be used for professional advancement. Requirements and eligibilities are unique to each program. Funds for writers to practice their craft *are* available; the key is knowing where to look. Become familiar with these two resources available in most large public libraries: *Annual Register of Grant Support* (National Register Publishing Co., Inc., 3004 Glenview Rd., Wilmette IL 60091) and *Foundation Grants to Individuals* (Foundation Center, 79 5th Ave., New York, NY 10003). The former is a guide to grant and fellowship support programs in government, public and private foundations, companies, professional associations, and special interest groups. A detailed subject index will lead you to writing-related programs. The Foundation Center directory lists approximately 1,000 foundations and application procedures for grants offered to individuals. Included are scholarships, fellowships, residencies, grants to needy writers, and a bibliography of other funding information.

If you don't win the first contests or fellowships you apply for, don't get discouraged. Some entries can be so close in merit that judges must reread each one numerous times. In all contests, judges weigh what is said in an entry (content) *and* how it is said (form). Analyze the content and form of your writing *before* judges do.

AAAS SOCIO-PSYCHOLOGICAL PRIZE, American Association for the Advancement of Science, 1333 H. St. NW, Washington DC 20005. Assistant to the Executive Officer: C. Borras. Psychology/social sciences/sociology.

AAAS-WESTINGHOUSE SCIENCE JOURNALISM AWARDS, American Association for the Advancement of Science, 1515 Massachusetts Ave. NW, Washington DC 20005. (202)467-4483. Administrator: Grayce A. Finger. Science, technology and engineering (newspaper, magazine, radio and TV).

ACTF STUDENT PLAYWRITING AWARDS, Producing Director, American College Theatre Festival, John F. Kennedy Center for the Performing Arts, Washington DC 20566. (202)254-3437. Student written play produced by participating college.

‡**MAUDE ADAMS PLAYWRITING COMPETITION**, Stephens College, Columbia MO 65215. (314)876-7193. Artistic Director: Addison Myers. Estab. 1984-85. Full-length plays written by women, dealing with women's issues, with leading roles for women.

AID TO INDIVIDUAL ARTISTS FELLOWSHIP, Ohio Arts Council, 727 E. Main St., Columbus OH 43205. (614)466-2613. Contact: Susan Dickson. Nonfiction, fiction, criticism, poetry and plays. (Ohio resident, nonstudent).

ALBERTA NEW NOVELIST COMPETITION, Alberta Culture, Film and Literary Arts, 12th Fl., CN Tower, Edmonton, Alberta T5J 0K5 Canada. (403)427-2554. Open only to unpublished Alberta resident authors.

ALBERTA NON-FICTION AWARD, Alberta Culture, Film and Literary Arts, 12 Fl., CN Tower, Edmonton, Alberta T5J 0K5 Canada. (403)427-2554. Nonfiction book by Alberta author published in calendar year.

THE NELSON ALGREN AWARD, *Chicago* Magazine, 3 Illinois Center, 303 E. Wacker Dr., Chicago IL 60601. (312)565-5000. Award Director: Christine Newman. Unpublished short story.

‡**THE AMERICAN BOOK AWARDS**, Before Columbus Foundation, Suite D, 1446 6th St., Berkeley CA 94710. (415)527-1586. Director: Gundars Strads. Previously published books by contemporary American authors.

‡**AMERICAN MINORITY PLAYWRIGHT'S FESTIVAL**, The Group Theatre Company, 3940 Brooklyn Ave. NE, Seattle WA 98105. (206)545-4969. Director: Ruben Sierra. Estab. 1984. One-act and full-length plays by minority playrights.

AMERICAN-SCANDINAVIAN FOUNDATION/TRANSLATION PRIZE, American-Scandinavian Foundation, 127 E. 73rd St., New York NY 10021. (212)879-9779. Contact: Publishing Division. Contemporary Scandinavian fiction and poetry translations.

AMERICAN SPEECH-LANGUAGE-HEARING ASSOCIATION (ASHA), NATIONAL MEDIA AWARD, 10801 Rockville Pike, Rockville MD 20852. (301)897-5700. Speech-language pathology and audiology (radio, TV, newspaper, magazine).

‡**AMY WRITING AWARDS**, The Amy Foundation, Box 16091, Lansing MI 48901. (517)323-3181. President: James Russell. Previously published religious articles in the secular media.

‡**ANNUAL DELACORTE PRESS PRIZE FOR AN OUTSTANDING FIRST YOUNG ADULT NOVEL**, Delacorte Press Books for Young Readers, 245 E. 47th St., New York NY 10017. (212)605-3555. Unpublished contemporary young adult (fiction) book.

ANNUAL INTERNATIONAL NARRATIVE CONTEST, Poets and Patrons, Inc., 13942 Keeler Ave., Crestwood IL 60445. Chairman: Mary Mathison. Narrative poetry.

ANNUAL INTERNATIONAL POETRY CONTEST, Poet's Study Club of Terre Haute, Indiana, 826 S. Center, Terre Haute IN 47804. President: Esther Alman. Serious poetry, light verse, and traditional haiku.

‡**ANNUAL INTERNATIONAL SHAKESPEAREAN SONNET CONTEST**, The Poets' Club of Chicago, Agnes W. Tatera, 2546 Atlantic St., Franklin Park IL 60131. (312)455-4771. Chairman: Agnes W. Tatera. "Classic" Shakespearean sonnets.

THE ANNUAL NATIONAL BIBLE WEEK EDITORIAL CONTEST, The Laymen's National Bible Committee Inc., 815 2nd Ave., New York NY 10017. (212)687-0555. Contact: Executive Director. Unpublished editorial (journalism students only).

ANNUAL NATIONAL ONE ACT PLAYWRITING CONTEST, Dubuque Fine Arts Players, 1089 S. Grandview, Dubuque IA 52001. Contest Director: Cheri Kraska. Unpublished one-act plays.

‡**ANNUAL NJ POETRY CONTEST**, NJIT Alumni Association, NJ Institute of Technology, Newark NJ 07102. (201)596-3449. Contest/Award Director: Dr. Herman A. Estrin. Poetry by elementary, junior high, secondary, and college students.

RUBY LLOYD APSEY PLAYWRITING AWARD, University of Alabama, Department of Theater and Dance, University Station, Birmingham AL 35294. (215)934-3236. Contest Director: Dr. Rick J. Plummer. Unpublished full length plays by New American playwrights.

ASSOCIATION FOR EDUCATION IN JOURNALISM AWARDS, Magazine Division, Loyola College, Baltimore MD 21210. Professor of Journalism: Andrew Ciofalo. Unpublished nonfiction magazine article, research paper on magazine journalism, and magazine design.

‡**VINCENT ASTOR MEMORIAL LEADERSHIP ESSAY CONTEST**, U.S. Naval Institute, Prebel Hall, U.S. Naval Academy, Annapolis MD 21402. (301)268-6110. Award Director: James A. Barber, Jr. Essays on the topic of leadership (junior officers and officer trainees).

THE AUTHOR OF THE YEAR AWARD, American Society of Journalists and Authors, 1501 Broadway, New York NY 10036. (212)997-0947. Executive Secretary: Marci Vitous-Hurwood. Nonfiction book or body of work nominated by a member of ASJA.

THE AXIOS AWARD, Axios Newsletter, Inc., 800 S. Euclid Ave., Fullerton CA 92632. (714)526-2131. Contest/Award Director: Daniel John Gorham. Best article published in a daily or weekly secular newspaper about Orthodox Catholic religion in America.

‡**BALTIMORE PLAYWRIGHTS' FESTIVAL**, Baltimore Playwrights' Festival, 8530 Dogwood Rd., Baltimore MD 21207. (301)597-4709. Producer: Tim Evans. Plays by Baltimore playwrights.

‡**BANTA AWARD**, Wisconsin Library Association/Banta Foundation of the George Banta Company, Inc., 1922 University Ave., Madison WI 53705. (608)231-1513. Award Director: Faith B. Miracle, Administrator, WLA. Published book by a Wisconsin author published during the previous year.

THE ALTHEA BANTREE MYSTERY CONTEST, Winston-Derek Publishers, Box 90883, Nashville TN 37209. (615)329-1319; 356-7384. Contest/Award Director: James W. Peebles, publisher. Unpublished mystery book.

BITTERROOT MAGAZINE POETRY CONTEST, Contact: Menke Katz, Editor-in-Chief, *Bitterroot*, Spring Glen NY 12483. Poetry.

BLACK WARRIOR REVIEW LITERARY AWARDS, *Black Warrior Review*, The University of Alabama, Box 2936, University AL 35486. (205)348-4518. Contact: Editor. Unpublished poetry and fiction.

BOLLINGEN PRIZE IN POETRY OF THE YALE UNIVERSITY LIBRARY, Yale University Library, New Haven CT 06520. (203)436-0236. Secretary, Yale Administrative Committee: David E. Schoonover. American poetry (book).

BOWLING WRITING COMPETITION, American Bowling Congress, Public Relations, 5301 S. 76th St., Greendale WI 53129. Director: Dave DeLorenzo, Public Relations Manager. Feature, editorial, local association and news.

‡**JAMES W. BROWN PUBLICATION AWARD**, ECT Foundation, 1126 16th St. NW, Washington DC 20036. (202)466-4780. Director: Jerrold E. Kemp, Ph.D. "For an outstanding nonperiodic publication in the field of educational technology, bearing a 1984 or 1985 publication date." Not restricted to books or print.

‡**ARLEIGH BURKE ESSAY CONTEST**, U.S. Naval Institute, Prebel Hall, U.S. Naval Academy, Annapolis MD 21402. (301)268-6110. Award Director: James A. Barber, Jr. Essay on advancement of professional, literary, and scientific knowledge in the naval and maritime services.

‡**CALIFORNIA BOOK AWARDS CONTEST**, Commonwealth Club of California, 681 Market St., San Francisco CA 94105. (415)362-4903. Executive Director: Michael J. Brassington. Published books by California authors.

‡**CANADA COUNCIL CHILDREN'S LITERATURE PRIZE**, Canada Council, Box 1047, Ottawa, Ontario K1P 5V8 Canada. (613)237-3400. Contact: Katherine Berg. Awards to encourage published Canadian writers of children's books and illustrators of books for young people.

‡**CANADA COUNCIL TRANSLATION PRIZES**, Canada Council, Box 1047, Ottawa, Ontario K1P 5V8 Canada. (613)237-3400. Contact: Katherine Berg. The best translations of Canadian works: one for a translation from English into French and one for a translation from French into English. *The books must be written and translated by Canadians.*

‡**CANADA-AUSTRALIA LITERARY PRIZE**, Canada Council, Box 1047, Ottawa, Ontario K1P 5V8 Canada. (613)237-3400. Head of Writing and Publishing Section: Naim Kattan. Awarded annually in alternate years to an English-language Australian or Canadian writer for the author's complete works.

‡**CANADA-FRENCH COMMUNITY OF BELGIUM LITERARY PRIZE**, Canada Council, Box 1047, Ottawa, Ontario K1P 5V8 Canada. (613)237-3400. Head of Writing and Publishing Section: Naim Kattam. Awarded annually in alternate years to a French-language Belgian or Canadian writer for the author's complete works.

‡**CANADA-SWITZERLAND LITERARY PRIZE**, Canada Council, Box 1047, Ottawa, Ontario K1P 5V8 Canada. (613)237-3400. Head of Writing and Publishing Section: Naim Kattan. Awarded annually in alternate years to a Canadian or Swiss writer for a work of poetry, fiction, drama or nonfiction published in French during the preceding eight years.

‡**MELVILLE CANE AWARD**, Poetry Society of America, 15 Gramercy Park S., New York NY 10003. (212)254-9268. Award Director: Dennis Stone. Published book of poems or prose work on a poet or poetry. Publishers only may submit.

RUSSELL L. CECIL ARTHRITIS WRITING AWARDS, Arthritis Foundation, 1314 Spring St. NW, Atlanta GA 30309. (404)872-7100. Contact: Public Relations Department. Medical and features (news stories, articles, and radio/TV scripts).

CHAMPION TUCK AWARDS, Administered by: The Amos Tuck School of Business Administration, Dartmouth College, Hanover NH 03755. (603)643-5596. Contest/Award Director: Ms. Jan Brigham Bent. Business and economics (newspapers, magazines, syndicates, wire services, TV and radio).

CHILDREN'S SCIENCE BOOK AWARDS, New York Academy of Sciences, 2 E. 63rd St., New York NY 10021. (212)838-0230. Public Relations Director: Ann E. Collins. General or trade science books for children under 17 years.

‡**GERTRUDE B. CLAYTOR MEMORIAL AWARD**, Poetry Society of America, 15 Gramercy Park S., New York NY 10003. (212)254-9628. Award Director: Dennis Stone. Poem in any form on the American scene or character. Members only.

‡**FRANK AND ETHEL S. COHEN AWARD**, National Jewish Book Awards—Jewish Thought, Jewish Book Council, 15 E. 26th St., New York NY 10010. (212)532-4949. Director: Ruth S. Frank. Work dealing with some aspect of Jewish thought.

COLLEGIATE POETRY CONTEST, *The Lyric*, 307 Dunton Dr. SW, Blacksburg VA 24060. Editor: Leslie Mellichamp. Unpublished poems (32 lines or less) by fulltime undergraduates in 4-year U.S. or Canadian colleges.

THE BERNARD F. CONNERS PRIZE FOR POETRY, *The Paris Review*, 541 E. 72nd St., New York NY 10021. Poetry Editor: Editorial Office. Unpublished poetry over 300 lines.

ALBERT B. COREY PRIZE IN CANADIAN-AMERICAN RELATIONS, Office of the Executive Director, American Historical Association, 400 A St. SE, Washington DC 20003. History, Canadian-U.S. relations or history of both countries (book).

‡**GUSTAV DAVIDSON MEMORIAL AWARD**, Poetry Society of America, 15 Gramercy Park S., New York NY 10003. (212)254-9628. Award Director: Dennis Stone. Sonnet or sequence in traditional forms. Members only.

‡**MARY CAROLYN DAVIES MEMORIAL AWARD**, Poetry Society of America, 15 Gramercy Park S., New York NY 10003. (212)254-9628. Award Director: Dennis Stone. Unpublished poem suitable for setting to music. Members only.

‡**ALICE FAY DI CASTAGNOLA AWARD**, Poetry Society of America, 15 Gramercy Park S., New York NY 10003. (212)254-9628. Award Director: Dennis Stone. Manuscript in progress: poetry, prose on poetry or verse-drama. Members only.

‡**EMILY DICKINSON AWARD**, Poetry Society of America, 15 Gramercy Park S., New York NY 10003. (212)254-9628. Award Director: Dennis Stone. Poem inspired by Emily Dickinson. Members only.

EDUCATOR'S AWARD, Box 1589, Austin TX 78767. Executive Director: Delta Kappa Gamma Society International. Education, teaching (book by woman or 2 women from country in which Society is established).

‡**WILLIAM AND JANICE EPSTEIN AWARD**, National Jewish Book Award—Fiction, Jewish Book Council, 15 E. 26th St., New York NY 10010. (212)532-4949. Director: Ruth S. Frank. Novel or collection of short stories of Jewish interest.

‡**MARIE-LOUISE ESTERNAUX POETRY SCHOLARSHIP CONTEST**, The Brooklyn Poetry Circle, 61 Pierrepont St., Brooklyn NY 11201. (718)875-8736. Contest Chairman: Gabrielle Lederer. Poetry by students.

JOHN K. FAIRBANK PRIZE IN EAST ASIAN HISTORY, Committee Chairman, American Historical Association, 400 A St. SE, Washington DC 20003. Book on East Asian history.

‡**NORMA FARBER FIRST BOOK AWARD**, Poetry Society of America, 15 Gramercy Park S., New York NY 10003. (212)254-9628. Award Director: Dennis Stone. Estab. 1984. Book of original poetry. Publishers only.

‡**FOLIO FICTION/POETRY AWARDS**, Folio, Dept. of Literature , American University, Washington DC 20016. (202)885-2971. Director: Ziba Rashidian. Estab. 1984. Fiction and poetry.

‡**CONSUELO FORD AWARD**, Poetry Society of America, 15 Gramercy Park S., New York NY 10003. (212)254-9628. Award Director: Dennis Stone. Unpublished lyric. Members only.

THE FORUM AWARD, Atomic Industrial Forum, 7101 Wisconsin Ave., Bethesda MA 20814. Contest Coordinator: Gloria Brooks. Nuclear energy (print and electronic media).

GLCA NEW WRITERS AWARDS IN POETRY AND FICTION, Great Lakes Colleges Association, Albion College, Albion MI 49224. (517)629-3030. Director: James W. Cook. Published poetry or fiction.

GUIDEPOSTS MAGAZINE YOUTH WRITING CONTEST, Guideposts Associates, Inc., 747 3rd Ave., New York NY 10017. Senior Editor: MaryAnn O'Roark. Memorable true experience of 1,200 words, preferably spiritual in nature. Unpublished first person story by high school juniors or seniors or students in equivalent grades overseas.

NATE HASELTINE MEMORIAL FELLOWSHIPS IN SCIENCE WRITING, Council for the Advancement of Science Writing, Inc., 618 North Elmwood, Oak Park IL 60302. Executive Director: William J. Cromie. Science journalism.

‡**ERNEST AND LEICESTER HEMINGWAY JOURNALISM AWARDS**, The Hemingway Days Festival, % Doug Edelstein, 325 N. 82nd St., Seattle WA 98103. (206)783-8295. Director: Doug Edelstein. Estab. 1985. News features, news, sports and arts reporting, and photojournalism by students.

ERNEST HEMINGWAY FOUNDATION AWARD, P.E.N. American Center, 568 Broadway, New York NY 10012. First-published novel or short story collection by American author.

‡**CECIL HEMLEY MEMORIAL AWARD**, Poetry Society of America, 15 Gramercy Park S., New York NY 10003. (212)254-9628. Award Director: Dennis Stone. Unpublished lyric poem on a philosophical theme. Members only.

SIDNEY HILLMAN PRIZE AWARD, Sidney Hillman Foundation, Inc., 15 Union Square, New York NY 10003. (212)242-0700. Executive Director: Joyce D. Miller. Social/economic themes related to ideals of Sidney Hillman (daily or periodical journalism, nonfiction, radio and TV).

HONOLULU MAGAZINE FICTION CONTEST, *Honolulu Magazine*, 35 Merchant St., Honolulu HI 96813. Contact: Pat Pitzer. Stories under 25 typewritten pages with a Hawaiian theme, setting and/or characters.

HOW-TO-DO-IT CONTEST, The Krantz Company Publishers, Inc., 2210 N. Burling, Chicago IL 60614. (312)472-4900. Publisher: Les Krantz. Reference book material (original question-and-answer combinations, or questions only and answers only).

‡**THE ROY W. HOWARD AWARDS**, The Scripps-Howard Foundation, 1100 Central Trust Tower, Cincinnati OH 45202. (513)977-3037. Public service reporting.

‡**ILLINOIS STATE FINE ARTS PLAYWRITING AWARD**, Illinois State University, Theatre Department, Normal IL 61761. (309)438-8783. Directors: Dr. John W. Kirk and Daniel Wilhelm. Previously unproduced full-length plays. Award plus production of winning play.

INTERNATIONAL FILM LITERATURE AWARDS, International Film Literature Society, Box 12193, La Jolla CA 92037. Narrative, criticism and technical.

INTERNATIONAL IMITATION HEMINGWAY COMPETITION, Harry's Bar & American Grill, 2020 Avenue of the Stars, Los Angeles CA 90067. (213)277-2333. Contest/Award Director: Mark S. Grody, Grody/Tellem Communications, Inc., Suite 200, 9100 S. Sepulveda Blvd., Los Angeles CA 90045. (213)417-3038. Unpublished one-page parody of Hemingway.

‡**INTERNATIONAL READING ASSOCIATION CHILDREN'S BOOK AWARD**, International Reading Association, Box 8139, 800 Barksdale Rd., Newark DE 19714-8139. (302)731-1600. Director: IRA Children's Book Award Subcommittee. First or second children's book (fiction or nonfiction).

INTERNATIONAL SHAKESPEAREAN SONNET CONTEST, 2546 Atlantic, Franklin Park IL 60131. Contest Chairman: Agnes Wathall Tatera. Unpublished Shakespearean sonnet by nonmembers of Poets Club of Chicago.

‡**IOWA ARTS COUNCIL LITERARY AWARDS**, Iowa Arts Council, State Capitol Complex, Des Moines IA 50319. (515)281-4451. Director: Iowa Arts Council. Estab. 1984. Unpublished fiction and poetry by Iowa writers (legal residents).

IOWA SCHOOL OF LETTERS AWARD FOR SHORT FICTION, Iowa School of Letters, Department of English/EPB, University of Iowa, Iowa City IA 52242. (319)353-3181. Award Director: John Leggett. Unpublished collection of short stories.

JOSEPH HENRY JACKSON/JAMES D. PHELAN LITERARY AWARDS, 8th Floor, 500 Washington St., San Francisco CA 94111. (415)392-0600. Assistant Coordinator: Susan Kelly. Jackson: unpublished, partly completed book-length fiction, nonfiction, short story or poetry by author with 3-year consecutive residency in N. California or Nevada prior to submissions. Age 20-35. Phelan: unpublished, incomplete work of fiction, nonfiction, short story, poetry or drama by California-born author. Age 20-35.

JACKSONVILLE UNIVERSITY PLAYWRITING CONTEST, College of Fine Arts, Jacksonville University, Jacksonville FL 32211. (904)744-3950. Director: Davis Sikes. Unproduced one-act and full-length plays.

ANSON JONES AWARD, c/o Texas Medical Association, 1801 N. Lamar Blvd., Austin TX 78701. (512)477-6704. Health (Texas newspaper, magazine, radio and TV).

‡**MARGO JONES PLAYWRITING COMPETITION**, Texas Woman's University, Department of Music & Drama, Box 23865, Denton TX 76204. (817)383-3586. Contest Chairman: Lewis Shena. Every other year. Unproduced plays for or about women.

‡**JUVENILE BOOK AWARDS**, Friends of American Writers, Box 1051, Park Ridge IL 60068. (312)527-1715. Award Director: Jean Morrison. Published juvenile book.

THE JANET HEIDINGER KAFKA PRIZE, English Department/Writers Workshop, 127 Lattimore Hall, University of Rochester, Rochester NY 14627. (716)275-2344. Chairman: Prof. Rowland L. Collins. Administrative Secretary: Patty Miller. Book-length fiction (novel, short story or experimental writing) by U.S. woman citizen submitted by publishers.

‡**KALEIDOSCOPE INTERNATIONAL POETRY, FICTION, AND ART AWARDS**, United Cerebral Palsy and Services for the Handicapped, 326 Locust St., Akron OH 44302. (216)762-9755, ext. 474 or 475. Contest/Award Director: Gail Willmott. Unpublished poetry, fiction and art by professional and amateur writers and artists with disabilities.

THE AGA KHAN PRIZE FOR FICTION, Editorial Office, *The Paris Review*, 541 E. 72nd St., New York NY 10021. Unpublished short story.

MARC A. KLEIN PLAYWRITING AWARD, Department of Theatre, Case Western Reserve University, 2070 Adelbert Rd., Cleveland OH 44106. (216)368-2858. Unpublished, professionally unproduced full length plays, evening of related short plays, or full length musical by students in American college or university.

‡**KNOWLEDGE INDUSTRY PUBLICATIONS, INC. AWARD FOR LIBRARY LITERATURE**, donated by Knowledge Industry Publications, Inc., Administered by American Library Association, 50 E. Huron, Chicago IL 60611. (312)944-6780. Outstanding contribution to library literature.

‡**SARAH H. KUSHNER MEMORIAL AWARD**, National Jewish Book Award—Scholarship, Jewish Book Council, 15 E. 26th St., New York NY 10010. (212)532-4949. Director: Ruth S. Frank. Book which makes an original contribution to Jewish learning.

‡**RUTH LAKE MEMORIAL AWARD**, Poetry Society of America, 15 Gramercy Park S., New York NY 10003. (212)254-9628. Award Director: Dennis Stone. Estab. 1984. Unpublished poem of retrospection.

LAMONT POETRY SELECTION, Academy of American Poets, 177 E. 87th St., New York NY 10128. (212)427-5665. Contest/Award Director: Nancy Schoenberger. Second book of poems, unpublished and submitted by publisher in manuscript form. (American citizens.)

STEPHEN LEACOCK AWARD FOR HUMOUR, The Stephen Leacock Associates, Box 854, Orillia, Ontario L3V 6K8 Canada. (705)325-6546. Chairman of Award Committee: Mrs. Jean Dickson. Humorous works by Canadian authors.

NORMAN LEAR AWARD FOR ACHIEVEMENT IN COMEDY PLAYWRITING, Producing Director, American College Theatre Festival, John F. Kennedy Center for the Performing Arts, Washington DC 20566. (202)254-3437. Plays produced by participating ACTF college or university.

JERRY LEWIS/MDA WRITING AWARDS, Craig H. Wood, Director, Department of Public Health Education, Muscular Dystrophy Association, 810 7th Ave., New York NY 10019. Works contributing to public understanding of muscular dystrophy and related neuromuscular diseases (all print media).

‡**ELIAS LIEBERMAN STUDENT POETRY AWARD**, Poetry Society of America, 15 Gramercy Park S., New York NY 10003. (212)254-9628. Award Director: Dennis Stone. Unpublished poem by student (grades 9-12).

‡**JOSEPH W. LIPPINCOTT AWARD**, Donated by Joseph W. Lippincott, Jr., Administered by American Library Association, 50 E. Huron, Chicago IL 60611. (312)944-6780. For distinguished service to the profession of librarianship (notable published professional writing).

‡**LOFT-MCKNIGHT WRITERS AWARD**, The Loft, 2301 E. Franklin Ave., Minneapolis MN 55406. (612)341-0431. Director: Susan Broadhead. Poetry and Creative Prose. Eight awards for Minnesota writers.

‡**LOFT-MENTOR SERIES**, The Loft, 2301 Franklin Ave., Minneapolis MN 55406. (612)341-0431. Director: Susan Broadhead. Poetry and fiction by Minnesota writers.

‡**LENORE MARSHALL POETRY PRIZE**, The New Hope Foundation, Inc. and *The Nation*, 445 Park Ave., New York NY 10022. (212)702-2311. Award Director: Harold Taylor. Write *The Nation*, 72 5th Ave., New York NY 10011. Previously published poetry.

‡**JOHN MASEFIELD MEMORIAL AWARD**, Poetry Society of America, 15 Gramercy Park S., New York NY 10003. (212)254-9628. Award Director: Dennis Stone. Unpublished narrative poem in English.

MASSACHUSETTS ARTISTS FELLOWSHIP, The Artists Foundation, Inc., 110 Broad St., Boston MA 02110. (617)482-8100. Funded by the Massachusetts Council on the Arts and Humanities. Director: Lucine A. Folgueras. Poetry, fiction, nonfiction and playwriting. (Massachusetts residents.)

‡**LUCILLE MEDWICK MEMORIAL AWARD**, Poetry Society of America, 15 Gramercy Park S., New York NY 10003. (212)254-9628. Award Director: Dennis Stone. Original poem on a humanitarian theme. Members only.

‡**THE EDWARD J. MEEMAN AWARDS**, The Scripps-Howard Foundation, 1100 Central Trust Tower, Cincinnati, OH 45202. (513)977-3037. Conservation Reporting.

MELCHER BOOK AWARD, Unitarian Universalist Association, 25 Beacon St., Boston MA 02108. Staff Liaison: Rev. Mark W. Harris. Religious liberalism (book).

MENCKEN AWARDS, Free Press Association, Box 1743, Apple Valley CA 92307. (415)834-6880. Contest/Award Director: Jeff Riggenbach. FPA Executive Director: Michael Grossberg, (619)242-4899. Defense of human rights and individual liberties (news story or investigative report, feature story, essay or review, editorial or op-ed column, editorial cartoon; and book).

KENNETH W. MILDENBERGER MEDAL, Modern Language Association, 62 5th Ave., New York NY 10011. Teaching foreign language and literatures (book or article).

JAMES MOONEY AWARD, The University of Tennessee Press/The Southern Anthropological Society, Department of Anthropology, University of North Carolina, Greensboro NC 27412. Contact: Harriet J. Kupferer. Unpublished book-lengh ms describing and interpreting New World people or culture—prehistoric, historic or contemporary.

FRANK LUTHER MOTT-KAPPA TAU ALPHA RESEARCH AWARD IN JOURNALISM, 107 Sondra Ave., Columbia MO 65202. (314)443-3521. Chief, Central Office: William H. Taft. Research in journalism (book).

MS PUBLIC EDUCATION AWARDS CONTEST, National Multiple Sclerosis Society, 205 E. 42nd St., New York NY 10017. Contact: Public Relations Director. Reporting on facts and consequences of multiple sclerosis (newspaper, magazine, radio or TV).

‡**NATIONAL JEWISH BOOK AWARD—BIOGRAPHY**, Dr. Moses Leo Gitelson Award, Jewish Book Council, 15 E. 26th St., New York NY 10010. (212)532-4949. Director: Ruth S. Frank. Book about a Jew who has made a contribution to the Jewish people.

NATIONAL JEWISH BOOK AWARD—CHILDREN'S LITERATURE, William (Zev) Frank Memorial Award, Jewish Book Council, 15 E. 26th St., New York NY 10010. (212)532-4949. Director: Ruth S. Frank. Children's book on Jewish theme.

NATIONAL JEWISH BOOK AWARD—FICTION, William and Janice Epstein Award, 15 E. 26th St., New York NY 10010. (212)532-4949. Director: Ruth S. Frank. Jewish fiction (novel or short story collection).

NATIONAL JEWISH BOOK AWARD—HOLOCAUST, Leon Jolson Award, Jewish Book Council, 15 E. 26th St., New York NY 10010. (212)532-4949. Director: Ruth S. Frank. Nonfiction book concerning the Holocaust.

‡**NATIONAL JEWISH BOOK AWARD—ILLUSTRATED CHILDREN'S BOOK**, Marcia and Louis Posner Award, Jewish Book Council, 15 E. 26th St., New York NY 10010. (212)532-4949. Director: Ruth S. Frank. Author and illustrator of a children's book on a Jewish theme.

‡**NATIONAL JEWISH BOOK AWARD—ISRAEL**, Morris J. Kaplun Memorial Award, Jewish Book Council, 15 E. 26th St., New York NY 10010. (212)532-4949. Director: Ruth S. Frank. Nonfiction work about the State of Israel.

‡**NATIONAL JEWISH BOOK AWARD—JEWISH HISTORY**, Gerrard and Ella Berman Award, Jewish Book Council, 15 E. 26th St., New York NY 10010. (212)532-4949. Director: Ruth S. Frank. Book of Jewish history.

NATIONAL JEWISH BOOK AWARD—JEWISH THOUGHT, Frank & Ethel S. Cohen Award, 15 E. 26th St., New York NY 10010. (212)532-4949. Director: Ruth S. Frank. Book dealing with some aspect of Jewish thought, past or present.

‡**NATIONAL JEWISH BOOK AWARD—SCHOLARSHIP**, Sarah H. Kushner Memorial Award, Jewish Book Council, 15 E. 26th St., New York NY 10010. (212)532-4949. Director: Ruth S. Frank. Book which makes an original contribution to Jewish learning.

‡**NATIONAL JEWISH BOOK AWARD—VISUAL ARTS**, Jewish Book Council, 15 E. 26th St., New York NY 10010. (212)532-4949. Director: Ruth S. Frank. Book about Jewish art.

‡**NATIONAL JEWISH BOOK AWARD—YIDDISH LITERATURE**, The Workmen's Circle Award, Jewish Book Council, 15 E. 26th St., New York NY 10010. (212)532-4949. Director: Ruth S. Frank. Book of literary merit in the Yiddish language.

‡**NATIONAL ONE-ACT PLAY CONTEST**, (formerly Great American Play Contest), Actors Theatre of Louisville, 316 W. Main St., Louisville KY 40202. (502)584-1265. Director: Julie Crutcher. Previously unproduced (professionally) one-act plays. "Entries must *not* have had an Equity or Equity-waiver production."

NATIONAL PLAY AWARD, Box 71011, Los Angeles CA 90071. (213)629-3762. Assistant Literary Manager: Emily Schiller. Unpublished, nonprofessionally produced plays.

NATIONAL PLAYWRIGHT COMPETITION, Unicorn Theatre, 3514 Jefferson, Kansas City MO 64111. (816)531-7529. Unpublished, unproduced plays. (U.S. residents only.)

NATIONAL SOCIETY OF PROFESSIONAL ENGINEERS JOURNALISM AWARDS, 1420 King St., Alexandria VA 22314. (703)684-2852. PR Director: Leslie Collins. Engineering and technology in contemporary life (articles in general interest magazines and newspapers).

ALLAN NEVINS PRIZE, Professor Kenneth T. Jackson, Secretary-Treasurer, Society of American Historians, 610 Fayerweather Hall, Columbia University, New York NY 10027. American history (nominated doctoral dissertations on arts, literature, science and American biographies).

‡**NEW PLAY FESTIVAL**, Colony/Studio Theatre, 1944 Riverside Dr., Los Angeles CA 90039. Award Director: Theresa Bailey. Estab. 1984. Unpublished, unproduced play. Send SASE.

NEW WRITERS AWARDS, Great Lakes Colleges Association, c/o English Department, Albion College, Albion MI 49224. (517)629-3030. Director: James W. Cook. Poetry or fiction (first book).

NEW YORK STATE HISTORICAL ASSOCIATION MANUSCRIPT AWARD, Box 800, Cooperstown NY 13326. (607)547-2508. Director of Publications: Dr. Wendell Tripp. Unpublished book-length monograph on New York State history.

NEWCOMEN AWARDS IN BUSINESS HISTORY, c/o *Business History Review*, Harvard Business University, Gallatin D-126, Soldiers Field, Boston MA 02163. (617)495-6154. Editor: Richard S. Tedlow. Business history article.

NMMA DIRECTORS AWARD, National Marine Manufacturers Association, 353 Lexington Ave., New York NY 10016. (212)684-6622. Boating and allied water sports.

NORTH AMERICAN ESSAY CONTEST FOR YOUNG MEN AND WOMEN OF GOODWILL, *The Humanist Magazine*, 7 Harwood Dr., Box 146, Amherst NY 14226. (716)839-5080. Contest/Award Director: Lloyd Morain. Unpublished essay by writers age 29 or younger.

OGLEBAY INSTITUTE, TOWNGATE THEATRE PLAYWRITING CONTEST, Oglebay Park, Wheeling WV 26003. (304)242-4200. Contest Director: Jennifer Coffield. Unpublished, nonprofessionally produced full length plays.

OPEN CIRCLE THEATRE PLAYWRIGHTS AWARD, Goucher College, Towson MD 21204. Director: Barry Knower. Unpublished, unproduced plays. (50% of major roles must be for women.)

THE C.F. ORVIS WRITING CONTEST, The Orvis Company, Inc., Manchester VT 05254. (802)362-3622. Contest/Award Director: Tom Rosenbauer. Outdoor writing about upland bird hunting and fly fishing (magazine and newspaper).

OSCARS IN AGRICULTURE, DeKalb AgResearch, Inc., Sycamore Rd., DeKalb IL 60115. (815)758-3461. Director of Corporate Public Relations: Ron Scherer. Agricultural news reporting (newspaper, magazine, TV and radio).

FRANCIS PARKMAN PRIZE, Professor Kenneth T. Jackson, Secretary, Society of American Historians, 610 Fayerweather Hall, Columbia University, New York NY 10027. Colonial or national U.S. history (book).

‡**THE ALICIA PATTERSON FOUNDATION FELLOWSHIP PROGRAM FOR JOURNALISTS**, The Alicia Patterson Foundation, Suite 320, 655 15th St. NW, Washington DC 20005. (813)962-6060. Contest/Award Director: Helen McMaster Coulson. One-year grants awarded to working journalists with five year's experience to pursue independent projects of significant interest.

‡**PEN MEDAL FOR TRANSLATION**, PEN American Center, 568 Broadway, New York NY 10012. (212)334-1660. Translators nominated by the PEN Translation Committee.

‡**PEN/NELSON ALGREN FICTION AWARD**, PEN American Center, 568 Broadway, New York NY 10012. (212)334-1660. "For the best uncompleted novel or short story collection by an American writer who needs financial assistance to finish the work."

‡**PEN PUBLISHER CITATION**, PEN American Center, 568 Broadway, New York NY 10012. (212)334-1660. "Awarded every two years to a publisher who has throughout his career, given distinctive and continuous service." Nominated by the PEN Executive Board.

‡**PEN/ROGER KLEIN AWARD FOR EDITING**, PEN American Center, 568 Broadway, New York NY 10012. (212)334-1660. "Given every two years to an editor of trade books who has an outstanding record of recognizing talents." Nominated by authors, agents, publishers and editors.

‡**PEN/SOUTHWEST HOUSTON DISCOVERY AWARDS**, Pen/Southwest, Dept. of English, University of Houston, Houston TX 77004. Poetry and fiction. Six month (at least) residents of Houston/Metro area with unpublished (book form) work.

‡**PEN SYNDICATED FICTION PROJECT**, Box 6303, Washington DC 20015. (301)229-0933. Director: Richard Harteis. Short fiction.

PEN TRANSLATION PRIZE, PEN American Center, 568 Broadway, New York NY 10012. Contact: Chairman, Translation Committee. Book-length translation into English. (No technical, scientific or reference.)

‡**PEN WRITING AWARDS FOR PRISONERS**, PEN American Center, 568 Broadway, New York NY 10012. (212)334-1660. "Awarded to the authors of the best poetry, plays, short fiction and nonfiction received from prison writers in the U.S."

THE MAXWELL PERKINS PRIZE, Charles Scribner's Sons, 115 5th Ave., New York NY 10003. (212)614-1300. Unpublished non-genre fiction (first novel).

PLAYWRITING FOR CHILDREN AWARD, Community Children's Theatre, 8021 E. 129th Terrace, Grandview MO 64030. (816)761-5775. Unpublished plays for grades 1-6.

‡**RENATO POGGIOLI TRANSLATION AWARD**, PEN American Center, 568 Broadway, New York NY 10012. (212)334-1660. "Given to encourage a beginning and promising translator who is working on a first book length translation from Italian into English."

PULITZER PRIZES, Secretary, The Pulitzer Prize Board, 702 Journalism, Columbia University, New York NY 10027. Awards for journalism, letters, drama and music in U.S. newspapers, and in literature, drama and music by Americans.

‡**PULP PRESS INTERNATIONAL 3-DAY NOVEL COMPETITION**, Pulp Press (Vancouver) Publishers, Suite 202, 986 Homer St., Vancouver, British Columbia V6R 2P1 Canada. (604)687-4233. Director: F.H. Eger. Novel written in three days.

ERNIE PYLE MEMORIAL AWARD, Scripps-Howard Foundation, 1100 Central Trust Tower, Cincinnati OH 45202. (513)977-3037. Human-interest reporting.

REAL ESTATE JOURNALISM ACHIEVEMENT COMPETITION, National Association of Realtors, 777 14th St. NW, Washington DC 20005. Contact: Lou Dombrowski or Dr. Paul Snider, Bradley University, Peoria IL 61625. Real estate reporting, writing and broadcasting.

RECREATION VEHICLE INDUSTRY ASSOCIATION DISTINGUISHED ACHIEVEMENT IN RV JOURNALISM AWARD, Recreation Vehicle Industry Assn., Box 2999, 1896 Preston White Dr., Reston VA 22090. (703)620-6003. National Director of Public Relations: Gary M. LaBella. RV industry.

‡**REDBOOK'S NEW SHORT STORY CONTEST**, Redbook Magazine, 224 W. 57th St., New York NY 10019. Fiction Editor: Kathy Sagan. Short stories by writers who have not previously published fiction in a major publication.

FOREST A. ROBERTS PLAYWRITING AWARD, In cooperation with Shiras Institute, Forest A. Roberts Theatre, Northern Michigan University, Marquette MI 49855. (906)227-2553. Award Director: Dr. James A. Panowski. Unpublished, unproduced plays.

‡**MARY ROBERTS RINEHART FUND**, George Mason University, Fairfax VA 22030. (703)323-2220. Address mail to Director, MRR Fund, Department of English. Nominated drama, poetry, fiction and nonfiction by beginning writers.

‡**THE CARL SANDBURG LITERARY ARTS AWARDS**, The Friends of the Chicago Public Library, 78 E. Washington St., Chicago IL 60611. (812)269-2922. Director; Lucia Adams. Chicago writers of fiction, nonfiction, poetry, and children's literature.

‡**SCHOLASTIC/SMITH-CORONA SHORT STORY WRITING AWARDS CONTEST**, Scholastic Inc., 730 Broadway, New York NY 10003. (212)505-3000. Fiction, nonfiction, poetry and drama (grades 7-12).

ROBERT LIVINGSTON SCHUYLER PRIZE, Committee Chairman, American Historical Association, 400 A St. SE, Washington DC 20003. Modern British, British Imperial, and British Commonwealth history by American citizen.

‡**THE CHARLES M. SCHULZ AWARD**, The Scripps-Howard Foundation, 1100 Central Trust Tower, Cincinnati OH 45202. (513)977-3037. Cartoonists.

SCIENCE-WRITING AWARD IN PHYSICS AND ASTRONOMY, Public Information Division, American Institute of Physics, 335 E. 45th St., New York NY 10017. Physics and astronomy work. (One award open to physicists, astronomers or members of AIP and affiliated societies, other award goes to professional writers in physics and astronomy.)

THE SCRIBNER CRIME NOVEL AWARD, Charles Scribner's Sons, 115 Fifth Ave., New York NY 10003. (212)614-1300. Unpublished first crime novel.

MINA P. SHAUGHNESSY MEDAL, Modern Language Association, 62 5th Ave., New York NY 10011. Research in teaching of English language and literature (book or article).

‡**SHELLEY MEMORIAL AWARD**, Poetry Society of America, 15 Gramercy Park S., New York NY 10003. (212)254-9628. Award Director: Dennis Stone. By nomination only to a living American poet.

SINCLAIR PRIZE FOR FICTION, Sinclair Research Ltd., Suite 800, 50 Staniford St., Boston MA 02114. (617)742-4826. Director: Mary Reinman. Full-length novel.

BRYANT SPANN MEMORIAL PRIZE, c/o History Dept., Indiana State University, Terre Haute IN 47809. Social criticism in the tradition of Eugene V. Debs.

‡**SPUR AWARDS (WESTERN WRITERS OF AMERICA, INC.)**, WWA, Box 1611, Laramie WI 82070. (307)742-3010. Director: Jean Mead. Ten categories of western: novel, historical novel, nonfiction book, juvenile nonfiction, juvenile fiction, nonfiction article, fiction short story, best TV script, movie screenplay, cover art. Also, Medicine Pipe Bearer's Award for best first novel.

STANLEY DRAMA AWARD, Wagner College, Staten Island NY 10301. (212)390-3256. Award Director: J.J. Boies. Unpublished and nonprofessionally produced plays by American playwrights.

‡**THE WALKER STONE AWARDS**, The Scripps-Howard Foundation, 1100 Central Trust Tower, Cincinnati OH 45202. (513)977-3037. Editorial writing.

JESSE STUART CONTEST, Seven, 3630 N.W. 22, Oklahoma City OK 73107-2893. Unpublished poems in the Jesse Stuart tradition.

MARVIN TAYLOR PLAYWRITING AWARD, (formerly *Cummings-Taylor Playwriting Award*), Sierra Repertory Theatre, Box 3030, Sonora CA 95370. (209)532-3120. Producing Director: Dennis C. Jones. Full-length plays.

‡**SYDNEY TAYLOR CHILDREN'S BOOK AWARDS**, Association of Jewish Libraries, #1512, 122 E. 42nd St., New York NY 10168. Contact: Chairperson of AJL Book Award Committee. Jewish picture book or upper elementary-level fiction.

THE TEN BEST "CENSORED" STORIES OF 1985, Project Censored—Sonoma State University, Rohnert Park CA 94928. (707)664-2149. Award Director: Carl Jensen, Ph.D. Current published, nonfiction stories of national social significance that have been overlooked or under-reported by the news media.

TOURNAMENT GAMING WRITING AWARDS, International Gaming Promotions, Inc., #107, 20201 Sherman Way, Canoga Park CA 91306. (800)426-4226/(818)998-2121. Senior Vice President, Marketing: John Romero. Tournament gaming (consumer magazine article).

‡**THE TRANSLATION CENTER AWARDS—NATIONAL & INTERNATIONAL**, The Translation Center, 307A Mathematics Bldg., Columbia University, New York NY 10027. (212)280-2305. Executive Director: Diane G.H. Cook. Outstanding translations of a book-length literary work.

UFO RESEARCH AWARD, Fund for UFO Research, Box 277, Mt. Rainier MD 20712. (301)779-8683. Contact: Executive Committee, Fund for UFO Research. Unscheduled cash awards for published works on UFO phenomena research or public education.

‡**CELIA B./WAGNER AWARD**, Poetry Society of America, 15 Gramercy Park St. S., New York NY 10003. (212)254-9628. Award Director: Dennis Stone. Unpublished poem.

EDWARD LEWIS WALLANT BOOK AWARD, Mrs. Irving Waltman, 3 Brighton Rd., West Hartford CT 06117. Published fiction with significance for the American Jew (novel or short stories).

WICHITA STATE UNIVERSITY PLAYWRITING CONTEST, Wichita State University Theatre, WSU, Box 31, Wichita KS 67208. (316)689-3185. Contest/Award Director: Bela Kiralyfalvi. Unpublished, unproduced one-act and full-length plays. (Graduate and undergraduate U.S. college students.)

BELL I. WILEY PRIZE, National Historical Society, 2245 Kohn Rd., Box 8200, Harrisburg PA 17105. (717)657-9555, ext. 3301. Civil War and Reconstruction nonfiction (book).

‡**WILLIAM CARLOS WILLIAMS AWARD**, Poetry Society of America, 15 Gramercy Park S., New York NY 10003. (212)254-9628. Award Director: Dennis Stone. Small press, nonprofit, or university press book of poetry submitted by publisher.

‡**THE EDWARD WILLIS SCRIPPS AWARD**, The Scripps-Howard Foundation, 1100 Central Trust Tower, Cincinnati OH 45202. (513)977-3037. Service to the First Amendment.

‡**H.W. WILSON LIBRARY PERIODICAL AWARD**, donated by H.W. Wilson Company, Administered by the American Library Association, 50 E. Huron, Chicago IL 60611. (312)944-6780. Periodical published by a local, state, or regional library, library group, or association in U.S. or Canada.

WISCONSIN ARTS BOARD FELLOWSHIP PROGRAM, 107 S. Butler St., Madison WI 53703. (608)266-0190. Director of Grants Programs. Awards for artistic works and activities for professional advancement. (Wisconsin writers.)

WORLD HUNGER MEDIA AWARDS, World Hunger Year/Kenny & Marianne Rogers, 350 Broadway, New York NY 10013. (212)226-2714. Director: Bill Ayres. Critical issues of domestic and world hunger (newspaper, periodical, film, TV, radio, photojournalism, book and cartoon, plus special achievement).

CAPTAIN DONALD T. WRIGHT AWARD, Southern Illinois University, Edwardsville IL 62026. Contact: John A. Regnell. Maritime transportation (newspaper and magazine, book, photos and photo essays, tapes, videotapes and films).

WRITER'S DIGEST CREATIVE WRITING COMPETITION, *Writer's Digest*, 9933 Alliance Rd., Cincinnati OH 45242. Unpublished article, short story, script and poetry.

WRITERS GUILD OF AMERICA WEST AWARDS, Allen Rivkin, Public Relations, Writers Guild of America West, 8955 Beverly Blvd., Los Angeles CA 90048. Scripts (screen, TV and radio). Members only.

‡**WRITERS OF THE FUTURE CONTEST**, L. Ron Hubbard, #343, 2210 Wilshire Blvd., Santa Monica CA 90403. (213)466-3310. Award Director: Fred Harris of Author Services, Inc. Unpublished science fiction and fantasy.

Appendix

The Business of Freelancing _____

The circumstance which gives authors
an advantage above all these great masters, is
this, that they can multiply their originals;
or rather, can make copies of their works,
to what number they please, which shall
be as valuable as the originals.
—Joseph Addison

Experienced freelancers will tell you this is a tough business, and it is. You have to invest time and money into proposals and manuscripts with no guarantees of acceptance. But the craft of writing also has advantages: You can research a subject and develop three stories using the research. You can sell second serial (reprint) rights to a story you sold last year.

Yes, this business where originals are as valuable as reproductions gives writers an edge, but this doesn't mean that editors want mass-produced photocopied, simultaneous and printout submissions. To be successful in this business, you must create *an original* (story, book, script) each time you write. You also must know the rules. Every profession has them. They may not be written rules, but every pro in the field knows them. The writing business is no different. Send a manuscript on yellow paper, and editors know you've been writing more for yourself than for readers. Whether you write books, gags, or short fiction, many of the same rules apply, like enclosing a self-addressed, stamped envelope with all submissions. This appendix includes these general rules of the writing trade. They are guidelines that publishing professionals follow—tips and treatments that editors expect you to know. Learn these rules first (they won't hinder your creativity), then call on editors (in writing, of course).

Manuscript Mechanics

Without manuscript mechanics, the most gifted work might get tossed aside by an editor who refuses to read hand-writing. A manuscript in a fancy typeface or with coffee-stained pages is no way to show your creativity. These basic rules will help you to submit your *creativity* in its best form to an editor.

Type of Paper. The paper you use must measure 8½x11 inches. That's a standard size and editors are adamant—they don't want offbeat colors and sizes.

There's a wide range of white, 8½x11 papers. The cheaper ones are wood content. They will suffice, but they are not recommended. Your best bet is a good 25 percent cotton fiber content paper. It has quality feel, smoothness, shows type neatly, and holds up under erasing. Editors almost unanimously discourage the use of erasable bond for manuscripts, as it tends to smear when handled. Don't use less than a 16-pound bond paper, and 20-pound is preferred.

File Copies. Always make a carbon or photocopy of your manuscript before you send the manuscript off to a publisher. You might want to make several photocopies while the original manuscript is fresh and crisp looking—as insurance against losing a submission in the mails, and as a means of circulating the same manuscript to other editors for reprint sales after the original has been accepted for publication. (Inform editors that the manuscript offered for reprint should *not* be used before it has first appeared in the original publication buying it, of course.) Some writers keep their original manuscript as a file copy, and submit a good-quality photocopy of the manuscript to an editor, with a personal note explaining that it is *not* a simultaneous or multiple submission. (The quality of photocopies varies from ones with gray streaks to those that look like the original manuscript. Visit print shops in your area until you find one with a copier that makes *perfect* copies.) Some writers tell the editor that he may toss the photocopied manuscript if it is of no interest to him, and reply with a self-addressed postcard (also enclosed). This costs a writer some photocopy expense, but saves on the postage bill—and may speed the manuscript review process in some editorial offices.

Type Characters. Another firm rule for manuscripts is to always type double space, using either elite or pica type. The slightly larger pica type is easier to read and many editors prefer it, but they don't object to elite. They *do* dislike (and often will refuse) hard-to-read or unusual typewritten characters, such as script, italics, Old English, all capitals, or unusual letter styles.

Page Format. Do not use a cover sheet; nor should you use a binder—unless you are submitting a play or television or movie script. Instead, in the upper left corner of page one list your name, address and phone number on four single-spaced lines. In the upper right corner, on three single-spaced lines, indicate the approximate word count for the manuscript, the rights you are offering for sale, and your copyright notice (© 1986 Chris Jones). It is *not* necessary to indicate that this is page one. Its format is self-evident.

Now, flip the lever to double-space and center the title in capital letters halfway down the page. To center, set the tabulator to stop in the exact left-right center of the page. Count the letters in the title (including spaces and punctuation) and backspace half that number. Centered one double-space under that, type "by" and centered one double-space under that, your name or pseudonym.

Now, after the title and byline block, drop down three double-spaces, paragraph indent and start your story.

Margins should be about 1¼ inches on all sides of each full page of typewritten manuscript. Paragraph indentation is five or six letter spaces, consistently.

On every page after the first, type your last name, a dash, and the page number in the upper left corner (page two, for example, would be: Jones—2). Then drop down two double-spaces and begin copy. If you are using a pseudonym, type your real name, followed by your pen name in parentheses, then a dash and the page number in the upper left corner of every page after page one. (page two, for example, would be: Jones (Smith)—2)

Carry on just as you have on the other pages after page one. After your last word and period on the final page, however, skip three double-spaces and then center the words "The End" or, more commonly, the old telegrapher's symbol—30—meaning the same thing.

If you are submitting novel chapters, leave one third of the first page of each chapter blank before typing the title. Subsequent pages should include in the upper

Jones--2

Title of Manuscript (optional)

Begin the second page, and all following pages, in this manner--
with a page-number line (as above) that includes your name, in case
loose manuscript pages get shuffled by mistake. You may include the
title of your manuscript or a shortened version of the title to identify
the Jones manuscript this page 2 belongs to.

Chris Jones
1234 My Street
Anytown, U.S.A.
Tel. 123/456-7890

About 3,000 words
First Serial Rights
©1986 Chris Jones

YOUR STORY OR NOVEL TITLE HERE

by
Chris Jones

The manuscript begins here—about halfway down the first page.
It should be cleanly typed, double spaced, using either elite or
pica type. Use one side of the paper only, and leave a margin of
about 1-1/4 inches on all four sides.

NEATNESS COUNTS. Here are sample pages of a manuscript ready for submission to an editor. If the author uses a pseudonym, it should be placed on the title page only in the byline position; the author's real name must always appear in the top left corner of the title page—for manuscript mailing and payment purposes. On subsequent pages, list the real name, then the pen name in parentheses, followed by a dash and the page number.

left margin the author's last name, a shortened form of the book's title, and a chapter number. Use arabic numerals for chapter titles.

How to Estimate Wordage. To estimate wordage, count the exact number of words on the first three pages of your manuscript (in manuscripts up to 25 pages), divide the total by 3 and multiply the result by the number of pages. Carry the total to the nearest 100 words. For example, if you have a 12-page manuscript with totals of 303, 316 and 289 words on the first three pages, divide your total of 908 by 3 to get 302. Now multiply 302 x 12 pages and you get 3,624. Your approximate wordage, therefore, will be 3,600 words. On manuscripts over 25 pages, count five pages instead of three, then follow the same process, dividing by 5 instead of 3.

Special Points to Remember. Always use a good, dark black (*not* colored) typewriter ribbon and clean your keys frequently. If the enclosures in the letters a, b, d, e, g, etc. get inked-in, your keys need cleaning. Keep your manuscript neat *always*. Occasional retyping over erasures is acceptable, but strikeovers are bad and give a manuscript a sloppy, careless appearance. Large white-out splotches (to hide typos) make your work look amateurish. Sloppy typing is viewed by many editors as a hint of sloppy work habits—and the likelihood of careless research and writing. Strive for a clean, professional-looking manuscript that reflects pride in your work.

Computer-related Submissions. Because of the increased efficiency they afford the writing, revising and editing process, computers (word processors) are a tool of the writing trade. Hard-copy computer printouts and disk submissions are the result of the computer revolution's impact on writers.

Most editors are receptive to computer printout submissions if the type produces letter-quality; double-spaced with wide margins; and generally easy-to-read pages. Fewer editors at this point are ready to accept disk submissions because some computer systems are not compatible with others. Manuscripts submitted in disk form will likely become more popular with writers and editors as the interfacing of equipment becomes more sophisticated. Those editors who welcome disk submissions often request that a hard copy of the manuscript accompany the disk and that the writer make prior arrangements before submitting a disk.

Many listings in this edition of *Writer's Market* include information about computer-related submissions. If no information is given, it usually means the editor will not accept computer-related submissions. Check with an editor before sending a computer printout or disk submission.

Mailing Your Manuscript. Except when working on assignment from a magazine, or when under contract to do a book for a publisher, always enclose a self-addressed return envelope and the correct amount of postage with your manuscript. Manuscript pages should be held together with a paper clip only—never stapled together. When submitting poetry, the poems should be typed single space (double space between stanzas), one poem per page. Long poems requiring more than a page should be on sheets paper-clipped together.

Most editors won't object if manuscripts under six pages are folded in thirds and letter-mailed. However, there is a marked *preference* for flat mailing (in large envelopes) of manuscripts of six or more pages. You will need two 9x12 gummed or clasped mailing envelopes: one for the return of the manuscript and any accompanying material, and another to send out the manuscript, photos and return envelope. It is acceptable to fold the 9x12 return envelope in half to fit inside the outer envelope. To prevent accidental loss of stamps, affix—don't paperclip—them to the return envelope.

Mark your envelope, as desired with FIRST CLASS MAIL, or SPECIAL FOURTH CLASS RATE: MANUSCRIPT. First Class mail costs more but ensures better handling and faster delivery. Special Fourth Class mail is handled the same as Parcel Post, so wrap it well. Also, the Special Fourth Class Rate only applies in the U.S., and to manuscripts that weigh one pound or more (otherwise, there is no price break).

For lighter weight manuscripts, First Class mail is recommended because of the better speed and handling. First Class mail is handled the same as Air Mail and is forwarded or returned automatically; however, Special Fourth Class Rate mail is not.

To make sure you get your submission back if undeliverable, print "Return Postage Guaranteed" under your return address.

For foreign publications and publishers, including the Canadian markets, always enclose an International Reply Coupon (IRC), determined by the weight of the manuscript at the post office.

Insurance is available, but payable only on typing fees or the tangible value of what is in the package, i.e., writing paper, so your best insurance is to keep a copy of what you send.

Cover Letters. At the Special Fourth Class rate, you may enclose a personal letter with your manuscript, but you must also add enough First Class postage to cover the letter and mark FIRST CLASS LETTER ENCLOSED on the outside.

In most cases, a brief cover letter is helpful in personalizing the submission. Nothing you say will make the editor decide in your favor (the manuscript must stand by itself in that regard), so don't use the letter to make a sales pitch. Tell an editor (concisely) something about yourself, your publishing history, or any particular qualifications you have for writing the enclosed manuscript. If you are doing an exposé on, say, "missing funds" at city hall—it would be useful to point out that you have worked as a village treasurer for six years in another town. If you have queried the editor on the article earlier, he probably already has the background information—so the note should be a brief reminder: "Here is the piece on city hall's missing funds that we discussed earlier. I look forward to hearing from you at your earliest convenience."

If the manuscript is a photocopy, indicate whether it is a simultaneous submission. An editor is likely to assume it is, unless you tell him otherwise—and many are offended by writers using this marketing tactic (though when agents use it, that seems to be OK).

When submitting a manuscript to a newspaper—even the Sunday magazine section—include a cover note inquiring about the paper's rates for freelance submissions. Newspaper editors are deluged regularly by PR offices and "free" writers who submit material for ego and publicity purposes. Make sure your submission is not part of that crowd, or you may find it in print without an acknowledgment—much less a check.

Query Letters. If you have an article idea that seems "right" for a particular publication, you should contact the editor with a query. A query letter is a powerful tool. It can open doors or deny entry to the published land. Though no query alone will sell a manuscript, a bad one may squelch your chances of even a cursory look from an editor. A good query letter can be your right of passage.

Granted, the specifics of a query depend on your manuscript content, the audience you hope to reach, and the particular slant you are taking. But some general guidelines may help you structure your book or article proposal in a way that reflects your professionalism.

● A query letter should inform and excite an editor—not only about an article/book idea, but about the prospect of your writing the manuscript.

● The lead paragraph may either succinctly capsule the idea, your slant and intent; or show the editor the topic and your style with a representative sample. (The latter type of lead paragraph would be double-spaced; with the rest of the query single-spaced.)

● Subsequent paragraphs should provide examples, names of people you intend to interview, and facts and anecdotes that support the writing of the manuscript. All of this should verify your ability/qualifications to do it.

● The closing paragraph might include a direct request to do the article/book; it may specify the date the manuscript can be completed and possibly suggest a proposed length.

In general, query letters are single-spaced; and whenever possible, they should be limited to one typed page. Address the current editor by name. Published writing samples and a list of credits may also be attached, if appropriate. See the Query Checklist on page 986 for a summary of the essentials in preparing a query.

Query Checklist

Use this checklist to get your story ideas from the thinking stage to the marketplace. Check the appropriate box as you complete each step.

☐ ☐ ☐ ☐ ☐ 1. Read what other writers have written on your idea. (Consult The *Subject Guide to Books in Print* and the *Readers' Guide to Periodical Literature* in any library.)

☐ ☐ ☐ ☐ ☐ 2. Develop and research your idea with one or two publications or publishers in mind.

☐ ☐ ☐ ☐ ☐ 3. Decide which aspect of the subject you will focus on—the more specific, the better—and which publisher needs material on this subject.

☐ ☐ ☐ ☐ ☐ 4. Ask yourself:
What type of manuscript will I offer to write— a how-to, nostalgic, or personality piece, for example? Whom will I interview for the information? What can I give readers that other writers can't give *on this subject?*

☐ ☐ ☐ ☐ ☐ 5. Write a query letter that subtly sells your slant on the idea and your writing ability. (Answer the above questions in your query.) Give the editor a "flavor" of the piece you'll be writing; a sample paragraph or lead is helpful.

☐ ☐ ☐ ☐ ☐ 6. Retype and proofread the query until it is perfect (i.e., no misspellings, typos, or white-out blots, etc.). Photocopy the query for your files.

☐ ☐ ☐ ☐ ☐ 7. Send the query letter with a self-addressed, stamped envelope to the editor.

☐ ☐ ☐ ☐ ☐ 8. Continue writing queries on other subjects. (Don't badger the editor with additional letters and phone calls.)

☐ ☐ ☐ ☐ ☐ 9. If the editor likes your idea, write the article or book to his/her specifications.

☐ ☐ ☐ ☐ ☐10. If you get a rejection slip, re-slant your idea for another publisher. Try another idea, maybe. Writers, as salespeople, sometimes get turned down. Well-thought-out projects will eventually sell. Keep writing.

Submitting Photos by Mail. When submitting black and white prints with your manuscript, send 8x10 glossies unless the editor indicates otherwise. Stamp or print your name, address and phone number on the back of each print or contact sheet. Don't use a heavy felt tip pen because the ink will seep through the print.

Buy some sturdy 9x12 envelopes. Your photo dealer should have standard print mailers in stock; some may be pre-stamped with "Photos—Do Not Bend" and contain two cardboard inserts. You can also pick up corrugated cardboard inserts from your local grocery store. Place your print(s) between two cardboard inserts, wrap two rubber bands around the bundle, and enclose it with your manuscript in the envelope.

When sending many prints (say, 25-50 for a photo book), mail them in a sturdy cardboard box; 8x10 print paper boxes are perfect. Add enough cardboard inserts to fill the carton after the prints and manuscript are in place, and cover the box with wrapping paper. Send rare or extremely valuable photos only when an editor specifically requests them; then send them in a fiberboard mailing case with canvas straps, available at most photo stores. Tell the editor to return the photos in the same case or return the empty case itself if the photos are kept.

For color transparencies, 35mm is the universally accepted size. Few buyers will look at color prints. (Check each market listing individually for exact preferences from editors). To mail transparencies, use slotted acetate sheets, which hold twenty slides and offer protection from scratches, moisture, dirt and dust—available in standard sizes from most photo supply houses. Do not use glass mounts. Put your name, address, and phone number on each transparency. Mail the transparencies just as you would prints, using corrugated cardboard. If a number of sheets is being sent, use a cardboard box. Because transparencies are irreplaceable (unless you have internegatives or duplicates made), insure the package.

Photo Captions. Prints and transparencies should always be captioned when submitted for consideration with a manuscript. For prints, type the caption on a sheet of paper and tape it to the bottom of the back of the print. The caption should fold over the front of the photo so that the buyer can fold it back for easy reading. Masking tape allows the editor to easily remove the copy for typesetting.

Enclosing return postage with photos sent through the mail is more than a professional courtesy; it also helps assure that you'll get the photos back.

Mailing Book Manuscripts. Do not bind your book manuscript pages in any way. They should be mailed loose in a box (a ream-size stationery box is perfect) without binding. To ensure a safe return, enclose a self-addressed label and suitable postage in stamps clipped to the label. If your manuscript is returned, it will either come back in your original box, or—increasingly likely today—in an insulated bag-like mailer, with your label and postage used thereon. Many publishing houses open the box a manuscript is mailed in, and toss the box (if it has not already been damaged in the mails, or in the opening); they then read and circulate the manuscript as necessary for editorial consideration, and finally route it through the mail room back to you with a letter or rejection slip. This kind of handling makes it likely that a freshly typed manuscript will be in rough shape after one or two submissions. So it is wise to have several photocopies made of a book-length manuscript while it is still fresh—and to circulate those to publishers, rather than risk an expensive retyping job in the midst of your marketing effort. As mentioned above, indicate in a cover note that the submission is not a multiple submission if such is the case.

Book manuscripts can be mailed Fourth Class Manuscript Rate, but that can be slow and have an additional mauling effect on the package in the mails. When doing so, if you include a letter, state this on the outer wrapping and add appropriate postage to your manuscript postal rate. Most writers use First Class, secure in the feeling that their manuscript is in an editorial office within a few days. Some send book manuscripts using the United Parcel Service, which can be less expensive than First Class mail when you drop the package off at UPS yourself. The drawback here is that UPS cannot legally carry First Class mail, so you will have to send your cover letter a few days before giving UPS the manuscript, and both will arrive at about the same

Postage by the Page

By Carolyn Hardesty

Writers have the satisfaction of "finishing" their work several times. After the relief of completing the first draft, each revision and draft and eventually the final typing give a temporary sensation of being done. But the *finishing* feels most complete when you seal the envelope, write *First Class* on it, and tuck it into the mail slot.

How often is this last stage delayed by a 20-minute wait behind customers who are stamp collectors or who have ten letters to certify? Writers, who have more ideas than time, don't need that added frustration.

The chart below can simplify the postal process and save you time. Postage rates are listed by numbers of pages (using 20-pound paper) for first-class packages up to 12 ounces. After the first ounce (22¢), the increments are 17¢. The post office sells a convenient 39¢ stamp and also 17¢ stamps, so a stock of those denominations will allow you to stamp and mail your manuscripts in any dropbox as easily at noon or midnight.

For poets and writers mailing very short pieces, there is a 10¢ assessment for mailing a large envelope which weighs two ounces or less.

See the glossary for more information about registered and certified mail, return receipt, international reply coupons, and express mail.

FIRST-CLASS POSTAGE RATES

ounces	9x12 envelope, 9x12 SASE number of pages	9x12 SASE (for return trips) number of pages	first-class postage
2	1 to 4	3 to 8	$ .39
3	5 to 10	9 to 12	.56
4	11 to 16	13 to 19	.73
5	17 to 21	20 to 25	.90
6	22 to 27	26 to 30	1.07
7	28 to 32	31 to 35	1.24
8	33 to 38	36 to 41	1.41
9	39 to 44	42 to 46	1.58
10	45 to 49	47 to 52	1.75
11	50 to 55	53 to 57	1.92
12	56 to 61	58 to 63	2.09

For short manuscripts or long queries, use a business-size envelope and up to five pages with a 22¢ stamp. If you are including a business-size SASE, four pages is the limit.

● First class packages weighing more than 12 ounces are charged according to geographical zones. This is true also for all weights of fourth class (or book rate) mail.

● Four captionless 5x7 photographs or two 8x10 photographs will increase the weight of your package by one ounce.

● Insurance (for typing and production costs) is 50¢ for up to a $25 liability; $1.10 covers costs to $50; and $1.40 takes care of costs to $100.

● Certified mail costs 75¢.

● International Reply Coupons (IRCs) for Canadian and overseas submissions are generally available only at larger post offices but are essential when you contact publishers overseas.

Carolyn Hardesty, as a freelance writer, teaching assistant and graduate student, doesn't have time for post office lines. This chart helps her—and will help you—avoid delays and "overstamping." She is pursuing a master of arts degree in writing at the University of Iowa.

time. Check with UPS in your area to see if it has benefits for you. The cost depends on the weight of your manuscript and the delivery distance.

The tips and recommendations made here are based upon what editors prefer. Give editors what they prefer and you won't be beginning with a strike or two against you before the manuscript is read.

The Waiting Game. The writer who sends off a story, article or book manuscript to an editor should turn immediately to other ideas and try to forget about the submission. Unless you are on assignment, or under contract to do a book—in which case, a phone call to your editor saying the manuscript is in the mail is quite appropriate—it's best to use your time productively on other writing projects. But one day you realize it's been too long. According to the *Writer's Market* listing, your editor responds to submissions in a maximum of four weeks—and it's been six already, and you haven't heard a word. Will inquiring about it jeopardize a possible sale? Are they really considering it, or has the editor had an accident and your manuscript is at the bottom of a huge stack of unread mail?

If you have had no report from a publisher by the maximum reporting time given in a *WM* listing, allow six weeks' grace period and then write a brief letter to the editor asking if your manuscript (give the title, a brief description, and the date you mailed it) has in fact reached his office. If so, is it still under consideration? Your concern at this point is the mails: Is the manuscript safely delivered? Don't act impatiently with an editor—who may be swamped, or short-staffed, or about to give your manuscript a second reading. Be polite and professional. Enclose another SASE to expedite a reply. This is usually enough to stir a decision if matters are lagging in an editorial office, even during rush season (which is year-round).

If you still hear nothing from a publisher one month after your follow-up, send the editor a short note asking if he received your previous follow-up, and include a photocopy of that second letter. If, after another month, you are still without word, send a polite letter saying that you are withdrawing the manuscript from consideration (include the title, date of submission, and dates of follow-up correspondence), and ask that the manuscript be returned immediately in the SASE your original correspondence included.

Rejection. It is possible you will get a quick response from an editor in the form of a rejection. Rejection slips or letters should not be taken as a *personal* rejection. Direct your energy toward writing manuscripts, not writing "attack" letters.

When your disappointment comes from not being paid for an article, try to analyze the situation as objectively as possible. The decision to challenge an editor shouldn't be a hasty one.

Many times, a writer and editor will agree on an assignment via the phone. It is difficult to know who misled whom when the agreement is not in writing. If an editor says he is interested in seeing the story you propose, chances are the editor does not consider this a commitment for the publication to buy the piece. Unless a specific assignment is given, most articles are written on speculation—at the writer's risk. The editor has a right to say, "no, thank you," unless a definite promise was made.

Should I Fight or Forget an Editor?

Some writers say yes to the former, *definitely* fight for your rights. Others say no; they'd rather spend time on new projects. "Personally, I don't like to fester over an 'unfair' deal—get on with living, forget it, bite the bullet," said one prolific author. "One of the joys of being a writer is freedom; one of the problems of being a writer is freedom, so I can't tell others what to do."

The American Society of Journalists and Authors (ASJA) has an editor-writer relations committee, pointed out another writer, "which is very helpful when you need to threaten an editor with *clout.*"

Many writers feel their insistence that editors pay their bills helps not only themselves but all writers. "Go to all lengths . . . Not only does this end your own seethings (inward) but also makes it a bit easier for your fellow writer," said one ASJA member who has collected more than $61,000 for members from nonpaying or slow-paying markets. "The bastards must not be allowed to think they can get away with it."

Some writers have turned to collection agencies, although they may only recoup 50 percent of the fees as they pay the agency the other half. Small claims court is a more economical option if the magazine is in the same state in which you live but should only be pursued if you have written documentation that you have earned the payment and that you have unsuccessfully tried to obtain payment. Of course, even if you win the case, you may have further complications in collecting the payment.

"I filed suit (because the work had already been published); the case was handsomely settled out of court," pointed out one writer. "Many writers new to the business worry about getting a reputation for making trouble. My attitude is who'd want to work with a dishonest editor again anyway."

One writer we know continues to write for a well-known national magazine that reneges on its promises—because a byline in the publication is valuable to her career.

Unfortunately sometimes the writer is last in line for payment—after the phone company, the printer, and salaried employees. In other cases payment problems can occur inadvertently. Before you accuse an editor of being dishonest, make sure there isn't a logical explanation for the check not arriving at your home.

Also, consider that the editor may have little control over the publisher's issuance of checks. If you've developed a good working relationship with an editor (and have been paid for assignments), then checks start arriving later than usual and you get less than the maximum payment for a cover story, say, a magazine may be heading toward bankruptcy or extinction. The editor will have made promises to you, but actually it may be the publisher who has reneged on the promises. Good editors will abandon ship (pardon the cliché) when they learn that the publisher isn't backing their promises with payment. But these editors usually get the blame for the publisher's shortcomings.

Many editors get into this business as writers, then are promoted to associate editor, articles editor, or perhaps editor. Many editors *are* writers on the weekends. Trust editors as you would any business associate (not blindly but with an objective eye). An encounter with a dishonest editor does not mean all transactions will end that way. Most editors can be trusted. (Sometimes we've received complaints *and* complimentary letters about an editor or market. In these *rare* cases, we may include the listing but will monitor the market closely for possible exclusion from our next book.)

The Business of Writing

A nine-page manuscript may not look "expensive," but when you add up the long-distance calls, travel, and writing time, you see it's a valuable product. While readers, and to some extent editors, are oblivious to these background tasks, the Internal Revenue Service need not be. Such costs can become deductible writing expenses at income tax time. Because the tax law could change in 1986, you'll want to watch for IRS changes. At press time, changes had not been finalized.

For the Records. Though the deadline for filing your tax return is April 15, you should maintain careful records all year. To arrive at verifiable figures, you will need two things: *records and receipts.* For tax purposes, good records are not only helpful; they are *required* by law. Receipts are the foundation that careful recordkeeping is built upon.

At tax time each year, a freelance writer normally reports his business activities on tax Schedule C ("Profit or Loss From Business or Profession"); the resulting figure for income is entered on Form 1040. In addition, if your writing or editing work nets you $400 or more in earnings, you must file a Schedule SE and pay self-employment tax, which makes you eligible for Social Security benefits. Furthermore, if you think your taxes from freelancing will be $100 or more, you are required to pay your taxes in quarterly installments. To do this, you file a declaration of estimated tax using Form 1040-ES ("Declaration Voucher") and use the envelopes the IRS provides to mail in your estimated taxes every three months.

It's not as complicated as it may sound, but one thing is certain: to document all these tax liabilities at the end of the year, you must have accurate records.

Tax laws don't require any particular type of records, as long as they are permanent, accurate and complete, and they clearly establish income, deductions, credits, etc. It's remarkably easy to overlook deductible expenses unless you record them at the time they are paid and keep receipts for them. Since some assets are subject to depreciation (typewriter, desk, files, tape recorder, camera equipment, etc.), you also need records of the purchase prices you used to determine depreciation allowances.

Finally, you need good records in case the IRS audits you and asks you to explain items reported on your return. Memos, scribbled notes, or sketchy records that merely approximate income, deductions, or other pertinent items affecting your taxes are simply *not* adequate. You must have a record supported by sales slips, invoices, receipts, bank deposit slips, canceled checks, and other documents.

Records for Credit Purposes. You and the IRS are not the only ones interested in the well-being of your business. Banks, credit organizations, suppliers of materials, and others often require information on the condition of your finances when you apply for credit—if, for example, you want to buy a house.

In fact, freelance writers, in the eyes of many lending institutions, might as well be totally unemployed. Some writers have taken on full-time jobs just to qualify for financing for a home, even when the "steady" job might produce less income than freelancing.

A Simple Bookkeeping System. There are almost as many ways of keeping records as there are recordkeepers to keep them. For a freelance writer, normally a simple type of "single-entry" bookkeeping that requires only one account book to record the flow of income and expense is completely adequate. At the heart of this single-entry system is the journal. It is an accounting book, available at any stationery store (the *Writer's Digest Diary* can be used, too), in which all the everyday transactions of your freelance business are recorded. Each transaction is set forth clearly, including the date, a description of the transaction, and the amount entered in the proper column—either "income" or "expense."

Income entries will include funds you receive, either by cash or check. Expense entries might include payments you make for writing supplies, photocopying, postage, repairs, dues paid to writers' organizations, travel expenses, books and magazine subscriptions, photo developing and printing, etc.—whatever you have to spend as a business expense.

The Receipt File. For each income entry you make, keep a copy of a receipt, an invoice, or other record to substantiate that entry. For each expense entry, keep a canceled check, a receipt, or other document. By keeping your record complete with some type of document to support *every* entry, your record is foolproof.

A partitioned, envelope-type folder works well for keeping receipts in order. If a receipt does not clearly indicate which entry it refers to, make a note on it and date it before filing it. That way, you can locate it quickly.

Business Banking. To record your income as accurately as possible, it is best to deposit all the money you receive in a separate bank account. This will give you deposit slips to verify the entries in your journal. Furthermore, you should make all payments by check, if possible, so that your business expenses will be well documented. If you have to pay cash, keep receipts on file.

Any record must be retained as long as it may be material to the administration of any law. Statutes of limitations for various legal purposes vary from state to state, but if you keep your records on file for seven to ten years, you will seldom run into difficulty. Records supporting items on a tax return should be kept for at least three years, although keeping them indefinitely is a good idea.

What's Deductible. Among your deductible expenses, don't overlook the following writing-related costs:

• **All writing supplies**, including paper, carbons, pens, ribbons, envelopes, copying costs, postage, photo developing and printing costs, and recording tapes.
• **Repairs and maintenance of writing equipment**, including typewriter, word processor, tape recorder and camera.
• **Courses and conferences attended to enhance you as a professional writer.** It's important to realize, though, that you can't deduct courses you take to *become* a writer. The IRS rule is that courses must be "refresher" or professionally improving in nature to count. Besides deducting the costs of these, also deduct mileage (at 20.5¢ a mile)—or actual car expenses, whichever is greater—cost of tickets for public transportation; cost of hotel/motel rooms; and costs of meals.
• **Courses taken as research on subjects you are writing about.** To establish that a course is for research, it would help if you had documentation from the potential publisher of your writings—such as a favorable response to a query. Even if the magazine should not publish what you write, the response will show the research was done in good faith.
• **Writing books, magazines and other references.**
• **Dues paid for membership in writers' organizations.**

Date	Description	Expense		Income	
Jan. 4	Box of floppies	$30	00		
6	Supply Mart - 1 ream of paper	$6	95		
6	Postage - Story sent to Analog		90¢		
8	Economic Bulletin - for March article & photos			$550	00
10	Pat's Bookstore - 1986 Writer's Market	$19	95		
13	Wright Corp. - for editing 4th quarter newsletter			$300	00
15	Renewal of WD subscription	$17	00		
18	Pat's - 20 manila envelopes	$4	00		
21	Mountain Press - for editing Survival Handbook			$575	00
21	Devphoto - for developing photos for Am. Horse J. article	$11	95		
23	1986 Poet's Market	$16	95		
28	Fee for Southern Writer's Conference	$30	00		
30	American Horse Journal for special issue article			$275	00
	Jan. TOTALS	$137	70	$1,700	00

A typical single-entry page in a bookkeeping journal that records a freelance writer's income and expense transactions.

• **Home office expenses.** In the past, writers using a portion of their home dining room or living room have been allowed to deduct a percentage of home costs as "office" expenses. This is no longer allowed. To take a home office deduction today, you must have a portion of your dwelling set aside *solely for writing on a regular basis.* The same rule applies to a separate structure on your property. For example, you may not use a portion of your garage for writing and a portion for parking your car. If your car goes in, your home office expense is out.

If you rent a five-room apartment for $300 a month and use one room exclusively for writing, you are entitled to deduct one-fifth of the rent which comes to $60 a month, or $720 a year. Add to this one-fifth of your heating bill and one-fifth of your electric bill and watch the deductions mount up. Keep a list, too, of long-distance phone bills arising from your writing.

If you own your home and use one room for writing, you can deduct the allocated expenses of operating that room. Among these allowable expenses are interest on mortgage, real estate taxes, repairs or additions to the home, cost of utilities, home insurance premiums, and depreciation on the room.

If you own a seven-room house with one room used for writing, one-seventh of the total cost of the house can be depreciated, as well as one-seventh of the above mentioned expenses.

There is a limit to home office expenses. You may not exceed in deductible expenses the amount of your gross income. If you made $1,000 last year, you can't deduct any more than that in home office expenses—no matter how much they came to. Just $1,000 in this case.

• **Mileage.** Take 20.5¢ a mile for the first 15,000 miles you travel on writing-related missions and 11¢ a mile for miles traveled over 15,000. Or you may take the actual cost of operating your car—gas, oil, tires, maintenance and depreciation. (See below for figuring depreciation.) If you use your car 100 percent for writing, the total cost of operating it is deductible. Compare mileage deduction to cost deduction, and use the one that gives you the bigger break.

What May Be Depreciated. You can count depreciation of your typewriter, desk, chair, lamps, tape recorder, files, camera equipment, photocopier, word processor, or anything else related to your writing which costs a considerable amount of money and which has a useful life of more than one year.

You have a couple of ways to recover these capital expenses. For most property placed into service after 1980, costs can be recovered in a relatively short period of time using the Accelerated Cost Recovery System (ACRS). Under this system, eligible capital expenses can be recovered by applying pre-determined percentages over a 3-, 5-, or 10-year period, depending on the category into which your property falls. Most of a writer's tangible property would likely be considered 3- or 5-year property. The accelerated cost recovery of 3-year property is 25% of its original cost in the first year; 38% in the second year; 37% in the third year. For 5-year recovery property, deductions are 15% the first year; 22% the second year; and 21% for each of the last 3 years.

An additional deduction called an investment tax credit (ITC) has been subject to considerable change in the last few years. Consult your tax adviser for information that is up-to-date and pertinent to your situation.

The IRS gives you yet another option for recovering your capital expenses. For tax years beginning after 1981, you may deduct up to $5,000 of normally depreciable property in the year you buy the typewriter, word processor or whatever. However, if you elect to take this deduction, you forfeit the investment tax credit.

There are other options, requirements and regulations that can affect the figuring of your taxes. It's wise to consult with a tax professional who is aware of the current percentages and category definitions involved in figuring your taxes. It will be important to calculate your tax both ways—using the $5,000 deduction and the ACRS/tax investment credit combination—in deciding which method best fits your situation.

Self-Employment Earnings. If after deductions you earn $400 or more, you are required to pay a Social Security tax of 11.8% of the first $39,600 of your earnings. And you must fill out and submit a Schedule SE (for "self-employment"). Finally, save your rejection slips. Though they may be unpleasant reminders, keep them in a folder. Look at them as professional communiques from publishers, not personal rejection letters. If you are subjected to a tax audit, these letters will help establish you as a working writer.

Rights and the Writer

"We find that writers and editors define rights in different ways," said our letter inviting editors (actually their publications) to be listed in this 1986 edition. "To eliminate any misinterpretations, make sure your answer is consistent with the following definitions."

Read on, and you'll see how we define each right—and you'll see the definitions upon which editors (we hope) updated the *rights* information in their listings.

Every so often, we hear from a writer who is confused because an editor claims to not ever acquire or buy rights. The truth is, any time an editor buys a story or asks you for permission to publish a story in return for contributor copies, this editor is asking you for *rights* (even when he doesn't use the word, rights). Occasionally people start magazines on their area of expertise (say, crafts or stamp collecting) but don't have extensive knowledge of publishing terms and practices. If you sense that an editor is interested in getting stories but doesn't seem to know what his and the writer's responsibilities are as to rights, be wary. In such a case, you'll want to explain what rights you're offering (in very basic terms) and if you expect additional payment for subsequent use of your work.

Selling Rights to Your Writing. The Copyright Law which went into effect January 1978 said writers were only selling one-time rights to their work unless they agreed otherwise in writing with a publisher. In some cases, however, a writer may have little say in the rights sold to an editor. The beginning writer, in fact, can jeopardize a sale by arguing with an editor who is likely to have other writers on call who are eager to please. As long as there are more writers than there are markets, this situation will remain the same.

As a writer acquires skill, reliability, and professionalism on the job, however, that writer becomes more valued to editors—and rights become a more important consideration. Though a beginning writer will accept modest payment just to get in print, an experienced writer soon learns that he cannot afford to give away good writing just to see a byline. At this point a writer must become concerned with selling reprints of articles already sold to one market, or using sold articles as chapters in a book on the same topic, or seeking markets for the same material overseas, offering work to TV or the movies. Such dramatic rights can be meaningful for both fiction and nonfiction writers.

What Editors Want. You should strive to keep as many rights to your work as you can from the outset, because before you can resell any piece of writing you must own the rights to negotiate. If you have sold "all rights" to an article, for instance, it can be reprinted *without* your permission, and without additional payment to you. Many writers will not deal with editors who buy all rights. What an editor buys will determine whether you can resell your own work. Here is a list of the rights most editors and publishers seek.

● **First Serial Rights.** The word serial does not mean publication in installments, but refers to the fact that libraries call periodicals "serials" because they are published in serial or continuing fashion. *First serial rights* means the writer offers the newspaper or magazine (both of which are periodicals) the right to publish the article, story or poem the first time in the periodical. All other rights to the material belong to the writer. Variations on this right are, for example, First North American Serial rights. Some magazines use this purchasing technique to obtain the right to publish first in both America and Canada since many American magazines are circulated in Canada. If an editor had purchased only First U.S. Serial Rights, a Canadian magazine could come out with prior or simultaneous publication of the same material. When material is excerpted from a book which is to be published and it appears in a magazine or newspaper prior to book publication, this is also called First Serial Rights.

- **First North American Serial Rights.** Magazine publishers which distribute in both the United States and Canada frequently buy these first rights which cover publication in both countries.
- **One-Time Rights.** This differs from First Serial Rights in that the buyer has no guarantee he will be the first to publish the work. One-time rights most often applies to photos, but occasionally writing, too.
- **Second Serial (Reprint) Rights.** This gives a newspaper or magazine the opportunity to print an article, poem or story after it has already appeared in another newspaper or magazine. The term is also used to refer to the sale of part of a book to a newspaper or magazine after a book has been published, whether or not there has been any first serial publication (income derived from second serial rights to book material is often shared 50/50 by author and book publisher).
- **All Rights.** Some magazines, either because of the top prices they pay for material, or the fact that they have book publishing interests or foreign magazine connections, buy All Rights. A writer who sells an article, story or poem to a magazine under these terms, forfeits the right to use his material in its present form elsewhere himself. If he signs a "work-for-hire" agreement, he signs away all rights and the copyright to the company making the assignment. If the writer thinks he may want to use his material later (perhaps in book form), he must avoid submitting to these types of markets, or refuse payment and withdraw his material if he discovers it later. Ask the editor whether he is willing to buy only first rights instead of all rights before you agree to an assignment or a sale. Some editors will reassign rights to a writer after a given period—say, one year. It's worth an inquiry in writing.
- **Simultaneous Rights.** This term covers articles and stories which are sold to publications (primarily religious magazines) which do not have overlapping circulations. A Catholic publication, for example, might be willing to buy Simultaneous Rights to a Christmas story which they like very much, even though they know a Presbyterian magazine may be publishing the same story in one of its Christmas issues. Publications which will buy simultaneous rights indicate this fact in their listings in *Writer's Market*. Always advise an editor when the material you are sending is a simultaneous submission.
- **Foreign Serial Rights.** Can you resell a story you have had published in America to a foreign magazine? If you sold only First U.S. Serial Rights to the American magazine, yes, you are free to market your story abroad. Of course, you must contact a foreign magazine that buys material which has previously appeared in an American periodical.
- **Syndication Rights.** This is a division of serial rights. For example, a book publisher may sell the rights to a newspaper syndicate to print a book in twelve installments in, say, each of twenty United States newspapers. If they did this prior to book publication it would be syndicating First Serial Rights to the book. If they did this after book publication, they would be syndicating Second Serial Rights to the book. In either case, the syndicate would be taking a commission on the sales it made to newspapers, so the remaining percentage would be split between author and publisher.
- **Subsidiary Rights.** The rights, other than book publication rights, should be included in a book contract, such as serial rights, dramatic rights, translation rights, etc.
- **Dramatic, Television and Motion Picture Rights.** This means the writer is selling his material for use on the stage, in television, or in the movies. Often a one-year "option" to buy such rights is offered (generally for 10% of the total price); the interested party then tries to sell the idea to other people—actors, directors, studios or television networks, etc.—who become part of the project, which then becomes a script. Some properties are optioned over and over again, but fail to become dra-

matic productions. In such cases, the writer can sell his rights again and again—as long as there is interest in the material. Though dramatic, TV and motion picture rights are more important to the fiction writer than to the nonfiction writer, producers today are increasingly interested in "real-life" material; many biographies and articles are being dramatized.

Book rights will be covered by the contract submitted to the writer by a book publisher. The writer does not indicate any such rights offered on the first page of his manuscript.

Communicate and Clarify. Before submitting material to a market, check its listing in this book to see what rights are purchased. Most editors will discuss rights they wish to purchase before an exchange of money occurs. Some buyers are adamant about what rights they will accept; others will negotiate. In any case, the rights purchased should be stated specifically *in writing* sometime during the course of the sale, usually in a letter or memo of agreement. If no rights are transferred in writing, and the material is sold for use in a collective work (that is, a work that derives material from a number of contributors), you are authorizing unlimited use of the piece in that work or updates of the work or later collective works in the same series. Thus, you can't collect reprint fees if the rights weren't spelled out in advance, in writing.

Give as much attention to the rights you haven't sold as you do the rights you have sold. Be aware of the rights you retain, with an eye for additional sales.

Whatever rights you sell or don't sell, make sure all parties involved in any sale understand the terms of the sale. Clarify what is being sold *before* any actual sale, and do it in writing. Communication, coupled with these guidelines and some common sense, will preclude misunderstandings with editors over rights.

Keep in mind, too, that if there is a change in editors from the edition of *Writer's Market* you're using, the rights bought may also change.

Copyrighting Your Writing. The copyright law, effective since January 1, 1978, protects your writing, unequivocally recognizes the creator of the work as its owner, and grants the creator all the rights, benefits and *privileges* that ownership entails.

In other words, the moment you finish a piece of writing—whether it be a short story, article, novel, poem or even paragraph—the law recognizes that only you can decide how it is to be used.

This law gives writers power in dealing with editors and publishers, but they should understand how to use that power. They should also understand that certain circumstances can complicate and confuse the concept of ownership. Writers must be wary of these circumstances, or risk losing ownership of their work.

Here are answers to frequently asked questions about copyright law:

● **To what rights am I entitled under copyright law?** The law gives you, as creator of your work, the right to print, reprint and copy the work; to sell or distribute copies of the work; to prepare "derivative works"—dramatizations, translations, musical arrangement, novelizations, etc.; to record the work; and to perform or display literary, dramatic or musical works publicly. These rights give you control over how your work is used, and assure you (in theory) that you receive payment for any use of your work.

If, however, you create the work as a "work-for-hire," you *do not* own any of these rights. The person or company that commissioned the work-for-hire owns the copyright. The work-for-hire agreement will be discussed in more detail later.

● **When does copyright law take effect, and how long does it last?** A piece of writing is copyrighted the moment it is put to paper. Protection lasts for the life of the author plus 50 years, thus allowing your heirs to benefit from your work. For material written by two or more people, protection lasts for the life of the last survivor plus 50 years. The life-plus-50 provision applies if the work was created or registered with the Copyright Office after Jan. 1, 1978, when the updated copyright law took effect. The old law protected works for a 28-year term, and gave the copyright owner the option to renew the copyright for an additional 28 years at the end of that term. Works copyrighted under the old law that are in their second 28-year term automatically receive an additional 19 years of protection (for a total of 75 years). Works in their first term also receive the 19-year extension, but must still be renewed when the first term ends.

If you create a work anonymously or pseudonymously, protection lasts for 100 years after the work's creation, or 75 years after its publication, whichever is shorter. The life-plus-50 coverage takes effect, however, if you reveal your identity to the Copyright Office any time before the original term of protection runs out.

Works created on a for-hire basis are also protected for 100 years after the work's creation or 75 years after its publication, whichever is shorter.

● **Must I register my work with the Copyright Office to receive protection?** No. Your work is copyrighted whether or not you register it, although registration offers certain advantages. For example, you must register the work before you can bring an infringement suit to court. You can register the work *after* an infringement has taken place, and *then* take the suit to court, but registering after the fact removes certain rights from you. You can sue for actual damages (the income or other benefits lost as a result of the infringement), but you can't sue for statutory damages and you can't recover attorney's fees unless the work has been registered with the Copyright Office *before* the infringement took place. Registering before the infringement also allows you to make a stronger case when bringing the infringement to court.

If you suspect that someone might infringe on your work, register it. If you doubt that an infringement is likely (and infringements are relatively rare), you might save yourself the time and money involved in registering the material.

● **I have an article that I want to protect fully. How do I register it?** Request the proper form from the Copyright Office. Send the completed form, a $10 registration fee, and one copy (if the work is unpublished; two if it's published) of the work to the Register of Copyrights, Library of Congress, Washington, D.C. 20559. You needn't register each work individually. A group of articles can be registered simultaneously (for a single $10 fee) if they meet these requirements: They must be assembled in orderly form (simply placing them in a notebook binder is sufficient); they must bear a single title ("Works by Chris Jones," for example); they must represent the work of one person (or one set of collaborators); and they must be the subject of a single claim to copyright. No limit is placed on the number of works that can be copyrighted in a group.

● **If my writing is published in a "collective work"—such as a magazine—does the publication handle registration of the work?** Only if the publication owns the piece of writing. Although the copyright notice carried by the magazine covers its contents, you must register any writing to which *you* own the rights if you want the additional protection registration provides.

Collective works are publications with a variety of contributors. Magazines, newspapers, encyclopedias, anthologies, etc., are considered collective works. If you sell something to a collective work, state specifically—*in writing*—what rights you're selling. If you don't, you are automatically selling the nonexclusive rights to use the writing in the collective work and in any succeeding issues or revisions of it. For example, a magazine that buys your article without specifying in writing the rights purchased can reuse the article in that magazine—without paying you. The same is true for other collective works, so always detail *in writing* what rights you are selling before actually making the sale.

When contributing to a collective work, ask that your copyright notice be placed on or near your published manuscript (if you still own the manuscript's rights). Prominent display of your copyright notice on published work has two advantages: It signals to readers and potential reusers of the piece that it belongs to you, and not to the collective work in which it appears; and it allows you to register all published work bearing such notice with the Copyright Office as a group for a single $10 fee. A published work *not* bearing notice indicating you as copyright owner can't be included in a group registration.

Display of copyright notice is especially important when contributing to an uncopyrighted publication—that is, a publication that doesn't display a copyright symbol and doesn't register with the Copyright Office. You risk losing copyright protection on material that appears in an uncopyrighted publication. Also, you have no legal recourse against a person who infringes on something that is published without appropriate copyright notice. That person has been misled by the absence of the copyright notice and can't be held liable for his infringement. Copyright protection remains in force on material published in an uncopyrighted publication without benefit of copyright notice if the notice was left off only a few copies, if you asked (in writing) that the notice be included and the publisher didn't comply, or if you register the work and make a reasonable attempt to place the notice on any copies that haven't been distributed after the omission was discovered.

Official notice of copyright consists of the symbol ©, the word "Copyright," or the abbreviation "Copr."; the name of the copyright owner or owners; and the year date of first publication (for example, "© 1986 Chris Jones").

● **Under what circumstances should I place my copyright notice on unpublished works that haven't been registered?** Place official copyright notice on the first page of *any* manuscript, a procedure intended not to stop a buyer from stealing your material (editorial piracy is very rare, actually), but to demonstrate to the editor that you understand your rights under copyright law, that you own that particular manuscript, and that you want to retain your ownership after the manuscript is published. Seeing this notice, an editor might be less apt to try to buy all rights from you. Remember, you want to retain your rights to any writing.

● **How do I transfer copyright?** A transfer of copyright, like the sale of any property, is simply an exchange of the property for payment. The law stipulates, however, that the transfer of any exclusive rights (and the copyright is the most exclusive of exclusive rights) must be made in writing to be valid. Various types of exclusive rights exist, as outlined above. Usually it is best not to sell your copyright. If you do, you lose control over the use of the manuscript, and forfeit future income from its use.

● **What is a "work-for-hire assignment"?** This is a work that another party commissions you to do. Two types of work-for-hire works exist: Work done as a regular employee of a company, and commissioned work that is specifically called a "work-for-hire" in writing at the time of assignment. The phrase "work-for-hire" or something close must be used in the written agreement, though you should watch for similar phrasings. The work-for-hire provision was included in the new copyright law so that no writer could unwittingly sign away his copyright. The phrase "work-for-hire" is a bright red flag warning the writer that the agreement he is about to enter into will result in loss of rights to any material created under the agreement.

Some editors offer work-for-hire agreements when making assignments, and expect writers to sign them routinely. By signing them, you forfeit the potential for additional income from a manuscript through reprint sales, or sale of other rights. Be careful, therefore, in signing away your rights in a "work-for-hire" agreement. Many articles written as works-for-hire or to which all rights have been sold are never resold, but if you retain the copyright, you might try to resell the article—something you wouldn't be motivated to do if you forfeited your rights to the piece.

● **Can I get my rights back if I sell all rights to a manuscript, or if I sell the copyright itself?** Yes. You or certain heirs can terminate the transfer of rights 40 years after creation or 35 years after publication of a work by serving written notice to the person to whom you transferred rights wihin specified time limits. Consult the Copyright Office for the procedural details. This may seem like a long time to wait, but remember that some manuscripts remain popular (and earn royalties and other fees) for much longer than 35 years.

● **Must all transfers be in writing?** Only work-for-hire agreements and transfers of exclusive rights *must* be in writing. However, getting any agreement in writing before the sale is wise. Beware of other statements about what rights the buyer purchases that may appear on checks, writer's guidelines or magazine mastheads. If the publisher makes such a statement elsewhere, you might insert a phrase like "No statement pertaining to purchase of rights than the one detailed in this letter—including masthead statements or writer's guidelines—applies to this agreement" into the letter that outlines your rights agreement. Some publishers put their terms in writing on the back of a check that, when endorsed by the writer, becomes in their view a "contract." If the terms on the back of the check do not agree with the rights you are selling, then change the endorsement to match the rights you have sold before signing the check for deposit. Contact the editor to discuss this difference in rights.

• **Are ideas and titles copyrightable?** No. Nor can information be copyrighted. Only the actual expression of ideas or information can be copyrighted. You can't copyright the idea to do a solar energy story, and you can't copyright information about building solar energy converters. But you can copyright the article that results from that idea and that information.

• **Where can I get more information about copyright law?** Write the Copyright Office (Library of Congress, Washington, D.C. 20559) for a free Copyright Information Kit. Call (not collect) the Copyright Public Information Office at (202)287-8700 weekdays between 8:30 a.m. and 5 p.m. if you need forms for registration of a claim to copyright. The Copyright Office will answer specific questions but won't provide legal advice. For more information about copyright and other laws, consult the latest edition of *Law and the Writer*, edited by Kirk Polking and Leonard S. Meranus (Writer's Digest Books).

How Much Should I Charge?

The jobs that writers can dream up for extra income while waiting for checks from publishers are limited only by their imaginations. New Hampshire writer Joyce Maynard wrote a note to the Cunard Lines entertainment division offering her services as a lecturer on writing aboard ship. She got a form reply acknowledging her letter and nothing more. Months later, she got a phone call from the entertainment coordinator of the *Queen Elizabeth 2*. Could she and her husband be ready to set sail for England, first class, all expenses paid, in 10 days?

On the other coast, two freelance writers in Los Angeles have successfully operated a Rent-a-Fan Club. For a fee, they show up with some associates at airports, restaurants or birthday parties and impersonate a 1950s style fan club for the unsuspecting *star*. Writers in less flamboyant parts of the country have used their lyric writing skills to create special birthday or anniversary songs for singing telegrams.

If you're a less gregarious writer, there are still hundreds of other writing jobs waiting for you within reach of a local phone call.

What follows is a list of writing jobs you might want to consider—and rates that have been reported to us by freelancers doing similar work in various parts of the United States. The rates in your own marketplace may be higher or lower, depending on demand and other local variables. Consider the rates quoted here as guidelines, not fixed fees.

How do you find out what the local going rate is? If possible, contact writers or friends in a related business or agency that employs freelancers to find out what has been paid for certain kinds of jobs in the past. Or try to get the prospective client to quote his budget for a specific project before you name your price.

When setting your own fees, keep two factors in mind: (1)how much you think the client is willing or able to pay for the job; and (2)how much you want to earn for your time. For example, if something you write helps a businessman get a $50,000 order or a school board to get a $100,000 grant, that may influence your fees. How much you want to earn for your time should take into consideration not only an hourly rate for the time you spend writing, but also the time involved in meeting with the client, doing research, and, where necessary, handling details with a printer or producer. One way to figure your hourly rate is to determine what an annual salary might be for a staff person to do the same job you are bidding on, and figure an hourly wage on that. If, for example, you think the buyer would have to pay a staff person $20,000 a year, divide that by 2,000 (approximately 40 hours per week for 50 weeks) and you will arrive at $10 an hour. Then add another 20% to cover the amount of fringe benefits that an employer normally pays in Social Security, unemployment insurance, paid vacations, hospitalization, retirement funds, etc. Then add another dollars-per-hour figure to cover your actual overhead expense for office space, equipment, supplies; plus time spent on professional meetings, readings, and making unsuccessful proposals. (Add up one year's expense and divide by the number of hours per year you work on freelancing. In the beginning you may have to adjust this to avoid pricing yourself out of the market.)

Regardless of the method by which you arrive at your fee for the job, be sure to get a letter of agreement signed by both parties covering the work to be done and the fee to be paid.

You will, of course, from time to time handle certain jobs at less than desirable rates because they are for a cause you believe in, or because the job offers additional experience or exposure to some profitable client for the future. Some clients pay hourly rates; others pay flat fees for the job. Both kinds of rates are listed when the data were available so you have as many pricing options as possible. More details on many of the freelance jobs listed below are contained in *Jobs for Writers*, edited by Kirk Polking (Writer's Digest Books)—which tells how to get writing jobs, how to handle them most effectively, and how to get a fair price for your work.

Advertising copywriting: Advertising agencies and the advertising departments of large companies need part-time help in rush seasons. Newspapers, radio and TV stations also need copywriters for their smaller business customers who do not have an agency. Depending on the client and the job, the following rates could apply: $10-$65 per hour, $100 and up per day, $200 and up per week, $100-$500 as a monthly retainer. Flat-fee-per-ad rates could range from $25-$500 depending upon size and kind of client.

Annual reports: A brief report with some economic information and an explanation of figures, $20-$35 per hour; a report that must meet Securities and Exchange Commission (SEC) standards and reports that use legal language could bill at $40-$65 per hour. Some writers who provide copywriting and editing services charge flat fees ranging from $1,500-$10,000.

Anthology editing: variable advance plus 3%-15% of royalties. Flat-fee-per-manuscript rates could range from $500-$5,000 or more if it consists of complex, technical material.

Article manuscript critique: 3,000 words, $30.

Arts reviewing: for weekly newspapers, $15-35; for dailies, $45 and up; for Sunday supplements, $100-$400; regional arts events summaries for national trade magazines, $35-$100.

Associations: miscellaneous writing projects, small associations, $5-$15 per hour; larger groups, up to $60 per hour; or a flat fee per project, such as $250-$500 for 10-12 page magazine articles, or $500-$1,500 for a 10-page booklet.

Audio cassette scripts: $150 for 20 minutes, assuming written from existing client materials; no additional research or meetings; otherwise $75-$100 per minute, $750 minimum.

Audiovisuals: Audiovisual writing: $100-$200 per scripted minute. Includes rough draft, editing conference with client, and final shooting script. For consulting, research, producing, directing, soundtrack oversight, etc., $300 per day plus travel and expenses.

Book, as-told-to (ghostwriting): author gets full advance and 50% of author's royalties; subject gets 50%. Hourly rate for subjects who are self-publishing ($10-$35 per hour).

Book, ghostwritten, without as-told-to credit: For clients who are either self-publishing or have no royalty publisher lined up, $5,000 to $30,000 with one-fourth down payment, one-fourth when book half finished, one-fourth at three quarters mark and last fourth of payment when manuscript completed; or chapter by chapter.

Book content editing: $10-$50 per hour and up; $600-$3,000 per manuscript, based on size and complexity of the project.

Book copyediting: $7.50-$20 per hour and up; occasionally $1 per page.

Book indexing: $8-$18 per hour; $1.50 per printed book page; or flat fee.

Book jacket blurb writing: $60-$75 for selling front cover copy plus inside and back cover copy summarizing content and tone of the book.

Book manuscript criticism: $125 for outline and first 20,000 words.

Book manuscript reading, nonspecialized subjects: $20-$50 for a half page summary and recommendation. *Specialized subject:* $100-$350 and up, depending on complexity of project.

Book proofreading: $6-$18 per hour and up; sometimes 60¢-75¢ per page.

Book proposal consultation: $25-$35 per hour.

Book proposal writing: $300-$1,000 or more depending on length and whether client provides full information or writer must do some research.

Book query critique: $50 for letter to publisher and outline.

Book research: $5-$20 per hour and up, depending on complexity.

Book reviews: byline and the book only, on small newspapers; to $25-$150 on larger publications.

Book rewriting: $12-$30 per hour; sometimes $5 per page. Some writers have combination ghostwriting and rewriting short-term jobs for which the pay could be $350 per day and up. Some participate in royalties on book rewrites.

Brochures: $200-$7,500 depending on client (small nonprofit organization to large corporation), length, and complexity of job.

Business booklets, announcement folders: writing and editing, $25-$1,000 depending on size, research, etc.

Business facilities brochure: 12-16 pages, $1,000-$4,000.

Business letters: such as those designed to be used as form letters to improve customer relations, $20 per hour for small businesses; $200-$500 per form letter for corporations.

Business meeting guide and brochure: 4 pages, $150; 8-12 pages, $300.

Business writing: On the local or national level, this may be advertising copy, collateral materials, speechwriting, films, public relations or other jobs—see individual entries on these subjects for details. General business writing rates could range from $20-$50 per hour; $100-$200 per day, plus expenses.

Catalogs for business: $60-$75 per printed page; more if many tables or charts must be reworked for readability and consistency.

Collateral materials for business: see business booklets, catalogs, etc.

Comedy writing for night club entertainers: *Gags only,* $2-$25 each. *Routines:* $100-$1,000 per minute. Some new comics may try to get a five-minute routine for $150; others will pay $2,500 for a five-minute bit from a top writer.

Commercial reports for businesses, insurance companies, credit agencies: $6-$10 per page; $5-$20 per report on short reports.

Company newsletters and inhouse publications: writing and editing 2-4 pages, $200-$500; 12-32 pages, $1,000-$2,000. Writing, $8-$40 per hour; editing, $8-$35 per hour.

Church history: $200-$1,000 for writing 15 to 50 pages.

Consultation on communications: $250 per day plus expenses for nonprofit, social service and religious organizations; $400 per day to others.

Consultation to business: on writing, PR, $25-$50 per hour.

Consumer complaint letters: $25 each.

Contest judging: short manuscripts, $5 per entry; with one-page critique, $10-$25. Overall contest judging: $100-$500.

Corporate history: $1,000-$20,000, depending on length, complexity and client resources.

Corporate profile: up to 3,000 words, $1,250-$2,500.

Dance criticism: $25-$400 per article (see also Arts reviewing.)

Direct-mail catalog copy: $10-$50 per page for 3-20 blocks of copy per page of a 24-48 page catalog.

Direct-mail packages: copywriting direct mail letter, response card, etc., $300-$3,000 depending on writer's skill, reputation.

Direct response card on a product: $250.

Editing: see book editing, company newsletters, magazines, etc.

Educational consulting and educational grant and proposal writing: $250-$750 per day and sometimes up to 5-10% of the total grant funds depending on whether writing only is involved or also research and design of the project itself.

Encyclopedia articles: entries in some reference books, such as biographical encyclopedias, 500-2,000 words and pay ranges from $60-$80 per 1,000 words. Specialists' fees vary.

English teachers—lay reading for: $4-$6 per hour.

Family histories: See histories, family.

Filmstrip script: See audiovisual.

Financial presentation for a corporation: 20-30 minutes, $1,500-$4,500.

Flyers for tourist attractions, small museums, art shows: $25 and up for writing a brief bio, history, etc.

Fund-raising campaign brochure: $5,000 for 20 hours' research and 30 hours to write, get it approved, lay out and produce with printer.

Gags: see comedy writing.

Genealogical research: $5-$25 per hour.

Ghostwriting: $15-$40 per hour; $5-$10 per page, $200 per day plus expenses. Ghostwritten professional and trade journal articles under someone else's byline, $250-$3,000. Ghostwritten books: see book, as-told-to (ghostwriting and book, ghostwritten, without as-told-to credit).

Ghostwriting a corporate book: 6 months' work, $13,000-$25,000.

Ghostwriting speeches: see speeches.

Government public information officer: part-time, with local governments, $10-$15 per hour; or a retainer for so many hours per period.

Histories, family: fees depend on whether the writer need only edit already prepared notes or do extensive research and writing; and the length of the work, $500-$5,000.

Histories, local: centennial history of a local church, $25 per hour for research through final manuscript for printer.

House organ editing: see company newsletters and inhouse publications.

Industrial product film: $1,000 for 10-minute script.

Industrial promotions: $15-$40 per hour. See also business writing.

Job application letters: $10-$25.

Lectures to local librarians or teachers: $50-$100.

Lectures to school classes: $25-$75; $150 per day.

Lectures at national conventions by well-known authors: $1,500-$10,000 and up, plus expenses; less for panel discussions.

Lectures at regional writers' conferences: $300 and up, plus expenses.

Magazine, city, calendar of events column: $150.

Magazine column: 200 words, $25. Larger circulation publications pay more.

Magazine editing: religious publications, $200-$500 per month.

Magazine stringing: 20¢-$1 per word based on circulation. Daily rate: $100-$200 plus expenses; weekly rate: $750 plus expenses. Also $7.50-$35 per hour plus expenses.

Manuscript consultation on book proposals: $25-$35 per hour.

Manuscript criticism: $20 per 16-line poem; $30 per article or short story of up to 3,000 words; book outlines and sample chapters of up to 20,000 words, $125.

Manuscript typing: 65¢-$1.25 per page with one copy.

Market research survey reports: $10 per report; $15-$30 per hour; writing results of studies or reports, $500-$1,200 per day.

Medical editing: $15-$30 per hour.

Medical proofreading: $10-$20 per hour.

Medical writing: $15-$80 per hour.
New product release: $300-$500 plus expenses.
Newsletters: see company newsletters and retail business newsletters.
Newspaper column, local: 80¢ per column inch to $5 for a weekly; $7.50 for dailies of 4,000-6,000 circulation; $10-$12.50 for 7,000-10,000 dailies; $15-$20 for 11,000-25,000 dailies; and $25 and up for larger dailies.
Newspaper feature: 35¢ to $1.50 per column inch for a weekly.
Newspaper feature writing, part-time: $1,000 a month for an 18-hour week.
Newspaper reviews of art, music, drama: see arts reviewing.
Newspaper stringing: 50¢-$2.50 per column inch up to $5 per column inch for some national publications. Also publications like *National Enquirer* pay lead fees up to $250 for tips on page one story ideas.
Newspaper ads for small business: $25 for a small, one-column ad, or $10 per hour and up.
Novel synopsis for film producer: $150 for 5-10 pages typed single-spaced.
Obituary copy: where local newspapers permit lengthier than normal notices paid for by the funeral home (and charged to the family), $15. Writers are engaged by funeral homes.
Opinion research interviewing: $4-$6 per hour or $15-$25 per completed interview.
Party toasts, limericks, place card verses: $1.50 per line.
Permission fees to publishers to reprint article or story: $75-$500; 10¢-15¢ per word; less for charitable organizations.
Photo brochures: $700-$15,000 flat fee for photos and writing.
Poetry criticism: $20 per 16-line poem.
Political writing: see public relations and speechwriting.
Press background on a company: $500-$1,200 for 4-8 pages.
Press kits: $500-$3,000.
Press release: 1-3 pages, $50-$200.
Printers' camera-ready typewritten copy: negotiated with individual printers, but see also manuscript typing services.
Product literature: per page, $100-$150.
Programmed instruction consultant fees: $300-$700 per day; $50 per hour.
Programmed instruction materials for business: $50 per hour for inhouse writing and editing; $500-$700 a day plus expenses for outside research and writing. *Alternate method:* $2,000-$5,000 per hour of programmed training provided, depending on technicality of subject.
Public relations for business: $200-$500 per day plus expenses.
Public relations for conventions: $500-$1,500 flat fee.
Public relations for libraries: small libraries, $5-$10 per hour; larger cities, $35 an hour and up.
Public relations for nonprofit or proprietary organizations: small towns, $100-$500 monthly retainers.
Public relations for politicians: small town, state campaigns, $10-$50 per hour; incumbents, congressional, gubernatorial, and other national campaigns, $25-$100 per hour.
Public relations for schools: $10 per hour and up in small districts; larger districts have full-time staff personnel.
Radio advertising copy: small towns, up to $5 per spot; $20-$65 per hour; $100-$250 per week for a four- to six-hour day; larger cities, $250-$400 per week.
Radio continuity writing: $5 per page to $150 per week, part-time.
Radio documentaries: $200 for 60 minutes, local station.
Radio editorials: $10-$30 for 90-second to two-minute spots.
Radio interviews: for National Public Radio, up to 3 minutes, $25; 3-10 minutes, $40-$75; 10-60 minutes, $125 to negotiable fees. Small radio stations would pay approximately 50% of the NPR rate; large stations, double the NPR rate.
Readings by poets, fiction writers: $25-$600 depending on the author.
Record album cover copy: $100-$250 flat fee.

Recruiting brochure: 8-12 pages, $500-$1,500.
Research for writers or book publishers: $10-$30 an hour and up. Some quote a flat fee of $300-$500 for a complete and complicated job.
Restaurant guide features: short article on restaurant, owner, special attractions, $15; interior, exterior photos, $15.
Résumé writing: $50-$150 per résumé.
Retail business newsletters for customers: $175-$300 for writing four-page publications. Some writers work with a local printer and handle production details as well, billing the client for the total package. Some writers also do their own photography.
Rewriting: copy for a local client, $27.50 per hour.
Sales brochure: 12-16 pages, $750-$3,000.
Sales letter for business or industry: $150-$500 for one or two pages.
Script synopsis for agent or film producer: $75 for 2-3 typed pages, single-spaced.
Scripts for nontheatrical films for education, business, industry: prices vary among producers, clients, and sponsors and there is no standardization of rates in the field. Fees include $75-$120 per minute for one reel (10 minutes) and corresponding increases with each successive reel; approximately 10% of the production cost of films that cost the producer more than $1,500 per release minute.
Services brochure: 12-18 pages, $1,250-$2,000.
Shopping mall promotion: $500 monthly retainer up to 15% of promotion budget for the mall.
Short story manuscript critique: 3,000 words, $30.
Slide film script: See audiovisuals.
Slide presentation: including visual formats plus audio, $1,000-$1,500 for 10-15 minutes.
Slide/single image photos: $75 flat fee.
Slide/tape script: $75-$100 per minute, $750 minimum.
Software manual writing: $15-$50 per hour for research and writing.
Special news article: for a business's submission to trade publication, $250-$400 for 1,000 words.
Special occasion booklet: Family keepsake of a wedding, anniversary, Bar Mitzvah, etc., $115 and up.
Speech for owners of a small business: $100 for six minutes.
Speech for owners of larger businesses: $500-$3,000 for 10-30 minutes.
Speech for local political candidate: $150-$250 for 15 minutes.
Speech for statewide candidate: $500-$800.
Speech for national candidate: $1,000 and up.
Syndicated newspaper column, self-promoted: $2-$8 each for weeklies; $5-$25 per week for dailies, based on circulation.
Teaching adult education course: $10-$60 per class hour.
Teaching adult seminar: $350 plus mileage and per diem for a 6- or 7-hour day; plus 40% of the tuition fee beyond the sponsor's breakeven point.
Teaching college course or seminar: $15-$70 per class hour.
Teaching creative writing in school: $15-$60 per hour of instruction, or $1,200 for a 10-session class of 25 students; less in recessionary times.
Teaching journalism in high school: proportionate to salary scale for full-time teacher in the same school district.
Teaching home-bound students: $5 per hour.
Technical typing: $1-$4 per double-spaced page.
Technical writing: $15-$50 per hour.
Trade journal ad copywriting: $250-$500.
Trade journal article: for business client, $500-$1,500.
Translation, commercial: a final draft in one of the common European languages, 2½-4½¢ per English word.
Translation for government agencies: $20-$60 per 1,000 foreign words into English.

Translation, literary: $40-$60 per thousand English words.

Translation through translation agencies: less 33⅓% for agency commission.

TV documentary: 30-minute five-six page proposal outline, $250 and up; 15-17 page treatment, $1,000 and up; less in smaller cities.

TV editorials: $35 and up for 1-minute, 45 seconds (250-300 words).

TV information scripts: short 5- to 10-minute scripts for local cable TV stations, $10-$15 per hour.

TV instruction taping: $150 per 30-minute tape; $25 residual each time tape is sold.

TV news film still photo: $3-$6 flat fee.

TV news story: $16-$25 flat fee.

TV filmed news and features: from $10-$20 per clip for 30-second spot; $15-$25 for 60-second clip; more for special events.

TV, national and local public stations: $35-$100 per minute down to a flat fee of $100-$500 for a 30- to 60-minute script.

TV scripts: (Teleplay only), 60 minutes, prime time, Writers Guild rates effective 3/1/85-2/28/86: $9,985; 30 minutes, $7,402.

Video script: See audiovisuals.

Writer-in-schools: Arts council program, $130 per day; $475 per week. Personal charges vary from $25 per day to $100 per hour depending on school's ability to pay.

Writer's workshop: lecturing and seminar conducting, $100 per hour to $500 per day plus expenses; local classes, $50 per student for 10 sessions.

Waiting for the Good News

Perhaps the greatest lesson which the lives
of literary men teach us is told in a single word: Wait.
—Henry Wadsworth Longfellow

In most occupations, people get paid for their work; they get praised and later honored at retirement dinners; they have health plans in case they get sick.

As a writer, you don't get scheduled rewards. Still, you wait for the phone to ring. You wait for the mailman. You wait for the time when editors buy your work. The secret, unfortunately, is to wait but to expect nothing. You'll have more time to write what is important; you'll not be disappointed.

Each day, the mail delivery at *Writer's Market* brings letters from writers, angry that they have not heard from a magazine or book publisher. Some writers, to get an editor's attention, will file a postal complaint or write to a newspaper's consumer help column. Some writers insult, and even threaten, an editor. Yes, that writer will get the editor's attention. No, that editor won't want to work with that writer.

What many writers don't realize (and what few editors will admit) is that their publishers don't have budgets to handle hundreds and sometimes thousands of submissions and correspondences with writers.

"To answer each writer's query as *I* want to, I'd be writing letters at midnight after a 14-hour day," said one editor. "The sad part is knowing that writers who have written to me are working past midnight, too."

In many editorial offices, the mail sits until after deadline; sometimes deadlines for several projects overlap.

That's why you'll want to go on to your next story after you've put one in the mail. In most cases, editors do not ignore your submissions. Six months response time can mean 180 days of waiting for a writer; that's just one book cycle for the editor.

Because you don't get prompt acceptances from an editor does not say your work won't sell. William Kennedy's *Ironweed* was turned down by 13 top publishers before Viking agreed to publish the book. It won the 1984 Pulitzer Prize for literature.

When you think editors are overlooking your work or ignoring your letters, keep in mind these quirks of the writing business.

- Editorial decisions are subjective. Editors want to discover the next Ernest Hemingway or William Kennedy. Sometimes the best work is ahead of its time. Literary scholars estimate that 80 years must pass before they can say who the great literary people of an age were.

- Manuscripts and queries sometimes are circulated among several editors in a company. This takes time. While the editors may not inform you of this practice, your manuscript may be under serious consideration.

- Editors are greatly outnumbered by writers. If a writer spends three hours on a detailed query and cover letter, the editor will *never* be able to reciprocate that amount of time. "If only editors would drop me a short note, I'd be satisfied," writers frequently say. The problem is that even brief notes take time and probably would seem like an incomplete response to the writer.

- Editors also get inquiries from writers that demand research time. In some cases, writers ask editors for information that is available in any library.

- Many writers expect a response from an editor because they spent 44¢ in postage to ask for a response. In theory, a self-addressed, stamped envelope *says* the writer would like the courtesy of a reply. In practice, editors find themselves owing the courtesy of a reply to more people than their schedules can accommodate. Some editors write notes to writers; others, who need 40 to 60 hours a week to write, edit, and get their books to press, can't correspond with every writer. Most editors do value writers' work, though they may not tell you this in a note.

Wait, as Longfellow suggests; don't quit writing. The breakthrough that most writers hope for—a book contract or byline in a top magazine—may come with the next story you write. It might not come or might come posthumously. It will never come if you let rejection and nonresponse affect what you put on paper.

One writer told *Writer's Market* that "I wish I could go back in time and tell the little kid who was sweating away on that second-hand typewriter that his father bought him for 10 bucks not to worry that he was going to make it."

Now he is glad he didn't know he would succeed. "If I had gotten some magic assurance and on the strength of that taken it easy because I was going to make it, I might not have."

That person, now a published author, still writes up to 14 hours a day. You've probably read his books, short stories and articles. His name? Isaac Asimov.

Waiting for the good news from an editor, you can develop more ideas. When the news is bad (a "no, thank you"), you can send this material to another editor. If no news arrives after repeated letters, send a certified letter withdrawing your work; send your writing elsewhere (there are more than 4,000 markets in this book). The good news is that you can be waiting and writing at the same time.

Glossary

Advance. A sum of money that a publisher pays a writer(s) prior to the publication of a book. It is usually paid in installments, such as one-half on signing the contract; one-half on delivery of a complete and satisfactory manuscript. The advance is paid against the royalty money that will be earned by the book.

All Rights. See "Rights and the Writer" in the appendix.

Assignment. Editor asks a writer to do a specific article for which he usually names a price for the completed manuscript.

B&W. Abbreviation for black & white photograph.

Beat. A specific subject area regularly covered by a reporter, such as the police department or education or the environment. It can also mean a scoop on some news item.

Bimonthly. Every two months. See also *semimonthly*.

Bionote. A sentence or brief paragraph about the writer at the bottom of the first or last page on which an article or short story appears in a publication. A bionote may also appear on a contributors' page where the editor discusses the writers contributing to that particular edition.

Biweekly. Every two weeks.

Blue-penciling. Editing a manuscript.

Book auction. Selling the rights (i.e. paperback, movie, etc.) of a hardback book to the highest bidder. A publisher or agent may initiate the auction.

Book packager. Draws all the elements of a book together, from the initial concept to writing and marketing strategies, then sells the book package to a book publisher and/or movie producer.

Broadside. An oversized sheet or a one-page poster with illustration and text (poetry, fiction or nonfiction).

Caption. Originally a title or headline over a picture but now a description of the subject matter of a photograph, including names of people where appropriate. Also called cutline.

Certified mail. Costs 75¢. Such mail travels with other mail but must be signed for at its destination. See also *return receipt*.

Chapbook. A small booklet, usually paperback, of poetry, ballads or tales.

Clean copy. Free of errors, cross-outs, wrinkles, smudges.

Clippings. News items of possible interest to trade magazine editors.

Clips. Samples, usually from newspapers or magazines, of a writer's (your) *published* work.

Closed captioned. Visually capsulating certain programs for the hearing impaired, with the aid of a special decoder that is attached to a television receiver.

Coffee table book. A general interest book, not necessarily timely, but one that sustains interest over a long period of time. It could be on art, music, collectibles, and similar topics. It is not news-related and not necessarily read at one sitting. In short, it's a publication you'd be proud to have on your coffee table as a conversation piece.

Column inch. All the type contained in one inch of a typeset column.

Compatible. The condition which allows one type of computer/word processor to share information or communicate with another type of machine.

Concept. A statement that summarizes a screenplay or teleplay—before the outline or treatment is written.

Contributor's copies. Copies of the issues of a magazine sent to an author in which his/her work appears.

Co-publishing. An arrangement (usually contractual) in which author and publisher share publication costs and profits.

Copyediting. Editing the manuscript for grammar, punctuation and printing style as opposed to subject content.

Copyright. A means to protect an author's work. See "Rights and the Writer."

Correspondent. Writer away from the home office of a newspaper or magazine who regularly provides it with copy.

Cover letter. A brief letter, accompanying a complete manuscript, especially useful if responding to an editor's request for a manuscript. A cover letter may also accompany a proposal or query. (A cover letter is *not* a query letter; the query is a detailed proposal for a story or book.)

Cutline. See *caption*.

Diorama. An advertising term referring to an elaborate, three-dimensional, miniature display.

Disk. A round, flat magnetic plate on which computer data may be stored.

Docudrama. A fictional film rendition of recent newsmaking events and people.

Dot-matrix. Printed type where individual characters are composed of a matrix or pattern of tiny dots.

El-hi. Elementary to high school.

Epigram. A short, witty, sometimes paradoxical saying.

Erotica. Usually fiction that is sexually-oriented; although it could be art on the same theme.

Express mail. For $10.75, the post office will guarantee next-day delivery to a specific address. This cost covers up to two pounds; to five is $12.85. The "next-day guarantee" depends upon the points of departure and destination as well as post office schedules.

Fair use. A provision of the copyright law that says short passages from copyrighted material may be used without infringing on the owner's rights.

Feature. An article giving the reader background information on the news. Also used by magazines to indicate a lead article or distinctive department.

Filler. A short item used by an editor to "fill" out a newspaper column or a page in a magazine. It could be a timeless news item, a joke, an anecdote, some light verse or short humor, a puzzle, etc.

First North American serial rights. See "Rights and the Writer."

Formula story. Familiar theme treated in a predictable plot structure—such as boy meets girl, boy loses girl, boy gets girl.

Gagline. The caption for a cartoon, or the cover teaser line and the punchline on the inside of a studio greeting card.

Ghostwriter. A writer who puts into literary form, an article, speech, story or book based on another person's ideas or knowledge.

Glossy. A black and white photograph with a shiny surface as opposed to one with a non-shiny matte finish.

Gothic novel. One in which the central character is usually a beautiful young girl, the setting is an old mansion or castle; there is a handsome hero and a real menace, either natural or supernatural.

Hard copy. The printed copy (usually on paper) of a computer's output.

Hardware. All the mechanically-integrated components of a computer that are not software. Circuit boards, transistors, and the machines that are the actual computer are the hardware.

Honorarium. A token payment. It may be a very small amount of money, or simply a byline and copies of the publication in which your material appears.

Illustrations. May be photographs, old engravings, artwork. Usually paid for separately from the manuscript. See also *package sale*.

Interactive fiction. Works of fiction in book or computer software format in which the reader determines the path that the story will take. The reader chooses from several alternatives at the end of a "chapter," and this determines the structure of the story. Interactive fiction features multiple plots and endings.

International Reply Coupon (IRC). Must be included with manuscripts to Canadian and overseas publishers to ensure return reply. Coupons cost 65¢ each, and one is sufficient for an ounce moving at surface rate; two are recommended for an air-mail return.

Invasion of privacy. Cause for suits against some writers who have written about persons (even though truthfully) without their consent.

Kill fee. A portion of the agreed-on price for a complete article that was assigned but which was subsequently cancelled.

Letter-quality submissions. Computer printout that looks like a typewritten manuscript.

Libel. A false accusation; or any published statement or presentation that tends to expose another to public contempt, ridicule, etc. Defenses are truth; fair comment on the matter of public interest; and privileged communication—such as a report of legal proceedings or a client's communication to his lawyer.

Little magazine. Publications of limited circulation, usually on literary or political subject matter.

Machine language. Symbols that can be used directly by a computer.

Magazette. A periodical published on an electronic 5¼" diskette.

Microcomputer. A small computer system capable of performing various specific tasks with data it receives. Personal computers are microcomputers.

Militaria. Articles having to do with the military (i.e.: uniforms, buttons, medals).

Miniseries. Special television programs with continuing plot lines and a series of episodes.

Model release. A paper signed by the subject of a photograph (or his guardian, if a juvenile) giving the photographer permission to use the photograph, editorially or for advertising purposes or for some specific purpose as stated.

Modem. A small electrical box that plugs into the serial card of a computer, used to transmit data from one computer to another, usually via telephone lines. The word, modem, comes from combining the beginnings of *mo*dulator-*dem*odulator.

Monograph. Thoroughly detailed and documented, scholarly study, concerning a singular subject.

Ms. Abbreviation for manuscript.

Mss. Abbreviation for more than one manuscript.

Multiple submissions. Some editors of nonoverlapping circulation magazines, such as religious publications, are willing to look at manuscripts which have also been submitted to other editors at the same time. See individual listings. No multiple submissions should be made to larger markets paying good prices for original material, unless it is a query on a highly topical article requiring an immediate response and that fact is so stated in your letter.

Newsbreak. A newsbreak can be a small newsworthy story added to the front page of a newspaper at press time or can be a magazine news item of importance to readers.

Novelette. A short novel, or a long short story; 7,000 to 15,000 words approximately.

Offprint. Copies of an author's article taken "out of issue" before a magazine is bound and given to the author in lieu of monetary payment. An offprint could then be used by the writer as a published clip/writing sample.

One-time rights. See "Rights and the Writer."

Outline. Of a book is usually a summary of its contents in five to fifteen double-spaced pages; often in the form of chapter headings with a descriptive sentence or two under each one to show the scope of the book. Of a screenplay or teleplay is a scene-by-scene narrative description of the story (10-15 pages for a ½-hour teleplay; 15-25 pages for a 1-hour teleplay; 25-40 pages for a 90-minute teleplay; 40-60 pages for a 2-hour feature film or teleplay).

Over-the-transom. Refers to unsolicited material submitted to a book publisher, magazine editor, etc., by a freelance writer. These submissions are said to come in "over-the-transom."

Package sale. The editor wants to buy manuscript and photos as a "package" and pay for them in one check.

Page rate. Some magazines pay for material at a fixed rate per published page, rather than so much per word.

Payment on acceptance. The editor sends you a check for your article, story or poem as soon as he reads it and decides to publish it.

Payment on publication. The editor decides to buy your material but doesn't send you a check until he publishes it.

Pen name. The use of a name other than your legal name on articles, stories, or books where you wish to remain anonymous. Simply notify your post office and bank that you are using the name so that you'll receive mail and/or checks in that name.

Photo feature. A feature in which the emphasis is on the photographs rather than any accompanying written material.

Photocopied submissions. Submitting *photocopies* of an original manuscript; are acceptable to some editors instead of the author's sending his original manuscript. See also *multiple submissions*.

Plagiarism. Passing off as one's own the expression of ideas and words of another writer.

Postal Money Order. Available at all post offices. Useful for writers who send longer manuscripts to publishers outside the United States since they are more economical than International Reply Coupons (IRCs). Money orders up to $25 may be purchased for 75 cents.

Program. A series of instructions written in symbols and codes that a computer "reads" to perform a specific task.

Public domain. Material which was either never copyrighted or whose copyright term has run out.

Publication not copyrighted. Publication of an author's work in such a publication places it in the public domain, and it cannot subsequently be copyrighted. See "Rights and the Writer."

Query. A letter to an editor aimed to get his interest in an article you want to write.

Rebus. Stories, quips, puzzles, etc., in juvenile magazines that convey words or syllables with pictures, objects, or symbols whose names resemble the sounds of the intended words.

Registered mail. Costs $3.60 beyond first-class postage. The fee covers the costs of special handling which includes the package's being signed in and out of every office it travels through.

Reporting time. The number of days, weeks, etc., it takes an editor to report back to the author on his query or manuscript.

Reprint rights. See "Rights and the Writer."

Return receipt. Available for 70¢ with either certified or registered mail. A postcard attached to your package will be signed at the destination and mailed back to you.

Round-up article. Comments from, or interviews with, a number of celebrities or experts on a single theme.

Royalties, standard hardcover book. 10% of the retail price on the first 5,000 copies sold; 12½% on the next 5,000 and 15% thereafter.

Royalties, standard mass paperback book. 4 to 8% of the retail price on the first 150,000 copies sold.

Royalties, trade paperback book. No less than 6% of list price on first 20,000 copies; 7½% thereafter.

SAE. Self-addressed envelope.

SASE. Self-addressed, stamped envelope.

Screenplay. Script for a film intended to be shown in theatres.

Second serial rights. See "Rights and the Writer."

Semimonthly. Twice a month.

Semiweekly. Twice a week.

Serial. Published periodically, such as a newspaper or magazine.

Sidebar. A feature presented as a companion to a straight news report (or main magazine article) giving sidelights on human-interest aspects, (or) sometimes elucidating just one aspect of the story.

Simultaneous submissions. Submissions of the same article, story or poem to several publications at the same time.

Slant. The approach of a story or article so as to appeal to the readers of a specific magazine. Does, for example, this magazine always like stories with an upbeat ending? Or does that one like articles aimed only at the blue-collar worker?

Slides. Usually called transparencies by editors looking for color photographs.

Slush pile. A collective term for the stack of unsolicited, or misdirected manuscripts received by an editor or book publisher.

Software. Programs and related documentation for use with a particular computer system.

Speculation. The editor agrees to look at the author's manuscript with no assurance that it will be bought.

Stringer. A writer who submits material to a magazine or newspaper from a specific geographical location.

Style. The way in which something is written—for example, short, punchy sentences of flowing, narrative description, or heavy use of quotes of dialogue.

Subsidiary rights. All those rights, other than book publishing rights included in a book contract—such as paperback, book club, movie rights, etc.

Subsidy publisher. A book publisher who charges the author for the cost to typeset and print his book, the jacket, etc., as opposed to a royalty publisher which pays the author.

Syndication rights. A book publisher may sell the rights to a newspaper syndicate to print a book in installments in one or more newspapers.

Synopsis. Of a book is a summary of its contents. Of a screenplay or teleplay is a summary of the story. See *Outline*.

Tabloids. Newspaper format publication on about half the size of the regular newspaper page, such as *National Enquirer*.

Tagline. A tagline has two definitions in the writing world: a caption for a photo or an editorial comment appended to a filler in a magazine such as those used in *The New Yorker*.

Tearsheet. Page from a magazine or newspaper containing your printed story, article, poem or ad.

Teleplay. A dramatic story written to be performed on television.

Transparencies. Positive color slides; not color prints.

Treatment. Synopsis of a proposed television or film script (40-60 pages for a 2-hour feature film or teleplay). More detailed than an outline.

Uncopyrighted publication. Publication of an author's work in such a publication potentially puts it in the public domain.

Unsolicited manuscript. A story, article, poem or book that an editor did not specifically ask to see.

User friendly. Easy to handle and use. Refers to computer hardware designed with the user in mind.

Vanity publisher. See *subsidy publisher*.

W.W. A notation used by some editors meaning "wrong word."

Word processor. A computer that produces typewritten copy via automated typing, text-editing, and storage and transmission capabilities.

Index

H

L

N

X Y

Z

Other Books of Interest

Computer Books
   The Complete Guide to Writing Software User Manuals, by Brad M. McGehee (paper) $14.95
   The Photographer's Computer Handbook, by B. Nadine Orabona (paper) $14.95
General Writing Books
   Beginning Writer's Answer Book, edited by Polking and Bloss $14.95
   Getting the Words Right: How to Revise, Edit and Rewrite, by Theodore A. Rees Cheney $13.95
   How to Become a Bestselling Author, by Stan Corwin $14.95
   How to Get Started in Writing, by Peggy Teeters $10.95
   How to Write a Book Proposal, by Michael Larsen $9.95
   How to Write While You Sleep, by Elizabeth Ross $12.95
   If I Can Write, You Can Write, by Charlie Shedd $12.95
   International Writers' & Artists' Yearbook (paper) $12.95
   Law & the Writer, edited by Polking & Meranus (paper) $10.95
   Knowing Where to Look: The Ultimate Guide to Research, by Lois Horowitz $16.95
   Make Every Word Count, by Gary Provost (paper) $7.95
   Teach Yourself to Write, by Evelyn Stenbock (paper) $9.95
   The 29 Most Common Writing Mistakes & How to Avoid Them, by Judy Delton $9.95
   Writer's Block & How to Use It, by Victoria Nelson $12.95
   Writer's Encyclopedia, edited by Kirk Polking $19.95
   Writer's Market, edited by Paula Deimling $19.95
   Writer's Resource Guide, edited by Bernadine Clark $16.95
   Writing for the Joy of It, by Leonard Knott $11.95
   Writing From the Inside Out, by Charlotte Edwards (paper) $9.95
Magazine/News Writing
   Complete Guide to Writing Nonfiction, by the American Society of Journalists & Authors $24.95
   The Craft of Interviewing, by John Brady $9.95
   How to Write & Sell the 8 Easiest Article Types, by Helene Schellenberg Barnhart $14.95
   Magazine Writing Today, by Jerome E. Kelley $10.95
   Newsthinking: The Secret of Great Newswriting, by Bob Baker $11.95
   Stalking the Feature Story, by William Ruehlmann $9.95
   Write On Target, by Connie Emerson $12.95
Fiction Writing
   Creating Short Fiction, by Damon Knight (paper) $8.95
   Fiction Is Folks: How to Create Unforgettable Characters, by Robert Newton Peck $11.95
   Fiction Writer's Help Book, by Maxine Rock $12.95
   Fiction Writer's Market, edited by Jean Fredette $17.95
   Handbook of Short Story Writing, by Dickson and Smythe (paper) $7.95
   How to Write Best-Selling Fiction, by Dean R. Koontz $13.95
   How to Write Short Stories that Sell, by Louise Boggess (paper) $7.95
   One Way to Write Your Novel, by Dick Perry (paper) $6.95
   Secrets of Successful Fiction, by Robert Newton Peck $8.95
   Storycrafting, by Paul Darcy Boles $14.95
   Writing Romance Fiction—For Love And Money, by Helene Schellenberg Barnhart $14.95
   Writing the Novel: From Plot to Print, by Lawrence Block (paper) $8.95
Special Interest Writing Books
   The Children's Picture Book: How to Write It, How to Sell It, by Ellen E. M. Roberts $17.95
   Complete Book of Scriptwriting, by J. Michael Straczynski $14.95
   Confession Writer's Handbook, by Florence K. Palmer $9.95
   The Craft of Comedy Writing, by Sol Saks $14.95
   The Craft of Lyric Writing, by Sheila Davis $16.95
   Guide to Greeting Card Writing, edited by Larry Sandman (paper) $7.95

How to Make Money Writing Fillers, by Connie Emerson (paper) $8.95
How to Write a Cookbook and Get It Published, by Sara Pitzer $15.95
How to Write a Play, by Raymond Hull $13.95
How to Write and Sell Your Personal Experiences, by Lois Duncan $10.95
How to Write and Sell (Your Sense of) Humor, by Gene Perret $12.95
How to Write "How-To" Books and Articles, by Raymond Hull (paper) $8.95
How to Write the Story of Your Life, by Frank P. Thomas $12.95
Mystery Writer's Handbook, by The Mystery Writers of America (paper) $8.95
On Being a Poet, by Judson Jerome $14.95
Poet's Handbook, by Judson Jerome $11.95
Poet's Market, by Judson Jerome $16.95
Programmer's Market, edited by Brad McGehee (paper) $16.95
Sell Copy, by Webster Kuswa $11.95
Successful Outdoor Writing, by Jack Samson $11.95
Travel Writer's Handbook, by Louise Zobel (paper) $9.95
TV Scriptwriter's Handbook, by Alfred Brenner (paper) $9.95
Writing After 50, by Leonard L. Knott $12.95
Writing and Selling Science Fiction, by Science Fiction Writers of America (paper) $7.95
Writing for Children & Teenagers, by Lee Wyndham (paper) $9.95
Writing for Regional Publications, by Brian Vachon $11.95
Writing for the Soaps, by Jean Rouverol $14.95
Writing to Inspire, by Gentz, Roddy, et al $14.95

The Writing Business

Complete Guide to Self-Publishing, by Tom & Marilyn Ross $19.95
Complete Handbook for Freelance Writers, by Kay Cassill $14.95
Editing for Print, by Geoffrey Rogers $14.95
Freelance Jobs for Writers, edited by Kirk Polking (paper) $7.95
How to Be a Successful Housewife/Writer, by Elaine Fantle Shimberg $10.95
How to Get Your Book Published, by Herbert W. Bell $15.95
How to Understand and Negotiate a Book Contract or Magazine Agreement, by Richard Balkin $11.95
How You Can Make $20,000 a Year Writing, by Nancy Hanson (paper) $6.95
The Writer's Survival Guide: How to Cope with Rejection, Success and 99 Other Hang-Ups of the Writing Life, by Jean and Veryl Rosenbaum $12.95

To order directly from the publisher, include $2.00 postage and handling for 1 book and 50¢ for each additional book. Allow 30 days for delivery.

Writer's Digest Books, Department B
9933 Alliance Road, Cincinnati OH 45242
Prices subject to change without notice.

Notes

Notes

Notes

Notes

Notes